Pocket
Italian Dictionary

2004 **Second Edition**

Italian ·····❯ English
English ·····❯ Italian

Editors
Pat Bulhosen
Francesca Logi
Loredana Riu

OXFORD
UNIVERSITY PRESS

OXFORD
UNIVERSITY PRESS

Great Clarendon Street, Oxford OX2 6DP

Oxford University Press is a department of the University of Oxford.
It furthers the University's objective of excellence in research, scholarship,
and education by publishing worldwide in

Oxford New York

Auckland Bangkok Buenos Aires Cape Town Chennai
Dar es Salaam Delhi Hong Kong Istanbul Karachi Kolkata
Kuala Lumpur Madrid Melbourne Mexico City Mumbai Nairobi
São Paulo Shanghai Taipei Tokyo Toronto

Oxford is a registered trade mark of Oxford University Press
in the UK and in certain other countries

Published in the United States
by Oxford University Press Inc., New York

First published 1997
Reissued with new cover 2000

This second edition 2004

British Library Cataloguing in Publication Data
Data available

Library of Congress Cataloging in Publication Data
Data available
ISBN 0-19-860896-9

1

Typeset in Nimrod, Arial and Meta by Morton Word Processing Ltd
Printed in Great Britain by Clays Ltd, Bungay, Suffolk

Preface / Prefazione

This dictionary has been designed to meet the needs of students, tourists and all those who require quick and reliable answers to their translation questions. It provides clear guidance on selecting the most appropriate translation, illustrative examples to help with construction and usage, and precise information on grammar and style.

Focussing on everyday, idiomatic Italian and English, both spoken and written, this easy-to-use dictionary also offers generous treatment of business and computing vocabulary. Its up-to-the-minute coverage and wealth of accurate translations make it an ideal reference tool and study aid.

This second edition also offers a wide range of supplementary materials such as an A-Z of Italian life and culture, a calendar of festive days in Italy, a correspondence section containing model letters to help with personal and business letter-writing in Italian, and a grammar summary.

Questo dizionario è stato creato per soddisfare le esigenze degli studenti, dei turisti e di tutti coloro che hanno bisogno di risposte rapide e sicure ai problemi di traduzione. Il lettore è guidato con chiarezza nella scelta del termine più appropriato, con esempi di uso della lingua e con indicazioni precise di grammatica e di stile.

Basandosi sull'uso contemporaneo dell'inglese e dell'italiano, scritto e parlato, questo dizionario di facile consultazione dedica particolare attenzione al lessico dell'informatica e degli affari. Attuale e aggiornato, con abbondante e precisa terminologia, rappresenta uno strumento di consultazione ideale e un valido sussidio didattico.

Questa seconda edizione contiene anche un vasto repertorio di materiali aggiuntivi: un supplemento su aspetti della civiltà britannica e statunitense, un calendario di giorni festivi nel Regno Unito e negli Stati Uniti, una sezione di corrispondenza che propone lettere-modello in inglese e note di grammatica.

List of contributors / Hanno collaborato

First edition/Prima edizione

Editors/Redazione
Debora Mazza
Jane Goldie
Donatella Boi
Francesca Logi
Peter Terrell
Sonia Tinagli-Baxter
Carla Zipoli

Allan Cameron
Michela Masci
Ilaria Panuccio

Copy editors/Segreteria di redazione
Alice Grandison
Mary Rigby
Daphne Trotter

Project management by/A cura di
LEXUS

Second edition/Seconda edizione

Pat Bulhosen
Francesca Logi
Loredana Riu

Contents / Indice

Introduction / Introduzione

Here is some basic information on the way the entries in this dictionary are organized.

A swung dash ~ is used to replace the headword within the entry.

Compounds are listed in alphabetical order. Remember this when looking for a word. The entry 'password', for example, is entered alphabetically – at some distance from the entry 'pass'. Likewise 'paintbrush' and 'paintpot' will have 'painter', 'pain threshold' and 'painting' entered in between.

Indicators are provided to guide the user to the best translation for a specific sense of a word. Types of indicator are:

field labels (see the list on p x), which indicate a general area of usage (commercial, computing, photography etc);

sense indicators, eg: **bore** *n* (*of gun*) calibro *m*; (*person*) seccatore, -trice *mf*;

typical subjects of verbs, eg: **bond** *vt* ‹*glue*› attaccare;

typical objects of verbs, placed after the translation of the verb, eg: **boost** *vt* stimolare ‹*sales*›; sollevare ‹*morale*›;

nouns that typically go together with certain adjectives, eg: **rich** *a* ricco; ‹*food*› pesante.

1, **2**, etc mean that the same word is being translated as a different part of speech, eg. **partition** **1** *n* ... **2** *vt* ...

A solid black square is used to

Ecco le informazioni essenziali su come sono organizzate le voci nel dizionario.

Un trattino ondulato ~ è utilizzato al posto del lemma all'interno della voce.

I vocaboli composti sono in ordine alfabetico. È importante ricordarlo quando si cerca la parola che interessa. La voce 'password', ad esempio, essendo in ordine alfabetico, compare a una certa distanza dopo la voce 'pass'. Per la stessa ragione fra 'paintbrush' and 'paintpot' compaiono 'painter', 'pain threshold' e 'painting'.

Degli indicatori vengono forniti per indirizzare l'utente verso la traduzione corrispondente al senso voluto di una parola. I tipi di indicatori sono:

etichette semantiche (vedi la lista a p x), indicanti l'ambito specifico in cui la parola viene generalmente usata in quel senso (commercio, informatica, fotografia ecc);

indicatori di significato, es.: **redazione** *nf* (*ufficio*) editorial office; (*di testi*) editing;

soggetti tipici di verbi, es.: **trovarsi** *vr* ‹*luogo*› be;

complementi oggetti tipici di verbi, collocati dopo la traduzione dello stesso verbo, es: **superare** *vt* overtake ‹*veicolo*›; pass ‹*esame*›;

sostantivi che ricorrono tipicamente con certi aggettivi, es.: **solare** *a* ‹*energia, raggi*› solar; ‹*crema*› sun.

1, **2**, ecc indicano che la stessa

identify phrasal verbs, eg ∎ **strip down** *vt* ... Phrasal verbs are listed in alphabetical order directly after the main verb. So 'strip down' comes after 'strip' and before 'strip cartoon'.

English pronunciation is given for the Italian user in the International Phonetic Alphabet (see p ix).

Italian stress is shown by a ' placed in front of the stressed syllable in a word.

Square brackets are used around parts of an expression which can be omitted without altering the sense.

parola viene tradotta come una diversa parte del discorso, es. **calcolatore** ⓵ *a* ... ⓶ *nm* ...

Un quadratino nero viene utilizzato per indicare i phrasal verbs, ad esempio: ∎ **strip down** *vt* ... I phrasal verbs si trovano in ordine alfabetico immediatamente dopo il verbo principale. Così 'strip down' viene subito dopo 'strip' e subito prima di 'strip cartoon'.

La pronuncia inglese è data usando l'Alfabetico Fonetico Internazionale (vedi p ix).

L'accento tonico nelle parole italiane è indicato dal segno ' collocato davanti alla sillaba accentata.

Delle parentesi quadre racchiudono parti di espressioni che possono essere omesse senza alterazioni di senso.

Proprietary terms / Marche depositate

This dictionary includes some words which are, or are asserted to be, proprietary names or trademarks. Their inclusion does not imply that they have acquired for legal purposes a non-proprietary or general significance, nor is any other judgment implied concerning their legal status. In cases where the editor has some evidence that a word is used as a proprietary name or trademark this is indicated by the symbol ®, but no judgment concerning the legal status of such words is made or implied thereby.

Questo dizionario include alcune parole che sono o vengono considerate nomi di marche depositate. La loro presenza non implica che abbiano acquisito legalmente un significato generale, né si suggerisce alcun altro giudizio riguardo il loro stato giuridico. Qualora il redattore abbia trovato testimonianza dell'uso di una parola come marca depositata, questa è stata contrassegnata dal simbolo ®, ma nessun giudizio riguardo lo stato giuridico di tale parola viene espresso o suggerito in tal modo.

Pronunciation of Italian

Vowels

a	is broad like *a* in *father*: **casa**.
e	has two sounds: closed like *ey* in *they*: **sera**; open like *e* in *egg*: **sette**.
i	is like *ee* in *feet*: **venire**.
o	has two sounds: closed like *o* in *show*: **bocca**; open like *o* in *dog*: **croma**.
u	is like *oo* in *moon*: **luna**.

When two or more vowels come together each vowel is pronounced separately: **buono**; **baia**.

Consonants

b, **d**, **f**, **l**, **m**, **n**, **p**, **t**, **v** are pronounced as in English. When these are double they are sounded distinctly: **bello**.

c	before **a**, **o**, or **u** and before consonants is like *k* in *king*: **cane**.
	before **e** or **i** is like *ch* in *church*: **cena**.
ch	is also like *k* in *king*: **chiesa**.
g	before **a**, **o**, or **u** is hard like *g* in *got*: **gufo**.
	before **e** or **i** is like *j* in *jelly*: **gentile**.
gh	is like *g* in *gun*: **ghiaccio**.
gl	when followed by **a**, **e**, **o**, or **u** is like *gl* in *glass*: **gloria**.
gli	is like *lli* in *million*: **figlio**.
gn	is like *ni* in *onion*: **bagno**.
h	is silent.
ng	is like *ng* in *finger* (not *singer*): **ringraziare**.
r	is pronounced distinctly.
s	between two vowels is like *s* in *rose*: **riso**.
	at the beginning of a word it is like *s* in *soap*: **sapone**.
sc	before *e* or *i* is like *sh* in *shell*: **scienza**.
z	sounds like *ts* within a word: **fazione**; like *dz* at the beginning: **zoo**.

The stress is shown by the sign **'** printed before the stressed syllable.

Pronuncia inglese

Simboli fonetici

Vocali e dittonghi

æ	b*a*d	ʊ	p*u*t	aʊ	n*ow*
ɑ:	*ah*	u:	t*oo*	aʊə	fl*our*
e	w*e*t	ə	*a*go	ɔɪ	c*oin*
ɪ	s*i*t	ɜ:	w*or*k	ɪə	h*ere*
i:	s*ee*	eɪ	m*a*de	eə	h*air*
ɒ	g*o*t	əʊ	h*o*me	ʊə	p*oor*
ɔ:	d*oo*r	aɪ	f*i*ve		
ʌ	c*u*p	aɪə	f*ire*		

Consonanti

b	*b*oy	l	*l*eg	t	*t*en
d	*d*ay	m	*m*an	tʃ	*ch*ip
dʒ	pa*g*e	n	*n*ew	θ	*th*ree
f	*f*oot	ŋ	si*ng*	ð	*th*is
g	*g*o	p	*p*en	v	*v*erb
h	*h*e	r	*r*un	w	*w*et
j	*y*es	s	*s*peak	z	hi*s*
k	*c*oat	ʃ	*sh*ip	ʒ	plea*s*ure

Note:
' precede la sillaba accentata.
La vocale nasale in parole quali *nuance* è indicata nella trascrizione fonetica
come õ: nju:õs.

Abbreviations / Abbreviazioni

adjective	adj	aggettivo	masculine or feminine	mf	maschile o femminile
abbreviation	abbr	abbreviazione	military	Mil	militare
administration	Admin	amministrazione	music	Mus	musica
adverb	adv	avverbio	noun	n	sostantivo
aeronautics	Aeron	aeronautica	nautical	Naut	nautica
American	Am	americano	old use	old	antiquato
anatomy	Anat	anatomia	pejorative	pej	peggiorativo
archaeology	Archaeol	archeologia	personal	pers	personale
architecture	Archit	architettura	photography	Phot	fotografia
astrology, astronomy	Astr	astrologia, astronomia	physics	Phys	fisica
attributive	attrib	attributo	plural	pl	plurale
automobiles	Auto	automobile	politics	Pol	politica
auxiliary	aux	ausiliario	possessive	poss	possessivo
biology	Biol	biologia	past participle	pp	participio passato
botany	Bot	botanica	prefix	pref	prefisso
British English	Br	inglese britannico	preposition	prep	preposizione
Chemistry	Chem	chimica	present tense	pres	presente
commerce	Comm	commercio	pronoun	pron	pronome
computers	Comput	informatica	psychology	Psych	psicologia
conjunction	conj	congiunzione	past tense	pt	tempo passato
cooking	Culin	cucina		qcno	qualcuno
definite article	def art	articolo determinativo		qcsa	qualcosa
	ecc	eccetera	proprietary term	®	marca depositata
economics	Econ	economia	rail	Rail	ferrovia
electricity	Electr	elettricità	reflexive	refl	riflessivo
et cetera	etc		religion	Relig	religione
feminine	f	femminile	relative pronoun	rel pron	pronome relativo
familiar	fam	familiare	somebody	sb	
figurative	fig	figurato	school	Sch	scuola
finance	Fin	finanza	singular	sg	singolare
formal	fml	formale	slang	sl	gergo
geography	Geog	geografia	something	sth	
geology	Geol	geologia	suffix	suff	suffisso
grammar	Gram	grammatica	technical	Techn	tecnico
humorous	hum	umoristico	telephone	Teleph	telefono
indefinite article	indef art	articolo indeterminativo	theatrical	Theat	teatrale
			television	TV	televisione
interjection	int	interiezione	typography	Typ	tipografia
interrogative	inter	interrogativo	university	Univ	università
invariable (no plural form)	inv	invariabile	auxiliary verb	v aux	verbo ausiliare
			intransitive verb	vi	verbo intransitivo
			reflexive verb	vr	verbo riflessivo
journalism	Journ	giornalismo	transitive verb	vt	verbo transitivo
law	Jur	legge/giuridico	transitive and intransitive	vt/i	verbo transitivo e intransitivo
literary	liter	letterario	vulgar	vulg	volgare
masculine	m	maschile			
mathematics	Math	matematica	cultural equivalent	≈	equivalenza culturale
mechanics	Mech	meccanica			
medicine	Med	medicina			
meteorology	Metereol	meteorologia			

a (*ad* *before vowel*) *prep* to; (stato in luogo, tempo, età) at; (con mese, città) in; (mezzo, modo) by; **dire qualcosa a qualcuno** tell somebody something; **alle tre** at three o'clock; **a vent'anni** at the age of twenty; **a Natale** at Christmas; **a dicembre** in December; **ero al cinema** I was at the cinema; **vivo a Londra** I live in London; **a due a due** two by two; **a piedi** on *or* by foot; **maglia a maniche lunghe** long-sleeved sweater; **casa a tre piani** house with three floors; **giocare a tennis** play tennis; **50 km all'ora** 50 km an hour; **2 euro al chilo** 2 euros a kilo; **al mattino/alla sera** in the morning/evening; **a venti chilometri/due ore da qui** twenty kilometres/two hours away

'abaco *nm* abacus

a'bate *nm* abbot

abbacchia'mento *nm* fam dejection

abbacchi'ato *adj* fam dejected, downhearted

ab'bacchio *nm* [young] lamb. **abbacchio alla romana** spring lamb

abbaci'nare *vt* dazzle, blind; fig deceive

abbagli'ante ① *adj* dazzling ② *nm* headlight, high-beam Am; **mettere gli abbaglianti** put the headlights on full beam

abbagli'are *vt* dazzle

ab'baglio *nm* blunder; **prendere un ∼** make a blunder

abbaia'mento *nm* barking

abbai'are *vi* bark

abba'ino *nm* dormer window; (mansarda) loft

abbando'nare *vt* abandon; leave ⟨*luogo*⟩; give up ⟨*piani ecc*⟩; **∼ il campo** Mil desert in the face of the enemy

abbando'narsi *vr* let oneself go; **∼ a** give oneself up to ⟨*ricordi ecc*⟩

abbando'nato *adj* abandoned

abban'dono *nm* abandoning; fig abandon; (stato) neglect

abbarbi'carsi *vr* **∼ a** cling to

abbassa'mento *nm* (di temperatura, acqua, prezzi) drop

abbas'sare *vt* lower; turn down ⟨*radio, TV*⟩; **∼ i fari** dip the headlights

abbas'sarsi *vr* stoop; ⟨*sole ecc*⟩ sink; fig demean oneself

ab'basso ① *adv* below ② *int* down with

abba'stanza *adv* enough; (alquanto) quite; **∼ nuovo** newish; **ne ho ∼!** I've had enough!, I'm fed up!

ab'battere *vt* demolish; shoot down ⟨*aereo*⟩; put down ⟨*animale*⟩; topple ⟨*regime*⟩; (fig: demoralizzare) dishearten

ab'battersi *vr* (cadere) fall; fig be discouraged; **∼ a terra/al suolo** fall down

abbatti'mento *nm* (morale) despondency

abbat'tuto *adj* despondent, down-in-the-mouth

abba'zia *nf* abbey

abbelli'mento *nm* embellishment

abbel'lire *vt* embellish

abbel'lirsi *vr* adorn oneself

abbeve'rare *vt* water

abbevera'toio *nm* drinking trough

abbiccì *nm inv* fig rudiments *pl*; **l'∼ di** the ABC of

abbi'ente *adj* well-to-do

abbi'etto *adj* despicable, abject

abbiglia'mento *nm* clothes *pl*; (industria) clothing industry, fam rag trade. **abbigliamento da bambino** children's wear. **abbigliamento da donna** ladies' wear. **abbigliamento per uomo** menswear. **abbigliamento sportivo** sportswear

abbigli'are *vt* dress

abbigli'arsi *vr* dress up

abbina'mento *nm* combining

abbi'nare *vt* combine; match ⟨*colori*⟩

abbindo'lare *vt* cheat

abbocca'mento *nm* interview; (conversazione) talk

abboc'care *vi* bite; ⟨*tubi*⟩ join; fig swallow the bait

abboc'cato *adj* ⟨*vino*⟩ fairly sweet

abbof'farsi = ABBUFFARSI

abbona'mento *nm* subscription; (ferroviario ecc) season-ticket; **fare l'∼** take out a subscription. **abbonamento all'autobus** bus pass. **abbonamento mensile** monthly ticket. **abbonamento alla televisione** television licence

abbo'nare *vt* make a subscriber

abbo'narsi *vr* subscribe (**a** to); take out a season-ticket (**a** for) ⟨*teatro, stadio*⟩

abbo'nato, -a *nmf* subscriber

abbon'dante *adj* abundant; ⟨*quantità*⟩ copious; ⟨*nevicata*⟩ heavy; ⟨*vestiario*⟩ roomy; **∼ di** abounding in

abbondante'mente *adv* ⟨*mangiare*⟩ copiously

abbon'danza *nf* abundance

abbon'dare *vi* abound

abbor'dabile *adj* ⟨*persona*⟩ approachable; ⟨*prezzo*⟩ reasonable

abbor'daggio *nm* Mil boarding

abbor'dare *vt* board ⟨*nave*⟩; approach ⟨*persona*⟩; (fam: attaccar bottone a) chat up; tackle ⟨*compito ecc*⟩

abbotto'nare *vt* button up

abbotto'nato *adj* fig tight-lipped

abbottona'tura *nf* [row of] buttons; **con ~ da donna/uomo** ⟨*giacca*⟩ that buttons on the left/right

abboz'zare ① *vt* sketch [out] ⟨*disegno*⟩; draft ⟨*documento*⟩; **~ un sorriso** give a little smile
② *vi* fam (rassegnarsi) resign oneself

ab'bozzo *nm* (di disegno) sketch; (di documento) draft

abbracci'are *vt* embrace; hug, embrace ⟨*persona*⟩; take up ⟨*professione*⟩; fig include

ab'braccio *nm* hug

abbrevi'are *vt* shorten; (ridurre) curtail; abbreviate ⟨*parola*⟩

abbreviazi'one *nf* abbreviation

abbron'zante *nm* suntan lotion

abbron'zare *vt* bronze; tan ⟨*pelle*⟩

abbron'zarsi *vr* get a tan

abbron'zato *adj* tanned

abbronza'tura *nf* [sun]tan

abbrusto'lire *vt* toast; roast ⟨*caffè ecc*⟩

abbruti'mento *nm* brutalization

abbru'tire *vt* brutalize; ⟨*lavoro*⟩ stultify

abbru'tirsi *vr* become brutalized

abbuf'farsi *vr* fam stuff oneself

abbuf'fata *nf* fam blowout

abbuo'nare *vt* reduce; fig overlook ⟨*mancanza, errore*⟩

abbu'ono *nm* allowance; Sport handicap

abdi'care *vi* abdicate

abdicazi'one *nf* abdication

aber'rante *adj* aberrant

aberrazi'one *nf* aberration

abe'taia *nf* wood of fir trees

a'bete *nm* fir

abi'etto *adj* despicable

abiezi'one *nf* degradation

abige'ato *nm* Jur cattle-stealing, rustling

'abile *adj* able; (idoneo) fit; (astuto) clever

abilità *nf inv* ability; (idoneità) fitness; (astuzia) cleverness

abili'tante *adj* **corso abilitante** [officially recognized] training course

abili'tare *vt* qualify

abili'tato *adj* qualified

abilitazi'one *nf* qualification; (titolo) diploma

abil'mente *adv* ably; (con astuzia) cleverly

abis'sale *adj* abysmal

a'bisso *nm* abyss

abi'tabile *adj* inhabitable

abitabilità *nf* fitness for human habitation; **licenza di ~** document certifying that a building is fit for human habitation

abi'tacolo *nm* Auto passenger compartment

abi'tante *nmf* inhabitant

abi'tare *vi* live

abi'tato ① *adj* inhabited
② *nm* built-up area

abitazi'one *nf* house; **crisi delle abitazioni** housing problem

abi'tino *nm* Relig scapular

'abito *nm* (da donna) dress; (da uomo) suit; **abiti** *pl* clothes. **abito da ballo** ball dress. **abito da cerimonia** formal dress. **abito da cocktail** cocktail dress. **abito mentale** mentality. **'abito scuro'** (su inviti) 'black tie'. **abito da sera** evening dress. **abito talare** cassock. **abito da uomo** suit

abitu'ale *adj* usual, habitual

abitual'mente *adv* usually

abitu'are *vt* accustom

abitu'arsi *vr* **~ a** get used to

abitu'ato *adj* **~ a** used to

abitudi'nario, -a ① *adj* of fixed habits
② *nmf* person of fixed habits

abi'tudine *nf* habit; **d'~** usually; **per ~** out of habit; **avere l'~ di fare qualcosa** be in the habit of doing something; **abitudini** *pl* customs

abiu'rare *vt* renounce

abla'tivo *nm* ablative

abluzi'oni *nfpl* **fare le ~** wash

abnegazi'one *nf* self-sacrifice

ab'norme *adj* abnormal

abo'lire *vt* abolish; repeal ⟨*legge*⟩

abolizi'one *nf* abolition; (di legge) repeal

abolizio'nismo *nm* abolitionism

abolizio'nista *adj & nmf* abolitionist

abomi'nevole *adj* abominable

abo'rigeno, -a *adj & nmf* aboriginal

abor'rire *vt* abhor

abor'tire *vi* miscarry; (volontariamente) have an abortion; fig fail

abor'tista *adj* pro-choice

abor'tivo *adj* abortive

a'borto *nm* miscarriage; (volontario) abortion

abrasi'one *nf* abrasion

abra'sivo *adj & nm* abrasive

abro'gare *vt* repeal

abroga'tivo *adj* **referendum**
 abrogativo referendum to repeal a law

abrogazi'one *nf* repeal

abruz'zese ① *adj* Abruzzi *attrib*
 ② *nmf* person from the Abruzzi
 ③ *nm* Abruzzi dialect

'abside *nf* apse

abu'lia *nf* apathy

a'bulico *adj* apathetic

abu'sare *vi* ∼ **di** abuse; over-indulge in
 ⟨*alcol*⟩; (approfittare di) take advantage of;
 (violentare) rape

abusi'vismo *nm* large-scale abuse.
 abusivismo edilizio building without
 planning permission

abu'sivo *adj* illegal

a'buso *nm* abuse; 'ogni ∼ sarà punito'
 'penalty for misuse'. **abuso di
 confidenza** breach of confidence. **abusi**
 pl **sessuali** sexual abuse

a.C. *abbr* (**avanti Cristo**) BC

a'cacia *nf* acacia

'acaro *nm* Zool mite

'acca *nf* fam **non ho capito un'**∼ I
 understood damn all

acca'demia *nf* academy. **Accademia
 di Belle Arti** Academy of Fine Arts.
 accademia militare military academy

acca'demico, -a ① *adj* academic
 ② *nmf* academician

acca'dere *vi* happen; **accada quel che
 accada** come what may

acca'duto *nm* event

accalappia'cani *nm inv* dog-catcher

accalappi'are *vt* catch; fig allure

accal'care *vt* cram together

accal'carsi *vr* crowd

accal'darsi *vr* get overheated; (per fatica)
 get hot; fig get excited

accal'dato *adj* overheated; (per fatica)
 hot; fig excited

accalo'rarsi *vr* get excited

accampa'mento *nm* camp

accam'pare *vt* fig put forth

accam'parsi *vr* camp

accani'mento *nm* tenacity; (odio) rage

acca'nirsi *vr* persist; (infierire) rage

accanita'mente *adv* ⟨*odiare*⟩ fiercely;
 ⟨*insistere*⟩ persistently; ⟨*lavorare*⟩
 assiduously

acca'nito *adj* persistent; ⟨*odio*⟩ fierce;
 ⟨*fumatore*⟩ inveterate; ⟨*lavoratore*⟩
 assiduous

ac'canto *adv* near; ∼ **a** *prep* next to; **la
 ragazza della porta** ∼ the girl next door

accanto'nare *vt* set aside; Mil billet

accaparra'mento *nm* hoarding; Comm
 cornering

accapar'rare *vt* hoard

accapar'rarsi *vr* grab; corner
 ⟨*mercato*⟩

accaparra|'tore, -trice *nmf* hoarder

accapigli'arsi *vr* scuffle; (litigare)
 squabble

accappa'toio *nm* bathrobe; (per spiaggia)
 beachrobe

accappo'nare *vt* fare ∼ **la pelle a
 qualcuno** make somebody's flesh creep

accarez'zare *vt* caress, stroke; fig
 cherish

accartocci'are *vt* scrunch up

accartocci'arsi *vr* curl up

acca'sarsi *vr* get married

accasci'arsi *vr* flop down; fig lose heart

accata'stare *vt* pile up

accatti'vante *adj* beguiling

accatti'varsi *vr* ∼ **le simpatie/la
 stima/l'affetto di qualcuno** gain
 somebody's sympathy/respect/affection

accatto'naggio *nm* begging

accat'tone, -a *nmf* beggar

accaval'lare *vt* cross ⟨*gambe*⟩

accaval'larsi *vr* pile up; fig overlap

acce'cante *adj* ⟨*luce*⟩ blinding

acce'care ① *vt* blind
 ② *vi* go blind

ac'cedere *vi* access; ∼ **a** enter;
 (acconsentire) comply with; Comput access

accele'rare ① *vi* accelerate
 ② *vt* speed up, accelerate; ∼ **il passo**
 quicken one's pace

accele'rata *nf* sudden acceleration

accele'rato *adj* rapid

accelera'tore *nm* accelerator.
 acceleratore grafico Comput graphics
 accelerator

accelerazi'one *nf* acceleration

ac'cendere *vt* light; turn on, switch on
 ⟨*luce, TV ecc*⟩; fig inflame; **ha da** ∼? have
 you got a light?

ac'cendersi *vr* catch fire; (illuminarsi)
 light up; fig become inflamed; ⟨*TV,
 computer*⟩ turn on, switch on

accendi'gas *nm inv* gas lighter; (su
 cucina) automatic ignition

accen'dino *nm* lighter

accendi'sigari *nm inv* cigar-lighter

accen'nare ① *vt* indicate; hum
 ⟨*melodia*⟩; give a hint of ⟨*sorriso*⟩
 ② *vi* ∼ **a** beckon to; fig hint at; (far l'atto di)
 make as if to; **accenna a piovere** it looks
 like rain

ac'cenno *nm* gesture; (con il capo) nod; fig
 hint

accensi'one *nf* lighting; (di motore)
 ignition

accen'tare *vt* accent; (con accento tonico)
 stress

accentazi'one *nf* accentuation

ac'cento *nm* accent; (tonico) stress. **accento acuto** acute [accent]. **accento circonflesso** circumflex [accent]. **accento grave** grave [accent]

accentra'mento *nm* centralizing

accen'trare *vt* centralize

accentra'tore *adj* ‹persona› who refuses to delegate; ‹politica› of centralization

accentu'are *vt* accentuate

accentu'arsi *vr* become more noticeable

accentu'ato *adj* marked

accerchia'mento *nm* surrounding

accerchi'are *vt* surround

accerchi'ato *adj* surrounded

accer'tabile *adj* ascertainable

accerta'mento *nm* check; **accertamenti** *pl* [medici] tests

accer'tare *vt* ascertain; (controllare) check; assess ‹reddito›

ac'ceso *adj* lighted; ‹radio, TV ecc› on; ‹colore› bright

acces'sibile *adj* accessible; ‹persona› approachable; ‹spesa› reasonable

ac'cesso *nm* access; (Med: di rabbia) fit; 'vietato l'∼' 'no entry'; '∼ riservato a ...' 'access restricted to ...'. **accesso diretto** Comput direct access. **accesso disabili** wheelchair access. **accesso a Internet** Comput Internet access. **accesso multiplo** Comput multi-access. **accesso remoto** Comput remote access

accessori'ato *adj* accessorized

acces'sorio ①*adj* accessory; (secondario) of secondary importance ②*nm* accessory; ‹accessori *pl* (rifiniture) fittings. **accessori** *pl* **per il bagno** bathroom fittings. **accessori** *pl* **moda** fashion accessories

ac'cetta *nf* hatchet

accet'tabile *adj* acceptable

accet'tare *vt* accept; (aderire a) agree to

accettazi'one *nf* acceptance; (luogo) reception; [banco] accettazione check-in [desk]; accettazione [bagagli] check-in

ac'cetto *adj* agreeable; **essere bene ∼** be very welcome

accezi'one *nf* meaning

acchiap'pare *vt* catch

+acchiotto *suff* lupacchiotto *nm* wolf cub; (affettuoso) baby wolf; **orsacchiotto** *nm* teddy bear; **fessacchiotto** *nm* nitwit

ac'chito *nm* **di primo ∼** at first

acciac'care *vt* crush; fig prostrate

acciac'cato, -a *adj* **essere ∼** ache all over

acci'acco *nm* infirmity; **acciacchi** (*pl:* afflizioni) aches and pains

acciaie'ria *nf* steelworks

acci'aio *nm* steel. **acciaio inossidabile** stainless steel

acciambel'larsi *vr* curl up

acciden'tale *adj* accidental

accidental'mente *adv* accidentally

acciden'tato *adj* ‹terreno› uneven

acci'dente *nm* accident; Med stroke; **non capisce/non vede un ∼** fam he doesn't understand/can't see a damn thing; **mandare un ∼ a qualcuno** fam tell somebody to go to hell

acci'denti *int* fam damn!; **∼ a te!** damn you!, blast you!

ac'cidia *nf* sloth

accigli'arsi *vr* frown

accigli'ato *adj* frowning

ac'cingersi *vr* **∼ a** be about to

+accio *suff* **erbaccia** *nf* weed; **donnaccia** *nf* tart; **faticaccia** *nf* hard slog; **lavoraccio** *nm* (lavoro faticoso) helluva job fam; (lavoro malfatto) botched job; **fattaccio** *nm* hum foul deed; **parolaccia** *nf* swear word; **avaraccio** *nm* skinflint

acciotto'lato *nm* cobbled paving, cobblestones *pl*

acci'picchia *int* good Lord!

acciuf'fare *vt* catch

acci'uga *nf* anchovy

accla'mare *vt* applaud; (eleggere) acclaim

acclamazi'one *nf* applause

acclima'tare *vt* acclimatize

acclima'tarsi *vr* get acclimatized

acclimatazi'one *nf* acclimatization

ac'cludere *vt* enclose

ac'cluso *adj* enclosed

accocco'larsi *vr* squat

acco'darsi *vr* tag along

accogli'ente *adj* welcoming; (confortevole) cosy

accogli'enza *nf* welcome

ac'cogliere *vt* receive; (con piacere) welcome; (contenere) hold

accol'lare *vt* **∼ qualcosa a qualcuno** fig saddle somebody with something

accol'larsi *vr* take on ‹responsabilità, debiti, doveri›

accol'lato *adj* ‹maglia› high-necked

accoltel'lare *vt* knife

accoman'dante *nmf* Jur sleeping partner

accomanda'tario, -a *nmf* Jur general partner

accoman'dita *nf* Jur limited partnership. **accomandita per azioni** limited partnership based on shares

accomia'tare *vt* dismiss

accomia'tarsi *vr* take one's leave (**da of**)

accomoda'mento *nm* arrangement

accomo'dante *adj* accommodating

accomo'dare *vt* (*riparare*) mend; (*disporre*) arrange

accomo'darsi *vr* make oneself at home; **si accomodi!** come in!; (*si sieda*) take a seat!

accompagna'mento *nm* accompaniment; (*seguito*) retinue

accompa'gnare *vt* accompany; ∼ **qualcuno a casa** see somebody home; ∼ **qualcuno alla porta** show somebody to the door; ∼ **qualcuno con lo sguardo** follow somebody with one's eyes

accompa'gnarsi *vr* ⟨*cibi, colori ecc*⟩ go [well] together; ∼ **con** *o* **a qualcuno** accompany somebody

accompagna|'tore, -trice *nmf* companion; (*di comitiva*) escort; Mus accompanist. ∼ **turistico** tour guide

accomu'nare *vt* pool

acconci'are *vt* arrange

acconci'arsi *vr* do one's hair

acconcia'tura *nf* hairstyle; (*ornamento*) headdress; '**acconciature**' 'ladies' hairdresser'

accondiscen'dente *adj* too obliging

accondiscen'denza *nf* excessive desire to please

accondi'scendere *vi* ∼ **a** condescend to; comply with ⟨*desiderio*⟩; (*acconsentire*) consent to

acconsen'tire *vi* consent

acconten'tare *vt* satisfy

acconten'tarsi *vr* be content (**di** with)

ac'conto *nm* deposit; **in** ∼ on account; **lasciare un** ∼ leave a deposit. **acconto di dividendo** interim dividend

accop'pare *vt* fam bump off

accoppia'mento *nm* coupling; (*di animali*) mating

accoppi'are *vt* couple; mate ⟨*animali*⟩

accoppi'arsi *vr* pair off; ⟨*animali*⟩ mate

accoppi'ata *nf* (*scommessa*) bet placed on two horses for first and second place; **sono una strana** ∼ they make strange bedfellows; **accoppiata vincente** fig winning combination

accoppia'tore *nm* **accoppiatore acustico** Comput acoustic coupler

acco'rato *adj* sorrowful

accorci'are *vt* shorten

accorci'arsi *vr* get shorter

accor'dare *vt* concede; match ⟨*colori ecc*⟩; Mus tune

accor'darsi *vr* agree

accorda|'tore, -trice *nmf* Mus tuner

ac'cordo *nm* agreement; Mus chord; (*armonia*) harmony; **andare d'**∼ get on well; **d'**∼**!** agreed!; **essere d'**∼ agree; **in** ∼ **con** in collusion with; **prendere accordi con qualcuno** make arrangements with somebody. **accordo collettivo** joint agreement

ac'corgersi *vr* ∼ **di** notice; (*capire*) realize

accorgi'mento *nm* shrewdness; (*espediente*) device

accorpa'mento *nm* amalgamation

accor'pare *vt* amalgamate

ac'correre *vi* hasten

accorta'mente *adv* astutely

accor'tezza *nf* (*previdenza*) forethought

ac'corto *adj* shrewd; **mal** ∼ incautious

accosta'mento *nm* (*di colori*) combination

acco'stare *vt* draw close to; approach ⟨*persona*⟩; put ajar ⟨*porta ecc*⟩

acco'starsi *vr* ∼ **a** come near to

accovacci'arsi *vr* crouch, squat down

accovacci'ato *adj* squatting

accoz'zaglia *nf* jumble; (*di persone*) mob

accoz'zare *vt* ∼ **colori** mix colours that clash

accredi'tabile *adj* reliable

accredita'mento *nm* credit. **accreditamento tramite bancogiro** Bank Giro Credit

accredi'tare *vt* confirm ⟨*notizia*⟩; Comm credit

accredi'tato *adj* accredited; ⟨*notizia*⟩ reliable

ac'crescere *vt* increase

ac'crescersi *vr* grow larger

accresci'mento *nm* increase

accresci'tivo *adj* augmentative

accucci'arsi *vr* ⟨*cane*⟩ lie down; ⟨*persona*⟩ crouch

accu'dire *vi* ∼ **a** attend to

accumu'lare *vt* accumulate

accumu'larsi *vr* pile up, accumulate

accumula'tore *nm* accumulator; Auto, Comput battery

accumulazi'one *nf* accumulation

ac'cumulo *nm* (*di merce*) build-up

accurata'mente *adv* carefully

accura'tezza *nf* care

accu'rato *adj* careful

ac'cusa *nf* accusation; Jur charge; **essere in stato di** ∼ Jur have been charged; **mettere qualcuno sotto** ∼ Jur charge somebody; **la Pubblica Accusa** Jur the public prosecutor

accu'sare *vt* accuse; Jur charge; complain of ⟨*dolore*⟩; ∼ **ricevuta di** Comm acknowledge receipt of

accusa'tivo *nm* Gram accusative

accu'sato, -a *nmf* accused

accusa'tore ① *adj* accusing ② *nm* Jur prosecutor

a'cerbo *adj* sharp; (non maturo) unripe

'acero *nm* maple

a'cerrimo *adj* implacable

ace'tato *nm* acetate

a'ceto *nm* vinegar. **aceto di vino** wine vinegar

ace'tone *nm* nail polish remover

ace'tosa *nf* Culin [edible] sorrel

aceto'sella *nf* Bot sorrel

A.C.I. *nf abbr* (**Automobile Club d'Italia**) Italian Automobile Association, ≈ AAA Am, ≈ RAC Br

acidità *nf* acidity. **acidità di stomaco** acid stomach

'acido ① *adj* acid; ⟨persona⟩ sour ② *nm* acid. ~ **cloridrico** hydrochloric acid

a'cidulo *adj* slightly sour

'acino *nm* berry; (chicco) grape

'acme *nf* acme

'acne *nf* acne

'acqua *nf* water; fare ~ Naut leak; ~ in bocca! fig mum's the word!; avere l'~ alla gola, essere con l'~ alla gola fig be pushed for time; ho fatto un buco nell'~ fig I had no luck whatsoever; in cattive acque in deep water; navigare in cattive acque be in financial difficulties. **acqua calda** hot water. **acqua di Colonia** eau de Cologne. **acqua corrente** running water. **acqua dolce** fresh water. **acqua minerale** mineral water. **acqua minerale gassata** fizzy mineral water. **acqua naturale** still mineral water. **acqua potabile** drinking water. **acqua del rubinetto** tap water. **acqua salata** salt water. **acqua saponata** suds. **acqua tonica** tonic water

acqua'forte *nf* etching

acqua'gym *nf* aquarobics

ac'quaio *nm* sink

acquama'rina *adj* aquamarine

acqua'plano *nm* hydroplane

acqua'ragia *nf* white spirit

acqua'rello *nm* watercolour

a'cquario *nm* aquarium, fish tank; Astr Aquarius

acquartie'rare *vt* Mil billet

acqua'santa *nf* holy water

acquasanti'era *nf* font

acqua'scivolo *nm* water slide

acqua'scooter *nm inv* water-scooter

a'cquata *nf* fam downpour

a'cquatico *adj* aquatic; **sport acquatico** water sport

acquat'tarsi *vr* crouch

acqua'vite *nf* brandy

acquaz'zone *nm* downpour

acque'dotto *nm* aqueduct

'acqueo *adj* **vapore** ~ steam, water vapour

acque'rello *nm* watercolour

acquicol'tura *nf* aquaculture

acquie'scente *adj* acquiescent

acquie'tare *vt* appease; calm ⟨dolore⟩

acquie'tarsi *vr* calm down

acqui'rente *nmf* purchaser

acqui'sire *vt* acquire

acqui'sito *adj* acquired

acquisizi'one *nf* attainment

acqui'stare *vt* purchase; (ottenere) acquire; ~ in ⟨prestigio, bellezza⟩ gain in

a'cquisto *nm* purchase; **uscire per acquisti** go shopping; **fare acquisti** shop; **ufficio acquisti** purchasing department. **acquisto rateale** hire purchase, HP, installment plan Am; **acquisto d'impulso** impulse buy. **acquisto a termine** Fin forward buying

acqui'trino *nm* marsh

acquo'lina *nf* far venire l'~ in bocca a qualcuno make somebody's mouth water; ho l'~ in bocca my mouth is watering

a'cquoso *adj* watery

'acre *adj* acrid; (al gusto) sour; fig harsh

a'credine *nf* acridness; (al gusto) sourness; fig harshness

acre'mente *adv* acridly

a'crilico *nm* acrylic

a'critico *adj* acritical

a'crobata *nmf* acrobat

acro'batico *adj* acrobatic

acroba'zia *nf* acrobatics *pl*

acroba'zie *nfpl* acrobatics; **fare** ~ fig do acrobatics

a'cronimo *nm* acronym

a'cropoli *nf* acropolis

acu'ire *vt* sharpen

acu'irsi *vr* become more intense

a'culeo *nm* sting; Bot prickle

a'cume *nm* acumen

acumi'nato *adj* pointed

a'custica *nf* acoustics *pl*

acustica'mente *adv* acoustically

a'custico *adj* acoustic

acuta'mente *adv* shrewdly

acu'tezza *nf* acuteness; fig shrewdness; (di suoni) shrillness

acutiz'zare *vt* aggravate (dolore)

acutiz'zarsi *vr* become worse

a'cuto ① *adj* sharp; ⟨suono⟩ shrill; ⟨freddo, odore⟩ intense; Gram, Math, Med acute ② *nm* Mus high note

ad (*before vowel*) *prep* = A

A.D. *abbr* Pol (**Alleanza Democratica**) Democratic Alliance

adagi'are *vt* lay down

adagi'arsi *vr* lie down

a'dagio ① *adv* slowly
② *nm* Mus adagio; (proverbio) adage

ada'mitico *adj* in costume ~ in one's birthday suit, stark naked

adat'tabile *adj* adaptable

adattabilità *nf* adaptability

adatta'mento *nm* adaptation; **avere spirito di ~** be adaptable. **adattamento cinematografico** film adaptation, adaptation for the cinema

adat'tare *vt* adapt; (aggiustare) fit

adat'tarsi *vr* adapt

adatta'tore *nm* adaptor

a'datto *adj* suitable (**a** for): (giusto) right

addì *adv* ~ **15 settembre 1995** on 15th September 1995

addebita'mento *nm* debit. **addebitamento diretto** direct debit

addebi'tare *vt* debit; fig ascribe ⟨colpa⟩

ad'debito *nm* charge

addensa'mento *nm* thickening; (di persone) gathering

adden'sare *vt* thicken

adden'sarsi *vr* thicken; (affollarsi) gather

adden'tare *vt* bite

adden'trarsi *vr* penetrate

ad'dentro *adv* deeply; **essere ~ in** be in on

addestra'mento *nm* training. **addestramento iniziale** basic training

adde'strare *vt* train

adde'strarsi *vr* train

addestra|'tore, -trice *nmf* trainer

ad'detto, -a ① *adj* assigned
② *nmf* employee; (diplomatico) attaché. **adetti** *pl* **ai lavori** persons involved in the work; **'vietato l'ingresso ai non addetti ai lavori** 'staff only'. **addetto commerciale** salesman. **addetto culturale** cultural attaché. **addetto stampa** information officer, press officer. **addetto ai traslochi** removal man

addi'accio *nm* **dormire all'~** sleep in the open

addi'etro *adv* (indietro) back; (nel passato) before

ad'dio *nm* & *int* goodbye. **addio al celibato** stag night, stag party. **addio al nubilato** hen night. **cena d'addio** farewell dinner

addirit'tura *adv* (perfino) even; (assolutamente) absolutely; ~! really!

ad'dirsi *vr* ~ **a** suit

addi'tare *vt* point at; (per identificare) point out; fig point to

addi'tivo *adj & nm* additive

addizio'nale ① *adj* additional
② *nf* (imposta) surtax

addizional'mente *adv* additionally

addizio'nare *vt* add [up]

addiziona'trice *nf* adding machine

addizi'one *nf* addition

addob'bare *vt* decorate

ad'dobbo *nm* decoration

addol'cire *vt* sweeten; tone down ⟨colore⟩; fig soften

addol'cirsi *vr* fig mellow

addolo'rare *vt* grieve

addolo'rarsi *vr* be upset (**per** by)

addolo'rato *adj* pained, distressed

ad'dome *nm* abdomen

addomesti'care *vt* tame

addomestica|'tore, -trice *nmf* tamer

addomi'nale ① *adj* abdominal
② *nmpl* **addominali** abdominals

addormen'tare *vt* put to sleep

addormen'tarsi *vr* go to sleep

addormen'tato *adj* asleep; fig slow

addos'sare *vt* ~ **a** (appoggiare) lean against; (attribuire) lay on

addos'sarsi *vr* (ammassarsi) crowd; shoulder ⟨responsabilità ecc⟩

ad'dosso *adv* on; ~ **a** *prep* on; (molto vicino) right next to; **andare/venire ~ a qualcuno** run into somebody; **mettere gli occhi ~ a qualcuno/qualcosa** hanker after somebody/something; **non mettermi le mani ~!** keep your hands off me!; **stare ~ a qualcuno** fig be on somebody's back; **farsela ~** (fam: bisogni corporali) dirty oneself; (pipì) wet oneself

ad'durre *vt* produce ⟨prova, documento⟩; give ⟨pretesto, esempio⟩

adegua'mento *nm* adjustment

adegu'are *vt* adjust

adegu'arsi *vr* conform

adeguata'mente *adv* suitably

adegua'tezza *nf* suitability

adegu'ato *adj* suitable; ~ **a** suited to, suitable for

a'dempiere *vt* fulfil

adempi'mento *nm* fulfilment

adem'pire *vt* fulfil

ade'noidi *nfpl* adenoids

a'depto, -a *nmf* adherent

ade'rente ① *adj* adhesive; ⟨vestito⟩ tight
② *nmf* follower

ade'renza *nf* adhesion; **aderenze** *pl* connections

ade'rire *vi* ~ **a** stick to, adhere to; support ⟨sciopero, petizione⟩; agree to ⟨richiesta⟩

adesca'mento *nm* Jur soliciting

ade'scare *vt* bait; fig entice

adesca'trice *nf* fille de joie

adesi'one *nf* adhesion; fig agreement

ade'sivo ⏹ *adj* adhesive
⏹ *nm* sticker; Auto bumper sticker

a'desso *adv* now; (poco fa) just now; (tra poco) any moment now; **da** ∼ **in poi** from now on; **per** ∼ for the moment; **fino** ∼ up till now

adia'cente *adj* adjacent; ∼ **a** next to

adia'cenze *nfpl* adjacent areas

adi'bire *vt* ∼ **a** put to use as

'adipe *nm* adipose tissue

adi'poso *adj* adipose

adi'rarsi *vr* get irate

adi'rato *adj* irate

a'dire *vt* resort to; ∼ **le vie legali** take legal proceedings; ∼ **la successione** Jur take possession of an inheritance

'adito *nm* **dare** ∼ **a** give rise to

ADM *nfpl abbr* (**Armi di Distruzione di Massa**) WMD

adocchi'are *vt* eye; (con desiderio) covet

adole'scente *adj & nmf* adolescent *attrib*

adole'scenza *nf* adolescence

adolescenzi'ale *adj* adolescent

adombra'mento *nm* darkening

adom'brare *vt* darken; fig veil

adom'brarsi *vr* (offendersi) take offence

adope'rare *vt* use

adope'rarsi *vr* take trouble

ado'rabile *adj* adorable

ado'rare *vt* adore

adorazi'one *nf* adoration; **in** ∼ adoring

ador'nare *vt* adorn

a'dorno *adj* adorned (**di** with)

adot'tare *vt* adopt

adot'tivo *adj* adoptive

adozi'one *nf* adoption

adrena'lina *nf* adrenalin

adri'atico ⏹ *adj* Adriatic
⏹ *nm* **l'Adriatico** the Adriatic

adu'lare *vt* flatter

adula|'tore, -trice *nmf* flatterer

adula'torio *adj* sycophantic

adulazi'one *nf* flattery

a'dultera *nf* adulteress

adulte'rare *vt* adulterate

adulte'rato *adj* adulterated

adulte'rino *adj* adulterous

adul'terio *nm* adultery

a'dultero ⏹ *adj* adulterous
⏹ *nm* adulterer

a'dulto, -a *adj & nmf* adult; (maturo) mature

adu'nanza *nf* assembly

adu'nare *vt* gather

adu'nata *nf* Mil parade

a'dunco *adj* hooked

adunghi'are *vt* claw

ae'rare *vt* air ⟨*stanza*⟩

aera'tore *nm* ventilator

aerazi'one *nf* ventilation

a'ereo ⏹ *adj* aerial; (dell'aviazione) air *attrib*
⏹ *nm* aeroplane, plane; **andare in** ∼ fly. **aereo da carico** cargo plane. **aereo da guerra** warplane. **aereo di linea** airliner. **aereo navetta** shuttle. **aereo a reazione** jet [plane]

ae'robica *nf* aerobics

ae'robico *adj* aerobic

aerodi'namica *nf* aerodynamics *sg*

aerodi'namico *adj* aerodynamic

aero'grafo *nm* airbrush

aero'gramma *nm* aerogram[me]

aero'linea *nf* airline

aero'mobile *nm* aircraft

aeromo'dello *nm* model aircraft

aero'nautica *nf* aeronautics; Mil Air Force

aero'nautico *adj* aeronautical

aerona'vale *adj* air and sea *attrib*

aero'plano *nm* aeroplane

aero'porto *nm* airport

aeroportu'ale *adj* airport *attrib*

aero'scalo *nm* cargo and servicing area

aero'sol *nm inv* aerosol. **apparecchio per aerosol** vaporizer

aerospazi'ale *adj* aerospace *attrib*

aero'statico *adj* **pallone aerostatico** aerostat

ae'rostato *nm* aerostat

aerostazi'one *nf* air terminal

aerosti'ere *nm* balloonist

aero'via *nf* air corridor

A.F. *abbr* (**alta frequenza**) HF

'afa *nf* sultriness

af'fabile *adj* affable

affabilità *nf* affability

affaccen'darsi *vr* busy oneself (**a** with)

affacci'arsi *vr* show oneself; ∼ **alla finestra** appear at the window

affacen'dato *adj* busy

affa'mare *vt* starve [out]

affa'mato *adj* starving

affan'nare *vt* leave breathless

affan'narsi *vr* busy oneself; (agitarsi) get worked up

affan'nato *adj* breathless; **dal respiro** ∼ wheezy

af'fanno *nm* breathlessness; fig worry; **essere in** ∼ **per** be anxious about

affannosa'mente *adv* breathlessly

affan'noso *adj* exhausting; **respiro ~** heavy breathing

af'fare *nm* matter; (occasione) bargain; Comm transaction, deal; **pensa agli affari tuoi** mind your own business; **non sono affari tuoi** fam it's none of your business; **fare affari d'oro** have a field day; **affari** *pl* business; **d'affari** ⟨uomo, cena, viaggio⟩ business; **affari** *pl* **esteri** foreign affairs; **ministro degli affari esteri** Foreign Secretary Br, Secretary of State Am

affa'rismo *nm* pej wheeling and dealing

affa'rista *nmf* wheeler-dealer

affasci'nante *adj* fascinating; ⟨persona, sorriso⟩ bewitching

affasci'nare *vt* bewitch; fig charm

affastel'lare *vt* tie up in bundles

affatica'mento *nm* fatigue

affati'care *vt* tire; (sfinire) exhaust

affati'carsi *vr* tire oneself out; (affannarsi) strive

affati'cato *adj* fatigued, suffering from fatigue; **~ dal troppo lavoro** overworked

af'fatto *adv* completely; **non ... ~** not ... at all; **niente ~!** not at all!

affer'mare *vt* affirm; (sostenere) assert

affer'marsi *vr* establish oneself

affermativa'mente *adv* in the affirmative

afferma'tivo *adj* affirmative

affer'mato *adj* established

affermazi'one *nf* assertion; (successo) achievement

affer'rare *vt* seize; catch ⟨oggetto⟩; (capire) grasp; **~ al volo** fig be quick on the uptake

affer'rarsi *vr* **~ a** grasp at, clutch at

affet'tare *vt* slice; (ostentare) affect

affet'tato ① *adj* sliced; ⟨sorriso, maniere⟩ affected ② *nm* cold meat, sliced meat

affetta'trice *nf* bacon-slicer

affettazi'one *nf* affectation

affet'tivo *adj* affective; **rapporto affettivo** emotional tie

af'fetto[1] *nm* affection; **con ~** affectionately; **gli affetti familiari** family ties

af'fetto[2] *adj* **~ da** suffering from

affettuosa'mente *adv* affectionately

affettuosi'tà *nf inv* (gesto) affectionate gesture

affettu'oso *adj* affectionate

affezio'narsi *vr* **~ a** grow fond of

affezio'nato *adj* devoted, attached (**a** to)

affezi'one *nf* affection; Med ailment

affian'care *vt* put side by side; Mil flank; fig support

affian'carsi *vr* come side by side; fig stand together, stand shoulder to shoulder; **~ a qualcuno** fig help somebody out

affiata'mento *nm* harmony

affia'tarsi *vr* get on well together

affia'tato *adj* close-knit; **una coppia affiatata** a very close couple

affibbi'are *vt* **~ qualcosa a qualcuno** saddle somebody with something; **~ un pugno a qualcuno** let fly at somebody

affi'dabile *adj* reliable, dependable

affidabilità *nf* reliability, dependability

affida'mento *nm* (Jur: dei minori) custody; **fare ~ su qualcuno** rely on somebody; **non dare ~ (a qualcuno)** not inspire confidence (in somebody)

affi'dare *vt* entrust

affi'darsi *vr* **~ a** rely on

affida'tario *adj* (famiglia) foster

af'fido *nm* **un bambino in ~** a foster child

affievoli'mento *nm* weakening

affievo'lirsi *vr* grow weak

af'figgere *vt* affix

affilacol'telli *nm inv* knife sharpener

affi'lare *vt* sharpen

affili'are *vt* affiliate

affili'arsi *vt* become affiliated

affiliazi'one *nf* affiliation

affi'nare *vt* sharpen; (perfezionare) refine

affinché *conj* so that, in order that

af'fine *adj* similar

affinità *nf inv* affinity

affiora'mento *nm* emergence; Naut surfacing

affio'rare *vi* emerge; fig come to light

affissi'one *nf* bill-posting; **'divieto di ~'** 'stick no bills'

af'fisso *nm* bill; Gram affix

affitta'camere ① *nm inv* landlord ② *nf inv* landlady

affit'tare *vt* (dare in affitto) let; (prendere in affitto) rent. **affittasi** to let, for rent

af'fitto *nm* rent; **contratto d'~** lease; **dare in ~** let; **prendere in ~** rent

affittu'ario, -a *nmf* Jur lessee

af'fliggere *vt* torment

af'fliggersi *vr* distress oneself

af'flitto *adj* distressed

afflizi'one *nf* distress; fig affliction

afflosci'are *vt* **la pioggia ha afflosciato le foglie** the rain has made the leaves go all limp

afflosci'arsi *vr* become floppy; (accasciarsi) flop down

afflu'ente *adj & nm* tributary

afflu'enza *nf* flow; (di gente) crowd

afflu'ire *vi* flow; fig pour in

af'flusso *nm* influx

affoga'mento *nm* drowning

affo'gare *vt/i* drown; Culin poach; ~ **in** fig be swamped with

affo'garsi *vr* (suicidarsi) drown oneself

affo'gato ① *adj* ⟨persona⟩ drowned; ⟨uova⟩ poached ② *nm* **affogato al caffè** ice cream with hot espresso poured over it

affolla'mento *nm* crowd

affol'lare *vt* crowd

affol'larsi *vr* crowd

affol'lato *adj* crowded

affonda'mento *nm* sinking

affon'dare *vt/i* sink

affon'darsi *vr* sink

affossa'mento *nm* (avvallamento) pothole; fig burial

affran'care *vt* redeem ⟨bene⟩; stamp ⟨lettera⟩; free ⟨schiavo⟩

affran'carsi *vr* free oneself

affran'cato *adj* ⟨lettera⟩ stamped; ⟨schiavo⟩ freed; **già ~** ⟨busta⟩ prepaid

affranca'trice *nf* franking machine, franker

affranca'tura *nf* stamping; (di spedizione) postage. **affrancatura a carico del destinatario** freepost. **affrancatura per l'estero** postage abroad

af'franto *adj* prostrate with grief, grief-stricken; (esausto) worn out

affre'scare *vt* paint a fresco on

af'fresco *nm* fresco

affret'tare *vt* speed up

affret'tarsi *vr* hurry

affrettata'mente *adv* hastily

affret'tato *adj* ⟨passo⟩ fast; ⟨decisione⟩ hasty; ⟨lavoro⟩ rushed

affron'tare *vt* face; confront ⟨nemico⟩; meet ⟨spese⟩

affron'tarsi *vr* clash

af'fronto *nm* affront, insult; **fare un ~ a qualcuno** insult somebody

affumi'care *vt* fill with smoke; Culin smoke

affumi'cato *adj* ⟨prosciutto, formaggio⟩ smoked; ⟨lenti, vetro⟩ tinted

affuso'lare *vt* taper [off]

affuso'lato *adj* tapering

Af'ganistan *nm* Afghanistan

af'gano *adj & nmf* Afghani, Afghan

AFI *nm abbr* (**Alfabeto Fonetico Internazionale**) IPA

aficio'nado, -a *nmf* aficionado

'afide *nm* aphid

'afono *adj* (rauco) hoarse

afo'risma *nm* aphorism

a'foso *adj* sultry

'Africa *nf* Africa. **Africa orientale** East Africa. **Africa nera** Black Africa. **Africa del Nord** North Africa

afri'cano, -a *adj & nmf* African

afri'kaans *nm* Afrikaans

afroameri'cano, -a *adj & nmf* Afro-American

afroasi'atico *adj* Afro-Asian

afroca'ribico *adj* Afro-Caribbean

afrocu'bano *adj* Afro-Cuban

afrodi'siaco *adj & nm* aphrodisiac

a'genda *nf* diary. **agenda elettronica** personal organizer, electronic organizer; **agenda da tavolo** desk diary

agen'dina *nf* pocket-diary

a'gente *nm* agent; **agenti** *pl* atmosferici atmospheric agents. **agente di cambio** stockbroker. **agente di custodia** prison warder. **agente del fisco** assessor. **agente immobiliare** estate agent, realtor Am. **agente marittimo** shipping agent. **agente di polizia** police officer. **agente segreto** secret agent. **agente teatrale** theatrical agent; (di compagnia) impresario. **agente di viaggio** travel agent

agen'zia *nf* agency; (filiale) branch office; (di banca) branch. **agenzia di collocamento** employment exchange. **agenzia immobiliare** estate agency, realtor Am. **agenzia matrimoniale** dating agency. **agenzia pubblicitaria** advertising agency. **agenzia di recupero crediti** debt collection agency. **agenzia di stampa** news agency, press agency. **agenzia di viaggi** travel agency

agevo'lare *vt* facilitate

agevolazi'one *nf* facilitation. **agevolazioni** *pl* **fiscali** tax breaks

a'gevole *adj* easy; ⟨strada⟩ smooth

agevol'mente *adv* easily

aggan'ciare *vt* hook up; Rail couple

aggan'ciarsi *vr* ⟨vestito⟩ hook up; ~ **a** ⟨maglia⟩ catch on; ⟨rimorchio⟩ hook onto

ag'gancio *nm* Aeron docking

ag'geggio *nm* gadget

agget'tivo *nm* adjective

agghiacci'ante *adj* terrifying

agghiacci'are *vt* fig ~ **qualcuno** make somebody's blood run cold

agghiacci'arsi *vr* freeze

agghin'dare *vt* fam dress up

agghin'darsi *vr* fam doll oneself up

agghin'dato *adj* dressed up; ⟨sala⟩ decorated; ⟨fig: stile⟩ stilted

aggiornabilità *nf* Comput upgradability

aggiorna'mento *nm* update; (azione) updating; **corso di ~** refresher course

aggior'nare *vt* (rinviare) postpone; (mettere a giorno) bring up to date, update

aggior'narsi *vr* get up to date
aggior'nato *adj* up-to-date; ⟨*versione*⟩ updated
aggio'taggio *nm* Jur manipulation of the market
aggira'mento *nm* Mil outflanking
aggi'rare *vt* surround; (fig: ingannare) trick
aggi'rarsi *vr* hang about; ∼ **su** ⟨*discorso ecc*⟩ be about; ⟨*somma*⟩ be around
aggiudi'care *vt* award; (all'asta) knock down
aggiudi'carsi *vr* win
aggi'ungere *vt* add
aggi'unta *nf* addition; **in** ∼ in addition
aggiun'tare *vt* splice
aggiun'tivo *adj* supplementary
aggi'unto ① *adj* added
② *adj & nm* (assistente) assistant
aggiu'stare *vt* mend; (sistemare) settle; (fam: mettere a posto) fix; **ora l'aggiusto io** fig I'll sort him out
aggiu'starsi *vr* adapt; (mettersi in ordine) tidy oneself up; (decidere) sort things out; ⟨*tempo*⟩ clear up
aggiusta'tina *nf* **dare un'**∼ a neaten
agglomera'mento *nm* conglomeration
agglome'rante *nm* binder
agglome'rato *nm* built-up area
aggrap'pare *vt* grasp
aggrap'parsi *vr* ∼ a cling to
aggrava'mento *nm* worsening; (di pena) increase
aggra'vante Jur ① *nf* aggravation
② *adj* aggravating; **circostanza aggravante** aggravation
aggra'vare *vt* (peggiorare) make worse; increase ⟨*pena*⟩; (appesantire) weigh down
aggra'varsi *vr* worsen
ag'gravio *nm* **aggravio fiscale** tax burden
aggrazi'ato *adj* graceful
aggre'dire *vt* attack
aggre'gare *vt* add; (associare a un gruppo ecc) admit
aggre'garsi *vr* ∼ a join
aggre'gato ① *adj* associated
② *nm* aggregate; (di case) block
aggregazi'one *nf* (di persone) gathering
aggressi'one *nf* aggression; (atto) attack. **aggressione a mano armata** armed assault
aggressività *nf* aggressiveness
aggres'sivo *adj* aggressive
aggres'sore *nm* aggressor
aggrin'zare, aggrinzire *vt* wrinkle
aggrin'zirsi *vr* wrinkle
aggrot'tare *vt* ∼ **le ciglia/la fronte** frown
aggrovigli'are *vt* tangle

aggrovigli'arsi *vr* get entangled; fig get complicated
aggrovigli'ato *adj* entangled; fig confused
agguan'tare *vt* catch
agguan'tarsi *vr* ∼ a grasp
aggu'ato *nm* ambush; (tranello) trap; **stare in** ∼ lie in wait; **tendere un** ∼ **a qualcuno** set an ambush for somebody
agguer'rito *adj* fierce
agiata'mente *adv* comfortably
agia'tezza *nf* comfort
agi'ato *adj* ⟨*persona*⟩ well off; ⟨*vita*⟩ comfortable
a'gibile *adj* ⟨*palazzo*⟩ fit for human habitation
agibilità *nf* fitness for human habitation
'agile *adj* agile
agilità *nf* agility
agil'mente *adv* agilely
'agio *nm* ease; **mettersi a proprio** ∼ make oneself at home
a'gire *vi* act; ⟨*comportarsi*⟩ behave; (funzionare) work; ∼ **su** affect
agi'tare *vt* shake; wave ⟨*mano*⟩; (fig: turbare) trouble; **'**∼ **prima dell'uso'** 'shake before using'
agi'tarsi *vr* toss about; (essere inquieto) be restless; ⟨*mare*⟩ get rough
agi'tato *adj* restless; ⟨*mare*⟩ rough
agita|'tore, -trice *nmf* (persona) agitator
agitazi'one *nf* agitation; **mettere in** ∼ **qualcuno** send somebody into a flat spin
'agli = A + GLI
'aglio *nm* garlic
a'gnello *nm* lamb
agno'lotti *nmpl* ravioli *sg*
a'gnostico, -a *adj & nmf* agnostic
'ago *nm* needle; **a 9 aghi** ⟨*stampante*⟩ 9-pin. **ago di pino** pine-needle
ago'gnare *vt* liter yearn for, thirst for
ago'nia *nf* agony
ago'nismo *nm* competitiveness
ago'nistica *nf* competition
ago'nistico *adj* competitive
agoniz'zante *adj* in one's death throes
agoniz'zare *vi* be on one's deathbed
agopun|'tore, -trice *nmf* acupuncturist
agopun'tura *nf* acupuncture
agorafo'bia *nf* agoraphobia
ago'rafobo, -a *nmf* agoraphobic
agostini'ano, -a *adj & nmf* Augustinian
a'gosto *nm* August
a'graria *nf* agriculture
a'grario ① *adj* agricultural
② *nm* landowner
a'greste *adj* rustic

a'gricolo *adj* agricultural

agricol'tore *nm* farmer

agricol'tura *nf* agriculture.
agricoltura biologica organic farming

agri'foglio *nm* holly

agrimen'sore *nm* land-surveyor

agritu'rismo *nm* farm holidays,
agrotourism

'agro¹ *adj* sour; all'∼ Culin pickled

'agro² *nm* countryside around a town

agroalimen'tare *adj* food *attrib*

agro'dolce *adj* bitter-sweet; Culin sweet-
and-sour; in ∼ sweet and sour

agrono'mia *nf* agronomy

a'gronomo, -a *nmf* agriculturalist

agropasto'rale *adj* based on farming

a'grume *nm* citrus fruit; (pianta) citrus
tree

agru'meto *nm* citrus plantation

aguz'zare *vt* sharpen; ∼ le orecchie
prick up one's ears; ∼ la vista look hard

aguz'zino *nm* slave-driver; (carceriere)
jailer

a'guzzo *adj* pointed

ah *int* ah!; ah, davvero? oh really?

ahi *int* ow!

ahimè *int* alas!

'ai = A + I

'aia *nf* threshing-floor

'Aia *nf* L'∼ The Hague

Aids *nm* Aids

AIE *abbr* (Associazione Italiana
degli Editori) association of Italian
publishers

air bag *nm inv* Auto air bag

ai'rone *nm* heron

air terminal *nm inv* air terminal

ai'tante *adj* sturdy

aiu'ola *nf* flowerbed

aiu'tante ① *nmf* assistant
② *nm* Mil adjutant. aiutante di campo
aide-de-camp

aiu'tare *vt* help

ai'uto *nm* help, aid; (assistente) assistant;
dare un ∼ lend a hand; venire in ∼ a
qualcuno come to somebody's rescue; ∼!
help!; aiuti *pl* alimentari food aid. aiuti *pl*
umanitari relief supplies. aiuto
chirurgo assistant surgeon. aiuto
domestico mother's help. aiuto
infermiere nursing auxiliary. aiuto in
linea Comput on-line help

aiz'zare *vt* incite; ∼ contro set on

al = A + IL

'ala *nf* wing; fare ∼ make way; avere le ali
ai piedi fig run like the wind; tarpare le ali
a qualcuno fig clip somebody's wings. ala
destra/sinistra (in calcio) right/left wing

ala'bastro *nm* alabaster

'alacre *adj* brisk

alam'bicco *nm* alembic

a'lano *nm* Great Dane

a'lare *nm* firedog; apertura alare
wingspan

A'laska *nf* Alaska

'alba *nf* dawn

alba'nese *adj & nmf* Albanian

Alba'nia *nf* Albania

'albatro *nm* albatross

albeggi'are *vi* dawn

albe'rare *vi* line with trees ⟨strada⟩

albe'rato *adj* wooded; ⟨viale⟩ tree-lined

albera'tura *nf* Naut masts *pl*

albe'rello *nm* sapling

alber'gare ① *vt* ⟨edificio⟩ accommodate
② *vi* liter lodge

alberga|'tore, -trice *nmf* hotel-keeper

alberghi'ero *adj* hotel *attrib*

al'bergo *nm* hotel. albergo diurno
hotel where rooms are rented during the
daytime. albergo a 3 stelle 3-star hotel

'albero *nm* tree; Naut mast; Mech shaft.
albero a camme camshaft. albero a
foglie caduche deciduous tree. albero
da frutto fruit tree. albero
genealogico family tree. albero a
gomiti crankshaft. albero della
gomma rubber tree. albero maestro
Naut mainmast. albero di Natale
Christmas tree. albero di
trasmissione Mech transmission shaft,
prop shaft

albi'cocca *nf* apricot

albi'cocco *nm* apricot (tree)

al'bino *nm* albino

'albo *nm* register; (libro ecc) album; (per
avvisi) notice board

album *nm inv* album. album da
colorare colouring book. album da
disegno sketch-book

al'bume *nm* albumen

albu'mina *nf* albumin

alca'lino *adj* alkaline

'alce *nm* elk

alchi'mia *nf* alchemy

alchi'mista *nm* alchemist

'alcol *nm* alcohol; Med spirit; (liquori forti)
spirits *pl*; darsi all'∼ take to drink. alcol
denaturato meths, surgical spirit.
alcol etilico ethyl alcohol

alcolicità *nf* alcohol content

al'colico ① *adj* alcoholic
② *nm* alcoholic drink

alco'lismo *nm* alcoholism

alco'lista *nmf* alcoholic

alcoliz'zato, -a *adj & nmf* alcoholic

alco'test® *nm inv* breathalyser® Br,
breathalyzer®

al'cova *nf* alcove

al'cun, alcuno *adj & pron* any; **non ha** ∼ **amico** he hasn't any friends, he has no friends; **alcuni** *pl* some, a few; **alcuni suoi amici** some of his friends

aldilà *nm* next world, hereafter

alea'torio *adj* unpredictable; Jur aleatory

aleggi'are *vi* ⟨*brezza*⟩ blow gently; ⟨*profumo*⟩ waft

a'letta *nf* Mech fin

alet'tone *nm* Aeron aileron; Auto stabilizer

'alfa *nf inv* alpha

alfa'betico *adj* alphabetical

alfabetizzazi'one *nf* **alfabetizzazione della popolazione** teaching people to read and write; **tasso di alfabetizzazione** literacy rate

alfa'beto *nm* alphabet. **Alfabeto Fonetico Internazionale** International Phonetic Alphabet. **alfabeto Morse** Morse code

alfanu'merico *adj* alphanumeric

alfi'ere *nm* (negli scacchi) bishop

al'fine *adv* eventually, in the end

'alga *nf* weed; **alghe** *pl* **marine** seaweed

'algebra *nf* algebra

Al'geri *nf* Algiers

Alge'ria *nf* Algeria

alge'rino, -a *adj & nmf* Algerian

algocol'tura *nf* seaweed farming

algo'ritmo *nm* algorithm

ali'ante *nm* glider

'alibi *nm inv* alibi

a'lice *nf* anchovy

alie'nabile *adj* Jur alienable

alie'nare *vt* alienate

alie'narsi *vr* become estranged; ∼ **le simpatie di qualcuno** lose somebody's good will

ali'enato, -a ① *adj* alienated ② *nmf* lunatic

alienazi'one *nf* alienation

a'lieno, -a ① *nmf* alien ② *adj* **è** ∼ **da invidia** envy is foreign *or* alien to him

alimen'tare ① *vt* feed; fig foment ② *adj* food *attrib*; ⟨*abitudine*⟩ dietary ③ *nmpl* **alimentari** foodstuffs

alimenta'tore *nm* power unit. **alimentatore automatico di documenti** automatic paper feed

alimentazi'one *nf* feeding; (cibo) food; (elettrica, a gas ecc) supply

ali'mento *nm* food; **alimenti** *pl* food; Jur alimony

a'liquota *nf* share; (di imposta) rate. **aliquota minima** basic rate; **ad** ∼ **zero** zero-rated

ali'scafo *nm* hydrofoil

'alito *nm* breath; **alito cattivo** bad breath

ali'tosi *nf inv* halitosis

all. *abbr* **(allegato)** encl

'alla = A + LA

allaccia'mento *nm* connection

allacci'are *vt* fasten ⟨*cintura*⟩; lace up ⟨*scarpe*⟩; do up ⟨*vestito*⟩; (collegare) connect; form ⟨*amicizia*⟩

allacci'arsi *vr* do up, fasten ⟨*vestito, cintura*⟩

allaga'mento *nm* flooding

alla'gare *vt* flood

alla'garsi *vr* to become flooded

allampa'nato *adj* lanky

allarga'mento *nm* (di strada, ricerche) widening

allar'gare *vt* widen; open ⟨*braccia, gambe*⟩; let out ⟨*vestito ecc*⟩; fig extend

allar'garsi *vr* to widen

allar'mante *adj* alarming

allar'mare *vt* alarm

allar'mato *adj* panicky, alarmed

al'larme *nm* alarm; **dare l'**∼ raise the alarm; **mettere in** ∼ **qualcuno** alarm somebody; **far scattare il campanello d'**∼ set the alarm bells ringing; **falso allarme** fig false alarm. **allarme aereo** air-raid siren; (suono) air-raid warning. **allarme antifumo** smoke alarm. **allarme antincendio** fire alarm. **allarme rosso** red alert

allar'mismo *nm* alarmism

allar'mista *nmf* alarmist

allatta'mento *nm* (di animale) suckling; (di neonato) feeding

allat'tare *vt* suckle ⟨*animale*⟩; feed ⟨*neonato*⟩; ∼ **artificialmente** bottle feed

'alle = A + LE

alle'anza *nf* alliance. **Alleanza Democratica** Pol Democratic Alliance. **Alleanza Nazionale** Pol National Alliance

alle'are *vt* unite

alle'arsi *vr* form an alliance

alle'ato, -a ① *adj* allied ② *nmf* ally

alle'gare¹ *vt* Jur allege

alle'gare² *vt* (accludere) enclose; set on edge ⟨*denti*⟩

alle'gato ① *adj* enclosed; Comput attached ② *nm* enclosure; Comput attachment; **in** ∼ attached, appended

allegazi'one *nf* Jur allegation

alleggeri'mento *nm* alleviation

allegge'rire *vt* lighten; fig alleviate

allegge'rirsi *vr* become lighter; (vestirsi leggero) put on lighter clothes

allego'ria *nf* allegory

alle'gorico *adj* allegorical

allegra'mente *adv* breezily

alle'gria *nf* gaiety

al'legro ① *adj* cheerful; ‹*colore*› bright; (brillo) tipsy
② *nm* Mus allegro

alle'luia *int* hallelujah

allena'mento *nm* training

alle'nare *vt* train

alle'narsi *vr* train

allena|'tore, -trice *nmf* trainer, coach

allen'tare *vt* loosen; fig relax

allen'tarsi *vr* become loose; Mech work loose

aller'gia *nf* allergy

al'lergico *adj* allergic

aller'gologo, -a *nmf* allergist

al'lerta *nf* stare ~ be alert, be on the alert; **essere in stato di** ~ Mil be in a state of alert; **mettere in stato di** ~ put on the alert

allesti'mento *nm* preparation; **in** ~ in preparation. **allestimento scenico** Theat set

alle'stire *vt* prepare; stage ‹*spettacolo*›; Naut fit out

allet'tante *adj* alluring; **poco** ~ unattractive

allet'tare *vt* entice

allet'tato *adj* bed-bound, laid up

alleva'mento *nm* breeding; (processo) bringing up; (luogo) farm; (per piante) nursery; **pollo di allevamento** battery chicken. **allevamento in batteria** battery farming. **allevamento a terra** free-range farming; **pollo/uova di allevamento a terra** free-range chicken/eggs

alle'vare *vt* bring up ‹*bambini*›; breed ‹*animali*›; grow ‹*piante*›

alleva|'tore, -trice *nmf* breeder

allevia'mento *nm* alleviation

allevi'are *vt* alleviate; fig lighten

alli'bito *adj* astounded; **rimanere** ~ be astounded

allibra'tore *nm* bookmaker

allie'tare *vt* gladden

allie'tarsi *vr* rejoice

alli'evo, -a ① *nmf* pupil
② *nm* Mil cadet

alliga'tore *nm* alligator

allinea'mento *nm* alignment

alline'are *vt* line up; Typ align; Fin adjust

alline'arsi *vr* line up; fig fall into line; ~ **con qualcuno** fig align oneself with somebody

alline'ato *adj* lined up; **i paesi non allineati** the non-aligned states

'allo = A + LO

allo'care *vt* allocate

al'locco[1] *nm* tawny owl

al'locco[2]**, -a** *nmf* fig idiot

allocuzi'one *nf* speech

al'lodola *nf* [sky]lark

alloggi'are ① *vt* ‹*persona*› put up; ‹*casa*› provide accommodation for; Mil billet
② *vi* put up, stay; Mil be billeted

al'loggio *nm* (appartamento) flat, apartment Am; Mil billet. **alloggio popolare** council flat

allontana'mento *nm* removal

allonta'nare *vt* move away; (licenziare) dismiss; avert ‹*pericolo*›

allonta'narsi *vr* go away

allopa'tia *nf* Med allopathy

al'lora *adv* then; (a quel tempo) at that time; (in tal caso) in that case; ~ ~ just then; **d'**~ **in poi** from then on; **e** ~? what now?; (e con ciò?) so what?; **fino** ~ until then

allorché *conj* when, as soon as

al'loro *nm* laurel; Culin bay; **dormire sugli allori** rest on one's laurels

'alluce *nm* big toe

alluci'nante *adj* fam incredible; **sostanza allucinante** hallucinogen

alluci'nato, -a *nmf* person who suffers from hallucinations; fam space cadet

allucina'torio *adj* hallucinatory

allucinazi'one *nf* hallucination

allucino'geno *adj* ‹*sostanza*› hallucinatory

al'ludere *vi* ~ **a** allude to

allu'minio *nm* aluminium

allu'naggio *nm* moon-landing

allu'nare *vi* land on the moon

allun'gabile *adj* ‹*tavolo*› extending

allun'gare *vt* lengthen; stretch out ‹*mano*›; stretch ‹*gamba*›; extend ‹*tavolo*›; (diluire) dilute; ~ **il collo** crane one's neck; ~ **il muso** pull a long face; ~ **il passo** quicken one's step; ~ **le mani su qualcuno** touch somebody up; (picchiare) start fighting with somebody; ~ **uno schiaffo a qualcuno** slap somebody

allun'garsi *vr* grow longer; (crescere) grow taller; (sdraiarsi) lie down, stretch out

allun'gato *adj* ‹*forma*› elongated

al'lungo *nm* (nel calcio) pass; (nella corsa) spurt; (nel pugilato) lunge

allusi'one *nf* allusion

allu'sivo *adj* allusive

alluvio'nale *adj* alluvial

alluvio'nato *adj* ‹*popolazione*› flooded out; ‹*territorio*› flooded

alluvi'one *nf* flood

alma'nacco *nm* almanac. **almanacco nobiliare** peerage

al'meno *adv* at least; **[se]** ~ **venisse il sole!** if only the sun would come out!

a'logena *nf* halogen lamp

a'logeno ① *nm* halogen
② *adj* **lampada alogena** halogen lamp

a'lone *nm* halo

alo'pecia *nf* Med alopecia

al'paca *nm inv* alpaca

al'pestre *adj* Alpine

'Alpi *nfpl* **le** ~ the Alps

alpi'nismo *nm* mountaineering

alpi'nista *nmf* mountaineer

alpi'nistico *adj* mountaineering *attrib*

al'pino ① *adj* Alpine
② *nm* Mil **gli alpini** the Alpine troops

al'quanto ① *adj* a certain amount of
② *adv* rather

Al'sazia *nf* Alsace

alt *int* stop; **intimare l'**~ give the order to halt

alta'lena *nf* swing; (tavola in bilico) see-saw

altale'nare *vi* fig vacillate

alta'mente *adv* highly

al'tare *nm* altar

alta'rino *nm* **scoprire gli altarini di qualcuno** reveal somebody's guilty secrets

alte'rabile *adj* which can be changed, alterable

alte'rare *vt* alter; adulterate ⟨*vino*⟩; (falsificare) falsify

alte'rarsi *vr* be altered; ⟨*cibo*⟩ go bad; ⟨*merci*⟩ deteriorate; (arrabbiarsi) get angry

alte'rato *adj* ⟨*suono*⟩ distorted; ⟨*viso*⟩ careworn; ⟨*cibo*⟩ spoilt; ⟨*vino*⟩ adulterated; (arrabbiato) angry

alterazi'one *nf* alteration; (di vino) adulteration

al'terco *nm* altercation

alte'rigia *nf* haughtiness

alter'nanza *nf* alternation; (in agricoltura) rotation; Pol regular change in government

alter'nare *vt* alternate

alter'narsi *vr* alternate

alterna'tiva *nf* alternative

alterna'tivo *adj* alternate; **medicina alternativa** alternative medicine

alter'nato *adj* alternating

alterna'tore *nm* Electr alternator

al'terno *adj* alternate; **a giorni alterni** every other day

al'tero *adj* haughty

al'tezza *nf* height; (profondità) depth; (suono) pitch; (di tessuto) width; (titolo) Highness; **essere all'**~ **di** be on a level with; fig be up to. **altezza libera di passaggio** headroom

altezzosa'mente *adv* haughtily

altezzosità *nf* haughtiness

altez'zoso *adj* haughty

al'ticcio *adj* tipsy, merry

al'timetro *nm* altimeter

altipi'ano *nm* plateau

altiso'nante *adj* high-sounding

alti'tudine *nf* altitude

'alto ① *adj* high; (di statura) tall; (profondo) deep; ⟨*suono*⟩ high-pitched; ⟨*tessuto*⟩ wide; Geog northern; **a notte alta** in the middle of the night; **avere degli alti e bassi** have some ups and downs; **di** ~ **bordo** high-class; **di** ~ **rango** high-ranking; **ad alta definizione** high-definition; **ad alta fedeltà** high-fidelity; **ad** ~ **livello** high-level; **a voce alta, ad alta voce** in a loud voice; ⟨*leggere*⟩ aloud; **essere in** ~ **mare** be on the high seas; fig be all at sea. **alta borghesia** *nf* gentry. **alta finanza** *nf* high finance. **alta frequenza** *nf* high frequency. **alta moda** *nf* high fashion. **alta pressione** *nf* (meteorologica) high pressure. **alta società** *nf* high society. **alta tensione** *nf* high voltage. **alto commissariato** *nm* High Commission. **alto medioevo** *nm* Dark Ages. **alto tradimento** *nm* high treason
② *adv* high; **in** ~ ⟨*essere*⟩ at the top; ⟨*guardare*⟩ up; **mani in** ~**!** hands up!; **dall'**~ from above; **guardare qualcuno dall'**~ **in basso** look down on somebody

altoate'sino *adj* South Tyrolean

alto'forno *nm* blast furnace

altolà *int* halt there!

altolo'cato *adj* highly placed

altopar'lante *nm* loudspeaker

altopi'ano *nm* plateau

altret'tanto ① *adj* & *pron* as much; (*pl*) as many
② *adv* likewise; **buona fortuna! –grazie,** ~ good luck! –thank you, the same to you

altri'menti *adv* otherwise

'altro ① *adj* other; **un** ~**, un'altra** another; **l'altr'anno** last year; **l'**~ **ieri** the day before yesterday; **domani l'**~ the day after tomorrow; **l'ho visto l'**~ **giorno** I saw him the other day
② *pron* other [one]; **un** ~**, un'altra** another [one]; **ne vuoi dell'**~**?** would you like some more?; **l'un l'**~ one another; **nessun** ~ nobody else; **gli altri** (la gente) other people
③ *nm* something else; **non fa** ~ **che lavorare** he does nothing but work; **desidera** ~**?** (in negozio) anything else?; **più che** ~**, sono stanco** I'm tired more than anything; **se non** ~ at least; **senz'**~ certainly; **tra l'**~ what's more; ~ **che!** absolutely!

altroché *adv* absolutely!

altroi'eri *nm* **l'**~ the day before yesterday

al'tronde: **d'**~ *adv* on the other hand

al'trove *adv* elsewhere

al'trui ① *adj* other people's
② *nm* other people's belongings *pl*

altru'ismo *nm* altruism

altruista *nmf* altruist

al'tura *nf* high ground; Naut deep sea

a'lunno, -a *nmf* pupil

alve'are *nm* hive

'alveo *nm* bed

alzabandi'era *nm inv* flag-raising

alzacri'stallo *nm* Auto window winder

al'zare *vt* lift, raise; (costruire) build; Naut hoist; ~ **le spalle** shrug one's shoulders; ~ **i tacchi** fig take to one's heels; ~ **la voce** raise one's voice; ~ **il volume** turn up the volume

al'zarsi *vr* (in piedi) stand up; (da letto) get up; ⟨vento, temperatura⟩ rise

al'zata *nf* lifting; (aumento) rise; (da letto) getting up; Archit elevation. **alzata di spalle** shrug of the shoulders

alza'taccia *nf* fam **fare un'**~ get up at the crack of dawn

al'zato *adj* up

A.M. *abbr* (**aeronautica militare**) Air Force

a'mabile *adj* lovable; ⟨vino⟩ sweet

amabilità *nf* kindness

amabil'mente *adv* kindly

a'maca *nf* hammock

a'malgama *nm* amalgam

amalga'mare *vt* amalgamate

amalga'marsi *vr* amalgamate

ama'nita *nf* Bot amanita

a'mante ① *adj* ~ **di** fond of
② *nmf* fig lover. **amante degli animali** animal lover. **amante della lettura** book lover
③ *nm* lover
④ *nf* mistress

amara'mente *adv* bitterly

ama'ranto ① *nm* Bot amarant[h]us; (colore) rich purple
② *adj* rich purple

a'mare *vt* love; be fond of ⟨musica, sport ecc⟩

amareggia'mento *nm* bitterness

amareggi'are *vt* embitter

amareggi'arsi *vr* become embittered

amareggi'ato *adj* embittered

ama'rena *nf* sour black cherry

ama'retto *nm* macaroon

ama'rezza *nf* bitterness; (dolore) sorrow

a'maro ① *adj* bitter
② *nm* bitterness; (liquore) bitters *pl*

ama'rognolo *adj* rather bitter

a'mato, -a ① *adj* loved
② *nmf* beloved

ama|'tore, -trice *nmf* lover

a'mazzone *nf* (in mitologia) Amazon; **all'**~ side saddle

Amaz'zonia *nf* Amazonia

amaz'zonico *adj* Amazonian

ambasce'ria *nf* diplomatic mission

ambasci'ata *nf* embassy; (messaggio) message

ambascia|'tore, -trice ① *nm* ambassador
② *nf* ambassadress

ambe'due *adj* & *pron* both

ambi'destro *adj* ambidextrous

ambien'tale *adj* environmental

ambienta'lismo *nm* environmentalism

ambienta'lista *adj* & *nmf* environmentalist

ambienta'mento *nm* acclimatization

ambien'tare *vt* acclimatize; set ⟨storia, film ecc⟩

ambien'tarsi *vr* get acclimatized

ambi'ente *nm* environment; (stanza) room

ambiguità *nf inv* ambiguity; (di persona) shadiness

am'biguo *adj* ambiguous; ⟨persona⟩ shady

am'bire *vi* ~ **a** aspire to

am'bito¹ *adj* ⟨lavoro, incarico⟩ much sought-after

'ambito² *nm* sphere

ambiva'lente *adj* ambivalent

ambiva'lenza *nf* ambivalence

ambizi'one *nf* ambition

ambizi'oso *adj* ambitious

amblio'pia *nf* lazy eye

'ambo ① *adj inv* both
② *nm* (in tombola, lotto) double

'ambra *nf* amber

am'brato *adj* amber

ambu'lante *adj* wandering; **venditore ambulante** hawker

ambu'lanza *nf* ambulance

ambulatori'ale *adj* **essere trattato con intervento** ~ have day surgery

ambula'torio *nm* (di medico) surgery; (di ospedale) out-patients' [department]. **ambulatorio dentistico** dental clinic

Am'burgo *nf* Hamburg

a'meba *nf* amoeba

a'mebico *adj* amoebic

'amen *int* amen; **e allora** ~! well, so be it!

amenità *nf inv* (facezia) pleasantry

a'meno *adj* pleasant

amenor'rea *nf* Med amenorrhoea

A'merica *nf* America. **America centrale** Central America. **America**

Latina Latin America. **America del Nord/Sud** North/South America

america'nata *nf* (pej: film) American rubbish

america'nismo *nm* Americanism; (patriottismo) flag-waving

americaniz'zarsi *vr* become Americanized

ameri'cano, **-a** *adj & nmf* American

ame'rindio *adj* Native American

ame'tista *nf* amethyst

ami'anto *nm* asbestos

ami'chevole *adj* friendly

ami'cizia *nf* friendship; **fare ～ con qualcuno** make friends with somebody; **amicizie** *pl* (amici) friends

a'mico, **-a** ① *adj* ⟨parola, persona⟩ friendly ② *nmf* friend. **amico del cuore** bosom friend. **amico d'infanzia** childhood friend. **amico intimo** close friend. **amico di penna** penfriend, penpal

'amido *nm* starch

ammac'care *vt* dent ⟨metallo⟩; bruise ⟨frutto⟩

ammac'carsi *vr* ⟨metallo⟩ get dented; ⟨frutto⟩ bruise

ammac'cato *adj* ⟨metallo⟩ dented; ⟨frutto⟩ bruised

ammacca'tura *nf* dent; (livido) bruise

ammaestra'mento *nm* training

ammae'strare *vt* (istruire) teach; train ⟨animale⟩

ammae'strato *adj* trained

ammaestra|'tore, **-trice** *nmf* trainer

ammainabandi'era *nm inv* flag-lowering

ammai'nare *vt* lower ⟨bandiera⟩; furl ⟨vele⟩

amma'larsi *vr* fall ill

amma'lato, **-a** *adj* ill *nmf* sick person; (paziente) patient

ammali'are *vt* bewitch

ammali'ato *adj* bewitched

ammalia|'tore, **-trice** ① *adj* bewitching ② *nm* enchanter ③ *nf* enchantress

am'manco *nm* deficit

ammanet'tare *vt* handcuff

ammani'carsi *vr* fig acquire connections

ammani'cato *adj* **essere ～** have connections

ammanigli'arsi *vr* fig = AMMANICARSI

ammanigli'ato *adj* fig = AMMANICATO

amman'sire *vt* tame, domesticate ⟨animali⟩; fig pacify, placate

amman'sirsi *vr* ⟨animali⟩ become tame; fig calm down

amman'tarsi *vr* ⟨persona⟩ wrap oneself up in a cloak; **～ di** fig feign ⟨virtù⟩

amma'raggio *nm* splashdown

amma'rare *vi* put down on the sea; ⟨navicella spaziale⟩ splash down

ammassa'mento *nm* Mil build-up

ammas'sare *vt* amass

ammas'sarsi *vr* crowd together

am'masso *nm* mass; (mucchio) pile

ammat'tire *vi* go mad

ammazzacaffè *nm inv* liqueur

ammazza'fame *nm inv* stodge

ammaz'zare *vt* kill

ammaz'zarsi *vr* (suicidarsi, fig) kill oneself; (rimanere ucciso) be killed

am'menda *nf* amends *pl*; (multa) fine; **fare ～ di qualcosa** make amends for something

am'messo ① *pp di* AMMETTERE ② *conj* **～ che** supposing that

am'mettere *vt* admit; (riconoscere) acknowledge; (supporre) suppose; **ammettiamo che ...** let's suppose [that]...

ammez'zato *nm* (piano ammezzato) mezzanine

ammic'care *vi* wink

ammini'strare *vt* administer; (gestire) run

ammini'strarsi *vr* fig manage one's finances

amministra'tivo *adj* administrative

amministra|'tore, **-trice** *nmf* administrator; (di azienda) manager; (di società) director. **amministratore aggiunto** associate director. **amministratore del condominio** property manager. **amministratore delegato** managing director. **amministratore unico** sole director

amministrazi'one *nf* administration; **fatti di ordinaria ～** fig routine matters. **amministrazione aziendale** (studi) business studies. **amministrazione comunale** local council. **amministrazione controllata** receivership. **amministrazione pubblica** civil service. **amministrazione regionale** regional council

ammino'acido *nm* amino acid

ammi'rabile *adj* admirable

ammi'raglia *nf* flag-ship

ammiragli'ato *nm* admiralty

ammi'raglio *nm* admiral

ammi'rare *vt* admire

ammi'rato *adj* **restare/essere ～** be full of admiration

ammira|'tore, **-trice** *nmf* admirer

ammirazi'one *nf* admiration

ammis'sibile *adj* admissible

ammissibilità *nf* acceptability

ammissi'one *nf* admission; (approvazione) acknowledgement

ammobili'are *vt* furnish

ammobIll'ato *adj* furnished; **stanza ammobiliata** furnished room

ammoderna'mento *nm* modernization

ammoder'nare *vt* modernize

ammoder'narsi *vr* move with the times

am'modo ① *adj* proper ② *adv* properly

ammogli'are *vt* marry off

ammogli'arsi *vr* get married

ammogli'ato ① *adj* married ② *nm* married man

am'mollo *nm* **in** ∼ soaking; **mettere in** ∼ pre-soak

ammo'niaca *nf* ammonia

ammoni'mento *nm* warning; (di rimprovero) admonishment

ammo'nire *vt* warn; (rimproverare) admonish

ammoni'tore *adj* admonishing

ammonizi'one *nf* Sport warning; (rimprovero) admonishment

ammon'tare ① *vi* ∼ **a** amount to ② *nm* amount

ammonticchi'are *vt* heap up, pile up

ammonticchi'arsi *vr* pile up

ammor'bare *vt* (con odore) pollute; (con malattie) infect

ammorbi'dente *nm* (per panni) softener

ammorbi'dire *vt* soften

ammorbi'dirsi *vr* soften

ammorta'mento *nm* Comm amortization

ammor'tare *vt* pay off (spesa); Comm amortize (debito)

ammortiz'zare *vt* Comm = AMMORTARE; Mech damp

ammortizza'tore *nm* shock-absorber

ammosci'are *vt* make flabby

ammosci'arsi *vt* get flabby

ammucchi'are *vt* pile up

ammucchi'arsi *vr* pile up

ammucchi'ata *nf* (sl: orgia) orgy; **un'**∼ **di** (fam: ammasso) loads of

ammuf'fire *vi* go mouldy

ammuf'firsi *vr* go mouldy

ammuf'fito *adj* mouldy; fig stuffy

ammutina'mento *nm* mutiny

ammuti'narsi *vr* mutiny

ammuti'nato ① *adj* mutinous ② *nm* mutineer

ammuto'lire *vi* be struck dumb

ammuto'lirsi *vr* fall silent

amne'sia *nf* amnesia

amni'stia *nf* amnesty

amnisti'are *vt* amnesty

'amo *nm* hook; fig bait

amo'rale *adj* amoral

amoralità *nf* amorality

a'more *nm* love; **d'**∼ (canzone, film) love; **fare l'**∼ make love; **per l'amor di Dio/del cielo!** for heaven's sake!; **andare d'**∼ **e d'accordo** get on like a house on fire; **amor proprio** self-respect; **amor cortese** courtly love; **è un** ∼ (persona) he's/she's a darling; **per** ∼ **di** for the sake of; **amori** *pl* love affairs

amoreggi'are *vi* flirt

amo'revole *adj* loving

amorevol'mente *adv* lovingly

a'morfo *adj* shapeless; (persona) colourless, grey

amo'rino *nm* cherub

amorosa'mente *adv* lovingly

amo'roso *adj* loving; (sguardo ecc) amorous; (lettera, relazione) love *attrib*

am'pere *inv* ampere; **da 15** ∼ 15-amp

ampe'rometro *nm* ammeter

ampia'mente *adv* widely

ampi'ezza *nf* (di esperienza) breadth; (di stanza) spaciousness; (di gonna) fullness; (importanza) scale. **ampiezza di vedute** broadmindedness

'ampio *adj* ample; (esperienza) wide; (stanza) spacious; (vestito) loose; (gonna, descrizione) full; (pantaloni) baggy; **di ampie vedute** broadminded

am'plesso *nm* embrace

amplia'mento *nm* (di cosa, porto) enlargement; (di strada, conoscenze) broadening

ampli'are *vt* broaden, widen (strada, conoscenze); enlarge (casa)

ampli'arsi *vr* broaden, grow wider

amplifi'care *vt* amplify; fig magnify

amplifica'tore *nm* amplifier

amplificazi'one *nf* amplification

am'polla *nf* cruet

ampol'loso *adj* pompous

ampu'tare *vt* amputate

amputazi'one *nf* amputation

amu'leto *nm* amulet

A.N. *abbr* Pol (**Alleanza Nazionale**) National Alliance (right-wing party)

anabbagli'ante ① *adj* Auto dipped ② *nm* **anabbaglianti** *pl* dipped headlights

anaboliz'zante *nm* anabolic steroid

ana'cardi *nmpl* cashew nuts

ana'cardio *nm* cashew

ana'conda *nf* Zool anaconda

anacro'nismo *nm* anachronism

anacro'nistico *adj* anachronistic; **essere** ~ be an anachronism

anae'robico *adj* anaerobic

anafi'lassi *nf* anaphylaxis

anafi'lattico *adj* **shock anafilattico** Med anaphylactic shock

a'nagrafe *nf* (ufficio) registry office; (registro) register of births, marriages and deaths

ana'grafico *adj* **dati** *pl* **anagrafici** personal data

ana'gramma *nm* anagram

anal'colico ⓵ *adj* non-alcoholic ⓶ *nm* soft drink, non-alcoholic drink

a'nale *adj* anal

analfa'beta *adj* & *nmf* illiterate

analfabe'tismo *nm* illiteracy

anal'gesico *nm* painkiller

a'nalisi *nf inv* analysis; Med test; **in ultima** ~ in the final analysis. **analisi grammaticale/del periodo/logica** parsing. **analisi di mercato** market research. **analisi del percorso critico** critical path analysis. **analisi del sangue** blood test

ana'lista *nmf* analyst. **analista economico** economic analyst. **analista finanziario** business analyst

ana'litico *adj* analytical

analiz'zabile *adj* analysable

analiz'zare *vt* analyse; Med test, analyse

anal'lergico *adj* hypoallergenic

analoga'mente *adv* analogously

analo'gia *nf* analogy

ana'logico *adj* analogue

analo'gismo *nm* reasoning by analogy

a'nalogo *adj* analogous

anam'nesi *nf inv* medical history

'ananas *nm inv* pineapple

anar'chia *nf* anarchy

a'narchico, -a ⓵ *adj* anarchic ⓶ *nmf* anarchist

anar'chismo *nm* anarchism

A.N.A.S. *nf abbr* (**Azienda Nazionale Autonoma delle Strade**) national road maintenance authority

ana'tema *nm* anathema

anato'mia *nf* anatomy

ana'tomico *adj* anatomical; ‹sedia› contoured, ergonomic

'anatra *nf* duck. **anatra selvatica** mallard

ana'troccolo *nm* duckling

'anca *nf* hip; (di animale) flank

ance'strale *adj* ancestral

'anche *conj* also, too, as well; (persino) even; **parla** ~ **francese** he also speaks French, he speaks French too, he speaks French as well; ~ **se** even if

ancheggi'are *vi* wiggle one's hips

anchilo'sarsi *vr* fig stiffen up

anchilo'sato *adj* fig stiff

an'cora[1] *adv* still; (con negazione) yet; (di nuovo) again; (di più) some more; ~ **una volta** once more; **non** ~ not yet; ~ **esistente** extant; ~ **più bello** even more beautiful; ~ **una birra** another beer, one more beer

'ancora[2] *nf* anchor; **gettare l'**~ drop anchor. **ancora di salvezza** fig last hope

anco'raggio *nm* anchorage

anco'rare *vt* anchor

anco'rarsi *vr* anchor; drop anchor; ~ **a** fig cling to

Andalu'sia *nf* Andalusia

anda'luso, -a *adj* & *nmf* Andalusian

anda'mento *nm* (del mercato, degli affari) trend

an'dante ⓵ *adj* (corrente) current; (di poco valore) cheap ⓶ *nm* Mus andante

an'dare ⓵ *vi* go; (funzionare) work; (essere di moda) be in; ~ **via** (partire) leave; ‹macchia› come out; ~ **a piedi** walk; ~ **a sciare** go skiing; ~ **[bene]** (confarsi) suit; ‹taglia› fit; **ti va bene alle tre?** does three o'clock suit you?; **non mi va di mangiare** I don't feel like eating; ~ **di fretta** be in a hurry; ~ **fiero di** be proud of; ~ **di moda** be in fashion; **va per i 40 anni** he's nearly 40; **ma va' [là]!** come on!; **come va?** how are things?; ~ **a male** go off; ~ **a fuoco** go up in flames; ~ **perduto** be lost; **va spedito [entro] stamattina** it must be sent this morning; **ne va del mio lavoro** my job is at stake; **come è andata a finire?** how did it turn out?; **cosa vai dicendo?** what are you talking about?; **andarsene** go away; (morire) pass away ⓶ *nm* going; ~ **e venire** (andirivieni) comings and goings *pl*; **a lungo** ~ eventually; **a tutto** ~ at full speed; **con l'**~ **del tempo** with the passing of time

an'data *nf* going; (viaggio) outward journey; **biglietto di sola andata/di andata e ritorno** single/return [ticket]

anda'tura *nf* walk; (portamento) bearing; Naut tack; Sport pace

an'dazzo *nm* fam turn of events; **prendere un brutto** ~ turn nasty

'Ande *nfpl* **le** ~ the Andes

an'dino *adj* Andean

andirivi'eni *nm inv* comings and goings *pl*

'andito *nm* passage

An'dorra *nf* Andorra

an'drone *nm* entrance

andro'pausa *nf* male menopause

a'neddoto *nm* anecdote

ane'lare *vt* ~ **a** long for

a'nelito *nm* longing

a'nello *nm* ring; (di catena) link. **anello di fidanzamento** engagement ring. **anello d'oro** gold ring

ane'mia *nf* anaemia

a'nemico *adj* anaemic

a'nemone *nm* anemone

aneste'sia *nf* anaesthesia; (sostanza) anaesthetic. **anestesia peridurale** epidural

aneste'sista *nmf* anaesthetist

ane'stetico *adj & nm* anaesthetic

anestetiz'zare *vt* anaesthetize

a'neto *nm* dill

anfeta'mina *nf* amphetamine

an'fibi *nmpl* (scarponi) army boots

an'fibio ① *nm* amphibian ② *adj* amphibious

anfite'atro *nm* amphitheatre

'anfora *nf* amphora

an'fratto *nm* ravine

an'gelico *adj* angelic

'angelo *nm* angel. **angelo custode** guardian angel

anghe'ria *nf* harassment

an'gina *nf inv* **angina [pectoris]** angina [pectoris]

angi'ologo, -a *nmf* Med angiologist

anglica'nesimo *nm* Relig Anglicanism

angli'cano, -a *adj & nmf* Relig Anglican

angli'cismo *nm* Anglicism

angliciz'zare *vt* anglicize

anglo+ *pref* Anglo+

angloameri'cano, -a *nmf* Anglo-American

an'glofilo, -a *adj & nmf* Anglophile

an'glofono, -a *nmf* English-speaker

anglofran'cese *adj* Anglo-French

anglo'sassone *adj & nmf* Anglo-Saxon

An'gola *nf* Angola

ango'lano, -a *adj & nmf* Angolan

ango'lare *adj* angular

angolazi'one *nf* angle shot; fig point of view

angoli'era *nf* (mobile) corner cupboard

'angolo *nm* corner; Math angle; **dietro l'∼** round the corner; **fare ∼ con** ⟨negozio, casa⟩ be on the corner of. **angolo acuto** acute angle. **angolo [di] cottura** kitchenette. **angolo retto** right angle

ango'loso *adj* angular; ⟨carattere⟩ difficult to get on with

'angora *nf* **[lana d']angora** angora

an'goscia *nf* anguish

angosci'are *vt* torment

angosci'arsi *vr* (preoccuparsi) worry oneself sick, torment oneself

angosci'ato *adj* agonized

angosci'oso *adj* (disperato) anguished; (che dà angoscia) distressing

angu'illa *nf* eel

an'guria *nf* water-melon

an'gustia *nf* (ansia) anxiety; (penuria) poverty

angusti'are *vt* distress

angusti'arsi *vr* be distressed (**per** about)

angusti'ato *adj* distressed

an'gusto *adj* narrow

'anice *nm* anise; Culin aniseed; (liquore) anisette

ani'cino *nm* (biscotto) aniseed biscuit

ani'dride *nf* **anidride carbonica** carbon dioxide. **anidride solforosa** sulphur dioxide

'anima *nf* soul; **non c'era ∼ viva** there was not a soul about; **all'∼ !** good grief!; **mi fa dannare l'∼ !** he'll be the death of me!; **l' ∼ della festa** the life and soul of the party; **un'∼ in pena** a soul in torment; **volere un bene dell'∼ a qualcuno** love somebody to death; **la buon'∼ della zia** my late aunt, God rest her soul. **anima gemella** soul mate

ani'male *adj & nm* animal. **animali** *pl* **domestici** pets. **animali** *pl* **selvatici** wild animals

anima'lesco *adj* animal

anima'lista *nmf* animal rights activist

ani'mare *vt* give life to; (ravvivare) enliven; (incoraggiare) encourage

ani'marsi *vr* come to life; (accalorarsi) become animated

ani'mato *adj* animate; ⟨discussione⟩ animated; ⟨strada, paese⟩ lively

anima'|tore, -trice *nmf* leading spirit; Cinema animator

animazi'one *nf* animation; **con ∼** animatedly. **animazione elettronica** animatronics

ani'melle *nfpl* (di agnello, vitello) sweetbread

'animo *nm* (mente) mind; (indole) disposition; (cuore) heart; **perdersi d'∼** lose heart; **farsi ∼** take heart

animosa'mente *adv* with animosity

animosità *nf* animosity

ani'moso *adj* brave; (ostile) hostile

ani'setta *nf* anisette

'anitra *nf* duck

annacqua'mento *nm* fig watering down, dilution

annac'quare *vt* anche fig water down

annac'quato *adj* watered down; ⟨colore, resoconto⟩ insipid

annaffi'are *vt* water

annaffia'toio *nm* watering-can

an'nali *nmpl* annals; **restare negli** ∼ go down in history

anna'spare *vi* flounder

an'nata *nf* year; (importo annuale) annual amount; ⟨di vino⟩ vintage. **vino d'annata** vintage wine

annebbia'mento *nm* fog build-up; fig clouding

annebbi'are *vt* cloud ⟨vista, mente⟩

annebbi'arsi *vr* get misty; (in città, su autostrada) get foggy; ⟨vista, mente⟩ grow dim

annega'mento *nm* drowning

anne'gare *vt/i* drown

anne'rire *vt/i* blacken

anne'rirsi *vr* become black

an'nessi *nmpl* (costruzioni) outbuildings; **tutti gli** ∼ **e i connessi** all the appurtenances

annessi'one *nf* (di nazione) annexation

an'nesso ① *pp di* ANNETTERE ② *adj* attached; ⟨Stato⟩ annexed

an'nettere *vt* add; (accludere) enclose; annex ⟨Stato⟩

annichi'lire *vt* annihilate

anni'darsi *vr* nest

annienta'mento *nm* annihilation

annien'tare *vt* annihilate

annien'tarsi *vr* abase oneself

anniver'sario *adj & nm* anniversary. **anniversario di matrimonio** *o* **di nozze** wedding anniversary

'anno *nm* year; **Buon Anno!** Happy New Year!; **quanti anni ha?** how old are you?; **Tommaso ha dieci anni** Thomas is ten [years old]; **gli anni '30** the '30s. **anno accademico** academic year. **anno bisestile** leap year. **anno civile** calendar year. **anno giudiziario** law year. **anno luce** light year. **anno nuovo** New Year. **anno sabbatico** Univ sabbatical. **anni verdi** *pl* salad days

anno'dare *vt* knot; do up ⟨cintura⟩; fig form

anno'darsi *vr* become knotted

annoi'are *vt* bore; (recare fastidio) annoy

annoi'arsi *vr* get bored; (condizione) be bored

annoi'ato *adj* bored

an'noso *adj* ⟨questione⟩ age-old

anno'tare *vt* note down; annotate ⟨testo⟩

annotazi'one *nf* note

annove'rare *vt* number

annu'ale *adj* annual, yearly

annual'mente *adv* annually

annu'ario *nm* year-book

annu'ire *vi* nod; (acconsentire) agree

annulla'mento *nm* annulment; (di appuntamento) cancellation

annul'lare *vt* annul; cancel ⟨appuntamento⟩; (togliere efficacia a) undo; disallow ⟨gol⟩; (distruggere) destroy

annul'larsi *vr* cancel each other out

an'nullo *nm* (timbro) franking

annunci'are *vt* announce; (preannunciare) foretell

annuncia'|tore, -trice *nmf* announcer

annunciazi'one *nf* Annunciation

an'nuncio *nm* announcement; (pubblicitario) advertisement, ad; (notizia) news. **annunci** *pl* **economici** classified advertisements. **annunci** *pl* **mortuari** obituaries, death notices. **annuncio personale** personal ad. **annuncio pubblicitario** advertisement

'annuo *adj* annual, yearly

annu'sare *vt* sniff

annu'sata *nf* **dare un'**∼ **a** have a sniff at

annuvola'mento *nm* clouding over

annuvo'lare *vt* cloud

annuvo'larsi *vr* cloud over

'ano *nm* anus

a'nodino *adj* anodyne

'anodo *nm* anode

anoma'lia *nf* anomaly

a'nomalo *adj* anomalous

a'nonima *nf* **Anonima Alcolisti** Alcoholics Anonymous. **anonima sequestri** Italian criminal organization specializing in kidnapping

anoni'mato *nm* **mantenere l'**∼ remain anonymous

anonimità *nf* anonymity

a'nonimo, -a ① *adj* anonymous ② *nmf* unknown person; (pittore, scrittore) anonymous painter/writer

anores'sia *nf* Med anorexia

ano'ressico, -a *nmf* anorexic

anor'male ① *adj* abnormal ② *nmf* deviant, abnormal person

anormalità *nf inv* abnormality

ANSA *nf abbr* (**Agenzia Nazionale Stampa Associata**) Italian press agency

'ansa *nf* handle; (di fiume) bend

an'sante *adj* panting

an'sare *vi* pant

'ansia, ansietà *nf* anxiety; **stare/essere in** ∼ **per** be anxious about

ansi'mante *adj* breathless

ansi'mare *vi* gasp for breath

ansio'litico *nm* tranquillizer

ansi'oso *adj* anxious

'anta *nf* (di finestra) shutter; (di armadio) door

antago'nismo *nm* antagonism

antago'nista *nmf* antagonist

antago'nistico *adj* antagonistic

an'tartico *adj & nm* Antarctic

a

An'tartide nf Antarctica
ante'bellico adj pre-war
antece'dente ① adj preceding
② nm precedent
ante'fatto nm prior event
ante'guerra ① adj pre-war
② nm pre-war period
ante'nato, -a nmf ancestor
an'tenna nf Radio, TV aerial; (di animale)
antenna; Naut yard; **rizzare le antenne** fig
prick up one's ears. **antenna
parabolica** satellite dish. **antenna
radar** radar scanner
ante'porre vt put before
ante'prima nf preview; **vedere qualcosa
in** ~ have a sneak preview of something.
anteprima di stampa Comput print
preview
anteri'ore adj front attrib; (nel tempo)
previous
anterior'mente adv (nel tempo)
previously; (nello spazio) in front
antesi'gnano, -a nmf fig forerunner
anti+ pref anti+
antiabor'tista ① nmf antiabortionist
② adj antiabortion attrib
anti'acido nm antacid
antiade'rente adj ⟨padella⟩ nonstick
antia'ereo adj anti-aircraft attrib
antial'lergico adj hypoallergenic
antia'partheid adj inv antiapartheid
antia'tomico adj anti-nuclear; **rifugio
antiatomico** fallout shelter
antibat'terico adj antibacterial
antibi'otico adj & nm antibiotic
antibloc'caggio adj inv antilock attrib
anti'caglia nf (oggetto) piece of old junk
antical'care nm softener
antica'mente adv in ancient times,
long ago
anti'camera nf ante-room; **fare** ~ be
kept waiting
antichità nf inv antiquity; (oggetto)
antique
antici'clone nm anticyclone
antici'clonico adj ⟨area⟩ anti-cyclonic
antici'pare ① vt advance; Comm pay in
advance; (prevedere) anticipate; (prevenire)
forestall
② vi be early
anticipata'mente adv in advance
antici'pato adj upfront; **pagamento
anticipato** advance payment
anticipazi'one nf anticipation; (notizia)
advance news
an'ticipo nm advance; (caparra) deposit;
in ~ early; (nel lavoro) ahead of schedule;
giocare d' ~ Sport, fig anticipate the next
move

an'tico ① adj ancient; ⟨mobile ecc⟩
antique; (vecchio) old; **all'antica** old-
fashioned
② nm **gli antichi** the ancients
anticomu'nista adj & nmf anti-
communist
anticoncezio'nale adj & nm
contraceptive
anticonfor'mismo nm
unconventionality
anticonfor'mista nmf nonconformist
anticonfor'mistico adj
unconventional, nonconformist
anticonge'lante adj & nm anti-freeze
anticonsu'mismo nm anti-
consumerism
anti'corpo nm antibody
anticostituzio'nale adj
unconstitutional
anti'crimine adj inv ⟨squadra⟩ crime
attrib
antidemo'cratico adj undemocratic
antidepres'sivo nm antidepressant
antidiluvi'ano adj fig antediluvian
antidolo'rifico nm painkiller
anti'doping nm inv Sport dope test
an'tidoto nm antidote
anti'droga adj inv ⟨campagna⟩ anti-
drugs; ⟨squadra⟩ drug attrib
antie'stetico adj ugly
antifa'scismo nm anti-fascism
antifa'scista adj & nmf anti-fascist
an'tifona nf fig dull and repetitive
speech; **capire l'** ~ take the hint; **sempre la
stessa** ~ always the same old story
anti'forfora adj inv dandruff attrib
anti'fumo adj inv anti-smoking
anti'furto ① nm anti-theft device;
(allarme) alarm. **antifurto della
macchina** car alarm
② adj inv ⟨sistema⟩ anti-theft
anti'gelo ① adj inv anti-freeze
② nm antifreeze; (parabrezza) defroster
anti'gene nm antigen
antigi'enico adj unhygienic
anti-inflazi'one adj inv anti-inflation
An'tille nfpl **le** ~ the West Indies
an'tilope nf antelope
anti'mafia adj inv anti-Mafia
antimilita'rista ① adj inv anti-
militaristic, anti-war
② nmf anti-militarist
antin'cendio adj inv **allarme
antincendio** fire alarm; **porta
antincendio** fire door
anti'nebbia adj inv **[faro] antinebbia**
Auto foglamp, foglight
antine'vralgico ① adj pain-killing
② nm pain-killer

antinfiamma'torio *adj & nm* anti-inflammatory

antinflazio'nistico *adj* anti-inflationary

antinquina'mento *adj inv* anti-pollution

antinucle'are *adj* anti-nuclear

antio'rario *adj* anti-clockwise, counter-clockwise Am

antiparassi'tario *nm* insecticide

antiparlamen'tare *adj* unparliamentary

antipasti'era *nf* hors d'oeuvre dish

anti'pasto *nm* hors d'oeuvre, starter. **antipasti** *pl* **caldi** hot starters. **antipasti** *pl* **freddi** cold starters. **antipasti** *pl* **misti** variety of starters

antipa'tia *nf* antipathy

anti'patico *adj* unpleasant

an'tipodi *nmpl* Antipodes; **essere agli ∼** *fig* be poles apart

anti'polio ➊ *nf inv* (vaccino) polio vaccine; **fare l'∼** have a polio injection ➋ *adj* ⟨siero, vaccino⟩ polio *attrib*

antipopo'lare *adj* anti-working-class

antiproibizio'nismo *nm* anti-prohibitionism

antiproibizio'nista *adj & nmf* anti-prohibitionist

antiproi'ettile *adj inv* bullet-proof

antiquari'ato *nm* antique trade; **pezzo d'antiquariato** antique

anti'quario, -a *nmf* antique dealer

anti'quato *adj* antiquated

antiraz'zismo *nm* antiracism

antiraz'zista *adj* anti-racist

antiretrovi'rale *adj* antiretroviral

antireu'matico *adj & nm* anti-rheumatic

antiri'flesso *adj inv* antiglare

anti'ruggine ➊ *nm inv* rust-inhibitor ➋ *adj* anti-rust

anti'rughe *adj inv* anti-wrinkle *attrib*

anti'scasso *adj inv* ⟨porta⟩ burglar-proof

antisci'opero *adj inv* anti-strike

anti'scippo *adj inv* theft-proof

anti'scivolo *adj inv* nonskid

antise'mita *adj* anti-Semitic

antisemi'tismo *nm* anti-Semitism

anti'settico *adj & nm* antiseptic

antisinda'cale *adj* ⟨comportamento⟩ anti-trade-union

anti'sismico *adj* earthquake-proof

antisoci'ale *adj* anti-social

antiso'lare *adj & nm* suntan

antisommer'gibile ➊ *adj inv* anti-submarine ➋ *nm* submarine hunter

antista'minico *nm* antihistamine

anti'stante *prep* ∼ **a** in front of

anti'tarlo *nm inv* woodworm treatment

anti'tarmico *adj* mothproof

antiterro'rismo *nm* counter-terrorism

antiterro'rista *adj* antiterrorist

antiterro'ristico *adj* antiterrorist

an'titesi *nf inv* antithesis

antite'tanica *nf* tetanus injection

antite'tanico *adj* tetanus *attrib*

anti'tetico *adj* antithetical

anti'trust *adj* antitrust

antitumo'rale *adj* which stops the growth of tumours

anti'urto *adj* shockproof

antivaio'losa *nf* smallpox injection

anti'vipera *adj* **siero antivipera** snakebite antidote

antivi'rale *adj* anti-viral

anti'virus *nm inv* Comput antivirus software

antolo'gia *nf* anthology

an'tonimo *nm* antonym

antono'masia: **per ∼** *a* ⟨poeta⟩ quintessential

antra'cite *nf* anthracite; (colore) charcoal [grey]

'antro *nm* cavern

antro'pofago *adj* man-eating, cannibalistic

antropolo'gia *nf* anthropology

antropo'logico *adj* anthropological

antro'pologo, -a *nmf* anthropologist

anu'lare *nm* ring-finger

An'versa *nf* Antwerp

'anzi *conj* in fact; (o meglio) or better still; (al contrario) on the contrary

anzianità *nf* old age; (di servizio) seniority

anzi'ano, -a ➊ *adj* old, elderly; (di grado ecc) senior ➋ *nmf* elderly person

anziché *conj* rather than

anzi'tempo *adv* prematurely

anzi'tutto *adv* first of all

a'orta *nf* aorta

A'pache *mf inv* Apache

apar'theid *nf* apartheid

apar'titico *adj* unaligned

apa'tia *nf* apathy

a'patico *adj* apathetic

'ape *nf* bee. **ape regina** queen bee

aperi'tivo *nm* aperitif

aperta'mente *adv* openly

a'perto *adj* open; **all'aria aperta** in the open air; **all'∼** ⟨piscina⟩, teatro) open-air; **∼ a tutti** open to all comers; **rimanere a bocca aperta** be dumbfounded

aper'tura *nf* opening; (inizio) beginning; (ampiezza) spread; (di arco) span; Pol overtures *pl*; Phot aperture. **apertura alare** wing span. **apertura di credito** loan agreement. **apertura di credito presso un negozio** charge account. **apertura domenicale [dei negozi]** Sunday trading. **apertura mentale** openness

api'ario *nm* apiary

'**apice** *nm* apex; **l'∼ di** the acme of

apicol'|tore, **-trice** *nmf* beekeeper

apicol'tura *nf* beekeeping

a'plomb *nm inv* (di un abito) hang; fig aplomb, self-assuredness

ap'nea *nf* **immersione in apnea** free diving

Apoca'lisse *nf* **l'∼** the Apocalypse

apoca'littico *adj* apocalyptic

a'pocrifo *adj* apocryphal

apo'geo *nm* apogee

a'polide ① *adj* stateless ② *nmf* stateless person

apo'litico *adj* apolitical

A'pollo *nm* Apollo

apolo'geta *nmf* apologist (**di** for)

apolo'gia *nf* apologia; (celebrazione) eulogy. **apologia di reato** condoning of a criminal act

apoples'sia *nf* apoplexy

apo'plettico *adj* apoplectic

a'postolo *nm* apostle

apostro'fare *vt* (mettere un apostrofo a) write with an apostrophe; reprimand ⟨persona⟩

a'postrofo *nm* apostrophe

apote'osi *nf* apotheosis

appaga'mento *nm* fulfilment

appa'gare *vt* satisfy

appa'garsi *vr* **∼ di** be satisfied with

appa'gato *adj* sated

appai'are *vt* pair; mate ⟨animali⟩

appallotto'lare *vt* roll into a ball

appallotto'larsi *vr* ⟨gatto⟩ curl up in a ball; ⟨farina⟩ become lumpy

appal'tare *vt* contract out; **∼ a imprese esterne** outsource

appalta'tore *nm* contractor

ap'palto *nm* contract; **dare in ∼** contract out; **appalto a imprese esterne** outsourcing; **gara di appalto** call for tenders

appan'naggio *nm* (in denaro) annuity; fig prerogative

appan'nare *vt* mist ⟨vetro⟩; dim ⟨vista⟩

appan'narsi *vr* mist over; ⟨vista⟩ grow dim

appa'rato *nm* apparatus; (apparecchiamento) array; (pompa) display.

apparato digerente digestive system. **apparato scenico** set

apparecchi'are ① *vt* prepare ② *vi* lay the table Br, set the table

apparecchia'tura *nf* (impianti) equipment

appa'recchio *nm* apparatus; (congegno) device; (radio, TV ecc) set; (aeroplano) aircraft; (telefono) phone. **apparecchio acustico** hearing aid

appa'rente *adj* apparent

apparente'mente *adv* apparently

appa'renza *nf* appearance; **in ∼** apparently

appa'rire *vi* appear; (sembrare) look

appari'scente *adj* striking; pej gaudy

apparizi'one *nf* apparition

apparta'mento *nm* flat, apartment Am. **appartamento ammobiliato** furnished flat. **appartamento in multiproprietà** timeshare

appar'tarsi *vr* withdraw

appar'tato *adj* secluded

apparte'nente *adj* **∼ a** belonging to

apparte'nenza *nf* membership

apparte'nere *vi* belong

appassio'nante *adj* (storia, argomento) exciting

appassio'nare *vt* excite; (commuovere) move

appassio'narsi *vr* **∼ a** become excited by

appassio'nato *adj* passionate; **∼ di** (entusiastico) fond of

appas'sire *vi* wither

appas'sirsi *vr* fade

appas'sito *adj* faded

appel'larsi *vr* **∼ a** a appeal to

ap'pello *nm* appeal; (chiamata per nome) rollcall; (esami) exam session; **fare l'∼** call the roll

ap'pena ① *adv* just; (a fatica) hardly ② *conj* [non] **∼** as soon as, no sooner ... than; **∼ prima di** just before

ap'pendere *vt* hang [up]

appendi'abiti *nm inv* hat-stand, hallstand

appen'dice *nf* appendix; **romanzo d'appendice** novel serialized in a magazine or newspaper

appendi'cite *nf* appendicitis

Appen'nini *nmpl* **gli ∼** the Apennines

appen'ninico *adj* Apennine

appesan'tire *vt* weigh down

appesan'tirsi *vr* become heavy

ap'peso ① *pp di* APPENDERE ② *adj* hanging; (impiccato) hanged

appe'tito *nm* appetite; **aver ∼** be hungry; **buon ∼!** enjoy your meal!

appeti'toso *adj* appetizing; fig tempting

appezza'mento *nm* plot of land

appia'nare *vt* level; fig smooth over

appia'narsi *vr* improve

appiat'tire *vt* flatten

appiat'tirsi *vr* flatten oneself; fig level out

appic'care *vt* ~ il fuoco a set fire to

appicci'care [1] *vt* stick; ~ a (fig: appioppare) palm off on [2] *vi* be sticky

appicci'carsi *vr* stick; ⟨cose⟩ stick together; ~ a qualcuno fig stick to somebody like glue

appiccica'ticcio *adj* sticky; fig clingy

appicci'cato *adj* stare ~ a qualcuno be all over somebody

appicci'coso *adj* sticky; fig clingy

appie'dato *adj* sono ~ I don't have the car; sono rimasto ~ I was stranded

appi'eno *adv* fully

appigli'arsi *vr* ~ a get hold of; fig stick to

ap'piglio *nm* fingerhold; (per piedi) foothold; fig pretext

appiop'pare *vt* ~ a palm off on; (fam: dare) give; ~ un ceffone a qualcuno slap somebody

appiso'larsi *vr* doze off

applau'dire *vt/i* applaud

ap'plauso *nm* applause

appli'cabile *adj* applicable

appli'care *vt* apply; enforce ⟨legge ecc⟩

appli'carsi *vr* apply oneself

appli'cato [1] *nmf* (impiegato) senior clerk [2] *adj* (nel ricamo) appliqué; matematica applicata applied mathematics

applica'tore *nm* applicator

applicazi'one *nf* application; (di legge) enforcement. applicazioni *pl* tecniche handicrafts

appoggi'are *vt* lean (a against); (mettere) put; (sostenere) back

appoggi'arsi *vr* ~ a lean against; fig rely on

appoggi'ato *adj* leaning (su on; contro, a against)

ap'poggio *nm* support; appoggi *pl* fig influential contacts

appollai'arsi *vr* fig perch

ap'porre *vt* affix

appor'tare *vt* bring; (causare) cause; ~ delle modifiche a qualcosa modify something

ap'porto *nm* contribution

apposita'mente *adv* (specialmente) especially; fatto ~ purpose-made

ap'posito *adj* proper

apposizi'one *nf* apposition

ap'posta *adv* on purpose; (espressamente) specially; neanche a farlo ~! what a coincidence!

apposta'mento *nm* ambush; (caccia) lying in wait

appo'stare *vt* post ⟨soldati⟩

appo'starsi *vr* lie in wait

ap'prendere *vt* understand; (imparare) learn

apprendi'mento *nm* learning. apprendimento assistito dal computer computer-aided learning

appren'dista *nmf* apprentice

apprendi'stato *nm* apprenticeship

apprensi'one *nf* apprehension; essere in ~ per be anxious about

appren'sivo *adj* apprehensive

ap'presso *adv & prep* (vicino) near; (dietro) behind; come ~ as follows

appre'stare *vt* prepare

appre'starsi *vr* get ready

apprez'zabile *adj* appreciable

apprezza'mento *nm* appreciation; (giudizio) opinion

apprez'zare *vt* appreciate

apprez'zato *adj* appreciated

ap'proccio *nm* approach

appro'dare *vi* land; ~ a fig come to; non ~ a nulla come to nothing

ap'prodo *nm* landing; (luogo) landing-stage

approfit'tare *vi* take advantage (di of), profit (di by)

approfitta'|tore, -trice *nmf* chancer

approfondi'mento *nm* deepening; di ~ ⟨corso⟩ advanced

approfon'dire *vt* broaden, widen ⟨indagine, conoscenze⟩

approfon'dirsi *vr* ⟨divario⟩ widen

approfon'dito *adj* ⟨studio, ricerca⟩ in-depth

appron'tare *vt* get ready, prepare

appropri'arsi *vr* ~ a (essere adatto a) suit; ~ di take possession of; ~ indebitamente di embezzle, misappropriate

appropri'ato *adj* appropriate

appropriazi'one *nf* Jur appropriation. appropriazione indebita Jur embezzlement

approssi'mare *vt* ~ per eccesso/difetto round up/down

approssi'marsi *vr* draw near

approssimativa'mente *adv* approximately

approssima'tivo *adj* approximate

approssimazi'one *nf* approximation

appro'vare *vt* approve of; approve ⟨legge⟩

a

approvazi'one *nf* approval

approvvigiona'mento *nm* supplying; **approvvigionamenti** *pl* provisions

approvvigio'nare *vt* supply

approvvigio'narsi *vr* stock up

appunta'mento *nm* appointment; fam date; **fissare un** ~, **prendere un** ~ make an appointment; **darsi** ~ decide to meet

appun'tare *vt* (annotare) take notes; (fissare) fix; (con spillo) pin; (appuntire) sharpen

appun'tarsi *vr* ~ **su** ‹*teoria*› be based on

appun'tato *nm* (carabiniere) lowest rank in the Carabinieri

ap'puntel'larsi *vr* (sostenersi) support oneself

ap'pun'tino *adv* meticulously

appun'tire *vt* sharpen

appun'tito *adj* ‹*matita*› sharp; ‹*mento*› pointed

ap'punto[1] *nm* note; (piccola critica) niggle

ap'punto[2] *adv* exactly; **per l'~!** exactly!; **stavo** ~ **dicendo ...** I was just saying ...

appura'mento *nm* verification

appu'rare *vt* verify

a'pribile *adj* that can be opened; **tettuccio apribile** Auto sun roof

apribot'tiglie *nm inv* bottle-opener

a'prile *nm* April; **primo d'aprile** April Fool's Day

aprio'ristico *adj* a priori

a'prire *vt* open; turn on ‹*luce, acqua ecc*›; (con chiave) unlock; open up ‹*ferita ecc*›; ~ **le ostilità** Mil commence hostilities; **apriti cielo!** heavens above!

a'prirsi *vr* open; (spaccarsi) split; (confidarsi) confide (**con** in)

apri'scatole *nm inv* tin opener, Br, can opener

APT *abbr* (**Azienda di Promozione Turistica**) Tourist Board

aqua'planing *nm* **andare in** ~ aquaplane

'aquila *nf* eagle; **non è un'~!** fig he's no genius!

aqui'lino *adj* aquiline

aqui'lone *nm* (giocattolo) kite

aqui'lotto *nm* (piccolo dell'aquila) eaglet

AR *abbr* (**andata e ritorno**) return [ticket]; *abbr* (**avviso di ricevimento**) return receipt for registered letters

ara'besco *nm* arabesque; hum scribble

A'rabia *nf* Arabia. **l'Arabia Saudita** Saudi Arabia

'arabo, -a [1] *adj* Arab; ‹*lingua*› Arabic [2] *nmf* Arab [3] *nm* (lingua) Arabic

arabo-israeli'ano *adj* Arab-Israeli

a'rachide *nf* peanut

arago'nese *adj* Aragonese

ara'gosta *nf* lobster

a'raldica *nf* heraldry

a'raldico *adj* heraldic

a'raldo *nm* herald

aran'ceto *nm* orange grove

a'rancia *nf* orange; **succo d'arancia** orange juice

aranci'ata *nf* orangeade

a'rancio *nm* orange (tree); (colore) orange

aranci'one *adj & nm* orange

a'rare *vt* plough

ara'tore *nm* ploughman

a'ratro *nm* plough

ara'tura *nf* ploughing

a'razzo *nm* tapestry

arbi'traggio *nm* Comm arbitrage; Sport refereeing; Jur arbitration

arbi'trare *vt* arbitrate in; Sport referee

arbitrarietà *nf* arbitrariness

arbi'trario *adj* arbitrary

arbi'trato *nm* arbitration

ar'bitrio *nm* will; **è un** ~ it's very high-handed

'arbitro *nm* arbiter; (Sport: nel calcio, boxe) referee, ref fam; (nel baseball, tennis, cricket) umpire

arboricol'tura *nf* arboriculture

ar'busto *nm* shrub

'arca *nf* ark; (cassa) chest. **l'~ di Noè** Noah's Ark

ar'caico *adj* archaic

arca'ismo *nm* archaism

ar'cangelo *nm* archangel

ar'cano [1] *adj* mysterious [2] *nm* mystery

ar'cata *nf* arch; (serie di archi) arcade

archeolo'gia *nf* archaeology

archeo'logico *adj* archaeological

arche'ologo, -a *nmf* archaeologist

ar'chetipo *nm* archetype

ar'chetto *nm* Mus bow

archi'tettare *vt* fig devise; **cosa state architettando?** fig what are you plotting?

archi'tetto *nm* architect. **architetto d'interni** interior designer

archit'tonico *adj* architectural

architet'tura *nf* anche Comput architecture

archi'trave *nm* lintel

archivi'abile *adj* that can be filed

archivi'are *vt* file, archive; Jur close

archiviazi'one *nf* filing; (Jur: di caso) closing. **archiviazione dati** data storage

ar'chivio *nm* archives *pl*; Comput file

archi'vista *nmf* filing clerk

archi'vistica *nf* rules governing the keeping of archives and records

ARCI *nf abbr* (**Associazione Ricreativa Culturale Italiana**) Italian cultural and leisure association

arci'duca *nm* archduke

arcidu'chessa *nf* archduchess

arci'ere *nm* archer

ar'cigno *adj* grim

arci'one *nm* saddle

arci'pelago *nm* archipelago

arci'vescovo *nm* archbishop

'**arco** *nm* arch; Math arc; (arma, Mus) bow; **nell'**∼ **di una giornata/due mesi** in the space of a day/two months. **arco rampante** flying buttress. **arco temporale** time-frame

arcoba'leno *nm* rainbow

arcu'are *vt* bend; ∼ **la schiena** ⟨gatto⟩ arch its back

arcu'arsi *vr* bend

arcu'ato *adj* bent; ⟨schiena di gatto⟩ arched

ar'dente *adj* burning; fig ardent. **camera ardente** chapel of rest

ardente'mente *adv* ardently

'**ardere** *vt/i* burn. **legna da ardere** firewood

ar'desia *nf* slate

ardi'mento *nm* boldness

ar'dire ① *vi* dare ② *nm* (coraggio) daring, boldness; (sfrontatezza) impudence

ar'dito *adj* daring; (coraggioso) bold; (sfacciato) impudent

ar'dore *nm* (calore) heat; fig ardour

'**arduo** *adj* arduous; (ripido) steep

'**area** *nf* area; (superficie) surface. **area fabbricabile** building land. **area di rigore** (in calcio) penalty area, penalty box. **area di servizio** service area. **area soggetta a vincoli ambientali** conservation area. **area [di sosta] per roulotte** trailer park Am, caravan site. **area di sviluppo** growth area

a'rena *nf* arena

are'naria *nf* sandstone

are'narsi *vr* run aground; ⟨fig: trattative⟩ reach deadlock; **mi sono arenato** I'm stuck

are'nile *nm* stretch of sand

areo'plano *nm* aeroplane

'**argano** *nm* winch

argen'tato *adj* silver-plated

ar'genteo *adj* silvery

argente'ria *nf* silver[ware]

argenti'ere *nm* silversmith

Argen'tina *nf* Argentina

argen'tina *nf* (maglia) round-necked pullover

argen'tino[1] *adj* silvery

argen'tino[2], **-a** *adj & nmf* Argentinian

ar'gento *nm* silver; **d'**∼ silver. **argento vivo** Chem quicksilver

ar'gilla *nf* clay

argil'loso *adj* ⟨terreno⟩ clayey; (simile all'argilla) clay-like

argi'nare *vt* embank; fig hold in check, contain

'**argine** *nm* embankment; (diga) dike; **fare** ∼ **a** fig hold in check, contain

argomen'tare *vi* argue

argo'mento *nm* argument; (motivo) reason; (soggetto) subject

argu'ire *vt* deduce

arguta'mente *adv* (con astuzia) shrewdly; (con facezia) wittily

ar'guto *adj* witty; (astuto) shrewd

ar'guzia *nf* wit; (battuta) witticism; (astuzia) shrewdness

'**aria** *nf* air; (aspetto) appearance; Mus tune; Auto choke; **avere l'**∼**...** look ...; **mandare all'**∼ **qualcosa** fig ruin something; **andare all'**∼ fig fall through; **a tenuta d'**∼ draughtproof; **avere la testa per** ∼ fig be absent-minded, have one's head in the clouds; **che** ∼ **tirava?** fig what was the atmosphere like?; **cambiare** ∼ fig have a change of scene; **cambia** ∼ **!** hum get out of here!. **corrente d'aria** draught; **aria-aria** *adj inv* Mil air-to-air. **aria condizionata** air-conditioning. **aria-terra** *adj inv* air-to-ground

ari'ano *adj* Aryan

arida'mente *adv* without emotion

aridità *nf* aridity

'**arido** *adj* arid

arieggi'are *vt* air; ∼ **una stanza** give a room an airing

arieggi'ato *adj* airy

ari'ete *nm* ram; (strumento) battering-ram; **Ariete** Astr Aries

ari'etta *nf* (brezza) breeze

a'ringa *nf* herring

ari'oso *adj* ⟨locale⟩ light and airy

'**arista** *nf* chine of pork

aristo'cratico, **-a** ① *adj* aristocratic ② *nmf* aristocrat

aristocra'zia *nf* aristocracy

arit'metica *nf* arithmetic

arit'metico *adj* arithmetical

arlec'chino *nm* Harlequin; fig buffoon

'**arma** *nf* weapon; (forze armate) [armed] forces; **armi** *pl* arms; **chiamare alle armi** call up; **sotto le armi** in the army; **alle prime armi** fig inexperienced, fledg[e]lling; **prendere/deporre le armi** take up arms/ put down one's arms; **passare qualcuno** ⋯⋗

a

per le armi execute somebody; confrontarsi ad armi pari compete on an equal footing. **arma bianca** knife. **arma a doppio taglio** fig double-edged sword. **arma da fuoco** firearm. **arma di distruzione di massa** weapon of mass destruction. **arma impropria** makeshift weapon. **arma segreta** fig secret weapon. **armi** pl **nucleari** nuclear weapons

armadi'etto nm locker, cupboard; (in aereo) overhead locker. **armadietto del bagno** bathroom cabinet. **armadietto dei medicinali** medicine cabinet

arma'dillo nm armadillo

ar'madio nm cupboard; (guardaroba) wardrobe. **armadio a muro** fitted cupboard

armamen'tario nm tools pl; fig paraphernalia

arma'mento nm armament, weaponry; Naut fitting out

ar'mare vt arm; (equipaggiare) fit out; Archit reinforce

ar'marsi vr arm oneself (**di** with)

ar'mata nf army; (flotta) fleet

ar'mato adj armed; **rapina a mano armata** armed robbery

arma'tore nm shipowner

arma'tura nf framework; (impalcatura) scaffolding; (di guerriero) armour

armeggi'are vi fig manoeuvre

Ar'menia nf Armenia

ar'meno, -a adj & nmf Armenian

arme'ria nf Mil armoury

armi'stizio nm armistice

armo'nia nf harmony

ar'monica nf armonica [a bocca] mouth-organ

ar'monico adj harmonic

armoniosa'mente adv harmoniously

armoni'oso adj harmonious

armoniz'zare ① vt harmonize ② vi match

armoniz'zarsi vr ‹colori› go together, match

ar'nese nm tool; (oggetto) thing; (congegno) gadget; **male in** ~ in bad condition

'arnia nf beehive

a'roma nm aroma; **aromi** pl herbs; **aromi** pl **naturali/artificiali** natural/artificial flavourings

aromatera'pia nf aromatherapy

aro'matico adj aromatic

aromatiz'zare vt flavour

'arpa nf harp

ar'peggio nm arpeggio

ar'pia nf harpy

arpi'one nm hook; (pesca) harpoon

ar'pista nmf harpist

arrabat'tarsi vr do all one can

arrabbi'arsi vr get angry

arrabbi'ato adj angry

arrabbia'tura nf rage; **prendersi un'**~ fly into a rage

arraf'fare vt grab

arraf'fone nm fam thief

arrampi'carsi vr climb [up]; ~ **sugli specchi** fig clutch at straws

arrampi'cata nf climb

arrampica|'tore, -trice nmf climber. **arrampicatore sociale** social climber

arran'care vi limp, hobble; fig struggle, limp along

arrangia'mento nm arrangement

arrangi'are vt arrange

arrangi'arsi vr manage; ~ **alla meglio** get by; **arrangiati!** get on with it!

arrangia|'tore, -trice nmf Mus arranger

arra'parsi vr vulg get randy

arre'care vt bring; (causare) cause

arreda'mento nm interior decoration; (l'arredare) furnishing; (mobili ecc) furnishings pl

arre'dare vt furnish

arreda|'tore, -trice nmf interior designer

ar'redo nm furnishings pl

arrem'baggio nm **lanciarsi all'**~ fig stampede

Ar'rendersi vr surrender; ~ **all'evidenza dei fatti** face facts

arren'devole adj ‹persona› yielding

arrendevo'lezza nf softness

arre'stare vt arrest; (fermare) stop

arre'starsi vr halt

ar'resto nm stop; Jur arrest; **la dichiaro in [stato d']** ~ you are under arrest; **mandato di arresto** warrant. **arresto cardiaco** heart failure, cardiac arrest. **arresti** pl **domiciliari** Jur house arrest

arretra'mento nm withdrawal

arre'trare ① vt withdraw; pull back ‹giocatore› ② vi withdraw

arre'trato ① adj (paese ecc) backward; (Mil: posizione) rear; **numero arretrato** (di rivista) back number **del lavoro** ~ a backlog of work ② nm (di stipendio) back pay; **essere in** ~ be behind schedule; **arretrati** pl arrears. **arretrati** pl **di paga** back pay

arricchi'mento nm enrichment

arric'chire vt enrich

arric'chirsi vr get rich

arric'chito, -a nmf nouveau riche

arricciaca'pelli nm inv tongs

arricci'are vt curl; ~ **il naso** turn up one's nose

ar'ridere *vi* ∼ **a qualcuno** ⟨*sorte*⟩ smile on somebody

ar'ringa *nf* Jur closing address

arrin'gare *vt* harangue

arrischi'arsi *vr* dare

arrischi'ato *adj* risky; (imprudente) rash

arri'vare *vi* arrive; ∼ **a** (raggiungere) reach; (ridursi) be reduced to

arri'vato, -a ① *adj* successful; **ben** ∼**!** welcome!
② *nmf* successful person; **il primo/ secondo** ∼ (in gara) the first/second to finish

arrive'derci *int* goodbye; ∼ **a domani** see you tomorrow

arri'vismo *nm* social climbing; (nel lavoro) careerism

arri'vista *nmf* social climber; (nel lavoro) careerist

ar'rivo *nm* arrival; Sport finish; ∼ **previsto per le ore ...** expected time of arrival ...

arro'gante *adj* arrogant

arro'ganza *nf* arrogance

arro'garsi *vr* ∼ **il diritto di fare qualcosa** take it upon oneself to do something; ∼ **il merito** take the credit

arrossa'mento *nm* reddening

arros'sare *vt* make red, redden ⟨*occhi*⟩

arros'sarsi *vr* go red

arros'sire *vi* blush, go red

arro'stire *vt* roast; toast ⟨*pane*⟩; (ai ferri) grill

arro'stirsi *vr* fig broil

ar'rosto *adj* & *nm* roast; **molto fumo e niente** ∼ fig all show and no substance. **arrosto d'agnello** roast lamb

arro'tare *vt* sharpen; (fam: investire) run over

arro'tino *nm* knife-sharpener

arroto'lare *vt* roll up

arroton'dare *vt* round; Math ecc round off; ∼ **lo stipendio** supplement one's income

arroton'darsi *vr* become round; ⟨*persona*⟩ get plump

arrovel'larsi *vr* ∼ **il cervello** rack one's brains

arroven'tare *vt* make red-hot

arroven'tarsi *vr* become red-hot

arroven'tato *adj* red-hot; ⟨*fig: discorso*⟩ fiery

arruf'fare *vt* ruffle; fig confuse

arruf'farsi *vr* become ruffled

arruf'fato *adj* ⟨*capelli*⟩ dishevelled, tousled

arruffia'narsi *vr* ∼ **[con] qualcuno** fig butter somebody up

arruggi'nire *vt* rust

arruggi'nirsi *vr* go rusty; fig (fisicamente) stiffen up; ⟨*conoscenze*⟩ go rusty

arruggi'nito *adj* rusty

arruola'mento *nm* enlistment

arruo'lare *vt/i* enlist

arruo'larsi *vr* enlist

arse'nale *nm* arsenal; (cantiere) [naval] dockyard

ar'senico *nm* arsenic

'arso ① *pp di* ARDERE
② *adj* burnt; (arido) dry

ar'sura *nf* burning heat; (sete) parching thirst

art déco *nf* art decò

'arte *nf* art; (abilità) craftsmanship; **senza** ∼ **né parte** incapable; **nome d'arte** professional name. **arte drammatica** dramatics; **le belle arti** *pl* the fine arts. **arti** *pl* **figurative** figurative arts. **arti** *pl* **dello spettacolo** performing arts

arte'fare *vt* adulterate ⟨*vino*⟩; disguise ⟨*voce*⟩

arte'fatto *adj* fake; ⟨*vino*⟩ adulterated

ar'tefice ① *nm* craftsman; fig author
② *nf* craftswoman

ar'teria *nf* artery. **arteria [stradale]** arterial road

arterio'sclerosi *nf* arteriosclerosis, hardening of the arteries

arterioscle'rotico *adj* senile

arteri'oso *adj* Anat arterial

'Artico *nm* l'∼ the Arctic

'artico *adj* Arctic

artico'lare ① *adj* articular
② *vt* articulate; (suddividere) divide

artico'larsi *vr* fig ∼ **in** consist of

artico'lato *adj* Auto articulated; fig well-constructed

articolazi'one *nf* Anat articulation

ar'ticolo *nm* article; **articoli** *pl* **per la casa** household goods; **articoli** *pl* **per la cucina** kitchenware; **articoli** *pl* **di marca** brand name goods; **articoli** *pl* **da regalo** gifts; **articoli** *pl* **da spiaggia** beach gear; **articoli** *pl* **sportivi** sports gear; **negozio di articoli sportivi** sports shop; **articoli** *pl* **vari** sundries. **articolo civetta** Comm loss leader. **articolo determinativo** Gram definite article. **articolo di fondo** leader, leading article. **articolo indeterminativo** Gram indefinite article. **articolo di prima pagina** Journ cover story. **articolo principale** Journ lead story

'Artide *nf* l'∼ the Arctic [region]

artifici'ale *adj* artificial

artifici'ere *nm* Mil explosives expert, bomb disposal expert

arti'ficio *nm* artifice; (affettazione) affectation

artificiosità *nf* artificiality

artifici'oso *adj* artful; (affettato) affected

artigi'ana *nf* craftswoman

artigia'nale *adj* made by hand; hum amateurish

artigianal'mente *adv* with craftsmanship; hum amateurishly

artigia'nato *nm* craftsmanship; (ceto) craftsmen *pl*

artigi'ano *nm* craftsman

artigli'ato *adj* with claws

artigli'ere *nm* artilleryman

artiglie'ria *nf* artillery. **artiglieria antiaerea** flak

ar'tiglio *nm* claw; fig clutch; **sfoderare gli artigli** fig show one's claws

ar'tista *nmf* artist

artistica'mente *adv* artistically

ar'tistico *adj* artistic

arti'stoide *adj* arty

art nouveau *nf* art nouveau

'arto *nm* limb

ar'trite *nf* arthritis

ar'tritico, -a *nmf* arthritic

ar'trosi *nf* rheumatism

arzigogo'lato *adj* fantastic, bizarre

ar'zillo *adj* sprightly

a'scella *nf* armpit

ascen'dente ① *adj* ascending ② *nm* (antenato) ancestor; (influenza) ascendancy; Astr ascendant

ascen'denza *nf* ancestry

a'scendere *vi* ascend

ascensi'one *nf* ascent; **l'Ascensione** the Ascension

ascen'sore *nm* lift, elevator Am

a'scesa *nf* ascent; (al trono) accession; (al potere) rise

a'scesi *nf* asceticism

a'scesso *nm* abscess

a'sceta *nmf* ascetic

a'scetico *adj* ascetic

'ascia *nf* axe

asciugabianche'ria *nm inv* (stenditoio) clothes horse; (macchina) tumble-drier

asciugaca'pelli *nm inv* hair dryer, hairdrier

asciuga'mano *nm* towel. **asciugamano di carta** paper towel

asciu'gare *vt* dry; ~ **le stoviglie** do the drying-up

asciu'garsi *vr* dry oneself; (diventare asciutto) dry up; ~ **le mani** dry one's hands

asciuga'trice *nf* tumble dryer

asci'utto *adj* dry; (magro) wiry; ⟨risposta⟩ curt; **essere all'**~ fig be hard up

ascol'tare ① *vt* listen to ② *vi* listen

ascolta|**'tore, -trice** *nmf* listener

a'scolto *nm* listening; **dare** ~ **a** listen to; **essere in** ~ Radio be listening; **mettersi in** ~ Radio tune in; **prestare** ~ listen

a'scrivere *vt* (attribuire) ascribe; ~ **a** (annoverare) number among

asessu'ato *adj* asexual

a'settico *adj* aseptic

asfal'tare *vt* asphalt

asfal'tato *adj* tarmac

a'sfalto *nm* asphalt

asfis'sia *nf* asphyxia

asfissi'ante *adj* ⟨caldo⟩ oppressive; ⟨fig: persona⟩ annoying

asfissi'are *vt* asphyxiate; fig annoy

'Asia *nf* Asia. **Asia Minore** Asia Minor

asi'ago *nm* full-fat white cheese

asi'atico, -a *adj & nmf* Asian

a'silo *nm* shelter; (d'infanzia) nursery school. **asilo infantile** day nursery. **asilo nido** day nursery. **asilo politico** political asylum

asim'metrico *adj* asymmetric[al]

a'sincrono *adj* asynchronous

'asino *nm* donkey; (fig: persona stupida) ass; Sch dunce; **qui casca l'**~**!** fig that's where it falls down!

'asma *nf* asthma

a'smatico *adj* asthmatic

asoci'ale *adj* asocial

'asola *nf* buttonhole

a'sparagi *nmpl* asparagus *sg*

aspara'gina *nf* Bot asparagus fern

a'sparago *nm* asparagus

a'spergere *vt* ~ **con/di** sprinkle with

asperità *nf inv* harshness; (di terreno) roughness

asper'sorio *nm* aspergillum, holy-water sprinkler

aspet'tare ① *vt* wait for; (prevedere) expect; ~ **un bambino** be expecting [a baby]; **fare** ~ **qualcuno** keep somebody waiting ② *vi* wait

aspet'tarsi *vr* expect

aspetta'tiva *nf* expectation; (nel lavoro) leave of absence; **all'altezza delle aspettative** up to expectations; **inferiore alle aspettative** not up to expectations. **aspettativa per malattia** sick leave. **aspettativa per maternità** maternity leave

a'spetto[1] *nm* look; (di problema) aspect; **di bell'**~ good-looking

a'spetto[2] *nm* **sala d'aspetto** waiting room

'aspic *nm* aspic

aspi'rante ① *adj* aspiring; ⟨pompa⟩ suction *attrib*

② *nmf* (a un posto) applicant; (al trono) aspirant; **gli aspiranti al titolo** the contenders for the title

aspira'polvere *nm inv* vacuum cleaner; **passare l'~** vacuum, hoover

aspi'rare **①** *vt* inhale; Mech suck in; (con elettrodomestici) vacuum, hoover
② *vi* ~ **a** aspire to

aspi'rato *adj* aspirate

aspira'tore *nm* extractor fan

aspirazi'one *nf* inhalation; Mech suction; (ambizione) ambition

aspi'rina® *nf* aspirin

aspor'tare *vt* take away

a'sporto **da ~** take-away

aspra'mente *adv* (duramente) severely

a'sprezza *nf* (al gusto) sourness; (di clima) severity; (di carattere, parole, suono) harshness; (di odore) pungency; (di litigio) bitterness

a'sprigno *adj* slightly sour

'aspro *adj* ⟨al gusto⟩ sour; ⟨clima⟩ severe; ⟨suono, parole⟩ harsh; ⟨odore⟩ pungent; ⟨litigio⟩ bitter

assaggi'are *vt* taste

assaggia|'tore, -trice *nmf* taster

assag'gini *nmpl* Culin samples

as'saggio *nm* tasting; (piccola quantità) taste; (fig: campione) sample

as'sai *adv* very; (moltissimo) very much; (abbastanza) enough

assa'lire *vt* attack

assali|'tore, -trice *nmf* assailant

assal'tare *vt* Mil attack, charge; hold up (banca, treno)

assalta'tore *nm* hold-up man

as'salto *nm* attack; **d'~** ⟨giornalismo⟩ aggressive; **prendere d'~** storm ⟨città⟩; fig mob ⟨persona⟩; hold up ⟨banca⟩

assapo'rare *vt* savour

assas'sina *nf* murderess

assassi'nare *vt* murder, assassinate; fig murder

assas'sinio *nm* murder, assassination

assas'sino **①** *adj* murderous
② *nm* murderer

'asse **①** *nf* board. **asse da stiro** ironing board.
② *nm* Techn axle; Math axis

assecon'dare *vt* satisfy; (favorire) support; **~ i capricci di qualcuno** indulge somebody's every whim; **~ i desideri di qualcuno** comply with somebody's wishes

assedi'are *vt* besiege

assedi'ato *adj* besieged

as'sedio *nm* siege

assegna'mento *nm* allotment; **fare ~ su** rely on

asse'gnare *vt* allot; award ⟨premio⟩

assegna'tario, -a *nmf* recipient

assegnazi'one *nf* (di alloggio, denaro, borsa di studio) allocation; (di premio) award

as'segno *nm* allowance; (bancario) cheque; **contro ~** cash on delivery; **pagare con un ~** pay by cheque. **assegno circolare** bank draft. **assegni familiari** *pl* family allowance. **assegno post-datato** post-dated cheque. **assegno sbarrato** crossed cheque. **assegno non trasferibile** cheque made out to "account payee only". **assegno turistico** traveller's cheque. **assegno a vuoto** bad cheque, dud cheque

assem'blaggio *nm* assemblage

assem'blare *vt* assemble

assem'blea *nf* assembly; (adunanza) gathering. **assemblea generale annuale** Annual General Meeting, AGM

assembra'mento *nm* gathering

assem'brare *vt* gather

assen'nato *adj* sensible

as'senso *nm* assent

assen'tarsi *vr* go away; (da stanza) leave the room

as'sente **①** *adj* absent; (distratto) absent-minded
② *nmf* absentee

assente'ismo *nm* absenteeism

assente'ista *nmf* frequent absentee

assen'tire *vi* acquiesce (**a** in)

as'senza *nf* absence; (mancanza) lack. **assenza di gravità** zero gravity. **assenze** *pl* **ingiustificate** (a scuola) truancy

asse'rire *vi* assert

asser|'tore, -trice *nmf* supporter

asserragli'arsi *vr* barricade oneself

asser'tivo *adj* assertive

asservi'mento *nm* subservience

asser'vire *vt* fig enslave

asser'virsi *vr* fig be subservient

asserzi'one *nf* assertion

assesso'rato *nm* [council] department

asses'sore *nm* councillor

assesta'mento *nm* settlement

asse'stare *vt* arrange; **~ un colpo** deal a blow

asse'starsi *vr* settle oneself

asse'stato *adj* **ben ~** well-judged

asse'tato *adj* parched

as'setto *nm* order; Naut, Aeron trim; **in ~ di guerra** on a war footing; **cambiare l'~ territoriale dell'Europa** change the map of Europe

assi'cella *nf* lath

assicu'rabile *adj* insurable

assicu'rare *vt* assure; Comm insure; register ‹*posta*›; (fissare) secure; (accertare) ensure

assicu'rarsi *vr* (con contratto) insure oneself; (legarsi) fasten oneself; ~ **che** make sure that

assicu'rata *nf* registered letter

assicura'tivo *adj* insurance *attrib*

assicu'rato *adj* insured; **lettera assicurata** registered letter

assicura‖'tore, -trice ① *nmf* insurance agent
② *adj* insurance; **società assicuratrice** insurance company

assicurazi'one *nf* assurance; (contratto) insurance; **fare un'~** take out insurance. **assicurazione multirischi** blanket cover. **assicurazione sanitaria** medical insurance. **assicurazione di viaggio** travel insurance

assidera'mento *nm* exposure

asside'rarsi *vr* fam be frozen; Med be suffering from exposure

asside'rato *adj* Med suffering from exposure; fam frozen

assidua'mente *adv* assiduously

assiduità *nf* assiduity

as'siduo *adj* assiduous; ‹*cliente*› regular

assi'eme *adj* [together] with

assil'lante *adj* ‹*persona, pensiero*› nagging

assil'lare *vt* pester

assil'larsi *vr* torment oneself

as'sillo *nm* worry

assimi'lare *vt* assimilate

assimilazi'one *nf* assimilation

assi'oma *nm* axiom

assio'matico *adj* axiomatic

As'siria *nf* Assyria

as'sise *nfpl* assizes; **Corte d'Assise** Court of Assize[s]

assi'stente *nmf* assistant. **assistente sociale** social worker. **assistente sociosanitario** care worker. **assistente universitario** assistant lecturer. **assistente di volo** flight attendant

assi'stenza *nf* assistance; (presenza) presence. **assistenza alla clientela** customer care. **assistenza medica** medical care. **assistenza ospedaliera** hospital treatment. **assistenza sanitaria** health care. **assistenza sociale** social work

assistenzi'ale *adj* welfare

assistenzia'lismo *nm* abuse of the welfare state

as'sistere ① *vt* assist; (curare) nurse
② *vi* ~ **a** (essere presente) be present at; watch (spettacolo ecc)

assi'stito *adj* ~ **da computer** computer-aided

'asso *nm* ace; **piantare in** ~ leave in the lurch. **asso nella manica** trump card

associ'are *vt* join; (collegare) associate

associ'arsi *vr* join forces; Comm enter into partnership; ~ **a** join; subscribe to (giornale ecc)

associ'ato, -a ① *adj* associate
② *nmf* partner

associazi'one *nf* association. **associazione di categoria** trade-union. **associazione per delinquere** criminal organization. **Associazione Europea di Libero Scambio** European Free Trade Association. **associazione in partecipazione** Comm joint venture

associazio'nismo *nm* Pol excessive tendency to form associations; Psych associationism

asso'dare *vt* ascertain ‹*verità*›

assogget'tare *vt* subject

assogget'tarsi *vr* submit

asso'lato *adj* sunny

assol'dare *vt* recruit

as'solo *nm* Mus solo

as'solto *pp di* ASSOLVERE

assoluta'mente *adv* absolutely

assolu'tismo *nm* absolutism

assolu'tista *nmf* absolutist

assolu'tistico *adj* absolutist

asso'luto *adj* absolute

assolu'torio *adj* **formula assolutoria** acquittal

assoluzi'one *nf* acquittal; Relig absolution

as'solvere *vt* perform ‹*compito*›; Jur acquit; Relig absolve

assolvi'mento *nm* performance

assomigli'are *vi* ~ **a** be like, resemble

assomigli'arsi *vr* resemble each other

assom'marsi *vr* combine; ~ **a qualcosa** add to something

asso'nanza *nf* assonance

asson'nato *adj* drowsy

asso'pirsi *vr* doze off

assor'bente *adj & nm* absorbent. **assorbente igienico** sanitary towel

assor'bire *vt* absorb

assor'dante *adj* deafening

assor'dare *vt* deafen

assorti'mento *nm* assortment

assor'tire *vt* match ‹*colori*›

assor'tito *adj* assorted; ‹*colori, persone*› matched

as'sorto *adj* engrossed

assottiglia'mento *nm* thinning; (aguzzamento) sharpening

assottigli'are *vt* make thin; (aguzzare) sharpen; (ridurre) reduce

assottigli'arsi *vr* grow thin; ⟨finanze⟩ be whittled away

assue'fare *vt* accustom

assue'farsi *vr* ∼ **a** get used to

assue'fatto *adj* (a caffè, aspirina) immune to the effects; (a droga) addicted

assuefazi'one *nf* (a caffè, aspirina) immunity to the effects; (a droga) addiction

as'sumere *vt* assume; take on ⟨impiegato⟩ ∼ **informazioni** make inquiries

as'sunto ① *pp di* ASSUMERE ② *nm* task

assunzi'one *nf* (di impiegato) employment; **l'Assunzione** Relig Assumption

assurdità *nf inv* absurdity; **dire delle** ∼ talk nonsense

as'surdo *adj* absurd

'asta *nf* pole; Mech bar; Comm auction; **a mezz'**∼ at half-mast. **asta di livello [dell'olio]** Auto dip-stick

a'stemio *adj* abstemious

aste'nersi *vr* abstain (**da** from)

astensi'one *nf* abstention

astensio'nismo *nm* persistent abstention

astensio'nista *nmf* persistent abstainer

astensio'nistico *adj* **tendenza astensionistica** tendency to abstain

aste'nuto, **-a** *nmf* abstainer

aste'risco *nm* asterisk

aste'roide *nm* asteroid

'astice *nm* crayfish

asti'cella *nf* stick; (in salto in alto) bar

astig'matico *adj* astigmatic

astigma'tismo *nm* astigmatism

asti'nenza *nf* abstinence; **crisi di astinenza** withdrawal symptoms

'astio *nm* rancour; **avere** ∼ **contro qualcuno** bear somebody a grudge

asti'oso *adj* resentful

a'stragalo *nm* anklebone

'astrakan *nm* astrakhan

astrat'tezza *nf* abstractness

astrat'tismo *nm* abstractionism

a'stratto *adj* abstract

astrin'gente *adj* & *nm* astringent

'astro *nm* star

+astro *suff* **giovinastro** *nm* lout; **giallastro** *adj* yellowish; **dolciastro** *adj* sweetish

astro'fisica *nf* astrophysics

astro'fisico, **-a** ① *adj* astrophysical ② *nmf* astrophysicist

astrolo'gia *nf* astrology

astro'logico *adj* astrological

a'strologo, **-a** *nmf* astrologer

astro'nauta *nmf* astronaut

astro'nautica *nf* astronautics

astro'nave *nf* spaceship

astrono'mia *nf* astronomy

astro'nomico *adj* (anche fig) astronomic, astronomical

a'stronomo, **-a** *nmf* astronomer

astrusità *nf* abstruseness

a'struso *adj* abstruse

a'stuccio *nm* case

a'stuto *adj* shrewd; (furbo) cunning

a'stuzia *nf* shrewdness; (azione) trick

a'tavico *adj* atavistic

ate'ismo *nm* atheism

ate'lier *nm inv* (di alta moda) atelier; (di artista) [artist's] studio

A'tene *nf* Athens

ate'neo *nm* university

ateni'ese *adj* & *nmf* Athenian

'ateo, **-a** *adj* & *nmf* atheist

a'tipico *adj* atypical

at'lante *nm* atlas; **i monti dell'Atlante** the Atlas Mountains

at'lantico *adj* Atlantic; **l'[Oceano] Atlantico** the Atlantic [Ocean]

at'leta *nmf* athlete

a'tletica *nf* athletics *sg*. **atletica leggera** track and field events. **atletica pesante** weight-lifting, boxing, wrestling, etc

a'tletico *adj* athletic

atle'tismo *nm* athleticism

atmo'sfera *nf* atmosphere

atmo'sferico *adj* atmospheric

a'tollo *nm* atoll

a'tomica *nf* atom bomb

a'tomico *adj* atomic

atomiz'zare *vt* atomize

atomizza'tore *nm* atomizer

'atomo *nm* atom

'atono *adj* unstressed

'atrio *nm* entrance hall, lobby

a'troce *adj* atrocious; ⟨terrible⟩ dreadful

atroce'mente *adv* atrociously

atrocità *nf inv* atrocity

atro'fia *nf* atrophy

atrofiz'zare *vt* atrophy

atrofiz'zarsi *vr* Med, fig atrophy

attac'cabile *adj* attachable

attaccabot'toni *nmf inv* [crashing] bore

attacca'brighe *nmf inv* troublemaker

attacca'mento *nm* attachment

attac'cante ① *adj* attacking ② *nm* Sport forward

attacca'panni *nm inv* [coat-]hanger; (a muro) [clothes-]hook

attac'care ① *vt* attach; (legare) tie; (appendere) hang; (cucire) sew on; (contagiare) pass on; (assalire) attack; (iniziare) start ② *vi* stick; (diffondersi) catch on

attac'carsi *vr* cling; (affezionarsi) become attached; (litigare) quarrel

attacca'ticcio *adj* sticky; fig clinging and tiresome

attac'cato *adj* stuck

attacca'tura *nf* junction. **attaccatura dei capelli** hairline

attac'chino *nm* billposter

at'tacco *nm* attack; (punto d'unione) junction; (accesso) fit. **attacco aereo** air attack. **attacco cardiaco** heart attack. **attacco epilettico** epileptic fit

attanagli'are *vt* (fig: tormentare) haunt

attar'darsi *vr* stay late; (indugiare) linger

attec'chire *vi* take; (moda ecc) catch on

atteggia'mento *nm* attitude

atteggi'are *vt* assume

atteggi'arsi *vr* ~ a pose as

attem'pato *adj* elderly

atten'darsi *vr* camp, pitch camp

atten'dente *nm* Mil batman

at'tendere ① *vt* wait for ② *vi* ~ a attend to

atten'dersi *vr* expect

atten'dibile *adj* reliable

attendibilità *nf* reliability

atte'nersi *vr* ~ a stick to

attenta'mente *adv* attentively

atten'tare *vi* ~ a make an attempt on

atten'tato *nm* act of violence; (politico) assassination attempt; ~ alla vita di attempted murder of. **attentato dinamitardo** bombing

attenta|'tore, -trice *nmf* attacker; (a scopo politico) terrorist

at'tento *adj* attentive; (accurato) careful; ~! look out!; **stare** ~ pay attention; 'attenti al cane' 'beware of the dog'

attenu'ante *nf* extenuating circumstance

attenu'are *vt* attenuate; (minimizzare) minimize; subdue (colori ecc); calm (dolore); soften ‹colpo›

attenu'arsi *vr* diminish

attenuazi'one *nf* lessening

attenzi'one *nf* attention; (cura) care; **fare** ~ be careful; ~! watch out!; ~, **prego** your attention, please; **coprire di attenzioni** lavish attention on

atter'raggio *nm* landing. **atterraggio di fortuna** emergency landing

atter'rare ① *vt* knock down ② *vi* land

atter'rire *vt* terrorize

atter'rirsi *vr* be terrified

at'tesa *nf* waiting; (aspettativa) expectation; **in** ~ **di** waiting for

at'teso *pp di* ATTENDERE

atte'stabile *adj* certifiable

atte'stare *vt* state; (certificare) certify

atte'stato *nm* certificate

attestazi'one *nf* certificate; (dichiarazione) declaration

'Attica *nf* Attica

'attico[1] *nm* (lingua) Attic

'attico[2] *nm* (appartamento) penthouse

at'tiguo *adj* adjacent

attil'lato *adj* ‹vestito› close-fitting

'attimo *nm* second; **un** ~! just a sec!; **in un** ~ in double-quick time; **non ho avuto un** ~ **di respiro** I haven't had time to draw breath

atti'nente *adj* ~ a pertaining to

at'tingere *vt* draw; fig obtain

atti'rare *vt* attract

atti'rarsi *vr* draw ‹attenzione›; incur ‹odio›

attitudi'nale *nm* **test attitudinale** aptitude test

atti'tudine *nf* (disposizione) aptitude; (atteggiamento) attitude

atti'vare *vt* activate

attivazi'one *nf* setting in motion, turning on; Phys, Chem activation

atti'vismo *nm* activism

atti'vista *nmf* activist

attività *nf inv* activity; Comm assets *pl.* **attività fisse** *pl* fixed assets. **attività liquide** *pl* Comm liquid assets

at'tivo ① *adj* active; Comm productive ② *nm* assets *pl*

attiz'zare *vt* poke; fig stir up

attizza'toio *nm* poker

'atto *nm* act; (azione) action; Comm, Jur deed; (certificato) certificate; **fare** ~ **di presenza** put in an appearance; **mettere in** ~ put into action; **atti** *pl* (di società ecc) proceedings. **atti** *pl* **di libidine violenta** indecent assault. **atti** *pl* **osceni** gross indecency. **atto di vendita** bill of sale

+attolo *suff* **vermiciattolo** *nm* slimy individual

at'tonito *adj* astonished

attorcigli'are *vt* twist

attorcigli'arsi *vr* get twisted

at'tore *nm* actor

attorni'are *vt* surround

attorni'arsi *vr* ~ **di** surround oneself with

at'torno ① *adv* around, about ② *prep* ~ a around, about

attrac'care *vt/i* dock

attra'ente *adj* attractive

at'trarre *vt* attract

at'trarsi *vr* be attracted to each other

attrat'tiva *nf* charm, attraction

attraversa'mento *nm* (di strada) crossing. **attraversamento pedonale** pedestrian crossing, crosswalk Am

attraver'sare *vt* cross; (passare) go through

attra'verso *prep* through; (obliquamente) across

attrazi'one *nf* attraction. **attrazioni** *pl* **turistiche** tourist attractions

attrez'zare *vt* equip; Naut rig

attrez'zarsi *vr* kit oneself out

attrezza'tura *nf* equipment; Naut rigging. **attrezzatura da campeggio** camping equipment

at'trezzo *nm* tool; **attrezzi** *pl* equipment; Sport appliances *pl*

attribu'ibile *adj* attributable

attribu'ire *vt* attribute

attribu'irsi *vr* ascribe to oneself; ∼ **il merito di** claim credit for

attri'buto *nm* attribute

attribuzi'one *nf* attribution

at'trice *nf* actress

at'trito *nm* friction

attrup'pare *vt* assemble

attrup'parsi *vr* gather

attu'abile *adj* feasible

attuabilità *nf* viability

attu'ale *adj* present; (di attualità) topical; (effettivo) actual

attualità *nf* topicality; (avvenimento) news; **programma di attualità** current affairs programme

attualiz'zare *vt* update

attual'mente *adv* at present

attu'are *vt* carry out

attu'ario, -a *nmf* actuary

attu'arsi *vr* be realized

attua'tore *nm* Techn actuator

attuazi'one *nf* carrying out

attuti'mento *nm* (di colpo) softening; (di suoni) muffling

attu'tire *vt* deaden; ∼ **il colpo** soften the blow

au'dace *adj* daring, bold; (insolente) audacious

au'dacia *nf* daring, boldness; (insolenza) audacity

audiapprendi'mento *nm* audio-based learning

'audience *nf inv* (telespettatori) audience

'audio *nm* audio

audiocas'setta *nf* audio cassette

audio'leso *adj* hearing-impaired

audio'libro *nm* audiobook, talking book

audio'metrico *adj* Med aural

audiovi'sivo *adj* audiovisual

'auditing *nm* auditing

audi'torio *nm* auditorium

audizi'one *nf* audition; Jur hearing

'auge *nm* height; **essere in** ∼ be popular

augu'rare *vt* wish

augu'rarsi *vr* hope

au'gurio *nm* wish; (presagio) omen; **auguri!** all the best!; (a Natale) Happy Christmas!; **tanti auguri** best wishes

au'gusto *adj* august

'aula *nf* classroom; Univ lecture-hall; (sala) hall; **silenzio in** ∼! silence in court!. **aula bunker** (in tribunale) secure courtroom. **aula magna** Univ great hall. **aula del tribunale** courtroom

aumen'tare *vt/i* increase; ∼ **di peso** gain weight

au'mento *nm* increase; (di stipendio) [pay] rise. **aumento di prezzo** price increase

'aureo *adj* golden

au'reola *nf* halo

au'rora *nf* dawn. **aurora boreale** aurora borealis, Northern Lights

auscul'tare *vt* Med auscultate

ausili'are *adj & nmf* auxiliary

auspi'cabile *adj* è ∼ **che ...** it is to be hoped that ...

auspi'care *vt* hope for

au'spicio *nm* omen; **auspici** *pl* (protezione) auspices; **è di buon** ∼ it is a good omen

austerità *nf* austerity

au'stero *adj* austere

Austra'lasia *nf* Australasia

au'strale *adj* southern

Au'stralia *nf* Australia

australi'ano, -a *adj & nmf* Australian

'Austria *nf* Austria

au'striaco, -a *adj & nmf* Austrian

austroun'garico *adj* Austro-Hungarian

autar'chia *nf* autarchy

au'tarchico *adj* autarchic

aut aut *nm inv* either-or [choice]

autenti'care *vt* authenticate

autenti'cato *adj* certified

autenticità *nf* authenticity

au'tentico *adj* authentic; (vero) true

au'tismo *nm* autism

au'tista *nm* driver

au'tistico *adj* autistic

'auto *nf inv* car; **viaggiare in** ∼ travel by car. **auto blindata** armour-plated car. **auto a quattro ruote motrici** four-wheel drive car. **auto sportiva** sports car. **auto a trazione anteriore** front- ···⟶

wheel drive car. **auto usata** second-hand car

auto+ *pref* self+

autoabbron'zante ① *nm* self-tan ② *adj* self-tanning

autoaccesso'rista *nmf* car accessory supplier

autoade'sivo ① *adj* self-adhesive ② *nm* sticker

autoaffermazi'one *nf* self-assertion

autoambu'lanza *nf* ambulance

autoa'nalisi *nf* self-analysis

autoartico'lato *nm* articulated lorry

autobiogra'fia *nf* autobiography

autobio'grafico *adj* autobiographical

auto'blinda *nf* armoured car

auto'bomba *nf* car-bomb

auto'botte *nf* tanker

'autobus *nm inv* bus

auto'carro *nm* lorry

autocertificazi'one *nf* self-certification

autoci'sterna *nf* tanker

auto'clave *nf* (contenitore ad alta pressione) autoclave; (idraulica) surge tank

autocombusti'one *nf* spontaneous combustion

autocommiserazi'one *nf* self-pity

autocompiaci'mento *nm* smugness, self-satisfaction

autocompiaci'uto *adj* smug, self-satisfied

autoconcessio'nario *nm* car dealer

autocon'trollo *nm* self-control

au'tocrate *nm* autocrat

auto'cratico *adj* autocratic

auto'critica *nf* self-criticism

au'toctono *adj* native, aboriginal

autode'nuncia *nf* spontaneous confession

autodeterminazi'one *nf* self-determination

autodi'datta ① *adj* self-taught ② *nmf* self-educated person, autodidact

autodi'fesa *nf* self-defence

autodisci'plina *nf* self-discipline

autodi'struggersi *vr* self-destruct, auto-distruct

autodistrut'tivo *adj* self-destructive

autodistruzi'one *nf* self-destruction

autoferrotranvi'ario *adj* public transport *attrib*

autoferrotranvi'eri *nmpl* public transport workers

autoffi'cina *nf* garage

autofinanzia'mento *nm* self-financing

autofinanzi'arsi *vr* be self-financing; ⟨persona⟩ use one's own finance

autogesti'one *nf* self-management

autoge'stirsi *vr* ⟨operai, studenti⟩ be self-managing

autoge'stito *adj* self-managed

auto'gol *nm inv* Sport own goal

autogo'verno *nm* home rule, self-rule

au'tografo *adj* & *nm* autograph

auto'grill *nm inv* motorway café

autogrù *nf inv* breakdown truck, recovery vehicle

autogui'dato *adj* homing *attrib*

autoim'mune *adj* autoimmune

autoiro'nia *nf* self-mockery

autola'vaggio *nm* car wash

autolesi'one *nf* self-inflicted wound

autolesio'nismo *nm* self-harm; fig self-destruction

autolesio'nistico *adj* self-destructive

auto'linea *nf* bus line

au'toma *nm* robot

automatica'mente *adv* automatically

auto'matico ① *adj* automatic; **auto con cambio** ~ automatic ② *nm* (bottone) press-stud; (fucile) automatic

automatiz'zare *vt* automate

automatizzazi'one *nf* automation

automazi'one *nf* automation

auto'mezzo *nm* motor vehicle; **uscita automezzi** motor vehicles exit

auto'mobile *nf* [motor] car. **automobile da corsa** racing car

automobi'lina *nf* toy car

automobi'lismo *nm* motoring

automobi'lista *nmf* motorist

automobi'listico *adj* ⟨industria⟩ automobile *attrib*

automodel'lismo *nm* model car making; (collezione) model car collecting

autono'leggio *nm* car rental

autonoma'mente *adv* autonomously

autono'mia *nf* autonomy; Auto range; (di laptop, cellulare) battery life

au'tonomo *adj* autonomous

auto'parco *nm* (insieme di auto) fleet of cars

autopat'tuglia *nf* patrol car

auto'pista *nf* [fairground] race track

auto'pompa *nf* fire engine

auto'psia *nf* autopsy

autopunizi'one *nf* self-punishment

auto'radio *nf inv* car radio; (veicolo) radio car

au'tore, -trice *nmf* author; (di pitture) painter; (di furto ecc) perpetrator; **quadro d'**~ genuine master

autoregolamentazi'one *nf* self-regulation

autore'parto *nm* Mil mechanized unit

auto'revole *adj* authoritative; (che ha influenza) influential

autorevo'lezza *nf* authority

autoriduzi'one *nf* protest which takes the form of paying less than the requisite amount

autori'messa *nf* garage

autoriparazi'oni *nfpl* '∼' 'car repairs', 'auto repairs'

autorità *nf inv* authority

autori'tario *adj* autocratic

autorita'rismo *nm* authoritarianism

autori'tratto *nm* self-portrait

autoriz'zare *vt* authorize

autorizzazi'one *nf* authorization

auto'scatto *nm* Phot automatic shutter release

auto'scontro *nm inv* bumper car

autoscu'ola *nf* driving school

autosno'dato *nm* articulated bus

autosoc'corso *nm* breakdown service; (veicolo) breakdown van, breakdown truck

auto'starter *nm inv* Auto self-starter

auto'stop *nm* hitch-hiking, hitching; fare l'∼ hitch-hike, hitch

autostop'pista *nmf* hitch-hiker

auto'strada *nf* motorway, highway Am. **autostrada dell'informazione** information superhighway. **autostrada a pedaggio** toll motorway. **Autostrada del Sole** Highway of the Sun (connecting Milan and Reggio Calabria)

autostra'dale *adj* motorway *attrib*, highway *attrib* Am

autosuffici'ente *adj* self-sufficient

autosuffici'enza *nf* self-sufficiency

autosuggesti'one *nf* autosuggestion

autotrasporta|'tore, -trice *nmf* haulier, carrier

autotra'sporto *nm* road haulage

auto'treno *nm* articulated lorry, roadtrain

autove'icolo *nm* motor vehicle

auto'velox *nm inv* speed camera

autovet'tura *nf* motor vehicle

autun'nale *adj* autumnal; ⟨giornata, vestiti⟩ autumn *attrib*

au'tunno *nm* autumn

aval'lare *vt* endorse, back ⟨cambiale⟩: fig endorse

a'vallo *nm* endorsement

avam'braccio *nm* forearm

avam'posto *nm* Mil forward position

A'vana *nf* Havana

a'vana ① *nm inv* (sigaro) Havana [cigar]; (colore) tobacco, dark brown
② *adj inv* ⟨colore⟩ tobacco-coloured, dark brown

avangu'ardia *nf* vanguard; fig avant-garde; **essere all'∼** be in the forefront; Techn be at the leading edge; **d'∼** avant-garde

avansco'perta *nf* reconnaissance; **andare in ∼** reconnoitre

avanspet'tacolo *nm* **da ∼** in poor taste

a'vanti ① *adv* (in avanti) forward; (davanti) in front; (prima) before; ∼! (entrate) come in!; (suvvia) come on!; '∼' (su semaforo) 'cross now', 'walk' Am; ∼ **diritto** straight ahead; **più ∼** further on; **va' ∼!** go ahead!; **andare ∼** (precedere) go ahead; ⟨orologio⟩ be fast; ∼ **e indietro** backwards and forwards
② *adj* (precedente) before
③ *prep* ∼ **a** before; (in presenza di) in the presence of

avanti'eri *adv* the day before yesterday

avan'treno *nm* front axle assembly

avanza'mento *nm* progress; (promozione) promotion

avan'zare ① *vi* advance; (progredire) progress; (essere d'avanzo) be left [over]
② *vt* advance; (superare) surpass; (promuovere) promote

avan'zarsi *vr* advance; (avvicinarsi) approach

avan'zata *nf* advance

avan'zato *adj* advanced; (nella notte) late; in età avanzata elderly

a'vanzo *nm* remainder; Comm surplus; **avanzi** *pl* (rovine) remains; (di cibo) left-overs. **avanzo di galera** jailbird

ava'raccio *nm* Scrooge

ava'ria *nf* (di motore) engine failure

avari'arsi *vr* spoil

avari'ato *adj* ⟨frutta, verdura⟩ rotten; ⟨carne⟩ tainted

ava'rizia *nf* avarice

a'varo, -a ① *adj* stingy
② *nmf* miser

a'vena *nf* oats *pl*

a'vere ① *vt* have; (ottenere) get; (indossare) wear; (provare) feel; **ho trent'anni** I'm thirty; **ha avuto il posto** he got the job; ∼ **fame/freddo** be hungry/cold; **ho mal di denti** I've got toothache; **cos'ha a che fare con lui?** what has it got to do with him?; ∼ **da fare** be busy; ∼ **luogo** take place; **che hai?** what's the matter with you?; **nei hai per molto?** will you be long?; **quanti ne abbiamo oggi?** what date is it today?; **avercela con qualcuno** have it in for somebody
② *v aux* have; **non l'ho visto** I haven't seen him; **lo hai visto?** have you seen him?; **l'ho visto ieri** I saw him yesterday
③ *nm* **averi** *pl* wealth *sg*

avia|'tore, -trice *nmf* aviator

aviazi'one *nf* aviation; Mil Air Force

avicol'tura *nm* poultry farming

avida'mente *adv* avidly

avidità *nf* avidness

'avido *adj* avid

avi'ere *nm* aircraft[s]man

avio'getto *nm* jet [plane]

avio'linea *nf* airline

aviotraspor'tato *adj* airborne

avitami'nosi *nf* vitamin deficiency

a'vito *adj* ancestral

'avo, **-a** *nmf* ancestor

avo'cado *nm inv* avocado

a'vorio *nm* ivory

a'vulso *adj* ~ **dal contesto** fig taken out of context

Avv. *abbr* (**avvocato**) lawyer

avva'lersi *vr* avail oneself (di of)

avvalla'mento *nm* depression

avvalo'rare *vt* bear out ‹tesi›; endorse ‹documento›; (accrescere) enhance

avvam'pare *vi* flare up; (arrossire) blush

avvantaggi'are *vt* favour

avvantaggi'arsi *vr* ~ **di** benefit from; (approfittare) take advantage of

avve'dersi *vr* (accorgersi) notice; (capire) realize

avve'duto *adj* shrewd

avvelena'mento *nm* poisoning

avvele'nare *vt* poison

avvele'narsi *vr* poison oneself

avvele'nato *adj* poisoned

avve'nente *adj* attractive

avve'nenza *nf* attraction, charm

avveni'mento *nm* event

avve'nire ① *vi* happen; (aver luogo) take place
② *nm* future

avveni'rismo *nm* excessive confidence in the future

avveni'ristico *adj* futuristic

avven'tarsi *vr* fling oneself

avventata'mente *adv* recklessly

avven'tato *adj* ‹decisione› rash

avven'tizio *adj* (personale) temporary; (guadagno) casual

av'vento *nm* advent; Relig Advent

avven'tore *nm* regular customer

avven'tura *nf* adventure; (amorosa) affair; **d'~** ‹film› adventure *attrib*

avventu'rarsi *vr* venture

avventuri'ero, **-a** ① *nm* adventurer
② *nf* adventuress

avventu'rismo *nm* adventurism

avventu'ristico *adj* adventurist

avventu'roso *adj* adventurous

avve'rabile *adj* ‹previsione› that may come true

avve'rarsi *vr* come true

av'verbio *nm* adverb

avver'sare *vt* oppose

avver'sario, **-a** ① *adj* opposing
② *nmf* opponent

avversi'one *nf* aversion

avversità *nf inv* adversity

av'verso *adj* (sfavorevole) adverse; (contrario) averse

avver'tenza *nf* (cura) care; (avvertimento) warning; (avviso) notice; (premessa) foreword; **avvertenze** *pl* (istruzioni) instructions

avver'tibile *adj* (disagio) perceptible

avverti'mento *nm* warning

avver'tire *vt* warn; (informare) inform; (sentire) feel

avvertita'mente *adv* deliberately

avvez'zare *vt* accustom

avvez'zarsi *vr* accustom oneself

av'vezzo *adj* ~ **a** used to

avvia'mento *nm* starting; Comm goodwill

avvi'are *vt* start

avvi'arsi *vr* set out

avvi'ato *adj* under way; **bene** ~ thriving

avvicenda'mento *nm* (in agricoltura) rotation; (nel lavoro) replacement; (delle stagioni) change

avvicen'dare *vt* rotate

avvicen'darsi *vr* take turns, alternate

avvicina'mento *nm* approach

avvici'nare *vt* bring near; approach ‹persona›

avvici'narsi *vr* come nearer, approach; **avvicinarsi a** come nearer to, approach

avvi'lente *adj* demoralizing; (umiliante) humiliating

avvili'mento *nm* despondency; (degradazione) degradation

avvi'lire *vt* dishearten; (degradare) degrade

avvi'lirsi *vr* lose heart; (degradarsi) degrade oneself

avvi'lito *adj* disheartened; (degradato) degraded

avvilup'pare *vt* envelop

avvilup'parsi *vr* wrap oneself up; (aggrovigliarsi) get entangled

avvinaz'zato *adj* drunk

avvin'cente *adj* ‹libro ecc› enthralling

av'vincere *vt* enthral

avvinghi'are *vt* clutch

avvinghi'arsi *vr* cling

av'vio *nm* start-up; **dare l'~ a qualcosa** get something under way; **prendere l'~** get under way

avvi'saglia *nf* (di malattia) first sign

avvi'sare *vt* inform; (mettere in guardia) warn

av'viso *nm* notice; (annuncio) announcement; (avvertimento) warning; (pubblicitario) advertisement; **a mio ~** in my opinion. **avviso di accreditamento** advice slip. **avviso a cura del ministero della salute** government health warning. **avviso di chiamata in linea** call waiting. **avviso di garanzia** Jur notification that one is to be the subject of a legal enquiry

avvista'mento *nm* sighting

avvi'stare *vt* catch sight of; **~ terra** make landfall

avvi'tare *vt* screw in; screw down ⟨coperchio⟩

avvi'tarsi *vr* ⟨aereo⟩ go into a spin

avvi'tata *nf* (di aereo) spin

avviz'zire *vi* wither

avviz'zito *adj* withered

avvo'cato *nm* lawyer; fig advocate. **avvocato del diavolo** devil's advocate

avvoca'tura *nf* legal profession; (insieme di avvocati) lawyers

av'volgere *vt* wrap [up]

av'volgersi *vr* wrap oneself up

avvol'gibile *nm* roller blind

avvolgi'mento *nm* winding

av'volto *adj* **~ in** wrapped in

avvol'toio *nm* vulture

aza'lea *nf* azalea

Azerbaigi'an *nm* Azerbaijan

azerbaigi'ano, -a *adj & nmf* Azerbaijani

azi'enda *nf* business, firm. **azienda agricola** farm. **azienda elettrica** electricity board. **azienda a partecipazioni statali** enterprise in which the government has a shareholding. **azienda di soggiorno** tourist bureau

azien'dale *adj* ⟨politica, dirigente⟩ company *attrib*; ⟨giornale⟩ in-house

azienda'listico *adj* company *attrib*

azio'nabile *adj* which can be operated

aziona'mento *nm* operation

azio'nare *vt* operate

azio'nario *adj* share *attrib*; **mercato azionario** share market

azi'one *nf* action; Fin share; **d'~** ⟨romanzo, film⟩ action[-packed]; **ad ~ ritardata** delayed action. **azione sindacale** industrial action

azio'nista *nmf* shareholder

a'zoto *nm* nitrogen

az'teco, -a *adj & nmf* Aztec

azzan'nare *vt* seize with its teeth; sink its teeth into ⟨gamba⟩

azzar'dare *vt* risk

azzar'darsi *vr* dare

azzar'dato *adj* risky; (precipitoso) rash

az'zardo *nm* hazard; **gioco d'azzardo** game of chance

azzec'care *vt* hit; (fig: indovinare) guess

azzera'mento *nm* setting to zero; fig **corso di azzeramento** remedial classes *pl*

azze'rare *vt* reset

azzi'mato *adj* dapper

'azzimo *adj* unleavened

azzit'tire *vt* silence, hush

azzit'tirsi *vr* go quiet, fall silent

azzop'pare *vt* lame

Az'zorre *nfpl* **le ~** the Azores

azzuf'farsi *vr* come to blows

azzur'rato *adj* ⟨lenti⟩ blue-tinted

az'zurro *adj & nm* blue; **principe azzurro** Prince Charming; **gli azzurri** the Italian national team

azzur'rognolo *adj* bluish

Bb

babà *nm inv* **~ al rum** rum baba

bab'beo ① *adj* foolish ② *nm* idiot

'babbo *nm* fam dad, daddy. **Babbo Natale** Father Christmas

bab'buccia *nf* slipper

babbu'ino *nm* baboon

ba'bordo *nm* Naut port side

baby boom *nm* baby boom

baby'sitter *nmf inv* baby-sitter; **fare il/la ~** babysit, do baby-sitting

ba'cato *adj* worm-eaten; **avere il cervello ~** have a slate loose

'bacca *nf* berry

baccalà *nm inv* dried salted cod

bac'cano *nm* din

bac'cello *nm* pod

bac'chetta *nf* rod; (magica) wand; (di direttore d'orchestra) baton; (di tamburo) drumstick

ba'checa *nf* showcase; (in ufficio) notice board. **bacheca elettronica** Comput bulletin board

bacia'mano *nm* kiss on the hand; **fare il** ∼ **a qualcuno** kiss somebody's hand

baci'are *vt* kiss

baci'arsi *vr* kiss [each other]

ba'cillo *nm* bacillus

baci'nella *nf* basin; (contenuto) basinful

ba'cino *nm* basin; Anat pelvis; (di porto) dock; (di minerali) field. **bacino carbonifero** coalfield. **bacino d'utenza** catchment area

'**bacio** *nm* kiss; **bacio sulla bocca** kiss on the lips

backgammon *nm* backgammon

'**baco** *nm* worm. **baco da seta** silkworm

'**bacon** *nm* bacon

ba'cucco *adj* **un vecchio** ∼ a senile old man

'**bada** *nf* **tenere qualcuno a** ∼ keep somebody at bay

ba'dare *vi* take care (**a** of); (fare attenzione) look out; **bada ai fatti tuoi!** mind your own business!

ba'dia *nf* abbey

ba'dile *nm* shovel

'**badminton** *nm* badminton

'**baffi** *nmpl* moustache *sg*; (di animale) whiskers; **mi fa un baffo** I don't give a damn; **ridere sotto i** ∼ laugh up one's sleeve

baf'futo *adj* moustached

ba'gagli *nmpl* luggage, baggage; **ritiro bagagli** baggage claim

bagagli'aio *nm* Rail luggage van, baggage car Am; Auto boot

ba'gaglio *nm* luggage, baggage; Mil kit; **un** ∼ a piece of luggage. **bagaglio a mano** hand-luggage, hand-baggage. **bagaglio in eccesso, bagaglio eccedente** excess baggage

baga'rino *nm* ticket tout

baga'tella *nf* trifle; Mus bagatelle

baggia'nata *nf* piece of nonsense; **non dire baggianate** don't talk nonsense

Bagh'dad *nf* Baghdad

bagli'ore *nm* glare; (improvviso) flash; (fig: di speranza) glimmer

bagna'cauda *nf* vegetables (especially raw) in an oil, garlic and anchovy sauce typical of Piedmont

ba'gnante *nmf* bather

ba'gnare *vt* wet; (inzuppare) soak; (immergere) dip; (innaffiare) water; ⟨mare, lago⟩ wash; ⟨fiume⟩ flow through

ba'gnarsi *vr* get wet; (al mare ecc) swim, bathe; '**vietato** ∼' 'no bathing'

bagnasci'uga *nm inv* edge of the water, waterline

ba'gnato *adj* wet; **bagnato fradicio** soaked

ba'gnino, -a *nmf* life guard

'**bagno** *nm* bath; (stanza) bathroom; (gabinetto) toilet; (al mare) swim, bathe; **bagni** *pl* (stabilimento) lido; **fare il** ∼ have a bath; (nel mare ecc) [have a] swim, bathe; **andare in** ∼ go to the bathroom, go to the toilet; **mettere a** ∼ soak; **con** ∼ ⟨camera⟩ en suite. **bagno oculare** eyebath. **bagno rivelatore** Phot developing bath. **bagno di sangue** bloodbath. **bagno di sviluppo** Phot developing bath. **bagno turco** Turkish bath

bagnoma'ria *nm* **cuocere a** ∼ cook in a double saucepan

bagnoschi'uma *nm inv* bubble bath, foam bath

ba'guette *nf inv* French loaf, baguette

Ba'hamas *nfpl* **le** ∼ the Bahamas

Bah'rain *nm* Bahrain, Bahrein

'**baia** *nf* bay

baio'netta *nf* bayonet

'**baita** *nf* mountain chalet

bala'ustra, balau'strata *nf* balustrade

balbet'tare *vt/i* stammer; ⟨bambino⟩ babble

balbet'tio *nm* stammering; (di bambino) babble

bal'buzie *nf* stutter

balbuzi'ente ① *adj* stuttering ② *nmf* stutterer

Bal'cani *nmpl* Balkans

bal'canico *adj* Balkan

balco'nata *nf* Theat balcony, dress circle

balcon'cino *nm* **reggiseno a balconcino** underwired bra

bal'cone *nm* balcony

baldac'chino *nm* canopy; **letto a baldacchino** four-poster bed

bal'danza *nf* boldness

baldan'zoso *adj* bold

bal'dorla *nf* revelry; **far** ∼ have a riotous time

Bale'ari *nfpl* **le [isole]** ∼ the Balearics, the Balearic Islands

ba'lena *nf* whale

bale'nare *vi* lighten; fig flash; **mi è balenata un'idea** I've just had an idea

bale'niera *nf* whaler

ba'leno *nm* **in un** ∼ in a flash

balenot'tera *nf* **balenottera azzurra** blue whale

ba'lera *nf* dance hall

ba'lestra *nf* crossbow

'**balia**[1] *nf* wetnurse

ba'lia[2] *nf* **in** ∼ **di** at the mercy of

ba'listico *adj* ballistic; **perito balistico** ballistics expert

'**balla** *nf* bale; (fam: frottola) tall story

bal'labile *adj* essere ∼ be good for dancing to

bal'lare *vi* dance; andare a ∼ go dancing

bal'lata *nf* ballad

balla'toio *nm* (nelle scale) landing

balle'rino, -a ① *nmf* dancer; (classico) ballet dancer

② *nf* (classica) ballet dancer, ballerina

bal'letto *nm* ballet

bal'lista *nmf* fam bullshitter

'ballo *nm* dance; (il ballare) dancing; **sala da ballo** ballroom; **essere in** ∼ ⟨lavoro, vita⟩ be at stake; ⟨persona⟩ be committed; **tirare qualcuno in** ∼ involve somebody. **ballo liscio** ballroom dancing. **ballo in maschera** masked ball

ballonzo'lare *vi* skip about

ballot'taggio *nm* second count [of votes]

balne'are *adj* bathing *attrib*; **stagione balneare** swimming season; **stazione balneare** seaside resort

balneazi'one *nf* 'divieto di balneazione' 'no bathing'

ba'lordo *adj* foolish; (stordito) stunned; **tempo** ∼ nasty weather

bal'samico *adj* ⟨aria⟩ balmy

'balsamo *nm* balsam; (per capelli) conditioner; (lenimento) remedy

'baltico *adj* Baltic; **il [mar] Baltico** The Baltic [Sea]

balu'ardo *nm* bulwark

'balza *nf* crag; (di abito) flounce

bal'zano *adj* (idea) weird

bal'zare *vi* bounce; (saltare) jump; ∼ **in piedi** leap to one's feet

'balzo *nm* bounce; (salto) jump; **prendere la palla al** ∼ fig seize an opportunity

bam'bagia *nf* cotton wool; **vivere nella** ∼ fig be in clover

bam'bina *nf* little girl; (piccola) baby; **ha avuto una** ∼ she had a [baby] girl

bambi'naia *nf* nursemaid, nanny

bambi'nata *nf* childish thing to do/say

bam'bino *nm* child; (appena nato) baby; **avere un** ∼ have a baby; (maschio) have a [baby] boy; **bambini** *pl* children, kids; (piccoli) babies. **bambino prodigio** child prodigy

bambi'none, -a *nmf* pej big *or* overgrown child

bam'boccio *nm* chubby child; (sciocco) simpleton; (fantoccio) rag doll

'bambola *nf* doll

bambo'lotto *nm* male doll

bambù *nm* bamboo

ba'nale *adj* banal

banalità *nf inv* banality

banaliz'zare *vt* trivialize

ba'nana *nf* banana

ba'nano *nm* banana (tree)

'banca *nf* bank. **banca d'affari** merchant bank, investment bank. **banca [di] dati** databank. **Banca Europea per la Ricostruzione e lo Sviluppo** European Bank for Reconstruction and Development. **banca degli occhi** eye bank. **banca del sangue** blood bank. **banca dello sperma** sperm bank

banca'rella *nf* stall

bancarel'lista *nmf* stallholder

ban'cario, -a ① *adj* banking *attrib*; **trasferimento bancario** bank transfer

② *nmf* bank employee

banca'rotta *nf* bankruptcy; **fare** ∼ go bankrupt

banchet'tare *vi* banquet

ban'chetto *nm* banquet

banchi'ere *nm* banker

ban'china *nf* Naut quay; (in stazione) platform; (di strada) path. **banchina spartitraffico** central reservation, median strip Am. **banchina non transitabile** soft verge

ban'chisa *nf* floe

'banco *nm* (di scuola) desk; (di negozio) counter; (di officina) bench; (di gioco, banca) bank; (di mercato) stall; (degli imputati) dock; **sotto** ∼ under the counter; **medicinale da banco** over the counter medicines. **banco dei formaggi** (in supermercato) cheese counter; (in mercato) cheese stall. **banco di ghiaccio** ice floe. **banco informazioni** information desk. **banco di nebbia** fog bank. **banco di sabbia** sandbank

'bancomat® *nm inv* (sportello) autobank, cashpoint, cash dispenser, cash point, cash machine, hole-in-the-wall; (carta) bank card, cash card

ban'cone *nm* counter; (in bar) bar

banco'nota *nf* banknote, bill Am; **banconote** *pl* paper currency

'banda *nf* band; (di delinquenti) gang. **banda d'atterraggio** Aeron landing strip. **banda larga** Comput broadband. **banda passante** bandwidth. **banda rumorosa** rumble strip

ban'dana *nf* bandanna

banderu'ola *nf* weathercock; Naut pennant

bandi'era *nf* flag; **cambiare** ∼ change sides, switch allegiances

bandie'rina *nf* (nel calcio) corner flag

bandie'rine *nfpl* bunting

ban'dire *vt* banish; (pubblicare) publish; fig dispense with ⟨formalità, complimenti⟩

ban'dista *nmf* bandsman

bandi'tismo *nm* banditry

ban'dito *nm* bandit

bandi'tore *nm* (di aste) auctioneer

'**bando** *nm* proclamation. **bando di concorso** job advertisement (published in an official gazette for a job for which a competitive examination has to be sat)

bang *nm inv* wham. **bang sonico** sonic boom

Bangla'desh *nm* Bangladesh

bar *nm inv* bar

'**bara** *nf* coffin

ba'racca *nf* hut; (catapecchia) hovel; **mandare avanti la** ～ keep the ship afloat

barac'cato, -a [1] *adj* living in a shanty town
[2] *nmf* shanty town dweller

barac'chino *nm* (di gelati, giornali) kiosk; Radio CB radio

barac'cone *nm* (roulotte) circus caravan; (in luna park) booth; (fig: organizzazione) lumbering great dinosaur of an organization

barac'copoli *nf inv* shanty town

bara'onda *nf* chaos; **non fare** ～ don't make a mess

ba'rare *vi* cheat

'**baratro** *nm* chasm

barat'tare *vt* barter

ba'ratto *nm* barter

ba'rattolo *nm* jar; (di latta) tin

'**barba** *nf* beard; (fam: noia) bore; **farsi la** ～ shave; **in** ～ **a** in spite of; **è una** ～ (noia) it's boring

barbabi'etola *nf* beetroot; **barbabietole** *pl* beetroot. **barbabietola da zucchero** sugar beet

Bar'bados *nfpl* **le** ～ Barbados

barbagi'anni *nm inv* barn owl

bar'barico *adj* barbaric

bar'barie *nf inv* barbarity

barba'rismo *nm* barbarism

'**barbaro** [1] *adj* barbarous
[2] *nm* barbarian

'**barbecue** *nm inv* barbecue, BBQ

bar'betta *nf* Naut painter

barbi'ere *nm* barber; (negozio) barber's

bar'biglio *nm* barb

barbi'turico *nm* barbiturate

bar'bone, -a [1] *nm* (vagabondo) vagrant; (cane) poodle
[2] *nf* bag lady

bar'boso *adj* fam boring

barbu'gliare *vi* mumble

bar'buto *adj* bearded

'**barca** *nf* boat; **una** ～ **di** fig a lot of. **barca a motore** motorboat. **barca da pesca** fishing boat. **barca a remi** rowing boat, rowboat Am. **barca di salvataggio** lifeboat. **barca a vela** sailing boat, sailboat Am

barcai'olo *nm* boatman

barcame'narsi *vr* manage

barca'rola *nf* Mus barcarole

Barcel'lona *nf* Barcelona

barcol'lare *vi* stagger

barcol'loni *adv* **camminare** ～ stagger

bar'cone *nm* barge; (di ponte) pontoon

bar'dare *vt* harness

bar'darsi *vr* hum dress up

barda'tura *nf* (per cavallo) harness

ba'rella *nf* stretcher

barelli'ere *nm* stretcher-bearer

'**Barents** *nm* **mare di Barents** Barents Sea

ba'rese *adj* from Bari

bari'centro *nm* centre of gravity

ba'rile *nm* barrel

bari'lotto *nm* fig tub of lard

ba'rista [1] *nm* barman
[2] *nf* barmaid

ba'ritono *nm* baritone

bar'lume *nm* glimmer; **un** ～ **di speranza** a glimmer of hope

'**barman** *nm inv* barman

'**baro** *nm* cardsharp

ba'rocco *adj & nm* baroque

ba'rometro *nm* barometer

baro'nale *adj* baronial

ba'rone *nm* baron; **i baroni** fig the top brass

baro'nessa *nf* baroness

'**barra** *nf* bar; (lineetta) oblique; Naut tiller. **barra delle applicazioni** Comput task bar. **barra dei menu** Comput menu bar. **barra di navigazione** navigation bar. **barra retroversa** backslash. **barra di rimorchio** tow bar. **barra di scorrimento** Comput scroll bar. **barra spaziatrice** space bar. **barra di stato** Comput status bar. **barra degli strumenti** Comput tool bar. **barra di titolo** Comput title bar; **barre** *pl* **laterali antintrusione** Auto side impact bars

bar'rage *nm inv* Sport jump-off

bar'rare *vt* block off ⟨strada⟩

barri'care *vt* barricade

barri'cata *nf* barricade

barri'era *nf* barrier; (stradale) road-block; Geol reef. **barriera corallina** coral reef. **barriera linguistica** language barrier. **barriera razziale** colour bar. **barriera del suono** sound barrier

bar'rire *vi* trumpet

bar'rito *nm* trumpeting

ba'ruffa *nf* scuffle; **far** ～ quarrel

barzel'letta *nf* joke; ～ **sporca** *o* **spinta** dirty joke

basa'mento *nm* base; Geol bedrock

ba'sare *vt* base

ba'sarsi *vr* ~ **su** be based on; **mi baso su ciò che ho visto** I'm going on [the basis of] what I saw

'basco, -a ① *adj & nmf* Basque ② *nm* (copricapo) beret

'base *nf* basis; (fondamento) foundation; Mil base; Pol rank and file; **a** ~ **di** containing; **in** ~ **a** on the basis of. **base di controllo** ground control. **base [di] dati** database. **base d'intesa** common ground. **base logica** logical basis. **base navale** naval base

'baseball *nm* baseball

ba'setta *nf* sideburn

basi'lare *adj* basic

ba'silica *nf* basilica

Basili'cata *nf* Basilicata

ba'silico *nm* basil

ba'sista *nm* grass roots politician; (di un crimine) mastermind

'basket *nm* basketball

bas'sezza *nf* lowness; (di statura) shortness; (viltà) vileness

bas'sista *nmf* bassist

'basso ① *adj* low; (di statura) short; ⟨acqua⟩ shallow; ⟨televisione⟩ quiet; (vile) despicable; **parlare a bassa voce** speak quietly, speak in a low voice, **la bassa Italia** southern Italy ② *nm* lower part; Mus bass [guitar]; **guardare in** ~ look down

basso'fondo *nm* (pl **bassifondi**) shallows; **bassifondi** *pl* (quartieri poveri) slums

bassorili'evo *nm* bas-relief

bas'sotto *nm* dachshund

ba'stardo, -a ① *adj* bastard; (di animale) mongrel ② *nmf* bastard; (animale) mongrel

ba'stare *vi* be enough; (durare) last; **basta!** that's enough!, that'll do!; **basta che** (purché) provided that; **basta così** that's enough; **basta così?** is that enough?, will that do?; (in negozio) will there be anything else?; **basta andare alla posta** you only have to go to the post office; **basta che tu lo faccia bene** make sure you do it well

Basti'an con'trario *nm* contrary old so-and-so

basti'mento *nm* ship; (carico) cargo

basti'one *nm* bastion

basto'nare *vt* beat

basto'nata *nf* **dare una** ~ **a** beat with a stick

baston'cino *nm* (da sci) ski pole. **bastoncino di pesce** fish finger, fish stick Am

ba'stone *nm* stick; (da golf) club; (da passeggio) walking stick. **bastone da hockey** hockey stick

ba'tosta *nf* blow

bat'tage *nm inv* battage **pubblicitario** media hype

bat'taglia *nf* battle; (lotta) fight

battagli'are *vi* battle; fig fight

bat'taglio *nm* (di campana) clapper; (di porta) knocker

battagli'one *nm* battalion

bat'tello *nm* boat; (motonave) steamer

bat'tente *nm* (di porta) wing; (di finestra) shutter; (battaglio) knocker

'battere ① *vt* beat; hit, knock ⟨testa, spalla⟩; (percorrere) scour; thresh ⟨grano⟩; break ⟨record⟩ ② *vi* (bussare, urtare) knock; ⟨cuore⟩ beat; ⟨ali ecc⟩ flap; Tennis serve; ~ **a macchina** type; ~ **gli occhi** blink; ~ **il piede** tap one's foot; ~ **le mani** clap [one's hands]; ~ **le ore** strike the hours

bat'teri *nmpl* bacteria

batte'ria *nf* battery; Mus drums *pl*; (Sport: eliminatoria) heat. **batteria a bottone** button battery

bat'terico *adj* bacterial

bat'terio *nm* bacterium

batteriolo'gia *nf* bacteriology

batterio'logico *adj* bacteriological

batte'rista *nmf* drummer

'battersi *vr* fight

bat'tesimo *nm* baptism, christening

battez'zare *vt* baptize, christen

battiba'leno *nm* **in un** ~ in a flash

batti'becco *nm* squabble

batticu'ore *nm* palpitation; **mi venne il** ~ I was scared

bat'tigia *nf* water's edge

batti'mano *nm* applause

batti'panni *nm inv* carpetbeater

batti'scopa *nm inv* skirting board

batti'stero *nm* baptistery

batti'strada *nm inv* outrider; (di pneumatico) tread; Sport pacesetter

battitap'peto *nm inv* carpet sweeper

'battito *nm* (alle tempie) throbbing; (di orologio) ticking; (della pioggia) beating. **battito cardiaco** heartbeat

batti'tore, -trice *nmf* Sport batsman

bat'tuta *nf* beat; (colpo) knock; (spiritosaggine) wisecrack; (osservazione) remark; Mus bar; Tennis service; Theat cue; (dattilografia) stroke. **battuta d'arresto** setback

ba'tuffolo *nm* flock

ba'ule *nm* trunk

bau'xite *nf* bauxite

'bava *nf* dribble; (di cane ecc) slobber; **aver la** ~ **alla bocca** foam at the mouth

bava'glino *nm* bib

ba'vaglio *nm* gag

bava'rese *nf* ice-cream cake with milk, eggs and cream

'bavero *nm* collar

ba'zar *nm inv* bazaar

ba'zooka *nm inv* bazooka

baz'zecola *nf* trifle

bazzi'care *vt/i* haunt

baz'zotto *adj* soft-boiled

be'arsi *vr* delight (**di** in)

beata'mente *adv* blissfully

beatifi'care *vt* beatify

beati'tudine *nf* bliss

be'ato *adj* blissful; Relig blessed; ∼ **te!** lucky you!

beauty-'case *nm inv* toilet bag

bebè *nm inv* baby

bec'caccia *nf* woodcock

bec'care *vt* peck; fig catch

bec'carsi *vr* (litigare) quarrel

bec'cata *nf* beakful; (colpo) peck

beccheggi'are *vi* pitch

bec'chime *nm* birdseed

bec'chino *nm* gravedigger

'becco *nm* beak; (di caffettiera ecc) spout; **chiudi il** ∼ fam shut your trap; **non ha il** ∼ **di un quattrino** fam he's skint; **restare a** ∼ **asciutto** fam end up with nothing. **becco Bunsen** Bunsen [burner]. **becco a gas** gas burner

bec'cuccio *nm* spout

'beeper *nm inv* beeper

be'fana *nf* legendary old woman who brings presents to children on Twelfth Night; (giorno) Twelfth Night; (donna brutta) old witch

'beffa *nf* hoax; **farsi beffe di qualcuno** mock somebody

bef'fardo *adj* derisory; ⟨persona⟩ mocking

bef'fare *vt* mock

bef'farsi *vr* ∼ **di** make fun of

beffeggi'are *vt* taunt

'bega *nf* quarrel; **è una bella** ∼ it's really annoying

be'gonia *nf* begonia

beh *int* well

'beige *adj inv & nm* beige

Bei'rut *nf* Beirut

be'lare *vi* bleat

be'lato *nm* bleating

'belga *adj & nmf* Belgian

'Belgio *nm* Belgium

Bel'grado *nf* Belgrade

Be'lize *nm* Belize

'bella *nf* (in carte, Sport) decider; (innamorata) sweetheart. **bella di giorno** Bot morning glory. **bella di notte** fig lady of the night

bel'lezza *nf* beauty; **che** ∼**!** how lovely!; **per** ∼ (per decorazione) for decoration; **chiudere/finire in** ∼ end on a high note; **la** ∼ **di tre mesi/500 euro** all of three months/500 euros

belli'cismo *nm* warmongering

belli'cistico *adj* warmongering

'bellico *adj* war attrib; **periodo bellico** wartime

bellicosità *nf* belligerence

belli'coso *adj* warlike

bellige'rante *adj & nmf* belligerent

bellige'ranza *nf* belligerence

bellim'busto *nm* dandy

'bello ① *adj* nice; (di aspetto) beautiful; ⟨uomo⟩ handsome; (moralmente) good; **cosa fai di** ∼ **stasera?** what are you up to tonight?; **oggi fa** ∼ it's a nice day today; **una bella cifra** a lot; **un bel piatto di pasta** a big plate of pasta; **nel bel mezzo** right in the middle; **un bel niente** absolutely nothing; **bell'e fatto** over and done with; **bell'amico sei!** fine friend you are!; **questa è bella!** that's a good one!; **bel voto** good mark; **il bel mondo** the beautiful people; **le belle arti** the fine arts ② *nm* (bellezza) beauty; (innamorato) sweetheart; **sul più** ∼ at the crucial moment; **il** ∼ **è che** ... the funny thing is that ...

beltà *nf* liter beauty

'belva *nf* wild beast

be'molle *nm* Mus flat

ben ▶ BENE

benché *conj* though, although

'benda *nf* bandage; (per occhi) blindfold

ben'dare *vt* bandage; blindfold ⟨occhi⟩

bendi'sposto *adj* **essere** ∼ **verso** be well-disposed towards

'bene ① *adv* well; **ben** ∼ thoroughly; ∼**!** good!; **star** ∼ (di salute) be well; ⟨vestito, stile⟩ suit; (finanziariamente) be well off; **non sta** ∼ (non è educato) it's not nice; **sta/va** ∼**!** all right!; **ti sta** ∼**!** [it] serves you right!; **voler** ∼ **a** love; **di** ∼ **in meglio** better and better; **fare** ∼ (aver ragione) do the right thing; **fare** ∼ **a** ⟨cibo⟩ be good for; **una persona per** ∼ a good person; **per** ∼ ⟨fare⟩ properly; **è ben difficile** it's very difficult; **ben cotto** well done; **come tu ben sai** as you well know; **lo credo** ∼**!** I can well believe it! ② *nm* good; **per il tuo** ∼ for your own good; **beni** *pl* (averi) property *sg*; **un** ∼ **di famiglia** a family heirloom. **beni ambientali** *pl* environment. **beni di consumo** *pl* consumer products, consumer goods. **beni culturali** *pl* cultural heritage. **beni immobili** *pl* real estate, realty Am. **beni mobili** *pl* movables

benedet'tino *adj & nm* Benedictine

bene'detto *adj* blessed

bene'dire *vt* bless; **mandare qualcuno a farsi** ∼ fam tell somebody to get lost

benedizi'one *nf* blessing

benedu'cato *adj* well-mannered

benefat|'tore, **-trice** *nmf* benefactor; benefactress

benefi'care *vt* help

benefi'cenza *nf* charity

benefici'are *vi* ∼ **di** profit by

benefici'ario, **-a** *adj & nmf* beneficiary

bene'flcio *nm* benefit; **con** ∼ **di inventario** with reservations. **beneficio accessorio** perquisite

be'nefico *adj* beneficial; (di beneficenza) charitable

'Benelux *nm* Benelux

beneme'renza *nf* benevolence

bene'merito *adj* worthy

bene'placito *nm* consent, approval

be'nessere *nm* well-being

bene'stante ① *adj* well off ② *nmf* well-off person

bene'stare *nm* consent

benevo'lenza *nf* benevolence

be'nevolo *adj* benevolent

ben'fatto *adj* well-made

Ben'gala *nm* Bengal

ben'godi *nm* **il paese di** ∼ a land of plenty

benia'mino *nm* favourite

be'nigno *adj* kindly; Med benign

Be'nin *nm* Benin

beninfor'mato ① *adj* well-informed ② *npl* **i beninformati** those in the know

benintenzio'nato, **-a** ① *adj* well-meaning ② *nmf* well-meaning person

benin'teso *adv* needless to say, of course; ∼ **che** ... of course, ...

be'nissimo *int* fine

benpen'sante *adj & nmf* self-righteous

bensì *conj* but rather

benser'vito *nm* **dare il** ∼ **a qualcuno** give somebody the sack

benve'nuto *adj & nm* welcome; **benvenuta! welcome!

ben'visto *adj* **essere** ∼ **(da qualcuno)** go down well (with somebody)

benvo'lere *vt* **farsi** ∼ **da qualcuno** win somebody's affection; **prendere a** ∼ **qualcuno** take a liking to somebody; **essere benvoluto da tutti** be well-liked by everyone

benvo'luto *adj* well-liked

ben'zene *nm* benzene

ben'zina *nf* petrol, gas Am; **far** ∼ get petrol. **benzina avio** aviation fuel. **benzina con piombo** leaded petrol.

benzina senza piombo *o* **verde** leadfree petrol, unleaded petrol. **benzina super** four-star petrol, premium gas Am

benzi'naio, **-a** *nmf* petrol station attendant, gas station attendant Am

be'one, **-a** *nmf* fam boozer

'berbero, **-a** *adj & nmf* Berber

'bere ① *vt* drink; (assorbire) absorb; fig swallow; ∼ **una tazza di tè** have a cup of tea ② *nm* drinking; **da** ∼ **e da mangiare** food and drink

berga'motto *nm* bergamot

'Bering *nm* **il mare di** ∼ the Bering Sea; **lo stretto di** ∼ the Bering Straits

ber'lina *nf* Auto saloon; **mettere alla** ∼ **qualcuno** ridicule somebody

berli'nese ① *nmf* Berliner ② *adj* Berlin *attrib*

Ber'lino *nm* Berlin. **Berlino Est** East Berlin

Ber'muda *nfpl* **le** ∼ the Bermudas

ber'muda *nmpl* (pantaloni) Bermuda shorts

'Berna *nf* Berne

ber'noccolo *nm* bump; (disposizione) flair

ber'retto *nm* beret, cap. **berretto a pompon** bobble hat

bersagli'are *vt* fig bombard

ber'saglio *nm* target

bescia'mella *nf* béchamel, white sauce

be'stemmia *nf* swearword; (maledizione) oath; (sproposito) blasphemy

bestemmi'are *vi* swear

'bestia *nf* animal; (persona brutale) beast; (persona sciocca) fool; **andare in** ∼ fam blow one's top; **lavorare come una** ∼ slave away. **bestia nera** fig pet hate

besti'ale *adj* bestial; 〈espressione, violenza〉 brutal; fam: 〈freddo, fame〉 terrible; **fa un caldo/freddo** ∼ it's dreadfully hot/cold

bestialità *nf inv* bestiality; fig nonsense

besti'ame *nm* livestock

betabloc'cante *nm* betablocker

Be'tlemme *nf* Bethlehem

betoni'era *nf* concrete mixer

'bettola *nf* fig dive

be'tulla *nf* birch. **betulla bianca** silver birch

be'vanda *nf* drink. **bevanda alcolica** alcoholic drink

bevi|'tore, **-trice** *nmf* drinker

be'vuta *nf* drink

be'vuto pp di BERE

Bhu'tan *nm* Bhutan

bi+ *pref* bi+

bi'ada *nf* fodder

bianche'ria *nf* linen. **biancheria per la casa** household linen. **biancheria** ···▷

intima underwear; (da donna) lingerie.
biancheria da letto bed linen

bian'chetto *nm* whitener

bi'anco, -a ① *adj* white; ⟨foglio⟩ blank;
voce bianca treble voice
② *nmf* white
③ *nm* white; **mangiare in** ∼ eat bland
food; **andare in** ∼ fam not score; **in** ∼ **e
nero** ⟨film, fotografia⟩ black and white,
monochrome; **passare una notte in** ∼
have a sleepless night. **bianco sporco**
off white. **bianco d'uovo** egg white

biancomangi'are *nm* blancmange

bian'core *nm* (bianchezza) whiteness

bianco'segno *nm* Jur blank document
bearing a signature

bianco'spino *nm* hawthorn

biasci'care *vt* (mangiare) eat noisily;
(parlare) mumble

biasi'mare *vt* blame

biasi'mevole *adj* blameworthy

bi'asimo *nm* blame

'Bibbia *nf* Bible

bibe'ron *nm inv* [baby's] bottle

'bibita *nf* [soft] drink. **bibita alcolica**
alcopop. **bibita gasata** fizzy drink

'biblico *adj* biblical

bibliogra'fia *nf* bibliography

biblio'grafico *adj* bibliographical

biblio'teca *nf* library; (mobile) bookcase

bibliote'cario, -a *nmf* librarian

bicame'rale *adj* two-chamber *attrib*,
bicameral

bicarbo'nato *nm* bicarbonate.
bicarbonato di sodio bicarbonate of
soda

bicchie'rata *nf* glassful

bicchi'ere *nm* glass

bicchie'rino *nm* fam tipple

bicente'nario *nm* bicentenary

'bici *nf* fam bike

bici'cletta *nf* bicycle, bike; **andare in** ∼
cycle, go by bike; (saper portare la bicicletta)
ride a bicycle. **bicicletta da corsa**
racer

bi'cipite *nm* biceps

bi'cocca *nf* hovel

bico'lore *adj* two-coloured

bidè *nm inv* bidet

bi'dello, -a *nmf* janitor, [school]
caretaker

bidirezio'nale *adj* bidirectional

bido'nare *vt* con, swindle; **farsi** ∼ be
conned

bido'nata *nf* fam swindle

bi'done *nm* bin; (fam: truffa) swindle; **fare
un** ∼ **a qualcuno** fam stand somebody up.
bidone dell'immondizia, **bidone**

della spazzatura rubbish bin, trash
can Am

bidon'ville *nf inv* shantytown

bi'eco *adj* callous

bi'ella *nf* connecting rod

Bielo'russia *nf* Belarus

bielo'russo, -a *adj & nmf* Belorussian

bien'nale *adj* biennial

bi'ennio *nm* two-year period

bi'erre *nfpl* (Brigate Rosse) Red Brigades

bi'etola *nf* beet

bifo'cale *adj* bifocal

bi'folco, -a *nmf* fig boor

bifor'carsi *vr* fork

biforcazi'one *nf* fork

bifor'cuto *adj* forked

biga'mia *nf* bigamy

'bigamo, -a ① *adj* bigamous
② *nmf* bigamist

big bang *nm* big bang

bighello'nare *vi* loaf around

bighel'lone *nm* loafer

bigiotte'ria *nf* costume jewellery;
(negozio) jeweller's

bigliet'taio *nm* booking clerk; (sui treni)
ticket-collector

bigliette'ria *nf* ticket-office; Theat box-
office. **biglietteria automatica** ticket
vending machine

bigli'etto *nm* ticket; (lettera breve) note;
(cartoncino) card; (di banca) banknote.
biglietto di sola andata single
[ticket]. **biglietto di andata e ritorno**
return [ticket]. **biglietto di auguri** card.
biglietto chilometrico ticket allowing
travel up to a maximum specified
distance. **biglietto collettivo** group
ticket. **biglietto elettronico** e-ticket.
biglietto giornaliero day pass.
biglietto d'ingresso entrance ticket.
biglietto d'invito invitation card.
biglietto della lotteria lottery ticket.
biglietto da visita business card

bigliet'tone *nm* (fam: soldi) big one

bignè *nm inv* puff. **bignè alla crema**
cream puff

bigo'dino *nm* roller

bi'gotto *nm* bigot

bi'kini *nm inv* bikini

bi'lancia *nf* scales *pl*; (di orologio, Comm)
balance; Bilancia Astr Libra. **bilancia
commerciale** balance of trade.
bilancia da cucina kitchen scales
bilancia dei pagamenti balance of
payments. **bilancia pesapersone**
scales

bilanci'are *vt* balance; fig weigh

bilancia'tura *nf* **bilanciatura
gomme** wheel-balancing

bilanci'ere *nm* (in sollevamento pesi) bar-bell; (di orologio) balance wheel

bi'lancio *nm* budget; Comm balance [sheet]; **fare il** ~ balance the books; fig take stock; **chiudere il** ~ **in attivo/passivo** to end the financial year in profit/with a loss. **bilancio patrimoniale** balance sheet. **bilancio preventivo** budget

bilate'rale *adj* bilateral

'**bile** *nf* bile; fig rage

bili'ardo *nm* billiards *sg*

'**bilico** *nm* equilibrium; **in** ~ in the balance

bi'lingue *adj* bilingual

bilingu'ismo *nm* bilingualism

bili'one *nm* billion

bili'oso *adj* bilious

bilo'cale ① *adj* two-room ② *nm* two-room flat

'**bimbo, -a** *nmf* child. ~ **in fasce** babe in arms

bimen'sile *adj* fortnightly Br, twice-monthly

bime'strale *adj* bimonthly

bi'mestre *nm* two months

bi'nario *nm* track; (piattaforma) platform

bi'nocolo *nm* binoculars *pl.*

bi'nomio *nm* binomial

bio+ *pref* bio+

bioagricol'tore *nm* organic farmer

bioagricol'tura *nf* organic farming

bio'chimica *nf* biochemistry

bio'chimico, -a ① *nmf* biochemist ② *adj* biochemical

biodegra'dabile *adj* biodegradable

biodiversità *nf* biodiversity

bio'etica *nf* bioethics

bio'fisica *nf* biophysics

biogra'fia *nf* biography

bio'grafico *adj* biographical

bi'ografo, -a *nmf* biographer

bioingegne'ria *nf* bioengineering

biolo'gia *nf* biology

biologica'mente *adv* biologically

bio'logico *adj* biological; ⟨agricoltura⟩ organic

bi'ologo, -a *nmf* biologist

bi'onda *nf* blonde. **bionda ossigenata** peroxide blonde. **bionda platinata** platinum blonde

bi'ondo ① *adj* blond ② *nm* fair colour; (uomo) fair-haired man. **biondo cenere** ash blond. **biondo platino** platinum blonde

bi'onico *adj* bionic

bio'psia *nf* biopsy

bio'ritmo *nm* biorhythm

bio'sfera *nf* biosphere

bi'ossido *nm* dioxide. **biossido di carbonio** carbon dioxide

biotecnolo'gia *nf* biotechnology

bioterro'rismo *nm* bioterrorism

bip *nm inv* blip

bipar'titico *adj* bipartisan

biparti'tismo *nm* two-party system

bipar'tito ① *adj* bipartite, two-party *attrib* ② *nm* two-party coalition

bipartizi'one *nf* division into two parts

bipo'lare *adj* Electr bipolar; Pol dominated by two large parties

bipola'rismo *nm* Pol system in which the numerous parties line up behind two main parties

bipolarizzazi'one *nf* Pol tendency towards 'bipolarismo'

bi'posto *adj inv* & *nm inv* two-seater

'**birba** *nf*, **birbante** *nm* rascal, rogue

birbo'nata *nf* trick

bir'bone *adj* wicked

birdie *nm inv* (golf) birdie

biri'chino, -a ① *adj* naughty ② *nmf* little devil

bi'rillo *nm* skittle; (di segnaletica stradale) traffic cone

Bir'mania *nf* Burma

bir'mano, -a *adj* & *nmf* Burmese

'**birra** *nf* beer; **a tutta** ~ fig flat out. **birra chiara** lager; **birra grande** ≈ pint. **birra piccola** ≈ half-pint. **birra scura** dark beer, brown ale Br

birre'ria *nf* beer-house; (fabbrica) brewery

bis *nm inv* encore

bi'saccia *nf* haversack

bi'sbetica *nf* shrew

bi'sbetico *adj* bad-tempered

bisbigli'are *vt/i* whisper

bi'sboccia *nf* **fare** ~ make merry

'**bisca** *nf* gambling-house

Bi'scaglia *nf* **il golfo di** ~ the Bay of Biscay

'**biscia** *nf* snake

biscotti'era *nf* biscuit barrel, biscuit tin

bi'scotto *nm* biscuit. **biscotto per cani** dog-biscuit

bisessu'ale *adj* & *nmf* bisexual

bise'stile *adj* **anno** ~ leap year

bisettima'nale *adj* twice-weekly

biset'trice *nf* bisector

bisezi'one *nf* bisection

bisil'labico *adj* two-syllable *attrib*, bisyllabic

bi'slacco *adj* peculiar

bi'slungo *adj* oblong

bi'snonno, -a ① *nm* great-grandfather

2▶ *nf* great-grandmother

biso'gnare *vi* **bisogna agire subito** we must act at once; **bisogna farlo** it is necessary to do it; **non bisogna scongelarlo** you don't need to defrost it

bi'sogno *nm* need; (povertà) poverty; **aver ~ di** need

biso'gnoso *adj* needy; (povero) poor; **~ di** in need of

bi'sonte *nm* bison

bi'stecca *nf* steak. **bistecca di cavallo** horsemeat steak. **bistecca ai ferri** grilled steak. **bistecca alla fiorentina** large grilled beef steak

bi'sticci *nmpl* bickering

bisticci'are *vi* quarrel

bi'sticcio *nm* quarrel; (gioco di parole) pun

bistrat'tare *vt* mistreat

bistrò *nm inv* bistro

'bisturi *nm inv* scalpel

bi'sunto *adj* very greasy

bit *nm inv* bit

bito'nale *adj* two-tone

bi'torzolo *nm* lump

'bitter *nm inv* bitter aperitif

bi'tume *nm* bitumen

bivac'care *vi* bivouac

bi'vacco *nm* bivouac

'bivio *nm* crossroads; (di strada) fork

bizan'tino *adj* Byzantine

'bizza *nf* tantrum; **fare le bizze** ‹bambini› play up

bizzar'ria *nf* eccentricity

biz'zarro *adj* bizarre

biz'zeffe *adv* **a ~** galore

'blackjack *nm* blackjack

blan'dire *vt* soothe; (allettare) flatter

'blando *adj* mild

bla'sfemo *adj* blasphemous

bla'sone *nm* coat of arms

blate'rare *vi* blather; **~ di qualcosa** burble on about something

'blatta *nf* cockroach

'bleso *adj* lisping

blin'dare *vt* armour-plate

blin'dato *adj* armoured

'blinker *nm inv* blinker

'blister *nm inv* blister pack

blitz *nm inv* blitz

bloc'care *vt* block; (isolare) cut off; Mil blockade; Comm freeze; stop ‹assegno›; **~ l'accesso a** seal off

bloc'carsi *vr* Mech jam

blocca'sterzo *nm* steering lock

bloc'cato *adj* blocked

bloc'chetto *nm* **blocchetto per appunti** memo pad **blocchetto di biglietti** book of tickets

'blocco *nm* block; Mil blockade; (dei fitti) restriction; (di carta) pad; (unione) coalition; **in ~** Comm in bulk. **blocco chiamate** Teleph call barring. **blocco per appunti** notepad. **blocco psicologico** mental block. **blocco stradale** road-block

block-notes *nm inv* memo pad

blu *adj inv & nm* blue

blu'astro *adj* bluish

blue chip *nf inv* Fin blue chip

blue-'jeans *nmpl* jeans

bluff *nm inv* (carte, fig) bluff

bluf'fare *vi* (carte, fig) bluff

'blusa *nf* blouse

'boa 1▶ *nm* boa [constrictor]; (sciarpa) [feather] boa
2▶ *nf* Naut buoy

bo'ato *nm* rumbling

bo'bina *nf* spool; (di film) reel; Electr coil

bobi'nare *vt* spool

'bocca *nf* mouth; **a ~ aperta** fig dumbfounded; **in ~ al lupo!** fam break a leg!; **fare la respirazione ~ a ~ a qualcuno** give somebody mouth to mouth resuscitation, give somebody the kiss of life; **essere di ~ buona** eat anything; fig be easily satisfied; **essere sulla ~ di tutti** be the talk of the town. **bocca del camino** chimneybreast. **bocca di leone** snapdragon

boccac'cesco *adj* licentious

boc'caccia *nf* grimace; **far boccacce** make faces

boc'caglio *nm* nozzle

boc'cale *nm* jug; (da birra) mug

bocca'porto *nm* Naut hatch

bocca'scena *nm inv* proscenium

boc'cata *nf* (di fumo) puff; **prendere una ~ d'aria** get a breath of fresh air

boc'cetta *nf* small bottle

boccheggi'are *vi* gasp

boc'chino *nm* cigarette holder; (di pipa, Mus) mouthpiece

'boccia *nf* (palla) bowl; **bocce** *pl* (gioco) bowls *sg*; **giocare a bocce** play bowls

bocci'are *vt* (agli esami) fail; (respingere) reject; (alle bocce) hit; **essere bocciato** fail; (ripetere) repeat a year

boccia'tura *nf* failure

bocci'olo *nm* bud

'boccolo *nm* ringlet

boccon'cino *nm* morsel

boc'cone *nm* mouthful; (piccolo pasto) snack

boc'coni *adv* face down[wards]

Bo'emia *nf* Bohemia

bo'emo, -a *adj & nmf* Bohemian

bo'ero, -a *nmf* Afrikaner

bofonchi'are *vi* grumble

boh *int* dunno

'**boia** *nm* executioner; **fa un freddo** ∼ fam it's brass-monkey weather; **ho un sonno** ∼ fam I can't keep my eyes open

boi'ata *nf* fam rubbish

boicot'taggio *nm* boycotting

boicot'tare *vt* boycott

bo'lero *nm* bolero

'**bolgia** *nf* (caos) bedlam

'**bolide** *nm* meteor; **passare come un** ∼ shoot past [like a rocket]

Bo'livia *nf* Bolivia

bolivi'ano, -a *adj & nmf* Bolivian

'**bolla** *nf* bubble; (vescica, in tappezzeria) blister; **finire in una** ∼ **di sapone** go up in smoke. **bolla di accompagnamento** packing list. **bolla d'aria** (in acqua) air bubble. **bolla di consegna** packing list

bol'lare *vt* stamp; fig brand

bol'lato *adj* fig branded; **carta bollata** paper with stamp showing payment of duty

bol'lente *adj* boiling [hot]

bol'letta *nf* bill; **essere in** ∼ be hard up

bollet'tino *nm* bulletin; Comm list. **bollettino d'informazione** fact sheet. **bollettino meteorologico** weather report. **bollettino ufficiale** gazette

bolli'latte *nm inv* milk pan

bol'lino *nm* coupon

bol'lire *vt/i* boil

bol'lito *nm* boiled meat

bolli'tore *nm* boiler; (per l'acqua) kettle

bolli'tura *nf* boiling

'**bollo** *nm* stamp; Auto tax disc

bol'lore *nm* boil; (caldo) intense heat; fig ardour

Bo'logna *nf* Bologna

bolo'gnese *nmf* person from Bologna; **spaghetti alla bolognese** spaghetti bolognese

'**bomba** *nf* bomb; **a prova di** ∼ bomb-proof; **tornare a** ∼ get back to the point. **bomba atomica** nuclear bomb. **bomba intelligente** smart bomb. **bomba a mano** hand grenade. **bomba molotov** petrol bomb. **bomba ad orologeria** time bomb. **bomba sporca** dirty bomb

bombarda'mento *nm* shelling; (con aerei) bombing; fig bombardment. **bombardamento aereo** air raid

bombar'dare *vt* shell; (con aerei) bomb; fig bombard; ∼ **a tappeto** carpet-bomb

bombardi'ere *nm* bomber

bom'bato *adj* domed

'**bomber** *nm inv* bomber jacket

bom'betta *nf* bowler [hat]

'**bombo** *nm* bumblebee

'**bombola** *nf* cylinder. **bombola di gas** gas bottle, gas cylinder

bombo'letta *nf* spray can

bombo'lone *nm* doughnut

bomboni'era *nf* wedding keep-sake

bo'naccia *nf* Naut calm

bonacci'one, -a ① *nmf* good-natured person

② *adj* good-natured

bo'nario *adj* kindly

bo'nifica *nf* land reclamation

bonifi'care *vt* reclaim

bo'nifico *nm* Comm discount. **bonifico [bancario]** [credit] transfer

bontà *nf* goodness; (gentilezza) kindness

'**bonus-'malus** *nm inv* Auto car-insurance policy with no claims bonus clause

'**boogie** *nm* boogie

'**bookmaker** *nm inv* bookmaker

'**boomerang** *nm inv* boomerang

boot *nm* Comput boot-up; **eseguire il** ∼ boot up

'**bora** *nf* cold north-east wind in the upper Adriatic

borbot'tare *vi* mumble; (stomaco) rumble

borbot'tio *nm* mumbling; (di stomaco) rumbling

'**borchia** *nf* stud

borchi'ato *adj* studded

bor'dare *vt* border

bor'data *nf* Naut broadside

borda'tura *nf* border

bor'deaux ① *nm inv* (vino) claret, Bordeaux

② *adj inv* (colore) claret

bor'dello *nm* brothel; fig bedlam; (disordine) mess

bor'dino *nm* narrow border

'**bordo** *nm* border; (estremità) edge; **a** ∼ Aeron, Naut on board; **d'alto** ∼ ⟨prostituta⟩ high-class. **bordo d'attacco** Aeron leading edge

bor'dura *nf* border

bor'gata *nf* hamlet

bor'ghese *adj* bourgeois; ⟨abito⟩ civilian; **in** ∼ in civilian dress; ⟨poliziotto⟩ in plain clothes

borghe'sia *nf* middle classes *pl*

'**borgo** *nm* village; (quartiere) district

'**boria** *nf* conceit

bori'oso *adj* conceited

bor'lotto *nm* **[fagiolo] borlotto** pinto bean

'**Borneo** *nm* Borneo

boro'talco *nm* talcum powder

bor'raccia *nf* flask

'**Borsa** *nf* **Borsa [valori]** Stock Exchange

'**borsa** *nf* bag; (borsetta) handbag. **borsa dell'acqua calda** hot-water bottle. ···⊱

borsa frigo cool-box. **borsa della spesa** shopping bag. **borsa di studio** scholarship. **borsa termica** cool bag. **borsa da viaggio** travel bag

borsai'olo nm pickpocket

bor'seggio nm pickpocketing

borsel'lino nm purse

bor'sello nm (portamonete) purse; (borsetto) man's handbag

bor'setta nf handbag

bor'setto nm man's handbag

bor'sino nm Fin dealing room

bor'sista nmf Fin speculator; Sch scholarship holder

bor'sone nm carryall

bo'scaglia nf woodlands pl

boscai'olo nm woodman; (guardaboschi) forester

bo'schetto nm grove

'bosco nm wood

bo'scoso adj wooded

'Bosnia nf Bosnia

bos'niaco, -a adj & nmf Bosnian

Bosnia-Erzego'vina nf Bosnia-Herzegovina

boss nm inv **boss mafioso** Mafia boss

'bosso nm boxwood

'bossolo nm cartridge case

Bot nm abbr (**Buoni Ordinari Del Tesoro**) T-bills

bo'tanica nf botany

bo'tanico ① adj botanical ② nm botanist

'botola nf trapdoor

Bot'swana nm Botswana

'botta nf blow; (rumore) bang; **fare a botte** come to blows. **botta e risposta** fig thrust and counter-thrust

botta'trice nf monkfish

'botte nf barrel

bot'tega nf shop; (di artigiano) workshop

botte'gaio, -a nmf shopkeeper

botte'ghino nm Theatr box-office; (del lotto) lottery-shop

bot'tiglia nf bottle; **in ~** bottled

bottiglie'ria nf wine shop

bot'tino nm loot; Mil booty

'botto nm bang; **di ~** all of a sudden

bot'tone nm button; Bot bud. **bottone di carica** winder

botu'lismo nm botulism

'bourbon nm bourbon

bo'vini nmpl cattle

bo'vino adj bovine; **carne bovina** beef

'bowling nm bowling, tenpin bowling Br

box nm inv (per cavalli) loosebox; (recinto per bambini) play-pen

'boxe nf boxing

'boxer nmpl jockey shorts

'bozza nf draft; Typ proof; (bernoccolo) bump. **bozza in colonna** galley [proof]. **bozza definitiva** page proof. **bozza impaginata** page proof. **bozza di stampa** page proof

boz'zetto nm sketch

'bozzolo nm cocoon

BR nfpl abbr (**Brigate Rosse**) Red Brigades

brac'care vt hunt

brac'cetto nm a ~ arm in arm

bracci'ale nm bracelet; (fascia) armband

braccia'letto nm bracelet; (di orologio) watch-strap. **braccialetto identificativo** identity bracelet

bracci'ante nm day labourer

bracci'ata nf (nel nuoto) stroke

'braccio nm (pl nf **braccia**) arm; (di fiume, pl **bracci**) arm. **braccio di ferro** arm wrestling

bracci'olo nm (di sedia) arm[rest]; (da nuoto) armband

'bracco nm hound

bracconi'ere nm poacher

'brace nf embers pl; **alla ~** char-grilled

'brache nfpl (fam: pantaloni) britches; **calare le ~** fig chicken out

braci'ere nm brazier

braci'ola nf chop. **braciola di maiale** pork chop

'brado adj allo stato ~ in the wild

braille nm Braille

brain-'storming nm inv brainstorming

'brama nf longing

bra'mare vt long for

bra'mino nm Brahmin

bramo'sia nf yearning

'branca nf branch

'branchia nf gill

'branco nm (di cani) pack; (pej: di persone) gang

branco'lare vi grope

'branda nf camp-bed

bran'dello nm scrap; **a brandelli** in tatters

bran'dina nf cot

bran'dire vt brandish

'brandy nm brandy

'brano nm piece; (di libro) passage

bran'zino nm sea bass

bra'sare vt braise

bra'sato nm braised beef with herbs

Bra'sile nm Brazil

brasili'ano, -a adj & nmf Brazilian

bra'vata nf bragging

'bravo adj good; (abile) clever; (coraggioso) brave; ~! well done!

bra'vura *nf* skill

'breccia *nf* breach; **sulla** ~ fig very successful, at the top

brecci'ame *nm* loose chipping *pl*

bre'saola *nf* dried, salted beef sliced thinly and eaten cold

Bre'tagna *nf* Brittany

bre'tella *nf* shoulder-strap; (strada) link road; Mech brace; **bretelle** *pl* (di calzoni) braces, suspenders Am

'bretone *adj* & *nmf* Breton

'breve *adj* brief, short; **in** ~ briefly; **tra** ~ shortly

brevet'tare *vt* patent

bre'vetto *nm* patent; (attestato) licence

brevità *nf* shortness

'brezza *nf* breeze

bricco'nata *nf* dirty trick

bric'cone *nm* blackguard; hum rascal

'briciola *nf* crumb; fig grain

'briciolo *nm* fragment; **non hai un** ~ **di cervello!** you don't have an ounce of common sense!

bridge *nm* (carte) bridge

'briga *nf* (fastidio) trouble; (lite) quarrel; **attaccar** ~ pick a quarrel; **prendersi la** ~ **di fare qualcosa** go to the trouble of doing something

brigadi'ere *nm* (dei Carabinieri) sergeant

brigan'taggio *nm* highway robbery

bri'gante *nm* bandit; hum rogue

bri'gare *vi* to intrigue

bri'gata *nf* brigade; (gruppo) group

briga'tista *nmf* Pol member of the Red Brigades

'briglia *nf* rein; **a** ~ **sciolta** at full gallop; fig at breakneck speed

bril'lante ① *adj* brilliant; (scintillante) sparkling ② *nm* diamond

brillan'tina *nf* brilliantine

bril'lare *vi* shine; ⟨metallo⟩ glitter; (scintillare) sparkle

'brillo *adj* tipsy

'brina *nf* hoar-frost

brin'dare *vi* toast; ~ **a qualcuno** drink a toast to somebody

'brindisi *nm inv* toast

'brio *nm* vivacity

bri'oche *nf inv* croissant

bri'oso *adj* vivacious

'briscola *nf* (seme) trumps

bri'tannico *adj* British

'brivido *nm* shiver; (di paura ecc) shudder; (di emozione) thrill; **avere i brividi** have the shivers; **dare i brividi a qualcuno** give somebody the shivers

brizzo'lato *adj* ⟨capelli, barba⟩ greying

'brocca *nf* jug

broc'cato *nm* brocade

'broccoli *nmpl* broccoli *sg*

bro'daglia *nf* pej dishwater

'brodo *nm* broth; (per cucinare) stock. **brodo di manzo** beef tea. **brodo di pollo** chicken broth; (per cucinare) chicken stock. **brodo ristretto** consommé. **brodo vegetale** clear broth; (per cucinare) vegetable stock

'broglio *nm* **broglio elettorale** gerrymandering

'broker *nmf inv* broker. **broker d'assicurazioni** insurance broker

'bromo *nm* Chem bromine

bro'muro *nm* bromide

bronchi'ale *adj* bronchial

bron'chite *nf* bronchitis

bron'chitico *adj* chesty

'broncio *nm* sulk; **fare il** ~ sulk

bronto'lare *vi* grumble; ⟨tuono ecc⟩ rumble; ~ **contro qualcuno/qualcosa** grumble or grouch about somebody/ something

bronto'lio *nm* grumbling; (di tuono, stomaco) rumbling

bronto'lone, -a *nmf* grumbler

'bronzo *nm* bronze; **una faccia di** ~ fam a brass neck

bros'sura *nf* **edizione in brossura** paperback

bru'care *vt* ⟨pecora⟩ graze

bruciacchi'are *vt* scorch

bruci'ante *adj* burning

brucia'pelo *adv* **a** ~ point-blank

bruci'are ① *vt* burn; (scottare) scald; (incendiare) set fire to ② *vi* burn; (scottare) scald

bruci'arsi *vr* burn oneself

bruci'ato *adj* burnt; fig burnt-out

brucia'tore *nm* burner

brucia'tura *nf* burn

bruci'ore *nm* burning sensation

'bruco *nm* grub

'brufolo *nm* spot, pimple

brufo'loso *adj* spotty, pimply

brughi'era *nf* heath

bruli'care *vi* swarm

bruli'chio *nm* swarming

'brullo *adj* bare

'bruma *nf* mist

Bru'nei *nm* Brunei

'bruno *adj* brown; ⟨occhi, capelli⟩ dark

brusca'mente *adv* (di colpo) suddenly; (in tono brusco) sharply

bru'schetta *nf* toasted bread rubbed with garlic and sprinkled with olive oil

'brusco *adj* sharp; (persona) brusque, abrupt; (improvviso) sudden

bru'sio *nm* buzzing
bru'tale *adj* brutal
brutalità *nf inv* brutality
brutaliz'zare *vt* brutalize
'bruto *adj & nm* brute
brut'tezza *nf* ugliness
'brutto *adj* ugly; ⟨*tempo, tipo, situazione, affare*⟩ nasty; (cattivo) bad. **brutta copia** *nf* rough copy. ~ **tiro** *nm* dirty trick
brut'tura *nf* ugly thing
bub'bone *nm* Med swelling
'buca *nf* hole; (avvallamento) hollow. **buca delle lettere** letter-box
buca'neve *nm inv* snowdrop
bucani'ere *nm* buccaneer
bu'care ① *vt* make a hole in; (pungere) prick; punch ⟨*biglietti*⟩ ② *vi* have a puncture
'Bucarest *nf* Bucharest
bu'carsi *vr* prick oneself; (con droga) shoot up
buca'tini *nmpl* pasta similar to spaghetti but thicker and hollow
bu'cato *nm* washing; **fare il ~** do the washing
'buccia *nf* peel, skin; **bucce** *pl* (di frutta) parings. **buccia di banana** banana skin
bucherel'lare *vt* riddle
bucherel'lato *adj* pitted
'buco *nm* hole. **buco della serratura** keyhole
bu'colica *nf* bucolic
bu'colico *nm* bucolic
'Budda *nm* Buddha
bud'dista *nmf* Buddhist
bu'dello *nm* (pl *nf* **budella**) bowel
'budget *nm inv* budget. **budget provvisorio** minibudget
budge'tario *adj* budgetary
bu'dino *nm* pudding
'bue *nm* (pl **buoi**) ox
'bufalo *nm* buffalo
bu'fera *nf* storm; (di neve) blizzard
bufferiz'zato *adj* Comput buffered
buf'fet *nm inv* snack bar; (mobile) sideboard; (pasto) buffet
buf'fetto *nm* cuff
'buffo ① *adj* funny; Theat comic ② *nm* funny thing
buffo'nata *nf* (scherzo) joke
buf'fone *nm* buffoon; **fare il ~** play the fool
bu'gia *nf* lie; ~ **pietosa** white lie
bugi'ardo, -a ① *adj* lying ② *nmf* liar
bugi'gattolo *nm* cubby-hole
'buio ① *adj* dark

② *nm* darkness; **al ~** in the dark; ~ **pesto** pitch dark
'bulbo *nm* bulb; (dell'occhio) eyeball
Bulga'ria *nf* Bulgaria
'bulgaro, -a *adj & nmf* Bulgarian
buli'mia *nf* bulimia
bu'limico *nmf* bulimic
'bullo *nm* bully
bul'lone *nm* bolt
'bunker *nm inv* bunker
buona'fede *nf* good faith
buo'nanima *nf* **la ~ di mio zio** my late uncle, God rest his soul
buona'notte *int* good night
buona'sera *int* good evening
buonco'stume *nf* Vice Squad
buondì *int* good day
buon'giorno *int* good morning; (di pomeriggio) good afternoon
buon'grado *nm* **di ~** willingly
buongu'staio, -a *nmf* gourmet, foodie fam
buon'gusto *nm* good taste
bu'ono ① *adj* good; ⟨momento⟩ right; **dar ~** (convalidare) accept; **alla buona** easygoing; ⟨cena⟩ informal; **buona fortuna!** good luck!; **buona notte/sera** good night/evening; **buon compleanno/Natale!** happy birthday/merry Christmas!; **buon viaggio!** have a good trip!; **buon appetito!** enjoy your meal!; ~ **senso** common sense; **di buon'ora** early; **a buon mercato** cheap; **una buona volta** once and for all; **buona parte di** the best part of; **tre ore buone** three good hours ② *nm* good; (in film) goody; (tagliando) voucher; (titolo) bond; **con le buone** gently. **buono acquisto** gift token. **buono sconto** money-off-coupon ③ *nmf* **buono, -a a nulla** dead loss
buontem'pone, -a *nmf* happy-go-lucky person
buonu'more *nm* good temper
buonu'scita *nf* retirement bonus; (di dirigente) golden handshake
buratti'naio *nm* puppeteer
burat'tino *nm* puppet
'burbero *adj* surly; (nei modi) rough
bu'rino, -a *nmf* hick
Bur'kina 'Faso *nm* Burkina (Faso)
'burla *nf* joke; **fare una ~ a** play a trick on; **per ~** for fun
bur'lare *vt* make a fool of
bur'larsi *vr* ~ **di** make fun of
bu'rocrate *nm* bureaucrat
burocra'tese *nm* gobbledygook
buro'cratico *adj* bureaucratic
burocra'zia *nf* bureaucracy
bu'rotica *nf* office automation

bur'rasca *nf* storm
burra'scoso *adj* stormy
'burro *nm* butter. **burro di arachidi** peanut butter
bur'rone *nm* ravine
Bu'rundi *nm* Burundi
bus *nm inv* Comput bus. **bus locale** local bus
bu'scare *vt* catch; **buscarle** fam get a hiding
bu'scarsi *vr* catch
bus'sare *vt* knock
'bussola *nf* compass; **perdere la ~** lose ones bearings
'busta *nf* envelope; (astuccio) case. **busta affrancata** business reply envelope. **busta a finestra** window envelope.

busta imbottita Jiffy bag®, padded envelope. **busta paga** pay-packet
busta'rella *nf* bribe
bu'stina *nf* (di tè) tea bag; (per medicine) sachet
'busto *nm* bust; (indumento) girdle; **a mezzo ~** half-length
bu'tano *nm* Calor gas®
buttafu'ori *nm inv* bouncer
but'tare *vt* throw; **~ giù** (demolire) knock down; (inghiottire) gulp down; scribble down ‹scritto›; fam put on ‹pasta›; (scoraggiare) dishearten; **~ via** throw away
but'tarsi *vr* throw oneself; (saltare) jump
butte'rato *adj* pitted
buz'zurro *nm* fam yokel
byte *nm inv* Comput byte

b
c

Cc

c.a. *abbr* (**cortese attenzione**) attn.
caba'ret *nm inv* cabaret
cabaret'tistico *adj* cabaret *attrib*
ca'bina *nf* Naut, Aeron cabin; (al mare) beach hut; (di funivia) [cable] car. **cabina elettorale** polling booth. **cabina di pilotaggio** cockpit; (di aereo di linea) flight deck. **cabina di prova** fitting room. **cabina telefonica** telephone box Br, phone booth
cabi'nato *nm* cabin cruiser
ca'blaggio *nm* Electr wiring
ca'blato *adj* ‹messaggio› cable *attrib*
cablo'gramma *nm* cablegram
cabo'taggio *nm* Naut coastal navigation
cabrio'let *nm inv* Auto convertible
ca'cao *nm* cocoa
ca'care *vi* vulg have a crap
caca'toa *nm inv* cockatoo
'cacca *nf* fam poo, number two
'cacchio *nm* fam hell; **ma che ~ fai/dici?** fam what the hell are you doing/saying?
'caccia ① *nf* hunt; (con fucile) shooting; (inseguimento) chase; (selvaggina) game ② *nm inv* Aeron fighter; Naut destroyer; **andare a ~** go hunting. **caccia alla balena** whaling. **caccia grossa** big game. **caccia all'uomo** man-hunt. **caccia alla volpe** fox hunting
cacciabombardi'ere *nm* Aeron fighter-bomber
cacciagi'one *nf* game
cacci'are ① *vt* hunt; (mandar via) chase away; (scacciare) drive out; (ficcare) shove;

caccia [fuori] I soldi! fam out with the money!; **~ un urlo** fam let out a yell ② *vi* go hunting
cacci'arsi *vr* (nascondersi) hide; (andare a finire) get to; **~ nei guai** get into trouble
caccia'tora *nf* alla **~** *a* Culin chasseur
caccia'tore, -trice *nmf* hunter. **cacciatore di dote** gold digger. **cacciatore di frodo** poacher. **cacciatore di taglie** bounty hunter. **cacciatore di teste** Comm head-hunter
cacciatorpedini'ere *nm inv* destroyer
caccia'vite *nm inv* screwdriver
cacci'ucco *nm* **cacciucco alla livornese** soup of seafood, tomato and wine served with bread
cache-'sexe *nm inv* thong
ca'chet *nm inv* Med capsule; (colorante) colour rinse; (stile) cachet
'cachi ① *nm inv* persimmon ② *adj inv* (colore) khaki
'cacio *nm* (formaggio) cheese
caci'otta *nf* creamy, fairly soft cheese
'caco *nm* fam persimmon
cacofo'nia *nf* cacophony
'cactus *nm inv* cactus
cada'uno *adj* each
ca'davere *nm* corpse
cada'verico *adj* fig deathly pale
ca'dente *adj* falling; ‹casa› crumbling
ca'denza *nf* cadence; (ritmo) rhythm; Mus cadenza
caden'zare *vt* give rhythm to

caden'zato adj measured

ca'dere vi fall; ⟨capelli ecc⟩ fall out; (capitombolare) tumble; ⟨vestito ecc⟩ hang; **far ∼** (di mano) drop; **∼ dal sonno** feel very sleepy; **lasciar ∼** drop; **∼ dalle nuvole** fig be taken aback; **∼ dalla finestra** fall out of the window

ca'detto nm cadet

ca'duta nf fall; fig downfall. **caduta dei capelli** hair loss. **caduta libera** freefall. **caduta massi** rockfall; (avviso) falling rocks

ca'duto nm **i caduti** the dead; **monumento ai caduti** war memorial

caffè nm inv coffee; (locale) café. **caffè corretto** espresso with a dash of liqueur. **caffè Internet** cybercafe, Internet café. **caffè lungo** weak black coffee. **caffè macchiato** coffee with a dash of milk. **caffè ristretto** extra-strong espresso coffee. **caffè solubile** instant coffee

caffe'ina nf caffeine

caffel'latte nm inv white coffee

caffette'ria nf coffee bar

caffetti'era nf coffee-pot. **caffettiera a stantuffo** cafetière

cafo'naggine nf boorishness

cafo'nata nf boorishness

ca'fone, **-a** nmf boor

cafone'ria nf (comportamento) boorishness; **è stata una ∼** it was boorish

ca'gare vi vulg crap; **va' a ∼!** go and get stuffed!

cagio'nare vt cause

cagio'nevole adj delicate

cagli'are vi curdle

cagli'arsi vr curdle

cagli'ata nf curd cheese

caglia'tura nf curdling

'cagna nf bitch

ca'gnara nf fam din

ca'gnesco adj **guardare qualcuno in ∼** scowl at somebody

ca'gnetto nm lapdog

C.A.I. nm abbr (**Club Alpino Italiano**) Italian mountain sports association

cai'mano nm cayman

'caio nm so-and-so

'Cairo nm **il ∼** Cairo

'cala nf creek

cala'brese adj & nmf Calabrian

Ca'labria nf Calabria

cala'brone nm hornet

cala'maio nm inkpot

calama'retto nm small squid

cala'mari nmpl squid sg

cala'maro nm squid

cala'mita nf magnet

calamità nf inv calamity; **∼ pl naturali** natural disasters

calami'tare vt draw ⟨attenzione⟩

ca'lante adj waning

ca'lare **1** vi come down; ⟨vento⟩ drop; (diminuire) fall; (tramontare) set; **∼ di peso** lose weight; **∼ di tono** fig drag **2** vt (abbassare) lower; (nei lavori a maglia) decrease **3** nm (di luna) waning

ca'larsi vr lower oneself

ca'lata nf (invasione) invasion

'calca nf throng

cal'cagno nm (pl f **calcagna**) heel; **stare alle calcagna di qualcuno** fig follow somebody around

cal'care[1] nm limestone

cal'care[2] vt tread; (premere) press [down]; **∼ la mano** fig exaggerate; **∼ le orme di qualcuno** fig follow in somebody's footsteps; **∼ le scene** fig tread the boards

'calce[1] nf lime. **calce viva** quicklime

'calce[2] nm **in ∼** at the foot of the page

calce'struzzo nm concrete

cal'cetto nm Sport five-a-side [football]; (da tavolo) table football

calci'are vt kick

calcia'tore nm footballer

calcifi'carsi vr calcify

calcificazi'one nf calcification

cal'cina nf mortar

calci'naccio nm (pezzo di intonaco) flake of plaster; (pezzo di muro) piece of rubble

'calcio[1] nm kick; Sport football; (di arma da fuoco) butt; **dare un ∼ a** kick; **giocare a ∼** play football. **calcio d'angolo** corner [kick]. **calcio di punizione** free kick. **calcio di rigore** penalty [kick]

'calcio[2] nm Chem calcium

calcio-mer'cato nm inv transfer market

'calco nm (con carta) tracing; (arte) cast

calco'lare vt calculate; (considerare) consider

calco'lato adj calculated

calcola'tore **1** adj calculating **2** nm calculator; (macchina elettronica) computer. **calcolatore digitale** (calcolatrice) calculator

calcola'trice nf calculating machine

'calcolo nm calculation; Med stone; **per ∼** fig out of self-interest; **mi sono fatto i calcoli** fig I've weighed up the pros and cons. **calcolo approssimativo** guesstimate. **calcolo biliare** gallstone. **calcolo renale** kidney stone

cal'daia nf boiler. **caldaia ad accumulo** storage heater

caldar'rosta nf roast chestnut

caldeggi'are vt support

'caldo ① *adj* warm; (molto caldo) hot; ⟨*situazione, zona*⟩ dangerous; ⟨*notizie*⟩ latest; **non gli fa né** ∼ **né freddo** fig he doesn't give a damn; **ondata di caldo** heatwave; **tavola calda** snack bar ② *nm* heat; **avere** ∼ be warm, be hot; **fa** ∼ it's warm, it's hot

caleido'scopio *nm* kaleidoscope

calen'dario *nm* calendar. **calendario sportivo** sporting calendar

ca'lesse *nm* gig

cali'brare *vt* calibrate

cali'brato *adj* calibrated; fig balanced; **taglie** *pl* **calibrate** clothes for non-standard sizes

'calibro *nm* calibre; (strumento) callipers *pl*; **di grosso** ∼ ⟨*persona*⟩ top *attrib*

'calice *nm* goblet; Relig chalice

californi'ano, -a *adj & nmf* Californian

ca'ligine *nm* fog; (industriale) smog

call-girl *nf inv* call girl

calligra'fia *nf* handwriting; (cinese) calligraphy

calli'grafico *adj* **perizia calligrafica** handwriting analysis

cal'ligrafo, -a *nmf* calligrapher

cal'lista *nmf* chiropodist

'callo *nm* corn; **fare il** ∼ **a** become hardened to

cal'loso *adj* callous

'calma *nf* calm; **mantenere la** ∼ keep calm; **prendersela con** ∼ fig take it easy; **fare qualcosa con** ∼ take one's time doing something

cal'mante ① *adj* calming ② *nm* sedative

cal'mare *vt* calm [down]; (lenire) soothe

cal'marsi *vr* calm down; ⟨*vento*⟩ drop; ⟨*dolore*⟩ die down

calmie'rare *vt* control the prices of

calmi'ere *nm* price control

'calmo *adj* calm

'calo *nm* Comm fall; (di volume) shrinkage; (di peso) loss; **in** ∼ dwindling

ca'lore *nm* heat; (moderato) warmth; **in** ∼ (di animale) on heat

calo'ria *nf* calorie

ca'lorico *adj* calorific

calo'rifero *nm* radiator

calorosa'mente *adv* warmly

calorosità *nf* fig warmth

calo'roso *adj* warm

ca'lotta *nf* **calotta cranica** skullcap. **calotta glaciale** icecap. **calotta polare** polar icecap

calpe'stare *vt* trample [down]; fig trample on ⟨*diritti, sentimenti*⟩; **'vietato** ∼ **l'erba'** 'keep off the grass'

calpe'stio *nm* (passi) footsteps *pl*; (rumore) stamping

ca'lunnia *nf* slander

calunni'are *vt* slander

calunni'oso *adj* slanderous

ca'lura *nf* heat

cal'vario *nm* Calvary; fig trial

calvi'nismo *nm* Calvinism

calvi'nista *nmf* Calvinist

cal'vizie *nf* baldness

'calvo *adj* bald

'calza *nf* (da reggicalze) stocking; (da uomo) sock. **calza della befana** ≈ Christmas stocking

calza'maglia *nf* tights *pl*; (per danza) leotard

cal'zante *adj* fig fitting

cal'zare ① *vt* (indossare) wear; (mettersi) put on ② *vi* fit; ∼ **a pennello** ⟨*indumenti*⟩ fit like a glove

calza'scarpe *nm inv* shoehorn

calza'tura *nf* footwear; **calzature** *pl* footwear *sg*

calzaturi'ficio *nm* shoe factory

cal'zetta *nf* ankle sock; **è una mezza** ∼ fig he's no use

calzet'tone *nm* knee-length woollen sock

cal'zino *nm* sock

calzo'laio *nm* shoe mender

calzole'ria *nf* (negozio) shoe shop

calzon'cini *nmpl* shorts. **calzoncini da bagno** swimming trunks

cal'zone *nm* Culin folded pizza with tomato, mozzarella etc inside

cal'zoni *nmpl* trousers, pants Am. **calzoni alla cavallerizza** jodhpurs

camale'onte *nm* chameleon

cambi'ale *nf* Comm bill of exchange

cambia'mento *nm* change

cambi'are ① *vt* change; move ⟨*casa*⟩; (fare cambio di) exchange; ∼ **canale** TV switch over; ∼ **rotta** Naut alter course; ∼ **l'aria in una stanza** air a room; ∼ **sesso** have a sex change ② *vi* change; (fare cambio) exchange

cambi'arsi *vr* change

cambiava'lute *nm* bureau de change

'cambio *nm* change; (Comm, scambio) exchange; Mech gear; **dare il** ∼ **a qualcuno** relieve somebody; **in** ∼ **di** in exchange for. **cambio della guardia** changeover. **cambio dell'olio** oil change

Cam'bogia *nf* Cambodia

cambogi'ano, -a *adj & nmf* Cambodian

cam'busa *nf* pantry

ca'melia *nf* camellia

'camera *nf* room; (mobili) [bedroom] suite; Camera Pol, Comm Chamber. **camera ammobiliata** bedsit. **camera** ···▸

ardente chapel of rest. **camera d'aria** inner tube. **camera blindata** strong room. **Camera di Commercio** Chamber of Commerce. **Camera dei Comuni** House of Commons. **Camera dei Deputati** ≈ House of Commons. **Camera dei Lord** House of Lords. **Camera dei Rappresentanti** House of Representatives. **camera doppia** double room. **camera a gas** gas chamber. **camera da letto** bedroom. **camera a due letti** twin room. **camera matrimoniale** double room. **camera oscura** darkroom. **camera degli ospiti** guest room. **camera singola** single room

came'rata¹ *nf* (dormitorio) dormitory; Mil barrack room

came'rata² *nmf* mate

camera'tesco *adj* comradely

camera'tismo *nm* comradeship

cameri'era *nf* maid; (di ristorante) waitress; (in albergo) chamber-maid

cameri'ere *nm* manservant; (di ristorante) waiter

came'rino *nm* dressing-room

came'ristico *adj* Mus chamber

'Camerun *nm* il ~ Cameroon

'camice *nm* overall

camice'ria *nf* shirt shop

cami'cetta *nf* blouse

ca'micia *nf* shirt; **essere nato con la ~** fig be born lucky. **uovo in camicia** poached egg. **camicia di forza** strait-jacket. **camicia nera** Blackshirt. **camicia da notte** nightdress; (da uomo) nightshirt

camici'aio *nm* (venditore) shirtseller; (sarto) shirtmaker

camici'ola *nf* vest

cami'netto *nm* fireplace. **caminetto alimentato a carbone** coalfire

ca'mino *nm* chimney; (focolare) fireplace, hearth

'camion *nm inv* lorry Br, truck. **camion della nettezza urbana** dust-cart Br, garbage truck Am

camion'cino *nm* van

camio'netta *nf* jeep

camio'nista *nmf* lorry driver Br, truck driver

'camma *nf* cam; **albero a camme** Auto camshaft

cam'mello ① *nm* camel; (tessuto) camel-hair
② *adj inv* (colore) camel

cam'meo *nm* cameo

cammi'nare *vi* walk; ⟨auto, orologio⟩ go; ~ **avanti e indietro** pace up and down

cammi'nata *nf* walk; **fare una ~** go for a walk

cam'mino *nm* way; **essere in ~** be on the way; **mettersi in ~** set out; **cammin facendo** on the way

camo'milla *nf* camomile; (bevanda) camomile tea

camo'millarsi *vr sl* camomillati! don't get your knickers in a twist!, cool it!

Ca'morra *nf* local mafia

camor'rista *nmf* member of the 'Camorra'

ca'moscio *nm* chamois; (pelle) suede

cam'pagna *nf* country; (paesaggio) countryside; Comm, Mil campaign; **in ~** in the country. **campagna elettorale** election campaign. **campagna promozionale** promotional campaign, marketing campaign. **campagna pubblicitaria** publicity campaign

campa'gnola *nf* Auto cross-country vehicle

campa'gnolo, -a ① *adj* rustic
② *nm* countryman
③ *nf* countrywoman

cam'pale *adj* field *attrib*; **giornata campale** fig strenuous day

cam'pana *nf* bell; (di vetro) belljar; **a ~** bellshaped; **essere sordo come una ~** be as deaf as a doorpost; **sentire anche l'altra ~** fig hear the other side of the story; **vivere sotto una ~ di vetro** fig be mollycoddled; **campane** *pl* **eoliche** wind chimes; **campane** *pl* **a morto** death knell

campa'naccio *nm* cowbell

campa'naro *nm* bell-ringer

campa'nella *nf* (di tenda) curtain ring

campa'nello *nm* door-bell; (cicalino) buzzer

Cam'pania *nf* Campania

campa'nile *nm* bell tower

campani'lismo *nm* parochialism

campani'lista *nmf* person with a parochial outlook

campani'listico *adj* parochial

cam'panula *nf* Bot campanula

cam'pare *vi* live; (a stento) get by; **tirare a ~** fig live from day to day

cam'pato *adj* ~ **in aria** unfounded

campeggi'are *vi* camp; (spiccare) stand out

campeggia|'tore, -trice *nmf* camper

cam'peggio *nm* camping; (terreno) campsite; **andare in ~** go camping; **fare ~ libero** camp in the wild. **campeggio per roulotte** caravan site

'camper *nm inv* camper (van)

cam'pestre *adj* rural

Campi'doglio *nm* Capitol

'camping *nm inv* campsite

campiona'mento *nm* sampling

campio'nario ① *nm* [set of] samples

⟨2⟩ *adj* **fiera campionaria** trade fair

campio'nato *nm* championship. **Campionato Mondiale di Calcio** World Cup

campiona'tura *nf* (di merce) range of samples; (in statistica) sampling. **campionatura casuale** random sample

campi'one *nm* champion; Comm sample; (esemplare) specimen; **indagine campione** (in statistica) sample. **campione gratuito** free sample; '∼ **senza valore**' 'sample, no commercial value'

campio'nessa *nf* ladies' champion

'campo *nm* field; (accampamento) camp; Mil encampment; **abbandonare il** ∼ Mil desert in the face of the enemy; fig throw in the towel; **a tutto** ∼ fig wide-ranging; **avere** ∼ **libero** fig have a free hand; **giocare a tutto** ∼ Sport cover the entire pitch. **campo d'aviazione** airfield. **campo base** base camp. **campo di battaglia** battlefield. **campo da calcio** football pitch. **campo di concentramento** concentration camp. **campo in erba** grass court. **campo da golf** golf course. **campo di grano** cornfield. **campo da hockey** hockey field. **campo di mais** cornfield. **campo di prigionia** prison camp. **campo profughi** refugee camp. **campo sportivo** sports ground. **campo di sterminio** death camp. **campo in superficie dura** hard court. **campo da tennis** tennis court

campo'santo *nm* cemetery

'campus *nm inv* (di università) campus

camuf'fare *vt* disguise

camuf'farsi *vr* disguise oneself

ca'muso *adj* naso ∼ snub nose

'Canada *nm* Canada

cana'dese *adj & nmf* Canadian

ca'naglia *nf* scoundrel; (plebaglia) rabble

ca'nale *nm* channel; (artificiale) canal. **Canal Grande** Gran Canal. **canale della Manica** English Channel. **canale di scolo** dyke

canaliz'zare *vt* channel ⟨acque, energie⟩

canalizzazi'one *nf* channelling; (rete) pipes *pl*

'canapa *nf* hemp. **canapa indiana** (droga) cannabis

Ca'narie *nfpl* **le** ∼ the Canaries

cana'rino *nm* canary

ca'nasta *nf* (gioco) canasta

cancel'labile *adj* erasable; ⟨impegno, incontro⟩ which can be cancelled

cancel'lare *vt* cross out; (con la gomma) rub out; fig wipe out; (annullare) cancel; Comput delete, erase

cancel'larsi *vr* be erased, be wiped out

cancel'lata *nf* railings *pl*

cancel'lato *adj* cancelled

cancella'tura *nf* erasure

cancellazi'one *nf* cancellation; Comput deletion

cancelle'ria *nf* chancellery; (articoli per scrivere) stationery

cancel'letto *nm* hash sign

cancelli'ere *nm* chancellor; (di tribunale) clerk

cancel'lino *nm* duster

can'cello *nm* gate

cance'rogeno **⟨1⟩** *nm* carcinogen **⟨2⟩** *adj* carcinogenic

cance'roso *adj* cancerous

can'crena *nf* gangrene; **andare in** ∼ become gangrenous

cancre'noso *adj* gangrenous

'cancro *nm* cancer; **Cancro** Astr Cancer; **tropico del Cancro** Tropic of Cancer

candeggi'are *vt* bleach

candeg'gina *nf* bleach

can'deggio *nm* bleaching

can'dela *nf* candle; Auto spark plug; **a lume di** ∼ by candle-light; ⟨cena⟩ candlelit; **tenere la** ∼ fig play gooseberry; **il gioco non vale la** ∼ the game is not worth the candle. **candela magica** sparkler

cande'labro *nm* candelabra

cande'letta *nf* Med pessary

candeli'ere *nm* candlestick

cande'line *nfpl* candles

cande'lotto *nm* (di dinamite) stick. **candelotto lacrimogeno** tear gas grenade

candida'mente *adv* innocently

candi'dare *vt* put forward as a candidate

candi'darsi *vr* stand as a candidate

candi'dato, -a *nmf* candidate

candida'tura *nf* Pol candidacy; (per lavoro) application

'candido *adj* snow-white; (sincero) candid; (puro) pure

can'dito **⟨1⟩** *adj* candied **⟨2⟩** *nm* piece of candied fruit

can'dore *nm* whiteness; fig innocence

'cane *nm* dog; (di arma da fuoco) cock; **un tempo da cani** foul weather; **fa un freddo** ∼ it's bitterly cold; **non c'era un** ∼ fig there wasn't a soul about; **solo come un** ∼ fig all on one's own; **essere come** ∼ **e gatto** fig fight like cat and dog; **essere un** ∼ ⟨attore, cantante⟩ be appalling, be a dog sl; **fatto da cani** fig ⟨lavoro⟩ botched; **mangiare da cani** fig eat very badly; **figlio di un** ∼ fam son of a bitch. **cane da caccia** hunting dog. **cane per ciechi** guide-dog. **cane da corsa** greyhound. **cane da guardia** guard-dog. **cane** ···⟩

lupo alsatian. **cane poliziotto** police dog. **cane da salotto** lapdog. **cane sciolto** fig maverick

ca'nestro *nm* basket; **fare ~** score a basket

'canfora *nf* camphor

cangi'ante *adj* iridescent; **seta cangiante** shot silk

can'guro *nm* kangaroo

ca'nicola *nf* scorching heat

ca'nile *nm* kennel; (di allevamento) kennels *pl.* **canile municipale** dog pound

ca'nino *adj & nm* canine

ca'nizie *nm* white hair

'canna *nf* reed; (da zucchero) cane; (di fucile) barrel; (bastone) stick; (di bicicletta) crossbar; (asta) rod; (fam: hashish) joint; **povero in ~** destitute. **canna fumaria** flue. **canna da pesca** fishing-rod. **canna da zucchero** sugar cane

cannabis *nf* cannabis

can'nella *nf* cinnamon

cannel'loni *nmpl* **cannelloni al forno** rolls of pasta stuffed with meat and baked in the oven

can'neto *nm* bed of reeds

can'nibale *nm* cannibal

canniba'lismo *nm* cannibalism

cannocchi'ale *nm* telescope

can'noli *nmpl* **cannoli alla siciliana** cylindrical pastries filled with ricotta and candied fruit

canno'nata *nf* cannon shot; **è una ~** fig it's brilliant

cannon'cino *nm* (dolce) cream horn

can'none *nm* cannon; fig ace

cannoneggia'mento *nm* cannonade

cannoni'era *nf* gunboat

cannoni'ere *nm* (soldato) gunner; (calciatore) top goal scorer

can'nuccia *nf* [drinking] straw; (di pipa) stem

ca'noa *nf* canoe

cano'ismo *nm* canoeing

'canone *nm* canon; (del telefono) standing charge; (affitto) rent; **equo canone** rent set by law

ca'nonica *nf* manse

ca'nonico *nm* canon

canoniz'zare *vt* canonize

canonizzazi'one *nf* canonization

ca'noro *adj* melodious

ca'notta *nf* (estiva) vest top

canot'taggio *nm* canoeing; (voga) rowing

canotti'era *nf* vest, singlet

canotti'ere *nm* oarsman

ca'notto *nm* [rubber] dinghy

cano'vaccio *nm* (trama) plot; (straccio) duster; (per ricamo) canvas

can'tante *nmf* singer. **cantante lirico** opera-singer

can'tare *vt/i* sing; **~ vittoria** fig crow; **fare ~ qualcuno** sl make somebody talk; **me le ha cantate** fam he told me off

canta'storie *nmf inv* story-teller

can'tata *nf* Mus cantata

can'tato *adj* sung

cantau'|tore, -trice *nmf* singer-song-writer

canticchi'are *vt* sing softly; (a bocca chiusa) hum

'cantico *nm* hymn

canti'ere *nm* yard; Naut shipyard; (di edificio) construction site. **cantiere navale** naval dockyard; (per piccole imbarcazioni) boatyard

cantie'ristica *nf* construction

canti'lena *nf* singsong; (ninna-nanna) lullaby

can'tina *nf* cellar; (per vini) wine cellar; (osteria) wine shop

'canto[1] *nm* singing; (canzone) song; Relig chant; (poesia) poem. **canto di Natale** *o* **natalizio** Christmas carol. **canto degli uccelli** birdsong

'canto[2] *nm* (angolo) corner; (lato) side; **dal ~ mio** for my part; **d'altro ~** on the other hand

canto'nale *adj* cantonal

canto'nata *nf* **prendere una ~** fig be sadly mistaken

can'tone *nm* canton; (angolo) corner

can'tore *nm* chorister

can'tuccio *nm* nook; **stare in un ~** fig hold oneself aloof

ca'nuto *adj* liter whitehaired

canzo'nare *vt* tease

canzona'torio *adj* teasing

canzona'tura *nf* teasing

can'zone *nf* song. **canzone d'amore** love song

canzo'netta *nf* fam pop song

canzoni'ere *nm* songbook

'caos *nm* chaos

ca'otico *adj* chaotic

C.A.P. *nm abbr* (**Codice di Avviamento Postale**) post code, zip code Am

cap. *abbr* (**capitolo**) chap., chapter

ca'pace *adj* able; (esperto) skilled; ⟨stadio, contenitore⟩ big; **~ di** (disposto a) capable of; **è ~ a cantare?** can he sing?

capacità *nf inv* ability; (attitudine) skill; (capienza) capacity. **capacità d'assorbimento** absorbency. **capacità di credito** creditworthiness. **capacità di memorizzazione** retentiveness.

capacità produttiva production capacity. **capacità di resistenza** staying power

capaci'tarsi *vr* ∼ **di** (rendersi conto) understand; (accorgersi) realize

ca'panna *nf* hut

capan'nello *nm* knot of people; **fare** ∼ **intorno a qualcuno/qualcosa** gather round somebody/something

ca'panno *nm* **capanno degli attrezzi** garden shed. **capanno da spiaggia** beach hut, cabana

capan'none *nm* shed; Aeron hangar

caparbietà *nf* obstinacy

ca'parbio *adj* obstinate

ca'parra *nf* deposit

capa'tina *nf* short visit; **fare una** ∼ **in città/da qualcuno** pop into town/in on somebody

ca'pello *nm* hair; **non torcere un** ∼ **a qualcuno** fig not lay a finger on somebody; **capelli** *pl* (capigliatura) hair *sg*; **lavarsi/asciugarsi i capelli** wash/dry one's hair; **avere i capelli a spazzola** have a crew-cut; **spaccare il** ∼ **in quattro** split hairs; **averne fin sopra i capelli** fig be fed up to the back teeth; **mettersi le mani nei capelli** fig tear one's hair out; **capelli** *pl* **d'angelo** vermicelli

capel'lone *nm* long-haired type, hippie

capel'luto *adj* hairy; **cuoio capelluto** scalp

ca'pestro *nm* noose; **contratto capestro** strait-jacket of a contract

capez'zale *nm* bolster; fig bedside

ca'pezzolo *nm* nipple

capi'ente *adj* capacious

capi'enza *nf* capacity

capiglia'tura *nf* hair

capil'lare *adj* capillary

ca'pire *vt* understand; **non capisco** I don't understand; ∼ **male** misunderstand; **si capisce!** naturally!; **sì, ho capito** yes, I see

capi'tale ① *adj* Jur capital; (principale) main
② *nf* (città) capital
③ *nm* Comm capital. **capitale di avviamento** start-up capital. **capitale azionario** Fin equity capital, share capital. **capitale di investimento** investment capital. **capitale di rischio** venture capital. **capitale sociale** Fin share capital

capita'lismo *nm* capitalism

capita'lista *nmf* capitalist

capita'listico *adj* capitalist

capitaliz'zare *vt* capitalize

capitalizzazi'one *nf* capitalization

capita'nare *vt* lead (rivolta); Sport captain

capitane'ria *nf* **capitaneria di porto** port authorities *pl*

capi'tano *nm* captain. **capitano di lungo corso** Naut captain

capi'tare *vi* (giungere per caso) come; (accadere) happen

'**capite**: **pro** ∼ *adv* per capita

capi'tello *nm* Archit capital

capito'lare *vi* capitulate

capitolazi'one *nf* capitulation

ca'pitolo *nm* chapter

capi'tombolo *nm* headlong fall; **fare un** ∼ tumble down

'**capo** *nm* head; (chi comanda) boss fam; (di vestiario) item; Geog cape; (in tribù) chief; (parte estrema) top; **a** ∼ (in dettato) new paragraph; **da** ∼ over again; **giramento di** ∼ dizziness; **mal di** ∼ headache; **in** ∼ **a un mese** within a month; **non ha né** ∼ **né coda** ‹*discorso, ragionamento*› I can't make head nor tail of it. **capo d'abbigliamento** item of clothing. **capo d'accusa** Jur charge, count. **capo di bestiame** head of cattle. **Capo di Buona Speranza** Cape of Good Hope. **capo reparto** head of department. **il Capo Verde** Cape Verde

capo'banda *nm* Mus band-master; (di delinquenti) ringleader

capocameri'ere, -a ① *nm* head waiter
② *nf* head waitress

ca'pocchia *nf* **capocchia di spillo** pinhead

ca'poccia *nm* (fam: testa) nut

capocci'one, -a *nmf* fam brainbox

capo'classe *nmf* ≈ form captain

capocor'data *nmf* (alpinista) leader

capocu'oco, -a *nmf* head cook

Capo'danno *nm* New Year's Day

capofa'miglia *nm* head of the family

capoffi'cina *nm* head mechanic

capo'fitto *nm* **a** ∼ headlong

capo'giro *nm* giddiness

capo'gruppo *nm* group leader

capola'voro *nm* masterpiece

capo'linea *nm* terminus

capo'lino *nm* **fare** ∼ peep in

capo'lista *nmf* Sport league leaders *pl*; Pol candidate whose name appears first on the list

capolu'ogo *nm* main town

capo'mafia *nm* Mafia boss

capo'mastro *nm* master builder

capo'rale *nm* lance-corporal

capore'parto *nmf* department head, head of department

capo'sala *nf inv* Med ward sister

capo'saldo *nm* stronghold

capo'scalo *nm* airline manager

capo'squadra *nm inv* foreman; Sport team captain

capostazi'one *nm inv* stationmaster

capo'stipite *nmf* (di famiglia) progenitor; (di esemplare) archetype

capo'tavola *nmf* (persona) head of the table; **sedere a** ∼ sit at the head of the table

capo'treno *nm* guard

ca'potta *nf* top

capot'tare *vi* somersault

capouf'ficio *nmf* department head

capo'verso *nm* first line; Jur paragraph

capo'volgere *vt* overturn; fig reverse

capo'volgersi *vr* overturn; ⟨barca⟩ capsize; fig be reversed

capovolgi'mento *nm* turnaround

capo'volto ① *pp di* CAPOVOLGERE ② *adj* upside down

'cappa *nf* cloak; (di camino) cowl; (di cucina) hood

cappa'santa *nf* Culin scallop

cap'pella *nf* chapel. **la Cappella Sistina** the Sistine Chapel

cappel'lano *nm* chaplain

cappel'letti *nmpl* small filled pasta parcels

cappelli'era *nf* hatbox

cappel'lino *nm* **cappellino di carta** party hat

cap'pello *nm* hat; **tanto di** ∼! I take my hat off to you! **cappello a cilindro** top hat. **cappello da cow boy** stetson, cowboy hat **cappello di feltro** homburg. **cappello di paglia** straw hat. **cappello da sole** sun hat

'cappero *nm* caper; **capperi!** fam gosh!

'cappio *nm* noose; **avere il** ∼ **al collo** fig have a millstone round one's neck; ⟨marito⟩ be henpecked

cap'pone *nm* capon

cap'potto *nm* [over] coat

cappuc'cino *nm* (frate) Capuchin [friar]; (bevanda) white coffee

cap'puccio *nm* hood; (di penna stilografica) cap

'capra *nf* goat; **salvare** ∼ **e cavoli** fig run with the hare and hunt with the hounds

ca'pretto *nm* kid

ca'priccio *nm* whim; (bizzarria) freak; **fare i capricci** have tantrums

capricci'oso *adj* capricious; ⟨bambino⟩ naughty

Capri'corno *nm* Astr Capricorn

capri'foglio *nm* honeysuckle

ca'prino *nm* goat's cheese

capri'ola *nf* somersault

capriolo *nm* roe (deer)

'capro *nm* [billy-]goat. **capro espiatorio** scapegoat

ca'prone *nm* [billy-] goat

'capsula *nf* capsule; (di proiettile) cap; (di dente) crown

cap'tare *vt* Radio, TV pick up; catch ⟨attenzione⟩

C.A.R. *nm abbr* (**Centro Addestramento Reclute**) basic training camp

cara'bina *nf* carbine

carabini'ere *nm* carabiniere; **Carabinieri** *pl* Italian police force (which is a branch of the army)

ca'raffa *nf* carafe

Ca'raibi *nmpl* (zona) Caribbean *sg*; (isole) Caribbean Islands; **il mar dei** ∼ the Caribbean [Sea]

cara'ibico *adj* Caribbean

cara'mella *nf* sweet. **caramella alla menta** mint

cara'mello *nm* caramel

ca'rato *nm* carat

ca'rattere *nm* character; (caratteristica) characteristic; **di buon** ∼ good-natured; **in** ∼ **con** (intonato) in keeping with; **è una persona di** ∼ (deciso) he's got character. **carattere jolly** Comput wild card. **carattere tipografico** typeface

caratte'rino *nm* difficult nature

caratte'rista ① *nm* character actor ② *nf* character actress

caratte'ristico, -a ① *adj* characteristic; (pittoresco) quaint ② *nf* characteristic

caratteriz'zare *vt* characterize

caratterizzazi'one *nf* characterization

cara'tura *nf* carats; Comm part-ownership

'caravan *nm inv* caravan

carboi'drato *nm* carbohydrate

car'bonchio *nm* anthrax

carbon'cino *nm* (per disegno) charcoal

car'bone *nm* coal; **stare sui carboni ardenti** fig be on tenterhooks. **carbone fossile** anthracite

carbo'nifero *adj* carboniferous

car'bonio *nm* carbon. **carbonio 14** carbon-14

carboniz'zare *vt* burn to a cinder, burn to a crisp; **è morto carbonizzato** he was burned to death

carboniz'zato *adj* charred

carbu'rante *nm* fuel

carbu'rare ① *vt* carburize ② *vi* fig be firing on all four cylinders; **il motore carbura male** the mixture is wrong

carbura'tore *nm* carburettor

carburazi'one *nf* carburation

car'cassa nf carcass; fig old wreck

carce'rario adj prison attrib

carce'rato, -a nmf prisoner

carcerazione nf imprisonment

'carcere nm prison; (punizione) imprisonment. **carcere di massima sicurezza** maximum security prison

carceri'ere, -a nmf gaoler

carci'noma nm carcinoma

carcio'fino nm baby artichoke

carci'ofo nm artichoke

cardel'lino nm goldfinch

car'diaco adj cardiac; **disturbo cardiaco** heart disease

'cardigan nm inv cardigan

cardi'nale adj & nm cardinal

'cardine nm hinge

cardiochi'rurgo nm heart surgeon

cardiolo'gia nf cardiology

cardi'ologo nm heart specialist

cardio'patico, -a nmf person suffering from a heart complaint

cardio'tonico nm heart stimulant

cardiovasco'lare adj cardiovascular

'cardo nm thistle

ca'rena nf Naut bottom

care'naggio nm **bacino di carenaggio** dry dock

ca'rente adj ∼ **di** lacking in

ca'renza nf lack; (scarsità) scarcity

care'stia nf famine; (mancanza) dearth

ca'rezza nf stroke; (di madre, amante) caress; **fare una** ∼ **a** stroke; (madre, amante) caress

carez'zare vt stroke; ⟨madre, amante⟩ caress

carez'zevole adj fig sweet

'cargo nm inv (nave) cargo boat, freighter; (aereo) cargo plane, freight plane

cari'are vt decay

cari'arsi vi decay

cari'ato adj decayed

'carica nf office; Mil, Electr charge; fig drive; **dotato di una forte** ∼ **di simpatia** really likeable. **carica esplosiva** payload

caricabatte'ria nm inv battery charger

cari'care vt load ⟨camion, software⟩; Mil, Electr charge; wind up ⟨orologio⟩

cari'carsi vr Electr charge [up]; ∼ **di lavoro** take on too much work

cari'cato adj fig affected

carica'tore nm (per proiettile) magazine; (per diapositive) carousel

carica'tura nf caricature

caricatu'rale adj grotesque

caricatu'rista nmf caricaturist

'carico ① adj loaded (di with); ⟨colore⟩ strong; ⟨orologio⟩ wound [up]; ⟨batteria⟩ charged ② nm load; (di nave) cargo; (il caricare) loading; **avere un** ∼ **di lavoro** have a heavy workload; **testimone a** ∼ Jur witness for the prosecution; **a** ∼ **di** Comm to be charged to; ⟨persona⟩ dependent on. **carico utile** payload

'carie nf [tooth] decay

caril'lon nm inv musical box

carino adj pretty, nice-looking; (piacevole) agreeable

ca'risma nm charisma

cari'smatico adj charismatic

carità nf charity; **per** ∼**!** (come rifiuto) God forbid!

carita'tevole adj charitable

car'linga nf fuselage

car'lino nm pug

carnagi'one nf complexion

car'naio nm fig shambles

car'nale adj carnal; **cugino carnale** first cousin

'carne nf flesh; (alimento) meat; **di** ∼ meaty. **carne macinata** mince, ground beef Am. **carne di maiale** pork. **carne di manzo** beef. **carne di vitella** veal

car'nefice nm executioner

carnefi'cina nf slaughter

carne'vale nm carnival

carneva'lesco adj carnival

car'nivoro ① nm carnivore ② adj carnivorous

car'noso adj fleshy

'caro, -a ① adj dear; **cari saluti** kind regards ② nmf fam darling, dear; **i miei cari** my nearest and dearest

ca'rogna nf carcass; fig bastard

caro'sello nm merry-go-round

ca'rota nf carrot

caro'vana nf caravan; (di veicoli) convoy

caro'vita nm high cost of living

'carpa nf carp

car'paccio nm finely sliced raw beef with oil, lemon and slivers of Parmesan

Car'pazi nmpl i ∼ the Carpathians

carpenti'ere nm carpenter

car'pire vt seize; (con difficoltà) extort

car'pone, carponi adv on all fours; **camminare** ∼ crawl

car'rabile adj suitable for vehicles; **passo** ∼ = passo carraio

car'raio adj passo ∼ entrance to driveway, garage etc where parking is forbidden

carreggi'ata nf roadway; **doppia carreggiata** dual carriageway, divided ⋯⟩

highway Am; **rimettersi in** ~ fig straighten oneself out

carrel'lata *nf* TV pan; (fig: di notizie) round-up

car'rello *nm* trolley; (di macchina da scrivere) carriage; Aeron undercarriage; Cinema, TV dolly. **carrello d'atterraggio** Aeron landing gear. **carrello dei dolci** dessert trolley. **carrello portabagagli** luggage trolley, baggage cart Am.

carrello della spesa shopping trolley

car'retta *nf* (veicolo vecchio) old banger; **tirare la** ~ fig plod along

car'retto *nm* cart

carri'era *nf* career; **di gran** ~ at full speed; **fare** ~ get on

carrie'rismo *nm* careerism

carrie'rista *nmf* **è un** ~ his career is all that matters

carri'ola *nf* wheelbarrow

'**carro** *nm* cart. **carro armato** tank. **carro attrezzi** breakdown vehicle, tow truck, wrecker Am. **carro funebre** hearse. **carro merci** truck

car'rozza *nf* carriage; Rail coach, car. **carrozza bagagliaio** Rail guard's van. **carrozza belvedere** Rail observation car. **carrozza cuccette** sleeping car. **carrozza fumatori** Rail smoker. **carrozza letti** Rail sleeping car. **carrozza ristorante** Rail restaurant car, buffet car

carroz'zella *nf* (per bambini) pram; (per invalidi) wheelchair

carrozze'ria *nf* bodywork; (officina) bodyshop

carrozzi'ere *nm* panel beater

carroz'zina *nf* pram; (pieghevole) push-chair, stroller Am

carroz'zone *nm* (di circo) caravan; (fig: organizzazione) slow-moving great monster of an organization

car'ruba *nf* carob

car'rubo *nm* carob

car'rucola *nf* pulley

carta *nf* paper; (da gioco) card; (statuto) charter; Geog map. **carta di addebito** charge card. **carta d'argento** senior citizens' railcard. **carta assegni** cheque card. **carta assorbente** blotting-paper. **carta carbone** carbon paper. **carta di credito** credit card. **carta crespata** crepe paper. **carta di debito** debit card. **carta fedeltà** loyalty card. **carta geografica** map. **carta d'identità** identity card. **carta igienica** toilet-paper. **carta d'imbarco** boarding pass, boarding card. **carta intelligente** smart card. **carta da lettere** writing-paper. **carta millimetrata** graph paper. **carta da pacchi** wrapping paper. **carta da parati** wallpaper. **carta da regali** giftwrap. **carta di riso** rice

paper. **carta smerigliata** emery paper. **carta stagnola** silver paper, silver foil; Culin aluminium foil. **carta straccia** waste paper. **carta stradale** road map. **carta termica** thermal paper. **carta topografica** ≈ Ordnance Survey Map. **carta velina** tissue-paper. **carta verde** Auto green card. **carta vetrata** sandpaper. **carta dei vini** wine-list

cartacar'bone *nf* carbon paper

car'taccia *nf* waste paper

car'taceo *adj* paper

carta'modello *nm* pattern

cartamo'neta *nf* paper money

carta'pecora *nf* vellum

carta'pesta *nf* papier mâché

carta'straccia *nf* waste paper

cartave'trare *vt* sand [down]

car'teggio *nm* correspondence

car'tella *nf* (per documenti ecc) briefcase; (di cartoncino) folder; (di scolaro) satchel, schoolbag. **cartella clinica** medical record

cartel'lina *nf* document wallet, folder

cartel'lino *nm* (etichetta) label; (dei prezzi) price-tag; (di presenza) time-card; **timbrare il** ~ clock in; (all'uscita) clock out

car'tello *nm* sign; (pubblicitario) poster; (stradale) road sign; (di protesta) placard; (Comm, di droga) cartel

cartel'lone *nm* poster; Theat bill. **cartellone pubblicitario** billboard

cartello'nista *nmf* poster designer

cartello'nistica *nf* poster designing

carti'era *nf* paper-mill

carti'lagine *nf* cartilage

cartina *nf* (geografica) map; (per sigarette) cigarette paper. **cartina di tornasole** litmus paper

car'toccio *nm* paper bag; **al** ~ Culin baked in foil

cartogra'fia *nf* cartography

car'tografo *nm* cartographer

carto'laio, -a *nmf* stationer

cartole'ria *nf* stationer's [shop]

cartolibre'ria *nf* stationer's and book shop

carto'lina *nf* postcard. **cartolina postale** postcard. **cartolina [precetto]** call-up papers

carto'mante *nmf* fortune-teller

carton'cino *nm* (materiale) card; (biglietto) card

car'tone *nm* cardboard; (arte) cartoon. **cartone animato** [animated] cartoon. **cartone ondulato** corrugated cardboard. **cartone di uova** egg box

car'tuccia *nf* cartridge; **mezza** ~ fig weakling. **cartuccia d'inchiostro** ink cartridge

'casa *nf* house; (abitazione propria) home; (ditta) firm; **amico di** ~ family friend; **andare a** ~ go home; **uscire di** ~ leave the house; **essere di** ~ be like one of the family; **fatto in** ~ home-made; ~ **per** ~ house-to-house. **casa d'aste** auction house. **casa di correzione** ≈ reform school. **casa di cura** nursing home. **casa del custode** gatehouse. **casa famiglia** care home. **casa madre** Comm parent company. **casa di mode** fashion house. **casa in multiproprietà** timeshare. **casa popolare** council house. **casa rifugio** women's refuge. **casa di riposo** old people's home, retirement home. **casa dello studente** hall of residence. **casa per le vacanze** holiday home

ca'sacca *nf* military coat; (giacca) jacket

ca'saccio: **a** ~ *adv* at random; **sparare a** ~ **su qualcuno/qualcosa** take a potshot at somebody/something

ca'sale *nm* (gruppo di case) hamlet; (casolare) farmhouse

casa'linga *nf* housewife

casa'lingo [1] *adj* domestic; (fatto in casa) home-made; (amante della casa) home-loving; (semplice) homely [2] *nm* **casalinghi** *pl* household goods

casa'nova *nm inv* (donnaiolo) Casanova

ca'sata *nf* family

ca'sato *nm* family name

ca'scante *adj* falling; (floscio) flabby

ca'scare *vi* fall [down]

ca'scata *nf* (di acqua) waterfall

casca|'tore, -trice [1] *nm* stuntman [2] *nf* stuntwoman

cas'chetto *nm* [capelli a] caschetto bob

ca'scina *nf* farm building

casci'nale *nm* farmhouse

'casco *nm* crash-helmet; (asciugacapelli) [hair-]drier. **casco di banane** bunch of bananas. **Caschi blu** *pl* Mil Blue Helmets, Blue Berets

caseggi'ato *nm* block of flats Br, apartment block

casei'ficio *nm* dairy

ca'sella *nf* pigeon-hole. **casella postale** post office box, PO box; (elettronica) mailbox

casel'lante *nmf* (per treni) signalman; (in autostrada) toll collector

casel'lario *nm* (mobile) filing cabinet; (di documenti) file. **casellario giudiziario** record of convictions; **avere il** ~ **giudiziario vuoto** have no criminal record

ca'sello *nm* (di autostrada) [motorway] toll booth

case'reccio *adj* home-made

ca'serma *nf* barracks *pl*; **da** ~ ⟨linguaggio⟩ barrack room *attrib*.

caserma dei Carabinieri military police station. **caserma dei pompieri**, **caserma dei vigili del fuoco** fire station

caser'mone *nm pej* barracks *pl*

cash and carry *nm inv* cash-and-carry

casi'nista *nmf fam* muddler

ca'sino *nm fam* (bordello) brothel; (fig sl: confusione) racket; (disordine) mess; **un** ~ **di** loads of; **è un** ~ (complicato) it's too complicated

casinò *nm inv* casino

ca'sistica *nf* (classificazione) record of occurrences

'caso *nm* chance; (fatto, circostanza, Med, Gram) case; **a** ~ at random; ~ **mai** if need be; **far** ~ **a** pay attention to; **non far** ~ **a** take no account of; **per** ~ by chance. **caso [giudiziario]** [legal] case, court case. **caso urgente** Med emergency case

caso'lare *nm* farmhouse

'caspita *int* good gracious

'cassa *nf* till; (di legno) crate; Comm cash; (luogo di pagamento) cash desk; (mobile) chest; (istituto bancario) bank. **cassa automatica prelievi** cash dispenser, automatic teller. **cassa comune** kitty **cassa continua** cash machine. **cassa da morto** coffin. **cassa di risparmio** savings bank. **cassa toracica** ribcage

cassa'forte *nf* safe

cassa'panca *nf* linen chest

cas'sata *nf* ice-cream cake

cas'sero *nm* Naut quarterdeck

casseru'ola *nf* saucepan

cas'setta *nf* case; (per registratore) cassette; **far buona** ~ Theatr be good box-office. **cassetta degli attrezzi** toolbox. **cassetta delle lettere** postbox, letterbox. **cassetta delle offerte** charity box. **cassetta portapane** breadbin. **cassetta portavalori** cash box. **cassetta del pronto soccorso** first-aid kit. **cassetta di sicurezza** strong-box, safe-deposit box

cas'setto *nm* drawer; (di fotocopiatrice ecc) tray. **cassetto di inserimento [dei] fogli** paper feed tray

casset'tone *nm* chest of drawers

cassi'ere, -a *nmf* cashier; (di supermercato) checkout assistant, checkout operator; (di banca) teller

cassinte'grato, -a *nmf* person who has been laid off

cas'sone *nm* (cassa) chest; (per acqua) cofferdam

casso'netto *nm* rubbish bin, wheelie bin, trash can Am

'casta *nf* caste

ca'stagna *nf* chestnut; **prendere qualcuno in** ~ fig catch somebody in the act. **castagna d'India** horse chestnut

casta'gnaccio nm tart from Tuscany made with chestnut flour

casta'gneto nm chestnut grove

ca'stagno nm chestnut[-tree]

casta'gnola nf (petardo) firecracker

ca'stano adj chestnut; ‹occhi, capelli› brown

ca'stello nm castle; (impalcatura) scaffold. **castello incantato** enchanted castle. **castello di sabbia** sandcastle

casti'gare vt punish

casti'gato adj (casto) chaste; ‹abito, atteggiamento› prim and proper

ca'stigo nm punishment

castità nf chastity

'casto adj chaste

ca'storo nm beaver

ca'strante adj fig frustrating

ca'strare vt castrate

ca'strato adj castrated; (inibito) inhibited; (cantante) castrato

castrazi'one nf gelding

ca'strone nm gelding

castrone'ria nf fam rubbish

'casual nm inv casual wear

casu'ale adj chance attrib

casual'mente adv by chance

ca'supola nf little house

cata'clisma nm fig upheaval

cata'comba nf catacomb

cata'falco nm catafalque

cata'fascio nm andare a ~ go to rack and ruin

cata'litico adj **marmitta catalitica** Auto catalytic converter

catali'zzare vt fig heighten

cataliz'zato adj Auto fitted with a catalytic converter

catalizza'tore ① adj Phys catalysing; **centro ~** fig catalyst ② nm Auto catalytic converter; fig catalyst

catalo'gabile adj which can be listed

catalo'gare vt catalogue

catalogazi'one nf cataloguing

cata'logna nf type of chicory with large leaves

ca'talogo nm catalogue

catama'rano nm (da diporto) catamaran

cata'pecchia nf hovel; fam dump

cata'pulta nf catapult

catapul'tare vt (scaraventare fuori) eject

catapul'tarsi vr (precipitarsi) dive

catarifran'gente nm reflector

ca'tarro nm catarrh

catar'roso adj ‹voce› catarrhal

ca'tarsi nf inv catharsis

ca'tartico adj cathartic

ca'tasta nf pile

cata'stale adj **registro catastale** land registry; **rendita catastale** revenue from landed property

ca'tasto nm land register

ca'tastrofe nf catastrophe

cata'strofico adj catastrophic

catastro'fismo nm catastrophe theory

catch nm all-in wrestling

cate'chismo nm catechism

catego'ria nf category

cate'gorico adj categorical

categoriz'zare vt categorize

ca'tena nf chain. **catena montuosa** mountain range. **catene da neve** pl [snow] chains

cate'naccio nm bolt

cate'nella nf (collana) chain; (di orologio) watch chain; **tirare la ~** (del gabinetto) flush, pull the plug

cate'nina nf chain

cate'ratta nf cataract

ca'terva nf **una ~ di** heaps of, loads of

ca'tetere nm catheter

'catgut nm inv catgut

cati'nella nf basin; **piovere a catinelle** bucket down

ca'tino nm basin

ca'todico adj cathode; **raggi catodici** cathode rays

ca'torcio nm fam old wreck

catra'mare vt tar

ca'trame nm tar

'cattedra nf (tavolo di insegnante) desk; (di università) chair

catte'drale nf cathedral

catte'dratico, -a ① nmf professor ② adj ‹pedante› pedantic; ‹insegnamento› university attrib

catti'veria nf wickedness; (azione) wicked action; **fare una ~ a qualcuno** be nasty to somebody

cattività nf captivity

cat'tivo adj bad; ‹bambino› naughty

cattocomu'nista nmf Catholic-communist

cattoli'cesimo nm Catholicism

cat'tolico, -a adj & nmf [Roman] Catholic

cat'tura nf capture

cattu'rare vt capture

cau'casico, -a nmf Caucasian

'Caucaso nm **il ~** the Caucasus

cauccìù nm rubber

'causa nf cause; Jur lawsuit; **far ~ a qualcuno** sue somebody. **causa di forza maggiore** circumstances beyond one's control; (in assicurazione) act of God

cau'sale *adj* causal

cau'sare *vt* cause

'caustico *adj* caustic

cauta'mente *adv* cautiously

cau'tela *nf* caution

caute'lare *vt* protect

caute'larsi *vr* take precautions

cauteriz'zare *vt* cauterize

cauterizzazi'one *nf* cauterization

'cauto *adj* cautious

cauzi'one *nf* security; (per libertà provvisoria) bail; (deposito) deposit

cav. *abbr* (**cavaliere**) Kt, Knight

'cava *nf* quarry; fig mine

caval'care *vt* ride; (stare a cavalcioni) sit astride

caval'cata *nf* ride; (corteo) cavalcade

cavalca'via *nm* flyover

cavalci'oni: a ∼ *adv* astride

cavali'ere *nm* rider; (titolo) knight; (accompagnatore) escort; (al ballo) partner

cavalle'resco *adj* chivalrous

cavalle'ria *nf* chivalry; Mil cavalry

cavalle'rizzo, -a ① *nm* horseman ② *nf* horsewoman

caval'letta *nf* grasshopper

caval'letto *nm* trestle; (di macchina fotografica) tripod; (di pittore) easel

caval'lina *nf* (ginnastica) horse; (gioco) leapfrog; **correre la** ∼ fig pursue a life of pleasure

caval'lino *adj* equine

ca'vallo *nm* horse; (misura di potenza) horsepower; (scacchi) knight; (dei pantaloni) crotch; **a** ∼ on horseback; **andare a** ∼ go horse-riding. **cavallo di battaglia** war horse. **cavallo a dondolo** rocking-horse. **cavallo da tiro** carthorse. **cavallo di Troia** Trojan horse

caval'lona *nf* pej ungainly female

caval'lone *nm* (ondata) roller

caval'luccio *nm* **cavalluccio marino** sea horse

ca'vare *vt* take out; (di dosso) take off; **cavarsela** get away with it; **se la cava bene** he's/she's doing all right

cavasti'vali *nm inv* bootjack

cava'tappi *nm inv* corkscrew

ca'veau *nm inv* (di banca) vault

ca'verna *nf* cave

caver'nicolo, -a *nmf* cave dweller

caver'noso *adj* ⟨voce⟩ deep

ca'vetto *nm* Electr lead

ca'vezza *nf* halter; **mettere la** ∼ **al collo a qualcuno** put somebody on a tight rein

'cavia *nf* guinea-pig

cavi'ale *nm* caviar

ca'viglia *nf* ankle

cavil'lare *vi* quibble

ca'villo *nm* quibble

cavil'loso *adj* pettifogging

cavità *nf inv* cavity

'cavo ① *adj* hollow ② *nm* cavity; (di metallo) cable; Naut rope. **televisione via cavo** cable TV. **cavo di collegamento** [connecting] cable. **cavo seriale** serial cable. **cavo di spiegamento** ripcord

cavo'lata *nf* fam rubbish; **non dire cavolate** fam don't talk rubbish; **non fare cavolate** fam don't act like an idiot

cavo'letto *nm* **cavoletto di Bruxelles** Brussels sprout

cavolfi'ore *nm* cauliflower

'cavolo *nm* cabbage; ∼! fam sugar!; **non ho capito un** ∼ fam I understood bugger-all; **che** ∼ **succede?** what the heck is going on?. **cavolo cappuccio** spring cabbage

caz'zata *nf* vulg shit; **non dire cazzate** don't talk shit; **non fare cazzate** don't fuck things up

'cazzo *vulg* ① *nm* prick ② *int* fuck!; **non capisce un** ∼ he doesn't understand a fucking thing; **non me ne importa un** ∼! I don't give a fuck!; **sono cazzi miei!** it's my fucking business!

caz'zotto *nm* punch; **prendere qualcuno a cazzotti** beat somebody up

cazzu'ola *nf* trowel

CB *nf abbr* (**banda cittadina**) CB

cc *abbr* (**centimetri cubi**) cc

c/c *abbr* (**conto corrente**) c/a

CCT *nm abbr* (**Certificato di Credito del Tesoro**) T-bill

CD *nm inv* CD

CD-ROM *nm inv* CD-Rom

ce ① *pers pron* (a noi) us; **ce lo ha dato** he gave it to us ② *adv* there; **ce ne sono molti** there are many; **ce ne vuole!** it takes some doing!

cec'chino *nm* sniper; Pol MP who votes against his own party

'cece *nm* chickpea

Ce'cenia *nf* Chechnya

cecità *nf* blindness

'ceco, -a *adj* & *nmf* Czech; **la Repubblica Ceca** the Czech Republic

Cecoslo'vacchia *nf* Czechoslovakia

cecoslo'vacco, -a *adj* & *nmf* Czechoslovak

'cedere ① *vi* (arrendersi) surrender; (concedere) yield; (sprofondare) subside ② *vt* give up; make over ⟨proprietà ecc⟩

ce'devole *adj* ⟨terreno ecc⟩ soft; fig yielding

ce'diglia *nf* cedilla

cedi'mento *nm* (di terreno) subsidence

'cedola *nf* coupon

cedo'lino *nm* (dello stipendio) wage slip

'cedro *nm* (albero) cedar; (frutto) citron

C.E.E. *nf abbr* (**Comunità Economica Europea**) E[E]C

cefa'lea *nf* headache

ce'falo *nm* mullet

'ceffo *nm* (muso) snout; (pej: persona) mug

cef'fone *nm* slap

ce'lare *vt* conceal

ce'larsi *vr* conceal oneself

ce'lato *adj* concealed

cele'brare *vt* celebrate, observe ⟨festività⟩

celebra'tivo *adj* celebratory

celebrazi'one *nf* celebration

'celebre *adj* famous

celebrità *nf inv* celebrity

'celere ① *adj* swift; **corso celere** crash course
② *nf* (polizia) flying squad

celerità *nf* speed; **con ~** speedily

ce'leste ① *adj* (divino) heavenly
② *adj & nm* (colore) pale blue

celesti'ale *adj* celestial

celi'bato *nm* celibacy

'celibe ① *adj* single
② *nm* bachelor

'cella *nf* cell. **cella frigorifera** cold store. **cella di isolamento** solitary confinement

+cello *suff* **monticello** *nm* mound; **praticello** *nm* small meadow

'cellofan *nm inv* cellophane; Culin cling film

cellofa'nare *vt* wrap in cling film

'cellula *nf* cell. **cellula fotoelettrica** electronic eye

cellu'lare ① *nm* (telefono) mobile (phone), cell phone
② *adj* **furgone cellulare** police van; **telefono cellulare** mobile (phone)

cellu'lite *nf* cellulite

cellu'litico *adj* full of cellulite

cellu'loide *adj* celluloid; **il mondo della ~** fig the celluloid world

cellu'losa *nf* cellulose

'Celsius *adj inv* Celsius

'celta *nm* Celt

'celtico *adj* Celtic

'cembalo *nm* Mus cembalo, harpsichord

cemen'tare *vt* cement

cementifi'care *vt* turn into a cement jungle

cementificazi'one *nf* turning into a cement jungle

cementi'ficio *nm* cement factory

ce'mento *nm* cement. **cemento armato** reinforced concrete

'cena *nf* dinner; (leggera) supper; (festa) dinner party

ce'nacolo *nm* circle

ce'nare *vi* have dinner; **~ fuori** eat out

'cencio *nm* rag; (per spolverare) duster; **bianco come un ~** white as a sheet

cenci'oso *adj* in rags

'cenere *nf* ash; (di carbone ecc) cinders *pl*; **le Ceneri** *pl* Ash Wednesday

Cene'rentola *nf* Cinderella

ce'netta *nf* (cena semplice) informal dinner; (cena intima) romantic dinner

'cenno *nm* sign; (col capo) nod; (con la mano) wave; (allusione) hint; (breve resoconto) mention; **far ~ di sì** nod

ce'none *nm* **il ~ di Capodanno/Natale** special New Year's Eve/Christmas Eve dinner

ceno'tafio *nm* cenotaph

censi'mento *nm* census

cen'sire *vt* take a census of

CENSIS *nm abbr* (**Centro Studi Investimenti Sociali**) national opinion research institute

cen'sore *nm* censor

cen'sura *nf* censorship

censu'rare *vt* censor

centelli'nare *vt* sip; fig measure out carefully

cente'nario, -a ① *adj & nmf* centenarian
② *nm* (commemorazione) centenary

centen'nale *adj* centennial

centesimo ① *adj* hundredth
② *nm* hundredth; (di dollaro, euro) cent; **non avere un ~** be penniless

cen'tigrado *adj* centigrade

cen'tilitro *nm* centilitre

cen'timetro *nm* centimetre

centi'naia *nfpl* hundreds

centi'naio *nm* hundred

'cento *adj & nm* a *or* one hundred; **per ~** percent

centodi'eci *nm* a *or* one hundred and ten; **~ e lode** Univ ≈ first class honours

centome'trista *nmf* Sport one hundred metres runner

cento'mila *nm* a *or* one hundred thousand

cen'trale ① *adj* central
② *nf* (di azienda ecc) head office. **centrale atomica** atomic power station. **centrale elettrica** power station, power plant. **centrale idroelettrica** hydroelectric power station. **centrale nucleare** nuclear power station. **centrale operativa** (di polizia)

operations room. **centrale telefonica** [telephone] exchange

centra'lina nf Teleph switchboard; (apparecchiatura) junction box

centralinista nmf (switchboard/ telephone) operator

centra'lino nm Teleph exchange; (di albergo ecc) switchboard

centra'lismo nm centralism

centraliz'zare vt centralize

cen'trare vt ~ qualcosa hit something in the centre; (fissare nel centro) centre; fig hit on the head (idea)

cen'trato adj ⟨tiro, colpo⟩ well-aimed; fig ⟨osservazione⟩ right on target

centrat'tacco nm Sport centre forward

cen'trifuga nf spin-drier. **centrifuga [asciugaverdure]** shaker. **centrifuga elettrica** juice extractor

centrifu'gare vt Techn centrifuge; ⟨lavatrice⟩ spin

cen'trino nm doily

cen'trismo nm Pol centrism

cen'trista adj Pol centrist

'centro nm centre; in ~ ⟨essere⟩ in town; ⟨andare⟩ into town. **centro di accoglienza** detention centre. **centro di attrazione** focal point. **centro città** city centre, midtown Am. **centro commerciale** shopping centre, mall. **centro di costi** Comm cost centre. **centro culturale** arts centre. **centro di gravità** centre of gravity. **centro di informazioni turistiche** tourist information office. **centro operativo** Mil operations room. **centro polisportivo** sports centre. **centro di riabilitazione** halfway house. **centro sociale** community centre. **centro sportivo** leisure centre. **centro storico** old town

centrocam'pista nm Sport midfield player, midfielder

centro'campo nm midfield

centro'destra nm inv Pol centre right

centromedi'ano nm Sport centre half

centrosi'nistra nm inv Pol centre left

centro'tavola nm inv centre-piece

centupli'care vt fig multiply

'ceppo nm (di albero) stump; (da ardere) log; (fig: gruppo) stock

'cera nf wax; (aspetto) look. **cera d'api** beeswax. **cera per auto** car wax. **cera per il pavimento** floor-polish

cera'lacca nf sealing-wax

ce'ramica nf (arte) ceramics; (materia) pottery; (oggetto) piece of pottery

cera'mista nmf ceramicist

ce'rata nf (giacca) waxed jacket

ce'rato adj ⟨tela⟩ waxed

cerbi'atto nm fawn

cerbot'tana nf blowpipe

'cerca nf andare in ~ di look for

cercaper'sone nm inv beeper; chiamare con il ~ beep

cer'care ① vt look for
② vi ~ di try to

cerca|'tore, -'trice nmf **cercatore d'oro** gold seeker

'cerchia nf circle. **cerchia familiare** family circle

cerchi'are vt circle, draw a circle around ⟨parola⟩

cerchi'ato adj ⟨occhi⟩ black-ringed

cerchi'etto nm (per capelli) hairband

'cerchio nm circle; (giocattolo) hoop

cerchi'one nm alloy wheel

cere'ale nm cereal

cerea'licolo adj grain attrib, cereal attrib

cere'brale adj cerebral

'cereo adj waxen

ce'retta nf depilatory wax; **fare la ~** wax

cer'foglio nm chervil

ceri'monia nf ceremony. **cerimonia inaugurale** induction ceremony. **cerimonia nuziale** marriage ceremony. **cerimonia di premiazione** awards ceremony

cerimoni'ale nm ceremonial

cerimoni'ere nm master of ceremonies

cerimoni'oso adj ceremonious

ce'rino nm [wax] match

cerni'era nf hinge; (di borsa) clasp. **cerniera lampo** zip[-fastener], zipper Am

'cernita nf selection

'cero nm candle

ce'rone nm greasepaint

ce'rotto nm [sticking] plaster. **cerotto callifugo** corn plaster. **cerotto [transdermico] alla nicotina** nicotine patch

certa'mente adv certainly

cer'tezza nf certainty

certifi'care vt certify

certifi'cato nm certificate. **certificato medico** doctor's note, sick note. **certificato di morte** death certificate

certificazi'one nf certification. **certificazione di bilancio** Fin auditors' report

'certo ① adj certain; ⟨notizia⟩ definite; (indeterminativo) some; **sono ~ di riuscire** I am certain to succeed; **a una certa età** at a certain age; **certi giorni** some days; **un ~ signor Giardini** a Mr Giardini; **una certa Anna** somebody called Anna; **certa gente** pej some people; **ho certi dolori!** I'm in ···⟩

such pain!; **certi** *pron pl* some; (alcune persone) some people

2) *adv* of course; **sapere per** ～ know for certain, know for sure; **di** ～ surely; ～ **che ... surely ...**

cer'tosa *nf* Carthusian monastery

certo'sino *nm* Carthusian [monk]; **pazienza certosina** exceptional patience

cer'tuni *pron* some

ce'rume *nm* earwax

cer'vello *nm* brain; **avere un** ～ **da gallina** be a bird-brain

cervel'lone, -a *nmf* hum brainbox

cervel'lotico *adj* (macchinoso) over-elaborate

cervi'cale *adj* cervical

'cervice *nf* cervix

'cervo *nm* deer

ce'sareo *adj* Med Caesarean; **parto cesareo** Caesarean

cesel'lare *vt* chisel

cesel'lato *adj* chiselled

cesella'tura *nf* chiselling

ce'sello *nm* chisel

ce'soie *nfpl* shears

'cespite *nm* source of income

ce'spuglio *nm* bush

cespugli'oso *adj* ⟨terreno⟩ bushy

ces'sare **1)** *vi* stop, cease **2)** *vt* stop

ces'sate *nm* **cessate il fuoco** ceasefire

ces'sato *adj* ～ **allarme/pericolo** all clear

cessazi'one *nf* cessation. **cessazione d'esercizio** closing down

cessi'one *nf* handover

'cesso *nm* sl (gabinetto) bog, john Am; (fig: locale, luogo) dump

'cesta *nf* [large] basket

ce'stello *nm* (di lavatrice) drum

cesti'nare *vt* throw away; bin ⟨lettera⟩ turn down ⟨proposta⟩

ce'stino *nm* [small] basket; (per la carta straccia) waste-paper basket

'cesto *nm* basket. **cesto della biancheria** linen basket

ce'sura *nf* caesura

ce'taceo *nm* cetacean

'ceto *nm* [social] class

'cetra *nf* lyre

cetrio'lino *nm* gherkin

cetri'olo *nm* cucumber

cfr *abbr* (**confronta**) cf

C.G.I.L. *nf abbr* (**Confederazione Generale Italiana del Lavoro**) trades union organization

'Chad *nm* Chad

cha'let *nm inv* chalet

cham'pagne *nm inv* champagne

'chance *nf inv* chance

chape'ron *nm inv* chaperone

char'lotte *nf inv* ice-cream cake with fresh cream, biscuits and fruit

'charter *nm inv* charter plane; **volo charter** charter flight

che **1)** *rel pron* (persona: soggetto) who; (persona: oggetto) whom; (cosa, animale) which; **questa è la casa** ～ **ho comprato** this is the house [that] I've bought; **il** ～ **mi sorprende** which surprises me; **dal** ～ **deduco che ...** from which I gather that ...; **avere di** ～ **vivere** have enough to live on; **grazie! –non c'è di che!** thank you –don't mention it; **il giorno** ～ **ti ho visto** fam the day I saw you

2) *inter adj* what; (esclamativo: con aggettivo) how; (con nome) what a; ～ **macchina prendiamo, la tua o la mia?** which car are we taking, yours or mine?; ～ **bello!** how nice!; ～ **idea!** what an idea!; ～ **bella giornata!** what a lovely day!

3) *inter pron* what; **a** ～ **pensi?** what are you thinking about?

4) *conj* that; (con comparazioni) than; **credo** ～ **abbia ragione** I think [that] he is right; **era così commosso** ～ **non riusciva a parlare** he was so moved, [that] he couldn't speak; **aspetto** ～ **telefoni** I'm waiting for him to phone; **è da un po'** ～ **non lo vedo** it's been a while since I saw him; **mi piace più Roma** ～ **Milano** I like Rome better than Milan; ～ **ti piaccia o no** whether you like it or not; ～ **io sappia** as far as I know

'checca *nf* fam queen

checché *pron* whatever

check-'in *nm inv* check-in; **fare il** ～ check in

check-'up *nm inv* Med check-up; **fare un** ～ have a check-up

cheese'burger *nm inv* cheeseburger

'chef *nm inv* chef

'chela *nf* nipper

chemiotera'pia *nf* chemotherapy, chemo fam

chemisi'er *nm inv* chemise

chero'sene *nm* paraffin

cheru'bino *nm* cherub

che'tare *vt* quieten

che'tarsi *vr* quieten down

cheti'chella: **alla** ～ *adv* silently

'cheto *adj* quiet

chi **1)** *rel pron* whoever; (coloro che) people who; **ho trovato** ～ **ti può aiutare** I found somebody who can help you; **c'è** ～ **dice che ...** some people say that ...; **senti** ～ **parla!** look who's talking!

2) *inter pron* (soggetto) who; (oggetto, con preposizione) whom; (possessivo) **di** ～ whose; ～ **sei?** who are you?; ～ **hai incontrato?**

who did you meet?, whom did you meet? fml; **di** ~ **sono questi libri?** whose books are these?; **con** ~ **parli?** who are you talking to?, to whom are you talking? fml; **a** ~ **lo dici!** tell me about it!

chi'acchiera nf chat; (pettegolezzo) gossip; **chiacchiere** pl chitchat; **far quattro chiacchiere** have a chat

chiacchie'rare vi chat; (far pettegolezzi) gossip

chiacchie'rato adj **essere** ~ ⟨persona⟩ be the subject of gossip

chi'acchiere nfpl (dolci) sweet pastries fried and sprinkled with icing sugar

chiacchie'rone, -a ① adj talkative ② nmf chatterbox

chia'mare vt call; (far venire) send for; **come ti chiami?** what's your name?; **mi chiamo Roberto** my name is Robert; ~ **alle armi** call up; **mandare a** ~ send for; ~ **a rapporto** debrief

chia'marsi vr be called

chia'mata nf call; Mil call-up. **chiamata a carico del destinatario** reverse charge call, transferred charge call. **chiamata interurbana** long-distance call. **chiamata in teleselezione** direct dialling, toll call Am. **chiamata urbana** local call

chi'appa nf fam cheek

chiara'mente adv clearly

chia'rezza nf clarity; (limpidezza) clearness

chiarifi'care vt clarify

chiarifica'tore adj clarificatory

chlarificazi'one nf clarification

chiari'mento nm clarification

chia'rire vt make clear; (spiegare) clear up

chia'rirsi vr become clear

chi'aro adj clear; (luminoso) bright; ⟨colore⟩ light; ⟨capelli⟩ fair

chia'rore nm glimmer

chiaro'scuro nm (tecnica) chiaroscuro

chiaroveg'gente ① adj clear-sighted ② nmf clairvoyant

chi'asso nm din

chiassosa'mente adv (rumorosamente) rowdily; (vistosamente) gaudily

chias'soso adj (rumoroso) rowdy; (vistoso) gaudy

chi'atta nf canal boat, canal barge

chi'ave nf key; **chiudere a** ~ lock. **chiave dell'accensione** ignition key. **chiave di basso** Mus bass clef. **chiave inglese** monkey-wrench. **chiave [inglese] a rullino** adjustable spanner

chia'vetta nf (in tubi) key

chiavi'stello nm latch

chi'azza nf stain. **chiazza di petrolio** oil-slick

chiaz'zare vt stain

chiaz'zato adj dappled

chic adj inv chic

chicches'sia pron anybody

chicchirichì nm inv cock-a-doodle-doo

'chicco nm grain; (di caffè) bean; (d'uva) grape. **chicco di caffè** coffee bean. **chicco di grandine** hailstone. **chicco d'orzo** barleycorn

chi'edere vt ask; (per avere) ask for; (esigere) demand; ~ **notizie di** ask after

chi'edersi vr wonder

chieri'chetto nm altar boy

chi'erico nm cleric

chi'esa nf church. **Chiesa anglicana** Church of England

chi'esto pp di CHIEDERE

chif'fon nm chiffon

'chiglia nf keel

chi'gnon nm inv bun

'chilo nm kilo

chilo'grammo nm kilogram[me]

chilo'hertz nm inv kilohertz

chilome'traggio nm Auto ≈ mileage

chilo'metrico adj in kilometres; fig endless

chi'lometro nm kilometre

'chilowatt nm inv kilowatt

chilowat'tora nm inv kilowatt hour

chi'mera nf fig illusion

'chimica nf chemistry. **chimica organica** organic chemistry

'chimico, -a ① adj chemical ② nmf chemist

chi'mono nm kimono

'china nf (declivio) slope; **inchiostro di china** Indian ink

chi'nare vt lower

chi'narsi vr stoop

chincaglie'rie nfpl knick-knacks

chinesitera'pia nf physiotherapy

chi'nino nm quinine

'chino adj bent

chi'notto nm sparkling soft drink

chintz nm chintz

chi'occia nf sitting hen

chi'occiola nf snail; Comput at sign, @. **scala a chiocciola** spiral staircase

chio'dato adj **pneumatici chiodati** snow tyres; **scarpe chiodate** shoes with crampons

chi'odo nm nail; (idea fissa) obsession. **chiodo di garofano** clove

chi'oma nf [head of] hair; (fogliame) foliage

chi'osco nm kiosk; (per giornali) news-stand

chi'ostro nm cloister

chip *nm inv* **chip [di silicio]** chip

'chipset *nm inv* chipset

chiro'mante *nmf* fortune teller, palmist

chiroman'zia *nf* palmistry

chiro'pratIco, **-a** *nmf* chiropractor

chirur'gia *nf* surgery. **chirurgia endoscopica** keyhole surgery. **chirurgia estetica** cosmetic surgery

chirurgica'mente *adv* surgically

chi'rurgico *adj* surgical

chi'rurgo *nm* surgeon

chissà *adv* who knows; ~ **quando arriverà** I wonder when he will arrive

chi'tarra *nf* guitar. **chitarra acustica** acoustic guitar. **chitarra basso** bass guitar

chitar'rista *nmf* guitarist

chi'udere ① *vt* shut, close; (con chiave) lock; turn off, switch off ⟨luce ecc⟩; turn off ⟨acqua⟩; (per sempre) close down ⟨negozio, fabbrica ecc⟩; (recingere) enclose; **chiudi il becco!** shut up!
② *vi* shut, close; (con chiave) lock up

chi'udersi *vr* shut; ⟨tempo⟩ cloud over; ⟨ferita⟩ heal over; fig withdraw into oneself

chi'unque ① *pron* anyone, anybody ② *rel pron* whoever

chi'usa *nf* enclosure; (di canale) lock; (conclusione) close

chi'uso ① pp di CHIUDERE ② *adj* closed, shut; ⟨tempo⟩ overcast; ⟨persona⟩ reserved; '~ **per turno**' 'closing day'

chiu'sura *nf* closing; (sistema) lock; (allacciatura) fastener; '~ **settimanale il lunedì**' 'closed on Mondays'. **chiusura centralizzata** Auto central locking. **chiusura lampo** zip, zipper Am

ci ① *pron* (personale) us; (riflessivo) ourselves; (reciproco) each other; (a ciò, di ciò ecc) about it; **non ci disturbare** don't disturb us; **aspettateci** wait for us; **ci ha detto tutto** he told us everything; **ci consideriamo ...** we consider ourselves ...; **ci laviamo le mani** we wash our hands; **ci odiamo** we hate each other; **non ci penso mai** I never think about it; **pensaci!** think about it!
② *adv* (qui) here; (lì) there; (moto per luogo) through it; **ci siamo** here we are; **ci siete?** are you there?; **ci siamo passati tutti** we all went through it; **c'è** there is; **ci vuole pazienza** it takes patience; **non ci vedo/ sento** I can't see/hear

C.ia *abbr* (**compagnia**) Co.

cia'batta *nf* slipper

ciabat'tare *vi* shuffle

ciabat'tino *nm* cobbler

ci'ac *nm inv* Cinema ~ **si gira!** action!

ci'alda *nf* wafer

cial'trone *nm* (mascalzone) scoundrel; (fannullone) wastrel

ciam'bella *nf* Culin ring-shaped cake; (salvagente) lifebelt; (gonfiabile) rubber ring

ci'ance *nfpl* yapping

cianci'are *vi* gossip

cianfru'saglie *nfpl* knick-knacks

cia'notico *adj* ⟨viso⟩ puce

cia'nuro *nm* cyanide

ci'ao *int fam* (all'arrivo) hello!, hi!; (alla partenza) bye-bye!, cheerio!

ciar'lare *vi* chat

ciarla'tano *nm* charlatan

ciarli'ero *adj* (loquace) talkative

cia'scuno ① *adj* each ② *pron* everyone, everybody; (distributivo) each [one]; **per** ~ each

ci'bare *vt* feed

ci'barie *nfpl* provisions

ci'barsi *vr* eat; ~ **di** live on

ciber'netica *nf* cybernetics

ciber'netico *adj* cybernetic

ciber'spazio *nm* cyberspace

'cibo *nm* food; **non toccare** ~ leave one's food untouched; **non ha toccato** ~ **da ieri** he hasn't had a bite to eat since yesterday. **cibo per animali** pet food; **cibi** *pl* **precotti** ready meals

ci'cala *nf* cicada

cica'lino *nm* buzzer

cica'trice *nf* scar

cicatriz'zante *nm* ointment

cicatriz'zare *vi* heal [up]

cicatriz'zarsi *vr* heal [up]

cicatrizzazi'one *nf* healing

'cicca *nf* cigarette end; (fam: sigaretta) fag; (fam: gomma) [chewing] gum

cic'chetto *nm fam* (bicchierino) nip; (rimprovero) telling-off

'ciccia *nf fam* fat, flab

cicci'one, **-a** *nmf fam* fatty, fatso

cice'rone *nm* guide

cicla'mino *nm* cyclamen

ciclica'mente *adv* cyclically

'ciclico *adj* cyclical

ci'clismo *nm* cycling

ci'clista *nmf* cyclist

'ciclo *nm* cycle; (di malattia) course. **ciclo economico** business cycle

ciclo'cross *nm* cyclo-cross

ciclomo'tore *nm* moped

ci'clone *nm* cyclone

ci'clonico *adj* cyclonic

ciclosti'lare *vt* duplicate

ciclosti'lato ① *nm* duplicate [copy] ② *adj* duplicate

ci'cogna *nf* stork

ci'coria *nf* chicory

ci'cuta *nf* hemlock

ci'eco, -a ① *adj* blind
② *nmf* blind man; blind woman; **i parzialmente ciechi** the partially sighted

ciel'lino *nmf* Pol member of the Comunione e Liberazione movement

ci'elo *nm* sky; Relig heaven; **al settimo ∼** in seventh heaven; **santo ∼!** good heavens!

'cifra *nf* figure; (somma) sum; (monogramma) monogram; (codice) code; **una ∼ sl** like crazy

ci'frare *vt* embroider with a monogram; (codificare) code

ci'frato *adj* monogrammed; (codificato) coded

'ciglio *nm* (bordo) edge; (degli occhi) eyelash; **ciglia** *pl* eyelashes

'cigno *nm* swan

cigo'lante *adj* squeaky

cigo'lare *vt* squeak

cigo'lio *nm* squeak

'Cile *nm* Chile

ci'lecca *nf* far ∼ miss

ci'leno, -a *adj & nmf* Chilean

cili'egia *nf* cherry

cili'egio *nm* cherry[-tree]

cilin'drata *nf* cubic capacity, c.c.; **macchina di grossa ∼** highpowered car

ci'lindro *nm* cylinder; (cappello) top hat, topper

'cima *nf* top; (fig: persona) genius; **in ∼ a** at the top of; **da ∼ a fondo** from top to bottom. **cima alla genovese** baked veal stuffed with chicken and chopped vegetables, served cold. **cime di rapa** *pl* turnip greens

ci'melio *nm* relic; **cimeli** *pl* memorabilia

cimen'tare *vt* put to the test

cimen'tarsi *vr* (provare) try one's hand; **∼ in** (arrischiarsi) venture into

'cimice *nf* bug; (puntina) drawing pin, thumbtack Am

cimini'era *nf* chimney; Naut funnel

cimi'tero *nm* cemetery. **cimitero delle macchine** breaker's yard

ci'mosa *nf* selvage, selvedge

ci'murro *nm* distemper

'Cina *nf* China

cincial'legra *nf* great tit

cincia'rella *nf* blue tit

cincillà *nm inv* chinchilla

cin cin *int* cheers!

cincischi'are *vi* fiddle

cincischi'arsi *vr* mess around

'cine *nm* fam cinema

cine'asta *nmf* film maker

Cinecittà *nf* (stabilimento) film complex in the suburbs of Rome

cine'club *nm inv* film club

ci'nefilo, -a *nmf* cinemagoer, film buff

cinegior'nale *nm* newsreel

cinema *nm inv* cinema, movie theater Am. **cinema d'essai** arts cinema

cine'matica *nf* kinematics

cinematogra'fare *vt* film

cinematogra'fia *nf* cinematography

cinemato'grafico *adj* film *attrib*

cinema'tografo *nm* cinema

cine'presa *nf* cine-camera

ci'nereo *adj* ashen

ci'nese *adj & nmf* Chinese

cinese'rie *nfpl* chinoiserie

cine'teca *nf* (raccolta) film collection

ci'netica *nf* kinetics

ci'netico *adj* kinetic

'cingere *vt* (circondare) surround

'cinghia *nf* strap; (cintura) belt. **cinghia del ventilatore** fanbelt. **cinghia della ventola** fanbelt

cinghi'ale *nm* wild boar; **pelle di cinghiale** pigskin

cinghi'ata *nf* lash

cingo'lato ① *adj* (mezzi) caterpillar *attrib*
② *nm* caterpillar

'cingolo *nm* Mech belt

cinguet'tare *vi* twitter

cinguet'tio *nm* twittering

cinica'mente *adv* cynically

'cinico *adj* cynical

ci'niglia *nf* (tessuto) chenille

ci'nismo *nm* cynicism

ci'nofilo *adj* ⟨unità⟩ dog-loving

cin'quanta *adj & nm* fifty

cinquanten'nale *nm* fiftieth anniversary

cinquan'tenne *adj & nmf* fifty-year-old

cinquan'tesimo *adj & nm* fiftieth

cinquan'tina *nf* una ∼ di about fifty

'cinque *adj & nm* five

cinquecen'tesco *adj* sixteenth-century

cinque'cento ① *adj* five hundred
② *nm* il **Cinquecento** the sixteenth century

cinque'mila *adj & nm* five thousand

cin'quina *nf* (in tombola) five in a row

'cinta *nf* (di pantaloni) belt; **muro di cinta** [boundary] wall

cin'tare *vt* enclose

'cintola *nf* (di pantaloni) belt

cin'tura *nf* belt. **cintura nera** black belt. **cintura di salvataggio** lifebelt. **cintura di sicurezza** Aeron, Auto seat belt

cintu'rato *nm* Auto radial tyre

cintu'rino *nm* cinturino
[dell'orologio] watch-strap; (di metallo)
bracelet

ciò *pron* this; that; ~ **che** what; ~
nondimeno nevertheless

ci'occa *nf* lock

ciocco'lata *nf* chocolate; (bevanda) [hot]
chocolate. **cioccolata in polvere**
drinking chocolate

cioccola'tino *nm* chocolate

ciocco'lato *nm* chocolate. **cioccolato
fondente** plain chocolate, dark
chocolate. **cioccolato al latte** milk
chocolate. **cioccolato da pasticceria**
cooking chocolate

cioè *adv* that is

ciondo'lare *vi* dangle

ciondo'lio *nm* dangling

ci'ondolo *nm* pendant

ciondo'loni *adv* fig hanging about

cionono'stante *adv* nonetheless

ci'otola *nf* bowl

ci'ottolo *nm* pebble; **ciottoli** *pl* (in spiaggia)
shingle

ci'piglio *nm* frown; **con** ~ with a frown

ci'polla *nf* onion; (bulbo) bulb

cipol'lotto *nm* green onion

ci'presso *nm* cypress

'cipria *nf* [face] powder

cipri'ota *adj* & *nmf* Cypriot

'Cipro *nm* Cyprus

'circa *adv* & *prep* about

cir'cense *adj* circus *attrib*

'circo *nm* circus

circo'lare ① *adj* circular
② *nf* circular; (di metropolitana) circle line
③ *vi* circulate

circola'torio *adj* Med circulatory

circolazi'one *nf* circulation; (traffico)
traffic

'circolo *nm* circle; (società) club. **circolo
del golf** golf-club. **Circolo polare
antartico** Antarctic Circle. **Circolo
polare artico** Arctic Circle. **circolo
sociale** social club

circon'cidere *vt* circumcise

circoncisi'one *nf* circumcision

circon'dare *vt* surround

circon'dario *nm* (amministrativo)
administrative district; (vicinato)
neighbourhood

circon'darsi *vr* ~ **di** surround oneself
with

circonfe'renza *nf* circumference.
circonferenza del collo collar size.
circonferenza dei fianchi hip
measurement. **circonferenza [della]
vita** waist measurement

circon'flesso *adj* **e con l'accento** ~
circumflex e

circonvallazi'one *nf* ring road

circo'scritto ① pp di CIRCOSCRIVERE
② *adj* limited

circo'scrivere *vt* circumscribe

circoscrizio'nale *adj* area

circoscrizi'one *nf* area.
circoscrizione elettorale
constituency

circo'spetto *adj* wary

circospezi'one *nf* **con** ~ warily

circo'stante *adj* surrounding

circo'stanza *nf* circumstance;
(occasione) occasion

circostanzi'ato *adj* circumstantial

circu'ire *vt* (ingannare) trick

circuite'ria *nf* circuitry

cir'cuito *nm* circuit

circumnavi'gare *vt* circumnavigate

circumnavigazi'one *nf*
circumnavigation

ci'rillico *adj* Cyrillic

cir'ripede *nm* barnacle

cir'rosi *nf* cirrhosis

Cisgior'dania *nf* West Bank

C.I.S.L. *nf abbr* (**Confederazione
Italiana Sindacati Lavoratori**) trades
union organization

C.I.S.N.A.L. *nf abbr* (**Confederazione
Italiana Sindacati Nazionali dei
Lavoratori**) trades union organization

'cispa *nf* (nell'occhio) sleep

ci'sposo *adj* bleary-eyed

ci'sterna *nf* cistern; (serbatoio) tank

'cisti *nf inv* cyst

cisti'fellea *nf* gall bladder

ci'stite *nf* cystitis

C.I.T. *nm abbr* (**Compagnia Italiana
Turismo**) Italian tourist organization

ci'tare *vt* (riportare brani ecc) quote; (come
esempio) cite; Jur summons

citazi'one *nf* quotation; Jur summons *sg*

citofo'nare *vt* buzz

ci'tofono *nm* entry phone; (in ufficio, su
aereo ecc) intercom

cito'logico *adj* cytological

'citrico *adj* citric

ci'trullo, -a *nmf* fam dimwit

città *nf inv* town; (grande) city. **Città del
Capo** Cape Town. **città dormitorio**
dormitory town. **città fantasma** ghost
town. **città giardino** garden city. **Città
del Vaticano** Vatican City

citta'della *nf* citadel

citta'dina *nf* town

cittadi'nanza *nf* citizenship;
(popolazione) citizens *pl*

citta'dino, -a *nmf* citizen; (abitante di città)
city dweller

ciucci'are *vt* fam suck

ci'uccio *nm* fam dummy

ci'uco *nm* ass

ci'uffo *nm* tuft

ci'urma *nf* Naut crew

ciur'maglia *nf* (gentaglia) rabble

ci'vetta *nf* owl; (fig: donna) flirt; **[auto]** civetta unmarked police car

civet'tare *vi* flirt

civette'ria *nf* flirtatiousness, coquettishness

civettu'olo *adj* flirtatious, coquettish

'civico *adj* civic

ci'vile ① *adj* civil ② *nm* civilian

civi'lista *nmf* (avvocato) specialist in civil law

civiliz'zare *vt* civilize

civiliz'zarsi *vr* become civilized

civiliz'zato *adj* ⟨paese⟩ civilized

civilizzazi'one *nf* civilization

civil'mente *adv* civilly

civiltà *nf inv* civilization; (cortesia) civility

ci'vismo *nm* public spirit

CL *nf abbr* (**Comunione e Liberazione**) young Catholics association

cl *abbr* (**centilitro**) centilitre(s)

'clacson *nm inv* horn

clacso'nare *vi* beep the horn, hoot

cla'more *nm* clamour; **fare ∼ cause a** sensation

clamorosa'mente *adv* ⟨sbagliare⟩ sensationally

clamo'roso *adj* noisy; ⟨sbaglio⟩ sensational

clan *nm inv* clan; fig clique

clandestina'mente *adv* secretly

clandestinità *nf* secrecy; **vivere nella ∼ live underground**

clande'stino *adj* clandestine; **movimento ∼ underground movement; passeggero ∼ stowaway**

'claque *nf inv* claque

clarinet'tista *nmf* clarinettist

clari'netto *nm* clarinet

'classe *nf* class; (aula) classroom; **di prima ∼ first-class. classe economica** economy class. **classe operaia** working class. **classe turistica** tourist class

classicheggi'ante *adj* classical

classi'cismo *nm* classicism

classi'cista *nmf* classicist

'classico ① *adj* classical; (tipico) classic ② *nm* classic

classifica *nf* classification; Sport league. **classifica dei singoli** singles charts

classifi'cabile *adj* classifiable

classifi'care *vt* classify

classifi'carsi *vr* be placed

classifica'tore *nm* (cartella) folder; (mobile) filing cabinet

classificazi'one *nf* classification

clas'sista ① *adj* class-conscious ② *nmf* class-conscious person

claudi'cante *adj* lame

'clausola *nf* clause. **clausola penale** Jur, Comm penalty clause. **clausola di recesso** Jur, Comm escape clause

claustrofo'bia *nf* claustrophobia

claustro'fobico *adj* claustrophobic

clau'sura *nf* Relig cloistered life; **di ∼** ⟨suora⟩ cloistered; **essere in ∼** fig shut oneself up; **vivere in ∼** fig live like a hermit

'clava *nf* club

clavicemba'lista *nmf* harpsichord player

clavi'cembalo *nm* harpsichord

cla'vicola *nf* collar-bone

clavi'cordo *nm* clavichord

cle'mente *adj* merciful; ⟨tempo⟩ mild

cle'menza *nf* mercy, clemency

clep'tomane *nmf* kleptomaniac

cleptoma'nia *nf* kleptomania

cleri'cale *adj* clerical

'clero *nm* clergy

cles'sidra *nf* hourglass

clic *nm inv* Comput click; **fare ∼ su** click on; **fare doppio ∼** double-click

clic'care *vi* Comput click; **∼ su** click on

cliché *nm inv* cliché

click ≈ CLIC

cli'ente *nmf* client; (di negozio) customer

clien'tela *nf* customers *pl*, clientele; (di avvocato) clientele

cliente'lare *adj* Pol nepotistic

cliente'lismo *nm* nepotism

'clima *nm* climate

clima'terio *nm* climacteric

climatica'mente *adv* climatically

cli'matico *adj* climatic; **stazione climatica** health resort

climatizza'tore *nm* air conditioner

climatizzazi'one *nf* air conditioning

'clinica *nf* clinic. **clinica di allergologia** allergy clinic. **clinica odontoiatrica** dental clinic. **clinica ostetrica** maternity hospital. **clinica psichiatrica** mental hospital

'clinico ① *adj* clinical ② *nm* clinician

clip *nf inv* paper-clip; (di orecchino) clip

cli'stere *nm* Med enema

clo'aca *nf* sewer

'**cloche** *nf inv* cloche hat
clo'nare *vt* clone
clonazi'one *nf* cloning
'**clone** *nm* clone
clo'rato *adj* chlorate
'**cloro** *nm* chlorine
cloro'filla *nf* chlorophyll
clorofluorocar'buro *nm* chlorofluorocarbon, CFC
cloro'formio *nm* chloroform
clou *adj inv* momenti ~ highlights
club *nm inv* club. **club per i giovani** youth club. **club sportivo** sports club
club-'sandwich *nm inv* club sandwich
cm *abbr* (**centimetro**) cm
CNR *nm abbr* (**Consiglio Nazionale delle Ricerche**) national research council
Co. *abbr* (**compagnia**) Co
coabi'tare *vi* live together
coabitazi'one *nf* (di razze) coexistence
coadiu|'tore, **-trice** *nmf* (in ufficio) assistant
coadiu'vare *vt* cooperate with
coagu'lante *nm* coagulant
coagu'lare *vt* coagulate
coagu'larsi *vr* coagulate
coagulazi'one *nf* coagulation
coalizi'one *nf* coalition
coaliz'zare *vt* fig unite
coaliz'zarsi *vr* unite
co'atto *adj* Jur compulsory
co'balto *nm* cobalt; (colore) cobalt blue
COBAS *nmpl abbr* (**Comitati di Base**) independent trade unions
'**cobra** *nm inv* cobra
'**Coca**® *nf* Coke®
Coca 'cola® *nf* Coca Cola
coca'ina *nf* cocaine
cocai'nomane *nmf* cocaine addict
coc'carda *nf* rosette
cocchi'ere *nm* coachman
coc'chio *nm* coach
'**coccige** *nm* coccyx
cocci'nella *nf* ladybird
'**coccio** *nm* earthenware; (frammento) fragment
cocciu'taggine *nf* stubbornness
cocciuta'mente *adv* stubbornly
cocci'uto *adj* stubborn
'**cocco** *nm* coconut palm; fam love; **noce di cocco** coconut
coccodè *nm inv* cluck
cocco'drillo *nm* crocodile
cocco'lare *vt* cuddle
co'cente *adj* (sole) burning; (lacrime, delusione) bitter

'**cocker** *nm inv* **cocker [spaniel]** cocker spaniel
'**cocktail** *nm inv* (ricevimento) cocktail party
co'comero *nm* watermelon
co'cuzzolo *nm* top; (di testa, cappello) crown
'**coda** *nf* tail; (di abito) train; (fila) queue; (di traffico) tailback; **fare la** ~ queue [up], stand in line Am. **coda di cavallo** (acconciatura) pony tail. **coda dell'occhio** corner of one's eye. **coda di paglia** guilty conscience
co'dardo, **-a** ① *adj* cowardly ② *nmf* coward
co'dazzo *nm* train
code'ina *nf* codeine
co'desto *adj* that
codice *nm* code; **in** ~ (messaggio) coded, in code; **mettere in** ~ encode. **codice di avviamento postale** postal code, zip code Am. **codice a barre** bar-code. **codice civile** civil code. **codice fiscale** National Insurance number Br, tax code. **codice penale** penal code. **codice PIN** PIN. **codice della strada** highway code
codi'cillo *nm* codicil
co'difica *nf* coding
codifi'care *vt* encode; codify (legge)
codifica|'tore, **-trice** *nmf* Comput encoder
codificazi'one *nf* encoding; (di legge) codification
co'dini *nmpl* bunches
coeffici'ente *nm* coefficient
coercizi'one *nf* coercion
coe'rente *adj* consistent
coe'renza *nf* consistency
coesi'one *nf* cohesion
coe'sistere *vi* coexist
coe'sivo *adj* cohesive
coe'taneo, **-a** *adj & nmf* contemporary
cofa'netto *nm* casket
'**cofano** *nm* (forziere) chest; Auto bonnet, hood Am
cofirma'tario, **-a** *nmf* cosignatory
coge'stire *vt* co-manage
cogi'tare *vi* ponder
'**cogliere** *vt* pick; (sorprendere) catch; (afferrare) seize; (colpire) hit; ~ **la palla al balzo** seize the opportunity; ~ **di sorpresa** take by surprise
co'glione *nm* vulg ball; (sciocco) dickhead; **rompere i coglioni a qualcuno** get on somebody's tits
'**Cognac** *nm* cognac
co'gnato, **-a** ① *nm* brother-in-law ② *nf* sister-in-law

cognizi'one *nf* knowledge; **con ∼ di causa** on an informed basis

cognome *nm* surname, second name. **cognome da ragazza/da nubile** maiden name

cogu'aro *nm* cougar

'coi = CON + I

coi'bente *adj* insulating

coinci'denza *nf* coincidence; (di treno ecc) connection

coin'cidere *vi* coincide

coinqui'lino *nm* flatmate

coin'volgere *vt* involve

coinvolgi'mento *nm* involvement

coin'volto *adj* involved

'coito *nm* coitus

col = CON + IL

colà *adv* there

cola'brodo *nm inv* strainer; **ridotto a un ∼** fam full of holes

cola'pasta *nm inv* colander

co'lare ① *vt* strain; (versare lentamente) drip
② *vi* (gocciolare) drip; (perdere) leak; **∼ a picco** Naut sink

co'lata *nf* (di metallo) casting; (di lava) flow

colazi'one *nf* (del mattino) breakfast; (di mezzogiorno) lunch; **far ∼** have breakfast/lunch. **prima colazione** breakfast. **colazione di lavoro** working lunch. **colazione al sacco** packed lunch

col'bacco *nm* fur hat

co'lei *pron f* the one

co'lera *nm* cholera

coleste'rolo *nm* cholesterol

colf *nf inv abbr* (**collaboratrice familiare**) home help

colibrì *nm inv* humming-bird

'colica *nf* colic

co'lino *nm* [tea] strainer

'colla *nf* glue; (di farina) paste. **colla di pesce** gelatine

collabo'rare *vi* collaborate; **∼ con** (polizia) co-operate with; **∼ a** (rivista) contribute to

collabora|'tore, -trice *nmf* collaborator; (di rivista) contributor. **collaboratrice familiare** domestic help

collaborazi'one *nf* collaboration; (con polizia) co-operation

collaborazio'nista *nmf* collaborator

col'lage *nm inv* collage

col'lana *nf* necklace; (serie) series. **collana di perle** pearl necklace

col'lant *nmpl* tights. **collant velati** sheer tights

col'lante *adj* adhesive

col'lare *nm* collar

colla'rino *nm* dog collar

col'lasso *nm* collapse. **collasso cardiaco** syncope. **collasso renale** kidney failure

collate'rale *adj* collateral

collau'dare *vt* test

collauda|'tore, -trice *nmf* tester

col'laudo *nm* test

collazio'nare *vt* collate

'colle *nm* hill; (passo) pass

col'lega *nmf* colleague

colle'gabile *adj* compatible (**a** with)

collega'mento *nm* connection; Mil liaison; Radio ecc link. **collegamento dati** data link. **collegamento ipertestuale** hyperlink. **collegamento in rete** networking

colle'gare *vt* connect

colle'garsi *vr* TV, Radio link up (**a** with); (Comput: a una rete ecc) go on line (**a** to)

collegi'ale ① *nmf* boarder ② *adj* (responsabilità, decisione) collective

col'legio *nm* (convitto) boarding-school. **collegio elettorale** constituency

'collera *nf* anger; **andare in ∼** get angry

col'lerico *adj* irascible

col'letta *nf* collection

collettività *nf inv* community

collet'tivo ① *adj* collective; (interesse) general; **biglietto collettivo** group ticket ② *nm* (studentesco, femminista) collective

col'letto *nm* collar

collet'tore *nm* (di fognatura) main sewer

collezio'nare *vt* collect

collezi'one *nf* collection. **collezione invernale** winter collection

collezio'nismo *nm* collecting

collezio'nista *nmf* collector. **collezionista di francobolli** stamp collector

colli'mare *vi* coincide

col'lina *nf* hill

colli'nare *adj* hill *attrib*

colli'netta *nf* knoll

colli'noso *adj* (terreno) hilly

col'lirio *nm* eyewash

collisi'one *nf* collision

'collo *nm* neck; (pacco) package; **a ∼ alto** high-necked; **a rotta di ∼** breakneck. **collo del piede** instep

colloca'mento *nm* placing; (impiego) employment

collo'care *vt* place

collo'carsi *vr* take one's place

collocazi'one *nf* placing

colloqui'ale *adj* (termine) colloquial; (tono) informal

col'loquio *nm* conversation; (udienza ecc) interview; (esame) oral [exam]

col'loso *adj* glutinous

col'lottola *nf* nape

collusi'one *nf* collusion

colluttazi'one *nf* scuffle

col'mare *vt* fill; bridge ⟨*divario*⟩; ~ qualcuno di gentilezze overwhelm somebody with kindness

'colmo ① *adj* full; un cucchiaio ~ a heaped spoonful
② *nm* top; fig height; al ~ della disperazione in the depths of despair; questo è il ~! (con indignazione) this is the last straw!; (con stupore) I don't believe it!; per ~ di sfortuna to crown it all

+colo *suff* poetucolo second rate poet

co'lomba *nf* dove. **colomba pasquale** dove-shaped cake with candied fruit eaten at Easter

colom'baccio *nm* wood pigeon

colom'baia *nf* dovecote

Co'lombia *nf* Colombia

colombi'ano *adj & nmf* Colombian

co'lombo *nm* pigeon; **colombi** *pl* (innamorati) lovebirds

Co'lonia *nf* Cologne; [acqua di] **colonia** [eau de] Cologne

colonia *nf* colony; (per bambini) holiday camp, summer camp

coloni'ale *adj* colonial

colonia'lista *nmf* colonialist

co'lonico *adj* ⟨terreno, casa⟩ farm *attrib*

coloniz'zare *vt* colonize

colonizza|'tore, -trice *nmf* colonizer

colonizzazi'one *nf* colonization

co'lonna *nf* column; (di auto) tailback. **colonna sonora** sound-track. **colonna vertebrale** spine

colon'nato *nm* colonnade

colon'nello *nm* colonel

colon'nina *nf* (distributore) petrol pump, gas pump Am

co'lono *nm* tenant farmer

colo'rante *nm* colouring. **colorante alimentare** food colouring

colo'rare *vt* colour; colour in ⟨disegno⟩

co'lore *nm* colour; (carte) suit; a colori in colour; di ~ coloured; farne di tutti i colori get up to all sorts of mischief; passarne di tutti i colori go through hell; diventare di tutti i colori fig turn scarlet. **colore a olio** oil paint. **colore primario** primary colour

colori'ficio *nm* paint and dyes shop

colo'rito ① *adj* coloured; ⟨viso⟩ rosy; ⟨racconto, linguaggio⟩ colourful
② *nm* complexion

co'loro *pron pl* the ones

colos'sale *adj* colossal

Colos'seo *nm* Coliseum

co'losso *nm* colossus

'colpa *nf* fault; (biasimo) blame; (colpevolezza) guilt; (peccato) sin; **dare la** ~ **a** blame; **essere in** ~ be at fault; **per** ~ **di** because of; **è** ~ **mia** it's my fault

col'pevole ① *adj* guilty
② *nmf* culprit

col'pire *vt* hit, strike; fig strike; ~ **nel segno** hit the nail on the head

'colpo *nm* blow; (di arma da fuoco) shot; (urto) knock; (emozione) shock; Med, Sport stroke; (furto) robbery; **di** ~ suddenly; **far** ~ make a strong impression; **far venire un** ~ **a qualcuno** fig give somebody a fright; **perdere colpi** ⟨motore⟩ keep missing; **a** ~ **d'occhio** at a glance; **a** ~ **sicuro** for certain. **colpo d'aria** chill. **colpo basso** blow below the belt. **colpo di frusta** Med whiplash injury. **colpo di grazia** kiss of death. **colpo da maestro** masterstroke. **colpo di scena** sensational development. **colpo di sole** sunstroke. **colpi di sole** *pl* (su capelli) highlights. **colpo di Stato** coup [d'état]. **colpo di telefono** ring, call; **dare un** ~ **di telefono a qn** give somebody a ring or call. **colpo di testa** [sudden] impulse. **colpo di vento** gust of wind

col'poso *adj* omicidio ~ manslaughter

coltel'lata *nf* stab

coltelle'ria *nf* cutlery shop

col'tello *nm* knife; **avere il** ~ **dalla parte del manico** have the upper hand. **coltello per il pane** breadknife. **coltello a serramanico** jackknife

colti'vare *vt* cultivate

coltiva|'tore, -trice *nmf* farmer

coltivazi'one *nf* farming; (di piante) growing. **coltivazione intensiva** intensive farming

'colto ① *pp di* COGLIERE
② *adj* cultured

'coltre *nf* blanket

col'tura *nf* cultivation. **coltura alternata** crop rotation

co'lui *pron m* the one

'colza *nf* Bot (oilseed) rape

'coma *nm inv* coma; **in** ~ in a coma; **in** ~ **irreversibile** brain dead

comanda'mento *nm* commandment

coman'dante *nm* commander; Naut, Aeron captain

coman'dare ① *vt* command; Mech control; ~ **a qualcuno di fare qualcosa** order somebody to do something
② *vi* be in charge

co'mando *nm* command; (di macchina) control

co'mare *nf* (pettegola) gossip

coma'toso *adj* Med comatose

combaci'are *vi* fit together; ⟨*testimonianze*⟩ concur

combattente ① *adj* fighting ② *nm* combatant. **ex combattente** ex-serviceman. **combattente per la libertà** freedom fighter

com'battere *vt/i* fight

combatti'mento *nm* fight; Mil battle; **fuori ~** (pugilato) knocked out

combat'tuto *adj* ⟨*gara*⟩ hard fought; (tormentato) torn; ⟨*discussione*⟩ heated

combi'nare *vt/i* arrange; (mettere insieme) combine; (fam: fare) do; **cosa stai combinando?** what are you doing?

combi'narsi *vr* combine; (mettersi d'accordo) come to an agreement

combinazi'one *nf* combination; (caso) coincidence; **per ~** by chance

com'briccola *nf* gang

combu'stibile ① *adj* combustible ② *nm* fuel

combusti'one *nf* combustion

com'butta *nf* gang; **in ~** in league

'come ① *adv* like; (in qualità di) as; (interrogativo, esclamativo) how; **questo vestito è ~ il tuo** this dress is like yours; **~?** pardon?; **~ stai?** how are you?; **~ va?** how are things?; **~ mai?** how come?; **~?** what?; **non sa ~ fare** he doesn't know what to do; **~ sta bene!** how well he looks!; **~ no!** that will be right!; **~ tu sai** as you know; **fa' ~ vuoi** do as you like; **~ se** as if ② *conj* (non appena) as soon as

come'done *nm* blackhead

co'meta *nf* comet

'comfort *nm inv* comfort; **con tutti i ~** with all mod cons

'comico ① *adj* comical; ⟨*teatro, attore*⟩ comic ② *nm* funny side; (attore) comic actor, comedian ③ *nf* comedienne; (attrice) comic actress, comedienne; (a torte in faccia) slapstick sketch

co'mignolo *nm* chimney-pot

cominci'are *vt/i* begin, start; **a ~ da oggi** from today; **per ~** to begin with; **cominciamo bene!** we're off to a fine start!

comi'tato *nm* committee. **comitato consultivo** advisory committee. **comitato direttivo** steering committee. **comitato esecutivo** executive committee. **comitato di gestione** management committee

comi'tiva *nf* party, group

co'mizio *nm* meeting. **comizio elettorale** election rally

'comma *nm* (capoverso) paragraph

com'mando *nm inv* commando

com'media *nf* comedy; (opera teatrale) play; fig sham. **commedia musicale** musical

commedi'ante ① *nm* comic actor; fig pej phoney ② *nf* comic actress; fig pej phoney

commedi'ografo, -a *nmf* playwright

commemo'rare *vt* commemorate

commemorazi'one *nf* commemoration. **commemorazione dei defunti** (2 novembre) All Soul's Day

commenda'tore *nm* commander

commen'sale *nmf* fellow diner

commen'tare *vt* comment on; (annotare) annotate

commen'tario *nm* commentary

commenta'|tore, -trice *nmf* commentator

com'mento *nm* comment; TV, Radio commentary. **commento musicale** music

commerci'ale *adj* commercial; ⟨*relazioni, trattative*⟩ trade; ⟨*attività*⟩; business; **centro commerciale** shopping centre

commerci'alista *nmf* business consultant; (contabile) accountant, certified public accountant Am

commercializ'zare *vt* market; pej commercialize

commercializzazi'one *nf* marketing; pej commercialization. **commercializzazione di massa** mass-marketing

commerci'ante *nmf* trader, merchant; (negoziante) shopkeeper. **commerciante all'ingrosso** wholesaler. **commerciante di oggetti d'arte** art dealer

commerci'are *vi* **~ in** deal in

com'mercio *nm* commerce; (internazionale) trade; (affari) business; **in ~** (prodotto) on sale. **commercio al dettaglio** *o* **al minuto** retail trade. **commercio all'ingrosso** wholesale trade.

com'messo, -a ① *pp di* COMMETTERE ② *nmf* shop assistant; **commessi** *pl* counter staff. **commesso viaggiatore** commercial traveller ③ *nf* (ordine) order

comme'stibile ① *adj* edible ② *nm* commestibili *pl* groceries

com'mettere *vt* commit; make ⟨*sbaglio*⟩; **~ un reato** commit an offence

commi'ato *nm* leave; **prendere ~ da** take leave of

commise'rare *vt* commiserate

commise'rarsi *vr* feel sorry for oneself

commissari'ato *nm* (di polizia) police station

commis'sario *nm* ≈ [police] superintendent; (membro di commissione) commissioner; Sport steward; Comm commission agent. **commissario di bordo** purser; **commissario capo** chief superintendent. **commissario d'esame** examiner. **commissario di gara** race official, steward. **commissario tecnico** (della nazionale) national team manager

commissi'one *nf* (incarico) errand; (comitato, percentuale) commission; (Comm: di merce) order; **commissioni** *pl* (acquisti) **fare commissioni** go shopping. **commissione d'esame** board of examiners. **Commissione Europea** European Commission. **commissione d'inchiesta** court of inquiry

commit'tente *nmf* purchaser

com'mosso [1] pp di COMMUOVERE [2] *adj* moved

commo'vente *adj* moving

commozi'one *nf* emotion. **commozione cerebrale** concussion

commu'overe *vt* touch, move

commu'oversi *vr* be touched

commu'tare *vt* change; Jur commute

commuta'tore *nm* Electr commutator

commutazi'one *nf* (di pena) commutation

comò *nm inv* chest of drawers

comoda'mente *adv* comfortably

como'dino *nm* bedside table

comodità *nf inv* comfort; (convenienza) convenience

'comodo [1] *adj* comfortable; (conveniente) convenient; (spazioso) roomy; (facile) easy; **stia comodo!** don't get up!; **far ~** be useful [2] *nm* comfort; **fare il proprio ~** do as one pleases; **prendila con ~!** take it easy!

Co'more *nfpl* **le (isole) ~** Comoros

'compact disc *nm inv* compact disc

compae'sano, -a [1] *nm* fellow countryman [2] *nf* fellow countrywoman

com'pagine *nf* (squadra) team

compa'gnia *nf* company; (gruppo) party; **fare ~ a qualcuno** keep somebody company; **essere di ~** be sociable. **compagnia aerea** airline. **compagnia di bandiera** (aerea) national airline. **compagnia low cost** budget airline, no frills airline

com'pagno, -a *nmf* companion; (Comm, Sport, in coppia) partner; Pol comrade. **compagno di classe** classmate. **compagno di scuola** schoolmate, schoolfriend. **compagno di squadra** team-mate. **compagno di viaggio** fellow traveller

compa'rabile *adj* comparable

compa'rare *vt* compare

compara'tivo *adj & nm* comparative

comparazi'one *nf* comparison

com'pare *nm* sidekick

compa'rire *vi* appear; (spiccare) stand out; **~ in giudizio** appear in court

com'parso, -a [1] pp di COMPARIRE [2] *nf* appearance; Cinema extra; Theat walk-on

compartecipazi'one *nf* sharing; (quota) share

comparti'mento *nm* compartment; (amministrativo) department

compas'sato *adj* calm and collected

compassi'one *nf* compassion; **aver ~ per** feel pity for; **far ~** arouse pity

compassio'nevole *adj* compassionate

com'passo *nm* [pair of] compasses *pl*

compa'tibile *adj* (conciliabile) compatible; (scusabile) excusable

compatibilità *nf* compatibility

compatibil'mente *adv* **~ con i miei impegni** if my commitments allow

compati'mento *nm* **un'aria di ~** air of condescension

compa'tire *vt* pity; (scusare) make allowances for

compatri'ota *nmf* compatriot

compat'tezza *nf* (di materia) compactness; (fig: di partito) solidarity

com'patto *adj* compact; (denso) dense; (solido) solid; fig united

compendi'are *vt* (fare un sunto) summarize

com'pendio *nm* outline; (sunto) synopsis; (libro) compendium

compene'trare *vt* pervade

compen'sare *vt* compensate; (supplire) make up for

compen'sarsi *vr* balance each other out

compen'sato *nm* (legno) plywood

compensazi'one *nf* compensation

com'penso *nm* compensation; (retribuzione) remuneration; **in compenso** (in cambio) in return; (d'altra parte) on the other hand; (invece) instead

'compera *nf* purchase; **far compere** do some shopping

compe'rare *vt* buy

compe'tente *adj* competent; ⟨ufficio⟩ appropriate

compe'tenza *nf* competence; (responsabilità) responsibility; **competenze** *pl* (onorari) fees

com'petere *vi* compete; **~ a** ⟨compito⟩ be the responsibility of

competitività *nf* competitiveness

competi'tivo *adj* ⟨prezzo, carattere⟩ competitive

competi|'tore, -trice *nmf* competitor

competizi'one *nf* competition

compia'cente *adj* obliging

compia'cenza *nf* obligingness; **avere la ∼ di ...** be so obliging as to ...

compia'cere *vt/i* please

compia'cersi *vr* (congratularsi) congratulate; **∼ di** (degnarsi) condescend to

compiaci'mento *nm* satisfaction; pej smugness

compiaci'uto *adj* satisfied; ⟨aria, sorriso⟩ smug

compi'angere *vt* pity; (per lutto ecc) sympathize with

'compiere *vt* (concludere) complete; commit ⟨delitto⟩; **∼ gli anni** have one's birthday

'compiersi *vr* end; (avverarsi) come true

compi'lare *vt* compile; fill in ⟨modulo⟩

compila|'tore, -trice *nmf* compiler

compilazi'one *nf* compilation

compi'mento *nm* completion; **portare a ∼ qualcosa** conclude something

com'pire *vt* = COMPIERE

compi'tare *vt* spell

'compito[1] *nm* task; (dovere) duty; Sch homework; **fare i compiti** do one's homework

com'pito[2] *adj* polite

compiu'tezza *nf* completeness

compi'uto *adj* **avere 30 anni compiuti** be over 30

comple'anno *nm* birthday

complemen'tare *adj* complementary; (secondario) subsidiary

comple'mento *nm* complement; Mil draft. **complemento oggetto** Gram direct object

comples'sato *adj* hung-up

complessità *nf* complexity

complessiva'mente *adv* on the whole; (in totale) altogether

comples'sivo *adj* comprehensive; (totale) total

com'plesso[1] *adj* complex; (difficile) complicated [2] *nm* complex, hang up fam; Psych complex; (di cantanti ecc) group; (di circostanze, fattori) combination; **in ∼** on the whole; (in totale) altogether. **complesso di inferiorità** inferiority complex

completa'mente *adv* completely

completa'mento *nm* completion

comple'tare *vt* complete

comple'tezza *nf* completeness

com'pleto[1] *adj* complete; (pieno) full [up]; **al ∼** ⟨teatro⟩ sold out; ⟨albergo⟩ full; **'∼ '** 'no vacancies'; **la famiglia al ∼** the whole family [2] *nm* (vestito) suit; (insieme di cose) set

compli'care *vt* complicate

compli'carsi *vr* become complicated

compli'cato complicated

complicazi'one *nf* complication; **salvo complicazioni** all being well

'complice [1] *nmf* accomplice [2] *adj* ⟨sguardo⟩ knowing

complicità *nf* complicity

complimen'tare *vt* compliment

complimen'tarsi *vr* **∼ con** congratulate

compli'mento *nm* compliment; **complimenti** *pl* (ossequi) regards; (congratulazioni) congratulations; **fare complimenti** stand on ceremony

complot'tare *vi* plot

com'plotto *nm* plot

compo'nente [1] *adj & nm* component [2] *nmf* member

componen'tistica *nf* (per auto, elettronica) accessories *pl*

compo'nibile *adj* ⟨cucina⟩ fitted; ⟨mobili⟩ modular

componi'mento *nm* composition; (letterario) work

com'porre *vt* compose; (sistemare) put in order; Typ set; lay out ⟨salma⟩; settle (lite)

com'porsi *vr* **∼ di** be made up of

comportamen'tale *adj* behavioural

comporta'mento *nm* behaviour

compor'tare *vt* (implicare) involve

compor'tarsi *vr* behave

com'posito *adj* Chem, Phot composite

composi|'tore, -trice *nmf* composer; Typ compositor

composizi'one *nf* composition. **composizione floreale** flower arrangement

com'posta *nf* stewed fruit; (concime) compost

compo'stezza *nf* composure

com'posto [1] *pp di* COMPORRE [2] *adj* ⟨parola⟩ compound; **essere ∼ da** consist of, comprise; **stai ∼!** sit properly! [3] *nm* Chem compound; Culin mixture

com'prare *vt* buy; (fig: corrompere) buy off, bribe

compra|'tore, -trice *nmf* buyer

compra'vendita *nf* buying and selling; **atto di compravendita** deed of sale

com'prendere *vt* understand; (includere) comprise

compren'donio *nm* **essere duro di ∼** be slow on the uptake

compren'sibile *adj* understandable

comprensibil'mente *adv* understandably

comprensi'one *nf* understanding

compren'sivo *adj* understanding; (che include) inclusive

com'preso [1] pp di COMPRENDERE
[2] adj included; **tutto compreso** ⟨prezzo⟩
all-in; **da lunedì a venerdì** ∼ Monday to
Friday inclusive

com'pressa nf compress; (pastiglia)
tablet

compressi'one nf compression.
compressione dati Comput data
compression

com'presso [1] pp di COMPRIMERE
[2] adj compressed

compres'sore nm (rullo) steamroller

compri'mario, -a [1] nm Theat
supporting actor
[2] nf supporting actress

com'primere vt press; (reprimere)
repress; Comput compress

compro'messo [1] pp di
COMPROMETTERE
[2] nm compromise; (contratto) preliminary
but binding agreement

compromet'tente adj compromising

compro'mettere vt compromise

compropri'età nf multiple ownership

comproprie'tario, -a nmf joint owner

compro'vare vt prove

com'punto adj contrite

compunzi'one nf compunction

compu'tare vt calculate; (addebitare)
estimate

com'puter nm inv computer.
computer da casa home computer

computeriz'zare vt computerize

computeriz'zato adj computerized

computerizzazi'one nf
computerization

computiste'ria nf book-keeping

'computo nm calculation

comu'nale adj municipal

co'mune [1] adj common; ⟨parti⟩
communal, common; ⟨amico⟩ mutual;
(ordinario) ordinary
[2] nm municipality; **in** ∼ shared; **fuori del**
∼ out of the ordinary; **avere qualcosa in**
∼ have something in common
[3] nf collective farm; commune

comu'nella nf **fare** ∼ form a clique

comune'mente adv commonly

comuni'cante adj interconnecting

comuni'care vt communicate; pass on
⟨malattia⟩; Relig administer Communion
to

comuni'carsi vr receive Communion

comunica'tiva nf communicativeness

comunica'tivo adj communicative

comuni'cato nm communiqué.
comunicato commerciale Radio
commercial. **comunicato stampa**
press release

comunicazi'one nf communication;
Teleph [phone] call; **avere la** ∼ get through;
dare la ∼ **a qualcuno** put somebody
through. **comunicazione dati** Comput
data communications

comuni'one nf communion; Relig [Holy]
Communion

comu'nismo nm communism

comu'nista adj & nmf communist

comu'nità nf inv community.
Comunità [Economica] Europea
European [Economic] Community.
Comunità degli Stati Indipendenti
Commonwealth of Independent States.
comunità terapeutica rehabilitation
centre

co'munque [1] conj however
[2] adv anyhow

con prep with; (mezzo) by; ∼ **facilità**
easily; ∼ **mia grande gioia** to my great
delight; **è gentile** ∼ **tutti** he is kind to
everyone; **col treno** by train; ∼ **questo**
tempo in this weather

co'nato nm **conato di vomito**
retching

'conca nf basin; (valle) dell

concate'nare vt link together

concate'narsi vr ⟨idee⟩ be connected

concatenazi'one nf connection

'concavo adj concave

con'cedere vt grant; award ⟨premio⟩;
(ammettere) admit

con'cedersi vr allow oneself ⟨pausa⟩;
treat oneself to ⟨lusso, vacanza⟩

concentra'mento nm concentration

concen'trare vt concentrate

concen'trarsi vr concentrate

concen'trato [1] adj concentrated
[2] nm concentrate. **concentrato di**
pomodoro tomato pureé

concentrazi'one nf concentration

con'centrico adj concentric

concepi'mento nm conception

conce'pire vt conceive ⟨bambino⟩;
(capire) understand; (figurarsi) conceive of;
devise ⟨piano ecc⟩

con'cernere vt concern

concer'tare vt Mus harmonize;
(organizzare) arrange

concer'tarsi vr agree

concer'tista nmf concert performer

con'certo nm concert; (composizione)
concerto. **concerto rock** rock concert

concessio'nario nm agent

concessi'one nf concession

con'cesso pp di CONCEDERE

con'cetto nm concept; (opinione) opinion

concet'toso adj cerebral

concezi'one nf conception; (idea)
concept

con'chiglia *nf* [sea] shell. **conchiglia del pellegrino** scallop shell, **conchiglia di san Giacomo** scallop shell

'concia *nf* tanning; (di tabacco) curing

conci'are *vt* tan; cure ⟨*tabacco*⟩; ∼ qualcuno per le feste give somebody a good hiding

conci'arsi *vr* (sporcarsi) get dirty; (vestirsi male) dress badly

conci'ato *adj* ⟨*pelle, cuoio*⟩ tanned; essere ∼ come un barbone look like something the cat dragged in

concili'abile *adj* compatible

concili'abolo *nm* private meeting

concili'ante *adj* conciliatory

concili'are *vt* reconcile; pay ⟨*contravvenzione*⟩; (favorire) induce

concili'arsi *vr* go together; (mettersi d'accordo) become reconciled

conciliazi'one *nf* reconciliation; Jur settlement

con'cilio *nm* Relig council; (riunione) assembly

conci'maia *nf* dunghill

conci'mare *vt* feed ⟨*pianta*⟩

con'cime *nm* manure; (chimico) fertilizer

concisi'one *nf* conciseness

con'ciso *adj* concise

conci'tato *adj* excited

concitta'dino, -a *nmf* fellow citizen

concla'mato *adj* Med full blown

con'clave *nm* conclave

con'cludere *vt* conclude; (finire con successo) successfully complete

con'cludersi *vr* come to an end

conclusi'one *nf* conclusion; in ∼ (insomma) in short

conclu'sivo *adj* conclusive

con'cluso *pp di* CONCLUDERE

concomi'tante *adj* contributory

concomi'tanza *nf* (di circostanze, fatti) combination; in ∼ con combined with, in conjunction with

concor'danza *nf* agreement

concor'dare ① *vt* agree [on]; Gram make agree
② *vi* (sul prezzo) agree

concor'dato *nm* agreement; Jur, Comm composition

con'corde *adj* in agreement; (unanime) unanimous

con'cordia *nf* concord

concor'rente ① *adj* concurrent; (rivale) competing
② *nmf* Comm, Sport competitor; (candidato) candidate; (a quiz, concorso di bellezza) contestant

concor'renza *nf* competition. **concorrenza sleale** unfair competition

concorrenzi'ale *adj* competitive

con'correre *vi* (contribuire) combine; (andare insieme) go together; (competere) compete

con'corso ① *pp di* CONCORRERE
② *nm* competition; **fuori** ∼ not in the official competition. **concorso di bellezza** beauty contest. **concorso di circostanze** combination of circumstances. **concorso di colpa** contributory negligence. **concorso ippico** showjumping event. **concorso a premi** prize-winning competition. **concorso in reato** Jur complicity. **concorso per titoli** competition in which exam results are not the sole criterion

concreta'mente *adv* concretely

concre'tare, concretizzare *vt* put into concrete form

con'creto *adj* concrete; in ∼ in concrete terms

concu'bina *nf* concubine

concussi'one *nf* acceptance of a bribe

con'danna *nf* sentence; pronunziare una ∼ hand down a sentence. **condanna a morte** death sentence. **condanna penale** prison sentence

condan'nare *vt* (disapprovare) condemn; Jur sentence

condan'nato, -a ① *adj* (destinato) forced
② *nmf* prisoner

con'densa *nf* condensation

conden'sare *vt* condense

conden'sarsi *vr* condense

condensa'tore *nm* Electr condenser

condensazi'one *nf* condensation

condi'mento *nm* seasoning; (salsa) dressing. **condimento per insalata** salad dressing

con'dire *vt* flavour; dress ⟨*insalata*⟩

condiscen'dente *adj* indulgent; pej condescending; (arrendevole) compliant

condiscen'denza *nf* indulgence; pej condescension; (arrendevolezza) compliance

con'dito *adj* Culin seasoned

condi'videre *vt* share

condizio'nale ① *adj & nm* conditional
② *nf* Jur suspended sentence

condiziona'mento *nm* Psych conditioning

condizio'nare *vt* condition

condizionata'mente *adv* conditionally

condizio'nato *adj* conditional (da on); **aria condizionata** air-conditioning

condiziona'tore *nm* air conditioner

condizi'one *nf* condition; a ∼ che on condition that; **condizioni** *pl* di credito credit terms. **condizione imprescindibile** precondition

condogli'anze *nfpl* condolences; **fare le ~ a** offer one's condolences to

'condom *nm inv* condom

condomini'ale *adj* ⟨spese⟩ common; ⟨riunione⟩ tenants' *attrib*

condo'minio *nm* joint ownership; (edificio) condominium

condo'mino, -a *nmf* joint owner

condo'nare *vt* remit

con'dono *nm* remission

con'dotta *nf* conduct, (circoscrizione di medico) country practice; (di gara ecc) management; (tubazione) pipe

con'dotto ① pp di CONDURRE ② *adj* **medico condotto** country doctor ③ *nm* pipe; Anat duct. **condotto dell'aria** air duct. **condotto sotterraneo** culvert

condu'cente *nmf* driver. **conducente di autobus** bus driver

con'durre *vt* lead; drive ⟨veicoli⟩ (accompagnare) take; conduct ⟨gas, elettricità ecc⟩; (gestire) run; **~ a termine** complete; **~ delle indagini** carry out an investigation

con'dursi *vr* behave

condut‖'tore, -trice ① *nmf* TV presenter; (di veicolo) driver ② *nm* Electr conductor

condut'tore *adj* **filo conduttore** leitmotif

condut'tura *nf* duct. **conduttura del gas** gas main

conduzi'one *nf* conduction

confabu'lare *vi* have a confab

confa'cente *adj* suitable

con'farsi *vr* **confarsi a** suit

confederazi'one *nf* confederation. **Confederazione elvetica** Swiss Confederation

confe'renza *nf* (discorso) lecture; (congresso) conference. **conferenza stampa** press conference, news conference

conferenzi'ere, -a *nmf* lecturer, speaker

confe'rire ① *vt* (donare) confer ② *vi* (consultarsi) confer

con'ferma *nf* confirmation; **dare ~** confirm

confer'mare *vt* confirm

confes'sare *vt* confess

confes'sarsi *vr* confess

confessio'nale ① *adj* ⟨segreto⟩ of the confession ② *nm* confessional

confessi'one *nf* confession

confes'sore *nm* confessor

con'fetto *nm* (di mandorla) sugared almond

confet'tura *nf* jam

confezionare *vt* manufacture; make ⟨abiti⟩ package ⟨merci⟩; **~ sottovuoto** vacuum-pack

confezio'nato *adj* ⟨vestiti⟩ off-the-peg; ⟨gelato⟩ wrapped

confezi'one *nf* manufacture; (di abiti) making; (di pacchi) packaging; **di ~** ⟨abiti⟩ off-the-peg; **confezioni** *pl* clothes. **confezione economica** economy pack, economy size. **confezione famiglia** family size. **confezione multipla** multipack. **confezione regalo** gift set. **confezione da sei** (di bottiglie, lattine) six-pack

confic'care *vt* thrust

confic'carsi *vr* lodge

confic'cato *adj* **~ in** lodged in, embedded in

confi'dare ① *vt* confide ② *vi* **~ in** trust

confi'darsi *vr* **~ con** confide in

confi'dente ① *adj* confident ② *nmf* confidant; (informatore) informer

confi'denza *nf* confidence; (familiarità) familiarity; **prendersi delle confidenze** take liberties

confidenzi'ale *adj* confidential; ⟨tono⟩ familiar; **in via ~** confidentially

configu'rare *vt* Comput configure

configurazi'one *nf* configuration

confi'nante *adj* neighbouring

confi'nare ① *vt* (relegare) confine ② *vi* **~ con** border on

confi'narsi *vr* (ritirarsi) withdraw

confi'nato ① *adj* confined ② *nm* prisoner

CONFIN'DUSTRIA *nf abbr* (**Confederazione generale dell'Industria Italiana**) ≈ CBI

con'fine *nm* border; (tra terreni) boundary

con'fino *nm* political exile

con'fisca *nf* (di proprietà) confiscation

confi'scare *vt* confiscate

conflagrazi'one *nf* conflagration

con'flitto *nm* conflict. **conflitto aereo** air war

conflittu'ale *adj* adversarial

conflittualità *nf* adversarial nature

conflu'enza *nf* confluence; (di strade) junction

conflu'ire *vi* ⟨fiumi⟩ flow together; ⟨strade⟩ meet

con'fondere *vt* confuse; (imbarazzare) embarrass

con'fondersi *vr* (mescolarsi) mingle; (sbagliarsi) be mistaken

confor'mare *vt* standardize (**a** in line with)

confor'marsi *vr* conform

conformazi'one *nf* conformity (**a** with); (del terreno) nature

con'forme *adj* standard

conforme'mente *adv* accordingly

confor'mismo *nm* conformity

confor'mista *nmf* conformist

conformità *nf* (a norma) conformity (**a** with); **in ∼ a** in accordance with, in conformity with

confor'tante *adj* comforting

confor'tare *vt* comfort

confor'tevole *adj* (comodo) comfortable

con'forto *nm* comfort; **a ∼ di** ⟨una tesi⟩ in support of; **conforti** *pl* **religiosi** last rites

confra'telli *nmpl* brethren

confra'ternita *nf* brotherhood

confron'tare *vt* compare

con'fronto *nm* comparison; **in ∼ a** by comparison with; **nei tuoi confronti** towards you; **senza ∼** far and away, by far. **confronto diretto** head to head

confusio'nario *adj* ⟨persona⟩ muddle-headed

confusi'one *nf* confusion; (baccano) racket; (disordine) mess; (imbarazzo) embarrassment

con'fuso ① *pp di* CONFONDERE ② *adj* confused; (indistinto) indistinct; (imbarazzato) embarrassed

confu'tare *vt* confute

conge'dare *vt* dismiss; Mil discharge

conge'darsi *vr* take one's leave

con'gedo *nm* leave; **essere in ∼** be on leave. **congedo malattia** sick leave. **congedo [di] maternità** maternity leave. **congedo [di] paternità** paternity leave

conge'gnare *vt* devise; (mettere insieme) assemble

con'gegno *nm* device

congelamento *nm* freezing; Med frostbite. **congelamento dei prezzi** price freeze

conge'lare *vt* freeze

conge'lato *adj* ⟨cibo⟩ deep-frozen

congela'tore *nm* freezer

congeni'ale *adj* congenial

con'genito *adj* congenital

congestio'nare *vt* congest

congestio'nato *adj* ⟨traffico⟩ congested; ⟨viso⟩ flushed

congesti'one *nf* congestion

conget'tura *nf* conjecture

congi'ungere *vt* join, connect; join ⟨mani⟩; combine ⟨sforzi⟩

congi'ungersi *vr* join, connect

congiunti'vite *nf* conjunctivitis

congiun'tivo *nm* subjunctive

congi'unto ① *pp di* CONGIUNGERE ② *adj* joined; ⟨azione⟩ joint; ⟨forze, sforzo⟩ combined ③ *nm* relative

congiun'tura *nf* junction; (situazione) situation

congiuntu'rale *adj* economic

congiunzi'one *nf* Gram conjunction

congi'ura *nf* conspiracy

congiu'rare *vi* conspire

conglome'rato *nm* conglomerate; fig conglomeration; (da costruzione) concrete

'Congo *nm* Congo

congo'lese *adj & nmf* Congolese

congratu'larsi *vr* **∼ con qualcuno per** congratulate somebody on

congratulazi'oni *nfpl* congratulations

con'grega *nf* band

congre'gare *vt* gather

congre'garsi *vr* congregate

congregazi'one *nf* congregation

congres'sista *nmf* convention participant

con'gresso *nm* congress, convention; (americano) Congress. **Congresso Nazionale Africano** African National Congress

'congrua *nf* stipend

'congruo *adj* proper; (giusto) fair

conguagli'are *vt* balance

congu'aglio *nm* balance

coni'are *vt* coin

conia'tura *nf* coinage

coniazi'one *nf* coinage

'conico *adj* conical

co'nifera *nf* conifer

co'niglia *nf* female rabbit, doe

conigli'era *nf* rabbit hutch

conigli'etta *nf* bunny girl

conigli'etto *nm* bunny

co'niglio *nm* rabbit

coniu'gale *adj* marital; ⟨vita⟩ married

coniu'gare *vt* conjugate

coniu'garsi *vr* get married; Gram conjugate

coniu'gato *adj* (sposato) married

coniugazi'one *nf* conjugation

'coniuge *nmf* spouse

connazio'nale *nmf* compatriot

connessi'one *nf* connection. **connessione a banda larga** broadband connection

con'nesso *pp di* CONNETTERE

con'nettere ① *vt* connect ② *vi* think rationally

con'nettersi *vr* (Comput: a Internet) log on (a to)

connet'tore *nm* connector

conni'vente *adj* conniving

conno'tare *vt* connote

conno'tato *nm* distinguishing feature; **connotati** *pl* description; **rispondere ai connotati** fit the description; **cambiare i connotati a qualcuno** hum re-arrange somebody's face

con'nubio *nm* fig union

'cono *nm* cone

cono'scente *nmf* acquaintance

cono'scenza *nf* knowledge; (persona) acquaintance; (sensi) consciousness; **perdere ~** lose consciousness; **riprendere ~** regain consciousness, come to. **conoscenza di lavoro** business contact

co'noscere *vt* know; (essere a conoscenza di) be acquainted with; (fare la conoscenza di) meet; **~ qualcosa a fondo** know something inside out

conosci|'tore, -trice *nmf* connoisseur

conosci'uto ① pp di CONOSCERE ② *adj* well-known

con'quista *nf* conquest

conqui'stare *vt* conquer; fig win

conquista'tore *nm* conqueror; fig ladykiller

consa'crare *vt* consecrate; ordain ⟨*sacerdote*⟩; (dedicare) dedicate

consa'crarsi *vr* devote oneself

consa'crato *adj* ⟨*suolo*⟩ hallowed

consacrazi'one *nf* consecration

consangu'ineo, -a *nmf* blood relation

consa'pevole *adj* conscious

consapevo'lezza *nf* consciousness

consapevol'mente *adv* consciously

conscia'mente *adv* consciously

'conscio *adj* conscious

consecu'tivo *adj* consecutive; (seguente) next

con'segna *nf* delivery; (merce) consignment; (custodia) care; (di prigioniero) handover; (Mil: ordine) orders *pl*; (Mil: punizione) confinement to barracks; **pagamento alla consegna** cash on delivery. **consegna della posta** mail delivery

conse'gnare *vt* deliver; Mil confine to barracks; hand over ⟨*prigioniero, chiavi*⟩

consegna'tario *nm* consignee

consegu'ente *adj* consequent

consegu'enza *nf* consequence; **di ~** (perciò) consequently; ⟨*agire, comportarsi*⟩ accordingly

consegui'mento *nm* achievement

consegu'ire ① *vt* achieve ② *vi* follow

con'senso *nm* consent; (della popolazione) consensus

consensu'ale *adj* consensus-based

consen'tire ① *vi* consent ② *vt* allow

consenzi'ente *adj* consenting

con'serto *adj* **a braccia conserte** with one's arms folded

con'serva *nf* preserve; (di frutta) jam; (di agrumi) marmalade. **conserva di pomodoro** tomato sauce

conser'vare *vt* preserve; (mantenere) keep; **~ in frigo** keep refrigerated; **~ in luogo asciutto** keep dry

conser'varsi *vr* keep; **~ in salute** keep well

conserva|'tore, -trice *adj & nmf* Pol conservative; **partito conservatore** Conservative Party, Tory Party Br

conserva'torio *nm* conservatory, school of music

conservato'rismo *nm* conservatism

conservazi'one *nf* preservation; **a lunga ~** long-life

con'sesso *nm* assembly

conside'rare *vt* consider; (stimare) regard

conside'rato *adj* (stimato) esteemed

considerazi'one *nf* consideration; (osservazione, riflessione) remark; (stima) respect

conside'revole *adj* considerable

consigli'abile *adj* advisable

consigli'are *vt* advise; (raccomandare) recommend

consigli'arsi *vr* **~ con qualcuno** ask somebody's advice

consigli'ere, -a *nmf* adviser; (membro di un consiglio) councillor. **consigliere d'amministrazione** board member. **consigliere delegato** managing director

con'siglio *nm* advice; (ente) council; **un ~** a piece of advice. **consiglio d'amministrazione** board of directors. **consiglio di guerra** war cabinet. **consiglio d'istituto** parent-teacher association. **consiglio dei ministri** Cabinet. **consiglio scolastico** education committee. **Consiglio di Sicurezza** (dell'ONU) Security Council. **Consiglio Superiore della Magistratura** body responsible for ensuring the independence of the judiciary

con'simile *adj* similar

consi'stente *adj* substantial; (spesso) thick; fig ⟨*argomento*⟩ solid

consi'stenza *nf* consistency; (spessore) thickness; (fig: di argomento) solidity

con'sistere *vi* **~ in** consist of

consoci'arsi *vr* go into partnership

consoci'ata *nf* (azienda) subsidiary

consociati'vismo *nm* excessive tendency to form associations

consoci'ato *nm* associate

con'socio, -a *nmf* fellow-member

conso'lante *adj* consoling

conso'lare¹ *adj* consular

conso'lare² *vt* console

conso'larsi *vr* console oneself

conso'lato *nm* consulate

consolazi'one *nf* consolation

'console¹ *nm* consul

con'sole² *nf inv* (tastiera) console. **console per videogiochi** games console

consolida'mento *nm* consolidation

consoli'dare *vt* consolidate

consoli'darsi *vr* consolidate

consommé *nm inv* consommé

conso'nante *nf* consonant

conso'nanza *nf* consonance

'consono *adj* appropriate (a to), suitable (a for)

con'sorte *nmf* consort

con'sorzio *nm* consortium

con'stare *vi* ~ **di** consist of; (risultare) appear; **a quanto mi consta** as far as I know; **mi consta che ...** seemingly ...;

consta'tare *vt* ascertain

constatazi'one *nf* statement of fact

consu'eto ① *adj* usual ② *nm* **più del** ~ more than usual

consuetudi'nario *adj* ⟨diritto⟩ common; ⟨persona⟩ set in one's ways

consue'tudine *nf* habit; (usanza) custom

consu'lente *nmf* consultant. **consulente aziendale** management consultant; (azienda) management consultancy. **consulente matrimoniale** marriage guidance counsellor

consu'lenza *nf* consultancy

consul'tare *vt* consult

consul'tarsi *vr* ~ **con** consult with

consultazi'one *nf* consultation

consul'tivo *adj* consultative

con'sulto *nm* consultation

consul'torio *nm* free clinic providing treatment for sexual problems and advice

consu'mare *vt* (usare) consume; wear out ⟨abito, scarpe⟩; consummate ⟨matrimonio⟩; commit ⟨delitto⟩

consu'marsi *vr* consume; ⟨abito, scarpe⟩ wear out; (struggersi) pine; '**da** ~ **preferibilmente entro il ...**' 'best before ...'

consu'mato *adj* ⟨politico⟩ consummate; ⟨scarpe, tappeto⟩ worn [out]

consuma|'tore, -trice *nmf* consumer

consumazi'one *nf* consumption; (bibita) drink; (spuntino) snack; (di matrimonio) consummation; (di delitto) commission

consu'mismo *nm* consumerism

consu'mista *nmf* consumerist

con'sumo *nm* consumption; (uso) use; **generi di consumo** consumer goods. **consumo [di carburante]** [fuel] consumption

consun'tivo *nm* **bilancio consuntivo** balance sheet; **fare il** ~ **di** fig take stock of

con'sunto *adj* well-worn

conta'balle *nmf* fam storyteller

con'tabile ① *adj* book-keeping ② *nmf* accountant

contabilità *nf inv* accounting; (ufficio) accounts department; **tenere la** ~ keep the accounts. **contabilità di gestione** management accounts. **contabilità in partita doppia** double entry book-keeping

contachi'lometri *nm inv* mileometer, odometer Am

conta'dino, -a *nmf* farm-worker, agricultural labourer; (proprietario) farmer; (medievale) peasant

contagi'are *vt* infect; **la sua allegria contagia tutti** his cheerfulness is very contagious

contagi'ato *adj* infected

con'tagio *nm* contagion

contagi'oso *adj* contagious

conta'giri *nm inv* rev counter

conta'gocce *nm inv* dropper; **dare qualcosa col** ~ fig dole something out in dribs and drabs

contami'nare *vt* contaminate

contaminazi'one *nf* contamination. **contaminazione incrociata** cross-contamination

contami'nuti *nm inv* timer

con'tante *nm* cash; **pagare in contanti** pay cash

con'tare ① *vt* count; (tenere conto di) take into account; **devi** ~ **un'ora per Il viaggio** you have to allow an hour for the journey ② *vi* count; ~ **di fare qualcosa** plan to do something

conta'scatti *nm inv* Teleph time-unit counter

con'tato *adj* ⟨giorni, ore⟩ numbered

conta'tore *nm* meter. **contatore del gas** gas meter

contat'tare *vt* contact

con'tatto *nm* contact; **essere in** ~ **con** be in touch or contact with; **mettersi in** ~ **con** contact, get in touch with

'conte *nm* count, earl Br

con'tea *nf* county

conteggi'are ① *vt* include ② *vi* calculate

con'teggio *nm* calculation. **conteggio alla rovescia** countdown

con'tegno *nm* behaviour; (atteggiamento) attitude; **darsi un** ∼ pull oneself together

conte'gnoso *adj* dignified

contem'plare *vt* contemplate; (fissare) gaze at

contempla'tivo *adj* contemplative

contemplazi'one *nf* contemplation

con'tempo *nm* **nel** ∼ in the meantime

contemporanea'mente *adv* at the same time

contempo'raneo, -a *adj & nmf* contemporary

conten'dente *nmf* competitor

con'tendere ① *vi* compete; (litigare) quarrel ② *vt* dispute

con'tendersi *vr* ∼ **qualcosa** compete for something

conte'nere *vt* contain; (reprimere) repress

conte'nersi *vr* contain oneself

conteni'tore *nm* container

conten'tabile *adj* **facilmente** ∼ easy to please

conten'tare *vt* please

conten'tarsi *vr* ∼ **di** be content with

conten'tezza *nf* happiness

conten'tino *nm* placebo

con'tento *adj* glad; (soddisfatto) happy

conte'nuto *nm* contents *pl*; (di libro, testo) content

contenzi'oso ① *adj* contentious ② *nm* dispute; (ufficio) legal department

con'tesa *nf* disagreement; Sport contest

con'teso ① *pp di* CONTENDERE ② *adj* contested

con'tessa *nf* countess

conte'stare *vt* contest; Jur give notification of ⟨contravvenzione⟩; ∼ **un reato a qualcuno** charge somebody with an offence

contesta|'tore, -trice ① *nmf* person who is anti-authority ② *adj* anti-authority

contestazi'one *nf* (disputa) dispute; (protesta) protest; (di contravvenzione) notification

con'testo *nm* context

con'tiguo *adj* adjacent

continen'tale *adj* continental

conti'nente *nm* continent

conti'nenza *nf* continence

contin'gente *nm* contingent; (quota) quota

contin'genza *nf* contingency

continua'mente *adv* (senza interruzione) continuously; (frequentemente) continually

continu'are *vt/i* continue; (riprendere) resume; ∼ **gli studi** stay on at school

continua'tivo *adj* on-going, continuous

continuazi'one *nf* continuation

continuità *nf* continuity

con'tinuo *adj* continuous; (molto frequente) continual; **di** ∼ continuously; (frequentemente) continually; **corrente continua** direct current

con'tinuum *nm inv* continuum

'conto *nm* calculation; (in banca, negozio) account; (di ristorante ecc) bill, check Am; (stima) consideration; **a conti fatti** all things considered; **ad ogni buon** ∼ in any case; **di poco/nessun** ∼ of little/no importance; **in fin dei conti** when all's said and done; **per** ∼ **di** on behalf of; **per** ∼ **mio** (a mio parere) in my opinion; (da solo) on my own; **per** ∼ **terzi** for a third party; **sul** ∼ **di qualcuno** ⟨voci, informazioni⟩ about somebody; **far** ∼ **di** (supporre) suppose; (proporsi) intend; **far** ∼ **su** rely on; **fare i propri conti** do one's accounts; **fare i conti con qualcuno** fig sort somebody out; **fare i conti in tasca a qualcuno** estimate how much somebody is worth; **fare i conti senza l'oste** forget the most important thing; **render** ∼ **a qualcuno di qualcosa** be accountable to somebody for something; **rendersi** ∼ **di qualcosa** realize something; **starsene per** ∼ **proprio** be on one's own; **tener** ∼ **di qualcosa** take something into account; **tenere da** ∼ **qualcosa** look after something. **conto in banca** bank account. **conto congiunto** joint account. **conto corrente** current account, checking account Am. **conto [corrente] comune** joint account. **conto corrente postale** Giro account. **conto profitti e perdite** profit and loss account. **conto alla rovescia** countdown. **conto spese** expense account

con'torcere *vt* twist

con'torcersi *vr* twist about

contor'nare *vt* surround

con'torno *nm* contour; Culin vegetables *pl*

contorsi'one *nf* contortion

contorsio'nista *nmf* contortionist

con'torto ① *pp di* CONTORCERE ② *adj* twisted

contrabban'dare *vt* smuggle

contrabbandi'ere, -a *nmf* smuggler

contrab'bando *nm* contraband

contrabbas'sista *nmf* double bass player

contrab'basso *nm* double bass

contraccambi'are *vt* return

contrac'cambio *nm* return

contraccet'tivo *nm* contraceptive

contraccezi'one *nf* contraception

contrac'colpo *nm* rebound; (di arma da fuoco) recoil; fig repercussion

con'trada *nf* (rione) district

contrad'detto *pp di* CONTRADDIRE

contrad'dire *vt* contradict

contraddi'stinguere *vt* differentiate, distinguish

contraddi'stinto ① *pp di* CONTRADDISTINGUERE ② *adj* ~ **da** distinguished by

contraddit'torio *adj* contradictory

contraddizi'one *nf* contradiction

contra'ente *nmf* contracting party

contra'ereo *adj* anti-aircraft

contraf'fare *vt* disguise

contraf'fatto ① *pp di* CONTRAFFARE ② *adj* disguised

contraffazi'one *nf* disguising

contraf'forte *nm* buttress

con'tralto ① *nm* counter-tenor ② *nf* contralto

contrap'peso *nm* counterbalance

contrap'porre *vt* (confrontare) compare; ~ **A a B** counter B with A

contrap'porsi *vr* be in opposition; ~ **a** contrast with; (opporsi a) be opposed to

contrap'punto *nm* Mus counterpoint

contraria'mente *adv* ~ **a** contrary to; ~ **a me** unlike me

contrari'are *vt* oppose; (infastidire) annoy

contrari'arsi *vr* get annoyed

contrarietà *nf inv* adversity; (ostacolo) set-back

con'trario ① *adj* contrary, opposite; ⟨direzione⟩ opposite; ⟨esito, vento⟩ unfavourable ② *nm* contrary, opposite; **al** ~ on the contrary

con'trarre *vt* contract

contrasse'gnare *vt* mark

contras'segno *nm* mark; **[in]** ~ ⟨spedizione⟩ cash on delivery, COD. **contrassegno IVA** VAT receipt

contra'stante *adj* contrasting

contra'stare ① *vt* oppose; (contestare) contest ② *vi* contrast; ⟨colori⟩ clash

con'trasto *nm* contrast; (di colori) clash; (litigio) dispute

contrattac'care *vt* counter-attack

contrat'tacco *nm* counter-attack

contrat'tare *vt/i* negotiate; (mercanteggiare) bargain

contrattazi'one *nf* contravention; (salariale) bargaining. **contrattazione di azioni** share dealing

contrat'tempo *nm* hitch

con'tratto ① *pp di* CONTRARRE

② *nm* contract. **contratto di lavoro** employment contract. **contratto a termine** fixed-term contract. **contratti a termine** *pl* Fin futures

contrattu'ale *adj* contractual

contravve'nire *vi* contravene a law

contravvenzi'one *nf* (multa) fine

contrazi'one *nf* contraction; (di prezzi) reduction

contribu'ente *nmf* contributor; (del fisco) taxpayer

contribu'ire *vi* contribute

contribu'tivo *adj* contributory

contri'buto *nm* contribution; **contributi** *pl* **pensionistici** pension contributions

con'trito *adj* contrite

'contro ① *prep* against; ~ **di me** against me ② *nm* **il pro e il** ~ the pros and cons *pl*

contro'battere *vt* counter

controbilanci'are *vt* counterbalance

controcor'rente ① *adj* ⟨idee, persona⟩ nonconformist ② *adv* upriver; fig upstream; **andare** ~ fig swim against the tide

controcul'tura *nf* counterculture

contro'curva *nf* second bend

contro'esodo *nm* massive return from holiday

controfa'gotto *nm* double bassoon

controffen'siva *nf* counter-offensive

controfi'gura *nf* stand-in

controfi'letto *nm* sirloin

contro'firma *nf* countersignature

controfir'mare *vt* countersign

controindicazi'one *nf* Med contraindication

controinterroga'torio *nm* cross-examination

control'labile *adj* ⟨emozione⟩ controllable; Tech which can be monitored

control'lare *vt* control; (verificare) check

control'larsi *vr* control oneself

control'lato *adj* controlled

con'troller *nm inv* Fin controller

con'trollo *nm* control; (verifica) check; Med check-up; **perdere il** ~ **di** lose control of. **controllo degli armamenti** arms control. **controllo automatico della velocità** automatic speed check. **controllo bagagli** baggage control. **controllo biglietti** ticket inspection. **controllo dei cambi** exchange control. **controllo del credito** credit control. **controllo delle nascite** birth control. **controllo ortografico** Comput spellchecker; **fare il** ~ **ortografico** spellcheck. **controllo passaporti** passport control. **controllo [di] qualità** ···⟩

quality control. **controllo radar della velocità** radar speed check

control'lore *nm* controller; (sui treni ecc) [ticket] inspector. **controllore di volo** air-traffic controller

contro'luce *nf* in ～ against the light

contro'mano *adv* in the wrong direction

contromi'sura *nf* countermeasure

contropar'tita *nf* compensation; in ～ in return

contropi'ede *nm* Sport breakaway; **prendere in** ～ fig catch off guard

controprodu'cente *adj* counter-productive

contro'prova *nf* cross-check; **fare la** ～ **di qualcosa** cross-check something

con'trordine *nm* counter order; **salvo contrordini** unless I/you hear to the contrary

contro'senso *nm* contradiction in terms

controspio'naggio *nm* counterespionage

controten'denza *nf* countertrend

controva'lore *nm* equivalent

contro'vento *adv* against the wind

contro'versia *nf* controversy; Jur dispute

contro'verso *adj* controversial

contro'voglia *adv* unwillingly

contu'mace *adj* Jur in default, absent

contu'macia *nf* default; in ～ in one's absence

contun'dente *adj* ⟨corpo, arma⟩ blunt

contur'bante *adj* perturbing

contur'bare *vt* perturb

contusi'one *nf* bruise

con'tuso *nm* person suffering from cuts and bruises

convale'scente *adj* & *nmf* convalescent

convale'scenza *nf* convalescence; **essere in** ～ be convalescing

con'valida *nf* ratification; (di nomina) confirmation; (di biglietto) validation

convali'dare *vt* ratify; confirm ⟨nomina⟩; validate ⟨atto, biglietto⟩

con'vegno *nm* meeting; (congresso) convention, congress

conve'nevole *adj* suitable

conve'nevoli *nmpl* pleasantries

conveni'ente *adj* convenient; (vantaggioso) advantageous; ⟨prezzo⟩ attractive

conveni'enza *nf* convenience; (interesse) advantage; (di prezzo) attractiveness

conve'nire ① *vi* agree; (riunirsi) gather; (essere opportuno) be convenient; **ci conviene andare** it's better to go; **non mi**

conviene stancarmi I'd better not tire myself out
② *vt* agree [on]

conven'ticola *nf* clique

con'vento *nm* (di suore) convent; (di frati) monastery

conve'nuto *adj* agreed

convenzio'nale *adj* conventional

convenzio'nato *adj* ⟨prezzo⟩ controlled

convenzi'one *nf* convention

conver'gente *adj* converging

conver'genza *nf* convergence

con'vergere *vi* converge

con'versa *nf* lay sister

conver'sare *vi* converse

conversa'tore, -trice *nmf* conversationalist

conversazi'one *nf* conversation

conversi'one *nf* conversion

con'verso *pp di* CONVERGERE

conver'tibile *nf* Auto convertible

conver'tire *vt* convert

conver'tirsi *vr* convert

conver'tito, -a ① *adj* converted
② *nmf* convert

converti'tore *nm* converter

con'vesso *adj* convex

convezi'one *nf* convection

convin'cente *adj* convincing

con'vincere *vt* convince

con'vinto *adj* convinced

convinzi'one *nf* conviction

convi'tato *nm* guest

con'vitto *nm* boarding school

convi'vente ① *nm* common-law husband
② *nf* common-law wife

convi'venza *nf* cohabitation

con'vivere *vi* live together

convivi'ale *adj* convivial

convo'care *vt* summon; Jur summons; convene ⟨riunione⟩

convocazi'one *nf* summoning; Jur summoning; (atto) summons; (riunione) meeting

convogli'are *vt* convey; ⟨navi⟩ convoy

con'voglio *nm* convoy; (ferroviario) train

convolare *vi* ～ **a giuste nozze** hum tie the knot

convulsa'mente *adv* convulsively

convulsi'one *nf* convulsion; fig fit

convul'sivo *adj* Med convulsive; ⟨riso⟩ hysterical

coope'rare *vi* co-operate

coopera'tiva *nf* co-operative

cooperazi'one *nf* co-operation

coordina'mento *nm* co-ordination

coordi'nare *vt* co-ordinate

coordi'nata *nf* Math co-ordinate; **coordinate** *pl* (su mappa) grid reference; **coordinate** *pl* **bancarie** bank details

coordi'nato ① *adj* co-ordinated ② *nm* (intimo) lingerie set

coordina|'tore, -trice *nmf* co-ordinator

coordinazi'one *nf* co-ordination. **coordinazione occhio-mano** hand-eye coordination

co'perchio *nm* lid; (copertura) cover

co'perta *nf* blanket; (copertura) cover; Naut deck. **coperta elettrica** electric blanket

coper'tina *nf* cover; (di libro) dust-jacket

co'perto ① *pp di* COPRIRE ② *adj* covered; (vestito) wrapped up; ⟨cielo⟩ overcast; ⟨piscina⟩ indoor ③ *nm* (a tavola) place; (prezzo del coperto) cover charge; **al ∼** under cover

coper'tone *nm* tarpaulin; (gomma) tyre

coper'tura *nf* cover; (azione) covering; (di strada) surfacing; (di malefatta) cover-up. **copertura globale** blanket coverage

'copia *nf* copy; **bella/brutta ∼** fair/rough copy; **essere la ∼ spiccicata di qualcuno** be the spitting image of somebody. **copia su carta** hard copy. **copia pirata** pirate copy. **copia di riserva** Comput backup copy.

'copia e in'colla *nm inv* Comput copy and paste; **fare un ∼** copy and paste

copi'are *vt* copy

copia'trice *nf* copier

copi'lota *nmf* co-pilot; (di auto) co-driver

copi'one *nm* Cinema, TV script

copi'oso *adj* copious

'coppa *nf* (calice) goblet; (bicchiere) glass; (per gelato ecc) dish; Sport cup. **coppa [di] gelato** ice-cream (served in a dish). **coppa del mondo** World Cup

cop'petta *nf* (di ceramica, vetro) bowl; (di gelato) small tub

'coppia *nf* couple; (in carte, voga) pair

co'prente *adj* ⟨cipria, vernice⟩ thick; ⟨collant⟩ opaque

copri'capo *nm* head covering

coprifu'oco *nm* curfew

copri'letto *nm* bedspread

copri'mozzo *nm* hub-cap

copriobiet'tivo *nm* lens cap

copripiu'mino *nm* duvet cover

co'prire *vt* cover; drown [out] ⟨suono⟩; hold ⟨carica⟩

co'prirsi *vr* (vestirsi) cover oneself up; (vestirsi pesante) dress warmly; fig cover up; (proteggersi) cover oneself; ⟨cielo⟩ become overcast

copritei'era *nm* tea cosy

co-protago'nista *nmf* Cinema co-star

'coque: **alla ∼** *adj* ⟨uovo⟩ soft-boiled

co'raggio *nm* bravery, courage; (sfacciataggine) nerve; **∼!** chin up!

coraggiosa'mente *adv* bravely, courageously

coraggi'oso *adj* brave, courageous

co'rale *adj* choral

co'rallo *nm* coral

co'rano *nm* Koran

co'razza *nf* armour; (di animali) shell

coraz'zata *nf* battleship

coraz'zato *adj* ⟨nave⟩ armour-plated

corazza'tura *nf* armour plate, armour plating

corazzi'ere *nm* cuirassier

corbelle'ria *nf* piece of nonsense; **dire corbellerie** talk nonsense

'corda *nf* cord; (spago, Mus) string; (fune) rope; (cavo) cable; **essere giù di ∼** be down; **dare ∼ a qualcuno** encourage somebody; **tagliare la ∼** cut and run; **tenere qualcuno sulla ∼** keep somebody on tenterhooks; **corde** *pl* **vocali** vocal cords. **corda per il bucato** washing line

cor'data *nf* roped party

cordi'ale ① *adj* cordial; **cordiali saluti** best wishes ② *nm* (bevanda) cordial

cordialità *nf inv* cordiality; **∼** *pl* (saluti) best wishes

'cordless *nm inv* Teleph cordless (phone)

cor'doglio *nm* grief; (lutto) mourning

cor'done *nm* cord; (schieramento) cordon. **cordone ombelicale** umbilical cord. **cordone sanitario** cordon sanitaire

Corea *nf* Korea. **Corea del Nord** North Korea. **Corea del Sud** South Korea

core'ano, -a *adj & nmf* Korean

coreogra'fare *vt* coreograph

coreogra'fia *nf* choreography; **fare la ∼ di** choreograph

core'ografo, -a *nmf* choreographer

Corfù *nf* Corfu

cori'aceo *adj* tough

cori'andoli *nmpl* (di carta) confetti *sg*

cori'andolo *nm* (spezia) coriander

cori'care *vt* put to bed

cori'carsi *vr* go to bed

Co'rinto *nf* Corinth

co'rista *nmf* choir member

'corna ▶ CORNO

cor'nacchia *nf* crow

corna'musa *nf* bagpipes *pl*

'cornea *nf* cornea

'corner *nm inv* corner; **salvarsi in ∼** fig have a lucky escape

cor'netta *nf* Mus cornet; (del telefono) receiver

cor'netto *nm* (brioche) croissant. ∼ **acustico** ear trumpet

cor'nice *nf* frame. **cornice a giorno** clip frame

cornici'one *nm* cornice

cornifi'care *vt* fam cheat on

'corno *nm* (pl f **corna**) horn; **fare le corna a qualcuno** fam cheat on somebody; **fare le corna** (per scongiuro) ≈ touch wood; **un** ∼**!** you must be joking!; (per niente) nonsense!. **corno da caccia** French horn

Corno'vaglia *nf* Cornwall

cornu'copia *nf* cornucopia

cor'nuto ① *adj* horned ② *nm* (fam: marito tradito) cuckold; (insulto) bastard

'coro *nm* chorus; Relig choir

co'rolla *nf* corolla

corol'lario *nm* corollary

co'rona *nf* crown; (di fiori) wreath; (rosario) rosary

corona'mento *nm* (di sogno) fulfilment; (di carriera) crowning achievement

coro'nare *vt* fulfil ⟨sogno⟩

coro'nario *adj* ⟨arteria⟩ coronary

cor'petto *nm* bodice

'corpo *nm* body; (Mil, diplomatico) corps *inv*; [a] ∼ a ∼ Mil hand to hand; **lottare** [a] ∼ a ∼ have a punch-up, slug it out; **dare** ∼ a **qualcosa** give substance to something; **buttarsi a** ∼ **morto in qualcosa** throw oneself desperately into something; **andare di** ∼ move one's bowels. **corpo di ballo** corps de ballet. **corpo estraneo** foreign body. **corpo insegnante** teaching staff. **corpo del reato** murder weapon

corpo'rale *adj* corporal

corporati'vismo *nm* corporatism

corpora'tura *nf* build

corporazi'one *nf* corporation

cor'poreo *adj* bodily

cor'poso *adj* full-bodied

corpu'lento *adj* stout

'corpus *nm inv* corpus

cor'puscolo *nm* corpuscle

corre'dare *vt* (di note) supply (**di** with); **corredato di curriculum** accompanied by a CV

corre'dino *nm* (per neonato) layette

cor'redo *nm* (nuziale) trousseau; (di informazioni ecc) set

correggere *vt* correct; lace ⟨bevanda⟩; ∼ **le bozze** proof-read

corre'lare *vt* correlate

cor'rente ① *adj* running; (in vigore) current; (frequente) everyday; ⟨inglese ecc⟩ fluent

② *nf* current; (d'aria) draught; **essere al** ∼ **di qualcosa** be aware of something; **tenersi al** ∼ keep up to date (**di** with). **corrente continua** direct current. **corrente trasversale** cross current

corrente'mente *adv* ⟨parlare⟩ fluently; (comunemente) commonly

'correre ① *vi* run; (affrettarsi) hurry; Sport race; ⟨notizie⟩ circulate; **lascia** ∼**!** let it go!; ∼ **dietro a** run after; **tra loro non corre buon sangue** there is bad blood between them

② *vt* run; ∼ **un pericolo** run a risk; **corre voce che** ... there's a rumour that ...

correspon'sabile *nmf* person jointly responsible

corresponsi'one *nf* payment

corretta'mente *adv* correctly; ⟨sedersi, mangiare⟩ properly; ⟨trattare, fare qualcosa⟩ right

corret'tivo *nm* corrective

cor'retto ① *pp di* CORREGGERE ② *adj* correct; ⟨caffè⟩ with a drop of alcohol

corret|'tore, -trice ① *nmf* **correttore di bozze** proof-reader ② *nm* **correttore grammaticale** Comput grammar checker. **correttore ortografico** Comput spellchecker

correzi'one *nf* correction. **correzione di bozze** proof-reading. **correzione errori** Comput error correction

cor'rida *nf* bullfight

corri'doio *nm* corridor; Aeron aisle

corri|'dore, -trice *nmf* (automobilistico) driver; (ciclista) cyclist; (a piedi) runner

corri'era *nf* coach, bus

corri'ere *nm* courier; (posta) mail; (spedizioniere) carrier. **corriere della droga** drug mule

corri'mano *nm* banister

corrispet'tivo *nm* amount due

corrispon'dente ① *adj* corresponding ② *nmf* correspondent. **corrispondente estero** foreign correspondent

corrispon'denza *nf* correspondence; **tenersi in** ∼ **con** correspond with; **per** ∼ ⟨fare un corso⟩ by correspondence; **corso per corrispondenza** correspondence course; **vendite per corrispondenza** mail-order [shopping]

corri'spondere *vi* correspond; ⟨stanza⟩ communicate; ∼ **a** (contraccambiare) return

corri'sposto *adj* ⟨amore⟩ reciprocated

corrobo'rare *vt* strengthen; fig corroborate

cor'rodere *vt* corrode

cor'rodersi *vr* corrode

cor'rompere *vt* corrupt; (con denaro) bribe

corrosi'one *nf* corrosion

corro'sivo *adj* corrosive

cor'roso pp di CORRODERE

cor'rotto ① pp di CORROMPERE ② *adj* corrupt

corrucci'arsi *vr* be vexed

corrucci'ato *adj* vexed

corru'gare *vt* wrinkle; ~ **la fronte** knit one's brows

corrut'tela *nf* depravity

corruzi'one *nf* corruption; (con denaro) bribery

'corsa *nf* running; (rapida) dash; Sport race; (di treno ecc) journey; **di** ~ at a run; **di gran** ~ in a great hurry; **fare una** ~ (sbrigarsi) run, hurry. **corsa agli armamenti** arms race. **corsa ciclistica** cycle race. **corsa ippica** horse race. **corsa all'oro** gold rush. **corsa a ostacoli** obstacle race. **corsa piana** flat racing. **corsa semplice** one way [ticket]

cor'sia *nf* gangway; (di ospedale) ward; Aut lane; (di supermercato) aisle. **corsia autobus** bus lane. **corsia d'emergenza** Aut hard shoulder. **corsia di sorpasso** fast lane, outside lane

'Corsica *nf* Corsica

cor'sivo *nm* italics *pl*; **in** ~ in italics

'corso ① pp di CORRERE ② *nm* course; (strada) main street; Comm circulation; (in borsa) price, quotation; **essere in** ~ be underway; **lavori in** ~ work in progress; **nel** ~ **di** during; **avere** ~ **legale** be legal tender. **corso d'acqua** waterway. **corso per corrispondenza** correspondence course; **corso di formazione** training course. **corso di formazione professionale** vocational course. **corso full immersion** immersion course. **corso del giorno** current daily price. **corso di laurea** degree course. **corso serale** evening class; **corsi** *pl* **di studio a distanza** distance learning

'corte *nf* [court] yard; (Jur, regale) court; **fare la** ~ **a qualcuno** court somebody. **corte d'appello** court of appeal. **Corte d'assise** crown court. **Corte di cassazione** supreme court of appeal. **Corte dei conti** National Audit Office. **Corte europea per i diritti dell'uomo** European Court of Human Rights. **Corte europea di giustizia** European Court of Justice. **corte di giustizia** court of law

cor'teccia *nf* bark

corteggia'mento *nm* courtship

corteggi'are *vt* court

corteggia'tore *nm* admirer

cor'teo *nm* procession. **corteo di auto** motorcade. **corteo funebre** funeral cortège. **corteo nuziale** bridal party

cor'tese *adj* courteous

corte'sia *nf* courtesy; **per** ~ please

cortigi'ano, -a ① *nmf* courtier ② *nf* courtesan

cor'tile *nm* courtyard

cor'tina *nf* curtain; (schermo) screen

'corto *adj* short; **per farla corta** to cut a long story short; **a** ~ **di** short of, hard up for. **corto circuito** *nm* short [circuit]

cortome'traggio *nm* Cinema short

cor'vino *adj* jet-black

'corvo *nm* raven

'cosa ① *nf* thing; (faccenda) matter ② *inter, rel pron* what; **[che]** ~ what; **nessuna** ~ nothing; **ogni** ~ everything; **per prima** ~ first of all; **tante cose** [so] many things; (augurio) all the best; ~**?** what?; ~ **hai detto?** what did you say?; **le cose le vanno bene** she's doing all right

'cosca *nf* clan

'coscia *nf* thigh; Culin leg; **cosce** *pl* **di rana** frogs' legs

cosci'ente *adj* conscious

cosci'enza *nf* conscience; (consapevolezza) consciousness; **mettersi la** ~ **a posto** salve one's conscience

coscienziosa'mente *adv* conscientiously

coscienzi'oso *adj* conscientious

cosci'otto *nm* leg

co'scritto *nm* conscript

coscrizi'one *nf* conscription

così ① *adv* so; (in questo modo) like this, like that; (perciò) therefore; **le cose stanno** ~ that's how things stand; **fermo** ~**!** hold it!; **proprio** ~**!** exactly!; **basta** ~**!** that will do!; **ah, è** ~**?** it's like that, is it?; ~ ~ so-so; **e** ~ **via** and so on; **per** ~ **dire** so to speak; **più di** ~ any more; **una** ~ **cara ragazza!** such a nice girl!; **è stato** ~ **generoso da aiutarti** he was kind enough to help you ② *conj* (allora) so ③ *adj inv* (tale) like that, such; **una ragazza** ~ a girl like that, such a girl

cosicché *conj* and so

cosid'detto *adj* so-called

co'smesi *nf* beauty treatment

co'smetico ① *adj* cosmetic ② *nm* **cosmetici** *pl* cosmetics; (trucchi) make-up

'cosmico *adj* cosmic

'cosmo *nm* cosmos

cosmo'nauta *nmf* cosmonaut

cosmopo'lita *adj* cosmopolitan

co'spargere *vt* sprinkle; (disseminare) scatter; ~ **il pavimento di cera** spread wax on the floor

co'spetto *nm* **al** ~ **di** in the presence of

co'spicuo *adj* conspicuous; ⟨somma ecc⟩ considerable

cospi'rare *vi* conspire, plot

cospira|'tore, -trice *nmf* conspirator, plotter

cospirazi'one *nf* conspiracy, plot

'**costa** *nf* coast, coastline; Anat rib; **sotto** ~ inshore. **Costa d'Avorio** Ivory Coast. **Costa Azzurra** Côte d'Azur. **Costa Smeralda** Emerald coast (in Sardinia)

costà *adv* there

co'stante *adj & nf* constant

co'stanza *nf* constancy

co'stare *vi* cost; **quanto costa?** how much is it?; **costi quel che costi** whatever the cost

'**Costa 'Rica** *nm* Costa Rica

co'stata *nf* chop. **costata [di manzo]** rib steak

co'stato *nm* ribs *pl*

costeggi'are *vt* (per mare) coast; (per terra) skirt

co'stei *pers pron* (soggetto) she; (complemento) her

costellazi'one *nf* constellation

coster'nato *adj* dismayed

costernazi'one *nf* consternation

costi'era *nf* stretch of coast

costi'ero *adj* coastal

co'stine *nfpl* (di maiale) spare ribs

'**costing** *nm* costing

costi'pato *adj* constipated; **essere** ~ (raffreddato) have a bad cold

costipazi'one *nf* constipation; (raffreddore) bad cold

costitu'ire *vt* constitute; (essere) be; (formare) form; (nominare) appoint

costitu'irsi *vr* ‹criminale› give oneself up

costituzio'nale *adj* constitutional

costituzional'mente *adv* Pol constitutionally

costituzi'one *nf* constitution; (formazione) formation

'**costo** *nm* cost; **a nessun** ~ on no account; **a** ~ **di perdere la salute** at the cost of one's health; **sotto** ~ at less than cost price; **costi** *pl* **di gestione** administration costs; **costi** *pl* **di spedizione** freight charges. **costo del denaro** Fin cost of money. **costo unitario** unit cost. **costo della vita** cost of living

'**costola** *nf* rib; (di libro) spine; **stare alle costole di qualcuno** follow somebody around

costo'letta *nf* cutlet

co'storo *pron* (soggetto) they; (complemento) them

co'stoso *adj* costly

co'stretto pp di COSTRINGERE

co'stringere *vt* force, compel

costrit'tivo *adj* coercive

costrizi'one *nf* compulsion

costru'ire *vt* build, construct

costrut'tivo *adj* constructive

costruzi'one *nf* building, construction; (edificio) building

co'stui *pers pron* (soggetto) he; (complemento) him

co'stume *nm* (usanza) custom; (indumento) costume; **costumi** *pl* (morale) morals. **costume da bagno** swim-suit; (da uomo) swimming trunks. **costume intero** one-piece. **costume tradizionale** traditional costume

costu'mista *nmf* wardrobe assistant

cote'chino *nm* spiced pork sausage

co'tenna *nf* pigskin; (della pancetta) rind. ~ **arrostita** crackling

co'togna *nf* quince

coto'letta *nf* cutlet. **cotoletta alla milanese** veal cutlet in breadcrumbs

coto'nato *adj* ‹capelli› back-combed

co'tone *nm* cotton. **cotone idrofilo** cotton wool, absorbent cotton Am

cotoni'ficio *nm* cotton mill

'**cotta** *nf* Relig surplice; (fam: innamoramento) crush; **prendere una** ~ **per qualcuno** fam have a crush on somebody

'**cottimo** *nm* piece-work

'**cotto** ① pp di CUOCERE ② *adj* done; (fam: innamorato) in love; (sbronzo) drunk; **ben** ~ well cooked; ‹carne› underdone; **troppo** ~ overcooked; ‹carne› overdone

cotton fi'oc® *nm inv* cotton bud

cot'tura *nf* cooking

'**country** *nm* country and western

cou'pon *nm inv* coupon

cou'scous *nm inv* couscous

co'vare *vt* hatch; sicken for ‹malattia›; harbour ‹rancore›

co'vata *nf* brood

'**covo** *nm* den

co'vone *nm* sheaf

cow-'boy *nm inv* cowboy

'**cozza** *nf* mussel. **cozze alla marinara** *pl* moules marinière

coz'zare *vi* ~ **contro** bump into

'**cozzo** *nm* fig clash

C.P. *abbr* (**Casella Postale**) PO Box

crac *nm inv* crack; (di tessuto) rip

crack *nm* (droga) crack

Cra'covia *nf* Cracow

'**crafen** *nm inv* cream doughnut

'**crampo** *nm* cramp

'**cranio** *nm* skull

cra'tere *nm* crater

cra'vatta *nf* tie; (a farfalla) bow-tie

cre'anza *nf* manners *pl*; **mala ∼** bad manners

cre'are *vt* create; **∼ assuefazione** be habit-forming

creatività *nf* creativity

crea'tivo *adj* creative

cre'ato *nm* creation

crea|'tore, -trice *nmf* creator; **andare al ∼** go to meet one's maker

crea'tura *nf* creature; (bambino) baby; **povera ∼!** poor thing!

creazi'one *nf* creation

cre'dente *nmf* believer

cre'denza *nf* belief; Comm credit; (mobile) sideboard

credenzi'ali *nfpl* credentials

'credere ① *vt* believe; (pensare) think ② *vi* ∼ **in** believe in; **credo di sì** I think so; **non ti credo** I don't believe you; **non posso crederci!** I can't believe it!

'credersi *vr* think oneself to be; **si crede uno scrittore** he flatters himself he is a writer

cre'dibile *adj* credible, believable

credibilità *nf* credibility

credi'tizio *adj* credit attrib

'credito *nm* credit; (stima) esteem; **comprare a ∼** buy on credit; **dare ∼ a qualcosa** give credence to something; **fare ∼** give credit. **credito all'esportazione** export credit. **credito inesigibile** bad debt

credi|'tore, -trice *nmf* creditor

'credo *nm inv* credo

credulità *nf* credulity

'credulo *adj* credulous

credu'lone, -a *nmf* simpleton

'crema *nf* cream; (di uova e latte) custard. **crema base per il trucco** vanishing cream. **crema depilatoria** depilatory [cream]. **crema detergente** cleansing cream. **crema idratante** moisturizer. **crema per le mani** hand cream. **crema pasticciera** confectioner's custard. **crema per la pelle** skin cream. **crema protettiva** barrier cream. **crema solare** suntan lotion. **crema per il viso** face cream

cremagli'era *nf* ratchet

cre'mare *vt* cremate

crema'torio *nm* crematorium

cremazi'one *nf* cremation

crème cara'mel *nf* crème caramel

creme'ria *nf* dairy (also selling ice cream and cakes)

Crem'lino *nm* Kremlin

cre'moso *adj* creamy

cren *nm* horseradish

'crepa *nf* crack

cre'paccio *nm* cleft; (di ghiacciaio) crevasse

crepacu'ore *nm* heart-break

crepa'pelle: a ∼ *adv* fit to burst

cre'pare *vi* crack; (fam: morire) kick the bucket; **∼ dal ridere** laugh fit to burst

crepa'tura *nf* crevice

crêpe *nf inv* pancake

crepi'tare *vi* crackle

crepi'tio *nm* crackling

cre'puscolo *nm* twilight

cre'scendo *nm* crescendo

cre'scenza *nf* creamy white cheese

'crescere ① *vi* grow; (aumentare) increase, grow ② *vt* (allevare) bring up; (aumentare) increase

cresci'one *nm* watercress

'crescita *nf* growth; (aumento) increase, growth

cresci'uto *pp di* CRESCERE

'cresima *nf* confirmation

cresi'mare *vt* confirm

cre'spato *adj* crinkly

cre'spella *nf* pancake

'crespo ① *adj* ⟨capelli⟩ frizzy ② *nm* crêpe

'cresta *nf* crest; (cima) peak; **abbassare la ∼** become less cocky; **alzare la ∼** become cocky; **sulla ∼ dell'onda** on the crest of a wave

'creta *nf* clay

'Creta *nf* Crete

cre'tese *adj & nmf* Cretan

creti'nata *nf* something stupid; **dire cretinate** talk nonsense

cre'tino, -a ① *adj* stupid ② *nmf* idiot

C.R.I. *abbr* (**Croce Rossa Italiana**) Italian Red Cross

'cribbio *int* gosh!, golly!

cric *nm inv* jack

'cricca *nf* gang

'cricco *nm* jack

cri'ceto *nm* hamster

'cricket *nm* cricket

crimi'nale *adj & nmf* criminal

criminalità *nf* crime. **criminalità organizzata** organized crime

'crimine *nm* crime

criminolo'gia *nf* criminology

crimi'nologo, -a *nmf* criminologist

crimi'noso *adj* criminal

'crine *nm* horsehair

crini'era *nf* mane

crino'lina *nf* crinoline

crioge'nia *nf* cryogenics

'cripta *nf* crypt

crip'tare *vt* encrypt

crisan'temo *nm* chrysanthemum

'**crisi** *nf inv* crisis; Med fit; **essere in** ∼ **di astinenza** be having withdrawal symptoms, be cold turkey fam. **crisi di nervi** hysterics. **crisi del settimo anno** seven-year itch

cristal'lino [1] *adj* crystal clear [2] *nm* crystalline lens

cristalliz'zare *vt* crystallize

cristalliz'zarsi *vr* crystallize; fig ⟨*parola, espressione*⟩ become part of the language

cri'stallo *nm* crystal

Cristia'nesimo *nm* Christianity

cristianità *nf* Christendom

cristi'ano, **-a** *adj & nmf* Christian

'**Cristo** *nm* Christ; **avanti** ∼ BC; **dopo** ∼ AD; **un povero c**∼ a poor beggar

cri'terio *nm* criterion; (buon senso) [common] sense

'**critica** *nf* criticism; (recensione) review; **fare la** ∼ **di** review ⟨*film, libro*⟩. **critica letteraria** literary criticism

criti'care *vt* criticize

'**critico** [1] *adj* critical [2] *nm* critic. **critico letterario** literary critic

criti'cone, **-a** *nmf* fault finder

crittazi'one *nf* **crittazione [dei] dati** Comput data encryption

crivel'lare *vt* riddle (**di** with)

cri'vello *nm* sieve

cro'ato, **-a** *adj & nmf* Croatian, Croat

Cro'azia *nf* Croatia

croc'cante [1] *adj* crisp [2] *nm* type of crunchy nut biscuit

croc'chetta *nf* croquette

'**crocchia** *nf* bun

'**crocchio** *nm* cluster

'**croce** *nf* cross; **a occhio e** ∼ roughly; **fare testa e** ∼ toss a coin; **fare o mettere una** ∼ **sopra qualcosa** fig forget about something; **mettere in** ∼ (criticare) crucify; (tormentare) nag nonstop. **Croce Rossa** Red Cross

croceros'sina *nf* Red Cross nurse

croce'via *nm inv* crossroads *sg*

croci'ata *nf* crusade

croci'ato [1] *adj* cruciform [2] *nm* crusader

cro'cicchio *nm* crossroads *sg*

croci'era *nf* cruise; **velocità di crociera** cruising speed

croci'figgere *vt* crucify

crocifissi'one *nf* crucifixion

croci'fisso [1] pp di CROCIFIGGERE [2] *adj* crucified [3] *nm* crucifix

crogio'larsi *vr* bask

crogi'olo *nm* crucible; fig melting pot

crogiu'olo *nm* = CROGIOLO

crois'sant *nm inv* croissant

crol'lare *vi* collapse; ⟨*prezzi*⟩ slump

'**crollo** *nm* collapse; (dei prezzi) slump

'**croma** *nf* quaver

cro'mato *adj* chromium-plated

'**cromo** *nm* chrome

cromo'soma *nm* chromosome

'**cronaca** *nf* chronicle; (di giornale) news; TV, Radio commentary; **fatto di** ∼ news item. **cronaca mondana** gossip column. **cronaca nera** crime news

'**cronico** *adj* chronic

cro'nista *nmf* reporter; (di partita) commentator

croni'storia *nf* chronicle

cro'nografo *nm* chronograph

cronolo'gia *nf* chronology

cronologica'mente *adv* chronologically

crono'logico *adj* chronological

cronome'traggio *nm* timing

cronome'trare *vt* time

cronome'trista *nmf* Sport timekeeper

cro'nometro *nm* chronometer; Sport stopwatch

cross *nm* (corsa campestre) cross-country; (motocross) motocross

cros'sista *nmf* scrambler; (a piedi) cross-country runner

'**crosta** *nf* crust; (di formaggio) rind; (di ferita) scab; (quadro) daub

cro'staceo *nm* shellfish

cro'stata *nf* tart. **crostata di frutta** fruit tart. **crostata di mele** apple pie

cro'stino *nm* croûton; **crostini** *pl* pieces of toasted bread served as a starter

croupi'er *nmf inv* croupier

crucci'are *vt* torment

crucci'arsi *vr* torment oneself

'**cruccio** *nm* torment

cruci'ale *adj* crucial

cruci'verba *nm inv* crossword [puzzle]

cru'dele *adj* cruel

crudel'mente *adv* cruelly

crudeltà *nf inv* cruelty

'**crudo** *adj* raw; ⟨*linguaggio*⟩ crude

cru'ento *adj* bloody

crumi'raggio *nm* strike-breaking

cru'miro *nm* blackleg, scab

'**crusca** *nf* bran

cru'scotto *nm* dashboard

C.S.I. *nf abbr* (**Comunità degli Stati Indipendenti**) CIS

'**Cuba** *nf* Cuba

cu'bano, **-a** *adj* & *nmf* Cuban

cu'betto *nm* **cubetto di ghiaccio** ice cube

'cubico *adj* cubic

cu'bismo *nm* cubism

cu'bista *adj* & *nmf* cubist

cubi'tale *adj* **a caratteri cubitali** in enormous letters

'cubo *nm* cube

cuc'cagna *nf* abundance; (baldoria) merry-making; **paese della ∼** land of plenty

cuc'cetta *nf* (su un treno) couchette; Naut berth

cucchiai'ata *nf* spoonful

cucchia'ino *nm* teaspoon; (contenuto) teaspoon[ful]

cucchi'aio *nm* spoon; **un ∼** a spoon[ful] (di of); **al ∼** ⟨dolce⟩ creamy. **cucchiaio di legno** wooden spoon. **cucchiaio da minestra** soup-spoon. **cucchiaio da tavola** tablespoon; (contenuto) tablespoon[ful]

cucchiai'one *nm* serving spoon

'cuccia *nf* basket; (in giardino) kennel; **[fa' la] ∼!** down!

cuccio'lata *nf* litter

'cucciolo *nm* puppy

cu'cina *nf* kitchen; (il cucinare) cooking; (cibo) food; (apparecchio) cooker; **far da ∼** cook; **libro di cucina** cook[ery] book. **cucina casalinga** home cooking. **cucina componibile** fitted kitchen. **cucina a gas** gas cooker

cuci'nare *vt* cook

cuci'nino *nm* kitchenette

cu'cire *vt* sew; **macchina da cucire** sewing-machine; **cucilo a macchina** do it on the machine

cu'cito *nm* sewing

cuci'tura *nf* seam

cucù *nm inv* cuckoo; **∼!** peekaboo!

'cuculo *nm* cuckoo

cuffia *nf* bonnet; (ricevitore) headphones *pl.* **cuffia da bagno** bathing cap. **cuffia con microfono** (per telefonino) headset

cu'gino, **-a** *nmf* cousin

'cui *pron* rel (persona: con prep) who[m]; (cose, animali: con prep) which; (tra articolo e nome) whose; **la persona con ∼ ho parlato** the person I spoke to, the person to whom I spoke fml; **la ditta per ∼ lavoro** the company I work for, the company for which I work; **l'amico il ∼ libro è stato pubblicato** the friend whose book was published; **in ∼** (dove) where; (quando) that; **per ∼** (perciò) so; **la città in ∼ vivo** the city I live in, the city where I live; **il giorno in ∼ l'ho visto** the day [that] I saw him

cu'latta *nf* breech

culi'naria *nf* cookery

culi'nario *adj* culinary

'culla *nf* cradle

cul'lare *vt* rock; fig cherish ⟨sogno, speranza⟩

cul'larsi *vr* **∼ nella speranza di** liter cherish the fond hope that

culmi'nante *adj* culminating

culmi'nare *vi* culminate

'culmine *nm* peak

'culo *nm* vulg arse; (fortuna) luck; **prendere qualcuno per il ∼** take the piss out of somebody

'culto *nm* cult; Relig religion; (adorazione) worship

cul'tura *nf* culture. **cultura generale** general knowledge. **cultura di massa** mass culture

cultu'rale *adj* cultural

cultu'rismo *nm* body-building

cultu'rista *nmf* body-builder

cu'mino *nm* **cumino nero** cumin

cumula'tivo *adj* cumulative; ⟨prezzo⟩ all-in, all-inclusive; **biglietto cumulativo** group ticket

'cumulo *nm* pile; (mucchio) heap; (nuvola) cumulus

'cuneo *nm* wedge

cu'netta *nf* gutter

cu'nicolo *nm* tunnel

cu'ocere ① *vt* cook; fire ⟨ceramica⟩ ② *vi* cook; ⟨ceramica⟩ fire

cu'oco, **-a** *nmf* cook

cu'oia *nfpl* **tirare le ∼** fam kick the bucket

cu'oio *nm* leather. **cuoio capelluto** scalp

cu'ore *nm* heart; **cuori** *pl* (carte) hearts; **di [buon] ∼** ⟨persona⟩ kind-hearted; **di tutto ∼** wholeheartedly; **ti ringrazio di tutto ∼** many thanks; **nel profondo del ∼** in one's heart of hearts; **nel ∼ della notte** in the middle of the night; **senza ∼** heartless; **mettersi il ∼ in pace** come to terms with it; **parlare a ∼ aperto** have a heart-to-heart (con with); **stare a ∼ a qualcuno** be very important to somebody. **∼ tenero** (persona) softy

cupa'mente *adv* darkly

cupi'digia *nf* greed

Cu'pido *nm* Cupid

'cupo *adj* gloomy; ⟨voce⟩ deep

'cupola *nf* dome; **a ∼** domed

'cura *nf* care; (amministrazione) management; Med treatment; **aver ∼ di** look after; **a ∼ di** ⟨libro⟩ edited by; **in ∼** under treatment; **fare delle cure termali** take the waters. **cura dimagrante** diet. **cura della fertilità** fertility treatment

cu'rabile *adj* curable

cu'rante *adj* **medico curante** GP, doctor

cu'rare *vt* take care of, look after; Med treat; (guarire) cure; edit ⟨*testo*⟩

cu'rarsi *vr* take care of oneself, look after oneself; **~ dei fatti propri** mind one's own business

cu'rato *nm* parish priest

cura|'tore, -trice *nmf* trustee; (di testo) editor. **curatore fallimentare** official receiver

'curcuma *nf* turmeric

curcu'mina *nf* turmeric

'curdo, -a ⓵ *nmf* Kurd ⓶ *adj* Kurdish

'curia *nf* curia

curio'saggine *nf* nosiness

curio'sare *vi* be curious; (mettere il naso) pry (**in** into); (nei negozi) look around

curiosità *nf inv* curiosity

curi'oso ⓵ *adj* curious; (strano) odd, curious ⓶ *nm* busybody

'curling *nm* Sport curling

cur'ricolo *nm* curriculum

cur'riculum *nm inv* curriculum

'curry *nm inv* curry. **curry in polvere** curry powder

cur'sore *nm* Comput cursor

'curva *nf* curve; (stradale) bend. **curva a**

gomito dogleg. **curva di apprendimento** learning curve

cur'vare *vt/i* bend, curve

cur'varsi *vr* bend, curve

'curvo *adj* curved; (piegato) bent

cusci'netto *nm* pad; Mech bearing. **cuscinetto puntaspilli** pincushion. **cuscinetto a sfere** ball bearing

cu'scino *nm* cushion; (guanciale) pillow. **cuscino gonfiabile** air cushion

cu'scus *nm inv* couscous

'cuspide *nf* spire

cu'stode *nm* caretaker; (di abitazione) concierge; (di fabbrica) guard; (di museo) custodian. **~ giudiziario** official receiver

cu'stodia *nf* care; Jur custody; (astuccio) case; **ottenere la ~ di** get custody of. **custodia cautelare** remand

custo'dire *vt* keep; (badare) look after

cu'taneo *adj* skin *attrib*

'cute *nf* skin

cu'ticola *nf* cuticle

'cutter *nm inv* cutter

CV *abbr* (**cavallo vapore**) hp

cyber'spazio *nm* cyberspace

cy'clette® *nf inv* exercise bicycle

Dd

da *prep* from; (con verbo passivo) by; (moto a luogo) to; (moto per luogo) through; (stato in luogo) at; (temporale) since; (continuativo) for; (causale) with; (in qualità di) as; (con caratteristica) with; (come) like; **da Roma a Milano** from Rome to Milan; **staccare un quadro dalla parete** take a picture off the wall; **i bambini dai 5 ai 10 anni** children between 5 and 10; **vedere qualcosa da vicino/lontano** see something from up close/from a distance; **amato da tutti** loved by everybody; **scritto da** written by; **andare dal panettiere** go to the baker's; **passo da te più tardi** I'll come over to your place later; **passiamo da qui** let's go this way; **un appuntamento dal dentista** an appointment at the dentist's; **il treno passa da Venezia** the train goes through Venice; **dall'anno scorso** since last year; **vivo qui da due anni** I've been living here for two years; **da domani** from tomorrow; **piangere dal dolore** cry with pain; **ho molto da fare** I have a lot to do; **occhiali da sole** sunglasses; **qualcosa da mangiare** something to eat; **un uomo dai capelli**

scuri a man with dark hair; **è un oggetto da poco** it's not worth much; **da solo** alone; **l'ho fatto da solo** I did it by myself; **si è fatto da sé** he is a self-made man; **vive da re** he lives like a king; **non è da lui** it's not like him

dab'bene *adj* honest

dac'capo *adv* again; (dall'inizio) from the beginning

dacché *conj* since

dada'ismo *nm* (arte) Dadaism

dada'ista *adj & nmf* Dadaist

'dado *nm* dice; Culin stock cube; Techn nut. **dado ad alette** wing nut

daf'fare *nm* work

'dagli = DA + GLI

dai[1] = DA + I

dai[2] *int* come on!; **~, non fare così!** come on, don't be like that!; **~, sbrigati!** come on, get a move on!

'daino *nm* deer; (pelle) buckskin

dal = DA + IL

'dalia *nf* dahlia

'dalla = DA + LA
'dalle = DA + LE
'dallo = DA + LO
'dalmata *nm* (cane) Dalmatian
Dal'mazia *nf* Dalmatia
dal'tonico *adj* colour-blind
'dama *nf* lady; (nei balli) partner; (gioco) draughts. **dama di compagnia** lady's companion. **dama di corte** lady-in-waiting
dama'scato *adj* damask
da'masco *nm* (tessuto) damask
dame'rino *nm* (bellimbusto) dandy
dami'gella *nf* (di sposa) bridesmaid
damigi'ana *nf* demijohn
dam'meno *adv* **non essere** ∼ be no less good (**di** than)
DAMS *nm abbr* (**Discipline delle Arti, della Musica e dello Spettacolo**) (corso di laurea) degree in fine art, music and drama
da'naro *nm* = DENARO
dana'roso *adj* loaded
da'nese ① *adj* Danish ② *nmf* Dane ③ *nm* (lingua) Danish
Dani'marca *nf* Denmark
dan'nare *vt* damn; **far** ∼ **qualcuno** drive somebody mad
dan'narsi *vr* fig wear oneself out; ∼ **l'anima (a fare qualcosa)** wear oneself out (doing something)
dan'nato, -a ① *adj* damned, damn fam ② *nmf* damned person; **lavorare/studiare come un** ∼ fig work/study like mad
dannazi'one *nf* damnation
danneggia'mento *nm* damage
danneggi'are *vt* damage; (nuocere) harm
danneggi'ato *adj* Jur injured
'danno *nm* damage; (a persona) harm; **danni** *pl* damage; **danni** *pl* **alla struttura portante** structural damage
dan'noso *adj* harmful
dan'tesco *adj* Dantean, Dantesque
danubi'ano *adj* Danubian
Da'nubio *nm* Danube
'danza *nf* dance; (il danzare) dancing. ∼ **folcloristica** country dancing
dan'zante *adj* **serata danzante** dance
dan'zare *vi* dance
danza|'tore, -trice *nmf* dancer. **danzatrice del ventre** belly dancer
dapper'tutto *adv* everywhere
dap'poco *adj* worthless
dap'prima *adv* at first
Darda'nelli *nmpl* **i** ∼ the Dardanelles
'dardo *nm* dart
'dare ① *vt* give; sit (esame); have (festa); ∼ **qualcosa a qualcuno** give somebody

something; ∼ **da mangiare a qualcuno** give somebody something to eat; ∼ **fuoco a qualcosa** set fire to something; ∼ **il benvenuto a qualcuno** welcome somebody; ∼ **la buonanotte a qualcuno** say good night to somebody; ∼ **del tu/del lei a qualcuno** address somebody as "tu/lei"; ∼ **del cretino a qualcuno** call somebody an idiot; ∼ **qualcosa per scontato** take something for granted; ∼ **fastidio a** annoy; **cosa danno alla TV stasera?** what's on TV tonight?; **darle a qualcuno** (picchiare) give somebody a walloping ② *vi* ∼ **nell'occhio** be conspicuous; ∼ **alla testa** go to one's head; ∼ **su** (finestra, casa) look on to; ∼ **sui o ai nervi a qualcuno** get on somebody's nerves ③ *nm* Comm debit
'darsena *nf* dock
'darsi *vr* (scambiarsi) give each other; ∼ **da fare** get down to it; **si è dato tanto da fare!** he went to so much trouble!; ∼ **a** (cominciare) take up; ∼ **al bere** take to drink; ∼ **per** (malato) pretend to be; ∼ **per vinto** give up; **può** ∼ maybe
darvini'ano *adj* Darwinian
darvi'nista *nmf* Darwinist
'data *nf* date; **di lunga** ∼ old established. **data di emissione** date of issue. **data di nascita** date of birth. **data di scadenza** expiry date; (su alimenti) best before date
data'base *nm inv* database. **database relazionale** relational database
da'tabile *adj* datable
da'tare *vt* date; **a** ∼ **da** as from
da'tario *nm* (su orologio) calendar
da'tato *adj* dated
da'tivo *nm* dative
'dato ① *adj* given; (dedito) addicted; ∼ **che** seeing that, given that ② *nm* datum; **dati** *pl* data. **dato di fatto** well established fact
da'tore *nm* giver. **datore di lavoro** employer
'dattero *nm* date
dattilogra'fare *vt/i* type; ∼ **a tastiera cieca** touch-type
dattilogra'fia *nf* typing. **dattilografia a tastiera cieca** touch-typing
datti'lografo, -a *nmf* typist
dattilo'scritto *adj* (copia) typewritten, typed
dat'torno *adv* **togliersi** ∼ clear off
da'vanti ① *adv* before; (dirimpetto) opposite; (di fronte) in front ② *adj inv* front ③ *nm* front; ∼ **di dietro** (maglia) back-to-front; ∼ **a** *prep* before, in front of; **passare** ∼ **a** pass, go past
davan'zale *nm* window sill

da'vanzo *adv* ce n'è ~ there is more than enough

dav'vero *adv* really; **per** ~ in earnest; **dici** ~? honestly?

dazi'ario *adj* excise

'dazio *nm* duty; (ufficio) customs *pl*. **dazi doganali** *pl* customs duties. **dazio d'importazione** import duty

D.C. *nf abbr* (**Democrazia Cristiana**) Christian Democratic Party

d.C. *abbr* (**dopo Cristo**) AD

D.D.T. *nm* (insetticida) DDT

'dea *nf* goddess

deambula'torio *adj* ambulatory

debel'lare *vt* defeat

debili'tante *adj* weakening

debili'tare *vt* weaken

debili'tarsi *vr* become debilitated

debilitazi'one *nf* debilitation

debita'mente *adv* duly

'debito ① *adj* due; **a tempo** ~ in due course
② *nm* debt. **debito pubblico** national debt

debi|'tore, -trice *nmf* debtor

'debole ① *adj* weak; ⟨*luce*⟩ dim; ⟨*suono*⟩ faint
② *nm* weak point; **avere un** ~ **per qualcuno** have a soft spot for somebody; **avere un** ~ **per qualcosa** have a weakness for something

debo'lezza *nf* weakness

debor'dare *vi* overflow

debosci'ato *adj* debauched

debrai'ata *nf* Auto declutching

debut'tante ① *adj* beginner
② *nmf* beginner; (attore) actor/actress making his/her début

debut'tare *vi* make one's début

de'butto *nm* début

'decade *nf* period of ten days

deca'dente *adj* decadent

decaden'tismo *nm* decadence

deca'denza *nf* decline; Jur loss

deca'dere *vi* lapse

decadi'mento *nm* (delle arti) decline

deca'duto *adj* ⟨*persona*⟩ impoverished; ⟨*decreto, norma*⟩ no longer in force

decaffei'nato ① *adj* decaffeinated
② *nm* decaffeinated coffee, decaf fam

deca'grammo *nm* decagram

decal'care *vt* trace

decalcifi'carsi *vr* become brittle

decalcificazi'one *nf* (condizione) brittle bones

decalcoma'nia *nf* transfer

de'calitro *nm* decalitre

de'calogo *nm* fig rule book

de'cametro *nm* decametre

de'cano *nm* dean

decan'tare *vt* (lodare) praise

decapi'tare *vt* decapitate; behead ⟨*condannato*⟩

decapitazi'one *nf* decapitation; beheading

decappot'tabile *adj* convertible

decappot'tare *vt* take down the hood of

'decathlon *nm* decathlon

de'cedere *vi* (morire) die

dece'duto *adj* deceased

decele'rare *vt/i* slow down, decelerate

decelerazi'one *nf* deceleration

decen'nale ① *adj* ten-yearly
② *nm* (anniversario) tenth anniversary

de'cenne *adj* ⟨*bambino*⟩ ten-year-old

de'cennio *nm* decade

de'cente *adj* decent

decente'mente *adv* decently

decentraliz'zare *vt* decentralize

decentra'mento *nm* decentralization

decen'trare *vt* decentralize

de'cenza *nf* decency

de'cesso *nm* death, decease fml; **atto di decesso** death certificate

'decibel *nm inv* decibel

de'cidere *vt* decide; settle ⟨*questione*⟩

de'cidersi *vr* make up one's mind

deci'frabile *adj* decipherable

deci'frare *vt* decipher; (documenti cifrati) decode

decifrazi'one *nf* deciphering

de'cigrado *nm* tenth of a degree

deci'grammo *nm* decigram

de'cilitro *nm* decilitre

deci'male *adj* decimal

deci'mare *vt* decimate

de'cimetro *nm* decimetre

'decimo *adj & nm* tenth

de'cina *nf* Math ten; **una** ~ **di** (circa dieci) about ten

decisa'mente *adv* definitely, decidedly

decisio'nale *adj* decision-making

decisi'one *nf* decision; **prendere una** ~ make *or* take a decision; **con** ~ decisively

decisio'nismo *nm* tendency to make decisions without consulting others

decisio'nista *nmf* person who does not consult others before making decisions

deci'sivo *adj* decisive

de'ciso ① *pp di* DECIDERE
② *adj* decided

decla'mare *vt/i* declaim

declama'torio *adj* ⟨*stile*⟩ declamatory

declas'sare *vt* downgrade

decli'nabile *adj* Gram declinable; ⟨*offerta*⟩ that can be refused

decli'nare ① *vt* decline; turn down, refuse ⟨*invito*⟩; ∼ **ogni responsabilità** disclaim all responsibility
② *vi* go down; ⟨tramontare⟩ set

declinazi'one *nf* Gram declension

de'clino *nm* decline; **in** ∼ ⟨*popolarità*⟩ on the decline

de'clivio *nm* downward slope

dé'co *adj inv* Art Deco

de'coder *nm inv* TV set-top box

deco'difica *nf* decoding

decodifi'care *vt* decode

decodifica'tore *nm* TV descrambler

decodificazi'one *nf* decoding

decol'lare *vi* take off

décolle'té ① *adj inv* low cut
② *nm inv* low neckline

de'collo *nm* take-off

decolonizzazi'one *nf* decolonization

decolo'rante *nm* bleach

decolo'rare *vt* bleach

decolorazi'one *nf* bleaching

decom'porre *vt* decompose

decom'porsi *vr* decompose

decomposizi'one *nf* decomposition

decompressi'one *nf* decompression

decom'primere *vt* decompress

deconcen'trarsi *vr* become distracted

deconge'lare *vt* defrost

decongestio'nare *vt* Med, fig relieve congestion in

decontami'nare *vt* Techn decontaminate

decontaminazi'one *nf* decontamination

decontrazi'one *nf* relaxation

deco'rare *vt* decorate

decora'tivo *adj* decorative

deco'rato *adj* ⟨ornato⟩ decorated

decora|'tore, -trice *nmf* decorator

decorazi'one *nf* decoration.
decorazione floreale flower arranging

de'coro *nm* decorum

decorosa'mente *adv* decorously

deco'roso *adj* dignified

decor'renza *nf* ∼ **dal** ... with effect from ..., effective from...

de'correre *vi* pass; **a** ∼ **da** with effect from

de'corso ① *pp di* DECORRERE
② *nm* passing; Med course

decre'mento *nm* decrease

de'crepito *adj* decrepit

decre'scente *adj* decreasing

de'crescere *vi* decrease; ⟨*prezzi*⟩ go down; ⟨*acque*⟩ subside

decre'tare *vt* decree; ∼ **lo stato d'emergenza** declare a state of emergency

de'creto *nm* decree. **decreto ingiuntivo** decree. **decreto legge** decree which has the force of law. **decreto legislativo** decree requiring the approval of Parliament

decre'tone *nm* Pol portmanteau bill

de'cubito *nm* **piaghe da decubito** bedsores

decur'tare *vt* reduce

decurtazi'one *nf* reduction

'dedalo *nm* maze

'dedica *nf* dedication

dedi'care *vt* dedicate

dedi'carsi *vr* dedicate oneself

'dedito *adj* ∼ **a** given to; ⟨assorto⟩ engrossed in; addicted to ⟨*vizi*⟩

dedizi'one *nf* dedication

de'dotto ① *pp di* DEDURRE
② *adj* deduced

dedu'cibile *adj* ⟨*tassa*⟩ allowable

de'durre *vt* deduce; ⟨sottrarre⟩ deduct

dedut'tivo *adj* deductive

deduzi'one *nf* deduction

défail'lance *nf inv* ⟨cedimento⟩ collapse

defal'care *vt* deduct

defalcazi'one *nf* deduction

defe'care *vi* defecate

defecazi'one *nf* defecation

defene'strare *vt* fig remove from office

defe'rente *adj* deferential

defe'renza *nf* deference

deferi'mento *nm* referral

defe'rire *vt* Jur remit

defezio'nare *vi* ⟨abbandonare⟩ defect

defezi'one *nf* defection

defezio'nista *nmf* defector

defici'ente ① *adj* ⟨mancante⟩ deficient; Med mentally deficient
② *nmf* mental defective; pej half-wit

defici'enza *nf* deficiency; ⟨lacuna⟩ gap; Med mental deficiency

'deficit *nm inv* deficit, shortfall; **essere in** ∼ be in deficit

defici'tario *adj* ⟨*bilancio*⟩ deficit *attrib*; ⟨*sviluppo*⟩ insufficient

defi'larsi *vr* ⟨scomparire⟩ slip away; ∼ **da qualcosa** sneak away from something

défi'lé *nm inv* fashion show

defi'nibile *adj* definable; ∼ **dall'utente** Comput user-definable

defi'nire *vt* define; ⟨risolvere⟩ settle

definitiva'mente *adv* for good

defini'tivo *adj* definitive

defi'nito *adj* definite

definizi'one *nf* definition; ⟨soluzione⟩ settlement

defiscaliz'zare *vt* abolish the tax on

defiscalizzazi'one *nf* abolition of tax

defla'grare *vt* (esplodere) explode

deflagrazi'one *nf* (esplosione) explosion

deflazio'nare *vt* deflate

deflazi'one *nf* deflation

deflazio'nistico *adj* deflationary

deflet'tore *nm* Auto quarterlight

deflu'ire *vi* ⟨liquidi⟩ flow away; ⟨persone⟩ stream out

de'flusso *nm* (di marea) ebb

defogli'ante ① *adj* defoliating ② *nm* defoliant

deforestazi'one *nf* deforestation

defor'mante *adj* artrite ∼ acute arthritis

defor'mare *vt* deform ⟨arto⟩; fig distort

defor'marsi *vr* lose its shape

defor'mato *adj* warped

deformazi'one *nf* (di fatti) distortion; è una ∼ professionale put it down to the job

de'forme *adj* deformed

deformità *nf inv* deformity

deframmen'tare *vt* defragment, fam defrag

defrau'dare *vt* defraud

de'funto, -a *adj & nmf* deceased

degene'rare *vi* degenerate

degenera'tivo *adj* ⟨processo⟩ degenerative

degene'rato *adj* degenerate

degenerazi'one *nf* degeneration

de'genere *adj* degenerate

de'gente ① *adj* bedridden ② *nmf* patient

de'genza *nf* confinement. **degenza ospedaliera** stay in hospital

'degli = DI + GLI

deglu'tire *vt* swallow

deglutizi'one *nf* swallowing

de'gnare *vt* ∼ qualcuno/qualcosa di uno sguardo deign or condescend to look at somebody/something

de'gnarsi *vr* deign, condescend

'degno *adj* worthy; (meritevole) deserving. **degno di lode** praiseworthy. **degno di nota** noteworthy

degrada'mento *nm* degradation

degra'dante *adj* demeaning

degra'dare *vt* degrade

degra'darsi *vr* lower oneself; ⟨città⟩ fall into a state of disrepair

degradazi'one *nf* degradation

de'grado *nm* deterioration. **degrado ambientale** environmental damage. **degrado urbano** urban blight, urban decay

degu'stare *vt* taste

degustazi'one *nf* tasting. **degustazione di vini** wine tasting

'dei = DI + I

deindiciz'zare *vt* deindex

déjà vu *nm inv* déjà vu

del = DI + IL

dela|'tore, -trice *nmf* [police] informer

delazi'one *nf* informing

'delega *nf* proxy; **legge** ∼ law that does not require Parliamentary approval

dele'gante *nmf* Jur representative

dele'gare *vt* delegate

dele'gato *nm* delegate

delegazi'one *nf* delegation

delegitti'mare *vt* delegitimize

dele'terio *adj* harmful

del'fino *nm* dolphin; (stile di nuoto) butterfly [stroke]; **nuotare a** ∼ do the butterfly

de'libera *nf* bylaw

delibe'rante *adj* ⟨organo⟩ decision making

delibe'rare *vt/i* deliberate; ∼ **su/in** rule on/in

deliberata'mente *adv* deliberately

delibe'rato *adj* (intenzionale) deliberate

delicata'mente *adv* delicately

delica'tezza *nf* delicacy; (fragilità) frailty; (tatto) tact

deli'cato *adj* delicate; ⟨salute⟩ frail; ⟨suono, colore⟩ soft

delimi'tare *vt* define

delimita'tivo *adj* defining

delimitazi'one *nf* definition

deline'are *vt* outline

deline'arsi *vr* be outlined; fig take shape

deline'ato *adj* outlined

delineazi'one *nf* outline

delinqu'ente *nmf* delinquent. **delinquente minorile** young offender. **delinquente recidivo** habitual offender

delinqu'enza *nf* delinquency. **delinquenza minorile** juvenile crime

delinquenzi'ale *adj* criminal

de'linquere *vi* commit a criminal act; **associazione per delinquere** conspiracy [to commit a crime]; **istigazione a delinquere** incitement to crime

de'liquio *nm* cadere in ∼ swoon

deli'rante *adj* Med delirious; (assurdo) insane; (sfrenato) frenzied

deli'rare *vi* be delirious

de'lirio *nm* delirium; fig frenzy; **mandare/andare in** ∼ fig send/go into a frenzy

de'litto *nm* crime. **delitto passionale** crime of passion

delittu'oso *adj* criminal

de'lizia *nf* delight

delizi'are *vt* delight

delizi'arsi *vr* ∼ **di** delight in

delizi'oso *adj* delightful; (cibo) delicious

'della = DI + LA

'delle = DI + LE

'dello = DI + LO

'delta *nm inv* delta

delta'plano *nm* hang-glider; **fare** ∼ **go** hang-gliding

deluci'dare *vt* fig clarify

delucidazi'one *nf* clarification

delu'dente *adj* disappointing

de'ludere *vt* disappoint

delusi'one *nf* disappointment

de'luso *adj* disappointed; **essere** ∼ **di** qualcosa/qualcuno be disillusioned with something/somebody

dema'gogico *adj* popularity-seeking, demagogic

dema'gogo *nm* demagogue

deman'dare *vt* entrust

demani'ale *adj* ⟨proprietà⟩ government attrib

de'manio *nm* government property

demar'care *vt* demarcate

demarcazi'one *nf* demarcation; **linea di demarcazione** demarcation line

de'mente *adj* demented

de'menza *nf* dementia. **demenza senile** senile dementia

demenzi'ale *adj* (assurdo) zany

de'merito *nm* **nota di** ∼ demerit mark

demilitariz'zare *vt* demilitarize

demilitarizzazi'one *nf* demilitarization

demistifi'care *vt* debunk

demistifica|'tore, -trice *nmf* debunker

demistifica'torio *adj* debunking

demistificazi'one *nf* debunking

demitiz'zare *vt* demythologize

demitizzazi'one *nf* demythologization

democratica'mente *adv* democratically

demo'cratico *adj* democratic

democratiz'zare *vt* democratize

democra'zia *nf* democracy

democristi'ano, -a *adj & nmf* Christian Democrat

'demodisk *nm inv* Comput demo disk

demogra'fia *nf* demography

demo'grafico *adj* demographic; **incremento demografico** increase in population

demo'lire *vt* demolish

demo'lito *adj* demolished

demolizi'one *nf* demolition

'demone *nm* demon

demo'niaco *adj* demonic

de'monio *nm* demon

demoniz'zare *vt* demonize

demonizzazi'one *nf* demonization

demoraliz'zante *adj* demoralizing

demoraliz'zare *vt* demoralize

demoraliz'zarsi *vr* become demoralized

demoraliz'zato *adj* demoralized

de'mordere *vi* give up

demoti'vare *vt* demotivate

demoti'varsi *vr* become demotivated

demoti'vato *adj* demotivated

demotivazi'one *nf* demotivation

de'nari *nmpl* (nelle carte) diamonds

de'naro *nm* money. **denaro virtuale** e-cash

denatu'rato *adj* **alcol denaturato** methylated spirits

denazionaliz'zare *vt* denationalize

deni'grare *vt* denigrate

denigra|'tore, -trice ① *adj* denigrating ② *nmf* denigrator

denigra'torio *adj* denigratory

denigrazi'one *nf* denigration

denomi'nare *vt* name

denomi'narsi *vr* be named

denomina'tivo *adj* denominative

denomina'tore *nm* denominator

denominazi'one *nf* denomination. **denominazione di origine controllata** mark guaranteeing the quality of a wine

deno'tare *vt* denote

denotazi'one *nf* denotation

densa'mente *adv* densely

densità *nf* density. **ad alta/bassa densità di popolazione** densely/ sparsely populated

'denso *adj* thick, dense

den'tale *adj* dental

den'tario *adj* dental

den'tata *nf* bite

den'tato *adj* ⟨lama⟩ serrated

denta'tura *nf* teeth *pl*; Techn serration

'dente *nm* tooth; (di forchetta) prong; (di montagna) jagged peak; **al** ∼ Culin just slightly firm; **lavarsi i denti** brush one's teeth. **dente del giudizio** wisdom tooth. **dente di latte** milk tooth. **dente di leone** Bot dandelion

'dentice *nm* dentex (type of sea bream)

denti'era *nf* dentures *pl*, false teeth *pl*; **mettersi la** ∼ put one's false teeth in

denti'fricio *nm* toothpaste

den'tista *nmf* dentist

'dentro ① *adv* in, inside; (in casa) indoors; **da** ~ from within; **qui** ~ in here; **metter** ~ (fam: in prigione) lock up, put inside ② *prep* in, inside; (di tempo) within, by ③ *nm* inside

denucleariz'zare *vt* denuclearize

denucleariz'zato *adj* nuclear-free, denuclearized

denuclearizzazi'one *nf* denuclearization

denu'dare *vt* bare

denu'darsi *vr* strip

de'nuncia *nf* denunciation; (alla polizia) reporting; **fare una** ~ draw up a report. **denuncia dei redditi** income tax return

denunci'are *vt* denounce; (accusare) report

de'nunzia = DENUNCIA

denu'trito *adj* underfed

denutrizi'one *nf* malnutrition

deodo'rante *adj* & *nm* deodorant. **deodorante antitraspirante** antiperspirant. **deodorante per ambienti** air-freshener. **deodorante a sfera** roll-on

deodo'rare *vt* deodorize

deontolo'gia *nf* (etica professionale) code of conduct

depenaliz'zare *vt* decriminalize

depenalizzazi'one *nf* decriminalization

dépen'dance *nf inv* outbuilding

depe'ribile *adj* perishable

deperi'mento *nm* wasting away; (di merci) deterioration

depe'rire *vi* waste away

depe'rito *adj* wasted

depi'lare *vt* depilate

depi'larsi *vr* shave ⟨gambe⟩; pluck ⟨sopracciglia⟩

depila'tore ① *adj* depilatory ② *nm* (apparecchio) hair remover

depila'torio *adj* depilatory

depilazi'one *nf* hair removal. **depilazione diatermica** electrolysis

depi'staggio *nm* fig diversionary manoeuvre

depi'stare *vt* fig throw off the track

dépli'ant *nm inv* brochure, leaflet

deplo'rabile *adj* deplorable

deplo'rare *vt* deplore; (dolersi di) grieve over

deplo'revole *adj* deplorable

depoliticiz'zare *vt* depoliticize

de'porre *vt* put down; lay down ⟨armi⟩; lay ⟨uova⟩; (togliere da una carica) depose; (testimoniare) testify

depor'tare *vt* deport

depor'tato, -a *nmf* deportee

deportazi'one *nf* deportation

deposi'tante *nmf* Fin depositor

deposi'tare *vt* Fin deposit; (lasciare in custodia) leave; (in magazzino) store

deposi'tario, -a *nmf* (di segreto) repository

deposi'tarsi *vr* settle

de'posito *nm* deposit; (luogo) warehouse; Mil depot. **deposito d'armi** arms dump. **deposito bagagli** left-luggage office, baggage checkroom Am. **deposito bagagli automatico** left-luggage lockers. **deposito bancario** deposit account. **deposito bancario vincolato** fixed term deposit account

deposizi'one *nf* deposition; (da una carica) removal

de'posto *adj* deposed

depotenzi'are *vt* weaken

depra'vare *vt* deprave

depra'vato *adj* depraved

depravazi'one *nf* depravity

depre'cabile *adj* appalling

depre'care *vt* deprecate

depre'dare *vt* plunder

depressio'nario *adj* **area depressionaria** Meteorol area of low pressure

depressi'one *nf* depression; **area di depressione** Meteorol area of low pressure; Econ depressed area

depres'sivo *adj* depressive

de'presso ① *pp di* DEPRIMERE ② *adj* depressed

depressuriz'zare *vt* depressurize

depressurizzazi'one *nf* depressurization

deprezza'mento *nm* depreciation

deprez'zare *vt* depreciate

deprez'zarsi *vr* depreciate

depri'mente *adj* depressing

de'primere *vt* depress

de'primersi *vr* get depressed

deprivazi'one *nf* deprivation

depu'rare *vt* purify

depu'rarsi *vr* be purified

depura'tore *nm* purifier

depurazi'one *nf* purification; (di detriti) effluent

depu'tare *vt* delegate

depu'tato, -a *nmf* ≈ Member of Parliament, MP

deputazi'one *nf* deputation

dequalifi'care *vt* disqualify

dequalifi'carsi *vr* disqualify oneself

dequalificazi'one *nf* disqualification

deraglia'mento *nm* derailment

deragli'are *vi* go off the lines; **far ~** derail

deraglia'tore *nm* derailleur gears *pl*

dera'pare *vi* Auto skid; ⟨*sciatore*⟩ sideslip

derattiz'zare *vt* clear of rats

derattizzazi'one *nf* rodent control

'derby *nm inv* Sport local derby

deregolamen'tare *vt* Comm deregulate

deregolamentazi'one *nf* deregulation

dere'litto *adj* derelict

deresponsabiliz'zare *vt* deprive of responsibility

deresponsabiliz'zarsi *vr* abdicate responsibility

deresponsabilizzazi'one *nf* depriving of responsibility

dere'tano *nm* backside, bottom

de'ridere *vt* deride

derisi'one *nf* derision

deri'sorio *adj* derisory

de'riva *nf* drift; **andare alla ~** drift

deri'vabile *adj* derivable

deri'vare ① *vi* **~ da** (provenire) derive from
   ② *vt* derive; (sviare) divert

deri'vata *nf* Math derivative

deri'vato ① *adj* derived
   ② *nm* by-product

derivazi'one *nf* derivation; (di fiume) diversion

derma'tite *nf* dermatitis

dermatolo'gia *nf* dermatology

dermato'logico *adj* dermatological

derma'tologo, **-a** *nmf* dermatologist

derma'tosi *nf* dermatosis

dermoprotet'tivo *adj* ⟨*crema*⟩ skin *attrib*; ⟨*azione*⟩ protective

'deroga *nf* dispensation

dero'gare *vi* **~ a** depart from

deroga'torio *adj* derogatory

der'rata *nf* merchandise. **derrate alimentari** *pl* foodstuffs

deru'bare *vt* rob

deru'bato *adj* robbed

desaliniz'zare *vt* desalinate

desalinizzazi'one *nf* desalination

desapare'cido *nmf* (pl **~s**) disappeared man/woman, desaparecido

descolarizzazi'one *nf* deschooling

descrit'tivo *adj* descriptive

de'scritto *pp di* DESCRIVERE

de'scrivere *vt* describe

descri'vibile *adj* describable

descrizi'one *nf* description

desensibiliz'zare *vt* desensitize

desensibilizzazi'one *nf* desensitization

de'sertico *adj* desert

de'serto ① *adj* uninhabited
   ② *nm* desert

deside'rabile *adj* desirable

deside'rare *vt* wish; (volere) want; (intensamente) long for; (bramare) desire; **desidera?** what would you like?, can I help you?; **lasciare a ~** leave a lot to be desired

deside'rato *adj* intended

desi'derio *nm* wish; (brama) desire; (intenso) longing

deside'roso *adj* desirous; (bramoso) longing

desi'gnare *vt* appoint, designate; (fissare) fix

desi'gnato *adj* designate *attrib*

designazi'one *nf* appointment

de'signer *nmf inv* designer

desi'nare ① *vi* dine
   ② *nm* dinner

desi'nenza *nf* ending

de'sistere *vi* **~ da** desist from

'desktop 'publishing *nm* desktop publishing, DTP

deso'lante *adj* distressing

deso'lare *vt* distress

deso'lato *adj* desolate; (spiacente) sorry; **siamo desolati di dovervi comunicare che ...** (in lettere) we are sorry to have to inform you that ...

desolazi'one *nf* desolation

'despota *nm* despot

desqua'marsi *vr* flake off

desquamazi'one *nf* flaking off

destabiliz'zante *adj* destabilizing

destabiliz'zare *vt* destabilize

destabilizzazi'one *nf* destabilization

de'stare *vt* waken; fig awaken

de'starsi *vr* waken; fig awaken

desti'nare *vt* destine; (nominare) appoint; (assegnare) assign; (indirizzare) address

destina'tario *nm* (di lettera, pacco) addressee

desti'nato *adj* **essere ~ a fare qualcosa** be destined *or* fated to do something

destinazi'one *nf* destination; fig purpose; **con ~ Parigi** ⟨*aereo, treno*⟩ destined for Paris

de'stino *nm* destiny; (fato) fate

destitu'ire *vt* dismiss

destitu'ito *adj* **~ di** devoid of

destituzi'one *nf* dismissal

'desto *adj* liter awake

'destra *nf* (parte) right; (mano) right hand; **prendere a ~** turn right; **a ~** ⟨*essere*⟩ on the right; ⟨*andare*⟩ to the right; **la prima a ~** the first on the right; **sulla ~** on the ⋯

right-hand side; **di** ∼ Pol right wing; **la** ∼ Pol the Right

destreggi'are *vi* manoeuvre

destreggi'arsi *vr* manoeuvre

de'strezza *nf* dexterity; (abilità) skill

'destro *adj* right; (abile) skilful

de'stroide *adj* Pol right-wing

destruttu'rato *adj* (incoerente) unstructured

desu'eto *adj* obsolete

de'sumere *vt* (congetturare) infer; (ricavare) obtain

desu'mibile *adj* inferable

detas'sare *vt* abolish the tax on

detassazi'one *nf* abolition of tax

detei'nato *adj* tannin free

dete'nere *vt* hold; ⟨polizia⟩ detain

deten'tivo *adj* **pena detentiva** custodial sentence

deten|'tore, -trice *nmf* holder. **detentore del titolo** titleholder

dete'nuto, -a *nmf* prisoner

detenzi'one *nf* detention

deter'gente ① *adj* cleaning; ⟨latte, crema⟩ cleansing ② *nm* detergent; (per la pelle) cleanser

deteriora'mento *nm* deterioration

deterio'rare *vt* cause to deteriorate ⟨cibo, relazione⟩

deterio'rarsi *vr* deteriorate

determi'nabile *adj* determinable

determinabilità *nf* determinability

determi'nante *adj* decisive

determi'nare *vt* determine

determi'narsi *vr* ∼ **a** resolve to

determina'tezza *nf* determination

determina'tivo *adj* ⟨articolo⟩ definite; **pronome** ∼ determiner

determi'nato *adj* (risoluto) determined; (particolare) specific; (stabilito) certain

determinazi'one *nf* determination; (decisione) decision

determi'nismo *nm* determinism

deter'rente *adj & nm* deterrent

deter'sivo *nm* detergent. **detersivo biologico** biological powder. **detersivo per bucato** washing powder. **detersivo per i piatti** washing-up liquid, dishwashing liquid *Am*

dete'stare *vt* detest, hate

dete'starsi *vr* hate oneself

deto'nare *vi* detonate

detona'tore *nm* detonator

detonazi'one *nf* detonation

detra'ibile *adj* deductible

de'trarre *vt* deduct (da from)

de'tratto ① pp di DETRARRE ② *adj* deducted

detrat|'tore, -trice *nmf* detractor

detrazi'one *nf* deduction; (da tasse) tax allowance

detri'mento *nm* detriment; **a** ∼ **di** to the detriment of

de'trito *nm* debris; **detriti** *pl* (di fiume) detritus. **detrito di falda** scree

detroniz'zare *vt* dethrone

'detta *nf* **a** ∼ **di** according to

dettagli'ante *nmf* Comm retailer

dettagli'are *vt* detail

dettagliata'mente *adv* in detail

det'taglio *nm* detail; **al** ∼ Comm retail

det'tame *nm* dictate; **i dettami della moda** the dictates of fashion

det'tare *vt* dictate; ∼ **legge** fig lay down the law

det'tato *nm* Sch dictation

detta'tura *nf* dictation

'detto ① pp di DIRE ② *adj* said; (chiamato) called; (soprannominato) nicknamed; ∼ **fatto** no sooner said than done ③ *nm* ∼ **[popolare]** saying

detur'pare *vt* disfigure

deturpazi'one *nf* disfigurement

deumidifi'care *vt* dehumidify

deumidifica'tore *nm* dehumidifier

deumidificazi'one *nf* dehumidification

devalutazi'one *nf* devaluation

deva'stante *adj* devastating

deva'stare *vt* devastate

deva'stato *adj* devastated

devasta|'tore, -trice ① *adj* destructive; fig devastating ② *nmf* destroyer

devastazi'one *nf* devastation; fig ravages *pl*

devi'ante *adj* deviant

devi'anza *nf* deviance

devi'are ① *vi* deviate ② *vt* divert

devi'ato *adj* ⟨mente⟩ warped

deviazi'one *nf* deviation; (stradale) diversion; **fare una** ∼ Auto make a detour

devitaliz'zare *vt* kill the nerve of, devitalize *fml*

devitalizzazi'one *nf* killing of the nerve, devitalization *fml*

devo'luto ① pp di DEVOLVERE ② *adj* devolved

devoluzi'one *nf* devolution

de'volvere *vt* devolve; ∼ **qualcosa in beneficenza** give something to charity

devota'mente *adv* devoutly

de'voto *adj* devout; (affezionato) devoted

devozi'one *nf* devotion

dg *abbr* (**decigrammi**) decigrams

di *prep* of; (partitivo) some; (scritto da) by; ⟨*parlare, pensare ecc*⟩ about; (con causa, mezzo) with; (con provenienza) from; (in comparazioni) than; (con infinito) to; **la casa di mio padre/dei miei genitori** my father's/ my parents' house; **compra del pane** buy some bread; **hai del pane?** do you have any bread?; **un film di guerra** a war film; **piangere di dolore** cry with pain; **coperto di neve** covered with snow; **sono di Genova** I'm from Genoa; **uscire di casa** leave one's house; **mi è uscito di mente** it slipped my mind; **più alto di te** taller than you; **è ora di partire** it's time to go; **crede di aver ragione** he thinks he's right; **dire di sì** say yes; **di domenica** on Sundays; **di sera** in the evening; **una pausa di un'ora** an hour's break; **un corso di due mesi** a two-month course

dia'bete *nm* diabetes

dia'betico, -a *adj & nmf* diabetic

diabolica'mente *adv* devilishly

dia'bolico *adj* diabolic[al]

di'acono *nm* deacon

dia'critico *adj* diacritic

dia'dema *nm* diadem; (di donna) tiara

di'afano *adj* diaphanous

dia'framma *nm* diaphragm; (divisione) screen

di'agnosi *nf inv* diagnosis

dia'gnostica *nf* Med diagnostics

diagnosti'care *vt* diagnose

dia'gnostici *nmpl* Comput diagnostics

dia'gnostico *adj* diagnostic

diago'nale *adj & nf* diagonal

diagonal'mente *adv* diagonally

dia'gramma *nm* diagram. **diagramma a barre** bar chart. **diagramma di flusso** flowchart

dialet'tale *adj* dialect *attrib*; **poesia dialettale** poetry in dialect

dialettaleggi'ante *adj* dialect *attrib*

dia'lettica *nf* dialectics

dia'lettico *adj* dialectic

dia'letto *nm* dialect

di'alisi *nf* dialysis

dialo'gante *adj* **unità dialogante** Comput interactive terminal

dialo'gare ①️ *vt* write the dialogue for ⟨*scena*⟩ ②️ *vi* ∼ **con** converse with

dialo'gato *adj* in dialogue

dialo'ghista *nmf* (scrittore) dialogue writer

di'alogo *nm* dialogue

dia'mante *nm* diamond

diaman'tifero *adj* diamond bearing

diametral'mente *adv* diametrically

di'ametro *nm* diameter

di'amine *int* **che** ∼ **...** what on earth ...

di'apason *nm inv* (per accordatura) tuning fork

diaposi'tiva *nf* slide

di'aria *nf* daily allowance

di'ario *nm* diary. **diario di bordo** logbook. **diario di classe** class register

dia'rista *nmf* (scrittore) diarist

diar'rea *nf* diarrhoea

di'aspora *nf* Diaspora

dia'triba *nf* diatribe

diavole'ria *nf* (azione) devilment; (marchingegno) weird contraption

diavo'letto *nm* imp; (hum: bambino) little devil

di'avolo *nm* devil; **va' al** ∼! fam go to hell!; **che** ∼ **fai?** fam what the hell are you doing?

di'battere *vt* debate

di'battersi *vr* struggle

dibattimen'tale *adj* Jur of the hearing

dibatti'mento *nm* (discussione) debate; Jur hearing

di'battito *nm* debate; (meno formale) discussion

dica'stero *nm* office

di'cembre *nm* December

dice'ria *nf* rumour

dichia'rare *vt* state; (ufficialmente) declare; ∼ **colpevole** Jur convict; **niente da** ∼? anything to declare?

dichia'rarsi *vr* (in amore) declare one's love; ∼ **soddisfatto** declare oneself satisfied; **si dichiara innocente** he says he's innocent; ∼ **a favore di qualcosa** declare oneself in favour of something; **si dichiara che ...** (in documenti) it is hereby declared that ...; ∼ **vinto** acknowledge defeat

dichia'rato *adj* avowed

dichiarazi'one *nf* statement; (documento, di guerra, d'amore) declaration; **fare una** ∼ (ufficialmente) make a statement. **dichiarazione dei diritti** Pol bill of rights. **dichiarazione doganale** customs declaration. **dichiarazione dei redditi** [income] tax return

dician'nove *adj & nm* nineteen

dicianno'venne *adj & nmf* nineteen-year-old

dicianno'vesimo *adj & nm* nineteenth

dicias'sette *adj & nm* seventeen

diciasset'tenne *adj & nmf* seventeen-year-old

diciasset'tesimo *adj & nm* seventeenth

diciot'tenne *adj & nmf* eighteen-year-old

diciot'tesimo *adj & nm* eighteenth

dici'otto *adj & nm* eighteen

dici'tura *nf* wording

dicoto'mia *nf* dichotomy

didasca'lia *nf* (di film) subtitle; (di illustrazione) caption; Theat stage direction

dida'scalico *adj* ‹letteratura› didactic

di'dattica *nf* didactics

didattica'mente *adv* didactically

di'dattico *adj* didactic; ‹televisione› educational

di'dentro *adv* inside

didi'etro ① *adv* behind ② *nm* hum hindquarters *pl*

di'eci *adj & nm* ten

dieci'mila *adj & nm* ten thousand

die'cina = DECINA

di'eresi *nf* diaeresis

'diesel *adj & nm inv* diesel

di'esis *nm inv* sharp

di'eta *nf* diet; a ~ on a diet

die'tetica *nf* dietetics

die'tetico *adj* diet

die'tista *nmf* dietician

die'tologo *nmf* dietician

di'etro ① *adv* behind ② *prep* behind; (dopo) after ③ *adj* back; ‹zampe› hind ④ *nm* back; **le stanze di** ~ the back rooms; **le zampe di** ~ the hind legs

dietro'front *nm inv* about-turn; fig U-turn; ~! about turn!

dietrolo'gia *nf* investigative journalism

di'fatti *adv* in fact

di'fendere *vt* defend

di'fendersi *vr* defend oneself; (fam: cavarsela) get by

difen'dibile *adj* defendable, defensible

difen'siva *nf* stare sulla ~ be on the defensive

difen'sivo *adj* defensive

difen'sore ① *adj* avvocato difensore defence counsel ② *nm* defender. **difensore civico** ombudsman

di'fesa *nf* defence; **prendere le difese di qualcuno** come to somebody's defence. **difesa civile** Civil Defence

di'feso ① pp di DIFENDERE ② *adj* defended; (luogo) sheltered

difet'tare *vi* be defective; ~ di lack

difet'tivo *adj* defective

di'fetto *nm* defect; (morale) fault, flaw; (mancanza) lack; (in tessuto, abito) flaw; **essere in** ~ be at fault; **far** ~ be lacking. **difetto di pronuncia** speech impediment

difet'toso *adj* defective; ‹abito› flawed

diffa'mare *vt* (con parole) slander; (per iscritto) libel

diffama|'tore, -trice *nmf* slanderer; (per iscritto) libeller

diffama'torio *adj* slanderous; (per iscritto) libellous

diffamazi'one *nf* slander; (scritta) libel

diffe'rente *adj* different

differente'mente *adv* differently

diffe'renza *nf* difference; **a** ~ **di** unlike; **non fare** ~ make no distinction (**fra** between). **differenza di fuso orario** time difference

differenzi'abile *adj* differentiable

differenzi'ale *adj & nm* differential

differenzi'are *vt* differentiate

differenzi'arsi *vr* ~ **da** differ from

differenzi'ato *adj* differentiated

differenziazi'one *nf* differentiation

diffe'ribile *adj* postponable

diffe'rire ① *vt* postpone ② *vi* be different

diffe'rita *nf* in ~ TV prerecorded

dif'ficile ① *adj* difficult; (duro) hard; (improbabile) unlikely ② *nm* difficulty

difficil'mente *adv* with difficulty

difficoltà *nf inv* difficulty; **trovarsi in** ~ be in trouble; **mettere qualcuno in** ~ put somebody on the spot. **difficoltà d'apprendimento** special needs; **bambini con** ~ **d'apprendimento** children with special needs

dif'fida *nf* warning

diffi'dare ① *vi* ~ **di** distrust ② *vt* warn

diffi'dente *adj* mistrustful

diffi'denza *nf* mistrust

dif'fondere *vt* spread; diffuse ‹calore, luce ecc›

dif'fondersi *vr* spread

difformità *nf inv* deformation; (di opinioni) difference of opinion

diffusa'mente *adv* at length

diffusi'one *nf* diffusion; (di giornale) circulation

dif'fuso ① pp di DIFFONDERE ② *adj* common; ‹malattia› widespread; ‹luce› diffuse

diffu'sore *nm* (per asciugacapelli) diffuser

difi'lato *adv* straight; (subito) straightaway

di'fronte *adj inv & adv* opposite; ~ **all'ingresso** in front of the entrance; (dall'altro lato della strada) opposite the entrance

difte'rite *nf* diphtheria

'diga *nf* dam; (argine) dike

dige'rente *adj* alimentary

dige'ribile *adj* digestible

digeribilità *nf* digestibility

dige'rire *vt* digest; fam stomach

digesti'one *nf* digestion

dige'stivo [1] *adj* digestive
[2] *nm* digestive; (dopo cena) liqueur

Digi'one *nf* Dijon

digi'tale [1] *adj* digital; (delle dita) finger *attrib*
[2] *nf* (fiore) foxglove

digitaliz'zare *vt* digitalize

digitalizzazi'one *nf* digitalizing

digi'tare *vt* key in ⟨dati⟩

digiu'nare *vi* fast

digi'uno [1] *adj* essere ∼ have an empty stomach
[2] *nm* fast; a ∼ ⟨bere ecc⟩ on an empty stomach

dignità *nf* dignity

digni'tario *nm* dignitary

dignitosa'mente *adv* with dignity

digni'toso *adj* dignified

DIGOS *nf abbr* (**Divisione Investigazioni Generali e Operazioni Speciali**) ≈ riot police

digressi'one *nf* digression

dIgri'gnare *vi* ∼ i denti grind one's teeth

digros'sare *vt* fig impart basic concepts to

dik'tat *nm inv* (trattato) diktat

dila'gare *vi* flood; fig spread

dilani'are *vt* tear to pieces

dilapi'dare *vt* squander

dilapidazi'one *nf* squandering

dila'tare *vt* dilate

dila'tarsi *vr* dilate; ⟨legno⟩ swell; ⟨metallo, gas⟩ expand

dila'tato *adj* dilated; ⟨legno⟩ swollen; ⟨metallo, gas⟩ expanded

dilatazi'one *nf* dilation; (di legno) swelling; (di metallo, gas) expansion

dilazio'nabile *adj* postponable

dilazio'nare *vt* delay

dilazi'one *nf* delay

dileggi'are *vt* mock

dilegu'are *vt* disperse

dilegu'arsi *vr* disappear

di'lemma *nm* dilemma

dilet'tante *nmf* amateur

dilettan'tesco *adj* amateurish

dilettan'tismo *nm* amateurism

dilettan'tistico *adj* amateurish

dilet'tare *vt* delight

dilet'tarsi *vr* ∼ di delight in

dilet'tevole *adj* delightful

di'letto, -a [1] *adj* beloved
[2] *nm* (piacere) delight
[3] *nmf* (persona) beloved

dili'gente *adj* diligent; ⟨lavoro⟩ accurate

dili'genza *nf* diligence

dilu'ente *nm* Techn diluent; (per vernici) thinner

dilu'ire *vt* dilute

diluizi'one *nf* dilution

dilun'gare *vt* prolong

dilun'garsi *vr* ∼ su dwell on ⟨argomento⟩

diluvi'are *vi* pour [down]

di'luvio *nm* downpour; fig flood. il ∼ universale the Flood

dima'grante *adj* slimming, diet

dimagri'mento *nm* loss of weight

dima'grire *vi* lose weight

dima'grirsi *vr* lose weight

dime'nare *vt* wave; wag ⟨coda⟩

dime'narsi *vr* be agitated

dimensio'nare *vt* fig get into proportion

dimensi'one *nf* dimension; (misura) size

dimenti'canza *nf* forgetfulness; (svista) oversight; per ∼ accidentally

dimenti'care *vt* forget; l'ho dimenticato a casa I left it at home

dimenti'carsi *vr* ∼ [di] forget

dimentica'toio *nm* andare/finire nel ∼ hum fall into oblivion

di'mentico *adj* ∼ di (che non ricorda) forgetful of; (non curante) oblivious of

dimessa'mente *adv* modestly

di'messo [1] pp di DIMETTERE
[2] *adj* humble; (trasandato) shabby; ⟨voce⟩ low

dimesti'chezza *nf* familiarity

di'mettere *vt* dismiss; (da ospedale ecc) discharge

di'mettersi *vr* resign

dimez'zare *vt* halve

diminu'ire *vt/i* diminish; (in maglia) decrease

diminu'ito *adj* Mus diminished

diminu'tivo *adj* & *nm* diminutive

diminuzi'one *nf* decrease; (riduzione) reduction; in ∼ dwindling

dimissio'nario [1] *adj* outgoing
[2] *nmf* outgoing chairman/president etc

dimissi'oni *nfpl* resignation *sg*; dare le ∼ resign

di'mora *nf* residence

dimo'rare *vi* reside

dimo'strabile *adj* demonstrable

dimostrabilità *nf* demonstrability

dimo'strante *nmf* demonstrator

dimo'strare *vt* demonstrate; (provare) prove; (mostrare) show

dimo'strarsi *vr* prove [to be]

dimostra'tivo *adj* demonstrative

dimostrazi'one *nf* demonstration; Math proof

di'namica *nf* dynamics; ∼ dei fatti sequence of events

di'namico *adj* dynamic

dina'mismo *nm* dynamism

dlnami'tardo, -a [1] *adj* **attentato dinamitardo** bomb attack
[2] *nmf* bomber

dina'mite *nf* dynamite

'dinamo *nf inv* dynamo

di'nanzi [1] *adv* in front
[2] *prep* ∼ a in front of

'dinaro *nm* (moneta) dinar

dina'stia *nf* dynasty

di'nastico *adj* dynastic

din'don *nm inv* dingdong

'dingo *nm inv* (cane) dingo

dini'ego *nm* denial

dinocco'lato *adj* lanky

dino'sauro *nm* dinosaur

din'torni *nmpl* outskirts; **nei ∼ di** in the vicinity of

din'torno *adv* around

'dio *nm* (pl **dei**) god; **Dio** God; **Dio mio!** my God!

dioce'sano *adj* diocesan

di'ocesi *nf inv* diocese

dioni'siaco *adj* Dionysian

dios'sina *nf* dioxin

diot'tria *nf* dioptre

dipa'nare *vt* wind into a ball; fig unravel

diparti'mento *nm* department

dipen'dente [1] *adj* depending
[2] *nmf* employee

dipen'denza *nf* dependence; (edificio) annexe

di'pendere *vi* ∼ da depend on; (provenire) derive from; **dipende** it depends

di'pingere *vt* paint; (descrivere) describe

di'pinto [1] *pp di* DIPINGERE
[2] *adj* painted
[3] *nm* painting

di'ploma *nm* diploma

diplo'mare *vt* graduate

diplo'marsi *vr* graduate

diplomatica'mente *adv* diplomatically

diplo'matico [1] *adj* diplomatic
[2] *nm* diplomat; (pasticcino) millefeuille (with alcohol)

diplo'mato [1] *nmf* person with school qualification
[2] *adj* qualified

diploma'zia *nf* diplomacy

di'porto *nm* **imbarcazione da** ∼ pleasure craft

dirada'mento *nf* thinning out

dira'dare *vt* thin out; make less frequent ⟨visite⟩

dira'darsi *vr* thin out; ⟨nebbia⟩ clear

dira'mare *vt* issue

dira'marsi *vr* branch out

diramazi'one *nf* (di strada, fiume) fork; (di albero, impresa) branch; (di ordine) issuing

'dire [1] *vt* say; (raccontare, riferire) tell; ∼ quello che si pensa speak one's mind; **voler ∼** mean; **volevo ben ∼!** I wondered!; **∼ di sì/no** say yes/no; **si dice che ...** rumour has it that ...; **come si dice "casa" in inglese?** what's the English for "casa"?; **questo nome mi dice qualcosa** the name rings a bell; **che ne dici di ...?** how about ...?; **non c'è che ∼** there's no disputing that; **e ∼ che ...** to think that ...; **a dir poco/tanto** at least/most
[2] *vi* ∼ bene/male di speak highly/ill of somebody; **dica pure** (in negozio) how can I help you?; **dici sul serio?** are you serious?; **per modo di ∼** as it were

di'retta *nf* TV live broadcast; **in ∼** live

diretta'mente *adv* directly

diret'tissima *nf* (strada) main route; **per ∼** Jur ⟨processare⟩ without going through the normal procedures

diret'tissimo *nm* fast train

diret'tiva *nf* directive; **direttive** *pl* (indicazioni) guidelines

diret'tivo [1] *adj* (dirigente) management *attrib*, managerial
[2] *nm* Pol executive

di'retto [1] *pp di* DIRIGERE
[2] *adj* direct; **il mio ∼ superiore** my immediate superior; **∼ a** (inteso) meant for; **essere ∼ a** be heading for; **in diretta** ⟨trasmissione⟩ live
[3] *nm* (treno) through train

diret'tore *nm* manager; (più in alto nella gerarchia) director; (di scuola) headmaster. **direttore amministrativo** company secretary. **direttore artistico** artistic director. **direttore del carcere** prison governor. **direttore di filiale** branch manager. **direttore di gara** referee. **direttore generale** managing director, chief executive officer. **direttore di giornale** newspaper editor. **direttore d'istituto** Univ department head. **direttore d'orchestra** conductor. **direttore del personale** personnel manager/director. **direttore di produzione** production manager/ director. **direttore spirituale** spiritual advisor. **direttore sportivo** team manager. **direttore tecnico** Sport manager. **direttore di zona** area manager, regional director

diret'trice *nf* manageress; (di scuola) headmistress; (indirizzo) guiding principle

direzio'nale *adj* directional

direzio'nare *vt* direct

direzi'one *nf* direction; (di società) management; Sch headmaster's/

headmistress's office (*primary school*); **in ~ nord** (traffico) northbound; **'tutte le direzioni'** Auto 'all routes'

diri'gente ① *adj* ruling ② *nmf* executive. **dirigente d'azienda** company director. **dirigente di partito** Pol party leader

diri'genza *nf* (gestione) management; (i dirigenti) top management; Pol leadership. **dirigenza aziendale** business management

dirigenzi'ale *adj* management *attrib*, managerial

di'rigere *vt* direct; conduct ⟨*orchestra*⟩; run ⟨*impresa*⟩

di'rigersi *vr* **~ verso** head for

diri'gibile *nm* airship

dirim'petto ① *adv* opposite ② *prep* **~ a** facing

di'ritto¹ ① *adj* straight; (destro) right ② *adv* straight; **andare ~** go straight on; **sempre ~** straight ahead, straight on ③ *nm* right side; Tennis forehand; **fare un ~** (a maglia) knit one

di'ritto² *nm* right; Jur law. **diritti degli animali** *pl* animal rights. **diritti d'autore** *pl* royalties. **diritti civili** *pl* civil rights. **diritti di prelievo** *pl* Fin drawing rights. **diritti umani** *pl* human rights. **diritto civile** civil law. **diritto commerciale** commercial law. **diritto penale** criminal law. **diritto di voto** right to vote, suffrage

dirit'tura *nf* straight line; fig honesty. **~ d'arrivo** Sport, fig home straight

diroc'cato *adj* tumbledown

dirom'pente *adj* anche fig explosive

dirotta'mento *nm* hijacking

dirot'tare ① *vt* reroute ⟨*treno, aereo*⟩; (illegalmente) hijack; divert ⟨*traffico*⟩ ② *vi* alter course

dirotta'|tore, -trice *nmf* hijacker, (solo di aereo) skyjacker

di'rotto *adj* ⟨*pioggia*⟩ pouring; ⟨*pianto*⟩ uncontrollable; **piovere a ~** rain heavily

di'rupo *nm* precipice

di'sabile ① *adj* disabled ② *nmf* disabled person

disabili'tare *vt* disable

disabi'tato *adj* uninhabited

disabitu'arsi *vr* **~ a** get out of the habit of

disac'cordo *nm* disagreement

disadatta'mento *nm* maladjustment

disadat'tato, -a ① *adj* maladjusted ② *nmf* misfit

disa'dorno *adj* unadorned

disaffezi'one *nf* disaffection

disa'gevole *adj* (scomodo) uncomfortable; (difficile) inconvenient

disagi'ato *adj* poor; ⟨*vita*⟩ hard; (scomodo) uncomfortable

di'sagio *nm* discomfort; (difficoltà) inconvenience; (imbarazzo) embarrassment, uneasiness; **sentirsi a ~** feel uncomfortable; **disagi** *pl* (privazioni) hardships

di'samina *nf* close examination

disamora'mento *nm* estrangement

disanco'rare *vt* Fin de-link

disappro'vare *vt* disapprove of

disapprovazi'one *nf* disapproval

disap'punto *nm* disappointment; **con suo grande ~** [much] to his chagrin

disarcio'nare *vt* unseat

disar'mante *adj* fig disarming

disar'mare *vt/i* disarm

disar'mato *adj* disarmed; fig defenceless

di'sarmo *nm* disarmament

disartico'lato *adj* fig disjointed

disa'strato, -a ① *adj* devastated ② *nmf* victim (of flood, earthquake ecc)

di'sastro *nm* disaster; (fam: grande confusione) mess; (fam: persona) disaster area. **disastro aereo** air crash

disastrosa'mente *adv* disastrously

disa'stroso *adj* disastrous

disat'tento *adj* inattentive

disattenzi'one *nf* inattention; (svista) oversight

disatti'vare *vt* de-activate

disa'vanzo *nm* deficit

disavve'duto *adj* thoughtless

disavven'tura *nf* misadventure

disavver'tenza *nf* inadvertence

di'sbrigo *nm* dispatch

di'scapito *nm* **a ~ di** to the detriment of

di'scarica *nf* scrap-yard

di'scarico *nm* (di merce) unloading; **prova a discarico** evidence for the defence; **testimone a discarico** witness for the defence

discen'dente ① *adj* descending ② *nmf* descendant

discen'denza *nf* descent; (discendenti) descendants *pl*

di'scendere ① *vi* (dal treno) get off; (da cavallo) dismount; (sbarcare) land; **~ da** (trarre origine da) be a descendant of ② *vt* descend

discen'sore *nm* (attrezzo) karabiner

di'scepolo, -a *nmf* disciple

di'scernere *vt* discern

discerni'mento *nm* discernment

di'scesa *nf* descent; (pendio) slope; **~ in picchiata** (di aereo) nosedive; **essere in ~** ⟨*strada*⟩ go downhill. **discesa libera** (in sci) downhill race

disce'sista *nmf* (sciatore) downhill skier

di'sceso pp di DISCENDERE

di'schetto nm Comput diskette

dischi'udere vt open; (svelare) disclose

dischi'udersi vr open up

di'scinto adj scantily dressed

disci'ogliere vt dissolve; thaw ⟨neve⟩; (fondersi) melt

disci'olto pp di DISCIOGLIERE

disci'plina nf discipline

discipli'nare ① adj disciplinary ② vt discipline

discipli'nato adj disciplined

disc-'jockey nm inv disc jockey, DJ

'disco nm disc; Sport discus; Mus record; ernia del disco slipped disc. **disco a 33 giri** LP. **disco a 45 giri** single. **disco fisso** Comput fixed disk, hard disk. **disco dei freni** brake disc. **disco master** Comput master disk. **disco rigido** Comput hard disk. **disco volante** flying saucer

discogra'fia nf (insieme di incisioni) discography; (industria) record industry

disco'grafico ① adj ⟨industria⟩ record attrib, recording; ⟨mercato, raccolta⟩ record attrib; **casa discografica** record company, recording company ② nmf record producer

'discolo ① nmf rascal ② adj unruly

di'scolpa nf clearing; **a sua ~ si deve dire che ...** in his defence it must be said that ...

discol'pare vt clear

discol'parsi vr clear oneself

disco'noscere vt deny; disown ⟨figlio⟩

discontinuità nf (nel lavoro) irregularity; (di stile) unevenness

discon'tinuo adj intermittent; fig ⟨impegno, rendimento⟩ uneven

discopa'tia nf disc problems pl

discor'dante adj discordant

discor'danza nf discordance; **essere in ~** clash

discor'dare vi ⟨opinioni⟩ conflict

di'scorde adj clashing

di'scordia nf discord; (dissenso) dissension

di'scorrere vi talk (**di** about)

discor'sivo adj colloquial

di'scorso ① pp di DISCORRERE ② nm speech; (conversazione) talk. **discorso indiretto** indirect speech. **discorso di ringraziamento** vote of thanks

di'scosto ① adj distant ② adv far away; **stare ~** stand apart

disco'teca nf disco; (raccolta) record library

discote'caro, -a nmf pej disco freak

di'scount nm inv discount store

discredi'tare vt discredit

di'scredito nm discredit

discre'pante adj contradictory

discre'panza nf discrepancy

di'screto adj discreet; (moderato) moderate; (abbastanza buono) fairly good

discrezionalità nf discretion

discrezi'one nf discretion; (giudizio) judgement; **a ~ di** at the discretion of

discrimi'nante ① adj extenuating ② nf Jur extenuating circumstances pl

discrimi'nare vt discriminate

discrimina'tivo adj ⟨provvedimento⟩ discriminatory

discrimina'torio adj ⟨atteggiamento⟩ discriminatory

discriminazi'one nf discrimination. **discriminazione in base all'età** age discrimination. **discriminazione sessuale** sexual discrimination

discussi'one nf discussion; (alterco) argument; **messa in ~** questioning

di'scusso ① pp di DISCUTERE ② adj controversial

di'scutere ① vt discuss; (formale) debate; (litigare) argue ② vi **~ su qualcosa** discuss something

discu'tibile adj debatable; ⟨gusto⟩ questionable

disde'gnare vt disdain

di'sdegno nm disdain

disde'gnoso adj disdainful

di'sdetta nf retraction; (sfortuna) bad luck; Comm cancellation

di'sdetto pp di DISDIRE

disdi'cevole adj unbecoming

di'sdire vt retract; (annullare) cancel

disedu'care vt have a bad effect on

diseduca'tivo adj bad for children

dise'gnare vt draw; (progettare) design

disegna|'tore, -trice nmf designer. **disegnatore di moda** fashion designer

di'segno nm drawing; (progetto, linea) design. **disegno di legge** bill. **disegno in scala** scale drawing. **disegno tecnico** technical drawing. **disegno dal vero** life drawing

diser'bante ① nm herbicide, weed-killer ② adj herbicidal, weed-killing

diser'bare vt weed

disere'dare vt disinherit

disere'dato ① adj dispossessed ② nmf **i diseredati** the dispossessed

diser'tare vt/i desert; **~ la scuola** stay away from school

diser'tore nm deserter

diserzi'one nf desertion

disfaci'mento *nm* decay; fig decline; **in** ~ decaying; fig in decline

di'sfare *vt* undo; strip ⟨*letto*⟩; (smantellare) take down; (annientare) defeat; ~ **le valigie** unpack [one's bags]

di'sfarsi *vr* fall to pieces; (sciogliersi) melt; ~ **di** (liberarsi di) get rid of

di'sfatta *nf* defeat

disfat'tismo *nm* defeatism

disfat'tista *adj & nmf* defeatist

di'sfatto *adj* fig worn out

disfunzio'nale *adj* dysfunctional

disfunzi'one *nf* disorder

disge'lare *vt/i* thaw

disge'larsi *vr* thaw

di'sgelo *nm* thaw

disgi'ungere *vt* disconnect

disgi'unto *adj* ⟨*firme*⟩ separate

di'sgrazia *nf* misfortune; (incidente) accident; (sfavore) disgrace

disgraziata'mente *adv* unfortunately

disgrazi'ato, **-a** ① *adj* unfortunate ② *nmf* wretch

disgrega'mento *nm* disintegration

disgre'gare *vt* break up

disgre'garsi *vr* disintegrate

disgrega'tivo *adj* disintegrating

disgrega'tore *adj* disintegrating

disgregazi'one *nf* (di società) break-up

disgu'ido *nm* **disguido postale** mistake in delivery

disgu'stare *vt* disgust

disgu'starsi *vr* ~ **di** be disgusted by

di'sgusto *nm* disgust

disgustosa'mente *adv* disgustingly; ~ **dolce** nauseatingly sweet

disgu'stoso *adj* disgusting

disidra'tante *adj* dehydrating

disidra'tare *vt* dehydrate

disidra'tarsi *vr* become dehydrated

disidra'tato *adj* dehydrated

disidratazi'one *nf* dehydration

disil'ludere *vt* disenchant, disillusion

disil'ludersi *vr* become disenchanted, become disillusioned

disillusi'one *nf* disenchantment, disillusionment

disil'luso *adj* disenchanted, disillusioned

disimbal'laggio *nm* unpacking

disimbal'lare *vt* unpack

disimpa'rare *vt* forget

disimpe'gnare *vt* release; (compiere) fulfil; redeem ⟨*oggetto dato in pegno*⟩

disimpe'gnarsi *vr* disengage oneself; (cavarsela) manage

disim'pegno *nm* (locale) vestibule; (disinteresse) lack of interest

disimpi'ego *nm* re-allocation; (di truppe) reassignment

disincagli'are *vt* Naut refloat

disincagli'arsi *vr* Naut float off

disincan'tato *adj* (disilluso) disillusioned, disenchanted

disincar'nato *adj* disembodied

disincenti'vante *adj* demotivating

disincenti'vare *vt* demotivate

disincen'tivo *nm* disincentive

disincroci'are *vt* uncross

disinfe'stare *vt* disinfest

disinfestazi'one *nf* disinfestation

disinfet'tante *adj & nm* disinfectant

disinfet'tare *vt* disinfect

disinfezi'one *nf* disinfection

disinfiam'marsi *vr* become less inflamed

disinflazio'nare *vt* disinflate

disinflazi'one *nf* disinflation

disinflazio'nistico *adj* disinflationary

disinfor'mato *adj* uninformed

disinformazi'one *nf* lack of information; (informazione erronea) misinformation

disingan'nare *vt* disabuse

disin'ganno *nm* disillusion

disini'birsi *vr* lose one's inhibitions

disini'bito *adj* uninhibited

disinne'scare *vt* defuse

disin'nesco *nm* (di bomba) bomb disposal

disinne'stare *vt* disengage

disinne'starsi *vr* disengage

disin'nesto *nm* disengagement

disinquina'mento *nm* cleaning up

disinqui'nare *vt* clean up

disinse'rire *vt* disconnect

disinse'rito *adj* disconnected

disinte'grare *vt* disintegrate

disinte'grarsi *vr* disintegrate

disintegrazi'one *nf* disintegration

disinteressa'mento *nm* lack of interest

disinteres'sarsi *vr* ~ **di** take no interest in

disinteressata'mente *adv* without interest; (senza secondo fine) disinterestedly

disinteres'sato *adj* uninterested; (senza secondo fine) disinterested

disinte'resse *nm* indifference; (oggettività) disinterestedness

disintossi'care *vt* detoxify

disintossi'carsi *vr* come off drugs; ⟨*alcolizzato*⟩ dry out, detox

disintossicazi'one *nf* giving up alcohol/drugs, detox; **programma di** ~ detox programme

disinvolta'mente *adv* in a relaxed way

disin'volto *adj* relaxed

disinvol'tura *nf* confidence

disi'stima *nf* lack of respect

disles'sia *nf* dyslexia

di'slessico *adj* dyslexic

disli'vello *nm* difference in height; fig inequality

disloca'mento *nm* Mil posting

dislo'care *vt* Mil post

dismenor'rea *nf* dysmenorrhoea

dismi'sura *nf* excess; a ∼ excessively

disobbedi'ente *adj* disobedient

disobbe'dire *vt* disobey

disoccu'pato, -a ① *adj* unemployed ② *nmf* unemployed person

disoccupazi'one *nf* unemployment

disonestà *nf* dishonesty

diso'nesto *adj* dishonest

disono'rare *vt* dishonour

disono'rato *adj* dishonoured

diso'nore *nm* dishonour

di'sopra ① *adv* above ② *adj* upper ③ *nm* top

disordi'nare *vt* disarrange

disordinata'mente *adv* untidily

disordi'nato *adj* untidy; (sregolato) immoderate

di'sordine *nm* disorder, untidiness; (sregolatezza) debauchery

disores'sia *nf* eating disorder

disor'ganico *adj* inconsistent

disorganiz'zare *vt* disorganize

disorganiz'zato *adj* disorganized

disorganizzazi'one *nf* disorganization

disorienta'mento *nm* disorientation

disorien'tare *vt* disorientate

disorien'tarsi *vr* lose one's bearings

disorien'tato *adj* fig bewildered

disos'sare *vt* bone

disos'sato *adj* boned

di'sotto ① *adv* below ② *adj* lower ③ *nm* bottom

di'spaccio *nm* dispatch

dispa'rato *adj* disparate

'dispari *adj* odd, uneven

dispa'rire *vi* disappear

disparità *nf inv* disparity

di'sparte *adv* in ∼ apart; stare in ∼ stand aside

di'spendio *nm* expenditure; pej waste

dispendiosa'mente *adv* extravagantly

dispendi'oso *adj* expensive

di'spensa *nf* pantry; (distribuzione) distribution; (mobile) cupboard; Jur exemption; Relig dispensation; (pubblicazione periodica) number

dispen'sare *vt* distribute; (esentare) exonerate

dispen'sario *nm* dispensary

di'spenser *nm inv* display rack; (confezione) dispenser

dispe'rare *vi* despair (di of)

dispe'rarsi *vr* despair

disperata'mente *adv* ⟨piangere⟩ desperately; ⟨studiare⟩ like mad

dispe'rato *adj* desperate; ⟨tentativo⟩ last-ditch

disperazi'one *nf* despair

di'sperdere *vt* scatter, disperse

di'sperdersi *vr* scatter, disperse

dispersi'one *nf* dispersion; (di truppe) dispersal

disper'sivo *adj* disorganized

di'sperso ① *pp di* DISPERDERE ② *adj* scattered; (smarrito) lost ③ *nm* missing soldier

di'spetto *nm* spite; a ∼ di in spite of; fare un ∼ a qualcuno spite somebody

dispet'toso *adj* spiteful

dispia'cere ① *nm* upset; (rammarico) regret; (dolore) sorrow; (preoccupazione) worry ② *vi* mi dispiace I'm sorry; non mi dispiace I don't dislike it; se non ti dispiace if you don't mind

dispiaci'uto *adj* sorry

dispie'gare *vt* unfold

dispie'garsi *vr* unfurl

dispo'nibile *adj* available; (gentile) helpful

disponibilità *nf* availability; (gentilezza) helpfulness. **disponibilità correnti** *pl* Fin current assets

di'sporre ① *vt* arrange ② *vi* dispose; (stabilire) order; ∼ di have at one's disposal

di'sporsi *vr* (in fila) line up

disposi'tivo *nm* device. **dispositivo di emergenza** emergency button/handle. **dispositivo di puntamento** Comput pointing device

disposizi'one *nf* disposition; (ordine) order; (libera disponibilità) disposal

di'sposto ① *pp di* DISPORRE ② *adj* ready; (incline) disposed; **essere ben disposto verso** be favourably disposed towards

dispotica'mente *adv* despotically

di'spotico *adj* despotic

dispo'tismo *nm* despotism

dispregia'tivo *adj* disparaging

disprez'zabile *adj* despicable

disprez'zare *vt* despise
di'sprezzo *nm* contempt
'disputa *nf* dispute
dispu'tare *vi* dispute; (gareggiare) compete
dispu'tarsi *vr* ~ **qualcosa** contend for something
disqui'sire *vi* discourse
disquisizi'one *nf* disquisition
dissa'crante *adj* debunking
dissa'crare *vt* debunk
dissacra|'tore, -trice *nmf* debunker
dissacra'torio *adj* debunking
dissacrazi'one *nf* debunking
dissangua'mento *nm* loss of blood; fig impoverishment
dissangu'are *vt* bleed; fig bleed dry
dissangu'arsi *vr* bleed; fig become impoverished
dissangu'ato *adj* bloodless; fig impoverished
dissa'pore *nm* disagreement
dissec'care *vt* dry up
dissec'carsi *vr* dry up
dissemi'nare *vt* disseminate; (notizie) spread
dissen'nato *adj* ⟨politica⟩ senseless
dis'senso *nm* dissent; (disaccordo) disagreement
dissente'ria *nf* dysentery
dissen'tire *vi* disagree (**da** with)
disseppelli'mento *nm* exhumation
disseppel'lire *vt* exhume ⟨cadavere⟩; disinter ⟨rovine⟩; fig unearth
dissertazi'one *nf* dissertation
disser'vizio *nm* poor service
disse'stare *vt* upset; Comm damage
disse'stato *adj* ⟨strada⟩ uneven; ⟨azienda⟩ shaky
dis'sesto *nm* ruin
disse'tante *adj* thirst-quenching
disse'tare *vt* ~ **qualcuno** quench somebody's thirst
disse'tarsi *vr* quench one's thirst
dissezio'nare *vr* dissect
dissezi'one *nf* dissection
dissi'dente *adj* & *nmf* dissident
dissi'denza *nf* dissidence
dis'sidio *nm* disagreement
dis'simile *adj* unlike, dissimilar
dissimu'lare *vt* conceal
dissimu'lato *adj* concealed
dissimula|'tore, -trice *nmf* dissembler
dissimulazi'one *nf* concealment
dissi'pare *vt* dissipate; (sperperare) squander

dissi'parsi *vr* ⟨nebbia⟩ clear; ⟨dubbio⟩ disappear
dissipa'tezza *nf* dissipation
dissi'pato *adj* dissipated
dissipa'tore *nm* **dissipatore termico** heat sink
dissipazi'one *nf* squandering
dissoci'abile *adj* separable
dissoci'are *vt* dissociate
dissoci'arsi *vr* dissociate oneself
dissoci'ato, -a ① *adj* Pol dissenting ② *nmf* Pol dissenter
dissociazi'one *nf* Pol dissociation
dissoda'mento *nm* tillage
disso'dare *vt* till
dis'solto *pp* di DISSOLVERE
disso'lubile *adj* dissoluble
dissolu'tezza *nf* dissoluteness
dissolu'tivo *adj* divisive
disso'luto *adj* dissolute
dissol'venza *nf* (di immagine) fade-out, dissolve
dis'solvere *vt* dissolve; (disperdere) dispel
dis'solversi *vr* dissolve; (disperdersi) clear
disso'nante *adj* dissonant
disso'nanza *nf* dissonance
dissotterra'mento *nm* disinterment
dissotter'rare *vt* disinter ⟨bara⟩; fig resurrect ⟨rancore⟩
dissua'dere *vt* dissuade
dissuasi'one *nf* dissuasion
dissua'sivo *adj* dissuasive
distacca'mento *nm* Mil detachment
distac'care *vt* detach; Sport leave behind
distac'carsi *vr* be detached
distac'cato *adj* ⟨tono, voce⟩ expressionless
di'stacco *nm* detachment; (separazione) separation; Sport lead
di'stante ① *adj* far away; fig ⟨person⟩ detached ② *adv* far away
di'stanza *nf* distance
distanzia'mento *nm* spacing [out]; Sport outdistancing
distanzi'are *vt* space out; Sport outdistance
di'stare *vi* be distant; **quanto dista?** how far is it?; **Roma dista 20 chilometri da qui** Rome is 20 kilometres away, Rome is 20 kilometres from here
di'stendere *vt* stretch out ⟨parte del corpo⟩; (spiegare) spread; (deporre) lay
di'stendersi *vr* stretch; (sdraiarsi) lie down; (rilassarsi) relax
distensi'one *nf* stretching; (rilassamento) relaxation; Pol dètente

disten'sivo *adj* relaxing

di'stesa *nf* expanse

di'steso pp di DISTENDERE

distil'lare *vt/i* distil

distil'lato ① *adj* distilled
② *nm* distillate

distillazi'one *nf* distillation

distille'ria *nf* distillery

di'stinguersi *vr* (per bravura ecc) distinguish oneself; **si distingue dagli altri per ...** it is distinguished from the others by ...

distin'guibile *adj* distinguishable

di'stinguo *nm inv* distinction

di'stinta *nf* Comm list. **distinta di pagamento** receipt. **distinta di versamento** paying-in slip

distinta'mente *adv* (separatamente) individually, separately; (chiaramente) clearly; (in modo elegante) in a distinguished way; **vi saluto ∼** Yours truly

distin'tivo ① *adj* distinctive
② *nm* badge

di'stinto ① pp di DISTINGUERSI
② *adj* distinct; (signorile) distinguished; **distinti saluti** Yours faithfully

distinzi'one *nf* distinction

di'stogliere *vt* ∼ **da** (allontanare) remove from; (dissuadere) dissuade from

di'stolto pp di DISTOGLIERE

di'storcere *vt* twist; distort ⟨suono⟩

di'storcersi *vr* sprain ⟨caviglia⟩

distorsi'one *nf* Med sprain; (alterazione) distortion

di'storto *adj* warped; ⟨suono⟩ distorted

di'strarre *vt* distract; (divertire) amuse

di'strarsi *vr* (deconcentrarsi) be distracted; (svagarsi) amuse oneself; **non ti distrarre!** pay attention!

distratta'mente *adv* absently

di'stratto ① pp di DISTRARRE
② *adj* absentminded; (disattento) inattentive

distrazi'one *nf* absent-mindedness; (errore) inattention; (svago) amusement; **errore di distrazione** absent-minded mistake

di'stretto *nm* district

distrettu'ale *adj* district *attrib*

distribu'ire *vt* distribute; (disporre) arrange; deal ⟨carte⟩

distribu'tore *nm* distributor; (di benzina) petrol pump, gas pump Am; (automatico) slot machine. **distributore automatico di biglietti** ticket machine. **distributore di bevande** drinks dispenser. **distributore di monete** change machine

distribuzi'one *nf* distribution

distri'care *vt* disentangle

distri'carsi *vr* fig get out of it

distro'fia *nf* **distrofia muscolare** muscular dystrophy

di'strofico *adj* dystrophic

di'struggere *vt* destroy

di'struggersi *vr* **si distrugge col bere** he is destroying himself with drink; **la macchina si è distrutta** the car has been written off

distruttività *nf* destructiveness

distrut'tivo *adj* destructive; ⟨critica⟩ negative

di'strutto ① pp di DISTRUGGERE
② *adj* destroyed; **un uomo ∼** a broken man

distrut'tore *nm* **distruttore di documenti** paper shredder

distruzi'one *nf* destruction

distur'bare *vt* disturb; (sconvolgere) upset

distur'barsi *vr* trouble oneself; **non si disturbi** please don't trouble yourself

distur'bato *adj* Med ⟨mente⟩ disordered; ⟨intestino⟩ upset

di'sturbo *nm* bother; (indisposizione) trouble; Med problem; Radio, TV interference; **disturbi** *pl* Radio, TV static. **disturbo da deficit dell'attenzione** attention deficit disorder. **disturbi di stomaco** *pl* stomach trouble

disubbidi'ente *adj* disobedient

disubbidi'enza *nf* disobedience

disubbi'dire *vi* ∼ **a** disobey

disuguagli'anza *nf* disparity; (eterogeneità) irregularity

disugu'ale *adj* unequal; (eterogeneo) irregular

disumanità *nf* inhumanity

disu'mano *adj* inhuman

disuni'one *nf* disunity

disu'nire *vt* divide

di'suso *nm* **cadere in ∼** fall into disuse

di'tale *nm* thimble

di'tata *nf* poke; (impronta) finger-mark

'dito *nm* (pl *nf* **dita**) finger; (di vino, acqua) finger. **dito del piede** toe

'ditta *nf* firm. **ditta di vendita per corrispondenza** mail order firm

dit'tafono *nm* dictaphone

ditta'tore *nm* dictator

dittatori'ale *adj* dictatorial

ditta'tura *nf* dictatorship

dit'tongo *nm* diphthong

diu'retico *adj* diuretic

di'urno *adj* daytime; **spettacolo diurno** matinée

'diva *nf* diva

diva'gare *vi* digress

divagazi'one *nf* digression. **divagazione sul tema** digression

divam'pare *vi* burst into flames; fig spread like wildfire

di'vano *nm* settee, sofa. **divano letto** sofa bed

divari'care *vt* open

divari'carsi *vr* splay

divari'cata *nf* splits *pl*

divari'cato *adj* ⟨gambe, braccia⟩ splayed

di'vario *nm* discrepancy; **un ∼ di opinioni** a difference of opinion

di'vellere *vt* (sradicare) uproot

di'velto pp di DIVELLERE

dive'nire *vi* = DIVENTARE

diven'tare *vi* become; (lentamente) grow; (rapidamente) turn

dive'nuto pp di DIVENIRE

di'verbio *nm* squabble

diver'gente *adj* divergent

diver'genza *nf* divergence.
  divergenza di opinioni difference of opinion

di'vergere *vi* diverge

diversa'mente *adv* (altrimenti) otherwise; (in modo diverso) differently

di'versi *adj & pron* (parecchi) several

diversifi'care *vt* diversify

diversifi'carsi *vr* differ; be different

diversifi'cato *adj* broad-based

diversificazi'one *nf* diversification

diversi'one *nf* diversion

diversità *nf inv* diversity; **ci sono molte ∼** there are many differences

diver'sivo ① *adj* diversionary ② *nm* diversion

di'verso *adj* different

diver'tente *adj* amusing

diver'ticolo *nm* digression

diverti'mento *nm* fun, amusement; **buon ∼!** enjoy yourself!, have fun!

diver'tire *vt* amuse

diver'tirsi *vr* enjoy oneself, have fun

diver'tito *adj* amused

divi'dendo *nm* dividend

di'videre *vt* divide; (condividere) share

di'vidersi *vr* (separarsi) separate

divi'eto *nm* prohibition. **'divieto di pesca'** 'fishing prohibited'; **'divieto di sosta'** 'no parking'

divina'mente *adv* divinely

divinco'larsi *vr* wriggle

divinità *nf inv* divinity

di'vino *adj* divine

di'visa *nf* uniform; Fin currency

divi'sibile *adj* divisible

divisi'one *nf* division

divisio'nismo *nm* (in arte) pointillism

di'vismo *nm* worship; (atteggiamento) superstar mentality

di'viso ① pp di DIVIDERE ② *adj* divided

divi'sore *nm* divisor

divi'sorio *adj* dividing; **muro divisorio** partition wall

'divo, -a *nmf* star

divo'rare *vt* devour

divo'rarsi *vr* **∼ da** be consumed with

divorzi'are *vi* divorce

divorzi'ato, -a *nmf* divorcee

di'vorzio *nm* divorce

divul'gare *vt* divulge; (rendere popolare) popularize

divul'garsi *vr* spread

divulga'tivo *adj* popular

divulgazi'one *nf* spread; (di cultura, scienza) popularization

dizio'nario *nm* dictionary. **dizionario dei sinonimi** thesaurus

dizi'one *nf* diction

DJ *nm inv* DJ

DNA *nm inv* DNA

do *nm* Mus (chiave, nota) C

D.O.C. *abbr* (**Denominazione di Origine Controllata**) mark guaranteeing the quality of a wine

'doccia *nf* shower; (grondaia) gutter; **fare la ∼** have a shower, shower

doccia'tura *nf* Med douche

do'cente ① *adj* teaching ② *nmf* teacher; (di università) lecturer

do'cenza *nf* university teacher's qualification

D.O.C.G. *abbr* (**Denominazione di Origine Controllata e Garantita**) mark guaranteeing the high quality of a wine

'docile *adj* docile

docilità *nf* docility

documen'tare *vt* document

documen'tario *adj & nm* documentary

documen'tarsi *vr* gather information (su about)

documen'tato *adj* well-documented; ⟨persona⟩ well-informed

documentazi'one *nf* documentation

docu'mento *nm* document; **documenti** *pl* papers. **documento d'identità** ID

dodeca'fonico *adj* Mus dodecaphonic

Dodecan'neso *nm* **il ∼** the Dodecanese

dodi'cenne *adj & nmf* twelve-year-old

dodi'cesimo *adj & nm* twelfth

'dodici *adj & nm* twelve

do'gana *nf* customs *pl*; (dazio) duty.
  dogana merci customs for freight.
  dogana passeggeri passenger customs

doga'nale *adj* customs *attrib*

dogani'ere *nm* customs officer

'doglie *nfpl* labour pains

'dogma *nm* dogma

dog'matico *adj* dogmatic

dogma'tismo *nm* dogmatism

'dolce ① *adj* sweet; ⟨clima⟩ mild; ⟨voce, consonante⟩ soft; ⟨acqua⟩ fresh ② *nm* (portata) dessert; (torta) cake; **non mangio dolci** I don't eat sweet things; **dolci** *pl* **della casa** (in menu) home-made cakes

dolce'mente *adv* sweetly

dolce'vita *adj inv* (maglione) rollneck

dol'cezza *nf* sweetness; (di clima) mildness

dolci'ario *adj* confectionery

dolci'astro *adj* sweetish

dolcifi'cante ① *nm* sweetener ② *adj* sweetening

dolcifica'tore *nm* (per acqua) softener

dolci'umi *nmpl* sweets

do'lente *adj* painful; (spiacente) sorry; **punto ~** sore point

do'lere *vi* ache, hurt; (dispiacere) regret

do'lersi *vr* regret; (protestare) complain; **~ di** be sorry for

'dollaro *nm* dollar

'dolly *nm inv* Cinema, TV dolly

'dolmen *nm inv* dolmen

'dolo *nm* Jur malice; (truffa) fraud

Dolo'miti *nfpl* **le ~** the Dolomites

dolo'mitico *adj* Dolomite, of the Dolomites

dolo'rante *adj* aching

do'lore *nm* pain; (morale) sorrow; **avere dei dolori** be in pain. **dolori post-partum** *pl* after-pains

dolorosa'mente *adv* painfully

dolo'roso *adj* painful

do'loso *adj* malicious

do'manda *nf* question; (richiesta) request; (scritta) application; Comm demand; **~ e offerta** supply and demand; **fare una ~ (a qualcuno)** ask (somebody) a question. **domanda di impiego** job application. **domanda riconvenzionale** counterclaim. **domanda trabocchetto** trick question

doman'dare *vt* ask; (esigere) demand; **~ qualcosa a qualcuno** ask somebody for something

doman'darsi *vr* wonder

do'mani ① *adv* tomorrow; **~ sera** tomorrow evening; **a ~** see you tomorrow ② *nm* **il ~** the future

do'mare *vt* tame; fig control ⟨emozioni⟩

doma|'tore, -trice *nmf* tamer. **domatore di cavalli** horsebreaker

domat'tina *adv* tomorrow morning

doma'tura *nf* (di cavallo) breaking

do'menica *nf* Sunday; **di ~** on Sundays. **Domenica delle Palme** Palm Sunday

domeni'cale *adj* Sunday *attrib*

domeni'cano *adj* Dominican

do'mestico, -a ① *adj* domestic; **le pareti domestiche** one's own four walls ② *nm* servant ③ *nf* maid

domicili'are *adj* **arresti domiciliari** Jur house arrest; **perquisizione domiciliare** Jur house search

domicili'arsi *vr* settle

domi'cilio *nm* domicile; (abitazione) home; **recapitiamo a ~** we do home deliveries

domi'nante *adj* ⟨nazione, colore⟩ dominant; ⟨caratteri⟩ chief; ⟨opinione⟩ prevailing; ⟨motivo⟩ main

domi'nanza *nf* Biol, Zool dominance

domi'nare ① *vt* dominate; (controllare) control ② *vi* rule; (prevalere) be dominant

domi'narsi *vr* control oneself

domina|'tore, -trice ① *adj* domineering ② *nmf* ruler

dominazi'one *nf* domination

Domi'nica *nf* Dominica

domini'cano *adj* **la Repubblica Dominicana** the Dominican Republic

do'minio *nm* control; Pol dominion; (ambito) field; **di ~ pubblico** common knowledge

'domino *nm* (gioco) dominoes

don *nm* (ecclesiastico) Father

do'nare ① *vt* give; donate ⟨sangue, organo⟩ ② *vi* **~ a** (giovare esteticamente) suit

do'narsi *vr* dedicate oneself

dona|'tore, -trice *nmf* donor. **donatore di organi** organ donor. **donatore del seme** sperm donor

donazi'one *nf* donation

dondo'lare ① *vt* swing; (cullare) rock ② *vi* sway

dondo'larsi *vr* swing

dondo'lio *nm* rocking

'dondolo *nm* swing; **cavallo/sedia a ~** rocking-horse/chair

dongio'vanni *nm inv* Romeo, Don Juan

'donna *nf* woman; **fare la prima ~** act like a prima donna; **'donne'** 'ladies'. **donna d'affari** businesswoman. **donna delle pulizie** cleaner. **donna di servizio** domestic help. **donna di vita** (prostituta) lady of the night

don'naccia *nf pej* hussy

donnai'olo *nm* womanizer

donnicci'ola *nf* fig old woman

'donnola *nf* weasel

'dono *nm* gift

'doping nm Sport drug-taking; **fa uso di ∼** he takes drugs

'dopo ① prep after; (a partire da) since ② adv after; afterwards; (più tardi) later; (in seguito) later on; **∼ di me** after me

dopo'barba nm inv aftershave

dopo'cena nm inv evening

dopodiché adv after which

dopodo'mani adv the day after tomorrow

dopogu'erra nm inv post-war period

dopola'voro nm inv working man's club

dopo'pranzo nm inv afternoon

dopo'sci adj & nm inv après-ski

doposcu'ola nm inv after-school activities pl

dopo-'shampoo ① nm inv conditioner ② adj inv conditioning

dopo'sole ① nm inv aftersun cream ② adj inv aftersun

dopo'tutto adv after all

doppi'aggio nm dubbing

doppia'mente adv (in misura doppia) doubly

doppi'are vt Naut double; Sport lap; Cinema dub

doppia|'tore, -trice nmf dubber

doppi'etta nf (fucile) double-barrelled shotgun; Auto double-declutch; (in calcio) two goals; (in pugilato) one-two

doppi'ezza nf duplicity

'doppio ① adj & adv double. **doppia nazionalità** dual nationality. **doppi vetri** double glazing. **doppio clic** Comput double click; **fare un ∼ su** double-click on. **doppio fallo** Tennis double fault. **doppio gioco** double-dealing. **doppio mento** double chin. **doppio senso** double entendre ② nm double, twice the quantity; Tennis doubles pl. **doppio misto** Tennis mixed doubles

doppio'fondo nm Naut double hull; (in valigia) false bottom

doppiogio'chista nmf double-dealer

doppi'one nm duplicate

doppio'petto adj double-breasted

dop'pista nmf Tennis doubles player

do'rare vt gild; Culin brown

do'rato adj gilt; (color oro) golden

dora'tura nf gilding

'dorico adj Archit Doric

do'rifora nf Colorado beetle

dormicchi'are vi doze

dormigli'one, -a nmf sleepyhead; fig lazybones

dor'mire vi sleep; (essere addormentato) be asleep; fig be asleep; **andare a ∼** go to bed; **∼ come un ghiro** sleep like a log; **∼ in**

piedi fig be half asleep; (essere stanco) be dead tired; **dormirci sopra** sleep on it

dor'mita nf good sleep; **fare una bella ∼** have a good sleep

dormi'tina nf nap

dormi'torio nm dormitory. **dormitorio pubblico** night shelter

dormi'veglia nm essere nel ∼ be half asleep

dor'sale ① adj dorsal ② nf (di monte) ridge

dor'sista nmf backstroke swimmer

'dorso nm back; (di libro) spine; (di monte) crest; (nel nuoto) backstroke; **a ∼ di cavallo** on horseback

do'saggio nm dosage; fig weighing; **sbagliare il ∼** get the amount wrong

do'sare vt dose; fig measure; **∼ le parole** weigh one's words

do'sato adj measured

dosa'tore nm measuring jug

'dose nf dose; **∼ eccessiva** overdose; **in buona ∼** fig in good measure

dos'sier nm inv (raccolta di dati, fascicolo) file

'dosso nm (dorso) back; (su strada) bump **levarsi di ∼ gli abiti** take off one's clothes. **dosso di rallentamento** road hump, speed hump

do'tare vt endow; (di accessori) equip

do'tato adj ⟨persona⟩ gifted; (fornito) equipped

dotazi'one nf (attrezzatura) equipment; (mezzi finanziari) endowment; **avere qualcosa in ∼** be equipped with something

'dote nf dowry; (qualità) gift

dott. abbr (**dottore**) Dr.

'dotto ① adj learned ② nm scholar; Anat duct

dotto'rale adj doctoral; pej pedantic

dotto'rando, -a nmf postgraduate student

dotto'rato nm doctorate

dot'tor|e, ∼'essa nmf doctor

dot'trina nf doctrine

dott.ssa abbr (**dottoressa**) Dr.

double-'face adj inv reversible

'dove adv where; **di ∼ sei?** where do you come from; **fin ∼?** how far?; **per ∼?** which way?

do'vere ① vi (obbligo) have to, must; **devo andare** I have to go, I must go; **devo venire anch'io?** do I have to come too?; **avresti dovuto dirmelo** you should have told me, you ought to have told me; **devo sedermi un attimo** I must sit down for a minute, I need to sit down for a minute; **dev'essere successo qualcosa** something must have happened; **come si deve** properly

② *vt* (essere debitore di, derivare) owe; **essere dovuto a** be due to

③ *nm* duty; **per** ~ out of duty; **rivolgersi a chi di** ~ apply to the appropriate authorities

dove'roso *adj* right and proper, only right

do'vizia *nf* **con** ~ **di particolari** in great detail

do'vunque **①** *adv* (dappertutto) everywhere; (in qualsiasi luogo) anywhere **②** *conj* wherever

dovuta'mente *adv* duly

do'vuto *adj* due; (debito) proper; **essere** ~ **a** be attributable to; **ha fatto più del** ~ he did more than he had to

Down: **sindrome di** ~ *nf* Med Down's syndrome

doz'zina *nf* **una** ~ **di uova** a dozen eggs; **mezza** ~ **di uova** half a dozen eggs

dozzi'nale *adj* cheap

'draga *nf* (scavatrice) dredger

draga'mine *nf inv* minesweeper

dra'gare *vt* dredge

'drago *nm* dragon

'dramma *nm* drama; **fare un** ~ **di qualcosa** fig make a drama out of something

drammatica'mente *adv* dramatically

drammaticità *nf* dramatic force

dram'matico *adj* dramatic

drammatiz'zare *vt* dramatize

drammatizzazi'one *nf* dramatization

drammatur'gia *nf* (genere) drama

dramma'turgo *nm* playwright

dram'mone *nm* (film) tear-jerker, weepy

drappeggi'are *vt* drape

drap'peggio *nm* drapery

drap'pello *nm* Mil squad; (gruppo) band

'drappo *nm* (tessuto) cloth

drastica'mente *adv* drastically

'drastico *adj* drastic

dre'naggio *nm* drainage. **drenaggio di capitali** transfer of capital. **drenaggio fiscale** fiscal drag

dre'nare *vt* drain

'Dresda *nf* Dresden

dres'sage *nm inv* (gara) dressage

drib'blare *vt* (in calcio) dribble; fig dodge

'dribbling *nm inv* (in calcio) dribble

'dritta *nf* (mano destra) right hand; Naut starboard; (informazione) pointer, tip; **a** ~ **e a manca** (dappertutto) left, right and centre

dritta'mente *adv* (furbescamente) craftily

'dritto, -a **①** *adj* = DIRITTO¹ **②** *nmf* fam crafty so-and-so

'drive *nm inv* Comput drive

drive-'in *nm inv* drive-in

driz'zare *vt* straighten; (rizzare) prick up

driz'zarsi *vr* straighten [up]; (alzarsi) raise; **mi si sono drizzati i capelli** fig my hair stood on end

'droga *nf* drug. **droga leggera** soft drug. **droga pesante** hard drug

dro'gare *vt* drug

dro'garsi *vr* take drugs

drogato, -a **①** *adj* drugged **②** *nmf* drug addict

droghe'ria *nf* grocery

droghi'ere, -a *nmf* grocer

drome'dario *nm* dromedary

'druso *nmf* Druse

dua'lismo *nm* dualism; (contrasto) conflict

'dubbio **①** *adj* doubtful; (ambiguo) dubious **②** *nm* doubt; (sospetto) suspicion; **mettere in** ~ doubt; **essere fuori** ~ be beyond doubt; **essere in** ~ be doubtful

dubbiosa'mente *adv* doubtfully

dubbi'oso, dubitante *adj* doubtful

dubi'tare *vi* doubt; ~ **di** doubt; (diffidare) mistrust; **dubito che venga** I doubt whether he'll come

dubita'tivo *adj* (ambiguo) ambiguous

Du'blino *nf* Dublin

'duca *nm* duke

du'cale *adj* ducal

'duce *nm* (nel fascismo) Duce

du'chessa *nf* duchess

'due *adj* & *nm* two

duecen'tesco *adj* thirteenth-century

duecen'tesimo two hundredth

duecento *adj* & *nm* two hundred

duel'lante *nmf* dueller

duel'lare *vi* duel

du'ello *nm* duel

due'mila *adj* & *nm* two thousand

due'pezzi *nm inv* (bikini) bikini; (vestito) two-piece suit

du'etto *nm* duo; Mus duet

'dumping *nm* Fin dumping

'duna *nf* dune

dune 'buggy *nm inv* beach buggy

'dunque *conj* therefore; (allora) well [then]; **arrivare al** ~ get down to the nitty-gritty

'duo *nm inv* duo; Mus duet

duodeci'male *adj* duodecimal

duode'nale *adj* **ulcera** ~ duodenal ulcer

duo'deno *nm* duodenum

du'omo *nm* cathedral

'duplex *nm* Teleph party line

dupli'care *vt* duplicate

dupli'cato *nm* duplicate

duplicazi'one *nf* duplication

'duplice *adj* double; **in** ~ in duplicate

duplicità *nf* duplicity

dura'mente *adv* ⟨*lavorare*⟩ hard; ⟨*rimproverare*⟩ harshly

du'rante *prep* during

du'rare ① *vi* last; ⟨*cibo*⟩ keep; (resistere) hold out; **così non può** ∼ this can't go on any longer; ∼ **in carica** remain in office; **finché dura** as long as it lasts ② *vt* ∼ **fatica** sweat blood

du'rata *nf* duration. **durata del collegamento** on-line time. **durata di conservazione** shelf-life. **durata della vita** life span

dura'turo *adj* lasting

du'revole *adj* ⟨*pace*⟩ lasting, enduring

du'rezza *nf* hardness; (di carne) toughness; (di voce, padre) harshness

'duro, -a ① *adj* hard; ⟨*persona, carne*⟩ tough; ⟨*voce*⟩ harsh; ⟨*pane*⟩ stale; **tieni** ∼! (resistere) hang in there!; ∼ **d'orecchio** hard of hearing ② *nmf* (persona) tough person, toughie *fam*

du'rone *nm* hardened skin

'duttile *adj* ⟨*materiale*⟩ ductile; ⟨*carattere, persona*⟩ malleable

duttilità *nf* (di materiale) ductility; (di individuo) malleability

'duty free *nm inv* duty-free shop

DVD *nm inv* DVD

Ee

e *conj* and

eba'nista *nmf* cabinet-maker

'ebano *nm* ebony

eb'bene *conj* well [then]

eb'brezza *nf* inebriation; (euforia) elation; **guida in stato di** ∼ drink-driving; **l'**∼ **della velocità** the thrill of speed

'ebbro *adj* inebriated; ∼ **di gioia** delirious with joy

'ebete *adj* stupid

ebollizi'one *nf* boiling

e'braico *adj & nm* Hebrew

ebra'ismo *nm* Judaism

e'breo, -a ① *adj* Jewish ② *nm* Jew ③ *nf* Jewess

'Ebridi *nfpl* **le** ∼ the Hebrides

eca'tombe *nf* **fare un'**∼ wreak havoc

ecc *abbr* (**eccetera**) etc

eccì *int* atishoo

ecce'dente *adj* ⟨*peso, bagaglio*⟩ excess

ecce'denza *nf* excess; (d'avanzo) surplus; **avere qualcosa in** ∼ have an excess of something; **bagagli in** ∼ excess baggage. **eccedenza di cassa** surplus. **eccedenza di peso** excess weight

ec'cedere ① *vt* exceed ② *vi* go too far; ∼ **nel bere** drink to excess; ∼ **nel mangiare** overeat

eccel'lente *adj* excellent

eccel'lenza *nf* excellence; (titolo) Excellency; **per** ∼ par excellence

ec'cellere *vi* excel (in at)

eccentricità *nf inv* eccentricity

ec'centrico, -a *adj & nmf* eccentric

ecce'pire *vt* object to

eccessiva'mente *adv* excessively

eccessivo *adj* excessive

ec'cesso *nm* excess; **andare agli eccessi** go to extremes; **dare in eccessi** fly into a temper; **all'**∼ to excess. **eccesso di personale** over-manning. **eccesso di peso** excess weight. **eccesso di velocità** speeding

ec'cetera *adv* et cetera

ec'cetto *prep* except; ∼ **che** (a meno che) unless

eccettu'are *vt* except

eccezio'nale *adj* exceptional; **in via [del tutto]** ∼ as an exception

eccezional'mente *adv* exceptionally; (contrariamente alla regola) as an exception

eccezi'one *nf* exception; Jur objection; **a** ∼ **di** with the exception of; **d'**∼ exceptional

ec'chimosi *nf inv* bruising

ec'cidio *nm* massacre

ecci'tabile *adj* ⟨*persona, carattere*⟩ excitable

eccita'mento *nm* excitement

ecci'tante ① *adj* exciting; ⟨*sostanza*⟩ stimulant ② *nm* stimulant

ecci'tare *vt* excite; (sessualmente) excite, arouse

ecci'tarsi *vr* get excited; (sessualmente) become aroused *or* excited

ecci'tato *adj* excited; (sessualmente) excited, aroused; ∼ **da** flushed with

eccitazi'one *nf* excitement; (sessuale) arousal, excitement

ecclesi'astico ① *adj* ecclesiastical ② *nm* priest

'ecco *adv* (qui) here; (là) there; ∼! (con approvazione) that's right!; ∼ **qua!** (dando ⋯▸

qualcosa) here you are!; ∼ **la tua borsa**
here is your bag; ∼ **mio figlio** there is my
son; **eccomi** here I am; ∼ **fatto** there we
are; ∼ **perché** this is why; ∼ **tutto** that is
all

ec'come *adv & int* and how!

ECG *abbr* (**elettrocardiogramma**)
ECG

echeggi'are *vi* echo

e'clettico *adj* eclectic

eclet'tismo *nm* eclecticism

eclis'sare *vt* fig eclipse

eclis'sarsi *vr* (sparire) disappear

e'clissi *nf inv* eclipse. **eclissi di sole**
solar eclipse

'eco *nmf* (pl m **echi**) echo; **ha suscitato
una vasta** ∼ it caused a great stir

eco+ *pref* eco+; **eco-guerrigliero** eco-
warrier

ecogra'fia *nf* scan

ecolo'gia *nf* ecology

eco'logico *adj* ecological; ⟨*prodotto*⟩
environmentally friendly, eco-friendly

e'cologo, -a *nmf* ecologist

e commerci'ale *nf* ampersand

econo'mia *nf* economy; (scienza)
economics; **fare** ∼ economize (**di** on);
[**fatto**] **in** ∼ [done] on the cheap; **senza** ∼
unstintingly; **fare qualcosa senza** ∼ spare
no expense doing something. **economia
aziendale** business administration.
economia domestica Sch home
economics. **economia di mercato**
market economy. **economia di libero
mercato** free market. **economia
mista** mixed economy. **economia
sommersa** black economy

economicità *nf* economy

eco'nomico *adj* economic; (a buon
prezzo) cheap; (con pochi costi) economical;
difficoltà economiche financial difficulties;
classe economica economy class; **edizione
economica** paperback

econo'mie *nfpl* (risparmi) savings

econo'mista *nmf* economist

economiz'zare ① *vt* save ⟨*tempo,
denaro*⟩
② *vi* economize (**su** on)

economizza'tore *nm* Auto fuel
economizer

e'conomo, -a ① *adj* thrifty
② *nmf* (di collegio) bursar

ecosi'stema *nm* ecosystem

ecoterro'rismo *nm* ecoterrorism

e'cru *adj inv* fawn

Ecua'dor *nm* Ecuador

ecuadori'ano, -a *adj & nmf*
Ecuadorian

ecu'menico *adj* ecumenical

ec'zema *nm* eczema

ed *conj* ▸ E

e'dema *nm* oedema

'Eden *nm* Eden

'edera *nf* ivy

e'dicola *nf* [newspaper] kiosk

edifi'cabile *adj* ⟨*area, terreno*⟩ classified
as suitable for development

edifi'cante *adj* edifying

edifi'care *vt* build; (indurre al bene) edify

edi'ficio *nm* building; fig structure

e'dile ① *adj* building *attrib*
② *nm* **edili** *pl* construction workers

edi'lizia *nf* building trade

edi'lizio *adj* building *attrib*

Edim'burgo *nf* Edinburgh

E'dipo *nm* Oedipus; **complesso di Edipo**
Oedipus complex

edi'tare *vt* edit

'editing *nm* editing

'edito *adj* published

edi'|tore, -trice ① *adj* publishing
② *nmf* publisher; (curatore) editor

edito'ria *nf* publishing. **editoria
elettronica** desktop publishing,
electronic publishing. **editoria
telematica** online publishing

editori'ale ① *adj* publishing
② *nm* (articolo) editorial, leader

e'ditto *nm* edict

edizi'one *nf* edition; (di manifestazione)
performance; **in** ∼ **italiana** ⟨*film*⟩ dubbed
into Italian. **edizione ridotta**
abridgement, abridged version. **edizione
della sera** (di telegiornale) evening news.

edo'nismo *nm* hedonism

edo'nistico *adj* hedonistic

educagi'oco *nm* edutainment

edu'canda *nf* [convent school] boarder;
fig prim and proper girl

edu'care *vt* educate; (allevare) bring up

educa'tivo *adj* educational

edu'cato *adj* polite

educa'|tore, -trice *nmf* educator

educazi'one *nf* education; (di bambini)
upbringing; (buone maniere) [good] manners
pl; **bella** ∼! what manners! **educazione
fisica** physical education. **educazione
sessuale** sex education

edulco'rare *vt* ∼ **la pillola** sweeten the
pill

EED *abbr* (**elaborazione elettronica
[dei] dati**) EDP

e'felide *nf* freckle

effemi'nato *adj* effeminate

effe'rato *adj* brutal

efferve'scente *adj* effervescent;
(frizzante) fizzy; ⟨*aspirina*®⟩ soluble

effettiva'mente *adv* **è troppo tardi** –∼
it's too late –so it is

effet'tivo ① *adj* actual; (efficace) effective; ⟨*personale*⟩ permanent; Mil regular ② *nm* (somma totale) sum total

ef'fetto *nm* effect; (impressione) impression; (cambiale) bill; **fare ∼** ⟨*medicina*⟩ take effect; **fare ∼ su** have an effect on, affect; **in effetti** in fact; **a tutti gli effetti** to all intents and purposes; **ad effetto** ⟨*frase*⟩ catchy; **la vista del sangue mi fa ∼** I can't stand the sight of blood; **tiro con ∼** spin. **effetto boomerang** boomerang effect. **effetto di luce** trick of the light. **effetti personali** *pl* personal belongings, personal effects fml. **effetto ritardato** delayed effect. **effetto serra** greenhouse effect. **effetto sonoro** sound effect. **effetto speciale** Cinema, TV special effect

effettu'are *vt* effect; carry out ⟨*controllo, sondaggio*⟩

effettu'arsi *vr* take place; **'si effettua dal ... al ...'** 'this service is available from ... till ...'

effi'cace *adj* effective

effi'cacia *nf* effectiveness

effici'ente *adj* efficient

effici'enza *nf* efficiency; **in piena ∼** in full swing

ef'figie *nf* effigy

ef'fimero *adj* ephemeral

ef'flusso *nm* outflow

ef'fluvio *nm* stink

ef'fondersi *vr* **∼ in ringraziamenti** be profusive in one's thanks

effrazi'one *nf* **effrazione con scasso** Jur breaking and entering

effusi'one *nf* effusion

'Egadi *nfpl* **le [isole] ∼** the Egadi Islands

egemo'nia *nf* hegemony

E'geo *nm* **l'∼** the Aegean [Sea]

e'gida *nf* **sotto l'∼ di** under the aegis of

E'gitto *nm* Egypt

egizi'ano, -a *adj & nmf* Egyptian

e'gizio, -a *adj & nmf* Ancient Egyptian

'egli *pers pron* he; **∼ stesso** he himself

ego'centrico, -a ① *adj* egocentric ② *nmf* egocentric person

egocen'trismo *nm* egocentricity

ego'ismo *nm* selfishness

ego'ista ① *adj* selfish ② *nmf* selfish person

egoistica'mente *adv* selfishly

ego'istico *adj* selfish

Egr. *abbr* (**egregio**) **∼ Sig.** (su busta) Mr.

e'gregio *adj* distinguished; **Egregio Signore** Dear Sir

eguali'tario *adj & nm* egalitarian

eh *int* huh!

'ehi *int* hey!

ehilà *int* hi!

ehm *int* um

eiacu'lare *vi* ejaculate

eiaculazi'one *nf* ejaculation

eiet'tabile *adj* ⟨*sedile*⟩ ejector

eiezi'one *nf* Aeron ejection

'Eire *nf* Eire

elabo'rare *vt* elaborate; process ⟨*dati*⟩

elabo'rato ① *adj* elaborate ② *nm* (tabulato) preprinted form

elabora'tore *nm* **elaboratore [di testi]** word processor

elaborazi'one *nf* elaboration; (di dati) processing. **elaborazione elettronica [dei] dati** electronic data processing. **elaborazione sequenziale** Comput batch processing. **elaborazione [di] testi** word processing

elar'gire *vt* lavish

elasticità *nf* elasticity. **elasticità mentale** mental agility. **elasticità di movimento** litheness

elasticiz'zato *adj* ⟨*stoffa*⟩ elasticated

e'lastico ① *adj* elastic; ⟨*tessuto*⟩ stretch; ⟨*passo*⟩ springy; ⟨*orario, mente*⟩ flexible; ⟨*persona*⟩ easy-going; ⟨*morale*⟩ lax; **collant** *pl* **elastici** support tights ② *nm* elastic; (fascia) rubber band

'Elba *nf* Elba

eldo'rado *nm* eldorado

ele'fante *nm* elephant; **avere una memoria da ∼** have a memory like an elephant; **fare passi da ∼** thump about. **∼ marino** sea-elephant

elefan'tesco *adj* elephantine

elefan'tessa *nf* cow[-elephant]

elefan'tiaco *adj* (enorme) elephantine

ele'gante *adj* elegant

elegante'mente *adv* elegantly

ele'ganza *nf* elegance

e'leggere *vt* elect

eleg'gibile *adj* eligible

ele'gia *nf* elegy

elemen'tare *adj* elementary; **scuola elementare** primary school

ele'mento *nm* element; (componente) part; **trovarsi nel proprio ∼** be in one's element; **elementi** *pl* (fatti) data; (rudimenti) elements

ele'mosina *nf* charity; **chiedere l'∼** beg; **vivere d'∼** live on charity; **fare l'∼** give money to beggars

elemosi'nare *vt/i* beg

elen'care *vt* list

e'lenco *nm* list. **elenco [degli] abbonati** Teleph telephone directory. **elenco telefonico** telephone directory

elet'tivo *adj* ⟨*carica*⟩ elective

e'letto, -a ① *pp di* ELEGGERE ② *adj* chosen

3) *nmf* (nominato) elected member; **per pochi eletti** fig for the chosen few

eletto'rale *adj* electoral

elettora'lismo *nm* electioneering

eletto'rato *nm* electorate

elet|'tore, -trice *nmf* voter

elet'trauto *nm inv* electrics garage

elettri'cista *nm* electrician

elettricità *nf* electricity; **togliere l'~** cut the electricity off; **è mancata l'~** there was a power cut

e'lettrico *adj* electric

elettriz'zante *adj* ‹notizia, gara› electrifying

elettriz'zare *vt* fig electrify

elettriz'zato *adj* fig electrified

elettro+ *pref* electro+

elettrocardio'gramma *nm* electrocardiogram, ECG

elettrocuzi'one *nf* electrocution

e'lettrodo *nm* electrode

elettrodo'mestico *nm* [electrical] household appliance

elettroencefalo'gramma *nm* electroencephalogram

elettroesecuzi'one *nf* electrocution

elet'trogeno *adj* **gruppo elettrogeno** generator

elet'trolisi *nf* electrolysis

elettromo'tore *nm* electric motor

elettromo'trice *nf* electric train

elet'trone *nm* electron

elet'tronico, -a **1)** *adj* electronic **2)** *nf* electronics

elettroshocktera'pia *nf* electroshock therapy, electroshock treatment, EST

elettro'tecnica *nf* electrical engineering

elettro'tecnico *nm* electrical engineer

elettro'treno *nm* electric train

ele'vare *vt* raise; (promuovere) promote; (erigere) erect; (fig: migliorare) better; **~ al quadrato/cubo** square/cube

ele'varsi *vr* rise; ‹edificio› stand

ele'vato *adj* high; (fig: sentimento) lofty; **~ al cubo/al quadrato** cubed/squared; **~ a dieci** raised to the power of ten

eleva'tore *nm* fork-lift truck

elevazi'one *nf* elevation

elezi'one *nf* election; **elezioni** *pl* **amministrative** local council elections; **elezioni** *pl* **politiche** general election

eliambu'lanza *nf* air ambulance

'elica *nf* Naut screw, propeller; Aeron propeller; (del ventilatore) blade

eli'cottero *nm* helicopter

elimi'nabile *adj* which can be eliminated

elimi'nare *vt* eliminate

elimina'toria *nf* Sport [preliminary] heat

eliminazi'one *nf* elimination

'elio *nm* (gas) helium

eli'porto *nm* heliport

elisabetti'ano *adj & nmf* Elizabethan

é'lite *nf inv* élite

eli'tista *adj* élitist

'ella *pers pron* liter she; **~ stessa** she herself

el'lenico *adj* Hellenic

elle'nistico *adj* Hellenistic

ellepì *nm inv* LP

+ellino *suff* **campanellino** *nm* [small] bell; **fiorellino** *nm* [little] flower; **gonnellina** *nf* short skirt

el'lisse *nf* ellipse

el'lissi *nf inv* ellipsis

el'littico *adj* elliptical

+ello *suff* **finestrella** *nf* little window; **pecorella** *nf* woolly sheep; **saltello** *nm* skip

el'metto *nm* helmet

elogi'are *vt* praise

elogia'tivo *adj* laudatory

e'logio *nm* praise; (discorso, scritto) eulogy; **degno di ~** laudable, praiseworthy; **ti faccio i miei elogi per** congratulations on. **~ funebre** funeral oration

elo'quente *adj* eloquent; fig tell-tale

elo'quenza *nf* eloquence

El Salva'dor *nm* El Salvador; **nel Salvador** in El Salvador

e'ludere *vt* elude; evade ‹sorveglianza, controllo›

elusi'one *nf* **elusione fiscale** tax avoidance

elu'sivo *adj* elusive

el'vetico *adj* Swiss; **Confederazione Elvetica** Swiss Confederation

emaci'ato *adj* emaciated

e-mail *nf inv* e-mail; **mandare per ~ e-mail**, send by e-mail; **indirizzo ~ e-mail** address

ema'nare **1)** *vt* give off; pass ‹legge› **2)** *vi* emanate

emanazi'one *nf* giving off; (di legge) enactment

emanci'pare *vt* emancipate

emanci'parsi *vr* become emancipated

emanci'pato *adj* emancipated

emancipazi'one *nf* emancipation

emargi'nato *nm* marginalized person

emarginazi'one *nf* marginalization

ema'toma *nm* haematoma

em'bargo *nm* embargo. **embargo sulle armi** arms embargo

em'blema *nm* emblem

emble'matico *adj* emblematic

embo'lia *nf* embolism

'embolo *nm* embolus

embrio'nale *adj* Biol, fig embryonic; **allo stato** ∼ ⟨*progetto, idea*⟩ embryonic

embri'one *nm* embryo

emenda'mento *nm* amendment

emen'dare *vt* amend

emen'darsi *vr* reform

emer'gente *adj* emergent

emer'genza *nf* emergency; **in caso di** ∼ in an emergency; **di** ∼ (di riserva) stand-by; **uscita d'emergenza** emergency exit. **emergenza sanitaria** ambulance

e'mergere *vi* emerge; ⟨*sottomarino*⟩ surface; (distinguersi) stand out

e'merito *adj* ⟨*professore*⟩ emeritus; **un** ∼ **imbecille** a prize idiot

e'merso *pp di* EMERGERE

e'messo *pp di* EMETTERE

e'metico *adj* emetic

e'mettere *vt* emit; give out ⟨*luce, suono*⟩; let out ⟨*grido*⟩; (mettere in circolazione) issue

emi'crania *nf* migraine

emi'grare *vi* emigrate

emi'grato, -a *nmf* immigrant

emigrazi'one *nf* emigration

emi'nente *adj* eminent

emi'nenza *nf* eminence; **Sua Eminenza** His/Your Eminence. **eminenza grigia** éminence grise

emi'rato *nm* emirate; **Emirati** *pl* **Arabi Uniti** United Arab Emirates

e'miro *nm* emir

emi'sfero *nm* hemisphere

emis'sario *nm* emissary; (fiume) effluent

emissi'one *nf* emission; (di denaro, francobolli) issue; (trasmissione) broadcast; '∼ **del biglietto**' 'take your ticket here'

emit'tente ① *adj* issuing; (trasmittente) broadcasting ② *nf* Radio transmitter

'emmental *nm* Emmenthal

emofi'lia *nf* haemophilia

emofi'liaco, -a *nmf* haemophiliac

emoglo'bina *nf* haemoglobin

emorra'gia *nf* haemorrhage; **avere un'**∼ haemorrhage

emor'roidi *nfpl* haemorrhoids, piles

emo'statico *adj* haemostatic

emotiva'mente *adv* emotionally

emotività *nf* emotional make-up

emotivo *adj* emotional; **con turbe emotive** emotionally disturbed

emozio'nante *adj* exciting; (commovente) moving

emozio'nare *vt* excite; (commuovere) move

emozio'narsi *vr* become excited; (commuoversi) be moved

emozio'nato *adj* excited; (commosso) moved

emozi'one *nf* emotion; (agitazione) excitement

empietà *nf inv* impiety

'empio *adj* impious; (spietato) pitiless; (malvagio) wicked

em'pirico *adj* empirical

empi'rismo *nm* empiricism

empi'rista *nmf* empiricist

em'porio *nm* emporium; (negozio) general store

emù *nm inv* emu

emu'lare *vt* emulate

emulazi'one *nf* emulation. **emulazione di terminale** terminal emulation

emulsio'nare *vt* emulsify

emulsio'narsi *vr* emulsify

emulsi'one *nf* emulsion

ena'lotto *nm* weekly lottery

encefa'lite *nf* **encefalite spongiforme bovina** Bovine Spongiform Encephalopathy, BSE

encefalo'gramma *nm* encephalogram

en'ciclica *nf* encyclical

enciclope'dia *nf* encyclopaedia

enciclo'pedico *adj* ⟨*mente, cultura, dizionario*⟩ encyclopaedic

encomi'are *vt* commend

en'comio *nm* commendation

ende'mia *nf* (situazione) endemic

en'demico *adj* endemic

endocrinolo'gia *nf* endocrinology

endo'vena ① *nf inv* intravenous injection ② *adv* intravenously

endove'noso *adj* intravenous; **per via endovenosa** intravenously

ener'getico *adj* ⟨*risorse, crisi*⟩ energy *attrib*; ⟨*alimento*⟩ energy-giving

ener'gia *nf* energy; **pieno di** ∼ full of energy. **energia alternativa** alternative energy. **energia atomica** atomic energy. **energia elettrica** electricity. **energia eolica** windpower. **energia idroelettrica** hydroelectricity. **energia nucleare** nuclear energy, nuclear power. **energia solare** solar energy, solar power

energica'mente *adv* energetically

e'nergico *adj* energetic; (efficace) strong

ener'gumeno *nm* Neanderthal

'enfasi *nf* emphasis

en'fatico *adj* emphatic

enfatiz'zare *vt* emphasize

enfi'sema *nm* emphysema

e'nigma *nm* enigma

enig'matico *adj* enigmatic

enig'mistica *nf* puzzles *pl*

E.N.I.T. *nm abbr* (**Ente Nazionale Italiano per il Turismo**) Italian State Tourist Office

en'nesimo *adj* Math nth; fam umpteenth; **all'ennesima potenza** Math, fig to the nth power/degree

eno'logico *adj* wine attrib

e'norme *adj* enormous, great big fam; **è un'ingiustizia** ∼ it's enormously unfair

enorme'mente *adv* massively

enormità *nf inv* enormity; (assurdità) absurdity

eno'teca *nf* wine-tasting shop

eno'tera *nf* evening primrose

en pas'sant *adv* in passing

'ente *nm* board; (società) company; (in filosofia) being

ente'rite *nf* enteritis

entero'clisma *nm* Med enema

entità *nf inv* (filosofia) entity; (gravità) seriousness; (dimensione) extent

entomolo'gia *nf* entomology

entou'rage *nm inv* entourage

en'trambi *adj & pron* both

en'trare *vi* go in, enter; ∼ in go into; (stare in, trovar posto in) fit into; (arruolarsi) join; **entrarci** (avere a che fare) have to do with; **tu che c'entri?** what has it got to do with you?; **da che parte si entra?** how do you get in?; **fallo** ∼ (in ufficio, dal medico ecc) show him in; **'vietato** ∼**'** 'no entry'

en'trata *nf* entry, entrance. **entrata libera** admission free. **entrata di servizio** tradesman's entrance; **entrate** *pl* Comm takings; (reddito) income *sg*

entre'côte *nf inv* beef entrecôte

'entro *prep* (tempo) within; ∼ **oggi** by the end of today

entro'bordo *nm* (motore) inboard motor; (motoscafo) speedboat

entro'terra *nm inv* hinterland

entusia'smante *adj* fascinating, exciting

entusia'smare *vt* arouse enthusiasm in

entusia'smarsi *vr* be enthusiastic (**per** about)

entusi'asmo *nm* enthusiasm

entusi'asta ① *adj* enthusiastic ② *nmf* enthusiast

entusi'astico *adj* enthusiastic

enucle'are *vt* define

enume'rare *vt* enumerate

enumerazi'one *nf* enumeration

enunci'are *vt* enunciate

enunciazi'one *nf* enunciation

E'olie *nfpl* **le** ∼ the Aeolian Islands

epa'tite *nf* hepatitis

epi'centro *nm* epicentre

'epico *adj* epic

epide'mia *nf* epidemic

epi'dermide *nf* epidermis

epidu'rale *adj* (Med: anestesia) epidural

Epifa'nia *nf* Epiphany

epi'gramma *nm* epigram

epiles'sia *nf* epilepsy

epi'lettico, -a *adj & nmf* epileptic

e'pilogo *nm* epilogue

episco'pato *nm* episcopacy

epi'sodico *adj* episodic; **caso** ∼ one-off case

epi'sodio *nm* episode

e'pistola *nf* epistle

episto'lare *adj* epistolary

episto'lario *nm* correspondence, letters *pl*

epi'taffio *nm* epitaph

e'piteto *nm* epithet

'epoca *nf* age; (periodo) period; **a quell'**∼ in those days; **un avvenimento che ha fatto** ∼ an epoch-making event; **auto d'epoca** vintage car; **mobile d'epoca** period furniture

e'ponimo *adj* eponymous

epo'pea *nf* epic

ep'pure *conj* [and] yet

E.P.T. *abbr* (**Ente Provinciale per il Turismo**) Italian local tourist board

epu'rare *vt* purge; purify ⟨acqua⟩

epura'tore *nm* water purifier

epurazi'one *nf* purging; (di acqua) purification. **epurazione etnica** ethnic cleansing

equalizza'tore *nm* equalizer

e'quanime *adj* level-headed; (imparziale) impartial

equa'tore *nm* equator

equatori'ale *adj* equatorial

equazi'one *nf* equation

e'questre *adj* equestrian; **circo equestre** circus

equidi'stante *adj* equidistant

equi'latero *adj* equilateral

equili'brare *vt* balance

equili'brato *adj* (persona) well-balanced

equi'librio *nm* balance; (buon senso) common sense; (di bilancia) equilibrium

equili'brismo *nm* **fare** ∼ do a balancing act

equili'brista *nmf* tightrope walker

e'quino *adj* horse *attrib*

equi'nozio *nm* equinox

equipaggia'mento *nm* equipment

equipaggi'are *vt* equip; (di persone) man

equi'paggio *nm* crew; Aeron cabin crew. **equipaggio di volo** aircrew

equipa'rare *vt* make equal

equipa'rato *adj* equal

é'quipe *nf inv* team

equità *nf* equity

equitazione *nf* riding, horseriding, horseback riding Am

equiva'lente *adj & nm* equivalent

equiva'lenza *nf* equivalence

equiva'lere *vi* ~ **a** be equivalent to

equivo'care *vi* misunderstand

e'quivoco ① *adj* equivocal; (sospetto) suspicious; **un tipo** ~ a shady character ② *nm* misunderstanding; **a scanso di equivoci** to avoid any misunderstandings; **giocare sull'**~ equivocate

'equo *adj* fair, just

'era *nf* era. **era glaciale** Ice Age

'erba *nf* grass; (aromatica, medicinale) herb; **in** ~ ‹atleta, attore› budding. **erba cipollina** chives

er'baccia *nf* weed

er'baceo *adj* herbaceous

erbi'cida *nm* weedkiller

erbi'voro ① *adj* herbivorous ② *nm* herbivore

erbo'rista *nmf* herbalist

erboriste'ria *nf* herbalist's shop

er'boso *adj* grassy

Erco'lano *nf* Herculaneum

'Ercole *nm* Hercules

er'culeo *adj* ‹forza› herculean

e'rede ① *nm* heir ② *nf* heiress

eredità *nf inv* inheritance; Biol heredity

eredi'tare *vt* inherit

ereditarietà *nf* heredity

eredi'tario *adj* hereditary

erediti'era *nf* heiress

+erello *suff* furterello *nm* petty theft; **pioggerella** *nf* drizzle

ere'mita *nm* hermit

'eremo *nm* isolated place; fig retreat

ere'sia *nf* heresy

e'retico, -a ① *adj* heretical ② *nmf* heretic

e'retto ① *pp di* ERIGERE ② *adj* erect

erezi'one *nf* erection; (costruzione) building

ergasto'lano, -a *nmf* prisoner serving a life sentence, lifer fam

er'gastolo *nm* life sentence; (luogo) prison

ergono'mia *nf* ergonomics

ergo'nomico *adj* ergonomic

ergotera'pia *nf* occupational therapy

ergotera'pista *nmf* occupational therapist

'erica *nf* heather

e'rigere *vt* erect; (fig: fondare) found

eri'tema *nm* (cutaneo) inflammation; (solare) sunburn. **eritema da pannolini** nappy rash

Eri'trea *nf* Eritrea

eri'treo, -a *adj & nmf* Eritrean

ermafro'dito *adj & nm* hermaphrodite

ermel'lino *nm* ermine

ermetica'mente *adv* hermetically

er'metico *adj* hermetic; (a tenuta d'aria) airtight

'ernia *nf* hernia

e'rodere *vi* erode

e'roe *nm* hero

ero'gare *vt* distribute; (fornire) supply

erogazi'one *nf* supply

e'rogeno *adj* erogenous

eroica'mente *adv* heroically

e'roico *adj* heroic

ero'ina *nf* heroine; (droga) heroin

eroi'nomane *nmf* heroin addict

ero'ismo *nm* heroism

'eros *nm* Eros

erosi'one *nf* erosion

e'rotico *adj* erotic

ero'tismo *nm* eroticism

'erpice *nm* harrow

er'rante *adj* wandering

er'rare *vi* (vagare) wander; (sbagliare) be mistaken

er'rato *adj* (sbagliato) mistaken; **se non vado** ~ if I'm not mistaken

'erre *nf* **erre moscia** burr

erronea'mente *adv* mistakenly

er'rore *nm* error, mistake; (di stampa) misprint; **essere in** ~ be wrong. **errore giudiziario** miscarriage of justice. **errore di stampa** printing error, typo

'erta *nf* **stare all'**~ be on the alert

eru'dirsi *vr* get educated

eru'dito *adj* learned

erut'tare ① *vt* ‹vulcano› erupt ② *vi* (ruttare) belch

eruzi'one *nf* eruption; Med rash

Es *nm* Psych l'~ the id

es. *abbr* (**esempio**) eg.

esacer'bare *vt* exacerbate

esage'rare ① *vt* exaggerate; ~ **le cose** exaggerate things, go over the top ② *vi* exaggerate; (nel comportamento) go over the top; ~ **nel mangiare** eat too much

esagerata'mente *adv* excessively

esage'rato ① *adj* exaggerated; ‹prezzo› exorbitant ② *nm* **è un** ~ he exaggerates

esagerazi'one *nf* exaggeration; **è costato un'~** it cost the earth; **senza ~** with no exaggeration

esago'nale *adj* hexagonal

e'sagono *nm* hexagon

esa'lare ⟨1⟩ *vt* give off; **~ l'ultimo respiro** breathe one's last ⟨2⟩ *vi* emanate

esalazi'one *nf* emission; **esalazioni** *pl* fumes

esal'tare *vt* exalt; (entusiasmare) elate

esal'tarsi *vr* (entusiasmarsi) get excited (**per** about)

esal'tato ⟨1⟩ *adj* (fanatico) fanatical ⟨2⟩ *nm* fanatic

esaltazi'one *nf* exaltation; (in discorso) fervour

e'same *nm* examination, exam; **dare un ~** take *or* sit an exam; **prendere in ~** examine. **esame di ammissione** Sch entrance examination. **esame di coscienza** soul-searching. **esame di guida** driving test. **esami di maturità** ≈ A-levels. **esame orale** Sch, Univ viva. **esame del sangue** blood test. **esame della vista** eye test

esami'nando, -a *nmf* examinee

esami'nare *vt* examine

esamina|'tore, -trice *nmf* examiner

e'sangue *adj* bloodless

e'sanime *adj* lifeless

esaspe'rante *adj* exasperating

esaspe'rare *vt* exasperate

esaspe'rarsi *vr* get exasperated

esasperazi'one *nf* exasperation

esatta'mente *adv* exactly

esat'tezza *nf* exactness; (precisione) precision; (di risposta, risultato) accuracy

e'satto exact; (risposta, risultato) correct; ⟨orologio⟩ right; **hai l'ora esatta?** do you have the right time?; **sono le due esatte** it's two o'clock exactly

esat'tore *nm* collector. **esattore dei crediti** Fin debt collector. **esattore delle imposte** tax collector, tax man

esau'dire *vt* grant; fulfil ⟨speranze⟩

esauri'ente *adj* exhaustive

esauri'mento *nm* exhaustion; **'fino ad ~ delle scorte'** 'subject to availability'. **esaurimento nervoso** nervous breakdown

esau'rire *vt* exhaust

esau'rirsi *vr* exhaust oneself; ⟨merci ecc⟩ run out

esau'rito *adj* exhausted; ⟨merci⟩ sold out; ⟨libro⟩ out of print; **fare il tutto ~** ⟨spettacolo⟩ play to a full house; **'tutto ~'** 'sold out'

esazi'one *nf* collection. **esazione crediti** debt collection

'esca *nf* bait

escande'scenza *nf* outburst; **dare in escandescenze** lose one's temper

escava'tore *nm* excavator

escava'trice *nf* excavator

escla'mare *vi* exclaim

esclama'tivo *adj* exclamatory

esclamazi'one *nf* exclamation

e'scludere *vt* exclude; rule out ⟨possibilità, ipotesi⟩

esclusi'one *nf* exclusion; **senza ~ di colpi** ⟨attacco⟩ all-out

esclu'siva *nf* exclusive right, sole right; **in ~** exclusive

esclusiva'mente *adv* exclusively

esclusi'vista *nmf* exclusive agent

esclu'sivo *adj* exclusive

e'scluso ⟨1⟩ *pp di* ESCLUDERE ⟨2⟩ *adj* **non è ~ che ci sia** it's not out of the question that he'll be there; **esclusi i presenti** with the exception of those present; **esclusi sabati e festivi** except Saturdays and Sundays/holidays ⟨3⟩ *nm* outcast

escogi'tare *vt* contrive

escoriazi'one *nf* graze

escre'mento *nm* excrement; **escrementi** *pl* excrement

escursi'one *nf* (gita) excursion; (camminata) hike; (scorreria) raid. **escursione termica** difference between the lowest and the highest temperature in a 24 hours period

escursio'nismo *nm* hiking

ese'crabile *adj* abominable

ese'crare *vt* abhor

esecu'tivo *adj & nm* executive

esecu|'tore, -trice *nmf* executor; Mus performer

esecuzi'one *nf* execution; Mus performance. **esecuzione capitale** capital punishment

esegu'ibile *nm* Comput executable file

esegu'ire *vt* carry out; Jur execute; Mus perform

e'sempio *nm* example; **ad** *o* **per ~** for example; **dare l'~ a qualcuno** set somebody an example; **fare un ~** give an example

esem'plare ⟨1⟩ *adj* examplary ⟨2⟩ *nm* specimen; (di libro) copy

esemplifi'care *vt* exemplify

esen'tare *vt* exempt

esen'tarsi *vr* free oneself

esen'tasse *adj* tax-free

e'sente *adj* exempt. **esente da imposta** duty-free. **esente da IVA** VAT exempt

e'sequie *nfpl* funeral rites

eser'cente *nmf* shopkeeper

eserci'tare *vt* exercise; (addestrare) train; (fare uso di) exert; (professione) practise

eserci'tarsi *vr* practise; ~ **nella danza** practise dancing

eserci'tato *adj* ‹occhio› practised; **tenere la memoria esercitata** give one's memory some exercise

esercitazi'one *nf* exercise; Mil drill; (di musica, chimica) practical class

e'sercito *nm* army. **Esercito della Salvezza** Salvation Army

eser'cizio *nm* exercise; (pratica) practice; Comm financial year; (azienda) business; **essere fuori** ~ be out of practice; **nell'**~ **delle proprie funzioni** in the line of duty. **esercizio finanziario** financial year. **esercizio fiscale** fiscal year, tax year. **esercizi a terra** *pl* floor exercises. **esercizio tributario** fiscal year, tax year

esi'bire *vt* show off; produce ‹documenti›

esi'birsi *vr* Theat perform; fig show off

esibizi'one *nf* Theat performance; (di documenti) production. **esibizione in volo** Aeron air display

esibizio'nismo *nm* showing off

esibizio'nista *nmf* exhibitionist

esi'gente *adj* exacting; (pignolo) fastidious

esi'genza *nf* demand; (bisogno) need

e'sigere *vt* demand; (riscuotere) collect

e'siguo *adj* meagre

esila'rante *adj* exhilarating

esila'rare *vt* exhilarate

'esile *adj* slender; ‹voce› thin

esili'are *vt* exile

esili'arsi *vr* go into exile

esili'ato, -a ⓵ *adj* exiled ⓶ *nmf* exile

e'silio *nm* exile

e'simere *vt* release

e'simersi *vr* ~ **da** get out of

e'simio *adj* distinguished

esi'stente *adj* existing

esi'stenza *nf* existence

esistenzi'ale *adj* existential

esistenzia'lismo *nm* existentialism

e'sistere *vi* exist

esi'tante *adj* hesitating; ‹voce› faltering

esi'tare *vi* hesitate

esitazi'one *nf* hesitation

'esito *nm* result; **avere buon** ~ be a success

'esodo *nm* exodus

e'sofago *nm* oesophagus

esone'rare *vt* exempt

e'sonero *nm* exemption

esorbi'tante *adj* exorbitant

esorbi'tare *vi* ~ **da** exceed

esor'cismo *nm* exorcism

esor'cista *nmf* exorcist

esorciz'zare *vt* exorcize

esordi'ente *nmf* person making his/her début

e'sordio *nm* opening; (di attore) début

esor'dire *vi* début

esor'tare *vt* (pregare) beg; (incitare) urge

eso'terico *adj* esoteric

e'sotico *adj* exotic

espa'drillas *nfpl* espadrilles

e'spandere *vt* expand

e'spandersi *vr* expand; (diffondersi) extend

espan'dibile *adj* Comput upgradeable

espandibilità *nf* Comput upgradeability

espansi'one *nf* expansion; **in** ~ expanding

espansio'nista *nmf* expansionist

espansio'nistico *adj* expansionist

espan'sivo *adj* expansive; ‹persona› friendly

espatri'are *vi* leave one's country

espatri'ato, -a *nmf* expatriate, expat fam

e'spatrio *nm* expatriation

espedi'ente *nm* expedient; **vivere di espedienti** live by one's wits

e'spellere *vt* expel; send off ‹calciatore›

esperi'enza *nf* experience; **per** ~ ‹sapere, parlare› from experience; **non ha** ~ he doesn't have any experience

esperi'mento *nm* experiment

e'sperto, -a *adj & nmf* expert. **esperto di computer** computer expert

espi'are *vt* atone for

espia'torio *adj* expiatory

espi'rare *vt/i* breathe out

espirazi'one *nf* exhalation; (scadenza) expiry

espli'care *vt* carry on

esplicita'mente *adv* explicitly

e'splicito *adj* explicit

e'splodere ⓵ *vi* explode ⓶ *vt* ‹arma› fire

esplo'rare *vt* explore

esplora|'tore, -trice *nmf* explorer; **giovane esploratore** boy scout; **giovane esploratrice** girl guide

esplorazi'one *nf* exploration

esplosi'one *nf* explosion

esplo'sivo *adj & nm* explosive

espo'nente *nm* exponent; **2 all'**~ superscript 2

esponenzi'ale *adj* exponential

e'sporre *vt* expose; display ‹merci›; (spiegare) expound; exhibit ‹quadri ecc›

e'sporsi *vr* (compromettersi) compromise oneself; (al sole) expose oneself; (alle critiche) lay oneself open

espor'tare *vt* Comm, Comput export

esporta|'tore, -trice *nmf* exporter

esportazi'one *nf* export

espo'simetro *nm* light meter

esposi|'tore, -trice ① *nmf* exhibitor; ② *nm* display rack

esposizi'one *nf* (mostra) exhibition; (in vetrina) display; (spiegazione ecc) exposition; (posizione, fotografia) exposure; **con ~ a nord/sud** north-/south-facing. **esposizione a radiazioni** radiation exposure

e'sposto ① *pp di* ESPORRE ② *adj* exposed; ⟨merce⟩ on show; ⟨spiegato⟩ set out; **~ a nord/sud** north-/south-facing ③ *nm* submission

espressa'mente *adv* expressly; **non l'ha detto ~** he didn't put it in so many words

espressi'one *nf* expression

espressio'nismo *nm* expressionism

espressio'nista *adj & nmf* expressionist

espressio'nistico *adj* expressionistic

espres'sivo *adj* expressive

e'spresso ① *pp di* ESPRIMERE ② *adj* express ③ *nm* (lettera) special delivery; (treno) express train; (caffè) espresso; **per ~** ⟨spedire⟩ [by] express [post]; **piatto ~** meal made to order

e'sprimere *vt* express

e'sprimersi *vr* express oneself

espropri'are *vt* dispossess

espropriazi'one *nf* Jur expropriation

e'sproprio *nm* expropriation

espulsi'one *nf* expulsion

e'spulso *pp di* ESPELLERE

esqui'mese *adj & nmf* Eskimo

es'senza *nf* essence

essenzi'ale ① *adj* essential ② *nm* important thing; **l'~** (di teoria ecc) the bare bones; **l'~ è ...** (la cosa più importante) the main thing is ...

essenzial'mente *adv* essentially

'essere ① *vi* be; **c'è** there is; **ci sono** there are; **ci sono!** (ho capito) I've got it!; **ci siamo!** (siamo arrivati) here we are at last!; **non ce n'è più** there's none left; **c'è di che essere contenti** there's a lot to be happy about; **che ora è? –sono le dieci** what time is it? –it's ten o'clock; **chi è? –sono io** who is it? –it's me; **è stato detto che** it has been said that; **siamo in due** there are two of us; **questa camicia è da lavare** this shirt is to be washed; **non è da te** it's not like you; **~ di** belong to; (provenire da) be from; **~ per** (favorevole) be in favour of; **se fossi in te, ...** if I were you, ...; **sarà!** if you say so!; **come sarebbe a dire?** what are you getting at?

② *v aux* have; (in passivi) be; **siamo arrivati** we have arrived; **ci sono stato ieri** I was there yesterday; **sono nato a Torino** I was born in Turin; **è riconosciuto come...** he is recognized as ...

③ *nm* being; **~ umano** human being; **~ vivente** living creature

essic'care *vt* dry

essic'cato *adj* dried; ⟨noce di cocco⟩ desiccated

'esso, -a *pers pron* he; she; (cosa, animale) it

est *nm* east; **l'Est europeo** Eastern Europe

'estasi *nf* ecstasy; **andare in ~ per** go into raptures over

estasi'are *vt* enrapture

estasi'arsi *vr* go into raptures

e'state *nf* summer

e'statico *adj* ecstatic

estempo'raneo *adj* impromptu

e'stendere *vt* extend

e'stendersi *vr* spread; (allungarsi) stretch

estensi'one *nf* extension; (ampiezza) expanse; Mus range. **estensione del file** Comput file extension

esten'sivo *adj* extensive

estenu'ante *adj* exhausting

estenu'are *vt* exhaust

estenu'arsi *vr* exhaust oneself

'estere *nm* ester

esteri'ore *adj & nm* exterior

esteriorità *nf* outward appearance; **badare all'~** judge by appearances

esterioriz'zare *vt* externalize

esterior'mente *adv* externally; (di persone) outwardly

esterna'mente *adv* on the outside

ester'nare *vt* express, show

e'sterno, -a ① *adj* external; (scala) outside; **per uso ~** for external use only ② *nm* Archit exterior; (in film) location shot ③ *nmf* day-pupil

'estero ① *adj* foreign ② *nm* foreign countries *pl*; **all'~** abroad; **ministero degli esteri** ≈ Foreign Office Br, State Department Am

esterofi'lia *nf* xenophilia

este'rofilo *adj* xenophile

esterre'fatto *adj* horrified

e'steso ① *pp di* ESTENDERE ② *adj* extensive; (diffuso) widespread; **per ~** ⟨scrivere⟩ in full

e'steta *nmf* aesthete

e'stetica *nf* aesthetics

estetica'mente *adv* aesthetically

esteticità *nf* aestheticism

e'stetico *adj* aesthetic; ⟨*chirurgia, chirurgo*⟩ plastic

este'tismo *nm* (dottrina, carattere) aestheticism

este'tista *nmf* beautician

estima'tore, -trice *nmf* fan

'estimo *nm* estimate

e'stinguere *vt* extinguish; close ⟨*conto*⟩

e'stinguersi *vr* die out

e'stinto, -a ① pp di ESTINGUERE ② *nmf* deceased

estin'tore *nm* [fire] extinguisher

estinzi'one *nf* extinction; (di incendio) putting out

estir'pare *vt* uproot; extract ⟨*dente*⟩; fig eradicate ⟨*crimine, malattia*⟩

estirpazi'one *nf* eradication; (di dente) extraction

e'stivo *adj* summer *attrib*

'estone *adj & nm* Estonian

E'stonia *nf* Estonia

e'storcere *vt* extort

estorsi'one *nf* extortion

e'storto pp di ESTORCERE

estradizi'one *nf* extradition

estra'gone *nm* tarragon

estra'ibile *adj* removable

e'straneo, -a ① *adj* extraneous; (straniero) foreign ② *nmf* stranger

estrani'are *vt* estrange

estrani'arsi *vr* become estranged

estrapo'lare *vt* extrapolate

e'strarre *vt* extract; (sorteggiare) draw

e'stratto ① pp di ESTRARRE ② *nm* extract; (brano) excerpt; (documento) abstract. **estratto conto** statement [of account], bank statement

estrazi'one *nf* extraction; (a sorte) draw. **estrazione a premi** prize draw

estrema'mente *adv* extremely

estre'mismo *nm* extremism

estre'mista *nmf* extremist

estremità ① *nf inv* extremity; (di una corda) end; ② *pl* Anat extremities

e'stremo ① *adj* extreme; (ultimo) last; **misure estreme** drastic measures; **fare un** ∼ **tentativo** make one last try; **l'Estremo Oriente** the Far East; ∼ **saluto** Mil military funeral; **l'estrema unzione** last rites ② *nm* (limite) extreme; **all'**∼ in the extreme; **passare da un** ∼ **all'altro** go from one extreme to the other; **estremi** *pl* (di documento) main points; (di reato) essential elements; **essere agli estremi** be at the end of one's tether; **andare agli estremi** go to extremes; **essere all'**∼ **delle forze** have no strength left

'estro *nm* (disposizione artistica) talent; (ispirazione) inspiration; (capriccio) whim

e'strogeno *nm* oestrogen

estro'mettere *vt* expel

estromissi'one *nf* ejection

e'stroso *adj* talented; (capriccioso) unpredictable

estro'verso ① *adj* extroverted ② *nm* extrovert

estu'ario *nm* estuary

esube'rante *adj* exuberant

esube'ranza *nf* exuberance

e'subero *nm* **esubero cassa integrazione** voluntary redundancy

esu'lare *vi* ∼ **da** be beyond the scope of

'esule *nmf* exile

esul'tante *adj* exultant

esul'tanza *nf* exultation

esul'tare *vi* rejoice

esu'mare *vt* exhume

età *nf* age; **raggiungere la maggiore** ∼ come of age; **un uomo di mezz'**∼ a middle-aged man; **avere la stessa** ∼ be the same age; **che** ∼ **gli daresti?** how old would you say he was?; **fin dalla più tenera** ∼ from his/her etc earliest years; **in** ∼ **avanzata** of advanced years; **è senza** ∼ it's hard to tell his age. **età del bronzo** Bronze Age. **età della pensione** retirement age

e'tano *nm* ethane

eta'nolo *nm* ethanol

'etere *nm* ether. **etere etilico** ether

e'tereo *adj* ethereal

eterna'mente *adv* eternally

eternità *nf* eternity; **è un'**∼ **che non la vedo** I haven't seen her for ages

e'terno *adj* eternal; ⟨*questione, problema*⟩ age-old; fig ⟨*discorso, conferenza*⟩ never-ending; **in** ∼ *fam* for ever; **giurare amore** ∼ swear undying love; **un** ∼ **bambino** a child

etero'geneo *adj* diverse, heterogeneous

eterosessu'ale *adj & nmf* heterosexual

eterosessualità *nf* heterosexuality

'etica *nf* ethics

eti'chetta¹ *nf* label; (con il prezzo) price-tag

eti'chetta² *nf* (cerimoniale) etiquette

etichet'tare *vt* label

etichetta'trice *nf* labelling machine

etichetta'tura *nf* (operazione) labelling

'etico *adj* ethical

eti'lometro *nm* Breathalyzer®

etimolo'gia *nf* etymology

e'tiope *adj & nmf* Ethiopian

Eti'opia *nf* Ethiopia

eti'opico *adj* Ethiopian

'Etna nm Etna

et'nia nf ethnic group

'etnico adj ethnic

etnolo'gia nf ethnology

e'trusco adj & nmf Etruscan

'ettaro nm hectare

+ettino suff **cosettina** nf small thing; **è una cosettina da niente** it's nothing

'etto, **etto'grammo** nm hundred grams, quarter pound

+etto suff **cameretta** nf little bedroom; **scherzetto** nf prank; **piccoletto** nm pej shorty

et'tolitro nm hectolitre

euca'lipto nm eucalyptus

eucari'stia nf Eucharist

eufe'mismo nm euphemism

eufe'mistico adj euphemistic

eufo'ria nf elation; Med euphoria

eu'forico adj elated; Med euphoric

euge'netica nf eugenics

eu'nuco nm eunuch

EUR abbr (**euro**) e

Eur'asia nf Eurasia

eurasi'atico adj Eurasian

'EURATOM nf abbr (**Comunità Europea dell'Energia Atomica**) EURATOM

euro+ pref Euro+

'euro nm inv Fin euro

eurobbligazi'one nf Eurobond

euro'cheque nm inv Eurocheque

Euro'city nm inv Rail international intercity

eurodepu'tato nm Euro MP, MEP

eurodi'visa nf Eurocurrency

euro'dollaro nm Eurodollar

Eu'ropa nf Europe

europe'ismo nm Europeanism

euro'peo, **-a** adj & nmf European

euro'scettico nm Euro-sceptic

eutana'sia nf euthanasia

evacu'are vt evacuate

evacuazi'one nf evacuation

e'vadere ① vt evade; (sbrigare) deal with ② vi ~ **da** escape from

evane'scente adj vanishing

evan'gelico adj evangelical

evange'lista nm evangelist

evan'gelo nm = VANGELO

evapo'rare vi evaporate

evaporazi'one nf evaporation

evasi'one nf escape; (fiscale) evasion; fig escapism

evasiva'mente adv evasively

eva'sivo adj evasive

e'vaso, **-a** ① pp di EVADERE

② nmf fugitive

eva'sore nm **evasore fiscale** tax evader

eveni'enza nf eventuality; **in ogni ~** if need be

e'vento nm event

eventu'ale adj possible

eventualità nf inv eventuality; **in ogni ~** at all events; **nell'~ che** in the event that

eventual'mente adv if necessary

ever'sivo adj subversive

evi'dente adj evident

evidente'mente adv evidently

evi'denza nf evidence; **mettere in ~** emphasize; **mettersi in ~** make oneself conspicuous; **arrendersi all'~** face the facts

evidenzi'are vt highlight

evidenzia'tore nm (penna) highlighter

evi'rare vt emasculate

evi'tare vt avoid; (risparmiare) spare

'evo nm age

evo'care vt evoke

evolu'tivo adj evolutionary

evo'luto ① pp di EVOLVERE ② adj evolved; (progredito) progressive; ⟨civiltà, nazione⟩ advanced; **una donna evoluta** a modern woman

evoluzi'one nf evolution; (di ginnasta, aereo) circle

e'volvere vt develop

e'volversi vr evolve

ev'viva int hurray; **~ il Papa!** long live the Pope!; **gridare ~** cheer; **~ la modestia!** what modesty!

ex prep ex, former; **ex moglie** ex-wife

ex 'aequo adv **arrivare ~** come in joint first

ex-Jugo'slavia nf ex-Yugoslavia

ex-jugo'slavo adj & nmf ex-Yugoslav

ex 'libris nm inv bookplate

ex'ploit nm inv feat, exploit

'extra ① adj inv extra; ⟨qualità⟩ first-class ② nm inv extra

extracomuni'tario, **-a** ① adj non-EC, non-EU ② nmf immigrant from outside the EU

extraconiu'gale adj extramarital

extraeuro'peo adj non-European

extraparlamen'tare adj extraparliamentary

extrasco'lastico adj extra-curricular

extrasensori'ale adj extrasensory

extrater'restre nmf extra-terrestrial

extrauniversi'tario adj extramural

ex 'voto nm inv ex voto

Ff

fa[1] *nm inv* Mus (chiave, nota) F

fa[2] *adv* ago; **due mesi** ∼ two months ago

fabbi'sogno *nm* requirements *pl*, needs *pl*. **fabbisogno dello Stato** government spending estimates

'fabbrica *nf* factory

fabbri'cabile *adj* ‹area, terreno› that can be built on

fabbri'cante *nm* manufacturer. **fabbricante d'armi** arms manufacturer

fabbri'care *vt* build; (produrre) manufacture; (fig: inventare) fabricate

fabbri'cato *nm* building

fabbricazi'one *nf* manufacturing; (costruzione) building

'fabbro *nm* blacksmith

fac'cenda *nf* matter; **faccende** *pl* domestiche housework *sg*

faccendi'ere *nm* wheeler-dealer

fac'chino *nm* porter

'faccia *nf* face; (di foglio) side; ∼ **a** ∼ face to face; ∼ **tosta** cheek; **voltar** ∼ change sides; **di** ∼ (palazzo) opposite; **alla** ∼ **di** (fam: a dispetto di) in spite of; **alla** ∼**!** (stupore) bloody hell!

facci'ata *nf* façade; (di foglio) side; (fig: esteriorità) outward appearance

fa'cente *nmf* **facente funzioni** deputy

fa'ceto *adj* facetious; **tra Il serio e Il** ∼ half joking

fa'cezia *nf* (battuta) witticism

fa'chiro *nm* fakir

'facile *adj* easy; (affabile) easy-going; **essere** ∼ **alle critiche** be quick to criticize; **essere** ∼ **al riso** laugh a lot; ∼ **a farsi** easy to do; **è** ∼ **che piova** it's likely to rain

facilità *nf* ease; (disposizione) aptitude; **avere** ∼ **di parola** express oneself well. **facilità d'uso** ease of use, user-friendliness

facili'tare *vt* facilitate

facilitazi'one *nf* facility; **facilitazioni** *pl* Fin special terms; **facilitazioni** *pl* **di pagamento** easy terms; **facilitazioni** *pl* **creditizie** credit facilities

facil'mente *adv* (con facilità) easily; (probabilmente) probably

faci'lone *adj* slapdash

facilone'ria *nf* slapdash attitude

facino'roso *adj* violent

facoltà *nf inv* faculty; (potere) power; **essere nel pieno possesso delle proprie** ∼ be compos mentis

facolta'tivo *adj* optional; **fermata facoltativa** request stop

facol'toso *adj* wealthy

fac'simile *nm inv* facsimile

fac'totum [1] *nm inv* man Friday [2] *nf inv* girl Friday

'faggio *nm* beech

fagi'ano *nm* pheasant

fagio'lino *nm* French bean

fagi'olo *nm* bean; **a** ∼ ‹arrivare, capitare› at the right time. **fagiolo borlotto** borlotti bean. **fagiolo bianco di Spagna** runner bean, haricot bean

fagoci'tare *vt* gobble up ‹società›

fa'gotto *nm* bundle; Mus bassoon

Fahren'heit *adj* Fahrenheit

'faida *nf* feud

fal da te *nm* do-it-yourself, DIY

fa'ina *nf* weasel

fa'lange *nf* (dito, Mil) phalanx

fal'cata *nf* stride

'falce *nf* scythe. **falce e martello** (simbolo) the hammer and sickle

fal'cetto *nm* sickle

falci'are *vt* cut; fig mow down

falci'ata *nf* (quantità d'erba) swathe

falcia'trice *nf* [lawn]mower

'falco *nm* hawk

fal'cone *nm* falcon

'falda *nf* stratum; (di neve) flake; (di cappello) brim; (di cappotto, frac) coat-tails; (pendio) slope. **falda freatica** water table

fale'gname *nm* carpenter

falegname'ria *nf* carpentry

fa'lena *nf* moth

'Falkland *nfpl* **le [isole]** ∼ the Falklands

'falla *nf* leak

fal'lace *adj* deceptive

'fallico *adj* phallic

fallimen'tare *adj* disastrous; Jur bankruptcy

falli'mento *nm* Comm bankruptcy; fig failure

fal'lire [1] *vi* Comm go bankrupt; fig fail [2] *vt* miss ‹colpo›

fal'lito [1] *adj* unsuccessful [2] *adj* & *nm* bankrupt

'fallo *nm* fault; (errore) mistake; Sport foul; (imperfezione) flaw; **senza** ∼ without fail; ⋯⟩

cogliere in ~ catch red-handed; **mettere un piede in** ~ slip. **fallo di mano** (in calcio) handball

falò nm inv bonfire

fal'sare vt alter; (falsificare) falsify

falsa'riga nf **sulla** ~ **di** along the same lines as

fal'sario, -a nmf forger; (di documenti) counterfeiter

fal'setto nm falsetto

falsifi'care vt fake; (contraffare) forge

falsificazi'one nf (di documenti) falsification

falsità nf falseness

'**falso** 1 adj false; (sbagliato) wrong; ⟨opera d'arte ecc⟩ fake; ⟨gioielli, oro⟩ imitation; **essere un** ~ **magro** be fatter than one looks

2 nm forgery; **giurare il** ~ commit perjury. **falso in atto pubblico** forgery of a legal document

'**fama** nf fame; (reputazione) reputation

'**fame** nf hunger; **aver** ~ be hungry; **fare la** ~ barely scrape a living; **da** ~ ⟨stipendio⟩ miserly; **avere una** ~ **da lupo** be ravenous

fa'melico adj ravenous

famige'rato adj infamous

fa'miglia nf family. **famiglia affidataria** foster family, foster home

famili'are 1 adj family attrib; (ben noto) familiar; (senza cerimonie) informal

2 nm relative, relation

familiarità nf familiarity; (informalità) informality

familiariz'zarsi vr familiarize oneself

fa'moso adj famous

fa'nale nm lamp; Auto ecc light. **fanali posteriori** pl Auto rear lights

fana'lino nm **fanalino di coda** Auto tail light; **essere il** ~ **di coda** fig bring up the rear, be the back marker

fa'natico, -a 1 adj fanatical; **essere** ~ **di calcio/cinema** be a football/cinema fanatic

2 nmf fanatic

fana'tismo nm fanaticism

fanciul'lezza nf childhood

fanci'ullo, -a nmf liter young boy; young girl

fan'donia nf lie; **fandonie!** nonsense!

fan'fara nf fanfare; (complesso) brass band

fanfaro'nata nf brag; fanfaronate pl bragging

fanfa'rone, -a nmf braggart

fan'ghiglia nf mud

'**fango** nm mud

fan'goso adj muddy

fannul'lone, -a nmf idler

fantasci'enza nf science fiction

fanta'sia nf fantasy; (immaginazione) imagination; (capriccio) fancy; (di tessuto) pattern; **fantasie** pl (sciocchezze) moonshine

fantasi'oso adj ⟨stilista, ragazzo⟩ imaginative; ⟨resoconto⟩ improbable, fanciful

fan'tasma nm ghost; **essere il** ~ **di se stesso** be a shadow of one's former self; **città fantasma** ghost town; **governo fantasma** shadow cabinet

fantasti'care vi day-dream, fantasize

fantastiche'ria nf day-dream, fantasy

fan'tastico adj fantastic; ⟨racconto⟩ fantasy attrib

'**fante** nm infantryman; (nelle carte) jack

fante'ria nm infantry

fan'tino nm jockey

fan'toccio nm puppet

fanto'matico adj (inafferrabile) phantom attrib; (immaginario) mythical

fara'butto nm trickster

fara'ona nf (uccello) guinea-fowl

'**farcia** nf stuffing; (di torta) filling

far'cire vt stuff; fill ⟨torta⟩

far'cito adj stuffed; ⟨dolce⟩ filled

fard nm inv blusher

far'dello nm bundle; fig burden

'**fare** 1 vt do; make ⟨dolce, letto, ecc⟩; (recitare la parte di) play; (trascorrere) spend; ~ **una pausa/un sogno** have a break/a dream; ~ **colpo su** impress; ~ **paura a** frighten; ~ **piacere a** please; **farla finita** put an end to it; ~ **l'insegnante** be a teacher; ~**lo scemo** play the idiot; ~ **una settimana al mare** spend a week at the seaside; **3 più 3 fa 6** 3 and 3 makes 6; **quanto fa? —fanno 50 euro** how much is it? –it's 50 euros; **far** ~ **qualcosa a qualcuno** get somebody to do something; (costringere) make somebody do something; ~ **vedere** show; **fammi parlare** let me speak; **niente a che** ~ **con** nothing to do with; **non c'è niente da** ~ (per problema) there is nothing we/you etc can do; **fa caldo/buio** it's warm/dark; **non fa niente** it doesn't matter; **strada facendo** on the way; **farcela** (riuscire) manage

2 vi **fai in modo di venire** try and come; ~ **da** act as; ~ **per** make as if to; ~ **presto** be quick; **non fa per me** it's not for me

3 nm (comportamento) manner; **sul far del giorno** at daybreak

fa'retto nm spot[light]

far'falla nf butterfly

farfal'lino nm (cravatta) bow tie

farfugli'are vt mutter

fa'rina nf flour. **farina di ceci** chickpea flour, gram flour. **farina gialla** maize flour. **farina integrale** wholemeal flour. **farina lattea** powdered milk for babies. **farina d'ossa** bonemeal

fari'nacei nmpl starchy food sg

fa'ringe *nf* pharynx

farin'gite *nf* pharyngitis

fari'noso *adj* ‹neve› powdery; ‹mela› soft; ‹patata› floury

farma'ceutico *adj* pharmaceutical; **industria farmaceutica** pharmaceuticals industry

farma'cia *nf* pharmacy; (negozio) chemist's [shop]. **farmacia di turno** duty pharmacy

farma'cista *nmf* chemist, pharmacist

'farmaco *nm* drug; **essere sotto farmaci** be on medication

'faro *nm* Auto headlight; Aeron beacon; (costruzione) lighthouse; **abbassare i fari** dip one's headlights; **accendere i fari** switch on one's lights. **fari antinebbia** *pl* fog lamps. **fari posteriori** *pl* rear lights

farragi'noso *adj* confused

'farsa *nf* farce

far'sesco *adj* farcical

'farsi *vr* (diventare) get; (sl: drogarsi) shoot up; ∼ **avanti** come forward; ∼ **i fatti propri** mind one's own business; ∼ **la barba** shave; ∼ **la villa** fam buy a villa; ∼ **il ragazzo** fam find a boyfriend; ∼ **due risate** have a laugh; ∼ **male** hurt oneself; ∼ **un nome** make a name for oneself; **farsela sotto** fam wet oneself

Far 'west *nm* Wild West

fa'scetta *nf* strip; (per capelli) hair band; (di giornale) wrapper

'fascia *nf* band; (zona) area; (ufficiale) sash; (benda) bandage; (di smoking) cummerbund; (in statistica) bracket. **fascia per capelli** hair band. **fascia elastica** crepe bandage; (ventriera) girdle. **fascia d'età** age bracket, age group. **fascia d'ozono** ozone layer. **fascia di reddito** income bracket

fasci'are *vt* bandage; cling to ‹fianchi›

fasci'arsi *vr* bandage; ∼ **la testa prima di rompersela** worry about something that might never happen

fascia'tura *nf* dressing; (azione) bandaging

fascicola|'tore, -trice *nmf* sorter

fa'scicolo *nm* file; (di rivista) issue; (libretto) booklet

fa'scina *nf* faggot

'fascino *nm* fascination

fasci'noso *adj* charming

'fascio *nm* bundle; (di fiori) bunch. **fascio di luce** beam of light

fa'scismo *nm* fascism

fa'scista *adj & nmf* fascist

'fase *nf* phase; **il motore è fuori** ∼ the timing is wrong; **sono fuori** ∼ I'm not firing on all four cylinders; **essere in** ∼ **di miglioramento** be on the mend, be

recovering; **essere in** ∼ **di espansione** be expanding

fast 'food *nm inv* fast food; (ristorante) fast food restaurant

fa'stidio *nm* nuisance; (scomodo) inconvenience; **fastidi** *pl* (preoccupazioni) worries; (disturbi) troubles; **dar** ∼ **a qualcuno** bother somebody

fastidi'oso *adj* tiresome

'fasto *nm* pomp

fa'stoso *adj* sumptuous

fa'sullo *adj* bogus

'fata *nf* fairy

fa'tale *adj* fatal; (inevitabile) fated; **donna fatale** femme fatale

fata'lismo *nm* fatalism

fata'lista ① *nmf* fatalist
② *adj* fatalistic

fatalità *nf inv* fate; (caso sfortunato) misfortune

fatal'mente *adv* inevitably

fa'tato *adj* ‹anello, bacchetta› magic

fa'tica *nf* effort; (lavoro faticoso) hard work; (stanchezza, di metalli) fatigue; **a** ∼ with great difficulty; **è** ∼ **sprecata** it's a waste of time; **fare** ∼ **a fare qualcosa** find it difficult to do something; **senza [nessuna]** ∼ without [any] effort; **fare** ∼ **a finire qualcosa** struggle to finish something; **uomo di fatica** odd-job man

fati'caccia *nf* pain

fati'care *vi* toil; ∼ **a** (stentare) find it difficult to

fati'cata *nf* effort; (sfacchinata) grind

fati'coso *adj* tiring; (difficile) difficult

fati'scente *adj* crumbling

'fato *nm* fate

fat'taccio *nm hum* foul deed

fat'tezze *nfpl* features

fat'tibile *adj* feasible

fatti'specie *nf* **nella** ∼ in this case

'fatto ① *pp di* FARE; **ormai è fatta!** what's done is done
② *adj* made; ∼ **a mano/in casa** handmade/home-made; **essere ben** ∼ ‹persona› have a nice figure; **un uomo** ∼ a grown man
③ *nm* fact; (azione) action; (avvenimento) event; (faccenda) business, matter; **sa il** ∼ **suo** he knows his business; **le ho detto il** ∼ **suo** I told her what I thought of her; **di** ∼ in fact; **in** ∼ **di** as regards; ∼ **sta che** the fact remains that; **mettere di fronte al** ∼ **compiuto** present with a fait accompli

fat'tore *nm* (causa, Math) factor; (di fattoria) farm manager. **fattore di protezione solare** protection factor

fatto'ria *nf* farm; (casa) farmhouse

fatto'rino *nm* messenger [boy]. **fattorino d'albergo** bellboy

fattucchi'era *nf* witch

fat'tura *nf* (stile) cut; (lavorazione) workmanship; Comm invoice. **fattura di acquisto** purchase invoice. **fattura pro-forma** pro forma [invoice]. **fattura di vendita** sales invoice

fattu'rare *vt* invoice; (adulterare) adulterate

fattu'rato *nm* turnover, sales *pl*

fatturazi'one *nf* invoicing, billing

'fatuo *adj* fatuous

'fauci *nfpl* (di leone) maw *sg*, jaws *pl*

'fauna *nf* fauna

'fausto *adj* propitious

fau'tore *nm* supporter

'fava *nf* broad bean

fa'vella *nf* speech

fa'villa *nf* spark

'favo *nm* honeycomb

'favola *nf* fable; (fiaba) story; (oggetto di pettegolezzi) laughing-stock; **è una ~!** (meraviglia) it's divine!

favo'loso *adj* fabulous

fa'vore *nm* favour; **essere a ~ di** be in favour of; **per ~** please; **di ~** ‹condizioni, trattamento› preferential; **col ~ delle tenebre** under cover of darkness

favoreggia'mento *nm* Jur aiding and abetting

favo'revole *adj* favourable

favorevol'mente *adv* favourably

favo'rire *vt* favour; (promuovere) promote; **vuol ~?** (a cena, pranzo) will you have some?; (entrare) will you come in?; **favorisca alla cassa** please pay at the cash-desk; **favorisca i documenti** your papers please

favo'rito, **-a** *adj & nmf* favourite

fax *nm inv* fax; **inviare via ~** fax, send by fax. **fax a carta comune** plain paper fax

fa'xare *vt* fax

fazi'one *nf* faction

faziosità *nf* bias

fazi'oso *nm* sectarian

fazzolet'tino *nm* **fazzolettino [di carta]** [paper] tissue

fazzo'letto *nm* handkerchief, hanky; (da testa) headscarf

feb'braio *nm* February

'febbre *nf* fever; **avere la ~** have *o* run a temperature. **febbre da fieno** hay fever

febbrici'tante *adj* fevered

feb'brile *adj* feverish

febbril'mente *adv* feverishly

'feccia *nf* dregs *pl*

'fecola *nf* potato flour

fecon'dare *vt* fertilize

feconda'tore *nm* fertilizer

fecondazi'one *nf* fertilization. **fecondazione artificiale** artificial insemination. **fecondazione in vitro** in vitro fertilization, IVF

fe'condo *adj* fertile

'fede *nf* faith; (fiducia) trust; (anello) wedding ring; **in buona/mala ~** in good/ bad faith; **prestar ~ a** believe; **tener ~ alla parola** keep one's word; **aver ~ in qualcuno** have faith in somebody, believe in somebody; **degno di ~** reliable; **in ~** Yours faithfully

fe'dele ① *adj* faithful ② *nmf* believer, worshipper; (seguace) follower; **i fedeli** the faithful

fedel'mente *adv* faithfully

fedeltà *nf* faithfulness; **alta fedeltà** high fidelity

'federa *nf* pillowcase

fede'rale *adj* federal

federa'lismo *nm* federalism

federa'lista *adj* federalist

fede'rato *adj* federate

federazi'one *nf* federation

fe'difrago, **-a** ① *adj* faithless; *hum* two-timing ② *nm* faithless wretch; *hum* two-timer

fe'dina *nf* avere la ~ penale sporca/ pulita have a/no criminal record

fega'telli *nmpl* (di maiale) pork liver

fega'tino *nm* fegatini *pl* di pollo chicken livers

'fegato *nm* liver; fig guts *pl*; **mangiarsi il ~, rodersi il ~** be consumed with rage

'felce *nf* fern

fe'lice *adj* happy; (fortunato) lucky; **~ come una Pasqua** blissfully happy

felice'mente *adv* happily; (con successo) successfully

felicità *nf* happiness

felici'tarsi *vr* **~ con** congratulate

felicitazi'oni *nfpl* congratulations

fe'lino *adj* feline

'felpa *nf* (indumento) sweatshirt; (stoffa) felt

fel'pato *adj* brushed; ‹passo› stealthy

'feltro *nm* felt; (cappello) felt hat

'femmina *nf* female

femmi'nile ① *adj* feminine; ‹rivista, abbigliamento› women's; ‹sesso› female ② *nm* feminine

femminilità *nf* femininity

femmi'nismo *nm* feminism

'femore *nm* femur

'fendere *vt* split

fendi'nebbia *nm inv* fog lamp

fendi'tura *nf* split; (in roccia) crack

fe'nice *nf* phoenix

feni'cottero *nm* flamingo

fenome'nale *adj* phenomenal

fe'nomeno *nm* phenomenon

'feretro *nm* coffin

feri'ale *adj* weekday; **giorno feriale** weekday

'ferie *nfpl* holidays; **andare in** ∼ go on holiday; **prendere le** ∼ go on holiday; **prendere delle** ∼ take time off; **prendere un giorno di** ∼ take a day off

feri'mento *nm* wounding

fe'rire *vt* wound; (in incidente) injure; fig hurt

fe'rirsi *vr* injure oneself

fe'rita *nf* wound. **ferita d'arma da fuoco** gunshot wound

fe'rito ① *adj* wounded
② *nm* wounded person; Mil casualty; ∼ **grave** seriously injured person; **i feriti** the injured

feri'toia *nf* loophole; **feritoie** *pl* **per le schede di espansione** Comput expansion slots

'ferma *nf* Mil period of service

fermacal'zoni *nm inv* cycle clip

fermaca'pelli *nm inv* hair slide

ferma'carte *nm inv* paperweight

ferma'coda *nm inv* (di stoffa) scrunchie

fermacra'vatta *nm inv* tiepin

ferma'fogli *nm inv* bulldog clip

fer'maglio *nm* clasp; (spilla) brooch; (per capelli) hair slide

ferma'mente *adv* firmly

ferma'porta *nm inv* doorstop

fer'mare ① *vt* stop; (fissare) fix; Jur detain ② *vi* stop

fer'marsi *vr* stop

fer'mata *nf* stop; '∼ **prenotata**' 'bus stopping'; **senza fermate** (tragitto) non-stop. **fermata dell'autobus** bus stop. **fermata obbligatoria** compulsory stop. **fermata a richiesta** request stop

fermen'tare *vi* ferment

fermentazi'one *nf* fermentation

fer'mento *nm* ferment; (lievito) yeast; **essere in** ∼ be in/get into a tizzy

fer'mezza *nf* firmness

'fermo ① *adj* still; (veicolo) stationary; (stabile) steady; (orologio) not working; ∼! don't move!; ∼ **restando che ...** it being understood that ...; '∼ **per manutenzione**' 'closed for repairs'
② *nm* Jur detention; Mech catch; **in stato di fermo** in custody. **fermo immagine** TV freeze frame. **fermo posta** poste restante, general delivery Am

fer'net® *nm inv* bitter digestive liqueur

fe'roce *adj* fierce, ferocious; (bestia) wild; (freddo, dolore) unbearable

feroce'mente *adv* fiercely, ferociously

fe'rocia *nf* ferocity

fer'raglia *nf* scrap iron

ferra'gosto *nm* 15 August (bank holiday in Italy); (periodo) August holidays *pl*

ferra'menta *nfpl* ironmongery *sg*; **negozio di ferramenta** ironmonger's

fer'rare *vt* shoe (cavallo)

fer'rato *adj* ∼ **in** (preparato in) well up in

'ferreo *adj* iron

'ferro *nm* iron; (attrezzo) tool; (di chirurgo) instrument; **di** ∼ (memoria) excellent; (alibi) cast-iron; **salute di** ∼ iron constitution; **ai ferri** (bistecca) grilled; **essere ai ferri corti** be at daggers drawn; **mettere il paese a** ∼ **e fuoco** put a country to the sword; **i ferri del mestiere** the tools of the trade. **ferro battuto** wrought iron. **ferro da calza** knitting needle. **ferro di cavallo** horseshoe. **ferro da stiro** iron. **ferro a vapore** steam iron

fer'roso *adj* ferrous

ferro'vecchio *nm* scrap merchant

ferro'via *nf* railway, railroad Am; **Ferrovie** *pl* **dello Stato** Italian State Railways

ferrovi'ario *adj* railway *attrib*, railroad Am *attrib*

ferrovi'ere *nm* railwayman, railroad worker Am

'fertile *adj* fertile

fertilità *nf* fertility

fertiliz'zante *nm* fertilizer

fertilizzazi'one *nf* fertilization

fer'vente *adj* blazing; fig fervent

fervente'mente *adv* fervently

'fervere *vi* (preparativi); be well under way

fervida'mente *adv* fervently

'fervido *adj* fervent; **fervidi auguri** best wishes

fer'vore *nm* fervour; (di discussione) heat

'fesa *nf* (carne) rump

fesse'ria *nf* **dire/fare una** ∼ fam say/do something stupid

'fesso ① pp di FENDERE
② *adj* cracked; (fam: sciocco) foolish
③ *nm* (fam: idiota) fool; **far** ∼ **qualcuno** fam con somebody

fes'sura *nf* crack; (per gettone ecc) slot. **fessura [per la scheda] di espansione** Comput expansion slot

'festa *nf* feast; (giorno festivo) holiday; (compleanno) birthday; (ricevimento) party; fig joy; **fare** ∼ **a qualcuno** welcome somebody; **essere in** ∼ be on holiday; **far** ∼ celebrate; **della** ∼ (vestito, tovaglia) best; **conciare qualcuno per le feste** give somebody a sound thrashing; **le feste** (Natale, Capodanno ecc) the holidays. **festa di addio al celibato** stag night, stag party. **festa di addio al nubilato** hen party. **festa di compleanno** birthday ⋯

party. **festa della mamma** Mother's
Day, Mothering Sunday. **festa
mascherata** fancy dress party. **festa
nazionale** public holiday, legal holiday
Am. **festa del papà** Father's Day

festai'olo-a ① *adj* festive
② *nmf* party animal

festeggia'mento *nm* celebration;
(manifestazione) festivity; **festeggiamenti** *pl*
celebrations

festeggi'are *vt* celebrate; (accogliere
festosamente) give a hearty welcome to

fe'stino *nm* party

'festival *nm inv* festival. **festival
cinematografico** film festival

festività *nfpl* festivities

fe'stivo *adj* holiday; (lieto) festive; **festivi**
pl public holidays

fe'stone *nm* (nel cucito) scallop, scollop; (di
carta) paper chain

fe'stoso *adj* merry

fe'tente ① *adj* evil smelling; fig
revolting
② *nmf* fam bastard

fe'ticcio *nm* fetish

'feto *nm* foetus

fe'tore *nm* stench

'fetta *nf* slice; **a fette** sliced. **fetta
biscottata** slices of crispy toast-like
bread

fet'tina *nf* thin slice

fet'tuccia *nf* tape; (con nome) name tape

fettuc'cine *nfpl* ribbon-shaped pasta

feu'dale *adj* feudal

'feudo *nm* feud

fez *nm inv* fez

FFSS *abbr* (**Ferrovie dello Stato**)
Italian State Railways

fi'aba *nf* fairy-tale

fia'besco *adj* fairy-tale *attrib*

fi'acca *nf* weariness; (indolenza) laziness;
battere la ~ be sluggish

fiac'care *vt* weaken

fi'acco *adj* weak; (indolente) slack; (stanco)
weary; (partita) dull

fi'accola *nf* torch

fiacco'lata *nf* torchlight procession

fi'ala *nf* phial

fia'letta *nf* phial. **fialetta puzzolente**
stink bomb

fi'amma *nf* flame; Naut pennant; **in
fiamme** in flames; **andare in fiamme** go up
in flames; **dare alle fiamme** commit to the
flames; **alla** ~ Culin flambé; **le Fiamme
Gialle** body responsible for border control
and investigating fraud. **fiamma
ossidrica** blowtorch

fiam'mante *adj* flaming; **nuovo** ~
brand new

fiam'mata *nf* blaze

fiammeggi'are ① *vi* blaze
② *vt* singe (pollo)

fiam'mifero *nm* match

fiam'mingo, -a ① *adj & nm* Flemish
② *nmf* Fleming

fian'cata *nf* wing

fiancheggi'are *vt* border; fig support

fi'anco *nm* side; (di persona) hip; (di animale)
flank; Mil wing; **al mio** ~ by my side; ~ **a**
~ (lavorare) side by side

Fi'andre *nfpl* **le** ~ Flanders

fia'schetta *nf* hip flask

fiaschette'ria *nf* wine shop

fi'asco *nm* flask; fig fiasco; **fare** ~ be a
fiasco

fia'tare *vi* breathe; (parlare) breathe a
word

fi'ato *nm* breath; (vigore) stamina;
strumenti a ~ wind instruments; **avere il**
~ **corto** be short of breath; **senza** ~
breathlessly; **tutto d'un** ~ (bere, leggere)
all in one go

'fibbia *nf* buckle

'fibra *nf* fibre; **fibre** *pl* (alimentari) roughage.
fibre artificiali *pl* man-made fibres.
fibra ottica optical fibre; **a fibre ottiche**
(cavo) fibre optic. **fibra sintetica** man-
made fibre, synthetic. **fibra di vetro**
fibreglass

fi'broma *nm* fibroid

fi'broso *adj* fibrous

ficca'naso *nmf inv* nosey parker

fic'care *vt* thrust; drive (chiodo ecc); (fam:
mettere) shove

fic'carsi *vr* thrust oneself; (nascondersi)
hide; ~ **nei guai** get oneself into trouble

'fiche *nf inv* (gettone) chip

'fico[1] *nm* (albero) fig-tree; (frutto) fig. **fico
d'India** prickly pear; **non me ne importa
un** ~ [secco] fam I don't give a damn; **non
capisce un** ~ [secco] fam he doesn't
understand a bloody thing; **non vale un** ~
[secco] fam it's totally worthless

'fico[2]**, -a** ① *nmf* fam cool sort
② *adj* cool

fidanza'mento *nm* engagement;
rompere il ~ break off one's engagement,
break it off

fidan'zarsi *vr* get engaged

fidan'zata *nf* (ufficiale) fiancée; (innamorata)
girlfriend

fidan'zato *nm* (ufficiale) fiancé; (innamorato)
boyfriend

fi'darsi *vr* ~ **di** trust

fi'dato *adj* trustworthy

'fido ① *adj* (compagno) loyal
② *nm* devoted follower; Comm credit

fi'ducia *nf* confidence; **degno di** ~
trustworthy; **persona di** ~ reliable
person; **di** ~ (fornitore, banca) regular,

usual; **avere ∼ in se stessi** believe in oneself; **incarico di ∼** important job

fiduci'ario, -a ① *adj* ⟨*rapporto, transazione*⟩ based on trust ② *nmf* trustee

fiduci'oso *adj* hopeful

fi'ele *nm* bile; *fig* bitterness; **amaro come il ∼** bitter

fienagi'one *nf* haymaking

fie'nile *nm* barn

fi'eno *nm* hay

fi'era *nf* fair. **fiera commerciale** trade fair. **fiera del libro** book fair

fie'rezza *nf* (dignità) pride

fi'ero *adj* proud

fi'evole *adj* faint; ⟨*luce*⟩ dim

'fifa *nf* fam jitters; **aver ∼** have the jitters

fi'fone, -a *nmf* fam chicken, yellowbelly

FIGC *nf abbr* (**Federazione Italiana Gioco Calcio**) Italian Football Association

Figi *nfpl* **le isole ∼** Fiji

'figli *nmpl* children

'figlia *nf* daughter. **figlia unica** only child

figli'are *vi* ⟨*animale*⟩; calve

figli'astra *nf* stepdaughter

figli'astro *nm* stepson

'figlio *nm* son; (generico) child; **è ∼ d'arte** he was born in a trunk. **figlio adottivo** adopted child. **figlio di papà** spoilt brat. **figlio di puttana** vulg son of a bitch. **figlio unico** only child

figli'occia *nf* goddaughter

figli'occio *nm* godson

figli'ola *nf* girl

figlio'lanza *nf* offspring

figli'olo *nm* boy; **figlioli** *pl* children

'figo, -a *adj* ▶ FICO

fi'gura *nf* figure; (aspetto esteriore) shape; (illustrazione) illustration; (in carte da gioco) picture [card]; **far bella/brutta ∼** make a good/bad impression; **mi hai fatto fare una brutta ∼** you made me look a fool; **che ∼!** how embarrassing! **figura paterna** father figure. **figura retorica** figure of speech

figu'raccia *nf* bad impression

figu'rare ① *vt* represent; (simboleggiare) symbolize; (immaginare) imagine ② *vi* (far figura) cut a fine figure; (in lista) appear, figure; **∼ in testa al cartellone** Theat get top billing

figu'rarsi *vr* (immaginarsi) imagine; **figurati!** imagine that!; **posso? –[ma] figurati!** may I? –of course!

figura'tivo *adj* figurative

figu'rina *nf* (da raccolta) cigarette card; (statuetta) figurine

figuri'nista *nmf* dress designer

figu'rino *nm* fashion sketch

fi'guro *nm* **un losco ∼** a shady character

figu'rone *nm* **fare un ∼** make an excellent impression

fil *nm* **fil di ferro** wire

'fila *nf* line; (di soldati ecc) file; (di oggetti) row; (coda) queue; **di ∼** in succession; **fare la ∼** queue [up], stand in line Am; **in ∼ indiana** single file

fila'mento *nm* filament

fi'lanca® *nf* type of synthetic stretch fabric

fi'lante *adj* ⟨*formaggio*⟩ stringy; **stella filante** (di carta) streamer

filantro'pia *nf* philanthropy

filan'tropico *adj* philanthropic

fi'lantropo, -a *nmf* philanthropist

fi'lare ① *vt* spin; Naut pay out ② *vi* (andarsene) run away; ⟨*liquido*⟩ trickle; ⟨*ragionamento*⟩ hang together; **fila!** fam scram!; **∼ con** (fam: amoreggiare) go out with; **∼ dritto** toe the line ③ *nm* (di viti, alberi) row

filar'monica *nf* (orchestra) orchestra

filar'monico *adj* philharmonic

fila'strocca *nf* rigmarole; (per bambini) nursery rhyme

filate'lia *nf* philately, stamp collecting

fila'telico, -a *nmf* philatelist

fi'lato ① *adj* spun; (ininterrotto) running; (continuato) uninterrupted; **di ∼** (subito) immediately; **andare dritto ∼ a** go straight to ② *nm* yarn

fila|'tore, -trice *nmf* spinner

fila'tura *nf* spinning; (filanda) spinning mill

'file *nm inv* Comput file

filetta'tura *nf* (di vite) thread

fi'letto *nm* (bordo) border; ⟨*di vite*⟩ thread; Culin fillet. **filetto ai ferri** grilled fillet of beef

fili'ale ① *adj* filial ② *nf* Comm branch

filibusti'ere *nm* rascal

fili'forme *adj* stringy

fili'grana *nf* filigree; (su carta) watermark

fi'lippica *nf* invective

filip'pino, -a *adj & nmf* Filipino

film *nm inv* film. **film catastrofico** disaster movie. **film comico** comedy. **film drammatico** drama. **film di fantascienza** science fiction film. **film giallo** thriller. **film a lungometraggio** feature film. **film dell'orrore** horror film. **film poliziesco** detective film. **film verità** docudrama

fil'mare *vt* film

fil'mato ① *adj* filmed ② *nm* short film

fil'mina *nf* film strip

fil'mino *nm* cine film

'filo *nm* thread; (tessile) yarn; (metallico) wire; (di lama) edge; (venatura) grain; (di perle) string; (d'erba) blade; (di luce) ray; **un ∼ di** (poco) a drop of; **con un ∼ di voce** in a whisper; **per ∼ e per segno** in detail; **fare il ∼ a qualcuno** fancy somebody; **perdere il ∼** lose the thread; **essere appeso a un ∼** be hanging by a thread; **essere sul ∼ del rasoio** be on a knife-edge; **un ∼ d'aria** a breath of air; **un ∼ di speranza** a glimmer of hope. **filo interdentale** dental floss. **filo a piombo** plumb-line. **filo spinato** barbed wire

filo+ *pref* philo+

filoameri'cano *adj* pro-American

'filobus *nm inv* trolleybus

filocomu'nista *adj* pro-communist

filodiffusi'one *nf* rediffusion

filodram'matica *nf* amateur dramatic society

filolo'gia *nf* philology

filo'logico *adj* philological

fi'lologo, -a *nmf* philologist

filon'cino *nm* ≈ French stick

fi'lone *nm* vein; (di pane) long loaf, Vienna loaf

fi'loso *adj* stringy

filoso'fia *nf* philosophy

fi'losofo, -a *nmf* philosopher

fil'traggio *nm* filtering

fil'trare *vt* filter

'filtro *nm* filter. **filtro chiamate** Teleph call screening. **filtro dell'olio** oil filter

'filza *nf* string

fin ▶ FINO¹

fi'nale ① *adj* final
② *nm* end
③ *nf* Sport final

fina'lista *nmf* finalist

finalità *nf inv* finality; (scopo) aim

final'mente *adv* at last; (in ultimo) finally

fi'nanza *nf* finance; **Guardia di ∼** body of police officers responsible for border control and for investigating fraud; **intendenza di ∼** inland revenue office

finanzia'mento *nm* funding

finanzi'are *vt* fund, finance

finanzi'aria *nf* investment company; (holding) holding company; Jur finance bill

finanzi'ario *adj* financial

finanzia'|tore, -trice *nmf* backer

finanzi'ere *nm* financier; (guardia di finanza) customs officer

finché *conj* until; (per tutto il tempo che) as long as

'fine ① *adj* fine; (sottile) thin; ⟨udito, vista⟩ keen; (raffinato) refined

② *nf* end; **alla ∼** in the end; **alla fin ∼** after all; **in fin dei conti** when all's said and done; **che ∼ ha fatto Anna?** what became of Anna?; **che ∼ hanno fatto le chiavi?** where have the keys got to?; **senza ∼** endless. **fine settimana** weekend

③ *nm* aim; **andare a buon ∼** be successful; **to lo dico a fin di bene** I'm telling you for your own good

fi'nestra *nf* window. **finestra a battenti** casement window

fine'strella *nf* Comput box. **finestrella di aiuto** help window. **finestrella di dialogo** dialog box, dialogue box Br. **finestrella di messaggio** message box

fine'strino *nm* Rail, Auto window

fi'nezza *nf* fineness; (sottigliezza) thinness; (raffinatezza) refinement

'fingere *vt* pretend; feign ⟨affetto ecc⟩

'fingersi *vr* pretend to be

fini'menti *nmpl* finishing touches; (per cavallo) harness *sg*

fini'mondo *nm* end of the world; fig pandemonium

fi'nire *vt* finish, end; (smettere) stop; (diventare, andare a finire) end up; **finiscila!** stop it!

fi'nito *adj* finished; (abile) accomplished

fini'tura *nf* finish

finlan'dese ① *adj* Finnish
② *nmf* Finn
③ *nm* (lingua) Finnish

Fin'landia *nf* Finland

'fino¹ *prep* ∼ **a** till, until; (spazio) as far as; ∼ **all'ultimo** to the last; ∼ **alla nausea** ⟨ripetere, leggere⟩ ad nauseam; **fin da** (tempo) since; (spazio) from; **fin dall'inizio** from the beginning; **fin qui** as far as here; **fin troppo** too much; ∼ **a che punto** how far

'fino² *adj* fine; (acuto) subtle; (puro) pure

fi'nocchio *nm* fennel; (fam: omosessuale) poof

fi'nora *adv* so far, up till now

'finta *nf* pretence, sham; Sport feint; **far ∼ di** pretend to; **far ∼ di niente** act as if nothing had happened; **per ∼** (per scherzo) for a laugh

'finto, -a ① *pp di* FINGERE
② *adj* false; (artificiale) artificial; **finta pelle** fake leather; **fare il ∼ tonto** act dumb

finzi'one *nf* pretence

fi'occo *nm* bow; (di neve) flake; (nappa) tassel; Naut jib; **coi fiocchi** fig excellent; **fiocchi** *pl* **di avena** oatmeal; (cotti) porridge; **fiocchi** *pl* **di granoturco** cornflakes; **fiocchi** *pl* **di latte** cottage cheese. **fiocco di neve** snowflake

fi'ocina *nf* harpoon

fi'oco *adj* weak; ⟨luce⟩ dim

fi'onda *nf* catapult

fio'raio, **-a** *nmf* florist

fiorda'liso *nm* cornflower

fi'ordo *nm* fiord

fi'ore *nm* flower; **a fior d'acqua** on the surface of the water; **a fiori** flowery; **in ~** flowering; **fior di** (abbondanza) a lot of; **il fior ~ di** the cream of; **ha i nervi a fior di pelle** his nerves are on edge; **nel ~ degli anni** in one's prime; **è il suo ~ all'occhiello** that's feather in his cap; **suo figlio è il suo ~ all'occhiello** his son is his pride and joy. **fiori d'arancio** *pl* orange blossom. **fiore di campo** wild flower. **fior di latte** (formaggio) soft cheese. **fiore selvatico** wild flower. **fiori di zucca fritti** *pl* fried pumpkin flowers

fio'rente *adj* ⟨industria⟩ booming

fioren'tina *nf* (bistecca) T-bone steak

fioren'tino *adj* Florentine

fio'retto *nm* (scherma) foil; Relig act of mortification

fi'ori *nmpl* (nelle carte) clubs

fiori'era *nf* container

fio'rino *nm* **fiorino olandese** guilder

fio'rire *vi* flower; ⟨albero⟩ blossom; fig flourish

fio'rista *nmf* florist; (negozio) florist's

fiori'tura *nf* flowering; (di albero) blossoming; (insieme di fiori) flowers *pl*

fio'rone *nm* (fico) early fig

fi'otto *nm* (di sangue) spurt; **scorrere a fiotti** pour out; **piove a fiotti** the rain is pouring down

Fi'renze *nf* Florence

'firma *nf* signature; (nome) name

firma'mento *nm* firmament

fir'mare *vt* sign

firma'tario, **-a** *nmf* signatory

fir'mato *adj* ⟨quadro, lettera⟩ signed; ⟨abito, borsa⟩ designer *attrib*

fisar'monica *nf* accordion

fi'scale *adj* fiscal

fisca'lista *nmf* tax consultant

fiscaliz'zare *vt* finance with government funds

fischi'are ① *vi* whistle; **mi fischiano le orecchie** I've got a ringing noise in my ears; fig my ears are burning
② *vt* whistle; (in segno di disapprovazione) boo

fischi'ata *nf* whistle

fischiet'tare *vt* whistle

fischiet'tio *nm* whistling

fischi'etto *nm* whistle

'fischio *nm* whistle; **fischi** *pl* Theat booing; **prendere fischi per fiaschi** get hold of the wrong end of the stick

'fisco *nm* Inland Revenue Br, IRS Am; (tasse) taxation; **il ~** the taxman

'fisica *nf* physics. **fisica atomica** atomic physics. **fisica nucleare** nuclear physics

fisica'mente *adv* physically

'fisico, **-a** ① *adj* physical
② *nmf* physicist. **fisico nucleare** atomic scientist
③ *nm* physique

'fisima *nf* whim

fisiolo'gia *nf* physiology

fisio'logico *adj* physiological

fisi'ologo, **-a** *nmf* physiologist

fisiono'mia *nf* features *pl*, face; (di paesaggio) appearance

fisiotera'pia *nf* physiotherapy

fisiotera'pista *nmf* physiotherapist, physio fam

fissa'mente *adv* fixedly; (permanentemente) steadily

fis'sare *vt* fix, fasten; (guardare fissamente) stare at; arrange ⟨appuntamento, ora⟩

fis'sarsi *vr* (stabilirsi) settle; (fissare lo sguardo) stare; **~ su** (ostinarsi) set one's mind on; **~ di fare qualcosa** become obsessed with doing something

fissa'tivo *nm* Phot fixative

fis'sato, **-a** ① *adj* (al muro) fixed; ⟨prezzo⟩ agreed
② *nm* (persona) person with an obsession

fissa'tore *nm* hair spray

fissazi'one *nf* fixation; (ossessione) obsession

'fisso ① *adj* fixed; **un lavoro ~** a regular job; **senza fissa dimora** of no fixed abode; **avere una ragazza fissa** have a steady girlfriend
② *adv* fixedly; **guardare ~ negli occhi qualcuno** stare at somebody; ⟨innamorato⟩ gaze into somebody's eyes

fitotera'pia *nf* herbalism; (per piante) plant health

'fitta *nf* sharp pain

fit'tavolo *nm* tenant

fit'tizio *adj* fictitious

'fitto[1] ① *adj* thick; **~ di** full of
② *nm* depth

'fitto[2] *nm* (affitto) rent; **dare a ~** let; **prendere a ~** rent; (noleggiare) hire

fiu'mana *nf* swollen river; fig stream

fi'ume ① *nm* river; fig stream
② *adj inv* ⟨discussione⟩ endless, never-ending; **romanzo fiume** roman-fleuve

fiu'tare *vt* smell; ⟨animale⟩ scent; snort ⟨cocaina⟩

fi'uto *nm* [sense of] smell; fig nose

'flaccido *adj* flabby

fla'cone *nm* bottle

flagel'lare *vt* flog

flagellazi'one *nf* flagellation

fla'gello *nm* scourge

fla'grante *adj* flagrant; **in** ~ in the act

fla'menco *nm* flamenco

flan *nm inv* baked custard

fla'nella *nf* flannel

'flangia *nf* (su ruota) flange

flash *nm inv* Journ newsflash

flau'tista *nfm* flautist

'flauto *nm* flute **flauto diritto** recorder. **flauto traverso** flute

'flebile *adj* feeble

fle'bite *nf* phlebitis

flebo'clisi *nf inv* drip

'flemma *nf* calm; Med phelgm

flem'matico *adj* phlegmatic

fles'sibile *adj* flexible

flessibilità *nf* flexibility

flessi'one *nf* (del busto in avanti) forward bend; (a terra) sit-up; (delle ginocchia) kneebend; (di vendite, produzione) drop, fall

fles'sivo *adj* Gram inflected

'flesso [1] *pp di* FLETTERE [2] *adj* Gram inflected

flessu'oso *adj* supple

'flettere *vt* bend

flip-'flop *nm inv* flip flop

flir'tare *vi* flirt

F.lli *abbr* (**fratelli**) Bros.

'floppy disk *nm inv* floppy disk

'flora *nf* flora

'florido *adj* flourishing

florovivа'istica *nf* (attività) growing under glass

'floscio *adj* limp; (flaccido) flabby

'flotta *nf* fleet

flot'tiglia *nf* flotilla

flu'ente *adj* fluent

fluidità *nf* fluidity; (nel parlare) fluency

flu'ido *nm* fluid

flu'ire *vi* flow

fluore'scente *adj* fluorescent

fluore'scenza *nf* fluorescence

flu'oro *nm* fluorine

fluo'ruro *nm* fluoride

'flusso *nm* flow; Med flux; (del mare) flood-tide. **flusso e riflusso** ebb and flow. **flusso di cassa** cash flow

'flutti *nmpl* billows

fluttu'ante *adj* fluctuating

fluttu'are *vi* (prezzi) fluctuate; (moneta) float

fluttuazi'one *nf* fluctuation; (di moneta) floating

fluvi'ale *adj* river

fo'bia *nf* phobia

'fobico *adj* phobic

'foca *nf* seal

fo'caccia *nf* (pane) flat bread; (dolce) ≈ raisin bread

fo'cale *adj* (distanza, punto) focal

focaliz'zare *vt* get into focus (fotografia); focus (attenzione); define (problema)

'foce *nf* mouth

fo'chista *nm* stoker

foco'laio *nm* Med focus; fig centre

foco'lare *nm* hearth; (caminetto) fireplace; Techn furnace

fo'coso *adj* fiery

'fodera *nf* lining; (di libro) dust-jacket; (di poltrona ecc) loose cover

fode'rare *vt* line; cover (libro)

fode'rato *adj* lined; (libro) covered

'foga *nf* impetuosity

'foggia *nf* fashion; (maniera) manner; (forma) shape

foggi'are *vt* mould

'foglia *nf* leaf; (di metallo) foil; **mangiare la** ~ catch on. **foglia di alloro** bay leaf

fogli'ame *nm* foliage

fogliet'tino *nm* **fogliettino igienico** (per pannolini) nappy liner

fogli'etto *nm* (pezzetto di carta) piece of paper

'foglio *nm* sheet; (pagina) leaf; (di domanda, iscrizione) form. **foglio di carta** sheet of paper. **foglio elettronico** Comput spreadsheet. **foglio illustrativo** instruction leaflet. **foglio protocollo** foolscap. **foglio rosa** provisional driving licence. **foglio di via** expulsion order

'fogna *nf* sewer

fogna'tura *nf* sewerage

fohn *nm inv* hair dryer

fo'lata *nf* gust

fol'clore *nm* folklore

folclo'ristico *adj* folk; (bizzarro) weird

folgo'rante *adj* (idea) brilliant

folgo'rare [1] *vi* (splendere) shine [2] *vt* (con un fulmine) strike

folgo'rato *adj* fig thunderstruck

folgorazi'one *nf* (da fulmine, elettrica) electrocution; (fig: idea) brainwave

'folgore *nf* thunderbolt

'folio: in ~ *adj* folio

'folla *nf* crowd

'folle *adj* mad; (velocità) breakneck; **in** ~ Auto in neutral; **andare in** ~ Auto coast

folleggi'are *vi* paint the town red

folle'mente *adv* madly

fol'letto *nm* elf

fol'lia *nf* madness; **alla** ~ (amare) to distraction; **costare una** ~ cost the earth; **fare una** ~ go mad; **farei follie per lei** I'd do anything for her

'folto *adj* thick

fomen'tare *vt* stir up

fond'ale *nm* Theat backcloth. **fondale marino** sea bed

fonda'menta *nfpl* foundations

fondamen'tale *adj* fundamental

fondamenta'lismo *nm* fundamentalism

fondamenta'lista *nmf* fundamentalist

fonda'mento *nm* (di principio, teoria) foundation; **privo di** ∼ groundless, without foundation

fon'dant *nm inv* fondant

fon'dare *vt* establish; base ⟨*ragionamento, accusa*⟩

fon'darsi *vr* be based (**su** on)

fon'dato *adj* ⟨*ragionamento*⟩ well-founded; ∼ **su** based on

fondazi'one *nf* establishment; **fondazioni** *pl* (di edificio) foundations

fon'delli *nmpl* **prendere qualcuno per i** ∼ fam pull somebody's leg

fon'dente *adj* ⟨*cioccolato*⟩ dark

'fondere ① *vt* melt; fuse ⟨*metallo*⟩ ② *vi* melt; ⟨*metallo*⟩ fuse; ⟨*colori*⟩ blend

fonde'ria *nf* foundry

'fondersi *vr* melt; Comm merge

'fondo ① *adj* deep; **è notte fonda** it's the middle of the night ② *nm* bottom; (fine) end; (sfondo) background; (indole) nature; (somma di denaro) fund; (feccia) dregs *pl*; (terreno) land; [sci di] ∼ cross-country skiing; **andare a** ∼ ⟨*nave*⟩ sink; **in** ∼ after all; **in** ∼ **a** at the end/bottom of; **in** ∼ **in** ∼ deep down; **fino in** ∼ right to the end; ⟨*capire*⟩ thoroughly; **andare fino in** ∼ **a qualcosa** get to the bottom of something; **dar** ∼ **a** use up; **a doppio** ∼ false bottomed; **toccare il** ∼ touch bottom; fig hit rock bottom; **senza** ∼ bottomless; **fondi** *pl* (denaro) funds; (di caffè) grounds; **fondi** *pl* **di magazzino** old stock; **fondi** *pl* **neri** slush fund. **articolo di fondo** (in giornale) editorial; **fondo fiduciario** trust fund. **fondo [comune] di investimento** investment trust. **Fondo Monetario Internazionale** International Monetary Fund. **fondo pensione** pension fund. **fondo per la ricostruzione** disaster fund. **fondo sopravvenienze passive** contigency fund. **fondo stradale** road surface

fondo'tinta *nm inv* foundation [cream]

fon'due *nf* (di formaggio) fondue

fon'duta *nf* fondue

fo'nema *nm* phoneme

fo'netica *nf* phonetics

fo'netico *adj* phonetic

fonolo'gia *nf* phonology

fon'tana *nf* fountain; (di farina) well

fonta'nella *nf* drinking fountain; Anat fontanelle

'fonte ① *nf* spring; fig source ② *nm* font

fon'tina *nf* soft mature cheese often used in cooking

'football *nm* **football americano** American football

foraggi'are *vt* fodder

fo'raggio *nm* forage

fo'rare ① *vt* pierce; punch ⟨*biglietto*⟩ ② *vi* puncture

fo'rarsi *vr* ⟨*gomma, pallone*⟩ go soft

fora'tura *nf* puncture

'forbici *nfpl* scissors; **un paio di** ∼ a pair of scissors. **forbici da siepe** garden shears. **forbici a zigzag** pinking shears, pinking scissors

forbi'cina *nf* earwig; **forbicine** *pl* (per le unghie) nail scissors

for'bito *adj* erudite

'forca *nf* fork; (patibolo) gallows *pl*

for'cella *nf* fork; (per capelli) hairpin

for'chetta *nf* fork; **essere una buona** ∼ enjoy one's food

forchet'tata *nf* (quantità) forkful

forchet'tone *nm* carving fork

for'cina *nf* hairpin

'forcipe *nm* forceps *pl*

for'cone *nm* pitchfork

for'ense *adj* forensic

fo'resta *nf* forest. **foresta equatoriale** rain forest. **Foresta Nera** Black Forest

fore'stale *adj* forest *attrib*; **la Forestale** branch of the police with responsibility for national forests

foreste'ria *nf* guest rooms *pl*

foresti'ero, -a ① *adj* foreign ② *nmf* foreigner

for'fait *nm inv* fixed price; **dare** ∼ (abbandonare) give up; **prezzo [a] forfait** all-in price; **contratto [a] forfait** lump-sum contract

forfe'tario *adj* flat rate

'forfora *nf* dandruff

'forgia *nf* forge

forgi'are *vt* forge

'forma *nf* form; (sagoma) shape; Culin mould; (per scarpe) shoe tree; (di calzolaio) last; **essere in** ∼ be in good form; **in (gran)** ∼ (very) fit, on (top) form; **a** ∼ **di** in the shape of; **sotto** ∼ **di** in the form of; **forme** *pl* (del corpo) curves; (convenzioni) appearances

formag'giera *nf* [covered] cheese board

formag'gino *nm* processed cheese

for'maggio *nm* cheese. **formaggio erborinato** blue cheese

for'male *adj* formal

forma'lina *nf* formalin

forma'lismo *nm* formalism

forma'lista *nmf* formalist

formalità *nf inv* formality

formaliz'zare *vt* formalize

formaliz'zarsi *vr* stand on ceremony, be formal

formal'mente *adv* formally

'forma 'mentis *nf inv* way of thinking, mindset

for'mare *vt* form; dial ⟨*numero di telefono*⟩

for'marsi *vr* form; (svilupparsi) develop

for'mato *nm* size; (di libro, dischetto) format. **formato famiglia** economy pack, economy size. **formato tessera** ⟨*fotografia*⟩ passport-size

format'tare *vt* format

formattazi'one *nf* formatting

formazione *nf* formation; Sport line-up; in ∼ in the process of being formed. **formazione professionale** vocational training. **formazione professionale postlaurea** graduate training scheme

for'mella *nf* tile

for'mica[1] *nf* ant

'formica[2]® *nf* Formica

formi'caio *nm* anthill

formichi'ere *nm* anteater

formico'lare *vi* ⟨*braccio ecc*⟩ tingle; ∼ di be swarming with; **mi formicola la mano** I have pins and needles in my hand

formico'lio *nm* swarming; (di braccio ecc) pins and needles *pl*

formi'dabile *adj* (tremendo) formidable; (eccezionale) tremendous

for'mina *nf* mould

for'moso *adj* curvy

'formula *nf* formula; **assolvere con** ∼ **piena** acquit. **formula di cortesia** polite form of address

formu'lare *vt* formulate; (esprimere) express

formulazi'one *nf* formulation

for'nace *nf* furnace; (per laterizi) kiln

for'naio, -a *nmf* baker; (negozio) bakery

fornel'letto *nm* **fornelletto a gas** gas stove

for'nello *nm* stove; (di pipa) bowl. **fornello da campeggio** camping stove

fornicazi'one *nf* fornication

for'nire *vt* supply (di with); ∼ **qualcosa a qualcuno** supply somebody with something

for'nirsi *vr* ∼ **di** provide oneself with

forni'tore *nm* supplier. **fornitore di servizi [Internet]** [Internet] service provider

forni'tura *nf* supply; **forniture** *pl* **per ufficio** office supplies

'forno *nm* oven; (panetteria) bakery; **al** ∼ roast; **da** ∼ ⟨*stoviglie*⟩ ovenproof. **forno**

autopulente self-cleaning oven. **forno crematorio** cremator. **forno elettrico** electric oven. **forno a gas** gas oven. **forno a microonde** microwave [oven]

'foro *nm* hole; (romano) forum; (tribunale) [law] court

'forse *adv* perhaps, maybe; **essere in** ∼ be in doubt

forsen'nato, -a [1] *adj* mad [2] *nmf* madman; madwoman

'forte [1] *adj* strong; ⟨*colore*⟩ bright; ⟨*suono*⟩ loud; (resistente) tough; ⟨*spesa*⟩ considerable; ⟨*dolore*⟩ severe; ⟨*pioggia*⟩ heavy; (fam: simpatico) great; ⟨*taglia*⟩ large; **essere** ∼ **in qualcosa** be good at something

[2] *adv* strongly; ⟨*parlare*⟩ loudly; (velocemente) fast; ⟨*piovere*⟩ heavily [3] *nm* (fortezza) fort; (specialità) strong point

for'tezza *nf* fortress; (forza morale) fortitude

fortifi'care *vt* fortify

fortifi'cato *adj* ⟨*città*⟩ walled

for'tino *nm* Mil blockhouse

for'tissimo *adj* ⟨*caffè, liquore*⟩ extra-strong

for'tuito *adj* fortuitous; **incontro fortuito** chance encounter

for'tuna *nf* fortune; (successo) success; (buona sorte) luck; **atterraggio di** ∼ forced landing; **aver** ∼ be lucky; **buona** ∼! good luck!; **di** ∼ makeshift; **per** ∼ luckily; **hai una** ∼ **sfacciata!** fam you lucky blighter!

fortu'nale *nm* storm

fortunata'mente *adv* fortunately

fortu'nato *adj* lucky, fortunate; ⟨*impresa*⟩ successful

fortu'noso *adj* ⟨*giornata*⟩ eventful

fo'runcolo *nm* pimple; (grosso) boil

forunco'loso *adj* spotty

'forza *nf* strength; (potenza) power; (fisica) force; **di** ∼ by force; **a** ∼ **di** by dint of; **con** ∼ hard; ∼! come on!; **in** ∼ **di** under, in accordance with; ∼ **maggiore** circumstances beyond one's control; **la** ∼ **pubblica** the police; **le forze armate** the armed forces; **per** ∼ against one's will; (naturalmente) of course; **farsi** ∼ bear up; **mare** ∼ **8** force 8 gale; **bella** ∼! fam big deal!; **che** ∼! (che simpatico, divertente) cool eh?. **forza di gravità** [force of] gravity. **forza lavoro** workforce; **forze** *pl* **di mercato** market forces. **forza di volontà** will-power

for'zare *vt* force; (scassare) break open; (sforzare) strain

for'zato [1] *adj* forced; ⟨*sorriso*⟩ strained [2] *nm* convict

forza'tura *nf* (di cassaforte) forcing; **sostenere che ... è una** ∼ to maintain that ... is forcing things

forzi'ere *nm* coffer

for'zuto *adj* strong

fo'schia *nf* haze, mist

'fosco *adj* dark

fo'sfato *nm* phosphate

'fosforo *nm* phosphorus

'fossa *nf* pit; (tomba) grave. **fossa biologica** cesspool. **fossa comune** mass grave. **fossa dell'orchestra** orchestra pit

fos'sato *nm* (di fortificazione) moat

fos'setta *nf* (di guancia) dimple

'fossile *nm* fossil

'fosso *nm* ditch; Mil trench

'foto *nf inv* fam photo; **fare delle** ∼ take some photos

foto'camera *nf* camera. **fotocamera digitale** digital camera, fam digicam

foto'cellula *nf* photocell

fotocomposi'|tore, -trice *nmf* filmsetter

fotocomposizi'one *nf* filmsetting, photo-composition

foto'copia *nf* photocopy

fotocopi'are *vt* photocopy

fotocopia'trice *nf* photocopier

foto'finish *nm inv* photo finish

foto'genico *adj* photogenic

fotogiorna'lista *nmf* photojournalist

fotogra'fare *vt* photograph

fotogra'fia *nf* (arte) photography; (immagine) photograph; **fare fotografie** take photographs. **fotografia aerea** aerial photography

foto'grafico *adj* photographic; **macchina fotografica** camera

fo'tografo, -a *nmf* photographer; (negozio) photographer's

foto'gramma *nm* frame

fotoincisi'one *nf* photoengraving

fotomo'dello, -a *nmf* [photographer's] model

fotomon'taggio *nm* photomontage

foto'ottica *nf* camera shop and optician's

fotorepor'tage *nm inv* photo essay

fotore'porter *nmf inv* newspaper photographer; (di rivista) magazine photographer

fotori'tocco *nm* retouching

fotoro'manzo *nm* photo story

foto'sintesi *nf* photosynthesis

'fottere *vt* (sl: rubare) nick; (sl: imbrogliare) screw; vulg fuck, screw

'fottersene *vr* vulg not give a fuck; **va' a farti** ∼**!** vulg fuck off!

fot'tuto *adj* (sl: maledetto) bloody

fou'lard *nm inv* scarf

'foxhound *nm inv* foxhound

fox-'terrier *nm inv* fox terrier

fo'yer *nm inv* foyer

fra *prep* (in mezzo a due) between; (in un insieme) among; (tempo, distanza) in; **detto** ∼ **noi** between you and me; ∼ **sé e sé** to oneself; ∼ **l'altro** what's more; ∼ **breve** soon; ∼ **quindici giorni** in two weeks' time; ∼ **tutti, siamo in venti** there are twenty of us altogether

fracas'sare *vt* smash

fracas'sarsi *vr* shatter

fracas'sato *adj* smashed

fra'casso *nm* din; (di cose che cadono) crash

fracas'sone, -a *nmf* clumsy person

'fradicio *adj* (bagnato) soaked; **ubriaco** ∼ blind drunk

'fragile *adj* fragile; fig frail

fragilità *nf* fragility; fig frailty

'fragola *nf* strawberry

fra'gore *nm* uproar; (di cose rotte) clatter; (di tuono) rumble

frago'roso *adj* uproarious; ⟨tuono⟩ rumbling; ⟨suono⟩ clanging

fra'grante *adj* fragrant

fra'granza *nf* fragrance

frain'tendere *vt* misunderstand

frain'tendersi *vr* be at cross-purposes

frain'teso *pp di* FRAINTENDERE

frammen'tario *adj* fragmentary

fram'mento *nm* fragment

fram'misto *adj* ∼ **di** interspersed with

'frana *nf* landslide; (fam: persona) walking disaster area

fra'nare *vi* slide down

franca'mente *adv* frankly

france'scano *adj & nm* Franciscan

fran'cese **1** *adj* French **2** *nm* Frenchman; (lingua) French **3** *nf* Frenchwoman

france'sina *nf* (scarpa) brogue

fran'chezza *nf* frankness; **in tutta** ∼ in all honesty

fran'chigia *nf* **franchigia bagaglio** (per aereo) baggage allowance

'Francia *nf* France

'franco[1] *adj* frank; Comm free; **farla franca** get away with something; **parlare** ∼ speak frankly. **franco a bordo** free on board. **franco domicilio** delivered free of charge. **franco fabbrica** ex-works; **franco di porto** carriage free, carriage paid

'franco[2] *nm* (moneta) franc

franco'bollo *nm* stamp

franco-cana'dese *adj & nmf* French Canadian

fran'cofono *adj* Francophone, French-speaking

Franco'forte *nf* Frankfurt

fran'gente *nm* (onda) breaker; (scoglio) reef; (fig: momento difficile) crisis; **in quel ~** in the circumstances

fran'getta *nf* fringe

'frangia *nf* fringe

frangi'flutti *nm inv* bulwark

frangi'vento *nm* windbreak

fra'noso *adj* subject to landslides

fran'toio *nm* olive-press

frantu'mare *vt* shatter

frantu'marsi *vr* shatter

fran'tumi *nmpl* splinters; **in ~** smashed; **andare in ~** be smashed to smithereens

frappè *nm inv* milkshake

frap'porre *vt* interpose

frap'porsi *vr* intervene

fra'sario *nm* vocabulary; (libro) phrase book

'frasca *nf* [leafy] branch; **saltare di palo in ~** jump from subject to subject

'frase *nf* sentence; (espressione) phrase. **frase fatta** cliché

fraseolo'gia *nf* phrases *pl*

'frassino *nm* ash [tree]

frastagli'are *vt* make jagged

frastagl'iato *adj* jagged

frastor'nare *vt* daze

frastor'nato *adj* dazed

frastu'ono *nm* racket

'frate *nm* friar; (monaco) monk

fratel'lanza *nf* brotherhood

fratellastro *nm* step brother, half-brother

fratel'lino *nm* little brother

fra'tello *nm* brother; **fratelli** *pl* (fratello e sorella) brother and sister; Relig brethren. **fratello gemello** twin brother. **fratello di sangue** blood brother

fraternità *nf* brotherhood

fraterniz'zare *vi* fraternize

fra'terno *adj* brotherly

fratri'cida ① *adj* fratricidal ② *nm* fratricide

frat'taglie *nfpl* (di pollo ecc) giblets

frat'tanto *adv* in the meantime

frat'tura *nf* fracture

frattu'rare *vt* break

frattu'rarsi *vr* break

fraudo'lento *adj* fraudulent

frazi'one *nf* fraction; (borgata) hamlet; (paese) administrative division of a municipality

'freccia *nf* arrow; Auto indicator

frecci'ata *nf* (osservazione pungente) cutting remark

fredda'mente *adv* coldly

fred'dare *vt* cool; (fig: con sguardo, battuta) cut down; (uccidere) kill

fred'dezza *nf* coldness

'freddo *adj & nm* cold; **aver ~** be cold; **fa ~** it's cold; **a ~** (sparare) in cold blood; (lavare) in cold water

freddo'loso *adj* sensitive to cold, chilly

fred'dura *nf* pun

fre'gare *vt* rub; (fam: truffare) cheat; (fam: rubare) swipe; **fregarsene** fam not give a damn; **me ne frego!** I don't give a damn!; **chi se ne frega!** what the heck!

fre'garsi *vr* rub (occhi, mani)

fre'gata *nf* rub; (nave) frigate

frega'tura *nf* fam (truffa) swindle; (delusione) letdown

'fregio *nm* Archit frieze; (ornamento) decoration

'fregola *nf* rutting; **avere la ~ di fare qualcosa** fam have a craze for doing something

fre'mente *adj* quivering

'fremere *vi* quiver

'fremito *nm* quiver

fre'nare ① *vt* brake; fig restrain; hold back (lacrime, impazienza) ② *vi* brake

fre'narsi *vr* check oneself

fre'nata *nf* **fare una ~ brusca** hit the brakes

frene'sia *nf* frenzy; (desiderio smodato) craze

frenetica'mente *adv* frantically

fre'netico *adj* frantic

'freno *nm* brake; fig check; **togliere il ~** release the brake; **usare il ~** apply the brake; **tenere a ~** restrain; **tenere a ~ la lingua** hold one's tongue; **porre un ~ a** fig rein in; **freni** *pl* **a disco** disc brakes. **freno a mano** handbrake. **freno a pedale** footbrake

frequen'tare *vt* frequent; attend (scuola ecc); mix with (persone); **non ci frequentiamo più** we don't see each other any more

fre'quente *adj* frequent; **di ~** frequently

fre'quenza *nf* frequency; (assiduità) attendance

'fresa *nf* mill

fre'sare *vt* mill

fre'schezza *nf* freshness; (di temperatura) coolness

'fresco ① *adj* fresh; (temperatura) cool; **~ di studi** fresh out of school; **stai ~!** fam you're for it!; **se ti vede stai ~** fam you're done for if he sees you ② *nm* coolness; **far ~** be cool; **mettere/tenere in ~** put/keep in a cool place; **al ~** (fam: in prigione) inside

fre'scura *nf* cool

'fresia *nf* freesia

'fretta *nf* hurry, haste; **aver ~** be in a hurry; **far ~ a qualcuno** hurry somebody; **in ~ e furia** in a great hurry; **andarsene in ~** rush away; **senza [nessuna] ~** at your/his etc leisure

frettolosa'mente *adv* hurriedly

fretto'loso *adj* ⟨persona⟩ hasty; ⟨lavoro⟩ rushed, hurried

fri'abile *adj* crumbly

fricas'sea *nf* stewed meat served with an egg and lemon sauce

'friggere ① *vt* fry; **vai a farti ~!** get lost! ② *vi* sizzle; **~ di impazienza** be on tenterhooks

friggi'trice *nf* electric chip pan

frigidità *nf* frigidity

'frigido *adj* frigid

fri'gnare *vi* whine

fri'gnone, -a *nmf* whiner

'frigo *nm inv* fridge

frigo'bar *nm inv* minibar

frigocongela'tore *nm* fridge-freezer

frIgo'rIfero ① *adj* refrigerating; ⟨camion⟩ refrigerated ② *nm* refrigerator

fringu'ello *nm* chaffinch

'frisbee® *nm inv* frisbee

frit'tata *nf* omelette

frit'tella *nf* fritter; (fam: macchia d'unto) grease stain

'fritto ① *pp di* FRIGGERE ② *adj* fried; **essere ~** be done for ③ *nm* fried food. **fritto misto** mixed fried fish/vegetables

frit'tura *nf* (pietanza) fried dish. **frittura di pesce** variety of fried fish

frivo'lezza *nf* frivolity

'frivolo *adj* frivolous

frizio'nare *vt* rub

frizi'one *nf* friction; Mech clutch; (di pelle) rub

friz'zante *adj* fizzy; ⟨vino⟩ sparkling; ⟨aria⟩ bracing

'frizzo *nm* gibe

fro'dare *vt* defraud

'frode *nf* fraud. **frode fiscale** tax evasion; **con la ~** Jur under false pretences

frol'lino *nm* (biscotto) ≈ shortbread biscuit

'frollo *adj* tender; ⟨selvaggina⟩ high; ⟨persona⟩ spineless; **pasta frolla** short[crust] pastry

'fronda *nf* [leafy] branch; fig rebellion

fron'doso *adj* leafy

fron'tale *adj* frontal; ⟨scontro⟩ head-on

'fronte ① *nf* forehead; (di edificio) front; **di ~** opposite; **di ~ a** opposite, facing; (a paragone) compared with ② *nm* Mil, Pol front; **far ~ a** face

fronteggi'are *vt* face

fronte'spizio *nm* title page

fronti'era *nf* frontier, border

fron'tone *nm* pediment

'fronzolo *nm* frill

'frotta *nf* swarm; (di animali) flock

'frottola *nf* fib; **frottole** *pl* nonsense *sg*

fru'gale *adj* frugal

fru'gare ① *vi* rummage ② *vt* search

fru'ire *vi* **~ di** make use of, take advantage of

frul'lare ① *vt* Culin whisk ② *vi* ⟨ali⟩ whirr

frul'lato *nm* **frullato di frutta** fruit drink with milk and crushed ice

frulla'tore *nm* [electric] mixer

frul'lino *nm* whisk

fru'mento *nm* wheat

frusci'are *vi* rustle

fru'scio *nm* rustle; (radio, giradischi) ground noise; (di acque) murmur

'frusta *nf* whip; (frullino) whisk

fru'stare *vt* whip

fru'stata *nf* lash

fru'stino *nm* riding crop

fru'strare *vt* frustrate

fru'strato *adj* frustrated

frustrazi'one *nf* frustration

'frutta *nf* fruit; **negozio di ~ e verdura** greengrocer's. **frutta esotica** exotic fruit, tropical fruit. **frutta fresca di stagione** seasonal fruit. **frutta secca** nuts *pl*

frut'tare ① *vi* bear fruit; Comm give a return ② *vt* yield

frut'teto *nm* orchard

frutticol'tore *nm* fruit farmer

frutticol'tura *nf* fruit farming, fruit growing

frutti'era *nf* fruit bowl

frut'tifero *adj* ⟨albero⟩ fruit-bearing; Fin ⟨deposito⟩ interest-bearing

frutti'vendolo, -a *nmf* greengrocer

'frutto *nm* anche fig fruit; Fin yield; **frutti di bosco** *pl* fruits of the forest; **frutti di mare** *pl* seafood *sg*. **frutto della passione** passion fruit

fruttu'oso *adj* profitable

FS *abbr* (**Ferrovie dello Stato**) Italian State Railways

f.to *abbr* (**firmato**) signed

fu *adj* (defunto) late; **il fu signor Rossi** the late Mr Rossi

fuci'lare *vt* shoot, execute by firing squad

fucilazi'one *nf* execution [by firing squad]

fu'cile *nm* rifle. **fucile ad aria compressa** air rifle. **fucile a canne mozze** sawn-off shotgun

fuci'lata *nf* shot

fu'cina *nf* forge

'fuco *nm* kelp

'fucsia *nf* fuchsia

'fuga *nf* escape; (perdita) leak; (di ciclisti) breakaway; Mus fugue; **darsi alla** ∼ take to flight; **mettere qualcuno in** ∼ put somebody to flight. **fuga di cervelli** brain drain. **fuga di gradini** flight of steps. **fuga di notizie** leak. **fuga romantica** elopement

fu'gace *adj* fleeting

fug'gevole *adj* short-lived

fuggi'asco, -a *nmf* fugitive

fuggi'fuggi *nm* stampede

fug'gire *vi* flee; ⟨innamorati⟩ elope; fig fly

fuggi'tivo, -a *nmf* fugitive

'fulcro *nm* fulcrum

ful'gore *nm* splendour

fu'liggine *nf* soot

fuliggi'noso *adj* sooty

full *nm inv* (nel poker) full house

fulmi'nante *adj* ⟨sguardo⟩ withering; **è morto di leucemia** ∼ he died very soon after contracting leukaemia

fulmi'nare *vt* strike by lightning; (con sguardo) look daggers at; (con scarica elettrica) electrocute

fulmi'narsi *vr* burn out

fulmi'nato *adj* **rimanere** ∼ electrocute oneself

'fulmine *nm* lightning; **colpo di fulmine** fig love at first sight; **un** ∼ **a ciel sereno** a bolt from the blue

ful'mineo *adj* rapid; ⟨sguardo⟩ withering

'fulvo *adj* tawny

fumai'olo *nm* funnel; (di casa) chimney

fu'mante *adj* ⟨minestra, tazza⟩ steaming

fu'mare *vt/i* smoke; (in ebollizione) steam; **'vietato** ∼' 'no smoking'

fu'mario *adj* (canna) flue

fu'mata *nf* (segnale) smoke signal

fuma|'tore, -trice *nmf* smoker; **non fumatori** ⟨scompartimento⟩ non-smoker, non-smoking

fu'metto *nm* comic strip; **fumetti** *pl* comics

'fumo *nm* smoke; (vapore) steam; fig hot air; **andare in** ∼ vanish; **vendere** ∼ put on an act; **cercava di vendere** ∼ it was all hot air; **fumi** *pl* (industriali) fumes; **sotto i fumi dell'alcol** under the influence of alcohol. **fumo passivo** passive smoking

fu'mogeno *adj* **cortina fumogena** smoke screen

fu'moso *adj* ⟨ambiente⟩ smoky; ⟨discorso⟩ vague

funambo'lesco *adj* acrobatic

fu'nambolo, -a *nmf* tightrope walker

'fune *nf* rope; (cavo) cable

'funebre *adj* funeral; (cupo) gloomy

fune'rale *nm* funeral

fu'nereo *adj* ⟨aria⟩ funereal

fu'nesto *adj* sad

'fungere *vi* ∼ **da** act as

'fungo *nm* mushroom; Bot, Med fungus; **funghi** *pl* Bot fungi. **fungo atomico** mushroom cloud. **fungo commestibile** edible mushroom

funico'lare *nf* funicular [railway]

funi'via *nf* cableway

funzio'nale *adj* functional

funzionalità *nf* functionality

funziona'mento *nm* functioning

funzio'nare *vi* work, function; ∼ **da** (fungere da) act as

funzio'nario *nm* official. **funzionario statale** civil servant

funzi'one *nf* function; (carica) office; Relig service; **entrare in** ∼ take up office; **mettere in** ∼ ⟨motore⟩ start up; **vivere in** ∼ **di** live for

fu'oco *nm* fire; (fisica, fotografia) focus; **far** ∼ fire; **dar** ∼ **a** set fire to; **andare a** ∼ go up in flames; **prendere** ∼ catch fire; **a** ∼ **vivo** ⟨cuocere⟩ on a high heat; **a** ∼ **lento** ⟨cuocere⟩ on a low heat; **'vietato accendere fuochi'** 'no campfires'; **fuochi** *pl* **d'artificio** fireworks. **fuoco amico** friendly fire. **fuoco di paglia** nine-days' wonder; **fuochi** *pl* **pirotecnici** pyrotechnics

fuorché *prep* except

fu'ori ① *adv* out; (all'esterno) outside; (all'aperto) outdoors; ∼! fam get out!; ∼ **i soldi!** fork up!; **andare di** ∼ (traboccare) spill over; **essere** ∼ **di sé** be beside oneself; **essere in** ∼ (sporgere) stick out; **far** ∼ fam get rid of; **fuori commercio** not for sale; ∼ **luogo** (inopportuno) out of place; ∼ **mano** out of the way; ∼ **moda** old-fashioned; ∼ **pasto** between meals; ∼ **pericolo** out of danger; ∼ **programma** unscheduled; ∼ **questione** out of the question; **fuori uso** out of use ② *nm* outside

fuori'bordo *nm* speedboat (with outboard motor), powerboat

fuori'campo *adj inv* Cinema ⟨voce⟩ off-screen

fuori'classe *nmf inv* champion

fuoricombatti'mento *nm* knockout

fuorigi'oco *nm & adv* offside

fuori'legge *nmf inv* outlaw

fuori'pista *nm* (sci) off-piste skiing

fuori'serie ① *adj* custom-made ② *nf inv* Auto custom-built model

fuori'strada *nm inv* off-road vehicle, off-roader

fuoriu'scita *nf* (perdita) leak

fuoriu'scito, **-a** *nmf* exile

fuorvi'are ① *vt* lead astray
② *vi* go astray

furbacchi'one *nm* crafty old devil

fur'bastro, **-a** *nmf* crafty devil

furbe'ria *nf* cunning

fur'besco *adj* sly, cunning

fur'bizia *nf* cunning

'**furbo** *adj* sly, cunning; (intelligente) clever;
(astuto) shrewd; **bravo** ∼! nice one!; **fare il**
∼ try to be clever

fu'rente *adj* furious

fu'retto *nm* ferret

fur'fante *nm* scoundrel

furgon'cino *nm* delivery van

fur'gone *nm* van. **furgone postale**
mail van

'**furia** *nf* fury; (fretta) haste; **a** ∼ **di** by dint
of; **andare su tutte le furie** fly into a rage

furi'bondo *adj* furious

furi'ere *nm* Mil quartermaster

furiosa'mente *adv* furiously

furi'oso *adj* furious; ⟨litigio⟩ violent

fu'rore *nm* fury; (veemenza) frenzy; **far** ∼
be all the rage

furoreggi'are *vi* be a great success

furtiva'mente *adv* covertly, stealthily

fur'tivo *adj* furtive, stealthy

'**furto** *nm* theft; **commettere un** ∼ steal; **è
un** ∼! fig it's daylight robbery!. **furto**

d'auto car theft. **furto di minore
entità** petty theft. **furto con scasso**
burglary

'**fusa** *nfpl* **fare le** ∼ purr

fu'scello *nm* (di legno) twig; (di paglia)
straw; **sei un** ∼ you're as light as a
feather

fu'seaux *nmpl* leggings

fu'sibile *nm* fuse

fu'silli *nmpl* pasta twirls

fusi'one *nf* fusion; Comm merger

'**fuso** ① pp di FONDERE
② *adj* melted
③ *nm* spindle; **a** ∼ spindle-shaped. **fuso
orario** time zone

fusoli'era *nf* fuselage

fu'stagno *nm* corduroy

fu'stella *nf* (talloncino) part of packaging
on prescribed medicine returned by the
pharmacist to claim a refund

fusti'gare *vt* flog; fig castigate

fu'stino *nm* (di detersivo) box

'**fusto** *nm* stem; (tronco) trunk; (recipiente di
metallo) drum; (di legno) barrel. **fusto del
letto** bedstead

'**futile** *adj* futile

futilità *nf* futility

futu'rismo *nm* futurism

futu'rista *nmf* futurist

fu'turo *adj* & *nm* future; **predire il** ∼ tell
fortunes, foretell. **futuro anteriore** Gram
future perfect

Gg

gabardine *nf* (tessuto) gabardine

gab'bare *vt* cheat

gab'barsi *vr* ∼ **di** make fun of

'**gabbia** *nf* cage; (da imballaggio) crate.
gabbia dell'ascensore lift cage.
gabbia degli imputati dock. **gabbia
toracica** rib cage

gabbi'ano *nm* [sea]gull. **gabbiano
comune** common gull

gabi'netto *nm* (di medico) consulting
room; Pol cabinet; (toilette) toilet; (laboratorio)
laboratory; **andare al** ∼ go to the toilet;
gabinetti *pl* **pubblici** public convenience

'**Gabon** *nm* Gabon

ga'elico *nm* Gaelic

'**gaffa** *nf* boathook

'**gaffe** *nf inv* blunder

gagli'ardo *adj* vigorous

gai'ezza *nf* gaiety

'**gaio** *adj* cheerful

'**gala** *nf* gala

ga'lante *adj* gallant

galante'ria *nf* gallantry

galantu'omo *nm* (pl **galantuomini**)
gentleman

ga'lassia *nf* galaxy

gala'teo *nm* [good] manners *pl*; (trattato)
book of etiquette

gale'otto *nm* (rematore) galley-slave;
(condannato) convict

ga'lera *nf* (nave) galley; fam slammer

'**galla** *nf* Bot gall; **a** ∼ afloat; **venire a** ∼
surface

galleggi'ante ① *adj* floating ·
② *nm* craft; (boa) float

galleggi'are *vi* float

galle'ria *nf* (traforo) tunnel; (d'arte) gallery;
Theat circle; (arcata) arcade; **prima galleria** ···⟩

dress circle. **galleria aerodinamica** wind tunnel

'Galles *nm* Wales

gal'lese ⟨1⟩ *adj* Welsh
⟨2⟩ *nm* Welshman; (lingua) Welsh
⟨3⟩ *nf* Welshwoman

gal'letta *nf* cracker

gal'letto *nm* cockerel; **fare il ~** show off, impress the girls

'gallico *adj* Gallic

gal'lina *nf* hen

galli'nella *nf* **gallinella d'acqua** moorhen

gal'lismo *nm* machismo

'gallo *nm* cock. **gallo cedrone** capercaillie

gal'lone *nm* stripe; (misura) gallon

galop'pante *adj* galloping

galop'pare *vi* gallop

galop'pino *nm* fare da ~ a qualcuno fam be somebody's gopher

ga'loppo *nm* gallop; **al ~** at a gallop

galvaniz'zare *vt* galvanize

'gamba *nf* leg; (di lettera) stem; **darsela a gambe** take to one's heels; **essere in ~** (essere forte) be strong; (capace) be smart

gam'bale *nm* (di stivale) bootleg

gamba'letto *nm* pop sock

gambe'retti *nmpl* shrimps. **gamberetti in salsa rosa** prawn cocktail

'gambero *nm* prawn; (di fiume) crayfish

gambe'roni *nmpl* king prawns

'Gambia *nf* the Gambia

gambiz'zare *vt* kneecap

'gambo *nm* stem; (di pianta) stalk

ga'mella *nf* billy

game 'point *nm inv* game point

ga'mete *nm* gamete

'gamma *nf* Mus scale; fig range. **gamma d'onda** waveband. **gamma di prezzi** price range. **gamma di prodotti** product range

ga'nascia *nf* jaw; **ganasce** *pl* **del freno** brake shoes

'gancio *nm* hook

'Gange *nm* Ganges

'ganghero *nm* **uscire dai gangheri** fig get into a temper

'gangster *nm inv* gangster

'gara *nf* competition; (di velocità) race; **fare a ~** compete. **gara d'appalto** call for tenders. **gara a cronometro** time trial

ga'rage *nm inv* garage

gara'gista *nmf* garage owner

ga'rante *nmf* guarantor

garan'tire *vt* guarantee; (rendersi garante) vouch for; (assicurare) assure

garan'tirsi *vr* **~ contro, ~ da** guard against, insure against

garan'tismo *nm* protection of civil liberties

garan'tito *adj* guaranteed

garan'zia *nf* guarantee; **in ~** under guarantee. **garanzia collaterale** collateral. **garanzia di rimborso** money-back guarantee. **garanzia a vita** lifetime guarantee

gar'bare *vi* like; **non mi garba** I don't like it

gar'bato *adj* courteous

'garbo *nm* courtesy; (grazia) grace; **con ~** graciously

gar'buglio *nm* muddle

gar'denia *nf* gardenia

gareggi'are *vi* compete

garga'nella *nf* **a ~** from the bottle

garga'rismo *nm* gargle; **fare i gargarismi** gargle

ga'ritta *nf* sentry box

ga'rofano *nm* carnation; **chiodo di garofano** clove

gar'retto *nm* shank

gar'rire *vi* chirp

gar'rotta *nf* garrotte

'garrulo *adj* garrulous

'garza *nf* gauze

gar'zone *nm* boy. **garzone di stalla** stable-boy

gas *nm inv* gas; **dare ~** Auto accelerate; **a ~** gas-fired; **a tutto ~** flat out. **gas asfissiante** poisonous gas. **gas esilarante** laughing gas. **gas lacrimogeno** tear gas. **gas nobile** inert gas. **gas propellente** propellant. **gas di scarico** *pl* exhaust fumes

gas'dotto *nm* natural gas pipeline

ga'solio *nm* diesel oil. **gasolio invernale** diesel containing anti-freeze

ga'sometro *nm* gasometer

gas'sare *vt* aerate; (uccidere col gas) gas

gas'sato ⟨1⟩ *adj* gassy; ⟨bevanda⟩ fizzy
⟨2⟩ *nf* lemonade

gas'soso, -a *adj* gassy

'gastrico *adj* gastric

ga'strite *nf* gastritis

gastroente'rite *nf* gastro-enteritis

gastrono'mia *nf* gastronomy

gastro'nomico *adj* gastronomic[al]

ga'stronomo, -a *nmf* gourmet

'gatta *nf* **una ~ da pelare** a headache

gatta'buia *nf hum* clink

gatta'iola *nf* catflap

gat'tino, -a *nmf* kitten

'gatto, -a *nmf* cat; **c'erano solo quattro gatti** there were only a few people. **gatto delle nevi** snowmobile. **gatto a nove**

code cat-o'-nine-tails. **gatto selvatico** wildcat

gat'toni *adv* on all fours

gat'tuccio *nm* dogfish

gau'dente *adj* pleasure-loving

'**gaudio** *nm* joy

ga'vetta *nf* mess tin; **fare la ∼** rise through the ranks

gay *adj inv* gay

Gaza *nf* **la striscia di ∼** Gaza strip

ga'zebo *nm inv* gazebo

'**gazza** *nf* magpie

gaz'zarra *nf* racket; **fare ∼** make a racket

gaz'zella *nf* gazelle; Auto police car

gaz'zetta *nf* gazette. **Gazzetta Ufficiale** official journal

gazzet'tino *nm* (titolo) title page; (rubrica) page

gaz'zosa *nf* clear lemonade

GB *abbr* (**Gran Bretagna**) GB

'**geco** *nm* gecko

ge'lare *vt/i* freeze; **far ∼ il sangue** make somebody's blood run cold

ge'lata *nf* frost

gela'taio, -a [1] *nmf* ice-cream seller [2] *nm* (negozio) ice-cream shop

gelate'ria *nf* ice-cream parlour

gelati'era *nf* ice-cream maker

gela'tina *nf* gelatine; (dolce) jelly. **gelatina di frutta** fruit jelly

gelati'noso *adj* gelatinous

ge'lato [1] *adj* frozen [2] *nm* ice-cream. **gelato alla vaniglia** vanilla ice-cream

'**gelido** *adj* freezing

'**gelo** *nm* (freddo intenso) freezing cold; (brina) frost; fig chill

ge'lone *nm* chilblain

gelosa'mente *adv* jealously

gelo'sia *nf* jealousy

ge'loso *adj* jealous

'**gelso** *nm* mulberry[-tree]

gelso'mino *nm* jasmine

gemel'laggio *nm* twinning

gemel'lare [1] *vt* twin [2] *adj* twin

ge'mello, -a *adj & nmf* twin; **gemelli** *pl* (di polsino) cuff-link. **gemelli** *pl* **monozigoti** identical twins; **Gemelli** *pl* Astr Gemini *sg*

'**gemere** *vi* groan

'**gemito** *nm* groan

'**gemma** *nf* gem; Bot bud

gemmolo'gia *nf* gemmology

gen'darme *nm* gendarme

'**gene** *nm* gene

genealo'gia *nf* genealogy

genea'logico *adj* genealogical

gene'rale[1] *adj* general; **in ∼** (tutto sommato) in general, on the whole; **parlando in ∼** generally speaking

gene'rale[2] *nm* Mil general. **generale di divisione** major-general

generalità *nf inv* (qualità) generality, general nature; (maggior parte) majority; **∼** *pl* (dati) particulars *pl*

generaliz'zare *vt* generalize

generalizzazi'one *nf* generalization

general'mente *adv* generally

gene'rare *vt* give birth to; (causare) breed; Techn generate

genera'tore *nm* Techn generator

generazio'nale *adj* generation *attrib*

generazi'one *nf* generation; **di ∼ in ∼** from generation to generation

'**genere** *nm* kind; Biol genus; Gram gender; (letterario, artistico) genre; (prodotto) product; **cose del ∼** such things; **il ∼ umano** mankind; **in ∼** generally; **generi** *pl* **alimentari** provisions; **generi** *pl* **di prima necessità** essentials

generica'mente *adv* generically

ge'nerico *adj* generic; **medico generico** general practitioner

'**genero** *nm* son-in-law

generosa'mente *adv* generously

generosità *nf* generosity

gene'roso *adj* generous

'**genesi** *nf* genesis

genetica'mente *adv* genetically; **∼ modificato** genetically modified

ge'netico, -a [1] *adj* genetic [2] *nf* genetics

gene'tlsta *nmf* geneticist

gen'giva *nf* gum

geni'ale *adj* ingenious; liter (congeniale) congenial

geni'ere *nm* Mil sapper

'**genio** *nm* genius; **andare a ∼** be to one's taste. **genio civile** civil engineering. **genio incompreso** misunderstood genius. **genio [militare]** Engineers

geni'tale [1] *adj* genital [2] *nm* genitali *pl* genitals

geni'tore *nm* parent

gen'naio *nm* January

geno'cidio *nm* genocide

ge'noma *nm* genome

geno'teca *nf* gene library

'**Genova** *nf* Genoa

geno'vese *adj* Genoese

gen'taglia *nf* rabble

'**gente** *nf* people *pl*

gen'tile *adj* kind; **Gentile Signore** (in lettere) Dear Sir

genti'lezza *nf* kindness; **per** ~ (per favore) please

gentil'mente *adv* kindly

gentilu'omo (pl **gentiluomini**) *nm* gentleman

genu'flettersi *vr* kneel down

genuina'mente *adv* genuinely

genu'ino *adj* genuine; ⟨cibo, prodotto⟩ natural

genzi'ana *nf* gentian

geo'fisica *nf* geophysics

geo'fisico, -a *nmf* geophysician

geogra'fia *nf* geography

geo'grafico *adj* geographical

ge'ografo, -a *nmf* geographer

geolo'gia *nf* geology

geo'logico *adj* geological

ge'ologo, -a *nmf* geologist

ge'ometra *nmf* surveyor

geome'tria *nf* geometry

geometrica'mente *adv* geometrically

geo'metrico *adj* geometric[al]

geopo'litico *adj* geopolitical

Ge'orgia *nf* Georgia

geo'termico *adj* geothermal, geothermic

ge'ranio *nm* geranium

gerar'chia *nf* hierarchy

gerarchica'mente *adv* hierarchically

ge'rarchico *adj* hierarchic[al]

ger'billo *nm* gerbil

ge'rente ① *nm* manager ② *nf* manageress

'gergo *nm* jargon; (dei giovani) slang. **gergo burocratico** bureaucratic jargon

geri'atra *nmf* geriatrician

geria'tria *nf* geriatrics

geri'atrico *adj* geriatric

'gerla *nf* wicker basket

Ger'mania *nf* Germany. **Germania [dell']Est** East Germany. **Germania [dell']Ovest** West Germany

ger'manico *adj* Germanic

'germe *nm* germ; (fig: principio) seed. **germe di grano** wheat germ

germogli'are *vi* sprout

ger'moglio *nm* sprout; **in** ~ Bot sprouting; **germogli** *pl* **di soia** beansprouts

gero'glifico *nm* hieroglyph; **geroglifici** *pl* hieroglyphics

geron'tologo, -a *nmf* gerontologist

ge'rundio *nm* gerund

Gerusa'lemme *nf* Jerusalem

ges'setto *nm* chalk

'gesso *nm* chalk; (Med, scultura) plaster

ge'staccio *nm* ≈ V-sign

gestazi'one *nf* gestation

gestico'lare *vi* gesticulate

gestio'nale *adj* management *attrib*

gesti'one *nf* management. **gestione aziendale** business management. **gestione dei dati** Comput data management. **gestione disco** Comput disk management. **gestione dell'energia** energy resource management. **gestione del flusso di cassa** cashflow management. **gestione patrimoniale** financial management

ge'stire *vi* manage; ~ **male** mishandle

ge'stirsi *vr* budget one's time and money

'gesto *nm* gesture; (azione: pl f **gesta**) deed

ge'store *nm* manager

Gesù *nm* Jesus. **Gesù bambino** baby Jesus

gesu'ita *nm* Jesuit

gesu'itico *adj* Jesuit *attrib*

get'tare *vt* throw; (scagliare) fling; (emettere) spout; Techn, fig cast; ~ **via** throw away

get'tarsi *vr* throw oneself; ~ **in** ⟨fiume⟩ flow into

get'tata *nf* throw; Techn casting

'gettito *nm* **gettito fiscale** tax revenue

'getto *nm* throw; (di liquidi, gas) jet; **a** ~ **continuo** in a continuous stream; **di** ~ straight off

getto'nato *adj* ⟨canzone⟩ popular

get'tone *nm* token; (per giochi) counter; **a** ~ coin operated

gettoni'era *nf* coin box

'geyser *nm inv* geyser

'Ghana *nm* Ghana

ghe'pardo *nm* cheetah

'gheppio *nm* kestrel

gher'mire *vt* grasp

'ghette *nfpl* (per neonato) leggings

ghettiz'zare *vt* ghettoize

'ghetto *nm* ghetto

ghiacci'aia *nf* glacier

ghiacci'aio *nm* glacier

ghiacci'are *vt/i* freeze

ghiacci'ato *adj* frozen; (freddissimo) ice-cold

ghi'accio *nm* ice; Auto black ice. **ghiaccio secco** dry ice

ghiacci'olo *nm* icicle; (gelato) ice lolly

ghi'aia *nf* gravel

ghiai'oso *adj* gritty

ghi'anda *nf* acorn

ghian'daia *nf* jay

ghi'andola *nf* gland. **ghiandola pituitaria** pituitary gland. **ghiandola sudoripara** sweat gland. **ghiandola surrenale** adrenal gland

ghigliot'tina *nf* guillotine

ghi'gnare *vi* sneer

'ghigno *nm* sneer

ghi'otto *adj* greedy, gluttonous; (appetitoso) appetizing

ghiot'tone, **-a** *nmf* glutton

ghiottone'ria *nf* (caratteristica) gluttony; (cibo) tasty morsel

ghiri'goro *nm* flourish

ghir'landa *nf* (corona) wreath; (di fiori) garland

'ghiro *nm* dormouse; **dormire come un** ∼ sleep like a log

'ghisa *nf* cast iron

già *adv* already; (un tempo) formerly; ∼! indeed!; ∼ **da ieri** since yesterday

gi'acca *nf* jacket. **giacca a vento** windcheater

giacché *conj* since

giac'cone *nm* jacket

gia'cenza *nf* **giacenze** *pl* **di magazzino** unsold stock

gia'cere *vi* lie

giaci'mento *nm* deposit. **giacimento di petrolio** oil deposit

gia'cinto *nm* hyacinth

gi'ada *nf* jade

giaggi'olo *nm* iris

giagu'aro *nm* jaguar

gial'lastro *adj* yellowish

gi'allo *adj & nm* yellow; [libro] giallo crime novel; [film] giallo thriller. **giallo dell'uovo** egg yolk

Gia'maica *nf* Jamaica

giamai'cano, **-a** *adj & nmf* Jamaican

Giap'pone *nm* Japan

giappo'nese *adj & nmf* Japanese

gi'ara *nf* jar

giardi'naggio *nm* gardening

giardini'ere, **-a** ➊ *nmf* gardener. **giardiniera di verdure** diced, mixed vegetables, cooked and pickled ➋ *nf* Auto estate car

giar'dino *nm* garden. **giardino d'infanzia** kindergarten. **giardino pensile** roof-garden; **giardini** *pl* **pubblici** park. **giardino zoologico** zoo

giarretti'era *nf* garter

Gi'ava *nf* Java

giavel'lotto *nm* javelin

Gi'buti *nf* Djibouti

gi'gante *nm* giant

gigan'tesco *adj* gigantic

gigantogra'fia *nf* blow-up

'giglio *nm* lily

gilè *nm inv* waistcoat

gin *nm inv* gin

gin'cana *nf* gymkhana

ginecolo'gia *nf* gynaecology

gineco'logico *adj* gynaecological

gine'cologo, **-a** *nmf* gynaecologist

gi'nepro *nm* juniper

gi'nestra *nf* broom

Gi'nevra *nf* Geneva

gingil'larsi *vr* fiddle; (perder tempo) potter

gin'gillo *nm* plaything; (ninnolo) knick-knack

gin'nasio *nm* (scuola) grammar school

gin'nasta *nmf* gymnast

gin'nastica *nf* gymnastics; (esercizi) exercises *pl*. **ginnastica ritmica** eurhythmics

ginocchi'ata *nf* **prendere una** ∼ bang one's knee

ginocchi'era *nf* knee-pad

gi'nocchio *nm* (*pl m* **ginocchi** *o f* **ginocchia**) knee; **in** ∼ on one's knees, kneeling; **mettersi in** ∼ kneel down; (per supplicare) go down on one's knees; **al** ∼ ⟨gonna⟩ knee-length

ginocchi'oni *adv* kneeling

gio'care *vt/i* play; (giocherellare) toy; (puntare) stake; (ingannare) trick; ∼ **a calcio/ a pallavolo** play football/volleyball; ∼ **d'astuzia** be crafty; ∼ **d'azzardo** gamble; ∼ **In Borsa** speculate on the Stock Exchange; ∼ **in casa** Sport, fig play on one's home ground, play at home

gio'carsi *vr* ∼ **la carriera** throw one's career away

gioca'|tore, **-trice** *nmf* player; (d'azzardo) gambler

gio'cattolo *nm* toy

giocherel'lare *vi* toy; (nervosamente) fiddle

giocherel'lone *adj* skittish

gi'oco *nm* game; (di bambini, Techn) play; (d'azzardo) gambling; (scherzo) joke; (insieme di pezzi ecc) set; **essere in** ∼ be at stake; **fare il doppio** ∼ **con qualcuno** double-cross somebody; **è un** ∼ **da ragazzi** fam it's a cinch. **gioco elettronico** computer game; **giochi** *pl* **della gioventù** nation-wide sports tournament for children. **gioco dell'oca** snakes and ladders; **Giochi** *pl* **Olimpici** Olympic Games; **giochi** *pl* **online** on-line gaming. **gioco di parole** play on words. **gioco di pazienza** game of manual skill. **gioco di prestigio** conjuring trick. **gioco di società** board game

giocoli'ere *nm* juggler

gio'coso *adj* playful

gi'ogo *nm* yoke

gi'oia *nf* joy; (gioiello) jewel; (appellativo) sweetie

gioielle'ria *nf* jeweller's [shop]

gioi'elli *nmpl* jewellery

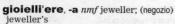

gioielli'ere, **-a** *nmf* jeweller; (negozio) jeweller's

gioi'ello *nm* jewel

gioiosa'mente *adv* joyfully

gioi'oso *adj* joyful

gio'ire *vi* ~ **per** rejoice at

Gior'dania *nf* Jordan

gior'dano, **-a** *adj & nmf* Jordanian

giorna'laio, **-a** *nmf* newsagent, newsdealer

gior'nale *nm* [news]paper; (diario) journal. **giornale di bordo** logbook. **giornale gratuito** freebie. **giornale del mattino** morning paper. **giornale radio** radio news. **giornale della sera** evening paper

giornali'ero ① *adj* daily
② *nm* (per sciare) day pass

giorna'lino *nm* comic

giorna'lismo *nm* journalism

giorna'lista *nmf* journalist

giornal'mente *adv* daily

gior'nata *nf* day; **buona** ~! have a good day!; **in** ~ today; **a** ~ ⟨essere pagato⟩ on a day-to-day basis; **vivere alla** ~ live from day to day. **giornata lavorativa** working day

gi'orno *nm* day; **al** ~ per day; **al** ~ **d'oggi** nowadays; **di** ~ by day; **in pieno** ~ in broad daylight; **un** ~ **sì, un** ~ **no** every other day; ~ **per** ~ day by day. **giorno di chiusura** closing day. **giorno delle elezioni** polling day. **giorno fatidico** (importante) D-day. **giorno feriale** weekday. **giorno festivo** public holiday. **giorno del giudizio** Judgement Day. **giorno dei morti** All Souls' day. **giorno di paga** payday

gi'ostra *nf* merry-go-round

gio'strarsi *vr* manage

giova'mento *nm* **trarre** ~ **da** derive benefit from

gi'ovane ① *adj* young; (giovanile) youthful
② *nm* youth; young man; **giovani** *pl* young people
③ *nf* girl, young woman

giova'nile *adj* youthful; ⟨scritto⟩ early

giova'notto *nm* young man

gio'vare *vi* ~ **a** be useful to; (far bene a) be good for

gio'varsi *vr* ~ **di** avail oneself of

Gi'ove *nm* Jupiter, Jove

giovedì *nm inv* Thursday; **di** ~ on Thursdays. **giovedì grasso** last Thursday before Lent. **giovedì santo** Maundy Thursday

gioventù *nf* youth; (i giovani) young people *pl*; ~ **bruciata** young drop-outs *pl*

giovi'ale *adj* jovial

giovi'nezza *nf* youth

gi'rabile *adj* ⟨assegno⟩ endorsable

gira'dischi *nm inv* record-player

gi'raffa *nf* giraffe; Cinema boom

gira'mondo *nmf inv* globetrotter; **da** ~ globetrotting

gi'randola *nf* (fuoco d'artificio) Catherine wheel; (giocattolo) windmill; (banderuola) weathercock

gi'rare ① *vt* turn; (andare intorno, visitare) go round; Comm endorse; Cinema shoot
② *vi* turn; ⟨aerei, uccelli⟩ circle; (andare in giro) wander; ~ **sotto** ... Comput run under ...; **mi gira la testa** I feel dizzy; **far** ~ **la testa a qualcuno** make somebody's head spin; **far** ~ **le scatole a qualcuno** fam drive somebody round the twist; ~ **al largo** steer clear

girar'rosto *nm* spit

gi'rarsi *vr* turn [round]

gira'sole *nm* sunflower

gi'rata *nf* turn; Comm endorsement; (in macchina ecc) ride; **fare una** ~ (a piedi) go for a walk; (in macchina) go for a ride

gira'volta *nf* spin; fig U-turn

gi'rello *nm* (per bambini) babywalker; Culin topside

gi'revole *adj* revolving; **ponte girevole** swing bridge

gi'rino *nm* tadpole

'giro *nm* turn; (circolo) circle; (percorso) round; (viaggio) tour; (passeggiata) short walk; (in macchina) drive; (in bicicletta) ride; (circolazione di denaro) circulation; **andare a fare un** ~ (a piedi) go for a stroll; (in macchina) go for a drive; (in bicicletta) go for a cycle ride; **fare il** ~ **di** go round; **nel** ~ **di un mese/anno** within a month/year; **prendere in** ~ **qualcuno** pull somebody's leg; **sentir dire in** ~ **qualcosa** hear something on the grapevine; **a** ~ **di posta** by return mail. **giro d'affari** Comm turnover. **giro in barca** boat trip. **giro guldato** guided tour. **giro [della] manica** armhole; **giri** *pl* **al minuto** revs per minute, rpm. **giro d'onore** lap of honour; **giri** *pl* **di parole** beating about the bush. **giro di pista** lap. **giro di prova** trial lap. **giro turistico** sightseeing tour. **giro vita** waist measurement. **giro di vite** fig clampdown

giro'collo *nm* choker; **a** ~ roundneck

gi'rone *nm* round. **girone di andata** first half of the season. **girone di ritorno** second half of the season

gironzo'lare *vi* wander about

giro'tondo *nm* ring-a-ring-o'-roses

girova'gare *vi* wander about

gi'rovago *nm* wanderer

'gita *nf* trip; **andare in** ~ go on a trip. **gita didattica** field trip. **gita organizzata** package tour. **gita in**

pullman coach trip. **gita scolastica** school trip

gi'tano, -a *nmf* gipsy

gi'tante *nmf* tripper

giù *adv* down; (sotto) below; (dabbasso) downstairs; **a testa in** ∼ (a capofitto) headlong; **essere** ∼ (di morale) be down, be depressed; (di salute) be run down; ∼ **di corda** down; ∼ **di lì, su per** ∼ more or less; **non andare** ∼ **a qualcuno** stick in somebody's craw

gi'ubba *nf* jacket; Mil tunic

giub'botto *nm* bomber jacket, jerkin. **giubbotto antiproiettile** bulletproof vest. **giubbotto di pelle** leather jacket. **giubbotto di salvataggio** lifejacket

gi'ubilo *nm* rejoicing

giudi'care *vt* judge; (ritenere) consider

gi'udice *nm* judge. **giudice conciliatore** justice of the peace. **giudice di gara** umpire. **giudice di linea** linesman. **giudice di pace** Justice of the Peace, JP

giudizi'ario *adj* legal, judicial

giu'dizio *nm* judg[e]ment; (opinione) opinion; (senno) wisdom; (processo) trial; (sentenza) sentence; **mettere** ∼ become wise. **giudizio universale** Last Judgement

giudizi'oso *adj* sensible

gi'ugno *nm* June

glugu'lare *nf* jugular

giul'lare *nm* jester

giu'menta *nf* mare

giun'chiglia *nf* jonquil

gi'unco *nm* reed

gi'ungere ①️ *vi* arrive; ∼ **a** (riuscire) succeed in; **mi giunge nuovo** it's news to me ②️ *vt* (unire) join

gi'ungla *nf* jungle. **giungla d'asfalto** concrete jungle

gi'unta *nf* addition; **per** ∼ in addition. **giunta comunale** district council. **giunta [militare]** [military] junta

gi'unto ①️ pp di GIUNGERE ②️ *nm* Mech joint. **giunto sferico** ball-and-socket joint

giun'tura *nf* joint

giuo'care, giu'oco = GIOCARE, GIOCO

giura'mento *nm* oath; **sotto** ∼ under oath; **prestare** ∼ take the oath. **giuramento d'Ippocrate** Hippocratic oath

giu'rare *vt/i* swear

giu'rato, -a ①️ *adj* sworn ②️ *nmf* juror

giu'ria *nf* jury

giu'ridico *adj* legal

giurisdizi'one *nf* jurisdiction

giurispru'denza *nf* jurisprudence

giu'rista *nmf* jurist

giu'stezza *nf* justness

giustifi'care *vt* justify

giustifi'carsi *vr* justify oneself; ∼ **di** *o* **per qualcosa** give an explanation for something

giustificazi'one *nf* justification

giu'stizia *nf* justice; **farsi** ∼ **da sé** take the law into one's own hands

giustizi'are *vt* execute

giustizi'ere *nm* executioner

gi'usto ①️ *adj* just, fair; (adatto) right; (esatto) exact ②️ *nm* (uomo retto) just man; (cosa giusta) right ③️ *adv* exactly; ∼ **ora** just now

glaci'ale *adj* glacial

gladia'tore *nm* gladiator

gla'diolo *nm* gladiolus

'glassa *nf* Culin icing

glau'coma *nm* glaucoma

gli ①️ def art *m pl* the; ▶ IL ②️ *pers pron* (a lui) [to] him; (a esso) [to] it; (a loro) [to] them; **non** ∼ **credo** I don't believe him/them

glice'mia *nf* glycaemia

glice'rina *nf* glycerine

'glicine *nm* wisteria

gli'elo *pron* (a lui) to him; (a lei) to her; (a loro) to them; (a Lei, forma di cortesia) to you; ∼ **prestai** I lent it to him/her etc; **gliel'ho chiesto** I've asked him/her etc

glie'ne *pron* (di ciò) of it; ∼ **ho dato un po'** I gave him/her/them/you some [of it]; ∼ **ho parlato** I've talked to him/her etc about it

glis'sare *vi* avoid the issue; ∼ **su qualcosa** skate over something

glo'bale *adj* global; fig overall

globalizzazi'one *nf* globalization

global'mente *adv* globally

'globo *nm* globe. **globo oculare** eyeball. **globo terrestre** globe

'globulo *nm* globule; Med corpuscle. **globulo bianco** white cell, white corpuscle. **globulo rosso** red cell, red corpuscle

'gloria *nf* glory

glori'arsi *vr* ∼ **di** be proud of

glorifi'care *vt* glorify

gloriosa'mente *adv* gloriously

glori'oso *adj* glorious

'glossa *nf* gloss

glos'sario *nm* glossary

glottolo'gia *nf* linguistics

glu'cosio *nm* glucose

glutam'mato *nm* **glutammato di sodio** monosodium glutamate

'gluteo *nm* buttock

'gnocchi *nmpl* (di patate) small flour and potato dumplings

'gnomo *nm* gnome

'gnorri *nm* fare lo ~ play dumb

goal *nm inv* goal; **fare un** ~ score *or* get a goal

'gobba *nf* hump

'gobbo, -a ① *adj* hunchbacked ② *nmf* hunchback

goc'cetto *nm* pick-me-up

'goccia *nf* drop; (di sudore) bead; **è stata l'ultima** ~ it was the last straw. **goccia di pioggia** raindrop. **goccia di rugiada** dewdrop

goccio'lare *vi* drip

goccio'lio *nm* dripping

go'dere *vi* (sl: sessualmente) come; ~ **di qualcosa** enjoy something, make the most of something

go'dersi *vr* ~ **qualcosa** enjoy something; **godersela** have a good time

godi'mento *nm* enjoyment

gof'faggine *nf* awkwardness

goffa'mente *adv* awkwardly

'goffo *adj* awkward

go-'kart *nm inv* go-kart

'gola *nf* throat; (ingordigia) gluttony; Geog gorge; (di camino) flue; **avere mal di** ~ have a sore throat; **far** ~ **a qualcuno** tempt somebody

go'letta *nf* schooner

golf *nm inv* jersey; Sport golf

gol'fino *nm* jumper

'golfo *nm* gulf

goli'ardico *adj* student *attrib*

golosità *nf inv* greediness; (cibo) tasty morsel

go'loso *adj* greedy

'golpe *nm inv* coup

go'mena *nf* painter

gomi'tata *nf* nudge; **dare una** ~ **a qualcuno** elbow somebody

'gomito *nm* elbow; **alzare il** ~ (fam: bere) raise one's elbow; ~ **a** ~ (lavorare) side by side

go'mitolo *nm* ball

'gomma *nf* rubber; (colla) gum; (pneumatico) tyre; **avere una** ~ **a terra** have a flat. **gomma arabica** gum arabic. **gomma da masticare** chewing gum. **gomma di scorta** spare tyre

gommapi'uma® *nf* foam rubber

gom'mino *nm* rubber tip

gom'mista *nm* tyre specialist

gom'mone *nm* [rubber] dinghy

gom'moso *adj* chewy

'gondola *nf* gondola

gondoli'ere *nm* gondolier

gonfa'lone *nm* banner

gonfi'abile *adj* inflatable

gonfi'are ① *vi* swell ② *vt* blow up; pump up (pneumatico); (esagerare) exaggerate

gonfi'arsi *vr* swell; (acque) rise

'gonfio *adj* swollen; (pneumatico) inflated

gonfi'ore *nm* swelling

gongo'lante *adj* overjoyed

gongo'lare *vi* be overjoyed

goni'ometro *nm* protractor

'gonna *nf* skirt. **gonna pantalone** culottes *pl*. **gonna a pieghe** pleated skirt. **gonna a portafoglio** wrapover skirt

gonor'rea *nf* gonorrh[o]ea

'gonzo *nm* simpleton

gorgheggi'are *vi* warble

gor'gheggio *nm* warble

'gorgo *nm* whirlpool

gorgogli'ante *adj* burbling, gurgling

gorgogli'are *vi* gurgle

gor'goglio *nm* burble

gorgon'zola *nm* strong, soft blue cheese

go'rilla *nm inv* gorilla; (guardia del corpo) bodyguard, minder

'gota *nf* cheek

'gotico *adj* & *nm* Gothic

'gotta *nf* gout

gover'nante *nf* housekeeper

gover'nare *vt* govern; (dominare) rule; (dirigere) manage; (curare) look after

governa'tivo *adj* government

governa'tore *nm* governor

go'verno *nm* government; (dominio) rule; **al** ~ in power. **governo ombra** shadow government

'gozzo *nm* (di animale) crop; Med goitre; fam throat

gozzovigli'are *vi* eat, drink and be merry

gracchi'are *vi* caw; fig (persona) screech

'gracchio *nm* caw

graci'dare *vi* croak

'gracile *adj* delicate

gra'dasso *nm* braggart

gradata'mente *adv* gradually

gradazi'one *nf* gradation. **gradazione alcolica** alcohol[lic]content. **a bassa gradazione alcolica** (birra) low-alcohol

gra'devole *adj* agreeable

gradevol'mente *adv* pleasantly, agreeably

gradi'ente *nm* gradient

gradi'mento nm liking; **indice di gradimento** Radio, TV popularity rating; **non è di mio ~** it's not to my liking

gradi'nata nf flight of steps; (di stadio, teatro) tiers pl

gra'dino nm step

gra'dire vt like; (desiderare) wish

gra'dito adj pleasant; (bene accetto) welcome

'grado nm degree; (rango) rank; **di buon ~** willingly; **essere in ~ di fare qualcosa** be in a position to do something; (essere capace a) be able to do something; **per gradi** ⟨procedere⟩ by degrees

gradu'ale adj gradual

gradual'mente adv gradually

gradu'are vt graduate

gradu'ato ① adj graded; (provvisto di scala graduata) graduated ② nm Mil noncommissioned officer

gradua'toria nf list

graduazi'one nf graduation

'graffa nf clip; (segno grafico) brace

graf'fetta nf staple

graffi'are vt scratch

graffia'tura nf scratch

'graffio nm scratch

gra'fia nf [hand]writing; (ortografia) spelling

'grafica nf graphics; (disciplina) graphics, graphic design. **grafica pubblicitaria** commercial art

grafica'mente adv in graphics, graphically

'grafico ① adj graphic ② nm graph; (persona) graphic designer. **grafico a torta** pie chart

gra'fite nf graphite

gra'fologo, -a nmf graphologist

gra'migna nf weed

gram'matica nf grammar

grammati'cale adj grammatical

grammatical'mente adv grammatically

gram'matico nm grammarian

'grammo nm gram[me]

gram'mofono nm gramophone

gran ▶ GRANDE

'grana nf grain; (formaggio) parmesan; (fam: seccatura) trouble; (fam: soldi) readies pl

gra'naio nm barn

gra'nata nf Mil grenade; (frutto) pomegranate

granati'ere nm Mil grenadier

gra'nato nm garnet

Gran Bre'tagna nf Great Britain

gran'cassa nf bass drum

gran'cevola nf spiny spider crab

'granchio nm crab; (fig: errore) blunder; **prendere un ~** make a blunder

grandango'lare nm wide-angle lens

gran'dangolo nm wide-angle lens

'grande ① (a volte gran) adj (ampio) large; (grosso) big; (alto) tall; (largo) wide; (fig: senso morale) great; (grandioso) grand; (adulto) grown-up; **~ e grosso** beefy; **ho una gran fame** I'm very hungry; **fa un gran caldo** it's very hot; **in ~** on a large scale; **in gran parte** to a great extent; **non è un gran che** it is nothing much; **di gran carriera** hotfoot; **un gran ballo** a grand ball; **alla ~** sl in a big way ② nmf (persona adulta) grown-up; (persona eminente) great man/woman

grandeggi'are vi **~ su** tower over; (darsi arie) show off

gran'dezza nf greatness; (ampiezza) largeness; (larghezza) width, breadth; (dimensione) size; (fasto) grandeur; (prodigalità) lavishness; **a ~ naturale** life-size

grandi'nare vi hail; **grandina** it's hailing

'grandine nf hail

grandlosità nf grandeur

grandi'oso adj grand

gran'duca nm grand duke

grandu'cato nm grand duchy

grandu'chessa nf grand duchess

gra'nello nm grain; (di frutta) pip

gra'nita nf crushed ice drink

gra'nlto nm granite

'grano nm grain; (frumento) wheat. **grano di pepe** peppercorn. **grano saraceno** buckwheat

gran[o]'turco nm corn

'granulo nm granule

'grappa nf very strong, clear spirit distilled from grapes; (morsa) cramp

'grappolo nm bunch. **grappolo d'uva** bunch of grapes

gras'setto nm bold [type]

gras'sezza nf fatness; (untuosità) greasiness

'grasso ① adj fat; ⟨cibo⟩ fatty; (unto) greasy; ⟨terreno⟩ rich; (grossolano) coarse ② nm fat; (sostanza) grease; **a basso contenuto di grassi** low-fat; **senza grassi** nonfat, fat-free

gras'soccio adj plump

gras'sone, -a nmf dumpling

'grata nf grating

gra'tella nf Culin grill

gra'ticcio nm (per piante) trellis; (stuoia) rush matting

gra'ticola nf Culin grill

gra'tifica nf bonus

gratificazi'one nf satisfaction

gra'tin *nm inv* gratin. **gratin di patate** potatoes with grated cheese

grati'nare *vt* cook au gratin

grati'nato *adj* au gratin

'gratis *adv* free

grati'tudine *nf* gratitude

'grato *adj* grateful; (gradito) pleasant

gratta'capo *nm* trouble

grattaci'elo *nm* skyscraper

'gratta e 'vinci *nm inv* scratch card

grat'tare ① *vt* scratch; (raschiare) scrape; (grattugiare) grate; (fam: rubare) pinch ② *vi* grate

grat'tarsi *vr* scratch oneself

grat'tugia *nf* grater

grattugi'are *vt* grate

gratuita'mente *adv* free [of charge]

gra'tuito *adj* free [of charge]; (ingiustificato) gratuitous

gra'vare ① *vt* burden ② *vi* ~ **su** weigh on

'grave *adj* (pesante) heavy; (serio) serious; (difficile) hard; ⟨voce, suono⟩ low; (fonetica) grave; **essere** ~ (gravemente ammalato) be seriously ill

grave'mente *adv* seriously, gravely

gravi'danza *nf* pregnancy. **gravidanza extrauterina** ectopic pregnancy. **gravidanza indesiderata** unwanted pregnancy

'gravido *adj* pregnant

gravità *nf* seriousness; Phys gravity

gravi'tare *vi* gravitate

gra'voso *adj* onerous

'grazia *nf* grace; (favore) favour; Jur pardon; **entrare nelle grazie di qualcuno** get into somebody's good books; **ministero di grazia e giustizia** Ministry of Justice

grazi'are *vt* pardon

'grazie *int* thank you!, thanks!; ~ **mille!** many thanks!, thanks a lot!; ~ **a Dio/al cielo!** thank God/goodness!; ~ **a** thanks to

grazi'oso *adj* charming; (carino) pretty

'Grecia *nf* Greece

'greco, -a *adj* & *nmf* Greek. **greco antico** (lingua) classical Greek

gre'gario ① *adj* gregarious ② *nm* (ciclismo) supporting rider

'gregge *nm* flock

'greggio ① *adj* raw ② *nm* (petrolio) crude [oil]

grembi'ale, **grembi'ule** *nm* apron

'grembo *nm* lap; (utero) womb; fig bosom

gre'mire *vt* pack

gre'mirsi *vr* become crowded (**di** with)

gre'mito *adj* packed

'gretto *adj* stingy; (di vedute ristrette) narrow minded

'greve *adj* heavy

'grezzo *adj* = GREGGIO

gri'dare ① *vi* shout; (di dolore) scream; ⟨animale⟩ cry ② *vt* shout; ~ **qualcosa ai quattro venti** shout something from the rooftops

'grido *nm* (pl m **gridi** o pl f **grida**) shout, cry; (di animale) cry; **all'ultimo** ~ the latest fashion; **scrittore di** ~ celebrated writer. **grido d'aiuto** cry for help. **grido di battaglia** battle cry

'grigio *adj* & *nm* grey. **grigio perla** pearl grey

'griglia *nf* grill; **alla** ~ grilled; **cuocere alla** ~ grill

grigli'ata *nf* barbecue. **grigliata mista** mixed grill. **grigliata di pesce** grilled fish

gril'letto *nm* trigger

'grillo *nm* cricket; (fig: capriccio) whim

grimal'dello *nm* picklock

'grinfia *nf* fig clutch

'grinta *nf* grit

grin'toso *adj* determined

'grinza *nf* wrinkle; (di stoffa) crease; **non fare una** ~ fig ⟨ragionamento⟩ be flawless

grip'pare *vi* Mech seize up

gri'sou *nm* firedamp

gris'sino *nm* bread-stick

'grizzly *nm inv* grizzly

groenlan'dese ① *adj* of Greenland ② *nmf* Greenlander

Groen'landia *nf* Greenland

'groggy *adj inv* punch-drunk

'gronda *nf* eaves *pl*

gron'daia *nf* gutter

gron'dare *vi* pour; (essere bagnato fradicio) be dripping wet

'groppa *nf* back

'groppo *nm* knot; **avere un** ~ **alla gola** have a lump in one's throat

gros'sezza *nf* size; (spessore) thickness

gros'sista *nmf* wholesaler

'grosso ① *adj* big, large; (spesso) thick; (grossolano) coarse; (grave) serious ② *nm* big part; (massa) bulk; **farla grossa** do a stupid thing

grossolanità *nf inv* (qualità) coarseness; (di errore) grossness; (gesto) boorishness

grosso'lano *adj* coarse; ⟨errore⟩ gross; ⟨comportamento⟩ boorish

grosso'modo *adv* roughly

'grotta *nf* cave, grotto

grot'tesco *adj* & *nm* grotesque

grovi'era *nmf* Gruyère

gro'viglio *nm* tangle; fig muddle

gru *nf inv* (uccello, edilizia) crane

'gruccia *nf* (stampella) crutch; (per vestito) hanger. **gruccia appendiabiti** clotheshanger

grufo'lare *vi* root
gru'gnire *vi* grunt
gru'gnito *nm* grunt
'grugno *nm* snout
'grullo *adj* silly
'grumo *nm* clot; (di farina ecc) lump
gru'moso *adj* lumpy
'grunge *nm* grunge
'gruppo *nm* group; (comitiva) party. **gruppo d'azione** action group. **gruppo pop** pop group. **gruppo sanguigno** blood group. **gruppo di sostegno** support group. **gruppo di utenti** user group
gruvi'era *nmf* = GROVIERA
'gruzzolo *nm* nest-egg
guada'gnare *vt* earn; gain ⟨*tempo, forza ecc*⟩
guada'gnarsi *vr* ~ **da vivere** earn a living
gua'dagno *nm* gain; (profitto) profit; (entrate) earnings *pl*; **guadagni** *pl* **illeciti** ill-gotten gains
gu'ado *nm* ford; **passare a** ~ ford
gua'ina *nf* sheath; (busto) girdle
gu'aio *nm* trouble; **che** ~! that's just brilliant!; **essere nei guai** be in a fix; **guai a te se lo tocchi!** don't you dare touch it!
gua'ire *vi* yelp
gua'ito *nm* yelp; **guaiti** *pl* yelping
gu'ancia *nf* cheek
guanci'ale *nm* pillow
gu'anto *nm* glove. **guanto da forno** oven glove. **guanto di spugna** face cloth
guan'tone *nm* mitt; **guantoni** *pl* [da boxe] boxing gloves
guarda'boschi *nm inv* forester
guarda'caccia *nm inv* gamekeeper
guarda'coste *nm inv* coastguard
guarda'linee *nm inv* Sport linesman
guarda'macchine *nmf* car-park attendant
guarda'parco *nm inv* park ranger
guar'dare ① *vt* look at; (osservare) watch; (badare a) look after; ⟨*finestra*⟩ look out on; ~ **la televisione** watch television ② *vi* look; (essere orientato verso) face; ~ **in su** look up
guarda'roba *nm inv* wardrobe; (di locale pubblico) cloakroom
guardarobi'ere, **-a** *nmf* cloakroom attendant
guar'darsi *vr* look at oneself; ~ **da** beware of; (astenersi) refrain from
gu'ardia *nf* guard; (poliziotto) policeman; (vigilanza) watch; **essere di** ~ be on guard; ⟨*medico*⟩ be on duty; **fare la** ~ **a** keep guard over; **mettere in** ~ **qualcuno** warn somebody; **stare in** ~ be on one's guard.

guardia carceraria prison warder, prison officer. **guardia del corpo** bodyguard, minder. **Guardia di finanza** body of police officers responsible for border control and for investigating fraud. **guardia forestale** forest ranger. **guardia medica** duty doctor
guardi'ano, **-a** *nmf* caretaker. **guardiano notturno** night watchman. **guardiano dello zoo** zoo keeper
guar'dingo *adj* cautious
guardi'ola *nf* gatekeeper's lodge
guarigi'one *nf* recovery
gua'rire ① *vt* cure ② *vi* recover; ⟨*ferita*⟩ heal [up]
gua'rito *adj* cured
guari|'tore, **-trice** *nmf* healer
guarnigi'one *nf* garrison
guar'nire *vt* trim; Culin garnish
guarnizi'one *nf* trimming; Culin garnish; Mech gasket. **guarnizione del freno** brake lining
guasta'feste *nmf inv* spoilsport
gua'stare *vt* spoil; (rovinare) ruin; break ⟨*meccanismo*⟩
gua'starsi *vr* spoil; (andare a male) go bad; ⟨*tempo*⟩ change for the worse; ⟨*meccanismo*⟩ break down
gu'asto ① *adj* broken; ⟨*ascensore, telefono*⟩ out of order; ⟨*auto*⟩ broken down; ⟨*cibo, dente*⟩ bad ② *nm* breakdown; (danno) damage; **ho un** ~ **alla macchina** my car's not working. **guasto al motore** engine failure
Guate'mala *nm* Guatemala
guazza'buglio *nm* muddle
guaz'zare *vi* wallow
gu'ercio *adj* cross-eyed
gu'erra *nf* war; (tecnica bellica) warfare; **la grande** ~ the Great War, World War I. **guerra batteriologica** germ warfare. **guerra biologica** biological warfare. **guerra civile** civil war. **guerra fredda** Cold War. **guerra del Golfo** Gulf War. **guerra lampo** blitzkrieg. **guerra mondiale** world war. **prima guerra mondiale** World War I, WW1. **seconda guerra mondiale** World War II, WW2. **guerra dei prezzi** price war. **guerra di secessione** American Civil War
guerrafon'daio, **-a** *nmf* warmonger
guerreggi'are *vi* wage war
guer'resco *adj* (di guerra) war; (bellicoso) warlike
guerri'ero *nm* warrior
guer'riglia *nf* guerrilla warfare
guerrigli'ero, **-a** *nmf* guerrilla
'gufo *nm* owl
'guglia *nf* spire
gu'ida *nf* guide; (direzione) guidance; (comando) leadership; (elenco) directory; Auto ⋯⋗

driving; (tappeto) runner; **chi era alla ~?**
who was driving?; **essere alla ~ di** fig be
the head of; **fare da ~** be a guide (**a** to).
guida commerciale trade directory.
guida a destra right-hand drive. **guida
a sinistra** left-hand drive. **guida
telefonica** phone book, telephone
directory. **guida turistica** tourist guide
gui'dare vt guide; Auto drive; steer
‹nave›; **~ a passo d'uomo** drive at
walking speed
guida|'tore, -trice nmf driver.
guidatore della domenica Sunday
driver
Gui'nea nf Guinea
Gui'nea-Bis'sau nf Guinea-Bissau
Gui'nea Equato'riale nf Equatorial
Guinea
guin'zaglio nm leash

gu'isa nf **a ~ di** like
guiz'zare vi dart; ‹luce› flash
gu'izzo nm dart; (di luce) flash
'gulag nm inv Gulag
'gulasch nm goulash
'guru nm inv high priest
'guscio nm shell; (di cellulare) fascia
gu'stare ⓵ vt taste
⓶ vi like
'gusto nm taste; (piacere) liking; **mangiare
di ~** eat heartily; **prenderci ~** come to
enjoy it, develop a taste for it; **al ~ di
pistacchio** pistachio flavoured; **buon ~**
good taste
gu'stoso adj tasty; fig delightful
guttu'rale adj guttural
Gu'yana nf Guyana

Hh

'habitat nm inv habitat
habitué nmf inv regular [customer]
'hacker nmf inv Comput hacker
Ha'iti nf Haiti
haiti'ano, -a adj & nmf Haitian
'halal adj halal
hall nf inv foyer; (di stazione) concourse
ham'burger nm inv hamburger.
hamburger vegetariano veggie burger
'handicap nm inv handicap
handicap'pare vt handicap
handicap'pato, -a ⓵ adj disabled
⓶ nmf disabled person. **handicappato
mentale** mentally handicapped person
'hangar nm inv hangar
'hard[-core] adj hard core
hard 'disk nm inv hard disk
hard 'rock nm hard rock
'hardware nm inv Comput hardware
'harem nm inv harem
'hashish nm hashish
hawa'iano, -a adj & nmf Hawaiian

'Hawaii nfpl **le ~** Hawaii
'heavy metal nm Mus heavy metal
henné nm henna
'herpes nm inv herpes; (su labbra) cold
sore. **herpes zoster** shingles
'hi-fi nm inv hi-fi
high 'tech nf high tech
'Himalaia nm Himalayas pl
'hinterland nm inv hinterland
'hippy adj & nmf inv hippy
'hit parade nf inv hit parade, charts pl
HIV nm HIV
'hockey nm hockey. **hockey su
ghiaccio** ice hockey. **hockey su prato**
field hockey
'holding nf inv holding company
hollywoo'diano adj Hollywood
Hong 'Kong nf Hong Kong
'hostess nf inv (air) stewardess
hot 'dog nm inv hot dog
'hotel nm inv hotel
'humus nm humus

Ii

i def art mpl the; ▶ IL

i'ato nm hiatus

i'berico *adj* Iberian

iber'nare *vi* hibernate

ibernazi'one *nf* hibernation

i'bisco *nm* hibiscus

ibri'dare *vt* interbreed

ibridazi'one *nf* interbreeding

'ibrido *adj & nm* hybrid

'iceberg *nm inv* iceberg; **la punta dell'~** fig the tip of the iceberg

i'cona *nf* icon

iconiz'zare *vt* iconize

icono'clasta *adj & nmf* iconoclast

icono'clastico *adj* iconoclastic

id'dio *nm* God

i'dea *nf* idea; (opinione) opinion; (ideale) ideal; (indizio) inkling; (piccola quantità) hint; (intenzione) intention; **cambiare ~** change one's mind; **neanche per ~!** not on your life!; **chiarirsi le idee** get one's ideas straight; **dare l'~ di ...** give the impression that ...; **essere dell'~ che ...** be of the opinion that ...; **non ne ho ~!** I've no idea!. **Idea fissa** obsession

ide'ale *adj & nm* ideal

idea'lista *nmf* idealist

idealiz'zare *vt* idealize

ide'are *vt* conceive

idea|'tore, -trice *nmf* originator

'idem *adv* the same

identica'mente *adv* identically

i'dentico *adj* identical

identifi'cabile *adj* identifiable

identifi'care *vt* identify

identifica'tivo *nm* **identificativo del chiamante** caller identification

identificazi'one *nf* identification

identi'kit® *nm inv* identikit. **identikit elettronico** e-fit

identità *nf inv* identity

ideo'gramma *nm* ideogram

ideolo'gia *nf* ideology

ideologica'mente *adv* ideologically

ideo'logico *adj* ideological

idillica'mente *adv* idyllically

i'dillico *adj* idyllic

i'dillio *nm* idyll

idi'oma *nm* language

idio'matico *adj* idiomatic; **espressione idiomatica** idiom, idiomatic expression

idiosincra'sia *nf* fig aversion; Med allergy

idi'ota ① *adj* idiotic
② *nmf* idiot

idio'zia *nf* idiocy; **dire/fare un'~** do/say something stupid; **dire idiozie** talk nonsense; **non fare idiozie!** don't act daft!

idola'trare *vt* worship

idoleggi'are *vt* idolize

'idolo *nm* idol

idoneità *nf* suitability; Mil fitness; **esame di idoneità** qualifying examination

i'doneo *adj* **~ a** suitable for; Mil fit for

i'drante *nm* hydrant; (tubo) hose; (usato dalla polizia) water cannon

idra'tante *adj* ‹crema› moisturizing

idra'tare *vt* hydrate; ‹cosmetico› moisturize

idratazi'one *nf* moisturizing

i'draulico ① *adj* hydraulic
② *nm* plumber

'idrico *adj* water *attrib*

idrocar'buro *nm* hydrocarbon

idroelettricità *nf* hydroelectricity

idroe'lettrico *adj* hydroelectric

i'drofilo *adj* **cotone ~** cotton wool, absorbent cotton Am

idrofo'bia *nf* rabies *sg*

i'drofobo *adj* rabid; fig furious

i'drofugo *adj* water-repellent

i'drogeno *nm* hydrogen

idrogra'fia *nf* hydrography

i'drolisi *nf* hydrolysis

idromas'saggio *nm* (sistema) whirlpool bath; **vasca con ~** jacuzzi®

idro'mele *nm* mead

idrorepel'lente *adj & nm* water-repellent

idroso'lubile *adj* water-soluble

idrotera'pia *nf* hydrotherapy

idrovo'lante *nm* seaplane

i'druro *nm* hydride

i'ella *nf* fam bad luck; **portare ~** be bad luck

iel'lato *adj* fam jinxed, plagued by bad luck

i'ena *nf* hyena

i'eri *adv* yesterday; **~ l'altro, l'altro ~** the day before yesterday; **il giornale di ~** yesterday's paper; **~ mattina** yesterday evening

ietta|'tore, -trice *nmf* jinx

ietta'tura *nf* (sfortuna) bad luck

igi'ene *nf* hygiene; **ufficio d'igiene** ≈ Public Health Service. **igiene mentale** mental health. **igiene personale** personal hygiene. **igiene pubblica** public health

igienica'mente *adv* hygienically

igi'enico *adj* hygienic

igie'nista *nmf* hygienist

ig'loo *nm inv* igloo

i'gname *nm* yam

i'gnaro *adj* unaware

i'gnifugo *adj* flame-retardant, fire-retardant

i'gnobile *adj* despicable

ignobil'mente *adv* despicably

igno'minia *nf* disgrace

igno'rante ➀ *adj* ignorant ➁ *nmf* ignoramus

igno'ranza *nf* ignorance; **Ignoranza crassa** crass ignorance

igno'rare *vt* (non sapere) be unaware of; (trascurare) ignore; **essere ignorato** go unheeded

i'gnoto *adj* unknown

i'guana *nf* iguana

il *def art m* the; **il latte fa bene** milk is good for you; **il signor Magnetti** Mr Magnetti; **il dottor Piazza** Doctor Piazza; **ha il naso grosso** he's got a big nose; **ha gli occhi azzurri** he's got blue eyes; **mettiti il cappello** put your hat on; **il lunedì** on Mondays; **il 2004** 2004; **costa 5 euro il chilo** it costs 5 euros a kilo

'ilare *adj* merry

ilarità *nf* hilarity

i'leo *nm* hipbone

illangui'dire *vi* grow weak

illazi'one *nf* inference

illecita'mente *adv* illicitly

il'lecito *adj* illicit

ille'gale *adj* illegal

illegalità *nf* illegality

illegal'mente *adv* illegally

illeg'gibile *adj* illegible; ‹libro› unreadable

illegittimità *nf* illegitimacy

ille'gittimo *adj* illegitimate

il'leso *adj* unhurt, uninjured

illette'rato, -a *adj & nmf* illiterate

illi'bato *adj* chaste

illimitata'mente *adv* indefinitely

illimi'tato *adj* unlimited

illivi'dire ➀ *vt* bruise ➁ *vi* (per rabbia) turn livid

illogica'mente *adv* illogically

il'logico *adj* illogical

il'ludere *vt* deceive

il'ludersi *vr* deceive oneself

illumi'nare *vt* light up; fig enlighten; **~ a giorno** floodlight

illumi'narsi *vr* light up

illuminazi'one *nf* lighting; fig enlightenment. **illuminazione a gas** gas lighting. **illuminazione al neon** strip lighting

Illumi'nismo *nm* Enlightenment

illusi'one *nf* illusion; **farsi illusioni** delude oneself. **illusione ottica** optical illusion

illusio'nismo *nm* conjuring

illusio'nista *nmf* conjurer

il'luso, -a ➀ *pp di* ILLUDERE ➁ *adj* deluded

➂ *nmf* day-dreamer

illu'sorio *adj* illusory

illu'strare *vt* illustrate

illustra'tivo *adj* illustrative

illustra|'tore, -trice *nmf* illustrator

illustrazi'one *nf* illustration. **illustrazione a colori/in bianco e nero** colour/black and white illustration

il'lustre *adj* distinguished

imbacuc'care *vt* wrap up

imbacuc'carsi *vr* wrap up

imbacuc'cato *adj* wrapped up

imbal'laggio *nm* packing

imbal'lare *vt* pack; Auto race

imballa|'tore, -trice *nmf* packer

imbalsa'mare *vt* embalm; stuff ‹animale›

imbalsa'mato *adj* embalmed; ‹animale› stuffed

imbambo'lato *adj* vacant

imban'dito *adj* ‹tavola› covered with food

imbaraz'zante *adj* embarrassing

imbaraz'zare *vt* embarrass; (ostacolare) encumber

imbaraz'zato *adj* embarrassed

imba'razzo *nm* embarrassment; (ostacolo) hindrance; **trarre qualcuno d' ~** help somebody out of a difficulty; **avere l'~ della scelta** be spoilt for choice. **imbarazzo di stomaco** indigestion.

imbarba'rire *vt* barbarize

imbarba'rirsi *vr* become barbarized

imbarca'dero *nm inv* landing-stage

imbar'care *vt* embark; (fam: rimorchiare) score; **~ acqua** ship water

imbar'carsi *vr* go on board; fig embark (in on)

imbarcazi'one *nf* boat. **imbarcazione da pesca** fishing boat. **imbarcazione di salvataggio** lifeboat

im'barco *nm* boarding; (banchina) landing-stage; '**~ immediato**' 'now boarding'

imbastar'dire *vt* debase

imbastar'dirsi *vr* become debased

imba'stire *vt* tack, baste; fig sketch

imbasti'tura *nf* tacking, basting

im'battersi *vr* **~ in** run into

imbat'tibile *adj* unbeatable

imbat'tuto *adj* unbeaten

imbavagli'are *vt* gag

imbec'cata *nf* Theat prompt

imbe'cille ➀ *adj* stupid ➁ *nmf* Med imbecile

imbellet'tarsi *vr* hum doll oneself up

imbel'lire *vt* embellish

im'berbe *adj* beardless; fig inexperienced

imbestia'lire *vi* fly into a rage; **far ~ qualcuno** drive somebody crazy

imbestia'lirsi *vr* fly into a rage

imbestia'lito *adj* enraged

im'bevere *vt* imbue (**di** with)

im'beversi *vr* absorb

imbe'vibile *adj* undrinkable

imbe'vuto *adj* **~ di** ⟨*acqua*⟩ soaked in; ⟨*nozioni*⟩ imbued with

imbian'care ① *vt* whiten ② *vi* turn white

imbian'chino *nm* [house] painter

imbion'dire ① *vt* bleach ② *vi* become bleached

imbion'dirsi *vr* become bleached

imbizzar'rire *vr* become restless; (arrabbiarsi) become angry

imbizzar'rirsi *vi* become restless; (arrabbiarsi) become angry

imboc'care *vt* feed; (entrare) enter; fig prompt

imbocca'tura *nf* opening; (ingresso) entrance; (Mus: di strumento) mouthpiece

im'bocco *nm* entrance

imboni'mento *nm* spiel

imboni'tore *nm* clever talker

imborghe'sire *vi* become middle class

imborghe'sirsi *vr* become middle class

imbo'scare *vt* hide

imbo'scarsi *vr* Mil shirk military service

imbo'scata *nf* ambush

imbo'scato *nm* draft dodger

imbottiglia'mento *nm* traffic jam

imbottigli'are *vt* bottle

imbottigli'arsi *vr* get snarled up in a traffic jam

imbottigli'ato *adj* ⟨*vino, acqua*⟩ bottled; ⟨*auto*⟩ stuck in a traffic jam, snarled up; **nave imbottigliata** ship in a bottle

imbot'tire *vt* stuff; pad (giacca); Culin fill

imbot'tirsi *vr* **~ di** (fig, di pasticche) stuff oneself with

imbot'tita *nf* quilt

imbot'tito *adj* ⟨*spalle*⟩ padded; ⟨*cuscino*⟩ stuffed; ⟨*panino*⟩ filled

imbotti'tura *nf* stuffing; (di giacca) padding; Culin filling

imbraca'tura *nf* harness

imbracci'are *vt* shoulder ⟨*fucile*⟩; grasp ⟨*scudo*⟩

imbra'nato *adj* clumsy

imbrat'tare *vt* mark

imbrat'tarsi *vr* dirty oneself

imbrigli'are *vt* bridle ⟨*cavallo*⟩; dam ⟨*acque*⟩

imbroc'care *vt* hit; **imbroccarla giusta** hit the nail on the head

imbrogli'are *vt* muddle; (raggirare) cheat; **~ le carte** fig confuse the issue

imbrogli'arsi *vr* get tangle; (confondersi) get confused

im'broglio *nm* tangled; (pasticcio) mess; (inganno) trick

imbrogli'one, -a *nmf* cheat

imbronci'are *vi* sulk

imbronci'arsi *vr* sulk

imbronci'ato *adj* sulky

imbru'nire *vi* get dark; **all'~** at dusk

imbrut'tire ① *vt* make ugly ② *vi* become ugly

imbu'care *vt* post, mail; (nel biliardo) pot

imbu'cato *adj* fam **è ~** he only got the job because of who he knows

imbufa'lirsi *vr* hit the roof

imbur'rare *vt* butter

im'buto *nm* funnel

i'mene *nm* hymen

imi'tare *vt* imitate

imita|'tore, -trice *nmf* imitator, impersonator

imitazi'one *nf* imitation; **'diffidare delle imitazioni'** 'beware of imitations'

immaco'lato *adj* spotless, immaculate; **l'immacolata Concezione** the Immaculate Conception

immagazzi'nare *vt* store

immagi'nare *vt* imagine; (supporre) suppose; **s'immagini!** don't mention it!

immagi'nario *adj* imaginary

immaginazi'one *nf* imagination; **è frutto della tua ~** it's a figment of your imagination

im'magine *nf* image; (rappresentazione, Idea) picture. **immagine aziendale** corporate image. **immagine della marca** brand image. **immagine speculare** mirror image

immagi'noso *adj* full of imagery

immalinco'nire *vt* sadden

immalinco'nirsi *vr* grow melancholy

imman'cabile *adj* unfailing

immancabil'mente *adv* without fail

im'mane *adj* huge; (orribile) terrible

imma'nente *adj* immanent

immangi'abile *adj* inedible

immatrico'lare *vt* register

immatrico'larsi *vr* ⟨*studente*⟩ matriculate

immatrico'lato *adj* registered

immatricolazi'one *nf* registration; (di studente) matriculation

immaturità *nf* immaturity

imma'turo *adj* unripe; ⟨*persona*⟩ immature; (precoce) premature

immedesi'marsi *vr* **~ in** identify oneself with

immedesimazi'one *nf* identification
immediata'mente *adv* immediately
immedia'tezza *nf* immediacy
immedi'ato *adj* immediate; **nell'~ futuro** in the immediate future
immemo'rabile *adj* immemorial
im'memore *adj* oblivious
immensa'mente *adv* enormously
immensità *nf* immensity
im'menso *adj* immense
immensu'rabile *adj* immeasurable
im'mergere *vt* immerse
im'mergersi *vr* plunge; ‹*sommergibile*› dive; **~ in** immerse oneself in
immeritata'mente *adv* undeservedly
immeri'tato *adj* undeserved
immeri'tevole *adj* undeserving
immersi'one *nf* immersion; (di sommergibile, palombaro) dive. **immersione [subacquea]** skin diving, scuba diving
im'merso pp di IMMERGERE
im'mettere *vt* introduce
im'mettersi *vr* introduce oneself
immi'grante *adj & nmf* immigrant
immi'grare *vi* immigrate
immi'grato, -a *nmf* immigrant
immigrazi'one *nf* immigration. **immigrazione interna** migration
immi'nente *adj* imminent
immi'nenza *nf* imminence
immischi'are *vt* involve
immischi'arsi *vr* **~ in** meddle in
immi'scibile *adj* immiscible
immis'sario *nm* tributary
immissi'one *nf* insertion; Techn intake; (introduzione) introduction. **immissione [di] dati** data entry
im'mobile *adj* motionless
im'mobili *nmpl* real estate
immobili'are *adj* **società immobiliare** building society, savings and loan Am
immobilità *nf* immobility
immobiliz'zare *vt* immobilize; Comm tie up
immobiliz'zato *adj* immobilized. **immobilizzato a letto** confined to bed
immobilizza'tore *nm* **immobilizzatore elettronico** Auto immobilizer
immobilizzazi'one *nf* immobilization; Fin fixed asset; **spese d'~** capital expenditure
immoderata'mente *adv* immoderately
immode'rato *adj* immoderate
immo'destia *nf* immodesty
immo'desto *adj* immodest

immo'lare *vt* sacrifice
immo'larsi *vr* sacrifice oneself
immondez'zaio *nm* rubbish tip
immon'dizia *nf* filth; (spazzatura) rubbish
Im'mondo *adj* filthy
immo'rale *adj* immoral
immoral'mente *adv* immorally
immorta'lare *vt* immortalize
immor'tale *adj* immortal
immortalità *nf* immortality
immoti'vato *adj* unjustified, unmotivated
im'moto *adj* motionless
im'mune *adj* exempt; Med immune
immunità *nf* immunity. **immunità diplomatica** diplomatic immunity. **immunità parlamentare** parliamentary privilege
immuniz'zare *vt* immunize
immunizzazi'one *nf* immunization
immunodefici'enza *nf* immunodeficiency
immunodepres'sivo *adj & nm* immunodepressant
immunolo'gia *nf* immunology
immuno'logico *adj* immunological
immuso'nirsi *vr* sulk
immuso'nito *adj* sulky
immu'tabile *adj* unchangeable
immu'tato *adj* unchanging
impacchet'tare *vt* wrap up
impacci'are *vt* hamper; (disturbare) inconvenience; (imbarazzare) embarrass
impacciata'mente *adv* awkwardly
impacci'ato *adj* embarrassed; (goffo) awkward
im'paccio *nm* embarrassment; (ostacolo) hindrance; (situazione difficile) awkward situation; **trarsi d'~** get out of an awkward situation
im'pacco *nm* compress
impadro'nirsi *vr* **~ di** take possession of; (fig: imparare) master
impa'gabile *adj* priceless
impagi'nare *vt* paginate
impaginazi'one *nf* pagination
impagli'are *vt* stuff ‹*animale*›
impa'lare *vt* impale
impa'lato *adj* fig stiff
impalca'tura *nf* scaffolding; fig structure
impal'lare *vt* snooker
impalli'dire *vi* turn pale; (fig: perdere d'importanza) pale into insignificance
impalli'nare *vt* riddle with bullets
impal'pabile *adj* impalpable; ‹*tessuto*› gossamer-like
impa'nare *vt* Culin bread

impa'nato *adj* breaded

impanta'narsi *vr* get bogged down

impape'rarsi *vr* falter, stammer

impappi'narsi *vr* falter, stammer

impa'rare *vt* learn; ~ **a proprie spese** learn to one's cost

impara'ticcio *nm* half-baked

impareggi'abile *adj* incomparable

imparen'tarsi *vr* ~ **con** become related to

imparen'tato *adj* related

'impari *adj* unequal; (dispari) odd

impar'tire *vt* impart

imparzi'ale *adj* impartial

imparzialità *nf* impartiality

im'passe *nf inv* impasse

impas'sibile *adj* impassive; **con aria ~** impassively

impa'stare *vt* Culin knead; blend ‹colori›

impasta'tura *nf* kneading

impastic'carsi *vr* pop pills

impasticci'are *vt* make a mess of

im'pasto *nm* Culin dough; (miscuglio) mixture

im'patto *nm* impact. **impatto ambientale** environmental impact

impau'rire *vt* frighten

impau'rirsi *vr* get frightened

im'pavido *adj* fearless

impazi'ente *adj* impatient; ~ **di fare qualcosa** eager to do something

impazien'tirsi *vr* lose patience

impazi'enza *nf* impatience

impaz'zata *nf* **all'~** at breakneck speed

impaz'zire *vi* go mad; ‹maionese› separate; **far ~ qualcuno** drive somebody mad; ~ **per** be crazy about; **da ~** ‹mal di testa› blinding

impaz'zito *adj* crazed

impec'cabile *adj* impeccable

impeccabil'mente *adv* impeccably

impedi'mento *nm* hindrance; (ostacolo) obstacle

impe'dire *vt* (impacciare) hinder; (ostruire) obstruct; ~ **di** prevent from; ~ **a qualcuno di fare qualcosa** prevent somebody [from] doing something

impe'gnare *vt* (dare in pegno) pawn; (vincolare) bind; (prenotare) reserve; (assorbire) take up

impe'gnarsi *vr* apply oneself; ~ **a fare qualcosa** commit oneself to doing something

impegna'tiva *nf* referral

impegna'tivo *adj* binding; ‹lavoro› demanding

impe'gnato *adj* politically committed

im'pegno *nm* engagement; Comm commitment; (zelo) care; **con ~** with dedication; **ho un ~** I'm doing something

impego'larsi *vr* ~ **in** become enmeshed in

impel'lente *adj* pressing

impene'trabile *adj* impenetrable

impen'narsi *vr* ‹cavallo› rear; fig bristle

impen'nata *nf* (di prezzi) sharp rise; (di cavallo) rearing; (di moto) wheelie; (di aereo) climb

impen'sabile *adj* unthinkable

impen'sato *adj* unexpected

impensie'rire *vt* worry

impensie'rirsi *vr* worry

impe'rante *adj* prevailing

impe'rare *vi* reign

impera'tivo *adj & nm* imperative

impera|'tore, -trice ① *nm* emperor ② *nf* empress

impercet'tibile *adj* imperceptible

impercettibil'mente *adv* imperceptibly

imperdo'nabile *adj* unforgivable

imperfetta'mente *adv* imperfectly

imper'fetto *adj & nm* imperfect

imperfezi'one *nf* imperfection

imperi'ale *adj* imperial

imperia'lismo *nm* imperialism

imperia'lista *adj & nmf* imperialist

imperia'listico *adj* imperialistic

imperi'oso *adj* imperious; (impellente) urgent

imperi'turo *adj* immortal

impe'rizia *nf* lack of skill

imper'lare *vt* bead

imperma'lire *vt* offend

imperma'lirsi *vr* take offence

imperme'abile ① *adj* ‹orologio› waterproof; ‹terreno› impermeable ② *nm* raincoat

imperni'are *vt* pivot; (fondare) base

imperni'arsi *vr* ~ **su** be based on

im'pero *nm* empire; (potere) rule; **stile impero** empire style

imperscru'tabile *adj* inscrutable

imperso'nale *adj* impersonal

imperso'nare *vt* personify; (interpretare) act [the part of]

imper'territo *adj* undaunted, undeterred

imperti'nente *adj* impertinent

imperti'nenza *nf* impertinence

impertur'babile *adj* imperturbable

impertur'bato *adj* unperturbed

imperver'sare *vi* rage

im'pervio *adj* inaccessible

'impeto *nm* impetus; (impulso) impulse; (slancio) transport

impet'tito *adj* stiff

impetuosa'mente *adv* impetuously

impetu'oso *adj* impetuous; ⟨*vento*⟩ blustering

impiallacci'are *vt* veneer

impiallacci'ato *adj* veneered

impian'tare *vt* install; set up ⟨*azienda*⟩

impi'anto *nm* plant; (sistema) system; (operazione) installation. **impianto di amplificazione** public address system, PA system. **impianto audio** sound system. **impianto elettrico** electrical system; **impianti** *pl* **fissi** fixtures and fittings. **impianto radio** Auto car stereo system. **impianto di rilavorazione [di scorie nucleari]** reprocessing plant. **impianto di riscaldamento** heating system. **impianto stereo** hi-fi

impia'strare *vt* plaster; (sporcare) dirty

impia'strarsi *vr* get dirty; ∼ **le mani** get one's hands dirty

impi'astro *nm* poultice; ⟨*persona noiosa*⟩ bore; (pasticcione) cack-handed person

impiccagi'one *nf* hanging

impic'care *vt* hang

impic'carsi *vr* hang oneself

impic'cato, -a ⓵ *nm* hanged man ⓶ *nf* hanged woman

impicci'arsi *vr* meddle

im'piccio *nm* hindrance; (seccatura) bother

impicci'one, -a *nmf* nosey parker

impie'gare *vt* employ; (usare) use; spend ⟨*tempo, denaro*⟩; Fin invest; **l'autobus ha impiegato un'ora** it took the bus an hour

impie'garsi *vr* get [oneself] a job

impiega'tizio *adj* clerical

impie'gato, -a *nmf* employee; (di ufficio) office worker. **impiegato di banca** bank clerk. **impiegato di concetto** administrative employee. **impiegato in prova** probationer. **impiegato statale** civil servant

impi'ego *nm* employment; (posto) job; Fin investment; **pubblico impiego** public sector. **impiego fisso** permanent job. **impieghi** *pl* **saltuari** odd jobs, casual employment. **impiego temporaneo** temporary job

impieto'sire *vt* move to pity

impieto'sirsi *vr* be moved to pity

impie'toso *adj* pitiless

impie'trito *adj* petrified

impigli'are *vt* entangle

impigli'arsi *vr* get entangled

impi'grire *vt* make lazy

impi'grirsi *vr* get lazy

impi'lare *vt* stack

impingu'are *vt* fig fill

impiom'bare *vt* seal ⟨*cassa, porta*⟩

impla'cabile *adj* implacable

implemen'tare *vt* implement

impli'care *vt* implicate; (sottintendere) imply

impli'carsi *vr* become involved

implicazi'one *nf* implication

implicita'mente *adv* implicitly

im'plicito *adj* implicit

implo'rante *adj* imploring

implo'rare *vt* implore

implorazi'one *nf* entreaty

implosi'one *nf* implosion

impolli'nare *vt* pollinate

impollinazi'one *nf* pollination

impoltro'nire *vt* make lazy

impoltro'nirsi *vr* become lazy

impolve'rare *vt* cover with dust

impolve'rarsi *vr* get covered with dust

impolve'rato *adj* dusty

impoma'tare *vt* put brilliantine on

impoma'tarsi *vr* put brilliantine on ⟨*capelli*⟩

imponde'rabile *adj* imponderable; ⟨*causa, evento*⟩ unpredictable

impo'nente *adj* imposing

impo'nenza *nf* impressiveness

impo'nibile ⓵ *adj* taxable ⓶ *nm* taxable income

impopo'lare *adj* unpopular

impopolarità *nf* unpopularity

imporpo'rarsi *vr* turn red

im'porre *vt* impose; (ordinare) order

im'porsi *vr* assert oneself; (aver successo) be successful; ∼ **di** (prefiggersi di) set oneself the task of

impor'tante ⓵ *adj* important ⓶ *nm* important thing

impor'tanza *nf* importance; **di vitale** ∼ crucially important

impor'tare ⓵ *vt* Comm, Comput import; (comportare) cause ⓶ *vi* matter; (essere necessario) be necessary; **non importa!** it doesn't matter!; **non me ne importa niente!** I couldn't care less!

importa|'tore, -trice ⓵ *adj* importing ⓶ *nmf* importer

importazi'one *nf* importation; (merce importata) import

import-'export *nm inv* import-export

im'porto *nm* amount

importu'nare *vt* pester; ∼ **qualcuno per qualcosa** pester somebody for something

impor'tuno *adj* troublesome; (inopportuno) untimely

imposizi'one *nf* imposition; (imposta) tax

imposses'sarsi *vr* ∼ **di** seize
impos'sibile ① *adj* impossible.
② *nm* **fare l'**∼ do absolutely all one can
impossibilità *nf* impossibility
im'posta¹ *nf* tax. **imposta fondiaria** land tax. **imposta patrimoniale** property tax. **imposta sul reddito** income tax. **imposta sui redditi di capitale** capital gains tax. **imposta sulle società** corporation tax. **imposta supplementare** surtax. **imposta sul valore aggiunto** value added tax
im'posta² *nf* (di finestra) shutter
impo'stare *vt* (progettare) plan; (basare) base; Mus pitch; (imbucare) post, mail; set out ⟨domanda, problema⟩
impostazi'one *nf* planning; (di voce) pitching; **impostazioni** *pl* Comput, Teleph settings
im'posto *pp di* IMPORRE
impo'store, -a *nmf* impostor
impo'stura *nf* imposture
impo'tente *adj* powerless; Med impotent
impo'tenza *nf* powerlessness; Med impotence
impoveri'mento *nm* impoverishment
impove'rire *vt* impoverish
impove'rirsi *vr* become poor; ⟨risorse⟩ become depleted; ⟨linguaggio⟩ become impoverished
imprati'cabile *adj* impracticable; ⟨strada⟩ impassable
impraticabilità *nf* **per** ∼ **del terreno/ delle strade** because of the state of the pitch/roads
imprati'chire *vt* train
imprati'chirsi *vr* ∼ **in,** ∼ **a** get practice in
impre'care *vi* curse
imprecazi'one *nf* curse
impreci'sabile *adj* indeterminable
impreci'sato *adj* indeterminate
imprecisi'one *nf* inaccuracy
impre'ciso *adj* inaccurate
impre'gnare *vt* impregnate; (imbevere) soak; fig imbue
impre'gnarsi *vr* become impregnated with
imprendi|'tore, -trice *nmf* entrepreneur
imprenditori'ale *adj* entrepreneurial
imprepa'rato *adj* unprepared
im'presa *nf* undertaking; (gesta) exploit; ⟨azienda⟩ firm. **impresa edile** property developer. **impresa familiare** family business. **impresa di pompe funebri** undertakers, funeral directors. **impresa pubblica** state-owned company. **impresa di traslochi** removals firm Br

impre'sario *nm* impresario; (appaltatore) contractor. **impresario di pompe funebri** undertaker, funeral director, mortician Am. **impresario teatrale** theatre manager
imprescin'dibile *adj* inescapable
impressio'nabile *adj* impressionable
impressio'nante *adj* impressive; (spaventoso) frightening
impressio'nare *vt* impress; (spaventare) frighten; expose ⟨foto⟩
impressio'narsi *vr* be affected; (spaventarsi) be frightened
impressi'one *nf* impression; (sensazione) sensation; (impronta) mark; **far** ∼ **a qualcuno** upset somebody; **dare l'**∼ **di essere ...** give the impression of being ...
impressio'nismo *nm* impressionism
impressio'nista *adj & nmf* impressionist
impressio'nistico *adj* impressionistic
im'presso ① *pp di* IMPRIMERE
② *adj* printed
impre'stare *vt* lend
impreve'dibile *adj* unforeseeable; ⟨persona⟩ unpredictable
imprevedibil'mente *adv* unexpectedly
imprevi'dente *adj* improvident
impre'visto ① *adj* unforeseen
② *nm* unforeseen event; **salvo imprevisti** all being well
imprigiona'mento *nm* imprisonment
imprigio'nare *vt* imprison
im'primere *vt* impress; (stampare) print; (comunicare) impart; **rimanere impresso a qualcuno** stick in somebody's mind
impro'babile *adj* unlikely, improbable; **è** ∼ **che ci sia** he is unlikely to be there
improbabilità *nf* improbability
improdut'tivo *adj* unproductive
im'pronta *nf* impression; (di dito) print; fig mark. **impronta digitale** fingerprint; **impronte** *pl* **genetiche** genetic fingerprinting. **impronta del piede** footprint
impron'tato *adj* ∼ **all'ironia** tinged with irony
impronunci'abile *adj* unpronounceable
impro'perio *nm* insult; **improperi** *pl* abuse *sg*
impropo'nibile *adj* unrealistic
im'proprio *adj* improper
improro'gabile *adj* which cannot be extended
improvvisa'mente *adv* suddenly
improvvi'sare *vt/i* improvise
improvvi'sarsi *vr* turn oneself into a
improvvi'sata *nf* surprise

improvvi'sato *adj* ⟨*discorso*⟩ unrehearsed

improvvisazi'one *nf* improvisation

improv'viso *adj* unexpected, sudden; all'∼ unexpectedly, suddenly

impru'dente *adj* imprudent

imprudente'mente *adv* imprudently

impru'denza *nf* imprudence

impu'dente *adj* impudent

impudente'mente *adv* impudently

impu'denza *nf* impudence

impu'dico *adj* immodest

impu'gnare *vt* grasp; Jur contest

impugna'tura *nf* grip; (manico) handle. **impugnatura a due mani** two-handed grip

impulsiva'mente *adv* impulsively

impulsività *nf* impulsiveness

impul'sivo *adj* impulsive

im'pulso *nm* impulse; **agire d'**∼ act on impulse

impune'mente *adv* with impunity

impunità *nf* impunity

impu'nito *adj* unpunished

impun'tarsi *vr* fig dig one's heels in

impun'tura *nf* stitching

impuntu'rare *vt* backstitch

impurità *nf inv* impurity

im'puro *adj* impure

impu'tabile *adj* attributable (**a** to); Jur indictable

impu'tare *vt* attribute; Jur charge

impu'tato, -a *nmf* accused

imputazi'one *nf* charge. **imputazione di omicidio** murder charge

imputri'dire *vi* putrefy

imputri'dito *adj* putrefied

in *prep* in; (moto a luogo) to; (su) on; (dentro) within; (mezzo) by; (con materiale) made of; **essere in casa/ufficio** be at home/at the office; **in mano/tasca** in one's hand/ pocket; **in fondo alla strada/borsa** at the bottom of the street/bag; **andare in Francia/campagna** go to France/the country; **salire in treno** get on the train; **versa la birra nel bicchiere** pour the beer into the glass; **in alto** up there; **in giornata** within the day; **nel 1997** in 1997; **una borsa in pelle** a bag made of leather, a leather bag, **alzarsi in piedi** stand up; **in macchina** ⟨*viaggiare, venire*⟩ by car; **in contanti** [in] cash; **in vacanza** on holiday; **di giorno in giorno** from day to day; **se fossi in te** if I were you; **siamo in sette** there are seven of us

inabbor'dabile *adj* unapproachable

i'nabile *adj* incapable; (fisicamente) unfit

inabilità *nf* incapacity

inabi'tabile *adj* uninhabitable

inacces'sibile *adj* inaccessible; ⟨*persona*⟩ unapproachable

inaccet'tabile *adj* unacceptable

inaccettabilità *nf* unacceptability

inacer'barsi *vr* grow bitter

inacer'bire *vt* embitter; exacerbate ⟨*rapporto*⟩

inaci'dire *vt* turn sour

inaci'dirsi *vr* go sour; ⟨*persona*⟩ become embittered

ina'datto *adj* unsuitable

inadegua'tezza *nf* inadequacy

inadegu'ato *adj* inadequate

inadempi'ente *nmf* defaulter

inadempi'enza *nf* nonfulfilment (**a** of). **inadempienza contrattuale** breach of contract

inadempi'mento *nm* nonfulfilment

inaffer'rabile *adj* elusive

inaffi'dabile *adj* untrustworthy

inaffon'dabile *adj* unsinkable

ina'lare *vt* inhale

inala'tore *nm* inhaler

inalazi'one *nf* inhalation

inalbe'rare *vt* hoist

inalbe'rarsi *vr* ⟨*cavallo*⟩ rear [up]; (adirarsi) lose one's temper

inalie'nabile *adj* inalienable

inalte'rabile *adj* unchanging; ⟨*colore*⟩ fast

inalte'rato *adj* unchanged

inami'dare *vt* starch

inami'dato *adj* starched

inammis'sibile *adj* inadmissible

inamovi'bile *adj* ⟨*disco ecc*⟩ non-removable

inanel'lato *adj* bejewelled

inani'mato *adj* inanimate; (senza vita) lifeless

inappa'gabile *adj* unsatisfiable

inappaga'mento *nm* nonfulfilment

inappa'gato *adj* unfulfilled

inappel'labile *adj* final

inappe'tenza *nf* lack of appetite

inappli'cabile *adj* inapplicable

inappropri'ato *adj* inapt

inappun'tabile *adj* faultless

inar'care *vt* arch; raise ⟨*sopracciglia*⟩

inar'carsi *vr* ⟨*legno*⟩ warp; ⟨*ripiano*⟩ sag; ⟨*linea*⟩ curve

inari'dire *vt* parch; empty of feelings ⟨*persona*⟩

inari'dirsi *vr* dry up; ⟨*persona*⟩ become empty of feelings

inarre'stabile *adj* unstoppable

inartico'lato *adj* inarticulate

inascol'tato *adj* unheard

inaspettata'mente *adv* unexpectedly

inaspet'tato *adj* unexpected

inaspri'mento *nm* (di carattere) embitterment; (di conflitto) worsening

ina'sprire *vt* embitter

ina'sprirsi *vr* become embittered

inattac'cabile *adj* unassailable; (irreprensibile) irreproachable

inatten'dibile *adj* unreliable

inat'teso *adj* unexpected

inattività *nf* inactivity

inat'tivo *adj* inactive

inattu'abile *adj* impracticable

inau'dito *adj* unheard of

inaugu'rale *adj* inaugural; **cerimonia inaugurale** official opening; **viaggio inaugurale** maiden voyage

inaugu'rare *vt* inaugurate; open ⟨*mostra*⟩; unveil ⟨*statua*⟩; christen ⟨*lavastoviglie ecc*⟩

inaugurazi'one *nf* inauguration; (di mostra) opening; (di statua) unveiling

Inavve'duto *adj* inadvertent; (sbadato) careless

inavver'tenza *nf* inadvertence

inavvertita'mente *adv* inadvertently

inavvici'nabile *adj* unapproachable

in'breeding *nm inv* inbreeding

'inca *adj & nmf* (pl **inca** *o* **incas**) Inca

incagli'are ① *vi* ground ② *vt* hinder

incagli'arsi *vr* run aground

in'caglio *nm* running aground; fig obstacle

incalco'labile *adj* incalculable

incal'lirsi *vr* grow callous; (abituarsi) become hardened

incal'lito *adj* callous; (abituato) hardened

incal'zante *adj* ⟨*ritmo*⟩ driving; ⟨*richiesta*⟩ urgent; ⟨*crisi*⟩ imminent

incal'zare *vt* pursue; fig press

incame'rare *vt* appropriate

incammi'nare *vt* get going; (fig: guidare) set off

incammi'narsi *vr* set out

incanala'mento *nm* canalization; fig channelling

incana'lare *vt* canalize; fig channel

incana'larsi *vr* converge on

incancel'labile *adj* indelible

incande'scente *adj* incandescent; ⟨*discussione*⟩ burning

incande'scenza *nf* incandescence

incan'tare *vt* enchant

incan'tarsi *vr* stand spellbound; (incepparsi) jam

incanta|'tore, -trice *nmf* enchanter; enchantress. **incantatore di serpenti** snake charmer

incan'tesimo *nm* spell

incan'tevole *adj* enchanting

in'canto *nm* spell; fig delight; (asta) auction; **come per ~** as if by magic

incanu'tire *vt* turn white

incanu'tito *adj* white

inca'pace *adj* incapable; **incapace d'intendere e di volere** Jur unfit to plead

incapacità *nf* incapability

incapo'nirsi *vr* be set

incap'pare *vi* ~ in run into

incappucci'arsi *vr* wrap up

incappretta'mento *nm* method of trussing up a victim by the ankles

incapricci'arsi *vr* ~ di take a fancy to

incapsu'lare *vt* seal; crown ⟨*dente*⟩

incarce'rare *vt* imprison

incarcerazi'one *nf* imprisonment

incari'care *vt* charge

incari'carsi *vr* take upon oneself; **me ne incarico io** I will see to it

incari'cato, -a ① *adj* in charge ② *nmf* representative. **incaricato d'affari** chargé d'affaires

in'carico *nm* charge; **per ~ di** on behalf of

incar'nare *vt* embody

incar'narsi *vr* become incarnate

incarnazi'one *nf* incarnation

incarta'mento *nm* documents *pl*

incartapeco'rito *adj* shrivelled up

incar'tare *vt* wrap [in paper]

incasel'lare *vt* pigeonhole

incasi'nato *adj* fam ⟨*vita*⟩ screwed up; ⟨*stanza*⟩ messed up

incas'sare *vt* pack; Mech embed; (incastonare) set; (riscuotere) cash; take ⟨*colpo*⟩

incas'sato *adj* set; ⟨*fiume*⟩ deeply embanked

in'casso *nm* collection; (introito) takings *pl*

incasto'nare *vt* set

incasto'nato *adj* embedded; ⟨*anello*⟩ inset (di with)

incastona'tura *nf* setting

inca'strare *vt* fit in; (fam: in situazione) corner

inca'strarsi *vr* fit, interlock

in'castro *nm* joint; **a ~** ⟨*pezzi*⟩ interlocking. **incastro a coda di rondine** dovetail joint

incate'nare *vt* chain

incatra'mare *vt* tar

incatti'vire *vt* turn nasty

incauta'mente *adv* imprudently

in'cauto *adj* imprudent

inca'vare *vt* hollow out

inca'vato *adj* hollow

incava'tura *nf* hollow

in'cavo *nm* hollow; (scanalatura) groove

incavo'larsi *vr* fam get shirty

incavo'lato *adj* fam shirty

in'cedere fml ① *vi* advance solemnly
② *nm* solemn gait

incendi'are *vt* set fire to; fig inflame

incendi'ario, -a ① *adj* incendiary; fig
⟨discorso⟩ inflammatory; fig ⟨bellezza⟩
sultry
② *nmf* arsonist

incendi'arsi *vr* catch fire

in'cendio *nm* fire. **incendio doloso**
arson; incendi *pl* dolosi cases of arson

inceneri'mento *nm* incineration;
(cremazione) cremation

incene'rire *vt* burn to ashes; (cremare)
cremate

incene'rirsi *vr* be burnt to ashes

inceneri'tore *nm* incinerator

in'censo *nm* incense

incensu'rabile *adj* irreproachable

incensu'rato *adj* blameless; **essere ~**
Jur have a clean record

incenti'vare *vt* motivate

incen'tivo *nm* incentive. **incentivo
fiscale** tax incentive

incen'trarsi *vr* **~ su** centre on

incep'pare *vt* block; fig hamper

incep'parsi *vr* jam

ince'rata *nf* oilcloth

incerot'tato *adj* with a plaster on

incer'tezza *nf* uncertainty

in'certo ① *adj* uncertain, unsure
② *nm* uncertainty; **sono gli incerti del
mestiere** that's the way it goes in this
business

incespi'care *vi* (inciampare) stumble

inces'sante *adj* unceasing

incessante'mente *adv* incessantly

in'cesto *nm* incest

incestu'oso *adj* incestuous

in'cetta *nf* buying up; **fare ~ di** stockpile

inchi'esta *nf* investigation; **fare un'~**
conduct an inquiry. **inchiesta
giudiziaria** criminal investigation.
inchiesta parlamentare
parliamentary inquiry

inchi'nare *vt* bow

inchi'narsi *vr* bow

in'chino *nm* bow; (di donna) curtsy

inchio'dare *vt* nail; nail down
⟨coperchio⟩; **~ a letto** ⟨malattia⟩ confine to
bed

inchi'ostro *nm* ink. **inchiostro di
china** Indian ink. **inchiostro
simpatico** invisible ink. **inchiostro di
stampa** newsprint

inciam'pare *vi* stumble; **~ in** trip over;
(imbattersi) run into

inci'ampo *nm* hindrance

inciden'tale *adj* incidental

inci'dente *nm* (episodio) incident;
(infortunio) accident. **incidente aereo**
plane crash. **incidente d'auto** car
accident. **incidente sul lavoro**
industrial accident. **incidente stradale**
road accident

inci'denza *nf* incidence

in'cidere ① *vt* cut; (arte) engrave;
(registrare) record
② *vi* **~ su** (gravare) weigh upon

in'cinta *adj* pregnant

incipi'ente *adj* incipient

incipri'are *vt* powder

incipri'arsi *vr* powder one's face

in'circa *adv* **all'~** more or less

incisi'one *nf* incision; (arte) engraving;
(acquaforte) etching; (registrazione) recording

inci'sivo ① *adj* incisive
② *nm* (dente) incisor

in'ciso *nm* **per ~** incidentally

inci'sore *nm* engraver

incita'mento *nm* incitement

inci'tare *vt* incite

inci'vile *adj* uncivilized; (maleducato)
impolite

inciviltà *nf* barbarism; (maleducazione)
rudeness

inclassifi'cabile *adv* unclassifiable

incle'mente *adj* harsh

incle'menza *nf* harshness

incli'nabile *adj* reclining

incli'nare ① *vt* tilt
② *vi* **~ a** be inclined to

incli'narsi *vr* ⟨torre⟩ lean; ⟨aereo⟩ tilt

incli'nato *adj* tilted; ⟨terreno⟩ sloping

inclinazi'one *nf* slope, inclination

in'cline *adj* inclined

in'cludere *vt* include; (allegare) enclose

inclusi'one *nf* inclusion

inclu'sivo *adj* inclusive

in'cluso ① pp di INCLUDERE
② *adj* included; (compreso) inclusive;
(allegato) enclosed

incoe'rente *adj* (contraddittorio)
inconsistent

incoerente'mente *adv* inconsistently

incoe'renza *nf* inconsistency

in'cognita *nf* unknown quantity

in'cognito ① *adj* unknown
② *nm* in **~** incognito

incol'lare *vt* stick; (con colla liquida) glue; Comput paste

incol'larsi *vr* stick to; ~ **a qualcuno** stick close to somebody

incolla'tura *nf* (nell'ippica) neck

incolle'rirsi *vr* lose one's temper

incolle'rito *adj* enraged

incol'mabile *adj* ⟨differenza⟩ unbridgeable; ⟨vuoto⟩ unfillable

incolon'nare *vt* line up

inco'lore *adj* colourless

incol'pare *vt* blame

in'colto *adj* uncultivated; ⟨persona⟩ uneducated

in'colume *adj* unhurt

incom'bente *adj* impending

incom'benza *nf* task

in'combere *vi* ~ **su** hang over; ~ **a** (spettare) be incumbent on

incombu'stibile *adj* noncombustible

incominci'are *vt/i* begin, start

Incommensu'rabile *adj* immeasurable

incomo'dare *vt* inconvenience

incomo'darsi *vr* trouble

in'comodo ① *adj* uncomfortable; (inopportuno) inconvenient
② *nm* inconvenience; **fare il terzo** ~ play gooseberry

incompa'rabile *adj* incomparable

incompa'tibile *adj* incompatible

incompatibilità *nf inv* incompatibility. **incompatibilità di carattere** incompatibility

incompe'tente *adj* incompetent

incompe'tenza *nf* incompetence

incompi'uto *adj* unfinished

incom'pleto *adj* incomplete

incompren'sibile *adj* incomprehensible, unintelligible

incomprensibil'mente *adv* incomprehensibly

incomprensi'one *nf* lack of understanding; (malinteso) misunderstanding

incom'preso *adj* misunderstood

inconce'pibile *adj* inconceivable

inconcili'abile *adj* irreconcilable

inconclu'dente *adj* inconclusive; ⟨persona⟩ ineffectual

incondizionata'mente *adv* unconditionally

incondizio'nato *adj* unconditional

inconfes'sabile *adj* unmentionable

inconfon'dibile *adj* unmistakable

inconfondibil'mente *adv* unmistakably

inconfu'tabile *adj* irrefutable

inconfutabil'mente *adv* irrefutably

incongru'ente *adj* inconsistent

incongru'enza *nf* incongruity

in'congruo *adj* inadequate

inconsa'pevole *adj* unaware; (inconscio) unconscious

inconsapevol'mente *adv* unwittingly

inconscia'mente *adv* unconsciously

in'conscio *adj & nm* Psych unconscious

inconsegu'ente *adj* **essere** ~ be a non sequitur

inconside'rabile *adj* negligible

inconside'rato *adj* inconsiderate

inconsi'stente *adj* insubstantial; ⟨notizia ecc⟩ unfounded

inconsi'stenza *nf* (di ragionamento, prove) flimsiness

inconso'labile *adj* inconsolable

inconsu'eto *adj* unusual

incon'sulto *adj* rash

incontami'nato *adj* uncontaminated

inconte'nibile *adj* irrepressible

inconten'tabile *adj* insatiable; (esigente) hard to please

inconte'stabile *adj* indisputable

inconte'stato *adj* unchallenged

inconti'nente *adj* incontinent

inconti'nenza *nf* incontinence

incon'trare *vt* meet; encounter, meet with ⟨difficoltà⟩

incon'trario: **all'**~ *adv* the other way around; (in modo sbagliato) the wrong way around

incon'trarsi *vr* meet; ~ **con qualcuno** meet somebody

Incontra'stabile *adj* incontrovertible

incontra'stato *adj* undisputed

in'contro ① *nm* meeting; (casuale) encounter; (di calcio, rugby) match; (di tennis) game; (di pugilato) fight. **incontro al vertice** summit meeting
② *prep* ~ **a** towards; **andare** ~ **a qualcuno** go to meet somebody; fig meet somebody half way

incontrol'labile *adj* uncontrollable

incontrollata'mente *adv* uncontrollably

inconveni'ente *nm* drawback

incoraggia'mento *nm* encouragement

incoraggi'ante *adj* encouraging

incoraggi'are *vt* encourage

incor'nare *vt* gore

incornici'are *vt* frame

incornicia'tura *nf* framing

incoro'nare *vt* crown

incoronazi'one *nf* coronation

incorpo'rare *vt* incorporate; (mescolare) blend

incorpo'rarsi vr blend; ⟨territori⟩ merge

incoreg'gibile adj incorrigible

in'correre vt ∼ in incur; ∼ **nel pericolo di ...** run the risk of ...

incorrut'tibile adj incorruptible

incosci'ente ⓵ adj unconscious; (irresponsabile) reckless ⓶ nmf irresponsible person

incosci'enza nf unconsciousness; (irresponsabilità) recklessness

inco'stante adj changeable; ⟨persona⟩ fickle

inco'stanza nf changeableness; (di persona) fickleness

incostituzio'nale adj unconstitutional

incostituzionalità nf unconstitutionality

incre'dibile adj incredible, unbelievable

incredibil'mente adv incredibly, unbelievably

incredulità nf incredulity

in'credulo adj incredulous

incremen'tale adj Comput, Math incremental

incremen'tare vt increase; (intensificare) step up

incre'mento nm increase. **incremento demografico** population growth. **incremento produttivo** increase in production

incresci'oso adj regrettable

incre'spare vt ruffle; wrinkle ⟨tessuto⟩; make frizzy ⟨capelli⟩; ∼ **la fronte** frown

incre'sparsi vr ⟨acqua⟩ ripple; ⟨tessuto⟩ wrinkle; ⟨capelli⟩ go frizzy

incrimi'nabile adj indictable

incrimi'nante adj incriminating

incrimi'nare vt indict; fig incriminate

incriminazi'one nf indictment

incri'nare vt crack; fig affect ⟨amicizia⟩

incri'narsi vr crack; ⟨amicizia⟩ be affected

incrina'tura nf crack

incroci'are ⓵ vt cross ⓶ vi Naut, Aeron cruise

incroci'arsi vr cross; ⟨razze⟩ interbreed

incroci'ato adj crossover

incrocia'tore nm cruiser

in'crocio nm crossing; (di strade) crossroads sg

incrol'labile adj indestructible

incro'stare vt encrust

incrostazi'one nf encrustation

incuba'trice nf incubator

incubazi'one nf incubation

'incubo nm nightmare; **da** ∼ nightmarish

in'cudine nf anvil

incul'care vt inculcate

incune'are vt wedge

incune'arsi vr slot in

incune'ato adj Med impacted

incu'pirsi vr fig darken

incu'rabile adj incurable

incu'rante adj careless

in'curia nf negligence

incurio'sire vt make curious

incurio'sirsi vr become curious

incursi'one nf raid. **incursione aerea** air raid, airstrike

incurva'mento nm bending

incur'vare vt bend

incur'varsi vr bend

incurva'tura nf bending

in'cusso pp di INCUTERE

incusto'dito adj unguarded

in'cutere vt arouse; ∼ **spavento a qualcuno** strike fear into somebody

'indaco nm indigo

indaffa'rato adj busy

inda'gare vt/i investigate

indaga'tore adj ⟨sguardo⟩ enquiring

in'dagine nf research; (giudiziaria) investigation. **indagine demoscopica** public opinion poll. **indagine di mercato** market survey

indebi'tare vt get into debt

indebi'tarsi vr get into debt

in'debito adj undue

indeboli'mento nm weakening

indebo'lire vt weaken

indebo'lirsi vr weaken

inde'cente adj indecent

indecente'mente adv indecently

inde'cenza nf indecency; (vergogna) disgrace

indeci'frabile adj indecipherable

indecisi'one nf indecision

inde'ciso adj undecided

indecli'nabile adj indeclinable

indeco'roso adj indecorous

inde'fesso adj tireless

indefi'nibile adj indefinable

indefi'nito adj indefinite

indefor'mabile adj crushproof

in'degno adj unworthy

inde'lebile adj indelible

indelebil'mente adv indelibly

indelicata'mente adv indiscreetly

indelica'tezza nf indelicacy; (azione) tactless act

indeli'cato adj indiscreet; (grossolano) indelicate

indemagli'abile adj ladderproof

indemoni'ato adj possessed

in'denne *adj* uninjured; (da malattia) unaffected

inden'nità *nf inv* allowance; (per danni) compensation. **indennità di accompagnamento** mobility allowance. **indennità di contingenza** cost-of-living allowance. **indennità di disoccupazione** job seeker's allowance. **indennità di fine rapporto** severance payment. **indennità di malattia** sickpay. **indennità parlamentare** MP's salary. **indennità di trasferimento** relocation allowance. **indennità di trasferta** travel allowance

indenniz'zare *vt* compensate

inden'nizzo *nm* compensation

indero'gabile *adj* binding

indescri'vibile *adj* indescribable

indescrivibil'mente *adv* indescribably

indeside'rabile *adj* undesirable

indeside'rato *adj* ⟨figlio, ospite⟩ unwanted

indetermi'nabile *adj* indeterminable

indetermina'tezza *nf* vagueness

indetermina'tivo *adj* indefinite

indetermi'nato *adj* indeterminate

'India *nf* India

indi'ano, -a *adj & nmf* Indian; **in fila indiana** in single file. **indiano d'America** American Indian

indiavo'lato *adj* possessed; (vivace) wild

indi'care *vt* show, indicate; (col dito) point at; (far notare) point out; (consigliare) advise

indicativa'mente *adv* as an idea; **può dirmi quanto costa** ∼? can you give me an idea of the price?

indica'tivo ① *adj* indicative; ⟨prezzo, cifra⟩ rough
② *nm* Gram indicative

indica'tore *nm* indicator; Techn gauge; (prontuario) directory. **indicatore di direzione** indicator light. **indicatore economico** economic indicator. **indicatore [del livello] dell'olio** oil gauge. **indicatore di velocità** speedometer

indicazi'one *nf* indication; (istruzione) direction. **indicazione stradale** road sign

'indice *nm* (dito) forefinger; (lancetta) pointer; (di libro, statistica) index; (fig: segno) sign. **indice di ascolto** audience rating. **indice azionario** share index. **indice di gradimento** popularity rating. **indice di mortalità** death rate. **indice di natalità** birth rate

indi'cibile *adj* inexpressible

indiciz'zare *vt* index-link

indiciz'zato *adj* index-linked

indicizzazi'one *nf* indexing

indietreggi'are *vi* draw back; Mil withdraw

indi'etro *adv* back, behind; **all'** ∼ backwards; **essere** ∼ be behind; (mentalmente) be backward; (con pagamenti) be in arrears; (di orologio) be slow; **fare marcia** ∼ reverse; **rimandare** ∼ send back; **rimanere** ∼ be left behind; **torna** ∼! come back!

indifen'dibile *adj* indefensible

indi'feso *adj* undefended; (inerme) helpless

indiffe'rente *adj* indifferent; **mi è** ∼ it's all the same to me

indifferente'mente *adv* (senza fare distinzioni) without distinction; (con indifferenza) indifferently; **funziona** ∼ **con i due programmi** it works equally well with either program

indiffe'renza *nf* indifference

in'digeno, -a ① *adj* indigenous
② *nmf* native

indi'gente *adj* needy, poverty-stricken

indi'genza *nf* poverty

indigesti'one *nf* indigestion

indi'gesto *adj* indigestible

indi'gnare *vt* make indignant

indi'gnarsi *vr* be indignant

indi'gnato *adj* indignant

indignazi'one *nf* indignation

indimenti'cabile *adj* unforgettable

'indio, -a ① *adj* Indian
② *nmf* (mpl **indii** o **indios**) Indian

indipen'dente *adj* independent; ⟨economicamente⟩ self-supporting

indipendente'mente *adv* independently; ∼ **da** regardless of

indipen'denza *nf* independence

in'dire *vt* announce

indiretta'mente *adv* indirectly

indi'retto *adj* indirect

indiriz'zare *vt* address; (mandare) send; (dirigere) direct

indiriz'zario *nm* mailing list

indiriz'zarsi *vr* direct one's steps

indi'rizzo *nm* address; (direzione) direction. **indirizzo di consegna** delivery address. **'indirizzo del destinatario'** 'addressee'. **indirizzo di memoria** Comput memory address. **'indirizzo del mittente'** 'sender's address'. **indirizzo di posta elettronica** e-mail address

indisci'plina *nf* lack of discipline

indiscipli'nato *adj* undisciplined

indi'screto *adj* indiscreet; **in modo** ∼ indiscreetly

indiscrezi'one *nf* indiscretion

indiscriminata'mente *adv* indiscriminately

indiscrimi'nato *adj* indiscriminate

indi'scusso *adj* unquestioned

indiscu'tibile *adj* unquestionable

indiscutibil'mente *adv* unquestionably

indispen'sabile *adj* essential; ⟨*persona*⟩ indispensable

indispet'tire *vt* irritate

indispet'tirsi *vr* get irritated

indi'sporre *vt* anger

indisposizi'one *nf* indisposition

indi'sposto ① *pp di* INDISPORRE ② *adj* indisposed

indisso'lubile *adj* indissoluble

indissolubil'mente *adv* indissolubly

indistin'guibile *adj* indiscernible

indistinta'mente *adv* without exception

indi'stinto *adj* indistinct

indistrut'tibile *adj* indestructible

indistur'bato *adj* undisturbed

in'divia *nf* endive

individu'abile *adj* detectable

individu'ale *adj* individual

individua'lista *nmf* individualist

individua'listico *adj* individualistic

individualità *nf* individuality

individu'are *vt* individualize; (localizzare) locate; (riconoscere) single out

indi'viduo *nm* individual

indivi'sibile *adj* indivisible

indivisibilità *nf* indivisibility

indi'viso *adj* undivided

indizi'are *vt* throw suspicion on

indizi'ario *adj* circumstantial

indizi'ato, -a ① *adj* suspected ② *nmf* suspect

in'dizio *nm* sign; Jur circumstantial evidence

Indo'cina *nf* Indochina

indoeuro'peo *adj* Indo-European

'indole *nf* nature

indo'lente *adj* indolent

indo'lenza *nf* indolence

indolenzi'mento *nm* stiffness, ache

indolen'zire *vt* stiffen up

indolen'zirsi *vr* stiffen up, go stiff

indolen'zito *adj* stiff

indo'lore *adj* painless

indo'mabile *adj* untameable

indo'mani *nm* l'~ the following day

in'domito *adj* untamed

Indo'nesia *nf* Indonesia

indonesi'ano, -a *adj & nmf* Indonesian

indo'rare *vt* gild; ~ la pillola sugar the pill

indos'sare *vt* wear; (mettere addosso) put on

indossa|'tore, -trice ① *nm* [male] model ② *nf* model

in'dotto *pp di* INDURRE

indottri'nare *vt* indoctrinate

indovi'nare *vt* guess; (predire) foretell

indovi'nato *adj* successful; (scelta) well-chosen

indovi'nello *nm* riddle

indo'vino, -a *nmf* fortune-teller

indù *adj inv & nmf inv* Hindu

indubbia'mente *adv* undoubtedly

in'dubbio *adj* undoubted

indubi'tabile *adj* indubitable

indubitabil'mente *adv* indubitably

indugi'are *vi* linger

indugi'arsi *vr* linger

in'dugio *nm* delay

indu'ismo *nm* Hinduism

indul'gente *adj* indulgent

indul'genza *nf* indulgence

in'dulgere *vi* ~ a indulge in

in'dulto ① *pp di* INDULGERE ② *nm* Jur pardon

indu'mento *nm* garment; indumenti *pl* clothes. indumenti intimi *pl* underwear

induri'mento *nm* hardening

indu'rire *vt* harden

indu'rirsi *vr* harden

in'durre *vt* induce; ~ qualcuno a fare induce somebody to do; ~ in tentazione lead into temptation

in'dustria *nf* industry. industria dell'abbigliamento clothing industry, fam rag trade. industria leggera light industry. industria pesante heavy industry. industria dello spettacolo show business, entertainment industry, fam showbiz. industria terziaria service industry. industria tessile textile industry, textiles

industri'ale ① *adj* industrial; zona industriale industrial estate ② *nmf* industrialist

industrializ'zare *vt* industrialize

industrializ'zato *adj* industrialized

industrializzazi'one *nf* industrialization

industrial'mente *adv* industrially

industri'arsi *vr* ~ per guadagnare qualcosa set to and earn some money

industriosa'mente *adv* industriously

industri'oso *adj* industrious

indut'tivo *adj* inductive

indut'tore *nm* inductor

induzi'one *nf* induction

inebe'tire *vt* daze

inebe'tito *adj* stunned

inebri'ante *adj* intoxicating, exciting

inebri'are *vt* intoxicate

inebri'arsi *vr* become inebriated

inecce'pibile *adj* unexceptionable

i'nedia *nf* starvation

i'nedito *adj* unpublished

inedu'cato *adj* impolite

inef'fabile *adj* inexpressible

ineffi'cace *adj* ineffective

ineffici'ente *adj* inefficient

ineffici'enza *nf* inefficiency

ineguagli'abile *adj* incomparable

ineguaglianza *nf* inequality

ineguagli'ato *adj* unequalled

inegu'ale *adj* unequal; ⟨*superficie*⟩ uneven

inelut'tabile *adj* inescapable

inenar'rabile *adj* indescribable

inequivo'cabile *adj* unequivocal

inequivocabil'mente *adv* unequivocally

ine'rente *adj* ∼ **a** inherent in

inerente'mente *adv* ∼ **a** concerning

i'nerme *adj* defenceless

inerpi'carsi *vr* ∼ **su** clamber up

i'nerte *adj* inactive; Phys inert

i'nerzia *nf* inactivity; Phys inertia

inesat'tezza *nf* inaccuracy

ine'satto *adj* inaccurate; (erroneo) incorrect; (non riscosso) uncollected

inesau'ribile *adj* inexhaustible

inesi'stente *adj* non-existent

inesi'stenza *nf* non-existence

ineso'rabile *adj* inexorable

inesorabil'mente *adv* inexorably

inesperi'enza *nf* inexperience

ine'sperto *adj* inexperienced

inespli'cabile *adj* inexplicable

inesplicabil'mente *adv* inexplicably

inesplo'rato *adj* undiscovered

ine'sploso *adj* unexploded

inespres'sivo *adj* expressionless

inespri'mibile *adj* inexpressible

inespu'gnabile *adj* impregnable

ineste'tismo *nm* blemish

inesti'mabile *adj* inestimable

inestin'guibile *adj* ⟨*sete*⟩ insatiable; ⟨*odio*⟩ undying

inestir'pabile *adj* impossible to eradicate

inestri'cabile *adj* inextricable

inestricabil'mente *adv* inextricably

inetti'tudine *nf* ineptitude

i'netto *adj* inept; ∼ **a** unsuited to

ine'vaso *adj* ⟨*pratiche, corrispondenza*⟩ pending

inevi'tabile *adj* inevitable

inevitabil'mente *adv* inevitably

in ex'tremis *adv* ⟨*segnare un gol*⟩ in the nick of time; (prima di morire) in extremis

i'nezia *nf* trifle

infagot'tare *vt* wrap up

infagot'tarsi *vr* wrap [oneself] up

infal'libile *adj* infallible

infa'mante *adj* defamatory

infa'mare *vt* defame

infama'torio *adj* defamatory

in'fame *adj* infamous; (fam: orrendo) awful, shocking

in'famia *nf* infamy

infan'gare *vt* cover with mud; fig sully

infan'garsi *vr* get muddy

infanti'cida *nmf* infanticide

infanti'cidio *nm* infanticide

infan'tile *adj* ⟨*letteratura, abbigliamento*⟩ children's *attrib*; ⟨*ingenuità*⟩ childlike; pej childish

in'fanzia *nf* childhood; (bambini) children *pl*; prima infanzia infancy

infar'cire *vt* stuff (di with)

infari'nare *vt* flour; ∼ **di** sprinkle with

infarina'tura *nf* fig smattering

in'farto *nm* heart attack

infasti'dire *vt* irritate

infasti'dirsi *vr* get irritated

infati'cabile *adj* untiring

infaticabil'mente *adv* tirelessly

in'fatti *conj* as a matter of fact; (veramente) indeed

infatu'arsi *vr* ∼ **di** become infatuated with

infatu'ato *adj* infatuated

infatuazi'one *nf* infatuation

in'fausto *adj* ill-omened

infecondità *nf* infertility

infe'condo *adj* infertile

infe'dele *adj* unfaithful

infedeltà *nf* unfaithfulness

infe'lice *adj* unhappy; (inappropriato) unfortunate; (cattivo) bad

infelicità *nf* unhappiness

infel'trire *vi* matt

infel'trirsi *vr* matt

infel'trito *adj* matted

inferi'ore ① *adj* (più basso) lower; ⟨*qualità*⟩ inferior ② *nmf* inferior

inferiorità *nf* inferiority

infe'rire *vt* infer; strike ⟨*colpo*⟩

inferme'ria *nf* infirmary; (di nave, scuola) sickbay

infermi'ere, -a [1] *nm* [male] nurse [2] *nf* nurse

infermità *nf* sickness. **infermità mentale** mental illness

in'fermo, -a [1] *adj* sick [2] *nmf* invalid

infer'nale *adj* infernal; (spaventoso) hellish

in'ferno *nm* hell; **va' all'∼!** go to hell!

infero'cirsi *vr* become fierce

inferri'ata *nf* grating

infervo'rare *vt* arouse enthusiasm in

infervo'rarsi *vr* get excited

infe'stare *vt* infest

infestato *adj* infested; **∼ dai fantasmi** haunted

infestazi'one *nf* infestation

infet'tare *vt* infect

infet'tarsi *vr* become infected

infet'tivo *adj* infectious

in'fetto *adj* infected

infezi'one *nf* infection

infiac'chire *vt/i* weaken

infiac'chirsi *vr* weaken

infiam'mabile *adj* [in]flammable

infiam'mare *vt* set on fire; Med, fig inflame

infiam'marsi *vr* catch fire; Med become inflamed

infiammazi'one *nf* Med inflammation

infia'scare *vt* bottle

infici'are *vt* Jur invalidate

in'fido *adj* treacherous

infie'rire *vi* (imperversare) rage; **∼ su** attack furiously

in'figgere *vt* drive

in'figgersi *vr* **∼ in** penetrate

infi'lare *vt* thread; (mettere) insert; (indossare) put on

infi'larsi *vr* slip on ⟨*vestito*⟩ **∼ in** (introdursi) slip into

infil'trarsi *vr* infiltrate

infil'trato, -a *nmf* infiltrator

infiltrazi'one *nf* infiltration; (d'acqua) seepage; (Med: iniezione) injection

infil'zare *vt* pierce; (infilare) string; (conficcare) stick

'infimo *adj* lowest

in'fine *adv* finally; (insomma) in short

infin'gardo *adj* slothful

infinità *nf* infinity; **un'∼ di** masses of

infinita'mente *adv* infinitely

infinitesi'male *adj* infinitesimal

infi'nito [1] *adj* infinite; Gram infinitive [2] *nm* infinite; Gram infinitive; Math infinity; **all'∼** endlessly

infinocchi'are *vt* fam hoodwink

infiocchet'tare *vt* tie up with ribbons

infiore'scenza *nf* inflorescence

infischi'arsi *vr* **∼ di** not care about; **me ne infischio** fam I couldn't care less

in'fisso [1] pp di INFIGGERE [2] *nm* fixture; (di porta, finestra) frame

infit'tire *vt/i* thicken

infit'tirsi *vr* thicken

inflazi'one *nf* inflation. **inflazione galoppante** galloping inflation. **inflazione strisciante** creeping inflation

inflazio'nistico *adj* inflationary

infles'sibile *adj* inflexible

inflessibilità *nf* inflexibility

inflessi'one *nf* inflection, inflexion

in'fliggere *vt* inflict

in'flitto pp di INFLIGGERE

influ'ente *adj* influential

influ'enza *nf* influence; Med influenza; **prendere l'∼** catch the flu. **influenza gastrointestinale** gastric flu

influen'zabile *adj* ⟨*mente, opinione*⟩ impressionable

influen'zare *vt* influence

influen'zato *adj* **essere ∼** (con febbre) have the flu

influ'ire *vi* **∼ su** influence

in'flusso *nm* influence

info'carsi *vr* catch fire; ⟨*viso*⟩ go red; ⟨*discussione*⟩ become heated

info'gnarsi *vr* fam get into a mess

infol'tire *vt/i* thicken

infon'dato *adj* unfounded

in'fondere *vt* instil

infor'care *vt* fork ⟨*fieno*⟩; get on ⟨*bici*⟩; put on ⟨*occhiali*⟩

inforca'tura *nf* crotch

infor'male *adj* informal

infor'mare *vt* inform

infor'marsi *vr* inquire (di about)

infor'matica *nf* information technology, IT, computer science

infor'matico *adj* computer *attrib*

informa'tivo *adj* informative

infor'mato *adj* informed; **male ∼** ill-informed

inform|'tore, -trice *nmf* (di polizia) informer. **informatore medico scientifico** representative of a pharmaceutical company

informazi'one *nf* information; **un'∼** a piece of information; **informazioni** *pl* information; **servizio informazioni** enquiries. **informazione genetica** genetic code. **informazione riservata** confidential information; **informazioni** *pl*

sbagliate misinformation; **informazioni** *pl* **sulla viabilità** travel news

in'forme *adj* shapeless

infor'nare *vt* put into the oven

infortu'narsi *vr* have an accident

infortu'nato, -a ① *adj* injured ② *nmf* injured person; **gli infortunati** the injured

infor'tunio *nm* accident. **infortunio sul lavoro** industrial accident

infortu'nistica *nf* study of industrial accidents

infos'sarsi *vr* sink; ⟨guance, occhi⟩ become hollow

infos'sato *adj* sunken, hollow

infradici'are *vt* drench

infradici'arsi *vr* get drenched; (diventare marcio) rot

infra'dito *nmpl* (scarpe) flip-flops

in'frangere *vt* break; (in mille pezzi) shatter

in'frangersi *vr* break; (in mille pezzi) shatter

infran'gibile *adj* unbreakable

in'franto ① *pp di* INFRANGERE ② *adj* shattered; fig ⟨cuore⟩ broken

infra'rosso *adj* infra-red

infrasettima'nale *adj* midweek

infrastrut'tura *nf* infrastructure

infrazi'one *nf* offence. **infrazione al codice della strada** traffic offence

infredda'tura *nf* cold

infreddo'lirsi *vr* feel cold

infreddo'lito *adj* cold

infre'quente *adj* infrequent

infruttu'oso *adj* fruitless

infuo'care *vt* make red-hot

infuo'cato *adj* burning

infu'ori *adv* all'~ outwards; all'~ **di** except; **denti** ~ buck teeth

infuri'are *vi* rage

infuri'arsi *vr* fly into a rage

infuri'ato *adj* blustering

infusi'one *nf* infusion

in'fuso ① *pp di* INFONDERE ② *nm* infusion

Ing. *abbr* **ingegnere**

ingabbi'are *vt* cage; (fig: mettere in prigione) jail

ingaggi'are *vt* engage; sign up ⟨calciatori ecc⟩; begin ⟨lotta, battaglia⟩

in'gaggio *nm* engagement; (di calciatore) signing [up]

ingan'nare *vt* deceive; (essere infedele a) be unfaithful to; ~ **l'attesa** kill time

ingan'narsi *vr* deceive oneself; **se non m'inganno** if I am not mistaken

ingan'nevole *adj* deceptive

in'ganno *nm* deceit; (frode) fraud; **trarre in** ~ deceive

ingarbugli'are *vt* entangle; (confondere) confuse

ingarbugli'arsi *vr* get entangled; (confondersi) become confused

ingarbu'gliato *adj* confused

inge'gnarsi *vr* do one's best; ~ **per vivere** try to scrape a living

inge'gnere *nm* engineer. **ingegnere aeronautico** aeronautical engineer. **ingegnere civile** civil engineer. **ingegnere edile** structural engineer. **ingegnere meccanico** mechanical engineer. **ingegnere minerario** mining engineer. **ingegnere navale** marine engineer

ingegne'ria *nf* engineering. **ingegneria aeronautica** aeronautical engineering. **ingegneria civile** civil engineering. **ingegneria edile** structural engineering. **ingegneria genetica** genetic engineering. **ingegneria meccanica** mechanical engineering

in'gegno *nm* brains *pl*; (genio) genius; (abilità) ingenuity

ingegnosa'mente *adv* ingeniously

ingegnosità *nf* ingenuity

inge'gnoso *adj* ingenious

ingelo'sire *vt* make jealous

ingelo'sirsi *vr* become jealous

in'gente *adj* huge

ingenua'mente *adv* artlessly

ingenuità *nf* ingenuousness

in'genuo *adj* ingenuous; (credulone) naïve

inge'renza *nf* interference

inge'rire *vt* swallow

inges'sare *vt* put in plaster

ingessa'tura *nf* plaster, plaster cast

Inghil'terra *nf* England

inghiot'tire *vt* swallow

in'ghippo *nm* trick

ingial'lire *vt* turn yellow

ingial'lirsi *vr* turn yellow

ingial'lito *adj* yellowed

ingigan'tire ① *vt* magnify; blow up out of proportion ⟨problema⟩ ② *vi* take on gigantic proportions

ingigan'tirsi *vr* take on gigantic proportions

inginocchi'arsi *vr* kneel [down]

inginocchi'ato *adj* kneeling

inginocchia'toio *nm* prie-dieu

ingioiel'larsi *vr* put on one's jewels

ingioiel'lato *adj* bejewelled

ingiù *adv* down; all'~ downwards; **a testa** ~ head downwards

ingi'ungere *vt* order

ingiunzi'one nf injunction, court order. ∼ **di pagamento** final demand

ingi'uria nf insult; (torto) wrong; (danno) damage

ingiuri'are vt insult; (fare un torto a) wrong

ingiuri'oso adj insulting

ingiusta'mente adv unjustly

ingiustifi'cabile adj unjustifiable; ⟨comportamento⟩ indefensible

ingiustifi'cato adj unjustified

ingiu'stizia nf injustice

ingi'usto adj unjust

in'glese ① adj English
② nm Englishman; (lingua) English; **gli inglesi** the English
③ nf Englishwoman

inglori'oso adj inglorious

ingob'bire vi become stooped

ingoi'are vt swallow

ingol'fare vt flood ⟨motore⟩

ingol'farsi vr fig get involved; ⟨motore⟩ flood

ingol'lare vt gulp down

ingom'brante adj cumbersome

ingom'brare vt clutter up; fig cram ⟨mente⟩

in'gombro nm encumbrance; **essere d'**∼ be in the way

ingor'digia nf greed

in'gordo adj greedy

ingor'gare vt block

ingor'garsi vr be blocked [up]

in'gorgo nm blockage; (del traffico) jam

ingoz'zare vt gobble up; (nutrire eccessivamente) stuff; fatten ⟨animali⟩

ingoz'zarsi vr stuff oneself (**di** with)

ingra'naggio nm gear; fig mechanism

ingra'nare ① vt engage
② vi be in gear

ingrandi'mento nm enlargement

ingran'dire vt enlarge; (esagerare) magnify

ingran'dirsi vr become larger; (aumentare) increase

ingrandi'tore nm Phot enlarger

ingras'saggio nm greasing, lubrication

ingras'sare ① vt fatten [up]; Mech lubricate, grease
② vi put on weight

ingras'sarsi vr put on weight

in'grasso nm **mettere all'**∼ force-feed

ingrati'tudine nf ingratitude

in'grato adj ungrateful; (sgradevole) thankless

ingrazi'arsi vr ingratiate oneself with

ingredi'ente nm ingredient

in'gresso nm entrance; (accesso) admittance; (sala) hall; Comput input **ingresso gratuito** o **libero** admission free; '**vietato l'**∼' 'no entry'; 'no admittance'. **ingresso degli artisti** stage door. **ingresso principale** main entrance. **ingresso di servizio** tradesmen's entrance. **ingresso/uscita** Comput input/output. **ingresso video** Techn video input

ingros'sare ① vt make big; (gonfiare) swell
② vi grow big; (gonfiare) swell

ingros'sarsi vr grow big; (gonfiare) swell

in'grosso: **all'**∼ adv wholesale

inguai'arsi vr get into trouble

inguai'nare vt sheathe

ingual'cibile adj crease-resistant

ingua'ribile adj incurable

inguaribil'mente adv incurably

'inguine nm groin

ingurgi'tare vt gulp down

ini'bire vt inhibit; (vietare) forbid

ini'bito adj inhibited

inibi'tore nm suppressant

inibizi'one nf inhibition; (divieto) prohibition

iniet'tare vt inject

iniet'tarsi vr ∼ **di sangue** ⟨occhi⟩ become bloodshot

iniezi'one nf injection. **iniezione endovenosa** intravenous injection. **iniezione intramuscolare** intramuscular injection

inimic'arsi vr ∼ **qualcuno** make an enemy of somebody

inimi'cizia nf enmity

inimi'tabile adj inimitable

inimmagi'nabile adj unimaginable

ininfiam'mabile adj nonflammable

inintelli'gibile adj unintelligible

ininterrotta'mente adv continuously

ininter'rotto adj continuous

iniquità nf inv iniquity

i'niquo adj iniquitous

inizi'ale adj & nf initial

inizial'mente adv initially

inizi'are ① vt begin; (avviare) open; ∼ **a fare qualcosa** begin doing something; ∼ **qualcuno a qualcosa** initiate somebody in something
② vi begin

inizia'tiva nf initiative; **prendere l'**∼ take the initiative. **iniziativa privata** private enterprise

inizi'ato, -a nmf initiated

inizia'|tore, -trice nmf initiator

iniziazi'one nf initiation

i'nizio *nm* beginning, start; **dare ~ a** start; **avere ~** get under way

innaffi'are *vt* water

innaffia'toio *nm* watering-can

innal'zare *vt* raise; (erigere) erect

innal'zarsi *vr* rise

innamo'rarsi *vr* fall in love (**di** with)

innamo'rato, -a ① *adj* in love ② *nm* boyfriend ③ *nf* girlfriend

in'nanzi ① *adv* (stato in luogo) in front; (di tempo) ahead; (avanti) forward; (prima) before; **d'ora ~** from now on ② *prep* (prima) before; **~ a** in front of; **~ tutto = innanzitutto**

innanzi'tutto *adv* (soprattutto) above all; (per prima cosa) first of all

in'nato *adj* innate

innatu'rale *adj* unnatural

inne'gabile *adj* undeniable

innegabil'mente *adv* undeniably

inneggi'are *vi* praise

innervo'sire *vt* make nervous

innervo'sirsi *vr* get irritated

inne'scare *vt* prime

in'nesco *nm* primer

inne'stare *vt* graft; Mech engage; (inserire) insert

in'nesto *nm* graft; Mech clutch; Electr connection

inneva'mento *nm* snowfall. **innevamento artificiale** snow-making

inne'vato *adj* covered in snow

'inno *nm* hymn. **inno nazionale** national anthem

inno'cente *adj* innocent; Jur not guilty

innocente'mente *adv* innocently

inno'cenza *nf* innocence

in'nocuo *adj* innocuous

inno'vare *vt* update

innova'tivo *adj* innovative

innova'tore *adj* trail-blazing

innovazi'one *nf* innovation

innume'revole *adj* innumerable

+ino *suff* fratellino *nm* little brother; sorellina *nf* little sister; freddino *adj* (piuttosto freddo) chilly; bellino *adj* (abbastanza bello) pretty; benino *adv* (così così) not bad; pochino *adv* (troppo poco) not enough; un pochino a little bit

inocu'lare *vt* inoculate

ino'doro *adj* odourless

inoffen'sivo *adj* inoffensive, harmless; ⟨animale⟩ harmless

inol'trare *vt* forward

inol'trarsi *vr* advance

inol'trato *adj* late

i'noltre *adv* besides

i'noltro *nm* forwarding

inon'dare *vt* flood

inondazi'one *nf* flood

inope'roso *adj* idle

inopi'nabile *adj* unimaginable

inoppor'tuno *adj* untimely

inor'ganico *adj* inorganic

inorgo'glire *vt* make proud

inorgo'glirsi *vr* become proud

inorri'dire ① *vt* horrify ② *vi* be horrified

inospi'tale *adj* inhospitable

inosser'vato *adj* unobserved; (non rispettato) disregarded; **passare ~** go unnoticed

inossi'dabile *adj* stainless

'inox *adj inv* ⟨acciaio⟩ stainless; ⟨pentole⟩ stainless steel

'input *nm inv* **input dati** data input

inqua'drare *vt* frame; fig set

inqua'drarsi *vr* **~ in** fit into

inquadra'tura *nf* framing

inqualifi'cabile *adj* unspeakable

inquie'tante *adj* unnerving

inquie'tare *vt* worry

inquie'tarsi *vr* get worried; (impazientirsi) get cross

inqui'eto *adj* restless; (preoccupato) worried

inquie'tudine *nf* anxiety

inqui'lino, -a *nmf* tenant

inquina'mento *nm* pollution. **inquinamento acustico** noise pollution. **inquinamento atmosferico** air pollution. **inquinamento delle prove** Jur tampering with the evidence

inqui'nare *vt* pollute

inqui'nato *adj* polluted

inqui'rente *adj* Jur ⟨magistrato⟩ examining; ⟨commissione⟩ of investigation

inqui'sire *vt/i* investigate

inqui'sito ① *adj* under investigation ② *nm* person under investigation

inquisi'tore, -trice ① *adj* inquiring ② *nmf* inquisitor

inquisi'torio *adj* questioning

inquisizi'one *nf* inquisition

insabbi'are *vt* bury

insabbi'arsi *vr* run aground

insa'lata *nf* salad. **insalata belga** Belgian endive. **insalata di mare** seafood salad. **insalata mista** mixed salad. **insalata di riso** rice salad. **insalata russa** Russian salad

insalati'era *nf* salad bowl

insa'lubre *adj* unhealthy

insa'nabile *adj* incurable

insangui'nare *vt* stain with blood

insangui'nato *adj* blood-stained

insapo'nare *vt* soap

insapo'narsi *vr* soap oneself

insapo'nata *nf* soaping

insa'pore *adj* tasteless

insapo'rire *vt* flavour

insa'puta *nf* all'~ di unknown to

in'saturo *adj* unsaturated

insazi'abile *adj* insatiable

inscato'lare *vt* can

inscatola'trice *nf* canning machine

insce'nare *vt* stage

inscin'dibile *adj* inseparable

in'scrivere *vt* Math inscribe

insec'chire *vt/i* wither

insedia'mento *nm* installation

insedi'are *vt* install

insedi'arsi *vr* install oneself

in'segna *nf* sign; (bandiera) flag; (decorazione) decoration; (emblema) insignia *pl*; (stemma) symbol. **insegna luminosa** neon sign

insegna'mento *nm* teaching

inse'gnante ① *adj* teaching ② *nmf* teacher. **insegnante di matematica** maths teacher. **insegnante di sostegno** tutor. **insegnante tirocinante** student teacher

inse'gnare *vt/i* teach; ~ qualcosa a qualcuno teach somebody something

insegui'mento *nm* pursuit

insegu'ire *vt* pursue

insegui|'tore, -trice *nmf* pursuer

inselvati'chire ① *vt* make wild ② *vi* grow wild

inselvati'chirsi *vr* grow wild

insemi'nare *vt* inseminate

inseminazi'one *nf* insemination. **inseminazione artificiale** artificial insemination

insena'tura *nf* inlet

insensata'mente *adv* senselessly

insen'sato *adj* senseless; (folle) crazy

insen'sibile *adj* fig insensitive; **avere le gambe insensibili** have no feeling in one's legs

insensibilità *nf* lack of feeling; fig insensitivity

insepa'rabile *adj* inseparable

inseri'mento *nm* insertion

inse'rire *vt* insert, place ‹annuncio›; Electr connect

inse'rirsi *vr* ~ in get into

inseri'tore *nm* **inseritore fogli (singoli)** (single) sheetfeed

in'serto *nm* file; (in un giornale) supplement; (in un film ecc) insert

inservi'ente *nmf* attendant

inserzi'one *nf* insertion; (avviso) advertisement; **inserzioni** *pl* classified ads

inserzio'nista *nmf* advertiser

insetti'cida *nm* insecticide

insetti'fugo *nm* insect repellent

in'setto *nm* insect

insicu'rezza *nf* insecurity

insi'curo *adj* insecure

in'sidia *nf* trick; (tranello) snare

insidi'are *vt/i* lay a trap for

insidi'oso *adj* insidious

insi'eme ① *adv* together; (contemporaneamente) at the same time ② *prep* ~ a [together] with ③ *nm* whole; (completo) outfit; Theat ensemble; Math set; **nell'**~ as a whole; **tutto** ~ (in una volta) at one go

insie'mistica *nf* set theory

in'signe *adj* renowned

insignifi'cante *adj* insignificant

insi'gnire *vt* decorate

insin'cero *adj* insincere

insinda'cabile *adj* final

insinu'ante *adj* insinuating

insinu'are *vt* insinuate

insinu'arsi *vr* penetrate; ~ **in** fig creep into

insinuazi'one *nf* insinuation

in'sipido *adj* insipid

insi'stente *adj* insistent

insistente'mente *adv* repeatedly

insi'stenza *nf* insistence

in'sistere *vi* insist; (perseverare) persevere

'insito *adj* inherent

insoddisfa'cente *adj* unsatisfactory

insoddi'sfatto *adj* unsatisfied; (scontento) dissatisfied

insoddisfazi'one *nf* dissatisfaction

insoffe'rente *adj* intolerant

insoffe'renza *nf* intolerance

insolazi'one *nf* sunstroke

inso'lente *adj* rude, insolent

insolente'mente *adv* insolently

inso'lenza *nf* rudeness, insolence; (commento) insolent remark

insolita'mente *adv* unusually

in'solito *adj* unusual

inso'lubile *adj* insoluble

inso'luto *adj* unsolved; (non pagato) unpaid

insol'vente *adj* Jur insolvent

insol'venza *nf* insolvency

insol'vibile *adj* insolvent

in'somma *adv* in short; ~! well!

inson'dabile *adj* unfathomable

in'sonne *adj* sleepless

in'sonnia *nf* insomnia

insonno'lito *adj* sleepy

insonoriz'zare *vt* soundproof

insonoriz'zato *adj* soundproofed

insoppor'tabile *adj* unbearable

insoppri'mibile *adj* unsuppressible

insor'genza *nf* onset

in'sorgere *vi* revolt, rise up; ⟨*problema*⟩ arise

insormon'tabile *adj* ⟨*ostacolo, difficoltà*⟩ insurmountable

in'sorto ① pp di INSORGERE ② *adj* rebellious ③ *nm* rebel

insospet'tabile *adj* unsuspected

insospet'tire ① *vt* make suspicious ② *vi* become suspicious

insospet'tirsi *vr* becomes suspicious

insoste'nibile *adj* untenable; (insopportabile) unbearable

insostitu'ibile *adj* irreplaceable

insoz'zare *vt* dirty

inspe'rabile *adj* hopeless; (insperato) unhoped-for

inspe'rato *adj* unhoped-for

inspie'gabile *adj* inexplicable

inspiegabil'mente *adv* inexplicably

inspi'rare *vt* breathe in

in'stabile *adj* unstable; (variabile) unsettled

instabilità *nf* instability; (di tempo) changeability

instal'lare *vt* install

instal'larsi *vr* (in casa, lavoro) settle in

installa|'tore, -trice *nmf* fitter

installazi'one *nf* installation; **installazioni** *pl* **di bordo** on-board equipment

instan'cabile *adj* untiring

instancabil'mente *adv* tirelessly

instau'rare *vt* found

instau'rarsi *vr* become established

instaurazi'one *nf* foundation

instra'dare *vt* direct

in'sù: all'∼ *adv* upwards; **naso all'**∼ turned-up nose

insubordi'nato *adj* insubordinate

insubordinazi'one *nf* insubordination

insuc'cesso *nm* failure

insudici'are *vt* dirty

insudici'arsi *vr* get dirty

insuffici'ente ① *adj* insufficient; (inadeguato) inadequate ② *nf* Sch fail

insufficiente'mente *adv* insufficiently

insuffici'enza *nf* insufficiency; (inadeguatezza) inadequacy; Sch fail.

insufficienza cardiaca cardiac insufficiency. **insufficienza di prove** lack of evidence

insu'lare *adj* insular

insu'lina *nf* insulin

in'sulso *adj* insipid; (sciocco) silly

insul'tare *vt* insult

in'sulto *nm* insult; **coprire qualcuno di insulti** heap abuse on somebody

insupe'rabile *adj* insuperable; (eccezionale) incomparable

insurrezi'one *nf* insurrection

insussi'stente *adj* groundless

intac'cabile *adj* subject to corrosion; fig open to criticism

intac'care *vt* nick; (corrodere) corrode; draw on ⟨*capitale*⟩; (danneggiare) damage

intagli'are *vt* carve

in'taglio *nm* carving

intan'gibile *adj* untouchable

in'tanto *adv* meanwhile; (per ora) for the moment; (avversativo) but; ∼ **che** while

intarsi'are *vt* inlay

intarsi'ato *adj* ∼ **di** inset with

in'tarsio *nm* inlay

intasa'mento *nm* (ostruzione) blockage; (ingorgo) traffic jam

inta'sare *vt* block, clog

inta'sarsi *vr* become blocked

inta'sato *adj* blocked

inta'scare *vt* pocket

in'tatto *adj* intact

intavo'lare *vt* start

inte'gerrimo *adj* of integrity

inte'grale *adj* whole; **edizione integrale** unabridged edition; **pane integrale** wholemeal bread; **versione integrale** (di film) uncut version; (di romanzo) unabridged version

integra'lista *nmf* fundamentalist

integral'mente *adv* fully

inte'grante *adj* integral

inte'grare *vt* integrate; (aggiungere) supplement

inte'grarsi *vr* integrate

integra'tivo *adj* supplementary, additional; **esame integrativo** test taken by pupil wishing to transfer from arts to a scientific stream etc

integra'tore *nm* **integratore alimentare** dietary supplement

integrazi'one *nf* integration

integrità *nf* integrity

'integro *adj* complete; (retto) upright

intelaia'tura *nf* framework

intellet'tivo *adj* intellectual

intel'letto *nm* intellect

intellettu'ale *adj* & *nmf* intellectual

intellettual'mente *adv* intellectually

intelli'gente *adj* intelligent

intelligente'mente *adv* intelligently

intelli'genza *nf* intelligence. **intelligenza artificiale** artificial intelligence

intelli'ghenzia *nf* intelligentsia

intelli'gibile *adj* intelligible

intelligibil'mente *adv* intelligibly

intelligi'oco *nm* computer game

intempe'rante *adj* intemperate

intempe'ranza *nf* intemperance; **intemperanze** *pl* excesses

intem'perie *nfpl* bad weather

intempe'stivo *adj* untimely

inten'dente *nm* superintendent

inten'denza *nf* **intendenza di finanza** inland revenue office

in'tendere *vt* (comprendere) understand; (udire) hear; (avere intenzione) intend; (significare) mean; **[siamo] intesi?** is that clear?

in'tendersi *vr* (capirsi) understand each other; **~ di** (essere esperto in) have a good knowledge of; **intendersela con** (fam: avere una relazione con) have it off with

intendi'mento *nm* understanding; (intenzione) intention

intendi'|tore, -trice *nmf* connoisseur; **intenditori** *pl* cognoscenti

intene'rire *vt* soften; (commuovere) touch

intene'rirsi *vr* be touched

intensa'mente *adv* intensely

intensifi'care *vt* intensify

intensifi'carsi *vr* intensify

intensità *nf* intensity

intensiva'mente *adv* intensively

inten'sivo *adj* intensive; **terapia intensiva** intensive care

in'tenso *adj* intense

inten'tare *vt* start up; **~ causa contro qualcuno** bring *or* institute proceedings against somebody

inten'tato *adj* **non lasciare nulla di ~** try everything

in'tento ① *adj* engrossed (**a** in) ② *nm* purpose

intenzio'nale *adj* intentional

intenzio'nato *adj* **essere ~ a fare qualcosa** have the intention of doing something

intenzi'one *nf* intention; **senza ~** unintentionally; **avere ~ di fare qualcosa** intend to do something, have the intention of doing something

intera'gire *vi* interact

intera'mente *adv* completely, entirely

interat'tivo *adj* interactive

interazi'one *nf* interaction

interca'lare ① *nm* stock phrase ② *vt* insert ‹*esclamazione*›

intercambi'abile *adj* interchangeable

interca'pedine *nf* cavity

inter'cedere *vi* intercede

intercessi'one *nf* intercession

intercet'tare *vt* intercept; tap ‹*telefono*›

intercettazi'one *nf* interception. **~ telefonica** telephone tapping

inter'city *nm inv* inter-city

intercomuni'cante *adj* [inter]communicating

interconfessio'nale *adj* interdenominational

intercon'nettere *vt* interconnect

intercontinen'tale *adj* intercontinental

inter'correre *vi* ‹*tempo*› elapse; (esistere) exist

interco'stale *adj* intercostal

interden'tale *adj* between the teeth; **filo interdentale** dental floss

inter'detto ① *pp di* INTERDIRE ② *adj* astonished; (proibito) forbidden; **rimanere ~** be taken aback; **lasciare qualcuno ~** astonish somebody, dumbfound somebody ③ *nm* Relig interdict

interdipartimen'tale *adj* interdepartmental

interdipen'dente *adj* interdependent

interdipen'denza *nf* interdependence

inter'dire *vt* ban; (nel calcio) intercept; Jur deprive of civil rights; Relig interdict; **~ a qualcuno di fare qualcosa** forbid somebody to do something

interdiscipli'nare *adj* interdisciplinary

interdizi'one *nf* ban; (nel calcio) interception; Relig interdict. **interdizione giudiziale** appointment of a legal guardian to a person of unsound mind. **interdizione legale** legally imposed ban. **interdizione dai pubblici uffici** ban on taking public office

interessa'mento *nm* interest

interes'sante *adj* interesting; **essere in stato ~** be pregnant

interes'sare ① *vt* interest; (riguardare) concern ② *vi* **~ a** interest; **non mi interessa** I'm not interested; (non mi importa) I don't care, it doesn't matter to me

interes'sarsi *vr* **~ a** take an interest in; **~ di** take care of

interes'sato *adj* (attento) interested; pej self-interested; **diretto ~** person concerned

inte'resse *nm* interest; **fare qualcosa per ~** do something out of self-interest; **essere nell'~ di qualcuno** be in somebody's interest; **un ∼ del 4%** 4% interest. **interesse attivo** interest charge. **interesse maturato** accrued interest. **interesse privato in atti di ufficio** abuse of public office. **interesse a tasso variabile** floating rate interest

interes'senza *nf* Econ profit-sharing

inter'faccia *nf* interface. **interfaccia grafica** graphics interface. **interfaccia uomo/macchina** man/machine interface. **interfaccia utente** user interface

interfacci'are *vt* interface

interfacci'arsi *vr* interface

interfe'renza *nf* interference

interfe'rire *vi* interfere

inter'fono *nm* intercom

interga'lattico *adj* intergalactic

interiet'tivo *adj* interjectory

interiezi'one *nf* interjection

'interim *nm inv* (incarico) temporary appointment; (periodo) interim; **ad ∼** on a temporary basis; ⟨*presidente*⟩ acting

interi'ora *nfpl* entrails

interi'ore *adj* inner

interioriz'zare *vt* internalize

interior'mente *adv* (nella parte interiore) internally; (emotivamente) inwardly

inter'linea *nf* line spacing; Typ leading. **interlinea doppia** double spacing

interline'are 🅵 *vt* space out 🅶 *adj* line *attrib*

interlocu'tore, -trice *nmf* speaker, interlocutor *fml*; **il mio ∼** the person I am/was speaking to

inter'ludio *nm* interlude

intermedi'ario, -a *adj & nmf* intermediary; Econ middleman

intermediazi'one *nf* (intervento) mediation

inter'medio *adj* in-between

inter'mezzo *nm* Theat, Mus intermezzo

intermi'nabile *adj* interminable

interministeri'ale *adj* interdepartmental

intermissi'one *nf* intermission

intermit'tente *adj* intermittent; ⟨*vulcano*⟩ dormant

intermit'tenza *nf* **a ∼** intermittent

interna'mente *adv* internally

interna'mento *nm* internment; (in manicomio) committal

inter'nare *vt* intern; (in manicomio) commit [to a mental institution]

inter'nato, -a 🅵 *adj* interned 🅶 *nmf* internee 🅷 *nm* boarding school

internazio'nale *adj* international

internazional'mente *adv* internationally

'Internet *nf* Internet; **in ∼** on the Internet; **via ∼** through the Internet. **∼ point** Internet kiosk

inter'nista *nmf* internist

in'terno 🅵 *adj* internal; Geog inland; (interiore) inner; ⟨*politica*⟩ national; **alunno ∼** boarder 🅶 *nm* interior; (di condominio) flat; Teleph extension; Cinema interior shot; **all'∼** inside; **ministero degli interni** Ministry of the Interior, ≈ Home Office

in'tero 🅵 *adj* whole, entire; Math whole; (intatto) intact; (completo) complete; **per ∼** in full 🅶 *nm* (totalità) whole

interparlamen'tare *adj* interparliamentary

interpar'titico *adj* cross-party

interpel'lanza *nf* parliamentary question

interpel'lare *vt* consult

interpel'lato, -a *nmf* person being questioned

interperso'nale *adj* interpersonal

interplane'tario *adj* interplanetary

interpo'lare *vt* interpolate

inter'porre *vt* interpose; use ⟨*influenza*⟩; **∼ ostacoli a** put obstacles in the way of

inter'porsi *vr* intervene; **∼ tra** come between

inter'posto *adj* **per interposta persona** through a third party

interpre'tare *vt* interpret; Mus perform; **∼ male** misinterpret

interpretari'ato *nm* interpreting

interpretazi'one *nf* interpretation; Mus performance

in'terprete *nmf* interpreter; Mus performer

interpunzi'one *nf* punctuation

inter'rare *vt* (seppellire) bury; (riempire) fill in; lay underground ⟨*cavo, tubo*⟩; plant ⟨*pianta, seme*⟩

inter'rato *nm* basement

interregio'nale *nm* long-distance train, stopping at most stations

interro'gante *nmf* questioner

interro'gare *vt* question; Sch examine

interrogativa'mente *adv* ⟨*guardare*⟩ inquiringly

interroga'tivo 🅵 *adj* interrogative; (sguardo) questioning; **punto interrogativo** question mark 🅶 *nm* question

interro'gato *adj* ⟨*studente*⟩ examinee; Jur person questioned

interroga'torio *adj & nm* questioning

interrogazi'one *nf* question; Sch oral [test]. **interrogazione ciclica** polling. **interrogazione parlamentare** parliamentary question

inter'rompere vt interrupt; (sospendere) stop; cut off ‹collegamento›

inter'rompersi vr break off

interrut'tore nm switch. **interruttore a reostato** dimmer

interruzi'one nf interruption; **senza ∼** non-stop. **interruzione della corrente** power cut. **interruzione di gravidanza** termination of pregnancy

interscambi'abile adj interchangeable

inter'scambio nm import-export trade

interse'care vt intersect

interse'carsi vr intersect

intersezi'one nf intersection

inter'stizio nm interstice

interur'bana nf long-distance call

interur'bano adj inter-city; **telefonata interurbana** long-distance call

interval'lare vt space out

inter'vallo nm interval; (spazio) space; (in ufficio) tea/coffee break; TV, Sch break; **fare un ∼** have a break; **a intervalli regolari** at regular intervals. **intervallo del pranzo** lunch hour, lunch break. **intervallo pubblicitario** commercial break

interve'nire vi intervene; (Med: operare) operate; **∼ a** take part in

inter'vento nm intervention; (presenza) presence; (chirurgico) operation; **pronto intervento** emergency services; **un ∼ a cuore aperto** open-heart surgery

inter'vista nf interview. **intervista esclusiva** exclusive interview

intervi'stare vt interview

intervi'stato, -a nmf interviewee

intervista│'tore, -trice nmf interviewer

in'tesa nf understanding; **d'∼** ‹cenno› of acknowledgement

in'teso, -a ① pp di INTENDERE
② adj **resta ∼ che ...** needless to say, ...; **∼ a** meant to; **[siamo] intesi!** agreed!
③ nf understanding

in'tessere vt weave together

inte'stare vt head; write one's name and address at the top of ‹lettera›; Comm register

inte'starsi vr **∼ a fare qualcosa** take it into one's head to do something

intesta'tario, -a nmf holder

intestazi'one nf heading; (su carta da lettere) letterhead

intesti'nale adj intestinal

inte'stino ① adj ‹lotte› internal
② nm intestine. **intestino crasso** large intestine. **intestino tenue** small intestine

intiepi'dire vt (scaldare) warm; cool ‹passione, desiderio›

intiepi'dirsi vr cool [down]; (scaldarsi) warm [up]; ‹fede› wane

intima'mente adv ‹conoscere› intimately

inti'mare vt order; **∼ l'alt** give the order to halt; **∼ l'alt a qualcuno** order somebody to stop

intimazi'one nf order. **intimazione di sfratto** eviction notice

intimida'torio adj threatening, intimidating

intimidazi'one nf intimidation

intimi'dire vt intimidate

intimi'dirsi vr be overwhelmed with shyness

intimità nf intimacy, togetherness

'intimo ① adj intimate; (interno) innermost; ‹amico› close
② nm (amico) close friend; (dell'animo) heart

intimo'rire vt frighten

intimo'rirsi vr get frightened

intimo'rito adj frightened

in'tingere vt dip

in'tingolo nm sauce; (pietanza) stew

intiriz'zire vt numb

intiriz'zirsi vr grow numb

intiriz'zito adj **essere ∼** (dal freddo) be perished

intito'lare vt entitle; (dedicare) dedicate

intito'larsi vr be called

intolle'rabile adj intolerable

intolle'rante adj intolerant

intona'care vt plaster

intonaca'tore nm plasterer

in'tonaco nm plaster. **intonaco a pinocchino** pebbledash

into'nare vt start to sing; tune ‹strumento›; match ‹colori›

into'narsi vr match

into'nato adj ‹persona› able to sing in tune; ‹voce, strumento› in tune; ‹colore› matching

intonazi'one nf (inflessione) intonation; ‹ironica› tone; (cantando) ability to sing in tune

in'tonso adj ‹libro› untouched

inton'tire ① vt ‹botta› stun, daze; ‹gas› make dizzy; fig stun
② vi go ga-ga

inton'tito adj dazed; fig stunned; ‹con l'età› ga-ga

intop'pare vi **∼ in** run into

in'toppo nm **c'è un ∼** something's come up

in'torno ① adv around
② prep **∼ a** around; (circa) about; **∼ al mondo** round-the-world

intorpi'dire vt numb

intorpi'dirsi vr become numb

intorpi'dito *adj* torpid
intossi'care *vt* poison
intossi'carsi *vr* be poisoned
intossicazi'one *nf* poisoning.
 intossicazione alimentare food
 poisoning
intra-azien'dale *adj* in-house
intradu'cibile *adj* untranslatable
intralci'are *vt* hamper
in'tralcio *nm* hitch; **essere d'~ (a
 qualcuno/qualcosa)** be a hindrance (to
 somebody/something)
intrallaz'zare *vi* intrigue
intral'lazzo *nm* racket
intramon'tabile *adj* timeless
intramusco'lare *adj* intramuscular
intra'net *nf inv* intranet
intransi'gente *adj* intransigent,
 uncompromising
intransi'genza *nf* intransigence
intransi'tivo *adj* intransitive
intrappolato *adj* **rimanere ~** be
 trapped
intrapren'dente *adj* enterprising
intrapren'denza *nf* initiative
intra'prendere *vt* undertake
intrat'tabile *adj* very difficult
intratte'nere *vt* entertain
intratte'nersi *vr* linger
intratteni'mento *nm* entertainment
intrave'dere *vt* catch a glimpse of;
 (presagire) foresee
intrecci'are *vt* interweave; plait
 ⟨capelli, corda⟩; **~ le mani** clasp one's
 hands
Intrecci'arsi *vr* intertwine; (aggrovigliarsi)
 become tangled
in'treccio *nm* (trama) plot; (di nastri, strade)
 tangle
in'trepido *adj* intrepid
intri'cato *adj* tangled
intri'gante ① *adj* intriguing
 ② *nmf* schemer
intri'gare ① *vt* entangle; (incuriosire)
 intrigue
 ② *vi* be intriguing
intri'garsi *vr* become entangled;
 (immischiarsi) meddle
in'trigo *nm* plot; **intrighi** *pl* plotting; (di
 corte) intrigues
intrinseca'mente *adv* intrinsically
in'trinseco *adj* intrinsic
in'triso *adj* **~ di** soaked with; fig imbued
 with
intri'stire *vt* sadden
intri'stirsi *vr* grow sad
intro'durre *vt* introduce; (inserire) insert;
 ~ a (iniziare a) introduce to

intro'dursi *vr* get in; **~ in** get into
introdut'tivo *adj* ⟨pagine, discorso⟩
 introductory
introduzi'one *nf* introduction
in'troito *nm* income, revenue; (incasso)
 takings *pl*
intro'mettere *vt* introduce
intro'mettersi *vr* interfere; (interporsi)
 intervene
intromissi'one *nf* intervention
introspet'tivo *adj* introspective
intro'vabile *adj* unobtainable
intro'verso, -a ① *adj* introverted
 ② *nmf* introvert
intrufo'larsi *vr* sneak in
in'truglio *nm* concoction
intrusi'one *nf* intrusion
in'truso, -a *nmf* intruder
intu'ibile *adj* deducible
intu'ire *vt* perceive
intuitiva'mente *adv* intuitively
intui'tivo *adj* intuitive
in'tuito *nm* intuition
intuizi'one *nf* intuition
inu'mano *adj* inhuman
inu'mare *vt* inter
inumi'dire *vt* dampen; moisten ⟨labbra⟩
inumi'dirsi *vr* become damp
i'nutile *adj* useless; (superfluo)
 unnecessary
inutilità *nf* uselessness
inutiliz'zabile *adj* unusable
inutiliz'zato *adj* unused
inutil'mente *adv* fruitlessly
inva'dente *adj* intrusive
in'vadere *vt* invade; (affollare) overrun
inva'ghirsi *vr* **~ di** take a fancy to
invali'cabile *adj* impassable; **'limite ~'**
 Mil 'no access beyond this point'
invali'dare *vt* invalidate
invalidità *nf* disability; Jur invalidity
in'valido, -a ① *adj* invalid; (handicappato)
 disabled
 ② *nmf* disabled person; **gli invalidi** the
 handicapped. **invalido di guerra**
 disabled ex-serviceman. **invalido del
 lavoro** industrial accident victim
in'vano *adv* in vain
invari'abile *adj* invariable
invariabil'mente *adv* invariably
invari'ato *adj* unchanged
invasi'one *nf* invasion
in'vaso *pp di* INVADERE
inva'sore ① *adj* invading
 ② *nm* invader
invecchia'mento *nm* (di vino)
 maturation
invecchi'are *vt/i* age

in'vece *adv* instead; (anzi) but; ∼ **di** instead of

inve'ire *vi* ∼ **contro** inveigh against

invele'nito *adj* embittered

inven'dibile *adj* unsaleable

inven'duto *adj* unsold

inven'tare *vt* invent

inventari'are *vt* make an inventory of

inven'tario *nm* inventory

inven'tato *adj* made-up

inven'tiva *nf* inventiveness

inven'tivo *adj* inventive

inven|'tore, **-trice** *nmf* inventor

invenzi'one *nf* invention

inver'nale *adj* wintry; **sport** *pl* **invernali** winter sports

in'verno *nm* winter

invero'simile *adj* improbable

inverosimil'mente *adv* incredibly

inversa'mente *adv* inversely; ∼ **proporzionale** in inverse proportion

inversi'one *nf* inversion; Mech reversal; fare un'∼ a U do a U-turn. **inversione di fondo** Comput reverse video. **inversione di tendenza** turnaround

in'verso ① *adj* inverse; (opposto) opposite ② *nm* opposite

inverte'brato *adj & nm* invertebrate

inver'tire *vt* reverse; (capovolgere) turn upside-down

investi'gare *vt* investigate

investiga|'tore, **-trice** *nmf* investigator. **investigatore privato** private investigator, private eye

investigazi'one *nf* investigation

investi'mento *nm* investment; (incidente) crash

inve'stire *vt* invest; (urtare) collide with; (travolgere) run over; ∼ **qualcuno di** invest somebody with

Investi'tura *nf* investiture

invete'rato *adj* inveterate

invet'tiva *nf* invective

invi'are *vt* send

invi'ato, **-a** *nmf* envoy; (di giornale) correspondent. **inviato di pace** peace envoy

in'vidia *nf* envy

invidi'are *vt* envy

invidi'oso *adj* envious

invigo'rire *vt* invigorate

invigo'rirsi *vr* become strong

invin'cibile *adj* invincible

in'vio *nm* dispatch; Comput enter

invio'labile *adj* inviolable

invipe'rirsi *vr* get nasty

invipe'rito *adj* furious

invischi'arsi *vr* get involved (**in** in)

invi'sibile *adj* invisible

invisibilità *nf* invisibility

invi'tante *adj* ⟨piatto, profumo⟩ enticing

invi'tare *vt* invite

invi'tato, **-a** *nmf* guest

in'vito *nm* invitation

invo'care *vt* invoke; (implorare) beg

invocazi'one *nf* invocation

invogli'are *vt* tempt; (indurre) induce

invogli'arsi *vr* ∼ **di** take a fancy to

involga'rire *vt* vulgarize

involontaria'mente *adv* involuntarily

involon'tario *adj* involuntary

invol'tini *nmpl* stuffed rolls (of meat, pastry)

in'volto *nm* parcel; (fagotto) bundle

in'volucro *nm* wrapping

invo'luto *adj* involved

invulne'rabile *adj* invulnerable

inzacche'rare *vt* splash with mud

inzup'pare *vt* soak; (intingere) dip

inzup'parsi *vr* get soaked

'io ① *pers pron* I; **sono io** it's me; **l'ho fatto io [stesso]** I did it myself ② *nm* **l'io** the ego

i'odio *nm* iodine

i'one *nm* ion

i'onico *adj* Ionic

l'onio *nm* **lo** ∼ the Ionian [Sea]

iono'sfera *nf* ionosphere

i'osa: **a** ∼ *adv* in abundance

iperattività *nf* hyperactivity

iperat'tivo *adj* hyperactive

i'perbole *nf* hyperbole

iper'critico *adj* hypercritical

ipermer'cato *nm* hypermarket

iper'metrope *adj* long-sighted

ipersen'sibile *adj* hypersensitive

ipertensi'one *nf* high blood pressure

iper'testo *nm* Comput hypertext

iperte'stuale *adj* **collegamento ipertestuale** hyperlink

iperventi'lare *vi* hyperventilate

ip'nosi *nf* hypnosis

ipnotera'pia *nf* hypnotherapy

ip'notico *adj* hypnotic

ipno'tismo *nm* hypnotism

ipnotiz'zare *vt* hypnotize

ipoaller'genico *adj* hypoallergenic

ipoca'lorico *adj* low-calorie

ipo'centro *nm* focus

ipocon'dria *nf* hypochondria

ipocon'driaco, **-a** *adj & nmf* hypochondriac

ipocri'sia *nf* hypocrisy

i'pocrita ① *adj* hypocritical

2 *nmf* hypocrite
ipocrita'mente *adv* hypocritically
ipo'dermico *adj* hypodermic
i'pofisi *nf* pituitary gland
ipo'teca *nf* mortgage
ipote'cabile *adj* mortgageable
ipote'care *vt* mortgage
ipote'cario *adj* mortgage *attrib*
ipote'nusa *nf* hypotenuse
ipo'termia *nf* hypothermia
i'potesi *nf inv* hypothesis; (caso, eventualità) eventuality; **nella migliore delle** ∼ at best; **nella peggiore delle** ∼ if the worst comes to the worst
ipo'tetico *adj* hypothetical
ipotiz'zare *vt* hypothesize
'ippico, -a **1** *adj* horse *attrib* **2** *nf* riding
ippoca'stano *nm* horse-chestnut
ip'podromo *nm* racecourse
ippo'potamo *nm* hippopotamus
'ipsilon *nf inv* [the letter] y
'ira *nf* anger
ira'scibile *adj* irascible
i'rato *adj* irate
'iride *nf* Anat iris; (arcobaleno) rainbow
'iris *nm inv* Bot iris
Ir'landa *nf* Ireland. **Irlanda del Nord** Northern Ireland
irlan'dese **1** *adj* Irish **2** *nm* Irishman; (lingua) Irish **3** *nf* Irishwoman
iro'nia *nf* irony
i'ronico *adj* ironic[al]
irradi'are *vt/i* radiate
irradiazi'one *nf* radiation
irraggiun'gibile *adj* unattainable
irragio'nevole *adj* unreasonable; (speranza, timore) irrational; (assurdo) absurd
irranci'dire *vi* go rancid
irrazio'nale *adj* irrational
irrazionalità *adj* irrationality
irrazional'mente *adv* irrationally
irre'ale *adj* unreal
irrea'listico *adj* unrealistic
irrealiz'zabile *adj* unattainable
irrealtà *nf* unreality
irrecupe'rabile *adj* irrecoverable
irrecu'sabile *adj* incontrovertible
irredi'mibile *adj* irredeemable
irrefre'nabile *adj* uncontrollable
irrefu'tabile *adj* irrefutable
irrego'lare *adj* irregular
irregolarità *nf inv* irregularity; (di terreno) unevenness; Sport foul

irregolar'mente *adv* (frequentare) irregularly; (comportarsi) erratically; (disporre) unevenly
irremo'vibile *adj* fig adamant
irrepa'rabile *adj* irreparable
irrepe'ribile *adj* (persona) not to be found; **sarò irreperibile** I'm not going to be contactable
irrepren'sibile *adj* irreproachable
irrepri'mibile *adj* irrepressible
irrequi'eto *adj* restless
irresi'stibile *adj* irresistible
irresistibil'mente *adv* irresistibly
irreso'luto *adj* irresolute
irrespon'sabile *adj* irresponsible
irresponsabilità *nf* irresponsibility
irrestrin'gibile *adj* preshrunk
irre'tire *vt* seduce
irrever'sibile *adj* irreversible
irreversibil'mente *adv* irrevocably
irrevo'cabile *adj* irrevocable
irrevocabil'mente *adv* irreversibly
irricono'scibile *adj* unrecognizable
irridu'cibile *adj* irreducible
irri'gare *vt* irrigate; (fiume) flow through
irrigazi'one *nf* irrigation
irrigidi'mento *nm* (di muscoli) stiffening; (di disciplina) tightening
irrigi'dire *vt* stiffen up
irrigi'dirsi *vr* stiffen up
irrile'vante *adj* unimportant
irrimedi'abile *adj* irreparable
irrimediabil'mente *adv* irreparably
irripe'tibile *adj* unrepeatable
irri'solto *adj* unresolved
irri'sorio *adj* derisive; (insignificante) derisory
irri'tabile *adj* irritable
irri'tante *adj* aggravating, annoying
irri'tare *vt* irritate, annoy
irri'tarsi *vr* get annoyed
irri'tato *adj* irritated, annoyed; (gola) sore
irritazi'one *nf* irritation
irrive'renza *nf* (qualità) irreverence; (azione) irreverent action
irrobu'stire *vt* fortify
irrobu'stirsi *vr* get stronger
ir'rompere *vi* burst (in into)
irro'rare *vt* sprinkle
irrorazi'one *nf* (di piante) crop spraying
irru'ente *adj* impetuous
irruvi'dire *vt* roughen
irruvi'dirsi *vr* become rough
irruzi'one *nf* raid; fig eruption; **fare** ∼ **in** burst into
ir'suto *adj* shaggy

'irto adj bristly

i'scritto, -a ① pp di ISCRIVERE
② adj registered
③ nmf member; **per** ~ in writing

i'scrivere vt register

i'scriversi vr ~ **a** register at, enrol at
⟨scuola⟩; join ⟨circolo ecc⟩

iscrizi'one nf registration; (epigrafe)
inscription

i'slamico adj Islamic

isla'mismo nm Islam

l'slanda nf Iceland

islan'dese ① adj Icelandic
② nmf Icelander

'ismi nmpl isms

i'sobara nf isobar

'isola nf island; **le isole britanniche** the
British Isles; **l'**~ **di Man** Isle of Man.
isola deserta desert island. **isola
pedonale** traffic island. **isola
spartitraffico** traffic island

iso'lano, -a ① adj insular
② nmf islander

iso'lante ① adj insulating
② nm insulator

iso'lare vt isolate; Mech, Electr insulate;
(acusticamente) soundproof

iso'lato ① adj isolated
② nm (di appartamenti) block

isolazio'nismo nm isolationism

iso'metrico adj isometric

i'soscele adj isosceles

is'panico adj Hispanic

ispessi'mento nm thickening

ispes'sire vt thicken

ispes'sirsi vr thicken

ispetto'rato nm inspectorate

ispet'tore nm inspector. **ispettore
capo** chief inspector. **ispettore di
polizia** police inspector. **ispettore
scolastico** inspector of schools.
ispettore delle tasse tax inspector.
ispettore di zona Comm area manager

ispezio'nare vt inspect

ispezi'one nf inspection; (di nave)
boarding

'ispido adj bristly

ispi'rare vt inspire; suggest ⟨idea,
soluzione⟩

ispi'rarsi vr ~ **a** be based on

ispi'rato adj inspired

ispirazi'one nf inspiration; (idea) idea

Isra'ele nm Israel

israeli'ano, -a adj & nmf Israeli

is'sare vt hoist

ist. abbr (**istituto**) dept

istan'taneo, -a ① adj instantaneous
② nf snapshot

i'stante nm instant; **all'**~ instantly

i'stanza nf petition. **istanza di
divorzio** petition for divorce

isterecto'mia nf hysterectomy

i'sterico adj hysterical; **attacco isterico**
hysterics pl

iste'rismo nm hysteria. **isterismo di
massa** mass hysteria

isti'gare vt instigate; ~ **qualcuno al male**
incite somebody to evil

istiga|'tore, -trice nmf instigator

istigazi'one nf instigation; ~ **a
delinquere** incitement to crime

istintiva'mente adv instinctively

istin'tivo adj instinctive

i'stinto nm instinct; **d'**~ instinctively.
istinto di conservazione instinct of
self-preservation. **istinto materno**
maternal instinct

istitu'ire vt institute; (fondare) found;
initiate ⟨manifestazione⟩

isti'tuto nm institute; Sch secondary
school; Univ department. **istituto di
bellezza** beauty salon. **istituto
commerciale** business college. **istituto
di credito** bank. **istituto per
l'infanzia** children's home. **istituto
tecnico professionale** technical
college

istitu|'tore, -trice nmf (insegnante) tutor;
(fondatore) founder

istituzio'nale adj institutional

istituzionaliz'zare vt institutionalize

istituzionaliz'zarsi vr become an
institution

istituzionalizzazi'one nf
institutionalization

istituzi'one nf institution; **le istituzioni**
state institutions

'istmo nm isthmus

isto'gramma nm bar chart

istolo'gia nf histology

istra'dare vt divert; fig guide (**a** towards)

'istrice nm porcupine

istri'one nm clown; Theat sl ham

istru'ire vt instruct; (addestrare) train;
(informare) inform; Jur prepare

istru'ito adj well-educated

istrut'tivo adj instructive, enlightening

istrut|'tore, -trice nmf instructor,
giudice istruttore examining
magistrate. **istruttore di guida** driving
instructor. **istruttore di nuoto**
swimming instructor

istrut'toria nf Jur investigation

istruzi'one nf instruction; Sch
education; **ministero della pubblica
istruzione** Department of Education.
istruzioni pl **per l'uso** instructions for
use

istupi'dire vt stupefy

I'talia *nf* Italy
itali'ano, **-a** *adj & nmf* Italian
itine'rante *adj* wandering; ⟨*mostra*⟩ touring; ⟨*spettacolo*⟩ travelling
itine'rario *nm* route, itinerary. **itinerario turistico** tourist route
itte'rizia *nf* jaundice

'ittico *adj* fishing *attrib*
i'uta *nf* jute
I.V.A. *nf abbr* (**imposta sul valore aggiunto**) VAT; **I.V.A. compresa** inclusive of VAT, VAT inclusive
'ivi *adv* (linguaggio burocratico) therein

Jj

ja'bot *nm inv* jabot
jack *nm inv* jack
ja'cquard *adj inv* (nella maglia) jacquard
'jais *nm* jet
'jam-session *nf inv* jam-session
jazz *nm* jazz
jaz'zista *nmf* jazz player
jeep *nf inv* jeep
'jersey *nm* jersey
jet *nm inv* jet. **jet privato** private jet
jet-'set *nm* jet set
'jingle *nm inv* jingle
'jodel *nm inv* yodel
'jogging *nm* jogging
joint 'venture *nf inv* Comm joint

venture
'jolly ① *nm inv* (carta da gioco) joker ② *adj* Comput **carattere jolly** wildcard [character]
'joystick *nm inv* joystick
Jugo'slavia *nf* Yugoslavia
jugo'slavo, **-a** *adj & nmf* Yugoslav[ian]
ju'jitsu *nm* ju-jitsu
juke'box *nm inv* juke box
jumbo-jet *nm inv* jumbo jet
junghi'ano, **-a** *adj & nmf* Jungian
'junior ① *adj inv* junior ② *nm* (pl **juniores**) junior
'juta *nf* jute

Kk

kafki'ano *adj* Kafkan, Kafkaesque
ka'jal *nm inv* kohl
'kaki ① *adj inv* khaki ② *nm inv* persimmon
Kala'hari *nm* il ∼ the Kalahari [Desert]
ka'pok *nm* kapok
ka'putt *adj inv* kaput
kara'kiri *nm* fare ∼ commit hara-kiri
kara'oke *nm inv* karaoke; **apparecchio per** ∼ karaoke machine
kara'te *nm* karate
kart *nm inv* go-kart
kar'tismo *nm* go-karting; **fare del** ∼ go go-karting
'kasher *adj inv* kosher
'Kashmir *nm* Kashmir
ka'yak *nm inv* kayak
Ka'zakistan *nm* Kazakhstan

KB Comput *abbr* (**kilobyte**) K, KB
Kbyte Comput *abbr* (**kilobyte**) kbyte
'Kenya *nm* Kenya
ker'messe *nf inv* fair; fig rowdy celebration
kero'sene *nm* paraffin
'ketchup *nm* ketchup
kg *abbr* (**chilogrammo**) kg
kib'butz *nm inv* kibbutz
'killer *nmf inv* assassin, hit man
'kilo *nm* kilo
kilt *nm inv* kilt
ki'mono *nm inv* kimono
kinesitera'pia *nf* physiotherapy
Kir'ghizistan *nm* Kyrgyzstan
kit *nm inv* **kit di aggiornamento** upgrade kit. **kit multimediale** multimedia kit

kitsch *adj inv* kitschy
'kiwi *nm inv* kiwi
'kleenex® *nm inv* Kleenex
km *abbr* (**chilometro**) km
km/h *abbr* (**chilometro**) kph
kmq *abbr* (**chilometro quadrato**) km²
ko'ala *nm inv* koala
koso'varo -a *adj & nmf* Kosovan

'Kosovo *nm* Kosovo
'krapfen *nm inv* doughnut
'kripton *nm* krypton
'Kurdistan *nm* Kurdistan
kuwaiti'ano *nm* Kuwaiti
kW *abbr* (**kilowatt**) kW
K-'way® *nm inv* cagoule
kWh *abbr* (**kilowatt all'ora**) kWh

Ll

l' *def art mf* (*before vowel*) the; ▶ IL
lì *adv* there; **fin lì** as far as there; **giù di lì**
thereabouts; **lì per lì** there and then; **la
cosa è finita lì** that was the end of it
la ① *def art f* the; ▶ IL
② *pron* (oggetto, riferito a persona) her; (riferito
a cosa, animale) it; (forma di cortesia) you
③ *nm inv* Mus (chiave, nota) A
là *adv* there; **di là** (in quel luogo) in there; (da
quella parte) that way; **eccolo là!** there he
is!; **farsi più in là** (far largo) make way; **là
dentro** in there; **là fuori** out there; **[ma] va'
là!** come off it!; **più in là** (nel tempo) later
on; (nello spazio) further on
'labbro *nm* (pl *nf* **labbra**) lip; **pendere
dalle labbra di qualcuno** hang on
somebody's every word. **labbro
leporino** harelip
labi'ale *adj & nf* labial
'labile *adj* fleeting
labiolet'tura *nf* lip-reading
labi'rinto *nm* labyrinth; (di sentieri ecc)
maze
labora'torio *nm* laboratory; (di negozio,
officina ecc) workshop. **laboratorio
linguistico** language lab
laboriosa'mente *adv* laboriously
labori'oso *adj* (operoso) industrious;
(faticoso) laborious
labra'dor *nm inv* labrador
labu'rista ① *adj* Labour
② *nmf* member of the Labour Party
'lacca *nf* lacquer; (per capelli) hairspray
lac'care *vt* lacquer
lacchè *nm inv* lackey
'laccio *nm* noose; (lazo) lasso; (trappola)
snare; (stringa) lace. **laccio emostatico**
tourniquet
lace'rante *adj* (grido) earsplitting
lace'rare *vt* tear; lacerate (carne)
lace'rarsi *vr* tear
lacerazi'one *nf* laceration
'lacero *adj* torn; (cencioso) ragged

la'conico *adj* laconic
'lacrima *nf* tear; (goccia) drop
lacri'male *adj* (condotto, ghiandola) tear
attrib
lacri'mare *vi* weep
lacri'mevole *adj* tear-jerking
lacri'mogeno *adj* **gas lacrimogeno**
tear gas
lacri'moso *adj* tearful
la'cuna *nf* gap
lacu'noso *adj* (preparazione, resoconto)
incomplete
la'custre *adj* lake *attrib*
lad'dove *conj* whereas
'ladro, -a ① *adj* thieving
② *nmf* thief; **al ∼!** stop thief!
ladro'cinio *nm* theft
la'druncolo *nm* petty thief
'lager *nm inv* concentration camp
laggiù *adv* down there; (lontano) over
there
'lagna *nf* (fam: persona) moaning Minnie;
(film) bore
la'gnanza *nf* complaint
la'gnarsi *vr* moan, whinge; (protestare)
complain (di about)
la'gnoso *adj* (persona) moaning,
whining; (film) weepy
'lago *nm* lake. **lago di Garda** Lake
Garda. **lago di sangue** pool of blood
la'guna *nf* lagoon
lagu'nare *adj* lagoon *attrib*
laiciz'zare *vt* laicize
'laico, -a ① *adj* lay; (vita) secular
② *nm* layman
③ *nf* laywoman
'lama ① *nf* blade; **a doppia ∼** (rasoio)
twin-blade
② *nm inv* (animale) llama
lambic'carsi *vr* **∼ il cervello** rack one's
brains
lam'bire *vt* lap

lamé *nm* lamé

la'mella *nf* (di fungo) lamella; (di metallo, plastica) sheet

lamen'tare *vt* lament

lamen'tarsi *vr* moan; ~ **di** (lagnarsi) complain about

lamen'tela *nf* complaint

lamen'tevole *adj* mournful; (pietoso) pitiful

la'mento *nm* moan

la'metta *nf* **lametta [da barba]** razor blade

lami'era *nf* sheet metal. **lamiera ondulata** corrugated iron

'lamina *nf* foil. **lamina d'oro** gold leaf

lami'nare *vt* laminate

lami'naria *nf* kelp

lami'nato ① *adj* laminated ② *nm* laminate; (tessuto) lamé

'lampada *nf* lamp. **lampada abbronzante** sunlamp. **lampada alogena** halogen lamp. **lampada da comodino** beside lamp. **lampada a gas** gas lamp. **lampada a olio** oil lamp. **lampada a pila** torch. **lampada da soffitto** overhead light. **lampada da tavolo** table lamp

lampa'dario *nm* chandelier

lampa'dato *nm* sl sun-bed freak

lampa'dina *nf* light bulb

lam'pante *adj* clear

lam'para *nf* light used when fishing at night

lampeg'giante *adj* flashing

lampeggi'are *vi* flash

lampeggia'tore *nm* Auto indicator

lampi'one *nm* street lamp

'lampo *nm* flash of lightning; (luce) flash; **lampi** *pl* lightning *sg*; **cerniera lampo** zip [fastener], zipper Am. **lampo di genio** stroke of genius. **lampo al magnesio** magnesium flash

lam'pone *nm* raspberry

'lana *nf* wool; **di** ~ woollen. **lana d'acciaio** steel wool. **lana grossa** double knitting [wool]. **lana merino** botany wool. **lana vergine** new wool. **lana di vetro** glass wool

lan'cetta *nf* pointer; (di orologio) hand. **lancetta dei minuti** minute hand. **lancetta delle ore** hour hand. **lancetta dei secondi** second hand

'lancia *nf* (arma) spear, lance; Naut launch. **lancia di salvataggio** lifeboat

lanciafi'amme *nm inv* flamethrower

lancia'missili *nm inv* missile launcher

lancia'palle *adj inv* **macchina lanciapalle** ball launcher for tennis practice

lancia'razzi ① *adj inv* **pistola lanciarazzi** Very pistol ② *nm inv* rocket launcher

lanci'are *vt* throw; (da un aereo) drop; launch ⟨missile, prodotto, attacco⟩; give ⟨grido⟩; Comput run ⟨file⟩; ~ **uno sguardo a** glance at; ~ **in alto** throw up

lanci'arsi *vr* fling oneself; (intraprendere) launch out

lanci'nante *adj* piercing

'lancio *nm* throwing; (da aereo) drop; (di missile, prodotto) launch; (Comput: di file) running. **lancio del disco** discus [throwing]. **lancio del giavellotto** javelin [throwing]. **lancio col paracadute** (di persona) parachute jump; (di pacco) airdrop, parachute drop. **lancio del peso** putting the shot, shot put

'landa *nf* moor

languida'mente *adv* languidly

'languido *adj* languid; (debole) feeble

langu'ore *nm* languor; (spossatezza) listlessness. **languore di stomaco** hunger pangs *pl*

lani'ero *adj* wool; **industria laniera** wool industry

lani'ficio *nm* woollen mill

lano'lina *nf* lanolin

la'noso *adj* woolly

lan'terna *nf* lantern; (faro) lighthouse

la'nugine *nf* down

'Laos *nm* Laos

lapalissi'ano *adj* obvious

laparosco'pla *nf* laparoscopy

lapi'dare *vt* stone; fig demolish

lapi'dario *adj* (conciso) terse; **arte lapidaria** stone carving

'lapide *nf* tombstone; (commemorativa) memorial tablet

'lapis *nm inv* pencil

lapi'slazzuli *nm inv* lapis lazuli

'lappa *nf* Bot burr

Lap'ponia *nf* Lapland

'lapsus *nm inv* lapse, error. **lapsus freudiano** Freudian slip

'laptop *nm inv* laptop

lardel'lare *vt* Culin lard

'lardo *nm* lard

larga'mente *adv* (ampiamente) widely

largheggi'are *vi* ~ **in** be free with

lar'ghezza *nf* width; (di spalle) breadth; fig liberality. **larghezza di vedute** broad-mindedness

'largo ① *adj* wide; (ampio) broad; ⟨abito⟩ loose; (liberale) liberal; (abbondante) generous; **stare alla larga** keep away; ~ **di manica** fig generous; ~ **di spalle** broad-shouldered; **a gambe larghe** with one's legs wide apart; **di larghe vedute** broad-minded

[2] *nm* width; **andare al** ∼ Naut go out to sea; **fare** ∼ make room; **farsi** ∼ make one's way; **al** ∼ **di** off the coast of

'**larice** *nm* larch

la'ringe *nf* larynx

larin'gite *nf* laryngitis

'**larva** *nf* larva; (persona emaciata) shadow. **larva di pidocchio** nit

la'sagne *nfpl* lasagne *sg*

'**lasca** *nf* roach

lasciapas'sare *nm inv* pass

lasci'are *vt* leave; (rinunciare) give up; (rimetterci) lose; (smettere di tenere) let go [of]; (concedere) let; ∼ **a desiderare** leave a lot to be desired; ∼ **di fare qualcosa** (smettere) stop doing something; **lascia perdere!** forget it!; **lascialo venire, lascia che venga** let him come

lasci'arsi *vr* (reciproco) leave each other, split up; ∼ **andare** let oneself go

'**lascito** *nm* legacy

la'scivo *adj* lascivious

'**laser** *adj* & *nm inv* [**raggio**] **laser** laser [beam]

lasertera'pia *nf* laser treatment

lassa'tivo *adj* & *nm* laxative

las'sismo *nm* laxity

'**lasso** *nm* **lasso di tempo** period of time

lassù *adv* up there

'**lastra** *nf* slab; (di ghiaccio) sheet; (di metallo, Phot) plate; (radiografia) X-ray [plate]. **lastra di pietra** paving slab, paving stone. **lastra di vetro** plate glass

lastri'care *vt* pave

lastri'cato *nm* pavement

'**lastrico** *nm* paving; **sul** ∼ on one's beam-ends

la'tente *adj* latent

late'rale *adj* side *attrib*; Med, Techn ecc lateral; **via** ∼ side street

lateral'mente *adv* sideways

late'rizi *nmpl* bricks

'**latice** *nm* latex

latifon'dista *nmf* big landowner

lati'fondo *nm* large estate

lati'nismo *nm* Latinism

la'tino *adj* & *nm* Latin

latino-ameri'cano, -a *adj* & *nmf* Latin American

lati'tante [1] *adj* in hiding
[2] *nmf* fugitive [from justice]

lati'tanza *nf* **darsi alla** ∼ go into hiding

lati'tudine *nf* latitude

'**lato** [1] *adj* **in senso** ∼ broadly speaking
[2] *nm* side; (aspetto) aspect; **a** ∼ **di** beside; **dal** ∼ **mio** (punto di vista) for my part;

d'altro ∼ fig on the other hand. **lato B** B side

la'tore, -trice *nmf* Comm bearer

la'trare *vi* bark

la'trato *nm* barking

la'trina *nf* latrine

'**latta** *nf* (materiale) tin; (recipiente) tin, can

lat'taio, -a [1] *nm* milkman
[2] *nf* milkwoman

lat'tante [1] *adj* breast-fed
[2] *nmf* suckling

'**latte** *nm* milk. **latte acido** sour milk. **latte condensato** condensed milk, evaporated milk. **latte detergente** cleansing milk. **latte di gallina** eggnog. **latte intero** whole milk, full-cream milk. **latte a lunga conservazione** long-life milk. **latte materno** mother's milk, breast milk. **latte parzialmente scremato** semi-skimmed milk. **latte in polvere** powdered milk. **latte scremato** skimmed milk. **latte di soia** soya milk

lat'teo *adj* milky; **dieta lattea** milk diet; **la Via Lattea** the Milky Way

latte'ria *nf* dairy

'**lattice** *nm* latex

latti'cello *nm* buttermilk

latti'cini *nmpl* dairy products

latti'era *nf* milk jug

lattigi'noso *adj* milky

lat'tina *nf* can, tin can

lat'tosio *nm* lactose

lat'tuga *nf* lettuce. **lattuga romana** cos lettuce

'**laudano** *nm* laudanum

'**laurea** *nf* degree; **prendere la** ∼ graduate. **laurea breve** degree that takes less than the standard period of time. **laurea in Lettere** arts degree

laure'ando, -a *nmf* final-year student

laure'are *vt* confer a degree on

laure'arsi *vr* graduate

laure'ato, -a *adj* & *nmf* graduate

'**lauro** *nm* laurel

'**lauto** *adj* lavish; ∼ **guadagno** handsome profit

'**lava** *nf* lava

la'vabile *adj* washable. **lavabile in lavastoviglie** dishwasher-safe

la'vabo *nm* wash-basin

lavacri'stallo *nm* windscreen wiper

la'vaggio *nm* washing. **lavaggio automatico** (per auto) carwash. **lavaggio del cervello** brainwashing. **lavaggio a secco** dry-cleaning

la'vagna *nf* slate; Sch blackboard. **lavagna a fogli mobili** flipchart. **lavagna luminosa** overhead projector, OHP

lava'macchine *nmf inv* car washer

la'vanda *nf* wash; Bot lavender; **gli hanno fatto la ~ gastrica** he had his stomach pumped

lavan'daia *nf* washerwoman

lavande'ria *nf* laundry. **lavanderia automatica** launderette

lavan'dino *nm* sink; (hum: persona) bottomless pit

lavapi'atti *nmf inv* dishwasher

la'vare *vt* wash; **~ i piatti** wash up; **~ a secco** dry-clean; **~ a mano** wash by hand; **~ i panni** do the washing

la'varsi *vr* wash, have a wash; **~ i denti** brush one's teeth; **~ le mani/il viso** wash one's hands/face; **~ la testa** o **i capelli** wash one's hair

lava'secco *nmf inv* dry-cleaner's

lavasto'viglie *nf inv* dishwasher

la'vata *nf* wash; **darsi una ~** have a wash. **lavata di capo** *fig* scolding

lava'tivo, -a *nmf* idler

lava'trice *nf* washing-machine

lava'vetri *nm inv* squeegee

la'vello *nm* kitchen sink

'lavico *adj* formed by lava

la'vina *nf* snowslide

lavo'rante *nmf* worker

lavo'rare [1] *vi* work; **~ di fantasia** (sognare) day-dream [2] *vt* work; knead ⟨pasta ecc⟩; till ⟨la terra⟩; **~ a maglia** knit; **~ troppo** overwork

lavora'tivo *adj* working; **giorno lavorativo** workday; **settimana lavorativa** working week

lavo'rato *adj* ⟨pietra, legno⟩ carved; ⟨cuoio⟩ tooled; ⟨metallo⟩ wrought; ⟨golf⟩ patterned; ⟨terra⟩ cultivated

lavora|'tore, -trice [1] *nmf* worker. **lavora|tore a domicilio** outworker, homeworker [2] *adj* working

lavorazi'one *nf* manufacture; (di terra) working; (del terreno) cultivation. **lavorazione [artigianale]** workmanship. **lavorazione del metallo** metalwork. **lavorazione in serie** mass production

lavo'rio *nm* intense activity

la'voro *nm* work; (faticoso, sociale) labour; (impiego) job; **andare al ~** go to work; **essere senza ~** be out of work; **mettersi al ~ (su qualcosa)** set to work (on something); **ministero dei lavori pubblici** Department of Public Works; **lavori** *pl* **di casa** housework; **lavori** *pl* **in corso** roadworks **lavori** *pl* **forzati** hard labour *sg*; **lavori** *pl* **stradali** roadworks. **ministero del lavoro** Department of Employment. **lavoro a domicilio** homeworking. **lavoro di gruppo** Sch working in

groups, group work. **lavoro interinale** temping. **lavoro a maglia** knitting. **lavoro nero** moonlighting. **lavoro part time** part-time job. **lavoro straordinario** overtime. **lavoro teatrale** play. **lavoro a tempo pieno** full-time job

lazza'rone *nm* rascal

le [1] *def art fpl* the; ▸IL [2] *pers pron* (oggetto) them; (a lei) her; **le hai parlato?** did you talk to her? (forma di cortesia) you

'leader [1] *nm inv* leader [2] *adj inv* leading; **prodotto leader** market leader

le'ale *adj* loyal

leal'mente *adv* loyally

lealtà *nf* loyalty

'leasing *nm inv* lease-purchase, leasing

'lebbra *nf* leprosy

lecca 'lecca *nm inv* lollipop

leccapi'edi *nmf inv* pej bootlicker

lec'care *vt* lick; *fig* suck up to

lec'carsi *vr* lick; (fig: agghindarsi) doll oneself up; **da ~ i baffi** mouth-watering

lec'cata *nf* lick

lec'cato *adj* ⟨persona⟩ dressed to kill

'leccio *nm* holm oak

leccor'nia *nf* delicacy

lecita'mente *adv* lawfully

'lecito *adj* lawful; (permesso) permissible

'ledere *vt* damage; Med injure

'lega *nf* league; (di metalli) alloy; **far ~ con qualcuno** take up with somebody. **lega doganale** customs union

le'gaccio *nm* string; (delle scarpe) shoelace

le'gale [1] *adj* legal [2] *nm* lawyer

legalità *nf* legality

legaliz'zare *vt* authenticate; (rendere legale) legalize

legalizzazi'one *nf* legalization

legal'mente *adv* legally

le'game *nm* tie; (amoroso) liaison; (connessione) link. **legame di parentela** family relationship. **legame di sangue** blood relationship. **legame sentimentale** emotional relationship

lega'mento *nm* Med ligament

le'gare [1] *vt* tie; tie up ⟨persona⟩; tie together ⟨due cose⟩; (unire, rilegare) bind; alloy ⟨metalli⟩; (connettere) connect; **legarsela al dito** *fig* bear a grudge [2] *vi* (far lega) get on well

le'garsi *vr* bind oneself; **~ a qualcuno** become attached to somebody

lega'tario, -a *nmf* legatee

le'gato *nm* legacy; Relig legate

lega'tura *nf* tying; (di libro) binding

legazi'one *nf* legation

le'genda *nf* legend, key

'legge *nf* law; (parlamentare) act; **a norma di ~** by law. **legge marziale** martial law

leg'genda *nf* legend; (didascalia) key

leggen'dario *adj* legendary

'leggere *vt/i* read; **~ male** (sbagliato) misread

legge'rezza *nf* lightness; (frivolezza) frivolity; (incostanza) fickleness

legger'mente *adv* slightly

leg'gero *adj* light; ⟨*bevanda*⟩ weak; (lieve) slight; (frivolo) frivolous; (incostante) fickle; **~ come una piuma** [as] light as a feather; **alla leggera** lightly

leggi'adro *adj* liter graceful

leg'gibile *adj* ⟨*scrittura*⟩ legible; ⟨*stile*⟩ readable

leg'gio *nm* lectern; Mus music stand

legife'rare *vi* legislate

legio'nario *nm* legionary

legi'one *nf* legion

legisla'tivo *adj* legislative

legisla'tore *nm* legislator

legisla'tura *nf* legislature

legislazi'one *nf* legislation

legittima'mente *adv* legitimately

legittimità *nf* legitimacy

le'gittimo *adj* legitimate; (giusto) proper; **legittima difesa** self-defence

'legna *nf* firewood

le'gnaia *nf* woodshed

le'gname *nm* timber

le'gnata *nf* blow with a stick

'legno *nm* wood; **di ~** wooden; **legni** *pl* Mus woodwind. **legno compensato** plywood

le'gnoso *adj* woody; (di legno) wooden; ⟨*gambe*⟩ stiff; ⟨*movimento*⟩ wooden

le'gume *nm* pod

'lei *pers pron* (soggetto) she; (oggetto, con prep) her; (forma di cortesia) you; **lo ha fatto ~ stessa** she did it herself

'lembo *nm* edge; (di terra) strip

'lemma *nm* headword

'lemming *nm inv* lemming

'lena *nf* vigour

'lendine *nm* nit

le'nire *vt* soothe

lenta'mente *adv* slowly

'lente *nf* lens. **lente a contatto** contact lens; **mettersi le lenti a contatto** put in one's contact lenses. **lente a contatto morbida** soft lens. **lente a contatto rigida** hard lens. **lente d'ingrandimento** magnifying glass. **lente semi-rigida** gas-permeable lens

len'tezza *nf* slowness

len'ticchia *nf* lentil

len'tiggine *nf* freckle

'lento *adj* slow; (allentato) slack; ⟨*abito*⟩ loose

'lenza *nf* fishing-line

len'zuolo *nm* sheet; **le lenzuola** the sheets. **lenzuolo con gli angoli** fitted sheet. **lenzuolo funebre** shroud

leon'cino *nm* lion cub

le'one *nm* lion; Astr Leo. **leone marino** sea lion

leo'nessa *nf* lioness

leo'pardo *nm* leopard

lepo'rino *adj* **labbro leporino** harelip

'lepre *nf* hare

le'protto *nm* leveret

'lercio *adj* filthy

lerci'ume *nm* filth

'lesbica *nf* lesbian

'lesbico *adj* lesbian

lesi'nare ① *vt* grudge
② *vi* be stingy

lesio'nare *vt* damage

lesi'one *nf* lesion; (danno) damage. **lesione cerebrale** brain damage. **lesione interna** internal injury. **lesioni** *pl* **personali** grievous bodily harm, GBH

'leso ① pp di LEDERE
② *adj* injured; **lesa maestà** high treason

les'sare *vt* boil

lessi'cale *adj* lexical

'lessico *nm* vocabulary

lessicogra'fia *nf* lexicography

lessi'cografo, -a *nmf* lexicographer

'lesso ① *adj* boiled
② *nm* boiled meat

'lesto *adj* quick; ⟨*mente*⟩ sharp. **lesto di mano** light-fingered

le'tale *adj* lethal

leta'maio *nm* dunghill; fig pigsty

le'tame *nm* dung

le'targico *adj* lethargic

le'targo *nm* lethargy; (di animali) hibernation

le'tizia *nf* joy

'lettera *nf* letter; **alla ~** literally; **eseguire qualcosa alla ~** carry out something to the letter; **lettere** *pl* (letteratura) literature *sg*; Univ Arts; **dottore in lettere** BA, Bachelor of Arts. **lettera d'accompagnamento** covering letter. **lettera d'amore** love letter. **lettera assicurata** registered letter. **lettera di cambio** bill of exchange. **lettera di credito** letter of credit. **lettera maiuscola** capital [letter]. **lettera minuscola** small letter. **lettera di presentazione** letter of introduction. **lettera raccomandata** recorded delivery letter. **lettera di scuse** letter of apology. **lettera di trasporto aereo** air waybill

lette'rale *adj* literal

letteral'mente *adv* literally

lette'rario *adj* literary

lette'rato ① *adj* well-read ② *nm* scholar; **letterati** *pl* literati

lettera'tura *nf* literature. **letteratura pulp** pulp fiction

letti'era *nf* (per gatto) litter

let'tiga *nf* stretcher

let'tino *nm* cot; Med couch. **lettino [pieghevole]** camp bed

'letto *nm* bed; andare a ∼ go to bed; [ri]fare il ∼ make the bed. **letto a castello** bunkbed. **letto di fiume** river bed. **letti** *pl* **gemelli** twin beds. **letto matrimoniale** double bed. **letto a una piazza** single bed. **letto a due piazze** double bed. **letto singolo** single bed

Let'tonia *nf* Latvia

letto'rato *nm* (corso) tutorial

let|'tore, -trice ① *nmf* reader; Univ language assistant ② *nm* Comput disk drive. **lettore di CD** CD player, CD system. **lettore [di] CD-ROM** CD-Rom drive. **lettore di codice a barre** barcode reader, scanner. **lettore di compact disc** compact disc player. **lettore di disco** disk drive. **lettore di floppy** floppy [disk] drive. **lettore di minidisc** minidisc player. **lettore di MP3** MP3 player

let'tura *nf* reading

leuce'mia *nf* leukaemia

'leva *nf* lever; Mil call-up; **nuove leve** *pl* new blood, young blood; **far** ∼ lever. **leva del cambio** gear lever. **leva di comando** control lever

le'vante *nm* East; (vento) east wind

leva'punti *nm inv* staple remover

le'vare *vt* (alzare) raise; (togliere) take away; (rimuovere) take off; (estrarre) pull out, lift, abolish ⟨divieto, tassa⟩; ∼ **di mezzo qualcosa** get something out of the way

le'varsi *vr* move (da away from); ⟨vento⟩ get up; ⟨sole⟩ rise; ∼ **di mezzo** get out of the way

le'vata *nf* rising; (di posta) collection

leva'taccia *nf* fare una ∼ get up at the crack of dawn

leva'toio *adj* **ponte levatoio** drawbridge

leva'trice *nf* midwife

leva'tura *nf* intelligence

levi'gare *vt* smooth; (con carta vetro) rub down

levi'gato *adj* ⟨superficie⟩ polished; ⟨pelle⟩ smooth

leviga'trice *nf* sander

levi'tare *vi* levitate

levitazi'one *nf* levitation

Le'vitico *nm* Leviticus

levri'ero *nm* greyhound. **levriero afgano** Afghan hound

lezi'one *nf* lesson; Univ lecture; (rimprovero) rebuke. **lezione di guida** driving lesson. **lezione di italiano** Italian lesson, Italian class

lezi'oso *adj* ⟨stile, modi⟩ affected

'lezzo *nm* stench

li *pers pron mpl* them

li'ana *nf* liana

liba'nese *adj* & *nmf* Lebanese

Li'bano *nm* Lebanon

'libbra *nf* (peso) pound

li'beccio *nm* south-west wind

li'bello *nm* libel

li'bellula *nf* dragon-fly

libe'rale ① *adj* liberal; (generoso) generous ② *nmf* liberal

libera'lismo *nm* liberalismo **[económico]** economic liberalism

liberalità *nf* generosity

liberal'mente *adv* liberally

libe'rare *vt* free; release ⟨prigioniero⟩ vacate ⟨stanza⟩; (salvare) rescue

libe'rarsi *vr* ⟨stanza⟩ become vacant; Teleph become free; (da impegno) get out of it; ∼ **di** get rid of

libera|'tore, -trice ① *adj* liberating ② *nmf* liberator

libera'torio *adj* liberating. **pagamento liberatorio** full and final payment

liberazi'one *nf* liberation; **la Liberazione** (ricorrenza) Liberation Day. **liberazione della donna** women's liberation, women's lib

Li'beria *nf* Liberia

libe'rismo *nm* free trade

'libero *adj* free; ⟨strada⟩ clear; ∼ **come l'aria** free as a bird. **libero arbitrio** *nm* free will. **libero docente** *nm* qualified university lecturer. **libero professionista** *nm* self-employed person

libertà *nf* freedom; (di prigioniero) release; ∼ *pl* (confidenze) liberties; **prendersi la** ∼ **di fare qualcosa** take the liberty of doing something. **libertà di espressione** freedom of speech. **libertà di parola** free speech. **libertà di pensiero** freedom of thought. **libertà provvisoria** Jur bail. **libertà di stampa** freedom of the press. **libertà vigilata** probation

liber'tino, -a ① *adj* dissolute, libertine ② *nmf* libertine

'liberty *nm* & *adj inv* Art Nouveau

'Libia *nf* Libya

'libico, **-a** adj & nmf Libyan

li'bidine nf lust

libidi'noso adj lustful

li'bido nf libido

libra'io nm bookseller

libre'ria nf (negozio) bookshop; (mobile) bookcase

li'bretto nm booklet; Mus libretto. **libretto degli assegni** cheque book. **libretto di circolazione** logbook. **libretto d'istruzioni** instruction booklet. **libretto di risparmio** savings account; (documento) passbook, savings book. **libretto universitario** book held by students which records details of their exam performances

'libro nm book. **libro bianco** White Paper. **libro dei canti** hymn-book. **libro contabile** account book. **libro degli esercizi** workbook. **libro giallo** crime novel. **libro mastro** Comm ledger. **libro paga** payroll. **libro di ricette** cookbook, recipe book; **libri** pl **sociali** company's books. **libro tascabile** paperback. **libro di testo** course book

li'cantropo nm werewolf

lice'ale ⓵ nmf secondary-school student ⓶ adj secondary-school attrib

li'cenza nf licence; (permesso) permission; Mil leave; Sch school-leaving certificate; **essere in** ∼ be on leave. **licenza di caccia** hunting licence. **licenza di esportazione** export licence. **licenza matrimoniale** marriage licence. **licenza di pesca** fishing licence. **licenza poetica** poetic licence. **licenza di porto d'armi** gun licence

licenzia'mento nm dismissal, lay-off

licenzi'are vt dismiss, sack fam; (conferire un diploma) grant a school-leaving certificate to

licenzi'arsi vr (da un impiego) resign; (accomiatarsi) take one's leave

licenzi'oso adj licentious

li'ceo nm secondary school, high school. **liceo classico** secondary school with an emphasis on humanities. **liceo scientifico** secondary school with an emphasis on sciences

li'chene nm lichen

'lido nm beach

'Liechtenstein nm Liechtenstein

lieta'mente adv happily

li'eto adj glad; (evento) happy; **molto** ∼! pleased to meet you!. **lieto fine** happy ending

li'eve adj light; (debole) faint; (trascurabile) slight

lievi'tare ⓵ vi rise ⓶ vt leaven

li'evito nm yeast. **lievito in polvere** baking powder

lift nm inv liftboy

'lifting nm inv face-lift

'ligio adj **essere** ∼ **al dovere** have a sense of duty

li'gnaggio nm lineage

'ligneo adj wooden

'lilla nm (colore) lilac

lillà nm Bot lilac

'lima nf file

limacci'oso adj slimy

li'manda nf dab

li'mare vt file

lima'tura nf (atto) filing; (residui) filings pl

'limbo nm limbo

li'metta nf **limetta [da unghie]** nail file; (di carta) emery board

limi'tare ⓵ nm threshold ⓶ vt limit

limi'tarsi vr ∼ **a fare qualcosa** restrict oneself to doing something; ∼ **in qualcosa** cut down on something

limitata'mente adv to a limited extent

limita'tivo adj limiting

limi'tato adj limited

limitazi'one nf limitation

'limite ⓵ adj (caso) extreme ⓶ nm limit; (confine) boundary; **entro certi limiti** within certain limits. **limite di credito** credit limit, credit ceiling. **limite di sopportazione** breaking point. **'limite di sosta'** 'restricted parking'. **limite di tempo** time limit. **limite di velocità** speed limit; **rispettare il** ∼ **di velocità** keep to the speed limit

li'mitrofo adj neighbouring

'limo nm slime

limo'nata nf (bibita) lemonade; (succo) lemon juice. **limonata amara** bitter lemon

li'mone nm lemon; (albero) lemon tree

'limpido adj clear; (occhi) limpid

'lince nf lynx

linci'are vt lynch

'lindo adj neat; (pulito) clean

'linea nf line; (di autobus, aereo) route; (di metropolitana) line; (di abito) cut; (di auto, mobile) design; (fisico) figure; **in** ∼ **d'aria** as the crow flies; **è caduta la** ∼ I've been cut off; **in** ∼ **di massima** as a rule; **a grandi linee** in outline; **mantenere la** ∼ keep one's figure; **in** ∼ Comput on-line; **in prima** ∼ in the front line; **mettersi in** ∼ line up. **nave di linea** liner; **volo di linea** scheduled flight. **linea aerea** airline. **linea d'arrivo** Sport finishing line. **linea commutata** Teleph switched line. **linea di confine** boundary. **linea continua** unbroken line. **linea dedicata** dedicated line. **linea di demarcazione** border line. **linea ferroviaria** railway line. **linea di fondo** baseline. **linea**

d'immersione water line. **linea laterale** Sport touch line. **linee** *pl* **della mano** lines of the hand. **linea di marea** tidemark. **linea mediana** Sport halfway line. **linea di partenza** Sport starting line. **linea principale** Rail main line. **linea punteggiata** dotted line. **linea secondaria** Rail branch line. **linea di tiro** line of fire. **linea tratteggiata** broken line

linea'menti *nmpl* features

line'are *adj* linear; ⟨*discorso*⟩ to the point; ⟨*ragionamento*⟩ consistent

line'etta *nf* (tratto lungo) dash; (d'unione) hyphen

'linfa *nf* Anat lymph; Bot sap. **linfa vitale** fig life blood

lin'fatico *adj* Anat lymphatic

linfoghi'andola *nf* lymph gland

linfo'nodo *nm* lymph node

linge'rie *nf* lingerie

lin'gotto *nm* ingot

'lingua *nf* tongue; (linguaggio) language; **avere la ~ lunga** fig have a big mouth. **lingua d'arrivo** target language. **lingua moderna** modern language. **lingua morta** dead language. **lingua di partenza** source language. **lingua straniera** foreign language

lingu'accia *nf* (persona) backbiter; **fare le linguacce** put one's tongue out (**a** at)

lingu'aggio *nm* language. **linguaggio infantile** baby-talk. **linguaggio per la marcatura di ipertesti** Comput hypertext markup language. **linguaggio dei segni** sign language

lingu'etta *nf* (di scarpa) tongue; (di busta) flap; Mus reed; (da tirare) tab

lingu'ista *nmf* linguist

lingu'istica *nf* linguistics

lingu'istico *adj* linguistic

'lino *nm* Bot flax; (tessuto) linen

li'noleum *nm* linoleum

liofiliz'zare *vt* freeze-dry

liofiliz'zato *adj* freeze dried

li'pide *nm* lipid

liposuzi'one *nf* liposuction

li'quame *nm* slurry

lique'fare *vt* liquefy; (sciogliere) melt

lique'farsi *vr* liquefy; (sciogliersi) melt

liqui'dare *vt* liquidate; settle ⟨*conto*⟩; pay off ⟨*debiti*⟩; clear ⟨*merce*⟩; (fam: uccidere) get rid of

liquida'tore *nm* liquidator

liquidazi'one *nf* liquidation; (di conti) settling; (di merce) clearance sale. **liquidazione totale [per cessata attività]** closing-down sale

'liquido *adj* & *nm* liquid. **liquido dei freni** brake fluid. **liquido scongelante** Auto de-icer. **liquido tergicristallo** screen wash

liqui'gas® *nm* Calor gas®

liqui'rizia *nf* liquorice

li'quore *nm* liqueur; **liquori** *pl* (superalcolici) liquors

'lira *nf* (ex moneta italiana) lira; (moneta di vari paesi) pound; Mus lyre. **lira sterlina** pound sterling

'lirico, -a ① *adj* lyrical; ⟨*poesia*⟩ lyric; ⟨*cantante, musica*⟩ opera *attrib* ② *nf* lyric poetry; Mus opera

li'rismo *nm* lyricism

'lisca *nf* fishbone; **avere la ~** (fam: nel parlare) have a lisp

lisci'are *vt* smooth; (accarezzare) stroke

'liscio *adj* smooth; ⟨*capelli*⟩ straight; ⟨*liquore*⟩ neat, straight; ⟨*acqua minerale*⟩ still; **passarla liscia** get away with it

li'seuse *nf inv* bed jacket

'liso *adj* worn [out]

'lista *nf* list; (striscia) strip; **fare una ~** make out a list. **lista di attesa** waiting list; **in ~ di attesa** on the waiting list; Aeron on stand-by. **lista elettorale** list of candidates. **lista degli invitati** guest list. **lista nera** blacklist. **lista di nozze** wedding list. **lista della spesa** shopping list. **lista dei vini** wine list

li'stare *vt* edge; Comput list

li'stino *nm* list. **listino di borsa** Stock-Exchange list. **listino dei cambi** exchange rates *pl*. **listino [dei] prezzi** price list

Lit. *abbr* (**lire italiane**) Italian lire

lita'nia *nf* litany

'litchi *nm inv* lychee

'lite *nf* quarrel; (baruffa) row; Jur lawsuit

liti'gante *nmf* Jur litigant

liti'gare *vi* quarrel; Jur litigate

li'tigio *nm* quarrel

litigi'oso *adj* quarrelsome

'litio *nm* lithium

litogra'fia *nf* (procedimento) lithography; (stampa) lithograph

li'tografo, -a *nmf* lithographer

lito'rale ① *adj* coastal ② *nm* coast

lito'raneo *adj* coastal

'litro *nm* litre

Litu'ania *nf* Lithuania

litu'ano, -a *adj* & *nmf* Lithuanian

litur'gia *nf* liturgy

li'turgico *adj* liturgical

li'uto *nm* lute

li'vella *nf* level. **livella a bolla d'aria** spirit level

livella'mento *nm* levelling out, levelling off

livel'lare *vt* level

livel'larsi *vr* level out

livella'tore *adj* levelling

livella'trice *nf* bulldozer

li'vello *nm* level; **passaggio a livello** level crossing; **sotto/sul** ∼ **del mare** below/above sea level; **ad alto** ∼ ⟨*conferenza, trattative*⟩ top-level, high-level; **a più livelli** multilevel. **livello di guardia** danger level. **livello di magazzino** stock level. **livello occupazionale** level of employment

'livido ① *adj* livid; (per il freddo) blue; (per una botta) black and blue. **livido di rabbia** livid
② *nm* bruise

li'vore *nm* spite

Li'vorno *nf* Leghorn

li'vrea *nf* livery

'lizza *nf* lists *pl*; **essere in** ∼ **per qualcosa** be in the running for something

lo ① *def art m* (*before s + consonant, gn, ps, z*) the; ▸ IL
② *pron* (riferito a persona) him; (riferito a cosa) it; **non lo so** I don't know

'lobbia *nf* Homburg [hat]

lob'bismo *nm* lobbying

lob'bista *nmf* lobbyist

'lobby *nf inv* lobby

lo'belia *nf* lobelia

'lobo *nm* lobe

loboto'mia *nf* lobotomy

lo'cale ① *adj* local
② *nm* (stanza) room; (treno) local train; **locali** *pl* (edifici) premises. **locale notturno** nightclub

località *nf* locality. **località balneare** seaside resort. **località turistica** tourist resort. **località di villeggiatura** holiday resort

localiz'zare *vt* localize; (reperire) locate

localiz'zarsi *vr* ∼ **in** be located in

localiz'zato *adj* localized

localizzazi'one *nf* localization; (reperimento) location

local'mente *adv* locally

lo'canda *nf* inn

locandi'ere, -a *nmf* innkeeper

locan'dina *nf* bill, poster

loca'tario, -a *nmf* tenant. **locatario residente** sitting tenant

loca'tivo *adj* Gram locative; Jur rental

loca'tore, -trice ① *nm* landlord
② *nf* landlady

locazi'one *nf* tenancy

locomo'tiva *nf* locomotive. **locomotiva a vapore** steam engine

locomo'tore *nm* locomotive, engine

locomozi'one *nf* locomotion; **mezzi di locomozione** means of transport

'loculo *nm* burial niche

lo'custa *nf* locust

locuzi'one *nf* expression

lo'dare *vt* praise

'lode *nf* praise; **degno di lode** praiseworthy; **laurea con lode** first-class degree

'loden *nm inv* (cappotto) loden [coat]; (stoffa) loden

lo'devole *adj* praiseworthy

'lodola *nf* lark

loga'ritmo *nm* logarithm

'loggia *nf* loggia; (massonica) lodge

loggi'one *nm* gallery, gods *pl*

'logica *nf* logic

logica'mente *adv* (in modo logico) logically; (ovviamente) of course

logicità *nf* logic

'logico *adj* logical

lo'gistica *nf* logistics

lo'gistico *adj* logistic[al]

'logo *nm inv* logo

logope'dia *nf* speech therapy

logope'dista *nmf* speech therapist

logo'rante *adj* ⟨*attesa, esperienza*⟩ wearing

logo'rare *vt* wear out; (sciupare) waste

logo'rarsi *vr* wear out; ⟨*persona*⟩ wear oneself out

logo'rio *nm* wear and tear; (stress) stress

'logoro *adj* worn-out

logor'roico *adj* loquacious

lom'baggine *nf* lumbago

Lombar'dia *nf* Lombardy

lom'bardo *adj* Lombardy *attrib*

lom'bare *adj* lumbar

lom'bata *nf* loin. **lombata di manzo** sirloin

'lombo *nm* Anat loin

lom'brico *nm* earthworm

londi'nese ① *adj* London *attrib*
② *nmf* Londoner

'Londra *nf* London

long-'drink *nm inv* long drink

longevità *nf* longevity

lon'gevo *adj* long-lived

longhe'rone *nm* strut

longi'lineo *adj* rangy

longitudi'nale *adj* lengthwise

longitudinal'mente *adv* lengthwise

longi'tudine *nf* longitude

long 'playing *nm inv* LP, long-playing record

lontana'mente *adv* distantly; (vagamente) vaguely; **neanche** ∼ not for a moment

lonta'nanza *nf* distance; (separazione) separation; **in** ~ in the distance

lon'tano ① *adj* far; (distante) distant; (nel tempo) far-off, distant; ⟨parente⟩ distant; (vago) vague; (assente) absent; **più** ~ further; **è** ~ **un paio di chilometri** it is a couple of kilometres away
   ② *adv* far [away]; **da** ~ from a distance; **tenersi** ~ **da** keep away from; **andare** ~ (allontanarsi) go away; (avere successo) go far

'lontra *nf* otter

'lonza *nf* (lombata) loin

lo'quace *adj* talkative

'lordo *adj* dirty; ⟨somma, peso⟩ gross; **al** ~ **di imposte** pre-tax

'loro¹ *pers pron pl* (soggetto) they; (oggetto) them; (forma di cortesia) you; **sta a** ~ it is up to them

'loro² ① (**il** ~ *m*, **la** ~ *f*, **i** ~ *mpl*, **le** ~ *fpl*) *poss adj* their; (forma di cortesia) your; **un** ~ **amico** a friend of theirs; (forma di cortesia) a friend of yours
   ② *poss pron* theirs; (forma di cortesia) yours; **i** ~ (famiglia) their folk

lo'sanga *nf* lozenge; **a losanghe** diamond-shaped

losca'mente *adv* suspiciously

'losco *adj* suspicious

'loto *nm* lotus

'lotta *nf* fight, struggle; (contrasto) conflict; Sport wrestling. **lotta di classe** class struggle. **lotta libera** all-in wrestling

lot'tare *vi* fight, struggle; Sport, fig wrestle

lotta|'tore, -trice *nmf* wrestler

lotte'ria *nf* lottery. **Lotteria di Stato** National Lottery

lottiz'zare *vt* divide up ⟨terreno⟩; fig parcel out

lottizzazi'one *nf* (di terreno) division into lots; fig parcelling out

'lotto *nm* [state] lottery; (porzione) lot; (di terreno) plot

lozi'one *nf* lotion. **lozione idratante** moisturizer. **lozione solare** suntan lotion

lubrifi'cante ① *adj* lubricating
   ② *nm* lubricant

lubrifi'care *vt* lubricate

luc'chetto *nm* padlock

lucci'cante *adj* sparkling

lucci'care *vi* sparkle

lucci'chio *nm* sparkle

lucci'cone *nm* **far venire i lucciconi** bring tears to the eyes

'luccio *nm* pike

'lucciola *nf* glow-worm; (fam: prostituta) lady of the night

'luce *nf* light; Auto highlight; **accendere/ spegnere la** ~ switch the light on/off; **far** ~ **su** fig shed light on; **dare alla** ~ give birth to; **venire alla** ~ come to light; **luci** *pl* **di arresto** Auto stop lights; **luci** *pl* **d'atterraggio** landing lights; **luci** *pl* **d'emergenza** Auto hazard [warning] lights, hazards. **luce della luna** moonlight; **luci** *pl* **di posizione** Auto sidelights; **luci** *pl* **posteriori** Auto rear-lights; **luci** *pl* **di retromarcia** Auto reversing lights. **luce del sole** sunlight. **luce stroboscopica** strobe

lu'cente *adj* shining

lucen'tezza *nf* shine

lucer'nario *nm* skylight

lu'certola *nf* lizard

lucida'labbra *nm inv* lip gloss

luci'dare *vt* polish

lucida'trice *nf* [floor-]polisher

'lucido ① *adj* shiny; ⟨pavimento, scarpe⟩ polished; (chiaro) clear; ⟨persona, mente⟩ lucid; ⟨occhi⟩ watery
   ② *nm* shine. **lucido [da scarpe]** [shoe] polish

lucra'tivo *adj* lucrative

'lucro *nm* lucre; **senza fini di** ~ non-profit-making, not-for-profit Am

luculli'ano *adj* ⟨pranzo⟩ lavish

ludo'teca *nf* playroom

'luglio *nm* July

'lugubre *adj* gloomy

'lui *pers pron* (soggetto) he; (oggetto, con prep) him; **lo ha fatto** ~ **stesso** he did it himself

lu'maca *nf* (mollusco) snail; fig slowcoach

'lume *nm* lamp; (luce) light; **a** ~ **di candela** by candlelight; **perdere il** ~ **della ragione** be beside oneself with rage

lumi'nare *nmf* luminary

lumi'narie *nfpl* illuminations

lumine'scente *adj* luminescent

lumine'scenza *nf* luminescence

lu'mino *nm* **lumino da notte** nightlight

luminosa'mente *adv* luminously

luminosità *nf* brightness

lumi'noso *adj* luminous; ⟨stanza, cielo ecc⟩ bright; **idea luminosa** brain wave

'luna *nf* moon; **chiaro di luna** moonlight; **avere la** ~ **storta** be in a bad mood. **luna di miele** honeymoon. **luna piena** full moon

'luna park *nm inv* fairground

lu'nare *adj* lunar

lu'naria *nf* moonstone

lu'nario *nm* almanac; **sbarcare il** ~ make [both] ends meet

lu'natico *adj* moody

lunedì *nm inv* Monday; **di** ~ on Mondays

lu'netta *nf* half-moon [shape]

lun'gaggine *nf* slowness

lunga'mente *adv* at great length

lun'ghezza *nf* length; di ∼ media medium-length. **lunghezza d'onda** wavelength

'lungi *adv* ero [ben] ∼ dall'immaginare che... I never dreamt for a moment that...

lungimi'rante *adj* far-seeing

lungimi'ranza *nf* far-sightedness

'lungo ① *adj* long; (diluito) weak; (lento) slow; a ∼ andare in the long run; saperla lunga be shrewd; andare per le lunghe drag on; di gran lunga by far; di lunga data long-term ② *nm* length ③ *prep* (durante) throughout; (per la lunghezza di) along

lungofi'ume *nm* riverside

lungo'lago *nm* lakeside

lungo'mare *nm* seafront

lungome'traggio *nm* feature film

lu'notto *nm* rear window. **lunotto termico** heated rear window

'lunula *nf* half-moon

lu'ogo *nm* place; (punto preciso) spot; (passo d'autore) passage; aver ∼ take place; dar ∼ a give rise to; fuori ∼ out of place; del ∼ ⟨usanze⟩ local. **luogo comune** cliché. **luogo di nascita** birthplace. **luogo natale** birthplace. **luogo pubblico** public place. **luogo di villeggiatura** holiday resort

luogote'nente *nm* Mil lieutenant

'lupa *nf* she-wolf

lu'para *nf* sawn-off shotgun

lu'petto *nm* Cub [Scout]

'lupo *nm* wolf. **lupo mannaro** werewolf

'luppolo *nm* hop

'lurido *adj* filthy

luri'dume *nm* filth

lu'singa *nf* flattery

lusin'gare *vt* flatter

lusin'garsi *vr* flatter oneself; (illudersi) fool oneself

lusinghi'ero *adj* flattering

lus'sare *vt* dislocate

lus'sarsi *vr* dislocate

lussazi'one *nf* dislocation

Lussem'burgo *nm* Luxembourg

'lusso *nm* luxury; di ∼ luxury *attrib*

lussuosa'mente *adv* luxuriously

lussu'oso *adj* luxurious

lussureggi'ante *adj* luxuriant

lus'suria *nf* lust

lussuri'oso *adj* dissolute

lu'strare *vt* polish

lu'strino *nm* sequin

'lustro ① *adj* shiny ② *nm* sheen; fig prestige; (quinquennio) five-year period

lute'rano *adj & nmf* Lutheran

'lutto *nm* mourning; parato a ∼ draped in black. **lutto stretto** deep mourning

luttu'oso *adj* mournful

Mm

m *abbr* (**metro**) m

ma *conj* but; (eppure) yet; ma! (dubbio) I don't know; (indignazione) really!; ma davvero? really?; ma va'? really?; ma sì! why not!; (certo che sì) of course!

'macabro *adj* macabre

macché *int* of course not!

macche'roni *nmpl* macaroni *sg*

macche'ronico *adj* ⟨italiano⟩ broken

'macchia¹ *nf* stain; (di diverso colore) spot; (piccola) speck; senza ∼ spotless; spargersi a ∼ d'olio spread rapidly. **macchia di colore** splash of colour. **macchia d'inchiostro** ink stain. **macchia di sangue** bloodstain

'macchia² *nf* (boscaglia) scrub; darsi alla ∼ take to the woods

macchi'are *vt* stain

macchi'arsi *vr* stain

macchi'ato ① *adj* ⟨caffè⟩ with a dash of milk; ⟨pelo⟩ spotted; ∼ di (sporco) stained with; ∼ d'inchiostro ink-stained, inky. ② *nm* (caffè) espresso with a dash of milk

macchi'etta *nf* spot

'macchina *nf* machine; (motore) engine; (automobile) car; in ∼ by car; giro in ∼ drive; cimitero delle macchine scrapyard. **macchina del caffè** coffee-maker. **macchina da cucire** sewing machine. **macchina per l'espresso** coffee machine. **macchina fotografica** camera. **macchina fototessere** photo booth. **macchina obliteratrice** ticket-stamping machine. **macchina da presa** cine camera. **macchina da scrivere** typewriter. **macchina sverniciante** paint stripper. **macchina utensile** machine tool. **macchina della verità** lie detector

macchinal'mente *adv* mechanically

macchi'nare *vt* plot

macchi'nario *nm* machinery

macchinazi'oni *nfpl* machinations, scheming

macchi'netta *nf* (per i denti) brace; (per il caffè) espresso coffee maker; (accendino) lighter

macchi'nista *nm* Rail engine driver; Naut engineer; Theat stagehand

macchi'noso *adj* complicated

Mace'donia *nf* Macedonia

mace'donia *nf* fruit salad

macel'laio, -a *nmf* butcher

macel'lare *vt* slaughter

macellazi'one *nf* slaughtering

macelle'ria *nf* butcher's [shop]

ma'cello *nm* (mattatoio) slaughterhouse; fig shambles *sg*; **andare al** ∼ fig go to the slaughter; **mandare al** ∼ fig send to his/her death

mace'rare *vt* macerate; fig distress

mace'rarsi *vr* be consumed

macerazi'one *nf* maceration

ma'cerie *nfpl* rubble *sg*; (rottami) debris *sg*

'**macero** *nm* pulping; (stabilimento) pulping mill

mach *nm inv* Mach

ma'chete *nm inv* machete

machia'vellico *adj* Machiavellian

ma'chismo *nm* machismo

'**macho** *adj inv* macho

ma'cigno *nm* boulder

maci'lento *adj* emaciated

'**macina** *nf* millstone

macinacaffè *nm inv* coffee mill

macina'pepe *nm inv* pepper mill

maci'nare *vt* mill

maci'nato ① *adj* ground ② *nm* (carne) mince

maci'nino *nm* mill; (hum: macchina) old banger

maciul'lare *vt* (stritolare) crush

'**macro** *nf inv* Comput macro

macrobi'otica *nf* **negozio di macrobiotica** health-food shop

macrobi'otico *adj* macrobiotic

macro'clima *nm* macroclimate

macro'cosmo *nm* macrocosm

macrofotogra'fia *nf* macrophotography

macro'scopico *adj* macroscopic

macu'lato *adj* spotted

Madaga'scar *nm* Madagascar

madami'gella *nf* young lady

'**madia** *nf* cupboard with a covered trough on top for making bread

'**madido** *adj* ∼ **di** damp with ⟨sudore⟩

Ma'donna *nf* Our Lady

mador'nale *adj* gross

'**madre** *nf* mother. **madre biologica** birth mother. **madre single** single mother

madre'lingua *adj inv* **inglese madrelingua** English native speaker

madre'patria *nf* native land

madre'perla *nf* mother-of-pearl

ma'drepora *nf* madrepore

madri'gale *nm* madrigal

ma'drina *nf* godmother

maestà *nf* majesty

maestosa'mente *adv* majestically

maestosità *nf* majesty

mae'stoso *adj* majestic

ma'estra *nf* teacher; Sch primary school teacher. **maestra d'asilo** kindergarten teacher. **maestra di canto** singing teacher. **maestra di piano** piano teacher. **maestra di sci** ski instructor

mae'strale *nm* northwest wind

mae'stranza *nf* workers *pl*

mae'stria *nf* mastery

ma'estro ① *nm* teacher; Sch primary school teacher; Mus maestro; (esperto) master; **colpo da maestro** masterstroke. **maestro d'asilo** kindergarten teacher. **maestro di canto** singing teacher. **maestro di cerimonie** master of ceremonies. **maestro di piano** piano teacher. **maestro di sci** ski instructor ② *adj* (principale) main; (di grande abilità) skilful

'**mafia** *nf* Mafia

mafi'oso ① *adj* of the Mafia ② *nm* member of the Mafia, Mafioso

'**maga** *nf* sorceress, magician

ma'gagna *nf* fault

ma'gari ① *adv* (forse) maybe ② *int* I wish! ③ *conj* (per esprimere desiderio) if only; (anche se) even if

magazzini'ere *nm* storeman, warehouseman

magaz'zino *nm* (deposito) warehouse; (in negozio) stockroom; (emporio) shop; **grande magazzino** department store. **magazzini** *pl* **portuali** naval stores

Magg. *abbr* (**maggiore**) Maj

mag'gese *nm* field lying fallow

'**maggio** *nm* May

maggio'lino *nm* May bug

maggio'rana *nf* marjoram

maggio'ranza *nf* majority

maggio'rare *vt* increase

maggior'domo *nm* butler

maggi'ore ① *adj* (di dimensioni, numero) bigger, larger; (superlativo) biggest, largest; ⋯⟶

(di età) older; (superlativo) oldest; (di importanza, Mus) major; (superlativo) greatest; **la maggior parte di** most; **la maggior parte del tempo** most of the time

2▸ *pron* (di dimensioni) the bigger, the larger; (superlativo) the biggest, the largest; (di età) the older; (superlativo) the oldest; (di importanza) the major; (superlativo) the greatest

3▸ *nm* Mil major; Aeron squadron leader

maggio'renne 1▸ *adj* of age
2▸ *nmf* adult

maggiori'tario *adj* (della maggioranza) majority; ⟨*sistema*⟩ first-past-the-post *attrib*

maggior'mente *adv* [all] the more; (più di tutto) most

'**Magi** *nmpl* **i re** ∼ the Magi

ma'gia *nf* magic; (trucco) magic trick

magica'mente *adv* magically

'**magico** *adj* magic

magi'stero *nm* (insegnamento) teaching; (maestria) skill; **facoltà di magistero** arts faculty

magi'strale *adj* masterly; **istituto magistrale** teacher-training college

magistral'mente *adv* in a masterly fashion

magi'strato *nm* magistrate

magistra'tura *nf* magistrature; **la** ∼ the Bench

'**maglia** *nf* stitch; (lavoro ai ferri) knitting; (tessuto) jersey; (di rete) mesh; (indumento intimo) vest; (esterno) top; (di calciatore) shirt; **fare la** ∼ knit. **maglia con cappuccio** fam hoody. **maglia diritta** knit. **maglia rosa** (ciclismo) ≈ yellow jersey. **maglia rovescia** purl

magli'aia *nf* knitter

maglie'ria *nf* knitwear

magli'etta *nf* **maglietta [a maniche corte]** tee-shirt

magli'ficio *nm* knitwear factory

ma'glina *nf* (tessuto) jersey

'**maglio** *nm* mallet

magli'one *nm* sweater, jumper. **maglione dolcevita** polo neck [jumper]. **maglione a girocollo** crew neck [sweater]. **maglione a V** V-neck [sweater]

'**magma** *nm* magma

ma'gnaccia *nm inv* fam pimp

ma'gnanimo *adj* magnanimous

ma'gnate *nm* magnate

ma'gnesia *nf* magnesia

ma'gnesio *nm* magnesium

ma'gnete *nm* magnet

magnetica'mente *adv* magnetically

ma'gnetico *adj* magnetic

magne'tismo *nm* magnetism

magne'tofono *nm* tape recorder

magnifica'mente *adv* magnificently

magnifi'cenza *nf* magnificence; (generosità) munificence

ma'gnifico *adj* magnificent; (generoso) munificent

magni'tudine *nf* Astr magnitude

'**magno** *adj* **aula magna** main hall

ma'gnolia *nf* magnolia

'**magnum** *nf inv* (bottiglia, pistola) magnum

'**mago** *nm* magician

ma'gone *nm* **avere il** ∼ be down; **mi è venuto il** ∼ I've got a lump in my throat

'**magra** *nf* low water

ma'grezza *nf* thinness

'**magro** *adj* thin; ⟨*carne*⟩ lean; (scarso) meagre; **magra consolazione** cold comfort

'**mai** *adv* never; (interrogativo, talvolta) ever; **caso** ∼ if anything; **caso** ∼ **tornasse** in case he comes back; **come** ∼? why?; **cosa** ∼? what on earth?; ∼ **più** never again; **più che** ∼ more than ever; **quando** ∼? whenever?; **quasi** ∼ hardly ever

mai'ale *nm* pig; (carne) pork. **maiale arrosto** roast pork

maia'lino *nm* piglet

'**mailing** *nm* direct mail, mailing

mai'olica *nf* majolica

maio'nese *nf* mayonnaise

'**mais** *nm* maize

mai'uscola *nf* capital [letter]; **bloc maiusc** (tasto) caps lock

mai'uscolo *adj* capital

mai'zena® *nf* cornflour

mal ▸ MALE

'**mala** *nf sl* **la** ∼ the underworld

malac'corto *adj* unwise

mala'fede *nf* bad faith

malaf'fare *nm* **gente di malaffare** shady characters *pl*

mala'llngua *nf* backbiter

mala'mente *adv* ⟨*ridotto*⟩ badly; ⟨*rispondere*⟩ rudely

malan'dato *adj* in bad shape; (di salute) in poor health

ma'lanimo *nm* ill will

ma'lanno *nm* misfortune; (malattia) illness; **prendersi un** ∼ catch something

mala'pena *adv* **a** ∼ hardly

ma'laria *nf* malaria

mala'ticcio *adj* sickly

ma'lato, -a 1▸ *adj* ill, sick; ⟨*pianta*⟩ diseased
2▸ *nmf* sick person. **malato di Aids** AIDS sufferer. **malato di cancro** cancer patient. **malato di mente** mentally ill person

malat'tia *nf* disease, illness; **ho preso due giorni di** ∼ I had two days off sick;

essere in ∼ be on sick leave. **malattia nervosa** nervous disease. **malattia venerea** venereal disease, VD

malaugurata'mente *adv* unfortunately

malaugu'rato *adj* ill-omened

malau'gurio *nm* bad *or* ill omen

mala'vita *nf* underworld

malavi'toso, -a *nmf* gangster

mala'voglia *nf* unwillingness; **di** ∼ unwillingly

Ma'lawi *nm* Malawi

malcapi'tato *adj* wretched

malce'lato *adj* ill-concealed

mal'concio *adj* battered

malcon'tento *nm* discontent

malco'stume *nm* immorality

mal'destro *adj* awkward; (inesperto) inexperienced

maldi'cente *adj* slanderous

maldi'cenza *nf* slander

maldi'sposto *adj* ill-disposed

Mal'dive *nfpl* Maldives

'male ① *adv* badly; **funzionare** ∼ not work properly; **star** ∼ be ill; **star** ∼ **a qualcuno** ‹vestito ecc› not suit somebody; **rimanerci** ∼ be hurt; **ho dormito** ∼ I didn't sleep well; **non c'è** ∼! not bad at all!
② *nm* evil; (dolore) pain, ache; (malattia) illness; (danno) harm; **distinguere il bene dal** ∼ know right from wrong; **andare a** ∼ go off; **aver** ∼ **a** have a pain in; **dove hai** ∼? where does it hurt?, where is the pain?; **far** ∼ **a qualcuno** (provocare dolore) hurt somebody; ‹cibo› be bad for somebody; **le cipolle mi fanno** ∼ onions don't agree with me; **mi fa** ∼ **la schiena** my back is hurting; **farsi** ∼ **alla schiena** hurt one's back. **mal d'aereo** airsickness. **mal d'aria** airsickness; **soffrire il mal d'aria** be airsick. **mal d'auto** carsickness. **mal di denti** toothache. **mal di gola** sore throat. **mal di mare** seasickness; **avere il mal di mare** be seasick. **mal d'orecchi** earache. **mal di pancia** stomach-ache. **mal di schiena** backache. **mal di testa** headache

maledetta'mente *adv* flipping

male'detto *adj* cursed; (orribile) awful

male'dire *vt* curse

maledizi'one *nf* curse; ∼! damn!

maleducata'mente *adv* rudely

maledu'cato *adj* ill-mannered

maleducazi'one *nf* rudeness

male'fatta *nf* misdeed

male'ficio *nm* witchcraft

ma'lefico *adj* ‹azione› evil; (nocivo) harmful

maleodo'rante *adj* foul-smelling

ma'lese *adj & nmf* Malaysian

Ma'lesia *nf* Malaysia

ma'lessere *nm* indisposition; fig uneasiness

ma'levolo *adj* malevolent

malfa'mato *adj* of ill repute

mal'fatto *adj* badly done; (malformato) ill-shaped

malfat'tore *nm* wrongdoer

mal'fermo *adj* unsteady; ‹salute› poor

malfor'mato *adj* misshapen

malformazi'one *nf* malformation

mal'gascio, -a *adj & nmf* Malagasy

malgo'verno *nm* misgovernment

mal'grado ① *prep* in spite of
② *conj* although

'Mali *nm* Mali

ma'lia *nf* spell

maligna'mente *adv* maliciously

mali'gnare *vi* malign

malignità *nf inv* malice; Med malignancy

ma'ligno *adj* malicious; (perfido) evil; Med malignant

malinco'nia *nf* melancholy

malinconica'mente *adv* melancholically

malin'conico *adj* melancholy

malincu'ore: a ∼ *adv* unwillingly, reluctantly

malinfor'mato *adj* misinformed

malintenzio'nato, -a *nmf* miscreant

malin'teso ① *adj* mistaken
② *nm* misunderstanding

ma'lizia *nf* malice; (astuzia) cunning; (espediente) trick

maliziosa'mente *adv* mischievously, naughtily

maliziosità *nf* naughtiness

malizi'oso *adj* (birichino) mischievous, naughty

malle'abile *adj* malleable

mal'leolo *nm* Anat malleolus

malleva'dore *nm* guarantor

'mallo *nm* husk

mal'loppo *nm* fam loot

malme'nare *vt* ill-treat

mal'messo *adj* (vestito male) shabbily dressed; ‹casa› poorly furnished; (fig: senza soldi) hard up

malnu'trito *adj* undernourished

malnutrizi'one *nf* malnutrition

'malo *adj* in ∼ **modo** badly

ma'locchio *nm* evil eye

ma'lora *nf* ruin; **della** ∼ awful; **andare in** ∼ go to ruin

ma'lore *nm* illness; **essere colto da** ∼ be suddenly taken ill

malri'dotto *adj* ⟨persona⟩ in a sorry state; ⟨auto, casa⟩ dilapidated, in a sorry state

mal'sano *adj* unhealthy

malsi'curo *adj* unsafe; (incerto) uncertain

'malta *nf* mortar

mal'tempo *nm* bad weather

mal'tese *adj & nmf* Maltese

'malto *nm* malt

mal'tosio *nm* maltose

maltratta'mento *nm* ill-treatment

maltrat'tare *vt* ill-treat

malu'more *nm* bad mood; **di** ∼ in a bad mood

'malva *adj inv* mauve

mal'vagio *adj* wicked

malvagità *nf inv* wickedness

malva'sia *nf* type of dessert wine

malversazi'one *nf* embezzlement

mal'visto *adj* unpopular (**da** with)

malvi'vente *nm* criminal

malvolenti'eri *adv* unwillingly

malvo'lere *vt* **farsi** ∼ make oneself unpopular; **prendere qualcuno a** ∼ take a dislike to somebody

'mamma *nf* mummy, mum; ∼ **mia!** good gracious!

mam'mario *adj* mammary

mam'mella *nf* breast

mam'mifero *nm* mammal

mam'mismo *nm* (del figlio) dependency on the mother figure; (della madre) excessive motherliness

mammogra'fia *nf* mammograph

'mammola *nf* violet

mammo'letta *nf* shrinking violet

mam'mone *nm* mummy's boy

mam'mut *nm inv* mammoth

ma'nata *nf* handful; (colpo) slap

'manca *nf* ▶ MANCO

manca'mento *nm* **avere un** ∼ faint

man'cante *adj* missing

man'canza *nf* lack; (assenza) absence; (insufficienza) shortage; (fallo) fault; (imperfezione) defect; **in** ∼ **d'altro** failing all else; **sento la sua** ∼ I miss him. **mancanza di tatto** lack of tact, indelicacy

man'care ① *vi* be lacking; (essere assente) be missing; (venir meno) fail; (morire) pass away; ∼ **di** be lacking in; ∼ **a** fail to keep ⟨promessa⟩; **mi manca casa** I miss home; **mi manchi** I miss you; **mi è mancato il tempo** I didn't have [the] time; **mi mancano 10 euro** I'm 10 euros short; **quanto manca alla partenza?** how long before we leave?; **è mancata la corrente** there was a power failure; **sentirsi** ∼ feel faint; **sentirsi** ∼ **il respiro** be unable to breathe [properly]

② *vt* miss ⟨bersaglio⟩; **è mancato poco che cadesse** he nearly fell

man'cato *adj* ⟨appuntamento⟩ missed; ⟨tentativo⟩ unsuccessful; ⟨occasione⟩ wasted

'manche *nf inv* heat

man'chevole *adj* defective

'mancia *nf* tip. ∼ **competente** reward

manci'ata *nf* handful

man'cino *adj* left-handed

'manco, -a ① *adj* left

② *nf* left hand

③ *adv* (nemmeno) not even

man'dante *nmf* (di delitto) instigator; Jur principal

manda'rancio *nm* clementine

man'dare *vt* send; (emettere) give off; utter ⟨suono⟩; ∼ **a chiamare** send for; ∼ **avanti la casa** run the house; ∼ **giù** (ingoiare) swallow

manda'rino *nm* Bot mandarin

man'data *nf* consignment; (di serratura) turn; **chiudere a doppia** ∼ double lock

manda'tario *nm* Jur agent

man'dato *nm* (incarico) mandate; Jur warrant. **mandato di comparizione [in giudizio]** subpoena. **mandato di pagamento** money order; **mandato di perquisizione** search warrant

man'dibola *nf* jaw

mando'lino *nm* mandolin

'mandorla *nf* almond; **a** ∼ ⟨occhi⟩ almond-shaped. **mandorla amara** bitter almond

mandor'lato *nm* nut brittle (type of nougat)

'mandorlo *nm* almond [tree]

man'dragola *nf* mandrake

'mandria *nf* herd

mandri'ano *nm* cowherd

man'drillo *nm* (scimmia) mandrill; (attrezzo) mandrel; fig fam goat

maneg'gevole *adj* easy to handle

maneggi'are *vt* handle

ma'neggio *nm* handling; (intrigo) plot; (scuola di equitazione) riding school

ma'nesco *adj* quick to hit out

ma'netta *nf* lever; **a tutta** ∼ flat out; **manette** *pl* handcuffs

man'forte *nm* **dare** ∼ **a qualcuno** support somebody

manga'nello *nm* truncheon

manga'nese *nm* manganese

mange'reccio *adj* edible

mangiacas'sette *nm inv* cassette player

mangia'dischi® *nm inv* portable record player

mangia'fumo *adj inv* candela ∼ air-purifying candle

mangia'nastri *nm inv* cassette player

mangi'are ① *vt/i* eat; (consumare) eat up; (corrodere) eat away; take ‹*scacchi, carte ecc*›; **dar da** ∼ **al gatto/cane** feed the cat/dog
② *nm* eating; (cibo) food; (pasto) meal

mangi'arsi *vr* ∼ **le parole** mumble; ∼ **le unghie** bite one's nails

mangia'soldi *adj inv* **macchinetta mangiasoldi** one-armed bandit

mangi'ata *nf* big meal; **farsi una bella** ∼ **di...** feast on...

mangia'toia *nf* manger

mangia|'tore, -trice *nmf* eater. **mangiatore di fuoco** fire-eater; **mangiatrice di uomini** maneater

man'gime *nm* fodder. **mangime per i polli** chicken feed

mangi'one, -a *nmf* fam glutton

mangiucchi'are *vt* nibble

'mango *nm* mango

man'grovia *nf* mangrove

man'gusta *nf* mongoose

ma'nia *nf* mania. **mania di grandezza** delusions of grandeur. **mania di persecuzione** persecution complex

mania'cale *adj* manic

ma'niaco, -a ① *adj* maniacal
② *nmf* maniac. **maniaco sessuale** sex maniac

ma'niaco-depres'sivo *adj & nmf* manic-depressive

'Manica *nf* **la** ∼ the [English] Channel

'manica *nf* sleeve; (fam: gruppo) band; **a maniche lunghe** long-sleeved; **senza maniche** sleeveless; **essere in maniche di camicia** be in shirt sleeves; **essere di** ∼ **larga** be generous; **essere di** ∼ **stretta** be strict. **manica a vento** wind sock

manica'retto *nm* tasty dish

maniche'ismo *nm* Manicheism

mani'chetta *nf* hose

mani'chino *nm* (da sarto, vetrina) dummy

'manico *nm* handle; Mus neck. **manico di scopa** broom handle

mani'comio *nm* mental home; (fam: confusione) tip

mani'cotto *nm* muff; Mech sleeve

mani'cure ① *nf* manicure
② *nmf inv* (persona) manicurist

mani'era *nf* manner; **in** ∼ **che** so that

manie'rato *adj* affected; ‹*stile*› mannered

manie'rismo *nm* mannerism

mani'ero *nm* manor

manifat'tura *nf* manufacture; (fabbrica) factory

manifatturi'ero *adj* manufacturing

manifesta'mente *adv* demonstrably, manifestly

manife'stante *nmf* demonstrator

manife'stare ① *vt* show; (esprimere) express
② *vi* demonstrate

manifes'tarsi *vr* show oneself

manifestazi'one *nf* show; (espressione) expression; (sintomo) manifestation; (dimostrazione pubblica) demonstration

mani'festo ① *adj* evident
② *nm* poster; (dichiarazione pubblica) manifesto

ma'niglia *nf* handle; (sostegno, in autobus ecc) strap

manipo'lare *vt* handle; (massaggiare) massage; (alterare) adulterate; fig manipulate

manipola|'tore, -trice ① *nmf* manipulator
② *adj* manipulative

manipolazi'one *nf* handling; (massaggio) massage; (alterazione) adulteration; fig manipulation

mani'scalco *nm* smith

'manna *nf* manna. **manna dal cielo** manna from heaven

man'naia *nf* (scure) axe; (da macellaio) cleaver

'mano *nf* hand; (strato di vernice ecc) coat; **alla** ∼ informal; **fuori** ∼ out of the way; **man** ∼ little by little; **man** ∼ **che** as; **sotto** ∼ to hand; **di seconda** ∼ secondhand; **a mani vuote** empty-handed; **a** ∼ ‹*scritto, ricamato, fatto*› by hand; ‹*trapano ecc*› hand[-held]; **dare una** ∼ **a qualcuno** give *or* lend somebody a hand; **ha le mani di pasta frolla** he is a butterfingers

mano'dopera *nf* labour

ma'nometro *nm* manometer, pressure gauge

mano'mettere *vt* tamper with; (violare) violate

ma'nopola *nf* (di apparecchio) knob; (guanto) mitten; (su autobus) handle

mano'scritto ① *adj* handwritten
② *nm* manuscript

mano'vale *nm* labourer

mano'vella *nf* handle; Techn crank. **manovella alzacristalli** winder

ma'novra *nf* manoeuvre; Rail shunting; **fare le manovre** Auto manoeuvre; **manovre** *pl* **di corridoio** lobbying

mano'vrabile *adj* manoeuvrable; fig ‹*persona*› easy to manipulate

mano'vrare ① *vt* (azionare) operate; fig manipulate ‹*persona*›
② *vi* manoeuvre

manro'vescio *nm* slap

man'sarda *nf* attic

mansio'nario *nm* job description

mansi'one *nf* task; (dovere) duty

mansu'eto *adj* meek; ⟨animale⟩ docile

'manta *nf* Zool manta

mante'cato ① *nm* soft ice cream ② *adj* creamy

man'tella *nf* cape

man'tello *nm* cloak; (soprabito, di animale) coat; (di neve) mantle

mante'nere *vt* (conservare) keep; (in buono stato, sostentare) maintain

mante'nersi *vr* ~ **in forma** keep fit

manteni'mento *nm* maintenance. **mantenimento dell'ordine pubblico** policing. **mantenimento della pace** Mil, Pol peacekeeping

mante'nuta *nf* kept woman

'mantice *nm* bellows *pl*; (di automobile) hood, top

'mantide *nf* mantis

man'tiglia *nf* mantilla

'manto *nm* cloak; (coltre) mantle

'Mantova *nf* Mantua

manto'vana *nf* (di tende) pelmet

manu'ale *adj & nm* manual. **manuale di conversazione** phrasebook. **manuale d'uso** user manual

manual'mente *adv* manually

ma'nubrio *nm* handle; (di bicicletta) handlebars *pl*; (per ginnastica) dumb-bell

manu'fatto *adj* manufactured

manutenzi'one *nf* maintenance; **un giardino che richiede poca** ~ **a** low-maintenance garden

'manzo *nm* steer; (carne) beef

maomet'tano *adj & nm* Muslim

Mao'metto *nm* Mohammed, Muhammad

ma'ori *adj inv & nmf inv* Maori

'mappa *nf* map

mappa'mondo *nm* globe

mar ▶ MARE

mara'chella *nf* prank

maragià *nm inv* maharajah

maran'tacea *nf* Bot arrowroot

mara'schino *nm* maraschino, sweet liqueur

ma'rasma *nm* fig decline

mara'tona *nf* marathon

marato'neta *nmf* marathon runner

'marca *nf* mark; Comm brand; (fabbricazione) make; (scontrino) ticket; **di** ~ branded. **marca da bollo** stamp showing that the necessary duties have been paid

mar'care *vt* mark; Sport score

marcata'mente *adv* markedly

mar'cato *adj* ⟨tratto, accento⟩ strong, marked

marca'tore *nm* (chi segna un gol) scorer; (chi marca un avversario) marker; (pennarello) marker pen

'Marche *nfpl* Marches

mar'chese, -a ① *nm* marquis ② *nf* marchioness

mar'chetta *nf* (assicurativa) National Insurance stamp; **fare marchette** fam be on the game

marchi'are *vt* brand

'marchio *nm* brand; (caratteristica) mark. **marchio depositato** registered trademark. **marchio di fabbrica** trademark, TM. **marchio registrato** registered trademark

'marcia *nf* march; Auto gear; Sport walk; **mettere in** ~ put into gear; **mettersi in** ~ start off; **cambiare** ~ change gear. **marcia a senso unico alternato** temporary one way system in operation. **marcia forzata** forced march. **marcia funebre** funeral march. **marcia indietro** reverse gear; **fare** ~ **indietro** reverse; fig back-pedal. **marcia nuziale** wedding march

marcia'longa *nf* (di sci) cross-country skiing race; (a piedi) long-distance race

marciapi'ede *nm* pavement, sidewalk Am; (di stazione) platform

marci'are *vi* march; (funzionare) go, work

marcia'|tore, -trice *nmf* walker

'marcio ① *adj* rotten ② *nm* rotten part; fig corruption

mar'cire *vi* go bad, rot

mar'cita *nf* water meadow

'marco *nm* (moneta) mark

marco'nista *nmf* radio operator

'mare *nm* sea; (luogo di mare) seaside; **sul** ~ ⟨casa⟩ at the seaside; ⟨città⟩ on the sea; **andare al** ~ go to the sea; **in alto** ~ on the high seas; **d'alto** ~ ocean-going; **essere in alto** ~ fig not know which way to turn. **mare Adriatico** Adriatic Sea; **mar Cinese** China Sea; **mar Ionio** Ionian Sea. **mare' d'Irlanda** Irish Sea; **mar Mediterraneo** Mediterranean; **mar Morto** Dead Sea; **mar Nero** Black Sea. **mare del Nord** North Sea; **mar Tirreno** Tyrrhenian Sea

ma'rea *nf* tide; **una** ~ **di** hundreds of; **alta/bassa marea** high/low tide. **marea montante** flood tide

mareggi'ata *nf* [sea] storm

mare'moto *nm* tidal wave, seaquake

maresci'allo *nm* (ufficiale) marshal; (sottufficiale) warrant officer

ma'retta *nf* choppiness; fig tension

marga'rina *nf* margarine

marghe'rita *nf* marguerite. **margherita settembrina** Michaelmas daisy

margheri'tina *nf* daisy

margi'nale *adj* marginal

marginaliz'zare *vt* marginalize

marginal'mente *adv* marginally

'margine *nm* margin; (orlo) brink; (bordo) border. **margine di errore** margin of error. **margine di sicurezza** safety margin. **margine di vendita** mark-up

mari'ano *adj* Relig Marian

ma'rina *nf* navy; (costa) seashore; (quadro) seascape. **marina mercantile** merchant navy. **marina militare** navy

mari'naio *nm* sailor. **marinaio d'acqua dolce** landlubber

mari'nare *vt* marinate; **~ la scuola** play truant

mari'naro *adj* seafaring

mari'nata *nf* marinade

mari'nato *adj* Culin marinated

ma'rino *adj* sea *attrib*, marine

mario'netta *nf* puppet

mari'tare *vt* marry

mari'tarsi *vr* get married

ma'rito *nm* husband

mari'tozzo *nm* currant bun

ma'rittimo *adj* maritime

mar'maglia *nf* rabble

marmel'lata *nf* jam; (di agrumi) marmalade

mar'mitta *nf* pot; Auto silencer. **marmitta catalitica** catalytic converter

'marmo *nm* marble

mar'mocchio *nm* fam brat

mar'moreo *adj* marble

marmoriz'zato *adj* marbled

mar'motta *nf* marmot

maroc'chino, -a *adj & nmf* Moroccan

Ma'rocco *nm* Morocco

ma'roso *nm* breaker

mar'rone ① *adj* brown ② *nm* brown; (castagna) chestnut; **marroni** *pl* **canditi** marrons glacés

'Marshall *nfpl* **le isole ~** Marshall Islands

mar'sina *nf* tails *pl*

marsupi'ale *nm* marsupial

mar'supio *nm* (borsa) bumbag

'Marte *nm* Mars

martedì *nm* Tuesday; **di ~** on Tuesdays. **martedì grasso** Shrove Tuesday

martel'lante *adj* ⟨mal di testa⟩ pounding, throbbing; **hanno fatto una pubblicità ~** they hyped the product, they bombarded the market with publicity

martel'lare ① *vt* hammer ② *vi* throb

martel'lata *nf* hammer blow

martel'letto *nm* (di giudice) gavel; (di pianoforte) hammer; (di medico) percussion hammer

martel'lio *nm* hammering

mar'tello *nm* hammer; (di battente) knocker. **~ pneumatico** pneumatic drill

marti'netto *nm* Mech jack

mar'tin pesca'tore *nm inv* kingfisher

'martire *nmf* martyr

mar'tirio *nm* martyrdom

'martora *nf* marten

martori'are *vt* torment

mar'xismo *nm* Marxism

mar'xista *adj & nmf* Marxist

marza'pane *nm* marzipan

marzi'ale *adj* martial

marzi'ano, -a *adj & nmf* Martian

'marzo *nm* March

mascal'zone *nm* rascal

ma'scara *nm inv* mascara

mascar'pone *nm* full-fat cream cheese often used for desserts

ma'scella *nf* jaw

'maschera *nf* mask; (costume) fancy dress; Cinema, Theat usher *m*, usherette *f*; (nella commedia dell'arte) stock character. **maschera antigas** gas mask. **maschera di bellezza** face pack. **maschera mortuaria** death mask. **maschera ad ossigeno** oxygen mask

maschera'mento *nm* masking; Mil camouflage

masche'rare *vt* mask; fig camouflage

masche'rarsi *vr* put on a mask; **~ da** dress up as

masche'rata *nf* masquerade

maschi'accio *nm* (ragazza) tomboy

ma'schile ① *adj* masculine; ⟨sesso⟩ male ② *nm* masculine [gender]

maschi'lismo *nm* male chauvinism

maschi'lista ① *adj* sexist ② *nm* male chauvinist

'maschio ① *adj* male; (virile) manly ② *nm* male; (figlio) son. **maschio dominante** alpha male

masco'lino *adj* masculine

ma'scotte *nf inv* mascot

maso'chismo *nm* masochism

maso'chista *adj & nmf* masochist

'massa *nf* mass; Electr earth, ground Am; **una ~** **[di gente]** a crowd [of people]

massa'crante *adj* gruelling

massa'crare *vt* massacre

mas'sacro *nm* massacre; fig mess

massaggi'are *vt* massage

massaggia|'tore, -trice ① *nm* masseur

2) *nf* masseuse

mas'saggio *nm* massage. **massaggio cardiaco** heart massage

mas'saia *nf* housewife

mas'sello **1)** *nm* (metallo) ingot **2)** *adj* ⟨legno⟩ solid

masse'rizie *nfpl* household effects

massiccia'mente *adv* on a big scale

massicci'ata *nf* hard core

mas'siccio **1)** *adj* massive; ⟨oro ecc⟩ solid; ⟨corporatura⟩ heavy **2)** *nm* massif

massifi'care *vt* de-individualize ⟨società⟩

massificazi'one *nf* de-individualization

'massima *nf* maxim; (temperatura) maximum

massi'male *nm* (assicurazione) limit of indemnity

massimiz'zare *vt* maximize

massimizzazi'one *nf* maximization

'massimo **1)** *adj* greatest; ⟨quantità⟩ maximum, greatest **2)** *nm* il ∼ the maximum; al ∼ at [the] most, as a maximum. **massimo storico** all-time high

'masso *nm* rock

mas'sone *nm* [Free]mason

massone'ria *nf* Freemasonry

mastecto'mia *nf* mastectomy

ma'stello *nm* wooden box for the grape or olive harvest

masteriz'zare *vt* ⟨CD, DVD⟩ burn

masterizza'tore *nm* **masterizzatore di CD** CD burner

masti'care *vt* chew; (borbottare) mumble

'mastice *nm* mastic, filler; (per vetri) putty

ma'stino *nm* mastiff

masto'dontico *adj* gigantic

ma'stoide *nm* mastoid

'mastro *nm* master; **libro mastro** ledger

mastur'barsi *vr* masturbate

masturbazi'one *nf* masturbation

ma'tassa *nf* skein

match 'point *nm inv* Tennis match point

matelassé *nm* quilting

mate'matica *nf* mathematics, maths, math Am. **matematica pura** pure mathematics

mate'matico, -a **1)** *adj* mathematical **2)** *nmf* mathematician

materas'sino *nm* small mattress. **materassino gonfiabile** air bed, lilo®

mate'rasso *nm* mattress. **materasso ad acqua** water bed. **materasso di gommapiuma** foam mattress. **materasso a molle** spring mattress

ma'teria *nf* matter; (materiale) material; (di studio) subject. **materia grigia** grey matter. **materia oscura** dark matter. **materia prima** raw material

materi'ale **1)** *adj* material; (grossolano) coarse **2)** *nm* material. **materiale da costruzione** building material. **materiale pubblicitario** publicity material. **materiale di scarto** waste material

materia'lismo *nm* materialism

materia'lista **1)** *adj* materialistic; **non** ∼ unworldly **2)** *nmf* materialist

materializ'zarsi *vr* materialize

material'mente *adv* physically

materna'mente *adv* maternally

mater'nità *nf* motherhood; **è alla prima** ∼ it's her first baby; **ospedale di maternità** maternity hospital

ma'terno *adj* maternal; **lingua materna** mother tongue

ma'tita *nf* pencil; **matite** *pl* **colorate** colour[ed] pencils. **matita emostatica** styptic pencil. **matita per gli occhi** eyeliner pencil

matriar'cale *adj* matriarchal

ma'trice *nf* matrix; (origini) roots *pl*; Comm counterfoil. **matrice attiva** Comput active matrix. **matrice passiva** Comput passive matrix

ma'tricola *nf* (registro) register; Univ fresher; **numero di matricola** (di studente) matriculation number

ma'trigna *nf* stepmother

matrimoni'ale *adj* matrimonial; **vita matrimoniale** married life

matri'monio *nm* marriage; (cerimonia) wedding. **matrimonio in bianco** unconsummated marriage; white wedding. **matrimonio civile** civil wedding. **matrimonio di convenienza** marriage of convenience. **matrimonio di fatto** common-law marriage

ma'trona *nf* matron

'matta *nf* (nelle carte) joker

mattacchi'one, -a *nmf* rascal

mat'tanza *nf* (di tonni) tuna fishing; fig killings *pl*

matta'toio *nm* slaughterhouse

matta'tore *nm* (artista) star performer

matte'rello *nm* rolling-pin

mat'tina *nf* morning; **la** ∼, **alla** ∼ in the morning; **domani** ∼ tomorrow morning; **ieri** ∼ yesterday morning

matti'nata *nf* morning; Theat matinée

mattini'ero *adj* **essere** ∼ be an early riser

mat'tino *nm* morning

'**matto**, **-a** [1] *adj* mad, crazy; Med insane; (falso) false; (opaco) matt. **matto da legare** barking mad; **avere una voglia matta di...** be dying for...
[2] *nm* madman
[3] *nf* madwoman

mat'tone *nm* brick; (libro) bore

matto'nella *nf* tile. **mattonella grezza** quarry tile

mattu'tino *adj* morning *attrib*

matu'rare *vt* ripen; Fin mature

maturazi'one *nf* ripening; Fin maturity; (fig: di idea ecc) gestation; **arrivare a** ~ ⟨frutta⟩ ripen; ⟨polizza⟩ mature

maturità *nf* maturity; Sch school-leaving certificate

ma'turo *adj* mature; ⟨frutto⟩ ripe

ma'tusa *nm* fam old fogey

Mauri'tania *sf* Mauritania

Mau'rizio *nf* [isola di] ~ Mauritius

mauso'leo *nm* mausoleum

maxi+ *pref* maxi+

'**mayday** *nm inv* Radio Mayday

'**mazza** *nf* club; (martello) hammer; (da baseball, cricket) bat. **mazza da golf** golf-club

maz'zata *nf* blow

maz'zetta *nf* (di banconote) bundle; (tangente) bribe

'**mazzo** *nm* bunch; (carte da gioco) pack

Mb *nm abbr* (**megabyte**) Comput Mb

me *pers pron* me; **me lo ha dato** he gave it to me; **secondo me** in my opinion; **fai come me** do as I do; **è più veloce di me** he is faster than me *or* faster than I am

me'andro *nm* meander

M.E.C. *nm abbr* (**Mercato Comune Europeo**) EEC

'**Mecca** *nf* **la** ~ Mecca

mec'canica *nf* mechanics. **meccanica quantistica** quantum mechanics

meccanica'mente *adv* mechanically

mec'canico [1] *adj* mechanical
[2] *nm* mechanic

mecca'nismo *nm* mechanism

meccanizza'zione *nf* mechanization

meccanogra'fia *nf* data processing

meccano'grafico *adj* data processing *attrib*

mece'nate *nmf* patron

mèche *nfpl* highlights; **farsi [fare] le** ~ have highlights put in, have one's hair streaked

me'daglia *nf* medal. **medaglia d'oro** (premio) gold medal; (atleta) gold medallist. **medaglia al valore** medal for valour

medagli'ere *nm* medal collection

medagli'one *nm* medallion; (gioiello) locket; **medaglioni** *pl* **di vitello** Culin medallions of veal

me'desimo *adj* same

'**media** *nf* average; Sch average mark; Math mean; **essere nella** ~ be in the mid-range

medi'ano [1] *adj* middle
[2] *nm* (calcio) half-back. **mediano di mischia** scrum half

medi'ante *prep* by

medi'are *vt* act as intermediary in

media'|tore, **-trice** *nmf* mediator; Comm middleman. **mediatore d'affari** business agent

mediazi'one *nf* mediation

medica'mento *nm* medicine

medi'care *vt* treat; dress ⟨ferita⟩

medi'cato *adj* ⟨shampoo⟩ medicated

medicazi'one *nf* medication; (di ferita) dressing

me'diceo *adj* from the period of the Medici, Medicean

medi'cina *nf* medicine. **medicina alternativa** alternative medicine, complementary medicine. **medicina del lavoro** occupational health. **medicina legale** forensic medicine, forensic science. **medicina popolare** folk medicine

medici'nale [1] *adj* medicinal
[2] *nm* medicine

'**medico** [1] *adj* medical
[2] *nm* doctor. **medico di base** general practitioner, GP. **medico di famiglia** family doctor. **medico generico** general practitioner, GP. **medico legale** forensic scientist. **medico di turno** duty doctor

medie'vale *adj* medieval

'**medio** [1] *adj* average; ⟨punto⟩ middle; ⟨statura⟩ medium; **scuola media** secondary school
[2] *nm* (dito) middle finger. **Medio Oriente** Middle East

medi'ocre *adj* mediocre; (scadente) poor

mediocre'mente *adv* indifferently

medio'evo *nm* Middle Ages *pl*

mediorien'tale *adj* middle-eastern

medita'bondo *adj* meditative

medi'tare [1] *vt* meditate; (progettare) plan; (considerare attentamente) think over
[2] *vi* meditate

medita'tivo *adj* meditative

meditazi'one *nf* meditation

mediter'raneo *adj* Mediterranean; **il [mar] Mediterraneo** the Mediterranean [Sea]

me'dusa *nf* jellyfish

'**megabyte** *nm inv* Comput megabyte

me'gafono *nm* megaphone

megaga'lattico *adj* gigantic

mega'lite *nm* megalith

mega'lomane *nmf* megalomaniac

me'gera *nf* hag

'meglio ① *adv* better; **tanto** ∼, ∼ **così** so much the better
② *adj* better; (superlativo) best
③ *nmf* best
④ *nf* **avere la** ∼ **su** have the better of; **fare qualcosa alla [bell'e]** ∼ do something as best one can
⑤ *nm* **fare del proprio** ∼ do one's best; **fare qualcosa il** ∼ **possibile** make an excellent job of something; **al** ∼ to the best of one's ability; **per il** ∼ for the best

'mela *nf* apple; **succo di mela** apple juice. **mela cotogna** quince

mela'grana *nf* pomegranate

mé'lange ① *nm* flecked wool
② *adj inv* ‹*lana*› flecked

mela'nina *nf* melanin

melan'zana *nf* aubergine, eggplant Am; **melanzane** *pl* **alla parmigiana** baked layers of aubergine, tomato and cheese

me'lassa *nf* molasses *sg*

me'lenso *adj* ‹*persona, film*› dull

me'leto *nm* apple orchard

mel'lifluo *adj* ‹*parole*› honeyed; ‹*voce*› sugary

'melma *nf* slime

mel'moso *adj* slimy

'melo *nm* apple [tree]

melo'dia *nf* melody

me'lodico *adj* melodic

melodi'oso *adj* melodious

melo'dramma *nm* melodrama

melodrammatica'mente *adv* melodramatically

melodram'matico *adj* melodramatic

melo'grano *nm* pomegranate tree

me'lone *nm* melon

mem'brana *nf* membrane

'membro *nm* member; (pl *nf* **membra** Anat) limb

memo'rabile *adj* memorable

'memore *adj* mindful; (riconoscente) grateful

me'moria *nf* memory; (oggetto ricordo) souvenir; **imparare a** ∼ learn by heart; **memorie** *pl* (biografiche) memoirs. **memoria cache** Comput cache memory. **memoria collettiva** folk memory. **memoria dinamica** Comput RAM. **memoria di massa** Comput mass storage. **memoria permanente** Comput non-volatile memory. **memoria di sola lettura** Comput read-only memory, ROM. **memoria a tampone** Comput buffer [memory]. **memoria volatile** Comput volatile memory

memori'ale *nm* memorial

memoriz'zare *vt* memorize; Comput save, store

mena'dito: **a** ∼ *adv* perfectly

me'nare *vt* lead; (fam: picchiare) hit; ∼ **la coda** ‹*cane*› wag its tail; ∼ **qualcuno per il naso** pull somebody's leg

mendi'cante *nmf* beggar, panhandler Am

mendi'care *vt/i* beg

menefre'ghista *adj* devil-may-care

mene'strello *nm* minstrel

me'ningi *nfpl* **spremersi le** ∼ rack one's brains

menin'gite *nf* meningitis

me'nisco *nm* meniscus

'meno ① *adv* less; (superlativo) least; (in operazioni, con temperatura) minus; ∼ **di** less than; **di** ∼ less; ∼ **moderno** less modern; **il** ∼ **moderno di tutti** the least modern of all; **far qualcosa alla** ∼ **peggio** do something as best one can; **fare a** ∼ **di qualcosa** do without something; **non posso fare a** ∼ **di ridere** I can't help laughing; ∼ **male!** thank goodness!; **sempre** ∼ less and less; **venir** ∼ (svenire) faint; **venir** ∼ **a qualcuno** ‹*coraggio*› fail somebody; **sono le tre** ∼ **un quarto** it's a quarter to three; **che tu venga o** ∼ whether you're coming or not; **quanto** ∼ at least
② *adj inv* less; (con nomi plurali) fewer
③ *nm* least; Math minus sign; **il** ∼ **possibile** as little as possible; **per lo** ∼ at least
④ *prep* except [for]
⑤ *conj* **a** ∼ **che** unless

meno'mare *vt* ‹*incidente*› maim

meno'mato, -a ① *adj* disabled
② *nmf* disabled person

meno'pausa *nf* menopause

'mensa *nf* table; Mil mess; (di azienda, scuola) canteen

men'sile ① *adj* monthly
② *nm* (stipendio) [monthly] salary; (rivista) monthly

mensilità *nf inv* monthly salary

mensil'mente *adv* monthly

'mensola *nf* bracket; (scaffale) shelf

'menta *nf* mint; **al gusto di** ∼ mint-flavoured. **menta piperita** peppermint. **menta verde** spearmint

men'tale *adj* mental

mentalità *nf inv* mentality. **mentalità ristretta** bigotry

'mente *nf* mind; **a** ∼ **fredda** in cold blood; **cosa ti è saltato in** ∼? what possessed you?; **venire in** ∼ **a qualcuno** occur to somebody

men'tina *nf* mint

men'tire *vi* lie

'mento *nm* chin

men'tolo *nm* menthol; **al** ∿ mentholated

'mentre *conj* (temporale) while; (invece) whereas

me'nu *nm inv* menu. **menu a discesa** Comput pull-down menu. **menu fisso** set menu. **menu a tendina** Comput pull-down menu, drop-down menu. **menu turistico** tourist menu

menzio'nare *vt* mention

menzi'one *nf* mention. **menzione speciale** special mention

men'zogna *nf* lie

mera'viglia *nf* wonder; **a** ∿ marvellously; **che** ∿! how wonderful!; **con mia grande** ∿ much to my amazement; **mi fa** ∿ **che...** I am surprised that...

meravigli'are *vt* surprise

meravigli'arsi *vr* ∿ **di** be surprised at

meravigliosa'mente *adv* marvellously

meravigli'oso *adj* marvellous, wonderful

mer'cante *nm* merchant. **mercante d'arte** art dealer. **mercante di schiavi** slave trader

mercanteggi'are *vi* trade; (sul prezzo) bargain

mercan'tile ① *adj* mercantile ② *nm* merchant ship

mercan'zia *nf* merchandise, goods *pl*

merca'tino *nm* (di quartiere) local street market; Fin unlisted securities market

mer'cato *nm* market; Fin market[place]; **a buon** ∿ ⟨comprare⟩ cheap[ly]; ⟨articolo⟩ cheap. **mercato all'aperto** street market. **mercato aperto** Econ open market. **mercato azionario** Fin equity market, share market. **mercato dei cambi** foreign exchange market. **Mercato Comune [Europeo]** [European] Common Market. **mercato coperto** covered market, indoor market. **mercato dell'eurovaluta** eurocurrency market. **mercato immobiliare** property market. **mercato libero** free market. **mercato di massa** mass market. **mercato nero** black market. **mercato del pesce** fish market. **mercato di prova** test market. **mercato al rialzo** Fin bull market. **mercato al ribasso** Fin bear market. **mercato specializzato** niche market. **mercato unico** Single Market

'merce *nf* goods *pl*, merchandise; **la** ∿ **venduta non si cambia senza lo scontrino** goods will not be exchanged without a receipt. **merce in conto vendita** sale or return goods. **merce deperibile** perishable goods

mercé *nf* **alla** ∿ **di** at the mercy of

merce'nario *adj & nm* mercenary

merceolo'gia *nf* study of commodities

merce'ria *nf* haberdashery; (negozio) haberdasher's

mercifi'care *vt* commercialize

mercificazi'one *nf* commercialization

mercoledì *nm inv* Wednesday; **di** ∿ on Wednesdays. **mercoledì delle Ceneri** Ash Wednesday

mer'curio *nm* mercury

me'renda *nf* afternoon snack; **far** ∿ have an afternoon snack

meridi'ana *nf* sundial

meridi'ano ① *adj* midday ② *nm* meridian

meridio'nale ① *adj* southern ② *nmf* southerner

meridi'one *nm* south

me'ringa *nf* meringue

merin'gata *nf* meringue pie

meri'tare *vt* deserve

meri'tato *adj* deserved

meri'tevole *adj* deserving

'merito *nm* merit; (valore) worth; **in** ∿ **a** as to; **per** ∿ **di** thanks to

merito'cratico *adj* meritocratic

meri'torio *adj* meritorious

merla'tura *nf* battlements *pl*

merlet'taia *nf* lacemaker

mer'letto *nm* lace

'merlo *nm* blackbird; **bravo** ∿! you fool!

mer'luzzo *nm* cod

'mero *adj* mere

mesca'lina *nf* mescaline

'mescere *vt* pour out

meschine'ria *nf* meanness

me'schino ① *adj* wretched; (gretto) mean ② *nm* wretch

'mescita *nf* wine shop

mescola'mento *nm* mixing

mesco'lanza *nf* mixture

mesco'lare *vt* mix; shuffle ⟨carte⟩; (confondere) mix up; blend ⟨tè, tabacco ecc⟩

mesco'larsi *vr* mix; (immischiarsi) meddle

mesco'lata *nf* (a carte) shuffle; Culin stir

'mese *nm* month. **mese civile** calendar month

me'setto *nm* **un** ∿ about a month, a month or so

'messa¹ *nf* Mass. **messa nera** black mass. **messa da requiem** requiem mass. **messa solenne** High Mass

'messa² *nf* (il mettere) putting. **messa in moto** Auto starting. **messa in piega** (di capelli) set; **farsi fare la** ∿ **in piega** have one's hair set. **messa a punto** adjustment. **messa in scena** production; fig production number. **messa a terra** earthing, grounding Am

messagge'ria *nf* **messaggeria elettronica** Comput messaging

messag'gero *nm* messenger

mes'saggio *nm* message. **messaggio di errore** Comput error message. **messaggio di testo** Teleph text message

mes'sale *nm* missal

'messe *nf* harvest

Mes'sia *nm* Messiah

messi'cano, **-a** *adj & nmf* Mexican

'Messico *nm* Mexico

messin'scena *nf* staging; fig act

'messo ① pp di METTERE ② *nm* messenger

mesti'ere *nm* trade; ‹*lavoro*› job; **essere del** ∼ be an expert, know one's trade

'mesto *adj* sad

'mestola *nf* (di cuoco) ladle; (di muratore) trowel

mestru'ale *adj* menstrual

mestruazi'one *nf* menstruation; **mestruazioni** *pl* period

'meta *nf* destination; fig aim

metà *nf inv* half; (centro) middle; **a** ∼ **prezzo** half price; **a** ∼ **strada** halfway; **a** ∼ **serata** halfway through the evening; **fare a** ∼ **con qualcuno** go halves with somebody, go fifty-fifty with somebody; **fare [a]** ∼ **e** ∼ go fifty-fifty, go halves

metabo'lismo *nm* metabolism

meta'carpo *nm* metacarpus

meta'done *nm* methadone

meta'fisica *nf* metaphysics

meta'fisico *adj* metaphysical

me'tafora *nf* metaphor

metaforica'mente *adv* metaphorically

meta'forico *adj* metaphorical

me'tallico *adj* metallic

metalliz'zato *adj* ‹grigio› metallic

me'tallo *nm* metal. **metallo vile** base metal

metal'loide *nm* metalloid

metallur'gia *nf* metallurgy

metal'lurgico *adj* metallurgical

metalmec'canico ① *adj* engineering ② *nm* engineering worker

meta'morfosi *nf inv* metamorphosis

me'tano *nm* methane

metano'dotto *nm* methane pipeline

meta'nolo *nm* methanol

me'tastasi *nf inv* metastasis

meta'tarso *nm* metatarsus

me'teora *nf* meteor

meteo'rite *nm* meteorite

meteorolo'gia *nf* meteorology

meteoro'logico *adj* meteorological

meteo'rologo *nm* meteorologist

me'ticcio, **-a** *nmf* half-caste

meticolosa'mente *adv* meticulously

metico'loso *adj* meticulous

me'tile *nm* methyl

me'todico *adj* methodical

meto'dista *adj & nmf* Methodist

'metodo *nm* method

metodolo'gia *nf* methodology

metodo'logico *adj* methodological

me'traggio *nm* length (in metres); **vendere a** ∼ sell by the metre

'metrico, **-a** ① *adj* metric; (in poesia) metrical ② *nf* metrics

'metro[1] *nm* metre; (nastro) tape measure. **metro cubo** cubic metre. **metro quadrato** square metre

'metro[2] *nf inv* fam underground, subway Am

me'tronomo *nm* metronome

metro'notte *nmf inv* night security guard

me'tropoli *nf inv* metropolis

metropoli'tana *nf* underground, subway Am

metropoli'tano *adj* metropolitan

'mettere *vt* put; (indossare) put on; (fam: installare) put in; ∼ **al mondo** bring into the world; ∼ **da parte** set aside; ∼ **fiducia** inspire trust; ∼ **qualcosa in chiaro** make something clear; ∼ **in mostra** display; ∼ **a posto** tidy up; ∼ **in vendita** put up for sale; ∼ **su** set up ‹casa, azienda›; **metter su famiglia** start a family; **ci ho messo un'ora** it took me an hour; **mettiamo che...** let's suppose that...

'mettersi *vr* (indossare) put on; (diventare) turn out; ∼ **a** start to; ∼ **con qualcuno** (fam: formare una coppia) start to go out with somebody; ∼ **a letto** go to bed; ∼ **a sedere** sit down; ∼ **in viaggio** set out

metti'foglio *nm* feeder

'mezza *nf* **è la** ∼ it's half past twelve; **sono le quattro e** ∼ it's half past four

mezza'dria *nf* sharecropping

mezza'luna *nf* half moon; (simbolo islamico) crescent; (coltello) two-handled chopping knife; **a** ∼ half-moon

mezza'manica *nf* **a** ∼ ‹maglia› short-sleeved; **mezzemaniche** *pl* pej lowest grade of clerks, pen-pushers

mezza'nino *nm* mezzanine

mez'zano, **-a** *adj* middle

mezza'notte *nf* midnight; **aspettare la** ∼ see in the New Year

mezz'asta: **a** ∼ *adv* at half mast

mezze'ria *nf* centre line

'mezzo[1] *adj* half; **di mezza età** middle aged; ∼ **blcchiere** half a glass; **una mezza idea** a vague idea; **siamo mezzi morti**

we're half dead; **sono le quattro e** ∼ it's half past four. **mezza cartuccia** *nf* runt. **mezza dozzina** *nf* half-dozen. **mezza età** *nf* middle age, midlife. **mezza giornata** *nf* half day. **mezzo guanto** *nm* mitt. **mezzo litro** *nm* half a litre. **mezz'ora** *nf* half an hour. **mezza pensione** *nf* half board. **mezza stagione** *nf* demi-season; **una giacca di** ∼ **stagione** a spring/autumn jacket. **mezza verità** *nf* half-truth.

2 *adv* (a metà) half; ∼ **addormentato** half asleep; ∼ **morto** half-dead; ∼ **morto di paura** petrified; ∼ **e** ∼ (così così) so so **3** *nm* (metà) half; (centro) middle; (per raggiungere un fine) means *sg*; **uno e** ∼ one and a half; **tre anni e** ∼ three and a half years; **in** ∼ **a** in the middle of; **il giusto** ∼ the happy medium; **levare di** ∼ clear away; **per** ∼ **di** by means of; **a** ∼ **posta** by mail; **via di** ∼ *fig* halfway house; (soluzione) middle way; **mezzi** *pl* (denaro) means *pl*; **mezzi** *pl* **di comunicazione di massa** mass media; **mezzi** *pl* **pubblici** public transport; **mezzi** *pl* **di trasporto** [means of] transport

mezzo'busto *nm* (statua) bust; TV talking head; **a** ∼ ⟨foto, ritratto⟩ half-length

mezzo'fondo *nm* middle-distance running

mezzogi'orno *nm* midday, noon; (sud) South; **il Mezzogiorno** Southern Italy. **mezzogiorno in punto** high noon

mezzo'sangue *nmf* crossbreed

mezzo'servizio *nm* **lavorare a** ∼ do part-time cleaning work

mi **1** *pers pron* me; (refl) myself; **mi ha dato un libro** he gave me a book; **non mi parla** he doesn't talk to me; **mi lavo le mani** I wash my hands; **eccomi** here I am **2** *nm* Mus (chiave, nota) E

'mia ▸ MIO

miago'lare *vi* miaow

miago'lio *nm* miaowing

mi'ao *nm* miaow

'mica¹ *nf* mica

'mica² *adv* fam (per caso) by any chance; **hai** ∼ **visto Paolo?** have you seen Paul, by any chance?; **non è** ∼ **bello** it is not at all nice; ∼ **male** not bad

'miccia *nf* fuse

micidi'ale *adj* deadly

'micio *nm* pussy cat

mi'cosi *nf inv* athlete's foot

mi'cotico *adj* fungal

microbiolo'gia *nf* microbiology

'microbo *nm* microbe

microchirur'gia *nf* microsurgery

micro'clima *nm* microclimate

microcom'puter *nm inv* microcomputer

micro'cosmo *nm* microcosm

micro'fiche *nf inv* microfiche

micro'film *nm inv* microfilm

micro'fisica *nf* microphysics

mi'crofono *nm* microphone. **microfono con la clip** clip-on microphone. **microfono spia** bugging device, bug. **microfono a stelo** boom microphone

microfotogra'fia *nf* Phot micrograph; (tecnica) micrography

microinfor'matica *nf* microcomputing

micro'onda *nf* microwave

microorga'nismo *nm* microorganism

microproces'sore *nm* microprocessor

micro'scheda *nf* microfiche

micro'scopico *adj* microscopic

micro'scopio *nm* microscope; **passare qualcosa al** ∼ *fig* examine something in microscopic detail

microse'condo *nm* microsecond

micro'solco *nm* (disco) long-playing record

micro'spia *nf* bug

mi'dollo *nm* (pl nf **midolla**, Anat) marrow; **fino al** ∼ ⟨bagnato⟩ through and through; ⟨corrotto⟩ to the core. **midollo osseo** bone marrow. **midollo spinale** spinal cord

'mie ▸ MIO

mi'ei ▸ MIO

mi'ele *nm* honey. **miele d'acacia** acacia honey

mi'etere *vt* reap

mietitrebbia'trice *nf* combine harvester

mieti'trice *nf* harvester

mieti'tura *nf* harvest

migli'aia *nfpl* thousands

migli'aio *nm* (pl nf **migliaia**) thousand; **a migliaia** in thousands

'miglio *nm* Bot millet; (misura: pl f **miglia**) mile. **miglia aeree** *pl* Br Air Miles, Am frequent-flyer miles. **miglio nautico** nautical mile. **miglia** *pl* **all'ora** miles per hour, mph. **miglio terrestre** mile

migliora'mento *nm* improvement

miglio'rare *vt/i* improve

migli'ore **1** *adj* better; (superlativo) the best; ∼ **amico** best friend; **i migliori auguri** best wishes **2** *nmf* **il/la** ∼ the best

miglio'ria *nf* improvement

mi'gnatta *nf* leech

'mignolo *nm* little finger, pinkie fam; (del piede) little toe

mi'gnon *adj inv* (bottiglie) miniature

mi'grare *vi* migrate

migra'tore *adj* migratory

migra'torio *adj* migratory

migrazi'one *nf* migration

'mila ▶ MILLE

mila'nese *adj & nmf* Milanese

Mi'lano *nf* Milan

miliar'dario, -a ① *nm* millionaire; (pluri-miliardario) billionaire ② *nf* millionairess; billionairess

mili'ardo *nm* billion

mili'are *adj* **pietra miliare** milestone

milio'nario, -a ① *nm* millionaire ② *nf* millionairess

mili'one *nm* million

milio'nesimo *adj & nm* millionth

mili'tante *adj & nmf* militant

mili'tanza *nf* militancy

mili'tare ① *vi* ~ **in** be a member of ⟨*un partito ecc*⟩ ② *adj* military ③ *nm* soldier; **fare il** ~ do one's military service. **militare di carriera** regular [soldier]. **militare di leva** National Serviceman

milita'rismo *nm* militarism

milita'rista *adj* militaristic

militariz'zare *vt* militarize

militas'solto *adj* having done National Service

'milite *nm* soldier

milite'sente *adj* exempt from National Service

mil'izia *nf* militia

millanta|'tore, -trice *nmf* boaster

'mille *adj & nm* (pl **mila**) a *or* one thousand; **due/tre mila** two/three thousand; ~ **grazie!** thanks a lot!; **millenovecentonovantaquattro** *nm* nineteen ninety-four

mille'foglie *nm inv* Culin vanilla slice

mil'lennio *nm* millennium

millepi'edi *nm inv* centipede

mil'lesimo *adj & nm* thousandth

milli'bar *nm inv* millibar

milli'grammo *nm* milligram

mil'lilitro *nm* millilitre

mil'limetro *nm* millimetre

'milza *nf* spleen

mi'mare ① *vt* mimic ⟨*persona*⟩ ② *vi* mime

mi'metico *adj* **tuta mimetica** camouflage; **animale mimetico** animal which has the ability to camouflage itself; **vernice mimetica** camouflage paint

mime'tismo *nm* ability to camouflage itself. **mimetismo politico** chameleon-like political traits

mimetiz'zare *vt* camouflage

mimetiz'zarsi *vr* camouflage oneself

'mimica *nf* mime. **mimica facciale** facial expressions *pl*

'mimico *adj* mimic

'mimo *nm* mime

mi'mosa *nf* mimosa

'mina *nf* mine; (di matita) lead

mi'naccia *nf* threat; **avere una** ~ **di aborto** come close to having a miscarriage. **minaccia di morte** death threat

minacci'are *vt* threaten

minacciosa'mente *adv* threateningly, menacingly

minacci'oso *adj* threatening; ⟨*onde*⟩ menacing

mi'nare *vt* mine; fig undermine

mina'reto *nm* minaret

mina'tore *nm* miner

mina'torio *adj* threatening

mine'rale *adj & nm* mineral

mineralo'gia *nf* mineralogy

mine'rario *adj* mining *attrib*

mi'nestra *nf* soup. **minestra in brodo** noodle soup. **minestra di verdure** vegetable soup

mine'strone *nm* minestrone (vegetable soup); (fam: insieme confuso) hotchpotch

mingher'lino *adj* skinny

'mini ① *nf inv* (gonna) mini ② *adj inv* mini

mini+ *pref* mini+

miniapparta'mento *nm* studio flat Br, studio apartment

minia'tura *nf* miniature

miniaturiz'zato *adj* miniaturized

mini'bus *nm inv* minibus

mini'disc *nm inv* minidisc

mini'disco *nm* minidisc

mini'era *nf* mine; **una** ~ **di notizie** a mine of information; **è una** ~ **di idee** he's full of ideas. **miniera a cielo aperto** opencast mine. **miniera d'oro** gold mine

mini'golf *nm* minigolf, miniature golf

mini'gonna *nf* miniskirt, mini

'minima *nf* (atmosferica) minimum temperature; Med minimum blood-pressure level; Mus minim

minima'lista *nmf* minimalist

minima'mente *adv* minimally

mini'market *nm inv* minimarket

minimiz'zare *vt* minimize, downplay

'minimo ① *adj* least, slightest; (il più basso) lowest; ⟨*salario, quantità ecc*⟩ minimum ② *nm* minimum; **girare al** ~ Auto idle; **toccare il** ~ **storico** be at an all-time low; **come** ~ at least, as a minimum

'minio *nm* red lead

ministeri'ale *adj* (di ministero) ministerial; (di governo) government

mini'stero *nm* ministry; (governo) government. **ministero dell'Ambiente e della Tutela del Territorio** ≈ Department of Natural Resources Am, ≈ Department of the Environment Br. **ministero degli [affari] Esteri** Foreign Office Br, State Department Am. **ministero della Difesa** Ministry of Defence Br, Department of Defense Am. **ministero di Grazia e Giustizia** Justice Department Am. **ministero degli Interni** Ministry of the Interior, ≈ Home Office. **ministero dell'Istruzione** Department for Education and Skills Br. **ministero del Lavoro e delle Politiche Sociali** ≈ Department for Work and Pensions. **ministero per le Politiche Agricole e Forestali** ≈ Department for Environment, Food, and Rural Affairs Br. **ministero della Salute** Department of Health

mi'nistro *nm* minister. **ministro della Difesa** Defence Minister Br, Defense Secretary Am. **ministro degli Esteri** Foreign Secretary Br, Secretary of State Am, foreign minister. **mInistro di GrazIa e Giustizia** Attorney General. **ministro dell'Interno** Home Secretary Br, Secretary of the Interior Am. **ministro del Lavoro** Employment Minister, Employment Secretary Br. **ministro del Tesoro** Chancellor of the Exchequer Br, Secretary of the Treasury Am

mini'tower *nm inv* Comput minitower

mino'ranza *nf* minority. **minoranza etnica** ethnic minority

mino'rato, -a ① *adj* disabled ② *nmf* disabled person

Mi'norca *nf* Menorca

mi'nore ① *adj* ⟨gruppo, numero⟩ smaller; (superlativo) smallest; ⟨distanza⟩ shorter; (superlativo) shortest; ⟨prezzo⟩ lower; (superlativo) lowest; (di età) younger; (superlativo) youngest; (di importanza) minor; (superlativo) least important ② *nmf* younger; (superlativo) youngest; Jur minor; **il ~ dei mali** the lesser of two evils; **i minori di 14 anni** children under 14

mino'renne ① *adj* under age ② *nmf* minor

minori'tario *adj* minority *attrib*

minu'etto *nm* minuet

mi'nuscolo, -a ① *adj* tiny, minuscule ② *nf* small letter

mi'nuta *nf* rough copy

minuta'mente *adv* ⟨esaminato⟩ in minute detail, minutely; ⟨lavorato, tritato⟩ finely

mi'nuto[1] *adj* minute; ⟨persona⟩ delicate; ⟨ricerca⟩ detailed; ⟨pioggia, neve⟩ fine; **al ~** Comm retail

mi'nuto[2] *nm* ⟨di tempo⟩ minute; **spaccare il ~** be dead on time; **minuti** *pl* **di recupero** Sport injury time

mi'nuzia *nf* trifle; **minuzie** *pl* minutiae

minuziosa'mente *adv* minutely

minuzi'oso *adj* minute, detailed; ⟨persona⟩ meticulous

'mio ① (il mio *m*, la mia *f*, i miei *mpl*, le mie *fpl*) *poss adj* my; **questa macchina è mia** this car is mine; **~ padre** my father; **un ~ amico** a friend of mine ② *poss pron* mine; **i miei** (genitori ecc) my folks

'miope *adj* short-sighted

mio'pia *nf* short-sightedness

'mira *nf* aim; (bersaglio) target; **prendere la ~** take aim; **prendere di ~ qualcuno** fig have it in for somebody

mi'rabile *adj* admirable

miraco'lato *adj* ⟨malato⟩ miraculously cured

mi'racolo *nm* miracle

miracolosa'mente *adv* miraculously

miraco'loso *adj* miraculous

mi'raggio *nm* mirage

mi'rare *vi* [take] aim; **~ alto** aim high

mi'rarsi *vr* (guardarsi) look at oneself

mi'riade *nf* myriad

mi'rino *nm* sight; Phot view-finder

'mirra *nf* myrrh

mir'tillo *nm* blueberry

'mirto *nm* myrtle

mi'santropo, -a *nmf* misanthropist

mi'scela *nf* mixture; ⟨di caffè, tabacco ecc⟩ blend

misce'lare *vt* mix

miscela'tore *nm* ⟨apparecchio⟩ blender; (di acqua) mixer tap

miscel'lanea *nf* miscellany

'mischia *nf* scuffle; (nel rugby) scrum

mischi'are *vt* mix; shuffle ⟨carte da gioco⟩

mischi'arsi *vr* mix; (immischiarsi) interfere

misco'noscere *vt* not appreciate

miscre'dente *nmf* heretic

mi'scuglio *nm* mixture; fig medley

mise'rabile *adj* wretched

misera'mente *adv* ⟨finire⟩ miserably; ⟨vivere⟩ in abject poverty; ⟨vestirsi⟩ shabbily

mi'seria *nf* poverty; (infelicità) misery; **guadagnare una ~** earn a pittance; **miserie** *pl* (disgrazie) misfortunes; **porca ~!** fam hell!

miseri'cordia *nf* mercy

misericordi'oso *adj* merciful

'misero *adj* (miserabile) wretched; (povero) poor; (scarso) paltry

mi'sfatto *nm* misdeed

mi'sogino *nm* misogynist

mis'saggio *nm* vision mixer

'**missile** *nm* missile. **missile cruise** cruise missile. **missile terra-aria** surface-to-air missile

missi'listico *adj* missile *attrib*

missio'nario, **-a** *nmf* missionary

missi'one *nf* mission. **missione di pace** peace mission

misteriosa'mente *adv* mysteriously

misteri'oso *adj* mysterious

mi'stero *nm* mystery

'**mistica** *nf* mysticism

misti'cismo *nm* mysticism

'**mistico** ① *adj* mystic[al] ② *nm* mystic

mistifi'care *vt* distort ⟨*verità*⟩

mistificazi'one *nf* (della verità) distortion

'**misto** ① *a* mixed; **scuola mista** mixed *or* co-educational school ② *nm* mixture; (di oggetti) miscellany. **misto lana** wool mixture; **misto lana/ cotone** wool/cotton mix

mi'sura *nf* measure; (dimensione) measurement; (taglia) size; (limite) limit; **su** ~ ⟨*abiti*⟩ made to measure; ⟨*mobile*⟩ custom-made; **a** ~ ⟨*andare, calzare*⟩ perfectly; **nella** ~ **in cui** insofar as. **misura di sicurezza** safety measure. **misura di capacità** unit of capacity. **misura di lunghezza** unit of length. **misura profilattica** prophylactic. **misure** *pl* **antidiscriminatorie** positive discrimination

misu'rare *vt* measure; try on ⟨*indumenti*⟩; (limitare) limit

misu'rarsi *vr* ~ **con** (gareggiare) compete with

misu'rato *adj* measured

misu'rino *nm* measuring spoon

'**mite** *adj* mild; ⟨*prezzo*⟩ moderate

'**mitico** *adj* mythical

miti'gare *vt* mitigate

miti'garsi *vr* calm down; ⟨*clima*⟩ become mild

'**mitilo** *nm* mussel

mitiz'zare *vt* mythicize

'**mito** *nm* myth

mitolo'gia *nf* mythology

mito'logico *adj* mythological

mi'tomane *nmf* compulsive liar

'**mitra** ① *nf* Relig mitre ② *nm inv* Mil machine-gun

mitragli'are *vt* machine-gun; ~ **di domande** fire questions at

mitraglia'trice *nf* machine-gun

mitt. *abbr* (**mittente**) sender

mitteleuro'peo *adj* Central European

mit'tente *nmf* sender

'**mixer** *nm inv* mixer

mne'monico *adj* mnemonic; **frase mnemonica** mnemonic

mo' *nm* **a mo' di** by way of ⟨*esempio, consolazione*⟩

'**mobile**[1] *adj* mobile; ⟨*volubile*⟩ fickle; (che si può muovere) movable; **beni** *pl* **mobili** movable personal estate; **squadra mobile** flying squad

'**mobile**[2] *nm* piece of furniture; **mobili** *pl* furniture *sg*. **mobile bar** drinks cabinet; **mobili** *pl* **da giardino** garden furniture; **mobili** *pl* **in stile** reproduction furniture

mo'bilia *nf* furniture

mobili'are *adj* ⟨*capitale*⟩ movable; ⟨*credito*⟩ medium-term; ⟨*mercato*⟩ share *attrib*; **patrimonio mobiliare** non-property assets

mobili'ere *nm* furniture dealer

mobili'ficio *nm* furniture factory

mo'bilio *nm* furniture

mobilità *nf* mobility. **mobilità del lavoro** labour mobility. **mobilità sociale** social mobility

mobili'tare *vt* mobilize

mobilitazi'one *nf* mobilization

'**moca** *nm inv* mocha

mocas'sino *nm* moccasin

mocci'coso, **-a** ① *adj* snotty ② *nmf* snottynosed kid; brat

'**moccolo** *nm* (di candela) candle-end; (moccio) snot

'**moda** *nf* fashion; **di** ~ in fashion; **andare di** ~ be in fashion; **alla** ~ ⟨*musica, vestiti*⟩ up to-date; **fuori** ~ unfashionable

mo'dale *adj* ⟨*verbo*⟩ modal

modalità *nf inv* formality. **modalità d'uso** instruction

modana'tura *nf* moulding

mo'della *nf* model

model'lante *adj* ⟨*gel per capelli*⟩ styling

model'lare *vt* model

model'lino *nm* model

model'lismo *nm* model-making; (collezionismo) collecting models

model'lista *nmf* model-maker; (moda) [fashion] designer

mo'dello *nm* model; ⟨*stampo*⟩ mould; (di carta) pattern; (modulo) form; (moda) male model. **modello CUD** ≈ P45. **modello in scala** scale model

'**modem** *nm inv* modem; **mandare per** ~ modem, send by modem

'**modem-fax** *nm inv* fax-modem

mode'rare *vt* moderate; (diminuire) reduce

mode'rarsi *vr* control oneself

moderata'mente *adv* moderately

mode'rato *adj* moderate

modera|'tore, **-trice** ① *nmf* (in tavola rotonda) moderator ② *adj* moderating

moderazi'one *nf* moderation

moderna'mente *adv* (in modo moderno) in a modern style

modernari'ato *nm* collecting 20th-century art and products

moder'nismo *nm* modernism

modernità *nf* modernity

moderniz'zare *vt* modernize

modernizzazi'one *nf* modernization

mo'derno *adj* modern

mo'destia *nf* modesty

mo'desto *adj* modest

'modico *adj* reasonable

mo'difica *nf* modification

modifi'care *vt* modify

modifi'cato *adj* modified. **modificato geneticamente** genetically modified

modifica'tore *nm* modifier

modificazi'one *nf* modification

mo'dista *nf* milliner

'modo *nm* way; (garbo) manners *pl*; (occasione) chance; Gram mood; **ad ogni ~** anyhow; **di ~ che** so that; **fare in ~ di** try to; **in che ~** (interrogativa) how; **in qualche ~** somehow; **in questo ~** like this. **modo di dire** idiom; **per ~ di dire** so to speak; **in ~ ottimistico/pessimistico/anormale** optimistically/pessimistically/abnormally

modu'lare *vt* modulate

modula'tore *nm* modulator. **modulatore di frequenza** frequency modulator

modulazi'one *nf* modulation **modulazione di frequenza** frequency modulation

'modulo *nm* form; ⟨lunare, di comando⟩ module. **modulo continuo** continuous paper. **modulo di domanda** application form. **modulo di iscrizione** enrolment form. **modulo di ordinazione** order form. **modulo di richiesta** claim form

'modus ope'randi *nm inv* modus operandi

'modus vi'vendi *nm inv* modus vivendi

mof'fetta *nf* skunk

'mogano *nm* mahogany

'mogio *adj* dejected

'moglie *nf* wife

moi'cano *adj* **taglio [di capelli] alla moicana** mohican [haircut]

mo'ine *nfpl* **fare le ~** behave in an affected way

'mola *nf* millstone; Mech grindstone

mo'lare *nm* molar

mo'lato *adj* ⟨vetro⟩ cut

mola'trice *nf* Mech grinder

Mol'davia *nf* Moldavia

'mole *nf* mass; (dimensione) size

mo'lecola *nf* molecule

moleco'lare *adj* molecular

mole'stare *vt* bother; (più forte) molest

molesta'|tore, -trice *nmf* molester

mo'lestia *nf* nuisance; **molestie** *pl* **sessuali** sexual harassment *sg*

mo'lesto *adj* bothersome

Mo'lise *nm* Molise

'molla *nf* spring; **molle** *pl* tongs; **prendere qualcuno con le molle** handle somebody with kid gloves

mol'lare ① *vt* let go; (fam: lasciare) leave; fam give ⟨ceffone⟩; Naut cast off ② *vi* cease; **mollala!** fam stop that!

'molle *adj* soft; (bagnato) wet

molleggi'are ① *vi* be springy ② *vt* spring

molleggi'arsi *vr* bend at the knees

mollegg'iato *adj* bouncy, springy

mol'leggio *nm* (di auto) suspension; (di letto) springs *pl*; (esercizio) knee-bends *pl*

mol'letta *nf* (per capelli) hairgrip, barrette Am; (per bucato) clothes-peg; **mollette** *pl* (per ghiaccio ecc) tongs

mollet'tone *nm* (per tavolo) padded table cloth

mol'lezza *nf* softness; **mollezze** *pl* fig luxury

mol'lica *nf* crumb

mol'liccio *adj* squidgy

mol'lusco *nm* mollusc

'molo *nm* pier; (banchina) dock

'molotov *adj inv* **bottiglia molotov** Molotov cocktail

mol'teplice *adj* manifold; (numeroso) numerous

molteplicità *nf* multiplicity

mol'tiplica *nf* (di bicicletta) gear ratio, gear wheel

moltipli'care *vt* multiply

moltipli'carsi *vr* multiply

moltiplica'tore *nm* multiplier

moltiplica'trice *nf* calculating machine

moltiplicazi'one *nf* multiplication

molti'tudine *nf* multitude

'molto ① *adj* a lot of; (con negazione e interrogazione) much, a lot of; (con nomi plurali) many, a lot of; **non ~ tempo** not much time, not a lot of time; **molte grazie** thank you very much ② *adv* very; (con verbi) a lot; (con avverbi) much; **~ stupido** very stupid; **~ bene, grazie** very well, thank you; **mangiare ~** eat a lot; **~ più veloce** much faster; **non mangiare ~** not eat a lot, not eat much ③ *pron* a lot; (molto tempo) a lot of time; (con negazione e interrogazione) much, a lot; (plurale) many; **non ne ho ~** I don't have much, I don't have a lot; **non ne ho molti** I don't have many, I don't have a lot; **non ci ····⫸**

metterò ∼ I won't be long; **fra non** ∼ before long; **molti** (persone) a lot of people; **eravamo in molti** there were a lot of us

momentanea'mente *adv* momentarily; **è** ∼ **assente** he's not here at the moment

momen'taneo *adj* momentary

mo'mento *nm* moment; **a momenti** (a volte) sometimes; (fra un momento) in a moment; **dal** ∼ **che** since; **per il** ∼ for the time being; **al** ∼ at the moment; **da un** ∼ **all'altro** ⟨cambiare idea ecc⟩ from one moment to the next; ⟨aspettare l'arrivo di qualcuno ecc⟩ at any moment

'**monaca** *nf* nun

'**Monaco** *nf* (di Baviera) Munich; **Principato di Monaco** Monaco

'**monaco** *nm* monk

mo'narca *nm* monarch

monar'chia *nf* monarchy

mo'narchico, -a ① *adj* monarchic ② *nmf* monarchist

mona'stero *nm* (di monaci) monastery; (di monache) convent

mo'nastico *adj* monastic

monche'rino *nm* stump

'**monco** *adj* maimed; (fig: troncato) truncated; ∼ **di un braccio** one-armed

mon'dana *nf* lady of the night

mondanità *nf* (gente) beau monde; ∼ *pl* pleasures of the world

mon'dano *adj* worldly; **vita mondana** social life

mon'dare *vt* (sbucciare) peel; shell ⟨piselli⟩; (pulire) clean

mondi'ale *adj* world *attrib*; ⟨scala⟩ worldwide; (fam: fantastico) fantastic; **di fama** ∼ world-famous

mondi'ali *nmpl* World Cup

mondial'mente *adv* ⟨operare⟩ worldwide; ∼ **noto** world-famous

mon'dina *nf* seasonal worker in the rice fields

'**mondo** *nm* world; **il bel** ∼ fashionable society; **un** ∼ (molto) a lot; **non è la fine del** ∼ it's not the end of the world; **è la fine del** ∼ (fam: fantastico) it's out the world; ∼ **cane!** fam damn!. **mondo accademico** academia. **mondo del lavoro** world of work. **mondo dei sogni** never-never land. **mondo dello spettacolo** show biz

mondovisi'one *nf* **in** ∼ transmitted worldwide

monelle'ria *nf* prank

mo'nello, -a *nmf* urchin

mo'neta *nf* coin; (denaro) money; (denaro spicciolo) [small] change. **moneta estera** foreign currency. **moneta [a corso] legale** legal tender. **moneta unica** single currency

mone'tario *adj* monetary

mongolfi'era *nf* hot air balloon

Mon'golia *nf* Mongolia

'**mongolo** *adj* Mongol

mo'nile *nm* jewel

'**monito** *nm* warning

'**monitor** *nm inv* monitor

monito'raggio *nm* monitoring

moni'tore *nm* monitor

mono'albero *adj inv* single-camshaft *attrib*

mono'blocco ① *nm* Auto cylinder block ② *adj inv* ⟨cucina⟩ fitted

mo'nocolo *nm* monocle

monoco'lore *adj* Pol one-party

monocro'matico *adj* monochrome

mono'dose *adj inv* individually packaged

monoga'mia *nf* monogamy

mo'nogamo *adj* monogamous

monogra'fia *nf* monograph

mono'gramma *nm* monogram

mono'kini *nm inv* monokini

mono'lingue *adj* monolingual

mono'lito *nm* monolith

monolo'cale *nm* studio flat Br, studio apartment

mo'nologo *nm* monologue

monoma'nia *nf* monomania

mononucle'osi *nf inv* **mononucleosi infettiva** glandular fever

monoparen'tale *adj* single-parent *attrib*

mono'pattino *nm* [child's] scooter

mono'petto *adj* single-breasted

mono'plano *nm* monoplane

mono'polio *nm* monopoly. **monopolio di Stato** state monopoly

monopoliz'zare *vt* monopolize

mono'posto *nm* single-seater

mono'reddito *adj* single-income *attrib*

monosac'caride *nm* monosaccharide

mono'sci *nm inv* monoski

monosil'labico *adj* monosyllabic

mono'sillabo ① *nm* monosyllable ② *adj* monosyllabic

mo'nossido *nm* **monossido di carbonio** carbon monoxide

monote'istico *adj* monotheistic

monotona'mente *adv* monotonously

monoto'nia *nf* monotony

mo'notono *adj* monotonous

mono'uso *adj* disposable

monou'tente *adj inv* single-user *attrib*

monovo'lume *nf* people carrier, multi-purpose vehicle

monsi'gnore *nm* monsignor

mon'sone nm monsoon

'monta nf Zool covering; (modo di cavalcare) riding style; **stallone da monta** stud horse

monta'carichi nm inv hoist

mon'taggio nm Mech assembly; Cinema editing; **scatola di montaggio** assembly kit; **catena di montaggio** production line

mon'tagna nf mountain; (zona) mountains pl. **Montagne** pl **Rocciose** Rocky Mountains. **montagne** pl **russe** roller coaster, big dipper

monta'gnoso adj mountainous

monta'naro, -a nmf highlander

mon'tano adj mountain attrib

mon'tante nm (di finestra, porta) upright; Fin total amount; (nel pugilato) upper cut

mon'tare vt/i mount; get on ‹veicolo›; (aumentare) rise; Mech assemble; frame ‹quadro›; Culin whip; edit ‹film›; (a cavallo) ride; fig blow up

mon'tarsi vr ~ **la testa** get big-headed

monta'scale nm inv stairlift

mon'tato, -a nmf fam poser

monta‖'tore, -trice nmf assembler

monta'tura nf Mech assembling; (di occhiali) frame; (di gioiello) mounting; fig exaggeration

'monte nm anche fig mountain; **a** ~ up stream; **andare a** ~ be ruined; **mandare a** ~ **qualcosa** ruin something. **Monte Bianco** Mont Blanc. **monte di pietà** pawnshop

Monte'negro nm Montenegro

monte'premi nm inv jackpot

mont'gomery nm inv duffel coat

mon'tone nm ram; **carne di montone** mutton

montu'oso adj mountainous

monumen'tale adj monumental

monu'mento nm monument. **monumento ai caduti** war memorial. **monumento commemorativo** memorial. **monumento nazionale** national monument

mo'plen® nm moulded plastic

mo'quette nf (tappeto) fitted carpet

'mora nf (di gelso) mulberry; (di rovo) blackberry

mo'rale ① adj moral ② nf morals pl; (di storia) moral ③ nm morale

mora'lista nmf moralist

mora'listico adj moralistic

moralità nf inv morality; (condotta) morals pl

moraliz'zare vt/i moralize

moral'mente adv morally

mora'toria nf moratorium

morbida'mente adv softly

morbi'dezza nf softness

'morbido adj soft

mor'billo nm measles sg

'morbo nm disease. **morbo di Alzheimer** Alzheimer's disease. **morbo di Creutzfeldt Jakob** Creutzfeldt-Jakob disease, CJD. **morbo della mucca pazza** mad cow disease

morbosa'mente adv morbidly

morbosità nf (qualità) morbidity

mor'boso adj morbid

'morchia nf sludge

mor'dace adj cutting

mor'dente adj biting

'mordere vt bite; (corrodere) bite into

mordicchi'are vt gnaw

mo'rello ① nm black horse ② adj blackish

mo'rena nf moraine

mo'rente adj dying

mo'resco adj Moorish

mor'fina nf morphine

morfi'nomane nmf morphine addict

morfolo'gia nf morphology

morfo'logico adj morphological

mori'bondo adj dying; ‹istituzione› moribund

morige'rato adj moderate

mo'rire vi die; fig die out; **fa un freddo da** ~ it's freezing cold, it's perishing; ~ **di noia** be bored to death; **c'era da** ~ **dal ridere** it was hilariously funny; **morir di fame** starve to death; fig starve

mor'mone nmf Mormon

mormo'rare vt/i murmur; ‹brontolare› mutter

mormo'rio nm murmuring; (lamentela) grumbling

'moro ① adj dark ② nm Moor

morosità nf default

mo'roso adj in arrears

'morra nf game for two players where each shouts a number at the same time as showing a number of fingers

'morsa nf vice; fig grip

'morse adj **alfabeto morse** Morse code

mor'setto nm clamp; (stringinaso) nose clip. **morsetto per batteria** battery lead connection

morsi'care vt bite

morsica'tura nf [snake] bite

'morso nm bite; (di cibo, briglia) bit; **i morsi della fame** hunger pangs

morta'della nf mortadella (type of salted pork)

mor'taio nm mortar

mor'tale adj mortal; (simile a morte) deadly; **di una noia** ~ deadly

mortalità *nf* mortality

mortal'mente *adv* ⟨*ferito*⟩ fatally; ⟨*offeso*⟩ mortally; ⟨*annoiato*⟩ to death; ~ **stanco** *fam* dead tired

morta'retto *nm* firecracker

'morte *nf* death; **non è la ~ di nessuno** it's not the end of the world; **lo odia a ~** *fam* she can't stand the sight of him; **annoiarsi a ~** *fam* be bored to death. **~ cerebrale** brain death

mortifi'cante *adj* mortifying

mortifi'care *vt* mortify

mortifi'carsi *vr* be mortified

mortifi'cato *adj* mortified

mortificazi'one *nf* mortification

'morto, -a ① *pp di* MORIRE
② *adj* dead; **~ di freddo** frozen to death; **stanco ~** dead tired
③ *nm* dead man
④ *nf* dead woman

mor'torio *nm* funeral

mo'saico *nm* mosaic

'Mosca *nf* Moscow

'mosca *nf* fly; (barba) goatee; **cadere come le mosche** be dropping like flies; **essere una ~ bianca** be a rarity; **non si sentiva volare una ~** you could have heard a pin drop. **mosca cieca** blindman's buff

mo'scato ① *adj* muscat; **noce moscata** nutmeg
② *nm* muscatel

mosce'rino *nm* midge; (fam: persona) midget

mo'schea *nf* mosque

moschetti'ere *nm* musketeer

mo'schetto *nm* musket

moschet'tone *nm* (in alpinismo) snaplink; (gancio) spring clip

moschi'cida ① *adj inv* **carta ~** fly paper
② *nm* fly spray

'moscio *adj* limp; **avere l'erre moscia** not be able to say one's rs properly

mo'scone *nm* bluebottle; (barca) pedalo

Mosè *nm* Moses

'mossa *nf* movement; (passo) move

'mosso ① *pp di* MUOVERE
② *adj* ⟨*mare*⟩ rough; ⟨*capelli*⟩ wavy; ⟨*fotografia*⟩ blurred

mo'starda *nf* mustard. **mostarda di Cremona** preserve made from candied fruit in grape must or sugar with mustard

'mostra *nf* show; (d'arte) exhibition; **far ~ di** pretend; **in ~** on show; **mettersi in ~** make oneself conspicuous; **far ~ di sé** show off; **far bella ~ di sé** look impressive. **mostra dell'artigianato** craft fair

'mostra-mer'cato *nf* trade fair

mo'strare *vt* show; (indicare) point out; (spiegare) explain; **~ di** (sembrare) seem; (fingere) pretend

mos'trarsi *vr* show oneself; (apparire) appear

mo'strina *nf* flash

'mostro *nm* monster; (fig: persona) genius. **mostro sacro** fig sacred cow

mostruosa'mente *adv* tremendously

mostru'oso *adj* monstrous; (incredibile) enormous

mo'tel *nm inv* motel

moti'vare *vt* cause; Jur justify

moti'vato *adj* ⟨*persona*⟩ motivated; ⟨*azione*⟩ justified

motivazi'one *nf* motivation; (giustificazione) justification

mo'tivo *nm* reason; (movente) motive; (in musica, letteratura) theme; (disegno) pattern, motif; **senza ~** for no reason; (senza giustificazione) unjustifiably. **motivo cachemire** paisley. **motivo a scacchi** chequered pattern

'moto ① *nm* motion; (esercizio) exercise; (gesto) movement; (sommossa) rising; **mettere in ~** start ⟨*motore*⟩. **moto ondoso** swell. **moto perpetuo** perpetual motion
② *nf inv* (motocicletta) motor bike

moto'carro *nm* three-wheeler

motoci'cletta *nf* motorcycle, motorbike. **motocicletta da corsa** racing motorbike, racer

motoci'clismo *nm* motorcycling

motoci'clista *nmf* motorcyclist, biker

moto'cross *nm* motocross, scrambling

motocros'sista *nmf* scrambler

moto'lancia *nf* motor launch

moto'nautica *nf* speedboat racing

moto'nave *nf* motor vessel

mo'tore ① *adj* motor *attrib*
② *nm* motor, engine; **con ~ turbo** turbocharged. **motore diesel** diesel engine. **motore a iniezione** fuel injection engine. **motore raffreddato ad aria** air-cooled engine. **motore a reazione** jet [engine]. **motore di ricerca** Comput search engine. **motore a scoppio** internal combustion engine

moto'retta *nf* motor scooter

moto'rino *nm* moped. **motorino d'avviamento** starter motor

mo'torio *adj* motor *attrib*

moto'rista *nmf* **motorista di bordo** flight engineer

motoriz'zare *vt* motorize

motoriz'zato *adj* Mil motorized

motorizzazi'one *nf* (ufficio) vehicle licensing office

moto'scafo *nm* motorboat

moto'sega *nf* chain saw

motove'detta *nf* patrol vessel, patrol boat

mo'trice *nf* engine

'motto *nm* motto; (facezia) witticism; (massima) saying

'mountain bike *nf inv* mountain bike

mouse *nm inv* Comput mouse

mousse *nf inv* Culin mousse. **mousse al cioccolato** chocolate mousse

mo'vente *nm* motive

mo'venze *nfpl* movements

movimen'tare *vt* enliven

movimen'tato *adj* lively

movi'mento *nm* movement; **essere sempre in** ∼ be always on the go. **movimento passeggeri e merci** passenger and freight traffic

Mozam'bico *nm* Mozambique

mozi'one *nf* motion. **mozione d'ordine** point of order

mozzafi'ato *adj inv* nail-biting

moz'zare *vt* cut off; dock ‹coda›; ∼ **il fiato a qualcuno** take somebody's breath away

mozza'rella *nf* mozzarella (mild, white cheese)

mozzi'cone *nm* (di sigaretta) stub

'mozzo ① *nm* Mech hub; Naut ship's boy ② *adj* ‹coda› truncated; ‹testa› severed

ms *abbr* (**manoscritto**) MS

'mucca *nf* cow; **morbo della mucca pazza** mad cow disease

'mucchio *nm* heap, pile; **un** ∼ **di** fig lots of

mucil'lagine *nf* Bot mucilage

'muco *nm* mucus

'muffa *nf* mould; **fare la** ∼ go mouldy

muf'fire *vi* go mouldy

muf'fola *nf* mitt

mu'flone *nm* Zool mouflon

mugghi'are *vi* ‹vento, mare› roar

mug'gire *vi* ‹mucca› moo, low; ‹toro› bellow

mug'gito *nm* moo; (di toro) bellow; (azione) mooing; bellowing

mu'ghetto *nm* lily of the valley

mugo'lare *vi* whine; ‹persona› moan

mugo'lio *nm* whining

mugu'gnare *vt* fam mumble

mulatti'era *nf* mule track

mu'latto, -a *nmf* mulatto

mu'leta *nf inv* muleta

muli'ebre *adj* liter feminine

muli'nare *vi* spin

muli'nello *nm* (d'acqua) whirlpool; (di vento) eddy; (giocattolo) windmill

mu'lino *nm* mill. **mulino a vento** windmill

'mulo *nm* mule

'multa *nf* fine. **multa per divieto di sosta** parking ticket

mul'tare *vt* fine

multico'lore *adj* multicoloured

multicultu'rale *adj* multicultural

multi'etnico *adj* multi-ethnic

multifo'cale *adj* ‹lente› varifocal. **occhiali multifocali** varifocals

multifunzio'nale *adj* multifunction[al]

multilate'rale *adj* multilateral

multi'lingue *adj inv* multilingual

multi'media *nmpl* multimedia

multimedi'ale *adj* multimedia *attrib*

multimedialità *nf* multimedia

multimiliar'dario, -a *nmf* multi-millionaire

multinazio'nale *adj & nf* multinational

'multiplo *adj & nm* multiple

multiproprietà *nf inv* time-share; **una casa in** ∼ a time-share

multiraz'ziale *adj* multi-racial

multi'sale *adj inv* **cinema multisale** multiplex [cinema]

multi'tasking *nm* Comput multitasking

multi'uso *adj inv* ‹utensile› all-purpose

'mummia *nf* mummy; (fig: persona) old fogey

mummifi'care *vt* mummify

'mungere *vt* milk

mungi'tura *nf* milking

munici'pale *adj* municipal

municipalità *nf inv* town council

muni'cipio *nm* town hall

munifi'cenza *nf* munificence, bounty

mu'nifico *adj* munificent

mu'nire *vt* fortify; ∼ **di** (provvedere) supply with; **munitevi di un carrello/cestino** please take a trolley/basket

munizi'oni *nfpl* ammunition *sg*

'munto *pp di* MUNGERE

mu'overe *vt* move; (suscitare) arouse

mu'oversi *vr* move; **muoviti!** hurry up!, come on!

'mura *nfpl* (di città) walls

mu'raglia *nf* wall

mu'rale *adj* mural; ‹pittura› wall *attrib*

mur'are *vt* wall up

mu'rario *adj* masonry *attrib*; **cinta muraria** walls *pl*; **opera muraria** masonry

mura'tore *nm* bricklayer; (con pietre) mason; (operaio edile) builder

mura'tura *nf* (di pietra) masonry, stonework; (di mattoni) brickwork

mu'rena *nf* moray eel

'muro nm wall; (di nebbia) bank; a ~
⟨armadio⟩ built-in. **muro divisorio**
partition wall. **muro di gomma** fig wall
of indifference; **fare ~ di gomma**
stonewall. **muro a intercapedine**
cavity wall. **Muro del pianto** Wailing
Wall. **muro portante** load-bearing wall.
muro del suono sound barrier

'musa nf anche fig muse

muschi'ato adj musky

'muschio nm musk; Bot moss

musco'lare adj muscular

muscola'tura nf muscles pl

'muscolo nm muscle

musco'loso adj muscular

mu'seo nm museum

museru'ola nf muzzle

'musica nf music. **musica gospel**
gospel music. **musica folk** folk [music]

'musical nm inv musical

musi'cale adj musical

musi'care vt set to music

musicas'setta nf cassette

musi'cista nmf musician

musicolo'gia nf musicology

'muso nm muzzle; (pej: di persona) mug; (di
aeroplano) nose; **fare il ~** sulk

mu'sone, -a adj & nmf sulker

'mussola nf muslin

mussul'mano, -a adj & nmf Muslim,
Moslem

'muta nf (cambio) change; (di penne) moult;
(di cani) pack; (per immersione subacquea)
wetsuit

muta'mento nm change

mu'tande nfpl pants

mutan'dine nfpl panties. **mutandine
da bagno** bathing trunks; (da donna)
bikini bottom

mutan'doni nmpl (da uomo) long johns;
(da donna) bloomers

mu'tante nmf mutant

mu'tare vt change

mutazi'one nf mutation

mu'tevole adj changeable

muti'lare vt mutilate

muti'lato, -a ① adj crippled
② nmf disabled person. **mutilato di
guerra** disabled ex-serviceman.
mutilato del lavoro person disabled at
work

mutilazi'one nf mutilation

mu'tismo nm dumbness; fig obstinate
silence

'muto adj dumb; (silenzioso) silent; (fonetica)
mute

'mutua nf [cassa] mutua sickness
benefit fund

mutu'abile adj ⟨farmaco⟩ prescribable
on the NHS

mutu'are vt borrow ⟨teoria, parola⟩

mutua'tario, -a nmf Fin borrower

mutu'ato, -a nmf ≈ NHS patient

'mutuo¹ adj mutual

'mutuo² nm loan; (per la casa) mortgage;
fare un ~ take out a mortgage; **società di
mutuo soccorso** friendly society **mutuo
ipotecario** mortgage

Nn

N° abbr (**numero**) No.

na'babbo nm nabob; **vivere da ~** live in
the lap of luxury

'nacchera nf castanet

na'dir nm nadir

'nafta nf naphtha; (per motori) diesel oil; **a
~ ⟨bruciatore⟩** oil-burning

'naia nf cobra; (sl: servizio militare) national
service

'nailon nm nylon

Na'mibia nf Namibia

na'nismo nm dwarfism

'nanna nf (sl: infantile) bye-byes; **andare a
~** go bye-byes; **fare la ~** sleep

'nano, -a adj & nmf dwarf

nanose'condo nm nanosecond

'napalm nm napalm

napole'tana nf (caffettiera) Neapolitan
coffee maker

napole'tano, -a adj & nmf Neapolitan

'Napoli nf Naples

'nappa nf tassel; (pelle) soft leather

narci'sismo nm narcissism

narci'sista adj & nmf narcissist

nar'ciso nm narcissus

nar'cosi nf general anaesthesia

nar'cotici nf Drug Squad

nar'cotico adj & nm narcotic

na'rice nf nostril

nar'rare vt tell

narra'tivo, -a ① adj narrative
② nf fiction

narra|'tore, **-trice** *nmf* narrator
narrazi'one *nf* narration; (racconto) story
na'sale *adj* nasal
na'scente *adj* budding
'nascere *vi* (venire al mondo) be born; (germogliare) sprout; (sorgere) rise; ∼ **da** fig arise from
'nascita *nf* birth
nasci'turo *nm* unborn child
na'scondere *vt* hide
na'scondersi *vr* hide
nascon'diglio *nm* hiding place
nascon'dino *nm* hide-and-seek
na'scosto ① pp di NASCONDERE ② *adj* hidden; **di** ∼ secretly; **ascoltare di** ∼ listen in on ‹*conversazione*›
na'sello *nm* (pesce) hake
'naso *nm* nose
na'sone *nm* big nose, hooter fam
'nassa *nf* lobster pot
'nastro *nm* ribbon; (di registratore ecc) tape. **nastro adesivo** adhesive tape, sticky tape. **nastro isolante** insulating tape. **nastro magnetico** magnetic tape, magtape fam. **nastro trasportatore** conveyor belt
Na'tale *nm* Christmas
na'tale *adj* ‹giorno, paese› of one's birth
na'tali *nmpl* parentage
natalità *nf* [number of] births, birthrate
nata'lizio *adj* (del Natale) Christmas *attrib*
na'tante ① *adj* floating ② *nm* craft
'natica *nf* buttock
na'tio *adj* native
Natività *nf* Nativity
na'tivo, **-a** *adj & nmf* native
'NATO *nf* Nato, NATO
'nato ① pp di NASCERE ② *adj* born; **uno scrittore** ∼ a born writer; **nata Rossi** née Rossi
na'tura *nf* nature; **pagare in** ∼ pay in kind; **di** ∼ **politica** of a political nature. **natura morta** still life
natu'rale *adj* natural; **al** ∼ ‹alimento› plain, natural; ∼**!** naturally, of course
natura'lezza *nf* naturalness
naturaliz'zare *vt* naturalize
natural'mente *adv* (ovviamente) naturally, of course
natu'rista *nmf* naturalist
natu'ristico *adj* naturist
naufra'gare *vi* be wrecked; ‹persona› be shipwrecked
nau'fragio *nm* shipwreck; fig wreck
'naufrago, **-a** *nmf* survivor
'nausea *nf* nausea; **avere la** ∼ feel sick

nausea'bondo *adj* nauseating
nause'are *vt* nauseate
'nautica *nf* navigation
'nautico *adj* nautical
na'vale *adj* naval
na'vata *nf* (centrale) nave; (laterale) aisle
'nave *nf* ship. **nave ammiraglia** flagship. **nave da carico** cargo boat. **nave cisterna** tanker. **nave da crociera** cruise liner. **nave fattoria** factory ship. **nave da guerra** warship. **nave di linea** liner. **nave passeggeri** passenger ship. **nave portacontainer** container ship. **nave spaziale** spaceship. **nave traghetto** ferry
na'vetta *nf* shuttle
navi'cella *nf* **navicella spaziale** nose cone
navi'gabile *adj* navigable
navi'gare *vi* sail; ∼ **in Internet** surf the Net, browse
naviga|'tore, **-trice** *nmf* navigator; (in Internet) surfer. **navigatore solitario** lone yachtsman. **navigatore spaziale** spaceman
navigazi'one *nf* navigation; **della** ∼ navigational
na'viglio *nm* fleet; (canale) canal
nazifa'scismo *nm* Nazi fascism
nazifa'scista *nmf* Nazi fascist
nazio'nale ① *adj* national ② *nf* Sport national team
naziona'lismo *nm* nationalism
naziona'lista *nmf* nationalist
nazionalità *nf inv* nationality
nazionaliz'zare *vt* nationalize
nazi'one *nf* nation; **Nazioni** *pl* **Unite** United Nations
na'zista *adj & nmf* Nazi
N.B. *abbr* (**nota bene**) NB
n.d.r. *abbr* (**nota del redattore**) editor's note
'n 'drangheta *nf* Calabrian Mafia
n.d.t. *abbr* (**nota del traduttore**) translator's note
NE *abbr* (**nord-est**) NE
ne ① *pron* (di lui) about him; (di lei) about her; (di loro) about them; (di ciò) about it; (da ciò) from that; (di un insieme) of it; (di un gruppo) of them; **ne sono contento** I'm happy about it; **non ne conosco nessuno** I don't know any of them; **ne ho** I have some; **non ne ho più** I don't have any left; ② *adv* from there; **ne vengo ora** I've just come from there; **me ne vado** I'm off; **ne va della mia reputazione** my reputation is at stake
né *conj* né... né... neither... nor...; **non ne ho il tempo né la voglia** I don't have either the time or the inclination; **né tu né io vogliamo andare** neither you nor I want ⠄⠂⊱

to go; **né l'uno né l'altro** neither [of them/ us]

ne'anche ① *adv* (neppure) not even; (senza neppure) without even
② *conj* (e neppure) neither...nor; **io non parlo inglese e lui** ~ I don't speak English, neither does he *or* and he doesn't either

'nebbia *nf* mist; (in città, autostrada) fog

nebbi'oso *adj* misty; ⟨città, autostrada⟩ foggy

nebuliz'zare *vt* atomize

nebulizza'tore *nm* atomizer; (per il naso) nasal spray

nebulizzazi'one *nf* atomizing; **fare delle nebulizzazioni** take nasal sprays

nebulosità *nf* vagueness

nebu'loso *adj* hazy; ⟨teoria⟩ nebulous; ⟨discorso⟩ woolly

necessaria'mente *adv* necessarily

neces'sario ① *adj* necessary
② *nm* **fare il** ~ do the necessary, do the needful

necessità *nf inv* necessity; (bisogno) need

necessi'tare *vi* ~ **di** need; (essere necessario) be necessary

necro'logio *nm* obituary

ne'cropoli *nf inv* necropolis

ne'crosi *nf* necrosis

ne'fando *adj* wicked

ne'fasto *adj* ill-omened

ne'frite *nf* nephritis

nefrolo'gia *nf* nephrology

ne'frologo, **-a** *nmf* nephrologist

ne'gabile *adj* deniable

ne'gare *vt* deny; (rifiutare) refuse; **essere negato per qualcosa** be no good at something

nega'tiva *nf* negative

nega'tivo *adj* negative

negazi'one *nf* negation; (diniego) denial; Gram negative

ne'gletto *adj* neglected

'negli = IN + GLI

negli'gente *adj* negligent

negli'genza *nf* negligence

negozi'abile *adj* negotiable

negozi'ante *nmf* dealer; (bottegaio) shopkeeper

negozi'are ① *vt* negotiate
② *vi* ~ **in** trade in, deal in

negozi'ati *nmpl* negotiations

ne'gozio *nm* shop. **negozio di abbigliamento** clothes shop. **negozio di alimentari** grocer's. **negozio di antiquariato** antique shop. **negozio duty free** duty-free shop. **negozio di ferramenta** hardware shop. **negozio**

giuridico legal transaction. **negozio di souvenir** gift shop

'negro, **-a** ① *adj* Negro, black
② *nmf* Negro, black; (scrittore) ghost writer; **come un** ~ ⟨lavorare⟩ like a slave

negro'mante *nmf* necromancer

'nei = IN + I

nel = IN + IL

'nella = IN + LA

'nelle = IN + LE

'nello = IN + LO

'nembo *nm* nimbus

ne'mesi *nf* nemesis

ne'mico, **-a** ① *adj* hostile
② *nmf* enemy

nem'meno *conj* not even

'nenia *nf* dirge; (per bambini) lullaby; (piagnucolio) wail

'neo *nm* mole; (applicato) beauty spot

neo+ *pref* neo+

neo'classico *adj* neoclassical

neocolonia'lismo *nm* neocolonialism

neofa'scismo *nm* neofascism

neola'tino *adj* Romance

neolaure'ato, **-a** *nmf* recent graduate

neo'litico *adj* Neolithic

neolo'gismo *nm* neologism

'neon *nm* neon

neo'nato, **-a** ① *adj* new born
② *nmf* newborn baby

neona'zismo *nm* Neonazism

neona'zista *adj* & *nmf* Neonazi

neozelan'dese ① *adj* New Zealand *attrib*
② *nmf* New Zealander

'Nepal *nm* Nepal

nep'pure *conj* not even

ne'rastro *adj* blackish

'nerbo *nm* (forza) strength; fig backbone; **senza** ~ effete

nerbo'ruto *adj* brawny

ne'retto *nm* Typ bold [type]

'nero ① *adj* black; (fam: arrabbiato) fuming
② *nm* black; **l'ho visto** ~ **su bianco** I've seen it in black and white; **mettere** ~ **su bianco** put in writing. **nero pieno** Typ solid. **nero di seppia** sepia

nerva'tura *nf* nerves *pl*; Bot veining; (di libro) band

ner'vetti *nmpl* chopped beef and veal with onions

ner'vino *adj* ⟨gas⟩ nerve *attrib*

'nervo *nm* nerve; Bot vein; **avere i nervi** be bad-tempered; **dare ai** *o* **sui nervi a qualcuno** get on somebody's nerves

nervo'sismo *nm* nerviness

ner'voso *adj* nervous, edgy; (irritabile) bad-tempered; **avere il** ~ be irritable; **esaurimento nervoso** nervous breakdown

'nespola *nf* medlar
'nespolo *nm* medlar[-tree]
'nesso *nm* link, connection
nes'suno ① *adj* no, not... any; (qualche) any; **non ho nessun problema** I don't have any problems, I have no problems; **non ha nessun valore** it hasn't any value, it has no value; **da nessuna parte** nowhere; **non lo trovo da nessuna parte** I can't find it anywhere; **in nessun modo** on no account; **per nessun motivo** for no reason; **nessuna notizia?** any news?
② *pron* nobody, no one, not... anybody, not... anyone; (qualcuno) anybody, anyone; **hai delle domande? –nessuna** do you have any questions? - none; ~ **di voi** none of you; ~ **dei due** (di voi due) neither of you; **non ho visto** ~ **dei tuoi amici** I haven't seen any of your friends; **c'è** ~**?** is anybody there?
'nesting *nm inv* Comput nesting
net *nm inv* Tennis net cord
'nettare[1] *nm* nectar
net'tare[2] *vt* clean
netta'rina *nf* nectarine
net'tezza *nf* cleanliness. **nettezza urbana** cleansing department
'netto *adj* clean; (chiaro) clear; Comm net; **di** ~ just like that
Net'tuno *nm* Neptune
nettur'bino *nm* dustman
'network *nm inv* network. **network televisivo** network television
'neuro *nf* neurological clinic
neuro+ *pref* neuro+
neurochirur'gia *nf* brain surgery
neurochi'rurgo *nm* brain surgeon
neurolo'gia *nf* neurology
neurologico *adj* neurological
neuropsichi'atra *nmf* neuropsychiatrist
neuropsichia'tria *nf* neuropsychiatry
neu'trale *adj & nm* neutral
neutralità *nf* neutrality
neutraliz'zare *vt* neutralize
'neutro ① *adj* neutral; Gram neuter ② *nm* Gram neuter
neu'trone *nm* neutron
ne'vaio *nm* snow-field
'neve *nf* snow
nevi'care *vi* snow; **nevica** it is snowing
nevi'cata *nf* snowfall
ne'vischio *nm* sleet
ne'voso *adj* snowy
nevral'gia *nf* neuralgia
ne'vralgico *adj* neuralgic; **punto nevralgico** nerve centre; (di questione ecc) crucial point
nevraste'nia *nf* neurasthenia

nevra'stenico *adj* neurasthenic; (irritabile) hot tempered
ne'vrite *nf* neuritis
ne'vrosi *nf inv* neurosis
ne'vrotico *adj* neurotic
'nibbio *nm* kite
Nica'ragua *nm* Nicaragua
nicara'guense *adj & nmf* Nicaraguan
'nicchia *nf* niche
nicchi'are *vi* shilly-shally
'nichel *nm* nickel
nichi'lista ① *nmf* nihilist ② *adj* nihilistic
nico'tina *nf* nicotine
nidi'ace *nm* nestling
nidi'ata *nf* brood
nidifi'care *vi* nest
nidifi'cato *adj* Comput nested
nidifIcazi'one *nf* Zool nesting
'nido *nm* nest; (giardino d'infanzia) crèche; a ~ **d'ape** ⟨tessuto⟩ honeycomb. **nido di uccello** bird's nest. **nido di vipere** fig nest of vipers
ni'ente ① *pron* nothing, not... anything; (qualcosa) anything; **non ho fatto** ~ **di male** I didn't do anything wrong, I did nothing wrong; **nient'altro?** anything else?; **grazie! –di** ~**!** thank you! –don't mention it!; **non serve a** ~ it is no use; **vuoi** ~**?** do you want anything?; **dal** ~ ⟨venire su⟩ from nothing; **da** ~ (poco importante) minor; (di poco valore) worthless
② *adj inv* fam ~ **pesci oggi** no fish today; **non ho** ~ **fame** I'm not the slightest bit hungry
③ *adv* **non fa** ~ (non importa) it doesn't matter; **per** ~ at all; ⟨litigare⟩ over nothing; ~ **affatto!** no way!
④ *nm* **un bel** ~ absolutely nothing, damn-all fam; **basta un** ~ **per spaventarlo** it doesn't take much to scare him
nientedi'meno, nientemeno ① *adv* ~ **che** no less than ② *int* fancy that!
'Niger *nm* Niger
Ni'geria *nf* Nigeria
neurochi'rurgo *nm* brain surgeon
night *nm inv* night club
'Nilo *nm* Nile
'ninfa *nf* nymph
nin'fea *nf* water lily
nin'fomane *nf* nymphomaniac; **da** ~ nymphomaniac
ninna'nanna *nf* lullaby
'ninnolo *nm* plaything; (fronzolo) knick-knack
ni'pote ① *nm* (di zii) nephew; (di nonni) grandson, grandchild; **nipoti** *pl* (collettivo) grandchildren, nephews and nieces

2 *nf* (di zii) niece; (di nonni) granddaughter, grandchild

nip'ponico *adj* Japanese

'**nisba** *pron* (sl: niente) zilch

'**nltldo** *adj* neat; (chiaro) clear

ni'trato *nm* nitrate

'**nitrico** *adj* nitric

ni'trire *vi* neigh

ni'trito *nm* (di cavallo) neigh; Chem nitrite

nitro+ *pref* nitro+

nitroglice'rina *nf* nitroglycerine

'**niveo** *adj* snow-white

N.N. *abbr* (**numeri**) Nos

NO *abbr* (**nord-ovest**) NW

no **1** *adv* no; **credo di no** I don't think so; **perché no?** why not?; **io no** not me; **sì o no?** yes or no?; **ha detto così, no?** he said so, didn't he?; **fa freddo, no?** it's cold, isn't it?; **se no** otherwise
2 *nm* no; (nelle votazioni) nay

nobil'donna *nf* noblewoman

'**nobile** **1** *adj* noble; **metallo ~** noble metal; **di animo ~** noble-minded
2 *nm* noble, nobleman
3 *nf* noble, noblewoman

nobili'are *adj* noble

nobiltà *nf* nobility

nobilu'omo *nm* (*pl* **nobiluomini**) nobleman

'**nocca** *nf* knuckle

nocci'ola *nf* hazelnut

noccio'line [americane] *nfpl* peanuts

nocci'olo[1] *nm* (albero) hazel

'**nocciolo**[2] *nm* stone; Phys core; fig heart; **il ~ della questione** the heart of the matter

'**noce** **1** *nf* walnut. **noce moscata** nutmeg. **noce pecan** pecan. **noce di vitello** veal with mushrooms
2 *nm* (legno) walnut; (albero) walnut [tree]

noce'pesca *nf* nectarine

no'cino *nm* walnut liqueur

no'civo *adj* harmful

no'dino *nm* veal chop

'**nodo** *nm* knot; fig lump; Comput node; **fare il ~ della cravatta** do up one's tie. **nodo alla gola** lump in the throat; **nodo della questione** crux of the matter. **nodo ferroviario** railway junction. **nodo piano** reef knot. **nodo scorsoio** slipknot

no'doso *adj* knotty

'**nodulo** *nm* nodule

Noè *nm* Noah

no-'global *adj* anti-globalization

'**nol** *pers pron* (soggetto) we; (oggetto, con prep) us; **chi è? –siamo ~** who is it? –it's us; **~ due** the two of us

'**noia** *nf* boredom; (fastidio) bother; (persona) bore; **dar ~** annoy

noi'altri *pers pron* we

noi'oso *adj* boring; (fastidioso) tiresome

noleggi'are *vt* hire; (dare a noleggio) hire out; charter ⟨nave, aereo⟩

no'leggio *nm* hire; (di nave, aereo) charter. **noleggio barche/biciclette/sci** boat/cycle/ski hire

'**nolo** *nm* hire; Naut freight; **a ~** for hire

'**nomade** **1** *adj* nomadic
2 *nmf* nomad

'**nome** *nm* name; Gram noun; **a ~ di** ⟨da parte di⟩ on behalf of; **di ~** by name; **farsi un ~** make a name for oneself; **nel ~ di...** in the name of.... **nome d'arte** professional name. **nome di battaglia** nom de guerre. **nome di battesimo** first name, Christian name, given name. **nome in codice** code name. **nome depositato** trade-name. **nome di dominio** Comput domain name. **nome per esteso** full name. **nome del file** filename. **nome proprio** proper name, proper noun. **nome da ragazza** maiden name. **nome da sposata** married name

no'mea *nf* reputation

nomencla'tura *nf* nomenclature

no'mignolo *nm* nickname

'**nomina** *nf* appointment; **di prima ~** newly appointed

nomi'nale *adj* nominal; Gram noun *attrib*

nomi'nare *vt* name; (menzionare) mention; (eleggere) appoint

nomina'tivo **1** *adj* nominative; Comm registered
2 *nm* nominative; (nome) name; **caso nominativo** nominative case

non *adv* not; **~ ti amo** I do not *or* don't love you; **~ c'è di che** not at all; **~ più** no longer

nonché *conj* (tanto meno) let alone; (e anche) as well as

nonconfor'mista *adj & nmf* nonconformist

nonconformità *nf* noncompliance

noncu'rante *adj* nonchalant; (negligente) indifferent

noncu'ranza *nf* nonchalance; (negligenza) indifference

nondi'meno *conj* nevertheless

'**nonna** *nf* grandmother, grandma fam, gran fam

'**nonno** *nm* grandfather, grandpa fam; **nonni** *pl* grandparents

non'nulla *nm inv* trifle

'**nono** *adj & nm* ninth

nono'stante **1** *prep* in spite of
2 *conj* although

non stop *adj inv & adv* nonstop

nontiscordardimé *nm inv* forget-me-not

nonvio'lento *adj* nonviolent

nonvio'lenza *nf* nonviolence

no 'profit *adj inv* non profit

nor'cino *nm* pig butcher

nord *nm* north; **del** ~ northern

nord-'est *nm* northeast; **a** ~ northeasterly; **del** ~ northeastern; **vento di nord-est** northeasterly [wind]

'nordico *adj* northern

nor'dista *adj & nmf* Yankee

nordocciden'tale *adj* northwestern

nordorien'tale *adj* northeastern

nord-'ovest *nm* northwest; **a** ~ northwesterly; **del** ~ northwestern **vento di nord-ovest** northwesterly [wind]

'norma *nf* norm; (regola) rule; (per l'uso) instruction; **a** ~ **di legge** according to law; **è buona** ~ it's advisable; **di** ~ as a rule, normally

nor'male ①*adj* normal ②*nm* **fuori del** ~ out of the ordinary; **superiore al** ~ above average

normalità *nf* normality; **rientrare nella** ~ be quite normal

normaliz'zare *vt* normalize

normal'mente *adv* normally

Norman'dia *nf* Normandy

nor'manno *adj* from Normandy; (storico) Norman

normativa *nf* regulations *pl*, laws *pl*

norma'tivo *adj* normative, prescriptive

nor'mografo *nm* stencil

nor'reno *adj* Norse

norve'gese *adj & nmf* Norwegian

Nor'vegia *nf* Norway

noso'comio *nm fml* hospital

nossi'gnore *adv* (assolutamente no) no way

nostal'gia *nf* (di casa, patria) homesickness; (del passato) nostalgia; **aver** ~ be homesick; **aver** ~ **di qualcuno** miss somebody

no'stalgico, -a ①*adj* nostalgic ②*nmf* reactionary

nostra ▸ NOSTRO

no'strale *adj* local

no'strano *adj* local; (fatto in casa) home-made

'nostre ▸ NOSTRO

'nostri ▸ NOSTRO

'nostro ① (il nostro *m*, la nostra *f*, i nostri *mpl*; le nostre *fpl*) *poss adj* our; **quella macchina è nostra** that car is ours; ~ **padre** our father; **un** ~ **amico** a friend of ours ②*poss pron* ours

no'stromo *nm* bo's'n, boatswain

'nota *nf* (segno) sign; (comunicazione, commento, Mus) note; (conto) bill; (lista) list; **degno di** ~ noteworthy; **prendere** ~ take note; **una** ~ **di colore** a touch of colour; **mettere in** ~ **qualcosa** add something to the list. **nota di accredito** Comm credit note; **note** *pl* **caratteristiche** distinguishing marks. **nota spese** expense account

no'tabile *adj & nm* notable

no'taio *nm* notary

no'tare *vt* (segnare) mark; (annotare) note down; (osservare) notice; **far** ~ **qualcosa** point something out; **farsi** ~ get oneself noticed; **nota bene che...** please note that...

notazi'one *nf* marking; (annotazione) notation

'notebook *nm inv* Comput notebook (PC)

'notes *nm inv* notepad

no'tevole *adj* (degno di nota) remarkable; (grande) considerable

no'tifica *nf* notification

notifi'care *vt* notify; Comm advise; ~ **un ordine di comparizione [in giudizio]** subpoena

notificazi'one *nf* notification

no'tizia *nf* **una** ~ a piece of news, some news; (informazione) a piece of information, some information; **le notizie** the news *sg*; **per avere** ~ **di** ⟨telefonare⟩ for news of; **non ha più dato notizie di sé** he hasn't been in touch since. **notizia di attualità** news item

notizi'ario *nm* news *sg*

'noto *adj* [well-]known; **rendere** ~ (far sapere) announce

notorietà *nf* fame; **raggiungere la** ~ become famous

no'torio *adj* well-known; *pej* notorious

not'tambulo *nm* night-bird

not'tata *nf* night; **far** ~ stay up all night

'notte *nf* night; **di** ~ at night; **a** ~ **fatta** when night had fallen; **la** ~ (durante la notte) at night; **buona** ~ good night; **fermarsi per la** ~ stay overnight; **peggio che andar di** ~ worse than ever; **prima** ~ **di nozze** wedding night. **notte in bianco** sleepless night

notte'tempo *adv* at night[-time]

not'turno *adj* nocturnal; ⟨servizio ecc⟩ night *attrib*; **in notturna** ⟨partita⟩ under flood-lights

'notula *nf* (conto) fee note

no'vanta *adj & nm* ninety

novan'tenne *adj & nmf* ninety year old

novan'tesimo *adj & nm* ninetieth

novan'tina *nf* about ninety

'nove *adj & nm* nine; **prova del** ~ Math casting out nines

nove'cento adj & nm nine hundred; **il Novecento** the twentieth century; **stile novecento** twentieth-century

no'vella nf short story

novelli'ere nm short-story writer

novel'lino, -a ① adj inexperienced ② nmf novice, beginner

no'vello adj new. **patate novelle** new potatoes

no'vembre nm November

nove'mila adj & nm nine thousand

no'vena nf novena

novi'lunio nm new moon

novità nf inv novelty; (notizie) news sg; **l'ultima** ~ (moda) the latest fashion

novizi'ato nm Relig novitiate; (tirocinio) apprenticeship

nozi'one nf notion; **perdere la** ~ **del tempo** lose track of time; **non avere la** ~ **del tempo** have no sense of time; **nozioni** pl rudiments; **poche nozioni di inglese** very basic English

nozio'nismo nm accumulation of facts

'nozze nfpl marriage sg; (cerimonia) wedding sg; **andare a** ~ (godersela) have a field day. **nozze d'argento** silver wedding [anniversary]. **nozze di diamante** diamond wedding [anniversary]. **nozze d'oro** golden wedding [anniversary].

'nube nf cloud. **nube di mistero** shroud of mystery. **nube tossica** toxic cloud

nubi'fragio nm cloudburst

'nubile ① adj unmarried ② nf unmarried woman

'nuca nf nape

nucle'are adj nuclear

'nucleo nm nucleus; (unità) unit. **nucleo familiare** family unit

nu'dismo nm nudism

nu'dista nmf nudist

nudità nf nudity, nakedness

'nudo adj naked; ⟨spoglio, terra⟩ bare; **a occhio** ~ to the naked eye; **verità nuda e cruda** naked truth; **a piedi nudi** barefoot

'nugolo nm large number

'nulla = NIENTE

nulla'osta nm inv permit

nullate'nente nm **i nullatenenti** the have-nots

nullità nf inv (persona) nonentity

'nullo adj Jur null and void

'nume nm numen

nume'rabile adj countable

nume'rale adj & nm numeral

nume'rare vt number

numera'tore nm Math numerator

numerazi'one nf numbering

nu'merico adj numerical

'numero nm number; (romano, arabo) numeral; (di scarpe) size; **fare** o **comporre il** ~ dial [the number]; **dare i numeri** fam be off one's head; **avere tutti i numeri per** have what it takes to. **numero arretrato** back issue. **numero cardinale** cardinal [number]. **numero di conto** account number. **numero decimale** decimal. **numero di fax** fax number. **numero intero** whole number. **numero ordinale** ordinal [number]. **numero d'ordine** Comm order number. **numero di previdenza sociale** ≈ National Insurance number. **numero di protocollo** reference number. **numero di telefono** phone number. **numero uno** number one. **numero verde** ≈ Freephone® number, toll-free number Am. **numero di volo** flight number

nume'roso adj numerous

numi'smatico adj numismatic

'nunzio nm nuncio

nu'ocere vi ~ **a** harm

nu'ora nf daughter-in-law

nuo'tare vi swim; fig wallow; ~ **come un pesce** swim like a fish; ~ **nell'oro** be stinking rich, be rolling in it

nuo'tata nf swim; **fare una** ~ have a swim

nuota|'tore, -trice nmf swimmer

nu'oto nm swimming; **stili** mpl **di** ~ swimming strokes

nu'ova nf piece of news; **buone nuove** good news; **nessuna** ~, **buona** ~ no news is good news

Nu'ova Cale'donia nf New Caledonia

Nu'ova Gui'nea nf New Guinea

nuova'mente adv again

Nu'ova Ze'landa nf New Zealand

nu'ovo adj new; **di** ~ again; **uscire di** ~ go/come back out, go/come out again; **mi risulta** ~ that's news to me; ~ **di pacca** o **zecca** brand new; **rimettere a** ~ give a new lease of life to; ~ **del mestiere** new to the job; **il** ~ **anno** [the] New Year. **nuova linfa** nf new blood. **nuovo stile** new look. **Nuovo Testamento** New Testament

'nursery nf nursery

nutri'ente adj nourishing

nutri'mento nm nourishment

nu'trire ① vt feed ⟨animale, malato, pianta⟩; harbour ⟨sentimenti⟩; cherish ⟨sogno⟩ ② vi (essere nutriente) be nourishing

nu'trirsi vr eat; ~ **di** fig live on

nutri'tivo adj nourishing, nutritional

nutrizi'one nf nutrition

'nuvola nf cloud; **avere la testa fra le nuvole** have one's head in the clouds;

vivere fra le nuvole live in cloud cuckoo land; **cadere dalle nuvole** be astounded
nuvo'loso *adj* cloudy

nuzi'ale *adj* nuptial; ⟨*vestito, anello ecc*⟩ wedding *attrib*; **pranzo nuziale** wedding breakfast

Oo

O *abbr* (**ovest**) W

o *conj* or; **o l'uno o l'altro** one or the other; either; **o... o...** either...or...

'oasi *nf inv* oasis

obbedi'ente = UBBIDIENTE

obbedi'enza = UBBIDIENZA

obbe'dire = UBBIDIRE

obbli'gare *vt* force, oblige

obbli'garsi *vr* ∼ **a** undertake to

obbli'gato *adj* obliged

obbligatoria'mente *adv* **fare qualcosa** ∼ be obliged to do something; **bisogna** ∼ **farlo** you absolutely have to do it

obbliga'torio *adj* compulsory

obbligazi'one *nf* obligation; Comm bond. **obbligazione a premio** premium bond

'obbligo *nm* obligation; (dovere) duty; **avere obblighi verso** be under an obligation to; **d'**∼ obligatory

ob'brobrio *nm* disgrace

obbrobri'oso *adj* disgraceful

obe'lisco *nm* obelisk

obe'rare *vt* overburden

obesità *nf* obesity

o'beso *adj* obese

obiet'tare *vt/i* object; ∼ **su** object to

obiettiva'mente *adv* objectively

obiettività *nf* objectivity

obiet'tivo ①*adj* objective ②*nm* objective; (scopo) object

obiet'tore *nm* objector. **obiettore di coscienza** conscientious objector

obiezi'one *nf* objection; **fare** ∼ **di coscienza** be a conscientious objector

obi'torio *nm* mortuary

o'blio *nm* oblivion

o'bliquo *adj* oblique; fig underhand

oblite'rare *vt* obliterate

oblò *nm inv* porthole

ob'lungo *adj* oblong

'oboe *nm* oboe

obsole'scenza *nf* obsolescence

obso'leto *adj* obsolete

'oca *nf* (pl **oche**) goose; (donna) silly girl

occasio'nale *adj* occasional

occasional'mente *adv* occasionally

occasi'one *nf* occasion; (buon affare) bargain; (motivo) cause; (opportunità) chance; **d'**∼ secondhand

occhi'aia *nf* eye socket; **occhiaie** *pl* shadows under the eyes

occhi'ali *nmpl* glasses, spectacles. **occhiali multifocali** varifocals. **occhiali scuri** dark glasses. **occhiali da sole** sunglasses. **occhiali da sole avvolgenti** wraparound sunglasses. **occhiali da vista** glasses, spectacles

occhia'luto *adj* wearing glasses

occhi'ata *nf* look; **dare un'**∼ **a** have a look at

occhieggi'are ①*vt* ogle ②*vi* (far capolino) peep

occhi'ello *nm* buttonhole; (asola) eyelet

'occhio *nm* eye; ∼**!** watch out!; ∼ **ai falsi** beware of imitations; **a quattr'occhi** in private; **abbassare gli occhi** look down, lower one's eyes; **sollevare gli occhi** look up, raise one's eyes; **tenere d'**∼ **qualcuno** keep an eye on somebody; **perdere d'**∼ lose sight of; **a** ∼ **[e croce]** roughly; **chiudere un** ∼ **(su qualcosa)** turn a blind eye (to something); **dare nell'**∼ attract attention; **pagare** *o* **spendere un** ∼ **[della testa]** pay an arm and a leg; **saltare agli occhi** be blindingly obvious. **occhio di falco** eagle eye. **occhio nero** (pesto) black eye. **occhio di pernice** (callo) corn

occhio'lino *nm* **fare l'**∼ **a qualcuno** wink at somebody, give somebody a wink

occiden'tale ①*adj* western ②*nmf* westerner

occidentaliz'zare *vt* westernize

occidentaliz'zarsi *vr* become westernized

occi'dente *nm* west; (paesi capitalisti) West

oc'cludere *vt* obstruct

occlusi'one *nf* occlusion

occor'rente ①*adj* necessary ②*nm* **l'occorrente** the necessary

occor'renza *nf* need; **all'**∼ if need be

oc'correre *vi* be necessary; **non occorre farlo** there is no need to do it

occulta'mento *nm* **occultamento di prove** concealment of evidence

n
o

occul'tare *vt* hide

occul'tismo *nm* occult

oc'culto *adj* hidden; (magico) occult

occu'pante *nmf* occupier; (abusivo) squatter

occu'pare *vt* occupy; spend ⟨tempo⟩; take up ⟨spazio⟩; (dar lavoro a) employ

occu'parsi *vr* occupy oneself; (trovare lavoro) find a job; ~ **di** (badare) look after; **occupati dei fatti tuoi!** mind your own business!

occu'pato *adj* engaged; ⟨persona⟩ busy; ⟨posto⟩ taken; **casa occupata** (alloggio abusivo) squat

occupazi'one *nf* occupation; Comm employment; (passatempo) pastime; **trovarsi un'~** (interesse) find oneself something to do

o'ceano *nm* ocean. **oceano Atlantico** Atlantic [Ocean]. **oceano Indiano** Indian Ocean. **oceano Pacifico** Pacific [Ocean]

'ocra *nf* ochre

'OCSE *nf abbr* (**Organizzazione per la Cooperazione e lo Sviluppo Economico**) OECD

ocu'lare *adj* ocular; ⟨testimone, bagno⟩ eye *attrib*

ocula'tezza *nf* care

ocu'lato *adj* ⟨scelta, persona⟩ prudent

ocu'lista *nmf* optician; (per malattie) ophthalmologist

od *conj* (davanti alla vocale o) or

'ode *nf* ode

odi'are *vt* hate; ~ **a morte** not be able to stand

odi'erno *adj* of today; (attuale) present

'odio *nm* hatred; **avere in** ~ hate

odi'oso *adj* hateful

odis'sea *nf* odyssey

o'dometro *nm* Auto milometer, odometer Am

odo'rare ① *vt* smell; (profumare) perfume ② *vi* ~ **di** smell of

odo'rato *nm* sense of smell

o'dore *nm* smell; (profumo) scent; **c'è** ~ **di...** there's a smell of...; **avere un buon/ cattivo** ~ smell nice/awful; **sentire** ~ **di** smell; **odori** *pl* Culin herbs

odo'roso *adj* fragrant

of'fendere *vt* offend; (ferire) injure

of'fendersi *vr* take offence

offen'siva *nf* Mil, fig offensive

offen'sivo *adj* offensive

offen'sore *nm* offender

offe'rente *nmf* offerer; (in aste) bidder; **il miglior** ~ the highest bidder

of'ferta *nf* offer; (donazione) donation; Comm supply; (nelle aste) bid; (di appalto) tender; **in** ~ **speciale** on special offer;

"offerte d'impiego" "situations vacant". **offerta pubblica di acquisto** takeover bid

of'ferto *pp di* OFFRIRE

offer'torio *nm* offertory

of'fesa *nf* offence

of'feso ① *pp di* OFFENDERE ② *adj* offended

offi'ciare *vt* officiate

offi'cina *nf* workshop. **officina [meccanica]** garage

offici'nale *adj* ⟨pianta⟩ medicinal

of'frire *vt* offer

of'frirsi *vr* offer oneself; ⟨occasione⟩ present itself; ~ **di fare qualcosa** offer to do something

off'set *nm inv* offset printing

off'shore *nm inv* (motoscafo) speedboat

offu'scare *vt* darken; fig dull ⟨memoria, bellezza⟩; blur ⟨vista⟩

offu'scarsi *vr* darken; fig ⟨memoria, bellezza⟩ fade away; ⟨vista⟩ become blurred

of'talmico *adj* ophthalmic

ogget'tistica *nf* manufacture and selling of household and gift items; (oggetti) household and gift items; **negozio di oggettistica** gift shop

oggettività *nf* objectivity

ogget'tivo *adj* objective

og'getto *nm* object; (argomento) subject. **oggetto sessuale** sex object. **oggetto** *pl* **smarriti** lost property, lost and found Am

'oggi *adv & nm* today; (al giorno d'oggi) nowadays; **da** ~ **in poi** from today on; ~ **[a] otto** a week today; **dall'**~ **al domani** overnight; **il giornale di** ~ today's paper; **al giorno d'**~ these days, nowadays

oggigi'orno *adv* nowadays

o'giva *nf* Mil warhead

'ogni *adj inv* every; (qualsiasi) any; ~ **tre giorni** every three days; **ad** ~ **costo** at any cost; **ad** ~ **modo** anyway; ~ **ben di Dio** all sorts of good things; ~ **cosa** everything; ~ **tanto** now and then; ~ **volta che** every time, whenever

o'gnuno *pron* everyone, everybody; ~ **di voi** each of you

ohibò *int* oh dear!

ohimè *int* oh dear!

o'kay *nm* **dare l'**~ **a qualcuno/qualcosa** give somebody/something the OK

'ola *nf inv* Mexican wave

O'landa *nf* Holland

olan'dese ① *adj* Dutch ② *nm* Dutchman; (lingua) Dutch; (formaggio) Edam ③ *nf* Dutchwoman

ole'andro *nm* oleander

ole'ato *adj* oiled; **carta oleata** greaseproof paper

oleo'dotto *nm* oil pipeline

ole'oso *adj* oily

ol'fatto *nm* sense of smell

oli'are *vt* oil

olia'tore *nm* oilcan

oli'era *nf* cruet

Olim'piadi *nfpl* Olympic games, Olympics

o'limpico *adj* Olympic

olim'pionico *adj* ⟨primato, squadra⟩ Olympic; **costume** ∼ Olympic swimming costume

+olino *suff* bestiolina *nf* (affettuoso) little creature; **macchiolina** *nf* spot; **pesciolino** *nm* little fish; **risolino** *nm* giggle; **sassolino** *nm* pebble; **strisciolina** *nf* thin strip; **magrolino** *adj* skinny

'olio *nm* oil; **sott'**∼ in oil; **colori a** ∼ oils; **quadro a** ∼ oil painting. **olio [di semi] di arachidi** groundnut oil. **olio essenziale** essential oil. **olio extravergine di oliva** extra-virgin olive oil. **olio di fegato di merluzzo** cod-liver oil. **olio di gomito** elbow grease. **olio lubrificante** lubricating oil. **olio di mais** corn oil. **olio minerale** mineral oil. **olio [del] motore** engine oil. **olio d'oliva** olive oil. **olio di semi** vegetable oil. **olio [di semi] di lino** linseed oil. **olio solare** suntan oil. **olio [di semi] di vinaccioli** grapeseed oil

o'liva *nf* olive

oli'vastro *adj* olive

oli'veto *nm* olive grove

oli'vetta *nf* toggle

o'livo *nm* olive tree

'olmo *nm* elm

olo'causto *nm* holocaust; **l'Olocausto** the Holocaust

o'lografo *adj* holograph

olo'gramma *nm* hologram

oltraggi'are *vt* offend

ol'traggio *nm* offence. **oltraggio al pudore** Jur gross indecency

oltraggi'oso *adj* offensive

ol'tranza *nf* ad ∼ to the bitter end

'oltre ① *adv* (di luogo) further; (di tempo) longer
② *prep* (nello spazio) beyond; (di tempo) later than; (più di) more than; (in aggiunta) besides; ∼ **a** (eccetto) except, apart from; **per** ∼ **due settimane** for more than two weeks; **una settimana e** ∼ a week and more

oltrecon'fine *adj* cross-border

oltre'mare *adv* overseas

oltre'modo *adv* extremely

oltrepas'sare *vt* go beyond; (eccedere) exceed; **oltrepassi il semaforo** go past the traffic lights; ∼ **il limite di velocità** break the speed limit; **'non** ∼**'** 'no trespassing'

OM *abbr* Radio (**onde medie**) MW

omacci'one *nm* bruiser

o'maggio *nm* homage; (dono) gift; **in** ∼ **con** free with. **omaggi** *pl* (saluti) respects

'Oman *nm* Oman

ombeli'cale *adj* umbilical; **cordone ombelicale** umbilical cord

ombe'lico *nm* navel

'ombra *nf* (zona) shade; (immagine oscura) shadow; **all'**∼ in the shade

ombreggi'are *vt* shade

ombreggia'ture *nfpl* shading

om'brello *nm* umbrella

ombrel'lone *nm* beach umbrella

om'bretto *nm* eye-shadow

om'broso *adj* shady; ⟨cavallo⟩ skittish; ⟨persona⟩ touchy

ome'lette *nf inv* omelette

ome'lia *nf* Relig sermon

omeopa'tla *nf* homeopathy

omeo'patico ① *adj* homeopathic
② *nm* homeopath

omertà *nf* conspiracy of silence

o'messo *pp di* OMETTERE

o'mettere *vt* omit

'OMG *nm abbr* (**Organismo Modificato Geneticamente**) GMO

omi'cida ① *adj* murderous, homicidal
② *nmf* murderer

omi'cidio *nm* murder. **omicidio colposo** manslaughter. **omicidio di massa** mass murder. **omicidio volontario** Jur culpable homicide

omissi'one *nf* omission

'omnibus *nm inv* omnibus

omofo'bia *nf* homophobia

omogeneiz'zare *vt* homogenize

omogeneiz'zato *adj* homogenized

omo'geneo *adj* homogeneous

o'mografo *nm* homograph

omolo'gare *vt* approve; **fare** ∼ **un testamento** prove a will

omologazi'one *nf* probate

o'monimo, -a ① *nmf* namesake
② *nm* (parola) homonym
③ *adj* of the same name

omosessu'ale *adj & nmf* homosexual

omosessualità *nf* homosexuality

'OMS *nf abbr* (**Organizzazione Mondiale della Sanità**) WHO

On. *abbr* (**onorevole**) MP, Hon.

'oncia *nf* ounce. **oncia fluida** fluid ounce

'onda *nf* wave; **andare in** ∼ TV, Radio go on the air; **seguire l'**∼ go with the crowd; **onde** *pl* **corte** short wave; **onde** *pl* **lunghe** long wave. **onda di maremoto** tidal ⋯⊹

wave; **onde** pl **medie** medium wave; **onde** pl **radio** radio waves. **onda d'urto** shock wave

on'data nf wave; **a ondate** in waves. **ondata di freddo** cold snap

'onde conj fml so that

ondeggi'are vi wave; ⟨barca⟩ roll

ondu'lato adj wavy

ondula'torio adj undulating

ondulazi'one nf undulation; (di capelli) wave

+one suff **cucchiaione** nm big spoon; **gattone** nm fat cat; **bacione** nm smacker; **bacioni** pl (in lettera) love and kisses; **omone** nm big guy; **nasone** nm big nose; **nebbione** nm dense fog, peasouper fam; **simpaticone** nm very friendly person; **lumacone** nm slowcoach; **testone** nm mule; **facilone** nm pej over-casual sort of person; **grassone** nm pej fat slob; **pigrone** nm lazy-bones sg; **chiacchierone** nm chatterbox; **criticone** nm nit-picker; **pasticcione** nm bungler

'onere nm burden

oner'oso adj onerous

onestà nf honesty; (rettitudine) integrity, honesty

o'nesto adj honest; (giusto) just

'ONG nf abbr (**organizzazione non governativa**) non-governmental organization

'onice nf onyx

o'nirico adj dream attrib

o'nisco nm slater

ONLUS nf abbr (**organizzazione non lucrativa di utilità sociale** non-profit organization

onnipo'tente adj omnipotent

onnipre'sente adj ubiquitous; Rel omnipresent

onnisci'ente adj omniscient

ono'mastico nm name day

onomato'pea nf onomatopoeia

onomato'peico adj onomatopoeic

ono'rabile adj honourable

ono'rare vt (fare onore a) be a credit to; honour ⟨promessa⟩

ono'rario ① adj honorary ② nm fee

ono'rarsi vr ~ **di** be proud of

ono'rato adj ⟨famiglia, professione⟩ respectable; **considerarsi** ~ **da qualcosa** consider oneself honoured by something; **l'onorata società** nf the Mafia

o'nore nm honour; **in** ~ **di** ⟨festa, ricevimento⟩ in honour of; **fare** ~ **a** do justice to ⟨pranzo⟩; **farsi** ~ **in** excel in; **a onor del vero** to tell the truth; **fare gli onori di casa** do the honours

ono'revole ① adj honourable ② nmf Member of Parliament

onorifi'cenza nf honour; (decorazione) decoration

ono'rifico adj honorary

'onta nf shame

on'tano nm alder

'O.N.U. nf abbr (**Organizzazione delle Nazioni Unite**) UN

opacità nf opaqueness, opacity

o'paco adj opaque; ⟨colori ecc⟩ dull; ⟨fotografia, rossetto⟩ matt

o'pale nf opal

'OPEC nf Opec, OPEC

'opera nf (lavoro) work; (azione) deed; Mus opera; (teatro) opera house; (ente) institution; **mettere in** ~ put into effect; **mettersi all'**~ get to work. **opera d'arte** work of art. **opera lirica** opera; **opere** pl **pubbliche** public works

ope'rabile adj operable

ope'raio, -a ① adj working ② nmf worker. **operaio edile** building worker. **operaio specializzato** skilled worker

ope'rare ① vt Med operate on; ~ **qualcuno al cuore** operate on somebody's heart; **farsi** ~ have an operation ② vi operate; (agire) work

opera'tivo, operatorio adj operating attrib

opera'tore, -trice nmf operator; TV cameraman. **operatore ecologico** refuse collector. **operatore sanitario** health worker. **operatore turistico** tour operator

operazi'one nf operation; Comm transaction. **operazione antidroga** anti-drug operation; **operazioni** pl **di soccorso** rescue operations. **operazione d'urgenza** emergency operation

ope'retta nf operetta

ope'roso adj industrious

opini'one nf opinion; **rimanere della propria** ~ still feel the same way. **opinione pubblica** public opinion, vox pop

oplà int oops

o'possum nm inv possum

'oppio nm opium

oppo'nente ① adj opposing ② nmf opponent

op'porre vt oppose; (obiettare) object; ~ **resistenza** offer resistance

op'porsi vr ~ **a** oppose

opportu'nismo nm expediency

opportu'nista nmf opportunist

opportunità nf inv opportunity; (l'essere opportuno) timeliness; **avere il senso dell'**~ have a sense of what is appropriate

oppor'tuno adj opportune; (adeguato) appropriate; **ritenere** ~ **fare qualcosa**

think it appropriate to do something; **il momento** ∼ the right moment

opposi'tore *nm* opposer

opposizi'one *nf* opposition; **d'**∼ ⟨*giornale, partito*⟩ opposition *attrib*; **in** ∼ in opposition

op'posto [1] pp di OPPORRE
[2] *adj* opposite; ⟨*opinioni*⟩ opposing
[3] *nm* opposite; **all'**∼ on the contrary

oppressi'one *nf* oppression

oppres'sivo *adj* oppressive

op'presso [1] pp di OPPRIMERE
[2] *adj* oppressed

oppres'sore *nm* oppressor

oppri'mente *adj* oppressive

op'primere *vt* oppress; (gravare) weigh down

op'pure *conj* otherwise, or [else]; **lunedì** ∼ **martedì** Monday or Tuesday

ops *int* oops

op'tare *vi* ∼ **per** opt for

'optional *nm inv* optional extra

opu'lento *adj* opulent

opu'lenza *nf* opulence

o'puscolo *nm* booklet; (pubblicitario) brochure

opzio'nale *adj* optional

opzi'one *nf* option

'ora[1] *nf* time; (unità) hour; **di buon'**∼ early; **che** ∼ **è?, che ore sono?** what time is it?; **a che** ∼**?** at what time?; **mezz'**∼ half an hour; **a ore** ⟨*lavorare, pagare*⟩ by the hour; **50 km all'**∼ 50 km an hour; **è** ∼ **di finirla!** that's enough now!; **a un'**∼ **di macchina** one hour by car; **non vedo l'**∼ **di vederti** I can't wait to see you; **fare le ore piccole** stay up until the small hours. ∼ **d'arrivo** arrival time. **ora di cena** dinnertime. **l'ora esatta** Teleph speaking clock. **ora legale** daylight saving time. **ora locale** local time. **ora di pranzo** lunchtime. **ora di punta, ore** *pl* **di punta** peak time; (per il traffico) rush hour. **ora solare** Greenwich Mean Time, GMT. **ora zero** Mil, fig zero hour

'ora[2] [1] *adv* now; (tra poco) presently; ∼ **come** ∼ just now, at the moment; **d'**∼ **in poi** from now on; **per** ∼ for the time being, for now;
[2] *conj* (dunque) now [then]; ∼ **che ci penso,...** now that I [come to] think about it...

o'racolo *nm* oracle

'orafo *nm* goldsmith

o'rale *adj & nm* oral; **per via** ∼ by mouth

ora'mai *adv* = ORMAI

o'rario [1] *adj* ⟨*tariffa*⟩ hourly; ⟨*segnale*⟩ time *attrib*; ⟨*velocità*⟩ per hour; **in senso** ∼ clockwise
[2] *nm* time; (tabella dell'orario) timetable, schedule Am; **essere in** ∼ be on time;

partire in ∼ leave on time; **lavorare fuori** ∼ work outside normal hours. **orario di apertura** opening hours *pl*. **orario di chiusura** closing time. **orario estivo** summer timetable. **orario ferroviario** railway timetable, railroad schedule Am. **orario flessibile** flexitime. **orario invernale** winter timetable. **orario di lavoro** working hours *pl*. **orario degli spettacoli** performance times *pl*. **orario di sportello** banking hours *pl*. **orario d'ufficio** business hours *pl*. **orario di visita** visiting hours *pl*, visiting time; (del medico) consulting hours *pl*. **orario di volo** flight time

o'rata *nf* gilthead

ora'|tore, -trice *nmf* orator; (conferenziere) speaker

ora'torio, -a [1] *adj* oratorical
[2] *nm* Mus oratorio
[3] *nmf* oratory

orazi'one *nf* Relig prayer

'orbita *nf* orbit; Anat [eye-]socket

'Orcadi *nfpl* Orkneys

or'chestra *nf* orchestra; (parte del teatro) pit. **orchestra da camera** chamber orchestra. **orchestra sinfonica** symphony orchestra

orche'strale [1] *adj* orchestral
[2] *nmf* member of an/the orchestra

orche'strare *vt* orchestrate

orchi'dea *nf* orchid

'orco *nm* ogre

'orda *nf* horde

or'digno *nm* device; (arnese) tool. **ordigno esplosivo** explosive device. **ordigno incendiario** incendiary device, firebomb

ordi'nale *adj & nm* ordinal

ordina'mento *nm* order; (leggi) rules *pl*

ordi'nanza *nf* (del sindaco) bylaw; **d'**∼ ⟨*soldato*⟩ on duty

ordi'nare *vt* (sistemare) arrange; (comandare) order; (prescrivere) prescribe; Relig ordain

ordi'nario [1] *adj* ordinary; (grossolano) common; ⟨*professore*⟩ with a permanent position; **di ordinaria amministrazione** routine
[2] *nm* ordinary; Univ professor; **fuori dell'**∼ out of the ordinary

ordi'nato *adj* (in ordine) tidy

ordinazi'one *nf* order; **fare un'**∼ place an order

'ordine *nm* order; (di avvocati, medici) association; **mettere in** ∼ put in order; tidy up ⟨*appartamento ecc*⟩; **di prim'**∼ first-class; **di terz'**∼ ⟨*film, albergo*⟩ third-rate; **di** ∼ **pratico/economico** ⟨*problema*⟩ of a practical/economic nature; **fino a nuovo** ∼ until further notice; **parola d'ordine** password. **ordine di acquisto** ⋯⟶

Comm purchase order. **ordine del giorno** agenda. **ordine di pagamento** banker's order. **ordine permanente** Fin standing order. **ordine pubblico** law and order. **ordini** pl **sacri** Holy Orders

or'dire vt (tramare) plot

orecchi'ette nfpl small pasta shells

orec'chino nm ear-ring; **orecchini** pl **con le clip** clip-ons

o'recchio nm (pl nf **orecchie**) ear; **avere** ∼ have a good ear; **esser duro d'**∼ be hard of hearing; **mi è giunto all'**∼ **che...** I've heard that...; **parlare all'**∼ **a qualcuno** whisper in somebody's ear; **suonare a** ∼ play by ear

orecchi'oni nmpl Med mumps sg

o'refice nm jeweller

orefice'ria nf (arte) goldsmith's art; (negozio) goldsmith's [shop]

'orfano, -a ① adj orphan ② nmf orphan

orfano'trofio nm orphanage

orga'netto nm barrel-organ; (a bocca) mouth-organ; (fisarmonica) accordion

or'ganico ① adj organic ② nm personnel

orga'nino nm hurdy-gurdy

orga'nismo nm organism; (corpo umano) body

orga'nista nmf organist

organizza|'tore, -trice nmf organizer

organiz'zare vt organize

organiz'zarsi vr get organized

organizza'tivo adj organizational

organizzazi'one nf organization. **organizzazione del servizio d'ordine** policing. **organizzazione studentesca** student union. **organizzazione umanitaria** relief agency, aid agency

'organo nm organ

or'gasmo nm orgasm; fig agitation

'orgia nf orgy

or'goglio nm pride

orgogli'oso adj proud

orien'tale adj eastern; (cinese ecc) oriental

orienta'mento nm orientation; **perdere l'**∼ lose one's bearings; **senso dell'**∼ sense of direction. **orientamento professionale** careers guidance. **orientamento scolastico** educational guidance

orien'tare vt orientate

orien'tarsi vr find one's bearings; (tendere) tend

ori'ente nm east. **l'Estremo Oriente** the Far East. **il Medio Oriente** the Middle East

orien'teering nm orienteering

o'rigano nm oregano

origi'nale ① adj original; (eccentrico) odd ② nm original

originalità nf originality

origi'nare vt/i originate

origi'nario adj (nativo) native

o'rigine nf origin; **in** ∼ originally; **aver** ∼ **da** originate from; **dare** ∼ **a** give rise to

origli'are vi eavesdrop

o'rina nf urine

ori'nale nm chamber-pot

ori'nare vi urinate

ori'undo adj native

orizzon'tale adj horizontal

orizzon'tare vt = ORIENTARE

oriz'zonte nm horizon

or'lare vt hem

orla'tura nf hem

'orlo nm edge; (di vestito ecc) hem

'orma nf track; (di piede) footprint; (impronta) mark

or'mai adv by now; (passato) by then; (quasi) almost

ormegg'iare vt moor

or'meggio nm mooring

ormo'nale adj hormonal

or'mone nm hormone

ornamen'tale adj ornamental

orna'mento nm ornament; **d'**∼ ⟨oggetto⟩ ornamental

or'nare vt decorate

or'narsi vr deck oneself

or'nato adj ⟨stile⟩ ornate

ornitolo'gia nf ornithology

orni'tologo, -a nmf ornithologist

ornito'rinco nm platypus

'oro nm gold; **d'**∼ gold; fig golden; **una persona d'**∼ a wonderful person. **oro nero** black gold

orologe'ria nf watchmaker

orologi'aio, -a nmf clockmaker, watchmaker

oro'logio nm (da polso, tasca) watch; (da tavolo, muro ecc) clock. **orologio biologico** biological clock. **orologio a carica automatica** self-winding watch. **orologio a cucù** cuckoo clock. **orologio digitale** digital clock. **orologio a pendolo** grandfather clock. **orologio da polso** wristwatch. **orologio al quarzo** quartz watch. **orologio a sveglia** alarm clock

o'roscopo nm horoscope

or'rendo adj awful, dreadful

or'ribile adj horrible

orribil'mente adv horribly

orripi'lante adj horrifying

or'rore *nm* horror; **avere qualcosa in ∼** hate something; **∼!** heck!; **film/romanzo dell'orrore** horror film/story

orsacchi'otto *nm* teddy bear

or'setto *nm* **orsetto lavatore** raccoon

'orso *nm* bear; (persona scontrosa) hermit. **orso bianco** polar bear. **orso bruno** brown bear

orsù *int* come now!

or'taggio *nm* vegetable

or'tensia *nf* hydrangea

or'tica *nf* nettle; **buttare qualcosa alle ortiche** fig fam chuck in

orti'caria *nf* nettle rash

orticol'tura *nf* horticulture

'orto *nm* vegetable plot

orto'dontico *adj* orthodontic

ortodon'zia *nf* orthodontics

ortodos'sia *nf* conformity

orto'dosso *adj* orthodox

ortofrut'ticolo *adj* **mercato ortofrutticolo** fruit and vegetable market

ortofrutticol'tore *nm* market gardener, truck farmer Am

ortofrutticol'tura *nf* market gardening

ortogo'nale *adj* perpendicular

ortogra'fia *nf* spelling

orto'grafico *adj* spelling *attrib*

orto'lano *nm* market gardener, truck farmer Am; (negozio) greengrocer's

ortope'dia *nf* orthopaedics

orto'pedico ① *adj* orthopaedic ② *nm* orthopaedic specialist

orzai'olo *nm* sty

or'zata *nf* barley-water

'orzo *nm* barley. **orzo perlato** pearl barley

osan'nato *adj* (esaltato) praised to the skies

o'sare *vt/i* dare; (avere audacia) be daring

oscenità *nf inv* obscenity

o'sceno *adj* obscene

oscil'lare *vi* swing; ⟨prezzi ecc⟩ fluctuate; Tech oscillate; (fig: essere indeciso) vacillate

oscillazi'one *nf* swinging; (di prezzi) fluctuation; Tech oscillation

oscura'mento *nm* darkening; (fig: di vista, mente) dimming; (totale) black-out

oscu'rare *vt* darken; fig obscure

oscu'rarsi *vr* get dark

oscurità *nf* darkness; (incomprensibilità) obscurity; **uscire dall'∼** fig emerge from obscurity; **morire nell'∼** fig die in obscurity

o'scuro *adj* dark; (triste) gloomy; (incomprensibile) obscure

o'smosi *nf* osmosis

ospe'dale *nm* hospital. **ospedale universitario** teaching hospital

ospedali'ero *adj* hospital *attrib*

ospi'tale *adj* hospitable

ospitalità *nf* hospitality; **non voglio abusare della tua ∼** I don't want to outstay my welcome

ospi'tare *vt* give hospitality to

'ospite ① *nm* (chi ospita) host; (chi viene ospitato) guest ② *nf* hostess; guest

o'spizio *nm* (per anziani) [old people's] home

ossa'tura *nf* bone structure; (di romanzo) structure, framework

'osseo *adj* bone *attrib*

osse'quente *adj* deferential; **∼ alla legge** law-abiding

ossequi'are *vt* pay one's respects to

os'sequio *nm* homage; **ossequi** *pl* respects

ossequi'oso *adj* obsequious

osser'vabile *adj* observable

osser'vante *adj* ⟨cattolico⟩ practising

osser'vanza *nf* observance

osser'vare *vt* observe; (notare) notice; keep ⟨ordine, silenzio⟩

osserva|'tore, -trice *nmf* observer

osserva'torio *nm* Astr observatory; Mil observation post

osservazi'one *nf* observation; (rimprovero) reproach

ossessio'nante *adj* haunting; ⟨persona⟩ nagging

ossessio'nare *vt* obsess; (infastidire) nag

ossessi'one *nf* obsession; (assillo) pain in the neck

osses'sivo *adj* obsessive; ⟨paura⟩ neurotic

os'sesso *adj* obsessed

os'sia *conj* that is

ossi'dabile *adj* liable to tarnish

ossi'dante *adj* tarnishing

ossi'dare *vt* oxidize

ossi'darsi *vr* oxidize

'ossido *nm* oxide. **ossido di carbonio** carbon monoxide. **ossido di zinco** zinc oxide

os'sidrico *adj* **fiamma ossidrica** blowlamp

ossige'nare *vt* oxygenate; (decolorare) bleach

ossige'narsi *vr* put back on its feet ⟨azienda⟩; **∼ i capelli** dye one's hair blonde

os'sigeno *nm* oxygen

'osso *nm* (Anat pl nf **ossa**) bone; **senz'∼** boneless. **osso mascellare** jawbone

osso'buco *nm* marrowbone

os'suto *adj* bony

ostaco'lare *vt* hinder, obstruct

ostaco'lista *nmf* hurdler

o'stacolo *nm* obstacle; Sport hurdle

o'staggio *nm* hostage; **prendere in ~** take hostage

o'stello *nm* **ostello della gioventù** youth hostel

osten'tare *vt* show off; **~ indifferenza** pretend to be indifferent

ostenta'mente *adv* ostentatiously

ostentazi'one *nf* ostentation

osteopo'rosi *nf inv* osteoporosis

oste'ria *nf* inn

oste'tricia *nf* obstetrics

o'stetrico, -a ① *adj* obstetric ② *nmf* obstetrician

'ostia *nf* host; (cialda) wafer

'ostico *adj* tough

o'stile *adj* hostile

ostilità *nf inv* hostility

osti'narsi *vr* ~ persist (a in)

osti'nato *adj* obstinate

ostinazi'one *nf* obstinacy

ostra'cismo *nm* ostracism

'ostrica *nf* oyster

ostro'goto *nm* **parlare ~** talk double Dutch

ostru'ire *vt* obstruct

ostruzi'one *nf* obstruction

ostruzio'nismo *nm* obstructionism; Sport obstruction. **ostruzionismo sindacale** work-to-rule

oto'rino *nm* ear, nose and throat *attrib*

otorinolaringoi'atra *nmf* ear, nose and throat specialist

'otre *nm* leather bottle

ottago'nale *adj* octagonal

ot'tagono *nm* octagon

ot'tanta *adj & nm* eighty

ottan'tenne *adj & nmf* eighty-year-old

ottan'tesimo *adj & nm* eightieth

ottan'tina *nf* about eighty

ot'tava *nf* octave

ot'tavo *adj & nm* eighth

otte'nere *vt* obtain; (più comune) get; (conseguire) achieve

ot'tetto *nm* Mus octet

'ottico, -a ① *adj* optic[al] ② *nmf* optician ③ *nf* (scienza) optics *sg*; (di lenti ecc) optics *pl*

otti'male *adj* optimum

ottima'mente *adv* very well

otti'mismo *nm* optimism

otti'mista *nmf* optimist

otti'mistico *adj* optimistic

ottimiz'zare *vt* optimize

'ottimo ① *adj* very good ② *nm* optimum; **essere all'~ della forma** be on top form

'otto *adj & nm* eight

+otto *suff* **bassotto** *adj* (piuttosto basso) quite short; **contadinotto** *nm* pej (sempliciotto) country bumpkin; **paesotto** *nm* hamlet; **leprotto** *nm* leveret; (affettuoso) baby hare; **pienotto** *adj* ⟨viso⟩ chubby

ot'tobre *nm* October

otto'cento *adj & nm* eight hundred; **l'Ottocento** the nineteenth century

ot'tone *nm* brass; **gli ottoni** Mus the brass

ottuage'nario, -a *adj & nmf* octogenarian

ot'tundere *vt* blunt

ottu'rare *vt* block; fill ⟨dente⟩

ottu'rarsi *vr* clog

ottura'tore *nm* Phot shutter

otturazi'one *nf* stopping; (di dente) filling

ot'tuso ① *pp di* OTTUNDERE ② *adj* obtuse

ouver'ture *nf inv* overture

o'vaia *nf* ovary

o'vale *adj & nm* oval

o'vatta *nf* cotton wool, absorbent cotton Am

ovat'tato *adj* ⟨suono, passi⟩ muffled

ovazi'one *nf* ovation

'ove *adv* liter where

over'dose *nf inv* overdose

'overdrive *nm inv* Auto overdrive

'ovest *nm* west

o'vile *nm* sheep-fold, pen

o'vino *adj* sheep *attrib*

ovoi'dale *adj* egg-shaped

ovo'via *nf* two-seater cable car

ovulazi'one *nf* ovulation

o'vunque *adv* = DOVUNQUE

ov'vero *conj* or; (cioè) that is

ovvia'mente *adv* obviously

ovvi'are *vi* ~ a qualcosa counter something

'ovvio *adj* obvious

ozi'are *vi* laze around

'ozio *nm* idleness; **stare in ~** idle about

ozi'oso *adj* idle; ⟨questione⟩ pointless

o'zono *nm* ozone; **buco nell'ozono** hole in the ozone layer

Pp

pacare *vt* calm

paca'tezza *nf* calm[ness]

pa'cato *adj* calm

'pacca *nf* slap

pac'chetto *nm* packet; (postale) parcel, package; (di sigarette) pack, packet. **pacchetto informativo** information pack. **pacchetto integrato** Comput integrated package. **pacchetto software** software package

'pacchia *nf* (fam: situazione) bed of roses

pacchia'nata *nf* è una ∼ it's so garish

pacchi'ano *adj* garish

'pacco *nm* parcel; (involto) bundle; **disfare un** ∼ unwrap a parcel; **fare un** ∼ make up a parcel; **pacchi** *pl* **postali** parcels, packages. **pacco bomba** parcel bomb. **pacco regalo** gift-wrapped package; **le faccio un** ∼ **regalo?** would you like it gift-wrapped?. **pacco umanitario** aid package

paccot'tiglia *nf* (roba scadente) junk, rubbish

'pace *nf* peace; **darsi** ∼ forget it; **fare** ∼ **con qualcuno** make it up with somebody; **lasciare in** ∼ **qualcuno** leave somebody in peace; **mettere** ∼ **fra** pacify, make [the] peace between; **andate in** ∼ Relig peace be with you; **in tempo di** ∼ in peacetime; **del tempo di** ∼ peacetime; **di** ∼ ⟨milizia⟩ peacekeeping; **firmare la** ∼ sign a peace treaty; **per amor di** ∼ for a quiet life

pace-'maker *nm inv* (apparecchio) pacemaker

pachi'derma *nm* (animale) pachyderm; fig thick-skinned person

pachi'stano, **-a** *nmf & adj* Pakistani

paci'ere *nm* peacemaker

pacifi'care *vt* reconcile; (mettere pace) pacify

pacificazi'one *nf* reconciliation

pa'cifico [1] *adj* pacific; (calmo) peaceful; **è** ∼ **che...** (comunemente accettato) it is clear that...
[2] *nm* **il Pacifico** the Pacific

paci'fismo *nm* pacifism

paci'fista *adj & nmf* pacifist

pacioc'cone, **-a** *nmf* fam chubby-chops

paci'ugo *nm* (poltiglia) mush

pa'dano *adj* **pianura padana** Po Valley

pa'della *nf* frying-pan; (per malati) bedpan; **cuocere in** ∼ fry; **dalla** ∼ **alla brace** out of the frying pan into the fire

padel'lata *nf* una ∼ **di** a frying-panful of

padigli'one *nm* pavilion. **padiglione auricolare** auricle

'Padova *nf* Padua

'padre *nm* father; **padri** *pl* (antenati) forefathers; **I padri della chiesa** the Church Fathers; **di** ∼ **in figlio** from father to son. **padre adottivo** (marito della madre) stepfather. **padre di famiglia** father, paterfamilias; **sono** ∼ **di famiglia** I have a family to look after. **padre spirituale** spiritual father

padre'nostro *nm* **il** ∼ the Lord's Prayer

padre'terno *nm* God Almighty

pa'drino *nm* godfather; ∼ **e madrina** godparents

padro'nale *adj* principal

padro'nanza *nf* mastery. **padronanza di sé** self-control

pa'drone, **-a** *nmf* master; mistress; (datore di lavoro) boss; (proprietario) owner. **padrone di casa** (di inquilini) landlord; landlady; (in ricevimento) master of the house; lady of the house

padroneggi'are *vt* master

padro'nesco *adj* domineering

padro'nissimo *adj* **essere** ∼ **di fare qualcosa** be quite at liberty to do something

pae'saggio *nm* scenery; (pittura) landscape. **paesaggio marino** seascape. **paesaggio montano** mountain landscape

paesag'gista *nmf* landscape architect

paesag'gistico *adj* landscape *attrib*

pae'sano, **-a** [1] *adj* country *attrib*
[2] *nmf* villager

pa'ese *nm* (nazione) country; (territorio) land; (villaggio) village; **il Bel Paese** Italy; **va' a quel** ∼**!** get lost!; **il mio** ∼ **natio** where I was born; **Paesi** *pl* **Bassi** Netherlands; **paesi** *pl* **dell'est** Eastern Bloc countries

paf'futo *adj* plump

pag. *abbr* (**pagina**) p.

'paga *nf* pay, wages *pl*

pa'gabile *adj* payable

pa'gaia *nf* paddle

paga'mento *nm* payment; **a** ∼ ⟨parcheggio⟩ which you have to pay to use. **pagamento anticipato** Comm advance payment. **pagamento alla consegna** cash on delivery, COD. **pagamento pedaggio** toll

paga'nesimo *nm* paganism

pa'gano, **-a** *adj* & *nmf* pagan

pa'gante *nmf* payer

pa'gare *vt/i* pay; ∼ **da bere a qualcuno** buy somebody a drink; **pagato in anticipo** prepaid, paid in advance; **te la faccio** ∼ you'll pay for this; **quanto pagherei per poter venire!** what I wouldn't give to be able to come!

pa'gella *nf* [school] report

pagg. *abbr* (**pagine**) pp.

pag'gio *nm* pageboy

'pagina *nf* page; **prima** ∼ Journ front page; ∼ **economica** financial news, financial pages; **Pagine** *pl* **gialle**® Yellow Pages®. **pagina mastra** master page. **pagina web** Comput web page

pagi'none *nm* centrefold

'paglia *nf* straw. **paglia e fieno** Culin mixture of ordinary and green tagliatelle

pagliac'cesco *adj* farcical

pagliac'cetto *nm* (per bambini) rompers *pl*; (da donna) camiknickers

pagliac'ciata *nf* farce

pagli'accio *nm* clown; **fare il** ∼ act *or* play the clown

pagli'aio *nm* haystack

paglie'riccio *nm* straw mattress

pagli'etta *nf* (cappello) boater; (per pentole) steel wool

pagli'uzza *nf* wisp of straw; (di metallo) particle

pa'gnotta *nf* [round] loaf

'pago *adj* satisfied

pa'goda *nf* pagoda

pa'guro *nm* hermit crab

pail'lard *nf inv* slice of grilled veal

pail'lette *nf inv* sequin

'paio *nm* (pl *nf* **paia**) pair; **un** ∼ (circa due) a couple; **un** ∼ **di** ⟨*scarpe, forbici*⟩ a pair of; **è un altro** ∼ **di maniche** *fig* that's a different kettle of fish

pai'olo *nm* copper pot

'Pakistan *nm* Pakistan

paki'stano, **-a** *adj* & *nmf* Pakistani

'pala *nf* shovel; (di remo, elica) blade; (di ruota) paddle; (di mulino) blade, vane. **pala d'altare** altar piece. **pala da fornaio** shovel. **pala meccanica** mechanical digger

pala'dino *nm* paladin; *fig* champion

pala'fitta *nf* pile-dwelling

palan'drana *nf* (abito largo) big long coat

pala'sport *nm inv* indoor sports arena

pa'late *nfpl* **a** ∼ ⟨*fare soldi*⟩ hand over fist

pa'lato *nm* palate

palaz'zetto *nm* **palazzetto dello sport** indoor sports arena

palaz'zina *nf* villa

pa'lazzo *nm* palace; (edificio) building. ∼ **comunale** town hall. **Palazzo Ducale** Doge's Palace. **palazzo delle esposizioni** exhibition centre. **palazzo di giustizia** law courts *pl*, courthouse. **palazzo dello sport** indoor sports arena

'palco *nm* (pedana) platform; Theat box; (palcoscenico) stage

palco'scenico *nm* stage

paleogra'fia *nf* palaeography

paleo'grafico *adj* palaeographical

pale'ografo, **-a** *nmf* palaeographer

paleo'litico *adj* palaeolithic

pale'sare *vt* disclose

pale'sarsi *vr* reveal oneself

pa'lese *adj* evident

Pale'stina *nf* Palestine

palesti'nese *adj* & *nmf* Palestinian

pa'lestra *nf* gymnasium, gym; (ginnastica) gymnastics *pl*

pa'letta *nf* spade; (per focolare) shovel. **paletta [della spazzatura]** dustpan

palet'tata *nf* shovelful

pa'letto *nm* peg

palin'sesto *nm* (documento) palimpsest; TV programme schedule

'palio *nm* (premio) prize; **il Palio** horse-race held at Siena

palis'sandro *nm* rosewood

paliz'zata *nf* fence

'palla *nf* ball; (proiettile) bullet; (fam: bugia) porkie; **prendere la** ∼ **al balzo** seize an opportunity; **essere una** ∼ sl be a drag; **che palle!** vulg this is a pain in the arse!, what a drag!. **palla da biliardo** billiard ball. **palla medica** medicine ball. **palla di neve** snowball. **palla al piede** *fig* millstone round one's neck

pallaca'nestro *nf* basketball

palla-'goal *nf* **hanno avuto molte palle-goal** they had a lot of goal-scoring opportunities

palla'mano *nf* handball

pallanuo'tista *nmf* water polo player

pallanu'oto *nf* water polo

pallavo'lista *nmf* volleyball player

palla'volo *nf* volleyball

palleggi'are *vi* (calcio) practise ball control; Tennis knock up

pal'leggio *nm* Sport warm-up

'pallet *nm inv* pallet

pallet'toni *nmpl* buckshot

pallia'tivo *nm* palliative

'pallido *adj* pale; **non ne ho la più pallida idea** I don't have the faintest *or* foggiest idea

pal'lina *nf* (di vetro) marble

pal'lino *nm* avere il ∿ del calcio be crazy about football, be football crazy

pallon'cino *nm* balloon; (lanterna) Chinese lantern; (fam: etilometro) Breathalyzer®

pal'lone *nm* ball; (calcio) football; (aerostato) balloon; **essere/andare nel** ∿ be/become confused. **pallone da calcio** football. **pallone gonfiato**: è un ∿ gonfiato he's so puffed-up. **pallone sonda** weather balloon

pallo'netto *nm* lob

pal'lore *nm* pallor

pal'loso *adj* sl boring

pal'lottola *nf* pellet; (proiettile) bullet. **pallottola dum-dum** dumdum bullet

pallottoli'ere *nm* abacus

'palma *nf* Bot palm. **palma da cocco** coconut palm. **palma da datteri** date palm

palmarès *nm inv* (di festival) award winners *pl*; (fig: i migliori) top names *pl*

pal'mato *adj* ⟨piede⟩ webbed

pal'mento *nm* **mangiava a quattro palmenti** he was really tucking in

pal'meto *nm* palm grove

palmi'pede *nm* web-footed animal

'palmo *nm* Anat palm; (misura) hand's breadth; **restare con un** ∿ **di naso** feel disappointed

'palo *nm* pole; (di sostegno) stake; (in calcio) goalpost; **fare il** ∿ ⟨ladro⟩ keep a lookout. **palo d'arrivo** (in ippica) finishing post **palo della luce** lamppost. **palo di partenza** (in ippica) starting post

palom'baro *nm* diver

pa'lombo *nm* dogfish

pal'pare *vt* feel

pal'pata *nf* **dare una** ∿ **a qualcosa** give something a feel

'palpebra *nf* eyelid

palpeggi'are *vt* feel

palpi'tare *vi* throb; (fremere) quiver

palpitazi'one *nf* palpitation; **avere le palpitazioni** have palpitations

'palpito *nm* throb; (del cuore) beat

paltò *nm inv* overcoat

pa'lude *nf* marsh, swamp

palu'doso *adj* marshy

pa'lustre *adj* marshy; ⟨piante, uccelli⟩ marsh *attrib*

'pampas *nfpl* pampas

'pamphlet *nm inv* pamphlet

pamphlet'tista *nmf* pamphleteer

'pampino *nm* vine leaf

pan *nm* ▶PANE

pana'cea *nf* panacea

pa'nache *nm inv* **far** ∿ (in ippica) fall

'Panama *nm* Panama; **il canale di** ∿ the Panama Canal

'panca *nf* bench; (in chiesa) pew

pancarré *nm* sliced bread

pan'cetta *nf* Culin bacon; (ciccia) paunch. **pancetta affumicata** smoked bacon

pan'chetto *nm* [foot]stool

pan'china *nf* garden seat; (in calcio) bench

'pancia *nf* belly, tummy fam; (di bottiglia, vaso) body; **mal di pancia** stomach-ache; **a** ∿ **piena/vuota** on a full/empty stomach; **metter su** ∿ develop a paunch; **a** ∿ **in giù** lying face down

panci'ata *nf* **prendere una** ∿ (in tuffo) do a belly flop

panci'era *nf* corset

panci'olle: **stare in** ∿ lounge about

panci'one *nm* (persona) pot belly

panci'otto *nm* waistcoat

panci'uto *adj* potbellied

'pancreas *nm inv* pancreas

pancre'atico *adj* pancreatic

'panda *nm inv* panda

pande'monio *nm* pandemonium

pan'dolce *nm* Christmas cake similar to panettone

pan'doro *nm* kind of sponge cake traditionally eaten at Christmas time

'pane *nm* bread; (pagnotta) loaf; (di burro) block. **pane casereccio** home-made bread. **pane a cassetta** sliced bread; **pan grattato** breadcrumbs *pl*. **pane integrale** wholemeal bread, granary bread. **pane nero** blackbread. **pane di segale** rye bread; **pan di Spagna** sponge cake. **pane tostato** toast

'panel *nm inv* (gruppo) panel

panette'ria *nf* bakery; (negozio) baker's [shop]

panetti'ere, -a *nmf* baker

panet'tone *nm* dome-shaped cake with sultanas and candied fruit eaten at Christmas

'panfilo *nm* yacht

pan'forte *nm* nougat-like spicy delicacy from Siena

'panico *nm* panic; **farsi prendere dal** ∿ panic

pani'ere *nm* basket; (cesta) hamper

pani'ficio *nm* bakery; (negozio) baker's [shop]

pani'naro, -a *nmf* preppie

pa'nino *nm* [bread] roll. **panino imbottito** filled roll. **panino al prosciutto** ham roll

panino'teca *nf* sandwich bar

'panna *nf* cream. **panna cotta** kind of creme caramel. **panna da cucina** ⋯⋗

[single] cream. **panna montata** whipped cream

'panne *nf* Mech in ∼ broken down; **restare in** ∼ break down

panneggi'ato *adj* draped

pan'neggio *nm* drapery

pan'nello *nm* panel. **pannello di controllo** control panel. **pannello solare** solar panel

'panno *nm* cloth; (di tavolo da gioco) baize; **panni** *pl* (abiti) clothes; **mettersi nei panni di qualcuno** fig put oneself in somebody's shoes

pan'nocchia *nf* (di granturco) cob

panno'lenci® *nm* brightly coloured felt

panno'lino *nm* (per bambini) nappy; (da donna) sanitary towel

pano'rama *nm* panorama; fig overview

pano'ramica *nf* (rassegna) overview

pano'ramico *adj* panoramic

panpe'pato *nm* type of gingerbread

pantacol'lant *nmpl* leggings

pantagru'elico *adj* ⟨pranzo⟩ gargantuan

pantalon'cini *nmpl* shorts. **pantaloncini da ciclista** cycling shorts. **pantaloncini corti** shorts

panta'loni *nmpl* trousers, pants Am. **pantaloni da sci** ski pants. **pantaloni della tuta** sweat pants. **pantaloni a tubo** drain-pipe trousers. **pantaloni a zampa d'elefante** bell-bottoms, flares

pan'tano *nm* bog

panta'noso *adj* marshy

pan'tera *nf* panther; (auto della polizia) high-speed police car. **pantera nera** black panther

pan'tofola *nf* slipper

pantofo'laio, -a *nmf* fig stay-at-home

panto'mima *nf* pantomime; fig act

pan'zana *nf* fib

'panzer *nm inv* Mil tank

pao'nazzo *adj* purple

'papa *nm* Pope; **a ogni morte di** ∼ fig once in a blue moon

papà *nm inv* dad[dy]

pa'paia *nf* pawpaw, papaya

pa'pale *adj* papal

papa'lina *nf* skull-cap

papa'razzo *nm* paparazzo

pa'pato *nm* papacy

pa'pavero *nm* poppy

'papera *nf* (errore) slip of the tongue

'papero *nm* gosling

pa'pilla *nf* **papilla gustativa** taste bud

papil'lon *nm inv* bow tie

pa'piro *nm* papyrus

'pappa *nf* (per bambini) baby food; **trovare la** ∼ **pronta** fig have everything ready and waiting

pappagal'lino *nm* budgerigar, budgie

pappa'gallo *nm* parrot

pappa'gorgia *nf* double chin

pappa'molle *nmf* wimp

pappar'delle *nfpl* strips of pasta usually served with a meat sauce

pap'parsi *vr* fam tuck away

pap'pone *nm* sl (mangione) pig; (sfruttatore) pimp

'paprica *nf* paprika

Pap test *nm inv* smear test, cervical smear

'Papua 'Nuova Gui'nea *nf* Papua New Guinea

'para *nf* **suole di** ∼ crepe soles

parà *nm inv* para

pa'rabola *nf* parable; (curva) parabola

para'bolico *adj* parabolic

para'brezza *nm inv* windscreen, windshield Am

paracadu'tare *vt* parachute

paracadu'tarsi *vr* parachute

paraca'dute *nm inv* parachute

paracadu'tismo *nm* parachuting. **paracadutismo ascensionale** parascending

paracadu'tista *nmf* parachutist

para'carro *nm* roadside post

para'digma *nm* Gram paradigm

paradi'siaco *adj* heavenly

para'diso *nm* paradise. **paradiso fiscale** tax haven. **paradiso terrestre** Eden, earthly paradise

parados'sale *adj* paradoxical

para'dosso *nm* paradox

para'fango *nm* mudguard

paraf'fina *nf* paraffin

parafra'sare *vt* paraphrase

pa'rafrasi *nf inv* paraphrase

para'fulmine *nm* lightning conductor

para'fuoco *nm inv* fireguard

pa'raggi *nmpl* neighbourhood *sg*

parago'nabile *adj* comparable (**a** to)

parago'nare *vt* compare

parago'narsi *vr* compare oneself

para'gone *nm* comparison; **a** ∼ **di** in comparison with; **non c'è** ∼! there's no comparison!

paragra'fare *vt* paragraph

pa'ragrafo *nm* paragraph

paraguai'ano, -a *adj & nmf* Paraguayan

Paragu'ay *nm* Paraguay

pa'ralisi *nf inv* paralysis

para'litico, -a *adj & nmf* paralytic

paraliz'zante *adj* crippling

paraliz'zare *vt* paralyse

paraliz'zato *adj* (dalla paura) transfixed

paral'lela *nf* parallel line; **è una ~ di...** ⟨*strada*⟩ it runs parallel to...; **parallele** *pl* parallel bars

parallela'mente *adv* in parallel

paralle'lismo *nm* parallelism

paral'lelo *adj & nm* parallel; **fare un ~ tra** draw a parallel between

parallelo'gramma *nm* parallelogram

para'lume *nm* lampshade

para'medico *nm* paramedic

para'mento *nm* hangings *pl*

pa'rametro *nm* parameter

paramili'tare *adj* paramilitary

pa'ranco *nm* block and tackle

para'noia *nf* paranoia

para'noico, -a *adj & nmf* paranoid

paranor'male *adj & nm* paranormal

para'occhi *nmpl* blinkers

parao'recchie *nm inv* earmuffs

parapen'dio *nm* paragliding

para'petto *nm* parapet

para'piglia *nm* turmoil

para'plegico, -a *adj & nmf* paraplegic

pa'rare ① *vt* (addobbare) adorn; (riparare) shield; save ⟨*tiro, pallone*⟩; ward off, parry ⟨*schiaffo, pugno*⟩
② *vi* (mirare) lead up to

pa'rarsi *vr* (abbigliarsi) dress up; (da pioggia, pugni) protect oneself; **~ dinanzi a qualcuno** appear in front of somebody

parasco'lastico *adj* ⟨*attività*⟩ extracurricular

para'sole *nm inv* parasol

paras'sita ① *adj* parasitic
② *nm* parasite

parassi'tario *adj* anche fig parasitic

parassi'tismo *nm* parasitism

parasta'tale *adj* government-controlled

para'stinchi *nm inv* shinpad, shinguard

pa'rata *nf* parade; (in calcio) save; (in scherma, pugilato) parry. **parata aerea** flypast

para'tia *nf* bulkhead

parauniversi'tario *adj* at university level

para'urti *nm inv* Auto bumper, fender Am. **parauarti** *pl* **tubolari rigidi** bull bars

para'vento *nm inv* screen

par'boiled *adj* **riso parboiled** parboiled rice

par'cella *nf* bill

parcheggi'are *vt* anche fig park; **~ in doppia fila** double-park

parcheggia'|'tore, -trice *nmf* parking attendant. **parcheggiatore abusivo** person who illegally earns money by looking after parked cars

par'cheggio *nm* parking; (posteggio) car park, parking lot Am. **parcheggio carta** Comput paper park. **parcheggio custodito** car park with attendant. **parcheggio incustodito** unattended car park. **parcheggio a pagamento** paying car park. **parcheggio sotterraneo** underground car park, underground parking garage Am

par'chimetro *nm* parking meter

'parco¹ *adj* sparing; (moderato) moderate; **essere ~ nel mangiare** eat sparingly

'parco² *nm* park. **parco di divertimenti** fun fair. **parco giochi** playground. **parco macchine** Auto fleet of cars. **parco naturale** wildlife park. **parco nazionale** national park. **parco regionale** [regional] wildlife park

pa'recchio ① *adj* quite a lot of; **parecchi** *pl* several, quite a lot of
② *pron* quite a lot; **parecchi** *pl* several, quite a lot
③ *adv* rather; (parecchio tempo) quite a time

pareggi'are ① *vt* level; (eguagliare) equal; Comm balance; **~ il bilancio** balance the budget
② *vi* draw; **hanno pareggiato nel secondo tempo** they equalized in the second half

pa'reggio *nm* Comm balance; Sport draw; **il gol del ~** the equalizer

paren'tado *nm* relatives *pl*; (vincolo di sangue) relationship

pa'rente *nmf* relative, relation. **parente acquisito** relation by marriage. **parente alla lontana** distant relation. **parente stretto** close relation

paren'tela *nf* relatives *pl*; (vincolo di sangue) relationship; **grado di parentela** degree of kinship

pa'rentesi *nf inv* parenthesis; (segno grafico) bracket; (fig: pausa) break; **aprire una ~** fig digress; **~ pl graffe** curly brackets; **~ pl quadre** square brackets; **tra ~ quadre** in square brackets; **~ pl tonde** round brackets; **fra ~,...** (a proposito) by the way,...

pa'reo *nm* (copricostume) sarong; **a ~** ⟨*gonna*⟩ wrap-around

pa'rere¹ *nm* opinion; **a mio ~** in my opinion; **essere del ~ che** be of the opinion that

pa'rere² *vi* seem; (pensare) think; **che te ne pare?** what do you think of it?; **pare di sì** it seems so; **mi pare che...** I think that...; **non mi par vero** I can't believe it; **mi pareva bene!** I thought as much!

pa'rete *nf* wall; (in alpinismo) face. **parete divisoria** partition wall

'pargolo *nf* liter child

'pari ① *adj inv* equal; ⟨*numero*⟩ even; **andare di ~ passo** keep pace; **essere ~** be even *or* quits; **arrivare ~** draw; **~ ~** ⋯⟶

⟨*copiare, ripetere*⟩ word for word; **fare ∼ o dispari** toss a coin
2 *nmf inv* equal, peer; **ragazza alla ∼** au pair [girl]; **lavorare alla ∼** work [as an] au pair; **mettersi in ∼ con qualcosa** catch up with something
3 *nm* (titolo nobiliare) peer

'**paria** *nm inv* pariah

parifi'cato *adj* ⟨*scuola*⟩ state-recognized

Pa'rigi *nf* Paris

pari'gino, -a *adj & nmf* Parisian

pa'riglia *nf* pair; **rendere la ∼ a qualcuno** give somebody tit for tat

parità *nf* equality; Tennis deuce; **a ∼ di condizioni/voti** if all circumstances/the votes are equal; **finire in ∼** ⟨*partita*⟩ end in a draw. **parità dei diritti** equal rights. **parità monetaria** monetary parity. **parità dei sessi** sexual equality, equality of the sexes

pari'tario *adj* parity *attrib*

'**parka** *nm inv* parka

parlamen'tare **1** *adj* parliamentary
2 *nmf* Member of Parliament
3 *vi* negotiate

parla'mento *nm* Parliament; **il Parlamento europeo** the European Parliament

par'lante *adj* ⟨*bambola, pappagallo*⟩ talking

parlan'tina *nf* **avere la ∼** be a chatterbox

par'lare *vt/i* speak, talk; speak ⟨*inglese, italiano*⟩; (confessare) talk; **∼ bene/male di qualcuno** speak well/ill of somebody; **∼ da solo** speak to oneself; **chi parla?** Teleph who's speaking?; **senti chi parla!** look who's talking!; **non parliamone più** let's forget about it; **non se ne parla nemmeno** don't even mention it!; **∼ a braccio** speak off the top of one's head; **far ∼ qualcuno** make somebody talk

par'lato *adj* ⟨*lingua*⟩ spoken

parla|'tore, -trice *nmf* speaker

parla'torio *nm* parlour; (in prigione) visiting room

parlot'tare *vi* mutter

parlot'tio *nm* muttering

parlucchi'are *vt* speak a little, have a smattering of ⟨*lingua*⟩

parmigi'ano *nm* Parmesan

paro'dia *nf* parody, send-up; **fare la ∼ di qualcuno** take somebody off

parodi'are *vt* parody, mimic

paro'distico *adj* ⟨*tono*⟩ parodying; **programma parodistico** take-off show

pa'rola *nf* word; (facoltà) speech; **è una ∼!** it is easier said than done!; **parole** *pl* (di canzone) words, lyrics; **rivolgere la ∼ a** address; **passare ∼** spread the word; **non fare ∼ di qualcosa con nessuno** not breathe a word of something to anybody; **ti credo sulla ∼** I'll take your word for it; **togliere la ∼ di bocca a qualcuno** take the words [right] out of somebody's mouth; **voler sempre l'ultima ∼** always want to have the last word; **dire due parole a qualcuno** have a word *or* chat with somebody; **di poche parole** ⟨*persona*⟩ of few words; **dare a qualcuno la propria ∼** give somebody one's word; **∼ per ∼** word for word; **in parole povere** crudely speaking. **parola chiave** keyword; **parole** *pl* **incrociate** crossword [puzzle]. **parola di moda** buzzword. **parola d'onore** word of honour. **parola d'ordine** password

paro'laccia *nf* swearword

paro'liere *nm* lyricist

paro'lina *nf* **dire due paroline a qualcuno** have a word *or* chat with somebody

paro'loni *nmpl* mumbo jumbo

paros'sismo *nm* paroxysm

paros'sistico *adj* Med paroxysmal

par'quet *nm inv* (pavimento) parquet flooring

parri'cida *nmf* parricide

parri'cidio *nm* parricide

par'rocchia *nf* parish

parrocchi'ale *adj* parish *attrib*

parrocchi'ano, -a *nmf* parishioner

'**parroco** *nm* parish priest

par'rucca *nf* wig

parrucchi'ere, -a *nmf* hairdresser

parruc'chino *nm* toupée, hairpiece

parsi'monia *nf* thrift

parsimoni'oso *adj* thrifty

'**parso** *pp di* PARERE[2]

'**parte** *nf* part; (lato) side; (partito) party; (porzione) share; (fazione) group; **a ∼** apart from; **in ∼** in part; **la maggior ∼ di** the majority of; **d'altra ∼** on the other hand; **da ∼** aside; (in disparte) to one side; **farsi da ∼** stand aside; **da ∼ di** from; (per conto di) on behalf of; **è gentile da ∼ tua** it is kind of you; **fare una brutta ∼ a qualcuno** behave badly towards somebody; **da che ∼ è...?** whereabouts is...?; **da una parte..., dall'altra...** on the one hand..., on the other hand...; **dall'altra ∼ di** on the other side of; **da nessuna ∼** nowhere; **da qualche ∼** somewhere; **da qualche altra ∼** somewhere else, elsewhere; **da tutte le parti** (essere) everywhere; **da questa ∼** (in questa direzione) this way; **da queste parti** hereabouts; **da un anno a questa ∼** for about a year now; **mettere qualcosa da ∼** put something aside; **essere dalla ∼ di qualcuno** be on somebody's side; **prendere le parti di qualcuno** take somebody's side; **dalla ∼ della ragione/del torto** in the right/the wrong; **essere ∼ in causa** be involved; **fare ∼ di** (appartenere a) be a member of; **fare la propria ∼** do one's share *or* bit; **mettere qualcuno a ~ di qualcosa** inform somebody of something; **prendere ~ a qualcosa** take part in something. **parte civile** plaintiff. **parte del discorso** part of speech

parteci'pante *nmf* participant

parteci'pare *vi* **~ a** participate in, take part in; (condividere) share in

partecipazi'one *nf* participation; (annuncio) announcement; Fin shareholding; (presenza) presence; **con la ~ [straordinaria] di...** featuring.... **partecipazione statale** (quota) state interest

par'tecipe *adj* participating

parteggi'are *vi* **~ per** side with

par'tenza *nf* departure; Sport start; **in ~ per** leaving for; **falsa partenza** false start

parti'cella *nf* particle

parti'cina *nf* bit part

parti'cipio *nm* participle. **participio passato** past participle. **participio presente** present participle

partico'lare [1] *adj* particular; (privato) private; (speciale) special, particular [2] *nm* detail, particular; **fin nei minimi particolari** down to the smallest detail; **in ~** (particolarmente) in particular

particolareggi'ato *adj* detailed

particolarità *nf inv* particularity; (dettaglio) detail

particolar'mente *adv* particularly

partigi'ano, **-a** *adj & nmf* partisan

par'tire *vi* leave; (aver inizio) start; (fam: rompersi) break; **a ~ da** [beginning] from; **~ molto bene** get off to a flying start; **~ in quarta** go off at half cock; **è partito** (fam: ubriaco) he's away

par'tita *nf* game; (incontro) match; Comm lot; (contabilità) entry; **dare ~ vinta a qualcuno** fig give in to somebody. **partita amichevole** friendly [match]. **partita di calcio** football match. **partita a carte** game of cards. **partita doppia** Comm double-entry book keeping. **partita di ritorno** Sport return match, rematch. **partita semplice** Comm single-entry book keeping

parti'tario *nm* Comm ledger. **partitario vendite** sales ledger

par'tito *nm* party; (scelta) choice; (occasione di matrimonio) match; **per ~ preso** out of sheer pig-headedness. **partito di governo** governing party. **partito di maggioranza** majority party. **partito politico** political party

partitocra'zia *nf* concentration of power in the hands of political parties to the detriment of parliamentary democracy

partizi'one *nf* (divisione) division; (Comput: di disco) partition

'**partner** *nmf inv* (in affari, coppia) partner

'**parto** *nm* childbirth; **un ~ facile** an easy birth *or* labour; **dolori** *pl* **del ~** labour pains; **morire di ~** die in childbirth. **parto cesareo** Caesarean. **parto in acqua** water birth. **parto indolore** natural childbirth. **parto pilotato** induction, induced labour. **parto prematuro** premature birth

partori'ente *nf* woman in labour

parto'rire *vt* anche fig give birth to

part-'time [1] *adj* part-time [2] *nm* **chiedere il ~** ask to work part-time

pa'rure *nf inv* (di gioielli) set of jewellery; (di biancheria intima) set of matching lingerie

par'venza *nf* appearance

parzi'ale *adj* partial

parzialità *nf* partiality; **fare ~ per qualcuno** be biased towards somebody

parzial'mente *adv* partially; (con parzialità) with bias; **parzialmente cieco** partially sighted; **parzialmente scremato** semi-skimmed

'**pascere** [1] *vi* ⟨mucche⟩ graze [2] *vt* graze on (erba)

pasci'uto *adj* **ben ~** plump

pasco'lare *vt* graze

'**pascolo** *nm* pasture

'**Pasqua** *nf* Easter; **l'isola di Pasqua** Easter Island

pa'squale *adj* Easter *attrib*

pa'squetta *nf* (lunedì di Pasqua) Easter Monday

'**passa**: **e ~** *adv* (e oltre) plus

pas'sabile *adj* passable

pas'saggio *nm* passage; (traversata) crossing; Sport pass; (su veicolo) lift, ride; **essere di ~** be passing through; **è stato un ~ obbligato** fig it was something essential, it had to be done. **passaggio a livello** level crossing, grade crossing Am. **passaggio pedonale** pedestrian crossing, crosswalk Am. **passaggio di proprietà** transfer of ownership, conveyancing

passamane'ria *nf* braid

passamon'tagna *nm inv* balaclava

pas'sante [1] *nmf* passer-by [2] *nm* (di cintura) loop [3] *adj* Tennis passing

passa'porto *nm* anche fig passport. **passaporto europeo** European passport, Europassport

pas'sare [1] *vi* pass; (attraversare) pass through; (far visita) call; (andare) go; (essere approvato) be passed; **~ davanti a qualcuno** go in front of somebody; **~ alla storia** go down in history; **~ di moda** go out of fashion; **mi è passato di mente** it slipped my mind; **~ sopra a qualcosa** pass over something; **~ per un genio/idiota** be taken for a genius/an idiot; **farsi ~ per qualcuno** ⋯⁚

pass oneself off as somebody; **passo!** (nelle carte) pass!; (per radio) over!

2 vt (far scorrere) pass over; (sopportare) go through; (al telefono) put through; Culin strain; pass ⟨esame, visita⟩; ∼ **in rivista** review; ∼ **qualcosa a qualcuno** pass something to somebody; **le passo il signor Rossi** Teleph I'll put you through to Mr Rossi; ∼ **qualcosa su qualcosa** ⟨crema, cera ecc⟩ give something a coat of something; ∼ **il limite** go over the limit; **passarsela bene** be well off; **come te la passi?** how are you doing?

3 nm col ∼ **del tempo** with the passing or passage of time

pas'sata nf (di vernice) coat; (spolverata) dusting; (occhiata) look

passa'tempo nm pastime

pas'sato **1** adj past; **l'anno** ∼ last year; **sono le tre passate** it's past or after three o'clock

2 nm past; Culin purée; Gram past tense; **in** ∼ in the past; **la musica del** ∼ the music of yesteryear. **passato di moda** old-fashioned. **passato prossimo** present perfect. **passato remoto** [simple] past. **passato di verdure** cream of vegetable soup

passaver'dure nm inv food mill

passavi'vande nm inv serving hatch

passeg'gero, -a **1** adj passing

2 nmf passenger. **passeggero in transito** transit passenger

passeggi'are vi walk, stroll

passeg'giata nf walk, stroll; (luogo) public walk; (in bicicletta) ride; **fare una** ∼ go for a walk

passeggia'trice nf streetwalker

passeg'gino nm pushchair, stroller Am

pas'seggio nm walk; (luogo) promenade; **andare a** ∼ go for a walk; **scarpe da passeggio** walking shoes

passe-par'tout nm inv master-key

passe'rella nf gangway; Aeron boarding bridge; (per sfilate) catwalk

'passero nm sparrow

passe'rotto nm (passero) sparrow

pas'sibile adj ∼ **di** liable to

passio'nale adj passionate; **delitto passionale** crime of passion

passi'one nf passion; **avere la** ∼ **del gioco** have a passion for gambling

passiva'mente adv passively

passività nf inv (inerzia) passiveness, passivity; Fin liabilities pl; ∼ pl **correnti** current liabilities

pas'sivo **1** adj passive

2 nm passive; Fin liabilities pl; **in** ∼ ⟨azienda⟩ in deficit; ⟨bilancio⟩ debit, in deficit

'passo nm step; (orma) footprint; (andatura) pace, step; (di libro) passage; (valico) pass; **a**

due passi da qui a stone's throw away; **a** ∼ **d'uomo** at walking pace; **di buon** ∼ at a spanking pace, at a cracking pace; **a passi felpati** stealthily; **di questo** ∼ at this rate; ∼ ∼ step by step; **fare due passi** go for a stroll; **allungare il** ∼ quicken one's pace, step out; **tornare sui propri passi** retrace one's steps; **fare un** ∼ **avanti** anche fig take a step forward; **fare un** ∼ **falso** fig make a wrong move; **di pari** ∼ fig hand in hand; **stare al** ∼ **con i tempi** keep up with the times, keep abreast of the times; **tenere il** ∼ keep up. **passo carrabile**, **passo carraio** driveway. **passo dell'oca** goose-step

'pasta nf (impasto per pane ecc) dough; (per dolci, pasticcino) pastry; (pastasciutta) pasta; (massa molle) paste; fig nature; **sono fatti della stessa** ∼ they're birds of a feather. **pasta e fagioli** very thick soup with blended borlotti beans and small pasta. **pasta al forno** pasta baked in white sauce with grated cheese. **pasta frolla** shortcrust pastry. **pasta al ragù** pasta with Bolognese sauce

pastasci'utta nf pasta

pa'stella nf batter

pa'stello nm pastel

pa'sticca nf pastille; (fam: pastiglia) pill

pasticce'ria nf cake shop, patisserie; (pasticcini) pastries pl; (arte) confectionery

pasticci'are **1** vi make a mess

2 vt make a mess of

pasticci'ere, -a nmf confectioner

pastic'cino nm little cake

pa'sticcio nm Culin pie; (lavoro disordinato) mess; **mettersi nei pasticci** get into trouble

pasticci'one, -a **1** nmf bungler

2 adj bungling

pasti'ficio nm pasta factory

pa'stiglia nf Med pill, tablet; (di menta) sweet. **pastiglia dei freni** Auto brake pad. **pastiglia per la gola** throat pastille. **pastiglia per la tosse** cough sweet

pa'stina nf small pasta shape. **pastina in brodo** noodle soup

'pasto nm meal; **fuori** ∼ between meals; **dare qualcosa in** ∼ **a** fig serve something up on a platter to ⟨pubblico, stampa⟩. **pasto pronto** TV dinner

pa'stora nf shepherdess

pasto'rale adj pastoral

pa'store nm shepherd; Relig pastor, vicar. **pastore scozzese** collie. **pastore tedesco** German shepherd, Alsatian

pasto'rizio adj sheep farming attrib

pastoriz'zare vt pasteurize

pastoriz'zato adj pasteurized

pastorizzazi'one nf pasteurization

pa'stoso adj doughy; fig mellow

pa'strocchio *nm* mess

pa'stura *nf* pasture; (per pesci) bait

pa'tacca *nf* (macchia) stain; (fig: oggetto senza valore) piece of junk

pa'tata *nf* potato. **patata americana** sweet potato; **patate** *pl* **arrosto** roast potatoes; **patate** *pl* **al cartoccio** jacket potatoes; **patate** *pl* **fritte** chips Br, French fries; **patate** *pl* **in insalata** potato salad; **patate** *pl* **lesse** boiled potatoes

pata'tine *nfpl* [potato] crisps, [potato] chips Am

pata'trac *nm inv* (crollo) crash

patch'work *nm inv* patchwork

pâté *nm inv* pâté. **pâté di fegato** liver pâté

pa'tella *nf* limpet

pa'tema *nm* anxiety

pa'tente *nf* licence; **prendere la** ~ get one's driving licence. **patente di guida** driving licence, driver's license Am

pater'nale *nf* scolding

paterna'lismo *nm* paternalism

paterna'lista *nm* paternalist

paterna'listico *adj* paternalistic

paternità *nf* paternity

pa'terno *adj* paternal; ⟨affetto ecc⟩ fatherly

pa'tetico *adj* pathetic; **cadere nel** ~ become over-sentimental

'pathos *nm* pathos

pa'tibolo *nm* gallows *sg*

pati'mento *nm* suffering

'patina *nf* patina; (sulla lingua) coating

'patio *nm* patio garden

pa'tire *vt/i* suffer

pa'tito, -a ① *adj* suffering ② *nmf* fanatic. **patito della musica** music lover

patolo'gia *nf* pathology. **patologia da radiazioni** radiation sickness. **patologia da sforzo ripetuto** repetitive strain injury, RSI

pato'logico *adj* pathological

pa'tologo, -a *nmf* pathologist

'patria *nf* native land; **amor di** ~ love of one's country

patri'arca *nm* patriarch

patriar'cale *adj* patriarchal

patriar'cato *nm* patriarchy

pa'trigno *nm* stepfather

patrimoni'ale *adj* property *attrib*

patri'monio *nm* estate

patri'ota *nmf* patriot

patri'ottico *adj* patriotic

patriot'tismo *nm* patriotism

pa'trizio, -a *adj & nmf* patrician

patroci'nante *adj* sponsoring

patroci'nare *vt* support

patro'cinio *nm* support; **sotto il** ~ **di** under the sponsorship of; Jur defended by. **patrocinio gratuito** legal aid

patro'nato *nm* patronage

pa'trono *nm* Relig patron saint; Jur counsel

'patta[1] *nf* (di tasca) flap

'patta[2] *nf* (pareggio) draw

patteggia'mento *nm* bargaining

patteggi'are *vt/i* negotiate

patti'naggio *nm* skating. **pattinaggio artistico** figure skating. **pattinaggio su ghiaccio** ice skating. **pattinaggio a rotelle** roller-skating

patti'nare *vi* skate; (auto) skid

pattina|'tore, -trice *nmf* skater

'pattino *nm* skate; Aeron skid. **pattino da ghiaccio** ice skate. **pattino a rotelle** roller skate

'patto *nm* deal; Pol pact; **a** ~ **che** on condition that; **scendere a patti, venire a patti** reach a compromise

pat'tuglia *nf* patrol; **essere di** ~ be on patrol. **pattuglia stradale** highway patrol Am, ≈ patrol car; police motorbike

pattu'ire *vt* negotiate

pat'tume *nm* rubbish

pattumi'era *nf* dustbin, trashcan Am

pa'ura *nf* fear; (spavento) fright; **aver** ~ be afraid; **mettere** ~ **a** frighten; **per** ~ **di** for fear of; **da** ~ (sl: libro, film) brilliant

pau'roso *adj* (che fa paura) frightening; (che ha paura) fearful; (fam: enorme) awesome

'pausa *nf* pause; (nel lavoro) break; **fare una** ~ pause; (nel lavoro) have a break. **pausa [per il] caffè** coffee break. **pausa [per il] pranzo** lunchbreak, lunch hour

pavida'mente *adv* timidly

'pavido ① *adj* cowardly ② *nm* coward

pavimen'tare *vt* pave ⟨strada⟩

pavimentazi'one *nf* paving

pavi'mento *nm* floor

pa'vone *nm* peacock

pavoneggi'arsi *vr* strut

pay tv *nf inv* pay TV

pazien'tare *vi* be patient

pazi'ente *adj & nmf* patient

paziente'mente *adv* patiently

pazi'enza *nf* patience; ~! never mind!; **perdere la** ~ lose one's patience

'pazza *nf* madwoman

pazza'mente *adv* madly

pazzerel'lone, -a *nmf* madcap

paz'zesco *adj* foolish; (esagerato) crazy

paz'zia *nf* madness; (azione) [act of] folly

'**pazzo** ① *adj* mad; fig crazy; **sei** ~? you must be crazy!, are you crazy?
② *nm* madman; **essere** ~ **di/per** be crazy about; ~ **di gioia** mad with joy; **da pazzi** fam crackpot; **darsi alla pazza gioia** live it up

paz'zoide *adj* fam whacky

P.C.I. *nm abbr* (**Partito Comunista Italiano**) Italian Communist Party

'**pecan** *nm inv* pecan

'**pecca** *nf* fault; **senza** ~ flawless

peccami'noso *adj* sinful

pec'care *vi* sin; ~ **di** be guilty of (ingratitudine)

pec'cato *nm* sin; ~ **che...** it's a pity that...; [**che**] ~! [what a] pity!. **peccato di gioventù** youthful folly

pecca|'tore, -trice *nmf* sinner

'**pece** *nf* pitch; **nero come la** ~ black as pitch

pechi'nese *nm* Pekin[g]ese

Pe'chino *nf* Beijing, Peking

'**pecora** *nf* sheep. **pecora nera** black sheep

peco'raio *nm* shepherd

peco'rella *nf* **cielo a pecorelle** sky full of fluffy white clouds. **pecorella smarrita** lost sheep

peco'rino *nm* (formaggio) sheep's milk cheese

peculi'are *adj* ~ **di** peculiar to

peculiarità *nf inv* peculiarity

pecuni'ario *adj* money *attrib*

pe'daggio *nm* toll

pedago'gia *nf* pedagogy

peda'gogico *adj* pedagogical

peda'gogo, -a *nmf* pedagogue

peda'lare *vi* pedal

peda'lata *nf* push on the pedals

pe'dale *nm* pedal. **pedale dell'acceleratore** gas pedal. **pedale del freno** brake pedal

pedalò *nm inv* pedalo

pe'dana *nf* footrest; Sport springboard

pe'dante *adj* pedantic

pedante'ria *nf* pedantry

pedan'tesco *adj* pedantic

pe'data *nf* (calcio) kick; (impronta) footprint

pede'rasta *nm* pederast

pe'destre *adj* pedestrian

pedi'atra *nmf* paediatrician

pedia'tria *nf* paediatrics

pedi'atrico *adj* paediatric

pedi'cure ① *nmf inv* chiropodist, podiatrist Am
② *nm* (cura dei piedi) pedicure

pedi'gree *nm inv* pedigree

pedi'luvio *nm* footbath

pe'dina *nf* (alla dama) piece; fig pawn

pedina'mento *nm* shadowing

pedi'nare *vt* shadow

pedofi'lia *nf* paedophilia

pe'dofilo, -a *nmf* paedophile

pedo'nale *adj* pedestrian

pe'done *nm* pedestrian

'**pedule** *nfpl* hiking boots

'**peeling** *nm inv* exfoliation treatment

'**peggio** ① *adv* worse; ~ **per te!** too bad!, tough!; **tanto** ~ too bad; ~ **di così** any worse; **la persona** ~ **vestita** the worst dressed person
② *adj* worse; **niente di** ~ nothing worse; **stare** ~ **di** be worse off than
③ *nm* **il** ~ **è che...** the worst of it is that...; **pensare al** ~ think the worst
④ *nf* **alla** ~ at worst; **avere la** ~ get the worst of it; **alla meno** ~ as best I can

peggiora'mento *nm* worsening

peggio'rare ① *vt* make worse, worsen
② *vi* get worse, worsen

peggiora'tivo *adj* pejorative

peggi'ore ① *adj* worse; (superlativo) worst; **nella** ~ **delle ipotesi** if the worst comes to the worst;
② *nmf* **il/la** ~ the worst

'**pegno** *nm* pledge; (nei giochi di società) forfeit; fig token; **dare qualcosa in** ~ pawn something; **in** ~ **d'amicizia** as a token of friendship

pelan'drone *nm* slob

pe'lare *vt* (spennare) pluck; (spellare) skin; (sbucciare) peel; (fam: spillare denaro) fleece

pe'larsi *vr* fam lose one's hair

pe'lati *nmpl* (pomodori) peeled tomatoes

pe'lato *adj* (calvo) bald

pel'lame *nm* skins *pl*

'**pelle** *nf* skin; (cuoio) leather; (buccia) peel; **avere la** ~ **d'oca** have goose-flesh; **non stare più nella** ~ be beside oneself; **salvare la** ~ save one's skin; **lasciarci la** ~ buy it; **essere** ~ **e ossa** be all skin and bones; **avere la** ~ **dura** be tough; **borsa di pelle** leather bag. **pelle scamosciata** suede

pellegri'naggio *nm* pilgrimage

pelle'grino, -a *nmf* pilgrim

pelle'rossa *nmf* Red Indian, Redskin

pellette'ria *nf* leather goods *pl*

pelli'cano *nm* pelican

pellicce'ria *nf* furrier's [shop]

pel'liccia *nf* fur; (indumento) fur [coat]

pellicci'aio, -a *nmf* furrier

pel'licola *nf* Phot, Cinema film. **pellicola a colori** colour film. **pellicola trasparente** Culin cling film

'**pelo** *nm* hair; (di animale) coat; (di lana) pile; **per un** ~ by the skin of one's teeth;

cavarsela per un ∼ have a narrow escape; **cercare il ∼ nell'uovo** nitpick

pe'loso adj hairy

'peltro nm pewter

pe'luche nm **giocattolo di peluche** soft toy; **orsetto di peluche** teddy bear

pe'luria nf down

'pelvico adj pelvic

'pena nf (punizione) punishment; (sofferenza) pain; (dispiacere) sorrow; (disturbo) trouble; **a mala ∼** hardly; **mi fa ∼** I pity him; **vale la ∼ andare** it is worth [while] going; **pene** pl **dell'inferno** hellfire. **pena di morte** death sentence

pe'nale adj criminal; **diritto penale** criminal law

pena'lista nmf criminal lawyer

penalità nf inv penalty

penaliz'zare vt penalize

penalizzazi'one nf (penalità) penalty

pe'nare vi suffer; (faticare) find it difficult

pen'daglio nm pendant

pen'dant nm inv **fare ∼ [con]** match

pen'dente [1] adj hanging; Comm outstanding [2] nm (ciondolo) pendant; **pendenti** pl drop earrings

pen'denza nf slope; Comm outstanding account

'pendere vi hang; (superficie) slope; (essere inclinato) lean

pen'dio nm slope; **in ∼** sloping

'pendola nf grandfather clock

pendo'lare [1] adj pendulum [2] nmf commuter

pendo'lino nm (treno) special, first class only, fast train

'pendolo nm pendulum; **orologio a pendolo** grandfather clock

'pene nm penis

pene'trante adj penetrating; (freddo) biting

pene'trare [1] vt/i penetrate; (trafiggere) pierce [2] vt (odore) get into [3] vi (entrare furtivamente) steal in

penetrazi'one nf penetration

penicil'lina nf penicillin

pe'nisola nf peninsula

peni'tente adj & nmf penitent

peni'tenza nf penitence; (punizione) penance; (in gioco) forfeit

penitenzi'ario nm penitentiary

'penna nf (per scrivere) pen; (di uccello) feather. **penna a feltro** felt-tip[ped pen]. **penna ottica** light pen. **penna a sfera** ball-point [pen]. **penna stilografica** fountain-pen

pen'nacchio nm plume

penna'rello nm felt-tip[ped pen]

'penne nfpl pasta quills

pennel'lare vt paint

pennel'lata nf brushstroke

pen'nello nm brush; **a ∼** (a perfezione) perfectly. **∼ da barba** shaving brush

pen'nino nm nib

pen'none nm (di bandiera) flagpole

pen'nuto adj feathered

pe'nombra nf half-light

pe'noso adj (fam: pessimo) painful

pen'sabile adj **non è ∼** it's unthinkable

pen'sare [1] vi think; **penso di sì** I think so; **∼ a** think of; remember to (chiudere il gas ecc); **pensa ai fatti tuoi!** mind your own business!; **ci penso io** I'll take care of it; **∼ di fare qualcosa** think of doing something; **a pensarci bene** on second thoughts; **∼ tra sé e sé** think to oneself; **pensarci su** think it over [2] vt think

pen'sata nf idea

pensa'tore, -trice nmf thinker

pensi'ero nm thought; (mente) mind; (preoccupazione) worry; **stare in ∼ per** be anxious about; **levarsi il ∼** to get something out of the way

pensie'roso adj pensive

'pensile [1] adj hanging; **giardino pensile** roof-garden [2] nm (mobile) wall unit

pensi'lina nf (di fermata d'autobus) bus shelter

pensio'nante nmf boarder; (ospite pagante) lodger

pensio'nato, -a [1] nmf pensioner [2] nm (per anziani) [old folks'] home; (per studenti) hostel

pensi'one nf pension; (albergo) boarding house; (vitto e alloggio) board and lodging; (da lavoro) retirement **andare in ∼** retire; **essere in ∼** be retired; **mezza pensione** half board. **pensione di anzianità** old-age pension. **pensione completa** full board. **pensione di invalidità** disability pension

pen'soso adj pensive

pen'tagono nm pentagon; **il Pentagono** the Pentagon

pen'tathlon nm pentathlon

Pente'coste nf Whitsun, Whit Sunday

penti'mento nm repentance

pen'tirsi vr **∼ di** repent of; (rammaricarsi) regret

penti'tismo nm turning informant

pen'tito nm terrorist or Mafioso turned informant

'pentola nf saucepan; (contenuto) potful. **pentola a pressione** pressure cooker

pento'lino nm saucepan

pe'nultimo *adj* last but one, penultimate

pe'nuria *nf* shortage

penzo'lare *vi* dangle

penzo'loni *adv* dangling

pe'onia *nf* peony

pepai'ola *nf* pepper pot

pe'pare *vt* pepper

pe'pato *adj* peppery

'pepe *nm* pepper; **grano di pepe** peppercorn. **pepe di Caienna** cayenne pepper. **pepe in grani** whole peppercorns. **pepe macinato** ground pepper; **pepe nero** black pepper

pepero'nata *nf* dish of peppers and tomatoes

peperon'cino *nm* chilli pepper

pepe'rone *nm* [sweet] pepper; **rosso come un ~** red as a beetroot; **peperoni** *pl* ripieni stuffed peppers. **peperone rosso** red pepper. **peperone verde** green pepper

pepi'era *nf* pepper pot; (macinino) pepper mill

pe'pita *nf* nugget

'peptico *adj* peptic

'per *prep* for; (attraverso) through; (stato in luogo) in, on; (distributivo) per; (mezzo, entro) by; (causa) with; (in qualità di) as; **mi è passato per la mente** it crossed my mind; **~ strada** on the street; **~ la fine del mese** by the end of the month; **in fila ~** due in double file; **l'ho sentito ~ telefono** I spoke to him on the phone; **~ iscritto** in writing; **~ caso** by chance; **~ esempio** for example; **ho aspettato ~ ore** I've been waiting for hours; **~ tutta la durata del viaggio** for the entire journey; **~ tempo** in time; **~ sempre** forever; **~ scherzo** as a joke; **gridare ~ il dolore** scream with pain; **vendere ~ diecimila euro** sell for ten thousand euros; **uno ~ volta** one at a time; **uno ~ uno** one by one; **venti ~ cento** twenty per cent; **~ fare qualcosa** [in order to] do something; **stare ~** be about to; **è troppo bello ~ essere vero** it's too good to be true

'pera *nf* pear; **farsi una ~** (sl: di eroina) shoot up

perbe'nismo *nm* prissiness

perbe'nista *adj inv* prissy

per'calle *nm* gingham

per'cento *adv* per cent

percentu'ale *nf* percentage

perce'pibile *adj* perceivable; (somma) payable

perce'pire *vt* perceive; (riscuotere) cash

percet'tibile *adj* perceptible

percettibil'mente *adv* perceptibly

percezi'one *nf* perception

perché [1] *conj* (in interrogative) why; (per il fatto che) because; (affinché) so that; **~ non vieni?** why don't you come?; **dimmi ~** tell me why; **~ no/si!** because!; **è troppo difficile ~ lo possa capire** it's too difficult for him to understand
[2] *nm inv* reason [why]; **senza un ~** without any reason

perciò *conj* so

per'correre *vt* cover (distanza); (viaggiare) travel

percor'ribile *adj* (strada) drivable, passable

percorribilità *nf* **percorribilità delle strade** road conditions *pl*

per'corso [1] pp di PERCORRERE
[2] *nm* (tragitto) course, route; (distanza) distance; (viaggio) journey. **percorso ecologico** nature trail. **percorso di guerra** assault course. **percorso a ostacoli** obstacle course. **percorso vascolare** cardiovascular circuit

per'cossa *nf* blow; **percosse** *pl* Jur assault and battery

per'cosso pp di PERCUOTERE

percu'otere *vt* strike

percussi'one *nf* percussion; **strumenti a ~** percussion instruments

percussio'nista *nmf* percussionist

per'dente *nmf* loser

'perdere [1] *vt* lose; (sprecare) waste; (non prendere) miss; (fig: vizio) ruin; **~ tempo** waste time; **lascia ~!** forget it!; **~ di vista** lose touch with
[2] *vi* lose; (recipiente) leak; **a ~** (vuoto) nonreturnable; **non avere niente da ~** have nothing to lose

'perdersi *vr* get lost; (reciproco) lose touch [with each other]

perdifi'ato: **a ~** *adv* (gridare) at the top of one's voice

perdigi'orno *nmf inv* idler

'perdita *nf* loss; (spreco) waste; (falla) leak; **a ~ d'occhio** as far as the eye can see; **chiudere in ~** (azienda) show a loss. **perdita di gas** gas leak. **perdita di sangue** loss of blood, bleeding. **perdita di tempo** waste of time

perdi'tempo *nm* waste of time

perdizi'one *nf* perdition

perdo'nare [1] *vt* forgive; (scusare) excuse; **mi perdoni se interrompo** sorry to interrupt, excuse me for interrupting; **per farsi ~** as an apology
[2] *vi* **~ a qualcuno** forgive somebody; **un male che non perdona** an incurable disease

per'dono *nm* forgiveness; Jur pardon; **chiedere ~** ask for forgiveness; (scusarsi) apologize

perdu'rare *vi* last; (perseverare) persist

perduta'mente *adv* hopelessly

per'duto ① pp di PERDERE
② adj lost; (rovinato) ruined

pe'renne adj everlasting; Bot perennial;
nevi perenni perpetual snow

perenne'mente adv perpetually

peren'torio adj peremptory

per'fetto ① adj perfect
② nm Gram perfect [tense]

perfezio'nare vt perfect; (migliorare)
improve

perfezio'narsi vr improve oneself;
(specializzarsi) specialize

perfezi'one nf perfection; alla ~ to
perfection

perfezio'nismo nm perfectionism

perfezio'nista nmf perfectionist

per'fidia nf wickedness; (atto) wicked act

'perfido adj treacherous; (malvagio)
perverse

per'fino adv even

perfo'rare vt pierce; punch ⟨schede⟩;
Mech drill

perfora'tore, -trice ① nmf punch-card
operator
② nm (apparecchio) punch. **perforatore
di schede** card punch

perforazi'one nf perforation; (di schede)
punching

per'formance nf inv Theat performance

perga'mena nf parchment

'pergola nf pergola

pergo'lato nm bower

periar'trite nf rheumatoid arthritis

perico'lante adj precarious; ⟨azienda⟩
shaky

pe'ricolo nm danger; (rischio) risk;
mettere in ~ endanger; essere fuori ~ be
out of danger. **pericolo pubblico**
danger to society. **pericolo di
valanghe** danger of avalanches

pericolosa'mente adv dangerously

pericolosità nf danger

perico'loso adj dangerous

peridu'rale nf epidural

perife'ria nf periphery; (di città) outskirts
pl; fig fringes pl

peri'ferica nf peripheral; ⟨strada⟩ ring
road. **periferica di input** Comput input
device

peri'ferico adj peripheral; ⟨quartiere⟩
outlying

pe'rifrasi nf inv circumlocution

perime'trale adj ⟨muro⟩ perimeter
attrib

pe'rimetro nm perimeter

peri'odico ① nm periodical
② adj periodical; ⟨vento, mal di testa,
numero⟩ recurring

pe'riodo nm period; Gram sentence.
periodo nero bad patch. **periodo di**

prova trial period. **periodo di
ripensamento** cooling-off period.
periodo di riposo breathing space.
periodo di transizione transitional
period, interim. **periodo di validità**
period of validity

peripe'zie nfpl misadventures

pe'rire vi perish

peri'scopio nm periscope

pe'rito, -a ① adj skilled
② nmf expert. **perito agrario**
agriculturalist. **perito di
assicurazione** Comm loss adjuster.
perito edile chartered surveyor. **perito
elettronico** electronics engineer

perito'nite nf peritonitis

pe'rizia nf skill; (valutazione) survey.
perizia medico-legale forensic tests

peri'zoma nm inv loincloth

'perla nf pearl. **perla coltivata**
cultured pearl

per'lina nf bead

perli'nato nm matchboard

perlo'meno adv at least

perlu'strare vt patrol

perlustrazi'one nf patrol; andare in ~
go on patrol

perma'loso adj touchy

perma'nente ① adj permanent
② nf perm; farsi [fare] la ~ have a perm

perma'nenza nf permanence; (soggiorno)
stay; in ~ permanently. **permanenza in
carica** tenure

perma'nere vi remain

perme'are vt permeate

perme'ato adj ~ di fig permeated with

per'messo ① pp di PERMETTERE
② nm permission; (autorizzazione) permit,
licence; Mil leave; [è] ~?, con ~ (posso
entrare?) may I come in?; (posso passare?)
excuse me. **permesso di lavoro** work
permit. **permesso di soggiorno**
residence permit

per'mettere vt allow, permit; potersi ~
qualcosa (finanziariamente) be able to afford
something

per'mettersi vr ~ di fare qualcosa
allow oneself to do something; come si
permette? how dare you?

permis'sivo adj permissive

permutazi'one nf exchange; Math
permutation

per'nacchia nf fam raspberry fam

per'nice nf partridge

pernici'oso adj pernicious

'perno nm pivot

pernot'tare vi stay overnight

'pero nm pear-tree

però conj but; (tuttavia) however

pe'rone nm Anat fibula

pero'rare *vt* plead

perpendico'lare *adj & nf* perpendicular

perpe'trare *vt* perpetrate

per'petua *nf* (di prete) priest's housekeeper

perpetu'are *vt* perpetuate

per'petuo *adj* perpetual

perplessità *nf inv* perplexity; (dubbio) doubt

per'plesso *adj* perplexed, puzzled

perqui'sire *vt* search

perquisizi'one *nf* search. **perquisizione domiciliare** search of the premises

persecu‖'tore, -trice *nmf* persecutor

persecuzi'one *nf* persecution

persegu'ire *vt* pursue

persegui'tare *vt* persecute

persegui'tato, -a *nmf* victim of persecution

perseve'rante *adj* persevering

perseve'ranza *nf* perseverance

perseve'rare *vi* persevere

'Persia *nf* Persia

persi'ana *nf* shutter. **persiana avvolgibile** roller shutter

persi'ano, -a *adj & nmf* Persian

'persico *adj* Persian

per'sino *adv* = PERFINO

persi'stente *adj* persistent; (dubbio) nagging

persi'stenza *nf* persistence

per'sistere *vi* persist; ~ **nel fare qualcosa** persist in doing something

'perso ① *pp di* PERDERE
② *adj* lost; **a tempo** ~ in one's spare time

per'sona *nf* person; (un tale) somebody; **di** ~, **in** ~ in person, personally; **per** ~ per person, a head; **per interposta** ~ through an intermediary; **curare la propria** ~ look after oneself, look after number one; **persone** *pl* people. **persona a carico** dependant. **persona di colore** black person. **persona giuridica** legal person. **persona di servizio** domestic

perso'naggio *nm* (persona di riguardo) personality; Theat ecc character

perso'nale ① *adj* personal
② *nm* staff; (aspetto) build. **personale di terra** ground crew

personalità *nf inv* personality

personaliz'zare *vt* customize (auto ecc); personalize (penna ecc)

personifi'care *vt* personify

personificazi'one *nf* personification

perspi'cace *adj* shrewd

perspi'cacia *nf* shrewdness

persua'dere *vt* convince; impress (critici); ~ **qualcuno a fare qualcosa** persuade somebody to do something

persuasi'one *nf* persuasion; **fare opera di** ~ **su qualcuno** try to persuade somebody

persuasività *nf* persuasiveness

persua'sivo *adj* persuasive

persu'aso *pp di* PERSUADERE

persua'sore *nm* persuader

per'tanto *conj* therefore

'pertica *nf* pole

perti'nace *adj* pertinacious

perti'nente *adj* relevant

per'tosse *nf* whooping cough

per'tugio *nm* opening

pertur'bare *vt* perturb

perturbazi'one *nf* disturbance. **perturbazione atmosferica** atmospheric disturbance

Perù *nm* Peru

peruvi'ano, -a *adj & nmf* Peruvian

per'vadere *vt* pervade

perva'sivo *adj* pervasive

per'vaso *pp di* PERVADERE

perven'ire *vi* reach; **far** ~ **qualcosa a qualcuno** send something to somebody

perversa'mente *adv* perversely

perversi'one *nf* perversion

perversità *nf inv* perversity

per'verso *adj* perverse

perver'tire *vt* pervert

perver'tirsi *vr* (gusti, costumi) become debased

perver'tito ① *adj* perverted
② *nm* pervert

pervi'cace *adj* obstinate

pervicace'mente *adv* obstinately

pervi'cacia *nf* obstinacy

per'vinca¹ *nm* (colore) blue with a touch of purple

per'vinca² *nf* Bot periwinkle

p.es. *abbr* (**per esempio**) e.g.

'pesa *nf* weighing; (bilancia) weighing machine; (per veicoli) weighbridge

pe'sante ① *adj* heavy; (stomaco) overfull; (accusa, ingiuria) serious; (noioso) boring; **andarci** ~ **con qualcuno** be heavy-handed with somebody
② *adv* (vestirsi) warmly

pesante'mente *adv* (cadere) heavily; (insultare) seriously

pesan'tezza *nf* heaviness

pesaper'sone *nm inv* scales

pe'sare ① *vt* weigh; ~ **le parole** weigh one's words
② *vi* weigh; (essere pesante) be heavy; ~ **su** fig lie heavy on

pe'sarsi *vr* weigh oneself

'pesca[1]*nf* (frutto) peach

'pesca[2]*nf* fishing; **andare a** ∼ go fishing.
pesca di beneficenza lucky dip.
pesca con la lenza angling. **pesca
subacquea** underwater fishing

pe'scare *vt* (andare a pesca di) fish for;
(prendere) catch; (fam: trovare) dig up, find;
guai se ti pesco! there will be trouble if I
catch you!

pesca'tore *nm* fisherman. **pescatore
di frodo** poacher. **pescatore di perle**
pearl diver

'pesce *nm* fish; **non sapere che pesci
pigliare** fig not know which way to turn;
prendere qualcuno a pesci in faccia fig
treat somebody like dirt; **sentirsi un** ∼
fuor d'acqua feel like a fish out of water.
pesce d'aprile! April Fool!. **pesce in
carpione** soused fish. **pesce al
cartoccio** fish baked in foil. **pesce
gatto** catfish. **pesce grosso** fig big fish.
pesce persico perch. **pesce piccolo**
fig small fry. **pesce rosso** goldfish.
pesce spada swordfish

pesce'cane *nm* shark

pesche'reccio *nm* fishing boat

pesche'ria *nf* fishmonger's [shop]

peschi'era *nf* fish-pond

'Pesci *nmpl* Astr Pisces

pescio'lino *nm* **pesciolino d'acqua
dolce** minnow

pesci'vendolo *nm* fishmonger

'pesco *nm* peach tree

pe'scoso *adj* teeming with fish

pe'seta *nf* peseta

pe'sista *nm* (in sollevamento pesi) weightlifter; (in lancio del peso) shot-putter

'peso *nm* weight; **essere di** ∼ **per
qualcuno** be a burden to somebody; **alzare
di** ∼ lift up in one go; **avere un** ∼ **sullo
stomaco** have a lead weight on one's
stomach; **di poco** ∼ (senza importanza) not
very important; **non dare** ∼ **a qualcosa**
not attach any importance to something.
peso massimo (nel pugilato) heavy
weight. **peso medio** (nel pugilato)
middleweight. **peso morto** dead weight.
peso netto net weight. **peso piuma**
(nel pugilato) featherweight **peso
specifico** specific gravity. **peso welter**
(nel pugilato) welterweight

pessi'mismo *nm* pessimism

pessi'mista [1] *nmf* pessimist
[2] *adj* pessimistic

pessimistica'mente *adv*
pessimistically

'pessimo *adj* very bad

pe'staggio *nm* beating-up

pe'stare *vt* tread on; (picchiare) beat;
crush ‹aglio, prezzemolo, uva›; ∼ **i piedi
[per terra]** stamp one's feet [on the
ground]; ∼ **un piede a qualcuno** tread on
somebody's foot

pe'stata *nf* bash; **dare una** ∼ **a un piede
a qualcuno** tread on somebody's foot

'peste *nf* plague; (persona) pest; **dire** ∼ **e
corna di qualcuno** tear somebody to bits.
peste bubbonica bubonic plague

pe'stello *nm* pestle

pesti'cida *nm* pesticide

pe'stifero *adj* (fastidioso) pestilential

pesti'lenza *nf* pestilence; (fetore) stench,
stink

pestilenzi'ale *adj* ‹odore, aria› noxious

'pesto [1] *adj* ground; **occhio pesto** black
eye
[2] *nm* basil and garlic sauce

'petalo *nm* petal

pe'tardo *nm* banger

petizi'one *nf* petition; **fare una** ∼ draw
up a petition

petro'dollaro *nm* petrodollar

petrol'chimico *adj* petrochemical

petroli'era *nf* [oil] tanker

petroli'ere *nm* oilman

petro'lifero *adj* oil-bearing

pe'trolio *nm* oil

pettego'lare *vi* gossip

pettego'lezzo *nm* piece of gossip;
pettegolezzi *pl* gossip *sg*; **far pettegolezzi**
gossip

pet'tegolo, -a [1] *adj* gossipy
[2] *nmf* gossip

petti'nare *vt* comb

petti'narsi *vr* comb one's hair

pettina'tura *nf* combing; (acconciatura)
hairstyle; ∼ **a caschetto** bob

'pettine *nm* comb

'petting *nm* petting

petti'nino *nm* (fermaglio) comb

petti'rosso *nm* robin [redbreast]

'petto *nm* chest; (seno) breast; **a doppio** ∼
double-breasted; **prendere qualcosa/
qualcuno di** ∼ face up to something/
somebody; **petti** *pl* **di pollo** chicken
breasts

petto'rale [1] *nm* Sport number; **pettorali**
pecs
[2] *adj* pectoral

petto'rina *nf* (di salopette) bib

petto'ruto *adj* ‹donna› full-breasted;
‹uomo› broad-chested

petu'lante *adj* impertinent

petu'lanza *nf* impertinence

pe'tunia *nf* petunia

'pezza *nf* cloth; (toppa) patch; (rotolo di
tessuto) roll; **trattare qualcuno come una** ∼
da piedi walk all over somebody. **pezza
d'appoggio** voucher. **pezza
giustificativa** voucher

pez'zato *adj* ‹cavallo, mucca› piebald

pez'zente *nmf* tramp; (avaro) miser

'pezzo *nm* piece; (parte) part; Mus piece; **un bel ∼ d'uomo** a fine figure of a man; **un ∼** (di tempo) some time; (di spazio) a long way; **al ∼** ‹costare› each; **essere a pezzi** (stanco) be shattered; **fare a pezzi** tear to shreds; **andare in mille pezzi** break into a thousand pieces; **cadere a pezzi** fall to pieces, fall to bits. **pezzo forte** centre-piece; **pezzi** *pl* **grossi** top brass. **pezzo grosso** bigwig, big shot. **pezzo di imbecille** stupid idiot. **pezzo di ricambio** spare [part]

pezzu'ola *nf* scrap of material

photo'fit® *nm inv* Photofit

pia'cente *adj* attractive

pia'cere ① *nm* pleasure; (favore) favour; **a ∼** as much as one likes; **per ∼!** please!; **∼ [di conoscerla]!** (nelle presentazioni) pleased to meet you!; **con ∼** with pleasure; **fare un ∼ a qualcuno** do somebody a favour ② *vi* **la Scozia mi piace** I like Scotland; **mi piacciono i dolci** I like sweets; **mi piacerebbe venire** I'd like to come; **faccio come mi pare e piace** I do as I please; **ti piace?** do you like it?; **lo spettacolo è piaciuto** the show was a success

pia'cevole *adj* pleasant

piacevol'mente *adv* agreeably

piaci'mento *nm* **a ∼** as much as you like

pia'dina *nf* unleavened focaccia bread

pi'aga *nf* sore; fig scourge; (fig: persona noiosa) pain; (fig: ricordo doloroso) wound

pia'gato *adj* covered with sores

piagni'steo *nm* whining

piagnuco'lare *vi* whimper

piagnuco'lio *nm* whimpering

piagnuco'loso *adj* maudlin

pi'alla *nf* plane

pial'lare *vt* plane

pialla'tura *nf* planing

pi'ana *nf* (pianura) plane

pianeggi'ante *adj* level

piane'rottolo *nm* landing

pia'neta *nm* planet

pi'angere ① *vi* cry; (disperatamente) weep; **mi piange il cuore** my heart bleeds; **mettersi a ∼ come una fontana** turn the waterworks on; **∼ sul latte versato** cry over split milk ② *vt* (lamentare) lament; (per un lutto) mourn; **∼ la morte di qualcuno** mourn somebody's death

pianifi'care *vt* plan

pianificazi'one *nf* planning. **pianificazione aziendale** corporate planning. **pianificazione familiare** family planning. **pianificazione territoriale** town-and-country planning

pia'nista *nmf* Mus pianist

pi'ano ① *adj* flat; (a livello) flush; (regolare) smooth; (facile) easy; **i 400 metri piani** the 400 metres flat race ② *adv* slowly; (con cautela) gently; (sottovoce) quietly; **andarci ∼** go carefully ③ *nm* plain; (di edificio) floor, storey; (livello) plane; (progetto) plan; Mus piano; **di primo ∼** first-rate; **primo piano** Phot close-up; **in primo ∼** in the foreground; **essere/mettersi in primo ∼** fig take/occupy centre-stage; **secondo piano** middle distance. **piano d'azione** action plan. **piano bar** piano bar. **piano d'emergenza** contingency plan. **piano di incentivi** incentive scheme. **piano di lavoro** work surface; (programma) work schedule. **piano di pensionamento** pension plan, pension scheme. **piano regolatore** town plan. **piano di sopra** upstairs. **piano di sotto** downstairs. **piano di studi** syllabus. **piano superiore** upper floor

piano'forte *nm* piano. **pianoforte a coda** grand [piano]. **pianoforte verticale** upright [piano]

pia'nola *nf* pianola

piano'terra *nm inv* ground floor, first floor Am

pi'anta *nf* plant; (del piede) sole; (disegno) plan; (di città) map; **di sana ∼** (totalmente) entirely; **in ∼ stabile** permanently. **pianta da appartamento** house-plant. **pianta stradale** road map

piantagi'one *nf* plantation

pianta'grane *nmf inv* fam **è un/una ∼** he's/she's bolshy

pian'tare *vt* plant; (conficcare) drive; pitch ‹tenda›; (fam: abbandonare) dump; **piantala!** fam stop it!; **piantato in** ‹spina, chiodo› embedded in; **∼ baracca e burattini** drop everything; (per sempre) chuck everything in

pian'tarsi *vr* plant oneself; (fam: lasciarsi) leave each other

pianta|'tore, -trice *nmf* planter

pianter'reno *nm* ground floor, first floor Am

pi'anto ① *pp di* PIANGERE ② *nm* crying; (disperato) weeping; (lacrime) tears *pl*

pianto'nare *vt* guard

pian'tone *nm* guard; **stare di ∼** stand guard; **mettere di ∼** put on guard. **piantone dello sterzo** Auto steering column

pia'nura *nf* plain. **pianura padana** Po valley

pi'astra *nf* plate; (lastra) slab; Culin griddle. **piastra elettronica** circuit board. **piastra madre** Comput motherboard. **piastra di registrazione** cassette deck

pia'strella *nf* tile

pia'strina *nf* Mil identity disc; Med platelet; Comput chip. **piastrina di riconoscimento** identity tag. **piastrina di silicio** silicon chip

piatta'forma *nf* platform. **piattaforma di lancio** launch pad. **piattaforma petrolifera** oil platform, offshore rig. **piattaforma rivendicativa** *o* **sindacale** union claims *pl*

piat'tino *nm* (di tazzina) saucer; (piatto piccolo) side plate

pi'atto ① *adj* flat; (monotono) dull ② *nm* plate; (da portata, vivanda) dish; (portata) course; (parte piatta) flat; (di giradischi) turntable; (di bilancia) pan; **piatti** *pl* Mus cymbals; **lavare i piatti** do the dishes, do the washing-up; **piatti** *pl* **da asporto** takeaway Br, carryout Am; **piatti** *pl* **caldi** hot dishes; **piatti** *pl* **di carne** meat dishes. **piatto fondo** soup plate. **piatto del giorno** dish of the day. **piatto piano** [ordinary] plate. **piatto di portata** serving dish, server. **piatto pronto** ready meal. **piatto unico** complete meal

pi'azza *nf* square; Comm market; **letto a una piazza** single bed; **letto a due piazze** double bed; **far ~ pulita** make a clean sweep; **mettere qualcosa in ~** fig make something public; **scendere in ~** fig take to the streets. **piazza d'armi** parade ground. **piazza del mercato** market square. **Piazza San Pietro** St Peter's Square

piazza'forte *nf* stronghold

piaz'zale *nm* large square

piazza'mento *nm* (in classifica) placing

piaz'zare *vt* place

piaz'zarsi *vr* Sport be placed; **~ secondo** come second, be placed second

piaz'zato *adj* ⟨cavallo⟩ placed; **ben ~** (robusto) well-built

piaz'zista ① *nm* salesman ② *nf* saleswoman

piaz'z[u]ola *nf* **piazz[u]ola di partenza** (nel golf) tee. **piazz[u]ola di sosta** pull-in

pic'cante *adj* hot; (pungente) sharp; (salace) spicy

pic'carsi *vr* (risentirsi) take offence; **~ di** (vantarsi di) claim to

pic'cata *nf* veal in sour lemon sauce

'picche *nfpl* (in carte) spades

picchet'taggio *nm* picketing

picchet'tare *vt* stake; ⟨scioperanti⟩ picket

pic'chetto *nm* picket

picchi'are ① *vt* hit; **~ la testa (contro qualcosa)** bang *or* hit one's head (against something) ② *vi* (bussare) knock; Aeron nosedive; **~ in testa** (motore) knock

picchi'arsi *vr* **~ il petto** beat one's breast

picchi'ata *nf* beating; Aeron nosedive; **scendere in ~** nosedive

picchi'ato *adj* (matto) touched

picchia'tore *nm* goon

picchiet'tare *vt* tap; (punteggiare) spot

picchiet'tato *adj* spotted

picchiet'tio *nm* tapping

'picchio *nm* woodpecker

pic'cino ① *adj* tiny; (gretto) mean; (di poca importanza) petty ② *nm* little one, child

piccion'cini *nmpl* fam lovebirds; **fare i ~** get all lovey-dovey

picci'one *nm* pigeon; **prendere due piccioni con una fava** kill two birds with one stone. **piccione viaggatore** carrier pigeon

'picco *nm* peak; **a ~** vertically; **colare a ~** sink

picco'lezza *nf* (di persona, ambiente) smallness; (grettezza) meanness; (inezia) trifle

'piccolo, -a ① *adj* small, little; ⟨vacanza, pausa⟩ little, short; (di statura) short; (gretto) petty ② *nmf* child, little one; **da ~** as a child; **in ~** in miniature; **nel mio ~** in my own small way

pic'cone *nm* pickaxe. **piccone da ghiaccio** ice pick

pic'cozza *nf* ice axe

pic'nic *nm inv* picnic

pi'docchio *nm* louse

pidocchi'oso ① *adj* flea-bitten; (fam: avaro) stingy ② *nm* fam miser

piè *nm inv* **a ~ di pagina** at the foot of the page; **saltare a ~ pari** skip; **ad ogni ~ sospinto** all the time, endlessly

pi'ede *nm* foot; (di armadio, letto) leg; **a piedi** on foot; **andare a piedi** walk; **a piedi nudi** barefoot; **avere i piedi piatti** have flat feet, be flat-footed; **a ~ libero** free; **in piedi** standing; **alzarsi in piedi** stand up; **in punta di piedi** on tiptoe; **ai piedi di** ⟨montagna⟩ at the foot of; **avere qualcuno ai propri piedi** have somebody at one's feet; **essere sul ~ di guerra** be ready for action; (nazione) be on war footing; **prendere ~** fig gain ground; ⟨moda⟩ catch on; **partire col ~ sbagliato** get off on the wrong foot; **mettere in piedi** (allestire) set up; **togliti dai piedi!** get out of the way!. **piede di insalata** head of lettuce. **piede di porco** (strumento) jemmy

pie'dino *nm* fare ∼ a qualcuno fam play footsie with somebody

piedi'stallo *nm* pedestal

pi'ega *nf* (piegatura) fold; (di gonna) pleat; (di pantaloni) crease; (grinza) wrinkle; (andamento) turn; **a pieghe** with pleats, pleated; **non fare una** ∼ (ragionamento) be flawless; (persona) not bat an eyelid; **prendere una brutta** ∼ get into bad ways

pie'gare ① *vt* fold; (flettere) bend ② *vi* bend

pie'garsi *vr* bend; ∼ **a** *fig* yield to

piega'tura *nf* folding; (piega) fold

pieghet'tare *vt* pleat

pieghet'tato *adj* pleated

pie'ghevole ① *adj* pliable; (tavolo) folding ② *nm* leaflet

Pie'monte *nm* Piedmont

piemon'tese *adj & nmf* Piedmontese

pi'ena *nf* (di fiume) flood; (folla) crowd

pi'eno ① *adj* full; (massiccio) solid; **in piena estate** in the middle of summer; **a pieni voti** (diplomarsi) ≈ with A-grades, with first class honours ② *nm* (colmo) height; (carico) full load; **in** ∼ (completamente) fully; **fare il** ∼ (di benzina) fill up; **nel** ∼ **delle forze** in top physical form

pie'none *nm* c'era il ∼ the place was packed

'piercing *nm inv* body piercing. **piercing all'ombelico** navel ring. **piercing nella lingua** tongue stud

pietà *nf* pity; (misericordia) mercy; **senza** ∼ (persona) pitiless; (spietatamente) pitilessly; **avere** ∼ **di qualcuno** take pity on somebody; **far** ∼ (far pena) be pitiful; (fam: essere orrendo) be useless

pie'tanza *nf* dish

pie'toso *adj* pitiful, merciful; (fam: pessimo) terrible

pi'etra *nf* stone. **pietra dura** semiprecious stone. **pietra preziosa** precious stone. **pietra dello scandalo** cause of the scandal

pie'traia *nf* scree

pie'trame *nm* stones *pl*

pietrifi'care *vt* petrify

pie'trina *nf* (di accendino) flint

pie'troso *adj* stony

'piffero *nm* fife

pigi'ama *nm* pyjamas *pl*, pajamas Am

'pigia 'pigia *nm inv* crowd, crush

pigi'are *vt* press

pigia'trice *nf* winepress

pigi'one *nf* rent; **dare a** ∼ let, rent out; **prendere a** ∼ rent

pigli'are *vt* (fam: afferrare) catch

'piglio *nm* air

pig'mento *nm* pigment

pig'meo, -a *adj & nmf* pygmy

'pigna *nf* cone. **pigna di abete** fir cone

pi'gnolo *adj* pedantic

pignora'mento *nm* Jur distraint

pigno'rare *vt* Jur distrain upon

pigo'lare *vi* chirp

pigo'lio *nm* chirping

pigra'mente *adv* lazily

pi'grizia *nf* laziness

'pigro *adj* lazy; (d'intelletto) slow

PIL *abbr* (**prodotto interno lordo**) GDP

'pila *nf* pile; Electr battery; (fam: lampadina tascabile) torch; (vasca) basin; **a pile** battery operated, battery powered

pi'lastro *nm* pillar

'pillola *nf* pill; **prendere la** ∼ be on the pill. **pillola del giorno dopo** morning-after pill

pi'lone *nm* pylon; (di ponte) pier

pi'lota ① *nmf* pilot; Auto driver. **pilota automatico** automatic pilot. **pilota di caccia** fighter pilot ② *adj inv* **progetto pilota** pilot project

pilo'taggio *nm* flying; **cabina di pilotaggio** flight deck

pilo'tare *vt* pilot; drive ⟨auto⟩

pinaco'teca *nf* art gallery

'Pinco Pal'lino *nm* so-and-so

pi'neta *nf* pine-wood

ping-'pong *nm* table tennis, ping-pong fam

'pingue *adj* fat

pingu'edine *nf* fatness

pingu'ino *nm* penguin; (gelato) choc ice on a stick

'pinna *nf* fin; (per nuotare) flipper

pin'nacolo *nm* pinnacle

'pino *nm* pine[-tree]. **pino marittimo** cluster pine, maritime pine

pi'nolo *nm* pine kernel

'pinta *nf* pint

pin-'up *nf inv* pin-up [girl]

'pinza *nf* pliers *pl*; Med forceps *pl*; **prendere qualcosa con le pinze** *fig* treat something cautiously

pin'zare *vt* (con pinzatrice) staple

pinza'trice *nf* stapler

pin'zette *nfpl* tweezers

pinzi'monio *nm* sauce for crudités

'pio *adj* pious; (benefico) charitable

piogge'rella *nf* drizzle

pi'oggia *nf* rain; (fig: di pietre, insulti) hail, shower; **sotto la** ∼ in the rain. **pioggia acida** acid rain. **pioggia radioattiva** radioactive fallout

pi'olo *nm* (di scala) rung

piom'bare ① *vi* fall heavily; ~ su fall upon; ~ all'improvviso nella stanza suddenly burst into the room ② *vt* ~ qualcuno nella disperazione plunge somebody into despair

piom'bino *nm* (sigillo) [lead] seal; (da pesca) sinker; (in tende) weight

pi'ombo *nm* lead; (sigillo) [lead] seal; a ~ plumb; **senza** ~ ‹*benzina*› unleaded; **avere un sonno di** ~ be a very heavy sleeper; **andare con i piedi di** ~ tread carefully; **anni di** ~ years when terrorism was at its height

pioni'ere, -a *nmf* pioneer

pi'oppo *nm* poplar

pior'rea *nf* pyorrhoea

pio'vano *adj* **acqua piovana** rainwater

pi'overe *vi* rain; ~ it's raining; ~ addosso a qualcuno ‹*guai, debiti*› rain down on somebody; [**su questo**] **non ci piove** fam that's for sure

pioviggi'nare *vi* drizzle

pio'voso *adj* rainy

pi'ovra *nf* octopus

pio'vuto *adj* ~ **dal cielo** fallen into one's lap

pipì *nf* **fare** [**la**] ~ pee, piddle; **andare a fare** [**la**] ~ go for a pee

'pipa *nf* pipe

pipe'rito *adj* **menta piperita** peppermint

pipi'strello *nm* bat

piqué *nm* piqué

'pira *nf* pyre

pi'ramide *nf* pyramid

pi'ranha *nm inv* piranha

pi'rata ① *nm* pirate. **pirata dell'aria** skyjacker. **pirata della strada** hit-and-run driver; (prepotente) road-hog ② *adj inv* pirate

pirate'ria *nf* piracy. **pirateria informatica** software piracy

pi'rite *nf* pyrite

piro'etta *nf* pirouette

pi'rofila *nf* (tegame) oven-proof dish

pi'rofilo *adj* heat-resistant

pi'romane *nmf* pyromaniac

piroma'nia *nf* pyromania

pi'roscafo *nm* steamer. **piroscafo di linea** liner

'piscia *nf* vulg piss

pisci'are *vi* vulg piss

pisci'ata *nf* vulg piss

pi'scina *nf* [swimming] pool. **piscina coperta** indoor [swimming] pool. **piscina gonfiabile** [inflatable] paddling pool. **piscina olimpionica** Olympic [swimming] pool. **piscina per il parto** birthing pool. **piscina scoperta** outdoor [swimming] pool, lido

pi'sello *nm* pea; (fam: pene) willie; **piselli** *pl* odorosi sweetpeas

piso'lino *nm* nap; **fare un** ~ have a nap

'pista *nf* track; Aeron runway, tarmac; (orma) footprint; (sci) slope, piste. **pista d'atterraggio** runway. **pista da ballo** dance floor. **pista ciclabile** cycle track. **pista da fondo** cross-country ski track. **pista di pattinaggio** ice rink. **pista per principianti** nursery slope. **pista di sci** ski slope, ski run, piste. **pista per slitte** toboggan run

pi'stacchio *nm* pistachio

pi'stola *nf* gun, pistol; (per spruzzare) spray-gun. **pistola a capsule** cap gun. **pistola a spruzzo** paint spray. **pistola a tamburo** revolver

pisto'lero *nm* gunslinger

pi'stone *nm* piston

'pitbull *nm inv* pitbull (terrier)

pi'tocco *nm* miser

pi'tone *nm* python

pitto'gramma *nm* pictogram

pit'tore, -trice *nmf* painter

pitto'resco *adj* picturesque

pit'torico *adj* pictorial

pit'tura *nf* painting; **pitture** *pl* **di guerra** warpaint. **pittura a guazzo** poster paint. **pittura rupestre** cave painting

pittu'rare *vt* paint

pitui'tario *adj* pituitary

più ① *adv* more; (superlativo) most; Math plus; ~ **importante** more important; **il** ~ **importante** the most important; ~ **caro/grande** dearer/bigger; **il** ~ **caro/grande** the dearest/biggest; **di** ~ more; **una coperta in** ~ an extra blanket; **non ho** ~ **soldi** I don't have any more money; **non vive** ~ **a Milano** he no longer lives in Milan; ~ **o meno** more or less; **il** ~ **lentamente possible** as slow as possible; **al** ~ **presto** as soon as possible; **per di** ~ what's more; **mai** ~! never again!; ~ **di** more than; **sempre** ~ more and more ② *adj* more; (superlativo) most; ~ **tempo** more time; **la classe con** ~ **alunni** the class with most pupils; ~ **volte** several times ③ *nm* most; Math plus sign; **il** ~ **è fatto** the worst is over; **parlare del** ~ **e del meno** make small talk; **i** ~ the majority

piuccheper'fetto *nm* pluperfect

pi'uma *nf* feather

piu'maggio *nm* plumage

piu'mato *adj* plumed

piu'mino *nm* (di cigni) down; (copriletto) eiderdown; (per cipria) powder-puff; (per spolverare) feather duster; (giacca) down jacket

piu'mone® *nm* duvet, continental quilt

piut'tosto *adv* rather; (invece) instead

'piva *nf* con le pive nel sacco emptyhanded

pi'vello *nm* fam greenhorn

'pivot *nm inv* (in pallacanestro) centre

'pizza *nf* pizza; Cinema reel; (fam: noia) bore. **pizza margherita** tomato and mozzarella pizza. **pizza marinara** pizza with tomato, oregano, garlic and anchovies. **pizza napoletana** pizza with tomato, mozzarella and anchovies. **pizza quattro stagioni** pizza with tomato, mozzarella, ham, mushrooms and artichokes

pizzai'ola: alla ∼ *adj* with tomatoes, garlic, and oregano

pizze'ria *nf* pizza restaurant, pizzeria

piz'zetta *nf* small pizza

piz'zetto *nm* (barba) goatee

pizzi'care ① *vt* pinch; (pungere) sting; (di sapore) taste sharp; (fam: sorprendere) catch; Mus pluck
② *vi* scratch; ⟨cibo⟩ be spicy

'pizzico, pizzi'cotto *nm* pinch

'pizzo *nm* lace; (di montagna) peak

pla'care *vt* placate; assuage ⟨fame, dolore⟩

pla'carsi *vr* calm down

'placca *nf* plate; (commemorativa, dentale) plaque; Med patch. **placca batterica** plaque

plac'care *vt* plate

plac'cato *adj* **placcato d'argento** silver-plated. **placcato d'oro** gold-plated

placca'tura *nf* plating

pla'cebo *nm inv* placebo; **effetto placebo** placebo effect

pla'centa *nf* placenta, afterbirth

'placido *adj* placid

pla'fond *nm inv* Comm ceiling

plafoni'era *nf* ceiling light

plagi'are *vt* plagiarize; pressure ⟨persona⟩

'plagio *nm* plagiarism

plaid *nm inv* tartan rug

pla'nare *vi* glide

'plancia *nf* Naut bridge; (passerella) gangplank

'plancton *nm* plankton

plane'tario ① *adj* planetary
② *nm* planetarium

pla'smare *vt* mould

'plastica *nf* (materia) plastic; Med plastic surgery; (arte) plastic art; **sacchetto di plastica** plastic bag

'plastico ① *adj* plastic; (rappresentazione) three-dimensional
② *nm* plastic model

'platano *nm* plane tree

pla'tea *nf* stalls *pl*; (pubblico) audience

'platino *nm* platinum

pla'tonico *adj* platonic

plau'sibile *adj* plausible; **poco** ∼ implausible

plausibilità *nf* plausibility

'plauso *nm* (consenso) approval

play'back *nm* **cantare in** ∼ mime

play'boy *nm inv* playboy

play'maker *nm inv* Sport playmaker

p.le *abbr* (**piazzale**) Sq.

ple'baglia *nf* pej mob

'plebe *nf* common people

ple'beo, -a *adj & nmf* plebeian

plebi'scito *nm* plebiscite

ple'nario *adj* plenary

pleni'lunio *nm* full moon

'plettro *nm* plectrum

pleu'rite *nf* pleurisy

'plico *nm* packet; **in** ∼ **a parte** under separate cover

plissé *adj inv* plissé; (gonna) accordeon pleated

plop *nm inv* plop; **fare** ∼ plop

plo'tone *nm* platoon; (di ciclisti) group. **plotone d'esecuzione** firing squad

'plotter *nm inv* Comput plotter. **plotter da tavolo** flatbed plotter

'plumbeo *adj* leaden

plum-'cake *nm inv* fruit cake

plu'rale *adj & nm* plural; **al** ∼ in the plural

pluralità *nf* (maggioranza) majority

pluridiscipli'nare *adj* multidisciplinary

plurien'nale *adj* ∼ **esperienza** many years' experience

plurigemel'lare *adj* ⟨parto⟩ multiple

pluripar'titico *adj* Pol multi-party

Plu'tone *nm* Pluto

plu'tonio *nm* plutonium

pluvi'ale *adj* rain *attrib*

pluvi'ometro *nm* rain gauge

pneu'matico ① *adj* pneumatic
② *nm* tyre. **pneumatico radiale** radial [tyre]

pneu'monia *nf* pneumonia

PNL *abbr* (**prodotto nazionale lordo**) GNP

Po *nm* Po

po' ▶ POCO

po'chette *nf inv* clutch bag

po'chino *nm* **un** ∼ a little bit

'poco ① *adj* little; ⟨tempo⟩ short; (con nomi plurali) few
② *pron* little; (poco tempo) a short time; (plurale) few
③ *nm* little; **un po'** a little [bit]; **un po' di** a little, some; (con nomi plurali) a few; **a** ∼ **a** ∼ little by little; **fra** ∼ soon; **per** ∼ (a poco

prezzo) cheap; (quasi) nearly; ~ **fa** a little while ago; **sono arrivato da** ~ I have just arrived; **un bel po'** quite a lot; **un bel po' di più/meno** quite a lot more/less; **un** ~ **di buono** a shady character **④** *adv* (con verbi) not much; (con avverbi, aggettivi) not very; **parla** ~ he doesn't speak much; **lo conosco** ~ I don't know him very well; ~ **spesso** not very often

po'dere *nm* farm

pode'roso *adj* powerful

'**podio** *nm* dais; Mus podium

po'dismo *nm* walking

po'dista *nmf* walker

po'ema *nm* poem. **poema epico** epic [poem]. **poema sinfonico** symphonic poem

poe'sia *nf* poetry; (componimento) poem

po'eta *nm* poet

poe'tessa *nf* poetess

po'etico *adj* poetic

poggiapi'edi *nm inv* footrest

poggi'are **①** *vt* lean; (posare) place **②** *vi* ~ **su** be based on

poggia'testa *nm inv* head-rest

'**poggio** *nm* hillock

poggi'olo *nm* balcony

'**poi** **①** *adv* (dopo) then; (più tardi) later [on]; (finalmente) finally; **d'ora in** ~ from now on; **questa** ~! well! **②** *nm* **pensare al** ~ think of the future

poiché *conj* since

pois *nm inv* **a** ~ polka-dot

'**poker** *nm* poker

po'lacco, -a **①** *adj* Polish **②** *nmf* Pole **③** *nm* (lingua) Polish

po'lare *adj* polar

polarità *nf inv* polarity

polariz'zare *vt* polarize

pola'roid® *nf inv* instant camera

'**polca** *nf* polka

po'lemica *nf* controversy

polemica'mente *adv* controversially

polemiciz'zare *vi* engage in controversy

po'lemico *adj* controversial

po'lenta *nf* cornmeal porridge

poli'clinico *nm* general hospital

policro'mia *nf* polychromy

po'licromo *adj* polychrome

poli'estere *nm* polyester

polieti'lene *nm* polyethylene

poliga'mia *nf* polygamy

poli'gamico *adj* polygamous

po'ligamo *adj* polygamous

poli'glotta *nmf* polyglot

po'ligono *nm* polygon; (di tiro) rifle range

po'limero *nm* polymer

Poli'nesia *nf* Polynesia

polinesi'ano *adj & nmf* Polynesian

'**polio[mie'lite]** *nf* polio[myelitis]

'**polipo** *nm* polyp

polisti'rolo *nm* polystyrene

poli'tecnico *nm* polytechnic

po'litica *nf* politics *sg*; (linea di condotta) policy; **fare** ~ be in politics; **darsi alla** ~ go into politics. **politica energetica** energy policy. **politica estera** foreign policy. **politica monetaria** monetary policy

politica'mente *adv* politically; ~ **corretto** politically correct, pc

politi'chese *nm* political jargon

politiciz'zare *vt* politicize

po'litico, -a **①** *adj* political **②** *nmf* politician

poliva'lente *adj* all-purpose

poli'zia *nf* police, police force. **polizia giudiziaria** Criminal Investigation Department, CID. **polizia scientifica** forensics. **polizia stradale** traffic police

polizi'esco *adj* police *attrib*; ‹romanzo, film› detective *attrib*

polizi'otto **①** *nm* policeman. **poliziotto in borghese** plain clothes policeman. **poliziotto privato** private detective **②** *adj* police *attrib*

'**polizza** *nf* policy. **polizza di assicurazione** insurance policy

pol'laio *nm* chicken run; (fam: luogo chiassoso) mad house

pol'lame *nm* poultry

polla'strella *nf* spring chicken; fig fam bird

polla'strello *nm* spring chicken

pol'lastro *nm* cockerel

polle'ria *nf* poultry butcher, poulterer

'**pollice** *nm* thumb, (unità di misura) inch

'**polline** *nm* pollen; **allergia al polline** hay fever

polli'vendolo, -a *nmf* poulterer

'**pollo** *nm* chicken; (fam: semplicione) simpleton; **far ridere i polli** be ridiculous. **pollo allevato a terra** free-range chicken. **pollo arrosto** roast chicken. **pollo di batteria** battery chicken. **pollo alla cacciatora** chicken chasseur

polmo'nare *adj* pulmonary

pol'mone *nm* lung. **polmone d'acciaio** iron lung

polmo'nite *nf* pneumonia

'**polo** *nm* pole; Sport polo; (maglietta) polo top; Pol party; (conservatori) Italian Conservatives. **polo magnetico** magnetic pole. **polo nord** North Pole. **polo sud** South Pole

Po'lonia *nf* Poland

'polpa *nf* pulp

pol'paccio *nm* calf

polpa'strello *nm* fingertip

pol'petta *nf* meatball

polpet'tone *nm* meatloaf. **polpettone sentimentale** fam hokum

'polpo *nm* octopus

pol'poso *adj* fleshy

pol'sino *nm* cuff

'polso *nm* pulse; Anat wrist; fig authority; **avere** ∼ be strict; **essere privo di** ∼ be soft

pol'tiglia *nf* mush

pol'trire *vi* lie around

pol'trona *nf* armchair; Theat seat in the stalls

pol'trone *adj* lazy

'polvere *nf* dust; (sostanza polverizzata) powder; **in** ∼ powdered; **sapone in polvere** soap powder. **polvere da sparo** gun powder

polveri'era *nf* gunpowder magazine; fig tinderbox

polve'rina *nf* (medicina) powder

polveriz'zare *vt* pulverize; (nebulizzare) atomize; smash, shatter ‹record›; ∼ **qualcuno** pulverize somebody

polve'rone *nm* cloud of dust

polve'roso *adj* dusty

po'mata *nf* ointment, cream. **pomata cicatrizzante** healing cream for cuts

pomel'lato *adj* dappled

po'mello *nm* knob; (guancia) cheek

pomeridi'ano *adj* afternoon *attrib*; **alle tre pomeridiane** at three in the afternoon, at three p.m.

pome'riggio *nm* afternoon; **buon** ∼! have a good afternoon!; **oggi** ∼ this afternoon; **questo** ∼ this afternoon

'pomice *nf* pumice

pomici'are *vi* fam snog, neck

pomici'ata *nf* fam snogging, necking

'pomo *nm* (oggetto) knob. **pomo d'Adamo** Adam's apple

pomo'doro *nm* tomato

'pompa *nf* pump; (sfarzo) pomp. **pompa della benzina** petrol pump, gas pump Am; **pompe** *pl* **funebri** (funzione) funeral

pom'pare *vt* pump; (gonfiare d'aria) pump up; (fig: esagerare) exaggerate; ∼ **fuori** pump out

pompei'ano, -a *adj & nmf* Pompeian

pom'pelmo *nm* grapefruit

pompi'ere *nm* fireman; **i pompieri** the fire brigade

pom'pon *nm inv* pompom

pom'poso *adj* pompous

'poncho *nm inv* poncho

ponde'rare *vt* ponder

ponde'roso *adj* ponderous

po'nente *nm* west

'ponte *nm* bridge; Naut deck; (impalcatura) scaffolding; **fare il** ∼ fig make a long weekend of it. **legge ponte** interim *or* bridging law; **governo ponte** interim government. **ponte aereo** airlift. **ponte auto** car deck. **ponte di coperta** main deck. **ponte levatoio** drawbridge. **ponte radio** radio link. **ponte dei Sospiri** Bridge of Sighs. **ponte di volo** flight deck

pon'tefice *nm* pontiff

pontifi'care *vi* pontificate

pontifi'cato *nm* pontificate

ponti'ficio *adj* papal

pon'tile *nm* jetty

'pony *nm inv* pony. **pony express** express delivery service

pool *nm inv* Comm consortium; (di giornalisti) team; (di esperti) pool, team. ∼ **genico** gene pool

pop'corn *nm* popcorn

'popelin *nm* poplin

popò [1] *nf* fam pooh
[2] *nm inv* fam bottie, bum

popo'lano *adj* of the [common] people

popo'lare [1] *adj* popular; (comune) common
[2] *vt* populate; **essere popolato da** (pieno di) be full by

popolarità *nf* popularity

popo'larsi *vr* get crowded

popolazi'one *nf* population

'popolo *nm* people

popo'loso *adj* populous

'poppa *nf* Naut stern; (mammella) breast; **a** ∼ astern

pop'pare *vt* suck

pop'pata *nf* (pasto) feed

poppa'toio *nm* [feeding-]bottle

popu'lista *nmf* populist

por'caio *nm* anche fig pigsty; **fare un** ∼ fam make a mess

por'cata *nf* load of rubbish; **porcate** *pl.* (fam: cibo) junk food; **fare una** ∼ **a qualcuno** play a dirty trick on somebody

porcel'lana *nf* porcelain, china. **porcellana fine** bone china

porcel'lino *nm* piglet. **porcellino d'India** guinea-pig

porche'ria *nf* dirt; (fig: cosa orrenda) piece of filth; (fam: robaccia) rubbish

por'chetta *nf* roast sucking pig

por'cile *nm* pigsty

por'cino [1] *adj* pig *attrib*
[2] *nm* (fungo) cep (edible mushroom)

'porco *nm* pig; (carne) pork

porco'spino *nm* porcupine

'porfido *nm* porphyry

'porgere *vt* give; (offrire) offer; ~ **orecchio** lend an ear; **porgo distinti saluti** (in lettera) I remain, yours sincerely

'porno *adj inv* porn

pornogra'fia *nf* pornography

porno'grafico *adj* pornographic

'poro *nm* pore

po'roso *adj* porous

'porpora *nf* purple

'porre *vt* put; (collocare) place; (supporre) suppose; ask ⟨domanda⟩; present ⟨candidatura⟩; ~ **una domanda a qualcuno** ask somebody a question; **poniamo [il caso] che...** let us suppose that...; ~ **fine** o **termine a** put an end to

'porro *nm* Bot leek; (verruca) wart

'porsi *vr* put oneself; ~ **a sedere** sit down; ~ **in cammino** set out

'porta *nf* door; Sport goal; (di città) gate; Comput port; ~ **a** ~ door-to-door; **mettere alla** ~ show somebody the door; **a porte chiuse** ⟨riunione, processo⟩ behind closed doors, in camera; **essere alle porte** (vicino) be on the doorstep. **porta a due battenti** double door[s]. **porta d'ingresso** front door. **porta parallela** Comput parallel port. **porta seriale** Comput serial port. **porta di servizio** tradesman's entrance. **porta di sicurezza** emergency exit. **porta per la stampante** Comput printer port. **porta a vento** swing-door

portaba'gagli *nm inv* (facchino) porter; (su treno ecc) luggage-rack; Auto boot, trunk Am; (sul tetto di un'auto) roof-rack

portabandi'era *nmf inv* standard-bearer

portabici'clette *nm inv* cycle rack

portabot'tiglie *nm inv* bottle rack, wine rack

porta'burro *nm inv* butter dish

porta'cenere *nm inv* ashtray

portachi'avi *nm inv* keyring

porta'cipria *nm inv* compact

portacon'tainer *nm inv* container truck

portadocu'menti *nm inv* document wallet

porta'erei *nf inv* aircraft carrier

portafi'nestra *nf* French window

porta'foglio *nm* wallet; (per documenti) portfolio; (ministero) ministry; **a** ~ ⟨gonna⟩ wrap-over

portafor'tuna ① *nm inv* lucky charm ② *adj inv* lucky

portagi'oie *nm inv* jewellery box

por'tale *nm* door; Comput portal

portama'tite *nm inv* pencil case

porta'mento *nm* deportment; (condotta) behaviour

porta'mina *nm inv* propelling pencil

portamo'nete *nm inv* purse

por'tante *adj* bearing *attrib*

portan'tina *nf* sedan-chair

portaom'brelli *nm inv* umbrella stand

porta'pacchi *nm inv* roof rack; (su bicicletta) luggage rack

porta'penne *nm inv* pencil case

por'tare *vt* (verso chi parla) bring; (lontano da chi parla) take; (sorreggere, Math) carry; (condurre) lead; (indossare) wear; (avere) bear; ~ **a spasso il cane** take the dog for a walk; ~ **a termine** bring to a close; ~ **avanti** carry on; ~ **bene/male** bring good/bad luck; ~ **bene/male gli anni** look young/old for one's age; ~ **fortuna** be lucky; ~ **rancore** bear a grudge; ~ **via** take away

portari'viste *nm inv* magazine rack

por'tarsi *vr* (trasferirsi) move; (comportarsi) behave

porta'sci *nm inv* ski rack

portasciuga'mano *nm* towel rail

portasiga'rette *nm inv* cigarette-case

porta'spilli *nm inv* pin-cushion

por'tata *nf* (di pranzo) course; Auto carrying capacity; (di arma) range; (fig: abilità) capability; **a** ~ **di mano** within reach; **alla** ~ **di tutti** accessible to all; (finanziariamente) within everybody's reach; **di grande** ~ (scoperta) with far-reaching consequences

por'tatile ① *adj* portable ② *nm* Comput laptop

por'tato *adj* ⟨indumento⟩ worn; (dotato) gifted; **essere** ~ **per qualcosa** have a gift for something; **essere** ~ **a** (tendere a) be inclined to

porta|'tore, -trice *nmf* bearer; **al** ~ to the bearer. **portatore di handicap** disabled person

portatovagli'olo *nm* napkin ring

portau'ovo *nm inv* egg-cup

porta'voce *nmf inv* spokesperson

por'tello *nm* hatch. **portello di sicurezza** escape hatch

por'tento *nm* marvel; (persona dotata) prodigy

porten'toso *adj* wonderful

port'folio *nm inv* (di fotografie ecc) portfolio

porti'cato *nm* portico

'portico *nm* portico

porti'era *nf* (di auto) door; (tendaggio) door curtain

porti'ere *nm* porter, doorman; Sport goalkeeper. **portiere di notte** night porter

porti'naio, **-a** *nmf* caretaker, concierge

portine'ria *nf* concierge's room; (di ospedale) porter's lodge

'**porto** [1] *pp di* PORGERE
[2] *nm* harbour; (complesso) port; (vino) port [wine]; (spesa di trasporto) carriage; **andare in ∼** succeed. **porto d'armi** gun licence. **porto container** container port. **porto fluviale** river port. **porto franco** free port. **porto marittimo** seaport

Porto'gallo *nm* Portugal

porto'ghese *adj & nmf* Portuguese

por'tone *nm* main door

portori'cano, **-a** *adj & nmf* Puerto Rican

Porto'rico *nm* Puerto Rico

portu'ale *nm* dock worker, docker

porzi'one *nf* portion

'**posa** *nf* laying; (riposo) rest; Phot exposure; (atteggiamento) pose; **mettersi in ∼** pose; **senza ∼** without rest

po'sare [1] *vt* put; (giù) put [down]
[2] *vi* (poggiare) rest; (per un ritratto) pose

po'sarsi *vr* alight; (sostare) rest; Aeron land

po'sata *nf* piece of cutlery; **posate** *pl* cutlery *sg*, flatware *sg* Am

po'sato *adj* sedate

po'scritto *nm* postscript

posi'tivo *adj* positive

posizio'nare *vt* position

posizi'one *nf* position; **farsi una ∼** get ahead; **prendere ∼** *fig* take a stand

posolo'gia *nf* dosage

po'sporre *vt* place after; (posticipare) postpone

po'sposto *pp di* POSPORRE

posse'dere *vt* possess, own

possedi'mento *nm* possession

posses'sivo *adj* possessive

pos'sesso *nm* possession, ownership; (bene) possession; **entrare in ∼ di** come into possession of; **essere in ∼ di** be in possession of; **prendere ∼ di** take possession of

posses'sore *nm* owner

pos'sibile [1] *adj* possible; **il più presto ∼** as soon as possible
[2] *nm* **fare [tutto] il ∼** do one's best

possibilità [1] *nf inv* possibility; (occasione) chance; **avere la ∼ di fare qualcosa** have the chance *or* opportunity to do something
[2] *nfpl* (mezzi) means

possi'dente *nmf* land-owner

'**posso** ▸ POTERE

'**posta** *nf* post, mail; (ufficio postale) post office; (al gioco) stake; **spese di ∼** postage; **per ∼** by post, by mail; **la ∼ in gioco è...** *fig* what's at stake is...; **a bella ∼** on

purpose; **Poste e Telecomunicazioni** [Italian] Post Office. **posta aerea** airmail. **posta centrale** main post office, central post office. **posta del cuore** agony column. **posta elettronica** electronic mail, e-mail; **spedire per ∼ elettronica** e-mail. **posta elettronica vocale** voicemail. **posta prioritaria** ≈ first-class mail

posta'giro *nm* postal giro

po'stale *adj* postal

postazi'one *nf* position; Mil emplacement

post'bellico *adj* postwar

postda'tare *vt* postdate ⟨assegno⟩

posteggi'are *vt/i* park

posteggia|'tore, **-trice** *nmf* parking attendant

po'steggio *nm* car-park, parking lot Am; (di taxi) taxi-rank

'**posteri** *nmpl* descendants

posteri'ore [1] *adj* back *attrib*, rear *attrib*; (nel tempo) later
[2] *nm* fam posterior; behind

posterità *nf* posterity

po'sticcio [1] *adj* artificial; (baffi, barba) false
[2] *nm* hair-piece

postici'pare *vt* postpone

po'stilla *nf* note; Jur rider

po'stino *nm* postman, mailman Am

postmo'derno *adj* postmodern

'**posto** [1] *pp di* PORRE
[2] *nm* place; (spazio) room; (impiego) job; Mil post; (sedile) seat; **a/fuori ∼** in/out of place; **prendere ∼** take up room; **sul ∼** on-site; **essere a ∼** ⟨casa, libri⟩ be tidy; **no grazie, sono a ∼** no thanks, I'm all right; **mettere a ∼** tidy ⟨stanza⟩; **fare ∼ a** make room for; **al ∼ di** (invece di) in place of, instead of. **posto di blocco** checkpoint. **posto di guardia** guard post. **posto di guida** driving seat. **posto di lavoro** job; Comput workstation; **posti** *pl* **in piedi** standing room. **posto di polizia** police station; **posti** *pl* **a sedere** seating, seats

post-'partum *adj* post-natal

'**postumo** [1] *adj* posthumous
[2] *nm* after-effect; **postumi** *pl* **della sbornia** hangover

po'tabile *adj* drinkable; **acqua potabile** drinking water; **non ∼** undrinkable

po'tare *vt* prune

po'tassa *nf* potash

po'tassio *nm* potassium

po'tente *adj* powerful; (efficace) potent

po'tenza *nf* power; (efficacia) potency. **potenza mondiale** world power. **potenza nucleare** nuclear power

potenzi'ale *adj & nm* potential

po'tere ① *nm* power; **al** ~ in power.
potere d'acquisto purchasing power,
spending power. **il quarto potere** the
fourth estate
② *vi* can, be able to; **posso entrare?** can I
come in?; (formale) may I come in?; **mi
spiace, non posso venire alla festa** I'm
sorry, I can't come to the party *or* I won't
be able to come to the party; **posso fare
qualche cosa?** can I do something?; **che tu
possa essere felice!** may you be happy!;
non ne posso più (sono stanco) I can't go
on; (sono stufo) I can't take any more; **può
darsi** perhaps; **può darsi che sia vero**
perhaps it's true; **potrebbe aver ragione**
he could be right, he might be right;
avresti potuto telefonare you could have
phoned, you might have phoned; **spero di
poter venire** I hope to be able to come;
senza poter telefonare without being able
to phone; **spero che potremo incontrarci
presto** I hope we can meet soon

potestà *nf* power

pot-pour'ri *nm inv* medley

'povero, -a ① *adj* poor; (semplice) plain;
~ **di** ⟨*paese, terreno*⟩ lacking in; **in parole
povere** in a few words
② *nf* poor woman
③ *nm* poor man; **i poveri** the poor

povertà *nf* poverty

pozi'one *nf* potion

'pozza *nf* pool

poz'zanghera *nf* puddle

'pozzo *nm* well; ⟨*minerario*⟩ pit. **pozzo
petrolifero** oil well. **pozzo di petrolio**
oil well. **pozzo di ventilazione** air
shaft

pp. *abbr* (**pagine**) pp

PP.TT. *abbr* (**Poste e
Telecomunicazioni**) [Italian] Post
Office

PR *nfpl abbr* PR

prêt-à-por'ter *nm* ready-to-wear
clothing

'Praga *nf* Prague

prag'matico *adj* pragmatic

prali'nato *adj* ⟨*mandorla, gelato*⟩
praline-coated

pram'matica *nf* **essere di** ~ be
customary

pranotera'pia *nf* laying on of hands

pran'zare *vi* lunch.

'pranzo *nm* lunch. **pranzo di lavoro**
business lunch, working lunch. **pranzo
della mensa scolastica** school lunch.
pranzo di nozze wedding breakfast

'prassi *nf* standard procedure

prate'ria *nf* grassland, prairie

'pratica *nf* practice; (esperienza)
experience; (documentazione) file; **avere** ~ **di
qualcosa** be familiar with something,
have experience of something; **mettere
qualcosa in** ~ put something into
practice; **far** ~ gain experience; **fare le
pratiche per** gather the necessary papers
for

prati'cabile *adj* practicable; ⟨*strada*⟩
passable

pratica'mente *adv* practically

prati'cante *nmf* apprentice; Relig
[regular] churchgoer

prati'care *vt* practise; (frequentare)
associate with; (fare) make

praticità *nf* practicality

'pratico *adj* practical; (esperto)
experienced, knowledgeable; (comodo)
convenient; **essere** ~ **di qualcosa** know
about something; **all'atto** ~ in practice

'prato *nm* meadow; (di giardino) lawn.
prato all'inglese lawn

preaccensi'one *nf* Auto pre-ignition

pre'ambolo *nm* preamble

preannunci'are *vt* give advance notice
of

prean'nuncio *nm* advance notice

preavvi'sare *vt* forewarn

preav'viso *nm* warning

precari'cato *adj* preloaded

precarietà *nf* frailty

pre'cario *adj* precarious

precauzi'one *nf* precaution; (cautela)
care

prece'dente ① *adj* previous
② *nm* precedent; **avere dei precedenti
penali** have a criminal record; **senza
precedenti** (successo) unprecedented

precedente'mente *adv* previously

prece'denza *nf* precedence; (di veicoli)
right of way; **dare la** ~ **a** give priority to;
Auto give way to; **avere la** ~ have priority;
Auto have right of way; ~ **assoluta** top
priority

pre'cedere *vt* precede

pre'cetto *nm* precept

precet|'tore, -trice *nmf* tutor

precipi'tare ① *vt* ~ **le cose** precipitate
events; ~ **qualcuno nella disperazione**
cast somebody into a state of despair
② *vi* fall headlong; (situazione, eventi) come
to a head

precipi'tarsi *vr* (gettarsi) throw oneself;
(affrettarsi) rush; ~ **a fare qualcosa** rush to
do something

precipitazi'one *nf* (fretta) haste;
⟨*atmosferica*⟩ precipitation

precipi'toso *adj* hasty; (avventato)
reckless; ⟨*caduta*⟩ headlong

preci'pizio *nm* precipice; **a** ~ headlong

preci'sabile *adj* specifiable

precisa'mente *adv* precisely

preci'sare *vt* specify; (spiegare) clarify; **ci tengo a ~ che...** I want to make the point that...

precisazi'one *nf* clarification

precisi'one *nf* precision

pre'ciso *adj* precise; ⟨*calcolo, risposta*⟩ accurate; ⟨*ore*⟩ sharp; (identico) identical

pre'cludere *vt* preclude

pre'cludersi *vr* ~ **ogni possibilità** preclude every possibility

pre'cluso pp di PRECLUDERE

pre'coce *adj* precocious; (prematuro) premature

precocità *nf* precociousness

precon'cetto ① *adj* preconceived ② *nm* prejudice

preconfezio'nato *adj* pre-packed

preconfigu'rato *adj* preconfigured

pre'correre *vt* (anticipare) anticipate; ~ **i tempi** be ahead of one's time

precorri|'tore, -trice *nmf* precursor, forerunner

pre'cotto *adj* ready-cooked. **precotto e surgelato** cook-chill

precur'sore *nm* forerunner, precursor

'preda *nf* prey; (bottino) booty; **essere in ~ al panico** be panic-stricken; **in ~ alle fiamme** engulfed in flames

pre'dare *vt* plunder

preda'tore *nm* predator

predeces'sore *nmf* predecessor

pre'della *nf* platform

predel'lino *nm* step

predesti'nare *vt* predestine

predesti'nato *adj* predestined, preordained

predestinazi'one *nf* predestination

predetermi'nare *vt* predetermine

predetermi'nato *adj* predetermined, preordained

pre'detto pp di PREDIRE

'predica *nf* sermon; fig lecture

predi'care *vt* preach

predi'cato *nm* predicate

predige'rito *adj* predigested

predi'letto, -a ① pp di PREDILIGERE ② *adj* favourite ③ *nmf* pet fam

predilezi'one *nf* predilection; **avere una ~ per** have a predilection for, be partial to

predi'ligere *vt* prefer

prediposizi'one *nf* predisposition; (al disegno ecc) bent (**a** for)

pre'dire *vt* foretell

predi'sporre *vt* arrange; ~ **qualcuno a qualcosa** Med predispose somebody to something; (preparare) prepare somebody for something

predi'sporsi *vr* ~ **a** prepare oneself for

predi'sposto, -a ① pp di PREDISPORRE ② *adj* arranged. **predisposto per la TV via cavo** cable-ready

predizi'one *nf* prediction

predomi'nante *adj* predominant

predomi'nare *vi* predominate

predo'minio *nm* predominance

pre'done *nm* robber

prefabbri'cato ① *adj* prefabricated ② *nm* prefabricated building

prefazi'one *nf* preface

prefe'renza *nf* preference; **di ~** preferably

preferenzi'ale *adj* preferential; **corsia preferenziale** bus and taxi lane

prefe'ribile *adj* preferable

preferibil'mente *adv* preferably

prefe'rire *vt* prefer

prefe'rito, -a *adj & nmf* favourite

pre'fetto *nm* prefect

prefet'tura *nf* prefecture

pre'figgere *vt* decide in advance, pre-arrange ⟨*termine*⟩

pre'figgersi *vr* ~ **uno scopo** set oneself an objective

prefigu'rare *vt* (anticipare) foreshadow

prefinanzia'mento *nm* bridging loan

prefis'sare *vt* pre-arrange ⟨*data, appuntamento*⟩

pre'fisso ① pp di PREFIGGERE ② *nm* prefix; Teleph [dialling] code

pre'gare ① *vi* Relig pray ② *vt* Relig pray to; (supplicare) beg; **farsi ~** need persuading; ~ **qualcuno di fare qualcosa** ask somebody to do something; **si prega di...** please...; **si prega di non...** please do not...; **si prega di non fumare** please refrain from smoking

pre'gevole *adj* valuable

preghi'era *nf* prayer; (richiesta) request

pregi'arsi *vr* **si pregia di non essere mai in ritardo** he prides himself on never being late

pre'giato *adj* esteemed; (prezioso) valuable

'pregio *nm* esteem; (valore) value; (di persona) good point; **di ~** valuable

pregiudi'care *vt* prejudice; (danneggiare) harm

pregiudi'cato ① *adj* prejudiced ② *nm* Jur previous offender

pregiu'dizio *nm* prejudice; (danno) detriment

pre'gnante *adj* (parola) pregnant, pregnant with meaning

'pregno *adj* (parola) pregnant; (pieno) full; ~ **di** ⟨*umidità*⟩ saturated with; ⟨*significato*⟩ pregnant with

'prego *int* (non c'è di che) don't mention it!; (per favore) please; ~? I beg your pardon?; **posso? –~** may I? –please do

pregu'stare *vt* look forward to

preinstal'lato *adj* preinstalled

prei'storia *nf* prehistory

prei'storico *adj* prehistoric

pre'lato *nm* prelate

prela'vaggio *nm* prewash

preleva'mento *nm* withdrawal

prele'vare *vt* withdraw ⟨soldi⟩; collect ⟨merci⟩; Med take

preli'evo *nm* (di soldi) withdrawal. **prelievo di sangue** blood sample

prelimi'nare ① *adj* preliminary ② *nm* **preliminari** *pl* preliminaries

pre'ludere *vi* ~ a herald

pre'ludio *nm* prelude

prema'man ① *nm inv* maternity dress ② *adj inv* maternity *attrib*

prematrimoni'ale *adj* premarital

prematura'mente *adv* prematurely

prema'turo, -a ① *adj* premature ② *nmf* premature baby

premedi'tare *vt* premeditate

premeditazi'one *nf* premeditation; **con ~** ⟨omicidio⟩ premeditated

'premere ① *vt* press; Comput hit ⟨tasto⟩ ② *vi* ~ **a** (importare) matter to; **mi preme sapere** I need to know; ~ **su** press on; push ⟨pulsante⟩; (fig: fare pressione su) put pressure on, pressure; ~ **per ottenere qualcosa** push for something

pre'messa *nf* introduction; **senza tante premesse** without further ado

pre'messo *pp di* PREMETTERE; ~ **che** bearing in mind that

pre'mettere *vt* (mettere prima) put before; **premetto che...** I want to make it clear first that...; ~ **un'introduzione a un libro** put an introduction at the beginning of a book

premi'are *vt* give a prize to; (ricompensare) reward

premi'ato *adj* award-winning

premiazi'one *nf* prize giving

premi'nente *adj* pre-eminent

premi'nenza *nf* pre-eminence

'premio *nm* prize; (ricompensa) reward; (di produzione ecc) bonus; Fin premium. **premio di assicurazione** insurance premium. **premio di consolazione** consolation prize; (ridicolo) booby prize. **premio di ingaggio** Sport signing fee. **premio di produzione** productivity bonus

premoni'tore *adj* ⟨sogno, segno⟩ premonitory

premonizi'one *nf* premonition

premu'nire *vt* fortify

premu'nirsi *vr* take protective measures; ~ **di** provide oneself with; ~ **contro** protect oneself against

pre'mura *nf* (fretta) hurry; (cura) care; **far ~ a qualcuno** hurry somebody up

premu'roso *adj* thoughtful

prena'tale *adj* antenatal

'prendere ① *vt* take; (afferrare) seize; catch ⟨treno, malattia, ladro, pesce⟩; have ⟨cibo, bevanda⟩; (far pagare) charge; (assumere) take on; (ottenere) get; (occupare) take up; (guadagnare) earn; ~ **informazioni** make inquiries; ~ **in giro qualcuno** pull somebody's leg; ~ **a calci/pugni** kick/ punch; **che ti prende?** what's got into you?; **quanto prende?** what do you charge?; ~ **una persona per un'altra** mistake a person for somebody else; **passare a ~ qualcuno** collect somebody, pick somebody up ② *vi* (voltare) turn; (attecchire) take root; (rapprendersi) set; ⟨fuoco⟩ catch, take; ~ **a destra/sinistra** turn right/left; ~ **a fare qualcosa** start doing something; **la colla non ha preso** the glue didn't take

'prendersi *vr* ~ **a pugni** come to blows; ~ **cura di** take care of ⟨ammalato⟩; **prendersela** take it to heart; **si prende troppo sul serio** he takes himself too seriously

prendi'sole *nm inv* sundress

preno'tare *vt* book, reserve

preno'tarsi *vr* ~ **per** put one's name down for

preno'tato *adj* booked, reserved

prenotazi'one *nf* booking, reservation. **prenotazione di gruppo** group booking

'prensile *adj* prehensile

preoccu'pante *adj* alarming

preoccu'pare *vt* worry

preoccu'parsi *vr* ~ worry (di about); ~ **di fare qualcosa** take the trouble to do something

preoccu'pato *adj* worried; (apprensivo) concerned

preoccupazi'one *nf* worry; (apprensione) concern

preopera'torio *adj* preoperative

prepagato-a ① *adj* prepaid ② *nm* Teleph pay-as-you-go

prepa'rare *vt* prepare; study for ⟨esame⟩; ~ **da mangiare** prepare a meal

prepa'rarsi *vr* get ready

prepara'tivi *nmpl* preparations

prepa'rato *nm* (prodotto) preparation

prepara'torio *adj* preparatory

preparazi'one *nf* preparation; (competenza) knowledge

prepensiona'mento *nm* early retirement

preponde'rante *adj* predominant, preponderant

preponde'ranza *nf* preponderance, prevalence

pre'porre *vt* place before

preposizi'one *nf* preposition

pre'posto ① pp di PREPORRE
② *adj* ~ a (addetto a) in charge of

prepo'tente ① *adj* overbearing
② *nmf* bully; fare il/la ~ con qualcuno bully somebody

prepo'tenza *nf* high-handedness

preprogram'mato *adj* Comput preprogrammed

pre'puzio *nm* foreskin, prepuce

preroga'tiva *nf* prerogative

'presa *nf* taking; (conquista) capture; (stretta) hold; (di cemento ecc) setting; Electr socket; (di gas, acqua) inlet, connection; (pizzico) pinch; **essere alle prese con** be struggling *or* grappling with; **a ~ rapida** ⟨cemento, colla⟩ quick-setting; **fare ~ su qualcuno** influence somebody.
macchina da presa cine camera. **presa d'aria** air vent.**presa in giro** leg-pull. **presa multipla** adaptor. **presa scart** scart connector

pre'sagio *nm* omen

presa'gire *vt* foretell

presa'lario *nm* maintenance grant

'presbite *adj* long-sighted

presbiteri'ano, -a *adj & nmf* Presbyterian

presbi'terio *nm* presbytery

pre'scelto *adj* selected

pre'scindere *vi* ~ da leave aside; **a ~ da** apart from

presco'lare *adj* pre-school; **in età ~** pre-school

pre'scritto pp di PRESCRIVERE

pre'scrivere *vt* prescribe

prescrizi'one *nf* prescription; (norma) rule; **cadere in ~** cease to be valid as a result of the statute of limitations

preselezi'one *nf* preliminary selection; (per il traffico) advance lane markings; Sport [qualifying] heats *pl*

presen'tare *vt* present; (far conoscere) introduce; show ⟨documento⟩; (inoltrare) submit

presen'tarsi *vr* present oneself; (farsi conoscere) introduce oneself; (a ufficio) attend; (alla polizia ecc) report; (come candidato) stand, run (**a** for); ⟨occasione⟩ occur; **~ bene/male** ⟨persona⟩ make a good/ bad impression; ⟨situazione⟩ look good/bad

presenta|'tore, -trice *nmf* presenter; (di notiziario) announcer. **presentatore di talk show** chatshow host

presentazi'one *nf* presentation; (per conoscersi) introduction; **fare le presentazioni** do the introductions; **dietro ~ di ricetta medica** on doctor's prescription only

pre'sente ① *adj* present; (attuale) current; (questo) this; **aver ~** remember
② *nm* present; **i presenti** those present
③ *nf* **allegato alla ~** (in lettera) enclosed

presenti'mento *nm* foreboding

pre'senza *nf* presence; (aspetto) appearance; **in ~ di, alla ~ di** in the presence of; **di bella ~** personable. **presenza di spirito** presence of mind

presenzi'are *vi* ~ **a** attend

pre'sepe, pre'sepio *nm* crib

preser'vare *vt* preserve; (proteggere) protect (**da** from)

preserva'tivo *nm* condom

preservazi'one *nf* preservation

'preside ① *nm* headmaster
② *nf* headmistress

presi'dente ① *nm* chairman; Pol president
② *nf* chairwoman; Pol president. **presidente del consiglio [dei ministri]** Prime Minister. **presidente della repubblica** President of the Republic

presiden'tessa *nf* chairwoman

presi'denza *nf* presidency; (di assemblea) chairmanship

presidenzi'ale *adj* presidential

presidi'are *vt* garrison

pre'sidio *nm* garrison

presi'edere *vt* preside over

'preso pp di PRENDERE

'pressa *nf* Mech press

press-'agent *mf inv* publicist, press agent

pres'sante *adj* urgent

pressap'poco *adv* about

pres'sare *vt* press

pressi'one *nf* pressure; **far ~ su** put pressure on; **essere sotto ~** fig be under pressure; **esercitare pressioni su qualcuno** put pressure on somebody; **a/di alta ~** high pressure. **pressione fiscale** tax burden. **pressione delle gomme** tyre pressure. **pressione del sangue** blood pressure

'presso ① *prep* near; (a casa di) with; (negli indirizzi) care of, c/o; ⟨lavorare⟩ for; **richiedere qualcosa ~ una società** request something from a company
② *nmpl* **pressi: nei pressi di...** in the neighbourhood *or* vicinity of...

pressoché *adv* almost

pressuriz'zare *vt* pressurize

pressuriz'zato *adj* pressurized

prestabi'lire *vt* arrange in advance

prestabi'lito *adj* agreed, predetermined

prestam'pato ① *adj* printed
② *nm* (modulo) form

pre'stante *adj* good-looking

pre'stanza *nf* good looks *pl*

pre'stare *vt* lend; ~ **attenzione** pay attention; ~ **aiuto** lend a hand; ~ **ascolto** lend an ear; ~ **fede a** give credence to; ~ **giuramento** take the oath; **farsi** ~ borrow (**da** from)

pre'starsi *vr* ⟨*frase*⟩ lend itself; ⟨*persona*⟩ offer

prestazi'one *nf* performance; **prestazioni** *pl* (servizi) services

prestigia|'tore, -trice *nmf* conjuror, conjurer

pre'stigio *nm* prestige; **gioco di prestigio** conjuring trick

prestigi'oso *nm* prestigious

'prestito *nm* loan; **dare in** ~ lend; **prendere in** ~ borrow. **prestito bancario** bank loan. **prestito con garanzia collaterale** collateral loan

'presto *adv* soon; (di buon'ora) early; (in fretta) quickly; **a** ~ see you soon; **al più** ~ as soon as possible; ~ **o tardi** sooner or later; **far** ~ be quick

pre'sumere *vt* presume; (credere) think

presu'mibile *adj* è ~ **che...** presumably, ...

pre'sunto *adj* ⟨colpevole⟩ presumed

presuntu'oso ① *adj* presumptuous
② *nmf* presumptuous person

presunzi'one *nf* presumption

presup'porre *vt* suppose; (richiedere) presuppose

presupposizi'one *nf* presupposition

presup'posto *nm* essential requirement

'prete *nm* priest

preten'dente ① *nmf* pretender
② *nm* (corteggiatore) suitor

pre'tendere ① *vt* (sostenere) claim; (esigere) demand
② *vi* ~ **a** claim to; ~ **di** (esigere) demand to

pretensi'one *nf* pretension

pretenzi'oso *adj* pretentious

preterintenzio'nale *adj* **omicidio preterintenzionale** manslaughter

pre'terito *nm* preterite

pre'tesa *nf* pretension; (esigenza) claim; **senza pretese** unpretentious

pre'teso *pp di* PRETENDERE

pre'testo *nm* pretext

pre'tore *nm* magistrate

pretta'mente *adv* decidedly

'pretto *adj* pure

pre'tura *nf* magistrate's court

preva'lente *adj* prevalent

prevalente'mente *adv* primarily, predominantly

preva'lenza *nf* prevalence

preva'lere *vi* prevail

pre'valso *pp di* PREVALERE

preve'dere *vt* foresee; forecast ⟨*tempo*⟩; ⟨*legge ecc*⟩ provide for

preve'nire *vt* precede; (evitare) prevent; (avvertire) forewarn

preventi'vare *vt* estimate; (aspettarsi) budget for

preven'tivo ① *adj* preventive; **bilancio preventivo** budget
② *nm* Comm estimate

preve'nuto *adj* forewarned; (maldisposto) prejudiced

prevenzi'one *nf* prevention; (preconcetto) prejudice

previ'dente *adj* provident

previ'denza *nf* foresight. **previdenza integrativa** supplementary social security, supplementary welfare Am. **previdenza sociale** social security, welfare Am

previdenzi'ale *adj* provident

'previo *adj* ~ **pagamento** on payment

previsi'one *nf* forecast; **in** ~ **di** in anticipation of; **previsioni** *pl* **del tempo** weather forecast

pre'visto ① *pp di* PREVEDERE
② *adj* foreseen
③ *nm* **più/meno/prima del** ~ more/less/earlier than expected

prezi'oso *adj* precious

prez'zemolo *nm* parsley

'prezzo *nm* price; [a] **metà** ~ half price; **a** ~ **ribassato** at a reduced price; **non aver** ~ fig be priceless. **prezzo d'acquisto** purchase price. **prezzo di costo** cost price. **prezzo al dettaglio** o **prezzo al minuto** retail price. **prezzo di fabbrica** factory price. **prezzo di favore** special price. **prezzo all'ingrosso** wholesale price. **prezzo intero** full price. **prezzo di listino** list price. **prezzo di mercato** market price. **prezzo d'offerta** offer price. **prezzo politico** subsidized price. **prezzo di riferimento** benchmark price. **prezzo scontato** sale price. **prezzo sorvegliato** controlled price. **prezzo stracciato** slashed price, drastically reduced price. **prezzo trattabile** price negotiable. **prezzo unitario** unit price. **prezzo di vendita** selling price

prigi'one *nf* prison; (pena) imprisonment; **mettere in** ~ imprison, put in prison

prigio'nia *nf* imprisonment

prigioni'ero, -a ① *adj* imprisoned
② *nmf* prisoner; **tenere** ~ **qualcuno** keep somebody prisoner. **prigioniero di** ⋯⋗

guerra prisoner of war, POW.

prigioniero politico political prisoner

'**prima** ① *adv* before; (più presto) earlier; (in anticipo) beforehand; (in primo luogo) first; **finiamo questo, ∼** let's finish this first; **puoi venire ∼?** (di giorni) can't you come any sooner?; (di ore) can't you come any earlier?; **∼ o poi** sooner or later; **quanto ∼** as soon as possible
② *prep* **∼ di** before; **∼ di mangiare** before eating; **∼ d'ora** before now
③ *conj* **∼ che** before; **∼ che posso** as soon as I can; **∼ possibile** asap
④ *nf* first class; Theat first night; Auto first [gear]. **prima elementare** first grade

pri'mario *adj* primary; (principale) principal

pri'mate *nm* primate

prima'tista *nmf* record-holder

pri'mato *nm* supremacy; Sport record

prima'vera *nf* spring

primave'rile *adj* spring *attrib*

primeggi'are *vi* excel

primi'tivo *adj* primitive; (originario) original

pri'mizie *nfpl* early produce *sg*

'**primo** ① *adj* first; (fondamentale) principal; (in importanza) main; (precedente tra due) former; (iniziale) early; (migliore) best
② *nm* first; **il ∼ d'aprile** April the first, April Fools' Day; **primi** *pl* **tempi** (i primi giorni) the beginning; **in un ∼ tempo** at first. **prima colazione** *nf* breakfast. **prima copia** *nf* master copy. **prima linea** *nf* Mil front line. **prima serata** *nf* prime time; **in prima serata trasmetteremo...** in the early evening slot we are bringing you...

primo'genito, -a *adj & nmf* first-born

primogeni'tura *nf* primogeniture; **vendere la ∼** sell one's birthright

primordi'ale *adj* primordial

'**primula** *nf* primrose

princi'pale ① *adj* main
② *nm* head, boss fam

princi'pato *nm* principality. **il Principato di Monaco** Monaco

'**principe** *nm* prince; **da ∼** princely. **principe ereditario** crown prince. **principe del foro** famous lawyer

princi'pesco *adj* princely

princi'pessa *nf* princess

principi'ante *nmf* beginner

principi'are *vt/i* begin, start

prin'cipio *nm* beginning; (concetto) principle; (causa) cause; **per ∼** on principle; **una questione di ∼** a matter of principle. **principio attivo** active ingredient

pri'ore *nm* prior

pri'ori: a ∼ ① *adv* ⟨decidere⟩ a priori; **farsi a ∼ un'opinione di** prejudge
② *adj* a priori

priorità *nf inv* priority

priori'tario *adj* having priority; ⟨obiettivo⟩ priority *attrib*; **la nostra scelta prioritaria** our decision, which must take priority

'**prisma** *nm* prism

'**privacy** *nf* privacy

pri'vare *vt* deprive

pri'varsi *vr* deprive oneself

privatiz'zare *vt* privatize

privatizzazi'one *nf* privatization

pri'vato, -a ① *adj* private
② *nmf* private citizen; **in ∼** in private; **ritirarsi a vita privata** withdraw from public life

privazi'one *nf* deprivation

privilegi'are *vt* privilege; (considerare più importante) favour

privi'legio *nm* privilege; **avere il ∼ di** have the privilege of; **questo saggio ha il ∼ della chiarezza** this essay has the merit of clarity

'**privo** *adj* **∼ di** devoid of; (mancante) lacking in

pro ① *prep* for
② *nm* advantage; **a che ∼?** what's the point?; **il ∼ e il contro** the pros and cons

pro'babile *adj* probable

probabilità *nf inv* probability; **avere buone ∼** have a fighting chance; **∼ di riuscita** chances of success

probabil'mente *adv* probably

pro'bante *adj* convincing

probità *nf* probity

pro'blema *nm* problem; **non c'è ∼** no problem

proble'matico *adj* problematic

pro'boscide *nf* trunk

procacci'are *vt* obtain

procacci'arsi *vr* obtain

pro'cace *adj* ⟨ragazza⟩ provocative

pro'cedere *vi* (in percorso, discorso) go on, proceed *fml*; (iniziare) start; **il lavoro procede bene** the work is going well; **∼ contro** Jur start legal proceedings against

procedi'mento *nm* process; Jur proceedings *pl*. **procedimento giudiziario** legal proceedings

proce'dura *nf* procedure. **procedura civile** civil proceedings *pl*. **procedura fallimentare** bankruptcy proceedings *pl*

procedu'rale *adj* procedural

proces'sare *vt* Jur try

processi'one *nf* procession

pro'cesso *nm* process; Jur trial; **essere sotto ∼** be on trial; **mettere sotto ∼** put

on trial. **processo di pace** peace
process

proces'sore *nm* Comput processor

processu'ale *adj* trial *attrib*

pro'cinto *nm* **essere in** ~ **di** be about to

proci'one *nm* raccoon

pro'clama *nm* proclamation

procla'mare *vt* proclaim

proclamazi'one *nf* proclamation

procrasti'nare *vt* liter postpone

procre'are *vt* procreate

procreazi'one *nf* procreation

pro'cura *nf* power of attorney; **per** ~ by
proxy. **Procura [della Repubblica]**
Public Prosecutor's office

procu'rare *vt/i* procure; (causare) cause;
(cercare) try

procura'tore *nm* attorney.
Procuratore Generale Attorney
General. **procuratore legale** lawyer.
procuratore della repubblica public
prosecutor

'prode *adj* brave

pro'dezza *nf* bravery

prodi'gare *vt* lavish

prodi'garsi *vr* do one's best

pro'diglo *nm* prodigy

prodigi'oso *adj* prodigious

'prodigo *adj* prodigal

prodi'torio *adj* treasonable

pro'dotto [1] pp di PRODURRE
[2] *nm* product; **prodotti** *pl* **agricoli** farm
produce *sg*; ~ **artigianale** *adj* made
by craftsmen; **prodotti** *pl* **di bellezza**
cosmetics. **prodotto derivato** by-
product; ~ **in fabbrica** *adj* factory-made.
prodotto finito end product, finished
product. **prodotto interno lordo** gross
domestic product. **prodotto nazionale
lordo** gross national product

pro'durre *vt* produce

pro'dursi *vr* ⟨attore⟩ play; (accadere)
happen, occur

produt'tore, -trice [1] *adj* producing.
produttore di petrolio oil-producing
[2] *nmf* producer

produttività *nf* productivity

produt'tivo *adj* productive; **poco** ~
unproductive

produzi'one *nf* production.
produzione in serie mass production

Prof. *abbr* (**professore**) Prof.

profa'nare *vt* desecrate

profanazi'one *nf* desecration

pro'fano [1] *adj* profane
[2] *nm* **i profani** *pl* the uninitiated

profe'rire *vt* utter

Prof.essa *abbr* (**Professoressa**) Prof.

profes'sare *vt* profess; practise
⟨professione⟩

professio'nale *adj* professional; **istituto
professionale** training college

professionalità *nf* professionalism

professi'one *nf* profession; **libera
professione** profession

professio'nismo *nm* professionalism

professio'nista *nmf* professional

professo'rale *adj* professorial

profes'sor|e, -essa *nmf* Sch teacher;
Univ lecturer; (titolare di cattedra) professor

pro'feta *nm* prophet

pro'fetico *adj* prophetic

profetiz'zare *vt* prophesy

profe'zia *nf* prophecy

pro'ficuo *adj* profitable

profi'lare *vt* outline; (ornare) border; Aeron
streamline

profi'larsi *vr* stand out

profi'lattico [1] *adj* prophylactic
[2] *nm* condom

pro'filo *nm* profile; (breve studio) outline; **di**
~ in profile. **profilo genetico** genetic
profiling

profite'roles *nmpl* profiteroles

profit'tare *vi* ~ **di** (avvantaggiarsi) profit
by; (approfittare) take advantage of

pro'fitto *nm* profit; (vantaggio) advantage;
mettere qualcosa a ~ turn something to
one's advantage; **trarre** ~ **da** (vantaggio)
derive benefit from

profonda'mente *adv* deeply,
profoundly

profondità *nf inv* depth; (del pensiero ecc)
depth, profundity; **in** ~ in depth;
passaggio in ~ Sport deep pass [down the
field]. **profondità di campo** Phot depth
of field

pro'fondo *adj* deep; ⟨pensiero ecc⟩
profound; ⟨cultura⟩ great

pro 'forma [1] *adj* routine; **fattura pro
forma** pro forma [invoice]
[2] *adv* as a formality
[3] *nm inv* formality

'profugo, -a *nmf* refugee

profu'mare [1] *vi* smell good; ~ **di** smell
of
[2] *vt* perfume

profu'marsi *vr* put on perfume

profumata'mente *adv* **pagare** ~ pay
through the nose

profu'mato *adj* ⟨fiore⟩ fragrant;
⟨fazzoletto ecc⟩ scented

profume'ria *nf* perfumery

pro'fumo *nm* perfume, scent

profusi'one *nf* profusion; **a** ~ in
profusion

pro'fuso *adj* profuse

pro'genie *nf* progeny

progeni|'tore, **-trice** *nmf* ancestor

proget'tare *vt* plan; plan, design ⟨costruzione⟩

progettazione *nf* planning, design. **progettazione assistita da computer** computer-aided design, CAD

proget'tista *nmf* designer

pro'getto *nm* plan; (di lavoro importante) project. **progetto di legge** bill. **progetto pilota** pilot scheme

prog'nosi *nf inv* prognosis; **in ~ riservata** on the danger list

pro'gramma *nm* programme; Comput program; **avere qualcosa in ~** have something planned, have something on; **programmi** *pl* **televisivi del mattino** breakfast TV. **programma antivirus** Comput antivirus program, antivirus software. **programma assemblatore** Comput assembler. **programma aziendale** business plan. **programma per la gestione dei file** Comput file manager. **programma di grafica** Comput graphics program. **programma politico** manifesto. **programma scolastico** syllabus. **programma di setup** Comput setup program. **programma di utilità** Comput utility program

program'mare *vt* programme; Comput program

program'mato *adj* ⟨sviluppo⟩ planned

programma|'tore, **-trice** *nmf* [computer] programmer

programmazi'one *nf* programming

progre'dire *vi* [make] progress

progres'sione *nf* progression

progres'sista *nmf* progressive

progres'sivo *adj* progressive

pro'gresso *nm* progress; **fare progressi** make progress

proi'bire *vt* forbid

proibi'tivo *adj* prohibitive

proibito *adj* forbidden; **è ~ fumare qui** it's no smoking here

proibizi'one *nf* prohibition

proibizio'nismo *nm* prohibition

proiet'tare *vt* project; show ⟨film⟩

proi'ettile *nm* bullet

proiet'tore *nm* projector; Auto headlight. **proiettore per diapositive** slide projector

proiezi'one *nf* projection. **proiezione di diapositive** slide show

'prole *nf* offspring

proletari'ato *nm* proletariat

prole'tario *adj & nm* proletarian

prolife'rare *vi* proliferate

pro'lifico *adj* prolific

prolissità *nf* prolixity, diffuseness

pro'lisso *adj* verbose, prolix

pro 'loco *nf* tourist office (in small towns)

'prologo *nm* prologue

pro'lunga *nf* extension

prolunga'mento *nm* extension

prolun'gare *vt* extend ⟨contratto, scadenza, strada⟩; prolong ⟨vita⟩; lengthen ⟨vita, strada⟩

prolun'garsi *vr* continue, go on; **~ su** (dilungarsi) dwell upon

prome'moria *nm* memo; (per se stessi) reminder, note; (formale) memorandum

pro'messa *nf* promise; **era già una ~ del...** he was already a promising new talent in...

pro'messo ① *pp di* PROMETTERE ② *adj* ⟨terra⟩ promised; **promessa sposa** *nf* betrothed. **promesso sposo** *nm* betrothed

promet'tente *adj* promising

pro'mettere *vt/i* promise

promi'nente *adj* prominent

promi'nenza *nf* prominence

promiscuità *nf* promiscuity

pro'miscuo *adj* promiscuous

promon'torio *nm* promontory

pro'mosso ① *pp di* PROMUOVERE ② *adj* Sch who has gone up a year; Univ who has passed an exam

promo|'tore, **-trice** *nmf* promoter

promozio'nale *adj* promotional; **vendita promozionale** special offer

promozi'one *nf* promotion

promul'gare *vt* promulgate

promulgazi'one *nf* promulgation

promu'overe *vt* promote; Sch move up a class; **essere promosso** Sch, Univ pass one's exams

proni'pote ① *nm* (di bisnonno) great-grandson; (di prozio) great-nephew; **pronipoti** *pl* great-grandchildren ② *nf* (di bisnonno) great-granddaughter; (di prozio) great-niece

pro'nome *nm* pronoun

pronomi'nale *adj* pronominal

pronosti'care *vt* forecast, predict

pronostica|'tore, **-trice** *nmf* forecaster

pro'nostico *nm* forecast

pron'tezza *nf* readiness; (rapidità) quickness. **prontezza di riflessi** quick reflexes *pl*; **con ~ di spirito** quick-wittedly

'pronto *adj* ready; (rapido) quick; **~!** Teleph hello!; **tenersi ~ (per qualcosa)** be ready (for something); **pronti, attenti, via!** (in gare) ready! steady! go!; **a pronta cassa** cash on delivery. **pronto intervento** *nm* emergency service. **pronto soccorso** *nm* first aid; (in ospedale) accident and emergency, A&E

prontu'ario *nm* handbook

pro'nuncia *nf* pronunciation

pronunci'are *vt* pronounce; (dire) utter; deliver ⟨*discorso*⟩

pronunci'arsi *vr* (su un argomento) give one's opinion; ~ **a favore/contro qualcosa** pronounce oneself in favour of/against something

pronunci'ato *adj* pronounced; (prominente) prominent

pro'nunzia = PRONUNCIA

pronunzi'are = PRONUNCIARE

propa'ganda *nf* propaganda. **propaganda elettorale** electioneering. **propaganda di partito** party political propaganda

propa'gare *vt* propagate

propa'garsi *vr* spread

propagazi'one *nf* propagation

prope'deutico *adj* introductory

propel'lente *nm* propellant

pro'pendere *vi* ~ **per** be in favour of

propensi'one *nf* inclination, propensity

pro'penso ⨍1⨎ pp di PROPENDERE ⨍2⨎ *adj* **essere** ~ **a fare qualcosa** be inclined to do something

propi'nare *vt* administer

pro'pizio *adj* favourable

proponi'mento *nm* resolution

pro'porre *vt* propose; (suggerire) suggest

pro'porsi *vr* set oneself ⟨*obiettivo, meta*⟩; ~ **di** intend to

proporzio'nale *adj* proportional

proporzio'nare *vt* proportion

proporzio'nato *adj* proportioned

proporzi'one *nf* proportion

pro'posito *nm* intention; **ho fatto il** ~ **di...** I have made the decision to...; **a** ~ by the way; **a** ~ **di** with regard to; **di** ~ (apposta) on purpose; **capitare a** ~, **giungere a** ~ come at just the right time; **propositi** *pl* **per l'anno nuovo** New Year's resolutions

proposizi'one *nf* clause; (frase) sentence

pro'posta *nf* proposal, suggestion. **proposta di legge** bill. **proposta di matrimonio** [marriage] proposal

pro'posto pp di PROPORRE

propria'mente *adv* ~ **detto** in the strict sense of the word

proprietà *nf inv* property; (diritto) ownership; (correttezza) propriety; **essere di** ~ **di qualcuno** be somebody's property. **proprietà collettiva** collective ownership. **proprietà immobiliare** property. **proprietà di linguaggio** correct use of language. **proprietà privata** private property

proprie'taria *nf* owner; (di casa affittata) landlady

proprie'tario *nm* owner; (di casa affittata) landlord

'proprio ⨍1⨎ *adj* one's [own]; (caratteristico) typical; (appropriato) proper ⨍2⨎ *adv* just; (veramente) really; **non** ~ not really, not exactly; (affatto) not... at all ⨍3⨎ *pron* one's own ⨍4⨎ *nm* one's own; **lavorare in** ~ be one's own boss; **mettersi in** ~ set up on one's own

propu'gnare *vt* support

propulsi'one *nf* propulsion; **a** ~ **atomica** atomic[-powered]. **propulsione a getto** jet propulsion

propul'sore *nm* propeller

'prora *nf* Naut prow

'proroga *nf* extension

proro'gabile *adj* extendable

proro'gare *vt* extend

pro'rompere *vi* burst out

'prosa *nf* prose

pro'saico *adj* prosaic

pro'sciogliere *vt* release; Jur acquit

prosciogli'mento *nm* release

pro'sciolto pp di PROSCIOGLIERE

prosciu'gare *vt* dry up; (bonificare) reclaim

prosciu'garsi *vr* dry up

prosci'utto *nm* ham. **prosciutto cotto** cooked ham. **prosciutto crudo** type of dry-cured ham, Parma ham

pro'scritto, -a ⨍1⨎ pp di PROSCRIVERE ⨍2⨎ *nmf* exile

pro'scrivere *vt* exile, banish

proscrizi'one *nf* exile, banishment

prosecuzi'one *nf* continuation

prosegui'mento *nm* continuation; **buon** ~! (viaggio) have a good journey!; (festa) enjoy the rest of the party!

prosegu'ire ⨍1⨎ *vt* continue ⨍2⨎ *vi* go on, continue

pro'selito *nm* convert

prospe'rare *vi* prosper

prosperità *nf* prosperity

'prospero *adj* prosperous; (favorevole) favourable

prospe'roso *adj* flourishing; (ragazza) buxom

prospet'tare *vt* show

prospet'tarsi *vr* seem

prospet'tiva *nf* perspective; (panorama) view; fig prospect

pro'spetto *nm* (vista) view; (facciata) façade; (tabella) table

prospici'ente *adj* facing

prossima'mente *adv* soon

prossimità *nf* proximity; **in** ~ **di** near

'prossimo, -a ⨍1⨎ *adj* near; (seguente) next; (molto vicino) close; **l'anno** ~ next ⋯⋗

year; ~ **venturo** next; **essere ~ a fare qualcosa** be about to do something ② *nmf* neighbour

'prostata *nf* prostate

prostitu'irsi *vr* prostitute oneself

prosti'tuta *nf* prostitute

prostituzi'one *nf* prostitution

pro'strare *vt* prostrate

pro'strarsi *vr* prostrate oneself

pro'strato *adj* prostrate

protago'nista *nmf* protagonist; **ruolo/ attore non ~** supporting role/actor

pro'teggere *vt* protect; (favorire) favour; **~ da sovrascrittura** write-protect

pro'teico *adj* protein *attrib*; **molto ~** rich in protein

prote'ina *nf* protein

pro'tendere *vt* stretch out

pro'tendersi *vr* (in avanti) lean out

pro'teso pp di PROTENDERE

pro'testa *nf* protest; (dichiarazione) protestation

prote'stante *adj & nmf* Protestant

prote'stare *vt/i* protest

prote'starsi *vr* ~ **innocente** protest one's innocence

protet'tivo *adj* protective

pro'tetto, -a ① pp di PROTEGGERE ② *adj* protected; **non ~** unprotected. **protetto da password** password-protected

protetto'rato *nm* protectorate

protet'|tore, -trice ① *nmf* protector; (sostenitore) patron ② *nm* (di prostituta) pimp

protezi'one *nf* protection. **protezione aerea** air cover. **protezione dell'ambiente** environmental protection. **protezione antivirus** virus protection. **protezione civile** civil defence

protocol'lare ① *adj* (visita) protocol ② *vt* register

proto'collo *nm* protocol; (registro) register; **carta protocollo** official stamped paper. **protocollo di gestione remota della posta elettronica** IMAP. **protocollo Internet** Internet protocol. **protocollo per il trasferimento di file** file transfer protocol. **protocollo per il trasferimento di ipertesti** hypertext transfer protocol

pro'totipo *nm* prototype

pro'trarre *vt* protract; (differire) postpone

pro'trarsi *vr* go on, continue

pro'tratto pp di PROTRARRE

protube'rante *adj* protuberant

protube'ranza *nf* protuberance

'prova *nf* test; (dimostrazione) proof; (tentativo) try, attempt; (di abito) fitting; Sport heat; Theat rehearsal; (bozza) proof; **prove** *pl* evidence; **fino a ~ contraria** until I'm told otherwise; **in ~** (assumere) for a trial period; **mettere alla ~** put to the test; **a ~ di bomba** bombproof; **a ~ di ladro** burglarproof. **prova del fuoco** fig acid test. **prova generale** dress rehearsal. **prova medico-legale** forensic evidence

pro'vare *vt* test; (dimostrare) prove; (tentare) try; try on ‹abiti ecc›; (sentire) feel; Theat rehearse; **prova!** just try!

pro'varsi *vr* try

proveni'enza *nf* origin

prove'nire *vi* ~ **da** come from

pro'vento *nm* proceeds *pl*

prove'nuto pp di PROVENIRE

pro'verbio *nm* proverb

pro'vetta *nf* test-tube; **bambino in provetta** test-tube baby

pro'vetto *adj* skilled

pro'vincia *nf* province

provinci'ale *adj* provincial; **strada provinciale** B road, secondary road

pro'vino *nm* specimen; Cinema screen test

provo'cante *adj* provocative

provo'care *vt* provoke; (causare) cause

provoca'|tore, -trice *nmf* troublemaker

provoca'torio *adj* provocative, confrontational

provocazi'one *nf* provocation

provo'lone *nm* type of cheese with a slightly smoked flavour

provve'dere *vi* ~ **a** provide for

provvedi'mento *nm* measure; (previdenza) precaution. **provvedimento disciplinare** disciplinary measure

provvedito'rato *nm* **provveditorato agli studi** education department

provvedi'tore *nm* **provveditore agli studi** director of education

provvi'denza *nf* providence

provvidenzi'ale *adj* providential

provvigi'one *nf* Comm commission; **lavorare a ~** work on commission

provvi'sorio *adj* provisional; **in via provvisoria** provisionally, for the time being

prov'vista *nf* supply

pro'zia *nf* great-aunt

pro'zio *nm* great-uncle

'prua *nf* Naut prow

pru'dente *adj* prudent

pru'denza *nf* prudence; **per ~** as a precaution

prudenzi'ale *adj* prudential

'prudere *vi* itch

'prugna *nf* plum. **prugna secca** prune. **prugna selvatica** damson

'prugno *nm* plum[-tree]

'prugnolo *nm* sloe

prurigi'noso *adj* itchy

pru'rito *nm* itch

P.S. *abbr* (**Pubblica Sicurezza**) police

pseu'donimo *nm* pseudonym

psica'nalisi *nf* psychoanalysis

psicana'lista *nmf* psychoanalyst

psicanaliz'zare *vt* psychoanalyse

'psiche *nf* psyche

psiche'delico *adj* psychedelic

psichi'atra *nmf* psychiatrist

psichia'tria *nf* psychiatry

psichi'atrico *adj* psychiatric

'psichico *adj* mental

psico'farmaco *nm* drug that affects the mind

psicolo'gia *nf* psychology

psico'logico *adj* psychological

psi'cologo, -a *nmf* psychologist

psico'patico, -a ① *adj* psychopathic ② *nmf* psychopath

psicopedago'gia *nf* educational psychology

psi'cosi *nf inv* psychosis

psicoso'matico *adj* psychosomatic

psicotera'peuta *nmf* psychotherapist

psicotera'pista *nmf* psychotherapist

psi'cotico, -a *adj & nmf* psychotic

PT *abbr* (**Posta e Telegrafi**) PO

puàh *int* yuck!

pub *nm inv* pub

pubbli'care *vt* publish

pubblicazi'one *nf* publication; **pubblicazioni** *pl* (di matrimonio) banns. **pubblicazione periodica** periodical

pubbli'cista *nmf* Journ correspondent

pubblicità *nf inv* publicity, advertising; (annuncio) advertisement, advert; **fare ~ a qualcosa** advertise something; **piccola pubblicità** small advertisements

pubblici'tario *adj* advertising

'pubblico ① *adj* public; **scuola pubblica** state school ② *nm* public; (spettatori) audience; **in ~** in public; **grande ~** general public; **Pubblica Sicurezza** police. **pubblico ministero** public prosecutor. **pubblico ufficiale** civil servant

'pube *nm* pubis

pubertà *nf* puberty

pu'dico *adj* modest

pu'dore *nm* modesty

pue'rile *adj* children's; pej childish

'puerpera *nf* new mother

puerpe'rale *adj* of childbirth, puerperal *fml*; ⟨depressione⟩ postnatal

puer'perio *nm* postnatal period

pugi'lato *nm* boxing

'pugile *nm* boxer

'Puglia *nf* Apulia

pugli'ese *adj & nmf* Apulian

pugna'lare *vt* stab

pugna'lata *nf* stab

pu'gnale *nm* dagger

'pugno *nm* fist; (colpo) punch; (manciata) fistful; (fig: numero limitato) handful; **dare un ~ a** a punch; **di proprio ~** ⟨scrivere⟩ in one's own hand; **fare a pugni** ⟨colori⟩ clash; **tenere in ~** ⟨situazione⟩ have under control; have in the palm of one's hand ⟨persona⟩; **un ~ in un occhio** fig an eyesore. **pugno di ferro** iron fist

'pula *nf* sl la ~ the fuzz

'pulce *nf* flea; (microfono) bug; **mettere la ~ nell'orecchio a qualcuno** sow a doubt in somebody's mind

pul'cino *nm* chick; (nel calcio) junior

pu'ledra *nf* filly

pu'ledro *nm* foal, colt

pu'leggia *nf* pulley

pu'lire *vt* clean; **~ a secco** dry-clean; **far ~ qualcosa** have something cleaned

puliscipi'edi *nm inv* boot scraper

pu'lito *adj* clean

puli'tura *nf* cleaning

puli'zia *nf* (il pulire) cleaning; (l'essere pulito) cleanliness; **pulizie** *pl* housework; **fare le pulizie** do the cleaning. **pulizia personale** personal hygiene

'pullman *nm inv* coach; (urbano) bus; **gita in ~** coach trip

pull'over *nm inv* pullover

pul'mino *nm* minibus

'pulpito *nm* pulpit

pul'sante *nm* button; Electr [push-]button. **pulsante di accensione** on/off switch. **pulsante di alimentazione** power switch

pul'sare *vi* pulsate

pulsazi'one *nf* pulsation

pul'viscolo *nm* dust

'puma *nm inv* puma

'punching 'bag *nf inv* punchbag

pun'gente *adj* prickly; ⟨insetto⟩ stinging; ⟨odore ecc⟩ sharp

'pungere *vt* prick; ⟨insetto⟩ sting; **~ qualcuno sul vivo** cut somebody to the quick

pungersi *vr* prick oneself; **~ un dito** prick one's finger

pungigli'one *nm* sting

pungo'lare *vt* goad

pu'nire *vt* punish

puni'tivo *adj* punitive

punizi'one *nf* punishment; Sport penalty; (in calcio) free kick. **punizione corporale** corporal punishment

'punta *nf* point; (estremità) tip; (di monte) peak, top; (un po') pinch; (di matita) point; · **doppie punte** (di capelli) split ends; **di ~** ⟨ore⟩ peak; ⟨personaggio⟩ leading

pun'tare ① *vt* point; (spingere con forza) push; (scommettere) bet; (fam: appuntare) fasten

② *vi* **~ su** fig rely on; (scommettere) bet on; **~ verso** (dirigersi) head for; **~ a** aspire to; **punta e clicca** Comput point and click

punta'spilli *nm inv* pincushion

pun'tata *nf* (di una storia) instalment; (televisiva) episode; (al gioco) stake, bet; (breve visita) flying visit; **a puntate** serialized, in instalments; **fare una ~ a/in** pop over to ⟨luogo⟩

puntaggia'tura *nf* punctuation

pun'teggio *nm* score

puntel'lare *vt* prop

pun'tello *nm* prop

punteru'olo *nm* awl

pun'tiglio *nm* spite; (ostinazione) obstinacy

puntigli'oso *adj* punctilious, pernickety *pej*

pun'tina *nf* (di giradischi) stylus. **puntina da disegno** drawing pin, thumb tack Am

pun'tine *nfpl* Aut puntine [platinate] points

pun'tino *nm* dot; **a ~** perfectly; ⟨cotto⟩ to a T; **puntini** *pl* [di sospensione] suspension points

'punto *nm* point; (in cucito, Med) stitch; (in punteggiatura) full stop; **in che ~?** where, exactly?; **di ~ in bianco** all of a sudden; **essere sul ~ di fare qualcosa** be on the point of doing something, be about to do something; **in ~** sharp; **mettere a ~** put right; fig fine-tune; tune up ⟨motore⟩; **messa a ~** fine tuning; **due punti** colon; **punti** *pl* **cardinali** points of the compass. **punto cieco** blind spot. **punto di congelamento** freezing point. **punto croce** cross-stitch. **punto debole** weak spot. **punto di domanda** question mark. **punto di ebollizione** boiling point. **punto esclamativo** exclamation mark. **punto di fuga** vanishing point. **punto di fusione** melting point. **punto d'incontro** meeting-point. **punto di infiammabilità** flashpoint. **punto interrogativo** question mark. **punto morto** fig stand-off. **punto nero** (comedone) blackhead. **punto di pareggio** Fin breakeven point. **punto di partenza** starting point. **punto di riferimento** landmark; (per la qualità) benchmark. **punto di rottura** breaking point. **punto a smerlo** blanket stitch. **punto [di] vendita** point of sale, outlet;

pubblicità al ~ [di] vendita point-of-sale publicity. **punto e virgola** semicolon. **punto di vista** point of view

puntu'ale *adj* punctual; **essere ~** be punctual, be on time

puntualità *nf* punctuality

puntualiz'zare *vt* make clear, clarify

puntual'mente *adv* punctually, on time; (come al solito) as usual

pun'tura *nf* (di ago ecc) prick; Med puncture; (iniezione) injection; (fitta) stabbing pain. **puntura d'ape** bee sting. **puntura d'insetto** insect bite. **puntura di spillo** pinprick. **puntura di zanzara** mosquito bite

punzecchi'are *vt* prick; fig tease

punzo'nare *vt* Techn punch, stamp

pun'zone *nm* punch

può ▶ POTERE; **~ darsi** maybe, perhaps

'pupa *nf* doll

pu'pazzo *nm* puppet. **pupazzo di neve** snowman

pup'illa *nf* Anat pupil

pu'pillo, -a *nmf* Jur ward; (di professore) favourite

purché *conj* provided

'pure ① *adv* too, also; (concessivo) **fate ~!** please do!; **io ~** me too; **è venuto ~ lui** he came too, he also came

② *conj* (tuttavia) yet; (anche se) even if; **pur di** just to

purè *nm* purée. **purè di patate** mashed potatoes, creamed potatoes

pu'rezza *nf* purity

'purga *nf* purge

pur'gante *nm* laxative

pur'gare *vt* purge

purga'torio *nm* purgatory

purifi'care *vt* purify

purificazi'one *nf* purification

pu'rista *nmf* purist

puri'tano, -a *adj* & *nmf* Puritan

'puro *adj* pure; ⟨vino ecc⟩ undiluted; **per ~ caso** by sheer chance, purely by chance. **puro cotone** *nm* pure cotton, 100% cotton; **pura lana vergine** *nf* pure new wool; **pura seta** *nf* pure silk

puro'sangue *adj* & *nm* thoroughbred

pur'troppo *adv* unfortunately

pus *nm* pus

'pustola *nf* pimple

puti'ferio *nm* uproar

putre'fare *vi* putrefy

putre'farsi *vr* putrefy

putre'fatto *adj* rotten

putrefazi'one *nf* putrefaction

'putrido *adj* putrid

putt *nm inv* putt

put'tana *nf* vulg whore

'puzza *nf* stink; **avere la ~ sotto il naso** be sniffy

puz'zare *vi* anche fig stink; **~ di bruciato** fig smell fishy; **~ d'imbroglio** stink; **~ di corruzione** stink of corruption; **questa storia mi puzza** the story stinks

'puzzo *nm* stink

'puzzola *nf* polecat

puzzo'lente *adj* stinking

puz'zone *nm* fam bastard

p.zza *abbr* (**piazza**) Sq.

Qq

Qatar *nm* Qatar

QI *abbr* (**quoziente di intelligenza**) IQ

qua *adv* here; **da un anno in ~** for the last year; **da quando in ~?** since when?; **di ~** this way; **di ~ di** on this side of; **~ dentro** in here; **~ sotto** under here; **~ vicino** near here; **~ e là** here and there

'quacchero, -a *nmf* Quaker

qua'derno *nm* exercise book; (per appunti) notebook. **quaderno a quadretti** maths exercise book. **quaderno a righe** lined exercise book

quadrango'lare *adj* ⟨forma⟩ quadrangular; **incontro quadrangolare** Sport four-sided tournament

qua'drangolo *nm* quadrangle

qua'drante *nm* quadrant; (di orologio) dial

qua'drare ① *vt* square; ⟨contabilità⟩ balance
② *vi* fit in

qua'drato ① *adj* square; (equilibrato) level-headed
② *nm* square; (nel pugilato) ring; **al ~** squared

quadra'tura *nf* Math squaring; (di bilancio) balancing

quadret'tare *vt* divide into small squares

quadret'tato *adj* squared; ⟨carta⟩ graph attrib; ⟨tessuto⟩ check, checked

qua'dretto *nm* square; (piccolo quadro) small picture; **a quadretti** ⟨tessuto⟩ check

quadricro'mia *nf* four-colour printing

quadrien'nale *adj* (che dura quattro anni) four-year; (ogni quattro anni) four-yearly

quadri'foglio *nm* four-leaf clover

qua'driglia *nf* square dance

quadri'latero *nm* quadrilateral

quadri'mestre *nm* (periodo) four-month period; Sch term

quadrimo'tore *nm* four-engined plane

quadri'nomio *nm* Math quadrinomial

quadripar'tito ① *adj* four-party
② *nm* (politica) four-party government

quadri'plegico *adj* quadriplegic

'quadro *nm* picture, painting; (quadrato) square; (fig: scena) sight; (tabella) table; Theat scene; (dirigente) executive; **fare il ~ della situazione** outline the situation; **fuori ~** Cinema, TV out of shot; **quadri** *pl* (carte) diamonds; **a quadri** ⟨tessuto, giacca, motivo⟩ check, checked. **quadro clinico** case history. **quadro di comando** control panel; **quadri** *pl* **direttivi** senior management. **quadro di distribuzione** Electr switchboard; **quadri** *pl* **intermedi** middle management. **quadro degli interruttori** switch panel. **quadro degli strumenti** instrument panel

qua'drupede *nm* quadruped

quadrupli'care *vt* quadruple

quadrupli'carsi *vr* quadruple

qua'druplice *adj* quadruple

'quadruplo *adj & nm* quadruple

quaggiù *adv* down here

'quaglia *nf* quail

'qualche *adj* (alcuni) a few, some; (un certo) some; (in interrogative) any; **ho ~ problema** I have a few problems, I have some problems; **~ tempo fa** some time ago; **hai ~ libro italiano?** have you any Italian books?; **posso prendere ~ libro?** can I take some books?; **in ~ modo** somehow; **in ~ posto** somewhere; **~ volta** sometimes; **~ cosa = qualcosa**

qualche'duno *pron* somebody, someone

qual'cosa *pron* something; (in interrogative) anything; **qualcos'altro** something else; **vuoi qualcos'altro?** would you like anything else?; **~ di strano** something strange; **vuoi ~ da mangiare?** would you like something to eat?; **vuoi ~ da bere?** would you like something to drink?, would you like something to drink?

qual'cuno *pron* someone, somebody; (in interrogative) anyone, anybody; (alcuni) some; (in interrogative) any; **qualcun altro** someone else, somebody else; **c'è qualcun altro che aspetta?** is anybody else waiting?; **ho letto ~ dei suoi libri** I've read some of his books; **conosci ~ dei suoi amici?** do you know any of his friends?

'quale ① *adj* which; (indeterminato) what; (come) as, like; ~ **macchina è la tua?** which car is yours?; ~ **motivo avrà di parlare così?** what reason would he have to speak like that?; ~ **onore!** what an honour!; **città quali Venezia** towns like Venice; ~ **che sia la tua opinione** whatever you may think
② *pron inter* which [one]; ~ **preferisci?** which [one] do you prefer?
③ *pron rel* **il/la** ~ (persona) who; (animale, cosa) that, which; (oggetto: con prep) whom; (oggetto: animale, cosa) which; **ho incontrato tua madre, la** ~ **mi ha detto...** I met your mother who told me...; **l'ufficio nel** ~ **lavoro** the office in which I work; **l'uomo con il** ~ **parlavo** the man to whom I was speaking
④ *adv* (come) as

qua'lifica *nf* qualification; (titolo) title

qualifi'cabile *adj* qualifiable

qualifi'care *vt* qualify; (definire) define

qualifi'carsi *vr* be placed

qualifica'tivo *adj* qualifying

qualifi'cato *adj* ⟨operaio⟩ semi-skilled

qualificazi'one *nf* qualification

qualità *nf inv* quality; (specie) kind; **in** ~ **di** in one's capacity as; **di prima** ~ high quality; **di ottima/cattiva** ~ top/poor quality

qualitativa'mente *adv* qualitatively

qualita'tivo *adj* qualitative

qua'lora *conj* in case

qualsiasi, qualunque *adj* any; (non importa quale) whatever; (ordinario) ordinary; **dammi una penna** ~ give me any pen [whatsoever]; **farei** ~ **cosa** I would do anything; ~ **cosa io faccia** whatever I do; ~ **persona** anyone, anybody; **in** ~ **caso** in any case; **uno** ~ any one, whichever; **l'uomo qualunque** the man in the street; **vivo in una casa** ~ I live in an ordinary house

qualunqu'ismo *nm* lack of political views

qualunqu'ista *nmf* (menefreghista) person with no political views

'quando *conj & adv* when; **da** ~ **ti ho visto** since I saw you; **da** ~ **esci con lui?** how long have you been going out with him?; **da** ~ **in qua?** since when?; ~**... ** ~**...** sometimes..., sometimes...; **continua ad insistere** ~ **sa di avere torto** he keeps on insisting even when he knows he's wrong

quantifi'cabile *adj* quantifiable

quantifi'care *vt* quantify

quantità *nf inv* quantity, amount; **una** ~ **di** (gran numero) a great deal of

quantitativa'mente *adv* quantitatively

quantita'tivo ① *nm* amount
② *adj* quantitative

'quanto ① *adj inter* how much; (con nomi plurali) how many; (in esclamazione) what a lot of; (tempo) how long; **quanti anni hai?** how old are you?
② *adj rel* as much...as; (tempo) as long as; (con nomi plurali) as many... as; **prendi** ~ **denaro ti serve** take as much money as you need; **prendi quanti libri vuoi** take as many books as you like
③ *pron inter* how much; (quanto tempo) how long; (plurale) how many; **quanti ne abbiamo oggi?** what date is it today?
④ *pron rel* as much as; (quanto tempo) as long as; (plurale) as many as; **prendine** ~/ **quanti ne vuoi** take as much/as many as you like; **stai** ~ **vuoi** stay as long as you like; **questo è** ~ that's it
⑤ *adv inter* how much; (quanto tempo) how long; ~ **sei alto** how tall are you?; ~ **hai aspettato?** how long did you wait for?; ~ **costa?** how much is it?; ~ **mi dispiace!** I'm so sorry!; **quant'è bello!** how nice!
⑥ *adv rel* as much as; **lavoro** ~ **posso** I work as much as I can; **è tanto intelligente** ~ **bello** he's as intelligent as he's good-looking; **in** ~ (in qualità di) as; (poiché) since; ~ **a** as for; **in** ~ **a me** as far as I'm concerned; **per** ~ however; **per** ~ **ne sappia** as far as I know; **per** ~ **mi riguarda** as far as I'm concerned; **per** ~ **mi sia simpatico** much as I like him; ~ **prima** (al più presto) as soon as possible

quan'tunque *conj* although

qua'ranta *adj & nm* forty

quaran'tena *nf* quarantine

quaran'tenne ① *adj* forty-year-old; (sulla quarantina) in his/her forties
② *nmf* forty-year-old; (sulla quarantina) person in his/her forties

quaran'tennio *nm* period of forty years

quaran'tesimo *adj & nm* fortieth

quaran'tina *nf* **una** ~ about forty

qua'resima *nf* Lent

quar'tetto *nm* quartet

quarti'ere *nm* district, area; Mil quarters *pl*; **quartieri** *pl* **alti** smart districts; **quartieri** *pl* **bassi** poor areas. **quartiere cinese** China-town. **quartiere dormitorio** dormitory town. **quartiere generale** headquarters. **quartiere a luci rosse** red light area. **quartiere residenziale** residential area

quar'tino *nm* (strumento musicale) instrument similar to a clarinet; Typ quarto; (di vino) quarter litre

'quarto ① *adj* fourth
② *nm* fourth; (quarta parte) quarter; **le sette e un** ~ [a] quarter past seven, [a] quarter after seven Am; **a tre quarti** (giacca, maniche) three-quarter length; **quarti** *pl* **di finale** quarter-finals. **quarto d'ora** quarter of an hour
③ *nf* (marcia) fourth [gear]

quarto'genito, -a *nmf* fourth child

quar'tultimo, **-a** *adj & nmf* fourth last

'quarzo *nm* quartz; **al ~** quartz. **quarzo rosa** rose quartz

'quasi ① *adv* almost, nearly; **~ mai** hardly ever
② *conj* (come se) as if; **~ ~ sto a casa** I'm tempted to stay home

quassù *adv* up here

qua'terna *nf* (lotto, tombola) set of four winning numbers

quater'nario *nm* (era) Quaternary

'quatto *adj* crouching; (silenzioso) silent; **starsene ~ ~** keep very quiet

quattordi'cenne *adj & nmf* fourteen-year-old

quattordi'cesimo *adj & nm* fourteenth

quat'tordici *adj & nm* fourteen

quat'trini *nmpl* money *sg*, dosh *sg fam*

'quattro *adj & nm* four; **dirne ~ a qualcuno** give somebody a piece of one's mind; **farsi in ~** (per qualcuno/per fare qualcosa) go to a lot of trouble (for somebody/to do something); **in ~ e quattr'otto** in a flash. **~ per ~** *nf inv* Auto four-wheel drive [vehicle], four-by-four; **a ~ tempi** Auto four-stroke

quat'trocchi *adv* **a ~** in private

quattrocen'tesco *adj* fifteenth-century

quattro'cento *adj & nm* four hundred; **il Quattrocento** the fifteenth century

quattro'mila *adj & nm* four thousand

Qué'bec *nm* Quebec

'quello ① *adj* that (*pl* those); **quell'albero** that tree; **quegli alberi** those trees; **quel cane** that dog; **quei cani** those dogs
② *pron* that [one] (*pl* those [ones]); **~ lì** that one over there; **~ che** the one that; (ciò che) what; **quelli che** the ones that, those that; **~ a destra** the one on the right

'quercia *nf* oak; **di ~** oak

que'rela *nf* [legal] action

quere'lante *nmf* plaintiff

quere'lare *vt* bring an action against

quere'lato, **-a** *nmf* defendant

que'sito *nm* question

questio'nare *vi* dispute

questio'nario *nm* questionnaire

quest'ione *nf* question; (faccenda) matter; (litigio) quarrel; **in ~** in doubt; **è fuori ~** it's out of the question; **è ~ di vita o di morte** it's a matter of life and death; **mettere qualcosa in ~** cast doubt on something; **una ~ personale** a personal matter

'questo ① *adj* this (*pl* these)
② *pron* this [one] (*pl* these [ones]); **~ qui**, **~ qua** this one here; **~ è quello che ha detto** that's what he said; **per ~** for this *or* that reason; **quest'oggi** today

que'store *nm* chief of police

'questua *nf* collection

que'stura *nf* police headquarters

qui ① *adv* here; **da ~ in poi**, **da ~ in avanti** from now on; **di ~ a una settimana** in a week's time; **fin ~** (nel tempo) up till now, until now; **~ dentro** in here; **~ sotto** under here; **~ vicino** *adv* near here
② *nm* **~ pro quo** misunderstanding

quie'scenza *nf* (di vulcano) dormancy; (pensione) retirement; **trattamento di quiescenza** retirement package

quie'tanza *nf* receipt

quie'tare *vt* calm

quie'tarsi *vr* calm down

qui'ete *nf* quiet; **disturbo della quiete pubblica** breach of the peace; **stato di quiete** Phys state of rest

qui'eto *adj* quiet

'quindi ① *adv* then
② *conj* therefore

quindi'cenne *adj & nmf* fifteen-year-old

quindi'cesimo *adj & nm* fifteenth

'quindici *adj & nm* fifteen; **~ giorni** a fortnight Br, two weeks *pl*

quindi'cina *nf* **una ~** about fifteen; **una ~ di giorni** a fortnight Br, two weeks *pl*

quindici'nale ① *adj* fortnightly Br, twice-monthly
② *nm* fortnightly magazine Br, twice-monthly magazine

quinquen'nale *adj* (che dura cinque anni) five-year; (ogni cinque anni) five-yearly

quin'quennio *nm* [period of] five years

'quinta *nf* Auto fifth [gear], overdrive

quin'tale *nm* a hundred kilograms

'quinte *nfpl* Theat wings

quintes'senza *nf* quintessence

quin'tetto *nm* quintet

'quinto *adj & nm* fifth

quintupli'care *vt* quintuple

quin'tuplo *adj* quintuple

qui'squilia *nf* trifle; **perdersi in quisquilie** get bogged down in details

quiz *nm inv* [gioco a] quiz quiz game. **quiz radiofonico** radio quiz

'quota *nf* quota; (rata) instalment; (altitudine) height; Aeron altitude, height; (ippica) odds *pl*; **perdere/prendere ~** lose/gain altitude *or* height; **da alta ~** high-flying. **quota fissa** fixed amount. **quota non imponibile** personal allowance. **quota di iscrizione** entry fee; (di club) membership fee. **quota di mercato** market share. **quota zero** sea level

quo'tare *vt* Comm quote

quo'tato *adj* quoted; **essere ~ in Borsa** be quoted on the Stock Exchange

quotazi'one *nf* quotation. **quotazione d'acquisto** buying rate. **quotazione** ···:

ufficiale (in Borsa) official quotation.
quotazione di vendita selling rate
quotidiana'mente *adv* daily
quotidi'ano ①︎ *adj* daily; (ordinario)
everyday

②︎ *nm* daily [paper]
'quoto *nm* Math quotient
quozi'ente *nm* quotient. **quoziente
d'intelligenza** intelligence quotient, IQ.
quoziente di purezza purity

Rr

ra'barbaro *nm* rhubarb
'rabbia *nf* rage; (ira) anger; Med rabies *sg*;
che ∼! what a nuisance!; **mi fa** ∼ it
makes me angry
'rabbico *adj* ⟨virus⟩ rabies *attrib*
rab'bino *nm* rabbi
rabbiosa'mente *adv* furiously
rabbi'oso *adj* hot-tempered; Med rabid;
(violento) violent
rabboc'care *vt* top up ⟨fiasco⟩
rabbo'nire *vt* pacify
rabbo'nirsi *vr* calm down
rabbrivi'dire *vi* shudder; (di freddo)
shiver
rabbuf'fare *vt* reprimand; ruffle
⟨capelli⟩
rab'buffo *nm* reprimand
rabbui'arsi *vr* get dark; ⟨viso⟩ darken
rabdo'mante *nmf* water diviner
rabdoman'zia *nf* water divining
raccapez'zare *vt* put together
raccapez'zarsi *vr* see one's way ahead
raccapricci'ante *adj* horrifying
raccatta'palle ①︎ *nm inv* ball boy
②︎ *nf inv* ball girl
raccat'tare *vt* pick up
rac'chetta *nf* racket. **racchetta da
neve** snowshoe. **racchetta da ping
pong** table-tennis bat. **racchetta da
sci** ski stick, ski pole. **racchetta da
tennis** tennis racket
'racchio *adj* fam ugly
racchi'udere *vt* contain
rac'cogliere *vt* pick; (da terra) pick up;
(mietere) harvest; (collezionare) collect;
(radunare) gather; win ⟨voti ecc⟩; (dare asilo a)
take in
rac'cogliersi *vr* gather; (concentrarsi)
collect one's thoughts
raccogli'mento *nm* concentration
raccogli|'tore, -trice ①︎ *nmf* collector
②︎ *nm* **raccoglitore a fogli mobili**
ring-binder
rac'colta *nf* collection; (di scritti)
compilation; (del grano ecc) harvesting;
(adunata) gathering; **chiamare a** ∼ call *or*

gather together. **raccolta
differenziata** collection of items for
recycling. **raccolta di fondi** fund-
raising
rac'colto, -a ①︎ pp di RACCOGLIERE
②︎ *adj* (rannicchiato) hunched; (intimo) cosy;
(concentrato) engrossed
③︎ *nm* (mietitura) harvest
raccoman'dabile *adj* advisable; **poco**
∼ ⟨persona⟩ shady
raccoman'dare *vt* recommend; (affidare)
entrust
raccoman'darsi *vr* (implorare) beg
raccoman'data *nf* letter sent by
recorded delivery, certified mail Am; **per**
∼ by recorded delivery. **raccomandata
con ricevuta di ritorno** letter sent by
recorded delivery with acknowledgement
of receipt
raccoman'data-e'spresso *nf*
express recorded delivery service
raccomandazi'one *nf*
recommendation
raccomo'dare *vt* repair
raccon'tare *vt* tell
rac'conto *nm* story. **racconto
dell'orrore** horror story
raccorci'are *vt* shorten
raccorci'arsi *vr* become shorter;
⟨giorni⟩ draw in
raccor'dare *vt* join
rac'cordo *nm* connection; ⟨stradale⟩
feeder. **raccordo anulare** ring road.
raccordo autostradale motorway
junction Br, intersection. **raccordo
ferroviario** siding. **raccordo a
gomito** elbow
ra'chitico *adj* rickety; (poco sviluppato)
stunted
racimo'lare *vt* scrape together
'racket *nm inv* racket
'rada *nf* Naut roads *pl*
'radar *nm inv* radar; **uomo radar** air
traffic controller
radden'sare *vt* thicken
radden'sarsi *vr* thicken
raddob'bare *vt* refit

rad'dobbo *nm* refit

raddol'cire *vt* sweeten; fig soften

raddol'cirsi *vr* become milder; ⟨*carattere*⟩ mellow

raddoppia'mento *nm* doubling

raddoppi'are *vt* double; increase twofold

rad'doppio *nm* doubling, twofold increase; (equitazione) gallop; (biliardo) double

raddriz'zabile *adj* which can be straightened

raddriz'zare *vt* straighten

raddrizza'tore *nm* (di corrente) rectifier

ra'dente *adj* grazing, shaving; **tiro radente** Mil grazing fire; Sport low shot just skimming the surface; **volo radente** Aeron hedge-hopping

'radere *vt* shave; graze ⟨*muro*⟩; ∼ **al suolo** raze [to the ground]

'radersi *vr* shave

radi'ale *adj* radial

radi'ante ① *adj* radiant ② *nm* Math radian

radi'are *vt* strike off; ∼ **dall'albo** strike off ⟨*medico*⟩; debar ⟨*avvocato*⟩

radia'tore *nm* radiator

radiazi'one *nf* radiation. **radiazione nucleare** nuclear radiation

'radica *nf* briar

radi'cale ① *adj* radical ② *nm* Gram root; Pol radical

radical'mente *adv* radically

radi'carsi *vr* ∼ **in** be rooted in

radi'cato *adj* deep-seated

ra'dicchio *nm* chicory

ra'dice *nf* root; **mettere [le] radici** ⟨*pianta*⟩ take root; fig put down roots. **radice quadrata** square root

'radio ① *nf inv* radio; **via** ∼ by radio; **contatto radio** radio contact; **ponte radio** radio link. **radio pirata** pirate radio. **radio portatile** portable radio. **radio ricevente** receiver. **radio [a] transistor** transistor radio. **radio trasmittente** transmitter ② *nm* Chem radium

radioama‖'tore, **-trice** *nmf* radio ham

radioascolta‖'tore, **-trice** *nmf* listener

radioassi'stito *adj* radio-assisted

radioattività *nf* radioactivity

radioat'tivo *adj* radioactive

radiobiolo'gia *nf* radiobiology

radio'bussola *nf* radio compass

radiocoman'dare *vt* operate by remote control

radiocoman'dato *adj* remote-controlled, radio-controlled

radio'cronaca *nf* radio commentary; **fare la** ∼ **di** commentate on

radiocro'nista *nmf* radio reporter

radiodiffusi'one *nf* broadcasting

radio'faro *nm* radio beacon

radio'fonico *adj* radio *attrib*

radiofre'quenza *nf* radio frequency

radiogo'niometro *nm* direction finder, radiogoniometer

radiogra'fare *vt* X-ray

radiogra'fia *nf* X-ray [photograph]; (radiologia) radiography; **fare una** ∼ ⟨*paziente*⟩ have an X-ray; ⟨*dottore*⟩ take an X-ray

radio'lina *nf* transistor

radiolocaliz'zare *vt* locate by radar

radiolo'gia *nf* radiology

radi'ologo, **-a** *nmf* radiologist

radio'onda *nf* radio wave

radioregistra'tore *nm* **radioregistratore portatile** portable radio cassette recorder

radiosco'pia *nf* Med radioscopy

radio'scopico *adj* radioscopic

radi'oso *adj* radiant

radio'spia *nf* bug

radio'sveglia *nf* radio alarm, clock radio

radio'taxi *nm inv* radio taxi

radiote'lefono *nm* radio-telephone; (privato) cordless [phone]

radiotelevi'sivo *adj* broadcasting *attrib*

radiotera'pia *nf* radiotherapy

radiotra'smettere *vt* radio

radiotrasmetti'tore *nm* radio

radiotrasmit'tente *nf* radio station

'rado *adj* sparse; (non frequente) rare; **di** ∼ seldom

radu'nare *vt* gather [together]

radu'narsi *vr* gather [together]

radu'nata *nf* gathering. **radunata sediziosa** seditious assembly

ra'duno *nm* meeting; Sport rally

ra'dura *nf* clearing

'rafano *nm* horseradish

raffazzo'nato *adj* ⟨*discorso, lavoro*⟩ botched

raf'fermo *adj* stale

'raffica *nf* gust; (di armi da fuoco) burst; (di domande, insulti) barrage

raffigu'rare *vt* represent

raffigurazi'one *nf* representation

raffi'nare *vt* refine

raffinata'mente *adv* elegantly

raffina'tezza *nf* refinement

raffi'nato *adj* refined

raffine'ria *nf* refinery. **raffineria di petrolio** oil refinery

rafforza'mento *nm* reinforcement; (di muscolatura, carattere) strengthening

raffor'zare *vt* reinforce

rafforza'tivo ① *adj* Gram intensifying ② *nm* Gram intensifier

raffredda'mento *nm* (processo) cooling; di ∼ cooling. **raffreddamento ad acqua** water-cooling. **raffreddamento ad aria** air-cooling

raffred'dare *vt* cool

raffred'darsi *vr* get cold; (prendere un raffreddore) catch a cold; ⟨sentimento, passione⟩ cool [off]

raffred'dato *adj* **essere** ∼ ⟨persona⟩ have a cold

raffred'dore *nm* cold; **avere il** ∼ have a cold. **raffreddore da fieno** hay fever

raf'fronto *nm* comparison

'rafia *nf* raffia

Rag. *abbr* **ragioniere**

ra'gazza *nf* girl; (fidanzata) girlfriend; **nome da ragazza** maiden name. **ragazza copertina** cover girl. **ragazza madre** unmarried mother. **ragazza alla pari** au pair [girl]. **ragazza squillo** call girl

ragaz'zata *nf* prank

ra'gazzo *nm* boy; (fidanzato) boyfriend; **da** ∼ (da giovane) as a boy. **ragazzo padre** unmarried father. **ragazzo di strada** guttersnipe. **ragazzo di vita** rent boy

ragge'lare *vt* fig freeze

ragge'larsi *vr* fig turn to ice

raggi'ante *adj* radiant

raggi'era *nf* (di ruota) spokes *pl*; **a** ∼ with a pattern like spokes radiating from a centre

'raggio *nm* ray; Math radius; (di ruota) spoke; **a raggi infrarossi** infrared. **raggio d'azione** range. **raggio laser** laser beam. **raggio di luna** moonbeam. **raggio di sole** ray of sunshine, sunbeam. **raggio di speranza** ray of hope. **raggio ultravioletto** ultraviolet ray; **raggi** *pl* **X** X-rays

raggi'rare *vt* trick, deceive

rag'giro *nm* trick, con trick

raggi'ungere *vt* reach; (conseguire) achieve

raggiun'gibile *adj* ⟨luogo⟩ within reach

raggiungi'mento *nm* attainment

raggomito'lare *vt* wind

raggomito'larsi *vr* curl up

raggranel'lare *vt* scrape together

raggrin'zire *vt* wrinkle

raggrin'zirsi *vr* wrinkle

raggru'mare *vt* curdle ⟨latte⟩

raggru'marsi *vr* ⟨latte⟩ curdle

raggruppa'mento *nm* (gruppo) group; (azione) grouping; Comm groupage

raggrup'pare *vt* group together

ragguagli'are *vt* compare; (informare) inform

raggu'aglio *nm* comparison; (informazione) information

ragguar'devole *adj* considerable

'ragia *nf* resin; **acqua** ∼ turpentine

ragià *nm inv* rajah

ragiona'mento *nm* reasoning; (discussione) discussion. **ragionamento per assurdo** reductio ad absurdum

ragio'nare *vi* reason; (discutere) discuss

ragio'nato *adj* ⟨argomento⟩ reasoned; ⟨cruciverba⟩ cryptic

ragi'one *nf* reason; (ciò che è giusto) right; **a** ∼ **o a torto** rightly or wrongly; **aver** ∼ be right; **perdere la** ∼ go out of one's mind; **a ragion veduta** after due consideration; **prenderle/darle di santa** ∼ get/give a good walloping; **ragion d'essere** raison d'être. **ragione di scambio** terms of trade. **ragione sociale** company name; **ragion di Stato** reasons *pl* of State

ragione'ria *nf* accountancy; (scuola) secondary school which provides training in accountancy

ragio'nevole *adj* reasonable

ragionevol'mente *adv* reasonably

ragioni'ere, -a *nmf* accountant

ra'glan *adj inv* ⟨manica⟩ raglan

ragli'are *vi* bray

'raglio *nm* bray

ragna'tela *nf* cobweb, web, spider web

'ragno *nm* spider

ragù *nm inv* meat sauce

RAI *nf abbr* (**Radio Audizioni Italiane**) Italian public broadcasting company

'raid *nm inv* raid

'raion® *nm* rayon®

ra'lenti *nm* **al** ∼ in slow motion

rallegra'menti *nmpl* congratulations

ralle'grare *vt* gladden

ralle'grarsi *vr* rejoice; ∼ **con qualcuno** congratulate somebody

rallenta'mento *nm* slowing down

rallen'tare *vt/i* slow down; (allentare) slacken

rallen'tarsi *vr* slow down

rallenta'tore *nm* (su strada) speed bump; **al** ∼ in slow motion

'rally *nm inv* rally

RAM *nf* RAM

ramai'olo *nm* ladle

raman'zina *nf* reprimand

ra'mare *vt* stake ⟨pianta⟩

ra'marro *nm* (animale) type of lizard

ra'mato *adj* ⟨capelli⟩ copper[-coloured], coppery

'rame *nm* copper; **color** ∼ copper-coloured

ramifi'care *vi* ⟨pianta⟩ put out branches

ramifi'carsi *vr* ⟨pianta⟩ put out branches; ⟨strada, fiume ecc⟩ branch; ⟨teoria⟩ ramify, branch

ramificazi'one *nf* ramification

ra'mino *nm* rummy

rammari'carsi *vr* ∼ **di** regret; (lamentarsi) complain (**di** about)

ram'marico *nm* regret

rammen'dare *vt* darn

ram'mendo *nm* darning

rammen'tare *vt* remember; ∼ **qualcosa a qualcuno** (richiamare alla memoria) remind somebody of something

rammen'tarsi *vr* remember

rammol'lire *vt* soften

rammol'lirsi *vr* go soft

rammol'lito, -a *nmf* wimp

'ramo *nm* branch

ramo'scello *nm* twig

'rampa *nf* (di scale) flight. **rampa d'accesso** slip road. **rampa di carico** loading ramp. **rampa di lancio** launch[ing] pad

ram'pante *adj* ⟨leone, cavallo⟩ rampant; **giovane** ∼ yuppie

rampi'cante ① *adj* climbing ② *nm* Bot creeper

ram'pino *nm* hook; fig pretext

ram'pollo *nm* hum brat; (discendente) descendant

ram'pone *nm* harpoon; (per scarpe) crampon

'rana *nf* frog; (nel nuoto) breaststroke; **uomo rana** frogman

ranch *nm inv* ranch

'rancido *adj* rancid

'rancio *nm* rations *pl*

ran'core *nm* rancour, resentment; **serbare** ∼ **verso qualcuno** bear somebody a grudge

'randa *nf* mainsail

ran'dagio *adj* stray

randel'lata *nf* blow with a club

ran'dello *nm* club

'rango *nm* rank

rannicchi'arsi *vr* huddle up

rannuvola'mento *nm* clouding over

rannuvo'larsi *vr* cloud over

ra'nocchio *nm* frog

ranto'lare *vi* wheeze

'rantolo *nm* wheeze; (di moribondo) death rattle

ra'nuncolo *nm* buttercup

'rapa *nf* turnip

ra'pace *adj* rapacious; ⟨uccello⟩ predatory

rapa'nello *nm* radish

ra'pare *vt* crop

ra'parsi *vr* fam have one's head shaved

'rapida *nf* rapids *pl*

rapida'mente *adv* quickly, rapidly

rapidità *nf* speed

'rapido ① *adj* fast, quick; ⟨guarigione, sviluppo⟩ rapid ② *nm* (treno) express [train]

rapi'mento *nm* (crimine) kidnapping

ra'pina *nf* robbery, hold-up fam. **rapina a mano armata** armed robbery. **rapina in banca** bank robbery

rapi'nare *vt* rob

rapina'tore *nm* robber. **rapinatore di banca** bank robber

ra'pire *vt* abduct; (per riscatto) kidnap; (fig: estasiare) ravish

ra'pito, -a ① *adj* abducted; (per riscatto) kidnapped; (estasiato) rapt ② *nmf* kidnap victim

rapi'tore, -trice *nmf* kidnapper

rappacifi'care *vt* pacify

rappacifi'carsi *vr* be reconciled, make it up

rappacificazi'one *nf* reconciliation

'rapper *nmf inv* Mus rapper

rappez'zare *vt* patch up

rappor'tare *vt* reproduce ⟨disegno⟩; (confrontare) compare

rap'porto *nm* report; (connessione) relation; (legame) relationship; Math, Techn ratio; **rapporti** *pl* relations, relationship; **essere in buoni rapporti** be on good terms; **rapporti** *pl* **d'affari** business relations. **rapporto di amicizia** friendship; **avere un** ∼ **di amicizia con qualcuno** be friends with somebody. **rapporto di lavoro** working relationship. **rapporto di parentela** family relationship; **avere un** ∼ **di parentela con qualcuno** be related to somebody; **rapporti** *pl* **prematrimoniali** premarital sex. **rapporto prezzo-prestazioni** price/performance ratio. **rapporto prezzo-qualità** value for money; **rapporti** *pl* **sessuali** sexual intercourse. **rapporto di trasmissione** Auto gear

rap'prendersi *vr* set; ⟨latte⟩ curdle

rappre'saglia *nf* reprisal

rappresen'tante *nmf* representative. **rappresentante di classe** class representative. **rappresentante di commercio** sales representative, [sales] rep fam. **rappresentante sindacale** trade union representative

rappresen'tanza *nf* delegation; Comm agency; **spese di rappresentanza** entertainment expenses; **di** ∼ ⋯⟫

⟨*appartamento, macchina*⟩ company
attrib. **rappresentanza esclusiva** sole
agency. **rappresentanza legale** legal
representation. **rappresentanza
proporzionale** proportional
representation, PR

rappresen'tare *vt* represent; Theat
perform

rappresenta'tiva *nf* representatives *pl*

rappresenta'tivo *adj* representative

rappresentazi'one *nf* representation;
(spettacolo) performance

rap'preso *pp di* RAPPRENDERSI

rapso'dia *nf* rhapsody

'raptus *nm inv* fit of madness

rara'mente *adv* rarely, seldom

rare'fare *vt* rarefy

rare'farsi *vr* rarefy

rare'fatto *adj* rarefied

rarità *nf inv* rarity

'raro *adj* rare

ra'sare *vt* shave; trim ⟨*siepe ecc*⟩

ra'sarsi *vr* shave

ra'sato *adj* shaved

rasa'tura *nf* shaving

raschia'mento *nm* Med curettage

raschi'are *vt* scrape; (togliere) scrape off

raschi'arsi *vr* ∼ **la gola** clear one's
throat

rasen'tare *vt* go close to

ra'sente *prep* very close to

'raso ① *pp di* RADERE
② *adj* smooth; (colmo) full to the brim;
⟨*barba*⟩ close-cropped; ∼ **terra** close to the
ground; **un cucchiaio** ∼ a level spoonful
③ *nm* satin

ra'soio *nm* razor. **rasoio elettrico**
electric shaver. **rasoio a mano libera**
cut-throat razor

'raspa *nf* rasp

'raspo *nm* (di uva) small bunch

ras'segna *nf* review; (mostra) exhibition;
(musicale, cinematografica) festival; **passare in**
∼ review; Mil inspect

rasse'gnare *vt* present

rasse'gnarsi *vr* resign oneself

rassegnata'mente *adv* with
resignation

rasse'gnato *adj* ⟨*persona, aria, tono*⟩
resigned

rassegnazi'one *nf* resignation

rassere'nare *vt* clear; fig cheer up

rassere'narsi *vr* become clear; fig cheer
up

rasset'tare *vt* tidy up; (riparare) mend

rassicu'rante *adj* ⟨*persona, parole,
presenza*⟩ reassuring

rassicu'rare *vt* reassure

rassicurazi'one *nf* reassurance

rasso'dare *vt* harden; fig strengthen

rassomigli'ante *adj* similar

rassomigli'anza *nf* resemblance

rassomigli'are *vi* ∼ a resemble

rastrella'mento *nm* (di fieno) raking;
(perlustrazione) combing

rastrel'lare *vt* rake; (perlustrare) comb

rastrelli'era *nf* rack; (per biciclette)
bicycle rack; (scolapiatti) [plate] rack

ra'strello *nm* rake

'rata *nf* instalment; (di mutuo) mortgage
repayment; **pagare a rate** pay by
instalments; **comprare qualcosa a rate**
buy something on hire purchase, buy
something on the installment plan Am

rate'ale *adj* by instalments; **pagamento
rateale** payment by instalments; **vendita
rateale** hire purchase

rate'are, rateizzare *vt* divide into
instalments

ra'tifica *nf* Jur ratification

ratifi'care *vt* Jur ratify

'ratto¹ *nm* liter (rapimento) abduction

'ratto² *nm* (roditore) rat. **ratto comune**
black rat

rattop'pare *vt* patch

rat'toppo *nm* patch

rattrap'pire *vt* make stiff

rattrap'pirsi *vr* become stiff

rattri'stare *vt* sadden

rattri'starsi *vr* become sad

rau'cedine *nf* hoarseness

'rauco *adj* hoarse

rava'nello *nm* radish

ravi'oli *nmpl* ravioli *sg*

ravve'dersi *vr* mend one's ways

ravvi'are *vt* tidy ⟨*capelli, stanza*⟩

ravvicina'mento *nm* (tra persone)
reconciliation; Pol rapprochement

ravvici'nare *vt* bring closer; (riconciliare)
reconcile

ravvici'narsi *vr* be reconciled

ravvi'sare *vt* recognize

ravvi'vare *vt* revive; fig brighten up

ravvi'varsi *vr* revive

rav'volgere *vt* roll up

rav'volgersi *vr* wrap oneself up

'rayon® *nm* rayon

razio'cinio *nm* rational thought; (buon
senso) common sense

razio'nale *adj* rational

razionalità *nf* (raziocinio) rationality; (di
ambiente) functional nature

razionaliz'zare *vt* rationalize
⟨*programmi, metodi, spazio*⟩

razional'mente *adv* (con raziocinio)
rationally

raziona'mento *nm* rationing

razio'nare *vt* ration
razi'one *nf* ration
'razza *nf* race; (di cani ecc) breed; (genere) kind; **che ~ di idiota!** fam what an idiot!
raz'zia *nf* raid
razzi'ale *adj* racial
raz'zismo *nm* racism
raz'zista *adj & nmf* racist
'razzo *nm* rocket. **razzo da segnalazione** flare
razzo'lare *vi* ⟨polli⟩ scratch about
re *nm inv* king; (Mus: chiave, nota) D; **Re** *pl* **Magi** Wise Men
rea'gente *adj & nm* reactant
rea'gire *vi* react
re'ale *adj* real; (di re) royal
rea'lismo *nm* realism
rea'lista *nmf* realist; (fautore del re) royalist
realistica'mente *adv* realistically
rea'listico *adj* realistic
realiz'zabile *adj* feasible
realiz'zare *vt* (attuare) carry out, realize; Comm make; score ⟨gol, canestro⟩; (rendersi conto di) realize
realiz'zarsi *vr* come true; (nel lavoro ecc) fulfil oneself
realiz'zato *adj* ⟨persona⟩ fulfilled
realizzazi'one *nf* realization; (di sogno, persona) fulfilment. **realizzazione scenica** production
rea'lizzo *nm* (vendita) proceeds *pl*; (riscossione) yield
real'mente *adv* really
realtà *nf inv* reality; **in ~** in reality; (a dire il vero) actually. **realtà virtuale** virtual reality
re'ame *nm* realm
re'ato *nm* crime, criminal offence; **reati** *pl* **informatici** computer crime. **reato minore** minor offence
reattività *nf* reactivity; (a farmaco) reaction
reat'tivo *adj* reactive
reat'tore *nm* reactor; Aeron jet [aircraft]. **reattore nucleare** atomic reactor
reazio'nario, -a *adj & nmf* reactionary
reazi'one *nf* reaction; **a ~** ⟨motore, aereo⟩ jet. **reazione a catena** chain reaction. **reazione chimica** chemical reaction
'rebus *nm inv* rebus; (enigma) puzzle
recapi'tare *vt* deliver
re'capito *nm* address; (consegna) delivery; **in caso di mancato ~... if undelivered... recapito a domicilio** home delivery. **recapito telefonico** contact telephone number
re'care *vt* bear; (produrre) cause

re'carsi *vr* go
re'cedere *vi* recede; fig give up
recensi'one *nf* review
recen'sire *vt* review
recen'sore *nm* reviewer
re'cente *adj* recent; **di ~** recently
recente'mente *adv* recently
re'ception *nf inv* reception [desk]
re'ceptionist *nmf* receptionist
recessi'one *nf* recession
reces'sivo *adj* Biol recessive; Econ recessionary
re'cesso *nm* recess
re'cidere *vt* cut off
reci'diva *nf* Jur recidivism; Med relapse; **furto con ~** repeat offence of theft
recidività *nf* recidivism
reci'divo, -a ① *adj* Med recurrent ② *nmf* repeat offender, persistent offender, recidivist *fml*; **è ~** fig he's lapsed back into his old ways
recin'tare *vt* close off
re'cinto *nm* enclosure; (per animali) pen; (per bambini) playpen. **recinto delle grida** Fin [trading] floor. **recinto del peso** (ippica) weigh-in room
recinzi'one *nf* (azione) enclosure; (muro) wall; (rete) wire fence; (cancellata) railings *pl*
recipi'ente *nm* container
re'ciproco *adj* reciprocal
re'ciso ① pp di RECIDERE ② *adj* (risoluto) definite
'recita *nf* performance. **recita scolastica** school play
re'cital *nm inv* recital
reci'tare ① *vt* recite; Theat act; play ⟨ruolo⟩ ② *vi* act; **~ a soggetto** improvise
recitazi'one *nf* recitation; Theat acting; **scuola di ~** drama school
recla'mare ① *vi* protest ② *vt* claim
ré'clame *nf inv* advertising; (avviso pubblicitario) advertisement
reclamiz'zare *vt* advertise
re'clamo *nm* complaint; **ufficio reclami** complaints department
recli'nabile *adj* reclining; **sedile reclinabile** reclining seat
recli'nare *vt* tilt ⟨sedile⟩; lean ⟨capo⟩
reclusi'one *nf* imprisonment
re'cluso, -a ① *adj* secluded ② *nmf* prisoner
'recluta *nf* recruit
recluta'mento *nm* recruitment
reclu'tare *vt* recruit
re'condito *adj* secluded; (intimo) secret

'record ① *nm inv* record; **a tempo di ~** in record time
  ② *adj inv* ⟨*cifra*⟩ record *attrib*

recrimi'nare *vi* recriminate

recriminazi'one *nf* recrimination

recrude'scenza *nf* Med fresh outbreak; fig (di violenza) renewed outbreak; (di criminalità) upsurge

recupe'rare ① *vt* recover; rehabilitate ⟨*tossicodipendente*⟩; make up ⟨*ore di assenza*⟩; **~ il tempo perduto** make up for lost time
  ② *vi* catch up

re'cupero *nm* recovery; (di tossicodipendenti) rehabilitation; (salvataggio) rescue; **corso di recupero** additional classes *pl*; **materiali di recupero** recycled material; **(che possono essere recuperati)** recyclable material; **[minuti di] recupero** Sport injury time; **partita di recupero** rematch. **recupero crediti** debt collection. **recupero [dei] dati** data recovery

redargu'ire *vt* rebuke

re'datto *pp di* REDIGERE

redat'|tore, -trice *nmf* editor; (di testo) writer. **redattore capo** editor in chief

redazi'one *nf* (ufficio) editorial office; (di testi) editing

redditività *nf* earning power

reddi'tizio *adj* profitable

'reddito *nm* income; **a basso ~** ⟨*famiglia*⟩ low income. **imposta sul reddito** income tax. **reddito complessivo** gross income. **reddito imponibile** taxable income. **reddito non imponibile** non-taxable income. **reddito da lavoro** earned income; **redditi** *pl* **occasionali** casual earnings. **reddito pubblico** government revenue

re'dento *pp di* REDIMERE

reden'tore *nm* redeemer

redenzi'one *nf* redemption

re'digere *vt* write; draw up ⟨*documento*⟩

re'dimere *vt* redeem

re'dimersi *vr* redeem oneself

redi'mibile *adj* ⟨*titoli*⟩ redeemable

redin'gote *nf inv* frock-coat; **abito a redingote** fitted button-through dress

'redini *nfpl* reins

redi'vivo *adj* restored to life

'reduce ① *adj* **~ da** back from
  ② *nmf* survivor

refe'rendum *nm inv* referendum

refe'renza *nf* reference

referenzi'ato *adj* with references

re'ferto *nm* report. **referto medico** medical report

refet'torio *nm* refectory

reflazio'nare *vt* Econ reflate

reflazi'one *nf* Econ reflation

'reflex *nm inv* reflex camera

'refluo *nm* effluent

refrat'tario *adj* refractory; **essere ~ a** fig be insensitive to ⟨*sentimenti*⟩; **sono ~ alla matematica** maths are a closed book to me

refrige'rante *adj* cooling *attrib*

refrige'rare *vt* refrigerate

refrigerazi'one *nf* refrigeration

refur'tiva *nf* stolen goods *pl*

re'fuso *nm* Typ literal, typo

rega'lare *vt* give

re'gale *adj* regal

re'galo ① *nm* present, gift; **articoli da regalo** gifts
  ② *adj* **confezione regalo** gift set

re'gata *nf* regatta

'reggae *nm* Mus reggae

reg'gente *nmf* regent

reg'genza *nf* regency

'reggere ① *vt* (sorreggere) bear; (tenere in mano) hold; (dirigere) run; (governare) govern; Gram take
  ② *vi* (resistere) hold out; (durare) last; fig stand

'reggersi *vr* stand

'reggia *nf* royal palace

reggi'calze *nm inv* suspender belt

reggi'mento *nm* regiment; (fig: molte persone) army

reggi'petto, reggiseno *nm* bra

re'gia *nf* Cinema direction; Theat production

re'gime *nm* regime; (dieta) diet; (di fiume) rate of flow; **a ~ torrentizio** in spate; **a pieno ~** ⟨*funzionare*⟩ at full speed. **regime alimentare** diet. **regime fiscale** tax system. **regime di giri** (di motore) revs per minute, rpm. **regime militare** military regime. **regime monetario aureo** gold standard. **regime di vita** lifestyle

re'gina *nf* queen; **ape regina** queen bee. **regina madre** queen mother

'regio *adj* royal

regio'nale *adj* regional

regiona'lismo *nm* (parola) regionalism

regional'mente *adv* regionally

regi'one *nf* region

re'gista *nmf* Cinema, TV director; Theat producer

regi'strare *vt* register; Comm enter; (incidere su nastro) tape, record; (su disco) record

registra'tore *nm* recorder; (magnetofono) tape-recorder. **registratore di cassa** cash register. **registratore a cassette** tape recorder, cassette recorder. **registratore di volo** flight recorder

registrazi'one *nf* registration; Comm entry; (di programma) recording; **sala di registrazione** recording studio.
registrazione [dei] dati data capture

re'gistro *nm* register; (ufficio) registry. **registro di bordo** log. **registro di cassa** ledger. **registro di classe** class register; **registro linguistico** register

re'gnare *vi* reign

'regno *nm* kingdom; (sovranità) reign. **regno animale** animal kingdom. **Regno Unito** United Kingdom. **regno vegetale** plant kingdom

'regola *nf* rule; **essere in** ∼ be in order; ⟨persona⟩ have one's papers in order; **a** ∼ **d'arte** in a workmanlike fashion

rego'labile *adj* ⟨velocità, luminosità⟩ adjustable

regola'mento *nm* regulation; Comm settlement. **regolamento di conti** settling of scores

rego'lare ① *adj* regular
② *vt* regulate; (ridurre, moderare) limit; (sistemare) settle

regolarità *nf* regularity

regolariz'zare *vt* settle ⟨debito⟩; regularize ⟨situazione⟩

rego'larsi *vr* (agire) act; (moderarsi) control oneself

rego'lata *nf* **darsi una** ∼ pull oneself together

regola'tore, -trice ① *adj* **piano regolatore** urban development plan
② *nmf* regulator

'regolo *nm* ruler. **regolo calcolatore** slide-rule

regre'dire *vi* Biol, Psych regress

regressi'one *nf* regression

regres'sivo *adj* regressive

re'gresso *nm* decline

reincar'narsi *vr* ∼ **in...** be reincarnated as...

reincarnazi'one *nf* reincarnation

reinseri'mento *nm* (di persona) reintegration

reinser'irsi *vr* (in ambiente) reintegrate

reinstal'lare *vt* reinstall

reinte'grare *vt* restore

reinven'tare *vt* reinvent

reinvesti'mento *nm* reinvestment

reinve'stire *vt* reinvest ⟨soldi⟩

reite'rare *vt* reiterate

reiterazi'one *nf* reiteration

re'lais *nm inv* relay

relativa'mente *adv* relatively; ∼ **a** as regards

relatività *nf* relativity

rela'tivo *adj* relative

rela|'tore, -trice *nmf* (in una conferenza) speaker; (di tesi) supervisor

re'lax *nm* relaxation

relazi'one *nf* relation; (di lavoro ecc) relationship; (rapporto amoroso) [love] affair; (resoconto) report; **pubbliche relazioni** *pl* public relations. **relazione extraconiugale** extramarital relationship; **relazioni** *pl* **industriali** industrial relations

rele'gare *vt* relegate

relegazi'one *nf* relegation

religi'one *nf* religion

religi'oso, -a ① *adj* religious
② *nm* monk
③ *nf* nun

re'liquia *nf* relic

reliqui'ario *nm* reliquary

re'litto *nm* wreck

re'mainder *nm inv* (libro) remainder

re'make *nm inv* remake

re'mare *vi* row

rema|'tore, -trice *nmf* rower

remini'scenza *nf* reminiscence

remissi'one *nf* remission; (sottomissione) submissiveness. **remissione del debito** remission of debt. **remissione di querela** withdrawal of an action

remissiva'mente *adv* submissively

remis'sivo *adj* submissive

re'mix *nm inv* Mus remix

'remo *nm* oar

'remora *nf* **senza remore** without hesitation

re'moto *adj* remote

remo'vibile *adj* removable

remune'rare *vt* remunerate

remunera'tivo *adj* remunerative

remunerazi'one *nf* remuneration

re'nale *adj* renal, kidney *attrib*

'rendere *vt* (restituire) return; (esprimere) render; (fruttare) yield; (far diventare) make

'rendersi *vr* become; ∼ **conto di qualcosa** realize something; ∼ **utile** make oneself useful

rendi'conto *nm* report

rendi'mento *nm* rendering; (produzione) yield

'rendita *nf* income; (dello Stato) revenue; **vivere di** ∼ fig rest on one's laurels. **rendita vitalizia** life annuity

'rene *nm* kidney. **rene artificiale** kidney machine

'reni *nfpl* (schiena) back

reni'tente ① *adj* **essere** ∼ **a** ⟨consigli di qualcuno⟩ be loath to accept; refuse to obey ⟨legge⟩
② *nm* **renitente alla leva** person who fails to report for military service after being called up, draft dodger Am

'renna *nf* reindeer (*pl inv*); (pelle) buckskin

'**Reno** *nm* Rhine

'**reo, -a** ① *adj* guilty
② *nmf* criminal. **reo confesso** self-confessed criminal

Rep. *abbr* (**repubblica**) Rep.

re'**parto** *nm* department; Mil unit; **reparti** *pl* **d'assalto** Mil assault troops. **reparto d'attacco** Sport attack. **reparto difensivo** Sport defence. **reparto grandi ustionati** Med burns unit. **reparto di massima sicurezza** secure unit. **reparto maternità** maternity ward. **reparto radiologia** X-ray unit

repel'**lente** *adj* repulsive

repen'**taglio** *nm* **mettere a** ∼ risk

repentina'**mente** *adv* suddenly

repen'**tino** *adj* sudden

reper'**ibile** *adj* available; **non è** ∼ (perduto) it's not to be found

reperibi'**lità** *nf* availability

repe'**rire** *vt* trace ⟨fondi⟩

re'**perto** *nm* **reperto archeologico** find. **reperto giudiziario** exhibit

reper'**torio** *nm* repertory; (elenco) index; **immagini** *pl* **di repertorio** archive footage

re'**play** *nm inv* [instant] replay

'**replica** *nf* reply; (obiezione) objection; (copia) replica; Theat repeat performance

repli'**care** *vt* reply; Theat repeat

repor'**tage** *nm inv* report

repressi'**one** *nf* repression

repres'**sivo** *adj* repressive

re'**presso** *pp di* REPRIMERE

re'**primere** *vt* repress

re'**pubblica** *nf* republic. **Repubblica Ceca** Czech Republic. **Repubblica Centrafricana** Central African Repblic. **Repubblica Dominicana** Dominican Republic. **Repubblica d'Irlanda** Republic of Ireland, Irish Republic. **repubblica parlamentare** parliamentary republic. **Repubblica Popolare cinese** People's Republic of China. **repubblica presidenziale** presidential-style republic. **Repubblica Slovacca** Slovakia

repubbli'**cano, -a** *adj & nmf* republican

repu'**tare** *vt* consider

repu'**tarsi** *vr* consider oneself

reputazi'**one** *nf* reputation

'**requiem** *nm inv* requiem

requi'**sire** *vt* requisition

requi'**sito** *nm* requirement

requisi'**toria** *nf* (arringa) closing speech

requisizi'**one** *nf* requisition

'**resa** *nf* surrender; Comm rendering. **resa dei conti** rendering of accounts. **resa incondizionata** unconditional surrender

re'**scindere** *vt* cancel

'**residence** *nm inv* residential hotel

resi'**dente** *adj & nmf* resident

resi'**denza** *nf* residence; (soggiorno) stay. **residenza protetta** sheltered accomodation

residenzi'**ale** *adj* residential; **zona residenziale** residential district

re'**siduo** ① *adj* residual
② *nm* remainder; **residui** *pl* **industriali** industrial waste

'**resina** *nf* resin

resi'**stente** *adj* resistant. **resistente all'acqua** water resistant

resi'**stenza** *nf* resistance; (fisica) stamina; Electr resistor; **la Resistenza** the Resistance. **resistenza passiva** passive resistance. **resistenza a pubblico ufficiale** resisting arrest

re'**sistere** *vi* ∼ [a] resist; (a colpi, scosse) stand up to; ∼ **alla pioggia/al vento** be rain/wind-resistant

'**reso** *pp di* RENDERE

reso'**conto** *nm* report. **resoconto annuale** annual report

respin'**gente** *nm* Rail buffer

re'**spingere** *vt* repel; (rifiutare) reject; (bocciare) fail

re'**spinto** *pp di* RESPINGERE

respi'**rare** *vt/i* breathe

respira'**tore** *nm* respirator. **respiratore artificiale** life support machine. **respiratore [a tubo]** snorkel

respira'**torio** *adj* respiratory

respirazi'**one** *nf* breathing; Med respiration. **respirazione artificiale** artificial respiration. **respirazione assistita** life support. **respirazione bocca a bocca** mouth-to-mouth resuscitation, kiss of life

re'**spiro** *nm* breath; (il respirare) breathing; fig respite. **respiro di sollievo** sigh of relief

respon'**sabile** ① *adj* responsible (**di** for); Jur liable
② *nmf* person responsible. **responsabile della gestione del portafoglio fondi di investimento** investment manager. **responsabile della produzione** production manager. **responsabile delle risorse umane** human resources manager

responsabi'**lità** *nf inv* responsibility; Jur liability. **responsabilità civile** Jur civil liability. **responsabilità limitata** limited liability. **responsabilità penale** criminal liability

responsabiliz'**zare** *vt* give responsibility to ⟨dipendente⟩; give a sense of responsibility to ⟨gente⟩

responsabil'**mente** *adv* responsibly

re'**sponso** *nm* response

'ressa *nf* crowd

re'stante ① *adj* remaining
  ② *nm* remainder

re'stare *vi* = RIMANERE

restau'rare *vt* restore

restaura|'tore, -trice *nmf* restorer

restaurazi'one *nf* restoration

re'stauro *nm* (riparazione) repair; (arte) restoration

re'stio *adj* restive; ~ **a** reluctant to

restitu'ibile *adj* returnable

restitu'ire *vt* return; (reintegrare) restore

restituzi'one *nf* return; Jur restitution

'resto *nm* rest, remainder; (saldo) balance; (denaro) change; **resti** *pl* (avanzi) remains; **del** ~ besides

re'stringere *vt* contract; take in ⟨vestiti⟩; (limitare) restrict; shrink ⟨stoffa⟩

re'stringersi *vr* contract; (farsi più vicini) close up; ⟨stoffa⟩ shrink

restringi'mento *nm* (di tessuto) shrinkage. **restringimento del campo visivo** Med tunnel vision

restrit'tivo *adj* restrictive

restrizi'one *nf* restriction

resurrezi'one *nf* resurrection

resusci'tare ① *vt* revive; resuscitate ⟨moribondo⟩
  ② *vi* ⟨Cristo⟩ rise again; fig revive

re'taggio *nm* legacy

re'tata *nf* round-up

'rete *nf* net; (sistema) network; ⟨televisiva⟩ channel; (in calcio, hockey) goal; fig trap; (per la spesa) string bag; **la Rete** (Internet) the net, the web. **rete commutata pubblica** Teleph switched public network. **rete di distribuzione** Comm distribution network. **rete locale** Comput local [area] network, LAN. **rete di protezione** (per acrobata) safety net. **rete stradale** road network. **rete telematica** communications network. **rete televisiva satellitare** satellite channel. **rete televisiva via cavo** cable company

reti'cente *adj* reticent

reti'cenza *nf* reticence

retico'lato *nm* grid; (rete metallica) wire netting

re'ticolo *nm* network. **reticolo geografico** grid

re'tina¹ *nf* (per capelli) hair net

'retina² *nf* Anat retina

re'tino *nm* net

retorica'mente *adv* rhetorically

re'torico, -a ① *adj* rhetorical; **domanda retorica** rhetorical question; **figura retorica** figure of speech
  ② *nf* rhetoric

re'trattile *adj* ⟨punta⟩ retractable

retribu'ire *vt* remunerate

retribu'tivo *adj* salary *attrib*

retribuzi'one *nf* remuneration

'retro ① *adv* behind; **vedi** ~ see over
  ② *nm inv* back. **retro di copertina** outside back cover

retroat'tivo *adj* retroactive

retrobot'tega *nm inv* back shop

retro'cedere ① *vi* retreat
  ② *vt* Mil demote; Sport relegate

retrocessi'one *nf* Sport relegation

retroda'tare *vt* backdate, predate

retro'fit *nm inv* Auto retrofitted catalytic converter

re'trogrado *adj* retrograde; fig old-fashioned; Pol reactionary

retrogu'ardia *nf* Mil rearguard

retro'gusto *nm* after-taste

retro'marcia *nf* reverse [gear]

retro'scena *nm inv* Theat backstage; **i** ~ fig the real story

retrospettiva'mente *adv* retrospectively

retrospet'tivo *adj* retrospective

retro'stante *adj* **il palazzo** ~ the building behind

retro'via *nf* Mil area behind the front lines

retro'virus *nm inv* retrovirus

retrovi'sore *nm* rear-view mirror

'retta¹ *nf* Math straight line; (di collegio, pensionato) fee

'retta² *nf* **dar** ~ **a qualcuno** take somebody's advice

rettango'lare *adj* rectangular

ret'tangolo ① *adj* right-angled
  ② *nm* rectangle

ret'tifica *nf* rectification

rettifi'care *vt* rectify

'rettile *nm* reptile

retti'lineo ① *adj* rectilinear; (retto) upright
  ② *nm* Sport back straight

retti'tudine *nf* rectitude

'retto ① *pp di* REGGERE
  ② *adj* straight; fig upright; (giusto) correct; **angolo retto** right angle
  ③ *nm* rectum

ret'tore *nm* Relig rector; Univ chancellor

reu'matico *adj* rheumatic

reuma'tismi *nmpl* rheumatism

reve'rendo *adj* reverend

rever'sibile *adj* reversible

revisio'nare *vt* revise; Comm audit; Auto overhaul

revisi'one *nf* revision; Comm audit; Auto overhaul. **revisione di bilancio** audit. **revisione di bozze** proof-reading. ┄┄╎╍

revisione dello stipendio salary review

revisio'nismo *nm* Pol revisionism

revisio'nista *adj* ⟨*politica*⟩ revisionist

revi'sore *nm* (di conti) auditor; (di bozze) proofreader; (di traduzioni) reviser

re'vival *nm inv* revival

'revoca *nf* repeal

revo'care *vt* repeal

revolve'rata *nf* revolver shot

rhythm and blues *nm* rhythm and blues, R & B

riabbas'sare *vt* lower again

riabbas'sarsi *vr* ⟨*acque*⟩ recede; ⟨*temperatura*⟩ fall again

riabbotto'nare *vt* button up again

riabbracci'are *vt* (abbracciare di nuovo) embrace again; (fig: rivedere) see again

riabili'tare *vt* rehabilitate

riabilitazi'one *nf* rehabilitation; **centro di riabilitazione** rehabilitation centre

riabitu'are *vt* ~ qualcuno a qualcosa reaccustom somebody to something, get somebody used to something again

riabitu'arsi *vr* ~ a qualcosa get used to something again, reaccustom oneself to something

riac'cendere *vt* switch on again ⟨*luce, TV*⟩; rekindle, revive ⟨*interesse, passione*⟩; rekindle ⟨*fuoco*⟩

riac'cendersi *vr* ⟨*luce*⟩ come back on; ⟨*interesse, passione*⟩ rekindle, revive

riaccensi'one *nf* la continua ~ continual switching on and off

riaccer'tare *vt* reassess

riacqui'stare *vt* buy back; regain ⟨*libertà, prestigio*⟩; recover ⟨*vista, udito*⟩

riacutiz'zarsi *vr* get worse again

riadatta'mento *nm* readjustment

riadat'tare *vt* convert ⟨*stanza*⟩; alter ⟨*indumento*⟩

riadat'tarsi *vr* readjust

riaddormen'tare *vt* get [back] to sleep again

riaddormen'tarsi *vr* fall asleep again

riadope'rare *vt* reuse

riaffacci'arsi *vr* (alla finestra) appear again; ⟨*idea*⟩ surface again

riaffermare *vt* reaffirm, reassert

riaffon'dare *vi* sink again

riaffron'tare *vt* deal with again ⟨*situazione*⟩; take up again ⟨*argomento*⟩

riagganci'are ① *vt* replace ⟨*ricevitore*⟩; ~ **la cornetta** hang up
② *vi* hang up

riaggre'garsi *vr* regroup

riallac'ciare *vt* refasten; reconnect ⟨*corrente*⟩; renew ⟨*amicizia*⟩

riallar'gare *vt* widen again ⟨*tunnel, strada*⟩

riallinea'mento *nm* realignment

rialline'are *vt* realign

rialloggi'are *vt* rehouse

rial'zare ① *vt* raise
② *vi* rise

rial'zarsi *vr* get up again

rial'zato *adj* **piano rialzato** mezzanine

ri'alzo *nm* rise; **al** ~ Fin bullish. **rialzo dei prezzi** price rise

ria'mare *vt* ~ qualcuno reciprocate somebody's love, love somebody back

riamma'larsi *vr* fall ill again

riam'mettere *vt* readmit ⟨*socio, studente*⟩

rian'dare *vi* return

riani'mare *vt* Med resuscitate; (ridare forza a) revive; (ridare coraggio a) cheer up

riani'marsi *vr* regain consciousness; (riprendere forza) revive; (riprendere coraggio) cheer up

rianimazi'one *nf* intensive care [unit]; **sala di rianimazione** intensive care unit

rianno'dare *vt* retie ⟨*filo*⟩; renew ⟨*rapporti*⟩

riaper'tura *nf* reopening

riappa'rire *vi* reappear

riap'pendere *vt* replace ⟨*cornetta*⟩; ~ [il telefono] hung up

riappiso'larsi *vr* doze off again

riappropri'arsi *vr* ~ di take back

ria'prire *vt* reopen

ria'prirsi *vr* reopen

ri'armo *nm* rearmament

ri'arso *adj* parched

riascol'tare *vt* listen to again

riasse'gnare *vt* reallocate

riassicu'rare *vt* reinsure

riassicurazi'one *nf* reinsurance

riassorbi'mento *nm* reabsorption

riassor'bire *vt* reabsorb

rias'sumere *vt* re-employ, take on again ⟨*impiegato*⟩; (ricapitolare) resume

riassu'mibile *adj* (riepilogabile) which can be summarized, summarizable

riassun'tivo *adj* summarizing

rias'sunto ① pp di RIASSUMERE
② *nm* summary

riattac'care ① *vt* ~ **il telefono** hang up
② *vi* (al telefono) hang up

riatti'vare *vt* reactivate ⟨*processo*⟩; reintroduce, bring back ⟨*servizio*⟩; start up again, restart ⟨*congegno*⟩; stimulate ⟨*circolazione sanguigna*⟩

ria'vere *vt* get back; regain ⟨*salute, vista*⟩

ria'versi *vr* recover

riavvicina'mento *nm* (tra persone) reconciliation; (tra paesi) rapprochement

riavvici'nare *vt* fig reconcile ⟨*paesi, persone*⟩

riavvici'narsi *vr* (riconciliarsi) be reconciled, make it up fam

riav'volgere *vt* rewind

riba'dire *vt* (confermare) reaffirm

ri'balta *nf* flap; Theat footlights *pl*; fig limelight

ribal'tabile *adj* tip-up

ribal'tare *vt/i* tip over; Naut capsize

ribal'tarsi *vr* tip over; Naut capsize

ribas'sare ① *vt* lower
② *vi* fall

ribas'sato *adj* reduced

ri'basso *nm* fall; (sconto) discount

ri'battere ① *vt* (a macchina) retype; (controbattere) deny
② *vi* answer back

ribattez'zare *vt* rename

ribel'larsi *vr* rebel

ri'belle ① *adj* rebellious
② *nmf* rebel

ribelli'one *nf* rebellion

'ribes *nm* (rosso) redcurrant; (nero) blackcurrant

ribol'lire *vi* (fermentare) ferment; fig seethe

ri'brezzo *nm* disgust; far ∼ a disgust

ribut'tante *adj* repugnant

ribut'tare *vt* (buttare di nuovo) throw back

rica'dere *vi* fall back; (nel peccato ecc) lapse; (pendere) hang [down]; ∼ **su** (riversarsi) fall on

rica'duta *nf* relapse; **avere una** ∼ to have a relapse

rical'care *vt* trace

ricalci'trante *adj* recalcitrant

ricalco'lare *vt* recalculate

rica'mare *vt* embroider

rica'mato *adj* embroidered

ri'cambi *nmpl* spare parts

ricambi'are *vt* return; reciprocate ⟨*sentimento*⟩; ∼ **qualcosa a qualcuno** repay somebody for something

ri'cambio *nm* replacement; Biol metabolism; **pezzo di ricambio** spare [part]

ri'camo *nm* embroidery

ricandi'dare *vt* (a elezioni) put forward as a candidate again

ricandi'darsi *vr* (a elezioni) stand again

ricapito'lare *vt* sum up; **ricapitoliamo** let's recap

ricapitolazi'one *nf* summary, recap fam

ri'carica *nf* (di sveglia) winder; (di batteria) recharging; (di penna) refill; (di fucile) reloading; Teleph top-up card

ricari'cabile *adj* rechargeable

ricari'care *vt* reload ⟨*macchina fotografica, fucile, camion*⟩; recharge ⟨*batteria*⟩; Comput reboot; rewind ⟨*orologio*⟩

ricat'tare *vt* blackmail

ricatta|'tore, -trice *nmf* blackmailer

ricatta'torio *adj* blackmail *attrib*

ri'catto *nm* blackmail. **ricatto morale** moral blackmail, emotional blackmail

rica'vare *vt* get; (ottenere) obtain; (dedurre) draw

rica'vato *nm* proceeds *pl*

ri'cavo *nm* proceeds *pl*

ricca'mente *adv* lavishly

ric'chezza *nf* wealth; fig richness; **ricchezze** *pl* riches

'riccio ① *adj* curly
② *nm* curl; (animale) hedgehog. **riccio di mare** sea-urchin

'ricciolo *nm* curl

riccio'luto *adj* curly

ricci'uto *adj* ⟨*barba*⟩ curly; ⟨*persona*⟩ curly-haired

'ricco, -a ① *adj* rich. **ricco sfondato** fam filthy rich
② *nmf* rich person; **i ricchi** the rich

ri'cerca *nf* search; (indagine) investigation; (scientifica) research; Sch project. **ricerca avanzata** Comput advanced search. **ricerca sul campo** field work. **ricerca di mercato** market research. **ricerca operativa** operational research

ricer'care *vt* search for; (fare ricerche su) research

ricer'cata *nf* wanted woman

ricercata'mente *adv* ⟨*vestire*⟩ with refinement; ⟨*parlare*⟩ in a refined way

ricerca'tezza *nf* refinement

ricer'cato ① *adj* sought-after; (raffinato) refined
② *nm* (dalla polizia) wanted man

ricerca|'tore, -trice *nmf* researcher

ricetrasmit'tente *nf* transceiver, two-way radio

ri'cetta *nf* Culin recipe; Med prescription

ricet'tacolo *nm* receptacle

ricet'tario *nm* (di cucina) recipe book; (di medico) prescription pad

ricetta|'tore, -trice *nmf* receiver of stolen goods, fence fam

ricettazi'one *nf* receiving [stolen goods]

rice'vente ① *adj* ⟨*apparecchio, stazione*⟩ receiving
② *nmf* receiver

ri'cevere *vt* receive; (dare il benvenuto) welcome; (di albergo) accommodate

ricevi'mento *nm* receiving; (accoglienza) welcome; (trattenimento) reception

ricevi'tore *nm* receiver. **ricevitore delle imposte** tax man. **ricevitore del lotto** lottery ticket agent

ricevito'ria *nf* **ricevitoria delle imposte** ≈ Inland Revenue. **ricevitoria del lotto** agency authorized to sell lottery tickets

rice'vuta *nf* receipt. **ricevuta d'acquisto** proof of purchase. **ricevuta doganale** docket. **ricevuta fiscale** tax receipt. **ricevuta di ritorno** acknowledgement of receipt. **ricevuta di versamento** receipt (given for bills etc paid at the Post Office)

rice'vuto *int* roger

ricezi'one *nf* Radio, TV reception

richia'mare *vt* (al telefono) call back; (far tornare) recall; (rimproverare) rebuke; (attirare) draw; ∼ **alla mente** call to mind

richi'amo *nm* recall; (attrazione) call

richie'dente *nmf* applicant

richi'edere *vt* ask for; (di nuovo) ask again for; ∼ **a qualcuno di fare qualcosa** ask *or* request somebody to do something

richi'esta *nf* request; Comm demand. **richiesta di indennizzo** claim for damages

richi'esto *adj* sought-after

ri'chiudere *vt* shut again, close again

ri'chiudersi *vr* ⟨ferita⟩ heal; ⟨porta⟩ shut again, close again

rici'clabile *adj* recyclable

rici'claggio *nm* recycling; (di denaro) laundering

rici'clare *vt* recycle ⟨carta, vetro⟩; launder ⟨denaro sporco⟩

rici'clarsi *vr* retrain; (cambiare lavoro) change one's line of work

rici'clato *adj* recycled

'ricino *nm* **olio di ricino** castor oil

ricogni'tore *nm* reconnaissance plane

ricognizi'one *nf* Mil reconnaissance

ricolle'gare *vt* (collegare di nuovo) reconnect

ricolle'garsi *vr* ∼ **a** ⟨evento, fatto⟩ relate to, tie up with

ricol'mare *vt* fill to the brim

ri'colmo *adj* full

ricominci'are *vt/i* start again; ∼ **da capo** start all over again

ricompa'rire *vi* reappear

ricom'parsa *nf* reappearance

ricom'pensa *nf* reward

ricompen'sare *vt* reward

ricom'porre *vt* (riscrivere) rewrite; (ricostruire) reform; Teleph redial; Typ reset

ricom'porsi *vr* regain one's composure

ricomposi'zione *nf* Teleph **ricomposizione automatica dell'ultimo numero** redial facility

riconcili'are *vt* reconcile

riconcili'arsi *vr* be reconciled

riconciliazi'one *nf* reconciliation

riconfer'mare *vt* reappoint

ricongi'ungere *vt* reunite

ricongi'ungersi *vr* become reunited

ricono'scente *adj* grateful

ricono'scenza *nf* gratitude

rico'noscere *vt* recognize; (ammettere) acknowledge

ricono'scibile *adj* recognizable

riconosci'mento *nm* recognition; (ammissione) acknowledgement; (per la polizia) identification. **riconoscimento vocale** Comput voice recognition

riconosci'uto *adj* recognized

ricon'quista *nf* reconquest

riconqui'stare *vt* Mil reconquer

ricon'segna *nf* return

riconse'gnare *vt* return

riconside'rare *vt* rethink

ricontrol'lare *vt* double-check

riconversi'one *nf* Econ restructuring

ricopi'are *vt* recopy

rico'prire *vt* re-cover; (rivestire) coat; (di insulti) shower (**di** with); hold ⟨carica⟩; ∼ **qualcuno di attenzioni** lavish attention on somebody

ricor'dare *vt* remember; (richiamare alla memoria) recall; (far ricordare) remind; (rassomigliare) look like

ricor'darsi *vr* ∼ **[di]** remember; ∼ **di fare qualcosa** remember to do something

ri'cordo *nm* memory; (oggetto) memento; (di viaggio) souvenir; **ricordi** *pl* (memorie) memoirs. ∼ **di famiglia** family heirloom

ricor'reggere *vt* correct again

ricor'rente *adj* recurrent

ricor'renza *nf* recurrence; (anniversario) anniversary

ri'correre *vi* recur; (accadere) occur; ⟨data⟩ fall; ∼ **a** have recourse to; (rivolgersi a) turn to

ri'corso ① pp di RICORRERE ② *nm* recourse; Jur appeal

ricostitu'ente *nm* tonic

ricostitu'ire *vt* re-establish

ricostru'ire *vt* reconstruct

ricostruzi'one *nf* reconstruction

ricove'rare *vt* give shelter to; ∼ **in ospedale** admit to hospital, hospitalize

ricove'rato, -a *nmf* hospital patient

ri'covero *nm* shelter; (ospizio) home

ricre'are *vt* recreate; (ristorare) restore

ricre'arsi *vr* amuse oneself

ricrea'tivo *adj* recreational

ricreazi'one *nf* recreation; Sch break, playtime

ri'credersi *vr* change one's mind

ri'crescere *vi* grow again

ricu'cire *vt* sew up; stitch up ⟨*ferita*⟩

ricupe'rare, ricupero = RECUPERARE, RECUPERO

ri'curvo *adj* bent

ricu'sare *vt* refuse

ridacchi'are *vi* giggle

ri'dare *vt* give back, return

rida'rella *nf* giggles *pl*

ridefi'nire *vt* redefine

ri'dente *adj* (piacevole) pleasant

'ridere *vi* laugh; ~ **di** (deridere) laugh at

ride'stare *vt* reawaken ⟨*ricordo, sentimento*⟩

ri'detto *pp di* RIDIRE

ridicoliz'zare *vt* ridicule

ri'dicolo *adj* ridiculous

ridimensiona'mento *nm* restructuring

ridimensio'nare *vt* restructure ⟨*azienda*⟩; *fig* get into perspective

ridi'pingere *vt* repaint

ri'dire *vt* repeat; **trova sempre da** ~ he's always finding fault; **hai qualcosa da** ~? do you have something to say?; **se non hai niente da** ~,... if you've no objection...

ridi'scendere *vi* go back down

ridistribu'ire *vt* redistribute

ridistribuzi'one *nf* redistribution

ridon'dante *adj* redundant

ri'dosso: **a** ~ **di** *adv* behind

ri'dotto ① *pp di* RIDURRE
② *nm* Theat foyer
③ *adj* reduced **essere** ~ **male** be worn out

ri'durre *vt* reduce

ri'dursi *vr* diminish; ~ **a fare qualcosa** be reduced to doing something; ~ **a** ⟨*problema*⟩ come down to

ridut'tivo *adj* reductive

ridut'tore *nm* Electr adaptor

riduzi'one *nf* reduction. **riduzione cinematografica** film adaptation. **riduzione della pena** reduced sentence. **riduzione di prezzo** price cut. **riduzione teatrale** adaptation for the theatre

riedifi'care *vt* rebuild

rieducazi'one *nf* (di malato) rehabilitation

rie'leggere *vt* re-elect

rielezi'one *nf* re-election

rie'mergere *vi* resurface

riem'pire *vt* fill [up]; fill in ⟨*moduli ecc*⟩

riem'pirsi *vr* fill [up]

riempi'tivo ① *adj* filling
② *nm* filler

rien'tranza *nf* recess

rien'trare *vi* go/come back in; (tornare) return; (piegare indentro) recede; ~ **in** (far parte) fall within

ri'entro *nm* return; (di astronave) re-entry

riepilo'gare *vt* recapitulate

rie'pilogo *nm* summing-up

rie'same *nm* reassessment

riesami'nare *vt* reappraise

ri'essere *vi* **ci risiamo!** here we go again!

riesu'mare *vt* exhume

rievo'care *vt* (commemorare) commemorate; recall ⟨*passato*⟩

rievocazi'one *nf* (commemorazione) commemoration; (ricordo) recollection

rifaci'mento *nm* remake

ri'fare *vt* do again; (creare) make again; (riparare) repair; (imitare) imitate; make ⟨*letto*⟩

ri'farsi *vr* (rimettersi) recover; (vendicarsi) get even; ~ **una vita/carriera** make a new life/career for oneself; ~ **il trucco** touch up one's makeup; ~ **di** make up for

ri'fatto *pp di* RIFARE

riferi'mento *nm* reference

rife'rire ① *vt* report; ~ **a** attribute to
② *vi* make a report

rife'rirsi *vr* ~ **a** refer to

rifi'lare *vt* (tagliare a filo) trim; (fam; affibbiare) saddle

rifi'nire *vt* finish off

rifini'tura *nf* finish

rifio'rire *vi* blossom again; *fig* flourish again

rifiu'tare *vt* refuse; ~ **di fare qualcosa** refuse to do something

rifi'uto *nm* refusal; **acque** *pl* **di** ~ waste water; **rifiuti** *pl* (immondizie) rubbish; **rifiuti** *pl* **industriali** industrial waste; **rifiuti** *pl* **urbani** urban waste

riflessi'one *nf* reflection; (osservazione) remark

rifles'sivo *adj* thoughtful; Gram reflexive

ri'flesso ① *pp di* RIFLETTERE
② *nm* (luce) reflection; Med reflex; **per** ~ indirectly

ri'flettere ① *vt* reflect
② *vi* think (**su** about)

ri'flettersi *vr* be reflected

riflet'tore *nm* reflector; (proiettore) search-light

ri'flusso *nm* ebb

rifocil'lare *vt* restore

rifocil'larsi *vr* liter, hum take some refreshment

rifondazi'one *nf* refounding. **Rifondazione Comunista** diehard Communist party

ri'fondere *vt* (rimborsare) refund

ri'forma *nf* reform; Relig reformation; Mil exemption on medical grounds

rifor'mare *vt* re-form; (migliorare) reform; Mil declare unfit for military service

riforma|'tore, -trice *nmf* reformer

rifor'mato *adj* ⟨chiesa⟩ Reformed; ⟨recluta, soldato⟩ unfit for military service

riforma'torio *nm* reformatory

riformat'tare *vt* Comput reformat

rifor'mista *adj* & *nmf* reformist

riformu'lare *vt* recast

riforni'mento *nm* supply; (scorta) stock; (di combustibile) refuelling; **stazione di rifornimento** petrol station

rifor'nire *vt* restock; ∼ **di** provide with

rifor'nirsi *vr* restock, stock up (**di** with)

ri'frangere *vt* refract

ri'fratto pp di RIFRANGERE

rifrazi'one *nf* refraction

rifug'gire ① *vt* shun ⟨gloria, celebrità⟩ ② *vi* escape again; ∼ **da** fig shun

rifugi'arsi *vr* take refuge

rifugi'ato, -a *nmf* refugee

ri'fugio *nm* shelter; (nascondiglio) hideaway, safe house. **rifugio antiaereo** bomb shelter. **rifugio antiatomico** fallout shelter

'riga *nf* line; (fila) row; (striscia) stripe; (scriminatura) parting; (regolo) rule; **a righe** (stoffa) striped; ⟨quaderno⟩ ruled; **mettersi in** ∼ line up

ri'gaglie *nfpl* (interiora) giblets

ri'gagnolo *nm* rivulet

ri'gare ① *vt* rule ⟨foglio⟩ ② *vi* ∼ **dritto** behave well

riga'toni *nmpl* small ridged pasta tubes

rigatti'ere *nm* junk dealer

rigene'rante *adj* regenerative

rigene'rare *vt* regenerate

riget'tare *vt* (gettare indietro) throw back; (respingere) reject; (vomitare) throw up

ri'getto *nm* rejection

ri'ghello *nm* ruler

rigida'mente *adv* rigidly

rigidità *nf* rigidity; (di clima) severity; (severità) strictness. **rigidità cadaverica** rigor mortis

'rigido *adj* rigid; (freddo) severe; (severo) strict

rigi'rare ① *vt* turn again; (ripercorrere) go round; fig twist ⟨argomentazione⟩ ② *vi* walk about

rigi'rarsi *vr* turn round; (nel letto) turn over

ri'giro *nm* (imbroglio) trick

'rigo *nm* line; Mus staff

ri'goglio *nm* bloom

rigogliosa'mente *adv* luxuriantly

rigogli'oso *adj* luxuriant

rigonfia'mento *nm* swelling

rigonfi'are *vt* reinflate

ri'gonfio *adj* swollen

ri'gore *nm* rigours *pl*; **a rigor di logica** strictly speaking; **calcio di rigore** penalty [kick]; **area di rigore** penalty area; **essere di** ∼ be compulsory

rigorosa'mente *adv* ⟨giudicare⟩ severely; ⟨seguire istruzioni⟩ exactly; **vestito** ∼ **in giacca e cravatta** wearing the obligatory jacket and tie

rigo'roso *adj* (severo) strict; (scrupoloso) rigorous

rigover'nare *vt* wash up

riguada'gnare *vt* regain, win back ⟨stima⟩; win more ⟨tempo, punti⟩

riguar'dare *vt* look at again; (considerare) regard; (concernere) concern; **per quanto riguarda...** with regard to...

riguar'darsi *vr* take care of oneself

rigu'ardo *nm* care; (considerazione) consideration; **nei riguardi di** towards; ∼ **a** with regard to

rigurgi'tante *adj* ∼ **di** swarming with

rigurgi'tare ① *vt* regurgitate ② *vi* ∼ **di** fig be swarming with

ri'gurgito *nm* regurgitation; (fig: di xenofobia, nazionalismo ecc) resurgence

rilanci'are ① *vt* throw back ⟨palla⟩; (di nuovo) throw again; increase ⟨offerta⟩; revive ⟨moda⟩; relaunch ⟨prodotto⟩ ② *vi* (a carte) raise the stakes; **rilancio di dieci** I'll raise you ten

ri'lancio *nm* (di offerta) increase; (di prodotto) re-launch

rilasci'are *vt* (concedere) grant; (liberare) release; issue ⟨documento⟩

rilasci'arsi *vr* relax

ri'lascio *nm* release; (di documento) issue

rilassa'mento *nm* relaxation. **rilassamento cutaneo** sagging of the skin

rilas'sare *vt* relax

rilas'sarsi *vr* relax

rilas'sato *adj* relaxed

rile'gare *vt* bind ⟨libro⟩

rile'gato *adj* bound

rilega|'tore, -trice *nmf* bookbinder

rilega'tura *nf* binding

ri'leggere *vt* reread

ri'lento: **a** ∼ *adv* slowly

rileva'mento *nm* survey; Comm buyout. **rilevamento dirigenti** management buyout, MBO

rile'vante *adj* considerable

rile'vanza *nf* significance

rile'vare *vt* (trarre) get; (mettere in evidenza) point out; (notare) notice; (in topografia) survey; Comm take over; Mil relieve

rilevazi'one *nf* (statistica) survey

rili'evo *nm* relief; Geog elevation; (in topografia) survey; (importanza) importance;

(osservazione) remark; **mettere in** ∼
qualcosa point something out

rilut'tante *adj* reluctant

rilut'tanza *nf* reluctance, unwillingness

'**rima** *nf* rhyme; **far** ∼ **con qualcosa**
rhyme with something; **rispondere a
qualcuno per le rime** give somebody as
good as one gets. **rima alternata**
alternate rhyme. **rima baciata** rhyming
couplet

riman'dare *vt* (posporre) postpone;
(mandare indietro) send back; (mandare di
nuovo) send again; (far ridare un esame) make
resit an examination

ri'mando *nm* return; (in un libro) cross-
reference

rimaneggia'mento *nm* rejig

rimaneggi'are *vt* rejig, recast

rima'nente ① *adj* remaining
② *nm* remainder

rima'nenza *nf* remainder; **rimanenze** *pl*
remnants; **rimanenze** *pl* **di magazzino**
unsold stock

rima'nere *vi* stay remain; (essere d'avanzo)
be left; (venirsi a trovare) be; (restare stupito) be
astonished; (restare d'accordo) agree; ∼
senza parole be speechless

rimangi'are *vt* (mangiare di nuovo) have
again, eat again

rimangi'arsi *vr* ∼ **la parola** break one's
promise

rimar'care *vt* remark

rimar'chevole *adj* remarkable

ri'mare *vt/i* rhyme

rimargi'nare *vt* heal

rimargi'narsi *vr* heal

ri'masto pp di RIMANERE

rima'sugli *nmpl* (di cibo) leftovers

rimbal'zare *vi* rebound; (proiettile)
ricochet; **far** ∼ bounce

rim'balzo *nm* rebound; (di proiettile)
ricochet

rimbam'bire ① *vi* be in one's dotage
② *vt* stun

rimbam'bito *adj* in one's dotage

rimbec'care *vi* retort

rimbecil'lire *vt* make brain-dead

rimbecil'lito *adj* (stupido) brain-dead;
(frastornato) stunned

rimboc'care *vt* turn up; roll up
(maniche); tuck in (coperte); ∼ **le coperte
a qualcuno** tuck somebody into bed

rimboc'carsi *vr* ∼ **le maniche** roll up
one's sleeves

rimbom'bare *vi* boom, resound

rim'bombo *nm* boom

rimbor'sabile *adj* reclaimable

rimbor'sare *vt* reimburse, repay

rim'borso *nm* reimbursement,
repayment. **rimborso d'imposta** tax

rebate. **rimborso spese** reimbursement
of expenses

rimboschi'mento *nm* reafforestation
Br, reforestation

rim'brotto *nm* reproach

rimedi'abile *adj* (errore) which can be
remedied

rimedi'are *vi* ∼ **a** remedy; make up for
(errore); (procurare) scrape up

ri'medio *nm* remedy

rimesco'lare *vt* mix [up]; shuffle
(carte); (rivangare) rake up; **mi fa** ∼ **il
sangue** it makes my blood boil

rimesco'lio *nm* (turbamento) shock

ri'messa *nf* (per veicoli) garage; (per aerei)
hangar; (per autobus) depot; (di denaro)
remittance; (di merci) consignment.
rimessa laterale Sport throw-in

ri'messo pp di RIMETTERE

rime'stare *vt* stir well

ri'mettere *vt* (a posto) put back; (restituire)
return; (affidare) entrust; (perdonare) remit;
(rimandare) put off; (vomitare) bring up; ∼ **in
gioco** (nel calcio) throw in; ∼ **in moto**
restart; **rimetterci** (fam: perdere) lose [out]

ri'mettersi *vr* (ristabilirsi) recover; (tempo)
clear up; ∼ **a** start again

'**rimmel**® *nm inv* mascara

rimoder'nare *vt* modernize

ri'monta *nf* Sport recovery

rimon'tare ① *vt* (risalire) go up; Mech
reassemble
② *vi* remount; ∼ **a** (risalire) go back to

rimorchi'are *vt* tow; fam pick up
(ragazza)

rimorchia'tore *nm* tug[boat]

ri'morchio *nm* tow; (veicolo) trailer

ri'mordere *vt* **mi rimorde la coscienza** fig
it's preying on my conscience

ri'morso *nm* remorse

rimo'stranza *nf* complaint

rimo'vibile *adj* removable

rimozi'one *nf* removal; (da un incarico)
dismissal. **rimozione forzata** illegally
parked vehicles removed at owner's
expense

rimpagi'nare *vt* regret

rim'pallo *nm* bounce

rim'pasto *nm* Pol reshuffle

rimpatri'are ① *vt* repatriate
② *vi* return home

rimpatri'ata *nf* reunion

rim'patrio *nm* repatriation

rim'piangere *vt* regret

rimpi'anto ① pp di RIMPIANGERE
② *nm* regret

rimpiat'tino *nm* hide-and-seek

rimpiaz'zare *vt* replace

rimpi'azzo *nm* replacement

rimpiccioli'mento *nm* shrinkage

rimpiccio'lire ① *vt* make smaller ② *vi* become smaller

rimpinz'are *vt* ~ di stuff with

rimpin'zarsi *vr* stuff oneself

rimpol'pare *vt* (ingrassare) fatten up; fig pad out (*scritto*)

rimprove'rare *vt* reproach; ~ qualcosa a qualcuno reproach somebody for something

rim'provero *nm* reproach

rimugi'nare *vt* liter rummage; fig ~ su brood over

rimune'rare *vt* remunerate

rimunera'tivo *adj* remunerative

rimunerazi'one *nf* remuneration

ri'muovere *vt* remove

ri'nascere *vi* be reborn, be born again

rinascimen'tale *adj* Renaissance

Rinasci'mento *nm* Renaissance

ri'nascita *nf* rebirth

rincal'zare *vt* (sostenere) support; (rimboccare) tuck in

rin'calzo *nm* support; rincalzi *pl* Mil reserves

rincantucci'arsi *vr* hide oneself away in a corner

rinca'rare ① *vt* increase the price of ② *vi* become more expensive

rin'caro *nm* price increase

rincar'tare *vt* rewrap

rinca'sare *vi* return home

rinchi'udere *vt* shut up

rinchi'udersi *vr* shut oneself up

rincon'trare *vt* meet again

rincon'trarsi *vr* meet [each other] again

rin'correre *vt* run after

rin'corsa *nf* run-up

rin'corso *pp di* RINCORRERE

rin'crescere *vi* mi rincresce di non... I'm sorry *or* I regret that I can't...; se non ti rincresce if you don't mind; rincresce vedere... it's sad to see...

rincresci'mento *nm* regret

rincresci'uto *pp di* RINCRESCERE

rincreti'nire ① *vt* make brain-dead ② *vi* go brain-dead

rincu'lare *vi* (arma) recoil; (cavallo) shy

rin'culo *nm* recoil

rincuo'rare *vt* encourage

rincuo'rarsi *vr* take heart

rinfacci'are *vt* ~ qualcosa a qualcuno throw something in somebody's face

rinfode'rare *vt* sheathe

rinfor'zare *vt* strengthen; (rendere più saldo) reinforce

rinfor'zarsi *vr* become stronger

rin'forzo *nm* reinforcement; fig support; rinforzi *pl* Mil reinforcements

rinfran'care *vt* reassure

rinfre'scante *adj* cooling

rinfre'scare ① *vt* cool; (rinnovare) freshen up ② *vi* get cooler

rinfre'scarsi *vr* freshen [oneself] up

rin'fresco *nm* light refreshment; (ricevimento) party

rin'fusa *nf* alla ~ at random

ringalluz'zire ① *vt* make cocky ② *vi* get cocky

ringhi'are *vi* snarl

ringhi'era *nf* railing; (di scala) banisters *pl*

ringhi'oso *adj* snarling

ringiova'nire ① *vt* rejuvenate (*pelle, persona, vestito*) make look younger ② *vi* become young again; (sembrare) look young again

ringrazia'mento *nm* thanks *pl*

ringrazi'are *vt* thank

rinne'gare *vt* disown

rinne'gato, -a *nmf* renegade

rinno'vabile *adj* renewable; (risorsa, foresta) sustainable

rinnova'mento *nm* renewal; (di edifici) renovation

rinno'vare *vt* renew; renovate (*edifici*)

rinno'varsi *vr* be renewed; (ripetersi) recur, happen again

rin'novo *nm* renewal

rinoce'ronte *nm* rhinoceros

rino'mato *adj* renowned

rinsal'dare *vt* consolidate

rinsa'vire *vi* come to one's senses

rinsec'chire *vi* shrivel up

rinsec'chito *adj* shrivelled up

rinta'narsi *vr* hide oneself away; (animale) retreat into its den

rintoc'care *vi* (compana) toll; (orologio) strike

rin'tocco *nm* toll; (di orologio) stroke

rinton'tire *vt* anche fig stun

rinton'tito *adj* (stordito) dazed

rintracci'are *vt* trace

rintro'nare ① *vt* stun ② *vi* boom

rintuz'zare *vt* blunt; (ribattere) retort; (reprimere) repress

ri'nuncia *nf* renunciation

rinunci'are *vi* ~ a renounce, give up

rinuncia'tario *adj* defeatist

ri'nunzia, rinunziare = RINUNCIA, RINUNCIARE

rinveni'mento *nm* (di reperti) discovery; (di refurtiva) recovery

rinve'nire ① *vt* find
② *vi* (riprendere i sensi) come round;
(ridiventare fresco) revive

rinvi'are *vt* put off; (mandare indietro)
return; (in libro) refer; ∼ **a giudizio** indict

rinvigo'rire *vt* strengthen

rin'vio *nm* Sport goal kick; (in libro) cross-reference; (di appuntamento) postponement;
(di merce) return. **rinvio a giudizio**
indictment

rioccu'pare *vt* reoccupy

rio'nale *adj* local

ri'one *nm* district

riordina'mento *nm* reorganization

riordi'nare *vt* tidy [up]; (ordinare di nuovo)
reorder

riorganiz'zare *vt* reorganize

riorganizzazi'one *nf* reorganization

R.I.P. *abbr* (**riposi in pace**) RIP

ripa'gare *vt* repay

ripa'rare ① *vt* (proteggere) shelter,
protect; (aggiustare) repair; (porre rimedio)
remedy
② *vi* ∼ **a** make up for

ripa'rarsi *vr* take shelter

ripa'rato *adj* ⟨luogo⟩ sheltered

riparazi'one *nf* repair; fig reparation

ripar'lare *vi* **ne riparliamo stasera** we'll
talk about it again tonight

ri'paro *nm* shelter; (rimedio) remedy

ripar'tire ① *vt* (dividere) divide
② *vi* leave again

ripartizi'one *nf* division

ripas'sare ① *vt* recross; (rivedere) revise
② *vi* pass again

ripas'sata *nf* (spolverata) quick dust;
(stirata) quick iron; (di vernice) second coat;
(fam: rimprovero) telling-off; **dar una** ∼ **a**
⟨lezione⟩ revise

ri'passo *nm* (di lezione) revision

ripensa'mento *nm* second thoughts *pl*

ripen'sare *vi* ∼ **a** think back to;
ripensarci (cambiare idea) change one's
mind; **ripensaci!** think again!

riper'correre *vt* (con la memoria) go back
over; trace ⟨storia⟩; ∼ **la strada fatta** go
back the way one came

riper'cosso *pp di* RIPERCUOTERE

ripercu'otere *vt* strike again

ripercu'otersi *vr* ⟨suono⟩ reverberate;
∼ **su qualcosa** (fig: avere conseguenze)
impact on something

ripercussi'one *nf* repercussion

ripe'scare *vt* (recuperare) fish out;
(ritrovare) find again

ripe'tente *nmf* student who is repeating
a year

ri'petere *vt* repeat

ri'petersi *vr* ⟨evento⟩ recur; ⟨persona⟩
repeat oneself

ripeti'tore *nm* TV relay

ripetizi'one *nf* repetition; (di lezione)
revision; (lezione privata) private lesson

ripetuta'mente *adv* repeatedly

ri'piano *nm* (di scaffale) shelf; (terreno
pianeggiante) terrace

ri'picca, ri'picco *nf* spite; **fare
qualcosa per** ∼ do something out of spite

ripida'mente *adv* steeply

'ripido *adj* steep

ripie'gare ① *vt* refold; (abbassare) lower
② *vi* (indietreggiare) retreat

ripie'garsi *vr* bend; ⟨sedile⟩ fold

ripi'ego *nm* expedient; (via d'uscita) way
out

ripi'eno ① *adj* full; Culin stuffed
② *nm* filling; Culin stuffing

ripiom'bare *vi* (per terra) fall down again;
∼ **nella disperazione** sink back into
despair

ripopo'lare *vt* repopulate

ripopo'larsi *vr* be repopulated

ri'porre *vt* put back; (mettere da parte) put
away; (collocare) place; repeat ⟨domanda⟩

ripor'tare *vt* (restituire) bring/take back;
(riferire) report; (subire) suffer; Math carry;
win ⟨vittoria⟩; transfer ⟨disegno⟩

ripor'tarsi *vr* go back; (riferirsi) refer

ri'porto *nm* (su abito, scarpa) appliqué; ∼ **di
4** Math carry 4; **cane da riporto** gun dog,
retriever; **nascondere la calvizie con un** ∼
comb one's hair over a bald spot

ripo'sante *adj* restful

ripo'sare ① *vi* rest
② *vt* put back

ripo'sarsi *vr* rest

ripo'sato *adj* ⟨mente⟩ fresh; ⟨viso⟩ rested

ri'poso *nm* rest; **andare a** ∼ retire; ∼! Mil
at ease!; **giorno di riposo** day off

ripo'stiglio *nm* cupboard

ri'posto *pp di* RIPORRE

ri'prendere *vt* take again; (prendere
indietro) take back; (riconquistare) recapture;
(ricuperare) recover; (ricominciare) resume;
(rimproverare) reprimand; take in ⟨cucitura⟩;
Cinema shoot

ri'prendersi *vr* recover; (correggersi)
correct oneself

ri'presa *nf* resumption; (ricupero)
recovery; Theat revival; Cinema shot; Auto
acceleration; Mus repeat. **ripresa aerea**
bird's-eye view; **riprese** *pl* Cinema filming

ripresen'tare *vt* resubmit ⟨domanda,
certificato⟩; reintroduce ⟨problema,
persona⟩

ripresen'tarsi *vr* (a ufficio) go/come back
again; (come candidato) stand again, run
again; ⟨occasione⟩ arise again; ⟨problema⟩
come up again, reappear; (a esame) resit

ri'preso *pp di* RIPRENDERE

ripristi'nare *vt* restore

ripro'dotto pp di RIPRODURRE

ripro'durre *vt* reproduce

ripro'dursi *vr* Biol reproduce; ⟨*fenomeno*⟩ happen again, recur

riprodut'tivo *adj* reproductive

riproduzi'one *nf* reproduction. **'riproduzione vietata'** 'copyright'

ripro'mettersi *vr* (intendere) intend

ripro'porre *vt* put forward again

ripro'porsi *vr* ∼ **di fare qualcosa** intend to do something; (come candidato) stand again; ⟨*problema*⟩ come up again, reappear

ri'prova *nf* confirmation; **a** ∼ **di** as confirmation of

ripro'vare *vt/i* retry

riprovazi'one *nf* **riprovazione generale** outcry

riprove'vole *adj* reprehensible

ripubbli'care *vt* republish

ripudi'are *vt* repudiate

ripu'gnante *adj* repugnant

ripu'gnanza *nf* disgust

ripu'gnare *vi* ∼ **a** disgust

ripu'lire *vt* clean [up]; fig polish

ripu'lita *nf* quick clean; **darsi una** ∼ have a wash and brushup

ripulsi'one *nf* repulsion

ripul'sivo *adj* repulsive

ri'quadro *nm* square; (pannello) panel

riqualifi'care *vt* reskill ⟨*lavoratori*⟩

riqualifica'zione *nf* retraining

ri'sacca *nf* undertow

ri'saia *nf* rice field, paddy field

risa'lire ① *vt* go back up ② *vi* ∼ **a** (nel tempo) date back to; (individuare) trace ⟨*colpevole*⟩

risa'lita *nf* ascent; **impianto di risalita** ski lift

risal'tare *vi* (emergere) stand out

ri'salto *nm* prominence; (rilievo) relief

risana'mento *nm* reclamation, redevelopment

risa'nare *vt* heal; (bonificare) reclaim; redevelop ⟨*area, quartiere*⟩

risa'puto *adj* well-known

risar'cibile *adj* refundable

risarci'mento *nm* compensation

risar'cire *vt* indemnify; **mi hanno risarcito i danni** they compensated me for the damage

ri'sata *nf* laugh

riscalda'mento *nm* heating. **riscaldamento autonomo** central heating (for one flat). **riscaldamento centralizzato** central heating system for whole block of flats

riscal'dare *vt* heat; warm ⟨*persona*⟩

riscal'darsi *vr* warm up

riscat'tabile *adj* redeemable

riscat'tare *vt* ransom

riscat'tarsi *vr* redeem oneself

ri'scatto *nm* ransom; (morale) redemption

rischia'rare *vt* light up; brighten ⟨*colore*⟩

rischia'rarsi *vr* light up; ⟨*cielo*⟩ clear up

rischi'are ① *vt* risk ② *vi* run the risk; ∼ **inutilmente** take needless risks

'rischio *nm* risk; **a** ∼ ⟨*soggetti*⟩ at-risk; **a basso** ∼ low-risk

rischi'oso *adj* risky

risciac'quare *vt* rinse

risci'acquo *nm* rinse

risciò *nm inv* rickshaw

riscon'trare *vt* (confrontare) compare; (verificare) verify; (rilevare) find

ri'scontro *nm* comparison; (verifica) verification; (Comm: risposta) reply

risco'prire *vt* rediscover

ri'scossa *nf* revolt; (riconquista) recovery

riscossi'one *nf* collection

ri'scosso pp di RISCUOTERE

ri'scrivere *vt* (scrivere di nuovo) rewrite; (rispondere) write back

riscri'vibile *adj* rewritable

riscu'otere *vt* shake; (percepire) draw; (ottenere) gain; cash ⟨*assegno*⟩

riscu'otersi *vr* rouse oneself

risen'tire ① *vt* hear again; (provare) feel ② *vi* ∼ **di** feel the effect of

risen'tirsi *vr* (offendersi) take offence

risentita'mente *adv* resentfully

risen'tito *adj* resentful

ri'serbo *nm* reserve; **mantenere il** ∼ remain tight-lipped

ri'serva *nf* reserve; (di caccia, pesca) reserve; Sport substitute, reserve; **di** ∼ spare; **senza riserve** wholeheartedly ⟨*accettare, appoggiare*⟩. **riserva di caccia** game reserve. **riserva indiana** Indian reservation. **riserva naturale** wildlife reserve

riser'vare *vt* reserve; (prenotare) book; (per occasione) keep

riser'varsi *vr* (ripromettersi) plan for oneself ⟨*cambiamento*⟩; **mi riservo la sorpresa** I want it to be a surprise

riserva'tezza *nf* reserve

riser'vato *adj* reserved; (confidenziale) classified; **'**∼ **ai clienti dell'albergo'** 'for hotel guests only'; **'**∼ **carico'** 'loading only'

ri'sguardo *nm* endpaper

ri'siedere *vi* ∼ **a** reside in

'risma *nf* ream; fig kind

'riso[1] [1] pp di RIDERE
[2] *nm* (pl nf **risa**) laughter; (singolo) laugh
'riso[2] *nm* (cereale) rice. **riso integrale** brown rice

riso'lino *nm* giggle

risolle'vare *vt* raise again; raise ⟨*morale*⟩; raise again, bring up again ⟨*problema, questione*⟩; increase, improve ⟨*sorti*⟩

risolle'varsi *vr* (da terra) rise again; fig pick up

ri'solto pp di RISOLVERE

risoluta'mente *adv* energetically

risolu'tezza *nf* determination

risolu'tivo *adj* (determinante) decisive; **scelta risolutiva** solution

riso'luto *adj* resolute, determined

risoluzi'one *nf* resolution

ri'solvere *vt* resolve; Math solve

ri'solversi *vr* (decidersi) decide; ∼ **in** turn into

riso'nanza *nf* resonance; **aver** ∼ fig arouse great interest. **risonanza magnetica** magnetic resonance, magnetic resonance imaging

riso'nare *vi* resound; (rimbombare) echo

ri'sorgere *vi* rise again

risorgi'mento *nm* revival; **il Risorgimento** the Risorgimento

ri'sorsa *nf* resource; (espediente) resort; **risorse** *pl* **energetiche** energy resources; **risorse** *pl* **naturali** natural resources; **risorse** *pl* **umane** human resources

ri'sorto pp di RISORGERE

ri'sotto *nm* risotto. **risotto alla marinara** sea-food risotto. **risotto alla milanese** risotto with saffron

ri'sparmi *nmpl* (soldi) savings

risparmi'are *vt* save; (salvare) spare

risparmia'|tore, -trice *nmf* saver

ri'sparmio *nm* saving. **risparmio energetico** energy saving

rispecchi'are *vt* reflect

rispe'dire *vr* send back, return

rispet'tabile *adj* respectable

rispettabilità *nf* respectability

rispet'tare *vt* respect; **farsi** ∼ command respect

rispet'tivo *adj* respective

ri'spetto *nm* respect; ∼ **a** as regards; (a paragone di) compared to

rispettosa'mente *adv* respectfully

rispet'toso *adj* respectful

risplen'dente *adj* shining

ri'splendere *vi* shine

rispon'dente *adj* ∼ **a** in keeping with

rispon'denza *nf* correspondence

ri'spondere *vi* answer; (rimbeccare) answer back; (obbedire) respond; ∼ **a** reply to; ∼ **di** (rendersi responsabile) answer for

rispo'sare *vt* remarry

rispo'sarsi *vr* remarry

ri'sposta *nf* answer, reply; (reazione) response; **senza risposta** unanswered ⟨*domanda, lettera*⟩

ri'sposto pp di RISPONDERE

rispun'tare *vi* ⟨*persona, sole*⟩ reappear

'rissa *nf* brawl

ris'soso *adj* pugnacious

ristabi'lire *vt* re-establish

ristabi'lirsi *vr* (in salute) recover

rista'gnare *vi* stagnate; (sangue) coagulate

ri'stagno *nm* stagnation

ri'stampa *nf* reprint; (azione) reprinting

ristam'pare *vt* reprint

risto'rante *nm* restaurant

risto'rare *vt* refresh

risto'rarsi *vr* liter take some refreshment; (riposarsi) take a rest

ristora'|tore, -trice [1] *nmf* (proprietario di ristorante) restaurateur; (fornitore) caterer [2] *adj* refreshing

ri'storo *nm* refreshment; (sollievo) relief; **servizio di ristoro** refreshments *pl*

ristret'tezza *nf* narrowness; (povertà) poverty; **vivere in ristrettezze** live in straitened circumstances

ri'stretto [1] pp di RESTRINGERE [2] *adj* narrow; (condensato) condensed; (limitato) restricted; **di idee ristrette** narrow-minded

ristruttu'rante *adj* ⟨*cosmetico*⟩ conditioning

ristruttu'rare *vt* Comm restructure; renovate ⟨*casa*⟩; repair ⟨*capelli*⟩

ristrutturazi'one *nf* Comm restructuring; (di casa) renovation

risucchi'are *vt* suck in

ri'succhio *nm* whirlpool; (di corrente) undertow

risul'tare *vi* result; (riuscire) turn out

risul'tato *nm* result; **risultati** *pl* **parziali** (di elezioni) preliminary results; (di partite) half-time results

risuo'nare [1] *vt* play again ⟨*pezzo musicale*⟩; ring again ⟨*campanello*⟩ [2] *vi* ⟨*grida, parola*⟩ echo; Phys resonate

risurrezi'one, risuscitare = RESURREZIONE, RESUSCITARE

risvegli'are *vt* reawaken ⟨*interesse*⟩

risvegli'arsi *vr* wake up; ⟨*natura*⟩ awake; ⟨*desiderio*⟩ be aroused

ri'sveglio *nm* waking up; (dell'interesse) revival; (del desiderio) arousal

ri'svolto *nm* (di giacca) lapel; (di pantaloni) turn-up, cuff *Am*; (di manica) cuff; (di tasca) flap; (di libro) inside flap

ritagli'are *vt* cut out

ri'taglio *nm* cutting; (di stoffa) scrap

ritar'dare ① *vi* be late; ⟨*orologio*⟩ be slow
② *vt* delay; slow down ⟨*progresso*⟩; (differire) postpone

ritarda'tario, -a *nmf* latecomer

ritar'dato ① pp di RITARDARE
② *adj* delayed; **a scoppio** ∼ delayed action *attrib*; Psych retarded

ri'tardo *nm* delay; **essere in** ∼ be late; ⟨*volo*⟩ be delayed

ri'tegno *nm* reserve

ritem'prare *vt* restore

rite'nere *vt* retain; deduct ⟨*somma*⟩; (credere) believe

riten'tare *vt* try again

rite'nuta *nf* (sul salario) deduction.
ritenuta d'acconto tax deducted in advance from payments made to self-employed people. **ritenuta diretta** taxation at source. **ritenuta alla fonte** taxation at source, deduction at source

ritenzi'one *nf* Med retention

riti'rare *vt* throw back ⟨*palla*⟩; (prelevare) withdraw; (riscuotere) draw; collect ⟨*pacco*⟩

riti'rarsi *vr* withdraw; ⟨*stoffa*⟩ shrink; (da attività) retire; ⟨*marea*⟩ recede

riti'rata *nf* retreat; (WC) toilet

ri'tiro *nm* withdrawal; Relig retreat; (da attività) retirement. **ritiro bagagli** baggage reclaim

'ritmica *nf* rhythmic gymnastics

ritmica'mente *adv* rhythmically

'ritmico *adj* rhythmic[al]

'ritmo *nm* rhythm; **a** ∼ **serrato** at a cracking pace

'rito *nm* rite; **di** ∼ customary. **rito funebre** funeral service

ritoc'care *vt* (correggere) touch up

ri'tocco *nm* alteration; **ritocchi** *pl* Phot retouching

ri'torcersi *vr* ∼ **contro qualcuno** boomerang on somebody

ritor'nare *vi* return; (andare/venire indietro) go/come back; (ricorrere) recur; (ridiventare) become again

ritor'nello *nm* refrain

ri'torno *nm* return

ritorsi'one *nf* retaliation

ri'torto *adj* ⟨*filo, cavo*⟩ twisted

ritra'durre *vt* (tradurre di nuovo) retranslate

ri'trarre *vt* (ritirare) withdraw; (distogliere) turn away; (rappresentare) portray

ritra'smettere *vt* TV show again, re-broadcast

ritrat'tabile *adj* ⟨*accusa*⟩ which can be withdrawn

ritrat'tare *vt* retract, withdraw ⟨*dichiarazione*⟩

ritrattazi'one *nf* withdrawal, retraction

ritrat'tista *nmf* portrait painter

ri'tratto ① pp di RITRARRE
② *nm* portrait

ritrazi'one *nf* retraction

ritrosa'mente *adv* shyly

ritro'sia *nf* shyness

ri'troso *adj* (timido) shy; **a** ∼ backwards; ∼ **a** reluctant to

ritrova'mento *nm* (azione) finding; (cosa) find

ritro'vare *vt* find [again]; regain ⟨*salute*⟩

ritro'varsi *vr* meet; (di nuovo) meet again; (capitare) find oneself; (raccapezzarsi) see one's way

ritro'vato *nm* discovery

ri'trovo *nm* meeting-place. **ritrovo notturno** night club

'ritto *adj* upright; (diritto) straight

ritu'ale *adj & nm* ritual

ritual'mente *adv* ritually

riunifi'care *vt* reunify

riunifi'carsi *vr* be reunited

riunificazi'one *nf* reunification

riuni'one *nf* meeting; (dopo separazione) reunion. **riunione del corpo insegnante** staff meeting. **riunione dei genitori (degli alunni)** parents' evening

riu'nire *vt* (unire) join together; (radunare) gather

riu'nirsi *vr* be reunited; (adunarsi) meet

riu'sare *vt* reuse

riusc'ire *vi* (aver successo) succeed; (in matematica ecc) be good (**in** at); (aver esito) turn out; **le è riuscito simpatico** she found him likeable

riu'scita *nf* (esito) result; (successo) success

ri'uso *nm* reuse

riutiliz'zare *vt* reuse

'riva *nf* (di mare, lago) shore; (di fiume) bank; **in** ∼ **al mare** on the seashore

rivacci'nare *vt* revaccinate

ri'vale *nmf* rival

rivaleggi'are *vi* compete (**con** with)

rivalità *nf inv* rivalry

ri'valsa *nf* revenge; **prendersi una** ∼ **su qualcuno** take revenge on somebody

rivalu'tare *vt* reappraise

rivalutazi'one *nf* revaluation

rivan'gare *vt* dig up again

rive'dere *vt* see again; revise ⟨*lezione*⟩; review ⟨*accordo*⟩; (verificare) check

rive'dibile *adj* ‹accordo› reviewable; ‹recluta› temporarily unfit

rive'lare *vt* reveal

rive'larsi *vr* (dimostrarsi) turn out

rivela'tore ① *adj* revealing ② *nm* Techn detector. **rivelatore di mine** mine detector

rivelazi'one *nf* revelation

ri'vendere *vt* resell

rivendi'care *vt* claim

rivendicazi'one *nf* claim

ri'vendita *nf* (negozio) shop. **rivendita autorizzata** authorized retailer

rivendi∥'tore, -trice *nmf* retailer. **rivenditore autorizzato** authorized retailer

riverbe'rare *vt* reflect ‹luce›

ri'verbero *nm* reverberation; (bagliore) glare

rive'renza *nf* reverence; (inchino) curtsy; (di uomo) bow

rive'rire *vt* respect; (ossequiare) pay one's respects to

rivernici'are *vt* repaint; ‹con smalto› revarnish

river'sare *vt* pour

river'sarsi *vr* ‹fiume› flow

river'sibile *adj* = REVERSIBLE

rivesti'mento *nm* covering

rive'stire *vt* (rifornire di abiti) clothe; (ricoprire) cover; (internamente) line; hold ‹carica›

rive'stirsi *vr* get dressed again

rive'stito *adj* ~ **di** covered with

rivi'era *nf* coast; (in corsa a ostacoli) water jump; **la ~ ligure** the Italian Riviera

ri'vincita *nf* Sport return match; (vendetta) revenge

rivis'suto *pp di* RIVIVERE

ri'vista *nf* review; (pubblicazione) magazine; Theat revue; **passare in ~** review. **rivista patinata** glossy magazine

rivitaliz'zare *vt* revitalize

rivitalizzazi'one *nf* revitalization

ri'vivere ① *vi* come to life again; (riprendere le forze) revive ② *vt* relive

'rivo *nm* stream

rivo'lere *vt* (volere di nuovo) want again; (volere indietro) want back

ri'volgere *vt* turn; (indirizzare) address

ri'volgersi *vr* turn round; **~ a** (indirizzarsi) turn to

rivolgi'mento *nm* upheaval

ri'volta *nf* revolt

rivol'tante *adj* revolting, disgusting

rivol'tare *vt* turn [over]; (mettendo l'interno verso l'esterno) turn inside out; (sconvolgere) upset

rivol'tarsi *vr* (ribellarsi) revolt

rivol'tella *nf* revolver

ri'volto *pp di* RIVOLGERE

rivol'toso, -a *nmf* rebel, insurgent

rivoluzio'nare *vt* revolutionize

rivoluzio'nario, -a *adj & nmf* revolutionary

rivoluzi'one *nf* revolution; (fig: disordine) chaos. **rivoluzione francese** French Revolution. **rivoluzione industriale** Industrial Revolution

riz'zare *vt* raise; (innalzare) erect; prick up ‹orecchie›

riz'zarsi *vr* stand up; ‹capelli› stand on end; ‹orecchie› prick up

'roaming *nm* Teleph **roaming internazionale** roaming

'roast-beef *nm inv* roast beef

'roba *nf* stuff; (personale) belongings *pl*, stuff; (faccenda) thing; (sl: droga) drugs *pl*; **~ da matti!** absolute madness!. **roba da bere** drink. **roba da lavare** washing. **roba da mangiare** food, things to eat. **roba da stirare** ironing

ro'baccia *nf* rubbish

robi'vecchi *nm inv* second-hand dealer

ro'bot *nm inv* robot; (da cucina) food processor

ro'botica *nf* robotics

ro'botico *adj* robotic

robotiz'zato *adj* robotic, robotized

robu'stezza *nf* sturdiness, robustness; (forza) strength

ro'busto *adj* sturdy, robust; (forte) strong

rocambo'lesco *adj* incredible

'rocca *nf* fortress

rocca'forte *nf* stronghold

rocchetti'era *nf* winder

roc'chetto *nm* reel

'roccia *nf* rock; (sport) rock-climbing

rock *nm* rock [music]. **rock acrobatico** rock 'n' roll

'roco *adj* throaty

ro'daggio *nm* running in

'Rodano *nm* Rhone

ro'dare *vt* run in

ro'deo *nm* rodeo

'rodere *vt* gnaw; (corrodere) corrode

'rodersi *vr* ~ **da** (logorarsi) be consumed with

rodi'tore *nm* rodent

rodo'dendro *nm* rhododendron

'rogito *nm* Jur deed

'rogna *nf* scabies *sg*; fig nuisance

ro'gnone *nm* Culin kidney

ro'gnoso *adj* scabby

'rogo *nm* (supplizio) stake; (per cadaveri) pyre

rol'lare ① *vt* roll ‹sigaretta›

[2] *vi* ⟨aereo, nave⟩ roll

ROM *nf* Comput ROM

rom *adj inv* & *nmf inv* (zingaro) Roma, Romany

'Roma *nf* Rome

Roma'nia *nf* Romania

ro'manico *adj* Romanesque

ro'mano, -a *adj* & *nmf* Roman

romantica'mente *adv* romantically

romanti'cismo *nm* romanticism

ro'mantico *adj* romantic

ro'manza *nf* romance

roman'zare *vt* fictionalize

roman'zato *adj* romanticized, fictionalized

roman'zesco *adj* fictional; (stravagante) wild, unrealistic

roman'zetto *nm* **romanzetto rosa** novelette

romanzi'ere *nm* novelist

ro'manzo [1] *adj* Romance
[2] *nm* novel; (storia incredibile romantica) romance. **romanzo d'appendice** serial story. **romanzo giallo** thriller. **romanzo sceneggiato** novel adapted for television/radio

rom'bare *vi* rumble

'rombo *nm* rumble; Math rhombus; (pesce) turbot

romboi'dale *adj* rhomboid, diamond-shaped

'rompere *vt* break; break off ⟨relazione⟩; **non ~ [le scatole]!** (fam: seccare) don't be a pain [in the neck]!

'rompersi *vr* break; **~ una gamba** break one's leg

rompi'capo *nm* nuisance; (indovinello) puzzle

rompi'collo *nm* daredevil; **a ~** at breakneck speed

rompighi'accio *nm inv* ice-breaker

rompi'mento *nm* fam pain

rompi'scatole *nmf inv* fam pain

'ronda *nf* rounds *pl*

ron'della *nf* Mech washer

'rondine *nf* swallow

ron'done *nm* swift

ron'fare *vi* (russare) snore; (fare le fusa) purr

ron'zare *vi* buzz; **~ attorno a qualcuno** fig hang about somebody

ron'zino *nm* jade

ron'zio *nm* buzz

'rosa [1] *nf* rose. **rosa rampicante** rambler, rambling rose. **rosa selvatica** wild rose. **rosa dei venti** wind rose
[2] *adj* & *nm inv* (colore) pink

ro'saio *nm* rosebush

ro'sario *nm* rosary

ro'sato [1] *adj* rosy
[2] *nm* (vino) rosé

'rosbif = ROAST-BEEF

rosé *nm inv* rosé

'roseo *adj* pink

ro'seto *nm* rose garden

ro'setta *nf* (coccarda) rosette; Mech washer

rosicchi'are *vt* nibble; (rodere) gnaw

rosma'rino *nm* rosemary

'roso *pp di* RODERE

roso'lare *vt* brown

roso'lato *adj* sauté

roso'lia *nf* German measles *sg*

ro'sone *nm* rosette; (apertura) rose window

'rospo *nm* toad

ros'setto *nm* lipstick

'rosso *adj* & *nm* red; **diventare ~** go red; **ha i capelli rossi** she's a redhead; **passare col ~** go through a red light, jump a red light. **rosso mattone** *adj* brick red. **rosso sangue** *adj* blood red. **rosso scarlatto** *adj* scarlet. **rosso d'uovo** [egg] yolk. **rosso vermiglio** *adj* vermilion

ros'sore *nm* redness; (della pelle) flush

rosticce'ria *nf* shop selling cooked meat and other prepared food

'rostro *nm* rostrum; (becco) bill

ro'tabile *adj* **strada rotabile** carriageway

ro'taia *nf* rail; (solco) rut

ro'tante *adj* rotating

ro'tare *vt/i* rotate

rota'tiva *nf* rotary press

rota'torio *adj* rotary

rotazi'one *nf* rotation; (di personale) turnover. **rotazione delle colture** crop rotation

rote'are *vt/i* roll

ro'tella *nf* small wheel; (di mobile) castor

roto'calco *nm* (sistema) rotogravure; ⟨rivista⟩ illustrated magazine

roto'lare *vt/i* roll

roto'larsi *vr* roll [about]

roto'lio *nm* rolling

'rotolo *nm* roll; (di pergamena) scroll; **andare a rotoli** go to rack and ruin. **rotolo di carta igienica** toilet roll

roto'loni *adv* **cadere ~** tumble

ro'tonda *nf* roundabout, traffic circle Am

rotondità *nf inv* (qualità) roundness; **~ pl** (curve femminili) curves *pl*, curvaceousness

ro'tondo, -a [1] *adj* round
[2] *nf* (spiazzo) terrace

ro'tore *nm* rotor

'rotta[1] *nf* Naut, Aeron course; **far ~ per** set a course for; **fuori ~** off course; **in ~ di collisione** on a collision course '**rotta**² *nf* **a ∼ di collo** at breakneck speed; **essere in ∼ con** be on bad terms with

rotta'maio *nm* junkyard

rot'tame *nm* scrap; *fig* wreck

'**rotto** ① *pp di* ROMPERE
② *adj* broken; (stracciato) torn

rot'tura *nf* break; **che ∼ di scatole!** *fam* what a pain!

'**rotula** *nf* kneecap

rou'lette *nf inv* roulette. **roulette russa** Russian roulette

rou'lotte *nf inv* caravan, trailer Am

rou'tine *nf inv* routine; **di ∼** ‹operazioni, controlli› routine

ro'vente *adj* scorching

'**rovere** *nm* (legno) oak

rovescia'mento *nm* overthrow

rovesci'are *vt* (buttare a terra) knock over; (sottosopra) turn upside down; (rivoltare) turn inside out; spill ‹liquido› overthrow ‹governo›; reverse ‹situazione›

rovesci'arsi *vr* (capovolgersi) overturn; (riversarsi) pour

ro'vescio ① *adj* (contrario) reverse; **alla rovescia** (capovolto) upside down; (con l'interno all'esterno) inside out
② *nm* reverse; (nella maglia) purl; (di pioggia) downpour; *Tennis* backhand

ro'vina *nf* ruin; (crollo) collapse; **in ∼** in ruins

rovi'nare ① *vt* ruin; (guastare) spoil
② *vi* crash

rovi'narsi *vr* be ruined; ‹persona› ruin oneself

rovi'nato *adj* ruined

ro'vine *nfpl* ruins

rovi'noso *adj* ruinous

rovi'stare *vt* ransack

'**rovo** *nm* bramble

rozza'mente *adv* crudely

roz'zezza *nf* indelicacy

'**rozzo** *adj* rough

R.R. *abbr* (**ricevuta di ritorno**) acknowledgement of receipt

R.U. *abbr* (**Regno Unito**) UK

'**ruba** *nf* **andare a ∼** sell like hot cakes

rubacchi'are *vt* pilfer

rubacu'ori *nm inv* heart-throb

ru'bare *vt* steal

rubi'condo *adj* ruddy

rubi'netto *nm* tap, faucet Am

ru'bino *nm* ruby

ru'bizzo *adj* spry

'**rublo** *nm* rouble

ru'brica *nf* (in giornale) column; (in programma televisivo) TV report; (quaderno con indice) address book. **rubrica degli annunci personali** personal column.

rubrica dei cuori solitari lonely hearts' column. **rubrica sportiva** sports column. **rubrica degli spettacoli** listings. **rubrica telefonica** telephone and address book.

'**rucola** *nf* rocket

'**rude** *adj* rough

'**rudere** *nm* ruin

ru'dezza *nf* bluntness

rudimen'tale *adj* rudimentary

rudi'menti *nmpl* rudiments

ruffi'ana *nf* procuress

ruffi'ano *nm* pimp; (adulatore) bootlicker

'**ruga** *nf* wrinkle

'**ruggine** *nf* rust; **fare la ∼** go rusty

ruggi'noso *adj* rusty

rug'gire *vi* roar

rug'gito *nm* roar

rugi'ada *nf* dew

ru'goso *adj* wrinkled

rul'lare *vi* roll; *Aeron* taxi

rul'lino *nm* film

rul'lio *nm* rolling; *Aeron* taxiing

'**rullo** *nm* roll; *Techn* roller

rum *nm* rum

ru'meno, -a *adj & nmf* Romanian

rumi'nante *nm* ruminant

rumi'nare *vi* ruminate

ru'more *nm* noise; *fig* rumour

rumoreggi'are *vi* rumble

rumorosa'mente *adv* noisily

rumo'roso *adj* noisy; (sonoro) loud

ru'olo *nm* *Theat* role; **di ∼** on the staff. **ruolo delle imposte** tax notice. **ruolo primario/secondario** major/minor role

ru'ota *nf* wheel; **andare a ∼ libera** free-wheel; **fare la ∼** do a cartwheel. **ruota dentata** cogwheel. **ruota di scorta** spare wheel. **ruota di stampa** (di stampante) print wheel. **ruota del timone** helm

'**rupe** *nf* cliff

ru'pestre *adj* ‹pittura› rock *attrib*

ru'pia *nf* rupee

ru'rale *adj* rural

ru'scello *nm* stream

'**ruspa** *nf* bulldozer

ru'spante *adj* free-range

rus'sare *vi* snore

'**Russia** *nf* Russia

'**russo, -a** ① *adj & nmf* Russian
② *nm* (lingua) Russian

'**rustico** *adj* rural; ‹carattere› rough

'**ruta** *nf* *Bot* rue

rut'tare *vi* belch, burp

rut'tino *nm* (di bambino) burp

'**rutto** *nm* belch, burp

'**ruvido** *adj* coarse

ruzzo'lare *vi* tumble down

ruzzo'lone *nm* tumble; **cadere ruzzoloni**

tumble down, tumble [helter-skelter]

'**Rwanda** *nm* Rwanda

Ss

S. *abbr* (**santo, santa**) St.; *abbr* (**sud**) south

'**sabato** *nm* Saturday; **di** ∼ on Saturdays

sab'batico *adj* sabbatical; **anno sabbatico** sabbatical [year]

'**sabbia** *nf* sand; **sabbie** *pl* **mobili** quicksand

sabbi'are *vt* sandblast

sabbia'tura *nf* (di vetro, metallo) sandblasting; (terapeutica) sand-bath

sabbi'oso *adj* sandy

sabo'taggio *nm* sabotage

sabo'tare *vt* sabotage

sabota|'tore, -trice *nmf* saboteur

'**sacca** *nf* bag. **sacca di resistenza** pocket of resistance. **sacca da viaggio** travel[ling]-bag, duffel bag

sacca'rina *nf* saccharin

sac'cente ① *adj* conceited ② *nmf* know-all, know-it-all Am

saccente'ria *nf* conceit

saccheggi'are *vt* sack; hum plunder ⟨frigo⟩

saccheggia|'tore, -trice *nmf* plunderer

sac'cheggio *nm* sack

sac'chetto *nm* bag. **sacchetto di plastica** plastic bag. **sacchetto per la spazzatura** bin liner, bin bag

'**sacco** *nm* sack; Anat sac; (contenuto) sack[ful]; **mettere nel** ∼ fig swindle; **un** ∼ (moltissimo) a lot; **un** ∼ **di** (gran quantità) lots of; **un** ∼ **di soldi** shedloads of money fam. **sacco a pelo** sleeping-bag. **sacco postale** mail-bag

saccope'lista *nmf* backpacker

sacer'dote *nm* priest

sacer'dozio *nm* priesthood

sacra'mento *nm* sacrament

sacrifi'cale *adj* sacrificial

sacrifi'care *vt* sacrifice

sacrifi'carsi *vr* sacrifice oneself

sacrifi'cato *adj* sacrificed; (non valorizzato) wasted

sacri'ficio *nm* sacrifice

sacri'legio *nm* sacrilege

sa'crilego *adj* sacrilegious

'**sacro** ① *adj* sacred; **la Sacra Bibbia** the Holy Bible ② *nm* Anat sacrum

sacro'santo *adj* sacrosanct; (verità) gospel; (diritto) sacred

'**sadico, -a** ① *adj* sadistic ② *nmf* sadist

sa'dismo *nm* sadism

sa'etta *nf* arrow; (fulmine) thunderbolt; **correre come una** ∼ run like the wind

sa'fari *nm inv* safari

'**saga** *nf* saga

sa'gace *adj* shrewd

sa'gacia *nf* sagacity

sag'gezza *nf* wisdom

saggia'mente *adv* sagely

saggi'are *vt* test

'**saggio**[1] *nm* (scritto) essay; (prova) proof; (di metallo) assay; (campione) sample; (esempio) example

'**saggio**[2] ① *adj* wise ② *nm* (persona) sage

sag'gista *nmf* essayist

sag'gistica *nf* non-fiction

Sagit'tario *nm* Astr Sagittarius

'**sago** = SAGÙ

'**sagoma** *nf* shape; (profilo) outline; (in falegnameria) template; **che** ∼! fam what a character!

sago'mare *vt* make according to a template

'**sagra** *nf* festival

sa'grato *nm* churchyard

sagre'stano *nm* sacristan

sagre'stia *nf* sacristy

sagù *nm* sago

Sa'hara *nm* Sahara

'**sala** *nf* hall; (salotto) living room; (per riunioni ecc) room; (di cinema) cinema. **sala arrivi** arrivals lounge. **sala d'aspetto** waiting room. **sala d'attesa** waiting room. **sala da ballo** ballroom. **sala di comando** control room. **sala conferenze** conference hall. **sala giochi** amusement arcade, games room. **sala d'imbarco** departure lounge. **sala di lettura** reading room. **sala macchine** engine room. **sala**

operatoria operating theatre Br, operating room Am. **sala parto** delivery room. **sala da pranzo** dining room. **sala professori** staff room, common room. **sala di regia** Radio, TV control room. **sala di ricevimento** function room. **sala riunioni** conference room. **sala da tè** tea shop

sa'lace *adj* salacious

sa'lame *nm* salami *sg*

salame'lecchi *nmpl* **fare** ~ bow and scrape; **prendi quello che vuoi senza tanti** ~ don't stand on ceremony, take what you want

sala'moia *nf* brine

sa'lare *vt* salt

salari'ato *nm* wage earner

sa'lario *nm* wages *pl*

salas'sare *vt* Med bleed; fig bleed dry

sa'lasso *nm* bleeding; **essere un** ~ fig cost a fortune

sala'tini *nmpl* savouries (eaten with aperitifs)

sa'lato *adj* salty; (costoso) dear; **acqua salata** salt water

sal'ciccia *nf* = SALSICCIA

sal'dare *vt* weld; set ⟨osso⟩; pay off ⟨debito⟩; settle ⟨conto⟩; ~ **a stagno** solder

sal'darsi *vr* ⟨osso⟩ knit; ⟨ferita⟩ heal

saldat'rice *nf* soldering iron

salda'tura *nf* soldering; (giunzione) join

'saldo ① *adj* firm, unshaken; (resistente) strong; ~ **come una roccia** solid as a rock; **essere** ~ **nei propri principi** stick to one's principles
② *nm* (pagamento) settlement; Comm balance; (di conto corrente) bank balance; **saldi** *pl* sale; **i** ~ **di fine stagione** the end of season sales; **in** ~ ⟨essere⟩ on sale; ⟨comprato⟩ in a sale. **saldo iniziale** opening balance

'sale *nm* salt; **non ha** ~ **in zucca** fam he hasn't got an ounce of common sense; **restare di** ~ be struck dumb [with astonishment]; **sali** *pl* Med smelling salts; **sali** *pl* **da bagno** bath salts. **sale da cucina** cooking salt. **sale fino** table salt. **sale grosso** cooking salt. **sale marino** sea salt. **sali e tabacchi** *pl* (negozio) tobacconist's shop

'salice *nm* willow. **salice piangente** weeping willow

sali'ente *adj* outstanding; **i punti salienti** the main points, the highlights

sali'era *nf* salt-cellar

sa'lina *nf* salt-works *sg*

salinità *nf* saltiness

sa'lino *adj* saline

sa'lire ① *vi* go/come up; (levarsi) rise; (su treno ecc) get on; (in macchina) get in
② *vt* go/come up ⟨scale⟩

sa'lita *nf* climb; (aumento) rise; **in** ~ uphill

sa'liva *nf* saliva

sali'vare ① *vt* salivate
② *adj* ⟨ghiandola⟩ salivary

salmi *nm* **in** ~ marinated and slowly cooked in the marinade

'salma *nf* corpse

sal'mastro ① *adj* brackish
② *nm* salt air

salmi'strare *vt* Culin cure

'salmo *nm* psalm

sal'mone *nm & adj inv* salmon. **salmone affumicato** smoked salmon

salmo'nella *nf* salmonella

sa'lone *nm* (salotto) living room; (di parrucchiere) salon. **salone dell'automobile** motor show. **salone di bellezza** beauty parlour. **salone del libro** book fair

salo'pette *nf inv* dungarees *pl*

salotti'ero *adj pej* mundane; **discorso salottiero** small talk

salot'tino *nm* bower

sa'lotto *nm* drawing room; (soggiorno) sitting room; (mobili) [three-piece] suite; **fare** ~ chat. **salotto letterario** literary salon

sal'pare ① *vi* sail
② *vt* ~ **l'ancora** weigh anchor

'salsa *nf* sauce; Mus salsa. **salsa di pomodoro** tomato sauce. **salsa di rafano** horseradish sauce. **salsa di soia** soy sauce. **salsa tartara** tartar sauce

sal'sedine *nf* saltiness

sal'siccia *nf* sausage

salsi'era *nf* sauce-boat, gravy boat

sal'tare ① *vi* jump; (venir via) come off; (balzare) leap; (esplodere) blow up; **saltar fuori** spring from nowhere; ⟨oggetto cercato⟩ turn up; **è saltato fuori che …** it emerged that …; ~ **fuori con …** come out with …; **salta agli occhi** (è evidente) it hits you; ~ **in aria** blow up; ~ **in mente** spring to mind
② *vt* jump [over]; skip ⟨pasti, lezioni⟩; Culin sauté

sal'tato *adj* Culin sautéed

saltel'lare *vi* hop; (di gioia) skip

saltim'banco *nm* acrobat

saltim'bocca *nm inv* slice of veal rolled with ham and sage and shallow-fried

'salto *nm* jump; (balzo) leap; (dislivello) drop; (fig: omissione, lacuna) gap; **fare un** ~ **da** (visitare) drop in on; **in un** ~ fig in a jiffy; **fare i salti mortali** fig go to great lengths; **fare quattro salti** fam go dancing; **fare un** ~ **nel buio** fig take a leap in the dark. **salto in alto** high jump. **salto con l'asta** pole-vault. **salto con** ⋯⟩

l'elastico bungee jump. **salto con la corda** skipping. **salto in lungo** long jump. **salto pagina** Comput page down. **salto di qualità** quality leap

saltuaria'mente *adv* occasionally, from time to time

saltu'ario *adj* desultory. **lavoro saltuario** casual work

sa'lubre *adj* healthy

salume'ria *nf* delicatessen

sa'lumi *nmpl* cold cuts

salumi'ere *nm* person who sells cold meat

salu'tare ① *vt* greet; (congedandosi) say goodbye to; (portare i saluti a) give one's regards to; Mil salute; **ti saluto!** fam cheerio!
② *adj* healthy

salu'tarsi *vr* (all'arrivo) greet each other; (alla partenza) say goodbye to each other

sa'lute *nf* health; **godere di ottima** ∼ be in the best of health, enjoy excellent health; **in** ∼ in good health; ∼**!** (dopo uno starnuto) bless you!; (a un brindisi) cheers!.
salute di ferro iron constitution

salu'tista *nmf* health fanatic; (dell'Esercito della Salvezza) Salvationist

sa'luto *nm* greeting; (di addio) goodbye; Mil salute; **saluti** *pl* (ossequi) regards

'salva *nf* salvo; **sparare a salve** shoot blanks; **a salve** ⟨*pistola*⟩ loaded with blank cartridges

salvacon'dotto *nm* safe-conduct

salvada'naio *nm* money box

salva'gente *nm* lifebelt; (a giubbotto) lifejacket; (ciambella) rubber ring; (spartitraffico) traffic island

salvaguar'dare *vt* protect, safeguard

salvaguar'darsi *vr* protect oneself

salvagu'ardia *nf* safeguard

sal'vare *vt* save; (proteggere) protect; ∼ **la faccia** save face; ∼ **la pelle** save one's skin

sal'varsi *vr* save oneself

salva'schermo *nm inv* Comput screen saver

salva'slip *nm inv* panty-liner

salva'taggio *nm* rescue; Naut salvage; Comput saving; **battello di salvataggio** lifeboat

salva'vita *nm inv* Electr circuit breaker

'salve ▶ SALVA

salva|'tore, -trice *nmf* saviour

sal'vezza *nf* safety; Relig salvation. **ancora di salvezza** fig salvation

'salvia *nf* sage

salvi'etta *nf* serviette

'salvo ① *adj* safe
② *nm* **trarre in** ∼ rescue
③ *prep* except [for]

④ *conj* ∼ **che** (a meno che) unless; (eccetto che) except that

samari'tano, -a *adj & nmf* Samaritan; **un buon** ∼ a good Samaritan

'samba *nf* samba

sam'buca *nf* sambuca

sam'buco *nm* elder

Sa'moa *nfpl* **Samoa Occidentali** Western Samoa

san *nm* (before proper names starting with a consonant) saint; ▶ SANTO

sa'nabile *adj* curable

sa'nare *vt* heal; (bonificare) reclaim; ∼ **il bilancio** balance the books

sana'toria *nf* decree legitimizing a situation which is in principle illegal

sana'torio *nm* sanatorium

san'cire *vt* sanction

'sandalo *nm* sandal; Bot sandalwood

sandi'nista *adj & nmf* Sandinista

'sandwich *nm inv* sandwich. **uomo sandwich** sandwich-man

san'gallo *nm* (tessuto) broderie anglaise

san'gria *nf* sangria

'sangue *nm* blood; **a** ∼ **freddo** in cold blood; **al** ∼ Culin rare; **appena al** ∼ Culin medium-rare; **farsi cattivo** ∼ **per** worry about; **iniettato di** ∼ ⟨*occhio*⟩ bloodshot; **all'ultimo** ∼ ⟨*lotta*⟩ to the death; **di** ∼ **blu** blue-blooded; **perdere** ∼ **dal naso** have a nose bleed; **sudare** ∼ sweat blood.
sangue freddo composure

sangue'misto *nm* half-caste

sangu'igno *adj* blood *attrib*

sangui'naccio *nm* Culin black pudding

sangui'nante *adj* bleeding

sangui'nare *vi* bleed

sangui'nario *adj* bloodthirsty

sangui'noso *adj* bloody

sangui'suga *nf* leech

sanità *nf* soundness; (salute) health; **ministero della sanità** Department of Health. **sanità di costumi** morality. **sanità mentale** sanity, mental health

sani'tario ① *adj* sanitary; **servizio sanitario** health service
② *nm* doctor

San Ma'rino *nm* San Marino

'sano *adj* sound; (salutare) healthy; ∼ **come un pesce** as fit as a fiddle. **sano di mente** sane

'sansa *nf* husk

San Sil'vestro *nm* New Year's Eve

santifi'care *vt* sanctify

santità *nf* sainthood

'santo, -a ① *adj* holy; (con nome proprio) saint; **Sant'Antonio** St Anthony; **San Francesco d'Assisi** St Francis of Assisi; **di santa ragione** in no uncertain terms

s

2 *nmf* saint. **santo patrono**, **santa patrona** patron saint

san'tone *nm* guru

santo'reggia *nf* Bot savory

santu'ario *nm* sanctuary

san Valen'tino *nm* St Valentine's Day; **giorno di san Valentino** Valentine's Day

sanzio'nare *vt* sanction

sanzi'one *nf* sanction. **sanzione amministrativa** administrative sanction. **sanzione penale** legal sanction

sa'pere 1 *vt* know; (essere capace di) be able to; (venire a sapere) hear; **saperla lunga** know a thing or two; **non lo so** I don't know; **non so che farci** there's nothing I can do about it; ∼ **a memoria** know by heart; ∼ **il fatto proprio** know what one is talking about; **per quanto ne sappia** insofar as I know

2 *vi* ∼ **di** know about; (aver sapore di) taste of; (aver odore di) smell of; **saperci fare** know how to go about it; **saperci fare con i bambini** be good with children

3 *nm* knowledge

sapi'ente 1 *adj* wise; (esperto) expert
2 *nm* sage

sapiente'mente *adv* wisely; (abilmente) skilfully

sapien'tone *nm* smart alec[k]

sapi'enza *nf* wisdom

sa'pone *nm* soap; **bolla di** ∼ soap bubble; **finire in una bolla di** ∼ fig come to nothing. **sapone da barba** shaving soap. **sapone da bucato** washing soap

sapo'netta *nf* bar of soap

sapo'noso *adj* soapy

sa'pore *nm* taste; **sentire** ∼ **di** detect a hint of

saporita'mente *adv* ⟨condire⟩ skilfully; ⟨mangiare⟩ appreciatively; ⟨dormire⟩ soundly

sapo'rito *adj* tasty

sapu'tello, **-a** *adj & nm* sl know-all, know-it-all Am

sara'banda *nf* fig uproar

sara'ceno, **-a** *adj & nmf* Saracen; **grano saraceno** buckwheat

saraci'nesca *nf* roller shutter; (di chiusa) sluice gate

'sarago *nm* white bream

sar'casmo *nm* sarcasm

sarcastica'mente *adv* sarcastically

sar'castico *adj* sarcastic

sar'cofago *nm* sarcophagus

Sar'degna *nf* Sardinia

sar'dina *nf* sardine

'sardo, **-a** *adj & nmf* Sardinian

sar'donico *adj* sardonic

sarti'ame *nm* rigging

'sarto, **-a** 1 *nm* tailor
2 *nf* dressmaker

sarto'ria *nf* (da uomo) tailor's; (da donna) dressmaker's; (arte) couture

s.a.s. *abbr* **società in accomandita semplice**

sas'saia *nf* stony ground

sassai'ola *nf* hail of stones

sas'sata *nf* blow with a stone; **una** ∼ **ha rotto il vetro** a stone broke the window; **prendere a sassate** throw stones at, stone

'sasso *nm* stone; (ciottolo) pebble; **sono rimasto di** ∼ I was struck dumb [with astonishment]

sassofo'nista *nmf* saxophonist

sas'sofono *nm* saxophone

'sassone *nmf* Saxon; **genitivo sassone** Saxon genitive

sas'soso *adj* stony

'Satana *nm* Satan

sa'tanico *adj* satanic

sa'tellite *adj inv & nm* satellite; **città satellite** satellite town

sati'nare *vt* glaze; polish ⟨metallo⟩

sati'nato *adj* glazed; ⟨metallo⟩ polished

'satira *nf* satire

sa'tirico *adj* satirical

satol'lare *vt* hum stuff

sa'tollo *adj* hum replete, full

satu'rare *vt* saturate

saturazi'one *nf* saturation

satur'nismo *nm* lead poisoning

Sa'turno *nm* Saturn

'saturo *adj* saturated; (pieno) full

'S.A.U.B. *nf abbr* (**Struttura Amministrativa Unificata di Base**) Italian national health service

'sauna *nf* sauna

sa'vana *nf* savannah

savoi'ardo *nm* (biscotto) sponge finger

savoir-'faire *nm* expertise, know-how

sazi'are *vt* satiate

sazi'arsi *vr* ∼ **di** fig weary of, grow tired of

sazietà *nf* **mangiare a** ∼ eat one's fill

'sazio *adj* satiated

sbaciucchi'are *vt* smother with kisses

sbaciucchi'arsi *vr* kiss and cuddle

sbada'taggine *nf* carelessness; **è stata una** ∼ it was careless

sbadata'mente *adv* carelessly

sba'dato *adj* careless

sbadigli'are *vi* yawn

sba'diglio *nm* yawn

sba'fare *vt* sponge

sba'fata *nf* fam nosh; **farsi una** ∼ fam have a nosh-up

'sbaffo *nm* smear

'sbafo *nm* sponging; **a** ~ (gratis) without paying

sbagli'are [1] *vi* make a mistake; (aver torto) be wrong

[2] *vt* make a mistake in; ~ **strada** go the wrong way; ~ **numero** get the number wrong; Teleph dial a wrong number; **sbagliando s'impara** practice makes perfect

sbagli'arsi *vr* make a mistake; **ti sbagli** you're mistaken, you're wrong; ~ **di grosso** be totally wrong

sbagli'ato *adj* wrong

'sbaglio *nm* mistake; **per** ~ by mistake

sbale'strare *vt* fig disconcert

sbale'strato *adj* disconcerted

sbal'lare [1] *vt* unpack; fam screw up ⟨conti⟩

[2] *vi* fam go crazy

sbal'lato *adj* (squilibrato) unbalanced

'sballo *nm* fam scream; (per droga) trip; **da** ~ sl terrific

sballot'tare *vt* toss about

sbalordi'mento *nm* amazement

sbalor'dire [1] *vt* stun

[2] *vi* be stunned

sbalordi'tivo *adj* amazing

sbalor'dito *adj* stunned; **restare** ~ be stunned

sbal'zare [1] *vt* throw; (da una carica) dismiss

[2] *vi* bounce; (saltare) leap

'sbalzo *nm* bounce; (sussulto) jolt; (di temperatura) sudden change; **a sbalzi** in spurts; **a** ~ (a rilievo) embossed

sban'care *vt* bankrupt; excavate ⟨terreno⟩; ~ **il banco** break the bank

sbanda'mento *nm* Auto skid; Naut list; fig going off the rails

sban'dare *vi* Auto skid; Naut list

sban'darsi *vr* (disperdersi) disperse

sban'data *nf* skid; Naut list; **prendere una** ~ **per** develop a crush on

sban'dato, -a [1] *adj* mixed-up

[2] *nmf* mixed-up person

sbandie'rare *vt* wave; fig display

sbarac'care *vt/i* clear up

sbaragli'are *vt* rout

sba'raglio *nm* rout; **mettere allo** ~ rout

sbaraz'zare *vt* clear

sbaraz'zarsi *vr* ~ **di** get rid of

sbaraz'zino, -a [1] *adj* mischievous

[2] *nmf* scamp

sbar'bare *vt* shave

sbar'barsi *vr* shave

sbarba'tello, -a *adj & nmf* novice

sbar'care *vt/i* disembark; ~ **il lunario** make ends meet

'sbarco *nm* landing; (di merci) unloading

'sbarra *nf* bar; (di passaggio a livello) barrier. **sbarra spaziatrice** space bar

sbarra'mento *nm* barricade

sbar'rare *vt* bar; (ostruire) block; cross ⟨assegno⟩; (spalancare) open wide

sbar'retta *nf* oblique

sbatacchi'are *vt/i* bang, slam

'sbattere [1] *vt* bang; slam, bang ⟨porta⟩; (urtare) knock; Culin beat; flap ⟨ali⟩; shake ⟨tappeto⟩; ~ **le palpebre** blink

[2] *vi* bang; ⟨porta⟩ slam, bang; ~ **contro** knock against; **andare a** ~ **contro** run into

sbat'tersi *vr* sl rush around; **sbattersene di qualcosa** not give a toss about something

sbat'tuto *adj* tossed; Culin beaten; fig run down

sba'vare *vi* dribble; ⟨colore⟩ smear

sbava'tura *nf* smear; **senza sbavature** fig faultless

sbec'care *vt* chip

sbec'cato *adj* chipped

sbeffeggi'are *vt* mock

sbelli'carsi *vr* ~ **dalle risa** split one's sides [with laughter]

sben'dare *vt* unbandage

'sberla *nf* slap

sbevaz'zare *vi* fam tipple

sbia'dire *vt/i* fade

sbia'dirsi *vr* fade

sbia'dito *adj* faded; fig colourless

sbian'cante *nm* whitener

sbian'care *vt/i* whiten

sbian'carsi *vr* whiten

sbi'eco *adj* slanting; **di** ~ on the slant; ⟨guardare⟩ sidelong; **guardare qualcuno di** ~ look askance at somebody; **tagliare di** ~ cut on the bias

sbigot'tire [1] *vt* dismay

[2] *vi* be dismayed

sbigot'tirsi *vr* be dismayed

sbigot'tito *adj* dismayed

sbilanci'are [1] *vt* unbalance

[2] *vi* (perdere l'equilibrio) overbalance

sbilanci'arsi *vr* lose one's balance

sbi'lancio *nm* lack of balance; Comm deficit

sbirci'are *vt* cast sidelong glances at

sbirci'ata *nf* furtive glance

sbircia'tina *nf* **dare una** ~ **a** sneak a glance at

'sbirro *nm* pej cop

sbizzar'rirsi *vr* satisfy one's whims

sbloc'care *vt* unblock; Mech release; decontrol ⟨prezzi⟩

'sbobba *nf* fam pigswill

sboc'care *vi* ~ **in** ⟨fiume⟩ flow into; ⟨strada⟩ lead to; ⟨folla⟩ pour into

sboc'cato *adj* foul-mouthed

sbocci'are *vi* blossom

'sbocco *nm* flowing; (foce) mouth; Comm outlet

sbolo'gnare *vt* fam get rid of

'sbornia *nf* **prendere una** ∼ get drunk; **smaltire la** ∼ sober up

sbor'sare *vt* pay out

sbot'tare *vi* burst out

sbotto'nare *vt* unbutton

sbotto'narsi *vr* (fam: confidarsi) open up; ∼ **la camicia** unbutton one's shirt

sboz'zare *vt* draft; sketch out ⟨dipinto⟩

sbra'carsi *vr* put on something more comfortable; ∼ **dalle risate** fam kill oneself laughing

sbracci'arsi *vr* wave one's arms

sbracci'ato *adj* bare-armed; ⟨abito⟩ sleeveless

sbrai'tare *vi* bawl

sbra'nare *vt* tear to shreds *or* pieces

sbra'narsi *vr* tear each other to shreds

sbrat'tare *vt* clean up

sbrec'cato *adj* chipped

sbricio'lare *vt* crumble

sbricio'larsi *vr* crumble

sbri'gare *vt* expedite; (occuparsi di) attend to

sbri'garsi *vr* hurry up, be quick

sbriga'tivo *adj* hurried, quick

sbrigli'ato *adj* ⟨fantasia⟩ unbridled

sbri'nare *vt* defrost; Auto de-ice

sbrina'tore *nm* Auto de-icer; (di frigo) defrost button

sbrindel'lare *vt* tear to shreds

sbrindel'lato *adj* in rags

sbrodo'lare *vt* stain

sbrodo'lone, -a *nmf* messy eater

sbrogli'are *vt* disentangle

'sbronza *nf* fam **prendersi una** ∼ get drunk, get hammered fam

sbron'zarsi *vr* get drunk, get hammered fam

'sbronzo *adj* (ubriaco) drunk, hammered fam

sbruffo'nata *nf* boast

sbruf'fone, -a *nmf* boaster

sbu'care *vi* come out

sbucci'are *vt* peel; shell ⟨piselli⟩

sbucci'arsi *vr* graze oneself

sbuccia'tore *nm* parer

sbuccia'tura *nf* graze

sbudel'lare *vt* gut ⟨pesce⟩; draw ⟨pollo⟩; disembowel ⟨persona⟩

sbudel'larsi *vr* ∼ **dal ridere** die laughing

sbuf'fare *vi* snort; (per impazienza) fume

'sbuffo *nm* puff; **a** ∼ ⟨maniche⟩ puff *attrib*

sbugiar'dare *vt* show to be a liar

sbuz'zare *vt* fam gut ⟨pesce⟩; draw ⟨pollo⟩; disembowel ⟨persona⟩

'scabbia *nf* scabies *sg*

'scabro *adj* rough; ⟨terreno⟩ uneven; ⟨stile⟩ bald

sca'broso *adj* rough; ⟨terreno⟩ uneven; ⟨fig: questione⟩ difficult; ⟨scena⟩ offensive

scacchi'era *nf* chessboard

scacciapensi'eri *nm inv* Mus Jew's harp

scacci'are *vt* chase away

'scacco *nm* check; **scacchi** *pl* (gioco) chess; (pezzi) chessmen; **dare** ∼ **matto a** checkmate; **a scacchi** ⟨tessuto⟩ checked; **subire uno** ∼ fig suffer a humiliating defeat

sca'dente *adj* shoddy, low-quality

sca'denza *nf* (di contratto) expiry; (di progetto, candidatura) deadline; Comm maturity; **a breve/lunga** ∼ short-/long-term

scaden'zario *nm* schedule

sca'dere *vi* expire; ⟨valore⟩ decline; ⟨debito⟩ be due

sca'duto *adj* ⟨biglietto⟩ out-of-date

sca'fandro *nm* diving suit

scaffala'tura *nf* shelves *pl*, shelving

scaf'fale *nm* shelf; (libreria) bookshelf

'scafo *nm* hull

scagion'are *vt* exonerate

'scaglia *nf* scale; (di sapone) flake; (scheggia) chip

scagli'are *vt* fling

scagli'arsi *vr* fling oneself; ∼ **contro** fig rail against

scaglio'nare *vt* space out

scagli'one *nm* group; **a scaglioni** in groups. **scaglione di reddito** tax bracket

sca'gnozzo *nm* henchman

'scala *nf* staircase; (portatile) ladder; (Mus, misura) scale; **scale** *pl* stairs; **in** ∼ to scale; **modello in** ∼ scale model; **su larga** ∼ large-scale *attrib*. **scala allungabile** extension ladder. **scala antincendio** fire escape. **scala Beaufort** Beaufort scale. **scala a chiocciola** spiral staircase. **scala mobile** escalator; (dei salari) cost of living index. **scala Richter** Richter scale. **scala di servizio** backstairs. **scala di sicurezza** fire escape. **scala di valori** scale of values

sca'lare ① *adj* scalar ② *vt* climb; layer ⟨capelli⟩; (detrarre) deduct

sca'lata *nf* climb; (dell'Everest ecc) ascent; **fare delle scalate** go climbing

scala|'tore, -trice *nmf* climber

scalca'gnato *adj* down at heel

scalci'are *vi* kick

scalci'nato *adj* shabby

scalda'acqua *nm inv* water-heater

scalda'bagno *nm* water-heater

scalda'muscoli *nm inv* legwarmer

scal'dare *vt* heat

scal'darsi *vr* warm up; (eccitarsi) get excited

sca'leno *adj* scalene

sca'leo *nm* step-ladder

scal'fire *vt* scratch

scalfit'tura *nf* scratch

scali'nata *nf* flight of steps. **scalinata di piazza di Spagna** Spanish Steps

sca'lino *nm* step; (di scala a pioli) rung

scalma'narsi *vr* rush about; (nel parlare) get worked up

scalma'nato *adj* worked up; **è ~** (vivace) he can't sit still

'scalmo *nm* rowlock

'scalo *nm* slipway; Naut port of call; **fare ~ a** a call at; Aeron land at; **senza scalo** nonstop. **scalo merci** freight depot, goods yard. **scalo passeggeri** stopover

sca'logna *nf* fam bad luck

scalo'gnato *adj* fam unlucky

sca'logno *nm* Bot scallion

scalop'pina *nf* escalope

scal'pare *vt* scalp

scalpel'lare *vt* chisel

scalpel'lino *nm* stone-cutter

scal'pello *nm* chisel

scalpi'tare *vi* paw the ground; fig champ at the bit

scalpi'tio *nm* pawing of the ground

'scalpo *nm* scalp

scal'pore *nm* noise; **fare ~** fig cause a sensation

scal'trezza *nf* shrewdness

scal'trirsi *vr* get shrewder

'scaltro *adj* shrewd

scal'zare *vt* bare the roots of ⟨*albero*⟩; fig undermine; (da una carica) oust

'scalzo *adj & adv* barefoot

scambi'are *vt* exchange; **~ qualcuno per qualcun altro** mistake somebody for somebody else

scambi'arsi *vr* exchange; **~ i saluti** exchange greetings

scambi'evole *adj* reciprocal

'scambio *nm* exchange; Comm trade. **libero scambio** free trade. **scambio di persona** mistaken identity

scamici'ato *nf* pinafore [dress]

sca'morza *nf* soft cheese

scamosci'ato *adj* suede *attrib*

scampa'gnata *nf* trip to the country

scampa'nato *adj* ⟨*gonna*⟩ flared

scampanel'lata *nf* [loud] ring

scampanel'lio *nm* ringing

scampan'io *nm* peal[ing]

scam'pare *vt* save; (evitare) escape; **scamparla bella** have a lucky escape

scam'pato ① *adj* **lo ~ pericolo** the escape from danger ② *nmf* survivor

'scampi *nmpl* (crostaceo) scampi

'scampo *nm* escape; **non c'è ~** there's no way out

'scampolo *nm* remnant

scanala'tura *nf* groove

scandagli'are *vt* sound

scanda'lismo *nm* muckraking

scanda'listico *adj* sensational; ⟨*giornale*⟩ sensationalist

scandaliz'zare *vt* scandalize

scandaliz'zarsi *vr* be scandalized

'scandalo *nm* scandal

scanda'loso *adj* scandalous; ⟨*somma ecc*⟩ scandalous; ⟨*fortuna*⟩ outrageous

Scandi'navia *nf* Scandinavia

scan'dinavo, -a *adj & nmf* Scandinavian

scan'dire *vt* scan ⟨*verso*⟩; pronounce clearly ⟨*parole*⟩; **~ il tempo** beat time

scandi'tore *nm* **scanditore ottico** Comput optical scanner

scan'nare *vt* slaughter

scan'nello *nm* lectern

'scanner *nm inv* scanner. **scanner manuale** Comput handheld scanner. **scanner piatto** flatbed scanner

scanneriz'zare *vt* Comput scan

scansafa'tiche *nmf inv* lazybones *sg*

scan'sare *vt* shift; (evitare) avoid

scan'sarsi *vr* get out of the way

scan'sia *nf* shelves *pl*

scansi'one *nf* Comput scanning

'scanso *nm* **a ~ di** in order to avoid; **a ~ di equivoci** to avoid any misunderstanding

scanti'nato *nm* basement

scanto'nare *vi* turn the corner; (svignarsela) sneak off

scanzo'nato *adj* easy-going

scapacci'one *nm* smack

scape'strato *adj* dissolute

scapigli'ato *adj* dishevelled

'scapito *nm* loss; **a ~ di** to the detriment of

'scapola *nf* shoulder-blade

'scapolo *nm* bachelor

scappa'mento *nm* Auto exhaust

scap'pare *vi* escape; (andarsene) dash [off]; (sfuggire) slip; **mi scappa da ridere!** I want to burst out laughing; **mi scappa la pipì** I'm bursting, I need a pee; **mi ha fatto ~ la pazienza** he tried my patience a bit too far; **lasciarsi ~ l'occasione** let the opportunity slip; **scappar via** run off *or* away

scap'pata *nf* fam short visit

scappa'tella *nf* escapade; (infedeltà) fling

scappa'toia *nf* way out

scappel'lotto *nm* cuff

scarabeo[1] *nm* scarab beetle

scarabeo[2]® *nm* Scrabble®

scarabocchi'are *vt* scribble

scara'bocchio *nm* scribble

scara'faggio *nm* cockroach

scara'mantico *adj* ⟨gesto⟩ to ward off the evil eye

scaraman'zia *nf* superstition

scara'mazzo *adj* ⟨perla⟩ baroque

scara'muccia *nf* skirmish

scaraven'tare *vt* hurl

scarcas'sato *adj* fam: ⟨macchina⟩ beat-up

scarce'rare *vt* release [from prison]

scardi'nare *vt* unhinge

'scarica *nf* discharge; (di arma da fuoco) volley; fig shower; **una ~ di botte** a hail of blows

scaricaba'rili *nm* **fare a ~** blame each other

scari'care *vt* discharge; Comput download; unload ⟨arma, merci, auto⟩; fig unburden

scari'carsi *vr* ⟨fiume⟩ flow; ⟨orologio, batteria⟩ run down; fig unwind

scarica'tore *nm* loader; (di porto) docker

'scarico [1] *adj* unloaded; (vuoto) empty; ⟨orologio⟩ run-down; ⟨batteria⟩ flat; fig untroubled
[2] *nm* unloading; (di rifiuti) dumping; (di acqua) draining; (di sostanze inquinanti) discharge; (luogo) [rubbish] dump; Auto exhaust; (idraulico) drain; (tubo) waste pipe. **'divieto di scarico'** 'no dumping'; **tubo di scarico** waste pipe

scarlat'tina *nf* scarlet fever

scar'latto *adj* scarlet

scarmigli'ato *adj* ruffled

sca'rnire *vt* fig simplify

'scarno *adj* thin; ⟨fig: stile⟩ bare

sca'rogna, scarognato = SCALOGNA, ▶SCALOGNATO

sca'rola *nf* curly endive

'scarpa *nf* shoe; (fam: persona) dead loss; **fare le scarpe a qualcuno** fig double-cross somebody; **scarpe** *pl* **basse** flat shoes, flats; **scarpe** *pl* **da danza** ballet shoes; **scarpe** *pl* **da ginnastica** trainers, gym shoes; **scarpe** *pl* **col tacco** high heels; **scarpe** *pl* **col tacco a spillo** stilettos; **scarpe** *pl* **con la zeppa** platform shoes

scar'pata *nf* slope; (burrone) escarpment

scarpi'era *nf* shoe rack

scarpi'nare *vi* hike

scarpon'cino *nm* ankle boot. **scarponcino Clark**® desert boot

scar'pone *nm* boot. **scarpone da alpinismo** climbing boot. **scarponi** *pl* **da sci** ski boots. **scarponi** *pl* **da trekking** walking boots

scarroz'zare *vt/i* drive around

scarroz'zata *nf* fam trip

scarruf'fato *adj* ruffled

scarseggi'are *vi* be scarce; **~ di** (mancare) be short of

scar'sezza *nf* scarcity, shortage

scarsità *nf* shortage

'scarso *adj* scarce; (manchevole) short

scartabel'lare *vt* skim through

scarta'mento *nm* Rail gauge. **scartamento ridotto** narrow gauge

scar'tare [1] *vt* discard; unwrap ⟨pacco⟩; (respingere) reject
[2] *vi* (deviare) swerve

scartave'trare *vt* sand

'scarto *nm* scrap; (in carte) discard; (deviazione) swerve; (distacco) gap

scartocci'are *vt* unwrap

scar'toffie *nfpl* bumf, bumph

scas'sare *vt* break

scas'sato *adj* fam clapped out

scassi'nare *vt* force open; pick ⟨serratura⟩

scassina|'tore, -trice *nmf* burglar

'scasso *nm* (furto) house-breaking

scata'fascio = CATAFASCIO

scate'nare *vt* fig stir up ⟨folla⟩; arouse ⟨sentimenti⟩

scate'narsi *vr* break out; ⟨fig: temporale⟩ break; (fam: darsi alla pazza gioia) go crazy, go wild; (fam: infiammarsi) get excited

scate'nato *adj* crazy, wild; **pazzo ~** fam off his head

'scatola *nf* box; (di latta) can, tin Br; **in ~** ⟨cibo⟩ canned, tinned Br; **rompere le scatole a qualcuno** fam get on somebody's nerves; **a ~ chiusa** ⟨comprare⟩ sight unseen. **scatola del cambio** gearbox. **scatola nera** Aeron black box

scato'lame *nm* (cibo) canned food

scato'letta *nf* small box; (di cibo) tin

scato'logico *adj* scatological

scat'tante *adj* zippy

scat'tare *vi* go off; (balzare) spring up; (adirarsi) lose one's temper; take ⟨foto⟩

'scatto *nm* (balzo) spring; (d'ira) outburst; (di telefono) unit; (dispositivo) release; **a scatti** jerkily; **di ~** suddenly

scatu'rire *vi* spring

scaval'care *vt* jump over ⟨muretto⟩; climb over ⟨muro⟩; (fig: superare) overtake

sca'vare *vt* dig ⟨*buca*⟩; dig up ⟨*tesoro*⟩; excavate ⟨*città sepolta*⟩

scava'trice *nf* excavator

scavezza'collo *nm* daredevil

'scavo *nm* excavation

scazzot'tare *vt* fam beat up

scazzot'tata *nf* fam punch-up; **prendersi una** ∼ get beaten up

'scegliere *vt* choose, select

sce'icco *nm* sheikh

scelle'rato *adj* wicked

'scelta *nf* choice; (di articoli) range; ... **a** ∼ (in menu) choice of ...; **prendine uno a** ∼ take your choice *or* pick; **di prima** ∼ top-grade, choice; ⟨*albergo*⟩ first-rate; **di seconda** ∼ second grade; pej second-rate. **scelta multipla** multiple choice

'scelto ① pp di SCEGLIERE ② *adj* select; ⟨*merce ecc*⟩ choice. **tiratore scelto** marksman

sce'mare *vt/i* diminish

sce'menza *nf* silliness; (azione) silly thing to do/say; **non diciamo scemenze!** let's not be silly!

'scemo ① *adj* idiotic ② *nm* idiot

scempi'aggine *nf* foolish thing to do/say

'scempio *nm* havoc; (fig: di paesaggio) ruination; **fare** ∼ **di** play havoc with

'scena *nf* scene; (palcoscenico) stage; **entrare in** ∼ Theat go/come on [stage]; fig come on the scene; **fare** ∼ put on an act; **fare una** ∼ make a scene; **fare scene** make a fuss; **andare in** ∼ Theat: ⟨*spettacolo*⟩ be staged, be put on; **fare** ∼ **muta** not open one's mouth; **scomparire dalla** ∼ fig vanish from the scene; **mettere in** ∼ produce, stage; **messa in** ∼ production, staging; fig set-up

sce'nario *nm* scenery

sce'nata *nf* row, scene

'scendere ① *vi* go/come down; (da treno, autobus) get off; (da macchina) get out; ⟨*strada*⟩ slope; ⟨*notte, prezzi*⟩ fall ② *vt* go/come down ⟨*scale*⟩

scendi'letto *nm* bedside rug

sceneggi'are *vt* dramatize

sceneggi'ato *nm* television serial

sceneggia'tura *nf* screenplay

'scenico *adj* scenic

scenogra'fia *nf* set design

sce'nografo, -a *nmf* set designer

sce'riffo *nm* sheriff

scervel'larsi *vr* rack one's brains

scervel'lato *adj* brainless

'sceso pp di SCENDERE

scetti'cismo *nm* scepticism

'scettico, -a ① *adj* sceptical ② *nmf* sceptic

'scettro *nm* sceptre

'scheda *nf* card. **scheda audio** Comput sound card. **scheda elettorale** ballot-paper. **scheda di espansione** Comput expansion card. **scheda grafica** Comput graphics card. **scheda madre** Comput motherboard. **scheda magnetica** card key. **scheda perforata** punch card. **scheda di rete** Comput network card. **scheda sonora** Comput sound card. **scheda telefonica** phonecard. **scheda di valutazione scolastica** report card, school report. **scheda video** Comput video card

sche'dare *vt* file

sche'dario *nm* file; (mobile) filing cabinet

sche'dato, -a ① *adj* with a police record ② *nmf* person with a police record

sche'dina *nf* ≈ pools coupon; **giocare la** ∼ ≈ do the pools

'scheggia *nf* fragment; (di legno) splinter

scheggi'are *vt* splinter

scheggi'arsi *vr* chip; ⟨*legno*⟩ splinter

sche'letrico *adj* skeletal

'scheletro *nm* skeleton; **essere ridotto ad uno** ∼ be all skin and bones

'schema *nm* diagram; (abbozzo) outline; **uscire dagli schemi** break with tradition

schematica'mente *adv* schematically

sche'matico *adj* schematic

schematiz'zare *vt* present schematically

'scherma *nf* fencing

scher'maglia *nf* skirmish

scher'mirsi *vr* protect oneself

'schermo *nm* screen; **sul grande** ∼ on the big screen; **farsi** ∼ **con** shield oneself with. **schermo panoramico** wide screen. **schermo a sfioramento** Comput touch screen

scher'nire *vt* mock

'scherno *nm* mockery

scher'zare *vi* joke; (giocare) play; **c'è poco da** ∼! it's nothing to laugh about!

'scherzo *nm* joke; (trucco) trick; (effetto) play; Mus scherzo; **fare uno** ∼ **a qualcuno** play a joke on somebody; **giocare brutti scherzi (a qualcuno)** ⟨*memoria, vista*⟩ play tricks (on somebody); **per** ∼ for fun; **scherzi a parte** joking apart, seriously; **stare allo** ∼ take a joke. **scherzo di natura** freak of nature

scher'zoso *adj* playful

schiaccia'noci *nm inv* nutcrackers *pl*

schiacci'ante *adj* damning; ⟨*vittoria*⟩ crushing

schiacci'are *vt* crush; (in tennis ecc) smash; press ⟨*pulsante*⟩; crack ⟨*noce*⟩; ∼ **un pisolino** grab forty winks

schiacci'arsi *vr* get crushed

schiaccia'sassi *nf inv* steamroller

schiaf'fare *vt* fam shove

schiaffeggi'are *vt* slap

schi'affo *nm* slap; **dare uno ∼ a** slap; **avere una faccia da schiaffi** have the kind of face you'd love to take a swipe at. **schiaffo morale** slap in the face

schiamaz'zare *vi* make a racket; ⟨galline⟩ cackle

schia'mazzo *nm* din; **schiamazzi** *pl* notturni disturbing the peace

schian'tare ① *vt* break
② *vi* **schianto dalla fatica** I'm wiped out

schian'tarsi *vr* crash

'schianto *nm* crash; fam knock-out; ⟨divertente⟩ scream

schia'rire ① *vt* clear; (sbiadire) fade
② *vi* brighten up

schia'rirsi *vr* brighten up; **∼ la gola** clear one's throat; **∼ le idee** get things clear in one's head; (dopo aver bevuto) clear one's head

schia'rita *nf* sunny interval

schiat'tare *vi* burst; **∼ di invidia** be green with envy

schia'vista *nmf* slave-driver

schiavitù *nf* slavery

schi'avo, -a *nmf* slave

schi'ena *nf* back. **mal di schiena** backache

schie'nale *nm* (di sedia) back

schi'era *nf* Mil rank; (moltitudine) crowd

schiera'mento *nm* lining up; Mil battle line. **schieramento di forze** rallying of the troops

schie'rare *vt* draw up; rally ⟨forze⟩

schie'rarsi *vr* draw up; ⟨forze⟩ rally; **∼ dalla parte di qualcuno, ∼ con qualcuno** rally [in support] to somebody; **∼ contro qualcuno** rally in opposition to somebody

schiet'tezza *nf* frankness

schi'etto *adj* frank; (puro) pure

schi'fezza *nf* **è una ∼** it's disgusting; ⟨film, libro⟩ it's rubbish

schifil'toso *adj* fussy

'schifo *nm* disgust; **fare ∼** be disgusting; **è uno ∼!** it's disgusting!

schi'foso *adj* disgusting, yucky fam; (di cattiva qualità) rubbishy

schioc'care ① *vt* crack ⟨frusta⟩; snap, click ⟨dita⟩; click ⟨lingua⟩
② *vi* crack

schi'occo *nm* (di frusta) crack; (di bacio) smack; (di dita, lingua) click

schioppet'tata *nf* shot

schi'oppo *nm* fam rifle; **a un tiro di ∼** fig a stone's throw away

schiri'bizzo *nm* fam fancy; **se mi salta lo ∼ ...** if it takes my fancy ...

schi'udere *vt* open

schi'udersi *vr* open

schi'uma *nf* foam; (di sapone) lather; (di bucato) suds; (feccia) scum. **schiuma da barba** shaving foam

schiu'mare ① *vt* skim
② *vi* foam

schiuma'rola *nf* Culin skimmer

schiu'mogeno *adj* foaming

schiu'moso *adj* ⟨birra, crema⟩ frothy, foamy; ⟨liquido⟩ scummy

schi'uso *pp di* SCHIUDERE

schi'vare *vt* avoid

'schivo *adj* bashful

schizofre'nia *nf* schizophrenia

schizo'frenico, -a *adj & nmf* schizophrenic

schiz'zare ① *vt* squirt; (inzaccherare) splash; (abbozzare) sketch; **∼ qualcuno/ qualcosa di qualcosa** splatter somebody/ something with something
② *vi* spurt; **∼ via** fig scurry away

schiz'zato, -a *adj & nmf* fam loony

schizzi'noso *adj* squeamish

'schizzo *nm* squirt; (di fango) splash; (abbozzo) sketch

sci *nm inv* ski; (sport) skiing. **sci d'acqua, sci acquatico** water-skiing. **sci acrobatico** hot dogging. **sci di fondo** cross-country skiing

'scia *nf* wake; (di fumo ecc) trail; **sulla ∼ di qualcuno** following in somebody's footsteps

sci'abola *nf* sabre

sciabor'dare *vt/i* lap

sciabor'dio *nm* lapping

sciacal'laggio *nm* profiteering

scia'callo *nm* jackal; fig profiteer

sciac'quare *vt* rinse

sciac'quarsi *vr* rinse oneself

sci'acquo *nm* mouthwash

scia'gura *nf* disaster

sciagu'rato *adj* unfortunate; (scellerato) wicked

scialac'quare *vt* squander

scialacqua|'tore, -trice *nmf* squanderer

scia'lare *vi* spend money like water

sci'albo *adj* pale; fig dull

sci'alle *nm* shawl

scia'luppa *nf* dinghy. **scialuppa di salvataggio** lifeboat

sciaman'nato *adj* good-for-nothing

scia'mano *nm* shaman

scia'mare *vi* swarm

sci'ame *nm* swarm; **a sciami** in swarms

sci'ampo *nm* shampoo

scian'cato *adj* lame

sci'are *vi* ski; **andare a ∼** go skiing

sci'arpa *nf* scarf

sci'atica *nf* Med sciatica

scia|'tore, -trice *nmf* skier

sciatte'ria *nf* slovenliness

sci'atto *adj* slovenly; ⟨stile⟩ careless

sciat'tone, -a *nmf* slovenly person

'scibile *nm* knowledge; **lo ~ umano** the sum of human knowledge

scic'coso *adj* fam snazzy

scienti'fico *adj* scientific

sci'enza *nf* science; (sapere) knowledge; **avere la ~ infusa** be naturally talented; **scienze** *pl* **sociali** social science

scienzi'ato, -a *nmf* scientist

sci'ita *adj & nmf* Shiite

scilin'guagnolo *nm* fig **avere lo ~** be a chatterbox

'scimmia *nf* monkey

scimmiot'tare *vt* ape

scimpanzé *nm inv* chimpanzee, chimp

scimu'nito *adj* idiotic

'scindere *vt* separate; **~ in** break down into

'scindersi *vr* divide; **~ in** divide into

scin'tilla *nf* spark

scintil'lante *adj* sparkling

scintil'lare *vi* sparkle

scintil'lio *nm* sparkle

sciò *int* shoo!

scioc'cante *adj* shocking

scioc'care *vt* shock

scioc'chezza *nf* foolishness; (assurdità) foolish thing; **sciocchezze!** nonsense!

sci'occo *adj* foolish

sci'ogliere *vt* untie; undo, untie ⟨nodo⟩; (liberare) release; (liquefare) melt; dissolve ⟨contratto, qualcosa nell'acqua⟩; loosen up ⟨muscoli⟩

sci'ogliersi *vr* ⟨nodo⟩ come undone; (liquefarsi) melt; ⟨contratto⟩ be dissolved; ⟨pastiglia⟩ dissolve

sciogli'lingua *nm inv* tongue-twister

scio'lina *nf* ski wax

sciol'tezza *nf* agility; (disinvoltura) ease

sci'olto ① pp di SCIOGLIERE
② *adj* loose; (agile) agile; (disinvolto) easy; **versi** *pl* **sciolti** blank verse

sciope'rante *nmf* striker

sciope'rare *vi* go on strike, strike

sci'opero *nm* strike, industrial action; **in ~** on strike. **sciopero bianco** work-to-rule. **sciopero generale** general strike. **sciopero a singhiozzo** on-off strike

sciori'nare *vt* fig show off

sciovi'nismo *nm* chauvinism

sciovi'nista *nmf* Pol chauvinist

sciovi'nistico *adj* Pol chauvinistic

sci'pito *adj* insipid

scip'pare *vt* fam snatch; **~ qualcuno** snatch somebody's bag/bracelet etc

scippa|'tore, -trice *nmf* bag-snatcher

'scippo *nm* bag-snatching

sci'rocco *nm* sirocco

scirop'pato *adj* ⟨frutta⟩ in syrup

sci'roppo *nm* syrup

scirop'poso *adj* syrupy

'scisma *nm* schism

scissi'one *nf* division

scissio'nista *adj* breakaway *attrib*

'scisso pp di SCINDERE

sciupacchi'are *vt* spoil

sciupacchi'ato *adj* spoilt

sciu'pare *vt* spoil; (sperperare) waste

sciu'parsi *vr* get spoiled; (deperire) wear oneself out

sciu'pio *nm* waste

scivo'lare *vi* slide; (involontariamente) slip

'scivolo *nm* slide; Techn chute

scivo'lone *nm* fall; (fig: errore) blunder

scivo'loso *adj* slippery

scle'rosi *nf* sclerosis. **sclerosi multipla, sclerosi a placche** multiple sclerosis, MS

scoc'care ① *vt* fire ⟨freccia⟩; strike ⟨ore⟩
② *vi* ⟨scintilla⟩ shoot out; **sono scoccate le cinque** five o'clock has just struck

scocci'are *vt* fam (dare noia a) bother

scocci'arsi *vr* fam be bored; **mi sono scocciato di aspettare** I'm fed up with waiting

scocci'ato *adj* fam fed up

scoccia|'tore, -trice *nmf* nuisance

scoccia'tura *nf* fam nuisance

sco'della *nf* bowl

scodel'lare *vt* dish out, dish up

scodinzo'lare *vi* wag its tail

scogli'era *nf* cliff; (a fior d'acqua) reef

'scoglio *nm* rock; (fig: ostacolo) stumbling block

scoglio'nato *adj* vulg pissed off

scoi'attolo *nm* squirrel

scola'pasta *nm inv* colander

scolapi'atti *nm inv* dish drainer

sco'lara *nf* schoolgirl

sco'lare¹ ① *vt* drain; strain ⟨pasta, verdura⟩
② *vi* drip

sco'lare² *adj* school *attrib*; **in età ~** ⟨bambino⟩ school-age

scola'resca *nf* pupils *pl*

sco'laro *nm* schoolboy

sco'lastico *adj* school *attrib*; **gita scolastica** school trip

scoli'osi *nf* curvature of the spine

scollacci'ato *adj* low-cut

scol'lare *vt* cut away the neck of ⟨*abito*⟩; (staccare) unstick

scol'lato *adj* ⟨*abito*⟩ low-necked

scolla'tura *nf* neckline; ∼ **profonda** plunging neckline

scolle'gare *vt* disconnect

'**scollo** *nm* neckline. **scollo a V** V-neck

'**scolo** *nm* drainage

scolo'rare *vt* fade

scolori'mento *nm* fading

scolo'rire *vt* fade

scolo'rirsi *vr* fade

scolo'rito *adj* faded

scol'pire *vt* carve; (imprimere) engrave

scombi'nare *vt* upset

scombusso'lare *vt* muddle up

scom'messa *nf* bet

scom'messo *pp di* SCOMMETTERE

scom'mettere *vt* bet; **ci puoi** ∼! you bet!

scomo'dare *vt* trouble

scomo'darsi *vr* trouble

scomodità *nf inv* discomfort

'**scomodo** ① *adj* uncomfortable ② *nm* **essere di** ∼ **a qualcuno** be a trouble to somebody

scompagin'are *vt* mess up

scompa'gnare *vt* split

scompa'gnato *adj* odd

scompa'rire *vi* disappear; (morire) pass away

scom'parsa *nf* disappearance; (morte) death, passing

scom'parso, -a ① *pp di* SCOMPARIRE ② *adj* missing; (morto) departed ③ *nmf* missing person; (morto) departed

scomparti'mento *nm* compartment

scom'parto *nf* compartment. **scomparto freezer** freezer compartment

scompen'sare *vt* throw off balance

scom'penso *nm* imbalance. **scompenso cardiaco** cardiac insufficiency

scompigli'are *vt* disarrange

scom'piglio *nm* confusion

scompisci'arsi *vr fam* ∼ **[dalle risa]** wet oneself, split one's sides laughing

scom'porre *vt* break down; ruffle ⟨*capelli*⟩; (fig: turbare) upset

scom'porsi *vr* lose one's composure

scomposizi'one *nf* breaking down

scom'posto ① *pp di* SCOMPORRE ② *adj* (sguaiato) unseemly; (disordinato) untidy

sco'munica *nf* excommunication

scomuni'care *vt* excommunicate

sconcer'tante *adj* disconcerting; (che rende perplesso) bewildering, baffling

sconcer'tare *vt* disconcert; (rendere perplesso) bewilder, baffle

sconcer'tato *adj* disconcerted; (perplesso) bewildered, baffled

scon'cezza *nf* indecency

'**sconcio** ① *adj* indecent ② *nm* **è uno** ∼ **che ...** it's a disgrace that ...

sconclusio'nato *adj* incoherent

scon'dito *adj* unseasoned; (insalata) with no dressing

sconfes'sare *vt* disown

scon'figgere *vt* defeat

sconfi'nare *vi* cross the border; (in proprietà privata) trespass

sconfi'nato *adj* unlimited

scon'fitta *nf* defeat; **subire una** ∼ be defeated, suffer defeat

scon'fitto *pp di* SCONFIGGERE

sconfor'tante *adj* disheartening, discouraging

scon'forto *nm* discouragement; **farsi prendere dallo** ∼ get discouraged, get disheartened

sconge'lare *vt* thaw out ⟨*cibo*⟩; defrost ⟨*frigo*⟩

scongiu'rare *vt* beseech; (evitare) avert

scongi'uro *nm* **fare gli scongiuri** ≈ touch wood, knock on wood Am

scon'nesso ① *pp di* SCONNETTERE ② *adj* fig incoherent

scon'nettere *vt* disconnect

sconosci'uto, -a ① *adj* unknown ② *nmf* stranger

sconquas'sare *vt* smash; (sconvolgere) upset

sconsa'crare *vt* deconsecrate

sconsiderata'mente *adv* inconsiderately

sconsidera'tezza *nf* lack of consideration, thoughtlessness

sconside'rato *adj* inconsiderate, thoughtless

sconsigli'abile *adj* not advisable

sconsigli'are *vt* advise against

sconso'lato *adj* disconsolate

scon'tare *vt* discount; (dedurre) deduct; (pagare) pay off; serve ⟨*pena*⟩; ∼ **la propria colpa** pay for one's sins

scon'tato *adj* discounted; (ovvio) expected; ∼ **del 10%** with 10% discount; **era** ∼ it was to be expected; **dare qualcosa per** ∼ take something for granted

scon'tento ① *adj* displeased ② *nm* discontent

'**sconto** *nm* discount; **fare uno** ∼ give a discount. **sconto commerciale** trade discount

scon'trarsi *vr* clash; (urtare) collide

scon'trino *nm* ticket; (di cassa) receipt; '**munirsi dello** ∼ **alla cassa**' sign reminding customers that payment must be made at the cash desk beforehand

'**scontro** *nm* clash; (urto) collision. **scontro automobilistico** car crash. **scontro frontale** head-on collision. **scontro a fuoco** shootout

scontrosità *nf* surliness

scon'troso *adj* surly

sconveni'ente *adj* unprofitable; (scorretto) unseemly

sconvol'gente *adj* (sorprendente) mind-blowing; (inquietante) upsetting

scon'volgere *vt* upset; (mettere in disordine) disarrange

sconvolgi'mento *nm* upheaval

scon'volto ① pp di SCONVOLGERE ② *adj* distraught, upset

'**scooter** *nm inv* scooter

'**scopa** *nf* broom; (gioco di carte) type of card game

sco'pare *vt* sweep; vulg shag

sco'pata *nf* sweep; vulg shag; **dare una** ∼ **per terra** give the floor a sweep

scoperchi'are *vt* take the lid off ⟨pentola⟩; take the roof off ⟨casa⟩

sco'perta *nf* discovery

sco'perto ① pp di SCOPRIRE ② *adj* uncovered; (senza riparo) exposed; (conto) overdrawn; (spoglio) bare

'**scopo** *nm* aim; **a** ∼ **di** for the sake of; **allo** ∼ **di** in order to

sco'pone *nm* (gioco di carte) type of card game

scoppi'are *vi* burst; fig break out

scoppiet'tare *vi* crackle

'**scoppio** *nm* burst; (di guerra) outbreak; (esplosione) explosion; **a** ∼ **ritardato** ⟨bomba⟩ delayed action; **ha reagito a** ∼ **ritardato** he did a double take

sco'prire *vt* discover; (togliere la copertura a) uncover; unveil ⟨statua⟩; ∼ **gli altarini** fam reveal his/her etc guilty secrets

scoraggia'mento *nm* discouragement

scoraggi'ante *adj* discouraging

scoraggi'are *vt* discourage

scoraggi'arsi *vr* lose heart

scor'butico *adj* Med suffering from scurvy; (fig: scontroso) disagreeable

scor'buto *nm* Med scurvy

scorci'are *vt* shorten

scorcia'toia *nf* short cut

'**scorcio** *nm* (di cielo) patch; (in arte) foreshortening; **di** ∼ (vedere) from an angle. **scorcio panoramico** panoramic view. **scorcio del secolo** end of the century

scor'dare *vt* forget; ∼ **qualcosa a casa** leave something at home

scor'darsi *vr* forget; ∼ **di qualcosa** forget something

scor'dato *adj* Mus out of tune

scorda'tura *nf* Mus going out of tune

sco'reggia *nf* fam fart

scoreggi'are *vi* fam fart

'**scorfano** *nm* scorpion fish

'**scorgere** *vt* make out; (notare) notice

'**scoria** *nf* waste; (di carbone) slag; **scorie** *pl* **nucleari** nuclear waste

scor'nare *vt* fig humiliate

scor'narsi *vr* fig come a cropper

scor'nato *adj* fig hangdog

'**scorno** *nm* humiliation

scorpacci'ata *nf* bellyful; **fare una** ∼ **di** stuff oneself with

scorpi'one *nm* scorpion; Astr Scorpio

scorraz'zare *vi* run about

'**scorrere** ① *vt* (dare un'occhiata) glance through ② *vi* run; (scivolare) slide; (fluire) flow; Comput scroll; (attorno a un oggetto) wrap

scorre'ria *nf* raid

scorret'tezza *nf* (mancanza di educazione) bad manners *pl*

scor'retto *adj* incorrect; (sconveniente) improper

scor'revole *adj* **porta scorrevole** sliding door

scorri'banda *nf* raid; fig excursion

scorri'mento *nm* Comput scrolling; (attorno a un oggetto) wrapping

'**scorsa** *nf* glance; **dare una** ∼ **a** glance through

'**scorso** ① pp di SCORRERE ② *adj* last; **l'anno** ∼ last year

scor'soio *adj* **nodo scorsoio** noose

'**scorta** *nf* escort; (provvista) supply

scor'tare *vt* escort

scortecci'are *vt* debark ⟨albero⟩; strip ⟨muro⟩

scor'tese *adj* rude

scorte'sia *nf* rudeness

scorti'care *vt* skin

scortica'tura *nf* graze

'**scorto** pp di SCORGERE

'**scorza** *nf* peel; (crosta) crust; (corteccia) bark; fig exterior. **scorza d'arancia** orange peel

scorzo'nera *nf* salsify

sco'sceso *adj* steep

'**scossa** *nf* shake; Electr, fig shock; **prendere la** ∼ get an electric shock. **scossa elettrica** electric shock. **scossa sismica** earth tremor

'**scosso** ① pp di SCUOTERE ② *adj* shaken; (sconvolto) upset

scos'sone *nm* jolt

sco'stante *adj* off-putting

sco'stare *vt* push away

sco'starsi *vr* stand aside

scostu'mato *adj* dissolute; (maleducato) ill-mannered

Scotch® *nm* Scotch tape®

scoten'nare *vt* skin ⟨*maiale*⟩; scalp ⟨*persona*⟩

scot'tante *adj* ⟨*argomento*⟩ burning; ⟨*fig: notizia*⟩ sensational

scot'tare ① *vt* burn; (con liquido, vapore) scald; Culin blanch ② *vi* ⟨*bevanda, cibo*⟩ be too hot; ⟨*sole, pentola*⟩ be very hot

scot'tarsi *vr* burn oneself; (con liquido, vapore) scald oneself; (al sole) get sunburnt; fig get one's fingers burnt

scot'tato *adj* Culin blanched

scotta'tura *nf* burn; (da liquido) scald; fig painful experience. **scottatura solare** sunburn

'Scottex® *nm* paper towel

'scotto¹ *adj* overcooked

'scotto² *nm* score; **pagare lo ~ di qualcosa** pay for something

scout ① *adj inv* scout *attrib* ② *nmf inv* scout

scou'tismo *nm* scout movement

sco'vare *vt* (scoprire) discover

scovo'lino *nm* bottle brush; (per pipa) pipe cleaner

'Scozia *nf* Scotland

scoz'zese ① *adj* Scottish ② *nmf* Scot

'scrambler *nm* Radio, Teleph scrambler

screan'zato *adj* rude

scredi'tare *vt* discredit

scre'mare *vt* skim

screpo'lare *vt* chap

screpo'larsi *vr* get chapped; ⟨*intonaco*⟩ crack

screpo'lato *adj* chapped; ⟨*intonaco*⟩ cracked

screpola'tura *nf* crack

screzi'ato *adj* speckled

'screzio *nm* disagreement

scribacchi'are *vt* scribble

scribac'chino, -a *nmf* scribbler; ⟨*impiegato*⟩ penpusher

scricchio'lante *adj* creaky

scricchio'lare *vi* creak

scricchio'lio *nm* creaking

'scricciolo *nm* wren; fig delicate-looking creature

'scrigno *nm* casket

scrimina'tura *nf* parting

scriteri'ato *adj* empty-headed

'scritta *nf* writing; (su muro) graffiti

'scritto ① *pp di* SCRIVERE ② *adj* written; **~ col computer** word-processed; **~ a macchina** typed; **~ a mano** handwritten ③ *nm* writing; (lettera) letter

scrit'toio *nm* writing-desk

scrit'|tore, -trice *nmf* writer

scrit'tura *nf* writing; Relig scripture; (calligrafia) handwriting; **scritture** *pl* contabili account books. **scrittura privata** Jur legal document drawn up by an individual

scrittu'rare *vt* engage

scriva'nia *nf* desk

scri'vente *nmf* writer

'scrivere *vt* write; (descrivere) write about; **~ a macchina** type

scroc'care *vt* fam **~ a** sponge off

scrocchi'are *vi* crack

'scrocco¹ *nm* fam **a ~** without paying; **vivere a ~** sponge off other people

'scrocco² *nm* **coltello a scrocco** pocket knife; **serratura a scrocco** spring lock

scroc'cone, -a *nmf* fam sponger

'scrofa *nf* sow

scrol'lare *vt* shake; **~ le spalle** shrug one's shoulders; **~ la testa** shake one's head

scrol'larsi *vr* shake oneself; **~ qualcosa di dosso** shake something off

'scrolling *nm* Comput scrolling

scrosci'ante *adj* pouring; ⟨*applausi*⟩ thunderous

scrosci'are *vi* roar; ⟨*pioggia*⟩; pelt down

'scroscio *nm* roar; (di pioggia) pelting; **uno ~ di applausi** thunderous applause; **piovere a ~** lash down

scro'stare *vt* scrape

scro'starsi *vr* flake

scro'stato *adj* flaky

'scroto *nm* scrotum

'scrupolo *nm* scruple; (diligenza) care; **senza scrupoli** unscrupulous, without scruples; **farsi scrupoli per qualcosa** have scruples about something

scrupo'loso *adj* scrupulous

scru'tare *vt* scan; (indagare) search

scruta'tore *nm* (di voti) returning officer

scruti'nare *vt* scrutinize

scru'tinio *nm* (di voti) poll; Sch assessment of progress; **scrutini** *pl* Sch meeting of teachers to discuss pupils' work and assign marks. **scrutinio segreto** secret ballot

scu'cire *vt* unstitch; **scuci i soldi!** fig fam cough up [the money]!

S

scu'cirsi *vr* come unstitched; (fig: parlare) talk; **non si scuce** he won't talk

scuci'tura *nf* unstitching

scude'ria *nf* stable; **scuderie** *pl* mews

scu'detto *nm* Sport championship shield; (campionato) national championship

scudi'ero *nm* squire

scudisci'ata *nf* whipping

'scudo *nm* shield; **farsi** ∼ **con qualcosa** shield oneself with something

scuffi'are *vi* capsize

scu'gnizzo *nm* street urchin

sculacci'are *vt* spank

sculacci'ata *nf* spanking; **prendere a sculacciate** spank

sculacci'one *nm* spanking

sculet'tare *vi* wiggle one's hips

scul|'tore, -trice ① *nm* sculptor ② *nf* sculptress

scul'tura *nf* sculpture

scu'ola *nf* school. **scuola allievi ufficiali** cadet school. **scuola per bambini con difficoltà d'apprendimento** special school. **scuola elementare** primary school, grade school Am. **scuola guida** driving school. **scuola materna** day nursery. **scuola media** secondary school. **scuola media inferiore** secondary school (10-13), junior high school Am. **scuola media superiore** secondary school (13-18). **scuola dell'obbligo** compulsory education. **scuola privata** private school, public school Br. **scuola di sci** ski school. **scuola serale** evening school. **scuola statale** state school. **scuola superiore** secondary school

scu'otere *vt* shake

scu'otersi *vr* (destarsi) rouse oneself; ∼ **qualcosa di dosso** fig shake something off

'scure *nf* axe

scu'rire *vt/i* darken

'scuro ① *adj* dark ② *nm* darkness; (imposta) shutter

scur'rile *adj* scurrilous

'scusa *nf* apology; (giustificazione) excuse; (pretesto) pretext; **chiedere** ∼ apologize; **[chiedo]** ∼**!** [I'm] sorry!

scu'sare *vt* excuse

scu'sarsi *vr* apologize (**di** for); **[mi] scusi!** excuse me!; (chiedendo perdono) [I'm] sorry!

sdebi'tarsi *vr* repay the kindness

sde'gnare *vt* despise; (fare arrabbiare) enrage

sde'gnarsi *vr* become angry

sde'gnato *adj* indignant

'sdegno *nm* disdain; (ira) indignation

sde'gnoso *adj* disdainful

sden'tato *adj* toothless

sdipa'nare *vt* wind

sdogana'mento *nm* customs clearance

sdoga'nare *vt* clear through customs

sdolci'nato *adj* sentimental, schmaltzy

sdoppia'mento *nm* splitting. **sdoppiamento della personalità** split personality

sdoppi'are *vt* halve

sdrai'arsi *vr* lie down

'sdraio *nf* **[sedia a]** ∼ deckchair

sdrammatiz'zare ① *vt* take the heat out of ② *vi* take the heat out of the situation

sdruccio'lare *vi* slither

sdruccio'levole *adj* slippery

sdruccio'lone *nm* slip

SE *abbr* (**sud-est**) SE

se ① *conj* if; (interrogativo) whether, if; **se mai** (caso mai) if need be; **se mai telefonasse,...** should he call,..., if he calls,...; **se no** otherwise, or else; **se non altro** at least, if nothing else; **se pure** (sebbene) even though; (anche se) even if; **non so se sia vero** I don't know whether it's true, I don't know if it's true; **come se** as if; **se lo avessi saputo prima!** if only I had known before!; **e se andassimo fuori a cena?** how about going out for dinner? ② *nm inv* if; **non voglio né se né ma** I don't want any ifs or buts

sé *pers pron* oneself; (lui) himself; (lei) herself; (esso, essa) itself; (loro) themselves; **l'ha fatto da sé** he did it himself; **ha preso i soldi con sé** he took the money with him; **si sono tenuti le notizie per sé** they kept the news to themselves

se'baceo *adj* sebaceous

seb'bene *conj* although

'sebo *nm* sebum

sec. *abbr* (**secolo**) c.

'secca *nf* shallows *pl*; **in** ∼ (nave) grounded

sec'cante *adj* annoying

sec'care ① *vt* dry; (importunare) annoy ② *vi* dry up

sec'carsi *vr* dry up; (irritarsi) get annoyed

secca|'tore, -trice *nmf* nuisance

secca'tura *nf* bother; **dare una** ∼ **a qualcuno** trouble somebody, bother somebody; **non voglio seccature!** I don't want the bother!

secchi'ata *nf* bucketful

secchi'ello *nm* bucket. **secchiello del ghiaccio** ice bucket

'secchio *nm* bucket. **secchio della spazzatura** rubbish bin, trash can Am

sec'chione, -a *nmf* fam dweeb

'secco, -a ① *adj* dry; (disseccato) dried; (magro) thin; (brusco) curt; (preciso) sharp;

restare a ∼ be left penniless; **restarci** ∼ (fam: morire di colpo) be killed on the spot; **frutta secca** nuts *pl*
2 *nm* (siccità) drought; **lavare a** ∼ dry-clean

secessi'one *nf* secession. **guerra di secessione** War of Secession

seco'lare *adj* age-old; (laico) secular

'secolo *nm* century; (epoca) age; **è un** ∼ **che non lo vedo** fam I haven't seen him for ages *or* yonks

se'conda **1** *nf* Sch, Rail second class; Auto second [gear]
2 *prep* **a** ∼ **di** according to

secon'dario *adj* Jur collateral; **effetto** ∼ side effect

se'condo **1** *adj* second
2 *nm* second, sec fam; (secondo piatto) main course; **un** ∼**!** just a sec[ond]!
3 *prep* according to; ∼ **me** in my opinion

secondo'genito, -a *adj & nm* second-born

secrezi'one *nf* secretion

'sedano *nm* celery. **sedano rapa** celeriac

se'dare *vt* put down, suppress ⟨rivolta⟩; fig soothe

seda'tivo *adj & nm* sedative; **somministrare sedativi a** sedate

'sede *nf* seat; (centro) centre; Relig see; Comm head office; **in** ∼ **di esami** during the exams; **in separata** ∼ in private. **sede centrale** head office. **sede sociale** registered office

seden'tario *adj* sedentary

se'dere **1** *vi* sit
2 *nm* (deretano) bottom

se'dersi *vr* sit down

'sedia *nf* chair. **sedia a dondolo** rocking chair. **sedia elettrica** electric chair. **sedia da giardino** garden seat. **sedia girevole** swivel chair. **sedia a rotelle** wheelchair. **sedia a sdraio** deckchair

sedi'cenne *adj & nmf* sixteen-year-old

sedi'cente *adj* self-styled

sedi'cesimo, -a *adj & nm* sixteenth

'sedici *adj & nm* sixteen

se'dile *nm* seat

sedimen'tare *vi* leave a sediment

sedi'mento *nm* sediment

sedizi'one *nf* sedition

sedizi'oso *adj* seditious

se'dotto pp di SEDURRE

sedu'cente *adj* seductive; (allettante) enticing

se'durre *vt* seduce

se'duta *nf* session; (di posa) sitting; ∼ **stante** *adv* here and now

se'duto *adj* sitting

sedut|'tore, -trice **1** *nm* charmer
2 *nf* temptress

seduzi'one *nf* seduction

seg. *abbr* (**seguente**) foll.

'sega *nf* saw; vulg wank; **mezza** ∼ vulg tosser; **non capire una** ∼ vulg understand damn all. **sega circolare** circular saw. **sega a mano** handsaw. **sega a nastro** band saw

'segale *nf* rye. **pane di segale** rye bread

sega'ligno *adj* wiry

se'gare *vt* saw

sega'trice *nf* saw. **segatrice a nastro** band saw

sega'tura *nf* sawdust

'seggio *nm* seat. **seggio elettorale** polling station

seg'giola *nf* chair

seggio'lino *nm* seat; (da bambino) child seat. **seggiolino per auto** car seat. **seggiolino regolabile** adjustable seat

seggio'lone *nm* (per bambini) high chair

seggio'via *nf* chair lift

seghe'ria *nf* sawmill

se'ghetto *nm* hacksaw

segmen'tare *vt* segment

seg'mento *nm* segment

segna'carte *nm* bookmark

segna'lare *vt* signal; (annunciare) announce; (indicare) point out

segna'larsi *vr* distinguish oneself

segnalazi'one *nf* signals *pl*; (di candidato) recommendation. **segnalazione stradale** road signs *pl*

se'gnale *nm* signal; (stradale) sign. **segnale acustico** beep. **segnale d'allarme** alarm; (in treno) communication cord Br, emergency brake; fig warning sign . **segnale digitale** Comput digital signal. **segnale di libero** Teleph dialling tone. **segnale orario** Teleph time signal, speaking clock

segna'letica *nf* signals *pl*; '∼ **in rifacimento**' 'road signs being repainted'. **segnaletica orizzontale** painted road markings *pl*. **segnaletica stradale** road signs *pl*

segna'letico *adj* **dati segnaletici** description; **foto segnaletica** photograph used for identification purposes

segna'libro *nm* bookmark

segna'punti *nm inv* pegboard

se'gnare *vt* mark; (prendere nota) note; (indicare) indicate; Sport score; ∼ **la fine di qualcosa** sound the death knell for something; ∼ **il passo** mark time

se'gnarsi *vr* cross oneself

se'gnato *adj* marked

S

'**segno** nm sign; (traccia, limite) mark;
(bersaglio) target; **far** ∼ (col capo) nod; (con la
mano) beckon; **fare** ∼ **di no** (con la testa)
shake one's head; **fare** ∼ **di sì** (con la testa)
nod [one's head]; **lasciare il** ∼ leave a
mark; **non dare segni di vita** give no sign
of life; **oltrepassare il** ∼ fig overstep the
mark. **segno della croce** sign of the
cross. **segno premonitore** early
warning. **segno di sottolineatura**
underscore. **segno più** plus sign. **segno
zodiacale** sign of the Zodiac, birth sign,
star sign

segre'gare vt segregate

segre'garsi vr cut oneself off

segre'gato adj in isolation

segregazi'one nf segregation

segregazio'nistico adj segregated

segretari'ato nm secretariat

segre'tario, -a nmf secretary; **fare da** ∼
a qualcuno be somebody's secretary;
segretaria tuttofare girl Friday.
segretario bilingue bilingual
secretary. **segretario comunale** town
clerk. **segretario di direzione**
executive secretary. **segretario
personale** personal assistant, PA.
Segretario di Stato Secretary of State

segrete'ria nf (ufficio) administrative
office; (segretariato) secretariat. **segreteria
studenti** Univ admissions office.
segreteria telefonica answering
machine, answerphone

segre'tezza nf secrecy

se'greto adj & nm secret; **in** ∼ in secret

segu'ace nmf follower; **avere molti
seguaci** have a large following

segu'ente adj following, next

se'gugio nm bloodhound

segu'ire vt/i follow; (continuare) continue;
∼ **con lo sguardo** follow with one's eyes;
∼ **le orme di qualcuno** follow in
somebody's footsteps; ∼ **un corso** take a
course

segui'tare vt/i continue

'**seguito** nm retinue; (sequela) series;
(continuazione) continuation; **di** ∼ in
succession; **in** ∼ later on; **in** ∼ **a**
following; (a causa di) owing to; **al** ∼ in
his/her wake; **fare** ∼ **a** Comm follow up

'**sei** adj & nm six

sei'cento adj & nm six hundred; **il
Seicento** the seventeenth century

sei'mila adj & nm six thousand

'**selce** nf flint

sel'ciato nm paving

se'lenio nm selenium

selettività nf selectivity

selet'tivo adj selective; **memoria
selettiva** selective memory

selet'tore nm selector

selezio'nare vt select; '∼ **il numero'**
'dial [the number]'

selezi'one nf selection. **selezione
naturale** natural selection

self-con'trol nm self-control

self-'service adj & nm inv self-service

'**sella** nf saddle

sel'lare vt saddle

seltz nm soda water

'**selva** nf forest; (fig: di errori, capelli) mass;
(di ammiratori) horde

selvag'gina nf game

sel'vaggio, -a ① adj wild; (primitivo)
savage
② nmf savage

sel'vatico adj wild

selvicol'tura nf forestry

se'maforo nm traffic lights pl

se'mantica nf semantics

se'mantico adj semantic

sembi'anza nf semblance; **sembianze** pl
(di persona) appearance

sem'brare vi seem; (assomigliare) look
like; **che te ne sembra?** what do you
think?; **mi sembra che ...** I think ...;
sembra che vada bene it's fine, seemingly
or apparently

'**seme** nm seed; (di mela) pip; (di carte) suit;
(sperma) semen. **seme della discordia**
seeds pl of discord

se'mente nf seed

seme'strale adj ⟨corso⟩ six-month;
⟨pagamento⟩ six-monthly, half-yearly

se'mestre nm six months; Univ term,
semester Am

semia'perto adj half-open

semi'asse nm axle

semiauto'matico adj semiautomatic

semi'breve nf Mus semibreve

semi'cerchio nm semicircle

semicirco'lare adj semicircular

semicirconfe'renza nf semicircle

semicondut'tore adj & nm
semiconductor

semicon'vitto nm **scuola a
semiconvitto** school for dayboarders

semicosci'ente adj semi-conscious;
half-conscious

semi'croma nf Mus semiquaver

semifi'nale nf semifinal

semifina'lista nmf semifinalist

semi'freddo nm cold dessert
resembling ice cream

semilavo'rato ① adj semi-finished
② nm **semilavorati** pl semi-finished goods

semi'minima nf Mus crotchet

'**semina** nf sowing

semi'nare vt sow; fam shake off
⟨inseguitori⟩; ∼ **zizzania** cause trouble

semi'nario *nm* seminar; Relig seminary

semina'rista *nm* seminarist

seminfermità *nf* partial disability.
seminfermità mentale diminished
responsibility

seminter'rato *nm* basement

semi'nudo *adj* half-naked

semioscurità *nf* semi-darkness

semiprezi'oso *adj* semiprecious

semi'secco *adj* medium-dry

semi'serio *adj* semi-serious

se'mItico *adj* Semitic

semi'tono *nm* Mus semitone

sem'mai ⓵ *conj* in case
⓶ *adv* è lui, ∼, che ... if anyone, it's him
who...

'semola *nf* bran

semo'lato *adj* ⟨zucchero⟩ caster *attrib*

semo'lino *nm* semolina

'semplice *adj* simple; **in parole semplici**
in plain words

semplice'mente *adv* simply

semplici'otto, -a *nmf* simpleton

sempli'cistico *adj* simplistic

semplicità *nf* simplicity

semplifi'care *vt* simplify

'sempre *adv* always; (ancora) still; **per** ∼
for ever; ∼ **più** more and more; **pur** ∼
still, nevertheless

sempre'verde *adj & nm* evergreen

'senape *nf* mustard

se'nato *nm* senate

sena|'tore, -trice_nmf_ senator

'Senegal *nm* Senegal

se'nile *adj* senile

senilità *nf* senility

'senior ⓵ *adj inv* senior
⓶ *nmf* (pl **seniores**) Sport senior

'senno *nm* sense; **giudicare col** ∼ **del poi**
use hindsight

sennò *adv* otherwise, or else

sennonché *conj* but, except that;
(fuorché) but, except

'seno *nm* (petto) breast; Math sine; **in** ∼ **a**
in the bosom of

sen'sale *nm* broker

sen'sato *adj* sensible

sensazio'nale *adj* sensational

sensaziona'listico *adj* sensationalist

sensazi'one *nf* sensation; **fare** ∼
⟨notizia, scoperta⟩ cause a sensation

sen'sibile *adj* sensitive; (percepibile)
perceptible; (notevole) considerable; **mondo**
∼ tangible world

sensibilità *nf* sensitivity

sensibiliz'zare *vt* make more aware (**a**
of)

sensibil'mente *adv* appreciably

sensi'tivo ⓵ *adj* sensory
⓶ *nmf* sensitive person; (medium) medium

'senso *nm* sense; (significato) meaning;
(direzione) direction; **far** ∼ **a qualcuno**
make somebody shudder; **in** ∼ **orario/
antiorario** clockwise/anticlockwise; **ai
sensi della legge** in accordance with the
law; **non ha** ∼ it doesn't make sense;
avere il ∼ **degli affari** have good business
sense; **di buon** ∼ ⟨persona⟩ sensible;
senza ∼ meaningless; **in un certo** ∼ ... in
a sense *or* way ...; **perdere i sensi** lose
consciousness; **a** ∼ ⟨ripetere, tradurre⟩ in
general terms; **in** ∼ **opposto** in the
opposite direction; **a** ∼ **unico** ⟨strada⟩
one-way; **a doppio** ∼ [di marcia] ⟨strada⟩
two-way; **a doppio** ∼ ⟨parola, espressione⟩
with a double meaning. **senso
dell'umorismo** sense of humour;
'senso vietato' 'no entry'

sen'sore *nm* sensor

sensu'ale *adj* sensual

sensualità *nf* sensuality

sen'tenza *nf* sentence; (proverbio) saying;
pronunciare una ∼ hand down a sentence;
pronunciare la ∼ pronounce sentence

sentenzi'are *vi* pass judgment

senti'ero *nm* path. **sentiero luminoso
di avvicinamento** Aeron approach lights

sentimen'tale *adj* sentimental

sentimenta'lista *nmf* sentimentalist

sentimental'mente *adv*
sentimentally

senti'mento *nm* feeling; **essere fuori di**
∼ be out of one's mind

sen'tina *nf* Naut bilge

senti'nella *nf* sentry; **essere di** ∼ be on
guard

sen'tire ⓵ *vt* feel; (udire) hear; (ascoltare)
listen to; (gustare) taste; (odorare) smell
⓶ *vi* feel; (udire) hear; ∼ **caldo/freddo** feel
hot/cold

sen'tirsi *vr* feel; ∼ **di fare qualcosa** feel
like doing something; ∼ **bene/male** feel
well/ill; **sentirsela di fare qualcosa** feel up
to doing something

sen'tito *adj* (sincero) sincere; **per** ∼ **dire**
by hearsay

sen'tore *nm* inkling

'senza *prep* without; ∼ **ombrello** without
an umbrella; ∼ **correre** without running;
senz'altro certainly; ∼ **un soldo** penniless;
'∼ **conservanti**' 'no preservatives'; **fare** ∼
do without

senza'tetto *nm inv* **i** ∼ the homeless

'sepalo *nm* sepal

sepa'rare *vt* separate

sepa'rarsi *vr* separate; (prendere commiato)
part; ∼ **da** be separated from

separata'mente *adv* separately

separa'tista *nmf* separatist

sepa'rato *adj* separate

separazi'one *nf* separation. **separazione consensuale** separation by mutual consent. **separazione legale** legal separation

sepol'crale *adj* liter sepulchral

se'polcro *nm* sepulchre

se'polto ① *pp di* SEPPELLIRE ② *adj* buried; **morto e** ∼ fig dead and buried

sepol'tura *nf* burial; **dare** ∼ **a qualcuno** bury somebody

seppel'lire *vt* bury

seppel'lirsi *vr* fig cut oneself off

'seppia ① *nf* cuttle fish ② *adj inv* sepia

sep'pure *conj* even if

se'quela *nf* series, succession; (di insulti) string

se'quenza *nf* sequence

sequenzi'ale *adj* sequential

seque'strare *vt* (rapire) kidnap; (confiscare) confiscate; Jur impound

sequestra|'tore, -trice *nmf* kidnapper

se'questro *nm* Jur impounding; (di persona) kidnap[ping]

se'quoia *nf* sequoia

'sera *nf* evening, night; **di** ∼, **la** ∼ in the evening; **da** ∼ ⟨abito⟩ evening *attrib*; **alle 8 di** ∼ at 8 o'clock in the evening, at 8 o'clock at night; **buona** ∼! good evening!; **dalla mattina alla** ∼ from morning to night; **ieri** ∼ yesterday evening, last night; **questa** ∼ this evening, tonight

se'rale *adj* evening *attrib*

seral'mente *adv* every evening, every night

se'rata *nf* evening; (ricevimento) party. **serata danzante** dance. **serata di gala** gala night

ser'bare *vt* keep; harbour ⟨odio⟩; cherish ⟨speranza⟩

serba'toio *nm* tank. **serbatoio d'acqua** water tank. **serbatoio della benzina** petrol tank, gas tank Am

'Serbia *nf* Serbia

'serbo¹, -a ① *adj & nmf* Serbian ② *nm* (lingua) Serbian

'serbo² *nm* **mettere in** ∼ put aside

serbo-cro'ato *nmf* Serbo-Croat[ian]

sere'nata *nf* serenade

serenità *nf* serenity

se'reno *adj* serene; ⟨cielo⟩ clear; **un fulmine a ciel** ∼ fam bolt from the blue

ser'gente *nm* sergeant

'serial *nm inv* **serial [televisivo]** television serial

seri'ale *adj* serial

seria'mente *adv* seriously

'serico *adj* silk

'serie *nf inv* series; (complesso) set; Sport division; **fuori** ∼ custom-built; **produzione in** ∼ mass production. **serie A** (di calcio) ≈ Premier League. **serie B** (di calcio) ≈ First Division; **di** ∼ **B** fig second-rate. **serie numerica** numerical series

serietà *nf* seriousness

'serio *adj* serious; (degno di fiducia) reliable; **sul** ∼ seriously; (davvero) really

ser'mone *nm* sermon

sero'nina *nf* serotonin

'serpe *nf* liter viper

serpeggi'ante *adj* ⟨strada⟩ twisting, winding

serpeggi'are *vi* ⟨strada⟩ twist, wind; (fig: diffondersi) spread

ser'pente *nm* snake. **serpente a sonagli** rattlesnake. **serpente velenoso** poisonous snake

serpen'tina *nf* **a** ∼ twisting and turning, winding; **fare una** ∼ weave

'serra *nf* greenhouse. **effetto serra** greenhouse effect

ser'raglio *nm* harem

ser'randa *nf* shutter

ser'rare *vt* shut; (stringere) tighten; (incalzare) press on

ser'rata *nf* lockout

serra'tura *nf* lock

'server *nm inv* server. **server di posta** mail server. **server web** web server

ser'vibile *adj* usable

ser'vile *adj* servile

servi'lismo *nm* servility

ser'vire ① *vt* serve; (al ristorante) wait on ② *vi* serve; (essere utile) be of use; **non serve** it's no good; '∼ **freddo** 'serve chilled'

ser'virsi *vr* (di cibo) help oneself; ∼ **da** buy from; ∼ **di** use

servi|'tore *nm* retainer

servitù *nf* servitude; (personale di servizio) servants *pl*

servizi'evole *adj* obliging

ser'vizio *nm* service; (da caffè ecc) set; (di cronaca, sportivo) report; (in tennis) serve; **servizi** *pl* bathroom; **essere di** ∼ be on duty; **fare** ∼ ⟨autobus ecc⟩ run; **servizi** *pl* (terziario) services; **servizi** *pl* **bancari a domicilio** home banking; **servizi** *pl* **bancari via telefono** telephone banking; **servizi** *pl* **igienici** toilet block; **servizi** *pl* **di pronto intervento** emergency services; **servizi** *pl* **pubblici** (bagni) public toilets; **servizi** *pl* **sociali** welfare services. **donna di servizio** maid. **fuori servizio** ⟨bus⟩ not in service; ⟨ascensore⟩ out of order. **servizio bus navetta** courtesy bus. **servizio compreso** service charge included. **servizio escluso** not including service charge. **area di**

servizio service station. **servizio in camera** room service. **servizio civile** civilian duties done instead of national service. **servizio filmato** film report. **servizio di linea** passenger service. **servizio militare** military service. **servizio pubblico** utility company. **servizio al tavolo** waiter service. **servizio da tavola** dinnerware. **servizio traghetto** passenger ferry

'**servo**, **-a** nmf servant

servo'freno nm servo brake

servo'sterzo nm power steering

'**sesamo** nm sesame

ses'santa adj & nm sixty

sessan'tenne adj & nmf sixty-year-old

sessan'tesimo adj & nm sixtieth

sessan'tina nf una ∼ di about sixty

Sessan'totto nm protest movement of 1968

sessi'one nf session

ses'sista adj sexist

'**sesso** nm sex; fare ∼ sl have sex. **sesso forte** stronger sex. **gentil sesso** fair sex. **sesso sicuro** safe sex

sessu'ale adj sexual

sessualità nf sexuality

'**sesto**¹ adj & nm sixth

sesto² nm rimettere in ∼ put back on its feet ⟨azienda⟩; restore ⟨vestito⟩; recondition ⟨motore, auto⟩

set nm inv set

'**seta** nf silk; di ∼ silk attrib

setacci'are vt sieve

se'taccio nm sieve; **passare qualcosa al** ∼ fig go through something with a fine-tooth comb

'**sete** nf thirst; avere ∼ be thirsty. **sete di sangue** blood lust

'**setola** nf bristle

'**setta** nf sect

set'tanta adj & nm seventy

settan'tenne adj & nmf seventy-year-old

settan'tesimo adj & nm seventieth

settan'tina nf una ∼ di about seventy

set'tario adj sectarian

'**sette** adj & nm seven

sette'cento adj & nm seven hundred; **il Settecento** the eighteenth century

set'tembre nm September

settentrio'nale ① adj northern ② nmf northerner

settentri'one nm north

'**setter** nm inv setter

'**settico** adj septic

setti'mana nf week; **alla** ∼ per week; **a metà** ∼ midweek, half-way through the week. **settimana corta** five-day week. **settimana lavorativa** working week

settima'nale adj & nm weekly

setti'mino, **-a** ① adj born two months premature ② nmf baby born two months premature

'**settimo** adj & nm seventh

set'tore nm sector

settori'ale adj sector-based

severità nf severity

se'vero adj severe; (rigoroso) strict

se'vizia nf torture; **sevizie** pl torture sg

sevizi'are vt torture

Sey'chelles nfpl Seychelles

sezio'nare vt divide; Med dissect

sezi'one nf section; (reparto) department; Med dissection

sfaccen'dare vi bustle about

sfaccen'dato adj idle

sfaccet'tare vt cut

sfaccet'tato adj cut; fig many-sided, multifaceted

sfaccetta'tura nf cutting; fig facet

sfacchi'nare vi toil

sfacchi'nata nf drudgery

sfaccia'taggine nf cheek

sfacciata'mente adv cheekily

sfacci'ato adj cheeky, fresh Am

sfa'celo nm ruin; in ∼ in ruins

sfagio'lare vi fam non mi sfagiola it's/he's/she's not my cup of tea

sfal'darsi vr flake off

sfal'sare vt stagger; ∼ il tiro shoot wide

sfa'mare vt feed

sfa'marsi vt satisfy one's hunger, eat one's fill

sfarfal'lio nm (di schermo, luce) flicker

'**sfarzo** nm pomp

sfar'zoso adj sumptuous

sfa'sato adj fam confused; ⟨motore⟩ which needs tuning; **sentirsi** ∼ fam be out of sync[h]

sfasci'are vt unbandage; (fracassare) smash

sfasci'arsi vr fall to pieces

sfasci'ato adj beat-up

'**sfascio** nm ruin; andare allo ∼ go to rack and ruin

sfa'tare vt explode

sfati'cato adj lazy

'**sfatto** adj unmade

sfavil'lante adj sparkling

sfavil'lare vi sparkle

sfavo'revole adj unfavourable

sfavo'rire vt disadvantage, put at a disadvantage

sfeb'brare vi comincia a ∼ his temperature is starting to come down '**sfera** *nf* sphere. **sfera affettiva** area of feelings and emotions. **sfera celeste** celestial sphere. **sfera di cristallo** crystal ball. **sfera di influenza** sphere of influence

'**sferico** *adj* spherical

sfer'rare *vt* unshoe ‹*cavallo*›; give ‹*calcio, pugno*›

sferruz'zare *vi* knit

sfer'zare *vt* whip

sfer'zata *nf* whip; fig telling-off

sfian'cante *adj* wearing

sfian'care *vt* wear out

sfian'carsi *vr* wear oneself out

sfiata'toio *nm* blowhole

sfi'brare *vt* exhaust

sfi'brato *adj* exhausted

'**sfida** *nf* challenge

sfi'dare *vt* challenge

sfi'ducia *nf* mistrust

sfiduci'ato *adj* discouraged

'**sfiga** *nf* sl bloody bad luck; **avere ~** be bloody unlucky

sfi'gato, -a sl ⓵ *adj* bloody unlucky ⓶ *nmf* unlucky beggar

sfigu'rare ⓵ *vt* disfigure ⓶ *vi* (far brutta figura) look out of place

sfilacci'are *vt* fray

sfilacci'arsi *vr* fray

sfi'lare ⓵ *vt* unthread; (togliere di dosso) take off ⓶ *vi* ‹*truppe*› march past; (in parata) parade

sfi'larsi *vr* come unthreaded; ‹*collant*› ladder; take off ‹*pantaloni*›

sfi'lata *nf* parade; (sfilza) series. **sfilata di moda** fashion show

sfila'tino *nm* long, thin loaf

'**sfilza** *nf* string

'**sfinge** *nf* sphinx

sfi'nire *vt* wear out

sfi'nito *adj* worn out

sfio'rare *vt* skim; touch on ‹*argomento*›

sfio'rire *vi* wither; ‹*bellezza*› fade

sfis'sare *vt* cancel

'**sfitto** *adj* vacant

'**sfizio** *nm* whim, fancy; **togliersi uno ~** satisfy a whim

sfizi'oso *adj* nifty

sfo'cato *adj* out of focus

sfoci'are *vi* ~ **in** flow into

sfode'rare *vt* draw ‹*pistola, spada*›; fig show off ‹*cultura*›; ~ **un sorriso** smile insincerely

sfode'rato *adj* ‹*giacca*› unlined

sfo'gare *vt* vent

sfo'garsi *vr* give vent to one's feelings

sfoggi'are *vt/i* show off

'**sfoggio** *nm* show, display; **fare ~ di** show off

'**sfoglia** *nf* sheet of pastry. **pasta sfoglia** puff pastry

sfogli'are *vt* leaf through

sfogli'ata[1] *nf* flaky pastry with filling

sfogli'ata[2] *nf* dare una ~ a ‹*libro, giornale*› flick through

'**sfogo** *nm* outlet; fig outburst; Med rash; **dare ~ a** give vent to

sfolgo'rante *adj* blazing

sfolgo'rare *vi* blaze

sfolla'gente *nm inv* truncheon, billy Am

sfol'lare ⓵ *vt* clear ⓶ *vi* Mil be evacuated

sfol'lato, -a *nmf* evacuee

sfol'tire *vt* thin [out]; **farsi ~ i capelli** have one's hair thinned

sfon'dare ⓵ *vt* break down ⓶ *vi* (aver successo) make a name for oneself

'**sfondo** *nm* background; **un'aggressione a ~ politico/razziale** a politically/racially motivated attack

sfon'done *nm* fam blunder

sfor'mare *vt* pull out of shape ‹*tasche*›

sfor'marsi *vi* lose its shape; ‹*persona*› lose one's figure

sfor'mato *nm* Culin flan

sfor'nito *adj* ~ **di** ‹*negozio*› out of

sfor'tuna *nf* bad luck

sfortunata'mente *adv* unfortunately, unluckily

sfortu'nato *adj* unlucky

sfor'zare *vt* force

sfor'zarsi *vr* try hard

sfor'zato *adj* forced

'**sforzo** *nm* effort; (tensione) stress

'**sfottere** *vt* sl tease

sfracel'larsi *vr* smash; ~ **al suolo** crash to the ground

sfrangi'ato *adj* fringed

sfrat'tare *vt* evict

'**sfratto** *nm* eviction

sfrecci'are *vi* flash past

sfrega'mento *nm* fricton, rubbing

sfre'gare *vt* rub

sfregi'are *vt* slash

sfregi'ato, -a ⓵ *adj* scarred ⓶ *nmf* scarface

'**sfregio** *nm* slash

sfre'narsi *vr* run wild

sfre'nato *adj* wild

sfrigo'lio *nm* crackling

sfron'dare *vt* prune

sfron'tato *adj* shameless, brazen

sfrutta'mento *nm* exploitation

sfrut'tare *vt* exploit; take advantage of, make the most of ⟨*occasione*⟩

sfug'gente *adj* elusive; ⟨*mento*⟩ receding

sfug'gire ① *vi* escape; ∼ a escape [from]; **mi sfugge** it escapes me; **mi è sfuggito [di mente]** it [completely] slipped my mind; **mi è sfuggito di mano** I lost hold of it; **lasciarsi** ∼ **un'occasione** let an opportunity slip; **mi è sfuggito un rutto** I just came out with a belch; **gli è sfuggito un colpo dal fucile** the rifle just went off in his hands
② *vt* avoid

sfug'gita *nf* **di** ∼ in passing

sfu'mare ① *vi* (svanire) vanish; ⟨*colore*⟩ shade off
② *vt* soften ⟨*colore*⟩

sfuma'tura *nf* shade

sfuri'ata *nf* outburst [of anger]

sga'bello *nm* stool

sgabuz'zino *nm* cupboard

sgam'bato *adj* ⟨*costume da bagno*⟩ high-cut

sgambet'tare *vi* kick one's legs; (camminare) trot

sgam'betto *nm* **fare lo** ∼ **a qualcuno** trip somebody up

sganasci'arsi *vr* ∼ **dalle risa** roar with laughter

sganci'are *vt* unhook; Rail uncouple; drop ⟨*bombe*⟩; fam cough up ⟨*denaro*⟩

sganci'arsi *vr* become unhooked; fig get away

sganghe'rato *adj* ramshackle

sgar'bato *adj* rude

'sgarbo *nm* discourtesy; **fare uno** ∼ **a qualcuno** be rude to somebody; **ricevere uno** ∼ be treated rudely

sgargi'ante *adj* garish

sgar'rare *vi* be wrong; (da regola) stray from the straight and narrow

'sgarro *nm* mistake, slip

sga'sato *adj* flat

sgattaio'lare *vi* sneak away; ∼ **via** decamp

sge'lare *vt/i* thaw

'sghembo *adj* slanting; **a** ∼ obliquely

sghiacci'are *vt* defrost; thaw out ⟨*carne*⟩

sghignaz'zare *vi* laugh scornfully

sghiri'bizzo *nm* whim, fancy

sgob'bare *vi* slog; fam: ⟨*studente*⟩ swot

sgob'bone, -a *nmf* slogger; (fam: studente) swot

sgoccio'lare *vi* drip

sgoccio'lio *nm* dripping

sgo'larsi *vr* shout oneself hoarse

sgomb[e]'rare *vt* clear [out]

'sgombro ① *adj* clear

② *nm* (trasloco) removal; (pesce) mackerel

sgomen'tare *vt* dismay

sgomen'tarsi *vr* be dismayed

sgo'mento *nm* dismay

sgomi'nare *vt* defeat

sgom'mare *vi* make the tyres screech

sgom'mata *nf* screech of tyres

sgonfi'are *vt* deflate

sgonfi'arsi *vr* go down

'sgonfio *adj* flat

'sgorbio *nm* scrawl; (fig: vista sgradevole) sight

sgor'gare ① *vi* gush [out]
② *vt* flush out, unblock ⟨*lavandino*⟩

sgoz'zare *vt* ∼ **qualcuno** cut somebody's throat

sgra'devole *adj* disagreeable

sgra'dito *adj* unwelcome

sgraffi'are *vt* scratch

'sgraffio *nm* scratch

sgrammaticata'mente *adv* ungrammatically

sgrammati'cato *adj* ungrammatical

sgra'nare *vt* shell ⟨*piselli*⟩; open wide ⟨*occhi*⟩

sgra'nato *adj* grainy; ⟨*fagioli*⟩ shelled; ⟨*occhi*⟩ wide-open

sgran'chire *vt* stretch

sgran'chirsi *vr* stretch

sgranocchi'are *vt* munch

sgras'sare *vt* remove the grease from

'sgravio *nm* relief. **sgravio fiscale** tax relief

sgrazi'ato *adj* ungainly

sgreto'lare *vt* crumble

sgreto'larsi *vr* crumble

sgri'dare *vt* scold

sgri'data *nf* scolding

sgron'dare *vt* drain

sgros'sare *vt* rough-hew ⟨*marmo*⟩; fig polish

sguai'ato *adj* coarse

sgual'cire *vt* crumple

sgual'drina *nf* slut

sgu'ardo *nm* look; (breve) glance; **dare uno** ∼ **a** glance at ⟨*giornale, testo*⟩. **sguardo di insieme** overview

sguar'nito *adj* unadorned; (privo di difesa) undefended

'sguattero, -a *nmf* skivvy

sguaz'zare *vi* splash; (nel fango) wallow

'sguincio *nm* sidelong glance

sguinzagli'are *vt* unleash

sgusci'are ① *vt* shell
② *vi* (sfuggire) slip away; ∼ **fuori** slip out

'shaker *nm inv* shaker

shake'rare *vt* shake

S

'shampoo *nm inv* shampoo; ~ **e messa in piega** shampoo and set

'shopper *nm inv* carrier bag

'shuttle *nm inv* [space] shuttle

si¹ *pers pron* (riflessivo) oneself; (lui) himself; (lei) herself; (esso, essa) itself; (loro) themselves; (reciproco) each other; (tra più di due) one another; (impersonale) you, one *fml*; **lavarsi** wash [oneself]; **si è lavata** she washed [herself]; **lavarsi le mani** wash one's hands; **si è lavata le mani** she washed her hands; **si è mangiato un pollo intero** he ate an entire chicken by himself; **incontrarsi** meet each other; **la gente si aiuta a vicenda** people help one another; **si potrebbe pensare che ...** you might think that ..., one might think that ... *fml*; **non si sa mai** you never know, one never knows; **queste cose si dimenticano facilmente** these things are easily forgotten

si² *nm* Mus (chiave, nota) B

sì *adv* yes; **credo di sì** I believe so; **penso di sì** I think so; **ha detto di sì** she said yes; **sì?** really?; **sì che mi piace!** yes I do like it!

sia¹ ▶ ESSERE

sia² *conj* ~... ~... (entrambi) both... and...; (o l'uno o l'altro) either... or...; ~ **che venga,** ~ **che non venga** whether he comes or not; **voglio** ~ **questo che quello** I want both this one and that one; **verranno** ~ **Giuseppe** ~ **Giacomo** both Giuseppe and Giacomo are coming

sia'mese *adj* Siamese

Si'beria *nf* Siberia

sibi'lare *vi* hiss

sibil'lino *adj* sibylline

'sibilo *nm* hiss

si'cario *nm* hired killer

sicché *conj* (perciò) so [that]; (allora) then

siccità *nf* drought

sic'come *conj* as

Si'cilia *nf* Sicily

sicili'ano, -a *adj & nmf* Sicilian

sico'moro *nm* sycamore

si'cura *nf* safety catch; (di portiera) childproof lock

sicura'mente *adv* definitely; ~ **sarà arrivato** he must have arrived by now

sicu'rezza *nf* (certezza) certainty; (salvezza) safety; **di** ~ ⟨dispositivo⟩ safety *attrib*; **di massima** ~ top security. **uscita di sicurezza** emergency exit

si'curo ① *adj* (non pericoloso) safe; (certo) sure; ⟨saldo⟩ steady; Comm sound ② *adv* certainly ③ *nm* safety; **al** ~ safe; **andare sul** ~ play [it] safe; **di** ~ definitely; **di** ~ **sarà arrivato** he must have arrived; ~**!** sure!

'sidecar *nm inv* sidecar

siderur'gia *nf* iron and steel industry

side'rurgico *adj* iron and steel *attrib*

'sidro *nm* cider

si'epe *nf* hedge

si'ero *nm* serum

sieronega'tivo, -a ① *adj* HIV negative ② *nmf* person who is HIV negative

sieroposi'tivo, -a ① *adj* HIV positive ② *nmf* person who is HIV positive

Si'erra Le'one *nf* Sierra Leone

si'esta *nf* afternoon nap, siesta; **fare la** ~ have an afternoon nap

si'fone *nm* siphon

Sig. *abbr* (**signore**) Mr

Sig.a *abbr* (**signora**) Mrs, Ms

siga'retta *nf* cigarette; **pantaloni** *pl* **a** ~ drainpipes

'sigaro *nm* cigar

Sigg. *abbr* (**signori**) Messrs

sigil'lare *vt* seal

si'gillo *nm* seal

'sigla *nf* acronym; (iniziali) initials *pl*. **sigla musicale** signature tune

si'glare *vt* initial

Sig.na *abbr* (**signorina**) Miss, Ms

signifi'care *vt* mean

significa'tivo *adj* significant

signifi'cato *nm* meaning

si'gnora *nf* lady; (davanti a nome proprio) Mrs; (non sposata) Miss; (in lettere ufficiali) Dear Madam; **la** ~ **Rossi** Mrs Rossi; **il signor Vené e** ~ Mr and Mrs Vené

si'gnore *nm* gentleman; Relig lord; (davanti a nome proprio) Mr; **il signor Rossi** Mr Rossi

signo'rile *adj* gentlemanly; (di lusso) luxury

signo'rina *nf* young lady; (seguito da nome proprio) Miss; **la** ~ **Rossi** Miss Rossi

silenzia'tore *nm* silencer

si'lenzio *nm* silence. **silenzio di tomba** deathly hush

silenzi'oso *adj* silent

'silfide *nf* sylph

silhou'ette *nf inv* silhouette, outline; **che** ~**!** you're so slim!

si'licio *nm* **piastrina di silicio** silicon chip

sili'cone *nm* silicone

'sillaba *nf* syllable

silla'bario *nm* primer

sillaba'tore *nm* Comput hyphenation program

sillo'gismo *nm* syllogism

silu'rare *vt* torpedo

si'luro *nm* torpedo

simbi'osi *nf* symbiosis; **vivere in** ~ need each other, have a symbiotic relationship

simboleggi'are *vt* symbolize

sim'bolico *adj* symbolic[al]
simbo'lismo *nm* symbolism
simbo'lista *nmf* symbolist
'simbolo *nm* symbol
similarità *nf inv* similarity
'simile ① *adj* similar; (tale) such; è ∼ a... it's like..., it's similar to..., **qualcosa di** ∼ something similar
② *nm* (il prossimo) fellow human being, fellow man
simili'tudine *nf* Gram simile
simil'mente *adv* similarly
simil'pelle *nf* Leatherette®
simme'tria *nf* symmetry
sim'metrico *adj* symmetric[al]
simpa'tia *nf* liking; (compenetrazione) sympathy; **prendere qualcuno in** ∼ take a liking to somebody; **provare** ∼ **per** like
sim'patico *adj* nice. **inchiostro simpatico** invisible ink
simpatiz'zante *nmf* well-wisher
simpatiz'zare *vt* ∼ **con** take a liking to; ∼ **per qualcosa/qualcuno** lean towards something/somebody
sim'posio *nm* symposium
simu'lare *vt* simulate; feign ⟨*amicizia, interesse*⟩
simula'tore *nm* simulator
simulazi'one *nf* simulation. **simulazione di reato** Jur making of false accusations
simul'tanea *nf* **in** ∼ simultaneously
simul'taneo *adj* simultaneous
sina'goga *nf* synagogue
sincera'mente *adv* sincerely; (a dire il vero) honestly
since'rarsi *vr* make sure
sincerità *nf* sincerity
sin'cero *adj* sincere
'sincope *nf* syncopation; Med fainting fit
sincron'ia *nf* sync[h]
sincro'nismo *nm* synchronism
sincroniz'zare *vt* synchronize
sincroniz'zato *adj* synchronized; **essere ben** ∼ **con** be in sync[h] with
sincronizzazi'one *nf* synchronization
'sincrono *adj* synchronous
sinda'cabile *adj* arguable
sinda'cale *adj* [trade] union *attrib*, [labor] union Am
sindaca'lista *nmf* trade unionist, labor union member Am
sinda'care *vt* inspect
sinda'cato *nm* [trade] union, [labor] union Am; (associazione) syndicate. **sindacato di categoria** trade union
'sindaco *nm* mayor
'sindrome *nf* syndrome. **sindrome da colon irritabile** irritable bowel

syndrome. **sindrome di Down** Down's syndrome. **sindrome da edifici malsani** sick building syndrome. **sindrome premestruale** premenstrual syndrome, PMS. **sindrome respiratoria acuta severa** severe acute respiratory syndrome, SARS
sinfo'nia *nf* symphony
sin'fonico *adj* symphonic
Singa'pore *nf* Singapore
singhioz'zare *vi* (di pianto) sob
singhi'ozzo *nm* hiccup; (di pianto) sob; **avere il** ∼ have the hiccups
'single *nmf inv* single
singo'lare ① *adj* singular; (strano) peculiar
② *nm* Gram singular
singolar'mente *adv* individually; (stranamente) peculiarly
'singolo ① *adj* single
② *nm* individual; Mus single; Tennis singles *pl*; **un** ∼ **di successo** a hit single
si'nistra *nf* left; **a** ∼ on the left; **girare a** ∼ turn to the left; **la seconda a** ∼ the second on the left; **con la guida a** ∼ ⟨*auto*⟩ with left-hand drive; **la** ∼ Pol the left; **di** ∼ Pol left wing
sini'strare *vt* injure; damage ⟨*casa*⟩
sini'strato *adj* injured; ⟨*casa*⟩ damaged
si'nistro ① *adj* left[-hand]; (avverso) sinister
② *nm* accident
sini'strorso, -a *nmf* pej leftie
'sino *prep* = FINO[1]
si'nonimo ① *adj* synonymous
② *nm* synonym
sin'tassi *nf* syntax
sin'tattico *adj* syntactic[al]
'sintesi *nf* synthesis; (riassunto) summary
sin'tetico *adj* synthetic; (conciso) summary
sintetiz'zare *vt* summarize
sintetizza'tore *nm* synthesizer
sinto'matico *adj* symptomatic
'sintomo *nm* symptom
sinto'nia *nf* tuning; **in** ∼ on the same wavelength; **in** ∼ **con** in harmony with, in tune with
sintonizza'tore *nm* tuner
sinu'oso *adj* ⟨*strada*⟩ winding
sinu'site *nf* sinusitis
sio'nismo *nm* Zionism
sio'nista *adj & nmf* Zionist
si'pario *nm* curtain
si'rena *nf* siren; (di nave) hooter
'Siria *nf* Syria
siri'ano, -a *adj & nmf* Syrian
si'ringa *nf* syringe
'sismico *adj* seismic

s

si'smografo *nm* seismograph

sismolo'gia *nf* seismology

si'stema *nm* system; **non è ~!** that's no way to behave!. **sistema di amplificazione sonora** induction loop. **sistema di gestione banca dati** database management system, DBMS. **sistema immunitario** immune system. **Sistema Monetario Europeo** European Monetary System. **sistema nervoso** nervous system. **sistema operativo** Comput operating system. **sistema solare** solar system. **sistema di vita** way of life

siste'mare *vt* (mettere) put; tidy up ‹casa, camera›; (risolvere) sort out; (procurare lavoro a) fix up with a job; (trovare alloggio a) find accommodation for; (sposare) marry off; (fam: punire) sort out

siste'marsi *vr* settle down; (trovare un lavoro) find a job; (trovare alloggio) find accommodation; (sposarsi) marry

sistematica'mente *adv* systematically

siste'matico *adj* systematic

sistemazi'one *nf* arrangement; (di questione) settlement; (lavoro) job; (alloggio) accommodation; (matrimonio) marriage

siste'mista *nmf* Comput systems engineer

'sistole *nf* systole

'sit-in *nm inv* sit-in

'sito *nm* site. **sito web** Comput web site

situ'are *vt* place

situazi'one *nf* situation; **essere all'altezza della ~** be equal to the situation, be up to the situation

'skai *nm* Leatherette®

'skateboard *nm inv* skateboard

sketch *nm inv* sketch

ski-'lift *nm inv* ski tow

'skipper *nmf inv* skipper

slab'brare *vt* stretch out of shape ‹maglia, tasca›

slab'brato *adj* ‹maglia, tasca› shapeless

slacci'are *vt* unfasten; unlace ‹scarpe›

'slalom *nm inv* slalom; **a ~** slalom *attrib*

slanci'arsi *vr* hurl oneself

slanci'ato *adj* slender

'slancio *nm* impetus; (impulso) impulse; **agire di ~** act on impulse

sla'vato *adj* ‹carnagione› fair

'slavo *adj* Slav[onic]

sle'ale *adj* disloyal; **concorrenza sleale** unfair competition

slealtà *nf* disloyalty

sle'gare *vt* untie

sle'garsi *vr* untie oneself

slip *nmpl* underpants

'slitta *nf* sledge; (trainata) sleigh

slitta'mento *nm* (di macchina) skid; (fig: di riunione) postponement

slit'tare *vi* Auto skid; ‹riunione› be put off

slit'tata *nf* skid

slit'tino *nm* toboggan

'slogan *nm inv* slogan, rallying cry

slo'gare *vt* dislocate

slo'garsi *vr* **~ una caviglia** sprain one's ankle

slo'gato *adj* sprained

sloga'tura *nf* sprain

sloggi'are ① *vt* dislodge ② *vi* move out

slot *nm* **slot di espansione** Comput expansion slot

slot-ma'chine *nf inv* slot-machine, one-armed bandit

Slo'vacchia *nf* Slovakia

slo'vacco, -a *adj & nmf* Slovak

Slo'venia *nf* Slovenia

smacchi'are *vt* clean

smacchia'tore *nm* stain remover

'smacco *nm* humiliating defeat

smagli'ante *adj* dazzling

smagli'arsi *vr* ‹calza› ladder *Br*, run

smaglia'tura *nf* ladder *Br*, run

smagnetiz'zare *vt* demagnetize

smagnetiz'zatore *nm* demagnetizer

sma'grito *adj* thinner

smalizi'ato *adj* cunning

smal'tare *vt* enamel; glaze ‹ceramica›; varnish ‹unghie›

smal'tato *adj* enamelled; ‹ceramica› glazed; ‹unghie› varnished

smalta'tura *nf* enamelling; (di ceramica) glazing

smalti'mento *nm* disposal; (di merce) selling off; (di grassi) burning off. **smaltimento [dei] rifiuti** waste disposal

smal'tire *vt* burn off; (merce) sell off; fig get through ‹corrispondenza›; **~ la sbornia** sober up

'smalto *nm* enamel; (di ceramica) glaze; (per le unghie) nail varnish, nail polish

smance'ria *nf* **fare smancerie** be overpolite

smance'roso *adj* simpering

'smania *nf* fidgets *pl*; (desiderio) longing; **avere la ~ di** have a craving for

smani'are *vi* have the fidgets; **~ per** long for

smani'oso *adj* restless

smantella'mento *nm* dismantling

smantel'lare *vt* dismantle

smarri'mento *nm* loss; (psicologico) bewilderment

smar'rire *vt* lose; (temporaneamente) mislay

smar'rirsi *vr* get lost; (turbarsi) be bewildered

smar'rito *adj* lost; ⟨sguardo⟩ bewildered, lost

smasche'rare *vt* unmask

smasche'rarsi *vr* fig reveal oneself

SME *nm abbr* (**Sistema Monetario Europeo**) EMS

smem'brare *vt* dismember

smemo'rato, -a ① *adj* forgetful ② *nmf* scatterbrain

smen'tire *vt* deny

smen'tita *nf* denial

sme'raldo *nm & adj inv* emerald

smerci'are *vt* sell off

'smercio *nm* sale

smerigli'ato *adj* emery. **vetro smerigliato** frosted glass

sme'riglio *nm* emery

smer'lare *vt* scallop

'smerlo *nm* scallop

'smesso ① *pp di* SMETTERE ② *adj* ⟨abiti⟩ cast-off

'smettere *vt* stop; stop wearing ⟨abiti⟩; **smettila!** stop it!

smidol'lato *adj* spineless

smilitariz'zare *vt* demilitarize

'smilzo *adj* thin

sminu'ire *vt* diminish

sminu'irsi *vr* fig belittle oneself

sminuz'zare *vt* crumble; (fig: analizzare) analyse in detail

smista'mento *nm* clearing; (postale) sorting; **stazione di** ∼ shunting yard, marshalling yard. **smistamento rifiuti** sorting of waste

smi'stare *vt* sort; Mil post; Rail marshall

smisu'rato *adj* boundless; (esorbitante) excessive

smitiz'zare *vt* demythologize

smobili'tare *vt* demobilize

smobilitazi'one *nf* demobilization

smo'dato *adj* immoderate

smog *nm* smog

'smoking *nm inv* dinner jacket, tuxedo Am

smon'tabile *adj* jointed

smon'taggio *nm* disassembly

smon'tare ① *vt* take to pieces; (scoraggiare) dishearten; take down ⟨tenda⟩ ② *vi* (da veicolo) get off; (da cavallo) dismount; (dal servizio) go off duty

smon'tarsi *vr* lose heart

'smorfia *nf* grimace; (moina) simper; **fare smorfie** make faces

smorfi'oso *adj* affected

'smorto *adj* pale; ⟨colore⟩ dull

smor'zare *vt* dim ⟨luce⟩; tone down ⟨colori⟩; deaden ⟨suoni⟩; quench ⟨sete⟩

smor'zata *nf* Sport drop shot

'smosso *pp di* SMUOVERE

smotta'mento *nm* landslide

SMS *nm abbr* SMS message, text message; **mandare un** ∼ **a qualcuno** text somebody

'smunto *adj* emaciated

smu'overe *vt* shift; (commuovere) move

smu'oversi *vr* move; (commuoversi) be moved

smus'sare *vt* round off; (fig: attenuare) tone down

smus'sarsi *vr* go blunt

smussa'tura *nf* bevel

snack bar *nm inv* snack bar

snatu'rato *adj* inhuman

snazionaliz'zare *vt* denationalize

S.N.C. *abbr* **società in nome collettivo**

snel'lire *vt* slim down

snel'lirsi *vr* slim [down]

'snello *adj* slim

sner'vante *adj* enervating

sner'vare *vt* enervate

sner'varsi *vr* get exhausted

sni'dare *vt* drive out

snif'fare *vt* snort

snob'bare *vt* snub

sno'bismo *nm* snobbery

snoccio'lare *vt* stone; fig blurt out

snoccio'lato *adj* ⟨olive⟩ pitted, with the stones removed

sno'dabile *adj* jointed

sno'dare *vt* untie; (sciogliere) loosen

sno'darsi *vr* come untied; ⟨strada⟩ wind

sno'dato *adj* ⟨persona⟩ double-jointed; ⟨dita⟩ flexible

'snodo *nm* coupling. **snodo ferroviario** coupling

'snowboard *nm inv* snowboard; **fare** ∼ snowboard

SO *abbr* (**sud-ovest**) SW

soap 'opera *nf inv* soap [opera]

so'ave *adj* gentle

sobbal'zare *vi* jerk; (trasalire) start

sob'balzo *nm* jerk; (trasalimento) start

sobbar'carsi *vr* ∼ **a** undertake

sobbol'lire *vi* simmer

sob'borgo *nm* suburb

sobil'lare *vt* stir up

sobilla‖'tore, -trice *nm* instigator

sobrietà *nf* sobriety

'sobrio *adj* sober

soc'chiudere *vt* half-close

socchi'uso ① *pp di* SOCCHIUDERE

2 *adj* ⟨occhi⟩ half-closed; ⟨porta⟩ ajar

soc'combere *vi* succumb

soc'correre *vt* assist

soccorri'tore, **-trice** *nmf* rescue worker

soc'corso **1** pp di SOCCORRERE
2 *nm* assistance, help; **venire in** ~ come to help, come to the rescue; **venire in** ~ **a qualcuno** come to somebody's rescue; **soccorsi** *pl* help; (persone) rescuers; (dopo disastro) relief workers. **soccorso alpino** mountain rescue. **soccorso disastri** disaster relief. **soccorso stradale** breakdown service, wrecking service Am

socialdemo'cratico, **-a** **1** *adj* Social Democratic
2 *nmf* Social Democrat

socialdemocra'zia *nf* Social Democracy

soci'ale *adj* social

socia'lismo *nm* Socialism

socia'lista *adj* & *nmf* Socialist

socializ'zare *vi* socialize

società *nf inv* society; Comm company. **società in accomandita semplice** limited partnership. **società per azioni** public limited company, plc. **società dei consumi** consumer society. **società in nome collettivo** commercial partnership. **società fiduciaria** trust company. **società a responsabilità limitata** limited liability company. **società di telecomunicazioni** communications company

soci'evole *adj* sociable

'socio, **-a** *nmf* member; Comm partner

socioeco'nomico *adj* socio-economic

sociolo'gia *nf* sociology

socio'logico *adj* sociological

soci'ologo, **-a** *nmf* sociologist

'soda *nf* soda. **soda da bucato** washing soda

soda'lizio *nm* association, society

soddisfa'cente *adj* satisfactory

soddi'sfare *vt/i* satisfy; meet ⟨richiesta⟩; make amends for ⟨offesa⟩

soddi'sfatto **1** pp di SODDISFARE
2 *adj* satisfied

soddisfazi'one *nf* satisfaction

'sodo **1** *adj* hard; fig firm; ⟨uovo⟩ hard-boiled
2 *adv* hard; **dormire** ~ sleep soundly
3 *nm* **venire al** ~ get to the point

sofà *nm inv* sofa

soffe'rente *adj* (malato) ill

soffe'renza *nf* suffering

soffer'marsi *vr* pause; ~ **su** dwell on

sof'ferto pp di SOFFRIRE

soffi'are **1** *vt* blow; reveal ⟨segreto⟩; (rubare) pinch fam
2 *vi* blow

soffi'ata *nf* datti una ~ al naso blow your nose; **fare una** ~ **a qualcuno** fig sl tip somebody off, give somebody a tip-off

'soffice *adj* soft

soffi'etto *nm* bellows; **a** ~ ⟨borsa⟩ expanding. **soffietto editoriale** blurb

'soffio *nm* puff; Med murmur

sof'fitta *nf* attic

sof'fitto *nm* ceiling

soffoca'mento *nm* suffocation

soffo'cante *adj* suffocating

soffo'care *vt/i* choke; fig stifle

sof'friggere *vt* fry lightly

sof'frire *vt/i* suffer; (sopportare) bear; ~ **di** suffer from; ~ **di [mal di] cuore** suffer from *or* have a heart condition; ~ **la fame/il freddo** be hungry/cold

sof'fritto **1** pp di SOFFRIGGERE
2 *nm* fried ingredients *pl*

sof'fuso *adj* ⟨luce⟩ soft, suffused

sofisti'care **1** *vt* (adulterare) adulterate
2 *vi* (sottilizzare) quibble

sofisti'cato *adj* sophisticated

soft *adj inv* soft

'softcopy *nf* Comput soft copy

'soft-core **1** *nm* soft-core, soft porn
2 *adj inv* **pornografia soft-core** soft porn

'software *nm inv* software; **dei** ~ software packages. **software di accesso** access software. **software applicativo** application software. **software di autoapprendimento** tutorial package, tutorial software. **software di comunicazione** communications software, comms software. **software didattico** educational software. **software di gestione errori** error correction software. **software di OCR** OCR software. **software di sistema** system software

softwa'rista *nmf* Comput software engineer

soggettiva'mente *adv* subjectively

sogget'tivo *adj* subjective

sog'getto **1** *nm* subject; **cattivo** ~ bad sort
2 *adj* subject; **essere** ~ **a** be subject to

soggezi'one *nf* subjection; (rispetto) awe

sogghi'gnare *vi* sneer

sog'ghigno *nm* sneer

soggio'gare *vt* subdue

soggior'nare *vi* stay

soggi'orno *nm* stay; (stanza) living room. **permesso di soggiorno** residence permit

soggi'ungere *vt* add

'soglia *nf* threshold; **alle soglie di qualcosa** on the threshold of something. **soglia del dolore** pain threshold. **soglia di povertà** poverty line

'sogliola *nf* sole. **sogliola limanda** lemon sole

so'gnare *vt/i* dream; ∼ **a occhi aperti** daydream

so'gnarsi *vr* dream; **non te lo sogni neppure!** forget it!, don't even think of it!

sogna|'tore, -trice *nmf* dreamer

'sogno *nm* dream; **fare un** ∼ have a dream; **neanche per** ∼**!** not on your life!; **essere un** ∼ (bellissimo) be a dream; **una casa da** ∼ a dream house; **il mio** ∼ **nel cassetto** my secret dream

'soia *nf* soya

sol *nm* Mus (chiave, nota) G

so'laio *nm* attic

sola'mente *adv* only

so'lare *adj* ⟨energia, raggi⟩ solar; ⟨crema⟩ sun *attrib*

so'larium *nm inv* solarium

sol'care *vt* plough

'solco *nm* furrow; (di ruota) track; (di nave) wake; (di disco) groove

solda'tessa *nf* servicewoman

sol'dato *nm* soldier. **soldato semplice** private

'soldo *nm* **non ha un** ∼ he hasn't got a penny to his name; **senza un** ∼ penniless; **al** ∼ **di** in the pay of; **soldi** *pl* (denaro) money *sg*; **fare [i] soldi** make money; **prelevare dei soldi** withdraw money; **da quattro soldi** cheapo, nickel-and-dime Am

'sole *nm* sun; (luce del sole) sun[light]; **al** ∼ in the sun; **prendere il** ∼ sunbathe

sole'cismo *nm* solecism

soleggi'ato *adj* sunny

so'lenne *adj* solemn

solennità *nf* solemnity

so'lere *vi* be in the habit of; **come si suol dire** as they say

so'letta *nf* insole

sol'fato *nm* sulphate

sol'feggio *nm* sol-fa

'solfuro *nm* sulphur

soli'dale *adj* in agreement

solidarietà *nf* solidarity

solidifi'care *vt/i* solidify

solidifi'carsi *vr* solidify

solidità *nf* solidity; (di colori) fastness

'solido ① *adj* solid; (robusto) sturdy; ⟨colore⟩ fast; **in** ∼ Jur jointly and severally ② *nm* solid

soli'loquio *nm* soliloquy

so'lista ① *adj* solo ② *nmf* soloist

solita'mente *adv* usually

soli'tario ① *adj* solitary; (isolato) lonely ② *nm* (brillante) solitaire; (gioco di carte) patience, solitaire

'solito ① *adj* usual; **essere** ∼ **fare qualcosa** be in the habit of doing something ② *nm* the usual; **di** ∼ usually

soli'tudine *nf* solitude

solleci'tare *vt* speed up; urge ⟨persona⟩

sollecitazi'one *nf* (richiesta) request; (preghiera) entreaty

sol'lecito ① *adj* prompt ② *nm* reminder

solleci'tudine *nf* promptness; (interessamento) concern; **con la massima** ∼ Comm as soon as possible

solle'one *nm* noonday sun; (periodo) dog days of summer

solleti'care *vt* tickle

sol'letico *nm* tickling; **fare il** ∼ **a qualcuno** tickle somebody; **soffrire il** ∼ be ticklish

solleva'mento *nm* **sollevamento pesi** weightlifting

solle'vare *vt* lift; (elevare) raise; (confortare) comfort; ∼ **una questione** raise a question; ∼ **qualcuno da un incarico** relieve somebody of a responsibility

solle'varsi *vr* rise; (riaversi) recover

solle'vato *adj* relieved

solli'evo *nm* relief; **che** ∼**!** what a relief!

'solo, -a ① *adj* alone; (isolato) lonely; (unico) only; Mus solo; **da** ∼ by myself/ yourself/himself etc ② *nmf* **il** ∼, **la sola** the only one ③ *nm* Mus solo ④ *adv* only; ∼ **il sabato/la domenica** Saturdays/Sundays only, only on Saturdays/Sundays

sol'stizio *nm* solstice

sol'tanto *adv* only

so'lubile *adj* soluble; ⟨caffè⟩ instant

soluzi'one *nf* solution; Comm payment; **senza** ∼ **di continuità** without interruption; **in unica** ∼ Comm as a lump sum. **soluzione salina per lenti** soaking solution

sol'vente ① *nm* solvent. **solvente per lo smalto** nail varnish remover. **solvente per unghie** nail polish remover ② *adj* solvent. **reparto solvente** pay ward

solvibilità *nf* Fin solvency

'soma *nf* load. **bestia da soma** beast of burden

'somalo, -a *adj & nmf* Somali

so'maro *nm* ass, donkey; Sch dunce

so'matico *adj* somatic; **tratti somatici** physical features

somatiz'zare vt react psychosomatically to

som'brero nm sombrero

somigli'ante adj similar

somigli'anza nf resemblance

somigli'are vi ~ a look like, resemble

somigli'arsi vr be alike; **chi si somiglia si piglia** birds of a feather flock together

'somma nf sum; Math addition

som'mare vt add; (totalizzare) add up

sommaria'mente adv summarily

som'mario adj & nm summary

som'mato adj **tutto** ~ all things considered

somme'lier nm inv wine waiter

som'mergere vt submerge

sommer'gibile nm submarine

som'merso [1] pp di SOMMERGERE [2] nm Econ black economy

som'messo adj soft

sommini'strare vt administer

somministrazi'one nf administration; ~ **per via orale** to be taken orally

sommità nf inv summit

'sommo [1] adj highest; fig supreme [2] nm summit

som'mossa nf rising

sommozza'tore nm frogman

so'naglio nm bell

'sonar nm inv sonar

so'nata nf sonata; fig fam beating

'sonda nf Mech drill; (spaziale, Med) probe

son'daggio nm drilling; (spaziale, Med) probe; (indagine) survey. **sondaggio d'opinione** opinion poll

son'dare vt sound; (investigare) probe

so'netto nm sonnet

sonnambu'lismo nm sleepwalking

son'nambulo, -a nmf sleepwalker

sonnecchi'are vi doze

son'nifero nm sleeping-pill

'sonno nm sleep; **aver** ~ be sleepy; **morire di** ~ be dead tired, be dead on one's feet; **morto di** ~ (fam: stupido) zombie; **perdere il** ~ anche fig lose sleep. **sonno eterno** Relig eternal rest

sonno'lenza nf sleepiness

'sono ▶ ESSERE

sonoriz'zare vt add a soundtrack to

so'noro [1] adj resonant; (rumoroso) loud; ⟨onde, scheda⟩ sound attrib [2] nm (Tech: di film) soundtrack

sontu'oso adj sumptuous

sopo'rifero adj soporific

sop'palco nm platform. **soppalco abitabile** loft conversion

soppe'rire vi ~ a qualcosa provide for something

soppe'sare vt weigh up ⟨situazione⟩

soppi'atto: **di** ~ adv furtively

soppor'tare vt support; (tollerare) stand; bear ⟨dolore⟩

sopportazi'one nf patience

soppressi'one nf removal; (di legge) abolition; (di diritti, pubblicazione) suppression; (annullamento) cancellation

sop'presso pp di SOPPRIMERE

sop'primere vt get rid of; abolish ⟨legge⟩; suppress ⟨diritti, pubblicazione⟩; (annullare) cancel

'sopra [1] adv on top; (più in alto) higher [up]; (al piano superiore) upstairs; (in testo) above; **mettilo lì** ~ put it up there; **di** ~ upstairs; **dormirci** ~ fig sleep on it; **pensarci** ~ think about it; **vedi** ~ see above [2] prep ~ [a] on; (senza contatto, oltre) over; (riguardo a) about; **è** ~ **al tavolo, è** ~ **il tavolo** it's on the table; **il quadro è appeso** ~ **al camino** the picture is hanging over the fireplace; **il ponte passa** ~ **all'autostrada** the bridge crosses over the motorway; **è caduto** ~ **il tetto** it fell on the roof; **l'uno** ~ **l'altro** one on top of the other; (senza contatto) one above the other; **abita** ~ **di me** he lives upstairs from me; **i bambini** ~ **i dieci anni** children over ten; **20°** ~ **lo zero** 20 above zero; ~ **il livello del mare** above sea level; **rifletti** ~ **quello che è successo** think about what happened; **prendere** ~ **di sé la responsabilità di qualcosa** assume responsibility for something; **scaricare la colpa** ~ **qualcuno** put the blame on somebody; **non ha nessuno** ~ **di sé** he has nobody above him; **al di** ~ **di** over; **al di** ~ **di ogni sospetto** beyond suspicion [3] nm **il [di]** ~ the top

so'prabito nm overcoat

soprac'ciglio nm (pl nf **sopracciglia**) eyebrow

sopracco'perta nf (di letto) bedspread

sopraccoper'tina nf book jacket, dust jacket

soprad'detto adj above-mentioned

sopraele'vare vt raise

sopraele'vata nf elevated railway

sopraele'vato adj raised

sopraf'fare vt overwhelm

sopraf'fatto pp di SOPRAFFARE

sopraffazi'one nf abuse of power

sopraf'fino adj excellent; ⟨gusto, udito⟩ highly refined

sopraggi'ungere vi ⟨persona⟩ turn up; (accadere) happen; **è sopraggiunta la pioggia** and then it started to rain

soprallu'ogo nm inspection

sopram'mobile nm ornament

soprannatu'rale adj & nm supernatural

sopran'nome *nm* nickname
soprannomi'nare *vt* nickname
sopran'numero *adv* sono in ∼ there are too many of them; **ce ne sono 15 in** ∼ there are 15 too many of them, there are 15 of them too many
so'prano *nm* or *nf inv* soprano
soprappensi'ero *adv* lost in thought
sopras'salto *nm* di ∼ with a start
soprasse'dere *vi* ∼ a postpone
soprat'tassa *nf* surtax. **soprattassa postale** excess postage
soprat'tetto *nm* fly sheet
soprat'tutto *adv* above all
sopravvalu'tare *vt* overvalue; overestimate ⟨*forze*⟩
sopravvalutazi'one *nf* overvaluation; (di forze) overestimation
sopravve'nire *vi* turn up; (accadere) happen
soprav'vento *nm* fig upper hand; **prendere il** ∼ take the upper hand
sopravvis'suto, -a ①▷ pp di SOPRAVVIVERE
②▷ *adj* surviving
③▷ *nmf* survivor
sopravvi'venza *nf* survival
soprav'vivere *vi* survive; ∼ a outlive ⟨*persona*⟩
soprinten'dente *nmf* supervisor; (di museo ecc) keeper
soprinten'denza *nf* supervision; (ente) board
so'pruso *nm* abuse of power
soq'quadro *nm* **mettere a** ∼ turn upside down
sor'betto *nm* sorbet
sor'bire *vt* sip; fig put up with
'sorcio *nm* mouse; **far vedere i sorci verdi a qualcuno** give somebody a rough time
'sordido *adj* sordid; (avaro) stingy
sor'dina *nf* mute; **in** ∼ fig on the quiet
sordità *nf* deafness
'sordo, -a ①▷ *adj* deaf; ⟨*rumore, dolore*⟩ dull
②▷ *nmf* deaf person
sordo'muto, -a ①▷ *adj* deaf-and-dumb, deaf without speech
②▷ *nmf* deaf mute
so'rella *nf* sister. **sorella gemella** twin sister
sorel'lastra *nf* stepsister, half-sister
sor'gente *nf* spring; (fonte) source. **programma sorgente** Comput source program
'sorgere *vi* rise; fig arise
sormon'tare *vt* surmount
sorni'one *adj* sly

sorpas'sare *vt* surpass; (eccedere) exceed; overtake, pass Am ⟨*veicolo*⟩
sorpas'sato *adj* old-fashioned
sor'passo *nm* overtaking, passing Am
sorpren'dente *adj* surprising; (straordinario) remarkable
sorprendente'mente *adv* surprisingly
sor'prendere *vt* surprise; (cogliere in flagrante) catch
sor'prendersi *vr* be surprised; ∼ a fare qualcosa catch oneself doing something; **non c'è da** ∼ it's hardly surprising
sor'presa *nf* surprise; di ∼ by surprise; **provare** ∼ feel surprised
sor'preso pp di SORPRENDERE
sor'reggere *vt* support; (tenere) hold up
sor'reggersi *vr* support oneself
sor'retto pp di SORREGGERE
sorri'dente *adj* smiling
sor'ridere *vi* smile; **la fortuna mi ha sorriso** fortune smiled on me
sor'riso ①▷ pp di SORRIDERE
②▷ *nm* smile
sorseggi'are *vt* sip
'sorso *nm* sip; (piccola quantità) drop
'sorta *nf* sort; di ∼ whatever; **ogni** ∼ di all sorts of
'sorte *nf* fate; (caso imprevisto) chance; **tirare a** ∼ draw lots; **per buona** ∼ liter by good fortune
sorteggi'are *vt* draw lots for
sor'teggio *nm* draw
sorti'legio *nm* witchcraft
sor'tire ①▷ *vi* come out
②▷ *vt* bring about ⟨*effetto*⟩
sor'tlta *nf* Mil sortie; (battuta) witticism
'sorto pp di SORGERE
sorvegli'ante *nmf* keeper; (controllore) overseer
sorvegli'anza *nf* watch; Mil ecc surveillance. **sorveglianza tramite braccialetto elettronico** electronic tagging
sorvegli'are *vt* watch over; (controllare) oversee; ⟨*polizia*⟩ watch, keep under surveillance
sorvegli'ato, -a ①▷ *adj* under surveillance
②▷ *nmf* **sorvegliato speciale** person kept under special surveillance
sorvo'lare *vt* fly over; fig skip
SOS *nm inv* SOS
'sosia *nm inv* double
so'spendere *vt* hang; (interrompere) stop; (privare di una carica) suspend
sospensi'one *nf* suspension. **sospensione condizionale [della pena]** suspended sentence
sospen'sorio *nm* Sport jockstrap

so'speso ① pp di SOSPENDERE
② adj ⟨impiegato, alunno⟩ suspended; ~
a hanging from; ~ a un filo fig hanging by
a thread
③ nm in ~ pending; (emozionato) in
suspense

sospet'tare vt suspect

so'spetto ① adj suspicious
② nm suspicion; (persona) suspect; **al di
sopra di ogni** ~ above suspicion

sospet'toso adj suspicious

so'spingere vt drive

so'spinto pp di SOSPINGERE

sospi'rare ① vi sigh
② vt long for

so'spiro nm sigh

'sosta nf stop, stop-off; (pausa) pause;
senza ~ nonstop; '~ **autorizzata ...**'
'parking permitted for ...'.**'divieto di
sosta'** 'no parking'

sostan'tivo nm noun

so'stanza nf substance; **sostanze** pl
(patrimonio) property sg; **in** ~ to sum up; **la**
~ **della questione** the nub of the matter

sostanzi'oso adj substantial; ⟨cibo⟩
nourishing; **poco** ~ insubstantial

so'stare vi stop; (fare una pausa) pause

so'stegno nm support. **sostegno
morale** moral support

soste'nere vt support; (sopportare) bear;
(resistere) withstand; (affermare) maintain;
(nutrire) sustain; sit ⟨esame⟩; ~ **le spese**
meet the costs; ~ **delle spese** incur
expenditure; ~ **una carica** hold a position;
~ **una parte** play a role

soste'nersi vr support oneself

soste'nibile adj ⟨sviluppo, crescita⟩
sustainable

sosteni'|tore, -trice nmf supporter

sostenta'mento nm maintenance

soste'nuto ① adj ⟨stile⟩ formal;
⟨velocità⟩ high; ⟨mercato, prezzi⟩ steady
② nm **fare il** ~ be stand-offish

sostitu'ire vt substitute (**a** for), replace
(**con** with)

sostitu'irsi vr ~ **a** replace

sosti'tuto, -a ① nmf replacement,
stand-in
② nm (surrogato) substitute.

sostituzi'one nf substitution

sotta'ceto adj pickled; **sottaceti** pl
pickles

sot'tacqua adv underwater

sot'tana nf petticoat; (di prete) cassock

sotter'fugio nm subterfuge; **di** ~
secretly

sotter'raneo ① adj underground
② nm cellar

sotter'rare vt bury

sottigli'ezza nf slimness; fig subtlety

sot'tile adj thin; ⟨udito, odorato⟩ keen;
⟨osservazione, distinzione⟩ subtle

sotti'letta® nf cheese slice

sottiliz'zare vi split hairs

sottin'tendere vt imply

sottin'teso ① pp di SOTTINTENDERE
② nm allusion; **senza sottintesi** openly
③ adj implied

'sotto ① adv below; (più in basso) lower
[down]; (al di sotto) underneath; (al piano di
sotto) downstairs; **è lì** ~ it's underneath; ~
~ deep down; (di nascosto) on the quiet; **di**
~ downstairs; **mettersi** ~ fig get down to
it; **mettere** ~ (fam: investire) knock down;
fatti ~! fam get stuck in!
② prep ~ **[a]** under; (al di sotto di)
under[neath]; **il fiume passa** ~ **un ponte**
the river passes under[neath] a bridge; **è**
~ **il tavolo, è** ~ **al tavolo** it's under[neath]
the table; **abita** ~ **di me** he lives
downstairs from me; **i bambini** ~ **i dieci
anni** children under ten; **20°** ~ **zero** 20
below zero; ~ **il livello del mare** below sea
level; ~ **la pioggia** in the rain; ~
Elisabetta I under Elizabeth I; ~ **calmante**
under sedation; ~ **chiave** under lock and
key; ~ **condizione che ...** on condition
that ...; ~ **giuramento** under oath; ~
sorveglianza under surveillance; ~
Natale/gli esami around Christmas/exam
time; **al di** ~ **di** under; **andare** ~ **i 50
all'ora** do less than 50km an hour
③ nm **il [di]** ~ the bottom

sotto'banco adv ⟨vendere, comprare⟩
under the counter

sottobicchi'ere nm coaster

sotto'bosco nm undergrowth

sotto'braccio adv arm in arm

sottoccu'pato adj underemployed

sottochi'ave adv under lock and key

sotto'costo adj & adv at less than cost
price

sottodi'rectory nf inv Comput
subdirectory

sottoe'sporre vt underexpose

sotto'fondo nm background

sotto'gamba adv **prendere qualcosa** ~
take something lightly

sotto'gonna nf underskirt

sottoindi'cato adj undermentioned

sottoinsi'eme nm Math subset

sottoline'are vt underline; fig underline
⟨importanza⟩; emphasize ⟨forma degli
occhi ecc⟩

sot'tolio adv in oil

sotto'mano adv within reach

sottoma'rino adj & nm submarine

sotto'messo ① pp di SOTTOMETTERE
② adj (remissivo) submissive

sotto'mettere vt submit; subdue
⟨popolo⟩

sotto'mettersi *vr* submit

sottomissi'one *nf* submission

sottopa'gare *vt* underpay

sottopas'saggio *nm* underpass; (pedonale) subway

sottopi'atto *nm* place mat, table mat

sotto'porre *vt* submit; (costringere) subject

sotto'porsi *vr* submit oneself; ∼ **a** undergo

sotto'posto *pp di* SOTTOPORRE

sottoproletari'ato *nm* underclass

sotto'scala *nm* cupboard under the stairs

sotto'scritto ①*pp di* SOTTOSCRIVERE ②*nm* undersigned

sotto'scrivere *vt* sign; (approvare) sanction, subscribe to

sottoscrizi'one *nf* (petizione) petition; (approvazione) sanction; (raccolta di denaro) appeal

sottosegre'tario *nm* undersecretary

sotto'sopra *adv* upside-down

sotto'stante *adj* **la strada** ∼ the road below

sottosu'olo *nm* subsoil

sottosvilup'pato *adj* underdeveloped

sottosvi'luppo *nm* underdevelopment

sottote'nente *nm* second lieutenant; Naut sub-lieutenant

sotto'terra *adv* underground

sottotito'lato *adj* subtitled

sotto'titolo *nm* (di film, programma) subtitle; (in libro, giornale) subheading

sottovalu'tare *vt* underestimate

sotto'vento *adv* downwind

sotto'veste *nf* slip

sotto'voce *adv* in a low voice

sottovu'oto *adj* vacuum-packed

sotto'zero *adj inv* subzero

sot'trarre *vt* remove; embezzle ‹fondi›; Math subtract

sot'trarsi *vr* ∼ **a** escape from; avoid ‹responsabilità›

sot'tratto *pp di* SOTTRARRE

sottrazi'one *nf* removal; (di fondi) embezzlement; Math subtraction

sottuffici'ale *nm* non-commissioned officer; Naut petty officer

sou'brette *nf inv* showgirl

souf'flé *nm inv* soufflé

souve'nir *nm inv* souvenir. **negozio di souvenir** souvenir shop

so'vente *adv* liter often

soverchie'ria *nf* bullying; **fare soverchierie a** bully

so'vietico, -a *adj & nmf* Soviet

sovrabbon'danza *nf* overabundance

sovraccari'care *vt* overload

sovrac'carico ① *adj* overloaded (**di** with) ② *nm* overload

sovraffati'carsi *vr* overexert oneself

sovraffolla'mento *nm* overcrowding

sovralimen'tare *vt* overfeed

sovrannatu'rale *adj & nm* = SOPRANNATURALE

sovrannazio'nale *adj* supranational

so'vrano, -a ① *adj* sovereign; fig supreme ② *nmf* sovereign

sovrappopo'lato *adj* overpopulated

sovrap'porre *vt* superimpose

sovrap'porsi *vr* overlap

sovrapposizi'one *nf* superimposition

sovrapro'fitto *nm* excess profits

sovra'stare *vt* dominate; fig: ‹pericolo› hang over

sovrastrut'tura *nf* superstructre

sovratensi'one *nf* Electr overload, overvoltage

sovrecci'tarsi *vr* get overexcited

sovrecci'tato *adj* overexcited

sovresposizi'one *nf* Phot overexposure

sovrimpressi'one *nf* Phot double exposure

sovrinten'dente, sovrintendenza = SOPRINTENDENTE, SOPRINTENDENZA

sovru'mano *adj* superhuman

sovvenzio'nare *vt* subsidize

sovvenzio'nato ① *pp di* SOVVENZIONARE ② *adj* subsidized; ∼ **dallo Stato** state-funded

sovvenzi'one *nf* subsidy

sovver'sivo, -a *adj & nmf* subversive

sovver'tire *vt* subvert

'sozzo *adj* filthy

SP *nf abbr* (**strada provinciale**) secondary road

S.p.A. *abbr* (**società per azioni**) plc

spac'care *vt* split; chop ‹legna›; ∼ **il minuto** keep perfect time; ∼ **il muso a qualcuno** sl smash somebody's face in; **o la va o la spacca** it's all or nothing; **un sole che spacca le pietre** a sun hot enough to fry an egg

spac'carsi *vr* split

spacca'tura *nf* split

spacci'are *vt* deal in, push ‹droga›; ∼ **qualcosa per qualcosa** pass something off as something; **essere spacciato** be done for, be a goner

spacci'arsi *vr* ∼ **per** pass oneself off as

spaccia|'tore, -trice *nmf* (di droga) dealer, pusher; (di denaro falso) distributor

'spaccio *nm* (di droga) dealing; (negozio) shop

'**spacco** *nm* split

spacco'nate *nfpl* blustering

spac'cone, -a *nmf* boaster

'**spada** *nf* sword

spadac'cino *nm* swordsman

spadroneggi'are *vi* act the boss

spae'sato *adj* disorientated

spa'ghetti *nmpl* spaghetti *sg*.
spaghetti in bianco spaghetti with
butter, oil and cheese. **spaghetti alla
carbonara** spaghetti with egg, cheese
and diced bacon. **spaghetti al sugo**
spaghetti with a sauce

spa'ghetto *nm* (fam: spavento) fright

'**Spagna** *nf* Spain

spagno'letta *nf* spool

spa'gnolo, -a ① *adj* Spanish
② *nmf* Spaniard
③ *nm* (lingua) Spanish

'**spago** *nm* string; (fam: spavento) fright;
dare ∼ **a qualcuno** encourage somebody

spai'ato *adj* odd

spalan'care *vt* open wide

spalan'carsi *vr* open wide

spalan'cato *adj* wide open

spa'lare *vt* shovel

'**spalla** *nf* shoulder; (di comico) straight
man; **spalle** *pl* (schiena) back; **alzata di
spalle** shrug [of the shoulders]; **alle spalle
di** behind; **alle spalle di qualcuno** ⟨ridere⟩
behind somebody's back; **avere qualcuno/
qualcosa alle spalle** have somebody/
something behind one; **di** ∼ ⟨violino ecc⟩
second; **vivere alle spalle di qualcuno** live
off somebody; **con le spalle al muro** anche
fig with one's back to the wall; **voltare le
spalle** turn one's back

spal'lata *nf* push with the shoulder;
(alzata di spalle) shrug [of the shoulders]

spalleggi'are *vt* back up

spal'letta *nf* parapet

spalli'era *nf* back; (di letto) headboard;
(ginnastica) wall bars *pl*

spal'lina *nf* strap; (imbottitura) shoulder
pad; **senza spalline** strapless

spal'mare *vt* spread

spal'marsi *vr* cover oneself

spa'nato *adj* ⟨vite⟩ threadless

spanci'ata *nf* belly flop

'**spandere** *vt* spread; (versare) spill;
spendere e ∼ spend and spend

'**spandersi** *vr* spread

spandighi'aia *nm inv* gritter

'**spaniel** *nm inv* spaniel

spappo'lare *vt* crush

spa'rare *vt/i* shoot; **spararle grosse** talk
big; ∼ **fandonie** talk nonsense

spa'rarsi *vr* shoot oneself; **si è sparato
un colpo alla tempia** he shot himself in
the temple

spa'rata *nf* fam tall story

spa'rato *nm* (della camicia) dicky

spara'toria *nf* shooting. **sparatoria
da auto in corsa** drive-by shooting

sparecchi'are *vt* clear

spa'reggio *nm* Comm deficit; Sport play-
off

'**spargere** *vt* scatter; (diffondere) spread;
shed ⟨lacrime, sangue⟩

'**spargersi** *vr* spread

spargi'mento *nm* scattering; (di lacrime,
sangue) shedding. **spargimento di
sangue** bloodshed

spa'rire *vi* disappear; **sparisci!** get lost!,
scram!

sparizi'one *nf* disappearance

spar'lare *vi* ∼ **di** run down

'**sparo** *nm* shot. **sparo
d'avvertimento** warning shot

sparpagli'are *vt* scatter

sparpagli'arsi *vr* scatter

sparpagli'ato *adj* far-flung

'**sparso** ① *pp* di SPARGERE
② *adj* scattered; (sciolto) loose

sparti'neve *nm inv* snowplough

spar'tire *vt* share out; (separare) separate

spar'tirsi *vr* share

spar'tito *nm* Mus score

sparti'traffico *nm inv* traffic island; (di
autostrada) central reservation, median
strip Am

spartizi'one *nf* division

spa'ruto *adj* gaunt; ⟨gruppo⟩ small; ⟨peli,
capelli⟩ sparse

sparvi'ero *nm* sparrow-hawk

spasi'mante *nm* hum admirer

spasi'mare *vi* suffer agonies; ∼ **per** be
madly in love with

'**spasimo** *nm* spasm

spa'smodico *adj* spasmodic

spas'sarsi *vr* amuse oneself;
spassarsela have a good time

spassio'nato *adj* ⟨osservatore⟩
dispassionate, impartial

'**spasso** *nm* fun; **essere uno** ∼ be
hilarious; **andare a** ∼ go for a walk;
essere a ∼ be out of work

spas'soso *adj* hilarious

'**spastico** *adj* spastic

'**spatola** *nf* spatula

spau'racchio *nm* scarecrow; fig
bugbear

spau'rire *vt* frighten

spa'valdo *adj* defiant

spaventa'passeri *nm inv* scarecrow

spaven'tare *vt* frighten, scare

spaven'tarsi *vr* be frightened, be
scared

spa'vento *nm* fright; **brutto da fare** ~ incredibly ugly

spaven'toso *adj* frightening; (fam: enorme) incredible

spazi'ale *adj* spatial; (cosmico) space *attrib*

spazi'are ① *vt* space out ② *vi* range

spazien'tirsi *vr* lose [one's] patience

'spazio *nm* space. **spazio aereo** airspace. **spazio indietro** Comput backspace. **spazio di tempo** period of time. **spazio vitale** elbowroom. **spazio web** web space

spazi'oso *adj* spacious

spazio-tempo'rale *adj* spatiotemporal

spazzaca'mino *nm* chimney sweep

spazza'neve *nm inv* (anche sci) snowplough

spaz'zare *vt* sweep; ~ **via** sweep away; (fam: mangiare) devour

spazza'trice *nf* sweeper

spazza'tura *nf* (immondizia) rubbish

spaz'zino *nm* road sweeper; (netturbino) dustman, refuse collector

'spazzola *nf* brush; (di tergicristallo) blade; **capelli a** ~ crew cut

spazzo'lare *vt* brush

spazzo'larsi *vr* ~ **i capelli** brush one's hair

spazzo'lino *nm* small brush. **spazzolino da denti** toothbrush. **spazzolino per le unghie** nailbrush

spazzo'lone *nm* scrubbing brush

'speaker *nm inv* Radio, TV announcer

specchi'arsi *vr* look at oneself in a/the mirror; (riflettersi) be mirrored; ~ **in** qualcuno model oneself on somebody

specchi'ato *adj* **di specchiata onestà** of spotless integrity

specchi'etto *nm* small mirror. **specchietto laterale** wing mirror. **specchietto retrovisore** driving mirror, rear-view mirror

'specchio *nm* mirror. **specchio unilaterale** two-way mirror

speci'ale ① *adj* special ② *nm* TV special [programme]

specia'lista *nmf* specialist

specialità *nf inv* speciality, specialty

specializ'zare *vt* specialize

specializ'zarsi *vr* specialize

specializ'zato *adj* (operaio) skilled; **siamo specializzati in ...** we specialize in ...

special'mente *adv* especially

'specie *nf inv* (scientifico) species; (tipo) kind; **fare** ~ **a** surprise; **in** ~ especially. **specie a rischio** endangered species

specifi'care *vt* specify

specificata'mente *adv* specifically

spe'cifico *adj* specific

speci'oso *adj* specious

specu'lare¹ *vi* speculate; ~ **su** (indagare) speculate on; Fin speculate in

specu'lare² *adj* mirror *attrib*

specula'tivo *adj* speculative

specula'tore *nm* speculator

speculazi'one *nf* speculation

spe'dire *vt* send; ~ **per posta** mail, post Br; ~ **qualcuno all'altro mondo** send somebody to meet his/her maker

spe'dito ① pp di SPEDIRE ② *adj* quick; (parlata) fluent

spedizi'one *nf* (di lettere ecc) dispatch; Comm consignment, shipment; (scientifica) expedition

spedizioni'ere *nm* Comm freight forwarder

'spegnere *vt* put out; turn off, switch off (motore, luce, televisione); turn off (gas); quench, slake (sete)

'spegnersi *vr* go out; (morire) pass away

spegni'mento *nm* standby

spelacchi'ato *adj* (tappeto) threadbare; (cane) mangy

spe'lare *vt* remove the fur of (coniglio)

spe'larsi *vr* (cane, tappeto) moult

speleolo'gia *nf* potholing, speleology

spel'lare *vt* skin; fig fleece

spel'larsi *vr* (serpente) shed its skin; (per il sole) peel; **mi sono spellato un ginocchio** I grazed *or* skinned my knee

spe'lonca *nf* cave; fig dingy hole

spendacci'one, -a *nmf* spendthrift

'spendere *vt* spend; ~ **fiato** waste one's breath

spen'nare *vt* pluck; fam fleece (cliente)

spennel'lare ① *vt* brush ② *vi* paint

spensierata'mente *adv* blithely

spensiera'tezza *nf* lightheartedness

spensie'rato *adj* lighthearted, carefree

'spento ① pp di SPEGNERE ② *adj* off; (gas) out; (smorto) dull; (vulcano) extinct

spenzo'lare *vt* dangle

spe'ranza *nf* hope; **pieno di** ~ hopeful; **senza** ~ hopeless

spe'rare ① *vt* hope for; (aspettarsi) expect ② *vi* ~ **in** trust in; **spero di sì** I hope so

'sperdersi *vr* get lost

sper'duto *adj* lost; (isolato) secluded

spergiu'rare *vi* commit perjury

spergi'uro, -a ① *nmf* perjurer ② *nm* perjury

sperico'lato *adj* swashbuckling

sperimen'tale *adj* experimental

sperimen'tare *vt* experiment with; test (resistenza, capacità, teoria)

sperimen'tato *adj* ⟨*metodo*⟩ tried and tested

sperimentazi'one *nf* experimentation; ~ **sugli animali** animal testing

'**sperma** *nm* sperm

spermi'cida ① *adj* spermicidal ② *nm* spermicide

spero'nare *vt* ram

spe'rone *nm* spur

sperpe'rare *vt* squander

'**sperpero** *nm* waste, squandering

spersonaliz'zare *vt* depersonalize

spersonaliz'zarsi *vr* become depersonalized

spersonalizzazi'one *nf* depersonalization

'**spesa** *nf* expense; (acquisto) purchase; **andare a far spese** go shopping; **darsi a spese folli** go on a shopping spree; **fare la** ~ do the shopping; **fare le spese di** pay for; **a proprie spese** at one's own expense; **spese** *pl* **di amministrazione** handling charge; **spese** *pl* **bancarie** bank charges; **spese** *pl* **di capitale** capital expenditure; **spese** *pl* **a carico del destinatario** carriage forward; **spese** *pl* **di esercizio** business expenses; **spese** *pl* **extra** out-of-pocket expenses; **spese** *pl* **di gestione** operating costs; **spese** *pl* **di movimentazione** handling charge; **spese** *pl* **di spedizione** shipping costs; **spese** *pl* **di viaggio** travel expenses

spe'sare *vt* pay expenses for; **spesato dalla ditta** paid for by the company, on the company

spe'sato *adj* all-expenses-paid

'**speso** *pp di* SPENDERE

'**spesso**[1] *adj* thick

'**spesso**[2] *adv* often

spes'sore *nm* thickness; (fig: consistenza) substance

spet'tabile *adj* (Comm abbr **Spett.**) **Spettabile ditta Rossi** Messrs Rossi

spettaco'lare *adj* spectacular

spet'tacolo *nm* spectacle; (rappresentazione) show; **dare** ~ **di sé** make a spectacle *or* an exhibition of oneself; **il mondo dello** ~ show business. **spettacolo di burattini** Punch-and-Judy show. **spettacolo di varietà** variety show

spettaco'loso *adj* spectacular

spet'tanza *nf* concern

spet'tare *vi* ~ **a** be up to; ⟨*diritto*⟩ be due to

spetta|'tore, -trice *nmf* spectator; **spettatori** *pl* (di cinema ecc) audience *sg*

spettego'lare *vi* gossip

spetti'nare *vt* ~ **qualcuno** ruffle somebody's hair

spetti'narsi *vr* ruffle one's hair

spet'trale *adj* ghostly

'**spettro** *nm* ghost; (fig: della fame) spectre; Phys spectrum; **ad ampio** ~ ⟨*medicina*⟩ broad-spectrum

spezi'are *vt* add spices to, spice

spezi'ato *adj* spicy

'**spezie** *nfpl* spices

spez'zare *vt* break

spez'zarsi *vr* break

spezza'tino *nm* stew

spez'zato ① *adj* broken ② *nm* coordinated jacket and trousers

spezzet'tare *vt* break into small pieces

spez'zone *nm* Cinema clip, footage *no pl*; (bomba) cluster bomb

'**spia** *nf* spy; (della polizia) informer; (di porta) peep-hole; **fare la** ~ sneak. **spia di accensione** power-on light. **spia di attività dell'hard disk** Comput hard disk activity light. **spia della benzina** petrol gauge. **spia luminosa** warning light. **spia dell'olio** oil [warning] light

spiacci'care *vt* squash

spia'cente *adj* sorry

spia'cevole *adj* unpleasant

spi'aggia *nf* beach

spia'nare *vt* level; (rendere liscio) smooth; roll out ⟨*pasta*⟩; raze to the ground ⟨*edificio*⟩

spia'nata *nf* flat ground

spi'ano *nm* **a tutto** ~ flat out

spian'tato *adj* fig penniless

spi'are *vt* spy on; wait for ⟨*occasione ecc*⟩

spiattel'lare *vt* blurt out; shove ⟨*oggetto*⟩

spiaz'zare *vt* wrong-foot

spi'azzo *nm* (radura) clearing

spic'care ① *vt* ~ **un salto** jump; ~ **il volo** take flight ② *vi* stand out

spic'cato *adj* marked

'**spicchio** *nm* (di agrumi) segment; (di aglio) clove

spicci'arsi *vr* hurry up

spiccia'tivo *adj* speedy

'**spiccio** *adj* no-nonsense

'**spiccioli** *nmpl* change

'**spicciolo** *adj* (comune) banal; ⟨*denaro*⟩ in change

'**spicco** *nm* relief; **fare** ~ stand out; **di** ~ high-profile

'**spider** *nmf inv* open-top sports car

spie'dino *nm* kebab

spi'edo *nm* spit; **allo** ~ on a spit, spitroasted

spiega'mento *nm* deployment

spie'gare *vt* explain; open out ⟨*cartina*⟩; unfurl ⟨*vele*⟩

spie'garsi *vr* explain oneself; ⟨*vele, bandiere*⟩ unfurl; **non so se mi spiego** need I say more?; **mi sono spiegato?** (minaccia) do I make myself clear?; **non riesco a spiegarmi come ...** I can't understand how ...

spie'gato *adj* ⟨*ali*⟩ outspread; **a sirene spiegate** with sirens blaring; **a voce spiegata** at the top of one's voice; **a vele spiegate** under full sail, with all sails in the wind

spiegazi'one *nf* explanation; **venire a una ∼ con qualcuno** sort things out with somebody

spiegaz'zare *vt* crumple

spiegaz'zato *adj* crumpled

spieta'tezza *nf* ruthlessness

spie'tato *adj* ruthless

spiffe'rare ① *vt* blurt out ② *vi* ⟨*vento*⟩ whistle

'spiffero *nm* (corrente d'aria) draught

'spiga *nf* spike; Bot ear

spi'gato *adj* herringbone

spigli'ato *adj* self-possessed

'spigola *nf* sea bass

spigo'lare *vt* glean

'spigolo *nm* edge; (angolo) corner

'spilla *nf* (gioiello) brooch. **spilla da balia** safety pin. **spilla di sicurezza** safety pin

spil'lare *vt* tap

'spillo *nm* pin. **spillo di sicurezza** safety pin

spil'lone *nm* hatpin

spilluzzi'care *vt* pick at

spi'lorcio, -a ① *adj* stingy ② *nm* miser, skinflint

spilun'gone, -a *nmf* beanpole

'spina *nf* thorn; (di pesce) bone; Electr plug; **a ∼ di pesce** ⟨*tessuto, disegno*⟩ herringbone; ⟨*parcheggio*⟩ in two angled rows; **stare sulle spine** be on tenterhooks; **una ∼ nel fianco** a thorn in one's side. **spina dorsale** spine

spi'naci *nmpl* spinach

spi'nale *adj* spinal

spi'nato ① *adj* ⟨*filo*⟩ barbed ② *nm* (tessuto) herringbone

spi'nello *nm* (fam: droga) joint

'spingere *vt* push; fig drive

'spingersi *vr* (andare) proceed

'spinnaker *nm inv* spinnaker

spi'noso *adj* thorny

spi'notto *nm* Electr plug

'spinta *nf* push; (violenta) thrust; fig spur; **dare una ∼ a qualcuno/qualcosa** give somebody/something a push; **farsi largo a spinte** push one's way through

spinta'rella *nf* (fam: raccomandazione) **ha ottenuto il lavoro grazie alla ∼ dello zio**

his uncle got him the job by pulling a few strings

'spinto ① *pp di* SPINGERE ② *adj* ⟨*barzelletta, spettacolo*⟩ risqué

spin'tone *nm* shove

spio'naggio *nm* espionage, spying

spi'one, -a *nmf* tell-tale

spio'vente ① *adj* ⟨*tetto*⟩ sloping ② *nm* slope

spi'overe *vi* liter stop raining; (ricadere) fall; (scorrere) flow down

'spira *nf* coil

spi'raglio *nm* small opening; (soffio d'aria) breath of air; (raggio di luce) gleam of light

spi'rale ① *adj* spiral ② *nm* spiral; (negli orologi) hairspring; (anticoncezionale) coil; **a ∼** spiral-shaped

spi'rare *vi* (soffiare) blow; (morire) pass away

spiri'tato *adj* possessed; ⟨*espressione*⟩ wild

spiri'tismo *nm* spiritualism

spiri'tista *nmf* spiritualist

spiri'tistico *adj* spiritualist

'spirito *nm* spirit; (arguzia) wit; (intelletto) mind; **fare dello ∼** be witty; **persona di ∼** witty person; **sotto ∼** in brandy. **spirito civico** community spirit. **spirito di contraddizione** contrariness. **Spirito Santo** Holy Spirit, Holy Ghost

spirito'saggine *nf* witticism

spiri'toso *adj* witty

spiritu'ale *adj* spiritual

spiritual'mente *adv* spiritually

splen'dente *adj* shining; **denti bianchi splendenti** gleaming white teeth

'splendere *vi* shine

'splendido *adj* splendid

splen'dore *nm* splendour

'spocchia *nf* conceit

spocchi'oso *adj* conceited

spode'stare *vt* dispossess; depose ⟨*re*⟩

spoetiz'zare *vt* disenchant

'spoglia *nf* (di animale) skin; **spoglie** *pl* (salma) mortal remains; (bottino) spoils; **sotto false spoglie** under false pretences

spogli'are *vt* strip; (svestire) undress; (fare lo spoglio di) go through; **∼ qualcuno di un diritto** divest somebody of a right

spogliarel'lista *nmf* strip-tease artist, stripper

spoglia'rello *nm* strip-tease

spogli'arsi *vr* strip, undress

spoglia'toio *nm* (in piscina, palestra) locker room; Sport changing room; (guardaroba) cloakroom, checkroom Am

'spoglio ① *adj* undressed; ⟨*albero, muro*⟩ bare; **∼ di** (privo) stripped of ② *nm* (scrutinio) perusal

S

'**spoiler** *nm inv* Auto spoiler

'**spola** *nf* shuttle; **fare la** ~ shuttle

spo'**letta** *nf* spool

spolmo'**narsi** *vr* shout oneself hoarse

spol'**pare** *vt* take the flesh off; fig fleece

spolve'**rare** *vt* dust; fam devour ⟨*cibo*⟩

'**sponda** *nf* (di mare, lago) shore; (di fiume) bank; (bordo) edge. **sponda posteriore ribaltabile** Auto tailgate

sponsoriz'**zare** *vt* sponsor

sponsorizzazi'**one** *nf* sponsorship

spontaneità *nf* spontaneity

spon'**taneo** *adj* spontaneous

'**spooling** *nm* Comput spooling

spopola'**mento** *nm* depopulation

spopo'**lare** ① *vt* depopulate
② *vi* (avere successo) draw the crowds

spopo'**larsi** *vr* become depopulated

'**spora** *nf* spore

sporadica'**mente** *adv* sporadically

spo'**radico** *adj* sporadic

sporcacci'**one**, **-a** *nmf* dirty pig

spor'**care** *vt* dirty; (macchiare) soil

spor'**carsi** *vr* get dirty

spor'**cizia** *nf* dirt

'**sporco** ① *adj* dirty; (macchiato) soiled **avere la coscienza sporca** have a guilty conscience
② *nm* dirt

spor'**gente** *adj* jutting, protruding; **ha i denti sporgenti** fam she has goofy teeth

spor'**genza** *nf* projection

'**sporgere** ① *vt* stretch out; ~ **querela contro** take legal action against
② *vi* jut out

'**sporgersi** *vr* lean out

sport *nm inv* sport; **fare qualcosa per** ~ do something for fun. **sport** *pl* **estremi** extreme sports. **sport** *pl* **invernali** winter sports

'**sporta** *nf* shopping basket

spor'**tello** *nm* door; (di banca ecc) window. **sportello automatico** cash dispenser, cash point, cash machine, hole-in-the-wall. **sportello della biglietteria** ticket window. **sportello pacchi** parcels counter

spor'**tivo**, **-a** ① *adj* sports *attrib*; ⟨*persona*⟩ sporty
② *nm* sportsman
③ *nf* sportswoman

'**sporto** *pp di* SPORGERE

'**sposa** *nf* bride; **dare in** ~ give in marriage, give away; **prendere in** ~ marry

sposa'**lizio** *nm* wedding

spo'**sare** *vt* marry; fig espouse

spo'**sarsi** *vr* get married; ⟨*vino*⟩ go (**con** with)

spo'**sato** *adj* married

spo'**sini** *nmpl* newly-weds

'**sposo** *nm* bridegroom; **sposi** *pl* [**novelli**] newlyweds

spossa'**tezza** *nf* exhaustion

spos'**sato** *adj* exhausted, worn out

sposses'**sato** *adj* dispossessed

sposta'**mento** *nm* displacement. **spostamento d'aria** airflow

spo'**stare** *vt* move; (differire) postpone; (cambiare) change

spo'**starsi** *vr* move

spo'**stato**, **-a** ① *adj* ill-adjusted
② *nmf* (disadattato) misfit

spot *nm inv* **spot** [**pubblicitario**] commercial

S.P.R. *abbr* (**si prega rispondere**) RSVP

'**spranga** *nf* bar

spran'**gare** *vt* bar

'**sprazzo** *nm* (di colore) splash; (di luce) flash; fig glimmer

spre'**care** *vt* waste

'**spreco** *nm* waste

spre'**cone** *adj* spendthrift

spre'**gevole** *adj* despicable

spregia'**tivo** *adj* pejorative

'**spregio** *nm* contempt; **fare uno** ~ **a qualcuno** offend somebody

spregiudi'**cato** *adj* unprejudiced; pej unscrupulous

'**spremere** *vt* squeeze

'**spremersi** *vr* ~ **le meningi** rack one's brains

spremi'**aglio** *nm inv* garlic press

spremia'**grumi** *nm inv* lemon squeezer

spremili'**moni** *nm inv* lemon squeezer

spre'**muta** *nf* juice. **spremuta d'arancia** fresh orange juice, freshly squeezed orange juice

spre'**tato** *nm* former priest

sprez'**zante** *adj* contemptuous

sprigio'**nare** *vt* emit

sprigio'**narsi** *vr* burst out

sprint *nm inv* sprint; **fare uno** ~ put on a spurt

spriz'**zare** *vt/i* spurt; be bursting with ⟨*salute, gioia*⟩

sprofon'**dare** *vi* sink; (crollare) collapse

sprofon'**darsi** *vr* ~ **in** sink into; fig be engrossed in

spron *nm* ▶ SPRONE

spro'**nare** *vt* spur on

'**sprone** *nm* spur; (sartoria) yoke; **a spron battuto** instantly; **andare a spron battuto** go hell-for-leather

sproporzio'**nato** *adj* disproportionate

sproporzi'**one** *nf* disproportion

sproposi'tato *adj* full of blunders; (*enorme*) huge

spro'posito *nm* blunder; (*eccesso*) excessive amount; **a** ∼ inopportunely

sprovve'duto *adj* unprepared; ∼ **di** lacking in

sprov'visto *adj* ∼ **di** out of; lacking in ⟨*fantasia, pazienza*⟩; **alla sprovvista** unexpectedly

spruz'zare *vt* sprinkle; (*vaporizzare*) spray; (*inzaccherare*) spatter

spruzza'tore *nm* spray

'spruzzo *nm* spray; (di fango) splash

spudorata'mente *adv* shamelessly

spudora'tezza *nf* shamelessness

spudo'rato *adj* shameless

'spugna *nf* sponge; (*tessuto*) towelling

spu'gnoso *adj* spongy

'spuma *nf* foam; (*schiuma*) froth; Culin mousse

spu'mante *nm* sparkling wine, spumante

spumeggi'ante *adj* bubbly; ⟨*mare*⟩ foaming

spumeggi'are *vi* ⟨*champagne*⟩ bubble; ⟨*birra*⟩ foam

'spunta *nf* **segno di spunta** tick

spun'tare ① *vt* (rompere la punta di) break the point of; trim ⟨*capelli*⟩; check off ⟨*lista, elenco*⟩; **spuntarla** fig win ② *vi* ⟨*pianta*⟩ sprout; ⟨*capelli*⟩ begin to grow; (*sorgere*) rise; (*apparire*) appear

spun'tarsi *vr* get blunt

spun'tata *nf* trim

spun'tino *nm* snack

'spunto *nm* cue; fig starting point; **dare** ∼ **a** give rise to

spur'gare *vt* purge

spur'garsi *vr* Med expectorate

'spurio *adj* spurious

spu'tacchio *nm* spittle

spu'tare *vt/i* spit; spit out ⟨*cibo*⟩; ∼ **sentenze** pass judgement; ∼ **l'osso** sl spit it out

'sputo *nm* spit

'squadra *nf* (*gruppo*) team, squad; (di polizia ecc) squad; (da disegno) square; **lavoro di squadra** teamwork. **squadra del buoncostume** Vice Squad. **squadra mobile** Flying Squad. **squadra narcotici** Drug Squad. **squadra di soccorso** rescue team

squa'drare *vt* square; (*guardare*) look up and down

squa'driglia *nf*, **squadrigli'one** *nm* squadron

squa'drone *nm* squadron

squagli'are *vt* melt

squagli'arsi *vr* melt; **squagliarsela** (fam: svignarsela) steal out

squa'lifica *nf* disqualification

squalifi'care *vt* disqualify

'squallido *adj* squalid

squal'lore *nm* squalor

'squalo *nm* shark

'squama *nf* scale; (di pelle) flake

squa'mare *vt* scale

squa'marsi *vr* ⟨*pelle*⟩ flake off

squa'moso *adj* scaly; ⟨*pelle*⟩ flaky

squarcia'gola: **a** ∼ *adv* at the top of one's voice

squarci'are *vt* rip

'squarcio *nm* rip; (di ferita, in nave) gash; (di cielo) patch

squar'tare *vt* quarter; dismember ⟨*animale*⟩

squarta'tore *nm* **Jack lo** ∼ Jack the Ripper

squash *nm* squash

squas'sare *vt* shake

squattri'nato *adj* penniless

squaw *nf inv* squaw

squilib'rare *vt* unbalance

squili'brato, -a ① *adj* unbalanced ② *nmf* lunatic

squi'librio *nm* imbalance

squil'lante *adj* shrill

squil'lare *vi* ⟨*campana*⟩ peal; ⟨*tromba*⟩ blare; ⟨*telefono*⟩ ring

'squillo *nm* blare; Teleph ring

squinter'nato *adj* anche fig crazy

squisi'tezza *nf* refinement

squi'sito *adj* exquisite; (fam: pietanza) yummy

squit'tire *vi* ⟨*pappagallo*⟩, fig squawk; ⟨*topo*⟩ squeak

sradi'care *vt* uproot; eradicate ⟨*vizio, male*⟩

sragio'nare *vi* rave

sregola'tezza *nf* dissipation

srego'lato *adj* inordinate; (*dissoluto*) dissolute

s.r.l. *abbr* (**società a responsabilità limitata**) Ltd

sroto'lare *vt* uncoil

SS *abbr* (**strada statale**) national road; *abbr* (**Santissimo**) Most Holy

ss *abbr* (**seguenti**) following

sst *int* sh!

'stabile ① *adj* stable; (*permanente*) lasting; ⟨*saldo*⟩ steady. **compagnia stabile** Theat repertory company ② *nm* (*edificio*) building

stabili'mento *nm* factory; (*industriale*) plant; (*edificio*) establishment. **stabilimento balneare** lido

stabi'lire *vt* establish; (*decidere*) decide

stabi'lirsi *vr* settle

S

stabilità nf stability

stabi'lito adj established

stabiliz'zare vt stabilize

stabiliz'zarsi vr stabilize

stabilizza'tore nm stabilizer

stacano'vista nmf workaholic

stac'care ① vt detach; pronounce clearly ⟨parole⟩; (separare) separate; turn off ⟨corrente⟩; ~ **gli occhi da** take one's eyes off
② vi (fam: finire di lavorare) knock off

stac'carsi vr come off; ~ **da** break away from ⟨partito, famiglia⟩; **si stacca alle cinque** knocking off time is five o'clock

staccata'mente adv staccato

stac'cato adj Mus staccato

staccio'nata nf fence

'stacco nm gap

'stadio nm stadium, sports ground

'staffa nf stirrup; **perdere le staffe** fig fly off the handle

staf'fetta nf Sport relay [race]; Mil dispatch rider

staffet'tista nmf Sport relay runner

stagio'nale adj seasonal

stagio'nare vt season ⟨legno⟩; mature ⟨formaggio⟩

stagio'nato adj ⟨legno⟩ seasoned; ⟨formaggio⟩ matured

stagiona'tura nf (di legno) seasoning; (di formaggio) maturation, maturing

stagi'one nf season; **di** ~ in season; **fuori** ~ out of season. **alta/bassa stagione** high/low season. **stagione lirica** opera season. **stagione delle piogge** rainy season

stagli'arsi vr stand out

sta'gnante adj stagnant

sta'gnare ① vt (saldare) solder; (chiudere ermeticamente) seal
② vi ⟨acqua⟩ stagnate

'stagno ① adj (a tenuta d'acqua) watertight
② nm (acqua ferma) pond; (metallo) tin

sta'gnola nf tinfoil

stalag'mite nf stalagmite

stalat'tite nf stalactite

'stalla nf stable; (per buoi) cowshed

stalli'ere nm groom

stal'lone nm stallion

sta'mani, stamat'tina adv this morning

stam'becco nm ibex

stam'berga nf hovel

'stampa nf Typ printing; (giornali, giornalisti) press; (riproduzione) print; **stampe** (postale) printed matter. **stampa fronte retro** two-sided printing, duplex printing. **stampa scandalistica** gutter press, tabloid press

stam'pante nf printer. **stampante ad aghi** dot matrix [printer]. **stampante a getto d'inchiostro** inkjet [printer]. **stampante laser** laser [printer]. **stampante a matrice di punti** dot matrix [printer]. **stampante seriale** serial printer. **stampante termica** thermal printer

stam'pare vt print

stampa'tello nm block letters pl, block capitals pl

stam'pato ① adj printed
② nm leaflet; Comput hard copy, printout; (modulo) print; **stampati** pl (pubblicità) promotional literature

stam'pella nf crutch

stampigli'are vt stamp

stampiglia'tura nf stamping; (dicitura) stamp

stam'pino nm stencil

'stampo nm mould; **di vecchio** ~ ⟨persona⟩ of the old school

sta'nare vt drive out

stan'care vt tire; (annoiare) bore

stan'carsi vr get tired

stan'chezza nf tiredness

'stanco adj tired; ~ **di** ⟨stufo⟩ fed up with; ~ **morto** dead tired, knackered fam

stand nm inv stand

'standard adj & nm inv standard

standardiz'zare vt standardize

standardizzazi'one nf standardization

'stand-by adj inv stand-by

'stanga nf bar; (persona) beanpole

stan'gare vt fam fail ⟨studente⟩; (con le tasse ecc) clobber

stan'gata nf fig blow; (fam: nel calcio) big kick; **prendere una** ~ (fam: agli esami, economica) come a cropper

stan'ghetta nf (di occhiali) leg

sta'notte nf tonight; (la notte scorsa) last night

'stante prep on account of; **a sé** ~ separate

stan'tio adj stale

stan'tuffo nm piston

'stanza nf room; (metrica) stanza. **stanza dei giochi** games room. **stanza da pranzo** dining room

stanzia'mento nm allocation

stanzi'are vt allocate

stan'zino nm walk-in cupboard

stap'pare vt uncork

star nf inv (del cinema, dello sport) star

'stare vi (rimanere) stay; (abitare) live; (con gerundio) be; **sto solo cinque minuti** I'll stay only five minutes; **sto in piazza Peyron** I live in Peyron Square; **sta dormendo** he's sleeping; ~ **a** (attenersi) keep to; (spettare) be up to; ~ **bene** (economicamente) be well off; (di salute) be well; (addirsi) suit; **sta bene!** that's fine!; ~ **dietro a** (seguire) follow; (sorvegliare) keep an eye on; (corteggiare) run after; ~ **in piedi** stand; ~ **per** be about to; ~ **sempre a fare qualcosa** be always doing something; **ben ti sta!** it serves you right!; **come stai/sta?** how are you?; **lasciar** ~ leave alone; **starci** (essere contenuto) go into; (essere d'accordo) agree; **il 3 nel 12 ci sta 4 volte** 3 into 12 goes 4; **non sa** ~ **agli scherzi** he can't take a joke; ~ **su** (con la schiena) sit up straight; ~ **sulle proprie** keep oneself to oneself

'**starna** *nf* partridge

starnaz'zare *vi* quack; *fig* shriek

starnu'tire *vi* sneeze

star'nuto *nm* sneeze

'**starsene** *vr* (rimanere) stay

'**starter** *nm inv* choke

sta'sera *adv* this evening, tonight

'**stasi** *nf* stasis

sta'tale ① *adj* state *attrib* ② *nmf* state employee, civil servant ③ *nf* (strada) main road, trunk road

'**statico** *adj* static

sta'tista *nm* statesman

sta'tistica *nf* statistics *sg*

sta'tistico *adj* statistical

'**Stati 'Uniti [d'America]** *nmpl* **gli** ~ the United States [of America]

'**stato** ① *pp di* ESSERE, STARE ② *nm* state; (posizione sociale) position; *Jur* status; **lo Stato** *Pol* the state. **stato d'animo** frame of mind. **stato di attesa** *Comput* wait state. **stato civile** marital status. **stato cuscinetto** buffer state. **Stato Maggiore** *Mil* General Staff. **stato di salute** state of health

stato-nazi'one *nm* nation-state

'**statua** *nf* statue. **statua di cera** waxwork

statu'ario *adj* statuesque

statuni'tense ① *adj* United States *attrib*, US *attrib* ② *nmf* citizen of the United States, US citizen

sta'tura *nf* height; **di alta** ~ tall; **di bassa** ~ short; **di media** ~ of average height. **statura morale** moral stature

sta'tuto *nm* statute

stazio'nario *adj* stationary

stazi'one *nf* station; (città) resort. **stazione degli autobus** bus station. **stazione balneare** seaside resort. **stazione climatica** health resort. **stazione ferroviaria** railway station *Br*, train station. **stazione marittima** ferry terminal. **stazione master** *Comput* master station. **stazione multimediale** *Comput* multimedia station. **stazione dei pullman** coach station *Br*, bus station.

stazione radiofonica radio station. **stazione di servizio** petrol station *Br*, service station. **stazione slave** *Comput* slave station. **stazione spaziale** space station. **stazione termale** spa, health resort

'**stecca** *nf* stick; (di ombrello) rib; (da biliardo) cue; *Med* splint; (di sigarette) carton; (di reggiseno) stiffener; **fare una** ~ *Mus* fluff a note

stec'cato *nm* fence

stec'chino *nm* cocktail stick

stec'chito *adj* skinny; (rigido) stiff; (morto) stone cold dead

'**stele** *nf* stele

'**stella** *nf* star; **salire alle stelle** (prezzi) rise sky-high, rocket. **stella alpina** edelweiss. **stella cadente** shooting star. **stella del cinema** movie star. **stella cometa** comet. **stella filante** streamer. **stella di mare** starfish. **stella polare** Pole Star, North Star

stel'lare *adj* star *attrib*; (grandezza) stellar

stel'lato *adj* starry

stel'lina *nf* starlet

'**stelo** *nm* stem. **lampada a stelo** standard lamp *Br*, floor lamp

'**stemma** *nm* coat of arms

stempe'rare *vt* dilute

stempi'ato *adj* bald at the temples

sten'dardo *nm* standard

'**stendere** *vt* spread out; (appendere) hang out; (distendere) stretch [out]; (scrivere) write down

'**stendersi** *vr* stretch out

stendibianche'ria *nm inv* clothes horse

stendi'toio *nm* clothes horse

stenodattilogra'fia *nf* shorthand typing

stenodatti'lografo, -a *nmf* shorthand typist

stenogra'fare *vt* take down in shorthand

stenogra'fia *nf* shorthand

sten'tare *vi* ~ **a** find it hard to

sten'tato *adj* laboured

'**stento** *nm* (fatica) effort; **a** ~ with difficulty; **stenti** *pl* hardships, privations

'**step** *nm* step aerobics

'**steppa** *nf* steppe

'**sterco** *nm* dung

stereo[fonico] *adj* stereo[phonic]

stereo'scopico *adj* stereoscopic

stereoti'pato *adj* stereotyped; (sorriso) insincere

stere'otipo *nm* stereotype

'**sterile** *adj* sterile; (terreno) barren

sterilità *nf* sterility

steriliz'zare *vt* sterilize

sterilizzazi'one *nf* sterilization

ster'lina *nf* pound. **lira sterlina** [pound] sterling

stermi'nare *vt* exterminate

stermi'nato *adj* immense

ster'minio *nm* extermination

'sterno *nm* breastbone

ste'roide *nm* steroid

ster'paglia *nf* brushwood

ster'rare *vt* excavate; dig up ⟨strada⟩

ster'rato ① *adj* ⟨strada⟩ dug up ② *nm* excavation; (di strada) digging up

ster'zare *vi* steer

'sterzo *nm* steering; (volante) steering wheel

'steso *pp di* STENDERE

'stesso ① *adj* same; io ~ myself; tu ~ yourself; **me** ~ myself; **se** ~ himself; **in quel momento** ~ at that very moment; **è stato ricevuto dalla stessa regina** (in persona) he was received by the Queen herself; **tuo fratello** ~ **dice che hai torto** even your brother says you're wrong; **l'ho visto coi miei stessi occhi** I saw it with my own eyes; **con le mie stesse mani** with my own hands; **è venuto il giorno** ~ he came the same day, he came that very day; **lo farò oggi** ~ I'll do it straight away today ② *pron* **lo** ~ the same one; (la stessa cosa) the same; **fa lo** ~ it's all the same; **ci vado lo** ~ I'll go just the same

ste'sura *nf* drawing up; (documento) draft

steto'scopio *nm* stethoscope

'steward *nm inv* steward, air steward

stick *nm inv* **colla a stick** glue stick; **deodorante in stick** stick deodorant

stiepi'dire *vt* warm

'stigma *nm inv* stigma

'stigmate *nfpl* stigmata

sti'lare *vt* draw up

'stile *nm* style; **in grande** ~ in style; **essere nello** ~ **di qualcuno** be typical of somebody, be just like somebody. **stile libero** (nel nuoto) freestyle, crawl. **stile di vita** life style

sti'lista *nmf* [fashion] designer; (parrucchiere) stylist

stiliz'zato *adj* stylized

'stilla *nf* drop

stil'lare *vi* ooze

stilo'grafica *nf* fountain pen

stilo'grafico *adj* **penna stilografica** fountain pen

'stima *nf* esteem; (valutazione) estimate

sti'mare *vt* esteem; (valutare) estimate; (ritenere) consider

sti'marsi *vr* consider oneself

sti'mato *adj* well-thought-of

stimo'lante ① *adj* stimulating ② *nm* stimulant

stimo'lare *vt* stimulate; (incitare) incite

'stimolo *nm* stimulus; (fitta) pang

'stinco *nm* shin; **non è uno** ~ **di santo** fam he's no saint

'stingere *vt/i* fade

'stingersi *vr* fade

'stinto *pp di* STINGERE

sti'pare *vt* cram

sti'parsi *vr* crowd together

stipendi'are *vt* pay a salary to

stipendi'ato ① *adj* salaried ② *nm* salaried worker

sti'pendio *nm* salary. **stipendio base** basic salary. **stipendio iniziale** starting salary

'stipite *nm* doorpost

stipu'lare *vt* stipulate

stipulazi'one *nf* stipulation; (accordo) agreement

stira'mento *nm* sprain

sti'rare *vt* iron; (distendere) stretch

sti'rarsi *vr* (distendersi) stretch; pull ⟨muscolo⟩

stira'tura *nf* ironing

'stiro *nm* **ferro da stiro** iron

'stirpe *nf* stock

stiti'chezza *nf* constipation

'stitico *adj* constipated

'stiva *nf* Naut hold

sti'vale *nm* boot; **lo Stivale** (Italia) Italy; **stivali** *pl* **di gomma** Wellington boots, Wellingtons; **poeta dei miei stivali!** fam poet my eye!, poet my foot!

stiva'letto *nm* ankle boot

stiva'lone *nm* high boot; **stivaloni** *pl* **da caccia** hunting boots; **stivaloni** *pl* **di gomma** waders

sti'vare *vt* load

'stizza *nf* anger

stiz'zire *vt* irritate

stiz'zirsi *vr* become irritated

stiz'zito *adj* irritated

stiz'zoso *adj* peevish

stocca'fisso *nm* stockfish

stoc'cata *nf* stab; (battuta pungente) gibe

Stoc'colma *nf* Stockholm

stock *nm* Comm stock

'stock-car *nm inv* stock car

'stoffa *nf* material; fig stuff; **avere** ~ have what it takes

stoi'cismo *nm* stoicism

'stoico *adj & nm* stoic

sto'ino *nm* doormat

'stola *nf* stole

'stolido *adj* stolid

'stolto *adj* foolish

stoma'chevole *adj* revolting

'stomaco *nm* stomach. **mal di stomaco** stomachache

stoma'tite *nf* stomatitis

sto'nare ① *vt/i* sing/play out of tune ② *vi* (non intonarsi) clash

sto'nato *adj* out of tune; (discordante) clashing; (confuso) bewildered

stona'tura *nf* false note; (discordanza) clash

stop *nm inv* (segnale stradale) stop sign; (in telegramma) stop

stop'pare *vt* stop

'stopper *nm inv* Sport fullback

'stoppia *nf* stubble

stop'pino *nm* wick

stop'poso *adj* tough

'storcere *vt* twist

'storcersi *vr* twist

stor'dire *vt* stun; (intontire) daze

stor'dirsi *vr* dull one's senses

stor'dito *adj* stunned; (intontito) dazed; (sventato) heedless

'storia *nf* history; (racconto, bugia) story; (pretesto) excuse; **senza storie!** no fuss!; **fare [delle] storie** make a fuss. **storia d'amore** love story. **storia di vita vissuta** human interest story

'storico ① *adj* historical; (di importanza storica) historic ② *nm* historian

stori'ella *nf* fam little story

storiogra'fia *nf* historiography

stori'ografo *nm* historiographer

stori'one *nm* sturgeon

'stormo *nm* flock

stor'nare *vt* avert; transfer ⟨somma⟩

'storno *nm* starling

storpi'are *vt* cripple; mangle ⟨parole⟩

storpia'tura *nf* deformation

'storpio, -a ① *adj* crippled ② *nmf* cripple

'storta *nf* (distorsione) sprain; **prendere una ~ alla caviglia** sprain one's ankle

'storto ① *pp di* STORCERE ② *adj* crooked; (ritorto) twisted; ⟨gambe⟩ bandy; fig wrong

stor'tura *nf* deformity; **~ mentale** twisted way of thinking

sto'viglie *nfpl* crockery *sg*, flatware Am

'strabico *adj* cross-eyed; **essere ~** be cross-eyed, [have a] squint

strabili'ante *adj* astonishing

strabili'are *vt* astonish

stra'bismo *nm* squint

straboc'care *vi* overflow

strabuz'zare *vt* **~ gli occhi** goggle; **ha strabuzzato gli occhi** his eyes popped out of his head

straca'narsi *vr* fam work like a slave, slave away

stra'carico *adj* overloaded

strac'chino *nm* soft cheese from Lombardy

stracci'are *vt* tear; (fam: vincere) thrash

straccia'tella *nf* vanilla ice cream with chocolate chips

stracci'ato *adj* torn; ⟨persona⟩ in rags; ⟨prezzi⟩ slashed; **a un prezzo ~** at a knock-down price, dirt cheap

'straccio ① *adj* torn ② *nm* rag; (strofinaccio) cloth; **essere ridotto ad uno ~** feel like a wet rag

stracci'one *nm* tramp

stracci'vendolo *nm* ragman

stracol'larsi *vr* sprain

stra'cotto ① *adj* overdone; (fam: innamorato) head over heels ② *nm* stew

'strada *nf* road; (di città) street; (fig: cammino) way; **essere fuori ~** be on the wrong track; **fare ~** lead the way; **tener la macchina in ~** keep the car on the road; (parcheggiare) keep the car on the street; **su ~** ⟨trasportare⟩ by road; **farsi ~** (aver successo) make one's way [in the world]. **strada d'accesso** approach road. **strada camionabile** road for heavy vehicles. **strada maestra** main road. **strada pedonale** pedestrianized street. **strada principale** main road. **strada privata** private road. **strada secondaria** secondary road. **strada a senso unico** one-way street. **strada senza uscita** dead end, cul-de-sac. **strada di terra battuta** dirt track

stra'dale ① *adj* road *attrib* ② *nf* **la Stradale** fam traffic police

stra'dario *nm* street plan

stra'dina *nf* little street; (in campagna) little road

strafalci'one *nm* blunder

stra'fare *vi* overdo it, overdo things

stra'foro: di ~ *adv* on the sly

strafot'tente *adj* arrogant

strafot'tenza *nf* arrogance

'strage *nf* slaughter

stra'grande *adj* vast

stralci'are *vt* remove

'stralcio *nm* removal; (parte) extract

stralu'nare *vt* **~ gli occhi** open one's eyes wide

stralu'nato *adj* ⟨occhi⟩ staring; ⟨persona⟩ distraught

stramaz'zare *vi* fall heavily; **~ al suolo** crash to the ground

strambe'ria *nf* oddity

'strambo *adj* strange

strampa'lato *adj* odd

stra'nezza *nf* strangeness

strango'lare *vt* strangle

strani'ero, -a ① *adj* foreign ② *nmf* foreigner

'strano *adj* strange; ∼ **ma vero** surprisingly enough, funnily enough

straordinaria'mente *adv* extraordinarily

straordi'nario *adj* extraordinary; (notevole) remarkable; ⟨*edizione*⟩ special. **lavoro straordinario** overtime; **treno straordinario** special [train]

strapaz'zare *vt* ill-treat; scramble ⟨*uova*⟩

strapaz'zarsi *vr* tire oneself out

stra'pazzo *nm* strain; **da** ∼ fig worthless

strapi'eno *adj* overflowing

strapi'ombo *nm* projection; **a** ∼ sheer

strapo'tere *nm* overwhelming power

strappa'lacrime *adj inv* weepy

strap'pare *vt* tear; (per distruggere) tear up; pull out ⟨*dente, capelli*⟩; (sradicare) pull up; (estorcere) wring

strap'parsi *vr* get torn; (allontanarsi) tear oneself away; ∼ **i capelli** fig be tearing one's hair out

'strappo *nm* tear; (strattone) jerk; (fam: passaggio) lift; **fare uno** ∼ **alla regola** make an exception to the rule. **strappo muscolare** muscle strain

strapun'tino *nm* folding seat

strari'pare *vi* flood

strasci'care *vt* trail; shuffle ⟨*piedi*⟩; drawl ⟨*parole*⟩

'strascico *nm* train; fig after-effect

strasci'coni: **a** ∼ *adv* dragging one's feet

straseco'lare *vi* be amazed

strass *nm inv* rhinestone

strata'gemma *nm* stratagem

stra'tega *nmf* strategist

strate'gia *nf* strategy

stra'tegico *adj* strategic; **mossa strategica** strategic move

stratifi'care *vt* stratify

stratigra'fia *nf* Geol stratigraphy

'strato *nm* layer; (di vernice ecc) coat, layer; (roccioso, sociale) stratum. **strato di nuvole** cloud layer

strato'sfera *nf* stratosphere

strato'sferico *adj* stratospheric; fig sky-high

stravac'carsi *vr* fam slouch

stravac'cato *adj* fam slouching

strava'gante *adj* extravagant; (eccentrico) eccentric

strava'ganza *nf* extravagance; (eccentricità) eccentricity

stra'vecchio *adj* ancient

strave'dere *vt* ∼ **per** worship

stravizi'are *vi* indulge oneself

stra'vizio *nm* excess

stra'volgere *vt* twist; (turbare) upset

stravolgi'mento *nm* twisting

stra'volto *adj* distraught; (fam: stanco) done in

strazi'ante *adj* heartrending; ⟨*dolore*⟩ agonizing

strazi'are *vt* grate on ⟨*orecchie*⟩; break ⟨*cuore*⟩

'strazio *nm* agony; **essere uno** ∼ be agony; **che** ∼! fam it's awful!; ∼ **di qualcosa** fam: ⟨*attore, cantante*⟩ murder something

'streamer *nm inv* Comput streamer

'strega *nf* witch

stre'gare *vt* bewitch

stre'gone *nm* wizard

stregone'ria *nf* witchcraft

'stregua *nf* **alla** ∼ **di** in the same way as; **alla stessa** ∼ ⟨*giudicare*⟩ by the same yardstick; **a questa** ∼ at this rate

stre'mare *vt* exhaust

stre'mato *adj* exhausted

'stremo ① *adj* extreme ② *nm* **ridotto allo** ∼ at the end of one's tether

'strenna *nf* present

'strenuo *adj* strenuous

strepi'tare *vi* make a din

strepi'tio *nm* din, uproar

strepi'toso *adj* noisy; fig resounding

strepto'cocco *nm* Med streptococcus

streptomi'cina *nf* Med streptomycin

stress *nm* stress

stres'sante *adj* ⟨*lavoro, situazione*⟩ stressful

stres'sare *vt* put under stress, be stressful for

stres'sarsi *vr* get stressed

stres'sato *adj* stressed [out]

'stretta *nf* grasp, squeeze; (dolore) pang; **essere alle strette** be in dire straits; **mettere alle strette qualcuno** have somebody's back up against the wall; **provare una** ∼ **al cuore** feel a pang. **stretta di mano** handshake

stret'tezza *nf* narrowness; **strettezze** *pl* (difficoltà finanziarie) financial difficulties

'stretto ① pp di STRINGERE ② *adj* narrow; (serrato) tight; (vicino) close; ⟨*dialetto*⟩ broad; (rigoroso) strict; **lo** ∼ **necessario** the bare minimum ③ *nm* Geog strait. **stretto di Messina** Straits of Messina

stret'toia *nf* bottleneck; (fam: difficoltà) tight spot

stri'ato *adj* striped

stria'tura *nf* streak

stri'dente *adj* strident

'stridere *vi* squeak; fig clash

stri'dore *nm* screech

'stridulo *adj* shrill

strigli'are *vt* groom

strigli'ata *nf* grooming; fig dressing down

stril'lare *vi/t* scream

'strillo *nm* scream

stril'lone *nm* newspaper seller

strimin'zito *adj* skimpy; (magro) skinny

strimpel'lare *vt* strum

stri'nare *vt* singe, scorch

'stringa *nf* lace; Comput string

strin'gato *adj* fig terse

'stringere ① *vt* press; (serrare) squeeze; (tenere stretto) hold tight; take in ⟨abito⟩; (comprimere) be tight; (restringere) tighten; ~ la mano a shake hands with ② *vi* (premere) press

'stringersi *vr* (accostarsi) draw close (a to); (avvicinarsi) squeeze up

strip'pata *nf* fam nosh-up; **farsi una** ~ have a nosh-up

strip-'tease *nm inv* striptease

'striscia *nf* strip; (riga) stripe; **a strisce** striped; **strisce** *pl* **di mezzeria** Auto lane markings; **strisce** *pl* **[pedonali]** zebra crossing sg, crosswalk Am

strisci'are ① *vi* crawl; (sfiorare) graze ② *vt* drag ⟨piedi⟩

strisci'arsi *vr* ~ a rub against

strisci'ata *nf* scratch

'striscio *nm* graze; Med smear; **colpire di** ~ graze

strisci'one *nm* banner

strito'lare *vt* grind

strizzacer'velli *nmf inv* sl shrink

striz'zare *vt* squeeze; (torcere) wring [out]; ~ **l'occhio** wink

'strofa *nf* strophe

strofi'naccio *nm* cloth; (per spolverare) duster. **strofinaccio da cucina** tea towel. **strofinaccio per i piatti** dishtowel

strofi'nare *vt* rub

strofi'nio *nm* rubbing

strom'bare *vt* splay

strombaz'zare ① *vt* boast about ② *vi* hoot

strombaz'zata *nf* (di clacson) hoot

stron'care *vt* cut off; (reprimere) crush; (criticare) tear to shreds

stron'zate *nfpl* vulg crap

'stronzo *nm* vulg shit

stropicci'are *vt* rub; crumple ⟨vestito⟩

stropicci'ata *nf* rub

stro'piccio *nm* rubbing

stroppi'are *vt* **il troppo stroppia** enough is as good as a feast

stroz'zare *vt* strangle

strozza'tura *nf* strangling; (di strada) narrowing

strozzi'naggio *nm* loan-sharking

stroz'zino *nm* pej usurer; (truffatore) shark

struc'cante *nm* make-up remover

struc'carsi *vr* remove one's make-up

strug'gente *adj* all-consuming

'struggersi *vr* liter pine [away]; ~ **di invidia/desiderio** be consumed with envy/ desire

struggi'mento *nm* yearning

strumen'tale *adj* instrumental

strumentaliz'zare *vt* make use of

strumen'tario *nm* instruments pl

strumentazi'one *nf* instrumentation

strumen'tista *nm* instrumentalist

stru'mento *nm* instrument; (arnese) tool. **strumento a corda/fiato** string/wind instrument. **strumento musicale** musical instrument. **strumento a percussione** percussion instrument

strusci'are *vt* rub

strusci'arsi *vr* ⟨gatto⟩ rub itself; ⟨due innamorati⟩ caress each other; ~ **intorno a qualcuno** fam suck up to somebody

'strutto *nm* lard

strut'tura *nf* structure

struttu'rale *adj* structural

struttura'lismo *nm* structuralism

struttural'mente *adv* structurally

struttu'rare *vt* structure

strutturazi'one *nf* structuring

'struzzo *nm* ostrich

stuc'care *vt* plaster; (per decorazione) stucco; put putty in ⟨vetri⟩

stucca'tore *nm* plasterer; (decorativo) stucco worker

stucca'tura *nf* plastering; (decorativo) stucco work

stuc'chevole *adj* nauseating

'stucco *nm* plaster; (decorativo) stucco; (per vetro) putty; **rimanere di** ~ be thunderstruck

stu'dente, -essa *nmf* student; (di scuola) schoolboy; schoolgirl

studen'tesco *adj* student; (di scolaro) school *attrib*

studi'are *vt* study

studi'arsi *vr* ~ **di** try to

'studio *nm* studying; (stanza, ricerca) study; (di artista, TV ecc) studio; (di professionista) office. **studio cinematografico** film studio. **studio dentistico** dental surgery

studi'oso, -a ① *adj* studious

S

2⟩ *nmf* scholar

'**stufa** *nf* stove. **stufa elettrica** electric fire. **stufa a gas** gas fire. **stufa a legna** wood-[burning] stove

stu'fare *vt* Culin stew; (dare fastidio) bore

stu'farsi *vr* get bored

stu'fato *nm* stew

'**stufo** *adj* bored; **essere** ∼ **di** be bored with, be fed up with

stu'oia *nf* mat

stu'olo *nm* crowd

stupefa'cente 1⟩ *adj* amazing
2⟩ *nm* drug

stupe'fare *vt* stun

stu'pendo *adj* stupendous; ∼! brilliant!

stupi'daggine *nf* (azione) stupid thing; (cosa da poco) nothing; **non dire stupidaggini!** don't talk stupid!

stupi'data *nf* stupid thing

stupidità *nf* stupidity

'**stupido** *adj* stupid

stu'pire 1⟩ *vt* astonish
2⟩ *vi* be astonished

stu'pirsi *vr* be astonished

stu'pore *nm* amazement

stu'prare *vt* rape

stupra'tore *nm* rapist

'**stupro** *nm* rape

sturabot'tiglie *nm inv* corkscrew

sturalavan'dini *nm inv* plunger

stu'rare *vt* uncork; unblock ⟨*lavandino*⟩

stuzzica'denti *nm inv* toothpick

stuzzi'care *vt* prod [at]; pick ⟨*denti*⟩; poke ⟨*fuoco*⟩; (molestare) tease; whet ⟨*appetito*⟩

stuzzi'chino *nm* Culin appetizer

su 1⟩ *prep* on; (senza contatto) over; (riguardo a) about; (circa, intorno a) about, around; **le chiavi sono sul tavolo** the keys are on the table; **il quadro è appeso sul camino** the picture is hanging over the fireplace; **un libro sull'antico Egitto** a book on or about Ancient Egypt; **sarò lì sulle cinque** I'll be there about five, I'll be there around five; **è durato sulle tre ore** it lasted for about three hours; **costa sui 75 euro** it costs about 75 euros; **decidere sul momento** decide at the time; **su commissione** on commission; **su due piedi** on the spot; **su misura** made to measure; **uno su dieci** one out of ten; **stare sulle proprie** keep oneself to oneself; **sul mare** ⟨*casa*⟩ by the sea
2⟩ *adv* (sopra) up; (al piano di sopra) upstairs; (addosso) on; **andare su** go up; (al piano di sopra) go upstairs; **ho su il cappotto** I've got my coat on; **in su** ⟨*guardare*⟩ up; **dalla vita in su** from the waist up; **su!** come on!

sua'dente *adj* persuasive

sub *nmf inv* skin-diver

sub+ *pref* sub+

su'bacqueo, **-a** 1⟩ *adj* underwater
2⟩ *nmf* skin-diver

subaffit'tare *vt* sublet

subaf'fitto *nm* sublet; **in** ∼ sublet

suba'gente *nm* subagent

subal'terno *adj* & *nm* subordinate

subappal'tare *vt* subcontract

subappalta'|tore, **-trice** *nmf* subcontractor

subap'palto *nm* subcontract; **in** ∼ subcontracted; **dare in** ∼ subcontract; **prendere in** ∼ take on a subcontract basis

sub'buglio *nm* turmoil

sub'conscio *adj* & *nm* subconscious

subconti'nente *nm* subcontinent

subcosci'ente *adj* & *nm* subconscious

subdi'rectory *nf inv* Comput subdirectory

subdola'mente *adv* deviously

'**subdolo** *adj* devious, underhand

suben'trare *vi* ⟨*circostanze*⟩ come up; ∼ **a** take the place of

su'bentro *nm* changeover

subequatori'ale *adj* subequatorial

su'bire *vt* undergo; (patire) suffer

subis'sare *vt* fig ∼ **di** overwhelm with

subi'taneo *adj* sudden

'**subito** *adv* at once, immediately, right away; ∼ **dopo** straight after; **vengo** ∼ I'll be right there

subli'mare *vt* sublimate

su'blime *adj* sublime

sublimi'nale *adj* subliminal

sublingu'ale *adj* sublingual

sublo'care *vt* sublease

subloca'tario *nm* sublessor

sublocazi'one *nf* sublease

subnor'male *adj* subnormal

subodo'rare *vt* suspect

subordi'nare *vt* subordinate

subordi'nato, **-a** *adj* & *nmf* subordinate

su'bordine *nm* **in** ∼ second in order of importance

subrou'tine *nf* Comput subroutine

subsi'denza *nf* Geol subsidence

sub'strato *nm* substratum, substrate

subto'tale *nm* subtotal

subtropi'cale *adj* subtropical

subu'mano *adj* subhuman

subur'bano *adj* suburban

suc'cedere *vi* (accadere) happen; ∼ **a** (in carica) succeed; (venire dopo) follow; ∼ **al trono** succeed to the throne

suc'cedersi *vr* happen one after the other; **si sono succeduti molti** ... there was a series of ...

successi'one *nf* succession; **in** ∼ in succession

successiva'mente *adv* subsequently

succes'sivo *adj* successive; ⟨*mese, giorno*⟩ following

suc'cesso 1 *pp di* SUCCEDERE 2 *nm* success; (esito) outcome; (disco ecc) hit

succes'sone *nm* huge success

succes'sore *nm* successor

succhi'are *vt* suck [up]; ∼ **il sangue a qualcuno** *fig* bleed somebody dry

succhi'ello *nm* gimlet

succinta'mente *adv* succinctly

suc'cinto *adj* (conciso) concise; ⟨*abito*⟩ scanty

'succo *nm* juice; *fig* essence. **succo d'arancia** orange juice. **succo di frutta** fruit juice. **succo di limone** lemon juice

suc'coso *adj* juicy

'succube *nm* **essere** ∼ **di qualcuno** be totally dominated by somebody

succu'lento *adj* succulent

succur'sale *nf* branch [office]

sud *nm* south; **del** ∼ southern; **a** ∼ **di** [to the] south of

Su'dafrica *nm* South Africa

sudafri'cano *adj & nmf* South African

Suda'merica *nf* South America

sudameri'cano, -a *adj & nmf* South American

Su'dan *nm* **il** ∼ the Sudan

suda'nese *adj & nmf* Sudanese

su'dare *vi* sweat, perspire; (faticare) sweat blood; ∼ **freddo** be in a cold sweat; ∼ **sangue** sweat blood; **mi fa** ∼ **freddo** it brings me out in a cold sweat; ∼ **sette camicie** sweat blood

su'data *nf* anche *fig* sweat

suda'ticcio *adj* sweaty

su'dato *adj* sweaty; ⟨*vittoria*⟩ hard-won; ⟨*pane*⟩ hard-earned

sud'detto *adj* above-mentioned

'suddito, -a *nmf* subject

suddi'videre *vt* subdivide

suddivisi'one *nf* subdivision

su'd-est *nm* southeast

'sudicio *adj* dirty, filthy

sudici'ume *nm* dirt, filth

sudocciden'tale *adj* southwestern

sudorazi'one *nf* perspiring

su'dore *nm* sweat, perspiration; *fig* sweat; **in un bagno di** ∼ bathed in sweat; **con il** ∼ **della fronte** *fig* by the sweat of one's brow. **sudore freddo** cold sweat

sudo'riparo *adj* sweat *attrib*

su'd-ovest *nm* southwest

'sue ▸ SUO

suffici'ente 1 *adj* sufficient; (presuntuoso) conceited

2 *nm* bare essentials *pl*; Sch pass mark

suffici'enza *nf* sufficiency; (presunzione) conceit; Sch pass; **a** ∼ enough; **prendere la** ∼ get the pass-mark

suf'fisso *nm* suffix

sufflè *nm inv* Culin soufflé

suffra'getta *nf* suffragette

suf'fragio *nm* (voto) vote; **in** ∼ **di qualcuno** in homage to somebody. **suffragio universale** universal suffrage

suffu'migio *nm* inhalation

suggel'lare *vt* seal

suggeri'mento *nm* suggestion

sugge'rire *vt* suggest; Theat prompt

suggeri'tore, -trice *nmf* Theat prompter

suggestio'nabile *adj* suggestible

suggestio'nare *vt* influence

suggestio'nato *adj* influenced

suggesti'one *nf* influence

sugge'stivo *adj* suggestive; ⟨*musica ecc*⟩ evocative

'sughero *nm* cork

'sugli = SU + GLI

'sugo *nm* (di frutta) juice; (di carne) gravy; (salsa) sauce; (sostanza) substance

'sui = SU + I

sui'cida 1 *adj* suicidal 2 *nmf* suicide

suici'darsi *vr* commit suicide

sui'cidio *nm* anche *fig* suicide; **tentato** ∼ attempted suicide

su'ino 1 *adj* **carne suina** pork 2 *nm* swine

suite *nf inv* suite

sul = SU + IL

sulfa'midico *nm* sulphonamide/sulpha drug

sul'fureo *adj* sulphuric

'sulla = SU + LA

'sulle = SU + LE

'sullo = SU + LO

sul'tana *nf* (persona) sultana

sulta'nina *adj* **uva** ∼ sultana

sul'tano *nm* sultan

'sunto *nm* summary

'suo, -a 1 *poss adj* **il** ∼, **i suoi** his; (di cosa, animale) its; (forma di cortesia) your; **la sua, le sue** her; (di cosa, animale) its; (forma di cortesia) your; **questa macchina è sua** this car is his/hers; ∼ **padre** his/her/your father; **un** ∼ **amico** a friend of his/hers/ yours 2 *poss pron* **il** ∼, **i suoi** his; (di cosa, animale) its; (forma di cortesia) yours; **la sua, le sue** hers; (di cosa animale) its; (forma di cortesia) yours; **i suoi** his/her folk[s]

su'ocera *nf* mother-in-law

su'ocero *nm* father-in-law

su'oi ▸ suo

su'ola *nf* sole; **suole** *pl* **di para** crepe soles

su'olo *nm* ground; (terreno) soil. **suolo pubblico** public land

suo'nare ① *vt* Mus play; ring ⟨*campanello*⟩; sound ⟨*allarme, clacson*⟩; ⟨*orologio*⟩ strike ⟨*ore*⟩; ∼ **il clacson** sound the horn, hoot the horn; (fam: imbrogliare) do ② *vi* ⟨*campanello, telefono, sveglia*⟩ ring; ⟨*clacson*⟩ hoot; ⟨*sirena*⟩ go [off]; ⟨*giradischi*⟩ play

suo'nato *adj* fam bonkers

suona|'tore, -trice *nmf* player

suone'ria *nf* alarm; (di cellulare) ringtone

su'ono *nm* sound

su'ora *nf* nun; **Suor Maria** Sister Maria

'super *nf* 4-star [petrol], premium [gas] Am

super+ *pref* super+

supe'rabile *adj* surmountable

superal'colico ① *nm* spirit ② *adj* **bevande superalcoliche** spirits

supera'mento *nm* (di timidezza) overcoming; (di esame) success (**di** in)

supe'rare *vt* surpass; (eccedere) exceed; (vincere) overcome; overtake, pass Am ⟨*veicolo*⟩; pass ⟨*esame*⟩; ∼ **la barriera del suono** break the sound barrier; ∼ **se stessi** surpass oneself; **ha superato la trentina** he's over thirty

su'perbia *nf* haughtiness

su'perbo *adj* haughty; (magnifico) superb

super'donna *nf* superwoman

superdo'tato *adj* highly gifted, super-talented

superfici'ale ① *adj* superficial ② *nmf* superficial person

superficialità *nf* superficiality

super'ficie *nf* surface; (area) area; **in** ∼ on the surface; fig: ⟨*esaminare*⟩ superficially

su'perfluo *adj* superfluous

Super-'Io *nm* Psych superego

superi'ora *nf* superior; Relig mother superior

superi'ore ① *adj* superior; (di grado) senior; (più elevato) higher; (sovrastante) upper; (al di sopra) above ② *nm* superior

superiorità *nf* superiority

superla'tivo *adj & nm* superlative

supermer'cato *nm* supermarket

supermo'della *nf* supermodel

super'nova *nf* Astr supernova

superpetroli'era *nf* Naut supertanker

superpo'tenza *nf* superpower

super'sonico *adj* supersonic

su'perstite ① *adj* surviving ② *nmf* survivor

superstizi'one *nf* superstition

superstizi'oso *adj* superstitious

super'strada *nf* toll-free motorway. **superstrada informatica** information superhighway

superu'omo *nm* superman

supervalu'tare *vt* overvalue

supervalutazi'one *nf* overvaluation

supervisi'one *nf* supervision

supervi'sore *nm* supervisor

su'pino *adj* supine

suppel'lettili *nfpl* furnishings

suppergiù *adv* about

supplemen'tare *adj* additional, supplementary

supple'mento *nm* supplement. **supplemento illustrato** colour supplement. **supplemento rapido** express train supplement

sup'plente ① *adj* temporary ② *nmf* Sch supply teacher

sup'plenza *nf* temporary post

'supplica *nf* plea; (domanda) petition

suppli'care *vt* beg

suppli'chevole *adj* imploring

sup'plire ① *vt* replace ② *vi* ∼ **a** (compensare) make up for

sup'plizio *nm* torture

sup'porre *vt* suppose

supportare *vt* Comput support

sup'porto *nm* support. **supporto di sistema** Comput system support

supposizi'one *nf* supposition

sup'posta *nf* suppository

sup'posto *pp* di SUPPORRE

suppu'rare *vi* fester

suppurazi'one *nf* suppuration; **andare in** ∼ fester

suprema'zia *nf* supremacy

su'premo *adj* supreme

surclas'sare *vt* outclass

surf *nm inv* surfboard; (sport) surfboarding

sur'fista *nmf* surfer

surge'lare *vt* deep-freeze

surge'lato ① *adj* frozen ② *nm* **surgelati** *pl* frozen food *sg*

Suri'name *nm* Surinam

'surplus *nm* surplus

surre'ale *adj* surreal

surrea'lismo *nm* surrealism

surrea'lista *nmf* surrealist

surrea'listico *adj* surrealist

surre'nale *adj* adrenal

surriscal'dare *vt* overheat

surriscal'darsi *vr* overheat

surro'gato *nm* substitute

suscet'tibile *adj* touchy

suscettibilità *nf* touchiness

susci'tare *vt* stir up; arouse ⟨*ammirazione ecc*⟩

su'sina *nf* plum. **susina selvatica** damson

su'sino *nm* plumtree

su'spense *nf* suspense

sussegu'ente *adj* subsequent

sussegu'irsi *vr* follow one after the other

sussidi'are *vt* subsidize

sussidi'ario *adj* subsidiary

sus'sidio *nm* subsidy; (aiuto) aid. **sussidio didattico** study aid. **sussidio di disoccupazione** unemployment benefit. **sussidio di malattia** sickness benefit

sussi'ego *nm* haughtiness; **con ∼** haughtily

sussi'stenza *nf* subsistence

sus'sistere *vi* subsistı (essere valido) hold good

sussul'tare *vi* start; **far ∼ qualcuno** give somebody a start

sus'sulto *nm* start

sussur'rare *vt/i* whisper; **si sussurra che …** it is rumoured that …

sussur'rio *nm* murmur

sus'surro *nm* whisper

su'tura *nf* suture

sutu'rare *vt* suture

suv'via *int* come on!

sva'gare *vt* amuse

sva'garsi *vr* amuse oneself

'svago *nm* relaxation; (divertimento) amusement; **prendersi un po' di ∼** have a break

svaligi'are *vt* rob; burgle ⟨*casa*⟩

svalu'tare *vt* devalue; fig underestimate

svalu'tarsi *vr* lose value

svalutazi'one *nf* devaluation

svam'pito, -a *nmf* airhead

sva'nire *vi* vanish

sva'nito, -a ① *adj* ⟨*persona*⟩ absent-minded; ⟨*sapore, sogno*⟩ faded ② *nmf* absent-minded person

svantaggi'ato *adj* at a disadvantage; ⟨*bambino, paese*⟩ disadvantaged

svan'taggio *nm* disadvantage; **essere in ∼** Sport be losing; **in ∼ di tre punti** three points down; **in ∼ rispetto a qualcuno** at a disadvantage compared with somebody

svantaggi'oso *adj* disadvantageous

svapo'rare *vi* evaporate

svari'ato *adj* varied

svari'one *nm* blunder

sva'sare *vt* splay; flare ⟨*gonna*⟩

sva'sato *adj* ⟨*gonna*⟩ flared

svasa'tura *nf* flare

'svastica *nf* swastika

sve'dese ① *adj & nm* (lingua) Swedish ② *nmf* Swede

'sveglia *nf* (orologio) alarm [clock]; **∼!** get up!; **mettere la ∼** set the alarm [clock]. **sveglia automatica** alarm call. **sveglia telefonica** wake-up call

svegli'are *vt* wake up; fig awaken; **∼ l'appetito a qualcuno** whet somebody's appetite

svegli'arsi *vr* wake up

'sveglio *adj* awake; (di mente) alert, sharp

sve'lare *vt* reveal

svel'tezza *nf* speed; fig quick-wittedness

svel'tire *vt* quicken

svel'tirsi *vr* ⟨*persona*⟩ liven up

'svelto *adj* quick; (slanciato) svelte; **alla svelta** quickly; **a passo ∼** quickly

sve'narsi *vr* slash one's wrists; fig reduce oneself to poverty

'svendere *vt* undersell

'svendita *nf* [clearance] sale

sve'nevole *adj* sentimental

sveni'mento *nm* fainting fit

sve'nire *vi* faint; **da ∼** incredibly

sven'tare *vt* foil

sven'tato ① *adj* thoughtless ② *nmf* thoughtless person

'sventola *nf* slap. **orecchie a sventola** protruding ears, jug-handle ears fam

svento'lare *vt/i* wave

svento'larsi *vr* fan oneself

svento'lio *nm* flutter

sventra'mento *nm* disembowelment; (di pollo) gutting; (fig: di edificio) demolition ⟨*edificio*⟩

sven'trare *vt* disembowel; gut ⟨*pollo*⟩; fig demolish ⟨*edificio*⟩

sven'tura *nf* misfortune

sventu'rato *adj* unfortunate

sve'nuto *pp di* SVENIRE

svergi'nare *vt* deflower

svergo'gnato *adj* shameless

sver'nare *vi* winter

svernici'ante *nm* paint stripper

svernici'are *vt* strip

sve'stire *vt* undress

sve'stirsi *vr* undress, get undressed

svet'tare *vi* ⟨*albero, torre*⟩ stand out; **∼ verso il cielo** stretch skywards

'Svezia *nf* Sweden

svezza'mento *nm* weaning

svez'zare *vt* wean

svi'are *vt* divert; (corrompere) lead astray

svi'arsi *vr* fig go astray

svico'lare *vi* turn down a side street; (fig: dalla questione ecc) evade the issue; (fig: da una persona) dodge out of the way

svi'gnarsela *vr* slip away

svigo'rire *vt* emasculate

svili'mento *nm* debasement

svi'lire *vt* debase

svilup'pare *vt* develop

svilup'parsi *vr* develop

sviluppa|'tore, -trice *nmf* developer. **sviluppatore web** web developer

svi'luppo *nm* development. **paese in via di sviluppo** developing country

svinco'lare *vt* release; clear ⟨*merce*⟩; redeem ⟨*deposito*⟩

svinco'larsi *vr* free oneself

'svincolo *nm* clearance; (di autostrada) exit; ∼ **di un deposito cauzionale** redemption of a deposit

svioli'nata *nf* fawning

svisce'rare *vt* gut; fig dissect

svisce'rato *adj* ⟨*amore*⟩ passionate; (ossequioso) obsequious

'svista *nf* oversight

svi'tare *vt* unscrew

svi'tato *adj* (fam: matto) cracked, nutty

'Svizzera *nf* Switzerland

'svizzera *nf* (carne) hamburger

'svizzero, -a *adj & nmf* Swiss

svoglia'taggine *nf* laziness; (riluttanza) unwillingness

svogli'atamente *adv* half-heartedly; (senza energia) listlessly

svoglia'tezza *nf* half-heartedness; (mancanza di energia) listlessness

svogli'ato *adj* half-hearted; (senza energia) listless

svolaz'zante *adj* ⟨*capelli*⟩ wind-swept

svolaz'zare *vi* flutter

svolaz'zio *nm* flutter

'svolgere *vt* unwind; unwrap ⟨*pacco*⟩; (risolvere) solve; (portare a termine) carry out; (sviluppare) develop

'svolgersi *vr* (accadere) take place

svolgi'mento *nm* course; (sviluppo) development

'svolta *nf* turning; fig turning-point

svol'tare *vi* turn

'svolto pp di SVOLGERE

svuo'tare *vt* empty [out]; (fig: di significato) deprive

'Swaziland *nm* Swaziland

swing *nm* Mus swing

switch *nm* Comput switch

Tt

T *abbr* (**tabaccheria**) tobacconist

tabac'caio, -a *nmf* tobacconist

tabacche'ria *nf* tobacconist's (which also sells stamps, postcards etc)

ta'bacco *nm* tobacco; **tabacchi** *pl* cigarettes and tobacco

taba'gismo *nm* nicotine addiction

ta'bella *nf* table; (lista) list. **tabella di conversione** conversion table. **tabella di marcia** fig schedule. **tabella dei prezzi** price list. **tabella retributiva** salary scale

tabel'lina *nf* Math multiplication table

tabel'lone *nm* wall chart. **tabellone degli arrivi** arrivals board. **tabellone del canestro** backboard. **tabellone delle partenze** departures board. **tabellone segnapunti** scoreboard

taber'nacolo *nm* tabernacle

tabù *adj & nm inv* taboo

tabu'lare *vt* tabulate

tabu'lato *nm* Comput [data] printout

tabula'tore *nm* tabulator

tabulazi'one *nf* tabulation

TAC *nf inv abbr* (**tomografia assiale computerizzata**) CAT scan

'tacca *nf* notch; **di mezza** ∼ ⟨*attore, giornalista*⟩ second-rate

taccagne'ria *nf* penny-pinching

tac'cagno *adj* fam stingy

taccheggia|'tore, -trice *nmf* shoplifter

tac'cheggio *nm* shoplifting

tac'chetto *nm* Sport stud

tac'chino *nm* turkey

tacci'are *vt* ∼ **qualcuno di qualcosa** accuse somebody of something

'tacco *nm* heel; **alzare i tacchi** take to one's heels; **scarpe senza** ∼ flat shoes, flats; **colpo di tacco** backheel. **tacchi** *pl* **a spillo** stiletto heels, stilettos

taccu'ino *nm* notebook

ta'cere ① *vi* be silent ② *vt* say nothing about; **mettere a** ∼ **qualcosa** ⟨*scandalo*⟩ hush something up; **mettere a** ∼ **qualcuno** silence somebody

tachicar'dia *nf* tachycardia

ta'chigrafo *nm* tachograph

ta'chimetro *nm* speedometer

tacita'mente *adv* tacitly; (in silenzio) silently

'tacito *adj* tacit, unspoken; (silenzioso) silent

taci'turno *adj* taciturn

ta'fano *nm* horsefly

taffe'ruglio *nm* scuffle

taffettà *nm* taffeta

'taglla *nf* (riscatto) ransom; (ricompensa) reward; (statura) height; (di abiti) size; **per taglie forti** outsize, OS. **taglia unica** one size

taglia'carte *nm inv* paperknife

'taglia e in'colla *nm inv* cut and paste; **fare un** ~ cut and paste

taglia'erba *nm inv* lawnmower

tagliafu'oco ① *adj inv* **porta tagliafuoco** fire door; **striscia tagliafuoco** fire break ② *nm inv* (in bosco) fire break

tagli'ando *nm* coupon; **fare il** ~ ≈ put one's car in for its MOT. **tagliando di controllo** manufacturer's sticker; (da raccogliere) token. **tagliando controllo bagaglio** baggage claim sticker. **tagliando di garanzia** warranty

taglia'pasta ① *adj inv* **rotella** ~ pastry cutter ② *nm inv* pastry cutter

tagliapa'tate *nm inv* potato peeler

tagli'are ① *vt* cut; (attraversare) cut across; cut off ‹telefono, elettricità›; carve ‹carne›; mow ‹erba›; **farsi** ~ **i capelli** have a haircut, have one's hair cut; ~ **i viveri a qualcuno** stop somebody's allowance ② *vi* cut

tagli'arsi *vr* cut oneself; ~ **il dito** cut one's finger; ~ **i capelli** have a haircut, have one's hair cut

taglia'sigari *nm inv* cigar cutter

tagli'ata *nf* finely-cut beef fillet; **dare una** ~ **a qualcosa** give something a cut, cut something

tagli'ato *adj* (a pezzi) jointed; **essere** ~ **per qualcosa** fig be cut out for something

taglia'unghie *nm inv* nail clippers *pl*

taglieggi'are *vt* extort money from

tagli'ente ① *adj* sharp ② *nm* cutting edge

tagli'ere *nm* chopping board. ~ **per il pane** breadboard

taglie'rina *nf* (per carta) guillotine; (per foto) trimmer; (per metallo, vetro) cutter

'taglio *nm* cut; (di stoffa) length; (di capelli) [hair-]cut; (parte tagliente) cutting edge; **di** ~ edgeways; **a doppio** ~ fig double-edged. **taglio e cucito** dressmaking; **dacci un** ~! fam put a sock in it!. **taglio di carne** cut of meat. **taglio cesareo** Caesarean section. **taglio di personale** personnel cut. **taglio dei prezzi** price cutting. **taglio alla spesa** spending cut

tagli'ola *nf* trap

taglio'lini *nmpl* thin soup noodles

tagli'one *nm* **legge del taglione** an eye for an eye and a tooth for a tooth, law of talion

tagliuz'zare *vt* cut into small pieces

tail'leur *nm inv* [lady's] suit

Tai'wan *nf* Taiwan

ta'lare *adj* **prendere la veste** ~ take holy orders

talassotera'pia *nf* therapy based on seawater

'talco *nm* talcum powder, talc

'tale ① *adj* such a; (con nomi plurali) such; **c'è un** ~ **disordine** there is such a mess; **non accetto tali scuse** I won't accept such excuses; **è un** ~ **bugiardo!** he's such a liar!; **il rumore era** ~ **che non si sentiva nulla** there was so much noise you couldn't hear yourself think; **il** ~ **giorno** on such and such a day; **vai il tal giorno alla tal ora** go on such a day at such a time; **quel tal signore** that gentleman; ~ **padre** ~ **figlio** like father like son; ~ **quale** just like ② *pron* **un** ~ someone; **quel** ~ that man; **il tal dei tali** such and such a person

ta'lea *nf* cutting

ta'lento *nm* talent

'talent scout *nmf inv* talent scout

tali'smano *nm* talisman

tallo'nare *vt* be hot on the heels of

tallon'cino *nm* coupon. **talloncino del prezzo** price tag

tal'lone *nm* heel. **tallone di Achille** fig Achilles' heel. **tallone aureo** Econ gold standard

tal'mente *adv* so

ta'lora *adv* = TALVOLTA

'talpa *nf* mole

tal'volta *adv* sometimes

tamburel'lare *vi* (con le dita) drum; (pioggia) beat, drum

tambu'rello *nm* tambourine

tambu'rino *nm* drummer

tam'buro *nm* drum. **tamburo del freno** brake drum

tame'rice *nf* tamarisk

'tamia *nm inv* chipmunk

Ta'migi *nm* Thames

tampona'mento *nm* Auto collision; (di ferita) dressing; (di falla) plugging. **tamponamento a catena** pile-up

tampo'nare *vt* (urtare) crash into; plug (falla); dress (ferita)

tam'pone *nm* swab; (per timbri) pad; (per mestruazioni) tampon; (per treni, Comput) buffer

tam'tam *nm inv* bush telegraph

TAN *abbr* (**tasso annuale nominale**) Fin AER

'tana *nf* den

'tandem *nm inv* tandem; **in** ~ ⟨*lavorare*⟩ in tandem

'tanfo *nm* stench

'tanga *nm inv* tanga

tan'gente ① *adj* tangent
② *nf* tangent; (somma) bribe

tangen'topoli *nf* widespread corruption in Italy in the early 90s

tangenzi'ale *nf* orbital road

tan'gibile *adj* tangible

tangibil'mente *adv* tangibly

'tango *nm* tango

'tanica *nf* (contenitore) jerry can; (serbatoio di nave) tank. **tanica di benzina** petrol can

tan'nino *nm* tannin

tan'tino: **un** ~ *adv* a little [bit]

'tanto ① *adj* [so] much; (con nomi plurali) [so] many, [such] a lot of; ~ **tempo** [such] a long time; **non ha tanta pazienza** he doesn't have much patience; ~ **tempo quanto ti serve** as much time as you need; **tanti amici quanti parenti** as many friends as relatives
② *pron* much; (plurale) many; (tanto tempo) much time; **è un uomo come tanti** he's just an ordinary man; **tanti** (molte persone) many people; **non ci vuole così** ~ it doesn't take that long; ~ **quanto** as much as; **tanti quanti** as many as
③ *conj* (comunque) anyway, in any case
④ *adv* (così) so; (con verbi) so much; **è** ~ **debole che non sta in piedi** he's so weak that he can't stand; **è** ~ **ingenuo da crederle** he's naive enough to believe her; **di** ~ **in** ~ every now and then; ~ **l'uno come l'altro** both; ~ **quanto** as much as; **tre volte** ~ three times as much; **una volta** ~ once in a while; ~ **meglio così!** so much the better!; **tant'è** so much so; ~ **vale che andiamo a casa** we might as well go home; ~ **per cambiare** for a change

Tan'zania *nf* Tanzania

tapi'oca *nf* tapioca

ta'piro *nm* tapir

ta'pis rou'lant *nm inv* conveyor belt

'tappa *nf* (parte di viaggio) stage; **fare** ~ **a** break one's journey in

tappa'buchi *nm inv* stopgap

tap'pare *vt* plug; cork ⟨*bottiglia*⟩; ~ **la bocca a qualcuno** fam shut somebody up

tappa'rella *nf* fam roller blind; **tirar su la** ~ pull the blind up

tap'parsi *vr* ~ **gli occhi** cover one's eyes; ~ **il naso** hold one's nose; ~ **le orecchie** put one's fingers in one's ears

tappe'tino *nm* mat; Comput mouse mat. **tappetino antiscivolo** [anti-slip] safety bathmat. **tappetino da bagno** bathmat.

tap'peto *nm* carpet; (piccolo) rug; **andare al** ~ (pugilato) hit the canvas; **mandare qualcuno al** ~ knock somebody down; **bombardamento a tappeto** carpet bombing. **tappeto erboso** lawn. **tappeto persiano** Persian carpet. **tappeto stradale** road surface. **tappeto verde** (tavolo) card table. **tappeto volante** magic carpet

tappez'zare *vt* paper ⟨*pareti*⟩; (con manifesti) cover

tappezze'ria *nf* tapestry; (di carta) wallpaper; (arte) upholstery; **fare da** ~ fig be a wallflower

tappezzi'ere *nm* upholsterer; (imbianchino) decorator

'tappo *nm* plug; (di sughero) cork; (di metallo, per penna) top; (fam pej: persona piccola) dwarf. **tappo di bottiglia** bottle top. **tappo a corona** crown cap. **tappi** *pl* **per le orecchie** earplugs. **tappo salvagocce** anti-drip top. **tappo di scarico [della coppa]** sump drain plug. **tappo a strappo** ring-pull. **tappo a vite** screw top

'tara *nf* (difetto) flaw; (ereditaria) hereditary defect; (peso) tare

taran'tella *nf* tarantella

ta'rantola *nf* tarantula

ta'rare *vt* Techn calibrate; Comm discount

ta'rato *adj* Comm discounted; Techn calibrated; Med with a hereditary defect; fam crazy

tarchi'ato *adj* stocky

tar'dare ① *vi* be late
② *vt* delay

'tardi *adv* late; **al più** ~ at the latest; **più** ~ later [on]; **sul** ~ late in the day; **far** ~ (essere in ritardo) be late; (con gli amici) stay up late; **a più** ~ see you later; **svegliarsi troppo** ~ oversleep

tardiva'mente *adv* late

tar'divo *adj* late; ⟨*bambino*⟩ retarded

'tardo *adj* slow; ⟨*pomeriggio, mattinata*⟩ late

'targa *nf* plate; Auto numberplate

tar'gato *adj* **un'auto targata...** a car with the registration number...

targ'hetta *nf* (su porta) nameplate; (sulla valigia) name tag. **targhetta di circolazione** numberplate. **targhetta commemorativa** memorial plaque. **targhetta stradale** street sign

ta'riffa *nf* rate, tariff; **a** ~ **ridotta** Teleph offpeak. **tariffa aerea** airfare. **tariffa doganale** customs tariff. **tariffa**

ferroviaria [rail] fares. **tariffa interna** inland postage. **tariffa ore di punta** peak rate. **tariffa professionale** [professional] fee. **tariffa telefonica** telephone charges. **tariffa unica** flat rate

tarif'fario ① *adj* tariff *adv* ② *nm* price list

tar'larsi *vr* get worm-eaten

tar'lato *adj* worm-eaten

'tarlo *nm* woodworm

'tarma *nf* moth

tar'marsi *vr* get moth-eaten

tarmi'cida *nm* ≈ moth-repellent

ta'rocco *nm* tarot; **tarocchi** *pl* tarot

tar'pare *vt* clip

tartagli'are *vi* stutter

'tartaro *adj & nm* tartar; **salsa tartara** tartar[e] sauce

tarta'ruga *nf* tortoise; (di mare) turtle; (per pettine ecc) tortoiseshell

tartas'sare *vt* (angariare) harass

tar'tina *nf* canapé

tar'tufo *nm* truffle

'tasca *nf* pocket; (in borsa) compartment; **da ~** pocket *attrib*; **avere le tasche piene di qualcosa** fam have had a bellyful of something; **se ne è stato con le mani in ~** fig he didn't lift a finger [to help]. **tasca a battente** flap pocket. **tasca del nero** (di polpo, seppia) ink sac. **tasca da pasticciere** icing bag. **tasca tagliata** slit pocket. **tasca a toppa** patchpocket

ta'scabile ① *adj* pocket *attrib* ② *nm* paperback

tasca'pane *nm inv* haversack

ta'schino *nm* breast pocket

tassì *nm inv* taxi

'tassa *nf* tax; (d'iscrizione ecc) fee; (doganale) duty. **tassa di circolazione** road tax. **tassa di esportazione** export duty. **tassa d'iscrizione** registration fee. **tassa di soggiorno** tourist tax, visitors' tax; **tasse** *pl* **scolastiche** school fees; **tasse** *pl* **universitarie** tuition fees

tas'sabile *adj* taxable

tas'sametro *nm* meter

tas'sare *vt* tax

tassativa'mente *adv* without fail

tassa'tivo *adj* strict

tassazi'one *nf* taxation

tas'sello *nm* wedge; (di stoffa) gusset; (per legno, parete) rawlplug

tas'sista *nmf* taxi driver

'tasso¹ *nm* Bot yew; (animale) badger

'tasso² *Comm* rate. **tasso agevolato** cut rate; **prestito a ~ agevolato** soft loan. **tasso base** base rate. **tasso base di interesse** base lending rate. **tasso di cambio** exchange rate. **tasso di**

crescita growth rate. **tasso di disoccupazione** unemployment rate. **tasso d'inquinamento** pollution level. **tasso di interesse** interest rate. **tasso di mortalità** death rate. **tasso di sconto** discount rate

ta'stare *vt* feel; **~ il terreno** fig test the water *or* ground

tasti'era *nf* keyboard. **tastiera numerica** Comput numeric keypad. **telefono a tastiera** touch-tone telephone

tasti'erino *nm* **tastierino numerico** numeric keypad

tastie'rista *nmf* keyboarder

'tasto *nm* key; (tatto) touch. **tasto Alt** Alt key. **tasto di cancellazione** delete key. **tasto control** Comput control key. **tasto cursore** Comput cursor key. **tasto delicato** fig touchy subject. **tasto eject** eject button. **tasto escape** escape key. **tasto funzione** Comput function key. **tasto numerico** Comput numeric[al] key. **tasto di ritorno a margine** return key. **tasto tabulatore** tab [key]

ta'stoni: a ~ *adv* gropingly; **camminare a ~** grope around; **cercare qualcosa a ~** grope for something

'tattica *nf* tactics *pl*

'tattico *adj* tactical

'tattile *adj* tactile

'tatto *nm* (senso) touch; (accortezza) tact; **aver ~** be tactful

tatu'aggio *nm* tattoo

tatu'are *vt* tattoo

tautolo'gia *nf* tautology

tauto'logico *adj* tautological

'tavola *nf* table; (illustrazione) plate; (asse) plank; **saper stare a ~** have good table manners; **calmo come una ~** (mare) like a mill pond. **tavola calda** snackbar. **tavola fredda** salad bar. **tavola periodica degli elementi** periodic table. **tavola pitagorica** multiplication table. **tavola rotonda** fig round table. **tavola a vela** sailboard; **fare ~ a vela** sailboard, windsurf

tavo'lato *nm* (pavimento) wooden flooring

tavo'letta *nf* bar; (medicinale) tablet; **andare a ~** Auto drive flat out. **tavoletta di cioccolata** chocolate bar. **tavoletta grafica** Comput digitizing tablet

tavo'lino *nm* [small] table; (da salotto) coffee table

'tavolo *nm* table. **tavolo anatomico** mortuary table, slab fam. **tavolo da biliardo** pool table. **tavolo da cucina** kitchen table. **tavolo da gioco** card table. **tavolo operatorio** Med operating table. **tavolo da pranzo** dining-table

tavo'lozza *nf* palette

taxi *nm inv* taxi

'tazza *nf* cup; (del water) bowl. **tazza da caffè/tè** coffee-cup/teacup

taz'zina *nf* **tazzina da caffè** espresso coffee cup

TBC *nf abbr* (**tubercolosi**) TB

T.C.I. *abbr* (**Touring Club Italiano**) association promoting tourism nationally and internationally

te *pers pron* you; **te l'ho dato** I gave it to you

tè *nm inv* tea. **tè al latte** tea with milk. **tè al limone** lemon tea

tea'trale *adj* theatre *attrib*; (affettato) theatrical

te'atro *nm* theatre. **teatro all'aperto** open-air theatre. **teatro lirico** opera [house]. **teatro neorealista** kitchen sink drama. **teatro di posa** Cinema set. **teatro tenda** marquee for fashions shows, concerts etc.

'techno *nf* techno (music)

'tecnico, -a ① *adj* technical ② *nmf* technician. **tecnico elettronico** electronics engineer. **tecnico informatico** computer engineer. **tecnico delle luci** Cinema, TV gaffer. **tecnico delle riparazioni** repairman. **tecnico del suono** sound technician ③ *nf* technique

tec'nigrafo *nm* drawing board

tec'nocrate *nmf* technocrat

tec'nofobo *adj* technophobe

tecnolo'gia *nf* technology

tecno'logico *adj* technological

te'desco, -a *adj & nmf* German

'tedio *nm* tedium

tedi'oso *adj* tedious

'TEE *nm abbr* (**treno espresso transeuropeo**) Trans-Europe-Express [train]

te'game *nm* saucepan; **uova al tegame** fried eggs

'teglia *nf* baking tin

'tegola *nf* tile; fig blow

tei'era *nf* teapot

te'ina *nf* theine

tek *nm* teak

tel. *abbr* (**telefono**) tel.

'tela *nf* cloth; (per quadri, vele) canvas; Theat curtain. **tela cerata** oilcloth. **tela indiana** cheesecloth. **tela di iuta** hessian. **tela di lino** linen. **tela rigida** buckram

te'laio *nm* (di bicicletta, finestra) frame; Auto chassis; (per tessere) loom

'tele *nf* fam telly, TV

tele'camera *nf* television camera

telecoman'dato *adj* remote-controlled, remote control *attrib*

teleco'mando *nm* remote control

'Telecom I'talia *nf* Italian State telephone company

telecomunicazi'oni *nfpl* telecommunications, telecomms

teleconfe'renza *nf* teleconference

tele'cronaca *nf* [television] commentary; **fare la ~ di** commentate on. **telecronaca diretta** live [television] coverage. **telecronaca registrata** recording

telecro'nista *nmf* television commentator

tele'ferica *nf* cableway

tele'film *nm inv* film [made] for television. **telefilm a episodi** series

telefo'nare *vt/i* [tele]phone, ring

telefo'nata *nf* call, [tele]phone call; **fare una ~** make a phone call. **telefonata anonima** nuisance call. **telefonata a carico del destinatario** reverse charge [phone] call; **fare una ~ a carico [del destinatario]** reverse the charges. **telefonata interurbana** long-distance call. **telefonata di lavoro** business call. **telefonata in teleselezione** ≈ STD call. **telefonata urbana** local call

telefonica'mente *adv* by [tele]phone

tele'fonico *adj* [tele]phone *attrib*

telefo'nino *nm* mobile [phone]

telefo'nista *nmf* operator

te'lefono *nm* [tele]phone; **numero di telefono** [tele]phone number. **telefono amico** the Samaritans. **telefono azzurro** children in need help line. **telefono cellulare** cell[ular] [tele]phone, mobile. **telefono cordless** cordless [phone]. **telefono interno** intercom. **telefono a monete** pay phone. **telefono pubblico** public telephone. **telefono rosso** Mil, Pol hotline. **telefono a scatti** telephone with call charges based on time-units. **telefono a scheda** cardphone. **telefono a tastiera** push-button phone

tele'genico *adj* telegenic

telegior'nale *nm* television news

telegra'fare *vt* telegraph

telegra'fia *nf* telegraphy

telegrafica'mente *adv* (con telegrafo) by telegram

tele'grafico *adj* telegraphic; (risposta) monosyllabic; **sii ~** keep it brief

te'legrafo *nm* telegraph

tele'gramma *nm* telegram

telela'voro *nm* teleworking

tele'matica *nf* data communications, telematics

teleno'vela *nf* soap opera

teleobiet'tivo *nm* telephoto lens

telepa'tia *nf* telepathy

tele'patico *adj* telepathic

tele'quiz *nm inv* TV quiz programme

teleradiotra'smettere *vt* simulcast

telero'manzo *nm* television serial

tele'schermo *nm* television screen

tele'scopio *nm* telescope

telescri'vente *nf* telex [machine]

teleselet'tivo *adj* direct dialling

teleselezi'one *nf* subscriber trunk dialling, STD; **chiamare in ∼** call direct, dial direct. **teleselezione internazionale** international direct dialling

telespetta|'tore, -trice *nmf* viewer; **i telespettatori** the viewing public

tele'text *nm* Teletext

'telethon *nm* telethon

Tele'video *nm* Teletext, Ceefax

televisi'one *nf* television; **guardare la ∼** watch television; **alla ∼** on television. **televisione ad alta definizione** high-definition television. **televisione in bianco e nero** black and white television. **televisione via cavo** cable TV. **televisione a circuito chiuso** closed-circuit television, CCTV. **televisione a colori** colour television. **televisione satellitare** satellite television

televi'sivo *adj* television, TV *attrib*; **apparecchio televisivo** television set; **operatore televisivo** television cameraman

televi'sore *nm* television [set], TV [set]. **televisore portatile** portable [TV], portable [television set]. **televisore con schermo panoramico** wide-screen TV

'telex [1] *nm inv* telex [2] *adj inv* telex *attrib*

tel'lurico *adj* telluric

'telo *nm* [piece of] cloth. **telo da bagno** beach towel. **telo di salvataggio** rescue blanket

'tema *nm* theme; Sch essay

te'matica *nf* main theme

teme'rario *adj* reckless

te'mere [1] *vt* be afraid of [2] *vi* be afraid

tem'paccio *nm* filthy weather

'tempera *nf* tempera; (pittura) painting in tempera

temperama'tite *nm inv* pencil-sharpener

tempera'mento *nm* temperament

tempe'rare *vt* temper; sharpen (matita)

tempe'rato *adj* temperate

tempera'tura *nf* temperature. **temperatura ambiente** room temperature

tempe'rino *nm* penknife

tem'pesta *nf* storm. **tempesta magnetica** magnetic storm. **tempesta**

di neve snowstorm. **tempesta di sabbia** sandstorm

tempe'stare *vt* **∼ qualcuno di colpi** rain blows on somebody; **∼ qualcuno di domande** bombard somebody with questions

tempe'stato *adj* (anello, diadema) encrusted (**di** with)

tempestiva'mente *adv* quickly, in a short space of time

tempe'stivo *adj* timely, well-timed

tempe'stoso *adj* stormy

'tempia *nf* Anat temple

'tempio *nm* Relig temple

tem'pismo *nm* timing

'tempo *nm* time; (atmosferico) weather; Mus tempo; Gram tense; (di film) part; (di partita) half; **a suo ∼** in due course; **∼ fa** some time ago; **per molto ∼, per tanto ∼** for a long time; **tanto ∼ fa** a long time ago; **un ∼** once; **ha fatto il suo ∼** it's out of date; **a ∼ indeterminato** ⟨*contratto*⟩ permanent; **primo tempo** (di film, partita) first half. **tempo di accesso** Comput access time. **tempo di cottura** cooking time. **tempo di esposizione** Phot exposure time. **tempo libero** free time, leisure time. **tempo limite di accettazione** latest check-in time. **tempo di pace** peacetime. **tempo reale** Comput real time; **in tempo reale** real-time *attrib*. **tempo supplementare** extra time; Sport extra time, overtime Am; **andare ai tempi supplementari** Sport go into extra time

tempo'rale [1] *adj* temporal [2] *nm* [thunder]storm

temporanea'mente *adv* temporarily

tempo'raneo *adj* temporary

temporeggi'are *vi* play for time

tem'prare *vt* form

te'nace *adj* tenacious, strong-willed

tenace'mente *adv* tenaciously

te'nacia *nf* tenacity

te'naglia *nf* pincers *pl*

'tenda *nf* curtain; (per campeggio) tent; (tendone) awning; **tirare le tende** draw the curtains. **tenda della doccia** shower curtain. **tenda a ossigeno** oxygen tent

ten'denza *nf* tendency. **tendenza al rialzo/ribasso** Fin bull/bear market

tendenzial'mente *adv* by nature

tendenzi'oso *adj* tendentious

'tendere [1] *vt* (allargare) stretch [out]; (tirare) tighten; (porgere) hold out; fig lay ⟨*trappola*⟩ [2] *vi* **∼ a** aim at; (essere portato a) tend to

'tendersi *vr* tauten

'tendine *nm* tendon. **tendine d'Achille** Achille's tendon. **tendine del** ⋯⟶

garretto hamstring. **tendine del ginocchio** hamstring

ten'done *nm* awning. **tendone del circo** big top

ten'dopoli *nf inv* tent city

'tenebre *nfpl* darkness

tene'broso ① *adj* gloomy
② *nm* bel ~ dark and handsome man

te'nente *nm* lieutenant. **tenente colonnello** wing commander

tenera'mente *adv* tenderly

te'nere ① *vt* hold; (mantenere) keep; (gestire) run; (prendere) take; (seguire) follow; (considerare) consider
② *vi* hold; ~ **stretto** hold tight; ~ **a qualcosa** ⟨oggetto⟩ be fond of something; **tengo alla sua presenza** I very much want him to be there; ~ **per** ⟨squadra⟩ support

tene'rezza *nf* tenderness

'tenero *adj* tender

tene'rone, -a *nmf* softie

te'nersi *vr* hold on (a to); (in una condizione) keep oneself; ~ **indietro** stand back

'tenia *nf* tapeworm

'tennis *nm* tennis. **tennis da tavolo** table tennis

ten'nista *nmf* tennis player

te'nore *nm* standard; Mus tenor; **a ~ di legge** by law. **tenore di vita** standard of living

tensi'one *nf* tension; Electr voltage; **mettere sotto ~** energize; **in ~** under stress. **alta tensione** high voltage. **tensione premestruale** premenstrual tension, PMT

ten'tacolo *nm* tentacle

ten'tare *vt* attempt; (sperimentare) try; (indurre in tentazione) tempt; ~ **la strada di** make a foray *or* venture into

tenta'tivo *nm* attempt

ten'tato *adj* **tentato suicidio** suicide attempt

tentazi'one *nf* temptation

tentenna'mento *nm* wavering; **ha avuto dei tentennamenti** he wavered a bit

tenten'nare *vi* waver

ten'toni *adv* **cercare qualcosa a ~** grope for something

'tenue *adj* fine; (debole) weak; (esiguo) small; (leggero) slight

te'nuta *nf* (capacità) capacity; (Sport, resistenza) stamina; (possedimento) estate; (divisa) uniform; (abbigliamento) clothes *pl*; **a ~ d'aria** airtight. **tenuta di strada** road holding

teolo'gia *nf* theology

teo'logico *adj* theological

te'ologo *nm* theologian

teo'rema *nm* theorem

teo'ria *nf* theory

teorica'mente *adv* theoretically

te'orico *adj* theoretical

te'pore *nm* warmth

'teppa *nf* mob

tep'pismo *nm* hooliganism

tep'pista *nm* hooligan, yob fam

te'quila *nf* tequila

tera'peutico *adj* therapeutic

tera'pia *nf* therapy; **in ~** in therapy. **terapia genica** gene therapy. **terapia di gruppo** group therapy. **terapia ormonale sostitutiva** hormone replacement therapy, HRT. **terapia d'urto** shock treatment

tergicri'stallo *nm* windscreen wiper, windshield wiper Am

tergilu'notto *nm* rear windscreen wiper

tergiver'sante *adj* equivocating, pussyfooting fam

tergiver'sare *vi* equivocate, pussyfoot around fam

'tergo *nm* **a ~** behind; **segue a ~** please turn over, PTO

teri'lene® *nm* Terylene®

'terital® *nm* Terylene®

ter'male *adj* thermal; **stazione termale** spa

'terme *nfpl* thermal baths

'termico *adj* thermal; **borsa termica** cool bag

'terminal *nm inv* air terminal

termi'nale *adj & nm* terminal; **malato terminale** terminally ill person

termina'lista *nmf* computer operator

termi'nare *vt/i* end, finish

terminazi'one *nf* (fine) termination; Gram ending. **terminazione nervosa** nerve ending

'termine *nm* (limite) limit; (fine) end; (condizione, parola) term; (scadenza) deadline; **ai termini della legge...** under the terms of act...; **contratto a termine** fixed-term contract. **termine di paragone** Gram term of comparison. **termine ultimo** final deadline

terminolo'gia *nf* terminology

'termite *nf* termite

termoco'perta *nf* electric blanket

termogra'fia *nf* thermal imaging

ter'mometro *nm* thermometer

'termos *nm inv* thermos®

termosi'fone *nm* radiator; (sistema) central heating

ter'mostato *nm* thermostat

termotera'pia *nf* Med heat treatment

termoventila'tore *nm* fan heater

'terra *nf* earth; (regione) land; (terreno) ground; (argilla) clay; (cosmetico) bronzing powder; **a ~** (sulla costa) ashore; (installazioni) onshore; **essere a ~** (gomma) be flat; fig be at rock bottom; **per ~** on the ground; (su pavimento) on the floor; **sotto ~** underground; **far ~ bruciata** carry out a scorched earth policy. **terra promessa** Promised Land. **Terra Santa** Holy Land. **terra di Siena** sienna

terra'cotta *nf* terracotta; **vasellame di ~** earthenware

terra'ferma *nf* dry land

Terra'nova *nf* Newfoundland

terrapi'eno *nm* embankment

ter'razza *nf*, **ter'razzo** *nm* balcony

terremo'tato, -a ① *adj* (zona) affected by an earthquake
② *nmf* earthquake victim

terre'moto *nm* earthquake

ter'reno ① *adj* earthly
② *nm* ground; (suolo) soil; (proprietà terriera) land; **perdere/guadagnare ~** lose/gain ground. **terreno alluvionale** alluvial soil. **terreno di bonifica** reclaimed land. **terreno boschivo** woodland. **terreno edificabile** building land. **terreno di gioco** playing field. **terreno di scontro** battlefield

ter'restre *adj* terrestrial; ⟨superficie, diametro⟩ of the earth; **esercito terrestre** land forces *pl*

ter'ribile *adj* terrible

terribil'mente *adv* terribly

ter'riccio *nm* potting compost

'terrier *nm inv* terrier

terri'ero *adj* ⟨proprietario⟩ land *attrib*; ⟨aristocrazia⟩ landed; **proprietà** *pl* **terriere** landed property

terrifi'cante *adj* terrifying

territori'ale *adj* territorial; **acque territoriali** territorial waters

terri'torio *nm* territory

ter'rone, -a *nmf* pej bloody Southerner

ter'rore *nm* terror

terro'rismo *nm* terrorism

terro'rista *nmf* terrorist

terroriz'zare *vt* terrorize

'terso *adj* clear

'terza *nf* (marcia) third [gear]

ter'zetto *nm* trio

terzi'ario ① *adj* tertiary
② *nm* service sector, tertiary sector. **terziario avanzato** high technology, hi-tech sector

'terzo ① *adj* third; **di terz'ordine** ⟨locale, servizio⟩ third-rate; **fare il ~ grado a qualcuno** give somebody the third degree; **la terza età** the third age; **il ~ mondo** the Third World
② *nm* third; **terzi** *pl* Jur third party

terzo'genito, -a *nmf* third-born

ter'zultimo, -a *adj & nmf* third from last

'tesa *nf* brim

'teschio *nm* skull

'tesi *nf inv* thesis

'teso ① *pp di* TENDERE
② *adj* taut; fig tense

tesore'ria *nf* treasury

tesori'ere *nm* treasurer

te'soro *nm* treasure; (tesoreria) treasury; **ministro del Tesoro** Finance Minister; ≈ Chancellor of the Exchequer Br

'tessera *nf* card; (abbonamento all'autobus) season ticket; (di club) membership card. **tessera magnetica** swipe card. **tessera dei trasporti pubblici** travel card. **tessera di sconto** discount card

'tessere *vt* weave; hatch (complotto); **~ le lodi di qualcosa** sing the praises of something

tesse'rino *nm* travel card

'tessile ① *adj* textile
② *nm* **tessili** *pl* textiles; (operai) textile workers

tessi'tore, -trice *nmf* weaver

tessi'tura *nf* weaving

tes'suto ① *pp di* TESSERE
② *adj* woven; **~ a mano** hand-woven
③ *nm* fabric, material; Anat tissue. **tessuto sintetico** synthetic material. **tessuto di spugna** terry towelling

'test *nm inv* test; **test** *pl* **genetici** genetic testing

'testa *nf* head; (cervello) brain; **essere in ~ a** be ahead of; **in ~** Sport in the lead; **~ o croce?** heads or tails?; **fare a ~ o croce** spin a coin, toss a coin; **andare a ~ alta** hold one's head up. **testa di rapa** fam pinhead. **testa di sbarco** beachhead. **testa di serie** (squadra) seeded team. **testa del treno** front of the train

testa-'coda *nm inv* **fare un ~** spin right round

testa'mento *nm* will. **Antico Testamento** Relig Old Testament. **Nuovo Testamento** Relig New Testament

testar'daggine *nf* stubbornness

testarda'mente *adv* stubbornly

te'stardo *adj* stubborn

te'stare *vt* test

te'stata *nf* head; (intestazione) heading; (colpo) [head]butt. **testata nucleare** nuclear warhead

'teste *nmf* witness

'tester *nm inv* tester

te'sticolo *nm* testicle

testi'mone *nmf* witness; **essere ~ di qualcosa** witness something. **testimone** ⋯⋙

di Geova Jehovah's Witness.
testimone oculare eye witness
testi'monial *nmf inv* celebrity who endorses a product
testimoni'anza *nf* testimony; **falsa testimonianza** Jur perjury
testimoni'are ① *vt* testify to ② *vi* testify, give evidence
te'stina *nf* head; (di stampante) printhead. **testina di cancellazione** Comput erase head. **testina di lettura** Comput read head. **testina rotante** (di macchina da scrivere) golf-ball. **testina di vitello** Culin calf's head
'**testo** *nm* text; **far ~** be authoritative; **con ~ a fronte** ⟨*traduzione*⟩ with the original text on the opposite page
te'stone, -a *nmf* blockhead
testoste'rone *nm* testosterone
testu'ale *adj* textual
'**tetano** *nm* tetanus
te'traggine *nf* bleakness
tetra'pak® *nm* tetrapak
'**tetro** *adj* bleak
tetta'rella *nf* teat
'**tetto** *nm* roof; **abbandono del ~ coniugale** Jur desertion. **tetto apribile** (di auto) sun[shine] roof. **tetto a terrazza** flat roof
tet'toia *nf* roofing
tet'tuccio *nm* **tettuccio apribile** sun-roof
teu'tonico *adj* Teutonic
'**Tevere** *nm* Tiber
ti *pers pron* you; (riflessivo) yourself; **ti ha dato un libro** he gave you a book; **lavati le mani** wash your hands; **eccoti!** here you are!; **sbrigati!** hurry up!
ti'ara *nf* tiara
'**Tibet** *nm* Tibet
tic *nm inv* tic
ticchet'tare *vi* tick
ticchet'tio *nm* ticking
'**ticchio** *nm* tic; (ghiribizzo) whim
'**ticket** *nm inv* (per farmaco, analisi) prescription charges, amount paid by National Health patients
tie-break *nm inv* tie break[er]
tiepida'mente *adv* half-heartedly
ti'epido *adj* lukewarm; fig half-hearted
ti'fare *vi* **~ per** be a fan of
'**tifo** *nm* Med typhus; **fare il ~ per** (appoggiare) be a fan of
tifoi'dea *nf* typhoid
ti'fone *nm* typhoon
ti'foso, -a *nmf* fan
tight *nm inv* morning dress
'**tiglio** *nm* lime
'**tigna** *nf* ringworm

ti'grato *adj* **gatto tigrato** tabby [cat]
'**tigre** *nf* tiger
'**tilde** *nf* tilde
tim'ballo *nm* Culin pie
tim'brare *vt* stamp; **~ il cartellino** (all'entrata) clock in; (all'uscita) clock out
'**timbro** *nm* stamp; (di voce) tone. **timbro a secco** embossing stamp
time out *nm inv* Sport time-out
'**timer** *nm inv* timer
timida'mente *adv* timidly, shyly
timi'dezza *nf* timidity, shyness
'**timido** *adj* timid, shy
'**timo** *nm* thyme
ti'mone *nm* helm, rudder. **timone di direzione** (di aereo) rudder. **timone di quota** (di aereo) elevator
timoni'ere *nm* helmsman
timo'rato *adj* **~ di Dio** God-fearing
ti'more *nm* fear; (soggezione) awe
'**Timor 'Est** *nm* East Timor
timo'roso *adj* timorous
'**timpano** *nm* eardrum; Mus kettledrum; **timpani** *pl* Mus timpani, kettledrums; **rompere i timpani a qualcuno** fig shatter somebody's eardrums
ti'nello *nm* dining-room
'**tingere** *vt* dye; (macchiare) stain
'**tingersi** *vr* (viso, cielo) be tinged (**di** with); **~ i capelli** have one's hair dyed; (da solo) dye one's hair
'**tino** *nm*, '**tinozza** *nf* tub
'**tinta** *nf* dye; (colore) colour; **in ~ unita** plain, self-coloured
tinta'rella *nf* fam suntan
tintin'nare *vi* tinkle
'**tinto** *pp di* TINGERE
tinto'ria *nf* (negozio) cleaner's
tin'tura *nf* dyeing; (colorante) dye. **tintura di iodio** iodine
tipica'mente *adv* typically
'**tipico** *adj* typical
'**tipo** *nm* type; (fam: individuo) chap, guy
tipogra'fia *nf* printer's; (arte) typography
tipo'grafico *adj* typographic[al]
ti'pografo *nm* printer
tip tap *nm* tap dancing
ti'raggio *nm* draught
tiranneggi'are *vt* tyrannize
tiran'nia *nf* tyranny
ti'ranno, -a ① *adj* tyrannical ② *nmf* tyrant
tiranno'sauro *nm* tyrannosaurus
ti'rante *nm* rope
tirapi'edi *nm inv* pej hanger-on
tira'pugni *nm inv* knuckle-duster

ti'rare ①) *vt* pull; (gettare) throw; (nel calcio) kick; (tracciare) draw; (stampare) print; fam land ⟨*calci, pugni*⟩

②) *vi* pull; ⟨*vento*⟩ blow; ⟨*abito*⟩ be tight; ⟨*sparare*⟩ fire; **~ avanti** fig get by; **~ su** bring up ⟨*figli*⟩; (da terra) pick up; **tirar su [col naso]** sniffle

ti'rarsi *vr* **~ indietro** fig back out, pull out

tiras'segno *nm* target shooting; (alla fiera) rifle range

ti'rata *nf* (strattone) pull, tug; **in una ~ in** one go; **dare a qualcuno una ~ d'orecchi** fig give somebody a telling off

tira'tore *nm* shot. **tiratore scelto** marksman

tira'tura *nf* printing; (di giornali) circulation; (di libri) [print] run

tirchie'ria *nf* meanness

'tirchio *adj* mean

tiri'tera *nf* spiel

'tiro *nm* (lancio) throw; (azione) throwing; (sparo) shot; (azione) shooting; (scherzo) trick; **cavallo da tiro** draught horse. **tiro con l'arco** archery. **tiro al bersaglio** target practice. **tiro alla fune** tug-of-war. **tiro al piattello** clay pigeon shooting. **tiro in porta** shot at goal. **tiro a segno** rifle-range

tiroci'nante *nmf* trainee

tiro'cinio *nm* training

ti'roide *nf* thyroid

Tir'reno *nm* **il [mar] ~** the Tyrrhenian Sea

ti'sana *nf* herb[al] tea

'tisi *nf* consumption

ti'tanio *nm* titanium

tito'lare ①) *adj* permanent
②) *nmf* (proprietario) owner; (nel calcio) regular player; (Jur: di diritto) holder

'titolo *nm* title; ⟨*accademico*⟩ qualification; Comm security; **a ~ di** as; **a ~ di favore** as a favour; **titoli** *pl* (di giornale, telegiornale) headlines. **titoli** *pl* **di coda** closing credits. **titolo di credito** credit instrument. **titolo mondiale** world title. **titolo obbligazionario** bond. **titoli** *pl* **delle principali notizie** news headlines. **titolo in sovrimpressione** superimposed title. **titolo di Stato** government security. **titoli** *pl* **di studio** qualifications. **titoli** *pl* **di testa** Cinema, TV opening credits. **titolo a tutta pagina** banner headline

titu'bante *adj* hesitant

titu'banza *nf* hesitation

titu'bare *vi* hesitate

tivù *nf inv* fam TV, telly

'tizio, -a ①) *nm* so-and-so; **un ~** some man
②) *nf* **una tizia** some woman

tiz'zone *nm* brand

toc'cante *adj* touching

toc'care ①) *vt* touch; touch on ⟨*argomento*⟩; (tastare) feel; (riguardare) concern
②) *vi* **~ a** (capitare) happen to; **mi tocca aspettare** I'll have to wait; **tocca a te** it's your turn; (a pagare da bere) it's your round; **'non ~'** 'please do not touch'

tocca'sana *nm inv* panacea

toc'cato *adj* (fam: matto) touched

'tocco ①) *nm* touch; (di pennello, orologio) stroke; (di pane ecc) chunk; **il ~ finale** the finishing touches
②) *adj* fam crazy, touched

toc toc *nm inv* knock, knock

'toga *nf* toga; (accademica, di magistrato) gown

'togliere *vt* take off ⟨*coperta*⟩; (Math, da scuola) take away; quench ⟨*sete*⟩; take out, remove ⟨*tonsille, dente ecc*⟩; **~ qualcosa di mano a qualcuno** take something away from somebody; **~ qualcuno dai guai** get somebody out of trouble; **ciò non toglie che... nevertheless..., the fact remains that...; **farsi ~ le tonsille** have one's tonsils [taken] out

'togliersi *vr* take off ⟨*abito*⟩; **~ la vita** take one's [own] life; **~ di mezzo** get out of the way; **togliti dai piedi!** get out of the way!

'Togo *nm* Togo

toi'lette *nf inv* toilet; (mobile) dressing table

to'letta *nf* toilet; (mobile) dressing table

tolle'rante *adj* tolerant

tolle'ranza *nf* tolerance; **casa di tolleranza** brothel

tolle'rare *vt* tolerate

'tolto *pp di* TOGLIERE

to'maia *nf* upper

'tomba *nf* grave

tom'bino *nm* manhole cover

'tombola *nf* bingo; (caduta) tumble

to'mino *nm* goat-cheese

'tomo *nm* tome

tomogra'fia *nf* Med tomography. **tomografia assiale computerizzata** computerized axial tomography, CAT

'tonaca *nf* habit

to'nale *adj* tonal

tonalità *nf inv* Mus tonality

to'nante *adj* booming

'tondo ①) *adj* (cifra) round
②) *nm* circle

'toner *nm inv* toner

'tonfo *nm* thud; (in acqua) splash

'Tonga *nf* Tonga

'tonica *nf* Mus keynote

'tonico ①) *adj* ⟨*sillaba*⟩ stressed; ⟨*muscoli*⟩ well toned

2 *nm* tonic

tonifi'care *vt* tone up ⟨*muscoli*⟩

ton'nara *nf* tuna-fishing net

ton'nato *adj* **vitello tonnato** veal with a tuna and mayonnaise sauce

tonnel'laggio *nm* tonnage

tonnel'lata *nf* ton. **tonnellata corta americana** short ton, net ton

'**tonno** *nm* tuna [fish]

'**tono** *nm* tone

ton'sille *nfpl* tonsils

tonsil'lite *nf* tonsillitis

'**tonto** *adj* fam thick

top *nm inv* (indumento) sun-top

to'pazio *nm* topaz

'**topless** *nm inv* in ∼ topless

top 'model *nf inv* supermodel, top model

'**topo** *nm* mouse. **topo di albergo/appartamento** thief in a hotel/block of flats. **topo di biblioteca** bookworm. **topo domestico** domestic mouse

topogra'fia *nf* topography

topo'grafico *adj* topographic[al]

to'ponimo *nm* place name

topo'ragno *nm* shrew

'**toppa** *nf* (rattoppo) patch; (serratura) keyhole

to'race *nm* chest

to'racico *adj* thoracic; **gabbia toracica** rib cage

'**torba** *nf* peat

'**torbido** *adj* cloudy; fig troubled

'**torcere** *vt* twist; wring [out] ⟨*biancheria*⟩

'**torcersi** *vr* twist

'**torchio** *nm* press

'**torcia** *nf* torch. **torcia elettrica** torch

torci'collo *nm* stiff neck

'**tordo** *nm* thrush

to'rero *nm* bullfighter

To'rino *nf* Turin

tor'menta *nf* snowstorm

tormen'tare *vt* torment

tormen'tato *adj* tormented

tor'mento *nm* torment

torna'conto *nm* benefit

tor'nado *nm inv* tornado

tor'nante *nm* hairpin bend

tor'nare *vi* return, go/come back; (ridiventare) become again; ⟨*conto*⟩ add up; ∼ **a sorridere** smile again; ∼ **su** go back up

tor'neo *nm* tournament

'**tornio** *nm* lathe

'**torno** *nm* **togliersi di** ∼ get out of the way

'**toro** *nm* bull; Astr Taurus

tor'pedine *nf* torpedo

torpedini'era *nf* torpedo boat

tor'pore *nm* torpor

'**torre** *nf* tower; (scacchi) castle. **torre d'avorio** ivory tower. **torre di controllo** control tower. **torre di osservazione** observation tower. **torre pendente, torre di Pisa** Leaning Tower of Pisa

torrefazi'one *nf* roasting; (negozio) coffee retailer

tor'rente *nm* torrent, mountain stream; (fig: di lacrime) flood; (fig: di parole) torrent

torrenzi'ale *adj* torrential; **in regime** ∼ in spate

tor'retta *nf* turret

'**torrido** *adj* torrid, sweltering

torri'one *nm* keep

tor'rone *nm* nougat

torsi'one *nf* twisting; (in ginnastica) twist

'**torso** *nm* torso; (di mela, pera) core; **a** ∼ **nudo** bare-chested

'**torsolo** *nm* core

'**torta** *nf* cake; (crostata) tart. **torta di compleanno** birthday cake. **torta di mele** apple tart. **torta nuziale** wedding cake. **torta pasqualina** spinach pie

torti'era *nf* cake tin

tor'tino *nm* pie

'**torto** **1** pp di TORCERE **2** *adj* twisted **3** *nm* wrong; (colpa) fault; **aver** ∼ be wrong; **a** ∼ wrongly; **far** ∼ **a qualcuno** wrong somebody; fig not do somebody justice; **non hai tutti i torti** you're not altogether wrong

'**tortora** *nf* turtle-dove

tortuosa'mente *adv* tortuously

tortu'oso *adj* winding; (ambiguo) tortuous

tor'tura *nf* torture

tortu'rare *vt* torture

'**torvo** *adj* ⟨*sguardo*⟩ menacing

tosa'erba *nm inv* lawnmower

to'sare *vt* shear

tosasi'epi *nm inv* hedge trimmer

tosa'tura *nf* shearing

To'scana *nf* Tuscany

to'scano, -a *adj & nmf* Tuscan

'**tosse** *nf* cough

'**tossico** **1** *adj* toxic **2** *nm* poison

tossicodipen'denza *nf* drug addiction, drug habit

tossi'comane *nmf* drug addict, drug user

tos'sire *vi* cough

tosta'pane *nm inv* toaster. **tostapane a espulsione automatica** pop-up toaster

to'stare *vt* toast ‹*pane*›; roast ‹*caffe*›

'tosto ① *adv* (subito) soon
② *adj* fam cool; **faccia tosta** cheek

tot ① *adj inv* **una cifra** ~ such and such a figure
② *nm* **un** ~ so much

to'tale *adj* & *nm* total. **totale complessivo** grand total. **totale parziale** subtotal

totalità *nf* entirety; **la** ~ **dei presenti** all those present

totali'tario *adj* totalitarian

totaliz'zare *vt* total; score ‹*punti*›

totalizza'tore *nm* (per scommesse) totalizer, tote

total'mente *adv* totally

'totano *nm* squid

'totem *nm inv* totem pole

toto'calcio *nm* ≈ [football] pools *pl*

'touche *nf inv* touch line

tou'pet *nm inv* toupee

tournée *nf inv* tour

to'vaglia *nf* tablecloth

tovagli'etta *nf* **tovaglietta [all'americana]** place mat

tovagli'olo *nm* napkin. **tovagliolo di carta** paper napkin

'tozzo ① *adj* squat
② *nm* **tozzo di pane** stale piece of bread

tra = FRA

trabal'lante *adj* staggering; ‹*sedia*› rickety, wonky

trabal'lare *vi* stagger; ‹*veicolo*› jolt

tra'biccolo *nm* fam contraption; (auto) jalopy

traboc'care *vi* overflow

traboc'chetto *nm* trap

traca'gnotto *adj* dumpy

tracan'nare *vt* gulp down

'traccia *nf* track; (orma) footstep; (striscia) trail; (residuo) trace; fig sign

tracci'are *vt* trace; sketch out ‹*schema*›; draw ‹*linea*›

tracci'ato *nm* (schema) layout. **tracciato di gara** circuit

tra'chea *nf* windpipe, trachea

tra'colla *nf* shoulder-strap; **borsa a tracolla** shoulder-bag

tra'collo *nm* collapse

tradi'mento *nm* betrayal; Pol treason; **alto tradimento** high treason

tra'dire *vt* betray; be unfaithful to ‹*moglie, marito*›

tradi'|tore, -trice *nmf* traitor

tradizio'nale *adj* traditional

tradiziona'lista *nmf* traditionalist

tradizional'mente *adv* traditionally

tradizi'one *nf* tradition

tra'dotto *pp di* TRADURRE

tra'durre *vt* translate

tradut'|tore, -trice *nmf* translator. **traduttore elettronico** electronic phrasebook

traduzi'one *nf* translation. **traduzione consecutiva** consecutive interpreting. **traduzione simultanea** simultaneous interpreting

tra'ente *nmf* Comm drawer

trafe'lato *adj* breathless

traffi'cante *nmf* dealer, trafficker. **trafficante d'armi** arms dealer. **trafficante di droga** drug dealer

traffi'care *vi* (affaccendarsi) busy oneself; ~ **in** pej traffic in

'traffico *nm* traffic; Comm trade. **traffico aereo** air traffic. **traffico della droga** drug trafficking. **traffico ferroviario** rail traffic. **traffico di stupefacenti** drug trafficking

traffi'cone, -a *nmf* fam wheeler dealer

tra'figgere *vt* penetrate, pierce; fig pierce

tra'fila *nf* fig rigmarole

trafi'letto *nm* minor news item

trafo'rare *vt* bore, drill

tra'foro *nm* boring, drilling; (galleria) tunnel; **lavoro di traforo** fretwork

trafu'gare *vt* steal

tra'gedia *nf* tragedy

traghet'tare *vt* ferry

tra'ghetto *nm* ferrying; (nave) ferry

tragica'mente *adv* tragically

'tragico ① *adj* tragic
② *nm* (autore) tragedian

tra'gitto *nm* journey; (per mare) crossing

tragu'ardo *nm* finishing post; (meta) goal

traiet'toria *nf* trajectory

trai'nare *vt* drag; (rimorchiare) tow

tralasci'are *vt* interrupt; (omettere) leave out; ~ **di fare qualcosa** fail to do something, omit to do something

'tralcio *nm* Bot shoot

tra'liccio *nm* (tela) ticking; (graticcio) trellis

tra'lice: in ~ *adv* (tagliare) on the slant; (guardare) sideways

tralu'cente *adj* shining

tram *nm inv* tram, streetcar Am

'trama *nf* weft; (di film ecc) plot

traman'dare *vt* hand down

tra'mare *vt* weave; (macchinare) plot

tram'busto *nm* turmoil

trame'stio *nm* bustle

tramez'zino *nm* sandwich

tra'mezzo *nm* partition

'tramite ① *prep* through

2 *nm* link; **con il ∼ di** by means of; **fare da ∼** act as go-between

tramon'tana *nf* north wind

tramon'tare *vi* set; (declinare) decline

tra'monto *nm* sunset; (declino) decline

tramor'tire **1** *vt* stun
2 *vi* faint

trampoli'ere *nm* wader

trampo'lino *nm* springboard; (per lo sci) ski-jump. **trampolino di lancio** fig launch pad

'trampolo *nm* stilt

tramu'tare *vt* transform

trance *nf* trance; **essere in ∼** be in a trance

'trancia *nf* shears *pl*; (fetta) slice

tra'nello *nm* trap

trangugi'are *vt* gulp down

'tranne *prep* except

tranquilla'mente *adv* peacefully

tranquil'lante *nm* tranquillizer

tranquillità *nf* calm; (di spirito) tranquillity

tranquilliz'zare *vt* reassure

tran'quillo *adj* quiet; (pacifico) peaceful; (coscienza) easy; **stai ∼ !** (non preoccuparti) don't worry!

transa'tlantico **1** *adj* transatlantic
2 *nm* ocean liner

tran'satto pp di TRANSIGERE

transazi'one *nf* Comm transaction; Jur settlement

tran'senna *nf* (barriera) barrier

transessu'ale *nmf* transsexual

tran'setto *nm* transept

'transfert *nm inv* Psych transference

tran'sigere *vi* Jur reach a settlement; (cedere) compromise

tran'sistor *nm inv* fam transistor [radio]

transi'tabile *adj* passable

transi'tare *vi* pass

transi'tivo *adj* transitive

'transito *nm* transit; **'divieto di ∼'** 'no thoroughfare'; **diritto di transito** right of way. **'transito alterno'** 'temporary one-way system'

transi'torio *adj* transitory

transizi'one *nf* transition; **di ∼** transitional

tran'tran *nm* fam routine

tranvi'ere *nm* tram driver, streetcar driver Am

'trapano *nm* drill. **trapano elettrico** electric drill

trapas'sare **1** *vt* pierce, penetrate
2 *vi* (morire) pass away

trapas'sato *nm* pluperfect

tra'passo *nm* passage

trape'lare *vi* anche fig leak out

tra'pezio *nm* trapeze; Math trapezium

trapian'tare *vt* transplant

trapi'anto *nm* transplant. **trapianto di cuore** heart transplant

'trappola *nf* trap

tra'punta *nf* quilt

'trarre *vt* draw; (ricavare) obtain; **∼ in inganno** deceive

trasa'lire *vi* start

trasan'dato *adj* shabby

trasbor'dare **1** *vt* transfer; Naut tran[s]ship
2 *vi* change

tra'sbordo *nm* trans[s]hipment

trascenden'tale *adj* transcendental

tra'scendere **1** *vt* transcend
2 *vi* (eccedere) go too far

trasci'nare *vt* drag; (fig: entusiasmo) carry away; **∼ e rilasciare** Comput drag and drop

trasci'narsi *vr* drag oneself; (camminare piano) dawdle

tra'scorrere **1** *vt* spend
2 *vi* pass

tra'scritto pp di TRASCRIVERE

tra'scrivere *vt* transcribe

trascrizi'one *nf* transcription

trascu'rabile *adj* negligible

trascu'rare *vt* neglect; (non tenere conto di) disregard

trascurata'mente *adv* carelessly

trascura'tezza *nf* negligence

trascu'rato *adj* negligent; (curato male) neglected; (nel vestire) slovenly

traseco'lato *adj* amazed

trasferi'mento *nm* transfer; (trasloco) move. **trasferimento automatico** direct debit. **trasferimento bancario** bank transfer

trasfe'rire *vt* transfer

trasfe'rirsi *vr* move

tra'sferta *nf* transfer; (indennità) subsistence allowance; Sport away match; **in ∼** ‹impiegato› on secondment; **giocare in ∼** play away

trasfigu'rare *vt* transfigure

trasfor'mare *vt* transform; (in rugby) convert

trasfor'marsi *vr* be transformed; **∼ in** turn into

trasforma'tore *nm* transformer

trasformazi'one *nf* transformation; (in rugby) conversion

trasfor'mista *nmf* (artista) quick-change artist

trasfusi'one *nf* transfusion

trasgre'dire *vt* disobey; Jur infringe

trasgredi'trice *nf* transgressor

trasgressi'one *nf* infringement; (di ordine) failure to obey

trasgres'sivo *adj* intended to shock

trasgres'sore *nm* transgressor

tra'slato *adj* metaphorical

traslitte'rare *vt* transliterate

traslo'care ① *vt* move
② *vi* move [house]

traslo'carsi *vr* move [house]

tra'sloco *nm* move; **compagnia di trasloco** removal company

tra'smesso *pp di* TRASMETTERE

tra'smettere *vt* pass on; TV, Radio broadcast; Techn, Med transmit

trasmetti'tore *nm* transmitter

trasmis'sibile *adj* transmissible

trasmissi'one *nf* transmission; TV, Radio programme. **trasmissione dati** data transmission. **trasmissione via fax** fax transmission. **trasmissione radiofonica** radio programme. **trasmissione remota** remote transmission. **trasmissione televisiva** television programme

trasmit'tente ① *nm* transmitter
② *nf* broadcasting station

traso'gnare *vi* day-dream

traso'gnato *adj* dreamy

traspa'rente *adj* transparent

traspa'renza *nf* transparency; **in ~** against the light

traspa'rire *vi* show [through]

traspi'rare *vi* perspire; fig transpire

traspirazi'one *nf* perspiration

tra'sporre *vt* transpose

traspor'tare *vt* transport; **lasciarsi ~ da** get carried away by; **~ con ponte aereo** airlift

traspor'tato *adj* transported; **~ dall'aria** airborne

trasporta'tore *nm* conveyor; (società) transport company, road haulier

tra'sporto *nm* transport; (fig: passione) passion; **ministro dei trasporti** Ministry of Transport. **trasporto aereo** air freight. **trasporto ferroviario** rail transport. **trasporto pesante** heavy goods transport. **trasporti** *pl* **pubblici** public transport. **trasporto stradale** road transport, road haulage

trastul'lare *vt* amuse

trastul'larsi *vr* amuse oneself; (perdere tempo) fool around

trasu'dare ① *vt* ooze [with]
② *vi* ooze

trasver'sale *adj* transverse; **strada trasversale** cross street

trasversal'mente *adv* widthways

trasvo'lare ① *vt* fly over
② *vi* **~ su** fig skim over

trasvo'lata *nf* crossing [by air]

'tratta *nf* (traffico illegale) trade; Comm draft. **tratta bancaria** Fin banker's draft. **tratta delle bianche** white slave trade. **tratta documentaria** documentary bill

trat'tabile *adj* or nearest offer, o.n.o.

tratta'mento *nm* treatment. **trattamento automatico delle informazioni** electronic data processing, EDP. **trattamento di bellezza** beauty treatment. **trattamento di fine rapporto** severance pay. **trattamento dell'immagine** image processing **trattamento di riguardo** special treatment

trat'tante *adj* conditioning

trat'tare ① *vt* treat; (commerciare in) deal in; (negoziare) negotiate
② *vi* **~ di** deal with

trat'tario *nm* Comm drawee

trat'tarsi *vr* **di che si tratta?** what's it about?; **si tratta di...** it's about...

tratta'tive *nfpl* negotiations; **il tavolo delle ~** the negotiating table

trat'tato *nm* treaty; (opera scritta) treatise. **trattato di pace** peace treaty

tratteggi'are *vt* outline; (descrivere) sketch

tratte'nere *vt* (far restare) keep; hold (respiro, in questura); hold back ‹lacrime, riso›; (frenare) restrain; (da paga) withhold; **sono stato trattenuto** (ritardato) I got held up

tratte'nersi *vr* restrain oneself; (fermarsi) stay; **~ su** (indugiare) dwell on

tratteni'mento *nm* entertainment; (ricevimento) party

tratte'nuta *nf* deduction

trat'tino *nm* dash; (in parole composte) hyphen

'tratto ① *pp di* TRARRE
② *nm* (di spazio, tempo) stretch; (di penna) stroke; (linea) line; (brano) passage; **tratti** *pl* (lineamenti) features; **a tratti** at intervals; **ad un ~** suddenly

trat'tore *nm* tractor

tratto'ria *nf* restaurant

'trauma *nm* trauma

trau'matico *adj* traumatic

traumatiz'zante *adj* traumatic

traumatiz'zare *vt* traumatize

tra'vaglio *nm* labour; (angoscia) anguish

trava'sare *vt* decant

tra'vaso *nm* decanting

trava'tura *nf* beams *pl*

'trave *nf* beam. **trave a sbalzo** cantilever

tra'veggole *nfpl* **avere le ~** be seeing things

'travellers cheque *nm* inv traveller's cheque

t

tra'versa *nf* (nel calcio) crossbar; è una ~ di via Roma it's off via Roma, it crosses via Roma

traver'sare *vt* cross

traver'sata *nf* crossing

traver'sie *nfpl* misfortunes

traver'sina *nf* Rail sleeper

tra'verso ① *adj* crosswise ② *adv* di ~ crossways; **andare di ~** ⟨cibo⟩ go down the wrong way; **camminare di ~** not walk in a straight line; **guardare qualcuno di ~** look askance at somebody; **sapere per vie traverse** *fam* find out indirectly

traver'sone *nm* (in calcio) cross

travesti'mento *nm* disguise

trave'stire *vt* disguise

trave'stirsi *vr* disguise oneself

travesti'tismo *nm* transvestism, crossdressing

trave'stito ① *adj* disguised ② *nm* transvestite

travi'are *vt* lead astray

travisa'mento *nm* distortion

travi'sare *vt* distort

travol'gente *adj* overwhelming

tra'volgere *vt* sweep away; (sopraffare) overwhelm

tra'volto *pp di* TRAVOLGERE

trazi'one *nf* traction. **trazione anteriore/posteriore** front-/rear-wheel drive

tre *adj & nm* three

tre'alberi *nm inv* three-masted ship, three-master

trebbi'are *vt* thresh

trebbia'trice *nf* threshing machine.

'treccia *nf* plait, braid; (in maglia) cable; **a trecce** cable *attrib*

tre'cento *adj & nm* three hundred; **il Trecento** the fourteenth century

tredi'cesima *nf* extra month's salary paid as a Christmas bonus

tredi'cesimo, -a *adj & nm* thirteenth

'tredici *adj & nm* thirteen

'tregua *nf* truce; *fig* respite

'trekking *nm* trekking

tre'mante *adj* trembling, quivering; (per il freddo) shivering

tre'mare *vi* tremble, quiver; (di freddo) shiver

trema'rella *nf fam* jitters *pl*

tremenda'mente *adv* terribly, tremendously

tre'mendo *adj* terrible, tremendous; **ho una fame tremenda** I'm terribly hungry

tremen'tina *nf* turpentine

tre'mila *adj & nm* three thousand

'tremito *nm* tremble, quiver; (per il freddo) shiver

tremo'lare *vi* shake; (luce) flicker

tre'more *nm* trembling

'tremulo *adj* tremulous

tre'nino *nm* miniature railway

'treno *nm* train. **treno merci** freight train, goods train. **treno navetta** shuttle. **treno passeggeri** passenger train. **treno postale** mail train. **treno straordinario** special train

'trenta *adj & nm* thirty. **trenta e lode** Univ ≈ first-class honours

trentatré 'giri *nm inv* LP

tren'tenne *adj & nmf* thirty-year-old

tren'tesimo *adj & nm* thirtieth

tren'tina *nf* una ~ **di** about thirty

trepi'dare *vi* be anxious

'trepido *adj* anxious

treppi'ede *nm* tripod

'tresca *nf* intrigue; ⟨amorosa⟩ affair

'trespolo *nm* perch

triango'lare *adj* triangular

tri'angolo *nm* triangle. **triangolo delle Bermude** Bermuda Triangle. **triangolo equilatero** equilateral triangle. **triangolo isoscele** isosceles triangle. **triangolo rettangolo** right-angled triangle. **triangolo di segnalazione** warning triangle

tri'bale *adj* tribal

tribo'lare *vi* (soffrire) suffer; (fare fatica) go to a lot of trouble

tribolazi'one *nf* suffering

tri'bordo *nm* starboard

tribù *nf inv* tribe

tri'buna *nf* podium, dais; (per uditori) gallery; Sport stand. **tribuna coperta** stand. **tribuna riservata al pubblico** public gallery. **tribuna della stampa** press gallery

tribu'nale *nm* court. **tribunale fallimentare** bankruptcy court. **tribunale minorile** juvenile court. **tribunale penale internazionale** international criminal court, ICC

tribu'tare *vt* bestow, confer

tribu'tario *adj* tax *attrib*

tri'buto *nm* tribute; (tassa) tax

tri'checo *nm* walrus

tri'ciclo *nm* tricycle

trico'lore ① *adj* three-coloured ② *nm* (bandiera) Italian flag

tri'dente *nm* trident

tridimensio'nale *adj* three-dimensional

trien'nale *adj* (ogni tre anni) three-yearly; (lungo tre anni) three-year

tri'ennio *nm* three-year period

tri'fase *adj* three-phase

tri'foglio *nm* clover

trifo'lato *adj* sliced thinly and cooked with olive oil, parsley and garlic

tri'gemino *adj* **parto trigemino** birth of triplets

'triglia *nf* mullet

trigonome'tria *nf* trigonometry, trig *fam*

tri'lingue *adj* trilingual

tril'lare *vi* trill

'trillo *nm* trill

trilo'gia *nf* trilogy

trime'strale *adj* quarterly

tri'mestre *nm* quarter

'trina *nf* lace

trin'cea *nf* trench

trince'rare *vt* entrench

trincia'pollo *nm inv* poultry shears *pl*

trinci'are *vt* cut up

trincia'trice *nf* **trinciatrice di documenti** document shredder

Trini'dad e To'bago *nm* Trinidad and Tobago

Trinità *nf* Trinity

'trio *nm* trio

trion'fale *adj* triumphal

trionfal'mente *adv* triumphantly

trion'fante *adj* triumphant

trion'fare *vi* triumph (**su** over)

tri'onfo *nm* triumph

tri'pletta *nf* Sport hat trick

tripli'care *vt* triple

'triplice *adj* triple; **in ~ [copia]** in triplicate

'triplo ① *adj* treble, triple; **una somma tripla del previsto** an amount three times as much as forecast ② *nm* **il ~ (di)** three times as much (as)

'trippa *nf* tripe; (fam: pancia) belly

tripudi'are *vi* rejoice

tri'pudio *nm* jubilation

tris *nm* (gioco) noughts and crosses, tick-tack-toe Am

'triste *adj* sad; ⟨luogo⟩ gloomy

tri'stezza *nf* sadness; (di luogo) gloominess

'tristo *adj* nasty

trita'carne *nm inv* mincer

tritaghi'accio *nm inv* ice-crusher

tri'tare *vt* mince

trita'tutto *nm inv* (elettrico) [food] processor

'trito *adj* **~ e ritrito** well-worn, trite

tri'tolo *nm* TNT

tri'tone *nm* (mitologia) Triton; Zool newt

'trittico *nm* triptych

trit'tongo *nm* triphthong

tritu'rare *vt* chop finely

triumvi'rato *nm* triumvirate

tri'vella *nf* drill

trivel'lare *vt* drill

trivi'ale *adj* vulgar

tro'feo *nm* trophy

troglo'dita *nmf* (preistoria) cave-dweller; fig Neanderthal

'trogolo *nm* (per maiali) trough

'troia *nf* sow; vulg bitch; (sessuale) whore

'tromba *nf* trumpet; Auto horn; **partire in ~** dive in head first. **tromba d'aria** whirlwind. **tromba di Eustachio** Eustachian tube. **tromba di Falloppio** Fallopian tube. **tromba delle scale** stairwell

trom'bare ① *vt* vulg bonk; (fam: in esame) fail
② *vi* vulg bonk

trom'betta *nm* toy trumpet

trombetti'ere *nm* bugler

trombet'tista *nmf* trumpet-player

trom'bone *nm* trombone

trom'bosi *nf inv* thrombosis. **trombosi coronarica** coronary thrombosis. **trombosi venosa profonda** deep-vein thrombosis, DVT

tron'care *vt* sever; truncate ⟨parola⟩

tron'chese *nm* wire cutters *pl*

tronche'sino *nm* (per le unghie) nail clippers *pl*

tron'chetto *nm* **tronchetto natalizio** Yule log

'tronco ① *adj* truncated; **licenziare in ~** fire on the spot
② *nm* trunk; (di strada) section. **tronco d'albero** tree trunk. **tronco di cono** truncated cone

tron'cone *nm* stump

troneggi'are *vi* **~ su** tower over

'trono *nm* throne

tropi'cale *adj* tropical

'tropico *nm* tropic. **tropico del Cancro** Tropic of Cancer. **tropico del Capricorno** Tropic of Capricorn. **tropici** *pl* Tropics

'troppo ① *adj* too much; (con nomi plurali) too many
② *pron* too much; (plurale) too many; (troppo tempo) too long; **troppi** (troppa gente) too many people; **me ne hai dato ~** you gave me too much
③ *adv* too; (con verbi) too much; **~ stanco** too tired; **ho mangiato ~** I ate too much; **hai fame? –non ~** are you hungry? –not very; **sentirsi di ~** feel unwanted

'trota *nf* trout. **trota di mare** sea trout. **trota salmonata** salmon trout

trot'tare *vi* trot

trotterel'lare *vi* trot along; ⟨*bambino*⟩ toddle

'**trotto** *nm* trot; **andare al** ∼ trot

'**trottola** *nf* [spinning] top; (movimento) spin

troupe *nf inv* **troupe televisiva** camera crew

trousse *nf inv* (per trucco) make-up bag

tro'vare *vt* find; (scoprire) find out; (incontrare) meet; (ritenere) think; **andare a** ∼ go to see

trova'robe *nmf* (persona) props *sg*

tro'varsi *vr* find oneself; (luogo) be; (sentirsi) feel

tro'vata *nf* bright idea. **trovata pubblicitaria** advertising gimmick, publicity stunt

trova'tello, **-a** *nmf* foundling

truc'care *vt* make up; cook ⟨*libri contabili*⟩; soup up ⟨*motore*⟩; rig ⟨*partita, elezioni*⟩

truc'carsi *vr* put one's make-up on

truc'cato *adj* made-up; ⟨*libri contabili*⟩ cooked; ⟨*partita, elezioni*⟩ rigged; ⟨*motore*⟩ souped up

trucca|'**tore**, **-trice** *nmf* make-up artist

'**trucco** *nm* (cosmetici) make-up; (imbroglio) trick; **trucchi** *pl* **del mestiere** tricks of the trade

'**truce** *adj* fierce; ⟨*delitto*⟩ savage

truci'dare *vt* slay

trucio'lato *nm* chipboard

tru'ciolo *nm* shaving

trucu'lento *adj* ⟨*delitto*⟩ savage; ⟨*film*⟩ violent

'**truffa** *nf* fraud

truf'fare *vt* defraud

truffa|'**tore**, **-trice** *nmf* fraudster

'**trullo** *nm* traditional house with a conical roof found in Apulia

'**truppa** *nf* troops *pl*; (gruppo) group; **truppe** *pl* **d'assalto** assault troops; **truppe** *pl* **di terra** ground troops

T-shirt *nf inv* tee-shirt, T-shirt

tu *pers pron* you; **sei tu?** is that you?; **l'hai fatto tu?** did you do it yourself?; **a tu per tu** in private; **darsi del tu** use the familiar tu to each other

'**tua** ▸ TUO

'**tuba** *nf* Mus tuba; (cappello) top hat

tu'bare *vi* coo; ⟨*innamorati*⟩ bill and coo

tuba'tura *nf* piping

tubazi'one *nf* piping; **tubazioni** *pl* piping *sg*, pipes

tuberco'lina *nf* tuberculin

tuberco'losi *nf* tuberculosis

'**tubero** *nm* tuber

tube'rosa *nf* tuberose

tu'betto *nm* tube. **tubetto di colore** tube of paint

tu'bino *nm* (vestito) shift; (cappello) bowler; derby Am

'**tubo** *nm* pipe; Anat canal; **non ho capito un** ∼ **fam** I understood zilch. **tubo digerente** alimentary canal. **tubo a raggi catodici** cathode-ray tube. **tubo di scappamento** exhaust [pipe]. **tubo di scarico** waste pipe

tubo'lare *adj* tubular

'**tue** ▸ TUO

tuf'fare *vt* plunge

tuf'farsi *vr* dive; '**vietato** ∼' 'no diving'

tuffa|'**tore**, **-trice** *nmf* diver

'**tuffo** *nm* dive; (bagno) dip; **ho avuto un** ∼ **al cuore** my heart leapt into my mouth. **tuffo di testa** dive

'**tufo** *nm* tufa

tu'gurio *nm* hovel

tuli'pano *nm* tulip

'**tulle** *nm* tulle

tume'fatto *adj* swollen

tumefazi'one *nf* swelling

'**tumido** *adj* swollen

tu'more *nm* tumour. **tumore benigno** benign tumour. **tumore del collo dell'utero** cervical cancer. **tumore maligno** malignant tumour

tumulazi'one *nf* burial

'**tumulo** *nm* (di pietre) cairn

tu'multo *nm* turmoil; (sommossa) riot

tumultu'oso *adj* tumultuous

tung'steno *nm* tungsten

'**tunica** *nf* tunic

Tuni'sia *nf* Tunisia

tuni'sino *adj* & *nmf* Tunisian

'**tunnel** *nm inv* tunnel. **tunnel sotto la Manica** Channel Tunnel

'**tuo** ⓵ (**il** ∼ *m*, **la tua** *f*, **i tuoi** *mpl*, **le tue** *fpl*) *poss adj* your; **è tua questa macchina?** is this car yours?; **un** ∼ **amico** a friend of yours; ∼ **padre** your father ⓶ *poss pron* yours; **i tuoi** your folk

tu'oi ▸ TUO

tuo'nare *vi* thunder

tu'ono *nm* thunder

tu'orlo *nm* yolk

tu'racciolo *nm* stopper; (di sughero) cork

tu'rare *vt* block; cork ⟨*bottiglia*⟩

tu'rarsi *vr* become blocked; ∼ **le orecchie** stick one's fingers in one's ears; ∼ **il naso** hold one's nose

'**turba** *nf* (folla) rabble. **turba psichica** mental illness

turba'mento *nm* disturbance; (sconvolgimento) upsetting. **turbamento della quiete pubblica** breach of the peace

tur'bante *nm* turban

tur'bare *vt* upset

tur'barsi *vr* get upset

tur'bato *adj* upset

tur'bina *nf* turbine

turbi'nare *vi* whirl

'turbine *nm* whirl. **turbine di polvere** dust storm. **turbine di vento** whirlwind

'turbo *nm inv* turbo

turbocompres'sore *nm* Tech turbocharger

turbo'lento *adj* turbulent

turbo'lenza *nf* turbulence

turboreat'tore *nm* turbo-jet

tur'chese *adj & nmf* turquoise

Tur'chia *nf* Turkey

tur'chino *adj & nm* deep blue

'turco, -a ① *adj* Turkish ② *nmf* Turk; **fumare come un** ∼ smoke like a chimney; **bestemmiare come un** ∼ swear like a trooper ③ *nm* (lingua) Turkish; fig double Dutch

'turgido *adj* turgid

tu'rismo *nm* tourism

tu'rista *nmf* tourist

tu'ristico *adj* tourist *attrib*

tur'nista *nmf* shift-worker

'turno *nm* turn; **a** ∼ in turn; **fare a** ∼ take turns; **fare i turni** work shifts; **di** ∼ on duty. **turno eliminatorio** heat. **turno di giorno** day shift. **turno di guardia** guard duty. **turno di lavoro** shift. **turno di notte** night shift; **del turno di notte** night shift *attrib*; **fare il turno di notte** be on night shift

'turpe *adj* base

turpi'loquio *nm* foul language

'tuta *nf* overalls *pl*; **tuta da ginnastica** tracksuit. **tuta da lavoro** overalls *pl*. **tuta mimetica** camouflage. **tuta da sci** ski suit. **tuta spaziale** spacesuit. **tuta subacquea** wetsuit

tu'tela *nf* Jur guardianship; (protezione) protection. **tutela dell'ambiente** environmental protection

tute'lare *vt* protect

tu'tina *nf* sleepsuit; (da danza) leotard

tu|'tore, -trice *nmf* guardian

'tutta *nf* mettercela ∼ per fare qualcosa go flat out for something

tutta'via *conj* nevertheless, still

'tutto ① *adj* whole; (con nomi plurali) all; (ogni) every; **tutta la classe** the whole class, all the class; **tutti gli alunni** all the pupils; **a tutta velocità** at full speed; **ho aspettato** ∼ **il giorno** I waited all day [long]; **vestito di** ∼ **punto** all kitted out; **in** ∼ **il mondo** all over the world; **noi tutti** all of us; **era tutta contenta** she was delighted; **tutti e due** both; **tutti e tre** all three ② *pron* all; (tutte le cose) everything; (qualunque cosa) anything; **c'è ancora del dolce?** –no, **l'ho mangiato** ∼ is there still some cake? –no, I ate it all; **le finestre sono pulite, le ho lavate tutte** the windows are clean, I washed them all; **raccontami** ∼ tell me everything; **tutti** (tutta la gente) everybody; **lo sanno tutti** everybody knows; **è capace di** ∼ he's capable of anything; ∼ **compreso** all in; **del** ∼ quite; **in** ∼ altogether ③ *adv* completely; **tutt'a un tratto** all at once; **tutt'altro** not at all; **tutt'altro che...** anything but... ④ *nm* whole; **tentare il** ∼ **per** ∼ go for broke; ∼ **cómpreso** all-inclusive; ∼ **esaurito** Theat full house

tutto'fare *adj inv & nmf inv* **[impiegato] tuttofare** general handyman

tut'tora *adv* still

tutù *nm inv* tutu; (lungo) ballet dress

tv *nf inv* TV. **tv via cavo** cable TV. **tv digitale** digital (television) **tv interattiva** interactive TV

tweed *nm* tweed

Uu

ubbidi'ente *adj* obedient

ubbidiente'mente *adv* obediently

ubbidi'enza *nf* obedience

ubbi'dire *vi* ∼ (a) obey

ubi'cato *adj* located

ubicazi'one *nf* location

ubiquità *nf* **non ho il dono dell'**∼ I can't be in two places at once

ubria'care *vt* get drunk

ubria'carsi *vr* get drunk; ∼ **di** fig become intoxicated with

ubria'chezza *nf* drunkenness; **in stato di** ∼ inebriated; **in stato di** ∼ **molesta** drunk and disorderly

ubri'aco, **-a** ① *adj* drunk. **ubriaco fradicio** dead *or* blind drunk ② *nmf* drunk

ubria'cone ① *nm* drunkard ② *adj* un marito ~ a drunkard of a husband

uccelli'era *nf* aviary

uccel'lino *nm* baby bird

uc'cello *nm* bird; (vulg: pene) cock. **uccello acquatico** water fowl. **uccello da cacciagione** game bird. **uccello del malaugurio** bird of ill omen. **uccello notturno** night *or* nocturnal bird. **uccello del paradiso** bird of paradise. **uccello di passo** bird of passage. **uccello rapace** bird of prey

uc'cidere *vt* kill

uc'cidersi *vr* kill oneself; (morire) be killed

+uccio *suff* boccuccia *nf* pretty little mouth; calduccio *nm* cosy warmth; c'è un bel calduccio it's nice and cosy; tesoruccio *nm* sweetie; avvocatuccio *nm* pej small town lawyer; cosuccia *nf* trifle; è una cosuccia da niente it's nothing; doloruccio *nm* twinge; vestituccio *nm* pej skimpy little dress

uccisi'one *nf* killing

uc'ciso *pp di* UCCIDERE

ucci'sore *nm* killer

U'craina *nf* l' ~ the Ukraine

u'craino, **-a** *adj & nmf* Ukrainian

u'dente *adj* i non udenti the hearing-impaired

u'dibile *adj* audible

udi'enza *nf* audience; (colloquio) interview; Jur hearing. **udienza a porte chiuse** hearing in camera

u'dire *vt* hear

udi'tivo *adj* auditory

u'dito *nm* hearing

udi'|tore, **-trice** *nmf* listener; Sch unregistered student (allowed to sit in on lectures)

udi'torio *nm* audience

UE *abbr* (**Unione Europea**) EU

uff *int* phew!

'uffa *int* (con impazienza) come on!; (con tono seccato) damn!

uffici'ale ① *adj* official ② *nm* officer; (funzionario) official; **pubblico ufficiale** public official. **ufficiale dell'esercito** army officer. **ufficiale giudiziario** clerk of the court. **ufficiale sanitario** health officer. **ufficiale dello Stato civile** registrar

ufficialità *nf* official status

ufficializ'zare *vt* make official, officialize

ufficial'mente *adv* officially

uf'ficio *nm* office; (dovere) duty; (reparto) department; **andare in** ~ go to the office. **ufficio acquisti** purchasing department. **ufficio cambi** bureau de change, exchange bureau. **ufficio di collocamento** employment office, jobcentre Br. **Ufficio Dazi e Dogana** Customs and Excise. **ufficio funebre** Relig funeral service. **ufficio delle imposte** tax office. **ufficio informazioni** information office. **ufficio di informazioni turistiche** tourist information office *or* centre. **ufficio oggetti smarriti** lost property office, lost and found Am. **ufficio del personale** personnel department. **ufficio postale** post office. **ufficio prenotazioni** advance booking office. **ufficio della redazione** newspaper office. **ufficio del turismo** tourist office. **ufficio turistico** tourist office

ufficiosa'mente *adv* unofficially

uffici'oso *adj* unofficial, off-the-record

'ufo[1] *nm inv* UFO

'ufo[2] a ~ *adv* without paying

ufolo'gia *nf* ufology

U'ganda *nf* Uganda

ugan'dese *adj & nmf* Ugandan

uggiosità *nf* dullness

uggi'oso *adj* boring

uguagli'anza *nf* equality

uguagli'are *vt* make equal; (essere uguale) equal; (livellare) level

uguagli'arsi *vr* ~ a compare oneself to

ugu'ale ① *adj* equal; (lo stesso) the same; (simile) like; **due più due è** ~ **a quattro** two plus two equals four ② *nm* Math equals sign; **che non ha** ~ unequalled

ugual'mente *adv* equally; (malgrado tutto) all the same

'ulcera *nf* ulcer. **ulcera gastrica** gastric ulcer. **ulcera peptica** peptic ulcer

u'liva *nf* ▶ OLIVA

uli'veto *nm* olive grove

u'livo *nm* olive[-tree]

'ulna *nf* Anat ulna

ulteri'ore *adj* further

ulterior'mente *adv* further

ultima'mente *adv* lately

ulti'mare *vt* complete

ulti'matum *nm inv* ultimatum

ulti'missime *nfpl* Journ stop press, latest news *sg*

'ultimo ① *adj* last; ⟨notizie ecc⟩ latest; (più lontano) farthest; fig ultimate; ⟨prezzo⟩ rockbottom; l' ~ **piano** the top floor ② *nm* last; **fino all'** ~ to the last; **per** ~ at the end

ultimo'genito, **-a** *nmf* last-born

ultrà *nmf inv* Sport fanatical supporter
ultraleg'gero *nm* (aereo) microlight
ultramo'derno *adj* ultra-modern
ultrapi'atto *adj* ultra-thin
ultrapo'tente *adj* extra-strong
ultra'rapido *adj* extra-fast
ultraresi'stente *adj* extra-strong
ultrasen'sibile *adj* ultrasensitive
ultra'sonico *adj* ultrasonic
ultrasu'ono *nm* ultrasound
ultrater'reno *adj* ⟨vita⟩ after death
ultravio'letto *adj* ultraviolet
ulu'lare *vi* howl
ulu'lato *nm* howling; **gli ululati** the howls, the howling
umana'mente *adv* ⟨trattare⟩ humanely; ~ **impossibile** not humanly possible
uma'nesimo *nm* humanism
uma'nista *nmf* humanist
umanità *nf* humanity
umani'tario *adj* humanitarian
u'mano *adj* human; (benevolo) humane
'Umbria *nf* Umbria
'umbro, -a *adj & nmf* Umbrian
umet'tare *vt* moisten
umidifica'tore *nm* humidifier
umidità *nf* dampness; (di clima) humidity
'umido ➊ *adj* damp; ⟨clima⟩ humid; ⟨mani, occhi⟩ moist
➋ *nm* dampness; **in** ~ Culin stewed
umile *adj* humble
umili'ante *adj* humiliating
umili'are *vt* humiliate
umili'arsi *vr* humble oneself
umiliazi'one *nf* humiliation
umil'mente *adv* humbly
umiltà *nf* humility
u'more *nm* humour; (stato d'animo) mood; **di cattivo/buon** ~ in a bad/good mood
umo'rismo *nm* humour
umo'rista *nmf* humorist
umoristica'mente *adv* humorously
umo'ristico *adj* humorous
un ▶ UNO
un' ▶ UNO
'una ▶ UNO
u'nanime *adj* unanimous
unanime'mente *adv* unanimously
unanimità *nf* unanimity; **all'** ~ unanimously
unci'nare *vt* hook
unci'nato *adj* hooked; ⟨parentesi⟩ angle *attrib*
unci'netto *nm* crochet hook
un'cino *nm* hook
undi'cenne *adj & nmf* eleven-year-old

undi'cesimo *adj & nm* eleventh
'undici *adj & nm* eleven
'ungere *vt* grease; (sporcare) get greasy; Relig anoint; (blandire) flatter
'ungersi *vr* (con olio solare) oil oneself; ~ **le mani** get one's hands greasy
unghe'rese ➊ *adj & nmf* Hungarian
➋ *nm* (lingua) Hungarian
Unghe'ria *nf* Hungary
'unghia *nf* nail; (di animale) claw; **cadere sotto le unghie di qualcuno** fall into somebody's clutches. **unghia fessa** cloven hoof
unghi'ata *nf* (graffio) scratch
ungu'ento *nm* ointment
unica'mente *adv* only
unicellu'lare *adj* single-cell, unicellular
unicità *nf* uniqueness
'unico *adj* only; (singolo) single; (incomparabile) unique
uni'corno *nm* unicorn
unidimensio'nale *adj* one-dimensional
unidirezio'nale *adj* unidirectional
unifamili'are *adj* one-family
unifi'care *vt* unify
unificazi'one *nf* unification
unifor'mare *vt* level
unifor'marsi *vr* conform (a to)
uni'forme ➊ *adj* uniform
➋ *nf* uniform. **uniforme di gala** Mil mess dress
uniformità *nf* uniformity
unilate'rale *adj* unilateral
unilateral'mente *adv* unilaterally
uninomi'nale *adj* Pol single-candidate
uni'one *nf* union; (armonia) unity; **Unione economica e monetaria** Economic and Monetary Union. **Unione Europea** European Union. **Unione Monetaria Europea** European Monetary Union. **unione sindacale** trade union, labor union Am. **Unione Sovietica** Soviet Union
unio'nista *nmf* Pol Unionist
u'nire *vt* unite; (collegare) join; blend ⟨colori ecc⟩
u'nirsi *vr* unite; (collegarsi) join
'unisex *adj inv* unisex
u'nisono *nm* **all'** ~ in unison
unità *nf inv* unity; (Math, Mil, reparto ecc) unit; Comput drive. **unità di archivio dati** data storage device. **unità di backup a nastro** Comput tape backup drive. **unità centrale di elaborazione** Comput central processing unit, CPU. **unità floppy disk** Comput floppy disk drive. **unità di inizializzazione** Comput boot drive. **unità di memoria di massa** Comput mass storage device. **unità di misura** unit of measurement. ·····❯

unità a nastro magnetico Comput tapedrive. **unità periferica** Comput peripheral. **unità di produzione** factory unit. **unità socio-sanitaria locale** local health centre. **unità di visualizzazione** Comput visual display unit, VDU

uni'tario *adj* unitary; **prezzo unitario** unit price

u'nito *adj* united; ⟨tinta⟩ plain; ⟨comunità⟩ tight-knit

univer'sale *adj* universal

universaliz'zare *vt* universalize

universal'mente *adv* universally

università *nf inv* university

universi'tario, -a ① *adj* university *attrib*
② *nmf* (docente) university lecturer; (studente) undergraduate

uni'verso *nm* universe

u'nivoco *adj* unambiguous

uno, -a ① *art indef* a; (davanti a vocale o h muta) an; **un esempio** an example;
② *pron* one; **a ~ a ~** one by one; **~ alla volta** one at a time; **l'~ e l'altro** both [of them]; **né l'~ né l'altro** neither [of them]; **~ di noi** one of us; **~ fa quello che può** you do what you can
③ *adj* a, one
④ *nm* (numerale) one; (un tale) some man
⑤ *nf* some woman

'unto ① *pp* ▶ di UNGERE
② *adj* greasy
③ *nm* grease

untu'oso *adj* greasy

unzi'one *nf* **l'Estrema Unzione** Extreme Unction, last rites

u'omo *nm* (pl **uomini**) man; 'uomini' (bagni) 'gents', 'men's room'. **uomo d'affari** business man. **uomo di colore** black man. **uomo di fiducia** right-hand man. **uomo di mondo** man of the world. **uomo-oggetto** toy boy. **uomo delle pulizie** cleaner; **uomo sandwich** sandwich-man. **uomo di Stato** statesman. **uomo della strada** man on the street

u'ovo *nm* (pl f **uova**) egg; **uova** *pl* eggs; **uova al bacon** bacon and eggs. **uovo barzotto** o **bazzotto** soft-boiled egg. **uovo in camicia** poached egg. **uovo di Colombo** obvious simple solution. **uovo all'occhio di bue** fried egg. **uovo all'ostrica** raw egg. **uovo di Pasqua** Easter egg. **uova** *pl* **al prosciutto** ham and eggs. **uovo sodo** hard-boiled egg. **uovo strapazzato** scrambled egg. **uovo al tegamino** fried egg

upgra'dabile *adj* upgradeable

'upupa *nf inv* hoopoe

ura'gano *nm* hurricane

u'ranio *nm* uranium

U'rano *nm* Uranus

urba'nesimo *nm* urbanization

urba'nista *nmf* town planner

urba'nistica *nf* town planning

urba'nistico *adj* urban

urbaniz'zare *vt* urbanize

urbanizzazi'one *nf* urbanization

ur'bano *adj* urban; (cortese) urbane

u'rea *nf* urea

u'retra *nf* Anat urethra

ur'gente *adj* urgent

urgente'mente *adv* urgently

ur'genza *nf* urgency; **in caso d'~** in an emergency; **d'~** ⟨misura, chiamata⟩ emergency *attrib*; **operare d'~** perform an emergency operation on

'urgere *vi* be urgent

u'rina *nf* urine

uri'nare *vi* urinate

ur'lare *vi* shout, yell; ⟨cane, vento⟩ howl

'urlo *nm* (pl m **urli**, pl f **urla**) shout; (di cane, vento) howling

'urna *nf* urn; (elettorale) ballot box; **andare alle urne** go to the polls

urrà *int* hurrah!

URSS *nf abbr* (**Unione delle Repubbliche Socialiste Sovietiche**) USSR

ur'tare *vt* knock against; (scontrarsi) bump into; fig irritate

ur'tarsi *vr* collide; fig clash

'urto *nm* knock; (scontro) crash; (contrasto) conflict; fig clash; **d'~** ⟨misure, terapia⟩ shock

Uru'guay *nm* Uruguay

U.S.A. *nmpl* US[A] *sg*

usa e getta *adj inv* ⟨rasoio, siringa⟩ throw-away, disposable

u'sanza *nf* custom; (moda) fashion

u'sare ① *vt* use; (impiegare) employ; (esercitare) exercise; **~ fare qualcosa** be in the habit of doing something
② *vi* (essere di moda) be fashionable; **non si usa più** it is out of fashion; ⟨attrezzatura, espressione⟩ it's not used any more

u'sato ① *adj* used; (non nuovo) second-hand
② *nm* second-hand goods *pl*; **dell'~** second-hand

u'sbeco, -a *adj & nmf* Uzbekistani

u'scente *adj* ⟨presidente⟩ outgoing

usci'ere *nm* usher

'uscio *nm* door

u'scire *vi* come out; (andare fuori) go out; (sfuggire) get out; (essere sorteggiato) come up; ⟨giornale⟩ come out; **~ da** Comput exit from, quit; **~ di strada** leave the road

u'scita *nf* exit, way out; (spesa) outlay; (di autostrada) junction; (battuta) witty remark;

(in ginnastica artistica) dismount; **uscite** pl Fin outgoings; **essere in libera** ∼ be off duty. **uscita di servizio** back door. **uscita di sicurezza** emergency exit, fire exit

usi'gnolo nm nightingale

'uso nm use; (abitudine) custom; (usanza) usage; **fuori** ∼ out of use; **per** ∼ **esterno** ⟨medicina⟩ for external use only. **uso e dosi** use and dosage

us'saro nm hussar

U.S.S.L. nf abbr (**Unità Socio-Sanitaria Locale**) local health centre

ustio'narsi vr burn oneself

ustio'nato, -a ① nmf burns case ② adj burnt

usti'one nf burn; **ustioni di primo grado** first-degree burns

usu'ale adj usual

usual'mente adv usually

usucapi'one nf Jur usucaption

usufru'ire vi ∼ **di** take advantage of, make use of

usu'frutto nm Jur use, usufruct fml

usufruttu'ario, -a nmf user, usufructuary fml

u'sura nf usury

usu'raio nm usurer

usur'pare vt usurp

usurpa|'tore, -trice nmf usurper

u'tensile nm tool; Culin utensil; **cassetta degli utensili** tool box; **utensili** pl **da cucina** kitchen utensils

u'tente nmf user. **utente finale** end user. **utenti** pl **della strada** road users

u'tenza nf use; (utenti) users pl. **utenza finale** end users pl

ute'rino adj uterine

'utero nm womb

'utile ① adj useful ② nm Comm profit; **unire l'**∼ **al dilettevole** combine business with pleasure. **utile su cambi** foreign exchange gain. **utile sul capitale investito** return on investment

utilità nf usefulness, utility; Comput utility

utili'tario, -a ① adj utilitarian ② nf Auto small car

utilita'ristico adj utilitarian

u'tility nm inv utility

utiliz'zare vt utilize

utilizzazi'one nf utilization

uti'lizzo nm use

util'mente adv usefully

Uto'pia nf Utopia

uto'pista nmf Utopian

uto'pistico adj Utopian

UVA nmpl abbr (**ultravioletto prossimo**) UV

'uva nf grapes pl; chicco d'uva grape. **uva bianca** white grapes. **uva nera** black grapes. **uva passa** raisins pl. **uva sultanina** currants pl. **uva da tavola** [eating] grapes. **uva da vino** wine grapes

u'vetta nf raisins pl

uxori'cida ① nm wife-killer, uxoricide fml ② nf husband-killer

Uzbeki'stan nm Uzbekistan

Vv

va' ▶ ANDARE

va'cante adj vacant

va'canza nf holiday, vacation Am; [giorno di] ∼ holiday; (posto vacante) vacancy; **vacanze** pl holidays, vacation Am; Univ vacation, vac fam; **essere in** ∼ be on holiday/vacation; **prendersi una** ∼ take a holiday/vacation; **andare in** ∼ go on holiday/vacation; **è** ∼ it's a holiday. **vacanza avventura** adventure holiday **vacanze** pl **estive** summer holidays/vacation; **vacanze** pl **di Natale** Christmas holidays/vacation; **vacanze** pl **di Pasqua** Easter holidays/vacation; **vacanze** pl **scolastiche** school holidays/vacation

vacan'ziere, -a nmf vacationer Am, holidaymaker Br

'vacca nf cow. **vacca da latte** dairy cow

vac'caro, -a nf cowherd

vacci'nare vt vaccinate; **farsi** ∼ get vaccinated

vaccinazi'one nf vaccination

vac'cino nm vaccine

vacil'lante adj tottering; ⟨oggetto⟩ wobbly; ⟨luce⟩ flickering; fig wavering, faltering

vacil'lare vi totter; ⟨oggetto⟩ wobble; ⟨luce⟩ flicker; fig waver

'vacuo ① adj (vano) vain; fig empty ② nm vacuum

'vado ▶ ANDARE

vaffan'culo int vulg fuck off!

vagabon'daggio *nm* Jur vagrancy

vagabon'dare *vi* wander

vaga'bondo ① *adj* ‹cane› stray ② *nmf* tramp

vaga'mente *adv* vaguely

va'gante *adj* wandering; **mina vagante** floating mine; **proiettile vagante** stray bullet

va'gare *vi* wander

vagheggi'are *vt* long for

va'ghezza *nf* vagueness

va'gina *nf* vagina

vagi'nale *adj* vaginal

va'gire *vi* whimper

va'gito *nm* whimper

'vaglia *nm inv* money order. **vaglia bancario** bank draft. **vaglia cambiario** promissory note. **vaglia internazionale** international money order. **vaglia postale** postal order

vagli'are *vt* sift; fig weigh

'vaglio *nm* sieve

'vago *adj* vague

vagon'cino *nm* (di funivia) car. **vagoncino a piattaforma** flat[bed] wagon

va'gone *nm* (per passeggeri) carriage, car; (per merci) truck, wagon. **vagone bagagliaio** luggage van, baggage car Am. **vagone ferroviario** railway carriage Br, railroad car Am **vagone frigorifero** refrigerator van. **vagone letto** sleeper. **vagone postale** mail coach. **vagone ristorante** restaurant car, dining car

vai'olo *nm* smallpox

va'langa *nf* avalanche

val'chiria *nf* Valkyrie

val'dese *adj & nmf* Waldensian

va'lente *adj* skilful

va'lenza *nf* Chem valency; (fig: valore) value

va'lere ① *vi* be worth; (contare) count; ‹regola› apply (**per** to); (essere valido) be valid; **far ~ i propri diritti** assert one's rights; **farsi ~** assert oneself; **non vale!** that's not fair!; **tanto vale che me ne vada** I might as well go ② *vt* **~ qualcosa a qualcuno** (procurare) earn somebody something; **valerne la pena** be worth it; **vale la pena di vederlo** it's worth seeing; **valersi di** avail oneself of

valeri'ana *nf* valerian

va'lersi *vr* **valersi di** avail oneself of

va'levole *adj* valid

'valgo *adj* **alluce valgo** hallux valgus; **ginocchia** *pl* **valghe** knock knees

vali'care *vt* cross

'valico *nm* pass

valida'mente *adv* validly; (efficacemente) efficiently; ‹contribuire› effectively

validità *nf* validity; **con ~ illimitata** valid indefinitely

'valido *adj* valid; (efficace) efficient; ‹contributo› valuable

valige'ria *nf* (fabbrica) leather factory; (negozio) leather goods shop

vali'getta *nf* small case; (per attrezzi) box. **valigetta del pronto soccorso** first aid kit. **valigetta ventiquattrore** overnight bag

va'ligia *nf* suitcase; **fare le valigie** pack; fig pack one's bags. **valigia diplomatica** diplomatic bag

val'lata *nf* valley

'valle *nf* valley; **a ~** downstream

val'letta *nf* TV assistant

val'letto *nm* valet; TV assistant

'vallo *nm* wall; **il ~ di Adriano** Hadrian's Wall

val'lone[1] *nm* (valle) deep valley

val'lone[2], **-a** *adj & nmf* Walloon

va'lore *nm* value, worth; (merito) merit; (coraggio) valour; **valori** *pl* Comm securities; **di ~** (oggetto) valuable; **oggetti di valore** valuables; **di grande ~** of great value; ‹medico, scienziato› top *attrib*; **senza ~** worthless; **a ~ aggiunto** value-added. **valore bollato** revenue stamp. **valore contabile** book value. **valore effettivo** real value. **valore di mercato** market value, street value. **valore mobiliare** security. **valore nominale** nominal value. **valore di realizzo** break-up value. **valore di riscatto** surrender value

valoriz'zare *vt* (mettere in valore) use to advantage; (aumentare di valore) increase the value of; (migliorare l'aspetto di) enhance

valoriz'zarsi *vr* **il paese ha bisogno di ~ migliorando...** the country needs to enhance the value of its assets by improving...

valorosa'mente *adv* courageously

valo'roso *adj* courageous

'valso pp di VALERE

va'luta *nf* currency. **valuta a corso legale** legal tender. **valuta estera** foreign currency

valu'tare *vt* value; weigh up ‹situazione›

valu'tario *adj* ‹mercato, norme› currency *attrib*

valuta'tivo *adj* for evaluation, evaluative

valutazi'one *nf* valuation

'valva *nf* valve

'valvola *nf* valve; Electr fuse. **valvola a farfalla** butterfly valve. **valvola pneumatica** air valve. **valvola di sicurezza** anche fig safety valve

'valzer *nm inv* waltz

vamp *nf inv* vamp

vam'pata *nf* blaze; (di calore) blast; (al viso) flush

vam'piro *nm* vampire; fig bloodsucker

va'nadio *nm* vanadium

vanaglori'oso *adj* vainglorious

vana'mente *adv* (inutilmente) in vain; (con vanità) vainly

van'dalico *adj* atto ∼ act of vandalism

vanda'lismo *nm* vandalism

vandalizzare *vt* vandalize

vandalizzazione *nf* vandalizing

'vandalo, -a *nmf* vandal

vaneggia'mento *nm* delirium

vaneggi'are *vi* rave

va'nesio *adj* conceited

'vanga *nf* spade

van'gare *vt* dig

van'gata *nf* (quantità) spadeful; (azione) blow with a spade

van'gelo *nm* Gospel; (fam; verità) gospel [truth]

vanifi'care *vt* nullify

va'niglia *nf* vanilla

vanigli'ato *adj* ⟨zucchero⟩ vanilla

vanil'lina *nf* vanillin

vanità *nf* vanity

vanitosa'mente *adv* vainly

vani'toso *adj* vain

'vano ① *adj* vain
② *nm* (stanza) room; (spazio vuoto) hollow. **vano doccia** shower room. **vano portabagagli** Auto boot, trunk Am

van'taggio *nm* advantage; Sport lead; Tennis advantage; **trarre ∼ da qualcosa** derive benefit from something

vantaggiosa'mente *adv* advantageously

vantaggi'oso *adj* advantageous

van'tare *vt* praise; (possedere) boast

van'tarsi *vr* boast

vante'ria *nf* boasting; **vanterie** *pl* boasting

'vanto *nm* boast

'vanvera *nf* a ∼ at random; **parlare a ∼** talk nonsense

va'pore *nm* steam; (di benzina, cascata) vapour; **a ∼** steam *attrib*; **al ∼** Culin steamed; **battello a vapore** steamboat. **vapore acqueo** steam, water vapour

vapo'retto *nm* ferry

vapori'era *nf* steam engine

vaporiz'zare *vt* vaporize

vaporizza'tore *nm* spray

vapo'roso *adj* ⟨vestito⟩ filmy; **capelli** *pl* **vaporosi** big hair

va'rano *nm* monitor [lizard]

va'rare *vt* launch

var'care *vt* cross

'varco *nm* passage; **aspettare al ∼** lie in wait

vare'china *nf* bleach

vari'abile ① *adj* changeable, variable
② *nf* Math variable

variabilità *nf* changeableness, variability

varia'mente *adv* variously

vari'ante *nf* variant

vari'are *vt/i* vary; **∼ di umore** change one's mood

vari'ato *adj* varied

variazi'one *nf* variation

va'rice *nf* varicose vein

vari'cella *nf* chickenpox

vari'coso *adj* varicose

varie'gato *adj* variegated

varietà ① *nf inv* variety
② *nm inv* variety show

'vario *adj* varied; **vari** (parecchi) various, several; **varie ed eventuali** any other business

vario'pinto *adj* multicoloured

'varo *nm* launch

Var'savia Warsaw

vasaio *nm* potter

'vasca *nf* tub; (piscina) pool; (lunghezza) length. **vasca da bagno** bath. **vasca con idromassaggio** whirlpool bath. **vasca di sviluppo** Phot developing tank

va'scello *nm* vessel; **capitano di vascello** captain

va'schetta *nf* tub; Phot tray. **vaschetta per il ghiaccio** ice-tray

vasco'lare *adj* Anat, Bot vascular

vasecto'mia *nf* vasectomy

vase'lina *nf* Vaseline®

vasel'lame *nm* china. **vasellame d'oro/d'argento** gold/silver plate

va'setto *nm* small pot; (per marmellata) [jam] jar

'vaso *nm* pot; (da fiori) vase; Anat vessel; (per cibi) jar. **vaso da notte** chamberpot. **vaso sanguigno** blood vessel

vasocostrit'tore *adj* vasoconstrictor

vasodilata'tore *adj* vasodilator

vas'sallo *nm* vassal

vas'soio *nm* tray

vastità *nf* vastness

'vasto *adj* vast; **di vaste vedute** broadminded

Vati'cano *nm* Vatican

vati'cinio *nm* prophecy

vattela'pesca *adv* fam God knows

'vattene! go away!; ▶ ANDARE

VCR *abbr* (**videoregistratore**) VCR

ve *pers pron* you; **ve l'ho dato** I gave it to you

'**vecchia** *nf* old woman

vecchi'aia *nf* old age

'**vecchio, -a** ① *adj* old
② *nmf* old man; old woman; **i vecchi** old
people; ~ **mio** old man

'**veccia** *nf* vetch

'**vece** *nf* **in** ~ **di** in place of; **fare le veci di
qualcuno** take somebody's place

ve'**dente** *adj* **i non** ~ the visually
handicapped

ve'**dere** ① *vt* see; see, watch ⟨*film,
partita*⟩; **far** ~ show; **farsi** ~ show one's
face; **non si vede** ⟨*macchia, imperfezione*⟩
it doesn't show; **non veder l'ora di fare
qualcosa** be raring to go; **non poter** ~
qualcuno not be able to stand the sight of
somebody; **vederci doppio** have double
vision; **ne ho viste di tutti i colori** fig I've
really seen life; **da** ~ ⟨*film, spettacolo*⟩ not
to be missed; **questo è da** ~! that remains
to be seen!; **chi si vede!** *fam* look who it
is!
② *vi* see

ve'**dersi** *vr* see oneself; (reciproco) see
each other; **vedersela brutta** have a
narrow escape

ve'**detta** *nf* (luogo) lookout; *Naut* patrol
vessel

'**vedova** *nf* widow. **vedova nera** Zool
black widow [spider]

'**vedovo** *nm* widower

ve'**duta** *nf* view

vee'**mente** *adj* vehement

vege'**tale** *adj* & *nm* vegetable

vegetali'**ano** *adj* & *nmf* vegan

vegeta'**lismo** *nm* veganism

vege'**tare** *vi* vegetate

vegetaria'**nismo** *nm* vegetarianism

vegetari'**ano, -a** *adj* & *nmf* vegetarian

vegeta'**tivo** *adj* vegetative

vegetazi'**one** *nf* vegetation

'**vegeto** *adj* ▸ VIVO

veg'**gente** *nmf* clairvoyant

'**veglia** *nf* watch; **fare la** ~ keep watch.
veglia funebre vigil

vegli'**are** *vi* be awake; ~ **su** watch over

vegli'**one** *nm* **veglione di
Capodanno** New Year's Eve celebration

veico'**lare** ① *vt* carry ⟨*malattia*⟩
② *adj* ⟨*traffico*⟩ vehicular

ve'**icolo** *nm* vehicle. **veicolo pesante**
heavy goods vehicle, HGV. **veicolo
spaziale** spacecraft

'**vela** *nf* sail; Sport sailing; **andare a gonfie
vele** fig go beautifully; ⟨*affari*⟩ be booming;
far ~ set sail. **vela di taglio** mainsail

ve'**lare** *vt* veil; (fig: nascondere) hide

ve'**larsi** *vr* ⟨*vista*⟩ mist over; ⟨*voce*⟩ go
husky

velata'**mente** *adv* indirectly

ve'**lato** *adj* veiled; ⟨*occhi*⟩ misty; ⟨*collant*⟩
sheer

vela'**tura** *nf* sails *pl*

'**velcro**® *nm* velcro®

veleggi'**are** *vi* sail

ve'**leno** *nm* poison

velenosa'**mente** *adv* ⟨*rispondere*⟩
venomously

vele'**noso** *adj* poisonous; ⟨*frase*⟩
venomous

ve'**letta** *nf* (di cappello) veil

'**velico** *adj* ⟨*circolo*⟩ sailing *attrib*;
superficie velica sail area

veli'**ero** *nm* sailing ship

ve'**lina** *nf* **(carta) velina** tissue paper;
(copia) carbon copy

ve'**lista** ① *nm* yachtsman
② *nf* yachtswoman

ve'**livolo** *nm* aircraft

velleità *nf inv* foolish ambition

vellei'**tario** *adj* unrealistic

'**vello** *nm* fleece

vellu'**tato** *adj* velvety

vel'**luto** *nm* velvet. **velluto a coste**
corduroy

'**velo** *nm* veil; (di zucchero, cipria) dusting;
(tessuto) voile

ve'**loce** *adj* fast

veloce'**mente** *adv* quickly

velo'**cipede** *nm* penny-farthing

velo'**cista** *nmf* Sport sprinter

velocità *nf inv* speed; (Auto: marcia) gear;
a due ~ fig two-tier. **velocità di clock**
Comput clock speed. **velocità di
crociera** cruising speed. **velocità di
stampa** print speed

velociz'**zare** *vt* speed up

ve'**lodromo** *nm* cycle track

'**vena** *nf* vein; **essere in** ~ **di** be in the
mood for. **vena poetica** poetic mood

ve'**nale** *adj* venal; ⟨*persona*⟩ mercenary,
venal

ve'**nato** *adj* grainy

vena'**torio** *adj* hunting *attrib*

vena'**tura** *nf* (di legno) grain; (di foglia,
marmo) vein

ven'**demmia** *nf* grape harvest

vendemmi'**are** *vt* harvest

vendemmia|'**tore, -trice** *nmf*
grapepicker

'**vendere** *vt* sell

'**vendersi** *vr* sell oneself; '**vendesi** 'for
sale'

ven'**detta** *nf* revenge. **vendetta
trasversale** vendetta

vendi'**care** *vt* avenge

vendi'**carsi** *vr* take revenge, get one's
revenge; ~ **di qualcuno** take one's

vengeance on somebody; ~ **di qualcosa** take revenge for something

vendicativa'mente *adv* vindictively

vendica'tivo *adj* vindictive

vendica'|tore, -trice *nmf* avenger

'vendita *nf* sale; **in** ~ on sale. **vendita all'asta** sale by auction. **vendita di beneficenza** bring and buy sale. **vendita per corrispondenza** mail-order; **azienda di** ~ **per corrispondenza** mail-order company; **catalogo di** ~ **per corrispondenza** mail-order catalogue. **vendita al dettaglio** retailing. **vendita all'ingrosso** wholesaling. **vendita al minuto** retailing. **vendita porta a porta** door-to-door selling. **vendita a rate** hire purchase, installment plan *Am*; **vendite** *pl* **al dettaglio** retail sales

vendi'|tore, -trice *nmf* seller. **venditore ambulante** hawker, pedlar. **venditore al dettaglio** retailer. **venditore all'ingrosso** wholesaler. **venditore al mercato** market trader. **venditore al minuto** retailer

ven'duto *adj* ⟨*merce*⟩ sold; fig: ⟨*arbitro*⟩ bent; **arbitro** ~**!** whose side are you on, ref!

vene'rabile, vene'rando *adj* venerable

vene'rare *vt* revere

venerazi'one *nf* reverence

venerdì *nm inv* Friday; **di** ~ on Fridays. **Venerdì Santo** Good Friday

'Venere *nf* Venus

ve'nereo *adj* venereal

'Veneto *nm* Veneto

'veneto *adj* from the Veneto

Ve'nezia *nf* Venice

venezi'ano, -a ① *adj & nmf* Venetian ② *nf* ⟨*persiana*⟩ Venetian blind; *Culin* sweet bun

Vene'zuela *nm* Venezuela

venezue'lano, -a *adj & nmf* Venezuelan

'vengo ▶ VENIRE

veni'ale *adj* venial

ve'nire *vi* come; ⟨*riuscire*⟩ turn out; ⟨*costare*⟩ cost; (in passivi) be; **quanto viene?** how much is it?; **viene prodotto in serie** it's mass-produced; ~ **a sapere** learn; ~ **in mente** occur; **mi è venuto un dubbio** I've just had a doubt; **gli è venuta la febbre** he's got a temperature; ~ **meno** (svenire) faint; ~ **meno a un contratto** go back on a contract, renege on a contract; ~ **via** come away; (staccarsi) come off; **mi viene da piangere** I feel like crying; **vieni a prendermi** come and pick me up; **vieni a trovarmi** come and see me; **nei giorni a** ~ in [the] days to come

ve'noso *adj* venous

ven'taglio *nm* fan

ven'tata *nf* gust [of wind]; fig breath

ven'tenne *adj & nmf* twenty-year-old

ven'tesimo *adj & nm* twentieth

'venti *adj & nm* twenty

venti'lare *vt* ventilate, air; ~ **un'idea** give an idea an airing; **poco ventilato** ⟨*stanza*⟩ airless

ventila'tore *nm* fan

ventilazi'one *nf* ventilation

ven'tina *nf* una ~ (circa venti) about twenty

ventiquat'trore ① *nf inv* ⟨*valigetta*⟩ overnight bag ② *adv* ~ **su ventiquattro** ⟨*lavorare*⟩ round-the-clock; ⟨*aperto*⟩ 24 hours

'vento *nm* wind; **c'è molto** ~ it's very windy; **farsi** ~ fan oneself. **vento contrario** headwind. **vento di prua** headwind. **vento di traverso** crosswind

'ventola *nf* fan

vento'lina *nf* fan. **ventolina di raffreddamento** Comput cooling fan

ven'tosa *nf* sucker, suction pad

ven'toso *adj* windy

'ventre *nm* stomach; (fig: della Terra) bowels *pl*; **basso** ~ lower abdomen

ventrico'lare *adj* Med ventricular

ven'tricolo *nm* ventricle

ven'triloquo *nm* ventriloquist

ventu'nesimo *adj & nm* twenty-first

ven'tuno *adj & nm* twenty-one

ven'tura *nf* fortune; **andare alla** ~ trust to luck

ven'turo *adj* next

ve'nuta *nf* coming; ~ **meno a** breaking

'vera *nf* ⟨*anello*⟩ wedding ring

vera'mente *adv* really

ve'randa *nf* veranda

ver'bale ① *adj* verbal ② *nm* (di riunione) minutes *pl*. ~ **di contravvenzione** fine

verbal'mente *adv* verbally

ver'bena *nf* verbena

'verbo *nm* verb; **il Verbo** Relig the Word. **verbo ausiliare** auxiliary [verb]. **verbo modale** modal auxiliary. **verbo riflessivo** reflexive verb

ver'boso *adj* verbose

ver'dastro *adj* greenish

'verde ① *adj* green; ~ **d'invidia** green with envy ② *nm* green; (vegetazione) greenery; (semaforo) green light; **essere al** ~ be broke. **verde bottiglia** bottle green. **verde oliva** olive green. **verde pisello** pea green. **verde pubblico** public parks *pl*

verdeggi'ante *adj* liter verdant

verde'mare *adj & nm inv* sea-green

verde'rame *nm* verdigris

ver'detto *nm* verdict. **verdetto di assoluzione** not guilty verdict. **verdetto di condanna** guilty verdict

ver'done *nm* greenfinch

ver'dura *nf* vegetables *pl*; **una ~ a** vegetable; **verdure** *pl* **miste** mixed vegetables

'verga *nf* rod

ver'gato *adj* lined

vergi'nale *adj* virginal

'vergine ① *nf* virgin; Astr Virgo ② *adj* virgin; ‹cassetta› blank

verginità *nf* virginity

ver'gogna *nf* shame; (timidezza) shyness

vergo'gnarsi *vr* feel ashamed; (essere timido) feel shy

vergognosa'mente *adv* shamefully

vergo'gnoso *adj* ashamed; (timido) shy; (disonorevole) shameful

veridicità *nf* veracity

ve'rifica *nf* check. **verifica dei bilanci** audit. **verifica di cassa** cash check

verifi'cabile *adj* verifiable

verifi'care *vt* check; verify ‹teoria›

verifi'carsi *vr* come true

verifica|'tore, -trice *nmf* checker

ve'rismo *nm* realism

verità *nf inv* truth

veriti'ero *adj* truthful

'verme *nm* worm. **verme solitario** tapeworm

vermi'celli *nmpl* vermicelli *sg* (pasta thinner than spaghetti)

ver'mifugo ① *adj* vermifugal ② *nm* vermifuge

ver'miglio *adj & nm* vermilion

'vermut *nm* vermouth

ver'nacolo *nm* vernacular

ver'nice *nf* paint; (trasparente) varnish; (pelle) patent leather; fig veneer; '~ **fresca**' 'wet paint'. **vernice a spirito** spirit varnish

vernici'are *vt* paint; (con vernice trasparente) varnish

vernicia'tura *nf* painting; (con vernice trasparente) varnishing; (strato) paintwork; fig veneer

vernis'sage *nm inv* vernissage

'vero ① *adj* true; (autentico) real; (perfetto) perfect; **è ~?** is that so?; **~ e proprio** full-blown; **sei stanca, ~?** you're tired, aren't you; **non ti piace, ~?** you don't like it, do you?. **vero cuoio** real leather ② *nm* truth; (realtà) life

verosimigli'anza *nf* plausibility

vero'simile *adj* probable, likely

verosimil'mente *adv* probably

ver'ruca *nf* wart; (sotto la pianta del piede) verruca

versa'mento *nm* (pagamento) payment; (in banca) deposit

ver'sante *nm* slope

ver'sare ① *vt* pour; (spargere) shed; (rovesciare) spill; pay ‹denaro› (in banca) pay in ② *vi* (trovarsi) be

ver'sarsi *vr* spill; (sfociare) flow

ver'satile *adj* versatile

versatilità *nf* versatility

ver'sato *adj* (pratico) versed

ver'setto *nm* verse

versifica|'tore, -trice *nmf* versifier

versi'one *nf* version; (traduzione) translation. **'versione integrale'** (libro) 'unabridged version'; (film) 'uncut'. **versione originale** original version. **'versione ridotta'** 'abridged version'. **versione teatrale** dramatization

'verso¹ *nm* verse; (grido) cry; (gesto) gesture; (senso) direction; (modo) manner; **fare il ~ a qualcuno** ape somebody; **non c'è ~ di** there is no way of; **versi** *pl* **sciolti** blank verse

'verso² *prep* towards; (nei pressi di) round about; **~ dove?** which way?

'vertebra *nf* vertebra

verte'brale *adj* vertebral

verte'brato *nm* vertebrate

ver'tenza *nf* dispute. **vertenza sindacale** industrial dispute

'vertere *vi* **~ su** focus on

verti'cale ① *adj* vertical; (in parole crociate) down ② *nf* handstand; **fare la ~** do a handstand

vertical'mente *adv* vertically

'vertice *nm* summit; Math vertex; **conferenza al vertice** summit conference; **incontro al vertice** summit meeting

ver'tigine *nf* dizziness; Med vertigo; **vertigini** *pl* giddy spells; **avere le vertigini** feel dizzy

vertiginosa'mente *adv* dizzily

vertigi'noso *adj* dizzy; ‹velocità› breakneck; ‹prezzi› sky-high; ‹scollatura› plunging

'vescia *nf* puffball

ve'scica *nf* bladder; (sulla pelle) blister

'vescovo *nm* bishop

'vespa *nf* wasp

'Vespa® *nf* scooter, Vespa®

vespasi'ano *nm* urinal

'vespro *nm* vespers *pl*

ves'sare *vt* fml oppress

ves'sillo *nm* standard

ve'staglia *nf* dressing gown, robe Am

'veste *nf* dress; (rivestimento) covering; **in ~ di** in the capacity of; **in ~ ufficiale** in an official capacity. **veste da camera** dressing gown, robe Am. **veste editoriale** layout. **veste tipografica** typographical design

vesti'ario *nm* clothing

ve'stibolo *nm* hall

ve'stigio *nm* (pl m **vestigi**, pl f **vestigia**) trace

ve'stire *vt* dress

ve'stirsi *vr* get dressed; ∼ **da** dress up as a

ve'stito ① *adj* dressed
② *nm* (da uomo) suit; (da donna) dress; vestiti *pl* clothes. **vestito da sposa** wedding dress

vete'rano, **-a** *adj & nmf* veteran

veteri'nario, **-a** ① *adj* veterinary
② *nm* veterinary surgeon
③ *nf* veterinary science

'veto *nm* veto

ve'traio *nm* glazier

ve'trato, **-a** ① *adj* glazed
② *nf* big window; (in chiesa) stained-glass window; (porta) glass door

vetre'ria *nf* glass works

ve'trina *nf* [shop-]window; (mobile) display cabinet

vetri'nista *nmf* window dresser

ve'trino *nm* (di microscopio) slide

vetri'olo *nm* vitriol

'vetro *nm* glass; (di finestra, porta) pane. ∼ **di sicurezza** safety glass

vetro'resina *nf* fibreglass

ve'troso *adj* vitreous

'vetta *nf* peak

vet'tore *nm* vector

vetto'vaglie *nfpl* provisions

vet'tura *nf* coach; ⟨ferroviaria⟩ coach, carriage; Auto car. **vettura di cortesia** courtesy car. **vettura d'epoca** vintage car

vettu'rino *nm* coachman

vezzeggi'are *vt* fondle

vezzeggia'tivo *nm* pet name

'vezzo *nm* habit; (attrattiva) charm; vezzi *pl* (moine) affectation

vez'zoso *adj* charming; pej affected

VF *abbr* (**Vigili del Fuoco**) fire brigade, fire department Am

vi ① *pers pron* you; (riflessivo) yourselves; (reciproco) each other; (tra più persone) one another; **vi ho dato un libro** I gave you a book; **lavatevi le mani** wash your hands; **eccovi!** here you are!
② *adv* = CI

'via¹ *nf* street, road; fig way; Anat tract; in ∼ **di** in the course of; **per** ∼ **di** on account of; **per** ∼ **aerea** by airmail. **Via Lattea** Astr Milky Way. **via di mezzo** halfway

house. **via respiratoria** Anat airway. **via d'uscita** let-out

'via² ① *adv* away; (fuori) out; **andar** ∼ go away; ⟨macchia⟩ come off, come out; **e così** ∼ and so on; **e** ∼ **dicendo** and whatnot; ∼ ∼ **che** as
② *int* ∼! go away!; Sport go!; (andiamo) come on!; ∼, **non ci credo** come off it *or* come on, I don't believe it
③ *nm* starting signal

viabilità *nf* road conditions *pl*; (rete) road network; (norme) road and traffic laws *pl*

via'card *nf inv* motorway card

vi'ado *nm* (pl **viados**) rent boy

via'dotto *nm* viaduct

viaggi'are *vi* travel; **il treno viaggia con 20 minuti di ritardo** the train is 20 minutes late

viaggia|'tore, **trice** *nmf* traveller

vi'aggio *nm* journey; (breve) trip; **buon** ∼! safe journey!, have a good trip!; **fare un** ∼ go on a journey; **essere in** ∼ be underway; **mettersi in** ∼ get underway. **viaggio d'affari** business trip. **viaggio di lavoro** working trip **viaggio di nozze** honeymoon. **viaggio organizzato** package tour

vi'ale *nm* avenue; (privato) drive

via'letto *nm* path

via'vai *nm* coming and going

vi'brante *adj* vibrant

vi'brare *vi* vibrate; (fremere) quiver

vibra'tore *nm* vibrator

vibra'torio *adj* vibratory

vibrazi'one *nf* vibration

vi'cario *nm* vicar

'vice *nmf inv* deputy

vice+ *pref* vice+

vicecoman'dante *nm* Mil second in command

vicediret|'tore, **-trice** ① *nm* assistant manager
② *nf* assistant manageress

vi'cenda *nf* event; **a** ∼ (fra due) each other; (a turno) in turn[s]

vicendevol'mente *adv* each other

vice'preside *nmf* vice-principal

vicepresi'dente *nmf* vice-president; Comm vice-chairman, vice-president Am

vicepresi'denza *nf* vice-presidency; Sch deputy head's office

viceré *nm inv* viceroy

viceret'tore *nm* vice-chancellor

vice'versa *adv* vice versa

vi'chingo, **-a** *adj & nmf* Viking

vici'nanza *nf* nearness; vicinanze (*pl:* paraggi) neighbourhood

vici'nato *nm* neighbourhood; (vicini) neighbours *pl*

vi'cino, **-a** ① *adj* near; (accanto) next

2 *adv* near, close

3 *prep* ~ a near [to]

4 *nmf* neighbour. **vicino di casa** nextdoor neighbour

vicissi'tudine *nf* vicissitude

'**vicolo** *nm* alley. **vicolo cieco** anche *fig* blind alley

'**video** *nm inv* (musicale) video; (schermo) screen. **video interattivo** interactive video

video'camera *nf* camcorder

videocas'setta *nf* video, video cassette

videoci'tofono *nm* video entry phone, videophone

video'clip *nm inv* video clip

videoconfe'renza *nf* videoconference

video'disco *nm* videodisc

videogi'oco *nm* video game

video'leso, -a **1** *adj* visually handicapped, visually impaired
2 *nmf* visually handicapped person

videoregistra'tore *nm* videorecorder

videoscrit'tura *nf* word processing

videosorvegli'anza *nf* video surveillance

video'teca *nf* video library

video'tel® *nm* ≈ Videotex®

videote'lefono *nm* view phone

videotermi'nale *nm* visual display unit, VDU

vidi'mare *vt* authenticate

vi'eni ▸ VENIRE

Vi'enna *nf* Vienna

vien'nese *adj & nmf* Viennese

vie'tare *vt* forbid; ~ **qualcosa a qualcuno** forbid somebody something

vie'tato *adj* forbidden; **sosta vietata** no parking; ~ **fumare** no smoking; ~ **ai minori di 18 anni** ⟨*film*⟩ for over 18-year-olds only, X-rated

Vi'etnam *nm* Vietnam

vietna'mita *adj & nmf* Vietnamese

vi'gente *adj* in force

'**vigere** *vi* be in force

vigi'lante *adj* vigilant

vigi'lanza *nf* vigilance; (a scuola) supervision; (di polizia) surveillance. **vigilanza notturna** night security guards *pl*. **vigilanza urbana** traffic police (in towns)

vigi'lare **1** *vt* keep an eye on
2 *vi* keep watch

vigi'lato, -a **1** *adj* under surveillance
2 *nmf* person under police surveillance. **vigilato speciale** person under special police surveillance

'**vigile** **1** *adj* watchful
2 *nm* ~ [urbano] traffic policeman. **vigile del fuoco** fireman, firefighter. **vigili** *pl* **del fuoco** firemen, fire brigade,

fire service. **vigili** *pl* **urbani** traffic police (in towns)

vi'gilia *nf* eve; Relig fast. **vigilia di Natale** Christmas Eve

vigliacca'mente *adv* in a cowardly way

vigliacche'ria *nf* cowardice

vigli'acco, -a **1** *adj* cowardly
2 *nmf* coward

'**vigna** *nf*, **vi'gneto** *nm* vineyard

vi'gnetta *nf* cartoon

vignet'tista *nm* cartoonist

vi'gogna *nf* (tessuto) vicuña

vi'gore *nm* vigour; **entrare in** ~ come into force; **essere in** ~ be in force

vigorosa'mente *adv* energetically

vigo'roso *adj* vigorous

'**vile** *adj* cowardly; (abietto) vile

vili'pendio *nm* scorn, contempt

'**villa** *nf* villa

vil'laggio *nm* village. **villaggio olimpico** Olympic village. **villaggio residenziale** commuter town. **villaggio satellite** satellite village. **villaggio turistico** holiday village

villa'nia *nf* rudeness

vil'lano **1** *adj* rude
2 *nm* boor; (contadino) peasant

villeggi'ante *nmf* holidaymaker

villeggi'are *vi* spend one's holidays

villeggia'tura *nf* holiday[s] [*pl*]. vacation Am

vil'letta *nf* small detached house. **villetta bifamiliare** semi-detached house. **villette** *pl* **a schiera** terraced houses

vil'lino *nm* detached house

vil'loso *adj* hairy

vil'mente *adv* in a cowardly way; (in modo spregevole) contemptibly

viltà *nf* cowardice

'**vimine** *nm* wicker; **sedia di vimini** wicker chair

vi'naio, -a *nmf* wine merchant

'**vincere** *vt* win; (sconfiggere) beat; (superare) overcome

'**vincita** *nf* win; (somma vinta) winnings *pl*

vinci∣'tore, -trice **1** *nmf* winner; (di battaglia) victor, winner
2 *adj* winning, victorious

vinco'lante *adj* binding

vinco'lare *vt* bind; Comm tie up

vinco'lato *adj* Fin nonredeemable; **deposito vincolato** fixed deposit, term deposit

'**vincolo** *nm* bond

vi'nicolo *adj* wine attrib

vi'nile *nm* vinyl

vi'nilico *adj* vinyl

vinil'pelle® *nm* Leatherette®

'vino *nm* wine. **vino d'annata** vintage wine. **vino bianco** white wine; **vin brûlé** mulled wine. **vino della casa** house wine. **vino da dessert** dessert wine. **vino nuovo** new wine. **vino rosato** rosé [wine]. **vino rosé** rosé [wine]. **vino rosso** red wine. **vino spumante** sparkling wine. **vino da taglio** blending wine. **vino da tavola** table wine

vin'santo *nm* dessert wine from Tuscany

'vinto *pp* di VINCERE

vi'ola *nf* Bot violet; Mus viola. **viola del pensiero** Bot pansy

vio'laceo *adj* purplish; ⟨*labbra*⟩ blue

vio'lare *vt* violate

violazi'one *nf* violation. **violazione di contratto** breach of contract. **violazione di domicilio** breaking and entering

violen'tare *vt* rape

violente'mente *adv* violently

vio'lento *adj* violent

vio'lenza *nf* violence. **violenza carnale** rape

vio'letto, -a ① *adj* & *nm* (colore) violet ② *nf* violet

violi'nista *nmf* violinist

vio'lino *nm* violin

violon'cello *nm* cello

vi'ottolo *nm* path

'vipera *nf* viper

vi'raggio *nm* Phot toning; Naut, Aeron turn

vi'rale *adj* viral

vi'rare *vi* turn; ⟨*nave*⟩ put about; **virare di bordo** change course

vi'rata *nf* (di aereo) turning; (di nave) coming about; (nel nuoto) turn; fig change of direction

'virgola *nf* comma; Math [decimal] point; **punto e virgola** semicolon; **quattro ∼ due (4,2)** four point two (4.2)

virgo'lette *nfpl* inverted commas, quotation marks

vi'rile *adj* virile; (da uomo) manly

virilità *nf* virility; manliness

viril'mente *adv* in a manly way

vi'rologo *nm* virologist

virtù *nf inv* virtue; **in ∼ di** ⟨*legge*⟩ under

virtu'ale *adj* virtual

virtual'mente *adv* virtually

virtuo'sismo *nm* bravura

virtu'oso ① *adj* virtuous ② *nm* virtuoso

viru'lento *adj* virulent

'virus *nm inv* virus

visa'gista *nmf* beautician

visce'rale *adj* visceral; ⟨*odio*⟩ deep-seated; ⟨*reazione*⟩ gut

'viscere *nfpl* guts

'vischio *nm* mistletoe

vischi'oso *adj* viscous; (appiccicoso) sticky

'viscido *adj* slimy

vi'sconte *nm* viscount

viscon'tessa *nf* viscountess

vi'scoso *adj* viscous

vi'sibile *adj* visible

visi'bilio *nm* profusion; **andare in ∼** go into ecstasies

visibilità *nf* visibility; **scarsa visibilità** poor visibility

visi'era *nf* (di elmo) visor; (di berretto) peak

visio'nare *vt* examine; Cinema screen

visio'nario, -a *adj* & *nmf* visionary

visi'one *nf* vision; **prima visione** Cinema first showing; **seconda visione** re-release, second showing. **visione notturna** night vision

'visita *nf* visit; (breve) call; Med examination; **fare ∼ a qualcuno** pay somebody a visit. **visita di controllo** Med checkup. **visita di cortesia** courtesy visit. **visita doganale** customs inspection. **visita a domicilio** home visit, call-out, house call. **visita fiscale** tax inspection. **visita guidata** guided tour. **visita lampo** flying visit. **visita di leva** medical examination for military service

visi'tare *vt* visit; (brevemente) call on; Med examine

visita|'tore, -trice *nmf* visitor

visiva'mente *adv* visually

vi'sivo *adj* visual

'viso *nm* face. **viso pallido** paleface

vi'sone *nm* mink

'vispo *adj* lively

vis'suto ① *pp* di VIVERE ② *adj* experienced

'vista *nf* sight; (veduta) view; **a ∼ d'occhio** ⟨*crescere*⟩ visibly; ⟨*estendersi*⟩ as far as the eye can see; **in ∼ di** in view of; **perdere di ∼ qualcuno** lose sight of somebody; fig lose touch with somebody; **a prima ∼** at first sight. **vista sul mare** sea view

'visto ① *pp* di VEDERE ② *nm* visa. **visto di entrata** o **di ingresso** entry visa, entry permit. **visto d'uscita** exit visa. ③ *conj* **∼ che...** seeing that...

vistosa'mente *adv* conspicuously

vi'stoso *adj* showy; (notevole) considerable

visu'ale *adj* visual

visualiz'zare *vt* visualize; Comput display

visualizza'tore *nm* Comput display, VDU. **visualizzatore a cristalli liquidi** Comput liquid crystal display

visualizzazi'one *nf* Comput display

'**vita** *nf* life; (durata della vita) lifetime; Anat waist; **a ~** for life; **essere in fin di ~** be at death's door; **essere in ~** be alive; **fare la bella ~** lead the good life; **costo della vita** cost of living. **vita eterna** eternal life. **vita media** Biol life expectancy. **vita mondana** high life; **fare ~ mondana** lead the high life. **vita notturna** night life. **vita terrena** Relig life on earth

vi'taccia *nf* slog

vi'tale *adj* vital

vitalità *nf* vitality

vita'lizio ① *adj* life attrib ② *nm* [life] annuity

vita'mina *nf* vitamin

vita'minico *adj* vitamin-enriched

vitaminiz'zato *adj* vitamin-enriched

'**vite** *nf* Mech screw; Bot vine; **giro di vite** fig clampdown. **vite canadese** Virginia creeper. **vite di coda** Aeron tailspin. **vite perpetua** endless screw

vi'tella *nf* (animale) calf; (carne) veal

vi'tello *nm* calf; (carne) veal; (pelle) calfskin. **vitello di latte** milk-fed veal. **vitello tonnato** sliced veal with tuna, anchovy, oil and lemon sauce

vi'ticcio *nm* tendril

viticol'tore *nm* wine grower

viticol'tura *nf* wine growing

vi'tino *nm* narrow waist. **vitino di vespa** slender little waist

'**vitreo** *adj* vitreous; (sguardo) glassy

'**vittima** *nf* victim

'**vitto** *nm* food; (pasti) board. **vitto e alloggio** board and lodging

vit'toria *nf* victory

vittori'ano *adj* Victorian

vittoriosa'mente *adv* victoriously, triumphantly

vittori'oso *adj* victorious

vitupe'rare *vt* vituperate

vitu'perio *nm* insult

vi'uzza *nf* narrow lane

'**viva** *int* hurrah!; **~ la Regina!** long live the Queen!

vi'vace *adj* vivacious; (mente) lively; (colore) bright

vivace'mente *adv* vivaciously

vivacità *nf* vivacity; (di mente) liveliness; (di colore) brightness

vivaciz'zare *vt* liven up

vi'vaio *nm* nursery; (per pesci) pond; fig breeding ground

viva'mente *adv* (ringraziare) warmly

vi'vanda *nf* food; (piatto) dish

vi'vente ① *adj* living ② *nmpl* **i viventi** the living

'**vivere** ① *vi* live; **~ di** live on; **vive** Typ stet ② *vt* (passare) go through ③ *nm* life; **modo di vivere** way of life

'**viveri** *nmpl* provisions

vivida'mente *adv* vividly

'**vivido** *adj* vivid

vivi'paro *adj* viviparous

vivisezio'nare *vt* vivisect

vivisezi'one *nf* vivisection

'**vivo** ① *adj* alive; (vivente) living; (vivace) lively; (colore) bright. **vivo e vegeto** alive and kicking; **farsi ~** keep in touch; (arrivare) turn up ② *nm* **colpire qualcuno sul ~** cut somebody to the quick; **dal ~** (trasmissione) live; (disegnare) from life; **i vivi** the living

vizi'are *vt* spoil (bambino ecc); (guastare) vitiate

vizi'ato *adj* spoilt; (aria) stale

'**vizio** *nm* vice; (cattiva abitudine) bad habit; (difetto) flaw. **vizio capitale** deadly sin. **vizio di forma** legal technicality. **vizio procedurale** procedural error

vizi'oso *adj* dissolute; (difettoso) faulty; **circolo vizioso** vicious circle

'**vizzo** *adj* (pelle) wrinkled; (pianta) withered

V.le *abbr* (**viale**) Ave

vocabo'lario *nm* dictionary; (lessico) vocabulary

vo'cabolo *nm* word

vo'cale ① *adj* vocal ② *nf* vowel

vo'calico *adj* (corde) vocal; (suono) vowel attrib

vocazi'one *nf* vocation

'**voce** *nf* voice; (diceria) rumour; (di bilancio, dizionario) entry. **voce bianca** Mus treble voice. **voce fuori campo** voiceover

voci'are ① *vi* (spettegolare) gossip ② *nm* buzz of conversation

vocife'rare *vi* shout; **si vocifera che...** it is rumoured that...

'**vodka** *nf inv* vodka

'**voga** *nf* rowing; (lena) enthusiasm; (moda) vogue; **essere in ~** be in vogue

vo'gare *vi* row; **~ a bratto** scull; **~ di coppia** scull

voga'tore *nm* oarsman; (attrezzo) rowing machine

'**voglia** *nf* desire; (volontà) will; (sulla pelle) birthmark; **aver ~ di fare qualcosa** feel like doing something; **morire dalla ~ di qualcosa** be dying for something; **di buona ~** willingly

'**voglio** ▶ VOLERE

vogli'oso *adj* (occhi, persona) covetous; **essere ~ di qualcosa** want something

'voi *pers pron* you; **siete** ∼**?** is that you?; **l'avete fatto** ∼**?** did you do it yourselves?

voia'ltri *pers pron* you

vo'lano *nm* shuttlecock; Mech flywheel

vo'lant *nm inv* valance

vo'lante ① *adj* flying; ⟨*foglio*⟩ loose ② *nm* steering-wheel

volanti'nare *vi* hand out leaflets

volan'tino *nm* leaflet

vo'lare *vi* fly

vo'lata *nf* Sport final sprint; **di** ∼ in a rush

vo'latile ① *adj* ⟨*liquido*⟩ volatile ② *nm* bird

volatiliz'zarsi *vr* vanish

vol-au-'vent *nm inv* vol-au-vent

vo'lée *nf inv* Tennis volley

vo'lente *adj* ∼ **o nolente** whether you like it or not

volente'roso *adj* willing

volenti'eri *adv* willingly; ∼**!** with pleasure!

vo'lere ① *vt* want; (chiedere di) ask for; (aver bisogno di) need; **non voglio** I don't want to; **vuole che io faccia io** he wants me to do it; **fai come vuoi** do as you like; **se tuo padre vuole, ti porto al cinema if** your father agrees, I'll take you to the cinema; **questa pianta vuole molte cure** this plant needs a lot of care; **vorrei un caffè** I'd like a coffee; **la leggenda vuole che...** legend has it that...; **la vuoi smettere?** will you stop that!; **senza** ∼ without meaning to; **voler bene/male a qualcuno** love/have something against somebody; **voler dire** mean; **ci vuole il latte** we need milk; **ci vuole tempo/pazienza** it takes time/patience; **volerne a** have a grudge against; **vuoi... vuoi...** either... or... ② *nm* will; **voleri** *pl* wishes

vol'gare *adj* vulgar; (popolare) common

volgarità *nf inv* vulgarity; **dire** ∼ use vulgar language, be vulgar

volgariz'zare *vt* popularize

volgarizzazi'one *nf* popularization

volgar'mente *adv* (grossolanamente) vulgarly; (comunemente) commonly, popularly

'volgere *vt/i* turn

'volgersi *vr* turn [round]; ∼ **a** (dedicarsi) take up

'volgo *nm* common people

voli'era *nf* aviary

voli'tivo *adj* strong-minded

'volo *nm* flight; **al** ∼ ⟨*fare qualcosa*⟩ quickly; ⟨*prendere qualcosa*⟩ in mid-air; **alzarsi in** ∼ ⟨*uccello*⟩ take off; **in** ∼ airborne. **volo di andata** outward flight. **volo charter** charter flight. **volo diretto** direct flight. **volo di linea** scheduled flight. **volo nazionale**

domestic flight. **volo di ritorno** return flight. **volo strumentale** flying on instruments. **volo a vela** gliding

volontà *nf inv* will; (desiderio) wish; **a** ∼ ⟨*mangiare*⟩ as much as you like

volontaria'mente *adv* voluntarily

volon'tario ① *adj* voluntary ② *nm* volunteer

volonte'roso *adj* willing

'volpe *nf* fox

vol'pino ① *adj* ⟨*astuzia*⟩ fox-like ② *nm* (cane) Pomeranian

volt *nm inv* volt

'volta *nf* time; (turno) turn; (curva) bend; Archit vault; **4 volte 4** 4 times 4; **a volte, qualche** ∼ sometimes; **c'era una** ∼**...** once upon a time there was...; **una** ∼ once; **due volte** twice; **tre/quattro volte** three/four times; **una** ∼ **per tutte** once and for all; **una** ∼ **ogni tanto** every so often; **uno alla** ∼ one at a time; **alla** ∼ **di** in the direction of. **volta a botte** barrel vault. **volta celeste** vault of heaven. **volta cranica** cranial vault. **volta a crociera** groin vault. **volta a vela** ribbed vault. **volta a ventaglio** fan vault

volta'faccia *nm inv* volte-face

voltagab'bana *nmf inv* turncoat

vol'taggio *nm* voltage

vol'tare *vt/i* turn; (rigirare) turn round; (rivoltare) turn over; ∼ **pagina** fig turn over a new leaf

vol'tarsi *vr* turn [round]

volta'stomaco *nm* nausea; fig disgust

volteggi'are *vi* circle; (ginnastica) vault

'volto ① *pp di* VOLGERE ② *nm* face; **ha mostrato il suo vero** ∼ he revealed his true colours

vol'tura *nf* (catastale) transfer of property. ∼ **di contratto** transfer of contract

vo'lubile *adj* fickle

volubil'mente *adv* in a fickle way, inconstantly

vo'lume *nm* volume. **volume di gioco** Sport possession

volumi'noso *adj* voluminous

vo'luta *nf* (spirale) spiral; (di capitello) volute

voluta'mente *adv* deliberately

vo'luto *adj* deliberate, intended

voluttà *nf* voluptuousness

voluttu'ario *adj* non-essential; **beni** *pl* voluttuari non-essentials

voluttu'oso *adj* voluptuous

vomi'tare *vi* vomit, be sick

vomi'tevole *adj* nauseating

'vomito *nm* vomit

'vongola *nf* clam

vo'race *adj* voracious

vorace'mente *adv* voraciously

vo'ragine *nf* abyss

vor'rei ▶ VOLERE

'vortice *nm* whirl; (gorgo) whirlpool; (di vento) whirlwind

vorticosa'mente *adv* in whirls

'vostro ① (il ~ *m*, la vostra *f*, i vostri *mpl*, le vostre *fpl*) *poss adj* your; è vostra questa macchina? is this car yours?; un ~ amico a friend of yours; ~ padre your father
② *poss pron* yours; i vostri your folks

vo'tante *nmf* voter

vo'tare *vi* vote

votazi'one *nf* voting; Sch marks *pl*. **votazione di fiducia** Pol, fig vote of confidence. **votazione per alzata di mano** show of hands. **votazione a scrutinio segreto** secret ballot

'voto *nm* vote; Sch mark; Relig vow. **voto decisivo** casting vote. **voto per alzata di mano** show of hands

vs. *abbr* Comm (**vostro**) yours

'vudu *nm inv* voodoo

vul'canico *adj* volcanic

vul'cano *nm* volcano. **vulcano intermittente** dormant volcano. **vulcano spento** extinct volcano

vulne'rabile *adj* vulnerable

vulnerabilità *nf* vulnerability

'vulva *nf* vulva

vuo'tare *vt* empty

vuo'tarsi *vr* empty

vu'oto ① *adj* empty; (non occupato) vacant; ~ di (sprovvisto) devoid of
② *nm* empty space; Phys vacuum; fig void; assegno a ~ dud cheque; sotto ~ ⟨prodotto⟩ vacuum-packed. **vuoto d'aria** air pocket. **vuoto a perdere** no deposit. **vuoto a rendere** ⟨bottiglia⟩ returnable

Ww

W *abbr* (**viva**) long live

'wafer *nm inv* (biscotto) wafer

wagon-'lit *nm inv* sleeping car

walkie-'talkie *nm inv* walkie-talkie

'water *nm inv* toilet, loo fam

watt *nm inv* watt

wat'tora *nm inv* Phys watt-hour

WC *nm inv* WC

'web *nm inv* Web

web'cam *nf inv* web cam

web'master *nm inv* webmster

wee'kend *nm inv* weekend

'welter *adj & nm inv* (in pugilato) welterweight

'western ① *adj inv* cowboy *attrib*
② *nm inv* Cinema western

'whisky *nm inv* whisky. **whisky di malto** malt [whisky]

wind'surf *nm inv* (tavola) windsurf; (sport) windsurfing; **fare ~ windsurf**

windsur'fista *nmf* sailboarder, windsurfer

'würstel *nm inv* frankfurter

Xx

xenofo'bia *nf* xenophobia

xe'nofobo, -a ① *adj* xenophobic
② *nmf* xenophobe

'xeres *nm inv* sherry

xero'copia *nf* xerox

xeroco'piare *vt* photocopy

xerocopia'trice *nf* photocopier

xilofo'nista *nmf* xylophone player

'xilofono *nm* xylophone

Yy

yacht *nm inv* yacht
yak *nm inv* Zool yak
'yankee *nmf inv* Yank
'Yemen *nm* Yemen
yeme'nita *nmf* Yemeni
yen *nm inv* yen
'yeti *nm* yeti
'yiddish *adj & nm inv* Yiddish

'yoga *nm* yoga
② *adj inv* yoga *attrib*
'yogurt *nm inv* yoghurt
yogurti'era *nf* yoghurt-maker
'yorkshire *nm inv* (cane) Yorkshire terrier
yo-'yo® *nm inv* yo-yo®
yup'pismo *nm* yuppiedom

Zz

zaba[gl]ione *nm* zabaglione (dessert made from eggs, wine or marsala and sugar)
'zacchera *nf* (schizzo) splash of mud
zaf'fata *nf* whiff; (di fumo) cloud
zaffe'rano *nm* saffron
zaf'firo *nm* sapphire
'zagara *nf* orange-blossom
'zaino *nm* rucksack
Za'ire *nm* Zaire
'Zambia *nm* Zambia
'zampa *nf* leg; **a quattro zampe** (animale) four-legged; (carponi) on all fours; **zampe pl di gallina** fig crow's feet; **zampe pl posteriori** hind legs
zam'pata *nf* paw; **dare una ~ a** hit with its paw
zampet'tare *vi* scamper
zam'petto *nm* Culin knuckle
zampil'lante *adj* spurting
zampil'lare *vi* spurt
zam'pillo *nm* spurt
zam'pino *nm* paw; **mettere lo ~ in** fig have a hand in
zam'pogna *nf* bagpipe
zampo'gnaro *nm* piper
zam'pone *nfpl* stuffed pigs trotter usually served with lentils
'zangola *nf* churn
'zanna *nf* fang; (di elefante) tusk
zan'zara *nf* mosquito
zanzari'era *nf* (velo) mosquito net; (su finestra) insect screen
'zappa *nf* hoe; **darsi la ~ sui piedi** fig shoot oneself in the foot
zap'pare *vt* hoe

zap'pata *nf* **dare una ~ a** hit with a hoe
zappet'tare *vt* hoe
'zapping *nm* channel-hopping Br, channel-surfing Am; **fare lo ~** channel-hop Br, channel-surf Am
zar *nm inv* tzar
za'rina *nf* tzarina
za'rista *adj & nmf* tzarist
'zattera *nf* raft
zatte'roni *nmpl* (scarpe) wedge shoes
za'vorra *nf* ballast; fig dead wood
zavor'rare *vt* load with ballast
'zazzera *nf* mop of hair
'zebra *nf* zebra; **zebre pl** (passaggio pedonale) zebra crossing, crosswalk Am
ze'brato *adj* (tessuto) with black and white stripes
'zecca¹ *nf* mint; **nuovo di ~** brand-new
'zecca² *nf* (parassita) tick
zec'chino *nm* sequin; **oro zecchino** pure gold
ze'lante *adj* zealous
'zelo *nm* zeal
'zenit *nm* zenith
'zenzero *nm* ginger
'zeppa *nf* wedge
'zeppo *adj* packed full; **pieno ~ di** crammed *or* packed with
zer'bino *nm* doormat
'zero *nm* zero, nought; (in calcio) nil; Tennis love; **due a ~** (in partite) two nil; **ricominciare da ~** fig start again from scratch; **sparare a ~ su qualcuno** fig lay into somebody; **avere il morale sotto ~** fig be down in the dumps

'zeta *nf* zed, zee Am

'zia *nf* aunt

zibel'lino *nm* sable

zi'gano, -a *adj & nmf* gypsy

'zigolo *nm* Zool bunting

'zigomo *nm* cheekbone

zigri'nato *adj* ⟨*pelle*⟩ grained; ⟨*metallo*⟩ milled

zig'zag *nm inv* zigzag; **andare a** ∼ zigzag

Zim'babwe *nm* Zimbabwe

zim'bello *nm* decoy; (oggetto di scherno) laughing-stock

'zinco *nm* zinc

zinga'resco *adj* gypsy *attrib*

'zingaro, -a *nmf* gypsy

'zio *nm* uncle

'zippo *nm* sl lighter

zi'tella *nf* spinster; pej old maid

zitel'lona *nf* pej old maid

zit'tire ① *vi* fall silent ② *vt* silence

'zitto *adj* silent; **sta'** ∼**!** keep quiet!

ziz'zania *nf* (discordia) discord; **seminare** ∼ cause trouble

'zoccola *nf* vulg whore

'zoccolo *nm* clog; (di cavallo) hoof; (di terra) clump; (di parete) skirting board, baseboard Am; (di colonna) base. **zoccolo duro** Pol hard core. **zoccolo fesso** cloven foot, cloven hoof

zodia'cale *adj* of the zodiac; **segno zodiacale** sign of the zodiac, birth sign

zo'diaco *nm* zodiac

zolfa'nello *nm* match

'zolfo *nm* sulphur

'zolla *nf* clod

zol'letta *nf* sugar cube, sugar lump

'zombi *nmf inv* fig zombie

zom'pare *vi* sl bonk

'zona *nf* zone; (area) area. **zona calda** fig hot spot. **zona denuclearizzata** nuclear-free zone. **zona di depressione** area of low pressure. **zona disastrata** disaster area. **zona disco** area for parking discs only. **zona erogena** erogenous zone. **zona di esclusione aerea** air exclusion zone. **zona giorno** living area. **zona industriale** industrial estate. **zona notte** sleeping area. **zona d'ombra** fig twilight zone. **zona pedonale** pedestrian precinct. **zona a traffico limitato** restricted traffic area. **zona verde** green belt

zonizzazi'one *nf* zoning

'zonzo: a zonzo *adv* **andare a** ∼ stroll about

'zoo *nm inv* zoo

zoolo'gia *nf* zoology

zoo'logico *adj* zoological

zo'ologo, -a *nmf* zoologist

zoosa'fari *nm inv* safari park

zootec'nia *nf* animal husbandry

zoo'tecnico *adj* ⟨*progresso*⟩ in animal husbandry; **patrimonio zootecnico** livestock

zoppi'cante *adj* limping; fig shaky

zoppi'care *vi* limp; (essere debole) be shaky

'zoppo, -a ① *adj* lame ② *nmf* cripple

'zotico *adj* uncouth

zoti'cone *nm* boor

zu'ava *nf* **calzoni** *pl* **alla** ∼ plus-fours

'zucca *nf* marrow; (fam: testa) head; (fam: persona) thickie; **cos'hai in quella** ∼**?** haven't you got anything between your ears?

zuc'cata *nf* **prendere una** ∼ fam hit one's head

zucche'rare *vt* sugar

zucche'rato *adj* sugared; **non** ∼ ⟨*succo d'arancia ecc*⟩ unsweetened

zuccheri'era *nf* sugar bowl

zuccheri'ficio *nm* sugar refinery

zucche'rino ① *adj* sugary ② *nm* sugar cube, sugar lump; fig sweetener; **essere uno** ∼ fig ⟨*persona*⟩ be a softy; ⟨*cosa*⟩ be a cinch

'zucchero *nm* sugar. **zucchero di canna** cane sugar. **zucchero filato** candyfloss **zucchero greggio** brown sugar. **zucchero vanigliato** vanilla sugar. **zucchero a velo** icing sugar, confectioners' sugar Am

zucche'roso *adj* fig honeyed

zuc'chetto *nm* (cappello) beanie

zuc'china *nf* courgette, zucchini Am

zuc'chino *nm* courgette, zucchini Am

zuc'cone *nm* fam blockhead

zuc'cotto *nm* dessert made with sponge, cream, chocolate and candied fruit

'zuffa *nf* scuffle

zufo'lare *vt/i* whistle

'zufolo *nm* penny whistle

zu'mare *vi* zoom

zu'mata *nf* zoom

'zuppa *nf* soup. **zuppa inglese** trifle

zup'petta *nf* **fare** ∼ **[con]** dunk

zuppi'era *nf* soup tureen

'zuppo *adj* soaked

A-Z of Italian life and culture

agriturismo

A type of holiday on a farm. It was originally intended that the holiday-makers would help with work on the farm in some capacity, but nowadays this virtually never happens. **Agriturismo** also means the venue – the farmhouse – often renovated and refurbished specially for tourists. This type of holiday offers various activities, e.g. walking, horse-riding, and sometimes tennis, swimming, etc. Good food and the open-air lifestyle are the main attractions. It is becoming much more popular and therefore more expensive than it was at first.

anno scolastico

The Italian school year usually begins in mid-September and ends at the beginning of June (except for students who are taking exams). As well as a few days' holiday for the various civil and religious festivals, there are about ten days' holiday over Christmas, New Year, and Twelfth Night, plus a few days at Easter.

aperitivo

It is an Italian tradition to have an aperitif, which may or may not be alcoholic and is served with a few peanuts, olives, or other appetizers, to stimulate the appetite before lunch or dinner. It is often taken at a bar and many bars have their own, homemade aperitif, based on liqueurs and fruit juices. The aperitif also provides a chance to catch up with friends.

ASL

Stands for **Azienda Sanitaria Locale**. The National Health Service provides care for citizens through these various local health authorities.

autostrade

Italy has a network of motorways – toll roads with two or more lanes on each carriageway. The tolls paid for using motorways finance their construction, management, and maintenance. The tariff depends on the vehicle in which

you are travelling and the stretch of motorway concerned, the relative costs of construction and maintenance being taken into account (e.g. mountain stretches can be more expensive). Usually you take a ticket from the booth when joining the motorway and hand it in for payment at the other end. The maximum speed limit for cars is 130 km/hr (150 km/hr on some stretches).

Bancomat

This is the name of the system of automatic cash withdrawal, of the actual cash machine, and of the card itself. The same card is often used as both a credit card and a bancomat card, so when you pay with the card in a shop you are asked whether you want to use it as a credit card or bancomat card; if it is the latter you have to key in your PIN on a special keypad the cashier gives you, and the transaction will be treated as a debit card transaction.

bandiera arancione

The orange flag is the mark of environmental quality awarded by the Italian Touring Club in inland areas. The criteria for the awarding of the orange flag are the development of cultural heritage, protection of the environment, improvement of hospitality, and quality both of restoration and of local products.

bandiera blu

The blue flag is an award given to beaches and ports in the member countries of the FEE (Federation for Environmental Education). The criteria that have to be met are, for beaches, the quality of the water and the coast, safety measures and services, and the promotion of environmental education. For ports, the quality of the water in the harbour, safety and disposal services, and environmental information provided are taken into consideration.

bar

A real institution of Italian life and culture, the bar is the place where you can have breakfast (if you didn't have any at home), a mid-morning snack, an aperitif or a sandwich at lunchtime, or a coffee, a digestif or whatever at any time of the day or evening. Usually drinks are taken standing at the bar. In many bars there are also tables where you can sit and read the newspapers.

Bars also play an important role in the lives of sports fans as they meet there to watch football matches or other events on the television.

Biennale di Venezia

This is an international show for the visual arts, cinema, architecture, dance, music, and theatre. The visual arts section, which is held in the Gardens, still takes place every two years and often welcomes avant-garde artists. The first Biennial International Art exhibition was held in 1895. The section devoted to cinema takes place annually. The other sections take place at irregular intervals.

Bocconi

With its headquarters in Milan, the **Bocconi** commercial university is an extremely prestigious private university, with only one faculty – economics.

caffè

Coffee is the typical Italian drink. It can be drunk at any time of the day, at home or in a bar. You can have a quick coffee standing at the counter, or a more leisurely one whilst chatting at a table. In bars or restaurants you can order '**un caffè**' (normal), '**ristretto**' or '**lungo**' (weaker or stronger), '**macchiato**' (hot or cold, with a drop of milk), or '**corretto**' (with a drop of spirits). Also on offer are decaff and hot malt drinks ('**caffè d'orzo**').

calcio

Football is definitely the sport that Italians love most; it is the sport with the most supporters and also the most people who actually play at some level. And of course it is a sport in which Italian teams have always excelled. The national league is divided into Serie A, Serie B, and Serie C. Some of the most famous Italian teams are Juventus, Milan, Inter (also in Milan), Roma, and Lazio.

Camera dei Deputati

The legislative assembly that, along with the Senate, makes up the Italian Parliament. It is composed of 630 deputies, elected by universal direct suffrage by citizens over 18 years of age.

Campidoglio

One of the seven hills of classical Rome, the **Campidoglio** was the acropolis and religious centre of the ancient city and is now the headquarters of the City of Rome. The square was designed by Michelangelo, and three buildings which he also designed face onto it. In the centre there is the statue of Marcus Aurelius on horseback. One of the buildings is the home of the Capitoline museums.

Canton Ticino

This is the only canton of the Swiss Confederation which has Italian as its official language. It is also the only Swiss region located south of the Alps. The history, culture, and language of this area are intermingled with those of the neighbouring Italian regions.

carabinieri

A corps of the Italian army with the tasks of guaranteeing the safety of citizens and their property and ensuring that State laws are observed. As well as being a military police force and responsible for public safety, the **carabinieri** also function as judiciary police.

carnevale

This is the period before Lent running from Twelfth Night to Ash Wednesday. It is celebrated with fancy dress parties, confetti, and streamers, especially during the weekend running from '**giovedì grasso**' (the last Thursday) to '**martedì grasso**' (Shrove Tuesday), which is the final day. The Venice carnival is very famous, with its open-air shows and fancy-dress balls, and so is the Viareggio carnival with its parade.

carta d'identità

An identity document issued to all citizens aged 15 and over. It is valid for foreign travel within the countries of the European Union and to others with which they have individual international agreements. It is renewed every five years at the town hall. It has a photo and various details such as the bearer's address, height, and colour of eyes and hair, and you can choose whether to include your marital status and profession. An electronic card, the same size as a credit card, can be requested.

Cattolica
The 'Catholic university' is a prestigious private institute with faculties of humanities and sciences.

Cinecittà
A complex of all of the different cinematographic studios set up on the outskirts of Rome in 1937. It includes a large number of film studios as well as studios for soundtracking.

CNR
The National Research Council is a national public body which carries out and promotes research activities for the scientific, technological, economic, and social development of the country.

Colosseo
The name given in the Middle Ages to the 'colossal' Flavian Amphitheatre, the most famous monument of Ancient Rome, which was begun by Vespasian in about 75 AD and inaugurated by Titus in 80 AD. It is oval in shape and no less than 50,000 spectators could attend the bloody battles between gladiators and beasts that were put on there.

comune
Each province is subdivided into municipalities (**comuni**), each of which is run by a council and municipal committee headed by a mayor. The functions of the comune are mainly administrative.

consiglio dei ministri
A body composed of ministers and headed by the prime minister: it forms the government.

consultorio familiare
Social-health service set up in the mid-70s. It provides health education (including preventive medicine) in the fields of gynaecology and paediatrics, as well as advice and support for people with mental health or legal problems.

enoteca
A place where good local wines are offered for sale and often for tasting. In many enoteche you can also eat while tasting the wines.

festival dei due mondi
The Festival di Spoleto (in the province of Perugia) takes place each year from late June to mid-July. It hosts dance, theatre, opera, and music events to which the biggest world names are invited. There are often avant-garde productions. Since 1958 Spoleto has attracted a sophisticated international audience.

festival di San Remo
This Ligurian tourist resort has hosted the festival of Italian music every year since 1951. After a period of decline in the 1970s it has recently regained its popularity. Established singers take part but it is also often the launch pad for new talent.

foglio rosa
This is the provisional driving licence, which can be applied for at the minimum age (18 for cars) and is valid for six months.

Gazzetta dello Sport
This is the sports daily, printed on its characteristic pink paper. It was founded in Milan in 1896 and is the most widely-read sports newspaper in Italy. It organizes the '**giro d'Italia**'.

Gazzetta Ufficiale
The official newspaper of the Italian State, which publishes approved laws, decrees, and various official announcements.

gelato
Made with milk, sugar, eggs, and various other ingredients, this is an Italian speciality, perfect as a summer dessert but good at any time of the day or year. The hand-made variety, bought in '**gelaterie**', can be served in a dish or in a

cone, and there are dozens of flavours to choose from.

giornali

Among the main Italian dailies are 'Repubblica' and 'Corriere della Sera'. The daily financial paper is 'il Sole 24 ore'. The weekly magazines 'L'Espresso' and 'Panorama' deal with current affairs, politics, and culture. As well as Italian versions of international titles, the weekly magazines 'Grazia', 'Anna', and 'Donna Moderna' cater for women. 'Famiglia Cristiana' is the Catholic weekly. Of the gossip magazines, 'Novella 2000' is the most popular of the gossip magazines.

giro d'Italia

One of the most famous cycling races in the world. It takes place from mid-May to the beginning of June. The route changes every year, but the last stage always ends in Milan. The winner is awarded the pink jersey.

Informagiovani

As the name suggests, this is a service of information and guidance for young people. Promoted by local bodies, the various centres (and their web-sites) provide information about all areas of interest to young people: courses and training, job ads, culture, politics, voluntary work, travel, etc. The first centres opened in Turin and Milan in the early 1980s; now there are about 600 centres throughout Italy. In addition to supplying information, they carry out a role of 'listening' to young people and also promote projects created by young people for young people.

Internet

The Italians' name for the World Wide Web, which they use as an inexhaustible source of information on culture, society, and Italian current affairs. The major newspapers and television stations have their own web-sites, as do councils, museums, etc. The suffix for Italian sites is ".it".

laghi

The north of Italy is the area with the highest concentration of lakes, which includes the three largest and most famous: Lake Garda (the largest of all), Lake Maggiore, and Lake Como. The area's mild climate and luxuriant greenery have always held a great attraction for both Italians and foreigners. Some lakes are equipped for water sports, others offer luxurious hotels and health farms

maturità

This is the exam that students take at the end of the five years of secondary school, between the ages of 18 and 19. It consists of two written tests (one of which is Italian language) and two orals. Marks (the maximum is 60 out of 60) depend on both the result of the tests and the average marks achieved over the last three years. The diploma is a requirement for university entry and, depending upon the type of secondary school attended, it can be in science, classics, arts, technology, etc.

mercati

Every Italian town and city has its own market, either open-air or covered, where fruit, vegetables, cheeses, cooked meats, and other produce are sold. There is also a weekly market where you can buy clothes, bags, household goods, and other items. The prices are cheaper than in the shops and people often haggle over the goods displayed on the stalls.

Mezzogiorno

A term which means southern Italy, including Sicily and Sardinia. The South has a wealth of artistic treasures and beautiful countryside but economically it is less industrialized than the rest of Italy.

Mole Antonelliana

The Mole Antonelliana, an extremely unusual monument (167 m high), is the symbol of Turin. Destined to be a synagogue, the building was begun in 1863 but, following financial problems and arguments about its stability, it was not finished until 1889. Subsequently acquired by the city, it is now the home of the New Museum of the Cinema. A glass lift provides access to the steeple.

Mostra del cinema di Venezia

Also known as the Venice festival, this is the film section of the **Biennale**. It was started in the 1930s and takes place every year at the end of August at the Palazzo del Cinema on the Venice Lido. One of the largest film festivals in Europe (and indeed the world), it attracts films, actors, directors, and other technicians from around the world and the festival winners are awarded the Golden Lion.

negozi

The hours of opening for shops vary according to the type of shop and where it is located. In general, food shops open at about 8 a.m. and close at 7.30 p.m. with a lunch break from 12.30 to 3.30 p.m. Clothes shops, bookshops, etc. open from 9 a.m. until 12.30 or 1 p.m. and then again from 3.30 to 7.30 p.m. In summer the lunch break is longer and shops stay open until 8.00 p.m. Some supermarkets and department stores in the big cities are open all day. Weekly closing also varies according to the type of shop. A lot of shops close for holidays in mid-August, after the summer sales, then reopen with the new autumn-season stock.

Normale

The 'Scuola Normale Superiore di Pisa' was set up in the early 1800s as a branch of the Paris Ecole Normale. Today it is an extremely prestigious institute offering first degree courses and research doctorates in science and the humanities.

onomastico

This is the feast day of the saint whose name you bear. Although less important than your birthday, your saint's day is always celebrated with cards and sometimes with a small gift.

Palio di Siena

A popular event that takes place every year in Siena on 2nd July and 16th August. The **'contrade'** or quarters districts of the city fight for the **'palio'**, a banner, in a cut-throat race on horseback around the medieval Piazza del Campo. It has deep historical roots but is still passionately followed by the Sienese and is a huge attraction for tourists from all over the world. There is a spectacular historical procession in brightly coloured Renaissance costumes before the race.

parchi nazionali

In Italy there are about 20 national parks which cover 5% of the territory. These come under the control of the Ministry of the Environment and their objective is the protection and development of large areas which are of particular importance from the point of view of the environment and the landscape. The best-known are **'Gran Paradiso'**, the national parks in Abruzzi, Lazio and Molise National Park, and the National Park of the Maddalena Archipelago. The marine parks, which aim to protect stretches of sea, coast, and sometimes whole islands and archipelagos, are becoming increasingly important.

passeggiata

This typical Italian custom involves walking with your family or friends in the square or main street, or along the promenade. It usually takes place before you eat, on Saturday afternoon or Sunday morning, and in the summer it can also take place in the evening after dinner. Depending on the time and the weather, you can have an aperitif or an ice-cream. The purpose is to stretch your legs, chat, see who is around, and be seen.

patente a punti

Following reform of the Italian highway code, each driving licence is now given an initial value of 20 points, which are reduced if traffic offences are committed. For example, for the more serious offences (overtaking on a bend, drink driving, or driving while under the effect of drugs) 10 points are deducted; passing a red light costs you 6 points, while parking in an area reserved for public transport costs 2 points. Once the number of infringements committed has reduced the initial number of points to zero, the licence is withdrawn and the driving test has to be retaken. Drivers with the worst records are required to undergo courses of 're-education'. The points system is also applied to foreign citizens who are passing though Italy: the penalties are totted up and filed in a special register.

Pinocchio

The hero of the children's book *The adventures of Pinocchio* by Collodi (1826-90), Pinocchio is a wooden puppet whose nose grows whenever he tells a lie. After various tribulations, accompanied by such famous characters as Geppetto (the puppetmaker), the Blue Fairy, the Fire Eater, Lucignolo, and the whale, etc., Pinocchio is turned into a real boy. Adapted for television and as a cartoon, the story has also been reinterpreted from a sociological and psychoanalytical point of view.

presidente del consiglio

This is the title of the Italian prime minister, the head of the government and of the council of ministers. Nominated by the president of the republic, he proposes the ministers. He controls and is responsible for government policy.

presidente della repubblica

The head of state who represents the nation. He/she is elected by Parliament and remains in office for 7 years. As Italy is a parliamentary republic the duties of the president are: to enact laws, to dissolve parliament and call new elections when necessary, to nominate the prime minister and ratify his choice of the ministers, and to grant pardons. He/she also chairs the body which oversees the appointment of judges.

provincia

In Italy's system of local government, each province is made up of neighbouring municipalities, the most important of which acts as the provincial capital. Each province is served by a provincial council, a committee, and a president.

questura

Provincial headquarters of the police force. Thefts are reported to the **Questura** and passports renewed there.

Quirinale

A sixteenth-century building on the hill of the same name, now the residence of the president of the republic. It was formerly the summer residence of the popes and then of the kings of Italy.

RAI

The state radio and television company. There are three television channels, RAI 1, RAI 2, and RAI 3, and three radio stations, Radio 1, Radio 2, and Radio 3, with various programmes and differing political standpoints.

regione

Italy is subdivided into 20 regions, 5 of which have a certain amount of political autonomy. Each region is subdivided in its turn into provinces and municipalities. The regions can issue legislative standards. They also have administrative duties which can be delegated to the provinces and the municipalities. Each region is served by a council, a committee, and a regional president.

sagra

A popular festival on a particular theme such as wine, sausages, fish, or mushrooms, with a fair and market, which takes place in many villages once a year, sometimes more frequently.

San Marino

The republic of San Marino forms an enclave within Italian territory but is an independent sovereign state completely surrounded by Italian soil, lying between Emilia-Romagna and the Marche, not far from the Adriatic coast. At just over 60 km² in area, it is one of the smallest states in the world.

santo patrono

In Italy the worship of the saints is very strong. The patron saint of a town or community is considered to be its protector. His or her saint's day is a religious holiday on which schools, offices, and most shops are closed. It is celebrated with a special mass and processions. In towns and cities illuminations are put up and there are stalls and sometimes a fair, in a mixture of the sacred and the secular.

Scala

The **Teatro alla Scala**, the Milan opera house, is one of the most famous opera houses in the world. Built in 1776-78, it has recently undergone a programme of restoration, during which the **Teatro degli Arcimboldi**, outside the city, staged its productions.

scuola
The Italian system provides for primary schools, middle schools, and secondary schools. Primary school lasts for five years from the age of six, middle school lasts for three years, and secondary school for five. Primary and middle schools all follow the same curriculum but there are a number of different types of secondary schools: scientific, classical, linguistic, and artistic grammar schools, various technical and commercial institutes, and schools for training nursery school teachers.

senato
The upper house of the Italian Parliament. 315 senators are elected by universal suffrage by citizens over 25 years of age. Senators must be at least 40 years old. These 315 seats are elected on a regional basis, i.e. they are split between the regions in proportion to population. The elected senators are joined by ex-heads of state and life senators nominated by the president of the republic from people who have given exceptional service to the country in the scientific, social, artistic, or literary fields.

settimana bianca
A winter holiday spent with your family or school-friends in a ski resort.

sindaco
The mayor is the head of local government and is in power for four years. He chairs and represents the council and municipal committee.

spumante
A sparkling white wine, often seen as the poor relation of French champagne but also often greatly prized. It can be dry or sweet and always features on Italian Christmas, New Year, and party menus.

stabilimento balneare
A stretch of beach equipped with parasols, loungers, showers, huts, perhaps a swimming-pool, and a bar, that you must pay to go onto. These beach clubs vary from large and crowded to very chic and exclusive and from fairly basic to luxurious. Many of them organize sports tournaments, card games, beauty contests, and dances.

tabaccaio
The tobacconist sells cigarettes and tobacco and is also the only shop apart from the post office where you can buy revenue stamps and postage stamps. It also sells bus tickets and other products. Sometimes there is also a bar. Its sign features a white T on a black background.

Telecom Italia
One of the largest telephone companies for both land lines and mobile phones.

trattoria
A **trattoria** used to be distinguishable from a restaurant because it was simpler, often family-run, and less expensive. Nowadays it is merely a 'typical' local restaurant, serving traditional local dishes in a country-style setting. It can also be very sophisticated, and sometimes quite expensive.

tricolore
The Italian national flag: green, white, and red in vertical bands of equal width. It was designed at the end of 1700s and adopted as the flag of the republic after the Second World War.

Umbria Jazz
An annual jazz festival that takes place around the middle of July in Perugia, Umbria. The biggest names in Italian and international jazz give concerts and seminars, from late morning until late at night, in theatres, clubs, parks, the stadium, etc. For ten days Perugia becomes the city of music.

Valle dei Templi
An archaeological zone in the province of Agrigento that provides the most glorious evidence of Ancient Greek civilization in Sicily. The remains of many temples are to be found on a ridge

(not a valley as the name suggests), among the almond trees. Built in the Doric style in the 5th century BC, the temples were burnt down by the Carthaginians, restored by the Romans in the 1st century AD, then half-destroyed by earthquakes and plundered over the following centuries, so that the only one that now remains intact is the magnificent **Tempio della Concordia**.

Vaticano

The Vatican (also called the Vatican City) has been an independent state within the city of Rome and the seat of the Pope since 1929. The Vatican Palace which surrounds Saint Peter's church is the Pope's residence and houses artistic treasures such as the Sistine Chapel and Raphael's frescos, as well as museums.

vigile urbano

This policeman is a typically Italian figure. Among his duties is controlling the traffic, and therefore also levying fines, e.g. for parking in a no parking zone or riding a motorcycle without a helmet. He is also responsible for environmental protection and for ensuring that municipal regulations (such as correct opening hours and the prices charged in public businesses) are observed, and town laws respected. Finally, he also deals with social problems, such as abandoned children and the monitoring of refugees' and travellers' camps.

Calendar of traditions, festivals, and holidays in Italian-speaking countries

1st January – Capodanno
New Year's Day – a public holiday often spent getting over the excesses of New Year's Eve.

6th January – Epifania
Twelfth Night – a public holiday and religious festival celebrating the adoration of Jesus by the three kings. By popular tradition it is also the day when 'la Befana', an old woman on a broomstick, brings children gifts: they hang up their stockings the night before and in the morning find them full of sweets, cakes, and little presents or, if they have been naughty, coal (nowadays usually made of sugar).

14th February – San Valentino
As in other countries, a day for lovers, marked by flowers, chocolates, and candlelit dinners.

8th March – Festa delle donne
Since the 1970s Women's Day has been celebrated with sprays of mimosa and discussions on women's issues.

19th March – Festa del papà
St. Joseph's day is the day on which Italian fathers are celebrated.

1st April – Pesce d'aprile
April Fool's Day, when it is traditional to play jokes and tricks on people. Children have fun trying to stick paper fish onto people's backs without their noticing.

25th April – Anniversario della Liberazione
A public holiday, this is a day of official ceremonies to commemorate the liberation of Italy from Nazi occupation on 25th April 1945.

1st May – Festa del lavoro
Public holiday – a civil festival celebrating the workers of the world.

2nd June – Festa della Repubblica
Public holiday – a civil festival to commemorate the referendum of 2nd June 1946 which led to the proclamation of the Italian Republic.

15th August – l'Assunzione
Public holiday – a religious festival that also marks the peak of the summer holidays. Just before and after this date, also known as 'Ferragosto', people set off on or return from their holidays. The factories in the north are closed, as are many shops except for those in tourist areas.

1st November – I Santi/Ognissanti
Public holiday and religious festival celebrating all the saints. Typically, cakes made with nuts and raisins, which vary from region to region, are eaten during this festival. People go to the cemetery to take flowers for their dead loved ones, although the Festival of the Dead ('I Morti') is the following day, 2nd November, which is not a holiday.

8th December – L'immacolata Concezione
Public holiday and religious festival that celebrates the purity of the Virgin Mary.

24th December – La vigilia di Natale
Christmas Eve is not a public holiday although the schools are usually closed. Families get together, and often a large dinner is prepared. Afterwards people open their Christmas presents from under the tree. The faithful go to midnight Mass.

25th December – Natale
Christmas Day is a public holiday and one of the most important religious festivals. Families who did not open their presents the night before do so on Christmas morning. Children who believe in Father Christmas think that he has come down the chimney to bring their presents during the night. Families get together to eat a big dinner, typically including a capon and ending with panettone and a glass of spumante.

26th December – Santo Stefano
A public holiday during which Christmas celebrations continue.

31st December – San Silvestro
New Year's Eve – the celebration of the end of the old year and beginning of the new. It is a working day for many people, although students are on holiday, but in the evening there is usually a big meal and a party, either at home or in a restaurant. Typical dishes are lentils (which are said to bring wealth) and cotechino (a large pork sausage), and a great deal of champagne and spumante is drunk. On the stroke of midnight fireworks are set off. In days gone by it was traditional to throw crockery out of the window but this no longer happens, to avoid damage to parked cars and injury to people passing by.

Movable holidays

Giovedì grasso (the Thursday before Lent). Fancy dress parties are held and people traditionally eat pancakes and fried pastries.

Martedì grasso (Shrove Tuesday). In some regions schools are closed.

Mercoledì delle ceneri (Ash Wednesday) – a religious occasion that marks the beginning of Lent. Some people fast on this day.

Venerdì santo (Good Friday) – a religious occasion that is not a public holiday although some schools are closed.

Pasqua (Easter) – the most important Catholic festival, celebrating the resurrection of Christ. A popular saying goes: *'Natale con i tuoi, Pasqua con chi vuoi'* (Christmas with your family, Easter with whoever you want), and in fact Italians often take the opportunity of the holiday period to go away on holiday. Those who stay at home cook a big meal, usually of lamb because of its symbolic meaning. A **colomba** (dove-shaped cake) is the traditional Easter cake.

Pasquetta (Easter Monday) – a public holiday when people often go out for the day, to the sea, the mountains, or the countryside.

L'Ascensione (Ascension) – a religious festival celebrating the ascension of Christ to heaven. It falls on the Thursday 40 days after Easter.

Pentecoste (Whitsun) – a religious festival celebrating the descent of the holy spirit to the apostles. It falls 50 days after Easter.

Festa della mamma (Mothers' Day) is on the second Sunday in May. Cards are sent and sometimes a present: perfume, chocolates, or flowers, especially roses.

Vita e cultura britannica e statunitense dalla A alla Z

Air Force One
Nome del jet usato dal presidente degli Stati Uniti per i viaggi ufficiali.

Ascot
Cittadina del Berkshire famosa per le corse dei cavalli. Il *Royal Ascot* è una corsa della durata di quattro giorni che ha luogo ad Ascot in giugno. La manifestazione è tradizionalmente inaugurata dalla regina. Questo evento sportivo e sociale attira tutto il bel mondo ed è rinomato per la stravaganza dei cappelli indossati dalle signore.

the Ashes
Trofeo conquistato dalla squadra che risulta vincente in una serie di partite tra le nazionali di cricket inglese e australiana. Gli *ashes* (le ceneri) sono quelli dei paletti delle porte, "inumati" dopo la partita del 1882, quando l'Australia batté l'Inghilterra per la prima volta.

the Big Issue
Una rivista venduta per le strade dai senzatetto in molte grandi città della Gran Bretagna. Il contenuto della rivista è principalmente a tema sociale, ma compaiono anche interviste, recensioni discografiche e cinematografiche di buona qualità. I venditori comprano ad un certo prezzo la rivista presso uno dei centri di distribuzione e la rivendono ad un prezzo (più alto) concordato: il margine di guadagno consente loro di mantenersi senza dover mendicare.

the Boat Race
Gara di canottaggio annuale tra le squadre delle Università di Oxford e Cambridge. Ha luogo a Londra sul Tamigi, tra le località di Putney e Mortlake, e si svolge su un percorso di 6,8 km.

the Booker prize
Il premio letterario più prestigioso in Gran Bretagna, assegnato annualmente per la narrativa.

the British Museum
Museo nazionale rinomato in particolare per la collezione di arte egizia e per i marmi cosiddetti 'Elgin', provenienti dal Partenone ad Atene. L'edificio ospita inoltre la Biblioteca Nazionale Britannica.

Broadway
Via di New York famosa per i suoi teatri, il cui nome indica per estensione la zona circostante. Avere successo a Broadway è la massima aspirazione per un attore o una produzione teatrale.

Buckingham Palace
Residenza ufficiale della regina a Londra.

building society
Tipo di banca specializzata in mutui e prestiti per l'acquisto di immobili.

Cabinet
Il Consiglio dei ministri britannico è composto da circa 20 ministri (*ministers*) nominati dal Primo ministro (*Prime Minister*) e si riunisce settimanalmente per discutere questioni amministrative e politiche del governo. Ciascun ministro è responsabile di un settore particolare, mentre il Consiglio nel suo insieme decide della politica governativa e coordina le attività dei ministri. Anche il leader del partito di opposizione nomina un governo ombra (SHADOW CABINET) con funzioni direttive e di governo simile a quelle svolte dai ministri del partito al potere.

Cambridge Certificate
Un diploma che chi studia l'inglese come lingua straniera può conseguire presentandosi agli esami impostati dall'Università di Cambridge. I diplomi che certificano il livello di competenza della lingua sono tre: *First Certificate in English, Advanced Certificate in English* e *Certificate of Proficiency in English*.

Canterbury
Città del Kent (nel sud-est dell'Inghilterra). La sua cattedrale è la

sede dell'Arcivescovo di Canterbury, che è a capo della chiesa anglicana.

Capitol Hill

Collina a Washington sulla quale si trova il palazzo del Campidoglio o Parlamento. Il suo nome viene utilizzato anche per designare le istituzioni governative americane.

Cardiff Arms Park

Stadio di Cardiff, capitale del Galles, dove gioca in casa la squadra gallese di rugby.

Central Park

Vasto parco nel quartiere di Manhattan a New York, caro ai newyorkesi in quanto costituisce un'oasi di verde in una zona fortemente urbanizzata.

Chequers

Proprietà di campagna nel Buckinghamshire residenza di campagna ufficiale del Primo ministro, dove i capi di Stato esteri vengono intrattenuti in occasione di visite ufficiali e dove si svolgono gli incontri al vertice.

the City

Forma abbreviata di *The City of London*. Occupa l'insediamento originario di Londra e costituisce una *municipality* (unità amministrativa autonoma), con a capo il Lord Mayor (il sindaco di Londra). Il nome si riferisce anche al centro finanziario di Londra, sede di banche e altre istituzioni affini.

the Commonwealth

Gruppo di circa cinquanta nazioni indipendenti che facevano un tempo parte dell'Impero Britannico.

Congress

Il Congresso è l'organismo legislativo nazionale degli Stati Uniti. Si riunisce nel Campidoglio, sul CAPITOL HILL ed è composto da due camere: il Senato (SENATE) e la Camera dei Rappresentanti (HOUSE OF REPRESENTATIVES). Tutte le proposte di legge devono essere presentate per l'approvazione alle due Camere a cui fa seguito la promulgazione da parte del Presidente (PRESIDENT).

Covent Garden

In passato, mercato ortofrutticolo di Londra, recentemente ristrutturato in quartiere di negozi e bar. Il nome si riferisce anche alla Royal Opera House, sede della National Opera e del Royal Ballet.

Crown Court

In Inghilterra e Galles, tribunale penale competente nei reati di maggiore gravità.

Death Valley

Bacino desertico nell'est della California e nell'ovest del Nevada, la zona più calda e arida dell'America del Nord. È ufficialmente riconosciuto come parte del patrimonio nazionale.

Downing Street

Via del centro di Londra dove, al numero 10, si trova la residenza londinese ufficiale del primo ministro britannico, designata come *10 Downing Street* o *Number 10*. La residenza ufficiale del Chancellor of the Exchequer (ministro del tesoro) si trova accanto, al numero 11.

the Edinburgh Festival

Festival artistico con ricorrenza annuale che ha luogo a Edimburgo, capitale della Scozia. È il più grande festival nel suo genere in Europa, rinomato soprattutto per la qualità della musica e delle rappresentazioni teatrali, oltre che per le manifestazioni del cosiddetto *Fringe*, cioè il festival non ufficiale, che si svolge parallelamente.

fish and chips

Piatto nazionale britannico, consiste in pesce fritto dorato e patatine. Generalmente condito con sale e aceto è per lo più venduto come piatto da asporto, avvolto in un cartoccio.

Fleet Street

Via londinese dove aveva sede la maggior parte dei quotidiani britannici. Il suo nome viene usato per designare la stampa o i giornalisti britannici in generale.

Florence Nightingale

Infermiera inglese vissuta nel XIX secolo, famosa per l'opera prestata negli ospedali militari durante la guerra di Crimea. È considerata la fondatrice della professione infermieristica e la riformatrice delle condizioni ospedaliere. È conosciuta anche come la *Lady with the Lamp* (la signora con la lampada).

further education

In Gran Bretagna con il termine *further education* si intende generalmente l'istruzione fornita alle persone di età superiore ai 16 anni, età in cui cessa l'obbligo scolastico, che prepara al diploma di studi superiori o alla formazione professionale. Negli Stati Uniti il termine *further education* si usa anche per definire l'insegnamento universitario e parauniversitario che in Gran Bretagna è invece detto *higher education*.

the Grand National

La corsa di cavalli a ostacoli più importante, tenuta annualmente a Aintree, presso Liverpool. È un evento di portata nazionale che attira puntualmente un forte interesse. Sono molte le persone che puntano sui cavalli solo in occasione di questa corsa.

Guy Fawkes

Membro del gruppo di cospiratori che tentò di far saltare in aria il palazzo di Westminster (sede del Parlamento) e di uccidere il re Giacomo I nel 1605. La congiura fu sventata e Fawkes, sorpreso con la polvere da sparo, giustiziato. Questi avvenimenti vengono ricordati ogni anno durante la *Bonfire Night* (notte dei falò, 5 novembre) con fuochi d'artificio e roghi nei quali vengono bruciati fantocci chiamati *guys*.

Harley Street

Via londinese nota per l'alta concentrazione di studi medici specializzati.

Harrods

Celebre grande magazzino nel quartiere londinese di Knightsbridge, dove si dice si possa trovare di tutto. È rinomato anche il reparto di generi alimentari.

Henley-on-Thames

Piccola città sul Tamigi, nella contea dell'Oxfordshire. Deve la sua fama alla regata annuale, conosciuta come *Henley*, che ha qui luogo.

heritage centre

In Gran Bretagna gli *heritage centres* sono dei tipi di museo in cui vengono ricreati edifici, macchinari, mezzi di trasporto ecc. di determinati periodi storici, così che i visitatori possano osservare com'era la vita tanto tempo fa.

the Home Counties

Nome collettivo delle contee inglesi più vicine a Londra (Buckinghamshire, Essex, Hertfordshire, Kent, Surrey e Middlesex).

the House of Commons

La Camera dei Comuni (anche detta *the Commons*) è la camera bassa del parlamento britannico (HOUSES OF PARLIAMENT). I 635 deputati (MEMBERS OF PARLIAMENT) eletti a suffragio diretto si riuniscono per discutere questioni di politica interna ed estera e per votare sulle proposte di legge.

the House of Lords

La Camera dei Lords (anche detta *the Lords*) è la camera alta del parlamento britannico (HOUSES OF PARLIAMENT). I membri non sono eletti, ma occupano il seggio per diritto ereditario, per nomina o d'ufficio. Le funzioni della Camera dei Lord si sono andate riducendo nel tempo ed oggi sono limitate alla discussione e alla proposta di amendamenti alle leggi già approvate dalla Camera dei Comuni (HOUSE OF COMMONS). La Camera dei Lords è anche il supremo tribunale d'appello.

the Houses of Parliament

Il parlamento britannico è composto dalla Camera dei Comuni (HOUSE OF COMMONS) e dalla Camera dei Lords (HOUSE OF LORDS). Houses of Parliament è anche il nome del palazzo di Westminster (*Palace of Westminster*), il gruppo di edifici che sorgono sul Tamigi, dove si riuniscono le due Camere.

the House of Representatives

La Camera dei Rappresentanti è la camera bassa del parlamento (CONGRESS) degli Stati Uniti. È composta da 435 rappresentanti (REPRESENTATIVEs) eletti ogni due anni: ciascun Stato elegge un numero di rappresentanti proporzionale alla sua popolazione. La funzione della Camera è quella di proporre e approvare i disegni di legge.

interstate (highway)

Denominazione della rete stradale statunitense che attraversa il paese in lungo e in largo, oltre i confini statali. Le *interstate highways* (tutte a quattro corsie) sono segnalate da un cartello blu e rosso con una I (*interstate*) e un numero: quelle che attraversano il paese da est a ovest hanno numeri pari, quelle che lo attraversano da nord a sud numeri dispari. Ad esempio la I-80 va da New York alla California e la I-95 dal Maine alla Florida.

the Ivy League

Gruppo di prestigiose università negli Stati Uniti nord-orientali, che comprendono Harvard, Yale e Princeton.

Jack the Ripper

(Jack lo Squartatore)
Assassino di prostitute tristemente noto che operò nella zona est di Londra nel 1888. La sua identità non è stata mai scoperta.

Job Centre

Agenzia di collocamento statale che ha anche la funzione di assegnare i sussidi di disoccupazione.

John o'Groats

Paese nella costa nord-orientale della Scozia considerato l'estremità settentrionale della Gran Bretagna, con l'esclusione delle isole.

Land's End

Estremità sud-occidentale dell'Inghilterra che ricorre nell'espressione *from Land's End to John o'Groats* (da Land's End a John o'Groats, cioè tutta la Gran Bretagna).

the Last Night of the Proms

Concerto conclusivo della stagione dei *Proms* (concerti di musica classica) che ha luogo ogni anno alla Royal Albert Hall di Londra. Il concerto termina regolarmente con una serie di composizioni patriottiche di Elgar ed è caratterizzato da un certo fervore nazionalista e da un'atmosfera di festa.

L-driver – learner driver

Con questo termine in Gran Bretagna si indica chi sta imparando a guidare. I principianti, quando si trovano al volante, devono essere accompagnati da qualcuno che abbia la patente di guida (*driving licence*). Inoltre devono esporre, anteriormente e posteriormente al veicolo, una targa di pratica (*L-plate*) fin quando non abbiano superato l'esame di guida (*driving test*). La targa di pratica consiste in una quadrato autoadesivo bianco con una L rossa.

the Little League

Serie di squadre di baseball di paesi e cittadine degli Stati Uniti, formate da bambini.

Lloyd's

Associazione di assicuratori, i cosiddetti *names* (nomi), responsabili del pagamento degli indennizzi in caso di danni a edifici, navi o altre proprietà assicurate presso di loro.

the Loch Ness monster

Mostro leggendario che, secondo la tradizione, vivrebbe nelle acque del Loch Ness, nelle Highlands scozzesi. Il mostro, chiamato familiarmente *Nessie*, è oggetto di frequenti ricerche. Le fotografie più celebri mostrano una creatura dal collo lungo e con le pinne.

Lord's

Il campo di cricket più famoso del mondo, situato nella zona di St John's Wood a Londra.

Magistrates' Court

In Inghilterra e Galles, tribunale penale competente in reati minori.

the Met

La prestigiosa Metropolitan Opera House a New York. Per un cantante lirico, esibirsi al Met è testimonianza del riconoscimento internazionale.

Monty Python

Gruppo di comici britannici di culto degli anni '70, conosciuti per il loro umorismo demenziale. Hanno anche girato una serie di film.

motorway

In Gran Bretagna esiste una vasta rete autostradale libera. Le autostrade, normalmente a tre corsie per ogni senso di marcia e con un limite di velocità di 112 km/h, sono contrassegnate dalla lettera M (*motorway*) e da un numero.

MP – Member of Parliament
Ciascun membro della Camera dei Comuni (HOUSE OF COMMONS) che rappresenta uno dei 659 collegi elettorali dell'Inghilterra, Scozia, Galles e Irlanda del Nord.

Murrayfield
Stadio della squadra di rugby scozzese, a Edimburgo.

Napa Valley
Area della California settentrionale famosa per la produzione vinicola.

the National Health Service
Servizio sanitario nazionale del Regno Unito che comprende medici generici e ospedali. Fu fondato nel 1946.

National Insurance (NI)
In Gran Bretagna, sistema di contributi (*National Insurance Contributions*) che tutti i lavoratori e i datori di lavoro sono tenuti a versare per la previdenza sociale, (sussidi, pensioni, assistenza sanitaria). Tutti gli adulti hanno un numero di previdenza sociale (*National Insurance Number*).

the National Trust
Organizzazione che si occupa della conservazione del patrimonio storico e naturale del Regno Unito.

the Northern Ireland Assembly
Il nuovo parlamento dell'Irlanda del Nord ha sede a Belfast. È stato istituito nel 1998 dal governo laburista britannico nell'ambito di un maggiore decentramento del potere a favore di una più estesa autonomia della regione.

the Old Bailey
Il tribunale penale più importante in Inghilterra.

the Old Lady of Threadneedle Street
Soprannome della Banca d'Inghilterra, che si trova in Threadneedle Street, nel centro finanziario di Londra.

the Oval
Campo di cricket nel sud di Londra utilizzato per gli incontri internazionali.

page 3
Terza pagina di alcuni giornali popolari nella quale sono pubblicate fotografie di pin-up in pose provocanti.

Parliament
Il parlamento britannico è il massimo organo legislativo del Paese ed è composto dal sovrano, dalla Camera dei Lords (HOUSE OF LORDS) e dalla dalla Camera dei Comuni (HOUSE OF COMMONS).

the Pentagon
È il complesso di edifici a pianta pentagonale, presso Washington, sede del ministero della Difesa e delle Forze armate statunitensi. Spesso si usa il termine *The Pentagon* per riferirsi allo Stato maggiore, cioè i generali e i comandanti militari.

President
Negli Stati Uniti il presidente è il capo dello Stato, responsabile della politica estera e comandante in capo delle Forze armate. Il presidente ha la facoltà di nominare i giudici federali e i ministri ed è inoltre chiamato a promulgare le leggi approvate dal CONGRESS. Può rimanere in carica per un massimo di due legislature (*terms*) di quattro anni ciascuna.

Pulitzer Prize
È un premio molto prestigioso che viene assegnato ogni anno negli Stati Uniti ad una trentina fra giornalisti e scrittori che si sono distinti per il loro lavoro nel campo del giornalismo, della letteratura e della musica.

Queen's (o King's) Counsel
Avvocato di rango superiore, la cui nomina è effettuata su raccomandazione del Lord Chancellor (il ministro di Giustizia per l'Inghilterra e il Galles).

the Queen's Speech
Un discorso programmatico preparato dai ministri del governo britannico e letto dalla regina presso la Camera dei Lord (HOUSE OF LORDS) durante la cerimonia di apertura del parlamento che si tiene ogni anno in autunno. Il discorso è importante in quanto illustra il programma del governo per l'anno seguente. Viene trasmesso alla radio e alla TV.

Remembrance Sunday
La domenica più vicina all'11 novembre, anniversario della firma dell'armistizio

che concluse la prima guerra mondiale.
I caduti delle due guerre vengono
commemorati in questo giorno, in
particolare con una cerimonia davanti al
Cenotaph, il monumento ai caduti,
in Whitehall.

Representative

Ciascuno dei membri della Camera
dei Rappresentanti (HOUSE OF
REPRESENTATIVES) degli Stati
Uniti.

Robin Hood

Eroe leggendario, capo di una banda di
fuorilegge che, durante il medioevo,
viveva nella foresta di Sherwood, nel
Nottinghamshire. Robin Hood e i suoi
compagni erano noti per sottrarre ai
ricchi e donare ai poveri. Lady Marian
era la sua innamorata.

Scotland Yard

Nome popolare che la *Metropolitan Police*
(polizia londinese) trae dalla sua vecchia
sede. Il nome ufficiale della sede attuale è
New Scotland Yard.

the Scottish Parliament

Il parlamento scozzese si riunisce presso
l'*Holyrood House* a Edimburgo, capitale
della Scozia. È stato istituito nel 1999 in
seguito al risultato del referendum
(concesso dal partito laburista dopo la
vittoria elettorale del 1997 nell'ambito di
un maggiore decentramento del potere)
a favore di una più estesa autonomia della
regione.

the Senate

Il Senato è la camera alta del parlamento
(CONGRESS) degli Stati Uniti. È
composto da 100 senatori (SENATORS),
due per ogni Stato, che rimangono in
carica sei anni. Tutte le leggi devono
essere approvate dal Senato e dalla
Camera dei Rappresentanti (HOUSE OF
REPRESENTATIVES), ma il Senato ha
inoltre responsabilità speciali in materia
di politica estera e facoltà di
'consultazione e approvazione' delle
nomine effettuate dal presidente.

Senator

Ciascuno dei membri del Senato
(SENATE) degli Stati Uniti.

Shadow Cabinet > CABINET

Silicon Valley

Nome dato alla zona nella Santa Clara
Valley in California, vicino alle città di
San Francisco e San Josè, dove sorgono
numerose industrie elettroniche e
informatiche. Il nome deriva dal largo
uso del silicio (*silicon*) nell'elettronica.

the Smithsonian Institution

Questo nome si riferisce generalmente ad
un vasto gruppo di musei di Washington
che ospitano diverse collezioni, dall'arte
alle armi. La *Smithsonian Institution*,
che amministra i musei, è rinomata per
la ricerca scientifica.

the Square Mile

Un altro nome del centro finanziario di
Londra (*the City*).

the Stars and Stripes

La bandiera degli Stati Uniti ha tredici
strisce, sei bianche e sette rosse, e 50
stelle bianche (una per ogni Stato) in
campo blu.

the Star-Spangled Banner

L'inno nazionale degli Stati Uniti,
adottato ufficialmente nel 1931. Con
questo nome si designa talvolta anche la
bandiera americana.

Stratford-upon-Avon

Città nel sud-ovest dell'Inghilterra,
nota per aver dato i natali a William
Shakespeare e per ospitare la Royal
Shakespeare Company. Il nome viene
spesso abbreviato in Stratford.

the Super Bowl

Finale del campionato di football
americano.

Trooping the Colour

Parata militare che ha luogo in
Whitehall, a Londra, in onore del
compleanno ufficiale della regina
(8 giugno).

Turner Prize

Premio in denaro assegnato ogni anno
dalla Tate Gallery di Londra ad un artista
britannico sotto i 50 anni per un'opera di
arte moderna. Si tratta di un evento
culturale di rilievo in Gran Bretagna,
e i lavori dei quattro finalisti sono esposti
presso la Tate Gallery prima
dell'assegnazione del premio.

Twickenham

Stadio della squadra inglese di rugby.
Deriva il suo nome dalla zona della
periferia londinese così chiamata, che si
trova sulle rive del Tamigi, ad ovest della
città.

the Union Jack

La bandiera del Regno Unito,
formata dalla croce di San Giorgio a
rappresentare l'Inghilterra, quella di
Sant'Andrea per la Scozia e quella di
San Patrizio per l'Irlanda del Nord.
La parola *jack* è un termine nautico
con cui si indica una bandiera.

Wall Street

La strada di Manhattan a New York dove
hanno sede la borsa (*New York Stock
Exchange*) e gli uffici di numerosi istituti
finanziari. Spesso con il nome *Wall Street*
si intende la borsa valori stessa.

Watford

Cittadina che segna il confine
immaginario che, per gli abitanti di
Londra e del sud-est dell'Inghilterra,
li separa dal resto del paese.

the Welsh Assembly

Il parlamento gallese con sede a Cardiff,
capitale del Galles. È stato istituito nel
1999 in seguito al risultato del
referendum (concesso dal partito
laburista dopo la vittoria elettorale del
1997 nell'ambito di un maggiore
decentramento del potere) a favore di una
più estesa autonomia della regione.

Wembley

Stadio di calcio nazionale inglese, a
Londra. Ospita anche concerti di musica
pop e altre manifestazioni di vaste
proporzioni.

the West End

Area del centro di Londra rinomata per i
teatri, i cinema, i locali notturni, i negozi
e i ristoranti.

Westminster

Zona di Londra in cui si trova la sede del
Parlamento; il nome viene spesso usato
per indicare il Parlamento stesso.

the White House

(la Casa Bianca)
Residenza ufficiale del presidente degli
Stati Uniti, in Pennsylvania Avenue,
a Washington. Nel cuore della Casa
Bianca si trova l'*Oval Office* (ufficio
ovale), ufficio del presidente.

Whitehall

Via londinese vicino alla sede del
Parlamento, dove vari dipartimenti del
governo hanno i loro uffici; il nome
designa anche, per estensione,
la pubblica amministrazione.

Wimbledon

Zona della periferia londinese famosa
per ospitare l'*All England Tennis Club*,
dove ogni anno si svolge il celebre torneo
di tennis conosciuto sotto il nome di
Wimbledon.

Giorni festivi nel Regno Unito e negli Stati Uniti

1 gennaio
New Year's Day (Capodanno)
Giorno festivo, generalmente trascorso a riprendersi dai festeggiamenti della notte precedente.

2 gennaio
Giorno festivo in Scozia.

6 gennaio
Epiphany o **Twelfth night** (Epifania)
Non ci sono particolari tradizioni legate a questa giornata, ma molti in questo giorno disfano l'albero di Natale e mettono via le decorazioni natalizie.

25 gennaio
Burns Night
Ricorrenza della nascita del poeta scozzese Robert Burns (XVIII secolo). Gli scozzesi festeggiano con una cena detta *Burns Supper* il cui piatto forte si chiama *haggis* (intestino di pecora farcito con una miscela di avena, frattaglie, cipolle e spezie). Tradizionalmente, durante la cena accompagnata dal suono delle cornamuse, si beve whisky e si leggono ad alta voce brani delle poesie di Robert Burns.

2 febbraio
Groundhog Day
Giorno in cui, secondo la tradizione statunitense, la marmotta (*groundhog*) esce dalla sua tana sotterranea alla fine del letargo. Se c'è il sole e la marmotta vede la propria ombra si nasconderà nella tana e ci saranno altre sei settimane di cattivo tempo. Se non vede la propria ombra, si crede che la primavera comincerà presto.

14 febbraio
St Valentine's Day
Nel giorno di San Valentino gli innamorati si scambiano fiori e regali. Esiste inoltre la tradizione di inviare un biglietto anonimo alla persona per cui si prova una tenera simpatia.

1 marzo
St David's Day
Giorno di festa nazionale in Galles, di cui San Davide è il santo protettore.

17 marzo
St Patrick's Day
La festa di San Patrizio, patrono d'Irlanda, viene celebrata dagli irlandesi in tutto il mondo con musica, canti e grandi bevute.

1 aprile
April Fools' Day
Giornata in cui si fanno numerosi scherzi: le vittime di tali scherzi sono dette *April Fools*.

23 aprile
St George's Day
San Giorgio è il patrono d'Inghilterra.

4 luglio
Independence Day
In questo giorno di festa nazionale negli Stati Uniti si celebra l'approvazione della Dichiarazione d'Indipendenza (1776) con parate, spettacoli di fuochi artificiali e picnic. In moltissime case viene esposta la bandiera americana.

12 ottobre
Columbus Day
Giorno festivo negli Stati Uniti, ricorrenza della scoperta dell'America da parte di Cristoforo Colombo nel 1492.

31 ottobre
Hallowe'en (vigilia d'Ognissanti)
La notte della vigilia d'Ognissanti in cui, secondo un'antica credenza anglosassone, è possibile vedere i fantasmi. Oggi è festeggiata per lo più dai bambini, che ricavano lanterne dalle zucche svuotate, si mascherano e fanno il giro del vicinato per chiedere dolci e regalini con il *trick or treat* ('dolcetto o scherzetto').

5 novembre
Bonfire Night/Guy Fawkes
In Gran Bretagna si festeggia il fallimento della Congiura delle Polveri per far saltare in aria il Parlamento nel 1605. Ovunque si organizzano spettacoli di fuochi d'artificio e falò in cui viene bruciato un pupazzo rudimentale detto *guy* che rappresenta Guy Fawkes, uno dei cospiratori.

11 novembre
Remembrance Day,
Veteran's Day negli USA
Giornata in cui si commemorano i caduti di tutte le guerre e la firma dell'armistizio (1918) che mise fine alla prima guerra mondiale. In Gran Bretagna la ricorrenza è anche nota come *Poppy Day* (giorno del papavero), per l'usanza di portare un papavero rosso di stoffa o carta sul petto (dai campi di papaveri in cui morirono migliaia di soldati sui fronti francese e belga).

30 novembre
St Andrew's Day
Sant'Andrea è il patrono della Scozia.

25 dicembre
Christmas Day (giorno di Natale)
Giorno festivo. Per tradizione i familiari si scambiano i doni intorno all'albero la mattina di Natale e i bambini spesso trovano, al risveglio, una calza (*Christmas stocking*) piena di dolci e regalini lasciata da *Father Christmas*, anche chiamato *Santa Claus*.

26 dicembre
Boxing Day in Gran Bretagna,
St Stephen's Day in Irlanda. Giorno festivo.

31 dicembre
New Year's Eve (la notte di San Silvestro)
In Scozia si chiama **Hogmanay** ed è tradizione andare a trovare amici e vicini di casa per augurare loro pace e prosperità portando in dono un pezzo di carbone o del whisky o qualcosa da mangiare.

Letter-writing / Redazione di lettere

Holiday postcard

■ *This is an informal card so you use caro followed immediately by the name. This style is used for friends and relatives (Cara in the feminine: Cara Claudia, Cara nonna etc. Cari/Care is used in the plural: Cari cugini, Cari tutti, Cari Simonetta e Andrea, Care Letizia e Margherita).*

■ *To be more formal, add the person's title before their name: Sig., Sig.ra, or Dott., Ing., Prof.ssa etc. If you want to send a postcard to a family, address it to: Famiglia Tabucchi.*

Caro Paolo,

Saluti da Bath! Sono arrivata qui un paio di giorni fa ed è tutto bellissimo. Beh, a parte il tempo, ma si sa com'è il clima da queste parti. Ho visitato le terme romane e la cattedrale e tanti altri bei posti. Ovviamente non ho saputo resistere alla tentazione di prendere un classico tè all'inglese nell'elegante 'Pump Room'! Domani partenza per Londra e giovedì ritorno a Firenze.

Come va il nuovo lavoro? Ti chiamo appena posso.

Bacioni
  Stella

Paolo Tabucchi
via ① del Platano 29
50100 Firenze

■ *This ending is informal. Another way of ending a card is with saluti followed by your name or name and surname.*

① *In addresses the words via, viale, corso etc can be written with or without a capital letter. The house or building number comes after the name of the street rather than before it, and the postcode comes before the name of the town or city. For villages and small towns the name of the provincial capital should also be included, either in full or in its usual abbreviated form.*

Letters / Lettere

Cartolina dalle vacanze

■ L'inizio è molto semplice e informale: Dear, seguito dal nome di battesimo del destinatario.

■ Il nome del destinatario è qui preceduto dall'abbreviazione del titolo (Mr, Mrs, Miss o Ms, senza puntino). Segue poi l'indirizzo. In Gran Bretagna molte case hanno un nome che si mette per primo; viene poi il numero civico, seguito dalla via, dal nome della città (talvolta, nel caso di grandi città, preceduto da quello del quartiere) o del paese, seguiti dalla contea; è molto importante indicare il codice postale (postcode); nel caso di corrispondenza internazionale, segue ovviamente la nazione. Per gli Stati Uniti, dopo il numero e il nome della via, si indica la città, la sigla dello stato e il codice postale (zip code).

Mr John Spaline Jr
100 Irving Palace
New York, NY 10001
USA

Dear John

Greetings from Naples! Got here a couple of days ago, but already in love with the place (in spite of the traffic). Everything is so different and the food is delicious. We have visited the Archaeological Museum, the Cathedral and the Aquarium. Tomorrow we're visiting Hercolaneum and Pompeii and then on Thursday we head home. Hope ② your mother is fully recovered by now.

See you soon,

Mark and Juliet.

6.8.2004 ①

Mr J. Roberts
The Willows
49 North Terrace
Kings Barton
Nottinghamshire
NG8 42l
England

■ Formula di saluto informale, da usare per amici e parenti. In alternativa si può usare All the best, With love from, o semplicemente Love (from).

① Nelle cartoline e nelle lettere personali, sia gli americani che gli inglesi mettono la data in alto a destra.

② Nelle cartoline si usa spesso uno stile 'telegrafico', in cui i pronomi soggetto vengono omessi: Got here…e Hope you're…anziché We got here…e I hope you're…

Letters / Lettere

Christmas and New Year wishes (informal)

Natale 2004

Cari Teresa e Federico,

Buon Natale e Felice Anno Nuovo

Vi auguro con tutto il cuore un anno pieno di
belle sorprese e spero che ci sia al più presto
l'occasione di rivederci.

Un abbraccio a tutti e due,

Paola

■ You write the date like this on
greetings cards. For Easter you
write Pasqua and the year. For other
occasions (birthdays, etc.) you can
write the date in full: 6 febbraio 2004
with the number, the month without
a capital letter, then the year, or as a
number: 6/2/04.

■ Standard greeting for Christmas and
New Year cards.

Christmas and New Year wishes (formal)

On the envelope:

Gentile Dott. Bossi e famiglia

■ In Italy fewer people send Christmas
cards than in Great Britain.
Young people don't send them;
it's considered slightly formal.
If you send a present to someone
you might attach a card, but if you
exchange presents in person you
don't normally give them a card,
just wish them Buon Natale.
The same goes for birthdays.

Monza, Natale 2004

BUON NATALE E FELICE
ANNO NUOVO

I miei più sentiti auguri a Lei ①
e alla famiglia

Fausto Mameli

■ Inside greetings cards you can write
the place you are writing from in
front of the date.

① Lei is written with a capital letter in
more formal letters.

. . . .

Auguri di Buon Natale e Buon Anno

Su un biglietto:

> [Best wishes for a] Happy ① Christmas and
> a Prosperous New Year
>
> Best wishes for Christmas and the New Year
>
> Wishing you every happiness this Christmas
> and in the New Year

① *Oppure:* Merry.

In una lettera:

> 44 Louis Gardens
> London NW6 4GM
>
> December 20th 2003
>
> Dear Peter and Claire,
>
> First of all, a very happy Christmas and all the best for the New Year to you
> and the children. ② We hope you're all well ③ and that we'll see you again.
> It seems ages since we last met up.
>
> We've had a very eventful year. Last summer Gavin came off his bike and
> broke his arm and collarbone. Kathy scraped through her A Levels and is
> now at Sussex doing European Studies. Poor Tony was made redundant in
> October and is still looking for a job.
>
> Do come and see us next time you are over this way. Just give us a ring a
> couple of days before so we can fix something.
>
> All best wishes
>
> Tony and Ann

② *Oppure (se i figli sono adulti):* to you and your family.

③ *Oppure (informale):* flourishing.

Invitation to a wedding and wedding reception

Filippo Bartolini   Cristiana Tedeschi

Annunciano il loro matrimonio

Chiesa di S. Jacopo – Siena

Sabato 22 maggio 2005 – ore 16.30

Siena –   Volterra –
Via della Salute, 50   Via A. Diaz, 6

- Invitations to weddings are called 'partecipazioni' and are written or printed.

- Very formal invitations are sent out by the parents who are announcing their son's or daughter's wedding.

Filippo e Cristiana

dopo la cerimonia saranno lieti di salutare
parenti ed amici presso la
Villa Il Poggio
Via Marradi 45 – Siena

R.S.V.P.

Invitation to a christening

Invitations to parties are usually by word of mouth, while for weddings announcements are usually sent out.

Fabrizio Castelli e Katherine Ferguson
partecipano la nascita di Luigi

Vi invitano al suo battesimo nel Duomo di Barga
il 15 febbraio 2005 alle ore 12.00
e al rinfresco che seguirà alla Locanda da Gabriele
in località la Mocchia di Barga

RSVP tel. 0583 – 861042

- When a phone number is given after RSVP you reply to the invitation by phone.

Invito (informale)

- *La data si può anche scrivere nei modi seguenti: April 10, 10 April, 10th April. Il nome del mese è in maiuscolo.*

- *In alto a destra si indica il nome e l'indirizzo del mittente, e sotto si scrive la data.*

35 Winchester Drive
Stoke Gifford
Bristol
BS34 8PD

April 22nd 2003

Dear Luca,

Is there any chance of your coming to stay with us in the summer holidays? Roy and Debbie would be delighted if you could (as well as David and me, of course). We hope to go to North Wales at the end of July/beginning of August, and you'd be very welcome to come too. It's really beautiful up there. We'll probably take tents – I hope that's OK by you.

Let me know as soon as possible if you can manage it.

All best wishes

Rachel Hemmings

Invito (formale)

Invito a un matrimonio e al rinfresco

Mr and Mrs Peter Thompson
request the pleasure of your company
at the marriage of their daughter
Hannah Louise
to
Steven David Warner
at St Mary's Church, Little Bourton
on Saturday 22nd July 2001 at 2 p.m.
And afterwards at the Golden Cross Hotel, Billing

23 Santers Lane
Little Bourton
Northampton
NN6 1AZ

R.S.V.P

Letters / Lettere

Accepting an invitation (formal)

CARLO E BEATRICE BUOZZI

ringraziano calorosamente per il gentile invito
e sono lieti di poter partecipare.

Invitation (informal)

Cara Claudia

È un po' che non ci sentiamo ma spero che tutto vada bene, sia con Andrea che con l'università. Il 7 agosto è il mio compleanno e pensavo di fare una festa. Che ne dici ① di venire qui a Napoli? Naturalmente sei invitata a casa mia per qualche giorno e ne approfitteremo per fare un po' di chiacchiere e un po' di mare. Fammi sapere al più presto! Spero tanto che tu venga, da sola o accompagnata, se tu e Andrea siete ancora insieme. Il mio indirizzo email è grazia@hotmail.com.

Un bacione ② e a prestissimo,

Grazia

- Invitations to parties are usually made in person or on the phone, unless it's a really formal occasion.

① For a letter to a friend you use the 'tu' form.

② This affectionate ending is used with close friends or relatives. Other informal endings are Baci or Un abbraccio.

Accepting an invitation (informal)

24 aprile 2005

Cara Grazia

Quanto tempo! Scusa se non mi sono fatta più viva ma tra gli esami e altre storie il tempo è volato. Certo che vengo giù a Napoli. L'ultimo esame lo dovrei avere a fine luglio e non ho ancora programmato niente per le vacanze, tanto più che adesso sono sola (mollata da Andrea due mesi fa, ma senza troppi drammi). Ora che ci siamo rimesse in contatto prometto di non sparire e non vedo l'ora di rivederti di persona. Torno a studiare.

Un abbraccio,

Claudia

- In informal letters you write the date at the top but not your address.

- In replies to informal invitations you also use only the Christian name, the 'tu' form and an affectionate ending.

Letters / Lettere

Per accettare un invito (informale)

> Luca Vallerini
> viale Italia 78
> 20162 Milano
>
> 2 May 2003
>
> Dear Mrs Hemmings ①,
>
> Many thanks for your letter and kind invitation. Since I don't have anything fixed yet for the summer holidays, I'd be delighted to come. However I mustn't be away for more than four or five days since my mother hasn't been very well.
>
> You must let me know what I should bring. How warm is it in North Wales? Can you swim in the sea? Camping is fine as far as I'm concerned, we take our tents everywhere.
>
> Looking forward to seeing you soon.
>
> Yours ②,
>
> Luca

① Questa è la lettera che un ragazzo scrive alla madre di un amico e quindi, anche se il tono generale è informale, si apre in modo piuttosto formale.

② Altre formule per questo tipo di lettera: With best wishes, Yours sincerely, Kind/Kindest regards.

Risposta a un invito (formale)

> **Per accettare:** Richard Willis has great pleasure in accepting Mr and Mrs Peter Thompson's kind invitation to the marriage of their daughter Hannah Louise to Steven Warner at St Mary's Church, Little Bourton, on Saturday 22nd July.
>
> **Per declinare:** Richard Willis regrets that he is unable to accept Mr and Mrs Peter Thompson's kind invitation to ...., owing to a prior engagement.

■ Si ripetono i particolari dell'invito, ma in modo meno dettagliato.

■ Nel caso non si possa accettare l'invito è consigliabile scrivere una lettera ai genitori della sposa, specialmente se si conoscono di persona.

Letters / Lettere

Replying to a job advertisement

- When you don't know the name of the person use this style. If you are writing to a company you can also use Spett.le Ditta.

- In letters written in reply to an advertisement you should make specific reference to the advert: under oggetto you put the position you are applying for with the reference number or abbreviation, as well as the newspaper and date that the advert appeared.

Bristol, 25 settembre 2005

Grifoni S.p.a.
viale Marconi, 67
20100 Milano

Oggetto: ricerca programmatore
Rif. AB 067
Corriere della Sera 12.09.2005

Gentili Signori

Ho letto con molto interesse il Vostro annuncio apparso sul Corriere della Sera del 12 settembre scorso e Vi sarei grato se poteste inviarmi ulteriori informazioni riguardo la posizione in oggetto.

Attualmente sono impiegato presso un'azienda di Bristol ma il mio contratto termina alla fine del mese e vorrei approfittare di questa opportunità per lavorare a Milano. Come risulta dal curriculum vitae che allego alla presente, oltre a possedere i titoli e l'esperienza richiesti, ho vissuto per qualche tempo in Italia ed ho un'ottima conoscenza della lingua italiana.

Resto a disposizione per un eventuale colloquio nel momento che riterrete più opportuno e faccio presente che dal 6 ottobre prossimo sarò raggiungibile a Milano al seguente indirizzo:

via Indipendenza 7
20100 Milano
tel. 02 429.96.67

In attesa di un Vostro cortese riscontro porgo cordiali saluti

David Baker
67 Whiteley Avenue
Bristol, BS5 6TW
UK

- When you are writing you should always include your own address after the signature either on the right or on the left.

Risposta a un annuncio di lavoro

via Giolitti 32
00100 Rome

26 September 2005

The Personnel Manager ①
Patterson Software plc
Milton State
Bath BA6 8YZ

Dear Sir or Madam ①,

I am interested in the post of programmer advertised in The Guardian of 12 September and would be very grateful if you could send me further particulars. ②

I am currently working for the Sempo Corporation, but my contract finishes at the end of the month, and I would like ③ to come and work in England. As you can see from my CV (enclosed), I have an excellent command of English and also the required qualifications and experience.

I will be available for interview any time after 6th October, from which date I can be contacted at the following address in the UK:

     c/o Lewis
     51 Dexter Road
     London N7 6BW
     Tel. 0208 607 5512

I look forward to hearing from you. ④

Yours sincerely

Maria Luisa Bianchi

Encl.

① *Oppure:* Ms Angela Summers, … *se nell'inserzione compare* Reply to Angela Summers; *oppure* Dear Ms Summers, Dear Mrs Wright *se compare solo il cognome.*

② *Oppure:* and would like to apply for this position, *se l'annuncio è ben dettagliato.*

③ *Se al momento si è disoccupati si scrive invece:* I am currently looking for work and I would like…

④ *Oppure:* Thanking you in anticipation/advance.

Letters / Lettere

Curriculum Vitae

. . . .

CURRICULUM VITAE

Nome e cognome	Gina Allen
Luogo e data di nascita	Birmingham, 21 settembre 1981
Residenza	127 Chatterton Terrace Londra W10 4RT, Gran Bretagna
Telefono abitazione	+44 (0)20 8741390
Telefono cellulare	+44 776 63294031
Indirizzo di posta elettronica	gina.allen@aol.com
Stato civile	Nubile ①
Nazionalità	Britannica ②

FORMAZIONE

1996-1998	'A Levels' (equivalente al diploma di scuola secondaria superiore) in italiano, storia e storia dell'arte, presso il Fulham Sixth Form College
1998-1999	Soggiorno in Italia durante il quale ho seguito un corso di italiano per stranieri a Bologna.
1999-2002	Laurea in storia dell'arte, University of Westminster di Londra, con tesi sul Mantegna. Durante l'ultimo anno di corso ho fatto uno stage presso la casa d'aste Sotheby's.
autunno 2002	Corso trimestrale di ricerca fotografica.

ESPERIENZE LAVORATIVE

dal luglio 2004	Ricercatrice fotografica presso la casa editrice Zoom. Mi occupo della ricerca iconografica per le pubblicazioni d'arte.
2003-2004	Assistente presso l'archivio fotografico 'PhotoArt' di Londra, specializzato in immagini di Belle Arti.
1998-1999	Impiego part-time presso un'agenzia di viaggi di Bologna.
Conoscenze linguistiche	Inglese madrelingua - Italiano buono parlato e scritto
Conoscenze informatiche	Buone conoscenze. Esperienza di ISDN/Photoshop
Interessi	Fotografia, cinema, yoga, ciclismo

---

① *A single man would put* celibe. *Otherwise you could put* coniugato/a *(you can add, if it is relevant,* senza figli *or* un figlio *etc.),* divorziato/a, vedovo/a.

② *Italian men also have to add whether they have completed their military service.*

• •

Curriculum Vitae

CURRICULUM VITAE ①

Name:	Maria Luisa Bianchi
Address:	via Giolitti 32
	00100 Rome
	Italy
Telephone:	(+39) 06 243 53 94
Nationality:	Italian
Date of Birth:	11/3/73

EDUCATION:

1990-95	Degree Course in Information Technology and English at Università degli Studi of Rome.
1987-1991	Diploma di Maturità Scientifica (equivalent to A levels) at the Liceo Scientifico in Rome.

EMPLOYMENT:

1996-present	Program development engineer with Sempo Informatica, Rome, specializing in computer graphics.
1995-1996	Trainee programmer with Oregon-Italia, Rome.

FURTHER SKILLS:

Languages:	Italian (mother tongue),
	English (fluent, spoken and written),
	French (good).
Interests:	Travel, fashion, tennis.

Letters / Lettere

① Oppure: Resumé (inglese americano)

Inquiry to a tourist office

9 febbraio 2005

Azienda di promozione turistica
Piazza Duomo 2
07100 Sassari

Gentili Signori

Sto programmando di trascorrere le vacanze in Sardegna con la famiglia
e sarei grato se volessero inviarmi un elenco delle case vacanza e dei
campeggi nella zona di San Teodoro.

Grazie per l'attenzione.

Distinti saluti
Brian McGregor
16 Victoria Road
London
SW2 5HU
UK

■ *Standard formula for closing a formal letter.*

Lettera all'ufficio del turismo

■ *Formula standard nella corrispondenza commerciale quando non si conosce il nome del destinatario e non si sa se sia uomo o donna. Nel caso di una ditta o un ente si può anche scrivere* Dear Sirs *(come in questo caso, se la lettera fosse indirizzata.a* The Regional Tourist Office, *anziché a* The Manager).

> via Manzoni 9
> 16100 Genoa
> Italy
>
> 4th May 2005
>
> The Manager
> Regional Tourist Office
> 3 Virgin Road
> Canterbury
> CT1 3AA
>
> Dear Sir or Madam,
>
> Please send me a list of hotels and guesthouses in Canterbury in the medium price range.
>
> I would also like details of coach trips to local sights in the second half of August.
>
> Yours faithfully
>
> Antonio Brizzi

■ *Formula di saluto che si usa nelle lettere formali, quando non si conosce il nome del destinatario. Si chiudono così le lettere che si aprono con* Dear Sir or Madam, Dear Sirs, Dear Sir *o* Dear Madam.

Booking a hotel room

18 giugno 2004

Hotel La rosa
Corso del Partigiano, 56
22100 Como

Gentile Signora Pacini ①
In seguito alla conversazione telefonica di stamattina, le scrivo
per confermare la prenotazione di una camera doppia con bagno
② dall'8 al 12 luglio. Mia moglie ed io arriveremo nel tardo
pomeriggio di giovedì 8. Per ogni comunicazione urgente il mio
numero di telefono è +44 031 5790 3352.

Cordiali saluti
P. Bromfield
Cardross Gardens
Edinburgh
EH2 5EG
Gran Bretagna

① *Alternatively you
can write* Gentili
Signori *if you
don't know the
name of the
person you are
writing to.*

② *Or:* una camera
singola/con
doccia

Booking a place in a campsite

Campeggio 'Il Gabbiano'
Via del Parco
14100 Asti

5 maggio 2005

Egregi signori,

il Vostro campeggio mi è stato segnalato dall'Ufficio del
turismo di Asti. Vorrei prenotare una piazzola per la nostra
tenda dal 5 al 15 agosto. Preferirei un posto tranquillo,
possibilmente non troppo vicino al mini-market.

Resto in attesa di una Vostra conferma.

Cordiali saluti,

Mary J Stevens
55 Old Road
Wallingford OX10 5DH
Gran Bretagna

Letters / Lettere

Prenotazione di una camera d'albergo

The Manager   35 Prince Edward Road
Torbay Hotel   Oxford OX7 3AA
Dawlish
Devon   Tel. 01865 322435
EX37 2LR

                                       23rd April 2003

Dear Sir or Madam,

I saw your hotel listed in the Inns of Devon guide for last year,
and wish to reserve a double (or twin-bedded) room with
shower ① in a quiet position from August 2nd-11th (nine
nights), also a single room for my son.

If you have anything suitable for this period please let me know
the price and whether you require a deposit.

Yours faithfully,

Charles Fairhurst

① *Oppure:*
with bath/with
ensuite.

Prenotazione in un campeggio

                        22 Daniel Avenue
                        Caldwood
                        Leeds LS8 7RR

                        Tel. 01132 998767

                        25th April 2003

Mr Joseph Vale
Lakeside Park
Rydal
Cumbria
LA22 9RZ

Dear Mr Vale,

Your campsite was recommended to me by James Dallas, who
knows it from several visits ① . I and two friends would like to
come for a week from July 18th to 25th. Could you please reserve
us a pitch for one tent ② , preferably close to the shore ③ .

Please confirm the booking and let me know if you require a
deposit. Would you also be good enough to send me instructions on
how to reach you from the motorway.

Yours sincerely,

Frances Good

① *O se si è trovato
il nome del
campeggio in una
guida, un depliant
o su Internet:*
I found your site
in the Good
Camper's
Guide/the Tourist
Board's list/on a
website *ecc.*

② *Oppure:*
a pitch for one
caravan.

③ *Per una posizione
alternativa:*
in a shady/
sheltered spot.

Letters / Lettere

Cancelling a reservation

16 maggio 2005

Pensione La Torre
via Don Bosco 61
Chiusdino
Grosseto

Gentili Signori,
la settimana scorsa ho prenotato telefonicamente una camera
singola dal 6 al 12 giugno. Sono molto spiacente ma, per motivi
familiari, mi trovo costretta a rimandare il soggiorno in
Toscana e perciò a disdire la prenotazione.
Sperando di non aver arrecato troppo disturbo, porgo distinti
saluti.

Sally Lewis
56 Nelson Rd
Farnborough
GU14 9RK
Hants
UK

Per disdire una prenotazione

via Giotto 2
90100 Palermo
Italy

July 20th 2002

Mrs J. Warrington
Downlands
Steyning
West Sussex
BN44 6LZ

Dear Mrs Warrington,
Unfortunately I have to cancel my/our reservation for the
week of August 7th ①. Due to unforeseen circumstances ②,
I/we have had to abandon my/our holiday plans.
I very much regret having to cancel (at such a late stage) and
hope it does not cause you undue inconvenience.
Yours sincerely,

Carlo Rubini

① *Oppure:*
for the period
from August 7th
to 14th.

② *Altri possibili
motivi:*
Owing to my
father's sudden
death/my wife's
ilness/son's
hospitalization
ecc.

Sending an e-mail

The illustration shows a typical interface for sending e-mail.

File   Modifica   Visualizza   Messagio   Inserisci   Formato   ?

A: anna.rossi@hotmail.com
Da: gaia@yahoo.it
Oggetto   foto

Ciao Anna ①

ora che sono anch'io collegato ② a Internet sarà più facile comunicare! Allego ③ alcune foto delle vacanze in montagna. Ci siamo divertiti un sacco questa volta.

Un bacione ④

Gaia

① *The beginning changes according to how formal it is. You can use caro/cara or leave it out.*

② Collegata *if the person writing is a girl or woman.*

③ Allegare *means to enclose and also to attach in emails.*

④ *In more formal emails you can end with* 'Distinti saluti' *like in letters.*

Letters / Lettere

Email

File   Edit   View   Mail   Insert   Format   Help

Subject: click here to enter the subject

Dear Katie,

Just a quick note to let you know that I received your test email. I'm glad that we can communicate over the Internet and I look forward to receiving that attachment you promised me.

All the best,

Clare

a¹, A /eɪ/ (letter) a, A *f inv*; Mus la *m inv*

a² /ə/ ⓵ stressed /eɪ/ (before a vowel **an**) *indef art* un *m*, una *f*; (before s + consonant, *gn, ps, z*) uno; (before *nf* starting with vowel) un'; (each) a; **I am a lawyer** sono avvocato; **a tiger is a feline** la tigre è un felino; **a knife and fork** un coltello e una forchetta; **a Mr Smith is looking for you** un certo signor Smith ti sta cercando; **£2 a kilo/a head** due sterline al chilo/a testa
⓶ *n* Mus la *m inv*

A & E *n* Br *abbr* (**Accident and Emergency**) pronto soccorso *m*

A2 *n* ⟨*exam/course*⟩ esame *m* sostenuto al termine del secondo anno del biennio di preparazione agli A-Level

A4 *adj* A4

AA *n* Br *abbr* (**Automobile Association**) ≈ A.C.I. *m*; *abbr* **Alcoholics Anonymous**

AAA *n* Am *abbr* (**American Automobile Association**) ≈ A.C.I. *m*

aback /ə'bæk/ *adv* **be taken** ∼ essere preso in contropiede

abacus /'æbəkəs/ *n* (pl **-cuses**) abaco *m*

abandon /ə'bændən/ ⓵ *vt* abbandonare; (give up) rinunciare a
⓶ *n* abbandono *m*

abandoned /ə'bændnd/ *adj* abbandonato; ⟨*behaviour*⟩ dissoluto

abandonment /ə'bændnmənt/ *n* (of strike, plan etc) rinuncia *f*

abashed /ə'bæʃt/ *adj* imbarazzato

abate /ə'beɪt/ *vi* calmarsi

abattoir /'æbətwɑ:(r)/ *n* mattatoio *m*

abbess /'æbes/ *n* badessa *f*

abbey /'æbɪ/ *n* abbazia *f*

abbot /'æbət/ *n* abate *m*

abbreviate /ə'bri:vɪeɪt/ *vt* abbreviare

abbreviation /əbri:vɪ'eɪʃn/ *n* abbreviazione *f*

ABC ⓵ *n* (alphabet) alfabeto *m*; **the** ∼ **of** (basics) l'ABC *m inv* di
⓶ *n abbr* (**American Broadcasting Company**) rete *f* televisiva americana

abdicate /'æbdɪkeɪt/ ⓵ *vi* abdicare
⓶ *vt* rinunciare a

abdication /æbdɪ'keɪʃn/ *n* abdicazione *f*

abdomen /'æbdəmən/ *n* addome *m*

abdominal /əb'dɒmɪnl/ *adj* addominale

abduct /əb'dʌkt/ *vt* rapire

abduction /əb'dʌkʃn/ *n* rapimento *m*

abductor /əb'dʌktə(r)/ *n* rapitore, -trice *mf*

aberrant /ə'berənt/ *adj* ⟨*behaviour, nature*⟩ aberrante

aberration /æbə'reɪʃn/ *n* aberrazione *f*

abet /ə'bet/ *vt* (pt/pp **abetted**) aid and ∼ Jur essere complice di

abeyance /ə'beɪəns/ *n* **in** ∼ in sospeso; **fall into** ∼ cadere in disuso

abhor /əb'hɔ:(r)/ *vt* (pt/pp **abhorred**) aborrire

abhorrence /əb'hɒrəns/ *n* orrore *m*

abhorrent /əb'hɒrənt/ *adj* ripugnante

abide /ə'baɪd/ ⓵ *vt* (pt/pp **abided**) (tolerate) sopportare
⓶ **abide by** *vi* rispettare

abiding /ə'baɪdɪŋ/ *adj* perpetuo

ability /ə'bɪlətɪ/ *n* capacità *f inv*

abject /'æbdʒekt/ *adj* ⟨*poverty*⟩ degradante; ⟨*apology*⟩ umile; ⟨*coward*⟩ abietto

ablative /'æblətɪv/ *n* ablativo *m*

ablaze /ə'bleɪz/ *adj* in fiamme; **be** ∼ **with light** risplendere di luci

able /'eɪbl/ *adj* capace, abile; **be** ∼ **to do something** poter fare qualcosa; **were you** ∼ **to...?** sei riuscito a...?

able-bodied /-'bɒdɪd/ *adj* robusto; Mil abile

able seaman *n* marinaio *m* scelto

ably /'eɪblɪ/ *adv* abilmente

abnegation /æbnɪ'geɪʃn/ *n* (of rights, privileges) rinuncia *f*; (self-abnegation) abnegazione *f*

abnormal /æb'nɔ:ml/ *adj* anormale

abnormality /æbnɔ:'mælətɪ/ *n* anormalità *f inv*

abnormally /æb'nɔ:məlɪ/ *adv* in modo anormale

aboard /ə'bɔ:d/ *adv & prep* a bordo

abode /ə'bəʊd/ *n* dimora *f*

abolish /ə'bɒlɪʃ/ *vt* abolire

abolition /æbə'lɪʃn/ *n* abolizione *f*

abominable /ə'bɒmɪnəbl/ *adj* abominevole

abominably /ə'bɒmɪnəblɪ/ *adv* disgustosamente

abominate /ə'bɒmɪneɪt/ *vt* abominare

aboriginal /æbə'rɪdʒɪnl/ *adj & n* (native) aborigeno, -a *mf*, indigeno, -a *mf*

Aborigine /æbə'rɪdʒɪni:/ *n* aborigeno, -a *mf* d'Australia

abort /ə'bɔ:t/ *vt* fare abortire; fig annullare

abortion /əˈbɔːʃn/ n aborto m; **have an ~** abortire

abortionist /əˈbɔːʃnɪst/ n persona f che pratica aborti, specialmente clandestini

abortive /əˈbɔːtɪv/ adj ⟨attempt⟩ infruttuoso

abound /əˈbaʊnd/ vi abbondare (**in** di)

about /əˈbaʊt/ **1** adv (here and there) [di] qua e [di] là; (approximately) circa; **be ~** ⟨illness, tourists⟩ essere in giro; **be up and ~** essere alzato; **leave something lying ~** lasciare in giro qualcosa
2 prep (concerning) su; (in the region of) intorno a; (here and there in) per; **what is the book/the film ~?** di cosa parla il libro/il film?; **he wants to see you –what ~?** ti vuole vedere –a che proposito?; **talk/know ~** parlare/sapere di; **I know nothing ~ it** non ne so niente; **~ 5 o'clock** intorno alle 5; **travel ~ the world** viaggiare per il mondo; **be ~ to do something** stare per fare qualcosa; **how ~ going to the cinema?** e se andassimo al cinema?

about-face n, **about-turn** n dietro front m inv

above /əˈbʌv/ adv & prep sopra; **~ all** soprattutto

above-board adj onesto

above-ground adv in superficie

above-mentioned /-menʃnd/ adj suddetto

above-named /-neɪmd/ adj suddetto

abrasion /əˈbreɪʒn/ n (injury) abrasione f

abrasive /əˈbreɪsɪv/ **1** adj abrasivo; (remark) caustico
2 n abrasivo m

abreast /əˈbrest/ adv fianco a fianco; **come ~ of** allinearsi con; **keep ~ of** tenersi al corrente di

abridged /əˈbrɪdʒd/ adj ridotto

abridg[e]ment /əˈbrɪdʒmnt/ n (version) edizione f ridotta

abroad /əˈbrɔːd/ adv all'estero

abrupt /əˈbrʌpt/ adj brusco

abruptly /əˈbrʌptlɪ/ adv bruscamente

ABS n abbr (**anti-lock braking system**) ABS m inv

abscess /ˈæbsɪs/ n ascesso m

abscond /əbˈskɒnd/ vi fuggire

abseiling /ˈæbseɪlɪŋ/ n Br discesa f a corda doppia; **to go ~** fare discesa a corda doppia

absence /ˈæbsəns/ n assenza f, (lack) mancanza f

absent[1] /ˈæbsənt/ adj assente

absent[2] /æbˈsent/ vt **~ oneself** essere assente

absentee /æbsənˈtiː/ n assente mf

absenteeism /æbsənˈtiːɪzm/ n assenteismo m

absentee landlord n proprietario m che affitta una casa in cui non abita

absently /ˈæbsəntlɪ/ adv ⟨say, look⟩ distrattamente

absent-minded /-ˈmaɪndɪd/ adj distratto

absent-mindedly /-ˈmaɪndɪdlɪ/ adv distrattamente

absent-mindedness /-ˈmaɪndɪdnɪs/ n distrazione f

absolute /ˈæbsəluːt/ adj assoluto; **an ~ idiot** un perfetto idiota

absolutely /ˈæbsəluːtlɪ/ adv assolutamente; (fam: indicating agreement) esattamente; **~ not** assolutamente no

absolution /æbsəˈluːʃn/ n assoluzione f

absolve /əbˈzɒlv/ vt assolvere

absorb /əbˈsɔːb/ vt assorbire; **~ed in** assorto in

absorbency /əbˈsɔːbənsɪ/ n capacità f d'assorbimento

absorbent /əbˈsɔːbənt/ adj assorbente

absorbent cotton n Am cotone m idrofilo, ovatta f

absorbing /əbˈsɔːbɪŋ/ adj avvincente

absorption /əbˈsɔːpʃn/ n assorbimento m; (in activity) concentrazione f

abstain /əbˈsteɪn/ vi astenersi (**from** da)

abstemious /əbˈstiːmɪəs/ adj moderato

abstention /əbˈstenʃn/ n Pol astensione f

abstinence /ˈæbstɪnəns/ n astinenza f

abstract /ˈæbstrækt/ **1** adj astratto
2 n astratto m; (summary) estratto m

abstraction /əbˈstrækʃn/ n **an air of ~** un'aria distratta

absurd /əbˈsɜːd/ adj assurdo

absurdity /əbˈsɜːdətɪ/ n assurdità f inv

absurdly /əbˈsɜːdlɪ/ adv assurdamente

abundance /əˈbʌndəns/ n abbondanza f

abundant /əˈbʌndənt/ adj abbondante

abundantly /əˈbʌndəntlɪ/ adv **~ clear** più che chiaro

abuse[1] /əˈbjuːz/ vt (misuse) abusare di; (insult) insultare; (ill-treat) maltrattare

abuse[2] /əˈbjuːs/ n abuso m; (verbal) insulti mpl; (ill-treatment) maltrattamento m; **~ of power** sopraffazione f

abusive /əˈbjuːsɪv/ adj offensivo

abut /əˈbʌt/ vi (pt/pp **abutted**) confinare (**onto** con)

abysmal /əˈbɪzml/ adj fam pessimo; ⟨ignorance⟩ abissale

abyss /əˈbɪs/ n abisso m

a/c abbr (**account**) c/c

academia /ækəˈdiːmɪə/ n mondo m accademico

academic /ækə'demɪk/ **1** *adj* teorico; *⟨qualifications, system⟩* scolastico; **be ~** *⟨person⟩* avere predisposizione allo studio **2** *n* docente *mf* universitario, -a

academically /ækə'demɪklɪ/ *adv* *⟨gifted⟩* accademicamente

academician /əkædə'mɪʃn/ *n* accademico, -a *mf*

academy /ə'kædəmɪ/ *n* accademia *f*; (of music) conservatorio *m*

ACAS /'eɪkæs/ *n* Br *abbr* (**Advisory Conciliation and Arbitration Service**) organismo *m* pubblico di mediazione tra i lavoratori e i datori di lavoro

accede /ək'siːd/ *vi* **~ to** accedere a *⟨request⟩*; salire a *⟨throne⟩*

accelerate /ək'seləreɪt/ *vt/i* accelerare

acceleration /əkselə'reɪʃn/ *n* accelerazione *f*

accelerator /ək'seləreɪtə(r)/ *n* Auto, Comput acceleratore *m*

accent[1] /'æksənt/ *n* accento *m*

accent[2] /æk'sent/ *vt* accentare

accented /æk'səntɪd/ *adj* *⟨speech⟩* con accento marcato

accentuate /ək'sentjʊeɪt/ *vt* accentuare

accept /ək'sept/ *vt* accettare

acceptability /ækseptə'bɪlɪtɪ/ *n* ammissibilità *f*

acceptable /ək'septəbl/ *adj* accettabile

acceptance /ək'septəns/ *n* accettazione *f*

access /'ækses/ **1** *n* accesso *m* **2** *vt* Comput accedere a

accessible /ək'sesəbl/ *adj* accessibile

accession /æk'seʃn/ *n* *⟨to throne⟩* ascesa *f* al trono

accessory /ək'sesərɪ/ *n* accessorio *m*; Jur complice *mf*

accident /'æksɪdənt/ *n* incidente *m*; (chance) caso *m*; **by ~** per caso; (unintentionally) senza volere; **I'm sorry, it was an ~** mi dispiace, non l'ho fatto apposta

accidental /æksɪ'dentl/ *adj* *⟨meeting⟩* casuale; *⟨death⟩* incidentale; (unintentional) involontario

accidentally /æksɪ'dentəlɪ/ *adv* per caso; (unintentionally) inavvertitamente

accident-prone *adj* soggetto a incidenti

acclaim /ə'kleɪm/ **1** *n* acclamazione *f* **2** *vt* acclamare (**as** come)

acclimatization /əklaɪmətaɪ'zeɪʃn/ *n* acclimatazione *f*

acclimatize /ə'klaɪmətaɪz/ *vt* **become ~d** acclimatarsi

accolade /'ækəleɪd/ *n* riconoscimento *m*

accommodate /ə'kɒmədeɪt/ *vt* ospitare; (oblige) favorire

accommodating /ə'kɒmədeɪtɪŋ/ *adj* accomodante

accommodation /əkɒmə'deɪʃn/ *n* (place to stay) sistemazione *f*; **look for ~** cercare una sistemazione

accompaniment /ə'kʌmpənɪmənt/ *n* accompagnamento *m*

accompanist /ə'kʌmpənɪst/ *n* Mus accompagnatore, -trice *mf*

accompany /ə'kʌmpənɪ/ *vt* (pt/pp **-ied**) accompagnare

accomplice /ə'kʌmplɪs/ *n* complice *mf*

accomplish /ə'kʌmplɪʃ/ *vt* (achieve) concludere; realizzare *⟨aim⟩*

accomplished /ə'kʌmplɪʃt/ *adj* dotato; *⟨fact⟩* compiuto

accomplishment /ə'kʌmplɪʃmənt/ *n* realizzazione *f*; (achievement) risultato *m*: (talent) talento *m*

accord /ə'kɔːd/ **1** *n* (treaty) accordo *m*; **with one ~** tutti d'accordo; **of his own ~** di sua spontanea volontà **2** *vt* accordare

accordance /ə'kɔːdəns/ *n* **in ~ with** in conformità di *o* a

according /ə'kɔːdɪŋ/ *adv* **~ to** secondo

accordingly /ə'kɔːdɪŋlɪ/ *adv* di conseguenza

accordion /ə'kɔːdɪən/ *n* fisarmonica *f*

accost /ə'kɒst/ *vt* abbordare

account /ə'kaʊnt/ *n* conto *m*; (report) descrizione *f*; (of eyewitness) resoconto *m*; **~s** *pl* Comm conti *mpl*; **on ~ of** a causa di; **on no ~** per nessun motivo; **on this ~** per questo motivo; **on my ~** per causa mia; **of no ~** di nessuna importanza; **take into ~** tener conto di
■ **account for** *vt* (explain) spiegare; *⟨person⟩* render conto di; (constitute) costituire; (destroy) distruggere

accountability /əkaʊntə'bɪlɪtɪ/ *n* responsabilità *f*

accountable /ə'kaʊntəbl/ *adj* responsabile (**for** di)

accountancy /ə'kaʊntənsɪ/ *n* ragioneria *f*, contabilità *f*

accountant /ə'kaʊntənt/ *n* (bookkeeper) contabile *mf*; ragioniere, -a *mf* (consultant) commercialista *mf*

account book *n* libro *m* contabile

account director *n* account director *mf inv*

account holder /ə'kaʊnthəʊldə(r)/ *n* (with bank, credit company) titolare *mf* del conto

accounting /ə'kaʊntɪŋ/ *n* (field) ragioneria *f*; (auditing) contabilità *f*

accounting period *n* periodo *m* contabile

account number *n* numero *m* di conto

accounts department *n* [ufficio *m*] contabilità *f*

accounts payable *npl* conto *m* creditori diversi

accounts receivable *npl* conto *m* creditori diversi

accoutrements /ə'ku:trəmənts/ *npl* equipaggiamento *msg*

accredited /ə'kredɪtɪd/ *adj* accreditato

accretion /ə'kri:ʃn/ *n* accrescimento *m*

accrue /ə'kru:/ *vi* ‹interest› maturare

accumulate /ə'kju:mjʊleɪt/ **①** *vt* accumulare
② *vi* accumularsi

accumulation /əkju:mjʊ'leɪʃn/ *n* accumulazione *f*

accumulator /ə'kju:mjʊleɪtə(r)/ *n* Electr accumulatore *m*

accuracy /'ækjʊrəsɪ/ *n* precisione *f*

accurate /'ækjʊrət/ *adj* preciso

accurately /'ækjʊrətlɪ/ *adv* con precisione

accusation /ækjʊ'zeɪʃn/ *n* accusa *f*

accusative /ə'kju:zətɪv/ *adj & n* ~ [case] Gram accusativo *m*

accuse /ə'kju:z/ *vt* accusare; ~ somebody of doing something accusare qualcuno di fare qualcosa

accused /ə'kju:zd/ *n* the ~ l'accusato *m*, l'accusata *f*

accuser /ə'kju:zə(r)/ *n* accusatore, trice *mf*

accusing /ə'kju:zɪŋ/ *adj* accusatore

accusingly /ə'kju:zɪŋlɪ/ *adv* ‹say, point› in modo accusatorio

accustom /ə'kʌstəm/ *vt* abituare (to a)

accustomed /ə'kʌstəmd/ *adj* abituato; grow *or* get ~ to abituarsi a

ace /eɪs/ *n* (in cards) asso *m*; Tennis ace *m inv*

acerbic /ə'sɜ:bɪk/ *adj* acido

acetate /'æsɪteɪt/ *n* acetato *m*

ache /eɪk/ **①** *n* dolore *m*
② *vi* dolere, far male; ~ all over essere tutto indolenzito

achieve /ə'tʃi:v/ *vt* ottenere ‹success›; realizzare ‹goal, ambition›

achievement /ə'tʃi:vmənt/ *n* (feat) successo *m*

achiever /ə'tʃi:və(r)/ *n* persona *f* di successo

Achilles' heel /əkɪli:z'hi:l/ *n* tallone *m* di Achille

aching /'eɪkɪŋ/ *adj* ‹body, limbs› dolorante; an ~ void un vuoto incolmabile

acid /'æsɪd/ **①** *adj* acido
② *n* acido *m*

acid drop *n* caramella *f* agli agrumi

acidic /ə'sɪdɪk/ *adj* acido

acidity /ə'sɪdətɪ/ *n* acidità *f*

acid rain *n* pioggia *f* acida

acid stomach *n* Med acidità *f* di stomaco

acid test *n* fig prova *f* del fuoco

acknowledge /ək'nɒlɪdʒ/ *vt* riconoscere; rispondere a ‹greeting›; far cenno di aver notato ‹sb's presence›; ~ receipt of accusare ricevuta di; ~ defeat dichiararsi vinto

acknowledgement /ək'nɒlɪdʒmənt/ *n* riconoscimento *m*; send an ~ of a letter confermare il ricevimento di una lettera

acme /'ækmɪ/ *n* the ~ of l'apice *m* di

acne /'æknɪ/ *n* acne *f*

acorn /'eɪkɔ:n/ *n* ghianda *f*

acoustic /ə'ku:stɪk/ *adj* acustico

acoustically /ə'ku:stɪklɪ/ *adv* acusticamente

acoustic guitar *n* chitarra *f* acustica

acoustics /ə'ku:stɪks/ *npl* acustica *fsg*

acquaint /ə'kweɪnt/ *vt* ~ somebody with metter qualcuno al corrente di

acquaintance /ə'kweɪntəns/ *n* ‹person› conoscente *mf*; make sb's ~ fare la conoscenza di qualcuno

acquainted *adj* be ~ with conoscere ‹person›; essere a conoscenza di ‹fact›; get *or* become ~ with somebody fare conoscenza con qualcuno; get *or* become ~ with something familiarizzare con qualcosa

acquiesce /ækwɪ'es/ *vi* acconsentire (to, in a)

acquiescence /ækwɪ'esəns/ *n* acquiescenza *f*

acquiescent /ækwɪ'esənt/ *adj* arrendevole

acquire /ə'kwaɪə(r)/ *vt* acquisire

acquired /ə'kwaɪəd/ *adj* ‹characteristic› acquisito; it's an ~ taste è una cosa che si impara ad apprezzare

acquisition /ækwɪ'zɪʃn/ *n* acquisizione *f*

acquisitive /ə'kwɪzətɪv/ *adj* avido

acquit /ə'kwɪt/ *vt* (pt/pp **acquitted**) assolvere; ~ oneself well cavarsela bene

acquittal /ə'kwɪtəl/ *n* assoluzione *f*

acre /'eɪkə(r)/ *n* acro *m* (= 4 047 m²)

acreage /'eɪkərɪdʒ/ *n* superficie *f* in acri

acrid /'ækrɪd/ *adj* acre

acrimonious /ækrɪ'məʊnɪəs/ *adj* aspro

acrimony /'ækrɪmənɪ/ *n* asprezza *f*

acrobat /'ækrəbæt/ *n* acrobata *mf*

acrobatic /ækrə'bætɪk/ *adj* acrobatico

acrobatics /ækrə'bætɪks/ *npl* acrobazie *fpl*

acronym /'ækrənɪm/ *n* acronimo *m*

across /ə'krɒs/ **①** *adv* dall'altra parte; (wide) in larghezza; (not lengthwise) attraverso; (in crossword) orizzontale; **come ~ something** imbattersi in qualcosa; **go ~** attraversare

2 *prep* (crosswise) di traverso su; (on the other side of) dall'altra parte di

across-the-board **1** *adj* generale
2 *adv* in generale

acrylic /ə'krɪlɪk/ **1** *n* acrilico *m*
2 *attrib* ⟨garment⟩ acrilico

act /ækt/ **1** *n* atto *m*; (in variety show) numero *m*; **put on an ~** fam fare scena
2 *vi* agire; (behave) comportarsi; Theat recitare; (pretend) fingere; **~ as** fare da
3 *vt* recitare ⟨role⟩
■ **act for** *vi* agire per conto di
■ **act out** *vt* recitare ⟨part⟩; mettere in atto ⟨fantasy⟩
■ **act up** *vi* ⟨child, photocopier⟩ fare i capricci

acting /'æktɪŋ/ **1** *adj* ⟨deputy⟩ provvisorio
2 *n* Theat recitazione *f*; (profession) teatro *m*; **~ profession** professione *f* dell'attore

action /'ækʃn/ *n* azione *f*; Mil combattimento *m*; Jur azione *f* legale; **out of ~** ⟨machine⟩ fuori uso; **take ~** agire; **~!** Cinema ciac si gira!

action group *n* gruppo *m* d'azione
action-packed *adj* ⟨film⟩ d'azione
action painting *n* pittura *f* d'azione
action plan *n* piano *m* d'azione
action replay *n* replay *m inv*

activate /'æktɪveɪt/ *vt* attivare; (Chem, Phys) rendere attivo

active /'æktɪv/ *adj* attivo

active duty, **active service** *n* Mil **be on ~** ~ prestare servizio in zona di operazioni

actively /'æktɪvlɪ/ *adv* attivamente
activist /'æktɪvɪst/ *n* attivista *mf*
activity /æk'tɪvətɪ/ *n* attività *f inv*
activity holiday *n* Br vacanza *f* con attività ricreative

act of God *n* causa *f* di forza maggiore
actor /'æktə(r)/ *n* attore *m*
actress /'æktrəs/ *n* attrice *f*
actual /'æktʃʊəl/ *adj* (real) reale
actually /'æktʃʊəlɪ/ *adv* in realtà
actuary /'æktʃʊərɪ/ *n* attuario, -a *mf*
acumen /'ækjʊmən/ *n* acume *m*
acupuncture /'ækjʊpʌŋktʃə(r)/ *n* agopuntura *f*
acupuncturist /ækjʊ'pʌŋktʃərɪst/ *n* agopuntore, -trice *mf*
acute /ə'kjuːt/ *adj* acuto; ⟨shortage, hardship⟩ estremo
acute accent *n* accento *m* acuto
acute angle *n* angolo *m* acuto
acutely /ə'kjuːtlɪ/ *adv* acutamente; ⟨embarrassed, aware⟩ estremamente

AD *abbr* (**Anno Domini**) d.C.
ad /æd/ *n* pubblicità *f inv*; (in paper) inserzione *f*, annuncio *m*
adage /'ædɪdʒ/ *n* detto *m*, adagio *m*
adamant /'ædəmənt/ *adj* categorico (that sul fatto che)
Adam's apple /'ædəmz/ *n* pomo *m* di Adamo
adapt /ə'dæpt/ **1** *vt* adattare ⟨play⟩
2 *vi* adattarsi
adaptability /ədæptə'bɪlətɪ/ *n* adattabilità *f*
adaptable /ə'dæptəbl/ *adj* adattabile
adaptation /ædæp'teɪʃn/ *n* Theat adattamento *m*
adapter, **adaptor** /ə'dæptə(r)/ *n* adattatore *m*; (two-way) presa *f* multipla
add /æd/ **1** *vt* aggiungere; Math addizionare
2 *vt* addizionare
■ **add in** *vt* (include) includere
■ **add on** *vt* aggiungere
■ **add to** *vt* (fig: increase) aggravare
■ **add up** **1** *vt* addizionare ⟨figures⟩
2 *vi* addizionare; **it doesn't ~ up** fig non quadra; **~ up to** ammontare a
added /'ædɪd/ *adj* maggiore
adder /'ædə(r)/ *n* vipera *f*
addict /'ædɪkt/ *n* tossicodipendente *mf*; fig fanatico, -a *mf*
addicted /ə'dɪktɪd/ *adj* assuefatto (to a); **~ to drugs** tossicodipendente; **he's ~ to television** è videodipendente
addiction /ə'dɪkʃn/ *n* dipendenza *f*; (to drugs) tossicodipendenza *f*
addictive /ə'dɪktɪv/ *adj* **be ~** dare assuefazione
addition /ə'dɪʃn/ *adj* Math addizione *f*; (thing added) aggiunta *f*; **in ~** in aggiunta
additional /ə'dɪʃnəl/ *adj* supplementare
additionally /ə'dɪʃnəlɪ/ *adv* in più
additive /'ædɪtɪv/ *n* additivo *m*
addled /'ædld/ *adj* ⟨thinking⟩ confuso
add-on *adj* accessorio
address /ə'dres/ **1** *n* indirizzo *m*; (speech) discorso *m*; **form of ~** formula *f* di cortesia
2 *vt* indirizzare; (speak to) rivolgersi a ⟨person⟩; tenere un discorso a ⟨meeting⟩
address book *n* rubrica *f*
addressee /ædre'siː/ *n* destinatario, -a *mf*
adenoids /'ædənɔɪdz/ *npl* adenoidi *fpl*
adept /'ædept/ *adj* esperto, -a *mf* (**at** in)
adequate /'ædɪkwət/ *adj* adeguato
adequately /'ædɪkwətlɪ/ *adv* adeguatamente
ADHD *abbr* (**Attention Deficit and Hyperactivity Disorder**) disturbo *m* da deficit dell'attenzione con iperattività

a

adhere /əd'hɪə(r)/ *vi* aderire; ∼ **to** attenersi a ⟨*principles, rules*⟩

adherence /əd'hɪərəns/ *n* fedeltà *f*

adherent /əd'hɪərənt/ *n* (of doctrine) adepto, -a *mf*; (of policy) sostenitore, -trice *mf*; (of cult) seguace *mf*

adhesion /əd'hi:ʒn/ *n* adesione *f*

adhesive /əd'hi:sɪv/ ① *adj* adesivo ② *n* adesivo *m*

ad hoc /æd'hɒk/ *adj* ⟨*alliance, arrangement*⟩ ad hoc; ⟨*committee, legislation*⟩ apposito; **on an** ∼ ∼ **basis** secondo le esigenze del momento

adieu /ə'dju:/ *n* **bid somebody** ∼ dire addio a qualcuno

ad infinitum /ædɪnfɪ'naɪtəm/ *adv* ⟨*continue*⟩ all'infinito

adjacent /ə'dʒeɪsənt/ *adj* adiacente

adjective /'ædʒɪktɪv/ *n* aggettivo *m*

adjoin /ə'dʒɔɪn/ *vt* essere adiacente a

adjoining /ə'dʒɔɪnɪŋ/ *adj* adiacente

adjourn /ə'dʒɜːn/ *vt* aggiornare (**until** a)

adjournment /ə'dʒɜːnmənt/ *n* aggiornamento *m*

adjudge /ə'dʒʌdʒ/ *vt* Jur (decree) giudicare; aggiudicare ⟨*costs, damages*⟩

adjudicate /ə'dʒuːdɪkeɪt/ *vi* decidere; (in competition) giudicare

adjudicator /ə'dʒuːdɪkeɪtə(r)/ *n* giudice *m*, arbitro *m*

adjunct /'ædʒʌnkt/ *n* aggiunta *f*; (hum: person) appendice *f*

adjust /ə'dʒʌst/ ① *vt* modificare; regolare ⟨*focus, sound*⟩ ② *vi* adattarsi

adjustable /ə'dʒʌstəbl/ *adj* regolabile

adjustable spanner *n* chiave *f* [inglese] a rullino

adjustment /ə'dʒʌstmənt/ *n* adattamento *m*; Techn regolamento *m*

adjutant /'ædʒʊtənt/ *n* Mil aiutante *mf*

ad lib /æd'lɪb/ ① *adj* improvvisato ② *adv* a piacere ③ *vi* (pt/pp **ad libbed**) fam improvvisare

adman /'ædmæn/ *n* fam pubblicitario *m*

admin /'ædmɪn/ *n* Br fam amministrazione *f*

administer /əd'mɪnɪstə(r)/ *vt* amministrare; somministrare ⟨*medicine*⟩

administration /ədmɪnɪ'streɪʃn/ *n* amministrazione *f*; Pol governo *m*

administration costs *n* costi *mpl* di gestione

administrative /əd'mɪnɪstrətɪv/ *adj* amministrativo

administrator /əd'mɪnɪstreɪtə(r)/ *n* amministratore, -trice *mf*

admirable /'ædmərəbl/ *adj* ammirevole

admiral /'ædmərəl/ *n* ammiraglio *m*

admiralty /'ædmɪrəltɪ/ *n* Br ministero *m* della marina militare britannica

admiration /ædmə'reɪʃn/ *n* ammirazione *f*

admire /əd'maɪə(r)/ *vt* ammirare

admirer /əd'maɪrə(r)/ *n* ammiratore, -trice *mf*

admiring /əd'maɪrɪŋ/ *adj* ⟨*person*⟩ pieno d'ammirazione; ⟨*look*⟩ ammirativo

admiringly /əd'maɪrɪŋlɪ/ *adv* ⟨*look, say*⟩ con ammirazione

admissible /əd'mɪsəbl/ *adj* ammissibile

admission /əd'mɪʃn/ *n* ammissione *f*; (to hospital) ricovero *m*; (entry) ingresso *m*

admissions office *n* Univ segreteria *f* studenti

admit /əd'mɪt/ ① *vt* (pt/pp **admitted**) (let in) far entrare; (to hospital) ricoverare; (acknowledge) ammettere ② *vi* ∼ **to something** ammettere qualcosa

admittance /əd'mɪtəns/ *n* ammissione *f*; **'no** ∼**'** 'vietato l'ingresso'

admittedly /əd'mɪtɪdlɪ/ *adv* bisogna riconoscerlo

admonish /əd'mɒnɪʃ/ *vt* ammonire

admonition /ædmə'nɪʃn/ *n* ammonimento *m*

ad nauseam /æd'nɔːzɪæm/ *adv* ⟨*discuss, repeat*⟩ fino alla nausea

ado /ə'duː/ *n* **without more** ∼ senza ulteriori indugi

adolescence /ædə'lesns/ *n* adolescenza *f*

adolescent /ædə'lesnt/ *adj & n* adolescente *mf*

adopt /ə'dɒpt/ *vt* adottare; Pol scegliere ⟨*candidate*⟩

adopted /ə'dɒptɪd/ *adj* ⟨*son, daughter*⟩ adottivo

adoption /ə'dɒpʃn/ *n* adozione *f*

adoption agency *n* agenzia *f* di adozioni

adoptive /ə'dɒptɪv/ *adj* adottivo

adorable /ə'dɔːrəbl/ *adj* adorabile

adoration /ædə'reɪʃn/ *n* adorazione *f*

adore /ə'dɔː(r)/ *vt* adorare

adoring /ə'dɔːrɪŋ/ *adj* ⟨*fan*⟩ in adorazione; **she has an** ∼ **husband** ha un marito che la adora

adoringly /ə'dɔːrɪŋlɪ/ *adv* con adorazione

adorn /ə'dɔːn/ *vt* adornare

adornment /ə'dɔːnmənt/ *n* ornamento *m*

adrenalin /ə'drenəlɪn/ *n* adrenalina *f*

Adriatic /eɪdrɪ'ætɪk/ *adj & n* **the** ∼ **[Sea]** il mare Adriatico, l'Adriatico *m*

adrift /ə'drɪft/ *adj* alla deriva; **be** ∼ andare alla deriva; **come** ∼ staccarsi

adroit /ə'drɔɪt/ *adj* abile

adroitly /ə'drɔɪtlɪ/ *adv* abilmente

ADSL *abbr* **(Asymmetric Digital Subscriber Line)** ADSL *f*

adulation /ædjʊ'leɪʃn/ *n* adulazione *f*

adult /'ædʌlt/ *n* adulto, -a *mf*

Adult Education *n* Br ≈ corsi *mpl* serali

adulterate /ə'dʌltəreɪt/ *vt* adulterare ⟨wine⟩

adulterated /ə'dʌltəreɪtɪd/ *adj* ⟨wine⟩ adulterato

adulterous /ə'dʌltərəs/ *adj* ⟨relationship⟩ adulterino; ⟨person⟩ adultero

adultery /ə'dʌltərɪ/ *n* adulterio *m*

adulthood /'ædʌlthʊd/ *n* età *f* adulta

adult literacy classes *n* Br corso *m* di alfabetizzazione per adulti

advance /əd'vɑːns/ ① *n* avanzamento *m*; Mil avanzata *f*; (payment) anticipo *m*; **in ∼** in anticipo
② *vi* avanzare; (make progress) fare progressi
③ *vt* promuovere ⟨cause⟩; avanzare ⟨theory⟩; anticipare ⟨money⟩

advance booking *n* prenotazione *f* [in anticipo]

advance booking office *n* ufficio *m* prenotazioni

advanced /əd'vɑːnst/ *adj* avanzato

Advanced Level *n* Br Sch = A-LEVEL

advanced search *n* Comput ricerca *f* avanzata; **∼ option** opzione *f* ricerca avanzata

advancement /əd'vɑːnsmənt/ *n* promozione *f*

advance notice *n* preannuncio *m*

advance party *n* Mil avanguardia *f*

advance payment *n* Comm pagamento *m* anticipato

advance warning *n* preavviso *m*

advantage /əd'vɑːntɪdʒ/ *n* vantaggio *m*; **take ∼ of** approfittare di

advantageous /ædvən'teɪdʒəs/ *adj* vantaggioso

advent /'ædvent/ *n* avvento *m*; **A∼** Relig Avvento *m*

adventure /əd'ventʃə(r)/ *n* avventura *f*

adventure holiday *n* vacanza *f* avventura

adventure playground *n* Br parco *m* giochi

adventurer /əd'ventʃərə(r)/ *n* avventuriero, -a *mf*

adventuress /əd'ventʃərɪs/ *n* avventuriera *f*

adventurous /əd'ventʃərəs/ *adj* avventuroso

adverb /'ædvɜːb/ *n* avverbio *m*

adversary /'ædvəsərɪ/ *n* avversario, -a *mf*

adverse /'ædvɜːs/ *adj* avverso

adversity /əd'vɜːsətɪ/ *n* avversità *f*

advert /'ædvɜːt/ *n* fam = ADVERTISEMENT

advertise /'ædvətaɪz/ ① *vt* reclamizzare; mettere un annuncio per ⟨job, flat⟩
② *vi* fare pubblicità; (for job, flat) mettere un annuncio

advertisement /əd'vɜːtɪsmənt/ *n* pubblicità *f inv*; (in paper) inserzione *f*, annuncio *m*

advertiser /'ædvətaɪzə(r)/ *n* (in newspaper) inserzionista *mf*

advertising /'ædvətaɪzɪŋ/ ① *n* pubblicità *f*
② *attrib* pubblicitario

advertising agency *n* agenzia *f* pubblicitaria

advertising campaign *n* campagna *f* pubblicitaria

advertising executive *n* dirigente *mf* pubblicitario, -a

advertising industry *n* settore *m* pubblicitario

Advertising Standards Authority *n* Br organo *m* di controllo sulla pubblicità

advice /əd'vaɪs/ *n* consigli *mpl*; **piece of ∼** consiglio *m*

advice centre *n* centro *m* di consulenza

advice note *n* avviso *m*

advice slip *n* avviso *m* di accreditamento

advisability /ədvaɪzə'bɪlətɪ/ *n* opportunità *f*

advisable /əd'vaɪzəbl/ *adj* consigliabile

advise /əd'vaɪz/ *vt* consigliare; (inform) avvisare; **∼ somebody to do something** consigliare a qualcuno di fare qualcosa; **∼ somebody against something** sconsigliare qualcosa a qualcuno

advisedly /əd'vaɪzɪdlɪ/ *adv* ⟨say⟩ deliberatamente

adviser /əd'vaɪzə(r)/ *n* consulente *mf*

advisory /əd'vaɪzərɪ/ *adj* consultivo

advisory committee *n* comitato *m* consultivo

advisory service *n* servizio *m* di consulenza; **pensions/immigration/pregnancy ∼** servizio di consulenza in materia di pensioni/immigrazione/gravidanza

advocacy /'ædvəkəsɪ/ *n* appoggio *m*

advocate[1] /'ædvəkət/ *n* (supporter) fautore, -trice *mf*

advocate[2] /'ædvəkeɪt/ *vt* propugnare

Aegean /ɪ'dʒɪən/ *n* **the ∼** l'Egeo *m*

aegis /'iːdʒɪs/ *n* **under the ∼ of** sotto l'egida di

aeon /'iːən/ *n* **∼s ago** milioni *mpl* e milioni di anni fa

AER n abbr (**Annual Equivalence Rate**) TAN m

aerate /'eəreɪt/ vt aerare; addizionare anidride carbonica a ‹water›

aerial /'eərɪəl/ ① adj aereo ② n antenna f

aerial camera n macchina f fotografica per fotografie aeree

aerial photography n fotografia f aerea

aerial warfare n guerra f aerea

aerie /'eərɪ/ n Am (eyrie) nido m [d'aquila]

aerobatics /eərə'bætɪks/ npl (manoeuvres) acrobazie fpl aeree

aerobics /eə'rəʊbɪks/ n aerobica fsg

aerodrome /'eərədrəʊm/ n aerodromo m

aerodynamic /eərəʊdaɪ'næmɪk/ adj aerodinamico

aerodynamics /eərəʊdaɪ'næmɪks/ n aerodinamica f

aerogram[me] /'eərəʊgræm/ n aerogramma m

aeronautic[al] /eərə'nɔːtɪk[əl]/ adj aeronautico

aeronautic[al] engineer n ingegnere m aeronautico

aeronautic[al] engineering n ingegneria f aeronautica

aeronautics /eərə'nɔːtɪks/ n aeronautica f

aeroplane /'eərəpleɪn/ n aeroplano m

aerosol /'eərəsɒl/ n bomboletta f spray

aerospace /'eərəspeɪs/ ① n (industry) industria f aerospaziale ② attrib ‹engineer, company› aerospaziale

aesthete /'iːsθiːt/ n esteta mf

aesthetic /iːs'θetɪk/ adj estetico

aesthetically /iːs'θetɪklɪ/ adv ‹restore› con gusto; ‹satisfying› esteticamente

aestheticism /iːs'θetɪsɪzm/ n (taste) estetica f; (doctrine, quality) estetismo m

aesthetics /iːs'θetɪks/ n estetica f

afar /ə'fɑː(r)/ adv from ∼ da lontano

affable /'æfəbl/ adj affabile

affably /'æfəblɪ/ adv affabilmente

affair /ə'feə(r)/ n affare m; (scandal) caso m; (sexual) relazione f

affect /ə'fekt/ vt influire su; (emotionally) colpire; (concern) riguardare; (pretend) affettare

affectation /æfek'teɪʃn/ n affettazione f

affected /ə'fektɪd/ adj affettato

affectedly /ə'fektɪdlɪ/ adv ‹talk› con affettazione

affection /ə'fekʃn/ n affetto m

affectionate /ə'fekʃnət/ adj affettuoso

affectionately /ə'fekʃnətlɪ/ adv affettuosamente

affidavit /æfɪ'deɪvɪt/ n affidavit m inv (dichiarazione scritta e giurata davanti a un pubblico ufficiale)

affiliated /ə'fɪlɪeɪtɪd/ adj affiliato

affiliation /ə'fɪlɪ'eɪʃn/ n (process, state) affiliazione f; (link) legame m

affinity /ə'fɪnətɪ/ n affinità f inv

affinity card n carta f di credito destinata ad una causa sociale

affirm /ə'fɜːm/ vt affermare; Jur dichiarare solennemente

affirmative /ə'fɜːmətɪv/ ① adj affermativo ② n in the ∼ affermativamente

affix /ə'fɪks/ vt affiggere; apporre ‹signature›

afflict /ə'flɪkt/ vt affliggere

affliction /ə'flɪkʃn/ n afflizione f

affluence /'æflʊəns/ n agiatezza f

affluent /'æflʊənt/ adj agiato

afford /ə'fɔːd/ vt (provide) fornire; **be able to ∼ something** potersi permettere qualcosa

affordable /ə'fɔːdəbl/ adj abbordabile

affray /ə'freɪ/ n rissa f

affront /ə'frʌnt/ ① n affronto m ② vt fare un affronto a

Afghan /'æfgæn/ n (person) afgano, -a mf; (language) afgano m; (coat) pellicciotto m afgano

Afghan hound n levriero m afgano

Afghanistan /æf'gænɪstæn/ n Afganistan m

aficionado /æfɪsjə'nɑːdəʊ/ n aficionado, -a mf

afield /ə'fiːld/ adv further ∼ più lontano

aflame /ə'fleɪm/ adj & adv liter in fiamme, sfolgorante; **be ∼** ‹cheek;› essere in fiamme; **be ∼ with desire** ardere dal desiderio

afloat /ə'fləʊt/ adj a galla

afoot /ə'fʊt/ adj **there's something ∼** si sta preparando qualcosa

aforesaid /ə'fɔːsed/ adj Jur suddetto

afraid /ə'freɪd/ adj **be ∼** aver paura; **I'm ∼ not** purtroppo no; **I'm ∼ so** temo di sì; **I'm ∼ I can't help you** mi dispiace ma non posso esserle d'aiuto

afresh /ə'freʃ/ adv da capo

Africa /'æfrɪkə/ n Africa f

African /'æfrɪkən/ adj & n africano, -a mf

African-American n afroamericano, -a mf

Afrikaans /æfrɪ'kɑːns/ n afrikaans m

Afrikaner /æfrɪ'kɑːnə(r)/ n boero, -a mf

Afro-American /æfrəʊə'merɪkən/ adj & n afroamericano, -a mf

Afro-Caribbean /æfrəʊkærə'bɪən/ adj & n afrocaraibico, -a mf

aft /ɑːft/ *adv* Naut a poppa; (towards the stern) verso poppa

after /'ɑːftə(r)/ **1** *adv* dopo; **the day** ~ il giorno dopo; **be** ~ cercare
2 *prep* dopo; ~ **all** dopotutto; **the day** ~ **tomorrow** dopodomani
3 *conj* dopo che

afterbirth *n* residui *mpl* di placenta

aftercare *n* Med ospedalizzazione *f* domiciliare

after-dinner speaker *n* persona *f* invitata a tenere un discorso dopo una cena o un ricevimento

after-effect *n* conseguenza *f*

afterlife *n* vita *f* nell'aldilà

aftermath /'ɑːftəmɑːθ/ *n* conseguenze *fpl*; **the** ~ **of war** il dopoguerra; **in the** ~ **of** nel periodo successivo a

afternoon *n* pomeriggio *m*; **good** ~! buon giorno!

afternoon tea *n* merenda *f*

afterpains *npl* dolori *mpl* post-parto

after-sales service *n* servizio *m* assistenza clienti

after-school *adj* doposcuola; ~ **club/activities** club/attività doposcuola

aftershave *n* [lozione *f*] dopobarba *m inv*

aftershock *n* fig effetti *mpl*

aftersun *n* & *a* doposole *m inv.*

aftertaste *n* retrogusto *m*

after-tax *adj* ⟨profits, earnings⟩ al netto

afterthought *n* added as an ~ aggiunto in un secondo momento; **as an** ~, **why not...?** ripensandoci bene, perché non...?

afterwards /'ɑːftəwədz/ *adv* in seguito

again /ə'ɡeɪn/ *adv* di nuovo; **[then]** ~ (besides) inoltre; (on the other hand) d'altra parte; ~ **and** ~ continuamente

against /ə'ɡeɪnst/ *prep* contro

age /eɪdʒ/ **1** *n* età *f inv*; (era) era *f*; ~**s** fam secoli; ~**s ago** fam secoli fa; **what** ~ **are you?** quanti anni hai?; **be under** ~ non avere l'età richiesta; **he's two years of** ~ ha due anni
2 *vt/i* (pres p ageing) invecchiare

age bracket, **age group** *n* fascia *f* d'età

aged¹ /eɪdʒd/ *adj* ~ **two** di due anni

aged² /'eɪdʒɪd/ **1** *adj* anziano
2 *n* **the** ~ *pl* gli anziani

aged debt *n* Fin somma *f* in scadenza

age discrimination *n* discriminazione *f* in base all'età

ageing /'eɪdʒɪŋ/ **1** *n* invecchiamento *m*
2 *adj* ⟨person, population⟩ che sta invecchiando

ageism /'eɪdʒɪzm/ *n* discriminazione *f* contro chi non è più giovane

ageless /'eɪdʒlɪs/ *adj* senza età

agency /'eɪdʒənsɪ/ *n* agenzia *f*; **have the** ~ **for** essere un concessionario di

agency-fee *n* commissione *f*

agency-nurse *n* infermiere, -a *mf* privato, -a

agenda /ə'dʒendə/ *n* ordine *m* del giorno; **on the** ~ all'ordine del giorno; fig in programma

agent /'eɪdʒənt/ *n* agente *mf*

age-old *adj* secolare

age range *n* fascia *f* d'età

aggravate /'æɡrəveɪt/ *vt* aggravare; (annoy) esasperare

aggravating /'æɡrəveɪtɪŋ/ *adj* Jur aggravante; (fam: irritating) irritante

aggravation /æɡrə'veɪʃn/ *n* aggravamento *m*; (annoyance) esasperazione *f*

aggregate /'æɡrɪɡət/ **1** *adj* totale
2 *n* totale *m*; **on** ~ nel complesso

aggression /ə'ɡreʃn/ *n* aggressione *f*

aggressive /ə'ɡresɪv/ *adj* aggressivo

aggressively /ə'ɡresɪvlɪ/ *adv* aggressivamente

aggressiveness /ə'ɡresɪvnɪs/ *n* aggressività *f*

aggressor /ə'ɡresə(r)/ *n* aggressore *m*

aggrieved /ə'ɡriːvd/ *adj* risentito

aggro /'æɡrəʊ/ *n* fam aggressività *f*; (problems) grane *fpl*

aghast /ə'ɡɑːst/ *adj* inorridito

agile /'ædʒaɪl/ *adj* agile

agility /ə'dʒɪlətɪ/ *n* agilità *f*

agitate /'ædʒɪteɪt/ **1** *vt* mettere in agitazione; (shake) agitare
2 *vi* fig ~ **for** creare delle agitazioni per

agitated /'ædʒɪteɪtɪd/ *adj* agitato

agitation /ædʒɪ'teɪʃn/ *n* agitazione *f*

agitator /'ædʒɪteɪtə(r)/ *n* agitatore, -trice *mf*

AGM *n* abbr (annual general meeting) assemblea *f* generale annuale

agnostic /æɡ'nɒstɪk/ *adj* & *n* agnostico, -a *mf*

ago /ə'ɡəʊ/ *adv* fa; **a long time/a month** ~ molto tempo/un mese fa; **how long** ~ **was it?** quanto tempo fa è successo?

agog /ə'ɡɒɡ/ *adj* eccitato

agonize /'æɡənaɪz/ *vi* angosciarsi (over per)

agonized /'æɡənaɪzd/ *adj* ⟨expression, cry⟩ angosciato

agonizing /'æɡənaɪzɪŋ/ *adj* angosciante

agony /'æɡənɪ/ *n* agonia *f*; (mental) angoscia *f*; **be in** ~ avere dei dolori atroci

agony aunt *n* persona *f* chi tiene la posta del cuore in una rivista

agoraphobia /ægərə'fəʊbɪə/ n
agorafobia f

agoraphobic /ægərə'fəʊbɪk/ adj
agorafobo, -a mf

agree /ə'griː/ ① vt accordarsi su; ~ to
do something accettare di fare qualcosa;
~ that essere d'accordo [sul fatto] che
② vi essere d'accordo; ⟨figures⟩
concordare; (reach agreement) mettersi
d'accordo; (get on) andare d'accordo;
(consent) acconsentire (to a); it doesn't ~
with me mi fa male; ~ with something
(approve of) approvare qualcosa

agreeable /ə'griːəbl/ adj gradevole;
(willing) d'accordo

agreeably /ə'griːəblɪ/ adv (pleasantly)
piacevolmente; (amicably) in modo
amichevole

agreed /ə'griːd/ adj convenuto

agreement /ə'griːmənt/ n accordo m; in
~ d'accordo; reach ~ arrivare ad un
accordo

agricultural /ægrɪ'kʌltʃərəl/ adj
agricolo

agriculturalist /ægrɪ'kʌltʃərəlɪst/ n
agronomo, -a mf

agricultural show n fiera f agricola

agriculture /'ægrɪkʌltʃə(r)/ n
agricoltura f

agritourism /ægrɪ'tʊərɪzəm/ n
agriturismo m

agronomy /ə'grɒnəmɪ/ n agronomia f

aground /ə'graʊnd/ adv run ~ ⟨ship⟩
arenarsi

ah /ɑː/ int ~ well! (resignedly) va bene!

ahead /ə'hed/ adv avanti; be ~ of essere
davanti a; fig essere avanti rispetto a;
draw ~ passare davanti (of a); go on ~
cominciare ad andare; get ~ ⟨in life⟩
riuscire; go ~! fai pure!; look ~ pensare
all'avvenire; plan ~ fare progetti per
l'avvenire

aid /eɪd/ ① n aiuto m; in ~ of a favore di
② vt aiutare

aid agency n organizzazione f
umanitaria

aide n assistente mf

aid package n pacco m umanitario

Aids /eɪdz/ n AIDS m

Aids awareness n sensibilizzazione f
all'AIDS

aid worker n persona f che lavora per
un'organizzazione umanitaria

ailing /'eɪlɪŋ/ adj malato

ailment /'eɪlmənt/ n disturbo m

aim /eɪm/ ① n mira f; fig scopo m; take ~
prendere la mira
② vt puntare ⟨gun⟩ (at su)
③ vi mirare; ~ to do something aspirare
a fare qualcosa

aimless /'eɪmlɪs/ adj senza scopo

aimlessly /'eɪmlɪslɪ/ adv senza scopo

ain't /eɪnt/ fam = am not; are not; have
not; has not

air /eə(r)/ ① n aria f; be on the ~
⟨programme⟩ essere in onda; put on ~s
darsi delle arie; by ~ in aereo; (airmail) per
via aerea
② vt arieggiare; far conoscere ⟨views⟩; pej
sfoggiare ⟨knowledge⟩

air ambulance n aereo m ambulanza;
(helicopter) eliambulanza f

air attack n attacco m aereo

air bag n Auto air bag m inv

air bed n materassino m [gonfiabile]

airborne /'eəbɔːn/ adj (plane) in volo;
⟨troops⟩ aerotrasportato

airbrush n aerografo m

air bubble n (in liquid, plastic, wallpaper)
bolla f d'aria

air-conditioned adj con aria
condizionata

air conditioner n condizionatore m

air-conditioning n aria f condizionata

air-cooled adj ⟨engine⟩ raffreddato ad
aria

air cover n protezione f aerea

aircraft n aereo m

aircraft carrier n portaerei f inv

aircraft[s]man n Br aviere m

air crash n disastro m aereo

aircrew n equipaggio m di volo

air cushion n (inflatable cushion) cuscino
m gonfiabile; (of hovercraft) cuscino m d'aria

air disaster n disastro m aereo

air display n esibizione f in volo

airdrop n lancio m con paracadute

air duct n condotto m dell'aria

air exclusion zone n zona f di
esclusione aerea

airfare n tariffa f aerea

airfield n campo m d'aviazione

airflow n spostamento m d'aria

air force n aviazione f

airfreight n (goods) merce f spedita via
aerea; (method of transport) trasporto m
aereo; (charge) costo m per trasporto aereo

air-freshener n deodorante m per
ambienti

air gun n fucile m ad aria compressa.

airhead n fam svampito,-a mf

air hole n sfiatatoio m

air hostess n hostess f inv

airing /'eərɪŋ/ n give a room an ~
arieggiare una stanza; give an idea an ~
fig ventilare un'idea

airing cupboard n Br sgabuzzino m del
boiler dove viene riposta la biancheria ad
asciugare

airless /'eəlɪs/ *adj* ⟨*evening*⟩ senza vento; ⟨*room*⟩ poco ventilato

air letter *n* aerogramma *m*

airlift ① *vt* trasportare con ponte aereo ② *n* ponte *m* aereo

airline *n* compagnia *f* aerea

airliner *n* aereo *m* di linea

airlock *n* bolla *f* d'aria

airmail *n* posta *f* aerea

air marshal *n* Br maresciallo *m* d'aviazione

Air Miles® *npl* Br miglia *fpl* aeree

airplane *n* Am aereo *m*

air pocket *n* vuoto *m* d'aria

airport *n* aeroporto *m*

air power *n* potenza *f* aerea

air raid *n* incursione *f* aerea

air-raid shelter *n* rifugio *m* antiaereo

air-raid siren *n* allarme *m* aereo

air-raid warning *n* allarme *m* aereo

air rifle *n* fucile *m* ad aria compressa

air-sea rescue *n* salvataggio *m* dal mare con impiego di mezzi aerei

air shaft *n* (in mine) pozzo *m* di ventilazione

airship *n* dirigibile *m*

air show *n* (trade exhibition) salone *m* dell'aviazione; (flying show) manifestazione *f* aerea

airsickness *n* mal *m* d'aereo

air sock *n* manica *f* a vento

airspeed *n* velocità *f* relativa all'aria

airspeed indicator *n* indicatore *m* di velocità (su un aereo)

air steward *n* steward *m inv*

air stewardess *n* hostess *f inv*

airstream *n* corrente *f* d'aria

airstrike *n* incursione *f* aerea

airstrip *n* pista *f* d'atterraggio

air terminal *n* (in town, terminus) [air-]terminal *m inv*

airtight *adj* ermetico

airtime *n* Radio, TV spazio *m* radiofonico/televisivo

air-to-air *adj* ⟨*missile*⟩ aria-aria; ⟨*refuelling*⟩ in volo

air traffic *n* traffico *m* aereo

air-traffic controller *n* controllore *m* di volo

air travel *n* viaggi *mpl* in aereo

air valve *n* valvola *f* pneumatica

air vent *n* presa *f* d'aria

air vice-marshal *n* Br vice-maresciallo *m* dell'aviazione

air war *n* conflitto *m* aereo

airwaves *npl* Radio, TV onde *fpl* radio

airway *n* (route) rotta *f* aerea; (airline) compagnia *f* aerea; Anat via *f* respiratoria; (ventilating passage) pozzo *m* di ventilazione

air waybill *n* polizza *f* di carico aerea

airworthiness *n* idoneità *f* di volo

airworthy *adj* idoneo al volo

airy /'eərɪ/ *adj* (-ier, -iest) arieggiato; ⟨*manner*⟩ noncurante

airy-fairy /eərɪ'feərɪ/ *adj* Br fam ⟨*plan, person*⟩ fuori dalla realtà

aisle /aɪl/ *n* corridoio *m*; (in supermarket) corsia *f*; (in church) navata *f*

ajar /ə'dʒɑː(r)/ *adj* socchiuso

aka *abbr* (**also known as**) alias

akin /ə'kɪn/ *adj* ∼ **to** simile a

AI *n abbr* (**artificial intelligence**) I.A. *f*

alabaster /'æləbɑːstə(r)/ *n* alabastro *m*

alacrity /ə'lækrətɪ/ *n* alacrità *f inv*

alarm /ə'lɑːm/ ① *n* allarme *m*; set the ∼ (of alarm clock) mettere la sveglia; **in** ∼ in stato di allarme ② *vt* allarmare; **don't be** ∼**ed!** non si allarmi!

alarm bell *n* campanello *m* d'allarme; set the ∼ ∼s ringing *n* Br fig far scattare il campanello d'allarme

alarm call *n* Teleph sveglia *f* automatica

alarm clock *n* sveglia *f*

alarmed *adj* allarmato

alarming /ə'lɑːmɪŋ/ *adj* allarmante, preoccupante

alarmist /ə'lɑːmɪst/ *adj* & *n* allarmista *mf*

alas /ə'læs/ *int* ahimè

Albania /æl'beɪnɪə/ *n* Albania *f*

Albanian /æl'beɪnɪən/ ① *n* (person) albanese *mf*; (language) albanese *m* ② *adj* albanese

albatross /'ælbətrɒs/ *n* (also in golf) albatro *m*

albeit /ɔːl'biːɪt/ *adv* & *conj* benché

albino /æl'biːnəʊ/ *adj* & *n* albino, -a *mf*

album /'ælbəm/ *n* album *m inv*

albumen /'ælbjʊmɪn/ *n* Biol, Bot albume *m*

alchemist /'ælkɪmɪʃt/ *n* alchimista *m*

alchemy /'ælkɪmɪ/ *n* Chem, fig alchimia *f*

alcohol /'ælkəhɒl/ *n* alcol *m*

alcoholic /ælkə'hɒlɪk/ ① *adj* alcolico ② *n* alcolizzato, -a *mf*

Alcoholics Anonymous *n* Anonima *f* Alcolisti

alcoholism /'ælkəhɒlɪzm/ *n* alcolismo *m*

alcohol-related *adj* ⟨*illness, disease*⟩ legato al consumo di alcol

alcopop /'ælkəʊpɒp/ *n* bibita *f* alcolica

alcove /'ælkəʊv/ *n* alcova *f*

alder /'ɔːldə(r)/ *n* (tree, wood) ontano *m*

ale /eɪl/ n birra f

alert /ə'lɜ:t/ ① adj attento; (watchful) vigile ② n segnale m d'allarme; **be on the ~** stare allerta ③ vt allertare

alertness /ə'lɜ:tnɪs/ n (attentiveness) attenzione f; (liveliness) vivacità f

A-level n Br Sch **~s** ≈ esami mpl di maturità; **he got an ~ in history** ha portato storia alla maturità

Alexandria /ælɪg'zændrɪə/ n Alessandria f [d'Egitto]

alfalfa /æl'fælfə/ n erba f medicinale

alfresco /æl'freskəʊ/ adj & adv all'aperto

algae /'ældʒi:/ npl alghe fpl

algebra /'ældʒɪbrə/ n algebra f

Algeria /æl'dʒɪərɪə/ n Algeria f

Algerian /æl'dʒɪərɪən/ adj & n algerino, -a mf

Algiers /æl'dʒɪəz/ n Algeri f

algorithm /'ælgərɪðm/ n algoritmo m

alias /'eɪlɪəs/ ① n pseudonimo m ② adv alias

alibi /'ælɪbaɪ/ n alibi m inv

alien /'eɪlɪən/ ① adj straniero; fig estraneo ② n straniero, -a mf; (from space) alieno, -a mf

alienate /'eɪlɪəneɪt/ vt alienare

alienation /eɪlɪə'neɪʃn/ n alienazione f

alight[1] /ə'laɪt/ vi scendere; ⟨bird⟩ posarsi

alight[2] adj be **~** essere in fiamme; **set ~** dar fuoco a

align /ə'laɪn/ vt allineare

alignment /ə'laɪnmənt/ n allineamento m; **out of ~** non allineato

alike /ə'laɪk/ ① adj simile; **be ~** rassomigliarsi ② adv in modo simile; **look ~** rassomigliarsi; **summer and winter ~** sia d'estate che d'inverno

alimentary /ælɪ'mentərɪ/ adj ⟨system⟩ digerente; ⟨process⟩ digestivo

alimentary canal n tubo m digerente

alimony /'ælɪmənɪ/ n alimenti mpl

alive /ə'laɪv/ adj vivo; **~ with** brulicante di; **~ to** sensibile a; **~ and kicking** vivo e vegeto

alkali /'ælkəlaɪ/ n alcali m

alkaline /'ælkəlaɪn/ adj alcalino

all /ɔ:l/ ① adj tutto; **~ the children, ~ children** tutti i bambini; **~ day** tutto il giorno; **he refused ~ help** ha rifiutato qualsiasi aiuto; **for ~ that** (nevertheless) perciò; **in ~ sincerity** in tutta sincerità; **be ~ for** essere favorevole a ② pron tutto; **~ of you/them** tutti voi/ loro; **~ of it** tutto; **~ of the town** tutta la città; **~ but one** tutti tranne uno; **in ~** in tutto; **~ in ~** tutto sommato; **most of ~**

più di ogni altra cosa; **once and for ~** una volta per tutte; **~ being well** salvo complicazioni ③ adv completamente; **~ but** quasi; **~ at once** (at the same time) tutto in una volta; **~ at once, ~ of a sudden** all'improvviso; **~ too soon** troppo presto; **~ the same** (nevertheless) ciononostante; **~ the better** meglio ancora; **she's not ~ that good an actress** non è poi così brava come attrice; **~ in** tutto; fam esausto; **thirty/three ~** (in sport) trenta/tre pari; **~ over** (finished) tutto finito; (everywhere) dappertutto; **it's ~ right** (I don't mind) non fa niente; **I'm ~ right** (not hurt) non ho niente; **~ right!** va bene!; **be ~ that** fam esp Am essere in gamba

all-American adj ⟨record, champion⟩ americano; ⟨girl, boy, hero⟩ tipicamente americano

all-around adj ⟨improvement⟩ generale

allay /ə'leɪ/ vt placare ⟨suspicions, anger⟩

all-clear n Mil cessato m allarme/ pericolo; (from doctor) autorizzazione f; **give somebody the ~ ~** fig dare il via libera a qualcuno

all-consuming adj ⟨passion⟩ sfrenato; ⟨ambition⟩ smisurato

all-day adj ⟨event⟩ che dura tutto il giorno

allegation /ælɪ'geɪʃn/ n accusa f

allege /ə'ledʒ/ vt dichiarare

alleged /ə'ledʒd/ adj presunto

allegedly /ə'ledʒɪdlɪ/ adv a quanto si dice

allegiance /ə'li:dʒəns/ n fedeltà f

allegorical /ælɪ'gɒrɪkl/ adj allegorico

allegory /'ælɪgərɪ/ n allegoria f

all-embracing /-əm'breɪsɪŋ/ adj globale

allergic /ə'lɜ:dʒɪk/ adj allergico

allergist /'ælədʒɪst/ n allergologo, -a mf

allergy /'ælədʒɪ/ n allergia f

allergy clinic n clinica f di allergologia

alleviate /ə'li:vɪeɪt/ vt alleviare

alleviation /əli:vɪ'eɪʃn/ n alleviamento m, alleggerimento m

alley /'ælɪ/ n vicolo m; (for bowling) corsia f

alleyway /'ælɪweɪ/ n vicolo m

all-found adj £200 **~** 200 sterline inclusi vitto e alloggio

alliance /ə'laɪəns/ n alleanza f

allied /'ælaɪd/ adj alleato; (fig: related) connesso (**to** a)

alligator /'ælɪgeɪtə(r)/ n alligatore m

all-important adj essenziale

all in adj (Br fam: exhausted) distrutto; ⟨fee, price⟩ tutto compreso

all-inclusive adj (fee, price) tutto compreso

all-in-one adj ⟨garment⟩ in un pezzo solo

all-in wresting *n* Sport catch *m*

all-night *adj* ⟨*party, meeting*⟩ che dura tutta la notte; ⟨*radio station*⟩ che trasmette tutta la notte; ⟨*service*⟩ notturno

allocate /'æləkeɪt/ *vt* assegnare; distribuire ⟨*resources*⟩

allocation /ælə'keɪʃn/ *n* assegnazione *f*; (of resources) distribuzione *f*

all-or-nothing *adj* ⟨*approach, policy*⟩ senza vie di mezzo

allot /ə'lɒt/ *vt* (pt/pp **allotted**) distribuire

allotment /ə'lɒtmənt/ *n* distribuzione *f*; (share) parte *f*; (land) piccolo lotto *m* di terreno

all-out ① *adj* ⟨*effort*⟩ estremo; ⟨*attack*⟩ senza esclusione di colpi.
② *adv* go all out to do something/for something mettercela tutta per fare qualcosa/per qualcosa

all-over *adj* ⟨*tan*⟩ integrale

all over ① *prep* ~ ~ China in/per tutta la Cina; the news is ~ ~ the village lo sanno tutti in paese; be ~ ~ somebody (fawning over) stare appiccicato a qualcuno
② *adv* be trembling ~ ~ tremare tutto; that's Mary ~ ~! è proprio da Mary!
③ *adj* when it's ~ ~ (finished) quando è tutto finito

allow /ə'laʊ/ *vt* permettere; (grant) accordare; (reckon on) contare; (agree) ammettere; ~ somebody to do something permettere a qualcuno di fare qualcosa; you are not ~ed to... è vietato...; how much are you ~ed? qual è il limite?
▪ **allow for** *vt* tener conto di

allowable /ə'laʊəbl/ *adj* permissibile; Jur lecito; ⟨*tax*⟩ deducibile

allowance /ə'laʊəns/ *n* sussidio *m*; (Am: pocket money) paghetta *f*; (for petrol etc) indennità *f inv*; (of luggage, duty free) limite *m*; (for tax purposes) deduzione *f*; make ~s for essere indulgente verso ⟨*somebody*⟩; tener conto di ⟨*something*⟩

alloy /'ælɔɪ/ *n* lega *f*

alloy steel *n* lega *f* d'acciaio

alloy wheel *n* cerchione *m* in lega d'acciaio

all points bulletin *n* Am allarme *m* generale

all-powerful *adj* onnipotente

all-purpose *adj* ⟨*building*⟩ polivalente; ⟨*utensil*⟩ multiuso

all right ① *adj* is it ~ ~ if...? va bene se...?; is that ~ ~ with you? ti va bene?; sounds ~ ~ to me per me va bene; that's [quite] ~ ~ (it doesn't matter) non c'è problema; is my hair ~ ~? sono a posto i miei capelli?; it's ~ ~ for you! è facile per te!; she's ~ ~ (competent) è abbastanza brava; (attractive) non è niente male; (pleasant) è piuttosto simpatica; will you be

~ ~? (able to manage) te la caverai?; feel ~ ~ (well) sentirsi bene
② *adv* ⟨*function, see*⟩ bene; (not brilliantly) così così; can I? –~ ~ posso? –d'accordo; she's doing ~ ~ (in life) le cose le vanno bene; (in health) sta bene; (in activity) se la cava bene; she knows ~ ~! (without doubt) lei lo sa di sicuro!; ~ ~, ~ ~!, va bene! va bene!

all-risk *adj* ⟨*policy, cover*⟩ multirischi

all-round *adj* ⟨*improvement*⟩ generale; ⟨athlete⟩ completo

all-rounder /-'raʊndə(r)/ *n* be a good ~ essere versatile

allspice /'ɔːlspaɪs/ *n* pepe *m* della Giamaica

all square *adj* be ~ ~ ⟨*people*⟩ essere pari; ⟨*accounts*⟩ quadrare

all-time *adj* ⟨*record*⟩ assoluto, senza precedenti; the ~ greats (people) i grandi; ~ high massimo *m* storico; be at an ~ low ⟨*person, morale*⟩ essere a terra; ⟨*figures, shares*⟩ toccare il minimo storico

all told *adv* tutto sommato

allude /ə'luːd/ *vi* alludere

allure /ə'ljʊə(r)/ *n* attrattiva *f*

alluring /ə'ljʊrɪŋ/ *adj* allettante, affascinante

allusion /ə'luːʒn/ *n* allusione *f*

ally[1] /'ælaɪ/ *n* alleato, -a *mf*

ally[2] /ə'laɪ/ *vt* (pt/pp **-ied**) alleare; ~ oneself with allearsi con

almighty /ɔːl'maɪtɪ/ ① *adj* (fam: big) mega *inv*
② *n* the A~ l'Onnipotente *m*

almond /'ɑːmənd/ *n* mandorla *f*; (tree) mandorlo *m*

almost /'ɔːlməʊst/ *adv* quasi

alms /ɑːmz/ *npl* (liter) elemosina *fsg*

aloft /ə'lɒft/ *adv* in alto; Naut sull'alberatura; from ~ dall'alto

alone /ə'ləʊn/ ① *adj* solo; leave me ~! lasciami in pace!; let ~ (not to mention) figurarsi
② *adv* da solo

along /ə'lɒŋ/ ① *prep* lungo
② *adv* ~ with assieme a; all ~ tutto il tempo; come ~! (hurry up) vieni qui!; I'll bring it ~ lo porto lì; I'll be ~ in a minute arrivo tra un attimo; move ~ spostarsi; move ~! circolare!

alongside /əlɒŋ'saɪd/ ① *adv* lungo bordo
② *prep* lungo; work ~ somebody lavorare fianco a fianco con qualcuno

aloof /ə'luːf/ *adj* distante

aloud /ə'laʊd/ *adv* ad alta voce

alpaca /æl'pækə/ *n* alpaca *m inv*

alpha /'ælfə/ *n* (letter) alfa *f inv*; Br Univ ≈ trenta *m inv* e lode

alphabet /'ælfəbet/ *n* alfabeto *m*

alphabetical /ælfə'betɪkl/ adj alfabetico

alphabetically /ælfə'betɪklɪ/ adv in ordine alfabetico

alpha male n maschio m dominante

alpine /'ælpaɪn/ adj alpino

Alps /ælps/ npl Alpi fpl

already /ɔːl'redɪ/ adv già

alright /ɔːl'raɪt/ = ALL RIGHT

Alsace /æl'zæs/ n Alsazia f

Alsatian /æl'seɪʃn/ n (dog) pastore m tedesco

also /'ɔːlsəʊ/ adv anche; ∼, I need... inoltre, ho bisogno di...

altar /'ɔːltə(r)/ n altare m

altar boy n chierichetto m

altar cloth n tovaglia f da altare

altar piece n pala f d'altare

alter /'ɔːltə(r)/ ① vt cambiare; aggiustare ‹clothes› ② vi cambiare

alteration /ɔːltə'reɪʃn/ n modifica f

altercation /ɔːltə'keɪʃn/ n alterco m

alternate¹ /'ɔːltəneɪt/ ① vi alternarsi ② vt alternare

alternate² /ɔːl'tɜːnət/ adj alterno; on ∼ days a giorni alterni

alternately /ɔːl'tɜːnətlɪ/ adv in modo alterno; (Am: alternatively) alternativamente

alternating current /'ɔːltəneɪtɪŋ/ n corrente f alternata

alternation /ɔːltə'neɪʃn/ n alternanza f

alternative /ɔːl'tɜːnətɪv/ ① adj alternativo ② n alternativa f

alternative energy n energia f alternativa

alternatively /ɔːl'tɜːnətɪvlɪ/ adv alternativamente

alternative medicine n medicina f alternativa

alternative technology n tecnologia f alternativa

alternator /'ɔːltəneɪtə(r)/ n Electr alternatore m

although /ɔːl'ðəʊ/ conj benché, sebbene

altimeter /'æltɪmiːtə(r)/ n altimetro m

altitude /'æltɪtjuːd/ n altitudine f

Alt key /'ælt/ n Comput tasto m Alt

alto /'æltəʊ/ n contralto m

altogether /ɔːltə'geðə(r)/ adv (in all) in tutto; (completely) completamente; I'm not ∼ sure non sono del tutto sicuro

altruism /'æltrʊɪzm/ n altruismo m

altruistic /æltrʊ'ɪstɪk/ adj altruistico

aluminium /æljʊ'mɪnɪəm/ n Am **aluminum** /ə'luːmɪnəm/ n alluminio m

aluminium foil n carta f stagnola

alumna /ə'lʌmnə/ n Am Sch Univ ex allieva f

alumnus /ə'lʌmnəs/ n Am Sch Univ ex allievo m

always /'ɔːlweɪz/ adv sempre

Alzheimer's disease /'æltshaɪməz/ n morbo m di Alzheimer

am /æm/ ▶ BE

a.m. abbr (**ante meridiem**) del mattino

amalgam /ə'mælgəm/ n amalgama m

amalgamate /ə'mælgəmeɪt/ ① vt fondere ② vi fondersi

amalgamation /əmælgə'meɪʃn/ n fusione f; (of styles) amalgama m

amass /ə'mæs/ vt accumulare

amateur /'æmətə(r)/ ① n non professionista mf; pej dilettante mf ② attrib dilettante; ∼ dramatics filodrammatica f

amateurish /'æmətərɪʃ/ adj dilettantesco

amaze /ə'meɪz/ vt stupire

amazed /ə'meɪzd/ adj stupito

amazement /ə'meɪzmənt/ n stupore m; to her ∼ con suo grande stupore; in ∼ stupito

amazing /ə'meɪzɪŋ/ adj incredibile

amazingly /ə'meɪzɪŋlɪ/ adv incredibilmente

Amazon /'æməzən/ ① n (in myths) Amazzone f; (fig: strong woman) amazzone f; (river) Rio m delle Amazzoni ② attrib ‹basin, forest, tribe› amazzonico

ambassador /æm'bæsədə(r)/ n ambasciatore, -trice mf

ambassador-at-large n Am ambasciatore, -trice mf a disposizione

amber /'æmbə(r)/ ① n ambra f ② adj (colour) ambra inv

ambidextrous /æmbɪ'dekstrəs/ adj ambidestro

ambience /'æmbɪəns/ n atmosfera f

ambient /'æmbɪənt/ adj ‹temperature› ambiente inv; (noise) circostante

ambiguity /æmbɪ'gjuːətɪ/ n ambiguità f inv

ambiguous /æm'bɪgjʊəs/ adj ambiguo

ambiguously /æm'bɪgjʊəslɪ/ adv in modo ambiguo

ambition /æm'bɪʃn/ n ambizione f; (aim) aspirazione f

ambitious /æm'bɪʃəs/ adj ambizioso

ambivalence /æm'bɪvələns/ n ambivalenza f

ambivalent /æm'bɪvələnt/ adj ambivalente

amble /'æmb(ə)l/ vi camminare senza fretta

ambulance /'æmbjʊləns/ n ambulanza f

ambulance man *n* guidatore *m* di ambulanze

ambush /'æmbʊʃ/ **1** *n* imboscata *f* **2** *vt* tendere un'imboscata a

ameba /ə'mi:bə/ *n* Am ameba *f*

amen /ɑ:'men/ *int* amen

amenability /əmi:nə'bɪlɪtɪ/ *n* arrendevolezza *f*

amenable /ə'mi:nəbl/ *adj* conciliante; ∼ to sensibile a

amend /ə'mend/ **1** *vt* modificare **2** *npl* **make ∼s** fare ammenda (**for** di, per)

amendment /ə'mendmənt/ *n* modifica *f*

amenities /ə'mi:nətɪz/ *npl* comodità *fpl*

America /ə'merɪkə/ *n* America *f*

American /ə'merɪkən/ *adj & n* americano, -a *mf*

American Civil War *n* guerra *f* di secessione [americana]

American English *n* inglese *m* americano

American Indian *n* indiano, -a *mf* d'America

Americanism /ə'merɪkənɪzm/ *n* americanismo *m*

amethyst /'æməθɪst/ *n* (gem) ametista *f*

Amex /'æmeks/ *n abbr* (**American Stock Exchange**) Borsa *f* valori americana; *abbr* **American Express**

amiable /'eɪmɪəbl/ *adj* amabile

amicable /'æmɪkəbl/ *adj* amichevole

amicably /'æmɪkəblɪ/ *adv* amichevolmente

amid[st] /ə'mɪd[st]/ *prep* in mezzo a

amino acid /ə'mi:nəʊ/ *n* amminoacido *m*

amiss /ə'mɪs/ **1** *adj* **there's something ∼** c'è qualcosa che non va **2** *adv* **take something ∼** prendersela [a male]; **it won't come ∼** non sarebbe sgradito

ammo /'æməʊ/ *n abbr* (**ammunition**) munizioni *fpl*

ammonia /ə'məʊnɪə/ *n* ammoniaca *f*

ammunition /æmjʊ'nɪʃn/ *n* munizioni *fpl*

amnesia /æm'ni:zɪə/ *n* amnesia *f*

amnesty /'æmnəstɪ/ *n* amnistia *f*

amoeba /ə'mi:bə/ *n* ameba *f*

amoebic /ə'mi:bɪk/ *adj* ⟨dysentry⟩ amebico

amok /ə'mɒk/ *adv* **run ∼** essere in preda a furore; ⟨imagination⟩ scatenarsi

among[st] /ə'mʌŋ[st]/ *prep* tra, fra; **talk ∼ yourselves** parlate tra [di] voi

amoral /eɪ'mɒrəl/ *adj* amorale

amorality /eɪmə'rælətɪ/ *n* amoralità *f*

amorous /'æmərəs/ *adj* amoroso

amorphous /ə'mɔ:fəs/ *adj* Chem amorfo; ⟨ideas, plans⟩ confuso; ⟨shape, collection⟩ informe

amount /ə'maʊnt/ **1** *n* quantità *f inv*; (sum of money) montante *m* **2** *v* ■ **amount to** *vt* ammontare a; fig equivalere a

amp /æmp/ *n* ampere *m inv*

ampere /'æmpeə(r)/ *n* ampere *m inv*

ampersand /'æmpəsænd/ *n* e *f inv* commerciale

amphetamine /æm'fetəmi:n/ *n* anfetamina *f*

amphibian /æm'fɪbɪən/ *n* anfibio *m*

amphibious /æm'fɪbɪəs/ *adj* anfibio

amphitheatre /'æmfɪθi:ətə(r)/ *n* anfiteatro *m*

ample /'æmpl/ *adj* (large) grande; ⟨proportions⟩ ampio; (enough) largamente sufficiente

amplifier /'æmplɪfaɪə(r)/ *n* amplificatore *m*

amplify /'æmplɪfaɪ/ *vt* (pt/pp **-ied**) amplificare ⟨sound⟩

amply /'æmplɪ/ *adv* largamente

amputate /'æmpjʊteɪt/ *vt* amputare

amputation /æmpjʊ'teɪʃn/ *n* amputazione *f*

amputee /æmpjʊ'ti:/ *n* mutilato, -a *mf* (in seguito ad amputazione)

amuse /ə'mju:z/ *vt* divertire

amused /ə'mju:zd/ *adj* divertito

amusement /ə'mju:zmənt/ *n* divertimento *m*

amusement arcade *n* sala *f* giochi

amusement park *n* luna park *m inv*

amusing /ə'mju:zɪŋ/ *adj* divertente

an /ən/, stressed /æn/ ▶ A

anabolic steroid /ænə'bɒlɪk/ *n* anabolizzante *m*

anachronism /ə'nækrənɪzm/ *n* **be an ∼** ⟨object, custom⟩ essere anacronistico

anaemia /ə'ni:mɪə/ *n* anemia *f*

anaemic /ə'ni:mɪk/ *adj* anemico

anaerobic /æneə'rəʊbɪk/ *adj* anerobico

anaesthesia /ænəs'θi:zɪə/ *n* anestesia *f*

anaesthetic /ænəs'θetɪk/ *n* anestesia *f*; **give somebody an ∼** somministrare a qualcuno l'anestesia

anaesthetist /ə'ni:sθətɪst/ *n* anestesista *mf*

anaesthetize /ə'ni:sθətaɪz/ *vt* anestetizzare

anagram /'ænəgræm/ *n* anagramma *m*

analgesic /ænəl'dʒi:zɪk/ *adj & n* analgesico *m*

analogous /ə'næləgəs/ *adj* analogo

analog[ue] /'ænəlɒg/ *adj* analogico

analogy /ə'næləʤɪ/ n analogia f

analyse /'ænəlaɪz/ vt analizzare

analysis /ə'næləsɪs/ n analisi f inv

analyst /'ænəlɪst/ n analista mf

analytical /ænə'lɪtɪkl/ adj analitico

anaphylaxis /ænəfɪ'læksɪs/, **anaphylactic shock** /ænəfɪ'læktɪk/ n anafilassi f, shock m anafilattico

anarchic[al] /ə'nɑːkɪk[l]/ adj anarchico

anarchist /'ænəkɪst/ n anarchico, -a mf

anarchy /'ænəkɪ/ n anarchia f

anathema /ə'næθəmə/ n eresia f

anatomical /ænə'tɒmɪkl/ adj anatomico

anatomically /ænə'tɒmɪklɪ/ adv anatomicamente

anatomy /ə'nætəmɪ/ n anatomia f

ANC n abbr (**African National Congress**) Congresso m Nazionale Africano

ancestor /'ænsestə(r)/ n antenato, -a mf

ancestral /æn'sestrəl/ adj ancestrale; ⟨home⟩ avito

ancestry /'ænsestrɪ/ n antenati mpl

anchor /'æŋkə(r)/ **1** n ancora f **2** vi gettare l'ancora **3** vt ancorare

anchorage /'æŋkərɪʤ/ n ancoraggio m

anchorman /'æŋkəmæn/ n Radio, TV anchor man m inv; Sport staffettista m dell'ultima frazione

anchorwoman /'æŋkəwʊmən/ n Radio TV anchor woman f inv

anchovy /'æntʃəvɪ/ n acciuga f

ancient /'eɪnʃənt/ adj antico; fam vecchio; ~ **Rome** l'antica Roma f

ancillary /æn'sɪlərɪ/ adj ausiliario

and /ənd/, accentato /ænd/ conj e; ~ **so on** e così via; **two** ~ **two** due più due; **six hundred** ~ **two** seicentodue; **more** ~ **more** sempre più; **nice** ~ **warm** bello caldo; **try** ~ **come** cerca di venire; **go** ~ **get** vai a prendere

Andean /'ændɪən/ adj andino

Andes /'ændiːz/ npl **the** ~ le Ande

Andorra /æn'dɔːrə/ n Andorra f

anecdote /'ænɪkdəʊt/ n aneddoto m

anemone /ə'nemənɪ/ n Bot anemone m

anew /ə'njuː/ adv di nuovo

angel /'eɪnʤl/ n angelo m

angel cake n dolce m di pan di Spagna

angelfish /'eɪnʤlfɪʃ/ n angelo m di mare

angelic /æn'ʤelɪk/ adj angelico

anger /'æŋgə(r)/ **1** n rabbia f **2** vt far arrabbiare

angina [pectoris] /æn'ʤaɪnə('pektərɪs)/ n angina f pectoris

angle¹ /'æŋgl/ n angolo m; fig angolazione f; **at an** ~ storto

angle² vi pescare con la lenza; ~ **for** fig cercare di ottenere

angle bracket n Techn parentesi f inv uncinata

Anglepoise [lamp] /'æŋglpɔɪz/ n lampada f a braccio estensibile

angler /'æŋglə(r)/ n pescatore, -trice mf

Anglican /'æŋglɪkən/ adj & n anglicano, -a mf

anglicism /'æŋglɪsɪzm/ n anglicismo m

anglicize /'æŋglɪsaɪz/ vt anglicizzare

angling /'æŋglɪŋ/ n pesca f con la lenza

Anglo+ /'æŋgləʊ/ pref anglo+

Anglo-American adj & n angloamericano, -a mf

Anglophone /'æŋgləfəʊn/ adj & n anglofono, -a mf

Anglo-Saxon /æŋgləʊ'sæksn/ adj & n anglosassone mf

Angola /æŋ'gəʊlə/ n Angola f

angora /æn'gɔːrə/ n lana f d'angora

angrily /'æŋgrɪlɪ/ adv rabbiosamente

angry /'æŋgrɪ/ adj (-ier, -iest) arrabbiato; **get** ~ arrabbiarsi; ~ **with** or **at somebody** arrabbiato con qualcuno; ~ **at** or **about something** arrabbiato per qualcosa

anguish /'æŋgwɪʃ/ n angoscia f; **in** ~ in preda all'angoscia

anguished /'æŋgwɪʃt/ adj (suffering) straziante; ⟨person⟩ angosciato

angular /'æŋgjʊlə(r)/ adj angolare

animal /'ænɪm(ə)l/ adj & n animale m

animal experiment n esperimento m sugli animali

animal husbandry /'hʌzbəndrɪ/ n allevamento m

animal kingdom n regno m animale

animal lover n amante mf degli animali

animal product n prodotto m di origine animale

animal rights npl diritti mpl degli animali

animal rights activist n animalista mf

animal sanctuary n rifugio m per animali

animal testing n sperimentazione f sugli animali

animate¹ /'ænɪmət/ adj animato

animate² /'ænɪmeɪt/ vt animare

animated /'ænɪmeɪtɪd/ adj animato; ⟨person⟩ vivace

animation /ænɪ'meɪʃn/ n animazione f

animator /'ænɪmeɪtə(r)/ n (film cartoonist) animatore, -trice mf; (director) regista mf di film d'animazione

animatronics /æˈnɪməˈtrɒnɪks/ *n* animazione *f* elettronica

animosity /æˈnɪˈmɒsətɪ/ *n* animosità *f inv*

aniseed /ˈænɪsiːd/ *n* anice *f*

ankle /ˈæŋk(ə)l/ *n* caviglia *f*

anklebone *n* astragalo *m*

ankle-deep *adj* be ~ in mud *adj* essere nel fango fino alle caviglie

ankle-length *adj* (dress) alla caviglia

ankle sock *n* calzino *m*

annals /ˈænəlz/ *npl* go down in the ~ [of history] passare agli annali

annex /əˈneks/ *vt* annettere

annexation /ænekˈseɪʃn/ *n* (action) annessione *f*; (land annexed) territorio *m* annesso

annex[e] /ˈæneks/ *n* annesso *m*

annihilate /əˈnaɪəleɪt/ *vt* annientare

annihilation /ənaɪəˈleɪʃn/ *n* annientamento *m*

anniversary /ænɪˈvɜːsərɪ/ *n* anniversario *m*

Anno Domini /ænəʊˈdɒmɪnaɪ/ *adv* dopo Cristo

annotate /ˈænəteɪt/ *vt* annotare

announce /əˈnaʊns/ *vt* annunciare

announcement /əˈnaʊnsmənt/ *n* annuncio *m*

announcer /əˈnaʊnsə(r)/ *n* annunciatore, -trice *mf*

annoy /əˈnɔɪ/ *vt* dare fastidio a

annoyance /əˈnɔɪəns/ *n* seccatura *f*; (anger) irritazione *f*

annoyed *adj* irritato; get ~ irritarsi; ~ with somebody irritato con qualcuno; ~ at/about something irritato per qualcosa; ~ that irritato che

annoying /əˈnɔɪɪŋ/ *adj* fastidioso

annual /ˈænjʊəl/ **①** *adj* annuale; ⟨income⟩ annuo
② *n* Bot pianta *f* annua; (children's book) almanacco *m*

Annual General Meeting *n* assemblea *f* generale annuale

annually /ˈænjʊəlɪ/ *adv* annualmente; she earns £50,000~ guadagna 50.000 sterline all'anno

annual report *n* resoconto *m* annuale

annuity /əˈnjuːətɪ/ *n* annualità *f inv*

annul /əˈnʌl/ *vt* (pt/pp **annulled**) annullare

Annunciation /ənʌnsɪˈeɪʃn/ *n* Annunciazione *f*

anode /ˈænəʊd/ *n* anodo *m*

anodyne /ˈænədaɪn/ *adj* liter (bland) anodino; (inoffensive) innocuo

anoint /əˈnɔɪnt/ *vt* ungere

anomalous /əˈnɒmələs/ *adj* anomalo

anomaly /əˈnɒmənalɪ/ *n* anomalia *f*

anon /əˈnɒn/ *abbr* (**anonymous**) anonimo

anonymity /ænəˈnɪmətɪ/ *n* anonimità *f*

anonymous /əˈnɒnɪməs/ *adj* anonimo; remain ~ mantenere l'anonimato

anonymously /əˈnɒnɪməslɪ/ *adv* anonimamente

anorak /ˈænəræk/ *n* giacca *f* a vento

anorexia /ˈænəˈreksɪə/ *n* anoressia *f*

anorexic /ænəˈreksɪk/ *adj & n* anoressico, -a *mf*

another /əˈnʌðə(r)/ *adj & pron* ~ [one] un altro, un'altra; ~ day un altro giorno; in ~ way diversamente; ~ time un'altra volta; one ~ l'un l'altro

answer /ˈɑːnsə(r)/ **①** *n* risposta *f*; (solution) soluzione *f*
② *vt* rispondere a ⟨person, question, letter⟩; esaudire ⟨prayer⟩; ~ the door aprire la porta; ~ the telephone rispondere al telefono
③ *vi* rispondere
∎ **answer back** *vi* ribattere
∎ **answer for** *vt* rispondere di

answerable /ˈɑːnsərəbl/ *adj* responsabile; be ~ to somebody rispondere a qualcuno

answering machine *n* Teleph segreteria *f* telefonica

answering service *n* servizio *m* di segreteria telefonica

answerphone /ˈɑːnsəfəʊn/ *n* segreteria *f* telefonica

ant /ænt/ *n* formica *f*

antacid /æntˈæsɪd/ *adj & n* antiacido *m*

antagonism /ænˈtægənɪzm/ *n* antagonismo *m*

antagonistic /æntægəˈnɪstɪk/ *adj* antagonistico

antagonize /ænˈtægənaɪz/ *vt* provocare l'ostilità di

Antarctic /ænˈtɑːktɪk/ **①** *n* Antartico *m*
② *adj* antartico

Antarctica /ænˈtɑːktɪkə/ *n* Antartide *f*

Antarctic Circle *n* Circolo *m* polare antartico

Antarctic Ocean *n* mare *m* antartico

anteater /ˈæntiːtə(r)/ *n* formichiere *m*

antecedent /æntɪˈsiːdənt/ *n* (precedent) antecedente *m*; (ancestor) antenato, -a *mf*

antedate /æntɪˈdeɪt/ *vt* (put earlier date on) retrodatare; (predate) precedere

antediluvian /æntɪdɪˈluːvɪən/ *adj* antidiluviano

antelope /ˈæntɪləʊp/ *n* antilope *m*

antenatal /æntɪˈneɪtl/ *adj* prenatale

antenatal class *n* corso *m* di preparazione al parto

antenatal clinic n Br assistenza f medica prenatale

antenna /æn'tenə/ n antenna f

anterior /æn'tɪərɪə/ adj anteriore

anteroom /'æntɪ-/ n anticamera f

antheap /'ænθiːp/ = ANTHILL

anthem /'ænθəm/ n inno m

anthill /'ænθɪl/ n formicaio m

anthology /æn'θɒlədʒɪ/ n antologia f

anthracite /'ænθrəsaɪt/ n antracite f

anthrax /'ænθræks/ n (disease) carbonchio m; (pustule) pustola f di carbonchio

anthropological /ænθrəpə'lɒdʒɪkl/ adj antropologico

anthropologist /ænθrə'pɒlədʒɪst/ n antropologo, -a mf

anthropology /ænθrə'pɒlədʒɪ/ n antropologia f

anti /'æntɪ/ ① pref anti- ② prep be ~ essere contro

anti-abortion adj antiabortista

anti-abortionist n antiabortista mf

anti-aircraft adj antiaereo

anti-apartheid adj antiapartheid inv

antibacterial /æntɪbæk'tɪərɪəl/ adj antibatterico

antiballistic missile /æntɪbəlɪstɪk'mɪsaɪl/ n missile m antimissile

antibiotic /æntɪbaɪ'ɒtɪk/ n antibiotico m

antibody /'æntɪbɒdɪ/ n anticorpo m

anticipate /æn'tɪsɪpeɪt/ vt prevedere; (forestall) anticipare

anticipation /æntɪsɪ'peɪʃn/ n anticipo m; (excitement) attesa f; in ~ of in previsione di

anticlimax /æntɪ'klaɪmæks/ n delusione f

anticlockwise /æntɪ'klɒkwaɪz/ adj & adv in senso antiorario

antics /'æntɪks/ npl gesti mpl buffi

anticyclone /æntɪ'saɪkləʊn/ n anticiclone m

antidepressant /æntɪdɪ'pres(ə)nt/ adj & n antidepressivo m

antidote /'æntɪdəʊt/ n antidoto m

anti-establishment adj contestatario

antifreeze /'æntɪfriːz/ n antigelo m

antiglare /æntɪ'gleə(r)/ adj ⟨screen⟩ antiriflesso inv

antihistamine /æntɪ'hɪstəmiːn/ n antistaminico m

anti-inflammatory /-ɪn'flæmətrɪ/ adj & n antinfiammatorio m

anti-inflation adj anti-inflazione inv

anti-inflationary /-ɪn'fleɪʃnərɪ/ adj antinflazionistico

anti-lock adj antibloccaggio inv

antipathy /æn'tɪpəθɪ/ n antipatia f

antiperspirant /æntɪ'pɜːspɪrənt/ n deodorante m antitraspirante

antipodean /æntɪpə'diːən/ adj & n australiano, -a e/o neozelandese mf

Antipodes /æn'tɪpədiːz/ npl Br the ~ gli antipodi

antiquarian /æntɪ'kweərɪən/ adj antiquario; ~ bookshop negozio m di libri antichi

antiquated /'æntɪkweɪtɪd/ adj antiquato

antique /æn'tiːk/ ① adj antico ② n antichità f inv

antique dealer n antiquario, -a mf

antiques fair n fiera f dell'antiquariato

antique shop n negozio m d'antiquariato

antiques trade n antiquariato m

antiquity /æn'tɪkwətɪ/ n antichità f

anti-racism n antirazzismo m

anti-racist adj antirazzista

antiretroviral /æntɪ'retrəʊvaɪrəl/ adj antiretrovirale

anti-riot adj ⟨police⟩ antisommossa inv

anti-rust adj antiruggine inv

anti-Semitic /æntɪsɪ'mɪtɪk/ adj antisemita

anti-Semitism /æntɪ'semɪtɪzm/ n antisemitismo m

antiseptic /æntɪ'septɪk/ adj & n antisettico m

anti-skid adj antiscivolo inv

anti-smoking adj contro il fumo, antifumo

antisocial /æntɪ'səʊʃəl/ adj ⟨behaviour⟩ antisociale; ⟨person⟩ asociale

anti-terrorist adj antiterrorista

anti-theft adj ⟨lock, device⟩ antifurto inv; ⟨camera⟩ di sorveglianza; ~ steering lock bloccasterzo m

antithesis /æn'tɪθəsɪs/ n antitesi f

antitrust /æntɪ'trʌst/ adj antitrust inv

antivirus program /æntɪ'vaɪrəs/ n Comput programma m antivirus

antivirus software n Comput programma m antivirus

antivivisectionist /æntɪvɪvɪ'sekʃənɪst/ ① n antivivisezionista mf ② adj antivivisezionistico

anti-war adj antimilitarista

antlers /'æntləz/ npl corna fpl

antonym /'æntənɪm/ n antonimo m

Antwerp /'æntwɜːp/ n Anversa f

anus /'eɪnəs/ n ano m

anvil /'ænvɪl/ n incudine f

anxiety /æŋ'zaɪətɪ/ n ansia f

anxious /'æŋkʃəs/ adj ansioso

anxiously /'æŋkʃəslɪ/ adv con ansia

any /'enɪ/ **1** adj (no matter which) qualsiasi, qualunque; **have we ∼ wine/biscuits?** abbiamo del vino/dei biscotti?; **have we ∼ jam/apples?** abbiamo della marmellata/ delle mele?; **∼ colour/number you like** qualsiasi colore/numero ti piaccia; **we don't have ∼ wine/biscuits** non abbiamo vino/biscotti; **I don't have ∼ reason to lie** non ho nessun motivo per mentire; **for ∼ reason** per qualsiasi ragione **2** pron (some) né; (no matter which) uno qualsiasi; **I don't want ∼ [of it]** non ne voglio [nessuno]; **there aren't ∼** non ce ne sono; **have we ∼?** ne abbiamo?; **have you read ∼ of her books?** hai letto qualcuno dei suoi libri? **3** adv **I can't go ∼ quicker** non posso andare più in fretta; **is it ∼ better?** va un po' meglio?; **would you like ∼ more?** ne vuoi ancora?; **I can't eat ∼ more** non posso mangiare più niente

anybody /'enɪbʌdɪ/ pron chiunque; (after negative) nessuno; **∼ can do that** chiunque può farlo; **I haven't seen ∼** non ho visto nessuno

anyhow /'enɪhaʊ/ adv ad ogni modo, comunque; (badly) non importa come

anyone /'enɪwʌn/ pron = ANYBODY

anyplace /'enɪpleɪs/ adv Am = ANYWHERE

anything /'enɪθɪŋ/ pron qualche cosa, qualcosa; (no matter what) qualsiasi cosa; (after negative) niente; **take/buy ∼ you like** prendi/compra quello che vuoi; **I don't remember ∼** non mi ricordo niente; **he's ∼ but stupid** è tutto fuorché stupido; **I'll do ∼ but that** farò qualsiasi cosa, tranne quello

anytime /'enɪtaɪm/ adv **if at ∼ you feel lonely...** se mai ti dovessi sentire solo...; **he could arrive ∼ now** potrebbe arrivare da un momento all'altro; **∼ after 2 pm** a qualsiasi ora dopo le due; **at ∼ of the day or night** a qualsiasi ora del giorno o della notte; **∼ you like** quando vuoi

anyway /'enɪweɪ/ adv ad ogni modo, comunque

anywhere /'enɪweə(r)/ adv dovunque; (after negative) da nessuna parte; **put it ∼** mettilo dove vuoi; **I can't find it ∼** non lo trovo da nessuna parte; **∼ else** da qualche altra parte; **I don't want to go ∼ else** non voglio andare da nessun'altra parte

aorta /eɪ'ɔːtə/ n aorta f

Aosta /æ'ɒstə/ n Aosta f

apace /ə'peɪs/ adv liter rapidamente

apart /ə'pɑːt/ adv lontano; **live ∼** vivere separati; **100 miles ∼** lontani 100 miglia; **born 20 minutes ∼** nati a distanza di 20 minuti; **∼ from** a parte; **you can't tell them ∼** non si possono distinguere; **joking ∼** scherzi a parte

apartheid /ə'pɑːthaɪt/ n apartheid f

apartment /ə'pɑːtmənt/ n (Am: flat) appartamento m; **in my ∼** a casa mia

apartment block n stabile m

apartment house n stabile m

apathetic /æpə'θetɪk/ adj (by nature) apatico; **∼ about something/towards somebody** (from illness, depression) indifferente a qualcosa/nei confronti di qualcuno

apathy /'æpəθɪ/ n apatia f

ape /eɪp/ **1** n scimmia f **2** vt scimmiottare

Apennines /'æpənaɪnz/ npl **the ∼** gli Appennini

aperitif /ə'perəti:f/ n aperitivo m

aperture /'æpətʃə(r)/ n apertura f

apex /'eɪpeks/ n vertice m

aphid /'eɪfɪd/ n afide m

aphrodisiac /æfrə'dɪzɪæk/ adj & n afrodisiaco m

apiary /'eɪpɪərɪ/ n apiario m

apiece /ə'pi:s/ adv ciascuno

aplenty /ə'plentɪ/ adv **there were goals ∼** c'è stata una valanga di gol

apocalypse /ə'pɒkəlɪps/ n Apocalisse f; (disaster, destruction) apocalisse f

apocalyptic /əpɒkə'lɪptɪk/ adj apocalittico

apocryphal /ə'pɒkrɪfəl/ adj apocrifo

apogee /'æpədʒi:/ n apogeo m

apolitical /eɪpə'lɪtɪkl/ adj apolitico

Apollo /ə'pɒləʊ/ n also fig Apollo m

apologetic /əpɒlə'dʒetɪk/ adj ⟨air, remark⟩ di scusa; **be ∼** essere spiacente

apologetically /əpɒlə'dʒetɪklɪ/ adv per scusarsi

apologist /ə'pɒlədʒɪst/ n apologeta mf (for di)

apologize /ə'pɒlədʒaɪz/ vi scusarsi (for per)

apology /ə'pɒlədʒɪ/ n scusa f; fig **an ∼ for a dinner** una sottospecie di cena

apoplectic /æpə'plektɪk/ adj (furious) furibondo; ⟨fit, attack⟩ apoplettico

apoplexy /'æpəpleksɪ/ n Med apoplessia f; (rage) rabbia f

apostle /ə'pɒsl/ n apostolo m

apostrophe /ə'pɒstrəfɪ/ n apostrofo m

apotheosis /əpɒθɪ'əʊsɪs/ n apoteosi f inv

appal /ə'pɔːl/ vt (pt/pp **appalled**) sconvolgere

Appalachians /æpə'leɪtʃnz/ npl **the ∼** gli Appalachi

appalling /ə'pɔːlɪŋ/ adj sconvolgente; **he's an ∼ teacher** fig è un disastro come professore

appallingly /ə'pɔːlɪŋlɪ/ adv ⟨behave, treat⟩ orribilmente; **unemployment figures are ∼ high** il tasso di disoccupazione è ⋯⊱

spaventosamente alto; **furnished in** ∼ **bad taste** arredato con pessimo gusto

apparatus /ˌæpəˈreɪtəs/ *n* apparato *m*

apparel /əˈpærəl/ *n* abbigliamento *m*

apparent /əˈpærənt/ *adj* evidente; (seeming) apparente

apparently /əˈpærəntlɪ/ *adv* apparentemente

apparition /ˌæpəˈrɪʃn/ *n* apparizione *f*

appeal /əˈpiːl/ **①** *n* appello *m*; (attraction) attrattiva *f*
② *vi* fare appello; ∼ **to** (be attractive to) attrarre

appeal fund *n* raccolta *f* di fondi

appealing /əˈpiːlɪŋ/ *adj* attraente

appealingly /əˈpiːlɪŋlɪ/ *adv* (beseechingly) in modo supplichevole; (attractively) in modo attraente

appeal[s] court *n* corte *f* d'appello

appear /əˈpɪə(r)/ *vi* apparire; (seem) sembrare; (publication) uscire; Theat esibirsi; **he finally** ∼**ed at...** fam si è fatto finalmente vedere alle...; ∼ **in court** comparire in giudizio

appearance /əˈpɪərəns/ *n* apparizione *f*; (look) aspetto *m*; **to all** ∼**s** a giudicare dalle apparenze; **keep up** ∼**s** salvare le apparenze

appease /əˈpiːz/ *vt* placare

appeasement /əˈpiːzmənt/ *n* **a policy of** ∼ una politica troppo conciliante

append /əˈpend/ *vt* apporre (signature) (**to** a)

appendage /əˈpendɪdʒ/ *n* appendice *f*

appendicitis /əpendɪˈsaɪtɪs/ *n* appendicite *f*

appendix /əˈpendɪks/ *n* (of book) (pl **-ices** /-əsiːz/) appendice *f*; (pl **-es**) Anat appendice *f*

appertain /ˌæpəˈteɪn/ *vi* ∼ **to** essere pertinente a

appetite /ˈæpɪtaɪt/ *n* appetito *m*

appetite suppressant *n* pillola *f* antifame

appetizer /ˈæpɪtaɪzə(r)/ *n* (drink) aperitivo *m*; (starter) antipasto *m*; (biscuit, olive) stuzzichino *m*

appetizing /ˈæpɪtaɪzɪŋ/ *adj* appetitoso

applaud /əˈplɔːd/ *vt/i* applaudire

applause /əˈplɔːz/ *n* applauso *m*

apple /ˈæpl/ *n* mela *f*; **she's the** ∼ **of his eye** è la luce dei suoi occhi

apple core *n* torsolo *m* di mela

apple orchard *n* meleto *m*

applet /ˈæplət/ *n* Comput applet *f*

apple tree *n* melo *m*

appliance /əˈplaɪəns/ *n* attrezzo *m*; **[electrical]** ∼ elettrodomestico *m*

applicable /ˈæplɪkəbl/ *adj* **be** ∼ **to** essere valido per; **not** ∼ (on form) non applicabile

applicant /ˈæplɪkənt/ *n* candidato, -a *mf*

application /æplɪˈkeɪʃn/ *n* applicazione *f*; (request) domanda *f*; (for job) candidatura *f*; **on** ∼ su richiesta

application form *n* modulo *m* di domanda

applicator /ˈæplɪkeɪtə(r)/ *n* applicatore *m*

applied /əˈplaɪd/ *adj* applicato

appliqué /əˈpliːkeɪ/ **①** *n* applicazione *f*
② *attrib* (motif, decoration) applicato

apply /əˈplaɪ/ **①** *vt* (pt/pp **-ied**) applicare; ∼ **oneself** applicarsi; ∼ **the brakes** frenare
② *vi* applicarsi; (law) essere applicabile; ∼ **to** (ask) rivolgersi a; ∼ **for** fare domanda per (job etc)

appoint /əˈpɔɪnt/ *vt* nominare; fissare (time) **well** ∼**ed** ben equipaggiato

appointee /əpɔɪnˈtiː/ *n* incaricato, -a *mf*

appointment /əˈpɔɪntmənt/ *n* appuntamento *m*; (to job) nomina *f*; (job) posto *m*

apportion /əˈpɔːʃn/ *vt* ripartire, attribuire

apposite /ˈæpəzɪt/ *adj* appropriato

apposition /æpəˈzɪʃn/ *n* apposizione *f*

appraisal /əˈpreɪzəl/ *n* valutazione *f*; **make an** ∼ **of something** valutare qualcosa

appraise /əˈpreɪz/ *vt* valutare

appreciable /əˈpriːʃəbl/ *adj* sensibile

appreciably /əˈpriːʃəblɪ/ *adv* sensibilmente

appreciate /əˈpriːʃɪeɪt/ **①** *vt* apprezzare; (understand) comprendere
② *vi* (increase in value) aumentare di valore

appreciation /əpriːsɪˈeɪʃn/ *n* (gratitude) riconoscenza *f*; (enjoyment) apprezzamento *m*; (understanding) comprensione *f*; (in value) aumento *m*; **in** ∼ come segno di riconoscenza (**of** per)

appreciative /əˈpriːʃətɪv/ *adj* riconoscente

apprehend /æprɪˈhend/ *vt* arrestare

apprehension /æprɪˈhenʃn/ *n* arresto *m*; (fear) apprensione *f*

apprehensive /æprɪˈhensɪv/ *adj* apprensivo

apprehensively /æprɪˈhensɪvlɪ/ *adv* con apprensione

apprentice /əˈprentɪs/ *n* apprendista *mf*

apprenticeship /əˈprentɪsʃɪp/ *n* apprendistato *m*

apprise /əˈpraɪz/ *vt* fml informare (**of** di)

approach /əˈprəʊtʃ/ **①** *n* avvicinamento *m*; (to problem) approccio *m*; (access) accesso *m*; **make** ∼**es to** fare degli approcci con

2) *vi* avvicinarsi
3) *vt* avvicinarsi a; (with request) rivolgersi a; affrontare ⟨*problem*⟩

approachable /ə'prəʊtʃəbl/ *adj* accessibile

approach lights *npl* Aeron sentiero *m* luminoso di avvicinamento

approach path *n* Aeron rotta *f* di avvicinamento

approach road *n* strada *f* d'accesso

approbation /æprə'beɪʃn/ *n* approvazione *f*

appropriate[1] /ə'prəʊprɪət/ *adj* appropriato

appropriate[2] /ə'prəʊprɪeɪt/ *vt* appropriarsi di

appropriately /ə'prəʊprɪətlɪ/ *adv* (suitably) in modo appropriato; ⟨*sited*⟩ convenientemente; ⟨*designed, chosen, behave*⟩ adeguatamente

appropriation /əprəʊprɪ'eɪʃn/ *n* Am Comm stanziamento *m*; (Jur: removal) appropriazione *f*

approval /ə'pru:vl/ *n* approvazione *f*; on ∼ in prova

approve /ə'pru:v/ **1)** *vt* approvare **2)** *vi* ∼ of approvare ⟨*something*⟩ avere una buona opinione di ⟨*somebody*⟩

approving /ə'pru:vɪŋ/ *adj* ⟨*smile, nod*⟩ d'approvazione

approvingly /ə'pru:vɪŋlɪ/ *adv* con approvazione

approximate[1] /ə'prɒksɪmeɪt/ *vi* ∼ **to** avvicinarsi a

approximate[2] /ə'prɒksɪmət/ *adj* approssimativo

approximately /ə'prɒksɪmətlɪ/ *adv* approssimativamente

approximation /əprɒksɪ'meɪʃn/ *n* approssimazione *f*

APR *n* (annual percentage rate) tasso *m* percentuale annuo

apricot /'eɪprɪkɒt/ *n* albicocca *f*; ∼ **tree** albicocco *m*

April /'eɪprəl/ *n* aprile *m*; make an ∼ Fool of somebody fare un pesce d'aprile a qualcuno

April Fools' Day *n* il primo d'aprile *m*

apron /'eɪprən/ *n* grembiule *m*

apropos /'æprəpəʊ/ *adv* ∼ **[of]** a proposito [di]

apse /æps/ *n* abside *f*

apt /æpt/ *adj* appropriato; ⟨*pupil*⟩ dotato; be ∼ to do something avere tendenza a fare qualcosa

aptitude /'æptɪtju:d/ *n* disposizione *f*

aptitude test *n* test *m inv* attitudinale

aptly /'æptlɪ/ *adv* appropriatamente

Apulia /ə'pju:lɪə/ *n* Puglia *f*

aqualung /'ækwəlʌŋ/ *n* autorespiratore *m*

aquamarine /ækwəmə'ri:n/ *adj & n* acquamarina *f*

aquaplane /'ækwəpleɪn/ *vi* Sport praticare l'acquaplano; Br Auto andare in aquaplaning

aquarium /ə'kweərɪəm/ *n* acquario *m*

Aquarius /ə'kweərɪəs/ *n* Astr Acquario *m*; be ∼ essere dell'Acquario

aquarobics /ækwə'rəʊbɪks/ *n* acquagym *f inv*

aquatic /ə'kwætɪk/ *adj* acquatico

aqueduct /'ækwədʌkt/ *n* acquedotto *m*

aquiline /'ækwɪlaɪn/ *adj* ⟨*nose, features*⟩ aquilino

Arab /'ærəb/ *adj & n* arabo, -a *mf*

Arabia /ə'reɪbɪə/ *n* Arabia *f*

Arabian /ə'reɪbɪən/ *adj* arabo

Arabic /'ærəbɪk/ **1)** *adj* arabo; ∼ numerals numeri *mpl* arabi **2)** *n* arabo *m*

Arab-Israeli *adj* arabo-israeliano

arable /'ærəbl/ *adj* coltivabile

arbiter /'ɑ:bɪtə(r)/ *n* arbitro *m*

arbitrarily /ɑ:bɪ'trerɪlɪ/ *adv* arbitrariamente

arbitrary /'ɑ:bɪtrərɪ/ *adj* arbitrario

arbitrate /'ɑ:bɪtreɪt/ *vi* arbitrare

arbitration /ɑ:bɪ'treɪʃn/ *n* arbitraggio *m*

arbitrator /'ɑ:bɪtreɪtə(r)/ *n* arbitro *m*

arbour /'ɑ:bə(r)/ *n* pergolato *m*

arc /ɑ:k/ *n* arco *m*

arcade /ɑ:'keɪd/ *n* portico *m*; (shops) galleria *f*

arcane /ɑ:'keɪn/ *adj* arcano

arch /ɑ:tʃ/ **1)** *n* arco *m*; (of foot) dorso *m* del piede **2)** *vt* the cat ∼ed its back il gatto ha arcuato la schiena

archaeological /ɑ:kɪə'lɒdʒɪkl/ *adj* archeologico

archaeologist /ɑ:kɪ'ɒlədʒɪst/ *n* archeologo, -a *mf*

archaeology /ɑ:kɪ'ɒlədʒɪ/ *n* archeologia *f*

archaic /ɑ:'keɪk/ *adj* arcaico

archbishop /ɑ:tʃ'bɪʃəp/ *n* arcivescovo *m*

arched /ɑ:tʃt/ *adj* (eyebrows) arcuato

arch-enemy *n* acerrimo nemico *m*

archer /'ɑ:tʃə(r)/ *n* arciere *m*

archery /'ɑ:tʃərɪ/ *n* tiro *m* con l'arco

archetypal /ɑ:kɪ'taɪpl/ *adj* the ∼ hero il prototipo dell'eroe

archetype /'ɑ:kɪtaɪp/ *n* archetipo *m*

archipelago /ɑ:kɪ'peləgəʊ/ *n* arcipelago *m*

architect /'ɑ:kɪtekt/ *n* architetto *m*

architectural /ɑːkɪˈtektʃərəl/ *adj* architettonico

architecturally /ɑːkɪˈtektʃərəlɪ/ *adv* architettonicamente

architecture /ˈɑːkɪtektʃə(r)/ *n* architettura *f*

archive /ˈɑːkaɪv/ *vt* also Comput archiviare

archives /ˈɑːkaɪvz/ *npl* archivi *mpl*

archiving /ˈɑːkaɪvɪŋ/ *n* Comput archiviazione *f*

archway /ˈɑːtʃweɪ/ *n* arco *m*

Arctic /ˈɑːktɪk/ **1** *adj* artico **2** *n* the ∼ l'Artico

Arctic Circle *n* Circolo *m* polare artico

Arctic Ocean *n* mare *m* artico

ardent /ˈɑːdənt/ *adj* ardente

ardently /ˈɑːdəntlɪ/ *adv* ardentemente

ardour /ˈɑːdə(r)/ *n* ardore *m*

arduous /ˈɑːdjʊəs/ *adj* arduo

arduously /ˈɑːdjʊəslɪ/ *adv* con fatica, con difficoltà

are /ɑː(r)/ ▸ BE

area /ˈeərɪə/ *n* area *f*; (region) zona *f*; (fig: field) campo *m*

area code *n* prefisso *m* [telefonico]

area manager *n* direttore, -trice *mf* di zona

arena /əˈriːnə/ *n* arena *f*

aren't /ɑːnt/ = are not ▸ BE

Argentina /ɑːdʒənˈtiːnə/ *n* Argentina *f*

Argentine /ˈɑːdʒəntaɪn/ *adj* argentino

Argentinian /ɑːdʒənˈtɪnɪən/ *adj & n* argentino, -a *mf*

arguable /ˈɑːɡjʊəbl/ *adj* it's ∼ that... si può sostenere che...

arguably /ˈɑːɡjʊəblɪ/ *adv* he is ∼... è probabilmente...

argue /ˈɑːɡjuː/ **1** *vi* litigare (about su); (debate) dibattere; don't ∼! non discutere! **2** *vt* (debate) dibattere; (reason) ∼ that sostenere che

argument /ˈɑːɡjʊmənt/ *n* argomento *m*; (reasoning) ragionamento *m*; have an ∼ litigare

argumentative /ɑːɡjʊˈmentətɪv/ *adj* polemico

aria /ˈɑːrɪə/ *n* aria *f*

arid /ˈærɪd/ *adj* arido

aridity /əˈrɪdətɪ/ *n* also fig aridità *f*

Aries /ˈeəriːz/ *n* Astr Ariete *m*; be ∼ essere dell'Ariete

arise /əˈraɪz/ *vi* (pt **arose** pp **arisen**) ⟨opportunity, need, problem;⟩ presentarsi; (result) derivare

aristocracy /ærɪˈstɒkrəsɪ/ *n* aristocrazia *f*

aristocrat /ˈærɪstəkræt/ *n* aristocratico, -a *mf*

aristocratic /ærɪstəˈkrætɪk/ *adj* aristocratico

arithmetic /əˈrɪθmətɪk/ *n* aritmetica *f*

arithmetical /ærɪθˈmetɪkl/ *adj* aritmetico

ark /ɑːk/ *n* Noah's Ark l'Arca *f* di Noè

arm /ɑːm/ **1** *n* braccio *m*; (of chair) bracciolo *m*; ∼s *pl* (weapons) armi *fpl*; ∼ in ∼ a braccetto; up in ∼s fam furioso (about per); fig with open ∼s a braccia aperte **2** *vt* armare

armadillo /ɑːməˈdɪləʊ/ *n* armadillo *m*

armaments /ˈɑːməmənts/ *npl* armamenti *mpl*

armband /ˈɑːmbænd/ *n* (for swimmer) bracciolo *m* (per nuotare): (for mourner) fascia *f* al braccio

armchair /ˈɑːmtʃeə(r)/ *n* poltrona *f*

armchair traveller *n* persona *f* che si interessa di viaggi senza viaggiare

armed /ɑːmd/ *adj* armato

armed forces /ˈfɔːsɪz/ *npl* forze *fpl* armate

armed robbery *n* rapina *f* a mano armata

Armenia /ɑːˈmiːnɪə/ *n* Armenia *f*

Armenian /ɑːˈmiːnɪən/ *adj & n* (person) armeno, -a *mf*; (language) armeno *m*

armful /ˈɑːmfʊl/ *n* bracciata *f*

armhole /ˈɑːmhəʊl/ *n* giro *m* manica *inv*

armistice /ˈɑːmɪstɪs/ *n* armistizio *m*

Armistice Day *n* l'Anniversario *m* dell'Armistizio (1 nov. 1918)

armour /ˈɑːmə(r)/ *n* armatura *f*

armour-clad /-ˈklæd/ *adj* ⟨vehicle⟩ blindato; ⟨ship⟩ corazzato

armoured /ˈɑːməd/ *adj* ⟨vehicle⟩ blindato

armoured car *n* autoblinda[ta] *f*

armour plate, armour plating /ˈpleɪtɪŋ/ *n* corazzatura *f*

armour-plated /-ˈpleɪtɪd/ *adj* corazzato

armoury /ˈɑːmərɪ/ *n* (factory) fabbrica *f* d'armi; (store) arsenale *m*, armeria *f*

armpit /ˈɑːmpɪt/ *n* ascella *f*

armrest /ˈɑːmrest/ *n* bracciolo *m* (di sedia)

arms control *n* controllo *m* degli armamenti

arms dealer *n* trafficante *mf* d'armi

arms dump *n* deposito *m* d'armi

arms embargo *n* embargo *m* sulle armi

arms limitation *n* controllo *m* degli armamenti

arms manufacturer *n* fabbricante *mf* d'armi

arms race *n* corsa *f* agli armamenti

arms treaty *n* trattato *m* sul controllo degli armamenti

arm-twisting /'ɑːmtwɪstɪŋ/ *n* pressioni *fpl*

arm-wrestling *n* braccio *m* di ferro

army /'ɑːmɪ/ *n* esercito *m*; **join the ~** arruolarsi

A road *n* Br [strada *f*] statale *f*

aroma /ə'rəʊmə/ *n* aroma *f*

aromatherapy /ərəʊmə'θerəpɪ/ *n* aromaterapia *f*

aromatic /ærə'mætɪk/ *adj* aromatico

arose /ə'rəʊz/ ▸ARISE

around /ə'raʊnd/ ❶ *adv* intorno; **all ~** tutt'intorno; **I'm not from ~ here** non sono di qui; **he's not ~** non c'è
❷ *prep* intorno a; in giro per ⟨*room, shops, world*⟩

arousal /ə'raʊzl/ *n* eccitazione *f*

arouse /ə'raʊz/ *vt* svegliare; (sexually) eccitare

arpeggio /ɑːˈpedʒɪəʊ/ *n* arpeggio *m*

arrange /ə'reɪndʒ/ *vt* sistemare ⟨*furniture, books*⟩; organizzare ⟨*meeting*⟩; fissare ⟨*date, time*⟩; **~ to do something** combinare di fare qualcosa

arrangement /ə'reɪndʒmənt/ *n* (of furniture) sistemazione *f*; Mus arrangiamento *m*; (agreement) accordo; (of flowers) composizione *f*; **make ~s** prendere disposizioni; **I've made other ~s** ho preso altri impegni

array /ə'reɪ/ ❶ *n* (clothes) abbigliamento *m*; (of troops, people) schieramento *m*; (of numbers) tabella *f*; (of weaponry) apparato *m*: (of goods, products) assortimento *m*; Comput matrice *f*
❷ *vt* **~ed in ceremonial robes** abbigliato da gran cerimonia

arrears /ə'rɪəz/ *npl* arretrati *mpl*; **be in ~** essere in arretrato; **paid in ~** pagato a lavoro eseguito

arrest /ə'rest/ ❶ *n* arresto *m*; **under ~** in stato d'arresto
❷ *vt* arrestare

arresting /ə'restɪŋ/ *adj* (striking) che colpisce

arrival /ə'raɪvl/ *n* arrivo *m*; **new ~s** *pl* nuovi arrivati *mpl*

arrivals board *n* tabellone *m* degli arrivi

arrival(s) lounge *n* sala *f* arrivi

arrival time *n* ora *f* d'arrivo

arrive /ə'raɪv/ *vi* arrivare; **~ at** fig raggiungere

arrogance /'ærəg(ə)ns/ *n* arroganza *f*

arrogant /'ærəg(ə)nt/ *adj* arrogante

arrogantly /'ærəg(ə)ntlɪ/ *adv* con arroganza

arrow /'ærəʊ/ *n* freccia *f*

arrowhead /'ærəʊhed/ *n* punta *f* di freccia

arse /ɑːs/ *n* vulg culo *m*

■ **arse about**, **arse around** *vi* vulg coglioneggiare

arsenal /'ɑːsən(ə)l/ *n* arsenale *m*

arsenic /'ɑːsənɪk/ *n* arsenico *m*

arson /'ɑːsən/ *n* incendio *m* doloso

arsonist /'ɑːsənɪst/ *n* incendiario, -a *mf*

art /ɑːt/ *n* arte *f*; **work of ~** opera *f* d'arte; **~s and crafts** *pl* artigianato *m*; **the A~s** *pl* l'arte *f*; **A~s degree** Univ laurea *f* in Lettere

art collection *n* collezione *f* d'arte

art collector *n* collezionista *mf* d'arte

art college *n* ≈ accademia *f* di belle arti

art dealer *n* commerciante *mf* di oggetti d'arte

art deco *n* art déco *f*

artefact /'ɑːtɪfækt/ *n* manufatto *m*

arterial /ɑːˈtɪərɪəl/ *adj* Anat arterioso

arterial road *n* arteria *f* [stradale]

artery /'ɑːtərɪ/ *n* arteria *f*

art exhibition *n* mostra *f* d'arte

art form *n* forma *f* d'arte

artful /'ɑːtfl/ *adj* scaltro

artfully /'ɑːtfʊlɪ/ *adv* astutamente

art gallery *n* galleria *f* d'arte

arthritic /ɑːˈθrɪtɪk/ *adj & n* artritico, -a *mf*

arthritis /ɑːˈθraɪtɪs/ *n* artrite *f*

artichoke /'ɑːtɪtʃəʊk/ *n* carciofo *m*

article /'ɑːtɪkl/ *n* articolo *m*; **~ of clothing** capo *m* d'abbigliamento

articulate¹ /ɑːˈtɪkjʊlət/ *adj* ⟨*speech*⟩ chiaro; **be ~** esprimersi bene

articulate² /ɑːˈtɪkjʊleɪt/ *vt* scandire ⟨*words*⟩

articulated lorry /ɑːˈtɪkjʊleɪtɪd/ *n* autotreno *m*

articulately /ɑːˈtɪkjʊlətlɪ/ *adv* chiaramente

articulation /ɑːtɪkjʊ'leɪʃn/ *n* (pronunciation, Anat) articolazione *f*; (expression) espressione *f*

artifice /'ɑːtɪfɪs/ *n* artificio *m*

artificial /ɑːtɪˈfɪʃl/ *adj* artificiale

artificial insemination *n* inseminazione *f* artificiale

artificial intelligence *n* intelligenza *f* artificiale

artificiality /ɑːtɪfɪʃɪ'ælətɪ/ *n* artificiosità *f*

artificial limb *n* arto *m* artificiale

artificially /ɑːtɪˈfɪʃəlɪ/ *adv* artificialmente; ⟨*smile*⟩ artificiosamente

artificial respiration *n* respirazione *f* artificiale

artillery /ɑːˈtɪlərɪ/ *n* artiglieria *f*

artisan /ɑːtɪ'zæn/ *n* artigiano, -a *mf*

artist /'ɑːtɪst/ *n* artista *mf*

artiste /ɑːˈtiːst/ n Theat artista mf

artistic /ɑːˈtɪstɪk/ adj artistico

artistically /ɑːˈtɪstɪklɪ/ adv
artisticamente

artistry /ˈɑːtɪstrɪ/ n arte f, talento m

artless /ˈɑːtlɪs/ adj spontaneo

artlessly /ˈɑːtlɪslɪ/ adv ‹smile›
ingenuamente

art nouveau /ɑːnuːˈvəʊ/ adj & n liberty
m

art school n ≈ accademia f di belle arti

arts degree n laurea f in Lettere

arts funding n sovvenzioni fpl alle arti

arts student n studente, -essa mf di
Lettere

art student n studente, -essa mf di belle
arti

artwork /ˈɑːtwɜːk/ n illustrazioni fpl

arty /ˈɑːtɪ/ adj fam ‹person›
intellettualoide; ‹district› degli
intellettuali

Aryan /ˈeərɪən/ adj & n ariano, -a mf

AS n esame m sostenuto al termine del
primo anno del biennio di preparazione
agli A-Level

as /æz/ ① conj come; (since) siccome;
(while) mentre; **as he grew older**
diventando vecchio; **as you get to know
her** conoscendola meglio; **young as she is**
per quanto sia giovane
② prep come; **as a friend** come amico; **as
a child** da bambino; **as a foreigner** in
quanto straniero; **disguised as** travestito
da
③ adv **as well** (also) anche; **as soon as I
get home** [non] appena arrivo a casa; **as
quick as you** veloce quanto te; **as quick as
you can** più veloce che puoi; **as far as**
(distance) fino a; **as far as I'm concerned**
per quanto mi riguarda; **as long as** finché;
(provided that) purché

asap adv abbr (**as soon as possible**)
prima possibile

asbestos /æzˈbestɒs/ n amianto m

ascend /əˈsend/ ① vi salire
② vi salire a ‹throne›

ascendancy /əˈsend(ə)nsɪ/ n **gain the
~ over somebody** acquisire una posizione
dominante su qualcuno

ascendant /əˈsend(ə)nt/ n **be in the ~**
Astr essere in ascendente; fig ‹person›
essere in auge

Ascension /əˈsenʃn/ n Relig Ascensione
f

ascent /əˈsent/ n ascesa f

ascertain /æsəˈteɪn/ vt accertare

ascetic /əˈsetɪk/ adj & n ascetico, -a mf

asceticism /əˈsetɪsɪzm/ n ascesi f

ascribable /əˈskraɪbəbl/ adj attribuibile

ascribe /əˈskraɪb/ vt attribuire

aseptic /eɪˈseptɪk/ adj asettico

asexual /eɪˈseksjʊəl/ adj asessuale,
asessuato

ash¹ /æʃ/ n (tree) frassino m

ash² n cenere f

ashamed /əˈʃeɪmd/ adj **be/feel ~**
vergognarsi

ash blond adj biondo cenere

ashen /ˈæʃ(ə)n/ adj (complexion) cinereo

ashore /əˈʃɔː(r)/ adv a terra; **go ~**
sbarcare

ashtray n portacenere m

ash tree n frassino m

Ash Wednesday n mercoledì m inv
delle Ceneri

Asia /ˈeɪʒə/ n Asia f

Asia Minor n Asia f Minore

Asian /ˈeɪʒ(ə)n/ adj & n asiatico, -a mf;
(Br: Indian, Pakistani) indiano, -a mf

Asiatic /eɪʒɪˈætɪk/ adj asiatico

aside /əˈsaɪd/ ① adv **take somebody ~**
prendere qualcuno a parte; **put something
~** mettere qualcosa da parte; **~ from you**
Am a parte te; **~ from his injuries** Am a
parte le sue ferite
② n **in an ~** tra parentesi

asinine /ˈæsɪnaɪn/ adj sciocco

ask /ɑːsk/ ① vt fare ‹question›; (invite)
invitare; **~ somebody something**
domandare or chiedere qualcosa a
qualcuno; **~ somebody to do something**
domandare or chiedere a qualcuno di fare
qualcosa
② vi **~ about something** informarsi su
qualcosa;
■ **ask after** vt chiedere [notizie] di
‹somebody›
■ **ask for** vt chiedere ‹something›;
chiedere di ‹somebody›; **~ for trouble** fam
andare in cerca di guai
■ **ask in** vt **~ somebody in** invitare
qualcuno ad entrare
■ **ask out** vt **~ somebody out** chiedere a
qualcuno di uscire

askance /əˈskɑːns/ adv **look ~ at
somebody/something** guardare qualcuno/
qualcosa di traverso

askew /əˈskjuː/ adj & adv di traverso

asking price /ˈɑːskɪŋ/ n prezzo m
trattabile

asleep /əˈsliːp/ adj **be ~** dormire; **fall ~**
addormentarsi

asparagus /əˈspærəgəs/ n asparagi mpl

aspect /ˈæspekt/ n aspetto m

aspen /ˈæspən/ n pioppo m tremulo

aspersions /əˈspɜːʃnz/ npl **cast ~ on**
diffamare

asphalt /ˈæsfælt/ n asfalto m

asphyxia /æsˈfɪksɪə/ n asfissia f

asphyxiate /əsˈfɪksɪeɪt/ vt asfissiare

asphyxiation /əsfɪksɪˈeɪʃn/ n asfissia f

aspic /ˈæspɪk/ n aspic m inv

aspirate¹ /'æspəreɪt/ *vt* aspirare

aspirate² /'æspɪrət/ *adj* aspirato

aspirations /æspə'reɪʃnz/ *npl* aspirazioni *fpl*

aspire /ə'spaɪə(r)/ *vi* ~ to aspirare a

aspirin /'æsprɪn/ *n* aspirina® *f*

aspiring /ə'spaɪərɪŋ/ *adj* ~ authors/ journalists aspiranti scrittori/giornalisti

ass /æs/ *n* asino *m*

assailant /ə'seɪlənt/ *n* assalitore, -trice *mf*

assassin /ə'sæsɪn/ *n* assassino, -a *mf*

assassinate /ə'sæsɪneɪt/ *vt* assassinare

assassination /əsæsɪ'neɪʃn/ *n* assassinio *m*

assault /ə'sɔːlt/ **1** *n* Mil assalto *m*; Jur aggressione *f* **2** *vt* aggredire

assault and battery *n* Jur lesioni *fpl* personali

assault course *n* Mil percorso *m* di guerra

assemblage /ə'semblɪdʒ/ assemblaggio *m*

assemble /ə'sembl/ **1** *vi* radunarsi **2** *vi* radunare; Techn montare

assembler /ə'semblə(r)/ *n* (in factory) montatore, -trice *mf*; Comput [programma] *m*] assemblatore *m*

assembly /ə'semblɪ/ *n* assemblea *f*; Sch assemblea *f* giornaliera di alunni e professori di una scuola; Techn montaggio *m*

assembly line *n* catena *f* di montaggio

assent /ə'sent/ **1** *n* assenso *m* **2** *vi* acconsentire

assert /ə'sɜːt/ *vt* asserire; far valere ‹one's rights›; ~ oneself farsi valere

assertion /ə'sɜːʃn/ *n* asserzione *f*

assertive /ə'sɜːtɪv/ *adj* be ~ farsi valere

assertiveness /ə'sɜːtɪvnɪs/ *n* capacità *f* di farsi valere; lack of ~ scarsa sicurezza *f* di sé

assess /ə'ses/ *vt* valutare; (for tax purposes) stabilire l'imponibile di

assessment /ə'sesmənt/ *n* valutazione *f*; (of tax) accertamento *m*

assessor /ə'sesə(r)/ *n* (Jur, in insurance) perito *m*; (tax) agente *m* del fisco

asset /'æset/ *n* (advantage) vantaggio *m*; (person) elemento *m* prezioso. ~s *pl* beni *mpl*; (on balance sheet) attivo *msg*

asset stripping /'æsetstrɪpɪŋ/ *n* rilevamento *m* di un'azienda per rivenderne le single attività fisse

assiduity /æsɪ'djuːətɪ/ *n* assiduità *f*

assiduous /ə'sɪdjʊəs/ *adj* assiduo

assign /ə'saɪn/ *vt* assegnare

assignation /æsɪg'neɪʃn/ *n* hum appuntamento *m* galante

assignment /ə'saɪnmənt/ *n* (task) incarico *m*

assimilate /ə'sɪmɪleɪt/ *vt* assimilare; integrare ‹person›

assimilation /əsɪmɪ'leɪʃn/ *n* assimilazione *f*

assist /ə'sɪst/ *vt/i* assistere; ~ somebody to do something assistere qualcuno nel fare qualcosa

assistance /ə'sɪstəns/ *n* assistenza *f*

assistant /ə'sɪstənt/ *n* assistente *mf*; (in shop) commesso, -a *mf*

assistant manager *n* vicedirettore, -trice *mf*

assistant professor *n* Am Univ docente *mf* universitario, -a del grado più basso

associate¹ /ə'səʊʃɪeɪt/ **1** *vt* associare (with a); be ~d with something (involved in) essere coinvolto in qualcosa **2** *vi* ~ with frequentare

associate² /ə'səʊʃɪət/ **1** *adj* associato **2** *n* collega *mf*; (member) socio, -a *mf*

associate company *n* consociata *f*

associate director *n* Comm amministratore *m* aggiunto

associate editor *n* co-redattore, -trice *mf*

associate member *n* membro *m* associato

association /əsəʊsɪ'eɪʃn/ *n* associazione *f*

Association Football *n* [gioco *m* del] calcio *m*

assorted /ə'sɔːtɪd/ *adj* assortito

assortment /ə'sɔːtmənt/ *n* assortimento *m*

assuage /ə'sweɪdʒ/ *vt* liter alleviare

assume /ə'sjuːm/ *vt* presumere; assumere ‹control›; ~ office entrare in carica; assuming that you're right,... ammettendo che tu abbia ragione,...

assumption /ə'sʌmpʃn/ *n* supposizione *f*; on the ~ that partendo dal presupposto che; the A~ Relig l'Assunzione *f*

assurance /ə'ʃʊərəns/ *n* assicurazione *f*; (confidence) sicurezza *f*

assure /ə'ʃʊə(r)/ *vt* assicurare; he ~d me of his innocence mi ha assicurato di essere innocente

assured /ə'ʃʊəd/ *adj* sicuro

Assyria /ə'sɪrɪə/ *n* Assiria *f*

asterisk /'æstərɪsk/ *n* asterisco *m*

astern /ə'stɜːn/ *adv* a poppa

asteroid /'æstərɔɪd/ *n* asteroide *m*

asthma /'æsmə/ *n* asma *f*

asthmatic /æs'mætɪk/ *adj* asmatico

astigmatism /ə'stɪgmətɪzm/ *n* astigmatismo *m*

astonish /ə'stɒnɪʃ/ *vt* stupire

astonished /ə'stɒnɪʃt/ *adj* sorpreso

astonishing /ə'stɒnɪʃɪŋ/ *adj* stupefacente

astonishingly /ə'stɒnɪʃɪŋlɪ/ *adv* sorprendentemente

astonishment /ə'stɒnɪʃmənt/ *n* stupore *m*

astound /ə'staʊnd/ *vt* stupire

astounding /ə'staʊndɪŋ/ *adj* incredible

astrakhan /æstrə'kæn/ *n* astrakan *m*

astray /ə'streɪ/ *adv* go ∼ smarrirsi; (morally) uscire dalla retta via; **lead** ∼ traviare

astride /ə'straɪd/ ①⟩ *adv* [a] cavalcioni ②⟩ *prep* a cavalcioni di

astringent /ə'strɪndʒənt/ ①⟩ *adj* astringente; fig austero ②⟩ *n* astringente·*m*

astrologer /ə'strɒlədʒə(r)/ *n* astrologo, -a *mf*

astrological /æstrə'lɒdʒɪkl/ *adj* astrologico

astrology /ə'strɒlədʒɪ/ *n* astrologia *f*

astronaut /'æstrənɔ:t/ *n* astronauta *mf*

astronomer /ə'strɒnəmə(r)/ *n* astronomo, -a *mf*

astronomic /æstrə'nɒmɪk/ *adj* fig astronomico

astronomical /æstrə'nɒmɪkl/ *adj* also fig astronomico

astronomically /æstrə'nɒmɪklɪ/ *adv* ∼ expensive dal prezzo astronomico; **prices are** ∼ **high** i prezzi sono astronomici

astronomy /ə'strɒnəmɪ/ *n* astronomia *f*

astrophysicist /æstrəʊ'fɪzɪsɪst/ *n* astrofisico, -a *mf*

astrophysics /æstrəʊ'fɪzɪks/ *n* astrofisica *f*

astute /ə'stju:t/ *adj* astuto

astutely /ə'stju:tlɪ/ *adv* con astuzia

astuteness /ə'stju:tnɪs/ *n* astuzia *f*

asylum /ə'saɪləm/ *n* [political] ∼ asilo *m* politico; [lunatic] ∼ manicomio *m*

asylum-seeker /ə'saɪləmsi:kə(r)/ *n* persona *f* che chiede asilo politico

asymmetric[al] /æsɪ'metrɪk[l]/ *adj* asimmetrico

at /ət/ stressed *prep* /æt/ *adj*; **at the station/the market** alla stazione/al mercato; **at the office/the bank** in ufficio/banca; **at the beginning** all'inizio; **at john's** da John; **at the hairdresser's** dal parrucchiere; **at home** a casa; **at work** al lavoro; **at school** a scuola; **at a party/wedding** a una festa/un matrimonio; **at one o'clock** all'una; **at 50 km an hour** ai 50 all'ora; **at Christmas/Easter** a Natale/Pasqua; **at times** talvolta; **two at a time** due alla volta; **good at languages** bravo nelle lingue; **at sb's request** su richiesta

di qualcuno; **are you at all worried?** sei preoccupato?

atavistic /ætə'vɪstɪk/ *adj* atavico

ate /et/ ▶ EAT

atheism /'eɪθɪɪzm/ *n* ateismo *m*

atheist /'eɪθɪɪst/ *n* ateo, -a *mf*

atheistic /eɪθɪ'ɪstɪk/ *adj* ⟨principle⟩ ateistico; ⟨person⟩ ateo

Athenian /ə'θi:nɪən/ *adj* & *n* ateniese *mf*

Athens /'æθənz/ *n* Atene *f*

athlete /'æθli:t/ *n* atleta *mf*

athlete's foot *n* micosi *f*

athletic /æθ'letɪk/ *adj* atletico

athletics /æθ'letɪks/ *n* atletica *fsg*

Atlantic /ət'læntɪk/ *adj* & *n* the ∼ [Ocean] l'[Oceano *m*] Atlantico *m*

atlas /'ætləs/ *n* atlante *m*

Atlas Mountains *npl* Monti *mpl* dell'Atlante

ATM *n abbr* (**automatic teller machine**) cassa *f* continua di prelevamento

atmosphere /'ætməsfɪə(r)/ *n* atmosfera *f*

atmospheric /ætməs'ferɪk/ *adj* atmosferico

atom /'ætəm/ *n* atomo *m*

atom bomb *n* bomba *f* atomica

atomic /ə'tɒmɪk/ *adj* atomico

atomic physics *n* fisica *f* atomica

atomic power station *n* centrale *f* atomica

atomic reactor *n* reattore *m* nucleare

atomic scientist *n* fisico, -a *mf* nucleare

atomize /'ætəmaɪz/ *vt* atomizzare

atomizer /'ætəmaɪzə(r)/ *n* atomizzatore *m*

atone /ə'təʊn/ *vi* ∼ **for** pagare per

atonement /ə'təʊnmənt/ *n* espiazione *f*

at-risk *adj* a rischio; **the** ∼ **register** l'elenco dei soggetti a rischio

atrocious /ə'trəʊʃəs/ *adj* atroce; fam ⟨meal, weather⟩ abominevole

atrociously /ə'trəʊʃəslɪ/ *adv* atrocemente; ⟨rude etc⟩ terribilmente

atrocity /ə'trɒsətɪ/ *n* atrocità *f inv*

atrophy /'ætrəfɪ/ ①⟩ *n* Med atrofia *f* ②⟩ *vi* Med, fig atrofizzarsi

at sign *n* Comput chiocciola *f*

attach /ə'tætʃ/ *vt* attaccare; attribuire ⟨importance⟩; **be** ∼**ed to** fig essere attaccato a

attaché /ə'tæʃeɪ/ *n* addetto *m*

attaché case *n* ventiquattrore *f inv*

attached *adj* ⟨document⟩ allegato; (fond) ∼ **to** affezionato a

attachment /əˈtætʃmənt/ n (affection) attaccamento m; (accessory) accessorio m; Comput allegato m

attack /əˈtæk/ ① n attacco m; (physical) aggressione f
② vt attaccare; (physically) aggredire

attacker /əˈtækə(r)/ n assalitore, -trice mf; (critic) detrattore, -trice mf

attain /əˈteɪn/ vt realizzare ⟨ambition⟩; raggiungere ⟨success, age, goal⟩

attainable /əˈteɪnəbl/ adj ⟨ambition⟩ realizzabile; ⟨success⟩ raggiungibile

attainment /əˈteɪnmənt/ n (of knowledge) acquisizione f; (of goal) realizzazione f, raggiungimento m; (success) risultato m

attempt /əˈtempt/ ① n tentativo m
② vt tentare

attend /əˈtend/ ① vt essere presente a; (go regularly to) frequentare; (accompany) accompagnare; ⟨doctor⟩ avere in cura ② vi essere presente; (pay attention) prestare attenzione
■ **attend to** vt occuparsi di; (in shop) servire

attendance /əˈtendəns/ n presenza f

attendance record n (of MP, committee member, schoolchild) tasso m di presenza

attendance register n Sch registro m

attendant /əˈtendənt/ n guardiano, -a mf

attention /əˈtenʃn/ n attenzione f; ∼! Mil attenti!; **pay** ∼ prestare attenzione; **need** ∼ aver bisogno di attenzioni; ⟨skin, hair, plant⟩ dover essere curato; ⟨car, tyres⟩ dover essere riparato; **for the** ∼ **of** all'attenzione di

attention deficit disorder n Med disturbo m da deficit dell'attenzione

attention-seeking /əˈtenʃnsiːkɪŋ/
① n bisogno m di attirare l'attenzione
② adj ⟨person⟩ che cerca di attirare l'attenzione.

attention span n he has a very short ∼ ∼ non è capace di mantenere a lungo la concentrazione

attentive /əˈtentɪv/ adj ⟨pupil, audience⟩ attento; ⟨son⟩ premuroso

attentively /əˈtentɪvlɪ/ adv attentamente

attentiveness /əˈtentɪvnɪs/ n (concentration) attenzione f; (solicitude) sollecitudine f

attenuate /əˈtenjʊeɪt/ vt attenuare

attest /əˈtest/ vt/i attestare

attic /ˈætɪk/ n soffitta f

attic room n mansarda f

attic window n lucernario m

attire /əˈtaɪə(r)/ ① n abiti mpl
② vt vestire (**in** con)

attitude /ˈætɪtjuːd/ n atteggiamento m

attn. abbr (**attention**) c.a.

attorney /əˈtɜːnɪ/ n (Am: lawyer) avvocato m; **power of** ∼ delega f

Attorney General n Br ≈ Procuratore m Generale; Am ≈ Ministro m di Grazia e Giustizia

attract /əˈtrækt/ vt attirare

attraction /əˈtrækʃn/ n attrazione f; (feature) attrattiva f

attractive /əˈtræktɪv/ adj ⟨person⟩ attraente; ⟨proposal, price⟩ allettante

attractiveness /əˈtræktɪvnɪs/ n (of person, place) fascino m; (of proposal) carattere m allettante; (of investment) covenienza f

attributable /əˈtrɪbjʊtəbl/ adj (error, fall, loss) attribuibile; **be** ∼ **to** ⟨change, profit, success⟩ essere dovuto a

attribute¹ /ˈætrɪbjuːt/ n attributo m

attribute² /əˈtrɪbjuːt/ vt attribuire

attribution /ætrɪˈbjuːʃn/ n attribuzione f

attributive /əˈtrɪbjʊtɪv/ adj attributivo

attrition /əˈtrɪʃn/ n **war of** ∼ guerra f di logoramento

attune /əˈtjuːn/ vt **be** ∼**d to** (in harmony with) essere sintonizzato con; (accustomed to) essere abituato a

aubergine /ˈəʊbəʒiːn/ n melanzana f

auburn /ˈɔːbən/ adj castano ramato

auction /ˈɔːkʃn/ ① n asta f
② vt vendere all'asta

auctioneer /ɔːkʃəˈnɪə(r)/ n banditore m

auction house n casa f d'aste

auction rooms npl sala f d'aste

auction sale n vendita f all'asta

audacious /ɔːˈdeɪʃəs/ adj sfacciato; (daring) audace

audaciously /ɔːˈdeɪʃəslɪ/ adv sfacciatamente; (daringly) con audacia

audacity /ɔːˈdæsɪtɪ/ n sfacciataggine f; (daring) audacia f

audible /ˈɔːdəbl/ adj udibile

audience /ˈɔːdɪəns/ n Theat pubblico m; TV telespettatori mpl; Radio ascoltatori mpl; (meeting) udienza f

audience participation n partecipazione f del pubblico

audience ratings npl indici mpl di ascolto.

audience research n sondaggio m tra il pubblico

audio /ˈɔːdɪəʊ/ pref audio

audiobook n audiolibro m

audio cassette n audiocassetta f

audio system n impianto m stereo

audiotape n audiocassetta f

audiotyping n trascrizione f da audiocassetta

audio typist n dattilografo, -a mf (che trascrive registrazioni)

audiovisual adj audiovisivo

audit /ˈɔːdɪt/ ① n verifica f del bilancio ② vt verificare

auditing /ˈɔːdɪtɪŋ/ n auditing m inv

audition /ɔːˈdɪʃn/ ① n audizione f ② vi fare un'audizione

auditor /ˈɔːdɪtə(r)/ n revisore m di conti

auditorium /ɔːdɪˈtɔːrɪəm/ n sala f

auditory /ˈɔːdɪt(ə)rɪ/ adj acustico, uditivo

augment /ɔːgˈment/ vt aumentare

augur /ˈɔːgə(r)/ vi ~ well/ill essere di buon/cattivo augurio

August /ˈɔːgəst/ n agosto m

august /ɔːˈgʌst/ adj augusto

Augustinian /ɔːgəˈstɪnɪən/ adj agostiniano

aunt /ɑːnt/ n zia f

auntie, **aunty** /ˈɑːntɪ/ n fam zietta f

au pair /əʊˈpeə(r)/ n ~ [girl] ragazza f alla pari

aura /ˈɔːrə/ n aura f

aural /ˈɔːrəl/ ① adj uditivo; Sch ⟨comprehension, test⟩ orale; ⟨Med: test⟩ audiometrico
② n Sch esercizio m di comprensione ed espressione orale; Mus ≈ dettato m musicale

aurora australis/borealis /ɔːˈrɔːrəʊˈstrɑːlɪs///bɔːrɪˈɑːlɪs/ n aurora f australe/boreale

auspices /ˈɔːspɪsɪz/ npl under the ~ of sotto l'egida di

auspicious /ɔːˈspɪʃəs/ adj di buon augurio

Aussie /ˈɒzɪ/ adj & n fam australiano, -a mf

austere /ɒˈstɪə(r)/ adj austero

austerity /ɒˈsterətɪ/ n austerità f

Australasia /ɒstrəˈleɪʒə/ n Australasia f

Australia /ɒˈstreɪlɪə/ n Australia f

Australian /ɒˈstreɪlɪən/ adj & n australiano, -a mf

Austria /ˈɒstrɪə/ n Austria f

Austrian /ˈɒstrɪən/ adj & n austriaco, -a mf

Austro-Hungarian /ɒstrəʊhʌŋˈgeərɪən/ adj austroungarico

autarchy /ˈɔːtɑːkɪ/ n autarchia f

authentic /ɔːˈθentɪk/ adj autentico

authenticate /ɔːˈθentɪkeɪt/ vt autenticare

authenticity /ɔːθenˈtɪsətɪ/ n autenticità f

author /ˈɔːθə(r)/ n autore m

authoritarian /ɔːθɒrɪˈteərɪən/ adj autoritario

authoritative /ɔːˈθɒrɪtətɪv/ adj autorevole; ⟨manner⟩ autoritario

authority /ɔːˈθɒrətɪ/ n autorità f; (permission) autorizzazione f; who's in ~ here? chi è il responsabile qui?; be in ~ over avere autorità su; be an ~ on essere un'autorità in materia di

authorization /ɔːθəraɪˈzeɪʃn/ n autorizzazione f

authorize /ˈɔːθəraɪz/ vt autorizzare

authorized dealer /ˈɔːθəraɪzd/ rivenditore m autorizzato

autism /ˈɔːtɪzm/ n autismo m

autistic /ɔːˈtɪstɪk/ adj autistico

auto /ˈɔːtəʊ/ ① n Am fam auto f ② attrib ⟨industry⟩ automobilistico; ⟨workers⟩ dell'industria automobilistica

autobiographical /ɔːtəbaɪəˈgræfɪkl/ adj autobiografico

autobiography /ɔːtəbaɪˈɒgrəfɪ/ n autobiografia f

autocrat /ˈɔːtəkræt/ n autocrate m

autocratic /ɔːtəˈkrætɪk/ adj autocratico

autocue /ˈɔːtəʊkjuː/ n TV gobbo m

auto-destruct vi ⟨spacecraft, missile⟩ autodistruggersi

autograph /ˈɔːtəgrɑːf/ ① n autografo m ② vt autografare

autoimmune /ɔːtəʊˈmjuːn/ adj ⟨disease, system⟩ autoimmune

automate /ˈɔːtəmeɪt/ vt automatizzare

automatic /ɔːtəˈmætɪk/ ① adj automatico
② n (car) macchina f col cambio automatico; (washing machine) lavatrice f automatica

automatically /ɔːtəˈmætɪklɪ/ adv automaticamente

automatic pilot n (device) pilota m automatico; be on ~ ~ also fig viaggiare con il pilota automatico inserito

automatic teller machine /ˈtelə/ n cassa f continua di prelevamento

automation /ɔːtəˈmeɪʃn/ n automazione f

automaton /ɔːˈtɒmətən/ n automa m

automobile /ˈɔːtəməbiːl/ n automobile f

automotive /ɔːtəˈməʊtɪv/ adj (self-propelling) autopropulso; ⟨design, industry⟩ automobilistico

autonomous /ɔːˈtɒnəməs/ adj autonomo

autonomously /ɔːˈtɒnəməslɪ/ adv autonomamente

autonomy /ɔːˈtɒnəmɪ/ n autonomia f

autopilot /ˈɔːtəʊpaɪlət/ n Aeron, fig pilota m automatico

autopsy /ˈɔːtɒpsɪ/ n autopsia f

auto-suggestion /ɔːtəʊsəˈdʒestʃən/ n autosuggestione f

autumn /'ɔːtəm/ n autunno m

autumnal /ɔː'tʌmnl/ adj autunnale

auxiliary /ɔːg'zɪlɪərɪ/ **①** adj ausiliario **②** n ausiliare m

auxiliary nurse n infermiere, -a mf ausiliario, -a

auxiliary verb n ausiliare m

avail /ə'veɪl/ **①** n to no ∼ invano **②** vi ∼ oneself of approfittare di

availability /əveɪlə'bɪlətɪ/ n (option, service) disponibilità f; (of drugs) reperibilità f, disponibilità f; **subject to** ∼ **fino ad** esaurimento

available /ə'veɪləbl/ adj disponibile; ⟨book, record etc⟩ in vendita

avalanche /'ævəlɑːnʃ/ n valanga f

avant-garde /ævɑ̃'gɑːd/ **①** n avanguardia f **②** adj d'avanguardia

avarice /'ævərɪs/ n avidità f

avaricious /ævə'rɪʃəs/ adj avido

Ave abbr (**Avenue**) V.le

avenge /ə'vendʒ/ vt vendicare

avenger /ə'vendʒə(r)/ n vendicatore, -trice mf

avenging /ə'vendʒɪŋ/ adj vendicatore

avenue /'ævənjuː/ n viale m; fig strada f

average /'ævərɪdʒ/ **①** adj medio; (mediocre) mediocre **②** n media f; **on** ∼ in media; **above** ∼ superiore al normale **③** vt ⟨sales, attendance etc⟩ raggiungere una media di ■ **average out at** vt risultare in media

averse /ə'vɜːs/ adj **not be** ∼ **to something** non essere contro qualcosa

aversion /ə'vɜːʃn/ n avversione f (**to** per)

avert /ə'vɜːt/ vt evitare ⟨crisis⟩; distogliere ⟨eyes⟩

aviary /'eɪvɪərɪ/ n uccelliera f

aviation /eɪvɪ'eɪʃn/ n aviazione f

aviation fuel n benzina f avio

aviation industry n industria f aeronautica

aviator /'eɪvɪeɪtə(r)/ n aviatore, -trice mf

avid /'ævɪd/ adj avido (**for** di); ⟨reader⟩ appassionato

avidity /ə'vɪdətɪ/ n avidità

avidly /'ævɪdlɪ/ adv ⟨read, collect⟩ avidamente; ⟨support⟩ con entusiasmo

avocado /ævə'kɑːdəʊ/ n avocado m

avoid /ə'vɔɪd/ vt evitare

avoidable /ə'vɔɪdəbl/ adj evitabile

avoidance /ə'vɔɪdəns/ n ∼ **of one's duty** astensione f dal proprio dovere

avowed /ə'vaʊd/ adj dichiarato

avuncular /ə'vʌŋkʊlə(r)/ adj benevolo

await /ə'weɪt/ vt attendere

awake /ə'weɪk/ **①** adj sveglio; **wide** ∼ completamente sveglio **②** vi (pt **awoke**, pp **awoken**) svegliarsi

awaken /ə'weɪkn/ **①** vt svegliare **②** vi svegliarsi

awakening /ə'weɪknɪŋ/ n risveglio m

award /ə'wɔːd/ **①** n premio m; (medal) riconoscimento m; (of prize) assegnazione f **②** vt assegnare; ⟨hand over⟩ consegnare

award ceremony n cerimonia f di premiazione

award winner n vincitore, -trice mf di un premio

award-winning adj ⟨book, film, design⟩ premiato

aware /ə'weə(r)/ adj **be** ∼ **of** (sense) percepire; (know) essere conscio di; **become** ∼ **of** accorgersi di; (learn) venire a sapere di; **be** ∼ **that** rendersi conto che

awareness /ə'weənɪs/ n percezione f; (knowledge) consapevolezza f

awash /ə'wɒʃ/ adj inondato (**with** di)

away /ə'weɪ/ adv via; **go/stay** ∼ andare/ stare via; **he's** ∼ **from his desk/the office** non è alla sua scrivania/in ufficio; **far** ∼ lontano; **four kilometres** ∼ a quattro chilometri; **play** ∼ Sport giocare fuori casa

away game n partita f fuori casa

awe /ɔː/ n soggezione f; **stand in** ∼ **of somebody** avere soggezione di qualcuno

awe-inspiring adj maestoso

awesome /'ɔːsəm/ adj imponente

awful /'ɔːf(ə)l/ **①** adj terribile; **that's an** ∼ **pity** è un gran peccato **②** adv fam estremamente

awfully /'ɔːf(ʊ)lɪ/ adv terribilmente; ⟨pretty⟩ estremamente; **that's** ∼ **nice of you** è veramente gentile da parte tua; **thanks** ∼ grazie mille

awhile /ə'waɪl/ adv per un po'

awkward /'ɔːkwəd/ adj ⟨movement⟩ goffo; ⟨moment, situation⟩ imbarazzante; ⟨time⟩ scomodo

awkwardly /'ɔːkwədlɪ/ adv ⟨move⟩ goffamente; ⟨say⟩ con imbarazzo; **the meeting is** ∼ **timed** la riunione è ad un orario scomodo

awkwardness /'ɔːkwədnɪs/ n ⟨clumsiness⟩ goffaggine f; (inconvenience) scomodità f; (embarrassment) imbarazzo m; (delicacy of situation) delicatezza f

awl /ɔːl/ n (for wood etc) punteruolo m

awning /'ɔːnɪŋ/ n tendone m

awoke(n) /ə'wəʊk(ən)/ ▸ AWAKE

AWOL /'eɪwɒl/ adj & adv abbr (**absent without leave**) **be/go** ∼ Mil assentarsi senza permesso; hum volatilizzarsi

awry /ə'raɪ/ adv storto

axe /æks/ **①** n scure f; **have an** ∼ **to grind** fig avere il proprio tornaconto

a

b

2 *vt* (pres p **axing**) fare dei tagli a ⟨*budget*⟩; sopprimere ⟨*jobs*⟩; annullare ⟨*project*⟩

axiom /'æksɪəm/ *n* assioma *m*

axiomatic /æksɪə'mætɪk/ *adj* **it is ∼ that...** è indiscutibile che...

axis /'æksɪs/ *n* (pl **axes** /-siːz/) asse *m*

axle /'æksl/ *n* Techn asse *m*

ay[e] /aɪ/ **1** *adv* sì
2 *n* sì *m inv*

Azerbaijan /æzəbaɪ'dʒɑːn/ *n* Azerbaigiano *m*

Azerbaijani /æzəbaɪ'dʒɑːnɪ/ *adj & n* (person) azerbaigiano, -a *mf*; (language) azerbaigiano *m*

Azores /ə'zɔːz/ *npl* **the ∼** le Azzorre

Aztec /'æztek/ *adj & n* (person) azteco, -a *mf*; (language) azteco *m*

azure /'eɪʒə(r)/ *adj & n* azzurro *m*

Bb

b¹, B /biː/ *n* (letter) b, B *f inv*; Mus si *m inv*

b² *abbr* **born**

b. & b. *abbr* **bed and breakfast**

BA *abbr* **Bachelor of Arts**

BAA *n abbr* (**British Airports Authority**) ente *m* che gestisce gli aeroporti britannici

baa /bɑː/ **1** *vi* belare
2 *int* bee

babble /'bæbl/ *vi* farfugliare; ⟨*stream*⟩ gorgogliare

babe /beɪb/ *n* liter bimbo, -a *mf*; (fam: woman) ragazza *f*; (fam: form of address) bella *f*; **a ∼ in arms** un bimbo in fasce; fig uno sprovveduto

baboon /bə'buːn/ *n* babbuino *m*

baby /'beɪbɪ/ *n* bambino, -a *mf*; (fam: darling) tesoro *m*

baby bird *n* uccellino *m*

baby boom *n* baby boom *m inv*

baby boomer *n* persona *f* nata durante il baby boom

baby buggy *n* Br carrozzina *f*

baby carriage *n* Am carrozzina *f*

baby carrier *n* zaino *m* portabimbo *inv*

baby-faced *adj* ⟨*person*⟩ con la faccia da bambino

babyish /'beɪbɪɪʃ/ *adj* bambinesco

baby shower *n* Am festa *f* in cui si portano regali a una mamma in attesa

baby-sit *vi* fare da baby-sitter

baby-sitter *n* baby-sitter *mf*

baby-sitting *n* **do ∼** fare il/la baby-sitter

baby talk *n* linguaggio *m* infantile

baby tooth *n* dente *m* di latte

baby walker *n* girello *m*

babywear *n* abbigliamento *m* per bambini

bachelor /'bætʃələ(r)/ *n* scapolo *m*; **B∼ of Arts/Science** laureato, -a *mf* in lettere/in scienze

bachelor apartment, bachelor flat Br *n* appartamento *m* da scapolo

bachelorhood /'bætʃələhʊd/ *n* celibato *m*

bacillus /bə'sɪləs/ *n* (pl **-lli**) bacillo *m*

back /bæk/ **1** *n* schiena *f*; (of horse, hand) dorso *m*; (of chair) schienale *m*; (of house, cheque, page) retro *m*; (in football) difesa *f*; **at the ∼** in fondo; **in the ∼** Auto dietro; **stand ∼ to** stare in piedi schiena contro schiena; **∼ to front** (sweater) il davanti di dietro; **you've got it all ∼ to front** fig hai capito tutto all'incontrario; **at the ∼ of beyond** in un posto sperduto
2 *adj* posteriore; ⟨*taxes, payments*⟩ arretrato
3 *adv* indietro; (returned) di ritorno; **turn/move ∼** tornare/spostarsi indietro; **put it ∼ here/there** rimettilo qui/là; **∼ at home** di ritorno a casa; **I'll be ∼ in five minutes** torno fra cinque minuti; **I'm just ∼** sono appena tornato; **when do you want the book ∼?** quando rivuoi il libro?; **pay ∼** ripagare ⟨*somebody*⟩; restituire ⟨*money*⟩; **∼ in power** di nuovo al potere
4 *vt* (support) sostenere; (with money) finanziare; puntare su ⟨*horse*⟩; (cover the back of) rivestire il retro di
5 *vi* Auto fare retromarcia
■ **back away** *vi* tirarsi indietro
■ **back down** *vi* battere in ritirata
■ **back in** *vi* Auto entrare in retromarcia; ⟨*person*⟩; entrare camminando all'indietro
■ **back out** *vi* Auto uscire in retromarcia; ⟨*person;*⟩ uscire camminando all'indietro; fig tirarsi indietro (**of** da)
■ **back up** **1** *vt* sostenere; confermare ⟨*person's alibi*⟩; Comput fare una copia di salvataggio di; **be ∼ed up** ⟨*traffic*⟩ essere congestionato
2 *vi* Auto fare retromarcia

backache *n* mal *m* di schiena

backbench n Br Pol scanni mpl del Parlamento dove siedono i parlamentari ordinari

backbencher n Br Pol parlamentare mf ordinario, -a

backbiting n maldicenza f

backboard n (in basketball) tabellone m

back boiler n caldaia f (posta dietro un caminetto)

backbone n spina f dorsale

back-breaking adj massacrante

back burner n put something on the ~ ~ rimandare qualcosa

backchat n risposta f impertinente

backcloth n Theat fondale m; fig sfondo m

back comb vt cotonare

back copy n numero m arretrato

back cover n retro m di copertina

backdate vt retrodatare ⟨cheque⟩; ~d to valido a partire da

back door n porta f di servizio

backdrop n Theat fondale m; fig sfondo m

back-end n (rear) fondo m

backer /'bækə(r)/ n sostenitore, -trice mf; (with money) finanziatore, -trice mf

backfire vi Auto avere un ritorno di fiamma; fig ⟨plan⟩ fallire; **the joke** ~d on **him** lo scherzo si è ritorto contro di lui

backgammon n backgammon m

background n sfondo m; (environment) ambiente m

background noise n rumore m di sottofondo

background reading n letture fpl generali

backhand n Tennis rovescio m

backhanded adj ⟨compliment⟩ implicito

backhander n (fam: bribe) bustarella f

backing /'bækɪŋ/ n (support) supporto m; (material used) fondo m; Mus accompagnamento m; ~ **singer/vocals/ group** cantante/voci/gruppo d'accompagnamento

back issue n numero m arretrato

backlash /'bæklæʃ/ n fig reazione f opposta

backless /'bæklɪs/ adj ⟨dress⟩ scollato dietro

backlist n opere fpl pubblicate

backlog n ~ **of work** lavoro m arretrato

back marker n Sport ultimo, -a mf

back number n numero m arretrato

backpack n zaino m

backpacker n saccopelista mf

backpacking n go ~ viaggiare con zaino e sacco a pelo

back passage n Anat retto m

back pay n arretrato m di stipendio

back-pedal vi pedalare all'indietro; fig fare marcia indietro

back pocket n tasca f di dietro

backrest n schienale m

back room n stanza f sul retro

back room boys npl esperti mpl che lavorano dietro le quinte

back-scratcher n manina f grattaschiena inv

back seat n sedile m posteriore

back-seat driver n persona f che dà consigli non richiesti

backside n fam fondoschiena m inv

backslash n Typ backslash nm inv

back-space n Comput backspace m

back-stage adj & adv dietro le quinte

backstairs npl scale f di servizio

backstitch n impuntura f vi impunturare

backstop n Sport ricevitore m

backstory n vicende fpl passate

back straight n Sport rettilineo m

backstreet n vicolo m; attrib ⟨abortionist⟩ clandestino

backstroke n dorso m

backtalk n Am = backchat

backtrack vi tornare indietro; fig fare marcia indietro

back translation n traduzione f di una traduzione

backup n rinforzi mpl; Comput riserva f, backup m inv; **do a** ~ realizzare un backup

backup copy n copia f di riserva

backup light n Am luce f di retromarcia

backward /'bækwəd/ adj ⟨step⟩ indietro; ⟨child⟩ lento nell'apprendimento; ⟨country⟩ arretrato

backward-looking /'bækwədlʊkɪŋ/ adj retrogrado

backwards /'bækwədz/ adv (also Am: **backward**) indietro; ⟨fall, walk⟩ all'indietro; ~ **and forwards** avanti e indietro

backwater /'bækwɔːtə(r)/ n fig luogo m arretrato

backyard /bæk'jɑːd/ n cortile m; **not in my** ~ **yard** fam non a casa mia

bacon /'beɪk(ə)n/ n ≈ pancetta f

bacon-slicer /'beɪkənslaɪsə(r)/ n affettatrice f

bacteria /bæk'tɪərɪə/ npl batteri mpl

bacterial /bæk'tɪərɪəl/ adj batterico

bacteriology /bæktɪərɪ'ɒlədʒɪ/ n batteriologia f

bad /bæd/ adj (**worse, worst**) cattivo; ⟨weather, habit, news, accident⟩ brutto; ⟨apple etc⟩ marcio; **the light is** ~ non c'è ⋯⋗

una buona luce; **my eyesight is** ~ non ho una buona vista; **use** ~ **language** dire delle parolacce; **she's going through a** ~ **patch** sta attraversando un brutto periodo; **feel** ~ sentirsi male; (feel guilty) sentirsi in colpa; **have a** ~ **back** avere dei problemi alla schiena; **smoking is** ~ **for you** fumare fa male; **go** ~ andare a male; **that's just too** ~! pazienza!; **not** ~ niente male; **things have gone from** ~ **to worse** le cose sono andate di male in peggio

bad blood *n* there is ~ ~ **between them** tra loro non corre buon sangue

bad boy *n* ragazzaccio *m*

bad breath *n* alito *m* cattivo

bad cheque *n* assegno *m* a vuoto

bad debt *n* credito *m* inesigibile

baddie, **baddy** /'bædɪ/ *n* fam cattivo, -a *mf*

bade /bæd/ ▶ BID¹

bad faith *n* malafede *f*

badge /bædʒ/ *n* distintivo *m*

badger /'bædʒə(r)/ ① *n* tasso *m* ② *vt* tormentare

badly /'bædlɪ/ *adv* male; ⟨hurt⟩ gravemente; ~ **off** povero; ~ **behaved** maleducato; **need** ~ aver estremamente bisogno di

bad-mannered /-'mænəd/ *adj* maleducato

badminton /'bædmɪntən/ *n* badminton *m*

bad-tempered /-'tempəd/ *adj* irascibile

baffle /'bæfl/ *vt* confondere

baffled /'bæfld/ *adj* sconcertato

baffling /'bæflɪŋ/ *adj* sconcertante

BAFTA, **Bafta** /'bæftə/ *n abbr* (**British Academy of Film and Television Arts**) società *m* britannica delle arti cinematografiche e televisive

bag /bæg/ ① *n* borsa *f*; (of paper) sacchetto *m*; **old** ~ sl megera *f*; ~**s under the eyes** occhiaie *fpl*; ~**s of** fam un sacco di; **it's in the** ~ fig è fatta ② *vt* (pt/pp **bagged**) (fam: take) accaparrarsi; ~ **somebody a seat** tenere un posto a qualcuno

bagel /'beɪgəl/ *n* panino *m* a forma di ciambella

baggage /'bægɪdʒ/ *n* bagagli *mpl*

baggage allowance *n* franchigia *f* bagaglio

baggage car *n* Rail bagagliaio *m*

baggage carousel *n* nastro *m* trasportatore per ritiro bagagli

baggage check *n* controllo *m* bagagli

baggage handler *n* addetto, -a *mf* ai bagagli

baggage locker *n* armadietto *m* per deposito bagagli

baggage reclaim *n* ritiro *m* bagagli

baggy /'bægɪ/ *adj* ⟨clothes⟩ ampio

Baghdad /bæg'dæd/ *n* Baghdad *f*

bag lady *n* fam barbona *f*

bag person *n* fam barbone, -a *mf*

bagpipes *npl* cornamusa *fsg*

bag snatcher *n* scippatore, -trice *mf*

baguette /bæg'et/ *n* baguette *f inv*

Bahamas /bə'hɑːməz/ *npl* the ~ le Bahamas

Bahrain, **Bahrein** /bɑː'reɪn/ *n* Bahrein *m*

bail /beɪl/ *n* cauzione *f*; **on** ~ su cauzione ■ **bail out** ① *vt* Naut aggottare; ~ **somebody out** Jur pagare la cauzione per qualcuno; fig trarre qualcuno d'impaccio ② *vi* Aeron paracadutarsi

bail bond *n* Am Jur cauzione *f*

bailiff /'beɪlɪf/ *n* ufficiale *m* giudiziario; (of estate) fattore *m*

bait /beɪt/ ① *n* esca *f*; **rise to the** ~ abboccare [all'amo] ② *vt* innescare; (fig: torment) tormentare

baize /beɪz/ *n* panno *m* (di tavolo da gioco e da biliardo)

bake /beɪk/ ① *vt* cuocere al forno; (make) fare ② *vi* cuocersi al forno

baked beans /beɪkt'biːnz/ *n* Culin fagioli *mpl* al pomodoro

baked potato *n* patata *f* cotta al forno (con la buccia)

baker /'beɪkə(r)/ *n* fornaio, -a *mf*, panettiere, -a *mf*

baker's [shop] /'beɪkəz/ *n* panetteria *f*

bakery /'beɪkərɪ/ *n* panificio *m*, forno *m*

baking /'beɪkɪŋ/ *n* cottura *f* al forno

baking powder *n* lievito *m* in polvere

baking soda *n* Culin bicarbonato *m* di sodio

baking tin *n* teglia *f*

balaclava /bælə'klɑːvə/ *n* passamontagna *m inv*

balance /'bæləns/ ① *n* (equilibrium) equilibrio *m*; Comm bilancio *m*; (outstanding sum) saldo *m*; **[bank]** ~ saldo *m*; **be** or **hang in the** ~ fig essere in sospeso; **on** ~ tutto sommato ② *vt* bilanciare; equilibrare ⟨budget⟩; Comm fare il bilancio di ⟨books⟩ ③ *vi* bilanciarsi; Comm essere in pareggio

balanced /'bælənst/ *adj* equilibrato

balance of payments *n* bilancia *f* dei pagamenti

balance of power *n* Pol equilibrio *m* delle forze

balance of trade *n* bilancia *f* commerciale

balance sheet *n* bilancio *m* patrimoniale

balancing act /'bælənsɪŋ/ *n* fig do a ∼
∼ fare equilibrismo

balcony /'bælkənɪ/ *n* balcone *m*

bald /bɔ:ld/ *adj* ‹person› calvo; ‹tyre›
liscio; ‹statement› nudo e crudo; **go** ∼
perdere i capelli

balderdash /'bɔ:ldədæʃ/ *n* sciocchezze
fpl

balding /'bɔ:ldɪŋ/ *adj* **be** ∼ stare
perdendo i capelli

baldly /'bɔ:ldlɪ/ *adv* ‹state› in modo nudo
e crudo

baldness /'bɔ:ldnɪs/ *n* calvizie *f*

bale /beɪl/ *n* balla *f*

Balearic Islands /bælerˈærɪk/ *npl*
isole *fpl* Baleari

baleful /'beɪlfl/ *adj* malvagio; (sad) triste

balefully /'beɪlfʊlɪ/ *adv* con malvagità

balk /bɔ:lk/ **1** *vt* ostacolare
2 *vi* ∼ **at** ‹horse› impennarsi davanti a;
fig tirarsi indietro davanti a

Balkan /'bɔ:lkn/ *adj* dei Balcani

Balkans /'bɔ:lknz/ *npl* Balcani *mpl*

ball[1] /bɔ:l/ *n* palla *f*; (football) pallone *m*; (of
yarn) gomitolo *m*; **on the** ∼ fam sveglio

ball[2] *n* (dance) ballo *m*)

ballad /'bæləd/ *n* ballata *f*

ball and chain *n* palla *f* al piede

ball-and-socket joint *n* giunto *m*
sferico

ballast /'bæləst/ *n* zavorra *f*

ball-bearing *n* cuscinetto *m* a sfera

ballboy *n* Tennis raccattapalle *m inv*

ballcock *n* Techn galleggiante *m* (in
serbatoio)

ball control *n* controllo *m* della palla

ball dress *n* abito *m* da sera

ballerina /bælə'ri:nə/ *n* ballerina *f*
[classica]

ballet /'bæleɪ/ *n* balletto *m*; (art form)
danza *f*

ballet dancer *n* ballerino, -a *mf*
[classico, -a]

ballet dress *n* tutù *m inv*

ballet shoes *npl* scarpe *fpl* da danza

ballgame *n* gioco *m* con la palla; Am
partita *f* di baseball; **that's a whole
different** ∼ fig è tutto un altro paio di
maniche

ballgirl *n* Tennis raccattapalle *f inv*

ball gown *n* abito *m* da sera

ballistic /bə'lɪstɪk/ *adj* balistico

ballistics *n* balistica *fsg*

balloon /bə'lu:n/ *n* pallone *m*; Aeron
mongolfiera *f*

balloonist /bə'lu:nɪst/ *n* aeronauta *mf*

ballot /'bælət/ *n* votazione *f*

ballot box *n* urna *f*

ballot paper *n* scheda *f* di votazione

ballpark *n* Am stadio *m* di baseball

ballpark figure *n* fam cifra *f*
approssimativa

ball-point [pen] *n* penna *f* a sfera

ballroom *n* sala *f* da ballo

ballroom dancing *n* ballo *m* liscio

balls up vulg **1** *vi* incasinarsi
2 *vt* incasinare

ballyhoo /bælɪ'hu:/ *n* (publicity) battage *m
inv* pubblicitario; (uproar) baccano *m*

balm /bɑ:m/ *n* balsamo *m*

balmy /'bɑ:mɪ/ *adj* (**-ier, -iest**) mite;
(fam: crazy) strampalato

balsam /'bɒlsəm/ *n* (oily) balsamo *m*

Baltic /'bɔ:ltɪk/ *adj & n* **the** ∼ [**Sea**] il
[mar] Baltico

balustrade /bælə'streɪd/ *n* balaustra *f*

bamboo /bæm'bu:/ *n* bambù *m*

bamboozle /bæm'bu:zl/ *vt* (fam: mystify)
confondere

ban /bæn/ **1** *n* proibizione *f*
2 *vt* (pt/pp **banned**) proibire; ∼ **from**
espellere da ‹club›; **she was** ∼**ned from
driving** le hanno ritirato la patente

banal /bə'nɑ:l/ *adj* banale

banality /bə'nælətɪ/ *n* banalità *f inv*

banana /bə'nɑ:nə/ *n* banana *f*

banana republic *n* pej repubblica *f*
delle banane

banana skin *n* buccia *f* di banana

band /bænd/ *n* banda *f*; (stripe) nastro *m*;
(Mus: pop group) complesso *m*; (Mus: brass ∼)
banda *f*; Mil fanfara *f*
■ **band together** *vi* riunirsi

bandage /'bændɪdʒ/ **1** *n* benda *f*
2 *vt* fasciare
■ **bandage up** *vt* fasciare

Band-Aid® *n* Med cerotto *m*

bandanna, bandana /bæn'dænə/ *n*
bandana *f*

bandit /'bændɪt/ *n* bandito *m*

band leader *n* leader *mf* di un
complesso

bandmaster *n* capobanda *m* (di banda
musicale)

band saw *n* segatrice *f* a nastro

bandsman *n* bandista *m*

bandstand *n* palco *m* coperto
[dell'orchestra]

bandwagon *n* **jump on the** ∼ fig seguire
la corrente

bandy[1] /'bændɪ/ *vt* (pt/pp **-ied**)
scambiarsi ‹words›
■ **bandy about** *vt* far circolare

bandy[2] *adj* (**-ier, -iest**) **be** ∼ avere le
gambe storte

bandy-legged /-'legd/ *adj* con le gambe
storte

bane /beɪn/ *n* **she/it is the** ∼ **of my life!** è
la mia rovina!

bang /bæŋ/ **1** n (noise) fragore m; (of gun, firework) scoppio m; (blow) colpo m; **go with a** ~ fam essere una cannonata

2 adv ~ **in the middle of** fam proprio nel mezzo di; **go** ~ ⟨gun⟩ sparare; ⟨balloon⟩ esplodere

3 int bum!

4 vt battere ⟨fist⟩; battere su ⟨table⟩; sbattere ⟨door, head⟩

5 vi scoppiare; ⟨door⟩ sbattere

■ **bang about**, **bang around** vi far rumore

■ **bang into** vt sbattere contro

banger /'bæŋə(r)/ n (firework) petardo m; (fam: sausage) salsiccia f: **old** ~ (fam: car) macinino m

Bangladesh /bæŋglə'deʃ/ n Bangladesh m

Bangladeshi /bæŋglə'deʃɪ/ **1** adj del Bangladesh

2 n persona f del Bangladesh

bangle /'bæŋgl/ n braccialetto m

banish /'bænɪʃ/ vt bandire

banishment /'bænɪʃmənt/ n bando m

banister /'bænɪstə/ n ringhiera f

banjo /'bændʒəʊ/ n banjo m inv

bank¹ /bæŋk/ **1** n (of river) sponda f; (slope) scarpata f

2 vi Aeron inclinarsi in virata

bank² **1** n banca f

2 vt depositare in banca

3 vi ~ **with** avere un conto [bancario] presso

■ **bank on** vt contare su

bank account n conto m in banca

bank balance n saldo m

bank-book n libretto m di risparmio

bank borrowings npl prestiti mpl bancari

bank card n carta f assegni

bank charges npl spese fpl bancarie, commissioni fpl

bank clerk n bancario, -a mf

bank details npl coordinate fpl bancarie

banker /'bæŋkə(r)/ n banchiere m

banker's draft n tratta f bancaria

banker's order n ordine m di pagamento

Bank Giro Credit n Br accreditamento m tramite bancogiro

bank holiday n giorno m festivo

banking /'bæŋkɪŋ/ n bancario m

banking hours npl orario m di sportello (in banca)

bank manager n direttore, -trice mf di banca

banknote n banconota f

bank raid n rapina f in banca

bank robber n rapinatore, -trice mf di banca

bank robbery n rapina f in banca

bankroll **1** n finanziamento m

2 vt finanziare ⟨person, party⟩

bankrupt /'bæŋkrʌpt/ **1** adj fallito; **go** ~ fallire

2 n persona f che ha fatto fallimento

3 vt far fallire

bankruptcy /'bæŋkrʌptsɪ/ n bancarotta f

bankruptcy court n tribunale m fallimentare

bankruptcy proceedings npl procedura f fallimentare

bank statement n estratto m conto

bank transfer n bonifico m bancario

banner /'bænə(r)/ n stendardo m; (of demonstrators) striscione m

banner headline n titolo m a tutta pagina

banns /bænz/ npl Relig pubblicazioni fpl [di matrimonio]

banquet /'bæŋkwɪt/ n banchetto m

bantam /'bæntəm/ n gallo m bantam

banter /'bæntə(r)/ n battute fpl di spirito

baptism /'bæptɪzm/ n battesimo m; ~ **of fire** fig battesimo m del fuoco

Baptist /'bæptɪst/ adj & n battista mf

baptize /bæp'taɪz/ vt battezzare

bar /bɑː(r)/ **1** n sbarra f; Jur ordine m degli avvocati; (of chocolate) tavoletta f; (café) bar m inv; (counter) banco m; Mus battuta f; (fig: obstacle) ostacolo m; ~ **of soap/gold** saponetta f/lingotto m; **be called to the** ~ Jur entrare a far parte dell'ordine degli avvocati; **behind** ~**s** fam dietro le sbarre

2 vt (pt/pp **barred**) sbarrare ⟨way⟩; sprangare ⟨door⟩; escludere ⟨person⟩

3 prep tranne; ~ **none** in assoluto

barb /bɑːb/ n barbiglio m; (fig: remark) frecciata f

Barbados /bɑː'beɪdɒs/ n Barbados fsg

barbarian /bɑː'beərɪən/ n barbaro, -a mf

barbaric /bɑː'bærɪk/ adj barbarico

barbarism /'bɑːbərɪzm/ n (brutality, primitiveness) barbarie f inv; (error of style) barbarismo m

barbarity /bɑː'bærətɪ/ n barbarie f inv

barbarous /'bɑːbərəs/ adj barbaro

barbecue /'bɑːbɪkjuː/ **1** n barbecue m inv; (party) grigliata f, barbecue m inv

2 vt arrostire sul barbecue

barbed /bɑːbd/ adj ~ **wire** filo m spinato

barber /'bɑːbə(r)/ n barbiere m

barber's shop n barbiere m

barbiturate /bɑː'bɪtjʊrət/ n barbiturico m

bar chart n istogramma m

bar code n codice m a barre

bar-coded adj con codice a barre

bar code reader *n* lettore *m* di codice a barre

bard /bɑːd/ *n* liter bardo *m*

bare /beə(r)/ ① *adj* nudo; ⟨tree, room⟩ spoglio; ⟨floor⟩ senza moquette; **the ~ bones** l'essenziale *m*
② *vt* scoprire; mostrare ⟨teeth⟩

bareback *adv* senza sella

barefaced *adj* sfacciato

barefoot *adv* scalzo

bare-headed *adj* a capo scoperto

barely /ˈbeəlɪ/ *adv* appena

bareness /ˈbeənɪs/ *n* nudità *f*

bargain /ˈbɑːgɪn/ ① *n* (agreement) patto *m*; (good buy) affare *m*; **into the ~** per di più
② *vi* contrattare; (haggle) trattare
■ **bargain for** *vt* (expect) aspettarsi

bargain basement *n* reparto *m* occasioni

bargaining /ˈbɑːgɪnɪŋ/ ① *n* (over pay) contrattazione *f*
② *attrib* ⟨power, rights⟩ contrattuale; ⟨position⟩ di negoziato

barge /bɑːdʒ/ *n* barcone *m*
■ **barge in** *vi* fam (to room) piombare dentro; (into conversation) interrompere bruscamente; **~ into** piombare dentro a ⟨room⟩; venire addosso a ⟨person⟩

bargepole /ˈbɑːdʒpəʊl/ *n* **I wouldn't touch him/it with a ~** non lo toccherei nemmeno con un dito

barista /bəˈrɪstə/ *n* esp Am barista *mf*

baritone /ˈbærɪtəʊn/ *n* baritono *m*

bark¹ /bɑːk/ *n* (of tree) corteccia *f*

bark² ① *n* abbaio *m*
② *vi* abbaiare

barking /ˈbɑːkɪŋ/ ① *n* abbaio *m*
② *adj* ⟨dog⟩ che abbaia; ⟨cough, laugh⟩ convulso
③ *adv* **be ~ mad** Br fam essere matto da legare

barley /ˈbɑːlɪ/ *n* orzo *m*

barleycorn *n* orzo *m*; (grain) chicco *m* d'orzo

barley sugar *n* caramella *f* d'orzo

barley water *n* Br orzata *f*

barley wine *n* Br birra *f* molto forte

barmaid /ˈbɑːmeɪd/ *n* barista *f*

barman /ˈbɑːmən/ *n* barista *m*

barmy /ˈbɑːmɪ/ *adj* fam strampalato

barn /bɑːn/ *n* granaio *m*

barnacle /ˈbɑːnəkl/ *n* cirripede *m*

barn dance *n* ballo *m* tradizionale statunitense; (social gathering) festa *f* negli USA in cui si fanno balli tradizionali

barn owl *n* barbagianni *m* inv

barnstorming *adj* sensazionale

barnyard *n* aia *f*

barometer /bəˈrɒmɪtə(r)/ *n* barometro *m*

baron /ˈbærən/ *n* barone *m*

baroness /ˈbærənɪs/ *n* baronessa *f*

baronial /bəˈrəʊnɪəl/ *adj* baronale

baroque /bəˈrɒk/ *adj* & *n* barocco *m*

barracking /ˈbærəkɪŋ/ *n* fischi *mpl* e insulti *mpl*

barrack room ① *n* camerata *f*
② *attrib* pej ⟨language⟩ da caserma

barracks /ˈbærəks/ *npl* caserma *fsg*

barrage /ˈbærɑːʒ/ *n* (in river) [opera *f* di] sbarramento *m*; Mil sbarramento *m*; (fig: of criticism, abuse) sfilza *f*

barrage balloon *n* pallone *m* di sbarramento

barrel /ˈbærəl/ *n* barile *m*, botte *f*; (of gun) canna *f*

barrel organ *n* organetto *m* [a cilindro]

barren /ˈbærən/ *adj* sterile; ⟨landscape⟩ brullo

barrette /bæˈret/ *n* Am (for hair) molletta *f*

barricade /ˈbærɪkeɪd/ ① *n* barricata *f*
② *vt* barricare

barrier /ˈbærɪə(r)/ *n* barriera *f*; Rail cancello *m*; fig ostacolo *m*

barrier cream *n* crema *f* protettiva

barrier method *n* Med metodo *m* anticoncezionale meccanico

barrier reef *n* barriera *f* corallina

barring /ˈbɑːrɪŋ/ *prep* **~ accidents** salvo imprevisti

barrister /ˈbærɪstə(r)/ *n* avvocato *m*

barrow /ˈbærəʊ/ *n* carretto *m*; (wheel~) carriola *f*

bar stool *n* sgabello *m* da bar

bartender /ˈbɑːtendə(r)/ *n* barista *mf*

barter /ˈbɑːtə(r)/ *vi* barattare (**for** con)

base /beɪs/ ① *n* base *f*
② *adj* vile
③ *vt* basare; **be ~d on** basarsi su

baseball /ˈbeɪsbɔːl/ *n* baseball *m*

baseball cap *n* berretto *m* da baseball

base camp *n* campo *m* base inv

base form *n* (of verb) forma *f* non coniugata di un verbo

base lending rate *n* tasso *m* base inv di interesse

baseless /ˈbeɪslɪs/ *adj* infondato

baseline /ˈbeɪslaɪn/ *n* Tennis linea *f* di fondo; fig riferimento *m*

basement /ˈbeɪsmənt/ *n* seminterrato *m*

basement flat *n* appartamento *m* nel seminterrato

base metal *n* metallo *m* vile inv

base rate *n* tasso *m* base inv

bash /bæʃ/ ① *n* colpo *m* violento; **have a ~!** fam provaci!
② *vt* colpire [violentemente]; (dent) ammaccare; **~ed in** ammaccato
■ **bash down** *vt* sfondare ⟨door⟩

■ **bash into** vt imbattersi in ⟨person⟩; sbattere contro ⟨wall, tree⟩

bashful /'bæʃfl/ adj timido

bashfully /'bæʃfʊlɪ/ adv timidamente

bashing /'bæʃɪŋ/ n fam (beating) pestaggio m; (criticism) critica f feroce; (defeat) batosta f; **take a** ∼ prendere una batosta

basic /'beɪsɪk/ adj di base; ⟨condition, requirement⟩ basilare; ⟨living conditions⟩ povero; **my Italian is pretty** ∼ il mio italiano è abbastanza rudimentale; **the** ∼**s** (of language, science) i rudimenti; (essentials) l'essenziale m

basically /'beɪsɪklɪ/ adv fondamentalmente

basic rate n tariffa f minima; (in tax) aliquota f minima

basil /'bæzɪl/ n basilico m

basilica /bə'zɪlɪkə/ n basilica f

basin /'beɪsn/ n bacinella f; (wash-hand ∼) lavabo m; (for food) recipiente m; Geog bacino m

basinful /'beɪsɪnfʊl/ n bacinella f (contenuto)

basis /'beɪsɪs/ n (pl -ses /'beɪsɪːz/) base f

bask /bɑːsk/ vi crogiolarsi

basket /'bɑːskɪt/ n cestino m

basketball n pallacanestro f

basket chair n sedia m di vimini

basketwork n (objects) oggetti mpl in vimini; (craft) lavoro m artigianale di oggetti in vimini

Basle /bɑːl/ n Basilea f

Basque /bæsk/ adj & n (person) basco, -a mf; (language) basco m

bass /beɪs/ **①** adj basso; ∼ **voice** voce f di basso
② n basso m

bass-baritone n baritono m basso

bass clef n chiave f di basso

bass drum n grancassa f

basset hound /'bæsɪt/ n basset hound m inv

bass guitar n (chitarra f) basso m

bassist /'beɪsɪst/ n bassista mf

bassoon /bə'suːn/ n fagotto m

bastard /'bɑːstəd/ n (illegitimate child) bastardo, -a mf; sl figlio m di puttana

baste¹ /beɪst/ vt (sew) imbastire

baste² vt Culin ungere con grasso

bastion /'bæstɪən/ n bastione m

bat¹ /bæt/ **①** n mazza f; (for table tennis) racchetta f; **off one's own** ∼ fam tutto da solo
② vt (pt/pp **batted**) battere; **she didn't** ∼ **an eyelid** fig non ha battuto ciglio

bat² n Zool pipistrello m

batch /bætʃ/ n gruppo m; (of goods) partita f; (of bread) infornata f

batch file n Comput batch file m inv

batch processing /'prəʊsesɪŋ/ n Comput elaborazione f a gruppi

bated /'beɪtɪd/ adj **with** ∼ **breath** col fiato sospeso

bath /bɑːθ/ **①** n (pl ∼**s** /bɑːðz/) bagno m; (tub) vasca f da bagno; ∼**s** pl piscina f; **have a** ∼ fare un bagno
② vt fare il bagno a
③ vi fare il bagno

bathe /beɪð/ **①** n bagno m
② vi fare il bagno
③ vt lavare ⟨wound⟩

bather /'beɪðə(r)/ n bagnante mf

bathing /'beɪðɪŋ/ n bagni mpl

bathing cap n cuffia f

bathing costume n costume m da bagno

bathing hut n cabina f (al mare)

bathing suit n costume m da bagno

bathing trunks n calzoncini mpl da bagno

bath mat n tappetino m da bagno

bathrobe /'bæθrəʊb/ n accappatoio m

bathroom /'bæθruːm/ n (also: toilet) bagno m

bathroom cabinet n armadietto m del bagno

bathroom fittings npl accessori mpl per il bagno

bathroom scales npl bilancia f pesapersone

bath salts npl sali mpl da bagno

bath-towel n asciugamano m da bagno

bathtub n vasca f da bagno

baton /'bæt(ə)n/ n Mus bacchetta f

baton charge n Br carica f con lo sfollagente

baton round n Br proiettile m di gomma

batsman /'bætsmən/ n Sport battitore m

battalion /bə'tælɪən/ n battaglione m

batten /'bætn/ n assicella f

batter /'bætə(r)/ n Culin pastella f

battered /'bætəd/ adj ⟨car⟩ malandato; ⟨wife, baby⟩ maltrattato

battering /'bæt(ə)rɪŋ/ n **take a** ∼ (from bombs, storm, waves) essere colpito; (from other team) prendersi una batosta; (from other boxer) prenderle

battering ram n ariete m

battery /'bætərɪ/ n batteria f; (of torch, radio) pila f

battery charger n caricabatterie m inv

battery chicken n pollo m di allevamento in batteria

battery controlled adj a pile

battery farming n allevamento m in batteria

battery hen *n* gallina *f* d'allevamento in batteria

battery life *n* autonomia *f*

battery operated, battery powered *adj* a pile

battery pack *n* battery pack *m inv*

battle /'bæt(ə)l/ **1** *n* battaglia *f*; fig lotta *f* **2** *vi* fig lottare

battleaxe *n* fam virago *f inv*

battle cry *n* also fig grido *m* di battaglia

battle dress *n* uniforme *f* da combattimento

battlefield *n*, **battleground** *n* campo *m* di battaglia; fig terreno *m* di scontro

battle lines *npl* Mil schieramenti *mpl*

battlements /'bætlmənts/ *npl* bordo *m* merlato; (crenellations) merlatura *f*

battle order *n* also fig ordine *m* di battaglia

battle-scarred *adj* agguerrito; fig segnato dalla vita

battleship *n* corazzata *f*

batty /'bætɪ/ *adj* fam strampalato

bauble /'bɔ:b(ə)l/ *n* (ornament) gingillo *m*; (jewellery) ninnolo *m*

bawdiness /'bɔ:dɪnɪs/ *n* oscenità *f*

bawdy /'bɔ:dɪ/ *adj* (**-ier**, **-iest**) piccante

bawl /bɔ:l/ *vt/i* urlare
  ∎ **bawl out** *vt* fam urlare ⟨name, order⟩; fare una sfuriata a ⟨somebody⟩

bay[1] /beɪ/ *n* Geog baia *f*

bay[2] *n* keep at ∼ tenere a bada

bay[3] *n* Bot alloro *m*

bay[4] *n* (horse) baio *m*

bay leaf *n* foglia *f* d'alloro

bayonet /'beɪənet/ *n* baionetta *f*

bay window *n* bay window *f inv* (grande finestra sporgente)

bazaar /bə'zɑ:(r)/ *n* bazar *m inv*

bazooka /bə'zu:kə/ *n* bazooka *m inv*

BBC *n abbr* (**British Broadcasting Corporation**) BBC *f*

BBQ *abbr* (**barbecue**) barbecue *m inv*

BC *abbr* (**before Christ**) a.C.

BE *abbr* (**bill of exchange**) cambiale *f*

be /bi:/ **1** *vi* (pres **am, are, is, are**; pt **was, were**; pp **been**) essere; **he is a teacher** è insegnante, fa l'insegnante; **what do you want to be?** cosa vuoi fare?; **be quiet!** sta'zitto!; **I am cold/hot** ho freddo/caldo; **it's cold/hot, isn't it?** fa freddo/caldo, vero?; **how are you?** come stai?; **I am well** sto bene; **there is** c'è; **there are** ci sono; **I have been to Venice** sono stato a Venezia; **has the postman been?** è passato il postino?; **you're coming too, aren't you?** vieni anche tu, no?; **it's yours, is it?** è tuo, vero?; **was John there? – yes, he was** c'era John? – sì; **John wasn't there – yes he was!** John non c'era – sì che c'era!;

three and three are six tre più tre fanno sei; **he is five** ha cinque anni; **that will be £10, please** fanno 10 sterline, per favore; **how much is it?** quanto costa?; **that's £5 you owe me** mi devi 5 sterline
  2 *v aux* **I am coming/reading** sto venendo/leggendo; **I'm staying** (not leaving) resto; **I am being lazy** sono pigro; **I was thinking of you** stavo pensando a te; **you are not to tell him** non devi dirglielo; **you are to do that immediately** devi farlo subito
  3 *passive* essere; **I have been robbed** sono stato derubato

beach /bi:tʃ/ *n* spiaggia *f*

beach ball *n* pallone *m* da spiaggia

beach buggy *n* dune buggy *f inv*

beach-comber /-kəʊmə(r)/ *n* persona *f* che vive rivendendo gli oggetti trovati sulla spiaggia

beachhead *n* testa *f* di sbarco

beach hut *n* cabina *f* [da spiaggia]

beachrobe *n* accappatoio *m*

beachwear *n* abbigliamento *m* da spiaggia

beacon /'bi:k(ə)n/ *n* faro *m*; Naut, Aeron fanale *m*

bead /bi:d/ *n* perlina *f*

beady-eyed /bi:dɪ'aɪd/ *adj* (sharp-eyed) a cui non sfugge niente

beagle /'bi:g(ə)l/ *n* beagle *m inv*, bracchetto *m*

beak /bi:k/ *n* becco *m*

beaker /'bi:kə(r)/ *n* coppa *f*; (in laboratory) becher *m inv*

beam /bi:m/ **1** *n* trave *f*; (of light) raggio *m*
  2 *vi* irradiare; ⟨person⟩ essere raggiante; ∼ **at somebody** fare un gran sorriso a qualcuno

beaming /'bi:mɪŋ/ *adj* raggiante

bean /bi:n/ *n* fagiolo *m*; (of coffee) chicco *m*; **spill the** ∼**s** fam spiattellare tutto

bean bag *n* (seat) poltrona *f* imbottita di pallini di polistirolo

beanfeast *n* fam festa *f*

beanie /'bi:nɪ/ *n* zucchetto *m*

beanpole *n* (fig fam: tall thin person) spilungone, -a *mf*

beansprout *n* germoglio *m* di soia

bear[1] /beə(r)/ *n* orso *m*

bear[2] *v* (pt **bore** pp **borne**) **1** *vt* (endure) sopportare; mettere al mondo ⟨child⟩; (carry) portare; ∼ **in mind** tenere presente; ∼ **fruit** ⟨tree⟩ produrre; fig dare frutto
  2 *vi* ∼ **left/right** andare a sinistra/a destra
  ∎ **bear out** *vt* confermare ⟨story, statement⟩
  ∎ **bear with** *vt* aver pazienza con
  ∎ **bear up** *vi* tirare avanti

bearable /'beərəbl/ *adj* sopportabile

bear cub *n* cucciolo *m* di orso

beard /bɪəd/ *n* barba *f*; **have a** ∼ avere la barba

bearded /'bɪədɪd/ *adj* barbuto

bearer /'beərə(r)/ *n* portatore, -trice *mf*; (of passport) titolare *mf*

bearing /'beərɪŋ/ *n* portamento *m*; Techn cuscinetto *m* [a sfera]; **have a** ∼ **on** avere attinenza con; **get one's** ∼**s** orientarsi; **lose one's** ∼**s** perdere l'orientamento

bear market *n* Fin mercato *m* al ribasso

bearskin *n* (pelt) pelle *f* d'orso; (hat) colbacco *m* militare

beast /bi:st/ *n* bestia *f*; (fam: person) animale *m*

beastly /'bi:stlɪ/ *adj* (**-ier**, **-iest**) fam orribile

beat /bi:t/ ① *n* battito *m*; (rhythm) battuta *f*; (of policeman) giro *m* d'ispezione ② *vt* (pt **beat** pp **beaten**) battere; picchiare ⟨*person*⟩; ∼ **a retreat** Mil battere in ritirata; ∼ **it!** fam darsela a gambe!; **it** ∼**s me why...** fam non capisco proprio perché...

■ **beat back** *vt* respingere ⟨*flames, crowd*⟩

■ **beat down** ① *vt* buttare giù ⟨*door*⟩ ② *vi* ⟨*sun*⟩ battere a picco

■ **beat off** *vt* respingere ⟨*attacker*⟩

■ **beat out** *vt* domare ⟨*flames*⟩

■ **beat up** *vt* picchiare

beaten /'bi:tn/ *adj* off the ∼ **track** fuori mano

beatify /bɪ'ætɪfaɪ/ *vt* beatificare

beating /'bi:tɪŋ/ *n* bastonata *f*; **get a** ∼ (with fists) essere preso a pugni; ⟨*team, player*⟩ prendere una batosta

beating-up *n* fam pestaggio *m*

beat-up *adj* fam ⟨*car*⟩ sfasciato

beau /bəʊ/ *n* liter, hum spasimante *m*

Beaufort scale /'bəʊfət/ *n* scala *f* Beaufort

beautician /bju:'tɪʃn/ *n* estetista *mf*

beautiful /'bju:tɪfl/ *adj* bello; **the** ∼ **people** il bel mondo

beautifully /'bju:tɪfʊlɪ/ *adv* splendidamente

beautify /'bju:tɪfaɪ/ *vt* (pt/pp **-ied**) abbellire

beauty /'bju:tɪ/ *n* bellezza *f*

beauty contest *n* concorso *m* di bellezza

beauty editor *n* redattore, -trice *mf* di articoli di bellezza

beauty parlour *n* istituto *m* di bellezza

beauty queen *n* reginetta *f* di bellezza

beauty salon *n* istituto *m* di bellezza

beauty sleep *n* hum need one's ∼ ∼ aver bisogno delle proprie ore di sonno

beauty spot *n* neo *m*; (place) luogo *m* pittoresco

beaver /'bi:və(r)/ *n* castoro *m*

■ **beaver away** *vi* (fam: work hard) sgobbare

becalmed /bɪ'kɑ:md/ *adj* in bonaccia

became /bɪ'keɪm/ ▶ BECOME

because /bɪ'kɒz/ ① *conj* perché; (at start of sentence) poiché ② *adv* ∼ **of** a causa di

beck /bek/ *n* **be at sb's** ∼ **and call** dover essere a completa disposizione di qualcuno

beckon /'bekn/ *vt/i* ∼ **[to]** chiamare con un cenno

become /bɪ'kʌm/ *v* (pt **became**, pp **become**) ① *vt* diventare ② *vi* diventare; **what has** ∼ **of her?** che ne è di lei?

becoming /bɪ'kʌmɪŋ/ *adj* ⟨*clothes*⟩ bello

bed /bed/ *n* letto *m*; (of sea, lake) fondo *m*; (layer) strato *m*; (of flowers) aiuola *f*; **in** ∼ **a** letto; **go to** ∼ andare a letto

BEd *n abbr* (**bachelor of Education**) ≈ laurea *f* in magistero

bed and board *n* vitto e alloggio *m*

bed and breakfast *n* bed and breakfast *m*

bed base *n* fondo *m* del letto

bed bath *n* **give somebody a** ∼ ∼ lavare qualcuno a letto

bedbug *n* cimice *f*

bedchamber *n* camera *f* da letto

bedclothes *npl* lenzuola e coperte *fpl*

bedding /'bedɪŋ/ *n* biancheria *f* per il letto, materasso e guanciali

bed down *vi* coricarsi

bedeck /bɪ'dek/ *vt* ornare

bedevil /bɪ'devəl/ *vt* tormentare ⟨*person*⟩; intralciare ⟨*plans*⟩

bedfellow *n* **make strange** ∼**s** fig fare una strana coppia

bedhead *n* testata *f* del letto

bed jacket *n* liseuse *f inv*

bedlam /'bedləm/ *n* baraonda *f*

bed linen *n* biancheria *f* per il letto

bedpan /'bedpæn/ *n* padella *f*

bedraggled /bɪ'drægld/ *adj* inzaccherato

bedridden /'bedrɪdən/ *adj* allettato

bedrock /'bedrɒk/ *n* basamento *m*; fig fondamento *m*

bedroom /'bedru:m/ *n* camera *f* da letto

bedroom farce *n* Theat pochade *f inv*

bedroom slipper *n* pantofola *f*

bedroom suburb *n* Am città *f inv* dormitorio

bed-settee *n* divano *m* letto

bedside /'bedsaɪd/ *n* at his ∼ al suo capezzale

bedside lamp *n* abat-jour *m inv*

bedside manner *n* modo *m* di trattare i pazienti; **have a good** ∼ ∼ saperci fare con i pazienti

bedside rug *n* scendiletto *m*

bedside table *n* comodino *m*

bed sit *n*, **bed-sitter** *n*, **bedsitting-room** *n* camera *f* ammobiliata [fornita di cucina]

bedsock *n* calzino *m* da notte

bedsore *n* piaga *f* da decubito

bedspread *n* copriletto *m*

bedstead *n* fusto *m* del letto

bedtime *n* l'ora *f* di andare a letto

bedwetting *n* il bagnare il letto

bee /biː/ *n* ape *f*

beech /biːtʃ/ *n* faggio *m*

beef /biːf/ *n* manzo *m*

beefburger *n* hamburger *m inv*

beefeater *n* guardia *f* della Torre di Londra

beefsteak *n* bistecca *f*

beefsteak tomato *n* grosso pomodoro *m*

beef stew *n* stufato *m* di manzo

beef tea *n* brodo *m* di manzo

beefy /'biːfɪ/ *adj* ⟨flavour⟩ di manzo; fam ⟨man⟩ grande e grosso

beehive /'biːhaɪv/ *n* alveare *m*

bee-keeper *n* apicoltore, -trice *mf*

bee-keeping *n* apicoltura *f*

bee-line *n* make a ∼ for fam precipitarsi verso

been /biːn/ ▸ BE

beep /biːp/ ① *n* (of car) suono *m* di clacson; (of telephone) segnale *m* acustico; (of electronic device, radio) bip *m inv* ② *vi* ⟨car, driver⟩ clacsonare; ⟨device⟩ fare bip ③ *vt* (with beeper) chiamare con il cercapersone; ∼ **the horn** clacsonare

beeper /'biːpə(r)/ *n* cercapersone *m inv*

beer /bɪə(r)/ *n* birra *f*

beer belly *n* pancia *f* da beone

beer bottle *n* bottiglia *f* da birra

beer garden *n* giardino *m* di un pub

beer mat *n* sottobicchiere *m*

beer money *n* fam quattro soldi *mpl*

beerswilling *adj* pej ubriacone

beer tent *n* spazio *m* per incontri con mescita di birra

bee sting *n* puntura *f* d'ape

beeswax /'biːzwæks/ *n* cera *f* d'api

beet /biːt/ *n* (Am: beetroot) barbabietola *f*; [sugar] ∼ barbabietola *f* da zucchero

beetle /'biːtl/ *n* scarafaggio *m*

■ **beetle off** *vi* (fam: hurry away) scappare

beetroot /'biːtruːt/ *n* barbabietola *f*

befall /bɪ'fɔːl/ *vt* liter accadere a

befit /bɪ'fɪt/ *vt* liter addirsi a

befitting /bɪ'fɪtɪŋ/ *adj* ⟨modesty, honesty⟩ opportuno

before /bɪ'fɔː(r)/ ① *prep* prima di; **the day** ∼ **yesterday** ieri l'altro; ∼ **long** fra poco ② *adv* prima; **never** ∼ **have I seen...** non ho mai visto prima... ∼ **that** prima; ∼ **going** prima di andare ③ *conj* (time) prima che; ∼ **you go** prima che tu vada

beforehand /bɪ'fɔːhænd/ *adv* in anticipo

before tax *adj* ⟨profit, income⟩ lordo, al lordo di imposte

befriend /bɪ'frend/ *vt* trattare da amico

befuddle /bɪ'fʌdl/ *vt* confondere ⟨mind⟩

beg /beg/ ① *v* (pt/pp **begged**) *vi* mendicare ② *vt* pregare; chiedere ⟨favour, forgiveness⟩

began /bɪ'gæn/ ▸ BEGIN

beggar /'begə(r)/ *n* mendicante *mf*; **you lucky** ∼! che fortuna sfacciata!; **poor** ∼! povero cristo!; **you little** ∼! monellaccio!

beggarly /'begəlɪ/ *adj* ⟨existence, meal⟩ miserabile; ⟨wage⟩ da fame

begging bowl /'begɪŋ/ *n* ciotola *f* del mendicante

begging letter *n* lettera *f* che sollecita offerte in denaro

begin /bɪ'gɪn/ *vt/i* (pt **began** pp **begun**, pres p **beginning**) cominciare; **well, to** ∼ **with** dunque, per cominciare

beginner /bɪ'gɪnə(r)/ *n* principiante *mf*

beginning /bɪ'gɪnɪŋ/ *n* principio *m*

begonia /bɪ'gəʊnɪə/ *n* begonia *f*

begrudge /bɪ'grʌdʒ/ *vt* (envy) essere invidioso di; dare malvolentieri ⟨money⟩

beguile /bɪ'gaɪl/ *vt* (charm) affascinare; (cheat) ingannare

beguiling /bɪ'gaɪlɪŋ/ *adj* accattivante

begun /bɪ'gʌn/ ▸ BEGIN

behalf /bɪ'hɑːf/ *n* on ∼ of a nome di; on my ∼ a nome mio; say hello on my ∼ salutalo da parte mia

behave /bɪ'heɪv/ *vi* comportarsi; ∼ [oneself] comportarsi bene

behaviour /bɪ'heɪvjə(r)/ *n* comportamento *m*; (of prisoner, soldier) condotta *f*

behavioural /bɪ'heɪvjərəl/ *adj* comportamentale

behaviourist /bɪ'heɪvjərɪst/ *adj & n* comportamentista *mf*

behaviour pattern *n* modello *m* comportamentale

behead /bɪ'hed/ vt decapitare

beheld /bɪ'held/ ▶ BEHOLD

behind /bɪ'haɪnd/ **1** prep dietro; (with pronoun) dietro di; **be ∼ something** fig stare dietro qualcosa
2 adv dietro, indietro; (late) in ritardo; **a long way ∼** molto indietro; **in the car ∼** nella macchina dietro
3 n fam didietro m

behindhand /bɪ'haɪndhænd/ adv indietro

behold /bɪ'həʊld/ vt (pt/pp **beheld**) liter vedere

beholden /bɪ'həʊldn/ adj obbligato (**to** verso)

beholder /bɪ'həʊldə(r)/ n **beauty is in the eye of the ∼** è bello ciò che piace

beige /beɪʒ/ adj & n beige m inv

Beijing /beɪ'dʒɪŋ/ n Pechino f

being /'biːɪŋ/ n essere m; **come into ∼** nascere

Beirut /beɪ'ruːt/ n Beirut f

bejewelled /bɪ'dʒuːəld/ adj ingioiellato

Belarus /belə'ruːs/ n Bielorussia f

belated /bɪ'leɪtɪd/ adj tardivo

belatedly /bɪ'leɪtɪdlɪ/ adv tardi

belch /beltʃ/ **1** vi ruttare
2 vt ∼ [out] eruttare ⟨smoke⟩

beleaguered /bɪ'liːgəd/ adj ⟨city⟩ assediato; ⟨troops⟩ accerchiato; fig ⟨person⟩ tormentato; fig ⟨company⟩ in difficoltà

Belfast /bel'fɑːst/ n Belfast f

belfry /'belfrɪ/ n campanile m

Belgian /'beldʒən/ adj & n belga mf

Belgium /'beldʒəm/ n Belgio m

Belgrade /bel'greɪd/ n Belgrado f

belie /bɪ'laɪ/ vt (give false impression of) dissimulare; (disprove) smentire

belief /bɪ'liːf/ n fede f; (opinion) convinzione f

believable /bɪ'liːvəbl/ adj credibile

believe /bɪ'liːv/ vt/i credere
■ **believe in** vt avere fiducia in ⟨person⟩; credere a ⟨ghosts⟩

believer /bɪ'liːvə(r)/ n Relig credente mf; **be a great ∼ in** credere fermamente in

belittle /bɪ'lɪtl/ vt sminuire ⟨person, achievements⟩

belittling /bɪ'lɪtlɪŋ/ adj ⟨comment⟩ che sminuisce

Belize /be'liːz/ n Belize m

bell /bel/ n campana f; (on door) campanello m; **that rings a ∼** fig mi dice qualcosa

bell-bottoms npl pantaloni mpl a zampa d'elefante

bellboy /'belbɔɪ/ n Am fattorino m d'albergo

belle /bel/ n bella f

bellhop /'belhɒp/ n Am fattorino m d'albergo

belligerence /bɪ'lɪdʒərəns/ n bellicosità f; Pol belligeranza f

belligerent /bɪ'lɪdʒərənt/ adj belligerante; (aggressive) bellicoso

bell-jar n campana f di vetro

bellow /'beləʊ/ vi gridare a squarciagola; ⟨animal⟩ muggire
■ **bellow out** vt urlare ⟨name, order⟩

bellows /'beləʊz/ npl (for fire) soffietto m

bell-pull n (rope) cordone m di campanello

bell-push n pulsante m di campanello

bell-ringer n campanaro m

bell-shaped adj a campana

bell-tower n campanile m

belly /'belɪ/ n pancia f

bellyache /'belɪ/ **1** n fam mal m di pancia
2 vi fam lamentarsi

belly button n fam ombelico m

belly dancer n danzatrice f del ventre

belly flop n (in swimming) spanciata f

bellyful /'belɪfʊl/ n fam **have had a ∼ of something** avere le tasche piene di qualcosa

belong /bɪ'lɒŋ/ vi appartenere (**to** a); (be member) essere socio (**to** di)

belongings /bɪ'lɒŋɪŋz/ npl cose fpl

beloved /bɪ'lʌvɪd/ adj & n amato, -a mf

below /bɪ'ləʊ/ **1** prep sotto; (with numbers) al di sotto di
2 adv sotto, di sotto; Naut sotto coperta; **see ∼** vedi qui di seguito

belt /belt/ **1** n cintura f; (area) zona f; Techn cinghia f
2 vi (fam: rush) ∼ **along** filare velocemente
3 vt (fam: hit) picchiare
■ **belt out** vt cantare a squarciagola ⟨song⟩
■ **belt up** vi (in car) mettersi la cintura [di sicurezza]; ∼ **up!** (sl: be quiet) stai zitto!

bemoan /bɪ'məʊn/ vt lamentare

bemused /bɪ'mjuːzd/ adj confuso

bench /bentʃ/ n panchina f; (work∼) piano m da lavoro; **the B∼** Jur la magistratura

benchmark /'bentʃmɑːk/ n punto m di riferimento; Comput paragone m con un campione; (fin: price) prezzo m di riferimento

bench-test vt Comput testare

bend /bend/ **1** n curva f; (of river) ansa f; **round the ∼** fam fuori di testa
2 vt (pt/pp **bent**) piegare
3 vi piegarsi; ⟨road⟩ curvare; ∼ **[down]** chinarsi
■ **bend over** vi inchinarsi

beneath /bɪ'niːθ/ **1** prep sotto, al di sotto di; **he thinks it's ∼ him** fig pensa che

sia sotto al suo livello; ~ contempt
indegno
2) adv giù

Benedictine /benɪ'dɪkti:n/ adj & n Relig
benedettino m

benediction /benɪ'dɪkʃn/ n Relig
benedizione f

benefactor /'benɪfæktə(r)/ n
benefattore, -trice mf

beneficial /benɪ'fɪʃl/ adj benefico

beneficiary /benɪ'fɪʃərɪ/ n beneficiario,
-a mf

benefit /'benɪfɪt/ **1)** n vantaggio m;
(allowance) indennità f inv
2) vt (pt/pp **-fited**, pres p **-fiting**) giovare
a
3) vi trarre vantaggio (**from** da)

Benelux /'benɪlʌks/ **1)** n Benelux m
2) attrib ⟨countries, organization⟩ del
Benelux

benevolence /bɪ'nevələns/ n
benevolenza f

benevolent /bɪ'nevələnt/ adj benevolo

benevolently /bɪ'nevələntlɪ/ adv con
benevolenza

Bengal /beŋ'gɔ:l/ n Bengala m

benign /bɪ'naɪn/ adj benevolo; Med
benigno

benignly /bɪ'naɪnlɪ/ adv con benevolenza

Benin /be'ni:n/ n Benin m

bent /bent/ **1)** ▶ BEND
2) adj ⟨person⟩ ricurvo; (distorted) curvato;
(fam: dishonest) corrotto; be ~ on doing
something essere ben deciso a fare
qualcosa
3) n predisposizione f

benzene /'benzi:n/ n benzene m

benzine /'benzi:n/ n benzina f

bequeath /bɪ'kwi:ð/ vt lasciare in
eredità

bequest /bɪ'kwest/ n lascito m

berate /bɪ'reɪt/ vt fml redarguire

bereaved /bɪ'ri:vd/ n the ~ pl i
familiari del defunto

bereavement /bɪ'ri:vmənt/ n lutto m

bereft /bɪ'reft/ adj ~ of privo di

beret /'bereɪ/ n berretto m

Berlin /bɜ:'lɪn/ n Berlino f

Berliner /bɜ:'lɪnə(r)/ n berlinese mf

Bermuda /bə'mju:də/ n le Bermuda

Bermuda shorts npl bermuda m inv

Berne /bɜ:n/ n Berna f

berry /'berɪ/ n bacca f

berserk /bə'sɜ:k/ adj go ~ diventare
una belva

berth /bɜ:θ/ **1)** n (bed) cuccetta f;
(anchorage) ormeggio m; give a wide ~ to
fam stare alla larga da
2) vi ormeggiare

beseech /bɪ'si:tʃ/ vt (pt/pp **beseeched**
or **besought**) supplicare

beseeching /bɪ'si:tʃɪŋ/ adj implorante

beset /bɪ'set/ adj a country ~ by strikes
un paese vessato dagli scioperi

beside /bɪ'saɪd/ prep accanto a; ~
oneself fuori di sé

besides /bɪ'saɪdz/ **1)** prep oltre a
2) adv inoltre

besiege /bɪ'si:dʒ/ vt assediare

besotted /bɪ'sɒtɪd/ adj infatuato (with
di)

besought /bɪ'sɔ:t/ ▶ BESEECH

bespatter /bɪ'spætə(r)/ vt schizzare

bespectacled /bɪ'spektək(ə)ld/ adj con
gli occhiali

bespoke /bɪ'spəʊk/ adj ⟨suit⟩ su misura;
⟨tailor⟩ che lavora su ordinazione

best /best/ **1)** adj migliore; the ~ part of
a year la maggior parte dell'anno; ~
before Comm preferibilmente prima di; ~
wishes migliori auguri
2) n the ~ il meglio; (person) il/la
migliore; at ~ tutt'al più; all the ~! tanti
auguri!; do one's ~ fare del proprio
meglio; to the ~ of my knowledge per
quel che ne so; make the ~ of it cogliere il
lato buono della cosa
3) adv meglio, nel modo migliore; as ~ I
could come meglio ho potuto; like ~
preferire

best before date n data f di scadenza

best friend n migliore amico, -a mf

bestial /'bestɪəl/ adj also fig bestiale

bestiality /bestɪ'ælətɪ/ n bestialità f

best man n testimone m

bestow /bɪ'stəʊ/ vt conferire (on a)

best-seller /-'selə(r)/ n bestseller m inv

best-selling /-'selɪŋ/ adj ⟨novelist⟩ più
venduto

bet /bet/ **1)** n scommessa f
2) vt/i (pt/pp **bet** or **betted**)
scommettere

beta blocker /'bi:təblɒkə(r)/ n
betabloccante m

beta-test /'bi:tətest/ vt Comput testare la
versione beta di

Bethlehem /'beθlɪhem/ n Betlemme f

betray /bɪ'treɪ/ vt tradire

betrayal /bɪ'treɪəl/ n tradimento m

betrothal /bɪ'trəʊðl/ n fidanzamento m

betrothed /bɪ'trəʊðd/ n liter, hum
promesso sposo m; promessa sposa f; be
~ essere fidanzato

better /'betə(r)/ **1)** adj migliore, meglio;
get ~ migliorare; (after illness) rimettersi; I
waited the ~ part of a week ho aspettato
buona parte della settimana
2) adv meglio; ~ off meglio; (wealthier) più
ricco; all the ~ tanto meglio; the sooner
the ~ prima è meglio è; I've thought ~ of ⋯⟩

it ci ho ripensato; **you'd** ~ **stay** faresti
meglio a restare; **I'd** ~ **not** è meglio che
non lo faccia
3 *vt* migliorare; ~ **oneself** migliorare le
proprie condizioni

betting /'betɪŋ/ *n* (activity) scommesse *fpl*;
what's the ~ **that...?** quanto
scommettiamo che...?

betting shop *n* ricevitoria *f*
(dell'allibratore)

between /bɪ'twiːn/ **1** *prep* fra, tra; ~
you and me detto fra di noi; ~ **us** (together)
tra me e te
2 *adv* [in] ~ in mezzo; (time) frattempo

betwixt /bɪ'twɪkst/ *adv* be ~ **and**
between essere una via di mezzo

bevel /'bevl/ **1** *n* (edge) spigolo *m*
smussato; (tool) squadra *f* falsa
2 *vt* smussare ⟨*mirror, edge*⟩

beverage /'bevərɪdʒ/ *n* bevanda *f*

bevy /'bevɪ/ *n* frotta *f*

beware /bɪ'weə(r)/ *vi* guardarsi (**of** da);
~ **of the dog!** attenti al cane!

bewilder /bɪ'wɪldə(r)/ *vt* disorientare

bewildered /bɪ'wɪldəd/ *adj* ⟨*look,*
person⟩ perplesso, sconcertato

bewildering /bɪ'wɪldərɪŋ/ *adj*
sconcertante

bewilderment /bɪ'wɪldəmənt/ *n*
perplessità *f*

bewitch /bɪ'wɪtʃ/ *vt* stregare; fig
affascinare completamente

beyond /bɪ'jɒnd/ **1** *prep* oltre; ~ **reach**
irraggiungibile; ~ **doubt** senza alcun
dubbio; ~ **belief** da non credere; **it's** ~ **me**
fam non riesco proprio a capire
2 *adv* più in là

B film *n* film *m inv* di serie B

Bhutan /buː'tɑːn/ *n* Bhutan *m*

bias /'baɪəs/ **1** *n* (preference) preferenza *f*;
pej pregiudizio *m*
2 *vt* (pt/pp **biased**) (influence) influenzare

bias binding, **bias tape** /'baɪndɪŋ/ *n*
(in sewing) fettuccia *f* in sbieco

biased /'baɪəst/ *adj* parziale

bib /bɪb/ *n* bavaglino *m*

Bible /'baɪbl/ *n* Bibbia *f*

Bible Belt *n* zona *f* del sud degli USA,
dove predomina il fondamentalismo
protestante

biblical /'bɪblɪkl/ *adj* biblico

bibliographic[al] /bɪblɪə'græfɪk[l]/ *adj*
bibliografico

bibliography /bɪblɪ'ɒgrəfɪ/ *n*
bibliografia *f*

bicarbonate /baɪ'kɑːbəneɪt/ *n* ~ **of**
soda bicarbonato *m* di sodio

bicentenary /baɪsen'tiːnərɪ/ **1** *n*
bicentenario *m*
2 *attrib* ⟨*celebration, year*⟩ bicentenario

biceps /'baɪseps/ *n* bicipite *m*

bicker /'bɪkə(r)/ *vi* litigare

bickering /'bɪkərɪŋ/ *n* bisticci *mpl*

bicycle /'baɪsɪkl/ **1** *n* bicicletta *f*
2 *vi* andare in bicicletta

bicycle clip *n* molletta *f* (per pantaloni)

bicycle lane *n* pista *f* ciclabile

bicycle rack *n* (in yard) rastrelliera *f* per
biciclette; (on car) portabiciclette *m inv*

bid[1] /bɪd/ **1** *n* offerta *f*; (attempt) tentativo
m
2 *vt/i* (pt/pp **bid**, pres p **bidding**)
offrire; (in cards) dichiarare

bid[2] *vt* (pt **bade** or **bid**, pp **bidden** or
bid, pres p **bidding**) liter (command)
comandare; ~ **somebody welcome** dare il
benvenuto a qualcuno

bidder /'bɪdə(r)/ *n* offerente *mf*

bidding /'bɪdɪŋ/ *n* offerte *fpl* (durante
un'asta)

bide /baɪd/ *vt* ~ **one's time** aspettare il
momento buono

bidet /'biːdeɪ/ *n* bidè *m inv*

biennial /baɪ'enɪəl/ *adj* biennale

bier /bɪə(r)/ *n* catafalco *m*

bifocals /baɪ'fəʊklz/ *npl* occhiali *mpl*
bifocali

big /bɪg/ **1** *adj* (**bigger**, **biggest**) grande;
⟨*brother, sister*⟩ più grande; (fam: generous)
generoso; **make** ~ **money** fare i soldi
2 *adv* **talk** ~ fam spararle grosse

bigamist /'bɪgəmɪst/ *n* bigamo, -a *mf*

bigamous /'bɪgəməs/ *adj* bigamo

bigamy /'bɪgəmɪ/ *n* bigamia *f*

big bang *n* (in astronomy) big bang *m*

big business *n* le grandi imprese; **be** ~
~ essere un grosso affare

big cat *n* grosso felino *m*

big deal *n* fam ~ ~! bella forza!

big dipper *n* (Br: at fair) montagne *fpl*
russe

big game hunting *n* caccia *f* grossa

bighead *n* fam montato, -a *mf*, gasato, -a
mf

big-headed *adj* fam montato, gasato

big-hearted *adj* generoso

bigmouth *n* fam pej chiacchierone, -a *mf*;
he's such a ~! (indiscreet) ha una lingua
lunga!

big name *n* (in film, art) grosso nome *m*

big noise *n* fam pezzo *m* grosso

bigot /'bɪgət/ *n* fanatico, -a *mf*

bigoted /'bɪgətɪd/ *adj* di mentalità
ristretta

bigotry /'bɪgətrɪ/ *n* mentalità *f* ristretta

big screen *n* grande schermo *m*

big shot *n* fam pezzo *m* grosso

Big Smoke *n* Br hum Londra *f*

big time **1** *n* **make** or **hit the** ~ ~ fam
raggiungere il successo

2 *attrib* big-time ‹crook› di alto livello

big toe *n* alluce *m*

big top *n* ‹tent› tendone *m* del circo; (fig: circus) circo *m*

bigwig *n* fam pezzo *m* grosso

bike /baɪk/ **1** *n* fam bici *f inv*
2 *vi* andare in bici
3 *vt* mandare per corriere

biker /'baɪkə(r)/ *n* motociclista *mf*

biker['s] jacket /'baɪkə(z)dʒækɪt/ *n* fam giubbotto *m* di pelle

bikini /bɪ'kiːnɪ/ *n* bikini *m inv*

bilateral /baɪ'lætrəl/ *adj* bilaterale

bilberry /'bɪlbərɪ/ *n* mirtillo *m*

bile /baɪl/ *n* bile *f*

bilge /bɪldʒ/ *n* Naut (place) carena *f*; (substance) sentina *f*; (fam: nonsense) idiozie *fpl*

bilingual /baɪ'lɪŋgwəl/ *adj* bilingue

bilingual secretary *n* segretario, -a *mf* bilingue

bilious /'bɪljəs/ *adj* Med ~ attack attacco *m* di bile

bill¹ /bɪl/ **1** *n* fattura *f*; (In restaurant etc) conto *m*; (poster) manifesto *m*; Pol progetto *m* di legge; (Am: note) biglietto *m* di banca; Theat be top of the ~ essere in testa al cartellone
2 *vt* fatturare

bill² *n* (beak) becco *m*

billboard /'bɪlbɔːd/ *n* cartellone *m* pubblicitario

billet /'bɪlɪt/ **1** *n* Mil alloggio *m*
2 *vt* (pt/pp **billeted**) alloggiare (**on** presso)

billfold *n* Am portafoglio *m*

billiard ball *n* palla *f* da biliardo

billiards /'bɪljədz/ *n* biliardo *m*

billiard table /'bɪljəd/ tavolo *m* da biliardo

billing /'bɪlɪŋ/ *n* Comm fatturazione *f*; **get top** ~ Theat comparire in testa al cartellone

billion /'bɪljən/ *n* (thousand million) miliardo *m*; (old-fashioned Br: million million) mille miliardi *mpl*

billionaire /bɪljə'neə(r)/ *n* miliardario, -a *mf*

bill of exchange *n* cambiale *f*

bill of fare *n* menù *m inv*

bill of rights *n* dichiarazione *f* dei diritti

bill of sale *n* atto *m* di vendita

billow /'bɪləʊ/ **1** *n* (of smoke) nube *f*
2 *vi* alzarsi in volute
■ **billow out** *vi* (skirt, sail) gonfiarsi; (smoke, cloud) levarsi in volute

billposter /'bɪlpəʊstə(r)/ *n* attacchino *m*

billy /'bɪlɪ/ *n* (Am: truncheon) sfollagente *m inv*

billycan /'bɪlɪkæn/ *n* gamella *f*

billy goat *n* caprone *m*

bimbo /'bɪmbəʊ/ *n* pej fam bambolona *f*; **his latest** ~ la sua ultima amichetta

bin /bɪn/ *n* bidone *m*

binary /'baɪnərɪ/ *adj* binario

bin bag *n* sacco *m* per l'immondizia

bind /baɪnd/ *vt* (pt/pp **bound**) legare (**to** a); (bandage) fasciare; Jur obbligare

binder /'baɪndə(r)/ *n* (for papers) raccoglitore *m*; (for cement, paint) agglomerante *m*

binding /'baɪndɪŋ/ **1** *adj* ‹promise, contract› vincolante
2 *n* (of book) rilegatura *f*; (on ski) attacco *m*

binge /bɪndʒ/ **1** *n* fam have a ~ fare baldoria; (eat a lot) abbuffarsi
2 *vi* abbuffarsi (**on** di)

bingo /'bɪŋgəʊ/ *n* ≈ tombola *f*

bin liner *n* Br sacchetto *m* per la spazzatura

binoculars /bɪ'nɒkjʊləz/ *npl* [pair of] ~ binocolo *msg*

biochemist /baɪəʊ'kemɪst/ *n* biochimico, -a *mf*

biochemistry /baɪəʊ'kemɪstrɪ/ *n* biochimica *f*

biodegradable /baɪəʊdɪ'greɪdəbl/ *adj* biodegradabile

biodiversity /baɪəʊdaɪ'vɜːsətɪ/ *n* biodiversità *f*

bioengineering /baɪəʊendʒɪ'nɪərɪŋ/ *n* bioingegneria *f*

biographer /baɪ'ɒgrəfə(r)/ *n* biografo, -a *mf*

biographical /baɪə'græfɪkl/ *adj* biografico

biography /baɪ'ɒgrəfɪ/ *n* biografia *f*

biological /baɪə'lɒdʒɪkl/ *adj* biologico

biological clock *n* orologio *m* biologico

biologically /baɪə'lɒdʒɪklɪ/ *adv* biologicamente

biological powder *n* detersivo *m* biologico

biological warfare *n* guerra *f* biologica

biologist /baɪ'ɒlədʒɪst/ *n* biologo, -a *mf*

biology /baɪ'ɒlədʒɪ/ *n* biologia *f*

bionic /baɪ'ɒnɪk/ *adj* bionico

biopic /'baɪəʊpɪk/ *n* Cin film *m* basato su una biografia

biopsy /'baɪɒpsɪ/ *n* biopsia *f*

biorhythm /'baɪəʊrɪðəm/ *n* bioritmo *m*

biosphere /'baɪəʊsfɪə(r)/ *n* biosfera *f*

biotechnology /baɪəʊtek'nɒlədʒɪ/ *n* biotecnologia *f*

bioterrorism /baɪəʊ'terərɪzm/ *n* bioterrorismo *m*

b

bipartisan /baɪpɑːtɪˈzæn/ adj Pol bipartitico

bipartite /baɪˈpɑːtaɪt/ adj bipartito

birch /bɜːtʃ/ n (tree) betulla f

bird /bɜːd/ n uccello m; (fam: girl) ragazza f; **kill two ~s with one stone** prendere due piccioni con una fava

birdbrain /ˈbɜːdbreɪn/ n fam **he's such a ~** ha un cervello da gallina

bird call n cinguettio m

birdie /ˈbɜːdɪ/ n (in golf) birdie m

birdlike /ˈbɜːdlaɪk/ adj come un uccello

bird of paradise n uccello m del paradiso

bird of prey n [uccello m] rapace m

bird sanctuary n riserva f per uccelli

birdseed n becchime m

bird's eye view n veduta f panoramica dall'alto

bird's nest n nido m di uccello

bird's nest soup n zuppa f di nido di rondine

birdsong n canto m degli uccelli

birdwatcher n persona f che pratica il bird-watching

bird-watching n go ~ fare del bird-watching

Biro® /ˈbaɪrəʊ/ n biro® f inv

birth /bɜːθ/ n nascita f; **give ~** partorire; **give ~ to** partorire

birth certificate n certificato m di nascita

birth-control n controllo m delle nascite

birthday n compleanno m

birthday party n festa f di compleanno

birthing pool n piccola piscina f per il parto

birthmark n voglia f

birth mother n madre f biologica

birthplace n luogo m di nascita

birth-rate n natalità f

birthright n diritto m di nascita

births, marriages, and deaths npl annunci mpl di nascite, di matrimonio, mortuari (sul giornale)

births column n annunci mpl delle nascite (sul giornale)

birth sign n segno m zodiacale

biscuit /ˈbɪskɪt/ n biscotto m

biscuit barrel, biscuit tin n biscottiera f

bisect /baɪˈsekt/ vt dividere in due [parti]

bisexual /baɪˈseksjʊəl/ adj & n bisessuale mf

bishop /ˈbɪʃəp/ n vescovo m; Chess alfiere m

bistro /ˈbiːstrəʊ/ n bistrò m inv

bit[1] /bɪt/ n pezzo m; (smaller) pezzetto m; (for horse) morso m; Comput bit m inv; **a ~ of** un pezzo di ⟨cheese, paper⟩; un po' di ⟨time, rain, silence⟩; **~ by ~** poco a poco; **do one's ~** fare la propria parte

bit[2] ▶ BITE

bitch /bɪtʃ/ n cagna f; sl arpia f

bitchy /ˈbɪtʃɪ/ adj velenoso

bite /baɪt/ ① n morso m; (insect) ~ puntura f; (mouthful) boccone m ② vt (pt **bit**, pp **bitten**) mordere; ⟨insect⟩ pungere; **~ one's nails** mangiarsi le unghie ③ vi mordere; ⟨insect⟩ pungere ■ **bite off** vt staccare (con un morso)

biting /ˈbaɪtɪŋ/ adj ⟨wind, criticism⟩ pungente; ⟨remark⟩ mordace

bit part n Theat particina f

bitter /ˈbɪtə(r)/ ① adj amaro ② n Br birra f amara

bitter almond n mandorla f amara

bitter lemon n limonata f amara

bitterly /ˈbɪtəlɪ/ adv amaramente; **it's ~ cold** c'è un freddo pungente

bitterness /ˈbɪtənɪs/ n amarezza f

bittersweet /bɪtəˈswiːt/ adj liter agrodolce

bitty /ˈbɪtɪ/ adj Br fam frammentario

bitumen /ˈbɪtjʊmɪn/ n bitume m

bivouac /ˈbɪvʊæk/ ① n bivacco m ② vi bivaccare

bizarre /bɪˈzɑː(r)/ adj bizzarro

blab /blæb/ vi (pt/pp **blabbed**) cianciare

black /blæk/ ① adj nero; **be ~ and blue** essere coperto di lividi ② n nero m ③ vt boicottare ⟨goods⟩ ■ **black out** ① vt cancellare ② vi (lose consciousness) perdere coscienza

Black Africa n Africa f nera

Black American n negro, -a americano, -a mf

black and white n bianco e nero

blackball vt dare voto contrario a

black belt n cintura f nera

blackberry n mora f

blackberry bush n rovo m

blackbird n merlo m

blackboard n Sch lavagna f

black box n Aeron scatola f nera

black bread n pane m nero

blackcurrant n ribes m inv nero

blacken /ˈblækən/ vt annerire

black eye n occhio m nero

Black Forest gateau n dolce m a base di cioccolato, panna e ciliegie

black gold n fam oro m nero

blackguard /ˈblægəd/ n hum brigante m

blackhead n Med punto m nero

black-headed gull *n* gabbiano *m* comune

black humour umorismo *m* nero

black ice *n* ghiaccio *m* (sulla strada)

blacking /'blækɪŋ/ (Br: boycotting) boicottaggio *m*; (polish) lucido *m* nero (per scarpe)

blackish /'blækɪʃ/ *adj* nerastro

blackjack *n* blackjack *m*

blackleg *n* Br crumiro *m*

blacklist *vt* mettere sulla lista nera

blackmail *n* ricatto *m vt* ricattare

blackmailer *n* ricattatore, -trice *mf*

black mark *n* fig neo *m*

black market *n* borsa *f* nera

black marketeer *n* borsanerista *mf*

black mass *n* messa *f* nera

blackness /'blæknɪs/ *n* nero *m*; (evilness) cattiveria *f*; (of moods) scontrosità *f*

black-out *n* blackout *m inv*; **have a ~** Med perdere coscienza

black pepper *n* pepe *m* nero

black pudding *n* ≈ sanguinaccio *m*

Black Sea *n* Mar *m* Nero

black sheep *n* fig pecora *f* nera

Blackshirt *n* camicia *f* nera

blacksmith *n* fabbro *m*

black spot *n* fig luogo *m* conosciuto per gli incidenti stradali

black swan *n* cigno *m* nero

black tie *n* (on invitation) abito scuro

black widow [spider] *n* vedova *f* nera

bladder /'blædə(r)/ *n* Anat vescica *f*

blade /bleɪd/ *n* lama *f*; (of grass) filo *m*

blame /bleɪm/ ① *n* colpa *f*
② *vt* dare la colpa a; **~ somebody for doing something** dare la colpa a qualcuno per aver fatto qualcosa; **no one is to ~** non è colpa di nessuno

blameless /'bleɪmlɪs/ *adj* innocente

blameworthy /'bleɪmwɜ:ðɪ/ *adj* biasimevole

blanch /blɑ:ntʃ/ ① *vi* sbiancare
② *vt* Culin sbollentare

blancmange /blə'mɒnʒ/ *n* biancomangiare *m*

bland /blænd/ *adj* ⟨food⟩ insipido; ⟨person⟩ insulso

blandly /'blændlɪ/ *adv* ⟨say⟩ in modo piatto

blank /blæŋk/ ① *adj* bianco; ⟨look⟩ vuoto
② *n* spazio *m* vuoto; ⟨cartridge⟩ cartuccia *f* a salve
③ *vt* ignorare; **she completely ~ed me** mi ha completamente ignorato
■ **blank out** *vt* cancellare dalla memoria ⟨memory⟩

blank cheque *n* assegno *m* in bianco

blanket /'blæŋkɪt/ *n* coperta *f*; **wet ~** fam guastafeste *mf inv*

blanket box, **blanket chest** *n* Br cassapanca *f*

blanket cover *n* (in insurance) assicurazione *f* che copre tutti i rischi

blanket stitch *n* punto *m* di rinforzo

blankly /'blæŋklɪ/ *adv* (uncomprehendingly) con espressione attonita; (without expression) senza espressione

blank verse *n* versi *mpl* sciolti

blare /bleə(r)/ *vi* suonare a tutto volume
■ **blare out** *vt* strombazzare rumorosamente

blarney /'blɑ:nɪ/ *n* fam lusinga *f*

blasé /'blɑ:zeɪ/ *adj* blasé *inv*

blaspheme /blæs'fi:m/ *vi* bestemmiare

blasphemous /'blæsfəməs/ *adj* blasfemo

blasphemy /'blæsfəmɪ/ *n* bestemmia *f*

blast /blɑ:st/ ① *n* (gust) raffica *f*; (sound) scoppio *m*
② *vt* (with explosive) far saltare
③ *int* sl maledizione!
■ **blast off** *vi* ⟨rocket⟩ decollare

blasted /'blɑ:stɪd/ *adj* sl maledetto

blast furnace *n* altoforno *m*

blasting /'blɑ:stɪŋ/ *n* brillamento *m*

blast-off *n* (of missile) lancio *m*

blatant /'bleɪtənt/ *adj* sfacciato

blatantly /'bleɪtəntlɪ/ *adv* ⟨copy, disregard⟩ sfacciatamente; **it's ~ obvious** è lampante

blather /'blæðə(r)/ *vi* fam blaterare

blaze /bleɪz/ ① *n* incendio *m*; **a ~ of colour** un'esplosione *f* di colori
② *vi* ardere
■ **blaze down** *vi* ⟨sun⟩ essere cocente

blazer /'bleɪzə(r)/ *n* blazer *m inv*

blazing *adj* ⟨row⟩ acceso; ⟨fire⟩ violento; ⟨building⟩ in fiamme

bleach /bli:tʃ/ ① *n* decolorante *m*: (for cleaning) candeggina *f*, varecchina *f*
② *vt* sbiancare; ossigenare ⟨hair⟩

bleak /bli:k/ *adj* desolato; fig ⟨prospects, future⟩ tetro

bleakly /'bli:klɪ/ *adv* ⟨stare, say⟩ in modo tetro

bleakness /'bli:knɪs/ *n* (of weather) tetraggine *f*; (of surroundings, future) desolazione *f*

bleary-eyed /blɪərɪ'aɪd/ *adj* **be ~** avere gli occhi gonfi

bleat /bli:t/ ① *vi* belare
② *n* belato *m*

bleed /bli:d/ ① *v* (pt/pp **bled**) *vi* sanguinare
② *vt* spurgare ⟨brakes, radiator⟩

bleeding /'bli:dɪŋ/ **1** n perdita di sangue f; (heavy) emorragia f; (deliberate) salasso m
2 adj ‹wound, hand› sanguinante; sl = BLOODY

bleeding heart n fig pej cuore m troppo tenero

bleep /bli:p/ **1** n bip m
2 vi suonare
3 vt chiamare col cercapersone

bleeper /'bli:pə(r)/ n cercapersone m inv

blemish /'blemɪʃ/ n macchia f

blend /blend/ **1** n (of tea, coffee, whisky) miscela f; (of colours) insieme m
2 vt mescolare
3 vi ‹colours, sounds› fondersi (with con)
■ **blend in 1** vi ‹person› passare inosservato; ∼ **in with** mescolarsi con
2 vt ∼ **something in** mescolare qualcosa

blender /'blendə(r)/ n Culin frullatore m

blending /'blendɪŋ/ n (of coffees, whiskies) miscela f

bless /bles/ vt benedire

blessed /'blesɪd/ adj also sl benedetto

blessing /'blesɪŋ/ n benedizione f

blew /blu:/ ▶ BLOW²

blight /blaɪt/ **1** n Bot ruggine f
2 vt far avvizzire ‹plants›

blighter /'blaɪtə(r)/ (Br fam: annoying person) idiota mf; **you lucky** ∼ hai una fortuna sfacciata!; **poor** ∼ povero diavolo m

blimey /'blaɪmɪ/ int Br fam accidenti!

blind /blaɪnd/ **1** adj cieco; ∼ **man/woman** cieco/cieca
2 npl the ∼ i ciechi
3 vt accecare
4 n [roller] ∼ avvolgibile m; [Venetian] ∼ veneziana f

blind alley n vicolo m cieco

blind date n appuntamento m galante con una persona sconosciuta

blind drunk adj ubriaco fradicio

blindfold **1** adv con gli occhi bendati
2 adj be ∼ avere gli occhi bendati
3 n benda f
4 vt bendare gli occhi a

blinding /'blaɪndɪŋ/ adj ‹light› accecante; ‹headache› da impazzire, tremendo

blindingly /'blaɪndɪŋlɪ/ adv ‹shine› in modo accecante; **be** ∼ **obvious** essere così lampante

blindly /'blaɪndlɪ/ adv ciecamente

blind-man's buff n moscacieca f

blindness /'blaɪndnɪs/ n cecità f

blind spot n (in car, on hill) punto m privo di visibilità; (in eye) punto m cieco; (fig: point of ignorance) punto m debole

blind trust n blind trust m

blink /blɪŋk/ vi sbattere le palpebre; ‹light› tremolare

blinkered /'blɪŋkəd/ adj ‹attitude, approach› ottuso; **be** ∼ avere i paraocchi

blinkers /'blɪŋkəz/ npl paraocchi mpl

blinking /'blɪŋkɪŋ/ n (of light) intermittenza f; (of eye) battere m

blip /blɪp/ n (on screen) segnale m luminoso a intermittenza; (on graph, line) piccola irregolarità f; (sound) ticchettio m; (hitch) intoppo m

bliss /blɪs/ n Rel beatitudine f; (happiness) felicità f

blissful /'blɪsfʊl/ adj beato; (happy) meraviglioso

blissfully /'blɪsfəlɪ/ adv beatamente; ∼ **ignorant** beatamente ignaro

blister /'blɪstə(r)/ **1** n Med vescica f; (in paint) bolla f
2 vi ‹paint› formare una bolla/delle bolle

blistering /'blɪst(ə)rɪŋ/ **1** n (of skin) vescica f; (of paint) bolle fpl
2 adj ‹sun› scottante; ‹heat› soffocante; ‹attack, criticism› feroce

blister pack n blister m inv

blithe /blaɪð/ adj (cheerful) gioioso; (nonchalant) spensierato

blithely /'blaɪðlɪ/ adv (nonchalantly) spensieratamente

blitz /blɪts/ n bombardamento m aereo; **have a** ∼ **on something** fig darci sotto con qualcosa

blitzkrieg /'blɪtskri:g/ n guerra f lampo

blizzard /'blɪzəd/ n tormenta f

bloated /'bləʊtɪd/ adj gonfio

blob /blɒb/ n goccia f

bloc /blɒk/ n Pol blocco m

block /blɒk/ **1** n blocco m; (building) isolato m; (building ∼) cubo m (per giochi di costruzione); ∼ **of flats** palazzo m
2 vt bloccare
■ **block out** vt coprire ‹light, sun›
■ **block up** vt bloccare

blockade /blɒ'keɪd/ **1** n blocco m
2 vt bloccare

blockage /'blɒkɪdʒ/ n ostruzione f

block and tackle n paranco m

block book vt prenotare in blocco

block booking n prenotazione f in blocco

block-buster n (fam: book, film) successone m; Mil bomba f potente

block capital n in ∼ s in stampatello

blockhead n fam testone, -a mf

blockhouse n Mil fortino m

block letters npl stampatello m

block vote n voto m per delega

block voting n votazione f per delega

blog /blɒg/ n Comput blog m

blogger /'blɒgə(r)/ n Comput blogger m

bloke /bləʊk/ n fam tizio m

blonde /blɒnd/ **1** adj biondo

② *n* bionda *f*

blood /blʌd/ *n* sangue *m*

blood-and-thunder *adj* ‹novel, film› pieno di sangue

blood bank *n* banca *f* del sangue

blood bath *n* bagno *m* di sangue

blood blister *n* vescica *f* di sangue

blood brother *n* fratello *m* di sangue

blood cell, blood corpuscle *n* globulo *m*

blood count *n* esame *m* emocromocitometrico

blood-curdling *adj* raccapricciante

blood donor *n* donatore, -trice *mf* di sangue

blood group *n* gruppo *m* sanguigno

bloodhound *n* segugio *m*

bloodless /'blʌdlɪs/ *adj* (pale) esangue; (revolution, coup) senza spargimento di sangue

blood-letting *n* Med salasso *m*; (killing) spargimento *m* di sangue

blood lust *n* sete *f* di sangue

blood money *n* compenso versato ad un killer o delatore

blood orange *n* arancia *f* sanguigna

blood poisoning *n* setticemia *f*

blood pressure *n* pressione *f* del sangue

blood-red *adj* rosso sangue *inv*

blood relative *n* parente *mf* consanguineo, -a

bloodshed *n* spargimento *m* di sangue

bloodshot *adj* iniettato di sangue

blood sports *npl* sport *mpl* cruenti

bloodstained *adj* macchiato di sangue

bloodstream *n* sangue *m*

bloodsucker *n* also fig sanguisuga *f*

blood test *n* analisi *f inv* del sangue

bloodthirsty *adj* assetato di sangue

blood transfusion *n* trasfusione *f* del sangue

blood type *n* gruppo *m* sanguigno

blood vessel *n* vaso *m* sanguigno

bloody /'blʌdɪ/ **①** *adj* (-ier, -iest) insanguinato; sl maledetto
② *adv* sl ~ **easy/difficult** facile/difficile da matti; ~ **tired/funny** stanco/divertente da morire; **you** ~ **well will!** e, accidenti, lo farai!

bloody-minded /blʌdɪ'maɪndɪd/ *adj* scorbutico

bloom /bluːm/ **①** *n* fiore *m*; **in** ~ (of flower) sbocciato; (of tree) in fiore
② *vi* fiorire; fig essere in forma smagliante

bloomer /'bluːmə(r)/ *n* fam papera *f*

bloomers /'bluːməz/ *npl* mutandoni *mpl* da donna

blooming /'bluːmɪŋ/ *adj* fam maledetto

blossom /'blɒsəm/ **①** *n* fiori *mpl* (d'albero); (single one) fiore *m*
② *vi* sbocciare
■ **blossom out** *vi* fig trasformarsi

blot /blɒt/ *n* also fig macchia *f*
■ **blot out** *vt* (pt/pp **blotted**) fig cancellare

blotch /blɒtʃ/ *n* macchia *f*

blotchy /'blɒtʃɪ/ *adj* chiazzato

blotter /'blɒtə(r)/ *n* tampone *m* di carta assorbente; (Am: police) registro *m* di polizia

blotting paper /'blɒtɪŋ/ *n* carta *f* assorbente

blotto /'blɒtəʊ/ *adj* fam ubriaco fradicio

blouse /blaʊz/ *n* camicetta *f*

blow¹ /bləʊ/ *n* colpo *m*

blow² *v* (pt **blew**, pp **blown**) **①** *vi* ‹wind› soffiare; ‹fuse› saltare
② *vt* (fam: squander) sperperare; ~ **one's nose** soffiarsi il naso; ~ **one's top** fam andare in bestia
■ **blow away** **①** *vt* far volar via ‹papers›
② *vt* ‹papers› volare via
■ **blow down** **①** *vt* abbattere
② *vi* abbattersi al suolo
■ **blow off** **①** *vt* ‹wind› portar via
② *vi* ‹hat, roof› volare via
■ **blow out** **①** *vt* (extinguish) soffiare
② *vi* ‹candle› spegnersi
■ **blow over** **①** *vt* ‹wind› buttare giù
② *vi* ‹storm› passare; fig ‹fuss, trouble› dissiparsi
■ **blow up** **①** *vt* (inflate) gonfiare; (enlarge) ingrandire ‹photograph›; (shatter by explosion) far esplodere
② *vi* esplodere

blow-by-blow *adj* ‹account› particolareggiato

blow-dry *vt* asciugare con l'asciugacapelli

blowfly *n* moscone *m* (della carne)

blowhole *n* (of whale) sfiatatoio *m*

blowlamp *n* fiamma *f* ossidrica

blown /bləʊn/ ▶ BLOW²

blowout *n* Elec corto circuito *m*; (in oil or gas well) fuga *f*; (of tyre) scoppio *m*; (fam: meal) abbuffata *f*

blowpipe *n* cerbottana *f*

blowtorch *n* cannello *m* ossidrico

blow-up **①** *n* Phot ingrandimento *m*
② *adj* ‹doll, toy, dinghy› gonfiabile

blowy /'bləʊɪ/ *adj* ventoso

blowzy /'blaʊzɪ/ *adj* pej ‹woman› volgarmente appariscente

BLT *n abbr* (**bacon, lettuce, and tomato**) sandwich *m* con bacon, lattuga e pomodoro

blubber /'blʌbə(r)/ **①** *n* (of whale) grasso *m* di balena; (fam: of person) ciccia *f*
② *vi* fam piagnucolare

bludgeon /'blʌdʒən/ *vt* manganellare

blue /blu:/ ① *adj* (pale) celeste; (navy) blu *inv*; (royal) azzurro; **feel** ~ essere giù di corda; ~ **with cold** livido per il freddo; **once in a** ~ **moon** una volta ogni morte di papa
② *n* blu *m inv*; **the** ~**s** Music il blues; **have the** ~**s** essere giù di corda; **out of the** ~ inaspettatamente; **a bolt from the** ~ un fulmine a ciel sereno

bluebell *n* giacinto *m* di bosco

Blue Berets *npl* Mil Caschi blu *mpl*

blueberry *n* mirtillo *m*

blue blood *n* sangue *m* blu

blue-blooded *adj* di sangue blu

bluebottle *n* moscone *m*

blue cheese *n* formaggio *m* erborinato

blue chip *adj* ‹company› di altissimo livello; ‹investment› sicuro

blue-collar job *n* lavoro *m* manuale

blue-collar worker *n* operaio *m*

blue-eyed *adj* con gli occhi azzurri

blue-eyed boy *n* Br fig fam prediletto *m*

blue film *n* film *m* a luci rosse

blue jeans *npl* blue jeans *mpl inv*

blue light *n* (on emergency vehicles) luce *f* delle auto della polizia

blueness /'blu:nɪs/ *n* azzurro *m*

blue pencil *n* go through something with the ~ ~ (censor) censurare qualcosa; (edit) fare una revisione di qualcosa

blueprint *n* fig progetto *m*

blue rinse *n* she's had a ~ ~ si è tinta i capelli color grigio argentato

blue-stocking *n* pej [donna] intellettualoide *f*

blue tit *n* cinciarella *f*

Bluetooth® *n* Bluetooth® *m*

blue whale *n* balenottera *f* azzurra

bluff /blʌf/ ① *n* bluff *m inv*
② *vi* bluffare

bluish /'blu:ɪʃ/ *adj* bluastro, azzurrognolo

blunder /'blʌndə(r)/ ① *n* gaffe *f inv*
② *vi* fare una/delle gaffe

blundering /'blʌnd(ə)rɪŋ/ *adj* ~ idiot rimbecillito *m*

blunt /blʌnt/ *adj* spuntato; ‹person› reciso

bluntly /'blʌntlɪ/ *adv* schiettamente

bluntness /'blʌntnɪs/ *n* (of manner) rudezza *f*; (of person) brutale schiettezza *f*

blur /blɜ:(r)/ ① *n* It's all a ~ fig è tutto confuso
② *vt* (pt/pp **blurred**) rendere confuso

blurb /blɜ:b/ *n* soffietto *m* editoriale

blurred /blɜ:d/ *adj* ‹vision, photo› sfocato

blurt /blɜ:t/ *v*
■ **blurt out** *vt* spifferare

blush /blʌʃ/ ① *n* rossore *m*

② *vi* arrossire

blusher /'blʌʃə(r)/ *n* fard *m inv*

bluster /'blʌstə(r)/ *n* (showing off) sbruffonata *f*

blustering /'blʌst(ə)rɪŋ/ ① *n* (rage) sfuriata *f*; (boasting) spacconata *f*
② *adj* (angry) infuriato; (boastful) sbruffone

blustery /'blʌst(ə)rɪ/ *adj* ‹wind› furioso; ‹day, weather› molto ventoso

blu-tak® /'blu:tæk/ *n* blu-tak® *m*

B movie *n* film *m inv* di serie B

BO *n* fam puzza *f* di sudore

boa /'bəʊə/ *n* boa *m inv*

boa constrictor /kən'strɪktə(r)/ boa *m inv*

boar /bɔ:(r)/ *n* cinghiale *m*

board /bɔ:d/ ① *n* tavola *f*; (for notices) tabellone *m*; (committee) assemblea *f*; ~ **(of directors)** consiglio *m* (di amministrazione); **full** ~ Br pensione *f* completa; **half** ~ Br mezza pensione *f*; ~ **and lodging** vitto e alloggio *m*; **go by the** ~ fam andare a monte
② *vt* Naut, Aeron salire a bordo di
③ *vi* ‹passengers› salire a bordo; ~ **with** stare a pensione da
■ **board up** *vt* sbarrare con delle assi

boarder /'bɔ:də(r)/ *n* pensionante *mf*; Sch convittore, -trice *mf*

board game *n* gioco *m* da tavolo

boarding /'bɔ:dɪŋ/ *n* Aeron, Naut imbarco *m*; (by customs officer) ispezione *f*; Mil abbordaggio *m*

boarding card *n* carta *f* di imbarco

boarding house *n* pensione *f*

boarding party *n* squadra *f* d'ispezione

boarding school *n* collegio *m*

board meeting *n* riunione *f* del consiglio di amministrazione

boardroom *n* sala *f* consiglio, sala *f* riunioni del consiglio di amministrazione

boardwalk *n* Am (by sea) lungomare *m*

boast /bəʊst/ ① *vi* vantarsi **(about** di)
② *vt* vantare

boaster /'bəʊstə(r)/ *n* sbruffone, -a *mf*

boastful /'bəʊstfʊl/ *adj* vanaglorioso

boat /bəʊt/ *n* barca *f*; (ship) nave *f*

boater /'bəʊtə(r)/ *n* (hat) paglietta *f*

boat-hook *n* gaffa *f*

boathouse /'bəʊthaʊs/ *n* rimessa *f* [per imbarcazioni]

boating /'bəʊtɪŋ/ ① *n* canottaggio *m*
② *adj* ‹accident› di navigazione

boating trip *n* traversata *f* per mare

boatload *n* carico *m*; ~**s of tourists** navi *fpl* cariche di turisti

boatswain /'bəʊs(ə)n/ *n* nostromo *m*

boatyard *n* cantiere *m* per imbarcazioni

bob /bɒb/ ① *n* (hairstyle) caschetto *m*

2 *vi* (pt/pp **bobbed**) (also ~ **up and down**) andare su e giù

bobbin /'bɒbɪn/ *n* bobina *f*

bobble hat /'bɒblhæt/ *n* berretto *m* a pompon

bobby /'bɒbɪ/ *n* Br fam poliziotto *m*

bobcat /'bɒbkæt/ *n* lince *f*

bobsleigh /'bɒbsleɪ/, **bobsled** /'bɒbsled/ **1** *n* bob *m inv* **2** *vi* andare sul bob

bode /bəʊd/ *vi* ~ **well/ill** essere di buono/cattivo augurio

bodge /bɒdʒ/ Br = BOTCH

bodice /'bɒdɪs/ *n* corpetto *m*

bodily /'bɒdɪlɪ/ **1** *adj* fisico **2** *adv* (forcibly) fisicamente

body /'bɒdɪ/ *n* corpo *m*; (organization) ente *m*; (amount: of poems etc) quantità *f*; **over my dead** ~! fam devi passare prima sul mio corpo!

body blow *n* deal a ~ ~ **to** fig assestare un duro colpo a

bodyboarding *n* bodyboarding *m inv*

bodybuilder *n* culturista *mf*

body-building *n* culturismo *m*

bodyguard *n* guardia *f* del corpo

body heat *n* calore *m* del corpo

body language *n* linguaggio *m* del corpo

body odour *n* fam puzza *f* di sudore

body piercing *n* piercing *m inv*

body politic *n* corpo *m* sociale

body shop *n* autocarrozzeria *f*

body snatching *n* furto *m* dei cadaveri

body stocking, **body suit** *n* body *m inv*

body warmer *n* gilet *m inv* imbottito

bodywork *n* Auto carrozzeria *f*

boffin /'bɒfɪn/ *n* Br fam scienziato *m*

bog /bɒg/ *n* palude *f*
■ **bog down** *vt* (pt/pp **bogged**) get ~**ged down** impantanarsi

bogey /'bəʊgɪ/ *n* (evil spirit) spirito *m* malvagio; (to frighten people) spauracchio *m*

boggle /'bɒg(ə)l/ *vi* **the mind** ~**s** non posso neanche immaginarlo

boggy /'bɒgɪ/ *adj* (swampy) paludoso; (muddy) fangoso

bog-standard *adj* fam ordinario

bogus /'bəʊgəs/ *adj* falso

bohemian /bəʊ'hi:mɪən/ *adj* ‹lifestyle, person› bohémien

boil¹ /bɔɪl/ *n* Med foruncolo *m*

boil² **1** *n* **bring/come to the** ~ portare/arrivare ad ebollizione **2** *vi* [far] bollire **3** *vi* bollire; (fig: with anger) ribollire; **the water** or **kettle's** ~**ing** l'acqua bolle

■ **boil away** *vi* ‹water› evaporare
■ **boil down to** *vi* fig ridursi a
■ **boil over** *vi* straboccare (bollendo)
■ **boil up** *vt* far bollire

boiler /'bɔɪlə(r)/ *n* caldaia *f*

boiler house *n* caldaia *f*

boiler room *n* locale *m* per la caldaia

boiler suit *n* tuta *f*

boiling /'bɔɪlɪŋ/ *adj* ‹water› bollente; **it's** ~ **in here!** qui si bolle!

boiling hot *adj* fam ‹liquid› bollente; ‹day› torrido

boiling point *n* punto *m* di ebollizione

boisterous /'bɔɪstərəs/ *adj* chiassoso

bold /bəʊld/ **1** *adj* audace **2** *n* Typ neretto *m*

boldly /'bəʊldlɪ/ *adv* audacemente

boldness /'bəʊldnɪs/ *n* audacia *f*

Bolivia /bə'lɪvɪə/ *n* Bolivia *f*

bollard /'bɒlɑːd/ *n* colonnina *m* di sbarramento al traffico

Bolognese /bɒlə'neɪz/ *n* ragù *m*

boloney /bə'ləʊnɪ/ *n* fam idiozie *fpl*

bolshy /'bɒlʃɪ/ *adj* Br fam (on one occasion) brontolone; **he's/she's** ~ (by temperament) è un/una piantagrane; **get** ~ fare [delle] storie

bolster /'bəʊlstə(r)/ **1** *n* cuscino *m* (cilindrico) **2** *vt* ~ **[up]** sostenere

bolt /bəʊlt/ **1** *n* (for door) catenaccio *m*; (for fixing) bullone *m* **2** *vt* fissare [con bulloni] (**to** a); chiudere col chiavistello ‹door›; ingurgitare ‹food› **3** *vt* svignarsela; ‹horse› scappar via **4** *adv* ~ **upright** diritto come un fuso

bolt-hole *n* Br rifugio *m*

bomb /bɒm/ **1** *n* bomba *f* **2** *vt* bombardare
■ **bomb along** *vi* (fam: move quickly) sfrecciare

bombard /bɒm'bɑːd/ *vt* also fig bombardare

bombardment /bɒm'bɑːdmənt/ *n* bombardamento *m*

bombastic /bɒm'bæstɪk/ *adj* ampolloso

bomb attack *n* bombardamento *m*

bomb blast *n* esplosione *f*

bomb disposal *n* disinnesco *m*

bomb disposal expert *n* artificiere *m*

bomb disposal squad *n* squadra *f* artificieri

bomber /'bɒmə(r)/ *n* Aviat bombardiere *m*; (person) dinamitardo *m*

bomber jacket *n* bomber *m inv*

bombing /'bɒmɪŋ/ *n* Mil bombardamento *m*; (by terrorists) attentato *m* dinamitardo

bombproof *adj* a prova di bomba

bombscare n stato m di allarme per la presunta presenza di una bomba

bombshell n (fig: news) bomba f; **blonde** ∼ bionda f esplosiva

bomb shelter n rifugio m antiaereo

bombsite n zona f bombardata; (fig: mess) campo f di battaglia

Bomb Squad n squadra f artificieri

bona fide /bəʊnə'faɪdɪ/ adj ‹member, refugee› autentico; ‹attempt› genuino; ‹offer› serio

bonanza /bə'nænzə/ n (windfall) momento m di prosperità; (in mining) filone m d'oro/ d'argento

bond /bɒnd/ ① n fig legame m; Comm obbligazione f
② vt ‹glue› attaccare

bondage /'bɒndɪdʒ/ n schiavitù f

bonded warehouse /'bɒndɪd/ n magazzino m doganale

bonding /'bɒndɪŋ/ n (between mother and baby) legame m madre-figlio; **male** ∼ solidarietà f maschile

bone /bəʊn/ ① n osso m; (of fish) spina f
② vt disossare ‹meat›; togliere le spine da ‹fish›

bone china n porcellana f fine

boned /bəʊnd/ adj ‹joint, leg, chicken› disossato; ‹fish› senza lische; ‹corset, bodice› con le stecche

bone-dry adj secco

bonehead n fam cretino, -a mf

bone idle adj fam fannullone

boneless /'bəʊnlɪs/ adj ‹chicken› disossato; ‹chicken breast› senz'osso; ‹fish› senza lische

bone marrow n midollo m osseo

bone-marrow transplant n trapianto m di midollo osseo

bonemeal n farina f d'ossa

bonfire /'bɒnfaɪə(r)/ n falò m inv

Bonfire Night n Br sera f del 5 novembre festeggiata con falò e fuochi d'artificio

bonk /bɒŋk/ vt sl scopare

bonkers /'bɒŋkəz/ adj fam suonato

bonnet /'bɒnɪt/ n cuffia f; (of car) cofano m

bonus /'bəʊnəs/ n (individual) gratifica f; (production ∼) premio m; (life insurance) dividendo m; **a** ∼ fig qualcosa in più

bonus point n five ∼ ∼s un bonus di cinque punti

bony /'bəʊnɪ/ adj (-ier, -iest) ossuto; ‹fish› pieno di spine

boo /buː/ ① interj (to surprise or frighten) bu! ② vt/i fischiare

boob /buːb/ ① n (fam: mistake) gaffe f inv; (breast) tetta f
② vi fam fare una gaffe

booboo /'buːbuː/ n fam gaffe f inv

booby prize /'buːbɪ/ n premio m di consolazione per il peggior contendente

booby trap ① n Mil ordigno m che esplode al contatto; (joke) trabocchetto m
② vt Mil mettere un ordigno esplosivo in

boogie /'buːgɪ/ n fam boogie m

booing /'buːɪŋ/ n fischi mpl

book /bʊk/ ① n libro m; (of tickets) blocchetto m; **keep the** ∼s Comm tenere la contabilità; **be in sb's bad/good** ∼s essere nel libro nero/nelle grazie di qualcuno; **do something by the** ∼ seguire strettamente le regole
② vt (reserve) prenotare; (for offence) multare
③ vi (reserve) prenotare

bookable /'bʊkəbl/ adj ‹event, ticket› che si può prenotare; ‹offence› che può essere multato

bookbinder n rilegatore, -trice mf

bookbinding n rilegatura f

bookcase n libreria f

book club n club m inv del libro

book-ends npl reggilibri mpl

book fair n fiera f del libro

bookie /'bʊkɪ/ n fam bookmaker m inv, allibratore m

booking /'bʊkɪŋ/ n (Br: reservation) prenotazione f; **make a** ∼ fare una prenotazione; **get a** ∼ (Br: from referee) ricevere un'ammonizione

booking clerk n Br impiegato, -a mf in un ufficio prenotazioni

booking form n Br modulo m di prenotazione

booking office n biglietteria f

bookish /'bʊkɪʃ/ adj ‹person› secchione

book jacket n sopraccoperta f

bookkeeper n contabile mf

bookkeeping n contabilità f

booklet /'bʊklɪt/ n opuscolo m

book lover n amante mf della lettura

bookmaker n allibratore m

bookmark n segnalibro m

bookplate n ex libris m inv

bookrest n leggio m

bookseller n libraio, -a mf

bookshelf n (single) scaffale f; (bookcase) libreria f

bookshop n libreria f

bookstall n edicola f

bookstore n Am libreria f

book token n Br buono m acquisto per libri

bookworm n topo m di biblioteca

boom /buːm/ ① n Comm boom m inv: (upturn) impennata f; (of thunder, gun) rimbombo m

2 *vi* ⟨*thunder, gun*⟩ rimbombare; fig prosperare

boomerang /'bu:məræŋ/ **1** *n* boomerang *m inv*
2 *vi* ~ **on somebody** ⟨*plan*⟩ ritorcersi contro qualcuno

boomerang effect *n* effetto *m* boomerang

booming /'bu:mɪŋ/ *adj* ⟨*sound*⟩ sonoro; ⟨*voice*⟩ tonante; ⟨*economy*⟩ fiorente; ⟨*demand, exports, sales*⟩ in crescita

boom microphone *n* microfono *m* a stelo

boon /bu:n/ *n* benedizione *f*

boor /bʊə(r)/ *n* zoticone *m*

boorish /'bʊərɪʃ/ *adj* maleducato

boost /bu:st/ **1** *n* spinta *f*
2 *vt* stimolare ⟨*sales*⟩; sollevare ⟨*morale*⟩; far crescere ⟨*hopes*⟩

booster /'bu:stə(r)/ *n* Med dose *f* supplementare

boot /bu:t/ **1** *n* stivale *m*; (up to ankle) stivaletto *m*; (football) scarpetta *f*; (climbing) scarpone *m*; Auto portabagagli *m inv*
2 *vt* Comput mettere in funzione
■ **boot out** *vt* fam cacciare
■ **boot up** Comput **1** *vi* caricarsi
2 *vt* caricare

boot black *n* lustrascarpe *mf inv*

boot drive *n* Comput unità *f inv* di inizializzazione

bootee /bu:'ti:/ *n* (knitted) babbuccia *f* di lana; (leather) stivaletto *m*

booth /bu:ð/ *n* (for phoning, voting) cabina *f*; (at market) bancarella *f*

bootlace *n* laccio *m*, stringa *f*

bootlegger *n* Am contrabbandiere *m* di alcolici

bootlicker *n* leccapiedi *mf inv*

bootmaker *n* calzolaio *m*

boot polish *n* lucido *m* da scarpe

boot scraper *n* puliscipiedi *m inv*

bootstrap *n* (on boot) linguetta *f* calzastivali; Comput lancio *m*; **pull oneself up by one's ~s** riuscire con le proprie forze

boot-up *n* Comput boot *m inv*

booty /'bu:tɪ/ *n* bottino *m*

booze /bu:z/ *n* fam alcolici *mpl*

boozer /'bu:zə(r)/ *n* fam (person) beone, -a *mf*;(Br: pub) bar *m inv*

booze-up *n* bella bevuta *f*

boozy /'bu:zɪ/ *adj* fam ⟨*laughter*⟩ da ubriaco; ⟨*meal*⟩ in cui si beve molto

bop /bɒp/ fam **1** *n* (blow) colpo *m*
2 *vt* dare un colpo a
3 *vi* Br (dance) ballare

border /'bɔ:də(r)/ **1** *n* bordo *m*; (frontier) frontiera *f*; (in garden) bordura *f*
2 *vt* confinare con; fig essere ai confini di

■ **border on** *vt* confinare con ⟨*country, land*⟩; essere al limite di ⟨*madness, hysteria*⟩

border dispute *n* (fight) conflitto *m* al confine; (disagreement) contesa *f* sul confine

border guard *n* guardia *f* di frontiera

borderline *n* linea *f* di demarcazione; ~ **case** caso *m* dubbio

border raid *n* incursione *f*

bore¹ /bɔ:(r)/ ▶ BEAR²

bore² *vt* Techn forare

bore³ **1** *n* (of gun) calibro *m*; (person) seccatore, -trice *mf*; (thing) seccatura *f*
2 *vt* annoiare

bored /bɔ:d/ *adj* annoiato, stufo; **be ~ (to tears** or **to death)** annoiarsi (da morire)

boredom /'bɔ:dəm/ *n* noia *f*

boring /'bɔ:rɪŋ/ *adj* noioso

born /bɔ:n/ **1** *pp* be ~ nascere; **I was ~ in 1963** sono nato nel 1963
2 *adj* nato; **a ~ liar/actor** un bugiardo/un attore nato

born-again *adj* convertito alla chiesa evangelica

borne /bɔ:n/ ▶ BEAR²

Borneo /'bɔ:nɪəʊ/ *n* Borneo *m*

borough /'bʌrə/ *n* municipalità *f inv*

borough council *n* Br ≈ comune *m*

borrow /'bɒrəʊ/ *vt* prendere in prestito (**from** da); **can I ~ your pen?** mi presti la tua penna?

borrower /'bɒrəʊə(r)/ *n* debitore, -trice *mf*

borrowing /'bɒrəʊɪŋ/ *n* prestito *m*; **increase in ~** Fin aumento *m* dell'indebitamento

borrowing costs *n* Fin costo *m* del denaro

borstal /'bɔ:stəl/ *n* Br riformatorio *m*

Bosnia /'bɒznɪə/ *n* Bosnia *f*

Bosnia-Herzegovina /-hɜ:tsəgəʊ'vi:nə/ *n* Bosnia-Erzegovina *f*

Bosnian /'bɒznɪən/ *adj & n* bosniaco, -a *mf*

bosom /'bʊzm/ *n* seno *m*

bosom buddy, **bosom friend** *n* fam amico, -a *mf* del cuore

boss /bɒs/ **1** *n* direttore, -trice *mf*
2 *vt* (also ~ **about**) comandare a bacchetta

bossy /'bɒsɪ/ *adj* autoritario

bosun /'bəʊsən/ *n* nostromo *m*

botanical /bə'tænɪkl/ *adj* botanico

botanist /'bɒtənɪst/ *n* botanico, -a *mf*

botany /'bɒtənɪ/ *n* botanica *f*

botch /bɒtʃ/ *vt* fare un pasticcio con

both /bəʊθ/ **1** *adj & pron* tutti e due, entrambi
2 *adv* ~ **men and women** sia uomini che donne; ~ **[of] the children** tutti e due i ⋯⟩

bambini; **they are** ∼ **dead** sono morti
entrambi; ∼ **of them** tutti e due

bother /'bɒðə(r)/ **1** *n* preoccupazione *f*;
(minor trouble) fastidio *m*; **it's no** ∼ non c'è
problema
2 *int* fam che seccatura!
3 *vt* (annoy) dare fastidio a; (disturb)
disturbare
4 *vi* preoccuparsi (**about** di); **don't** ∼
lascia perdere

Botswana /bɒt'swɑːnə/ *n* Botswana *m*

bottle /'bɒt(ə)l/ **1** *n* bottiglia *f*; (baby's)
biberon *m inv*
2 *vt* imbottigliare
■ **bottle up** *vt* fig reprimere

bottle bank *n* contenitore *m* per la
raccolta del vetro

bottle-feed *vt* allattare col biberon

bottle-feeding *n* allattamento *m* col
biberon

bottle green *adj & n* verde *m* bottiglia
inv

bottleneck *n* fig ingorgo *m*

bottle-opener *n* apribottiglie *m inv*

bottle top *n* tappo *m* di bottiglia

bottle-washer *n* hum **chief cook and** ∼
tuttofare *mf inv*

bottom /'bɒtm/ **1** *adj* ultimo; **the** ∼
shelf l'ultimo scaffale in basso
2 *n* (of container) fondo *m*; (of river) fondale
m; (of hill) piedi *mpl*; (buttocks) sedere *m*; **at**
the ∼ in fondo; **at the** ∼ **of the page** in
fondo alla pagina; **get to the** ∼ **of** fig
vedere cosa c'è sotto
■ **bottom out** *vi* ⟨inflation,
unemployment etc⟩ assestarsi

bottom drawer *n* fig corredo *m*

bottom gear *n* Br Auto prima *f*

bottomless /'bɒtəmlɪs/ *adj* senza fondo

bottom line *n* Fin utile *m*; **that's the** ∼
∼ (decisive factor) la questione è tutta qui

botulism /'bɒtjʊlɪzm/ *n* botulismo *m*

bouffant /'buːfã/ *adj* ⟨hair, hairstyle⟩
cotonato; ⟨sleeve⟩ a sbuffo

bough /baʊ/ *n* ramoscello *m*

bought /bɔːt/ ▶ BUY

boulder /'bəʊldə(r)/ *n* masso *m*

bounce /baʊns/ **1** *vi* rimbalzare; fam
⟨cheque⟩ essere respinto
2 *vt* far rimbalzare ⟨ball⟩
■ **bounce back** *vi* fig riprendersi;
⟨email⟩ tornare indietro

bouncer /'baʊnsə(r)/ *n* fam buttafuori *m*
inv

bouncy /'baʊnsɪ/ *adj* ⟨ball⟩ che rimbalza
bene; ⟨mattress, walk⟩ molleggiato; fig
⟨person⟩ esuberante

bound¹ /baʊnd/ **1** *n* balzo *m*
2 *vi* balzare

bound² **1** ▶ BIND

2 *adj* ∼ **for** ⟨ship⟩ diretto a; **be** ∼ **to do**
(likely) dovere fare per forza; (obliged) essere
costretto a fare

boundary /'baʊndərɪ/ *n* limite *m*

boundless /'baʊndlɪs/ *adj* illimitato

bounds /baʊndz/ *npl* fig limiti *mpl*; **out of**
∼ fuori dai limiti

bounty /'baʊntɪ/ *n* (gift) dono *m*;
(generosity) munificenza *f*

bounty hunter *n* cacciatore *m* di taglie

bouquet /bʊ'keɪ/ *n* mazzo *m* di fiori; (of
wine) bouquet *m*

bourbon /'bʊəbən/ *n* bourbon *m inv*

bourgeois /'bʊəʒwɑː/ *adj* pej borghese

bourgeoisie /bʊəʒwɑː'ziː/ *n* borghesia *f*

bout /baʊt/ *n* Med attacco *m*; Sport
incontro *m*

boutique /buː'tiːk/ *n* negozio *m*; **fashion**
∼ negozio *m* di abbigliamento

bovine /'bəʊvaɪn/ *adj* bovino

bow¹ /bəʊ/ *n* (weapon) arco *m*; Mus
archetto *m*; (knot) nodo *m*

bow² /baʊ/ **1** *n* inchino *m*
2 *vi* inchinarsi
3 *vt* piegare ⟨head⟩
■ **bow out** *vi* (withdraw) ritirarsi (**of** da)

bow³ /baʊ/ *n* Naut prua *f*

bowel /'baʊəl/ *n* intestino *m*; **have a** ∼
movement andare di corpo; ∼**s** *pl*
intestini *mpl*

bower /'baʊə(r)/ *n* (in garden) pergolato *m*;
(liter: chamber) salottino *m*

bowl¹ /bəʊl/ *n* (for soup, cereal) scodella *f*;
(of pipe) fornello *m*

bowl² **1** *n* (ball) boccia *f*
2 *vt* lanciare
3 *vi* Cricket servire; (in bowls) lanciare
■ **bowl along** *vi* (in car etc) andare
spedito
■ **bowl over** *vt* buttar giù; (fig: leave
speechless) lasciare senza parole

bow-legged /bəʊ'legd/ *adj* dalle gambe
storte

bowler¹ /'bəʊlə(r)/ *n* Cricket lanciatore *m*;
Bowls giocatore *m* di bocce

bowler² *n* ∼ **[hat]** bombetta *f*

bowling /'bəʊlɪŋ/ *n* gioco *m* delle bocce

bowling alley /'bəʊlɪŋælɪ/ *n* pista *f* da
bowling

bowling green *n* prato *m* da bocce

bowls /bəʊlz/ *n* gioco *m* delle bocce

bowstring *n* corda *f* d'arco

bow tie *n* cravatta *f* a farfalla

bow window *n* bow window *f inv*

box¹ /bɒks/ *n* scatola *f*; Theat palco *m*

box² **1** *vi* Sport fare il pugile
2 *vt* ∼ **sb's ears** dare uno scapaccione a
qualcuno

boxer /'bɒksə(r)/ *n* pugile *m*

boxer shorts *npl* boxer *mpl*

boxing /'bɒksɪŋ/ *n* pugilato *m*

Boxing Day *n* Br [giorno *m* di] Santo Stefano *m*

box number *n* casella *f*

box office *n* Theat botteghino *m*

boxroom *n* Br sgabuzzino *m*

boxwood *n* bosso *m*

boy /bɔɪ/ *n* ragazzo *m*; (younger) bambino *m*

boy band *n* boy band *f inv*

boycott /'bɔɪkɒt/ ① *n* boicottaggio *m* ② *vt* boicottare

boyfriend /'bɔɪfrend/ *n* ragazzo *m*

boyhood /'bɔɪhʊd/ *n* (childhood) infanzia *f*; (adolescence) adolescenza *f*

boyish /'bɔɪɪʃ/ *adj* da ragazzino

boy scout *n* boy scout *m inv*

bpm *abbr* (**beats per minute**) bpm *mpl*

bps *abbr* (**bits per second**) Comput bps *mpl*

BR *abbr* (**British Rail**) ente *m* ferroviario britannico, ≈ FS

bra /brɑː/ *n* reggiseno *m*

brace /breɪs/ ① *n* sostegno *m*; (dental) apparecchio *m* ② *vt* ~ **oneself** fig farsi forza (**for** per affrontare)

bracelet /'breɪslɪt/ *n* braccialetto *m*

braces /'breɪsɪz/ *npl* bretelle *fpl*

bracing /'breɪsɪŋ/ *adj* tonificante

bracken /'brækn/ *n* felce *f*

bracket /'brækɪt/ ① *n* mensola *f*; (group) categoria *f*; Typ parentesi *f inv* ② *vt* mettere fra parentesi

brackish /'brækɪʃ/ *adj* salmastro

bradawl /'brædɔːl/ *n* punteruolo *m*

brag /bræg/ *vi* (pt/pp **bragged**) vantarsi (**about** di)

bragging /'brægɪŋ/ *n* vanterie *fpl*

Brahmin /'brɑːmɪn/ *n* Relig bramino *m*

braid /breɪd/ *n* (edging) passamano *m*

braille /breɪl/ *n* braille *m*

brain /breɪn/ *n* cervello *m*; ~**s** *pl* fig testa *fsg*

brainbox *n* fam capoccione *m*

brainchild *n* invenzione *f* personale

brain damage *n* lesione *f* cerebrale

brain-dead *adj* Med cerebralmente morto; fig senza cervello

brain death *n* morte *f* cerebrale

brain drain *n* fuga *f* di cervelli

brainless /'breɪnlɪs/ *adj* senza cervello

brain scan *n* scansione *m inv* del cervello

brain scanner *n* scanner *m inv* (per il cervello)

brainstorm *n* Med, fig eccesso *m* di pazzia; (Am: brainwave) lampo *m* di genio

brainstorming session *n* brainstorming *m inv*

brains trust *n* brain trust *m inv*, gruppo *m* di esperti

brain surgeon *n* neurochirurgo *m*

brain surgery *n* neurochirurgia *f*

brain teaser *n* fam rompicapo *m*

brainwash *vt* fare il lavaggio del cervello a

brainwashing *n* lavaggio *m* del cervello

brainwave *n* lampo *m* di genio

brainy /'breɪnɪ/ *adj* (**-ier, -iest**) intelligente

braise /breɪz/ *vt* brasare

brake /breɪk/ ① *n* freno *m* ② *vi* frenare

brake block *n* pastiglia *f*

brake disc *n* disco *m* dei freni

brake drum *n* tamburo *m* del freno

brake fluid *n* liquido *m* dei freni

brake-light *n* stop *m inv*

brake lining *n* guarnizione *f* del freno

brake pad *n* ganascia *f* del freno

brake pedal *n* pedale *m* del freno

bramble /'bræmb(ə)l/ *n* rovo *m*; (fruit) mora *f*

bran /bræn/ *n* crusca *f*

branch /brɑːntʃ/ ① *n* also fig ramo *m*; Comm succursale *f*; filiale *f*; (of bank) agenzia *f*; **our Oxford St** ~ (of store) il negozio di Oxford St ② *vi* ‹road› biforcarsi ▪ **branch off** *vi* biforcarsi ▪ **branch out** *vi* ~ **out into** allargare le proprie attività nel ramo di

branch line *n* linea *f* secondaria

branch manager *n* (of bank) direttore, -trice *mf* di agenzia; (of company) direttore, -trice *mf* di filiale; (of shop) direttore, -trice *mf* di succursale

branch office *n* filiale *f*; (of bank) agenzia *f*

brand /brænd/ ① *n* marca *f*; (on animal) marchio *m* ② *vt* marcare ‹animal›; fig tacciare (**as** di)

branded /'brændɪd/ *adj* ‹goods› di marca

brand image *n* brand image *f*

brandish /'brændɪʃ/ *vt* brandire

brand leader *n* marca *f* leader *inv*

brand name *n* marca *f*

brand-new *adj* nuovo fiammante

brandy /'brændɪ/ *n* brandy *m inv*

brash /bræʃ/ *adj* sfrontato

brass /brɑːs/ *n* ottone *m*; **the** ~ Mus gli ottoni *mpl*; **top** ~ fam pezzi *mpl* grossi

brass band *n* banda *f* (di soli ottoni)

b

brassiere /'bræzɪə(r)/ n fml, Am reggiseno m

brass instrument n Mus ottone m

brass neck n Br fam faccia f tosta

brass rubbing n ricalco m di iscrizione tombale o commemorativa

brassy /'brɑːsɪ/ adj (-ier, -iest) fam volgare

brat /bræt/ n pej marmocchio, -a mf

bravado /brə'vɑːdəʊ/ n bravata f

brave /breɪv/ ① adj coraggioso ② vt affrontare

bravely /'breɪvlɪ/ adv con coraggio

bravery /'breɪvərɪ/ n coraggio m

bravo /brɑː'vəʊ/ int bravo!

bravura /brə'vjʊərə/ n virtuosismo m

brawl /brɔːl/ ① n rissa f ② vi azzuffarsi

brawn /brɔːn/ n Culin ≈ soppressata f

brawny /'brɔːnɪ/ adj muscoloso

bray vi ⟨donkey⟩ ragliare

brazen /'breɪzn/ adj sfrontato
■ **brazen out** vt affrontare con piglio sicuro

brazier /'breɪzɪə(r)/ n braciere m

Brazil /brə'zɪl/ n Brasile m

Brazilian /brə'zɪlɪən/ adj & n brasiliano, -a mf

Brazil [nut] n noce f del Brasile

breach /briːtʃ/ ① n (of law) violazione f; (gap) breccia f; (fig: in party) frattura f ② vt recedere ⟨contract⟩

breach of contract n Jur inadempienza f contrattuale

breach of promise n Jur inadempienza f a una promessa di matrimonio

breach of the peace n Jur violazione f dell'ordine pubblico

breach of trust n Jur abuso m di fiducia

bread /bred/ n pane m; **a slice of ~ and butter** una fetta di pane imburrato

bread and butter n fig fonte f di guadagno principale

breadbasket n cestino m per il pane; fig granaio m

breadbin n Br cassetta f portapane inv

breadboard n tagliere m per il pane

breadcrumbs npl briciole fpl; Culin pangrattato m

breadfruit n frutto m dell'albero del pane

breadknife n coltello m per il pane

breadline n be on the ~ essere povero in canna

bread roll n panino m

breadstick n filoncino m

breadth /bredθ/ n larghezza f

breadwinner /'bredwɪnə(r)/ n quello, -a mf che porta i soldi a casa

break /breɪk/ ① n rottura f; (interval) intervallo m; (interruption) interruzione f; (fam: chance) opportunità f inv
② vt (pt **broke**, pp **broken**) rompere; (interrupt) interrompere; ~ **one's arm** rompersi un braccio
③ vi rompersi; ⟨day⟩ spuntare; ⟨storm⟩ scoppiare; ⟨news⟩ diffondersi; ⟨boy's voice⟩ cambiare
■ **break away** vi scappare; fig chiudere (from con)
■ **break down** ① vi ⟨machine, car⟩ guastarsi; ⟨negotiations⟩ interrompersi; (in tears) scoppiare in lacrime
② vt sfondare ⟨door⟩; ripartire ⟨figures⟩
■ **break in** vi ⟨burglar⟩ introdursi
■ **break into** vt introdursi con la forza in; forzare ⟨car⟩
■ **break off** ① vt rompere ⟨engagement⟩
② vi ⟨part of whole⟩ rompersi; (when speaking) interrompersi
■ **break out** vi ⟨argument, war⟩ scoppiare
■ **break through** vi ⟨sun⟩ spuntare
■ **break up** ① vt far cessare ⟨fight⟩; disperdere ⟨crowd⟩
② vi ⟨crowd⟩ disperdersi; ⟨marriage⟩ naufragare; ⟨couple⟩ separarsi; Sch iniziare le vacanze

breakable /'breɪkəbl/ adj fragile

breakage /'breɪkɪdʒ/ n rottura f

breakaway /'breɪkəweɪ/ ① n (from person) separazione f, allontanamento m; (from organization) scissione f; Sport contropiede m
② attrib ⟨faction, group, state⟩ separatista

breakdown /'breɪkdaʊn/ n (of car, machine) guasto m; Med esaurimento m nervoso; (of figures) analisi f inv

breaker /'breɪkə(r)/ n (wave) frangente m

breaker's yard n Auto cimitero m delle macchine

break even vi andare in pareggio

break-even point n punto m di pareggio, punto m di equilibrio

breakfast /'brekfəst/ n [prima] colazione f

breakfast bar n tavolo m a penisola

breakfast bowl n scodella f per i cereali

breakfast cereals npl cereali mpl per la colazione

breakfast television, breakfast TV n programmi mpl televisivi del mattino

break free vi fuggire

break-in n irruzione f

breaking /'breɪkɪŋ/ n (of glass, seal, contract) rottura f; (of bone) frattura f; (of law, treaty) violazione f; (of voice) cambiamento m; (of promise) venuta f meno; (of horse) domatura *f*; (of link, sequence, tie) interruzione *f*

breaking and entering /ˈbreɪkɪŋənd ˈentərɪŋ/ *n* Jur effrazione *f* con scasso

breaking point *n* Techn punto *m* di rottura; fig limite *m* di sopportazione

breakneck *adj* ⟨pace, speed⟩ a rotta di collo

break-out *n* (from prison) evasione *f*

breakpoint *n* Tennis breakpoint *m inv*

breakthrough *n* (discovery) scoperta *f*; (in negotiations) passo *m* avanti

break-up *n* (of family, company) disgregazione *f*; (of alliance, relationship) rottura *f*; (of marriage) dissoluzione *f*

breakwater *n* frangiflutti *m inv*

breast /brest/ *n* seno *m*

breastbone *n* sterno *m*

breastfeed *vt* allattare al seno

breast pocket *n* taschino *m*

breast-stroke *n* nuoto *m* a rana

breath /breθ/ *n* respiro *m*, fiato *m*; **out of ∼** senza fiato; **under one's ∼** sottovoce; **a ∼ of air** un filo d'aria

breathalyse /ˈbreθəlaɪz/ *vt* sottoporre alla prova del palloncino

breathalyser® Br, **breathalyzer®** /ˈbreθəlaɪzə(r)/ *n* alcoltest *m inv*

breathe /briːð/ *vt/i* respirare; **∼ a sigh of relief** tirare un sospiro di sollievo
■ **breathe in** ① *vi* inspirare
② *vt* respirare ⟨scent, air⟩
■ **breathe out** *vt/i* espirare

breather /ˈbriːðə(r)/ *n* pausa *f*

breathing /ˈbriːðɪŋ/ *n* respirazione *f*

breathing apparatus *n* respiratore *m*

breathing space *n* (respite) tregua *f*; **give oneself a ∼** riprendere fiato

breathless /ˈbreθlɪs/ *adj* senza fiato

breathlessly /ˈbreθlɪslɪ/ *adv* senza fiato

breathtaking /ˈbreθteɪkɪŋ/ *adj* mozzafiato

breathtakingly /ˈbreθteɪkɪŋlɪ/ *adv* **∼ audacious** di un'audacia stupefacente; **∼ beautiful** di una bellezza mozzafiato

breath test *n* prova *f* del palloncino

bred /bred/ ▶BREED

breech /briːtʃ/ *n* Med natiche *fpl*; (of gun) culatta *f*

breed /briːd/ ① *n* razza *f*
② *vt* (pt/pp **bred**) allevare; (give rise to) generare
③ *vi* riprodursi

breeder /ˈbriːdə(r)/ *n* allevatore, -trice *mf*

breeding /ˈbriːdɪŋ/ *n* allevamento *m*; fig educazione *f*

breeding ground *n* zona *f* di riproduzione; fig terreno *m* fertile

breeding period, breeding season *n* stagione *f* di riproduzione

breeze /briːz/ *n* brezza *f*

breeze block *n* Br mattone *m* fatto con scorie di coke

breezily /ˈbriːzɪlɪ/ *adv* (confidently) con sicurezza; (casually) con disinvoltura; (cheerfully) allegramente

breezy /ˈbriːzɪ/ *adj* ventoso

brevity /ˈbrevətɪ/ *n* brevità *f*

brew /bruː/ ① *n* infuso *m*
② *vt* mettere in infusione ⟨tea⟩; produrre ⟨beer⟩
③ *vi* fig ⟨trouble⟩ essere nell'aria

brewer /ˈbruːə(r)/ *n* birraio *m*

brewery /ˈbruərɪ/ *n* fabbrica *f* di birra

brew-up *n* Br fam tè *m inv*

briar /ˈbraɪə(r)/ *n* rosa *f* selvatica; (heather) erica *f*; (thorns) rovo *m*; (pipe) pipa *f* in radica

bribe /braɪb/ ① *n* (money) bustarella *f*; (large sum of money) tangente *f*
② *vt* corrompere

bribery /ˈbraɪbərɪ/ *n* corruzione *f*

brick /brɪk/ *n* mattone *m*
■ **brick up** *vt* murare

brickbat *n* fig critica *f* spietata

brick-built *adj* di mattoni

bricklayer *n* muratore *m*

bricklaying *n* muratura *f*

brick red *adj* rosso mattone *inv*

bricks-and-mortar *adj* ⟨company, business⟩ di tipo tradizionale

brickwork *n* muratura *f* di mattoni

brickworks *n* fabbrica *f* di mattoni

bridal /ˈbraɪdl/ *adj* nuziale

bridal party *n* corteo *m* nuziale

bridal suite *n* camera *f* nuziale

bridal wear *n* confezioni *fpl* da sposa

bride /braɪd/ *n* sposa *f*

bridegroom /ˈbraɪdgruːm/ *n* sposo *m*

bridesmaid /ˈbraɪdzmeɪd/ *n* damigella *f* d'onore

bridge¹ /brɪdʒ/ ① *n* ponte *m*; (of nose) setto *m* nasale; (of spectacles) ponticello *m*
② *vt* fig colmare ⟨gap⟩

bridge² *n* Cards bridge *m*

bridge-building *n* costruzione *f* di ponti provvisori; fig mediazione *f*

bridging loan /ˈbrɪdʒɪŋ/ *n* Br Fin pre-finanziamento *m*, credito *m* provvisorio

bridle /ˈbraɪd(ə)l/ *n* briglia *f*

bridle path, bridleway /ˈbraɪd(ə)lweɪ/ *n* sentiero *m* per cavalli

brief¹ /briːf/ *adj* breve; **in ∼** in breve

brief² ① *n* istruzioni *fpl*; (Jur: case) causa *f*
② *vt* dare istruzioni a; Jur affidare la causa a

briefcase /'bri:fkeɪs/ n cartella f

briefing /'bri:fɪŋ/ n briefing m inv

briefly /'bri:flɪ/ adv brevemente; **briefly,...** in breve,...

briefness /'bri:fnɪs/ n brevità f

briefs /bri:fs/ npl slip m inv

brigade /brɪ'geɪd/ n brigata f

brigadier /brɪgə'dɪə(r)/ n generale m di brigata

bright /braɪt/ adj ⟨metal, idea⟩ brillante; ⟨day, room, future⟩ luminoso; (clever) intelligente; ∼ **red** rosso m acceso

brighten /'braɪt(ə)n/ v ∼ **[up]** ① vt ravvivare; rallegrare ⟨person⟩ ② vi ⟨weather⟩ schiarirsi; ⟨face⟩ illuminarsi; ⟨person⟩ rallegrarsi

brightly /'braɪtlɪ/ adv ⟨shine⟩ intensamente; ⟨smile⟩ allegramente

brightness /'braɪtnɪs/ n luminosità f; (intelligence) intelligenza f

bright spark n Br fam genio m

bright young things npl Br i giovani di belle speranze

brill /brɪl/ ① n Zool rombo m liscio ② adj Br fam fantastico

brilliance /'brɪljəns/ n luminosità f; (of person) genialità f

brilliant /'brɪljənt/ adj (very good) eccezionale; (very intelligent) brillante; ⟨sunshine⟩ splendente

brilliantly /'brɪljəntlɪ/ adv ⟨shine⟩ intensamente; ⟨perform⟩ in modo eccezionale

Brillo pad® /'brɪləʊ/ n paglietta f d'acciaio

brim /brɪm/ n bordo m; (of hat) tesa f
■ **brim over** vi (pt/pp **brimmed**) traboccare

brine /braɪn/ n salamoia f

bring /brɪŋ/ vt (pt/pp **brought**) portare ⟨person, object⟩
■ **bring about** vt causare
■ **bring along** vt portare [con sé]
■ **bring back** vt restituire ⟨something borrowed⟩; reintrodurre ⟨hanging⟩; fare ritornare in mente ⟨memories⟩
■ **bring down** vt portare giù; fare cadere ⟨government⟩; fare abbassare ⟨price⟩
■ **bring forward** vt anticipare ⟨meeting, date⟩; **the meeting has been brought forward to this afternoon** la riunione è stata anticipata al pomeriggio
■ **bring in** vt introdurre ⟨legislation⟩; **his job ∼s in £30,000 a year** guadagna 30.000 sterline all'anno
■ **bring off** vt ∼ **something off** riuscire a fare qualcosa
■ **bring on** vt (cause) provocare
■ **bring out** vt (emphasize) mettere in evidenza; pubblicare ⟨book⟩

■ **bring round** vt portare; (persuade) convincere; far rinvenire ⟨unconscious person⟩
■ **bring up** vt (vomit) rimettere; allevare ⟨children⟩; tirare fuori ⟨question, subject⟩

bring and buy sale n Br vendita f di beneficenza

brink /brɪŋk/ n orlo m; **on the ∼ of disaster** sull'orlo del disastro

brinkmanship /'brɪŋkmənʃɪp/ n strategia f del rischio calcolato

brisk /brɪsk/ adj svelto; ⟨person⟩ sbrigativo; ⟨trade, business⟩ redditizio; ⟨walk⟩ a passo spedito

brisket /'brɪskɪt/ n Culin punta f di petto

briskly /'brɪsklɪ/ adv velocemente; ⟨say⟩ frettolosamente; ⟨walk⟩ di buon passo

bristle /'brɪsl/ ① n setola f ② vi bristling with pieno di

bristly /'brɪslɪ/ adj ⟨chin⟩ ispido

Britain /'brɪtn/ n Gran Bretagna f

British /'brɪtʃ/ ① adj britannico; ⟨ambassador⟩ della Gran Bretagna ② npl the ∼ il popolo britannico

British Airports Authority n ente m che gestisce gli aeroporti britannici

British Broadcasting Corporation n ente m radio-televisivo nazionale britannico

British Columbia n Columbia f Britannica

Britisher /'brɪtɪʃə(r)/ n Am britannico, -a mf

British Gas n Br società f del gas britannica

British Isles npl Isole fpl Britanniche

British Rail n ente m ferroviario britannico

British Telecom n Br società f britannica di telecomunicazioni

Briton /'brɪtən/ n cittadino, -a britannico, -a mf

Brittany /'brɪtənɪ/ n Bretagna f

brittle /'brɪtl/ adj fragile

brittle-bone disease n decalcificazione f ossea, osteoporosi f

broach /brəʊtʃ/ vt toccare ⟨subject⟩

B road n Br ≈ strada f provinciale

broad /brɔːd/ adj ampio; ⟨hint⟩ chiaro; ⟨accent⟩ marcato. **two metres ∼** largo due metri; **in ∼ daylight** in pieno giorno

broadband n Comput banda f larga; **on ∼** a banda larga; **∼ connection** connessione f a banda larga

broad-based /'beɪst/ adj ⟨coalition, education⟩ diversificato; ⟨approach, campaign⟩ su larga scala; ⟨consensus⟩ generale

broad bean n fava f

broadcast /'brɔːdkæst/ ① n trasmissione f

② *vt/i* (pt/pp **-cast**) trasmettere

broadcaster /'brɔːdkæstə(r)/ *n*
giornalista *mf* radiotelevisivo, -a

broadcasting /'brɔːdkæstɪŋ/ *n*
diffusione *f* radiotelevisiva; **be in ~**
lavorare per la televisione/radio

broad-chested *adj* con il torace
robusto

broaden /'brɔːdn/ ① *vt* allargare; **~**
one's horizons allargare i propri orizzonti
② *vi* allargarsi

broadly /'brɔːdlɪ/ *adv* largamente; **~**
[speaking] generalmente

broad-minded /-'maɪndɪd/ *adj* di larghe
vedute

broadness /'brɔːdnɪs/ *n* larghezza *f*

broadsheet *n* quotidiano *m* di grande
formato

broad-shouldered *adj* con le spalle
larghe

broadside *n* (Naut: of ship) fiancata *f*;
(enemy fire) bordata *f*; *n* (criticism) attacco *m*;
deliver a ~ lanciare un attacco *adv* di
fianco

brocade /brə'keɪd/ *n* broccato *m*

broccoli /'brɒkəlɪ/ *n inv* broccoli *mpl*

brochure /'brəʊʃə(r)/ *n* opuscolo *m*;
(travel ~) dépliant *m inv*

brogue /'brəʊg/ *n* (shoe) scarpa *m* da
passeggio; (accent) cadenza *f* dialettale

broil /brɔɪl/ ① *vt* Culin cuocere alla griglia
⟨meat⟩
② *vi* cuocere alla griglia; fig arrostire

broiler /'brɔɪlə(r)/ *n* (chicken) pollastro *m*;
(Am: grill) griglia *f*

broke /brəʊk/ ① ▶ BREAK
② *adj* fam al verde

broken /'brəʊk(ə)n/ ① ▶ BREAK
② *adj* rotto; **~ English** inglese *m* stentato

broken-down *adj* ⟨machine⟩ guasto;
⟨wall⟩ pericolante

broken heart *n* cuore *m* infranto; **die**
of a ~ ~ essere distrutto da una
delusione amorosa

broken-hearted /-'hɑːtɪd/ *adj* affranto

broken home *n* he comes from a **~ ~** i
suoi sono divisi

broken marriage *n* matrimonio *m*
fallito

broker /'brəʊkə(r)/ *n* broker *m inv*

brokerage /'brəʊkərɪdʒ/ *n* (fee, business)
intermediazione *f*

broking /'brəʊkɪŋ/ *n* attività *f* di
intermediazione

brolly /'brɒlɪ/ *n* fam ombrello *m*

bromide /'brəʊmaɪd/ *n* (in pharmacy
printing) bromuro *m*; (fig: comment) banalità *f*
inv

bronchial /'brɒŋkɪəl/ *adj* ⟨infection⟩
bronchiale; ⟨wheeze, cough⟩ di petto

bronchitis /brɒŋ'kaɪtɪs/ *n* bronchite *f*

bronze /brɒnz/ ① *n* bronzo *m*
② *attrib* di bronzo

Bronze Age *n* età *f* del Bronzo

brooch /brəʊtʃ/ *n* spilla *f*

brood /bruːd/ ① *n* covata *f*; (hum: children)
prole *f*
② *vi* covare; fig rimuginare

brooding /'bruːdɪŋ/ *adj* ⟨person, face⟩
pensieroso; ⟨landscape⟩ sinistro

broody /'bruːdɪ/ *adj* (depressed)
pensieroso; **feel ~** Br fam ⟨woman⟩
desiderare un figlio

broody hen *n* chioccia *f*

brook[1] /brʊk/ *n* ruscello *m*

brook[2] *vt* sopportare

broom /bruːm/ *n* scopa *f*; Bot ginestra *f*

broom cupboard *n* ripostiglio *m*

broom handle *n* Br manico *m* di scopa

broomstick *n* manico *m* di scopa

Bros. *abbr* (**brothers**) F.lli

broth /brɒθ/ *n* brodo *m*

brothel /'brɒθ(ə)l/ *n* bordello *m*

brother /'brʌðə(r)/ *n* fratello *m*

brotherhood /'brʌðəhʊd/ *n* (bond)
fratellanza *f*; (of monks) confraternita *f*

brother-in-law *n* (pl **brothers-in-law**)
cognato *m*

brotherly /'brʌðəlɪ/ *adj* fraterno

brought /brɔːt/ ▶ BRING

brow /braʊ/ *n* fronte *f*; (eyebrow)
sopracciglio *m*; (of hill) cima *f*

browbeat /'braʊbiːt/ *vt* (pt **-beat**, pp
-beaten) intimidire

brown /braʊn/ ① *adj* marrone; castano
⟨hair⟩
② *n* marrone *m*
③ *vt* rosolare ⟨meat⟩
④ *vi* ⟨meat⟩ rosolarsi

brown ale *n* Br birra *f* scura

brown bear *n* orso *m* bruno

brown bread *n* pane *m* integrale

browned-off /braʊnd'ɒf/ *adj* Br fam stufo
(with di)

brown envelope *n* busta *f* di carta da
pacchi

Brownie /'braʊnɪ/ *n* coccinella *f* (negli
scout)

brownie point *n* fam punto *m* di merito

brownish /'braʊnɪʃ/ *adj* sul marrone

brownout *n* Am oscuramento *m* parziale

brown owl *n* allocco *m*

brown paper *n* carta *f* da pacchi

brown rice *n* riso *m* integrale

brown-skinned /-'skɪnd/ *adj* scuro di
pelle

brownstone *n* (Am: house) palazzo *m* in
arenaria

brown sugar *n* Culin zucchero *m* greggio

browse /brauz/ **1** *v* vi (read) leggicchiare; (in shop) curiosare; (on Internet) navigare
2 *vt* visitare ⟨*Internet, web site*⟩

browser /'brauzə(r)/ *n* (Comput: program) browser *m inv*; (in shop) persona *f* che curiosa

bruise /bru:z/ **1** *n* livido *m*; (on fruit) ammaccatura *f*
2 *vt* ammaccare ⟨*fruit*⟩; ~ **one's arm** farsi un livido sul braccio

bruised /bru:zd/ *adj* (physically) contuso; ⟨*eye*⟩ pesto; ⟨*fruit*⟩ ammaccato; ⟨*ego, spirit*⟩ ferito

bruiser /'bru:zə(r)/ *n* fam omaccione *m*

bruising /'bru:zɪŋ/ **1** *n* livido *m*, contusione *f*
2 *adj* ⟨*game*⟩ violento; (emotionally) ⟨*remark*⟩ pesante; ⟨*campaign, encounter*⟩ traumatizzante; ⟨*defeat*⟩ cocente

brunch /brʌntʃ/ *n* brunch *m inv*

Brunei /bru:'naɪ/ *n* Brunei *m*

brunette /bru:'net/ *n* bruna *f*

brunt /brʌnt/ *n* **bear the ~ of something** subire maggiormente qualcosa

brush /brʌʃ/ **1** *n* spazzola *f*; (with long handle) spazzolone *m*; (for paint) pennello *m*; (bushes) boscaglia *f*; (fig: conflict) breve scontro *m*
2 *vt* spazzolare ⟨*hair*⟩; lavarsi ⟨*teeth*⟩; scopare ⟨*stairs, floor*⟩
■ **brush against** *vt* sfiorare
■ **brush aside** *vt* fig ignorare
■ **brush off** *vt* spazzolare; (with hands) togliere; ignorare ⟨*criticism*⟩
■ **brush up** *vt/i* fig ~ up [on] rinfrescare

brush-off *n* fam **give somebody the ~** mandare qualcuno a quel paese

brushstroke *n* pennellata *f*

brushup *n* Br **have a [wash and] brushup** darsi una ripulita

brushwood *n* sterpaglie *fpl*

brushwork *n* tocco *m*

brusque /brusk/ *adj* brusco

brusquely /'bruskli/ *adv* bruscamente

Brussels /'brʌsəlz/ *n* Bruxelles *f*

Brussels sprouts *npl* cavolini *mpl* di Bruxelles

brutal /'bru:t(ə)l/ *adj* brutale

brutality /bru:'tælətɪ/ *n* brutalità *f inv*

brutalize /'bru:təlaɪz/ *vt* brutalizzare

brutally /'bru:təlɪ/ *adv* brutalmente

brute /bru:t/ *n* bruto *m*; ~ **force** forza *f* bruta

brutish /'bru:tɪʃ/ *adj* da bruto

BS *abbr* Am **Bachelor of Science**

BSc *abbr* **Bachelor of Science**

BSE *n abbr* (**bovine spongiform encephalitis**) encefalite *f* bovina spongiforme

B side *n* (of record) lato *m* B

BST *abbr* (**British Summer Time**) ora *f* legale in Gran Bretagna

B2B /bi:tə'bi:/ *abbr* (**business to business**) ⟨*trade, directory*⟩ B2B

bubble /'bʌbl/ *n* bolla *f*; (in drink) bollicina *f*

bubble bath *n* bagnoschiuma *m inv*

bubble car *n* Br fam auto *f* monoposto a tre ruote

bubblegum *n* gomma *f* da masticare

bubble pack *n* Br (for pills) blister *m inv*; (for small item) involucro *m* di plastica

bubble wrap *n* plastica *f* a bolle

bubbling /'bʌblɪŋ/ **1** *n* (sound) gorgoglio *m*
2 *adj* che ribolle

bubbly /'bʌblɪ/ **1** *n* fam champagne *m inv*, spumante *m*
2 *adj* ⟨*liquid*⟩ effervescente; ⟨*personality*⟩ spumeggiante

bubonic plague /bju:bɒnɪk'pleɪg/ *n* peste *f* bubbonica

buccaneer /bʌkə'nɪə(r)/ *n* bucaniere *m*

Bucharest /bju:kə'rest/ *n* Bucarest *f*

buck¹ /bʌk/ **1** *n* maschio *m* del cervo; (rabbit) maschio *m* del coniglio
2 *vi* ⟨*horse*⟩ saltare a quattro zampe

buck² *n* Am fam dollaro *m*

buck³ *n* **pass the ~** scaricare la responsabilità
■ **buck up** **1** *vi* fam tirarsi su; (hurry) sbrigarsi
2 *vt* **you'll have to ~ your ideas up** fam dovresti darti una regolata

bucket /'bʌkɪt/ **1** *n* secchio *m*; **kick the ~** (fam: die) crepare
2 *vi* **it's ~ing down** fam piove a catinelle

bucketful /'bʌkɪtfʊl/ *n* secchio *m*

bucket seat *n* Auto, Aeron sedile *m* anatomico

bucket shop *n* Br fam agenzia *f* di viaggi che vende biglietti a prezzi scontati

bucking bronco /bʌkɪŋ'brɒŋkəʊ/ *n* cavallo *m* da rodeo

buckle /'bʌkl/ **1** *n* fibbia *f*
2 *vt* allacciare
3 *vi* ⟨*shelf*⟩ piegarsi; ⟨*wheel*⟩ storcersi
■ **buckle down** *vi* (to work) mettersi sotto
■ **buckle in** *vt* legare

buckram *n* tela *f* rigida

buckshot *n* pallettoni *mpl*

buckskin *n* pelle *f* di daino

buck teeth *npl* denti *mpl* da coniglio

buckwheat *n* grano *m* saraceno

bucolic /bjʊ'kɒlɪk/ *adj & n* bucolico *m*

bud /bʌd/ *n* bocciolo *m*

Buddha /'bʊdə/ n Budda m inv

Buddhism /'bʊdɪzm/ n buddismo m

Buddhist /'bʊdɪst/ adj & n buddista mf

budding /'bʌdɪŋ/ adj Bot (into leaf) in germoglio; (into flower) in boccio; ⟨athlete, champion, artist⟩ in erba; ⟨talent, romance⟩ nascente; ⟨career⟩ promettente

buddy /'bʌdɪ/ n fam amico, -a mf

budge /bʌdʒ/ **1** vt spostare
2 vi spostarsi
■ **budge over**, **budge up** vi fam farsi più in là

budgerigar /'bʌdʒərɪgɑː(r)/ n cocorita f

budget /'bʌdʒɪt/ **1** n bilancio m; (allotted to specific activity) budget m inv; **I'm on a** ∼ cerco di limitare le spese
2 vi (pt/pp **budgeted**) prevedere le spese; ∼ **for something** includere qualcosa nelle spese previste

budgetary /'bʌdʒɪt(ə)rɪ/ adj budgetario; ∼ **year** esercizio m finanziario

budget day n Br Pol giorno m della presentazione del bilancio dello Stato

budgie /'bʌdʒɪ/ n fam = BUDGERIGAR

buff /bʌf/ **1** adj (colour) [color] camoscio
2 n [color m] camoscio m; fam fanatico, -a mf
3 vt lucidare

buffalo /'bʌfələʊ/ n (inv or pl **-es**) bufalo m

buffer /'bʌfə(r)/ n Rail respingente m; Comput buffer m inv; **old** ∼ fam vecchio bacucco m

buffer state n stato m cuscinetto inv

buffer zone n zona f cuscinetto inv

buffet[1] /'bʊfeɪ/ n (meal, in station) buffet m inv

buffet[2] /'bʌfɪt/ vt (pt/pp **buffeted**) sferzare

buffet car n Br Rail carrozza f ristorante

buffoon /bə'fuːn/ n buffone, -a mf

bug /bʌg/ **1** n (insect) insetto m; Comput bug m inv; (fam: device) cimice f
2 vt (pt/pp **bugged**) fam installare delle microspie in ⟨room⟩; mettere sotto controllo ⟨telephone⟩; (fam: annoy) scocciare

bugbear /'bʌgbeə(r)/ n (problem, annoyance) spauracchio m

bugger /'bʌgə(r)/ fam **1** n bastardo m
2 int merda!
■ **bugger about**, **bugger around** fam
1 vi (behave stupidly) fare il cretino
2 vt ∼ **somebody about** creare problemi a qualcuno
■ **bugger off** vi (fam: go away) andarsene; ∼ **off!** vai a farti friggere!

bugging device /'bʌgɪŋ/ n microfono m spia

buggy /'bʌgɪ/ n **[baby]** ∼ passeggino m

bugle /'bjuːg(ə)l/ n tromba f

bugler /'bjuːglə(r)/ n trombettiere m

build /bɪld/ **1** n (of person) corporatura f
2 vt/i (pt/pp **built**) costruire
■ **build on** vt aggiungere ⟨extra storey⟩; sviluppare ⟨previous work⟩
■ **build up 1** vt ∼ **up one's strength** rimettersi in forza
2 vi ⟨pressure, traffic⟩ aumentare; ⟨excitement, tension⟩ crescere

builder /'bɪldə(r)/ n (company) costruttore m; (worker) muratore m

builder's labourer n muratore m

builder's merchant n fornitore m di materiale da costruzione

building /'bɪldɪŋ/ n edificio m

building block n (child's toy) pezzo m delle costruzioni; (basic element) componente m

building contractor n imprenditore m edile

building land n terreno m edificabile

building materials npl materiali mpl da costruzione

building permit n licenza f edilizia

building plot n terreno m edificabile

building site n cantiere m [di costruzione]

building society n istituto m di credito immobiliare

building trade n edilizia f

building worker n Br muratore m

build-up n (increase) aumento m; (in tension, of gas, in weapons) accumulo m; (publicity) battage m inv pubblicitario; **give something a good** ∼ (publicity) fare buona pubblicità a qualcosa

built /bɪlt/ ▶ BUILD

built-in adj ⟨unit⟩ a muro; fig ⟨feature⟩ incorporato

built-up adj region urbanizzato; ∼ **area** centro m abitato

bulb /bʌlb/ n bulbo m; Electr lampadina f

bulbous /'bʌlbəs/ adj grassoccio

Bulgaria /bʌl'geərɪə/ n Bulgaria f

Bulgarian /bʌl'geərɪən/ adj & n bulgaro, -a mf

bulge /bʌldʒ/ **1** n rigonfiamento m; **it shows all my** ∼**s** mette in evidenza tutti i miei cuscinetti [di grasso]
2 vi esser gonfio (**with** di); ⟨stomach, wall⟩ sporgere; ⟨eyes, with surprise⟩ uscire dalle orbite

bulging /'bʌldʒɪŋ/ adj gonfio; ⟨eyes⟩ sporgente

bulimia [nervosa] /bʊ'lɪmɪə(nɜː'vəʊsə)/ n bulimia f

bulimic /bʊ'lɪmɪk/ adj & n bulimico, -a mf

bulk /bʌlk/ n volume m; (greater part) grosso m; **in** ∼ in grande quantità; (loose) sfuso

bulk-buy vt/i comprare in grandi quantità

bulk-buying n acquisto m in grande quantità

bulk carrier n mezzo m per il trasporto di rinfuse

bulkhead n Naut, Aeron paratia f

bulky /'bʌlkɪ/ adj voluminoso

bull /bʊl/ n toro m; **take the ∼ by the horns** fig prendere il toro per le corna

bull bars npl Auto paraurti mpl tubolari rigidi

bulldog n bulldog m inv

bulldog clip n fermafogli m inv

bulldoze vt (knock down) demolire [con bulldozer]; (clear) spianare [con bulldozer]; (fig: force) costringere

bulldozer /'bʊldəʊzə(r)/ n bulldozer m inv

bullet /'bʊlɪt/ n pallottola f

bulletin /'bʊlɪtɪn/ n bollettino m

bulletin board n Comput bacheca f elettronica

bulletproof /'bʊlɪtpruːf/ adj antiproiettile inv; ⟨vehicle⟩ blindato

bulletproof vest giubbotto m antiproiettile

bullfight /'bʊlfaɪt/ n corrida f

bullfighter /'bʊlfaɪtə(r)/ n torero m

bullfighting /'bʊlfaɪtɪŋ/ n corride fpl

bullion /'bʊlɪən/ n **gold ∼** oro m in lingotti

bullish /'bʊlɪʃ/ adj (optimistic) ottimistico; ⟨market, shares, stocks⟩ al rialzo

bull market n Fin mercato m al rialzo

bullock /'bʊlək/ n manzo m

bullring /'bʊlrɪŋ/ n arena f

bull's-eye /'bʊlzaɪ/ n centro m del bersaglio; **score a ∼** fare centro

bully /'bʊlɪ/ ① n prepotente mf
② vt fare il/la prepotente con

bullying /'bʊlɪŋ/ n prepotenze fpl

bulrush /'bʊlrʌʃ/ n giunco m di palude

bulwark /'bʊlwək/ n Mil, fig baluardo m; Naut parapetto m; (breakwater) frangiflutti m inv

bum¹ /bʌm/ n sl sedere m

bum² n Am fam vagabondo, -a mf
■ **bum around** vi fam vagabondare

bumbag /'bʌmbæg/ n Br fam marsupio m

bumble-bee /'bʌmblbiː/ n calabrone m

bumbling /'bʌmblɪŋ/ adj ⟨attempt⟩ maldestro; ⟨person⟩ inconcludente

bumf /bʌmf/ n (Br: toilet paper) carta f igienica; (fam: documents) scartoffie fpl

bump /bʌmp/ ① n botta f; (swelling) bozzo m, gonfiore m; (in road) protuberanza f
② vt sbattere

■ **bump into** vt sbattere contro; (meet) imbattersi in

■ **bump off** vt fam far fuori

■ **bump up** vt fam [far] aumentare ⟨prices, salaries⟩

bumper /'bʌmpə(r)/ ① n Auto paraurti m inv
② adj abbondante

bumper car n autoscontro m

bumph /bʌmf/ n = BUMF

bumpkin /'bʌmpkɪn/ n **country ∼** zoticone, -a mf

bumptious /'bʌmpʃəs/ adj presuntuoso

bumpy /'bʌmpɪ/ adj ⟨road⟩ accidentato; ⟨flight⟩ turbolento

bun /bʌn/ n focaccina f (dolce); (hair) chignon m inv

bunch /bʌntʃ/ n (of flowers, keys) mazzo m; (of bananas) casco m; (of people) gruppo m; **∼ of grapes** grappolo m d'uva

bundle /'bʌndl/ ① n fascio m; (of money) mazzetta f; **a ∼ of nerves** fam un fascio di nervi
② vt **∼ [up]** affastellare

bundled software /'bʌndld-/ n Comput software m inv in bundle

bung /bʌŋ/ vt fam (throw) buttare
■ **bung up** vt (block) otturare

bungalow /'bʌŋgələʊ/ n bungalow m inv

bungee jump /'bʌndʒɪdʒʌmp/ n salto m con l'elastico

bungee jumping /'bʌndʒɪdʒʌmpɪŋ/ n salto m da ponti, grattacieli, ecc. con un cavo elastico attaccato alla caviglia

bungle /'bʌŋgl/ vt fare un pasticcio di

bunion /'bʌnjən/ n Med callo m all'alluce

bunk /bʌŋk/ ① n cuccetta f; **do a ∼** fam svignarsela
② vi **∼ off/∼ off school** fam marinare la scuola

bunk beds npl letti mpl a castello

bunker /'bʌŋkə(r)/ n (for coal) carbonaia f; (golf) ostacolo m; Mil bunker m inv

bunkum /'bʌŋkəm/ n fandonie fpl

bunny /'bʌnɪ/ n fam coniglietto m

Bunsen [burner] /'bʌnsən[bɜːnə(r)]/ n becco m Bunsen

bunting /'bʌntɪŋ/ n (flags on ship) gran pavese m; Zool zigolo m

buoy /bɔɪ/ n boa f
■ **buoy up** vt fig sostenere ⟨prices⟩; tirare su ⟨person⟩

buoyancy /'bɔɪənsɪ/ n galleggiabilità f

buoyancy aid n salvagente m

buoyant /'bɔɪənt/ adj ⟨boat⟩ galleggiante; ⟨water⟩ che aiuta a galleggiare; fig ⟨person⟩ allegro; ⟨prices⟩ in aumento

burble /'bɜːb(ə)l/ ① n (of stream) gorgoglio m; (of voices) borbottio m

2 *vi* ⟨*stream*⟩ gorgogliare; ~ **on about something** ⟨*person*⟩ blaterare di qualcosa

burbling /'bɜːblɪŋ/ **1** *n* (of stream) gorgoglio *m*; (rambling talk) borbottio *m*
2 *adj* ⟨*stream*⟩ gorgogliante; ⟨*voice*⟩ che borbotta

burden /'bɜːdn/ **1** *n* carico *m*
2 *vt* caricare

burdensome /'bɜːdnsəm/ *adj* gravoso

bureau /'bjʊərəʊ/ *n* (pl **-x** /'bjʊərəʊz/ or ~**s**) (desk) scrivania *f*; (office) ufficio *m*

bureaucracy /bjʊə'rɒkrəsɪ/ *n* burocrazia *f*

bureaucrat /'bjʊərəkræt/ *n* burocrate *mf*

bureaucratic /bjʊrə'krætɪk/ *adj* burocratico

burgeon /'bɜːdʒən/ *vi* ⟨*plant*⟩ germogliare; (fig: flourish) fiorire; (fig: multiply) moltiplicarsi rapidamente, crescere rapidamente

burgeoning /'bɜːdʒənɪŋ/ *adj* fiorente

burger /'bɜːgə(r)/ *n* hamburger *m inv*

burger bar *n* fast-food *m inv*

burglar /'bɜːglə(r)/ *n* svaligiatore, -trice *mf*

burglar alarm *n* antifurto *m inv*

burglarize /'bɜːgləraɪz/ *vt* Am svaligiare

burglar-proof *adj* a prova di ladro

burglary /'bɜːglərɪ/ *n* furto *m* con scasso

burgle /'bɜːgl/ *vt* svaligiare; **they have been** ~**d** sono stati svaligiati

Burgundy /'bɜːgəndɪ/ **1** *n* Borgogna *f*; burgundy (wine) borgogna *m inv*
2 *adj* (colour) rosso scuro

burial /'berɪəl/ *n* sepoltura *f*

burial ground *n* cimitero *m*

Burkina [Faso] /bɜːkinə ('fæsəʊ)/ *n* Burkina Faso *m*

burlesque /bɜː'lesk/ *n* parodia *f*

burly /'bɜːlɪ/ *adj* (**-ier**, **-iest**) corpulento

Burma /'bɜːmə/ *n* Birmania *f*

Burmese /bɜː'miːz/ *adj* & *n* birmano, -a *mf*

burn /bɜːn/ **1** *n* bruciatura *f*
2 *vt* (pt/pp **burnt** or **burned**) bruciare; ~ **one's boats** or **bridges** fig tagliarsi i ponti alle spalle; Comput masterizzare ⟨*CD, DVD*⟩
3 *vi* bruciare
▪ **burn down** *vt/i* bruciare
▪ **burn out** *vi* fig esaurirsi
▪ **burn up** *vt* fig bruciare ⟨*calories, energy*⟩

burned-out *adj* = BURNT-OUT

burner /'bɜːnə(r)/ *n* (on stove) bruciatore *m*

burning /'bɜːnɪŋ/ **1** *n* (setting on fire) incendio *m*; **I can smell** ~! sento odore di bruciato!

2 *adj* ⟨*ember, coal*⟩ acceso; (on fire) in fiamme; fig ⟨*fever, desire*⟩ bruciante; **a** ~ **sensation** una sensazione di bruciore; **a** ~ **question** una questione scottante

burnish /'bɜːnɪʃ/ *vt* lucidare

burns unit *n* Med reparto *m* grandi ustionati

burnt /bɜːnt/ ▸ BURN

burnt-out *adj* ⟨*building, car*⟩ distrutto dalle fiamme; fig ⟨*person*⟩ sfinito

burp /bɜːp/ **1** *n* fam rutto *m*
2 *vi* fam ruttare

burr /bɜː(r)/ *n* Bot lappa *f*; (in language) erre *f* moscia

burrow /'bʌrəʊ/ **1** *n* tana *f*
2 *vt* scavare ⟨*hole*⟩

bursar /'bɜːsə(r)/ *n* economo, -a *mf*

bursary /'bɜːsərɪ/ *n* borsa *f* di studio

burst /bɜːst/ **1** *n* (of gunfire, energy, laughter) scoppio *m*; (of speed) scatto *m*
2 *vt* (pt/pp **burst**) far scoppiare; ~ **its banks** ⟨*river*⟩ rompere gli argini
3 *vi* scoppiare; ~ **into tears** scoppiare in lacrime; ~ **into flames** andare in fiamme; **she** ~ **into the room** ha fatto irruzione nella stanza; **be** ~**ing at the seams** ⟨*room*⟩ scoppiare
▪ **burst in** *vi* (enter suddenly) fare irruzione
▪ **burst out** *vi* ~ **out laughing/crying** scoppiare a ridere/piangere

Burundi /bʊ'rʊndɪ/ *n* Burundi *m*

bury /'berɪ/ *vt* (pt/pp **-ied**) seppellire; (hide) nascondere

bus /bʌs/ **1** *n* autobus *m inv*, pullman *m inv*; (long distance) pullman *m inv*, corriera *f*
2 *vt* (pt/pp **bussed**) trasportare in autobus

busby /'bʌzbɪ/ *n* colbacco *m* militare

bus conductor *n* ≈ bigliettaio *m*

bus conductress *n* ≈ bigliettaia *f*

bus driver *n* conducente *mf* di autobus

bush /bʊʃ/ *n* cespuglio *m*; (land) boscaglia *f*

bushed /bʊʃt/ *adj* (fam: tired) distrutto

bushel /'bʊʃ(ə)l/ *n* hide one's light under a ~ essere troppo modesto; Am fam ~s of un sacco di

bushfighting *n* Mil guerriglia *f*

bushfire *n* incendio *m* in aperta campagna

bush telegraph *n* fig hum tamtam *m inv*

bushy /'bʊʃɪ/ *adj* (**-ier**, **-iest**) folto

busily /'bɪzɪlɪ/ *adv* con grande impegno

business /'bɪznɪs/ *n* affare *m*; Comm affari *mpl*; (establishment) attività *f* di commercio; **on** ~ per affari; **he has no** ~ **to** non ha alcun diritto di; **mind one's own** ~ farsi gli affari propri; **that's none of your** ~ non sono affari tuoi

business activity n attività f inv economica; (of single company) attività f inv aziendale

business analyst n analista mf finanziario, -a

business associate n socio, -a mf

business call n (phone call) telefonata f di lavoro; (visit) appuntamento m di lavoro

business card n biglietto m da visita

business centre n centro m affari

business class n Aeron business class f inv

business college n scuola f di amministrazione aziendale

business contact n contatto m di lavoro

business cycle n ciclo m economico

business deal n operazione f commerciale

business expenses npl spese fpl di lavoro

business failures npl chiusura f di aziende

business hours npl (in office) orario m d'ufficio; (of shop) orario m d'apertura

business-like adj efficiente

business lunch n pranzo m di lavoro or d'affari

businessman /'bɪznɪsmən/ n uomo m d'affari

business management n amministrazione f aziendale

business park n centro m affari

business plan n piano m economico; (of single company) programma m aziendale

business premises npl sede f di un'azienda

business proposition n proposta f d'affari

business reply envelope n busta f affrancata

business school n scuola f di amministrazione aziendale

business software n software m per l'ufficio

business studies npl economia f e commercio

business suit n (for man) abito m scuro

business trip n viaggio m di lavoro

businesswoman /'bɪznɪswʊmən/ n donna f d'affari

busk /bʌsk/ vi Br ⟨singer⟩ cantare per strada; ⟨musician⟩ suonare per strada

busker /'bʌskə(r)/ n suonatore, -trice mf ambulante

bus lane n corsia f autobus

busload /'bʌsləʊd/ n a ∼ of tourists una comitiva di turisti; by the ∼ in massa

busman's holiday /bʌsmənz'hɒlɪdeɪ/ n Br vacanze fpl passate a fare quello che si fa normalmente

bus pass n abbonamento m all'autobus

bus route n percorso m dell'autobus

bus shelter n pensilina f alla fermata dell'autobus

bus station n stazione f degli autobus

bus stop n fermata f d'autobus

bust[1] /bʌst/ n busto m; (chest) petto m

bust[2] ① adj fam rotto; go ∼ fallire ② vt (pt/pp **busted** or **bust**) fam far scoppiare ③ vi scoppiare

bustle /'bʌsl/ n (activity) trambusto m ■ **bustle about** vi affannarsi

bustling /'bʌslɪŋ/ adj animato

bust size n circonferenza f del torace

bust-up n fam lite f

busy /'bɪzɪ/ ① adj (-ier, -iest) occupato; ⟨day, time⟩ intenso; ⟨street⟩ affollato; (with traffic) pieno di traffico; be ∼ doing essere occupato a fare ② vt ∼ oneself darsi da fare

busybody /'bɪzɪbɒdɪ/ n ficcanaso m f inv

but /bʌt/, ① atono /bət/ conj ma ② prep eccetto, tranne; **nobody** ∼ **you** nessuno tranne te; ∼ **for** (without) se non fosse stato per; **the last** ∼ **one** il penultimo; **the next** ∼ **one** il secondo ③ adv soltanto; **there were** ∼ **two** ce n'erano soltanto due

butane /'bju:teɪn/ n butano m

butch /bʊtʃ/ adj fam ⟨man⟩ macho inv; ⟨woman⟩ mascolino

butcher /'bʊtʃə(r)/ ① n macellaio m ② vt macellare; fig massacrare

butcher's [shop] /'bʊtʃəz[ʃɒp]/ n macelleria f

butchery /'bʊtʃərɪ/ n (trade) macelleria f; (slaughter) massacro m

butler /'bʌtlə(r)/ n maggiordomo m

butt /bʌt/ ① n (of gun) calcio m; (of cigarette) mozzicone m; (for water) barile m; (fig: target) bersaglio m ② vt dare una testata a; ⟨goat⟩ dare un'incornata a ■ **butt in** vi interrompere

butter /'bʌtə(r)/ ① n burro m ② vt imburrare ■ **butter up** vt fam arruffianarsi

butter-bean n fagiolo m bianco

buttercup n ranuncolo m

butter dish n portaburro m inv

butter-fingered adj con le mani di pasta frolla

butter-fingers n fam mani fpl di pasta frolla

butterfly /'bʌtəflaɪ/ n farfalla f

butterfly net n retino m per farfalle

butterfly nut *n* dado *m* ad alette

butterfly stroke *n* nuoto *m* a farfalla

buttermilk /ˈbʌtəmɪlk/ *n* latticello *m*

butterscotch /ˈbʌtəskɒtʃ/ *n* caramella *f* dura a base di burro e zucchero

buttocks /ˈbʌtəks/ *npl* natiche *fpl*

button /ˈbʌtn/ ① *n* bottone *m*; (on mouse, of status bar) pulsante *m*
② *vt* ~ **[up]** abbottonare
③ *vi* ~ **[up]** abbottonarsi

button battery *n* batteria *f* a bottone

button-down *adj* ⟨collar⟩ button down, coi bottoni; ⟨shirt⟩ con il colletto coi bottoni, button down

buttonhole *n* occhiello *m*, asola *f*

buttonhook *n* asola *f*, occhiello *m*

button mushroom *n* piccolo champignon *m inv*

buttress /ˈbʌtrɪs/ ① *n* contrafforte *m*
② *vt* fig sostenere

buxom /ˈbʌksəm/ *adj* formosa

buy /baɪ/ ① *n* good/bad ~ buon/cattivo acquisto *m*
② *vt* (pt/pp **bought**) comprare; ~ **somebody a drink** pagare da bere a qualcuno; **I'll ~ this one** (drink) questo lo offro io
■ **buy into** *vt* (accept) accettare
■ **buy off** *vt* (bribe) comprare
■ **buy out** *vt* rilevare la quota di ⟨one's partner⟩
■ **buy up** *vt* (buy all of) accaparrarsi

buyer /ˈbaɪə(r)/ *n* compratore, -trice *mf*

buyout /ˈbaɪaʊt/ *n* Comm rilevamento *m*

buzz /bʌz/ ① *n* ronzio *m*; **give somebody a ~** fam (on phone) dare un colpo di telefono a qualcuno; (excite) mettere in fermento qualcuno
② *vi* ronzare
③ *vt* ~ **somebody** chiamare qualcuno col cicalino
■ **buzz off** *vi* fam levarsi di torno

buzzard /ˈbʌzəd/ *n* poiana *f*

buzzer /ˈbʌzə(r)/ *n* cicalino *m*

buzzing /ˈbʌzɪŋ/ ① *n* (of buzzer) trillo *m*; (of insects) ronzio *m*
② *adj* ⟨party, atmosphere, town⟩ molto animato

buzzword /ˈbʌzwɜːd/ *n* fam parola *f* di moda

by /baɪ/ ① *prep* (near, next to) vicino a; (at the latest) per; **by Mozart** di Mozart; **he was run over by a bus** è stato investito da un autobus; **by oneself** da solo; **by the sea** al mare; **by sea** via mare; **by car/bus** in macchina/autobus; **by day/night** di giorno/notte; **by the hour/metre** a ore/metri; **six metres by four** sei metri per quattro;; **he won by six metres** ha vinto di sei metri; **I missed the train by a minute** ho perso il treno per un minuto; **I'll be home by six** sarò a casa per le sei; **by this time next week** a quest'ora tra una settimana; **he rushed by me** mi è passato accanto di corsa
② *adv* **she'll be here by and by** sarà qui fra poco; **by and by the police arrived** poco dopo è arrivata la polizia; **by and large** nel complesso; **put by** mettere da parte; **go/pass by** passare

bye /baɪ/ *int* fam ciao!

bye-bye /ˈbaɪbaɪ/ *int* fam ciao, arrivederci; **go ~s** Br (baby talk) andare a fare la nanna

by-election *n* elezione *f* straordinaria indetta per coprire una carica rimasta vacante in Parlamento

Byelorussia /bjeləʊˈrʌʃə/ *n* Bielorussia *f*

Byelorussian /bjeləʊˈrʌʃn/ *adj* & *n* bielorusso

bygone *adj* passato

by-law *n* legge *f* locale

by-line *n* (In newspaper) nome *m* dell'autore; Sport linea *f* laterale

bypass ① *n* circonvallazione *f*; Med by-pass *m inv*
② *vt* evitare

by-product *n* sottoprodotto *m*

by-road *n* strada *f* secondaria

bystander *n* spettatore, -trice *mf*

byte /baɪt/ *n* Comput byte *m inv*

byway *n* strada *f* secondaria

byword *n* **be a ~ for** essere sinonimo di

by-your-leave *n* **without so much as a ~** senza neanche chiedere il permesso

Byzantine /bɪˈzæntaɪn/ *adj* bizantino

c¹, C /siː/ *n* (letter) c, C *f inv*; (Br Sch: grade) voto *m* scolastico corrispondente alla sufficienza; Mus do *m inv*

c², C *abbr* (**Celsius, centigrade**) C; *abbr* (**cent(s)**) c; *abbr* (**circa**) ca

C4 /siːˈfɔː(r)/ *abbr* Br (**channel four**) rete *f* televisiva britannica

CA Br *abbr* (**Chartered Accountant**) [dottore *m*] commercialista *m*; Am *abbr* (**California**) Cal; *abbr* (**Central America**) America *f* centrale

CAA *n* Br *abbr* (**Civil Aviation Authority**) organismo *m* di controllo dell'aviazione civile

CAB *n* Br *abbr* (**Citizens' Advice Bureau**) ufficio *m* di consulenza legale gratuita per i cittadini

cab /kæb/ *n* taxi *m inv*; (of lorry, train) cabina *f*

cabana /kəˈbɑːnə/ *n* (Am: hut) cabina *f* da spiaggia

cabaret /ˈkæbəreɪ/ *n* cabaret *m inv*

cabbage /ˈkæbɪdʒ/ *n* cavolo *m*

cabby /ˈkæbɪ/ *n fam* tassista *mf*

cab driver *n* tassista *mf*

cabin /ˈkæbɪn/ *n* (of plane, ship) cabina *f*; (hut) capanna *f*

cabin boy *n* mozzo *m*

cabin crew *n* Aeron equipaggio *m*

cabin cruiser *n* cabinato *m*

cabinet /ˈkæbɪnɪt/ *n* armadietto *m*; [display] ∼ vetrina *f*; C∼ Pol consiglio *m* dei ministri

cabinet-maker *n* ebanista *mf*

cabinet meeting *n* Br riunione *f* del governo

cabinet minister *n* Br ministro *m*

cabinet reshuffle *n* Br rimpasto *m* ministeriale

cable /ˈkeɪb(ə)l/ *n* cavo *m*; (TV) TV *f* via cavo; this channel is only available on ∼ questo canale è disponibile solo sulla TV via cavo

cable car *n* cabina *f* (della funivia)

cable company *n* rete *f* televisiva via cavo

cablegram *n* cablogramma *m*

cable-knit *adj* ⟨*sweater*⟩ a trecce

cable railway *n* funicolare *f*

cable-ready *adj* predisposto per la TV via cavo

cable television *n* televisione *f* via cavo

cable TV *n* TV *f inv* via cavo

cableway *n* (for people) funivia *f*

caboodle /kəˈbuːdl/ *n fam* the whole ∼ baracca e burattini

cab rank, cab stand *n* posteggio *m* dei taxi

cache /kæʃ/ *n* nascondiglio *m*; ∼ of arms deposito *m* segreto di armi

cache memory *n* Comput memoria *f* cache

cachet /ˈkæʃeɪ/ *n* prestigio *m*

cackle /ˈkækl/ *vi* ridacchiare

cacophony /kəˈkɒfənɪ/ *n* cacofonia *f*

cactus /ˈkæktəs/ *n* (pl **-ti** /ˈkæktaɪ/ or **-tuses**) cactus *m inv*

CAD /kæd/ *n abbr* (**computer-aided design**) CAD *m inv*

cadaver /kəˈdɑːvə(r)/ *n* cadavere *m*

cadaverous /kəˈdævərəs/ *adj* cadaverico

CADCAM /ˈkædkæm/ *n abbr* (**computer-aided design and computer-aided manufacture**) CADCAM *m inv*

caddie /ˈkædɪ/ *n* portabastoni *m inv*

caddy /ˈkædɪ/ *n* [**tea-**] ∼ barattolo *m* del tè

cadence /ˈkeɪdəns/ *n* cadenza *f*

cadet /kəˈdet/ *n* cadetto *m*

cadet corps *n* Mil corpo *m* dei cadetti

cadet school *n* scuola *f* allievi ufficiali

cadge /kædʒ/ *vt/i fam* scroccare

cadre /ˈkɑːdr(ə)/ *n* Admin, Pol quadri *mpl*

CAE *n abbr* (**computer-aided engineering**) CAE *m inv*

Caesarean, Caesarian /sɪˈzeərɪən/ *n* parto *m* cesareo

café /ˈkæfeɪ/ *n* caffè *m inv*

cafeteria /kæfəˈtɪərɪə/ *n* tavola *f* calda

cafetière /kæfəˈtjeə(r)/ *n* caffettiera *f* a stantuffo

caffeine /ˈkæfiːn/ *n* caffeina *f*

cage /keɪdʒ/ *n* gabbia *f*

cage bird *n* uccello *m* da gabbia

cagey /ˈkeɪdʒɪ/ *adj fam* riservato (**about** su)

cagoule /kəˈguːl/ *n* Br K-way® *m inv*

cahoots /kəˈhuːts/ *npl fam* be in ∼ essere in combutta

cairn /keən/ *n* (of stones) tumulo *m* di pietre

Cairo /ˈkaɪrəʊ/ *n* il Cairo

cajole /kəˈdʒəʊl/ *vt* persuadere con le lusinghe

cake /keɪk/ *n* torta *f*; (small) pasticcino *m*; ∼ of soap saponetta *f*; it was a piece of ∼ *fam* è stato un gioco da ragazzi; you can't have your ∼ and eat it *fig* non si può avere la botte piena e la moglie ubriaca; sell like hot ∼s andare a ruba

caked /keɪkt/ *adj* incrostato (**with** di)

cake mix *n* miscela *f* per torte

cake shop *n* pasticceria *f*

cake tin *n* (for baking) tortiera *f*; (for storing) scatola *f* di latta (per torte)

CAL *abbr* (**computer-assisted learning**) CAL *m*

Calabria /kəˈlæbrɪə/ *n* Calabria *f*

Calabrian /kəˈlæbrɪən/ *adj & n* calabrese

calamine lotion /ˈkæləmaɪn/ *n* lozione *f* alla calamina

calamitous /kə'læmɪtəs/ *adj* disastroso

calamity /kə'læmətɪ/ *n* calamità *f inv*

calcify /'kælsɪfaɪ/ *vi* calcificarsi

calcium /'kælsɪəm/ *n* calcio *m*

calculate /'kælkjʊleɪt/ *vt* calcolare

calculated /'kælkjʊleɪtɪd/ *adj* ⟨risk, insult, decision⟩ calcolato; ⟨crime⟩ premeditato

calculating /'kælkjʊleɪtɪŋ/ *adj* fig calcolatore

calculating machine *n* calcolatrice *f*

calculation /kælkjʊ'leɪʃn/ *n* calcolo *m*

calculator /'kælkjʊleɪtə(r)/ *n* calcolatrice *f*

calculus /'kælkjʊləs/ *n* Math, Med calcolo *m*

calendar /'kælɪndə(r)/ *n* calendario *m*

calendar month *n* mese *m* civile

calendar year *n* anno *m* civile

calf[1] /kɑ:f/ *n* (pl **calves**) vitello *m*

calf[2] *n* (pl **calves**) Anat polpaccio *m*

calfskin /'kɑ:fskɪn/ *n* [pelle *f* di] vitello *m*

calibrate /'kælɪbreɪt/ *vt* calibrare ⟨instrument⟩; tarare ⟨scales⟩

calibre /'kælɪbə(r)/ *n* calibro *m*

calico /'kælɪkəʊ/ *n* cotone *m* grezzo

California /kælɪ'fɔ:nɪə/ *n* California *f*

Californian /kælɪ'fɔ:nɪən/ *adj & n* californiano, -a *mf*

CALL *n abbr* (computer-assisted language learning) CALL *m inv*

call /kɔ:l/ **①** *n* grido *m*; Teleph telefonata *f*; (visit) visita *f*; **be on** ~ ⟨doctor⟩ essere di guardia; **good/bad** ~ fam buona/pessima idea

② *vt* chiamare; indire ⟨strike⟩; **be ~ed** chiamarsi

③ *vi* chiamare; ~ **[in or round]** passare

■ **call back** *vt/i* richiamare

■ **call by** *vi* (make brief visit) passare

■ **call for** *vt* (ask for) chiedere; (require) richiedere; (fetch) passare a prendere

■ **call in ①** *vi* (make brief visit) passare

② *vt* chiamare ⟨patient, client⟩; interpellare ⟨expert⟩

■ **call off** *vt* richiamare ⟨dog⟩; disdire ⟨meeting⟩; revocare ⟨strike⟩

■ **call on** *vt* chiamare; (appeal to) fare un appello a; (visit) visitare

■ **call out** *vt/i* chiamare ad alta voce

■ **call together** *vt* riunire

■ **call up** *vt* Mil chiamare alle armi; Teleph chiamare

callback facility /'kɔ:lbæk/ *n* Teleph servizio *m* telefonico che permette di individuare il numero che ha chiamato

call barring *n* blocco *m* chiamate

call box *n* cabina *f* telefonica

call centre Br, **call center** Am *n* call center *m inv*

caller /'kɔ:lə(r)/ *n* visitatore, -trice *mf*; Teleph persona *f* che telefona

caller identification *n* identificativo *m* del chiamante

call-girl *n* call-girl *f inv*, [ragazza *f*] squillo *f inv*

calligrapher /kə'lɪgrəfə(r)/ *n* calligrafo, -a *mf*

calligraphy /kə'lɪgrəfɪ/ *n* calligrafia *f*

calling /'kɔ:lɪŋ/ *n* vocazione *f*

calliper /'kælɪpə(r)/ *n* (for measuring) calibro *m*; (leg support) tutore *m*

callisthenics /kælɪs'θenɪks/ *n* ginnastica *f*

callous /'kæləs/ *adj* insensibile

callousness /'kæləsnɪs/ *n* insensibilità *f*

call-out *n* (doctor) visita *f* a domicilio; (plumber, electrician) chiamata *f*

call-out charge *n* costo *m* della chiamata

callow /'kæləʊ/ *adj* immaturo

call screening *n* filtro *m* chiamate

call sign *n* Radio segnale *m* di chiamata

call-up *n* Mil chiamata *f* alle armi

call-up papers *npl* cartolina *f* precetto

call waiting *n* avviso *m* di chiamata in linea

calm /kɑ:m/ **①** *adj* calmo

② *n* calma *f*

■ **calm down ①** *vt* calmare

② *vi* calmarsi

calmly /'kɑ:mlɪ/ *adv* con calma

calmness /'kɑ:mnɪs/ *n* calma *f*

Calor gas® /'kælə/ *n* Br liquigas® *m inv*

calorie /'kælərɪ/ *n* caloria *f*

calorific /kælə'rɪfɪk/ *adj* calorico

calve /kɑ:v/ *vi* figliare

calves /kɑ:vz/ *npl* ▶ CALF[1] & CALF[2]

cam /kæm/ *n* Techn camma *f*

camaraderie /kæmə'rædərɪ/ *n* cameratismo *m*

camber /'kæmbə(r)/ *n* curvatura *f*

Cambodia /kæm'bəʊdɪə/ *n* Cambogia *f*

Cambodian /kæm'bəʊdɪən/ *adj & n* cambogiano, -a *mf*

camcorder /'kæmkɔ:də(r)/ *n* videocamera *f*

came /keɪm/ ▶ COME

camel /'kæml/ *n* cammello *m*

camel hair *n* cammello *m*

camellia /kə'mi:lɪə/ *n* camelia *f*

cameo /'kæmɪəʊ/ *n* cammeo *m*

cameo role *n* Theat, Cinema breve apparizione *f*

camera /'kæmərə/ *n* macchina *f* fotografica; TV telecamera *f*

camera crew *n* troupe *f inv* televisiva

cameraman /'kæmərəmæn/ n
operatore m [televisivo], cameraman m
inv

Cameroon /'kæməruːn/ n il Camerun

camisole /'kæmɪsəʊl/ n canotta f

camomile /'kæməmaɪl/ n camomilla f

camouflage /'kæməflɑːʒ/ ❶ n
mimetizzazione f
❷ vt mimetizzare

camp[1] /kæmp/ ❶ n campeggio f; Mil
campo m
❷ vi campeggiare; Mil accamparsi

camp[2] adj (affected) affettato

campaign /kæm'peɪn/ ❶ n campagna f
❷ vi fare una campagna

campaigner /kæm'peɪnə(r)/ n
partecipante mf a una campagna

campaign trail n be on the ～ ～ fare
la campagna elettorale

campaign worker n Br Pol membro m
dello staff di una campagna elettorale

camp bed n letto m da campo

camper /'kæmpə(r)/ n campeggiatore,
-trice mf; Auto camper m inv

campfire /'kæmpfaɪə(r)/ n fuoco m di
bivacco

camphor /'kæmfə(r)/ n canfora f

camping /'kæmpɪŋ/ n campeggio m

camping equipment n attrezzatura f
da campeggio

camping gas n gas m inv da
campeggio

camping holiday n vacanza f in tenda

camping site n campeggio m

camping stool n Br sgabello m
pieghevole

camping stove n fornello m da
campeggio

campsite /'kæmpsaɪt/ n campeggio m

campus /'kæmpəs/ n (pl **-puses**) Univ
città f universitaria, campus m inv

camshaft /'kæmʃɑːft/ n albero m a
camme

can[1] /kæn/ ❶ n (for petrol) latta f; (tin)
scatola f; ～ of beer lattina f di birra
❷ vt mettere in scatola

can[2] /kæn/, unstressed /kən/ v aux (pres
can; pt could) (be able to) potere; (know
how to) sapere; I cannot or can't go non
posso andare; he could not or couldn't go
non poteva andare; she can't swim non sa
nuotare; I ～ smell something burning
sento odor di bruciato

Canada /'kænədə/ n Canada m

Canadian /kə'neɪdɪən/ adj & n canadese
mf

canal /kə'næl/ n canale m

canal boat, **canal barge** n chiatta f

canapé /'kænəpeɪ/ n canapè m inv

Canaries /kə'neərɪz/ npl Canarie fpl

canary /kə'neərɪ/ n canarino m

cancel /'kænsl/ ❶ v (pt/pp **cancelled**)
vt disdire ⟨meeting, newspaper⟩; revocare
⟨contract, order⟩; annullare ⟨reservation,
appointment, stamp⟩
❷ vi ⟨guest, host⟩ annullare

cancellation /kænsə'leɪʃn/ n (of meeting,
contract) revoca f; (in hotel, restaurant, for flight)
cancellazione f

cancer /'kænsə(r)/ n cancro m; C～ Astr
Cancro m

cancerous /'kænsərəs/ adj canceroso

cancer patient n malato,-a mf di
cancro

cancer research n ricerca f sul
cancro

candelabra /kændə'lɑːbrə/ n
candelabro m

candid /'kændɪd/ adj franco

candidacy /'kændɪdəsɪ/ n Pol
candidatura f

candidate /'kændɪdət/ n candidato, -a
mf

candidly /'kændɪdlɪ/ adv francamente

candied /'kændɪd/ adj candito

candle /'kænd(ə)l/ n candela f

candlelight /'kænd(ə)llaɪt/ n by ～ a
lume di candela

candlelit dinner /'kænd(ə)llɪt/ n cena
f a lume di candela

candlestick /'kænd(ə)lstɪk/ n
portacandele m inv

candlewick bedspread
/'kænd(ə)lwɪk/ n copriletto m inv di
ciniglia

candour /'kændə(r)/ n franchezza f

candy /'kændɪ/ n Am caramella f; a [piece
of] ～ una caramella

candyfloss /'kændɪflɒs/ n zucchero m
filato

candy-striped /straɪpt/ adj (blue) a
righe bianche e celesti; (pink) a righe
bianche e rosa

cane /keɪn/ ❶ n (stick) bastone m; Sch
bacchetta f
❷ vt prendere a bacchettate ⟨pupil⟩

cane sugar n zucchero m di canna

canine /'keɪnaɪn/ adj canino

canine tooth n canino m

canister /'kænɪstə(r)/ n barattolo m

cannabis /'kænəbɪs/ n cannabis f

canned /kænd/ adj in scatola; ～ music
fam musica f registrata

cannibal /'kænɪbl/ n cannibale mf

cannibalism /'kænɪbəlɪzm/ n
cannibalismo m

cannibalize /'kænɪbəlaɪz/ vt riciclare
parti di

cannon /'kænən/ n inv cannone m

cannon ball n palla f di cannone

cannon fodder *n* carne *f* da cannone, carne *f* da macello

cannot /'kænɒt/ ▶ CAN²

canny /'kænɪ/ *adj* astuto

canoe /kə'nu:/ ⟨1⟩ *n* canoa *f*
⟨2⟩ *vi* andare in canoa

canoeing /kə'nu:ɪŋ/ *n* canoismo *m*

canon /'kænən/ *n* (rule) canone *m*; (person) canonico *m*

canonization /kænənaɪz'zeɪʃn/ *n* canonizzazione *f*

canonize /'kænənaɪz/ *vt* canonizzare

canoodle /kə'nu:dl/ *vi* fam sbaciucchiarsi

can-opener *n* apriscatole *m inv*

canopy /'kænəpɪ/ *n* baldacchino *f*; (of parachute) calotta *f*

cant /kænt/ *n* (hypocrisy) ipocrisia *f*; (jargon) gergo *m*

can't /kɑ:nt/ = CANNOT ▶ CAN²

cantankerous /kæn'tæŋkərəs/ *adj* stizzoso

cantata /kæn'tɑ:tə/ *n* Mus cantata *f*

canteen /kæn'ti:n/ *n* mensa *f*; ~ of cutlery servizio *m* di posate

canter /'kæntə(r)/ ⟨1⟩ *n* piccolo galoppo *m*
⟨2⟩ *vi* andare a piccolo galoppo

cantilever /'kæntɪli:və(r)/ *n* cantilever *m inv*, trave *f* a sbalzo

cantonal /'kæntənəl/ *adj* cantonale

canvas /'kænvəs/ *n* tela *f*; (painting) dipinto *m* su tela

canvass /'kænvəs/ *vi* Pol fare propaganda elettorale

canvasser /'kænvəsə(r)/ *n* propagandista *mf* elettorale (porta a porta)

canvassing /'kænvəsɪŋ/ *n* (door to door for votes) propaganda *f* porta a porta; (door to door for sales) vendita *f* porta a porta

canyon /'kænjən/ *n* canyon *m inv*

canyoning /'kænjənɪŋ/ *n* canyoning *m inv*

cap /kæp/ ⟨1⟩ *n* berretto *m*; (nurse's) cuffia *f*; (top, lid) tappo *m*
⟨2⟩ *vt* (pt/pp **capped**) (fig: do better than) superare

capability /keɪpə'bɪlətɪ/ *n* capacità *f*

capable /'keɪpəbl/ *adj* capace; (skilful) abile; be ~ of doing something essere capace di fare qualcosa

capably /'keɪpəblɪ/ *adv* con abilità

capacious /kə'peɪʃəs/ *adj* ⟨pocket, car boot⟩ capace

capacity /kə'pæsətɪ/ *n* capacità *f*; (function) qualità *f*; in my ~ as in qualità di

cape¹ /keɪp/ *n* (cloak) cappa *f*

cape² *n* Geog capo *m*

Cape of Good Hope *n* Capo *m* di Buona Speranza

caper¹ /'keɪpə(r)/ ⟨1⟩ *vi* saltellare
⟨2⟩ *n* fam birichinata *f*

caper² *n* Culin cappero *m*

Cape Town *n* Città *f* del Capo

Cape Verde /vɜ:d/ *n* Capo Verde *m*

capful /'kæpfʊl/ *n* tappo *m*

cap gun *n* pistola *f* a capsule

capillary /kə'pɪlərɪ/ *adj* & *n* capillare *m*

capital /'kæpɪtl/ *n* (town) capitale *f*; (money) capitale *m*; (letter) lettera *f* maiuscola

capital allowances *npl* detrazioni *mpl* per ammortamento

capital city *n* capitale *f*

capital expenditure *n* spese *fpl* in conto capitale; (personal) spese *fpl* di capitale

capital gains tax *n* imposta *f* sui redditi di capitale

capital goods *npl* beni *mpl* strumentali

capital-intensive *adj* ad uso intensivo di capitale

capital investment *n* investimento *m* di capitale

capitalism /'kæpɪtəlɪzm/ *n* capitalismo *m*

capitalist /'kæpɪtəlɪst/ *adj* & *n* capitalista *mf*

capitalize /'kæpɪtəlaɪz/ *vi* ~ on fig trarre vantaggio da

capital letter *n* lettera *f* maiuscola

capital punishment *n* pena *f* capitale

capital spending *n* spese *fpl* in conto capitale

capital transfer tax *n* imposta *f* sui trasferimenti di capitale

capitulate /kə'pɪtjʊleɪt/ *vi* capitolare

capitulation /kəpɪtjʊ'leɪʃn/ *n* capitolazione *f*

capon /'keɪpɒn/ *n* cappone *m*

caprice /kə'pri:s/ *n* (whim) capriccio *m*

capricious /kə'prɪʃəs/ *adj* capriccioso

Capricorn /'kæprɪkɔ:n/ *n* Astr Capricorno *m*

caps /kæps/ *npl abbr* (**capital letters**) maius. *fpl*

capsicum /'kæpsɪkəm/ *n* peperone *m*

capsize /kæp'saɪz/ ⟨1⟩ *vi* capovolgersi
⟨2⟩ *vt* capovolgere

caps lock *n* Comput bloccamaiuscole *m inv*

capstan /'kæpstən/ *n* argano *m*

capsule /'kæpsju:l/ *n* capsula *f*

captain /'kæptɪn/ ⟨1⟩ *n* capitano *m*
⟨2⟩ *vt* comandare ⟨team⟩

caption /'kæpʃn/ *n* intestazione *f*; (of illustration) didascalia *f*

captious /'kæpʃəs/ *adj* ⟨remark⟩ ipercritico

captivate /'kæptɪveɪt/ *vt* incantare

captive /'kæptɪv/ **①** *adj* prigioniero; **hold/take** ∼ tenere/fare prigioniero **②** *n* prigioniero, -a *mf*

captivity /kæp'tɪvətɪ/ *n* prigionia *f*; (animals) cattività *f*

captor /'kæptə(r)/ *n* (of person) persona *f* che tiene prigioniero qualcuno; (of person for ransom) rapitore, -trice *mf*

capture /'kæptʃə(r)/ **①** *n* cattura *f* **②** *vt* catturare; attirare ⟨attention⟩

car /kɑ:(r)/ *n* macchina *f*; **by** ∼ in macchina

carafe /kə'ræf/ *n* caraffa *f*

car alarm *n* antifurto *m* della macchina

caramel /'kærəməl/ *n* (sweet) caramella *f* al mou; Culin caramello *m*

carat /'kærət/ *n* carato *m*

caravan /'kærəvæn/ *n* roulotte *f inv*; (horsedrawn) carovana *f*

caravan site *n* area *f* per roulotte

caraway /'kærəweɪ/ *n* (plant) cumino *m* dei prati

carbohydrate /kɑ:bə'haɪdreɪt/ *n* carboidrato *m*

carbolic /kɑ:'bɒlɪk/ *adj* (soap) al fenolo

car bomb *n* autobomba *f*

carbon /'kɑ:bən/ *n* carbonio *m*: (paper) carta *f* carbone; (copy) copia *f* in carta carbone

carbon copy *n* copia *f* in carta carbone; (fig: person) ritratto *m*

carbon-date *vt* datare con il carbonio 14

carbon dating *n* datazione *f* con il carbonio 14

carbon dioxide *n* anidride *f* carbonica

carbon filter *n* filtro *m* al carbone

carbon monoxide *n* monossido *m* di carbonio

carbon paper *n* carta *f* carbone

car boot sale *n* Br mercatino *m* di oggetti usati, esposti nei bagagliai delle macchine

carbuncle /'kɑ:bʌŋk(ə)l/ *n* Med foruncolo *m*

carburettor /kɑ:bjʊ'retə(r)/ *n* carburatore *m*

carcass /'kɑ:kəs/ *n* carcassa *f*

carcinogen /kɑ:'sɪnədʒən/ *n* cancerogeno *m*

carcinogenic /kɑ:smə'dʒenɪk/ *adj* cancerogeno

car crash *n* scontro *m* automobilistico

card /kɑ:d/ *n* (for birthday, Christmas etc) biglietto *m* di auguri; (playing ∼) carta *f*

[da gioco]; (membership ∼) tessera *f*; (business ∼) biglietto *m* da visita; (credit ∼) carta *f* di credito; Comput scheda *f*

cardboard /'kɑ:dbɔ:d/ *n* cartone *m*

cardboard box *n* scatola *f* di cartone; (large) scatolone *m*

cardboard city *n* fam zona *f* in cui vivono i senzatetto

car deck *n* (on ferry) ponte *m* auto

card game *n* gioco *m* di carte

cardiac /'kɑ:dɪæk/ *adj* cardiaco

cardiac arrest *n* arresto *m* cardiaco

cardigan /'kɑ:dɪgən/ *n* cardigan *m inv*

cardinal /'kɑ:dɪnl/ **①** *adj* cardinale; ∼ **number** numero *m* cardinale **②** *n* Relig cardinale *m*

card index *n* schedario *m*

cardiologist /kɑ:dɪ'ɒlədʒɪst/ *n* cardiologo, -a *mf*

cardiology /kɑ:dɪ'ɒlədʒɪ/ *n* cardiologia *f*

cardiovascular /kɑ:dɪə'væskjʊlə(r)/ *adj* cardiovascolare

card key *n* scheda *f* magnetica

cardphone *n* telefono *m* a scheda

card table *n* tappeto *m* verde

card trick *n* trucco *m* con le carte

care /keə(r)/ **①** *n* cura *f*; (caution) attenzione *f*; (worry) preoccupazione *f*; ∼ **of** (on letter abbr **c/o**) presso; **take** ∼ (be cautious) fare attenzione; **bye, take** ∼ ciao, stammi bene; **take** ∼ **of** occuparsi di; **be taken into** ∼ essere preso in custodia da un ente assistenziale; **'[handle] with** ∼' 'fragile' **②** *vi* ∼ **about** interessarsi di; ∼ **for** (feel affection for) volere bene a; (look after) aver cura di; **I don't** ∼ **for chocolate** non mi piace il cioccolato; **I don't** ∼ non me ne importa; **who** ∼**s?** chi se ne frega?; **for all I** ∼ per quello che me ne importa

care assistant *n* Br Med assistente *mf* a domicilio

career /kə'rɪə(r)/ **①** *n* carriera *f*; (profession) professione *f*; ∼ **woman** *n* donna in carriera **②** *vi* andare a tutta velocità

career break *n* pausa *f* nella carriera

career move *n* passo *m* utile per un avanzamento di carriera

careers adviser *n* consulente *mf* di orientamento professionale

careers office *n* centro *m* di orientamento professionale

careers service *n* servizio *m* di orientamento professionale

carefree /'keəfri:/ *adj* spensierato

careful /'keəfʊl/ *adj* attento; ⟨driver⟩ prudente

carefully /'keəfʊlɪ/ *adv* con attenzione

care home *n* casa *f* famiglia

careless /'keəlɪs/ *adj* irresponsabile; (in work) trascurato; ‹*work*› fatto con poca cura; ‹*driver*› distratto

carelessly /'keəlɪslɪ/ *adv* negligentemente

carelessness /'keəlɪsnɪs/ *n* trascuratezza *f*

carer /'keərə(r)/ *n* Br (relative) familiare *m* che assiste un anziano o un handicappato; (professional) assistente *mf* a domicilio

caress /kə'res/ ➀ *n* carezza *f* ➁ *vt* accarezzare

caretaker /'keəteɪkə(r)/ *n* custode *mf*; (in school) bidello *m*

care worker *n* assistente *mf* sociosanitario

careworn /'keəwɔːn/ *adj* ‹*face*› segnato dalle preoccupazioni

car ferry *n* traghetto *m* (per il trasporto di auto)

car-free *adj* ‹*environment*› senza macchine

cargo /'kɑːgəʊ/ *n* (pl **-es**) carico *m*

cargo plane *n* aereo *m* da carico

cargo ship *n* nave *f* da carico

car hire *n* autonoleggio *m*

Caribbean /kærɪ'biːən/ ➀ *n* the ∼ (sea) il Mar *m* dei Caraibi ➁ *adj* caraibico

caricature /'kærɪkətjʊə(r)/ ➀ *n* caricatura *f* ➁ *vt* fare una caricatura di

caricaturist /'kærɪkətjʊərɪst/ *n* caricaturista *mf*

caring /'keərɪŋ/ *adj* ‹*parent*› premuroso; ‹*attitude*› altruista; **the ∼ professions** le attività assistenziali

carjack /'kɑːdʒæk/ *vt* furto *m* d'auto con minaccia o violenza al conducente

carjacker /'kɑːdʒækə(r)/ *n* chi effettua un furto d'auto con minaccia o violenza al conducente

carjacking /'kɑːdʒækɪŋ/ *n* furto *m* d'auto con aggressione al conducente

carload /'kɑːləʊd/ *n* a ∼ of people un'automobile *f* piena di persone

carnage /'kɑːnɪdʒ/ *n* carneficina *f*

carnal /'kɑːn(ə)l/ *adj* carnale

carnation /kɑː'neɪʃn/ *n* garofano *m*

carnival /'kɑːnɪvl/ *n* carnevale *m*

carnivore /'kɑːnɪvɔː(r)/ *n* carnivoro *m*

carnivorous /kɑː'nɪvərəs/ *adj* carnivoro

carob /'kærəb/ *n* (pod) carruba *f*; (tree) carrubo *m*

carol /'kærəl/ *n* [**Christmas**] ∼ canto *m* natalizio; ∼ **concert** concerto *m* natalizio; **go ∼ singing** andare a cantare le canzoni natalizie per le strade

carousel /kærʊ'sel/ *n* (merry-go-round) giostra *f*; (for luggage) nastro *m* trasportatore; (for slides) caricatore *m* circolare

carp[1] /kɑːp/ *n inv* carpa *f*

carp[2] *vi* lamentarsi; ∼ **at** trovare da ridire su

car park *n* parcheggio *m*

carpenter /'kɑːpəntə(r)/ *n* falegname *m*

carpentry /'kɑːpəntrɪ/ *n* falegnameria *f*

carpet /'kɑːpɪt/ ➀ *n* tappeto *m*; (wall-to-wall) moquette *f inv*; **be on the ∼** fig essere ammonito ➁ *vt* mettere la moquette in ‹*room*›

carpet-bomb *vt* bombardare a tappeto

carpet fitter *n* artigiano *m* che mette in opera la moquette

carpet slipper *n* pantofola *f*

carpet sweeper *n* battitappeto *m inv*

carpet tile *n* riquadro *m* di moquette

car phone *n* telefono *m* in macchina

car radio *n* autoradio *f inv*

carriage /'kærɪdʒ/ *n* carrozza *f*; (of typewriter) carrello *m*; (of goods) trasporto *m*; (cost) spese *fpl* di trasporto; (bearing) portamento *m*; ∼ **paid** Comm franco di porto

carriage clock *n* orologio *m* da tavolo

carriageway /'kærɪdʒweɪ/ *n* strada *f* carrozzabile; **north-bound** ∼ carreggiata *f* nord

carrier /'kærɪə(r)/ *n* (company) impresa *f* di trasporti; Aeron compagnia *f* di trasporto aereo; (of disease) portatore *m*

carrier [bag] *n* borsa *f* [per la spesa]

carrier pigeon *n* piccione *m* viaggiatore

carrot /'kærət/ *n* carota *f*

carry /'kærɪ/ *v* (pt/pp **-ied**) ➀ *vt* portare; (transport) trasportare; Math riportare; **get carried away** fam lasciarsi prender la mano ➁ *vi* ‹*sound*› trasmettersi

■ **carry forward** *vt* riportare ‹*balance, figure*›

■ **carry off** *vt* portare via; vincere ‹*prize*›

■ **carry on** ➀ *vi* continuare; (fam: make scene) fare delle storie; ∼ **on with something** continuare qualcosa; ∼ **on with somebody** fam intendersela con qcno ➁ *vt* mantenere ‹*business*›; ∼ **on doing something** continuare a fare qualcosa

■ **carry out** *vt* portare fuori; eseguire ‹*instructions, task*›; mettere in atto threat; effettuare ‹*experiment, survey*›

carryall *n* Am borsone *m*

carrycot /'kærɪkɒt/ *n* porte-enfant *m inv*

carry-on *n* fam (complicated procedure) impresa *f*; (bad behaviour) storie *fpl*

carryout *n* Am piatti *mpl* da asporto

car seat *n* (for baby or child) seggiolino *m* per auto

carsick /ˈkɑːsɪk/ *adj* be ~ avere il mal d'auto

cart /kɑːt/ **1** *n* carretto *m*; **put the ~ before the horse** fig mettere il carro davanti ai buoi
2 *vt* (fam: carry) portare

cartel /kɑːˈtel/ *n* cartello *m*

car theft *n* furto *m* d'auto

carthorse /ˈkɑːthɔːs/ *n* cavallo *m* da tiro

cartilage /ˈkɑːtɪlɪdʒ/ *n* Anat cartilagine *f*

cartographer /kɑːˈtɒgrəfə(r)/ *n* cartografo, -a *mf*

cartography /kɑːˈtɒgrəfɪ/ *n* cartografia *f*

carton /ˈkɑːt(ə)n/ *n* scatola *f* di cartone; (for drink) cartone *m*; (of cream, yoghurt) vasetto *m*; (of cigarettes) stecca *f*

cartoon /kɑːˈtuːn/ *n* vignetta *f*; (strip) vignette *fpl*; (film) cartone *m* animato; (in art) bozzetto *m*

cartoonist /kɑːˈtuːnɪst/ *n* vignettista *mf*; (for films) disegnatore, -trice *mf* di cartoni animati

cartridge /ˈkɑːtrɪdʒ/ *n* cartuccia *f*; (for film) bobina *f*; (of record player) testina *f*

cartwheel /ˈkɑːtwiːl/ *n* (of cart) ruota *f* di carro; (in gymnastics) ruota *f*; **do a ~** (in gymnastics) fare la ruota

carve /kɑːv/ *vt* scolpire; tagliare ‹meat›
■ **carve out** *vt* crearsi ‹name, reputation, market›
■ **carve up** *vt* spartire ‹estate, territory, proceeds›

carving /ˈkɑːvɪŋ/ *n* scultura *f*

carving knife *n* trinciante *m*

car wash *n* autolavaggio *m inv*

car worker *n* operaio, -a *mf* dell'industria automobilistica

Casanova /ˈkæsənəʊvə/ *n* Casanova *m inv*

cascade /kæsˈkeɪd/ **1** *vi* scendere a cascata
2 *n* cascata *f*

case¹ /keɪs/ *n* caso *m*; **in any ~** in ogni caso; **in that ~** in questo caso; **just in ~** per sicurezza; **in ~ he comes** nel caso in cui venisse; **in ~ of emergency** in caso d'emergenza

case² *n* (container) scatola *f*; (crate) cassa *f*; (for spectacles) astuccio *m*; (suitcase) valigia *f*; (for display) vetrina *f*

case history *n* Med cartella *f* clinica

casement window /ˈkeɪsmənt/ *n* finestra *f* a battenti

casenotes *npl* pratica *f*

case study *n* analisi *f inv*

casework *n* do ~ occuparsi di assistenza sociale

cash /kæʃ/ **1** *n* denaro *m* contante; (fam: money) contanti *mpl*; **pay [in] ~** pagare in contanti; ~ **on delivery** pagamento alla consegna
2 *vt* incassare ‹cheque›
■ **cash in** *vt* riscuotere ‹bond, policy›; Am incassare ‹check›
■ **cash in on** *vt* fam approfittarsi di

cash-and-carry *n* cash and carry *m inv*

cashback *n* contanti *mpl* che si possono richiedere alla cassa di un negozio quando si effettua un pagamento con carta di debito

cash box *n* cassetta *f* portavalori

cash card *n* bancomat® *m inv*

cash desk *n* cassa *f*

cash dispenser *n* sportello *m* automatico, cassa *f* automatica

cashew [nut] /kəˈʃuː/ *n* anacardio *m*

cash flow *n* flusso *m* di cassa; ~ ~ **difficulties** difficoltà *fpl* di flusso di cassa; ~ ~ **management** gestione *f* del flusso di cassa

cashier /kæˈʃɪə(r)/ *n* cassiere, -a *mf*

cashless /ˈkæʃlɪs/ *adj* ‹society, transaction› basato sull'uso di carte di credito, assegni ecc. anziché sul contante

cash machine *n* (sportello) bancomat® *m inv*

cashmere /ˈkæʃmɪə(r)/ *n* cachemire *m inv*

cash on delivery *n* pagamento *m* alla consegna

cashpoint *n* (sportello) bancomat® *m inv*

cash register *n* registratore *m* di cassa

casing /ˈkeɪsɪŋ/ *n* (of machinery) rivestimento *m*; (of gearbox) scatola *f*; (of tyre) copertone *m*

casino /kəˈsiːnəʊ/ *n* casinò *m inv*

cask /kɑːsk/ *n* barile *m*

casket /ˈkɑːskɪt/ *n* scrigno *m*; (Am: coffin) bara *f*

casserole /ˈkæsərəʊl/ *n* casseruola *f*; (stew) stufato *m*

cassette /kəˈset/ *n* cassetta *f*

cassette deck *n* piastra *f* di registrazione

cassette player *n* mangiacassette *m inv*

cassette recorder *n* registratore *m* (a cassette)

cassette tape *n* cassetta *f*

cassock /ˈkæsək/ *n* tonaca *f*

cast /kɑːst/ **1** *n* (throw) lancio *m*; (mould) forma *f*; Theat cast *m inv*; **[plaster] ~** Med ingessatura *f*
2 *vt* (pt/pp **cast**) dare ‹vote›; Theat assegnare le parti di ‹play›; fondere ‹metal›; (throw) gettare; (shed) sbarazzarsi di; ~ **an actor as** dare ad un attore il

ruolo di; ∼ **a glance at** lanciare uno sguardo a

■ **cast off** ① *vi* Naut sganciare gli ormeggi

② *vt* (in knitting) diminuire

■ **cast on** *vt* (in knitting) avviare

castanets /ˌkæstə'nets/ *npl* nacchere *fpl*

castaway /'kɑːstəweɪ/ *n* naufrago, -a *mf*

caste /kɑːst/ *n* casta *f*

caster /'kɑːstə(r)/ *n* (wheel) rotella *f*

caster sugar *n* zucchero *m* raffinato

casting /'kɑːstɪŋ/ *n* casting *m inv*

casting director *n* direttore *m* del casting

casting vote *n* voto *m* decisivo

cast iron ① *n* ghisa *f*

② *adj* **cast-iron** di ghisa; fig solido

castle /'kɑːsl/ *n* castello *m*; (in chess) torre *f*

cast-offs *npl* abiti *mpl* smessi

castor /'kɑːstə(r)/ *n* (wheel) rotella *f*

castor oil *n* olio *m* di ricino

castor sugar *n* zucchero *m* raffinato

castrate /kæ'streɪt/ *vt* castrare

castration /kæ'streɪʃn/ *n* castrazione *f*

castrato /kæs'trɑːtəʊ/ *n* castrato *m*

casual /'kæʒʊəl/ *adj* (chance) casuale; remark senza importanza; ⟨glance⟩ di sfuggita; ⟨attitude, approach⟩ disinvolto; ⟨chat⟩ informale; ⟨clothes⟩ casual *inv*; ⟨work⟩ saltuario; ∼ **wear** abbigliamento *m* casual

casualize /'kæʒʊəlaɪz/ *vt* impiegare con contratto a termine ⟨labour⟩

casually /'kæʒʊəlɪ/ *adv* ⟨dress⟩ casual; ⟨meet⟩ casualmente

casualty /'kæʒʊəltɪ/ *n* (injured person) ferito *m*; (killed) vittima *f*

casualty [department] *n* pronto soccorso *m*

cat /kæt/ *n* gatto *m*; pej arpia *f*

catacombs /'kætəkuːmz/ *npl* catacombe *fpl*

catalogue /'kætəlɒg/ ① *n* catalogo *m*
② *vt* catalogare

catalyst /'kætəlɪst/ *n* Chem & fig catalizzatore *m*

catalytic converter /kætə'lɪtɪk/ *n* Auto marmitta *f* catalitica

catamaran /kætəmə'ræn/ *n* catamarano *m*

catapult /'kætəpʌlt/ ① *n* catapulta *f*; (child's) fionda *f*
② *vt* fig catapultare

cataract /'kætərækt/ *n* Med cataratta *f*

catarrh /kə'tɑː(r)/ *n* catarro *m*

catastrophe /kə'tæstrəfɪ/ *n* catastrofe *f*

catastrophic /kætə'strɒfɪk/ *adj* catastrofico

cat burglar *n* Br scassinatore, -trice *mf* acrobata

catch /kætʃ/ ① *n* (of fish) pesca *f*; (fastener) fermaglio *m*; (on door) fermo *m*; (on window) gancio *m*; (fam: snag) tranello *m*
② *vt* (pt/pp **caught**) acchiappare ⟨ball⟩; (grab) afferrare; prendere ⟨illness, fugitive, train⟩; ∼ **a cold** prendersi un raffreddore; ∼ **sight of** scorgere; **I caught him stealing** l'ho sorpreso mentre rubava; ∼ **one's finger in the door** chiudersi il dito nella porta; ∼ **sb's eye** or **attention** attirare l'attenzione di qualcuno
③ *vi* ⟨fire⟩ prendere; (get stuck) impigliarsi

■ **catch on** *vi* fam (understand) afferrare; (become popular) diventare popolare

■ **catch out** *vt* (show to be wrong) prendere in castagna

■ **catch up** ① *vt* raggiungere
② *vi* recuperare; ⟨runner⟩ riguadagnare terreno; ∼ **up with** raggiungere ⟨somebody⟩; mettersi in pari con ⟨work⟩

catch-all *adj* ⟨term⟩ polivalente; ⟨clause⟩ che comprende tutte le possibilità

catching /'kætʃɪŋ/ *adj* contagioso

catchment area /'kætʃmənt/ *n* bacino *m* d'utenza

catchphrase /'kætʃfreɪz/ *n* tormentone *m*

catch-22 situation /kætʃtwentɪ'tuː/ *n* situazione *f* senza uscita

catchword /'kætʃwɜːd/ *n* slogan *m inv*

catchy /'kætʃɪ/ *adj* (-ier, -iest) orecchiabile

catechism /'kætɪkɪzm/ *n* catechismo *m*

categorical /kætɪ'gɒrɪkl/ *adj* categorico

categorically /kætə'gɒrɪlkɪ/ *adv* categoricamente

categorize /'kætɪgəraɪz/ *vt* categorizzare

category /'kætɪgərɪ/ *n* categoria *f*

cater /'keɪtə(r)/ ① *vi* ∼ **for** provvedere a ⟨needs⟩; fig venire incontro alle esigenze di
② *vt* occuparsi del rinfresco di ⟨party⟩

caterer /'keɪtərə(r)/ *n* persona *f* che si occupa di ristorazione

catering /'keɪtərɪŋ/ *n* (trade) ristorazione *f*; (food) rinfresco *m*

caterpillar /'kætəpɪlə(r)/ *n* bruco *m*

caterwaul /'kætəwɔːl/ *vi* miagolare

catfish *n* pesce *m* gatto

catflap *n* gattaiola *f*

catgut *n* catgut *m inv*

cathedral /kə'θiːdrl/ *n* cattedrale *f*

Catherine wheel /'kæθ(ə)rɪn/ *n* girandola *f*

catheter /'kæθɪtə(r)/ *n* catetere *m*

cathode-ray tube /kæθəʊd'reɪ/ *n* tubo *m* a raggi catodici

Catholic /'kæθəlɪk/ *adj* & *n* cattolico, -a *mf*

Catholicism /kə'θɒlɪsɪzm/ n cattolicesimo m

catkin /'kætkɪn/ n Bot amento m

cat litter n lettiera f del gatto

catnap vi ① fare un pisolino ② n pisolino m

cat-o'-nine-tails n gatto m a nove code

CAT scan n TAC f

cat's-eye n Br catarifrangente m (inserito nell'asfalto)

catsuit n tuta f

cattery /'kætərɪ/ n pensione f per gatti

cattle /'kæt(ə)l/ npl bestiame msg

cattle grid n recinto m metallico che impedisce al bestiame di accedere a una strada

cattle market n mercato m del bestiame; fig fam ‹for sexual encounters› locale m dove la gente va per rimorchiare

cattle shed n stalla f

catty /'kætɪ/ adj (-ier, -iest) dispettoso

catwalk /'kætwɔːk/ n passerella f

Caucasian /kɔː'keɪʒ(ə)n/ ① n (Geog: inhabitant) caucasico, -a mf; (white person) bianco, -a mf ② Geog caucasico; ‹race, man› bianco

caught /kɔːt/ ▶ CATCH

cauldron /'kɔːldrən/ n calderone m

cauliflower /'kɒlɪflaʊə(r)/ n cavolfiore m

cauliflower cheese n cavolfiori mpl gratinati

causal /'kɔːzəl/ adj causale

cause /kɔːz/ ① n causa f; (reason) motivo m; **good ~** buona causa ② vt causare; **~ somebody to do something** far fare qualcosa a qualcuno

causeway /'kɔːzweɪ/ n strada f sopraelevata

caustic /'kɔːstɪk/ adj caustico

cauterize /'kɔːtəraɪz/ vt cauterizzare

caution /'kɔːʃn/ ① n cautela f; (warning) ammonizione f ② vt mettere in guardia; Jur ammonire

cautionary /'kɔːʃ(ə)nərɪ/ adj ‹tale› di ammonimento

cautious /'kɔːʃəs/ adj cauto

cautiously /'kɔːʃəslɪ/ adv cautamente

cavalcade /kævəl'keɪd/ n sfilata f

cavalier /kævə'lɪə(r)/ ① adj noncurante ② n **C~** sostenitore, -trice mf di Carlo I durante la guerra civile inglese

cavalry /'kævəlrɪ/ n cavalleria f

cave /keɪv/ n caverna f
■ **cave in** vi ‹roof› crollare; (fig: give in) capitolare

caveat /'kævɪæt/ n avvertimento m

cave dweller n cavernicolo, -a mf

caveman n cavernicolo m

cave painting n pittura f rupestre

caver /'keɪvə(r)/ n speleologo, -a mf

cavern /'kævən/ n caverna f

caviare /'kævɪɑː(r)/ n caviale m

caving /'keɪvɪŋ/ n speleologia f

cavity /'kævətɪ/ n cavità f inv; (in tooth) carie f inv

cavity wall insulation n isolamento m per muri a intercapedine

cavort /kə'vɔːt/ vi saltellare

caw /kɔː/ ① n (noise) gracchio m ② vi gracchiare

cayenne pepper /'kaɪen/ n pepe m di Caienna

cayman /'keɪmən/ n caimano m

CB ① n abbr (**Citizens' Band**) CB f inv ② attrib ‹equipment, radio, wavelength› CB

CBI n abbr Br (**Confederation of British Industry**) ≈ Confindustria f

cc abbr (**cubic centimetre**) cc m; (**carbon copy**) cc

CCJ n abbr Br (**County Court Judgement**) sentenza f del tribunale di contea

CCTV abbr (**closed-circuit television**) televisione f a circuito chiuso

CD n abbr (**Civil Defence**) difesa f civile; abbr (**compact disc**) CD m inv; Am abbr (**Congressional District**) circoscrizione f del Congresso; abbr (**corps diplomatique**) CD m inv

CD burner, CD writer n masterizzatore m di CD

CD-I abbr (**compact disc interactive**) CD-I m

CD player n lettore m [di] compact, lettore m di CD

CD-R abbr (**compact disc recordable**) CD-R m

CD-Rom /si:di:'rɒm/ n CD-Rom m inv

CD-Rom drive n lettore m CD-Rom

CD-RW abbr (**compact disc rewritable**) CD-RW m

cease /si:s/ ① n without **~** incessantemente ② vt/i cessare

ceasefire /'si:sfaɪə(r)/ n cessate il fuoco m inv

ceaseless /'si:slɪs/ adj incessante

ceaselessly /'si:slɪslɪ/ adv incessantemente

cedar /'si:də(r)/ n cedro m

cede /si:d/ vt cedere

cedilla /sə'dɪlə/ n cedilla f

ceiling /'si:lɪŋ/ n soffitto m; fig tetto m [massimo]

celebrate /'selɪbreɪt/ ① vt festeggiare ‹birthday, victory›

2 *vi* far festa

celebrated /'selɪbreɪtɪd/ *adj* celebre (**for** per)

celebration /selɪ'breɪʃn/ *n* celebrazione *f*

celebrity /sɪ'lebrətɪ/ *n* celebrità *f inv*

celeriac /sɪ'lerɪæk/ *n* sedano *m* rapa

celery /'selərɪ/ *n* sedano *m*

celestial /sɪ'lestɪəl/ *adj* celestiale

celibacy /'selɪbəsɪ/ *n* celibato *m*

celibate /'selɪbət/ *adj* ⟨*man*⟩ celibe; ⟨*woman*⟩ nubile

cell /sel/ *n* cella *f*; Biol cellula *f*

cellar /'selə(r)/ *n* scantinato *m*; (for wine) cantina *f*

cellist /'tʃelɪst/ *n* violoncellista *mf*

cello /'tʃeləʊ/ *n* violoncello *m*

Cellophane® /'seləfeɪn/ *n* cellophane® *m inv*

cellphone /'selfəʊn/ *n* [telefono *m*] cellulare *m*

cellular phone /seljʊlə'fəʊn/ *n* [telefono *m*] cellulare *m*

cellulite /'seljʊlaɪt/ *n* cellulite *f*

celluloid /'seljʊlɔɪd/ *n* celluloide *f*

Celsius /'selsɪəs/ *adj* Celsius

Celt /kelt/ *n* celta *mf*

Celtic /'keltɪk/ *adj* celtico

cement /sɪ'ment/ **1** *n* cemento *m*; (adhesive) mastice *m*
2 *vt* cementare; (stick) attaccare col mastice; fig consolidare

cement mixer *n* betoniera *f*

cemetery /'semətrɪ/ *n* cimitero *m*

cenotaph /'senətæf/ *n* cenotafio *m*

censor /'sensə(r)/ **1** *n* censore *m*
2 *vt* censurare

censorship /'sensəʃɪp/ *n* censura *f*

censure /'senʃə(r)/ **1** *n* biasimo *m*
2 *vt* biasimare

census /'sensəs/ *n* censimento *m*

cent /sent/ *n* (coin) centesimo *m*

centenary /sen'ti:nərɪ/ *n*, Am
centennial /sen'tenɪəl/ *n* centenario *m*

center /'sentə(r)/ *n* Am = CENTRE

centigrade /'sentɪgreɪd/ *adj* centigrado

centilitre /'sentɪli:tə(r)/ *n* centilitro *m*

centimetre /'sentɪmi:tə(r)/ *n* centimetro *m*

centipede /'sentɪpi:d/ *n* centopiedi *m inv*

central /'sentrəl/ *adj* centrale

Central African Republic *n* Repubblica *f* Centrafricana

Central America *n* America *f* centrale

central heating *n* riscaldamento *m* autonomo

centralize /'sentrəlaɪz/ *vt* centralizzare

central locking *n* Auto chiusura *f* centralizzata

centrally /'sentrəlɪ/ *adv* al centro; ∼ **heated** con riscaldamento autonomo

central nervous system *n* sistema *m* nervoso centrale

central processing unit *n* Comput unità *f inv* centrale di elaborazione

central reservation *n* Auto banchina *f* spartitraffico *inv*

centre Br, **center** Am /'sentə(r)/ **1** *n* centro *m*
2 *vt* (pt/pp **centred**) centrare
■ **centre on**, **centre around** *vt* ⟨*activities, life*⟩ imperniarsi su; ⟨*industry, people*⟩ incentrarsi su; ⟨*thoughts*⟩ concentrarsi su

centrefold *n* (pin-up picture) paginone *m*; (model) pin-up *f inv*

centre forward *n* centravanti *m inv*

centre ground Br, **center ground** Am *n* fig centro *m*

centre half *n* Sport centromediano *m*

centre of gravity *n* centro *m* di gravità

centrepiece *n* (of table) centrotavola *m*; (fig: of exhibition) pezzo *m* forte

centre spread *n* paginone *m*

centre stage *n* Theat centro *m* della scena; **stand** ∼ ∼ tenersi al centro della scena; **take/occupy** ∼ ∼ fig essere/ mettersi in primo piano

centrifugal /sentrɪ'fju:gl/ *adj* ∼ **force** forza *f* centrifuga

century /'sentʃərɪ/ *n* secolo *m*

CEO *n abbr* (**Chief Executive Officer**) direttore, -trice *mf* generale

ceramic /sɪ'ræmɪk/ *adj* ceramico

ceramics /sɪ'ræmɪks/ *n* (art) ceramica *fsg*; (objects) ceramiche *fpl*

cereal /'sɪərɪəl/ *n* cereale *m*

cerebral /'serɪbrl/ *adj* cerebrale

cerebral palsy /'pɔːlzɪ/ *n* paralisi *f* cerebrale

ceremonial /serɪ'məʊnɪəl/ **1** *adj* da cerimonia
2 *n* cerimoniale *m*

ceremonially /serɪ'məʊnɪəlɪ/ *adv* secondo il rituale

ceremonious /serɪ'məʊnɪəs/ *adj* cerimonioso

ceremoniously /serɪ'məʊnɪəslɪ/ *adv* in modo cerimonioso

ceremony /'serɪmənɪ/ *n* cerimonia *f*; **without** ∼ senza cerimonie

cert /sɜːt/ *n* Br fam **it's a [dead]** ∼**!** ci puoi scommettere!

certain /'sɜːtn/ *adj* certo; **for** ∼ di sicuro; **make** ∼ accertarsi; **he is** ∼ **to win** è certo di vincere; **it's not** ∼ **whether he'll come** non è sicuro che venga

certainly /'sɜːtnlɪ/ *adv* certamente; ∼ not! no di certo!

certainty /'sɜːtntɪ/ *n* certezza *f*; it's a ∼ è una cosa certa

certifiable /'sɜːtɪfaɪəbl/ *adj* ⟨*verifiable statement, evidence*⟩ dimostrabile; (mad) pazzo

certificate /sə'tɪfɪkət/ *n* certificato *m*

certified /'sɜːtɪfaɪd/ *adj* autenticato

certified mail *n* Am (lettera) raccomandata *f*

certified public accountant *n* Am ≈ commercialista *mf*

certify /'sɜːtɪfaɪ/ *vt* (pt/pp **-ied**) certificare; (declare insane) dichiarare malato di mente

certitude /'sɜːtɪtjuːd/ *n* certezza *f*

cervical /'sɜːvɪkl/ *adj* cervicale

cervical cancer *n* tumore *m* del collo dell'utero

cervical smear *n* Pap test *m inv*, striscio *m*

cervix /'sɜːvɪks/ *n* cervice *f* uterina, collo *m* dell'utero

cessation /se'seɪʃn/ *n* cessazione *f*.

cesspool /'sespuːl/ *n* pozzo *m* nero

cf. *abbr* (**compare**) cf, cfr

CFC *n abbr* (**chlorofluorocarbon**) CFC *m inv*

CFC-free *adj* ⟨*product, spray*⟩ senza CFC

CFE *abbr* **College of Further Education**

CGI *abbr* Comput (**common graphical interface**) CGI *f*

Chad /tʃæd/ *n* Chad *m*

chafe /tʃeɪf/ *vt* irritare

chaff /tʃɑːf/ *n* pula *f*

chaffinch /'tʃæfɪntʃ/ *n* fringuello *m*

chagrin /'ʃægrɪn/ *n* much to his ∼ con suo grande dispiacere

chain /tʃeɪn/ **1)** *n* catena *f*
2) *vt* incatenare ⟨*prisoner*⟩; attaccare con la catena ⟨*dog*⟩ (to a)
■ **chain up** *vt* legare alla catena ⟨*dog*⟩

chain gang *n* gruppo *m* di prigionieri incatenati

chain letter *n* lettera *f* della catena di Sant'Antonio

chain mail *n* cotta *f* di maglia

chain reaction *n* reazione *f* a catena

chain saw *n* motosega *f*

chain-smoke *vi* fumare una sigaretta dopo l'altra

chain-smoker *n* fumatore, -trice *mf* accanito, -a

chain store *n* negozio *m* appartenente ad una catena

chair /tʃeə(r)/ **1)** *n* sedia *f*; Univ cattedra *f*
2) *vt* presiedere

chairlift /'tʃeəlɪft/ *n* seggiovia *f*

chairman /'tʃeəmən/ *n* presidente *m*; ∼ **and managing director** presidente *m* direttore generale

chairperson /'tʃeəpɜːs(ə)n/ *n* presidente *m*, -essa *f*

chairwoman /'tʃeəwʊmən/ *n* presidentessa *f*

chalet /'ʃæleɪ/ *n* chalet *m inv*; (in holiday camp) bungalow *m inv*

chalice /'tʃælɪs/ *n* Relig calice *m*

chalk /tʃɔːk/ *n* gesso *m*

chalky /'tʃɔːkɪ/ *adj* gessoso

challenge /'tʃælɪndʒ/ **1)** *n* sfida *f*; Mil intimazione *f*
2) *vt* sfidare; Mil intimare il chi va là a; fig mettere in dubbio ⟨*statement*⟩

challenger /'tʃælɪndʒə(r)/ *n* sfidante *mf*

challenging /'tʃælɪndʒɪŋ/ *adj* ⟨*job*⟩ impegnativo

chamber /'tʃeɪmbə(r)/ *n* C∼ **of Commerce** Camera *f* di commercio

chambermaid *n* cameriera *f* ai piani

chamber music *n* musica *f* da camera

chamber orchestra *n* orchestra *f* da camera

chamber pot *n* vaso *m* da notte

chambers /'tʃeɪmbəz/ *n pl* Jur studio *m* [legale]

chameleon /kə'miːlɪən/ *n* also fig camaleonte *m*

chamois[1] /'ʃæmwɑː/ *n inv* (animal) camoscio *m*

chamois[2] /'ʃæmɪ/ *n* ∼**[-leather]** [pelle *f* di] camoscio *m*

champagne /ʃæm'peɪn/ *n* champagne *m inv*

champion /'tʃæmpɪən/ **1)** *n* Sport campione *m*; (of cause) difensore *m*, difenditrice *f*
2) *vt* (defend) difendere; (fight for) lottare per

championship /'tʃæmpɪənʃɪp/ *n* Sport campionato *m*

chance /tʃɑːns/ **1)** *n* caso *m*; (possibility) possibilità *f inv*; (opportunity) occasione *f*; by ∼ per caso; take a ∼ provarci; give somebody a second ∼ dare un'altra possibilità a qualcuno
2) *attrib* fortuito
3) *vt* if you ∼ to see him se ti capita di vederlo; I'll ∼ it fam corro il rischio

chancel /'tʃɑːnsəl/ *n* Archit coro *m*

chancellor /'tʃɑːnsələ(r)/ *n* cancelliere *m*; Univ rettore *m*; C∼ of the Exchequer ≈ ministro *m* del tesoro

chancy /'tʃɑːnsɪ/ *adj* rischioso

chandelier /ʃændə'lɪə(r)/ *n* lampadario *m*

chandler /'tʃɑːndlə(r)/ *n* fornitore *m* navale

change /tʃeɪndʒ/ **1** n cambiamento m; (money) resto m; (small coins) spiccioli mpl; for a ∼ tanto per cambiare; **have a** ∼ **of heart** cambiare idea; **a** ∼ **of clothes** un cambio di vestiti; ∼ **of address** cambiamento m d'indirizzo; **a** ∼ **of scene** also fig un cambiamento di scena; **the** ∼ **[of life]** la menopausa
2 vt cambiare; (substitute) scambiare (for con); ∼ **one's clothes** cambiarsi [i vestiti]; ∼ **trains** cambiare treno
3 vi cambiare; (∼ clothes) cambiarsi; **all** ∼**!** stazione terminale!
■ **change down** vi Auto passare alla marcia inferiore
■ **change up** vi Auto passare alla marcia superiore

changeability /tʃeɪndʒə'bɪlɪtɪ/ n (of weather) instabilità f

changeable /'tʃeɪndʒəbl/ adj mutevole; ‹weather› variable

changeless /'tʃeɪndʒlɪs/ adj ‹appearance› inalterabile; ‹character› costante; ‹law, routine› immutabile

change machine n distributore m di monete

changeover /'tʃeɪndʒəʊvə(r)/ n (time period) periodo m di transizione; (transition) passaggio m; (of leaders) subentro m; (of employees, guards) cambio m; (Sport: in relay) passaggio m del testimone; (Sport: of ends) cambiamento m

changing /'tʃeɪndʒɪŋ/ adj in mutamento

changing-room n camerino m; (for sports) spogliatoio m

channel /'tʃænl/ **1** n canale m; **the [English] C**∼ la Manica
2 vt (pt/pp **channelled**) ∼ **one's energies into something** convogliare le proprie energie in qualcosa

channel ferry n traghetto m attraverso la Manica

channel-hop vi Br fare lo zapping

channel-hopping n Br zapping m inv

Channel Islands npl Isole fpl del Canale

channel-surf vi Am fare lo zapping

channel-surfing n Am zapping m inv

Channel Tunnel n tunnel m inv sotto la Manica

chant /tʃɑːnt/ **1** n cantilena f; (of demonstrators) slogan m inv di protesta
2 vt cantare; ‹demonstrators› gridare
3 vi ‹demonstrators› gridare slogan di protesta

chaos /'keɪɒs/ n caos m

chaotic /keɪ'ɒtɪk/ adj caotico

chap /tʃæp/ n fam tipo m

chapel /'tʃæpl/ n cappella f

chaperone, **chaperon** /'ʃæpərəʊn/
1 n chaperon m inv
2 vt fare da chaperon a ‹somebody›

chaplain /'tʃæplɪn/ n cappellano m

chapped /tʃæpt/ adj ‹skin, lips› screpolato

chapter /'tʃæptə(r)/ n capitolo m

char[1] /tʃɑː(r)/ n fam donna f delle pulizie

char[2] vt (pt/pp **charred**) (burn) carbonizzare

character /'kærɪktə(r)/ n carattere m; (in novel, play) personaggio m; **that's out of** ∼ non è da te/lui; **quite a** ∼ fam un tipo particolare

character actor n caratterista mf

character assassination n denigrazione f

characteristic /kærəktə'rɪstɪk/ **1** adj caratteristico
2 n caratteristica f

characteristically /kærəktə'rɪstɪklɪ/ adv tipicamente

characterization /kærɪktəraɪ'zeɪʃn/ n caratterizzazione f

characterize /'kærɪktəraɪz/ vt caratterizzare

character reference n referenze fpl (relative al carattere)

charade /ʃə'rɑːd/ n farsa f; ∼**s** sciarada fsg

charcoal /'tʃɑːkəʊl/ n carbonella f

charge /tʃɑːdʒ/ **1** n (cost) prezzo m; Electr, Mil carica f; Jur accusa f; **free of** ∼ gratuito; **be in** ∼ essere responsabile (**of** di); **take** ∼ assumersi la responsabilità; **take** ∼ **of** occuparsi di
2 vt far pagare ‹free›; far pagare a ‹person›; Electr, Mil caricare; Jur accusare (**with** di); ∼ **somebody for something** far pagare qualcosa a qualcuno; **what do you** ∼**?** quanto prende?; ∼ **it to my account** lo addebiti sul mio conto
3 vi (attack) caricare

charge account n (in store) apertura m di credito presso un negozio

charge card n (credit card) carta f di addebito; (store card) carta f di credito [di un negozio]

charged /tʃɑːdʒd/ adj Phys carico; **emotionally** ∼ ‹atmosphere› carico di emozione

chargé d'affaires /ʃɑːʒeɪdæ'feə(r)/ n incaricato m d'affari

charge hand n caposquadra mf

charge nurse n caposala mf

char-grilled /-'grɪld/ adj alla brace

chariot /'tʃærɪət/ n cocchio m

charisma /kə'rɪzmə/ n carisma m

charismatic /kærɪz'mætɪk/ adj carismatico

charitable /'tʃærɪtəbl/ adj caritatevole; (kind) indulgente

charity /'tʃærətɪ/ n carità f; (organization) associazione f di beneficenza; **concert** ···ʒ

given for ∼ concerto *m* di beneficenza;
live on ∼ vivere di elemosina
charity box *n* (in church) cassetta *f* delle
offerte
charity shop *n* negozio *m* dell'usato a
scopo di beneficenza
charity work *n* lavoro *m* volontario
(per beneficenza)
charlady /'tʃɑ:leɪdɪ/ *n* Br donna *f* delle
pulizie
charlatan /'ʃɑ:lətən/ *n* ciarlatano, -a *mf*
charm /tʃɑ:m/ ① *n* fascino *m*; (object)
ciondolo *m*
② *vt* affascinare
charmer /'tʃɑ:mə(r)/ *n* he's a real ∼ è
un vero seduttore
charming /'tʃɑ:mɪŋ/ *adj* affascinante
charmingly /'tʃɑ:mɪŋlɪ/ *adv* in modo
affascinante
charred /tʃɑ:d/ *adj* carbonizzato
chart /tʃɑ:t/ *n* carta *f* nautica; (table)
tabella *f*
charter /'tʃɑ:tə(r)/ ① *n* ∼ [flight] [volo
m] charter *m inv*
② *vt* noleggiare
chartered accountant *n*
commercialista *mf*
chartered flight *n* Br volo *m* charter
inv
chartered surveyor *n* Br perito *m*
edile
charter plane *n* Br charter *m inv*
charwoman /'tʃɑ:wʊmən/ *n* donna *f*
delle pulizie
chase /tʃeɪs/ ① *n* inseguimento *m*; **give
∼** mettersi all'inseguimento
② *vt* inseguire
■ **chase away, chase off** *vt* cacciare
via
■ **chase up** *vt* fam cercare
chaser /'tʃeɪsə(r)/ *n* (fam: drink) liquore *m*
bevuto dopo la birra
chasm /'kæz(ə)m/ *n* abisso *m*
chassis /'ʃæsɪ/ *n* (pl **chassis** /'ʃæsɪz/)
telaio *m*
chaste /tʃeɪst/ *adj* casto
chasten /'tʃeɪs(ə)n/ *vt* castigare; **they
looked suitably ∼ed** avevano l'aria
mortificata
chastise /tʃæ'staɪz/ *vt* castigare
chastity /'tʃæstətɪ/ *n* castità *f*
chat /tʃæt/ ① *n* chiacchierata *f*; **have a
∼ with** fare quattro chiacchiere con;
Comput chat *f inv*
② *vi* (pt/pp **chatted**) chiacchierare;
Comput chattare
■ **chat up** *vt* abbordare
chatline *n* Teleph chat line *f inv*
chatroom *n* Comput chat room *f inv*
chat show *n* talk show *m inv*

chatshow host *n* presentatore, -trice
mf di talk show
chattel /'tʃæt(ə)l/ *n* Jur **goods and ∼s**
beni *mpl* mobili
chatter /'tʃætə(r)/ ① *n* chiacchiere *fpl*
② *vi* chiacchierare; ⟨teeth⟩ battere
chatterbox /'tʃætəbɒks/ *n* fam
chiacchierone, -a *mf*
chatty /'tʃætɪ/ *adj* (**-ier, -iest**)
chiacchierone; ⟨style⟩ familiare
chauffeur /'ʃəʊfə(r)/ *n* autista *mf*
chauvinism /'ʃəʊvɪnɪzm/ *n* sciovinismo
m
chauvinist /'ʃəʊvɪnɪst/ *n* sciovinista *mf*;
male ∼ fam maschilista *m*
cheap /tʃi:p/ ① *adj* a buon mercato;
⟨rate⟩ economico; (vulgar) grossolano; (of
poor quality) scadente
② *adv* a buon mercato
cheapen /'tʃi:p(ə)n/ *vt* ∼ **oneself**
screditarsi
cheaply /'tʃi:plɪ/ *adv* a buon mercato
cheap rate *adj & adv* Teleph a tariffa
ridotta
cheat /tʃi:t/ ① *n* imbroglione, -a *mf*; (at
cards) baro *m*
② *vt* imbrogliare; ∼ **somebody out of
something** sottrarre qualcosa a qualcuno
con l'inganno
③ *vi* imbrogliare; (at cards) barare
■ **cheat on** *vt* fam tradire ⟨wife⟩
Chechnya /tʃetʃ'njɑ:/ *n* Cecenia *f*
check[1] /tʃek/ ① *adj* ⟨pattern⟩ a quadri
② *n* disegno *m* a quadri
check[2] ① *n* verifica *f*; (of tickets) controllo
m; (in chess) scacco *m*; (Am: bill) conto *m*;
(Am: cheque) assegno *m*; (Am: tick) segnetto
m; **keep a ∼ on** controllare; **keep in ∼**
tenere sotto controllo
② *vt* verificare; controllare ⟨tickets⟩;
(restrain) contenere; (stop) bloccare
③ *vi* controllare; ∼ **on something**
controllare qualcosa
■ **check in** ① *vi* registrarsi all'arrivo
(in albergo); Aeron fare il check-in
② *vt* registrare all'arrivo (in albergo)
■ **check off** *vt* spuntare ⟨item on list⟩
■ **check out** ① *vi* (of hotel) saldare il
conto
② *vt* (fam: investigate) controllare
■ **check up** *vi* accertarsi
■ **check up on** *vt* prendere
informazioni su
checked /tʃekt/ *adj* a quadri
checkbook *n* Am libretto *m* d'assegni
checkered /'tʃekəd/ *adj* Am ⟨cloth,
pattern⟩ a quadretti; ⟨career⟩ con alti e
bassi
checkers /'tʃekəz/ *n* Am dama *f*
check-in *n* accettazione *f*, check-in *m*
inv

check-in desk *n* banco *m* dell'accettazione, banco *m* del check-in

checking account /'tʃekɪŋ/ *n* Am conto *m* corrente

check-in time *n* check-in *m inv*

checklist *n* lista *f* di controllo

check mark *n* Am segnetto *m*

checkmate *int* scacco matto!

checkout *n* (in supermarket) cassa *f*

checkout assistant, checkout operator *n* Br cassiere, -a *mf*

checkpoint *n* posto *m* di blocco

checkroom *n* Am deposito *m* bagagli

check-up *n* Med visita *f* di controllo, check-up *m inv*

cheddar /'tʃedə(r)/ *n* formaggio *m* semi-stagionato

cheek /tʃiːk/ *n* guancia *f*; (impudence) sfacciataggine *f*

cheekbone /'tʃiːkbəʊn/ *n* zigomo *m*

cheekily /'tʃiːkɪlɪ/ *adv* sfacciatamente

cheeky /'tʃiːkɪ/ *adj* sfacciato

cheep /tʃiːp/ *vi* pigolare

cheer /tʃɪə(r)/ ① *n* evviva *m inv*; **three** ∼**s** tre urrà; ∼**s!** salute!; (goodbye) arrivederci; (thanks) grazie ② *vt/i* acclamare
▪ **cheer up** ① *vt* tirare su [di morale] ② *vi* tirarsi su [di morale]; ∼ **up!** su con la vita!

cheerful /'tʃɪəfʊl/ *adj* allegro

cheerfully /'tʃɪəfʊlɪ/ *adv* allegramente; **I could** ∼ **strangle him!** lo strangolerei volentieri!

cheerfulness /'tʃɪəfʊlnɪs/ *n* allegria *f*

cheerily /'tʃɪərɪlɪ/ *adv* allegramente

cheering /'tʃɪərɪŋ/ *n* acclamazione *f*

cheerio /tʃɪərɪ'əʊ/ *int* fam arrivederci

cheerleader /'tʃɪəliːdə(r)/ *n* leader *mf* dei tifosi

cheerless /'tʃɪəlɪs/ *adj* triste, tetro

cheery /'tʃɪərɪ/ *adj* allegro

cheese /tʃiːz/ *n* formaggio *m*
▪ **cheese off** *vt* fam be ∼d off with one's job essere stufo del proprio lavoro; **I'm really** ∼**d off about it** ne ho le scatole piene

cheeseboard *n* (object) vassoio *m* dei formaggi; (selection) piatto *m* di formaggi

cheeseburger *n* cheeseburger *m inv*

cheesecake *n* dolce *m* al formaggio

cheesecloth *n* mussola *f*, tela *f* indiana

cheese counter *n* banco *m* dei formaggi

cheesy /'tʃiːzɪ/ *adj* ⟨smell⟩ di formaggio; ⟨grin⟩ smagliante

cheetah /'tʃiːtə/ *n* ghepardo *m*

chef /ʃef/ ① *n* cuoco, -a *mf*, chef *m inv* ② *vi* (pt/pp **cheffed**) fam fare lo chef

chemical /'kemɪkl/ ① *adj* chimico ② *n* prodotto *m* chimico

chemically /'kemɪklɪ/ *adv* chimicamente

chemise /ʃə'miːz/ *n* (undergarment) sottoveste *f inv*; (dress) chemisier *m inv*

chemist /'kemɪst/ *n* (pharmacist) farmacista *mf*; (scientist) chimico, -a *mf*

chemistry /'kemɪstrɪ/ *n* chimica *f*

chemist's [shop] *n* farmacia *f*

chemotherapy /kiːməʊ'θerəpɪ/ *n* chemioterapia *f*

cheque /tʃek/ *n* assegno *m*

chequebook /'tʃekbʊk/ *n* libretto *m* degli assegni

cheque card *n* carta *f* assegni

chequer /'tʃekə(r)/ *n* (square) scacco *m*; (pattern) motivo *m* a scacchi; (in game) pedina *f*

chequered /'tʃekəd/ *adj* (patterned) a scacchi; fig ⟨career, history⟩ movimentato

chequers /'tʃekəz/ *n* dama *f*

cherish /'tʃerɪʃ/ *vt* curare teneramente; (love) avere caro; nutrire ⟨hope⟩

cherry /'tʃerɪ/ *n* ciliegia *f*; (tree) ciliegio *m*

cherry brandy *n* cherry-brandy *m inv*

cherry-pick *vt* scegliere accuratamente

cherry tree *n* ciliegio *m*

cherub /'tʃerəb/ *n* cherubino *m*

chervil /'tʃɜːvɪl/ *n* cerfoglio *m*

chess /tʃes/ *n* scacchi *mpl*

chessboard *n* scacchiera *f*

chessman *n* pezzo *m* degli scacchi

chessplayer *n* scacchista *mf*

chess set *n* scacchi *mpl*

chest /tʃest/ *n* petto *m*; (box) cassapanca *f*; **get something off one's** ∼ fig levarsi un peso [dallo stomaco]

chest freezer *n* freezer *m inv* orizzontale, congelatore *m* orizzontale

chestnut /'tʃesnʌt/ *n* castagna *f*; (tree) castagno *m*

chest of drawers *n* cassettone *m*, comò *m inv*

chesty /'tʃestɪ/ *adj* ⟨person⟩ che soffre di bronchite; ⟨cough⟩ bronchitico

chew /tʃuː/ *vt* masticare
▪ **chew over** *vt* (fam: think about carefully) rimuginare su

chewing gum /'tʃuːɪŋ/ *n* gomma *f* da masticare

chewy /'tʃuːɪ/ *adj* ⟨meat⟩ legnoso; ⟨toffee⟩ gommoso

chic /ʃiːk/ *adj* chic *inv*

chick /tʃɪk/ *n* pulcino *m*; (fam: girl) ragazza *f*

chicken /'tʃɪkn/ ① *n* pollo *m* ② *attrib* ⟨soup, casserole⟩ di pollo

3 *adj* fam fifone
■ **chicken out** *vi* fam he ∼ed out gli è
venuta fifa
chicken breast *n* petto *m* di pollo
chicken curry *n* pollo *m* al curry
chicken feed *n* mangime *m* per i polli;
(fam: paltry sum) miseria *f*
chicken livers *npl* fegatini *mpl* di
pollo
chicken noodle soup *n* vermicelli
mpl in brodo di pollo
chickenpox *n* varicella *f*
chicken wire *n* rete *f* metallica (a
maglia esagonale)
chick flick *n* fam film *m inv* mirato ad
un pubblico femminile
chick lit *n* fam romanzi *mpl* mirati ad un
pubblico femminile
chickpea /'tʃɪkpiː/ *n* cece *m*
chicory /'tʃɪkəri/ *n* cicoria *f*
chief /tʃiːf/ **1** *adj* principale
2 *n* capo *m*
chief executive *n* direttore, -trice *mf*
generale
chief executive officer *n* direttore,
-trice *mf* generale
chief inspector *n* (Br: of police)
ispettore *m* capo
chiefly /'tʃiːflɪ/ *adv* principalmente
chief of police *n* capo *m* della polizia
Chief of Staff *n* Mil capo *m* di stato
maggiore; (of the White House) segretario *m*
generale
chief superintendent *n* (Br: of police)
commissario *m* capo
chiffon /'ʃɪfɒn/ **1** *n* chiffon *m*
2 *adj* ⟨dress, scarf⟩ di chiffon
chilblain /'tʃɪlbleɪn/ *n* gelone *m*
child /tʃaɪld/ *n* (pl ∼**ren**) bambino, -a *mf*;
(son/daughter) figlio, -a *mf*
child abuse *n* violenza *f* sui minori;
(sexual) violenza *f* sessuale sui minori
childbearing *n* gravidanza *f*; **of** ∼ **age**
in età feconda
child benefit *n* Br assegni *mpl* familiari
childbirth *n* parto *m*
childcare *n* (bringing up children)
educazione *f* dei bambini; (nurseries etc)
strutture *fpl* di assistenza ai bambini
childhood /'tʃaɪldhʊd/ *n* infanzia *f*
childish /'tʃaɪldɪʃ/ *adj* infantile
childishness /'tʃaɪldɪʃnɪs/ *n* puerilità *f*
childless /'tʃaɪldlɪs/ *adj* senza figli
childlike /'tʃaɪldlaɪk/ *adj* ingenuo
child-minder *n* baby-sitter *mf inv*
child molester *n* molestatore, -trice *mf*
di bambini
child prodigy *n* bambino prodigio

child-proof *adj* ⟨container⟩ a prova di
bambino; ∼ **lock** sicura *f* a prova di
bambino
children /'tʃɪldrən/ *npl* ▶ CHILD
children's home *n* istituto *m* per
l'infanzia
child seat *n* seggiolino *m* per bambini
Chile /'tʃɪlɪ/ *n* Cile *m*
Chilean /'tʃɪlɪən/ *adj* & *n* cileno, -a *mf*
chill /tʃɪl/ **1** *n* freddo *m*; (illness)
infreddatura *f*
2 *vt* raffreddare
■ **chill out** *vi* (relax) rilassarsi
chilli /'tʃɪlɪ/ *n* (pl **-es**) ∼ **[pepper]**
peperoncino *m*
chilly /'tʃɪlɪ/ *adj* freddo
chime /tʃaɪm/ *vi* suonare
chimera /kɪ'mɪərə/ *n* (beast, idea) chimera
f
chimney /'tʃɪmnɪ/ *n* camino *m*
chimneybreast *n* bocca *f* del camino
chimney-pot *n* comignolo *m*
chimney-sweep *n* spazzacamino *m*
chimp /tʃɪmp/ *n* fam scimpanzé *m*
chimpanzee /tʃɪmpæn'ziː/ *n*
scimpanzé *m inv*
chin /tʃɪn/ *n* mento *m*
China /'tʃaɪnə/ *n* Cina *f*
china *n* porcellana *f*
China Sea *n* Mar *m* Cinese
China tea *n* tè *m inv* cinese
Chinatown *n* quartiere *m* cinese
Chinese /tʃaɪ'niːz/ *adj* & *n* cinese *mf*;
(language) cinese *m*; **the** ∼ *pl* i cinesi
Chinese lantern *n* lanterna *f* cinese
chink[1] /tʃɪŋk/ *n* (slit) fessura *f*
chink[2] **1** *n* (noise) tintinnio *m*
2 *vi* tintinnare
chinos /'tʃiːnəʊz/ *npl* pantaloni *mpl*
cachi di cotone
chintz /tʃɪnts/ *n* chintz *m inv*
chip /tʃɪp/ **1** *n* (fragment) scheggia *f*; (in
china, paintwork) scheggiatura *f*; Comput chip
m inv; (in gambling) fiche *f inv*; ∼**s** *pl* Br Culin
patatine *fpl* fritte; Am Culin patatine *fpl*;
have a ∼ **on one's shoulder** avere un
complesso di inferiorità
2 *vt* (pt/pp **chipped**) (damage) scheggiare
■ **chip in** fam *vi* intromettersi; (with money)
contribuire
chipboard /'tʃɪpbɔːd/ *n* truciolato *m*
chipmunk /'tʃɪpmʌŋk/ *n* tamia *m inv*
chip pan *n* friggitrice *f*
chipped /tʃɪpt/ *adj* (damaged) scheggiato
chippings /'tʃɪpɪŋz/ *npl* (on road) breccia
f; 'loose ∼' 'attenzione: breccia'
chippy /'tʃɪpɪ/ *n* (Br fam: chip shop) negozio
m di fish and chips

chip shop n Br negozio m di fish and chips

chiropodist /kɪ'rɒpədɪst/ n podiatra mf inv

chiropody /kɪ'rɒpədɪ/ n podiatria f

chiropractor /'kaɪərəʊpræktə(r)/ n chiropratico, -a mf

chirp /tʃɜːp/ vi cinguettare; ⟨cricket⟩ fare cri cri

chirpy /'tʃɜːpɪ/ adj fam pimpante

chisel /'tʃɪzl/ ① n scalpello m
② vt (pt/pp **chiselled**) scalpellare

chit /tʃɪt/ n bigliettino m

chitchat /'tʃɪ(t)tʃæt/ n fam chiacchiere fpl; **spend one's time in idle ∼** fam perdere tempo in chiacchiere

chivalrous /'ʃɪvlrəs/ adj cavalleresco

chivalrously /'ʃɪvlrəslɪ/ adv con cavalleria

chivalry /'ʃɪvlrɪ/ n cavalleria f

chives /tʃaɪvz/ npl erba f cipollina

chlorine /'klɔːriːn/ n cloro m

chlorofluorocarbon /klɔːrəʊfluərəʊ'kɑːb(ə)n/ n clorofluorocarburo m

chloroform /'klɒrəfɔːm/ n cloroformio m

chlorophyll /'klɒrəfɪl/ n clorofilla f

choc ice /'tʃɒk aɪs/ n Br gelato m ricoperto di cioccolato

chock /tʃɒk/ n zeppa f

chock-a-block /tʃɒkə'blɒk/, **chock-full** /tʃɒk'fʊl/ adj pieno zeppo

chocolate /'tʃɒkələt/ n cioccolato m; (drink) cioccolata f; **a ∼** un cioccolatino

choice /tʃɔɪs/ ① n scelta f
② adj scelto

choir /'kwaɪə(r)/ n coro m

choirboy /'kwaɪəbɔɪ/ n corista m

choirgirl /'kwaɪəgɜːl/ n corista f

choke /tʃəʊk/ ① n Auto aria f
② vt/i soffocare; **I ∼d on a fishbone** mi è rimasta in gola una lisca
■ **choke back** vt soffocare ⟨tears, sob⟩

choker /'tʃəʊkə(r)/ n girocollo m

cholera /'kɒlərə/ n colera m

cholesterol /kə'lestərɒl/ n colesterolo m

chomp /tʃɒmp/ v
■ **chomp on** vt fam masticare rumorosamente

choose /tʃuːz/ vt/i (pt **chose**, pp **chosen**) scegliere; **∼ to do something** scegliere di fare qualcosa; **as you ∼** come vuoi

choos[e]y /'tʃuːzɪ/ adj fam difficile

chop /tʃɒp/ ① n (blow) colpo m (d'ascia); Culin costata f; **get the ∼** fam ⟨employee⟩ essere licenziato; ⟨project⟩ essere bocciato
② vt (pt/pp **chopped**) tagliare

■ **chop down** vt abbattere ⟨tree⟩
■ **chop off** vt spaccare

chopper /'tʃɒpə(r)/ n accetta f; fam elicottero m

chopping block n ceppo m; **put one's head on the ∼ ∼** fig esporsi a rischi

chopping board n tagliere m

chopping knife n coltello m

choppy /'tʃɒpɪ/ adj increspato

chopsticks /'tʃɒpstɪks/ npl bastoncini mpl cinesi

choral /'kɔːrəl/ adj corale; **∼ society** coro m

chord /kɔːd/ n Mus corda f

chore /tʃɔː(r)/ n corvè f inv; [household] **∼s** faccende fpl domestiche

choreograph /'kɒrɪəgrɑːf/ vt coreografare

choreographer /kɒrɪ'ɒgrəfə(r)/ n coreografo, -a mf

choreography /kɒrɪ'ɒgrəfɪ/ n coreografia f

chorister /'kɒrɪstə(r)/ n corista mf

chortle /'tʃɔːtl/ vi ridacchiare

chorus /'kɔːrəs/ n coro m; (of song) ritornello m

chorus girl n ballerina f di varietà

chose, chosen /tʃəʊz/, /'tʃəʊzn/
▶ CHOOSE

chowder /'tʃaʊdə(r)/ n zuppa m di pesce

chow mein /tʃaʊ'meɪn/ n piatto m cinese di spaghettini fritti con gamberetti, ecc. e verdure

Christ /kraɪst/ n Cristo m; **∼ Almighty!** fam porca miseria!

christen /'krɪs(ə)n/ vt battezzare

christening /'krɪsnɪŋ/ n battesimo m

Christian /'krɪstʃən/ adj & n cristiano, -a mf

Christianity /krɪstɪ'ænətɪ/ n cristianesimo m

Christian name n nome m di battesimo

Christmas /'krɪsməs/ ① n Natale m
② attrib di Natale

Christmas box n Br mancia f natalizia

Christmas card n biglietto m d'auguri di Natale

Christmas carol n canto m natalizio, canto m di Natale

Christmas cracker n tubo m di cartone colorato contenente una sorpresa

Christmas Day n il giorno di Natale

Christmas Eve n la vigilia di Natale

Christmas present n regalo m di Natale

Christmas stocking n calza f (per i doni di Babbo Natale)

Christmas tree n albero m di Natale

chrome /krəʊm/ *n*, **chromium** /'krəʊmɪəm/ *n* cromo *m*

chromium-plated /-'pleɪtɪd/ *adj* cromato

chromosome /'krəʊməsəʊm/ *n* cromosoma *m*

chronic /'krɒnɪk/ *adj* cronico

chronicle /'krɒnɪkl/ *n* cronaca *f*

chronological /krɒnə'lɒdʒɪkl/ *adj* cronologico

chronologically /krɒnə'lɒdʒɪklɪ/ *adv* ⟨ordered⟩ in ordine cronologico

chrysalis /'krɪsəlɪs/ *n* crisalide *f*

chrysanthemum /krɪ'sænθəməm/ *n* crisantemo *m*

chubby /'tʃʌbɪ/ *adj* (**-ier, -iest**) paffuto

chuck /tʃʌk/ *vt* fam buttare
∎ **chuck in** *vt* fam mollare ⟨job, boyfriend⟩
∎ **chuck out** *vt* fam buttare via ⟨object⟩; buttare fuori ⟨person⟩
∎ **chuck up** *vt* fam = CHUCK in

chuckle /'tʃʌk(ə)l/ *vi* ridacchiare

chuffed /tʃʌft/ *adj* fam felice come una Pasqua

chug /tʃʌg/ *vi* **the train** ~**ged into/out of the station** il treno è entrato nella/uscito dalla stazione sbuffando

chum /tʃʌm/ *n* fam amico, -a *mf*

chummy /'tʃʌmɪ/ *adj* fam **be** ~ **with** essere amico di

chump /tʃʌmp/ *n* fam zuccone *m*, -a *f*; Culin braciola *f*

chunk /tʃʌnk/ *n* grosso pezzo *m*

chunky /'tʃʌŋkɪ/ *adj* ⟨sweater⟩ di lana grossa; ⟨jewellery⟩ massiccio; fam ⟨person⟩ tarchiato

Chunnel /'tʃʌnl/ *n* Br fam tunnel *m inv* sotto la Manica

church /tʃɜːtʃ/ *n* chiesa *f*

churchgoer *n* praticante *mf*

church hall *n* sala *f* parrocchiale

churchyard /'tʃɜːtʃjɑːd/ *n* cimitero *m*

churlish /'tʃɜːlɪʃ/ *adj* sgarbato

churn /tʃɜːn/ ➊ *n* zangola *f*; (for milk) bidone *m*
➋ *vt* fare ⟨butter⟩; far rivoltare ⟨stomach⟩
∎ **churn out** *vt* sfornare ⟨novels, products⟩
∎ **churn up** *vt* agitare ⟨water⟩

chute /ʃuːt/ *n* scivolo *m*; (for rubbish) canale *m* di scarico

chutney /'tʃʌtnɪ/ *n* salsa *f* piccante a base di frutti e spezie

CIA *n abbr* Am (**Central Intelligence Agency**) CIA *f*

cicada /sɪ'kɑːdə/ *n* cicala *f*

CID *abbr* **Criminal Investigation Department**

cider /'saɪdə(r)/ *n* sidro *m*

cigar /sɪ'gɑː(r)/ *n* sigaro *m*

cigarette /sɪgə'ret/ *n* sigaretta *f*

cigarette butt, cigarette end *n* cicca *f*, mozzicone *m* di sigaretta

cigarette lighter *n* accendino *m*

cinch /sɪntʃ/ *n* fam **it's a** ~ è un gioco da ragazzi

cinder /'sɪndə(r)/ *n* (glowing) brace *f*; **burn something to a** ~ carbonizzare qualcosa

Cinderella /sɪndə'relə/ *n* Cenerentola *f*

cinder track *n* pista *f* di cenere

cine-camera /'sɪnɪ-/ *n* cinepresa *f*

cine-film *n* filmino *m* a passo ridotto

cinema /'sɪnɪmə/ *n* cinema *m inv*

cinema complex *n* cinema *m inv* multisale

cinemagoer /'sɪnɪməgəʊə(r)/ *n* (spectator) spettatore, -trice *mf*; (regular) cinefilo, -a *mf*

cinematography /sɪnəmə'tɒgrəfɪ/ *n* cinematografia *f*

cinnamon /'sɪnəmən/ *n* cannella *f*

cipher /'saɪfə(r)/ *n* (code) cifre *fpl*; fig nullità *f inv*

circa /'sɜːkə/ *prep* circa

circle /'sɜːkl/ ➊ *n* cerchio *m*; Theat galleria *f*; **in a** ~ in cerchio
➋ *vt* girare intorno a; cerchiare ⟨mistake⟩
➌ *vi* descrivere dei cerchi

circuit /'sɜːkɪt/ *n* circuito *m*; (lap) giro *m*

circuit board *n* circuito *m* stampato

circuit breaker *n* salvavita *m*

circuitous /sə'kjuːɪtəs/ *adj* ~ **route** percorso *m* lungo e indiretto

circular /'sɜːkjʊlə(r)/ *adj* & *n* circolare *f*; ~ **letter** *n* circolare *f*

circular saw *n* sega *f* circolare

circulate /'sɜːkjʊleɪt/ ➊ *vt* far circolare
➋ *vi* circolare

circulation /sɜːkjʊ'leɪʃn/ *n* circolazione *f*; (of newspaper) tiratura *f*

circulatory /sɜːkjʊ'leɪtərɪ/ *adj* Med circolatorio

circumcise /'sɜːkəmsaɪz/ *vt* circoncidere

circumcision /sɜːkəm'sɪʒn/ *n* circoncisione *f*

circumference /ʃə'kʌmfərəns/ *n* circonferenza *f*

circumflex /'sɜːkəmfleks/ *n* accento *m* circonflesso

circumnavigate /sɜːkəm'nævɪgeɪt/ *vt* doppiare ⟨cape⟩; circumnavigare ⟨world⟩

circumnavigation /sɜːkəmnævɪ'geɪʃn/ *n* circumnavigazione *f*

circumspect /'sɜːkəmspekt/ *adj* circospetto

circumspectly /'sɜːkəmspektlɪ/ *adv* in modo circospetto

circumstance /'sɜːkəmstəns/ n circostanza f; **~s** pl (financial) condizioni fpl finanziarie

circumstantial /sɜːkəm'stænʃl/ adj Jur ‹evidence› indiziario; (detailed) circostanziato

circus /'sɜːkəs/ n circo m

cirrhosis /sɪ'rəʊsɪs/ n cirrosi f inv

CIS abbr (**Commonwealth of Independent States**) CSI f

cistern /'sɪstən/ n (tank) cisterna f; (of WC) serbatoio m

citadel /'sɪtədel/ n cittadella f

cite /saɪt/ vt citare

citizen /'sɪtɪzn/ n cittadino, -a mf; (of town) abitante mf

Citizens' Advice Bureau n ufficio m di consulenza legale gratuita per i cittadini

citizen's arrest n arresto m effettuato da un privato cittadino

citizens' band n Radio banda f cittadina

citizenship /'sɪtɪznʃɪp/ n cittadinanza f

citric acid /sɪtrɪk'æsɪd/ acido m citrico

citrus /'sɪtrəs/ n **~** [fruit] agrume m

city /'sɪtɪ/ n città f inv; **the C~** la City [di Londra]

city centre n Br centro m [della città]

city slicker n fam cittadino m sofisticato

civic /'sɪvɪk/ 1 adj civico 2 **~s** npl educazione fsg civica

civic centre n centro m municipale

civil /'ʃɪvl/ a civile

civil engineer n ingegnere m civile

civil engineering n ingegneria f civile

civilian /sɪ'vɪljən/ 1 adj civile; in **~** clothes in borghese 2 n civile mf

civility /sɪ'vɪlətɪ/ n cortesia f

civilization /sɪvɪlaɪ'zeɪʃn/ n civiltà f inv

civilize /'sɪvɪlaɪz/ vt civilizzare

civilized /'sɪvɪlaɪzd/ adj ‹country› civilizzato; ‹person, behaviour› civile; become **~** civilizzarsi

civil law n diritto m civile

civil liability n Jur responsabilità f inv civile

civil liberty n libertà f inv civile

civilly /'sɪvɪlɪ/ adv civilmente

civil rights npl 1 diritti mpl civili 2 attrib ‹march, activist› per i diritti civili

civil servant n impiegato, -a mf statale

Civil Service n pubblica amministrazione f

civil war n guerra f civile

civil wedding n matrimonio m civile

civvies /'sɪvɪz/ npl fam in **~** in borghese

CJD n abbr (**Creutzfeldt-Jakob disease**) morbo m di Creutzfeldt Jakob

cl abbr (**centilitre(s)**) cl

clad /klæd/ adj vestito (in di)

cladding /'klædɪŋ/ n rivestimento m

claim /kleɪm/ 1 n richiesta f; (right) diritto m; (assertion) dichiarazione f; lay **~** to something rivendicare qualcosa 2 vt richiedere; reclamare ‹lost property›; rivendicare ‹ownership›; **~** that sostenere che
■ **claim back** vt reclamare ‹money›

claimant /'kleɪmənt/ n richiedente mf; (to throne) pretendente mf

claim form n modulo m di richiesta

clairvoyant /kleə'vɔɪənt/ n chiaroveggente mf

clam /klæm/ n Culin vongola f
■ **clam up** vi zittirsi

clamber /'klæmbə(r)/ vi arrampicarsi

clammy /'klæmɪ/ adj (**-ier, -iest**) appiccicaticcio

clamour /'klæmə(r)/ 1 n (noise) clamore m; (protest) rimostranza f 2 vi **~** for chiedere a gran voce

clamp /klæmp/ 1 n morsa f 2 vt ammorsare; Auto mettere i ceppi bloccaruote a
■ **clamp down** vi fam essere duro
■ **clamp down on** vt reprimere

clampdown n fig giro m di vite

clan /klæn/ n clan m inv

clandestine /klæn'destɪn/ adj clandestino

clang /klæŋ/ n suono m metallico

clanger /'klæŋə(r)/ n fam gaffe f inv

clank /klæŋk/ 1 n rumore m metallico 2 vi fare un rumore metallico

clannish /'klænɪʃ/ adj pej ‹family, profession› chiuso

clap /klæp/ 1 n give somebody a **~** applaudire qualcuno; **~** of thunder tuono m 2 vt/i (pt/pp **clapped**) applaudire; **~** one's hands applaudire

clapboard /'klæpbɔːd/ 1 n Am rivestimento m di legno 2 attrib Am rivestito di legno

clapped out /klæpt/ adj fam (past it) sfinito; (exhausted) stanco morto; ‹car, machine› scassato

clapping /'klæpɪŋ/ n applausi mpl

claptrap /'klæptræp/ n fam sciocchezze fpl

claret /'klærət/ n claret m inv

clarification /klærɪfɪ'keɪʃn/ n chiarimento m

clarify /'klærɪfaɪ/ vt/i (pt/pp **-ied**) chiarire

clarinet /klærɪ'net/ n clarinetto m

clarinettist /klærɪ'netɪst/ n clarinettista mf

clarity /'klærətɪ/ n chiarezza f

clash /klæʃ/ ① n scontro m; (noise) fragore m
② vi scontrarsi; ⟨colours⟩ stonare; ⟨events⟩ coincidere

clasp /klɑːsp/ ① n chiusura f
② vt agganciare; (hold) stringere

class /klɑːs/ ① n classe f; (lesson) corso m
② vt classificare

class-conscious adj classista

class-consciousness n classismo m

classic /'klæsɪk/ ① adj classico
② n classico m; ~s pl Univ lettere fpl classiche

classical /'klæsɪk(ə)l/ adj classico

classification /klæsɪfɪ'keɪʃn/ n classificazione f

classified adj (secret) riservato

classified ad /klæsɪfaɪd'æd/ n annuncio m

classified section n pagina f degli annunci

classify /'klæsɪfaɪ/ vt (pt/pp -led) classificare

classmate n compagno, -a mf di classe

classroom n aula f

class system n sistema m classista

classy /'klɑːsɪ/ adj (-ier, -iest) fam d'alta classe

clatter /'klætə(r)/ ① n fracasso m
② vi far fracasso

clause /klɔːz/ n clausola f; Gram proposizione f

claustrophobia /klɒstrə'fəʊbɪə/ n claustrofobia f

claustrophobic /klɒstrə'fəʊbɪk/ adj claustrofobico

clavichord /'klævɪkɔːd/ n clavicordo m

clavicle /'klævɪkl/ n clavicola f

claw /klɔː/ ① n artiglio m; (of crab, lobster & Techn) tenaglia f
② vt ⟨cat⟩ graffiare

clay /kleɪ/ n argilla f

clayey /'kleɪɪ/ adj ⟨soil⟩ argilloso

clay pigeon shooting n tiro m al piattello

clean /kliːn/ ① adj pulito, lindo
② adv completamente
③ vt pulire ⟨shoes, windows⟩; ~ one's teeth lavarsi i denti; **have a coat** ~ed portare un cappotto in lavanderia
■ **clean out** vt ripulire ⟨room⟩; **be** ~ed **out** (fig: have no money) essere senza un soldo
■ **clean up** ① vt pulire
② vi far pulizia

clean-cut adj ⟨image, person⟩ rispettabile

cleaner /'kliːnə(r)/ n uomo m, donna f delle pulizie; (substance) detersivo m; **[dry]** ~'s lavanderia f, tintoria f

cleaning /'kliːnɪŋ/ n pulizia f; **do the** ~ fare le pulizie

cleaning lady n donna f delle pulizie

cleaning product n detergente m

cleanliness /'klenlɪnɪs/ n pulizia f

clean-living /-'lɪvɪŋ/ ① n vita f integra
② adj ⟨person⟩ integro

cleanse /klenz/ vt pulire

cleanser /'klenzə(r)/ n detergente m

clean-shaven /-'ʃeɪvən/ adj sbarbato

clean sheet n **start with a** ~ ~ fig voltare pagina

cleansing cream /'klenzɪŋ/ n latte m detergente

clear /klɪə(r)/ ① adj chiaro; ⟨conscience⟩ pulito; ⟨road⟩ libero; ⟨profit, advantage, majority⟩ netto; ⟨sky⟩ sereno; ⟨water⟩ limpido; ⟨glass⟩ trasparente; **make something** ~ mettere qualcosa in chiaro; **have I made myself** ~? mi sono fatto capire?; **I'm not** ~ **about what I have to do** non mi è ben chiaro quello che devo fare; **five** ~ **days** cinque giorni buoni; **be in the** ~ essere a posto
② adv **stand** ~ **of** allontanarsi da; **keep** ~ **of** tenersi alla larga da
③ vt sgombrare ⟨room, street⟩; sparecchiare ⟨table⟩; (acquit) scagionare; (authorize) autorizzare; scavalcare senza toccare ⟨fence, wall⟩; guadagnare ⟨sum of money⟩; passare ⟨Customs⟩; ~ **one's throat** schiarirsi la gola
④ vi ⟨face, sky⟩ rasserenarsi; ⟨fog⟩ dissiparsi
■ **clear away** vt metter via
■ **clear off** vi fam filar via
■ **clear out** ① vt sgombrare
② vi fam filar via
■ **clear up** ① vt (tidy) mettere a posto; chiarire ⟨mystery⟩
② vi ⟨weather⟩ schiarirsi

clearance /'klɪərəns/ n (space) spazio m libero; (authorization) autorizzazione f; (Customs) sdoganamento m

clearance sale n liquidazione f

clear-cut adj ⟨plan, division⟩ ben definito; ⟨problem, rule⟩ chiaro; ⟨difference, outline⟩ netto; **the matter is not so** ~ la faccenda non è così semplice

clear-headed /-'hedɪd/ adj lucido

clearing /'klɪərɪŋ/ n radura f

clearly /'klɪəlɪ/ adv chiaramente

clear-out n ripulita f

clear-sighted /-'saɪtɪd/ adj perspicace

clearway /'klɪəweɪ/ n Auto strada f con divieto di sosta

cleavage /'kliːvɪdʒ/ n (woman's) décolleté m inv

cleave /kliːv/ vt spaccare

cleaver /'kli:və(r)/ n mannaia f

clef /klef/ n Mus chiave f

cleft /kleft/ n fenditura f

clemency /'klemənsɪ/ n clemenza f

clement /'klemənt/ adj clemente

clench /klentʃ/ vt serrare

clergy /'klɜ:dʒɪ/ npl clero m

clergyman /'klɜ:dʒɪmən/ n ecclesiastico m

cleric /'klerɪk/ n ecclesiastico m

clerical /'klerɪkl/ adj impiegatizio; Relig clericale

clerical assistant n impiegato, -a mf

clerk /klɑ:k/, Am /klɜ:k/ n impiegato, -a mf; (Am: shop assistant) commesso, -a mf

clever /'klevə(r)/ adj intelligente; (skilful) abile

cleverly /'klevəlɪ/ adv intelligentemente; (skilfully) abilmente

cliché /'kli:ʃeɪ/ n cliché m inv

clichéd /'kli:ʃeɪd/ adj ⟨idea, technique⟩ convenzionale; ⟨art, music⟩ stereotipato; ~ **expression** frase f fatta

click /klɪk/ 1 vi scattare; (Comput: with mouse) cliccare
2 n (Comput: with mouse) clic m inv
■ **click on** vt Comput cliccare su

client /'klaɪənt/ n cliente mf

clientele /kli:ɒn'tel/ n clientela f

cliff /klɪf/ n scogliera f

cliffhanger /'klɪfhæŋə(r)/ n **it was a real** ~ ci ha lasciato in sospeso

climate /'klaɪmət/ n clima f

climatic /klaɪ'mætɪk/ adj climatico

climax /'klaɪmæks/ n punto m culminante

climb /klaɪm/ 1 n salita f
2 vt scalare ⟨mountain⟩; arrampicarsi su ⟨ladder, tree⟩
3 vi arrampicarsi; (rise) salire; ⟨road⟩ salire
■ **climb down** vi scendere; (from ladder, tree) scendere; fig tornare sui propri passi
■ **climb over** vt scavalcare ⟨fence, wall⟩
■ **climb up** vt salire su ⟨hill⟩

climber /'klaɪmə(r)/ n alpinista mf; (plant) rampicante m

climbing /'klaɪmɪŋ/ adj rampicante

climbing boot n scarpone m da alpinismo

climbing expedition n scalata f

climbing frame n struttura f su cui possono arrampicarsi i bambini

clinch /klɪntʃ/ 1 vt fam concludere ⟨deal⟩
2 n (in boxing) clinch m inv

clincher /'klɪntʃə(r)/ n (fam: act, remark) fattore m decisivo; (argument) argomento m decisivo

cling /klɪŋ/ vi (pt/pp **clung**) aggrapparsi; (stick) aderire

cling film n pellicola f trasparente

clingy /'klɪŋɪ/ adj ⟨dress⟩ attillato; ⟨person⟩ appiccicoso

clinic /'klɪnɪk/ n ambulatorio m

clinical /'klɪnɪkl/ adj clinico

clinically /'klɪnɪklɪ/ adv clinicamente

clink /klɪŋk/ 1 n tintinnio m; (fam: prison) galera f
2 vi tintinnare

clip¹ /klɪp/ 1 n fermaglio m; (jewellery) spilla f
2 vt (pt/pp **clipped**) attaccare

clip² 1 n (extract) taglio m
2 vt obliterare ⟨ticket⟩

clipart n clip art f inv

clipboard n fermablocco m

clip-clop /'klɪpklɒp/ n rumore m fatto dagli zoccoli dei cavalli

clip frame n cornice f a giorno

clip-on adj ⟨bow tie⟩ con la clip

clip-on microphone n microfono m con la clip

clip-ons npl (earrings) orecchini mpl con le clip

clippers /'klɪpəz/ npl (for hair) rasoio m; (for hedge) tosasiepi m inv; (for nails) tronchesina f

clipping /'klɪpɪŋ/ n (from newspaper) ritaglio m

clique /kli:k/ n cricca f

cliquey, cliquish /'kli:kɪ/, /'kli:kɪʃ/ adj ⟨atmosphere⟩ esclusivo; ⟨profession, group⟩ chiuso

cloak /kləʊk/ n mantello m

cloak-and-dagger adj ⟨film⟩ d'avventura; (surreptitious) clandestino

cloakroom n guardaroba m inv; (toilet) bagno m

cloakroom attendant n (Br: at toilets) addetto, -a mf ai bagni; (in hotel) guardarobiere, -a mf

cloakroom ticket n scontrino m del guardaroba

clobber /'klɒbə(r)/ 1 n fam armamentario m
2 vt (fam: hit) colpire; (defeat) stracciare

cloche /klɒʃ/ n (in garden) campana f di vetro

cloche hat n cloche f inv

clock /klɒk/ n orologio m; (fam: speedometer) tachimetro m
■ **clock in**, **clock on** vi attaccare
■ **clock out**, **clock off** vi staccare

clock face n quadrante m

clockmaker n orologiaio, -a mf

clock radio n radiosveglia f

clock speed n Comput velocità f di clock

clock tower n torre f dell'orologio

clock-watch *vi* guardare continuamente l'orologio

clockwise *adj & adv* in senso orario

clockwork *n* **1** meccanismo *m*; **like ~** fam alla perfezione **2** *attrib* a molla

clod /klɒd/ *n* zolla *f*

clog /klɒg/ **1** *n* zoccolo *m* **2** *vt* (pt/pp **clogged**) **~ [up]** intasare ⟨*drain*⟩; inceppare ⟨*mechanism*⟩ **3** *vi* ⟨*drain*⟩ intasarsi

cloister /'klɔɪstə(r)/ *n* chiostro *m*

clone /kləʊn/ **1** *n* Biol, Comput, fig clone *m* **2** *vt* clonare

cloning /'kləʊnɪŋ/ *n* clonazione *f*

close[1] /kləʊs/ **1** *adj* vicino; ⟨*friend*⟩ intimo; ⟨*weather*⟩ afoso; **have a ~ shave** fam scamparla bella; **be ~ to somebody** essere unito a qualcuno **2** *adv* vicino; **~ by** vicino; **it's ~ on five o'clock** sono quasi le cinque

close[2] /kləʊz/ **1** *n* fine *f*; **draw to a ~** concludere **2** *vt* chiudere **3** *vi* chiudersi; ⟨*shop*⟩ chiudere ■ **close down** **1** *vt* chiudere **2** *vi* ⟨*TV station*⟩ interrompere la trasmissione; ⟨*factory*⟩ chiudere ■ **close in** *vi* ⟨*mist*⟩ calare; ⟨*enemy*⟩ avvicinarsi da ogni lato ■ **close up** **1** *vi* (come closer together) stringersi; ⟨*shop*⟩ chiudere **2** *vt* (bring closer together) avvicinare; chiudere ⟨*shop*⟩

close combat *n* corpo a corpo *m inv*

close-cropped /-'krɒpt/ *adj* ⟨*hair*⟩ rasato

closed-circuit television /kləʊzdsɜ:kɪt-telɪ'vɪʒən/ *n* televisione *f* a circuito chiuso

closed shop /kləʊzd'ʃɒp/ *n* azienda *f* che assume solo personale aderente ad un dato sindacato

close-fitting /kləʊs'fɪtɪŋ/ *adj* ⟨*garment*⟩ attillato

close-knit /kləʊs'nɪt/ *adj* fig ⟨*family, group*⟩ affiatato

closely /'kləʊslɪ/ *adv* da vicino; ⟨*watch, listen*⟩ attentamente

close-run *adj* ⟨*race, competition*⟩ combattutissimo

close season /kləʊs/ *n* stagione *f* di chiusura della caccia e della pesca

closet /'klɒzɪt/ *n* Am armadio *m*

close-up /'kləʊs-/ *n* primo piano *m*

closing /'kləʊzɪŋ/ *adj* ⟨*stages, minutes, words, scene*⟩ ultimo

closing date *n* data *f* di scadenza

closing-down sale *n* liquidazione *f* totale [per cessata attività]

closing time *n* orario *m* di chiusura

closure /'kləʊʒə(r)/ *n* chiusura *f*

clot /klɒt/ **1** *n* grumo *m*; (fam: idiot) tonto, -a *mf* **2** *vi* (pt/pp **clotted**) ⟨*blood*⟩ coagularsi

cloth /klɒθ/ *n* (fabric) tessuto *m*; (duster etc) straccio *m*

clothe /kləʊð/ *vt* vestire

clothes /kləʊðz/ *npl* vestiti *mpl*, abiti *mpl*

clothes-brush *n* spazzola *f* per abiti

clotheshanger *n* gruccia *f* appendiabiti

clothes horse *n* stendibiancheria *m inv*

clothes-line *n* corda *f* stendibiancheria

clothes peg *n* molletta *f* per bucato

clothes shop *n* negozio *m* di abbigliamento

clothing /'kləʊðɪŋ/ *n* abbigliamento *m*

clotted cream /'klɒtɪd/ *n* Br panna *f* rappresa (ottenuta scaldando il latte)

cloud /klaʊd/ *n* nuvola *f* ■ **cloud over** *vi* rannuvolarsi

cloudburst /'klaʊdbɜ:st/ *n* acquazzone *m*

cloudy /'klaʊdɪ/ *adj* (**-ier, -iest**) nuvoloso; ⟨*liquid*⟩ torbido

clout /klaʊt/ **1** *n* fam colpo *m*; (influence) impatto *m* (**with** su) **2** *vt* fam colpire

clove /kləʊv/ *n* chiodo *m* di garofano; **~ of garlic** spicchio *m* d'aglio

cloven foot, cloven hoof /'kləʊvən/ *n* (of animal) zoccolo *m* fesso; (of devil) piede *m* biforcuto

clover /'kləʊvə(r)/ *n* trifoglio *m*

clover leaf *n* raccordo *m* di due autostrade

clown /klaʊn/ **1** *n* pagliaccio *m* **2** *vi* **~ [about/around]** fare il pagliaccio

club /klʌb/ **1** *n* club *m inv*; (weapon) clava *f*; Sport mazza *f*; **~s** *pl* (Cards) fiori *mpl* **2** *vt* (pt/pp **clubbed**) *vt* bastonare ■ **club together** *vi* unirsi

club car *n* Am carrozza *f* ferroviaria con sala bar

club class *n* business class *f inv*

club foot *n* piede *m* deformato

clubhouse *n* (for socializing) circolo *m*; (Am: for changing) spogliatoio *m*

club sandwich *n* club-sandwich *m inv*

cluck /klʌk/ *vi* chiocciare

clue /klu:/ *n* indizio *m*; (in crossword) definizione *f*; **I haven't a ~** fam non ne ho idea

clued-up /klu:d'ʌp/ *adj* Br fam ben informato

clueless /'klu:lɪs/ *adj* Br fam incapace

clump /klʌmp/ *n* gruppo *m*

c

■ **clump about**, **clump around** *vi* (walk noisily) camminare con passo pesante

clumsily /'klʌmzɪlɪ/ *adv* in modo maldestro; ⟨*remark*⟩ senza tatto

clumsiness /'klʌmzɪnɪs/ *n* goffaggine *f*

clumsy /'klʌmzɪ/ *adj* (**-ier**, **-iest**) maldestro; ⟨*tool*⟩ scomodo; ⟨*remark*⟩ senza tatto

clung /klʌŋ/ ▶ CLING

cluster /'klʌstə(r)/ ① *n* gruppo *m*
② *vi* raggrupparsi (**round** intorno a)

clutch /klʌtʃ/ ① *n* stretta *f*; Auto frizione *f*; **be in sb's ～es** essere in balia di qualcuno
② *vt* stringere; (grab) afferrare
③ *vi* ～ **at** afferrare

clutch bag *n* pochette *f inv*

clutch cable *n* cavo *m* della frizione

clutter /'klʌtə(r)/ ① *n* caos *m*
② *vt* ～ [**up**] ingombrare

cm *abbr* (**centimetre**) cm

CND *n abbr* (**Campaign for Nuclear Disarmament**) campagna *f* per il disarmo nucleare

Co. *abbr* (**company**) C., C.ia; **and ～** hum e compagnia; *abbr* (**county**) contea *f*

c/o *abbr* (**care of**) c/o, presso

coach /kəʊtʃ/ ① *n* pullman *m inv*; Rail vagone *m*; (horse-drawn) carrozza *f*; Sport allenatore, -trice *mf*
② *vt* far esercitare; Sport allenare

coach party *n* Br gruppo *m* di gitanti (in pullman)

coach station *n* Br stazione *f* dei pullman

coach trip *n* viaggio *m* in pullman

coachwork *n* Br carrozzeria *f*

coagulate /kəʊ'ægjʊleɪt/ *vi* coagularsi

coagulation /kəʊægjʊ'leɪʃn/ *n* coagulazione *f*

coal /kəʊl/ *n* carbone *m*

coalfield *n* bacino *m* carbonifero

coal fire *n* caminetto *m* alimentato a carbone

coalition /kəʊə'lɪʃn/ *n* coalizione *f*

coal-mine *n* miniera *f* di carbone

coalminer *n* minatore *m*

coal scuttle *n* secchio *m* del carbone

coal seam *n* giacimento *m* di carbone

coarse /kɔːs/ *adj* grossolano; ⟨*joke*⟩ spinto

coarse-grained /-'greɪnd/ *adj* ⟨*texture*⟩ a grana grossa

coarsely /'kɔːslɪ/ *adv* ⟨*ground*⟩ grossolanamente; ⟨*joke*⟩ in modo spinto

coast /kəʊst/ ① *n* costa *f*
② *vi* (freewheel) scendere a ruota libera; Auto scendere in folle

coastal /'kəʊstəl/ *adj* costiero

coaster /'kəʊstə(r)/ *n* (mat) sottobicchiere *m inv*

coastguard /'kəʊs(t)gɑːd/ *n* guardia *f* costiera

coastline /'kəʊstlaɪn/ *n* litorale *m*

coat /kəʊt/ ① *n* cappotto *m*; (of animal) manto *m*; (of paint) mano *f*; ～ **of arms** stemma *f*
② *vt* coprire; (with paint) ricoprire

coat-hanger *n* gruccia *f*

coat-hook *n* gancio *m* [appendiabiti]

coating /'kəʊtɪŋ/ *n* rivestimento *m*; (of paint) stato *m*

coat rack *n* attaccapanni *m* a muro

coat-tails *npl* falde *fpl*; **be always hanging on sb's ～** attaccarsi sempre alle falde di qualcuno

coax /kəʊks/ *vt* convincere con le moine

cob /kɒb/ *n* (of corn) pannocchia *f*

cobble /'kɒbl/ *vt* ～ **together** raffazzonare

cobbler /'kɒblə(r)/ *n* ciabattino *m*

cobblestones /'kɒbəlstəʊnz/ *npl* acciottolato *msg*

cobra /'kəʊbrə/ *n* cobra *m inv*

cobweb /'kɒbweb/ *n* ragnatela *f*

cocaine /kə'keɪn/ *n* cocaina *f*

coccyx /'kɒksɪks/ *n* coccige *m*

cock /kɒk/ ① *n* gallo *m*; (any male bird) maschio *m*; vulg cazzo *m*
② *vt* sollevare il grilletto di ⟨*gun*⟩; ～ **its ears** ⟨*animal*⟩ drizzare le orecchie
■ **cock up** fam ① *vt* incasinare
② *vi* incasinarsi

cock-a-doodle-doo /kɒkədu:d(ə)l'du:/ *int* chicchirichì!

cock-a-hoop *adj* fam al settimo cielo

cock-and-bull story *n* fam panzana *f*

cockatoo /kɒkə'tu:/ *n* cacatoa *m inv*

cockcrow /'kɒkkrəʊ/ *n* **at ～** al primo canto del gallo

cocked hat /kɒkt'hæt/ *n* fam **knock somebody/something into a ～ ～** schiacciare qualcuno/qualcosa

cockerel /'kɒkərəl/ *n* galletto *m*

cocker spaniel /'kɒkə(r)/ *n* cocker *m inv* [spaniel]

cock-eyed /-'aɪd/ *adj* fam storto; (absurd) assurdo

cockfighting /'kɒkfaɪtɪŋ/ *n* combattimenti *mpl* di galli

cockle /'kɒkl/ *n* cardio *m*

cockney /'kɒknɪ/ *n* (dialect) dialetto *m* londinese; (person) abitante *mf* dell'est di Londra

cockpit /'kɒkpɪt/ *n* Aeron cabina *f*

cockroach /'kɒkrəʊtʃ/ *n* scarafaggio *m*

cocksure /kɒk'ʃʊə(r)/ *adj* ⟨*person, manner, attitude*⟩ presuntuoso

cocktail /'kɒkteɪl/ *n* cocktail *m inv*

cocktail bar n [cocktail] bar m inv

cocktail dress n abito m da cocktail m inv

cocktail party n cocktail-party m inv

cocktail shaker n shaker m inv

cocktail stick n stecchino m

cock-up n sl **make a** ∼ fare un casino (of con)

cocky /'kɒkɪ/ adj (**-ier**, **-iest**) fam presuntuoso

cocoa /'kəʊkəʊ/ n cacao m

coconut /'kəʊkənʌt/ n noce f di cocco

coconut palm n palma f di cocco

coconut shy n Br tiro m al bersaglio in cui si devono abbattere noci di cocco

cocoon /kə'ku:n/ n bozzolo m

COD abbr (**cash on delivery**) pagamento m alla consegna

cod /kɒd/ n inv merluzzo m

coddle /'kɒd(ə)l/ vt coccolare

code /kəʊd/ n codice m

coded /'kəʊdɪd/ adj codificato

codeine /'kəʊdi:n/ n codeina f

code name n nome m in codice

codeword n parola f d'ordine

coding /'kəʊdɪŋ/ n Comput codifica f

cod-liver oil n olio m di fegato di merluzzo

coeducational /kəʊedjʊ'keɪʃənəl/ adj misto

coefficient /kəʊɪ'fɪʃənt/ n coefficiente m

coerce /kəʊ'ɜ:s/ vt costringere

coercion /kəʊ'ɜ:ʃn/ n coercizione f

coexist /kəʊɪg'zɪst/ vi coesistere

coexistence /kəʊɪg'zɪstəns/ n coesistenza f

C of E abbr (**Church of England**) Chiesa f anglicana

coffee /'kɒfɪ/ n caffè m inv

coffee bar n caffè m inv, bar m inv

coffee bean n chicco m di caffè

coffee break n pausa f per il caffè

coffee grinder n macinacaffè m inv

coffee machine n (in café) macchina f per l'espresso

coffee-maker n (on stove) caffettiera f; (electric) macchina f per il caffè (con il filtro)

coffee morning n Br riunione m mattutina in cui viene servito il caffè

coffee percolator n (on stove) caffettiera f; (electric) macchina f per il caffè (con il filtro)

coffee-pot n caffettiera f

coffee shop n torrefazione f; (café) caffè m inv, bar m inv

coffee table n tavolino m

coffer /'kɒfə(r)/ n forziere m

coffin /'kɒfɪn/ n bara f

cog /kɒg/ n Techn dente m

cogent /'kəʊdʒənt/ adj convincente

cogitate /'kɒdʒɪteɪt/ vi cogitare

cognac /'kɒnjæk/ n Cognac m

cognoscenti /kɒnə'ʃentɪ/ npl intenditori mpl

cogwheel /'kɒgwi:l/ n ruota f dentata

cohabit /kəʊ'hæbɪt/ vi Jur convivere

coherent /kəʊ'hɪərənt/ adj coerente; (when speaking) logico

cohesion /kəʊ'hi:ʒən/ n coesione f

cohort /'kəʊhɔ:t/ n fig seguito m

coil /kɔɪl/ ① n rotolo m; Electr bobina f; ∼s pl spire fpl ② vt ∼ [up] avvolgere

coin /kɔɪn/ ① n moneta f ② vt coniare ⟨word⟩

coinage /'kɔɪnɪdʒ/ n (of coins, currency) coniatura f; (word, phrase) neologismo m

coin box n (pay phone) telefono m a monete; (on pay phone, in laundromat) gettoniera f

coincide /kəʊɪn'saɪd/ vi coincidere

coincidence /kəʊ'ɪnsɪdəns/ n coincidenza f

coincidental /kəʊɪnsɪ'dentl/ adj casuale

coincidentally /kəʊɪnsɪ'dentlɪ/ adv casualmente

coin operated adj a gettone

Coke® /kəʊk/ n Coca® f

coke n [carbone m] coke m

Col. abbr (**Colonel**) Col. m

colander /'kʌləndə(r)/ n Culin colapasta m inv

cold /kəʊld/ ① adj freddo; **I'm** ∼ ho freddo; **get** ∼ **feet** farsi prendere dalla fifa ② n freddo m; Med raffreddore m

cold-blooded /-'blʌdɪd/ adj spietato

cold calling n Comm visita f senza preavviso

cold comfort n magra consolazione f

cold frame n telaio m coperto di vetro per proteggere le piante dal gelo

cold-hearted /-'hɑ:tɪd/ adj insensibile

coldly /'kəʊldlɪ/ adv fig freddamente

cold meat n salumi mpl

coldness /'kəʊldnɪs/ n freddezza f

cold shoulder n ① **give somebody the** ∼ ∼ snobbare qualcuno ② vt trattare freddamente

cold snap n ondata f di freddo

cold sore n herpes m inv

cold store n cella f frigorifera

cold sweat n sudore m freddo; **bring somebody out in a** ∼ ∼ far sudare freddo qualcuno

cold turkey *n* (reaction) crisi *f inv* di astinenza; **be ∼ ∼** avere una crisi di astinenza; **quit ∼ ∼** smettere di colpo di drogarsi

Cold War *n* guerra *f* fredda

coleslaw /'kəʊslɔ:/ *n* insalata *f* di cavolo crudo, cipolle e carote in maionese

colic /'kɒlɪk/ *n* colica *f*

collaborate /kə'læbəreɪt/ *vi* collaborare; **∼ on something** collaborare a qualcosa

collaboration /kəlæbə'reɪʃn/ *n* collaborazione *f*; (with enemy) collaborazionismo *m*

collaborator /kə'læbəreɪtə(r)/ *n* collaboratore, -trice *mf*; (with enemy) collaborazionista *mf*

collage /kɒ'lɑ:ʒ/ *n* collage *m inv*; (film) montaggio *m*

collapse /kə'læps/ ⓵ *n* crollo *m* ⓶ *vi* ⟨person⟩ svenire; ⟨roof, building⟩ crollare

collapsible /kə'læpsəbl/ *adj* pieghevole

collar /'kɒlə(r)/ *n* colletto *m*; (for animal) collare *m*

collarbone /'kɒləbəʊn/ *n* clavicola *f*

collar size *n* taglia *f* di camicia

collate /kə'leɪt/ *vt* collazionare

collateral /kə'lætərəl/ *n* garanzia *f* collaterale; **put up ∼** offrire una garanzia collaterale

collateral loan *adj* Fin prestito *m* con garanzia collaterale

colleague /'kɒli:g/ *n* collega *mf*

collect /kə'lekt/ ⓵ *vt* andare a prendere ⟨person⟩; ritirare ⟨parcel, tickets⟩; riscuotere ⟨taxes⟩; raccogliere ⟨rubbish⟩; (as hobby) collezionare ⓶ *vi* riunirsi ⓷ *adv* **call ∼** Am telefonare a carico del destinatario

collected /kə'lektɪd/ *adj* controllato

collection /kə'lekʃn/ *n* collezione *f*; (in church) questua *f*; (of rubbish) raccolta *f*; (of post) levata *f*

collective /kə'lektɪv/ *adj* collettivo

collective bargaining *n* contrattazione *f* collettiva

collective farm *n* comune *f*

collective noun *n* nome *m* collettivo

collective ownership *n* comproprietà *f*

collector /kə'lektə(r)/ *n* (of stamps etc) collezionista *mf*

collector's item *n* pezzo *m* da collezionista

college /'kɒlɪdʒ/ *n* istituto *m* parauniversitario; **C∼ of ...** Scuola *f* di ...

college of education *n* Br ≈ facoltà *f* *inv* di magistero

college of further education *n* Br istituto *m* parauniversitario

collide /kə'laɪd/ *vi* scontrarsi

collie /'kɒlɪ/ *n* pastore *m* scozzese, collie *m inv*

colliery /'kɒlɪərɪ/ *n* miniera *f* di carbone

collision /kə'lɪʒn/ *n* scontro *m*; **be on a ∼ course** essere in rotta di collisione

colloquial /kə'ləʊkwɪəl/ *adj* colloquiale

colloquialism /kə'ləʊkwɪəlɪzm/ *n* espressione *f* colloquiale

colloquially /kə'ləʊkwɪəlɪ/ *adv* colloquialmente

colloquium /kə'ləʊkwɪəm/ *n* colloquio *m*

collude /kə'l(j)u:d/ *vi* complottare

collusion /kə'l(j)u:ʒn/ *n* collusione *f*; **in ∼ with** in accordo con

cologne /kə'ləʊn/ *n* colonia *f*

Colombia /kə'lɒmbɪə/ *n* Colombia *f*

Colombian /kə'lɒmbɪən/ *adj & n* colombiano, -a *mf*

colon /'kəʊlən/ *n* due punti *mpl*; Anat colon *m inv*

colonel /'kɜ:nl/ *n* colonnello *m*

colonial /kə'ləʊnɪəl/ *adj* coloniale

colonialist /kə'ləʊnɪəlɪst/ *adj & n* colonialista *mf*

colonization /kɒlənaɪ'zeɪʃn/ *n* colonizzazione *f*

colonize /'kɒlənaɪz/ *vt* colonizzare

colonizer /'kɒlənaɪzə(r)/ *n* colonizzatore, -trice *mf*

colonnade /kɒlə'neɪd/ *n* colonnato *m*

colony /'kɒlənɪ/ *n* colonia *f*

Colorado beetle /kɒlə'rɑ:dəʊ/ *n* dorifora *f*

colossal /kə'lɒsl/ *adj* colossale

colour /'kʌlə(r)/ ⓵ *n* colore *m*; (complexion) colorito *m*; **∼s** *pl* (flag) bandiera *fsg*; **show one's true ∼s** fig buttare giù la maschera; **in ∼** a colori; **off ∼** fam giù di tono ⓶ *vt* colorare; **∼ [in]** colorare ⓷ *vi* (blush) arrossire

colour bar *n* discriminazione *f* razziale

colour-blind *adj* daltonico

colour code *vt* distinguere per mezzo di colori diversi

coloured /'kʌləd/ ⓵ *adj* colorato; ⟨person⟩ di colore ⓶ *n* (person) persona *f* di colore

colour fast *adj* dai colori resistenti

colour film *n* film *m inv* a colori

colourful /'kʌləfʊl/ *adj* pieno di colore

colouring /'kʌlərɪŋ/ *n* (of plant, animal) colorazione *f*; (complexion) colorito *m*; (dye: for hair) tinta *f*; (for food) colorante *m*

colouring book *n* album *m inv* da colorare

colourless /'kʌləlɪs/ adj incolore

colour photo[graph] n fotografia f a colori

colour scheme n [combinazione f di] colori mpl

colour sense n senso m del colore

colour supplement n supplemento m illustrato a colori

colour television n televisione f a colori

colt /kəʊlt/ n puledro m

column /'kɒləm/ n colonna f

columnist /'kɒləmnɪst/ n giornalista mf che cura una rubrica

coma /'kəʊmə/ n coma m inv

comatose /'kəʊmətəʊz/ adj Med in stato comatoso

comb /kəʊm/ ① n pettine m; (for wearing) pettinino m
② vt pettinare; (fig: search) setacciare; ~ one's hair pettinarsi i capelli
■ **comb through** vt setacciare ⟨files, desk⟩

combat /'kɒmbæt/ ① n combattimento m
② vt (pt/pp **combated**) combattere

combat jacket n giubba f da combattimento

combination /kɒmbɪ'neɪʃn/ n combinazione f

combine[1] /kəm'baɪn/ ① vt unire; ~ a job with being a mother conciliare il lavoro con il ruolo di madre
② vi ⟨chemical elements⟩ combinarsi

combine[2] /'kɒmbaɪn/ n Comm associazione f

combined /kəm'baɪnd/ adj combinato

combine [harvester] n mietitrebbia f

combustible /kəm'bʌstəbl/ adj combustibile

combustion /kəm'bʌstʃn/ n combustione f

come /kʌm/ vi (pt **came**, pp **come**) venire; **after coming all this way** dopo tutta questa strada; **where do you ~ from?** da dove vieni?; ~ **to** (reach) arrivare a; **that ~s to £10** fanno 10 sterline; **I've ~ to appreciate her** ho finito per apprezzarla; **I don't know what the world is coming to** mi chiedo dove andremo a finire; ~ **into money** ricevere dei soldi; **that's what comes of being ...** ecco cosa significa essere...; ~ **true/open** verificarsi/aprirsi; ~ **first** arrivare primo; fig venire prima di tutto; ~ **in two sizes** esistere in due misure; **the years to ~** gli anni a venire; **how ~?** fam come mai?
■ **come about** vi succedere
■ **come across** ① vi ~ **across as being** fam dare l'impressione di essere
② vt (find) imbattersi in

■ **come after** vt (follow) venire dopo; (chase, pursue) inseguire
■ **come along** vi venire; ⟨job, opportunity⟩ presentarsi; (progress) andare bene
■ **come apart** vi smontarsi; (break) rompersi
■ **come at** vt (attack) avventarsi su
■ **come away** vi venir via; ⟨button, fastener⟩ staccarsi
■ **come back** vi ritornare
■ **come before** vt (precede) precedere; (be more important than) venire prima di
■ **come by** ① vi passare
② vt (obtain) avere
■ **come down** vi scendere; ~ **down to** (reach) arrivare a; **the situation comes down to...** la situazione si riduce a...; **don't ~ down too hard on her** vacci piano con lei; ~ **down with flu** prendersi l'influenza
■ **come forward** vi farsi avanti
■ **come in** vi entrare; (in race) arrivare; ⟨tide⟩ salire; ~ **in with somebody** (in an undertaking) associarsi a qualcuno
■ **come in for** vt ~ **in for criticism** essere criticato
■ **come into** vt (inherit) ereditare ⟨money, inheritance⟩
■ **come off** ① vi staccarsi; (take place) esserci; (succeed) riuscire
② vt ~ **off it!** non farmi ridere!
■ **come on** vi (make progress) migliorare; ~ **on!** (hurry) dai!; (indicating disbelief) ma va là!
■ **come out** vi venir fuori; ⟨book, sun⟩ uscire; ⟨stain⟩ andar via; ⟨homosexual⟩ rivelare la propria omosessualità; ~ **out [on strike]** scioperare
■ **come out with** vt venir fuori con ⟨joke, suggestion⟩
■ **come over** vi venire; **what's ~ over you?** cosa ti prende?
■ **come round, come around** vi venire; (after fainting) riaversi; (change one's mind) farsi convincere
■ **come through** ① vi ⟨news⟩ arrivare
② vt attraversare ⟨operation⟩
■ **come to** vi (after fainting) riaversi.
■ **come under** vi trovarsi sotto
■ **come up** vi salire; ⟨sun⟩ sorgere; ⟨plant⟩ crescere; ⟨name, subject⟩ venir fuori; ⟨job, opportunity⟩ presentarsi; **something came up** (I was prevented) ho avuto un imprevisto
■ **come up against** vt incontrare
■ **come up to** vt (reach) arrivare a; essere all'altezza di ⟨expectations⟩
■ **come up with** vt tirar fuori

come-back n ritorno m

comedian /kə'miːdɪən/ n [attore m] comico m

comedienne /kəmiːdɪ'en/ n attrice f comica

come-down n passo m indietro

comedy /'kɒmədɪ/ n commedia f

comer /'kʌmə(r)/ n open to all ~s aperto a tutti; take on all ~s battersi contro tutti gli sfidanti

comet /'kɒmɪt/ n cometa f

come-uppance /kʌm'ʌpəns/ n get one's ~ fam avere quel che si merita

comfort /'kʌmfət/ **1** n benessere m; (consolation) conforto m; all the ~s tutti i comfort
2 vt confortare

comfortable /'kʌmfətəbl/ adj comodo; be ~ ⟨person⟩ stare comodo; fig (in situation) essere a proprio agio; (financially) star bene

comfortably /'kʌmfətəblɪ/ adv comodamente

comforting /'kʌmfətɪŋ/ adj confortante

comfort station n Am bagno m pubblico

comfy /'kʌmfɪ/ adj fam comodo

comic /'kɒmɪk/ **1** adj comico
2 n comico, -a mf; (periodical) fumetto m

comical /'kɒmɪk(ə)l/ adj comico

comically /'kɒmɪk(ə)lɪ/ adv comicamente

comic book n giornalino m [a fumetti]

comic relief n provide some ~ ~ Theat fare una parentesi comica; fig sdrammatizzare

comic strip n striscia f di fumetti

coming /'kʌmɪŋ/ **1** adj promettente
2 n venuta f; ~s and goings viavai m

comma /'kɒmə/ n virgola f

command /kə'mɑːnd/ **1** n also Comput comando m; (order) ordine m; (mastery) padronanza f; in ~ al comando
2 vt ordinare; comandare ⟨army⟩

commandant /'kɒməndænt/ n Mil comandante m

commandeer /kɒmən'dɪə(r)/ vt requisire

commander /kə'mɑːndə(r)/ n comandante m

commanding /kə'mɑːndɪŋ/ adj ⟨view⟩ imponente; ⟨lead⟩ dominante

commanding officer n comandante m

commandment /kə'mɑːndmənt/ n comandamento m

commando /kə'mɑːndəʊ/ n commando m inv

command performance n Br Theat serata f di gala (su richiesta del capo di stato)

commemorate /kə'meməreɪt/ vt commemorare

commemoration /kəmemə'reɪʃn/ n commemorazione f

commemorative /kə'memərətɪv/ adj commemorativo

commence /kə'mens/ vt/i cominciare

commencement /kə'mensmənt/ n inizio m

commend /kə'mend/ vt complimentarsi con (on per); (recommend) raccomandare (to a)

commendable /kə'mendəbl/ adj lodevole

commendation /kɒmen'deɪʃn/ n elogio m; (for bravery) riconoscimento m

commensurate /kə'menʃərət/ adj proporzionato (with a)

comment /'kɒment/ **1** n commento m; no ~! no comment!
2 vi fare commenti (on su)

commentary /'kɒməntrɪ/ n commento m; [running] ~ (on radio, TV) cronaca f diretta

commentate /'kɒmənteɪt/ vt ~ on TV, Radio fare la cronaca di
■ **commentate on** vt fare la radiocronaca/telecronaca di ⟨sporting event⟩

commentator /'kɒmənteɪtə(r)/ n cronista mf

commerce /'kɒmɜːs/ n commercio m

commercial /kə'mɜːʃl/ **1** adj commerciale
2 n TV pubblicità f inv

commercial break n spot m inv [pubblicitario], interruzione f pubblicitaria

commercialism /kə'mɜːʃ(ə)lɪzm/ n pej affarismo m

commercialize /kə'mɜːʃ(ə)laɪz/ vt commercializzare

commercial law n diritto m commerciale

commercially /kə'mɜːʃ(ə)lɪ/ adv commercialmente

command centre Br, **command center** Am n centro m di comando

commercial traveller n commesso m viaggiatore

commiserate /kə'mɪzəreɪt/ vi esprimere il proprio rincrescimento (with a)

commissar /kɒmɪ'sɑː(r)/ n commissario m

commission /kə'mɪʃn/ **1** n commissione f; receive one's ~ Mil essere promosso ufficiale; out of ~ fuori uso
2 vt commissionare; Mil promuovere ufficiale; ~ a painting from somebody, ~ somebody to do a painting commissionare un dipinto a qualcuno

commissionaire /kəmɪʃə'neə(r)/ n portiere m

commissioner /kə'mɪʃənə(r)/ n commissario m; C~ for Oaths ≈ notaio m

commit /kə'mɪt/ vt (pt/pp committed) commettere; (to prison, hospital) affidare (to a); impegnare ⟨funds⟩; ~ oneself ···⟩

impegnarsi; ∼ **something to memory**
imparare qualcosa a memoria

commitment /kəˈmɪtmənt/ n impegno
m; (involvement) compromissione f

committed /kəˈmɪtɪd/ adj impegnato

committee /kəˈmɪtɪ/ n comitato m

commodity /kəˈmɒdətɪ/ n prodotto m

commodore /ˈkɒmədɔː(r)/ n
commodoro m

common /ˈkɒmən/ **1** adj comune;
(vulgar) volgare
2 n prato m pubblico; **have in** ∼ avere in
comune; **House of C**∼**s** Camera f dei
Comuni

common cold n raffreddore m

commoner /ˈkɒmənə(r)/ n persona f
non nobile

common ground n fig terreno m
d'intesa

common-law n diritto m
consuetudinario

common-law husband n convivente
m (more uxorio)

common-law marriage n
matrimonio m di fatto

common-law wife n convivente f
(more uxorio)

commonly /ˈkɒmənlɪ/ adv
comunemente

Common Market n Mercato m
Comune

common-or-garden adj ordinario

commonplace adj banale

common-room n sala f dei professori/
degli studenti

commonsense n buon senso m

Commonwealth n **1** Br
Commonwealth m inv
2 attrib ⟨country, Games⟩ del
Commonwealth

**Commonwealth of Independent
States** n Comunità f degli stati
indipendenti

commotion /kəˈməʊʃn/ n confusione f

communal /ˈkɒmjʊnəl/ adj comune

commune /ˈkɒmjuːn/ **1** n comune f
2 /kəˈmjuːn/ vi ∼ **with** essere in
comunione con ⟨nature⟩; comunicare con
person

communicable /kəˈmjuːnɪkəbl/ adj
⟨disease⟩ trasmissibile

communicate /kəˈmjuːnɪkeɪt/ vt/i
comunicare

communication /kəmjuːnɪˈkeɪʃn/ n
comunicazione f; (of disease) trasmissione
f; **be in** ∼ **with somebody** essere in
contatto con qualcuno; ∼**s** pl (technology)
telecomunicazioni fpl

communication cord n fermata f
d'emergenza

communications company n
società f di telecomunicazioni

communications satellite n
satellite m per telecomunicazioni

communications software n
software m di comunicazione

communication studies /ˈstʌdɪz/ n
studi mpl di comunicazione

communicative /kəˈmjuːnɪkətɪv/ adj
comunicativo

Communion /kəˈmjuːnɪən/ n [Holy] ∼
comunione f

communiqué /kəˈmjuːnɪkeɪ/ n
comunicato m stampa

Communism /ˈkɒmjʊnɪzm/ n
comunismo m

Communist /ˈkɒmjʊnɪst/ adj & n
comunista mf

Communist Party n partito m
communista

community /kəˈmjuːnətɪ/ n comunità f

community care n cura f fuori
dell'ambito ospedaliero

community centre n centro m sociale

community policing n polizia f di
quartiere

community service n servizio m
civile (in sostituzione di pene per reati
minori)

community spirit n spirito m civico

commute /kəˈmjuːt/ **1** vi fare il
pendolare
2 vt Jur commutare

commuter /kəˈmjuːtə(r)/ n pendolare
mf

commuter belt n zona f suburbana
abitata dai pendolari

commuter train n treno m dei
pendolari

Comoros /ˈkɒmərəʊz/ npl the ∼
(Islands) le (isole) Comore fpl

compact[1] /kəmˈpækt/ adj compatto

compact[2] /ˈkɒmpækt/ n portacipria m
inv

compact disc n compact disc m inv

compact disc player n lettore m di
compact disc

companion /kəmˈpænjən/ n compagno,
-a mf

companionable /kəmˈpænjənəbl/ adj
⟨person⟩ socievole; ⟨silence⟩ non pesante

companionship /kəmˈpænjənʃɪp/ n
compagnia f

company /ˈkʌmpənɪ/ n compagnia f;
(guests) ospiti mpl; **I didn't know you had**
∼ pensavo che fossi solo

company brochure n opuscolo m
dell'azienda

company car n macchina f della ditta

company director *n* dirigente *mf* d'azienda

company letterhead *n* carta *f* intestata dell'azienda

company pension scheme *n* piano *m* di pensionamento aziendale

company policy *n* politica *f* aziendale

company secretary *n* direttore, -trice *mf* amministrativo, -a

comparable /'kɒmpərəbl/ *adj* paragonabile

comparative /kəm'pærətɪv/ **①** *adj* comparativo; (relative) relativo **②** *n* Gram comparativo *m*

comparatively /kəm'pærətɪvlɪ/ *adv* relativamente

compare /kəm'peə(r)/ **①** *vt* paragonare (with/to a) **②** *vi* it can't ∼ non ha paragoni

comparison /kəm'pærɪsn/ *n* paragone *m*

compartment /kəm'pɑːtmənt/ *n* compartimento *m*; Rail scompartimento *m*

compass /'kʌmpəs/ *n* bussola *f*

compasses /'kʌmpəsɪz/ *npl* pair of ∼ compasso *msg*

compassion /kəm'pæʃn/ *n* compassione *f*

compassionate /kəm'pæʃənət/ *adj* compassionevole

compatible /kəm'pætəbl/ *adj* compatibile; be ∼ ⟨people⟩ avere caratteri compatibili

compatriot /kəm'pætrɪət/ *n* compatriota *mf*

compel /kəm'pel/ *vt* (pt/pp **compelled**) costringere

compelling /kəm'pelɪŋ/ *adj* ⟨reason, argument⟩ convincente; ⟨performance, film, speaker⟩ avvincente

compendium /kəm'pendɪəm/ *n* (handbook) compendio *m*; (Br: box of games) scatola *f* di giochi

compensate /'kɒmpənseɪt/ **①** *vt* risarcire **②** *vi* ∼ for fig compensare di

compensation /kɒmpən'seɪʃn/ *n* risarcimento *m*; (fig: comfort) consolazione *f*

compère /'kɒmpeə(r)/ *n* presentatore, -trice *mf*

compete /kəm'piːt/ *vi* competere; (take part) gareggiare

competence /'kɒmpɪtəns/ *n* competenza *f*

competent /'kɒmpɪtənt/ *adj* competente

competition /kɒmpə'tɪʃn/ *n* concorrenza *f*; (contest) gara *f*

competitive /kəm'petɪtɪv/ *adj* competitivo; ∼ prices prezzi *mpl* concorrenziali

competitor /kəm'petɪtə(r)/ *n* concorrente *mf*

compilation /kɒmpɪ'leɪʃn/ *n* compilazione *f*; (collection) raccolta *f*

compile /kəm'paɪl/ *vt* compilare

complacency /kəm'pleɪsənsɪ/ *n* compiacimento *m*

complacent /kəm'pleɪsənt/ *adj* compiaciuto

complacently /kəm'pleɪsəntlɪ/ *adv* con compiacimento

complain /kəm'pleɪn/ *vi* lamentarsi (about di); (formally) reclamare; ∼ of Med accusare

complaint /kəm'pleɪnt/ *n* lamentela *f*; (formal) reclamo *m*; Med disturbo *m*

complement[1] /'kɒmplɪmənt/ *n* complemento *m*; with a full ∼ of 25 con un effettivo al completo di 25

complement[2] /'kɒmplɪment/ *vt* complementare; ∼ each other complementarsi a vicenda

complementary /kɒmplɪ'mentərɪ/ *adj* complementare

complementary medicine *n* medicina *f* alternativa

complete /kəm'pliːt/ **①** *adj* completo; (utter) finito **②** *vt* completare; compilare ⟨form⟩

completely /kəm'pliːtlɪ/ *adv* completamente

completion /kəm'pliːʃn/ *n* fine *f*

complex /'kɒmpleks/ *adj* & *n* complesso *m*

complexion /kəm'plekʃn/ *n* carnagione *f*; that puts a different ∼ on the matter questo mette la questione in una luce nuova

complexity /kəm'pleksətɪ/ *n* complessità *f inv*

compliance /kəm'plaɪəns/ *n* accettazione *f*; (with rules) osservanza *f*; in ∼ with in osservanza a ⟨law⟩; conformemente a ⟨request⟩

compliant /kəm'plaɪənt/ *adj* accondiscendente; Comput conforme; ∼ with conforme a

complicate /'kɒmplɪkeɪt/ *vt* complicare

complicated /'kɒmplɪkeɪtɪd/ *adj* complicato

complication /kɒmplɪ'keɪʃn/ *n* complicazione *f*

complicity /kəm'plɪsətɪ/ *n* complicità *f*

compliment /'kɒmplɪmənt/ **①** *n* complimento *m*; ∼s *pl* omaggi *mpl* **②** *vt* complimentare

complimentary /kɒmplɪ'mentərɪ/ *adj* complimentoso; (given free) in omaggio

comply /kəm'plaɪ/ *vi* (pt/pp **-ied**) ∼ with conformarsi a

component /kəm'pəʊnənt/ adj & n ~
[part] componente m

compose /kəm'pəʊz/ vt comporre; ~
oneself ricomporsi; be ~d of essere
composto da

composed /kəm'pəʊzd/ adj (calm)
composto

composer /kəm'pəʊzə(r)/ n
compositore, -trice mf

composite /'kɒmpəzɪt/ adj composto;
⟨style⟩ composito

composition /kɒmpə'zɪʃn/ n
composizione f; (essay) tema m

compos mentis /kɒmpɒs'mentɪs/ adj
nel pieno possesso delle proprie facoltà

compost /'kɒmpɒst/ n composta f

composure /kəm'pəʊʒə(r)/ n calma f

compound[1] /kəm'paʊnd/ vt (make worse)
aggravare

compound[2] /'kɒmpaʊnd/ [1] adj
composto
[2] n Chem composto m; Gram parola f
composta; (enclosure) recinto m

compound fracture n frattura f
esposta

compound interest n interesse m
composto

comprehend /kɒmprɪ'hend/ vt
comprendere

comprehensible /kɒmprɪ'hensəbl/ adj
comprensibile

comprehensibly /kɒmprɪ'hensəblɪ/
adv comprensibilmente

comprehension /kɒmprɪ'henʃn/ n
comprensione f

comprehensive /kɒmprɪ'hensɪv/ adj
& n comprensivo; ~ [school] scuola f
media in cui gli allievi hanno capacità
d'apprendimento diverse

comprehensive insurance n Auto
polizza f casco

compress[1] /'kɒmpres/ n compressa f

compress[2] /kəm'pres/ vt also Comput
comprimere

compressed air /kəm'prest/ n aria f
compressa

compression /kəm'preʃn/ n
compressione f

comprise /kəm'praɪz/ vt comprendere;
(form) costituire

compromise /'kɒmprəmaɪz/ [1] n
compromesso m
[2] vt compromettere
[3] vi fare un compromesso

compromising /'kɒmprəmaɪzɪŋ/ adj
⟨situation⟩ compromettente

compulsion /kəm'pʌlʃn/ n desiderio m
irresistibile

compulsive /kəm'pʌlsɪv/ adj Psych
patologico; ~ eating voglia f ossessiva di
mangiare

compulsory /kəm'pʌlsərɪ/ adj
obbligatorio; ~ subject materia f
obbligatoria

compulsory purchase n Br
espropriazione f (per pubblica utilità)

compunction /kəm'pʌŋkʃn/ n liter
scrupolo m

computation /kɒmpjʊ'teɪʃn/ n calcolo
m

computer /kəm'pjuːtə(r)/ n computer m
inv

computer-aided adj assistito da
computer

computer-aided design n
progettazione f assistita da computer

computer-aided learning n
apprendimento m assistito dal computer

**computer-assisted language
learning** n apprendimento m della
lingua assistito dal computer

computer crime n reati mpl
informatici

computer dating n possibilità f di
incontrare l'anima gemella tramite
agenzie in rete

computer dating service n servizio
m di ricerca dell'anima gemella in rete

computer engineer n tecnico m
informatico

computer error n errore m
informatico

computer game n gioco m su
computer; ~ ~s intelligiochi mpl

computer graphics n grafica f
computerizzata

computer hacker n pirata m
informatico

computerization /kəmpjuːtəraɪ'zeɪʃn/
n computerizzazione f

computerize /kəm'pjuːtəraɪz/ vt
computerizzare

computer-literate adj che sa usare il
computer

computer operator n terminalista mf

computer program n programma m
[informatico]

computer programmer n
programmatore, -trice mf di computer

computer science n informatica f

computer scientist n esperto, -a mf
di informatica

computer virus n virus m inv [su
computer]

computing /kəm'pjuːtɪŋ/ n informatica
f

comrade /'kɒmreɪd/ n camerata m; Pol
compagno, -a mf

comradeship /'kɒmreɪdʃɪp/ n
cameratismo m

con[1] /kɒn/ ▶PRO

con² ① *n* fam fregatura *f*
② *vt* (pt/pp **conned**) fam fregare

concave /'kɒnkeɪv/ *adj* concavo

conceal /kən'si:l/ *vt* nascondere

concealment /kən'si:lmənt/ *n*
dissimulazione *f*

concede /kən'si:d/ *vt* (admit) ammettere;
(give up) rinunciare a; lasciar fare ⟨goal⟩

conceit /kən'si:t/ *n* presunzione *f*

conceited /kən'si:tɪd/ *adj* presuntuoso

conceivable /kən'si:vəbl/ *adj*
concepibile

conceive /kən'si:v/ ① *vt* Biol concepire
② *vi* aver figli; ~ **of** fig concepire

concentrate /'kɒnsəntreɪt/ ① *vt*
concentrare
② *vi* concentrarsi
③ *n* concentrato *m*

concentration /kɒnsən'treɪʃn/ *n*
concentrazione *f*

concentration camp *n* campo *m* di
concentramento

concentric /kən'sentrɪk/ *adj*
concentrico

concept /'kɒnsept/ *n* concetto *m*

conception /kən'sepʃn/ *n* concezione *f*;
(idea) idea *f*

conceptual /kən'septjʊəl/ *adj*
concettuale

concern /kən'sɜ:n/ ① *n* preoccupazione
f; Comm attività *f inv*
② *vt* (be about, affect) riguardare; (worry)
preoccupare; ~ **oneself with** preoccuparsi
di; **as far as I am** ~**ed** per quanto mi
riguarda

concerned /kən'sɜ:nd/ *adj* (worried)
preoccupato; **be** ~ **about** essere
preoccupato per; (involved) interessato; **all
(those)** ~ tutti gli interessati

concerning /kən'sɜ:nɪŋ/ *prep* riguardo
a

concert /'kɒnsət/ *n* concerto *m*

concerted /kən'sɜ:tɪd/ *adj* collettivo

concert hall *n* sala *f* da concerti

concertina /kɒnsə'ti:nə/ *n* piccola
fisarmonica *f*

concert master *n* Am primo violino *m*

concerto /kən'tʃeətəʊ/ *n* concerto *m*

concession /kən'seʃn/ *n* concessione *f*;
(reduction) sconto *m*

concessionary /kən'seʃənrɪ/ *adj*
(reduced) scontato

conciliate /kən'sɪlɪeɪt/ *vt* blandire

conciliation /kənsɪlɪ'eɪʃn/ *n*
conciliazione *f*

conciliator /kən'sɪlɪeɪtə(r)/ *n*
mediatore, -trice *mf*

conciliatory /kən'sɪlɪətrɪ/ *adj*
conciliatorio

concise /kən'saɪs/ *adj* conciso

concisely /kən'saɪslɪ/ *adv* in modo
conciso

conciseness /kən'saɪsnɪs/ *n* concisione
f

conclude /kən'klu:d/ ① *vt* concludere
② *vi* concludersi

concluding /kən'klu:dɪŋ/ *adj* finale,
conclusivo

conclusion /kən'klu:ʒn/ *n* conclusione
f; **in** ~ per concludere

conclusive /kən'klu:sɪv/ *adj* definitivo

conclusively /kən'klu:sɪvlɪ/ *adv* in
modo definitivo

concoct /kən'kɒkt/ *vt* confezionare; fig
inventare

concoction /kən'kɒkʃn/ *n* mistura *f*;
(drink) intruglio *m*

concord /'kɒŋkɔ:d/ *n* concordia *f*

concordance /kən'kɔ:dəns/ *n* accordo
m; (index) concordanze *fpl*; **be in** ~ **with**
essere in accordo con

concourse /'kɒŋkɔ:s/ *n* atrio *m*

concrete /'kɒŋkri:t/ ① *adj* concreto
② *n* calcestruzzo *m*
③ *vt* ricoprire di calcestruzzo

concrete jungle *n* giungla *f* d'asfalto

concrete mixer *n* betoniera *f*

concur /kən'kɜ:(r)/ *vi* (pt/pp
concurred) essere d'accordo

concurrently /kən'kʌrəntlɪ/ *adv*
contemporaneamente

concuss /kən'kʌs/ *vt* **be** ~**ed** avere una
commozione cerebrale

concussion /kən'kʌʃn/ *n* commozione *f*
cerebrale

condemn /kən'dem/ *vt* condannare;
dichiarare inagibile ⟨building⟩

condemnation /kɒndem'neɪʃn/ *n*
condanna *f*

condensation /kɒnden'seɪʃn/ *n*
condensazione *f*

condense /kən'dens/ ① *vt* condensare;
Phys condensare
② *vi* condensarsi

condensed milk /kəndenst'mɪlk/ *n*
latte *m* condensato

condescend /kɒndɪ'send/ *vi* degnarsi

condescending /kɒndɪ'sendɪŋ/ *adj*
condiscendente

condescendingly /kɒndɪ'sendɪŋlɪ/
adv in modo condiscendente

condiment /'kɒndɪmənt/ *n* condimento
m

condition /kən'dɪʃn/ ① *n* condizione *f*;
on ~ **that** a condizione che
② *vt* Psych condizionare

conditional /kən'dɪʃənəl/ ① *adj*
⟨acceptance⟩ condizionato; Gram
condizionale; **be** ~ **on** essere condizionato
da
② *n* Gram condizionale

conditionally /kən'dɪʃənəlɪ/ *adv*
condizionatamente

conditioner /kən'dɪʃənə(r)/ *n* balsamo
m; (for fabrics) ammorbidente *m*

conditioning /kən'dɪʃənɪŋ/ **1** *n* (of hair)
balsamo *m*; Psych condizionamento *m*
2 *adj* ‹*shampoo, lotion etc*› trattante

condole /kən'dəʊl/ *vi* fare le
condoglianze (**with** a)

condolences /kən'dəʊlənsɪz/ *npl*
condoglianze *fpl*

condom /'kɒndəm/ *n* preservativo *m*

condo[minium] /'kɒndəʊ/,
/kɒndə'mɪnɪəm/ *n* Am condominio *m*

condone /kən'dəʊn/ *vt* passare sopra a

conducive /kən'dju:sɪv/ *adj* be ∼ to
contribuire a

conduct[1] /'kɒndʌkt/ *n* condotta *f*

conduct[2] /kən'dʌkt/ *vt* condurre;
dirigere ‹*orchestra*›

conduction /kən'dʌkʃn/ *n* conduzione *f*

conductor /kən'dʌktə(r)/ *n* direttore *m*
d'orchestra; (of bus) bigliettaio *m*; Phys
conduttore *m*

conductress /kən'dʌktrɪs/ *n* bigliettaia
f

cone /kəʊn/ *n* cono *m*; Bot pigna *f*; Auto
birillo *m*
■ **cone off** *vt* be ∼d off Auto essere
chiuso da birilli

confection /kən'fekʃn/ *n* (cake, dessert)
dolce *m*; a ∼ of (combination) una
combinazione di

confectioner /kən'fekʃənə(r)/ *n*
pasticciere, -a *mf*

confectionery /kən'fekʃənərɪ/ *n*
pasticceria *f*

confederation /kənfedə'reɪʃn/ *n*
confederazione *f*

confer /kən'fɜ:(r)/ **1** *v* (pt/pp
conferred) *vt* conferire (**on** a)
2 *vi* (discuss) conferire

conference /'kɒnfərəns/ *n* conferenza *f*

conference room *n* sala *f* riunioni

confess /kən'fes/ **1** *vt* confessare
2 *vi* confessare; Relig confessarsi

confession /kən'feʃn/ *n* confessione *f*

confessional /kən'feʃənəl/ *n*
confessionale *m*

confessor /kən'fesə(r)/ *n* confessore *m*

confetti /kən'fetɪ/ *n* coriandoli *mpl*

confide /kən'faɪd/ *vt* confidare
■ **confide in** *vt* ∼ **in somebody** fidarsi di
qualcuno

confidence /'kɒnfɪdəns/ *n* (trust) fiducia
f; (self-assurance) sicurezza *f* di sé; (secret)
confidenza *f*; **in** ∼ in confidenza

confidence trick *n* truffa *f*

confidence trickster
/'kɒnfɪdənstrɪkstə(r)/ *n* imbroglione, -a *mf*

confident /'kɒnfɪdənt/ *adj* fiducioso;
(self-assured) sicuro di sé

confidential /kɒnfɪ'denʃl/ *adj*
confidenziale

confidentiality /kɒnfɪdenʃɪ'ælətɪ/ *n*
riservatezza *f*

confidentially /kɒnfɪ'denʃəlɪ/ *adv*
confidenzialmente

confidently /'kɒnfɪdəntlɪ/ *adv* con aria
fiduciosa; **we** ∼ **expect to win** siamo
fiduciosi nella vittoria

confine /kən'faɪn/ *vt* rinchiudere; (limit)
limitare; **be** ∼**d to bed** essere confinato a
letto

confined /kən'faɪnd/ *adj* ‹*space*› limitato

confinement /kən'faɪnmənt/ *n*
detenzione *f*; Med parto *m*

confines /'kɒnfaɪnz/ *npl* confini *mpl*

confirm /kən'fɜ:m/ *vt* confermare; Relig
cresimare

confirmation /kɒnfə'meɪʃn/ *n* conferma
f; Relig cresima *f*

confirmed /kən'fɜ:md/ *adj* incallito; ∼
bachelor scapolo *m* impenitente

confiscate /'kɒnfɪskeɪt/ *vt* confiscare

confiscation /kɒnfɪs'keɪʃn/ *n* confisca
f

conflagration /kɒnflə'greɪʃn/ *n*
conflagrazione *f*

conflate /kən'fleɪt/ *vt* fondere

conflict[1] /'kɒnflɪkt/ *n* conflitto *m*

conflict[2] /kən'flɪkt/ *vi* essere in
contraddizione

conflicting /kən'flɪktɪŋ/ *adj*
contraddittorio

confluence /'kɒnfluəns/ *n* (of rivers)
confluenza *f*; fig convergenza *f*

conform /kən'fɔ:m/ *vi* ‹*person*›
conformarsi; ‹*thing*› essere conforme (**to**
a)

conformist /kən'fɔ:mɪst/ *n* conformista
mf

conformity /kən'fɔ:mɪtɪ/ *n* conformità *f*;
Relig ortodossia *f*; **in** ∼ **with** in conformità
a

confound /kən'faʊnd/ *vt* (perplex)
confondere; (show to be wrong) confutare

confounded /kən'faʊndɪd/ *adj* fam
maledetto

confront /kən'frʌnt/ *vt* affrontare; **the
problems** ∼**ing us** i problemi che
dobbiamo affrontare

confrontation /kɒnfrʌn'teɪʃn/ *n*
confronto *m*

confrontational /kɒnfrʌn'teɪʃənl/ *adj*
provocatorio

confuse /kən'fju:z/ *vt* confondere

confused /kən'fju:zd/ *adj* ‹*presentation,
idea*› ingarbugliato

confusing /kən'fju:zɪŋ/ *adj* che confonde

confusion /kən'fju:ʒn/ *n* confusione *f*

congeal /kən'dʒi:l/ *vi* ‹*blood*› coagularsi

congenial /kən'dʒi:nɪəl/ *adj* congeniale

congenital /kən'dʒenɪtl/ *adj* congenito

congested /kən'dʒestɪd/ *adj* congestionato

congestion /kən'dʒestʃn/ *n* congestione *f*

congestion charge *n* pedaggio *m* per circolare nelle strade del centro di Londra

conglomerate /kən'glɒmərət/ *n* conglomerato *m*

Congo /'kɒŋgəʊ/ *n* Congo *m*

Congolese /kɒŋgə'li:z/ *adj & n* congolese *mf*

congratulate /kən'grætjʊleɪt/ *vt* congratularsi con (on per)

congratulations /kəngrætjʊ'leɪʃnz/ *npl* congratulazioni *fpl*

congregate /'kɒŋgrɪgeɪt/ *vi* radunarsi

congregation /kɒŋgrɪ'geɪʃn/ *n* Relig assemblea *f*

congress /'kɒŋgres/ *n* congresso *m*

congressman /'kɒŋgresmən/ *n* Am Pol membro *m* del congresso

conical /'kɒnɪkl/ *adj* conico

conifer /'kɒnɪfə(r)/ *n* conifera *f*

conjecture /kən'dʒektʃə(r)/ **①** *n* congettura *f*
② *vt* congetturare
③ *vi* fare congetture

conjugal /'kɒndʒʊgl/ *adj* coniugale

conjugate /'kɒndʒʊgeɪt/ *vt* coniugare

conjugation /kɒndʒʊ'geɪʃn/ *n* coniugazione *f*

conjunction /kən'dʒʌŋkʃn/ *n* congiunzione *f*; **in ~ with** insieme a

conjunctivitis /kəndʒʌŋktɪ'vaɪtɪs/ *n* congiuntivite *f*

conjure up /'kʌndʒə(r)/ *vt* evocare ‹*image*›; tirar fuori dal nulla ‹*meal*›

conjuring /'kʌndʒərɪŋ/ *n* giochi *mpl* di prestigio

conjuring trick /'kʌndʒərɪŋ/ *n* gioco *m* di prestigio

conjuror, conjurer /'kʌndʒərə(r)/ *n* prestigiatore, -trice *mf*

conk /kɒŋk/ *vi* **~ out** fam ‹*machine*› guastarsi; ‹*person*› crollare

conker /'kɒŋkə(r)/ *n* fam castagna *f* (d'ippocastano)

conman /'kɒnmæn/ *n* fam truffatore *m*

connect /kə'nekt/ **①** *vt* collegare; **be ~ed with** avere legami con; (be related to) essere imparentato con; **be well ~ed** aver conoscenze influenti
② *vi* essere collegato (**with** a); ‹*train*› fare coincidenza

connecting /kə'nektɪŋ/ *adj* ‹*room*› di comunicazione

connecting flight *n* coincidenza *f*

connection /kə'nekʃn/ *n* (between ideas) nesso *m*; (in travel) coincidenza *f*; Electr, Comput collegamento *m*; **in ~ with** con riferimento a; **~s** (people) conoscenze *fpl*

connector /kə'nektə(r)/ *n* Comput connettore *m*

connivance /kə'naɪvəns/ *n* connivenza *f*

connive /kə'naɪv/ *vi* **~ at** essere connivente in

connoisseur /kɒnə'sɜ:(r)/ *n* intenditore, -trice *mf*

connotation /kɒnə'teɪʃn/ *n* connotazione *f*

connote /kə'nəʊt/ *vt* evocare; (in linguistics) connotare

conquer /'kɒŋkə(r)/ *vt* conquistare; fig superare ‹*fear*›

conqueror /'kɒŋkərə(r)/ *n* conquistatore *m*

conquest /'kɒŋkwest/ *n* conquista *f*

conscience /'kɒnʃəns/ *n* coscienza *f*

conscientious /kɒnʃɪ'enʃəs/ *adj* coscienzioso

conscientiously /kɒnsɪ'enʃəslɪ/ *adv* coscienziosamente

conscientious objector /əb'dʒektə(r)/ *n* obiettore *m* di coscienza

conscious /'kɒnʃəs/ *adj* conscio; ‹*decision*› meditato; **[fully] ~** cosciente; **be/become ~ of something** rendersi conto di qualcosa

consciously /'kɒnʃəslɪ/ *adv* consapevolmente

consciousness /'kɒnʃəsnɪs/ *n* consapevolezza *f*; Med conoscenza *f*

conscript¹ /'kɒnskrɪpt/ *n* coscritto *m*

conscript² /kən'skrɪpt/ *vt* Mil chiamare alle armi; **~ somebody to do something** fig reclutare qualcuno per fare qualcosa

conscription /kən'skrɪpʃn/ *n* coscrizione *f*, leva *f*

consecrate /'kɒnsɪkreɪt/ *vt* consacrare

consecration /kɒnsɪ'kreɪʃn/ *n* consacrazione *f*

consecutive /kən'sekjʊtɪv/ *adj* consecutivo

consecutively /kən'sekjʊtɪvlɪ/ *adv* consecutivamente

consensus /kən'sensəs/ *n* consenso *m*

consent /kən'sent/ **①** *n* consenso *m*
② *vi* acconsentire

consequence /'kɒnsɪkwəns/ *n* conseguenza *f*; (importance) importanza *f*

consequent /'kɒnsɪkwənt/ *adj* conseguente

consequently /'kɒnsɪkwəntlɪ/ adv di conseguenza

conservation /kɒnsə'veɪʃn/ n conservazione f

conservation area n area f soggetta a vincoli ambientali

conservationist /kɒnsə'veɪʃənɪst/ n fautore, -trice mf della tutela ambientale

conservatism /kən'sɜ:vətɪzm/ n conservatorismo m

conservative /kən'sɜ:vətɪv/ ① adj conservativo; ⟨estimate⟩ ottimistico; C∼ Pol adj conservatore
② n conservatore, -trice mf

Conservative Party n partito m conservatore

conservatory /kən'sɜ:vətrɪ/ n spazio m chiuso da vetrate adiacente alla casa

conserve /kən'sɜ:v/ vt conservare

consider /kən'sɪdə(r)/ vt considerare; ∼ doing something considerare la possibilità di fare qualcosa

considerable /kən'sɪdərəbl/ adj considerevole

considerably /kən'sɪdərəblɪ/ adv considerevolmente

considerate /kən'sɪdərət/ adj pieno di riguardo

considerately /kən'sɪdərətlɪ/ adv con riguardo

consideration /kənsɪdə'reɪʃn/ n considerazione f; (thoughtfulness) attenzione f; (respect) riguardo m; (payment) compenso m; **take into** ∼ prendere in considerazione

considering /kən'sɪdərɪŋ/ prep considerando; ∼ **that** considerando che

consign /kən'saɪn/ vt affidare

consignment /kən'saɪnmənt/ n consegna f

consist /kən'sɪst/ vi ∼ **of** consistere di

consistency /kən'sɪstənsɪ/ n coerenza f; (density) consistenza f

consistent /kən'sɪstənt/ adj coerente; ⟨loyalty⟩ costante; **be** ∼ **with** far pensare a

consistently /kən'sɪstəntlɪ/ adv coerentemente; ⟨late, loyal⟩ costantemente

consolation /kɒnsə'leɪʃn/ n consolazione f

consolation prize n premio m di consolazione

console /kən'səʊl/ vt consolare

consolidate /kən'sɒlɪdeɪt/ vt consolidare

consolidation /kənsɒlɪ'deɪʃn/ n (of knowledge, position) consolidamento m

consoling /kən'səʊlɪŋ/ adj consolante

consonant /'kɒnsənənt/ n consonante f

consort¹ /'kɒnsɔ:t/ n consorte mf

consort² /kən'sɔ:t/ vi ∼ **with** frequentare

consortium /kən'sɔ:tɪəm/ n consorzio m

conspicuous /kən'spɪkjʊəs/ adj facilmente distinguibile; **be** ∼ **by one's absence** brillare per la propria assenza

conspicuously /kən'spɪkjʊəslɪ/ adv ⟨dressed⟩ vistosamente; ⟨placed⟩ in evidenza; ⟨silent, empty⟩ in modo evidente

conspiracy /kən'spɪrəsɪ/ n cospirazione f

conspirator /kən'spɪrətə(r)/ n cospiratore, -trice mf

conspire /kən'spaɪə(r)/ vi cospirare

constable /'kʌnstəbl/ n agente m [di polizia]

constabulary /kən'stæbjʊlərɪ/ n Br polizia f

constancy /'kɒnstənsɪ/ n costanza f

constant /'kɒnstənt/ adj costante

constantly /'kɒnstəntlɪ/ adv costantemente

constellation /kɒnstə'leɪʃn/ n costellazione f

consternation /kɒnstə'neɪʃn/ n costernazione f

constipated /'kɒnstɪpeɪtɪd/ adj stitico

constipation /kɒnstɪ'peɪʃn/ n stitichezza f

constituency /kən'stɪtjʊənsɪ/ n collegio m elettorale di un deputato nel Regno Unito

constituent /kən'stɪtjʊənt/ n costituente m; Pol elettore, -trice mf

constitute /'kɒnstɪtju:t/ vt costituire

constitution /kɒnstɪ'tju:ʃn/ n costituzione f

constitutional /kɒnstɪ'tju:ʃənl/ ① adj costituzionale
② n passeggiata f salutare

constitutionally /kɒnstɪ'tju:ʃənəlɪ/ adv Pol costituzionalmente; (innately) di costituzione

constrain /kən'streɪn/ vt costringere

constraint /kən'streɪnt/ n costrizione f; (restriction) restrizione f; (strained manner) disagio m

constrict /kən'strɪkt/ vt ⟨tight jacket⟩ stringere

constriction /kən'strɪkʃn/ n (of chest, throat) senso m di oppressione; (constraint) costrizione f; (of blood vessel) restrizione f

construct /kən'strʌkt/ vt costruire

construction /kən'strʌkʃn/ n costruzione f; (interpretation) interpretazione f; **under** ∼ in costruzione

construction engineer n ingegnere m edile

construction paper n Am cartoncino m

construction site n cantiere m

construction worker n [operaio m] edile m

constructive /kən'strʌktɪv/ *adj*
costruttivo

constructively /kən'strʌktɪvlɪ/ *adv* in
modo costruttivo

construe /kən'stru:/ *vt* interpretare

consul /'kɒnsl/ *n* console *m*

consular /'kɒnsjʊlə(r)/ *adj* consolare

consulate /'kɒnsjʊlət/ *n* consolato *m*

consult /kən'sʌlt/ *vt* consultare

consultancy /kən'sʌltənsɪ/ **1** *n* (advice)
consulenza *f*; (firm) ufficio *m* di consulenza;
Br Med posto *m* di specialista; **do** ∼ fare
il/la consulente
2 *attrib* ⟨*fees, service, work*⟩ di
consulenza

consultant /kən'sʌltənt/ *n* consulente
mf; Med specialista *mf*

consultation /kɒnsl'teɪʃn/ *n*
consultazione *f*; Med consulto *m*

consultative /kən'sʌltətɪv/ *adj* di
consulenza

consulting hours /kən'sʌltɪŋ/ *npl* Med
orario *m* di visita

consulting room *n* Med ambulatorio *m*

consumable /kən'sju:məbl/ *n* bene *m*
di consumo

consume /kən'sju:m/ *vt* consumare

consumer /kən'sju:mə(r)/ *n*
consumatore, -trice *mf*

consumer advice *n* consigli *mpl* ai
consumatori

consumer confidence *n* fiducia *f* del
consumatore

consumer goods *npl* beni *mpl* di
consumo

consumerism /kən'sju:mərɪzm/ *n*
consumismo *m*

consumer organization *n*
organizzazione *f* per la tutela dei
consumatori

consumer products *npl* beni *mpl* di
consumo

consumer protection *n* tutela *f* dei
consumatori

consumer society *n* società *f inv*
consumista, società *f inv* dei consumi

consuming /kən'sju:mɪŋ/ *adj* ⟨*passion*⟩
struggente; ⟨*urge*⟩ pressante; ⟨*hatred*⟩
insaziabile

consummate /'kɒnsjʊmeɪt/ *vt*
consumare

consummation /kɒnsjʊ'meɪʃn/ *n*
consumazione *f*

consumption /kən'sʌmpʃn/ *n* consumo
m

cont. /kɒnt/ *abbr* (**continued**) segue

contact /'kɒntækt/ **1** *n* contatto *m*;
(person) conoscenza *f*
2 *vt* mettersi in contatto con

contactable /'kɒntæktəbl/ *adj* ⟨*person*⟩
reperibile

contact lenses *npl* lenti *fpl* a contatto

contagious /kən'teɪdʒəs/ *adj* contagioso

contain /kən'teɪn/ *vt* contenere; ∼
oneself controllarsi

container /kən'teɪnə(r)/ *n* recipiente *m*;
(for transport) container *m inv*

container port *n* porto *m* container

container ship *n* [nave *f*] portacontainer *f inv*

container truck *n* [autocarro *m*]
portacontainer *m inv*

contaminate /kən'tæmɪneɪt/ *vt*
contaminare

contamination /kəntæmɪ'neɪʃn/ *n*
contaminazione *f*

contd *abbr* (**continued**) segue

contemplate /'kɒntəmpleɪt/ *vt*
contemplare; (consider) considerare; ∼
doing something considerare di fare
qualcosa

contemplation /kɒntəm'pleɪʃn/ *n*
contemplazione *f*

contemplative /kən'templətɪv/ *adj*
contemplativo

contemporaneous
/kəntempə'reɪnɪəs/ *adj* contemporaneo
(**with** a)

contemporaneously
/kəntempə'reɪnɪəslɪ/ *adv*
contemporaneamente (**with** a)

contemporary /kən'tempərərɪ/ *adj & n*
contemporaneo, -a *mf*

contempt /kən'tempt/ *n* disprezzo *m*;
beneath ∼ più che vergognoso; ∼ **of court**
oltraggio *m* alla Corte

contemptible /kən'tem(p)təbl/ *adj*
spregevole

contemptuous /kən'tem(p)tjʊəs/ *adj*
sprezzante

contemptuously /kən'tem(p)tjʊəslɪ/
adv sprezzantemente

contend /kən'tend/ **1** *vi* ∼ **with**
occuparsi di
2 *vt* (assert) sostenere

contender /kən'tendə(r)/ *n* concorrente
mf

content¹ /'kɒntent/ *n* contenuto *m*

content² /kən'tent/ **1** *adj* soddisfatto
2 *n* **to one's heart's** ∼ finché se ne ha
voglia
3 *vt* ∼ **oneself** accontentarsi (**with** di)

contented /kən'tentɪd/ *adj* soddisfatto

contentedly /kən'tentɪdlɪ/ *adv* con aria
soddisfatta

contention /kən'tenʃn/ *n* (assertion)
opinione *f*

contentious /kən'tenʃəs/ *adj* ⟨*subject*⟩
controverso; ⟨*view*⟩ discutibile; ⟨*person,
group*⟩ polemico

contentment /kən'tentmənt/ n
soddisfazione f

contents /'kɒntents/ npl contenuto m

contest[1] /'kɒntest/ n gara f

contest[2] /kɒn'test/ vt contestare
⟨statement⟩; impugnare ⟨will⟩; Pol
⟨candidates⟩ contendersi; ⟨one candidate⟩
aspirare a

contestant /kən'testənt/ n concorrente
mf

context /'kɒntekst/ n contesto m

continent /'kɒntɪnənt/ n continente m;
the C∼ l'Europa f continentale

continental /kɒntɪ'nentl/ adj
continentale

continental breakfast n prima
colazione f a base di pane, burro,
marmellata, croissant ecc

continental quilt n piumone m

contingency /kən'tɪndʒənsɪ/ n
eventualità f inv

contingency fund n fondo m
sopravvenienze passive

contingency plan n piano m
d'emergenza

contingent /kən'tɪndʒənt/ [1] adj be ∼
on dipendere da
[2] n Mil contingente m

continual /kən'tɪnjʊəl/ adj continuo

continually /kən'tɪnjʊəlɪ/ adv
continuamente

continuation /kəntɪnjʊ'eɪʃn/ n
continuazione f

continue /kən'tɪnju:/ [1] vt continuare;
∼ doing or to do something continuare a
fare qualcosa; to be ∼d continua
[2] vi continuare

continued /kən'tɪnju:d/ adj continuo

continuity /kɒntɪ'nju:ətɪ/ n continuità f

continuity announcer n
annunciatore, -trice mf

continuity girl n segretaria f di
produzione

continuous /kən'tɪnjʊəs/ adj continuo

continuously /kən'tɪnjʊəslɪ/ adv
continuamente

continuum /kən'tɪnjʊəm/ n continuum
m inv

contort /kən'tɔ:t/ vt contorcere

contortion /kən'tɔ:ʃn/ n contorsione f

contortionist /kən'tɔ:ʃənɪst/ n
contorsionista mf

contour /'kɒntʊə(r)/ n contorno m; (line)
curva f di livello

contraband /'kɒntrəbænd/ n
contrabbando m

contraception /kɒntrə'sepʃn/ n
contraccezione f; use ∼ ricorrere alla
contraccezione

contraceptive /kɒntrə'septɪv/ adj & n
contraccettivo m

contract[1] /'kɒntrækt/ n contratto m

contract[2] /kən'trækt/ [1] vi (get smaller)
contrarsi
[2] vt contrarre ⟨illness⟩

contraction /kən'trækʃn/ n
contrazione f

contract killer n sicario m

contractor /kən'træktə(r)/ n
imprenditore, -trice mf

contractual /kən'træktjʊəl/ adj
contrattuale

contract work n lavoro m su
commissione

contract worker n lavoratore, -trice
mf con contratto a termine

contradict /kɒntrə'dɪkt/ vt contraddire

contradiction /kɒntrə'dɪkʃn/ n
contraddizione f

contradictory /kɒntrə'dɪktərɪ/ adj
contraddittorio

contraflow /'kɒntrəfləʊ/ n utilizzazione
f di una corsia nei due sensi di marcia
durante lavori stradali

contraindication /kɒntrəɪndɪ'keɪʃn/ n
controindicazione f

contralto /kən'træltəʊ/ n contralto m

contraption /kən'træpʃn/ n fam
aggeggio m

contrariness /kən'treərɪnɪs/ n spirito
m di contraddizione

contrariwise /kən'treərɪwaɪz/ adv
(conversely) d'altra parte, d'altro canto; (in
the opposite direction) in direzione opposta

contrary[1] /'kɒntrərɪ/ [1] adj contrario
[2] adv ∼ to contrariamente a
[3] n contrario m; on the ∼ al contrario

contrary[2] /kən'treərɪ/ adj disobbediente

contrast[1] /'kɒntrɑ:st/ n contrasto m

contrast[2] /kən'trɑ:st/ [1] vt confrontare
[2] vi contrastare

contrasting /kən'trɑ:stɪŋ/ adj
contrastante

contravene /kɒntrə'vi:n/ vt trasgredire

contravention /kɒntrə'venʃn/ n
trasgressione f

contribute /kən'trɪbju:t/ vt/i
contribuire

contribution /kɒntrɪ'bju:ʃn/ n
contribuzione f; (what is contributed)
contributo m

contributor /kən'trɪbjʊtə(r)/ n
contributore, -trice mf

contributory /kən'trɪbjʊtərɪ/ adj
⟨factor⟩ concomitante; be ∼ to
contribuire a

con trick n raggiro m, truffa f

contrite /kən'traɪt/ adj contrito

contrive /kən'traɪv/ vt escogitare; ~ **to
do something** riuscire a fare qualcosa

contrived /kən'traɪvd/ adj ⟨style, effect⟩
artificioso; ⟨plot, ending⟩ forzato;
⟨incident, meeting⟩ non fortuito

control /kən'trəʊl/ **1** n controllo m; ~**s**
pl (of car, plane) comandi mpl; **get out of** ~
sfuggire al controllo
2 vt (pt/pp **controlled**) controllare; ~
oneself controllarsi

control column n Aeron cloche f inv

control key n Comput tasto m di
controllo

controlled /kən'trəʊld/ adj ⟨explosion,
performance, person⟩ controllato; **Labour-**
~ dominato dai laburisti

controller /kən'trəʊlə(r)/ n controllore
m; Fin controllore m [della gestione]; Radio,
TV direttore, -trice mf

control panel n (on machine) quadro m
dei comandi; (for plane) quadro m di
comando

control room n sala f di comando;
Radio, TV sala f di regia

control tower n torre f di controllo

controversial /kɒntrə'vɜːʃl/ adj
controverso

controversy /'kɒntrəvɜːsɪ/ n
controversia f

conundrum /kə'nʌndrəm/ n enigma m

conurbation /kɒnɜː'beɪʃn/ n
conturbazione f

convalesce /kɒnvə'les/ vi essere in
convalescenza

convalescence /kɒnvə'lesəns/ n
convalescenza f

convalescent /kɒnvə'lesənt/ adj
convalescente

convalescent home n
convalescenziario m

convection /kən'vekʃn/ n convezione f

convector /kən'vektə(r)/ n ~ **[heater]**
convettore m

convene /kən'viːn/ **1** vt convocare
2 vi riunirsi

convener /kən'viːnə(r)/ n (organizer)
organizzatore, -trice mf; (chair) presidente
m

convenience /kən'viːnɪəns/ n
convenienza f; **[public]** ~ gabinetti mpl
pubblici; **with all modern** ~**s** con tutti i
comfort

convenience foods npl cibi mpl
precotti

convenience store n negozio m
aperto fino a tardi

convenient /kən'viːnɪənt/ adj comodo;
be ~ **for somebody** andar bene per
qualcuno; **if it is** ~ **[for you]** se ti va bene

conveniently /kən'viːnɪəntlɪ/ adv
comodamente; ~ **located** in una posizione
comoda

convent /'kɒnvənt/ n convento m

convention /kən'venʃn/ n convenzione
if; (assembly) convegno m

conventional /kən'venʃnəl/ adj
convenzionale

conventionally /kən'venʃnəlɪ/ adv
convenzionalmente

convention centre n palazzo m dei
congressi

convent school n scuola f retta da
religiose

converge /kən'vɜːdʒ/ vi convergere

conversant /kən'vɜːsənt/ adj ~ **with**
pratico di

conversation /kɒnvə'seɪʃn/ n
conversazione f

conversational /kɒnvə'seɪʃnəl/ adj di
conversazione

conversationalist /kɒnvə'seɪʃnəlɪst/
n conversatore, -trice mf

converse¹ /kən'vɜːs/ vi conversare

converse² /'kɒnvɜːs/ n inverso m

conversely /'kɒnvɜːslɪ/ adv viceversa

conversion /kən'vɜːʃn/ n conversione f

conversion rate n [tasso m di] cambio
m

conversion table n tabella f di
conversione

convert¹ /'kɒnvɜːt/ n convertito, -a mf

convert² /kən'vɜːt/ vt convertire (**into**
in); sconsacrare ⟨church⟩

converter /kən'vɜːtə(r)/ n Electr
convertitore m

convertible /kən'vɜːtəbl/ **1** adj
convertibile
2 n Auto macchina f decappottabile

convex /'kɒnveks/ adj convesso

convey /kən'veɪ/ vt portare; trasmettere
⟨idea, message⟩

conveyance /kən'veɪəns/ n trasporto
m; (vehicle) mezzo m di trasporto

conveyancing /kən'veɪənsɪŋ/ n Jur
passaggio m di proprietà

conveyor /kən'veɪə(r)/ n (of goods,
persons) trasportatore m

conveyor belt n nastro m
trasportatore

convict¹ /'kɒnvɪkt/ n condannato, -a mf

convict² /kən'vɪkt/ vt giudicare
colpevole

conviction /kən'vɪkʃn/ n condanna f;
(belief) convinzione f; **previous** ~
precedente m penale

convince /kən'vɪns/ vt convincere

convincing /kən'vɪnsɪŋ/ adj
convincente

convincingly /kən'vɪnsɪŋlɪ/ *adv* in modo convincente

convivial /kən'vɪvɪəl/ *adj* conviviale

convoluted /'kɒnvəluːtɪd/ *adj* contorto

convoy /'kɒnvɔɪ/ *n* convoglio *m*

convulse /kən'vʌls/ *vt* sconvolgere; **be ~d with laughter** contorcersi dalle risa

convulsion /kən'vʌlʃn/ *n* convulsione *f*

convulsive /kən'vʌlsɪv/ *adj* convulso; Med convulsivo

convulsively /kən'vʌlsɪvlɪ/ *adv* convulsamente

coo /kuː/ *vi* tubare

cooing /'kuːɪŋ/ *n* (of bird, lovers) tubare *m inv*

cook /kʊk/ **1** *n* cuoco, -a *mf*
2 *vt* cucinare; **is it ~ed?** è cotto? **~ the books** fam truccare i libri contabili
3 *vi* ⟨food⟩ cuocere; ⟨person⟩ cucinare
■ **cook up** *vt* (fam) inventare ⟨excuse, story etc⟩

cookbook /'kʊkbʊk/ *n* libro *m* di cucina

cook-chill *adj* ⟨foods, products⟩ precotto e surgelato

cooked meats /kʊkt'miːts/ *npl* salumi *mpl*

cooker /'kʊkə(r)/ *n* cucina *f*; (apple) mela *f* da cuocere

cookery /'kʊkərɪ/ *n* cucina *f*

cookery book *n* libro *m* di cucina

cookie /'kʊkɪ/ *n* Am biscotto *m*

cooking /'kʊkɪŋ/ *n* cucina *f*; **be good at ~** saper cucinare bene; **do the ~** cucinare

cooking apple *n* mela *f* da cuocere

cooking chocolate *n* cioccolato *m* da pasticceria

cooking foil *n* carta *f* stagnola

cooking salt *n* sale *m* da cucina

cooking time *n* tempo *m* di cottura

cool /kuːl/ **1** *adj* fresco; (calm) calmo; (unfriendly) freddo; (fam: excellent or attractive) fantastico; **a ~ T-shirt** una maglietta fantastica; **'I won!' '~!'** 'ho vinto!' 'fantastico!'
2 *n* fresco *m*; **keep/lose one's ~** mantenere/perdere la calma
3 *vt* rinfrescare
4 *vi* rinfrescarsi
■ **cool down** **1** *vi* ⟨soup, tea etc⟩ raffreddarsi; (fig: become calm) calmarsi
2 *vt* raffreddare ⟨soup, tea etc⟩; (fig) calmare

cool bag *n* Br borsa *f* frigo

cool-box *n* borsa *f* termica

cool-headed *adj* equilibrato

cooling /'kuːlɪŋ/ **1** *n* raffreddamento *m*
2 *adj* ⟨agent⟩ refrigerante; ⟨system, tower⟩ di raffreddamento; ⟨drink, swim⟩ rinfrescante

cooling-off period *n* (in industrial relations) periodo *m* di tregua [sindacale]; Comm fase *f* di riflessione

coolly /'kuːllɪ/ *adv* freddamente

coolness /'kuːlnɪs/ *n* freddezza *f*

coop /kuːp/ **1** *n* stia *f*
2 *vt* **~ up** rinchiudere

co-op /'kəʊɒp/ *n abbr* (**cooperative**) cooperativa *f*

cooperate /kəʊ'ɒpəreɪt/ *vi* cooperare

cooperation /kəʊɒpə'reɪʃn/ *n* cooperazione *f*

cooperative /kəʊ'ɒpərətɪv/ *adj & n* cooperativa *f*

co-opt /kəʊ'ɒpt/ *vt* eleggere

coordinate /kəʊ'ɔːdɪmeɪt/ *vt* coordinare

coordinated /kəʊ'ɔːdɪmeɪtɪd/ *adj* coordinato

coordinates *npl* (clothes) coordinato *m sg*

coordination /kəʊɔː'dɪneɪʃn/ *n* coordinazione *f*

coordinator /kəʊ'ɔːdɪmeɪtə(r)/ *n* coordinatore, -trice *mf*

co-owner /kəʊ'əʊnə(r)/ *n* comproprietario, -a *mf*

cop /kɒp/ *n* fam poliziotto *m*

co-parent /kəʊ'peərənt/ *vt* condividere la responsabilità dell'educazione dei figli

co-parenting /kəʊ'peərəntɪŋ/ *n* condivisione *f* della responsabilità dell'educazione dei figli

cope /kəʊp/ *vi* fam farcela; **can she ~ by herself?** ce la fa da sola?; **~ with** farcela con; **I couldn't ~ with five kids** non ce la farei con cinque bambini

Copenhagen /kəʊpən'heɪgən/ *n* Copenhagen *f*

copier /'kɒpɪə(r)/ *n* fotocopiatrice *f*

co-pilot /'kəʊpaɪlət/ *n* copilota *m*

copious /'kəʊpɪəs/ *adj* abbondante

copiously /'kəʊpɪəslɪ/ *adv* abbondantemente

cop-out *n* fam (evasive act) bidone *m*; (excuse) scappatoia *f*

copper[1] /'kɒpə(r)/ **1** *n* rame *m*: **~s** pl monete fpl da uno o due penny
2 *attrib* di rame

copper[2] *n* fam poliziotto *m*

copper beech *n* faggio *m* rosso

copper-coloured *adj* [color] rame *inv*; ⟨hair⟩ ramato

copperplate *n* calligrafia *f* ornata

coppice /'kɒpɪs/ *n*, **copse** /kɒps/ *n* boschetto *m*

co-property /'kəʊprɒpətɪ/ *n* comproprietà *f inv*

copulate /'kɒpjʊleɪt/ *vi* accoppiarsi

copulation /kɒpjʊ'leɪʃn/ *n* copulazione *f*

copy /'kɒpɪ/ **1** *n* copia *f*

2 *vt* (pt/pp **-ied**) copiare
■ **copy down** *vt* = COPY
■ **copy out** *vt* = COPY
copybook *n* blot one's ∼ rovinarsi la reputazione
copycat **1** *n* pej fam copione, -a *mf*
2 *adj* ⟨crime, murder⟩ ispirato da un altro
copy editor *n* segretario, -a *mf* di redazione
copyright *n* diritti *mpl* d'autore
copy-typist *n* dattilografo, -a *mf*
copywriter *n* copywriter *mf inv*
coquetry /'kɒkɪtrɪ/ *n* civetteria *f*
coquettish /kɒ'ketɪʃ/ *adj* civettuolo
coral /'kɒrəl/ *n* corallo *m*
coral island *n* isola *f* di corallo
coral pink *adj* & *n* rosa *m inv* corallo
coral reef *n* barriera *f* corallina
cord /kɔːd/ *n* corda *f*; (thinner) cordoncino *m*; (fabric) velluto *m* a coste; ∼s *pl* pantaloni *mpl* di velluto a coste
cordial /'kɔːdɪəl/ **1** *adj* cordiale
2 *n* analcolico *m*
cordially /'kɔːdɪəlɪ/ *adv* con tutto il cuore
cordless /'kɒːdlɪs/ *adj* ⟨phone, kettle⟩ cordless
cordless telephone *adj* telefono *m* cordless
cordon /'kɔːdn/ *n* cordone *m* (di persone)
■ **cordon off** *vt* bloccare
corduroy /'kɔːdərɔɪ/ *n* velluto *m* a coste
core /kɔː(r)/ *n* (of apple, pear) torsolo *m*; (fig: of organization) cuore *m*; (of problem, theory) nocciolo *m*
core curriculum *n* materie *fpl* fondamentali (del programma scolastico)
co-respondent /kəʊrɪ'spɒndənt/ *n* Jur correo, -a *mf* in adulterio
Corfu /kɔː'fuː/ *n* Corfù *f*
coriander /kɒrɪ'ændə(r)/ *n* coriandolo *m*
cork /kɔːk/ *n* sughero *m*; (for bottle) turacciolo *m*
corkage /'kɔːkɪdʒ/ *n* somma *f* pagata a un ristorante per servire una bottiglia di vino portata da fuori
corker /'kɔːkə(r)/ *n* Br fam (story) storia *f* strabiliante; (stroke, shot) tiro *m* da maestro
corkscrew /'kɔːkskruː/ *n* cavatappi *m inv*
corkscrew curls *npl* boccoli *mpl*
corn[1] /kɔːn/ *n* grano *m*; (Am: maize) granturco *m*
corn[2] *n* Med callo *m*
corncob /'kɔːnkɒb/ *n* pannocchia *f* [di mais]
cornea /'kɔːnɪə/ *n* cornea *f*

corned beef /kɔːnd'biːf/ *n* manzo *m* sotto sale
corner /'kɔːnə(r)/ **1** *n* angolo *m*; (football) calcio *m* d'angolo, corner *m inv*
2 *vt* fig bloccare; Comm accaparrarsi ⟨market⟩
corner shop *n* negozio *m* di quartiere
cornerstone /'kɔːnəstəʊn/ *n* pietra *f* angolare
cornet /'kɔːnɪt/ *n* Mus cornetta *f*; (for ice-cream) cono *m*
cornfield /'kɔːnfiːld/ *n* campo *m* di grano; (sweetcorn) campo *m* di mais
cornflour /'kɔːnflaʊə(r)/ *n* farina *f* finissima di mais
cornflower /'kɔːnflaʊə(r)/ *n* fiordaliso *m*
cornice /'kɔːnɪs/ *n* (inside) cornice *f*; (outside) cornicione *m*
Cornish pasty /kɔːnɪʃ'pæstɪ/ *n* fagottino *m* di pasta sfoglia ripieno di carne e verdura
corn oil *n* olio *m* di mais
corn on the cob *n* pannocchia *f* cotta
corn plaster *n* [cerotto *m*] callifugo *m*
cornstarch /n Am fecola *f* di mais
cornucopia /kɔːnjʊ'kəʊpɪə/ *n* cornucopia *f*; fig abbondanza *f*
Cornwall /'kɔːnwɔːl/ *n* Cornovaglia *f*
corny /'kɔːnɪ/ *adj* (**-ier**, **-iest**) fam ⟨joke, film⟩ scontato; ⟨person⟩ banale; (sentimental) sdolcinato
corollary /kə'rɒlərɪ/ *n* corollario *m*
coronary /'kɒrənərɪ/ **1** *adj* coronario
2 *n* ∼ **[thrombosis]** trombosi *f* coronarica
coronation /kɒrə'neɪʃn/ *n* incoronazione *f*
coroner /'kɒrənə(r)/ *n* coroner *m inv* (nel diritto britannico, ufficiale incaricato delle indagini su morti sospette)
coronet /'kɒrənet/ *n* coroncina *f*
corporal[1] /'kɔːpərəl/ *n* Mil caporale *m*
corporal[2] *adj* corporale; ∼ **punishment** punizione *f* corporale
corporate /'kɔːpərət/ *adj* ⟨decision, policy, image⟩ aziendale; ∼ **life** la vita in un'azienda
corporate hospitality *n* omaggi *mpl* offerti dalla ditta ai clienti importanti
corporate identity *n* logo *m* dell'azienda
corporate image *n* immagine *f* aziendale
corporate lawyer *n* legale *mf* specializzato, -a in diritto aziendale
corporate planning *n* pianificazione *f* aziendale
corporate raider *n* finanziere *m* d'assalto

corporation /kɔːpəˈreɪʃn/ n ente m; (of town) ≈ consiglio m comunale

corporation tax n Br imposta f sul reddito delle aziende

corps /kɔː(r)/ n (pl **corps** /kɔːz/) corpo m

corps de ballet /kɔːdəˈbæleɪ/ n corpo m di ballo

corpse /kɔːps/ n cadavere m

corpulent /ˈkɔːpjʊlənt/ adj corpulento

corpus /ˈkɔːpəs/ n (of words) corpus m inv

corpuscle /ˈkɔːpʌsl/ n globulo m

correct /kəˈrekt/ **1** adj corretto; be ∼ ⟨person⟩ aver ragione; ∼! esatto! **2** vt correggere

correcting fluid n bianchetto m

correction /kəˈrekʃn/ n correzione f

corrective /kəˈrektɪv/ n correttivo m

correctly /kəˈrektlɪ/ adv correttamente

correlate /ˈkɒrəleɪt/ **1** vt correlare **2** vi essere correlato

correlation /kɒrəˈleɪʃn/ n correlazione f

correspond /kɒrɪˈspɒnd/ vi corrispondere (to a); ⟨two things⟩ corrispondere; (write) scriversi

correspondence /kɒrɪˈspɒndəns/ n corrispondenza f

correspondence course n corso m per corrispondenza

correspondent /kɒrɪˈspɒndənt/ n corrispondente mf

corresponding /kɒrɪˈspɒndɪŋ/ adj corrispondente

correspondingly /kɒrɪˈspɒndɪŋlɪ/ adv in modo corrispondente

corridor /ˈkɒrɪdɔː(r)/ n corridoio m

corroborate /kəˈrɒbəreɪt/ vt corroborare

corrode /kəˈrəʊd/ **1** vt corrodere **2** vi corrodersi

corrosion /kəˈrəʊʒn/ n corrosione f

corrugated /ˈkɒrəgeɪtɪd/ adj ondulato

corrugated iron n lamiera f ondulata

corrupt /kəˈrʌpt/ **1** adj corrotto **2** vt corrompere

corruption /kəˈrʌpʃn/ n corruzione f

corset /ˈkɔːsɪt/ n & s pl busto m

Corsica /ˈkɔːsɪkə/ n Corsica f

Corsican /ˈkɔːsɪkən/ adj & n corso, -a mf

cortège /kɔːˈteɪʒ/ n [funeral] ∼ corteo m funebre

cosh /kɒʃ/ n randello m

co-signatory /kəʊˈsɪgnətrɪ/ n cofirmatario, -a mf

cosily /ˈkəʊzɪlɪ/ adv ⟨sit, lie⟩ in modo confortevole

cosiness /ˈkəʊzɪnɪs/ n (of room) comodità f; (intimacy) intimità f

cos lettuce /kɒs/ n lattuga f romana

cosmetic /kɒzˈmetɪk/ **1** adj cosmetico **2** n ∼s pl cosmetici mpl

cosmetic surgery n chirurgia f estetica

cosmic /ˈkɒzmɪk/ adj cosmico

cosmonaut /ˈkɒzmənɔːt/ n cosmonauta mf

cosmopolitan /kɒzməˈpɒlɪtən/ adj cosmopolita

cosmos /ˈkɒzmɒs/ n cosmo m

Cossack /ˈkɒsæk/ adj & n cosacco, -a mf

cosset /ˈkɒsɪt/ vt coccolare

cost /kɒst/ **1** n costo m; ∼s pl Jur spese fpl processuali; at all ∼s a tutti i costi; I learnt to my ∼ ho imparato a mie spese **2** vt (pt/pp **cost**) costare; it ∼ me £20 mi è costato 20 sterline **3** vt (pt/pp **costed**) ∼ [out] stabilire il prezzo di

co-star /ˈkəʊstɑː/ **1** n Cinema, Theat co-protagonista mf **2** vi/t film ∼ring X and Y un film con X e Y come protagonisti

Costa Rica /kɒstəˈriːkə/ n Costa Rica m

cost centre n centro m di costi

cost-cutting n tagli mpl sulle spese; as a ∼ exercise [come misura] per ridurre le spese

cost-effective adj conveniente

cost-effectiveness n convenienza f

costing /ˈkɒstɪŋ/ n (process) determinazione f dei costi; (discipline) costing m inv

costly /ˈkɒstlɪ/ adj -ier, -iest costoso

cost of living n costo m della vita

cost-of-living index n indice m del costo della vita

cost price n prezzo m di costo

costume /ˈkɒstjuːm/ n costume m

costume drama n dramma m storico

costume jewellery n bigiotteria f

cosy /ˈkəʊzɪ/ **1** adj -ier, -iest ⟨pub, chat⟩ intimo; it's nice and ∼ in here si sta bene qui **2** n tea ∼ copriteiera m inv

cot /kɒt/ n lettino m; (Am: camp bed) branda f

cot death n Br morte f inspiegabile di un neonato nel sonno

Côte d'Azur /kəʊtdæˈzʊə(r)/ n Costa f Azzurra

cottage /ˈkɒtɪdʒ/ n casetta f

cottage cheese n fiocchi mpl di latte

cottage hospital n Br piccolo ospedale m (in zona rurale)

cottage industry n attività f inv artigianale basata sul lavoro a domicilio

cottage loaf n pagnotta f casereccia

cottage pie *n* Br pasticcio *m* di patate e carne macinata

cotton /'kɒtn/ ① *n* cotone *m*
② *attrib* di cotone
■ **cotton on** *vi* fam capire

cotton bud *n* cotton fioc® *m inv*

cotton mill *n* cotonificio *m*

cotton reel *n* rocchetto *m*, spagnoletta *f*

cotton wool *n* Br cotone *m* idrofilo

couch /kaʊtʃ/ *n* divano *m*

couchette /kuːˈʃet/ *n* cuccetta *f*

couch potato *n* pantofolaio, -a *mf*

cougar /'kuːgə(r)/ *n* coguaro *m*

cough /kɒf/ ① *n* tosse *f*
② *vi* tossire
■ **cough up** *vt/i* sputare; (fam: pay) sborsare

cough mixture *n* sciroppo *m* per la tosse

could /kʊd/ atono, /kəd/ *v aux* (▶ also CAN²) ∼ **I have a glass of water?** potrei avere un bicchier d'acqua?; **I ∼n't do it even if I wanted** non potrei farlo nemmeno se lo volessi; **I ∼n't care less** non potrebbe importarmene di meno; **he ∼n't have done it without help** non avrebbe potuto farlo senza aiuto; **you ∼ have phoned** avresti potuto telefonare

council /'kaʊnsl/ *n* consiglio *m*

council estate *n* Br complesso *m* di case popolari

council house *n* casa *f* popolare

council housing *n* Br case *fpl* popolari

councillor /'kaʊnsələ(r)/ *n* consigliere, -a *mf*

council tax *n* imposta *f* locale sugli immobili

counsel /'kaʊnsl/ ① *n* consigli *mpl*; Jur avvocato *m*
② *vt* (pt/pp **counselled**) consigliare a ⟨*person*⟩

counselling /'kaʊnsəlɪŋ/ ① *n* (psychological) terapia *f* [psichiatrica]; Sch orientamento *m* scolastico; **careers ∼** orientamento *m* professionale
② *attrib* ⟨*group, centre, service*⟩ di assistenza

counsellor /'kaʊnsələ(r)/ *n* consigliere, -a *mf*

count¹ /kaʊnt/ *n* (nobleman) conte *m*

count² ① *n* conto *m*; **keep ∼** tenere il conto
② *vt/i* contare
■ **count against** *vt* ⟨*inexperience, police record*⟩ deporre a sfavore di
■ **count among** *vt* ∼ **somebody among one's friends** annoverare qualcuno tra i propri amici
■ **count in** *vt* (include) includere; **∼ me in!** io ci sto!
■ **count on** *vt* contare su

■ **count out** *vt* contare ⟨*money*⟩; **∼ me out!** fate senza di me!
■ **count up** ① *vt* contare
② *vi* ∼ **to ten** contare fino a dieci

countable /'kaʊntəbl/ *adj* ⟨*noun*⟩ numerabile

countdown /'kaʊntdaʊn/ *n* conto *m* alla rovescia

countenance /'kaʊntənəns/ ① *n* espressione *f*
② *vt* approvare

counter¹ /'kaʊntə(r)/ *n* banco *m*; (in games) gettone *m*

counter² ① *adv* ∼ **to** contro, in contrasto a; **go ∼ to something** andare contro qualcosa
② *vt/i* opporre ⟨*measure, effect*⟩; parare ⟨*blow*⟩

counteract /kaʊntərˈækt/ *vt* neutralizzare

counter-attack *n* contrattacco *m*

counterbalance /'kaʊntəbæləns/ ① *n* contrappeso *m*
② *vt* controbilanciare

counter-claim *n* replica *f*

counter-clockwise Am ① *adj* antiorario
② *adv* in senso antiorario

counter-culture /'kaʊntəkʌltʃə(r)/ *n* controcultura *f*

counter-espionage *n* controspionaggio *m*

counterfeit /'kaʊntəfɪt/ ① *adj* contraffatto
② *n* contraffazione *f*
③ *vt* contraffare

counterfoil /'kaʊntəfɔɪl/ *n* matrice *f*

counter-inflationary /-ɪnˈfleɪʃənərɪ/ *adj* antinflazionistico

counter-insurgency /-ɪnˈsɜːdʒənsɪ/ *attrib* per reprimere un'insurrezione

counter-intelligence *n* controspionaggio *m*

countermeasure /'kaʊntəmeʒə(r)/ *n* contromisura *f*

counter-offensive *n* controffensiva *f*

counterpane /'kaʊntəpeɪn/ *n* copriletto *m*

counterpart /'kaʊntəpɑːt/ *n* equivalente *mf*

counterpoint /'kaʊntəpɔɪnt/ *n* contrappunto *mf*

counter-productive *adj* controproduttivo

countersign /'kaʊntəsaɪn/ *vt* controfirmare

countersignature *n* controfirma *f*

counter staff *n* commessi *mpl*

counter-terrorism *n* antiterrorismo *m*

countess /'kaʊntɪs/ *n* contessa *f*

countless /ˈkaʊntlɪs/ adj innumerevole

countrified /ˈkʌntrɪfaɪd/ adj ⟨person⟩ campagnolo

country /ˈkʌntrɪ/ n nazione f, paese m; (native land) patria f; (countryside) campagna f; in the ~ in campagna; go to the ~ andare in campagna; Pol indire le elezioni politiche

country and western n country m inv

country bumpkin n pej buzzurro, -a mf

country club n club m inv sportivo e ricreativo in campagna

country cousin n pej provinciale mf

country dancing n danza f folcloristica

country house n villa f di campagna

countryman n uomo m di campagna; (fellow ~) compatriota m

country music n country m inv

countryside n campagna f

countrywide adj & adv in tutto il paese

county /ˈkaʊntɪ/ n contea f (unità amministrativa britannica)

county council n Br Pol consiglio m di contea

county court n Br Jur tribunale m di contea

coup /ku:/ n Pol colpo m di stato

couple /ˈkʌpl/ n coppia f; a ~ of un paio di

coupon /ˈku:pɒn/ n tagliando m; (for discount) buono m sconto

courage /ˈkʌrɪdʒ/ n coraggio m

courageous /kəˈreɪdʒəs/ adj coraggioso

courageously /kəˈreɪdʒəslɪ/ adv coraggiosamente

courgette /kʊəˈʒet/ n zucchino m

courier /ˈkʊrɪə(r)/ n corriere m; (for tourists) guida f

course /kɔ:s/ n Sch corso m; Naut rotta f; Culin portata f; (for golf) campo m; ~ of treatment Med serie f inv di cure; of ~ naturalmente; in the ~ of durante; in due ~ a tempo debito; ~ of action linea f d'azione

course book n libro m di testo

coursework /kɔ:swɜ:k/ n Sch, Univ esercitazioni fpl scritte che contano per la media

court /kɔ:t/ ① n tribunale m; Sport campo m; take somebody to ~ citare qualcuno in giudizio
② vt fare la corte a ⟨woman⟩; sfidare ⟨danger⟩; ~ing couples coppiette fpl

court case n caso m giudiziario

court circular n bollettino quotidiano f di corte

courteous /ˈkɜ:tɪəs/ adj cortese

courteously /ˈkɜ:tɪəslɪ/ adv cortesemente

courtesy /ˈkɜ:təsɪ/ n cortesia f

courtesy bus n servizio m bus navetta

courtesy car n vettura f di cortesia

courthouse /ˈkɔ:thaʊs/ n Jur palazzo m di giustizia, tribunale m

courtier /ˈkɔ:tɪə(r)/ n cortigiano, -a mf

court martial ① n (pl ~s martial) corte f marziale
② court-martial vt (pt ~led) portare davanti alla corte marziale

court of inquiry n commissione f d'inchiesta

court of law n Jur corte f di giustizia

court order n Jur ingiunzione f

courtroom n Jur aula f [di tribunale]

courtship /ˈkɔ:tʃɪp/ n corteggiamento m

courtyard /ˈkɔ:tjɑ:d/ n cortile m

cousin /ˈkʌzn/ n cugino, -a mf

cove /kəʊv/ n insenatura f

covenant /ˈkʌvənənt/ n (agreement) accordo m; (payment agreement) impegno m scritto a pagare

cover /ˈkʌvə(r)/ ① n copertura f; (of cushion, to protect something) fodera f; (of book, magazine) copertina f; take ~ mettersi al riparo; under separate ~ a parte
② vt coprire; foderare ⟨cushion⟩; Journ fare un servizio su
■ **cover for** vt (replace) sostituire ⟨somebody⟩
■ **cover up** vt coprire; fig soffocare ⟨scandal⟩
■ **cover up for** vt fare da copertura a ⟨somebody⟩

coverage /ˈkʌvərɪdʒ/ n Journ it got a lot of ~ i media gli hanno dedicato molto spazio

cover charge n coperto m

covered market /ˈkʌvəd/ n mercato m coperto

covered wagon n carro m coperto

cover girl n ragazza f copertina

covering /ˈkʌv(ə)rɪŋ/ n copertura f; (for floor) rivestimento m; ~ of snow strato m di neve

covering fire n fuoco m di copertura

covering letter n lettera f d'accompagnamento

cover note n (from insurance company) polizza f provvisoria

cover story n (in paper) articolo m di prima pagina

covert /ˈkəʊvɜ:t/ adj ⟨threat⟩ velato; ⟨operation⟩ segreto; ⟨glance⟩ furtivo

covertly /ˈkəʊvɜ:tlɪ/ adv furtivamente; ⟨operate⟩ in segreto

cover-up n messa f a tacere

cover version n Mus versione f non originale

covet /'kʌvɪt/ vt bramare

covetous /'kʌvətəs/ adj avido

covetously /'kʌvətəslɪ/ adv avidamente

cow /kaʊ/ n vacca f, mucca f

coward /'kaʊəd/ n vigliacco, -a mf

cowardice /'kaʊədɪs/ n vigliaccheria f

cowardly /'kaʊədlɪ/ adj da vigliacco

cowbell /'kaʊbel/ n campanaccio m

cowboy /'kaʊbɔɪ/ n cowboy m inv; fig fam buffone m

cower /'kaʊə(r)/ vi acquattarsi

cowherd /'kaʊhɜːd/ n vaccaro m

cowhide /'kaʊhaɪd/ n (leather) vacchetta f

cowl /kaʊl/ n cappuccio m

cowlick /'kaʊlɪk/ n fam ciocca f ribelle

cowl neck n collo m ad anello

cowpat /'kaʊpæt/ n sterco m di vacca

cowshed /'kaʊʃed/ n stalla f

cox /kɒks/ n **coxswain** /'kɒks(ə)n/ n timoniere, -a mf

coy /kɔɪ/ adj falsamente timido; (flirtatiously) civettuolo; **be ∼ about something** essere evasivo su qualcosa

coyly /'kɔɪlɪ/ adv con falsa modestia; ⟨flirtatiously⟩ con civetteria

cozy /'kəʊzɪ/ adj Am = COSY

CPU n abbr (**central processing unit**) CPU f inv

crab /kræb/ n granchio m

crab apple n mela f selvatica

crack /kræk/ **①** n (in wall) crepa f; (in china, glass, bone) incrinatura f; (noise) scoppio m; (fam: joke) battuta f; **have a ∼** (try) fare un tentativo **②** adj (fam: best) di prim'ordine **③** vt incrinare ⟨china, glass⟩; schiacciare ⟨nut⟩; decifrare ⟨code⟩ fam risolvere ⟨problem⟩; **∼ a joke** fam fare una battuta **④** vt ⟨china, glass⟩ incrinarsi; ⟨whip⟩ schioccare

■ **crack down** vi fam prendere seri provvedimenti

■ **crack down on** vt fam prendere seri provvedimenti contro

■ **crack up** vi crollare

crackdown /'krækdaʊn/ n misure fpl (on contro)

cracked /krækt/ adj ⟨plaster⟩ crepato; ⟨skin⟩ screpolato; ⟨rib⟩ incrinato; (fam: crazy) svitato

cracker /'krækə(r)/ n (biscuit) cracker m inv; (fireware) petardo m; [Christmas] ∼ cilindro m di cartone contenente una sorpresa che produce una piccola esplosione quando viene aperto

crackers /'krækəz/ adj fam matto

cracking /'krækɪŋ/ adj Br fam eccellente; **at a ∼ pace** a ritmo incalzante

crackle /'krækl/ vi crepitare

crackling /'kræklɪŋ/ n (on radio) disturbo m; (of foil, cellophane) sfregamento m; (of fire) crepitio m; (crisp pork) cotenna f arrostita

crackpot /'krækpɒt/ fam **①** n pazzo, -a mf **②** adj da pazzi

cradle /'kreɪdl/ n culla f

cradle-snatcher n fam **he's/she's a ∼** se la intende con i ragazzini/le ragazzine

craft¹ /krɑːft/ n inv (boat) imbarcazione f

craft² n mestiere m; (technique) arte f

craft fair n mostra f dell'artigianato

craftily /'krɑːftɪlɪ/ adv con astuzia

craftsman /'krɑːftsmən/ n artigiano m

craftsmanship /'krɑːftsmənʃɪp/ n maestria f

crafty /'krɑːftɪ/ adj (**-ier, -iest**) astuto

crag /kræg/ n rupe f

craggy /'krægɪ/ adj scosceso; ⟨face⟩ dai lineamenti marcati

cram /kræm/ **①** v (pt/pp **crammed**) vt stipare (**into** in) **②** vi (for exams) sgobbare

crammer /'kræmə(r)/ n (Br fam: school) ≈ istituto m di recupero

cramp /kræmp/ n crampo m

cramped /kræmpt/ adj ⟨room⟩ stretto; ⟨handwriting⟩ appiccicato; **it's a bit ∼ in here** si sta un po' stretti qui

crampon /'kræmpən/ n rampone m

cranberry /'krænbərɪ/ n Culin mirtillo m rosso

crane /kreɪn/ **①** n (at docks, bird) gru f inv **②** vt **∼ one's neck** allungare il collo

cranium /'kreɪnɪəm/ n cranio m

crank¹ /kræŋk/ n tipo, -a mf strampalato, -a

crank² n Techn manovella f

crankshaft /'kræŋkʃɑːft/ n albero m a gomiti

cranky /'kræŋkɪ/ adj strampalato; (Am: irritable) irritabile

cranny /'krænɪ/ n fessura f

crap /kræp/ n sl (faeces) merda f; (film, book etc) schifezza f; (nonsense) stronzate fpl; **have a ∼** cacare

crappy /'kræpɪ/ adj sl di merda

crash /kræʃ/ **①** n (noise) fragore m; Auto, Aeron incidente m; Comm crollo m; Comput crash m inv **②** vi schiantarsi (**into** contro); ⟨plane⟩ precipitare **③** vt schiantare ⟨car⟩

■ **crash out** vi (sl: go to sleep) crollare; (on sofa etc) dormire

crash barrier n guardrail m inv

crash course n corso m intensivo

crash diet n dieta f drastica

crash-helmet n casco m

crash-land *vi* fare un atterraggio di fortuna

crash-landing *n* atterraggio *m* di fortuna

crass /kræs/ *adj* ⟨*ignorance*⟩ crasso

crate /kreɪt/ *n* (for packing) cassa *f*

crater /'kreɪtə(r)/ *n* cratere *m*

cravat /krə'væt/ *n* foulard *m inv*

crave /kreɪv/ *vt* morire dalla voglia di

craving /'kreɪvɪŋ/ *n* voglia *f* smodata

crawl /krɔːl/ **①** *n* (swimming) stile *m* libero; **do the** ～ nuotare a stile libero; **at a** ～ a passo di lumaca
② *vi* andare carponi; ～ **with** brulicare di

crawler lane /'krɔːlə/ *n* Auto corsia *f* riservata al traffico lento

crayfish /'kreɪfɪʃ/ *n* gambero *m* d'acqua dolce

crayon /'kreɪən/ *n* pastello *m* a cera; (pencil) matita *f* colorata

craze /kreɪz/ *n* mania *f*

crazed /kreɪzd/ *adj* ⟨*china, glaze*⟩ screpolato; ⟨*animal, person*⟩ impazzito; **power-**～ ubriaco di potere

crazy /'kreɪzɪ/ *adj* (**-ier, -iest**) matto; **be** ～ **about** andar matto per

crazy golf *n* Br minigolf *m inv*

crazy paving *n* Br pavimentazione *f* a mosaico irregolare

creak /kriːk/ **①** *n* scricchiolio *m*
② *vi* scricchiolare

creaky /'kriːkɪ/ *adj* ⟨*leather*⟩ che cigola; ⟨*door, hinge*⟩ cigolante; ⟨*joint, bone, floorboard*⟩ scricchiolante; fig fam ⟨*alibi, policy*⟩ traballante

cream /kriːm/ **①** *n* crema *f*; (fresh) panna *f*
② *adj* ⟨*colour*⟩ [bianco] panna *inv*
③ *vt* Culin sbattere
■ **cream off** *vt* accaparrarsi ⟨*top pupils, scientists etc*⟩

cream cheese *n* formaggio *m* cremoso

cream cracker *n* Br cracker *m inv*

cream puff *n* sfogliatina *f* alla panna *inv*

cream soda *n* soda *f* aromatizzata alla vaniglia

cream tea *n* Br tè *m inv* servito con pasticcini da mangiare con marmellata e panna

creamy /'kriːmɪ/ *adj* (**-ier, -iest**) cremoso

crease /kriːs/ **①** *n* piega *f*
② *vt* stropicciare
③ *vi* stropicciarsi

crease-resistant *adj* che non si stropiccia

create /kriː'eɪt/ *vt* creare

creation /kriː'eɪʃn/ *n* creazione *f*

creative /kriː'eɪtɪv/ *adj* creativo

creative director *n* direttore, -trice *mf* creativo, -a

creative writing *n* (school subject) composizione *f*

creativity /kriːeɪ'tɪvətɪ/ *n* creatività *f*

creator /kriː'eɪtə(r)/ *n* creatore, -trice *mf*

creature /'kriːtʃə(r)/ *n* creatura *f*

creature comforts *npl* comodità *fpl*; **like one's** ～ ～ amare le proprie comodità

crèche /kreʃ/ *n* asilo *m* nido *inv*

credence /'kriːdəns/ *n* credito *m*; **give** ～ **to something** (believe) dare credito a qualcosa

credentials /krɪ'denʃlz/ *npl* credenziali *fpl*

credibility /kredə'bɪlətɪ/ *n* credibilità *f*

credible /'kredəbl/ *adj* credibile

credit /'kredɪt/ **①** *n* credito *m*; (honour) merito *m*; **take the** ～ **for** prendersi il merito di
② *vt* accreditare; ～ **somebody with something** Comm accreditare qualcosa a qualcuno; fig attribuire qualcosa a qualcuno

creditable /'kredɪtəbl/ *adj* lodevole

credit balance *n* saldo *m* attivo

credit card *n* carta *f* di credito

credit control *n* controllo *m* del credito

credit facilities *npl* facilitazioni *fpl* creditizie

credit limit *n* limite *m* di credito

credit note *n* Comm nota *f* di accredito

creditor /'kredɪtə(r)/ *n* creditore, -trice *mf*

credits /'kredɪts/ *npl* titoli *mpl* di coda

credit side *n* on the ～ ～ tra i lati positivi

credit squeeze *n* stretta *f* creditizia

credit terms *npl* condizioni *fpl* di credito

credit transfer *n* bonifico *m*

creditworthiness /'kredɪ(t)wɜːðɪnɪs/ *n* capacità *f* di credito

creditworthy /'kredɪ(t)wɜːðɪ/ *adj* meritevole di credito

credulity /krɪ'djuːlətɪ/ *n* credulità *f*; **strain sb's** ～ essere ai limiti della credibilità

credulous /'kredjʊləs/ *adj* credulo

creed /kriːd/ *n* credo *m inv*

creek /kriːk/ *n* insenatura *f*; (Am: stream) torrente *m*; **up the** ～ (fam: in trouble) nei guai

creep /kriːp/ **①** *vi* (pt/pp **crept**) muoversi furtivamente
② *n* fam tipo *m* viscido; **it gives me the** ～**s** mi fa venire i brividi

creeper /'kriːpə(r)/ *n* pianta *f* rampicante

creepy /'kriːpɪ/ *adj* che fa venire i brividi

creepy-crawly /-'krɔːlɪ/ *n* fam insetto

cremate /krɪ'meɪt/ *vt* cremare

cremation /krɪ'meɪʃn/ *n* cremazione *f*

crematorium /kremə'tɔːrɪəm/ *n* crematorio *m*

crepe /kreɪp/ *n* (fabric) crespo *m*

crepe bandage *n* fascia *f* elastica

crepe paper *n* carta *f* crespata

crepe soles *npl* suole *fpl* di para

crept /krept/ ▶ CREEP

crescendo /krɪ'ʃendəʊ/ *n* Mus crescendo *m*; **reach a** ~ fig ⟨noise, protests⟩ raggiungere il picco; ⟨campaign⟩ raggiungere il culmine

crescent /'kresənt/ *n* mezzaluna *f*

crescent moon *n* mezzaluna *f*

cress /kres/ *n* crescione *m*

crest /krest/ *n* cresta *f*; (coat of arms) cimiero *m*; **be on the** ~ **of a wave** essere sulla cresta dell'onda

crestfallen /'krestfɔːlən/ *adj* mogio

Crete /kriːt/ *n* Creta *f*

Creutzfeldt-Jakob disease /krɔɪtsfelt'jækɒb/ *n* morbo *m* di Creutzfeldt Jakob

crevasse /krɪ'væs/ *n* crepaccio *m*

crevice /'krevɪs/ *n* crepa *f*

crew /kruː/ *n* equipaggio *m*; (gang) équipe *f inv*

crew cut *n* capelli *mpl* a spazzola

crew neck *n* girocollo *m*

crew neck sweater *n* maglione *m* a girocollo

crib¹ /krɪb/ *n* (for baby) culla *f*

crib² *vt/i* (pt/pp **cribbed**) fam copiare

cribbage /'krɪbɪdʒ/ *n* gioco *m* di carte

crick /krɪk/ *n* ~ **in the neck** torcicollo *m*

cricket¹ /'krɪkɪt/ *n* (insect) grillo *m*

cricket² *n* cricket *m*

cricketer /'krɪkɪtə(r)/ *n* giocatore *m* di cricket

crime /kraɪm/ *n* crimine *m*; (criminality) criminalità *f*; **it's a** ~ fig è un delitto

crime of passion *n* delitto *m* passionale

crime prevention *n* prevenzione *f* della criminalità

criminal /'krɪmɪnl/ ① *adj* criminale; ⟨law, court⟩ penale ② *n* criminale *mf*

criminal charges *npl* **face** ~ ~ essere imputato

criminal investigation *n* inchiesta *f* giudiziaria

Criminal Investigation Department *n* Br ≈ polizia *f* giudiziaria

criminal justice *n* sistema *m* penale

criminal law *n* diritto *m* penale

criminally insane /'krɪmɪnəlɪ/ *adj* pazzo criminale

criminal offence *n* reato *m*

criminal record *n* **have a/no** ~ ~ avere la fedina penale sporca/pulita

criminology /krɪmɪ'nɒlədʒɪ/ *n* criminologia *f*

crimp /krɪmp/ *vt* pieghettare ⟨fabric⟩; increspare ⟨pastry⟩; arricciare ⟨hair⟩

crimson /'krɪmz(ə)n/ *adj* cremisi *inv*

cringe /krɪndʒ/ *vi* (cower) acquattarsi; (at bad joke etc) fare una smorfia

crinkle /'krɪŋk(ə)l/ ① *vt* spiegazzare ② *vi* spiegazzarsi

crinkly /'krɪŋklɪ/ *adj* ⟨paper, material⟩ crespato; ⟨hair⟩ crespo

cripple /'krɪpl/ ① *n* storpio, -a *mf* ② *vt* storpiare; fig danneggiare

crippled /'krɪpld/ *adj* ⟨person⟩ storpio; ⟨ship⟩ danneggiato

crippling /'krɪplɪŋ/ *adj* ⟨taxes, debts⟩ esorbitante; ⟨disease⟩ devastante; ⟨strike, effect⟩ paralizzante

crisis /'kraɪsɪs/ *n* (pl **-ses** /'kraɪsiːz/) crisi *f inv*

crisp /krɪsp/ *adj* croccante; ⟨air⟩ frizzante; ⟨style⟩ incisivo

crispbread /'krɪs(p)bred/ *n* crostini *mpl* di pane

crisps /krɪsps/ *npl* patatine *fpl*

crispy /'krɪspɪ/ *adj* croccante

crɪss-cross /'krɪs-/ *adj* a linee incrociate

criterion /kraɪ'tɪərɪən/ *n* (pl **-ria** /kraɪ'tɪərɪə/) criterio *m*

critic /'krɪtɪk/ *n* critico, -a *mf*

critical /'krɪtɪkl/ *adj* critico

critically /'krɪtɪklɪ/ *adv* in modo critico; ~ **ill** gravemente malato

critical path analysis *n* analisi *f inv* del percorso critico

criticism /'krɪtɪsɪzm/ *n* critica *f*; **he doesn't like** ~ non ama le critiche

criticize /'krɪtɪsaɪz/ *vt* criticare

croak /krəʊk/ *vi* gracchiare; ⟨frog⟩ gracidare

Croatia /krəʊ'eɪʃə/ *n* Croazia *f*

crochet /'krəʊʃeɪ/ ① *n* lavoro *m* all'uncinetto ② *vt* fare all'uncinetto

crochet-hook *n* uncinetto *m*

crock /krɒk/ *n* fam **old** ~ (person) rudere *m*; (car) macinino *m*

crockery /'krɒkərɪ/ *n* terrecotte *fpl*

crocodile /'krɒkədaɪl/ *n* coccodrillo *m*

crocodile tears *npl* lacrime *fpl* di coccodrillo

crocus /ˈkrəʊkəs/ n (pl -es) croco m

croft /krɒft/ n piccola fattoria f

croissant /ˈkrwæsɑ̃/ n cornetto m, croissant m inv

crone /krəʊn/ n pej vecchiaccia f

crony /ˈkrəʊnɪ/ n compare m

crook /krʊk/ n (fam: criminal) truffatore, -trice mf

crooked /ˈkrʊkɪd/ adj storto; ⟨limb⟩ storpiato; (fam: dishonest) disonesto; ~ **deal** fregatura f

croon /kru:n/ vt/i canticchiare

crop /krɒp/ ① n raccolto m; fig quantità f inv
② v (pt/pp **cropped**)
③ vt coltivare
■ **crop up** vi fam presentarsi

crop rotation n rotazione f delle colture

crop spraying /ˈkrɒpspreɪɪŋ/ n irrorazione f

croquet /ˈkrəʊkeɪ/ n croquet m

croquette /krəʊˈket/ n crocchetta f

cross /krɒs/ ① adj (annoyed) arrabbiato; **talk at** ~ **purposes** fraintendersi
② n croce f; Bot, Zool incrocio m
③ vt sbarrare ⟨cheque⟩; incrociare ⟨road, animals⟩; ~ **oneself** farsi il segno della croce; ~ **one's arms** incrociare le braccia; ~ **one's legs** accavallare le gambe; **keep one's fingers** ~**ed for somebody** tenere le dita incrociate per qualcuno; **it** ~**ed my mind** mi è venuto in mente
④ vi (go across) attraversare; ⟨lines⟩ incrociarsi
■ **cross off** vt (from list) depennare
■ **cross out** vt sbarrare; (from list) depennare

crossbar n (of goal) traversa f; (on bicycle) canna f

cross-border adj oltreconfine

crossbow n balestra f

crossbred adj ibrido

crossbreed vt ibridare, incrociare ⟨animals, plants⟩ n (animal) incrocio m, ibrido m

cross-Channel adj attraverso la Manica; ⟨ferry⟩ che attraversa la Manica

cross-check n controprova f vt fare la controprova di

cross-contamination n contaminazione f incrociata

cross-country n Sport corsa f campestre

cross-country skiing n sci m di fondo

cross-court adj ⟨shot, volley⟩ diagonale

cross-cultural adj multiculturale

crosscurrent n corrente f trasversale

cross-dressing n travestitismo m

cross-examination n controinterrogatorio m

cross-examine vt sottoporre a controinterrogatorio

cross-eyed /ˈkrɒsaɪd/ adj strabico

crossfire n fuoco m incrociato

crossing /ˈkrɒsɪŋ/ n (for pedestrians) passaggio m pedonale; (sea journey) traversata f

cross-legged /krɒsˈlegd/ adj & adv con le gambe incrociate

crossly /ˈkrɒslɪ/ adv con rabbia

crossover adj ⟨straps⟩ incrociato

cross-party adj ⟨talks, committee⟩ interpartitico

cross-purposes npl **we are at** ~ non ci siamo capiti

cross-question vt interrogare ⟨person⟩

cross-reference n rimando m

crossroads n incrocio m; **reach a** ~ fig arrivare a un bivio

cross-section n sezione f; (of community) campione m

cross-stitch n punto m croce

crosswalk n Am attraversamento m pedonale

crosswind n vento m di traverso

crosswise adv in diagonale

crossword n ~ **[puzzle]** parole fpl crociate

crotch /krɒtʃ/ n Anat inforcatura f; (in trousers) cavallo m

crotchet /ˈkrɒtʃɪt/ n Mus semiminima f

crotchety /ˈkrɒtʃətɪ/ adj irritabile

crouch /kraʊtʃ/ vi accovacciarsi

croupier /ˈkru:pɪə(r)/ n croupier m inv

crouton /ˈkru:tɒn/ n crostino m

crow /krəʊ/ ① n corvo m; **as the** ~ **flies** in linea d'aria
② vi cantare

crowbar /ˈkrəʊbɑ:/ n piede m di porco

crowd /kraʊd/ ① n folla f
② vt affollare
③ vi affollarsi

crowd control n controllo m della folla

crowded /ˈkraʊdɪd/ adj affollato

crowd-puller /ˈkraʊdpʊlə(r)/ n (event) grande attrazione f

crowd scene n Cinema, Theat scena f di massa

crown /kraʊn/ ① n corona f
② vt incoronare; incapsulare ⟨tooth⟩

Crown court n Br Jur ≈ corte f d'Assise

crowning glory /ˈkraʊnɪŋ/ n culmine m; **her hair is her** ~ i capelli sono il suo punto forte

crown jewels npl gioielli mpl della corona

crown prince n principe m ereditario

crow's feet /krəʊz'fiːt/ *npl* (on face) zampe *fpl* di gallina

crow's nest /krəʊz'nest/ *n* coffa *f*

crucial /'kruːʃl/ *adj* cruciale

crucially /'kruːʃəlɪ/ *adv* ~ **important** di vitale importanza

crucifix /'kruːsɪfɪks/ *n* crocifisso *m*

crucifixion /kruːsɪ'fɪkʃn/ *n* crocifissione *f*

crucify /'kruːsɪfaɪ/ *vt* (pt/pp **-ied**) crocifiggere

crude /kruːd/ *adj* ⟨oil⟩ greggio; ⟨language⟩ crudo; ⟨person⟩ rozzo

crudely /'kruːdlɪ/ *adv* (vulgarly) in modo crudo; (simply) schematicamente; (roughly: assembled) sommariamente; ⟨painted, made⟩ rozzamente; ~ **speaking** in parole povere

crudity /'kruːdətɪ/ *n* (vulgarity) volgarità *f*

cruel /'kruːəl/ *adj* (**-ler**, **-lest**) crudele (**to** verso)

cruelly /'kruːəlɪ/ *adv* con crudeltà

cruelty /'kruːəltɪ/ *n* crudeltà *f*

cruelty-free *adj* ⟨cosmetics⟩ non testato sugli animali

cruise /kruːz/ ① *n* crociera *f*
② *vi* fare una crociera; ⟨car⟩ andare a velocità di crociera

cruise liner *n* nave *f* da crociera

cruise missile *n* missile *m* cruise *inv*

cruiser /'kruːzə(r)/ *n* Mil incrociatore *m*; (motor boat) motoscafo *m*

cruising speed /'kruːzɪŋ/ *n* velocità *m* *inv* di crociera

crumb /krʌm/ *n* briciola *f*

crumble /'krʌmbl/ ① *vt* sbriciolare
② *vi* sbriciolarsi; ⟨building, society⟩ sgretolarsi

crumbling /'krʌmblɪŋ/ *adj* fatiscente

crumbly /'krʌmblɪ/ *adj* friabile

crummy /'krʌmɪ/ *adj* fam (substandard) scadente; (Am: unwell) malato

crumpet /'krʌmpɪt/ *n* Culin focaccina *f* da tostare e mangiare con burro e marmellata

crumple /'krʌmpl/ ① *vt* spiegazzare
② *vi* spiegazzarsi

crunch /krʌntʃ/ ① *n* fam **when it comes to the** ~ quando si viene al dunque
② *vt* sgranocchiare
③ *vi* ⟨snow⟩ scricchiolare

crunchy /'krʌntʃɪ/ *adj* ⟨vegetables, biscuits⟩ croccante

crusade /kruː'seɪd/ *n* crociata *f*

crusader /kruː'seɪdə(r)/ *n* crociato *m*

crush /krʌʃ/ ① *n* (crowd) calca *f*; **have a** ~ **on somebody** essersi preso una cotta per qualcuno
② *vt* schiacciare; sgualcire ⟨clothes⟩

crushed ice /krʌʃt'aɪs/ *n* ghiaccio *m* tritato

crushed velvet *n* velluto *m* stazzonato

crushing /'krʌʃɪŋ/ *adj* ⟨defeat, weight, blow⟩ schiacciante; ⟨blow⟩ tremendo

crust /krʌst/ *n* crosta *f*

crustacean /krʌ'steɪʃn/ *n* crostaceo *m*

crusty /'krʌstɪ/ *adj* ⟨bread⟩ croccante; (irritable) scontroso

crutch /krʌtʃ/ *n* gruccia *f*; Anat inforcatura *f*

crux /krʌks/ *n* fig punto *m* cruciale; ~ **of the matter** nodo *m* della questione

cry /kraɪ/ ① *n* grido *m*; ~ **for help** grido d'aiuto; **have a** ~ farsi un pianto; **a far** ~ **from** fig tutta un'altra cosa rispetto a
② *vi* (pt/pp **cried**) (weep) piangere; (call) gridare

■ **cry off** *vi* (Br: cancel) disdire

■ **cry out** *vi* (shout) urlare

cryogenics /kraɪə'dʒenɪks/ *n* criogenia *f*

crypt /krɪpt/ *n* cripta *f*

cryptic /'krɪptɪk/ *adj* criptico

cryptically /'krɪptɪklɪ/ *adv* ⟨say, speak⟩ in modo enigmatico; ~ **worded** espresso in maniera sibillina

crystal /'krɪstl/ *n* cristallo *m*; (glassware) cristalli *mpl*

crystal ball *n* sfera *f* di cristallo

crystal clear *adj* ⟨water, sound⟩ cristallino; **let me make it** ~ ~ lasciatemelo spiegare chiaramente

crystal-gazing /'krɪstlgeɪzɪŋ/ *n* predizione *f* del futuro (con la sfera di cristallo)

crystallize /'krɪstəlaɪz/ *vi* (become clear) concretizzarsi

CS gas *n* Br gas *m* *inv* lacrimogeno

CST *abbr* Am (**Central Standard Time**) ora *f* solare della zona centrale dell'America settentrionale

C2C /siːtəˈsiː/ *abbr* (**consumer to consumer**) C2C

cub /kʌb/ *n* (animal) cucciolo *m*; **C~** [Scout] lupetto *m*

Cuba /'kjuːbə/ *n* Cuba *f*

Cuban /'kjuːbən/ *adj & n* cubano -a, *mf*

cubby-hole /'kʌbɪ-/ *n* (compartment) scomparto *m*; (room) ripostiglio *m*

cube /kjuːb/ *n* cubo *m*

cubic /'kjuːbɪk/ *adj* cubico

cubicle /'kjuːbɪkl/ *n* cabina *f*

cubism /'kjuːbɪzm/ *n* cubismo *m*

cubist /'kjuːbɪst/ *adj & n* cubista *mf*

cub reporter *n* cronista *mf* alle prime armi

cuckoo /'kʊkuː/ *n* cuculo *m*

cuckoo clock *n* orologio *m* a cucù

cucumber /'kjuːkʌmbə(r)/ *n* cetriolo *m*

cud /kʌd/ n also fig **chew the** ∼ ruminare

cuddle /'kʌd(ə)l/ **1** vt coccolare
2 vi ∼ **up to** starsene accoccolato insieme a
3 n **have a** ∼ ⟨child⟩ farsi coccolare; ⟨lovers⟩ abbracciarsi

cuddly /'kʌd(ə)lɪ/ adj tenerone; (wanting cuddles) coccolone

cuddly toy n peluche m inv

cudgel /'kʌdʒl/ n randello m

cue[1] /kju:/ n segnale m; Theat battuta f d'entrata

cue[2] n (in billiards) stecca f

cue ball n pallino m

cuff /kʌf/ **1** n polsino m; (Am: turn-up) orlo m; (blow) scapaccione m; **off the** ∼ improvvisando
2 vt dare una pacca a

cuff link n gemello m

cuisine /kwɪ'zi:n/ n cucina f; **haute** ∼ /əʊt/ haute cuisine f

cul-de-sac /'kʌldəsæk/ n vicolo m cieco

culinary /'kʌlɪnərɪ/ adj culinario

cull /kʌl/ vt scegliere ⟨flowers⟩ (kill) selezionare e uccidere

culminate /'kʌlmɪneɪt/ vi culminare

culmination /kʌlmɪ'neɪʃn/ n culmine m

culottes /kju:'lɒts/ npl gonna fsg pantalone

culpable /'kʌlpəbl/ adj colpevole

culpable homicide n Jur omicidio m colposo

culprit /'kʌlprɪt/ n colpevole mf

cult /kʌlt/ n culto m

cultivate /'kʌltɪveɪt/ vt coltivare; fig coltivarsi ⟨person⟩

cultivated /'kʌltɪveɪtɪd/ adj ⟨soil⟩ lavorato; ⟨person⟩ colto

cultural /'kʌltʃərəl/ adj culturale

cultural attaché n addetto m culturale

culture /'kʌltʃə(r)/ n cultura f

cultured /'kʌltʃəd/ adj colto

cultured pearl n perla f coltivata

culture shock n shock m inv culturale

culture vulture n fam fanatico, -a mf di cultura

culvert /'kʌlvət/ n condotto m sotterraneo

cumbersome /'kʌmbəsəm/ adj ingombrante

cumin /'kju:mɪn/ n cumino m nero

cummerbund /'kʌməbʌnd/ n fascia f (dello smoking)

cumulative /'kju:mjʊlətɪv/ adj cumulativo

cunning /'kʌnɪŋ/ **1** adj astuto
2 n astuzia f

cup /kʌp/ n tazza f; (prize, of bra) coppa f

cupboard /'kʌbəd/ n armadio m

cupboard love n Br hum amore m interessato

cupboard space n spazio m negli armadi

Cup Final n finale f di coppa

cupful /'kʌpfʊl/ n tazza f (contenuto)

Cupid /'kju:pɪd/ n Cupido m

cupola /'kju:pələ/ n Archit cupola f

cup tie n Br partita f eliminatoria

cur /kɜ:(r)/ n (pej: dog) cagnaccio m

curable /'kjʊərəbl/ adj curabile

curate /'kjʊərət/ n curato m

curator /kjʊə'reɪtə(r)/ n direttore, -trice mf (di museo)

curb /kɜ:b/ vt tenere a freno

curd cheese /kɜ:d/ n cagliata f

curdle /'kɜ:dl/ vi coagularsi

cure /kjʊə(r)/ **1** n cura f
2 vt curare; (salt) mettere sotto sale; (smoke) affumicare

cure-all n toccasana m inv, panacea f

curfew /'kɜ:fju:/ n coprifuoco m

curio /'kjʊərɪəʊ/ n curiosità f inv

curiosity /kjʊərɪ'ɒsətɪ/ n curiosità f

curious /'kjʊərɪəs/ adj curioso

curiously /'kjʊərɪəslɪ/ adv curiosamente

curl /kɜ:l/ **1** n ricciolo m
2 vt arricciare
3 vi arricciarsi
■ **curl up** vi raggomitolarsi

curler /'kɜ:lə(r)/ n bigodino m

curling /'kɜ:lɪŋ/ n Sport curling m

curly /'kɜ:lɪ/ adj (**-ier, -iest**) riccio

curly-haired, curly-headed /-'heəd/, /-'hedɪd/ adj (tight curls) dai capelli crespi; (loose curls) riccio

currant /'kʌrənt/ n (dried) uvetta f

currency /'kʌrənsɪ/ n valuta f; (of word) ricorrenza f; **foreign** ∼ valuta f estera

current /'kʌrənt/ **1** adj corrente
2 n corrente f

current account n Br conto m corrente

current affairs npl attualità f

current assets npl Fin disponibilità fpl correnti

current liabilities npl Fin passività fpl correnti

currently /'kʌrəntlɪ/ adv attualmente

curriculum /kə'rɪkjʊləm/ n programma m di studi

curriculum vitae /'vi:taɪ/ n curriculum vitae m inv

curry /'kʌrɪ/ **1** n curry m inv; (meal) piatto m al curry
2 vt (pt/pp **-ied**) ∼ **favour with somebody** cercare d'ingraziarsi qualcuno

curry powder n curry m in polvere

curse /kɜːs/ ① n maledizione f; (oath)
imprecazione f
② vt maledire
③ vi imprecare

cursor /'kɜːsə(r)/ n cursore m

cursor keys npl tasti mpl cursore

cursory /'kɜːsərɪ/ adj sbrigativo

curt /kɜːt/ adj brusco

curtail /kə'teɪl/ vt ridurre

curtailment /kə'teɪlmənt/ n (of rights,
freedom) limitazione f; (of expenditure, service)
riduzione f; (of holiday) interruzione f

curtain /'kɜːtn/ n tenda f; Theat sipario m
■ **curtain off** vt separare con una tenda

curtain call n Theat chiamata f alla
ribalta

curtly /'kɜːtlɪ/ adv bruscamente

curtsy, curtsey /'kɜːtsɪ/ ① n inchino
m
② vi (pt/pp -ied) fare l'inchino

curvaceous /kɜː'veɪʃəs/ adj formoso

curve /kɜːv/ ① n curva f
② vi curvare; ~ to the right/left curvare a
destra/sinistra

curved /kɜːvd/ adj curvo

curvy /'kɜːvɪ/ adj (-ier, -iest) ⟨woman⟩
formoso

cushion /'kʊʃn/ ① n cuscino m
② vt attutire; (protect) proteggere

cushy /'kʊʃɪ/ adj (-ier, -iest) fam facile

custard /'kʌstəd/ n (liquid) crema f
pasticcera

custard cream n Br biscotto m farcito
alla crema

custard pie n torta f alla crema (nei
film comici)

custard tart n torta f alla crema

custodial sentence /kʌ'stəʊdɪəl/ n
condanna f ad una pena detentiva

custodian /kʌ'stəʊdɪən/ n custode mf

custody /'kʌstədɪ/ n (of child) custodia f;
(imprisonment) detenzione f preventiva

custom /'kʌstəm/ n usanza f; Jur
consuetudine f; Comm clientela f

customary /'kʌstəmərɪ/ adj (habitual)
abituale; it's ~ to... è consuetudine...

custom-built /-'bɪlt/ adj ⟨house⟩ ad hoc

custom car n vettura f personalizzata

customer /'kʌstəmə(r)/ n cliente mf

customer care n assistenza f alla
clientela

customer feedback n feedback m
inv dai clienti

customer relations npl rapporto m
con i clienti

customer service n assistenza f ai
clienti

customize /'kʌstəmaɪz/ vt
personalizzare

custom-made /-'meɪd/ adj su misura

customs /'kʌstəmz/ npl dogana f

Customs and Excise n Br ufficio m
Dazi e Dogana

customs clearance n sdoganamento
m

customs declaration n
dichiarazione f doganale

customs duties npl dazi mpl doganali

customs hall n dogana f

customs officer n doganiere m,
guardia f di finanza

cut /kʌt/ ① n (with knife etc, of clothes) taglio
m; (reduction) riduzione f; (in public spending)
taglio m
② vt/i (pt/pp cut, pres p cutting)
tagliare; (reduce) ridurre; ~ one's finger
tagliarsi il dito; ~ sb' hair tagliare i
capelli a qualcuno
③ vi (with cards) alzare
■ **cut away** vt tagliar via
■ **cut back** vt tagliare ⟨hair⟩; potare
⟨hedge⟩; (reduce) ridurre
■ **cut back on** vt (reduce) ridurre
■ **cut down** vt abbattere ⟨tree⟩; (reduce)
ridurre
■ **cut in** ① vt Auto tagliare la strada; (into
conversation) interrompere
② vt ~ somebody in on a deal dare una
percentuale a qualcuno
■ **cut off** vt tagliar via; (disconnect)
interrompere; fig isolare; I was ~ off Teleph
la linea è caduta
■ **cut out** vt ritagliare; (delete) eliminare;
be ~ out for fam essere tagliato per; ~ it
out! fam dacci un taglio!
■ **cut short** vt interrompere ⟨holiday,
discussion⟩
■ **cut up** vt (slice) tagliare a pezzi

cut-and-dried adj ⟨answer, solution⟩
ovvio; I like everything to be ~ mi piace
che tutto sia ben chiaro e definito

cut and paste ① n taglia e incolla m
② vt tagliare e incollare

cut and thrust n the ~ ~ ~ of debate
gli scambi mpl animati del dibattito

cutback /'kʌtbæk/ n riduzione f; (in
government spending) taglio m

cute /kjuːt/ adj fam (in appearance) carino;
(clever) acuto

cut glass n vetro m intagliato

cuticle /'kjuːtɪkl/ n cuticola f

cutlery /'kʌtlərɪ/ n posate fpl

cutlet /'kʌtlɪt/ n cotoletta f

cut-off n (upper limit) limite m [massimo]

cut-off date n data f di scadenza

cut-off point n limite m; Comm data f di
scadenza

cut-offs npl (jeans) jeans mpl tagliati

cut-out n (outline) ritaglio m

cut-price adj a prezzo ridotto; ⟨shop⟩
che fa prezzi ridotti

cutter /'kʌtə(r)/ n (ship) cutter m inv; (on ship) lancia f; (for metal, glass) taglierina f

cut-throat ① n assassino, -a mf
② adj ‹competition› spietato

cut-throat razor n Br rasoio m da barbiere

cutting /'kʌtɪŋ/ ① adj ‹remark› tagliente
② n (from newspaper) ritaglio m; (of plant) talea f

cutting edge n (blade) filo m; **be at the** ~ ~ fig essere all'avanguardia

cuttingly /'kʌtɪŋlɪ/ adv ‹speak› in maniera tagliente

cutting room n Cinema **end up on the** ~ ~ **floor** essere tagliato in fase di montaggio

CV n abbr (**Curriculum Vitae**) CV m

cwt abbr (**hundredweight**) Br ≈ 50 kg, Am ≈ 45 kg

cyanide /'saɪənaɪd/ n cianuro m

cybercafe /'saɪbəkæfeɪ/ n caffè m Internet

cyberculture /'saɪbəkʌltʃə(r)/ n cybercultura f

cybernetics /saɪbə'netɪks/ n cibernetica f

cyberspace /'saɪbəspeɪs/ n ciberspazio m

cyclamen /'sɪkləmən/ n ciclamino m

cycle /'saɪk(ə)l/ ① n ciclo m; (bicycle) bicicletta f, fam bici f inv
② vi andare in bicicletta

cycle clip n fermacalzoni m inv

cycle lane n pista f ciclabile

cycle race n corsa f ciclistica

cycle rack n portabiciclette m inv

cycle track, **cycle path** n pista f ciclabile

cyclical /'saɪklɪkl/ adj ciclico

cycling /'saɪklɪŋ/ n ciclismo m

cycling holiday n Br vacanza f in bicicletta; **go on a** ~ ~ fare una vacanza in bicicletta

cycling shorts npl pantaloncini mpl da ciclista

cyclist /'saɪklɪst/ n ciclista mf

cyclo-cross /'saɪkləʊ-/ n ciclocross m inv

cyclone /'saɪkləʊn/ n ciclone m

cygnet /'sɪgnɪt/ n cigno m giovane

cylinder /'sɪlɪndə(r)/ n cilindro m

cylindrical /sɪl'lɪndrɪkl/ adj cilindrico

cymbals /'sɪmblz/ npl Mus piatti mpl

cynic /'sɪnɪk/ n cinico, -a mf

cynical /'sɪnɪk(ə)l/ adj cinico

cynically /'sɪnɪklɪ/ adv cinicamente

cynicism /'sɪnɪsɪzm/ n cinismo m

cypress /'saɪprəs/ n cipresso m

Cypriot /'sɪprɪət/ adj & n cipriota mf

Cyprus /'saɪprəs/ n Cipro m

Cyrillic /sɪ'rɪlɪk/ adj cirillico

cyst /sɪst/ n ciste f

cystitis /sɪ'staɪtɪs/ n cistite f

Czar, **czar** /zɑː(r)/ n zar m inv

Czech /tʃek/ adj & n ceco, -a mf

Czechoslovak /tʃekə'sləʊvæk/ adj cecoslovacco

Czechoslovakia /tʃekəslə'vækɪə/ n Cecoslovacchia f

Czech Republic n Repubblica f Ceca

Dd

d¹, D /diː/ n (letter) d, D f inv; Mus re m inv

d² abbr (**died**) morto

dab /dæb/ ① n colpetto m; **a** ~ **of** un pochino di
② vt (pt/pp **dabbed**) toccare leggermente ‹eyes›
■ **dab on** vt mettere un po' di ‹paint etc›

dabble /'dæbl/ vi ~ **in something** fig occuparsi di qualcosa a tempo perso

dachshund /'dækshʊnd/ n bassotto m

dad[dy] /'dæd[ɪ]/ n fam papà m inv, babbo m

daddy-long-legs n zanzarone m [dei boschi]; (Am: spider) ragno m

daffodil /'dæfədɪl/ n giunchiglia f

daft /dɑːft/ adj sciocco

dagger /'dægə(r)/ n stiletto m; Typ croce f; **be at** ~**s drawn** fam essere ai ferri corti

dahlia /'deɪlɪə/ n dalia f

daily /'deɪlɪ/ ① adj giornaliero
② adv giornalmente
③ n (newspaper) quotidiano m; (fam: cleaner) donna f delle pulizie

daintily /'deɪntɪlɪ/ adv delicatamente

dainty /'deɪntɪ/ adj (**-ier**, **-iest**) grazioso; ‹movement› delicato

dairy /'deərɪ/ n caseificio m; (shop) latteria f

dairy cow n mucca f da latte

dairyman /'deərɪmən/ n (on farm) operaio m addetto all'allevamento di mucche [da latte]; (Am: farmer) allevatore m

dairy products npl latticini mpl

dais /'deɪɪs/ n pedana f

daisy /'deɪzɪ/ n margheritina f; (larger) margherita f

dale /deɪl/ n liter valle f

dally /'dælɪ/ vi (pt/pp -ied) stare a gingillarsi

dam /dæm/ ① n diga f
② vt (pt/pp **dammed**) costruire una diga su

damage /'dæmɪdʒ/ ① n danno m (to a); ~s pl Jur risarcimento msg
② vt danneggiare; fig nuocere a

damage limitation exercise n manovra f per contenere i danni

damaging /'dæmɪdʒɪŋ/ adj dannoso

damask /'dæməsk/ n damasco m

dame /deɪm/ n liter dama f; Am sl donna f

dammit /'dæmɪt/ int Br fam accidenti!

damn /dæm/ ① adj fam maledetto
② adv ⟨lucky, late⟩ maledettamente
③ n I don't care or give a ~ fam non me ne frega un accidente
④ vt dannare

damnation /dæm'neɪʃn/ ① n dannazione f
② int fam accidenti!

damnedest /'dæmdɪst/ ① n do one's ~ (to do) (fam: hardest) fare del proprio meglio (per fare)
② adj it was the ~ thing (surprising) era la cosa più straordinaria

damning /'dæmɪŋ/ adj schiacciante

damp /dæmp/ ① adj umido
② n umidità f
③ vt = DAMPEN

dampen /'dæmpən/ vt inumidire; fig raffreddare ⟨enthusiasm⟩

damper /'dæmpə(r)/ n the news put a ~ on the evening fam la notizia ha raggelato l'atmosfera della serata

dampness /'dæmpnɪs/ n umidità f

damson /'dæmzən/ n (fruit) susina f selvatica, prugna f selvatica

dance /dɑːns/ ① n ballo m
② vt/i ballare
■ **dance about, dance up and down** vi saltellare qua e là

dance hall n sala f da ballo

dance music n musica f da ballo

dancer /'dɑːnsə(r)/ n ballerino, -a mf

dancing /'dɑːnsɪŋ/ n ballo m

dandelion /'dændɪlaɪən/ n dente m di leone

dandruff /'dændrʌf/ n forfora f

Dane /deɪn/ n danese mf; **Great** ~ danese m

danger /'deɪndʒə(r)/ n pericolo m; **in/out of** ~ in/fuori pericolo

danger level n livello m di guardia

danger list n **on the** ~ ~ in prognosi riservata; **off the** ~ ~ fuori pericolo

danger money n indennità f di rischio

dangerous /'deɪndʒərəs/ adj pericoloso

dangerously /'deɪndʒərəslɪ/ adv pericolosamente; ~ **ill** in pericolo di vita

danger signal n also fig segnale m di pericolo

dangle /'dæŋgl/ ① vi penzolare; fig **leave somebody dangling** lasciare qualcuno in sospeso
② vt far penzolare

Danish /'deɪnɪʃ/ ① adj danese
② n (language) danese m

Danish pastry n dolce m di pasta sfoglia contenente pasta di mandorle, mele ecc

dank /dæŋk/ adj umido e freddo

Danube /'dænjuːb/ n Danubio m

dapper /'dæpə(r)/ adj azzimato

dappled /'dæp(ə)ld/ adj ⟨grey, horse⟩ pomellato; ⟨sky⟩ screziato; ⟨shade, surface⟩ chiazzato

dare /deə(r)/ ① vt/i osare; (challenge) sfidare (to a); ~ [to] **do something** osare fare qualcosa; I ~ **say!** molto probabilmente!
② n sfida f

daredevil /'deədevl/ n spericolato, -a mf

daring /'deərɪŋ/ ① adj audace
② n audacia f

dark /dɑːk/ ① adj buio; ~ **blue/brown** blu/marrone scuro; **It's getting** ~ sta cominciando a fare buio; ~ **horse** fig (in race, contest) vincitore m imprevisto; (not much known about) misterioso m; **keep something** ~ fig tenere qualcosa nascosto
② n **after** ~ col buio; **in the** ~ al buio; **keep somebody in the** ~ fig tenere qualcuno all'oscuro

Dark Ages n alto Medioevo m

dark chocolate n cioccolato m fondente

darken /'dɑːkn/ ① vt oscurare
② vi oscurarsi

dark-eyed /-'aɪd/ adj ⟨person⟩ dagli occhi scuri

dark glasses npl occhiali mpl scuri

darkly /'dɑːklɪ/ adv ⟨mutter, hint⟩ cupamente

dark matter n materia f oscura

darkness /'dɑːknɪs/ n buio m

darkroom /'dɑːkruːm/ n camera f oscura

dark-skinned adj ⟨person⟩ dalla pelle scura

darling /'dɑːlɪŋ/ ① *adj* adorabile; **my ~** Joan carissima Joan

② *n* tesoro *m*; **be a ~ and...** sii gentile e...

darn /dɑːn/ *vt* rammendare

darning needle /'dɑːnɪŋ/ *n* ago *m* da rammendo

dart /dɑːt/ ① *n* dardo *m*; (in sewing) pince *f inv*; **~s** *sg* (game) freccette *fpl*

② *vi* lanciarsi

dartboard /'dɑːtbɔːd/ *n* bersaglio *m* [per freccette]

dash /dæʃ/ ① *n* Typ trattino *m*; (in Morse) linea *f*; **a ~ of milk** un goccio di latte; **make a ~ for** lanciarsi verso

② *vi* **I must ~** devo scappare

③ *vt* far svanire ⟨*hopes*⟩; (hurl) gettare

■ **dash off** ① *vi* scappar via

② *vt* (write quickly) buttare giù

■ **dash out** *vi* uscire di corsa

dashboard /'dæʃbɔːd/ *n* cruscotto *m*

dashing /'dæʃɪŋ/ *adj* (bold) ardito; (in appearance) affascinante

DAT *abbr* (**digital audio tape**) DAT *f inv*

data /'deɪtə/ *npl* & *sg* dati *mpl*

databank *n* banca *f* di dati

database *n* banca *f* dati, database *m inv*

database management system *n* sistema *m* di gestione di data base

data capture *n* registrazione *f* di dati

data communications *npl* comunicazione *f* dati, telematica *f*

data compression *n* compressione *f* dati

data disk *n* dischetto *m* di dati

data entry *n* immissione *f* [di] dati

data file *n* file *m inv* dati

data handling *n* manipolazione *f* [di] dati

data input *n* input *m* dati

data link *n* collegamento *m* dati

data processing *n* elaborazione *f* [di] dati

data protection *n* protezione *f* dati

data protection act *n* Jur legge *f* britannica per la salvaguardia delle informazioni personali

data retrieval *n* recupero *m* dati

data security *n* sicurezza *f* dei dati

data storage *n* archiviazione *f* dati

data storage device *n* unità *f* archivio dati

data transmission *n* trasmissione *f* dati

date[1] /deɪt/ *n* (fruit) dattero *m*

date[2] ① *n* data *f*; (meeting) appuntamento *m*; **to ~** fino ad oggi; **out of ~** (not fashionable) fuori moda; (expired) scaduto; ⟨*information*⟩ non aggiornato; **make a ~**

with somebody dare un appuntamento a qualcuno; **be up to ~** essere aggiornato

② *vt/i* datare; (go out with) uscire con

■ **date back to** *vt* risalire a

dated /'deɪtɪd/ *adj* fuori moda; ⟨*language*⟩ antiquato

date line *n* linea *f* [del cambiamento] di data

date of issue *n* data *f* di emissione

date rape *n* stupro *m* perpetrato da persona nota alla vittima

date stamp *n* (mark) timbro *m* con la data

dating agency /'deɪtɪŋ/ *n* agenzia *f* matrimoniale

dative /'deɪtɪv/ *n* dativo *m*

daub /dɔːb/ *vt* imbrattare ⟨*walls*⟩

daughter /'dɔːtə(r)/ *n* figlia *f*

daughter-in-law *n* (pl **daughters-in-law**) nuora *f*

daunt /dɔːnt/ *vt* scoraggiare; **nothing ~ed** per niente scoraggiato

daunting /'dɔːntɪŋ/ *adj* ⟨*task, prospect*⟩ poco allettante; ⟨*person*⟩ che intimidisce; **I'm faced with a ~ amount of work** mi aspetta una quantità di lavoro preoccupante; **it can be (quite) ~** può essere (piuttosto) allarmante

dauntless /'dɔːntlɪs/ *adj* intrepido

dawdle /'dɔːdl/ *vi* bighellonare; (over work) cincischiarsi

dawn /dɔːn/ ① *n* alba *f*; **at ~** all'alba

② *vi* albeggiare; **it ~ed on me** fig mi è apparso chiaro

dawn raid *n* (police) raid *m* della polizia all'alba; (stock market) dawn raid *m inv*

day /deɪ/ *n* giorno *m*; (whole day) giornata *f*; (period) epoca *f*; **~ by ~** giorno per giorno; **~ after ~** giorno dopo giorno; **these ~s** oggigiorno; **In those ~s** a quei tempi; **it's had its ~** fam ha fatto il suo tempo

day-boy *n* Br Sch alunno *m* esterno

daybreak *n* **at ~** allo spuntar del giorno

day-care *n* (for young children) scuola *f* materna

day centre *n* centro *m* di accoglienza

day-dream ① *n* sogno *m* ad occhi aperti

② *vi* sognare ad occhi aperti

day-girl *n* Sch alunna *f* esterna

daylight *n* luce del giorno *f*

daylight robbery *n* fam **it's ~ ~** è un furto!

daylight saving time *n* ora *f* legale

day nursery *n* (0–3 years) asilo *m* nido; (3–6 years) scuola *f* materna

day off *n* giorno *m* di riposo

day pass *n* biglietto *m* giornaliero

day release n giorno m di congedo settimanale dal lavoro da dedicare a corsi di formazione

day return n (ticket) biglietto m di andata e ritorno con validità giornaliera

day school n scuola f che non fornisce alloggio

daytime n giorno m; **in the ~** di giorno

daytime TV n programmi mpl televisivi trasmessi durante il giorno

day-to-day adj quotidiano; **on a ~ basis** giorno per giorno

day trader n day trader m inv

day trading n day trading m inv

day trip n gita f (di un giorno)

day tripper n gitante mf

daze /deɪz/ n **in a ~** stordito; fig sbalordito

dazed /deɪzd/ adj stordito; fig sbalordito

dazzle /ˈdæzl/ vt abbagliare

dazzling /ˈdæzlɪŋ/ adj abbagliante

DBMS n abbr (**database management system**) DBMS m

D-day n Mil D-day m inv; (important day) giorno m fatidico

deacon /ˈdiːk(ə)n/ n diacono m

dead /ded/ **1** adj morto; (numb) intorpidito; **~ and buried** morto e sepolto **~ body** morto m; **~ centre** pieno centro m

2 adv **~ tired** stanco morto; **~ slow/easy** lentissimo/facilissimo; **you're ~ right** hai perfettamente ragione; **stop ~** fermarsi di colpo; **be ~ on time** essere in perfetto orario

3 n **the ~** pl i morti; **in the ~ of night** nel cuore della notte

deaden /ˈded(ə)n/ vt attutire ⟨sound⟩; calmare ⟨pain⟩

dead end **1** n vicolo m cieco **2** attrib dead-end ⟨job⟩ senza prospettive

dead heat n **it was a ~ ~** è finita a pari merito

deadline n scadenza f

deadlock n **reach ~** fig giungere ad un punto morto

dead loss n fam (person) buono, -a mf a nulla; (thing) oggetto m inutile

deadly /ˈdedlɪ/ adj (**-ier, -iest**) mortale; (fam: dreary) barboso; **~ sins** peccati mpl capitali

dead on arrival adj Med deceduto durante il trasporto

deadpan adj impassibile; ⟨humour⟩ all'inglese

dead ringer n fam **be a ~ ~ for somebody** essere la copia spiccicata di qualcuno

Dead Sea n Mar m Morto

dead weight n (fig: burden) peso m morto

dead wood n Br fig zavorra f

deaf /def/ adj sordo; **~ and dumb** sordomuto

deaf aid n apparecchio m acustico

deafen /ˈdef(ə)n/ vt assordare; (permanently) render sordo

deafening /ˈdefənɪŋ/ adj assordante

deaf mute adj & n sordomuto, -a mf

deafness /ˈdefnɪs/ n sordità f

deaf without speech adj sordomuto, -a mf

deal /diːl/ **1** n (agreement) patto m; (in business) accordo m; **whose ~?** (Cards) a chi tocca dare le carte?; **a good** or **great ~** molto; **get a raw ~** fam ricevere un trattamento ingiusto

2 vt (pt/pp **dealt** /delt/) (in cards) dare; **~ somebody a blow** dare un colpo a qualcuno

■ **deal in** vt trattare in

■ **deal out** vt ⟨hand out⟩ distribuire

■ **deal with** vt (handle) occuparsi di; trattare con ⟨company⟩; (be about) trattare di; **that's been ~t with** è stato risolto

dealer /ˈdiːlə(r)/ n commerciante mf; (in drugs) spacciatore, -trice mf

dealership /ˈdiːləʃɪp/ n Comm concessione f

dealing /ˈdiːlɪŋ/ n (in drugs) traffico m, spaccio m

dealing room n Fin borsino m

dealings /ˈdiːlɪŋz/ npl **have ~ with** avere a che fare con

dean /diːn/ n decano m; Univ preside mf di facoltà

dear /dɪə(r)/ **1** adj caro; (in letter) Caro; (formal) Gentile

2 n caro, -a mf

3 int **oh ~!** Dio mio!

dearly /ˈdɪəlɪ/ adv ⟨love⟩ profondamente; ⟨pay⟩ profumatamente

dearth /dɜːθ/ n penuria f

death /deθ/ n morte f

deathbed n letto m di morte

death camp n campo m di sterminio

death certificate n certificato m di morte

death duty n tassa f di successione

death knell n campane fpl a morto; fig tramonto m

death list n lista f dei bersagli (di un assassino)

deathly /ˈdeθlɪ/ **1** adj **~ silence** silenzio m di tomba

2 adv **~ pale** di un pallore cadaverico

death mask n maschera f mortuaria

death penalty n pena f di morte

death rate n tasso m di mortalità

death ray n raggio m mortale

death row /rəʊ/ *n* Am braccio *m* della morte

death sentence *n* also fig condanna *f* a morte

death's head *n* teschio *m*

death threat *n* minaccia *f* di morte

death throes *npl* also fig agonia *f*

death toll *n* bilancio *m* delle vittime

death trap *n* trappola *f* mortale

death warrant *n* ordine *m* di esecuzione di una condanna a morte

death wish *n* desiderio *m* di morire

debacle /deɪ'bɑ:k(ə)l/ *n* sfacelo *m*

debar /dɪ'bɑ:(r)/ *vt* (pt/pp **debarred**) escludere

debase /dɪ'beɪs/ *vt* degradare

debatable /dɪ'beɪtəbl/ *adj* discutibile

debate /dɪ'beɪt/ ① *n* dibattito *m*
② *vt* discutere; (in formal debate) dibattere
③ *vi* ~ **whether to**... considerare se...

debauchery /dɪ'bɔ:tʃərɪ/ *n* dissolutezza *f*

debenture bond /dɪ'bentʃə(r)/ *n* obbligazione *f* non garantita

debilitating /dɪ'bɪlɪteɪtɪŋ/ *adj* ‹disease› debilitante

debility /dɪ'bɪlətɪ/ *n* debilitazione *f*

debit /'debɪt/ ① *n* debito *m*
② *vt* (pt/pp **debited**) Comm addebitare ‹sum, account›

debit card *n* carta *f* di debito

debonair /debə'neə(r)/ *adj* ‹person› elegante e cortese

debrief /di:'bri:f/ *vt* chiamare a rapporto; **be** ~**ed** ‹defector, freed hostage› essere interrogato; ‹diplomat, agent› essere chiamato a rapporto

debriefing /di:'bri:fɪŋ/ *n* (of hostage, defector) interrogatorio *m*

debris /'debri:/ *n* macerie *fpl*

debt /det/ *n* debito *m*; **be in** ~ avere dei debiti

debt collection *n* esazione *f* crediti

debt collection agency *n* agenzia *f* di recupero crediti

debt collector *n* esattore *m* dei crediti

debtor /'detə(r)/ *n* debitore, -trice *mf*

debug /di:'bʌg/ *vt* (pt/pp **debugged**) Comput correggere gli errori di; togliere i microfoni spia da ‹room›

debunk /dɪ'bʌŋk/ *vt* ridicolizzare · ‹theory, myth›

début /'deɪbu:/ *n* debutto *m*

decade /'dekeɪd/ *n* decennio *m*

decadence /'dekədəns/ *n* decadenza *f*

decadent /'dekədənt/ *adj* decadente

decaffeinated /di:'kæfɪneɪtɪd/ *adj* decaffeinato

decalitre /'dekəli:tə(r)/ *n* decalitro *m*

decametre /'dekəmi:tə(r)/ *n* decametro *m*

decamp /dɪ'kæmp/ *vi* sgattaiolare via; ~ **with something** (steal) squagliarsela con qualcosa

decant /dɪ'kænt/ *vt* travasare

decanter /dɪ'kæntə(r)/ *n* caraffa *f* (di cristallo)

decapitate /dɪ'kæpɪteɪt/ *vt* decapitare

decathlon /dɪ'kæθlɒn/ *n* decathlon *m inv*

decay /dɪ'keɪ/ ① *n* (also fig) decadenza *f*; (rot) decomposizione *f*; (of tooth) carie *f inv*
② *vi* imputridire; (rot) decomporsi; ‹tooth› cariarsi

deceased /dɪ'si:st/ ① *adj* defunto
② *n* **the** ~ il defunto; la defunta

deceit /dɪ'si:t/ *n* inganno *m*

deceitful /dɪ'si:tfʊl/ *adj* falso

deceitfully /dɪ'si:tfʊlɪ/ *adv* falsamente

deceive /dɪ'si:v/ *vt* ingannare

decelerate /di:'seləreɪt/ *vi* decelerare

deceleration /di:selə'reɪʃn/ *n* decelerazione *f*

December /dɪ'sembə(r)/ *n* Dicembre *m*

decency /'di:sənsɪ/ *n* decenza *f*

decent /'di:sənt/ *adj* decente; (respectable) rispettabile; **very** ~ **of you** molto gentile da parte tua

decently /'di:səntlɪ/ *adv* decentemente; (kindly) gentilmente

decentralization /di:sentrəlaɪ'zeɪʃn/ *n* decentramento *m*

decentralize /di:'sentrəlaɪz/ *vt* decentrare

deception /dɪ'sepʃn/ *n* inganno *m*

deceptive /dɪ'septɪv/ *adj* ingannevole

deceptively /dɪ'septɪvlɪ/ *adv* ingannevolmente; **it looks** ~ **easy** sembra facile ma non lo è

decibel /'desɪbel/ *n* decibel *m inv*

decide /dɪ'saɪd/ ① *vt* decidere; **that's** ~**d then** siamo d'accordo, allora
② *vi* decidere (**on** di)
■ **decide on** *vt* scegliere ‹date, outfit, course of action›

decided /dɪ'saɪdɪd/ *adj* risoluto

decidedly /dɪ'saɪdɪdlɪ/ *adv* risolutamente; (without doubt) senza dubbio

decider /dɪ'saɪdə(r)/ *n* (point) punto *m* decisivo; (goal) goal *m inv* decisivo; (game) spareggio *m*

deciduous /dɪ'sɪdjʊəs/ *adj* a foglie decidue

decigram[me] /'desɪgræm/ *n* decigrammo *m*

decilitre /'desɪli:tə(r)/ *n* decilitro *m*

decimal /'desɪml/ ① *adj* decimale
② *n* numero *m* decimale

decimal point *n* virgola *f*

decimal system *n* sistema *m* decimale

decimate /'desɪmeɪt/ *vt* decimare

decimetre /'desɪmiːtə(r)/ *n* decimetro *m*

decipher /dɪ'saɪfə(r)/ *vt* decifrare

decision /dɪ'sɪʒn/ *n* decisione *f*

decision-maker /dɪ'sɪʒnmeɪkə(r)/ *n* persona *f* che ama o ha il potere di prendere decisioni

decision-making /dɪ'sɪʒnmeɪkɪŋ/ *n* be good/bad at ∼ saper/non saper prendere decisioni; ∼ **process** *n* processo *m* decisionale

decisive /dɪ'saɪsɪv/ *adj* decisivo

decisively /dɪ'saɪsɪvlɪ/ *adv* con decisione

deck[1] /dek/ *vt* abbigliare

deck[2] *n* Naut ponte *m*; **on** ∼ in coperta; **top** ∼ (of bus) piano *m* di sopra; ∼ **of cards** mazzo *m*

deckchair /'dektʃeə(r)/ *n* [sedia *f* a] sdraio *f inv*

declaration /deklə'reɪʃn/ *n* dichiarazione *f*

declare /dɪ'kleə(r)/ *vt* dichiarare; **anything to** ∼? niente da dichiarare?; ∼ **one's love** dichiararsi

declassify /diː'klæsɪfaɪ/ *vt* rimuovere dai vincoli di segretezza ⟨*document, information*⟩

declension /dɪ'klenʃn/ *n* declinazione *f*

decline /dɪ'klaɪn/ [1] *n* declino *m* [2] *vt* also Gram declinare [3] *vi* (decrease) diminuire; ⟨*health*⟩) deperire; (say no) rifiutare

declutch /diː'klʌtʃ/ *vi* Br lasciare la frizione

decode /diː'kəʊd/ *vt* decifrare; Comput decodificare

decoding /diː'kəʊdɪŋ/ *n* decodifica *f*, decodificazione *f*

décolleté /deɪ'kɒlteɪ/ *adj* décolleté *inv*, scollato

decompose /diːkəm'pəʊz/ *vi* decomporsi

decomposition /diːkɒmpə'zɪʃn/ *n* scomposizione *f*

decompress /diːkəm'pres/ *vt* decomprimere

decompression /diːkəm'preʃn/ *n* decompressione *f*

decontaminate /diːkən'tæmɪneɪt/ *vt* decontaminare

décor /'deɪkɔː(r)/ *n* decorazione *f*; (including furniture) arredamento *m*

decorate /'dekəreɪt/ *vt* decorare; (paint) pitturare; (wallpaper) tappezzare

decoration /dekə'reɪʃn/ *n* decorazione *f*

decorative /'dekərətɪv/ *adj* decorativo

decorator /'dekəreɪtə(r)/ *n* painter and ∼ imbianchino *m*

decorous /'dekərəs/ *adj* decoroso

decorously /'dekərəslɪ/ *adv* decorosamente

decorum /dɪ'kɔːrəm/ *n* decoro *m*

decoy[1] /'diːkɔɪ/ *n* esca *f*

decoy[2] /dɪ'kɔɪ/ *vt* adescare

decrease[1] /'diːkriːs/ *n* diminuzione *f*; **be on the** ∼ essere in diminuzione

decrease[2] /dɪ'kriːs/ *vt/i* diminuire

decreasing /dɪ'kriːsɪŋ/ *adj* in diminuzione

decreasingly /dɪ'kriːsɪŋlɪ/ *adv* sempre meno

decree /dɪ'kriː/ [1] *n* decreto *m* [2] *vt* decretare

decrepit /dɪ'krepɪt/ *adj* decrepito

decriminalization /diːkrɪmɪnəlaɪ'zeɪʃn/ *n* depenalizzazione *f*

decriminalize /diː'krɪmɪnəlaɪz/ *vt* depenalizzare

dedicate /'dedɪkeɪt/ *vt* dedicare

dedicated /'dedɪkeɪtɪd/ *adj* ⟨person⟩ scrupoloso

dedication /dedɪ'keɪʃn/ *n* dedizione *f*; (in book) dedica *f*

deduce /dɪ'djuːs/ *vt* dedurre (**from** da)

deduct /dɪ'dʌkt/ *vt* dedurre

deduction /dɪ'dʌkʃn/ *n* deduzione *f*

deed /diːd/ *n* azione *f*; Jur atto *m* di proprietà

deed of covenant *n* Jur accordo *m* accessorio ad un contratto immobiliare

deed poll *n* change one's name by ∼ ∼ cambiare nome con un atto unilaterale

deem /diːm/ *vt* ritenere

deep /diːp/ *adj* profondo; **go off the** ∼ **end** fam arrabbiarsi

deepen /'diːpn/ [1] *vt* approfondire; scavare più profondamente ⟨*trench*⟩ [2] *vi* approfondirsi; fig ⟨*mystery*⟩ infittirsi

deep-fat-fryer *n* friggitrice *f*

deepfelt *adj* profondo

deep-freeze *n* congelatore *m*

deep-fried *adj* fritto (in molto olio)

deep-frozen *adj* surgelato

deep-fry *vt* friggere (in molto olio)

deeply *adv* profondamente

deep-rooted *adj* ⟨habit, prejudice⟩ radicato

deep-sea *adj* ⟨exploration, diving⟩ in profondità; ⟨fisherman, fishing⟩ d'alto mare

deep-sea diver *n* palombaro *m*

deep-seated *adj* radicato

deep-set *adj* ⟨eyes⟩ infossato

deep South *n* Am il profondo Sud

deep-vein thrombosis n trombosi f venosa profonda

deer /dɪə(r)/ n inv cervo m

de-escalate /diː'eskəleɪt/ vt ridurre ⟨crisis, violence⟩

deface /dɪ'feɪs/ vt sfigurare ⟨picture⟩; deturpare ⟨monument⟩

defamation /defə'meɪʃn/ n diffamazione f

defamatory /dɪ'fæmətərɪ/ adj diffamatorio

default /dɪ'fɔːlt/ ❶ n (Jur: non-payment) morosità f; (failure to appear) contumacia f; Comput default m inv; **win by** ∼ Sport vincere per abbandono dell'avversario; **in** ∼ **of** per mancanza di
❷ adj ∼ **drive** Comput lettore m di default
❸ vi (not pay) venir meno ad un pagamento; Comput ∼ **to something** ritornare all'impostazione di default

defeat /dɪ'fiːt/ ❶ n sconfitta f
❷ vt sconfiggere; (frustrate) vanificare ⟨attempts⟩; **that** ∼**s the object** questo fa fallire l'obiettivo

defeatist /dɪ'fiːtɪst/ adj & n disfattista mf

defecate /'defəkeɪt/ vi defecare

defect[1] /dɪ'fekt/ vi Pol fare defezione

defect[2] /'diːfekt/ n difetto m

defective /dɪ'fektɪv/ adj difettoso

defector /dɪ'fektə(r)/ n (from party) defezionista mf; (from country) fuor[i]uscito, -a mf

defence /dɪ'fens/ n difesa f

defenceless /dɪ'fenslɪs/ adj indifeso

Defence Minister n ministro m della difesa

defend /dɪ'fend/ vt difendere; (justify) giustificare

defendant /dɪ'fendənt/ n Jur imputato, -a mf

defender /dɪ'fendə(r)/ n difensore m, -ditrice f

defensive /dɪ'fensɪv/ ❶ adj difensivo
❷ n difensiva f; **on the** ∼ sulla difensiva

defer /dɪ'fɜː(r)/ ❶ vt (pt/pp **deferred**) (postpone) rinviare
❷ vi ∼ **to somebody** rimettersi a qualcuno

deference /'defərəns/ n deferenza f

deferential /defə'renʃl/ adj deferente

deferentially /defə'renʃəlɪ/ adv con deferenza

deferment, deferral /dɪ'fɜːmənt/, /dɪ'fɜːrəl/ n (postponement) rinvio m

defiance /dɪ'faɪəns/ n sfida f; **in** ∼ **of** sfidando

defiant /dɪ'faɪənt/ adj ⟨person⟩ ribelle; ⟨gesture, attitude⟩ di sfida

defiantly /dɪ'faɪəntlɪ/ adv con aria di sfida

deficiency /dɪ'fɪʃənsɪ/ n insufficienza f

deficient /dɪ'fɪʃənt/ adj insufficiente; **be** ∼ **in** mancare di

deficit /'defɪsɪt/ n deficit m inv

defile /dɪ'faɪl/ vt fig contaminare

define /dɪ'faɪn/ vt definire

defined adj ⟨role⟩ definito

definite /'defnɪt/ adj definito; (certain) ⟨answer, yes⟩ definitivo; ⟨improvement, difference⟩ netto; **he was** ∼ **about it** è stato chiaro in proposito

definite article n (grammatical) articolo m determinativo

definitely /'defnɪtlɪ/ adv sicuramente

definition /defɪ'nɪʃn/ n definizione f

definitive /dɪ'fɪnətɪv/ adj definitivo

deflate /dɪ'fleɪt/ vt sgonfiare

deflation /dɪ'fleɪʃn/ n Comm deflazione f

deflationary /dɪ'fleɪʃənrɪ/ adj deflazionistico

deflect /dɪ'flekt/ vt deflettere

deformed /dɪ'fɔːmd/ adj deforme

deformity /dɪ'fɔːmətɪ/ n deformità f inv

DEFRA abbr Br (**Department for Environment, Food, and Rural Affairs**) ≈ Ministero m per le Politiche Agricole e Forestali

defrag /'diːfræg/ vt fam deframmentare

defragment /'diːfrægment/ vt Comput deframmentare

defraud /dɪ'frɔːd/ vt defraudare

defray /dɪ'freɪ/ vt fml sostenere

defrost /diː'frɒst/ vt sbrinare ⟨fridge⟩; scongelare ⟨food⟩

deft /deft/ adj abile

deftly /'deftlɪ/ adv con destrezza

deftness /'deftnɪs/ n destrezza f

defunct /dɪ'fʌŋkt/ adj morto e sepolto; ⟨law⟩ caduto in disuso

defuse /diː'fjuːz/ vt disinnescare; calmare ⟨situation⟩

defy /dɪ'faɪ/ vt (pt/pp **-ied**) (challenge) sfidare; resistere a ⟨attempt⟩; (not obey) disobbedire a

degenerate[1] /dɪ'dʒenəreɪt/ vi degenerare; ∼ **into** fig degenerare in

degenerate[2] /dɪ'dʒenərət/ adj degenerato

degeneration /dɪdʒenə'reɪʃn/ n degenerazione f

degenerative /dɪ'dʒenərətɪv/ adj degenerativo

degradation /degrə'deɪʃn/ n (debasement) degradazione f; (of culture) deterioramento m; (squalor) desolazione f

degrade /dɪ'greɪd/ vt (humiliate) degradare ⟨person⟩; (damage) deteriorare ⟨environment⟩

degrading /dɪ'greɪdɪŋ/ adj degradante

degree /dɪ'gri:/ *n* grado *m*; Univ laurea *f*; **20 ~s** 20 gradi; **not to the same ~** non allo stesso livello

degree ceremony *n* Br Univ cerimonia *f* di consegna delle lauree

degree course *n* Br Univ corso *m* di laurea

dehydrate /di:haɪ'dreɪt/ *vt* disidratare

dehydrated /di:haɪ'dreɪtɪd/ *adj* disidratato

dehydration /di:haɪ'dreɪʃn/ *n* disidratazione *f*

de-ice /di:'aɪs/ *vt* togliere il ghiaccio da

de-icer /di:'aɪsə(r)/ *n* (mechanical) sbrinatore *m*; (chemical) liquido *m* scongelante

deign /deɪn/ *vi* **~ to do something** degnarsi di fare qualcosa

deity /'di:ətɪ/ *n* divinità *f inv*

déjà vu /deɪʒɑ:'vu:/ *n* déjà vu *m inv*

dejected /dɪ'dʒektɪd/ *adj* demoralizzato

dejectedly /dɪ'dʒektɪdlɪ/ *adv* con aria demoralizzata

dejection /dɪ'dʒekʃn/ *n* abbacchiamento *m*

delay /dɪ'leɪ/ **①** *n* ritardo *m* **without ~** senza indugio
② *vt* ritardare **be ~ed** ⟨*person*⟩ essere trattenuto; ⟨*train, aircraft*⟩ essere in ritardo
③ *vi* indugiare

delayed action /dɪ'leɪd/ *adj* ad azione ritardata; ⟨*bomb*⟩ a scoppio ritardato

delegate¹ /'delɪgət/ *n* delegato, -a *mf*

delegate² /'delɪgeɪt/ *vt* delegare

delegation /delɪ'geɪʃn/ *n* delegazione *f*

delete /dɪ'li:t/ *vt* cancellare

delete [key] *n* tasto *m* di cancellazione

deletion /dɪ'li:ʃn/ *n* cancellatura *f*

deliberate¹ /dɪ'lɪbərət/ *adj* deliberato; (slow) posato

deliberate² /dɪ'lɪbəreɪt/ *vi/i* deliberare

deliberately /dɪ'lɪbərətlɪ/ *adv* deliberatamente; (slowly) in modo posato

deliberation /dɪlɪbə'reɪʃn/ *n* deliberazione *f*; **with ~** in modo posato

delicacy /'delɪkəsɪ/ *n* delicatezza *f*; (food) prelibatezza *f*

delicate /'delɪkət/ *adj* delicato

delicately /'delɪkətlɪ/ *adv* ⟨*handle, phrase*⟩ con delicatezza; ⟨*crafted, flavoured*⟩ con raffinatezza

delicatessen /delɪkə'tesn/ *n* negozio *m* di specialità gastronomiche

delicious /dɪ'lɪʃəs/ *adj* delizioso

delight /dɪ'laɪt/ **①** *n* piacere *m*
② *vt* deliziare
③ *vi* **~ in** dilettarsi con

delighted /dɪ'laɪtɪd/ *adj* lieto

delightful /dɪ'laɪtfʊl/ *adj* delizioso

delineate /dɪ'lɪnɪeɪt/ *vt* also fig delineare

delineation /dɪlɪnɪ'eɪʃn/ *n* delineazione *f*

delinquency /dɪ'lɪŋkwənsɪ/ *n* delinquenza *f*

delinquent /dɪ'lɪŋkwənt/ **①** *adj* delinquente
② *n* delinquente *mf*

delirious /dɪ'lɪrɪəs/ *adj* **be ~** delirare; (fig: very happy) essere pazzo di gioia

delirium /dɪ'lɪrɪəm/ *n* delirio *m*

deliver /dɪ'lɪvə(r)/ *vt* consegnare; recapitare ⟨*post, newspaper*⟩; tenere ⟨*speech*⟩; dare ⟨*message*⟩; tirare ⟨*blow*⟩; (set free) liberare; **~ a baby** far nascere un bambino

deliverance /dɪ'lɪv(ə)rəns/ *n* liberazione *f*

delivery /dɪ'lɪvərɪ/ *n* consegna *f*; (of post) distribuzione *f*; Med parto *m*; **cash on ~** pagamento *m* alla consegna

delivery address *n* indirizzo *m* del destinatario

delivery man *n* fattorino *m*

delivery room *n* Med sala *f* parto

delta /'deltə/ *n* delta *m inv*

delude /dɪ'lu:d/ *vt* ingannare; **~ oneself** illudersi

deluge /'delju:dʒ/ **①** *n* diluvio *m*
② *vt* (fig: with requests etc) inondare

delusion /dɪ'lu:ʒn/ *n* illusione; **~s of grandeur** mania *f* di grandezza

de luxe /də'lʌks/ *adj* di lusso

delve /delv/ *vi* **~ into** (into pocket etc) frugare in; (into notes, the past) fare ricerche in

demagnetize /di:'mægnətaɪz/ *vt* smagnetizzare

demand /dɪ'mɑ:nd/ **①** *n* richiesta *f*; Comm domanda *f*; **in ~** richiesto; **on ~** a richiesta
② *vt* esigere (**of/from** da)

demanding /dɪ'mɑ:ndɪŋ/ *adj* esigente

demanning /di:'mænɪŋ/ *n* Br taglio *m* di personale

demarcation /di:mɑ:'keɪʃn/ *n* demarcazione *f*

demean /dɪ'mi:n/ *vt* **~ oneself** abbassarsi (**to** a)

demeaning /dɪ'mi:nɪŋ/ *adj* degradante

demeanour /dɪ'mi:nə(r)/ *n* comportamento *m*

demented /dɪ'mentɪd/ *adj* demente

dementia /dɪ'menʃə/ *n* demenza *f*

demerara [sugar] /demə'reərə/ *n* zucchero *m* grezzo di canna

demilitarization /di:mɪlɪtəraɪ'zeɪʃn/ *n* demilitarizzazione *f*

demilitarize /di:'mɪlɪtəraɪz/ *vt* smilitarizzare

demise /dɪ'maɪz/ n decesso m

demister /di:'mɪstə(r)/ n Auto sbrinatore m

demo /'deməʊ/ n (pl ∼s) fam manifestazione f

demobilize /di:'məʊbəlaɪz/ vt Mil smobilitare

democracy /dɪ'mɒkrəsɪ/ n democrazia f

democrat /'deməkræt/ n democratico, -a mf

democratic /demə'krætɪk/ adj democratico

democratically /demə'krætɪklɪ/ adv democraticamente

demo disk n Comput demo disk m inv

demographic /demə'græfɪk/ adj demografico

demolish /dɪ'mɒlɪʃ/ vt demolire

demolition /demə'lɪʃn/ n demolizione f

demon /'di:mən/ n demonio m

demonic /dɪ'mɒnɪk/ adj ⟨aspect, power⟩ demoniaco

demonize /'di:mənaɪz/ vt demonizzare

demonstrable /'demənstrəbl/ adj dimostrabile

demonstrably /'demənstrəblɪ/ adv ⟨false, untrue⟩ manifestamente

demonstrate /'demənstreɪt/ 1 vt dimostrare; dare una dimostrazione dell'uso di ⟨appliance⟩
2 vi Pol manifestare

demonstration /demən'streɪʃn/ n dimostrazione f; Pol manifestazione f

demonstrative /dɪ'mɒnstrətɪv/ adj Gram dimostrativo; **be** ∼ essere espansivo

demonstrator /'demənstreɪtə(r)/ n Pol manifestante mf; (for product) dimostratore, -trice mf

demoralize /dɪ'mɒrəlaɪz/ vt demoralizzare

demoralizing /dɪ'mɒrəlaɪzɪŋ/ adj demoralizzante, avvilente

demote /dɪ'məʊt/ vt retrocedere di grado; Mil degradare

demur /dɪ'mɜ:/ 1 vi (pt/pp **demurred**) (complain) protestare; (disagree) obiettare
2 n without ∼ senza obiezioni

demure /dɪ'mjʊə(r)/ adj schivo

demurely /dɪ'mjʊəlɪ/ adv in modo schivo

den /den/ n tana f; (room) rifugio m

denationalize /di:'næʃ(ə)nəlaɪz/ vt denazionalizzare

denial /dɪ'naɪəl/ n smentita f

denier /'denɪə(r)/ n denaro m

denigrate /'denɪgreɪt/ vt denigrare

denigrating /'denɪgreɪtɪŋ/ adj denigratore

denim /'denɪm/ n [tessuto m] jeans m; ∼s pl [blue-]jeans mpl

Denmark /'denmɑ:k/ n Danimarca f

denomination /dɪnɒmɪ'neɪʃn/ n Relig confessione f; (money) valore f

denote /dɪ'nəʊt/ vt denotare

denounce /dɪ'naʊns/ vt denunciare

dense /dens/ adj denso; ⟨crowd, forest⟩ fitto; (stupid) ottuso

densely /'denslɪ/ adv ⟨populated⟩ densamente; ∼ **wooded** fittamente ricoperto di alberi

density /'densətɪ/ n densità f inv; (of forest) fittezza f

dent /dent/ 1 n ammaccatura f
2 vt ammaccare

dental /'dentl/ adj dei denti; ⟨treatment⟩ dentistico; ⟨hygiene⟩ dentale

dental appointment n appuntamento m dal dentista

dental clinic n (hospital) clinica f odontoiatrica; (part of hospital) reparto m odontoiatrico

dental floss n filo m interdentale

dental plate n dentiera f

dental surgeon n odontoiatra mf, medico m dentista

dental surgery n Br (premises) studio m dentistico; (treatment) visita f dentistica

dented /dentɪd/ adj ammaccato; ∼ **pride** orgoglio m ferito

dentist /'dentɪst/ n dentista mf

dentistry /'dentɪstrɪ/ n odontoiatria f

dentures /'dentʃəz/ npl dentiera fsg

denude /dɪ'nju:d/ vt denudare

denunciation /dɪnʌnsɪ'eɪʃn/ n denuncia f

Denver boot /'denvə/ n Am = WHEEL CLAMP

deny /dɪ'naɪ/ vt (pt/pp -**ied**) negare; (officially) smentire; ∼ **somebody something** negare qualcosa a qualcuno; **I can't** ∼**it** non posso negarlo

deodorant /di:'əʊdərənt/ n deodorante m

deodorize /di:'əʊdəraɪz/ vt deodorare

depart /dɪ'pɑ:t/ vi ⟨plane, train⟩ partire; liter ⟨person⟩ andare via; (deviate) allontanarsi (**from** da)

departed /dɪ'pɑ:tɪd/ adj (euph: dead) scomparso

department /dɪ'pɑ:tmənt/ n reparto m; Pol ministero m; (of company) sezione f; Univ dipartimento m

departmental /di:pɑ:t'mentl/ adj ⟨Pol: colleague, meeting⟩ di sezione; (in business) di reparto

department head n caporeparto mf; Univ direttore, -trice mf d'istituto

department manager n (of business) direttore, -trice mf di reparto; (of store) caporeparto mf inv

Department of Defense *n* Am ministero *m* della Difesa

Department of Energy *n* Am ≈ ministero *m* dell'Industria

Department of Health *n* ministero *m* della Sanità

Department of Social Security *n* Br ≈ Istituto *m* Nazionale della Previdenza Sociale

Department of the Environment *n* Br ministero *m* dell'Ambiente

Department of Trade and Industry *n* Br ministero *m* del Commercio e dell'Industria

department store *n* grande magazzino *m*

departure /dɪˈpɑːtʃə(r)/ *n* partenza *f*; (from rule) allontanamento *m*; **new** ∼ svolta *f*

departure gate *n* (at airport) uscita *f*

departure lounge *n* (at airport) sala *f* d'attesa

departure platform *n* Rail binario *m*

departures board *n* tabellone *m* delle partenze

depend /dɪˈpend/ *vi* dipendere (**on** da); (rely) contare (**on** su); **it all** ∼**s** dipende; ∼**ing on what he says** a seconda di quello che dice

dependability /dɪpendəˈbɪlətɪ/ *n* affidabilità *f*

dependable /dɪˈpendəbl/ *adj* fidato

dependant /dɪˈpendənt/ *n* persona *f* a carico

dependence /dɪˈpendəns/ *n* dipendenza *f*

dependent /dɪˈpendənt/ *adj* dipendente (**on** da)

depict /dɪˈpɪkt/ *vt* (in writing) dipingere; (with picture) rappresentare

depiction /dɪˈpɪkʃn/ *n* rappresentazione *f*

depilatory /dɪˈpɪlətərɪ/ *n* (cream) crema *f* depilatoria

deplete /dɪˈpliːt/ *vt* ridurre; **totally** ∼**d** completamente esaurito

depletion /dɪˈpliːʃn/ *n* (of resources, funds) impoverimento *m*

deplorable /dɪˈplɔːrəbl/ *adj* deplorevole

deplore /dɪˈplɔː(r)/ *vt* deplorare

deploy /dɪˈplɔɪ/ **①** *vt* Mil spiegare **②** *vi* schierarsi

deployment /dɪˈplɔɪmənt/ *n* schieramento *m*

depoliticize /diːpəˈlɪtɪsaɪz/ *vt* depoliticizzare

depopulate /diːˈpɒpjʊleɪt/ *vt* spopolare

depopulation /diːpɒpjʊˈleɪʃn/ *n* spopolamento *m*

deport /dɪˈpɔːt/ *vt* deportare

deportation /diːpɔːˈteɪʃn/ *n* deportazione *f*

deportee /diːpɔːˈtiː/ *n* deportato, -a *mf*

deportment /dɪˈpɔːtmənt/ *n* portamento *m*

depose /dɪˈpəʊz/ *vt* deporre

deposit /dɪˈpɒzɪt/ **①** *n* deposito *m*; (against damage) cauzione *f*; (first instalment) acconto *m* **②** *vt* depositare

deposit account *n* libretto *m* di risparmio; (without instant access) conto *m* vincolato

depositor /dɪˈpɒzɪtə(r)/ *n* Fin depositante *mf*

deposit slip *n* (in bank) distinta *f* di versamento

depot /ˈdepəʊ/ *n* deposito *m*; Am Rail stazione *f* ferroviaria

deprave /dɪˈpreɪv/ *vt* depravare

depraved /dɪˈpreɪvd/ *adj* depravato

depravity /dɪˈprævətɪ/ *n* depravazione *f*

deprecate /ˈdeprəkeɪt/ *vt* disapprovare

deprecatory /deprɪˈkeɪtərɪ/ *adj* (disapproving) di disapprovazione; (apologetic) di scusa

depreciate /dɪˈpriːʃɪeɪt/ *vi* deprezzarsi

depreciation /dɪpriːsɪˈeɪʃn/ *n* deprezzameto *m*

depress /dɪˈpres/ *vt* deprimere; (press down) premere

depressed /dɪˈprest/ *adj* depresso; ∼ **area** zona *f* depressa

depressing /dɪˈpresɪŋ/ *adj* deprimente

depression /dɪˈpreʃn/ *n* depressione *f*

depressive /dɪˈpresɪv/ **①** *adj* depressivo **②** *n* depresso, -a *mf*

depressurize /diːˈpreʃəraɪz/ *vi* depressurizzare

deprivation /deprɪˈveɪʃn/ *n* privazione *f*

deprive /dɪˈpraɪv/ *vt* ∼ **somebody of something** privare qualcuno di qualcosa

deprived /dɪˈpraɪvd/ *adj* ⟨area, childhood⟩ disagiato

dept *abbr* **department**

depth /depθ/ *n* profondità *f inv*: **in** ∼ ⟨study, analyse⟩ in modo approfondito; **in the** ∼**s of winter** in pieno inverno; **in the** ∼**s of despair** nella più profonda disperazione; **be out of one's** ∼ (in water) non toccare il fondo; fig sentirsi in alto mare

deputation /depjʊˈteɪʃn/ *n* deputazione *f*

deputize /ˈdepjʊtaɪz/ *vi* ∼ **for** fare le veci di

deputy /ˈdepjʊtɪ/ *n* vice *mf*; (temporary) sostituto, -a *mf*

deputy chairman *n* vicepresidente *m*

deputy leader n Br Pol sottosegretario m

deputy president n vicepresidente mf

deputy premier, **deputy prime minister** n Pol vice primo ministro m

derail /dɪˈreɪl/ vt be ∼ed ⟨train⟩ essere deragliato

derailleur gears /dɪˈreɪljə/ npl deragliatore msg

derailment /dɪˈreɪlmənt/ n deragliamento m

deranged /dɪˈreɪndʒd/ adj squilibrato

deregulate /diːˈregjʊleɪt/ vt deregolamentare ⟨market⟩

deregulation /diːregjʊˈleɪʃn/ n deregolamentazione f

derelict /ˈderəlɪkt/ adj abbandonato

deride /dɪˈraɪd/ vt deridere

derision /dɪˈrɪʒn/ n derisione f

derisive /dɪˈraɪsɪv/ adj derisorio

derisory /dɪˈraɪsərɪ/ adj ⟨laughter⟩ derisorio; ⟨offer⟩ irrisorio

derivation /derɪˈveɪʃn/ n derivazione f

derivative /dɪˈrɪvətɪv/ ① adj derivato ② n derivato m

derive /dɪˈraɪv/ ① vt (obtain) derivare; be ∼d from ⟨word⟩ derivare da ② vi ∼ from derivare da

dermatitis /dɜːməˈtaɪtɪs/ n dermatite f

dermatologist /dɜːməˈtɒlədʒɪst/ n dermatologo, -a mf

derogatory /dɪˈrɒgətrɪ/ adj ⟨comments⟩ peggiorativo

derrick /ˈderɪk/ n derrick m inv

derv /dɜːv/ n Br gasolio m

descaler /diːˈskeɪlə(r)/ n Br disincrostante m

descend /dɪˈsend/ ① vi scendere; be ∼ed from discendere da ② vt scendere da ■ **descend on** vt (attack) piombare su; (visit) capitare [all'improvviso]

descendant /dɪˈsendənt/ n discendente mf

descent /dɪˈsent/ n discesa f; (lineage) origine f

descrambler /diːˈskræmblə(r)/ n Teleph, TV decodificatore m

describe /dɪˈskraɪb/ vt descrivere

description /dɪˈskrɪpʃn/ n descrizione f; they had no help of any ∼ non hanno avuto proprio nessun aiuto

descriptive /dɪˈskrɪptɪv/ adj descrittivo; (vivid) vivido

desecrate /ˈdesɪkreɪt/ vt profanare

desecration /desɪˈkreɪʃn/ n profanazione f

desegregate /diːˈsegrɪgeɪt/ vt abolire la segregazione razziale in ⟨school⟩

deselect /diːsɪˈlekt/ vt Br be ∼ed non avere riconferma della candidatura alle elezioni da parte del proprio partito

desensitize /diːˈsensɪtaɪz/ vt desensibilizzare

desert¹ /ˈdezət/ ① n deserto m ② adj deserto; ∼ island isola f deserta

desert² /dɪˈzɜːt/ ① vt abbandonare ② vi disertare

desert boot n scarponcino m Clark®

deserted /dɪˈzɜːtɪd/ adj deserto

deserter /dɪˈzɜːtə(r)/ n Mil disertore m

desertion /dɪˈzɜːʃn/ n Mil diserzione f; (of family) abbandono m

deserts /dɪˈzɜːts/ npl get one's just ∼ ottenere ciò che ci si merita

deserve /dɪˈzɜːv/ vt meritare

deservedly /dɪˈzɜːvədlɪ/ adv meritatamente

deserving /dɪˈzɜːvɪŋ/ adj meritevole; ∼ cause opera f meritoria

desiccated /ˈdesɪkeɪtɪd/ adj essiccato; (pej: dried up) secco

design /dɪˈzaɪn/ ① n progettazione f; (fashion ∼, appearance) design m inv; (pattern) modello m; (aim) proposito m; have ∼s on aver mire su ② vt progettare; disegnare ⟨clothes, furniture, model⟩; be ∼ed for essere fatto per

designate /ˈdezɪgneɪt/ vt designare

designation /dezɪgˈneɪʃn/ n designazione f

design consultant n progettista mf

designer /dɪˈzaɪnə(r)/ n progettista mf; (of clothes) stilista mf; (Theat: of set) scenografo, -a mf

design fault n difetto m di concezione

design feature n prestazione f

designing /dɪˈzaɪnɪŋ/ adj pej calcolatore

desirable /dɪˈzaɪərəbl/ adj desiderabile

desire /dɪˈzaɪə(r)/ ① n desiderio m ② vt desiderare

desist /dɪˈzɪst/ vi desistere (**from** da)

desk /desk/ n scrivania f; (in school) banco m; (in hotel) reception f inv; (cash ∼) cassa f; (check-in ∼) check-in m inv

deskbound adj ⟨job⟩ sedentario

desk diary n agenda da tavolo

desk pad n (blotter) tampone m; (notebook) block-notes m inv

desktop n piano m della scrivania; (computer) [computer m inv] desktop m inv

desktop publishing n desktop publishing m inv, editoria f da tavolo

desolate /ˈdesələt/ adj desolato

desolation /desəˈleɪʃn/ n desolazione f

despair /dɪˈspeə(r)/ ① n disperazione f; in ∼ disperato; ⟨say⟩ per disperazione

② *vi* I ~ **of that boy** quel ragazzo mi fa disperare

desperate /'despərət/ *adj* disperato; **be** ~ ⟨*criminal*⟩ essere un disperato; **be** ~ **for something** morire dalla voglia di

desperately /'despərətlɪ/ *adv* disperatamente; **he said** ~ ha detto, disperato

desperation /despə'reɪʃn/ *n* disperazione *f*; **in** ~ per disperazione

despicable /dɪ'spɪkəbl/ *adj* disprezzevole

despise /dɪ'spaɪz/ *vt* disprezzare

despite /dɪ'spaɪt/ *prep* malgrado

despondency /dɪ'spɒndənsɪ/ *n* abbattimento *m*

despondent /dɪ'spɒndənt/ *adj* abbattuto

despot /'despɒt/ *n* despota *m*

despotism /'despətɪzm/ *n* dispotismo *m*

des res /dez'rez/ *n abbr* fam (**desirable residence**) abitazione *f* desiderabile

dessert /dɪ'zɜːt/ *n* dolce *m*

dessert spoon *n* cucchiaio *m* da dolce

dessert wine *n* vino *m* da dessert

destabilize /diː'steɪbɪlaɪz/ *vt* destabilizzare

destination /destɪ'neɪʃn/ *n* destinazione *f*

destine /'destɪn/ *vt* destinare; **be** ~**d for something** essere destinato a qualcosa; ~**d for each other** fatti l'uno per l'altra

destined /'destɪnd/ *adj* ~ **for Paris** ⟨*train, package*⟩ con destinazione Parigi; **it was** ~ **to happen** era destino che succedesse

destiny /'destɪnɪ/ *n* destino *m*

destitute /'destɪtjuːt/ *adj* bisognoso

destitution /destɪ'tjuːʃn/ *n* indigenza *f*

destroy /dɪ'strɔɪ/ *vt* distruggere

destroyer /dɪ'strɔɪə(r)/ *n* Naut cacciatorpediniere *m*

destruct /dɪ'strʌkt/ *vi* distruggersi

destruction /dɪ'strʌkʃn/ *n* distruzione *f*

destructive /dɪ'strʌktɪv/ *adj* distruttivo; fig ⟨*criticism*⟩ negativo

destructiveness /dɪ'strʌktɪvnɪs/ *n* distruttività *f*

desultory /'desəltrɪ/ *adj* ⟨*conversation*⟩ sconnesso; ⟨*friendship*⟩ incostante; ⟨*attempt*⟩ poco convinto

detach /dɪ'tætʃ/ *vt* staccare

detachable /dɪ'tætʃəbl/ *adj* separabile

detached /dɪ'tætʃt/ *adj* fig distaccato; ~ **house** villetta *f*

detached retina *n* Med retina *f* distaccata

detachment /dɪ'tætʃmənt/ *n* distacco *m*; Mil distaccamento *m*

detail /'diːteɪl/ **①** *n* particolare *m*, dettaglio *m*; **in** ~ particolareggiatamente **②** *vt* esporre con tutti i particolari; Mil assegnare

detail drawing *n* disegno *m* dettagliato

detailed /'diːteɪld/ *adj* particolareggiato, dettagliato

detain /dɪ'teɪn/ *vt* ⟨*police*⟩ trattenere; (delay) far ritardare

detainee /diːteɪ'niː/ *n* detenuto, -a *mf*

detect /dɪ'tekt/ *vt* individuare; (perceive) percepire

detectable /dɪ'tektəbl/ *adj* individuabile

detection /dɪ'tekʃn/ *n* scoperta *f*

detective /dɪ'tektɪv/ *n* investigatore, -trice *mf*

detective constable *n* Br agente *mf* della polizia giudiziaria

detective inspector *n* Br ispettore, -trice *mf* della polizia giudiziaria

detective story *n* racconto *m* poliziesco

detective work *n* indagini *fpl*

detector /dɪ'tektə(r)/ *n* (for metal) cercametalli *m inv*, metal detector *m inv*

detention /dɪ'tenʃn/ *n* detenzione *f*; Sch punizione *f*

detention centre *n* centro *m* di accoglienza

deter /dɪ'tɜː(r)/ *vt* (pt/pp **deterred**) impedire; ~ **somebody from doing something** impedire a qualcuno di fare qualcosa

detergent /dɪ'tɜːdʒənt/ *n* detersivo *m*

deteriorate /dɪ'tɪərɪəreɪt/ *vi* deteriorarsi

deterioration /dɪtɪərɪə'reɪʃn/ *n* deterioramento *m*

determination /dɪtɜːmɪ'neɪʃn/ *n* determinazione *f*

determine /dɪ'tɜːmɪn/ *vt* (ascertain) determinare; ~ **to** (resolve) decidere di

determined /dɪ'tɜːmɪnd/ *adj* deciso

determining /dɪ'tɜːmɪnɪŋ/ *adj* determinante

deterrent /dɪ'terənt/ *n* deterrente *m*

detest /dɪ'test/ *vt* detestare

detestable /dɪ'testəbl/ *adj* detestabile

detonate /'detəneɪt/ **①** *vt* far detonare **②** *vi* detonare

detonation /detə'neɪʃn/ *n* detonazione *f*

detonator /'detəneɪtə(r)/ *n* detonatore *m*

detour /'diːtʊə(r)/ *n* deviazione *f*

detox[1] /'diːtɒks/ *n* disintossicazione *f*

detox[2] /diː'tɒks/ **①** *vi* disintossicarsi **②** *vt* disintossicare

detoxify /diː'tɒksɪfaɪ/ *vt* disintossicare

detract /dɪˈtrækt/ *vi* ~ from sminuire ⟨*merit*⟩; rovinare ⟨*pleasure, beauty*⟩

detractor /dɪˈtræktə(r)/ *n* detrattore, -trice *mf*

detriment /ˈdetrɪmənt/ *n* to the ~ of a danno di

detrimental /detrɪˈmentl/ *adj* dannoso

detritus /dɪˈtraɪtəs/ *n* detriti *mpl*

deuce /djuːs/ *n* Tennis deuce *m inv*

devaluation /diːvæljʊˈeɪʃn/ *n* svalutazione *f*

devalue /diːˈvæljuː/ *vt* svalutare ⟨*currency*⟩

devastate /ˈdevəsteɪt/ *vt* devastare

devastated /ˈdevəsteɪtɪd/ *adj* fam sconvolto

devastating /ˈdevəsteɪtɪŋ/ *adj* devastante; ⟨*news*⟩ sconvolgente

devastation /devəˈsteɪʃn/ *n* devastazione *f*

develop /dɪˈveləp/ **1** *vt* sviluppare; contrarre ⟨*illness*⟩; (add to value of) valorizzare ⟨*area*⟩
2 *vi* svilupparsi; ~ into divenire

developer /dɪˈveləpə(r)/ *n* [property] ~ imprenditore, -trice *mf* edile

developing bath *n* Phot bagno *m* di sviluppo, bagno *m* rivelatore

developing country *n* paese *m* in via di sviluppo

developing tank *n* Phot vasca *f* di sviluppo

development /dɪˈveləpmənt/ *n* sviluppo *m*; (of vaccine etc) messa *f* a punto

development company *n* (for property) impresa *f* edile

deviant /ˈdiːvɪənt/ *adj* deviato

deviate /ˈdiːvɪeɪt/ *vi* deviare

deviation /diːvɪˈeɪʃn/ *n* deviazione *f*

device /dɪˈvaɪs/ *n* dispositivo *m*; leave somebody to his own ~s lasciare qualcuno per conto suo

devil /ˈdevl/ *n* diavolo *m*

devilish /ˈdev(ə)lɪʃ/ *adj* diabolico

devilishly /ˈdev(ə)lɪʃlɪ/ *adv* fig fam terribilmente

devil-may-care *adj* menefreghista

devilment /ˈdev(ə)lmənt/ *n* Br cattiveria *f*

devil's advocate *n* avvocato *m* del diavolo

devil worship *n* culto *m* satanico

devious /ˈdiːvɪəs/ *adj* ⟨*person*⟩ subdolo; ⟨*route*⟩ tortuoso

deviously /ˈdiːvɪəslɪ/ *adv* subdolamente

devise /dɪˈvaɪz/ *vt* escogitare

devoid /dɪˈvɔɪd/ *adj* ~ of privo di

devolution /diːvəˈluːʃn/ *n* (of power) decentramento *m*

devote /dɪˈvəʊt/ *vt* dedicare

devoted /dɪˈvəʊtɪd/ *adj* ⟨*daughter etc*⟩ affezionato; be ~ to something consacrarsi a qualcosa

devotedly /dɪˈvəʊtɪdlɪ/ *adv* con dedizione

devotee /devəˈtiː/ *n* appassionato, -a *mf*

devotion /dɪˈvəʊʃn/ *n* dedizione *f*; ~s *pl* Relig devozione *fsg*

devour /dɪˈvaʊə(r)/ *vt* divorare

devout /dɪˈvaʊt/ *adj* devoto

devoutly /dɪˈvaʊtlɪ/ *adv* Relig devotamente; (sincerely) fervidamente

dew /djuː/ *n* rugiada *f*

dewy /ˈdjuːɪ/ *adj* rugiadoso

dewy-eyed /-ˈaɪd/ *adj* (moved) con gli occhi lucidi; (naive) ingenuo

dexterity /dekˈsterətɪ/ *n* destrezza *f*

dexterous /ˈdekstrəs/ *adj* ⟨*person, movement*⟩ agile, destro; ⟨*hand*⟩ abile; ⟨*mind*⟩ acuto

dexterously /ˈdekstrəslɪ/ *adv* ⟨*move*⟩ agilmente; ⟨*manage*⟩ abilmente

DfES *abbr* Br (**Department for Education and Skills**) ≈ Ministero *m* dell'Istruzione

dg *abbr* (**decigram**) dg *m*

diabetes /daɪəˈbiːtiːz/ *n* diabete *m*

diabetic /daɪəˈbetɪk/ *adj & n* diabetico, -a *mf*

diabolical /daɪəˈbɒlɪkl/ *adj* diabolico

diabolically /daɪəˈbɒlɪklɪ/ *adv* (wickedly) diabolicamente; (fam: badly) orribilmente

diacritic /daɪəˈkrɪtrɪk/ *adj* (accent, mark) diacritico

diaeresis /daɪˈerɪsɪs/ *n* dieresi *f inv*

diagnose /ˈdaɪəgnəʊz/ *vt* diagnosticare

diagnosis /daɪəgˈnəʊsɪs/ *n* (pl **-oses** /daɪəgˈnəʊsiːz/) diagnosi *f inv*

diagnostic /daɪəgˈnɒstɪk/ *adj* diagnostico

diagnostics /daɪəgˈnɒstɪks/ *n* Med diagnostica *f*

diagonal /daɪˈægənl/ *adj & n* diagonale *f*

diagonally /daɪˈægənlɪ/ *adv* diagonalmente

diagram /ˈdaɪəgræm/ *n* diagramma *m*

dial /ˈdaɪəl/ **1** *n* (of clock, machine) quadrante *m*; Teleph disco *m* combinatore
2 *vi* (pt/pp **dialled**) Teleph fare il numero; ~ direct chiamare in teleselezione
3 *vt* fare ⟨*number*⟩

dialect /ˈdaɪəlekt/ *n* dialetto *m*

dialectic /daɪəˈlektɪk/ **1** *n* dialettica *f*
2 *adj* dialettico

dialectics /daɪəˈlektɪks/ *n* dialettica *f*

dialling code /ˈdaɪəlɪŋ/ *n* prefisso *m*

dialling tone *n* segnale *m* di linea libera

dialogue /'daɪəlɒg/ n dialogo m

dialogue box n Comput finestra f di dialogo

dial tone n Am Teleph segnale m di linea libera

dial-up adj ‹connection, access› dial-up

dialysis /daɪ'ælɪsɪs/ n dialisi f

dialysis machine n rene m artificiale

diameter /daɪ'æmɪtə(r)/ n diametro m

diametrically /daɪə'metrɪklɪ/ adv ~ opposed diametralmente opposto

diamond /'daɪəmənd/ n diamante m, brillante m; (shape) losanga f; ~s pl (in cards) quadri mpl

diamond jubilee n sessantesimo anniversario m

diamond-shaped adj romboidale

diamond wedding [anniversary] n nozze fpl di diamante

diaper /'daɪəpə(r)/ n Am pannolino m

diaphanous /daɪ'æfənəs/ adj diafano

diaphragm /'daɪəfræm/ n diaframma m

diarist /'daɪərɪst/ n (author) diarista mf; (journalist) giornalista mf di piccola cronaca

diarrhoea /daɪə'riːə/ n diarrea f

diary /'daɪərɪ/ n (for appointments) agenda f; (for writing in) diario m

diatribe /'daɪətraɪb/ n diatriba f

dice /daɪs/ ① n inv dadi mpl ② vt Culin tagliare a dadini

dicey /'daɪsɪ/ adj fam rischioso

dichotomy /daɪ'kɒtəmɪ/ n dicotomia f

dicky /'dɪkɪ/ ① n (shirt front) pettino m, sparato m ② adj Br fam ‹heart› malandato

dictate /dɪk'teɪt/ vt/i dettare

dictation /dɪk'teɪʃn/ n dettato m

dictator /dɪk'teɪtə(r)/ n dittatore m

dictatorial /dɪktə'tɔːrɪəl/ adj dittatoriale

dictatorship /dɪk'teɪtəʃɪp/ n dittatura f

diction /'dɪkʃn/ n dizione f

dictionary /'dɪkʃənrɪ/ n dizionario m

dictum /'dɪktəm/ n (maxim) massima f; (statement) affermazione f

did /dɪd/ ▶ DO

didactic /dɪ'dæktɪk/ adj didattico

diddle /'dɪdl/ vt fam gabbare

didn't /'dɪdnt/ = DID NOT

die[1] /daɪ/ n Techn (metal mould) stampo m; (for cutting) matrice f

die[2] vi (pres p **dying**) morire (**of** di); **be dying to do something** fam morire dalla voglia di fare qualcosa; **be dying for a drink** fam morire dalla voglia di bere qualcosa
■ **die away** vi ‹noise, applause› smorzarsi
■ **die down** vi calmarsi; ‹fire, flames› spegnersi

■ **die off** vi morire uno dopo l'altro

■ **die out** vi estinguersi; ‹custom› morire

diehard /'daɪhɑːd/ n (Pol: in party) fanatico, -a mf; (stubborn person) ultraconservatore mf

diesel /'diːzl/ n diesel m

diesel engine n motore m diesel

diesel train n treno m con locomotiva diesel

diet /'daɪət/ ① n regime m alimentare; (restricted) dieta f; **be on a** ~ essere a dieta ② vi essere a dieta

dietary /'daɪətrɪ/ adj ‹habit› alimentare

dietary fibre n fibre fpl alimentari

dietary supplement n integratore m dietetico

dietician /daɪə'tɪʃn/ n dietologo, -a mf

differ /'dɪfə(r)/ vi differire; (disagree) non essere d'accordo

difference /'dɪfrəns/ n differenza f; (disagreement) divergenza f

different /'dɪfrənt/ adj diverso, differente; (various) diversi; **be** ~ **from** essere diverso da

differential /dɪfə'renʃl/ ① adj differenziale ② n differenziale m

differentiate /dɪfə'renʃɪeɪt/ vt distinguere (**between** fra); (discriminate) discriminare (**between** fra); (make different) differenziare

differentiation /dɪfərenʃɪ'eɪʃn/ n differenziazione f

differently /'dɪfrəntlɪ/ adv in modo diverso; ~ **from** diversamente da

difficult /'dɪfɪkəlt/ adj difficile

difficulty /'dɪfɪkəltɪ/ n difficoltà f inv; **with** ~ con difficoltà

diffidence /'dɪfɪdəns/ n mancanza f di sicurezza

diffident /'dɪfɪdənt/ adj senza fiducia in se stesso

diffidently /'dɪfɪdəntlɪ/ adv senza fiducia in se stesso

diffuse[1] /dɪ'fjuːs/ adj diffuso; (wordy) prolisso

diffuse[2] /dɪ'fjuːz/ vt Phys diffondere

diffuseness /dɪ'fjuːsnɪs/ n (of organization) estensione f; (of argument) prolissità f

dig /dɪg/ ① n (poke) spinta f; (remark) frecciata f; Archaeol scavo m; ~s pl fam camera fsg ammobiliata ② vt/i (pp/pp **dug**, pres p **digging**) scavare ‹hole›; vangare ‹garden›; (thrust) conficcare; ~ **somebody in the ribs** dare una gomitata a qualcuno
■ **dig out** vt fig tirar fuori
■ **dig up** vt scavare ‹garden, street, object›; sradicare ‹tree, plant›; (fig: find) scovare

digest[1] /'daɪdʒest/ n compendio m

digest² /daɪ'dʒest/ vt digerire

digestible /daɪ'dʒestəbl/ adj digeribile

digestion /daɪ'dʒestʃn/ n digestione f

digestive /daɪ'dʒestɪv/ adj digestivo

digestive [biscuit] n Br biscotto m di farina integrale

digestive system n apparato m digerente

digestive tract n apparato m digerente

digger /'dɪgə(r)/ n Techn scavatrice f

diggings /'dɪgɪŋz/ npl (in archaeology) scavi mpl

digicam /'dɪdʒɪkæm/ n fam fotocamera f digitale

digit /'dɪdʒɪt/ n cifra f; (finger) dito m

digital /'dɪdʒɪtl/ adj digitale

digital [television] n TV f digitale

digital audio tape n audiocassetta f digitale

digital camera n fotocamera f digitale

digital clock n orologio m digitale

digital computer n computer m digitale

digitalize /'dɪdʒɪtəlaɪz/ vt digitalizzare

digitizer /'dɪdʒɪtaɪzə(r)/ n Comput tavoletta f grafica

dignified /'dɪgnɪfaɪd/ adj dignitoso

dignify /'dɪgnɪfaɪ/ vt nobilitare ⟨occasion, building⟩

dignitary /'dɪgnɪtərɪ/ n dignitario m

dignity /'dɪgnətɪ/ n dignità f

digress /daɪ'gres/ vi divagare

digression /daɪ'greʃn/ n digressione f

dike /daɪk/ n diga f

dilapidated /dɪ'læpɪdeɪtɪd/ adj cadente

dilapidation /dɪlæpɪ'deɪʃn/ n rovina f

dilate /daɪ'leɪt/ ① vt dilatare
② vi dilatarsi

dilation /daɪ'leɪʃn/ n dilatazione f

dilatory /'dɪlətərɪ/ adj dilatorio

dilemma /dɪ'lemə/ n dilemma m

dilettante /dɪlɪ'tæntɪ/ n dilettante mf

diligence /'dɪlɪdʒəns/ n diligenza f

diligent /'dɪlɪdʒənt/ adj diligente

dill /dɪl/ n aneto m

dilly-dally /'dɪlɪdælɪ/ vi (pt/pp -ied) fam tentennare

dilute /daɪ'lju:t/ vt diluire

dilution /daɪ'lju:ʃn/ n also fig diluizione f

dim /dɪm/ ① adj (dimmer, dimmest) ⟨light⟩ debole; (dark) scuro; ⟨prospect, chance⟩ scarso; (indistinct) impreciso; (fam: stupid) tonto
② vt/i (pt/pp **dimmed**) affievolire

dime /daɪm/ n Am moneta f da dieci centesimi

dimension /daɪ'menʃn/ n dimensione f

dime store n Am grande magazzino m con prezzi molto bassi

diminish /dɪ'mɪnɪʃ/ vt/i diminuire

diminished /dɪ'mɪnɪʃt/ adj ridotto; Mus diminuito; **on grounds of ~ responsibility** Jur per seminfermità mentale

diminutive /dɪ'mɪnjʊtɪv/ adj & n diminutivo m

dimly /'dɪmlɪ/ adv ⟨see, remember⟩ indistintamente; ⟨shine⟩ debolmente

dimmer /'dɪmə(r)/ n interruttore m a reostato

dimple /'dɪmpl/ n fossetta f

dimwit /'dɪmwɪt/ n fam stupido m

dim-witted /-'wɪtɪd/ adj fam stupido

din /dɪn/ n baccano m
■ **din into** vt ~ **something into somebody** ficcare qualcosa in testa a qualcuno

dine /daɪn/ vi pranzare

diner /'daɪnə(r)/ n (Am: restaurant) tavola f calda; **the last ~ in the restaurant** l'ultimo cliente nel ristorante

dingdong /'dɪŋdɒŋ/ n dindon m

dingdong battle n Br battibecco m

dinghy /'dɪŋgɪ/ n dinghy m; (inflatable) canotto m pneumatico

dingy /'dɪndʒɪ/ adj (-ier, -iest) squallido e tetro

dining car n carrozza f ristorante

dining hall n refettorio m

dining room n sala f da pranzo

dining table n tavolo m da pranzo

dinky /'dɪŋkɪ/ adj Br fam carino

dinner /'dɪnə(r)/ n cena f; (at midday) pranzo m

dinner dance n cena f danzante

dinner fork n forchetta f

dinner hour n Br Sch pausa f del pranzo

dinner jacket n smoking m inv

dinner knife n coltello m

dinner money n Br Sch soldi mpl dati dai genitori agli scolari per il pranzo

dinner party n cena f (con invitati)

dinner plate n piatto m piano

dinner service, dinner set n servizio m da tavola

dinner time n (evening) ora f di cena; (midday) ora f di pranzo

dinnerware /'dɪnəweə(r)/ n Am servizio m da tavola

dinosaur /'daɪnəsɔ:(r)/ n dinosauro m

dint /dɪnt/ n **by ~ of** a forza di

diocese /'daɪəsɪs/ n diocesi f inv

diode /'daɪəʊd/ n diodo m

dioxide /daɪ'ɒksaɪd/ n biossido m

dip /dɪp/ ① n (in ground) inclinazione f; Culin salsina f; **go for a ~** andare a fare una nuotata

2 *vt* (pt/pp **dipped**) (in liquid) immergere; abbassare ⟨*head, headlights*⟩
3 *vi* ⟨*land*⟩ formare un avvallamento
■ **dip into** *vt* scorrere ⟨*book*⟩

diphtheria /dɪfˈθɪərɪə/ *n* difterite *f*

diphthong /ˈdɪfθɒŋ/ *n* dittongo *m*

diploma /dɪˈpləʊmə/ *n* diploma *m*

diplomacy /dɪˈpləʊməsɪ/ *n* diplomazia *f*

diplomat /ˈdɪpləmæt/ *n* diplomatico, -a *mf*

diplomatic /dɪpləˈmætɪk/ *adj* diplomatico

diplomatically /dɪpləˈmætɪklɪ/ *adv* con diplomazia

diplomatic bag *n* valigia *f* diplomatica

diplomatic immunity *n* immunità *f* diplomatica

dippy /ˈdɪpɪ/ *adj* (fam: crazy, weird) pazzo

dipstick /ˈdɪpstɪk/ *n* Auto astina *f* dell'olio

dire /ˈdaɪə(r)/ *adj* ⟨*situation, consequences*⟩ terribile

direct /daɪˈrekt/ **1** *adj* diretto
2 *adv* direttamente
3 *vt* (aim) rivolgere ⟨*attention, criticism*⟩; (control) dirigere; fare la regia di ⟨*film, play*⟩; ∼ **somebody** (show the way) indicare la strada a qualcuno; ∼ **somebody to do something** ordinare a qualcuno di fare qualcosa

direct access *n* Comput accesso *m* diretto

direct current *n* corrente *m* continua

direct debit *n* addebitamento *m* diretto

direct dialling *n* teleselezione *f*

direct hit *n* Mil colpo *m* diretto

direction /dɪˈrekʃn/ *n* direzione *f*; (of play, film) regia *f*; ∼**s** *pl* indicazioni *fpl*; ∼**s for use** istruzioni *fpl* per l'uso

directional /daɪˈrekʃənəl/ *adj* direzionale

directive /daɪˈrektɪv/ *n* direttiva *f*

direct line *n* linea *f* diretta

directly /daɪˈrektlɪ/ **1** *adv* direttamente; (at once) immediatamente
2 *conj* [non] appena

direct mail *n* mailing *m inv*

directness /daɪˈrektnɪs/ *n* (of person, attitude) franchezza *f*; (of play, work, writing) chiarezza *f*

direct object *n* complemento *m* oggetto

director /dɪˈrektə(r)/ *n* Comm direttore, -trice *mf*; (of play, film) regista *mf*

directorate /daɪˈrektərət/ *n* (board) consiglio *m* d'amministrazione

director general *n* presidente *mf*

Director of Public Prosecutions *n* Br ≈ Procuratore *m* della Repubblica

directorship /dɪˈrektəʃɪp/ *n* posto *m* di direttore

directory /dɪˈrektərɪ/ *n* elenco *m*; Teleph elenco *m* [telefonico]; (of streets) stradario *m*

directory assistance *n* Am servizio *m* informazioni abbonati

directory enquiries *npl* Br servizio *m* informazioni abbonati

direct rule *n* Pol sottomissione *f* al governo centrale

direct speech *n* discorso *m* diretto

direct transfer *n* trasferimento *m* automatico

dirt /dɜːt/ *n* sporco *m*; ∼ **cheap** fam ad [un] prezzo stracciato

dirtiness /ˈdɜːtɪnɪs/ *n* (of person etc) sporcizia *f*

dirt track *n* (road) strada *f* sterrata; Sport pista *f* sterrata

dirty /ˈdɜːtɪ/ **1** *adj* (-**ier**, -**iest**) sporco
2 *vt* sporcare

dirty bomb *n* bomba *f* sporca

dirty-minded /-ˈmaɪndɪd/ *adj* fissato sul sesso

dirty trick *n* brutto scherzo *m*

dirty tricks *npl* Pol faccende *fpl* sporche

dirty weekend *n* fam weekend *m inv* clandestino con l'amante

dirty word *n* parolaccia *f*

disability /dɪsəˈbɪlətɪ/ *n* infermità *f inv*

disable /dɪˈseɪbl/ *vt* (make useless) mettere fuori uso ⟨*machine*⟩; (in accident) rendere invalido; Comput disabilitare; **be** ∼**d by arthritis** essere menomato dall'artrite

disabled /dɪˈseɪbld/ *adj* invalido

disabled access *n* (to public building etc) accesso *m* per gli invalidi

disabled driver *n* guidatore, -trice *mf* invalido, -a

disabled person *n* invalido, -a *mf*

disabuse /dɪsəˈbjuːz/ *vt* disingannare

disadvantage /dɪsədˈvɑːntɪdʒ/ *n* svantaggio *m*; **at a** ∼ in una posizione di svantaggio

disadvantaged /dɪsədˈvɑːntɪdʒd/ *adj* svantaggiato

disadvantageous /dɪsædvənˈteɪdʒəs/ *adj* svantaggioso

disaffected /dɪsəˈfektɪd/ *adj* disilluso

disagree /dɪsəˈgriː/ *vi* non essere d'accordo; ∼ **with** ⟨*food*⟩ far male a

disagreeable /dɪsəˈgriːəbl/ *adj* sgradevole

disagreement /dɪsəˈgriːmənt/ *n* disaccordo *m*; (quarrel) dissidio *m*

disallow /dɪsəˈlaʊ/ *vt* respingere; Sport annullare

disappear /dɪsəˈpɪə(r)/ *vi* scomparire

disappearance /dɪsə'pɪərəns/ *n* scomparsa *f*

disappoint /dɪsə'pɔɪnt/ *vt* deludere

disappointed /dɪsə'pɔɪntɪd/ *adj* deluso; I am ~ in you mi hai deluso

disappointing /dɪsə'pɔɪntɪŋ/ *adj* deludente

disappointment /dɪsə'pɔɪntmənt/ *n* delusione *f*

disapproval /dɪsə'pruːvəl/ *n* disapprovazione *f*

disapprove /dɪsə'pruːv/ *vi* disapprovare; ~ of somebody/something disapprovare qualcuno/qcsa

disapproving /dɪsə'pruːvɪŋ/ *adj* ⟨look, gesture⟩ di disapprovazione

disarm /dɪs'ɑːm/ ① *vt* disarmare ② *vi* Mil disarmarsi

disarmament /dɪs'ɑːməmənt/ *n* disarmo *m*

disarming /dɪs'ɑːmɪŋ/ *adj* ⟨frankness etc⟩ disarmante

disarrange /dɪsə'reɪndʒ/ *vt* scompigliare

disarray /dɪsə'reɪ/ *n* in ~ in disordine

disaster /dɪ'zɑːstə(r)/ *n* disastro *m*

disaster area *n* zona *f* disastrata; (fig: person) disastro *m*

disaster fund *n* fondi *mpl* a favore dei disastrati

disaster movie *n* film *m* *inv* catastrofico

disaster relief *n* soccorso *m* disastri

disaster victim *n* disastrato, -a *mf*

disastrous /dɪ'zɑːstrəs/ *adj* disastroso

disastrously /dɪ'zɑːstrəslɪ/ *adv* ⟨fail⟩ disastrosamente; ⟨end, turn out⟩ in modo catastrofico; go ~ wrong essere un disastro

disband /dɪs'bænd/ ① *vt* sciogliere; smobilitare ⟨troops⟩ ② *vi* sciogliersi; ⟨regiment⟩ essere smobilitato

disbelief /dɪsbɪ'liːf/ *n* incredulità *f*; in ~ con incredulità

disbelieve /dɪsbɪ'liːv/ *vt* non credere

disc /dɪsk/ *n* disco *m*; (CD) compact disc *m* *inv*

discard /dɪ'skɑːd/ *vt* scartare; (throw away) eliminare; scaricare ⟨boyfriend⟩

disc brakes *npl* Auto freni *mpl* a disco

discern /dɪ'sɜːn/ *vt* discernere

discernible /dɪ'sɜːnəbl/ *adj* discernibile

discerning /dɪ'sɜːnɪŋ/ *adj* perspicace

discharge[1] /'dɪstʃɑːdʒ/ *n* Electr scarica *f*; (dismissal) licenziamento *m*; Mil congedo *m*; (Med: of blood) emissione *f*; (of cargo) scarico *m*

discharge[2] /dɪs'tʃɑːdʒ/ ① *vt* scaricare ⟨battery, cargo⟩; (dismiss) licenziare; Mil

congedare; Jur assolvere ⟨accused⟩; dimettere ⟨patient⟩; ~ one's duty esaurire il proprio compito ② *vi* Electr scaricarsi

disciple /dɪ'saɪpl/ *n* discepolo *m*

disciplinarian /dɪsɪplɪ'neərɪən/ *n* persona *f* autoritaria

disciplinary /'dɪsɪplɪnərɪ/ *adj* disciplinare

discipline /'dɪsɪplɪn/ ① *n* disciplina *f* ② *vt* disciplinare; (punish) punire

disciplined /'dɪsɪplɪnd/ *adj* ⟨person, approach⟩ sistematico

disc jockey *n* disc jockey *m* *inv*

disclaim /dɪs'kleɪm/ *vt* negare

disclaimer /dɪs'kleɪmə(r)/ *n* rifiuto *m*

disclose /dɪs'kləʊz/ *vt* svelare

disclosure /dɪs'kləʊʒə(r)/ *n* rivelazione *f*

disco /'dɪskəʊ/ *n* discoteca *f*

discoloration /dɪskʌlə'reɪʃn/ *n* (process) scoloramento *m*; (spot) macchia *f* scolorita

discolour /dɪs'kʌlə(r)/ ① *vt* scolorire ② *vi* scolorirsi

discomfort /dɪs'kʌmfət/ *n* scomodità *f*; fig disagio *m*

disconcert /dɪskən'sɜːt/ *vt* sconcertare

disconcerting /dɪskən'sɜːtɪŋ/ *adj* sconcertante

disconnect /dɪskə'nekt/ *vt* disconnettere

disconsolate /dɪs'kɒnsələt/ *adj* sconsolato

discontent /dɪskən'tent/ *n* scontentezza *f*

discontented /dɪskən'tentɪd/ *adj* scontento

discontinue /dɪskən'tɪnjuː/ *vt* cessare, smettere; Comm sospendere la produzione di; ~d line fine *f* serie

discontinuity /dɪskɒntɪ'njuːɪtɪ/ *n* discontinuità *f*

discord /'dɪskɔːd/ *n* discordia *f*; Mus dissonanza *f*

discordant /dɪ'skɔːdənt/ *adj* ~ note nota *f* discordante

discothèque /'dɪskətek/ *n* discoteca *f*

discount[1] /'dɪskaʊnt/ *n* sconto *m*

discount[2] /dɪs'kaʊnt/ *vt* (not believe) non credere a; (leave out of consideration) non tener conto di

discount card *n* tessera *f* di sconto

discount flight *n* volo *m* a prezzo ridotto

discount store *n* discount *m* *inv*

discourage /dɪs'kʌrɪdʒ/ *vt* scoraggiare; (dissuade) dissuadere

discouragement /dɪs'kʌrɪdʒmənt/ *n* (despondency) scoraggiamento *m*; (disincentive) disincentivo *m*

discourse /'dɪskɔːs/ n discorso m
discourteous /dɪs'kɜːtɪəs/ adj scortese
discourteously /dɪs'kɜːtɪəslɪ/ adv
scortesemente
discover /dɪ'skʌvə(r)/ vt scoprire
discovery /dɪs'kʌvərɪ/ n scoperta f
discredit /dɪs'kredɪt/ ①n discredito m
②vt screditare
discreet /dɪ'skriːt/ adj discreto
discreetly /dɪ'skriːtlɪ/ adv
discretamente
discrepancy /dɪ'skrepənsɪ/ n
discrepanza f
discretion /dɪ'skreʃn/ n discrezione f
discriminate /dɪ'skrɪmɪneɪt/ vi
discriminare (**against** contro); ~ **between**
distinguere tra
discriminating /dɪ'skrɪmɪneɪtɪŋ/ adj
esigente
discrimination /dɪskrɪmɪ'neɪʃn/ n
discriminazione f; (quality) discernimento
m
discriminatory /dɪs'krɪmɪnətərɪ/ adj
discriminatorio, discriminativo
discus /'dɪskəs/ n disco m
discuss /dɪ'skʌs/ vt discutere; (examine
critically) esaminare
discussion /dɪ'skʌʃn/ n discussione f
discussion document,
discussion paper n documento m in
abbozzo
disdain /dɪs'deɪn/ ①n sdegno f
②vt sdegnare
disdainful /dɪs'deɪnfʊl/ adj sdegnoso
disease /dɪ'ziːz/ n malattia f
diseased /dɪ'ziːzd/ adj malato
disembark /dɪsem'bɑːk/ vi sbarcare
disembodied /dɪsem'bɒdɪd/ adj ⟨voices⟩
evanescente; ⟨head⟩ senza corpo; ⟨soul⟩
disincarnato
disenchant /dɪsen'tʃɑːnt/ vt
disincantare
disenchanted /dɪsen'tʃɑːntɪd/ adj
disincantato
disenchantment /dɪsen'tʃɑːntmənt/ n
disincanto m
disenfranchise /dɪsen'fræntʃaɪz/ vt
privare del diritto di voto
disengage /dɪsen'geɪdʒ/ vt
disimpegnare; disinnestare ⟨clutch⟩
disentangle /dɪsen'tæŋgəl/ vt
districare
disfavour /dɪs'feɪvə(r)/ n sfavore m; **fall
into** ~ perdere il favore
disfigure /dɪs'fɪgə(r)/ vt deformare
disgorge /dɪs'gɔːdʒ/ vt rigettare
disgrace /dɪz'greɪs/ ①n vergogna f; **fail
into** ~ cadere in disgrazia; **I am in** ~ sono
caduto in disgrazia; **it's a** ~ è una
vergogna

②vt disonorare
disgraceful /dɪz'greɪsfʊl/ adj
vergognoso
disgruntled /dɪs'grʌntld/ adj
malcontento
disguise /dɪs'gaɪz/ ①n travestimento
m; **in** ~ travestito
②vt contraffare ⟨voice⟩; dissimulare
⟨emotions⟩; ~**d as** travestito da
disgust /dɪs'gʌst/ ①n disgusto m: **in** ~
con aria disgustata
②vt disgustare
disgusting /dɪs'gʌstɪŋ/ adj disgustoso
dish /dɪʃ/ n piatto m; **do the** ~**es** lavare i
piatti
■ **dish out** vt (serve) servire; (distribute)
distribuire
■ **dish up** vt servire
dishcloth /'dɪʃklɒθ/ n strofinaccio m
dishearten /dɪs'hɑːt(ə)n/ vt scoraggiare
disheartening /dɪs'hɑːt(ə)nɪŋ/ adj
scoraggiante
dishevelled /dɪ'ʃevld/ adj scompigliato
dishonest /dɪs'ɒnɪst/ adj disonesto
dishonestly /dɪs'ɒnɪstlɪ/ adv
disonestamente
dishonesty /dɪs'ɒnɪstɪ/ n disonestà f
dishonour /dɪs'ɒnə(r)/ ①n disonore m
②vt disonorare ⟨family⟩; non onorare
⟨cheque⟩
dishonourable /dɪs'ɒnərəbl/ adj
disonorevole
dishonourably /dɪs'ɒnərəblɪ/ adv in
modo disonorevole
dishtowel n strofinaccio m per i piatti
dishwasher /'dɪʃwɒʃə(r)/ n lavapiatti f
inv
dishwasher-safe adj lavabile in
lavastoviglie
dishy /'dɪʃɪ/ adj (**-ier**, **est**) Br fam ⟨man,
woman⟩ fico, figo
disillusion /dɪsɪ'luːʒn/ vt disilludere
disillusioned /dɪsɪ'luːʒnd/ adj deluso
(**with** di)
disillusionment /dɪsɪ'luːʒnmənt/ n
disillusione f
disincentive /dɪsɪn'sentɪv/ n
disincentivo m
disinclined /dɪsɪn'klaɪnd/ adj riluttante
disinfect /dɪsɪn'fekt/ vt disinfettare
disinfectant /dɪsɪn'fektənt/ n
disinfettante m
disingenuous /dɪsɪn'dʒenjʊəs/ adj
⟨comment⟩ insincero; ⟨smile⟩ falso
disinherit /dɪsɪn'herɪt/ vt diseredare
disintegrate /dɪs'ɪntəgreɪt/ vi
disintegrarsi
disintegration /dɪsɪntɪ'greɪʃn/ n
disgregazione f

disinterested /dɪs'ɪntərestɪd/ *adj*
disinteressato

disjointed /dɪs'dʒɔɪntɪd/ *adj* sconnesso

disk /dɪsk/ *n* Comput disco *m*; (diskette)
dischetto *m*

disk drive *n* lettore *m* [di disco]

disk operating system
/'dɪskɒpəreɪtɪŋ/ *n* sistema *m* operativo su
disco

dislike /dɪs'laɪk/ ① *n* avversione *f*; **your
likes and** ∼**s** i tuoi gusti
② *vt* I ∼ **him/it** non mi piace; **I don't** ∼
him/it non mi dispiace

dislocate /'dɪsləkeɪt/ *vt* slogare; ∼ **one's
shoulder** slogarsi una spalla

dislocation /dɪslə'keɪʃn/ *n* (of hip, knee)
lussazione *f*

dislodge /dɪs'lɒdʒ/ *vt* sloggiare

disloyal /dɪs'lɔɪəl/ *adj* sleale

disloyally /dɪs'lɔɪəlɪ/ *adv* slealmente

disloyalty /dɪs'lɔɪəltɪ/ *n* slealtà *f*

dismal /'dɪzməl/ *adj* ⟨person⟩
abbacchiato; ⟨news, weather⟩ deprimente;
⟨performance⟩ mediocre

dismantle /dɪs'mæntl/ *vt* smontare
⟨tent, machine⟩; fig smantellare

dismay /dɪs'meɪ/ *n* sgomento *m*; **much to
my** ∼ con mio grande sgomento

dismayed /dɪs'meɪd/ *adj* sgomento

dismember /dɪs'membə(r)/ *vt* also fig
smembrare

dismiss /dɪs'mɪs/ *vt* licenziare
⟨employee⟩; (reject) scartare ⟨idea,
suggestion⟩

dismissal /dɪs'mɪsəl/ *n* licenziamento *m*

dismissive /dɪs'mɪsɪv/ *adj* ⟨person,
attitude⟩ sprezzante; **be** ∼ **of** essere
sprezzante verso

dismount /dɪs'maʊnt/ *vi* smontare

disobedience /dɪsə'biːdɪəns/ *n*
disubbidienza *f*

disobedient /dɪsə'biːdɪənt/ *adj*
disubbidiente

disobey /dɪsə'beɪ/ ① *vt* disubbidire a
⟨rule⟩
② *vi* disubbidire

disorder /dɪs'ɔːdə(r)/ *n* disordine *m*; Med
disturbo *m*

disordered /dɪs'ɔːdəd/ *adj* ⟨life⟩
disordinato; ⟨mind⟩ disturbato

disorderly /dɪs'ɔːdəlɪ/ *adj* disordinato;
⟨crowd⟩ turbolento; ∼ **conduct**
turbamento *m* della quiete pubblica

disorganization /dɪsɔːgənaɪ'zeɪʃn/ *n*
disorganizzazione *f*

disorganized /dɪs'ɔːgənaɪzd/ *adj*
disorganizzato

disorientate /dɪs'ɔːrɪənteɪt/ *vt*
disorientare

disorientation /dɪsɔːrɪen'teɪʃn/ *n*
disorientamento *m*

disown /dɪs'əʊn/ *vt* disconoscere; **I'll** ∼
you fam faccio finta di non conoscerti

disparaging /dɪ'spærɪdʒɪŋ/ *adj*
sprezzante

disparagingly /dɪ'spærɪdʒɪŋlɪ/ *adv*
sprezzantemente

disparate /'dɪspərət/ *adj* (different)
eterogeneo; ⟨incompatible⟩ disparato

disparity /dɪ'spærətɪ/ *n* disparità *f inv*

dispassionate /dɪ'spæʃənət/ *adj*
spassionato

dispassionately /dɪs'pæʃənətlɪ/ *adv*
spassionatamente

dispatch /dɪ'spætʃ/ ① *n* Comm
spedizione *f*; (Mil, report) dispaccio *m*; **with**
∼ con prontezza
② *vt* spedire; (kill) spedire al creatore

Dispatch Box *n* Br Pol postazione *f* da
cui parlano i ministri nel Parlamento
britannico

dispatch box *n* valigia *f* diplomatica

dispatch rider *n* staffetta *f*

dispel /dɪ'spel/ *vt* (pt/pp **dispelled**)
dissipare

dispensable /dɪ'spensəbl/ *adj*
dispensabile

dispensary /dɪ'spensərɪ/ *n* farmacia *f*

dispense /dɪ'spens/ *vt* distribuire; ∼
with fare a meno di

dispenser /dɪ'spensə(r)/ *n* (device)
distributore *m*

dispensing chemist /dɪ'spensɪŋ/ *n*
farmacista *mf*; (shop) farmacia *f*

dispensing optician *n* Br ottico *m*

dispersal /dɪ'spɜːsl/ *n* dispersione *f*

disperse /dɪ'spɜːs/ ① *vt* disperdere
② *vi* disperdersi

dispersion /dɪ'spɜːʃn/ *n* dispersione *f*

dispirited /dɪ'spɪrɪtɪd/ *adj* scoraggiato

displace /dɪs'pleɪs/ *vt* spostare

displaced person *n* profugo, -a *mf*

displacement /dɪs'pleɪsmənt/ *n*
spostamento *m*

display /dɪ'spleɪ/ ① *n* mostra *f*; Comm
esposizione *f*; (of feelings) manifestazione *f*;
pej ostentazione *f*; Comput display *m inv*
② *vt* mostrare; esporre ⟨goods⟩;
manifestare ⟨feelings⟩; Comput visualizzare

display advertisement *n* annuncio
m pubblicitario di grande formato

display cabinet, **display case** *n*
vetrina *f*

display rack *n* espositore *m*

display window *n* vetrina *f*

displease /dɪs'pliːz/ *vt* non piacere a; **be**
∼**d with** essere scontento di

displeasure /dɪs'pleʒə(r)/ *n* malcontento *m*; **incur sb's** ~ scontentare qualcuno

disposable /dɪ'spəʊzəbl/ *adj* (throwaway) usa e getta; ⟨*income*⟩ disponibile

disposal /dɪ'spəʊzl/ *n* (getting rid of) eliminazione *f*; **be at sb's** ~ essere a disposizione di qualcuno

dispose /dɪ'spəʊz/ *vi* ~ **of** (get rid of) disfarsi di; **be well** ~**d** essere ben disposto (**to** verso)

disposition /dɪspə'zɪʃn/ *n* disposizione *f*; (nature) indole *f*

dispossessed /dɪspə'zest/ *adj* ⟨*family*⟩ spossessato; ⟨*son*⟩ diseredato

disproportionate /dɪsprə'pɔːʃənət/ *adj* sproporzionato

disproportionately /dɪsprə'pɔːʃənətlɪ/ *adv* in modo sproporzionato

disprove /dɪs'pruːv/ *vt* confutare

dispute /dɪ'spjuːt/ ◻1 *n* disputa *f*; (industrial) contestazione *f* ◻2 *vt* contestare ⟨*statement*⟩

disqualification /dɪskwɒlɪfɪ'keɪʃn/ *n* squalifica *f*; (from driving) ritiro *m* della patente

disqualify /dɪs'kwɒlɪfaɪ/ *vt* escludere; Sport squalificare; ~ **somebody from driving** ritirare la patente a qualcuno

disquiet /dɪs'kwaɪət/ *n* inquietudine *f*

disquieting /dɪs'kwaɪətɪŋ/ *adj* allarmante

disregard /dɪsrɪ'gɑːd/ ◻1 *n* mancanza *f* di considerazione ◻2 *vt* ignorare

disrepair /dɪsrɪ'peə(r)/ *n* **fall into** ~ deteriorarsɪ; **in a state of** ~ in cattivo stato

disreputable /dɪs'repjʊtəbl/ *adj* malfamato

disrepute /dɪsrɪ'pjuːt/ *n* discredito *m*; **bring somebody into** ~ rovinare la reputazione a qualcuno

disrespect /dɪsrɪ'spekt/ *n* mancanza *f* di rispetto

disrespectful /dɪsrɪ'spektfʊl/ *adj* irrispettoso

disrespectfully /dɪsrɪ'spektfʊlɪ/ *adv* irrispettosamente

disrupt /dɪs'rʌpt/ *vt* creare scompiglio in; sconvolgere ⟨*plans*⟩

disruption /dɪs'rʌpʃn/ *n* scompiglio *m*; (of plans) sconvolgimento *m*

disruptive /dɪs'rʌptɪv/ *adj* ⟨*person, behaviour*⟩ indisciplinato

dissatisfaction /dɪ(s)sætɪs'fækʃn/ *n* malcontento *m*

dissatisfied /dɪ(s)'sætɪsfaɪd/ *adj* scontento

dissect /dɪ'sekt/ *vt* sezionare

dissection /dɪ'sekʃn/ *n* dissezione *f*

disseminate /dɪ'semɪneɪt/ *vt* divulgare

dissemination /dɪsemɪ'neɪʃn/ *n* divulgazione *f*

dissension /dɪ'senʃn/ *n* (discord) dissenso *m*

dissent /dɪ'sent/ ◻1 *n* dissenso *m* ◻2 *vi* dissentire

dissertation /dɪsə'teɪʃn/ *n* tesi *f inv*

disservice /dɪ(s)'sɜːvɪs/ *n* **do somebody/oneself a** ~ rendere un cattivo servizio a qualcuno/se stesso

dissidence /'dɪsɪdəns/ *n* dissidenza *f*

dissident /'dɪsɪdənt/ *n* dissidente *mf*

dissimilar /dɪ(s)'sɪmɪlə(r)/ *adj* dissimile (**to** da)

dissimilarity /dɪs(s)ɪmɪ'lærətɪ/ *n* diversità *f inv*

dissipate /'dɪsɪpeɪt/ *vt* dissipare ⟨*hope, enthusiasm*⟩

dissipated /'dɪsɪpeɪtɪd/ *adj* dissipato

dissipation *n* dissipatezza *f*, sregolatezza *f*

dissociate /dɪ'səʊʃɪeɪt/ *vt* dissociare; ~ **oneself from** dissociarsi da

dissolute /'dɪsəluːt/ *adj* dissoluto

dissolution /dɪsə'luːʃn/ *n* scioglimento *m*

dissolve /dɪ'zɒlv/ ◻1 *vt* dissolvere ◻2 *vi* dissolversi

dissonance /'dɪsənəns/ *n* dissonanza *f*

dissonant /'dɪsənənt/ *adj* Mus dissonante

dissuade /dɪ'sweɪd/ *vt* dissuadere

distance /'dɪstəns/ *n* distanza *f*; **it's a short** ~ **from here to the station** la stazione non è lontana da qui; **in the** ~ in lontananza; **from a** ~ da lontano

distance learning *n* corsi *mpl* di studio a distanza

distant /'dɪstənt/ *adj* distante; ⟨*relative*⟩ lontano

distantly /'dɪstəntlɪ/ *adv* ⟨*reply*⟩ con distacco

distaste /dɪs'teɪst/ *n* avversione *f*

distasteful /dɪs'teɪstfʊl/ *adj* spiacevole

distemper /dɪ'stempə(r)/ *n* (paint) tempera *f*; (in horses, dogs) cimurro *m*

distend /dɪ'stend/ *vi* dilatarsi

distil /dɪ'stɪl/ *vt* (pt/pp **distilled**) distillare

distillation /dɪstɪ'leɪʃn/ *n* distillazione *f*

distillery /dɪ'stɪlərɪ/ *n* distilleria *f*

distinct /dɪ'stɪŋkt/ *adj* chiaro; (different) distinto

distinction /dɪ'stɪŋkʃn/ *n* distinzione *f*; Sch massimo *m* dei voti

distinctive /dɪ'stɪŋktɪv/ *adj* caratteristico

distinctly /dɪ'stɪŋktlɪ/ *adv* chiaramente

distinguish /dɪ'stɪŋgwɪʃ/ *vt/i* distinguere; ~ **oneself** distinguersi

distinguishable /dɪ'stɪŋgwɪʃəbl/ *adj* distinguibile

distinguished /dɪ'stɪŋgwɪʃt/ *adj* rinomato; ⟨*appearance*⟩ distinto; ⟨*career*⟩ brillante

distinguishing /dɪ'stɪŋgwɪʃɪŋ/ *adj* ⟨*feature*⟩ distintivo

distort /dɪ'stɔːt/ *vt* distorcere

distortion /dɪ'stɔːʃn/ *n* distorsione *f*

distract /dɪ'strækt/ *vt* distrarre

distracted /dɪ'stræktɪd/ *adj* assente; (fam: worried) preoccupato

distracting /dɪ'stræktɪŋ/ *adj* che distrae; **I found the noise too** ~ il rumore mi disturbava troppo

distraction /dɪ'strækʃn/ *n* distrazione *f*; (despair) disperazione *f*; **drive somebody to** ~ portare qualcuno alla disperazione

distraught /dɪ'strɔːt/ *adj* sconvolto

distress /dɪ'stres/ ① *n* angoscia *f*; (pain) sofferenza *f*; (danger) difficoltà *f* ② *vt* sconvolgere; (sadden) affliggere

distressed /dɪ'strest/ *adj* (upset) turbato; (stronger) afflitto

distressing /dɪ'stresɪŋ/ *adj* penoso; (shocking) sconvolgente

distress signal *n* segnale *m* di richiesta di soccorso

distribute /dɪ'strɪbjuːt/ *vt* distribuire

distribution /dɪstrɪ'bjuːʃn/ *n* distribuzione *f*

distribution network *n* rete *f* di distribuzione

distributor /dɪ'strɪbjʊtə(r)/ *n* distributore *m*

district /'dɪstrɪkt/ *n* regione *f*; Admin distretto *m*

district attorney *n* Am procuratore. *m* distrettuale

district council *n* Br consiglio *m* distrettuale

district court *n* Am corte *f* distrettuale federale

district manager *n* direttore, -trice *mf* di zona

district nurse *n* infermiere, -a *mf* che fa visite a domicilio

distrust /dɪs'trʌst/ ① *n* sfiducia *f* ② *vt* non fidarsi di

distrustful /dɪs'trʌstfʊl/ *adj* diffidente

disturb /dɪ'stɜːb/ *vt* disturbare; (emotionally) turbare; spostare ⟨*papers*⟩

disturbance /dɪ'stɜːbəns/ *n* disturbo *m*; ~**s** *pl* (rioting etc) disordini *mpl*

disturbed /dɪ'stɜːbd/ *adj* turbato; [mentally] ~ malato di mente

disturbing /dɪ'stɜːbɪŋ/ *adj* inquietante

disuse /dɪs'juːs/ *n* **fall into** ~ cadere in disuso

disused /dɪs'juːzd/ *adj* non utilizzato

ditch /dɪtʃ/ ① *n* fosso *m* ② *vt* (fam: abandon) abbandonare ⟨*plan, car*⟩; piantare ⟨*lover*⟩

ditchwater /'dɪtʃwɔːtə(r)/ *n* **as dull as** ~ una barba

dither /'dɪðə(r)/ *vi* titubare

ditto /'dɪtəʊ/ *adv* idem; (in list) idem come sopra

ditto marks *npl* virgolette *fpl*

divan /dɪ'væn/ *n* divano *m*

dive /daɪv/ ① *n* tuffo *m*; Aeron picchiata *f*; (fam: place) bettola *f* ② *vi* tuffarsi; (when in water) immergersi; Aeron scendere in picchiata; (fam: rush) precipitarsi

dive-bomb *vt* Mil bombardare in picchiata

diver /'daɪvə(r)/ *n* (from board) tuffatore, -trice *mf*; (scuba) sommozzatore, -trice *mf*; (deep sea) palombaro *m*

diverge /daɪ'vɜːdʒ/ *vi* divergere

divergent /daɪ'vɜːdʒənt/ *adj* divergente

diverse /daɪ'vɜːs/ *adj* vario

diversify /daɪ'vɜːsɪfaɪ/ *vt/i* (pt/pp **-ied**) Comm diversificare

diversion /daɪ'vɜːʃn/ *n* deviazione *f*; (distraction) diversivo *m*

diversionary /daɪ'vɜːʃənərɪ/ *adj* ⟨*tactic, attack*⟩ diversivo

diversity /daɪ'vɜːsətɪ/ *n* varietà *f*

divert /daɪ'vɜːt/ *vt* deviare ⟨*traffic*⟩; distogliere ⟨*attention*⟩

divest /daɪ'vest/ *vt* privare (**of** di)

divide /dɪ'vaɪd/ ① *vt* dividere (**by** per); **six** ~**d by two** sei diviso due ② *vi* dividersi
■ **divide out** *vt* = DIVIDE
■ **divide up** *vt* = DIVIDE

dividend /'dɪvɪdend/ *n* dividendo *m*; **pay** ~**s** fig ripagare

divider /dɪ'vaɪdə(r)/ *n* (in room) divisorio *m*; (in file) cartoncino *m* separatore

dividers /dɪ'vaɪdəz/ *npl* compasso *m* a punte fisse

dividing /dɪ'vaɪdɪŋ/ *adj* ⟨*wall, fence*⟩ divisorio

dividing line *n* linea *f* di demarcazione

divine /dɪ'vaɪn/ *adj* divino

divinely /dɪ'vaɪnlɪ/ *adv* also fam divinamente

diving /'daɪvɪŋ/ *n* (from board) tuffi *mpl*; (scuba) immersione *f*

diving board *n* trampolino *m*

diving mask *n* maschera *f* [subacquea]

diving suit *n* muta *f*; (deep sea) scafandro *m*

divinity /dɪ'vɪnətɪ/ *n* divinità *f inv*; (subject) teologia *f*; (at school) religione *f*

divisible /dɪ'vɪzəbl/ *adj* divisibile (**by** per)

division /dɪ'vɪʒn/ *n* divisione *f*; (in sports league) serie *f*

divisional /dɪ'vɪʃənəl/ *adj* ‹*commander, officer*› di divisione

divisive /dɪ'vaɪsɪv/ *adj* ‹*policy*› che crea discordia; **be socially** ∼ creare delle divisioni sociali

divorce /dɪ'vɔːs/ ① *n* divorzio *m* ② *vt* divorziare da

divorced /dɪ'vɔːst/ *adj* divorziato; **get** ∼ divorziare

divorcee /dɪvɔː'siː/ *n* divorziato, -a *mf*

divulge /daɪ'vʌldʒ/ *vt* rendere pubblico
∎ **divvy up** *vt fam* = DIVIDE up

DIY *abbr* **do-it-yourself**

dizziness /'dɪzɪnɪs/ *n* giramenti *mpl* di testa

dizzy /'dɪzɪ/ *adj* (**-ier, -iest**) vertiginoso; **I feel** ∼ mi gira la testa

DJ *n abbr* (**disc jockey**) DJ *m inv*; Br *abbr* (**dinner jacket**) smoking *m inv*

Djibouti /dʒɪ'buːtɪ/ *n* Gibuti *f*

DNA ① *n abbr* (**deoxyribonucleic acid**) DNA *m inv* ② *attrib* ‹*testing*› del DNA

DNR *abbr* Am (**Department of Natural Resources**) ≈ Ministero *m* dell'Ambiente e della Tutela del Territorio; (**do not resuscitate**) non rianimare

do /duː/ ① *n* (pl **dos** or **do's**) fam festa *f* ② *vt* (3 sg pres tense **does**; pt **did**; pp **done**) fare; (fam: cheat) fregare; **do somebody out of something** (money) fregare qualcuno a qualcuno; (opportunity) defraudare qualcuno di qualcosa; **be done** Culin essere cotto; **well done** bravo; Culin ben cotto; **do the flowers** sistemare i fiori; **do the washing up** lavare i piatti; **do one's hair** farsi i capelli ③ *vi* (be suitable) andare; (be enough) bastare; **this will do** questo va bene; **that will do!** basta così!; **do well/badly** cavarsela bene/male; **how is he doing?** come sta? ④ *v aux* **do you speak Italian?** parli italiano?; **you don't like him, do you?** non ti piace, vero?; (expressing astonishment) non dirmi che ti piace!; **yes, I do** sì; (emphatic) invece sì; **no, I don't** no; **I don't smoke** non fumo; **don't you/doesn't he?** vero?; **so do I** anch'io; **do come in, John** entra, John; **how do you do?** piacere
∎ **do away with** *vt* abolire ‹*rule*›
∎ **do for** *vt* (ruin) rovinare
∎ **do in** *vt* (fam: kill) uccidere; farsi male a ‹*back*›; **done in** fam esausto
∎ **do up** *vt* (fasten) abbottonare; (renovate) rimettere a nuovo; (wrap) avvolgere

∎ **do with** *vt* **I could do with a spanner** mi ci vorrebbe una chiave inglese
∎ **do without** *vt* fare a meno di

d.o.b. *abbr* (**date of birth**) data *f* di nascita

docile /'dəʊsaɪl/ *adj* docile

dock¹ /dɒk/ *n* Jur banco *m* degli imputati

dock² ① *n* Naut bacino *m* ② *vi* entrare in porto; ‹*spaceship*› congiungersi

docker /'dɒkə(r)/ *n* portuale *m*

docket /'dɒkɪt/ ① *n* (Comm: label) etichetta *f*; (customs certificate) ricevuta *f* doganale ② *vt* Comm etichettare ‹*parcel, package*›

docking /'dɒkɪŋ/ *n* Naut ormeggio *m*; (of spaceshuttle) aggancio *m*

docks /dɒks/ *npl* porto *m*

dockworker /'dɒkwɜːkə(r)/ *n* portuale *m*

dockyard /'dɒkjɑːd/ *n* cantiere *m* navale

doctor /'dɒktə(r)/ ① *n* dottore *m*, dottoressa *f* ② *vt* alterare ‹*drink*›; castrare ‹*cat*›

doctorate /'dɒktərət/ *n* dottorato *m*

Doctor of Philosophy *n* titolare *mf* di un dottorato di ricerca

doctor's note /'dɒktəz/ *n* certificato *m* medico

doctrine /'dɒktrɪn/ *n* dottrina *f*

docudrama /'dɒkjʊdrɑːmə/ *n* film *m inv* verità

document /'dɒkjʊmənt/ *n* documento *m*

documentary /dɒkjʊ'mentərɪ/ *adj* & *n* documentario *m*

documentation /dɒkjʊmen'teɪʃn/ *n* documentazione *f*

document holder *n* (for keyboarder) leggio *m*

document wallet *n* (folder) cartellina *f*

doddery /'dɒdərɪ/ *adj fam* barcollante

doddle /'dɒd(ə)l/ *n* Br fam **it's a** ∼ è un gioco da ragazzi

dodge /dɒdʒ/ ① *n* fam trucco *m* ② *vt* schivare ‹*blow*›; evitare ‹*person*› ③ *vi* scansarsi; ∼ **out of the way** scansarsi

dodgems /'dɒdʒəmz/ *npl* autoscontro *msg*

dodgy /'dɒdʒɪ/ *adj* (**-ier, -iest**) (fam: dubious) sospetto

DOE *n* Br *abbr* (**Department of the Environment**) ministero *m* dell'Ambiente; Am *abbr* (**Department of Energy**) ≈ ministero *m* dell'Industria

doe /dəʊ/ *n* femmina *f* (di daino, renna, lepre); (rabbit) coniglia *f*

does /dʌz/ ▶ DO

doesn't /'dʌznt/ = DOES NOT

dog /dɒg/ ① *n* cane *m*

2 vt (pt/pp **dogged**) ⟨illness, bad luck⟩ perseguitare

dog biscuit n biscotto m per cani

dog breeder n allevatore, -trice mf di cani

dog collar n collare m (per cani); Relig fam collare m del prete

dog-eared /-ɪəd/ adj con le orecchie

dog-end n fam cicca f

dogfight n combattimento m di cani; Aeron combattimento m aereo

dogged /'dɒgɪd/ adj ostinato

doggedly /'dɒgɪdlɪ/ adv ostinatamente

doggy bag /'dɒgɪ/ n sacchetto m per portarsi a casa gli avanzi di un pasto al ristorante

doggy-paddle n fam nuoto m a cagnolino

dog handler n addestratore, -trice mf di cani

doghouse /'dɒghaʊs/ n Am canile m; **in the ~** Br & Am fam in disgrazia

dogma /'dɒgmə/ n dogma m

dogmatic /dɒg'mætɪk/ adj dogmatico

do-gooder /duː'gʊdə(r)/ n pej pseudo benefattore, -trice mf

dog-paddle n nuoto m a cagnolino

dogsbody n fam tirapiedi mf inv

dog tag n Am Mil fam piastrina f di riconoscimento

doh /dəʊ/ n Mus do m

doily /'dɔɪlɪ/ n centrino m

doing /'duːɪŋ/ n **it's none of my ~** non sono stato io; **this is her ~** questa è opera sua; **it takes some ~!** ce ne vuole!

do-it-yourself /duːɪtjə'self/ n fai da te m, bricolage m

do-it-yourself shop n negozio m di bricolage

doldrums /'dɒldrəmz/ npl **be in the ~** essere giù di corda; ⟨business⟩ essere in fase di stasi

dole /dəʊl/ n sussidio m di disoccupazione; **be on the ~** essere disoccupato

■ **dole out** vt distribuire

doleful /'dəʊlfl/ adj triste

dolefully /'dəʊlfʊlɪ/ adv tristemente

dole queue n Br coda f per riscuotere il sussidio di disoccupazione; (fig: number of unemployed) numero m dei disoccupati

doll /dɒl/ n bambola f

■ **doll up** vt fam **~ oneself up** mettersi in ghingheri

dollar /'dɒlə(r)/ n dollaro m

dollar bill n banconota f da un dollaro

dollar diplomacy n politica f di investimenti all'estero

dollar sign n simbolo m del dollaro

dollop /'dɒləp/ n fam cucchiaiata f

dolly /'dɒlɪ/ n (fam: doll) bambola f; Cinema, TV dolly m inv

Dolomites /'dɒləmaɪts/ npl Dolomiti mpl

dolphin /'dɒlfɪn/ n delfino m

domain /də'meɪn/ n dominio m

domain name n Comput nome m di dominio

dome /dəʊm/ n cupola f

domed /dəʊmd/ adj ⟨skyline, city⟩ ricco di cupole; ⟨roof, ceiling⟩ a cupola; ⟨forehead, helmet⟩ bombato

domestic /də'mestɪk/ adj domestico; Pol interno; Comm nazionale.

domestic animal n animale m domestico

domestic appliance n elettrodomestico m

domesticate /də'mestɪkeɪt/ vt addomesticare

domesticated /də'mestɪkeɪtɪd/ adj ⟨animal⟩ addomesticato

domestic flight n volo m nazionale

domestic help n collaboratore, -trice mf familiare

domesticity /dɒme'stɪsətɪ/ n ⟨home life⟩ vita f di famiglia; ⟨household duties⟩ faccende fpl domestiche

domestic servant n domestico, -a mf

domiciliary /dɒmɪ'sɪlɪərɪ/ adj ⟨visit, care⟩ a domicilio

dominance /'dɒmɪnəns/ n Biol, Zool dominanza f; (domination) predominio m; (numerical strength) preponderanza f

dominant /'dɒmɪnənt/ adj dominante

dominate /'dɒmɪneɪt/ vt/i dominare

domination /dɒmɪ'neɪʃn/ n dominio m

domineering /dɒmɪ'nɪərɪŋ/ adj autoritario

Dominica /də'mɪnɪkə/ n Dominica f

Dominican Republic /də'mɪnɪkən/ n Repubblica f Dominicana

dominion /də'mɪnjən/ n Br Pol dominio m inv

domino /'dɒmɪnəʊ/ n (pl **-es**) tessera f del domino; **~es** sg (game) domino m

don[1] /dɒn/ vt (pt/pp **donned**) liter indossare

don[2] n docente mf universitario, -a

donate /dəʊ'neɪt/ vt donare

donation /dəʊ'neɪʃn/ n donazione f

done /dʌn/ n ▶ DO

donkey /'dɒŋkɪ/ n asino m

donkey jacket n giacca f pesante

donkey's years fam **not for ~ ~** non da secoli

donkey-work n sgobbata f

donor /'dəʊnə(r)/ n donatore, -trice mf

donor card *n* tessera *f* del donatore di organi

don't /dəʊnt/ = DO NOT

doodle /'du:dl/ *vi* scarabocchiare

doom /du:m/ **①** *n* fato *m*; (ruin) rovina *f*
② *vt* be ~ed to failure essere destinato al fallimento

doomed /du:md/ *adj* ‹vessel› destinato ad affondare

doomsday /'du:mzdeɪ/ *n* giorno *m* del giudizio

doomwatch /'du:mwɒtʃ/ *n* catastrofismo *m*

door /dɔ:(r)/ *n* porta *f*; (of car) portiera *f*; out of ~s all'aperto

door bell *n* campanello *m*

doorman *n* portiere *m*

doormat *n* zerbino *m*

door plate *n* (of doctor etc) targa *f*

doorstep *n* gradino *m* della porta

doorstop *n* fermaporta *m inv*

door-to-door **①** *adj* ‹canvassing, selling› porta a porta
② *adv* ‹sell› porta a porta

doorway *n* vano *m* della porta

dope /dəʊp/ **①** *n* fam (drug) droga *f* leggera; (information) indiscrezioni *fpl*; (idiot) idiota *mf*
② *vt* drogare; Sport dopare

dope test *n* Sport antidoping *m inv*

dopey /'dəʊpɪ/ *adj* fam addormentato

dormant /'dɔ:mənt/ *adj* latente; ‹volcano› inattivo

dormer /'dɔ:mə(r)/ *n* ~ [window] abbaino *m*

dormitory /'dɔ:mɪtərɪ/ *n* dormitorio *m*

dormitory town *n* città *f inv* dormitorio

dormouse /'dɔ:maʊs/ *n* (pl **dormice** /'dɔ:maɪs/) ghiro *m*

dosage /'dəʊsɪdʒ/ *n* dosaggio *m*

dose /dəʊs/ *n* dose *f*

doss /dɒs/ *vi* sl accamparsi
■ **doss down** *vi* sistemarsi [a dormire]

dosser /'dɒsə(r)/ *n* barbone, -a *mf*

doss-house *n* dormitorio *m* pubblico

dot /dɒt/ *n* punto *m*; at 8 o'clock on the ~ alle 8 in punto

dotage /'dəʊtɪdʒ/ *n* be in one's ~ essere un vecchio rimbambito

dot-com /dɒt'kɒm/ **①** *adj* ‹company› che opera in Internet; ‹millionaire› arricchito grazie a Internet
② *n* azienda *f* che opera in Internet

dote /dəʊt/ *vi* ~ on stravedere per

dot matrix [printer] *n* stampante *f* a matrice di punti

dotted /'dɒtɪd/ *adj* ~ line linea *f* punteggiata; sign on the ~ line firmare

nell'apposito spazio; be ~ with essere punteggiato di

dotty /'dɒtɪ/ *adj* (-ier, -iest) fam tocco; ‹idea› folle

double /'dʌbl/ **①** *adj* doppio
② *adv* cost ~ costare il doppio; see ~ vedere doppio; ~ the amount la quantità doppia
③ *n* doppio *m*; (person) sosia *m inv*; ~s *pl* Tennis doppio *m*; at the ~ di corsa
④ *vt* raddoppiare; (fold) piegare in due
⑤ *vi* raddoppiare
■ **double back** *vi* (go back) fare dietro front
■ **double up** *vi* (bend over) piegarsi in due (with per); (share) dividere una stanza

double act *n* Theat, fig numero *m* eseguito da due attori

double-barrelled /-'bærəld/ *adj* ‹gun› a doppia canna

double-barrelled surname *n* cognome *m* doppio

double-bass *n* contrabbasso *m*

double bed *n* letto *m* matrimoniale

double bend *n* Auto doppia curva *f*

double bill *n* Theat rappresentazione *f* di due spettacoli

double bluff *n* atto *m* del dire la verità facendola sembrare una menzogna

double-book **①** *vi* ‹hotel, airline, company› fare prenotazioni doppie
② *vt* ~ a room/seat etc riservare la stessa camera/lo stesso posto a due persone

double-breasted *adj* a doppio petto

double-check **①** *vt/i* ricontrollare
② *n* double check ulteriore controllo *m*

double chin *n* doppio mento *m*

double-click *vi* Comput fare doppio click; ~ on fare doppio click su

double cream *n* Br ≈ panna *f* densa

double-cross *vt* ingannare

double cuff *n* polsino *m* con risvolto

double-dealing **①** *n* doppio gioco *m*
② *adj* doppio

double-decker *n* autobus *m inv* a due piani

double door[s] *n* [pl] porta *f* a due battenti

double Dutch *n* fam ostrogoto *m*

double-edged /-'edʒd/ *adj* also fig a doppio taglio

double entendre /du:blɑ̃'tɑ̃dr(ə)/ *n* doppio senso *m*

double entry book-keeping *n* contabilità *f* in partita doppia

double exposure *n* Phot sovrimpressione *f*

double fault *n* Tennis doppio fallo *m*

double feature n Cinema proiezione f di due film con biglietto unico

double-fronted /-'frʌntɪd/ adj ‹house› con due finestre ai lati della porta principale

double glazing n doppio vetro m

double-jointed adj ‹person, limb› snodato

double knitting [wool] n lana f grossa

double lock vt chiudere a doppia mandata

double-park vt/i parcheggiare in doppia fila

double-quick adv rapidissimamente adj in ~ time in un baleno

double room n camera f doppia

double saucepan n Br bagnomaria m inv

double spacing n Typ interlinea f doppia

double spread n Journ articolo m/ pubblicità f su due pagine

double standard n have ~ ~s usare metri diversi

double take n do a ~ ~ reagire a scoppio ritardato

double talk n pej discorso m ambiguo

double time n Am Mil marcia f forzata; be paid ~ ~ ricevere doppia paga per lo straordinario

double vision n have ~ ~ vederci doppio

double whammy n (fam: two bits of bad luck) sfortuna f doppia

double yellow line[s] n[pl] Br Aut due linee fpl gialle continue indicanti divieto di fermata e di sosta

doubly /'dʌblɪ/ adv doppiamente

doubt /daʊt/ **❶** n dubbio m
❷ vt dubitare di

doubtful /'daʊtfʊl/ adj dubbio; (having doubts) in dubbio

doubtfully /'daʊtfʊlɪ/ adv con aria dubbiosa

doubtless /'daʊtlɪs/ adv indubbiamente

douche /duːʃ/ n (Med: vaginal) irrigazione f

dough /dəʊ/ n pasta f; (for bread) impasto m; (fam: money) quattrini mpl

doughnut /'dəʊnʌt/ n bombolone m, krapfen m inv

dour /'dʊə(r)/ adj ‹mood, landscape› cupo; ‹person, expression› arcigno; ‹building› austero

douse /daʊs/ vt spegnere

dove /dʌv/ n colomba f

dovecot[e] /'dʌvkɒt/ n colombaia f

dovetail /'dʌvteɪl/ n Techn incastro m a coda di rondine

dowdy /'daʊdɪ/ adj (-ier, -iest) trasandato

down[1] /daʊn/ n (feathers) piumino m

down[2] **❶** adv giù; go/come ~ scendere; ~ there laggiù; sales are ~ le vendite sono diminuite; £50 ~ 50 sterline d'acconto; ~ 10% ridotto del 10% ~ with...! abbasso...!
❷ prep walk ~ the road camminare per strada; ~ the stairs giù per le scale; fall ~ the stairs cadere giù dalle scale; get that ~ you! fam butta giù!; be ~ the pub fam essere al pub
❸ vt bere tutto d'un fiato ‹drink›; ~ tools staccare; (in protest) interrompere il lavoro per protesta

down-and-out n spiantato, -a mf

downbeat adj (pessimistic) pessimistico; (laidback) distaccato

downcast adj abbattuto

downfall n caduta f; (of person) rovina f

downgrade vt (in seniority) degradare

down-hearted /-'hɑːtɪd/ adj scoraggiato

downhill adv in discesa; go ~ fig essere in declino

downhill skiing n sci m di fondo

down-in-the-mouth adj fam abbattuto

download vt Comput scaricare

down-market adj ‹newspaper, programme› rivolto al pubblico delle fasce basse; ‹products› dozzinale; ‹area› popolare; ‹hotel, restaurant› economico

down payment n deposito m

downpipe n Br tubo m di scolo

downplay vt minimizzare

downpour n acquazzone m

downright **❶** adj (absolute) totale; ‹lie› bell'e buono; (idiot) perfetto
❷ adv (completely) completamente

downs /daʊnz/ npl Br (hills) colline fpl di gesso nell'Inghilterra meridionale

downside /'daʊnsaɪd/ n svantaggio m

downside up adj & adv Am sottosopra

downsize /'daʊnsaɪz/ **❶** vt ‹company› ridurre l'organico di
❷ vi ridurre l'organico

Down's syndrome /'daʊnz/ n sindrome f di Down

downstairs adv al piano di sotto adj del piano di sotto

downstream adv a valle

down-to-earth adj (person) con i piedi per terra

downtown adv Am in centro

downtrodden /'daʊntrɒd(ə)n/ adj oppresso

downturn n (in economy) fase f discendente; (in career) svolta f negativa

down under *adv* fam in Australia e/o Nuova Zelanda

downward[s] /'daʊnwəd[z]/ ① *adj* verso il basso; ‹slope› in discesa ② *adv* verso il basso

downwind /daʊn'wɪnd/ *adv* sottovento

downy /'daʊnɪ/ *adj* (**-ier, -iest**) coperto di peluria

dowry /'daʊrɪ/ *n* dote *f*

doz *abbr* (**dozen**) dozzina *f*

doze /dəʊz/ ① *n* sonnellino *m* ② *vi* sonnecchiare
■ **doze off** *vi* assopirsi

dozen /'dʌzn/ *n* dozzina *f*; ~s of books libri a dozzine

DPhil *n abbr* (**Doctor of Philosophy**) titolare *mf* di un dottorato di ricerca

DPP *n* Br *abbr* (**Director of Public Prosecutions**) ≈ Procuratore *m* della Repubblica

Dr *abbr* (**doctor**) Dott. *m*, Dott.essa *f*; *abbr* (**drive**) ≈ via *f*

drab /dræb/ *adj* ‹colour› spento; ‹building› tetro; ‹life› scialbo

draft¹ /drɑːft/ ① *n* abbozzo *m*; Comm cambiale *f*; Am Mil leva *f* ② *vt* abbozzare; Am Mil arruolare
■ **draft in** *vt* chiamare ‹reinforcements, police›

draft² *n* Am = DRAUGHT

draft dodger /'dɒdʒə(r)/ *n* renitente *mf* alla leva

draftsman /'drɑːftsmən/ *n* Am = DRAUGHTSMAN

drag /dræg/ ① *n* fam scocciatura *f*; in ~ fam ‹man› travestito da donna ② *vt* (pt/pp **dragged**) trascinare; dragare ‹river›
■ **drag on** *vi* ‹time, meeting› trascinarsi
■ **drag out** *vt* tirare per le lunghe ‹discussion›; ~ something out of somebody tirar fuori qualcosa a qualcuno con le pinze
■ **drag up** *vt* (mention unnecessarily) tirare in ballo

drag and drop *vt* Comput trascinare e rilasciare

dragon /'drægən/ *n* drago *m*

dragonfly /'drægənflaɪ/ *n* libellula *f*

drag show *n* spettacolo *m* di travestiti

drain /dreɪn/ ① *n* tubo *m* di scarico; (grid) tombino *m*; the ~s le fognature; be a ~ on sb's finances prosciugare le finanze di qualcuno ② *vt* drenare ‹land, wound›; scolare ‹liquid, vegetables›; svuotare ‹tank glass, person› ③ *vi* [away] andar via; leave something to ~ lasciare qualcosa a scolare

drainage /'dreɪnɪdʒ/ *n* (system) drenaggio *m*; (of land) scolo *m*

draining board /'dreɪnɪŋ/ *n* scolapiatti *m inv*

drainpipe /'dreɪnpaɪp/ *n* tubo *m* di scarico

drainpipe trousers *npl* pantaloni *mpl* a tubo

drake /dreɪk/ *n* maschio *m* dell'anatra

drama /'drɑːmə/ *n* arte *f* drammatica; (play) opera *f* teatrale; (event) dramma *m*

dramatic /drə'mætɪk/ *adj* drammatico

dramatically /drə'mætɪklɪ/ *adv* in modo drammatico

dramatics /drə'mætɪks/ *npl* arte *f* drammatica; pej atteggiamento *m* teatrale

dramatist /'dræmətɪst/ *n* drammaturgo, -a *mf*

dramatization /dræmətaɪ'zeɪʃn/ *n* (for cinema) adattamento *m* cinematografico; (for stage) adattamento *m* teatrale; (for TV) adattamento *m* televisivo; (exaggeration) drammatizzazione *f*

dramatize /'dræmətaɪz/ *vt* adattare per il teatro; fig drammatizzare

drank /dræŋk/ ▶ DRINK

drape /dreɪp/ ① *n* Am tenda *f* ② *vt* appoggiare (**over** su)

drastic /'dræstɪk/ *adj* drastico

drastically /'dræstɪklɪ/ *adv* drasticamente

draught /drɑːft/ *n* corrente *f* [d'aria]

draught beer *n* birra *f* alla spina

draught-proof ① *adj* a tenuta d'aria ② *vt* tappare le fessure di

draughts /drɑːfts/ *n sg* (game) [gioco *m* della] dama *fsg*

draughtsman /'drɑːftsmən/ *n* disegnatore, -trice *mf*

draughty /'drɑːftɪ/ *adj* pieno di correnti d'aria; it's ~ c'è corrente

draw /drɔː/ ① *n* (attraction) attrazione *f*; Sport pareggio *m*; (in lottery) sorteggio *m* ② *vt* (pt **drew**, pp **drawn**) tirare; (attract) attirare; disegnare ‹picture›; tracciare ‹line›; ritirare ‹money›; attingere ‹water›; ~ lots tirare a sorte ③ *vi* ‹tea› essere in infusione; Sport pareggiare; ~ near avvicinarsi
■ **draw away** *vi* (go ahead) distanziarsi; (move off) allontanarsi
■ **draw back** ① *vt* tirare indietro; ritirare ‹hand›; tirare ‹curtains› ② *vi* (recoil) tirarsi indietro
■ **draw in** ① *vt* ritrarre ‹claws etc› ② *vi* ‹train› arrivare; ‹days› accorciarsi
■ **draw on** *vt* attingere a ‹savings, sb's experience›
■ **draw out** ① *vt* (pull out) tirar fuori; ritirare ‹money› ② *vi* ‹train› partire; ‹days› allungarsi
■ **draw up** ① *vt* redigere ‹document›; accostare ‹chair›; ~ oneself up [to one's full height] drizzarsi

2 *vi* (stop) fermarsi

drawback /'drɔːbæk/ *n* inconveniente *m*

drawbridge /'drɔːbrɪdʒ/ *n* ponte *m* levatoio

drawee /drɔːˈiː/ *n* trattario *m*

drawer /drɔː(r)/ *n* cassetto *m*; Fin traente *mf*

drawing /'drɔːɪŋ/ *n* disegno *m*

drawing board *n* tavolo *m* da disegno; fig **go back to the ~ ~** ricominciare da capo

drawing pin *n* puntina *f*

drawing rights *npl* Fin diritti *mf* di prelievo

drawing room *n* salotto *m*

drawl /drɔːl/ *n* pronuncia *f* strascicata

drawn /drɔːn/ ▶ DRAW

dread /dred/ **1** *n* terrore *m*
2 *vt* aver il terrore di

dreadful /'dredfʊl/ *adj* terribile

dreadfully /'dredfʊlɪ/ *adv* terribilmente

dream /driːm/ **1** *n* sogno *m*
2 *attrib* di sogno
3 *vt/i* (pt/pp **dreamt** /dremt/ or **dreamed**) sognare (**about/of** di)
■ **dream up** *vt* escogitare ⟨*plan, idea*⟩

dreamer /'driːmə(r)/ *n* (idealist) sognatore, -trice *mf*; (inattentive) persona *f* con la testa fra le nuvole

dream-world *n* **live in a ~** vivere tra le nuvole

dreamy /'driːmɪ/ *adj* fam ⟨*house etc*⟩ di sogno; ⟨*person*⟩ che è un sogno; (distracted) distratto; ⟨*sound, music*⟩ dolce

dreary /'drɪərɪ/ *adj* (**-ier, -iest**) tetro; (boring) monotono

dredge /dredʒ/ *vt/i* dragare
■ **dredge up** *vt* riesumare ⟨*the past*⟩

dredger /'dredʒə(r)/ *n* draga *f*

dregs /dregz/ *npl* feccia *fsg*

drench /drentʃ/ *vt* **get ~ed** inzupparsi

drenched /drentʃt/ *adj* zuppo

dress /dres/ **1** *n* (woman's) vestito *m*; (clothing) abbigliamento *m*
2 *vt* vestire; (decorate) adornare; Culin condire; Med fasciare; **~ oneself, get ~ed** vestirsi
3 *vi* vestirsi
■ **dress up** *vi* mettersi elegante; (in disguise) travestirsi (**as** da)

dress circle *n* Theat prima galleria *f*

dress designer *n* stilista *mf*

dresser /'dresə(r)/ *n* (furniture) credenza *f*; (Am: dressing table) toilette *f inv*

dressing /'dresɪŋ/ *n* Culin condimento *m*; Med fasciatura *f*

dressing down *n* fam sgridata *f*

dressing gown *n* vestaglia *f*

dressing room *n* (in gym) spogliatoio *m*; Theat camerino *m*

dressing table *n* toilette *f inv*

dressmaker *n* sarta *f*

dressmaking *n* confezioni *fpl* (per donna)

dress rehearsal *n* prova *f* generale

dress sense *n* **have ~ ~** saper abbinare i capi d'abbigliamento

dressy /'dresɪ/ *adj* (**-ier, -iest**) elegante

drew /druː/ ▶ DRAW

dribble /'drɪbl/ *vi* gocciolare; ⟨*baby*⟩ sbavare; Sport dribblare

dribs and drabs /'drɪbzən'dræbz/ *npl* **in ~** alla spicciolata

dried /draɪd/ *adj* ⟨*food*⟩ essiccato

drier /'draɪə(r)/ *n* asciugabiancheria *m inv*

drift /drɪft/ **1** *n* movimento *m* lento; ⟨*of snow*⟩ cumulo *m*; (meaning) senso *m*
2 *vi* (off course) andare alla deriva; ⟨*snow*⟩ accumularsi; fig ⟨*person*⟩ procedere senza meta
■ **drift apart** *vi* ⟨*people*⟩ allontanarsi l'uno dall'altro

drifter /'drɪftə(r)/ *n* persona *f* senza meta

driftwood /'drɪftwʊd/ *n* pezzi *mpl* di legno galleggianti

drill /drɪl/ **1** *n* trapano *m*; Mil esercitazione *f*
2 *vt* trapanare; Mil fare esercitare
3 *vi* Mil esercitarsi; **~ for oil** trivellare in cerca di petrolio

drily /'draɪlɪ/ *adv* seccamente

drink /drɪŋk/ **1** *n* bevanda *f*; (alcoholic) bicchierino *m*; **have a ~** bere qualcosa; **a ~ of water** un po' d'acqua
2 *vt/i* (pt **drank**, pp **drunk**) bere
■ **drink to** *vt* (toast) brindare a
■ **drink up** **1** *vt* finire
2 *vi* finire il bicchiere

drinkable /'drɪŋkəbl/ *adj* potabile

drink-driving *n* Br guida *f* in stato di ebbrezza

drinker /'drɪŋkə(r)/ *n* bevitore, -trice *mf*

drinking chocolate /'drɪŋkɪŋ/ *n* Br cioccolata *f* in polvere

drinking water *n* acqua *f* potabile

drink problem *n* Br **he has a ~ ~** beve

drinks cupboard *n* Br mobile *m* bar

drinks dispenser *n* Br distributore *m* di bevande

drinks machine *n* Br distributore *m* di bevande

drinks party *n* Br cocktail *m inv*

drip /drɪp/ **1** *n* gocciolamento *m*; (drop) goccia *f*; Med flebo *f inv*; (fam: person) mollaccione, -a *mf*
2 *vi* (pt/pp **dripped**) gocciolare

drip-dry *adj* che non si stira

drip-feed *n* flebo [clisi] *f inv*

dripping /'drɪpɪŋ/ ① n (from meat) grasso m d'arrosto
② adj ~ [wet] fradicio

drive /draɪv/ ① n (in car) giro m; (entrance) viale m; (energy) grinta f; Psych pulsione f; (organized effort) operazione f; Techn motore m; Comput lettore m, unità f inv
② vt (pt **drove** pp **driven**) portare ⟨person by car⟩; guidare ⟨car⟩; (Sport: hit) mandare; Techn far funzionare; ~ **somebody mad** far diventare matto qualcuno
③ vi guidare
■ **drive at** vt what are you driving at? dove vuoi arrivare?
■ **drive away** ① vt portare via in macchina; (chase) cacciare
② vi andare via in macchina
■ **drive back** ① vt respingere ⟨people, animals⟩; (in car) riportare
② vi ritornare in macchina
■ **drive in** ① vt piantare ⟨nail⟩
② vi arrivare [in macchina]
■ **drive off** ① vt portare via in macchina; (chase) cacciare
② vi andare via in macchina
■ **drive on** vi proseguire; ~ **on**! avanti!
■ **drive up** vi arrivare (in macchina)

drive-by shooting n sparatoria f da auto in corsa

drive-in adj ~ **cinema** cinema m inv drive-in

drivel /'drɪvl/ n fam sciocchezze fpl

driven /'drɪvn/ ▶DRIVE

driver /'draɪvə(r)/ n guidatore, -trice mf; (of train) conducente mf

driver's license n Am patente f di guida

drive-through n Am drive-in m inv

driveway /'draɪvweɪ/ n strada f d'accesso

driving /'draɪvɪŋ/ ① adj ⟨rain⟩ violento; ⟨force⟩ motore
② n guida f

driving force n spinta f; (person behind) forza f trainante

driving instructor n istruttore, -trice mf di guida

driving lesson n lezione f di guida

driving licence n patente f di guida

driving mirror n (rearview) specchietto m retrovisore

driving school n scuola f guida

driving seat n be in the ~ ~ essere alla guida

driving test n esame m di guida; take one's ~ ~ fare l'esame di guida

drizzle /'drɪzl/ ① n pioggerella f
② vi piovigginare

droll /drəʊl/ adj divertente

drone /drəʊn/ n (bee) fuco m: (sound) ronzio m

■ **drone on** vi (talk boringly) tirarla per le lunghe

drool /druːl/ vi sbavare; ~ **over something/somebody** fig fam sbavare per qualcosa/qualcuno

droop /druːp/ vi abbassarsi; ⟨flowers⟩ afflosciarsi

drop /drɒp/ ① n (of liquid) goccia f; (fall) caduta f; (in price, temperature) calo m
② vt (pt/pp **dropped**) far cadere; sganciare ⟨bomb⟩; (omit) omettere; (give up) abbandonare; ~ **the subject** cambiare discorso
③ vi cadere; ⟨price, temperature, wind⟩ calare; ⟨ground⟩ essere in pendenza
■ **drop behind** vi rimanere indietro
■ **drop by** vi = drop in
■ **drop in** vi passare
■ **drop off** ① vt depositare ⟨person⟩
② vi cadere; (fall asleep) assopirsi
■ **drop out** vi cadere; (from race, society) ritirarsi; ~ **out of school** lasciare la scuola

drop-dead adv fam ~ **gorgeous** stupendo

drop-down menu n Comput menu m inv a tendina

drop handlebars npl manubrio m ricurvo

drop-out n persona f contro il sistema sociale

droppings /'drɒpɪŋz/ npl sterco m

drop shot n Sport drop shot m inv, smorzata f

drop zone n (for supplies etc) zona f di lancio

drought /draʊt/ n siccità f

drove /drəʊv/ ▶DRIVE

droves /drəʊvz/ npl in ~ in massa

drown /draʊn/ ① vi annegare
② vt annegare; coprire ⟨noise⟩; **he was** ~ed è annegato

drowning /draʊnɪŋ/ n annegamento m

drowse /draʊz/ vi sonnecchiare; (be very sleepy) essere sonnolento

drowsiness /'draʊzɪnɪs/ n sonnolenza f

drowsy /'draʊzɪ/ adj sonnolento

drudgery /'drʌdʒərɪ/ n lavoro m pesante e noioso

drug /drʌg/ ① n droga f; Med farmaco m; take ~s drogarsi
② vt (pt/pp **drugged**) drogare

drug abuse n abuso m di stupefacenti

drug addict n tossicomane, -a mf

drug addiction n tossicodipendenza f

drug dealer n spacciatore, -trice mf [di droga]

drugged /drʌgd/ adj drogato

druggist /'drʌgɪst/ n Am farmacista mf

drug habit n tossicodipendenza f

drug mule n corriere m della droga

Drug Squad n Br [squadra f] narcotici f

drugs raid n operazione f antidroga

drugs ring n rete f di narcotrafficanti

drugstore /'drʌgstɔ:(r)/ n Am negozio m di generi vari, inclusi medicinali, che funge anche da bar; (dispensing) farmacia f

drug-taking n consumo m di stupefacenti; Sport doping m inv

drug test n Sport antidoping m inv

drug user n tossicomane, -a mf

drum /drʌm/ **1** n tamburo m; (for oil) bidone m; ~s pl (in pop group) batteria f **2** vi (pt/pp **drummed**) suonare un tamburo; (in pop group) suonare la batteria **3** vt ~ **something into somebody** fam ripetere qualcosa a qualcuno cento volte; ~ **one's fingers on the table** tamburellare con le dita sul tavolo

■ **drum up** vt ottenere ⟨business, customers, support⟩

drum kit n batteria f

drummer /'drʌmə(r)/ n percussionista mf; (in pop group) batterista mf

drumstick /'drʌmstɪk/ n bacchetta f; (of chicken, turkey) coscia f

drunk /drʌŋk/ **1** ▶ DRINK **2** adj ubriaco; **get** ~ urbiacarsi **3** n ubriaco, -a mf

drunkard /'drʌŋkəd/ n ubriacone, -a mf

drunken /'drʌŋkən/ adj ubriaco

drunken driving n guida f in stato di ebbrezza

dry /draɪ/ **1** adj (**drier**, **driest**) asciutto; ⟨climate, country⟩ secco **2** vt/i asciugare; ~ **one's eyes** asciugarsi le lacrime

■ **dry out** vi ⟨clothes⟩ asciugarsi; ⟨alcoholic⟩ disintossicarsi

■ **dry up** vi seccarsi; fig ⟨source⟩ prosciugarsi; (fam: be quiet) stare zitto; (do dishes) asciugare i piatti

dry cell n cella f a secco

dry-clean vt pulire a secco

dry-cleaner's n (shop) tintoria f

dryer /'draɪə/ n = DRIER

dry ice n ghiaccio m secco

drying-up /draɪɪŋ-/ n Br **do the** ~ asciugare i piatti

dryness /'draɪnɪs/ n secchezza f

dry rot n carie f del legno

DSS n Br abbr (**Department of Social Security**) (local office) ≈ Ufficio m della Previdenza Sociale; (ministry) ≈ Istituto m Nazionale della Previdenza Sociale

DTI n Br abbr (**Department of Trade and Industry**) ≈ ministero m del Commercio e dell'Industria

DTP n abbr (**desktop publishing**) DTP m

dual /'dju:əl/ adj doppio

dual carriageway n strada f a due carreggiate

dual nationality n doppia nazionalità f

dual-purpose adj a doppio uso

dub /dʌb/ vt (pt/pp **dubbed**) doppiare ⟨film⟩; (name) soprannominare

dubbing /'dʌbɪŋ/ n doppiaggio m

dubious /'dju:bɪəs/ adj dubbio; **be** ~ **about** avere dei dubbi riguardo

dubiously /'dju:bɪəslɪ/ adv ⟨look at⟩ con aria dubbiosa; (say) con esitazione

Dublin /'dʌblɪn/ n Dublino f

duchess /'dʌtʃɪs/ n duchessa f

duck /dʌk/ **1** n anatra f **2** vt (in water) immergere; ~ **one's head** abbassare la testa **3** vi abbassarsi

■ **duck out of** vt sottrarsi a ⟨task⟩

duckling /'dʌklɪŋ/ n anatroccolo m

duct /dʌkt/ n condotto m; Anat dotto m

dud /dʌd/ **1** adj Mil fam disattivato; ⟨coin⟩ falso; ⟨cheque⟩ a vuoto **2** n fam (banknote) banconota f falsa; (Mil: shell) granata f disattivata

due /dju:/ **1** adj dovuto; **be** ~ ⟨train⟩ essere previsto; **the baby is** ~ **next week** il bambino dovrebbe nascere la settimana prossima; ~ **to** (owing to) a causa di; **be** ~ **to** (causally) essere dovuto a; **I'm** ~ **to...** dovrei...; **in** ~ **course** a tempo debito **2** adv ~ **north** direttamente a nord

duel /'dju:əl/ n duello m

dues /dju:z/ npl quota f [di iscrizione]

duet /dju:'et/ n duetto m

duffel bag /dʌf(ə)l/ n sacca f da viaggio

duffel coat n montgomery m inv

dug /dʌg/ ▶ DIG

duke /dju:k/ n duca m

dull /dʌl/ **1** adj (overcast, not bright) cupo; (not shiny) opaco; ⟨sound⟩ soffocato; (boring) monotono; (stupid) ottuso **2** vt intorpidire ⟨mind⟩; attenuare ⟨pain⟩

dullness /'dʌlnɪs/ n (of life) monotonia f; (of company, conversation) noia f; (no shine) opacità f

dully /'dʌllɪ/ adv ⟨say, repeat⟩ monotonamente

duly /'dju:lɪ/ adv debitamente

dumb /dʌm/ adj muto; (fam: stupid) ottuso

■ **dumb down** vt abbassare il livello intellettuale di ⟨course, programme⟩

dumbfounded /dʌm'faʊndɪd/ adj sbigottito

dummy /'dʌmɪ/ n (tailor's) manichino m; (for baby) succhiotto m; (model) riproduzione f

dummy run n (trial) prova f

dump /dʌmp/ **1** n (for refuse) scarico m; (fam: town) mortorio m; **be down in the** ~s fam essere depresso

2 *vt* scaricare; (fam: put down) lasciare; (fam: get rid of) liberarsi di

dumping /'dʌmpɪŋ/ *n* Fin dumping *m inv*, esportazione *f* sottocosto; **no ~** divieto *m* di scarico

dumpling /'dʌmplɪŋ/ *n* gnocco *m*

dumpy /'dʌmpɪ/ *adj* (plump) tracagnotto

dunce /dʌns/ *n* zuccone, -a *mf*

dune /djuːn/ *n* duna *f*

dung /dʌŋ/ *n* sterco *m*

dungarees /dʌŋɡə'riːz/ *npl* tuta *fsg*

dungeon /'dʌndʒən/ *n* prigione *f* sotterranea

dunk /dʌŋk/ *vt* inzuppare

dunno /də'nəʊ/ fam (I don't know) boh

duo /'djuːəʊ/ *n* duo *m inv*; Mus duetto *m*

dupe /djuːp/ **1** *n* zimbello *m*
2 *vt* gabbare

duplicate[1] /'djuːplɪkət/ **1** *adj* doppio
2 *n* duplicato *m*; (document) copia *f*; **in ~** in duplicato

duplicate[2] /'djuːplɪkeɪt/ *vt* fare un duplicato di; ‹research› essere una ripetizione di ‹work›

duplicator /'djuːplɪkeɪtə(r)/ *n* duplicatore *m*

duplicity /djʊ'plɪsətɪ/ *n* duplicità *f*, doppiezza *f*

durable /'djʊərəbl/ *adj* resistente; ‹basis, institution› durevole

duration /djʊə'reɪʃn/ *n* durata *f*

duress /djʊə'res/ *n* costrizione *f*; **under ~** sotto minaccia

during /'djʊərɪŋ/ *prep* durante

dusk /dʌsk/ *n* crepuscolo *m*

dusky /'dʌskɪ/ *adj* ‹complexion› scuro

dust /dʌst/ **1** *n* polvere *f*
2 *vt* spolverare; (sprinkle) cospargere ‹cake› (with di)
3 *vi* spolverare

dustbin *n* pattumiera *f*

dustbin man *n* Br netturbino *m*

dust-cart *n* camion *m* della nettezza urbana

dust cover *n* (on book) sopraccoperta *f*; (on furniture) telo *m* di protezione

duster /'dʌstə(r)/ *n* strofinaccio *m*

dust-jacket *n* sopraccoperta *f*

dustman *n* spazzino *m*

dustpan *n* paletta *f* per la spazzatura

dust sheet *n* (on furniture) telo *m* di protezione

dusty /'dʌstɪ/ *adj* (**-ier, -iest**) polveroso

Dutch /dʌtʃ/ **1** *adj* olandese; **go ~** fam fare alla romana
2 *n* (language) olandese *m*; **the ~** *pl* gli olandesi

Dutch courage *n* spavalderia *f* ispirata dall'alcool

Dutchman /'dʌtʃmən/ *n* olandese *m*

dutiable /'djuːtɪəbl/ *adj* soggetto a imposta

dutiful /'djuːtɪfl/ *adj* rispettoso

dutifully /'djuːtɪfʊlɪ/ *adv* a dovere

duty /'djuːtɪ/ *n* dovere *m*; (task) compito *m*; (tax) dogana *f*; **be on ~** essere di servizio

duty chemist *n* farmacia *f* di turno

duty-free **1** *adj* esente da dogana
2 *n* duty-free *m inv*

duty-free allowance *n* limite *m* d'acquisto di merci esenti da dogana

duty roster, duty rota *n* tabella *f* dei turni

duvet /'duːveɪ/ *n* piumone *m*

duvet cover *n* Br copripiumone *m*

DVD *n abbr* (**digital video disc**) DVD *m*

DVT *abbr* (**deep-vein thrombosis**) TVP *f*

dwarf /dwɔːf/ **1** *n* (*pl* **-s** *or* **dwarves**) nano, -a *mf*
2 *vt* rimpicciolire

dweeb /dwiːb/ *n* esp Am: fam secchione, -a *mf*

dwell /dwel/ *vi* (pt/pp **dwelt**) liter dimorare
■ **dwell on** *vt* fig soffermarsi su

dweller /'dwelə(r)/ *n* **city/town ~** cittadino, -a *mf*

dwelling /'dwelɪŋ/ *n* abitazione *f*

dwindle /'dwɪndl/ *vi* diminuire

dwindling /'dwɪndlɪŋ/ *adj* (strength, health) in calo; ‹resources, audience, interest› in diminuzione

DWP *abbr* Br (**Department for Work and Pensions**) ≈ Ministero *m* del Lavoro e delle Politiche Sociali

dye /daɪ/ **1** *n* tintura *f*
2 *vt* (pres p **dyeing**) tingere

dyed-in-the-wool /daɪdɪnðə'wʊl/ *adj* inveterato

dying /'daɪɪŋ/ ▶ DIE[2]

dyke /daɪk/ *n* (to prevent flooding) diga *f*; (beside ditch) argine *m*; (Br: ditch) canale *m* di scolo

dynamic /daɪ'næmɪk/ *adj* dinamico

dynamics /daɪ'næmɪks/ *n* dinamica *fsg*

dynamism /daɪnə'mɪzm/ *n* dinamismo *m*

dynamite /'daɪnəmaɪt/ *n* dinamite *f*

dynamo /'daɪnəməʊ/ *n* dinamo *f inv*

dynasty /'dɪnəstɪ/ *n* dinastia *f*

dysentery /'dɪsəntrɪ/ *n* dissenteria *f*

dysfunctional /dɪs:fʌnkʃ(ə)nəl/ *adj* disfunzionale

dyslexia /dɪs'leksɪə/ *n* dislessia *f*

dyslexic /dɪs'leksɪk/ *adj* dislessico

Ee

e¹, **E** /iː/ n (letter) e, E f inv; Mus mi m
e² abbr (**euro**) EUR m
E abbr (**east**) E
each /iːtʃ/ **1** adj ogni
2 pron ognuno; £1 ∼ una sterlina ciascuno; **they love/hate** ∼ **other** si amano/odiano; **we lend** ∼ **other money** ci prestiamo i soldi; **bet on a horse** ∼ **way** puntare su un cavallo piazzato e vincente
eager /ˈiːgə(r)/ adj ansioso (**to do** di fare); ⟨pupil⟩ avido di sapere
eager beaver n fam **be an** ∼ ∼ essere pieno di zelo
eagerly /ˈiːgəlɪ/ adv ⟨wait⟩ ansiosamente; ⟨offer⟩ premurosamente
eagerness/ˈiːgənɪs/ n premura f
eagle /ˈiːgl/ n aquila f
eagle-eyed /ˈ-aɪd/ adj (sharp-eyed) che ha un occhio di falco
ear /ɪə(r)/ n orecchio m; (of corn) spiga f
earache /ˈɪəreɪk/ n mal m d'orecchi
eardrum /ˈɪədrʌm/ n timpano m
earl /ɜːl/ n conte m
ear lobe n lobo m dell'orecchio
early /ˈɜːlɪ/ **1** adj (**-ier, -iest**) (before expected time) in anticipo; ⟨spring⟩ prematuro; ⟨reply⟩ pronto; ⟨works, writings⟩ primo; **be here** ∼! sii puntuale!; **you're** ∼! sei in anticipo!; ∼ **morning walk** passeggiata f mattutina; **in the** ∼ **morning** la mattina presto; **in the** ∼ **spring** all'inizio della primavera
2 adv presto; (ahead of time) in anticipo; ∼ **in the morning** la mattina presto
early retirement n prepensionamento m; **take** ∼ andare in prepensionamento
early warning n **come as an** ∼ ∼ **of something** essere il segno premonitore di qualcosa
early warning system n Mil sistema m d'allarme avanzato
earmark /ˈɪəmɑːk/ vt riservare (**for** a)
earmuffs /ˈɪəmʌfs/ npl paraorecchie m inv
earn /ɜːn/ vt guadagnare; (deserve) meritare
earned income /ɜːnd/ n reddito m da lavoro
earner /ˈɜːnə(r)/ n (person) persona f che guadagna; **the main [revenue]** ∼ la principale fonte di sostentamento; **a nice little** ∼ fam un'ottima fonte di guadagno
earnest /ˈɜːnɪst/ **1** adj serio
2 n **in** ∼ sul serio

earnestly /ˈɜːnɪstlɪ/ adv con aria seria
earning power /ˈɜːnɪŋ/ n (of person) capacità f di guadagno; (of company) redditività f inv
earnings /ˈɜːnɪŋz/ npl guadagni mpl; (salary) stipendio m
ear, nose, and throat department n reparto m otorinolaringoiatrico
earphones npl cuffia fsg
earplug n (for noise) tappo m per le orecchie
ear-ring n orecchino m
earshot n **within** ∼ a portata d'orecchio; **he is out of** ∼ non può sentire
ear-splitting /ˈɪəsplɪtɪŋ/ adj ⟨scream, shout⟩ lacerante
earth /ɜːθ/ **1** n terra f; (of fox) tana f; **where/what on** ∼? dove/che diavolo?
2 vt Electr mettere a terra
earthenware /ˈɜːθnweə/ n terraglia f
earthly /ˈɜːθlɪ/ adj terrestre; **be no** ∼ **use** fam essere perfettamente inutile
earthquake n terremoto m
earth sciences npl scienze fpl della terra
earthshaking adj fam ⟨news⟩ sconvolgente; ⟨experience⟩ travolgente
earth tremor n scossa f sismica
earthwork n (embankment) terrapieno m; (excavation work) lavori mpl di scavo
earthworm n lombrico m
earthy /ˈɜːθɪ/ adj terroso; (coarse) grossolano
earwax /ˈɪəwæks/ n cerume m
earwig /ˈɪəwɪg/ n forbicina f
ease /iːz/ **1** n **at** ∼ a proprio agio; **at** ∼! Mil riposo!; **ill at** ∼ a disagio; **with** ∼ con facilità
2 vt calmare ⟨pain⟩; alleviare ⟨tension, shortage⟩; (slow down) rallentare; (loosen) allentare
3 vi ⟨pain, situation, wind⟩ calmarsi
■ **ease off 1** vi ⟨pain, pressure, tension⟩ attenuarsi
2 vt (remove gently) togliere con delicatezza
■ **ease up** vi = ease off
easel /ˈiːzl/ n cavalletto m
easily /ˈiːzɪlɪ/ adv con facilità; ∼ **the best** certamente il meglio
east /iːst/ **1** n est m; **to the** ∼ **of** a est di
2 adj dell'est
3 adv verso est
East Africa n Africa f orientale

East Berlin n Berlino f Est

eastbound adj ‹carriageway, traffic› diretto a est

East End n quartiere m nella zona est di Londra

Easter /'iːstə(r)/ n Pasqua f

easterly /'iːstəlɪ/ adj da levante

Easter egg n uovo m di Pasqua

Easter Monday n lunedì m dell'Angelo, Pasquetta f

eastern /'iːstən/ adj orientale

Eastern block n paesi mpl dell'est

Easter Sunday n [domenica f di] Pasqua f

East German n Pol tedesco, -a mf dell'est

East Germany n Pol Germania f est

East Indies npl Indie fpl orientali

East Timor /'tiːmɔː(r)/ n Timor Est m

eastward[s] /'iːstwəd[z]/ adv verso est

easy /'iːzɪ/ adj (-ier, -iest) facile; **take it** or **things** ∼ prendersela con calma; **take it** ∼**I** (don't get excited) calma!; **go** ∼ **with** andarci piano con

easy-care adj facilmente lavabile

easy chair n poltrona f

easy-going adj conciliante; **too** ∼ troppo accomodante

easy money n facili guadagni mpl

easy terms npl facilitazioni fpl di pagamento

eat /iːt/ vt/i (pt **ate**, pp **eaten**) mangiare
- **eat into** vt intaccare
- **eat out** vi mangiar fuori
- **eat up** vt mangiare tutto ‹food›; fig inghiottire ‹profits›

eatable /'iːtəbl/ adj mangiabile

eater /'iːtə(r)/ n (apple) mela f da tavola; **be a big** ∼ ‹person› essere una buona forchetta; **he's a fast** ∼ mangia sempre in fretta

eatery /'iːtərɪ/ n fam tavola f calda

eating apple n mela f non da cuocere

eating disorder n disoressia f

eating habits npl abitudini fpl alimentari

eau-de-Cologne /əʊdəkə'ləʊn/ n acqua f di colonia

eaves /iːvz/ npl cornicione msg

eavesdrop /'iːvzdrɒp/ vi (pt/pp **-dropped**) origliare; ∼ **on** ascoltare di nascosto

e-banking /'iːbæŋɪŋ/ n e-banking m

ebb /eb/ ① n (tide) riflusso m; **at a low** ∼ fig a terra
② vi rifluire; fig declinare

ebony /'ebənɪ/ n ebano m

EBRD n abbr (**European Bank for Reconstruction and Development**) BERS f

ebullient /ɪ'bʌlɪənt/ adj esuberante

e-business /'iːbɪznɪs/ n e-business m inv

EC n abbr (**European Community**) CE f

e-cash /'iːkæʃ/ n denaro m virtuale

eccentric /ek'sentrɪk/ adj & n eccentrico, -a mf

eccentricity /eksen'trɪsətɪ/ n eccentricità f inv

ecclesiastical /ɪkliːzɪ'æstɪkl/ adj ecclesiastico

ECG n abbr (**electrocardiogram**) ECG m

echo /'ekəʊ/ ① n (pl **-es**) eco f or m
② vt (pt/pp **echoed**, pres p **echoing**) echeggiare; ripetere ‹words›
③ vi risuonare (**with** di)

eclectic /ɪ'klektɪk/ n eclettico

eclipse /ɪ'klɪps/ ① n Astr eclissi f inv
② vt fig eclissare

eco+ /'iːkəʊ/ pref eco+

eco-friendly adj che rispetta l'ambiente

ecological /iːkə'lɒdʒɪkl/ adj ecologico

ecologist /ɪ'kɒlədʒɪst/ ① n ecologo, -a mf
② adj ecologico

ecology /ɪ'kɒlədʒɪ/ n ecologia f

e-commerce /'iːkɒmɜːs/ n e-commerce m inv

economic /iːkə'nɒmɪk/ adj economico

economical /iːkə'nɒmɪkl/ adj economico

economically /iːkə'nɒmɪklɪ/ adv economicamente; ‹thriftily› in economia; ∼ **priced** a prezzo economico

economic analyst n analista mf economico, -a

economics /iːkə'nɒmɪks/ n economia f

economist /ɪ'kɒnəmɪst/ n economista mf

economize /ɪ'kɒnəmaɪz/ vi economizzare (**on su**)

economy /ɪ'kɒnəmɪ/ n economia f

economy class n Aeron classe f turistica

economy drive n campagna f di risparmio

economy pack, economy size n confezione f economica inv

ecosystem /'iːkəʊsɪstəm/ n ecosistema m

ecoterrorism n ecoterrorismo m

eco-warrior n eco-guerrigliero, -a mf

ecstasy /'ekstəsɪ/ n estasi f inv; (drug) ecstasy f

ecstatic /ɪk'stætɪk/ adj estatico

ecstatically /ɪk'stætɪklɪ/ adv estaticamente

ectopic pregnancy /ek'tɒpɪk/ n
gravidanza f extrauterina

Ecuador /'ekwədɔ:(r)/ n Ecuador m

ecumenical /i:kjʊ'menɪkl/ adj
ecumenico

eczema /'eksɪmə/ n eczema m

eddy /'edɪ/ n vortice m

Eden /'i:d(ə)n/ n eden m, paradiso m
terrestre

edge /edʒ/ **1** n bordo m; (of knife) filo m;
(of road) ciglio m; **on** ~ con i nervi tesi;
have the ~ **on** fam avere un vantaggio su
2 vt bordare
■ **edge forward** vi avanzare lentamente

edgeways /'edʒweɪz/ adv di fianco; **I
couldn't get a word in** ~ non ho potuto
infilare neanche mezza parola nel
discorso

edging /'edʒɪŋ/ n bordo m

edgy /'edʒɪ/ adj (nervous) nervoso; (fam:
modern) all'avanguardia

edible /'edəbl/ adj commestibile; **this
pizza's not** ~ questa pizza è immangiabile

edict /'i:dɪkt/ n editto m

edifice /'edɪfɪs/ n edificio m

edify /'edɪfaɪ/ vt (pt/pp **-ied**) edificare

edifying /'edɪfaɪɪŋ/ adj edificante

Edinburgh /'edɪmb(ə)rə/ n Edimburgo f

edit /'edɪt/ vt (pt/pp **edited**) far la
revisione di ⟨text⟩; curare l'edizione di
⟨anthology, dictionary⟩; dirigere
⟨newspaper⟩; montare ⟨film⟩; editare
⟨tape⟩; ~**ed by** ⟨book⟩ a cura di
■ **edit out** vt tagliare

edition /ɪ'dɪʃn/ n edizione f

editor /'edɪtə(r)/ n (of anthology, dictionary)
curatore, -trice mf; (of newspaper) redattore,
-trice mf; (of film) responsabile mf del
montaggio

editorial /edɪ'tɔ:rɪəl/ **1** adj redazionale
2 n Journ editoriale m

EDP n abbr (**electronic data
processing**) EDP m, EED f

EDT abbr Am (**Eastern Daylight Time**)
ora f legale degli stati orientali
dell'America settentrionale

educate /'edjʊkeɪt/ vt istruire; educare
⟨public, mind⟩; **be** ~**d at Eton** essere
educato a Eton

educated /'edjʊkeɪtɪd/ adj istruito

education /edjʊ'keɪʃn/ n istruzione f;
(culture) cultura f, educazione f

educational /edjʊ'keɪʃnəl/ adj
istruttivo; ⟨visit⟩ educativo; ⟨publishing⟩
didattico

educationalist /edjʊ'keɪʃnəlɪst/ n
studioso, -a mf di pedagogia

educationally /edjʊ'keɪʃnəlɪ/ adv
⟨disadvantaged, privileged⟩ dal punto di
vista degli studi; ⟨useless, useful⟩ dal
punto di vista didattico

educational psychology n
psicopedagogia f, psicologia f
dell'educazione

educational television n televisione
f scolastica

education authority n Br autorità fpl
scolastiche

education committee n Br consiglio
m scolastico

education department n Br
ministero m della pubblica istruzione; (in
local government) provveditorato m agli
studi; (in university) istituto m di pedagogia

educative /'edjʊkətɪv/ adj educativo,
istruttivo

educator /'edjʊkeɪtə(r)/ n educatore,
··trice mf

Edwardian /ed'wɔ:dɪən/ n del regno di
Edoardo VII

EEA abbr (**European Economic Area**)
EEA f

EEC **1** n abbr (**European Economic
Community**) CEE f
2 attrib ⟨policy, directive⟩ della CEE

eel /i:l/ n anguilla f

eerie /'ɪərɪ/ adj (**-ier, -iest**) inquietante

efface /ɪ'feɪs/ vt cancellare

effect /ɪ'fekt/ **1** n effetto m; **in** ~ in
effetti; **take** ~ ⟨law⟩ entrare in vigore;
⟨medicine⟩ fare effetto
2 vt effettuare

effective /ɪ'fektɪv/ adj efficace; (striking)
che colpisce; (actual) di fatto; ~ **from** in
vigore a partire da

effectively /ɪ'fektɪvlɪ/ adv
efficacemente; (actually) di fatto

effectiveness /ɪ'fektɪvnɪs/ n efficacia f

effeminate /ɪ'femɪnət/ adj effeminato

effervescent /efə'vesnt/ adj
effervescente

effete /ɪ'fi:t/ adj ⟨person⟩ senza nerbo;
⟨civilization⟩ che ha fatto il suo tempo

efficacious /efɪ'keɪʃəs/ adj efficace

efficacy /'efɪkəsɪ/ n efficacia f

efficiency /ɪ'fɪʃənsɪ/ n efficienza f; (of
machine) rendimento m

efficient /ɪ'fɪʃənt/ adj efficiente

efficiently /ɪ'fɪʃəntlɪ/ adv
efficientemente

effigy /'efɪdʒɪ/ n effigie f

effluent /'eflʊənt/ **1** n (waste) refluo m;
(river) emissario m
2 attrib ⟨treatment, management⟩ dei
reflui

effort /'efət/ n sforzo m; **make an** ~
sforzarsi

effortless /'efətlɪs/ adj facile

effortlessly /'efətlɪslɪ/ adv con facilità

effrontery /ɪ'frʌntərɪ/ n sfrontatezza f

effusion /ɪ'fju:ʒn/ n (emotional) effusione f

effusive /ɪˈfjuːsɪv/ adj espansivo; ⟨speech⟩ caloroso

e-fit /ˈiːfɪt/ n identikit m inv elettronico

EFL ① n abbr (**English as a Foreign Language**) EFL m
② attrib ⟨teacher, course⟩ di inglese come lingua straniera

EFT n abbr **electronic funds transfer**

EFTA /ˈeftə/ n abbr (**European Free Trade Association**) EFTA f

e.g. abbr (**exempli gratia**) per es.

egalitarian /ɪɡælɪˈteərɪən/ adj egalitario

egg /eɡ/ n uovo m
■ **egg on** vt fam incitare

egg box n cartone m di uova

eggcup n portauovo m inv

egg custard n crema f pasticciera

egghead n pej fam intellettuale mf

eggplant n Am melanzana f

eggshaped /ˈeɡʃeɪpt/ adj ovale

eggshell n guscio m d'uovo

egg-timer n clessidra f per misurare il tempo di cottura delle uova

egg whisk n frusta f

egg white n albume m, bianco m d'uovo

egg yolk n tuorlo m, rosso m

ego /ˈiːɡəʊ/ n ego m

egocentric /iːɡəʊˈsentrɪk/ adj egocentrico

egoism /ˈeɡəʊɪzm/ n egoismo m

egoist /ˈeɡəʊɪst/ n egoista mf

egotism /ˈeɡəʊtɪzm/ n egotismo m

egotist /ˈeɡəʊtɪst/ n egotista mf

Egypt /ˈiːdʒɪpt/ n Egitto m

Egyptian /ɪˈdʒɪpʃn/ adj & n egiziano, -a mf

eiderdown /ˈaɪdədaʊn/ n (quilt) piumino m

eight /eɪt/ adj & n otto m

eighteen /eɪˈtiːn/ adj & n diciotto m

eighteenth /eɪˈtiːnθ/ adj & n diciottesimo, -a mf

eighth /eɪtθ/ adj & n ottavo, -a mf

eighties /ˈeɪtɪz/ npl (period) **the** ~ gli anni Ottanta mpl; (age) ottant'anni mpl; ▶ also FORTIES

eightieth /ˈeɪtɪɪθ/ adj & n ottantesimo, -a mf

eighty /ˈeɪtɪ/ adj & n ottanta m

Eire /ˈeərə/ n Repubblica f d'Irlanda

either /ˈaɪðə(r)/ ① adj & pron ~ [of them] l'uno o l'altro; **I don't like** ~ [of them] non mi piace né l'uno né l'altro; **on** ~ **side** da tutte e due le parti
② adv **I don't** ~ nemmeno io; **I don't like John or his brother** ~ non mi piace John e nemmeno suo fratello

③ conj ~ **John or his brother will be there** ci saranno o John o suo fratello; **I don't like** ~ **John or his brother** non mi piacciono né John né suo fratello; ~ **you go to bed or [else]**... o vai a letto o [altrimenti]...

ejaculate /ɪˈdʒækjʊleɪt/ ① vi eiaculare
② vt (exclaim) prorompere

ejaculation /ɪˈdʒækjʊleɪʃn/ n eiaculazione f; (exclamation) esclamazione f

eject /ɪˈdʒekt/ vt eiettare ⟨pilot⟩; espellere ⟨tape, drunk⟩

eject button n tasto m eject

ejection /ɪˈdʒekʃn/ n (of gases, waste, troublemaker) espulsione f; (of lava) emissione f; Aeron eiezione f

eke /iːk/ vt ~ **out** far bastare; (increase) arrotondare; ~ **out a living** arrangiarsi

elaborate¹ /ɪˈlæbərət/ adj elaborato

elaborate² /ɪˈlæbəreɪt/ vi entrare nei particolari (**on** di)

elaborately /ɪˈlæbərətlɪ/ adv in modo elaborato

elaboration /ɪlæbəˈreɪʃn/ n (of plan, theory) elaborazione f

elapse /ɪˈlæps/ vi trascorrere

elastic /ɪˈlæstɪk/ ① adj elastico
② n elastico m

elasticated /ɪˈlæstɪkeɪtɪd/ adj ⟨waistband, bandage⟩ elastico; ⟨material⟩ elasticizzato

elastic band n elastico m

elasticity /ɪlæsˈtɪsətɪ/ n elasticità f

elated /ɪˈleɪtɪd/ adj esultante

elation /ɪˈleɪʃn/ n euforia f

elbow /ˈelbəʊ/ n gomito m

elbow grease n fam olio m di gomito

elbow room n (room to move) spazio m vitale; **there isn't much** ~ ~ **in this kitchen** si è un po' allo stretto in questa cucina

elder¹ /ˈeldə(r)/ n (tree) sambuco m

elder² ① adj maggiore
② n **the** ~ il/la maggiore

elderberry /ˈeldəbərɪ/ n bacca f di sambuco

elderly /ˈeldəlɪ/ adj anziano

elder statesman n decano m della politica

eldest /ˈeldɪst/ ① adj maggiore
② n **the** ~ il/la maggiore

e-learning /ˈiːlɜːnɪŋ/ n Comput formazione f in rete

elect /ɪˈlekt/ ① adj **the president** ~ il futuro presidente
② vt eleggere; ~ **to do something** decidere di fare qualcosa

election /ɪˈlekʃn/ n elezione f

election campaign n campagna f elettorale

electioneering /ɪˈlekʃənɪərɪŋ/ n
(campaigning) propaganda f elettorale; pej
elettoralismo m

elective /ɪˈlektɪv/ adj ⟨office, official⟩
elettivo, eletto; (empowered to elect)
elettorale; Sch, Univ facoltativo; ~ **surgery**
interventi mpl chirurgici facoltativi

elector /ɪˈlektə(r)/ n elettore, -trice mf

electoral /ɪˈlektərəl/ adj elettorale

electoral roll n liste fpl elettorali

electorate /ɪˈlektərət/ n elettorato m

electric /ɪˈlektrɪk/ adj elettrico

electrical /ɪˈlektrɪkl/ adj elettrico

electrical engineer n elettrotecnico
m

electrical engineering n
elettrotecnica f

electrically /ɪˈlektrɪk(ə)lɪ/ adv ~ **driven**
[a motore] elettrico

electric blanket n termocoperta f

electric fire n stufa f elettrica

electrician /ɪlekˈtrɪʃn/ n elettricista m

electricity /ɪlekˈtrɪsətɪ/ n elettricità f

electricity board n Br azienda f
elettrica

electricity supply n alimentazione f
elettrica

electric shock n **get an ~** ~ prendere
la scossa

electric storm n temporale m

electrify /ɪˈlektrɪfaɪ/ vt (pt/pp **-ied**)
elettrificare; fig elettrizzare

electrifying /ɪˈlektrɪfaɪɪŋ/ adj fig
elettrizzante

electrocute /ɪˈlektrəkjuːt/ vt fulminare;
(execute) giustiziare sulla sedia elettrica

electrocution /ɪlektrəˈkjuːʃn/ n
elettrocuzione f

electrode /ɪˈlektrəʊd/ n elettrodo m

electrolysis /ɪlekˈtrɒlɪsɪs/ n Chem
elettrolisi f; (hair removal) depilazione f
diatermica

electron /ɪˈlektrɒn/ n elettrone m

electronic /ɪlekˈtrɒnɪk/ adj elettronico

electronic banking n servizi mpl
bancari telematici

electronic engineer n tecnico m
elettronico; (with diploma) perito m
elettronico; (with degree) ingegnere m
elettronico

electronic engineering n
ingegneria f elettronica

electronic eye n cellula f fotoelettrica

electronic funds transfer n sistemi
mpl telematici di trasferimento fondi

electronic mail n posta f elettronica

electronic organizer n Comput
agenda f elettronica

electronic publishing n editoria f
elettronica

electronics /ɪlekˈtrɒnɪks/ n elettronica
f

electronic tagging n sorveglianza f
tramite braccialetto elettronico

electro-shock therapy,
electroshock treatment
/ɪˈlektrəʊ-/ n terapia f elettroshock

elegance /ˈelɪgəns/ n eleganza f

elegant /ˈelɪgənt/ adj elegante

elegantly /ˈelɪgəntlɪ/ adv elegantemente

elegy /ˈelədʒɪ/ n elegia f

element /ˈelɪmənt/ n elemento m

elementary /elɪˈmentərɪ/ adj
elementare

elephant /ˈelɪfənt/ n elefante m

elephantine /elɪˈfæntaɪn/ adj ⟨person⟩
mastodontico

elevate /ˈelɪveɪt/ vt elevare

elevated adj ⟨language, rank⟩ elevato;
⟨walkway, railway⟩ soprelevato

elevation /elɪˈveɪʃn/ n elevazione f;
(height) altitudine f; (angle) alzo m

elevator /ˈelɪveɪtə(r)/ n Am ascensore m

eleven /ɪˈlevn/ adj & n undici m

eleven plus n (formerly) esame m di
ammissione alla scuola secondaria
inglese

elevenses /ɪˈlevənzɪz/ n Br fam pausa f
per il caffè (a metà mattina)

eleventh /ɪˈlevənθ/ adj & n undicesimo,
-a mf; **at the ~ hour** fam all'ultimo
momento

elf /elf/ n (pl **elves**) elfo m

elicit /ɪˈlɪsɪt/ vt ottenere

eligible /ˈelɪdʒəbl/ adj eleggibile; ~
young man buon partito; **be ~ for** aver
diritto a

eliminate /ɪˈlɪmɪneɪt/ vt eliminare

elimination /ɪlɪmɪˈneɪʃn/ n
eliminazione f; **by a process of ~**
procedendo per eliminazione

élite /eɪˈliːt/ n fior fiore m

élitist /ɪˈliːtɪst/ adj elitista

ellipse /ɪˈlɪps/ n ellisse f

elliptical /ɪˈlɪptɪk(ə)l/ adj also fig ellittico

elm /elm/ n olmo m

elocution /eləˈkjuːʃn/ n elocuzione f

elongate /ˈiːlɒŋgeɪt/ vt allungare

elongated /ˈiːlɒŋgeɪtɪd/ adj allungato

elope /ɪˈləʊp/ vi fuggire [per sposarsi]

elopement /ɪˈləʊpmənt/ n fuga f
romantica

eloquence /ˈeləkwəns/ n eloquenza f

eloquent /ˈeləkwənt/ adj eloquente

eloquently /ˈeləkwəntlɪ/ adv con
eloquenza

El Salvador /elˈsælvədɔː(r)/ n El
Salvador m; **in ~ ~** nel Salvador

else /els/ *adv* altro; **who** ∼**?** e chi altro?; **he did of course, who** ∼**?** l'ha fatto lui e chi, se no?; **nothing** ∼ nient'altro; **or** ∼ altrimenti; **someone** ∼ qualcun altro; **somewhere** ∼ da qualche altra parte; **anyone** ∼ chiunque altro; (as question) nessun'altro?; **anything** ∼ qualunque altra cosa; (as question) altro?

elsewhere /els'weə(r)/ *adv* altrove

elucidate /ɪ'lu:sɪdeɪt/ *vt* delucidare

elude /ɪ'lu:d/ *vt* eludere; (avoid) evitare; **the name** ∼**s me** il nome mi sfugge

elusive /ɪ'lu:sɪv/ *adj* elusivo

emaciated /ɪ'meɪsɪeɪtɪd/ *adj* emaciato

e-mail **①** *n* e-mail *f*, posta *f* elettronica **②** *vt* spedire per e-mail

e-mail account *n* account *m inv* di posta elettronica

e-mail address *n* indirizzo *m* di posta elettronica

emanate /'eməneɪt/ *vi* emanare

emancipate *vt* emancipare

emancipated /ɪ'mænsɪpeɪtɪd/ *adj* emancipato

emancipation /ɪmænsɪ'peɪʃn/ *n* emancipazione *f*; (of slaves) liberazione *f*

e-marketing /'i:mɑ:kɪtɪŋ/ *n* e-marketing *m inv*

emasculate /ɪ'mæskjʊleɪt/ *vt* evirare; fig svigorire

embalm /ɪm'bɑ:m/ *vt* imbalsamare

embankment /ɪm'bæŋkmənt/ *n* argine *m*; Rail massicciata *f*

embargo /em'bɑ:gəʊ/ *n* (pl **-es**) embargo *m*

embark /ɪm'bɑ:k/ *vi* imbarcarsi; ∼ **on** intraprendere

embarkation /embɑ:'keɪʃn/ *n* imbarco *m*

embarrass /em'bærəs/ *vt* imbarazzare

embarrassed /em'bærəst/ *adj* imbarazzato

embarrassing /em'bærəsɪŋ/ *adj* imbarazzante

embarrassment /em'bærəsmənt/ *n* imbarazzo *m*

embassy /'embəsɪ/ *n* ambasciata *f*

embed /ɪm'bed/ *vt* Comput integrare ⟨command⟩; ∼**ded in** ⟨gem⟩ incastonato in; ⟨plant⟩ piantato in; ⟨sharp object⟩ conficcato in; ⟨rock⟩ incluso in; ∼**ded** ⟨traditions, feelings⟩ radicato; **be** ∼**ded in** fig radicarsi in

embellish /ɪm'belɪʃ/ *vt* abbellire

embers /'embəz/ *npl* braci *fpl*

embezzle /ɪm'bezl/ *vt* appropriarsi indebitamente di

embezzlement /ɪm'bez(ə)lmənt/ *n* appropriazione *f* indebita

embitter /ɪm'bɪtə(r)/ *vt* amareggiare

emblem /'embləm/ *n* emblema *m*

emblematic /emblə'mætɪk/ *adj* emblematico

embodiment /ɪm'bɒdɪmənt/ *n* incarnazione *f*

embody /ɪm'bɒdɪ/ *vt* (pt/pp **-ied**) incorporare; ∼ **what is best in...** rappresentare quanto c'è di meglio di...

embolism /'embəlɪzm/ *n* Med embolia *f*

emboss /ɪm'bɒs/ *vt* sbalzare ⟨metal⟩; stampare in rilievo ⟨paper⟩

embossed /ɪm'bɒst/ *adj* in rilievo

embrace /ɪm'breɪs/ **①** *n* abbraccio *m* **②** *vt* abbracciare **③** *vi* abbracciarsi

embroider /ɪm'brɔɪdə(r)/ *vt* ricamare ⟨design⟩; fig abbellire

embroidery /ɪm'brɔɪdərɪ/ *n* ricamo *m*

embroil /ɪm'brɔɪl/ *vt* **become** ∼**ed in something** rimanere invischiato in qualcosa

embryo /'embrɪəʊ/ *n* embrione *m*

embryonic /'embrɪ'ɒnɪk/ *adj* Biol. fig embrionale

emend /ɪ'mend/ *vt* emendare

emerald /'emərəld/ *n* smeraldo *m*

emerge /ɪ'mɜ:dʒ/ *vi* emergere; (come into being: nation) nascere; ⟨sun, flowers⟩ spuntare fuori

emergence /ɪ'mɜ:dʒəns/ *n* emergere *m*; (of new country) nascita *f*

emergency /ɪ'mɜ:dʒənsɪ/ *n* emergenza *f*; **in an** ∼ in caso di emergenza

emergency ambulance service *n* pronto soccorso *m* autoambulanze

emergency case *n* Med caso *m* di emergenza

emergency centre *n* (for refugees etc) centro *m* di accoglienza; Med centro *m* di soccorso mobile

emergency exit *n* uscita *f* di sicurezza

emergency landing *n* Aeron atterraggio *m* di fortuna

emergency laws *npl* Pol leggi *fpl* straordinarie

emergency number *n* numero *m* di emergenza

emergency powers *npl* Pol poteri *mpl* straordinari

emergency rations *npl* viveri *mpl* di sopravvivenza

emergency service *n* Med servizio *m* di pronto soccorso

emergency services *npl* servizi *mpl* di pronto intervento

emergency surgery *n* **undergo** ∼ ∼ essere operato d'urgenza

emergency ward *n* [reparto *m* di] pronto soccorso *m*

emergency worker *n* addetto *m* a operazioni di soccorso

emergent /ɪ'mɜːdʒənt/ *adj* ‹industry, nation› emergente

emery board /'eməri/ *n* limetta *f* per le unghie di carta.

emery paper *n* carta *f* vetrata

emigrant /'emigrənt/ *n* emigrante *mf*

emigrate /'emigreit/ *vi* emigrare

emigration /emi'greiʃn/ *n* emigrazione *f*

eminence /'eminəns/ *n* (fame) eminenza *f*, gloria *f*; (honour) distinzione *f*; (hill) altura *f*

eminent /'eminənt/ *adj* eminente

eminently /'eminəntli/ *adv* eminentemente

emirate /'emiərət/ *n* emirato *m*

emissary /'emisəri/ *n* emissario *m* (**to** di)

emission /ɪ'mɪʃn/ *n* emissione *f*; (of fumes) esalazione *f*

emit /ɪ'mɪt/ *vt* (pt/pp **emitted**) emettere; esalare ‹fumes›

Emmy /'emi/ *n* Emmy *m*, Oscar *m inv* televisivo americano

emoticon /ɪ'məʊtɪkɒn/ *n* Comput emoticon *m inv*

emotion /ɪ'məʊʃn/ *n* emozione *f*

emotional /ɪ'məʊʃənəl/ *adj* denso di emozione; ‹person, reaction› emotivo; **become** ∼ avere una reazione emotiva; **don't get so** ∼ non lasciarti prendere dalle emozioni

emotionally /ɪ'məʊʃənəli/ *adv* ‹speak› emotivamente; ∼ **disturbed** con turbe emotive

emotionless /ɪ'məʊʃənlɪs/ *adj* impassibile

emotive /ɪ'məʊtɪv/ *adj* emotivo

empathize /'empəθaɪz/ *vi* ∼ **with somebody** immedesimarsi nei problemi di qualcuno

empathy /'empəθi/ *n* comprensione *f*

emperor /'empərə(r)/ *n* imperatore *m*

emphasis /'emfəsis/ *n* enfasi *f*; **put the** ∼ **on something** accentuare qualcosa

emphasize /'emfəsaiz/ *vt* accentuare ‹word, syllable›; sottolineare ‹need›

emphatic /ɪm'fætɪk/ *adj* categorico

emphatically /ɪm'fætɪkli/ *adv* categoricamente

empire /'empaɪə(r)/ *n* impero *m*

empirical /em'pɪrɪkl/ *adj* empirico

empiricism /em'pɪrɪsɪzm/ *n* empirismo *m*

employ /em'plɔɪ/ *vt* impiegare; fig usare ‹tact›

employable /em'plɔɪəbl/ *adj* ‹person› che ha i requisiti per svolgere un lavoro

employee /emplɔɪ'iː/ *n* impiegato, -a *mf*

employee buyout *n* rilevamento *m* dipendenti

employer /em'plɔɪə(r)/ *n* datore *m* di lavoro

employment /em'plɔɪmənt/ *n* occupazione *f*; (work) lavoro *m*

employment agency *n* ufficio *m* di collocamento

employment contract *n* contratto *m* di lavoro

employment exchange *n* agenzia *f* di collocamento

employment figures *npl* dati *mpl* sull'occupazione

Employment Minister, Employment Secretary *n* ministro *m* del lavoro

emporium /em'pɔːrɪəm/ *n* hum emporio *m*

empower /ɪm'paʊə(r)/ *vt* autorizzare; (enable) mettere in grado

empowerment /ɪm'paʊəmənt/ *n* empowerment *m inv*

empress /'emprɪs/ *n* imperatrice *f*

empties /'emptɪz/ *npl* vuoti *mpl*

emptiness /'emptɪnɪs/ *n* vuoto *m*

empty /'empti/ **1** *adj* vuoto; ‹promise, threat› vano **2** *vt* (pt/pp **-ied**) vuotare ‹container› **3** *vi* vuotarsi ∎ **empty out** *vt/i* = EMPTY

empty-handed /-'hændɪd/ *adj* ‹arrive, leave› a mani vuote

empty-headed /-'hedɪd/ *adj* scriteriato

EMS *n* *abbr* (**European Monetary System**) SME *m*

EMU *abbr* (**European Monetary Union**) UME *f*

emulate /'emjʊleɪt/ *vt* emulare

emulsify /ɪ'mʌlsɪfaɪ/ **1** *v* (pt/pp **-ied**) *vt* emulsionare **2** *vi* emulsionarsi

emulsion /ɪ'mʌlʃn/ *n* emulsione *f*

enable /ɪ'neɪbl/ *vt* ∼ **somebody to** mettere qualcuno in grado di

enact /ɪ'nækt/ *vt* Theat rappresentare; decretare ‹law›

enamel /ɪ'næml/ **1** *n* smalto *m* **2** *vt* (pt/pp **enamelled**) smaltare

enamelling /ɪ'næməlɪŋ/ *n* (process) smaltatura *f*; (art) decorazione *f* a smalto

enamoured /ɪ'næməd/ *adj* be ∼ of essere innamorato di

enc. *abbr* (**enclosures**) alleg.

encampment /ɪn'kæmpmənt/ *n* accampamento *m*

encapsulate /en'kæpsjʊleɪt/ *vt* (include) incapsulare; (summarize) sintetizzare

encase /en'keɪs/ *vt* rivestire (**in** di)

encash /enˈkæʃ/ vt Br incassare

encephalogram /enˈkefələgræm/ n encefalogramma m

enchant /ɪnˈtʃɑːnt/ vt incantare

enchanting /ɪnˈtʃɑːntɪŋ/ adj incantevole

enchantment /ɪnˈtʃɑːntmənt/ n incanto m

encircle /ɪnˈsɜːkl/ vt circondare

encl abbr (**enclosed; enclosure**) all.

enclave /ˈenkleɪv/ n enclave f inv; fig territorio m

enclose /ɪnˈkləʊz/ vt circondare ⟨land⟩; (in letter) allegare (**with** a)

enclosed /ɪnˈkləʊzd/ adj ⟨space⟩ chiuso; (in letter) allegato

enclosure /ɪnˈkləʊʒə(r)/ n (at zoo) recinto m; (in letter) allegato m

encode /ɪnˈkəʊd/ vt codificare

encoder /ɪnˈkəʊdə(r)/ n codificatore, -trice mf

encompass /ɪnˈkʌmpəs/ vt (Include) comprendere

encore /ˈɒŋkɔː(r)/ n & int bis m inv

encounter /ɪnˈkaʊntə(r)/ **1** n incontro m; (battle) scontro m **2** vt incontrare

encourage /ɪnˈkʌrɪdʒ/ vt incoraggiare; promuovere ⟨the arts, independence⟩

encouragement /ɪnˈkʌrɪdʒmənt/ n incoraggiamento m; (of the arts) promozione f

encouraging /ɪnˈkʌrɪdʒɪŋ/ adj incoraggiante; ⟨smile⟩ di incoraggiamento

encroach /ɪnˈkrəʊtʃ/ vt ∼ **on** invadere ⟨land, privacy⟩; abusare di ⟨time⟩; interferire con ⟨rights⟩

encrust /enˈkrʌst/ vt **be** ∼**ed with** ⟨ice⟩ essere incrostato di; ⟨jewels⟩ essere tempestato di

encrypt /enˈkrɪpt/ vt criptare

encumber /ɪnˈkʌmbə(r)/ vt **be** ∼**ed with** essere carico di ⟨children, suitcases⟩; essere ingombro di ⟨furniture⟩

encumbrance /ɪnˈkʌmbrəns/ n peso m

encyclop[a]edia /ɪnsaɪkləˈpiːdɪə/ n enciclopedia f

encyclop[a]edic /ɪnsaɪkləˈpiːdɪk/ adj enciclopedico

end /end/ **1** n fine f; (of box, table, piece of string) estremità f; (of town, room) parte f; (purpose) fine m; **in the** ∼ alla fine; **at the** ∼ **of May** alla fine di maggio; **at the** ∼ **of the street/garden** in fondo alla strada/al giardino; **on** ∼ (upright) in piedi; **for days on** ∼ per giorni e giorni; **for six days on** ∼ per sei giorni di fila; **put an** ∼ **to something** mettere fine a qualcosa; **make** ∼**s meet** fam sbarcare il lunario; **no** ∼ **of** fam un sacco di **2** vt/i finire

■ **end in** vt ⟨word⟩ terminare in; finire in ⟨failure, argument⟩

■ **end off** vt concludere ⟨meal, speech⟩

■ **end up** vi finire; ∼ **up doing something** finire col fare qualcosa

endanger /ɪnˈdeɪndʒə(r)/ vt rischiare ⟨one's life⟩; mettere a repentaglio ⟨somebody else, success of something⟩

endangered species /ɪnˈdeɪndʒəd/ n specie f a rischio

endear /ɪnˈdɪə(r)/ vt ∼ **oneself to somebody** conquistarsi la simpatia di qualcuno; ∼ **somebody to** conquistare a qualcuno la simpatia di

endearing /ɪnˈdɪərɪŋ/ adj accattivante

endearingly /ɪnˈdɪərɪŋlɪ/ adv ⟨smile⟩ in modo accattivante; ∼ **honest** di un'onestà disarmante

endearment /ɪnˈdɪəmənt/ n **term of** ∼ vezzeggiativo m

endeavour /ɪnˈdevə(r)/ **1** n tentativo m **2** vi sforzarsi (**to** di)

endemic /enˈdemɪk/ **1** adj endemico **2** n (situation) endemia f

ending /ˈendɪŋ/ n fine f; Gram desinenza f

endive /ˈendaɪv/ n indivia f

endless /ˈendlɪs/ adj interminabile; ⟨patience⟩ infinito

endlessly /ˈendlɪslɪ/ adv continuamente; ⟨patient⟩ infinitamente

endocrinology /endəʊkrɪˈnɒlədʒɪ/ n endocrinologia f

endorse /enˈdɔːs/ vt girare ⟨cheque⟩; ⟨sports personality⟩ fare pubblicità a ⟨product⟩; approvare ⟨plan⟩

endorsement /enˈdɔːsmənt/ n (of cheque) girata f; (of plan) conferma f; (on driving licence) registrazione f su patente di un'infrazione

endow /ɪnˈdaʊ/ vt dotare

endowment insurance /ɪnˈdaʊmənt/ n assicurazione f sulla vita che fornisce un reddito in caso di sopravvivenza

endpaper n risguardo m

end product n prodotto m finito

end result n risultato m finale

endurable /ɪnˈdjʊərəbl/ adj sopportabile

endurance /ɪnˈdjʊərəns/ n resistenza f; **it is beyond** ∼ è insopportabile

endurance test n prova f di resistenza

endure /ɪnˈdjʊə(r)/ **1** vt sopportare **2** vi durare

enduring /ɪnˈdjʊərɪŋ/ adj duraturo

end user n utente m finale

enema /ˈenɪmə/ n Med clistere m

enemy /ˈenəmɪ/ **1** n nemico, -a mf **2** attrib nemico

energetic /enəˈdʒetɪk/ adj energico

energetically /enəˈdʒetɪklɪ/ adv ⟨speak, promote, publicize⟩ vigorosamente; ⟨work, ⸱⸱⸱❖

exercise⟩ con energia; ⟨*deny*⟩
risolutamente

energize /'enədʒaɪz/ *vt* stimolare; Electr
alimentare [elettricamente]

energizing /'enədʒaɪzɪŋ/ *adj* ⟨*influence*⟩
stimolante

energy /'enədʒɪ/ *n* energia *f*

energy efficiency *n* razionalizzazione
f del consumo energetico

energy-efficient *adj* a consumo
ottimale di energia

energy policy *n* politica *f* energetica

energy resources *npl* risorse *fpl*
energetiche

energy saving *n* risparmio *m*
energetico

energy-saving *adj* ⟨*device*⟩ che fa
risparmiare energia; ⟨*measure*⟩ per
risparmiare energia

enervate /'enəveɪt/ *vt* snervare

enfold /en'fəʊld/ *vt* avvolgere

enforce /ɪn'fɔːs/ *vt* far rispettare ⟨*law*⟩

enforced /ɪn'fɔːst/ *adj* forzato

enforcement /ɪn'fɔːsmənt/ *n*
applicazione *f*; (of discipline) imposizione *f*

ENG *abbr* (**electronic news
gathering**) ENG *m*

engage /ɪn'geɪdʒ/ ① *vt* assumere ⟨*staff*⟩;
Theat ingaggiare; Auto ingranare ⟨*gear*⟩; ∼
somebody in conversation fare
conversazione con qualcuno
② *vi* Techn ingranare; ∼ in impegnarsi in

engaged /ɪn'geɪdʒd/ *adj* (in use, busy)
occupato; ⟨*person*⟩ impegnato; (to be
married) fidanzato; **get ∼** fidanzarsi (**to** con)

engaged tone *n* Br segnale *m* di
occupato

engagement /ɪn'geɪdʒmənt/ *n*
fidanzamento *m*; (appointment)
appuntamento *m*; Mil combattimento *m*

engagement ring *n* anello *m* di
fidanzamento

engagements book *n* agenda *f*

engaging /ɪn'geɪdʒɪŋ/ *adj* attraente

engender /ɪn'dʒendə(r)/ *vt* fig generare

engine /'endʒɪn/ *n* motore *m*; Rail
locomotrice *f*

engine drive *n* macchinista *m*

engineer /endʒɪ'nɪə(r)/ ① *n* ingegnere
m; (service, installation) tecnico *m*; Naut, Am
Rail macchinista *m*
② *vt* fig architettare

engineering /endʒɪ'nɪərɪŋ/ *n*
ingegneria *f*

engine failure *n* guasto *m* [al motore];
(in jet) avaria *f*

engine oil *n* olio *m* [del] motore

engine room *n* sala *f* macchine

engine shed *n* Rail deposito *m*

England /'ɪŋglənd/ *n* Inghilterra *f*

English /'ɪŋglɪʃ/ ① *adj* inglese; **the ∼
Channel** la Manica
② *n* (language) inglese *m*; **the ∼** *pl* gli
inglesi

English as a Foreign Language *n*
inglese *m* come lingua straniera

English as a Second Language *n*
inglese *m* come seconda lingua

Englishman *n* inglese *m*

English rose *n* donna *f* dalla bellezza
tipicamente inglese

English speaker *n* anglofono, -a *mf*

English-speaking *adj* anglofono

Englishwoman *n* inglese *f*

engrave /ɪn'greɪv/ *vt* incidere

engraving /ɪn'greɪvɪŋ/ *n* incisione *f*

engross /ɪn'grəʊs/ *vt* ∼ed in assorto in

engrossing /ɪn'grəʊsɪŋ/ *adj* avvincente

engulf /ɪn'gʌlf/ *vt* ⟨*fire, waves*⟩
inghiottire

enhance /ɪn'hɑːns/ *vt* accrescere
⟨*beauty, reputation*⟩; migliorare
⟨*performance*⟩

enigma /ɪ'nɪgmə/ *n* enigma *m*

enigmatic /enɪg'mætɪk/ *adj* enigmatico

enjoy /ɪn'dʒɔɪ/ *vt* godere di ⟨*good health*⟩;
∼ **oneself** divertirsi; **I ∼ cooking/painting**
mi piace cucinare/dipingere; **I ∼ed the
meal/film** mi è piaciuto il pranzo/il film;
∼ **your meal** buon appetito

enjoyable /ɪn'dʒɔɪəbl/ *adj* piacevole

enjoyment /ɪn'dʒɔɪmənt/ *n* piacere *m*

enlarge /ɪn'lɑːdʒ/ ① *vt* ingrandire
② *vi* ∼ **upon** dilungarsi su

enlargement /ɪn'lɑːdʒmənt/ *n*
ingrandimento *m*

enlarger /ɪn'lɑːdʒə(r)/ *n* Phot
ingranditore *m*

enlighten /ɪn'laɪtn/ *vt* illuminare

enlightened /ɪn'laɪtənd/ *adj*
progressista

enlightening /ɪn'laɪtnɪŋ/ *adj* istruttivo

enlightenment /ɪn'laɪtənmənt/ *n* The
E∼ l'Illuminismo *m*

enlist /ɪn'lɪst/ ① *vt* Mil reclutare; ∼ **sb's
help** farsi aiutare da qualcuno
② *vi* Mil arruolarsi

enliven /ɪn'laɪvn/ *vt* animare

enmesh /en'meʃ/ *vt* **become ∼ed in** fig
impegolarsi in

enmity /'enmətɪ/ *n* inimicizia *f*

ennoble /en'nəʊbl/ *vt* nobilitare

enormity /ɪ'nɔːmətɪ/ *n* enormità *f*

enormous /ɪ'nɔːməs/ *adj* enorme

enormously /ɪ'nɔːməslɪ/ *adv*
estremamente; ⟨*grateful*⟩ infinitamente

enough /ɪ'nʌf/ ① *adj & n* abbastanza; **I
didn't bring ∼ clothes** non ho portato
abbastanza vestiti; **have you had ∼?** (to
eat/drink) hai mangiato/bevuto

abbastanza?; I've had ∼**! fam ne ho abbastanza!; is that** ∼**? basta?; that's** ∼**!** basta così!; **£50 isn't** ∼ 50 sterline non sono sufficienti
2 *adv* abbastanza; **you're not working fast** ∼ non lavori abbastanza in fretta; **funnily** ∼ stranamente

enquire /ɪn'kwaɪə(r)/ *vi* domandare; ∼ **about** chiedere informazioni su

enquiring /ɪn'kwaɪərɪŋ/ *adj* ⟨look⟩ indagatore; ⟨mind⟩ avido di sapere

enquiry /ɪn'kwaɪərɪ/ *n* domanda *f*; (investigation) inchiesta *f*

enrage /ɪn'reɪdʒ/ *vt* fare arrabbiare

enrich /ɪn'rɪtʃ/ *vt* arricchire; (improve) migliorare ⟨vocabulary⟩

enrol /ɪn'rəʊl/ *vt* (pt/pp **-rolled**) (for exam, in club) iscriversi (**for, in** a)

enrolment /ɪn'rəʊlmənt/ *n* iscrizione *f*

ensconced /ɪn'skɒnst/ *adj* comodamente sistemato (**in** in)

ensemble /ɒn'sɒmbl/ *n* (clothing & Mus) complesso *m*

ensign /'ensaɪn/ *n* insegna *f*

enslave /ɪn'sleɪv/ *vt* render schiavo

ensue /ɪn'sjuː/ *vi* seguire; ∼ **from** sorgere da; **the ensuing discussion** la discussione che ne è seguita

en suite /ã'swiːt/ **1** *n* (bathroom) camera *f* con bagno annesso
2 *adj* ⟨bathroom⟩ annesso; ⟨room⟩ con bagno

ensure /ɪn'ʃʊə(r)/ *vt* assicurare; ∼ **that** ⟨person⟩ assicurarsi che; ⟨measure⟩ garantire che

ENT *n abbr* (**Ear Nose and Throat**) otorino *m*

entail /ɪn'teɪl/ *vt* comportare; **what does it** ∼**?** in che cosa consiste?

entangle /ɪn'tæŋgl/ *vt* **get** ∼**d in** rimanere impigliato in; fig rimanere coinvolto in

entanglement /ɪn'tæŋg(ə)lmənt/ *n* (emotional) legame *m* sentimentale; (complicated situation) pasticcio *m*

enter /'entə(r)/ **1** *vt* entrare in; iscrivere ⟨horse, runner in race⟩; cominciare ⟨university⟩; partecipare a ⟨competition⟩; Comput immettere ⟨data⟩; (write down) scrivere
2 *vi* entrare; Theat entrare in scena; (register as competitor) iscriversi; (take part) partecipare (**in** a)
3 *n* Comput invio *m*
■ **enter into** *vt* (begin) intavolare ⟨negotiations, an argument⟩

enteritis /entə'raɪtɪs/ *n* enterite *f*

enterprise /'entəpraɪz/ *n* impresa *f*; (quality) iniziativa *f*

enterprising /'entəpraɪzɪŋ/ *adj* intraprendente

entertain /entə'teɪn/ **1** *vt* intrattenere; (invite) ricevere; nutrire ⟨ideas, hopes⟩; prendere in considerazione ⟨possibility⟩
2 *vi* intrattenersi; (have guests) ricevere

entertainer /entə'teɪnə(r)/ *n* artista *mf*

entertaining /entə'teɪnɪŋ/ *adj* ⟨person⟩ di gradevole compagnia; ⟨evening, film, play⟩ divertente

entertainment /entə'teɪnmənt/ *n* (amusement) intrattenimento *m*

entertainment industry *n* l'industria *f* dello spettacolo

enthral /ɪn'θrɔːl/ *vt* (pt/pp **enthralled**) **be** ∼**led** essere affascinato (**by** da)

enthralling /ɪn'θrɔːlɪŋ/ *adj* ⟨novel, performance⟩ affascinante

enthuse /ɪn'θjuːz/ *vi* ∼ **over** entusiasmarsi per

enthusiasm /ɪn'θjuːzɪæzm/ *n* entusiasmo *m*

enthusiast /ɪn'θjuːzɪæst/ *n* entusiasta *mf*

enthusiastic /ɪnθjuːzɪ'æstɪk/ *adj* entusiastico

enthusiastically /ɪnθjuːzɪ'æstɪklɪ/ *adv* entusiasticamente

entice /ɪn'taɪs/ *vt* attirare

enticement /ɪn'taɪsmənt/ *n* (incentive) incentivo *m*

enticing /ɪn'taɪsɪŋ/ *adj* ⟨prospect, offer⟩ allettante; ⟨person⟩ seducente; ⟨food, smell⟩ invitante

entire /ɪn'taɪə(r)/ *adj* intero

entirely /ɪn'taɪəlɪ/ *adv* del tutto; **I'm not** ∼ **satisfied** non sono completamente soddisfatto

entirety /ɪn'taɪərətɪ/ *n* **in its** ∼ nell'insieme

entitle /ɪn'taɪtl/ *vt* dare diritto a; ∼ **somebody to something** dare a qualcuno il diritto di qualcosa

entitled /ɪn'taɪtld/ *adj* ⟨book⟩ intitolato; **be** ∼ **to something** aver diritto a qualcosa

entitlement /ɪn'taɪtlmənt/ *n* diritto *m*

entity /'entətɪ/ *n* entità *f*

entomology /entə'mɒlədʒɪ/ *n* entomologia *f*

entourage /'ɒntʊrɑːʒ/ *n* entourage *m inv*

entrails /'entreɪlz/ *npl* intestini *mpl*

entrance[1] /'entrəns/ *n* entrata *f*; Theat entrata *f* in scena; (right to enter) ammissione *f*; **'no** ∼**'** 'ingresso vietato'

entrance[2] /ɪn'trɑːns/ *vt* estasiare

entrance examination *n* esame *m* di ammissione

entrance fee *n* **how much is the** ∼ ∼**?** quanto costa il biglietto di ingresso?

entrance hall *n* (in house) ingresso *m*

entrance requirements npl
requisiti mpl di ammissione
entrance ticket n biglietto m
d'ingresso
entrancing /ɪnˈtrɑːnsɪŋ/ adj incantevole
entrant /ˈentrənt/ n concorrente mf
entreat /ɪnˈtriːt/ vt supplicare
entreatingly /ɪnˈtriːtɪŋlɪ/ adv ‹beg, ask›
in tono implorante
entreaty /ɪnˈtriːtɪ/ n supplica f
entrée /ˈɑːtreɪ/ n Br (starter) primo m; (Am:
main course) secondo m; **her wealth gave her
an ∼ into high society** il denaro le ha
aperto le porte dell'alta società
entrenched /ɪnˈtrentʃt/ adj ‹ideas,
views› radicato
entrepreneur /ɒntrəprəˈnɜː(r)/ n
imprenditore, -trice mf
entrepreneurial /ɒntrəprəˈnɜːrɪəl/ adj
imprenditoriale; **have ∼ skills** avere il
senso degli affari
entrust /ɪnˈtrʌst/ vt **∼ somebody with
something, ∼ something to somebody**
affidare qualcosa a qualcuno
entry /ˈentrɪ/ n ingresso m; (way in)
entrata f; (in directory etc) voce f; (in
appointment diary) appuntamento m; **'no ∼'**
'ingresso vietato'; Auto 'accesso vietato'
entry fee n quota f di iscrizione
entry form n modulo m di ammissione
entry permit n visto m di entrata
entryphone n citofono m
entry requirements npl requisiti mpl
di ammissione
entry visa n visto m di ingresso
entwine /ɪnˈtwaɪn/ vt also fig intrecciare
E-number n Br sigla f degli additivi
enumerate /ɪˈnjuːməreɪt/ vt enumerare
enumeration /ɪnjuːməˈreɪʃn/ n (list)
enumerazione f; (counting) conto m
enunciate /ɪˈnʌnsɪeɪt/ vt enunciare
enunciation /ɪnʌnsɪˈeɪʃn/ n (of principle,
facts) enunciazione f; (of word) articolazione
f
envelop /ɪnˈveləp/ vt (pt/pp
enveloped) avviluppare
envelope /ˈenvələʊp/ n busta f
enviable /ˈenvɪəbl/ adj invidiabile
envious /ˈenvɪəs/ adj invidioso
enviously /ˈenvɪəslɪ/ adv con invidia
environment /ɪnˈvaɪrənmənt/ n
ambiente m
environmental /ɪnvaɪrənˈmentl/ adj
ambientale
environmental health n salute f
pubblica
environmentalist /ɪnvaɪrənˈmentəlɪst/
n ambientalista mf
environmentally /ɪnvaɪrənˈmentəlɪ/
adv **∼ friendly** che rispetta l'ambiente

environmental scientist n studioso,
-a mf di ecologia applicata
Environmental Studies npl Br Sch
ecogeografia f e ecobiologia f
envisage /ɪnˈvɪzɪdʒ/ vt prevedere
envoy /ˈenvɔɪ/ n inviato, -a mf
envy /ˈenvɪ/ ① n invidia f
② vt (pt/pp **-ied**) **∼ somebody something**
invidiare qualcuno per qualcosa
enzyme /ˈenzaɪm/ n enzima m
EOF abbr Comput (**end of file**) EOF m
ephemeral /ɪˈfemərəl/ adj effimero
epic /ˈepɪk/ ① adj epico
② n epopea f
epicentre /ˈepɪsentə(r)/ n epicentro m
epidemic /epɪˈdemɪk/ n epidemia f
epidermis /epɪˈdɜːmɪs/ n epidermide f
epidural /epɪˈdjʊərəl/ n Med anestesia f
epidurale
epigram /ˈepɪɡræm/ n epigramma m
epilepsy /ˈepɪlepsɪ/ n epilessia f
epileptic /epɪˈleptɪk/ adj & n epilettico,
-a mf
epilogue /ˈepɪlɒɡ/ n epilogo m
Epiphany /ɪˈpɪfənɪ/ n Epifania f
episode /ˈepɪsəʊd/ n episodio m
episodic /epɪˈsɒdɪk/ adj episodico
epistle /ɪˈpɪsl/ n liter epistola f
epitaph /ˈepɪtɑːf/ n epitaffio m
epithet /ˈepɪθet/ n epiteto m
epitome /ɪˈpɪtəmɪ/ n epitome f
epitomize /ɪˈpɪtəmaɪz/ vt essere il
classico esempio di
epoch /ˈiːpɒk/ n epoca f
epoch-making adj che fa epoca
eponymous /ɪˈpɒnɪməs/ adj eponimo
EQ abbr (**graphic equalizer**) EQ m
equable /ˈekwəbl/ adj ‹climate›
temperato; ‹temperament› equilibrato
equably /ˈekwəblɪ/ adv con serenità
equal /ˈiːkwl/ ① adj ‹parts, amounts›
uguale; **of ∼ height** della stessa altezza;
be ∼ to the task essere all'altezza del
compito
② n pari m inv; **treat somebody as an ∼**
trattare qualcuno da pari a pari
③ vt (pt/pp **equalled**) (be same in quantity
as) essere pari a; (rival) uguagliare; **5 plus 5
∼s 10** 5 più 5 [è] uguale a 10
equality /ɪˈkwɒlətɪ/ n uguaglianza f
equalize /ˈiːkwəlaɪz/ vi Sport pareggiare
equalizer /ˈiːkwəlaɪzə(r)/ n Sport
pareggio m; **get the ∼** pareggiare
equally /ˈiːkwəlɪ/ adv ‹divide› in parti
uguali; **∼ intelligent** della stessa
intelligenza; **∼,...** allo stesso tempo ...
equal opportunities npl uguaglianza
f dei diritti

Equal Opportunities Commission n Br commissione f per l'uguaglianza dei diritti nei rapporti di lavoro

equal opportunity attrib ⟨legislation⟩ per l'uguaglianza dei diritti nei rapporti di lavoro; ⟨employer⟩ che applica l'uguaglianza dei diritti

equal rights npl parità f dei diritti

equals sign n segno m uguale

equanimity /ekwə'nɪmətɪ/ n equanimità f

equate /ɪ'kweɪt/ vt ∼ something with something equiparare qualcosa a qualcosa

equation /ɪ'kweɪʒn/ n Math equazione f

equator /ɪ'kweɪtə(r)/ n equatore m

equatorial /ekwə'tɔːrɪəl/ adj equatoriale

Equatorial Guinea n Guinea Equatoriale f

equestrian /ɪ'kwestrɪən/ adj equestre

equidistant /iːkwɪ'dɪstənt/ adj equidistante

equilateral /iːkwɪ'lætərəl/ adj equilatero

equilibrium /iːkwɪ'lɪbrɪəm/ n equilibrio m

equine /'ekwaɪn/ adj ⟨disease, species⟩ equino; ⟨features⟩ cavallino

equinox /'iːkwɪnɒks/ n equinozio m

equip /ɪ'kwɪp/ vt (pt/pp **equipped**) equipaggiare; attrezzare ⟨kitchen, office⟩

equipment /ɪ'kwɪpmənt/ n attrezzatura f

equitable /'ekwɪtəbl/ adj giusto

equity /'ekwətɪ/ n (justness) equità f; Comm azioni fpl

equity capital n Fin capitale m azionario

equity financing n Fin finaziamento m attraverso l'emissione di azioni

equity market n Fin mercato m azionario

equivalent /ɪ'kwɪvələnt/ ① adj equivalente; be ∼ to equivalere a ② n equivalente m

equivocal /ɪ'kwɪvəkl/ adj equivoco

equivocate /ɪ'kwɪvəkeɪt/ vi parlare in modo equivoco, giocare sull'equivoco

equivocation /ɪkwɪvə'keɪʃn/ n affermazione f equivoca; too much ∼ troppi equivoci

era /'ɪərə/ n età f; (geological) era f

eradicate /ɪ'rædɪkeɪt/ vt eradicare

erase /ɪ'reɪz/ vt cancellare

erase head n Comput testina f di cancellazione

eraser /ɪ'reɪzə(r)/ n gomma f [da cancellare]; (for blackboard) cancellino m

erasure /ɪ'reɪʒə(r)/ n (act) cancellazione f; (on paper) cancellatura f

erect /ɪ'rekt/ ① adj eretto ② vt erigere

erection /ɪ'rekʃn/ n erezione f

ergonomic /ɜːgə'nɒmɪk/ adj ergonomico; ⟨seat⟩ anatomico

ergonomics /ɜːgə'nɒmɪks/ n ergonomia f

Erie /'ɪərɪ/ n Lake E∼ il lago Erie

Eritrea /err'treɪə/ n Eritrea f

ERM n abbr **Exchange Rate Mechanism**

ermine /'ɜːmɪn/ n ermellino m

erode /ɪ'rəʊd/ vt ⟨water⟩ erodere; ⟨acid⟩ corrodere

erogenous /ɪ'rɒdʒɪnəs/ adj erogeno

erosion /ɪ'rəʊʒn/ n erosione f; (by acid) corrosione f

erotic /ɪ'rɒtɪk/ adj erotico

erotica /ɪ'rɒtɪkə/ npl (art) arte f erotica; (literature) letteratura f erotica; Cinema film mpl erotici

eroticism /ɪ'rɒtɪsɪzm/ n erotismo m

err /ɜː(r)/ vi errare; (sin) peccare

errand /'erənd/ n commissione f

errant /'erənt/ adj ⟨husband, wife⟩ infedele

erratic /ɪ'rætɪk/ adj irregolare; ⟨person, moods⟩ imprevedibile; ⟨exchange rate⟩ incostante

erroneous /ɪ'rəʊnɪəs/ adj erroneo

erroneously /ɪ'rəʊnɪəslɪ/ adv erroneamente

error /'erə(r)/ n errore m; in ∼ per errore

error message n Comput messaggio m di errore

ersatz /'ɜːsæts/ n surrogato m; ∼ tobacco surrogato del tabacco

erudite /'erʊdaɪt/ adj erudito

erudition /erʊ'dɪʃn/ n erudizione f

erupt /ɪ'rʌpt/ vi eruttare; ⟨spots⟩ spuntare; (fig: in anger) dare in escandescenze

eruption /ɪ'rʌpʃn/ n eruzione f; fig scoppio m

escalate /'eskəleɪt/ ① vi intensificarsi ② vt intensificare

escalation /eskə'leɪʃn/ n escalation f inv

escalator /'eskəleɪtə(r)/ n scala f mobile

escapade /'eskəpeɪd/ n scappatella f

escape /ɪ'skeɪp/ ① n fuga f; (from prison) evasione f; have a narrow ∼ cavarsela per un pelo ② vi ⟨prisoner⟩ evadere (**from** da); sfuggire (**from somebody** alla sorveglianza di qualcuno); ⟨animal⟩ scappare; ⟨gas⟩ fuoriuscire ③ vt ∼ notice passare inosservato; the name ∼s me mi sfugge il nome

escape·[key] *n* (tasto) escape *m inv*

escape chute *n* Aeron scivolo *m*

escape clause *n* clausola *f* di recesso

escapee /ɪskeɪˈpiː/ *n* evaso *m*

escape hatch *n* Naut portello *m* di sicurezza

escape route *n* (for fugitives) itinerario *m* di fuga; (in case of fire etc) percorso *m* di emergenza

escapism /ɪˈskeɪpɪzm/ *n* evasione *f* dalla realtà

escapologist /eskəˈpɒlədʒɪst/ *n* illusionista *mf* capace di liberarsi dalle catene

escarpment /esˈkɑːpmənt/ *n* scarpata *f*

eschew /ɪsˈtʃuː/ *vt* evitare ⟨*discussion*⟩; rifuggire ⟨*temptation*⟩; rifuggire da ⟨*violence*⟩

escort[1] /ˈeskɔːt/ *n* (of person) accompagnatore, -trice *mf*; Mil etc scorta *f*

escort[2] /ɪˈskɔːt/ *vt* accompagnare; Mil etc scortare

Eskimo /ˈeskɪməʊ/ *n* esquimese *mf*

esophagus /ɪˈsɒfəgəs/ *n* Am esofago *m*

esoteric /esəˈterɪk/ *adj* esoterico

ESP *n abbr* (**extrasensory perception**) ESP *f*; *n abbr* **English for Special Purposes**

esp *abbr* **especially**

especial /ɪˈspeʃl/ *adj* speciale

especially /ɪˈspeʃəlɪ/ *adv* specialmente; ⟨*kind*⟩ particolarmente

espionage /ˈespɪənɑːʒ/ *n* spionaggio *m*

espouse /ɪˈspaʊz/ *vt* abbracciare ⟨*cause*⟩

espresso /eˈspresəʊ/ *n* (coffee) espresso *m*

Esq Br *abbr* (**esquire**) **James McBride**, ∼ Egr. Sig. James McBride

essay /ˈeseɪ/ *n* saggio *m*; Sch tema *f*

essence /ˈesns/ *n* essenza *f*; **in** ∼ in sostanza

essential /ɪˈsenʃl/ **1** *adj* essenziale **2** *n* **the** ∼**s** *pl* l'essenziale *m*

essentially /ɪˈsenʃəlɪ/ *adv* essenzialmente

essential oil *n* olio *m* essenziale

est *abbr* (**established**) fondato nel

EST *abbr* Am (**Eastern Standard Time**) ora *f* solare degli stati orientali dell'America settentrionale

establish /ɪˈstæblɪʃ/ *vt* stabilire ⟨*contact, lead*⟩; fondare ⟨*firm*⟩; (prove) accertare; ∼ **oneself as** affermarsi come

established /ɪˈstæblɪʃt/ *adj* ⟨*way of doing something, view*⟩ generalmente accettato; ⟨*company*⟩ affidabile; ⟨*brand*⟩ riconosciuto; **a well** ∼ **fact** un dato di fatto; **the** ∼ **church** la religione di Stato

establishment /ɪˈstæblɪʃmənt/ *n* (firm) azienda *f*; **the E**∼ l'establishment *m*

estate /ɪˈsteɪt/ *n* tenuta *f*; (possessions) patrimonio *m*; (housing) quartiere *m* residenziale

estate agency *n* agenzia *f* immobiliare

estate agent *n* agente *m* immobiliare

estate car *n* giardiniera *f*

estate duty *n* Br imposta *f* di successione

esteem /ɪˈstiːm/ **1** *n* stima *f* **2** *vt* stimare; (consider) giudicare

ester /ˈestə(r)/ *n* estere *m*

estimate[1] /ˈestɪmət/ *n* valutazione *f*; Comm preventivo *m*; **at a rough** ∼ a occhio e croce

estimate[2] /ˈestɪmeɪt/ *vt* stimare

estimated time of arrival /ˈestɪmeɪtɪd/ *n* ora *f* prevista di arrivo

estimation /estɪˈmeɪʃn/ *n* (esteem) stima *f*; **in my** ∼ (judgement) a mio giudizio

Estonia /ɪˈstəʊnɪə/ *n* Estonia *f*

estrange /ɪˈstreɪndʒ/ *vt* estraniare; ∼**d from somebody** separato da qualcuno; **her** ∼**d husband** il marito da cui è separata

estrangement /ɪˈstreɪndʒmənt/ *n* disamoramento *m*

estuary /ˈestjʊərɪ/ *n* estuario *m*

ETA *n abbr* **estimated time of arrival**

et al /etˈæl/ *abbr* (**et alii**) e altri

etc /etˈsetərə/ *abbr* (**et cetera**) ecc

et cetera, etcetera /etˈsetərə/ *adv* eccetera

etch /etʃ/ *vt* incidere all'acquaforte; ∼**ed on her memory** fig impresso nella sua memoria

etching /ˈetʃɪŋ/ *n* acquaforte *f*

eternal /ɪˈtɜːnl/ *adj* eterno

eternal life *n* vita *f* eterna

eternally /ɪˈtɜːnəlɪ/ *adv* eternamente

eternal triangle *n* eterno triangolo *m*

eternity /ɪˈtɜːnətɪ/ *n* eternità *f*

ether /ˈiːθə(r)/ *n* etere *m*

ethereal /ɪˈθɪərɪəl/ *adj* etereo

ethic /ˈeθɪk/ *n* etica *f*

ethical /ˈeθɪkl/ *adj* etico

ethics /ˈeθɪks/ *n* etica *f*

Ethiopia /iːθɪˈəʊpɪə/ *n* Etiopia *f*

ethnic /ˈeθnɪk/ *adj* etnico

ethnically /ˈeθnɪklɪ/ *adv* etnicamente

ethnic cleansing *n* epurazione *f* etnica

ethnic minority *n* minoranza *f* etnica

ethnology /eθˈnɒlədʒɪ/ *n* etnologia *f*

ethos /ˈiːθɒs/ *n* **company** ∼ filosofia *f* dell'azienda

e-ticket /ˈiːtɪkɪt/ *n* Comput biglietto *m* elettronico

etiquette /ˈetɪket/ *n* etichetta *f*

etymology /etɪˈmɒlədʒɪ/ n etimologia f

EU n abbr (**European Union**) UE f

eucalyptus /juːkəˈlɪptəs/ n eucalipto m

eugenics /juːˈdʒenɪks/ n eugenetica f

eulogize /ˈjuːlədʒaɪz/ [1] vt fare il panegirico di
[2] vi ~ over something tessere le lodi di qualcosa

eulogy /ˈjuːlədʒɪ/ n elogio m

eunuch /ˈjuːnək/ n eunuco m

euphemism /ˈjuːfəmɪzm/ n eufemismo m

euphemistic /juːfəˈmɪstɪk/ adj eufemistico

euphemistically /juːfəˈmɪstɪklɪ/ adv eufemisticamente

euphoria /juːˈfɔːrɪə/ n euforia f

euphoric /juːˈfɒrɪk/ adj euforico

Eurasian /jʊˈreɪʒ(ə)n/ adj ⟨people, region⟩ eurasiatico

EURATOM /jʊrˈætəm/ n abbr (**European Atomic Energy Community**) EURATOM f

eurhythmics /jʊˈrɪðmɪks/ n ginnastica f ritmica

euro /ˈjʊərəʊ/ n euro m inv

eurobond n eurobbligazione f

Eurocheque n eurochèque m inv

Eurocrat /ˈjʊərəʊkræt/ n eurocrate mf

eurocurrency n eurovaluta f

Eurodollar n eurodollaro m

euromarket n euromercato m

Euro-MP n eurodeputato, -a mf

Europe /ˈjʊərəp/ n Europa f

European /jʊərəˈpɪən/ adj & n europeo, -a mf

European Bank for Reconstruction and Development n Banca f Europea per la Ricostruzione e lo Sviluppo

European Commission n Commissione f Europea

European Community n Comunità f Europea

European Court of Human Rights n Corte f europea per i diritti dell'uomo

European Court of Justice n Corte f europea di giustizia

European Economic Community n Comunità f Economica Europea

European Free Trade Association n Associazione f Europea di Libero Scambio

European Monetary System n Sistema m Monetario Europeo

European Monetary Union n Unione f Monetaria Europea

European Parliament n Parlamento m Europeo

European Union n Unione f Europea

Euro-sceptic n Br euroscettico, -a mf

euthanasia /juːθəˈneɪzɪə/ n eutanasia f

evacuate /ɪˈvækjʊeɪt/ vt evacuare ⟨building, area⟩

evacuation /ɪvækjʊˈeɪʃn/ n evacuazione f

evacuee /ɪvækjuˈiː/ n sfollato m

evade /ɪˈveɪd/ vt evadere ⟨taxes⟩; evitare ⟨the enemy, authorities⟩; ~ the issue evitare l'argomento

evaluate /ɪˈvæljʊeɪt/ vt valutare

evaluation /ɪvæljʊˈeɪʃn/ n valutazione f, stima f

evangelical /iːvænˈdʒelɪkl/ adj evangelico

evangelist /ɪˈvændʒəlɪst/ n evangelista m

evaporate /ɪˈvæpəreɪt/ vi evaporare; fig svanire

evaporated milk /ɪˈvæpəreɪtɪd/ n latte m condensato

evaporation /ɪvæpəˈreɪʃn/ n evaporazione f

evasion /ɪˈveɪʒn/ n evasione f

evasive /ɪˈveɪsɪv/ adj evasivo

evasively /ɪˈveɪsɪvlɪ/ adv in modo evasivo

eve /iːv/ n liter vigilia f

even /ˈiːvn/ [1] adj (level) piatto; (same, equal) uguale; (regular) regolare; ⟨number⟩ pari; **get ~ with** vendicarsi di; **now we're ~** adesso siamo pari
[2] adv anche, ancora; ~ **if** anche se; ~ **so** con tutto ciò; **not ~** nemmeno; ~ **bigger/ hotter** ancora più grande/caldo
[3] vt ~ **the score** Sport pareggiare
▪ **even out** vi livellarsi
▪ **even up** vt livellare

even-handed /-ˈhændɪd/ adj imparziale

evening /ˈiːvnɪŋ/ n sera f; (whole evening) serata f; **this ~** stasera; **in the ~** la sera

evening class n corso m serale

evening dress n (man's) abito m scuro; (woman's) abito m da sera

evening performance n spettacolo m serale

evening primrose n enotera f

evening star n Venere f

evenly /ˈiːvnlɪ/ adv ⟨distributed⟩ uniformemente; ⟨breathe⟩ regolarmente; ⟨divided⟩ in uguali parti

event /ɪˈvent/ n avvenimento m; (function) manifestazione f; Sport gara f; **in the ~ of** nell'eventualità di; **in the ~** alla fine

even-tempered /-ˈtempəd/ adj pacato

eventful /ɪˈventfʊl/ adj movimentato

eventing /ɪˈventɪŋ/ n Br concorso m ippico completo

eventual /ɪ'ventjʊəl/ *adj* the ~ winner was... alla fine il vincitore è stato...

eventuality /ɪventjʊ'ælətɪ/ *n* eventualità *f*

eventually /ɪ'ventjʊəlɪ/ *adv* alla fine; ~! finalmente!

ever /'evə(r)/ *adv* mai; **I haven't** ~... non ho mai...; **for** ~ per sempre; **hardly** ~ quasi mai; ~ **since** da quando; (since that time) da allora; ~ **so** fam veramente

evergreen /'evəgriːn/ *n* sempreverde *m*

everlasting /evə'lɑːstɪŋ/ *adj* eterno

every /'evrɪ/ *adj* ogni; ~ **one** ciascuno; ~ **other day** un giorno sì un giorno no

everybody /'evrɪbɒdɪ/ *pron* tutti *pl*

everyday /'evrɪdeɪ/ *adj* quotidiano, di ogni giorno

everyone /'evrɪwʌn/ *pron* tutti *pl*; ~ **else** tutti gli altri

everyplace /'evrɪpleɪs/ *adv* Am fam = EVERYWHERE

everything /'evrɪθɪŋ/ *pron* tutto; ~ **else** tutto il resto

everywhere /'evrɪweə(r)/ *adv* dappertutto; (wherever) dovunque

evict /ɪ'vɪkt/ *vt* sfrattare

eviction /ɪ'vɪkʃn/ *n* sfratto *m*

evidence /'evɪdəns/ *n* evidenza *f*; Jur testimonianza *f*; **give** ~ testimoniare

evident /'evɪdənt/ *adj* evidente

evidently /'evɪdəntlɪ/ *adv* evidentemente

evil /'iːvl/ ① *adj* cattivo ② *n* male *m*

evil-smelling /-'smelɪŋ/ *adj* puzzolente

evocative /ɪ'vɒkətɪv/ *adj* evocativo; **be** ~ **of** evocare

evoke /ɪ'vəʊk/ *vt* evocare

evolution /iːvə'luːʃn/ *n* evoluzione *f*

evolutionary /iːvə'luːʃn(ə)rɪ/ *adj* evolutivo

evolve /ɪ'vɒlv/ ① *vt* evolvere ② *vi* evolversi

ewe /juː/ *n* pecora *f*

ex /eks/ *n* (fam: former partner) ex *mf*

ex+ *pref* ex+

exacerbate /ɪg'sæsəbeɪt/ *vt* esacerbare ⟨situation⟩

exact /ɪg'zækt/ ① *adj* esatto ② *vt* esigere

exacting /ɪg'zæktɪŋ/ *adj* esigente

exactitude /ɪg'zæktɪtjuːd/ *n* esattezza *f*

exactly /ɪg'zæktlɪ/ *adv* esattamente; **not** ~ non proprio

exactness /ɪg'zæktnɪs/ *n* precisione *f*

exaggerate /ɪg'zædʒəreɪt/ *vt/i* esagerare

exaggerated /ɪg'zædʒəreɪtɪd/ *adj* esagerato; **he has an** ~ **sense of his own importance** si crede chissà chi

exaggeration /ɪgzædʒə'reɪʃn/ *n* esagerazione *f*

exalt /ɪg'zɔːlt/ *vt* elevare; (praise) vantare

exam /ɪg'zæm/ *n* esame *m*

examination /ɪgzæmɪ'neɪʃn/ *n* esame *m*; (of patient) visita *f*; (of wreckage) ispezione *f*

examination paper *n* testo *m* d'esame

examine /ɪg'zæmɪn/ *vt* esaminare; visitare ⟨patient⟩

examinee /ɪgzæmɪ'niː/ *n* esaminando *m*

examiner /ɪg'zæmɪnə(r)/ *n* Sch esaminatore, -trice *mf*

example /ɪg'zɑːmpl/ *n* esempio *m*; **for** ~ per esempio; **make an** ~ **of somebody** punire qualcuno per dare un esempio; **be an** ~ **to somebody** dare il buon esempio a qualcuno

exasperate /ɪg'zæspəreɪt/ *vt* esasperare

exasperation /ɪgzæspə'reɪʃn/ *n* esasperazione *f*

excavate /'ekskəveɪt/ *vt* scavare; Archaeol fare gli scavi di

excavation /ekskə'veɪʃn/ *n* scavo *m*

excavator /'ekskəveɪtə(r)/ *n* (machine) escavatrice *f*, escavatore *m*

exceed /ɪk'siːd/ *vt* eccedere

exceedingly /ɪk'siːdɪŋlɪ/ *adv* estremamente

excel /ɪk'sel/ ① *v* (pt/pp **excelled**) *vi* eccellere ② *vt* ~ **oneself** superare se stessi

excellence /'eksələns/ *n* eccellenza *f*

Excellency /'eksələnsɪ/ *n* (title) Eccellenza *f*

excellent /'eksələnt/ *adj* eccellente

excellently /'eksələntlɪ/ *adv* in modo eccellente

except /ɪk'sept/ ① *prep* eccetto, tranne; ~ **for** eccetto, tranne; ~ **that**... eccetto che... ② *vt* eccettuare

excepting /ɪk'septɪŋ/ *prep* eccetto, tranne

exception /ɪk'sepʃn/ *n* eccezione *f*; **take** ~ **to** fare obiezioni a

exceptional /ɪk'sepʃənəl/ *adj* eccezionale

exceptionally /ɪk'sepʃənəlɪ/ *adv* eccezionalmente

excerpt /'eksɜːpt/ *n* estratto *m*

excess /ɪk'ses/ *n* eccesso *m*; **in** ~ **of** oltre

excess baggage *n* bagaglio *m* eccedente

excess fare *n* supplemento *m*

excessive /ɪk'sesɪv/ *adj* eccessivo

excessively /ɪk'sesɪvlɪ/ *adv* eccessivamente

excess postage *n* soprattassa *f* postale

excess profits *npl* sovraprofitto *m*

exchange /ɪks'tʃeɪndʒ/ **①** *n* scambio *m*; Teleph centrale *f*; Comm cambio *m*; **[stock]** ～ borsa *f* valori; **in** ～ in cambio (**for** di) **②** *vt* scambiare (**for** con): cambiare ⟨money⟩; ～ **views** scambiarsi i punti di vista; ～ **contracts** fare il rogito **③** *vi* (on house purchase) fare il rogito

exchange control *n* controllo *m* dei cambi

exchange controls *npl* misure *fpl* di controllo dei cambi

exchange rate *n* tasso *m* di cambio

Exchange Rate Mechanism *n* meccanismo *m* di cambio dello Sme

exchequer /ɪks'tʃekə(r)/ *n* Pol tesoro *m*

excise¹ /'eksaɪz/ *n* dazio *m*

excise² /ek'saɪz/ *vt* recidere

excise duty *n* dazio *m*

excitable /ɪk'saɪtəbl/ *adj* eccitabile

excite /ɪk'saɪt/ *vt* eccitare

excited /ɪk'saɪtɪd/ *adj* eccitato; **get** ～ eccitarsi

excitedly /ɪk'saɪtɪdlɪ/ *adv* tutto eccitato

excitement /ɪk'saɪtmənt/ *n* eccitazione *f*

exciting /ɪk'saɪtɪŋ/ *adj* eccitante; ⟨story, film⟩ appassionante; ⟨holiday⟩ entusiasmante

excl *abbr* **excluding**

exclaim /ɪk'skleɪm/ *vt/i* esclamare

exclamation /eksklə'meɪʃn/ *n* esclamazione *f*

exclamation mark *n*, Am **exclamation point** *n* punto *m* esclamativo

exclude /ɪk'sklu:d/ *vt* escludere

excluding /ɪk'sklu:dɪŋ/ *pron* escluso

exclusion /ɪk'sklu:ʒn/ *n* esclusione *f*

exclusion zone *n* zona *f* proibita

exclusive /ɪk'sklu:sɪv/ *adj* ⟨rights, club⟩ esclusivo; ⟨interview⟩ in esclusiva; ～ **of**... ...escluso

exclusively /ɪk'sklu:sɪvlɪ/ *adv* esclusivamente

excommunicate /ekskə'mjun:nɪkeɪt/ *vt* scomunicare

excrement /'ekskrɪmənt/ *n* escremento *m*

excreta /ɪk'skri:tə/ *npl* escrementi *mpl*

excrete /ɪk'skri:t/ *vt* espellere; secernere ⟨liquid⟩

excretion /ɪk'skri:ʃn/ *n* (of animal, human) escremento *m*

excruciating /ɪk'skru:ʃIeɪtɪŋ/ *adj* atroce ⟨pain⟩; (fam: very bad) spaventoso

excursion /ɪk'skɜ:ʃn/ *n* escursione *f*

excusable /ɪk'skju:zəbl/ *adj* perdonabile

excuse¹ /ɪk'skju:s/ *n* scusa *f*

excuse² /ɪk'skju:z/ *vt* scusare; ～ **from** esonerare da; ～ **me!** (to get attention) scusi!; (to get past) permesso!, scusi!; (indignant) come ha detto?

ex-directory *adj* be ～ non figurare sull'elenco telefonico

exec /ɪg'zek/ *n* Am *abbrev fam* **executive**

execrable /'eksɪkrəbl/ *adj* esecrabile

executable file /'eksɪkju:təbl/ *n* Comput eseguibile *m*

execute /'eksɪkju:t/ *vt* eseguire; (put to death) giustiziare; attuare ⟨plan⟩

execution /eksɪ'kju:ʃn/ *n* esecuzione *f*; (of plan) attuazione *f*

executioner /eksɪ'kju:ʃənə(r)/ *n* boia *m inv*

executive /ɪg'zekjutɪv/ **①** *adj* esecutivo **②** *n* dirigente *mf*; Pol esecutivo *m*

executive committee *n* comitato *m* esecutivo

executive director *n* direttore, -trice *mf* [esecutivo, -a]

executive jet *n* jet *m inv* privato

executive producer *n* Cinema direttore, -trice *mf* di produzione

executive secretary *n* segretario, -a *mf* di direzione

executor /ɪg'zekjutə(r)/ *n* Jur esecutore, -trice *mf*

exemplary /ɪg'zemplərɪ/ *adj* esemplare

exemplify /ɪg'zemplɪfaɪ/ *vt* (pt/pp **-ied**) esemplificare

exempt /ɪg'zempt/ **①** *adj* esente **②** *vt* esentare (**from** da)

exemption /ɪg'zempʃn/ *n* esenzione *f*

exercise /'eksəsaɪz/ **①** *n* esercizio *m*; Mil esercitazione *f*; **physical** ～**s** ginnastica *f*; **take** ～ fare del moto; **you need more** ～ devi muoverti di più **②** *vt* esercitare ⟨muscles, horse⟩; portare a spasso ⟨dog⟩; usare ⟨patience⟩; mettere in pratica ⟨skills⟩ **③** *vi* esercitarsi; ～ **more** fare più moto

exercise bike *n* cyclette® *f inv*

exercise book *n* quaderno *m*

exert /ɪg'zɜ:t/ *vt* esercitare; ～ **oneself** sforzarsi

exertion /ɪg'zɜ:ʃn/ *n* sforzo *m*

ex gratia /eks'greɪʃə/ *adj* ⟨award, payment⟩ a titolo di favore

exhale /eks'heɪl/ *vt/i* esalare

exhaust /ɪg'zɔ:st/ *n* Auto scappamento *m*; (pipe) tubo *m* di scappamento

exhausted /ɪg'zɔ:stɪd/ *adj* esausto

exhaust fumes **①** *npl* fumi *mpl* di scarico *m* **②** *vt* esaurire

exhausting /ɪgˈzɔːstɪŋ/ *adj* estenuante; ⟨*climate, person*⟩ sfibrante

exhaustion /ɪgˈzɔːstʃn/ *n* esaurimento *m*

exhaustive /ɪgˈzɔːstɪv/ *adj* fig esauriente

exhibit /ɪgˈzɪbɪt/ ① *n* oggetto *m* esposto; Jur reperto *m*
② *vt* esporre; fig dimostrare

exhibition /eksɪˈbɪʃn/ *n* mostra *f*; (of strength, skill) dimostrazione *f*

exhibition centre *n* palazzo *m* delle esposizioni

exhibitionist /eksɪˈbɪʃənɪst/ *n* esibizionista *mf*

exhibitor /ɪgˈzɪbɪtə(r)/ *n* espositore, -trice *mf*

exhilarated /ɪgˈzɪləreɪtɪd/ *adj* rallegrato

exhilarating /ɪgˈzɪləreɪtɪŋ/ *adj* stimolante; ⟨*mountain air*⟩ tonificante

exhilaration /ɪgzɪləˈreɪʃn/ *n* allegria *f*

exhort /ɪgˈzɔːt/ *vt* esortare

exhume /ɪgˈzjuːm/ *vt* esumare

exile /ˈeksaɪl/ ① *n* esilio *m*; (person) esule *mf*
② *vt* esiliare

exist /ɪgˈzɪst/ *vi* esistere

existence /ɪgˈzɪstəns/ *n* esistenza *f*; in ~ esistente; be in ~ esistere

existential /egzɪˈstenʃ(ə)l/ *adj* esistenziale

existentialism /egzɪˈstenʃəlɪzm/ *n* esistenzialismo *m*

existing /ɪgˈzɪstɪŋ/ *adj* ⟨*policy, management, leadership*⟩ attuale; ⟨*laws, order*⟩ vigente

exit /ˈeksɪt/ ① *n* uscita *f*; Theat uscita *f* di scena
② *vi* Theat uscire di scena; Comput uscire (**from** da)

exit sign *n* cartello *m* di uscita

exodus /ˈeksədəs/ *n* esodo *m*

ex officio /eksəˈfɪʃɪəʊ/ *adj* ⟨*member*⟩ di diritto

exonerate /ɪgˈzɒnəreɪt/ *vt* esonerare

exorbitant /ɪgˈzɔːbɪtənt/ *adj* esorbitante

exorcism /ˈeksɔːsɪzm/ *n* esorcismo *m*

exorcist /ˈeksɔːsɪst/ *n* esorcista *mf*

exorcize /ˈeksɔːsaɪz/ *vt* esorcizzare

exotic /ɪgˈzɒtɪk/ *adj* esotico

exotica /ɪgˈzɒtɪkə/ *npl* oggetti *mpl* esotici

expand /ɪkˈspænd/ ① *vt* espandere; sviluppare ⟨*economy*⟩
② *vi* espandersi; Comm svilupparsi; ⟨*metal*⟩ dilatarsi
■ **expand on** *vt* (explain better) approfondire

expandable /ɪkˈspændəbl/ *adj* Comput ⟨*memory*⟩ espandibile

expanding /ɪkˈspændɪŋ/ *adj* ⟨*file*⟩ a soffietto *inv*; ⟨*population, sector*⟩ in espansione; ⟨*bracelet*⟩ allungabile

expanse /ɪkˈspæns/ *n* estensione *f*

expansion /ɪkˈspænʃn/ *n* espansione *f*; Comm sviluppo *m*; (of metal) dilatazione *f*

expansion board, **expansion card** *n* Comput scheda *f* di espansione

expansionist /ɪkˈspænʃənɪst/ *n & a* espansionista *mf*

expansion slot *n* Comput fessura *f* [per la scheda] di espansione, slot *m* di espansione

expansive /ɪkˈspænsɪv/ *adj* espansivo

expatriate /eksˈpætrɪət/ *n* espatriato, -a *mf*

expect /ɪkˈspekt/ *vt* aspettare ⟨*letter, baby*⟩; (suppose) pensare; (demand) esigere; I ~ **so** penso di sì; **we ~ to arrive on Monday** contiamo di arrivare lunedì; I **didn't ~ that** questo non me lo aspettavo; **she ~s too much from him** pretende troppo da lui; **be ~ing** essere in stato interessante

expectancy /ɪkˈspektənsɪ/ *n* aspettativa *f*

expectant /ɪkˈspektənt/ *adj* in attesa; ~ **mother** donna *f* incinta

expectantly /ɪkˈspektəntlɪ/ *adv* con impazienza

expectation /ekspekˈteɪʃn/ *n* aspettativa *f*, speranza *f*

expediency /ɪkˈspiːdɪənsɪ/ *n* (appropriateness) opportunità *f*; (self-interest) opportunismo *m*

expedient /ɪkˈspiːdɪənt/ ① *adj* conveniente
② *n* espediente *m*

expedite /ˈekspɪdaɪt/ *vt fml* accelerare

expedition /ekspɪˈdɪʃn/ *n* spedizione *f*

expeditionary /ekspɪˈdɪʃənərɪ/ *adj* Mil di spedizione

expeditionary force *n* corpo *m* di spedizione

expel /ɪkˈspel/ *vt* (pt/pp **expelled**) espellere

expend /ɪkˈspend/ *vt* consumare

expendable /ɪkˈspendəbl/ *adj* sacrificabile

expenditure /ɪkˈspendɪtʃə(r)/ *n* spesa *f*

expense /ɪkˈspens/ *n* spesa *f*; **business ~s** *pl* spese *fpl*; **at my ~** a mie spese; **at the ~ of** fig a spese di

expense account *n* conto *m* spese

expensive /ɪkˈspensɪv/ *adj* caro, costoso

expensively /ɪkˈspensɪvlɪ/ *adv* costosamente

experience /ɪkˈspɪərɪəns/ ① *n* esperienza *f*
② *vt* provare ⟨*sensation*⟩; avere ⟨*problem*⟩

experienced /ɪkˈspɪərɪənst/ *adj* esperto

experiment /ɪk'sperɪmənt/ ① *n*
esperimento
② /ɪk'sperɪment/ *vi* sperimentare
experimental /ɪksperɪ'mentl/ *adj*
sperimentale
experimentation /ɪksperɪmen'teɪʃn/ *n*
sperimentazione *f*; ∼ **with drugs**
esperienza *f* della droga
expert /'eksp3:t/ *adj & n* esperto, -a *mf*
expertise /eksp3:'ti:z/ *n* competenza *f*
expertly /'eksp3:tlɪ/ *adv* abilmente
expiate /'ekspɪeɪt/ *vt* espiare ⟨*crime,
sin*⟩; fare ammenda per ⟨*guilt*⟩
expiration /ekspɪ'reɪʃn/ *n* (end, exhalation)
espirazione *f*
expire /ɪk'spaɪə(r)/ *vi* scadere
expiry /ɪk'spaɪərɪ/ *n* scadenza *f*
expiry date *n* data *f* di scadenza
explain /ɪk'spleɪn/ *vt* spiegare
■ **explain away** *vt* (give reasons for)
trovare delle giustificazioni per
explanation /eksplə'neɪʃn/ *n*
spiegazione *f*
explanatory /ɪk'splænətərɪ/ *adj*
esplicativo
expletive /ɪk'spli:tɪv/ *n* imprecazione *f*
explicit /ɪk'splɪsɪt/ *adj* esplicito
explicitly /ɪk'splɪsɪtlɪ/ *adv*
esplicitamente
explode /ɪk'spləʊd/ ① *vi* esplodere
② *vt* fare esplodere
exploit[1] /'eksplɔɪt/ *n* impresa *f*
exploit[2] /ɪk'splɔɪt/ *vt* sfruttare
exploitation /eksplɔɪ'teɪʃn/ *n*
sfruttamento *m*
exploitative /ɪk'splɔɪtətɪv/ *adj* inteso a
sfruttare gli individui; ⟨*attitude, system*⟩ a
carattere di sfruttamento
exploration /eksplə'reɪʃn/ *n*
esplorazione *f*
exploratory /ɪk'splɒrətərɪ/ *adj*
esplorativo
explore /ɪk'splɔ:(r)/ *vt* esplorare; fig
studiare ⟨*implications*⟩
explorer /ɪk'splɔ:rə(r)/ *n* esploratore,
-trice *mf*
explosion /ɪk'spləʊʒn/ *n* esplosione *f*
explosive /ɪk'spləʊsɪv/ *adj & n*
esplosivo *m*
exponent /ɪk'spəʊnənt/ *n* esponente *mf*
exponential /ekspə'nenʃəl/ *adj*
esponenziale
export[1] /'ekspɔ:t/ *n* esportazione *f*
export[2] /ek'spɔ:t/ *vt* esportare
export agent *n* esportatore, -trice *mf*
export control *n* controllo *m* delle
esportazioni
export credit *n* credito *m*
all'esportazione

export drive *n* campagna *f* di
esportazione
export duty *n* tassa *f* di esportazione
export earnings *npl* ricavato *m* delle
esportazioni
exporter /ek'spɔ:tə(r)/ *n* esportatore,
-trice *mf*
export finance *n* finanziamento *m*
delle esportazioni
export-import company *n* azienda
di import-export
export licence *n* licenza *f* di
esportazione
export market *n* mercato *m* delle
esportazioni
export trade *n* commercio *m* di
esportazione
expose /ɪk'spəʊz/ *vt* esporre; ⟨*reveal*⟩
svelare; smascherare ⟨*traitor etc*⟩
exposée /ɪk'spəʊzeɪ/ *n* (of scandal)
rivelazioni *fpl*
exposition /ekspə'zɪʃn/ *n* (of facts)
esposizione *f*
exposure /ɪk'spəʊʒə(r)/ *n* esposizione *f*;
Med esposizione *f* prolungata al freddo/
caldo; (of crimes) smascheramento *m*; **24**
∼**s** Phot 24 pose
exposure meter *n* Phot esposimetro *m*
exposure time *n* Phot tempo *m* di
esposizione
expound /ɪk'spaʊnd/ *vt* esporre
express /ɪk'spres/ ① *adj* espresso
② *adv* ⟨*send*⟩ per espresso
③ *n* (train) espresso *m*
④ *vt* esprimere; ∼ **oneself** esprimersi
expression /ɪk'spreʃn/ *n* espressione *f*
expressionless /ɪk'spreʃənlɪs/ *adj*
⟨*tone, voice*⟩ distaccato; ⟨*playing*⟩ piatto;
⟨*eyes, face*⟩ inespressivo
expressive /ɪk'spresɪv/ *adj* espressivo
expressively /ɪk'spresɪvlɪ/ *adv*
espressamente
expulsion /ɪk'spʌlʃn/ *n* espulsione *f*
expurgate /'ekspəgeɪt/ *vt* espurgare
exquisite /ek'skwɪzɪt/ *adj* squisito
exquisitely /ek'skwɪzɪtlɪ/ *adv* ⟨*dressed,
written*⟩ in modo elegante e raffinato; ∼
beautiful di una bellezza fine
ex-serviceman /'s3:vɪsmən/ *n* ex-
combattente *m*
ex-servicewoman /'s3:vɪswʊmən/ *n*
ex-combattente *f*
extant /ɪk'stænt/ *adj* ancora esistente
extempore /ɪk'stempərɪ/ *adv* ⟨*speak*⟩
senza preparazione
extend /ɪk'stend/ ① *vt* prolungare ⟨*visit,
road*⟩; prorogare ⟨*visa, contract*⟩; ampliare
⟨*building, knowledge*⟩; (stretch out)
allungare; tendere ⟨*hand*⟩
② *vi* ⟨*garden, knowledge*⟩ estendersi

extendable /ɪk'stendəbl/ adj ‹cable›
allungabile; ‹contract› prorogabile

extension /ɪk'stenʃn/ n prolungamento
m; (of visa, contract) proroga f; (of treaty)
ampliamento m; (part of building) annesso m;
(length of cable) prolunga f; Teleph interno m;
~ **226** interno 226; (hair) ~s le extension

extension ladder n scala f allungabile

extension lead n Electr prolunga f

extensive /ɪk'stensɪv/ adj ampio, vasto

extensively /ɪk'stensɪvlɪ/ adv
ampiamente

extent /ɪk'stent/ n (scope) portata f; **to a
certain** ~ fino a un certo punto; **to such
an** ~ **that...** fino al punto che...

extenuating /ɪk'stenjʊetɪŋ/ adj ~
circumstances attenuanti fpl

exterior /ɪk'stɪərɪə(r)/ adj & n esterno m

exterminate /ɪk'stɜːmɪneɪt/ vt
sterminare

extermination /ɪkstɜːmɪ'neɪʃn/ n
sterminio m

external /ɪk'stɜːnl/ adj esterno; **for** ~
use only Med per uso esterno

externalize /ɪk'stɜːnəlaɪz/ vt
esteriorizzare

externally /ɪk'stɜːnəlɪ/ adv
esternamente

externals /ɪk'stɜːn(ə)lz/ npl apparenze
fpl

extinct /ɪk'stɪŋkt/ adj estinto

extinction /ɪk'stɪŋkʃn/ n estinzione f

extinguish /ɪk'stɪŋgwɪʃ/ vt estinguere

extinguisher /ɪk'stɪŋgwɪʃə(r)/ n
estintore m

extol /ɪk'stəʊl/ vt (pt/pp **extolled**)
lodare

extort /ɪk'stɔːt/ vt estorcere

extortion /ɪk'stɔːʃn/ n estorsione f

extortionate /ɪk'stɔːʃənət/ adj
esorbitante

extra /'ekstrə/ ① adj in più; ‹train›
straordinario; **an** ~ **£10** 10 sterline extra,
10 sterline in più
② adv in più; (especially) più; **pay** ~
pagare in più, pagare extra; ~ **strong/
busy** fortissimo/occupatissimo
③ n Theat comparsa f; ~s pl extra mpl

extra charge n supplemento m; **at no**
~ ~ senza ulteriori spese

extract¹ /'ekstrækt/ n estratto m

extract² /ɪk'strækt/ vt estrarre ‹tooth,
oil›; strappare ‹secret›; ricavare ‹truth›

extraction /ɪk'strækʃn/ n (process)
estrazione f; **of French** ~ di origine
francese

extractor [fan] /ɪk'stræktə(r)/ n
aspiratore m

extra-curricular /-kə'rɪkjʊlə(r)/ adj
extrascolastico

extradite /'ekstrədaɪt/ vt Jur estradare

extradition /ekstrə'dɪʃn/ n estradizione
f

extra-dry adj ‹sherry, wine› extra dry
inv

extra-fast adj ultrarapido

extra-large adj ‹pullover, shirt› extra
large inv

extramarital /ekstrə'mærɪtəl/ adj
extraconiugale

extramural /ekstrə'mjʊərəl/ adj Br Univ
‹course, lecture› organizzato
dall'università e aperto a tutti

extraneous /ɪk'streɪnɪəs/ adj (not
essential) inessenziale; ‹issue, detail›
superfluo

extraordinarily /ɪk'strɔːdɪnərɪlɪ/ adv
straordinariamente

extraordinary /ɪk'strɔːdɪnərɪ/ adj
straordinario

extrapolate /ɪk'stræpəleɪt/ vt arguire;
Math estrapolare

extrasensory perception
/ekstrə'sensərɪ/ n percezione f
extrasensoriale

extra-special adj eccezionale

extra-strong adj ‹thread› robustissimo;
‹coffee› fortissimo; ‹disinfectant, weed
killer› potentissimo; ‹paper›
ultraresistente inv

extraterrestrial /ekstrətɪ'restrɪəl/ n &
adj extraterrestre mf

extra time n tempo m supplementare;
play ~ ~ giocare i tempi supplementari

extravagance /ɪk'strævəgəns/ n (with
money) prodigalità f; (of behaviour)
stravaganza f

extravagant /ɪk'strævəgənt/ adj
spendaccione; (bizarre) stravagante; ‹claim›
esagerato

extravagantly /ɪk'strævəgəntlɪ/ adv
dispendiosamente

extravaganza /ɪkstrævə'gænzə/ n
rappresentazione f spettacolare

extra virgin olive oil n olio m
extravergine d'oliva

extreme /ɪk'striːm/ ① adj estremo
② n estremo m; **in the** ~ al massimo

extremely /ɪk'striːmlɪ/ adv
estremamente

extreme sports npl sport mpl estremi

extremism /ɪk'striːmɪzm/ n estremismo
m

extremist /ɪk'striːmɪst/ n estremista mf

extremity /ɪk'stremətɪ/ n (end) estremità
f inv

extricate /'ekstrɪkeɪt/ vt districare

extrovert /'ekstrəvɜːt/ n estroverso, -a
mf

exuberance /ɪg'zjuːbərəns/ n
esuberanza f

exuberant /ɪgˈzjuːbərənt/ *adj* esuberante

exude /ɪgˈzjuːd/ *vt* also fig trasudare

exult /ɪgˈzʌlt/ *vi* esultare

exultant /ɪgˈzʌltənt/ *adj* esultante; ⟨cry⟩ di esultanza

exultantly /ɪgˈzʌltəntlɪ/ *adv* con esultanza

ex-works *adj* ⟨price, value⟩ franco fabbrica

eye /aɪ/ **①** *n* occhio *m*; (of needle) cruna *f*; **keep an ～ on** tener d'occhio; **see ～ to ～** aver le stesse idee **②** *vt* (pt/pp **eyed**, pres p **ey[e]ing**) guardare ■ **eye up** *vt* adocchiare ⟨somebody⟩

eyeball *n* bulbo *m* oculare

eyebath *n* bagno *m* oculare

eyebrow *n* sopracciglio *m* (pl sopracciglia *f*)

eyebrow pencil *n* matita *f* per le sopracciglia

eye-catching /ˈaɪkætʃɪŋ/ *adj* che attira l'attenzione

eye contact *n* **avoid ～ ～ with somebody** evitare di incrociare lo sguardo di qualcuno; **try to make ～ ～ with somebody** tentare di incrociare lo sguardo di qualcuno

eyedrops *n pl* collirio *m*

eyeful /ˈaɪfʊl/ *n* **get an ～** (of something) avere gli occhi pieni (di qualcosa); (fam: good look) lustrarsi la vista

eyeglass *n* (monocle) monocolo *m*

eyeglasses *n pl* Am occhiali *mpl* [da vista]

eyelash *n* ciglio *m* (pl ciglia *f*)

eyelet /ˈaɪlɪt/ *n* occhiello *m*

eye-level *adj* ⟨grill, shelf⟩ all'altezza degli occhi

eyelid *n* palpebra *f*

eye liner *n* eye liner *m inv*

eye make-up *n* trucco *m* per gli occhi

eye-opener *n* rivelazione *f*

eyepatch *n* benda *f* per gli occhi

eye-shade *n* visiera *f*

eyeshadow *n* ombretto *m*

eyesight *n* vista *f*

eyesore *n* fam pugno *m* nell'occhio

eye strain *n* affaticamento *m* degli occhi

eye test *n* esame *m* della vista

eyewash *n* bagno *m* oculare; (fig: nonsense) fumo *m* negli occhi

eyewitness *n* testimone *mf* oculare

eyrie /ˈɪərɪ/ *n* nido *m* d'aquila

e-zine /ˈiːziːn/ *n* Comput e-zine *f inv*

Ff

F¹ *abbr* (**Fahrenheit**) F

f², **F** /ef/ *n* (letter) f, F *f inv*; Mus fa *m inv*

FA *n* Br abbr (**Football Association**) associazione *f* calcistica britannica, ≈ FIGC *f*

façade /fəˈsɑːd/ *n* (of building, person) facciata *f*

fable /ˈfeɪbl/ *n* favola *f*

fabric /ˈfæbrɪk/ *n* also fig tessuto *m*

fabricate /ˈfæbrɪkeɪt/ *vt* fabbricare; inventare ⟨story⟩

fabrication /fæbrɪˈkeɪʃn/ *n* invenzione *f*; (manufacture) fabbricazione *f*

fabric softener /sɒfnə(r)/ *n* ammorbidente *m*

fabulous /ˈfæbjʊləs/ *adj* fam favoloso

face /feɪs/ **①** *n* faccia *f*, viso *m*; (grimace) smorfia *f*; (surface) faccia *f*; (of clock) quadrante *m*; **pull ～s** far boccacce; **in the ～ of** di fronte a; **on the ～ of it** in apparenza

② *vt* essere di fronte a; (confront) affrontare; **～ north** ⟨house⟩ dare a nord; **～ the fact that** arrendersi al fatto che ■ **face up to** *vt* accettare ⟨facts⟩; affrontare ⟨person⟩

face flannel *n* ≈ guanto *m* di spugna

faceless /ˈfeɪslɪs/ *adj* anonimo

facelift /ˈfeɪslɪft/ *n* plastica *f* facciale

face pack *n* maschera *f* di bellezza

face powder *n* cipria *f*

face saving *adj* ⟨plan, solution⟩ per salvare la faccia

facet /ˈfæsɪt/ *n* sfaccettatura *f*; fig aspetto *m*

facetious /fəˈsiːʃəs/ *adj* spiritoso. **～ remarks** spiritosaggini *mpl*

face to face **①** *adj* ⟨meeting⟩ a quattr'occhi **②** *adv* ⟨be seated⟩ faccia a faccia; **meet somebody ～ ～ ～** avere un incontro a quattr'occhi con qualcuno; **come ～ ～ ～ with** trovarsi di fronte a

face value n (of money) valore m nominale; **take someone/something at ~** ~ fermarsi alle apparenze

facial /'feɪʃl/ ① adj facciale ② n trattamento m di bellezza al viso

facile /'fæsaɪl/ adj semplicistico

facilitate /fəˈsɪlɪteɪt/ vt rendere possibile; (make easier) facilitare

facilitator /fəˈsɪlɪteɪtə(r)/ n mediatore m

facility /fəˈsɪlətɪ/ n facilità f; **facilities** pl (of area, in hotel etc) attrezzature fpl; **credit facilities** pl facilitazioni fpl di pagamento

facing /'feɪsɪŋ/ prep ~ **the sea** ⟨house⟩ che dà sul mare; **the person ~ me** la persona di fronte a me

facsimile /fækˈsɪmɪlɪ/ n facsimile m

fact /fækt/ n fatto m; **in ~** infatti

fact finding adj ⟨mission, tour, trip⟩ di inchiesta

faction /'fækʃn/ n fazione f

factional /'fækʃnəl/ adj ⟨leader, activity⟩ di una fazione; ⟨fighting, arguments⟩ tra fazioni

factor /'fæktə(r)/ n fattore m

factory /'fæktərɪ/ n fabbrica f

factory farming n allevamento m su scala industriale

factory floor n (place) reparto m produzione; (workers) operai mpl

factory inspector n verificatore, -trice mf

factory made adj prodotto in fabbrica

factory shop n negozio m di vendita diretta dalla fabbrica al consumatore

factory unit n unità f inv di produzione

factory worker n operaio, -a mf

fact sheet n (one issue) prospetto m illustrativo; (periodical) bollettino m d'informazione

factual /'fæktʃʊəl/ adj **be ~** attenersi ai fatti

factually /'fæktʃʊəlɪ/ adv ⟨inaccurate⟩ dal punto di vista dei fatti

faculty /'fækəltɪ/ n facoltà f inv

fad /fæd/ n capriccio m

faddish /'fædɪʃ/ adj ⟨person⟩ sempre in preda a una nuova mania

fade /feɪd/ vi sbiadire; ⟨sound, light⟩ affievolirsi; ⟨flower⟩ appassire
■ **fade away** vi ⟨sound⟩ affievolirsi; (dying person) spegnersi
■ **fade in** vt cominciare in dissolvenza ⟨picture⟩
■ **fade out** vt finire in dissolvenza ⟨picture⟩

faded /'feɪdɪd/ adj ⟨clothing, carpet, colour⟩ sbiadito; ⟨flower, beauty⟩ appassito; ⟨glory⟩ svanito

faeces /'fiːsiːz/ npl feci fpl

fag /fæg/ n (chore) fatica f; (fam: cigarette) sigaretta f; (Am sl: homosexual) frocio m

fag end n fam mozzicone m di sigaretta, cicca f; (of day, decade, conversation) fine f; (of material) scampolo m

fagged /fægd/ adj ~ **out** fam stanco morto

faggot /'fægət/ n (meatball) polpetta f di carne; (firewood) fascina f

Fahrenheit /'færənhaɪt/ adj Fahrenheit

fail /feɪl/ ① n **without ~** senz'altro ② vi ⟨attempt⟩ fallire; ⟨eyesight, memory⟩ indebolirsi; ⟨engine, machine⟩ guastarsi; ⟨marriage⟩ andare a rotoli; (in exam) essere bocciato; **~ to do something** non fare qualcosa; **I tried but I ~ed** ho provato ma non ci sono riuscito; **a ~ed politician** un politico fallito ③ vt non superare ⟨exam⟩; bocciare ⟨candidate⟩; (disappoint) deludere; **words ~ me** mi mancano le parole; **unless my memory ~s me** se la memoria non mi tradisce

failing /'feɪlɪŋ/ ① n difetto m ② prep ~ **that** altrimenti

fail-safe adj ⟨device, system⟩ di sicurezza

failure /'feɪljə(r)/ n fallimento m; (mechanical) guasto m; (person) incapace mf

faint /feɪnt/ ① adj leggero; ⟨memory⟩ vago; **feel ~** sentirsi mancare ② n svenimento m ③ vi svenire

faint-hearted /-'hɑːtɪd/ adj timido

fainting fit /'feɪntɪŋ/ n svenimento m

faintly /'feɪntlɪ/ adv (slightly) leggermente

faintness /'feɪntnɪs/ n (physical) debolezza f

fair¹ /feə(r)/ n fiera f

fair² ① adj ⟨hair, person⟩ biondo; ⟨skin⟩ chiaro; ⟨weather⟩ bello; (just) giusto; (quite good) discreto; Sch abbastanza bene; **a ~ amount** abbastanza ② adv **play ~** fare un gioco pulito

fair copy n bella copia f

fairground /'feəgraʊnd/ n luna park m inv

fair-haired adj dai capelli chiari

fairly /'feəlɪ/ adv con giustizia; (rather) discretamente, abbastanza

fair-minded /feə'maɪndɪd/ adj equo

fairness /'feənɪs/ n giustizia f

fair play n fair play m inv

fair skinned /-'skɪnd/ adj di carnagione chiara

fairway n Naut via f d'acqua navigabile; (in golf) fairway m inv

fair weather friend n pej amico m finché tutto va bene

fairy /'feərɪ/ n fata f; **good ~** fata [buona]; **wicked ~** strega f

fairy godmother n fata f buona

fairy lights *npl* Br lampadine *fpl* colorate

fairy story, fairy-tale *n* fiaba *f*

faith /feɪθ/ *n* fede *f*; (trust) fiducia *f*; **in good/bad** ∼ in buona/mala fede

faithful /'feɪθfl/ *adj* fedele

faithfully /'feɪθfʊlɪ/ *adv* fedelmente; **yours** ∼ distinti saluti

faithfulness /'feɪθfʊlnɪs/ *n* fedeltà *f*

faith-healer /-hiːlə(r)/ *n* guaritore, -trice *mf*

faith healing /-hiːlɪŋ/ *n* guarigione *f* per fede

faithless /'feɪθlɪs/ *adj* ⟨friend, servant⟩ sleale; ⟨husband⟩ infedele

fake /feɪk/ **1** *adj* falso
  2 *n* falsificazione *f*; (person) impostore *m*
  3 *vt* falsificare; (pretend) fingere

falcon /'fɔːlkən/ *n* falcone *m*

Falklands /'fɔːkləndz/ *npl* le isole Falkland, le isole Malvine

fall /fɔːl/ **1** *n* caduta *f*; (in prices) ribasso *m*; (Am: autumn) autunno *m*; **have a** ∼ fare una caduta
  2 *vi* (pt **fell**, pp **fallen**) cadere; ⟨night⟩ scendere; ∼ **in love** innamorarsi
  ■ **fall about** *vi* (with laughter) morire dal ridere
  ■ **fall apart** *vi* ⟨table, car, house⟩ cadere a pezzi; ⟨shoes⟩ rompersi; fig ⟨person⟩ crollare
  ■ **fall back** *vi* indietreggiare; ⟨army⟩ ritirarsi
  ■ **fall back on** *vt* ritornare su
  ■ **fall behind** *vi* rimanere indietro; ∼ **behind with** Br *or* **in** Am essere indietro con ⟨work, project, payments⟩
  ■ **fall down** *vi* cadere; ⟨building⟩ crollare
  ■ **fall for** *vt* fam innamorarsi di ⟨person⟩; cascarci ⟨something, trick⟩
  ■ **fall in** *vi* caderci dentro; (collapse) crollare; Mil mettersi in riga; ∼ **in with** concordare con ⟨suggestion, plan⟩
  ■ **fall off** *vi* cadere; (diminish) diminuire
  ■ **fall open** *vi* ⟨book⟩ aprirsi (cadendo); ⟨robe⟩ aprirsi
  ■ **fall out** *vi* (quarrel) litigare; **his hair is** ∼**ing out** perde i capelli
  ■ **fall over** *vi* cadere
  ■ **fall through** *vi* ⟨plan⟩ andare a monte

fallacious /fə'leɪʃəs/ *adj* fallace

fallacy /'fæləsɪ/ *n* errore *m*

fallible /'fæləbl/ *adj* fallibile

Fallopian tube /fə'ləʊpɪən/ *n* tromba *f* di Falloppio

fallout /'fɔːlaʊt/ *n* pioggia *f* radioattiva

fallout shelter *n* rifugio *m* antiatomico

fallow /'fæləʊ/ *adj* **lie** ∼ essere a maggese

false /fɔːls/ *adj* falso

false alarm *n* falso allarme *m*

false bottom *n* doppio fondo *m*

falsehood /'fɔːlshʊd/ *n* menzogna *f*

falsely /'fɔːlslɪ/ *adv* falsamente

falseness /'fɔːlsnɪs/ *n* falsità *f*

false pretences *npl* under ∼ ∼ sotto false spoglie; Jur con la frode

false start *n* Sport falsa partenza *f*

false teeth *npl* dentiera *f*

falsetto /fɔːl'setəʊ/ **1** *n* (voice) falsetto *m* inv
  2 *adj* in falsetto

falsification /fɔːlsɪfɪ'keɪʃn/ *n* (of document, figures) falsificazione *f*: (of truth, facts) deformazione *f*

falsify /'fɔːlsɪfaɪ/ *vt* (pt/pp **-ied**) falsificare

falsity /'fɔːlsətɪ/ *n* falsità *f*

falter /'fɔːltə(r)/ *vi* vacillare; (making speech) esitare

faltering /'fɔːltərɪŋ/ *adj* ⟨economy⟩ vacillante; ⟨voice⟩ esitante

fame /feɪm/ *n* fama *f*

famed /feɪmd/ *adj* rinomato

familiar /fə'mɪljə(r)/ *adj* familiare; **be** ∼ **with** (know) conoscere; **become too** ∼ prendersi troppe confidenze

familiarity /fəmɪlɪ'ærətɪ/ *n* familiarità *f*

familiarize /fə'mɪlɪəraɪz/ *vt* familiarizzare; ∼ **oneself with something** familiarizzarsi con qualcosa

family /'fæməlɪ/ *n* famiglia *f*

family allowance *n* assegni *mpl* familiari

family circle *n* (group) cerchia *f* familiare; Am Theat seconda galleria *f*

family doctor *n* medico *m* di famiglia

family life *n* vita *f* familiare

family name *n* cognome *m*

family planning *n* pianificazione *f* familiare

family tree *n* albero *m* genealogico

family unit *n* nucleo *m* familiare

famine /'fæmɪn/ *n* carestia *f*

famished /'fæmɪʃt/ *adj* **be** ∼ fam avere una fame da lupo

famous /'feɪməs/ *adj* famoso

fan¹ /fæn/ **1** *n* ventilatore *m*; (handheld) ventaglio *m*
  2 *vt* (pt/pp **fanned**) far vento a; ∼ **oneself** sventagliarsi; fig ∼ **the flames** soffiare sul fuoco
  ■ **fan out** *vi* spiegarsi a ventaglio

fan² *n* (admirer) ammiratore, -trice *mf*, fan *mf*; Sport tifoso *m*; (of Verdi etc) appassionato, -a *mf*

fanatic /fə'nætɪk/ *n* fanatico, -a *mf*

fanatical /fə'nætɪkl/ *adj* fanatico

fanatically /fə'nætɪklɪ/ *adv* con fanatismo

fanaticism /fə'nætɪsɪzm/ n fanatismo m

fan belt n cinghia f per ventilatore

fanciful /'fænsɪfl/ adj fantasioso

fancy /'fænsɪ/ ① n fantasia f; I've taken a real ~ to him mi è molto simpatico; as the ~ takes you come ti pare
② adj fantasia inv
③ vt (believe) credere; (fam: want) aver voglia di; he fancies you fam gli piaci; ~ that! ma guarda un po'!

fancy dress n costume m

fancy dress party n festa f mascherata

fanfare /'fænfeə(r)/ n fanfara f

fang /fæŋ/ n zanna f; (of snake) dente m

fan heater n termoventilatore m

fanlight n lunetta f

fan mail n posta f dei fan

fantasize /'fæntəsaɪz/ vi fantasticare

fantastic /fæn'tæstɪk/ adj fantastico

fantasy /'fæntəsɪ/ n fantasia f

fanzine /'fænzi:n/ n fanzine f inv

FAQ abbr (**frequently asked questions**) FAQ fpl

far /fɑ:(r)/ ① adv lontano; (much) molto; by ~ di gran lunga; ~ away lontano; as ~ as the church fino alla chiesa; how ~ is it from here? quanto dista da qui?; as ~ as I know per quanto io sappia
② adj ⟨end, side⟩ altro; the F~ East l'Estremo Oriente m; in the ~ distance in lontananza

faraway /'fɑ:rəweɪ/ adj ⟨land⟩ lontano; ⟨look⟩ assente

farce /fɑ:s/ n farsa f

farcical /'fɑ:sɪkl/ adj ridicolo

fare /feə(r)/ n tariffa f; (food) vitto m

fare-dodger /-dɒdʒə(r)/ n passeggero, -a mf senza biglietto

farewell /feə'wel/ ① int liter addio!
② n addio m; ~ dinner cena f d'addio

far-fetched /-'fetʃt/ adj improbabile

far flung /-'flʌŋ/ adj (remote) remoto; (widely distributed) sparpagliato; ⟨network⟩ esteso

farm /fɑ:m/ ① n fattoria f, azienda f agricola
② vi fare l'agricoltore
③ vt coltivare ⟨land⟩
■ **farm out** vt dare in appalto ⟨work⟩

farmer /'fɑ:mə(r)/ n agricoltore m

farmers' market n vendita f diretta dal produttore agricolo al consumatore

farmhand /'fɑ:mhænd/ n bracciante m

farmhouse /'fɑ:mhaʊs/ n casa f colonica

farming /'fɑ:mɪŋ/ n agricoltura f

farm produce n prodotto m agricolo

farmyard /'fɑ:mjɑ:d/ n aia f

far-off adj lontano

far-reaching /-'ri:tʃɪŋ/ adj ⟨programme, plan, proposal⟩ di larga portata; ⟨effect, implication, change⟩ notevole

far-sighted /-'saɪtɪd/ adj ⟨policy⟩ lungimirante; (Am: long-sighted) presbite

fart /fɑ:t/ fam ① n scoreggia f
② vi scoreggiare

farther /'fɑ:ðə(r)/ ① adv più lontano
② adj at the ~ end of all'altra estremità di

farthest adj & adv = FURTHEST

fascia /'feɪʃɪə/ n Br (dashboard) cruscotto m; (for mobile phone) guscio m

fascinate /'fæsɪneɪt/ vt affascinare

fascinating /'fæsɪneɪtɪŋ/ adj affascinante

fascination /fæsɪ'neɪʃn/ n fascino m

fascism /'fæʃɪzm/ n fascismo m

fascist /'fæʃɪst/ adj & n fascista mf

fashion /'fæʃn/ ① n moda f; (manner) maniera f; in ~ di moda; out of ~ non più di moda
② vt modellare

fashionable /'fæʃ(ə)nəbl/ adj di moda; be ~ essere alla moda

fashionably /'fæʃ(ə)nəblɪ/ adv alla moda

fashion designer n stilista mf

fashion house n casa f di moda

fashion model n indossatore, -trice mf, modello, -a mf

fashion show n sfilata f di moda

fast¹ /fɑ:st/ ① adj veloce; ⟨colour⟩ indelebile; be ~ ⟨clock⟩ andare avanti
② adv velocemente; (firmly) saldamente; ~er! più in fretta!; be ~ asleep dormire profondamente

fast² ① n digiuno m
② vi digiunare

fasten /'fɑ:sn/ ① vt allacciare; chiudere ⟨window⟩; (stop flapping) mettere un fermo a
② vi allacciarsi

fastener /'fɑ:snə(r)/ n, **fastening** /'fɑ:snɪŋ/ n chiusura f

fast food ① n fast food m inv
② attrib ⟨chain⟩ di fast food; ~ ~ restaurant fast food m inv

fast forward ① n avanzamento m veloce
② vt far avanzare velocemente ⟨tape⟩
③ attrib ⟨key, button⟩ di avanzamento veloce

fast growing adj in rapida espansione

fastidious /fə'stɪdɪəs/ adj esigente

fast lane n Auto corsia f di sorpasso; life in the ~ ~ fig vita f frenetica

fast-talking adj ⟨salesperson⟩ che raggira con la sua parlantina

fast track n corsia f preferenziale

fast-track vt accelerare la carriera di ⟨somebody⟩

fat /fæt/ ① *adj* (**fatter, fattest**) ⟨*person, cheque*⟩ grasso; fam **that's a ~ lot of use** non serve a un accidente ② *n* grasso *m*

fatal /'feɪtl/ *adj* mortale; ⟨*error*⟩ fatale

fatalism /'feɪtəlɪzm/ *n* fatalismo *m*

fatalist /'feɪtəlɪst/ *n* fatalista *mf*

fatality /fə'tæləti/ *n* morte *f*

fatally /'feɪtəlɪ/ *adv* mortalmente

fate /feɪt/ *n* destino *m*

fated /'feɪtɪd/ *adj* destinato; **it was ~** era destino

fateful /'feɪtful/ *adj* fatidico

fat free *adj* magro

fat-head *n* fam zuccone, -a *mf*

father /'fɑːðə(r)/ ① *n* padre *m* ② *vt* generare ⟨*child*⟩

Father Christmas Babbo *m* Natale

father confessor *n* Relig confessore *m*

father figure *n* figura *f* paterna

fatherhood *n* paternità *f*

father-in-law *n* (pl **fathers-in-law**) suocero *m*

fatherland *n* patria *f*

fatherly /'fɑːðəlɪ/ *adj* paterno

Father's Day /'fɑːðəz/ *n* la festa del papà

fathom /'fæðəm/ ① *n* Naut braccio *m* ② *vt* ~ [**out**] comprendere

fatigue /fə'tiːg/ ① *n* fatica *f* ② *vt* affaticare

fatness /'fætnɪs/ *n* grassezza *f*

fatten /'fætn/ *vt* ingrassare ⟨*animal*⟩

fattening /'fætnɪŋ/ *adj* **cream is ~** la panna fa ingrassare

fatty /'fætɪ/ ① *adj* grasso ② *n* fam ciccione, -a *mf*

fatuous /'fætjuəs/ *adj* fatuo

faucet /'fɔːsɪt/ *n* Am rubinetto *m*

fault /fɔːlt/ ① *n* difetto *m*; Geol faglia *f*; Tennis fallo *m*; **be at ~** avere torto; **find ~ with** trovare da ridire su; **it's your ~** è colpa tua ② *vt* criticare

fault-finding /'fɔːltfaɪndɪŋ/ ① *n* (of person) atteggiamento *m* ipercritico; Techn localizzazione *f* del guasto ② *adj* ⟨*attitude*⟩ da criticone; ⟨*person*⟩ ipercritico

faultless /'fɔːltlɪs/ *adj* impeccabile

faultlessly /'fɔːltlɪslɪ/ *adv* impeccabilmente

faulty /'fɔːltɪ/ *adj* difettoso

fauna /'fɔːnə/ *n* fauna *f*

faux pas /fəʊ'pɑː/ *n* gaffe *f inv*

favour /'feɪvə(r)/ ① *n* favore *m*; **be in ~ of something** essere a favore di qualcosa; **do somebody a ~** fare un piacere a qualcuno ② *vt* (prefer) preferire

favourable /'feɪv(ə)rəbl/ *adj* favorevole

favourably /'feɪv(ə)rəblɪ/ *adv* favorevolmente

favourite /'feɪv(ə)rɪt/ ① *adj* preferito ② *n* preferito, -a *mf*; Sport favorito, -a *mf*

favouritism /'feɪv(ə)rɪtɪzm/ *n* favoritismo *m*

fawn /fɔːn/ ① *adj* fulvo ② *n* (animal) cerbiatto *m*

fax /fæks/ ① *n* (document, machine) fax *m inv*; **by ~** per fax ② *vt* faxare

fax machine *n* fax *m inv*

fax-modem *n* fax-modem *m inv*

fax number *n* numero *m* di fax

faze /feɪz/ *vt* fam scompaginare

FBI *n abbr* Am (**Federal Bureau of Investigation**) FBI *m*

FC *abbr* (**football club**) FC

fear /fɪə(r)/ ① *n* paura *f*; **no ~!** fam vai tranquillo! ② *vt* temere ③ *vi* ~ **for something** temere per qualcosa

fearful /'fɪəfl/ *adj* pauroso; (awful) terribile

fearless /'fɪəlɪs/ *adj* impavido

fearlessly /'fɪəlɪslɪ/ *adv* senza paura

fearsome /'fɪəsəm/ *adj* spaventoso

feasibility /fiːzɪ'bɪlətɪ/ *n* praticabilità *f*

feasible /'fiːzəbl/ *adj* fattibile; (possible) probabile

feast /fiːst/ ① *n* festa *f*; (banquet) banchetto *m* ② *vi* banchettare ∎ **feast on** *vt* godersi

feat /fiːt/ *n* impresa *f*

feather /'feðə(r)/ *n* piuma *f*; **you could have knocked me down with a ~** sono rimasto di sasso

feather-brained /-breɪnd/ *adj* che non ha un briciolo di cervello

feather duster *n* piumino *m* (per spolverare)

featherweight *n* peso *m* piuma *inv*

feature /'fiːtʃə(r)/ ① *n* (quality) caratteristica *f*; Journ articolo *m*; **~s** *pl* (of face) lineamenti *mpl* ② *vt* ⟨*film*⟩ avere come protagonista ③ *vi* (on a list etc) comparire

feature film *n* lungometraggio *m*

feature length film *n* lungometraggio *m*

February /'februərɪ/ *n* febbraio *m*

feces /'fiːsiːz/ *npl* feci *fpl*

feckless /'feklɪs/ *adj* inetto

fecund /'fekənd/ *adj* fecondo

fed /fed/ ① ▶ FEED ② *adj* **be ~ up** fam essere stufo (**with** di)

federal /'fed(ə)rəl/ *adj* federale

federalist /'fed(ə)rəlɪst/ *n* & *adj* federalista *mf*

Federal Republic of Germany *n* Repubblica *f* Federale Tedesca

federate /'fed(ə)rət/ *adj* federato

federation /fedə'reɪʃn/ *n* federazione *f*

fee /fiː/ *n* tariffa *f*; (lawyer's, doctor's) onorario *m*; (for membership, school) quota *f*

feeble /'fiːbl/ *adj* debole; ⟨excuse⟩ fiacco

feeble minded /-'maɪndɪd/ *adj* deficiente

feebleness /'fiːblnɪs/ *n* debolezza *f*

feed /fiːd/ **1** *n* mangiare *m*; (for baby) pappa *f*; **five ~s a day** cinque pasti al giorno
2 *vt* (pt/pp **fed**) dar da mangiare a ⟨animal⟩; (support) nutrire; **~ something into something** inserire qualcosa in qualcosa; **~ paper into the printer** alimentare la stampante con fogli
3 *vi* mangiare
■ **feed up** *vt* ingrassare ⟨somebody⟩

feedback /'fiːdbæk/ *n* controreazione *f*; (of information) reazione *f*, feedback *m*

feeder /'fiːdə(r)/ *n* (for printer, photocopier) mettifoglio *m inv*; (Br; bib) bavaglino *m*; (road) raccordo *m*

feeding bottle /'fiːdɪŋ/ *n* Br biberon *m inv*

feeding time *n* (in zoo) l'ora *f* del pasto degli animali

feel /fiːl/ **1** *vt* (pt/pp **felt**) sentire; (experience) provare; (think) pensare; (touch: searching) tastare; (touch: for texture) toccare
2 *vi* **~ soft/hard** essere duro/morbido al tatto; **~ hot/hungry** aver caldo/fame; **~ ill** sentirsi male; **I don't ~ like it** non ne ho voglia; **how do you ~ about it?** (opinion) che te ne pare?; **it doesn't ~ right** non mi sembra giusto
■ **feel for** *vt* (feel sympathy for) dispiacersi per
■ **feel up to** *vt* **~ up to doing something** sentirsi in grado di fare qualcosa; **I don't ~ up to it** non me la sento

feeler /'fiːlə(r)/ *n* (of animal) antenna *f*; **put out ~s** fig tastare il terreno

feel-good factor *n* sensazione *f* di benessere

feeling /'fiːlɪŋ/ *n* sentimento *m*; (awareness) sensazione *f*

fee paying *adj* ⟨school⟩ a pagamento, privato; ⟨parent, pupil⟩ che paga l'iscrizione (a una scuola privata)

feet /fiːt/ ▶ FOOT

feign /feɪn/ *vt* simulare

feint /feɪnt/ *n* finta *f*

feisty /'faɪstɪ/ *adj* Am (quarrelsome) stizzoso; (fam: lively) esuberante

felicitous /fə'lɪsɪtəs/ *adj* felice

feline /'fiːlaɪn/ *adj* felino

fell[1] /fel/ *vt* (knock down) abbattere

fell[2] ▶ FALL

fellow /'feləʊ/ *n* (of society) socio *m*; (fam: man) tipo *m*

fellow citizen *n* concittadino, -a *mf*

fellow countryman *n* compatriota *m*

fellow men *npl* prossimi *mpl*

fellowship /'feləʊʃɪp/ *n* cameratismo *m*; (group) associazione *f*; Univ incarico *m* di ricercatore, -trice *mf*

fellow traveller *n* compagno, -a *mf* di viaggio; Pol, fig compagno, -a *mf* di strada

felon /'felən/ *n* Jur criminale *mf*

felony /'felənɪ/ *n* delitto *m*

felt[1] /felt/ ▶ FEEL

felt[2] *n* feltro *m*

felt-tipped pen /-tɪpt'pen/ *n* pennarello *m*

female /'fiːmeɪl/ **1** *adj* femminile; **the ~ antelope** l'antilope femmina
2 *n* femmina *f*

feminine /'femɪnɪn/ **1** *adj* femminile
2 *n* Gram femminile *m*

femininity /femɪ'nɪnətɪ/ *n* femminilità *f*

feminist /'femɪnɪst/ *adj* & *n* femminista *mf*

fen /fen/ *n* zona *f* paludosa

fence /fens/ **1** *n* recinto *m*; (fam: person) ricettatore *m*
2 *vi* Sport tirar di scherma
■ **fence in** *vt* chiudere in un recinto

fencer /'fensə(r)/ *n* schermidore *m*

fencing /'fensɪŋ/ *n* steccato *m*; Sport scherma *f*

fend /fend/ *vi* **~ for oneself** badare a se stesso
■ **fend off** *vt* parare; difendersi da ⟨criticisms⟩

fender /'fendə(r)/ *n* parafuoco *m inv*; Naut parabordo *m*; (Am: on car) parafango *m*

fennel /'fenl/ *n* finocchio *m*

ferment[1] /'fɜːment/ *n* fermento *m*

ferment[2] /fə'ment/ **1** *vi* fermentare
2 *vt* far fermentare

fermentation /fɜːmen'teɪʃn/ *n* fermentazione *f*

fern /fɜːn/ *n* felce *f*

ferocious /fə'rəʊʃəs/ *adj* feroce

ferocity /fə'rɒsətɪ/ *n* ferocia *f*

ferret /'ferɪt/ *n* furetto *m*
■ **ferret about** *vi* curiosare; **~ about in** curiosare in
■ **ferret out** *vt* scovare

ferrous /'ferəs/ *adj* ferroso

ferry /'ferɪ/ **1** *n* traghetto *m*
2 *vt* (pt/pp **-ied**) traghettare

ferryman /'ferɪmən/ *n* traghettatore *m*

fertile /'fɜːtaɪl/ *adj* fertile

fertility /fɜː'tɪlətɪ/ *n* fertilità *f*

fertility drug *n* farmaco *m* contro la sterilità

fertility treatment *n* cura *f* della fertilità

fertilize /'fɜ:tɪlaɪz/ *vt* fertilizzare ⟨land, ovum⟩

fertilizer /'fɜ:tɪlaɪzə(r)/ *n* fertilizzante *m*

fervent /'fɜ:vənt/ *adj* fervente

fervour /'fɜ:və(r)/ *n* fervore *m*

fester /'festə(r)/ *vi* suppurare

festival /'festɪvl/ *n* Mus, Theat festival *m*; Relig festa *f*

festive /'festɪv/ *adj* festivo; ~ **season** periodo *m* delle feste natalizie

festivities /fe'stɪvətɪz/ *npl* festeggiamenti *mpl*

festoon /fe'stu:n/ *vt* ~ **with** ornare di

fetch /fetʃ/ *vt* andare/venire a prendere; (be sold for) raggiungere [il prezzo di]

fetching /'fetʃɪŋ/ *adj* attraente

fête /feɪt/ ① *n* festa *f*
② *vt* festeggiare

fetid /'fetɪd/ *adj* fetido

fetish /'fetɪʃ/ *n* feticcio *m*

fetter /'fetə(r)/ *vt* incatenare

fettle /'fetl/ *n* **in fine** ~ in buona forma

fetus /'fi:təs/ *n* (pl **-tuses**) feto *m*

feud /fju:d/ *n* faida *f*

feudal /'fju:dl/ *adj* feudale

fever /'fi:və(r)/ *n* febbre *f*

fevered /'fi:vəd/ *adj* ⟨brow⟩ febbricitante; ⟨imagination⟩ febbrile

feverish /'fi:vərɪʃ/ *adj* febbricitante; fig febbrile

fever pitch *n* **bring a crowd to** ~ ~ esaltare la folla

few /fju:/ ① *adj* pochi; **every** ~ **days** ogni due o tre giorni; **a** ~ **people** alcuni; ~ **people know that** poche persone lo sanno; ~**er reservations** meno prenotazioni; **the** ~**est number** il numero più basso
② *pron* pochi; ~ **of us** pochi di noi; **a** ~ alcuni; **quite a** ~ parecchi; ~**er than last year** meno dell'anno scorso

fez /fez/ *n* fez *m inv*

fiancé /fi'ɒnseɪ/ *n* fidanzato *m*

fiancée /fi'ɒnseɪ/ *n* fidanzata *f*

fiasco /fi'æskəʊ/ *n* fiasco *m*

fib /fɪb/ *n* storia *f*; **tell a** ~ raccontare una storia

fibber /'fɪbə(r)/ *n* fam contaballe *mf inv*

fibre /'faɪbə(r)/ *n* fibra *f*

fibreglass ① *n* fibra *f* di vetro
② *attrib* in fibra di vetro

fibre optic *adj* ⟨cable⟩ a fibre ottiche

fibre optics *n* fibra *f* ottica

fibroid /'faɪbrɔɪd/ ① *n* fibroma *m*
② *adj* fibroso

fibula /'fɪbjʊlə/ *n* Anat perone *m*

fiche /fi:ʃ/ *n* microscheda *f*

fickle /'fɪkl/ *adj* incostante

fiction /'fɪkʃn/ *n* **[works of]** ~ narrativa *f*: (fabrication) finzione *f*

fictional /'fɪkʃənəl/ *adj* immaginario

fictionalize /'fɪkʃənəlaɪz/ *vt* romanzare

fictitious /fɪk'tɪʃəs/ *adj* fittizio

fiddle /'fɪdl/ ① *n* fam violino *m*; (cheating) imbroglio *m*
② *vi* gingillarsi (**with** con)
③ *vt* fam truccare ⟨accounts⟩

fiddly /'fɪdlɪ/ *adj* intricato

fidelity /fɪ'delətɪ/ *n* fedeltà *f*

fidget /'fɪdʒɪt/ *vi* agitarsi

fidgety /'fɪdʒətɪ/ *adj* agitato

field /fi:ld/ *n* campo *m*

field day *n* **have a** ~ ~ ⟨press, critics⟩ godersela; (make money) fare affari d'oro

fielder /'fi:ldə(r)/ *n* Sport esterno *m*

field events *npl* atletica *fsg* leggera

field glasses *npl* binocolo *msg*

Field Marshal *n* feldmaresciallo *m*

field mouse *n* topo *m* campagnolo

field trip *n* gita *f* didattica

fieldwork *n* ricerche *fpl* sul terreno

fiend /fi:nd/ *n* demonio *m*

fiendish /'fi:ndɪʃ/ *adj* diabolico

fierce /fɪəs/ *adj* feroce

fiercely /'fɪəslɪ/ *adv* ferocemente

fierceness /'fɪəsnɪs/ *n* ferocia *f*

fiery /'faɪərɪ/ *adj* (**-ier, -iest**) focoso

fiesta /fɪ'estə/ *n* sagra *f*

fife /faɪf/ *n* piffero *m*

fifteen /fɪf'ti:n/ *adj & n* quindici *m*

fifteenth /fɪf'ti:nθ/ *adj & n* quindicesimo, -a *mf*

fifth /fɪfθ/ *adj & n* quinto, -a *mf*

fifties /'fɪftɪz/ *npl* (period) **the** ~ gli anni Cinquanta *mpl*; (age) cinquant'anni *mpl*; ▶ also **FORTIES**

fiftieth /'fɪftɪɪθ/ *adj & n* cinquantesimo, -a *mf*

fifty /'fɪftɪ/ *adj & n* cinquanta *m*

fifty-fifty ① *adj* **have a** ~ **chance** avere una probabilità su due
② *adv* **go** ~ fare [a] metà e metà; **split something** ~ dividersi qualcosa a metà

fig /fɪg/ *n* fico *m*

fig. *abbr* (**figure**) fig.

fight /faɪt/ ① *n* lotta *f*; (brawl) zuffa *f*; (argument) litigio *m*; (boxing) incontro *m*
② *vt* (pt/pp **fought**) also fig combattere
③ *vi* combattere; (brawl) azzuffarsi; (argue) litigare
■ **fight back** ① *vi* reagire
② *vt* frenare ⟨tears⟩
■ **fight for** *vt* lottare per ⟨freedom, independence⟩
■ **fight off** *vt* combattere ⟨cold⟩

fighter /'faɪtə(r)/ n combattente mf; Aeron caccia m inv; **he's a** ∼ ha uno spirito combattivo

fighter-bomber n cacciabombardiere m

fighter pilot n pilota m di cacciabombardiere

fighting /'faɪtɪŋ/ n combattimento m

fighting chance n have a ∼ ∼ avere buone probabilità

fighting fit adj in piena forma

figment /'fɪgmənt/ n it's a ∼ of your imagination questo è tutta una tua invenzione

fig tree n fico m

figurative /'fɪgərətɪv/ adj ⟨sense⟩ figurato; ⟨art⟩ figurativo

figuratively /'fɪgərətɪvlɪ/ adv ⟨use⟩ in senso figurato

figure /'fɪgə(r)/ ❶ n (digit) cifra f; (carving, sculpture, illustration, form) figura f; (body shape) linea f; ∼ **of speech** modo m di dire ❷ vi (appear) figurare ❸ vt (Am: think) pensare
■ **figure out** vt dedurre; capire ⟨person⟩

figurehead n figura f simbolica

figure of speech n modo m di dire; (literary device) figura f retorica

figure skating n pattinaggio m artistico

figurine /'fɪgəriːn/ n statuetta f

Fiji /'fiːdʒiː/ n Figi fpl

filament /'fɪləmənt/ n filamento m

filch /fɪltʃ/ vt fam rubacchiare

file[1] /faɪl/ ❶ n scheda f; (set of documents) incartamento m; (folder) cartellina f; Comput file m inv ❷ vt archiviare ⟨documents⟩

file[2] n (line) fila f; **in single** ∼ in fila

file[3] ❶ n Techn lima f ❷ vt limare

file cabinet n Am = FILING CABINET

file extension n Comput estensione f del file

file manager n Comput file manager m inv

filename n Comput nome m del file

file transfer protocol n Comput protocollo m per il trasferimento di file

filial /'fɪlɪəl/ adj filiale

filibuster /'fɪlɪbʌstə(r)/ n ostruzionismo m parlamentare

filigree /'fɪlɪgriː/ n filigrana f

filing /'faɪlɪŋ/ n archiviazione f

filing cabinet n schedario m, classificatore m

filing card n scheda f

filing clerk n archivista mf

filings /'faɪlɪŋz/ npl limatura fsg

filing system n sistema m di classificazione, sistema m di archivio

fill /fɪl/ ❶ n eat one's ∼ mangiare a sazietà ❷ vt riempire; otturare ⟨tooth⟩ ❸ vi riempirsi
■ **fill in** vt compilare ⟨form⟩
■ **fill in for** vt rimpiazzare someone
■ **fill in on** vt ∼ somebody in on something mettere qualcuno al corrente di qualcosa
■ **fill out** vt compilare ⟨form⟩
■ **fill up** ❶ vi ⟨room, tank⟩ riempirsi; Auto far il pieno ❷ vt riempire

filler /'fɪlə(r)/ n mastice m

fillet /'fɪlɪt/ ❶ n filetto m ❷ vt (pt/pp **filleted**) disossare

fillet steak n bistecca f di filetto

fill in n (fam: replacement) rimpiazzo m

filling /'fɪlɪŋ/ n Culin ripieno m; (of tooth) piombatura f

filling station n stazione f di rifornimento

filly /'fɪlɪ/ n puledra f

film /fɪlm/ ❶ n Cinema film m inv; Phot pellicola f; [cling] ∼ pellicola f per alimenti ❷ vt/i filmare

film buff n cinefilo, -a mf

film festival n festival m cinematografico

film-goer /'fɪlmgəʊə(r)/ n frequentatore, -trice mf di cinema

film industry n industria f cinematografica

filming /'fɪlmɪŋ/ n riprese fpl

filmset n allestimento m scenico

film star n star f inv, divo, -a mf

film studio n studio m cinematografico

filmy /'fɪlmɪ/ adj (thin: fabric, screen) trasparente; (thin) sottilissimo

filter /'fɪltə(r)/ ❶ n filtro m ❷ vt filtrare
■ **filter through** vi ⟨news⟩ trapelare

filter cigarette n sigaretta f con filtro

filter coffee n (ground coffee) caffè m macinato per filtro; (cup of coffee) caffè m inv fatto con il filtro

filter-paper n carta f da filtro

filter tip n filtro m; (cigarette) sigaretta f col filtro

filth /fɪlθ/ n sudiciume m

filthy /'fɪlθɪ/ adj (-ier, -iest) sudicio; ⟨language⟩ sconcio

filthy rich adj fam ricco sfondato

fin /fɪn/ n pinna f

final /'faɪnl/ ❶ adj finale; (conclusive) decisivo ❷ n Sport finale f; ∼s pl Univ esami mpl finali

finale /fɪˈnɑːlɪ/ n finale m

finalist /ˈfaɪnəlɪst/ n finalista mf

finality /faɪˈnælɪtɪ/ n finalità f

finalize /ˈfaɪnəlaɪz/ vt mettere a punto ⟨text⟩; definire ⟨agreement⟩

finally /ˈfaɪnəlɪ/ adv (at last) finalmente; (at the end) alla fine; (to conclude) per finire

finance /ˈfaɪnæns/ ① n finanza f ② vt finanziare

finance company, finance house n società f finanziaria

finance director n direttore, -trice mf finanziario, -a

finances npl finanze fpl

financial /faɪˈnænʃl/ adj finanziario

financially /faɪˈnænʃəlɪ/ adv finanziariamente

financial year n Br esercizio m [finanziario]

finch /fɪntʃ/ n fringuello m

find /faɪnd/ ① n scoperta f
② vt (pt/pp **found**) trovare; (establish) scoprire; ~ **somebody guilty** Jur dichiarare qualcuno colpevole
■ **find out** ① vt scoprire
② vi (enquire) informarsi

findings /ˈfaɪndɪŋz/ npl conclusioni fpl

fine[1] /faɪn/ ① n (penalty) multa f
② vt multare

fine[2] ① adj bello; (slender) fine; **he's** ~ (in health) sta bene
② adv bene; **that's cutting it** ~ non ci lascia molto tempo.
③ int [va] bene

fine art, fine arts npl belle arti fpl

finely /ˈfaɪnlɪ/ adv ⟨cut⟩ finemente

finery /ˈfaɪnərɪ/ n splendore m

finesse /fɪˈnes/ n finezza f

fine-tooth[ed] comb /-tuːˈθ[t]/ n **go over something with a** ~ ~ passare qualcosa al setaccio

fine-tune vt mettere a punto

fine tuning n messa f a punto

finger /ˈfɪŋɡə(r)/ ① n dito m (pl dita f)
② vt tastare

finger bowl n lavadita m inv

finger hole n Mus foro m

fingermark n ditata f

fingernail n unghia f

finger-paint vi dipingere con le dita

fingerprint n impronta f digitale

fingertip n punta f del dito; **have something at one's** ~s sapere qualcosa a menadito; (close at hand) avere qualcosa a portata di mano

finicky /ˈfɪnɪkɪ/ adj (person) pignolo; ⟨task⟩ intricato

finish /ˈfɪnɪʃ/ ① n fine f; (finishing line) traguardo m; (of product) finitura f; **have a good** ~ ⟨runner⟩ avere un buon finale

② vt finire; ~ **reading** finire di leggere
③ vi finire
■ **finish off** vt finire ⟨something⟩; (fam: exhaust) sfinire
■ **finish with** vt (no longer be using) finire (di adoperare); (end relationship with) lasciare
■ **finish up** vt finire ⟨drink, meal⟩

finishing line /ˈfɪnɪʃɪŋlaɪn/ n traguardo m

finishing touches /ˈtʌtʃɪz/ npl ritocchi mpl

finite /ˈfaɪnaɪt/ adj limitato

Finland /ˈfɪnlənd/ n Finlandia f

Finn /fɪn/ n finlandese mf

Finnish /ˈfɪnɪʃ/ ① adj finlandese
② n (language) finnico m

fiord /fjɔːd/ n fiordo m

fir /fɜː(r)/ n abete m

fir cone n pigna f (di abete)

fire /ˈfaɪə(r)/ ① n fuoco m; (forest, house) incendio m; **be on** ~ bruciare; **catch** ~ prendere fuoco; **set** ~ **to** dar fuoco a; **under** ~ sotto il fuoco
② vt cuocere ⟨pottery⟩; sparare ⟨shot⟩; tirare ⟨gun⟩; (fam: dismiss) buttar fuori
③ vi sparare (**at** a)

fire alarm n allarme m antincendio inv

firearm n arma f da fuoco

firebomb ① n ordigno m incendiario
② vt lanciare ordigni incendiari contro ⟨building⟩

fire brigade n vigili mpl del fuoco

fire door n porta f antincendio

fire drill n esercitazione f per l'evacuazione in caso di incendio

fire engine n autopompa f

fire escape n uscita f di sicurezza

fire exit n uscita f di sicurezza

fire extinguisher n estintore m

firefighter n vigile m del fuoco

fireguard n parafuoco m inv

fireman n pompiere m, vigile m del fuoco

fireplace n caminetto m

fireproof adj ⟨door⟩ antincendio, ⟨clothing⟩ ignifugo

fire-retardant /rɪˈtɑːdənt/ adj ⟨material⟩ ignifugo

fire service n vigili mpl del fuoco

fireside n **by** or **at the** ~ accanto al fuoco

fire station n caserma f dei pompieri

firewall n Comput firewall m inv

firewood n legna f (da ardere)

firework n fuoco m d'artificio; ~s pl (display) fuochi mpl d'artificio

firing line /ˈfaɪərɪŋ/ n **be in the** ~ essere sulla linea di tiro

firing squad n plotone m d'esecuzione

firm[1] /fɜːm/ n ditta f, azienda f

firm² *adj* fermo; ⟨*soil*⟩ compatto; (stable, properly fixed) solido; (resolute) risoluto

firmly /'fɜːmlɪ/ *adv* ⟨*hold*⟩ stretto; ⟨*say*⟩ con fermezza

first /fɜːst/ ① *adj & n* primo, -a *mf*; at ∼ all'inizio; who's ∼? chi è il primo?; from the ∼ [fin] dall'inizio
② *adv* ⟨*arrive, leave*⟩ per primo; (beforehand) prima; (in listing) prima di tutto, innanzitutto

first aid *n* pronto soccorso *m*

first-aid kit *n* cassetta *f* di pronto soccorso

first-class ① *adj* di prim'ordine; Rail di prima classe
② *adv* ⟨*travel*⟩ in prima classe

first cousin *n* cugino, -a *mf* di primo grado

first edition *n* prima edizione *f*

first floor *n* primo piano *m*; (Am: ground floor) pianterreno *m*

first grade *n* Am prima *f* elementare

firsthand *adj & adv* di prima mano

firstly /'fɜːstlɪ/ *adv* in primo luogo

first name *n* nome *m* di battesimo

first night *n* Theat prima *f*

first-rate *adj* ottimo

first time buyer *n* acquirente *mf* della prima casa

firth /fɜːθ/ *n* foce *f*

fiscal /'fɪskəl/ *adj* fiscale

fiscal year *n* Am esercizio *m* finanziario

fish /fɪʃ/ ① *n* pesce *m*
② *vt/i* pescare
■ **fish out** *vt* tirar fuori

fish and chips *n* pesce *m* fritto e patatine

fish and chip shop *n* friggitoria *f* dove si vende pesce fritto e patatine

fishbone /'fɪʃbəʊn/ *n* lisca *f*

fishbowl *n* boccia *f* dei pesci rossi

fisherman /'fɪʃəmən/ *n* pescatore *m*

fish farm *n* vivaio *m*

fish finger *n* bastoncino *m* di pesce

fishing /'fɪʃɪŋ/ *n* pesca *f*

fishing boat *n* peschereccio *m*

fishing rod *n* canna *f* da pesca

fish market *n* mercato *m* del pesce

fishmonger /'fɪʃmʌŋgə(r)/ *n* pescivendolo *m*

fishnet /'fɪʃnet/ *adj* ⟨*stockings*⟩ a rete

fish slice *n* paletta *f* per fritti

fish tank *n* acquario *m*

fishy /'fɪʃɪ/ *adj* (fam: suspicious) sospetto

fission /'fɪʃn/ *n* Phys fissione *f*

fist /fɪst/ *n* pugno *m*

fistful /'fɪstfʊl/ *n* manciata *f*, pugno *m*

fit¹ /fɪt/ *n* (attack) attacco *m*; (of rage) accesso *m*; (of generosity) slancio *m*

fit² *adj* (**fitter**, **fittest**) (suitable) adatto; (healthy) in buona salute; Sport in forma; **be** ∼ **to do something** essere in grado di fare qualcosa; ∼ **to eat** buono da mangiare; **keep** ∼ tenersi in forma; **do as you see** ∼ fai come ritieni meglio

fit³ ① *n* (of clothes) taglio *m*; it's a good ∼ ⟨*coat etc*⟩ ti/le sta bene
② *vi* (pt/pp **fitted**) (be the right size) andare bene; **it won't** ∼ (no room) non ci sta
③ *vt* (fix) applicare (**to** a); (install) installare; **it doesn't** ∼ **me** ⟨*coat etc*⟩ non mi va bene; ∼ **with** fornire di
■ **fit in** ① *vi* ⟨*person*⟩ adattarsi; **it won't** ∼ **in** (no room) non ci sta
② *vt* (in schedule, vehicle) trovare un buco per

fitful /'fɪtfl/ *adj* irregolare

fitfully /'fɪtfʊlɪ/ *adv* ⟨*sleep*⟩ a sprazzi

fitment /'fɪtmənt/ *n* ∼s (in house) impianti *mpl* fissi

fitness /'fɪtnɪs/ *n* (suitability) capacità *f*; [physical] ∼ forma *f*, fitness *m*

fitness programme *n* programma *m* di fitness

fitness video *n* video *m* di fitness

fitted /'fɪtɪd/ *adj* ⟨*wardrobe*⟩ a muro; ⟨*kitchen, bedroom*⟩ componibile; ⟨*jacket*⟩ attillato

fitted carpet *n* moquette *f inv*

fitted cupboard *n* armadio *m* a muro; (smaller) armadietto *m* a muro

fitted kitchen *n* cucina *f* componibile

fitted sheet *n* lenzuolo *m* con angoli

fitter /'fɪtə(r)/ *n* installatore, -trice *mf*

fitting /'fɪtɪŋ/ ① *adj* appropriato
② *n* (of clothes) prova *f*; Techn montaggio *m*; ∼s *pl* accessori *mpl*

fitting room *n* camerino *m*

five /faɪv/ *adj & n* cinque *m*

five-a-side *n* Br (football) calcio *m* a cinque

fiver /'faɪvə(r)/ *n* fam biglietto *m* da cinque sterline

fix /fɪks/ ① *n* (sl: drugs) pera *f*; **be in a** ∼ fam essere nei guai
② *vt* fissare; (repair) aggiustare; preparare ⟨*meal*⟩
■ **fix up** *vt* fissare ⟨*meeting*⟩

fixation /fɪk'seɪʃn/ *n* fissazione *f*

fixative /'fɪksətɪv/ *n* fissativo *m*

fixed /fɪkst/ *adj* fisso

fixed assets *npl* attività *fpl* fisse, immobilizzazioni *fpl*

fixed price *n* prezzo *m* a forfait

fixed-term contract *n* contratto *m* a tempo determinato

fixer /'fɪksə(r)/ *n* Phot fissatore *m*; (fam: person) trafficone, -a *mf*

fixture /'fɪkstʃə(r)/ *n* Sport incontro *m*: ∼s and fittings impianti *mpl* fissi

fizz /fɪz/ *vi* frizzare

fizzle /ˈfɪzl/ *vi* ∼ **out** finire in nulla

fizzy /ˈfɪzɪ/ *adj* gassoso

fizzy drink *n* bibita *f* gassata

fjord /fjɔːd/ *n* fiordo *m*

flab /flæb/ *n* fam ciccia *f* cascante

flabbergasted /ˈflæbəgɑːstɪd/ *adj* **be** ∼ rimanere a bocca aperta

flabby /ˈflæbɪ/ *adj* floscio

flag¹ /flæg/ *n* bandiera *f*

flag² *vi* (pt/pp **flagged**) cedere
■ **flag down** *vt* (pt/pp **flagged**) far segno di fermarsi a ⟨*taxi*⟩

flagellation /flædʒəˈleɪʃn/ *n* flagellazione *f*

flagon /ˈflægən/ *n* bottiglione *m*

flagpole /ˈflægpəʊl/ *n* asta *f* della bandiera

flagrant /ˈfleɪgrənt/ *adj* flagrante

flagship /ˈflægʃɪp/ *n* Naut nave *f* ammiraglia; fig fiore *m* all'occhiello

flagstone /ˈflægstəʊn/ *n* pietra *f* per lastricato

flail /fleɪl/ ① *n* (for threshing corn etc) correggiato *m*
② *vt* battere ⟨*corn*⟩
■ **flail about**, **flail around** *vi* ⟨*arms, legs*⟩ agitare

flair /fleə(r)/ *n* (skill) talento *m*; (style) stile *m*

flak /flæk/ *n* Mil artiglieria *f* antiaerea; (fig fam: criticism) valanga *f* di critiche; **take a lot of** ∼ subire molte critiche

flake /fleɪk/ ① *n* fiocco *m*
② *vi* ∼ **[off]** cadere in fiocchi

flaky /ˈfleɪkɪ/ *adj* a scaglie

flaky pastry *n* pasta *f* sfoglia

flamboyant /flæmˈbɔɪənt/ *adj* ⟨*personality*⟩ brillante; ⟨*tie*⟩ sgargiante

flame /fleɪm/ *n* fiamma *f*

flamenco /fləˈmeŋkəʊ/ *n* flamenco *m*

flamer /ˈfleɪmə(r)/ *n* Comput flamer *m*, utente *mf* email che manda messaggi offensivi

flame retardant /rɪtəˈdənt/ *adj* ⟨*substance, chemical*⟩ ignifugo; ⟨*furniture, fabric*⟩ ignifugato

flame-thrower /-θrəʊə(r)/ *n* Mil lanciafiamme *m inv*

flaming /ˈfleɪmɪŋ/ ① *adj* ⟨*row*⟩ acceso: ⟨*building*⟩ in fiamme
② *n* Comput flaming *m inv*, invio *m* di messaggi offensivi

flamingo /fləˈmɪŋgəʊ/ *n* fenicottero *m*

flammable /ˈflæməbl/ *adj* infiammabile

flan /flæn/ *n* [fruit] ∼ crostata *f*

flange /flændʒ/ *n* (on pipe etc) flangia *f*

flank /flæŋk/ ① *n* fianco *m*
② *vt* fiancheggiare

flannel /ˈflæn(ə)l/ *n* flanella *f*; (for washing) ≈ guanto *m* di spugna

flannelette /flænəˈlet/ *n* flanella *f* di cotone

flannels /ˈflæn(ə)lz/ *npl* (trousers) pantaloni *mpl* di flanella

flap /flæp/ ① *n* (of pocket, envelope) risvolto *m*; (of table) ribalta *f*; **in a** ∼ fam in grande agitazione
② *vi* (pt/pp **flapped**) sbattere; fam agitarsi
③ *vt* ∼ **its wings** battere le ali

flapjack /ˈflæpdʒæk/ *n* Br dolcetto *m* di fiocchi d'avena; Am frittella *f*

flare /fleə(r)/ *n* fiammata *f*; (device) razzo *m*
■ **flare up** *vi* ⟨*rash*⟩ venire fuori; ⟨*fire*⟩ fare una fiammata; ⟨*person, situation*⟩ esplodere

flared /fleəd/ *adj* ⟨*garment*⟩ svasato

flares /fleəz/ *npl* (trousers) pantaloni *mpl* a zampa d'elefante

flash /flæʃ/ ① *n* lampo *m*; **in a** ∼ fam in un attimo
② *vi* lampeggiare; ∼ **past** passare come un bolide
③ *vt* lanciare ⟨*smile*⟩; ∼ **one's headlights** lampeggiare; ∼ **a torch at** puntare una torcia su
■ **flash by** *vi* ⟨*person, years, landscape*⟩ passare come un lampo

flashback *n* scena *f* retrospettiva

flashbulb *n* Phot flash *m inv*

flashcard *n* Sch scheda *f* didattica

flasher /ˈflæʃə(r)/ *n* Auto lampeggiatore *m*

flash flood *n* alluvione *f* improvvisa

flashgun *n* Phot flash *m inv*

flashing /ˈflæʃɪŋ/ *adj* ⟨*light*⟩ lampeggiante

flashlight *n* Phot flash *m inv*; (Am: torch) torcia *f* [elettrica]

flashpoint *n* (trouble spot) punto *m* caldo; Chem punto *m* di infiammabilità

flashy /ˈflæʃɪ/ *adj* vistoso

flask /flɑːsk/ *n* fiasco *m*; (vacuum ∼) termos *m inv*

flat /flæt/ ① *adj* (**flatter**, **flattest**) piatto; ⟨*refusal*⟩ reciso; ⟨*beer*⟩ sgassato; ⟨*battery*⟩ scarico; ⟨*tyre*⟩ a terra; **A** ∼ Mus la bemolle
② *n* appartamento *m*; Mus bemolle *m*; (puncture) gomma *f* a terra

flat broke *adj* fam completamente al verde

flat feet *npl* piedi *mpl* piatti

flatfish *n* pesce *m* piatto

flat-footed /-ˈfʊtɪd/ *adj* **be** ∼ ∼ avere i piedi piatti

flat hunting *n* Br **go** ∼ ∼ andare in cerca di un appartamento

flatly /'flætlɪ/ *adv* ⟨*refuse*⟩
categoricamente

flatmate *n* Br persona *f* con cui si divide
un appartamento

flat out *adv* ⟨*drive, work*⟩ a tutto gas; **it
only does 120 kph** ∼ ∼ arriva a 120 km
all'ora andando a tutta manetta; **go** ∼ ∼
for something mettercela tutta per fare
qualcosa

flat racing *n* corse *fpl* piane

flat rate 1 *n* forfait *m inv*; (unitary rate)
tariffa *f* unica
2 *attrib* ⟨*fee, tax*⟩ forfettario

flat spin *n* Aeron virata *f* piatta; **be in a** ∼
∼ fam essere in fibrillazione

flatten /'flætn/ *vt* appiattire

flatter /'flætə(r)/ *vt* adulare

flattering /'flætərɪŋ/ *adj* ⟨*comments*⟩
lusinghiero; ⟨*colour, dress*⟩ che fa
sembrare più bello

flattery /'flætərɪ/ *n* adulazione *f*

flat tyre *n* gomma *f* a terra

flatulence /'flætjʊləns/ *n* flatulenza *f*

flaunt /flɔːnt/ *vt* ostentare

flautist /'flɔːtɪst/ *n* flautista *mf*

flavour /'fleɪvə(r)/ 1 *n* sapore *m*
2 *vt* condire; **chocolate** ∼**ed** al sapore di
cioccolato

flavour-enhancer /-ɪnhɑːnsə(r)/ *n*
esaltatore *m* dell'aroma

flavouring /'fleɪvərɪŋ/ *n* condimento *m*

flavourless /'fleɪvəlɪs/ *adj* insipido

flaw /flɔː/ *n* difetto *m*

flawed /flɔːd/ *adj* difettoso

flawless /'flɔːlɪs/ *adj* perfetto

flax /flæks/ *n* lino *m*

flaxen /'flæksən/ *adj* ⟨*hair*⟩ biondo
platino

flea /fliː/ *n* pulce *f*

flea-bitten /'fliːbɪtən/ *adj* infestato dalle
pulci; fig pidocchioso

flea market *n* mercato *m* delle pulci

fleapit *n* Br fam pej pidocchietto *m*

fleck /flek/ *n* macchiolina *f*

fled /fled/ ▸ FLEE

fledg[e]ling /'fledʒlɪŋ/ 1 *n* uccellino *m*
(che ha appena messo le ali)
2 *attrib* fig ⟨*democracy, enterprise*⟩
giovane; ⟨*party, group*⟩ alle prime armi

flee /fliː/ *vt/i* (pt/pp **fled**) fuggire (**from**
da)

fleece /fliːs/ 1 *n* pelliccia *f*
2 *vt* fam spennare

fleecy /'fliːsɪ/ *adj* ⟨*lining*⟩ felpato

fleet /fliːt/ *n* flotta *f*; (of cars) parco *m*

fleeting /'fliːtɪŋ/ *adj* **catch a** ∼ **glance of
something** intravedere qualcosa; **for a** ∼
moment per un attimo

Flemish /'flemɪʃ/ *adj* fiammingo

flesh /fleʃ/ *n* carne *f*; **in the** ∼ in persona;
one's own ∼ **and blood** il proprio sangue
■ **flesh out** *vt* dare più consistenza a
⟨*essay etc*⟩

flesh eating /-iːtɪŋ/ *adj* carnivoro

flesh wound *n* ferita *f* superficiale

fleshy /'fleʃɪ/ *adj* carnoso

flew /fluː/ ▸ FLY²

flex¹ /fleks/ *vt* flettere ⟨*muscle*⟩

flex² *n* Electr filo *m*

flexibility /fleksə'bɪlətɪ/ *n* flessibilità *f*

flexible /'fleksəbl/ *adj* flessibile

flexitime /'fleksɪtaɪm/ *n* orario *m*
flessibile

flick /flɪk/ *vt* dare un buffetto a; ∼
something off something togliere qualcosa
da qualcosa con un colpetto
■ **flick through** *vt* sfogliare

flicker /'flɪkə(r)/ *vi* tremolare

flick knife *n* Br coltello *m* a scatto

flier /'flaɪə(r)/ *n* = FLYER

flight¹ /flaɪt/ *n* (fleeing) fuga *f*; **take** ∼
darsi alla fuga

flight² *n* (flying) volo *m*; ∼ **of stairs** rampa
f

flight attendant *n* assistente *mf* di
volo

flight bag *n* bagaglio *m* a mano

flight deck *n* Aeron cabina *f* di
pilotaggio; Naut ponte *m* di volo

flight engineer *n* motorista *mf* di
bordo

flight lieutenant *n* Mil capitano *m*

flight path *n* traiettoria *f* di volo

flight recorder *n* registratore *m* di
volo

flighty /'flaɪtɪ/ *adj* (**-ier, -iest**) frivolo

flimsy /'flɪmzɪ/ *adj* (**-ier, -iest**)
⟨*material*⟩ leggero; ⟨*shelves*⟩ poco robusto;
⟨*excuse*⟩ debole

flinch /flɪntʃ/ *vi* (wince) sussultare; (draw
back) ritirarsi; ∼ **from a task** fig sottrarsi a
un compito

fling /flɪŋ/ 1 *n* **have a** ∼ (fam: affair) avere
un'avventura
2 *vt* (pt/pp **flung**) gettare
■ **fling away** *vt* gettar via
■ **fling open** *vt* spalancare ⟨*door,
window*⟩

flint /flɪnt/ *n* pietra *f* focaia; (for lighter)
pietrina *f*

flip /flɪp/ 1 *vt* (pt/pp **flipped**) dare un
colpetto a; buttare in aria ⟨*coin*⟩
2 *vi* fam uscire dai gangheri; (go mad)
impazzire
■ **flip through** *vt* sfogliare

flip chart *n* lavagna *f* a fogli mobili

flip-flop *n* (sandal) infradito *m inv*;
(Comput: device) flip-flop *m inv*,

multivibratore *m* bistabile; (Am: about face) voltafaccia *m inv*

flippant /'flɪpənt/ *adj* irriverente

flipper /'flɪpə(r)/ *n* pinna *f*

flipping /'flɪpɪŋ/ Br fam **1** *adj* maledetto **2** *adv* ⟨stupid, painful, cold⟩ maledettamente

flip side *n* (of record) retro *m*; (fig: other side) rovescio *m*

flirt /flɜːt/ **1** *n* civetta *f* **2** *vi* flirtare

flirtation /flɜː'teɪʃn/ *n* flirt *m inv*

flirtatious /flɜː'teɪʃəs/ *adj* civettuolo

flit /flɪt/ *vi* (pt/pp **flitted**) volteggiare

float /fləʊt/ **1** *n* galleggiante *m*; (in procession) carro *m*; (money) riserva *f* di cassa
2 *vi* galleggiare; Fin fluttuare
■ **float off** *vi* ⟨boat⟩ andare alla deriva: ⟨balloon⟩ volare via

floating /'fləʊtɪŋ/ *adj* ⟨bridge⟩ galleggiante; ⟨population⟩ fluttuante

floating rate interest *n* Fin interesse *m* a tasso variabile

floating voter *n* Pol elettore, -trice *mf* indeciso, -a

flock /flɒk/ **1** *n* gregge *m*; (of birds) stormo *m*
2 *vi* affollarsi

floe /fləʊ/ *n* banchisa *f*

flog /flɒg/ *vt* (pt/pp **flogged**) bastonare; (fam: sell) vendere

flood /flʌd/ **1** *n* alluvione *f*; (of river) straripamento *m*; (fig: of replies, letters, tears) diluvio *m*: **be in** ∼ ⟨river⟩ essere straripato
2 *vt* allagare
3 *vi* ⟨river⟩ straripare

flood control *n* prevenzione *f* delle inondazioni

flood damage *n* danno *m* provocato da un'inondazione

floodgate *n* chiusa *f*; **open the** ∼**s** fig spalancare le porte

floodlight **1** *n* riflettore *m*
2 *vt* (pt/pp **floodlit**) illuminare con riflettori

floodplain *n* pianura *f* alluvionale

flood tide *n* marea *f* montante

flood waters *npl* acque *fpl* alluvionali

floor /flɔː(r)/ **1** *n* pavimento *m*; (storey) piano *m*; (for dancing) pista *f*
2 *vt* (baffle) confondere; (knock down) stendere ⟨person⟩

floorboard *n* asse *f* del pavimento

floorcloth *n* straccio *m* per lavare il pavimento

floor exercises *npl* esercizi *mpl* a terra

floor manager *n* TV direttore, -trice *mf* di studio; Comm gerente *mf* di un negozio

floor polish *n* cera *f* per il pavimento

floor show *n* spettacolo *m* di varietà

floor space *n* superficie *f*; **we don't have the** ∼ non abbiamo lo spazio

flop /flɒp/ **1** *n* fam (failure) tonfo *m*; Theat fiasco *m*
2 *vi* (pt/pp **flopped**) (fam: fail) far fiasco
■ **flop down** *vi* accasciarsi

floppy /'flɒpɪ/ *adj* floscio

floppy disk *n* floppy disk *m inv*

floppy [disk] drive *n* lettore *m* di floppy

flora /'flɔːrə/ *n* flora *f*

floral /'flɔːrəl/ *adj* floreale

Florence /'flɒrəns/ *n* Firenze *f*

Florentine /'flɒrəntaɪn/ *adj* fiorentino

florid /'flɒrɪd/ *adj* ⟨complexion⟩ florido; ⟨style⟩ troppo ricercato

florist /'flɒrɪst/ *n* fioraio, -a *mf*

floss /flɒs/ **1** *n* filo *m* interdentale
2 *vt* ∼ **one's teeth** usare il filo interdentale
3 *vi* usare il filo interdentale

flotsam /'flɒtsəm/ *n* relitti *mpl* alla deriva

flounce /flaʊns/ **1** *n* balza *f*
2 *vi* ∼ **out** uscire con aria melodrammatica

flounder[1] /'flaʊndə(r)/ *vi* dibattersi; ⟨speaker⟩ impappinarsi

flounder[2] *n* (fish) passera *f* di mare

flour /'flaʊə(r)/ *n* farina *f*

flourish /'flʌrɪʃ/ **1** *n* gesto *m* drammatico; (scroll) ghirigoro *m*
2 *vi* prosperare
3 *vt* brandire

flourishing /'flʌrɪʃɪŋ/ *adj* ⟨industry, business⟩ fiorente; ⟨garden⟩ rigoglioso

floury /'flaʊərɪ/ *adj* farinoso

flout /flaʊt/ *vt* fregarsene di ⟨rules⟩

flow /fləʊ/ **1** *n* flusso *m*
2 *vi* scorrere; (hang loosely) ricadere

flow chart *n* diagramma *m* di flusso

flower /'flaʊə(r)/ **1** *n* fiore *m*
2 *vi* fiorire

flower arrangement *n* composizione *f* floreale

flower arranging *n* composizione *f* floreale

flower bed *n* aiuola *f*

flowered /'flaʊəd/ *adj* a fiori

flower garden *n* giardino *m* fiorito

flowering /'flaʊərɪŋ/ **1** *n* Bot fioritura *f*; (fig: development) espansione *f*
2 *adj* ⟨shrub, tree⟩ in fiore; **early/late** ∼ a fioritura precoce/tardiva

flowerpot *n* vaso *m* [per i fiori]

flower shop *n* fiorista *m*

flower show *n* mostra *f* floreale

flowery /'flaʊərɪ/ adj fiorito

flown /fləʊn/ ▶ FLY²

fl oz abbr **fluid ounces**

flu /flu:/ n influenza f

fluctuate /'flʌktjʊeɪt/ vi fluttuare

fluctuation /flʌktjʊ'eɪʃn/ n fluttuazione f

flue /flu:/ n (of chimney, stove) canna f fumaria

fluency /'flu:ənsɪ/ n (in speaking) competenza f; (in writing) speditezza f

fluent /'flu:ənt/ adj spedito; **speak ~ Italian** parlare correntemente l'italiano

fluently /'flu:əntlɪ/ adv speditamente

fluff /flʌf/ n peluria f

fluffy /'flʌfɪ/ adj (-ier, -iest) vaporoso; ⟨toy⟩ di peluche

fluid /'flu:ɪd/ ① adj fluido ② n fluido m

fluid ounce n oncia f fluida

fluke /flu:k/ n colpo m di fortuna

flummox /'flʌməks/ vt fam sbalestrare

flung /flʌŋ/ ▶ FLING

flunk /flʌŋk/ vt Am fam essere bocciato in

fluorescent /flʊə'resnt/ adj fluorescente

fluorescent lighting n luce f fluorescente

fluoride /'flʊəraɪd/ n fluoruro m

flurry /'flʌrɪ/ n (snow) raffica f; fig agitazione f

flush /flʌʃ/ ① n (blush) [vampata f di] rossore m
② vi arrossire
③ vt lavare con un getto d'acqua; **~ the toilet** tirare l'acqua
④ adj a livello (**with** di); (fam: affluent) pieno di soldi
∎ **flush out** vt snidare ⟨spy⟩

flushed /flʌʃt/ adj (cheeks) rosso; **~ with** eccitato da ⟨success⟩; raggiante di ⟨pride⟩

fluster /'flʌstə(r)/ vt agitare

flustered /'flʌstəd/ adj in agitazione; **get ~** mettersi in agitazione

flute /flu:t/ n flauto m

flutter /'flʌtə(r)/ ① n battito m
② vi svolazzare

flux /flʌks/ n **in a state of ~** in uno stato di flusso

fly¹ /flaɪ/ n (pl **flies**) mosca f

fly² ① vi (pt **flew**, pp **flown**) volare; (go by plane) andare in aereo; ⟨flag⟩ sventolare; (rush) precipitarsi; **~ open** spalancarsi
② vt pilotare ⟨plane⟩; trasportare [in aereo] ⟨troops, supplies⟩; volare con ⟨Alitalia etc⟩
∎ **fly away** vi volare via

fly³ n & **flies** pl (on trousers) patta f

flyaway /'flaɪəweɪ/ adj ⟨hair⟩ che non stanno a posto

fly-by-night adj ⟨person⟩ irresponsabile; ⟨company⟩ non affidabile

flycatcher /'flaɪkætʃə(r)/ n pigliamosche m inv

fly-drive adj con la formula aereo più auto

flyer /'flaɪə(r)/ n aviatore m; (leaflet) volantino m

fly-fishing n pesca f con la mosca

flying /'flaɪɪŋ/ n aviazione f

flying buttress n arco m rampante

flying colours: with ~ ~ a pieni voti

flying saucer n disco m volante

flying start n ottima partenza f; **get off to a ~ ~** partire benissimo

flying visit n visita f lampo inv

flyleaf n risguardo m

fly on the wall adj ⟨documentary⟩ con telecamera nascosta

flyover n cavalcavia m inv

fly-past n Br Aeron parata f aerea

flysheet n (handbill) volantino m; (of tent) soprattenda m inv

fly spray n moschicida m

FM abbr (**Frequency Modulation**) FM

foal /fəʊl/ n puledro m

foam /fəʊm/ ① n schiuma f; (synthetic) gommapiuma® f
② vi spumare; **~ at the mouth** far la bava alla bocca

foam bath n bagnoschiuma m

foam rubber n gommapiuma® f

fob /fɒb/ vt (pt/pp **fobbed**) **~ something off** affibbiare qualcosa (**on somebody** a qualcuno); **~ somebody off** liquidare qualcuno

focal /'fəʊkl/ adj focale

focal point n (of village, building) centro m di attrazione; (main concern) punto m centrale; (in optics) fuoco m; **the room lacks a ~ ~** nella stanza manca un punto che focalizzi l'attenzione

focus /'fəʊkəs/ ① n fuoco m; **in ~** a fuoco; **out of ~** sfocato
② vt (pt/pp **focused** or **focussed**) fig concentrare (**on** su)
③ vi **~ on something** Phot mettere a fuoco qualcosa; fig concentrarsi su qualcosa

fodder /'fɒdə(r)/ n foraggio m

foe /fəʊ/ n nemico, -a mf

foetal /'fi:tl/ adj fetale

foetid /'fetɪd/ adj fetido

foetus /'fi:təs/ n (pl **-tuses**) feto m

fog /fɒg/ n nebbia f

fog bank n banco m di nebbia

fogey /'fəʊgɪ/ n **old ~** persona f antiquata

foggy /'fɒgɪ/ adj (**foggier**, **foggiest**) nebbioso; **it's ~** c'è nebbia; **I haven't got**

the foggiest [idea] fam non ne ho la più pallida idea

foghorn /'fɒghɔːn/ n sirena f da nebbia

fog lamp, **foglight** /'fɒglaɪt/ n Auto [faro m] antinebbia m inv

foible /'fɔɪbl/ n punto m debole

foil[1] /'fɔɪl/ n lamina f di metallo

foil[2] vt (thwart) frustrare

foil[3] n (sword) fioretto m

foist /fɔɪst/ vt appioppare (**on somebody** a qualcuno)

fold[1] /'fəʊld/ n (for sheep) ovile m

fold[2] **①** n piega f
② vt piegare; ~ **one's arms** incrociare le braccia
③ vi piegarsi; (fail) crollare
■ **fold back** vt ripiegare ⟨sheets⟩; aprire ⟨shutters⟩
■ **fold in** vt incorporare ⟨flour, eggs⟩
■ **fold up** **①** vt ripiegare ⟨chair⟩
② vi essere pieghevole; fam ⟨business⟩ collassare

foldaway /'fəʊldəweɪ/ adj ⟨bed⟩ pieghevole; ⟨table⟩ estraibile

folder /'fəʊldə(r)/ n cartella f

folding /'fəʊldɪŋ/ adj pieghevole

folding seat n strapuntino m, sedile m pieghevole

folding stool n sgabello m pieghevole

fold-out n (in magazine) pieghevole m

foliage /'fəʊlɪɪdʒ/ n fogliame m

folk /fəʊk/ npl gente f; **my ~s** (family) i miei; **hello there ~s** ciao a tutti

folk dance n danza f popolare

folklore n folclore m

folk medicine n rimedio m della nonna

folk memory n memoria f collettiva

folk music n musica f folk

folk song n canto m popolare

folk wisdom n saggezza f popolare

follow /'fɒləʊ/ vt/i seguire; **it doesn't ~** non è necessariamente così; ~ **suit** fig fare lo stesso; **as ~s** come segue
■ **follow through** vt portare avanti ⟨project, idea⟩
■ **follow up** vt fare seguito a ⟨letter⟩

follower /'fɒləʊə(r)/ n seguace mf

following /'fɒləʊɪŋ/ **①** adj seguente
② n seguito m; (supporters) seguaci mpl
③ prep in seguito a

follow-on n seguito m

follow-up **①** n (of socialwork case) controllo m: (of patient, ex inmate) visita f di controllo; (film, record, single, programme) seguito m
② attrib ⟨survey, work, interview⟩ successivo; ~ **letter** lettera f che fa seguito

folly /'fɒlɪ/ n follia f

foment /fə'ment/ vt fig fomentare

fond /fɒnd/ adj affezionato; ⟨hope⟩ vivo; **be ~ of** essere appassionato di ⟨music⟩ **I'm ~ of...** ⟨food, person⟩ mi piace moltissimo...

fondle /'fɒndl/ vt coccolare

fondly /'fɒndlɪ/ adv ⟨hope⟩ ingenuamente

fondness /'fɒndnɪs/ n affetto m; (for things) amore m

font /fɒnt/ n fonte f battesimale; Typ carattere m di stampa

food /fuːd/ n cibo m; (for animals, groceries) mangiare m; **let's buy some ~** compriamo qualcosa da mangiare

food aid n aiuti mpl alimentari

foodie /'fuːdɪ/ n fam buongustaio, -a mf

food mixer n frullatore m

food poisoning n intossicazione f alimentare

food processor n tritatutto m inv elettrico

foodstuffs npl generi mpl alimentari

fool[1] /fuːl/ **①** n sciocco, -a mf; **she's no ~** non è una stupida; **make a ~ of oneself** rendersi ridicolo
② vt prendere in giro
③ vi ~ **around** giocare; ⟨husband, wife⟩ avere l'amante

fool[2] n Culin crema f

foolhardy /'fuːlhɑːdɪ/ adj temerario

foolish /'fuːlɪʃ/ adj stolto

foolishly /'fuːlɪʃlɪ/ adv scioccamente

foolishness /'fuːlɪʃnɪs/ n sciocchezza f

foolproof /'fuːlpruːf/ adj facilissimo

foolscap /'fuːlskæp/ n (Br: paper) carta f protocollo

foot /fʊt/ n (pl **feet**) piede m; (of animal) zampa f; (measure) piede (= 30,48 cm); **on ~** a piedi; **on one's feet** in piedi; **put one's ~ in it** fam fare una gaffe

footage /'fʊtɪdʒ/ n (piece of film) spezzone m; **news ~** servizio m [filmato]

foot-and-mouth disease n afta f epizootica

football n calcio m; (ball) pallone m

footballer n giocatore m di calcio

football pools npl totocalcio m

footbrake n freno m a pedale

footbridge n passerella f

foothills npl colline fpl pedemontane

foothold n punto m d'appoggio

footing n **lose one's ~** perdere l'appiglio; **on an equal ~** in condizioni di parità

footlights npl luci nfpl della ribalta

footloose and fancy-free adj libero come l'aria

footman n valletto m

footnote n nota f a piè di pagina

foot passenger *n* (on boat) passeggero, -a *mf*

footpath *n* sentiero *m*

footprint *n* orma *f*; (of machine) ingombro *m*

footrest *n* poggiapiedi *m inv*

footsore *adj* be ~ avere male ai piedi

footstep *n* passo *m*; follow in somebody's ~s fig seguire l'esempio di qualcuno

footstool *n* sgabellino *m*

footwear *n* calzature *fpl*

for /fə(r), *accentato*/fɔː(r)/ ① *prep* per; ~ this reason per questa ragione; I have lived here ~ ten years vivo qui da dieci anni; ~ supper per cena; ~ all that nonostante questo; what ~? a che scopo?; send ~ a doctor chiamare un dottore; fight ~ a cause lottare per una causa; go ~ a walk andare a fare una passeggiata; there's no need ~ you to go non c'è bisogno che tu vada; it's not ~ me to say non sta a me dirlo; now you're ~ it ora sei nei pasticci
② *conj* poiché, perché

forage /'fɒrɪdʒ/ ① *n* foraggio *m*
② *vi* ~ for cercare

foray /'fɒreɪ/ *n* Mil incursione *f*, make a ~ into (politics, acting) tentare la strada di

forbade /fə'bæd/ ▶FORBID

forbearance /fɔː'beərəns/ *n* pazienza *f*

forbearing /fɔː'beərɪŋ/ *adj* tollerante

forbid /fə'bɪd/ *vt* (pt **forbade**, pp **forbidden**) proibire

forbidden /fə'bɪd(ə)n/ *adj* ‹fruit, place› proibito

forbidding /fə'bɪdɪŋ/ *adj* ‹prospect› che spaventa; (stern) severo

force /fɔːs/ ① *n* forza *f*; in ~ in vigore; (in large numbers) in massa; come into ~ entrare in vigore; the [armed] ~s *pl* le forze armate
② *vt* forzare; ~ something on somebody ‹decision› imporre qualcosa a qualcuno; ‹drink› costringere qualcuno a fare qualcosa
■ **force back** *vt* trattenere ‹tears›
■ **force down** *vt* buttar giù (controvoglia) ‹food, drink›

forced /fɔːst/ *adj* forzato

forced landing *n* atterraggio *m* forzato

force-feed *vt* (pt/pp **-fed**) nutrire a forza

forceful /'fɔːsfʊl/ *adj* energico

forcefully /'fɔːsfʊlɪ/ *adv* ‹say, argue› con forza

forceps /'fɔːseps/ *npl* forcipe *m*

forcible /'fɔːsəbl/ *adj* forzato

forcibly /'fɔːsəblɪ/ *adv* forzatamente

ford /fɔːd/ ① *n* guado *m*
② *vt* guadare

fore /fɔː(r)/ *n* to the ~ in vista; come to the ~ salire alla ribalta

forearm /'fɔːrɑːm/ *n* avambraccio *m*

forebears /'fɔːbeəz/ *npl* antenati *mpl*

foreboding /fɔː'bəʊdɪŋ/ *n* presentimento *m*

forecast /'fɔːkɑːst/ ① *n* previsione *f*
② *vt* (pt/pp **forecast**) prevedere

forecaster /'fɔːkɑːstə(r)/ *n* pronosticatore, -trice *mf*; (economic) analista *mf* della congiuntura; (of weather) meteorologo, -a *mf*

forecourt *n* (of garage) spiazzo *m* [antistante]

forefathers *npl* antenati *mpl*

forefinger *n* [dito *m*] indice *m*

forefront *n* be in the ~ essere all'avanguardia

foregone *adj* be a ~ conclusion essere una cosa scontata

foreground *n* primo piano *m*

forehand *n* Tennis diritto *m*

forehead /'fɔːhed/, /'fɒrɪd/ *n* fronte *f*

foreign /'fɒrən/ *adj* straniero; ‹trade› estero; (not belonging) estraneo; he is ~ è uno straniero

foreign affairs *npl* affari *mpl* esteri

foreign body *n* corpo *m* estraneo

foreign correspondent *n* corrispondente *mf* estero

foreign currency *n* valuta *f* estera

foreigner /'fɒrənə(r)/ *n* straniero, -a *mf*

foreign exchange *n* (currency) valuta *f* estera

foreign exchange market *n* mercato *m* dei cambi

foreign language *n* lingua *f* straniera

foreign minister *n* ministro *m* degli Esteri

Foreign Office *n* Br ministero *m* degli [affari] Esteri

Foreign Secretary *n* Br Ministro *m* degli Esteri

foreleg /'fɔːleg/ *n* zampa *f* anteriore

foreman /'fɔːmən/ *n* caporeparto *m*

foremost /'fɔːməʊst/ ① *adj* principale
② *adv* first and ~ in primo luogo

forename /'fɔːneɪm/ *n* nome *m* di battesimo

forensic /fə'rensɪk/ *adj* ~ medicine medicina legale

forensic evidence *n* prova *f* medico-legale

forensic science *n* medicina *f* legale

forensic scientist *n* medico *m* legale

forensic tests *npl* perizia *f sg* medico-legale

forerunner /'fɔːrʌnə(r)/ *n* precursore *m*

foresee /fɔːˈsiː/ *vt* (pt **-saw**, pp **-seen**) prevedere

foreseeable /fɔːˈsiːəbl/ *adj* in the ~ future nel futuro immediato

foreshadow *vt* prevedere

foresight /ˈfɔːsaɪt/ *n* previdenza *f*

foreskin /ˈfɔːskɪn/ *n* Anat prepuzio *m*

forest /ˈfɒrɪst/ *n* foresta *f*

forestall /fɔːˈstɔːl/ *vt* prevenire

forester /ˈfɒrɪstə(r)/ *n* guardia *f* forestale

forest fire *n* incendio *m* nei boschi

forest ranger /ˈreɪndʒə(r)/ *n* Am guardia *f* forestale

forestry /ˈfɒrɪstrɪ/ *n* silvicoltura *f*

foretaste /ˈfɔːteɪst/ *n* pregustazione *f*

foretell /fɔːˈtel/ *vt* (pt/pp **-told**) predire

forethought /ˈfɔːθɔːt/ *n* accortezza *f*, previdenza *f*

forever /fəˈrevə(r)/ *adv* per sempre; he's ~ complaining si lamenta sempre

forewarn /fɔːˈwɔːn/ *vt* avvertire

foreword /ˈfɔːwɜːd/ *n* prefazione *f*

forfeit /ˈfɔːfɪt/ **1** *n* (in game) pegno *m*; Jur penalità *f*
2 *vt* perdere

forfeiture /ˈfɔːfɪtʃə(r)/ *n* (of right) perdita *f*; (of property) confisca *f*

forgave /fəˈgeɪv/ ▶ FORGIVE

forge[1] /fɔːdʒ/ *vi* ~ ahead ⟨*runner*⟩ lasciarsi indietro gli altri; fig farsi strada

forge[2] **1** *n* fucina *f*
2 *vt* fucinare; (counterfeit) contraffare

forger /ˈfɔːdʒə(r)/ *n* contraffattore *m*

forgery /ˈfɔːdʒərɪ/ *n* contraffazione *f*

forget /fəˈget/ *vt/i* (pt **-got**, pp **-gotten**) dimenticare; dimenticarsi di ⟨*language, skill*⟩; ~ oneself perdere la padronanza di sé

■ **forget about** *vt* dimenticarsi di

forgetful /fəˈgetful/ *adj* smemorato

forgetfulness /fəˈgetfulnɪs/ *n* smemoratezza *f*

forget-me-not *n* non-ti-scordar-di-mè *m inv*

forgettable /fəˈgetəbl/ *adj* ⟨*day, fact, film*⟩ da dimenticare

forgive /fəˈgɪv/ *vt* (pt **-gave**, pp **-given**) ~ somebody for something perdonare qualcuno per qualcosa

forgiveness /fəˈgɪvnɪs/ *n* perdono *m*

forgiving /fəˈgɪvɪŋ/ *adj* ⟨*person*⟩ indulgente

forgo /fɔːˈgəʊ/ *vt* (pt **-went**, pp **-gone**) rinunciare a

forgot(ten) /fəˈgɒt(n)/ ▶ FORGET

fork /fɔːk/ **1** *n* forchetta *f*; (for digging) forca *f*; (in road) bivio *m*
2 *vi* ⟨*road*⟩ biforcarsi; ~ right prendere a destra

■ **fork out** **1** *vt* fam sborsare
2 *vi* sborsare soldi

forked lightning /fɔːkt/ *n* fulmine *m* ramificato

fork-lift truck *n* elevatore *m*

forlorn /fəˈlɔːn/ *adj* ⟨*look*⟩ perduto; ⟨*place*⟩ derelitto; ~ hope speranza *f* vana

form /fɔːm/ **1** *n* forma *f*; (document) modulo *m*; Sch classe *f*
2 *vt* formare; formulare ⟨*opinion*⟩
3 *vi* formarsi

formal /ˈfɔːml/ *adj* formale

formal dress *n* abito *m* da cerimonia

formalin /ˈfɔːməlɪn/ *n* formalina *f*

formality /fɔːˈmælətɪ/ *n* formalità *f inv*

formally /ˈfɔːməlɪ/ *adv* in modo formale; (officially) ufficialmente

format /ˈfɔːmæt/ **1** *n* formato *m*
2 *vt* formattare ⟨*disk, page*⟩

formation /fɔːˈmeɪʃn/ *n* formazione *f*

formative /ˈfɔːmətɪv/ *adj* ~ years anni formativi

former /ˈfɔːmə(r)/ *adj* precedente; ⟨*PM, colleague*⟩ ex; the ~, the latter il primo, l'ultimo

formerly /ˈfɔːməlɪ/ *adv* precedentemente; (in olden times) in altri tempi

formidable /ˈfɔːmɪdəbl/ *adj* formidabile

formless /ˈfɔːmlɪs/ *adj* ⟨*mass*⟩ informe; ⟨*novel*⟩ che manca di struttura

form teacher *n* Br Sch ≈ coordinatore, -trice *mf* del consiglio di classe

formula /ˈfɔːjʊlə/ *n* (pl **-ae** /ˈfɔːmjʊliː/ or **-s**) formula *f*

formulate /ˈfɔːmjʊleɪt/ *vt* formulare

formulation /fɔːmjʊˈleɪʃn/ *n* formulazione *f*

fornication /fɔːnɪˈkeɪʃn/ *n* fornicazione *f*

forsake /fəˈseɪk/ *vt* (pt **-sook** /fəˈsʊk/, pp **-saken**) abbandonare

forseeable /fəˈsiːəbl/ *adj* in the ~ future in futuro per quanto si possa prevedere

forswear /fɔːˈsweə(r)/ *vt* (renounce) abiurare

fort /fɔːt/ *n* Mil forte *m*

forte /ˈfɔːteɪ/ *n* [pezzo *m*] forte *m*

forth /fɔːθ/ *adv* back and ~ avanti e indietro; and so ~ e così via

forthcoming /fɔːθˈkʌmɪŋ/ *adj* prossimo; (communicative) comunicativo; no response was ~ non arrivava nessuna risposta

forthright /ˈfɔːθraɪt/ *adj* schietto

forthwith /fɔːθˈwɪθ/ *adv* immediatamente

forties /ˈfɔːtɪz/ *npl* (period) the ~ gli anni Quaranta *mpl*; (age) quarant'anni *mpl*; a man in his ~ un quarantenne

fortieth /'fɔ:tɪɪθ/ *adj & n* quarantesimo, -a *mf*

fortification /fɔ:tɪfɪ'keɪʃn/ *n* fortificazione *f*

fortified /'fɔ:tɪfaɪd/ *adj* fortificato; ~ wine vino liquoroso; ~ with vitamins arricchito con vitamine

fortify /'fɔ:tɪfaɪ/ *vt* (pt/pp -ied) fortificare; fig rendere forte

fortitude /'fɔ:tɪtju:d/ *n* coraggio *m*

fortnight /'fɔ:tnaɪt/ *n* Br quindicina *f*

fortnightly /'fɔ:tnaɪtlɪ/ ① *adj* bimensile ② *adv* ogni due settimane

fortress /'fɔ:trɪs/ *n* fortezza *f*

fortuitous /fɔ:'tju:ɪtəs/ *adj* fortuito

fortunate /'fɔ:tʃənət/ *adj* fortunato; that's ~! meno male!

fortunately /'fɔ:tʃənətlɪ/ *adv* fortunatamente

fortune /'fɔ:tʃu:n/ *n* fortuna *f*

fortune cookie *n* Am biscottino *m* che racchiude un foglietto con una predizione

fortune-teller *n* indovino, -a *mf*

forty /'fɔ:tɪ/ *adj & n* quaranta *m*; have ~ winks fam fare un pisolino

forum /'fɔ:rəm/ *n* foro *m*

forward /'fɔ:wəd/ ① *adv* avanti; (towards the front) in avanti; move ~ andare avanti ② *adj* in avanti; (presumptuous) sfacciato ③ *n* Sport attaccante *m* ④ *vt* inoltrare ⟨letter⟩; spedire ⟨goods⟩

forward buying *n* Fin acquisto *m* a termine

forwarding address *n* indirizzo *m* a cui inoltrare la corrispondenza

forward-looking *adj* ⟨company, person⟩ lungimirante

forward planning *n* pianificazione *f* a lungo termine

forwards /'fɔ:wədz/ *adv* avanti

forward slash *n* slash *m inv*

fossil /'fɒs(ə)l/ *n* fossile *m*

fossil fuel *n* combustibile *m* fossile

fossilized /'fɒsɪlaɪzd/ *adj* fossile; ⟨ideas⟩ fossilizzato

foster /'fɒstə(r)/ *vt* allevare ⟨child⟩

foster child *n* figlio, -a *mf* in affidamento

foster family *n* famiglia *f* affidataria

foster home *n* famiglia *f* affidataria

foster mother *n* madre *f* affidataria

fought /fɔ:t/ ▶ FIGHT

foul /faʊl/ ① *adj* ⟨smell, taste⟩ cattivo; ⟨air⟩ viziato; ⟨language⟩ osceno; ⟨mood, weather⟩ orrendo ② *vt* inquinare ⟨water⟩; Sport commettere un fallo contro; ⟨nets, rope⟩ impigliarsi in ■ **foul up** *vt* (fam: spoil) mandare in malora

foul-mouthed /-'maʊðd/ *adj* sboccato

foul play ① *n* Jur delitto *m* ② *n* Sport fallo *m*

foul-smelling /-'smelɪŋ/ *adj* puzzo.

foul-up *n* pasticcio *m*

found[1] /faʊnd/ ▶ FIND

found[2] *vt* fondare

foundation /faʊn'deɪʃn/ *n* (basis) fondamento *m*; (charitable) fondazione *f*; ~s *pl* (of building) fondamenta *fpl*; lay the ~-stone porre la prima pietra

foundation course *n* Br Univ corso *m* propedeutico

founder[1] /'faʊndə(r)/ *n* fondatore, trice *mf*

founder[2] *vi* ⟨ship⟩ affondare

foundry /'faʊndrɪ/ *n* fonderia *f*

fount /faʊnt/ *n* Typ carattere *m* [stampa]

fountain /'faʊntɪn/ *n* fontana *f*

fountain pen *n* penna *f* stilografica

four /fɔ:(r)/ *adj & n* quattro *m*

four-by-four *n* (vehicle) quattro per quattro *f*

four four time *n* Mus quattro quarti

four-letter word *n* parolaccia *f*

four-poster [bed] *n* letto *m* a baldacchino

foursome /'fɔ:səm/ *n* quartetto *m*

four-star ① *adj* ⟨hotel, restaurant⟩ a quattro stelle ② *n* (petrol) super *f*

four-stroke *adj* ⟨engine⟩ a quattro tempi

fourteen /fɔ:'ti:n/ *adj & n* quattordici *m*

fourteenth /fɔ:'ti:nθ/ *adj & n* quattordicesimo, -a *mf*

fourth /fɔ:θ/ *adj & n* quarto, -a *mf*

fourthly /'fɔ:θlɪ/ *adv* in quarto luogo

fourth rate *adj* ⟨job, hotel, film⟩ di terz'ordine

four-wheel drive [vehicle] *n* quattro per quattro *m inv*

fowl /faʊl/ *n* pollame *m*

fox /fɒks/ ① *n* volpe *f* ② *vt* (puzzle) ingannare

fox cub *n* volpacchiotto *m*

fox fur *n* pelliccia *f* di volpe

foxglove *n* digitale *f*

foxhound *n* foxhound *m inv*

fox-hunt *n* caccia *f* alla volpe

fox hunting *n* caccia *f* alla volpe

fox terrier *n* fox-terrier *m inv*

foxtrot *n* fox-trot *m inv*

foxy /'fɒksɪ/ *adj* (-ier, -iest) (fam: sexy) sexy *inv*; (crafty) scaltro

foyer /'fɔɪeɪ/ *n* Theat ridotto *m*; (in hotel) salone *m* d'ingresso

fracas /'fræka:/ *n* baruffa *f*

fraction /'frækʃn/ *n* frazione *f*

fractionally /ˈfrækʃənəlɪ/ adv (slightly) leggermente

fracture /ˈfræktʃə(r)/ ①̵ n frattura f
②̵ vt fratturare
③̵ vi fratturarsi

fragile /ˈfrædʒaɪl/ adj fragile

fragment /ˈfrægmənt/ n frammento m

fragmentary /ˈfrægm(ə)ntərɪ/ adj frammentario

fragrance /ˈfreɪgrəns/ n fragranza f

fragrant /ˈfreɪgrənt/ adj fragrante

frail /freɪl/ adj gracile

frailty /ˈfreɪltɪ/ n (imperfection) debolezza f (of person: moral) fragilità f inv; (of person: physical) gracilità f; (of health, state) precarietà f inv

frame /freɪm/ ①̵ n (of picture, door, window) cornice f; (of spectacles) montatura f; Anat ossatura f; (structure, of bike) telaio m
②̵ vt incorniciare ⟨picture⟩; fig formulare; (sl: incriminate) montare

frame of mind n stato m d'animo

framework /ˈfreɪmwɜːk/ n struttura f; within the ~ of the law nell'ambito della legge

franc /fræŋk/ n franco m

France /frɑːns/ n Francia f

franchise /ˈfræntʃaɪz/ n Pol diritto m di voto; Comm franchigia f

Franciscan /frænˈsɪskən/ n francescano m

frank[1] /fræŋk/ vt affrancare ⟨letter⟩

frank[2] adj franco

Frankfurt /ˈfræŋkfɜːt/ n Francoforte f

frankfurter /ˈfræŋkfɜːtə(r)/ n würstel m inv

frankincense /ˈfræŋkɪnsens/ n incenso m

franking machine /ˈfræŋkɪŋ/ n affrancatrice f

frankly /ˈfræŋklɪ/ adv francamente

frantic /ˈfræntɪk/ adj frenetico; be ~ with worry essere agitatissimo

frantically /ˈfræntɪklɪ/ adv freneticamente

fraternal /frəˈtɜːnl/ adj fraterno

fraternity /frəˈtɜːnətɪ/ n (club) associazione f; (spirit, brotherhood) fratellanza f

fraud /frɔːd/ n frode f; (person) impostore m

fraudulent /ˈfrɔːdjʊlənt/ adj fraudolento

fraught /frɔːt/ adj ~ with pieno di

fray[1] /freɪ/ n mischia f

fray[2] vi sfilacciarsi

frayed /freɪd/ adj ⟨cuffs⟩ sfilacciato; ⟨nerves⟩ a pezzi

frazzle /ˈfræz(ə)l/ n be worn to a ~ essere ridotto uno straccio; burn something to a ~ carbonizzare qualcosa

freak /friːk/ ①̵ n fenomeno m; (person) scherzo m di natura; (fam: weird person) tipo m strambo
②̵ adj anormale
■ **freak out** vi (fam: lose control, go crazy) andar fuori di testa

freakish /ˈfriːkɪʃ/ adj strambo

freckle /ˈfrekl/ n lentiggine f

freckled /ˈfrekld/ adj lentigginoso

free /friː/ ①̵ adj (**freer, freest**) libero; ⟨ticket, copy⟩ gratuito; (lavish) generoso; ~ of charge gratuito; set ~ liberare; ~ with... Comm in omaggio per...
②̵ vt (pt/pp **freed**) liberare

free agent n persona f libera di agire come vuole

free and easy adj disinvolto

freebee, freebie /ˈfriːbɪ/ n fam (free gift) omaggio m; (trip) viaggio m gratuito; (newspaper) giornale m gratuito

freedom /ˈfriːdəm/ n libertà f

freedom fighter n combattente mf per la libertà

free enterprise n liberalismo m economico

free fall n caduta f libera

Freefone®, Freephone n numero m verde

free-for-all n (disorganized situation, fight) baraonda f

free gift n omaggio m

freehand adv a mano libera

freehold n proprietà f [fondiaria] assoluta

free house n Br pub m inv che non è legato a nessun produttore di birra

free-kick n calcio m di punizione

freelance adj & adv indipendente

freeloader n fam scroccone m

freely /ˈfriːlɪ/ adv liberamente; (generously) generosamente; I ~ admit that... devo ammettere che...

free market n economia f di libero mercato

Freemason n massone m

Freemasonry n massoneria f

Freephone n = FREEFONE

freephone number n numero m verde

freepost n Br affrancatura f a carico del destinatario

free-range adj ⟨eggs⟩ di allevamento a terra; ⟨hens⟩ allevato a terra

free-range egg n uovo m di gallina ruspante

free sample n campione m gratuito

free speech n libertà f di parola

free spirit n persona f che ama la sua indipendenza

free-standing *adj* ⟨*heater*⟩ non incassato; ⟨*statue*⟩ a tutto tondo; ⟨*lamp*⟩ a stelo

freestyle *n* stile *m* libero

free trade *n* libero scambio *m*

free trial period *n* periodo *m* di prova gratuito

freeware /'fri:weə/ *n* Comput freeware *m inv*

freeway *n* Am autostrada *f*

freewheel *vi* ⟨*car*⟩ (in neutral) andare in folle; (with engine switched off) andare a motore spento; ⟨*bicycle*⟩ andare a ruota libera

free will *n* of one's own ∼ di spontanea volontà

freeze /fri:z/ ☐ *vt* (pt **froze**, pp **frozen**) gelare; bloccare ⟨*wages*⟩
☐ *vi* ⟨*water*⟩ gelare; **it's freezing** si gela; **my hands are freezing** ho le mani congelate

freeze-dried *adj* liofilizzato

freeze-frame *n* (video) fermo *m* immagine

freezer /'fri:zə(r)/ *n* freezer *m inv*, congelatore *m*

freezer compartment *n* scomparto *m* freezer

freezing /'fri:zɪŋ/ ☐ *adj* gelido
☐ *n* **below** ∼ sotto zero

freezing cold *adj* gelido

freezing fog *n* nebbia *f* ghiacciata

freezing point *n* punto *m* di congelamento

freight /freɪt/ *n* carico *m*

freight charges *npl* costi *mpl* di spedizione

freighter /'freɪtə(r)/ *n* nave *f* da carico

freight forwarder *n* spedizioniere *m*

freight train *n* Am treno *m* merci

French /frentʃ/ ☐ *adj* francese
☐ *n* (language) francese *m*; **the** ∼ *pl* i francesi

French beans *npl* fagiolini *mpl* [verdi]

French bread *n* filone *m* (di pane)

French Canadian ☐ *n* canadese *mf* francofono, -a
☐ *adj* del Canada francofono

French doors *npl* porta-finestra *f inv*

French dressing *n* Br vinaigrette *f inv*

French fries *npl* patate *fpl* fritte

French horn *n* corno *m* da caccia

French kiss *n* bacio *m* profondo

French knickers *npl* culottes *fpl*

Frenchman *n* francese *m*

French polish *n* vernice *f* a olio e gommalacca

French-speaking *adj* francofono

French toast *n* pane *m* immerso nell'uovo sbattuto e fritto

French window *n* porta-finestra *f*

Frenchwoman *n* francese *f*

frenetic /frə'netɪk/ *adj* ⟨*activity*⟩ frenetico

frenzied /'frenzɪd/ *adj* frenetico

frenzy /'frenzɪ/ *n* frenesia *f*

frequency /'fri:kwənsɪ/ *n* frequenza *f*

frequent[1] /'fri:kwənt/ *adj* frequente

frequent[2] /frɪ'kwent/ *vt* frequentare

frequent-flyer miles *npl* Am miglia *fpl* aeree

frequently /'fri:kwəntlɪ/ *adv* frequentemente

fresco /'freskəʊ/ *n* affresco *m*

fresh /freʃ/ *adj* fresco; (new) nuovo; (Am: cheeky) sfacciato

fresh air *n* aria *f* fresca; **get some** ∼ prendere una boccata d'aria

freshen /'freʃn/ *vi* ⟨*wind*⟩ rinfrescare
■ **freshen up** ☐ *vt* dare una rinfrescata a
☐ *vi* rinfrescarsi

fresh-faced /-'feɪst/ *adj* dalla faccia giovanile

freshly /'freʃlɪ/ *adv* di recente

freshman /'freʃmən/ *n* Am matricola *f*; (fig: in congress, in firm) nuovo arrivato *m*

freshness /'freʃnɪs/ *n* freschezza *f*

freshwater /'freʃwɔ:tə(r)/ *adj* di acqua dolce

fret /fret/ *vi* (pt/pp **fretted**) inquietarsi

fretful /'fretfʊl/ *adj* irritabile

fretsaw /'fretsɔ:/ *n* seghetto *m* da traforo

fretwork /'fretwɜ:k/ *n* [lavoro *m* di] traforo *m*

Freudian slip /'frɔɪdɪən/ *n* lapsus *m inv* freudiano

friar /'fraɪə(r)/ *n* frate *m*

friction /'frɪkʃn/ *n* frizione *f*

Friday /'fraɪdeɪ/ *n* venerdì *m inv*

fridge /frɪdʒ/ *n* frigo *m*

fridge-freezer *n* frigocongelatore *m*

fried /fraɪd/ ☐ ▶ **FRY**[1]
☐ *adj* fritto; ∼ **egg** uovo *m* fritto

friend /frend/ *n* amico, -a *mf*

friendly /'frendlɪ/ *adj* (**-ier, -iest**) ⟨*relations, meeting, match*⟩ amichevole; ⟨*neighbourhood, smile*⟩ piacevole; ⟨*software*⟩ di facile uso; **be** ∼ **with** essere amico di

friendly fire *n* fuoco *m* amico

friendship /'frendʃɪp/ *n* amicizia *f*

frieze /fri:z/ *n* fregio *m*

frigate /'frɪgət/ *n* fregata *f*

fright /fraɪt/ *n* paura *f*; **take** ∼ spaventarsi

frighten /'fraɪt(ə)n/ *vt* spaventare

■ **frighten away** *vt* far scappare ⟨*bird, intruder*⟩

frightened /'fraɪtənd/ *adj* spaventato; be ~ aver paura (**of** di)

frightening /'fraɪt(ə)nɪŋ/ *adj* spaventoso

frightful /'fraɪtfl/ *adj* terribile

frightfully /'fraɪtfʊlɪ/ *adv* terribilmente

frigid /'frɪdʒɪd/ *adj* frigido

frigidity /frɪ'dʒɪdətɪ/ *n* freddezza *f*; Psych frigidità *f*

frill /frɪl/ *n* volant *m inv*

frilly /'frɪlɪ/ *adj* ⟨*dress*⟩ con tanti volant

fringe /frɪndʒ/ *n* frangia *f*; (of hair) frangetta *f*; (fig: edge) margine *m*

fringe benefits *npl* benefici *mpl* supplementari

frisk /frɪsk/ *vt* (search) perquisire

frisky /'frɪskɪ/ *adj* (**-ier, -iest**) vispo

fritter /'frɪtə(r)/ *n* frittella *f*

■ **fritter away** *vt* sprecare

frivolity /frɪ'vɒlətɪ/ *n* frivolezza *f*

frivolous /'frɪvələs/ *adj* frivolo

frizzy /'frɪzɪ/ *adj* (**-ier, -iest**) crespo

fro /frəʊ/ ▶ TO

frock /frɒk/ *n* abito *m*

frog /frɒg/ *n* rana *f*

frogman *n* uomo *m* rana *inv*

frogmarch *vt* Br portare via a forza

frogs' legs *npl* cosce *fpl* di rana

frogspawn *n* uova *fpl* di rana

frolic /'frɒlɪk/ *vi* (pt/pp **frolicked**) ⟨*lambs*⟩ sgambettare; fam ⟨*people*⟩ folleggiare

from /frɒm/ *prep* da; ~ **Monday** da lunedì; ~ **that day** da quel giorno; **he's** ~ **London** è di Londra; **this is a letter** ~ **my brother** questa è una lettera di mio fratello; **documents** ~ **the 16th century** documenti del XVI secolo; **made** ~ fatto con; **she felt ill** ~ **fatigue** si sentiva male dalla stanchezza; ~ **now on** d'ora in poi

front /frʌnt/ **①** *n* parte *f* anteriore; (fig: organization etc) facciata *f*; (of garment) davanti *m*; **sea** ~ lungomare *m*; Mil, Pol, Meteorol fronte *m*; **in** ~ **of** davanti a; **in** *or* **at the** ~ davanti; **to the** ~ avanti; **②** *adj* davanti; ⟨*page, row, wheel*⟩ anteriore

frontage /'frʌntɪdʒ/ *n* (of house) facciata *f*; **with ocean/river** ~ (access) prospiciente l'oceano/il fiume

frontal /'frʌntl/ *adj* frontale

front bench *n* Br Pol parlamentari *mpl* di maggiore importanza

front door *n* porta *f* d'entrata

front garden *n* giardino *m* sul davanti

frontier /'frʌntɪə(r)/ *n* frontiera *f*

front line *n* Mil prima linea *f*; **be in the** ~ ~ fig essere in prima linea

front of house *n* Br Theat foyer *m inv*

front page **①** *n* prima pagina *f*; **②** *adj* ⟨*picture, spread*⟩ in prima pagina

front runner *n* Sport concorrente *mf* in testa; (favourite) favorito, -a *mf*

front-wheel drive *n* trazione *f* anteriore

frost /frɒst/ *n* gelo *m*; **hoar** ~ brina *f*

frostbite /'frɒs(t)baɪt/ *n* congelamento *m*

frostbitten /'frɒs(t)bɪtən/ *adj* congelato

frosted /'frɒstɪd/ *adj* ~ **glass** vetro *m* smerigliato

frostily /'frɒstɪlɪ/ *adv* gelidamente

frosting /'frɒstɪŋ/ *n* Am Culin glassa *f*

frosty /'frɒstɪ/ *adj* (**-ier, -iest**) also fig gelido

froth /frɒθ/ **①** *n* schiuma *f*; **②** *vi* far schiuma

frothy /'frɒθɪ/ *adj* (**-ier, -iest**) schiumoso

frown /fraʊn/ **①** *n* cipiglio *m*; **②** *vi* aggrottare le sopracciglia

■ **frown on** *vt* disapprovare

froze /frəʊz/ ▶ FREEZE

frozen /'frəʊzn/ **①** ▶ FREEZE **②** *adj* ⟨*corpse, hand*⟩ congelato; ⟨*wastes*⟩ gelido; Culin surgelato; **I'm** ~ sono gelato

frozen food *n* surgelati *mpl*

frugal /'fru:gl/ *adj* frugale

frugally /'fru:gəlɪ/ *adv* frugalmente

fruit /fru:t/ *n* frutto *m*; (collectively) frutta *f*; **eat more** ~ mangia più frutta

fruit bowl *n* fruttiera *f*

fruit cake *n* dolce *m* con frutta candita

fruit cocktail *n* macedonia *f* [di frutta]

fruit drop *n* drop *m inv* alla frutta

fruiterer /'fru:tərə(r)/ *n* fruttivendolo, -a *mf*

fruit farmer *n* frutticoltore *m*

fruit fly *n* moscerino *m* della frutta

fruitful /'fru:tfʊl/ *adj* fig fruttuoso

fruit gum *n* caramella *f* alla frutta

fruition /fru:'ɪʃn/ *n* **come to** ~ dare dei frutti

fruit juice *n* succo *m* di frutta

fruitless /'fru:tlɪs/ *adj* infruttuoso

fruitlessly /'fru:tlɪslɪ/ *adv* senza risultato

fruit machine *n* macchinetta *f* mangiasoldi

fruit salad *n* macedonia *f* [di frutta]

fruity /'fru:tɪ/ *adj* ⟨*wine*⟩ fruttato

frump /frʌmp/ *n* donna *f* scialba

frumpy /'frʌmpɪ/ *adj* scialbo

frustrate /frʌ'streɪt/ *vt* frustrare; rovinare ⟨*plans*⟩

frustrated /frʌ'streɪtɪd/ *adj* frustrato

frustrating /frʌ'streɪtɪŋ/ *adj* frustrante

frustration /frʌ'streɪʃn/ *n* frustrazione *f*

fry¹ /fraɪ/ *n inv* small ~ fig pesce *m* piccolo

fry² *vt/i* (pt/pp **fried**) friggere

frying pan /'fraɪɪŋ/ *n* padella *f*

ft. *abbr* (**foot** *or* **feet**) piede, piedi

ftp *abbr* (**file transfer protocol**) Comput FTP *m*

fuchsia /'fjuːʃə/ *n* fucsia *f*

fuck /fʌk/ vulg **1** *vt/i* scopare
2 *n* I don't give a ~ me ne sbatto; **what the ~ are you doing?** che cazzo fai?
3 *int* cazzo!
■ **fuck off** *vi* (vulg) ~ **off!** vaffanculo!
■ **fuck up** *vt* (vulg: ruin) mandare a puttane

fucking /'fʌkɪŋ/ *adj* vulg del cazzo

fuddled /'fʌd(ə)ld/ *adj* (confused) confuso; (slightly drunk) brillo

fuddy-duddy /'fʌdɪdʌdɪ/ *n* fam matusa *mf inv*

fudge /fʌdʒ/ *n* caramella *f* a base di zucchero, burro e latte

fuel /'fjuːəl/ **1** *n* carburante *m*; fig nutrimento *m*
2 *vt* fig alimentare

fuel consumption *n* consumo *m* di carburante

fuel efficient *adj* economico

fuel injection *n* iniezione *f*

fuel injection engine *n* motore *m* a iniezione

fuel oil *n* nafta *f*

fuel pump *n* pompa *f* della benzina

fuel tank *n* serbatoio *m*

fuggy /'fʌgɪ/ *adj* (Br: smoky) fumoso

fugitive /'fjuːdʒɪtɪv/ *n* fuggiasco, -a *mf*

fugue /fjuːg/ *n* Mus fuga *f*

fulcrum /'fʊlkrəm/ *n* fulcro *m*

fulfil /fʊl'fɪl/ *vt* (pt/pp -**filled**) soddisfare ⟨conditions, need⟩; adempiere a ⟨promise⟩; realizzare ⟨dream, desire⟩; ~ **oneself** realizzarsi

fulfilling /fʊl'fɪlɪŋ/ *adj* soddisfacente

fulfilment /fʊl'fɪlmənt/ *n* **sense of** ~ senso *m* di appagamento

full /fʊl/ **1** *adj* pieno (**of** di); (detailed) esauriente; ⟨bus, hotel⟩ completo; ⟨skirt⟩ ampio; **at** ~ **speed** a tutta velocità; **in** ~ **swing** in pieno fervore
2 *adv* in pieno; **you know** ~ **well that** sai benissimo che
3 *n* **in** ~ per intero

full-back *n* difensore *m*

full beam *n* Auto [fari *mpl*] abbaglianti *mpl*

full blast *adv* fam **the TV was on** ~ ~ c'era la TV a manetta

full-blown /-'blaʊn/ *adj* ⟨epidemic⟩ vero a e proprio; ⟨disease⟩ conclamato

full board *n* pensione *f* completa

full-bodied /-'bɒdɪd/ *adj* ⟨wine⟩ corposo

full-cream milk *n* latte *m* intero

full-frontal *adj* ⟨photograph⟩ di nudo frontale

full house *n* Theat tutto esaurito *m inv*; (in poker) full *m inv*

full-length *adj* ⟨dress⟩ lungo; ⟨curtain⟩ lungo fino a terra; ⟨portrait⟩ intero; ~ ~ film lungometraggio *m*

full moon *n* luna *f* piena

full name *n* nome *m* per esteso

full price *n* prezzo *m* intero

full-scale *adj* ⟨model⟩ in scala reale; ⟨alert⟩ di massima gravità

full stop *n* punto *m*

full-time *adj* & *adv* a tempo pieno

fully /'fʊlɪ/ *adv* completamente; (in detail) dettagliatamente; ~ **booked** ⟨hotel, restaurant⟩ tutto prenotato

fully fledged /-'fledʒd/ *adj* ⟨bird⟩ che ha messo tutte le penne; ⟨lawyer⟩ con tutte le qualifiche; ⟨member⟩ a tutti gli effetti

fulsome /'fʊlsəm/ *adj* esagerato

fumble /'fʌmbl/ *vi* ~ **in** rovistare in; ~ **with** armeggiare con; ~ **for one's keys** rovistare alla ricerca delle chiavi
■ **fumble about** *vi* (in dark) andare a tentoni; ~ **in** rovistare in ⟨bag⟩

fume /fjuːm/ *vi* (be angry) essere furioso

fumes /fjuːmz/ *npl* fumi *mpl*; (from car) gas *mpl* di scarico

fumigate /'fjuːmɪgeɪt/ *vt* suffumicare

fun /fʌn/ *n* divertimento *m*; **for** ~ per ridere; **make** ~ **of** prendere in giro; **have** ~ divertirsi

function /'fʌŋkʃn/ **1** *n* funzione *f*; (event) cerimonia *f*
2 *vi* funzionare; ~ **as** (serve as) funzionare da

functional /'fʌŋkʃ(ə)nəl/ *adj* funzionale

function key *n* Comput tasto *m* [di] funzioni

function room *n* sala *f* di ricevimento

fund /fʌnd/ **1** *n* fondo *m*; fig pozzo *m*; ~**s** *pl* fondi *mpl*
2 *vt* finanziare

fundamental /fʌndə'mentl/ *adj* fondamentale

fundamentalist /fʌndə'mentəlɪst/ *n* fondamentalista *mf*

funding /'fʌndɪŋ/ *n* (financial aid) finanziamento *m*; (of debt) consolidamento *m*

fund-raiser /-reɪzə(r)/ *n* (person) promotore, -trice *mf* di raccolte di fondi; (event) manifestazione *f* per la raccolta di fondi

fund-raising /-reɪzɪŋ/ *n* raccolta *f* di fondi

funeral /'fjuːnərəl/ *n* funerale *m*

funeral directors *n* impresa *f* di pompe funebri

funeral home, funeral parlour Am *n* camera *f* ardente

funeral march *n* marcia *f* funebre

funeral service *n* rito *m* funebre

funereal /fjuːˈnɪərɪəl/ *adj* lugubre

funfair /ˈfʌnfeə(r)/ *n* luna park *m inv*

fungal /ˈfʌŋɡəl/ *adj* ⟨infection⟩ micotico

fungus /ˈfʌŋɡəs/ *n* (pl **-gi** /ˈfʌŋɡaɪ/) fungo *m*

funicular /fjuːˈnɪkjʊlə(r)/ *n* funicolare *f*

fun loving /ˈfʌnlʌvɪŋ/ *adj* ⟨person⟩ amante del divertimento

funnel /ˈfʌnl/ *n* imbuto *m*; (on ship) ciminiera *f*

funnily /ˈfʌnɪlɪ/ *adv* comicamente; (oddly) stranamente; ∼ **enough** strano a dirsi

funny /ˈfʌnɪ/ *adj* (**-ier, -iest**) buffo; (odd) strano

funny bone *n* osso *m* del gomito

funny business *n* fam affare *m* losco

fur /fɜː(r)/ *n* pelo *m*; (for clothing) pelliccia *f*; (in kettle) deposito *m*

fur coat *n* pelliccia *f*

furious /ˈfjʊərɪəs/ *adj* furioso

furiously /ˈfjʊərɪəslɪ/ *adv* furiosamente

furl /fɜːl/ *vt* serrare ⟨sail⟩

furnace /ˈfɜːnɪs/ *n* fornace *f*

furnish /ˈfɜːnɪʃ/ *vt* ammobiliare ⟨flat⟩; fornire ⟨supplies⟩

furnished /ˈfɜːnɪʃt/ *adj* ∼ **room** stanza *f* ammobiliata

furnishings /ˈfɜːnɪʃɪŋz/ *npl* mobili *mpl*

furniture /ˈfɜːnɪtʃə(r)/ *n* mobili *mpl*

furniture remover /rɪmuːvə(r)/ *n* Br impresa *f* di traslochi

furniture van *n* furgone *m* per i traslochi

furore /fjʊˈrɔːrɪ/ *n* (outrage, criticism) scalpore *m*; (acclaim) entusiasmo *m*

furred /fɜːd/ *adj* ⟨tongue⟩ impastato

furrow /ˈfʌrəʊ/ *n* solco *m*

furry /ˈfɜːrɪ/ *adj* ⟨animal⟩ peloso; ⟨toy⟩ di peluche

further /ˈfɜːðə(r)/ **1** *adj* (additional) ulteriore; **at the** ∼ **end** all'altra estremità;

until ∼ **notice** fino a nuovo avviso **2** *adv* più lontano; ∼,... inoltre,... ∼ **off** più lontano **3** *vt* promuovere

further education *n* istruzione *f* parauniversitaria

furthermore /fɜːðəˈmɔː(r)/ *adv* per di più

furthest /ˈfɜːðɪst/ **1** *adj* più lontano **2** *adv* più lontano; **the** ∼ **advanced of the students** lo studente più avanti

furtive /ˈfɜːtɪv/ *adj* furtivo

furtively /ˈfɜːtɪvlɪ/ *adv* furtivamente

fury /ˈfjʊərɪ/ *n* furore *m*

fuse¹ /fjuːz/ *n* (of bomb) detonatore *m*; (cord) miccia *f*

fuse² **1** *n* Electr fusibile *m* **2** *vt* fondere; Electr far saltare **3** *vi* fondersi; Electr saltare; **the lights have**∼**d** sono saltate le luci

fuse box *n* scatola *f* dei fusibili

fuselage /ˈfjuːzəlɑːʒ/ *n* Aeron fusoliera *f*

fuse wire *n* [filo *m* di] fusibile *m*

fusillade /ˈfjuːzɪlˈɑːd/ *n* Mil scarica *f*; fig raffica *f*

fusion /ˈfjuːʒn/ *n* fusione *f*

fuss /fʌs/ **1** *n* storie *fpl*; **make a** ∼ fare storie; **make a** ∼ **of** colmare di attenzioni **2** *vi* fare storie

fussy /ˈfʌsɪ/ *adj* (**-ier, -iest**) ⟨person⟩ difficile da accontentare; ⟨clothes etc⟩ pieno di fronzoli

fusty /ˈfʌstɪ/ *adj* che odora di stantio; ⟨smell⟩ di stantio

futile /ˈfjuːtaɪl/ *adj* inutile

futility /fjʊˈtɪlətɪ/ *n* futilità *f*

future /ˈfjuːtʃə(r)/ *adj* & *n* futuro; **in** ∼ **in** futuro

future perfect *n* futuro *m* anteriore

futures *npl* Fin contratti *mpl* a termine

futuristic /fjuːtʃəˈrɪstɪk/ *adj* futuristico

fuze /fjuːz/ *n* & *v* Am = FUSE

fuzz /fʌz/ *n* **the** ∼ (sl: police) la pula

fuzzy /ˈfʌzɪ/ *adj* (**-ier, -iest**) ⟨hair⟩ crespo; ⟨photo⟩ sfuocato

FYI *abbr* (**for your information**) per vostra informazione

Gg

g¹, G /dʒiː/ *n* (letter) g, G *f inv*; Mus sol *m inv*

g² *abbr* (**gram(s)**) g

G8 *n abbr* (**group of 8**) G8 *mpl*

gab /ɡæb/ *n* fam **have the gift of the** ∼ avere la parlantina

gabardine /gæbə'diːn/ n gabardine f

gabble /'gæb(ə)l/ vi parlare troppo in fretta

gable /'geɪb(ə)l/ n frontone m

Gabon /gə'bɒn/ n Gabon m

gad /gæd/ vi (pt/pp **gadded**) ∼ about andarsene in giro

gadget /'gædʒɪt/ n aggeggio m

Gaelic /'geɪlɪk/ adj & n gaelico m

gaff /gæf/ n Br fam **blow the** ∼ spifferare un segreto; **blow the** ∼ **on something** svelare la verità su qualcosa

gaffe /gæf/ n gaffe f inv

gaffer /'gæfə(r)/ n (Br: foreman) caposquadra m; (Br: boss) capo m; Cinema, TV tecnico m delle luci

gag /gæg/ ① n bavaglio m; (joke) battuta f ② vt (pt/pp **gagged**) imbavagliare

gaga /'gɑːgɑː/ adj fam rimbambito

gage /geɪdʒ/ n & vt Am = GAUGE

gaiety /'geɪətɪ/ n allegria f

gaily /'geɪlɪ/ adv allegramente

gain /geɪn/ ① n guadagno m; (increase) aumento m
② vt acquisire; ∼ **weight** aumentare di peso; ∼ **access** accedere
③ vi ‹clock› andare avanti
■ **gain on** vt guadagnare terreno su ‹runner, car›

gainful /'geɪnfʊl/ adj ∼ **employment** lavoro m remunerativo

gainsay /geɪn'seɪ/ vt contraddire ‹person›; contestare ‹argument›

gait /geɪt/ n andatura f

gala /'gɑːlə/ ① n gala f; **swimming** ∼ manifestazione f di nuoto
② attrib di gala

galaxy /'gæləksɪ/ n galassia f

gale /geɪl/ n bufera f

gale warning n avviso m di imminente bufera

gall /gɔːl/ n (impudence) impudenza f

gallant /'gælənt/ adj coraggioso; (chivalrous) galante

gallantly /'gæləntlɪ/ adv galantemente

gallantry /'gæləntrɪ/ n coraggio m

gall bladder n cistifellea f

gallery /'gælərɪ/ n galleria f

galley /'gælɪ/ n (ship's kitchen) cambusa f

galley [proof] n bozza f in colonna

Gallic /'gælɪk/ adj francese

galling /'gɔːlɪŋ/ adj irritante

gallivant /'gælɪvænt/ vi fam andare in giro

gallon /'gælən/ n gallone m (Br = 4,5 l; Am = 3,7 l)

gallop /'gæləp/ ① n galoppo m
② vi galoppare

gallows /'gæləʊz/ n forca f

gallstone /'gɔːlstəʊn/ n calcolo m biliare

galore /gə'lɔː(r)/ adv a bizzeffe

galvanize /'gælvənaɪz/ vt Techn galvanizzare; fig stimolare (**into** a)

Gambia /'gæmbɪə/ n Gambia m

gambit /'gæmbɪt/ n prima mossa f

gamble /'gæmbl/ ① n (risk) azzardo m
② vi giocare; (on Stock Exchange) speculare; ∼ **on** (rely) contare su

gambler /'gæmblə(r)/ n giocatore, -trice mf [d'azzardo]

gambling /'gæmblɪŋ/ n gioco m [d'azzardo]

gambol /'gæmb(ə)l/ vi saltellare

game /geɪm/ ① n gioco m; (match) partita f; (animals, birds) selvaggina f; ∼**s** pl Sch ≈ ginnastica f
② adj (brave) coraggioso; **are you** ∼? ti va?; **be** ∼ **for** essere pronto per

game bird n uccello m da cacciagione

gamekeeper n guardacaccia m inv

game park n = game reserve

game plan n tattica f

game point n Tennis game point m inv

game reserve n (for hunting) riserva f di caccia; (for preservation) parco m naturale [faunistico]

games console n console f per videogiochi

game show n ≈ quiz m inv televisivo

gamesmanship /'geɪmzmənʃɪp/ n stratagemmi mpl

games room n sala f giochi

games software n computer game m inv

game warden n guardacaccia m inv

gaming /'geɪmɪŋ/ n **on-line** ∼ giochi online

gaming laws npl leggi fpl che regolano il gioco d'azzardo

gaming machine n slot machine f inv

gaming zone n sito m su cui giocare online

gammon /'gæmən/ n coscia f di maiale affumicata

gamut /'gæmət/ n fig gamma f

gander /'gændə(r)/ n oca f maschio; **take a** ∼ **at something** fam dare un'occhiata a qualcosa

gang /gæŋ/ n banda f; (of workmen) squadra f
■ **gang up** vi far comunella (**on** contro)

gangland /'gæŋlænd/ n malavita f

gangleader /'gæŋliːdə(r)/ n capobanda mf inv

gangling /'gæŋglɪŋ/ adj spilungone

gangplank /'gæŋplæŋk/ n passerella f

gang rape n stupro m collettivo

gangrene /'gæŋgriːn/ n cancrena f

gangrenous /'gæŋgrɪnəs/ adj cancrenoso

gangster /'gæŋstə(r)/ n gangster m inv

gangway /'gæŋweɪ/ n passaggio m; Naut, Aeron passerella f

gaol /dʒeɪl/ ① n carcere m ② vt incarcerare

gaoler /'dʒeɪlə(r)/ n carceriere m

gap /gæp/ n spazio m; (in ages, between teeth) scarto m; (in memory) vuoto m; (in story) punto m oscuro

gape /geɪp/ vi stare a bocca aperta; (be wide open) spalancarsi; ∼ at guardare a bocca aperta

gaping /'geɪpɪŋ/ adj aperto

gap year n anno m sabbatico tra la fine della scuola superiore e l'inizio dell'università

garage /'gærɑ:ʒ/ n garage m inv; (for repairs) meccanico m; (for petrol) stazione f di servizio

garage mechanic n meccanico m

garage sale n vendita f di articoli usati a casa propria

garb /gɑ:b/ n tenuta f

garbage /'gɑ:bɪdʒ/ n immondizia f; (nonsense) idiozie fpl

garbage can n Am bidone m dell'immondizia

garbage truck n Am camion m della nettezza urbana

garbled /'gɑ:bld/ adj confuso

garden /'gɑ:dn/ ① n giardino m; [public] ∼s pl giardini mpl pubblici ② vi fare giardinaggio

garden centre n Br vivaio m (che vende anche articoli da giardinaggio)

garden city n città f inv giardino

gardener /'gɑ:dnə(r)/ n giardiniere, -a mf

garden flat n appartamento m al pianterreno o seminterrato che dà sul giardino

gardening /'gɑ:dnɪŋ/ n giardinaggio m

garden shears npl cesoie fpl

garden suburb n periferia f verde

garden-variety adj Am ⟨writer, book⟩ insignificante

gargle /'gɑ:gl/ ① n gargarismo m ② vi fare gargarismi

gargoyle /'gɑ:gɔɪl/ n gargouille f inv

garish /'geərɪʃ/ adj sgargiante

garland /'gɑ:lənd/ n ghirlanda f

garlic /'gɑ:lɪk/ n aglio m

garlic bread n pane m condito con aglio

garlic press n spremiaglio m inv

garment /'gɑ:mənt/ n indumento m

garnet /'gɑ:nɪt/ n granato m

garnish /'gɑ:nɪʃ/ ① n guarnizione f ② vt guarnire

garret /'gærɪt/ n soffitta f

garrison /'gærɪsn/ n guarnigione f

garrotte /gə'rɒt/ ① n Br garrotta f ② vt (strangle) strangolare

garrulous /'gærʊləs/ adj chiacchierone

garter /'gɑ:tə(r)/ n giarrettiera f; (Am: for man's socks) reggicalze m inv da uomo

gas /gæs/ ① n gas m inv; (Am fam: petrol) benzina f ② vt (pt/pp **gassed**) asfissiare ③ vi fam blaterare

gas burner n becco m a gas

gas chamber n camera f a gas

gas cooker n cucina f a gas

gaseous /'gæsɪəs/ adj gassoso

gas fire n stufa f a gas

gas-fired /-faɪəd/ adj ⟨boiler, water heater⟩ a gas

gash /gæʃ/ ① n taglio m ② vt tagliare; ∼ one's arm farsi un taglio nel braccio

gasket /'gæskɪt/ n Techn guarnizione f

gas main n conduttura f del gas

gas mask n maschera f antigas

gas meter n contatore m del gas

gasoline /'gæsəli:n/ n Am benzina f

gas oven n forno m a gas

gasp /gɑ:sp/ vi avere il fiato mozzato

gas pedal n Am pedale m dell'acceleratore

gas ring n Br (fixed) bruciatore m; (portable) fornelletto m [portatile]

gas station n Am distributore m di benzina

gassy /'gæsɪ/ adj ⟨drink⟩ gassato

gastric /'gæstrɪk/ adj gastrico

gastric flu n influenza f gastro-intestinale

gastric ulcer n ulcera f gastrica

gastritis /gæ'straɪtɪs/ n gastrite f

gastroenteritis /gæstrəʊentə'raɪtɪs/ n gastroenterite f

gastronomy /gæ'strɒnəmɪ/ n gastronomia f

gate /geɪt/ n cancello m; (at airport) uscita f

gâteau /'gætəʊ/ n torta f

gatecrash ① vt entrare senza invito a ② vi entrare senza invito

gatecrasher n intruso, -a mf

gatehouse n (to castle) corpo m di guardia; (to park) casa f del custode

gatekeeper n custode mf

gatepost n palo m del cancello

gateway n ingresso m

gather /'gæðə(r)/ ① vt raccogliere; (conclude) dedurre; (in sewing) arricciare; ∼ speed acquistare velocità; ∼ together ⋯⟩

radunare ⟨*people, belongings*⟩; (obtain gradually) acquistare
2 *vi* ⟨*people*⟩ radunarsi; **a storm is** ∼**ing** si sta preparando un acquazzone

gathering /'gæðərɪŋ/ *n* family ∼ ritrovo *m* di famiglia

GATT /gæt/ *abbr* (**General Agreement on Tariffs and Trade**) GATT *m*

gauche /gəʊʃ/ *adj* ⟨*person, attitude*⟩ impacciato; ⟨*remark*⟩ inopportuno

gaudy /'gɔːdɪ/ *adj* (**-ier, -iest**) pacchiano

gauge /geɪdʒ/ **1** *n* calibro *m*; Rail scartamento *m*; (device) indicatore *m* **2** *vt* misurare; fig stimare

gaunt /gɔːnt/ *adj* (thin) smunto

gauntlet /'gɔːntlɪt/ *n* throw down the ∼ lanciare il guanto della sfida

gauze /gɔːz/ *n* garza *f*

gave /geɪv/ ▶ GIVE

gawky /'gɔːkɪ/ *adj* (**-ier, -iest**) sgraziato

gawp /gɔːp/ *vi* ∼ (**at**) fam guardare con aria da ebete

gay /geɪ/ *adj* gaio; (homosexual) omosessuale; ⟨*bar, club*⟩ gay

Gaza strip /'gɑːzə/ *n* la striscia *f* di Gaza

gaze /geɪz/ **1** *n* sguardo *m* fisso **2** *vi* guardare; ∼ **at** fissare; ∼ **into space** avere lo sguardo perso nel vuoto

gazelle /gə'zel/ *n* gazzella *f*

gazette /gə'zet/ *n* (official journal) bollettino *m* ufficiale; (newspaper title) gazzetta *f*

gazetteer /gæzɪ'tɪə(r)/ *n* (book) dizionario *m* geografico; (part of book) indice *m* dei nomi geografici

gazump /gə'zʌmp/ *vt* Comm sl **we've been** ∼**ed** il proprietario della casa ha optato per un'offerta migliore dopo avere accettato la nostra

GB *abbr* (**Great Britain**) GB

GBH *n abbr* (**grievous bodily harm**) lesioni *fpl* personali gravi

GCSE *n* Br *abbr* (**General Certificate of Secondary Education**) esami *mpl* conclusivi della scuola dell'obbligo

GDP *n abbr* (**gross domestic product**) PIL *m*

gear /gɪə(r)/ **1** *n* equipaggiamento *m*; Techn ingranaggio *m*; Auto marcia *f*; **in** ∼ con la marcia innestata; **change** ∼ cambiare marcia **2** *vt* finalizzare (**to** a) **3** *vi* ∼ **up for** prepararsi per ⟨*election*⟩; ∼ **up to do something** prepararsi per fare qualcosa

gearbox /'gɪəbɒks/ *n* Auto scatola *f* del cambio

gear lever, **gearstick**, Am **gear shift** *n* leva *f* del cambio

gear wheel *n* moltiplica *f*

geese /giːs/ ▶ GOOSE

geezer /'giːzə(r)/ *n* sl tipo *m*

gel /dʒel/ *n* gel *m inv*

gelatine /'dʒelətɪn/ *n* gelatina *f*

gelatinous /dʒɪ'lætɪnəs/ *adj* gelatinoso

gelding /'geldɪŋ/ *n* (horse) castrone *m*; (castration) castrazione *f*

gelignite /'dʒelɪgnaɪt/ *n* gelatina *f* esplosiva

gem /dʒem/ *n* gemma *f*

Gemini /'dʒemɪnaɪ/ *n* Astr Gemelli *mpl*

gen /dʒen/ *n* Br fam informazioni *fpl*; **what's the** ∼ **on this?** cosa c'è da sapere su questo?

gender /'dʒendə(r)/ *n* Gram genere *m*

gene /dʒiːn/ *n* gene *m*

genealogy /dʒiːnɪ'ælədʒɪ/ *n* genealogia *f*

gene library *n* genoteca *f*

gene pool *n* pool *m* genetico

general /'dʒenrəl/ **1** *adj* generale **2** *n* generale *m*; **in** ∼ in generale

general election *n* elezioni *fpl* politiche

generalization /dʒenrəlaɪ'zeɪʃn/ *n* generalizzazione *f*

generalize /'dʒenrəlaɪz/ *vi* generalizzare

general knowledge *n* cultura *f* generale

generally /'dʒenrəlɪ/ *adv* generalmente

general practitioner *n* medico *m* generico

general public *n* [grande] pubblico *m*

general-purpose *adj* multiuso *inv*

general strike *n* sciopero *m* generale

generate /'dʒenəreɪt/ *vt* generare

generation /dʒenə'reɪʃn/ *n* generazione *f*

generation gap *n* gap *m inv* generazionale

generator /'dʒenəreɪtə(r)/ *n* generatore *m*

generic /dʒɪ'nerɪk/ *adj* ∼ **term** termine *m* generico

generosity /dʒenə'rɒsətɪ/ *n* generosità *f*

generous /'dʒenərəs/ *adj* generoso

generously /'dʒenərəslɪ/ *adv* generosamente

genesis /'dʒenəsɪs/ *n* fig genesi *f inv*

gene therapy *n* terapia *f* genica

genetic /dʒɪ'netɪk/ *adj* genetico

genetically modified /dʒɪ'netɪklɪ 'mɒdɪfaɪd/ *adj* ⟨*crops*⟩ modificato geneticamente

genetic engineering *n* ingegneria *f* genetica

genetic fingerprinting /'fɪŋgəprɪntɪŋ/ *n* impronte *fpl* genetiche

geneticist /dʒɪ'netɪsɪst/ *n* genetista *mf*

genetics /dʒɪˈnetɪks/ n genetica f

genetic testing n test mpl genetici

Geneva /dʒɪˈniːvə/ n Ginevra f

genial /ˈdʒiːnɪəl/ adj gioviale

genially /ˈdʒiːnɪəlɪ/ adv con giovialità

genie /ˈdʒiːnɪ/ n genio m

genitals /ˈdʒenɪtlz/ npl genitali mpl

genitive /ˈdʒenɪtɪv/ adj & n ∼ **[case]** genitivo m

genius /ˈdʒiːnɪəs/ n (pl **-uses**) genio m

Genoa /ˈdʒenəʊə/ n Genova f

genocide /ˈdʒenəsaɪd/ n genocidio m

genome /ˈdʒiːnəʊm/ n genoma m

genre /ˈʒɑ̃rə/ n genere m [letterario]

gent /dʒent/ n fam signore m; **the** ∼**s** sg il bagno per uomini

genteel /dʒenˈtiːl/ adj raffinato

gentle /ˈdʒentl/ adj delicato; ⟨breeze, tap, slope⟩ leggero

gentleman /ˈdʒentlmən/ n signore m; (well-mannered) gentiluomo m

gentleness /ˈdʒentlnɪs/ n delicatezza f

gently /ˈdʒentlɪ/ adv delicatamente

gentry /ˈdʒentrɪ/ n alta borghesia f

genuine /ˈdʒenjʊɪn/ adj genuino

genuinely /ˈdʒenjʊɪnlɪ/ adv ⟨sorry⟩ sinceramente

genus /ˈdʒiːnəs/ n Biol genere m

geographer /dʒɪˈɒɡrəfə(r)/ n geografo m

geographical /dʒɪəˈɡræfɪkl/ adj geografico

geographically /dʒɪəˈɡræfɪklɪ/ adv geograficamente

geography /dʒɪˈɒɡrəfɪ/ n geografia f

geological /dʒɪəˈlɒdʒɪkl/ adj geologico

geologist /dʒɪˈɒlədʒɪst/ n geologo, -a mf

geology /dʒɪˈɒlədʒɪ/ n geologia f

geometric[al] /dʒɪəˈmetrɪk[l]/ adj geometrico

geometry /dʒɪˈɒmɪtrɪ/ n geometria f

geophysics /dʒɪəʊˈfɪzɪks/ n geofisica f

geopolitical /dʒiːəʊpəˈlɪtɪkl/ adj geopolitico

Georgia /ˈdʒɔːdʒə/ n Georgia f

Georgian /ˈdʒɔːdʒən/ n & adj georgiano, -a mf; (language) georgiano m

geranium /dʒəˈreɪnɪəm/ n geranio m

gerbil /ˈdʒɜːbəl/ n gerbillo m

geriatric /dʒerɪˈætrɪk/ adj geriatrico

geriatrics /dʒerɪˈætrɪks/ n geriatria f

geriatric ward n reparto m geriatria

germ /dʒɜːm/ n germe m; ∼**s** pl microbi mpl

German /ˈdʒɜːmən/ n & adj tedesco, -a mf; (language) tedesco m

germane /dʒəˈmeɪn/ adj ⟨point, remark⟩ pertinente

Germanic /dʒəˈmænɪk/ adj germanico f

German measles n rosolia f

German shepherd n pastore m tedesco

Germany /ˈdʒɜːmənɪ/ n Germania f

germinate /ˈdʒɜːmɪneɪt/ vi germogliare

germ warfare n guerra f batteriologica

gerrymandering /ˈdʒerɪmænd(ə)rɪŋ/ n manipolazione f dei confini di una circoscrizione elettorale

gerund /ˈdʒerənd/ n gerundio m

gestate /dʒeˈsteɪt/ vi Biol essere incinta; fig maturare

gestation /dʒeˈsteɪʃən/ n gestazione f

gesticulate /dʒeˈstɪkjʊleɪt/ vi gesticolare

gesture /ˈdʒestʃə(r)/ n gesto m

get /ɡet/ **①** vt (pt/pp **got** pp Am also **gotten**, pres p **getting**) (receive) ricevere; (obtain) ottenere; trovare ⟨job⟩; (buy, catch, fetch) prendere; (transport, deliver to airport etc) portare; (reach on telephone) trovare; (fam: understand) comprendere; preparare ⟨meal⟩; ∼ **somebody to do something** far fare qualcosa a qualcuno

② vi (become) ∼ **tired/bored/angry** stancarsi/annoiarsi/arrabbiarsi; **I'm** ∼**ting hungry** mi sta venendo fame; ∼ **real!** fatti furbo!; ∼ **dressed/married** vestirsi/ sposarsi; ∼ **something ready** preparare qualcosa; ∼ **nowhere** non concludere nulla; **this is** ∼**ting us nowhere** questo non ci è di nessun aiuto; ∼ **to** (reach) arrivare a

■ **get about** vi ⟨person⟩ muoversi; ⟨rumour⟩ circolare

■ **get across** vt far capire ⟨message, meaning⟩; ∼ **something across to somebody** far capire qualcosa a qualcuno

■ **get ahead** vi (progress) fare progressi

■ **get along** vi = **get on**

■ **get along with** vt andare d'accordo con ⟨somebody⟩

■ **get around** vi = **get about**

■ **get at** vi (criticize) criticare; **I see what you're** ∼**ting at** ho capito cosa vuoi dire; **what are you** ∼**ting at?** dove vuoi andare a parare?

■ **get away** vi (leave) andarsene; (escape) scappare

■ **get away with** vt restare impunito per

■ **get behind with** vt rimanere indietro con

■ **get by** vi passare; (manage) cavarsela

■ **get down** **①** vi scendere; ∼ **down to work** mettersi al lavoro

② vt (depress) buttare giù

■ **get in** **①** vi entrare

② vt mettere dentro ⟨washing⟩; far venire ⟨plumber⟩

■ **get into** vt penetrare in ⟨building⟩; mettersi in ⟨trouble⟩; (squeeze into) entrare in ⟨dress⟩

■ **get off** ⬛1 *vi* scendere; (from work) andarsene; Jur essere assolto; ~ **off the bus/one's bike** scendere dal pullman/dalla bici

⬛2 *vt* (remove) togliere

■ **get on** *vi* salire; (be on good terms) andare d'accordo; (make progress) andare avanti; (in life) riuscire; ~ **on the bus/one's bike** salire sul pullman/sulla bici; **how are you ~ting on?** come va?

■ **get on with** *vt* andare d'accordo con ⟨*person*⟩; andare avanti in ⟨*work*⟩

■ **get out** ⬛1 *vi* uscire; (of car) scendere; ~ **out!** fuori!

⬛2 *vt* togliere ⟨*cork, stain*⟩

■ **get out of** *vt* (avoid doing) evitare

■ **get over** ⬛1 *vi* andare al di là

⬛2 *vt* fig riprendersi da ⟨*illness*⟩

■ **get round** ⬛1 *vt* aggirare ⟨*rule*⟩; rigirare ⟨*person*⟩

⬛2 *vi* **I never ~ round to it** non mi sono mai deciso a farlo

■ **get through** *vi* (on telephone) prendere la linea

■ **get together** ⬛1 *vi* (meet) incontrarsi

⬛2 *vt* mettere insieme ⟨*people, money, report*⟩

■ **get up** ⬛1 *vi* alzarsi; (climb) salire

⬛2 *vt* salire su; ~ **up a hill** salire su una collina

■ **get up to** *vt* combinare ⟨*mischief*⟩

getaway *n* fuga *f*

get-together *n* incontro *m* fra amici

get-up *n* tenuta *f*

get-up-and-go *n* dinamismo *m*

geyser /'giːzə(r)/ *n* scaldabagno *m*; Geol geyser *m inv*

G-force *n* forza *f* di gravità

Ghana /'gɑːnə/ *n* Ghana *m*

ghastly /'gɑːstlɪ/ *adj* (**-ier, -iest**) terribile; **feel ~** sentirsi da cani

gherkin /'gɜːkɪn/ *n* cetriolino *m*

ghetto /'getəʊ/ *n* ghetto *m*

ghetto blaster /blɑːstə(r)/ *n* fam radio-registratore *m* stereo portatile

ghost /gəʊst/ *n* fantasma *m*

ghostly /'gəʊstlɪ/ *adj* spettrale

ghost town *n* città *f inv* fantasma

ghost writer *n* negro *m*

ghoulish /'guːlɪʃ/ *adj* macabro

giant /'dʒaɪənt/ ⬛1 *n* gigante *m*

⬛2 *adj* gigante

gibberish /'dʒɪbərɪʃ/ *n* stupidaggini *fpl*

gibe /dʒaɪb/ ⬛1 *n* malignità *f inv*

⬛2 *vi* beffarsi (**at** di)

giblets /'dʒɪblɪts/ *npl* frattaglie *fpl*

giddiness /'gɪdɪnɪs/ *n* vertigini *fpl*

giddy /'gɪdɪ/ *adj* (**-ier, -iest**) vertiginoso; **feel ~** avere le vertigini

giddy spell *n* giramento *m* di testa

gift /gɪft/ *n* dono *m*; (made to charity) donazione *f*

gifted /'gɪftɪd/ *adj* dotato

gift shop *n* negozio *m* di souvenir

gift token *n* Br buono *m* acquisto

gift voucher *n* Br buono *m* acquisto

gift-wrap *vt* impacchettare in carta da regalo

gig /gɪg/ *n* Mus fam concerto *m*

gigantic /dʒaɪˈgæntɪk/ *adj* gigantesco

giggle /'gɪg(ə)l/ ⬛1 *n* risatina *f*

⬛2 *vi* ridacchiare

giggly /'gɪglɪ/ *adj* ⟨*person*⟩ che ha la ridarella

gild /gɪld/ *vt* dorare

gilding /'gɪldɪŋ/ *n* doratura *f*

gill /dʒɪl/ *n* (measure) quarto *m* di pinta

gills /gɪlz/ *npl* branchia *fsg*

gilt /gɪlt/ ⬛1 *adj* dorato

⬛2 *n* doratura *f*

gilt-edged stock /-edʒd/ *n* Fin investimento *m* sicuro

gimlet /'gɪmlɪt/ *n* succhiello *m*

gimmick /'gɪmɪk/ *n* trovata *f*

gimmicky /'gɪmɪkɪ/ *adj* ⟨*production*⟩ pieno di trovate a effetto

gin /dʒɪn/ *n* gin *m inv*

ginger /'dʒɪndʒə(r)/ ⬛1 *adj* rosso fuoco *inv*; ⟨*cat*⟩ rosso

⬛2 *n* zenzero *m*

ginger ale *n* bibita *f* gassata allo zenzero

ginger beer *n* bibita *f* allo zenzero

gingerbread *n* panpepato *m*

ginger-haired /-'heəd/ *adj* con i capelli rossi

gingerly /'dʒɪndʒəlɪ/ *adv* con precauzione

ginger nut, **ginger snap** *n* biscotto *m* allo zenzero

gingham /'gɪŋəm/ *n* tessuto *m* vichy

gin rummy *n* variante *f* del gioco del ramino

gipsy /'dʒɪpsɪ/ *n* = GYPSY

giraffe /dʒɪˈrɑːf/ *n* giraffa *f*

girder /'gɜːdə(r)/ *n* Techn trave *f*

girdle /'gɜːdl/ *n* cintura *f*; (corset) busto *m*

girl /gɜːl/ *n* ragazza *f*; (female child) femmina *f*

girl Friday *n* segretaria *f* tuttofare *inv*

girlfriend *n* amica *f*; (of boy) ragazza *f*

girl guide *n* Br giovane esploratrice *f*

girlish /'gɜːlɪʃ/ *adj* da ragazza

giro /'dʒaɪərəʊ/ *n* bancogiro *m*; (cheque) sussidio *m* di disoccupazione

girth /gɜːθ/ *n* circonferenza *f*

gist /dʒɪst/ *n* **the ~** la sostanza

give /gɪv/ ⬛1 *n* elasticità *f*

⬛2 *vt* (pt **gave**, pp **given**) dare; (as present) regalare (**to** a); fare ⟨*lecture,* *present, shriek*⟩; donare ⟨*blood*⟩; ~ **birth** partorire

3 *vi* (to charity) fare delle donazioni; (yield) cedere

■ **give away** *vt* dar via; (betray) tradire; (distribute) assegnare; ~ **away the bride** portare la sposa all'altare

■ **give back** *vt* restituire

■ **give in** *vt* consegnare

2 *vi* (yield) arrendersi

■ **give off** *vt* emanare

■ **give out** **1** *vi* ⟨*supplies, patience*⟩ esaurirsi; ⟨*engine, heart*⟩ fermarsi

2 *vt* (distribute) distribuire; diffondere ⟨*heat*⟩

■ **give over** *vi* ~ **over!** piantala!

■ **give up** **1** *vt* rinunciare a; ~ **oneself up** arrendersi

2 *vi* rinunciare

■ **give way** *vi* cedere; Auto dare la precedenza; (collapse) crollare

give-and-take *n* concessioni *fpl* reciproche

giveaway *n* **to be a dead** ~ essere un indizio ovvio

given /'gɪvn/ ▸ GIVE

given name *n* nome *m* di battesimo

GLA *n* Br *abbr* (**Greater London Authority**) organismo *m* di governo di Londra

glacier /'glæsɪə(r)/ *n* ghiacciaio *m*

glad /glæd/ *adj* contento (**of** di)

gladden /'glædn/ *vt* rallegrare

glade /gleɪd/ *n* radura *f*

gladiator /'glædɪeɪtə(r)/ *n* gladiatore *m*

gladiolus /glædɪ'əʊləs/ *n* gladiolo *m*

gladly /'glædlɪ/ *adv* volentieri

glamorize /'glæməraɪz/ *vt* rendere affascinante

glamorous /'glæmərəs/ *adj* affascinante

glamour /'glæmə(r)/ *n* fascino *m*

glance /glɑːns/ **1** *n* sguardo *m*

2 *vi* ~ **at** dare un'occhiata a

■ **glance off** *vt* ⟨*bullet, stone*⟩ rimbalzare contro

■ **glance up** *vi* alzare gli occhi

gland /glænd/ *n* ghiandola *f*

glandular /'glændjʊlə(r)/ *adj* ghiandolare

glandular fever *n* mononucleosi *f*

glare /gleə(r)/ **1** *n* bagliore *m*; (look) occhiataccia *f*

2 *vi* ~ **at** dare un'occhiataccia a

glaring /'gleərɪŋ/ *adj* sfolgorante; ⟨*mistake*⟩ madornale

glass /glɑːs/ *n* vetro *m*; (for drinking) bicchiere *m*

glass ceiling *n* barriera *f* invisibile che impedisce alle donne di avanzare nella carriera

glasses /'glɑːsɪz/ *npl* (spectacles) occhiali *mpl*

glasshouse /'glɑːshaʊs/ *n* serra *f*

glassy /'glɑːsɪ/ *adj* vitreo

glassy-eyed /-'aɪd/ *adj* (from drink, illness) che ha gli occhi vitrei

glaucoma /glɔː'kəʊmə/ *n* glaucoma *m*

glaze /gleɪz/ **1** *n* smalto *m*

2 *vt* mettere i vetri a ⟨*door, window*⟩; smaltare ⟨*pottery*⟩; Culin spennellare

glazed /gleɪzd/ *adj* ⟨*eyes*⟩ vitreo

glazier /'gleɪzɪə(r)/ *n* vetraio *m*

gleam /gliːm/ **1** *n* luccichio *m*

2 *vi* luccicare

gleaming /'gliːmɪŋ/ *adj* (clean) splendente; ~ **white teeth** denti bianchi splendenti

glean /gliːn/ *vt* racimolare ⟨*information*⟩

glee /gliː/ *n* gioia *f*

gleeful /'gliːfʊl/ *adj* gioioso

gleefully /'gliːfʊlɪ/ *adv* gioiosamente

glen /glen/ *n* vallone *m*

glib /glɪb/ *adj* pej insincero

glibly /'glɪblɪ/ *adv* pej senza sincerità

glide /glaɪd/ *vi* scorrere; (through the air) planare

glider /'glaɪdə(r)/ *n* aliante *m*

gliding /'glaɪdɪŋ/ *n* volo *m* a vela

glimmer /'glɪmə(r)/ **1** *n* barlume *m*

2 *vi* emettere un barlume

glimpse /glɪmps/ **1** *n* occhiata *f*; **catch a** ~ **of** intravedere

2 *vt* intravedere

glint /glɪnt/ **1** *n* luccichio *m*

2 *vi* luccicare

glisten /'glɪsn/ *vi* luccicare

glitch /glɪtʃ/ *n* Comput problema *m* tecnico

glitter /'glɪtə(r)/ *vi* brillare

gloat /gləʊt/ *vi* gongolare (**over** su)

global /'gləʊbl/ *adj* mondiale

globalization *n* globalizzazione *f*

global warming *n* riscaldamento *m* dell'atmosfera terrestre

globe /gləʊb/ *n* globo *m*; (as a map) mappamondo *m*

globe-trotting /-trɒtɪŋ/ **1** *n* viaggi *mpl* intorno al mondo

2 *adj* ⟨*life*⟩ da giramondo; ⟨*person*⟩ giramondo

globule /'glɒbjuːl/ *n* globulo *m*

gloom /gluːm/ *n* oscurità *f*; (sadness) tristezza *f*

gloomily /'gluːmɪlɪ/ *adv* (sadly) con aria cupa

gloomy /'gluːmɪ/ *adj* (**-ier**, **-iest**) cupo

glorify /'glɔːrɪfaɪ/ *vt* (pt/pp **-ied**) glorificare; **a glorified waitress** niente più che una cameriera

glorious /'glɔːrɪəs/ *adj* splendido; ⟨*deed, hero*⟩ glorioso

glory /'glɔːrɪ/ ① n gloria f; (splendour) splendore m; (cause for pride) vanto m
② vi ~ in vantarsi di

glory-hole n fam ripostiglio m

gloss /glɒs/ n lucentezza f
■ **gloss over** vt sorvolare su

glossary /'glɒsərɪ/ n glossario m

gloss paint n vernice f lucida

glossy /'glɒsɪ/ adj (-ier, -iest) lucido; ⟨paper⟩ patinato

glossy magazine n rivista f patinata

glottal stop /'glɒt(ə)l/ n occlusiva f glottale

glove /glʌv/ n guanto m

glove compartment n Auto cruscotto m

glove puppet n burattino m

glow /gləʊ/ ① n splendore m; (in cheeks) rossore m; (of candle) luce f soffusa
② vi risplendere; ⟨candle⟩ brillare; ⟨person⟩ avvampare

glower /'glaʊə(r)/ vi ~ (at) guardare in cagnesco

glowing /'gləʊɪŋ/ adj ardente; ⟨account⟩ entusiastico

glow-worm n lucciola f

glucose /'gluːkəʊs/ n glucosio m

glue /gluː/ ① n colla f
② vt incollare

glue sniffer n persona f che sniffa colla

glue-sniffing /-snɪfɪŋ/ n sniffare m la colla

glum /glʌm/ adj (**glummer**, **glummest**) tetro

glumly /'glʌmlɪ/ adv con aria tetra

glut /glʌt/ n eccesso m

glutinous /'gluːtɪnəs/ adj colloso

glutton /'glʌtən/ n ghiottone, -a mf

gluttonous /'glʌtənəs/ adj ghiotto

gluttony /'glʌtənɪ/ n ghiottoneria f

glycerine /'glɪsəriːn/ n glicerina f

GM abbr (**genetically modified**) MG

gm abbr (**gram**) g

GMO abbr (**genetically modified organism**) OGM m inv

GMT abbr (**Greenwich mean time**) GMT

gnarled /nɑːld/ adj nodoso

gnash /næʃ/ vt ~ one's teeth digrignare i denti

gnat /næt/ n moscerino m

gnaw /nɔː/ vt rosicchiare

gnome /nəʊm/ n gnomo m

GNP abbr (**gross national product**) PNL m

GNVQ n abbr Br (**General National Vocational Qualification**) diploma m di istituto tecnico

go /gəʊ/ ① n (pl **goes**) energia f; (attempt) tentativo m; on the **go** in movimento; at one **go** in una sola volta; it's your **go** tocca a te; make a **go** of it riuscire
② vi (pt **went**, pp **gone**) andare; (leave) andar via; (vanish) sparire; (become) diventare; (be sold) vendersi; **go** and see andare a vedere; **go** swimming/shopping andare a nuotare/fare spese; where's the time gone? come ha fatto il tempo a volare così?; it's all gone è finito; be going to do stare per fare; I'm not going to non ne ho nessuna intenzione; to **go** Am ⟨hamburgers etc⟩ da asporto; a coffee to **go** un caffè da portar via
■ **go about** ① vi andare in giro
② vt affrontare ⟨task⟩
■ **go after** vt (chase, pursue) correr dietro a
■ **go ahead** vi (event) aver luogo; **go** ahead with mandare avanti ⟨plans, wedding⟩
■ **go along** vi make something up as you **go** along inventare qualcosa mentre si va avanti
■ **go along with** vt concordare con ⟨person, view, plan⟩
■ **go around** vi ⟨rumour⟩ girare; **go** around with (person) andare in giro con
■ **go around together** vi ⟨people⟩ andare in giro insieme
■ **go away** vi andarsene
■ **go back** vi ritornare
■ **go back on** vt rimangiarsi ⟨promise⟩; tornare su ⟨decision⟩
■ **go by** vi passare
■ **go down** vi scendere; ⟨sun⟩ tramontare; ⟨ship⟩ affondare; ⟨swelling⟩ diminuire
■ **go for** vt andare a prendere; andare a cercare ⟨doctor⟩; (choose) optare per; (fam: attack) aggredire; he's not the kind I **go** for non è il genere che mi attira
■ **go in** vi entrare
■ **go in for** vt partecipare a ⟨competition⟩; darsi a ⟨tennis⟩
■ **go into** vt entrare in ⟨building⟩; (discuss) discutere
■ **go off** vi andarsene; ⟨alarm⟩ scattare; ⟨gun, bomb⟩ esplodere; ⟨food, milk⟩ andare a male; **go** off well riuscire
■ **go on** vi andare avanti; what's going on? cosa succede?
■ **go on at** vt fam scocciare
■ **go on with** vt (continue) andare avanti con
■ **go out** vi uscire; ⟨light, fire⟩ spegnersi
■ **go out with** vt uscire con somebody
■ **go over** ① vi andare
② vt (check) controllare
■ **go round** vi andare in giro; (visit) andare; (turn) girare; is there enough to **go** round? ce n'è abbastanza per tutti?
■ **go through** ① vi ⟨bill, proposal⟩ passare

2 *vt* (suffer) subire; (check) controllare; (read) leggere
- ■ **go through with** *vt* portare a termine ⟨*plan*⟩
- ■ **go under** *vi* passare sotto; ⟨*ship, swimmer*⟩ andare sott'acqua; (fail) fallire
- ■ **go up** *vi* salire; ⟨*Theat: curtain*⟩ aprirsi
- ■ **go with** *vt* accompagnare
- ■ **go without** **1** *vt* fare a meno di ⟨*supper; sleep*⟩
  2 *vi* fare senza

goad /gəʊd/ *vt* spingere (**into** a); (taunt) spronare

go-ahead **1** *adj* ⟨*person, company*⟩ intraprendente
2 *n* okay *m*

goal /gəʊl/ *n* porta *f*; (point scored) gol *m inv*; (in life) obiettivo *m*; **score a** ~ segnare

goalie /'gəʊlɪ/ fam, **goalkeeper** /'gəʊlkiːpə(r)/ *n* portiere *m*

goalpost /'gəʊlpəʊst/ *n* palo *m*

goat /gəʊt/ *n* capra *f*

goatee /gəʊ'tiː/ *n* pizzetto *m*

gobble /'gɒbl/ *vi* ⟨*turkey*⟩ fare glu glu
- ■ **gobble up** *vt* tranguiare

gobbledygook /'gɒb(ə)ldɪguːk/ *n* ostrogoto *m*

go-between *n* intermediario, -a *mf*

goblet /'gɒblɪt/ *n* calice *m*

goblin /'gɒblɪn/ *n* folletto *m*

gobsmacked /'gɒbsmækt/ *adj* Br fam **I was** ~ sono rimasto a bocca aperta

God, **god** /gɒd/ *n* Dio *m*, dio *m*

godchild *n* figlioccio, -a *mf*

goddamn *adj* maledetto

god-daughter *n* figlioccia *f*

goddess /'gɒdes/ *n* dea *f*

godfather *n* padrino *m*

god-fearing /-fɪərɪŋ/ *adj* timorato di Dio

god-forsaken /-fəseɪkən/ *adj* dimenticato da Dio

godless /'gɒdlɪs/ *adj* empio

godlike /'gɒdlaɪk/ *adj* divino

godly /'gɒdlɪ/ *adj* (**-ier, -iest**) pio

godmother *n* madrina *f*

godparents *npl* padrino *m* e madrina *f*

godsend *n* manna *f*

godson *n* figlioccio *m*

goer /'gəʊə(r)/ *n* Br **be a** ~ ⟨*car*⟩ essere una bomba

go-getter /'gəʊgetə(r)/ *n* persona *f* intraprendente

go-getting /-getɪŋ/ *adj* intraprendente

goggle /'gɒgl/ *vi* fam ~ **at** fissare con gli occhi sgranati

goggles *npl* occhiali *mpl*; (of swimmer) occhialini *mpl* [da piscina]: (of worker) occhiali *mpl* protettivi

going /'gəʊɪŋ/ **1** *adj* ⟨*price, rate*⟩ corrente; ~ **concern** azienda *f* florida
2 *n* it's hard ~ è una faticaccia; **while the** ~ **is good** finché si può

going-over *n* (cleaning) pulizia *f* da cima a fondo; (examination) revisione *f*; **the doctor gave me a thorough** ~ il dottore mi ha fatto una visita completa; **give somebody a** ~ (beat up) dare una manica di botte a qualcuno

goings-on *npl* avvenimenti *mpl*

go-kart /-kɑːt/ *n* go-kart *m inv*

go-karting /-kɑːtɪŋ/ *n* kartismo *m*; **go** ~ fare del kartismo

gold /gəʊld/ **1** *n* oro *m*
2 *adj* d'oro

gold-digger *n* fig cacciatore, -trice *mf* di dote

gold dust *n* polvere *f* d'oro; fig cosa *f* rara

golden /'gəʊldn/ *adj* dorato

golden handshake *n* Br buonuscita *f* (al termine di un rapporto di lavoro)

golden rule *n* regola *f* fondamentale

golden wedding *n* nozze *fpl* d'oro

goldfish *n inv* pesce *m* rosso

gold medal *n* medaglia *f* d'oro

gold medallist *n* (vincitore, -trice *mf* della) medaglia *f* d'oro

gold mine *n* miniera *f* d'oro

gold-plated /'pleɪtɪd/ *adj* placcato d'oro

gold rush *n* corsa *f* all'oro

goldsmith *n* orefice *m*

golf /gɒlf/ *n* golf *m*

golf club *n* circolo *m* di golf; (implement) mazza *f* da golf

golf course *n* campo *m* di golf

golfer /'gɒlfə(r)/ *n* giocatore, -trice *mf* di golf

golliwog /'gɒlɪwɒg/ *n* bambolotto *m* negro

gondola /'gɒndələ/ *n* gondola *f*

gondolier /gɒndə'lɪə(r)/ *n* gondoliere *m*

gone /gɒn/ ▶GO

goner /'gɒnə(r)/ *n* fam **be a** ~ essere spacciato

gong /gɒŋ/ *n* gong *m inv*

gonorrh[o]ea /gɒnə'rɪə/ *n* gonorrea *f*

good /gʊd/ **1** *adj* (**better, best**) buono; ⟨*child, footballer, singer*⟩ bravo; ⟨*holiday, film*⟩ bello; ~ **at** bravo in; **a** ~ **deal of anger** molta rabbia; **as** ~ **as** (almost) quasi; ~ **morning**, ~ **afternoon** buon giorno; ~ **evening** buona sera; ~ **night** buona notte; **have a** ~ **time** divertirsi
2 *n* bene *m*; **for** ~ per sempre; **do** ~ far del bene; **do somebody** ~ far bene a qualcuno; **it's no** ~ è inutile; **be up to no** ~ combinare qualcosa

goodbye /gʊd'baɪ/ *int* arrivederci

good-for-nothing ① n buono, -a mf a nulla
② adj her ∼ son quel buono a nulla di suo figlio
Good Friday n Venerdì m Santo
good-humoured /-'hjuːməd/ adj amichevole; ⟨remark, smile⟩ bonario
goodies /'gʊdɪz/ npl (fam: to eat) bontà fpl
good-looking /-'lʊkɪŋ/ adj bello
good-natured /-'neɪtʃəd/ adj be ∼ avere un buon carattere
goodness /'gʊdnɪs/ n bontà f; my ∼! santo cielo!; thank ∼! grazie al cielo!
goods /gʊdz/ npl prodotti mpl
goods train n treno m merci
good-time girl n (fun-loving) ragazza f allegra; (euph: prostitute) donnina f allegra
goodwill /gʊd'wɪl/ n buona f volontà; Comm avviamento m
goody /'gʊdɪ/ n (fam: person) buono m
goody bag n omaggi mpl consegnati ai visitatori di una fiera dalle aziende espositrici
goody-goody n santarellino, -a mf
gooey /'guːɪ/ adj fam appiccicaticcio; fig sdolcinato
goof /guːf/ vi fam cannare
goofy /'guːfɪ/ adj fam sciocco
google /'guːgl/ vi usare Google
goon /guːn/ n (clown) svitato m; (thug) picchiatore m
goose /guːs/ n (pl **geese**) oca f
gooseberry /'gʊzbərɪ/ n uva f spina
goose-flesh n, **goose-pimples** npl pelle fsg d'oca
goose-step n passo m dell'oca
gore¹ /gɔː(r)/ n sangue m
gore² vt incornare
gorge /gɔːdʒ/ ① n Geog gola f
② vt ∼ oneself ingozzarsi
gorgeous /'gɔːdʒəs/ adj stupendo
gorilla /gə'rɪlə/ n gorilla m inv
gormless /'gɔːmlɪs/ adj fam stupido
gorse /gɔːs/ n ginestrone m
gory /'gɔːrɪ/ adj (-ier, -iest) cruento
gosh /gɒʃ/ int fam caspita
gosling /'gɒzlɪŋ/ n ochetta f
go-slow n forma f di protesta che consiste in un rallentamento del ritmo di lavoro
gospel /'gɒspl/ n vangelo m
gospel music n musica f gospel
gospel truth n sacrosanta verità f
gossamer /'gɒsəmə(r)/ n (fabric) mussola f; (cobweb) fili mpl di ragnatela
gossip /'gɒsɪp/ ① n pettegolezzi mpl; (person) pettegolo, -a mf
② vi pettegolare
gossip column n cronaca f mondana

gossipy /'gɒsɪpɪ/ adj pettegolo
got /gɒt/ ▶ GET; have ∼ avere; have ∼ to do something dover fare qualcosa
Gothic /'gɒθɪk/ adj gotico
gotten /'gɒtn/ Am ▶ GET
gouge /gaʊdʒ/ vt ∼ out cavare
goulash /'guːlæʃ/ n gulash m inv
gourd /gʊəd/ n (fruit) zucca f
gourmet /'gʊəmeɪ/ n buongustaio, -a mf
gout /gaʊt/ n gotta f
govern /'gʌv(ə)n/ vt/i governare; (determine) determinare
governess /'gʌvənɪs/ n istitutrice f
governing adj ⟨party⟩ al potere; ⟨class⟩ dirigente; the ∼ body (school governors) il consiglio d'istituto
government /'gʌvnmənt/ n governo m
governmental /gʌvn'mentl/ adj governativo
government health warning n avviso m a cura del ministero della salute
government stocks npl titoli mpl di stato
governor /'gʌvənə(r)/ n governatore m; (of school) amministratore, -trice mf; (of prison) direttore, -trice mf; (fam: boss) capo m
gown /gaʊn/ n vestito m; Univ, Jur toga f
GP abbr **general practitioner**
GPA n abbr Am (**grade point average**) media f scolastica
grab /græb/ vt (pt/pp **grabbed**) ∼ [hold of] afferrare
Grace n his/your ∼ (duke) il signor duca; (archbishop) Sua Eccellenza; her/your ∼ (duchess) la signora duchessa
grace /greɪs/ n grazia f; (before meal) benedicite m inv; with good ∼ volentieri; say ∼ dire il benedicite; three days' ∼ tre giorni di proroga
graceful /'greɪsfʊl/ adj aggraziato
gracefully /'greɪsfʊlɪ/ adv con grazia
gracious /'greɪʃəs/ adj cortese; (elegant) lussuoso
gradation /grə'deɪʃn/ n gradazione f
grade /greɪd/ ① n livello m; Comm qualità f; Sch voto m; (Am Sch: class) classe f; Am = GRADIENT
② vt Comm classificare; Sch dare il voto a
grade crossing n Am passaggio m a livello
grade school n Am scuola f elementare
gradient /'greɪdɪənt/ n pendenza f
gradual /'grædʒʊəl/ adj graduale
gradually /'grædʒʊəlɪ/ adv gradualmente
graduate¹ /'grædʒʊət/ n laureato, -a mf
graduate² /'grædʒʊeɪt/ vi Univ laurearsi

graduated ···❖ gratification ···

graduated /'grædʒʊeɪtɪd/ *adj* ⟨*container*⟩ graduato

graduate training scheme *n* formazione *f* professionale postlaurea

graduation /grædʒʊ'eɪʃn/ *n* laurea *f*; (calibration) graduazione *f*

graduation ceremony *n* cerimonia *f* di consegna dei diplomi di laurea

graffiti /grə'fiːtɪ/ *npl* graffiti *mpl*

graffiti artist *n* pittore, -trice *mf* di graffiti

graft /grɑːft/ **1** *n* Bot, Med innesto *m*; (Med: organ) trapianto *m*; (fam: hard work) duro lavoro *m*; (fam: corruption) corruzione *f* **2** *vt* innestare; trapiantare ⟨*organ*⟩

grain /greɪn/ *n* (of sand, salt) granello *m*; (of rice) chicco *m*; (cereals) cereali *mpl*; (in wood) venatura *f*; **it goes against the** ~ fig è contro la mia/sua natura

grainy /'greɪnɪ/ *adj* ⟨*photograph*⟩ sgranato; ⟨*paintwork*⟩ granulato

gram /græm/ *n* grammo *m*

grammar /'græmə(r)/ *n* grammatica *f*

grammarian /grə'meərɪən/ *n* grammatico, -a *mf*

grammar school *n* ≈ liceo *m*

grammatical /grə'mætɪkl/ *adj* grammaticale

grammatically /grə'mætɪklɪ/ *adv* grammaticalmente

gran /græn/ *n* fam nonna *f*

granary /'grænərɪ/ *n* granaio *m*

granary bread *n* pane *m* integrale

grand /grænd/ *adj* grandioso; fam eccellente

grandad /'grændæd/ *n* fam nonno *m*

grandchild *n* nipote *mf*

granddaughter *n* nipote *f*

grandeur /'grændʒə(r)/ *n* grandiosità *f*

grandfather *n* nonno *m*

grandfather clock *n* pendolo *m* (che poggia a terra)

grandiose /'grændɪəʊs/ *adj* grandioso

grandma /'grændmɑː/ *n* nonna *f*

grandmother *n* nonna *f*

grandpa /'grændpɑː/ *n* nonno *m*

grandparents *npl* nonni *mpl*

grand piano *n* pianoforte *m* a coda

grand slam *n* vittoria *f* di tutte le fasi di una gara

grandson *n* nipote *m*

grandstand *n* tribuna *f*

grand total *n* totale *m* complessivo

granite /'grænɪt/ *n* granito *m*

granny /'grænɪ/ *n* fam nonna *f*

granny flat *n* Br appartamentino *m* indipendente per genitori anziani annesso all'abitazione principale

grant /grɑːnt/ **1** *n* (money) sussidio *m*; Univ borsa *f* di studio **2** *vt* accordare; (admit) ammettere; **take something for** ~**ed** dare per scontato qualcosa; **take somebody for** ~**ed** considerare quello che qualcuno fa come dovuto

granular /'grænjʊlə(r)/ *adj* granulare

granulated /'grænjʊleɪtɪd/ *adj* ~ **sugar** zucchero *m* semolato

granule /'grænjuːl/ *n* granello *m*

grape /greɪp/ *n* acino *m*; ~**s** *pl* uva *fsg*

grapefruit /'greɪpfruːt/ *n inv* pompelmo *m*

grapeseed oil /'greɪpsiːd/ *n* olio *m* di vinaccioli

grapevine /'greɪpvaɪn/ *n* vite *f*; **hear something on the** ~ sentir dire in giro qualcosa

graph /grɑːf/ *n* grafico *m*

graphic /'græfɪk/ *adj* grafico; (vivid) vivido

graphically /'græfɪklɪ/ *adv* graficamente; (vividly) vividamente

graphic design *n* grafica *f*

graphic designer *n* grafico, -a *mf*

graphics /'græfɪks/ *n* grafica *f*

graphics card *n* Comput scheda *f* grafica

graphics interface *n* Comput interfaccia *f* grafica

graphite /'græfaɪt/ *n* grafite *f*

graphologist /græ'fɒlədʒɪst/ *n* grafologo, -a *mf*

graph paper *n* carta *f* millimetrata

grapple /'græpl/ *vi* ~ **with** also fig essere alle prese con

grasp /grɑːsp/ **1** *n* stretta *f*; (understanding) comprensione *f* **2** *vt* afferrare

grasping /'grɑːspɪŋ/ *adj* avido

grass /grɑːs/ *n* erba *f*

grass court *n* campo *m* in erba

grasshopper *n* cavalletta *f*

grassland *n* prateria *f*

grassroots *npl* base *f*; **at the** ~ alla base

grass snake *n* biscia *f*

grassy /'grɑːsɪ/ *adj* erboso

grate¹ /greɪt/ *n* grata *f*

grate² **1** *vt* Culin grattugiare; ~ **one's teeth** far stridere i denti **2** *vi* stridere

grateful /'greɪtfl/ *adj* grato

gratefully /'greɪtfʊlɪ/ *adv* con gratitudine

grater /'greɪtə(r)/ *n* Culin grattugia *f*

gratification /grætɪfɪ'keɪʃn/ *n* soddisfazione *f*

gratified /'grætɪfaɪd/ adj appagato

gratify /'grætɪfaɪ/ vt (pt/pp **-ied**) appagare

gratifying /'grætɪfaɪɪŋ/ adj appagante

grating /'greɪtɪŋ/ n grata f

gratis /'grɑːtɪs/ adv gratis

gratitude /'grætɪtjuːd/ n gratitudine f

gratuitous /grə'tjuːɪtəs/ adj gratuito

gratuity /grə'tjuːətɪ/ n gratifica f

grave¹ /greɪv/ adj grave

grave² n tomba f

gravedigger /'greɪvdɪgə(r)/ n becchino m

gravel /'grævl/ n ghiaia f

gravelly /'grævəlɪ/ adj ⟨voice⟩ rauco

gravely /'greɪvlɪ/ adv gravamente

graven image /'greɪvən/ n idolo m

gravestone /'greɪvstəʊn/ n lapide f

graveyard /'greɪvjɑːd/ n cimitero m

gravitate /'grævɪteɪt/ vi gravitare

gravity /'grævətɪ/ n gravità f

gravy /'greɪvɪ/ n sugo m della carne

gravy boat n salsiera f

gray /greɪ/ adj Am = GREY

graze¹ /greɪz/ vi ⟨animal⟩ pascolare

graze² ① n escoriazione f
② vt (touch lightly) sfiorare; (scrape) escoriare; sbucciarsi ⟨knee⟩

grease /griːs/ ① n grasso m
② vt ungere

greasepaint /'griːspeɪnt/ n cerone m

greaseproof paper
/griːspruːf'peɪpə(r)/ n carta f oleata

greaser /'griːsə(r)/ n (motorcyclist) componente m di una banda giovanile di motociclisti

greasy /'griːsɪ/ adj (**-ier, -iest**) untuoso; ⟨hair, skin⟩ grasso

great /greɪt/ adj grande; (fam: marvellous) eccezionale

great-aunt n prozia f

great big adj enorme

Great Britain n Gran Bretagna f

Great Dane n danese m

great-grandchildren npl pronipoti mpl

great-grandfather n bisnonno m

great-grandmother n bisnonna f

great-great-grandchildren npl pronipoti mpl

greatly /'greɪtlɪ/ adv enormemente

greatness /'greɪtnɪs/ n grandezza f

great-uncle n prozio m

Grecian /'griːʃ(ə)n/ adj greco

Greece /griːs/ n Grecia f

greed /griːd/ n avidità f; (for food) ingordigia f

greedily /'griːdɪlɪ/ adv avidamente; ⟨eat⟩ con ingordigia

greedy /'griːdɪ/ adj (**-ier, -iest**) avido; (for food) ingordo

Greek /griːk/ adj & n greco, -a mf; (language) greco m

green /griːn/ ① adj verde; (fig: inexperienced) immaturo
② n verde m; (grass) prato m; (in golf) green m inv; ∼s pl verdura f; **the G∼s** pl Pol i verdi

green beans n fagiolini mpl

green belt n zona f verde intorno a una città

green card n carta f verde; Am permesso m di soggiorno

greenery /'griːnərɪ/ n verde m

green-eyed monster /-aɪd'mɒnstə(r)/ n gelosia f

greenfield site /'griːnfiːld/ n terreno m su cui non sono mai esistiti insediamenti urbani

greenfinch n verdone m

green fingers npl have ∼ ∼ avere il pollice verde

greenfly n afide m

greengage n susina f verde

greengrocer n fruttivendolo, -a mf

greenhorn n (new) novellino m; (gullible) pivello m

greenhouse n serra f

greenhouse effect n effetto m serra

Greenland n Groenlandia f

green light n fam verde m

green onion n Am cipollotto m

green salad n insalata f verde

greet /griːt/ vt salutare; (welcome) accogliere

greeting /'griːtɪŋ/ n saluto m; (welcome) accoglienza f

greetings card /'griːtɪŋz/ n biglietto m d'auguri

gregarious /grɪ'geərɪəs/ adj gregario; (person) socievole

gremlin /'gremlɪn/ n hum spirito m maligno

Grenada /grɪ'neɪdə/ n Grenada f

grenade /grɪ'neɪd/ n granata f

grenadier /grenə'dɪə(r)/ n Mil guardia f reale inglese

grew /gruː/ ▶ GROW

grey Br, **gray** Am /greɪ/ ① adj grigio; ⟨hair⟩ bianco
② n grigio m
③ vi diventare bianco
■ **grey out** vt Comput visualizzare con sfondo azzurro ombreggiato

grey area n zona f oscura

grey-haired /heəd/ adj dai capelli grigi

greyhound n levriero m

grey matter *n* (brain) materia *f* grigia

grey squirrel *n* scoiattolo *m* grigio

grid /grɪd/ *n* griglia *f*; (on map) reticolato *m*; Electr rete *f*.

griddle /'grɪd(ə)l/ *n* (for meat) piastra *f*

gridiron *n* griglia *f*; Am campo *m* di football americano

gridlock *n* (fig: deadlock) situazione *f* di stallo; (in traffic) imbottigliamento *m*

grid reference *n* coordinate *fpl*

grief /griːf/ *n* dolore *m*; **come to** ∼ ⟨plans⟩ naufragare

grief-stricken /-strɪkən/ *adj* affranto dal dolore

grievance /'griːvəns/ *n* lamentela *f*

grieve /griːv/ **①** *vt* addolorare
② *vi* essere addolorato

grievous /'griːvəs/ *adj* doloroso

grievous bodily harm *n* lesioni *fpl* personali gravi

grievously /'griːvəslɪ/ *adv* tristemente

grill /grɪl/ **①** *n* graticola *f*; (for grilling) griglia *f*; **mixed** ∼ grigliata *f* mista
② *vt* cuocere alla griglia; (interrogate) sottoporre al terzo grado
③ *vi* cuocere alla griglia

grille /grɪl/ *n* grata *f*

grim /grɪm/ *adj* (**grimmer, grimmest**) arcigno; ⟨determination⟩ accanito

grimace /'grɪməs/ **①** *n* smorfia *f*
② *vi* fare una smorfia

grime /graɪm/ *n* sudiciume *m*

grimly /'grɪmlɪ/ *adv* accanitamente

Grim Reaper *n* Morte *f*

grimy /'graɪmɪ/ *adj* (**-ier, -iest**) sudicio

grin /grɪn/ **①** *n* sorriso *m*
② *vi* (pt/pp **grinned**) fare un gran sorriso

grind /graɪnd/ **①** *n* (fam: hard work) sfacchinata *f*
② *vt* (pt/pp **ground**) macinare; affilare ⟨knife⟩; (Am: mince) tritare; ∼ **one's teeth** digrignare i denti

grindstone /'graɪndstəʊn/ *n* mola *f*; **keep one's nose to the** ∼ lavorare indefessamente

grip /grɪp/ **①** *n* presa *f*; fig controllo *m*: (bag) borsone *m*; **be in the** ∼ **of** essere in preda a; **get a** ∼ **of oneself** controllarsi
② *vt* (pt/pp **gripped**) afferrare; ⟨tyres⟩ far presa su; tenere avvinto ⟨attention⟩

gripe /graɪp/ *vi* (fam: grumble) lagnarsi

gripping /'grɪpɪŋ/ *adj* avvincente

grisly /'grɪzlɪ/ *adj* (**-ier, -iest**) raccapricciante

gristle /'grɪsl/ *n* cartilagine *f*

grit /grɪt/ **①** *n* graniglia *f*; (for roads) sabbia *f*; (courage) coraggio *m*
② *vt* (pt/pp **gritted**) spargere sabbia su ⟨road⟩; ∼ **one's teeth** serrare i denti

gritter /'grɪtə(r)/ *n* Br Auto spandighiaia *m inv*

gritty /'grɪtɪ/ *adj* (sandy) pieno di terra; (gravelly) ghiaioso; (hard, determined) grintoso; novel, film crudo

grizzle /'grɪzl/ *vi* piagnucolare

grizzly /'grɪzlɪ/ *n* (bear) grizzly *m inv*

groan /grəʊn/ **①** *n* gemito *m*
② *vi* gemere

grocer /'grəʊsə(r)/ *n* droghiere, -a *mf*

groceries /'grəʊsərɪz/ *npl* generi *mpl* alimentari

grocer's [shop] *n* drogheria *f*

groggy /'grɒgɪ/ *adj* (**-ier, -iest**) stordito; (unsteady) barcollante

groin /grɔɪn/ *n* Anat inguine *m*

groom /gruːm/ **①** *n* sposo *m*; (for horse) stalliere *m*
② *vt* strigliare ⟨horse⟩; fig preparare; **well-** ∼**ed** ben curato

groove /gruːv/ *n* scanalatura *f*

grope /grəʊp/ *vi* brancolare; ∼ **for** cercare a tastoni

gross /grəʊs/ **①** *adj* obeso; (coarse) volgare; (glaring) grossolano; ⟨salary, weight⟩ lordo
② *n inv* grossa *f*

gross domestic product *n* prodotto *m* interno lordo

gross indecency *n* Jur oltraggio *m* al pudore

grossly /'grəʊslɪ/ *adv* (very) enormemente

gross national product *n* prodotto *m* nazionale lordo

grotesque /grəʊ'tesk/ *adj* grottesco

grotesquely /grəʊ'tesklɪ/ *adv* in modo grottesco

grotto /'grɒtəʊ/ *n* (pl **-es**) grotta *f*

grotty /'grɒtɪ/ *adj* (**-ier, -iest**) fam ⟨flat, street⟩ squallido

grouch /graʊtʃ/ *vi* brontolare (**about** contro)

grouchy /'graʊtʃɪ/ *adj* brontolone

ground[1] /graʊnd/ ▸ GRIND

ground[2] **①** *n* terra *f*; Sport terreno *m*: (reason) ragione *f*; ∼**s** *pl* (park) giardini *mpl*: (of coffee) fondi *mpl*
② *vi* ⟨ship⟩ arenarsi
③ *vt* bloccare a terra ⟨aircraft⟩; Am Electr mettere a terra

ground control *n* base *f* di controllo

ground crew *n* personale *m* di terra

ground floor *n* pianterreno *m*

grounding /'graʊndɪŋ/ *n* base *f*

groundless /'graʊndlɪs/ *adj* infondato

groundnut oil *n* olio *m* d'arachidi

ground rules *npl* principi *mpl* fondamentali

groundsheet *n* telone *m* impermeabile

ground troops *npl* truppe *fpl* di terra

groundwork *n* lavoro *m* di preparazione

group /gru:p/ ① *n* gruppo *m*
② *vt* raggruppare
③ *vi* raggrupparsi

groupage /'gru:pɪdʒ/ *n* Comm raggruppamento *m*

group booking *n* prenotazione *f* di gruppo

group leader *n* capogruppo *m*

group therapy *n* terapia *f* di gruppo

group work *n* lavoro *m* di gruppo

grouse[1] /graʊs/ *n inv* gallo *m* cedrone

grouse[2] *vi fam* brontolare

grove /grəʊv/ *n* boschetto *m*

grovel /'grɒvl/ *vi* (pt/pp **grovelled**) strisciare

grovelling /'grɒv(ə)lɪŋ/ *adj* leccapiedi *inv*

grow /grəʊ/ ① *vi* (pt **grew**, pp **grown**) crescere; (become) diventare; ⟨unemployment, fear⟩ aumentare; ⟨town⟩ ingrandirsi
② *vt* coltivare; ∼ **one's hair** farsi crescere i capelli
■ **grow apart** *vi* ⟨friends, couple⟩ disamorarsi
■ **grow on** *vt* (fam: become pleasing to) **it'll** ∼ **on you** finirà per piacerti
■ **grow out of** *vt* **he's** ∼**n out of his jumper** il golf gli è diventato troppo piccolo
■ **grow up** *vi* crescere; ⟨town⟩ svilupparsi

growbag /'grəʊbæg/ *n* sacco *m* di terriccio dentro cui si coltivano piante

grower /'grəʊə(r)/ *n* coltivatore, -trice *mf*

growing pains /'grəʊɪŋ/ *npl* (of child) dolori *mpl* della crescita; (fig: of firm, project) difficoltà *fpl* iniziali nello sviluppo

growl /graʊl/ ① *n* grugnito *m*
② *vi* ringhiare

grown /grəʊn/ ① ▶ GROW
② *adj* adulto

grown-up *adj* & *n* adulto, -a *mf*

growth /grəʊθ/ *n* crescita *f*; (increase) aumento *m*; Med tumore *m*

growth area *n* area *f* di sviluppo

growth industry *n* industria *f* in rapida crescita

growth rate *n* tasso *m* di crescita

groyne /grɔɪn/ *n* Br pennello *m* (per difendere le spiagge dall'erosione)

grub /grʌb/ *n* larva *f*; (fam: food) mangiare *m*

grubby /'grʌbɪ/ *adj* (**-ier, -iest**) sporco

grudge /grʌdʒ/ ① *n* rancore *m*; **bear somebody a** ∼ portare rancore a qualcuno
② *vt* dare a malincuore

grudging /'grʌdʒɪŋ/ *adj* riluttante

grudgingly /'grʌdʒɪŋlɪ/ *adv* a malincuore

gruelling /'gru:əlɪŋ/ *adj* estenuante

gruesome /'gru:səm/ *adj* macabro

gruff /grʌf/ *adj* burbero

gruffly /'grʌflɪ/ *adv* in modo burbero

grumble /'grʌmbl/ *vi* brontolare (**at** contro)

grumpy /'grʌmpɪ/ *adj* (**-ier, -iest**) scorbutico

grunge /grʌndʒ/ *n* (dirt) lerciume *m*; (style) grunge *m inv*

grunt /grʌnt/ ① *n* grugnito *m*
② *vi* fare un grugnito

G-string *n* (garment) tanga *m inv*

guarantee /gærən'ti:/ ① *n* garanzia *f*
② *vt* garantire

guarantor /gærən'tɔ:(r)/ *n* garante *mf*

guard /gɑ:d/ ① *n* guardia *f*; (security) guardiano *m*; (on train) capotreno *m*; Techn schermo *m* protettivo; **be on** ∼ essere di guardia; **on one's** ∼ in guardia
② *vt* sorvegliare; (protect) proteggere
■ **guard against** *vt* guardarsi da

guard-dog *n* cane *m* da guardia

guarded /'gɑ:dɪd/ *adj* guardingo

guardian /'gɑ:dɪən/ *n* (of minor) tutore, -trice *mf*

guardian angel *n* also *fig* angelo *m* custode

guard of honour *n* guardia *f* d'onore

guardroom *n* corpo *m* di guardia

guard's van *n* Br Rail carrozza *f* bagagliaio

Guatemala /gwætə'mɑ:lə/ *n* Guatemala *m*

guava /'gwɑ:və/ *n* (fruit) guava *f*; (tree) albero *m* di guava

Guernsey /'gɜ:nzɪ/ *n* Guernsey *f*

guerrilla /gə'rɪlə/ *n* guerrigliero, -a *mf*

guerrilla warfare *n* guerriglia *f*

guess /ges/ ① *n* supposizione *f*
② *vt* indovinare
③ *vi* indovinare; (Am: suppose) supporre

guesstimate /'gestɪmət/ *n* calcolo *m* approssimativo

guesswork /'geswɜ:k/ *n* supposizione *f*

guest /gest/ *n* ospite *mf*; (in hotel) cliente *mf*

guest house *n* pensione *f*

guest room *n* camera *f* degli ospiti

guest worker *n* lavoratore *m* immigrato; lavoratrice *f* immigrata

guff /gʌf/ *n* (nonsense) stupidaggini *fpl*

guffaw /gʌ'fɔ:/ ① *n* sghignazzata *f*
② *vi* sghignazzare

guidance /'gaɪdəns/ *n* guida *f*; (advice) consigli *mpl*

guide /gaɪd/ ① *n* guida *f*; [Girl] G~ giovane esploratrice *f*
② *vt* guidare

guidebook /'gaɪdbʊk/ *n* guida *f* turistica

guided missile /'gaɪdɪd/ *n* missile *m* teleguidato

guide dog *n* cane *m* per ciechi

guided tour *n* giro *m* guidato

guidelines /'gaɪdlaɪmz/ *npl* direttive *fpl*

guiding principle /gaɪdɪŋ'prɪnsɪp(ə)l/ *n* direttrice *f*

guild /gɪld/ *n* corporazione *f*

guile /gaɪl/ *n* astuzia *f*

guileless /'gaɪllɪs/ *adj* senza malizia

guillotine /'gɪləti:n/ *n* ghigliottina *f*; (for paper) taglierina *f*

guilt /gɪlt/ *n* colpa *f*

guiltily /'gɪltɪlɪ/ *adv* con aria colpevole

guilty /'gɪltɪ/ *adj* (-ier, -iest) colpevole; have a ~ conscience avere la coscienza sporca

Guinea /'gɪnɪ/ *n* Guinea *f*

guinea /'gmɪ/ *n* ghinea *f*

Guinea-Bissau /-bɪ'saʊ/ *n* Guinea-Bissau *f*

guinea fowl faraona *f*

guinea pig *n* porcellino *m* d'India; (in experiments) cavia *f*

guise /gaɪz/ *n* in the ~ of sotto le spoglie di

guitar /gɪ'tɑ:(r)/ *n* chitarra *f*

guitarist /gɪ'tɑ:rɪst/ *n* chitarrista *mf*

Gulag /'gu:læg/ *n* gulag *m inv*

gulch /gʌltʃ/ *n* Am burrone *m*

gulf /gʌlf/ *n* Geog golfo *m*; fig abisso *m*

Gulf States *npl* gli stati *mpl* del Golfo

Gulf War *n* la guerra *f* del Golfo

gull /gʌl/ *n* gabbiano *m*

gullet /'gʌlɪt/ *n* esofago *m*; (throat) gola *f*

gullible /'gʌləbl/ *adj* credulone

gully /'gʌlɪ/ *n* burrone *m*; (drain) canale *m* di scolo

gulp /gʌlp/ ① *n* azione *f* di deglutire; (of food) boccone *m*; (of liquid) sorso *m*
② *vi* deglutire
■ **gulp down** *vt* trangugiare ⟨food⟩; scolarsi ⟨liquid⟩

gum[1] /gʌm/ *n* Anat gengiva *f*

gum[2] ① *n* gomma *f*; (chewing-gum) gomma *f* da masticare, chewing-gum *m inv*
② *vt* (pt/pp **gummed**) ingommare (**to** a)

gumboot /'gʌmbu:t/ *n* stivale *m* di gomma

gummed /gʌmd/ ① ▶ GUM[2]
② *adj* ⟨label⟩ adesivo

gumption /'gʌmpʃn/ *n* fam buon senso *m*

gumshoe /'gʌmʃu:/ *n* (fam: private investigator) investigatore *m* privato

gum tree *n* fam be up a ~ ~ essere in difficoltà

gun /gʌn/ *n* pistola *f*; (rifle) fucile *m*; (cannon) cannone *m*; he had a ~ era armato
■ **gun down** *vt* (pt/pp **gunned**) freddare

gun barrel *n* canna *f* di fucile

gunboat *n* cannoniera *f*

gun dog *n* cane *m* da caccia

gunfire *n* spari *mpl*; (of cannon) colpi *mpl* [di cannone]

gunge /gʌndʒ/ *n* Br poltiglia *f* [disgustosa]

gung-ho /gʌŋ'həʊ/ *adj* hum (eager for war) guerrafondaio; (overzealous) esaltato

gun laws *npl* leggi *fpl* sulle armi

gun licence *n* porto *m* d'armi

gunman /'gʌnmən/ *n* uomo *m* armato

gunner /'gʌnə(r)/ *n* artigliere *m*

gunpoint *n* hold somebody up at ~ assalire qualcuno a mano armata

gunpowder *n* polvere *f* da sparo

gunshot *n* colpo *m* [di pistola]

gunshot wound *n* ferita *f* d'arma da fuoco

gunslinger *n* pistolero *m*

gurgle /'gɜ:gl/ *vi* gorgogliare; ⟨baby⟩ fare degli urletti

guru /'gʊru:/ *n* guru *m inv*

gush /gʌʃ/ *vi* sgorgare; (enthuse) parlare con troppo entusiasmo (**over** di)
■ **gush out** *vi* sgorgare

gushing /'gʌʃɪŋ/ *adj* eccessivamente entusiastico

gusset /'gʌsɪt/ *n* gherone *m*

gust /gʌst/ *n* (of wind) raffica *f*

gusto /'gʌstəʊ/ *n* with ~ con trasporto

gusty /'gʌstɪ/ *adj* ventoso

gut /gʌt/ ① *n* intestino *m*; ~s *pl* pancia *f*; (fam: courage) fegato *m*
② *vt* (pt/pp **gutted**) Culin svuotare delle interiora; ~ted by fire sventrato da un incendio

gutsy /'gʌtsɪ/ *adj* (brave) coraggioso; (spirited) gagliardo

gutter /'gʌtə(r)/ *n* canale *m* di scolo; (on roof) grondaia *f*; fig bassifondi *mpl*

guttering /'gʌtərɪŋ/ *n* grondaie *fpl*

gutter press *n* stampa *f* scandalistica

guttersnipe /'gʌtəsnaɪp/ *n* ragazzo, -a *mf* di strada

guttural /'gʌtərəl/ *adj* gutturale

guv, guvnor /gʌv/, /'gʌvnə(r)/ *n* (Br fam: boss) capo *m*

guy /gaɪ/ *n* fam tipo *m*, tizio *m*

Guyana /gaɪ'ɑ:nə/ *n* Guyana *f*

Guy Fawkes Day /fɔ:ks/ *n* Br anniversario *m* del fallimento della Congiura delle Polveri (5 novembre)

guzzle /'gʌzl/ *vt* ingozzarsi con ⟨*food*⟩; he's ∼d the lot si è sbafato tutto

gym /dʒɪm/ *n* fam palestra *f*; (gymnastics) ginnastica *f*

gymkhana /dʒɪm'kɑːnə/ *n* manifestazione *f* equestre

gymnasium /dʒɪm'neɪzɪəm/ *n* palestra *f*

gymnast /'dʒɪmnæst/ *n* ginnasta *mf*

gymnastics /dʒɪm'næstɪks/ *n* ginnastica *f*

gym shoes *npl* scarpe *fpl* da ginnastica

gym-slip *n* Sch ≈ grembiule *m* (da bambina)

gynaecologist /gaɪnɪ'kɒlədʒɪst/ *n* ginecologo, -a *mf*

gynaecology /gaɪnɪ'kɒlədʒɪ/ *n* ginecologia *f*

gyp /dʒɪp/ *n* Br **my back is giving me** ∼ ho un terribile mal di schiena

gypsum /'dʒɪpsəm/ *n* gesso *m*

gypsy /'dʒɪpsɪ/ *n* zingaro, -a *mf*

gyrate /dʒaɪ'reɪt/ *vi* roteare

Hh

h, **H** /eɪtʃ/ *n* h, H *f inv*

ha! ha! /hɑː'hɑː/ *int* ah! ah!

haberdashery /hæbə'dæʃərɪ/ *n* merceria *f*; Am negozio *m* d'abbigliamento da uomo

habit /'hæbɪt/ *n* abitudine *f*; (Relig: costume) tonaca *f*; **be in the** ∼ **of doing something** avere l'abitudine di fare qualcosa

habitable /'hæbɪtəbl/ *adj* abitabile

habitat /'hæbɪtæt/ *n* habitat *m inv*

habitation /hæbɪ'teɪʃn/ *n* **unfit for human** ∼ inagibile

habit-forming /-fɔːmɪŋ/ *adj* **be** ∼ creare assuefazione

habitual /hə'bɪtjʊəl/ *adj* abituale; ⟨*smoker, liar*⟩ inveterato

habitually /hə'bɪtjʊəlɪ/ *adv* regolarmente

habitual offender *n* delinquente *mf* recidivo

hack¹ /hæk/ *n* (writer) scribacchino, -a *mf*

hack² *vt* tagliare; ∼ **to pieces** tagliare a pezzi

hacker /'hækə(r)/ *n* Comput pirata *m* informatico

hacking /'hækɪŋ/ *n* Comput pirateria *f* informatica

hacking cough *n* brutta tosse *f*

hackles /'hæk(ə)lz/ *npl* (on animal) pelo *m* del collo; (on bird) piumaggio *m* del collo; **make sb's** ∼ **rise** fig far imbestialire qualcuno

hackney cab /'hæknɪ/ *n* fml taxi *m inv*

hackneyed /'hæknɪd/ *adj* trito [e ritrito]

hacksaw /'hæksɔː/ *n* seghetto *m*

had /hæd/ ▶HAVE

haddock /'hædək/ *n inv* eglefino *m*

haematoma /hiːmə'təʊmə/ *n* ematoma *m*

haemoglobin /hiːmə'gləʊbɪn/ *n* emoglobina *f*

haemophilia /hiːmə'fɪlɪə/ *n* emofilia *f*

haemophiliac /hiːmə'fɪlɪæk/ *n* emofiliaco, -a *mf*

haemorrhage /'hemərɪdʒ/ *n* emorragia *f*

haemorrhoids /'hemərɔɪdz/ *npl* emorroidi *fpl*

hag /hæg/ *n* old ∼ vecchia befana *f*

haggard /'hægəd/ *adj* sfatto

haggis /'hægɪs/ *n* piatto *m* scozzese a base di frattaglie di pecora e avena

haggle /'hægl/ *vi* contrattare (**over** per)

Hague /heɪg/ *n* **the** ∼ l'Aia *f*

hail¹ /heɪl/ **1** *vt* salutare; far segno a ⟨*taxi*⟩
2 *vi* ∼ **from** provenire da

hail² **1** *n* grandine *f*
2 *vi* grandinare

hailstone /'heɪlstəʊn/ *n* chicco *m* di grandine

hailstorm /'heɪlstɔːm/ *n* grandinata *f*

hair /heə(r)/ *n* capelli *mpl*; (on body, of animal) pelo *m*; **wash one's** ∼ lavarsi i capelli

hairband *n* (rigid) cerchietto *m*; (elastic) fascia *f* [per capelli]

hairbrush *n* spazzola *f* per capelli

hair curler *n* arricciacapelli *m inv*

haircut *n* taglio *m* di capelli; **have a** ∼ farsi tagliare i capelli

hairdo *n* fam pettinatura *f*

hairdresser *n* parrucchiere, -a *mf*

hairdryer, **hairdrier** *n* fon *m inv*; (with hood) casco *m* (asciugacapelli)

hair gel *n* gel *m inv* [per capelli]

hairgrip *n* molletta *f*

hairless /ˈheəlɪs/ adj ⟨animal⟩ senza peli; ⟨body⟩, chin) glabro

hairline n (on head) attaccatura f dei capelli

hairline crack n incrinatura f sottilissima

hairline fracture n Med frattura f capillare

hairnet n retina f per capelli

hairpiece n toupet m inv

hairpin n forcina f

hairpin bend n tornante m, curva f a gomito

hair-raising /heəreɪzɪŋ/ adj terrificante

hair remover n crema f depilatoria

hairslide n Br fermacapelli m inv

hair-splitting /ˈheəsplɪtɪŋ/ n pedanteria f

hairspray n lacca f [per capelli]

hairstyle n acconciatura f

hairstylist n parrucchiere, -a mf

hair transplant n trapianto m di capelli

hairy /ˈheərɪ/ adj (**-ier, -iest**) peloso; (fam: frightening) spaventoso

Haiti /ˈheɪtɪ/ n Haiti m

Haitian /ˈheɪʃ(ə)n/ n & adj haitiano, -a mf; (language) haitiano m

hake /heɪk/ n inv nasello m

halal /hæˈlæl/ adj ⟨meat, butcher⟩ halal

halcyon days /ˈhælsɪən/ npl bei tempi mpl andati

hale /heɪl/ adj ∼ **and hearty** in piena forma

half /hɑːf/ ① n (pl **halves**) metà f inv; cut in ∼ tagliare a metà; one and a ∼ uno e mezzo; ∼ **a dozen** mezza dozzina; ∼ **an hour** mezz'ora
② adj mezzo; **[at]** ∼ **price** [a] metà prezzo
③ adv a metà; ∼ **past two** le due e mezza

half-and-half ① adj mezzo e mezzo
② adv a metà; **go** ∼ fare a metà

half-back n mediano m

half-baked adj fam che non sta in piedi

half board n mezza pensione f

half-breed n & adj mezzosangue mf inv

half-brother n fratellastro m

half-caste n meticcio, -a mf

half-century n mezzo secolo m

half cock n **go off at** ∼ partire col piede sbagliato

half-conscious adj semicosciente

halfcrown, half a crown n Br mezza corona f

half-cut adj (fam: drunk) ciucco

half day n mezza giornata f

half-dead adj also fig mezzo morto

half-dozen n mezza dozzina f

half fare n metà tariffa f

half-hearted /-ˈhɑːtɪd/ adj esitante

half-heartedly /-ˈhɑːtɪdlɪ/ adv senza entusiasmo

half hour n mezz'ora f

halfhourly adj & adv ogni mezz'ora

half-length adj ⟨portrait⟩ a mezzo busto

half-light n penombra f

half mast n **at** ∼ ∼ a mezz'asta

half measures npl mezze misure fpl

half-moon ① n mezzaluna f; (of fingernail) lunula f
② attrib ⟨spectacles⟩ a mezzaluna

half pay n metà stipendio m

halfpenny /ˈheɪpnɪ/ n Br mezzo penny m inv

half-pint n mezza pinta f (Br = 0,28 l, Am = 0,24 l); (beer) piccola f; fig mezza calzetta f

half price ① adj a metà prezzo
② adv [a] metà prezzo

half-sister n sorellastra f

half size ① n (of shoe) mezzo numero m
② adj ⟨copy⟩ ridotto della metà

half smile n mezzo sorriso m

half-starved adj mezzo morto di fame

half-term n vacanza f di metà trimestre

half-time n Sport intervallo m

half-truth n mezza verità f inv

halfway ① adj **the** ∼ **mark/stage** il livello intermedio
② adv a metà strada; **get** ∼ fig arrivare a metà

halfway house n (compromise) via f di mezzo; (rehabilitation centre) centro m di riabilitazione per ex detenuti

halfway line n Sport linea f mediana

halfwit n idiota mf

half-year ① n Fin, Comm semestre m
② attrib ⟨profit, results⟩ semestrale

half-yearly adj ⟨meeting, payment⟩ semestrale

halibut /ˈhælɪbət/ n inv ippoglosso m

halitosis /hælɪˈtəʊsɪs/ n alitosi f inv

hall /hɔːl/ n (entrance) ingresso m; (room) sala f; (mansion) residenza f di campagna

hallelujah /(h)ælɪˈluːjə/ int alleluia!

hallmark /ˈhɔːlmɑːk/ n marchio m di garanzia; fig marchio m

hallo /həˈləʊ/ int ciao!; (on telephone) pronto!; **say** ∼ **to** salutare

hall of residence n residenza f universitaria

hallowed /ˈhæləʊd/ adj ⟨ground⟩ consacrato; ⟨tradition⟩ sacro

Halloween /hæləʊˈiːn/ n vigilia f d'Ognissanti e notte delle streghe, celebrata soprattutto dai bambini

hallucinate /həˈluːsɪneɪt/ vi avere le allucinazioni

hallucination /həluːsɪˈneɪʃn/ n
allucinazione f

hallucinatory /həˈluːsɪnət(ə)rɪ/ adj
⟨drug⟩ allucinogeno

hallucinogen /həˈluːsɪnədʒən/ n
sostanza f allucinante

hallucinogenic /həluːsɪnəˈdʒenɪk/ adj
allucinogeno

hallway /ˈhɔːlweɪ/ n ingresso m

halo /ˈheɪləʊ/ n (pl **-es**) aureola f; Astr
alone m

halogen /ˈhælədʒən/ n alogeno m

halt /hɔːlt/ **1** n alt m inv; **come to a** ~
fermarsi; ⟨traffic⟩ bloccarsi
2 vi fermarsi; ~! alt!
3 vt fermare

halter /ˈhɔːltə(r)/ n (for horse) cavezza f

halter-neck n modello m con
allacciatura dietro il collo che lascia la
schiena scoperta

halting /ˈhɔːltɪŋ/ adj esitante

haltingly /ˈhɔːltɪŋlɪ/ adv con esitazione

halve /haːv/ vt dividere a metà; (reduce)
dimezzare

ham /hæm/ n prosciutto m; Theat attore,
-trice mf da strapazzo

hamburger /ˈhæmbɜːgə(r)/ n
hamburger m inv

ham-fisted /-ˈfɪstɪd/ adj Br fam maldestro

hamlet /ˈhæmlɪt/ n paesino m

hammer /ˈhæmə(r)/ **1** n martello m
2 vt martellare
3 vi ~ **at/on** picchiare a
■ **hammer in** vt piantare ⟨nail⟩
■ **hammer out** vt definire con grandi
sforzi ⟨agreement, policy⟩

hammer and sickle n falce f e
martello m

hammered /ˈhæməd/ adj (fam: drunk)
sbronzo

hammock /ˈhæmək/ n amaca f

hamper[1] /ˈhæmpə(r)/ n cesto m; [gift] ~
cestino m

hamper[2] vt ostacolare

hamster /ˈhæmstə(r)/ n criceto m

hamstring /ˈhæmstrɪŋ/ **1** n (of horse)
tendine m del garretto; (of human) tendine
m del ginocchio
2 vt fig rendere impotente

hand /hænd/ **1** n mano f; (of clock)
lancetta f; (writing) scrittura f; (worker)
manovale m; **all** ~**s** Naut l'equipaggio al
completo; **at** ~, **to** ~ a portata di mano;
by ~ a mano; **on the one** ~ da un lato; **on
the other** ~ d'altra parte; **out of** ~
incontrollabile; (summarily) su due piedi; **in**
~ in corso; ⟨situation⟩ sotto controllo;
(available) disponibile; **give somebody a** ~
dare una mano a qualcuno; ~ **in** ~ ⟨run,
walk⟩ mano nella mano; **go** ~ **in** ~ fig
andare di pari passo (**with** con)

2 vt porgere
■ **hand back** vt restituire ⟨something⟩
■ **hand down** vt tramandare
■ **hand in** vt consegnare
■ **hand on** vt passare
■ **hand out** vt distribuire
■ **hand over** vt passare; (to police)
consegnare

handbag n borsa f (da signora)

hand baggage n bagaglio m a mano

handball n pallamano f; (fault in football)
fallo m di mano; ~! mano!

handbasin n lavandino m

handbook n manuale m

handbrake n freno m a mano

handcart n carretto m

hand cream n crema f per le mani

handcuffs npl manette fpl

hand-dryer, hand-drier n
asciugamani m inv ad aria

hand-eye coordination n
coordinazione f occhio-mano

handful /ˈhændfʊl/ n manciata f; **be
[quite] a** ~ fam essere difficile da tenere a
freno

hand grenade n bomba f a mano

handgun n pistola f

hand-held adj a mano

handicap /ˈhændɪkæp/ n handicap m
inv

handicapped /ˈhændɪkæpt/ adj
mentally/physically ~ mentalmente/
fisicamente handicappato

handicraft /ˈhændɪkrɑːft/ n artigianato
m

handiwork /ˈhændɪwɜːk/ n opera f

handkerchief /ˈhæŋkətʃɪf/ n (pl **-s** &
-chieves) fazzoletto m

handle /ˈhændl/ **1** n manico m; (of door)
maniglia f; **fly off the** ~ fam perdere le
staffe
2 vt maneggiare; occuparsi di ⟨problem,
customer⟩; prendere ⟨difficult person⟩;
trattare ⟨subject⟩; **be good at handling
somebody** saperci fare con qualcuno

handlebar moustache
/hændlbaːməˈstaːʃ/ n baffi mpl a
manubrio

handlebars /ˈhændlbaːz/ npl manubrio
m

handler /ˈhændlə(r)/ n (of dog)
addestratore, -trice mf

handling /ˈhændlɪŋ/ n (touching, holding)
manipolazione f; (of weapon) maneggio m;
(dealing with) gestione f

handling charge n (for goods) spese fpl
di movimentazione; (administrative) spese fpl
di amministrazione

hand lotion n lozione f per le mani

hand-luggage n bagaglio m a mano

handmade adj fatto a mano

handout n (at lecture) foglio m informativo; (fam: money) elemosina f

handover n (of prisoner, ransom) consegna f; (of property, territory) cessione f; ~ **of power** passaggio m delle consegne

hand-pick vt scegliere ⟨produce⟩; selezionare con cura ⟨staff⟩

handrail n corrimano m

hand-reared /-ˈrɪəd/ adj ⟨animal⟩ allattato con il biberon

handset n Teleph ricevitore m

handshake n stretta f di mano

hand signal n Auto segnalazione f con la mano

hands-off adj ⟨policy⟩ di non intervento; ⟨manager⟩ che delega le responsabilità

handsome /ˈhænsəm/ adj bello; (fig: generous) generoso; ⟨salary⟩ considerevole

hands-on adj ⟨experience⟩ pratico; ⟨approach⟩ pragmatico; ⟨control⟩ diretto; ⟨manager⟩ che segue direttamente le varie attività

handspring n salto m sulle mani

handstand n verticale f

hand-to-hand adj & adv ⟨fight⟩ corpo a corpo

hand-to-mouth adj ⟨existence⟩ precario

hand towel n asciugamano m

hand-woven /-ˈwəʊvən/ adj tessuto a mano

handwriting n calligrafia f

handwritten adj scritto a mano

handy /ˈhændɪ/ adj (**-ier, -iest**) pratico; ⟨person⟩ abile; **have/keep** ~ avere/tenere a portata di mano

handyman /ˈhændɪmæn/ n tuttofare m inv

hang /hæŋ/ ①① vt (pt/pp **hung**) appendere ⟨picture⟩; (pt/pp **hanged**) impiccare ⟨criminal⟩; ~ **oneself** impiccarsi; ~ **wallpaper** tappezzare ②② vi (pt/pp **hung**) pendere; ⟨hair⟩ scendere ③③ n **get the** ~ **of it** fam afferrare

■ **hang about** vi gironzolare

■ **hang around** vi = HANG ABOUT

■ **hang back** vi (hesitate) esitare

■ **hang down** vi ⟨hem⟩ pendere

■ **hang on** vi tenersi stretto; (fam: wait) aspettare; Teleph restare in linea

■ **hang on to** vt tenersi stretto a; (keep) tenere

■ **hang out** ①① vi spuntare; **where does he usually** ~ **out?** fam dove bazzica di solito? ②② vt stendere ⟨washing⟩

■ **hang up** ①① vt appendere; Teleph riattaccare ②② vi essere appeso; Teleph riattaccare

hangar /ˈhæŋə(r)/ n hangar m inv

hanger /ˈhæŋə(r)/ n gruccia f

hanger-on n leccapiedi mf inv

hang-glider n deltaplano m

hang-gliding n deltaplano m

hanging /ˈhæŋɪŋ/ n (of person) impiccagione f; (curtain) tendaggio m; (on wall) arazzo m

hangman n boia m

hangover n postumi mpl della sbornia

hang-up n fam complesso m

hank /hæŋk/ n (of hair) ciocca f; (of wool etc) matassa f

hanker /ˈhæŋkə(r)/ vi ~ **after something** smaniare per qualcosa

hanky, hankie /ˈhæŋkɪ/ n fam fazzoletto m

hanky-panky /hæŋkɪˈpæŋkɪ/ n fam qualcosa m di losco

ha'penny /ˈheɪpnɪ/ n Br abbr (**halfpenny**) mezzo penny m inv

haphazard /hæpˈhæzəd/ adj a casaccio; **in a** ~ **fashion** a casaccio

haphazardly /hæpˈhæzədlɪ/ adv a casaccio

hapless /ˈhæplɪs/ adj sventurato

happen /ˈhæpn/ vi capitare, succedere; **as it** ~**s** per caso; **I** ~**ed to meet him** mi è capitato di incontrarlo; **what has** ~**ed to him?** cosa gli è capitato?; (become of) che fine ha fatto?

happening /ˈhæp(ə)nɪŋ/ n avvenimento m

happily /ˈhæpɪlɪ/ adv felicemente; (fortunately) fortunatamente

happiness /ˈhæpɪnɪs/ n felicità f

happy /ˈhæpɪ/ adj (**-ier, -iest**) contento, felice

happy ending n lieto fine m

happy-go-lucky adj spensierato

happy hour n ora f in cui nei pub le bevande vengono vendute a prezzi scontati

happy medium n giusto mezzo m

harangue /həˈræŋ/ vt ⟨morally⟩ fare un sermone a; ⟨politically⟩ arringare

harass /ˈhærəs/ vt perseguitare

harassed /ˈhærəst/ adj stressato

harassment /ˈhærəsmənt/ n persecuzione f; **sexual** ~ molestie fpl sessuali

harbinger /ˈhɑːbɪndʒə(r)/ n liter segnale m; (person) precursore m; precorritrice f

harbour /ˈhɑːbə(r)/ ①① n porto m ②② vt dare asilo a; nutrire ⟨grudge⟩

hard /hɑːd/ ①① adj ⟨question, problem⟩ difficile; **be** ~ **on somebody** ⟨person⟩ essere duro con qualcuno ②② adv ⟨work⟩ duramente; ⟨pull, hit, rain, snow⟩ forte; ~ **hit by unemployment** duramente colpito dalla disoccupazione; **take something** ~ non accettare qualcosa; **think** ~**!** pensaci bene!; **try** ~ mettercela ⋯❖

tutta; **try ∼er** metterci più impegno; **∼ done by** fam trattato ingiustamente

hard and fast adj ⟨rule, distinction⟩ preciso

hardback n edizione f rilegata

hardboard n truciolato m

hard-boiled /-'bɔɪld/ adj ⟨egg⟩ sodo

hard cash n contante m

hard copy n copia f stampata

hard core ① n (in construction) massicciata f; (of group, demonstrators) zoccolo m duro
② adj ⟨pornography, video⟩ hard-core; ⟨supporter, opponent⟩ irriducibile

hard court n campo m in superficie dura

hard disk n hard disk m inv, disco m rigido

hard drive n Comput hard drive m

hard drug n droga f pesante

hard-earned /-'ɜnd/ adj ⟨cash⟩ sudato

harden /'hɑːdn/ vi indurirsi

hardened adj ⟨criminal⟩ inveterato; ⟨drinker⟩ cronico

hard-faced /-'feɪst/ adj ⟨person⟩ dai tratti duri

hard-fought adj ⟨battle⟩ accanito

hard hat n casco m

hard-headed /-'hedɪd/ adj pratico; ⟨businessman⟩ dal sangue freddo

hardhearted /-'hɑːtɪd/ adj dal cuore duro

hard-hitting /-'hɪtɪŋ/ adj ⟨report, speech⟩ incisivo

hard labour n Br lavori mpl forzati

hard lens n lente f a contatto rigida

hardline ① adj ⟨policy, regime⟩ duro
② n linea f dura; **∼ lines!** che sfortuna!

hardliner n Pol fautore, -trice mf della linea dura

hard luck n sfortuna f

hard-luck story n **give somebody a ∼ ∼** raccontare a qualcuno le proprie disgrazie

hardly /'hɑːdlɪ/ adv appena; **∼ ever** quasi mai

hardness /'hɑːdnɪs/ n durezza f

hard-nosed /-'nəʊzd/ adj ⟨attitude, businessman, government⟩ duro

hard of hearing adj duro d'orecchio

hard-on n fam erezione f

hard porn n pornografia f hard-core

hard-pressed /-'prest/ adj in difficoltà; (for time) a corto di tempo

hard-pushed /-'pʊʃt/ adj (having problems) in difficoltà

hard rock n Mus hard rock m

hard sell n tecnica f di vendita aggressiva

hardship /'hɑːdʃɪp/ n avversità f inv

hard shoulder n Auto corsia f d'emergenza

hard up adj fam a corto di soldi; **∼ ∼ for something** a corto di qualcosa

hardware n ferramenta fpl; Comput hardware m inv

hardware shop n negozio m di ferramenta

hard-wearing /-'weərɪŋ/ adj resistente

hardwood n legno m duro

hard-working /-'wɜːkɪŋ/ adj **be ∼** essere un gran lavoratore

hardy /'hɑːdɪ/ adj (-ier, -iest) dal fisico resistente; ⟨plant⟩ che sopporta il gelo

hare /heə(r)/ n lepre f

hare-brained /'heəbreɪnd/ adj ⟨scheme⟩ da scervellati; ⟨person⟩ scervellato

harelip /heə'lɪp/ n labbro m leporino

harem /'hɑːriːm/ n serraglio m

hark /hɑːk/ v
■ **hark back** vt fig **∼ back to** ritornare su

haricot [bean] /'hærɪkəʊ/ n fagiolo m bianco

harm /hɑːm/ ① n male m; (damage) danni mpl; **out of ∼'s way** in un posto sicuro; **it won't do any ∼** non farà certo male
② vt far male a; (damage) danneggiare

harmful /'hɑːmfʊl/ adj dannoso

harmless /'hɑːmlɪs/ adj innocuo

harmonica /hɑː'mɒnɪkə/ n armonica f [a bocca]

harmonious /hɑː'məʊnɪəs/ adj armonioso

harmoniously /hɑː'məʊnɪəslɪ/ adv in armonia

harmonize /'hɑːmənaɪz/ vi fig armonizzare

harmony /'hɑːmənɪ/ n armonia f

harness /'hɑːnɪs/ ① n finimenti mpl; (of parachute) imbracatura f
② vt bardare ⟨horse⟩; sfruttare ⟨resources⟩

harp /hɑːp/ n arpa f
■ **harp on** vi fam insistere (**about** su)

harpist /'hɑːpɪst/ n arpista mf

harpoon /hɑː'puːn/ n arpione m

harpsichord /'hɑːpsɪkɔːd/ n clavicembalo m

harrow /'hærəʊ/ n erpice m

harrowing /'hærəʊɪŋ/ adj straziante

harry /'hærɪ/ vt (pursue, harass) assillare

harsh /hɑːʃ/ adj duro; ⟨light⟩ abbagliante

harshly /'hɑːʃlɪ/ adv duramente

harshness /'hɑːʃnɪs/ n durezza f

harvest /'hɑːvɪst/ ① n raccolta f; (of grapes) vendemmia f; (crop) raccolto m
② vt raccogliere

harvester /'hɑːvɪstə(r)/ n (person) mietitore, -trice mf; (machine) mietitrice f

harvest festival n festa f del raccolto

has /hæz/ ▶ HAVE

has-been /-biːn/ n fam (person) persona f che ha fatto il suo tempo; (thing) anticaglia f

hash /hæʃ/ n make a ∼ of fam fare un casino con

hash [sign] n cancelletto m

hashish /'hæʃɪʃ/ n hashish m

hassle /'hæsl/ [1] n fam rottura f [2] vt rompere le scatole a

hassock /'hæsək/ n cuscino m di inginocchiatoio

haste /heɪst/ n fretta f; make ∼ affrettarsi

hasten /'heɪsn/ [1] vi affrettarsi [2] vt affrettare

hastily /'heɪstɪlɪ/ adv frettolosamente

hasty /'heɪstɪ/ adj (-ier, -iest) frettoloso; ‹decision› affrettato

hat /hæt/ n cappello m

hatbox /'hætbɒks/ n cappelliera f

hatch[1] /hætʃ/ n (for food) sportello m passavivande inv; Naut boccaporto m

hatch[2] [1] vi ∼ [out] rompere il guscio; ‹egg› schiudersi [2] vt covare; tramare ‹plot› ■ **hatch up** vt tramare ‹plot›

hatchback /'hætʃbæk/ n Auto (car) tre/ cinque porte m inv; (door) porta f del bagagliaio

hatchet /'hætʃɪt/ n ascia f

hate /heɪt/ [1] n odio m [2] vt odiare

hateful /'heɪtfʊl/ adj odioso

hate mail n lettere fpl offensive o minatorie

hatpin /'hætpɪn/ n spillone m

hatred /'heɪtrɪd/ n odio m

hat-trick n tripletta f

haughtily /'hɔːtɪlɪ/ adv altezzosamente

haughty /'hɔːtɪ/ adj (-ier, -iest) altezzoso

haul /hɔːl/ [1] n (fish) pescata f; (loot) bottino m; (pull) tirata f [2] vt tirare; trasportare ‹goods› [3] vi ∼ on tirare

haulage /'hɔːlɪdʒ/ n trasporto m

haulier /'hɔːlɪə(r)/ n autotrasportatore m

haunch /hɔːntʃ/ n anca f

haunt /hɔːnt/ [1] n ritrovo m [2] vt frequentare; (linger in the mind) perseguitare; this house is ∼ed questa casa è abitata da fantasmi

haunted /'hɔːntɪd/ adj ‹house› infestato dai fantasmi; ‹look› tormentato

haunting /'hɔːntɪŋ/ adj ‹memory, melody› ossessionante

have /hæv/ [1] vt (3 sg pres tense **has**; pt/pp **had**) avere; fare ‹breakfast, bath, walk etc›; ∼ **a drink** bere qualcosa; ∼ **lunch/dinner** pranzare/cenare; ∼ **a rest** riposarsi; **I had my hair cut** mi sono tagliata i capelli; **we had the flat painted** abbiamo fatto tinteggiare la casa; **I had it made** l'ho fatto fare; ∼ **to do something** dover fare qualcosa; ∼ **him telephone me tomorrow** digli di telefonarmi domani; **he has** or **he's got two houses** ha due case; **you've got the money,** ∼**n't you?** hai i soldi, no? [2] v aux avere; (with verbs of motion & some others) essere; **I** ∼ **seen him** l'ho visto; **he has never been there** non ci è mai stato; [3] npl the ∼**s and the** ∼**-nots** i ricchi e i poveri

■ **have in** vt avere in casa/ufficio etc ‹builders etc›

■ **have off** vt fam **he's having it off with his secretary** si fa la segretaria

■ **have on** vt (be wearing) portare; (dupe) prendere in giro; **I've got something on tonight** ho un impegno stasera; **you're having me on!** tu mi stai prendendo in giro!

■ **have out** vt ∼ **it out with somebody** chiarire le cose con qualcuno; ∼ **a tooth out** farsi togliere un dente

haven /'heɪvn/ n fig rifugio m

haver /'heɪvə(r)/ vi (dither) titubare

haversack /'hævəsæk/ n zaino m

havoc /'hævək/ n strage f; **play** ∼ **with** fig scombussolare

haw /hɔː/ ▶ HUM

Hawaii /həˈwaɪɪ/ n le Hawaii

Hawaiian /həˈwaɪən/ n & adj hawaiano, -a mf; (language) hawaiano m

hawk[1] /hɔːk/ n falco m

hawk[2] vt vendere in giro

hawker /'hɔːkə(r)/ n venditore, -trice mf ambulante

hawkish /'hɔːkɪʃ/ adj Pol intransigente

hawthorn /'hɔːθɔːn/ n biancospino m

hay /heɪ/ n fieno m

hay fever n raffreddore m da fieno

hayloft n fienile m

haymaking n fienagione f

haystack n pagliaio m

haywire adj fam **go** ∼ dare i numeri; ‹plans› andare all'aria

hazard /'hæzəd/ [1] n (risk) rischio m [2] vt rischiare; ∼ **a guess** azzardare un'ipotesi

hazardous /'hæzədəs/ adj rischioso

hazard [warning] lights npl Auto luci fpl d'emergenza

haze /heɪz/ n foschia f

hazel /'heɪz(ə)l/ n nocciolo m; (colour) [color] m nocciola m

hazelnut /'heɪz(ə)lnʌt/ *n* nocciola *f*

hazy /'heɪzɪ/ *adj* (**-ier, -iest**) nebbioso; fig ⟨person⟩ confuso; ⟨memories⟩ vago

HDTV *abbr* (**high-definition television**) HDTV *f*

he /hi:/ *pron* lui; **he's tired** è stanco; **I'm going but he's not** io vengo, ma lui no

head /hed/ **1** *n* testa *f*; (of firm) capo *m*; (of primary school) direttore, -trice *mf*; (of secondary school) preside *mf*; (on beer) schiuma *f*; **use your** ∼! usa la testa!; **be off one's** ∼ essere fuori di testa; **have a good** ∼ **for business** avere il senso degli affari; **have a good** ∼ **for heights** non soffrire di vertigini; **10 pounds a** ∼ 10 sterline a testa; **20** ∼ **of cattle** 20 capi di bestiame; ∼ **first** a capofitto; ∼ **over heels in love** innamorato pazzo; ∼s **or tails?** testa o croce?
2 *vt* essere a capo di; essere in testa a ⟨list⟩; colpire di testa ⟨ball⟩
3 *vi* ∼ **for** dirigersi verso

headache *n* mal *m* di testa

headband *n* fascia *f* per capelli

head boy *n* Br Sch alunno *m* che rappresenta la scuola nelle manifestazioni ufficiali e che ha responsabilità speciali

head-butt *vt* dare una testata a

head case *n* fam **be a** ∼ ∼ essere matto da legare

head cold *n* raffreddore *m* di testa

headcount *n* **do a** ∼ contare i presenti

headdress *n* acconciatura *f*

header /'hedə(r)/ *n* colpo *m* di testa; (dive) tuffo *m* di testa; (on document) intestazione *f*

headfirst *adv* ⟨dive, fall⟩ di testa; ⟨rush into⟩ a testa bassa

headgear *n* copricapo *m*

head girl *n* Br Sch alunna *f* che rappresenta la scuola nelle manifestazioni ufficiali e che ha responsabilità speciali

headhunt *vt* cercare per assumere

headhunter *n* also Comm cacciatore, -trice *mf* di teste

headhunting *n* Comm ricerca *f* ad hoc di personale

heading *n* (in list etc) titolo *m*

headlamp *n* Auto fanale *m*

headland *n* promontorio *m*

headlight *n* Auto fanale *m*

headline *n* titolo *m*

headlong *adj & adv* a capofitto

head louse *n* pidocchio *m*

headmaster *n* (of primary school) direttore *m*; (of secondary school) preside *m*

headmistress *n* (of primary school) direttrice *f*; (of secondary school) preside *f*

head of department *n* capo *mf* reparto

head office *n* sede *f* centrale

head-on **1** *adj* ⟨collision⟩ frontale
2 *adv* frontalmente

headphones *npl* cuffie *fpl*

headquarters *npl* sede *fsg*; Mil quartier *msg* generale

headrest *n* poggiatesta *m inv*

headroom *n* sottotetto *m*; (of bridge) altezza *f* libera di passaggio

headscarf *n* foulard *m inv*, fazzoletto *m*

headset *n* cuffia *f* con microfono

headstand *n* **do a** ∼ fare la verticale

head start *n* **have a** ∼ ∼ partire avvantaggiato

headstone *n* (of grave) lapide *f*

headstrong *adj* testardo

head teacher *n* (of primary school) direttore, -trice *mf*; (of secondary school) preside *mf*

head-to-head *n* confronto *m* diretto ● *adj* diretto

head waiter *n* capocameriere *m*

headway *n* progresso *m*

headwind *n* vento *m* di prua

heady /'hedɪ/ *adj* che dà alla testa

heal /hi:l/ *vt/i* guarire

healer /'hi:lə(r)/ *n* guaritore, -trice *mf*; **time is a great** ∼ il tempo guarisce tutti i mali

healing /'hi:lɪŋ/ *adj* ⟨power, effect⟩ curativo; **the** ∼ **process** il processo di guarigione

health /helθ/ *n* salute *f*

health care *n* assistenza *f* sanitaria

health centre *n* Br ambulatorio *m*

health check *n* controllo *m*

health club *n* club *m* ginnico

health farm *n* centro *m* di rimessa in forma

health foods *npl* alimenti *mpl* macrobiotici

health-food shop *n* negozio *m* di macrobiotica

health hazard *n* pericolo *m* per la salute

healthily /'helθɪlɪ/ *adv* in modo sano

health insurance *n* assicurazione *f* contro malattie

health officer *n* ufficiale *m* sanitario

health resort *n* (in mountains, by sea) stazione *f* climatica; (spa town) stazione *f* termale

Health Service *n* (Br: for public) servizio *m* sanitario; (Am: Univ) infermeria *f*

health visitor *n* Br infermiere, -a *mf* che fa visite a domicilio

health warning *n* avviso *m* del ministero della sanità

healthy /'helθɪ/ *adj* (**-ier, -iest**) sano

heap /hi:p/ ① *n* mucchio *m*; ~s of fam un sacco di
② *vt* ~ **[up]** ammucchiare

heaped /hi:pt/ *adj* a ~ **spoonful** un cucchiaio colmo

hear /hɪə(r)/ *vt/i* (pt/pp **heard**) sentire; ~, ~! bravo!
■ **hear about** *vt* (learn of) sentir parlare di
■ **hear from** *vi* aver notizie di
■ **hear of** *vi* sentir parlare di; **he would not** ~ **of it** non ne ha voluto sentir parlare

hearing /'hɪərɪŋ/ *n* udito *m*; Jur udienza *f*

hearing aid *n* apparecchio *m* acustico

hearing-impaired /-ɪm'peəd/ *adj* audioleso

hearsay /'hɪəseɪ/ *n* **from** ~ per sentito dire

hearse /hɜ:s/ *n* carro *m* funebre

heart /hɑ:t/ *n* cuore *m*; ~s *pl* (Cards) cuori *mpl*; **at** ~ di natura; **by** ~ a memoria

heartache *n* pena *f*

heart attack *n* infarto *m*

heartbeat *n* battito *m* cardiaco

heartbreak *n* afflizione *f*

heartbreaking *adj* straziante

heart-broken *adj* **be** ~ avere il cuore spezzato

heartburn *n* mal *m* di stomaco

heart disease *n* malattia *f* cardiaca

hearten /'hɑ:t(ə)n/ *vt* rincuorare

heartening /'hɑ:t(ə)nɪŋ/ *adj* rincuorante

heart failure *n* arresto *m* cardiaco

heartfelt /'hɑ:tfelt/ *adj* di cuore

hearth /hɑ:θ/ *n* focolare *m*

hearthrug /'hɑ:θrʌg/ *n* tappeto *m* davanti al camino

heartily /'hɑ:tɪlɪ/ *adv* di cuore; ⟨eat⟩ con appetito; **be** ~ **sick of something** non poterne più di qualcosa

heartland /'hɑ:tlænd/ *n* (industrial, rural) cuore *m*; Pol roccaforte *f*

heartless /'hɑ:tlɪs/ *adj* spietato

heartlessly /'hɑ:tlɪslɪ/ *adv* in modo spietato

heart-lung machine *n* polmone *m* artificiale

heart rate *n* battito *m* cardiaco

heart-rending /-rendɪŋ/ *adj* ⟨sigh, story⟩ straziante

heart-searching *n* esame *m* di coscienza

heart surgeon *n* cardiochirurgo, -a *mf*

heartthrob *n* fam rubacuori *m inv*

heart-to-heart ① *n* conversazione *f* a cuore aperto
② *adj* a cuore aperto

heart transplant *n* trapianto *m* di cuore

heart-warming *adj* toccante

hearty /'hɑ:tɪ/ *adj* caloroso; ⟨meal⟩ copioso; ⟨person⟩ gioviale

heat /hi:t/ ① *n* calore *m*; Sport prova *f* eliminatoria
② *vt* scaldare
③ *vi* scaldarsi
■ **heat up** *vt* scaldare ⟨food, drink⟩; riscaldare ⟨room⟩

heated /'hi:tɪd/ *adj* ⟨swimming pool⟩ riscaldato; ⟨discussion⟩ animato

heater /'hi:tə(r)/ *n* (for room) stufa *f*; (for water) boiler *m inv*; Auto riscaldamento *m*

heath /hi:θ/ *n* brughiera *f*

heat haze *n* foschia *f* (dovuta all'afa)

heathen /'hi:ðn/ *adj* & *n* pagano, -a *mf*

heather /'heðə(r)/ *n* erica *f*

heating /'hi:tɪŋ/ *n* riscaldamento *m*

heat loss *n* perdita *f* di calore

heat-resistant *adj* resistente al calore

heat sink *n* dissipatore *m* termico

heatstroke *n* colpo *m* di sole

heat treatment *n* Med termoterapia *f*

heatwave *n* ondata *f* di calore

heave /hi:v/ ① *vt* tirare; (lift) tirare su; (fam: throw) gettare; emettere ⟨sigh⟩
② *vi* tirare; **my stomach** ~**d** avevo la nausea

heaven /'hev(ə)n/ *n* paradiso *m*; ~ **help you if...** Dio vi scampi se... **raise one's eyes to** ~ alzare gli occhi al cielo; **H**~**s!** santo cielo!

heavenly /'hev(ə)nlɪ/ *adj* celeste; fam delizioso

heaven-sent /-'sent/ *adj* ⟨opportunity⟩ provvidenziale

heavily /'hevɪlɪ/ *adv* pesantemente; ⟨smoke, drink etc⟩ molto

heaviness /'hevɪnɪs/ *n* pesantezza *f*

heavy /'hevɪ/ *adj* (**-ier, -iest**) pesante; ⟨traffic⟩ intenso; ⟨rain, cold⟩ forte; **be a** ~ **smoker/drinker** essere un gran fumatore/bevitore

heavy-duty *adj* ⟨equipment, shoes⟩ molto resistente

heavy goods vehicle *n* veicolo *m* pesante da trasporto

heavy-handed /-'hændɪd/ *adj* (severe) severo; (clumsy) maldestro

heavy industry *n* industria *f* pesante

heavy metal *n* Mus heavy metal *m*

heavyweight *n* peso *m* massimo

Hebrew /'hi:bru:/ *adj* & *n* ebreo

heck /hek/ fam ① *int* cavolo
② *n* **a** ~ **of a lot of** un sacco di; **what the** ~**!** chi se ne frega!; **what the** ~ **is going on?** che cavolo succede?

h

heckle /'hekl/ vt interrompere di continuo

heckler /'heklə(r)/ n disturbatore, -trice mf

hectare /'hekteə(r)/ n ettaro m

hectic /'hektɪk/ adj frenetico

hectoring /'hektərɪŋ/ adj prepotente

hedge /hedʒ/ **1** n siepe f
2 vi fig essere evasivo

hedge-clippers npl cesoie fpl

hedgehog n riccio m

hedgerow n siepe f

hedonism /'hi:dənɪzm/ n edonismo m

hedonistic /hi:də'nɪstɪk/ adj edonistico

heebie-jeebies /hi:bɪ'dʒi:bɪz/ npl fam
give somebody the ∼ far venire i brividi a qualcuno

heed /hi:d/ **1** n pay **∼ to** prestare ascolto a
2 vt prestare ascolto a

heedless /'hi:dlɪs/ adj noncurante

heel[1] /hi:l/ n tallone m; (of shoe) tacco m;
down at ∼ fig trasandato; **take to one's ∼s** fam darsela a gambe

heel[2] vi **∼ over** Naut inclinarsi

heel bar n calzolaio m

hefty /'heftɪ/ adj (**-ier, -iest**) massiccio

heifer /'hefə(r)/ n giovenca f

height /haɪt/ n altezza f; (of plane)
altitudine f; (of season, fame) culmine m

heighten /'haɪt(ə)n/ vt fig accrescere

heinous /'hi:nəs/ adj abominevole

heir /eə(r)/ n erede mf

heiress /eə'res/ n ereditiera f

heirloom /'eəlu:m/ n cimelio m di famiglia

heist /haɪst/ adj Am fam furto m; (armed) rapina f

held /held/ ▶ HOLD[2]

helicopter /'helɪkɒptə(r)/ n elicottero m

heliport /'helɪpɔ:t/ n eliporto m

helium /'hi:lɪəm/ n elio m

helix /'hi:lɪks/ n elica f

hell /hel/ **1** n inferno m; **go to ∼!** sl va' al diavolo!; **make sb's life ∼** rendere la vita infernale a qualcuno
2 int porca miseria!

hell-bent adj **∼ on doing something** deciso a tutti i costi a fare qualcosa

Hellenic /hɪ'lenɪk/ adj ellenico

hellfire /'helfaɪə(r)/ n pene fpl dell'inferno

hell-for-leather adv fam **go ∼** andare a spron battuto

hello /hə'ləʊ/ int & n = HALLO

Hell's angel n Hell's angel m inv

helm /helm/ n timone m; **at the ∼** fig al timone

helmet /'helmɪt/ n casco m

help /help/ **1** n aiuto m; (employee) aiuto m domestico; **that's no ∼** non è d'aiuto
2 vt aiutare; **∼ oneself to something** servirsi di qualcosa; **∼ yourself** (at table) serviti pure; **I could not ∼ laughing** non ho potuto trattenermi dal ridere; **it cannot be ∼ed** non c'è niente da fare; **I can't ∼ it** non ci posso far niente
3 vi aiutare
■ **help out 1** vt dare una mano a
2 vi dare una mano

help desk n help desk m inv

helper /'helpə(r)/ n aiutante mf

helpful /'helpfʊl/ adj (person) di aiuto; (advice) utile

helping /'helpɪŋ/ n porzione f

helping hand n **give somebody a ∼ ∼** dare una mano a qualcuno

helpless /'helplɪs/ adj (unable to manage) incapace; (powerless) impotente

helplessly /'helplɪslɪ/ adv con impotenza; (laugh) incontrollatamente

helpline n assistenza f telefonica

help window n Comput finestrella f di aiuto

helter-skelter /heltə'skeltə(r)/ **1** adv in fretta e furia
2 n scivolo m a spirale nei luna park

hem /hem/ **1** n orlo m
2 vt (pt/pp **hemmed**) orlare
■ **hem in** vt intrappolare

hemisphere /'hemɪsfɪə(r)/ n emisfero m

hemline /'hemlaɪn/ n orlo m

hemlock /'hemlɒk/ n cicuta f

hemophilia n Am = HAEMOPHILIA

hemp /hemp/ n canapa f

hen /hen/ n gallina f; (any female bird) femmina f

hence /hens/ adv (for this reason) quindi; (from now on) a partire da ora; (from here) da qui

henceforth /hens'fɔ:θ/ adv fml (from that time on) da allora in poi; (from now on) d'ora in poi

henchman /'hentʃmən/ n pej tirapiedi m inv

hen-coop n stia f

hen house n pollaio m

henna /'henə/ n hennè m

hen night n fam addio m al nubilato

hen party n fam festa f di addio al nubilato

henpecked /'henpekt/ adj tiranneggiato dalla moglie

hepatitis /hepə'taɪtɪs/ n epatite f

her /hɜː(r)/ **1** poss adj suo m, sua f, suoi mpl, sue fpl; **∼ job/house** il suo lavoro/la sua casa; **her mother/father** sua madre/suo padre
2 pers pron (direct object) la; (indirect object) le; (after prep) lei; **I know ∼** la conosco; **give**

~ the money dalle i soldi; **give it to ~** daglielo; **I came with ~** sono venuto con lei; **it's ~** è lei; **I've seen ~** l'ho vista; **I've seen ~, but not him** ho visto lei, ma non lui

herald /'herəld/ *vt* annunciare

heraldic /he'rældɪk/ *adj* araldico

heraldry /'herəldrɪ/ *n* araldica *f*

herb /hɜ:b/ *n* erba *f*

herbaceous /hɜ:'beɪʃəs/ *adj* erbaceo; **~ border** aiuola *f*

herbal /'hɜ:b(ə)l/ *adj* alle erbe

herbalist /'hɜ:bəlɪst/ *n* erborista *mf*

herbal tea *n* tisana *f*

herb garden *n* aromatario *m*

herbs /hɜ:bz/ *npl* (for cooking) aromi *mpl* [da cucina]; (medicinal) erbe *fpl*

herb tea *n* tisana *f*

herculean /hɜ:kjʊ'li:ən/ *adj* ⟨task⟩ erculeo

herd /hɜ:d/ ① *n* gregge *m*
② *vt* (tend) sorvegliare; (drive) far muovere; fig ammassare
■ **herd together** ① *vi* raggrupparsi
② *vt* raggruppare

here /hɪə(r)/ *adv* qui qua; **in ~** qui dentro; **come/bring ~** vieni/porta qui; **~ is...**, **~ are...** ecco...; **~ you are!** ecco qua!

hereabouts /hɪərə'baʊts/ Br, **hereabout** Am *adv* da queste parti

hereafter *adv* in futuro

here and now *adv* seduta stante *n* **the ~ ~ ~** il presente

hereby *adv* con la presente

hereditary /hɪ'redɪtərɪ/ *adj* ereditario

heredity /hɪ'redətɪ/ *n* ereditarietà *f*

heresy /'herəsɪ/ *n* eresia *f*

heretic /'herətɪk/ *n* eretico, -a *mf*

herewith /hɪə'wɪð/ *adv* Comm con la presente

heritage /'herɪtɪdʒ/ *n* eredità *f*

hermetic /hɜ:'metɪk/ *adj* ermetico

hermetically /hɜ:'metɪklɪ/ *adv* ermeticamente

hermit /'hɜ:mɪt/ *n* eremita *mf*

hernia /'hɜ:nɪə/ *n* ernia *f*

hero /'hɪərəʊ/ *n* (pl **-es**) eroe *m*

heroic /hɪ'rəʊɪk/ *adj* eroico

heroically /hɪ'rəʊɪklɪ/ *adv* eroicamente

heroin /'herəʊɪn/ *n* eroina *f* (droga)

heroin addict *n* eroinomane *mf*

heroine /'herəʊɪn/ *n* eroina *f*

heroism /'herəʊɪzm/ *n* eroismo *m*

heron /'herən/ *n* airone *m*

hero-worship ① *n* culto *m* degli eroi
② *vt* venerare

herpes /'hɜ:pi:z/ *n* herpes *m*

herring /'herɪŋ/ *n* aringa *f*

herringbone /'herɪŋbəʊn/ *adj* ⟨pattern⟩ spigato

hers /hɜ:z/ *poss pron* il suo *m*, la sua *f*, i suoi *mpl*, le sue *fpl*; **a friend of ~** un suo amico; **friends of ~** dei suoi amici; **that is ~** quello è suo; (as opposed to mine) quello è il suo

herself /hə'self/ *pers pron* (reflexive) si; (emphatic) lei stessa; (after prep) sé, se stessa; **she poured ~ a drink** si è versata da bere; **she told me so ~** me lo ha detto lei stessa; **she's proud of ~** è fiera di sé; **by ~** da sola

hesitant /'hezɪtənt/ *adj* esitante

hesitantly /'hezɪtəntlɪ/ *adv* con esitazione

hesitate /'hezɪteɪt/ *vi* esitare

hesitation /hezɪ'teɪʃn/ *n* esitazione *f*

hessian /'hesɪən/ *n* tela *f* di iuta

heterogeneous /hetərə'dʒi:nɪəs/ *adj* eterogeneo

heterosexual /hetərəʊ'sekʃʊəl/ *adj* eterosessuale

het up /het/ *adj* fam agitato

hew /hju:/ *vt* (pt **hewed**, pp **hewed** or **hewn**) spaccare

hexagon /'heksəgən/ *n* esagono *m*

hexagonal /hek'sægənl/ *adj* esagonale

hey /heɪ/ *int* ehi!

heyday /'heɪdeɪ/ *n* tempi *mpl* d'oro

hey presto /heɪ'prestəʊ/ *int* (magic) e voilà!

HGV *abbr* **heavy goods vehicle**

hi /haɪ/ *int* ciao!

hiatus /haɪ'eɪtəs/ *n* (pl **-tuses**) iato *m*

hibernate /'haɪbəneɪt/ *vi* andare in letargo

hibernation /haɪbə'neɪʃn/ *n* letargo *m*

hiccup /'hɪkʌp/ ① *n* singhiozzo *m*; (fam: hitch) intoppo *m*; **have the ~s** avere il singhiozzo
② *vi* fare un singhiozzo

hick /hɪk/ *n* Am fam buzzurro, -a *mf*

hick town *n* Am fam città *f inv* provinciale

hid /hɪd/, **hidden** /'hɪdn/ ▶ HIDE²

hide¹ /haɪd/ *n* (leather) pelle *f* (di animale)

hide² ① *vt* (pt **hid**, pp **hidden**) nascondere
② *vi* nascondersi

hide-and-seek *n* play **~** giocare a nascondino

hideaway /'haɪdəweɪ/ *n* (secluded place) rifugio *m*; (hiding place) nascondiglio *m*

hidebound /'haɪdbaʊnd/ *adj* (conventional) limitato

hideous /'hɪdɪəs/ *adj* orribile

hideously /'hɪdɪəslɪ/ *adv* orribilmente

hideout /'haɪdaʊt/ *n* nascondiglio *m*

hiding[1] /'haɪdɪŋ/ n (fam: beating) bastonata; (defeat) batosta f

hiding[2] n **go into** ~ sparire dalla circolazione

hiding place n nascondiglio m

hierarchic[al] /haɪə'rɑ:kɪk[l]/ adj gerarchico

hierarchy /'haɪərɑ:kɪ/ n gerarchia f

hieroglyphics /haɪərə'glɪfɪks/, **hieroglyphs** npl geroglifici mpl

hi-fi /'haɪfaɪ/ n abbr (**high fidelity**) hi-fi m inv; (set of equipment) impianto m hi-fi, stereo m inv

higgledy-piggledy /hɪgldɪ'pɪgldɪ/ adv alla rinfusa

high /haɪ/ ① adj alto; ‹meat› che comincia ad andare a male; ‹wind› forte; (on drugs) fatto; **it's** ~ **time we did something about it** è ora di fare qualcosa in proposito
② adv in alto; ~ **and low** in lungo e in largo
③ n massimo m; (temperature) massima f; **from on** ~ dall'alto; **be on a** ~ fam essere fatto

high and dry adj fig **leave somebody** ~ ~ ~ piantare in asso qualcuno

high-beam n Am abbagliante m

high-born adj nobile

highbrow adj & n intellettuale mf

high chair n seggiolone m

high-class adj ‹hotel, shop, car› d'alta classe; ‹prostitute› di alto bordo

high command n stato m maggiore

High Commission n alto commissariato m

High Commissioner n alto commissario m

High Court n ≈ Corte f Suprema

high-definition adj ad alta definizione

high-definition television n televisione f ad alta definizione

high diving n tuffo m

high-end adj ‹product, model› della fascia più alta

higher education /haɪəredjʊ'keɪʃn/ n istruzione f universitaria

higher mathematics n matematica f avanzata

highfaluting /haɪfə'lu:tɪŋ/ adj fam ‹ideas› pretenzioso; ‹language› pomposo

high fashion n alta moda f

high-fibre adj ‹diet› ricco di fibre

high-fidelity ① n alta fedeltà f
② adj ad alta fedeltà

high finance n alta finanza f

high-flier n (person) persona f che mira alto

high-flown adj ‹phrases› ampolloso

high-flying adj ‹aircraft› da alta quota; ‹career› ambizioso; ‹person› che mira alto

high-frequency adj alta frequenza f

High German n alto tedesco m

high-grade adj ‹oil, mineral, product› di prima qualità

high ground n collina f; **take the moral** ~ ~ assumere un atteggiamento moralistico

high-handed /-'hændɪd/ adj dispotico

high-handedly /-'hændɪdlɪ/ adv dispoticamente

highheeled /-hi:ld/ adj coi tacchi alti

high heels npl tacchi mpl alti

high jinks /dʒɪŋks/ npl baldoria f

high jump n salto m in alto

Highland games /haɪlənd/ n manifestazione f tradizionale scozzese con gare sportive e musicali

Highlands /'haɪləndz/ npl Highlands fpl (regione della Scozia del nord)

high-level adj ‹talks› ad alto livello; ‹official› di alto livello

high life n bella vita f

highlight /'haɪlaɪt/ ① vt (emphasize, with pen) evidenziare
② n (in art) luce f; (in hair) riflesso m, colpo m di sole; (of exhibition) parte f saliente; (of week, year) avvenimento m saliente; (of match, show) momento m clou

highlighter /'haɪlaɪtə(r)/ n (marker) evidenziatore m

highly /'haɪlɪ/ adv molto; **speak** ~ **of** lodare; **think** ~ **of** avere un'alta opinione di

highly-paid /-'peɪd/ adj ben pagato

highlystrung /-'strʌŋ/ adj nervoso

High Mass n messa f solenne

high-minded /-'maɪndɪd/ adj ‹person› di animo nobile

high-necked /-'nekt/ adj a collo alto

Highness /'haɪnɪs/ n altezza f; **Your** ~ Sua Altezza

high noon n mezzogiorno m in punto

high-performance adj ad alta prestazione

high-pitched /-'pɪtʃt/ adj ‹voice, sound› acuto

high point n momento m culminante

high-powered adj ‹car, engine› molto potente; ‹job› di alta responsabilità; ‹person› dinamico

high pressure ① n Meteorol alta pressione f
② attrib Techn ad alta pressione; ‹job› stressante

high priest n Relig gran sacerdote m; fig guru m inv

high priestess n Relig, fig gran sacerdotessa f

high-principled adj ⟨person⟩ di alti principi

high-profile adj ⟨politician, group⟩ di spicco; ⟨visit⟩ di grande risonanza

high-ranking adj di alto rango

high-rise ① adj ⟨building⟩ molto alto ② n edificio m molto alto

high road n strada f principale

high school n Am ≈ scuola f superiore; Br ≈ scuola f media e superiore

high sea n on the ∼ ∼s in alto mare

high season n alta stagione f

high society n alta società f

high-sounding /-'saʊndɪŋ/ adj ⟨title⟩ altisonante

high-speed adj ⟨train, film⟩ rapido

high-spirited adj pieno di brio

high spirits npl brio m

high spot n momento m culminante

high street n strada f principale

high-street shop n negozio m popolare

high-street spending n acquisto m di beni di consumo

high tea n pasto m pomeridiano servito insieme al tè

high tech /'tek/ n high tech f

high tide n alta marea f

high treason n alto tradimento m

high voltage n alta tensione f

highway /'haɪweɪ/ n public ∼ strada f pubblica

Highway Code n Br Codice m stradale

highwayman n brigante m

highway robbery n brigantaggio m

high wire n filo m (per acrobati)

hijack /'haɪdʒæk/ ① vt dirottare ② n dirottamento m

hijacker /'haɪdʒækə(r)/ n dirottatore, -trice mf

hijacking /'haɪdʒækɪŋ/ n dirottamento m

hike /haɪk/ ① n escursione f a piedi; (in price) aumento m ② vi fare un'escursione a piedi

hiker /'haɪkə(r)/ n escursionista mf

hiking /'haɪkɪŋ/ n escursionismo m

hiking boots npl pedule fpl

hilarious /hɪ'leərɪəs/ adj da morir dal ridere

hilarity /hɪ'lærətɪ/ n ilarità f

hill /hɪl/ n collina f; (mound) collinetta f; (slope) altura f

hill-billy /-bɪlɪ/ n Am montanaro m degli Stati Uniti sudorientali

hillock /'hɪlək/ n poggio m

hillside /'hɪlsaɪd/ n pendio m

hilltop /'hɪltɒp/ n sommità f inv di una collina

hilly /'hɪlɪ/ adj collinoso

hilt /hɪlt/ n impugnatura f; to the ∼ fam ⟨support⟩ fino in fondo; ⟨mortgaged⟩ fino al collo

him /hɪm/ pers pron (direct object) lo; (indirect object) gli; (with prep) lui; I know ∼ lo conosco; give ∼ the money dagli i soldi; give it to ∼ daglielo; I spoke to ∼ gli ho parlato; it's ∼ è lui; she loves ∼ lo ama; she loves ∼, not you ama lui, non te

Himalayas /hɪmə'leɪəz/ npl Himalaia msg

himself /hɪm'self/ pers pron (reflexive) si; (emphatic) lui stesso; (after prep) sé, se stesso; he poured ∼ out a drink si è versato da bere; he told me so ∼ me lo ha detto lui stesso; he's proud of ∼ è fiero di sé; by ∼ da solo

hind /haɪnd/ adj posteriore

hinder /'hɪndə(r)/ vt intralciare

hind legs npl zampe fpl posteriori

hindquarters /'haɪn(d)kwɔːtəz/ npl didietro m

hindrance /'hɪndrəns/ n intralcio m

hindsight /'haɪndsaɪt/ n with ∼ con il senno del poi

Hindu /'hɪnduː/ adj & n indù mf inv

Hinduism /'hɪnduɪzm/ n induismo m

hinge /hɪndʒ/ ① n cardine m ② vi ∼ on fig dipendere da

hint /hɪnt/ ① n (clue) accenno m; (advice) suggerimento m; (indirect suggestion) allusione f; (trace) tocco m ② vt ∼ that... far capire che... ③ vi ∼ at alludere a

hinterland /'hɪntəlænd/ n entroterra m inv, hinterland m inv

hip /hɪp/ n fianco m

hip bone n ileo m

hip flask n fiaschetta f

hippie /'hɪpɪ/ n hippy mf inv

hippo /'hɪpəʊ/ n fam ippopotamo m

hip pocket n tasca f posteriore

Hippocratic oath /hɪpə'krætɪk/ adj giuramento m d'Ippocrate

hippopotamus /hɪpə'pɒtəməs/ n (pl -muses or -mi /hɪpə'pɒtəmaɪ/) ippopotamo m

hip replacement n protesi f inv all'anca

hire /'haɪə(r)/ ① vt affittare; assumere ⟨person⟩; ∼ [out] affittare ② n noleggio m; 'for ∼' 'affittasi'

hire car n macchina f a noleggio

hire purchase n Br acquisto m rateale; on ∼ ∼ a rate

his /hɪz/ ① poss adj suo m, sua f, suoi mpl, sue fpl; ∼ job/house il suo lavoro/la ···}

high-principled ···} his · · ·

h

sua casa; ~ **mother/father** sua madre/suo padre

2) *poss pron* il suo *m*, la sua *f*, i suoi *mpl*, le sue *fpl*; **a friend of** ~ un suo amico; **friends of** ~ dei suoi amici; **that is** ~ questo è suo; (as opposed to mine) questo è il suo

Hispanic /hɪˈspænɪk/ *adj* ispanico

hiss /hɪs/ **1)** *n* sibilo *m*; (of disapproval) fischio *m*
2) *vt* fischiare
3) *vi* sibilare; (in disapproval) fischiare

historian /hɪˈstɔːrɪən/ *n* storico, -a *mf*

historic /hɪˈstɒrɪk/ *adj* storico

historical /hɪˈstɒrɪkl/ *adj* storico

historically /hɪˈstɒrɪklɪ/ *adv* storicamente

history /ˈhɪstərɪ/ *n* storia *f*; **make** ~ passare alla storia

histrionic /hɪstrɪˈɒnɪk/ *adj* istrionico

histrionics /hɪstrɪˈɒnɪks/ *npl* scene *fpl*

hit /hɪt/ **1)** *n* (blow) colpo *m*; (fam: success) successo *m*; **score a direct** ~ ⟨missile⟩ colpire in pieno
2) *vt* (pt/pp **hit**, pres p **hitting**) colpire; ~ **one's head on the table** battere la testa contro il tavolo; **the car** ~ **the wall** la macchina ha sbattuto contro il muro; ~ **the target** colpire il bersaglio; ~ **the nail on the head** fare centro; ~ **the roof** fam perdere le staffe
■ **hit back** *vi* ⟨retaliate⟩ ribattere
■ **hit off** *vt* ~ **it off** andare d'accordo
■ **hit on** *vt* fig trovare

hit-and-miss *adj* ⟨affair, undertaking⟩ imprevedibile; ⟨method⟩ a casaccio

hit-and-run *adj* ⟨raid, attack⟩ lampo *inv*; ⟨accident⟩ causato da un pirata della strada

hit-and-run driver *adj* pirata *m* della strada

hitch /hɪtʃ/ **1)** *n* intoppo *m*; **technical** ~ problema *m* tecnico
2) *vt* attaccare; ~ **a lift** chiedere un passaggio
■ **hitch up** *vt* tirarsi su ⟨trousers⟩

hitch-hike *vi* fare l'autostop

hitchhiker *n* autostoppista *mf*

hitch-hiking *n* autostop *m*

hi-tech *adj* ▶ HIGH TECH

hither /ˈhɪðə(r)/ *adv* ~ **and thither** di qua e di là

hitherto /hɪðəˈtuː/ *adv* finora

hit list *n* lista *f* degli obiettivi

hit man *n* sicario *m*

hit-or-miss *adj* **on a very** ~ **basis** all'improvvista

hit parade *n* hit parade *f inv*, classifica *f*

hit single *n* singolo *m* di successo

HIV *n abbr* (**human immunodeficiency virus**) HIV; ~ **positive** sieropositivo; ~ **negative** sieronegativo

hive /haɪv/ *n* alveare *m*; ~ **of industry** fucina *f* di lavoro
■ **hive off** *vt* Comm separare

HM *abbr* (**Her Majesty** *or* **His Majesty**) SM

HMS *abbr* **His/Her Majesty's Ship**

hoard /hɔːd/ **1)** *n* provvista *f*; (of money) gruzzolo *m*
2) *vt* accumulare

hoarding /ˈhɔːdɪŋ/ *n* palizzata *f*; (with advertisements) tabellone *m* per manifesti pubblicitari

hoar frost /ˈhɔː(r)/ *n* brina *f*

hoarse /hɔːs/ *adj* rauco

hoarsely /ˈhɔːslɪ/ *adv* con voce rauca

hoarseness /ˈhɔːsnɪs/ *n* raucedine *f*

hoary /ˈhɔːrɪ/ *adj* ⟨person⟩ con i capelli bianchi; ~ **old joke** barzelletta *f* vecchia

hoax /həʊks/ *n* scherzo *m*; (false alarm) falso allarme *m*

hoaxer /ˈhəʊksə(r)/ *n* burlone, -a *mf*

hob /hɒb/ *n* piano *m* di cottura

hobble /ˈhɒbl/ *vi* zoppicare

hobby /ˈhɒbɪ/ *n* hobby *m inv*

hobby horse *n* fig fissazione *f*

hobnailed /ˈhɒbneɪld/ *adj* ~ **boots** *pl* scarponi *mpl* chiodati

hobnob /ˈhɒbnɒb/ *v*
■ **hobnob with** *vt* (pt/pp **hobnobbed**) frequentare

hobo /ˈhəʊbəʊ/ *n* Am vagabondo, -a *mf*

hock /hɒk/ *n* vino *m* bianco del Reno

hockey /ˈhɒkɪ/ *n* hockey *m*

hocus-pocus /həʊkəsˈpəʊkəs/ *n* (trickery) trucco *m*

hod /hɒd/ *n* (for coal) secchio *m* del carbone; (for bricks) cassetta *f* (per trasportare mattoni)

hoe /həʊ/ **1)** *n* zappa *f*
2) *vt* (pres p **hoeing**) zappare

hog /hɒg/ **1)** *n* maiale *m*
2) *vt* (pt/pp **hogged**) fam monopolizzare

hog-tie /ˈhɒgtaɪ/ *vt* legare le quattro zampe di ⟨pig, cow⟩; Am fig ostacolare ⟨person⟩

hogwash /ˈhɒgwɒʃ/ *n* fam cretinate *fpl*

hoi polloi /hɔɪpʊˈlɔɪ/ *npl* plebaglia *fsg*

hoist /hɔɪst/ **1)** *n* montacarichi *m inv*; (fam: push) spinta *f* in su
2) *vt* sollevare; innalzare ⟨flag⟩; levare ⟨anchor⟩

hoity-toity /hɔɪtɪˈtɔɪtɪ/ *adj* fam altezzoso

hokum /ˈhəʊkəm/ *n* Am fam (sentimentality) polpettone *m* sentimentale; (nonsense) cretinate *fpl*

hold[1] /həʊld/ *n* Naut, Aeron stiva *f*

hold² ① *n* presa *f*; (fig: influence) ascendente *m*; **get ∼ of** trovare; procurarsi ⟨*information*⟩ ② *vt* (pt/pp **held**) tenere; ⟨*container*⟩ contenere; essere titolare di ⟨*licence, passport*⟩; trattenere ⟨*breath, suspect*⟩; mantenere vivo ⟨*interest*⟩; ⟨*civil servant etc*⟩ occupare ⟨*position*⟩; (retain) mantenere; **∼ sb's hand** tenere qualcuno per mano; **∼ one's tongue** tenere la bocca chiusa; **∼ somebody responsible** considerare qualcuno responsabile; **∼ that** (believe) ritenere che ③ *vi* tenere; ⟨*weather, luck*⟩ durare; ⟨*offer*⟩ essere valido; Teleph restare in linea; **I don't ∼ with the idea that...** fam non sono d'accordo sul fatto che...
■ **hold against** *vt* **∼ something against somebody** avercela con qualcuno per qualcosa
■ **hold back** ① *vt* rallentare ② *vi* esitare
■ **hold down** *vt* tenere a bada ⟨*somebody*⟩
■ **hold on** *vi* (wait) attendere; Teleph restare in linea
■ **hold on to** *vt* aggrapparsi a; (keep) tenersi
■ **hold out** ① *vt* porgere ⟨*hand*⟩; fig offrire ⟨*possibility*⟩ ② *vi* (resist) resistere
■ **hold to** *vt* **∼ somebody to something** far mantenere qualcosa a qualcuno
■ **hold up** *vt* tenere su; (delay) rallentare; (rob) assalire; **∼ one's head up** fig tenere la testa alta

holdall /'həʊldɔːl/ *n* borsone *m*

holder /'həʊldə(r)/ *n* titolare *mf*; (of record) detentore, -trice *mf*; (container) astuccio *m*

holding /'həʊldɪŋ/ *n* (land) terreno *m* in affitto; Comm azioni *fpl*

holding company *n* società *f inv* finanziaria

hold-up *n* ritardo *m*; (attack) rapina *f* a mano armata

hole /həʊl/ *n* buco *m*

hole-in-the-wall *n* fam sportello *m* del Bancomat®

holiday /'hɒlɪdeɪ/ ① *n* vacanza *f*; (public) giorno *m* festivo; (day off) giorno *m* di ferie; **go on ∼** andare in vacanza ② *vi* andare in vacanza

holiday home *n* casa *f* per le vacanze

holiday job *n* (Br: in summer) lavoretto *m* estivo

holiday-maker *n* vacanziere *mf*

holiday resort *n* luogo *m* di villeggiatura

holier-than-thou /həʊlɪəðən'ðaʊ/ *adj* ⟨*attitude*⟩ da santerellino

holiness /'həʊlɪnɪs/ *n* santità *f*; **Your H∼** Sua Santità

Holland /'hɒlənd/ *n* Olanda *f*

holler /'hɒlə(r)/ *vi* urlare (**at** contro)

hollow /'hɒləʊ/ ① *adj* cavo; ⟨*promise*⟩ a vuoto; ⟨*voice*⟩ assente; ⟨*cheeks*⟩ infossato ② *n* cavità *f inv*; (in ground) affossamento *m*
■ **hollow out** *vt* scavare

holly /'hɒlɪ/ *n* agrifoglio *m*

hollyhock /'hɒlɪhɒk/ *n* malvone *m*

holocaust /'hɒləkɔːst/ *n* olocausto *m*

hologram /'hɒləɡræm/ *n* ologramma *m*

holograph /'hɒləɡrɑːf/ *n* documento *m* olografo

hols /hɒlz/ *n* Br fam *abbr* (**holidays**) vacanze *fpl*

holster /'həʊlstə(r)/ *n* fondina *f*

holy /'həʊlɪ/ *adj* (**-ier, -est**) santo; ⟨*water*⟩ benedetto

Holy Bible *n* Sacra Bibbia *f*

Holy Land *n* Terra *f* Santa

Holy Scriptures sacre scritture *fpl*

Holy Ghost, **Holy Spirit** *n* Spirito *m* Santo

Holy Week *n* settimana *f* santa

homage /'hɒmɪdʒ/ *n* omaggio *m*; **pay ∼ to** rendere omaggio a

homburg /'hɒmbɜːɡ/ *n* cappello *m* di feltro

home /həʊm/ ① *n* casa *f*; (for children) istituto *m*; (for old people) casa *f* di riposo; (native land) patria *f* ② *adv* **at ∼** a casa; (football) in casa; **feel at ∼** sentirsi a casa propria; **come/go ∼** venire/andare a casa; **drive a nail ∼** piantare un chiodo a fondo. ③ *adj* domestico; ⟨*movie, video*⟩ casalingo; ⟨*team*⟩ ospitante; Pol nazionale

home address *n* indirizzo *m* di casa

home brew *n* (beer) birra *f* fatta in casa

home cinema [system], **home entertainment system** *n* (sistema di) home cinema *m*

homecoming *n* (return home) ritorno *m* a casa

home computer *n* computer *m inv* da casa

home cooking *n* cucina *f* casalinga

Home Counties *npl* contee *fpl* intorno a Londra

home economics *n* Sch economia *f* domestica

home front *n* (during war) fronte *m* interno; (in politics) politica *f* interna

home game *n* partita *f* in casa

home ground *n* **play on one's ∼ ∼** giocare in casa

home-grown /-'ɡrəʊn/ *adj* ⟨*produce*⟩ del proprio orto; fig nostrano

home help *n* aiuto *m* domestico (per persone non autosufficienti)

homeland *n* patria *f*
homeless /'həʊmlɪs/ *adj* senza tetto
home loan *n* mutuo *m* per la casa
homeloving /'həʊmlʌvɪŋ/ *adj* casalingo
homely /'həʊmlɪ/ *adj* (**-ier, -iest**) *adj*
semplice; ⟨*atmosphere*⟩ familiare; (Am; ugly)
bruttino
home-made *adj* fatto in casa
home market *n* mercato *m* interno
Home Office *n* Br ministero *m* degli
interni
homeopathic /həʊmɪə'pæθɪk/ *adj*
omeopatico
homeopathy /həʊmɪ'ɒpəθɪ/ *n*
omeopatia *f*
homeowner *n* proprietario, -a *mf*
immobiliare
home page *n* Comput home page *f inv*
home rule *n* autogoverno *m*
Home Secretary *n* Br ≈ ministro *m*
degli interni
home shopping *n* acquisti *mpl*
attraverso la televisione
homesick *adj* be ∼ avere nostalgia (**for**
di)
homesickness *n* nostalgia *f* di casa
homestead *n* fattoria *f*
home town *n* città *f inv* natia
home truth *n* tell somebody a few ∼
∼s dirne quattro a qualcuno
home video *n* filmato *m* di
videoamatore
homeward /'həʊmwəd/ ① *adj* di
ritorno
② *adv* ∼[s] verso casa; ∼ **bound** sulla
strada del ritorno; **travel** ∼[s] tornare a
casa
homework /'həʊmwɜːk/ *n* Sch compiti
mpl
homeworker /'həʊmwɜːkə(r)/ *n*
lavoratore, -trice *mf* a domicilio
homeworking /'həʊmwɜːkɪŋ/ *n* lavoro *m*
a domicilio
homey /'həʊmɪ/ *adj* (home-loving)
casalingo; (cosy) accogliente
homicidal /hɒmɪ'saɪdəl/ *adj* omicida
homicide /'hɒmɪsaɪd/ *n* (crime) omicidio
m
homily /'hɒmɪlɪ/ *n* omelia *f*
homing /'həʊmɪŋ/ *adj* ⟨*missile, device*⟩
autoguidato
homing pigeon piccione *f* homing
homoeopathic /həʊmɪə'pæθɪk/ *adj*
omeopatico
homoeopathy /həʊmɪ'ɒpəθɪ/ *n*
omeopatia *f*
homogeneous /hɒmə'dʒiːnɪəs/ *adj*
omogeneo
homogenize /hə'mɒdʒənaɪz/ *vt*
omogeneizzare

homogenous /hə'mɒdʒənəs/ *adj*
omogeneo
homograph /'hɒməɡrɑːf/ *n* omografo *m*
homonym /'hɒmənɪm/ *n* omonimo *m*
homophobia /həʊmə'fəʊbɪə/ *n*
omofobia *f*
homosexual /həʊmə'sekʃʊəl/ *adj* & *n*
omosessuale *mf*
homosexuality /həʊməsekʃʊ'ælɪtɪ/ *n*
omosessualità *f*
Hon. *abbr* (**Honourable**) On.
Honduras /hɒn'djʊərəs/ *n* Honduras *m*
hone /həʊn/ *vt* (sharpen) affilare; (perfect)
affinare
honest /'ɒnɪst/ *adj* onesto; ⟨*frank*⟩
sincero
honestly /'ɒnɪstlɪ/ *adv* onestamente;
(frankly) sinceramente; ∼! ma insomma!
honesty /'ɒnɪstɪ/ *n* onestà *f*; ⟨*frankness*⟩
sincerità *f*
honey /'hʌnɪ/ *n* miele *m*; (fam: darling)
tesoro *m*
honeycomb /'hʌnɪkəʊm/ *n* favo *m*
honeydew melon /'hʌnɪdjuː/ *n*
melone *m* (dalla buccia gialla)
honeymoon /'hʌnɪmuːn/ *n* luna *f* di
miele
honeysuckle /'hʌnɪsʌkl/ *n* caprifoglio
m
honey trap *n* trappola *f* tesa a qualcuno
servendosi di una collaboratrice graziosa
Hong Kong /hɒŋ'kɒŋ/ *n* Hong Kong *f*
honk /hɒŋk/ *vi* Auto clacsonare
honky-tonk /'hɒŋkɪtɒŋk/ *adj* ⟨*piano*⟩
honkytonky *inv*
honor /'ɒnə(r)/ *n* Am = HONOUR
honorary /'ɒnərərɪ/ *adj* onorario
honorific /ɒnə'rɪfɪk/ *adj* onorifico
honour /'ɒnə(r)/ ① *n* onore *m*
② *vt* onorare
honourable /'ɒnərəbl/ *adj* onorevole
honourably /'ɒnərəblɪ/ *adv* con onore
honours degree /'ɒnəz/ *n* ≈ diploma
m di laurea
hood /hʊd/ *n* cappuccio *m*; (of pram)
tettuccio *m*; (over cooker) cappa *f*; Am Auto
cofano *m*
hoodlum /'huːdləm/ *n* teppista *m*
hoodwink /'hʊdwɪŋk/ *vt* fam
infinocchiare
hoody, hoodie /'hʊdɪ/ *n* fam maglia *f*
con cappuccio
hoof /huːf/ *n* (pl ∼**s** or **hooves**) zoccolo
m
hoo-ha /'huːhɑː/ *n* fam **cause a** ∼ fare
scalpore
hook /hʊk/ ① *n* gancio *m*; (for crochet)
uncinetto *m*; (for fishing) amo *m*; **off the** ∼
Teleph staccato; fig fuori pericolo; **by** ∼ **or**
by crook in un modo o nell' altro

2 *vt* agganciare
3 *vi* agganciarsi

hookah /'hʊkə/ *n* narghilè *m inv*

hook and eye *n* gancino *m*

hooked /hʊkt/ *adj* ‹nose› adunco; ∼ **on**
(fam: drugs) dedito a; **be** ∼ **on skiing** essere
un fanatico dello sci

hooker /'hʊkə(r)/ *n* Am sl battona *f*

hookey /'hʊkɪ/ *n* **play** ∼ Am fam marinare
la scuola

hooligan /'huːlɪgən/ *n* teppista *f*

hooliganism /'huːlɪgənɪzm/ *n* teppismo
m

hoop /huːp/ *n* cerchio *m*

hoopla /'huːplɑː/ *n* (Br: at fair) lancio *m*
degli anelli (nei luna park); (Am: fuss)
trambusto *m*

hooray /hʊ'reɪ/ *int* & *n* = HURRAH

hoot /huːt/ **1** *n* colpo *m* di clacson; (of
siren) ululato *m*; (of owl) grido *m*; ∼**s of
laughter** risate *fpl*
2 *vi* ‹owl› gridare; ‹car› clacsonare;
‹siren› ululare; (jeer) fischiare

hooter /'huːtə(r)/ *n* (siren) sirena *f*; Auto
clacson *m inv*; (Br fam: nose) nasone *m*

hoover® /'huːvə(r)/ **1** *n* aspirapolvere *m
inv*
2 *vt* passare l'aspirapolvere su ‹carpet›;
passare l'aspirapolvere in ‹room›
3 *vi* passare l'aspirapolvere

hop¹ /hɒp/ *n* luppolo *m*

hop² **1** *n* saltello *m*: **catch somebody on
the** ∼ fam prendere qualcuno alla
sprovvista
2 *vi* (pt/pp **hopped**) saltellare; ∼ **it!** fam
tela!
■ **hop in** *vi* fam saltar su
■ **hop out** *vi* fam saltar giù; ∼ **out to the
shops** fare un salto ai negozi

hope /həʊp/ **1** *n* speranza *f*; **there's no** ∼
of that happening non c'è nessuna
speranza che succeda
2 *vi* sperare (**for** in); **I** ∼ **so/not** spero di
sì/no
3 *vt* ∼ **that** sperare che

hopeful /'həʊpfʊl/ *adj* pieno di speranza;
(promising) promettente; **be** ∼ **that** avere
buone speranze che

hopefully /'həʊpfʊlɪ/ *adv* con speranza;
(it is hoped) se tutto va bene

hopeless /'həʊplɪs/ *adj* senza speranze;
(useless) impossible; (incompetent) incapace

hopelessly /'həʊplɪslɪ/ *adv*
disperatamente; ‹inefficient, lost›
completamente

hopelessness /'həʊplɪsnɪs/ *n*
disperazione *f*

hopscotch /'hɒpskɒtʃ/ *n* campana *f*
(gioco)

horde /hɔːd/ *n* orda *f*

horizon /hə'raɪzn/ *n* orizzonte *m*; **on the**
∼ all'orizzonte

horizontal /hɒrɪ'zɒntl/ *adj* orizzontale

horizontal bar *n* sbarra *f* orizzontale

horizontally /hɒrɪ'zɒntəlɪ/ *adv*
orizzontalmente

hormonal /hɔː'məʊnəl/ *adj* ormonale;
(moody) lunatico

hormone /'hɔːməʊn/ *n* ormone *m*

hormone replacement therapy *n*
terapia *f* ormonale sostitutiva

horn /hɔːn/ *n* corno *m*; Auto clacson *m inv*

hornet /'hɔːnɪt/ *n* calabrone *m*

horn-rimmed /-rɪmd/ *adj* ‹spectacles›
con la montatura di tartaruga

horny /'hɔːnɪ/ *adj* calloso; (fam: sexually)
arrapato

horoscope /'hɒrəskəʊp/ *n* oroscopo *m*

horrendous /hə'rendəs/ *adj* spaventoso

horrible /'hɒrəbl/ *adj* orribile

horribly /'hɒrəblɪ/ *adv* orribilmente

horrid /'hɒrɪd/ *adj* orrendo

horrific /hə'rɪfɪk/ *adj* raccapricciante; fam
‹accident, prices, story› terrificante

horrify /'hɒrɪfaɪ/ *vt* (pt/pp **-ied**) far
inorridire; **I was horrified** ero inorridito

horrifying /'hɒrɪfaɪɪŋ/ *adj* terrificante

horror /'hɒrə(r)/ *n* orrore *m*

horror film *n* film *m inv* dell'orrore

horror story *n* racconto *m* dell'orrore

hors-d'œuvre /ɔː'dɜːvr/ *n* antipasto *m*

horse /hɔːs/ *n* cavallo *m*
■ **horse around** *vi* fare il pagliaccio

horseback *n* **on** ∼ a cavallo

horseback riding *n* Am equitazione *f*

horsebox *n* furgone *m* per il trasporto
dei cavalli

horse chestnut *n* ippocastano *m*

horsefly *n* tafano *m*

horsehair *n* crine *m* di cavallo

horseman *n* cavaliere *m*

horse manure *n* concime *m*

horseplay *n* gioco *m* pesante

horsepower *n* cavallo *m* [vapore]

horse race *n* corsa *f* ippica

horse racing *n* corse *fpl* di cavalli

horseradish *n* rafano *m*

horseradish sauce *n* salsa *f* di rafano

horseriding *n* equitazione *f*

horseshoe *n* ferro *m* di cavallo

horseshow *n* concorso *m* ippico

hors[e]y /'hɔːsɪ/ *adj* ‹person› che adora i
cavalli; ‹face› cavallino

horticultural /hɔːtɪ'kʌltʃʊrəl/ *adj* di
orticoltura

horticulture /'hɔːtɪkʌltʃə(r)/ *n*
orticoltura *f*

hose /həʊz/ *n* (pipe) manichetta *f*
■ **hose down** *vt* lavare con la
manichetta

hosepipe /'həʊzpaɪp/ *n* manichetta *f*

hosiery /'həʊʒərɪ/ *n* maglieria *f*

hospice /'hɒspɪs/ *n* (for the terminally ill) ospedale *m* per i malati in fase terminale

hospitable /hɒ'spɪtəbl/ *adj* ospitale

hospitably /hɒ'spɪtəblɪ/ *adv* con ospitalità

hospital /'hɒspɪtl/ *n* ospedale *m*

hospitality /hɒspɪ'tælɪtɪ/ *n* ospitalità *f*

hospitalize /'hɒspɪtəlaɪz/ *vt* ricoverare [in ospedale]

host[1] /həʊst/ *n* a ~ of una moltitudine di

host[2] *n* ospite *m*

host[3] *n* Relig ostia *f*

hostage /'hɒstɪdʒ/ *n* ostaggio *m*; **hold somebody** ~ tenere qualcuno in ostaggio

host country *n* paese *m* ospitante

hostel /'hɒstl/ *n* ostello *m*

hostess /'həʊstɪs/ *n* padrona *f* di casa; Aeron hostess *f inv*

hostile /'hɒstaɪl/ *adj* ostile

hostility /hɒ'stɪlɪtɪ/ *n* ostilità *f*; **hostilities** *pl* ostilità *fpl*

hot /hɒt/ *adj* (**hotter, hottest**) caldo; (spicy) piccante; **I am** *or* **feel** ~ ho caldo; **it is** ~ fa caldo; **in** ~ **water** fig nei guai

hot-air balloon *n* mongolfiera *f*

hotbed *n* fig focolaio *m*

hot-blooded /-'blʌdɪd/ *adj* ⟨person⟩ focoso; ⟨reaction⟩ passionale

hot cake *n* **sell like** ~ ~s andare a ruba

hotchpotch /'hɒtʃpɒtʃ/ *n* miscuglio *m*

hot cross bun *n* panino *m* dolce con spezie e uvette, tipicamente pasquale

hot dog *n* hot dog *m inv*

hotdogging *n* sci *m* acrobatico

hotel /həʊ'tel/ *n* hotel *m inv*, albergo *m*

hotelier /həʊ'telɪə(r)/ *n* albergatore, -trice *mf*

hotfoot *adv* hum ⟨go⟩ di gran carriera

hothead *n* persona *f* impetuosa

hot-headed /-'hedɪd/ *adj* impetuoso

hothouse *n* serra *f*

hotline *n* linea *f* diretta; Mil, Pol telefono *m* rosso

hotly /'hɒtlɪ/ *adv* fig accanitamente

hotplate *n* piastra *f* riscaldante

hot seat *n* **be in the** ~ essere in una posizione difficile

hotshot *n* fam persona *f* di successo; pej carrierista *mf*

hot spot *n* (trouble zone) zona *f* calda; (sunny place) luogo *m* assolato

hot tap *n* rubinetto *m* dell'acqua calda

hot-tempered /-'tempəd/ *adj* irascibile

hot-water bottle *n* borsa *f* dell'acqua calda

hound /haʊnd/ ⟨1⟩ *n* cane da caccia *m*

⟨2⟩ *vt* fig perseguire

hour /'aʊə(r)/ *n* ora *f*

hourglass /'aʊəɡlɑ:s/ *n* clessidra *f*

hourly /'aʊəlɪ/ ⟨1⟩ *adj* ad ogni ora; ⟨pay, rate⟩ a ora

⟨2⟩ *adv* ogni ora

house[1] /haʊs/ *n* casa *f*; Pol Camera *f*; Theat sala *f*; **at my** ~ a casa mia, da me

house[2] /haʊz/ *vt* alloggiare ⟨person⟩; incastrare ⟨machine⟩

houseboat *n* casa *f* galleggiante

housebound *adj* costretto in casa

housebreaking *n* furto *m* con scasso

house call *n* visita *f* a domicilio

household *n* casa *f*, famiglia *f*

household appliance *n* elettrodomestico *m*

householder *n* capo *m* di famiglia

household name *n* noto *m*

house husband *n* casalingo *m*

housekeeper *n* governante *f* di casa

housekeeping *n* governo *m* della casa; (money) soldi *mpl* per le spese di casa

House of Commons *n* Camera *f* dei Comuni

House of Lords *n* Camera *f* dei Lord

House of Representatives *n* Camera *f* dei Rappresentanti

house plant *n* pianta *f* da appartamento

house-proud *adj* orgoglioso della propria casa

Houses of Parliament *npl* Parlamento *m*

house-to-house *adj* ⟨search⟩ casa per casa

house-trained /-treɪnd/ *adj* che non sporca in casa

house-warming [party] *n* festa *f* di inaugurazione della nuova casa

housewife *n* casalinga *f*

housework *n* lavori *mpl* domestici

housing /'haʊzɪŋ/ *n* alloggio *m*; Techn alloggiamento *m*

housing estate *n* zona *f* residenziale

hovel /'hɒvl/ *n* tugurio *m*

hover /'hɒvə(r)/ *vi* librarsi; (linger) indugiare; ~ **on the brink of doing something** essere sul punto di fare qualcosa

hovercraft /'hɒvəkrɑːft/ *n* hovercraft *m inv*

how /haʊ/ *adv* come; ~ **are you?** come stai?; ~ **about a coffee/going on holiday?** che ne diresti di un caffè/di andare in vacanza?; ~ **do you do?** molto lieto!; ~ **old are you?** quanti anni hai?; ~ **long** quanto tempo; ~ **many** quanti; ~ **much** quanto; ~ **often** ogni quanto; **and** ~! eccome!; ~ **odd!** che strano!

however /haʊ'evə(r)/ *adv* (nevertheless) comunque; ~ **small** per quanto piccolo

howl /haʊl/ **1** *n* ululato *m* **2** *vi* ululare; (cry with laughter) singhiozzare

howler /'haʊlə(r)/ *n* fam strafalcione *m*

HP *abbr* **hire purchase**; *abbr* (**horse power**) C. V.

HQ *n* Mil *abbr* (**headquarters**) Q.G.

HR *abbr* (**human resources**) RU

HRT *abbr* (**hormone replacement therapy**) TOS *f*

HTML *abbr* (**hypertext markup language**) Comput HTML *m*

HTTP *abbr* (**hypertext transfer protocol**) Comput HTTP *m*

hub /hʌb/ *n* mozzo *m*; fig centro *m*

hubbub /'hʌbʌb/ *n* baccano *m*

hubcap /'hʌbkæp/ *n* coprimozzo *m*

huckleberry /'hʌklbərɪ/ *n* Am mirtillo *m* americano

huddle /'hʌdl/ *vi* ~ **together** rannicchiarsi l'uno contro l'altro

hue[1] /hju:/ *n* colore *m*

hue[2] *n* ~ **and cry** clamore *m*

huff /hʌf/ *n* **be in a/go into a** ~ fare il broncio

hug /hʌg/ **1** *n* abbraccio *m*; **give somebody a** ~ abbracciare qualcuno **2** *vt* (pt/pp **hugged**) abbracciare; (keep close to) tenersi vicino a; aggrapparsi a ⟨wall⟩

huge /hju:dʒ/ *adj* enorme

hugely /'hju:dʒlɪ/ *adv* enormemente

huh /hʌ/ *int* (inquiry) eh?; (in surprise) oh!

hulk /hʌlk/ *n* (of ship, tank etc) carcassa *f*

hulking /'hʌlkɪŋ/ *adj* fam grosso

hull /hʌl/ *n* Naut scafo *m*

hullabaloo /hʌləbə'lu:/ *n* fam (noise) trambusto *m*; (outcry) fracasso *m*

hullo /hə'ləʊ/ *int* = HALLO

hum /hʌm/ **1** *n* ronzio *m* **2** *vt* (pt/pp **hummed**) canticchiare **3** *vi* ⟨motor⟩ ronzare; fig fervere di attività; ~ **and haw** esitare

human /'hju:mən/ **1** *adj* umano **2** *n* essere *m* umano

human being *n* essere *m* umano

humane /hju:'meɪn/ *adj* umano

humanely /hju:'meɪnlɪ/ *adv* umanamente

human interest story *n* storia *f* di vita vissuta

humanitarian /hju:mænɪ'teərɪən/ *adj* & *n* umanitario, -a *mf*

humanities /hju:'mænɪtɪz/ *pl* Univ dottrine *fpl* umanistiche

humanity /hju:'mænətɪ/ *n* umanità *f*

human nature *n* natura *f* umana

human resources *npl* risorse *fpl* umane

human resources manager *n* responsabile *mf* delle risorse umane

humble /'hʌmbl/ **1** *adj* umile **2** *vt* umiliare

humbly /'hʌmblɪ/ *adv* umilmente

humbug /'hʌmbʌg/ *n* (nonsense) sciocchezze *fpl*; (dishonesty) falsità *f*; (Br: sweet) caramella *f* alla menta

humdrum /'hʌmdrʌm/ *adj* noioso

humid /'hju:mɪd/ *adj* umido

humidifier /hju:'mɪdɪfaɪə(r)/ *n* umidificatore *m*

humidity /hju:'mɪdətɪ/ *n* umidità *f*

humiliate /hju:'mɪlɪeɪt/ *vt* umiliare

humiliating /hju:'mɪlɪeɪtɪŋ/ *adj* avvilente

humiliation /hju:mɪlɪ'eɪʃn/ *n* umiliazione *f*

humility /hju:'mɪlətɪ/ *n* umiltà *f*

hummingbird /'hʌmɪŋbɜ:d/ *n* colibrì *m* *inv*

hummock /'hʌmək/ *n* (of earth) poggio *m*

hummus /'hʊməs/ *n* hummus *m*, purè *m* di ceci

humorist /'hju:mərɪst/ *n* umorista *mf*

humorous /'hju:mərəs/ *adj* umoristico

humorously /'hju:mərəslɪ/ *adv* con spirito

humour /'hju:mə(r)/ **1** *n* umorismo *m*; (mood) umore *m*; **have a sense of** ~ avere il senso dell' umorismo **2** *vt* compiacere

hump /hʌmp/ *n* protuberanza *f*; (of camel, hunchback) gobba *f*; **he's got the** ~ sl è di malumore

humpback[ed] bridge /'hʌm(p)bæk[t]/ *n* ponte *m* a schiena d'asino

humus /'hju:məs/ *n* humus *m*

hunch /hʌntʃ/ *n* (idea) intuizione *f*

hunchback /'hʌntʃbæk/ *n* gobbo, -a *mf*

hunched /hʌntʃt/ *adj* ~ **up** incurvato

hundred /'hʌndrəd/ **1** *adj* **one/a** ~ cento **2** *n* cento *m inv*; ~**s of** centinaia di

hundredfold /'hʌndrədfəʊld/ *adv* **increase a** ~ centuplicare

hundredth /'hʌndrədθ/ *adj* & *n* centesimo *m*

hundredweight /'hʌndrədweɪt/ *n* cinquanta chili *m*

hung /hʌŋ/ ▸ HANG

Hungarian /hʌŋ'geərɪən/ *n* & *adj* ungherese *mf*; (language) ungherese *m*

Hungary /'hʌŋgərɪ/ *n* Ungheria *f*

hunger /'hʌŋgə(r)/ *n* fame *f* ■ **hunger for** *vt* aver fame di

hunger strike *n* sciopero *m* della fame

hung-over *adj* be ~ avere i postumi della sbornia

hungrily /'hʌŋɡrɪlɪ/ *adv* con appetito

hungry /'hʌŋɡrɪ/ *adj* (**-ier, -iest**) affamato; **be** ~ aver fame

hung-up *adj* fam (tense) complessato; **be** ~ **on somebody/something** (obsessed) essere fissato con qualcuno/qualcosa

hunk /hʌŋk/ *n* grosso pezzo *m*; (fam: man) figo *m*

hunky-dory /hʌŋkɪ'dɔːrɪ/ *adj* fam perfetto

hunt /hʌnt/ **1** *n* caccia *f*
2 *vt* andare a caccia di ⟨*animal*⟩; dare la caccia a ⟨*criminal*⟩
3 *vi* andare a caccia; ~ **for** cercare

hunter /'hʌntə(r)/ *n* cacciatore *m*

hunting /'hʌntɪŋ/ *n* caccia *f*

hunt saboteur *n* Br sabotatore, -trice *mf* della caccia

huntsman /'hʌntsmən/ *n* (hunter) cacciatore *m*; (fox-hunter) cacciatore *m* di volpe

hurdle /'hɜːdl/ *n* Sport & fig ostacolo *m*

hurdler /'hɜːdlə(r)/ *n* ostacolista *mf*

hurdy-gurdy /hɜːdɪ'ɡɜːdɪ/ *n* organino *m*

hurl /hɜːl/ *vt* scagliare

hurly-burly /hɜːlɪ'bɜːlɪ/ *n* chiasso *m*

hurrah /hʊ'rɑː/ **hurray** /hʊ'reɪ/ **1** *int* urrà!
2 *n* urrà *m*

hurricane /'hʌrɪkən/ *n* uragano *m*

hurried /'hʌrɪd/ *adj* affrettato; ⟨*job*⟩ fatto in fretta

hurriedly /'hʌrɪdlɪ/ *adv* in fretta

hurry /'hʌrɪ/ **1** *n* fretta *f*; **be in a** ~ aver fretta
2 *vi* (pt/pp **-ied**) affrettarsi
■ **hurry up 1** *vi* sbrigarsi
2 *vt* mettere fretta a ⟨*person*⟩; accelerare ⟨*things*⟩

hurt /hɜːt/ **1** *n* male *m*
2 *vt* (pt/pp **hurt**) far male a; (offend) ferire
3 *vi* far male; **my leg** ~**s** mi fa male la gamba

hurtful /'hɜːtfʊl/ *adj* fig offensivo

hurtle /'hɜːtl/ *vi* ~ **along** andare a tutta velocità

husband /'hʌzbənd/ *n* marito *m*

hush /hʌʃ/ *n* silenzio *m*
■ **hush up** *vt* mettere a tacere

hushed /hʌʃt/ *adj* ⟨*voice*⟩ sommesso

hush-hush *adj* fam segretissimo

husky /'hʌskɪ/ *adj* (**-ier, -iest**) ⟨*voice*⟩ rauco

hussar /hʊ'zɑː(r)/ *n* ussaro *m*

hustings /'hʌstɪŋz/ *n* **on the** ~ in campagna elettorale

hustle /'hʌsl/ **1** *vt* affrettare

2 *n* attività *f* incessante; ~ **and bustle** trambusto *m*

hut /hʌt/ *n* capanna *f*

hutch /hʌtʃ/ *n* conigliera *f*

hyacinth /'haɪəsɪnθ/ *n* giacinto *m*

hybrid /'haɪbrɪd/ **1** *adj* ibrido
2 *n* ibrido *m*

hydrangea /haɪ'dreɪndʒə/ *n* ortensia *f*

hydrant /'haɪdrənt/ *n* **[fire]** ~ idrante *m*

hydraulic /haɪ'drɔːlɪk/ *adj* idraulico

hydrocarbon /haɪdrəʊ'kɑːbən/ *n* idrocarburo *m*

hydrochloric /haɪdrə'klɒrɪk/ *adj* ~ **acid** acido *m* cloridrico

hydroelectric /haɪdrəʊɪ'lektrɪk/ *adj* idroelettrico

hydroelectricity /haɪdrəʊlek'trɪsɪtɪ/ *n* energia *f* idroelettrica

hydroelectric power station *n* centrale *f* idroelettrica

hydrofoil /'haɪdrəfɔɪl/ *n* aliscafo *m*

hydrogen /'haɪdrədʒən/ *n* idrogeno *m*

hydrolysis /haɪ'drɒləsɪs/ *n* idrolisi *f*

hydrophobia /haɪdrə'fəʊbɪə/ *n* idrofobia *f*

hydroplane /'haɪdrəpleɪn/ *n* (boat) aliscafo *m*; (Am: seaplane) idrovolante *m*

hydrotherapy /haɪdrəʊ'θerəpɪ/ *n* idroterapia *f*

hyena /haɪ'iːnə/ *n* iena *f*

hygiene /'haɪdʒiːn/ *n* igiene *m*

hygienic /haɪ'dʒiːnɪk/ *adj* igienico

hygienically /haɪ'dʒiːnɪklɪ/ *adv* igienicamente

hymn /hɪm/ *n* inno *m*

hymn book *n* libro *m* dei canti

hype /haɪp/ *n* fam grande pubblicità *f*; **media** ~ battage *m* pubblicitario
■ **hype up** *vt* fam fare grande pubblicità a ⟨*film, star, book*⟩; (exaggerate) gonfiare

hyper /'haɪpə(r)/ *adj* fam eccitato

hyperactive /haɪpər'æktɪv/ *adj* iperattivo

hyperactivity /haɪpəræk'tɪvɪtɪ/ *n* iperattività *f*

hyperbole /haɪ'pɜːbəlɪ/ *n* iperbole *f*

hypercritical /haɪpə'krɪtɪkl/ *adj* ipercritico

hyperlink *n* Comput hyperlink *m inv*, collegamento *m* ipertestuale

hypermarket /'haɪpəmɑːkɪt/ *n* ipermercato *m*

hypersensitive /haɪpə'sensɪtɪv/ *adj* pej permaloso; (physically) ipersensibile

hypertension /haɪpə'tenʃn/ *n* ipertensione *f*

hypertext /'haɪpətekst/ *n* Comput ipertesto *m*

hypertext markup language *n* Comput linguaggio *m* per la marcatura di ipertesti

hypertext transfer protocol *n* Comput protocollo *m* per il trasferimento di ipertesti

hyperventilate /haɪpə'ventɪleɪt/ *vi* iperventilare

hyphen /'haɪfn/ *n* trattino *m*

hyphenate /'haɪfəneɪt/ *vt* unire con trattino

hypnosis /hɪp'nəʊsɪs/ *n* ipnosi *f*

hypnotherapy /hɪpnəʊ'θerəpɪ/ *n* ipnoterapia *f*

hypnotic /hɪp'nɒtɪk/ *adj* ipnotico

hypnotism /'hɪpnətɪzm/ *n* ipnotismo *m*

hypnotist /'hɪpnətɪst/ *n* ipnotizzatore, -trice *mf*

hypnotize /'hɪpnətaɪz/ *vt* ipnotizzare

hypoallergenic /haɪpəʊælə'dʒenɪk/ *adj* anallergico

hypochondria /haɪpə'kɒndrɪə/ *n* ipocondria *f*

hypochondriac /haɪpə'kɒndrɪæk/ *adj* & *n* ipocondriaco, -a *mf*

hypocrisy /hɪ'pɒkrəsɪ/ *n* ipocrisia *f*

hypocrite /'hɪpəkrɪt/ *n* ipocrita *mf*

hypocritical /hɪpə'krɪtɪkl/ *adj* ipocrita

hypocritically /hɪpə'krɪtɪklɪ/ *adv* ipocriticamente

hypodermic /haɪpə'dɜːmɪk/ *adj* & *n* ~ **[syringe]** siringa *f* ipodermica

hypotenuse /haɪ'pɒtənjuːz/ *n* ipotenusa *f*

hypothermia /haɪpəʊ'θɜːmɪə/ *n* ipotermia *f*

hypothesis /haɪ'pɒθəsɪs/ *n* ipotesi *f inv*

hypothetical /haɪpə'θetɪkl/ *adj* ipotetico

hypothetically /haɪpə'θetɪklɪ/ *adv* in teoria; ⟨*speak*⟩ per ipotesi

hysterectomy /hɪstə'rektəmɪ/ *n* isterectomia *f*

hysteria /hɪ'stɪərɪə/ *n* isterismo *m*

hysterical /hɪ'sterɪkl/ *adj* isterico

hysterically /hɪ'sterɪklɪ/ *adv* istericamente; ~ **funny** da morir dal ridere

hysterics /hɪ'sterɪks/ *npl* attacco *m* isterico

i¹, I /aɪ/ *n* (letter) i, I *f inv*

I² /aɪ/ *pron* io; **I'm tired** sono stanco; **he's going, but I'm not** lui va, ma io no

IAP *n abbr* (**internet access provider**) Comput IAP *m*

IBA *n abbr* (**Independent Broadcasting Authority**) organismo *m* indipendente di vigilanza sulla radiotelevisione

ibex /'aɪbeks/ *n* stambecco *m*

ICC *n abbr* (**International Criminal Court**) TPI *m*

ice /aɪs/ **①** *n* ghiaccio *m* **②** *vt* glassare ⟨*cake*⟩ ■ **ice over, ice up** *vi* ghiacciarsi

ice age *n* era *f* glaciale

ice axe *n* piccozza *f* per il ghiaccio

iceberg *n* iceberg *m inv*

icebox *n* Am frigorifero *m*

ice-breaker *n* Naut rompighiaccio *m inv*

ice bucket *n* secchiello *m* del ghiaccio

ice cap *n* calotta *f* glaciale

ice-cold *adj* ghiacciato

ice cream *n* gelato *m*

ice-cream parlour *n* gelateria *f*

ice-cream sundae *n* coppa *f* [di] gelato guarnita

ice cube *n* cubetto *m* di ghiaccio

ice dancer *n* ballerino, -a *mf* sul ghiaccio

ice floe *n* banco *m* di ghiaccio

ice hockey hockey *m* su ghiaccio

Iceland /'aɪslənd/ *n* Islanda *f*

Icelander /'aɪsləndə(r)/ *n* islandese *mf*

Icelandic /aɪs'lændɪk/ *adj* & *n* islandese *m*

ice lolly *n* ghiacciolo *m*

ice pack *n* impacco *m* di ghiaccio

ice pick *n* piccone *m* da ghiaccio

ice rink *n* pista *f* di pattinaggio

ice-skate *n* pattino *m* da ghiaccio

ice-skater pattinatore, -trice *mf* sul ghiaccio

ice-skating pattinaggio *m* sul ghiaccio

ice-tray *n* vaschetta *f* per il ghiaccio

icicle /'aɪsɪkl/ *n* ghiacciolo *m*

icily /'aɪsɪlɪ/ *adv* gelidamente

icing /'aɪsɪŋ/ *n* glassa *f*

icing sugar *n* zucchero *m* a velo

icon /'aɪkɒn/ *n* icona *f*

iconize /'aɪkənaɪz/ *vt* Comput iconizzare

ICT *n abbr* (**information and communication technology**) ICT *f*

icy /'aɪsɪ/ *adj* (**-ier, -iest**) ghiacciato; fig gelido

id /ɪd/ *n* the ∼ l'Es *m*

ID *n abbr* (**identification, identity**) documento *m* d'identità; ∼ **card** *n* carta *f* d'identità

idea /aɪ'dɪə/ *n* idea *f*; **I've no** ∼! non ne ho idea!

ideal /aɪ'dɪəl/ ① *adj* ideale
② *n* ideale *m*

idealism /aɪ'dɪəlɪzm/ *n* idealismo *m*

idealist /aɪ'dɪəlɪst/ *n* idealista *mf*

idealistic /aɪdɪə'lɪstɪk/ *adj* idealistico

idealize /aɪ'dɪəlaɪz/ *vt* idealizzare

ideally /aɪ'dɪəlɪ/ *adv* idealmente

identical /aɪ'dentɪkl/ *adj* identico

identical twin *n* gemello, -a *mf* monozigote

identifiable /aɪdentɪ'faɪəbl/ *adj* identificabile

identification /aɪdentɪfɪ'keɪʃn/ *n* identificazione *f*; (proof of identity) documento *m* di riconoscimento

identify /aɪ'dentɪfaɪ/ ① *vt* (pt/pp **-ied**) identificare
② *vi* ∼ **with** identificarsi con

identikit® /aɪ'dentɪkɪt/ *n* identikit *m inv*

identikit® **picture** *n* identikit *m inv*

identity /aɪ'dentətɪ/ *n* identità *f inv*

identity bracelet *n* braccialetto *m* identificativo

identity card *n* carta *f* d'identità

identity parade *n* confronto *m* all'americana

ideological /aɪdɪə'lɒdʒɪkl/ *adj* ideologico

ideology /aɪdɪ'ɒlədʒɪ/ *n* ideologia *f*

idiocy /'ɪdɪəsɪ/ *n* idiozia *f*

idiom /'ɪdɪəm/ *n* idioma *f*

idiomatic /ɪdɪə'mætɪk/ *adj* idiomatico

idiomatically /ɪdɪə'mætɪklɪ/ *adv* in modo idiomatico

idiosyncrasy /ɪdɪə'sɪŋkrəsɪ/ *n* idiosincrasia *f*

idiosyncratic /ɪdɪəsɪŋ'krætɪk/ *adj* particolare

idiot /'ɪdɪət/ *n* idiota *mf*

idiotic /ɪdɪ'ɒtɪk/ *adj* idiota

idle /'aɪd(ə)l/ ① *adj* (lazy) pigro, ozioso; (empty) vano; ⟨*machine*⟩ fermo
② *vi* oziare; ⟨*engine*⟩ girare a vuoto
■ **idle away** *vt* passare nell'ozio ⟨*day, time*⟩

idleness /'aɪd(ə)lnɪs/ *n* ozio *m*

idly /'aɪdlɪ/ *adv* oziosamente

idol /'aɪd(ə)l/ *n* idolo *m*

idolize /'aɪdəlaɪz/ *vt* idolatrare

idyll /'ɪdɪl/ *n* idillio *m*

idyllic /ɪ'dɪlɪk/ *adj* idillico

i.e. *abbr* (**id est**) cioè

if /ɪf/ *conj* se; **as if** come se

iffy /'ɪfɪ/ *adj* incerto

igloo /'ɪglu:/ *n* igloo *m inv*

ignite /ɪg'naɪt/ ① *vt* dar fuoco a
② *vi* prender fuoco

ignition /ɪg'nɪʃn/ *n* Auto accensione *f*

ignition key *n* chiave *f* d'accensione

ignoramus /ɪgnə'reɪməs/ *n* ignorante *mf*

ignorance /'ɪgnərəns/ *n* ignoranza *f*

ignorant /'ɪgnərənt/ *adj* (lacking knowledge) ignaro; (rude) ignorante

ignore /ɪg'nɔ:(r)/ *vt* ignorare

ill /ɪl/ ① *adj* ammalato; **feel** ∼ **at ease** sentirsi a disagio
② *adv* male
③ *n* male *m*

ill-advised /-əd'vaɪzd/ *adj* avventato

ill-bred /-'bred/ *adj* maleducato

ill-considered /-kən'sɪdəd/ *adj* ⟨*measure, remark*⟩ avventato

ill effect *n* effetto *m* negativo

illegal /ɪ'li:gl/ *adj* illegale

illegality /ɪlɪ'gælətɪ/ *n* illegalità *f*

illegally /ɪ'li:gəlɪ/ *adv* illegalmente

illegible /ɪ'ledʒəbl/ *adj* illeggibile

illegibly /ɪ'ledʒəblɪ/ *adv* in modo illeggibile

illegitimacy /ɪlɪ'dʒɪtɪməsɪ/ *n* illegittimità *f*

illegitimate /ɪlɪ'dʒɪtɪmət/ *adj* illegittimo

ill-equipped /-ɪ'kwɪpt/ *adj* non equipaggiato

ill-fated /-'feɪtɪd/ *adj* sfortunato

ill feeling *n* rancore *m*

ill-fitting *adj* ⟨*garment, shoe*⟩ che non va bene

ill-founded /-'faʊndɪd/ *adj* ⟨*argument, gossip*⟩ infondato

ill-gotten gains /ɪlgɒ(t)n'geɪnz/ *adj* guadagni *mpl* illeciti

ill health *n* problemi *mpl* di salute

illicit /ɪ'lɪsɪt/ *adj* illecito

illicitly /ɪ'lɪsɪtlɪ/ *adv* illecitamente

ill-informed /-ɪn'fɔ:md/ *adj* ⟨*person*⟩ male informato

illiteracy /ɪ'lɪtərəsɪ/ *n* analfabetismo *m*

illiterate /ɪ'lɪtərət/ *adj & n* analfabeta *mf*

ill-mannered /-'mænəd/ *adj* maleducato

illness /'ɪlnɪs/ *n* malattia *f*

illogical /ɪ'lɒdʒɪkl/ *adj* illogico

illogically /ɪ'lɒdʒɪklɪ/ *adv* illogicamente

ill-prepared /-prɪ'peəd/ *adj* impreparato

ill-timed /-'taɪmd/ *adj* ‹*arrival*›
inopportuno; ‹*campaign*› fatto al
momento sbagliato

ill-treat *vt* maltrattare

ill-treatment *n* maltrattamento *m*

illuminate /ɪ'lu:mɪneɪt/ *vt* illuminare

illuminated /ɪ'lu:mɪneɪtɪd/ *adj* ‹*sign*›
luminoso

illuminating /ɪ'lu:mɪneɪtɪŋ/ *adj*
chiarificatore

illumination /ɪlu:mɪ'neɪʃn/ *n*
illuminazione *f*

illuminations *npl* Br luminarie *fpl*

illusion /ɪ'lu:ʒn/ *n* illusione *f*; **be under
the ∼ that** avere l'illusione che

illusory /ɪ'lu:sərɪ/ *adj* illusorio

illustrate /'ɪləstreɪt/ *vt* illustrare

illustration /ɪlə'streɪʃn/ *n* illustrazione *f*

illustrative /'ɪləstrətɪv/ *adj* illustrativo

illustrator /'ɪləstreɪtə(r)/ *n* illustratore,
-trice *mf*

illustrious /ɪ'lʌstrɪəs/ *adj* illustre

ill will *n* malanimo *m*

image /'ɪmɪdʒ/ *n* immagine *f*; (exact
likeness) ritratto *m*

image-conscious *adj* attento
all'immagine

image maker *n* persona *f* che cura
l'immagine

image processing *n* trattamento *m*
dell'immagine

imagery /'ɪmɪdʒərɪ/ *n* immagini *fpl*

imaginable /ɪ'mædʒɪnəbl/ *adj*
immaginabile

imaginary /ɪ'mædʒɪnərɪ/ *adj*
immaginario

imagination /ɪmædʒɪ'neɪʃn/ *n*
immaginazione *f*, fantasia *f*; **it's your ∼** è
solo una tua idea

imaginative /ɪ'mædʒɪnətɪv/ *adj*
fantasioso

imaginatively /ɪ'mædʒɪnətɪvlɪ/ *adv* con
fantasia *or* immaginazione

imagine /ɪ'mædʒɪn/ *vt* immaginare;
(wrongly) inventare

IMAP *abbr* (**Internet mail access
protocol**) Comput protocollo *m* di gestione
remota della posta elettronica

imbalance /ɪm'bæləns/ *n* squilibrio *m*

imbecile /'ɪmbəsi:l/ *n* imbecille *mf*

imbibe /ɪm'baɪb/ ❶ *vt* ingerire; fig
assorbire
❷ *vi* hum bere

imbue /ɪm'bju:/ *vt* **∼d with** impregnato
di

IMF *n abbr* (**International Monetary
Fund**) FMI *m*

imitate /'ɪmɪteɪt/ *vt* imitare

imitation /ɪmɪ'teɪʃn/ *n* imitazione *f*

imitative /'ɪmɪtətɪv/ *adj* imitativo

imitator /'ɪmɪteɪtə(r)/ *n* imitatore, -trice
mf

immaculate /ɪ'mækjʊlət/ *adj*
immacolato

immaculately /ɪ'mækjʊlətlɪ/ *adv*
immacolatamente

immaterial /ɪmə'tɪərɪəl/ *adj* (unimportant)
irrilevante

immature /ɪmə'tʃʊə(r)/ *adj* immaturo

immeasurable /ɪ'meʒərəbl/ *adj*
incommensurabile

immediacy /ɪ'mi:dɪəsɪ/ *n* immediatezza
f

immediate /ɪ'mi:dɪət/ *adj* immediato;
‹*relative*› stretto; **in the ∼ vicinity** nelle
immediate vicinanze

immediately /ɪ'mi:dɪətlɪ/ ❶ *adv*
immediatamente; **∼ next to** subito
accanto a
❷ *conj* [non] appena

immemorial /ɪmɪ'mɔ:rɪəl/ *adj* **from time
∼** da tempo immemorabile

immense /ɪ'mens/ *adj* immenso

immensely /ɪ'menslɪ/ *adv*
immensamente

immensity /ɪ'mensətɪ/ *n* immensità *f*

immerse /ɪ'mɜ:s/ *vt* immergere; **be ∼d
in** fig essere immerso in

immersion /ɪ'mɜ:ʃn/ *n* immersione *f*

immersion course *n* Br corso *m* full
immersion

immersion heater *n* scaldabagno *m*
elettrico

immigrant /'ɪmɪgrənt/ *n* immigrante *mf*

immigrate /'ɪmɪgreɪt/ *vi* immigrare

immigration /ɪmɪ'greɪʃn/ *n*
immigrazione *f*

immigration control *n* controllo *m*
dell'immigrazione

imminence /'ɪmɪnəns/ *n* imminenza *f*

imminent /'ɪmɪnənt/ *adj* imminente

immobile /ɪ'məʊbaɪl/ *adj* immobile

immobilize /ɪ'məʊbɪlaɪz/ *vt*
immobilizzare

immobilizer /ɪ'məʊbɪlaɪzə(r)/ *n* Auto
immobilizzatore *m* elettronico

immoderate /ɪ'mɒdərət/ *adj* smodato

immodest /ɪ'mɒdɪst/ *adj* immodesto

immoral /ɪ'mɒrəl/ *adj* immorale

immorality /ɪmə'rælətɪ/ *n* immoralità *f*

immortal /ɪ'mɔ:tl/ *adj* immortale

immortality /ɪmɔ:'tælətɪ/ *n* immortalità
f

immortalize /ɪ'mɔ:təlaɪz/ *vt*
immortalare

immovable /ɪ'mu:vəbl/ *adj* fig
irremovibile

immune /ɪ'mjuːn/ adj immune (**to/from** da)

immune system n sistema m immunitario

immunity /ɪ'mjuːnətɪ/ n immunità f

immunization /ɪmjʊnaɪ'zeɪʃn/ n immunizzazione f

immunize /'ɪmjʊnaɪz/ vt immunizzare

immunodeficiency /ɪmjʊnəʊdɪ'fɪʃənsɪ/ n immunodeficienza f

immunodepressant /ɪmjʊnəʊdɪ'pres(ə)nt/ **1** adj immunodepressivo **2** n immunodepressivo m

immunology /ɪmjʊ'nɒlədʒɪ/ n immunologia f

immutable /ɪ'mjuːtəbl/ adj immutabile

imp /ɪmp/ n diavoletto m

impact /'ɪmpækt/ n impatto m

impacted /ɪm'pæktɪd/ adj ⟨tooth⟩ incluso; ⟨fracture⟩ incuneato

impair /ɪm'peə(r)/ vt danneggiare

impaired /ɪm'peəd/ adj hearing ~ audioleso: **visually** ~ videoleso

impale /ɪm'peɪl/ vt impalare

impalpable /ɪm'pælpəbl/ adj (intangible) impalpabile

impart /ɪm'pɑːt/ vt impartire

impartial /ɪm'pɑːʃəl/ adj imparziale

impartiality /ɪmpɑːʃɪ'ælətɪ/ n imparzialità f

impassable /ɪm'pɑːsəbl/ adj impraticabile

impasse /æm'pɑːs/ n fig impasse f inv

impassioned /ɪm'pæʃnd/ adj appassionato

impassive /ɪm'pæsɪv/ adj impassibile

impassively /ɪm'pæsɪvlɪ/ adv impassibilmente

impatience /ɪm'peɪʃns/ n impazienza f

impatient /ɪm'peɪʃnt/ adj impaziente

impatiently /ɪm'peɪʃntlɪ/ adv impazientemente

impeach /ɪm'piːtʃ/ vt accusare

impeccable /ɪm'pekəbl/ adj impeccabile

impeccably /ɪm'pekəblɪ/ adv in modo impeccabile

impede /ɪm'piːd/ vt impedire

impediment /ɪm'pedɪmənt/ n impedimento m; (in speech) difetto m

impel /ɪm'pel/ vt (pt/pp **impelled**) costringere; **feel ~led** to sentire l'obbligo di

impending /ɪm'pendɪŋ/ adj imminente

impenetrable /ɪm'penɪtrəbl/ adj impenetrabile

imperative /ɪm'perətɪv/ **1** adj imperativo

2 n Gram imperativo m

imperceptible /ɪmpə'septəbl/ adj impercettibile

imperfect /ɪm'pɜːfɪkt/ **1** adj imperfetto; (faulty) difettoso

2 n Gram imperfetto m

imperfection /ɪmpə'fekʃn/ n imperfezione f

imperial /ɪm'pɪərɪəl/ adj imperiale

imperialism /ɪm'pɪərɪəlɪzm/ n imperialismo m

imperialist /ɪm'pɪərɪəlɪst/ n imperialista mf

imperil /ɪm'perəl/ vt (pt/pp **imperilled**) mettere in pericolo

imperious /ɪm'pɪərɪəs/ adj imperioso

imperiously /ɪm'pɪərɪəslɪ/ adv in modo imperioso

impermeable /ɪm'pɜːmɪəbl/ adj impermeabile

impersonal /ɪm'pɜːsənəl/ adj impersonale

impersonate /ɪm'pɜːsəneɪt/ vt impersonare

impersonation /ɪmpɜːsə'neɪʃn/ n imitazione f

impersonator /ɪm'pɜːsəneɪtə(r)/ n imitatore, -trice mf

impertinence /ɪm'pɜːtɪnəns/ n impertinenza f

impertinent /ɪm'pɜːtɪnənt/ adj impertinente

imperturbable /ɪmpə'tɜːbəbl/ adj imperturbabile

impervious /ɪm'pɜːvɪəs/ adj ~ **to** fig indifferente a

impetuous /ɪm'petjʊəs/ adj impetuoso

impetuously /ɪm'petjʊəslɪ/ adv impetuosamente

impetus /'ɪmpɪtəs/ n impeto m

impiety /ɪm'paɪətɪ/ n Relig empietà f

impinge /ɪm'pɪndʒ/ v
■ **impinge on** vt (affect) influire su; (restrict) condizionare

impious /'ɪmpɪəs/ adj Relig empio

impish /'ɪmpɪʃ/ adj birichino

implacable /ɪm'plækəbl/ adj implacabile

implant¹ /ɪm'plɑːnt/ vt trapiantare; fig inculcare

implant² /'ɪmplɑːnt/ n trapianto m

implausible /ɪm'plɔːzəbl/ adj poco plausibile

implement¹ /'ɪmplɪmənt/ n attrezzo m

implement² /'ɪmplɪment/ vt mettere in atto

implementation /ɪmplɪmən'teɪʃn/ n (of law, policy, idea) attuazione f; Comput implementazione f

implicate /'ɪmplɪkeɪt/ vt implicare

implication /ˌɪmplɪˈkeɪʃn/ *n*
implicazione *f*; **by** ∼ implicitamente

implicit /ɪmˈplɪsɪt/ *adj* implicito;
(absolute) assoluto

implicitly /ɪmˈplɪsɪtlɪ/ *adv*
implicitamente; (absolutely) completamente

implied /ɪmˈplaɪd/ *adj* implicito,
sottinteso

implore /ɪmˈplɔː(r)/ *vt* implorare

imploring /ɪmˈplɔːrɪŋ/ *adj* implorante

implosion /ɪmˈpləʊʒn/ *n* implosione *f*

imply /ɪmˈplaɪ/ *vt* (pt/pp **-ied**) implicare;
what are you ∼**ing?** che cosa vorresti
insinuare?

impolite /ɪmpəˈlaɪt/ *adj* sgarbato

impolitely /ɪmpəˈlaɪtlɪ/ *adv*
sgarbatamente

import[1] /ˈɪmpɔːt/ *n* Comm importazione *f*;
(importance) importanza *f*; (meaning)
rilevanza *f*

import[2] /ɪmˈpɔːt/ *vt* importare

importance /ɪmˈpɔːtəns/ *n* importanza *f*

important /ɪmˈpɔːtənt/ *adj* importante

importation /ɪmpɔːˈteɪʃn/ *n* Comm
importazione *f*

import duty /ˈɪmpɔːt/ *n* dazio *m*
d'importazione

importer /ɪmˈpɔːtə(r)/ *n* importatore,
-trice *mf*

import-export /ˈɪmpɔːtˈekspɔːt/ *n*
import-export *m*

importing country /ɪmˈpɔːtɪŋ/ *n* paese
m di importazione

impose /ɪmˈpəʊz/ **1** *vt* imporre (**on** a)
2 *vi* imporsi; ∼ **on** abusare di

imposing /ɪmˈpəʊzɪŋ/ *adj* imponente

imposition /ɪmpəˈzɪʃn/ *n* imposizione *f*

impossibility /ɪmˈpɒsɪbɪlətɪ/ *n*
impossibilità *f*

impossible /ɪmˈpɒsəbl/ *adj* impossibile

impossibly /ɪmˈpɒsəblɪ/ *adv*
impossibilmente

impostor /ɪmˈpɒstə(r)/ *n* impostore, -a
mf

impotence /ˈɪmpətəns/ *n* impotenza *f*

impotent /ˈɪmpətənt/ *adj* impotente

impound /ɪmˈpaʊnd/ *vt* confiscare

impoverished /ɪmˈpɒvərɪʃt/ *adj*
impoverito

impracticable /ɪmˈpræktɪkəbl/ *adj*
impraticabile

impractical /ɪmˈpræktɪkl/ *adj* non
pratico

imprecise /ɪmprɪˈsaɪs/ *adj* impreciso

impregnable /ɪmˈpregnəbl/ *adj*
imprendibile

impregnate /ˈɪmpregneɪt/ *vt*
impregnare (**with** di); Biol fecondare

impresario /ɪmprɪˈsɑːrɪəʊ/ *n* (pl **-os**)
impresario *m* (di spettacoli)

impress /ɪmˈpres/ *vt* imprimere; fig
colpire (positivamente); ∼ **something**
[**up**]**on somebody** fare capire qualcosa a
qualcuno

impression /ɪmˈpreʃn/ *n* impressione *f*;
(imitation) imitazione *f*

impressionable /ɪmˈpreʃənəbl/ *adj*
⟨*child, mind*⟩ influenzabile

impressionism /ɪmˈpreʃənɪzm/ *n*
impressionismo *m*

impressionist /ɪmˈpreʃənɪst/ *n*
imitatore, -trice *mf*; (artist) impressionista
mf

impressionistic /ɪmpreʃəˈnɪstɪk/ *adj*
impressionista; ⟨*account*⟩ approssimativo

impressive /ɪmˈpresɪv/ *adj* imponente

imprint[1] /ˈɪmprɪnt/ *n* impressione *f*

imprint[2] /ɪmˈprɪnt/ *vt* imprimere; ∼**ed**
on my mind impresso nella mia memoria

imprison /ɪmˈprɪzən/ *vt* incarcerare

imprisonment /ɪmˈprɪzənmənt/ *n*
reclusione *f*

improbable /ɪmˈprɒbəbl/ *adj*
improbabile

impromptu /ɪmˈprɒmptjuː/ **1** *adj*
improvvisato
2 *adv* in modo improvvisato

improper /ɪmˈprɒpə(r)/ *adj* ⟨*use*⟩
improprio; ⟨*behaviour*⟩ scorretto

improperly /ɪmˈprɒpəlɪ/ *adv*
scorrettamente

impropriety /ɪmprəˈpraɪətɪ/ *n*
scorrettezza *f*

improve /ɪmˈpruːv/ *vt/i* migliorare
■ **improve** [**up**]**on** *vt* perfezionare

improvement /ɪmˈpruːvmənt/ *n*
miglioramento *m*

improvident /ɪmˈprɒvɪdənt/ *adj*
(heedless of the future) imprevidente

improvisation /ɪmprəvaɪˈzeɪʃn/ *n*
improvvisazione *f*

improvise /ˈɪmprəvaɪz/ *vt/i*
improvvisare

imprudent /ɪmˈpruːdənt/ *adj*
imprudente

impudence /ˈɪmpjʊdəns/ *n* sfrontatezza
f

impudent /ˈɪmpjʊdənt/ *adj* sfrontato

impudently /ˈɪmpjʊdəntlɪ/ *adv*
sfrontatamente

impulse /ˈɪmpʌls/ *n* impulso *m*; **on** [**an**]
∼ impulsivamente

impulse buy *n* acquisto *m* d'impulso

impulse buying *n* acquisti *mpl* fatti
d'impulso

impulsive /ɪmˈpʌlsɪv/ *adj* impulsivo

impulsively /ɪmˈpʌlsɪvlɪ/ *adv*
impulsivamente

impunity /ɪm'pju:nətɪ/ *n* with ~
impunemente

impure /ɪm'pjʊə(r)/ *adj* impuro

impurity /ɪm'pjʊərətɪ/ *n* impurità *f inv*;
impurities *pl* impurità *fpl*

impute /ɪm'pju:t/ *vt* imputare (**to** a)

in /ɪn/ **1** *prep* in; (with names of towns) a; **in
the garden** in giardino; **in the street** in or
per strada; **in bed/hospital** a letto/
all'ospedale; **in the world** nel mondo; **in
the rain** sotto la pioggia; **in the sun** al sole;
in this heat con questo caldo; **in summer/
winter** in estate/inverno; **in 1995** nel 1995;
in the evening la sera; **he's arriving in two
hours' time** arriva fra due ore; **deaf in one
ear** sordo da un orecchio; **in the army**
nell'esercito; **in English/Italian** in inglese/
italiano; **in ink/pencil** a penna/matita; **in
red** ⟨*dressed, circled*⟩ di rosso; **the man in
the raincoat** l'uomo con l'impermeabile; **in
a soft/loud voice** a voce bassa/alta; **one in
ten people** una persona su dieci; **in doing
this, he...** nel far questo,...; **in itself** in sé;
in that in quanto
2 *adv* (at home) a casa; (indoors) dentro;
he's not in yet non è ancora arrivato; **in
there/here** lì/qui dentro; **ten in all** dieci in
tutto; **day in, day out** giorno dopo giorno;
have it in for somebody fam avercela con
qualcuno; **send him in** fallo entrare; **come
in** entrare; **bring in the washing** portare
dentro i panni
3 *adj* (fam: in fashion) di moda
4 *n* **the ins and outs** i dettagli

in. *abbr* (**inch**) pollice *m*

inability /ɪnə'bɪlətɪ/ *n* incapacità *f*

inaccessible /ɪnæk'sesəbl/ *adj*
inaccessibile

inaccuracy /ɪn'ækjʊrəsɪ/ *n* inesattezza
f

inaccurate /ɪn'ækjʊrət/ *adj* inesatto

inaccurately /ɪn'ækjʊrətlɪ/ *adv* in
modo inesatto

inaction /ɪn'ækʃn/ *n* (not being active)
inazione *f*; (failure to act) inerzia *f*

inactive /ɪn'æktɪv/ *adj* inattivo

inactivity /ɪnæk'tɪvətɪ/ *n* inattività *f*

inadequacy /ɪn'ædɪkwəsɪ/ *n*
inadeguatezza *f*

inadequate /ɪn'ædɪkwət/ *adj*
inadeguato

inadequately /ɪn'ædɪkwətlɪ/ *adv*
inadeguatamente

inadmissible /ɪnæd'mɪsəbl/ *adj*
inammissibile

inadvertent /ɪnəd'vɜ:tənt/ *adj*
involontario

inadvertently /ɪnəd'vɜ:təntlɪ/ *adv*
inavvertitamente

inadvisable /ɪnæd'vaɪzəbl/ *adj*
sconsigliabile

inalienable /ɪn'eɪlɪənəbl/ *adj*
inalienabile

inane /ɪ'neɪn/ *adj* futile

inanely /ɪ'neɪnlɪ/ *adv* in modo vacuo

inanimate /ɪn'ænɪmət/ *adj* esanime

inanity /ɪ'nænətɪ/ *n* stupidità *f inv*

inapplicable /mə'plɪkəbl/ *adj*
inapplicabile

inappropriate /mə'prəʊprɪət/ *adj*
inadatto

inapt /ɪn'æpt/ *adj* (inappropriate)
inappropriato

inarticulate /mɑ:tɪkjʊlət/ *adj*
inarticolato

inasmuch /məz'mʌtʃ/ *conj* ~ **as** (insofar
as) in quanto; (seeing that) poiché

inattention /mə'tenʃn/ *n* disattenzione
f

inattentive /mə'tentɪv/ *adj* disattento

inaudible /ɪn'ɔ:dəbl/ *adj* impercettibile

inaudibly /ɪn'ɔ:dəblɪ/ *adv* in modo
impercettibile

inaugural /ɪ'nɔ:gjʊrəl/ *adj* inaugurale

inaugurate /ɪ'nɔ:gjʊreɪt/ *vt* inaugurare

inauguration /mɔ:gjʊ'reɪʃn/ *n*
inaugurazione *f*

inauspicious /mɔ:'spɪʃəs/ *adj* infausto

in-between *adj* intermedio

inborn /'mbɔ:n/ *adj* innato

inbred /m'bred/ *adj* congenito

inbreeding /m'bri:dɪŋ/ *n* (in animals)
inbreeding *m*; (in humans) unioni *mpl* fra
consanguinei

inbuilt /m'bɪlt/ *adj* ⟨*feeling*⟩ innato

Inc. *abbr* (**Incorporated**) Spa *f*

incalculable /m'kælkjʊləbl/ *adj*
incalcolabile

incandescence /mkæn'desəns/ *n* liter
incandescenza *f*

incandescent /mkæn'desənt/ *adj* liter
incandescente

incapable /m'keɪpəbl/ *adj* incapace

incapacitate /mkə'pæsɪteɪt/ *vt* rendere
incapace

incapacity /mkə'pæsətɪ/ *n* also Jur
incapacità *f*

incarcerate /m'kɑ:səreɪt/ *vt*
incarcerare

incarnate /m'kɑ:nət/ *adj* **the devil** ~ il
diavolo in carne e ossa

incarnation /mkɑ:'neɪʃn/ *n*
incarnazione *f*

incendiary /m'sendɪərɪ/ **1** *adj*
incendiario
2 *n* ~ **[bomb]** bomba *f* incendiaria

incendiary device *n* ordigno *m*
incendiario

incense[1] /'msens/ *n* incenso *m*-

incense[2] /m'sens/ *vt* esasperare

incensed /ɪnˈsenst/ *adj* furibondo

incentive /ɪnˈsentɪv/ *n* incentivo *m*

incentive scheme *n* piano *m* di incentivi

inception /ɪnˈsepʃn/ *n* inizio *m*

incessant /ɪnˈsesənt/ *adj* incessante

incessantly /ɪnˈsesəntlɪ/ *adv* incessantemente

incest /ˈɪnsest/ *n* incesto *m*

incestuous /ɪnˈsestjʊəs/ *adj* incestuoso

inch /ɪntʃ/ **1** *n* pollice *m* (= 2,54 cm)
2 *vi* ~ **forward** avanzare gradatamente

incidence /ˈɪnsɪdəns/ *n* incidenza *f*

incident /ˈɪnsɪdənt/ *n* incidente *m*

incidental /ɪnsɪˈdentl/ *adj* incidentale;
~ **expenses** spese *fpl* accessorie

incidentally /ɪnsɪˈdent(ə)lɪ/ *adv* incidentalmente; (by the way) a proposito

incident room *n* (for criminal investigation) centrale *f* operativa

incinerate /ɪnˈsɪnəreɪt/ *vt* incenerire

incinerator /ɪnˈsɪnəreɪtə(r)/ *n* inceneritore *m*

incipient /ɪnˈsɪpɪənt/ *adj* incipiente

incision /ɪnˈsɪʒn/ *n* incisione *f*

incisive /ɪnˈsaɪsɪv/ *adj* incisivo

incisor /ɪnˈsaɪzə(r)/ *n* incisivo *m*

incite /ɪnˈsaɪt/ *vt* incitare

incitement /ɪnˈsaɪtmənt/ *n* incitamento *m*

incivility /ɪnsɪˈvɪlətɪ/ *n* scortesia *f*

incl *abbr* **inclusive**; *abbr* **including**

inclement /ɪnˈklemənt/ *adj* inclemente

inclination /ɪnklɪˈneɪʃn/ *n* inclinazione *f*

incline[1] /ɪnˈklaɪn/ **1** *vt* inclinare; **be** ~**d to do something** essere propenso a fare qualcosa
2 *vi* inclinarsi

incline[2] /ˈɪnklaɪn/ *n* pendio *m*

include /ɪnˈkluːd/ *vt* includere

including /ɪnˈkluːdɪŋ/ *prep* incluso

inclusion /ɪnˈkluːʒn/ *n* inclusione *f*

inclusive /ɪnˈkluːsɪv/ **1** *adj* incluso; ~ **of** comprendente; **be** ~ **of** comprendere. **2** *adv* incluso

incognito /ɪnkɒgˈniːtəʊ/ *adv* incognito

incoherent /ɪnkəˈhɪərənt/ *adj* incoerente; (because drunk etc) incomprensibile

incoherently /ɪnkəˈhɪərəntlɪ/ *adv* incoerentemente; (because drunk etc) incomprensibilmente

income /ˈɪnkəm/ *n* reddito *m*

income bracket *n* fascia *f* di reddito

income tax *n* imposta *f* sul reddito

income tax return *n* dichiarazione *f* dei redditi

incoming /ˈɪnkʌmɪŋ/ *adj* in arrivo; ~ **tide** marea *f* montante

incommunicado /ɪnkəmjuːnɪˈkɑːdəʊ/ *adj* (involuntarily) segregato; **he's** ~ (in meeting) non vuole essere disturbato

incomparable /ɪnˈkɒmp(ə)rəbl/ *adj* incomparabile

incompatibility /ɪnkəmpætɪˈbɪlətɪ/ *n* incompatibilità *f*

incompatible /ɪnkəmˈpætəbl/ *adj* incompatibile

incompetence /ɪnˈkɒmpɪtəns/ *n* incompetenza *f*

incompetent /ɪnˈkɒmpɪtənt/ *adj* incompetente

incomplete /ɪnkəmˈpliːt/ *adj* incompleto

incomprehensible /ɪnkɒmprɪˈhensəbl/ *adj* incomprensibile

inconceivable /ɪnkənˈsiːvəbl/ *adj* inconcepibile

inconclusive /ɪnkənˈkluːsɪv/ *adj* inconcludente

incongruity /ɪnkɒŋˈgruːətɪ/ *n* (of appearance) contrasto *m*; (of situation) assurdità *f inv*

incongruous /ɪnˈkɒŋgrʊəs/ *adj* contrastante

inconsequential /ɪnkɒnsɪˈkwenʃl/ *adj* senza importanza

inconsiderate /ɪnkənˈsɪdərət/ *adj* trascurabile

inconsistency /ɪnkənˈsɪstənsɪ/ *n* incoerenza *f*

inconsistent /ɪnkənˈsɪstənt/ *adj* incoerente; **be** ~ **with** non essere coerente con

inconsistently /ɪnkənˈsɪstəntlɪ/ *adv* in modo incoerente

inconsolable /ɪnkənˈsəʊləbl/ *adj* inconsolabile

inconspicuous /ɪnkənˈspɪkjʊəs/ *adj* non appariscente

inconspicuously /ɪnkənˈspɪkjʊəslɪ/ *adv* modestamente

inconstancy /ɪnˈkɒnstənsɪ/ *n* incostanza *f*

inconstant /ɪnˈkɒnstənt/ *adj* ‹conditions› variabile; ‹lover› volubile

incontestable /ɪnkənˈtestəbl/ *adj* incontestabile

incontinence /ɪnˈkɒntɪnəns/ *n* incontinenza *f*

incontinent /ɪnˈkɒntɪnənt/ *adj* incontinente

inconvenience /ɪnkənˈviːnɪəns/ *n* scomodità *f*; (drawback) inconveniente *m*; **put somebody to** ~ dare disturbo a qualcuno

inconvenient /ɪnkənˈviːnɪənt/ *adj* scomodo; ‹time, place› inopportuno

inconveniently /ɪnkən'vi:nɪəntlɪ/ *adv* in modo inopportuno

incorporate /ɪn'kɔːpəreɪt/ *vt* incorporare; (contain) comprendere

Incorrect /ɪnkə'rekt/ *adj* incorretto

incorrectly /ɪnkə'rektlɪ/ *adv* scorrettamente

incorrigible /ɪn'kɒrɪdʒəbl/ *adj* incorreggibile

incorruptible /ɪnkə'rʌptəbl/ *adj* incorruttibile

increase[1] /'ɪnkri:s/ *n* aumento *m*; **on the** ~ in aumento

increase[2] /ɪn'kri:s/ *vt/i* aumentare

increased *adj* ⟨demand, risk⟩ maggiore

increasing /ɪn'kri:sɪŋ/ *adj* ⟨impatience etc⟩ crescente; ⟨numbers⟩ in aumento

increasingly /ɪn'kri:sɪŋlɪ/ *adv* sempre più

incredible /ɪn'kredəbl/ *adj* incredibile

incredibly /ɪn'kredəblɪ/ *adv* incredibilmente

incredulity /ɪnkrə'dju:lətɪ/ *n* incredulità *f*

incredulous /ɪn'kredjʊləs/ *adj* incredulo

increment /'ɪnkrɪmənt/ *n* incremento *m*

incremental /ɪnkrɪ'mentəl/ *adj* Comput, Math incrementale; ⟨effect, measures⟩ progressivo

incriminate /ɪn'krɪmɪneɪt/ *vt* Jur incriminare

incriminating /ɪn'krɪmɪneɪtɪŋ/ *adj* ⟨evidence⟩ incriminante

in-crowd *n* **be in with the** ~ frequentare gente alla moda

incubate /'ɪŋkjʊbeɪt/ *vt* incubare

incubation /ɪŋkjʊ'beɪʃn/ *n* incubazione *f*

incubation period *n* Med periodo *m* di incubazione

incubator /'ɪŋkjʊbeɪtə(r)/ *n* (for baby) incubatrice *f*

inculcate /'ɪŋkʌlkeɪt/ *vt* inculcare

incumbent /ɪn'kʌmbənt/ *adj* **be** ~ **on** somebody incombere a qualcuno

incur /ɪn'kɜː(r)/ *vt* (pt/pp **incurred**) incorrere; contrarre ⟨debts⟩

incurable /ɪn'kjʊərəbl/ *adj* incurabile

incurably /ɪn'kjʊərəblɪ/ *adv* incurabilmente

incursion /ɪn'kɜːʃn/ *n* incursione *f*

indebted /ɪn'detɪd/ *adj* obbligato (**to** verso)

indecency /ɪn'di:sənsɪ/ *n* oscenità *f*; (offence) atti *mpl* osceni; **gross** ~ atti *mpl* osceni

indecent /ɪn'di:sənt/ *adj* indecente

indecent assault *n* atti *mpl* di libidine violenta

indecent exposure *n* esibizionismo *m* (dei genitali)

indecipherable /ɪndɪ'saɪfərəbl/ *adj* indecifrabile

indecision /ɪndɪ'sɪʒn/ *n* indecisione *f*

indecisive /ɪndɪ'saɪsɪv/ *adj* indeciso

indecisiveness /ɪndɪ'saɪsɪvnɪs/ *n* indecisione *f*

indeed /ɪn'di:d/ *adv* (in fact) difatti; **yes** ~! sì, certamente!; ~ **I am/do** veramente!; **very much** ~ moltissimo; **thank you very much** ~ grazie infinite; ~? davvero?

indefatigable /ɪndɪ'fætɪgəbl/ *adj* instancabile

indefensible /ɪndɪ'fensəbl/ *adj* Mil indifendibile; (morally) ingiustificabile; (logically) insostenibile

indefinable /ɪndɪ'faɪnəbl/ *adj* indefinibile

indefinite /ɪn'defɪnɪt/ *adj* indefinito

indefinitely /ɪn'defɪnɪtlɪ/ *adv* indefinitamente; ⟨postpone⟩ a tempo indeterminato

indelible /ɪn'deləbl/ *adj* indelebile

indelibly /ɪn'deləblɪ/ *adv* in modo indelebile

indelicacy /ɪn'delɪkəsɪ/ *n* (tactlessness) mancanza *f* di tatto; (coarseness) rozzezza *f*

indelicate /ɪn'delɪkət/ *adj* (tactless) privo di tatto; (coarse) rozzo

indemnity /ɪn'demnətɪ/ *n* indennità *f inv*

indent[1] /'ɪndent/ *n* Typ rientranza *f* dal margine

indent[2] /ɪn'dent/ *vt* Typ fare rientrare dal margine

indentation /ɪnden'teɪʃn/ *n* (notch) intaccatura *f*

independence /ɪndɪ'pendəns/ *n* indipendenza *f*

Independence Day *n* Am = anniversario *m* dell'Indipendenza degli USA (4 luglio)

independent /ɪndɪ'pendənt/ *adj* indipendente

independently /ɪndɪ'pendəntlɪ/ *adv* indipendentemente

in-depth *adj* ⟨analysis, study, knowledge⟩ approfondito

indescribable /ɪndɪ'skraɪbəbl/ *adj* indescrivibile

indescribably /ɪndɪ'skraɪbəblɪ/ *adv* indescrivibilmente

indestructible /ɪndɪ'strʌktəbl/ *adj* indistruttibile

indeterminate /ɪndɪ't3:mɪnət/ *adj* indeterminato

index /'ɪndeks/ *n* indice *m*

indexation /ɪndek'seɪʃn/ *n* indicizzazione *f*

index card n scheda f

index finger n dito m indice

index-linked adj ⟨pension⟩ legato al costo della vita

India /'ɪndɪə/ n India f

Indian /'ɪndɪən/ **1** adj indiano; (American) indiano [d'America]
2 n indiano, -a mf; (American) indiano [d'America]

Indian elephant n elefante m indiano

Indian ink n inchiostro m di china

Indian Ocean n oceano m Indiano

Indian summer n estate f di San Martino

indicate /'ɪndɪkeɪt/ **1** vt indicare; (register) segnare
2 vi Auto mettere la freccia; ∼ left mettere la freccia a sinistra

indication /ɪndɪ'keɪʃn/ n indicazione f

indicative /ɪn'dɪkətɪv/ **1** adj be ∼ of essere indicativo di
2 n Gram indicativo m

indicator /'ɪndɪkeɪtə(r)/ n Auto freccia f

indict /ɪn'daɪt/ vt accusare

indictment /ɪn'daɪtmənt/ n Jur imputazione f

indie /'ɪndɪ/ **1** adj fam Cinema, Mus indipendente
2 n (band) gruppo m musicale legato a una casa discografica indipendente; (film) film m prodotto da una casa di produzione indipendente

indifference /ɪn'dɪf(ə)rəns/ n indifferenza f

indifferent /ɪn'dɪf(ə)rənt/ adj indifferente; (not good) mediocre

indifferently /ɪn'dɪf(ə)rəntlɪ/ adv in modo indifferente; (not well) in modo mediocre

indigenous /ɪn'dɪdʒɪnəs/ adj indigeno

indigestible /ɪndɪ'dʒestəbl/ adj indigesto

indigestion /ɪndɪ'dʒestʃn/ n indigestione f

indignant /ɪn'dɪgnənt/ adj indignato

indignantly /ɪn'dɪgnəntlɪ/ adv con indignazione

indignation /ɪndɪg'neɪʃn/ n indignazione f

indignity /ɪn'dɪgnətɪ/ n umiliazione f

indigo /'ɪndɪgəʊ/ n indaco m

indirect /ɪndaɪ'rekt/ adj indiretto

indirectly /ɪndaɪ'rektlɪ/ adv indirettamente

indirect speech n discorso m indiretto

indiscernible /ɪndɪ'sɜːnəbl/ adj indistinguibile

indiscreet /ɪndɪ'skriːt/ adj indiscreto

indiscretion /ɪndɪ'skreʃn/ n indiscrezione f

indiscriminate /ɪndɪ'skrɪmɪnət/ adj indiscriminato

indiscriminately /ɪndɪ'skrɪmɪnətlɪ/ adv senza distinzione

indispensable /ɪndɪ'spensəbl/ adj indispensabile

indisposed /ɪndɪ'spəʊzd/ adj indisposto

indisputable /ɪndɪ'spjuːtəbl/ adj indisputabile

indisputably /ɪndɪ'spjuːtəblɪ/ adv indisputabilmente

indistinct /ɪndɪ'stɪŋkt/ adj indistinto

indistinctly /ɪndɪ'stɪŋktlɪ/ adv indistintamente

indistinguishable /ɪndɪ'stɪŋgwɪʃəbl/ adj indistinguibile

individual /ɪndɪ'vɪdjʊəl/ **1** adj individuale
2 n individuo m

individualist /ɪndɪ'vɪdjʊəlɪst/ n individualista mf

individualistic /ɪndɪvɪdjʊə'lɪstɪk/ adj individualistico

individuality /ɪndɪvɪdjʊ'ælətɪ/ n individualità f

individually /ɪndɪ'vɪdjʊəlɪ/ adv individualmente

indivisible /ɪndɪ'vɪzəbl/ adj indivisibile

Indochina /ɪndəʊ'tʃaɪnə/ n Indocina f

indoctrinate /ɪn'dɒktrɪneɪt/ vt indottrinare

Indo-European /ɪndəʊjʊərə'pɪən/ adj indoeuropeo

indolence /'ɪndələns/ n indolenza

indolent /'ɪndələnt/ adj indolente

indomitable /ɪn'dɒmɪtəbl/ adj indomito

Indonesia /ɪndə'niːzjə/ n Indonesia f

Indonesian /ɪndə'niːzjən/ adj & n (person) indonesiano, -a mf; (language) indonesiano m

indoor /'ɪndɔː(r)/ adj interno; ⟨shoes⟩ per casa; ⟨plant⟩ da appartamento; ⟨swimming pool etc⟩ coperto

indoors /ɪn'dɔːz/ adv dentro; go ∼ andare dentro

indubitable /ɪn'djuːbɪtəbl/ adj indubitabile

indubitably /ɪn'djuːbɪtəblɪ/ adv indubitabilmente

induce /ɪn'djuːs/ vt indurre (to a); (produce) causare

inducement /ɪn'djuːsmənt/ n (incentive) incentivo m

induction /ɪn'dʌkʃn/ n (inauguration) introduzione f; (of labour) parto m indotto; Electr induzione f

induction ceremony n cerimonia f inaugurale

induction course n corso m introduttivo

induction loop n sistema m di amplificazione sonora

indulge /ɪn'dʌldʒ/ **1** vt soddisfare; viziare ⟨child⟩
2 vi ~ in concedersi

indulgence /ɪn'dʌldʒəns/ n lusso m; (leniency) indulgenza f

indulgent /ɪn'dʌldʒənt/ adj indulgente

industrial /ɪn'dʌstrɪəl/ adj industriale

industrial accident n infortunio m sul lavoro

industrial action n sciopero m; take ~ ~ scioperare

industrial dispute n vertenza f sindacale

industrial espionage n spionaggio m industriale

industrial estate n zona f industriale

industrialist /ɪn'dʌstrɪəlɪst/ n industriale mf

industrialized /ɪn'dʌstrɪəlaɪzd/ adj industrializzato

industrial relations npl relazioni fpl industriali

industrial tribunal n tribunale m competente per i conflitti di lavoro

industrial waste n rifiuti mpl industriali

industrious /ɪn'dʌstrɪəs/ adj industrioso

industriously /ɪn'dʌstrɪəslɪ/ adv in modo industrioso

industry /'ɪndəstrɪ/ n industria f; (zeal) operosità f

inebriated /ɪ'niːbrɪeɪtɪd/ adj ebbro

inedible /ɪn'edəbl/ adj immangiabile

ineffective /ɪnɪ'fektɪv/ adj inefficace

ineffectively /ɪnɪ'fektɪvlɪ/ adv inutilmente, invano

ineffectual /ɪnɪ'fektʃʊəl/ adj inutile; ⟨person⟩ inconcludente

inefficiency /ɪnɪ'fɪʃənsɪ/ n inefficienza f

inefficient /ɪnɪ'fɪʃnt/ adj inefficiente

ineligible /ɪn'elɪdʒəbl/ adj inadatto

inept /ɪ'nept/ adj inetto

ineptitude /ɪ'neptɪtjuːd/ n inettitudine f

inequality /ɪnɪ'kwɒlətɪ/ n ineguaglianza f

inert /ɪ'nɜːt/ adj inerte

inertia /ɪ'nɜːʃə/ n inerzia f

inescapable /ɪnɪ'skeɪpəbl/ adj inevitabile

inestimable /ɪn'estɪməbl/ adj inestimabile

inevitable /ɪn'evɪtəbl/ adj inevitabile

inevitably /ɪn'evɪtəblɪ/ adv inevitabilmente

inexact /ɪnɪg'zækt/ adj inesatto

inexcusable /ɪnɪk'skjuːzəbl/ adj imperdonabile

inexhaustible /ɪnɪg'zɔːstəbl/ adj inesauribile

inexorable /ɪn'eksərəbl/ adj inesorabile

inexorably /ɪn'egzərəblɪ/ adv inesorabilmente

inexpensive /ɪnɪk'spensɪv/ adj poco costoso

inexpensively /ɪnɪk'spensɪvlɪ/ adv a buon mercato

inexperience /ɪnɪk'spɪərɪəns/ n inesperienza f

inexperienced /ɪnɪk'spɪərɪənst/ adj inesperto

inexplicable /ɪnɪk'splɪkəbl/ adj inesplicabile

inexplicably /ɪnɪk'splɪkəblɪ/ adv inesplicabilmente, inspiegabilmente

inextricable /ɪnɪk'strɪkəbl/ adj inestricabile

inextricably /ɪnɪk'strɪkəblɪ/ adv inestricabilmente

infallibility /ɪnfælɪ'bɪlətɪ/ n infallibilità f

infallible /ɪn'fæləbl/ adj infallibile

infamous /'ɪnfəməs/ adj infame; ⟨person⟩ famigerato

infamy /'ɪnfəmɪ/ n infamia f

infancy /'ɪnfənsɪ/ n infanzia f; in its ~ fig agli inizi

infant /'ɪnfənt/ n bambino, -a mf piccolo, -a

infanticide /ɪn'fæntɪsaɪd/ n infanticidio m

infantile /'ɪnfəntaɪl/ adj infantile

infantry /'ɪnfəntrɪ/ n fanteria f

infant school n scuola f elementare per bambini dai 5 ai 7 anni

infatuated /ɪn'fætʃʊeɪtɪd/ adj infatuato (with di)

infatuation /ɪnfætʃʊ'eɪʃn/ n infatuazione f

infect /ɪn'fekt/ vt infettare; become ~ed ⟨wound⟩ infettarsi

infection /ɪn'fekʃn/ n infezione f

infectious /ɪn'fekʃəs/ adj infettivo

infer /ɪn'fɜː(r)/ vt (pt/pp inferred) dedurre (from da); (imply) implicare

inference /'ɪnfərəns/ n deduzione f

inferior /ɪn'fɪərɪə(r)/ **1** adj inferiore; ⟨goods⟩ scadente; (in rank) subalterno
2 n inferiore mf; (in rank) subalterno, -a mf

inferiority /ɪnfɪərɪ'ɒrətɪ/ n inferiorità f

inferiority complex n complesso m di inferiorità

infernal /ɪn'fɜːnl/ adj infernale

inferno /ɪn'fɜːnəʊ/ n inferno m

647

infertile /ɪnˈfɜːtaɪl/ *adj* sterile
infertility /ɪnfəˈtɪlətɪ/ *n* sterilità *f*
infest /ɪnˈfest/ *vt* be ∼ed with essere infestato di
infestation /ɪnfeˈsteɪʃn/ *n* infestazione *f*
infidelity /ɪnfɪˈdelətɪ/ *n* infedeltà *f inv*
infighting /ˈɪnfaɪtɪŋ/ *n* fig lotta *f* per il potere
infiltrate /ˈɪnfɪltreɪt/ *vt* infiltrare; Pol infiltrarsi in
infiltration /ɪnfɪlˈtreɪʃn/ *n* infiltrazione *f*
infinite /ˈɪnfɪnɪt/ *adj* infinito
infinitely /ˈɪnfɪnɪtlɪ/ *adv* infinitamente
infinitesimal /ɪnfɪnɪˈtesɪml/ *adj* infinitesimo
infinitive /ɪnˈfɪnətɪv/ *n* Gram infinito *m*
infinity /ɪnˈfɪnətɪ/ *n* infinità *f*
infirm /ɪnˈfɜːm/ *adj* debole
infirmary /ɪnˈfɜːm(ə)rɪ/ *n* infermeria *f*
infirmity /ɪnˈfɜːmətɪ/ *n* debolezza *f*
in flagrante delicto /ɪnfləɡræntɪdɪˈlɪktəʊ/ *adv* in flagrante
inflame /ɪnˈfleɪm/ *vt* infiammare
inflamed /ɪnˈfleɪmd/ *adj* infiammato; become ∼ infiammarsi
inflammable /ɪnˈflæməbl/ *adj* infiammabile
inflammation /ɪnfləˈmeɪʃn/ *n* infiammazione *f*
inflammatory /ɪnˈflæmətrɪ/ *adj* incendiario
inflatable /ɪnˈfleɪtəbl/ *adj* gonfiabile
inflate /ɪnˈfleɪt/ *vt* gonfiare
inflated /ɪnˈfleɪtɪd/ *adj* ⟨price, fee, claim⟩ eccessivo; ⟨style⟩ ampolloso; ⟨tyre⟩ gonfio; an ∼ ego un'alta opinione di sé
inflation /ɪnˈfleɪʃn/ *n* inflazione *f*
inflationary /ɪnˈfleɪʃənərɪ/ *adj* inflazionario
inflect /ɪnˈflekt/ *vt* flettere ⟨noun, adjective⟩; modulare ⟨voice⟩
inflected /ɪnˈflektɪd/ *adj* ⟨language⟩ flessivo; ⟨form⟩ flesso
inflection /ɪnˈflekʃn/ *n* (of voice) modulazione *f*
inflexible /ɪnˈfleksəbl/ *adj* inflessibile
inflexion /ɪnˈflekʃn/ *n* inflessione *f*
inflict /ɪnˈflɪkt/ *vt* infliggere (on a)
in-flight *adj* a bordo
influence /ˈɪnfluəns/ **1** *n* influenza *f*; use one's ∼ esercitare la propria influenza **2** *vt* influenzare
influential /ɪnfluˈenʃl/ *adj* influente
influenza /ɪnfluˈenzə/ *n* influenza *f*
influx /ˈɪnflʌks/ *n* affluenza *f*
info /ˈɪnfəʊ/ *n* fam informazione *f*

inform /ɪnˈfɔːm/ **1** *vt* informare; keep somebody ∼ed tenere qualcuno al corrente **2** *vi* ∼ against denunziare
informal /ɪnˈfɔːml/ *adj* informale; ⟨agreement⟩ ufficioso
informality /ɪnfəˈmælətɪ/ *n* informalità *f inv*
informally /ɪnˈfɔːməlɪ/ *adv* in modo informale
informant /ɪnˈfɔːmənt/ *n* informatore, -trice *mf*
information /ɪnfəˈmeɪʃn/ *n* informazioni *fpl*; a piece of ∼ un'informazione
information desk *n* banco *m* informazioni
information highway *n* autostrada *f* telematica
information officer *n* addetto, -a *mf* stampa
information pack *n* pacchetto *m* informativo
information processing *n* elaborazione *f* dati
information superhighway *n* Comput autostrada *f* dell'informazione
information system *n* sistema *m* informativo
information technology *n* informatica *f*
informative /ɪnˈfɔːmətɪv/ *adj* informativo; ⟨film, book⟩ istruttivo
informer /ɪnˈfɔːmə(r)/ *n* informatore, -trice *mf*; Pol delatore, -trice *mf*
infra-red /ɪnfrəˈred/ *adj* infrarosso
infrastructure /ˈɪnfrəstrʌktʃə(r)/ *n* infrastruttura *f*
infrequent /ɪnˈfriːkwənt/ *adj* infrequente
infrequently /ɪnˈfriːkwəntlɪ/ *adv* raramente
infringe /ɪnˈfrɪndʒ/ *vt* ∼ on usurpare
infringement /ɪnˈfrɪndʒmənt/ *n* violazione *f*
infuriate /ɪnˈfjʊərɪeɪt/ *vt* infuriare
infuriating /ɪnˈfjʊərɪeɪtɪŋ/ *adj* esasperante
infuse /ɪnˈfjuːz/ *vi* ⟨tea⟩ restare in infusione
infusion /ɪnˈfjuːʒn/ *n* (drink) infusione *f*; (of capital, new blood) afflusso *m*
ingenious /ɪnˈdʒiːnɪəs/ *adj* ingegnoso
ingenuity /ɪndʒɪˈnjuːətɪ/ *n* ingegnosità *f*
ingenuous /ɪnˈdʒenjʊəs/ *adj* ingenuo
ingest /ɪnˈdʒest/ *vt* ingerire ⟨food⟩; assimilare ⟨fact⟩
ingot /ˈɪŋɡət/ *n* lingotto *m*
ingrained /ɪnˈɡreɪnd/ *adj* (in person) radicato; ⟨dirt⟩ incrostato

ingratiate /ɪn'greɪʃɪeɪt/ vt ~ oneself with somebody ingraziarsi qualcuno

ingratitude /ɪn'grætɪtjuːd/ n ingratitudine f

ingredient /ɪn'griːdɪənt/ n ingrediente m

ingrowing /'ɪngrəʊɪŋ/ adj ⟨nail⟩ incarnito

inhabit /ɪn'hæbɪt/ vt abitare

inhabitable /ɪn'hæbɪtəbl/ adj abitabile

inhabitant /ɪn'hæbɪtənt/ n abitante mf

inhale /ɪn'heɪl/ ① vt aspirare; Med inalare
② vi inspirare; (when smoking) aspirare

inhaler /ɪn'heɪlə(r)/ n (device) inalatore ms

inherent /ɪn'hɪərənt/ adj inerente

inherit /ɪn'herɪt/ vt ereditare

inheritance /ɪn'herɪtəns/ n eredità f inv

inhibit /ɪn'hɪbɪt/ vt inibire

inhibited /ɪn'hɪbɪtɪd/ adj inibito

inhibition /ɪnhɪ'bɪʃn/ n inibizione f

inhospitable /ɪnhɒ'spɪtəbl/ adj inospitale

in-house adj ⟨training⟩ interno all'azienda; ⟨magazine⟩ aziendale

inhuman /ɪn'hjuːmən/ adj disumano

inhumanity /ɪnhjʊ'mænɪtɪ/ n disumanità f

inimitable /ɪ'nɪmɪtəbl/ adj inimitabile

iniquitous /ɪ'nɪkwɪtəs/ adj iniquo

initial /ɪ'nɪʃl/ ① adj iniziale
② n iniziale f
③ vt (pt/pp **initialled**) siglare

initially /ɪ'nɪʃəlɪ/ adv all'inizio

initiate /ɪ'nɪʃɪeɪt/ vt iniziare

initiation /ɪnɪʃɪ'eɪʃn/ n iniziazione f

initiative /ɪ'nɪʃətɪv/ n iniziativa f; take the ~ prendere l'iniziativa

inject /ɪn'dʒekt/ vt iniettare

injection /ɪn'dʒekʃn/ n iniezione f

in-joke n it's an ~ è una battuta tra di noi/loro

injunction /ɪn'dʒʌŋkʃn/ n ingiunzione f

injure /'ɪndʒə(r)/ vt ferire; (wrong) nuocere

injured /'ɪndʒəd/ ① adj ferito; Jur the ~ party la parte lesa
② npl the ~ i feriti

injury /'ɪndʒərɪ/ n ferita f; (wrong) torto m

injury time n Sport recupero m

injustice /ɪn'dʒʌstɪs/ n ingiustizia f; do somebody an ~ giudicare qualcuno in modo sbagliato

ink /ɪŋk/ n inchiostro m

ink-jet printer n stampante f a getto d'inchiostro

inkling /'ɪŋklɪŋ/ n sentore m

inky /'ɪŋkɪ/ adj macchiato d'inchiostro

inlaid /ɪn'leɪd/ adj intarsiato

inland /'ɪnlənd/ ① adj interno
② adv all'interno

Inland Revenue n fisco m

in-laws /'ɪnlɔːz/ npl fam parenti mpl acquisiti

inlay /'ɪnleɪ/ n intarsio m

inlet /'ɪnlet/ n insenatura f; Techn entrata f

inmate /'ɪnmeɪt/ n (of hospital) degente mf; (of prison) detenuto, -a mf

inn /ɪn/ n locanda f

innards /'ɪnədz/ npl fam frattaglie fpl

innate /ɪ'neɪt/ adj innato

inner /'ɪnə(r)/ adj interno

inner city ① n quartieri mpl nel centro di una città caratterizzati da problemi sociali
② attrib ⟨problems⟩ dell'area urbana con problemi sociali

inner ear n orecchio m interno

innermost /'ɪnəməʊst/ adj il più profondo

inner tube n camera f d'aria

innings /'ɪnɪŋz/ nsg (in cricket) turno m di battuta; **have had a good** ~ (Br fig: when leaving job etc) aver avuto una carriera lunga e gratificante; (when dead) aver avuto una vita lunga e piena di soddisfazioni

innkeeper /'ɪnkiːpə(r)/ n locandiere, -a mf

innocence /'ɪnəsəns/ n innocenza f

innocent /'ɪnəsənt/ adj innocente

innocently /'ɪnəsəntlɪ/ adv innocentemente

innocuous /ɪ'nɒkjʊəs/ adj innocuo

innovate /'ɪnəveɪt/ vi innovare

innovation /ɪnə'veɪʃn/ n innovazione f

innovative /'ɪnəvətɪv/ adj innovativo

innovator /'ɪnəveɪtə(r)/ n innovatore, -trice mf

innuendo /ɪnjʊ'endəʊ/ n (pl **-es**) insinuazione f

innumerable /ɪ'njuːmərəbl/ adj innumerevole

inoculate /ɪ'nɒkjʊleɪt/ vt vaccinare

inoculation /ɪnɒkjʊ'leɪʃn/ n vaccinazione f

inoffensive /ɪnə'fensɪv/ adj inoffensivo

inoperable /ɪn'ɒpərəbl/ adj inoperabile

inopportune /ɪn'ɒpətjuːn/ adj inopportuno

inordinate /ɪ'nɔːdɪnət/ adj smodato

inordinately /ɪ'nɔːdɪnətlɪ/ adv smodatamente

inorganic /ɔːr'gænɪk/ adj inorganico

in-patient n degente mf

input /'ɪnpʊt/ n input m inv, ingresso m

inquest /'ɪnkwest/ n inchiesta f

inquire /ɪnˈkwaɪə(r)/ **1** *vi* informarsi (**about** su); ~ **into** far indagini su **2** *vt* domandare

inquiring /ɪnˈkwaɪərɪŋ/ *adj* ⟨*mind*⟩ curioso; ⟨*look, voice*⟩ interrogativo

inquiry /ɪnˈkwaɪərɪ/ *n* domanda *f*; (investigation) inchiesta *f*

inquisitive /ɪnˈkwɪzətɪv/ *adj* curioso

inquisitively /ɪnˈkwɪzɪtɪvlɪ/ *adv* con molta curiosità

inroad /ˈɪnrəʊd/ *n* **make** ~**s into** intaccare ⟨*savings*⟩; cominciare a risolvere ⟨*problem*⟩

INS *n abbr* Am (**Immigration and Naturalization Service**) ufficio *m* immigrazione e naturalizzazione

insalubrious /ɪnsəˈluːbrɪəs/ *adj* (dirty) insalubre; (sleazy) sordido

insane /ɪnˈseɪn/ *adj* pazzo; fig insensato

insanitary /ɪnˈsænɪt(ə)rɪ/ *adj* malsano

insanity /ɪnˈsænətɪ/ *n* pazzia *f*

insatiable /ɪnˈseɪʃəbl/ *adj* insaziabile

inscribe /ɪnˈskraɪb/ *vt* iscrivere

inscription /ɪnˈskrɪpʃn/ *n* iscrizione *f*

inscrutable /ɪnˈskruːtəbl/ *adj* impenetrabile

insect /ˈɪnsekt/ *n* insetto *m*

insecticide /ɪnˈsektɪsaɪd/ *n* insetticida *m*

insect repellent *n* insettifugo *m*

insecure /ɪnsɪˈkjʊə(r)/ *adj* malsicuro; fig ⟨*person*⟩ insicuro

insecurity /ɪnsɪˈkjʊərətɪ/ *n* mancanza *f* di sicurezza

insemination /ɪnsemɪˈneɪʃn/ *n* inseminazione *f*

insensitive /ɪnˈsensɪtɪv/ *adj* insensibile

inseparable /ɪnˈsep(ə)rəbl/ *adj* inseparabile

insert[1] /ˈɪnsɜːt/ *n* inserto *m*

insert[2] /ɪnˈsɜːt/ *vt* inserire

insertion /ɪnˈsɜːʃn/ *n* inserzione *f*

inset /ˈɪnset/ **1** *n* (map, photo) dettaglio *m* **2** *adj* ~ **with** ⟨*necklace*⟩ incastonato di; ⟨*table*⟩ intarsiato di

inshore /ˈɪnʃɔː(r)/ **1** *adj* ⟨*current*⟩ diretta a riva; ⟨*fishing, waters, current*⟩ costiero; ⟨*wind*⟩ dal mare **2** *adv* ⟨*fish*⟩ sotto costa

inside /ɪnˈsaɪd/ **1** *n* interno *m*; ~**s** *pl* fam pancia *f* **2** *adv* dentro; ~ **out** a rovescio; (thoroughly) a fondo **3** *prep* dentro; (of time) entro

inside lane *n* Auto corsia *f* interna

inside leg *n* interno *m* della gamba

insider /ɪnˈsaɪdə(r)/ *n* persona *f* all'interno

insider dealer, **insider trader** *n* Fin persona *f* che pratica l'insider trading

insider dealing, **insider trading** /ˈdiːlɪŋ/, /ˈtreɪdɪŋ/ *n* Fin insider trading *m*

insidious /ɪnˈsɪdɪəs/ *adj* insidioso

insidiously /ɪnˈsɪdɪəslɪ/ *adv* insidiosamente

insight /ˈɪnsaɪt/ *n* intuito *m* (**into** per); **an** ~ **into** un quadro di

insignia /ɪnˈsɪgnɪə/ *npl* insegne *fpl*

insignificant /ɪnsɪgˈnɪfɪkənt/ *adj* insignificante

insincere /ɪnsɪnˈsɪə(r)/ *adj* poco sincero

insincerity /ɪnsɪnˈserətɪ/ *n* mancanza *f* di sincerità

insinuate /ɪnˈsɪnjʊeɪt/ *vt* insinuare

insinuation /ɪnsɪnjʊˈeɪʃn/ *n* insinuazione *f*

insipid /ɪnˈsɪpɪd/ *adj* insipido

insist /ɪnˈsɪst/ **1** *vi* insistere (**on** per) **2** *vt* ~ **that** insistere che

insistence /ɪnˈsɪstəns/ *n* insistenza *f*

insistent /ɪnˈsɪstənt/ *adj* insistente

insistently /ɪnˈsɪstəntlɪ/ *adv* insistentemente

insofar /ɪnsəˈfɑː(r)/ *conj* ~ **as** (to the extent that) nella misura in cui; (seeing that) in quanto; ~ **as I know** per quanto ne sappia

insole /ˈɪnsəʊl/ *n* soletta *f*

insolence /ˈɪnsələns/ *n* insolenza *f*

insolent /ˈɪnsələnt/ *adj* insolente

insolently /ˈɪnsələntlɪ/ *adv* con insolenza

insoluble /ɪnˈsɒljʊbl/ *adj* insolubile

insolvency /ɪnˈsɒlvənsɪ/ *n* insolvenza *f*

insolvent /ɪnˈsɒlvənt/ *adj* insolvente

insomnia /ɪnˈsɒmnɪə/ *n* insonnia *f*

insomniac /ɪnˈsɒmnɪæk/ *n* persona *f* che soffre di insonnia

insomuch /ɪnsəˈmʌtʃ/ *conj* ~ **as** (to the extent that) nella misura in cui; (seeing that) in quanto

inspect /ɪnˈspekt/ *vt* ispezionare; controllare ⟨*ticket*⟩

inspection /ɪnˈspekʃn/ *n* ispezione *f*; (of ticket) controllo *m*

inspector /ɪnˈspektə(r)/ *n* ispettore, -trice *mf*; (of tickets) controllore *m*

inspiration /ɪnspəˈreɪʃn/ *n* ispirazione *f*

inspire /ɪnˈspaɪə(r)/ *vt* ispirare

inspired /ɪnˈspaɪəd/ *adj* ⟨*person, performance*⟩ ispirato; ⟨*idea*⟩ luminosa

inspiring /ɪnˈspaɪərɪŋ/ *adj* ⟨*person, speech*⟩ entusiasmante

instability /ɪnstəˈbɪlətɪ/ *n* instabilità *f*

install /ɪnˈstɔːl/ *vt* installare; insediare ⟨*person*⟩

installation /ɪnstəˈleɪʃn/ *n* installazione *f*

instalment /ɪn'stɔːlmənt/ n Comm rata f;
(of serial) puntata f; (of publication) fascicolo
m

instance /'ɪnstəns/ n (case) caso m;
(example) esempio m; **in the first** ~ in
primo luogo; **for** ~ per esempio

instant /'ɪnstənt/ ① adj immediato; Culin
espresso
② n istante m

instantaneous /ɪnstən'teɪnɪəs/ adj
istantaneo

instant camera n polaroid® f inv

instant coffee n caffè m inv solubile

instantly /'ɪnstəntlɪ/ adv
immediatamente

instant replay n Sport replay m inv

instead /ɪn'sted/ adv invece; ~ **of doing**
anziché fare; ~ **of me** al mio posto; ~ **of
going** invece di andare

instep /'ɪnstep/ n collo m del piede

instigate /'ɪnstɪgeɪt/ vt istigare

instigation /ɪnstɪ'geɪʃn/ n istigazione f;
at his ~ dietro suo suggerimento

instigator /'ɪnstɪgeɪtə(r)/ n istigatore,
-trice mf

instil /ɪn'stɪl/ vt (pt/pp **instilled**)
inculcare (**into** in)

instinct /'ɪnstɪŋkt/ n istinto m

instinctive /ɪn'stɪŋktɪv/ adj istintivo

instinctively /ɪn'stɪŋktɪvlɪ/ adv
istintivamente

institute /'ɪnstɪtjuːt/ ① n istituto m
② vt istituire ⟨scheme⟩; iniziare ⟨search⟩;
intentare ⟨legal action⟩

institution /ɪnstɪ'tjuːʃn/ n istituzione f;
(home for elderly) istituto m per anziani; (for
mentally ill) istituto m per malati di mente

institutionalize /ɪnstɪ'tjuːʃənəlaɪz/ vt
istituzionalizzare

institutionalized /ɪnstɪ'tjuːʃənəlaɪzd/
adj ⟨racism, violence⟩ istituzionalizzato;
become ~ (officially established) essere
istituzionalizzato; **be** ~**d** ⟨person⟩ non
essere autonomo a causa di un lungo
soggiorno in ospedale psichiatrico

instruct /ɪn'strʌkt/ vt istruire; (order)
ordinare

instruction /ɪn'strʌkʃn/ n istruzione f;
~**s** pl (orders) ordini mpl

instruction book n libretto m di
istruzioni

instructive /ɪn'strʌktɪv/ adj istruttivo

instructor /ɪn'strʌktə(r)/ n istruttore,
-trice mf

instrument /'ɪnstrʊmənt/ n strumento
m

instrumental /ɪnstrʊ'ment(ə)l/ adj
strumentale; **be** ~ in contribuire a

instrumentalist /ɪnstrʊ'mentəlɪst/ n
strumentista mf

instrument panel n quadro m degli
strumenti

insubordinate /ɪnsə'bɔːdɪnət/ adj
insubordinato

insubordination /ɪnsəbɔːdɪ'neɪʃn/ n
insubordinazione f

insubstantial /ɪnsəb'stænʃəl/ adj
(unreal) irreale; ⟨evidence⟩ inconsistente;
⟨flimsy, building⟩ poco solido; ⟨meal⟩ poco
sostanzioso

insufferable /ɪn'sʌf(ə)rəbl/ adj
insopportabile

insufficient /ɪnsə'fɪʃənt/ adj
insufficiente

insufficiently /ɪnsə'fɪʃəntlɪ/ adv
insufficientemente

insular /'ɪnsjʊlə(r)/ adj.fig gretto

insulate /'ɪnsjʊleɪt/ vt isolare

insulating tape /'ɪnsjʊleɪtɪŋ/ n nastro
m isolante

insulation /ɪnsjʊ'leɪʃn/ n isolamento m

insulator /'ɪnsjʊleɪtə(r)/ n isolante m

insulin /'ɪnsjʊlɪn/ n insulina f

insult¹ /'ɪnsʌlt/ n insulto m

insult² /ɪn'sʌlt/ vt insultare

insuperable /ɪn'suːpərəbl/ adj
insuperabile

insurable value /ɪn'ʃʊərəbl/ n valore
m assicurabile

insurance /ɪn'ʃʊərəns/ n assicurazione
f

insurance broker n broker mf inv
d'assicurazioni

insurance claim n richiesta f di
indennizzo (ad assicurazione)

insurance policy n polizza f
d'assicurazione

insurance premium n premio m
assicurativo

insure /ɪn'ʃʊə(r)/ vt assicurare

insurgent /ɪn'sɜːdʒənt/ n rivoltoso, -a mf

insurmountable /ɪnsə'maʊntəbl/ adj
insormontabile

insurrection /ɪnsə'rekʃn/ n
insurrezione f

intact /ɪn'tækt/ adj intatto

intake /'ɪnteɪk/ n immissione f; (of food)
consumo m

intangible /ɪn'tændʒəbl/ adj intangibile

integral /'ɪntɪgrəl/ adj integrale

integrate /'ɪntɪgreɪt/ ① vt integrare
② vi integrarsi

integration /ɪntɪ'greɪʃn/ n integrazione
f

integrity /ɪn'tegrɪtɪ/ n integrità f

intellect /'ɪntəlekt/ n intelletto m

intellectual /ɪntə'lektjʊəl/ adj & n
intellettuale mf

intelligence ⋯⟶ interject

intelligence /ɪn'telɪdʒəns/ *n* intelligenza *f*; Mil informazioni *fpl*

intelligent /ɪn'telɪdʒənt/ *adj* intelligente

intelligently /ɪn'telɪdʒəntlɪ/ *adv* intelligentemente

intelligentsia /ɪntelɪ'dʒentsɪə/ *n* intellighenzia *f*

intelligible /ɪn'telɪdʒəbl/ *adj* intelligibile

intemperate /ɪn'temp(ə)rət/ *adj* ⟨*language, person*⟩ intemperante; ⟨*weather*⟩ rigido; ⟨*attack*⟩ violento

intend /ɪn'tend/ *vt* destinare; (have in mind) aver intenzione di; **be** ∼**ed for** essere destinato a

intended /ɪn'tendɪd/ **1** *adj* ⟨*visit, purchase*⟩ programmato; ⟨*result*⟩ voluto, desiderato
2 *n* her ∼ hum il suo fidanzato; **his** ∼ hum la sua fidanzata

intense /ɪn'tens/ *adj* intenso; ⟨*person*⟩ dai sentimenti intensi

intensely /ɪn'tenslɪ/ *adv* intensamente; (very) estremamente

intensification /ɪntensɪfɪ'keɪʃn/ *n* intensificazione *f*

intensify /ɪn'tensɪfaɪ/ **1** *v* (pt/pp **-ied**) *vt* intensificare
2 *vi* intensificarsi

intensity /ɪn'tensətɪ/ *n* intensità *f*

intensive /ɪn'tensɪv/ *adj* intensivo; ∼ **care** terapia *f* intensiva

intensive care [unit] *n* [reparto *m*] rianimazione *f*

intensively /ɪn'tensɪvlɪ/ *adv* intensivamente

intent /ɪn'tent/ **1** *adj* intento; ∼ **on** (absorbed in) preso da; **be** ∼ **on doing something** essere intento a fare qualcosa
2 *n* intenzione *f*; **to all** ∼**s and purposes** a tutti gli effetti

intention /ɪn'tenʃn/ *n* intenzione *f*

intentional /ɪn'tenʃənəl/ *adj* intenzionale

intentionally /ɪn'tenʃənəlɪ/ *adv* intenzionalmente

intently /ɪn'tentlɪ/ *adv* attentamente

inter /ɪn'tɜː(r)/ *vt* (pt/pp **interred**) fml interrare

interact /ɪntər'ækt/ *vi* ⟨*two factors, people*⟩ interagire; Comput dialogare

interaction /ɪntər'ækʃn/ *n* cooperazione *f*

interactive /ɪntər'æktɪv/ *adj* interattivo

interactive television *n* televisione *f* interattiva

interactive video *n* video *m* interattivo

interbreed /ɪntə'briːd/ **1** *vt* ibridare
2 *vi* incrociarsi

interbreeding /ɪntə'briːdɪŋ/ *n* ibridazione *f*

intercede /ɪntə'siːd/ *vi* intercedere (**on behalf of** a favore di)

intercept /ɪntə'sept/ *vt* intercettare

interchange /'ɪntətʃeɪndʒ/ *n* scambio *m*; Auto raccordo *m* [autostradale]

interchangeable /ɪntə'tʃeɪndʒəbl/ *adj* interscambiabile

intercity /ɪntə'sɪtɪ/ **1** *n* (Br: train) intercity *m inv*
2 *adj* intercity

intercom /'ɪntəkɒm/ *n* citofono *m*

interconnecting /ɪntəkə'nektɪŋ/ *adj* ⟨*rooms*⟩ comunicante

intercontinental /ɪntəkɒntɪ'nentəl/ *adj* intercontinentale

intercourse /'ɪntəkɔːs/ *n* (sexual) rapporti *mpl* [sessuali]

interdepartmental /ɪntədiːpɑːt'ment(ə)l/ *adj* Univ, Comm interdipartimentale; Pol interministeriale

interdependent /ɪntədɪ'pendənt/ *adj* interdipendente

interdisciplinary /ɪntədɪsɪ'plɪnərɪ/ *adj* interdisciplinare

interest /'ɪntrəst/ **1** *n* interesse *m*; **have an** ∼ **in** Comm essere cointeressato in; **be of** ∼ essere interessante
2 *vt* interessare
3 *adj* interessato

interest-bearing *adj* fruttifero

interested /'ɪntrəstɪd/ *adj* interessato

interest-free *adj* senza interessi

interest-free loan *n* prestito *m* senza interessi

interesting /'ɪnt(ə)rəstɪŋ/ *adj* interessante

interest rate *n* tasso *m* di interesse

interface /'ɪntəfeɪs/ **1** *n* Comput, fig interfaccia *f*
2 *vi* interfacciarsi
3 *vt* interfacciare

interfere /ɪntə'fɪə(r)/ *vi* interferire; ∼ **with** interferire con

interference /ɪntə'fɪərəns/ *n* interferenza *f*

interfering /ɪntə'fɪərɪŋ/ *adj* ⟨*person*⟩ impiccione

interim /'ɪntərɪm/ **1** *adj* temporaneo; ∼ **payment** acconto *m*
2 *n* **in the** ∼ nel frattempo

interior /ɪn'tɪərɪə(r)/ **1** *adj* interiore
2 *n* interno *m*

interior decorator *n* arredatore, -trice *mf*

interior designer *n* (of colours, fabrics etc) arredatore, -trice *mf*; (of walls, space) architetto *m* d'interni

interject /ɪntə'dʒekt/ *vt* intervenire

interjection /ɪntə'dʒekʃn/ n Gram
interiezione f; (remark) intervento m

interlink /ɪntə'lɪŋk/ vt connettere; **be
~ed with** essere connesso con

interlock /ɪntə'lɒk/ vi ⟨parts⟩ incastrarsi

interlocking /'ɪntəlɒkɪŋ/ adj a incastro

interloper /'ɪntələʊpə(r)/ n intruso, -a
mf

interlude /'ɪntəluːd/ n intervallo m

intermarry /ɪntə'mærɪ/ vi sposarsi tra
parenti; ⟨different groups⟩ contrarre
matrimoni misti

intermediary /ɪntə'miːdɪərɪ/ n
intermediario, -a mf

intermediate /ɪntə'miːdɪət/ adj
intermedio

interminable /ɪn'tɜːmɪnəbl/ adj
interminabile

intermission /ɪntə'mɪʃn/ n intervallo m

intermittent /ɪntə'mɪtənt/ adj
intermittente

intermittently /ɪntə'mɪtəntlɪ/ adv a
intermittenza

intern /ɪn'tɜːn/ vt internare

internal /ɪn'tɜːnl/ adj interno

internal combustion engine n
motore m a scoppio

internally /ɪn'tɜːnəlɪ/ adv internamente;
⟨deal with⟩ all'interno

international /ɪntə'næʃ(ə)nəl/ **1** adj
internazionale
2 n (game) incontro m internazionale;
(player) competitore, -trice mf in gare
internazionali

internationally /ɪntə'næʃ(ə)nəlɪ/ adv
internazionalmente; **it applies ~** ha
validità internazionale

international money order n vaglia
m inv postale internazionale

International Phonetic Alphabet
n Alfabeto m Fonetico Internazionale

international reply coupon n
tagliando m di risposta internazionale

internee /ɪntɜː'niː/ n internato, -a mf

internet /'ɪntənet/ n Internet m

Internet access n Comput accesso m
Internet

Internet access provider n Comput
fornitore m di accesso ai servizi Internet

Internet café n caffè m Internet

Internet kiosk n Internet point m inv

Internet protocol n Comput protocollo
m Internet

Internet service provider n Comput
fornitore m di servizi Internet

Internet user n utente mf di Internet

internist /ɪn'tɜːnɪst/ n Am internista mf

internment /ɪn'tɜːnmənt/ n
internamento m

interplay /'ɪntəpleɪ/ n azione f reciproca

interpolate /ɪn'tɜːpəleɪt/ vt interpolare

interpose /ɪntə'pəʊz/ vt (insert)
frapporre; interrompere con ⟨comment,
remark⟩

interpret /ɪn'tɜːprɪt/ **1** vt interpretare
2 vi fare l'interprete.

interpretation /ɪntɜːprɪ'teɪʃn/ n
interpretazione f

interpreter /ɪn'tɜːprɪtə(r)/ n interprete
mf

interpreting /ɪn'tɜːprɪtɪŋ/ n
interpretariato m

interrelated /ɪntərɪ'leɪtɪd/ adj ⟨facts⟩ in
correlazione

interrogate /ɪn'terəgeɪt/ vt interrogare

interrogation /ɪnterə'geɪʃn/ n
interrogazione f; (by police) interrogatorio
m

interrogative /ɪntə'rɒgətɪv/ adj & n ~
[pronoun] interrogativo m

interrupt /ɪntə'rʌpt/ vt/i interrompere

interruption /ɪntə'rʌpʃn/ n interruzione
f

intersect /ɪntə'sekt/ **1** vi intersecarsi
2 vt intersecare

intersection /ɪntə'sekʃn/ n
intersezione f; (of street) incrocio m

interspersed /ɪntə'spɜːst/ adj ~ with
inframmezzato di

interstate /'ɪntəsteɪt/ Am **1** n
superstrada f fra stati
2 adj ⟨commerce, links⟩ fra stati

intertwine /ɪntə'twaɪn/ vi attorcigliarsi

interval /'ɪntəvl/ n intervallo m; **bright
~s** pl schiarite fpl

intervene /ɪntə'viːn/ vi intervenire

intervention /ɪntə'venʃn/ n intervento
m

interview /'ɪntəvjuː/ **1** n Journ
intervista f; (for job) colloquio m [di lavoro]
2 vt intervistare

interviewee /ɪntəvjuː'iː/ n (on TV, radio,
in survey) intervistato, -a mf; (for job)
persona f sottoposta a un colloquio di
lavoro

interviewer /'ɪntəvjuːə(r)/ n
intervistatore, -trice mf

interwar adj **the ~ years** gli anni tra le
due guerre

interweave /ɪntə'wiːv/ vt intrecciare
⟨themes, threads⟩; mischiare ⟨rhythms⟩

intestinal /ɪnte'staɪml/ adj intestinale

intestine /ɪn'testɪn/ n intestino m

intimacy /'ɪntɪməsɪ/ n intimità f

intimate[1] /'ɪntɪmət/ adj intimo; **be ~
with** (sexually) avere relazioni intime con

intimate[2] /'ɪntɪmeɪt/ vt far capire; (imply)
suggerire

intimately /'ɪntɪmətlɪ/ adv intimamente

intimidate /ɪn'tɪmɪdeɪt/ vt intimidire

intimidating /adj/ ⟨behaviour, person⟩ intimidatorio; ⟨prospect⟩ impressionante

intimidation /ɪntɪmɪˈdeɪʃn/ n intimidazione f

into /ˈɪntə/, di fronte a una vocale /ˈɪntʊ/ prep dentro, in; **go** ~ **the house** andare dentro [casa] or in casa; **be** ~ (fam: like) essere appassionato di; **I'm not** ~ **that** questo non mi piace; **7** ~ **21 goes 3** il 7 nel 21 ci sta 3 volte; **translate** ~ **French** tradurre in francese; **get** ~ **trouble** mettersi nei guai

intolerable /ɪnˈtɒlərəbl/ adj intollerabile

intolerance /ɪnˈtɒlərəns/ n intolleranza f

intolerant /ɪnˈtɒlərənt/ adj intollerante

intonation /ɪntəˈneɪʃn/ n intonazione f

intone /ɪnˈtəʊn/ vt recitare ⟨prayer⟩

intoxicated /ɪnˈtɒksɪkeɪtɪd/ adj inebriato

intoxicating /ɪnˈtɒksɪkeɪtɪŋ/ adj ⟨drink⟩ alcolico; ⟨smell, sight⟩ inebriante

intoxication /ɪntɒksɪˈkeɪʃn/ n ebbrezza f

intractable /ɪnˈtræktəbl/ adj intrattabile; ⟨problem⟩ insolubile

intramural /ɪntrəˈmjʊərəl/ adj ⟨studies⟩ tenuto in sede

intranet /ˈɪntrənet/ n Comput intranet f

intransigence /ɪnˈtrænzɪdʒəns/ n intransigenza f

intransigent /ɪnˈtrænzɪdʒənt/ adj intransigente

intransitive /ɪnˈtrænzɪtɪv/ adj intransitivo

intransitively /ɪnˈtrænzɪtɪvlɪ/ adv intransitivamente

intrauterine device /ɪntrəjuːtəraɪndɪˈvaɪs/ n Med spirale f, dispositivo m anticoncezionale intrauterino

intravenous /ɪntrəˈviːnəs/ adj endovenoso

intravenous drip n flebo[clisi] f inv

intravenous drug user n tossicomane mf che si inietta in vena

intravenously /ɪntrəˈviːnəslɪ/ adv per via endovenosa

in-tray n vassoio m per pratiche e corrispondenza da evadere

intrepid /ɪnˈtrepɪd/ adj intrepido

intricacy /ˈɪntrɪkəsɪ/ n complessità f

intricate /ˈɪntrɪkət/ adj complesso

intrigue /ɪnˈtriːg/ **1** n intrigo m **2** vt intrigare **3** vi tramare

intriguing /ɪnˈtriːgɪŋ/ adj intrigante

intrinsic /ɪnˈtrɪnsɪk/ adj intrinseco

introduce /ɪntrəˈdjuːs/ vt presentare; (bring in, insert) introdurre

introduction /ɪntrəˈdʌkʃn/ n introduzione f; (to person) presentazione f; (to book) prefazione f

introductory /ɪntrəˈdʌktərɪ/ adj introduttivo

introspective /ɪntrəˈspektɪv/ adj introspettivo

introvert /ˈɪntrəvɜːt/ n introverso, -a mf

introverted /ˈɪntrəvɜːtɪd/ adj introverso

intrude /ɪnˈtruːd/ vi intromettersi

intruder /ɪnˈtruːdə(r)/ n intruso, -a mf

intrusion /ɪnˈtruːʒn/ n intrusione f

intrusive adj ⟨camera, question⟩ indiscreto

intuition /ɪntjʊˈɪʃn/ n intuito m

intuitive /ɪnˈtjuːɪtɪv/ adj intuitivo

intuitively /ɪnˈtjuːɪtɪvlɪ/ adv intuitivamente

inundate /ˈɪnəndeɪt/ vt fig inondare (**with** di)

inure /ɪnˈjʊə(r)/ vt become ~d to something assuefarsi a qualcosa

invade /ɪnˈveɪd/ vt invadere

invader /ɪnˈveɪdə(r)/ n invasore m

invalid[1] /ˈɪnvəlɪd/ n invalido, -a mf

invalid[2] /ɪnˈvælɪd/ adj non valido

invalidate /ɪnˈvælɪdeɪt/ vt invalidare

invaluable /ɪnˈvæljʊ(ə)bl/ adj prezioso; (priceless) inestimabile

invariable /ɪnˈveərɪəbl/ adj invariabile

invariably /ɪnˈveərɪəblɪ/ adv invariabilmente

invasion /ɪnˈveɪʒn/ n invasione f

invective /ɪnˈvektɪv/ n invettiva f

invent /ɪnˈvent/ vt inventare

invention /ɪnˈvenʃn/ n invenzione f

inventive /ɪnˈventɪv/ adj inventivo

inventor /ɪnˈventə(r)/ n inventore, -trice mf

inventory /ˈɪnvəntrɪ/ n inventario m

inverse /ɪnˈvɜːs/ **1** adj inverso **2** n inverso m

inversely /ɪnˈvɜːslɪ/ adv inversamente

invert /ɪnˈvɜːt/ vt invertire; **in** ~**ed commas** tra virgolette

invertebrate /ɪnˈvɜːtɪbrət/ adj & n invertebrato m

invest /ɪnˈvest/ **1** vt investire **2** vi fare investimenti; ~ **in** (fam: buy) comprarsi

investigate /ɪnˈvestɪgeɪt/ vt investigare

investigation /ɪnvestɪˈgeɪʃn/ n investigazione f

investigative journalism /ɪnˈvestɪgətɪv/ n dietrologia f

investiture /ɪnˈvestɪtʃə(r)/ n investitura f

investment /ɪn'vestmənt/ n
investimento m

investment capital n capitale m di
investimento

investment income n reddito m da
investimenti

investment manager n responsabile
mf della gestione del portafoglio fondi di
investimento

investment trust n fondo m comune
di investimento

investor /ɪn'vestə(r)/ n investitore, -trice
mf

inveterate /ɪn'vetərət/ adj inveterato

invidious /ɪn'vɪdɪəs/ adj ingiusto;
⟨position⟩ antipatico

invigilate /ɪn'vɪdʒɪleɪt/ vi Sch
sorvegliare lo svolgimento di un esame

invigilator /ɪn'vɪdʒɪleɪtə(r)/ n persona f
che sorveglia lo svolgimento di un esame

invigorate /ɪn'vɪgəreɪt/ vt rinvigorire

invigorating /ɪn'vɪgəreɪtɪŋ/ adj
tonificante

invincible /ɪn'vɪnsəbl/ adj invincibile

inviolable /ɪn'vaɪələbl/ adj inviolabile

invisible /ɪn'vɪzəbl/ adj invisibile

invisible ink n inchiostro m simpatico

invitation /ɪnvɪ'teɪʃn/ n invito m

invitation card n biglietto m d'invito

invite /ɪn'vaɪt/ vt invitare; (attract) attirare
▪ **invite in** vt invitare a entrare
▪ **invite round** vt invitare a casa

inviting /ɪn'vaɪtɪŋ/ adj invitante

in vitro fertilization
/ɪnviː'trəʊfɜːtɪlaɪ'zeɪʃn/ n fecondazione f in
vitro

invoice /'ɪnvɔɪs/ **1** n fattura f
2 vt ~ **somebody** emettere una fattura a
qualcuno

invoke /ɪn'vəʊk/ vt invocare

involuntarily /ɪn'vɒlʌntərɪlɪ/ adv
involontariamente

involuntary /ɪn'vɒləntrɪ/ adj
involontario

involve /ɪn'vɒlv/ vt comportare; (affect,
include) coinvolgere; (entail) implicare; **get
~d with somebody** legarsi a qualcuno;
(romantically) legarsi sentimentalmente a
qualcuno

involved /ɪn'vɒlvd/ adj complesso,

involvement /ɪn'vɒlvmənt/ n
coinvolgimento m

invulnerable /ɪn'vʌln(ə)rəbl/ adj
invulnerabile; ⟨position⟩ inattaccabile

inward /'ɪnwəd/ adj interno; ⟨thoughts
etc⟩ interiore

inward investment n Comm
investimento m di capitali stranieri

inward-looking /'ɪnwədlʊkɪŋ/ adj
⟨person⟩ egocentrico; ⟨society, policy⟩
chiuso

inwardly /'ɪnwədlɪ/ adv interiormente

inward[s] /'ɪnwəd[z]/ adv verso
l'interno

in-your-face adj fam aggressivo

iodine /'aɪədiːn/ n iodio m

Ionian Sea /aɪəʊnɪən/ n mar m Ionio

iota /aɪ'əʊtə/ n briciolo m

IOU abbr (**I owe you**) pagherò m inv

IPA n abbr (**International Phonetic
Alphabet**) AFI m

IQ abbr (**intelligence quotient**) Q.I. m

IRA abbr (**Irish Republican Army**)
I.R.A. f

Iran /ɪ'rɑːn/ n Iran m

Iranian /ɪ'reɪnɪən/ adj & n iraniano, -a
mf

Iraq /ɪ'rɑːk/ n Iraq m

Iraqi /ɪ'rɑːkɪ/ adj & n iracheno, -a mf

irascible /ɪ'ræsəbl/ adj irascibile

irate /aɪ'reɪt/ adj adirato

Ireland /'aɪələnd/ n Irlanda f

iris /'aɪrɪs/ n Anat iride f; Bot iris f inv

Irish /'aɪrɪʃ/ **1** adj irlandese
2 n the I~ pl gli irlandesi

Irishman /'aɪrɪʃmən/ n irlandese m

Irish Republic n Repubblica f
d'Irlanda

Irish sea n mare m d'Irlanda

Irishwoman /'aɪrɪʃwʊmən/ n irlandese
f

irk /ɜːk/ vt infastidire

irksome /'ɜːksəm/ adj fastidioso

iron /'aɪən/ **1** adj di ferro
2 n ferro m; (appliance) ferro m [da stiro]
3 vt/i stirare
▪ **iron out** vt eliminare stirando; fig
appianare

Iron Curtain n cortina f di ferro

iron fist n fig pugno m di ferro

ironic[al] /aɪ'rɒnɪk[l]/ adj ironico

ironing /'aɪənɪŋ/ n stirare m; (articles)
roba f da stirare; **do the ~** stirare

ironing board n asse f da stiro

iron lung n polmone m d'acciaio

ironmonger /'aɪənmʌŋgə(r)/ n ~'s
[shop] negozio m di ferramenta

irony /'aɪərənɪ/ n ironia f

irradiate /ɪ'reɪdɪeɪt/ vt irradiare

irrational /ɪ'ræʃənl/ adj irrazionale

irreconcilable /ɪ'rekənsaɪləbl/ adj
irreconciliabile

irrecoverable /ɪrɪ'kʌv(ə)rəbl/ adj
⟨debt, object⟩ irrecuperabile; ⟨loss⟩
irreparabile

irredeemable /ɪrɪ'diːməbl/ adj Fin
⟨shares, loan⟩ irredimibile; ⟨loss⟩

irreparabile; Relig ⟨sinner⟩ che non è redimibile

irrefutable /ɪrɪˈfjuːtəbl/ adj irrefutabile

irregular /ɪˈregʊlə(r)/ adj irregolare

irregularity /ɪregjʊˈlærətɪ/ n irregolarità f inv

irregularly /ɪˈregjʊləlɪ/ adv in modo irregolare

irrelevant /ɪˈreləvənt/ adj non pertinente

irreligious /ɪrɪˈlɪdʒəs/ adj irreligioso

irreparable /ɪˈrepərəbl/ adj irreparabile

irreparably /ɪˈrep(ə)rəblɪ/ adv irreparabilmente

irreplaceable /ɪrɪˈpleɪsəbl/ adj insostituibile

irrepressible /ɪrɪˈpresəbl/ adj irrefrenabile; ⟨person⟩ incontenibile

irreproachable /ɪrɪˈprəʊtʃəbl/ adj irreprensibile

irresistible /ɪrɪˈzɪstəbl/ adj irresistibile

irresolute /ɪˈrezəluːt/ adj irresoluto

irrespective /ɪrɪˈspektɪv/ adj ∼ of senza riguardo per

irresponsible /ɪrɪˈspɒnsəbl/ adj irresponsabile

irresponsibly /ɪrɪˈspɒnsəblɪ/ adv irresponsabilmente

irretrievable /ɪrɪˈtriːvəbl/ adj ⟨loss, harm⟩ irreparabile

irreverence /ɪˈrevərəns/ n irriverenza f

irreverent /ɪˈrevərənt/ adj irriverente

irreverently /ɪˈrevərəntlɪ/ adv in modo irriverente

irreversible /ɪrɪˈvɜːsəbl/ adj irreversibile

irreversibly /ɪrɪˈvɜːsɪblɪ/ adv irreversibilmente

irrevocable /ɪˈrevəkəbl/ adj irrevocabile

irrevocably /ɪˈrevəkəblɪ/ adv irrevocabilmente

irrigate /ˈɪrɪgeɪt/ vt irrigare

irrigation /ɪrɪˈgeɪʃn/ n irrigazione f

irritability /ɪrɪtəˈbɪlətɪ/ n irritabilità f

irritable /ˈɪrɪtəbl/ adj irritabile

irritable bowel syndrome n sindrome f da colon irritabile

irritant /ˈɪrɪtənt/ n sostanza f irritante; (fig: person) persona f irritante

irritate /ˈɪrɪteɪt/ vt irritare

irritated /ˈɪrɪteɪtɪd/ adj irritato, stizzito

irritating /ˈɪrɪteɪtɪŋ/ adj irritante

irritation /ɪrɪˈteɪʃn/ n irritazione f

IRS n abbr Am (**Internal Revenue Service**) fisco m

is /ɪz/ ▸ BE

Islam /ˈɪzlɑːm/ n Islam m

Islamic /ɪzˈlæmɪk/ adj islamico

island /ˈaɪlənd/ n isola f; (in road) isola f spartitraffico

islander /ˈaɪləndə(r)/ n isolano, -a mf

island hopping /ˈaɪləndhɒpɪŋ/ n go ∼ ∼ andare di isola in isola

isle /aɪl/ n liter isola f

Isle of Man n l'isola f di Man

isms /ˈɪz(ə)mz/ npl pej ismi mpl

isobar /ˈaɪsəbɑː(r)/ n isobara f

isolate /ˈaɪsəleɪt/ vt isolare

isolated /ˈaɪsəleɪtɪd/ adj isolato

isolation /aɪsəˈleɪʃn/ n isolamento m

isosceles /aɪˈsɒsəliːz/ adj isoscele

ISP n abbr (**Internet service provider**) Comput ISP m

Israel /ˈɪzreɪl/ n Israele m

Israeli /ɪzˈreɪlɪ/ adj & n israeliano, -a mf

issue /ˈɪʃuː/ ① n (outcome) risultato m; (of magazine) numero m; (of stamps etc) emissione f; (offspring) figli mpl; (matter, question) questione f; **at** ∼ in questione; **take** ∼ **with somebody** prendere posizione contro qualcuno ② vt distribuire ⟨supplies⟩; rilasciare ⟨passport⟩; emettere ⟨stamps, order⟩; pubblicare ⟨book⟩; **be** ∼**d with something** ricevere qualcosa ③ vi ∼ **from** uscire da

isthmus /ˈɪsməs/ n (pl **-muses**) istmo m

it /ɪt/ pron (direct object) lo m, la f; (indirect object) gli m, le f; **it's broken** è rotto/rotta; **will it be enough?** basterà?; **it's hot** fa caldo; **it's raining** piove; **it's me** sono io; **who is it?** chi è?; **it's two o'clock** sono le due; **I doubt it** ne dubito; **take it with you** prendilo con te; **give it a wipe** dagli una pulita

IT n abbr (**Information technology**) informatica f

Italian /ɪˈtæljən/ adj & n italiano, -a mf; (language) italiano m

italic /ɪˈtælɪk/ adj in corsivo

italics /ɪˈtælɪks/ npl corsivo msg; **in** ∼ in corsivo

Italy /ˈɪtəlɪ/ n Italia f

itch /ɪtʃ/ ① n prurito m ② vi avere prurito, prudere; **be** ∼**ing to** fam avere una voglia matta di

itching powder /ˈɪtʃɪŋ/ n polverina f che dà prurito

itchy /ˈɪtʃɪ/ adj che prude; **my foot is** ∼ ho prurito al piede; **have** ∼ **feet** fig avere la terra che scotta sotto i piedi

item /ˈaɪtəm/ n articolo m; (on agenda, programme) punto m; (on invoice) voce f; ∼ [**of news**] notizia f

itemize /ˈaɪtəmaɪz/ vt dettagliare ⟨bill⟩

itinerant /aɪˈtɪnərənt/ adj itinerante

itinerary /aɪˈtɪnərərɪ/ n itinerario m

ITN n abbr Br (**independent television**) rete f televisiva britannica

its /ɪts/ *poss pron* suo *m*, sua *f*, suoi *mpl*, sue *fpl*; ~ **mother/cage** sua madre/la sua gabbia

it's = it is, it has

itself /ɪt'self/ *pron* (reflexive) si; (emphatic) essa stessa; **the baby looked at** ~ **in the mirror** il bambino si è guardato nello specchio; **by** ~ da solo; **the machine in** ~ **is simple** la macchina di per sé è semplice

ITV *abbr* (**Independent Television**)

stazione *f* televisiva privata

IUD *n abbr* (**intrauterine device**) spirale *f*

IVF *n abbr* (**in vitro fertilization**) FIV *f*

ivory /'aɪvərɪ/ **1** *n* avorio *m* **2** *attrib* d'avorio

Ivory Coast *n* Costa *f* d'Avorio

ivory tower *n* fig torre *f* d'avorio

ivy /'aɪvɪ/ *n* edera *f*

Jj

j, J /dʒeɪ/ *n* (letter) j, J *f inv*

jab /dʒæb/ **1** *n* colpo *m* secco; (fam: injection) puntura *f*
2 *vt* (pt/pp **jabbed**) punzecchiare

jabber /'dʒæbə(r)/ *vi* borbottare

jack /dʒæk/ *n* Auto cric *m inv*; Teleph jack *m inv*; (in cards) fante *m*, jack *m inv*
■ **jack in** *vt* sl piantare ⟨job⟩
■ **jack up** *vt* Auto sollevare [con il cric]; fam aumentare di molto ⟨salary etc⟩

jackal /'dʒæk(ə)l/ *n* sciacallo *m*

jackboot /'dʒækbu:t/ *n* stivale *m* militare

jackdaw /'dʒækdɔ:/ *n* taccola *f*

jacket /'dʒækɪt/ *n* giacca *f*; (of book) sopraccoperta *f*

jacket potato *n* patata *f* cotta al forno con la buccia

jack-in-the-box *n* scatola *f* a sorpresa contenente un pupazzo a molla

jackknife /'dʒæknaɪf/ **1** *n* coltello *m* a serramanico
2 *vi* sbandare finendo di traverso rispetto al rimorchio

jackpot /'dʒækpɒt/ *n* premio *m* (di una lotteria); **win the** ~ vincere alla lotteria; **hit the** ~ fig fare un colpo grosso

jackrabbit /'dʒækræbɪt/ *n* lepre *f* americana

jade /dʒeɪd/ **1** *n* giada *f* **2** *attrib* di giada

jaded /'dʒeɪdɪd/ *adj* spossato

jagged /'dʒægɪd/ *adj* dentellato

jail /dʒeɪl/ = GAOL

jailbird *n* avanzo *m* di galera

jailbreak *n* evasione *f*

jail sentence *n* condanna *f* al carcere

jalopy /dʒə'lɒpɪ/ *n* fam vecchia carretta *f*

jam¹ /dʒæm/ *n* marmellata *f*

jam² **1** *n* Auto ingorgo *m*; (fam: difficulty) guaio *m*

2 *vt* (pt/pp **jammed**) (cram) pigiare; disturbare ⟨broadcast⟩; inceppare ⟨mechanism, drawer etc⟩; **be** ~**med** ⟨roads⟩ essere congestionato
3 *vi* ⟨mechanism⟩ incepparsi; ⟨window, drawer⟩ incastrarsi
■ **jam on** *vt* ~ **on the brakes** inchiodare

Jamaica /dʒə'meɪkə/ *n* Giamaica *f*

Jamaican /dʒə'meɪkən/ *adj & n* giamaicano, -a *mf*

jam jar *n* barattolo *m* per la marmellata

jam-packed *adj* fam pieno zeppo

jampot *n* vasetto *m* per la marmellata

jangle /'dʒæŋgl/ **1** *vt* far squillare **2** *vi* squillare

janitor /'dʒænɪtə(r)/ *n* (caretaker) custode *m*; (in school) bidello, -a *mf*

January /'dʒænjʊərɪ/ *n* gennaio *m*

Japan /dʒə'pæn/ *n* Giappone *m*

Japanese /dʒæpə'ni:z/ *adj & n* giapponese *mf*; (language) giapponese *m*

jar¹ /dʒɑ:(r)/ *n* (glass) barattolo *m*

jar² *vi* (pt/pp **jarred**) ⟨sound⟩ stridere

jargon /'dʒɑ:gən/ *n* gergo *m*

jarring /'dʒɑ:rɪŋ/ *adj* stridente

jasmine /'dʒæsmɪn/ *n* gelsomino *m*

jaundice /'dʒɔ:ndɪs/ *n* itterizia *f*

jaundiced /'dʒɔ:ndɪst/ *adj* fig inacidito

jaunt /dʒɔ:nt/ *n* gita *f*

jaunty /'dʒɔ:ntɪ/ *adj* (**-ier, -iest**) sbarazzino

javelin /'dʒævlɪn/ *n* giavellotto *m*

jaw /dʒɔ:/ **1** *n* mascella *f*; (bone) mandibola *f*
2 *vi* fam ciarlare

jawbone /'dʒɔ:bəʊn/ *n* Anat osso *m* mascellare

jawline *n* mento *m*

jay /dʒeɪ/ *n* ghiandaia *f*

jaywalker /'dʒeɪwɔ:kə(r)/ *n* pedone *m* indisciplinato

jazz /dʒæz/ n jazz m
- **jazz up** vt ravvivare

jazz band n complesso m di jazz

jazzy /'dʒæzı/ adj vistoso

jealous /'dʒeləs/ adj geloso

jealously /'dʒeləslı/ adv gelosamente

jealousy /'dʒeləsı/ n gelosia f

jeans /dʒiːnz/ npl [blue] jeans mpl

jeep /dʒiːp/ n jeep f inv

jeer /dʒıə(r)/ ① n scherno m
- ② vi schernire; ~ at prendersi gioco di
- ③ vt (boo) fischiare

jeering /'dʒıərıŋ/ n fischi mpl

jell /dʒel/ vi concretarsi

jellied /'dʒelıd/ adj ⟨eels⟩ in gelatina

Jell-o® /'dʒel-ʊ/ n Am dolce m di gelatina di frutta

jelly /'dʒelı/ n gelatina f

jelly baby n caramella f gommosa a forma di pupazzetto

jelly bean n caramella f di gelatina di frutta

jellyfish n medusa f

jemmy /'dʒemı/ n piede m di porco

jeopardize /'dʒepədaız/ vt mettere in pericolo

jeopardy /'dʒepədı/ n in ~ in pericolo

jerk /dʒɜːk/ ① n scatto m, scossa f
- ② vt scattare
- ③ vi sobbalzare; ⟨limb, muscle⟩ muoversi a scatti

jerkily /'dʒɜːkılı/ adv a scatti

jerkin /'dʒɜːkın/ n gilè m inv

jerky /'dʒɜːkı/ adj traballante

jerry-built /'dʒerıbılt/ adj pej costruito alla bell'e meglio

jersey /'dʒɜːzı/ n maglia f; Sport maglietta f; (fabric) jersey m

Jerusalem /dʒə'ruːsələm/ n Gerusalemme f

jest /dʒest/ ① n scherzo m; in ~ per scherzo
- ② vi scherzare

jester /'dʒestə(r)/ n buffone m

Jesuit /'dʒezjʊıt/ ① n gesuita m
- ② adj gesuitico

Jesus /'dʒiːzəs/ n Gesù m

jet¹ /dʒet/ n (stone) giaietto m

jet² n (of water) getto m; (nozzle) becco m; (plane) aviogetto m, jet m inv

jet-black adj nero ebano

jet engine n motore m a reazione

jet fighter n caccia m inv a reazione

jetfoil n aliscafo m

jet lag n scombussolamento m da fuso orario

jet-lagged adj be ~ soffrire di jet lag

jet-propelled adj a reazione

jet propulsion n propulsione f a getto

jet setter n be a ~ appartenere al jet set

jet ski n moto m d'acqua

jet-skier n persona m che fa moto d'acqua

jet-skiing n moto m d'acqua

jettison /'dʒetısn/ vt gettare a mare; fig abbandonare

jetty /'dʒetı/ n molo m

Jew /dʒuː/ n ebreo m

jewel /'dʒuːəl/ n gioiello m

jewelled /'dʒuːəld/ adj ornato di pietre preziose

jeweller /'dʒuːələ(r)/ n gioielliere m; ~'s [shop] gioielleria f

jewellery /'dʒuːəlrı/ n gioielli mpl

Jewess /'dʒuːıs/ n ebrea f

Jewish /'dʒuːıʃ/ adj ebreo

Jew's harp n Mus scacciapensieri m inv

jib /dʒıb/ vi (pt/pp **jibbed**) fig mostrarsi riluttante (at a)

jibe /dʒaıb/ n ▶ GIBE

jiffy /'dʒıfı/ n fam in a ~ in un batter d'occhio

Jiffy bag® n busta f imbottita

jig /dʒıg/ n Mus giga f (danza popolare)

jiggle /'dʒıg(ə)l/ vt scuotere

jigsaw /'dʒıgsɔː/ n ~ [puzzle] puzzle m inv

jilt /dʒılt/ vt piantare

jingle /'dʒıŋgl/ ① n (rhyme) canzoncina f pubblicitaria
- ② vi tintinnare
- ③ vt far tintinnare

jingoist /'dʒıŋgəʊıst/ n Pol sciovinista mf

jingoistic /dʒıŋgəʊ'ıstık/ adj Pol sciovinistico

jinx /dʒıŋks/ n fam (person) iettatore, -trice mf; it's got a ~ on it è iellato

jinxed /dʒıŋkst/ adj be ~ essere iellato

jitters /'dʒıtəz/ npl fam have the ~ aver una gran fifa

jittery /'dʒıtərı/ adj fam in preda alla fifa

jive /dʒaıv/ n (Am fam: talk) storie fpl

Jnr abbr **junior**

job /dʒɒb/ n lavoro m; this is going to be quite a ~ fam [questa] non sarà un'impresa facile; it's a good ~ that... meno male che...

jobcentre n ufficio m statale di collocamento

job creation scheme n Br programma m di creazione di posti di lavoro

job description n mansionario m

job-hunting n ricerca f impiego

jobless /'dʒɒblıs/ adj senza lavoro

job lot *n* (at auction) insieme *m* di oggetti disparati

job satisfaction *n* soddisfazione *f* nel lavoro

job security *n* sicurezza *f* di impiego

job seeker *n* persona *f* che cerca lavoro

job seeker's allowance *n* Br indennità *f* di disoccupazione

job-share **1** *n* (position) posto *m* condiviso
2 *attrib* ⟨scheme⟩ di condivisione del posto di lavoro

job-sharing *n* job sharing *m inv*

jockey /'dʒɒkɪ/ *n* fantino *m*

jockey shorts *npl* boxer *mpl*

jockstrap *n* sospensorio *m*

jocular /'dʒɒkjʊlə(r)/ *adj* scherzoso

jocularly /'dʒɒkjʊləlɪ/ *adv* scherzosamente

jodhpurs /'dʒɒdpəz/ *npl* calzoni *mpl* alla cavallerizza

Joe Bloggs /dʒəʊ'blɒgz/ *n* l'uomo qualunque

jog /'dʒɒg/ **1** *n* colpetto *m*; at a ∼ in un balzo; Sport go for a ∼ andare a fare jogging
2 *vt* (pt/pp **jogged**) (hit) urtare; ∼ sb's memory farlo ritornare in mente a qualcuno
3 *vi* Sport fare jogging
■ **jog along** *vi* fig tirare avanti

jogger /dʒɒgə(r)/ *n* persona *f* che fa jogging

jogging /'dʒɒgɪŋ/ *n* jogging *m*

john /dʒɒn/ *n* (Am fam: toilet) gabinetto *m*

John Bull *n* il tipico inglese

John Doe *n* Am uomo *m* non identificato

join /dʒɔɪn/ **1** *n* giuntura *f*
2 *vt* raggiungere, unire; raggiungere ⟨person⟩; (become member of) iscriversi a; entrare in ⟨firm⟩
3 *vi* ⟨roads⟩ congiungersi
■ **join in** *vi* partecipare
■ **join up** **1** *vi* Mil arruolarsi
2 *vt* unire
■ **join up with** *vt* (meet) raggiungere ⟨friends⟩; congiungersi a ⟨road; river⟩

joiner /'dʒɔɪnə(r)/ *n* falegname *m*

joint /dʒɔɪnt/ **1** *adj* comune
2 *n* articolazione *f*; (in wood, brickwork) giuntura *f*; Culin arrosto *m*; (fam: bar) bettola *f*; (sl: drug) spinello *m*

joint account *n* conto *m* [corrente] comune

joint agreement *n* accordo *m* collettivo

jointed /'dʒɔɪntɪd/ *adj* Culin ⟨chicken⟩ tagliato a pezzi; ⟨doll, puppet⟩ snodabile; ⟨rod, pole⟩ smontabile

joint effort *n* collaborazione *f*

joint honours *npl* Br Univ laurea *f* in due discipline

jointly /'dʒɔɪntlɪ/ *adv* unitamente

joint owner *n* comproprietario, -a *mf*

joint venture *n* joint venture *f inv*

joist /dʒɔɪst/ *n* travetto *m*

joke /dʒəʊk/ **1** *n* (trick) scherzo *m*; (funny story) barzelletta *f*
2 *vi* scherzare

joker /'dʒəʊkə(r)/ *n* burlone, -a *mf*; (in cards) jolly *m inv*

joking /'dʒəʊkɪŋ/ *n* ∼ apart scherzi a parte

jokingly /'dʒəʊkɪŋlɪ/ *adv* per scherzo

jollity /'dʒɒlətɪ/ *n* allegria *f*

jolly /'dʒɒlɪ/ **1** *adj* (**-ier**, **-iest**) allegro
2 *adv* fam molto

Jolly Roger /'rɒdʒə(r)/ *n* bandiera *f* dei pirati

jolt /dʒəʊlt/ **1** *n* scossa *f*, sobbalzo *m*
2 *vt* far sobbalzare
3 *vi* sobbalzare

Jordan /'dʒɔːdn/ *n* Giordania *f*; (river) Giordano *m*

Jordanian /dʒɔː'deɪnɪən/ *adj* & *n* giordano, -a *mf*

joss stick /'dʒɒs/ *n* bastoncino *m* d'incenso

jostle /'dʒɒsl/ *vt* spingere

jot /dʒɒt/ *n* nulla *f*
■ **jot down** *vt* (pt/pp **jotted**) annotare

jotter /'dʒɒtə(r)/ *n* taccuino *m*; (with a spine) quaderno *m*

jottings /'dʒɒtɪŋz/ *npl* annotazioni *fpl*

journal /'dʒɜːnl/ *n* giornale *m*; (diary) diario *m*

journalese /dʒɜːnə'liːz/ *n* gergo *m* giornalistico

journalism /'dʒɜːnəlɪzm/ *n* giornalismo *m*

journalist /'dʒɜːnəlɪst/ *n* giornalista *mf*

journey /'dʒɜːnɪ/ **1** *n* viaggio *m*
2 *vi* viaggiare

jovial /'dʒəʊvɪəl/ *adj* gioviale

jowl /dʒaʊl/ *n* (jaw) mascella *f*; (fleshy fold) guancia *f*; cheek by ∼ with somebody fianco a fianco con qualcuno

joy /dʒɔɪ/ *n* gioia *f*

joyful /'dʒɔɪfʊl/ *adj* gioioso

joyfully /'dʒɔɪfʊlɪ/ *adv* con gioia

joyless /'dʒɔɪlɪs/ *adj* ⟨occasion⟩ triste; ⟨marriage⟩ infelice

joypad *n* Comput joypad *m*

joyride *n* fam giro *m* con una macchina rubata

joyrider *n* fam persona *f* che ruba una macchina per andare a fare un giro

joyriding *n* giri *mpl* su una macchina rubata

joystick n Comput joystick m inv
JP n abbr Br (**Justice of the Peace**) giudice m di pace
Jr abbr **junior**
jubilant /'dʒu:bɪlənt/ adj giubilante
jubilation /dʒu:bɪ'leɪʃn/ n giubilo m
jubilee /'dʒu:bɪli:/ n giubileo m
Judaism /'dʒu:deɪɪzm/ n giudaismo m
judder /'dʒʌdə(r)/ vi vibrare violentemente
judge /dʒʌdʒ/ **①** n giudice m
② vt giudicare; (estimate) valutare; (consider) ritenere
③ vi giudicare (**by** da)
judgement, judgment /'dʒʌdʒmənt/ n giudizio m; Jur sentenza f
judicial /dʒu:'dɪʃl/ adj giudiziario
judiciary /dʒu:'dɪʃərɪ/ n magistratura f
judicious /dʒu:'dɪʃəs/ adj giudizioso
judo /'dʒu:dəʊ/ n judo m
jug /dʒʌg/ n brocca f; (small) bricco m
juggernaut /'dʒʌgənɔ:t/ n fam grosso autotreno m
juggle /'dʒʌgl/ vi fare giochi di destrezza
juggler /'dʒʌglə(r)/ n giocoliere, -a mf
jugular /'dʒʌgjʊlə(r)/ n giugulare f; **go straight for the** ~ fig colpire nel punto debole
juice /dʒu:s/ n succo m; ~ **extractor** n spremiagrumi m inv elettrico
juicy /'dʒu:sɪ/ adj (**-ier, -iest**) succoso; fam ⟨story⟩ piccante
ju-jitsu /dʒu:'dʒɪtsu:/ n jujitsu m
jukebox /'dʒu:kbɒks/ n juke-box m inv
July /dʒʊ'laɪ/ n luglio m
jumble /'dʒʌmbl/ **①** n accozzaglia f
② vt ~ [**up**] mischiare
jumble sale n vendita f di beneficenza
jumbo /'dʒʌmbəʊ/ n ~ [**jet**] jumbo jet m inv
jump /dʒʌmp/ **①** n salto m; (in prices) balzo m; (in horse racing) ostacolo m
② vi saltare; (with fright) sussultare; ⟨prices⟩ salire rapidamente; ~ **to conclusions** saltare alle conclusioni
③ vt saltare; ~ **the gun** fig precipitarsi; ~ **the queue** non rispettare la fila
■ **jump at** vt fig accettare con entusiasmo ⟨offer⟩
■ **jump back** vi fare un salto indietro
■ **jump down** vt ~ **down sb's throat** saltare addosso a qualcuno
■ **jump in** vi (to vehicle) saltar su
■ **jump on** vt saltare su ⟨bus, train, bike, horse⟩; (attack) aggredire ⟨somebody⟩
■ **jump out** vi saltare fuori; ~ **out of something** saltare giù da qualcosa ⟨window, train, bed⟩
■ **jump up** vi rizzarsi in piedi
jumped-up /dʒʌmpt'ʌp/ adj montato
jumper /'dʒʌmpə(r)/ n (sweater) golf m inv

jump jet n aeroplano m a decollo e atterraggio verticali
jump leads npl cavi mpl per batteria
jump-start vt far partire con i cavi da batteria
jumpsuit n tuta f
jumpy /'dʒʌmpɪ/ adj nervoso
junction /'dʒʌŋkʃn/ n (of roads) incrocio m; Rail nodo m ferroviario
juncture /'dʒʌŋktʃə(r)/ n **at this** ~ a questo punto
June /dʒu:n/ n giugno m
Jungian /'jʊŋɪən/ adj junghiano
jungle /'dʒʌŋgl/ n giungla f
junior /'dʒu:nɪə(r)/ **①** adj giovane; (in rank) subalterno; Sport junior inv
② n **the** ~**s** pl Sch i più giovani
junior doctor n assistente mf ospedaliero, -a
junior high school n Am scuola f media inferiore
junior minister n sottosegretario m
junior school n scuola f elementare
juniper /'dʒu:nɪpə(r)/ n ginepro m
junk /dʒʌŋk/ n cianfrusaglie fpl
junk food n fam cibo m poco sano, porcherie fpl
junkie /'dʒʌŋkɪ/ n sl tossico, -a mf
junk mail n posta f spazzatura
junk shop n negozio m di rigattiere
junkyard n (for scrap) rottamaio m; (for old cars) cimitero m delle macchine
junta /'dʒʌntə/ n giunta f militare
Jupiter /'dʒu:pɪtə(r)/ n Giove m
jurisdiction /dʒʊərɪs'dɪkʃn/ n giurisdizione f
jurisprudence /dʒʊrɪs'pru:dəns/ n giurisprudenza f
jurist /'dʒʊərɪst/ n giurista mf
juror /'dʒʊərə(r)/ n giurato, -a mf
jury /'dʒʊərɪ/ n giuria f
jury box n banco m dei giurati
jury duty n esp. Am = JURY SERVICE
jury service n **do** ~ far parte di una giuria popolare
just /dʒʌst/ **①** adj giusto
② adv (barely) appena; (simply) solo; (exactly) esattamente; ~ **as tall** altrettanto alto; ~ **as I was leaving** proprio quando stavo andando via; **I've** ~ **seen her** l'ho appena vista; **it's** ~ **as well** meno male; ~ **at that moment** proprio in quel momento; ~ **listen!** almeno ascolta!; **I'm** ~ **going** sto andando proprio ora
justice /'dʒʌstɪs/ n giustizia f; **do** ~ **to** rendere giustizia a
Justice Department n Am ministero m di Grazia e Giustizia

Justice of the Peace *n* giudice *m* di pace

justifiable /dʒʌstɪˈfaɪəbl/ *adj* giustificabile

justifiably /dʒʌstɪˈfaɪəblɪ/ *adv* in modo giustificato

justification /dʒʌstɪfɪˈkeɪʃn/ *n* giustificazione *f*

justified /ˈdʒʌstɪfaɪd/ *adj* ‹action› motivato

justify /ˈdʒʌstɪfaɪ/ *vt* (pt/pp **-ied**) giustificare

justly /ˈdʒʌstlɪ/ *adv* giustamente

justness /ˈdʒʌstnɪs/ *n* (of decision) giustezza *f*; (of claim, request) legittimità *f*

jut /dʒʌt/ *vi* (pt/pp **jutted**) ~ out

sporgere

jute /dʒuːt/ *n* iuta *f*

juvenile /ˈdʒuːvənaɪl/ ① *adj* giovanile; (childish) infantile; (for the young) per i giovani
② *n* giovane *mf*

juvenile crime *n* delinquenza *f* minorile

juvenile delinquency *n* delinquenza *f* minorile

juvenile delinquent *n* delinquente *mf* minorile

juvenile offender *n* Jur imputato, -a *mf* minorenne

juxtapose /dʒʌkstəˈpəʊz/ *vt* giustapporre

Kk

k¹, **K** /keɪ/ *n* (letter) k, K *f inv*

K² *abbr* (**kilo**) k; *abbr* (**kilobyte**) KB, Kbyte *m inv*; *abbr* **thousand pounds**; he earns £50 K guadagna 50 mila sterline

kale /keɪl/, **curly kale** *n* cavolo *m* riccio

kaleidoscope /kəˈlaɪdəskəʊp/ *n* caleidoscopio *m*

kangaroo /kæŋɡəˈruː/ *n* canguro *m*

kaput /kəˈpʊt/ *adj* fam kaputt *inv*

karaoke /kærɪˈəʊkɪ/ *n* karaoke *m inv*

karaoke machine *n* apparecchio *m* per il karaoke

karate /kəˈrɑːtɪ/ *n* karatè *m*

kart /kɑːt/ *n* kart *m inv*

Kashmir /kæʃˈmɪə(r)/ *n* Kashmir *m*

Kashmiri /kæʃˈmɪərɪ/ ① *adj* del Kashmir
② *n* nativo, -a *mf* del Kashmir

kayak /ˈkaɪæk/ *n* kayak *m inv*

Kazakhstan /kæzəkˈstɑːn/ *n* Kazakistan *m*

KB *n abbr* (**kilobyte**) KB, Kbyte *m inv*

kebab /kɪˈbæb/ *n* Culin spiedino *m* di carne

kedgeree /ˈkedʒərɪ/ *n* Br piatto *m* indiano a base di pesce, riso e uova

keel /kiːl/ *n* chiglia *f*
■ **keel over** *vi* capovolgersi

keen /kiːn/ *adj* (intense) acuto; ‹interest› vivo; ‹eager› entusiastico; ‹competition› feroce; ‹wind, knife› tagliente; ~ **on** entusiasta di; she's ~ on him le piace molto; be ~ to do something avere voglia di fare qualcosa

keenly /ˈkiːnlɪ/ *adv* intensamente

keenness /ˈkiːnnɪs/ *n* entusiasmo *m*

keep /kiːp/ ① *n* (maintenance) mantenimento *m*; (of castle) maschio *m*; for ~s per sempre
② *vt* (pt/pp **kept**) tenere; (not throw away) conservare; (detain) trattenere; mantenere ‹family, promise›; tenere ‹shop›; allevare ‹animals›; rispettare ‹law, rules›; ~ **something hot** tenere qualcosa in caldo; ~ **somebody waiting** far aspettare qualcuno; ~ **something to oneself** tenere qualcosa per sé;
③ *vi* (remain) rimanere; ‹food› conservarsi; ~ **calm** rimanere calmo; ~ **left/right** tenere la sinistra/la destra; ~ **[on] doing something** continuare a fare qualcosa
■ **keep at** *vt* (persevere with) ~ **at it!** non mollare!
■ **keep away** ① *vi* non avvicinarsi, stare alla larga
② *vt* tenere lontano
■ **keep away from** *vt* non avvicinarsi a ‹fire›; stare alla larga da ‹somebody›; ~ **somebody away from something** tener qualcuno lontano da qualcosa
■ **keep back** ① *vt* trattenere ‹person›; ~ **something back from somebody** tenere nascosto qualcosa a qualcuno
② *vi* tenersi indietro
■ **keep down** ① *vi* star giù
② *vt* mandar giù ‹food›; mantenere basso ‹prices, inflation etc›; ~ **one's voice down** non alzare la voce
■ **keep from** *vt* ~ **somebody from doing something** impedire a qualcuno di fare qualcosa; ~ **somebody from** impedire a qualcuno di ‹falling›; ~ **somebody from their work** distogliere qualcuno dal lavoro;

∼ **something from somebody** tenere nascosto qualcosa a qualcuno; ∼ **the truth from somebody** nascondere la verità a qualcuno

■ **keep in** *vt* (in school) trattenere oltre l'orario per punizione; reprimere ⟨*indignation, anger etc*⟩

■ **keep in with** *vt* mantenersi in buoni rapporti con

■ **keep off** *vt* (avoid) astenersi da ⟨*cigarettes, chocolate etc*⟩; evitare ⟨*delicate subject*⟩

■ **keep on** ① *vi* (continue one's journey) proseguire; fam assillare (**at somebody** qualcuno)
② *vt* non togliersi ⟨*coat, hat*⟩; tenere ⟨*employee*⟩

■ **keep out** ① *vt* tenere fuori; ∼ **out!** alla larga!
② *vt* non far entrare ⟨*person, animal*⟩

■ **keep out of** *vt* ⟨*person*⟩ non entrare in ⟨*place*⟩; tenersi fuori da ⟨*argument*⟩; ∼ **somebody out of** tenere qualcuno alla larga da ⟨*place*⟩; ∼ **me out of this!** lasciamene fuori!

■ **keep to** *vt* non deviare da ⟨*path, subject*⟩; ∼ **something to oneself** tenere qualcosa per sé

■ **keep up** ① *vi* ⟨*remain level*⟩ stare al passo; ⟨*rain, good weather*⟩ mantenersi
② *vt* (continue) continuare; (prevent from going to bed) tenere alzato; mantenere alto ⟨*prices*⟩; tener su ⟨*trousers*⟩

■ **keep up with** *vt* (in race) stare al passo con ⟨*person, fashion*⟩; ⟨*wages*⟩ seguire il corso di ⟨*inflation*⟩

keeper /'ki:pə(r)/ *n* custode *mf*

keep-fit *n* ginnastica *f*

keeping /'ki:pɪŋ/ *n* custodia *f*; **be in** ∼ **with** essere in armonia con

keepsake /'ki:pseɪk/ *n* ricordo *m*

keg /keg/ *n* barilotto *m*

kelp /kelp/ *n* laminaria *f*, fuco *m*

kennel /'kenl/ *n* canile *m*; ∼**s** *pl* (boarding) canile *m*; (breeding) allevamento *m* di cani

Kenya /'kenjə/ *n* Kenya *m*

Kenyan /'kenjən/ *adj & n* keniota *mf*

kept /kept/ ▶ KEEP

kerb /kɜ:b/ *n* bordo *m* del marciapiede

kernel /'kɜ:nl/ *n* nocciolo *m*

kerosene /'kerəsi:n/ *n* Am cherosene *m*

kestrel /'kestrəl/ *n* gheppio *m*

ketchup /'ketʃʌp/ *n* ketchup *m*

kettle /'ket(ə)l/ *n* bollitore *m*; **put the** ∼ **on** mettere l'acqua a bollire

kettledrum /'ket(ə)ldrʌm/ *n* timpano *m*

key /ki:/ ① *n* also Mus chiave *f*; (of piano, typewriter) tasto *m*
② *vt* ∼ **[in]** digitare ⟨*character*⟩; **could you** ∼ **this?** puoi battere questo?

keyboard *n* Comput, Mus tastiera *f*

keyboarder *n* tastierista *mf*

keyboard player *n* tastierista *mf*

keyboards *npl* Mus tastiere *fpl*

keyed-up /ki:d'ʌp/ *adj* (excited) teso; (anxious) estremamente agitato; (ready to act) psicologicamente preparato

keyhole *n* buco *m* della serratura

keyhole surgery *n* chirurgia *f* endoscopica

key money *n* (for apartment) somma *f* richiesta ad un affittuario quando si trasferisce nell'abitazione

keynote *n* Mus tonica *f*; (main theme) tema *m* principale

keynote speech *n* discorso *m* programmatico

keypad *n* Comput tastierino *m* numerico

keyring *n* portachiavi *m inv*

key signature *n* Mus armatura *f* di chiave

keystroke *n* Comput keystroke *m inv*

keyword *n* parola *f* chiave

kg *abbr* (**kilogram**) kg

khaki /'kɑːkɪ/ ① *adj* cachi *inv*
② *n* cachi *m*

kibbutz /kɪ'bʊts/ *n* (pl **-es** or **-im**) kibbutz *m inv*

kibosh /'kaɪbɒʃ/ *n* fam **put the** ∼ **on something** mandare all'aria qualcosa

kick /kɪk/ ① *n* calcio *m*; (fam: thrill) piacere *m*; **for** ∼**s** fam per spasso; **get a** ∼ **out of something** trovare un piacere incredibile in qualcosa
② *vt* dar calci a; ∼ **the bucket** fam crepare
③ *vi* ⟨*animal*⟩; scalciare; ⟨*person*⟩ dare calci

■ **kick around** *vi* fam ① essere in giro
② *vt* buttar giù ⟨*idea*⟩

■ **kick in** *vt* sfondare a calci ⟨*door*⟩

■ **kick off** *vi* Sport dare il calcio d'inizio; fam iniziare

■ **kick out** *vt* (fam: of school, club etc) sbatter fuori

■ **kick up** *vt* ∼ **up a row** fare una scenata

kickback /'kɪkbæk/ *n* fam tangente *f*

kick-off *n* Sport calcio *m* d'inizio; **for a** ∼ fam tanto per cominciare

kick-start *vt* mettere in moto ⟨*motorbike*⟩; rilanciare ⟨*economy*⟩

kid /kɪd/ ① *n* capretto *m*; (fam; child) ragazzino, -a *mf*
② *vt* (pt/pp **kidded**) fam prendere in giro.
③ *vi* fam scherzare

kid gloves *npl* guanti *mpl* di capretto; **handle somebody with** ∼ ∼ trattare qualcuno con i guanti

kidnap /'kɪdnæp/ *vt* (pt/pp **-napped**) rapire, sequestrare

kidnapper /'kɪdnæpə(r)/ *n* sequestratore, -trice *mf*, rapitore, -trice *mf*

kidnapping /'kɪdnæpɪŋ/ *n* rapimento *m*, sequestro *m* [di persona]

kidney /'kɪdnɪ/ *n* rene *m*; Culin rognone *m*

kidney bean *n* fagiolo *m* comune

kidney dialysis *n* dialisi *f*

kidney failure *n* collasso *m* renale

kidney machine *n* rene *m* artificiale

kidney-shaped /'kɪdnɪʃeɪpt/ *adj* a forma di fagiolo

kidney stone *n* calcolo *m* renale

kill /kɪl/ *vt* uccidere; fig metter fine a; ammazzare ⟨*time*⟩
■ **kill off** *vt* eliminare ⟨*people*⟩; distruggere ⟨*plants, insects*⟩

killer /'kɪlə(r)/ *n* assassino, -a *mf*; **it was a real** ~ fig è stato micidiale

killer instinct *n* istinto *m* di uccidere; fig spietatezza *f*

killer whale *n* orca *f*

killing /'kɪlɪŋ/ *n* uccisione *f*; (murder) omicidio *m*

killjoy /'kɪldʒɔɪ/ *n* guastafeste *mf inv*

kiln /kɪln/ *n* fornace *f*

kilo /'kiːləʊ/ *n* chilo *m*

kilobyte *n* kilobyte *m inv*

kilogram *n* chilogrammo *m*

kilohertz *n* chilohertz *m inv*

kilometre *n* chilometro *m*

kilowatt *n* chilowatt *m inv*

kilt /kɪlt/ *n* kilt *m inv* (gonnellino degli scozzesi)

kimono /kɪ'məʊnəʊ/ *n* kimono *m inv*, chimono *m inv*

kin /kɪn/ *n* congiunti *mpl*; **next of** ~ parente *m* stretto

kind¹ /kaɪnd/ *n* genere *m*, specie *f*; (brand, type) tipo *m*; **what** ~ **of car?** che tipo di macchina?; ~ **of** fam alquanto; **two of a** ~ due della stessa specie

kind² *adj* gentile, buono; ~ **to animals** amante degli animali; ~ **regards** cordiali saluti

kindergarten /'kɪndəɡɑːtn/ *n* asilo *m* infantile

kind-hearted /-'hɑːtɪd/ *adj* ⟨*person*⟩ di [buon] cuore

kindle /'kɪndl/ *vt* accendere

kindly /'kaɪndlɪ/ ① *adj* **-ier, -iest** benevolo
② *adv* gentilmente; (if you please) per favore

kindness /'kaɪndnɪs/ *n* gentilezza *f*

kindred /'kɪndrɪd/ *adj* **she's a** ~ **spirit** è la mia/sua/tua anima gemella

kinetic /kɪ'netɪk/ *adj* cinetico

kinetics /kɪ'netɪks/ *n* cinetica *f*

king /kɪŋ/ *n* re *m inv*

kingdom /'kɪŋdəm/ *n* regno *m*

kingfisher /'kɪŋfɪʃə(r)/ *n* martin *m inv* pescatore

kingly /'kɪŋlɪ/ *adj* also fig regale

king-sized /'kɪŋsaɪzd/ *adj* ⟨*cigarette*⟩ king-size *inv*, lungo; ⟨*bed*⟩ matrimoniale grande

kink /kɪŋk/ *n* attorcigliamento *m*

kinky /'kɪŋkɪ/ *adj* fam bizzarro

kinship /'kɪnʃɪp/ *n* (blood relationship) parentela *f*; (empathy) affinità *f*

kiosk /'kiːɒsk/ *n* chiosco *m*; Teleph cabina *f* telefonica

kip /kɪp/ ① *n* fam pisolino *m*; **have a** ~ schiacciare un pisolino
② *vi* (pt/pp **kipped**) fam dormire

kipper /'kɪpə(r)/ *n* aringa *f* affumicata

kirk /kɜːk/ *n* (Scottish) chiesa *f*

kiss /kɪs/ ① *n* bacio *m*
② *vt* baciare
③ *vi* baciarsi

kiss of death *n* colpo *m* di grazia

kiss of life *n* respirazione *f* bocca a bocca; **give somebody the** ~ ~ ~ fare la respirazione bocca a bocca a qualcuno

kissogram /'kɪsəɡræm/ *n* servizio *m* commerciale in cui un messaggio di auguri viene scherzosamente recapitato con un bacio da una ragazza in abiti succinti

kit /kɪt/ ① *n* equipaggiamento *m*, kit *m inv*; (tools) attrezzi *mpl*; (construction kit) pezzi *mpl* da montare, kit *m inv*
② *vt* (pt/pp **kitted**) ~ **out** equipaggiare

kitbag /'kɪtbæɡ/ *n* sacco *m* a spalla

kitchen /'kɪtʃɪn/ ① *n* cucina *f*
② *attrib* di cucina

kitchenette /kɪtʃɪ'net/ *n* cucinino *m*

kitchen foil *n* carta *f* di alluminio

kitchen garden *n* orto *m*

kitchen paper *n* carta *f* da cucina

kitchen roll *n* Scottex® *m inv*

kitchen scales *npl* bilancia *f* da cucina

kitchen sink *n* lavello *m*; **everything bar the** ~ fig proprio tutto quanto

kitchen-sink drama *n* teatro *m* neorealista

kitchen towel *n* Scottex® *m inv*

kitchen unit *n* elemento *m* componibile da cucina

kitchenware *n* (crockery) stoviglie *fpl*; (implements) utensili *mpl* da cucina

kite /kaɪt/ *n* aquilone *m*

kitemark /'kaɪtmɑːk/ *n* Br marchio *m* di conformità alle norme britanniche

kith /kɪθ/ *n* ~ **and kin** amici e parenti *mpl*

kitsch /kɪtʃ/ *n* kitsch *m inv*

kitten /'kɪtn/ *n* gattino *m*

kitty /'kɪtɪ/ *n* (money) cassa *f* comune

kiwi /'ki:wi:/ n Zool kiwi m inv
kiwi fruit n kiwi m inv
kleptomania /kleptə'meɪnɪə/ n cleptomania f
kleptomaniac /kleptə'meɪnɪæk/ n cleptomane mf
km abbr (**kilometre**) km
kmh abbr (**kilometres per hour**) km/h
knack /næk/ n tecnica f; **have the ∼ for doing something** avere la capacità di fare qualcosa
knapsack /'næpsæk/ n sacco m da montagna
knave /neɪv/ n (in cards) fante m; (rogue) furfante m
knead /ni:d/ vt impastare
knee /ni:/ n ginocchio m; **go down on one's ∼s to somebody** inginocchiarsi davanti qualcuno
kneecap /'ni:kæp/ n rotula f
knee-deep adj **the water was ∼** l'acqua arrivava alle ginocchia
kneel /ni:l/ vi (pt/pp **knelt**) **∼ [down]** inginocchiarsi; **be ∼ing** essere inginocchiato
knee-length adj ⟨boots⟩ alto; ⟨skirt⟩ al ginocchio; ⟨socks⟩ lungo
knee-pad n ginocchiera f
knees-up /'ni:zʌp/ n Br fam festa f
knell /nel/ n campana f a morto; **sound the death ∼ for something** segnare la fine di qualcosa
knelt /nelt/ ▸KNEEL
knew /nju:/ ▸KNOW
knickerbocker glory /nɪkəbɒkə'glɔːrɪ/ n coppa f [gelato] gigante
knickers /'nɪkəz/ npl mutandine fpl
knick-knacks /'nɪknæks/ npl ninnoli mpl
knife /naɪf/ ➊ n (pl **knives**) coltello m ➋ vt fam accoltellare
knife-edge n **be on a ∼** ⟨person⟩ trovarsi sul filo del rasoio; ⟨negotiations⟩ essere appeso a un filo
knifepoint n **at ∼** sotto la minaccia di un coltello
knife sharpener n affilacoltelli m inv
knight /naɪt/ ➊ n cavaliere m; (in chess) cavallo m ➋ vt nominare cavaliere
knighthood /'naɪthʊd/ n **receive a ∼** ricevere il titolo di cavaliere
knit /nɪt/ vt/i (pt/pp **knitted**) lavorare a maglia; **∼ one, purl one** un diritto, un rovescio; **∼ one's brow** aggrottare le sopracciglia
knitted /'nɪtɪd/ adj lavorato a maglia
knitting /'nɪtɪŋ/ n lavorare m a maglia; (product) lavoro m a maglia
knitting needle n ferro m da calza

knitwear /'nɪtweə(r)/ n maglieria f
knives /naɪvz/ npl ▸KNIFE
knob /nɒb/ n pomello m; (of stick) pomo m; (of butter) noce f
knobbly /'nɒblɪ/ adj nodoso; (bony) spigoloso
knock /nɒk/ ➊ n colpo m; **there was a ∼ at the door** hanno bussato alla porta ➋ vt bussare a ⟨door⟩; (fam: criticize) denigrare; **∼ a hole in something** fare un buco in qualcosa; **∼ one's head** battere la testa (**on** contro) ➌ vi (at door) bussare
■ **knock about** ➊ vt malmenare ➋ vi fam girovagare
■ **knock back** vt (fam: drink quickly) buttar giù tutto d'un fiato
■ **knock down** vt far cadere; (with fist) stendere con un pugno; (in car) investire; (demolish) abbattere; (fam: reduce) ribassare ⟨price⟩
■ **knock off** ➊ vt (fam: steal) fregare; (fam: complete quickly) fare alla bell'e meglio ➋ vi (fam: cease work) staccare
■ **knock out** vt eliminare; (make unconscious) mettere K.O.; (fam: anaesthetize) addormentare
■ **knock over** vt rovesciare; (in car) investire
■ **knock up** vt fam (prepare quickly) buttare giù; (sl: make pregnant) mettere incinta
knockabout n Sport **have a ∼** palleggiare
knock-down furniture n mobili mpl scomponibili
knock-down price n prezzo m stracciato
knocker /'nɒkə(r)/ n battente m; (critic) denigratore, -trice mf
knocking /'nɒkɪŋ/ n (on door) colpi mpl; Auto battito m in testa
knocking-off time /nɒkɪŋ'ɒf/ n **∼ ∼ is five o'clock** si stacca alle cinque
knock-kneed /-'ni:d/ adj con gambe storte
knock-on effect n implicazioni fpl
knock-out n knock-out m inv; **be a ∼** fig essere uno schianto
knoll /nəʊl/ n collinetta f
knot /nɒt/ ➊ n nodo m; **to tie the ∼** fam convolare a giuste nozze ➋ vt (pt/pp **knotted**) annodare; Br fam **get ∼ted!** vai a farti friggere!
knotty /'nɒtɪ/ adj (**-ier, -iest**) fam spinoso
know /nəʊ/ ➊ vt (pt **knew**, pp **known**) sapere; conoscere ⟨person, place⟩; (recognize) riconoscere; **get to ∼ somebody** conoscere qualcuno; **∼ how to swim** sapere nuotare; **∼ right from wrong** saper distinguere il bene dal male ➋ vi sapere; **did you ∼ about this?** lo sapevi?

③ *n* in the ~ fam al corrente
■ **know of** *vt* conoscere; **not that I ~ of** non che io sappia
know-all *n* fam sapientone, -a *mf*
know-how *n* know-how *m inv*
knowing /'nəʊɪŋ/ *adj* d'intesa
knowingly /'nəʊɪŋlɪ/ *adv* (intentionally) consapevolmente; ⟨*smile etc*⟩ con un aria d'intesa
knowledge /'nɒlɪdʒ/ *n* conoscenza *f*
knowledgeable, knowledgable /'nɒlɪdʒəbl/ *adj* ben informato
known /nəʊn/ ① ▶ KNOW
② *adj* noto
knuckle /'nʌkl/ *n* nocca *f*
■ **knuckle down** *vi* darci sotto (**to** con)
■ **knuckle under** *vi* sottomettersi
knuckle-duster *n* tirapugni *m inv*
koala [bear] /kəʊ'ɑːlə/ *n* koala *m inv*
Koran /kə'rɑːn/ *n* Corano *m*
Korea /kə'rɪə/ *n* Corea *f*
Korean /kə'rɪən/ *adj & n* coreano, -a *mf*;

(language) coreano *m*
kosher /'kəʊʃə(r)/ *adj* kasher *inv*
Kosovan /'kɒsəvn/ ① *adj* kosovaro
② *n* kosovaro, -a *mf*
Kosovo /'kɒsəvəʊ/ *n* Kosovo *m*
kowtow /kaʊ'taʊ/ *vi* piegarsi
kph *abbr* (**kilometres per hour**) km/h
kudos /'kjuːdɒs/ *n* fam gloria *f*
Kurd /'kɜːd/ ① *n* curdo, -a *mf*
② *adj* curdo
Kurdish /'kɜːdɪʃ/ *adj & n* (language) curdo *m*
Kurdistan /kɜːdɪ'stɑːn/ *n* Kurdistan *m*
Kuwait /kʊ'weɪt/ *n* Kuwait *m*
Kuwaiti /kʊ'weɪtɪ/ *adj & n* kuwaitiano, -a *mf*
kW *abbr* (**kilowatt**) kW
kWh *abbr* (**kilowatt-hour**) kWh
Kyrgyzstan /kɪəgɪ'stɑːn/ *n* Kirghizistan *m*

Ll

l, L /el/ *n* (letter) l, L *f inv*
L *abbr* (**lake**) L; *abbr* (**large**) L; *abbr* (**learner**) P; *abbr* (**left**) sinistra *f*; *abbr* (**line**) v; *abbr* (**litre(s)**) l
lab /læb/ *n* fam laboratorio *m*
lab assistant *n* assistente *mf* di laboratorio
lab coat *n* camice *m*
label /'leɪbl/ ① *n* etichetta *f*
② *vt* (pt/pp **labelled**) mettere un'etichetta a; fig etichettare ⟨*person*⟩
labelling /'leɪbəlɪŋ/ *n* (act) etichettatura *f*
labor /'leɪbə(r)/ *n & v* Am = LABOUR
laboratory /lə'bɒrətrɪ/ *n* laboratorio *m*
laborer /'leɪbərə(r)/ *n* Am = LABOURER
laborious /lə'bɔːrɪəs/ *adj* laborioso
laboriously /lə'bɔːrɪəslɪ/ *adv* in modo laborioso
labor union /'leɪbə/ *n* Am sindacato *m*
labour /'leɪbə(r)/ ① *n* lavoro *m*; (workers) manodopera *f*; Med doglie *fpl*; **be in ~** avere le doglie; **L~** Pol partito *m* laburista
② *attrib* Pol laburista
③ *vi* lavorare
④ *vt* ~ **the point** fig ribadire il concetto
labour camp *n* campo *m* di lavoro
laboured /'leɪbəd/ *adj* ⟨*breathing*⟩ affannato
labourer /'leɪbərə(r)/ *n* manovale *m*

labour exchange *n* old ufficio *m* di collocamento
labour force *n* manodopera *f*
labouring /'leɪbərɪŋ/ *n* lavoro *m* manuale
labour-intensive *adj* ad uso intensivo di lavoro; **be ~** richiedere molta manodopera
labour market *n* mercato *m* del lavoro
Labour Party *n* Partito *m* laburista
labour relations *npl* relazioni *fpl* industriali
labour-saving /'leɪbəseɪvɪŋ/ *adj* che fa risparmiare lavoro e fatica
labour ward *n* reparto *m* maternità
labrador /'læbrədɔː(r)/ *n* (dog) labrador *m inv*
lab technician *n* tecnico, -a *mf* di laboratorio
laburnum /lə'bɜːnəm/ *n* maggiociondolo *m*
labyrinth /'læbərɪnθ/ *n* labirinto *m*
lace /leɪs/ ① *n* pizzo *m*; (of shoe) laccio *m*
② *attrib* di pizzo
③ *vt* allacciare ⟨*shoes*⟩; correggere ⟨*drink*⟩
lacerate /'læsəreɪt/ *vt* lacerare
laceration /læsə'reɪʃn/ *n* lacerazione *f*
lace-up [shoe] *n* scarpa *f* stringata

lack /læk/ ① *n* mancanza *f*; ~ **of interest** disinteressamento *m*; ~ **of evidence** insufficienza *f* di prove
② *vt* **the programme** ~**s originality** il programma manca di originalità; **I** ~ **the time** mi manca il tempo
③ *vi* **be** ~**ing** mancare; **be** ~**ing in something** mancare di qualcosa

lackadaisical /lækə'deɪzɪkl/ *adj* senza entusiasmo

lackey /'lækɪ/ *n* lacchè *m inv*

lackluster /'læklʌstə(r)/ *adj* Am = LACKLUSTRE

lacklustre /'læklʌstə(r)/ *adj* scialbo

laconic /lə'kɒnɪk/ *adj* laconico

laconically /lə'kɒnɪklɪ/ *adv* laconicamente

lacquer /'lækə(r)/ *n* lacca *f*

lactate /læk'teɪt/ *vi* produrre latte

lactation /læk'teɪʃn/ *n* lattazione *f*

lacy /'leɪsɪ/ *adj* di pizzo

lad /læd/ *n* ragazzo *m*

ladder /'lædə(r)/ ① *n* scala *f*; (In tights) smagliatura *f*
② *vi* smagliarsi

ladderproof /'lædəpru:f/ *adj* ⟨stockings⟩ indemagliable

laddish /'lædɪʃ/ *adj* fam da ragazzacci

laden /'leɪdn/ *adj* carico (**with** di)

la-di-da /lɑ:dɪ'dɑ:/ *adj* affettato

ladle /'leɪdl/ ① *n* mestolo *m*
② *vt* ~ [**out**] versare (col mestolo)

lady /'leɪdɪ/ *n* signora *f*; (title) Lady *f*; **ladies** [room] *n* bagno *m* per donne

ladybird *n*, Am **ladybug** *n* coccinella *f*

lady-in-waiting /-weɪtɪŋ/ *n* dama *f* di corte

ladykiller *n* fam dongiovanni *m inv*

ladylike /'leɪdɪlaɪk/ *adj* signorile

lady mayoress *n* moglie *f* del Lord Mayor

Ladyship *n* her/your L~ (to aristocrat) ≈ Signora Contessa

lady's maid *n* cameriera *f* personale

lag[1] /læg/ *vi* (pt/pp **lagged**) ~ **behind** restare indietro

lag[2] *vt* (pt/pp **lagged**) isolare ⟨pipes⟩

lager /'lɑ:gə(r)/ *n* birra *f* chiara

lager lout *n* Br pej giovinastro *m* ubriaco

lagging /'lægɪŋ/ *n* (for pipes) materiale *m* isolante

lagoon /lə'gu:n/ *n* laguna *f*

laid /leɪd/ ▶ LAY[3]; **sl get** ~ scopare

laid-back *adj* fam rilassato

laid up *adj* be ~ essere allettato

lain /leɪn/ ▶ LIE[2]

lair /leə(r)/ *n* tana *f*

laird /leəd/ *n* (in Scotland) proprietario *m* terriero

laity /'leɪətɪ/ *n* laicato *m*

lake /leɪk/ *n* lago *m*; L~ **Garda** lago di Garda

lakeside /'leɪksaɪd/ ① *n* riva *f* del lago
② *attrib* ⟨café, scenery⟩ della/sulla riva del lago

lama /'lɑ:mə/ *n* lama *m inv*

lamb /læm/ *n* agnello *m*

lambast[e] /læm'beɪst/ *vt* biasimare ⟨person, organization⟩

lamb chop *n* cotoletta *f* d'agnello

lambskin *n* pelle *f* d'agnello

lambswool *n* lana *f* d'agnello, lambswool *m inv*

lame /leɪm/ *adj* zoppo; fig ⟨argument⟩ zoppicante; ⟨excuse⟩ traballante

lamé /'lɑ:meɪ/ *n* lamé *m*

lame duck *n* (person) inetto, -a *mf*; (firm) azienda *f* in cattive acque

lament /lə'ment/ ① *n* lamento *m*
② *vt* lamentare
③ *vi* lamentarsi

lamentable /'læməntəbl/ *adj* deplorevole

laminated /'læmɪneɪtɪd/ *adj* laminato

lamp /læmp/ *n* lampada *f*; (in street) lampione *m*

lampoon /læm'pu:n/ ① *n* satira *f*
② *vt* fare oggetto di satira

lamp-post *n* lampione *m*

lampshade /'læmpʃeɪd/ *n* paralume *m*

lance /lɑ:ns/ ① *n* lancia *f*
② *vt* Med incidere

lance corporal *n* appuntato *m*

lancet /'lɑ:nsɪt/ *n* Med bisturi *m inv*

land /lænd/ ① *n* terreno *m*; (country) paese *m*; (as opposed to sea) terra *f*; **plot of** ~ pezzo *m* di terreno
② *vt* Naut sbarcare; fam ⟨obtain⟩ assicurarsi; **be** ~**ed with something** fam ritrovarsi fra capo e collo qualcosa
③ *vi* Aeron atterrare; (fall) cadere; ~ **on one's feet** fig cadere in piedi
■ **land up** *vi* fam finire

land agent *n* (on estate) fattore *m*

land army *n* gruppo *m* di lavoratrici agricole durante la seconda guerra mondiale

landfall *n* Naut approdo *m*; **make** ~ (reach) approdare; (sight) avvistare terra

landfill site *n* discarica *f* in cui i rifiuti vengono interrati

landing /'lændɪŋ/ *n* Naut sbarco *m*; Aeron atterraggio *m*; (top of stairs) pianerottolo *m*

landing card *n* Aeron, Naut carta *f* di sbarco

landing craft *n* mezzo *m* da sbarco

landing gear *n* Aeron carrello *m* d'atterraggio

landing lights *npl* luci *fpl* d'atterraggio

landing party n Mil reparto m da sbarco

landing-stage n pontile m da sbarco

landing strip n pista f d'atterraggio

landlady n proprietaria f; (of flat) padrona f di casa

landlocked adj privo di sbocco sul mare

landlord n proprietario m; (of flat) padrone m di casa

landlubber /'lændlʌbə(r)/ n marinaio m d'acqua dolce

landmark n punto m di riferimento; fig pietra f miliare

land mass n continente m

landmine n Mil mina f terrestre

landowner n proprietario, -a mf terriero, -a

landscape n paesaggio m

landscape architect n paesaggista mf

landscape gardener n paesaggista mf

landslide n frana f; Pol valanga f di voti

landslip n smottamento m

lane /leɪn/ n sentiero m; Auto, Sport corsia f

lane closure n (on motorway) chiusura f di corsia

lane markings n (on road) [strisce fpl di] mezzeria f

langoustine /'lɒŋɡʊsti:n/ n scampo m

language /'læŋɡwɪdʒ/ n lingua f; (speech, style, Comput) linguaggio m

language barrier n barriera f linguistica

language laboratory n laboratorio m linguistico

languid /'læŋɡwɪd/ adj languido

languidly /'læŋɡwɪdlɪ/ adv languidamente

languish /'læŋɡwɪʃ/ vi languire

languor /'læŋɡə(r)/ n languore m

lank /læŋk/ adj ⟨hair⟩ liscio

lanky /'læŋkɪ/ adj (**-ier**, **-iest**) allampanato

lanolin /'lænəlɪn/ n lanolina f

lantern /'læntən/ n lanterna f

lanyard /'lænjəd/ n (Naut: rope) cima f

Laos /laʊs/ n Laos m

lap[1] /læp/ n grembo m

lap[2] [1] n (Sport, of journey) tappa f; ~ **of honour** giro m d'onore [2] vi (pt/pp **lapped**) ⟨water⟩ ~ **against** lambire [3] vt Sport doppiare

lap[3] vt (pt/pp **lapped**) ~ **up** bere avidamente; bersi completamente ⟨lies⟩; credere ciecamente a ⟨praise⟩

lap and shoulder belt n Auto, Aeron cintura f di sicurezza

laparoscope /'læpərəskəʊp/ n laparoscopio m

laparoscopy /læpə'rɒskəpɪ/ n laparoscopia f

lap belt n Auto, Aeron cintura f di sicurezza addominale

lapdog /'læpdɒg/ n cane m da salotto; **he's her** ~ è il suo cagnolino

lapel /lə'pel/ n bavero m

Lapland /'læplænd/ n Lapponia f

lapse /læps/ [1] n sbaglio m; (moral) sbandamento m [morale]; (of time) intervallo m [2] vi (expire) scadere; (morally) scivolare; ~ **into** cadere in

laptop /'læptɒp/ n ~ [**computer**] computer m inv portatile, laptop m inv

larceny /'lɑ:sənɪ/ n furto m

larch /lɑ:tʃ/ n larice m

lard /lɑ:d/ n strutto m

larder /'lɑ:də(r)/ n dispensa f

large /lɑ:dʒ/ adj & adv grande; ⟨number, amount⟩ grande, grosso; **by and** ~ in complesso; **at** ~ in libertà; (in general) ampiamente

large intestine n intestino m crasso

largely /'lɑ:dʒlɪ/ adv ~ **because of** in gran parte a causa di

largeness /'lɑ:dʒnɪs/ n grandezza f

large-scale adj ⟨map⟩ a grande scala; ⟨operation⟩ su larga scala

largesse /lɑ:'ʒes/ n generosità f

lark[1] /lɑ:k/ n (bird) allodola f

lark[2] n (joke) burla f
■ **lark about** vi giocherellare

larva /'lɑ:və/ n (pl **-vae** /'lɑ:vi:/) larva f

laryngitis /lærɪn'dʒaɪtɪs/ n laringite f

larynx /'lærɪŋks/ n laringe f

lasagne /lə'zænjə/ n lasagne fpl

lascivious /lə'sɪvɪəs/ adj lascivo

laser /'leɪzə(r)/ n laser m inv

laser disc n disco m laser

laser printer n stampante f laser

laser treatment n laserterapia f

lash /læʃ/ [1] n frustata f; (eyelash) ciglio m [2] vt (whip) frustare; (tie) legare fermamente
■ **lash out** vi attaccare; (spend) sperperare (**on** in)

lashings /'læʃɪŋz/ npl ~ **of** fam una marea di

lass /læs/ n ragazzina f

lasso /lə'su:/ n lazo m

last /lɑ:st/ [1] adj (final) ultimo; (recent) scorso; ~ **year** l'anno scorso; ~ **night** ieri sera; **at** ~ alla fine; **at** ~! finalmente!;

that's the ~ straw fam questa è l'ultima goccia
2 *n* ultimo, -a *mf*; **the ~ but one** il penultimo
3 *adv* per ultimo; (last time) l'ultima volta; **~ but not least** per ultimo ma non il meno importante
4 *vi* durare

last-ditch *adj* ⟨attempt⟩ disperato

lasting /'lɑːstɪŋ/ *adj* durevole

lastly /'lɑːstlɪ/ *adv* infine

last-minute *adj* all'ultimo minuto

last name *n* (surname) cognome *m*

last rites *npl* Relig estrema unzione *f*

Last Supper *n* Ultima Cena *f*

latch /lætʃ/ *n* chiavistello *m*; (on gate) saliscendi *m inv*; **leave the door on the ~** chiudere la porta senza far scattare la serratura
■ **latch on to** *vt* fissarsi con ⟨person, idea⟩

latchkey /'lætʃkiː/ *n* chiave *f* di casa

latchkey child *n* bambino *m* che ha le chiavi di casa in quanto i genitori lavorano

late /leɪt/ **1** *adj* (delayed) in ritardo; (at a late hour) tardo; (deceased) defunto; **it's ~** (at night) è tardi; **in ~ November** alla fine di novembre; **of ~** recentemente; **be a ~ developer** ⟨child⟩ essere lento nell'apprendimento
2 *adv* tardi; **stay up ~** stare alzati fino a tardi

latecomer /'leɪtkʌmə(r)/ *n* ritardatario, -a *mf*; (to political party etc) nuovo, -a arrivato, -a *mf*

late developer *n* (child) **be a ~** essere tardivo

lately /'leɪtlɪ/ *adv* recentemente

lateness /'leɪtnɪs/ *n* ora *f* tarda; (delay) ritardo *m*

late-night *adj* ⟨film⟩ ultimo; **it's ~ shopping on Thursdays** i negozi rimangono aperti fino a tardi il giovedì

latent /'leɪtnt/ *adj* latente

later /'leɪtə(r)/ **1** *adj* ⟨train⟩ che parte più tardi; ⟨edition⟩ più recente
2 *adv* più tardi; **~ on** più tardi, dopo

lateral /'lætərəl/ *adj* laterale

late riser /'raɪzə(r)/ *n* dormiglione, -a *mf*

latest /'leɪtɪst/ **1** *adj* ultimo; (most recent) più recente; **the ~ [news]** le ultime notizie
2 *n* **six o'clock at the ~** alle sei al più tardi

latex /'leɪteks/ *n* la[t]tice *m*

lath /læθ/ *n* assicella *f*

lathe /leɪð/ *n* tornio *m*

lather /'lɑːðə(r)/ **1** *n* schiuma *f*
2 *vt* insaponare

3 *vi* far schiuma

Latin /'lætɪn/ **1** *adj* latino
2 *n* latino *m*

Latin America *n* America *f* Latina

Latin American *n* & *adj* latino-americano *mf*

Latino /ləˈtiːnəʊ/ *n* Am latino-americano, -a *mf*

latitude /'lætɪtjuːd/ *n* Geog latitudine *f*; fig libertà *f* d'azione

latrine /ləˈtriːn/ *n* latrina *f*

latter /'lætə(r)/ **1** *adj* ultimo
2 *n* **the ~** quest'ultimo

latter-day *adj* moderno

latterly /'lætəlɪ/ *adv* ultimamente

lattice /'lætɪs/ *n* traliccio *m*

lattice window *n* finestra *f* con vetri a losanghe

lattice-work *n* intelaiatura *f* a traliccio

Latvia /'lætvɪə/ *n* Lettonia *f*

Latvian /'lætvɪən/ *adj* & *n* lettone *mf*; (language) lettone *m*

laudable /'lɔːdəbl/ *adj* lodevole

laudatory /'lɔːdətrɪ/ *adj* elogiativo

laugh /lɑːf/ **1** *n* risata *f*
2 *vi* ridere (**at/about** di); **~ at somebody** (mock) prendere in giro qualcuno
■ **laugh off** *vt* ridere di ⟨criticism⟩

laughable /'lɑːfəbɪ/ *adj* ridicolo

laughing gas /'lɑːfɪŋ/ *n* gas *m inv* esilarante

laughing stock *n* zimbello *m*

laughter /'lɑːftə(r)/ *n* risata *f*

launch¹ /lɔːntʃ/ *n* (boat) lancia *f*

launch² **1** *n* lancio *m*; (of ship) varo *m*
2 *vt* lanciare ⟨rocket, product⟩; varare ⟨ship⟩; sferrare ⟨attack⟩
■ **launch into** *vt* intraprendere ⟨career⟩; imbarcarsi in ⟨speech⟩

launcher /'lɔːntʃə(r)/ *n* lanciamissili *m inv*

launch[ing] pad /'lɔːntʃ[ɪŋ]/ *n* piattaforma *f* di lancio; fig trampolino *m* di lancio

launch pad *n* piattaforma *f* di lancio

launder /'lɔːndə(r)/ *vt* lavare e stirare; **~ money** fig riciclare denaro sporco

launderette /lɔːndəˈret/ *n* lavanderia *f* automatica

laundry /'lɔːndrɪ/ *n* lavanderia *f*; (clothes) bucato *m*

laureate /'lɒrɪət/ *adj* **poet ~** poeta *m* di corte; **Nobel ~** vincitore, -trice *mf* del Nobel

laurel /'lɒrəl/ *n* alloro *m*; **rest on one's ~s** fig dormire sugli allori

lav /læv/ *n* Br fam gabinetto *m*

lava /'lɑːvə/ *n* lava *f*

lavatorial /lævəˈtɔːrɪəl/ *adj* ⟨humour⟩ scatologico

lavatory /'lævətrɪ/ n gabinetto m

lavender /'lævəndə(r)/ n lavanda f

lavender blue adj color lavanda

lavish /'lævɪʃ/ ① adj copioso; (wasteful) prodigo; **on a ~ scale** su vasta scala
② vt **~ something on somebody** ricoprire qualcuno di qualcosa

lavishly /'lævɪʃlɪ/ adv copiosamente

law /'lɔ:/ n legge f; **study ~** studiare giurisprudenza, studiare legge; **take the ~ into one's own hands** farsi giustizia da sé; **~ of the jungle** legge della giungla

law-abiding /'lɔ:əbaɪdɪŋ/ adj che rispetta la legge

law and order n ordine m pubblico

lawbreaker /'lɔ:breɪkə(r)/ n persona f che infrange la legge

law court n tribunale m

lawful /'lɔ:fʊl/ adj legittimo

lawfully /'lɔ:fʊlɪ/ adv legittimamente

lawfulness /'lɔ:fʊlnɪs/ n legalità f

lawless /'lɔ:lɪs/ adj senza legge

lawmaker /'lɔ:meɪkə(r)/ n legislatore m

lawn /lɔ:n/ n prato m [all'inglese]

lawnmower /'lɔ:nməʊə(r)/ n tosaerba m inv

law school n facoltà f di giurisprudenza

lawsuit /'lɔ:su:t/ n causa f

lawyer /'lɔ:jə(r)/ n avvocato m

lax /læks/ adj negligente; ⟨morals etc⟩ lassista

laxative /'læksətɪv/ n lassativo m

laxity /'læksətɪ/ n lassismo m

lay¹ /leɪ/ adj laico; fig profano

lay² ▶ LIE²

lay³ ① vt (pt/pp **laid**) porre, mettere; apparecchiare ⟨table⟩
② vi ⟨hen⟩ fare le uova
■ **lay aside** vt mettere da parte
■ **lay down** vt posare; stabilire ⟨rules, conditions⟩
■ **lay in** vt farsi una scorta di ⟨coal, supplies etc⟩
■ **lay into** vt sl picchiare
■ **lay off** ① vt licenziare ⟨workers⟩
② vi (fam: stop) **~ off!** smettila!
■ **lay on** vt (organize) organizzare
■ **lay out** vt (display, set forth) esporre; (plan) pianificare ⟨garden⟩; (spend) sborsare; Typ impaginare
■ **lay up** vt **I was laid up in bed for a week** sono stato costretto a letto per una settimana

layabout /'leɪəbaʊt/ n fannullone, -a mf

lay-by n piazzola f di sosta

layer /'leɪə(r)/ n strato m

layette /leɪ'et/ n corredino m

layman /'leɪmən/ n profano m

lay-off n (permanent) licenziamento m; (temporary) sospensione f

layout /'leɪaʊt/ n disposizione f; Typ impaginazione f, layout m inv

lay preacher n predicatore m laico

laze /leɪz/ vi **~ [about]** oziare

lazily /'leɪzɪlɪ/ adv ⟨move, wander etc⟩ pigramente

laziness /'leɪzɪnɪs/ n pigrizia f

lazy /'leɪzɪ/ adj (-ier, -iest) pigro

lazybones /'leɪzɪbəʊnz/ n poltrone, -a mf

lazy eye n ambliopia f

lb abbr (**pound**) libbra

LCD n abbr (**liquid crystal display**) LCD m

lead¹ /led/ n piombo m; (of pencil) mina f

lead² /li:d/ ① n guida f; (leash) guinzaglio m; (flex) filo m; (clue) indizio m; Theat parte f principale; (distance ahead) distanza f (over su); **in the ~** in testa; **follow sb's ~** seguire l'esempio di qualcuno
② vt (pt/pp **led**) condurre; dirigere ⟨expedition, party etc⟩; (induce) indurre; **~ the way** mettersi in testa; **~ into temptation** indurre in tentazione
③ vi (be in front) condurre; (in race, competition) essere in testa
■ **lead astray** vt sviare
■ **lead away** vt portar via
■ **lead on** vt ingannare
■ **lead off** ① vi (begin) cominciare
② vt (take away) portare via
■ **lead to** vt portare a
■ **lead up to** vt preludere; **the period ~ing up to the election** il periodo precedente le elezioni; **what's this ~ing up to?** dove porta questo?

leaded /'ledɪd/ adj con piombo

leaded petrol Br, **leaded gasoline** Am n benzina f con piombo

leaden /'ledən/ adj di piombo

leader /'li:də(r)/ n capo m; (of orchestra) primo violino m; (in newspaper) articolo m di fondo

leadership /'li:dəʃɪp/ n direzione f, leadership f inv; **show ~** mostrare capacità di comando

leadership contest n elezione f alla direzione del partito

lead-free /'ledfri:/ adj senza piombo

lead-in /'li:dɪn/ n presentazione f

leading¹ /'li:dɪŋ/ adj principale

leading² /'ledɪŋ/ n Typ interlinea f

leading article n articolo m di fondo

leading edge n Aeron bordo m d'attacco; **at the ~ ~ of** (technology) all'avanguardia in

leading lady attrice f principale

leading light n personaggio m di spicco

leading man attore m principale

leading question n domanda f che influenza la risposta

lead poisoning n saturnismo m

lead story n articolo f principale

leaf /li:f/ n (pl **leaves**) foglia f; (of table) asse f; fig **take a ~ out of sb's book** imparare la lezione di qualcuno; **turn over a new ~** voltare pagina
■ **leaf through** vt sfogliare

leaflet /'li:flɪt/ n dépliant m inv; (advertising) dépliant m inv pubblicitario; (political) manifestino m

leafy /'li:fɪ/ adj ⟨tree⟩ ricco di foglie; ⟨wood⟩ molto verde; ⟨suburb, area⟩ ricco di verde

league /li:g/ n lega f; Sport campionato m; **be in ~ with** essere in combutta con

league table n classifica f del campionato

leak /li:k/ ① n (hole) fessura f; Naut falla f; (of gas & fig) fuga f
② vi colare; ⟨ship⟩ fare acqua; ⟨liquid, gas⟩ fuoriuscire
③ vt ~ **something to somebody** fig far trapelare qualcosa a qualcuno

leakage /'li:kɪdʒ/ n perdita f; (of gas & fig) fuga f

leaky /'li:kɪ/ adj che perde; Naut che fa acqua

lean¹ /li:n/ adj magro

lean² ① vt (pt/pp **leaned** or **leant** /lent/) appoggiare (**against/on** contro/su); ~ **one's elbows on the table** appoggiare i gomiti sul tavolo
② vi appoggiarsi (**against/on** contro/su); (not be straight) pendere; **be ~ing against** essere appoggiato contro; ~ **on somebody** (depend on) appoggiarsi a qualcuno; (fam: exert pressure on) stare alle calcagna di qualcuno
■ **lean back** vi sporgersi indietro
■ **lean forward** vi piegarsi in avanti
■ **lean out** vi sporgersi
■ **lean over** vi piegarsi
■ **lean towards** vt (favour) propendere per

leaning /'li:nɪŋ/ ① adj pendente; **the L~ Tower of Pisa** la torre di Pisa, la torre pendente
② n tendenza f

leanness /'li:nnɪs/ n magrezza f

lean-to n garage m inv adiacente alla casa

leap /li:p/ ① n salto m
② vi (pt/pp **leapt** /lept/ or **leaped**) saltare; **he leapt at it** fam l'ha preso al volo

leapfrog /'li:pfrɒg/ n cavallina f

leap year n anno m bisestile

learn /lɜ:n/ ① vt (pt/pp **learnt** or **learned**) imparare; ~ **to swim** imparare a nuotare; **I have ~ed that...** (heard) sono venuto a sapere che...; fig **he's ~t his lesson** ha imparato la lezione
② vi imparare; **as I've ~t to my cost** come ho imparato a mie spese

learned /'lɜ:nɪd/ adj colto

learner /'lɜ:nə(r)/ n also Auto principiante mf

learning /'lɜ:nɪŋ/ n cultura f

learning curve n curva f di apprendimento

learning difficulties npl (of schoolchildren) difficoltà fpl d'apprendimento

learning disability n difficoltà fpl d'apprendimento

lease /li:s/ ① n contratto m d'affitto; (rental) affitto m; **the job has given him a new ~ of life** grazie al lavoro ha ripreso gusto alla vita
② vt affittare

leasehold /'li:shəʊld/ n proprietà f in affitto

leaseholder /'li:shəʊldə(r)/ n titolare mf di un contratto d'affitto

leash /li:ʃ/ n guinzaglio m

leasing /'li:sɪŋ/ n (by company) leasing m; ~ **scheme** piano di leasing

least /li:st/ ① adj più piccolo; (smallest amount) meno; **you've got ~ luggage** hai meno bagagli di tutti
② n **the ~** il meno; **that's the ~ of my worries** questa è la cosa che mi preoccupa di meno; **at ~** almeno; **not in the ~** niente affatto
③ adv meno; **the ~ expensive wine** il vino meno caro

leather /'leðə(r)/ ① n pelle f; (of soles) cuoio m
② attrib di pelle/cuoio; ~ **jacket** giubbotto m di pelle

leathery /'leðərɪ/ adj (meat, skin) duro

leave /li:v/ ① n (holiday) congedo m; Mil licenza f; **on ~** in congedo/licenza; **take one's ~** accomiatarsi; ~ **of absence** aspettativa f
② vt (pt/pp **left**) lasciare; uscire da ⟨house, office⟩; (forget) dimenticare; **there is nothing left** non è rimasto niente; ~ **somebody in peace** lasciare in pace qualcuno
③ vi andare via; ⟨train, bus⟩ partire
■ **leave aside** vt (disregard) lasciare da parte
■ **leave behind** vt lasciare; (forget) dimenticare
■ **leave out** vt omettere; (not put away) lasciare fuori

leaves /li:vz/ ▶LEAF

leaving /'li:vɪŋ/ adj ⟨party, present⟩ d'addio

Lebanese /lebə'ni:z/ adj & n libanese mf

Lebanon /'lebənən/ n Libano m

lecher /'letʃə(r)/ n libertino m

lecherous /'letʃərəs/ adj lascivo

lechery /'letʃərɪ/ n lascivia f

lectern /'lektɜ:n/ n leggio m, scannello m

lecture /'lektʃə(r)/ **1** n conferenza f; Univ lezione f; (reproof) ramanzina f **2** vi fare una conferenza (**on** su); Univ insegnare (**on something** qualcosa) **3** vt ~ **somebody** rimproverare qualcuno

lecturer /'lektʃərə(r)/ n conferenziere, -a mf; Univ docente mf universitario, -a

lecture room n Br Univ aula f magna

lectureship /'lektʃəʃɪp/ n Br Univ docenza f universitaria

lecture theatre n Br Univ aula f magna

LED abbr (**light-emitting diode**) LED m inv

led /led/ ▶ LEAD²

ledge /ledʒ/ n cornice f; (of window) davanzale m

ledger /'ledʒə(r)/ n libro m mastro

leech /li:tʃ/ n sanguisuga f

leek /li:k/ n porro m

leer /lɪə(r)/ **1** n sguardo m libidinoso **2** vi ~ (**at**) guardare in modo libidinoso

lees /li:z/ npl (wine sediment) fondi mpl

leeway /'li:weɪ/ n fig libertà f di azione

left¹ /left/ ▶ LEAVE

left² **1** adj sinistro **2** adv a sinistra **3** n also Pol sinistra f: **on the** ~ **a** sinistra

left-hand adj di sinistra; **on the** ~ **side** sulla sinistra

left-hand drive adj ⟨car⟩ con la guida a sinistra

left-handed /-'hændɪd/ adj mancino; ⟨scissors etc⟩ per mancini

leftie /'leftɪ/ n sinistrorso, -a mf

leftist /'leftɪst/ adj & n sinistrorso, -a mf

left-luggage lockers npl deposito m bagagli automatico

left luggage [office] n deposito m bagagli

leftovers npl rimasugli mpl

left wing n Pol sinistra f; Sport ala f sinistra

left-wing adj Pol di sinistra

left-winger n Pol persona f di sinistra; Sport ala f sinistra

leg /leg/ **1** n gamba f; (of animal) zampa f; (of journey) tappa f; Culin (of chicken) coscia f; (of lamb) cosciotto m; **be on one's last** ~**s** ⟨machine⟩ funzionare per miracolo; **not have a** ~ **to stand on** non avere una ragione che regga **2** vt ~ **it** fam darsela a gambe

legacy /'legəsɪ/ n lascito m

legal /'li:gl/ adj legale; **take** ~ **action** intentare un'azione legale

legal adviser n consulente mf legale

legal aid n gratuito patrocinio m

legal eagle n hum principe m del foro

legal holiday n Am festa f nazionale

legality /lɪ'gælətɪ/ n legalità f

legalization /li:gəlaɪ'zeɪʃn/ n legalizzazione f

legalize /'li:gəlaɪz/ vt legalizzare

legally /'li:gəlɪ/ adv legalmente

legal proceedings npl procedimento m sg giudiziario

legal tender n valuta f a corso legale

legend /'ledʒənd/ n leggenda f

legendary /'ledʒəndərɪ/ adj leggendario

leggings /'legɪŋz/ npl (for baby) ghette fpl; (for woman) pantacollant mpl; (for man) gambali mpl

leggy /'legɪ/ adj ⟨person⟩ con le gambe lunghe

Leghorn /'leghɔ:n/ n Livorno f

legibility /ledʒə'bɪlətɪ/ n leggibilità f

legible /'ledʒəbl/ adj leggibile

legibly /'ledʒəblɪ/ adv in modo leggibile

legion /'li:dʒn/ n legione f

legionnaire /li:dʒə'neə(r)/ n Mil legionario m

legionnaire's disease n legionellosi f

legislate /'ledʒɪsleɪt/ vi legiferare

legislation /ledʒɪs'leɪʃn/ n legislazione f

legislative /'ledʒɪslətɪv/ adj legislativo

legislator /'ledʒɪsleɪtə(r)/ n legislatore m

legislature /'ledʒɪsleɪtʃə(r)/ n legislatura f

legitimacy /lɪ'dʒɪtɪməsɪ/ n (lawfulness) legittimità f; (of argument) validità f

legitimate /lɪ'dʒɪtɪmət/ adj legittimo; ⟨excuse⟩ valido

legitimately /lɪ'dʒɪtɪmətlɪ/ adv legittimamente

legitimize /lɪdʒɪtɪ'maɪz/ vt rendere legittimo

legless /'leglɪs/ adj senza gambe; (Br: drunk) ubriaco fradicio

leg-pulling n presa f in giro

legroom n spazio m per le gambe

leg warmer n scaldamuscoli m inv

legwork n fatica f; **do the** ~ fare da galoppino

leisure /'leʒə(r)/ n tempo m libero; **at your** ~ con comodo

leisure centre n centro m sportivo e ricreativo

leisurely /'leʒəlɪ/ adj senza fretta

leisure time n tempo m libero

leisurewear /'leʒəweə(r)/ n abbigliamento m per il tempo libero

lemming /'lemɪŋ/ n lemming m inv

lemon /'lemən/ n limone m

lemonade /leməˈneɪd/ n limonata f

lemon curd n crema f al limone

lemon juice n (drink) succo m di limone

lemon sole n sogliola f limanda

lemon squash n sciroppo m di limone

lemon tea n tè m inv al limone

lemon tree n limone m

lemon yellow ① n giallo m limone
② adj giallo limone

lend /lend/ vt (pt/pp **lent**) prestare; ~ **a hand** fig dare una mano; ~ **an ear** prestare ascolto; ~ **itself to** prestarsi a

lender /ˈlendə(r)/ n prestatore, -trice mf

lending library /ˈlendɪn/ n biblioteca f per il prestito

length /leŋθ/ n lunghezza f; (piece) pezzo m; (of wallpaper) parte f; (of visit) durata f; **at** ~ **a** lungo; (at last) alla fine

lengthen /ˈleŋθən/ ① vt allungare
② vi allungarsi

lengthways /ˈleŋθweɪz/ adv per lungo

lengthwise /ˈleŋθwaɪz/ adv longitudinale

lengthy /ˈleŋθɪ/ adj (**-ier, -iest**) lungo

lenience /ˈliːnɪəns/ n indulgenza f

lenient /ˈliːnɪənt/ adj indulgente

leniently /ˈliːnɪəntlɪ/ adv con indulgenza

lens /lenz/ n lente f; Phot obiettivo m; (of eye) cristallino m

lens cap n copriobiettivo m

Lent /lent/ n Quaresima f

lent ▸ LEND

lentil /ˈlentl/ n Bot lenticchia f

Leo /ˈliːəʊ/ n Astr Leone m

leopard /ˈlepəd/ n leopardo m

leopardskin /ˈlepədskɪn/ ① n pelle f di leopardo
② attrib di [pelle di] leopardo

leotard /ˈliːətɑːd/ n body m inv

leper /ˈlepə(r)/ n lebbroso, -a mf; fig appestato, -a mf

leprosy /ˈleprəsɪ/ n lebbra f

lesbian /ˈlezbɪən/ ① adj lesbico
② n lesbica f

lesbianism /ˈlezbɪənɪzm/ n lesbismo m

lesion /ˈliːʒn/ n lesione f

Lesotho /ləˈsuːtuː/ n Lesotho m

less /les/ ① adj meno di; ~ **and** ~ sempre meno;
② adv & prep meno
③ n meno m

lessee /leˈsiː/ n Jur affittuario, -a mf

lessen /ˈlesn/ vt/i diminuire

lesser /ˈlesə(r)/ adj minore; **the** ~ **of two evils** il minore fra i due mali

lesson /ˈlesn/ n lezione f; **teach somebody a** ~ fig dare una lezione a qualcuno

lessor /leˈsɔː/ n Jur locatore, -trice mf

lest /lest/ conj liter per timore che

let /let/ ① vt (pt/pp **let**, pres p **letting**) lasciare, permettere; (rent) affittare; ~ **alone** (not to mention) tanto meno; **'to** ~' 'affittasi'; ~ **us go** andiamo; ~ **somebody do something** lasciare fare qualcosa a qualcuno, permettere a qualcuno di fare qualcosa; ~ **me know** fammi sapere; **just** ~ **him try!** che ci provi solamente!; ~ **onself in for something** fam impelagarsi in qualcosa
② n Tennis colpo m nullo; (Br: lease) contratto m d'affitto
③ vi ~ **fly at somebody** aggredire qualcuno

■ **let down** vt sciogliersi ⟨hair⟩; abbassare ⟨blinds⟩; (lengthen) allungare; (disappoint) deludere; **don't** ~ **me down** conto su di te

■ **let go** ① vi mollare; ~ **go of** lasciare andare
② vt mollare ⟨rope, person⟩; ~ **somebody go** rilasciare ⟨prisoner⟩; licenziare ⟨employee⟩; ~ **oneself go** lasciarsi andare

■ **let in** vt far entrare

■ **let off** vt far partire; (not punish) perdonare; ~ **somebody off doing something** abbonare qualcosa a qualcuno; ~ **off steam** fig scaricarsi

■ **let on** vi sl **don't** ~ **on** non spifferare niente

■ **let out** vt far uscire; (make larger) allargare; emettere ⟨scream, groan⟩

■ **let through** vt far passare

■ **let up** vi fam diminuire

let-down n delusione f

lethal /ˈliːθl/ adj letale; ~ **dose** n dose f letale

lethargic /lɪˈθɑːdʒɪk/ adj apatico

lethargy /ˈleθədʒɪ/ n apatia f

let-out n fam via f d'uscita

letter /ˈletə(r)/ n lettera f

letter bomb n lettera f esplosiva

letter box n buca f per le lettere

letterhead n (heading) intestazione f; (paper) carta f intestata

lettering /ˈletərɪn/ n caratteri mpl

letter of apology n lettera f di scuse

letter of credit n Comm lettera f di credito

letter of introduction n lettera f di presentazione

lettuce /ˈletɪs/ n lattuga f

let-up n fam pausa f

leukaemia /luːˈkiːmɪə/ n leucemia f

level /ˈlevl/ ① adj piano; (in height, competition) allo stesso livello; ⟨spoonful⟩ raso; **draw** ~ **with somebody** affiancare qualcuno; **do one's** ~ **best** fare del proprio meglio
② n livello m; **on the** ~ fam giusto
③ vt (pt/pp **levelled**) livellare; (aim) puntare (**at** su)

■ **level off** *vi* ⟨*inflation, unemployment*⟩ stabilizzarsi

■ **level out** *vi* ⟨*surface*⟩ diventare pianeggiante; ⟨*aircraft*⟩ mettersi in orizzontale

■ **level with** *vt* (fam: be honest with) essere franco con

level crossing *n* passaggio *m* a livello

level-headed /-'hedɪd/ *adj* posato

level pegging *n* it's ∼ ∼ so far finora sono alla pari

lever /'li:və(r)/ *n* leva *f*

■ **lever off**, **lever up** *vt* sollevare (con una leva)

leverage /'li:vərɪdʒ/ *n* azione *f* di una leva; fig influenza *f*

leveret /'levərət/ *n* leprotto *m*

levitate /'levɪteɪt/ *vi* levitare

levity /'levətɪ/ *n* leggerezza *f*

levy /'levɪ/ *vt* (pt/pp **levied**) imporre ⟨*tax*⟩

lewd /lju:d/ *adj* osceno

lexical /'leksɪkəl/ *adj* lessicale

lexicographer /leksɪ'kɒɡrəfə(r)/ *n* lessicografo, -a *mf*

lexicographic /leksɪkə'ɡræfɪk/ *adj* lessicografico

lexicography /leksɪ'kɒɡrəfɪ/ *n* lessicografia *f*

lexicon /'leksɪkən/ *n* lessico *m*

liability /laɪə'bɪlətɪ/ *n* responsabilità *f*; (fam: burden) peso *m*; **liabilities** *pl* passività *fpl*

liable /'laɪəbl/ *adj* responsabile (**for** di); **be** ∼ **to** ⟨*rain, break etc*⟩ rischiare di; (tend to) tendere a

liaise /lɪ'eɪz/ *vi* fam essere in contatto

liaison /lɪ'eɪzɒn/ *n* contatti *mpl*; Mil collegamento *m*; (affair) relazione *f*

liar /'laɪə(r)/ *n* bugiardo, -a *mf*

Lib Dem /lɪb'dem/ Br Pol *abbr* Liberal Democrat

libel /'laɪbl/ **①** *n* diffamazione *f*
② *vt* (pt/pp **libelled**) diffamare

libellous Br, **libelous** Am *adj* diffamatorio

liberal /'lɪb(ə)rəl/ **①** *adj* (tolerant) di larghe vedute; (generous) generoso. **L**∼ *adj* Pol liberale
② *n* liberale *mf*

Liberal Democrat *n* Br Pol liberal-democratico, -a *mf*

liberalism /'lɪb(ə)rəlɪzm/ *n* liberalismo *m*

liberalization /lɪbərəlaɪ'zeɪʃn/ *n* (of trade) liberalizzazione *f*

liberalize /'lɪbərəlaɪz/ *vt* liberalizzare

liberally /'lɪbrəlɪ/ *adv* liberalmente

liberate /'lɪbəreɪt/ *vt* liberare

liberated /'lɪbəreɪtɪd/ *adj* ⟨*woman*⟩ emancipata

liberating /'lɪbəreɪtɪŋ/ *adj* liberatorio

liberation /lɪbə'reɪʃn/ *n* liberazione *f*; (of women) emancipazione *f*

liberator /'lɪbəreɪtə(r)/ *n* liberatore, -trice *mf*

Liberia /laɪ'bɪərɪə/ *n* Liberia *f*

libertarian /lɪbə'teərɪən/ *adj* & *n* liberale *mf*

libertarianism /lɪbə'teərɪənɪzm/ *n* liberalismo *m*

liberty /'lɪbətɪ/ *n* libertà *f*; **take the** ∼ **of doing something** prendersi la libertà di fare qualcosa; **take liberties** prendersi delle libertà; **be at** ∼ **to do something** essere libero di fare qualcosa

libido /lɪ'bi:dəʊ/ *n* libido *f inv*

Libra /'li:brə/ *n* Astr Bilancia *f*

librarian /laɪ'breərɪən/ *n* bibliotecario, -a *mf*

library /'laɪbrərɪ/ *n* biblioteca *f*

libretto /lɪ'bretəʊ/ *n* (pl **-tti** or **-ttos**) libretto *m* di opera

Libya /'lɪbɪə/ *n* Libia *f*

Libyan /'lɪbɪən/ *adj* & *n* libico, -a *mf*

lice /laɪs/ ▶LOUSE

licence /'laɪsns/ *n* licenza *f*; (for TV) canone *m* televisivo; (for driving) patente *f*; (freedom) sregolatezza *f*

licence number *n* numero *m* di targa

licence plate *n* targa *f*

license /'laɪsns/ *vt* autorizzare; **be** ∼**d** ⟨*car*⟩ avere il bollo; ⟨*restaurant*⟩ essere autorizzato alla vendita di alcolici

licensee /laɪsən'si:/ *n* titolare *mf* di licenza (per la vendita di alcolici)

licensing hours /'laɪsənsɪŋ/ *npl* Br orario *m* in cui è permessa la vendita di alcolici

licensing laws *npl* Br normativa *f sg* sulla vendita di alcolici

licentious /laɪ'senʃəs/ *adj* licenzioso

licentiousness /laɪ'senʃəsnɪs/ *n* licenziosità *f*

lichen /'laɪkən/ *n* Bot lichene *m*

lick /lɪk/ **①** *n* leccata *f*; **a** ∼ **of paint** una passata leggera di pittura
② *vt* leccare; (fam: defeat) battere; leccarsi ⟨*lips*⟩; fam ∼ **somebody into shape** rendere qualcuno efficiente

licorice /'lɪkərɪs/ *n* Am = LIQUORICE

lid /lɪd/ *n* coperchio *m*; (of eye) palpebra *f*; **keep the** ∼ **on something** fam non lasciare trapelare qualcosa

lido /'li:dəʊ/ *n* (beach) lido *m*; ⟨*Br: pool*⟩ piscina *f* scoperta

lie[1] /laɪ/ **①** *n* bugia *f*; **tell a** ∼ mentire
② *vi* (pt/pp **lied**, pres p **lying**) mentire

lie² *vi* (pt **lay**, pp **lain**, pres p **lying**) ⟨*person*⟩ sdraiarsi; ⟨*object*⟩ stare; (remain) rimanere; **leave something lying about** or **around** lasciare qualcosa in giro; **here ~s...** qui giace...; **~ low** tenersi nascosto
■ **lie around** ① *vi* ⟨*person*⟩ girellare ② *vt* girellare in ⟨*house*⟩
■ **lie back** *vi* (relax) rilassarsi
■ **lie down** *vi* sdraiarsi
■ **lie in** *vi* (stay in bed) rimanere a letto

Liechtenstein /ˈlɪktənstaɪn/ *n* Liechtenstein *m*

lie detector *n* macchina *f* della verità

lie-down *n* **have a ~** fare un riposino

lie-in *n* fam **have a ~** restare a letto fino a tardi

lieu /ljuː/ *n* **in ~ of** in luogo di

lieutenant /lefˈtenənt/ *n* tenente *m*

life /laɪf/ *n* (pl **lives**) vita *f*; **give one's ~ for somebody/one's country** dare la vita per qualcuno/la patria; **give one's ~ to** (devote oneself to) dedicare la propria vita a; **lose one's ~** perdere la vita; **for dear ~** per salvare la pelle; **not on your ~!** fam neanche morto!

life-and-death *adj* ⟨*struggle*⟩ disperato

lifebelt *n* salvagente *m*

lifeblood *n* fig linfa *f* vitale

lifeboat *n* lancia *f* di salvataggio; (on ship) scialuppa *f* di salvataggio

lifebuoy *n* salvagente *m*

life coach *n* life coach *mf* inv

life drawing *n* disegno *m* dal vero

life expectancy *n* vita *f* media

life form *n* forma *f* di vita

lifeguard *n* (on beach etc) bagnino, -a *mf*

life-imprisonment *n* ergastolo *m*

life insurance *n* assicurazione *f* sulla vita

life jacket *n* giubbotto *m* di salvataggio

lifeless /ˈlaɪflɪs/ *adj* inanimato

lifelike *adj* realistico

lifeline *n* sagola *f* di salvataggio

lifelong *adj* di tutta la vita

lifer /ˈlaɪfə(r)/ *n* fam ergastolano, -a *mf*

lifesaving /ˈlaɪfseɪvɪŋ/ *n* salvataggio *m*

life sentence *n* condanna *f* all'ergastolo

life-size[d] /ˈlaɪfsaɪz[d]/ *adj* a grandezza naturale

lifespan *n* durata *f* della vita

life story *n* biografia *f*

lifestyle *n* stile *m* di vita

lifestyle drug *n* medicinale *m* che migliora la qualità della vita

life support *n* Med respirazione *f* assistita; **on ~** attaccato al respiratore artificiale; **~ machine** respiratore artificiale

lifetime *n* vita *f*; **the chance of a ~** un'occasione unica; **~ guarantee** garanzia *f* a vita

lift /lɪft/ ① *n* ascensore *m*; Auto passaggio *m*; **give somebody a ~** dare un passaggio a qualcuno; **I got a ~** mi hanno dato un passaggio
② *vt* sollevare; revocare ⟨*restrictions*⟩; (fam: steal) rubare
③ *vi* ⟨*fog*⟩ alzarsi
■ **lift off** *vi* ⟨*rocket*⟩ partire
■ **lift up** *vt* sollevare

liftboy *n* Br lift *m* inv

lift-off *n* decollo *m* (di razzo)

ligament /ˈlɪgəmənt/ *n* Anat legamento *m*

light¹ /laɪt/ ① *adj* (not dark) luminoso; **~ green** verde chiaro
② *n* luce *f*; (lamp) lampada *f*; **in the ~ of** fig alla luce di; **have you got a ~?** ha da accendere?; **come to ~** essere rivelato
③ *vt* (pt/pp **lit** or **lighted**) accendere; (illuminate) illuminare
■ **light up** ① *vt* accendere ⟨*pipe*, *cigarette*⟩; illuminare ⟨*face*⟩; rischiarare ⟨*sky*⟩
② *vi* ⟨*face*⟩ illuminarsi

light² ① *adj* (not heavy) leggero; **make ~ of** non dare peso a
② *adv* **travel ~** viaggiare con poco bagaglio

light bulb *n* lampadina *f*

lighten¹ /ˈlaɪtn/ *vt* illuminare

lighten² *vt* alleggerire ⟨*load*⟩

light entertainment *n* varietà *m* inv

lighter /ˈlaɪtə(r)/ *n* accendino *m*

lighter fuel *n* (liquid) gas *m* inv da accendino

light-fingered /-ˈfɪŋgəd/ *adj* svelto di mano

light-headed /-ˈhedɪd/ *adj* sventato

light-hearted /-ˈhɑːtɪd/ *adj* spensierato

lighthouse *n* faro *m*

light industry *n* industria *f* leggera

lighting /ˈlaɪtɪŋ/ *n* illuminazione *f*

lightly /ˈlaɪtlɪ/ *adv* leggermente; ⟨*accuse*⟩ con leggerezza; ⟨*take something*⟩ alla leggera; (without concern) senza dare importanza alla cosa; **get off ~** cavarsela a buon mercato

lightness /ˈlaɪtnɪs/ *n* leggerezza *f*

lightning /ˈlaɪtnɪŋ/ *n* lampo *m*, fulmine *m*

lightning conductor *n* parafulmine *m*

lightning strike *n* sciopero *m* a sorpresa

light-pen *n* (for computer screen) penna *f* ottica

lightweight *adj* leggero *n* (in boxing) peso *m* leggero

light year n anno m luce; **it was ~ ~s ago** è stato secoli fa

like¹ /laɪk/ **①** adj simile

② prep come; **~ this/that** così; **what's he ~?** com'è?

③ conj (fam: as) come; (Am: as if) come se

like² **①** vt piacere, gradire; **I should** or **would ~** vorrei, gradirei; **I ~ him** mi piace; **I ~ this car** mi piace questa macchina; **I ~ dancing** mi piace ballare; **I ~ that!** fam questa mi è piaciuta!; **~ it or lump it!** abbozzala!

② n **~s and dislikes** pl gusti mpl

likeable /'laɪkəbl/ adj simpatico

likelihood /'laɪklɪhʊd/ n probabilità f

likely /'laɪklɪ/ **①** adj (-ier, -iest) probabile

② adv probabilmente; **not ~!** fam neanche per sogno!

like-minded /laɪk'maɪndɪd/ adj con gusti affini

liken /'laɪkən/ vt paragonare (**to** a)

likeness /'laɪknɪs/ n somiglianza f

likewise /'laɪkwaɪz/ adv lo stesso

liking /'laɪkɪŋ/ n gusto m; **is it to your ~?** è di suo gusto?; **take a ~ to somebody** prendere qualcuno in simpatia

lilac /'laɪlək/ **①** n lillà m

② adj lilla

Lilo® /'laɪləʊ/ n materassino m gonfiabile

lilting /'lɪltɪŋ/ adj cadenzato

lily /'lɪlɪ/ n giglio m

lily of the valley n mughetto m

lily pond n stagno m con ninfee

limb /lɪm/ n arto m

limber /'lɪmbə(r)/ vi **~ up** sciogliersi i muscoli

limbo /'lɪmbəʊ/ n (Relig, fig, dance) limbo m; **be in ~** ⟨person⟩ essere nel limbo del dubbio; ⟨future of something⟩ essere in sospeso

lime¹ /laɪm/ n (fruit) limetta f; (tree) tiglio m

lime² n calce f

lime-green adj & n verde m limone

limelight /'laɪmlaɪt/ n **be in the ~** essere molto in vista

limestone /'laɪmstəʊn/ n calcare m

limit /'lɪmɪt/ **①** n limite m; **be the ~** essere il colmo; **that's the ~!** fam questo è troppo!

② vt limitare (**to** a)

limitation /lɪmɪ'teɪʃn/ n limite m

limited /'lɪmɪtɪd/ adj ristretto

limited company n società f inv a responsabilità limitata

limited edition n (book, lithograph) edizione f limitata

limited liability n responsabilità f limitata

limitless /'lɪmɪtlɪs/ adj infinito

limousine /'lɪməziːn/ n limousine f inv

limp¹ /lɪmp/ **①** n andatura f zoppicante; **have a ~** zoppicare

② vi zoppicare

limp² adj floscio

limpet /'lɪmpɪt/ n **be like a ~** fig essere attaccaticcio

limpid /'lɪmpɪd/ adj limpido

limp-wristed /-'rɪstɪd/ adj pej effeminato

linchpin /'lɪntʃpɪn/ n (fig: essential element) perno m

line¹ /laɪn/ **①** n linea f; (length of rope, cord) filo m; (of writing) riga f; (of poem) verso m; (row) fila f; (wrinkle) ruga f; (of business) settore m; (Am: queue) coda f; **in ~ with** in conformità con; **bring into ~** mettere al passo ⟨structure, law⟩ nell'esercizio delle proprie funzioni; **~ of fire** linea f di tiro; **stand in ~** (Am: queue) fare la coda; **in ~ for** ⟨promotion etc⟩ in lista per; **on the ~** ⟨job, career⟩ in serio pericolo; **read between the ~s** fig leggere tra le righe

② vt segnare; fiancheggiare ⟨street⟩; foderare ⟨garment⟩

■ **line up** **①** vi allinearsi

② vt allineare

lineage /'lɪnɪɪdʒ/ n lignaggio m

linear /'lɪnɪə(r)/ adj lineare

lined¹ /laɪnd/ adj ⟨face⟩ rugoso; ⟨paper⟩ a righe

lined² adj ⟨garment⟩ foderato

line manager n line manager m inv

linen /'lɪnɪn/ **①** n lino m; (articles) biancheria f

② attrib di lino

linen basket n cesto m della biancheria

liner /'laɪnə(r)/ n nave f di linea

linesman /'laɪnzmən/ n Sport guardalinee m inv

line-up n (personnel, Sport) formazione f; (identification) confronto m all'americana

linger /'lɪŋɡə(r)/ vi indugiare

lingerie /'lãʒərɪ/ n biancheria f intima (da donna)

lingering /'lɪŋɡərɪŋ/ adj ⟨illness⟩ lento; ⟨look⟩ prolungato; ⟨doubt⟩ persistente

linguist /'lɪŋɡwɪst/ n linguista mf

linguistic /lɪŋ'ɡwɪstɪk/ adj linguistico

linguistically /lɪŋ'ɡwɪstɪklɪ/ adv linguisticamente

linguistics /lɪŋ'ɡwɪstɪks/ n linguistica fsg

lining /'laɪnɪŋ/ n (of garment) fodera f; (of brakes) guarnizione f

link /lɪŋk/ **①** n (of chain) anello m; fig legame m

2 *vt* collegare; ~ **arms** prendersi sottobraccio
■ **link up** *vi* unirsi (**with** a); TV collegarsi
linkage /'lɪŋkɪdʒ/ *n* (connection) connessione *f*; (in genetics) associazione *f*
link road *n* bretella *f*
links /lɪŋks/ *n or npl* campo *msg* da golf
link-up *n* collegamento *m*
lino /'laɪməʊ/ *n*, **linoleum** /lɪ'nəʊlɪəm/ *n* linoleum *m*
linseed oil /'lɪnsi:dɔɪl/ *n* olio *m* [di semi] di lino
lint /lɪnt/ *n* garza *f*
lintel /'lɪntəl/ *n* architrave *m*
lion /'laɪən/ *n* leone *m*; **get the** ~**'s share** fig prendersi la fetta più grossa
lion cub *n* leoncino *m*
lioness /'laɪənɪs/ *n* leonessa *f*
lip /lɪp/ *n* labbro *m* (*pl* labbra *f*); (edge) bordo *m*
lip gloss *n* lucidalabbra *m inv*
liposuction /'laɪpəʊsʌkʃn/ *n* liposuzione *f*
lip-read *vi* leggere le labbra
lip-reading *n* lettura *f* delle labbra
lipsalve *n* burro *m* [di] cacao
lip-service *n* pay ~ **to** approvare soltanto a parole
lipstick *n* rossetto *m*
liquefy /'lɪkwɪfaɪ/ **1** *v* (pt/pp **-ied**) *vt* liquefare
2 *vi* liquefarsi
liqueur /lɪ'kjʊə(r)/ *n* liquore *m*
liquid /'lɪkwɪd/ **1** *n* liquido *m*
2 *adj* liquido
liquidate /'lɪkwɪdeɪt/ *vt* liquidare
liquidation /lɪkwɪ'deɪʃn/ *n* liquidazione *f*; **go into** ~ Comm andare in liquidazione
liquidator /'lɪkwɪdeɪtə(r)/ *n* liquidatore, -trice *mf*
liquid crystal display *n* visualizzatore *m* a cristalli liquidi
liquidize /'lɪkwɪdaɪz/ *vt* rendere liquido
liquidizer /'lɪkwɪdaɪzə(r)/ *n* Culin frullatore *m*
liquor /'lɪkə(r)/ *n* bevanda *f* alcolica
liquorice /'lɪkərɪs/ *n* liquirizia *f*
liquor store *n* Am negozio *m* di alcolici
lira /'lɪərə/ *n* old lira *f*; **50,000 lire** 50.000 lire
lisp /lɪsp/ **1** *n* pronuncia *f* con la lisca; **have a** ~ parlare con la lisca
2 *vi* parlare con la lisca
list¹ /lɪst/ **1** *n* lista *f*
2 *vt* elencare
list² *vi* ⟨ship⟩ inclinarsi
listen /'lɪsn/ *vi* ascoltare; ~ **to** ascoltare
■ **listen in** *vi* (secretly) origliare; ~ **in on** ascoltare di nascosto ⟨conversation⟩

listener /'lɪs(ə)nə(r)/ *n* ascoltatore, -trice *mf*
listeria /lɪ'stɪərɪə/ *n* (illness) listeriosi *f*; (bacteria) listeria *f*
listings /'lɪstɪŋz/ *npl* rubrica *f* degli spettacoli
listless /'lɪstlɪs/ *adj* svogliato
listlessly /'lɪstlɪslɪ/ *adv* in modo svogliato
list price *n* prezzo *m* di listino
lit /lɪt/ ▶ LIGHT¹
litany /'lɪtənɪ/ *n* litania *f*
literacy /'lɪtərəsɪ/ *n* alfabetizzazione *f*
literal /'lɪtərəl/ *adj* letterale
literally /'lɪt(ə)rəlɪ/ *adv* letteralmente
literary /'lɪtərərɪ/ *adj* letterario
literary critic *n* critico, -a *mf* letterario, -a
literary criticism *n* critica *f* letteraria
literate /'lɪtərət/ *adj* be ~ saper leggere e scrivere
literati /'lɪtə'rɑːti:/ *npl* letterati *mpl*
literature /'lɪtrətʃə(r)/ *n* letteratura *f*
lithe /laɪð/ *adj* flessuoso
lithographer /lɪ'θɒɡrəfə(r)/ *n* litografo, -a *mf*
lithography /lɪ'θɒɡrəfɪ/ *n* litografia *f*
Lithuania /lɪθjʊ'eɪnɪə/ *n* Lituania *f*
Lithuanian /lɪθjʊ'eɪnɪən/ *adj & n* lituano, -a *mf*; (language) lituano *m*
litigation /lɪtɪ'ɡeɪʃn/ *n* causa *f* [giudiziaria]
litmus paper /'lɪtməs/ *n* cartina *f* di tornasole
litmus test *n* Chem test *m inv* con cartina di tornasole; fig prova *f* del nove
litre /'liːtə(r)/ *n* litro *m*
litter /'lɪtə(r)/ **1** *n* immondizie *fpl*; Zool figliata *f*
2 *vt* be ~**ed with something** essere ingombrato di qualcosa
litter-bin *n* bidone *m* della spazzatura
litterbug /'lɪtəbʌɡ/ *n* persona *f* che butta per terra cartacce e rifiuti
little /'lɪtl/ **1** *adj* piccolo; (not much) poco
2 *adv & n* poco *m*; **a** ~ un po'; **a** ~ **water** un po' d'acqua; **a** ~ **better** un po' meglio; ~ **by** ~ a poco a poco
little finger *n* mignolo *m* (della mano)
little-known *adj* poco noto
liturgical /lɪ'tɜːdʒɪkl/ *adj* liturgico
liturgy /'lɪtədʒɪ/ *n* liturgia *f*
live¹ /laɪv/ **1** *adj* vivo; ⟨ammunition⟩ carico; ~ **broadcast** trasmissione *f* in diretta; **be** ~ Electr essere sotto tensione
2 *adv* ⟨broadcast⟩ in diretta
live² /lɪv/ *vi* vivere; (reside) abitare
■ **live down** *vt* far dimenticare

■ **live for** vt vivere solo per ⟨one's work, family⟩

■ **live in** vi ⟨nanny, au-pair⟩ abitare sul posto di lavoro

■ **live off** vt vivere alle spalle di

■ **live on** ① vt vivere di
② vi sopravvivere

■ **live through** vt vivere

■ **live together** vi ⟨friends⟩ vivere insieme; ⟨lovers⟩ convivere

■ **live up** vt ~ it up far la bella vita

■ **live up to** vt essere all'altezza di

■ **live with** vt convivere con ⟨lover, situation⟩; vivere con ⟨mother etc⟩

lived-in /'lɪvdɪn/ adj have that ~ look ⟨room, flat⟩ avere un'aria vissuta

live-in adj ⟨maid, nanny⟩ che vive in casa

livelihood /'laɪvlɪhʊd/ n mezzi mpl di sostentamento

liveliness /'laɪvlɪnɪs/ n vivacità f

lively /'laɪvlɪ/ adj (-ier, -iest) vivace

liven /'laɪvn/ v

■ **liven up** /'laɪvn/ ① vt vivacizzare
② vi vivacizzarsi

liver /'lɪvə(r)/ n fegato m

liver pâté n pâté m inv di fegato

Liverpudlian /lɪvə'pʌdlɪən/ n ⟨born there⟩ originario, -a mf di Liverpool; ⟨living there⟩ abitante mf di Liverpool

livery /'lɪvərɪ/ n (uniform) livrea f

lives /laɪvz/ ▶ LIFE

livestock /'laɪvstɒk/ n bestiame m

live wire n fig be a ~ essere superdinamico

livid /'lɪvɪd/ adj fam livido

living /'lɪvɪŋ/ ① adj vivo
② n earn one's ~ guadagnarsi da vivere; the ~ pl i vivi

living room n soggiorno m

living will n dichiarazione f dell'interessato in cui si rifiuta l'accanimento terapeutico

lizard /'lɪzəd/ n lucertola f

llama /'lɑːmə/ n lama m

LLB abbr (**Bachelor of Laws**) laureato, -a mf in legge

load /ləʊd/ ① n carico m; ~s of fam un sacco di; that's a ~ off my mind mi sono tolto un peso [dallo stomaco]
② vt ~ [up] caricare

loaded /'ləʊdɪd/ adj carico; (fam: rich) ricchissimo; ~ question domanda f esplosiva f

loading bay /'ləʊdɪŋ/ n piazzola f di carico e scarico

loaf[1] /ləʊf/ n (pl **loaves**) pane m; (round) pagnotta f: use one's ~ (fam) pensare con il proprio cervello

loaf[2], ~ **about** or **around** vi oziare

loafer /'ləʊfə(r)/ n (idler) scansafatiche mf inv; (shoe) mocassino m

loan /ləʊn/ ① n prestito m; on ~ in prestito
② vt prestare

loan shark n fam strozzino, -a mf

loath /ləʊθ/ adj be ~ to do something essere restio a fare qualcosa

loathe /ləʊð/ vt detestare

loathing /'ləʊðɪŋ/ n disgusto m

loathsome /'ləʊðsəm/ adj disgustoso

loaves /ləʊvz/ ▶ LOAF[1]

lob /lɒb/ ① vt (pres p pt -bb-) lanciare in alto; Sport respingere a pallonetto
② n Sport pallonetto m

lobby /'lɒbɪ/ ① n atrio m; Pol gruppo m di pressione, lobby f inv
② v ~ for something fare pressioni per qualcosa

lobbying /'lɒbɪɪŋ/ n lobbismo m

lobbyist /'lɒbɪɪst/ n lobbista mf

lobe /ləʊb/ n (of ear) lobo m

lobelia /lə'biːlɪə/ n lobelia f

lobster /'lɒbstə(r)/ n aragosta f

lobster pot n nassa f per aragoste

local /'ləʊkl/ ① adj locale; under ~ anaesthetic sotto anestesia locale; I'm not ~ non sono del posto
② n abitante mf del luogo; (fam: public house) pub m inv locale

local authority n autorità f locale

local bus n bus m locale

local call n Teleph telefonata f urbana

local election n elezioni fpl amministrative

local government n autorità f inv locale

locality /ləʊ'kælətɪ/ n zona f

localized /'ləʊkəlaɪzd/ adj localizzato

locally /'ləʊkəlɪ/ adv localmente; ⟨live, work⟩ nei paraggi

local network n Comput rete f locale

locate /ləʊ'keɪt/ vt situare; trovare ⟨person⟩; be ~d essere situato

location /ləʊ'keɪʃn/ n posizione f; filmed on ~ girato in esterni

loch /lɒx/ n lago m

lock[1] /lɒk/ n (of hair) ciocca f

lock[2] ① n (on door) serratura f: (on canal) chiusa f
② vt chiudere a chiave; bloccare ⟨wheels⟩
③ vi chiudersi

■ **lock in** vt chiudere dentro

■ **lock out** vt chiudere fuori

■ **lock together** vi ⟨pieces⟩ incastrarsi

■ **lock up** ① vt (in prison) mettere dentro
② vi chiudere

locker /'lɒkə(r)/ n armadietto m

locker room n spogliatoio m

locket /'lɒkɪt/ n medaglione m

lockout *n* serrata *f*

locksmith *n* fabbro *m*

lock-up *n* (prison) guardina *f*

loco /'ləʊkəʊ/ *adj* (Br: crazy) toccato

locomotion /ləʊkə'məʊʃn/ *n* locomozione *f*

locomotive /ləʊkə'məʊtɪv/ *n* locomotiva *f*

locum /'ləʊkəm/ *n* sostituto, -a *mf*

locust /'ləʊkəst/ *n* locusta *f*

lodge /lɒdʒ/ **1** *n* (porter's) portineria *f*; (masonic) loggia *f*
2 *vt* presentare ⟨claim, complaint⟩; (with bank, solicitor) depositare; **be** ~**d** essersi conficcato
3 *vi* essere a pensione (**with** da); (become fixed) conficcarsi

lodger /'lɒdʒə(r)/ *n* inquilino, -a *mf*

lodgings /'lɒdʒɪŋ/ *npl* camere *fpl* in affitto

loft /lɒft/ *n* soffitta *f*

loft conversion *n* soppalco *f* abitabile

lofty /'lɒftɪ/ *adj* (**-ier**, **-iest**) alto; (haughty) altezzoso

log /lɒg/ **1** *n* ceppo *m*; Auto libretto *m* di circolazione; Naut giornale *m* di bordo; **sleep like a** ~ fam dormire come un ghiro **2** *vt* (pt/pp **logged**) registrare
■ **log in** *vi* aprire una sessione
■ **log off** *vi* disconnettersi
■ **log on** *vi* connettersi (**to a**)
■ **log out** *vi* chiudere una sessione

logarithm /'lɒgərɪðm/ *n* logaritmo *m*

logbook /'lɒgbʊk/ *n* Naut giornale *m* di bordo; Auto libretto *m* di circolazione

log cabin *n* capanna *f* di tronchi

logger /'lɒgə(r)/ *n* boscaiolo *m*

loggerheads /'lɒgəhedz/ *npl* **be at** ~ fam essere in totale disaccordo

logic /'lɒdʒɪk/ *n* logica *f*

logical /'lɒdʒɪkl/ *adj* logico

logically /'lɒdʒɪklɪ/ *adv* logicamente

logistics /lə'dʒɪstɪks/ *npl* logistica *f*

logo /'ləʊgəʊ/ *n* logo *m inv*

loin /lɔɪn/ *n* Culin lombata *f*

loin chop *n* lombatina *f*

loincloth /'lɔɪnklɒθ/ *n* perizoma *m*

loiter /'lɔɪtə(r)/ *vi* gironzolare

loll /lɒl/ *vi* ~ **about** (posture) stravaccarsi; (do nothing) starsene in panciolle

lollipop /'lɒlɪpɒp/ *n* lecca-lecca *m inv*

lollop /'lɒləp/ *vi* ⟨rabbit, person⟩ avanzare a balzi

lolly /'lɒlɪ/ *n* lecca-lecca *m inv*; (fam: money) quattrini *mpl*

Lombardy /'lɒmbədɪ/ *n* Lombardia *f*

London /'lʌndən/ **1** *n* Londra *f* **2** *attrib* londinese, di Londra

Londoner /'lʌndənə(r)/ *n* londinese *mf*

lone /ləʊn/ *adj* solitario

loneliness /'ləʊnlɪnɪs/ *n* solitudine *f*

lonely /'ləʊnlɪ/ *adj* (**-ier**, **-iest**) solitario; ⟨person⟩ solo

lonely hearts' column *n* rubrica *f* dei cuori solitari

loner /'ləʊnə(r)/ *n* persona *f* solitaria

lonesome /'ləʊnsəm/ *adj* solo

long¹ /lɒŋ/ **1** *adj* (**-er** /'lɒŋgə(r)/, **-est** /'lɒŋgɪst/) (lungo); **a** ~ **time** molto tempo; **a** ~ **way** distante; **in the** ~ **run** a lungo andare; (in the end) alla fin fine **2** *adv* a lungo, lungamente; **how** ~ **is it?** quanto è lungo?; ⟨in time⟩ quanto dura?; **all day** ~ tutto il giorno; **not** ~ **ago** non molto tempo fa; **before** ~ fra breve; **he's no** ~**er here** non è più qui; **as** or **so**~ **as** finché; (provided that) purché; **so** ~! fam ciao!; **will you be** ~? ti ci vuole molto?

long² *vi* ~ **for** desiderare ardentemente

long-awaited *adj* tanto atteso

long-distance *adj* a grande distanza; Sport di fondo; ⟨call⟩ interurbano

long division *n* divisione *f*

longevity /lɒn'dʒevətɪ/ *n* longevità *f*

long face *n* muso *m* lungo

longhand /'lɒŋhænd/ *n* **in** ~ in scrittura ordinaria

long-haul *attrib* su lunga distanza; ⟨plane⟩ per lunghi tragitti

longing /'lɒŋɪŋ/ **1** *adj* desideroso **2** *n* brama *f*

longingly /'lɒŋɪŋlɪ/ *adv* con desiderio

longitude /'lɒŋgɪtjuːd/ *n* Geog longitudine *f*

long jump *n* salto *m* in lungo

long-life milk *n* latte *m* a lunga conservazione

long-lived /-'lɪvd/ *adj* longevo

long-playing record *n* 33 giri *m inv*

long-range *adj* Mil, Aeron a lunga portata; ⟨forecast⟩ a lungo termine

long-sighted /-saɪtɪd/ *adj* presbite

long-sleeved /-'sliːvd/ *adj* a maniche lunghe

long-standing *adj* di vecchia data

long-suffering *adj* infinitamente paziente

long-term *adj* a lunga scadenza

long-time *adj* ⟨partner⟩ di lunga data

long wave *n* onde *fpl* lunghe

long-winded /-'wɪndɪd/ *adj* prolisso

loo /luː/ *n* fam gabinetto *m*

look /lʊk/ **1** *n* occhiata *f*; (appearance) aspetto *m*; [good] ~**s** *pl* bellezza *f*; **have a** ~ **at** dare un'occhiata a **2** *vi* guardare. (seem) sembrare; ~ **here!** mi ascolti bene!; ~ **at** guardare; ~ **for** cercare; ~ **somebody in the eye** guardare negli occhi qualcuno; ~ **somebody up and** ⋯⋫

down guardare qualcuno dall'alto in basso; ~ **a fool** fare la figura del cretino; ~ **young/old for one's age** portarsi bene/male gli anni; ~ **like** (resemble) assomigliare a; **it ~s as if it's going to rain** sembra che stia per piovere; ~ **sharp** (fam: hurry up) darsi una mossa
■ **look after** vt badare a
■ **look ahead** vi (think of the future) guardare al futuro
■ **look back** vi girarsi; (think of the past) guardare indietro
■ **look down** vi guardare in basso; ~ **down on somebody** fig guardare dall'alto in basso qualcuno
■ **look forward to** vt essere impaziente di
■ **look in on** vt passare da
■ **look into** vt (examine) esaminare
■ **look on** ①) vi (watch) guardare ②) vt ~ **on somebody/something as** (consider to be) considerare qualcuno/qualcosa come
■ **look on to** vt ⟨room⟩ dare su
■ **look out** ①) vi guardare fuori; (take care) fare attenzione; ~ **out!** attento! ②) vt cercare ⟨something for somebody⟩
■ **look out for** vt cercare
■ **look over** vt riguardare ⟨notes⟩; ispezionare ⟨house⟩
■ **look round** vi girarsi; (in shop, town etc) dare un'occhiata
■ **look through** vt dare un'occhiata a ⟨script, notes⟩
■ **look to** vt (rely on) contare su
■ **look up** ①) vi guardare in alto ②) vt cercare [nel dizionario] ⟨word⟩; (visit) andare a trovare
■ **look up to** vt fig rispettare
look-alike n sosia mf inv
looker-on /lʊkər'ɒn/ n (pl **lookers-on**) spettatore, -trice mf
look-in n Br fam **give somebody a ~** dare una chance a qualcuno; **get a ~** avere una chance
lookout /'lʊkaʊt/ n guardia f; (prospect) prospettiva f; **be on the ~ for** tenere gli occhi aperti per
loom[1] /lu:m/ n telaio m
loom[2] vi apparire; fig profilarsi
loony /'lu:nɪ/ adj & n fam matto, -a mf; ~ **bin** manicomio m
loop /lu:p/ n cappio m; (on garment) passante m
loophole /'lu:phəʊl/ n (in the law) scappatoia f
loopy /'lu:pɪ/ adj fam matto
loose /lu:s/ adj libero; ⟨knot⟩ allentato; ⟨page⟩ staccato; ⟨clothes⟩ largo; ⟨morals⟩ dissoluto; (inexact) vago; **be at a ~ end** non sapere cosa fare; **come ~** ⟨knot⟩ sciogliersi; **set ~** liberare
loose change n spiccioli mpl
loose chippings npl ghiaino m

loose-leaf notebook n raccoglitore m di fogli
loosely /'lu:slɪ/ adv scorrevolmente; ⟨defined⟩ vagamente
loosely knit adj ⟨group⟩ poco unito
loosen /'lu:sn/ vt sciogliere
■ **loosen up** ①) vt sciogliere ⟨muscles⟩ ②) vi (fam: relax) rilassarsi
loot /lu:t/ ①) n bottino m ②) vt/i depredare
looter /lu:tə(r)/ n saccheggiatore, -trice mf
looting /'lu:tɪŋ/ n saccheggio m
lop /lɒp/ vt ~ **off** (pt/pp **lopped**) potare
lope /ləʊp/ vi ~ **off** andarsene a passi lunghi
lop-eared /lɒpɪəd/ adj con le orecchie [a] penzoloni
lopsided /lɒp'saɪdɪd/ adj sbilenco
loquacious /lə'kweɪʃəs/ adj loquace
lord /lɔ:d/ n signore m; (title) Lord m; **House of L~s** Camera f dei Lord; **the L~'s Prayer** il Padrenostro; **good L~!** Dio Mio!
Lord Mayor n sindaco m della City di Londra
Lordship /'lɔ:dʃɪp/ n **your/his L~** (of noble) Sua Signoria; **your L~** (to judge) Signor Giudice
lore /lɔ:(r)/ n tradizioni fpl
lorry /'lɒrɪ/ n camion m inv
lorry driver n camionista mf
lose /lu:z/ ①) vt (pt/pp **lost**) perdere; ~ **heart** perdersi d'animo; ~ **one's inhibitions** disinibirsi; ~ **one's nerve** farsi prendere dalla paura; ~ **sight of** perdere di vista, perdere d' occhio; ~ **touch with** perdere di vista; ~ **track of time** perdere la nozione del tempo; ~ **weight** calare di peso ②) vi perdere; ⟨clock⟩ essere indietro
■ **lose out** vi rimetterci
loser /'lu:zə(r)/ n perdente mf
losing battle /'lu:zɪŋ/ n battaglia f persa
loss /lɒs/ n perdita f; ~**es** pl Comm perdite fpl; **be at a ~** essere perplesso; **be at a ~ for words** non trovare le parole; **make a ~** Comm subire una perdita
loss adjuster /'lɒsədʒʌstə(r)/ n Comm perito m di assicurazione
loss-leader n articolo m civetta
loss-making /'lɒsmeɪkɪŋ/ adj ⟨company⟩ in passivo; ⟨product⟩ che non vende
lost /lɒst/ ①) ▶ LOSE ②) adj perduto; **get ~** perdersi; **get ~!** fam va' a quel paese!
lost and found n Am oggetti mpl smarriti
lost property n Br oggetti mpl smarriti

lost property office *n* ufficio *m*
oggetti smarriti

lot¹ /lɒt/ (at auction) lotto *m*; (piece of land)
lotto *m*; **draw ~s** tirare a sorte

lot² *n* **the ~** il tutto; **a ~ of, ~s of** molti;
the ~ of you tutti voi; **it has changed a ~**
è cambiato molto

lotion *n* lozione *f*

lottery /'lɒtərɪ/ *n* lotteria *f*

lottery ticket *n* biglietto *m* della
lotteria

loud /laʊd/ **①** *adj* sonoro, alto; ⟨*colours*⟩
sgargiante
② *adv* forte; **out ~** ad alta voce

loud hailer /'heɪlə(r)/ *n* megafono *m*

loudly /'laʊdlɪ/ *adv* forte

loudspeaker /laʊd'spi:kə(r)/ *n*
altoparlante *m*

lounge /laʊndʒ/ **①** *n* salotto *m*; (in hotel)
salone *m*
② *vi* poltrire
▪ **lounge about** *vi* stare in panciolle

lounge suit *n* vestito *m* da uomo
(formale)

louse /laʊs/ *n* (pl **lice**) pidocchio *m*
▪ **louse up** *vt* (fam: ruin) guastare

lousy /'laʊzɪ/ *adj* (**-ier, -iest**) fam
schifoso

lout /laʊt/ *n* zoticone *m*

loutish /laʊtɪʃ/ *adj* rozzo

louvred /'lu:vəd/ *adj* ⟨*door, blinds*⟩ con le
gelosie

lovable /'lʌvəbl/ *adj* adorabile

love /lʌv/ **①** *n* amore *m*; (Tennis) zero *m*;
In ~ innamorato (**with** di)
② *vt* amare ⟨*person, country*⟩; **I ~**
watching tennis mi piace molto guardare
il tennis

love affair *n* relazione *f* [sentimentale]

lovebite *n* succhiotto *m*

love letter *n* lettera *f* d'amore

love life *n* vita *f* sentimentale

lovely /'lʌvlɪ/ *adj* (**-ier, -iest**) bello; (in
looks) bello, attraente; (in character)
piacevole; ⟨*meal*⟩ delizioso; **have a ~ time**
divertirsi molto

lovemaking *n* il fare l'amore

lover /'lʌvə(r)/ *n* amante *mf*

love song *n* canzone *f* d'amore

love story *n* storia *f* d'amore

lovey-dovey /lʌvɪ'dʌvɪ/ *adj* Br fam **get**
all ~ fare i piccioncini

loving /'lʌvɪŋ/ *adj* affettuoso

lovingly /'lʌvɪŋlɪ/ *adv* affettuosamente

low /ləʊ/ **①** *adj* basso; (depressed) giù *inv*
② *adv* basso; **feel ~** sentirsi giù
③ *n* minimo *m*; Meteorol depressione *f*; **at**
an all-time ~ ⟨*prices etc*⟩ al livello minimo

low-alcohol *adj* ⟨*beer*⟩ a bassa
gradazione alcolica

lowbrow /'ləʊbraʊ/ *adj* di scarsa cultura

low-budget *adj* ⟨*flight, airline*⟩ low-cost
inv

low-calorie *adj* ipocalorico

low-cost *adj* low-cost *inv*

low-cut *adj* ⟨*dress*⟩ scollato

low-down **①** *adj* fam ⟨*trick*⟩ mancino
② *n* (details) informazioni *fpl*

lower /'ləʊə(r)/ **①** *adj* & *adv* ▸ LOW
② *vt* abbassare; **~ oneself** abbassarsi

lower class **①** *adj* del ceto basso
② *n* ceto *m* basso

lowest common denominator
/'ləʊɪst/.../dɪ'nɒmɪneɪtə(r)/ *n* minimo
denominatore *m* comune

low-fat *adj* ⟨*diet*⟩ a basso contenuto di
grassi; ⟨*cheese, milk*⟩ magro

low gear *n* Auto marcia *f* bassa

low-grade *adj* di qualità inferiore

low-income *adj* ⟨*families*⟩ a basso
reddito

low-key *adj* fig moderato

lowlands *npl* pianure *fpl*

low-level *adj* ⟨*talks*⟩ informale;
⟨*radiation*⟩ debole; ⟨*bombing*⟩ a bassa
quota

lowly /'ləʊlɪ/ *adj* (**-ier, -iest**) umile

low-lying *adj* ⟨*land*⟩ a bassa quota

low-maintenance *adj* **a ~ garden** un
giardino che richiede poca manutenzione

low-paid *adj* ⟨*job, worker*⟩ mal pagato

low-priced *adj* a basso prezzo

low profile *n* **keep a ~** mantenere un
profilo basso

low-profile *adj* ⟨*campaign*⟩ di basso
profilo

low-quality *adj* scadente

low-risk *adj* a basso rischio

low season *n* bassa stagione *f*

low-tech *adj* a bassa tecnologia

low tide *n* bassa marea *f*

loyal /'lɔɪəl/ *adj* leale

loyally /'lɔɪəlɪ/ *adv* lealmente

loyalty /'lɔɪəltɪ/ *n* lealtà *f*

loyalty card *n* carta *f* fedeltà

lozenge /'lɒzɪndʒ/ *n* losanga *f*; (tablet)
pastiglia

LP *n abbr* (**long-playing record**) LP *m*
inv

L-plate *n* Br Auto cartello *m* che indica
che il conducente non ha ancora preso la
patente

LSD *n* LSD *m*

LST *abbr* (**local standard time**) ora *f*
locale

Ltd *abbr* (**Limited**) s.r.l.

lubricant /'lu:brɪkənt/ *n* lubrificante *m*

lubricate /'lu:brɪkeɪt/ *vt* lubrificare

lubrication /luːbrɪˈkeɪʃn/ *n*
lubrificazione *f*

lucid /ˈluːsɪd/ *adj ⟨explanation⟩* chiaro;
(sane) lucido

lucidity /luːˈsɪdətɪ/ *n* lucidità *f*; (of
explanation) chiarezza *f*

luck /lʌk/ *n* fortuna *f*; **bad ~** sfortuna *f*;
good ~! buona fortuna!

luckily /ˈlʌkɪlɪ/ *adv* fortunatamente

lucky /ˈlʌkɪ/ *adj* (**-ier, -iest**) fortunato;
be ~ essere fortunato; *⟨thing⟩* portare
fortuna

lucky charm *n* portafortuna *m inv*

lucky dip *n* pesca *f* di beneficenza

lucrative /ˈluːkrətɪv/ *adj* lucrativo

lucre /ˈluːkə(r)/ *n* (fam: money) soldi *mpl*

ludicrous /ˈluːdɪkrəs/ *adj* ridicolo

ludicrously /ˈluːdɪkrəslɪ/ *adv ⟨expensive,
complex⟩* eccessivamente

ludo /ˈluːdəʊ/ *n* Br gioco *m* da tavolo

lug /lʌg/ *vt* (pt/pp **lugged**) fam trascinare

luggage /ˈlʌgɪdʒ/ *n* bagaglio

luggage-rack *n* portabagagli *m inv*

luggage trolley *n* carrello *m*
portabagagli

luggage van *n* bagagliaio *m*

lughole /ˈlʌghəʊl/ *n* (Br fam: ear) orecchio
m

lugubrious /lʊˈguːbrɪəs/ *adj* lugubre

lukewarm /ˈluːkwɔːm/ *adj* tiepido; fig
poco entusiasta

lull /lʌl/ ① *n* pausa *f*
② *vt* **~ to sleep** cullare

lullaby /ˈlʌləbaɪ/ *n* ninnananna *f*

lumbago /lʌmˈbeɪgəʊ/ *n* lombaggine *f*

lumbar /ˈlʌmbə(r)/ *adj* lombare

lumber /ˈlʌmbə(r)/ ① *n* cianfrusaglie *fpl*;
(Am: timber) legname *m*
② *vt* fam **~ somebody with something**
affibbiare qualcosa a qualcuno

lumberjack /ˈlʌmbədʒæk/ *n*
tagliaboschi *m inv*

luminary /ˈluːmɪnərɪ/ *n* (fig: person)
luminare *mf*

luminous /ˈluːmɪnəs/ *adj* luminoso

lump[1] /lʌmp/ ① *n* (of sugar) zolletta *f*;
(swelling) gonfiore *m*; (in breast) nodulo *m*; (in
sauce) grumo *m*; **a ~ in one's throat** un
groppo alla gola
② *vt* **~ together** ammucchiare

lump[2] *vt* **~ it** fam **you'll just have to ~ it**
che ti piaccia o no è così

lump sugar *n* zucchero *m* in zollette

lump sum *n* somma *f* globale

lumpy /ˈlʌmpɪ/ *adj* (**-ier, -iest**) grumoso

lunacy /ˈluːnəsɪ/ *n* follia *f*

lunar /ˈluːnə(r)/ *adj* lunare

lunatic /ˈluːnətɪk/ *n* pazzo, -a *mf*

lunch /lʌntʃ/ ① *n* pranzo *m*; **she's gone
to ~** è andata a pranzo; **let's have ~
together sometime** pranziamo qualche
volta insieme
② *vi* pranzare

lunch box *n* cestino *m* del pranzo

lunchbreak *n* pausa *f* pranzo

luncheon /ˈlʌntʃn/ *n* (formal) pranzo *m*

luncheon meat *n* carne *f* in scatola

luncheon voucher *n* buono *m* pasto

lunch hour *n* pausa *f* pranzo

lunchtime /ˈlʌntʃtaɪm/ *n* ora *f* di pranzo

lung /lʌŋ/ *n* polmone *m*

lung cancer *n* cancro *m* al polmone

lunge /lʌndʒ/ *vi* lanciarsi (**at** su)

lurch[1] /lɜːtʃ/ *n* **leave in the ~** fam lasciare
nei guai

lurch[2] *vi* barcollare

lure /lʊə(r)/ ① *n* esca *f*; fig lusinga *f*
② *vt* adescare

lurid /ˈlʊərɪd/ *adj* (gaudy) sgargiante;
(sensational) sensazionalistico

lurk /lɜːk/ *vi* appostarsi

luscious /ˈlʌʃəs/ *adj* saporito; fig sexy
inv

lush /lʌʃ/ *adj* lussureggiante

lust /lʌst/ ① *n* lussuria *f*
② *vi* **~ after** desiderare [fortemente]

lustful /ˈlʌstfʊl/ *adj* lussurioso

lustre /ˈlʌstə(r)/ *n* lustro *m*

lusty /ˈlʌstɪ/ *adj* (**-ier, -iest**) vigoroso

lute /luːt/ *n* liuto *m*

luvvy, luvvie /ˈlʌvɪ/ *n* fam attore, -trice
mf pretenzioso

Luxembourg /ˈlʌksəmbɜːg/ *n* (city)
Lussemburgo *f*; (state) Lussemburgo *m*

luxuriant /lʌgˈʒʊərɪənt/ *adj*
lussureggiante, rigoglioso

luxuriantly /lʌgˈʒʊərɪəntlɪ/ *adv*
rigogliosamente

luxurious /lʌgˈʒʊərɪəs/ *adj* lussuoso

luxuriously /lʌgˈʒʊərɪəslɪ/ *adv*
lussuosamente

luxury /ˈlʌkʃərɪ/ ① *n* lusso *m*; **live in ~**
vivere nel lusso
② *attrib* di lusso

LV *abbr* **luncheon voucher**

LW *abbr* (**long wave**) OL

lychee /ˈlaɪtʃiː/ *n* litchi *m inv*

lych-gate /ˈlɪtʃ-/ *n* entrata *f* coperta di
un cimitero

lycra® /ˈlaɪkrə/ *n* lycra *f*

lying /ˈlaɪɪŋ/ ① ▶ LIE[1], ▶ LIE[2]
② *n* mentire *m*

lymph gland /ˈlɪmf/ *n* linfoghiandola *f*

lymph node *n* linfonodo *m*

lynch /lɪntʃ/ *vt* linciare

lynch mob *n* linciatori *mpl*

lynchpin /'lɪntʃpɪn/ n fig pilastro m
lynx /lɪŋks/ n lince f
lyric /'lɪrɪk/ adj lirico
lyrical /'lɪrɪkl/ adj lirico; (fam: enthusiastic)

entusiasta; ~ **poetry** n poesia f lirica
lyricism /'lɪrɪsɪzm/ n lirismo m
lyricist /'lɪrɪsɪst/ n paroliere, -a mf
lyrics /'lɪrɪks/ npl parole fpl

Mm

m¹, **M** /em/ n (letter) m, M f inv
m² abbr (**metre(s)**) m; abbr (**million**)
milione m; abbr (**mile(s)**) miglio
MA n abbr (**Master of Arts**) (diploma)
laurea f in lettere; (person) laureato, -a mf
in lettere; Am abbr **Massachusetts**
ma'am /mɑːm/ int signora; (to queen) Sua
Altezza
mac /mæk/ n fam impermeabile m
macabre /mə'kɑːbr/ adj macabro
macaroni /mækə'rəʊnɪ/ n maccheroni
mpl
macaroni cheese n maccheroni mpl
gratinati al formaggio
macaroon /mækə'ruːn/ n ≈ amaretto m
mace¹ /meɪs/ n (staff) mazza f
mace² n (spice) macis mf
Macedonia /mæsə'dəʊnɪə/ n Macedonia
f
machete /mə'ʃetɪ/ n machete m inv
Machiavellian /mækɪə'velɪən/ adj
machiavellico
machinations /mækɪ'neɪʃnz/
macchinazioni fpl
machine /mə'ʃiːn/ ① n macchina f
② vt (sew) cucire a macchina; Techn
lavorare a macchina
machine-gun n mitragliatrice f
machine operator n addetto, -a mf
alle macchine
machine-readable adj ⟨data, text⟩
leggibile dalla macchina
machinery /mə'ʃiːnərɪ/ n macchinario
m; fig meccanismo m
machine-stitch vt cucire a macchina
machine tool n macchina f utensile
machine translation n traduzione f
elettronica
machinist /mə'ʃiːnɪst/ n macchinista
mf; (on sewing machine) lavorante mf adetto,
-a alla macchina da cucire
machismo /mæ'kɪzməʊ/ n machismo m
macho /'mætʃəʊ/ adj macho inv
mackerel /'mækr(ə)l/ n inv sgombro m
mackintosh /'mækɪntɒʃ/ n
impermeabile m

macro /'mækrəʊ/ n Comput macro f inv
macrocosm /'mækrəʊkɒzm/ n
macrocosmo m
mad /mæd/ adj (**madder, maddest**)
pazzo, matto; (fam: angry) furioso (**at** con);
like ~ fam come un pazzo; **be ~ about**
somebody/something (fam: keen on) andare
matto per qualcuno/qualcosa
Madagascar /mædə'gæskə(r)/ n
Madagascar m
madam /'mædəm/ n signora f
mad cow disease n fam = BSE
madden /'mædən/ vt (make angry) far
diventare matto
maddening /mæd(ə)nɪŋ/ adj ⟨delay,
person⟩ esasperante
made /meɪd/ ▶ MAKE
Madeira cake /mə'dɪərə/ n pan m di
Spagna
made to measure adj [fatto] su
misura
made-up adj (wearing make-up) truccato;
⟨road⟩ asfaltata; ⟨story⟩ inventato
madhouse /'mædhaʊs/ n fam
manicomio m; **it's like a ~ in here!**
sembra di essere in un manicomio
madly /'mædlɪ/ adv fam follemente; **~ in**
love innamorato follemente
madman /'mædmən/ n pazzo m
madness /'mædnɪs/ n pazzia f
madonna /mə'dɒnə/ n madonna f
madwoman /'mædwʊmən/ n pazza f
mafia /'mæfɪə/ n also fig mafia f
mag /mæg/ n abbr **magazine**
magazine /mægə'ziːn/ n rivista f; Mil,
Phot magazzino m
maggot /'mægət/ n verme m
maggoty /'mægətɪ/ adj coi vermi
Magi /'meɪdʒaɪ/ npl **the M~** i Re Magi
magic /'mædʒɪk/ ① n magia f; (tricks)
giochi mpl di prestigio
② adj magico; ⟨trick⟩ di prestigio
magical /'mædʒɪkl/ adj magico
magic carpet n tappeto m volante
magician /mə'dʒɪʃn/ n mago, -a mf;
(entertainer) prestigiatore, -trice mf

magistrate /'mædʒɪstreɪt/ n magistrato m

magistrate's court n ≈ pretura f

magnanimity /mægnə'nɪmətɪ/ n magnanimità f

magnanimous /mæg'nænɪməs/ adj magnanimo

magnate /'mægneɪt/ n magnate m

magnesia /mæg'niːʃə/ n magnesia f

magnesium /mæg'niːzɪəm/ n magnesio m

magnet /'mægnɪt/ n magnete m, calamita f

magnetic /mæg'netɪk/ adj magnetico

magnetic resonance imaging n Med risonanza f magnetica

magnetic tape n nastro m magnetico

magnetism /'mægnətɪzm/ n magnetismo m

magnetize /'mægnətaɪz/ vt magnetizzare

magnification /mægnɪfɪ'keɪʃn/ n ingrandimento m

magnificence /mæg'nɪfɪsəns/ n magnificenza f

magnificent /mæg'nɪfɪsənt/ adj magnifico

magnificently /mæg'nɪfɪsəntlɪ/ adv magnificamente

magnify /'mægnɪfaɪ/ vt (pt/pp **-ied**) ingrandire; (exaggerate) ingigantire

magnifying glass /'mægnɪfaɪɪŋ/ n lente f d'ingrandimento

magnitude /'mægnɪtjuːd/ n grandezza f; (importance) importanza f; **a project of this** ~ un progetto di tale portata

magnolia /mæg'nəʊlɪə/ n (tree) magnolia f; (colour) crema m

magnum opus /mægnəm'ɒpəs/ n opera f principale

magpie /'mægpaɪ/ n gazza f

mahogany /mə'hɒgənɪ/ ① n mogano m ② attrib di mogano

maid /meɪd/ n cameriera f; old ~ pej zitella f

maiden /'meɪdn/ ① n liter fanciulla f ② adj ⟨speech, voyage⟩ inaugurale

maiden aunt n zia f zitella

maiden name n nome m da ragazza

mail /meɪl/ ① n posta f ② vt impostare

mailbag n sacco m postale

mail bomb n pacco m esplosivo (arrivato per posta)

mailbox n Am cassetta f delle lettere; (e-mail) casella f postale

mail coach n Rail vagone m postale

mail delivery n consegna f della posta

mailing /'meɪlɪŋ/ n (action) mailing m inv; (document) pubblicità f

mailing address n recapito m postale

mailing list n elenco m d'indirizzi per un mailing

mailman /'meɪlmən/ n Am postino m

mail order ① n vendita f per corrispondenza ② attrib ⟨business⟩ di vendita per corrispondenza; ⟨goods⟩ comprati per corrispondenza

mail-order catalogue n catalogo m di vendita per corrispondenza

mail-order firm n ditta f di vendita per corrispondenza

mail room n reparto m spedizioni

mail server n Comput server m inv di posta

mailshot n mailing m inv

mail train n treno m postale

mail van n (delivery vehicle) furgone m postale; (in train) vagone m postale

maim /meɪm/ vt menomare

main¹ /meɪn/ n (water; gas; electricity) conduttura f principale

main² ① adj principale; **the** ~ **thing is to...** la cosa essenziale è di... ② n **in the** ~ in complesso

main course n secondo m

main deck n ponte m di coperta

mainframe n Comput mainframe m inv

mainland n continente m

main line ① n Rail linea f principale ② attrib ⟨station, terminus, train⟩ della linea principale

mainly /'meɪnlɪ/ adv principalmente

main memory n Comput memoria f principale

main office n (of company) sede f centrale

main road n strada f principale

mainsail n randa f, vela f di taglio

mainstay n fig pilastro m

mainstream ① adj (conventional) tradizionale ② n corrente f principale

main street n via f principale

maintain /meɪn'teɪn/ vt mantenere; (keep in repair) curare la manutenzione di; (claim) sostenere

maintenance /'meɪntənəns/ n mantenimento m; (care) manutenzione f; (allowance) alimenti mpl

maintenance grant n (for student) presalario m

maintenance order n Br obbligo m degli alimenti

maisonette /meɪzə'net/ n appartamento m a due piani

maize /meɪz/ n granoturco m

Maj abbr (**Major**) Mag

majestic /mə'dʒestɪk/ adj maestoso

majestically /məˈdʒəestɪklɪ/ *adv*
maestosamente

majesty /ˈmædʒəstɪ/ *n* maestà *f inv*;
His/Her M~ Sua Maestà

major /ˈmeɪdʒə(r)/ **①** *adj* maggiore; ~
road strada *f* con diritto di precedenza
② *n* Mil, Mus maggiore *m*
③ *vi* Am ~ **in** specializzarsi in

Majorca /məˈjɔːkə/ *n* Maiorca *f*

major general *n* generale *m* di
divisione

majority /məˈdʒɒrɪtɪ/ *n* maggioranza *f*;
be in the ~ avere la maggioranza

make /meɪk/ **①** *n* (brand) marca *f*
② *vt* (pt/pp **made**) fare; (earn)
guadagnare; rendere ⟨*happy, clear*⟩;
prendere ⟨*decision*⟩; ~ **somebody laugh**
far ridere qualcuno; ~ **somebody do**
something far fare qualcosa a qualcuno;
~ **it** (to party, top of hill etc) farcela; **what time**
do you ~ **it?** che ore fai?
③ *vi* ~ **as if to** fare per
■ **make after** *vt* (chase) inseguire
■ **make do** *vi* arrangiarsi
■ **make for** *vt* dirigersi verso
■ **make good ①** *vi* riuscire
② *vt* compensare ⟨*loss*⟩; risarcire
⟨*damage*⟩
■ **make off** *vi* fuggire
■ **make off with** *vt* (steal) sgraffignare
■ **make out** *vt* (distinguish) distinguere;
(write out) rilasciare ⟨*cheque*⟩; compilare
⟨*list*⟩; (claim) far credere
■ **make over** *vt* cedere
■ **make up ①** *vt* (constitute) comporre;
(complete) completare; (invent) inventare;
(apply cosmetics to) truccare; fare ⟨*parcel*⟩; ~
up one's mind decidersi; ~ **it up** (after
quarrel) riconciliarsi
② *vi* (after quarrel) fare la pace
■ **make up for** *vt* compensare; ~ **up for**
lost time recuperare il tempo perso
■ **make up to** *vt* arruffianarsi

make-believe ① *adj* finto
② *n* finzione *f*

make-do-and-mend *vi* arrangiarsi col
poco che si ha

make-over *n* trasformazione *f*

maker /ˈmeɪkə(r)/ *n* fabbricante *mf*; **M**~
Relig Creatore *m*; **send somebody to meet**
his/her ~ spedire qualcuno all'altro
mondo

makeshift ① *adj* di fortuna
② *n* espediente *m*

make-up *n* trucco *m*; (character) natura *f*

make-up artist *n* truccatore, -trice *mf*

make-up bag *n* astuccio *m* per il
trucco

make-up remover *n* struccante *m*

making /ˈmeɪkɪŋ/ *n* (manufacture)
fabbricazione *f*; **be the** ~ **of** essere la
causa del successo di; **have the** ~**s of** aver
la stoffa di; **in the** ~ in formazione

maladjusted /mæləˈdʒʌstɪd/ *adj*
disadattato

maladjustment /mæləˈdʒʌstmənt/ *n*
disadattamento *m*

Malagasy /mæləˈgæzɪ/ *n* (native of
Madagascar) malgascio, -a *mf*; (language)
malgascio *m*

malaise /məˈleɪz/ *n* fig malessere *m*

malaria /məˈleərɪə/ *n* malaria *f*

Malawi /məˈlɑːwɪ/ *n* Malawi *m*

Malaysia /məˈleɪʒə/ *n* Malesia *f*

Malaysian /məˈleɪʒən/ *n & adj* malese
mf

Maldives /ˈmɔːldiːvz/ *npl* **the** ~ le
Maldive

male /meɪl/ **①** *adj* maschile
② *n* maschio *m*

male chauvinism *n* maschilismo *m*

male chauvinist [pig] *n* [sporco *m*]
maschilista *m*

male menopause *n* andropausa *f*

male model *n* indossatore *m*

male nurse *n* infermiere *m*

male voice choir *n* coro *m* maschile

malevolence /məˈlevələns/ *n*
malevolenza *f*

malevolent /məˈlevələnt/ *adj* malevolo

malformation /mælfɔːˈmeɪʃn/ *n*
malformazione *f*

malformed /mælˈfɔːmd/ *adj* malformato

malfunction /mælˈfʌŋkʃn/ **①** *n*
funzionamento *m* imperfetto
② *vi* funzionare male

Mali /ˈmɑːlɪ/ *n* Mali *m*

malice /ˈmælɪs/ *n* malignità *f*; **bear**
somebody ~ voler del male a qualcuno

malicious /məˈlɪʃəs/ *adj* maligno

maliciously /məˈlɪʃəslɪ/ *adv* con
malignità

malign /məˈlaɪn/ *vt* malignare su

malignancy /məˈlɪgnənsɪ/ *n* malignità *f*

malignant /məˈlɪgnənt/ *adj* maligno

malinger /məˈlɪŋgə(r)/ *vi* fingersi malato

malingerer /məˈlɪŋgərə(r)/ *n*
scansafatiche *mf inv*

mall /mæl/ *n* (shopping arcade, in suburb)
centro *m* commerciale; (Am: street) strada *f*
pedonale

mallard /ˈmælɑːd/ *n* germano *m* reale

malleable /ˈmælɪəbl/ *adj* malleabile

mallet /ˈmælɪt/ *n* martello *m* di legno

malnourished /mælˈnʌrɪʃt/ *adj*
malnutrito

malnutrition /mælnjʊˈtrɪʃn/ *n*
malnutrizione *f*

malpractice /mælˈpræktɪs/ *n*
negligenza *f*

malt /mɔːlt/ *n* malto *m*

Malta /ˈmɔːltə/ *n* Malta *f*

Maltese /mɔːlˈtiːz/ *adj & n* maltese *mf*

maltreat /mælˈtriːt/ *vt* maltrattare

maltreatment /mælˈtriːtmənt/ *n* maltrattamento *m*

malt whisky *n* whisky *m inv* di malto

mammal /ˈmæml/ *n* mammifero *m*

mammary /ˈmæmərɪ/ *adj* mammario

mammograph /ˈmæməɡrɑːf/ *n* mammografia *f*

mammoth /ˈmæməθ/ ① *adj* mastodontico
② *n* mammut *m inv*

man /mæn/ ① *n* (pl **men**) uomo *m*; (chess, draughts) pedina *f*; **the** ~ **in the street** l'uomo della strada; ~ **to** ~ da uomo a uomo
② *vt* (pt/pp **manned**) equipaggiare; far funzionare ⟨*pump*⟩; essere di servizio a ⟨*counter, telephones*⟩

manacle /ˈmænəkl/ *vt* ammanettare

manage /ˈmænɪdʒ/ ① *vt* dirigere; gestire ⟨*shop, affairs*⟩; (cope with) farcela; ~ **to do something** riuscire a fare qualcosa
② *vi* riuscire; (cope) farcela (**on** con)

manageable /ˈmænɪdʒəbl/ *adj* ⟨*hair*⟩ docile; ⟨*size*⟩ maneggevole

management /ˈmænɪdʒmənt/ *n* gestione *f*; **the** ~ la direzione

management accounting *n* contabilità *f* di gestione

management buyout *n* buyout *m inv* da parte dei manager, rilevamento *m* dirigenti

management consultancy *n* (firm) consulente *m* aziendale; (activity) consulenza *f* aziendale

management consultant *n* consulente *mf* aziendale

manager /ˈmænɪdʒə(r)/ *n* direttore *m*; (of shop, bar) gestore *m*; Sport manager *m inv*

manageress /mænɪdʒəˈres/ *n* direttrice *f*

managerial /mænɪˈdʒɪərɪəl/ *adj* ~ **staff** personale *m* direttivo

managing director /ˈmænɪdʒɪŋ/ *n* direttore, -trice *mf* generale

mandarin /ˈmændərɪn/ *n* ~ **[orange]** mandarino *m*

mandate /ˈmændeɪt/ *n* mandato *m*

mandatory /ˈmændətrɪ/ *adj* obbligatorio

mandolin /ˈmændəlɪn/ *n* mandolino *m*

mandrake /ˈmændreɪk/ *n* mandragola *f*

mane /meɪn/ *n* criniera *f*

manful /ˈmænfl/ *adj* coraggioso

manfully /ˈmænfʊlɪ/ *adv* coraggiosamente

manger /ˈmeɪndʒə(r)/ *n* mangiatoia *f*

mangle /ˈmæŋɡl/ *vt* (damage) maciullare

mango /ˈmæŋɡəʊ/ *n* (pl **-es**) mango *m*

mangrove /ˈmæŋɡrəʊv/ *n* mangrovia *f*

mangy /ˈmeɪndʒɪ/ *adj* ⟨*dog*⟩ rognoso

manhandle /ˈmænhændl/ *vt* malmenare

manhole /ˈmænhəʊl/ *n* botola *f*

manhole cover *n* tombino *m*

manhood /ˈmænhʊd/ *n* età *f* adulta; (quality) virilità *f*

man-hour *n* ora *f* lavorativa

manhunt /ˈmænhʌnt/ *n* caccia *f* all'uomo

mania /ˈmeɪnɪə/ *n* mania *f*

maniac /ˈmeɪnɪæk/ *n* maniaco, -a *mf*

manic /ˈmænɪk/ *adj* (obsessive) maniacale; (frenetic) frenetico

manic depression *n* psicosi *f inv* maniaco-depressiva

manic-depressive *adj* maniaco-depressivo

manicure /ˈmænɪkjʊə(r)/ ① *n* manicure *f inv*
② *vt* fare la manicure a

manicurist /ˈmænɪkjʊərɪst/ *n* manicure *f inv*

manifest /ˈmænɪfest/ ① *adj* manifesto
② *n* Comm manifesto *m*
③ *vt* manifestare; ~ **itself** manifestarsi

manifestation /mænɪfeˈsteɪʃn/ *n* manifestazione *f*

manifestly /ˈmænɪfestlɪ/ *adv* palesemente

manifesto /mænɪˈfestəʊ/ *n* manifesto *m*

manifold /ˈmænɪfəʊld/ *adj* molteplice

manipulate /məˈnɪpjuleɪt/ *vt* manipolare

manipulation /mənɪpjʊˈleɪʃn/ *n* manipolazione *f*

manipulative /məˈnɪpjʊlətɪv/ *adj* manipolatore

mankind /mænˈkaɪnd/ *n* genere *m* umano

manly /ˈmænlɪ/ *adj* virile

man-made *adj* artificiale; ~ **fibre** *n* fibra *f* sintetica

manna /ˈmænə/ *n* manna *f*: ~ **from heaven** fig manna *f* dal cielo

mannequin /ˈmænɪkɪn/ *n* manichino *m*

manner /ˈmænə(r)/ *n* maniera *f*: **in this** ~ in questo modo; **have no** ~**s** avere dei pessimi modi; **good/bad** ~**s** buone/cattive maniere

mannered /ˈmænəd/ *adj* pej manierato

mannerism /ˈmænərɪzm/ *n* affettazione *f*

mannish /ˈmænɪʃ/ *adj* mascolino

manoeuvrable /məˈnuːvrəbl/ *adj* manovrabile

manoeuvre /məˈnuːvə(r)/ ① *n* manovra *f*

2 *vt* fare manovra con ⟨*vehicle*⟩; manovrare ⟨*person*⟩

manor /'mænə(r)/ *n* maniero *m*

manpower /'mænpaʊə(r)/ *n* manodopera *f*

manse /mæns/ *n* canonica *f*

mansion /'mænʃn/ *n* palazzo *m*

manslaughter /'mænslɔ:tə(r)/ *n* omicidio *m* colposo

mantelpiece /'mæntlpi:s/ *n* mensola *f* di caminetto

mantis /'mæntɪs/ *n* mantide *f*

Mantua /'mæntjʊə/ *n* Mantova *f*

manual /'mænjʊəl/ **1** *adj* manuale **2** *n* manuale *m*

manufacture /mænjʊ'fæktʃə(r)/ **1** *vt* fabbricare **2** *n* manifattura *f*

manufacturer /mænjʊ'fæktʃərə(r)/ *n* fabbricante *m*

manure /mə'njʊə(r)/ *n* concime *m*

manuscript /'mænjʊskrɪpt/ *n* manoscritto *m*

Manx /mæŋks/ *n* (language) lingua *f* parlata nell'isola di Man; **the M∼** *pl* (people) gli abitanti dell'isola di Man

many /'menɪ/ *adj* & *pron* molti; **there are as ∼ boys as girls** ci sono tanti ragazzi quante ragazze; **as ∼ as 500** ben 500; **as ∼ as that** così tanti; **as ∼** altrettanti; **very ∼, a good/great ∼** moltissimi; **∼ a time** molte volte

many-sided /-'saɪdɪd/ *adj* ⟨*personality, phenomenon*⟩ sfaccettato

map /mæp/ *n* carta *f* geografica; (of town) mappa *f*
■ **map out** *vt* (pt/pp **mapped**) fig programmare

maple /'meɪpl/ *n* acero *m*

mar /mɑ:(r)/ *vt* (pt/pp **marred**) rovinare

marathon /'mærəθən/ *n* maratona *f*

marauder /mə'rɔ:də(r)/ *n* predone *m*

marble /'mɑ:bl/ **1** *n* marmo *m*; (for game) pallina *f* **2** *attrib* di marmo

March /mɑ:tʃ/ *n* marzo *m*

march **1** *n* marcia *f*; (protest) dimostrazione *f* **2** *vi* marciare **3** *vt* far marciare; **∼ somebody off** scortare qualcuno fuori

marcher /'mɑ:tʃə(r)/ *n* (in procession, band) persona *f* che marcia in una processione, in un corteo ecc; (in demonstration) dimostrante *mf*

marchioness /mɑ:ʃə'nes/ *n* marchesa *f*

march past *n* sfilata *f*

mare /'meə(r)/ *n* giumenta *f*

margarine /mɑdʒə'ri:n/ *n* margarina *f*

marge /mɑdʒ/ *n* (Br fam: margarine) margarina *f*

margin /'mɑdʒɪn/ *n* margine *m*

marginal /'mɑdʒɪnəl/ *adj* marginale

marginalize /'mɑ:dʒɪnəlaɪz/ *vt* marginalizzare

marginally /'mɑdʒɪnəlɪ/ *adv* marginalmente

marigold /'mærɪgəʊld/ *n* calendula *f*

marijuana /mærʊ'wɑ:nə/ *n* marijuana *f*

marina /mə'ri:nə/ *n* porticciolo *m*

marinade /mærɪ'neɪd/ **1** *n* marinata *f* **2** *vt* marinare

marine /mə'ri:n/ **1** *adj* marino **2** *n* (sailor) soldato *m* di fanteria marina

Marine Corps *n* i Marine

marine engineer *n* ingegnere *m* navale; (works in engine room) macchinista *m*

marionette /mærɪə'net/ *n* marionetta *f*

marital /'mærɪtl/ *adj* coniugale; **∼ status** stato *m* civile

maritime /'mærɪtaɪm/ *adj* marittimo

marjoram /'mɑ:dʒərəm/ *n* maggiorana *f*

mark¹ /mɑ:k/ *n* (currency) marco *m*

mark² **1** *n* (stain) macchia *f*; (sign, indication) segno *m*; Sch voto *m*; **be the ∼ of** designare **2** *vt* segnare; (stain) macchiare; Sch correggere; Sport marcare; **∼ time** Mil segnare il passo; fig non far progressi; **∼ my words** ricordati quello che dico
■ **mark down** *vt* (reduce the price of) ribassare
■ **mark out** *vt* delimitare; fig designare
■ **mark up** *vt* (increase the price of) aumentare

marked /mɑ:kt/ *adj* marcato

markedly /'mɑ:kɪdlɪ/ *adv* notevolmente

marker /'mɑ:kə(r)/ *n* (for highlighting) evidenziatore *m*; Sport marcatore *m* (of exam) esaminatore, -trice *mf*

marker pen *n* evidenziatore *m*

market /'mɑ:kɪt/ **1** *n* mercato *m* **2** *vt* vendere al mercato; (launch) commercializzare; **on the ∼** sul mercato

market analyst *n* analista *mf* di mercato

market day *n* giorno *m* di mercato

market economy *n* economia *f* di mercato

market forces *npl* forze *fpl* di mercato

market garden *n* orto *m*

market gardener *n* ortofrutticoltore, -trice *mf*

market gardening *n* ortofrutticoltura *f*

marketing /'mɑ:kɪtɪŋ/ *n* marketing *m*

marketing campaign *n* campagna *f* promozionale *or* pubblicitaria

marketing department *n* ufficio *m* marketing

marketing man *n* addetto, -a *mf* al marketing

marketing mix *n* mix *m inv* del marketing

marketing strategy *n* strategia *f* di marketing

market leader *n* (company, product) leader *m inv* del mercato

market place *n* (square, Fin) mercato *m*.

market price *n* prezzo *m* di mercato

market research *n* ricerca *f* di mercato

market square *n* piazza *f* del mercato

market stall *n* banco *m* del mercato

market survey *n* indagine *f* di mercato

market town *n* cittadina *f* dove si tiene il mercato

market trader *n* venditore, -trice *mf* al mercato

market value *n* valore *m* di mercato

markings /'mɑ:kɪŋz/ *npl* (on animal) colori *mpl*

marksman /'mɑ:ksmən/ *n* tiratore *m* scelto

marksmanship /'mɑ:ksmənʃɪp/ *n* abilità *f* nel tiro

mark-up *n* (margin) margine *m* di vendita; (price increase) aumento *m*

marmalade /'mɑ:məleɪd/ *n* marmellata *f* d'arance

maroon /mə'ru:n/ *adj* marrone rossastro

marooned /mə'ru:nd/ *adj* abbandonato

marquee /mɑ:'ki:/ *n* tendone *m*; (Am: awning) pensilina *f* con pubblicità

marquess /'mɑ:kwɪs/ *n* marchese *m*

marquetry /'mɑ:kɪtrɪ/ *n* intarsio *m*

marquis /'mɑ:kwɪs/ *n* marchese *m* ·

marriage /'mærɪdʒ/ *n* matrimonio *m*

marriage ceremony *n* cerimonia *f* nuziale

marriage certificate *n* certificato *m* di matrimonio

marriage guidance counsellor *n* consulente *mf* matrimoniale

marriage of convenience *n* matrimonio *m* di convenienza

married /'mærɪd/ *adj* sposato; ⟨life⟩ coniugale

marrow /'mærəʊ/ *n* Anat midollo *m*; (vegetable) zucca *f*

marrowbone /'mærəʊbəʊn/ *n* midollo *m* osseo

marry /'mærɪ/ ① *vt* (pt/pp **-led**) sposare; **get married** sposarsi
② *vi* sposarsi

Mars /mɑ:z/ *n* Marte *m*

marsh /mɑ:ʃ/ *n* palude *f*

marshal /'mɑ:ʃl/ ① *n* (steward) cerimoniere *m*
② *vt* (pt/pp **marshalled**) fig organizzare ⟨arguments⟩

Marshall Islands /'mɑ:ʃl/ *npl* **the ~** le isole Marshall

marshmallow /mɑ:ʃ'mæləʊ/ *n* caramella *f* gommosa e pastosa

marshy /'mɑ:ʃɪ/ *adj* paludoso

marsupial /mɑ:'su:pɪəl/ *n* marsupiale *m*

marten /'mɑ:tɪn/ *n* martora *f*

martial /'mɑ:ʃl/ *adj* marziale

Martian /'mɑ:ʃn/ *adj & n* marziano, -a *mf*

martinet /mɑ:tɪ'net/ *n* fanatico, -a *mf* della disciplina

martyr /'mɑ:tə(r)/ ① *n* martire *mf*
② *vt* martirizzare

martyrdom /'mɑ:tədəm/ *n* martirio *m*

martyred /'mɑ:təd/ *adj* fam da martire

marvel /'mɑ:vl/ ① *n* meraviglia *f*
② *vi* (pt/pp **marvelled**) meravigliarsi (at di)

marvellous /'mɑ:vələs/ *adj* meraviglioso

marvellously /'mɑ:vələslɪ/ *adv* meravigliosamente

Marxism /'mɑ:ksɪzm/ *n* marxismo *m*

Marxist /'mɑ:ksɪst/ *adj & n* marxista *mf*

marzipan /'mɑ:zɪpæn/ *n* marzapane *m*

mascara /mæ'skɑrə/ *n* mascara *m inv*

mascot /'mæskət/ *n* mascotte *f inv*

masculine /'mæskjʊlɪn/ ① *adj* maschile
② *n* Gram maschile *m*

masculinity /mæskjʊ'lɪnətɪ/ *n* mascolinità *f*

mash /mæʃ/ ① *n* Culin fam purè *m inv*
② *vt* impastare

mashed potatoes /mæʃt/ *npl* purè *m inv* di patate

mask /mɑ:sk/ ① *n* maschera *f*
② *vt* mascherare

masked ball /mɑ:skt'bɔl/ *n* ballo *m* in maschera

masking tape /'mɑ:skɪŋ/ *n* nastro *m* di carta adesiva

masochism /'mæsəkɪzm/ *n* masochismo *m*

masochist /'mæsəkɪst/ *n* masochista *mf*

Mason /'meɪsn/ *n* massone *m*

mason *n* muratore *m*

Masonic /mə'sɒnɪk/ *adj* massonico

masonry /'meɪsnrɪ/ *n* muratura *f*; **two tons of ~** due tonnellate di pietre

masquerade /mæskə'reɪd/ ① *n* fig mascherata *f*
② *vi* **~ as** (pose) farsi passare per

mass[1] /mæs/ *n* Relig messa *f*

mass² ① *n* massa *f*; ~**es of** fam un sacco di
② *vi* ammassarsi

massacre /'mæsəkə(r)/ ① *n* massacro *m*
② *vt* massacrare

massage /'mæsɑːʒ/ ① *n* massaggio *m*
② *vt* massaggiare; fig manipolare ⟨*statistics*⟩

masseur /mæ'sɜː(r)/ *n* massaggiatore *m*

masseuse /mæ'sɜːz/ *n* massaggiatrice *f*

mass grave *n* fossa *f* comune

mass hysteria *n* isterismo *m* di massa

massive /'mæsɪv/ *adj* enorme

massively /'mæsɪvlɪ/ *adv* estremamente

mass market ① *n* mercato *m* di massa
② *attrib* del mercato di massa

mass-marketing *n* commercializzazione *f* di massa

mass media *npl* mezzi *mpl* di comunicazione di massa, mass media *mpl*

mass murder *n* omicidio *m* di massa

mass murderer *n* omicida *mf* di massa

mass-produce *vt* produrre in serie

mass production *n* produzione *f* in serie

mass screening *n* Med controllo *m* su larga scala

mast /mɑːst/ *n* Naut albero *m*; (for radio) antenna *f*

master /'mɑːstə(r)/ ① *n* maestro *m*, padrone *m*; (teacher) professore *m*; (of ship) capitano *m*; **M**~ (boy) signorino *m*
② *vt* imparare perfettamente; avere padronanza di ⟨*language*⟩

master bedroom *n* camera *f* da letto principale

master builder *n* capomastro *m*

master copy *n* originale *m*

master disk *n* Comput disco *m* master

master key *n* passe-partout *m inv*

masterly /'mɑːstəlɪ/ *adj* magistrale

mastermind ① *n* cervello *m*
② *vt* ideare e dirigere

Master of Arts *n* (diploma) laurea *f* in lettere; (person) laureato, -a *mf* in lettere

master of ceremonies *n* (presenting entertainment) presentatore *m*; (of formal occasion) maestro *m* di cerimonie

Master of Science *n* (diploma) laurea *f* in discipline scientifiche; (person) laureato, -a *mf* in discipline scientifiche

masterpiece *n* capolavoro *m*

master plan *n* piano *m* generale

master race *n* razza *f* superiore

master stroke *n* colpo *m* da maestro

master tape *n* nastro *m* matrice

mastery /'mæstərɪ/ *n* (of subject) padronanza *f*

masticate /'mæstɪkeɪt/ *vi* masticare

masturbate /'mæstə'beɪt/ *vi* masturbarsi

masturbation /mæstə'beɪʃn/ *n* masturbazione *f*

mat /mæt/ *n* stuoia *f*: (on table) sottopiatto *m*

match¹ /mætʃ/ ① *n* Sport partita *f*; (equal) uguale *mf*; (marriage) matrimonio *m*; (person to marry) partito *m*; **be a good** ~ ⟨*colours*⟩) intonarsi bene; **be no** ~ **for** non essere dello stesso livello di
② *vt* (equal) uguagliare; (be like) andare bene con
③ *vi* intonarsi

match² *n* fiammifero *m*

matchbox /'mætʃbɒks/ *n* scatola *f* di fiammiferi

matching /'mætʃɪŋ/ *adj* intonato

matchmaker *n* **he's a successful** ~ (for couples) è stato l'artefice di molti matrimoni

match point *n* Tennis match point *m inv*

matchstick *n* fiammifero *m*

mate¹ /meɪt/ ① *n* compagno, -a *mf*; (assistant) aiuto *m*; Naut secondo *m*; (fam: friend) amico, -a *mf*
② *vi* accoppiarsi
③ *vt* accoppiare

mate² *n* (in chess) scacco *m* matto

material /mə'tɪərɪəl/ ① *n* materiale *m*; (fabric) stoffa *f*; **raw** ~**s** *pl* materie *fpl* prime
② *adj* materiale

materialism /mə'tɪərɪəlɪzm/ *n* materialismo *m*

materialistic /mətɪərɪə'lɪstɪk/ *adj* materialistico

materialize /mə'tɪərɪəlaɪz/ *vi* materializzarsi

maternal /mə'tɜːnl/ *adj* materno

maternity /mə'tɜːnətɪ/ *n* maternità *f*

maternity clothes *npl* abiti *mpl* pre-maman

maternity department *n* (in store) reparto *m* pre-maman

maternity hospital *n* maternità *f inv*

maternity leave *n* congedo *m* per maternità

maternity unit *n* reparto *m* maternità

maternity ward *n* maternità *f inv*

matey /'meɪtɪ/ *adj* fam amichevole

math /mæθ/ *n* Am matematica *f*

mathematical /mæθə'mætɪkl/ *adj* matematico

mathematically /mæθə'mætɪklɪ/ *adv* matematicamente

mathematician /mæθəmə'tɪʃn/ *n* matematico, -a *mf*

mathematics /mæθ'mætɪks/ n matematica *fsg*

maths /mæθs/ n fam matematica *fsg*

matinée /'mætɪneɪ/ n Theat matinée *f inv*

mating /'meɪtɪŋ/ n accoppiamento *m*

mating call n richiamo *m* [per l'accoppiamento]

mating season n stagione *f* degli amori

matriarchal /meɪtrɪ'ɑ:kl/ adj matriarcale

matriarchy /'meɪtrɪɑ:kɪ/ n matriarchia *f*

matrices /'meɪtrɪsi:z/ ▶ MATRIX

matriculate /mə'trɪkjʊleɪt/ vi immatricolarsi

matriculation /mətrɪkjʊ'leɪʃn/ n immatricolazione *f*

matrimonial /mætrɪ'məʊnɪəl/ adj matrimoniale

matrimony /'mætrɪmənɪ/ n matrimonio *m*

matrix /'meɪtrɪks/ n pl **matrices** /'meɪtrɪsi:z/ matrice *f*

matron /'meɪtrən/ n (of hospital) capoinfermiera *f*: (of school) governante *f*

matronly /'meɪtrənlɪ/ adj matronale

matron of honour n Br damigella *f* d'onore (sposata)

matt /mæt/ adj opaco

matted /'mætɪd/ adj ∼ **hair** capelli *mpl* tutti appiccicati tra loro

matter /'mætə(r)/ **①** n (affair) faccenda *f*; (question) questione *f*; (pus) pus *m*; (Phys: substance) materia *f*; **money** ∼s questioni *fpl* di soldi; **as a** ∼ **of fact** a dire la verità; **what is the** ∼? che cosa c'è?
② vi importare; ∼ **to somebody** essere importante per qualcuno; **it doesn't** ∼ non importa

matter-of-fact adj pratico

matting /'mætɪŋ/ n materiale *m* per stuoie

mattress /'mætrɪs/ n materasso *m*

maturation /mætʃʊ'reɪʃn/ n (of tree, body) sviluppo *m*: (of whisky, wine) invecchiamento *m*; (of cheese) stagionatura *f*

mature /mə'tʃʊə(r)/ **①** adj maturo; Comm in scadenza
② vi maturare
③ vt far maturare

mature student n Br persona *f* che riprende gli studi universitari dopo i 25 anni

maturity /mə'tʃʊərətɪ/ n maturità *f*; Comm maturazione *f*

maudlin /'mɔ:dlɪn/ adj ⟨song⟩ sdolcinato; ⟨person⟩ piagnucoloso

maul /mɔ:l/ vt malmenare

Maundy /'mɔ:ndɪ/ n ∼ **Thursday** giovedì *m* santo

Mauritania /mɒrɪ'teɪnɪə/ n Mauritania *f*

Mauritius /mə'rɪʃəs/ n [isola *f* di] Maurizio *f*

mausoleum /mɔ:sə'lɪəm/ n mausoleo *m*

mauve /məʊv/ adj malva

maverick /'mævərɪk/ n, adj anticonformista *mf*

mawkish /'mɔ:kɪʃ/ adj sdolcinato

max. abbr (**maximum**) max. *m*

maxi /'mæksɪ/ n (dress) vestito *m* alla caviglia; (skirt) gonna *f* alla caviglia

maxim /'mæksɪm/ n massima *f*

maximization /mæksɪmaɪ'zeɪʃn/ n massimizzazione *f*

maximize /'mæksɪmaɪz/ vt massimizzare ⟨profits, sales⟩; Comput ingrandire ⟨window⟩

maximum /'mæksɪməm/ **①** adj massimo; **ten minutes** ∼ dieci minuti al massimo
② n (pl **-ima**) massimo *m*

maximum security prison n carcere *m* di massima sicurezza

May /meɪ/ n maggio *m*

may v aux (only in present) potere; ∼ **I come in?** posso entrare?; **if I** ∼ **say so** se mi posso permettere; ∼ **you both be very happy** siate felici; **I** ∼ **as well stay** potrei anche rimanere; **it** ∼ **be true** potrebbe esser vero; **she** ∼ **be old, but...** sarà anche vecchia, ma...

maybe /'meɪbɪ/ adv forse, può darsi

May-bug n maggiolino *m*

Mayday n Radio mayday *m inv*

May Day n il primo maggio

mayhem /'meɪhem/ n **create** ∼ creare scompiglio

mayonnaise /meɪə'neɪz/ n maionese *f*

mayor /'meə(r)/ n sindaco *m*

mayoress /meə'res/ n sindaco *m*; (wife of mayor) moglie *f* del sindaco

maypole /'meɪpəʊl/ n palo *m* intorno al quale si balla durante la celebrazione del primo maggio

May queen n reginetta *f* di calendimaggio

maze /meɪz/ n labirinto *m*

Mb abbr (**megabyte**) MB *m inv*

MBA n abbr (**Master of Business Administration**) laurea *f inv* in economia e commercio

MBE n Br abbr (**Member of the Order of the British Empire**) onorificenza *f* britannica

MBO n abbr **management buyout**

MC n abbr (**Master of Ceremonies**) (in cabaret) presentatore *m*; (at banquet) maestro *m* delle cerimonie; Am *abbr* (**Member of Congress**) membro *m* del Congresso

McCoy /mə'kɔɪ/ *n* this whisky is the real ∼ questo è un vero whisky

MD *abbr* (**Managing Director**) direttore, -trice *mf* generale; *abbr* (**Doctor of Medicine**) dottore *m* in medicina; Am *abbr* **Maryland**

ME *n abbr* (**myalgic encephalomyelitis**) encefalomelite *f* mialgica; Am *abbr* **Maine**

me /miː/ *pers pron* (object) mi; (with preposition) me; **he knows me** mi conosce; **she called me, not you** ha chiamato me, non te; **give me the money** dammi i soldi; **give it to me** dammelo; **he explained it to me** me lo ha spiegato; **it's me** sono io

mead /miːd/ *n* idromele *m*

meadow /'medəʊ/ *n* prato *m*

meagre /'miːgə(r)/ *adj* scarso

meal¹ /miːl/ *n* pasto *m*; **did you enjoy your ∼?** ha mangiato bene?

meal² *n* (grain) farina *f*

meal ticket *n* (figʊ quality, qualification) fonte *f* di guadagno; **he's only a ∼ to her** le interessano solo i suoi soldi

mealy-mouthed /miːlɪ'maʊðd/ *adj* ambiguo

mean¹ /miːn/ *adj* avaro; (unkind) meschino; (low in rank) basso; (accommodation) misero

mean² ❶ *adj* medio ❷ *n* (average) media *f*; **Greenwich ∼ time** ora *f* media di Greenwich

mean³ *vt* (pt/pp **meant**) voler dire; (signify) significare; (intend) intendere; **I ∼ it** lo dico seriamente; **∼ well** avere buone intenzioni; **be ∼t for** (present) essere destinato a; (remark) essere riferito a

meander /mɪ'ændə(r)/ *vi* vagare

meaning /'miːnɪŋ/ *n* significato *m*

meaningful /'miːnɪŋfʊl/ *adj* significativo

meaningless /'miːnɪŋlɪs/ *adj* senza senso

meanness /'miːnnɪs/ *n* (with money) avarizia *f*; (unkindness) meschinità *f*

means /miːnz/ ❶ *n* mezzo *m*; **∼ of transport** mezzo *m* di trasporto; **by ∼ of** per mezzo di; **by all ∼!** certamente!; **by no ∼** niente affatto ❷ *npl* (resources) mezzi *mpl*; **∼ test** *n* accertamento *m* patrimoniale

meant /ment/ ▶ MEAN³

meantime /'miːntaɪm/ ❶ *n* **in the ∼** nel frattempo ❷ *adv* intanto

meanwhile /'miːnwaɪl/ *adv* intanto

measles /'miːzlz/ *nsg* morbillo *m*

measly /'miːzlɪ/ *adj* fam misero

measurable /'meʒərəbl/ *adj* misurabile

measure /'meʒə(r)/ ❶ *n* misura *f* ❷ *vt/i* misurare
■ **measure out** *vt* dosare (amount)
■ **measure up** *vi* fig avere i requisiti richiesti
■ **measure up to** *vt* fig essere all'altezza di

measured /'meʒed/ *adj* misurato

measurement /'meʒəmənt/ *n* misura *f*

measuring jug /'meʒərɪŋ/ *n* dosatore *m*

measuring spoon *n* misurino *m*

meat /miːt/ *n* carne *f*

meatball *n* Culin polpetta *f* di carne

meat-eater *n* (animal) carnivoro *m*; **I'm not a ∼** non mangio carne

meat hook *n* gancio *m* da macellaio

meat loaf *n* polpettone *m*

meat pie *n* tortino *m* di carne

meaty /'miːtɪ/ *adj* (**-ier**, **-iest**) di carne; fig sostanzioso

Mecca /'mekə/ *n* La Mecca

mechanic /mɪ'kænɪk/ *n* meccanico *m*

mechanical /mɪ'kænɪkl/ *adj* meccanico

mechanical engineering *n* ingegneria *f* meccanica

mechanically /mɪ'kænɪklɪ/ *adv* meccanicamente

mechanics /mɪ'kænɪks/ ❶ *n* meccanica *f* ❷ *npl* meccanismo *msg*

mechanism /'mekənɪzm/ *n* meccanismo *m*

mechanization /mekənaɪ'zeɪʃn/ *n* meccanizzazione *f*

mechanize /'mekənaɪz/ *vt* meccanizzare

medal /'medl/ *n* medaglia *f*

medallion /mɪ'dælɪən/ *n* medaglione *m*

medallist /'medəlɪst/ *n* vincitore, -trice *mf* di una medaglia

meddle /'medl/ *vi* immischiarsi (**in** in); (tinker) armeggiare (**with** con)

media /'miːdɪə/ ❶ *n* ▶ MEDIUM ❷ *npl* **the ∼** i mass media

median /'miːdɪən/ *adj* **∼ strip** Am banchina *f* spartitraffico

media studies *npl* scienze *fpl* delle comunicazioni

mediate /'miːdɪeɪt/ *vi* fare da mediatore

mediation /miːdɪ'eɪʃn/ *n* mediazione *f*

mediator /'miːdɪeɪtə(r)/ *n* mediatore, -trice *mf*

medic /'medɪk/ *n* (fam: doctor) medico *m*; (fam: student) studente, -essa *mf* di medicina; Mil fam infermiere, -a *mf* militare

medical /'medɪkl/ ❶ *adj* medico ❷ *n* visita *f* medica

medical care *n* assistenza *f* medica

medical check-up n controllo m
medico

medical examiner n Am =
PATHOLOGIST

medical history n anamnesi f inv

medical insurance n assicurazione f
sanitaria

medically /'medɪklɪ/ adv ∼ qualified
con qualifiche di medico; ∼ fit in buona
salute

medical officer n Mil ufficiale m
medico

medical profession n (occupation)
professione f del medico; (doctors collectively)
categoria f medica

medical student n studente, -essa mf
di medicina

medicated /'medɪkeɪtɪd/ adj medicato

medication /medɪ'keɪʃn/ n (drugs)
medicinali mpl; are you on any ∼? sta
prendendo delle medicine?

medicinal /mɪ'dɪsɪnl/ adj medicinale

medicine /'medsən/ n medicina f

medicine ball n palla f medica

medicine bottle n flacone m

medicine cabinet n armadietto m dei
medicinali

medicine man n stregone m

medieval /medɪ'iːvl/ adj medievale

mediocre /miːdɪ'əʊkə(r)/ adj mediocre

mediocrity /miːdɪ'ɒkrətɪ/ n mediocrità
f

meditate /'medɪteɪt/ vi meditare (on su)

meditative /'medɪtətɪv/ adj ⟨music,
person⟩ meditativo; ⟨mood, expression⟩
meditabondo

Mediterranean /medɪtə'reɪnɪən/ ① n
the ∼ [Sea] il [mare] Mediterraneo
② adj mediterraneo

medium /'miːdɪəm/ ① adj medio; Culin di
media cottura
② n mezzo m; (pl -s) (person) medium mf
inv

medium dry adj ⟨drink⟩ semisecco

medium-length adj ⟨book, film, hair⟩
di media lunghezza

medium-range adj ⟨missile⟩ di media
portata

medium-rare adj ⟨meat⟩ appena al
sangue

medium-sized /'miːdɪəmsaɪzd/ adj di
taglia media

medium wave n onde fpl medie

medley /'medlɪ/ n miscuglio m; Mus
miscellanea f

meek /miːk/ adj mite, mansueto

meekly /'miːklɪ/ adv docilmente

meet /miːt/ ① vt (pt/pp **met**) incontrare;
(at station, airport) andare incontro a; (for first

time) far la conoscenza di; pagare ⟨bill⟩;
soddisfare ⟨requirements⟩
② vi incontrarsi; ⟨committee⟩ riunirsi; ∼
with incontrare ⟨problem⟩; incontrarsi con
⟨person⟩
③ n raduno m (sportivo)
■ **meet up** vi ⟨people⟩ incontrarsi; ∼ up
with somebody incontrare qualcuno

meeting /'miːtɪŋ/ n riunione f, meeting
m inv; (large) assemblea f; (by chance)
incontro m; be in a ∼ essere in riunione

meeting-place n luogo m d'incontro

meeting-point n punto m d'incontro

mega+ /'megə/ pref mega+

megabyte /'megəbaɪt/ n Comput
megabyte m inv

megalith /'megəlɪθ/ n megalite m

megalomania /megələ'meɪnɪə/ n
megalomania f

megalomaniac /megələ'meɪnɪæk/ adj
& n megalomane mf

megaphone /'megəfəʊn/ n megafono m

melancholy /'melənkəlɪ/ ① adj
malinconico
② n malinconia f

mellow /'meləʊ/ ① adj ⟨wine⟩ generoso;
⟨sound, colour⟩ caldo; ⟨person⟩ dolce
② vi ⟨person⟩ addolcirsi

melodic /mɪ'lɒdɪk/ adj melodico

melodious /mɪ'ləʊdɪəs/ adj melodioso

melodrama /'melədrɑːmə/ n
melodramma m

melodramatic /melədrə'mætɪk/ adj
melodrammatico

melodramatically /melədrə'mætɪklɪ/
adv in modo melodrammatico

melody /'melədɪ/ n melodia f

melon /'melən/ n melone m

melt /melt/ ① vt sciogliere
② vi sciogliersi
■ **melt away** vi ⟨snow⟩ sciogliersi;
⟨crowd⟩ disperdersi; ⟨support⟩ venir meno
■ **melt down** vt fondere

meltdown /'meltdaʊn/ n (in nuclear
reactor) fusione f del nocciolo

melting point /'meltɪŋ/ n punto m di
fusione

melting pot n fig crogiuolo m

member /'membə(r)/ n membro m; be a
∼ of the family far parte della famiglia

member countries paesi mpl membri

Member of Congress n Am membro
m del Congresso

Member of Parliament deputato, -a
mf

**Member of the European
Parliament** n eurodeputato, -a mf

membership /'membəʃɪp/ n iscrizione
f; (members) soci mpl

membrane /'membreɪn/ n membrana f

memento /mɪˈmentəʊ/ n ricordo m

memo /ˈmeməʊ/ n promemoria m inv

memoirs /ˈmemwɑːz/ npl ricordi mpl

memo pad n blocchetto m

memorabilia /memərəˈbɪlɪə/ npl cimeli mpl

memorable /ˈmemərəbl/ adj memorabile

memorandum /meməˈrændəm/ n promemoria m inv

memorial /mɪˈmɔːrɪəl/ n monumento m

memorial service n funzione f commemorativa

memorize /ˈmeməraɪz/ vt memorizzare

memory /ˈmemərɪ/ n also Comput memoria f; (thing remembered) ricordo m; from ∼ a memoria; in ∼ of in ricordo di

men /men/ ▶ MAN

menace /ˈmenəs/ **1** n minaccia f; (nuisance) piaga f **2** vt minacciare

menacing /ˈmenəsɪŋ/ adj minaccioso

menacingly /ˈmenəsɪŋlɪ/ adv minacciosamente

mend /mend/ **1** vt riparare; (darn) rammendare **2** n on the ∼ in via di guarigione

menfolk /ˈmenfəʊk/ n uomini mpl

menial /ˈmiːnɪəl/ adj umile

meningitis /menɪnˈdʒaɪtɪs/ n meningite f

menopause /ˈmenəpɔːz/ n menopausa f

Menorca /mɪˈnɔːkə/ n Minorca f

men's room n toilette f inv degli uomini

menstruate /ˈmenstrʊeɪt/ vi mestruare

menstruation /menstrʊˈeɪʃn/ n mestruazione f

menswear /ˈmenzweə(r)/ n abbigliamento m per uomo

mental /ˈmentl/ adj mentale; (fam: mad) pazzo

mental arithmetic n calcolo m mentale

mental block n blocco m psicologico

mental health n (of person) salute f mentale

mental health care n assistenza f psichiatrica

mental home n clinica f psichiatrica

mental illness n malattia f mentale

mentality /menˈtælətɪ/ n mentalità f inv

mentally /ˈmentəlɪ/ adv mentalmente; ∼ ill malato di mente

mentholated /ˈmenθəleɪtɪd/ adj al mentolo

mention /ˈmenʃn/ **1** n menzione f **2** vt menzionare; **don't** ∼ **it** non c'è di che

mentor /ˈmentɔː(r)/ n mentore m

menu /ˈmenjuː/ n menu m inv

menu bar n Comput barra f dei menu

MEP n abbr (**Member of the European parliament**) eurodeputato, -a mf

mercantile /ˈmɜːkəntaɪl/ adj mercantile

mercenary /ˈmɜːsɪnərɪ/ **1** adj mercenario **2** n mercenario m

merchandise /ˈmɜːtʃəndaɪz/ n merce f

merchant /ˈmɜːtʃənt/ n commerciante mf

merchant bank n Br banca f d'affari

merchant banker n (owner) proprietario, -a mf di una banca d'affari; (executive) dirigente mf di banca d'affari

merchant navy n marina f mercantile

merciful /ˈmɜːsɪfl/ adj misericordioso

mercifully /ˈmɜːsɪfʊlɪ/ adv fam grazie a Dio

merciless /ˈmɜːsɪlɪs/ adj spietato

mercilessly /ˈmɜːsɪlɪslɪ/ adv senza pietà

mercurial /mɜːˈkjʊərɪəl/ adj fig volubile

mercury /ˈmɜːkjʊrɪ/ n mercurio m

mercy /ˈmɜːsɪ/ n misericordia f; **be at sb's** ∼ essere alla mercé or in balia di qualcuno

mercy killing n eutanasia f

mere /mɪə(r)/ adj solo

merely /ˈmɪəlɪ/ adv solamente

merest /ˈmɪərɪst/ adj minimo

merge /mɜːdʒ/ **1** vi fondersi **2** vt Comm fondere

merger /ˈmɜːdʒə(r)/ n fusione f

meridian /məˈrɪdɪən/ n meridiano m

meringue /məˈræŋ/ n meringa f

merit /ˈmerɪt/ **1** n merito m; (advantage) qualità f inv **2** vt meritare

mermaid /ˈmɜːmeɪd/ n sirena f

merrily /ˈmerɪlɪ/ adv allegramente

merriment /ˈmerɪmənt/ n baldoria f

merry /ˈmerɪ/ adj (**-ier**, **-iest**) allegro; **M**∼ **Christmas!** Buon Natale!; **make** ∼ far festa

merry-go-round n giostra f

merry-making /ˈmerɪmeɪkɪŋ/ n festa f

mesh /meʃ/ n maglia f

mesmerize /ˈmezməraɪz/ vt ipnotizzare

mesmerized /ˈmezməraɪzd/ adj fig ipnotizzato

mess /mes/ n disordine m, casino m fam; (trouble) guaio m; (something spilt) sporco m; Mil mensa f; **make a** ∼ **of** (botch) fare un pasticcio di

■ **mess about** **1** vi perder tempo; ∼ **about with** armeggiare con **2** vt prendere in giro ⟨person⟩

■ **mess up** *vt* mettere in disordine, incasinare fam; (botch) mandare all'aria

■ **mess with** *vt* (fam: interfere with) trafficare con ⟨*computer, radio etc*⟩; contrariare ⟨*person*⟩

message /'mesɪdʒ/ *n* messaggio *m*

message window *n* Comput finestra *f* di messaggio

messaging /'mesɪdʒɪŋ/ *n* messaggeria *f* elettronica

mess dress *n* Mil uniforme *f* di gala

messenger /'mesɪndʒə(r)/ *n* messaggero *m*

messenger boy *n* fattorino *m*

Messiah /mɪ'saɪə/ *n* Messia *m*

Messrs /'mesəz/ *npl* (on letter) ∼ Smith Spett. ditta Smith

messy /'mesɪ/ *adj* (**-ier, -iest**) disordinato; (in dress) sciatto

met /met/ ▸ MEET

metabolism /mɪ'tæbəlɪzm/ *n* metabolismo *m*

metal /'metl/ ① *n* metallo *m* ② *adj* di metallo

metal detector *n* metal detector *m inv*

metal fatigue *n* fatica *f* del metallo

metallic /mɪ'tælɪk/ *adj* metallico

metallurgy /mɪ'tælədʒɪ/ *n* metallurgia *f*

metal polish *n* lucido *m* per metalli

metalwork /'metlwɜːk/ *n* lavorazione *f* del metallo

metamorphose /metə'mɔːfəʊz/ ① *vt* trasformare ② *vi* trasformarsi (**into** in)

metamorphosis /metə'mɔːfəsɪs/ *n* (pl **-phoses** /metə'mɔːfəsiːz/) metamorfosi *f inv*

metaphor /'metəfə(r)/ *n* metafora *f*

metaphorical /metə'fɒrɪkl/ *adj* metaforico

metaphorically /metə'fɒrɪklɪ/ *adv* metaforicamente

metaphysical /metə'fɪzɪkl/ *adj* metafisico; (abstract) astruso

mete /miːt/ *v*
■ **mete out** *vt* dispensare ⟨*punishment, justice*⟩

meteor /'miːtɪə(r)/ *n* meteora *f*

meteoric /miːtɪ'ɒrɪk/ *adj* fig fulmineo

meteorite /'miːtɪəraɪt/ *n* meteorite *m*

meteorological /miːtɪərə'lɒdʒɪkl/ *adj* meteorologico

Meteorological Office *n* Ufficio *m* meteorologico

meteorologist /miːtɪə'rɒlədʒɪst/ *n* meteorologo, -a *mf*

meteorology /miːtɪə'rɒlədʒɪ/ *n* meteorologia *f*

meter[1] /'miːtə(r)/ *n* contatore *m*

meter[2] *n* Am = METRE

meter reader *n* persona *f* incaricata di leggere il contatore (di gas, elettricità)

methane /'miːθeɪn/ *n* metano *m*

method /'meθəd/ *n* metodo *m*

method acting *n* metodo *m* dell'Actors' Studio

method actor *n* attore *m* che segue il metodo dell'Actors' Studio

methodical /mɪ'θɒdɪkl/ *adj* metodico

methodically /mɪ'θɒdɪklɪ/ *adv* metodicamente

Methodist /'meθədɪst/ *n* metodista *mf*

methodology /meθə'dɒlədʒɪ/ *n* metodologia *f*

meths /meθs/ *n* fam alcol *m* denaturato

methyl /'miːθaɪl/ *n* metile *m*

methylated /'meθɪleɪtɪd/ *adj* ∼ **spirit(s)** alcol *m* denaturato

meticulous /mɪ'tɪkjʊləs/ *adj* meticoloso

meticulously /mɪ'tɪkjʊləslɪ/ *adv* meticolosamente

metre /'miːtə(r)/ *n* metro *m*

metric /'metrɪk/ *adj* metrico

metrication /metrɪ'keɪʃn/ *n* conversione *f* al sistema metrico

metronome /'metrənəʊm/ *n* metronomo *m*

metropolis /mɪ'trɒpəlɪs/ *n* metropoli *f inv*

metropolitan /metrə'pɒlɪtən/ *adj* metropolitano

metropolitan district *n* Br circoscrizione *f* amministrativa urbana

Metropolitan police *n* Br polizia *f* di Londra

mettle /'metl/ *n* coraggio *m*; **show one's** ∼ mostrare di che stoffa si è fatti

mew /mjuː/ ① *n* miao *m* ② *vi* miagolare

mews /mjuːz/ *n* Br (stables) scuderie *fpl*; (street) stradina *f*; (yard) cortile *m*

mews flat *n* Br piccolo appartamento *m* ricavato da vecchie scuderie

Mexican /'meksɪkən/ *adj & n* messicano, -a *mf*

Mexican wave *n* ola *f inv*

Mexico /'meksɪkəʊ/ *n* Messico *m*

mezzanine /'metsəniːn/ *n* mezzanino *m*

miaow /mɪ'aʊ/ ① *n* miao *m* ② *vi* miagolare

mice /maɪs/ ▸ MOUSE

Michaelmas /'mɪkəlməs/ *n* festa *f* di San Michele (29 settembre)

Michaelmas daisy *n* Br margherita *f* settembrina

Michaelmas Term *n* Br Univ primo trimestre *m*

mickey /'mɪkɪ/ *n* **take the** ∼ **out of** prendere in giro

Mickey Mouse *n* Topolino *m*

microbe /'maɪkrəʊb/ *n* microbo *m*

microchip /'maɪkrəʊtʃɪp/ *n* microchip *m inv*

microcomputer /'maɪkrəʊkəmpjuːtə(r)/ *n* microcomputer *m inv*

microcosm /'maɪkrəkɒzm/ *n* microcosmo *m*

microfilm *n* microfilm *m inv*

microlight *n* ultraleggero *m*

microlighting *n* volo *m* con l'ultraleggero

micromesh tights *npl* collant *mpl* velati

microphone *n* microfono *m*

microphysics *n* microfisica *f*

microprocessor *n* microprocessore *m*

microscope *n* microscopio *m*

microscopic *adj* microscopico

microsurgery *n* microchirurgia *f*

microwave *n* microonda *f*; (oven) forno *m* a microonde

mid /mɪd/ *adj* ~ **May** metà maggio; **in** ~ **air** a mezz'aria

midday /mɪd'deɪ/ *n* mezzogiorno *m*

middle /'mɪdl/ **①** *adj* di centro; **the M~ Ages** il medioevo; **the ~ class(es)** la classe media; **the M~ East** il Medio Oriente
② *n* mezzo *m*; **in the ~ of** ⟨*room, floor etc*⟩ in mezzo a; **in the ~ of the night** nel pieno della notte, a notte piena

middle-aged /-'eɪdʒd/ *adj* di mezza età

middle-age spread *n* pancetta *f* di mezza età

Middle America *n* (social group) ceto *m* medio americano a tendenza conservatrice

middlebrow *adj* ⟨*book*⟩ per il lettore medio; ⟨*person*⟩ con interessi culturali convenzionali

middle-class *adj* borghese

middle distance *n* Phot, Cinema secondo piano *m*; **gaze into the ~ ~** avere lo sguardo perso nel vuoto

middle-eastern *adj* mediorientale

Middle English *n* medio inglese *m*

middle finger *n* dito *m* medio

middle ground *n* Pol centro *m*; **occupy the ~ ~** adottare una posizione intermedia

middle-income *adj* ⟨*person, family, country*⟩ dal reddito medio

middleman /'mɪdlmæn/ *n* Comm intermediario *m*

middle manager *n* quadro *m* intermedio

middle-of-the-road *adj* (ordinary) ordinario; ⟨*policy*⟩ moderato

middle-size[d] /-saɪz[d]/ *adj* di misura media

middleweight *n* peso *m* medio

middling /'mɪdlɪŋ/ *adj* discreto

midfield /'mɪd'fiːld/ *n* centrocampo *m*

midfield player *n* centrocampista *m*

midge /mɪdʒ/ *n* moscerino *m*

midget /'mɪdʒɪt/ *n* nano, -a *mf*

Midlands /'mɪdləndz/ *npl* **the M~** l'Inghilterra *fsg* centrale

mid-life *n* mezza età *f*

mid-life crisis *n* crisi *f inv* di mezza età

midnight /'mɪdnaɪt/ *n* mezzanotte *f*

mid-range *attrib* ⟨*car*⟩ (in price) di prezzo medio; (in power) di media cilindrata; ⟨*hotel*⟩ intermedio

midriff /'mɪdrɪf/ *n* diaframma *m*

mid-season *adj* di metà stagione

midshipman /'mɪdʃɪpmən/ *n* Br cadetto *m* di marina; Am allievo *m* dell'Accademia Navale

midst /mɪdst/ *n* **in the ~ of** in mezzo a; **in our ~** fra di noi, in mezzo a noi

midstream /mɪd'striːm/ *adv* **in ~** (in river) nel mezzo della corrente; (fig: in speech) nel mezzo del discorso

midsummer /'mɪdsʌmə(r)/ *n* mezza estate *f*

Midsummer's Day *n* festa *f* di San Giovanni (24 giugno)

mid-term *attrib* Sch di metà trimestre; Pol a metà del mandato del governo

midtown *n* Am centro *m* (cittadino); **a ~ apartment** un appartamento in centro

midway /'mɪdweɪ/ *adv* a metà strada

midweek /mɪd'wiːk/ **①** *adj* di metà settimana
② *adv* a metà settimana

midwife /'mɪdwaɪf/ *n* ostetrica *f*

midwifery /'mɪdwɪfrɪ/ *n* ostetricia *f*

midwinter /mɪd'wɪntə(r)/ *n* pieno inverno *m*

miffed /mɪft/ *adj* fam seccato

might[1] /maɪt/ *v aux* **I ~** potrei; **will you come? – I ~** vieni? – può darsi; **it ~ be true** potrebbe essere vero; **I ~ as well stay** potrei anche restare; **he asked if he ~ go** ha chiesto se poteva andare; **you ~ have drowned** avresti potuto affogare; **you ~ have said so!** avresti potuto dirlo!

might[2] *n* potere *m*

mighty /'maɪtɪ/ **①** *adj* (**-ier, -iest**) potente
② *adv* fam molto

migraine /'miːgreɪn/ *n* emicrania *f*

migrant /'maɪgrənt/ **①** *adj* migratore
② *n* (bird) migratore, -trice *mf*; (person: for work) emigrante *mf*

migrate /maɪ'greɪt/ *vi* migrare

migration /maɪˈɡreɪʃn/ n migrazione f

migratory /maɪˈɡreɪtəri/ adj ‹animal›
migratore

mike /maɪk/ n fam microfono f

Milan /mɪˈlæn/ n Milano f

Milanese /mɪləˈniːz/ adj milanese

mild /maɪld/ adj ‹weather› mite; ‹person›
dolce; ‹flavour› delicato; ‹illness› leggero

mildew /ˈmɪldjuː/ n muffa f

mildly /ˈmaɪldlɪ/ adv moderatamente;
‹say› dolcemente; **to put it** ~ a dir poco,
senza esagerazione

mildness /ˈmaɪldnɪs/ n (of person, words)
dolcezza f; (of weather) mitezza f

mile /maɪl/ n miglio m (= 1,6 km); **~s**
nicer fam molto più bello; **~s too big** fam
eccessivamente grande

mileage /ˈmaɪlɪdʒ/ n chilometraggio m

mileage allowance n indennità f inv
di trasferta per chilometro

milestone /ˈmaɪlstəʊn/ n pietra f
miliare

milieu /mɪˈjɜː/ n ambiente m

militant /ˈmɪlɪtənt/ adj & n militante mf

militarism /ˈmɪlɪtərɪzm/ n militarismo
m

militarize /ˈmɪlɪtəraɪz/ vt militarizzare

military /ˈmɪlɪtrɪ/ adj militare

military academy n accademia f
militare

military policeman n agente m di
polizia militare

military service n servizio m militare

militate /ˈmɪlɪteɪt/ vi ~ **against** opporsi
a

militia /mɪˈlɪʃə/ n milizia f

milk /mɪlk/ ① n latte m
② vt mungere

milk chocolate n cioccolato m al latte

milk float n Br furgone m del lattaio

milk jug n bricco m del latte

milkman n lattaio m

milk pudding n budino m a base di
latte

milk shake n frappé m inv

milk train n primo treno m del mattino

milky /ˈmɪlkɪ/ adj (-ier, -iest) latteo; ‹tea
etc› con molto latte

Milky Way n Astr Via f Lattea

mill /mɪl/ ① n mulino m; (factory) fabbrica
f; (for coffee etc) macinino m
② vt macinare ‹grain›
■ **mill about, mill around** vi brulicare

millennium /mɪˈlenɪəm/ n millennio m

miller /ˈmɪlə(r)/ n mugnaio m

millet /ˈmɪlɪt/ n miglio m

milligram /ˈmɪlɪɡræm/ n milligrammo m

millimetre /ˈmɪlɪmiːtə(r)/ n millimetro
m

million /ˈmɪljən/ adj & n milione m; **a** ~
pounds un milione di sterline

millionaire /mɪljəˈneə(r)/ n miliardario,
-a mf

millipede /ˈmɪlɪpiːd/ n millepiedi m inv

millpond n **like a** ~ calmo come una
tavola

millstone n **a** ~ **round one's neck** fig un
peso

mill-wheel n ruota f di mulino

milometer /maɪˈlɒmɪtə(r)/ n Br ≈
contachilometri m inv

mime /maɪm/ ① n mimo m
② vt mimare

mime artist n mimo, a mf

mimic /ˈmɪmɪk/ ① n imitatore, -trice mf
② vt (pt/pp **mimicked**) imitare

mimicry /ˈmɪmɪkrɪ/ n mimetismo m

mimosa /mɪˈməʊzə/ n mimosa f

min. abbr (**minute**) min.; abbr minimum

minaret /mɪnəˈret/ n minareto m

mince /mɪns/ ① n carne f tritata
② vt Culin tritare; **not** ~ **words** parlare
senza mezzi termini

mincemeat /ˈmɪnsmiːt/ n miscuglio m
di frutta secca; **make** ~ **of** fig demolire

mince pie n pasticcino m a base di
frutta secca

mincer /ˈmɪnsə(r)/ n tritacarne m inv

mind /maɪnd/ ① n mente f; (sanity)
ragione f; **to my** ~ a mio parere; **give
somebody a piece of one's** ~ dire chiaro
e tondo a qualcuno quello che si pensa;
make up one's ~ decidersi; **have
something in** ~ avere qualcosa in mente;
bear something in ~ tenere presente
qualcosa; **have something on one's** ~
essere preoccupato; **have a good** ~ **to**
avere una grande voglia di; **I have
changed my** ~ ho cambiato idea; **be out
of one's** ~ essere fuori di sé
② vt (look after) occuparsi di; **I don't** ~ **the
noise** il rumore non dà fastidio; **I don't** ~
what we do non mi importa quello che
facciamo; ~ **the step!** attenzione al
gradino!
③ vi **I don't** ~ non mi importa; **never** ~!
non importa!; **do you** ~ **if...?** ti dispiace
se...?
■ **mind out** vi ~ **out!** [fai] attenzione!

mind-bending /-bendɪŋ/ adj ‹problem›
complicatissimo; ~ **drugs** psicofarmaci
mpl

mind-blowing /-bləʊɪŋ/ adj fam
sconvolgente

mind-boggling /-bɒɡlɪŋ/ adj fam
incredibile

minded /ˈmaɪndɪd/ adj **if you're so** ~ se
vuole

minder /ˈmaɪndə(r)/ n (Br: bodyguard)
gorilla m inv; (for child) baby-sitter mf inv

mindful /ˈmaɪndfʊl/ adj ~ **of** attento a

mindless /'maɪndlɪs/ adj noncurante

mind-reader n persona f che legge nel pensiero; **I'm not a ~** non leggo nel pensiero

mine¹ /maɪn/ poss pron il mio m, la mia f, i miei mpl, le mie fpl; **a friend of ~** un mio amico; **friends of ~** dei miei amici; **that is ~** questo è mio; (as opposed to yours) questo è il mio

mine² **1** n miniera f; (explosive) mina f **2** vt estrarre; Mil minare

mine-detector n rivelatore m di mine

minefield /'maɪnfiːld/ n also fig campo m minato

miner /'maɪnə(r)/ n minatore m

mineral /'mɪnərəl/ **1** n minerale m **2** adj minerale

mineral oil n (Am: paraffin) olio m minerale

mineral rights npl concessioni fpl minerarie

mineral water n acqua f minerale

minesweeper /'maɪnswiːpə(r)/ n dragamine m inv

mingle /'mɪŋgl/ vi ~ **with** mescolarsi a

mini /'mɪnɪ/ n ▶ MINISKIRT

mini+ pref mini+

miniature /'mɪnɪtʃə(r)/ **1** adj in miniatura **2** n miniatura f

miniature golf n minigolf m inv

miniature railway n trenino m

mini-budget n Br Pol budget m inv provvisorio

minibus n minibus m inv, pulmino m

minicab n taxi m inv

minidisc n minidisc m inv

minidisc player n lettore m di minidisc

minim /'mɪnɪm/ n Mus minima f

minimal /'mɪnɪməl/ adj minimo

minimalist adj minimalista

minimally /'mɪnɪməlɪ/ adv (very slightly) minimamente

minimarket /'mɪnɪmɑːkɪt/ n minimarket m inv

minimize /'mɪnɪmaɪz/ vt minimizzare

minimum /'mɪnɪməm/ **1** n (pl **-ima**) minimo m **2** adj minimo; **ten minutes ~** minimo dieci minuti

mining /'maɪnɪŋ/ **1** n estrazione f **2** attrib estrattivo

mining engineer n ingegnere m minerario

miniskirt /'mɪnɪskɜːt/ n minigonna f

minister /'mɪnɪstə(r)/ n ministro m; Relig pastore m

ministerial /mɪnɪ'stɪərɪəl/ adj ministeriale

minister of state n Br Pol titolo m di un parlamentare con competenze specifiche in seno a un ministero

ministry /'mɪnɪstrɪ/ n Pol ministero m; **the ~** Relig il ministero sacerdotale

mink /mɪŋk/ n visone m

minnow /'mɪnəʊ/ n (fish) pesciolino m d'acqua dolce

minor /'maɪnə(r)/ **1** adj minore **2** n minorenne mf

Minorca /mɪ'nɔːkə/ n Minorca f

minority /maɪ'nɒrətɪ/ n minoranza f; (age) minore età f

minority leader n Am Pol leader mf inv dell'opposizione

minority rule n governo m di minoranza

minor offence n Br reato m minore

minor road n strada f secondaria

minster /'mɪnstə(r)/ n (cathedral) cattedrale f

minstrel /'mɪnstrəl/ n menestrello m

mint¹ /mɪnt/ **1** n zecca f; fam patrimonio m **2** adj **in ~ condition** in condizione perfetta **3** vt coniare

mint² n (herb) menta f

mint-flavoured /-fleɪvəd/ adj al gusto di menta

minuet /mɪnjʊ'et/ n minuetto m

minus /'maɪnəs/ **1** prep meno; (fam: without) senza **2** n ~ **[sign]** meno m

minuscule /'mɪnəskjuːl/ adj minuscolo

minute¹ /'mɪnɪt/ n minuto m; **in a ~** (shortly) tra un minuto; **~s** pl (of meeting) verbale msg

minute² /maɪ'njuːt/ adj minuto; (precise) minuzioso

minute hand /'mɪnɪt/ n lancetta f dei minuti

minutely /maɪ'njuːtlɪ/ adv ⟨vary, differ⟩ di poco; ⟨describe, examine⟩ minuziosamente

minutiae /maɪ'njuːʃɪaɪ/ npl minuzie fpl

miracle /'mɪrəkl/ n miracolo m

miraculous /mɪ'rækjʊləs/ adj miracoloso

mirage /'mɪrɑːʒ/ n miraggio m

mire /'maɪə(r)/ n pantano m

mirror /'mɪrə(r)/ **1** n specchio m **2** vt rispecchiare

mirror image n (exact replica) copia f esatta; (inverse) immagine f speculare

mirth /mɜːθ/ n ilarità f

misadventure /mɪsæd'ventʃə(r)/ n disavventura f

misanthropist /mɪ'zænθrəpɪst/ n misantropo, -a mf

misapprehension /mɪsæprɪ'henʃn/ *n* malinteso *m*; **be under a** ∼ avere frainteso

misappropriate /mɪsə'prəʊprɪeɪt/ *vt* appropriarsi indebitamente di ⟨*funds*⟩

misbehave /mɪsbɪ'heɪv/ *vi* comportarsi male

misbehaviour /mɪsbɪ'heɪvjə(r)/ *n* comportamento *m* scorretto

miscalculate /mɪs'kælkjʊleɪt/ *vt/i* calcolare male

miscalculation /mɪskælkjʊ'leɪʃn/ *n* calcolo *m* sbagliato

miscarriage /'mɪskærɪdʒ/ *n* aborto *m* spontaneo; ∼ **of justice** errore *m* giudiziario

miscarry /mɪs'kærɪ/ *vi* abortire

miscellaneous /mɪsə'leɪnɪəs/ *adj* assortito

miscellany /mɪ'selənɪ/ *n* (of people, things) misto *m*; (anthology) miscellanea *f*

mischief /'mɪstʃɪf/ *n* malefatta *f*; (harm) danno *m*

mischievous /'mɪstʃɪvəs/ *adj* (naughty) birichino; (malicious) dannoso

mischievously /'mɪstʃɪvəslɪ/ *adv* in modo birichino

misconceived /mɪskən'siːvd/ *adj* ⟨*argument, project*⟩ sbagliato

misconception /mɪskən'sepʃn/ *n* concetto *m* erroneo

misconduct /mɪs'kɒndʌkt/ *n* cattiva condotta *f*

misconstrue /mɪskən'struː/ *vt* fraintendere

miscount /mɪs'kaʊnt/ *vt/i* contare male

misdeed /mɪs'diːd/ *n* misfatto *m*

misdemeanour /mɪsdɪ'miːnə(r)/ *n* reato *m*

misdirect /mɪsdaɪ'rekt/ *vt* mettere l'indirizzo sbagliato su ⟨*letter, parcel*⟩; dare istruzioni sbagliate a ⟨*jury*⟩; **the letter was** ∼**ed to our old address** la lettera ci è stata erroneamente spedita al vecchio indirizzo

miser /'maɪzə(r)/ *n* avaro *m*

miserable /'mɪzrəbl/ *adj* (unhappy) infelice; (wretched) miserabile; fig ⟨*weather*⟩ deprimente

miserably /'mɪzrəblɪ/ *adv* ⟨*live, fail*⟩ miseramente; ⟨*say*⟩ tristemente

miserly /'maɪzəlɪ/ *adj* avaro; ⟨*amount*⟩ ridicolo

misery /'mɪzərɪ/ *n* miseria *f*; (fam: person) piagnone, -a *mf*

misfire /mɪs'faɪə(r)/ *vi* ⟨*gun*⟩ far cilecca; ⟨*plan etc*⟩ non riuscire

misfit /'mɪsfɪt/ *n* disadattato, -a *mf*

misfortune /mɪs'fɔːtʃuːn/ *n* sfortuna *f*

misgivings /mɪs'gɪvɪŋz/ *npl* dubbi *mpl*

misguided /mɪs'gaɪdɪd/ *adj* fuorviato

mishandle /mɪs'hændl/ *vt* gestire male ⟨*operation, meeting*⟩; non prendere per il verso giusto ⟨*person*⟩; (roughly) maneggiare senza precauzioni ⟨*object*⟩; maltrattare ⟨*person, animal*⟩

mishap /'mɪshæp/ *n* disavventura *f*

mishear /mɪs'hɪə(r)/ *vt* sentire male

mishmash /'mɪʃmæʃ/ *n* fam guazzabuglio *m*

misinform /mɪsɪn'fɔːm/ *vt* informar male

misinformation /mɪsɪnfə'meɪʃn/ *n* informazioni *fpl* sbagliate

misinterpret /mɪsɪn'tɜːprɪt/ *vt* fraintendere

misinterpretation /mɪsɪntɜːprɪ'teɪʃn/ *n* interpretazione *f* sbagliata

misjudge /mɪs'dʒʌdʒ/ *vt* giudicar male; (estimate wrongly) valutare male

mislay /mɪs'leɪ/ *vt* (pt/pp **-laid**) smarrire

mislead /mɪs'liːd/ *vt* (pt/pp **-led**) fuorviare

misleading /mɪs'liːdɪŋ/ *adj* fuorviante

mismanage /mɪs'mænɪdʒ/ *vt* amministrare male

mismanagement /mɪs'mænɪdʒmənt/ *n* cattiva amministrazione *f*

mismatch /'mɪsmætʃ/ *n* discordanza *f*

misname /mɪs'neɪm/ *vt* dare il nome sbagliato a

misnomer /mɪs'nəʊmə(r)/ *n* termine *m* improprio

misogynist /mɪs'ɒdʒənɪst/ *n* misogino *m*

misplace /mɪs'pleɪs/ *vt* mettere in un posto sbagliato; ∼ **one's trust** riporre male la propria fiducia

misprint /'mɪsprɪnt/ *n* errore *m* di stampa

mispronounce /mɪsprə'naʊns/ *vt* pronunciare male

mispronunciation /mɪsprənʌnsɪeɪʃn/ *n* (act) pronuncia *f* sbagliata; (instance) errore *m* di pronuncia

misquote /mɪs'kwəʊt/ *vt* citare erroneamente

misread /mɪs'riːd/ *vt* leggere male ⟨*sentence, meter*⟩; (misinterpret) fraintendere ⟨*actions*⟩

misrepresent /mɪsreprɪ'zent/ *vt* rappresentare male

misrepresentation /mɪsreprɪzen'teɪʃn/ *n* (of facts, opinions) travisamento *m*

Miss /mɪs/ *n* (pl **-es**) signorina *f*

miss ① *n* colpo *m* mancato
② *vt* (fail to hit or find) mancare; perdere ⟨*train, bus, class*⟩; (feel the loss of) sentire la mancanza di; **I** ∼**ed that part** (failed to notice)

mi è sfuggita quella parte; ∼ **the point** non afferrare il punto

3] *vi* **but he** ∼**ed** (failed to hit) ma l'ha mancato

▪ **miss out** *vt* saltare, omettere

misshapen /mɪsˈʃeɪpən/ *adj* malformato

missile /ˈmɪsaɪl/ *n* missile *m*

missing /ˈmɪsɪŋ/ *adj* mancante; ⟨person⟩ scomparso; Mil disperso; **be** ∼ essere introvabile; ∼ **in action** Mil disperso

mission /ˈmɪʃn/ *n* missione *f*

missionary /ˈmɪʃənrɪ/ *n* missionario, -a *mf*

missive /ˈmɪsɪv/ *n* missiva *f*

misspell /mɪsˈspel/ *vt* (pt/pp **-spelt**, **-spelled**) sbagliare l'ortografia di

misspent /mɪsˈspent/ *adj* **a** ∼ **youth** una gioventù sprecata

mist /mɪst/ *n* (fog) foschia *f*; **because of the** ∼ **on the windows** a causa dei vetri appannati

▪ **mist over** *vi* ⟨eyes⟩ velarsi

▪ **mist up** *vi* appannarsi, annebbiarsi

mistake /mɪˈsteɪk/ **1]** *n* sbaglio *m*; **by** ∼ per sbaglio

2] *vt* (pt **mistook**, pp **mistaken**) sbagliare ⟨road, house⟩; fraintendere ⟨meaning, words⟩; ∼ **for** prendere per

mistaken /mɪˈsteɪkən/ *adj* sbagliato; **be** ∼ sbagliarsi; ∼ **identity** errore *m* di persona

mistakenly /mɪˈsteɪkənlɪ/ *adv* erroneamente

mister /ˈmɪstə(r)/ *n* signore *m*

mistletoe /ˈmɪsltəʊ/ *n* vischio *m*

mistranslate /mɪstrænzˈleɪt/ *vt* tradurre in modo sbagliato

mistranslation /mɪstrænzˈleɪʃn/ *n* traduzione *f* sbagliata

mistreat /mɪsˈtriːt/ maltrattare

mistreatment /mɪsˈtriːtmənt/ *n* maltrattamento *m*

mistress /ˈmɪstrɪs/ *n* padrona *f*; (teacher) maestra *f*; (lover) amante *f*

mistrust /mɪsˈtrʌst/ **1]** *n* sfiducia *f*

2] *vt* non aver fiducia in

misty /ˈmɪstɪ/ *adj* (**-ier**, **-iest**) nebbioso; *fig* indistinto

misty-eyed /-ˈaɪd/ *adj* ⟨look⟩ commosso; **he goes all** ∼ **about it** a parlarne si commuove

misunderstand /mɪsʌndəˈstænd/ *vt* (pt/pp **-stood**) fraintendere

misunderstanding /mɪsʌndəˈstændɪŋ/ *n* malinteso *m*

misuse[1] /mɪsˈjuːz/ *vt* usare male

misuse[2] /mɪsˈjuːs/ *n* cattivo uso *m*

mite /maɪt/ *n* Zool acaro *m*; (child) piccino, -a *mf*

mitigate /ˈmɪtɪgeɪt/ *vt* attenuare

mitigating /ˈmɪtɪgeɪtɪŋ/ *adj* attenuante

mitre Br, **miter** Am /ˈmaɪtə(r)/ *n* mitra *f*

mitt /mɪt/ *n* (no separate fingers) muffola *f*; (cut-off fingers) mezzo guanto *m*; (in baseball) guantone *m*; (fam: hand) mano *f*

mitten /ˈmɪtn/ *n* manopola *f*, muffola *f*

mix /mɪks/ **1]** *n* (combination) mescolanza *f*; Culin miscuglio *m*; (ready-made) preparato *m*

2] *vt* mischiare

3] *vi* mischiarsi; ⟨person⟩ inserirsi; ∼ **with** (associate with) frequentare

▪ **mix in** *vt* incorporare ⟨eggs, flour etc⟩

▪ **mix up** *vt* mescolare ⟨papers⟩; (confuse, mistake for) confondere

mixed /mɪkst/ *adj* misto

mixed ability *adj* ⟨class, teaching⟩ per alunni di capacità diverse

mixed bag *n* **it was a very** ∼ ∼ *fig* c'era un po' di tutto

mixed blessing *n* **be a** ∼ ∼ avere vantaggi e svantaggi

mixed doubles *npl* Tennis doppio *m* misto

mixed economy *n* economia *f* mista

mixed grill *n* grigliata *f* di carne mista

mixed marriage *n* matrimonio *m* misto

mixed-media *adj* multimediale

mixed metaphor *n* abbinamento *m* di parte di due o più metafore diverse con effetto comico

mixed race **1]** *adj* ⟨children⟩ con genitori di razze diverse

2] *n* **she's of** ∼ i suoi genitori sono di razze diverse

mixed-up *adj* ⟨person, emotions⟩ confuso

mixed vegetables *npl* verdure *fpl* miste

mixer /ˈmɪksə(r)/ *n* Culin frullatore *m*, mixer *m inv*; **he's a good** ∼ è un tipo socievole

mixing /ˈmɪksɪŋ/ *n* (of people, objects, ingredients) mescolamento *m*: Mus mixaggio *m*

mixture /ˈmɪkstʃə(r)/ *n* mescolanza *f*; (medicine) sciroppo *m*: Culin miscela *f*

mix-up *n* (confusion) confusione *f*: (mistake) pasticcio *m*

mm *abbr* (**millimetre(s)**) mm

MMS *abbr* (**multimedia messaging service**) MMS *m*

MO *abbr* (**medical officer**) ufficiale *m* medico; *abbr* (**money order**) vaglia *m inv* postale; Am *abbr* **Missouri**

moan /məʊn/ **1]** *n* lamento *m*

2] *vi* lamentarsi; (complain) lagnarsi

moat /məʊt/ *n* fossato *m*

mob /mɒb/ **1]** *n* folla *f*: (rabble) gentaglia *f*; (fam: gang) banda *f*

2] *vt* (pt/pp **mobbed**) assalire

mobile /ˈməʊbaɪl/ **1]** *adj* mobile

2 *n* composizione *f* mobile; (phone) [telefono *m*] cellulare *m*

mobile home *n* casa *f* roulotte

mobile library *n* Br biblioteca *f* itinerante

mobile phone *n* (telefono *m*) cellulare *m*, telefonino *m*

mobile shop *n* furgone *m* attrezzato per la vendita

mobility /məˈbɪlətɪ/ *n* mobilità *f*

mobility allowance *n* Br indennità *f* *inv* di accompagnamento

mobilization /məʊbɪlaɪˈzeɪʃn/ *n* mobilitazione *f*

mobilize /ˈməʊbɪlaɪz/ *vt* mobilitare

mocha /ˈmɒkə/ *n* moca *m* *inv*

mock /mɒk/ **1** *adj* finto
2 *vt* canzonare

mockery /ˈmɒkərɪ/ *n* derisione *f*; **a ~ of** una parodia di

mock-up *n* modello *m* in scala

MoD *n* *abbr* (**Ministry of Defence**) Br Ministero *m* della Difesa

modal /ˈməʊdl/ *adj* **~ auxiliary** verbo *m* modale

mod con /mɒdˈkɒn/ Br *abbr* (**modern convenience**) **all ~ ~s** tutti i comfort

mode /məʊd/ *n* modo *m*; Comput modalità *f*

model /ˈmɒdl/ **1** *n* modello *m*; [fashion] **~** indossatore, -trice *mf*, modello, -a *mf*
2 *adj* ⟨yacht, plane⟩ in miniatura; ⟨pupil, husband⟩ esemplare, modello
3 *vt* (*pt/pp* **modelled**) indossare ⟨clothes⟩
4 *vi* fare l'indossatore, -trice *mf*: (for artist) posare

modelling /ˈmɒd(ə)lɪŋ/ *n* (with clay etc) modellare *m* con la creta; (of clothes) professione *f* di indossatore; **do some ~** (for artist) fare il modello

modelling clay *n* creta *f* per modellare

modem /ˈməʊdem/ **1** *n* modem *m* *inv*
2 *vt* mandare per modem

moderate¹ /ˈmɒdəreɪt/ **1** *vt* moderare
2 *vi* moderarsi

moderate² /ˈmɒdərət/ **1** *adj* moderato
2 *n* Pol moderato, -a *mf*

moderately /ˈmɒdərətlɪ/ *adv* ⟨drink, speak etc⟩ moderatamente; ⟨good, bad etc⟩ relativamente

moderation /mɒdəˈreɪʃn/ *n* moderazione *f*; **in ~** con moderazione

modern /ˈmɒdn/ *adj* moderno

modern-day *adj* attuale

modernism /ˈmɒdənɪzm/ *n* modernismo *m*

modernity /məˈdɜːnətɪ/ *n* modernità *f*

modernization /mɒdənaɪˈzeɪʃn/ *n* modernizzazione *f*

modernize /ˈmɒdənaɪz/ *vt* modernizzare

modern languages *npl* lingue *fpl* moderne

modest /ˈmɒdɪst/ *adj* modesto

modesty /ˈmɒdɪstɪ/ *n* modestia *f*

modicum /ˈmɒdɪkəm/ *n* **a ~ of** un po' di

modification /mɒdɪfɪˈkeɪʃn/ *n* modificazione *f*

modifier /ˈmɒdɪfaɪə(r)/ *n* (in linguistics) modificatore *m*

modify /ˈmɒdɪfaɪ/ *vt* (*pt/pp* **-fied**) modificare

modular /ˈmɒdjʊlə(r)/ *adj* ⟨course⟩ a moduli; ⟨construction, furniture⟩ modulare

modulate /ˈmɒdjʊleɪt/ *vt/i* modulare

module /ˈmɒdjuːl/ *n* modulo *m*

modus operandi /məʊdəsɒpəˈrændiː/ *n* modus operandi *m* *inv*

mogul /ˈməʊgl/ *n* magnate *m*

Mohammed /məˈhæmɪd/ *n* Maometto *m*

mohican /məʊˈhiːkən/ *n* (hairstyle) taglio *m* [di capelli] alla moicana

moist /mɔɪst/ *adj* umido

moisten /ˈmɔɪsn/ *vt* inumidire

moisture /ˈmɔɪstʃə(r)/ *n* umidità *f*

moisturizer /ˈmɔɪstʃəraɪzə(r)/ *n* [crema *f*] idratante *m*

molar /ˈməʊlə(r)/ *n* molare *m*

molasses /məˈlæsɪz/ *n* Am melassa *f*

mold /məʊld/ Am = MOULD

Moldavia /mɒlˈdeɪvɪə/ *n* Moldavia *f*

mole¹ /məʊl/ *n* (on face etc) neo *m*

mole² *n* Zool talpa *f*

mole³ *n* (breakwater) molo *m*

molecular /məˈlekjʊlə(r)/ *adj* molecolare

molecule /ˈmɒlɪkjuːl/ *n* molecola *f*

molehill /ˈməʊlhɪl/ *n* monticello *m*

moleskin /ˈməʊlskɪn/ *n* (fur) pelliccia *f* di talpa

molest /məˈlest/ *vt* molestare

mollify /ˈmɒlɪfaɪ/ *vt* (*pt/pp* **-ied**) placare

mollusc /ˈmɒləsk/ *n* mollusco *m*

mollycoddle /ˈmɒlɪkɒdl/ *vt* tenere nella bambagia

molt /məʊlt/ Am = MOULT

molten /ˈməʊltən/ *adj* fuso

mom /mɒm/ *n* Am *fam* mamma *f*

moment /ˈməʊmənt/ *n* momento *m*; **at the ~** in questo momento

momentarily /məʊmənˈterɪlɪ/ *adv* (for an instant) per un momento; (Am: at any moment) da un momento all'altro; (Am; very soon) tra un momento

momentary /ˈməʊməntrɪ/ *adj* momentaneo

momentous /məˈmentəs/ *adj* molto importante

momentum /mə'mentəm/ n impeto m

Monaco /'mɒnəkəʊ/ n Principato m di Monaco

monarch /'mɒnək/ n monarca m

monarchist /'mɒnəkɪst/ n monarchico, -a mf

monarchy /'mɒnəkɪ/ n monarchia f

monastery /'mɒnəstrɪ/ n monastero m

monastic /mə'næstɪk/ adj monastico

Monday /'mʌndeɪ/ n lunedì m inv

monetary /'mʌnətrɪ/ adj monetario

money /'mʌnɪ/ n denaro m

money box n salvadanaio m

moneylender n usuraio m

moneymaker n (business) attività f redditizia; (product) prodotto m che rende bene

money order n vaglia m inv postale

Mongolia /mɒŋ'gəʊlɪə/ n Mongolia f

mongrel /'mʌŋgrəl/ n bastardino m

monitor /'mɒnɪtə(r)/ ①n Techn monitor m inv ②vt controllare

monk /mʌŋk/ n monaco m

monkey /'mʌŋkɪ/ n scimmia f
■ **monkey about with** vt (fam: interfere with) armeggiare con

monkey business n fam (fooling) scherzi mpl; (cheating) imbrogli mpl

monkey-nut n nocciolina f americana

monkey wrench n chiave f inglese a rullino

monkfish /'mʌŋkfɪʃ/ n bottatrice f

mono /'mɒnəʊ/ n mono m

monochrome /'mɒnəkrəʊm/ adj monocromatico; Cinema, TV in bianco e nero

monocle /'mɒnəkl/ n monocolo m

monogamous /mə'nɒgəməs/ adj monogamo

monogamy /mə'nɒgəmɪ/ n monogamia f

monogram /'mɒnəgræm/ n monogramma m

monograph /'mɒnəgrɑːf/ n monografia f

monolith /'mɒnəlɪθ/ n monolito m

monologue /'mɒnəlɒg/ n monologo m

monomania /mɒnə'meɪnɪə/ n monomania f

monoplane /'mɒnəpleɪn/ n monoplano m

monopolize /mə'nɒpəlaɪz/ vt monopolizzare

monopoly /mə'nɒpəlɪ/ n monopolio m

monoski /'mɒnəʊski:/ ①n monoscì m inv ②vi praticare il monoscì

monosodium glutamate /mɒnəsəʊdɪəm'gluːtəmeɪt/ n glutammato m di sodio

monosyllabic /mɒnəsɪ'læbɪk/ adj monosillabico

monosyllable /'mɒnəsɪləbl/ n monosillabo m

monotone /'mɒnətəʊn/ n speak in a ~ parlare con tono monotono

monotonous /mə'nɒtənəs/ adj monotono

monotonously /mə'nɒtənəslɪ/ adv in modo monotono

monotony /mə'nɒtənɪ/ n monotonia f

monsoon /mɒn'suːn/ n monsone m

monster /'mɒnstə(r)/ n mostro m

monstrosity /mɒn'strɒsətɪ/ n mostruosità f

monstrous /'mɒnstrəs/ adj mostruoso

montage /mɒn'tɑːʒ/ n montaggio m

Mont Blanc /mɒn'blã/ n Monte m Bianco

Montenegro /mɒntɪ'niːgrəʊ/ n Montenegro m

month /mʌnθ/ n mese m

monthly /'mʌnθlɪ/ ①adj mensile ②adv mensilmente ③n (periodical) mensile m

monument /'mɒnjʊmənt/ n monumento m

monumental /mɒnjʊ'mentl/ adj fig monumentale

monumentally /mɒnjʊ'mentəlɪ/ adv ⟨boring, ignorant⟩ enormemente

moo /mu:/ ①n muggito m ②vi (pt/pp **mooed**) muggire

mooch /mu:tʃ/ vi ~ about fam gironzolare; ~ about the house gironzolare per casa

mood /mu:d/ n umore m; **be in a good/ bad** ~ essere di buon/cattivo umore; **be in the** ~ **for** essere in vena di

moody /'mu:dɪ/ adj (-ier, -iest) (variable) lunatico; (bad-tempered) di malumore

moon /mu:n/ n luna f; **over the** ~ fam al settimo cielo
■ **moon about, moon around** vi (fam: wander aimlessly) gironzolare
■ **moon over** vt fam sospirare d'amore per ⟨somebody⟩

moonbeam n raggio m di luna

moon buggy n veicolo m lunare

moonlight ①n chiaro m di luna ②vi fam lavorare in nero

moonlighting n fam lavoro m nero

moonlit adj illuminato dalla luna

moonshine n (nonsense) fantasie fpl; (Am: liquor) liquore m di contrabbando

moor¹ /mʊə(r)/ n brughiera f

moor² vt Naut ormeggiare

moorhen /ˈmʊəhen/ n gallinella f d'acqua

mooring /ˈmʊərɪŋ/ n (place) ormeggio m; ∼s pl (chains) ormeggi mpl

Moorish /ˈmʊərɪʃ/ adj moresco

moorland /ˈmʊələnd/ n brughiera f

moose /muːs/ n (pl **moose**) alce m

moot /muːt/ adj it's a ∼ **point** è un punto controverso

mop /mɒp/ **1** n mocio® m inv; ∼ **of hair** zazzera f
2 vt (pt/pp **mopped**) lavare con il mocio®
■ **mop up** vt (dry) asciugare con il mocio®; (clean) pulire con il mocio®

mope /məʊp/ vi essere depresso
■ **mope about**, **mope around** vi trascinarsi

moped /ˈməʊped/ n ciclomotore m

moral /ˈmɒrəl/ **1** adj morale
2 n morale f

morale /məˈrɑːl/ n morale m; **be a** ∼ **booster** tirare su di morale

moral fibre n forza f morale

moralistic /mɒrəˈlɪstɪk/ adj moralistico

morality /məˈrælətɪ/ n moralità f

moralize /ˈmɒrəlaɪz/ vi moraleggiare

morally /ˈmɒrəlɪ/ adv moralmente

morals /ˈmɒrəlz/ npl moralità f

moratorium /mɒrəˈtɔːrɪəm/ n moratoria f

morbid /ˈmɔːbɪd/ adj morboso

more /mɔː(r)/ **1** adj più; **a few** ∼ **books** un po' più di libri; **some** ∼ **tea?** ancora un po' di tè?; **there's no** ∼ **bread** non c'è più pane; **there are no** ∼ **apples** non ci sono più mele; **one** ∼ **word and...** ancora una parola e...
2 pron di più; **would you like some** ∼? ne vuoi ancora?; **no** ∼, **thank you** non ne voglio più, grazie
3 adv più; ∼ **interesting** più interessante; ∼ **(and** ∼**) quickly** (sempre) più veloce; ∼ **than** più di; **I don't love him any** ∼ non lo amo più; **once** ∼ ancora una volta; ∼ **or less** più o meno; **the** ∼ **I see him, the** ∼ **I like him** più lo vedo, più mi piace

moreish /ˈmɔːrɪʃ/ adj fam **be** ∼ tirare per la gola

moreover /mɔːrˈəʊvə(r)/ adv inoltre

morgue /mɔːg/ n obitorio m

MORI /ˈmɔːrɪ/ n abbr (**Market Opinion Research Institute**) istituto m di sondaggio e ricerche di mercato

moribund /ˈmɒrɪbʌnd/ adj moribondo

morning /ˈmɔːnɪŋ/ n mattino m, mattina f; **spend the** ∼ **doing something** passare la mattinata facendo qualcosa; **in the** ∼ del mattino; (tomorrow) domani mattina

morning-after pill n pillola f del giorno dopo

morning coffee n caffè m inv del mattino

morning dress n tight m inv

morning sickness n nausea f mattutina

Moroccan /məˈrɒk(ə)n/ adj & n marocchino, -a mf

Morocco /məˈrɒkəʊ/ n Marocco m

morocco leather n marocchino m

moron /ˈmɔːrɒn/ n fam deficiente mf

morose /məˈrəʊs/ adj scontroso

morosely /məˈrəʊslɪ/ adv in modo scontroso

morphine /ˈmɔːfiːn/ n morfina f

morris dance /ˈmɒrɪs/ n danza f tradizionale inglese

Morse /mɔːs/ n ∼ **[code]** [codice m] Morse m

morsel /ˈmɔːsl/ n (food) boccone m

mortal /ˈmɔːtl/ adj & n mortale mf

mortal combat n duello m mortale

mortality /mɔːˈtælətɪ/ n mortalità f

mortally /ˈmɔːtəlɪ/ adv ‹wounded, offended› a morte; ‹afraid› da morire

mortar /ˈmɔːtə(r)/ n mortaio m

mortgage /ˈmɔːgɪdʒ/ **1** n mutuo m; (money raised on collateral of property) ipoteca f
2 vt ipotecare

mortgage rate n tasso m d'interesse sui mutui

mortgage relief n sgravio m fiscale sul mutuo

mortgage repayment n rata f del mutuo

mortician /mɔːˈtɪʃn/ n Am impresario, -a mf di pompe funebri

mortification /mɔːtɪfɪˈkeɪʃn/ n (of the flesh, embarrassment) mortificazione f

mortify /ˈmɔːtɪfaɪ/ vt (pt/pp **-ied**) mortificare

mortuary /ˈmɔːtjʊərɪ/ n camera f mortuaria

mosaic /məʊˈzeɪɪk/ n mosaico m

Moscow /ˈmɒskəʊ/ n Mosca f

Moselle /məʊˈzel/ n (wine) vino m della Mosella

Moses /ˈməʊzɪz/ n Mosè

Moslem /ˈmʊzlɪm/ adj & n musulmano, -a mf

mosque /mɒsk/ n moschea f

mosquito /mɒsˈkiːtəʊ/ n (pl **-es**) zanzara f

mosquito bite n puntura m di zanzara

mosquito net n zanzariera f

mosquito repellent n antizanzare m inv

moss /mɒs/ n muschio m

mossy /ˈmɒsɪ/ adj muschioso

most /məʊst/ ① *adj* (majority) la maggior parte di; **for the ~ part** per lo più ② *adv* più, maggiormente; (very) estremamente, molto; **the ~ interesting day** la giornata più interessante; **a ~ interesting day** una giornata estremamente interessante; **the ~ beautiful woman in the world** la donna più bella del mondo; **~ unlikely** veramente improbabile ③ *pron* **~ of them** la maggior parte di loro; **at [the] ~** al massimo; **make the ~ of** sfruttare al massimo; **~ of the time** la maggior parte del tempo

mostly /'məʊs(t)lɪ/ *adv* per lo più

MOT *n* Br revisione *f* obbligatoria di autoveicoli

motel /məʊ'tel/ *n* motel *m inv*

moth /mɒθ/ *n* falena *f*; [clothes-] **~** tarma *f*

mothball /'mɒθbɔːl/ *n* pallina *f* di naftalina

moth-eaten /-iːtən/ *adj* tarmato

mother /'mʌðə(r)/ ① *n* madre *f* ② *vt* fare da madre a

motherboard /'mʌðəbɔːd/ *n* scheda *f* madre

motherhood /'mʌðəhʊd/ *n* maternità *f*

Mothering Sunday /mʌðərɪŋ'sʌndeɪ/ *n* la festa della mamma

mother-in-law *n* (pl **mothers-in-law**) suocera *f*

motherland /'mʌðəlænd/ *n* patria *f*

motherless /'mʌðəlɪs/ *adj* orfano, -a *mf* di madre

motherly /'mʌðəlɪ/ *adj* materno

mother-of-pearl *n* madreperla *f*

mother's boy *n* mammone *m*

Mother's Day *n* la festa della mamma

mother's help *n* Br aiuto *m* domestico

mother-to-be *n* futura mamma *f*

mother tongue *n* madrelingua *f*

mothproof /'mɒθpruːf/ *adj* antitarmico

motif /məʊ'tiːf/ *n* motivo *m*

motion /'məʊʃn/ ① *n* moto *m*; (proposal) mozione *f*; (gesture) gesto *m* ② *vt/i* **~ [to] somebody to come in** fare segno a qualcuno di entrare

motionless /'məʊʃ(ə)nlɪs/ *adj* immobile

motionlessly /'məʊʃənlɪslɪ/ *adv* senza alcun movimento

motion picture ① *n* film *m inv* [per il cinema] ② *attrib* ⟨industry⟩ cinematografico

motivate /'məʊtɪveɪt/ *vt* motivare

motivated /'məʊtɪveɪtɪd/ *adj* ⟨person, student⟩ motivato; **politically/racially ~** ⟨act⟩ a sfondo politico/razziale

motivation /məʊtɪ'veɪʃn/ *n* motivazione *f*

motive /'məʊtɪv/ *n* motivo *m*

motley /'mɒtlɪ/ *adj* disparato

motor /'məʊtə(r)/ ① *n* motore *m*; (car) macchina *f* ② *adj* a motore; Anat motore ③ *vi* andare in macchina

Motorail /'məʊtəreɪl/ *n* treno *m* per trasporto auto

motorbike /'məʊtəbaɪk/ *n* fam moto *f inv*

motor boat *n* motoscafo *m*

motorcade /'məʊtəkeɪd/ *n* Am corteo *m* di auto

motor car *n* automobile *f*

motorcycle *n* motocicletta *f*

motorcycle escort *n* scorta *f* di motociclette

motorcycle messenger *n* corriere *m* in moto

motorcyclist *n* motociclista *mf*

motorhome *n* camper *m inv*; (towed) roulotte *f inv*

motoring /'məʊtərɪŋ/ *n* automobilismo *m*

motorist /'məʊtərɪst/ *n* automobilista *mf*

motor launch *n* motolancia *f*

motor mechanic *n* meccanico *m*

motormouth *n* fam chiacchierone, -a *mf*

motor oil *n* olio *m* lubrificante

motor racing *n* corse *fpl* automobilistiche

motor scooter *n* motorino *m*

motor vehicle *n* autoveicolo *m*

motorway *n* autostrada *f*

mottled /'mɒtld/ *adj* chiazzato

motto /'mɒtəʊ/ *n* (pl **-es**) motto *m*

mould[1] /'məʊld/ *n* (fungus) muffa *f*

mould[2] ① *n* stampo *m* ② *vt* foggiare; fig formare

moulder /'məʊldə(r)/ *vi* ⟨corpse, refuse⟩ andare in decomposizione

moulding /'məʊldɪŋ/ *n* Archit cornice *f*

mouldy /'məʊldɪ/ *adj* ammuffito; (fam: worthless) ridicolo

moult /məʊlt/ *vi* ⟨bird⟩ fare la muta; ⟨animal⟩ perdere il pelo

mound /maʊnd/ *n* mucchio *m*; (hill) collinetta *f*

mount /maʊnt/ ① *n* (horse) cavalcatura *f*; (of jewel, photo, picture) montatura *f* ② *vt* montare a ⟨horse⟩; salire su ⟨bicycle⟩; incastonare ⟨jewel⟩; incorniciare ⟨photo, picture⟩ ③ *vi* aumentare ■ **mount up** *vi* aumentare

mountain /'maʊntɪn/ *n* montagna *f*; **make a ~ out of a molehill** fare di una mosca un elefante

mountain bike *n* mountain bike *f inv*

mountain climbing *n* alpinismo *m*

mountaineer /maʊntɪ'nɪə(r)/ n
alpinista mf

mountaineering /maʊntɪ'nɪərɪŋ/ n
alpinismo m

mountainous /'maʊntɪnəs/ adj
montagnoso

mountain range n catena f montuosa

mountain top n cima f di montagna

mounted police /maʊntɪdpə'liːs/ n
polizia f a cavallo

mourn /mɔːn/ **1** vt lamentare
2 vi ~ for piangere la morte di

mourner /'mɔːnə(r)/ n persona f che
participa a un funerale

mournful /'mɔːnfʊl/ adj triste

mournfully /'mɔːnfʊlɪ/ adv tristemente

mourning /'mɔːnɪŋ/ n in ~ in lutto

mouse /maʊs/ n (pl **mice**) topo m;
Comput mouse m inv

mousehole n tana f di topi/di un topo

mouse mat n Comput tappetino m

mousetrap n trappola f [per topi]

mousse /muːs/ n Culin mousse f inv

moustache /mə'stɑːʃ/ n baffi mpl

mousy /'maʊsɪ/ adj ⟨colour⟩ grigio topo

mouth[1] /maʊð/ vt ~ **something** dire
qualcosa silenziosamente muovendo
solamente le labbra

mouth[2] /maʊθ/ n bocca f; (of river) foce f

mouthful /'maʊθfʊl/ n boccone m

mouth organ n armonica f [a bocca]

mouthpiece n imboccatura f; (fig:
person) portavoce m inv

mouth-to-mouth resuscitation n
respirazione f bocca a bocca

mouthwash n colluttorio m

mouthwatering /-wɔːtərɪŋ/ adj che fa
venire l'acquolina in bocca

movable /'muːvəbl/ adj movibile

move /muːv/ **1** n mossa f; (moving house)
trasloco m; **on the** ~ in movimento; **get a**
~ **on** fam darsi una mossa
2 vt muovere; (emotionally) commuovere;
spostare ⟨car, furniture⟩; (transfer)
trasferire; (propose) proporre; ~ **house**
traslocare
3 vi muoversi; (move house) traslocare;
don't ~! non muoverti!
■ **move about**, **move around** vi (in
house) muoversi; (in country) spostarsi
■ **move along** **1** vi andare avanti
2 vt muovere in avanti
■ **move away** **1** vi allontanarsi; (move
house) trasferirsi
2 vt allontanare
■ **move forward** vi avanzare vt spostare
avanti
■ **move in** vi (to a house) trasferirsi
■ **move off** vi ⟨vehicle⟩ muoversi
■ **move on** **1** vi (move to another place)
muoversi

2 vt ⟨police⟩ far circolare
■ **move on to** vt passare a ⟨new topic,
next question⟩
■ **move out** vi (of house) andare via
■ **move over** **1** vi spostarsi
2 vt spostare
■ **move up** vi muoversi; (advance, increase)
avanzare

movement /'muːvmənt/ n movimento
m; (of clock) meccanismo m

movie /'muːvɪ/ n film m inv; **go to the** ~s
andare al cinema

movie camera n cinepresa f

movie director n regista mf
cinematografico, -a

movie-goer n persona f che va al
cinema

movie star n stella f del cinema, star f
inv del cinema

movie theater n Am cinema m

moving /'muːvɪŋ/ adj mobile; (touching)
commovente

mow /məʊ/ vt (pt **mowed**, pp **mown** or
mowed) tagliare ⟨lawn⟩
■ **mow down** vt (destroy) sterminare

mower /'məʊə(r)/ n tosaerba m inv

Mozambique /məʊzæm'biːk/ n
Mozambico m

MP abbr (**Member of Parliament**)
deputato, -a mf

MP3 player n lettore m di MP3

mpg abbr (**miles per gallon**) miglia al
gallone

mph abbr (**miles per hour**) miglia
all'ora

MPV n abbr (**multi-purpose vehicle**)
MPV m

Mr /'mɪstə(r)/ n (pl **Messrs**) Signor m

Mrs /'mɪsɪz/ n Signora f

Ms /mɪz/ n Signora f (modo m formale di
rivolgersi ad una donna quando non si
vuole indicarla come sposata o nubile)

MS n abbr (**multiple sclerosis**) sclerosi
f a placche or multipla; abbr
(**manuscript**) ms; Am abbr **Mississippi**

MSc n abbr (**Master of Science**)
(diploma) laurea f in discipline scientifiche;
(person) laureato, -a mf in discipline
scientifiche

MST abbr Am (**Mountain Standard
Time**) tempo f medio della zona delle
Montagne Rocciose

Mt. abbr (**mount**) (in place names) M.

much /mʌtʃ/ adj, adv & pron molto; ~
as per quanto; **I love you just as** ~ **as
before/him** ti amo quanto prima/lui; **as** ~
as £5 million ben cinque milioni di
sterline; **as** ~ **as that** così tanto; **very** ~
tantissimo, moltissimo; ~ **the same** quasi
uguale

muck /mʌk/ *n* (dirt) sporcizia *f*; (farming) letame *m*; (fam: filth) porcheria *f*
■ **muck about** *vi* fam perder tempo; ∼ **about with** trafficare con
■ **muck in** *vi* fam dare una mano
■ **muck up** *vt* fam rovinare; (make dirty) sporcare

muckraking /'mʌkreɪkɪŋ/ *n* scandalismo *m*

mucky /'mʌkɪ/ *adj* (**-ier, -iest**) sudicio

mucus /'mju:kəs/ *n* muco *m*

mud /mʌd/ *n* fango *m*

muddle /'mʌdl/ **[1]** *n* disordine *m*; (mix-up) confusione *f*
[2] *vt* ∼ [**up**] confondere ⟨dates⟩
■ **muddle through** *vi* farcela alla bell'e meglio

muddle-headed /-'hedɪd/ *adj* ⟨plan⟩ confuso; ⟨person⟩ confusionario

muddy /'mʌdɪ/ *adj* (**-ier, -iest**) ⟨path⟩ fangoso; ⟨shoes⟩ infangato

mudflat *n* distesa *f* di fango

mudguard *n* parafango *m*

mud hut *n* capanna *f* di fango

mudpack *n* (for beauty treatment) maschera *f* di fango

mud pie *n* formina *f* di fango

mudslide *n* colata *f* di fango

mud-slinging /-slɪŋɪŋ/ *n* diffamazione *f*

muesli /'mju:zlɪ/ *n* muesli *m inv*

muffle /'mʌfl/ *vt* smorzare ⟨sound⟩
■ **muffle up** *vi* (for warmth) imbacuccarsi

muffler /'mʌflə(r)/ *n* sciarpa *f*; Am Auto marmitta *f*

mug[1] /mʌg/ *n* tazza *f*; (for beer) boccale *m*; (fam: face) muso *m*; (fam: simpleton) pollo *m*

mug[2] *vt* (pt/pp **mugged**) aggredire e derubare
■ **mug up** *vt* (fam: learn) imparare alla bell'e meglio

mugger /'mʌgə(r)/ *n* assalitore, -trice *mf*

mugging /'mʌgɪŋ/ *n* aggressione *f* per furto

muggy /'mʌgɪ/ *adj* (**-ier, -iest**) afoso

Muhammad /mə'hæmɪd/ *n* Maometto *m*

mulatto /mju:'lætəʊ/ *adj & n* Am mulatto, -a *mf*

mulberry /'mʌlb(ə)rɪ/ *n* Am (fruit) mora *f* di gelso; (tree) gelso *m*

mule[1] /mju:l/ *n* mulo *m*

mule[2] *n* (slipper) ciabatta *f*

mulish /'mju:lɪʃ/ *adj* testardo

mull /mʌl/ *vt* ∼ **over** rimuginare su

mulled /mʌld/ *adj* ∼ **wine** vin brûlé *m inv*

multi+ /'mʌltɪ/ *pref* multi+

multi-access *n* Comput accesso *m* multiplo

multichannel /mʌltɪ'tʃænəl/ *adj* ⟨television⟩ con molti canali

multicoloured /'mʌltɪkʌləd/ *adj* variopinto

multicultural /mʌltɪ'kʌltʃərəl/ *adj* multiculturale

multidisciplinary /mʌltɪdɪsɪ'plɪnərɪ/ *adj* Sch, Univ pluridisciplinare

multi-ethnic *adj* multietnico

multifaceted /mʌltɪ'fæsɪtɪd/ *adj* ⟨gemstone⟩ sfaccettato; ⟨career⟩ variegato; ⟨personality⟩ sfaccettato

multifunction /mʌltɪ'fʌŋkʃn/ *adj* multifunzionale

multigym /'mʌltɪdʒɪm/ *n* attrezzo *m* multiuso

multilateral /mʌltɪ'læt(ə)rəl/ *adj* Pol multilaterale

multilevel /'mʌltɪlevəl/ *adj* ⟨parking, access⟩ a più piani; ⟨analysis⟩ a più livelli

multilingual /mʌltɪ'lɪŋgwəl/ *adj* multilingue *inv*

multimedia /mʌltɪ'mi:dɪə/ **[1]** *n* multimedia *mpl*
[2] *adj* multimediale

multinational /mʌltɪ'næʃnəl/ **[1]** *adj* multinazionale
[2] *n* multinazionale *f*

multipack *n* confezione *f* multipla

multi-party /'mʌltɪpɑːtɪ/ *adj* ⟨government, system⟩ pluripartitico

multiplayer *adj* Comput ⟨game⟩ in multiplayer

multiple /'mʌltɪpl/ *adj & n* multiplo *m*

multiple choice *adj* scelta *f* multipla

multiple choice question *n* Sch test *m inv* a scelta multipla

multiple ownership *n* comproprietà *f*

multiple pileup *n* tamponamento *m* a catena

multiple sclerosis *n* sclerosi *f* a placche *or* multipla

multiple store *n* Br negozio *m* appartenente a una catena

multiplex /'mʌltɪpleks/ **[1]** *n* Teleph multiplex *m inv*; Cinema cinema *m inv* multisale
[2] *adj* Teleph in multiplex

multiplication /mʌltɪplɪ'keɪʃn/ *n* moltiplicazione *f*

multiply /'mʌltɪplaɪ/ **[1]** *vt* (pt/pp **-ied**) moltiplicare (**by** per)
[2] *vi* moltiplicarsi

multi-purpose *adj* ⟨tool, gadget⟩ multiuso *inv*; ⟨organization⟩ con più scopi

multi-purpose vehicle *n* monovolume *f*

multi-racial *adj* multirazziale

multi-storey *adj* ∼ **car park** parcheggio *m* a più piani

multitask *vi* ⟨person⟩ eseguire varie mansioni; ⟨computer⟩ eseguire il multitasking

multi-track *adj* ⟨*sound system*⟩ a più piste

multitude /'mʌltɪtjuːd/ *n* moltitudine *f*; **hide a ~ of sins** ⟨*rug etc*⟩ nascondere un sacco di magagne

multi-user *adj* ⟨*system, installation*⟩ multiutente

mum[1] /mʌm/ *adj* **keep ~** fam non aprire bocca

mum[2] *n* fam mamma *f*

mumble /'mʌmbl/ *vt/i* borbottare

mumbo-jumbo /mʌmbəʊ'dʒʌmbəʊ/ *n* (fam: speech, writing) paroloni *mpl*

mummy[1] /'mʌmɪ/ *n* fam mamma *f*

mummy[2] *n* Archaeol mummia *f*

mummy's boy *n* Br pej mammone *m*

mumps /mʌmps/ *n* orecchioni *mpl*

munch /mʌntʃ/ *vt/i* sgranocchiare

mundane /mʌn'deɪn/ *adj* (everyday) banale

municipal /mjʊ'nɪsɪpl/ *adj* municipale

munitions /mjʊ'nɪʃnz/ *npl* munizioni *fpl*

mural /'mjʊərəl/ *n* dipinto *m* murale

murder /'mɜːdə(r)/ ① *n* assassinio *m* ② *vt* assassinare; (fam: ruin) massacrare

murder case *n* caso *m* di omicidio

murder charge *n* imputazione *f* di omicidio

murderer /'mɜːdərə(r)/ *n* assassino, -a *mf*

murderess /'mɜːdəres/ *n* assassina *f*

murderous /'mɜːdərəs/ *adj* omicida

murky /'mɜːkɪ/ *adj* (**-ier, -iest**) oscuro

murmur /'mɜːmə(r)/ ① *n* mormorio *m* ② *vt/i* mormorare

murmuring /'mɜːmərɪŋ/ *n* mormorio *m*; **~s** *pl* (of discontent) segnali *mpl* di malcontento

muscle /'mʌsl/ *n* muscolo *m*
■ **muscle in** *vi* sl intromettersi (**to** in)

muscle strain *n* strappo *m* muscolare

muscular /'mʌskjʊlə(r)/ *adj* muscolare; (strong) muscoloso

muscular dystrophy /'dɪstrəfɪ/ *n* distrofia *f* muscolare

muse /mjuːz/ *vi* meditare (**on** su)

museum /mjuː'zɪəm/ *n* museo *m*

mushroom /'mʌʃrʊm/ ① *n* fungo *m* ② *vi* fig spuntare come funghi

mushroom cloud *n* fungo *m* atomico

mushy /'mʌʃɪ/ *adj* fig sdolcinato

music /'mjuːzɪk/ *n* musica *f*; (written) spartito *m*; **set to ~** musicare

musical /'mjuːzɪkl/ ① *adj* musicale; ⟨*person*⟩ dotato di senso musicale ② *n* commedia *f* musicale

musical box *n* carillon *m inv*

musical instrument *n* strumento *m* musicale

music box *n* carillon *m inv*

music centre *n* impianto *m* stereo

music hall *n* teatro *m* di varietà

musician /mjuː'zɪʃn/ *n* musicista *mf*

music lover *n* amante *mf* della musica

musicology /mjuːzɪ'kɒlədʒɪ/ *n* musicologia *f*

music stand *n* leggio *m*

music stool *n* sgabello *m* per pianoforte

music video *n* video clip *m inv*

musings /'mjuːzɪŋz/ *npl* riflessioni *fpl*

musk /mʌsk/ *n* muschio *m*

musket /'mʌskɪt/ *n* moschetto *m*

musketeer /mʌskə'tɪə(r)/ *n* moschettiere *m*

musky /'mʌskɪ/ *adj* muschiato

Muslim /'mʌzlɪm/ *adj & n* musulmano, -a *mf*

mussel /'mʌsl/ *n* cozza *f*

must /mʌst/ ① *v aux* (only in present) dovere; **you ~ not be late** non devi essere in ritardo; **she ~ have finished by now** (probability) deve aver finito ormai ② *n* **a ~** fam una cosa da non perdere

mustache /mə'stɑːʃ/ *n* Am = MOUSTACHE

mustard /'mʌstəd/ *n* senape *f*

muster /'mʌstə(r)/ *vt* radunare ⟨*troops*⟩; fare appello a ⟨*strength*⟩

musty /'mʌstɪ/ *adj* (**-ier, -iest**) stantio

mutant /'mjuːtənt/ *n & adj* mutante *mf*

mutate /mjuː'teɪt/ ① *vi* ⟨*cell, organism*⟩ subire una mutazione; **~ into** ⟨*alien, monster*⟩ trasformarsi in ② *vt* far subire una mutazione

mutation /mjuː'teɪʃn/ *n* Biol mutazione *f*

mute /mjuːt/ *adj* muto

muted /'mjuːtɪd/ *adj* smorzato

mutilate /'mjuːtɪleɪt/ *vt* mutilare

mutilation /mjuːtɪ'leɪʃn/ *n* mutilazione *f*

mutinous /'mjuːtɪnəs/ *adj* ammutinato

mutiny /'mjuːtɪnɪ/ ① *n* ammutinamento *m* ② *vi* (pt/pp **-ied**) ammutinarsi

mutter /'mʌtə(r)/ ① *n* borbottio *m* ② *vt/i* borbottare

mutton /'mʌtn/ *n* carne *f* di montone

mutual /'mjuːtjʊəl/ *adj* reciproco; (fam: common) comune

mutually /'mjuːtjʊəlɪ/ *adv* reciprocamente

Muzak® /'mjuːzæk/ *n* musica *f* di sottofondo

muzzle /'mʌzl/ ① *n* (of animal) muso *m*; (of firearm) bocca *f*; (for dog) museruola *f* ② *vt* fig mettere il bavaglio a

MW *abbr* (**medium wave**) OM

my /maɪ/ *poss adj* mio *m*, mia *f*, miei *mpl*, mie *fpl*; **my job/house** il mio lavoro/la mia casa; **my mother/father** mia madre/ mio padre

myalgic encephalomyelitis /maɪæ̃ldʒɪkensefələumaɪ'laɪtɪs/ n encefalomielite f mialgica

Myanmar /maɪæn'mɑ:(r)/ n Myanmar f

myopic /maɪ'ɒpɪk/ adj miope

myself /maɪ'self/ pers pron (reflexive) mi; (emphatic) me stesso; (after prep) me; **I've seen it ~** l'ho visto io stesso; **by ~** da solo; **I thought to ~** ho pensato tra me e me; **I'm proud of ~** sono fiero di me

mysterious /mɪ'stɪərɪəs/ adj misterioso

mysteriously /mɪ'stɪərɪəslɪ/ adv misteriosamente

mystery /'mɪstərɪ/ n mistero m; **~ [story]** racconto m del mistero

mystery play n mistero m (teatrale)

mystery tour n viaggio m con destinazione a sorpresa

mystic[al] /'mɪstɪk[l]/ adj mistico

mysticism /'mɪstɪsɪzm/ n misticismo m

mystification /mɪstɪfɪ'keɪʃn/ n disorientamento m

mystified /'mɪstɪfaɪd/ adj disorientato

mystify /'mɪstɪfaɪ/ vt disorientare

mystique /mɪ'sti:k/ n mistica f

myth /mɪθ/ n mito m

mythical /'mɪθɪkl/ adj mitico

mythological /mɪθə'lɒdʒɪkl/ adj mitologico

mythology /mɪ'θɒlədʒɪ/ n mitologia f

Nn

n¹, **N** /en/ n (letter) n, N f inv

N² abbr (**north**) N

n/a, **N/A** abbr (**not applicable**) non pertinente

nab /næb/ vt (pt/pp **nabbed**) fam beccare

nadir /'neɪdə(r)/ n nadir m; fig punto m più basso, fondo m

naff /næf/ adj Br fam banale

nag¹ /næg/ n (horse) ronzino m

nag² ① vt (pt/pp **nagged**) assillare ② vi essere insistente ③ n (person) brontolone, -a mf

nagging /'nægɪŋ/ adj ⟨pain⟩ persistente

nail /neɪl/ n chiodo m; (of finger, toe) unghia f; **on the ~** fam sull'unghia
■ **nail down** vt inchiodare; **~ somebody down to a time/price** far fissare a qualcuno un'ora/un prezzo

nail-biting /-baɪtɪŋ/ ① n abitudine f di mangiarsi le unghie ② adj ⟨match, finish⟩ mozzafiato inv; ⟨wait⟩ esasperante

nail brush n spazzolino m da unghie

nail clippers npl tronchesina m

nail file n limetta f da unghie

nail polish n smalto m [per unghie]

nail polish remover n acetone m, solvente m per unghie

nail scissors npl forbicine fpl da unghie

nail varnish n smalto m [per unghie]

nail varnish remover n solvente m per smalto

naïve /naɪ'i:v/ adj ingenuo

naïvely /naɪ'i:vlɪ/ adv ingenuamente

naïvety /naɪ'i:vtɪ/ n ingenuità f

naked /'neɪkɪd/ adj nudo; **with the ~ eye** a occhio nudo

nakedness /'neɪkɪdnɪs/ n nudità f

name /neɪm/ ① n nome m; **what's your ~?** come ti chiami?; **my ~ is Matthew** mi chiamo Matthew; **I know her by ~** la conosco di nome; **by the ~ of Bates** di nome Bates; **make a ~ for oneself** farsi un nome; **call somebody ~s** fam insultare qualcuno ② vt (to position) nominare; chiamare ⟨baby⟩; (identify) citare; **be ~d after** essere chiamato col nome di

name day n Relig onomastico m

name-drop vi he's always **~ping** si vanta sempre di conoscere persone famose

nameless /'neɪmlɪs/ adj senza nome

namely /'neɪmlɪ/ adv cioè

nameplate n targhetta f

namesake n omonimo, -a mf

name tag n targhetta f attaccata ad un oggetto con il nome del proprietario

name tape n fettuccia f attaccata ad un oggetto con il nome del proprietario

Namibia /nə'mɪbɪə/ n Namibia f

nanny /'nænɪ/ n bambinaia f

nanny goat n capra f

nanosecond /'nænəusekənd/ n fam nanosecondo m

nap /næp/ ① n pisolino m; **have a ~** fare un pisolino

2 *vi* **catch somebody** ~**ping** cogliere qualcuno alla sprovvista

napalm /'neɪpɑ:m/ *n* napalm *m*

nape /neɪp/ *n* ~ **[of the neck]** nuca *f*

napkin /'næpkɪn/ *n* tovagliolo *m*

Naples /'neɪp(ə)lz/ *n* Napoli *f*

nappy /'næpɪ/ *n* pannolino *m*

nappy liner *n* filtrante *m*

nappy rash *n* Br eritema *m* da pannolini

narcotic /nɑ:'kɒtɪk/ *adj & n* narcotico *m*

narcotics agent *n* Am agente *m* della squadra antidroga

narked /nɑ:kt/ *adj* fam scocciato

narrate /nə'reɪt/ *vt* narrare

narration /nə'reɪʃn/ *n* narrazione *f*

narrative /'nærətɪv/ **1** *adj* narrativo **2** *n* narrazione *f*

narrator /nə'reɪtə(r)/ *n* narratore, -trice *mf*

narrow /'nærəʊ/ **1** *adj* stretto; fig ⟨views⟩ ristretto; ⟨margin, majority⟩ scarso; **have a** ~ **escape** scamparla per un pelo **2** *vi* restringersi
■ **narrow down** *vt* (reduce) restringere

narrowly /'nærəʊlɪ/ *adv* ~ **escape death** evitare la morte per un pelo

narrow-minded /-'maɪndɪd/ *adj* di idee ristrette

nasal /'neɪzl/ *adj* nasale

nasal spray *n* spray *m inv* nasale

nastily /'nɑ:stɪlɪ/ *adv* (spitefully) con cattiveria

nasty /'nɑ:stɪ/ *adj* (**-ier, -iest**) ⟨smell, person, remark⟩ cattivo; ⟨injury, situation, weather⟩ brutto; **turn** ~ ⟨person⟩ diventare cattivo; ⟨situation⟩ mettersi male; ⟨weather⟩ volgere al brutto

nation /'neɪʃn/ *n* nazione *f*

national /'næʃən(ə)l/ **1** *adj* nazionale **2** *n* cittadino, -a *mf*

national anthem *n* inno *m* nazionale

National Curriculum *n* Br programma *m* scolastico ministeriale per il Galles e l'Inghilterra

national debt *n* debito *m* pubblico

National Front *n* Br partito *m* britannico di estrema destra

national grid *n* Electr rete *f* elettrica nazionale

National Health *n* Br servizio *m* nazionale di assistenza sanitaria

National Health Service *n* servizio *m* sanitario britannico

National Insurance *n* ≈ Previdenza *f* sociale

National Insurance number *n* numero *m* di Previdenza sociale

Nationalism /'næʃənəlɪzm/ *n* nazionalismo *m*

nationality /næʃə'nælɪtɪ/ *n* nazionalità *f inv*

nationalization /næʃənəlaɪ'zeɪʃn/ *n* nazionalizzazione

nationalize /'næʃənəlaɪz/ *vt* nazionalizzare

National Lottery *n* Lotteria *f* di Stato

nationally /'næʃənəlɪ/ *adv* a livello nazionale

national monument *n* monumento *m* nazionale

National Savings Bank *n* Br Cassa *f* di risparmio

national service *n* Br servizio *m* militare

National Trust *n* Br associazione *f* per la tutela del patrimonio culturale e ambientale in Gran Bretagna

nation state *n* stato-nazione *m*

nationwide /'neɪʃnwaɪd/ *adj* su scala nazionale

native /'neɪtɪv/ **1** *adj* nativo; (innate) innato **2** *n* nativo, -a *mf*; (local inhabitant) abitante *mf* del posto; (outside Europe) indigeno, -a *mf* **she's a** ~ **of Venice** è originaria di Venezia

Native American *adj & n* amerindio, -a *mf*

native land *n* paese *m* nativo

native language *n* lingua *f* madre

native speaker *n* persona *f* di madrelingua; **Italian** ~ ~**s** italiani madrelingua

Nativity /nə'tɪvətɪ/ *n* **the** ~ la Natività

Nativity play *n* rappresentazione sulla nascita di Gesù

Nato, NATO /'neɪtəʊ/ *n abbr* (**North Atlantic Treaty Organization**) NATO *f*

natter /'nætə(r)/ **1** *n* **have a** ~ fam fare quattro chiacchiere **2** *vi* fam chiacchierare

natty /'nætɪ/ *adj* fam (smart) chic *inv*; (clever) geniale

natural /'nætʃ(ə)rəl/ *adj* naturale

natural childbirth *n* parto *m* indolore

natural gas *n* metano *m*

natural history *n* storia *f* naturale

naturalist /'nætʃ(ə)rəlɪst/ *n* naturalista *mf*

naturalization /nætʃ(ə)rəlaɪ'zeɪʃn/ *n* naturalizzazione *f*

naturalize /'nætʃ(ə)rəlaɪz/ *vt* naturalizzare

naturally /'nætʃ(ə)rəlɪ/ *adv* (of course) naturalmente; (by nature) per natura

nature /'neɪtʃə(r)/ *n* natura *f*; **by** ~ per natura

nature conservancy *n* protezione *f* della natura

nature reserve *n* riserva *f* naturale

nature trail *n* percorso *m* ecologico

naturism /'neɪtʃərɪzm/ *n* nudismo *m*

naturist /'neɪtʃərɪst/ ① *n* naturista *mf* ② *adj* naturistico

naught /nɔːt/ *n* = NOUGHT

naughtily /'nɔːtɪlɪ/ *adv* male

naughtiness /'nɔːtɪnɪs/ *n* (of child, pet) birbanteria *f*; (of joke, suggestion) maliziosità *f inv*

naughty /'nɔːtɪ/ *adj* (-ier, -iest) monello; (slightly indecent) spinto

nausea /'nɔːzɪə/ *n* nausea *f*

nauseate /'nɔːzɪeɪt/ *vt* nauseare

nauseating /'nɔːzɪeɪtɪŋ/ *adj* nauseante

nauseatingly /'nɔːzɪeɪtɪŋlɪ/ *adv* ‹rich, sweet› disgustosamente

nauseous /'nɔːzɪəs/ *adj* I feel ∼ ho la nausea

nautical /'nɔːtɪkl/ *adj* nautico

nautical mile *n* miglio *m* marino

naval /'neɪvl/ *adj* navale

naval base *n* base *f* navale

naval dockyard *n* cantiere *m* navale militare

naval officer *n* ufficiale *m* di marina

naval station *n* base *f* navale

naval stores *npl* (depot) magazzini *mpl* della marina militare

nave /neɪv/ *n* navata *f* centrale

navel /'neɪvl/ *n* ombelico *m*

navel ring *n* piercing *m inv* all'ombelico

navigable /'nævɪgəbl/ *adj* navigabile

navigate /'nævɪgeɪt/ ① *vi* navigare; Auto fare da navigatore ② *vt* navigare su ‹river›

navigation /nævɪ'geɪʃn/ *n* navigazione *f*

navigational /nævɪ'geɪʃənəl/ *adj* ‹instruments› di navigazione; ‹science› della navigazione

navigator /'nævɪgeɪtə(r)/ *n* navigatore *m*

navvy /'nævɪ/ *n* manovale *m*

navy /'neɪvɪ/ ① *n* marina *f* ② ∼ [blue] *adj* blu scuro *inv* ③ *n* blu *m inv* scuro

nay /neɪ/ ① *adv* anzi ② *n* (negative vote) no *m*

Nazi /'nɑːtsɪ/ *n & adj* nazista *mf*

NB *abbr* (**nota bene = please note**) n.b. *m*

NBC *n abbr* (**National Broadcasting Company**) NBC *f* (rete nazionale televisiva statunitense)

NC Am *abbr* **North Carolina**

NCO *n abbr* (**non-commissioned officer**) sottufficiale *m*

ND Am *abbr* **North Dakota**

NE *abbr* (**north-east**) NE

Ne Am *abbr* **Nebraska**

Neapolitan /nɪə'pɒlɪtən/ *adj & n* napoletano, -a *mf*

near /nɪə(r)/ ① *adj* vicino; ‹future› prossimo; **the ∼est bank** la banca più vicina ② *adv* vicino; **draw ∼** avvicinarsi; **∼ at hand** a portata di mano ③ *prep* vicino a; **he was ∼ to tears** aveva le lacrime agli occhi ④ *vt* avvicinarsi a

nearby /nɪə'baɪ/ *adj & adv* vicino

near-death experience *n* esperienza *f* ultraterrena

Near East *n* Medio Oriente *m*

nearly /'nɪəlɪ/ *adv* quasi; **it's not ∼ enough** non è per niente sufficiente

near miss *n* have a ∼ ∼ ‹planes, cars› evitare per poco uno scontro

nearness /'nɪənɪs/ *n* vicinanza *f*

nearside *n* Auto (in Britain) lato *m* sinistro; (in America, rest of Europe) lato *m* destro

near-sighted /-'saɪtɪd/ *adj* Am miope

near-sightedness *n* miopia *f*

neat /niːt/ *adj* (tidy) ordinato; (clever) efficace; (undiluted) liscio

neaten /'niːtən/ *vt* riordinare ‹pile of papery›; dare un'aggiustatina a ‹tie, skirt›

neatly /'niːtlɪ/ *adv* ordinatamente; (cleverly) efficacemente

neatness /'niːtnɪs/ *n* (tidiness) ordine *m*

necessarily /nesə'serɪlɪ/ *adv* necessariamente

necessary /'nesəsərɪ/ *adj* necessario

necessitate /nɪ'sesɪteɪt/ *vt* rendere necessario

necessity /nɪ'sesətɪ/ *n* necessità *f inv*

neck /nek/ *n* collo *m*; (of dress) colletto *m*; ∼ **and** ∼ testa a testa

necking /'nekɪŋ/ *n* fam pomiciata *f*

necklace /'neklɪs/ *n* collana *f*

neckline *n* scollatura *f*

necktie *n* cravatta *f*

nectar /'nektə(r)/ *n* nettare *m*

nectarine /'nektərɪn/ *n* nettarina *f*

neé /neɪ/ *adj* ∼ **Brett** nata Brett

need /niːd/ ① *n* bisogno *m*; **be in ∼** essere bisognoso; **be in ∼ of** avere bisogno di; **if ∼ be** se ce ne fosse bisogno; **there is a ∼ for** c'è bisogno di; **there is no ∼ for that** non ce n'è bisogno; **there is no ∼ for you to go** non c'è bisogno che tu vada ② *vt* aver bisogno di; **I ∼ to know** devo saperlo; **it ∼s to be done** bisogna farlo ③ *v aux* **you ∼ not go** non c'è bisogno che tu vada; **∼ I come?** devo venire?

needful /'niːdfʊl/ ① *adj* necessario

2) *n* do the ∼ fare il necessario

needle /'niːdl/ 1) *n* ago *m*; (for knitting) uncinetto *m*; (of record player) puntina *f*
2) *vt* (fam: annoy) punzecchiare

needless /'niːdlɪs/ *adj* inutile

needlessly /'niːdlɪslɪ/ *adv* inutilmente

needlework /'niːdlwɜːk/ *n* cucito *m*

needs /niːdz/ *adv* ∼ must il dovere chiama

need-to-know *adj* we have a ∼ policy la nostra politica consiste nel tenere informati solo i diretti interessati

needy /'niːdɪ/ *adj* (**-ier,-iest**) bisognoso

negate /nɪ'geɪt/ *vt* (cancel out) annullare; mettere in forma negativa ‹sentence›; (contradict) contraddire; (deny) negare

negation /nɪ'geɪʃn/ *n* negazione *f*

negative /'negətɪv/ 1) *adj* negativo
2) *n* negazione *f*; Phot negativo *m*; in the ∼ Gram alla forma negativa

neglect /nɪ'glekt/ 1) *n* trascuratezza *f*; state of ∼ stato di abbandono
2) *vt* trascurare; he ∼ed to write non si è curato di scrivere

neglected /nɪ'glektɪd/ *adj* trascurato

neglectful /nɪ'glektfʊl/ *adj* negligente; be ∼ of trascurare

negligée /'neglɪʒeɪ/ *n* négligé *m inv*

negligence /'neglɪdʒəns/ *n* negligenza *f*

negligent /'neglɪdʒənt/ *adj* negligente

negligently /'neglɪdʒəntlɪ/ *adv* con negligenza

negligible /'neglɪdʒbl/ *adj* trascurabile

negotiable /nɪ'gəʊʃəbl/ *adj* ‹road› transitabile; Comm negoziabile; not ∼ ‹cheque› non trasferibile

negotiate /nɪ'gəʊʃɪeɪt/ 1) *vt* negoziare; Auto prendere ‹bend›
2) *vi* negoziare

negotiating /nɪ'gəʊʃɪeɪtɪŋ/ *adj* ‹rights› al negoziato; ‹team, committee› che conduce le trattative; ‹ploy, position› di negoziato; the ∼ table il tavolo delle trattative

negotiation /nɪgəʊʃɪ'eɪʃn/ *n* negoziato *m*

negotiator /nɪ'gəʊʃɪeɪtə(r)/ *n* negoziatore, -a *mf*

Negro /'niːgrəʊ/ *adj & n* (*pl* **-es**) negro, -a *mf*

neigh /neɪ/ *vi* nitrire

neighbour /'neɪbə(r)/ *n* vicino, -a *mf*

neighbourhood /'neɪbəhʊd/ *n* vicinato *m*; in the ∼ of nei dintorni di; fig circa

neighbourhood watch scheme *n* vigilanza *f* da parte della gente del quartiere

neighbouring /'neɪbərɪŋ/ *adj* vicino

neighbourly /'neɪbəlɪ/ *adj* amichevole

neither /'naɪðə(r)/ 1) *adj & pron* nessuno dei due, né l'uno né l'altro
2) *adv* ∼... nor né... né
3) *conj* nemmeno, neanche; ∼ do/did I nemmeno io

neo+ /'niːəʊ/ *pref* neo+

neologism /nɪ'ɒlədʒɪzm/ *n* neologismo *m*

neon /'niːɒn/ *n* neon *m*

neon light *n* luce *f* al neon

Nepal /nɪ'pɔːl/ *n* Nepal *m*

nephew /'nevjuː/ *n* nipote *m*

nephritis /nɪ'fraɪtəs/ *n* nefrite *f*

nepotism /'nepətɪzm/ *n* nepotismo *m*

Neptune /'neptjuːn/ *n* Nettuno *m*

nerve /nɜːv/ *n* nervo *m*; (fam: courage) coraggio *m*; (fam: impudence) faccia *f* tosta; lose one's ∼ perdersi d'animo; you've got a ∼ hai una bella faccia tosta!; live on one's ∼s vivere con i nervi a fior di pelle; be a bag of ∼s avere i nervi a fior di pelle

nerve-racking /'nɜːvrækɪŋ/ *adj* logorante

nerviness /'nɜːvɪnɪs/ *n* Br nervosismo *m*; Am grinta *f*

nervous /'nɜːvəs/ *adj* nervoso; he makes me ∼ mi mette in agitazione

nervous breakdown *n* esaurimento *m* nervoso

nervous energy *n* energia *f* in eccesso

nervously /'nɜːvəslɪ/ *adv* nervosamente

nervousness /'nɜːvəsnɪs/ *n* nervosismo *m*; (before important event) tensione *f*

nervous system *n* sistema *m* nervoso

nervous wreck *n* fascio *m* di nervi

nervy /'nɜːvɪ/ *adj* (**-ier, -iest**) nervoso; (Am: impudent) sfacciato

nest /nest/ 1) *n* nido *m*
2) *vi* fare il nido

nested /'nestɪd/ *adj* Comput nidificato

nest egg *n* gruzzolo *m*

nesting /'nestɪŋ/ 1) *n* Zool nidificazione *f*; Comput nesting *m inv*, nidificazione *f*
2) *attrib* ‹habit› di nidificare; ‹place› per nidificare; ‹season› della nidificazione

nestle /'nesl/ *vi* accoccolarsi
■ **nestle up to** *vt* accoccolarsi accanto a ‹somebody›

nestling /'nes(t)lɪŋ/ *n* nidiace *m*

net¹ /net/ 1) *n* rete *f*
2) *vt* (*pt/pp* **netted**) (catch) prendere (con la rete)

net² 1) *adj* netto; ∼ of VAT al netto dell'IVA
2) *vt* (*pt/pp* **netted**) incassare un utile netto di

netball /'netbɔːl/ *n* sport *m inv* femminile simile alla pallacanestro

net cord *n* corda *f* di rete; Tennis (shot) net *m inv*

Netherlands /'neðələndz/ *npl* the ∼ i Paesi Bassi

netiquette /'netɪket/ *n* Comput netiquette *f inv*

netspeak *n* Comput linguaggio *m* del net

netting /'netɪŋ/ *n* **[wire]** ∼ reticolato *m*

nettle /'netl/ *n* ortica *f*

net ton *n* Am tonnellata *f* corta americana

network /'netwɜːk/ *n* rete *f*

network card *n* Comput scheda *f* di rete

networked /'netwɜːkt/ *adj* Comput collegato in rete

networking /'netwɜːkɪŋ/ *n* (establishing contacts) stabilimento *m* di una rete di contatti; Comput collegamento *m* in rete

network television *n* Am network *m inv* televisivo

neuralgia /njʊə'rældʒə/ *n* nevralgia *f*

neuritis /njʊə'raɪtɪs/ *n* nevrite *f*

neurologist /njʊə'rɒlədʒɪst/ *n* neurologo, -a *mf*

neurology /njʊə'rɒlədʒɪ/ *n* neurologia *f*

neurosis /njʊə'rəʊsɪs/ *n* (pl **-oses** /njʊə'rəʊsiːz/) nevrosi *f inv*

neurosurgeon /'njʊərəsɜːdʒən/ *n* neurochirurgo *m*

neurotic /njʊə'rɒtɪk/ *adj* nevrotico

neurotically /njʊə'rɒtɪklɪ/ *adv* in modo ossessivo

neuter /'njuːtə(r)/ **①** *adj* gram neutro **②** *n* gram neutro *m* **③** *vt* sterilizzare

neutral /'njuːtrəl/ **①** *adj* neutro; (country, person) neutrale **②** *n* in ∼ Auto in folle

neutrality /njuː'trælətɪ/ *n* neutralità *f*

neutralize /'njuːtrəlaɪz/ *vt* neutralizzare

never /'nevə(r)/ *adv* [non...] mai; (fam: expressing disbelief) ma va'; ∼ **again** mai più; **well I** ∼**!** chi l'avrebbe detto!

never-ending *adj* interminabile

nevermore /nevə'mɔː(r)/ *adv* mai più

never-never *n* fam **buy something on the** ∼ comprare qualcosa a rate

never-never land *n* mondo *m* dei sogni

nevertheless /nevəðə'les/ *adv* tuttavia

new /njuː/ *adj* nuovo

New Age **①** *n* New Age *f inv* **②** *attrib* ⟨music, ideas, sect⟩ New Age *inv*

new blood *n* nuove leve *fpl*

newborn *adj* neonato

New Caledonia *n* Nuova Caledonia *f*

newcomer *n* nuovo, -a arrivato, -a *mf*

newfangled *adj* pej modernizzante

newfound *adj* nuovo

Newfoundland /'njuːfən(d)lənd/ *n* Terranova *f*

New Guinea *n* Nuova Guinea *f*

newish /'njuːɪʃ/ *adj* abbastanza nuovo

new-laid /'njuːleɪd/ *adj* fresco

new look **①** *adj* ⟨car, team⟩ nuovo; ⟨edition, show⟩ rinnovato; ⟨product⟩ dall'aspetto nuovo **②** *n* they have given the shop a completely ∼ ∼ hanno completamente rinnovato il negozio

newly /'njuːlɪ/ *adv* (recently) di recente

newly-built *adj* costruito di recente

newly-weds /'njuːlɪwedz/ *npl* sposini *mpl*

new moon *n* luna *f* nuova

newness /'njuːnɪs/ *n* novità *f*

news /njuːz/ *n* notizie *fpl*; TV telegiornale *m*; Radio giornale *m* radio; **piece of** ∼ notizia *f*

news agency *n* agenzia *f* di stampa

newsagent's *n* Br giornalaio *m* (che vende anche tabacchi, caramelle ecc)

news bulletin *n* notiziario *m*

newscast *n* Am notiziario *m*

newscaster *n* giornalista *mf* televisivo, -a/radiofonico, -a

news conference *n* conferenza *f* stampa *inv*

newsdealer *n* Am giornalaio, -a *mf*

news desk *n* (at newspaper) redazione *f*

news editor *n* caporedattore, -trice *mf* di servizi di cronaca

newsflash *n* notizia *f* flash

newsgroup *n* newsgroup *m inv*

news headlines *npl* TV titoli *mpl* delle principali notizie

news item *n* notizia *f* di attualità

newsletter *n* bollettino *m* d'informazione

newspaper /'njuːzpeɪpə(r)/ *n* giornale *m*; (material) carta *f* di giornale

newspaperman *n* giornalista *m*

newspaper office *n* ufficio *m* della redazione

newspaperwoman *n* giornalista *f*

newspeak /'njuːspiːk/ *n* Am giornalese *m*

newsprint *n* (paper) carta *f* da giornale; (ink) inchiostro *m* di stampa

newsreader *n* giornalista *mf* televisivo, -a/radiofonico, -a

newsreel *n* cinegiornale *m*

newsroom *n* redazione *f*

news sheet *n* bollettino *m*

newsstand *n* edicola *f*

news value *n* interesse *m* mediatico

newsworthy *adj* che merita di essere pubblicato

newsy /'njuːzɪ/ *adj* ‹*letter*› pieno di notizie

newt /njuːt/ *n* tritone *m*

new technology *n* nuova tecnologia *f*

New Testament *n* Nuovo Testamento *m*

new wave *n* & *adj* new wave *f inv*

New Year *n* (January 1st) Capodanno *m*; (next year) l'anno *m* nuovo; **Happy ~ ~!** buon anno!; **closed for ~ ~** chiuso per le feste di Capodanno; **see in the ~ ~** festeggiare il Capodanno

New Year Honours list *n* Br lista *f* delle persone che ricevono decorazioni il 1 gennaio

New Year's Day *n* Capodanno *m*

New Year's Eve *n* vigilia *f* di Capodanno

New Year's resolution *n* proposito *m* per l'anno nuovo

New Zealand /'ziːlənd/ *n* Nuova Zelanda *f*

New Zealander /'ziːləndə(r)/ *n* neozelandese *mf*

next /nekst/ ① *adj* prossimo; (adjoining) vicino; **who's ~?** a chi tocca?; **the ~ best thing would be to...** alternativamente la cosa migliore sarebbe di...; **~ to nothing** quasi niente; **the ~ day** il giorno dopo; **~ week** la settimana prossima; **the week after ~** fra due settimane; **the ~ thing I knew** la sola cosa che ho saputo dopo ② *adv* dopo; **when will you see him ~?** quando lo rivedi la prossima volta?; **~ to** accanto a ③ *n* seguente *mf*; **~ of kin** parente *m* prossimo

next door ① *adj* ‹*dog, bell*› dei vicini; ‹*office*› accanto *inv*; **the girl ~** also fig la ragazza della porta accanto ② *adv* ‹*live, move in*› nella casa accanto

next-door neighbour *n* vicino *m* di casa

nexus /'neksəs/ *n* (network) rete *f*

NF *n* Br Pol *abbr* **National Front**

NH Am *abbr* **New Hampshire**

NHS *n abbr* **National Health Service**

NI *n* Br *abbr* **National Insurance**) previdenza *f* sociale; *abbr* **(Northern Ireland)** Irlanda *f* del Nord

nib /nɪb/ *n* pennino *m*

nibble /'nɪbl/ *vt/i* mordicchiare ■ **nibble at, nibble on** *vt* = NIBBLE

Nicaragua /nɪkə'rægjʊə/ *n* Nicaragua *m*

nice /naɪs/ *adj* ‹*day, weather, holiday*› bello; ‹*person*› gentile, simpatico; ‹*food*› buono; **it was ~ meeting you** è stato un piacere conoscerla

nice-looking *adj* carino

nicely /'naɪslɪ/ *adv* gentilmente; (well) bene

niceties /'naɪsətɪz/ *npl* finezze *fpl*

niche /niːʃ/ *n* nicchia *f*

niche market *n* mercato *m* specializzato

nick /nɪk/ ① *n* tacca *f*; (on chin etc) taglietto *m*; (fam: prison) galera *f*; (fam: police station) centrale *f* [di polizia]; **in the ~ of the time** fam appena in tempo; **in good ~** fam in buono stato ② *vt* intaccare; (fam: steal) fregare; (fam: arrest) beccare; **~ one's chin** farsi un taglietto nel mento

nickel /'nɪkl/ *n* nichel *m*; Am moneta *f* da cinque centesimi

nickel-and-dime *adj* Am fam da quattro soldi

nickelodeon /nɪkl'əʊdɪən/ *n* (Am: juke box) juke box *m inv*

nickname /'nɪkneɪm/ ① *n* soprannome *m* ② *vt* soprannominare

nicotine /'nɪkətiːn/ *n* nicotina *f*

nicotine patch *n* cerotto *m* (transdermico) alla nicotina

niece /niːs/ *n* nipote *f*

nifty /'nɪftɪ/ *adj* fam (skilful) geniale; (attractive) sfizioso

Niger /'naɪdʒə(r)/ *n* Niger *m*

Nigeria /naɪ'dʒɪərɪə/ *n* Nigeria *f*

Nigerian /naɪ'dʒɪərɪən/ *adj* & *n* nigeriano, -a *mf*

niggardly /'nɪgədlɪ/ *adj* ‹*person*› tirchio; ‹*salary*› misero

niggle /'nɪgl/ fam ① *n* (complaint) cosetta *f* da ridire ② *vi* (complain) lamentarsi in continuazione ③ *vt* (irritate) dar fastidio a

niggling /'nɪglɪŋ/ *adj* ‹*detail*› insignificante; ‹*pain*› fastidioso; ‹*doubt*› persistente

night /naɪt/ ① *n* notte *f*; (evening) sera *f*; **at ~** la notte, di notte; (in the evening) la sera, di sera; **Monday ~** lunedì notte/sera; **work ~s** lavorare la notte ② *adj* di notte

nightcap *n* papalina *f*; (drink) bicchierino *m* bevuto prima di andare a letto

nightclub *n* locale *m* notturno, night[-club] *m inv*

nightclubbing *n* **go ~** andare nei night [club]

nightdress *n* camicia *f* da notte

nightfall *n* crepuscolo *m*

nightgown, fam **nightie** *n* camicia *f* da notte

nightingale /'naɪtɪŋgeɪl/ *n* usignolo *m*

nightlife *n* vita *f* notturna

night light *n* lumino *m* da notte

nightly /'naɪtlɪ/ ① *adj* di notte, di sera
② *adv* ogni notte, ogni sera

nightmare /'naɪtmeə(r)/ *n also fig*
incubo *m*

nightmarish /'naɪtmeərɪʃ/ *adj* da
incubo

night owl *n* nottambulo, -a *mf*

night porter *n* portiere *m* di notte

night school *n* scuola *f* serale

nightshade *n* Bot **deadly** ~ belladonna *f*

night shelter *n* dormitorio *m* pubblico

nightshift *n* (workers) turno *m* di notte;
be on the ~ fare il turno di notte

nightshirt *n* camicia *f* da notte (da
uomo)

nightspot *n* night club *m inv*

nightstand *n* Am comodino *m*

nightstick *n* (Am: truncheon) manganello
m

night-time *n* **at** ~ di notte, la notte

night vision *n* visione *f* notturna

nightwatchman *n* guardiano *m*
notturno

nightwear *n* indumenti *mpl* da notte

nil /nɪl/ *n* nulla *m*; Sport zero *m*

Nile /naɪl/ *n* Nilo *m*

nimble /'nɪmbl/ *adj* agile

nimbly /'nɪmblɪ/ *adv* agilmente

nincompoop /'nɪŋkəmpuːp/ *n* fam
scemo *m*

nine /naɪn/ *adj & n* nove *m*

ninepin /'naɪnpɪn/ *n* birillo *m*; **be falling
like** ~**s** ⟨troops, guards, candidates⟩
cadere come le mosche

nineteen /naɪn'tiːn/ *adj & n* diciannove
m

nineteenth /naɪn'tiːnθ/ *adj & n*
diciannovesimo, -a *mf*

nineties /'naɪntɪz/ *npl* (period) **the** ~ gli
anni Novanta *mpl*; (age) novant'anni *mpl*;
▸ *also* FORTIES

ninetieth /'naɪntɪɪθ/ *adj & n*
novantesimo, -a *mf*

nine-to-five ① *adj* ⟨job⟩ in un ufficio;
⟨routine⟩ dell'ufficio
② *adv* ⟨work⟩ dalle nove alle cinque

ninety /'naɪntɪ/ *adj & n* novanta *m*

ninth /naɪnθ/ *adj & n* nono, -a *mf*

nip /nɪp/ ① *n* pizzicotto *m*; (bite) morso *m*
② *vt* pizzicare; (bite) mordere; ~ **in the
bud** fig stroncare sul nascere
③ *vi* (fam: run) fare un salto

nipper /'nɪpə(r)/ *n* fam ragazzino, -a *mf*

nipple /'nɪpl/ *n* capezzolo *m*; (Am: on bottle)
tettarella *f*

nippy /'nɪpɪ/ *adj* (**-ier, -iest**) fam (cold)
pungente; (quick) svelto

nit /nɪt/ *n* (egg) lendine *m*; (larva) larva *f* di
pidocchio

nit-pick *vi* cercare il pelo nell'uovo

nitrate /'naɪtreɪt/ *n* nitrato *m*

nitric /'naɪtrɪk/ *adj* nitrico

nitrogen /'naɪtrədʒn/ *n* azoto *m*

nitty-gritty /nɪtɪ'grɪtɪ/ *n* fam **the** ~ il
nocciolo [della questione]; **get down to the**
~ arrivare al dunque

nitwit /'nɪtwɪt/ *n* fam imbecille *mf*

NJ Am *abbr* **New Jersey**

NM Am *abbr* **New Mexico**

no /nəʊ/ ① *adv* no
② *n* (pl **noes**) no *m invar*
③ *adj* nessuno; **I have no time** non ho
tempo; **in no time** in un baleno; **'no
parking'** 'sosta vietata'; **'no smoking'**
'vietato fumare'; **it's no go** è inutile

no., No. *abbr* (**number**) No.

Noah /'nəʊə/ *n* Noè *m*; ~**'s Ark** l'arca *f* di
Noè

nobility /nəʊ'bɪlətɪ/ *n* nobiltà *f*

noble /'nəʊbl/ *adj* nobile

nobleman /'nəʊblmən/ *n* nobile *m*

noble-minded /-'maɪndɪd/ *adj* di animo
nobile

noble savage *n* buon selvaggio *m*

nobly /'nəʊblɪ/ *adv* (selflessly)
generosamente; ~ **born** di nobili natali

nobody /'nəʊbədɪ/ ① *pron* nessuno; **he
knows** ~ non conosce nessuno; **he's** ~
important non è nessuno d'importante
② *n* **he's a** ~ non è nessuno

no claims bonus *n* abbuono *m* in
assenza di sinistri

nocturnal /nɒk'tɜːnl/ *adj* notturno

nod /nɒd/ ① *n* cenno *m* del capo; **give a**
~ fare un cenno col capo
② *vt* (pt/pp **nodded**) fare un cenno col
capo; (in agreement) fare di sì col capo
③ *vi* ~ **one's head** fare di sì col capo
■ **nod off** *vi* assopirsi

node /nəʊd/ *n* nodo *m*

nodule /'nɒdjuːl/ *n* nodulo *m*

no-go *adj* fam **it's** ~ non è possibile

no-go area *n* zona *f* calda a cui la
polizia può accedere solo con la forza

no-hoper /nəʊ'həʊpə(r)/ *n* persona *f*
senza prospettive

noise /nɔɪz/ *n* rumore *m*; (loud) rumore
m, chiasso *m*

noiseless /'nɔɪzlɪs/ *adj* silenzioso

noiselessly /'nɔɪzlɪslɪ/ *adv*
silenziosamente

noise level *n* intensità *f inv* del rumore

noise pollution *n* inquinamento *m*
acustico

noisily /'nɔɪzɪlɪ/ *adv* rumorosamente

noisy /'nɔɪzɪ/ *adj* (**-ier, -iest**) rumoroso

nomad /'nəʊmæd/ *n* nomade *mf*

nomadic /nəʊ'mædɪk/ *adj* nomade

nominal /'nɒmɪnl/ *adj* nominale

nominally /'nɒmɪnəlɪ/ *adv* nominalmente

nominate /'nɒmɪneɪt/ *vt* proporre come candidato; (appoint) designare

nomination /nɒmɪ'neɪʃn/ *n* nomina *f*; (person nominated) candidato, -a *mf*

nominative /'nɒmɪnətɪv/ *adj & n gram* ∼ **[case]** nominativo *m*

nominee /nɒmɪ'niː/ *n* persona *f* nominata

non+ /nɒn/ *pref* non+, in+

non-academic *adj* ⟨course⟩ pratico; ⟨staff⟩ non insegnante

non-addictive *adj* che non dà assuefazione

non-alcoholic *adj* analcolico

non-attendance *n* mancata presenza *f*

non-believer *n* non credente *mf*

nonchalant /'nɒnʃələnt/ *adj* disinvolto

nonchalantly /'nɒnʃələntlɪ/ *adv* in modo disinvolto

non-classified *adj* ⟨information⟩ non confidenziale

non-combustible *adj* incombustibile

non-commercial *adj* ⟨event, activity⟩ senza fini di lucro

non-commissioned /-kə'mɪʃnd/ *adj* ∼ **officer** sottufficiale *m*

non-committal /-kə'mɪtəl/ *adj* che non si sbilancia

non-compliance *n* (with standards) non conformità *f* (with a); (with orders) inadempienza *f* (with a)

nonconformist /nɒnkən'fɔːmɪst/ *adj & n* anticonformista *mf*

non-cooperation *n* non cooperazione *f*

non-denominational /-dɪnɒmɪ'neɪʃənl/ *adj* ⟨church⟩ ecumenico; ⟨school⟩ laico

nondescript /'nɒndɪskrɪpt/ *adj* qualunque

none /nʌn/ **1** *pron* (person) nessuno; (thing) niente; ∼ **of us** nessuno di noi; ∼ **of this** niente di questo; **there's** ∼ **left** non ce n'è più
2 *adv* **she's** ∼ **too pleased** non è per niente soddisfatta; **I'm** ∼ **the wiser** non ne so più di prima

non-EC *adj* ⟨national⟩ extracomunitario; ⟨country⟩ che non appartiene alla Comunità Europea

nonentity /nɒ'nentətɪ/ *n* nullità *f inv*

non-essentials /-ɪ'senʃlz/ *npl* (details) dettagli *mpl*; (objects) cose *fpl* accessorie

nonetheless /nʌnðə'les/ *adv* = NEVERTHELESS

non-event *n* delusione *f*

non-existent *adj* inesistente

non-family *adj* al di fuori della famiglia

non-fat *adj* magro; ⟨diet⟩ senza grassi

non-fiction *n* saggistica *f*

non-flammable *adj* non infiammabile

non-fulfilment *n* (of contract, obligation) inadempienza *f* (of a); (of desire) inappagamento *m*

non-infectious *adj* non infettivo

non-iron *adj* che non si stira

non-judgmental *adj* imparziale

non-league *adj* Sport fuori campionato

no-no *n* fam cosa *f* proibita; **that's a** ∼ è un argomento tabù

no-nonsense *adj* ⟨manner, attitude⟩ diretto; ⟨tone⟩ spiccio; ⟨look, policy⟩ pratico; ⟨person⟩ franco

non-partisan *adj* imparziale

non-party *adj* ⟨issue, decision⟩ apartitico; ⟨person⟩ indipendente

non-person *n* (insignificant person) nullità *f inv*; **officially, he is a** ∼ Pol ufficialmente non è mai esistito

nonplussed /nɒn'plʌst/ *adj* perplesso

non-professional *adj* dilettante

non-profit-making /-'prɒfɪtmeɪkɪŋ/ *adj* ⟨organization⟩ senza fini di lucro

non-redeemable *adj* Fin vincolato

non-refillable *adj* ⟨lighter, pen⟩ non ricaricabile; ⟨can, bottle⟩ non riutilizzabile

non-religious *adj* laico

non-resident **1** *adj* ⟨job, course⟩ non residenziale; Comput che non risiede in permanenza nella memoria centrale
2 *n* non residente *mf*

non-residential *adj* ⟨guest⟩ di passaggio; ⟨student, visitor⟩ non residente; ⟨caretaker⟩ che non alloggia sul posto; ⟨area⟩ non residenziale

non-returnable *adj* ⟨bottle⟩ a perdere

non-segregated *adj* ⟨area⟩ non segregato; ⟨society⟩ non segregazionista

nonsense /'nɒnsəns/ *n* sciocchezze *fpl*

nonsensical /nɒn'sensɪkl/ *adj* assurdo

non sequitur /nɒn'sekwɪtə(r)/ *n* affermazione *f* senza legame con quanto detto prima

non-skid *adj* antiscivolo *inv*

non-smoker *n* non fumatore, -trice *mf*; (compartment) scompartimento *m* non fumatori

non-smoking *adj* non fumatori *inv*

non-specialized *adj* non specializzato

non-starter *n* **be a** ∼ ⟨person⟩ non avere nessuna probabilità di riuscita; ⟨plan, idea⟩ essere destinato al fallimento

non-stick *adj* antiaderente

non-stop **1** *adj* ⟨talk, work, pressure, noise⟩ continuo; ⟨train⟩ diretto; ⟨journey⟩ senza fermate; ⟨flight⟩ senza scalo

② *adv* ⟨*work, talk*⟩ senza sosta; ⟨*travel, fly*⟩ senza scalo

non-swimmer *n* persona *f* che non sa nuotare

non-taxable *adj* non imponibile

non-union *adj* ⟨*person*⟩ non iscritto ad un sindacato; ⟨*company*⟩ non sindacalizzato

non-violent *adj* non violento

non-white, **non-White** *n* persona *f* di colore

noodles /'nu:dlz/ *npl* taglierini *mpl*

nook /nʊk/ *n* cantuccio *m*

noon /nu:n/ *n* mezzogiorno *m*; **at** ∼ a mezzogiorno

no one *pron* nessuno

noose /nu:s/ *n* nodo *m* scorsoio

nor /nɔ:(r)/ *adv* & *conj* né; ∼ **do I** neppure io

Nordic /'nɔ:dɪk/ *adj* nordico

norm /nɔ:m/ *n* norma *f*

normal /'nɔ:ml/ *adj* normale

normality /nɔ:'mælətɪ/ *n* normalità *f*

normally /'nɔ:məlɪ/ *adv* (usually) normalmente

Norman /'nɔ:mən/ ① *adj* normanno; ⟨*landscape village*⟩ della Normandia ② *n* normanno *m*

Norse /nɔ:s/ *adj* ⟨*mythology, saga*⟩ norreno

north /nɔ:θ/ ① *n* nord *m*; **to the** ∼ **of** a nord di ② *adj* del nord, settentrionale ③ *adv* a nord

North Africa *n* Africa *f* del Nord

North African *adj* & *n* nordafricano, -a *mf*

North America *n* America *f* del Nord

North American *adj* & *n* nordamericano, -a *mf*

Northants /nɔ:'θænts/ Br *abbr* **Northamptonshire**

northbound /'nɔ:θbaʊnd/ *adj* ⟨*traffic, carriageway*⟩ in direzione nord

Northd Br *abbr* **Northumberland**

north-east ① *adj* di nord-est, nordorientale ② *n* nord-est *m* ③ *adv* a nord-est; ⟨*travel*⟩ verso nord-est

north-easterly ① *adj* ⟨*point*⟩ a nord-est; ⟨*wind*⟩ di nord-est ② *n* vento *m* di nord-est

northeastern /nɔ:θ'i:stən/ *adj* nordorientale

northerly /'nɔ:ðəlɪ/ *adj* ⟨*direction*⟩ nord; ⟨*wind*⟩ del nord

northern /'nɔ:ðən/ *adj* del nord, settentrionale

Northern Ireland *n* Irlanda *f* del Nord

Northern Lights *npl* aurora *f* boreale

North Korea *n* Corea *f* del Nord

North Pole *n* polo *m* nord

North Sea *n* Mare *m* del Nord

North Star *n* stella *f* polare

northward[s] /'nɔ:θwəd[z]/ *adv* verso nord

north-west ① *adj* di nord-ovest, nordoccidentale ② *n* nord-ovest *m* ③ *adv* a nord-ovest; ⟨*travel*⟩ verso nord-ovest

north-westerly ① *adj* ⟨*point*⟩ a nord-ovest; ⟨*wind*⟩ di nord-ovest ② *n* vento *m* di nord-ovest

north-western *adj* nordoccidentale

Norway /'nɔ:weɪ/ *n* Norvegia *f*

Norwegian /nɔ:'wi:dʒn/ *adj* & *n* norvegese *mf*

nose /nəʊz/ *n* naso *m*
■ **nose about** *vi* curiosare

nosebleed /'nəʊzbli:d/ *n* emorragia *f* nasale

nosedive /'nəʊzdaɪv/ *n* Aeron picchiata *f*; **take a** ∼ fig ⟨*prices;*⟩ scendere vertiginosamente

nosey /'nəʊzɪ/ *adj* = NOSY

no-show *n* persona *f* che non si è presentata

nosily /'nəʊzɪlɪ/ *adv* in modo indiscreto

nostalgia /nɒ'stældʒɪə/ *n* nostalgia *f*

nostalgic /nɒ'stældʒɪk/ *adj* nostalgico

nostril /'nɒstrəl/ *n* narice *f*

nosy /'nəʊzɪ/ *adj* (**-ier, -iest**) fam ficcanaso *inv*

not /nɒt/ *adv* non; **he is** ∼ Italian non è italiano; **I hope** ∼ spero di no; ∼ **all of us have been invited** non siamo stati tutti invitati; **if** ∼ se no; ∼ **at all** niente affatto; ∼ **a bit** per niente; ∼ **even** neanche; ∼ **yet** non ancora; **in the** ∼ **too distant future** in un futuro non troppo lontano; ∼ **only... but also...** non solo... ma anche...

notable /'nəʊtəbl/ *adj* (remarkable) notevole

notably /'nəʊtəblɪ/ *adv* (in particular) in particolare

notary /'nəʊtərɪ/ *n* notaio *m*; ∼ **public** notaio *m*

notation /nəʊ'teɪʃn/ *n* notazione *f*

notch /nɒtʃ/ *n* tacca *f*
■ **notch up** *vt* (score) segnare

note /nəʊt/ ① *n* nota *f*; (short letter, banknote) biglietto *m*; (memo, written comment etc) appunto *m*; **of** ∼ ⟨*person*⟩ di spicco; ⟨*comments, event*⟩ degno di nota; **make a** ∼ **of** prendere nota di; **take** ∼ **of** (notice) prendere nota di ② *vt* (notice) notare; (write) annotare
■ **note down** *vt* annotare

notebook /'nəʊtbʊk/ *n* taccuino *m*

notebook [PC] *n* notebook *m inv*

noted /'nəʊtɪd/ *adj* noto, celebre (**for** per)

notepad *n* blocco *m* per appunti

notepaper *n* carta *f* da lettere

noteworthy *adj* degno di nota

nothing /'nʌθɪŋ/ **1** *pron* niente, nulla **2** *adv* niente affatto; **for** ~ (free, in vain) per niente; (with no reason) senza motivo; ~ **but** nient'altro che; ~ **much** poco o nulla; ~ **interesting** niente di interessante; **it's** ~ **to do with you** non ti riguarda

notice /'nəʊtɪs/ **1** *n* (on board) avviso *m*; (review) recensione *f*; (termination of employment) licenziamento *m*; [advance] ~ preavviso *m*; **two months'** ~ due mesi di preavviso; **at short** ~ con breve preavviso; **until further** ~ fino nuovo avviso; **give [in one's]** ~ ⟨*employee*⟩ dare le dimissioni; **give an employee** ~ dare il preavviso ad un impiegato; **take no** ~ **of** non fare caso a; **take no** ~! non farci caso! **2** *vt* notare

noticeable /'nəʊtɪsəbl/ *adj* evidente

noticeably /'nəʊtɪsəblɪ/ *adv* sensibilmente

noticeboard /'nəʊtɪsbɔːd/ *n* bacheca *f*

notification /nəʊtɪfɪ'keɪʃn/ *n* notifica *f*

notify /'nəʊtɪfaɪ/ *vt* (pt/pp **-ied**) notificare

notion /nəʊʃn/ *n* idea *f*, nozione *f*; **he hasn't the slightest** ~ **of time** gli manca completamente la nozione del tempo; ~**s** *pl* (Am: haberdashery) merceria *f*

notoriety /nəʊtə'raɪətɪ/ *n* notorietà *f*

notorious /nəʊ'tɔːrɪəs/ *adj* famigerato; **be** ~ **for** essere tristemente famoso per

notoriously /nəʊ'tɔːrɪəslɪ/ *adv* **they're** ~ **unreliable** tutti sanno che su di loro non si può mai fare affidamento

Notts /nɒts/ Br *abbr* **Nottinghamshire**

notwithstanding /nɒtwɪθ'stændɪŋ/ **1** *prep* malgrado **2** *adv* ciononostante

nougat /'nʌgət/ *n* torrone *m*

nought /nɔːt/ *n* zero *m*

noughts and crosses *n* tris *m*

noun /naʊn/ *n* nome *m*, sostantivo *m*

nourish /'nʌrɪʃ/ *vt* nutrire

nourishing /'nʌrɪʃɪŋ/ *adj* nutriente

nourishment /'nʌrɪʃmənt/ *n* nutrimento *m*

novel /'nɒvl/ **1** *adj* insolito **2** *n* romanzo *m*

novelette /nɒvə'let/ *n* (oversentimental) romanzetto *m* rosa

novelist /'nɒvəlɪst/ *n* romanziere, -a *mf*

novelty /'nɒvəltɪ/ *n* novità *f*; **novelties** *pl* (objects) oggettini *mpl*

November /nəʊ'vembə(r)/ *n* novembre *m*

novice /'nɒvɪs/ *n* novizio, -a *mf*

now /naʊ/ **1** *adv* ora, adesso; **by** ~ ormai; **just** ~ proprio ora; **right** ~ subito; ~ **and again,** ~ **and then** ogni tanto; ~, ~! su! **2** *conj* ~ [**that**] ora che, adesso che

nowadays /'naʊədeɪz/ *adv* oggigiorno

nowhere /'nəʊweə(r)/ *adv* in nessun posto, da nessuna parte

noxious /'nɒkʃəs/ *adj* nocivo

nozzle /'nɒzl/ *n* bocchetta *f*

nr *abbr* **near**

NSPCC *n* Br *abbr* (**National Society for the Prevention of Cruelty to Children**) Società *f* nazionale per la protezione dell'infanzia

NT *abbr* **New Testament**

nth /enθ/ *adj* Math, fig **to the** ~ **power/degree** all'ennesima potenza; **for the** ~ **time** per l'ennesima volta

nuance /'njuːɑ̃s/ *n* sfumatura *f*

nub /nʌb/ *n* **the** ~ **of the matter** il nocciolo della questione

nubile /'njuːbaɪl/ *adj* ⟨*attractive*⟩ desiderabile

nuclear /'njuːklɪə(r)/ *adj* nucleare

nuclear bomb *n* bomba *f* atomica

nuclear deterrent *n* deterrente *m* nucleare

nuclear energy *n* energia *f* nucleare

nuclear-free zone *n* Br zona *f* denuclearizzata

nuclear physics *n* fisica *f* nucleare

nuclear power *n* (energy) energia *f* nucleare; (country) potenza *f* nucleare

nuclear power station *n* centrale *f* nucleare

nuclear shelter *n* rifugio *m* antiatomico

nuclear waste *n* scorie *fpl* nucleari

nucleus /'njuːklɪəs/ *n* (pl **-lei** /'njuːklɪaɪ/) nucleo *m*

nude /njuːd/ **1** *adj* nudo **2** *n* nudo *m*; **in the** ~ nudo

nudge /nʌdʒ/ **1** *n* colpetto *m* di gomito **2** *vt* dare un colpetto col gomito a

nudism /'njuːdɪzm/ *n* nudismo *m*

nudist /'njuːdɪst/ *n* nudista *mf*

nudity /'njuːdətɪ/ *n* nudità *f*

nugget /'nʌgɪt/ *n* pepita *f*

nuisance /'njuːsəns/ *n* seccatura *f*; (person) piaga *f*; **what a** ~! che seccatura!

nuisance call *n* Teleph telefonata *f* anonima

null /nʌl/ *adj* ~ **and void** nullo

nullify /'nʌlɪfaɪ/ *vt* (pt/pp **-ied**) annullare

numb /nʌm/ **1** *adj* intorpidito; ~ **with cold** intirizzito dal freddo **2** *vt* intorpidire

number /'nʌmbə(r)/ **1** *n* numero *m*; **a** ~ **of people** un certo numero di persone

2 *vt* numerare; (include) annoverare

numbering /ˈnʌmbərɪŋ/ *n* numerazione *f*

number one *n* (most important) numero uno *m*; **look after ∼ ∼** (oneself) pensare prima di tutto a se stessi

number plate *n* targa *f*

numeracy /ˈnjuːmərəsɪ/ *n* **improve standards of ∼** migliorare il livello nel calcolo

numeral /ˈnjuːmərəl/ *n* numero *m*, cifra *f*

numerate /ˈnjuːmərət/ *adj* **be ∼** sapere far di calcolo

numerical /njuːˈmerɪkl/ *adj* numerico; **in ∼ order** in ordine numerico

numerically /njuːˈmerɪklɪ/ *adv* numericamente

numeric keypad /njuːˈmerɪk/ *n* Comput tastierino *m* numerico

numerous /ˈnjuːmərəs/ *adj* numeroso

nun /nʌn/ *n* suora *f*

nuptial /ˈʌpʃl/ **1** *adj* nuziale **2** **∼s** *npl* nozze *fpl*

nurse /nɜːs/ **1** *n* infermiere, -a *mf*; **children's ∼** bambinaia *f* **2** *vt* curare

nursemaid *n* bambinaia *f*

nursery /ˈnɜːsərɪ/ *n* stanza *f* dei bambini; (for plants) vivaio *m*; **[day] ∼** asilo *m*

nursery rhyme *n* filastrocca *f*

nursery school *n* scuola *f* materna

nursery slope *n* Br pista *f* per principianti

nurse's aid *n* Am aiuto infermiere, -a *mf*

nursing /ˈnɜːsɪŋ/ *n* professione *f* d'infermiere

nursing auxiliary *n* Br aiuto infermiere, -a *mf*

nursing home *n* casa *f* di cura per anziani

nurture /ˈnɜːtə(r)/ *vt* allevare; fig coltivare

nut /nʌt/ *n* noce *f*; Techn dado *m*; (fam: head) zucca *f*

nutcrackers /ˈnʌtkrækəz/ *npl* schiaccianoci *m inv*

nutmeg /ˈnʌtmeg/ *n* noce *f* moscata

nutrient /ˈnjuːtrɪənt/ *n* sostanza *f* nutritiva

nutrition /njuːˈtrɪʃn/ *n* nutrizione *f*

nutritional /njuːˈtrɪʃnəl/ *adj* nutritivo

nutritionist /njuːˈtrɪʃənɪst/ *n* nutrizionista *mf*

nutritious /njuːˈtrɪʃəs/ *adj* nutriente

nuts /nʌts/ *npl* frutta *f* secca; **be ∼** fam essere svitato

nutshell /ˈnʌtʃel/ *n* guscio *m* di noce; **in a ∼** fig in parole povere

nuzzle /ˈnʌzl/ *vt* ⟨horse, dog⟩ strofinare il muso contro

■ **nuzzle up** *vi* **∼ up against** *or* **to somebody** rannicchiarsi contro qualcuno

NV Am *abbr* **Nevada**

NVQ *n abbr* Br (**national vocational qualification**) diploma conseguito presso un istituto tecnico o professionale

NW *abbr* (**north-west**) NO

NY Am *abbr* **New York**

NYC Am *abbr* **New York City**

nylon /ˈnaɪlɒn/ **1** *n* nailon *m*: **∼s** *pl* calze *fpl* di nailon **2** *attrib* di nailon

nymph /nɪmf/ *n* ninfa *f*

nymphomaniac /nɪmfəˈmeɪmræk/ **1** *n* ninfomane *f* **2** *adj* da ninfomane

NZ *abbr* **New Zealand**

Oo

o,¹ O /əʊ/ *n* (letter) o, O *f inv*

O² /əʊ/ *n* Teleph zero *m*

oaf /əʊf/ *n* (pl **oafs**) zoticone, -a *mf*

oak /əʊk/ **1** *n* quercia *f* **2** *attrib* di quercia

OAP *abbr* (**old-age pensioner**) pensionato, -a *mf*

oar /ɔː(r)/ *n* remo *m*

oarsman /ˈɔːzmən/ *n* vogatore *m*

oasis /əʊˈeɪsɪs/ *n* (pl **oases** /əʊˈeɪsiːz/) oasi *f inv*

oatcake /ˈəʊtkeɪk/ *n* galletta *f* di avena

oath /əʊθ/ *n* giuramento *m*; (swear-word) bestemmia *f*

oatmeal /ˈəʊtmiːl/ *n* farina *f* d'avena

oats /əʊts/ *npl* avena *fsg*; Culin **[rolled] ∼** fiocchi *mpl* d'avena

obdurate /ˈɒbdjʊrət/ *adj* (stubborn) irremovibile; (hardhearted) insensibile

OBE *n* Br *abbr* (**Officer of the (Order of the) British Empire**) onorificenza *f* britannica

obedience /əˈbiːdɪəns/ *n* ubbidienza *f*

obedient /əˈbiːdɪənt/ *adj* ubbidiente

obediently /əˈbiːdɪəntlɪ/ *adv*
ubbidientemente

obelisk /ˈɒbəlɪsk/ *n* obelisco *m*

obese /əˈbiːs/ *adj* obeso

obesity /əˈbiːsətɪ/ *n* obesità *f*

obey /əˈbeɪ/ **①** *vt* ubbidire a; osservare
⟨*instructions, rules*⟩
② *vi* ubbidire

obituary /əˈbɪtjʊərɪ/ *n* necrologio *m*

object[1] /ˈɒbdʒɪkt/ *n* oggetto *m*; Gram
complemento *m* oggetto; **money is no** ∼ i
soldi non sono un problema

object[2] /əbˈdʒekt/ *vi* (be against) opporsi
(to a); ∼ **that...** obiettare che...

objection /əbˈdʒekʃn/ *n* obiezione *f*;
have no ∼ non avere niente in contrario

objectionable /əbˈdʒekʃ(ə)nəbl/ *adj*
discutibile; ⟨*person*⟩ sgradevole

objective /əbˈdʒektɪv/ **①** *adj* oggettivo
② *n* obiettivo *m*

objectively /əbˈdʒektɪvlɪ/ *adv*
obiettivamente

objectivity /ɒbdʒekˈtəvətɪ/ *n* oggettività
f

objector /əbˈdʒektə(r)/ *n* oppositore,
-trice *mf*

obligation /ɒblɪˈgeɪʃn/ *n* obbligo *m*; **be
under an** ∼ avere un obbligo; **without** ∼
senza impegno

obligatory /əˈblɪgətrɪ/ *adj* obbligatorio

oblige /əˈblaɪdʒ/ *vt* (compel) obbligare; (do
a small service for) fare una cortesia a; **much**
∼**d** grazie mille

obliging /əˈblaɪdʒɪŋ/ *adj* disponibile

oblique /əˈbliːk/ *adj* obliquo; fig indiretto;
∼ **[stroke]** *n* barra *f*

obliterate /əˈblɪtəreɪt/ *vt* obliterare

obliteration /əblɪtəˈreɪʃn/ *n* (of mark,
memory) rimozione *f*; (of city) annientamento
m

oblivion /əˈblɪvɪən/ *n* oblio *m*

oblivious /əˈblɪvɪəs/ *adj* **be** ∼ essere
dimentico (**of, to** di)

oblong /ˈɒblɒŋ/ **①** *adj* oblungo
② *n* rettangolo *m*

obnoxious /əbˈnɒkʃəs/ *adj* detestabile

oboe /ˈəʊbəʊ/ *n* oboe *m inv*

obscene /əbˈsiːn/ *adj* osceno; ⟨*profits,
wealth*⟩ vergognoso

obscenity /əbˈsenətɪ/ *n* oscenità *f inv*

obscure /əbˈskjʊə(r)/ **①** *adj* oscuro
② *vt* oscurare; (confuse) mettere in ombra

obscurity /əbˈskjʊərətɪ/ *n* oscurità *f*

obsequious /əbˈsiːkwɪəs/ *adj*
ossequioso

observable /əbˈzɜːvəbl/ *adj* (discernible)
percettibile

observance /əbˈzɜːvəns/ *n* (of custom)
osservanza *f*

observant /əbˈzɜːvənt/ *adj* attento

observation /ɒbzəˈveɪʃn/ *n*
osservazione *f*

observation car *n* carrozza *f*
belvedere

observation tower *n* torre *f* di
osservazione

observatory /əbˈzɜːvətrɪ/ *n* osservatorio
m

observe /əbˈzɜːv/ *vt* osservare; (notice)
notare; (keep, celebrate) celebrare

observer /əbˈzɜːvə(r)/ *n* osservatore,
-trice *mf*

obsess /əbˈses/ *vt* **be** ∼**ed by** essere
fissato con

obsession /əbˈseʃn/ *n* fissazione *f*

obsessive /əbˈsesɪv/ *adj* ossessivo

obsessively /əbˈsesɪvlɪ/ *adv*
ossessivamente

obsolescence /ɒbsəˈlesəns/ *n*
obsolescenza *f*; **built-in** ∼ obsolescenza *f*
programmata

obsolete /ˈɒbsəliːt/ *adj* obsoleto; ⟨*word*⟩
desueto; ⟨*idea*⟩ sorpassato

obstacle /ˈɒbstəkl/ *n* ostacolo *m*

obstacle course *n* Mil, fig percorso *m*
ad ostacoli

obstacle race *n* corsa *f* ad ostacoli

obstetrician /ɒbstəˈtrɪʃn/ *n* ostetrico,
-a *mf*

obstetrics /ɒbˈstetrɪks/ *n* ostetricia *f*

obstinacy /ˈɒbstɪnɪsɪ/ *n* ostinazione *f*

obstinate /ˈɒbstɪnət/ *adj* ostinato

obstinately /ˈɒbstɪntlɪ/ *adv*
ostinatamente

obstreperous /əbˈstrepərəs/ *adj*
turbolento

obstruct /əbˈstrʌkt/ *vt* ostruire; (hinder)
ostacolare

obstruction /əbˈstrʌkʃn/ *n* ostruzione *f*;
(obstacle) ostacolo *m*

obstructive /əbˈstrʌktɪv/ *adj* **be** ∼
⟨*person*⟩ creare dei problemi

obtain /əbˈteɪn/ **①** *vt* ottenere
② *vi* prevalere

obtainable /əbˈteɪnəbl/ *adj* ottenibile

obtrusive /əbˈtruːsɪv/ *adj* ⟨*object*⟩
stonato

obtuse /əbˈtjuːs/ *adj* ottuso

obverse /ˈɒbvɜːs/ *adj* **the** ∼ **side/face** (of
coin) l'altra faccia *f*

obviate /ˈɒbvɪeɪt/ *vt* fml ovviare a

obvious /ˈɒbvɪəs/ *adj* ovvio

obviously /ˈɒbvɪəslɪ/ *adv* ovviamente

occasion /əˈkeɪʒn/ **①** *n* occasione *f*;
(event) evento *m*; **on** ∼ talvolta; **on the** ∼
of in occasione di
② *vt* cagionare

occasional /əˈkeɪʒənl/ *adj* saltuario; **he
has the** ∼ **glass of wine** ogni tanto beve
un bicchiere di vino

occasionally /əˈkeɪʒənəlɪ/ *adv* ogni tanto

occult /ɒˈkʌlt/ *adj* occulto

occupancy /ˈɒkjʊpənsɪ/ *n* available for immediate ∼ libero immediatamente; change of ∼ cambio *m* di inquilino

occupant /ˈɒkjʊpənt/ *n* occupante *mf*; (of vehicle) persona *f* a bordo

occupation /ɒkjʊˈpeɪʃn/ *n* occupazione *f*; (job) professione *f*

occupational /ɒkjʊˈpeɪʃənəl/ *adj* professionale

occupational hazard *n* rischio *m* professionale

occupational health *n* medicina *f* del lavoro

occupational pension *n* Br pensione *f* di lavoro

occupational psychologist *n* psicologo, -a *mf* del lavoro

occupational therapist *n* ergoterapista *mf*

occupational therapy *n* ergoterapia *f*

occupier /ˈɒkjʊpaɪə(r)/ *n* residente *mf*

occupy /ˈɒkjʊpaɪ/ *vt* (pt/pp **occupied**) occupare; (keep busy) tenere occupato

occur /əˈkɜː(r)/ *vi* (pt/pp **occurred**) accadere; (exist) trovarsi; it ∼ red to me that mi è venuto in mente che

occurrence /əˈkʌrəns/ *n* (event) fatto *m*

ocean /ˈəʊʃn/ *n* oceano *m*

ocean-going /ˈəʊʃəngəʊɪŋ/ *adj* ⟨ship⟩ d'alto mare

ochre /ˈəʊkə(r)/ *n & adj* (colour) ocra *f*

o'clock /əˈklɒk/ *adv* it's 7 ∼ sono le sette; at 7 ∼ alle sette

octagon /ˈɒktəgən/ *n* ottagono *m*

octagonal /ɒkˈtægənl/ *adj* ottagonale

octave /ˈɒktɪv/ *n* Mus ottava *f*

octet /ɒkˈtet/ *n* Mus ottetto *m*

October /ɒkˈtəʊbə(r)/ *n* ottobre *m*

octogenarian /ɒktədʒɪˈneərɪən/ *n & adj* ottantenne *mf*

octopus /ˈɒktəpəs/ *n* (pl **-puses**) polpo *m*

oculist /ˈɒkjʊlɪst/ *n* oculista *mf*

OD *n abbr* (**overdose**) overdose *f inv*

odd /ɒd/ *adj* ⟨number⟩ dispari; (not of set) scompagnato; (strange) strano; forty ∼ quaranta e rotti; ∼ jobs lavoretti *mpl*; the ∼ one out l'eccezione *f*; at ∼ moments a tempo perso; have the ∼ glass of wine bere un bicchiere di vino ogni tanto

oddball /ˈɒdbɔːl/ *n* fam eccentrico, -a *mf*

odd bod /ˈɒdbɒd/ *n* Br fam tipo, -a *mf* strano, -a

oddity /ˈɒdətɪ/ *n* stranezza *f*

odd-job man *n* tuttofare *m inv*

odd jobs *npl* lavoretti *mpl*

oddly /ˈɒdlɪ/ *adv* stranamente; ∼ enough stranamente

oddment /ˈɒdmənt/ *n* (of fabric) scampolo *m*

odds /ɒdz/ *npl* (chances) probabilità *fpl*; at ∼ in disaccordo; ∼ and ends cianfrusaglie *fpl*; it makes no ∼ non fa alcuna differenza

odds-on *adj* be the ∼ favourite (in betting) essere il gran favorito; she has an ∼ chance of... ha molte probabilità di...; it is ∼ that è molto probabile che

ode /əʊd/ *n* ode *f*

odious /ˈəʊdɪəs/ *adj* odioso

odium /ˈəʊdɪəm/ *n* odio *m*

odometer /əʊˈdɒmɪtə(r)/ *n* Am contachilometri *m inv*, odometro *m*

odour /ˈəʊdə(r)/ *n* odore *m*

odourless /ˈəʊdəlɪs/ *adj* inodore

odyssey /ˈɒdɪsɪ/ *n* odissea *f*

OECD *n abbr* (**Organization for Economic Cooperation and Development**) OCSE *f*

oedema /ɪˈdiːmə/ *n* edema *m*

oesophagus /ɪˈsɒfəgəs/ *n* esofago *m*

oestrogen /ˈiːstrədʒən/ *n* estrogeno *m*

of /ɒv/ *prep* di; a cup of tea/coffee una tazza di tè/caffè; the hem of my skirt l'orlo della mia gonna; the summer of 1989 l'estate del 1989; the two of us noi due; made of di; that's very kind of you è molto gentile da parte tua; a friend of mine un mio amico; a child of three un bambino di tre anni; the fourth of January il quattro gennaio; within a year of their divorce a circa un anno dal loro divorzio; half of it la metà; the whole of the room tutta la stanza

off /ɒf/ **1** *prep* da; (distant from) lontano da; take £10 ∼ the price ridurre il prezzo di 10 sterline; ∼ the coast presso la costa; a street ∼ the main road una traversa della via principale; (near) una strada vicina alla via principale; get ∼ the ladder scendere dalla scala; get ∼ the bus scendere dall'autobus; leave the lid ∼ the saucepan lasciare la pentola senza il coperchio **2** *adv* ⟨button, handle⟩ staccato; ⟨light, machine⟩ spento; ⟨brake⟩ disinserito; ⟨tap⟩ chiuso; 'off' (on appliance) 'off'; 2 kilometres ∼ a due chilometri di distanza; a long way ∼ molto distante; (time) lontano; ∼ and on di tanto in tanto; with his hat/coat ∼ senza il cappotto/cappello; with the light ∼ a luce spenta; 20% ∼ 20% di sconto; be ∼ (leave) andar via; Sport essere partito; ⟨food⟩ essere andato a male; (all gone) essere finito; ⟨wedding, engagement⟩ essere cancellato; I'm ∼ drugs/alcohol ho smesso di drogarmi/bere; be ∼ one's food non avere appetito; she's ∼ today (on holiday) è in ferie oggi; (ill) è malata oggi; ⋯⟩

I'm ∼ home vado a casa; **you'd be better** ∼ **doing...** faresti meglio a fare...; **have a day** ∼ avere un giorno di vacanza; **drive/ sail** ∼ andare via

offal /'ɒfl/ n Culin frattaglie fpl

offbeat /'ɒfbiːt/ adj insolito

off-centre adj Br fuori centro

off chance n there's an ∼ ∼ that c'è una remota possibilità che; **just on the** ∼ ∼ **that** nella remota possibilità che

off colour adj (not well) giù di forma; ⟨joke, story⟩ sporco

offence /ə'fens/ n (illegal act) reato m; **give** ∼ offendere; **take** ∼ offendersi (**at** per)

offend /ə'fend/ vt offendere

offender /ə'fendə(r)/ n Jur colpevole mf

offensive /ə'fensɪv/ ① adj offensivo ② n offensiva f; **go on the** ∼ passare all'offensiva

offer /'ɒfə(r)/ ① n offerta f; **on special** ∼ in offerta speciale ② vt offrire; opporre ⟨resistance⟩; ∼ **somebody something** offrire qualcosa a qualcuno; ∼ **to do something** offrirsi di fare qualcosa

offering /'ɒfərɪn/ n offerta f

offer price n Comm prezzo m d'offerta

offertory /'ɒfətrɪ/ n Relig offertorio m

offhand /ɒf'hænd/ ① adj (casual) spiccio ② adv su due piedi

office /'ɒfɪs/ n ufficio m; (post, job) carica f

office automation n burotica f

office block n Br complesso m di uffici

office building n Br complesso m di uffici

office hours npl orario m di ufficio

office junior n fattorino, -a mf

office politics n intrighi mpl di ufficio

officer /'ɒfɪsə(r)/ n ufficiale m; (police) agente m [di polizia]

office worker n impiegato, -a mf

official /ə'fɪʃl/ ① adj ufficiale ② n funzionario, -a mf; Sport dirigente m

officialdom /ə'fɪʃəldəm/ n burocrazia f

officially /ə'fɪʃəlɪ/ adv ufficialmente

officiate /ə'fɪʃɪeɪt/ vi officiare

officious /ə'fɪʃəs/ adj autoritario

officiously /ə'fɪʃəslɪ/ adv in modo autoritario

offing /'ɒfɪn/ n **in the** ∼ in vista

off-key adj Mus stonato

off-licence n negozio m per la vendita di alcolici

off-limits adj off-limits inv

off-line adj Comput fuori linea inv, off-line inv

offload /ɒf'ləʊd/ vt scaricare

off-message adj Pol **be** ∼ non essere in linea con la politica del governo

off-peak adj ⟨travel⟩ fuori dagli orari di punta; ⟨electricity⟩ a tariffa notturna ridotta; ∼ **call** Teleph telefonata f a tariffa ridotta

offprint /'ɒfprɪnt/ n estratto m

off-putting /-pʊtɪn/ adj fam scoraggiante

off-road vi viaggiare in fuoristrada

off-roader /'ɒfrəʊdə(r)/, **off-road vehicle** n fuoristrada

off-screen ① adj ⟨voice, action⟩ fuoricampo inv; ⟨relationship⟩ nella vita privata ② adv nella vita privata

off-season adj ⟨losses⟩ di bassa stagione; ⟨cruise⟩ in bassa stagione

offset /'ɒfset/ vt (pt/pp **-set**, pres p **-setting**) controbilanciare

offset printing n offset m inv

offshoot /'ɒfʃuːt/ n ramo m; fig diramazione f

offshore /'ɒfʃɔː(r)/ adj ⟨wind⟩ di terra; ⟨company, investment⟩ offshore inv

offside /ɒf'saɪd/ adj Sport [in] fuori gioco; ⟨wheel etc⟩ (left) sinistro; (right) destro

offspring /'ɒfsprɪn/ n prole f

off-stage adv dietro le quinte

off-the-cuff adj ⟨remark⟩ spontaneo; ⟨speech⟩ improvvisato

off-the-peg adj ⟨garment⟩ prêt-à-porter inv, confezionato

off-the-record adj ⟨comment, statement⟩ ufficioso

off-the-shelf adj Comm standard inv

off-the-shoulder adj ⟨dress⟩ senza bretelle

off-the-wall adj fam ⟨sense of humour⟩ strano

off-white adj bianco sporco

often /'ɒfn/ adv spesso; **how** ∼ ogni quanto; **every so** ∼ una volta ogni tanto

ogle /'əʊgl/ vt mangiarsi con gli occhi

ogre /'əʊgə(r)/ n orco m

oh /əʊ/ int oh!; **oh dear** oh Dio!

OHMS Br abbr (**On Her/His Majesty's Service**) abbreviazione f apposta su corrispondenza ufficiale del governo britannico

OHP n abbr (**overhead projector**) lavagna f luminosa

oil /ɔɪl/ ① n olio m; (petroleum) petrolio m; (for heating) nafta f ② vt oliare

oil-burning adj ⟨stove, boiler⟩ a nafta

oil can n (applicator) oliatore m

oil change n cambio m dell'olio

oilcloth n tela f cerata

oilfield n giacimento m di petrolio

oil filter n filtro m dell'olio

oil-fired /-faɪəd/ adj ⟨furnace, heating⟩ a nafta

oil gauge *n* indicatore *m* [del livello] dell'olio

oil heater *n* stufa *f* a nafta

oil lamp *n* lampada *f* a olio

oil paint *n* colore *m* a olio

oil painting *n* pittura *f* a olio

oil pipeline *n* oleodotto *m*

oil pressure *n* pressione *f* dell'olio

oil producing /-prədjuːsɪŋ/ *adj* ‹country› produttore di petrolio

oil refinery *n* raffineria *f* di petrolio

oil rig *n* piattaforma *f* petrolifera, offshore *m inv*

oilseed rape /ˈɔɪlsiːd/ *n* colza *f*

oilskins *npl* indumenti *mpl* di tela cerata

oil slick *n* chiazza *f* di petrolio

oil spill *n* fuoriuscita *f* di petrolio

oil stove *n* stufa *f* a nafta

oil tank *n* (domestic) serbatoio *m* della nafta; (industrial) cisterna *f* della nafta

oil tanker *n* petroliera *f*

oil well *n* pozzo *m* petrolifero

oily /ˈɔɪlɪ/ *adj* (**-ier**, **-iest**) unto; fig untuoso

ointment /ˈɔɪntmənt/ *n* pomata *f*

OK, okay /əʊˈkeɪ/ **1** *int* va bene, o.k. **2** *adj* if that's OK **with you** se ti va bene; **she's OK** (well) sta bene; **is the milk still OK?** il latte è ancora buono? **3** *adv* (well) bene **4** *vt* (pt/pp **OK'd**, **okayed**) dare l'o.k. a

old /əʊld/ *adj* vecchio; ‹girlfriend› ex; **how ~ is she?** quanti anni ha?; **she is ten years ~** ha dieci anni

old age *n* vecchiaia *f*

old-age pension *n* Br pensione *f* di vecchiaia

old-age pensioner *n* pensionato, -a *mf*

old boy *n* Sch ex-allievo *m*

old country *n* paese *m* d'origine

olden /ˈəʊldən/ *adj* **the ~ days** i tempi andati

old-established /-ɪˈstæblɪʃt/ *adj* di lunga data

olde-worlde /əʊldɪˈwɜːldɪ/ *adj* hum dall'aria falsamente antica

old-fashioned /-ˈfæʃ(ə)nd/ *adj* antiquato

old favourite *n* (book, play) classico *m*; (song, film) vecchio successo *m*

old flame *n* fam vecchia fiamma *f*

old girl *n* ex-allieva *f*

Old Glory *n* bandiera *f* statunitense

old hand *n* **be an ~ ~ at something/at doing something** saperci fare con qualcosa/a fare qualcosa

old hat *adj* fam **be ~ ~** essere roba vecchia

oldie /ˈəʊldɪ/ *n* (person) vecchio, -a *mf*; (film, song) vecchio successo *m*

old lady *n* (elderly woman) signora *f* anziana; **my ~ ~** (mother) la mia vecchia; (wife) la mia signora

old maid *n* zitella *f*

old man *n* (elderly man) uomo *m* anziano; (old: dear chap) vecchio *m* mio; **my ~ ~** (father) il mio vecchio; (husband) mio marito *m*; **the ~ ~** (boss) il capo

old master *n* (work) dipinto *m* antico (specialmente di un pittore europeo del XIII-XVII secolo)

old people's home *n* casa *f* di riposo

old soldier *n* (former soldier) veterano *m*

Old Testament *n* Antico Testamento *m*

old-time *adj* di un tempo; **~ dancing** ballo *m* liscio

old-timer *n* veterano, -a *mf*

old wives' tale *n* superstizione *f*

old woman *n* (elderly lady) donna *f* anziana; **my ~ ~** (mother) mia madre *f*; (wife) la mia signora; **be an ~ ~** pej: man essere una donnicciola

olive /ˈɒlɪv/ **1** *n* (fruit, colour) oliva *f*; (tree) olivo *m* **2** *adj* d'oliva; (colour) olivastro

olive branch *n* fig ramoscello *m* d'olivo

olive green *adj & n* verde *m* oliva *inv*

olive grove *n* oliveto *m*

olive oil *n* olio *m* di oliva

olive-skinned /-ˈskɪnd/ *adj* olivastro

Olympic /əˈlɪmpɪk/ *adj* olimpico

Olympic Games, Olympics *npl* Olimpiadi *fpl*

Oman /əʊˈmɑːn/ *n* Oman *m*

ombudsman /ˈɒmbʊdzmən/ *n* difensore *m* civico

omelette /ˈɒmlɪt/ *n* omelette *f inv*

omen /ˈəʊmən/ *n* presagio *m*

ominous /ˈɒmɪnəs/ *adj* sinistro

omission /əˈmɪʃn/ *n* omissione *f*

omit /əˈmɪt/ *vt* (pt/pp **omitted**) omettere; **~ to do something** tralasciare di fare qualcosa

omnibus /ˈɒmnɪbəs/ *n* (bus) omnibus *m inv*

omnibus edition *n* Br TV replica *f* delle puntate precedenti

omnipotent /ɒmˈnɪpətənt/ *adj* onnipotente

omnipresent /ɑmnɪˈprez(ə)nt/ *adj* onnipresente

on /ɒn/ **1** *prep* su; (on horizontal surface) su, sopra; **on Monday** lunedì; **on Mondays** di lunedì; **on the first of May** il primo maggio; **on arriving** all'arrivo; **on one's** ⋯⟩

finger nel dito; **on foot** a piedi; **on the right/left** a destra/sinistra; **on the Rhine/Thames** sul Reno/Tamigi; **on the radio/television** alla radio/televisione; **on the bus/train** in autobus/treno; **go on the bus/train** andare in autobus/treno; **get on the bus/train** salire sull'autobus/sul treno; **on me** (with me) con me; **it's on me** fam tocca a me

2️⃣ *adv* (further on) dopo; (switched on) acceso; ⟨*brake*⟩ inserito; (in operation) in funzione; **'on'** (on machine) 'on'; **he had his hat/coat on** portava il cappello/cappotto; **without his hat/coat on** senza cappello/capotto; **with/without the lid on** con/senza coperchio; **be on** ⟨*film, programme, event*⟩ esserci; **it's not on** fam non è giusto; **be on at** fam tormentare (**to** per); **on and on** senza sosta; **on and off** a intervalli; **and so on** e così via; **go on** continuare; **stick on** attaccare; **sew on** cucire

on-board *adj* di bordo

once /wʌns/ 1️⃣ *adv* una volta; (formerly) un tempo; ∼ **upon a time there was** c'era una volta; **at** ∼ subito; (at the same time) contemporaneamente; ∼ **and for all** una volta per tutte
2️⃣ *conj* [non] appena

once-over *n* fam **give somebody/something the** ∼ (look, check) dare un'occhiata veloce a qualcuno/qualcosa

oncoming /'ɒnkʌmɪŋ/ *adj* che si avvicina dalla direzione opposta

one /wʌn/ 1️⃣ *adj* uno, una; **not** ∼ **person** nemmeno una persona
2️⃣ *n* uno *m*
3️⃣ *pron* uno; (impersonal) si; ∼ **another** l'un l'altro; ∼ **by** ∼ [a] uno a uno; ∼ **never knows** non si sa mai

one-armed bandit /wʌnɑːmd'bændɪt/ *n* slot-machine *f inv*

one-dimensional /-daɪ'menʃənəl/ *adj* unidimensionale; **be** ∼ fig ⟨*character*⟩ mancare di spessore

one-eyed /-'aɪd/ *adj* con un occhio solo

one-for-one *adj* = ONE-TO-ONE

one-handed /-'hændɪd/ *adv* ⟨*catch, hold*⟩ con una sola mano

one-horse town *n* fam cittadina *f* di provincia

one-legged /-'legɪd/ *adj* con una sola gamba

one-liner *n* battuta *f* d'effetto

one-man *adj* ⟨*bobsled*⟩ monoposto *inv*; ⟨*for one person*⟩; per una sola persona; **she's a** ∼ **woman** è una donna fedele; **it's a** ∼ **outfit/operation** manda avanti tutto da solo

one-man band *n* musicista *m* che suona più strumenti contemporaneamente; **be a** ∼ fig mandare avanti tutto da solo

one-off *adj* Br ⟨*experiment, order, deal*⟩ unico e irripetibile; ⟨*event, decision, offer, payment*⟩ eccezionale; ⟨*example, design*⟩ unico; ⟨*issue, magazine*⟩ speciale

one-parent family *n* famiglia *f* con un solo genitore

one-piece *adj* ∼ **swimsuit** costume intero

one-room flat, one-room apartment *n* monolocale *m*

one's /wʌnz/ *poss* **one has to look after** ∼ **health** ci si deve preoccupare della propria salute

oneself /wʌn'self/ *pron* (reflexive) si; (emphatic) sé, se stesso; **by** ∼ da solo; **be proud of** ∼ essere fieri di sé

one-shot *adj* Am = ONE-OFF

one-sided /-'saɪdɪd/ *adj* unilaterale

one-time *adj* ex *inv*

one-to-one *adj* ⟨*personal relationship*⟩ fra due persone; ⟨*private lesson*⟩ individuale; ⟨*correspondence*⟩ di uno a uno

one-upmanship /-'ʌpmənʃɪp/ *n* arte *f* di primeggiare

one-way *adj* ⟨*street*⟩ a senso unico; ⟨*ticket*⟩ di sola andata

one-woman *adj* **it's a** ∼ **outfit** manda avanti tutto da sola; **he's a** ∼ **man** è un uomo fedele

ongoing /'ɒngəʊɪŋ/ *adj* ⟨*process*⟩ continuo; ⟨*battle, saga*⟩ in corso

onion /'ʌnjən/ *n* cipolla *f*

on-line *adj* Comput in linea, on-line *inv*: **go** ∼ **to...** connettersi a...; ∼ **time** durata *f* del collegamento

onlooker /'ɒnlʊkə(r)/ *n* spettatore, -trice *mf*

only /'əʊnlɪ/ 1️⃣ *adj* solo; ∼ **child** figlio, -a *mf* unico, -a
2️⃣ *adv & conj* solo, solamente; ∼ **just** appena

on-message *adj* Pol **be** ∼ essere in linea con la politica del governo

o.n.o. Br *abbr* (**or nearest offer**) trattabile

on-off *adj* ⟨*button, control*⟩ di accensione

onrush /'ɒnrʌʃ/ *n* (of people, water) ondata *f*

on-screen *adj* sullo schermo

onset /'ɒnset/ *n* (beginning) inizio *m*

onshore /'ɒnʃɔː(r)/ *adj* ⟨*wind*⟩ di mare; ⟨*work*⟩ a terra

onside /ɒn'saɪd/ *adj & adv* Sport non in fuorigioco

on-site *adj* sul posto

onslaught /'ɒnslɔːt/ *n* attacco *m*

on-stage *adj & adv* in scena

on-target earnings *npl* guadagni *mpl* previsti incluse commissioni

on-the-job *adj* ⟨training⟩ in sede

on-the-spot *adj* ⟨advice, quotation⟩ immediato

onto /'ɒntu:/ *prep* (also **on to**) su

onus /'əʊnəs/ *n* the ~ **is on me** spetta a me la responsabilità (**to** di)

onward[s] /'ɒnwəd[z]/ *adv* in avanti; **from then** ~ da allora [in poi]

oodles /'u:dlz/ *n* fam un sacco

ooh /u:/ *int* oh!

oomph /u:mf/ *n* fam verve *f inv*

oops /u:ps/ *int* ops!

ooze /u:z/ *vi* fluire

op /ɒp/ *n* = OPERATION

opal /'əʊpl/ *n* opale *f*

opaque /əɪ'peɪk/ *adj* opaco

Opec, OPEC /'əʊpek/ *n abbr* (**Organization of petroleum Exporting Countries**) OPEC *f*

open /'əʊpən/ **1** *adj* aperto; (free to all) pubblico; ⟨job⟩ vacante; **in the** ~ **air** all'aperto

2 *n* **in the** ~ all'aperto; fig alla luce del sole

3 *vt* aprire

4 *vi* aprirsi; ⟨shop⟩ aprire; ⟨flower⟩ sbocciare

■ **open onto** *vt* ⟨door, window;⟩ dare su

■ **open out 1** *vi* ⟨road⟩ allargarsi; ⟨flower⟩ aprisi

2 *vt* aprire ⟨map, newspaper⟩

■ **open up 1** *vt* aprire

2 *vi* aprirsi

■ **open with** *vi* (start with) iniziare con

open-air *adj* ⟨pool, market, stage⟩ all'aperto

opencast mining *n* Br miniera *f* a cielo aperto

open competition *n* concorso *m*

open day *n* giorno *m* di apertura al pubblico

open-ended /-'endɪd/ *adj* ⟨relationship, question, contract⟩ aperto; ⟨stay⟩ a tempo indeterminato; ⟨period⟩ indeterminato; ⟨strategy⟩ flessibile

opener /'əʊpənə(r)/ *n* (for tins) apriscatole *m inv*; (for bottles) apribottiglie *m inv*

open government *n* politica *f* di trasparenza

open-handed /-'hændɪd/ *adj* generoso

open-heart surgery *n* intervento *m* a cuore aperto

open house *n* (Am: open day) giornata *f* di apertura al pubblico; **it's always** ~ ~ **at the Batemans'** i Bateman sono sempre molto ospitali

opening /'əʊpənɪŋ/ *n* apertura *f*; (beginning) inizio *m*; (job) posto *m* libero

opening balance *n* Fin saldo *m* iniziale

opening ceremony *n* cerimonia *f* inaugurale

opening hours *npl* orario *m* d'apertura

open learning *n* open learning *m inv*

openly /'əʊpənlɪ/ *adv* apertamente

open market *n* Econ mercato *m* aperto

open minded /-'maɪndɪd/ *adj* aperto; (broad-minded) di vedute larghe

open-mouthed /-'maʊðd/ *adj* bocca aperta

open-necked /-'nekt/ *adj* ⟨shirt⟩ col colletto sbottonato

openness /'əʊpənnɪs/ *n* (of government, atmosphere) trasparenza *f*: (candour) franchezza *f*; (receptiveness) apertura *f* mentale

open-plan *adj* a pianta aperta

open sandwich *n* tartina *f*

open scholarship *n* Univ borsa *f* di studio assegnata per concorso

open season *n* (in hunting) stagione *f* della caccia

open secret *n* segreto *m* di Pulcinella

open ticket *n* biglietto *m* aperto

Open University *n* Br Univ corsi *mpl* universitari per corrispondenza

open verdict *n* Jur verdetto *m* che dichiara non accertabili le cause della morte

opera /'ɒpərə/ *n* opera *f*

operable /'ɒpərəbl/ *adj* operabile

opera glasses *npl* binocolo *msg* da teatro

opera house *n* teatro *m* lirico

opera singer *n* cantante *mf* lirico, -a

operate /'ɒpəreɪt/ **1** *vt* far funzionare ⟨machine, lift⟩; azionare ⟨lever, brake⟩; mandare avanti ⟨business⟩

2 *vi* Techn funzionare; (be in action) essere in funzione; Mil, fig operare

■ **operate on** *vt* Med operare

operatic /ɒpə'rætɪk/ *adj* lirico, operistico

operating costs /'ɒpəreɪtɪŋ/ *npl* spese *fpl* di esercizio

operating instructions *npl* istruzioni *fpl* per l'uso

operating room *n* Am sala *f* operatoria

operating system *n* Comput sistema *m* operativo

operating table *n* Med tavolo *m* operatorio

operating theatre *n* Br sala *f* operatoria

operation /ɒpə'reɪʃn/ *n* operazione *f*; Tech funzionamento *m*: **in** ~ Techn in funzione; **come into** ~ fig entrare in funzione; ⟨law⟩ entrare in vigore; **have an** ~ Med subire un'operazione

operational /ˌɒpəˈreɪʃənəl/ *adj* operativo; ‹*law etc*› in vigore

operations room *n* Mil centro *m* operativo; (police) centrale *f* operativa

operative /ˈɒpərətɪv/ *adj* operativo

operator /ˈɒpəreɪtə(r)/ *n* (user) operatore, -trice *mf*; Teleph centralinista *mf*

operetta /ɒpəˈretə/ *n* operetta *f*

ophthalmic /ɒfˈθælmɪk/ *adj* oftalmico

opinion /əˈpɪnjən/ *n* opinione *f*; **in my ~** secondo me

opinionated /əˈpɪnɪəneɪtɪd/ *adj* dogmatico

opinion poll *n* sondaggio *m* di opinione

opium /ˈəʊpɪəm/ *n* oppio *m*

opponent /əˈpəʊnənt/ *n* avversario, -a *mf*

opportune /ˈɒpətjuːn/ *adj* opportuno

opportunist /ɒpəˈtjuːnɪst/ *n* opportunista *mf*

opportunistic /ɒpətjʊˈnɪstɪk/ *adj* opportunistico

opportunity /ɒpəˈtjuːnətɪ/ *n* opportunità *f inv*

oppose /əˈpəʊz/ *vt* opporsi a; **be ~d to something** essere contrario a qualcosa; **as ~d to** al contrario di

opposing /əˈpəʊzɪŋ/ *adj* avversario; (opposite) opposto

opposite /ˈɒpəzɪt/ **①** *adj* opposto; ‹*house*› di fronte; **~ number** fig controparte *f*; **the ~ sex** l'altro sesso **②** *n* contrario *m* **③** *adv* di fronte **④** *prep* di fronte a

opposition /ɒpəˈzɪʃn/ *n* opposizione *f*

oppress /əˈpres/ *vt* opprimere

oppression /əˈpreʃn/ *n* oppressione *f*

oppressive /əˈpresɪv/ *adj* oppressivo; ‹*heat*› opprimente

oppressor /əˈpresə(r)/ *n* oppressore *m*

opt /ɒpt/ *v*
■ **opt for** *vt* optare per
■ **opt out** *vi* dissociarsi (**of** da)

optic /ˈɒptɪk/ *adj* ‹*nerve, disc, fibre*› ottico

optical /ˈɒptɪkl/ *adj* ottico; **~ illusion** illusione *f* ottica

optician /ɒpˈtɪʃn/ *n* ottico, -a *mf*

optics /ˈɒptɪks/ *n* ottica *f*

optimism /ˈɒptɪmɪzm/ *n* ottimismo *m*

optimist /ˈɒptɪmɪst/ *n* ottimista *mf*

optimistic /ɒptɪˈmɪstɪk/ *adj* ottimistico

optimistically /ɒptɪˈmɪstɪklɪ/ *adv* ottimisticamente

optimize /ˈɒptɪmaɪz/ *vt* ottimizzare

optimum /ˈɒptɪməm/ **①** *adj* ottimale **②** *n* (pl **-ima**) optimum *m*

option /ˈɒpʃn/ *n* scelta *f*; Comm opzione *f*

optional /ˈɒpʃənəl/ *adj* facoltativo; **~ extras** optional *m inv*

opulence /ˈɒpjʊləns/ *n* opulenza *f*

opulent /ˈɒpjʊlənt/ *adj* opulento

opus /ˈəʊpəs/ *n* (pl **opuses** or **opera**) opera *f*

or /ɔː(r)/ *conj* o, oppure; (after negative) né; **or [else]** se no; **in a year or two** fra un anno o due

oracle /ˈɒrəkl/ *n* oracolo *m*

oral /ˈɔːrəl/ **①** *adj* orale **②** *n* fam esame *m* orale

orally /ˈɔːrəlɪ/ *adv* oralmente

orange /ˈɒrɪndʒ/ **①** *n* arancia *f*; (colour) arancione *m* **②** *adj* arancione

orangeade /ɒrɪndʒˈeɪd/ *n* aranciata *f*

orange blossom *n* fiori *mpl* d'arancio

orange juice *n* succo *m* d'arancia

orange peel *n* scorza *f* d'arancia

orange squash *n* Br succo *m* d'arancia (diluito in acqua)

orange tree *n* arancio *m*

oration /əˈreɪʃn/ *n* orazione *f*

orator /ˈɒrətə(r)/ *n* oratore, -trice *mf*

oratorio /ɒrəˈtɔːrɪəʊ/ *n* oratorio *m*

oratory /ˈɒrətrɪ/ *n* oratorio *m*

orbit /ˈɔːbɪt/ **①** *n* orbita *f* **②** *vt* orbitare

orbital /ˈɔːbɪtl/ *adj* **~ road** tangenziale *f*

orchard /ˈɔːtʃəd/ *n* frutteto *m*

orchestra /ˈɔːkɪstrə/ *n* orchestra *f*

orchestral /ɔːˈkestrəl/ *adj* orchestrale

orchestra pit *n* [fossa *f* dell']orchestra *f*

orchestrate /ˈɔːkɪstreɪt/ *vt* orchestrare

orchid /ˈɔːkɪd/ *n* orchidea *f*

ordain /ɔːˈdeɪn/ *vt* decretare; Relig ordinare

ordeal /ɔːˈdiːl/ *n* fig terribile esperienza *f*

order /ˈɔːdə(r)/ **①** *n* ordine *m*; Comm ordinazione *f*; **out of ~** ‹*machine*› fuori servizio; **in ~ that** affinché; **in ~ to** per; **take holy ~s** prendere i voti **②** *vt* ordinare
■ **order about**, **order around** *vt* (give orders to) impartire ordini a

order book *n* registro *m* degli ordini

order form *n* modulo *m* di ordinazione

orderly /ˈɔːdəlɪ/ **①** *adj* ordinato **②** *n* Mil attendente *m*; Med inserviente *m*

orderly officer *n* Mil attendente *m*

order number *n* numero *m* d'ordine

ordinal /ˈɔːdɪnəl/ *n* & *adj* ordinale *m*

ordinarily /ɔːdɪˈnerɪlɪ/ *adv* (normally) normalmente

ordinary /ˈɔːdɪnərɪ/ *adj* ordinario

ordination /ɔːdɪˈneɪʃn/ *n* Relig ordinazione *f*

ordnance /'ɔ:dnəns/ n Mil materiale m militare

Ordnance Survey n Br istituto m cartografico; ~ ~ **Map** carta f topografica dell'istituto cartografico

ore /ɔ:(r)/ n minerale m grezzo

oregano /ɒrɪ'gɑ:nəʊ/ n origano m

organ /'ɔ:gən/ n Anat Mus organo m

organ donor n Med donatore, -trice mf di organi

organic /ɔ:'gænɪk/ adj organico; (without chemicals) biologico

organically /ɔ:'gænɪklɪ/ adv organicamente; ~ **grown** coltivato biologicamente

organic chemistry n chimica f organica

organic farm n azienda f agricola specializzata in prodotti biologici

organic farming n agricoltura f biologica

organism /'ɔ:gənɪzm/ n organismo m

organist /'ɔ:gənɪst/ n organista mf

organization /ɔ:gənaɪ'zeɪʃn/ n organizzazione f

organizational /ɔ:gənaɪ'zeɪʃənəl/ adj ⟨ability, role⟩ organizzativo

organize /'ɔ:gənaɪz/ vt organizzare

organized crime /ɔ:gənaɪzd'kraɪm/ n criminalità f organizzata

organized labour n manodopera f organizzata

organizer /'ɔ:gənaɪzə(r)/ n organizzatore, -trice mf

organ transplant n Med trapianto m di organi

orgasm /'ɔ:gæzm/ n orgasmo m

orgy /'ɔ:dʒɪ/ n orgia f

Orient /'ɔ:rɪənt/ n Oriente m

oriental /ɔ:rɪ'entl/ **1** adj orientale; ~ **carpet** tappeto m persiano **2** n orientale mf

orientate /'ɔ:rɪənteɪt/ vt ~ **oneself** orientarsi

orientation /ɔ:rɪən'teɪʃn/ n orientamento m

orienteering /ɔ:rɪen'tɪərɪŋ/ n orientamento m

orifice /'ɒrɪfɪs/ n orifizio m

origin /'ɒrɪdʒɪn/ n origine f

original /ə'rɪdʒɪnl/ **1** adj originario; (not copied, new) originale **2** n originale m; **in the** ~ in versione originale

originality /ərɪdʒɪ'nælətɪ/ n originalità f

originally /ə'rɪdʒɪnəlɪ/ adv originariamente

originate /ə'rɪdʒɪneɪt/ vi ~ **in** avere origine in

originator /ə'rɪdʒɪneɪtə(r)/ n ideatore, -trice mf

Orkney /'ɔ:knɪ/ n (also Orkney Islands) Orcadi fpl

ornament /'ɔ:nəmənt/ n ornamento m; (on mantelpiece etc) soprammobile m

ornamental /ɔ:nə'mentl/ adj ornamentale

ornamentation /ɔ:nəmen'teɪʃn/ n decorazione f

ornate /ɔ:'neɪt/ adj ornato

ornithologist /ɔ:nɪ'θɒlədʒɪst/ n ornitologo, -a mf

ornithology /ɔ:nɪ'θɒlədʒɪ/ n ornitologia f

orphan /'ɔ:fn/ **1** n orfano, -a mf **2** vt rendere orfano; **be** ~**ed** rimanere orfano; **be** ~**ed by...** essere reso orfano da...

orphanage /'ɔ:fənɪdʒ/ n orfanotrofio m

orphaned /'ɔ:fənd/ adj rimasto orfano

orthodox /'ɔ:θədɒks/ adj ortodosso

orthopaedic /ɔɪθə'piːdɪk/ adj ortopedico

orthopaedics /ɔ:θə'piːdɪks/ n ortopedia f

OS abbr (**outsize**) per taglie forti

oscillate /'ɒsɪleɪt/ vi oscillare

osmosis /ɒz'məʊsɪs/ n osmosi f inv; **by** ~ per osmosi

ostensible /ɒ'stensəbl/ adj apparente

ostensibly /ɒ'stensəblɪ/ adv apparentemente

ostentation /ɒsten'teɪʃn/ n ostentazione f

ostentatious /ɒsten'teɪʃəs/ adj ostentato

ostentatiously /ɒsten'teɪʃəslɪ/ adv ostentatamente

osteopath /'ɒstɪəpæθ/ n osteopata mf

osteoporosis /ɒstɪəpə'rəʊsɪs/ n osteoporosi f

ostracism /'ɒstrəsɪzm/ n ostracismo m

ostracize /'ɒstrəsaɪz/ vt ostracizzare

ostrich /'ɒstrɪtʃ/ n struzzo m

OTE abbr (**on-target earnings**) guadagni mpl previsti incluse commissioni

other /'ʌðə(r)/ **1** adj, pron & n altro, -a mf; **the** ~ [**one**] l'altro, -a mf; **the** ~ **two** gli altri due; **two** ~**s** altri due; ~ **people** gli altri; **any** ~ **questions?** altre domande?; **every** ~ **day** (alternate days) a giorni alterni; **the** ~ **day** l'altro giorno; **the** ~ **evening** l'altra sera; **someone/ something or** ~ qualcuno/qualcosa **2** adv ~ **than him** tranne lui; **somehow or** ~ in qualche modo; **somewhere or** ~ da qualche parte

otherwise /'ʌðəwaɪz/ adv altrimenti; (differently) diversamente

other-worldly /ʌðə'wɜːldlɪ/ *adj* disinteressato alle cose materiali

OTT *abbr fam* (**over-the-top**) esagerato

otter /'ɒtə(r)/ *n* lontra *f*

OU *n* Br *abbr* (**Open University**) corsi *mpl* universitari per corrispondenza

ouch /aʊtʃ/ *int* ahi!

ought /ɔːt/ *v aux* I/we ~ **to stay** dovrei/dovremmo rimanere; **he** ~ **not to have done it** non avrebbe dovuto farlo; **that** ~ **to be enough** questo dovrebbe bastare

ounce /aʊns/ *n* oncia *f* (= 28,35 g)

our /'aʊə(r)/ *poss adj* il nostro *m*, la nostra *f*, i nostri *mpl*, le nostre *fpl*; ~ **mother/father** nostra madre/nostro padre

ours /'aʊəz/ *poss pron* il nostro *m*, la nostra *f*, i nostri *mpl*, le nostre *fpl*; **a friend of** ~ un nostro amico; **friends of** ~ dei nostri amici; **that is** ~ quello è nostro; (as opposed to yours) quello è il nostro

ourselves /aʊə'selvz/ *pers pron* (reflexive) ci; (emphatic) noi, noi stessi; **we poured** ~ **a drink** ci siamo versati da bere; **we heard it** ~ l'abbiamo sentito noi stessi; **we are proud of** ~ siamo fieri di noi; **by** ~ da soli

oust /aʊst/ *vt* rimuovere

out /aʊt/ ➀ *adv* fuori; (not alight) spento; **be** ~ ⟨flower⟩ essere sbocciato; ⟨workers⟩ essere in sciopero; ⟨calculation⟩ essere sbagliato; Sport essere fuori; (unconscious) aver perso i sensi; (fig: not feasible) essere fuori questione; **the sun is** ~ è uscito il sole; ~ **and about** in piedi; **get** ~! fam fuori!; **you should get** ~ **more** dovresti uscire più spesso; ~ **with it!** fam sputa il rospo!; **be** ~ **to have the intenzione di**; ➁ *prep* ~ **of** fuori da; ~ **of date** non aggiornato; ⟨passport⟩ scaduto; ~ **of order** guasto; ~ **of print/stock** esaurito; ~ **of sorts** indisposto; ~ **of tune** (singer) stonato; (instrument) scordato; **be** ~ **of bed/the room** fuori dal letto/dalla stanza; ~ **of breath** senza fiato; ~ **of danger** fuori pericolo; ~ **of work** disoccupato; **nine** ~ **of ten** nove su dieci; **be** ~ **of sugar/bread** rimanere senza zucchero/pane; **go** ~ **of the room** uscire dalla stanza

out-and-out *adj* ⟨success, failure⟩ totale; ⟨villain, liar⟩ vero e proprio

outback /'aʊtbæk/ *n* entroterra *m inv* australiano

outbid /aʊt'bɪd/ *vt* (pt/pp -**bid**. pres p -**bidding**) ~ **somebody** rilanciare l'offerta di qualcuno

outboard /'aʊtbɔːd/ *adj* ~ **motor** fuoribordo *m inv*

outbreak /'aʊtbreɪk/ *n* (of war) scoppio *m*; (of disease) insorgenza *f*

outbuilding /'aʊtbɪldɪŋ/ *n* costruzione *f* annessa

outburst /'aʊtbɜːst/ *n* esplosione *f*

outcast /'aʊtkɑːst/ *n* esule *mf*; (social) escluso *m*

outclass /aʊt'klɑːs/ *vt* surclassare

outcome /'aʊtkʌm/ *n* risultato *m*

outcrop /'aʊtkrɒp/ *n* affioramento *m*

outcry /'aʊtkraɪ/ *n* protesta *f*

outdated /aʊt'deɪtɪd/ *adj* sorpassato

outdo /aʊt'duː/ *vt* (pt -**did**, pp -**done**) superare

outdoor /'aʊtdɔː(r)/ *adj* ⟨life, sports⟩ all'aperto; ~ **swimming pool** piscina *f* scoperta

outdoors /aʊt'dɔːz/ *adv* all'aria aperta; **go** ~ uscire all'aria aperta

outer /'aʊtə(r)/ *adj* esterno

outer space *n* spazio *m* cosmico

outfit /'aʊtfɪt/ *n* equipaggiamento *m*; (clothes) completo *m*; (fam: organization) organizzazione *f*

outfitter /'aʊtfɪtə(r)/ *n* **men's** ~ **'s** negozio *m* di abbigliamento maschile

outflow /'aʊtfləʊ/ *n* (of money) uscite *fpl*

outgoing /'aʊtgəʊɪŋ/ ➀ *adj* (president) uscente; ⟨mail⟩ in partenza; (sociable) estroverso ➁ *npl* ~**s** uscite *fpl*

outgrow /aʊt'grəʊ/ *vi* (pt -**grew**, pp -**grown**) diventare troppo grande per

outhouse /'aʊthaʊs/ *n* costruzione *f* annessa

outing /'aʊtɪŋ/ *n* gita *f*

outlandish /aʊt'lændɪʃ/ *adj* stravagante

outlast /aʊt'lɑːst/ *vt* durare più a lungo di

outlaw /'aʊtlɔː/ ➀ *n* fuorilegge *mf inv* ➁ *vt* dichiarare illegale

outlay /'aʊtleɪ/ *n* spesa *f*

outlet /'aʊtlet/ *n* sbocco *m*; fig sfogo *m*; Comm punto *m* [di] vendita

outline /'aʊtlaɪn/ ➀ *n* contorno *m*; (summary) sommario *m* ➁ *vt* tracciare il contorno di; (describe) descrivere

outline agreement *n* abbozzo *m* di accordo

outlive /aʊt'lɪv/ *vt* sopravvivere a

outlook /'aʊtlʊk/ *n* vista *f*; (future prospect) prospettiva *f*; (attitude) visione *f*

outlying /'aʊtlaɪɪŋ/ *adj* ~ **areas** zone *fpl* periferiche

outmanoeuvre /aʊtmə'nuːvə(r)/ *vt* ~ **somebody** passare in vantaggio su qualcuno con un'abile manovra

outmoded /aʊt'məʊdɪd/ *adj* fuori moda

outnumber /aʊt'nʌmbə(r)/ *vt* superare in numero

out-of-body experience *n* esperienza *f* extracorporea

out of bounds *adj & adv* ⟨area⟩ vietato l'accesso

out-of-date *adj* ⟨*theory, concept*⟩ sorpassato; ⟨*ticket, passport*⟩ scaduto

out-of-pocket *adj* **be out of pocket** essere in perdita; **~ expenses** spese *fpl* extra

out-of-the-way *adj* ⟨*places*⟩ fuori mano

outpatient /ˈaʊtpeɪʃnt/ *n* paziente *mf* esterno, -a; **~s' department** ambulatorio *m*

outpost /ˈaʊtpəʊst/ *n* avamposto *m*

output /ˈaʊtpʊt/ *n* produzione *f*

outrage /ˈaʊtreɪdʒ/ **1** *n* oltraggio *m* **2** *vt* oltraggiare

outrageous /aʊtˈreɪdʒəs/ *adj* oltraggioso; ⟨*price*⟩ scandaloso

outrider /ˈaʊtraɪdə(r)/ *n* battistrada *m inv*

outright[1] /ˈaʊtraɪt/ *adj* completo; ⟨*refusal*⟩ netto

outright[2] /aʊtˈraɪt/ *adv* completamente; (at once) immediatamente; (frankly) francamente

outrun /aʊtˈrʌn/ *vt* superare

outsell /aʊtˈsel/ *vt* vendere meglio di ⟨*product*⟩

outset /ˈaʊtset/ *n* inizio *m*; **from the ~** fin dall'inizio

outside[1] /ˈaʊtsaɪd/ **1** *adj* esterno **2** *n* esterno *m*; **from the ~** dall'esterno; **at the ~** al massimo

outside[2] /aʊtˈsaɪd/ **1** *adv* all'esterno, fuori; (out of doors) fuori; **go ~** andare fuori **2** *prep* fuori da; (in front of) davanti a

outsider /aʊtˈsaɪdə(r)/ *n* estraneo, -a *mf*

outsize /ˈaʊtsaɪz/ *adj* smisurato; ⟨*clothes*⟩ per taglie forti

outskirts /ˈaʊtskɜːts/ *npl* sobborghi *mpl*

outsmart /aʊtˈsmɑːt/ *vt* essere più furbo di

outsource /ˈaʊtsɔːs/ *vt* appaltare a imprese esterne

outsourcing /ˈaʊtsɔːsɪŋ/ *n* appalto *m* a imprese esterne

outspoken /aʊtˈspəʊkn/ *adj* schietto

outspread /ˈaʊtspred/ *adj* ⟨*wings*⟩ spiegato; ⟨*arms, fingers*⟩ disteso

outstanding /aʊtˈstændɪŋ/ *adj* eccezionale; ⟨*landmark*⟩ prominente; (not settled) in sospeso

outstandingly /aʊtˈstændɪŋlɪ/ *adv* eccezionalmente; **~ good** eccezionale

outstay /aʊtˈsteɪ/ *vt* **~ one's s welcome** abusare dell'ospitalità di qualcuno

outstretched /ˈaʊtstretʃt/ *adj* allungato

outstrip /aʊtˈstrɪp/ *vt* (pt/pp **-stripped**) superare

out-tray *n* vassoio *m* per corrispondenza e pratiche evase

outvote /aʊtˈvəɪt/ *vt* mettere in minoranza

outward /ˈaʊtwəd/ **1** *adj* esterno; (journey) di andata **2** *adv* verso l'esterno

outwardly /ˈaʊtwədlɪ/ *adv* esternamente

outwards /ˈaʊtwədz/ *adv* verso l'esterno

outweigh /aʊtˈweɪ/ *vt* aver maggior peso di

outwit /aʊtˈwɪt/ *vt* (pt/pp **-witted**) battere in astuzia

outworker /ˈaʊtwɜːkə(r)/ *n* Br lavoratore, -trice *mf* a domicilio

outworn /aʊtˈwɔːn/ *adj* ⟨*outmoded*⟩ sorpassato

oval /ˈəʊvl/ **1** *adj* ovale **2** *n* ovale *m*

ovary /ˈəʊvərɪ/ *n* Anat ovaia *f*

ovation /əʊˈveɪʃn/ *n* ovazione *f*

oven /ˈʌvn/ *n* forno *m*

oven cleaner *n* detergente *m* per il forno

oven glove *n* guanto *m* da forno

ovenproof *adj* da forno

oven-ready *adj* pronto da mettere in forno

over /ˈəʊvə(r)/ **1** *prep* sopra; (across) al di là di; (during) durante; (more than) più di; **~ the phone** al telefono; **~ the page** alla pagina seguente; **all ~ Italy** in tutta [l']Italia; ⟨*travel*⟩ per l'Italia **2** *adv* Math col resto di; (ended) finito; **~ again** un'altra volta; **~ and ~** più volte; **~ and above** oltre a; **~ here/there** qui/là; **all ~** (everywhere) dappertutto; **it's all ~** è tutto finito; **I ache all ~** ho male dappertutto; **come/bring ~** venire/ portare; **turn ~** girare

over+ *pref* (too) troppo

overact /əʊvərˈækt/ *vi* strafare

overactive /əʊvərˈæktɪv/ *adj* ⟨*imagination*⟩ sbrigliato

overall[1] /ˈəʊvərɔːl/ *n* grembiule *m*

overall[2] /əʊvərˈɔːl/ **1** *adj* complessivo; (general) generale **2** *adv* complessivamente

overalls /ˈəʊvərɔːlz/ *npl* tuta *fsg* [da lavoro]

overarm /ˈəʊɪvərɑːm/ *adj & adv* ⟨*throw*⟩ col braccio al di sopra della spalla

overawe /əʊvərˈɔː/ *vt* fig intimidire

overbalance /əʊvəˈbæləns/ *vi* perdere l'equilibrio

overbearing /əʊvəˈbeərɪŋ/ *adj* prepotente

overblown /əʊvəˈbləʊn/ *adj* ⟨*style*⟩ ampolloso

overboard /ˈəʊvəbɔːd/ *adv* Naut in mare

overbook /əʊvəˈbʊk/ *vt* accettare un numero di prenotazioni superiore ai posti disponibili

overburden /əʊvə'bɜːdən/ vt
sovraccaricare (**with** di)

overcapacity /əʊvəkə'pæsətɪ/ n
eccesso m di capacità produttiva

overcast /'əʊvəkɑːst/ adj coperto

overcharge /əʊvə'tʃɑːdʒ/ **1** vt ~
somebody far pagare più del dovuto a
2 vi far pagare più del dovuto

overcoat /'əʊvəkəʊt/ n cappotto m

overcome /əʊvə'kʌm/ vt (pt **-came**, pp
-come) vincere; **be** ~ **by** essere
sopraffatto da

overcompensate /əʊvə'kɒmpənseɪt/
vi compensare eccessivamente

overconfident /əʊvə'kɒnfɪdənt/ adj
troppo sicuro di sé

overcook /əʊvə'kʊk/ vt cuocere troppo

overcrowded /əʊvə'kraʊdɪd/ adj
sovraffollato

overcrowding /əʊvə'kraʊdɪŋ/ n (in
transport) calca f; (in city, institution)
sovraffollamento m

overdo /əʊvə'duː/ vt (pt **-did**, pp **-done**)
esagerare; (cook too long) stracuocere; ~ **it**
(fam: do too much) strafare

overdose /'əʊvədəʊs/ n overdose f inv

overdraft /'əʊvədrɑːft/ n scoperto m;
have an ~ avere il conto scoperto

overdraw /əʊvə'drɔː/ vt (pt **-drew**, pp
-drawn) ~ **one's account** andare allo
scoperto; **be** ~**n by...** ⟨account⟩ essere
scoperto di...

overdressed /əʊvə'drest/ adj troppo
elegante

overdrive /'əʊvədraɪv/ n Auto overdrive
m inv

overdue /əʊvə'djuː/ adj in ritardo

overeat /əʊvər'iːt/ vi mangiare troppo

overemphasize /əʊvər'emfəsaɪz/ vt
esagerare ⟨importance⟩; dare troppo
rilievo a ⟨aspect, fact⟩

overenthusiastic
/əʊvərɪnθjuːzɪ'æstɪk/ adj troppo
entusiasta

overestimate /əʊvər'estɪmeɪt/ vt
sopravvalutare

overexcited /əʊvərɪk'saɪtɪd/ adj
sovreccitato; **get** ~ sovreccitarsi

overexert /əʊvərɪg'zɜːt/ vt ~ **oneself**
sovraffaticarsi

overexposure /əʊvərek'spəʊʒə(r)/ n
Phot sovresposizione f; (in the media)
attenzione f eccessiva da parte dei media

overfeed /əʊvə'fiːd/ vt sovralimentare
⟨child, pet⟩; concimare troppo ⟨plant⟩

overflow[1] /'əʊvəfləʊ/ n (water) acqua f
che deborda; (people) pubblico m in
eccesso; (outlet) scarico m

overflow[2] /əʊvə'fləʊ/ vi debordare

overgenerous /əʊvə'dʒenərəs/ adj
⟨amount⟩ troppo generoso

overgrown /əʊvə'grəʊn/ adj ⟨garden⟩
coperto di erbacce

overhang[1] /'əʊvəhæŋ/ n sporgenza f

overhang[2] /əʊvə'hæŋ/ **1** vi (pt/pp
-hung) sporgere
2 vt sovrastare

overhanging /əʊvə'hæŋɪŋ/ adj ⟨ledge,
cliff⟩ sporgente

overhaul[1] /'əʊvəhɔːl/ n revisione f

overhaul[2] /əʊvə'hɔːl/ vt Techn
revisionare

overhead[1] /əʊvə'hed/ adv in alto

overhead[2] /'əʊvəhed/ **1** adj aereo;
⟨railway⟩ sopraelevato; ⟨lights⟩ da soffitto
2 npl ~**s** spese fpl generali

overhead light n lampada f da soffitto

overhead locker n Aeron armadietto m
[per il bagaglio a mano]

overhead projector n lavagna f
luminosa

overhear /əʊvə'hɪə(r)/ vt (pt/pp **-heard**)
sentire per caso ⟨conversation⟩; **I** ~**d him
saying it** l'ho sentito per caso mentre lo
diceva

overheat /əʊvə'hiːt/ **1** vi Auto
surriscaldarsi
2 vt surriscaldare

over-indulge **1** vi eccedere
2 vt viziare ⟨child⟩

over-indulgence n (excess) eccesso m;
(laxity towards) indulgenza f eccessiva

overjoyed /əʊvə'dʒɔɪd/ adj felicissimo

overkill /'əʊvəkɪl/ n (exaggerated treatment)
esagerazione f

overland /'əʊvəlænd/ adj & adv via
terra; ~ **route** via f terrestre

overlap /əʊvə'læp/ **1** vi (pt/pp **-lapped**)
sovrapporsi
2 vt sovrapporre

overlay /əʊvə'leɪ/ vt ricoprire

overleaf /əʊvə'liːf/ adv sul retro

overload[1] /əʊvə'ləʊd/ vt sovraccaricare

overload[2] /'əʊvələʊd/ n Electr
sovratensioni fpl

overlook /əʊvə'lʊk/ vt dominare; (fail to
see, ignore) lasciarsi sfuggire

overly /'əʊvəlɪ/ adv eccessivamente

overmanned /əʊvə'mænd/ adj con
un'eccedenza di personale

overmanning /əʊvə'mænɪŋ/ n eccesso
m di personale

overmuch /əʊvə'mʌtʃ/ adv troppo

overnight[1] /'əʊvənaɪt/ adj notturno

overnight[2] /əʊvə'naɪt/ vt inviare
tramite sistemi di spedizione notturna
con consegna il mattino seguente ⟨goods⟩

overnight bag n piccola borsa f da
viaggio

overnight stay n sosta f per la notte

overpass /'əʊvəpɑːs/ n cavalcavia m inv

overpay ···⟩ overvalue ···

overpay /əʊvə'peɪ/ *vt* (pt/pp **-paid**)
strapagare

overplay /əɪvə'pleɪ/ *vt* (exaggerate)
esagerare

overpopulated /əʊvə'pɒpjʊleɪtɪd/ *adj*
sovrappopolato

overpower /əʊvə'paʊə(r)/ *vt* sopraffare

overpowering /əʊvə'paʊərɪŋ/ *adj*
insostenibile

overpriced /əʊvə'praɪst/ *adj* troppo
caro

overproduce /əʊvəprə'dju:s/ *vt*
produrre in eccesso

overqualified /əʊvə'kwɒlɪfaɪd/ *adj*
troppo qualificato

overrate /əʊvə'reɪt/ *vt* sopravvalutare

overrated /əʊvə'reɪtɪd/ *adj*
sopravvalutato

overreach /əʊvə'ri:tʃ/ *vt* ~ oneself
puntare troppo in alto

overreact /əʊvərɪ'ækt/ *vi* avere una
reazione eccessiva

overreaction /əʊvərɪ:'ækʃn/ *n* reazione
f eccessiva

override /əʊvə'raɪd/ *vt* (pt **-rode**, pp
-ridden) passare sopra a

overriding /əʊvə'raɪdɪŋ/ *adj* prevalente

overrule /əʊvə'ru:l/ *vt* annullare
⟨*decision*⟩; we were ~d by the chairman il
direttore ha prevalso su di noi

overrun /əʊvə'rʌn/ *vt* (pt **-ran**, pp **-run**,
pres p **-running**) invadere; oltrepassare
⟨*time*⟩; be ~ with essere invaso da

overseas[1] /əʊvə'si:z/ *adv* oltremare

overseas[2] /'əʊvəsi:z/ *adj* d'oltremare

oversee /əʊvə'si:/ *vt* (pt **-saw**, pp
-seen) sorvegliare

oversell /əʊvə'sel/ *vt* lodare
esageratamente ⟨*idea, plan*⟩

oversensitive /əʊvə'sensɪtɪv/ *adj*
⟨*person*⟩ ipersensibile

oversexed /əʊvə'sekst/ *adj* fam be ~
essere un maniaco/una maniaca del sesso

overshadow /əʊvə'ʃædəʊ/ *vt*
adombrare

overshoot /əʊvə'ʃu:t/ *vt* (pt/pp **-shot**)
oltrepassare

oversight /'əʊvəsaɪt/ *n* disattenzione *f*;
an ~ una svista

oversimplification
/əʊvəsɪmplɪfɪ'keɪʃn/ *n* semplificazione *f*
eccessiva

oversimplified /əʊvə'sɪmplɪfaɪd/ *adj*
semplicistico

oversimplify /əʊvə'sɪmplɪfaɪ/ *vt*
semplificare eccessivamente

oversize[d] /əʊvə'saɪz[d]/ *adj* più
grande del normale

oversleep /əʊvə'sli:p/ *vi* (pt/pp **-slept**)
svegliarsi troppo tardi

overspend /əʊvə'spend/ *vi* spendere
troppo

overspending /əʊvə'spendɪŋ/ *n* spese
fpl eccessive; Fin spese *fpl* superiori al
bilancio di previsione

overspill /'əʊvəspɪl/ **[1]** *n* (excess amount)
eccedenza *f*
[2] *attrib* ~ housing development città *f*
inv satellite; ~ population popolazione *f*
in eccesso

overstaffed /əʊvə'stɑ:ft/ *adj* be ~
avere personale in eccedenza

overstaffing /əʊvə'stɑ:fɪŋ/ *n* eccedenza
f di personale

overstate /əʊvə'steɪt/ *vt* esagerare; its
importance cannot be ~d la sua
importanza non sarà mai sottolineata a
sufficienza; ~ the case esagerare le cose

overstatement /əʊvə'steɪtmənt/ *n*
esagerazione *f*

overstay /əʊvə'steɪ/ *vt* ~ one's time
trattenersi troppo a lungo; ~ one's visa
trattenersi oltre la scadenza del visto

overstep /əʊvə'step/ *vt* (pt/pp
-stepped) ~ the mark oltrepassare ogni
limite

overstretched /əʊvə'stretʃt/ *adj*
⟨*person*⟩ sovraccarico [di lavoro]; ⟨*budget,
resources*⟩ sfruttato fino al limite

oversubscribed /əʊvəsəb'skraɪbd/ *adj*
⟨*share issue*⟩ sottoscritto in eccesso; ⟨*offer,
tickets*⟩ richiesto oltre la disponibilità

overt /əʊ'vɜ:t/ *adj* palese

overtake /əʊvə'teɪk/ *vt/i* (pt **-took**, pp
-taken) sorpassare

overtaking /əʊvə'teɪkɪŋ/ *n* sorpasso *m*;
no ~ divieto di sorpasso

overtax /əʊvə'tæks/ *vt* fig abusare di

over-the-counter *adj* ⟨*medicines*⟩
venduto senza ricetta

over-the-top *adj* fam esagerato; go over
the top esagerare

overthrow[1] /'əʊvəθrəʊ/ *n* Pol
rovesciamento *m*

overthrow[2] /əʊvə'θrəʊ/ *vt* (pt **-threw**,
pp **-thrown**) Pol rovesciare

overtime /'əʊvətaɪm/ **[1]** *n* lavoro
straordinario *m*
[2] *adv* work ~ fare lo straordinario

overtired /əʊvə'taɪəd/ *adj* sovraffaticato

overtly /əʊ'vɜ:tlɪ/ *adv* apertamente

overtone /'əʊvətəʊn/ *n* fig sfumatura *f*

overture /'əʊvətjʊə(r)/ *n* Mus preludio *m*;
~s *pl* fig approccio *msg*; make ~s to
mostrare un atteggiamento di apertura
verso

overturn /əʊvə'tɜ:n/ **[1]** *vt* ribaltare
[2] *vi* ribaltarsi

overvalue /əʊvə'vælju:/ *vt*
sopravvalutare ⟨*currency, property*⟩

o

overview /ˈəʊvəvjuː/ *n* visione *f* d'insieme

overweight /əʊvəˈweɪt/ *adj* sovrappeso

overwhelm /əʊvəˈwelm/ *vt* sommergere (**with** di); (with emotion) confondere

overwhelming /əʊvəˈwelmɪŋ/ *adj* travolgente; ‹*victory, majority*› schiacciante

overwhelmingly /əʊvəˈwelmɪŋlɪ/ *adv* ‹*vote, accept, reject*› con una maggioranza schiacciante; ‹*generous*› straordinariamente

overwork /əʊvəˈwɜːk/ **1** *n* lavoro *m* eccessivo
2 *vt* far lavorare eccessivamente
3 *vi* lavorare eccessivamente

overworked /əʊvəˈwɜːkt/ *adj* affaticato dal troppo lavoro

overwrite /əʊvəˈraɪt/ *vt* Comput registrare sopra a

overwrought /əʊvəˈrɔːt/ *adj* in stato di agitazione

ovulation /ɒvjʊˈleɪʃn/ *n* ovulazione *f*

ow /aʊ/ *int* ahi!

owe /əʊ/ *vt* also fig dovere (**[to] somebody** a qualcuno); ∼ **somebody something** dovere qualcosa a qualcuno

owing /ˈəʊɪŋ/ **1** *adj* be ∼ ‹*money*› essere da pagare
2 *prep* ∼ **to** a causa di

owl /aʊl/ *n* gufo *m*

own¹ /əʊn/ **1** *adj* proprio
2 *pron* a car of my ∼ una macchina per

conto mio; **on one's** ∼ da solo; **hold one's** ∼ **with** tener testa a; **get one's** ∼ **back** fam prendersi una rivincita

own² *vt* possedere; (confess) ammettere; **I don't** ∼ **it** non mi appartiene
■ **own up** *vi* confessare (**to something** qualcosa)

owner /ˈəʊnə(r)/ *n* proprietario, -a *mf*

owner-driver *n* persona *f* che guida un'auto di sua proprietà

owner-occupied /-ˈɒkjʊpaɪd/ *adj* abitato dal proprietario

owner-occupier *n* persona *f* che abita in una casa di sua proprietà

ownership /ˈəʊnəʃɪp/ *n* proprietà *f*

ox /ɒks/ *n* (*pl* **oxen**) bue *m* (*pl* buoi)

Oxbridge /ˈɒksbrɪdʒ/ *n* le università di Oxford e Cambridge

oxide /ˈɒksaɪd/ *n* ossido *m*

oxidize /ˈɒksɪdaɪz/ **1** *vt* ossidare
2 *vi* ossidarsi

oxygen /ˈɒksɪdʒən/ *n* ossigeno *m*

oxygen mask *n* maschera *f* ad ossigeno

oyster /ˈɔɪstə(r)/ *n* ostrica *f*

oz *abbr* (**ounce(s)**) oncia *f*

ozone /ˈəʊzəʊn/ *n* ozono *m*

ozone depletion *n* distruzione *f* dell'ozonosfera

ozone-friendly *adj* che non danneggia l'ozono

ozone layer *n* fascia *f* d'ozono

Pp

p, P /piː/ *n* (letter) p, P *f inv*; Br *abbr* **penny, pence**

p & p *n abbr* (**postage and packing**) spese *fpl* di spedizione

P45 *n* Br (form) ≈ modello CUD *m*

PA *abbr* (**personal assistant**) segretario, -a *mf* personale; Am *abbr* (**Pennsylvania**) Pennsylvania *f*

p.a. *abbr* (**per annum**) all'anno

pace /peɪs/ **1** *n* passo *m*; (speed) ritmo *m*; **keep** ∼ **with** camminare di pari passo con
2 *vi* ∼ **up and down** camminare avanti e indietro

pacemaker /ˈpeɪsmeɪkə(r)/ *n* Med pacemaker *m inv*; (runner) battistrada *m inv*

pace-setter *n* (athlete) battistrada *m inv*

Pacific /pəˈsɪfɪk/ *adj & n* the ∼ [Ocean] l'oceano *m* Pacifico, il Pacifico

pacifier /ˈpæsɪfaɪə(r)/ *n* Am ciuccio *m*, succhiotto *m*

pacifism /ˈpæsɪfɪzm/ *n* pacifismo *m*

pacifist /ˈpæsɪfɪst/ *n* pacifista *mf*

pacify /ˈpæsɪfaɪ/ *vt* (pt/pp **-led**) placare ‹*person*›; pacificare ‹*country*›

pack /pæk/ **1** *n* (of cards) mazzo *m*; (of hounds) muta *f*; (of wolves, thieves) branco *m*; (of cigarettes etc) pacchetto *m*; **a** ∼ **of lies** un mucchio di bugie
2 *vt* impacchettare ‹*article*›; fare ‹*suitcase*›; mettere in valigia ‹*swimsuit etc*›; (press down) comprimere; ∼**ed** (crowded) strapieno, pieno zeppo
3 *vi* fare i bagagli; **send somebody** ∼**ing** fam mandare qualcuno a quel paese
■ **pack in** *vt* fam mollare ‹*job*›; ∼ **it in!** (stop it) piantala!
■ **pack off** *vt* (send) spedire

■ **pack out** *vt* be ∼ed out ⟨*cinema, shops*⟩ essere strapieno, essere pieno zeppo

■ **pack up** [1] *vt* impacchettare
[2] *vi* fam ⟨*machine*⟩ guastarsi

package /'pækɪdʒ/ [1] *n* pacco *m*
[2] *vt* impacchettare

package deal *n* offerta *f* tutto compreso

package holiday *n* vacanza *f* organizzata

package tour *n* viaggio *m* organizzato

packaging /'pækɪdʒɪŋ/ *n* (materials) confezione *f*; (promotion: of product) presentazione *f* pubblicitaria

packed /pækt/ *adj* pieno zeppo; ∼ **with** pieno zeppo di

packed lunch *n* pranzo *m* al sacco

packer /'pækə(r)/ *n* (in factory) imballatore, -trice *mf*

packet /'pækɪt/ *n* pacchetto *m*; **cost a** ∼ fam costare un sacco

pack ice *n* banchisa *f*

packing /'pækɪŋ/ *n* imballaggio *m*

pact /pækt/ *n* patto *m*

pad[1] /pæd/ [1] *n* imbottitura *f*; (for writing) bloc-notes *m inv*, taccuino *m*; (fam: home) casa *f*
[2] *vt* (pt/pp **padded**) imbottire

pad[2] *vi* (pt/pp **padded**) camminare con passo felpato

■ **pad out** *vt* gonfiare

padded bra *n* reggiseno *m* imbottito

padded cell *n* cella *f* con le pareti imbottite

padded envelope *n* busta *f* imbottita

padded shoulders *npl* spalline *fpl* imbottite

padding /'pædɪŋ/ *n* imbottitura *f*; (in written work) fronzoli *mpl*

paddle /'pædl/ [1] *n* pagaia *f*; **go for a** ∼ sguazzare
[2] *vt* (row) spingere remando
[3] *vi* (wade) sguazzare

paddling pool *n* (public) piscina *f* per bambini; (inflatable) piscina *f* gonfiabile

paddock /'pædək/ *n* recinto *m*

padlock /'pædlɒk/ [1] *n* lucchetto *m*
[2] *vt* chiudere con lucchetto

padre /'pɑːdreɪ/ *n* padre *m*

Padua /'pædjʊə/ *n* Padova *f*

paediatric /piːdɪˈætrɪk/ *adj* pediatrico

paediatrician /piːdɪəˈtrɪʃn/ *n* pediatra *mf*

paediatrics /piːdɪˈætrɪks/ *n* pediatria *f*

paedophile /'piːdəʊfaɪl/ *n* pedofilo, -a *mf*

paedophilia /piːdəʊˈfɪlɪə/ *n* pedofilia *f*

pagan /'peɪɡən/ *adj & n* pagano, -a *mf*

paganism /'peɪɡənɪzm/ *n* paganesimo *m*

page[1] /peɪdʒ/ *n* pagina *f*

page[2] [1] *n* (boy) paggetto *m*; (in hotel) fattorino *m*
[2] *vt* far chiamare ⟨*person*⟩

pageant /'pædʒənt/ *n* parata *f*

pageantry /'pædʒəntrɪ/ *n* cerimoniale *m*

pageboy *n* (at wedding) paggio *m*

page proof *n* bozza *f* definitiva

pager /'peɪdʒə(r)/ *n* cercapersone *m inv*

page three *n* Br terza pagina *f* di quotidiano scandalistico inglese con una pin-up

page three girl *n* Br pin-up *f inv*

paid /peɪd/ [1] ▶ PAY
[2] *adj* ∼ **employment** lavoro *m* remunerato; **put** ∼ **to** mettere fine a

paid-up *adj* Br ⟨*member*⟩ che ha pagato la sua quota; ⟨*instalment*⟩ versato

pail /peɪl/ *n* secchio *m*

pain /peɪn/ [1] *n* dolore *m*; **be in** ∼ soffrire; **take** ∼**s to do something** fare il possibile per fare qualcosa; ∼ **in the neck** fam rottura *f* di scatole; ⟨*person*⟩ rompiscatole *mf inv*
[2] *vt* fig addolorare

pained /peɪnd/ *adj* addolorato

painful /'peɪnfʊl/ *adj* doloroso; (laborious) penoso

painfully /'peɪnfʊlɪ/ *adv* ∼ **shy** incredibilmente timido

painkiller /'peɪnkɪlə(r)/ *n* calmante *m*

painkilling /'peɪnkɪlɪŋ/ *adj* antinevralgico

painless /'peɪnlɪs/ *adj* indolore

painlessly /'peɪnlɪslɪ/ *adv* in modo indolore

painstaking /'peɪnzteɪkɪŋ/ *adj* minuzioso

paint /peɪnt/ [1] *n* pittura *f*; ∼**s** *pl* colori *mpl*
[2] *vt/i* pitturare; ⟨*artist*⟩ dipingere; ∼ **the town red** folleggiare

■ **paint over** *vt* (cover with paint) coprire di vernice

paintbox /'peɪntbɒks/ *n* scatola *f* di colori

paintbrush /'peɪntbrʌʃ/ *n* pennello *m*

painter /'peɪntə(r)/ *n* pittore, -trice *mf*; (decorator) imbianchino *m*

pain threshold *n* soglia *f* del dolore

painting /'peɪntɪŋ/ *n* pittura *f*; (picture) dipinto *m*

paintpot *n* latta *f* di pittura

paint remover *n* sverniciante *m*

paint roller *n* rullo *m*

paint spray *n* pistola *f* a spruzzo

paint stripper *n* (tool) macchina *f* sverniciante; (chemical) sverniciante *m*

paintwork *n* pittura *f*

pair /peə(r)/ n paio m; (of people) coppia f:
a ~ of trousers/scissors un paio di
pantaloni/forbici
- **pair off** vi mettersi in coppia
- **pair up** vi ⟨dancers⟩ fare coppia; (for
game) formare una coppia

paisley /'peɪzlɪ/ n motivo m cachemire
inv

pajamas /pə'dʒɑːməz/ npl Am pigiama
msg

Pakistan /pɑːkɪ'stɑːn/ n Pakistan m

Pakistani /pɑːkɪ'stɑːnɪ/ adj & n
pakistano, -a mf

pal /pæl/ n fam amico, -a mf
- **pal up** vi (fam: become friends) fare
amicizia (with con)

palace /'pælɪs/ n palazzo m

palaentology /pælɪən'tɒlədʒɪ/ n
paleontologia f

palaeontologist /pæɪən'tɒlədʒɪst/ n
paleontologo, -a mf

palatable /'pælətəbl/ adj gradevole al
gusto

palate /'pælət/ n palato m

palatial /pə'leɪʃl/ adj sontuoso

palaver /pə'lɑːvə(r)/ n (fam: fuss) storie
fpl

pale[1] /peɪl/ n (stake) palo m; **beyond the ~**
fig inaccettabile

pale[2] ① adj pallido
② vi impallidire; **~ into insignificance**
diventare insignificante

paleness /'peɪlnɪs/ n pallore m

Palestine /'pælɪstaɪn/ n Palestina f

Palestinian /pælə'stɪnɪən/ adj & n
palestinese mf

palette /'pælɪt/ n tavolozza f

palette knife n spatola f

paling /'peɪlɪŋ/ n (stake) palo m; (fence)
palizzata f

palisade /pælɪ'seɪd/ n (fence) palizzata f

pall /pɔːl/ ① n drappo m funebre; fig velo
m di tristezza; (of smoke) cappa f
② vi stufare

pallet /'pælɪt/ n pallet m inv

palliative /'pælɪətɪv/ n palliativo m

pallid /'pælɪd/ adj pallido

pallor /'pælə(r)/ n pallore m

palm /pɑːm/ n palmo m; (tree) palma f
- **palm off** vt **~ something off on
somebody** rifilare qualcosa a qualcuno

palmist /'pɑːmɪst/ n chiromante mf

palmistry /'pɑːmɪstrɪ/ n chiromanzia f

Palm Sunday n Domenica f delle
Palme

palmtop [computer] n Comput
palmtop m inv

palpable /'pælpəbl/ adj palpabile;
(perceptible) tangibile

palpate /pæl'peɪt/ vi palpare

palpitate /'pælpɪteɪt/ vi palpitare

palpitations /pælpɪ'teɪʃnz/ npl
palpitazioni fpl

paltry /'pɔːltrɪ/ adj (-ler, -lest)
insignificante

pampas /'pæmpəs/ n pampas fpl

pamper /'pæmpə(r)/ vt viziare

pamphlet /'pæmflɪt/ n opuscolo m

pan /pæn/ ① n tegame m, pentola f; (for
frying) padella f; (of scales) piatto m
② vt (pt/pp **panned**) (fam: criticize)
stroncare
- **pan out** vi (fam: develop) mettersi

panacea /pænə'siːə/ n panacea f

panache /pə'næʃ/ n stile m

Panama /'pænəmɑː/ n Panama m; **the ~
Canal** il canale di Panama

pancake /'pænkeɪk/ n crêpe f inv,
frittella f

Pancake Day n martedì m inv grasso

pancreas /'pæŋkrɪəs/ n pancreas m inv

panda /'pændə/ n panda m inv

panda car n macchina f della polizia

pandemonium /pændɪ'məʊnɪəm/ n
pandemonio m

pander /'pændə(r)/ vi **~ to somebody**
compiacere qualcuno

pane /peɪn/ n **~ [of glass]** vetro m

panel /'pænl/ n pannello m; (group of
people) giuria f; **~ of experts** gruppo m di
esperti; **~ of judges** giuria f

panelling /'pænəlɪŋ/ n pannelli mpl

panellist /'pænəlɪst/ n Radio, TV
partecipante mf

pan-fry vt friggere

pang /pæŋ/ n **~s of hunger** morsi mpl
della fame; **~s of conscience** rimorsi mpl
di coscienza

panhandler /'pænhændlə(r)/ n Am: fam
mendicante mf

panic /'pænɪk/ ① n panico m
② vi (pt/pp **panicked**) lasciarsi
prendere dal panico

panic button n fam **hit the ~ ~** farsi
prendere dal panico

panic buying n accaparramento m

panicky /'pænɪkɪ/ adj che si lascia
prendere dal panico facilmente

panic-stricken /'pænɪkstrɪkən/ adj in
preda al panico

pannier /'pænɪə(r)/ n (on bike) borsa f; (on
mule) bisaccia f

panorama /pænə'rɑːmə/ n panorama m

panoramic /pænə'ræmɪk/ adj
panoramico

pan scourer n paglietta f

pansy /'pænzɪ/ n viola f del pensiero;
(fam: effeminate man) finocchio m

pant /pænt/ vi ansimare

pantechnicon /pæn'teknɪkən/ n
furgone m per traslochi

panther /'pænθə(r)/ n pantera f

panties /'pæntɪz/ npl mutandine fpl

panting /'pæntɪŋ/ adj ansante

pantomime /'pæntəmaɪm/ n
pantomima f

pantry /'pæntrɪ/ n dispensa f

pants /pænts/ npl (underwear) mutande
fpl; (woman's) mutandine fpl; (trousers)
pantaloni mpl

panty girdle /'pæntɪ/ n guaina f

pantyhose n Am collant m inv

panty-liner n salvaslip m inv

papal /'peɪpl/ adj papale

paparazzi /pæpə'rætzɪ/ npl paparazzi
mpl

paper /'peɪpə(r)/ ① n carta f; (wallpaper)
carta f da parati; (newspaper) giornale m;
(exam) esame m scritto; (treatise) saggio m:
∼s pl (documents) documenti mpl; (for
identification) documento msg [d'identità]; on
∼ in teoria; **put down on** ∼ mettere per
iscritto
② attrib di carta; (version) su carta
③ vt tappezzare
■ **paper over** vt ∼ over the cracks
dissimulare le divergenze

paperback n edizione f economica

paper bank n contenitore m per la
raccolta della carta

paper boy n ragazzo m che recapita i
giornali a domicilio

paper chain n festone m di carta

paper chase n corsa f campestre in cui
i partecipanti seguono una scia di pezzetti
di carta

paper clip n graffetta f

paper currency n banconote fpl

paper feed tray n Comput vassoio m
della carta

paperknife n tagliacarte m inv

paper mill n cartiera f

paper money n cartamoneta f

paper napkin n tovagliolo m di carta

paper round n he does a ∼ ∼ recapita
i giornali a domicilio

paper shop n edicola f

paper shredder n distruttore m di
documenti

paper-thin adj sottilissimo

paper towel n (toilet) asciugamano m di
carta; (kitchen) carta f asciugatutto

paper-weight n fermacarte m inv

paperwork n lavoro m d'ufficio

papery /'peɪpərɪ/ adj ⟨texture, leaves⟩
cartaceo

paprika /pə'priːkə/ n paprica f

Papua New Guinea /'pæpjʊə/ n
Papua Nuova Guinea f

par /pɑː(r)/ n (in golf) par m inv; **on a** ∼
with alla pari con; **feel below** ∼ essere un
po' giù di tono

para¹ /'pærə/ n (paragraph) paragrafo m

para² n Br Mil para m inv

parable /'pærəbl/ n parabola f

parachute /'pærəʃuːt/ ① n paracadute
m inv
② vi lanciarsi col paracadute

parachute drop n (of supplies) lancio m
col paracadute

parachute jump n lancio m col
paracadute

parachuting /'pærəʃuːtɪŋ/ n
paracadutismo m

parachutist /'pærəʃuːtɪst/ n
paracadutista mf

parade /pə'reɪd/ ① n (military) parata f
militare; (display) sfoggio m
② vi sfilare
③ vt (show off) far sfoggio di

parade ground n piazza f d'armi

paradigm /'pærədaɪm/ n paradigma m

paradise /'pærədaɪs/ n paradiso m

paradox /'pærədɒks/ n paradosso m

paradoxical /pærə'dɒksɪkl/ adj
paradossale

paradoxically /pærə'dɒksɪklɪ/ adv
paradossalmente

paraffin /'pærəfɪn/ n paraffina f; (oil)
cherosene m

paragliding /'pærəglaɪdɪŋ/ n
parapendio m

paragon /'pærəgən/ n ∼ **of virtue**
modello m di virtù

paragraph /'pærəgrɑːf/ n paragrafo m

Paraguay /'pærəgwaɪ/ n Paraguay m

parallel /'pærəlel/ ① adj & adv parallelo
② n Geog, fig parallelo m; (line) parallelo f
③ vt essere paragonabile a

parallel bars npl parallele fpl

parallelogram /pærə'leləʊgræm/ n
Math parallelogramma m

parallel port n Comput porta f parallela

paralyse /'pærəlaɪz/ vt paralizzare

paralysis /pə'ræləsɪs/ n (pl **-ses**)
/pə'ræləsiːz/ paralisi f inv

paralytic /pærə'lɪtɪk/ adj ⟨person⟩
paralitico; ⟨arm, leg⟩ paralizzato; (Br fam;
drunk) ubriaco fradicio

paramedic /pærə'medɪk/ n paramedico
m

parameter /pə'ræmɪtə(r)/ n parametro
m

paramilitary /pærə'mɪlɪtrɪ/ ① n
appartenente mf ad un gruppo
paramilitare
② adj paramilitare

paramount /'pærəmaʊnt/ adj supremo;
be ∼ essere essenziale

paranoia /pærə'nɔɪə/ n paranoia f

paranoid /'pærənɔɪd/ adj paranoico

paranormal /pærə'nɔːməl/ adj & n paranormale m

parapet /'pærəpɪt/ n parapetto m

paraphernalia /pærəfə'neɪlɪə/ n armamentario m

paraphrase /'pærəfreɪz/ ① n parafrasi f inv
② vt parafrasare

paraplegic /pærə'pliːdʒɪk/ adj & n paraplegico, -a mf

parascending /'pærəsendɪŋ/ n Br paracadutismo m ascensionale

parasite /'pærəsaɪt/ n parassita mf

parasitic /pærə'sɪtɪk/ adj parassitario

parasol /'pærəsɒl/ n parasole m

paratrooper /'pærətruːpə(r)/ n paracadutista m

parboil /'pɑːbɔɪl/ vt scottare

parcel /'pɑːsl/ n pacco m
■ **parcel up** vt impacchettare ⟨clothes etc⟩

parcel bomb n pacco m bomba inv

parch /pɑːtʃ/ vt disseccare

parched /'pɑːtʃt/ adj ⟨land⟩ riarso; (thirsty) I'm ∼ sto morendo di sete

parchment /'pɑːtʃmənt/ n pergamena f

pardon /'pɑːdn/ ① n perdono m; Jur grazia f; ∼? prego?; I beg your ∼? fml chiedo scusa? I do beg your ∼ (sorry) chiedo scusa!
② vt perdonare; Jur graziare

pare /peə(r)/ vt (peel) pelare

parent /'peərənt/ n genitore m

parentage /'peərəntɪdʒ/ n natali mpl

parental /pə'rentl/ adj dei genitori

parent company n casa f madre

parenthesis /pə'renθəsɪs/ n (pl -ses /pə'renθəsiːz/) parentesi f inv

parenthood /'peərənthʊd/ n (fatherhood) paternità f; (motherhood) maternità f

parenting /'peərəntɪŋ/ n educazione f dei figli; ∼ **classes** corsi di sostegno pratico e psicologico per nuovi genitori

parents' evening n riunione f dei genitori degli alunni

parer /'peərə(r)/ n sbucciatore m

pariah /pə'raɪə/ n paria m

parings /'peərɪŋz/ npl (of fruit) bucce fpl; (of nails) ritagli mpl di unghie

Paris /'pærɪs/ n Parigi f

parish /'pærɪʃ/ n parrocchia f

parishioner /pə'rɪʃənə(r)/ n parrocchiano, -a mf

parish priest n (Catholic) parroco m; (Protestant) pastore m

Parisian /pə'rɪzɪən/ adj & n parigino, -a mf

parity /'pærətɪ/ n parità f

park /pɑːk/ ① n parco m
② vt Auto posteggiare, parcheggiare; ∼ oneself fam installarsi
③ vi posteggiare, parcheggiare

parka /'pɑːkə/ n parka m inv

park-and-ride n parcheggio m collegato al centro di una città da mezzi pubblici

parking /'pɑːkɪŋ/ n parcheggio m, posteggio m; 'no ∼' 'divieto di sosta'

parking attendant n parcheggiatore, -trice mf, posteggiatore, -trice mf

parking lot n Am posteggio m, parcheggio m

parking meter n parchimetro m

parking space n posteggio m, parcheggio m

parkland n parco m

park ranger, park warden n guardaparco m inv

parliament /'pɑːləmənt/ n parlamento m

parliamentary /pɑːlə'mentərɪ/ adj parlamentare

parlour /'pɑːlə(r)/ n salotto m

parochial /pə'rəʊkɪəl/ adj parrocchiale; fig ristretto

parochialism /pə'rəʊkɪəlɪzm/ n campanilismo m

parody /'pærədɪ/ ① n parodia f
② vt (pt/pp -ied) parodiare

parole /pə'rəʊl/ ① n on ∼ sulla parola; eligible for ∼ suscettibile di essere liberato sulla parola
② vt mettere in libertà sulla parola

paroxysm /'pærəksɪzm/ n accesso m

parquet floor /'pɑːkeɪ/ n parquet m

parquet flooring /'flɔːrɪŋ/ n parquet m inv

parrot /'pærət/ n pappagallo m

parry /'pærɪ/ vt (pt/pp -ied) parare ⟨blow⟩; (in fencing) eludere

parse /pɑːz/ vt fare l'analisi grammaticale di ⟨sentence⟩; Comput analizzare la sintassi di

parsimonious /pɑːsɪ'məʊnɪəs/ adj parsimonioso

parsing /'pɑːzɪŋ/ n analisi f grammaticale; Comput analisi f sintattica

parsley /'pɑːslɪ/ n prezzemolo m

parsnip /'pɑːsnɪp/ n pastinaca f

parson /'pɑːsn/ n pastore m

part /pɑːt/ ① n parte f; (of machine) pezzo m; for my ∼ per quanto mi riguarda; on the ∼ of da parte di; take sb's ∼ prendere le parti di qualcuno; take ∼ in prendere parte a
② adv in parte
③ vt ∼ one's hair farsi la riga
④ vi ⟨people⟩ separarsi; ∼ with separarsi da

part exchange *n* take in ∼ ∼ prendere indietro come pagamento parziale

partial /'pɑːʃl/ *adj* parziale; **be** ∼ **to** aver un debole per

partiality /pɑːʃɪ'ælətɪ/ *n* (liking) predilezione *f*

partially /'pɑːʃəlɪ/ *adv* parzialmente; ∼ **sighted** parzialmente cieco

participant /pɑː'tɪsɪpənt/ *n* partecipante *mf*

participate /pɑː'tɪsɪpeɪt/ *vi* partecipare (in a)

participation /pɑːtɪsɪ'peɪʃn/ *n* partecipazione *f*

participatory /pɑːtɪsɪ'peɪtərɪ/ *adj* partecipativo

participle /pɑː'tɪsɪpl/ *n* participio *m*; **present/past** ∼ participio presente/passato

particle /'pɑːtɪkl/ *n* Phys, Gram particella *f*

particular /pə'tɪkjʊlə(r)/ *adj* particolare; (precise) meticoloso; pej difficile; **in** ∼ in particolare

particularly /pə'tɪkjʊləlɪ/ *adv* particolarmente

particulars /pə'tɪkjʊləz/ *npl* particolari *mpl*

parting /'pɑːtɪŋ/ ① *n* separazione *f*; (in hair) scriminatura *f*
② *attrib* di commiato

partisan /pɑːtɪ'zæn/ *n* partigiano, -a *mf*

partition /pɑː'tɪʃn/ ① *n* (wall) parete *f* divisoria; Pol divisione *f*
② *vt* dividere
∎ **partition off** *vt* separare

partly /'pɑːtlɪ/ *adv* in parte

partner /'pɑːtnə(r)/ *n* Comm socio, -a *mf*; (sport, in relationship) compagno, -a *mf*

partnership /'pɑːtnəʃɪp/ *n* Comm società *f inv*

part of speech *n* categoria *f* grammaticale

part owner *n* comproprietario, -a *mf*

part payment *n* acconto *m*

partridge /'pɑːtrɪdʒ/ *n* pernice *f*

part-time *adj* & *adv* part time; **be** or **work** ∼ lavorare part time

part-way *adv* ∼ **through the evening** a metà serata

party /'pɑːtɪ/ *n* ricevimento *m*, festa *f*; (group) gruppo *m*; Pol partito *m*; Jur parte *f*; **be** ∼ **to** essere parte attiva in

party animal *n* festaiolo, -a *mf*

party dress *n* abito *m* da sera

party-goer *n* festaiolo, -a *mf*

party hat *n* cappellino *m* di carta

party leader *n* dirigente *m* di partito

party line *n* Teleph duplex *m inv*; Pol linea *f* del partito

party piece *n* pezzo *m* forte; **do one's** ∼ ∼ esibirsi nel proprio pezzo forte

party political broadcast *n* comunicato *m* di partito (trasmesso per radio o per televisione)

party politics *n* politica *f* di partito

party wall *n* muro *m* divisorio

pass /pɑːs/ ① *n* lasciapassare *m inv*; (in mountains) passo *m*; Sport passaggio *m*; (Sch: mark) [voto *m*] sufficiente *m*; **get a** ∼ Sch ottenere la sufficienza; **make a** ∼ **at** fam fare delle avances a
② *vt* passare; (overtake) sorpassare; (approve) far passare; (exceed) oltrepassare; fare ⟨remark⟩; esprimere ⟨judgement⟩; Jur pronunciare ⟨sentence⟩; ∼ **water** orinare; ∼ **the time** passare il tempo
③ *vi* passare; (in exam) essere promosso; **let something** ∼ fig lasciar correre qualcosa; ∼! (in game) passo!
∎ **pass as** *vt* = PASS FOR
∎ **pass away** *vi* mancare
∎ **pass by** *vi* (go past) passare
∎ **pass down** *vt* passare; fig trasmettere
∎ **pass for** *vt* (be accepted as) passare per
∎ **pass off** ① *vi* (disappear) passare; (take place) svolgersi
② *vt* ∼ **somebody/something off as** far passare qualcuno/qualcosa per
∎ **pass on** *vt* passare ⟨message, information⟩
∎ **pass on to** *vt* passare a ⟨new subject, next question⟩
∎ **pass out** *vi* fam svenire
∎ **pass over** ① *vt* (not mention) passare sopra a; ∼ **somebody over for promotion** non prendere in considerazione qualcuno per una promozione
② *vi* (die) spirare
∎ **pass round** *vt* far passare
∎ **pass through** *vt* attraversare
∎ **pass up** *vt* passare; (fam: miss) lasciarsi scappare

passable /'pɑːsəbl/ *adj* ⟨road⟩ praticabile; (satisfactory) passabile

passage /'pæsɪdʒ/ *n* passaggio *m*; (corridor) corridoio *m*; (voyage) traversata *f*

pass book *n* Fin libretto *m* di risparmio

passé /'pæseɪ/ *adj* pej sorpassato

passenger /'pæsɪndʒə(r)/ *n* passeggero, -a *mf*

passenger compartment *n* Br Auto abitacolo *m*

passenger ferry *n* traghetto *m*

passenger plane *n* aereo *m* passeggeri

passenger seat *n* posto *m* accanto al guidatore

passenger train *n* treno *m* passeggeri

passepartout /pæspɑː'tuː/ *n* (key, frame) passe-partout *m inv*

passer-by /pɑːsə'baɪ/ *n* (pl **-s-by**) passante *mf*

passing /'pɑːsɪŋ/ *adj* ⟨*motorist*⟩ di passaggio; ⟨*thought*⟩ di sfuggita; ⟨*reference*⟩ en passant; ⟨*resemblance*⟩ vago

passing place /'pɑːsɪŋ/ *n* piazzola *f* di sosta per consentire il transito dei veicoli nei due sensi

passing shot *n* Tennis passante *m*

passion /'pæʃn/ *n* passione *f*

passionate /'pæʃənət/ *adj* appassionato

passionately /'pæʃənətlɪ/ *adv* appassionatamente

passion fruit *n* frutto *m* della passione

passive /'pæsɪv/ *adj* & *n* passivo *m*

passively /'pæsɪvlɪ/ *adv* passivamente

passiveness /'pæsɪvnɪs/ *n* passività *f*

passive resistance *n* resistenza *f* passiva

passive smoking *n* fumo *m* passivo

pass-key *n* (master-key) passe-partout *m inv*; (for access) chiave *f*

pass mark *n* Sch [voto *m*] sufficiente *m*

Passover *n* Pasqua *f* ebraica

passport *n* passaporto *m*

password *n* parola *f* d'ordine

password-protected *adj* Comput ⟨*file, site*⟩ protetto da password

past /pɑːst/ ① *adj* passato; (former) ex; that's all ~ tutto questo è passato; in the ~ few days nei giorni scorsi; the ~ week la settimana scorsa
② *n* passato *m*
③ *prep* oltre; at ten ~ two alle due e dieci
④ *adv* oltre; go/come ~ passare

pasta /'pæstə/ *n* pasta [asciutta] *f*

paste /peɪst/ ① *n* pasta *f*; (dough) impasto *m*; (adhesive) colla *f*
② *vt* incollare
■ **paste down** *vt* incollare
■ **paste in** *vt* incollare
■ **paste up** *vt* affiggere ⟨*notice, poster*⟩

paste jewellery *n* bigiotteria *f*

pastel /'pæstl/ ① *n* pastello *m*
② *attrib* pastello

pasteurization /pɑːstʃəraɪ'zeɪʃn/ *n* pastorizzazione *f*

pasteurize /'pɑːstʃəraɪz/ *vt* pastorizzare

pasteurized /'pɑːstʃəraɪzd/ *adj* pastorizzato

pastille /'pæstɪl/ *n* pastiglia *f*

pastime /'pɑːstaɪm/ *n* passatempo *m*

pasting /'peɪstɪŋ/ *n* (fam: defeat, criticism) batosta *f*

past master *n* esperto, -a *mf*

pastor /'pɑːstə(r)/ *n* pastore *m*

pastoral /'pɑːstərəl/ *adj* pastorale

past participle *n* participio *m* passato

pastrami /pæ'strɑːmɪ/ *n* carne *m* di manzo affumicata

pastry /'peɪstrɪ/ *n* pasta *f*; **pastries** *pl* pasticcini *mpl*

past tense *n* passato *m*

pasture /'pɑːstʃə/ *n* pascolo *m*

pasty[1] /'pæstɪ/ *n* ≈ pasticcio *m*

pasty[2] /'peɪstɪ/ *adj* smorto

pat /pæt/ ① *n* buffetto *m*; (of butter) pezzetto *m*
② *adv* have something off ~ conoscere qualcosa a menadito
③ *vt* (pt/pp **patted**) dare un buffetto a; ~ somebody on the back fig congratularsi con qualcuno

patch /pætʃ/ ① *n* toppa *f*; (spot) chiazza *f*; (period) periodo *m*: not a ~ on fam molto inferiore a
② *vt* mettere una toppa su
■ **patch up** *vt* riparare alla bell'e meglio; appianare ⟨*quarrel*⟩

patchwork /'pætʃwɜːk/ *n* patchwork *m inv*; fig mosaico *m*

patchy /'pætʃɪ/ *adj* incostante

pâté /'pæteɪ/ *n* pâté *m inv*

patent /'peɪtnt/ ① *adj* palese
② *n* brevetto *m*
③ *vt* brevettare

patent leather *n* vernice *m*

patently /'peɪtəntlɪ/ *adv* in modo palese

paternal /pə'tɜːnl/ *adj* paterno

paternalism /pə'tɜːnəlɪzm/ *n* paternalismo *m*

paternalistic /pətɜːnə'lɪstɪk/ *adj* paternalistico

paternity /pə'tɜːnətɪ/ *n* paternità *f*

paternity leave *n* congedo *m* di paternità

paternity suit *n* causa *f* per il riconoscimento di paternità

path /pɑːθ/ *n* (pl ~s /pɑːðz/) sentiero *m*; (orbit) traiettoria *f*; fig strada *f*

pathetic /pə'θetɪk/ *adj* patetico; (fam: very bad) penoso

pathological /pæθə'lɒdʒɪkl/ *adj* patologico

pathologist /pə'θɒlədʒɪst/ *n* patologo, -a *mf*

pathology /pə'θɒlədʒɪ/ *n* patologia *f*

pathos /'peɪθɒs/ *n* pathos *m*

patience /'peɪʃns/ *n* pazienza *f*; (game) solitario *m*

patient /'peɪʃnt/ *adj* & *n* paziente *mf*

patiently /'peɪʃntlɪ/ *adv* pazientemente

patio /'pætɪəʊ/ *n* terrazza *f*

patio doors *npl* portafinestra *f*

patio garden *n* cortile *m*

patriarch /'peɪtrɪɑːk/ *n* patriarca *m*

patriarchal /peɪtrɪ'ɑːkəl/ *adj* patriarcale

patriarchy /'peɪtrɪɑːkɪ/ *n* patriarcato *m*

patriot /'pætrɪət/ *n* patriota *mf*

patriotic /pætrɪ'ɒtɪk/ *adj* patriottico

patriotism /'pætrɪətɪzm/ n patriottismo m

patrol /pə'trəʊl/ ①n pattuglia f
②vt/i pattugliare

patrol boat n motovedetta f

patrol car n autopattuglia f

patron /'peɪtrən/ n patrono m; (of charity) benefattore, -trice mf; (of the arts) mecenate mf; (customer) cliente mf

patronage /'pætrənɪdʒ/ n patrocinio m; (of shop etc) frequentazione f

patronize /'pætrənaɪz/ vt frequentare abitualmente; fig trattare con condiscendenza

patronizing /'pætrənaɪzɪŋ/ adj condiscendente

patronizingly /'pætrənaɪzɪŋlɪ/ adv con condiscendenza

patron saint n [santo, -a mf] patrono, -a mf

patter¹ /'pætə(r)/ ①n picchiettio m
②vi picchiettare

patter² n (of salesman) chiacchiere fpl

pattern /'pætn/ n motivo m; (for knitting, sewing, in behaviour) modello m

patterned /'pætənd/ adj ⟨material⟩ fantasia

paunch /pɔːntʃ/ n pancia f

pauper /'pɔːpə(r)/ n povero, -a mf

pause /pɔːz/ ①n pausa f
②vi fare una pausa

pave /peɪv/ vt pavimentare; ∼ the way preparare la strada (for a)

pavement /'peɪvmənt/ n marciapiede m

pavement café n caffè m con tavolini all'aperto

pavilion /pə'vɪljən/ n padiglione m; (Cricket) costruzione f annessa al campo da gioco con gli spogliatoi

paving /'peɪvɪŋ/ n lastricato m

paving slab, **paving stone** n lastra f di pietra

paw /pɔː/ ①n zampa f
②vt fam mettere le zampe addosso a

pawn¹ /pɔːn/ n (in chess) pedone m; fig pedina f

pawn² ①vt impegnare
②n in ∼ in pegno

pawnbroker /'pɔːnbrəʊkə(r)/ n prestatore, -trice mf su pegno

pawnshop /'pɔːnʃɒp/ n monte m di pietà

pawpaw /'pɔːpɔː/ n papaia f

pay /peɪ/ ①n paga f; in the ∼ of al soldo di
②vt (pt/pp **paid**) pagare; prestare ⟨attention⟩; fare ⟨compliment, visit⟩; ∼ cash pagare in contanti
③vi pagare; (be profitable) rendere; it doesn't ∼ to... fig è fatica sprecata...; ∼ in

instalments pagare a rate; ∼ through the nose fam pagare profumatamente
■ **pay back** vt ripagare
■ **pay for** vt pagare per
■ **pay in** vt versare
■ **pay off** ①vt saldare ⟨debt⟩
②vi fig dare dei frutti
■ **pay out** vt (spend) pagare
■ **pay up** vi pagare

payable /'peɪəbl/ adj pagabile; make ∼ to intestare a

pay cheque Br, **pay check** Am n assegno m della paga

payday n giorno m di paga

PAYE Br abbr (**pay-as-you-earn**) trattenute fpl fiscali alla fonte

payee /peɪ'iː/ n beneficiario m

payer /'peɪə(r)/ n pagante mf

paying-in slip /peɪɪŋ'ɪn/ n distinta f di versamento

payload /'peɪləʊd/ n (of bomb) carica f esplosiva; (of aircraft, ship) carico m utile

payment /'peɪmənt/ n pagamento m; ∼ by instalments pagamento m rateale

pay-packet n busta f paga inv

pay-per-view n pay per view f; ∼ programme/film un film/programma pay per view

payphone n telefono m pubblico

payroll n (list) libro m paga; (sum of money) paga f del personale; (employees collectively) personale m

payslip n busta f paga inv

pay television n pay tv f

PC abbr (**personal computer**) PC m inv; abbr (**police constable**) agente m di polizia

pc abbr (**per cent**) per cento; abbr (**politically correct**) politicamente corretto; abbr (**postcard**) cartolina f postale

pd Am abbr (**police department**) reparto m di polizia

PDF abbr (**portable document format**) Comput PDF m; a ∼ file un file PDF

PE n abbr (**physical education**) educazione f fisica

pea /piː/ n pisello m

peace /piːs/ n pace f; ∼ of mind tranquillità f

peaceable /'piːsəbl/ adj pacifico

peace envoy n mediatore, -trice mf

peaceful /'piːsfʊl/ adj calmo, sereno

peacefully /'piːsfʊlɪ/ adv in pace

peacekeeping ①n Mil Pol mantenimento m della pace
②attrib ⟨force, troops⟩ di mantenimento della pace

peacemaker n mediatore, -trice mf

peace process n processo m di pace

peacetime ① *n* tempo *m* di pace
② *attrib* ⟨*planning, government*⟩ del
tempo di pace; ⟨*army, alliance, training*⟩
in tempo di pace

peace treaty *n* trattato *m* di pace

peach /piːtʃ/ *n* pesca *f*; (tree) pesco *m*

peacock /'piːkɒk/ *n* pavone *m*

pea green *adj* verde pisello

peak /piːk/ *n* picco *m*; fig culmine *m*

peaked cap /piːkt/ *n* berretto *m* a
punta

peak hours *npl* ore *fpl* di punta

peak period *n* ora *f* di punta

peak rate *n* tariffa *f* ore di punta; ∼ ∼
calls Teleph chiamate a tariffa ore di punta

peak season *n* alta stagione *f*

peak time *n* = PRIME TIME

peaky /'piːkɪ/ *adj* malaticcio

peal /piːl/ *n* (of bells) scampanio *m*; ∼s of
laughter fragore *msg* di risate

peanut /'piːnʌt/ *n* nocciolina *f*
[americana]; ∼s *pl* fam miseria *fsg*

peanut butter *n* burro *m* di arachidi

pear /peə(r)/ *n* pera *f*; (tree) pero *m*

pearl /pɜːl/ *n* perla *f*

pearl barley *n* orzo *m* perlato

pearl-diver *n* pescatore, -trice *mf* di
perle

pearl grey ① *n* grigio *m* perla *inv*
② *adj* grigio perla *inv*

Pearly Gates /pɜːlɪ/ *npl* hum porte *fpl*
del paradiso

peasant /'peznt/ *n* contadino, -a *mf*

peat /piːt/ *n* torba *f*

pebble /'pebl/ *n* ciottolo *m*

pebble-dash *n* intonaco *m* a
pinocchino

pecan /'piːkən/ *n* (tree) pecan *m inv*; (nut)
noce *f* pecan *inv*

peck /pek/ ① *n* beccata *f*: (*kiss*) bacetto
m
② *vt* beccare; (kiss) dare un bacetto a
■ **peck at** *vi* beccare

pecking order /'pekɪŋ/ *n* gerarchia *f*

peckish /'pekɪʃ/ *adj* be ∼ fam avere un
languorino allo stomaco

pecs /peks/ fam, **pectorals** /'pektərəlz/
npl pettorali *mpl*

pectoral /'pektərəl/ *adj & n* pettorale *m*

peculiar /pɪ'kjuːlɪə(r)/ *adj* strano;
(special) particolare; ∼ **to** tipico di

peculiarity /pɪkjuːlɪ'ærətɪ/ *n* stranezza
f; (feature) particolarità *f inv*

peculiarly /pɪ'kjuːlɪəlɪ/ *adv*
singolarmente

pecuniary /pə'kjuːnɪərɪ/ *adj* pecuniario

pedagogical /pedə'gɒdʒɪkl/ *adj*
pedagogico

pedagogy /'pedəgɒdʒɪ/ *n* pedagogia *f*

pedal /'pedl/ ① *n* pedale *m*
② *vi* pedalare

pedal bin *n* pattumiera *f* a pedale

pedant /'pedənt/ *n* pedante *m*

pedantic /pɪ'dæntɪk/ *adj* pedante

pedantically /pɪ'dæntɪklɪ/ *adv* in modo
pedante

pedantry /'pedəntrɪ/ *n* pedanteria *f*

peddle /'pedl/ *vt* vendere porta a porta

pedestal /'pedɪstl/ *n* piedistallo *m*

pedestrian /pɪ'destrɪən/ ① *n* pedone *m*
② *adj* fig scadente

pedestrian crossing *n* passaggio *m*
pedonale

pedestrian precinct *n* zona *f*
pedonale

pediatrician /piːdɪə'trɪʃn/ *n* Am =
PAEDIATRICIAN

pedicure /'pedɪkjʊə(r)/ *n* pedicure *f inv*

pedigree /'pedɪgriː/ ① *n* pedigree *m inv*;
(of person) lignaggio *m*
② *attrib* ⟨*animal*⟩ di razza, con pedigree

pedlar, peddler /'pedlə(r)/ *n* old
venditore, -trice *mf* ambulante; **drug** ∼
spacciatore, -trice *mf* di droga

pedophile /'piːdəfaɪl/ *n* Am = PAEDOPHILE

pee /piː/ fam ① *vi* (pt/pp **peed**) fare la
pipì
② *n* go for a ∼ andare a fare la pipì

peek /piːk/ fam ① *vi* sbirciare
② *n* take a ∼ **at something** dare una
sbirciata a qualcosa

peekaboo /'piːkə'buː/ *int* cucù

peel /piːl/ ① *n* buccia *f*
② *vt* sbucciare
③ *vi* ⟨*nose etc*⟩ spellarsi; ⟨*paint*⟩ staccarsi
■ **peel off** ① *vt* togliersi ⟨*item of
clothing*⟩
② *vi* ⟨*wallpaper*⟩ staccarsi; ⟨*skin*⟩
squamarsi

peeler /'piːlə(r)/ *n* sbucciatore *m*

peelings /'piːlɪŋz/ *npl* bucce *fpl*

peep /piːp/ ① *n* sbirciata *f*
② *vi* sbirciare

peephole /'piːphəʊl/ *n* spioncino *m*

Peeping Tom /'piːpɪŋ/ *n* fam guardone
m

peer[1] /pɪə(r)/ *vi* ∼ **at** scrutare

peer[2] *n* nobile *m*; his ∼s *pl* (in rank) i suoi
pari; (in age) i suoi coetanei

peerage /'pɪərɪdʒ/ *n* Br Pol nobiltà *f*;
(book) almanacco *m* nobiliare; **be given a**
∼ essere elevato al rango di pari

peer group *n* (of same status) pari *mpl*; (of
same age) coetanei *mpl*; ∼ ∼ **pressure**
pressione *f* esercitata dal gruppo cui si
appartiene

peerless /'pɪəlɪs/ *adj* impareggiabile

peeved /piːvd/ *adj* fam irritato

peevish /'piːvɪʃ/ *adj* fam irritabile

peg /peg/ ① *n* (hook) piolo *m*; (for tent) picchetto *m*; (for clothes) molletta *f*; **off the** ~ fam prêt-a-porter ② *vt* (pt/pp **pegged**) fissare ⟨*prices*⟩; stendere con le mollette ⟨*washing*⟩

pegboard /'pegbɔːd/ *n* segnapunti *m inv*

pejorative /pɪ'dʒɒrətɪv/ *adj* peggiorativo

pejoratively /pɪ'dʒɒrətɪvlɪ/ *adv* in modo peggiorativo

peke /piːk/ *n* fam (dog) pechinese *m*

Peking /pɪːkɪŋ/ *n* Pechino *f*

pekin[g]ese /piːkɪ'niːz/ *n* pechinese *m*

pelican /'pelɪkən/ *n* pellicano *m*

pelican crossing *n* passaggio *m* pedonale con semaforo

pellet /'pelɪt/ *n* pallottola *f*

pell-mell /pel'mel/ *adv* alla rinfusa

pelmet /'pelmɪt/ *n* mantovana *f*

pelt[1] /pelt/ *n* (skin) pelliccia *f*

pelt[2] ① *vt* bombardare ② *vi* (fam: run fast) catapultarsi; (rain heavily) venir giù a fiotti ■ **pelt along** *vi* (move quickly) precipitarsi lungo ■ **pelt down** *vi* ⟨*rain*⟩ venir giù a fiotti

pelvis /'pelvɪs/ *n* Anat bacino *m*

pen[1] /pen/ *n* (for animals) recinto *m*

pen[2] *n* penna *f*; (ball-point) penna *f* a sfera

penal /'piːnl/ *adj* penale

penal code *n* codice *m* penale

penalize /'piːnəlaɪz/ *vt* penalizzare

penalty /'penltɪ/ *n* sanzione *f*; (fine) multa *f*; (in football) [calcio *m* di] rigore *m*

penalty area, **penalty box** *n* area *f* di rigore

penalty clause *n* Comm, Jur clausola *f* penale

penalty kick *n* [calcio *m* di] rigore *m*

penalty shoot-out *n* rigori *mpl*

penance /'penəns/ *n* penitenza *f*

pence /pens/ ▶ PENNY

penchant /'pɑ̃ʃɑ̃/ *n* debole *m*

pencil ① *n* /'pensl/ matita *f* ② *vt* (pt/pp **pencilled**) scrivere a matita ■ **pencil in** *vt* annotare provvisoriamente ⟨*date*⟩

pencil case *n* [astuccio *m*] portamatite *m inv*

pencil sharpener *n* temperamatite *m inv*

pendant /'pendənt/ *n* ciondolo *m*

pending /'pendɪŋ/ ① *adj* in sospeso ② *prep* in attesa di

pendulum /'pendjʊləm/ *n* pendolo *m*

penetrate /'penɪtreɪt/ *vt/i* penetrare

penetrating /'penɪtreɪtɪŋ/ *adj* ⟨*sound, stare*⟩ penetrante; ⟨*remark*⟩ acuto

penetration /penɪ'treɪʃn/ *n* penetrazione *f*

penfriend /'penfrend/ *n* amico, -a *mf* di penna

penguin /'pengwɪn/ *n* pinguino *m*

penicillin /penɪ'sɪlɪn/ *n* penicillina *f*

peninsula /pɪ'nɪnsjʊlə/ *n* penisola *f*

penis /'piːnɪs/ *n* pene *m*

penitence /'penɪtəns/ *n* penitenza *f*

penitent /'penɪtənt/ *adj & n* penitente *mf*

penitentiary /penɪ'tenʃərɪ/ *n* Am penitenziario *m*

penknife /'pennaɪf/ *n* temperino *m*

pen-name *n* pseudonimo *m*

pennant /'penənt/ *n* bandiera *f*

penniless /'penɪlɪs/ *adj* senza un soldo

penny /'penɪ/ *n* (pl **pence**; single coins **pennies**) penny *m*; Am centesimo *m*; **spend a** ~ fam andare in bagno; **the** ~**'s dropped!** fam ci è arrivato!

penny-farthing *n* velocipede *m*

penny-pinching /'penɪpɪntʃɪŋ/ ① *adj* taccagno ② *n* taccagneria *f*

penny whistle *n* zufolo *m*

pen-pusher *n* fam scribacchino, -a *mf*

pension /'penʃn/ *n* pensione *f* ■ **pension off** *vt* (force to retire) mandare in pensione

pensioner /'penʃənə(r)/ *n* pensionato, -a *mf*

pension fund *n* fondo *m* pensioni; (of an individual) fondo *m* pensione

pension scheme *n* piano *m* di pensionamento

pensive /'pensɪv/ *adj* pensoso

pentagon /'pentəgən/ *n* pentagono *m*; Am Pol **the P**~ il Pentagono

pentagonal /pen'tægənəl/ *adj* pentagonale

pentathlete /pen'tæθliːt/ *n* pentatleta *mf*

pentathlon /pen'tæθlɒn/ *n* pentathlon *m inv*

Pentecost /'pentɪkɒst/ *n* Pentecoste *f*

penthouse /'penthaʊs/ *n* attico *m*

pent-up /'pentʌp/ *adj* represso

penultimate /pɪ'nʌltɪmət/ *adj* penultimo

penury /'penjʊrɪ/ *n* miseria *f*

peony /'pɪənɪ/ *n* peonia *f*

people /'piːpl/ ① *npl* persone *fpl*, gente *fsg*; (citizens) popolo *msg*; **a lot of** ~ una marea di gente; **the** ~ la gente; **English** ~ gli inglesi; ~ **say** si dice; **for four** ~ per quattro ② *vt* popolare

people carrier *n* monovolume *f*

pep /pep/

P

■ **pep up** *vt* vivacizzare ⟨*party, conversation*⟩; tirare su ⟨*person*⟩

PEP /pep/ *abbr* Br (**personal equity plan**) piano *m* di investimento azionario personale

pepper /'pepə(r)/ **①** *n* pepe *m*; (vegetable) peperone *m*
② *vt* (season) pepare

peppercorn *n* grano *m* di pepe

peppercorn rent affitto *m* nominale

pepper mill *n* macinapepe *m inv*

peppermint *n* menta *f* piperita; (sweet) caramella *f* alla menta

pepper pot *n* pepiera *f*

pep pill /'peppɪl/ *n* fam stimolante *m*

pep talk *n* discorso *m* d'incoraggiamento

peptic /'peptɪk/ *adj* peptico

peptic ulcer *n* ulcera *f* peptica

per /pɜː(r)/ *prep* per

per annum /pər'ænəm/ *adv* all'anno

per capita /pə'kæpɪtə/ *adj & adv* pro capite

perceive /pə'siːv/ *vt* percepire; (interpret) interpretare

per cent *adv* per cento

percentage /pə'sentɪdʒ/ *n* percentuale *f*

perceptible /pə'septəbl/ *adj* percettibile; fig sensibile

perceptibly /pə'septɪblɪ/ *adv* percettibilmente; fig sensibilmente

perception /pə'sepʃn/ *n* percezione *f*

perceptive /pə'septɪv/ *adj* perspicace

perch[1] /pɜːtʃ/ **①** *n* pertica *f*
② *vi* ⟨*bird*⟩ appollaiarsi

perch[2] *n inv* (fish) pesce *m* persico

percolate /'pɜːkəleɪt/ *vi* infiltrarsi; ⟨*coffee*⟩ passare

percolator /'pɜːkəleɪtə(r)/ *n* caffettiera *f* a filtro

percussion /pə'kʌʃn/ *n* percussione *f*

percussion instrument *n* strumento *m* a percussione

percussionist /pə'kʌʃ(ə)nɪst/ *n* percussionista *mf*

peremptory /pə'remptərɪ/ *adj* perentorio

perennial /pə'renɪəl/ **①** *adj* perenne
② *n* pianta *f* perenne

perfect[1] /'pɜːfɪkt/ **①** *adj* perfetto
② *n* Gram passato *m* prossimo

perfect[2] /pə'fekt/ *vt* perfezionare

perfection /pə'fekʃn/ *n* perfezione *f*; **to ~** alla perfezione

perfectionism /pə'fekʃənɪzm/ *n* perfezionismo *m*

perfectionist /pə'fekʃ(ə)nɪst/ *adj & n* perfezionista *mf*

perfectly /'pɜːfɪktlɪ/ *adv* perfettamente

perfidious /pə'fɪdɪəs/ *adj* perfido

perforate /'pɜːfəreɪt/ *vt* perforare

perforated /'pɜːfəreɪtɪd/ *adj* perforato; ⟨*ulcer*⟩ perforante

perforation /pɜːfə'reɪʃn/ *n* perforazione *f*

perform /pə'fɔːm/ **①** *vt* compiere, fare; eseguire ⟨*operation, sonata*⟩; recitare ⟨*role*⟩; mettere in scena ⟨*play*⟩
② *vi* Theat recitare; Techn funzionare

performance /pə'fɔːməns/ *n* esecuzione *f*; (at theatre, cinema) rappresentazione *f*; Techn rendimento *m*

performance artist *n* performance artist *mf*

performance bonus *n* premio *m* di produttività

performance indicators *npl* indicatori *mpl* di performance

performance-related *adj* commensurato alla produttività

performer /pə'fɔːmə(r)/ *n* artista *mf*

performing arts /pə'fɔːmɪŋ/ *npl* arti *fpl* dello spettacolo

perfume /'pɜːfjuːm/ *n* profumo *m*

perfumed /'pɜːfjuːmd/ *adj* profumato

perfunctory /pə'fʌŋktərɪ/ *adj* superficiale

perhaps /pə'hæps/ *adv* forse

peril /'perɪl/ *n* pericolo *m*

perilous /'perɪləs/ *adj* pericoloso

perilously /'perɪləslɪ/ *adv* pericolosamente

perimeter /pə'rɪmɪtə(r)/ *n* perimetro *m*

period /'pɪərɪəd/ **①** *n* periodo *m*; (menstruation) mestruazioni *fpl*; Sch ora *f* di lezione; (full stop) punto *m* fermo
② *attrib* (costume) d'epoca; ⟨*furniture*⟩ in stile

periodic /pɪərɪ'ɒdɪk/ *adj* periodico

periodical /pɪərɪ'ɒdɪkl/ *n* periodico *m*, rivista *f*

periodically /pɪərɪ'ɒdɪklɪ/ *adv* periodicamente

period of notice *n* periodo *m* di preavviso

peripheral /pə'rɪfərəl/ **①** *adj* periferico
② *n* Comput periferica *f*

periphery /pə'rɪfərɪ/ *n* periferia *f*

periscope /'perɪskəʊp/ *n* periscopio *m*

perish /'perɪʃ/ *vi* (rot) deteriorarsi; (die) perire

perishable /'perɪʃəbl/ **①** *adj* deteriorabile
② **~s** *npl* merce *f* deperibile

perished /'perɪʃt/ *adj* (fam: freezing cold) **be ~** essere intirizzito

perishing /'perɪʃɪŋ/ *adj* fam **it's ~** fa freddo da morire

peritonitis /perɪtə'naɪtɪs/ *n* peritonite *f*

perjure /'pɜːdʒə(r)/ *vt* ~ oneself spergiurare

perjury /'pɜːdʒərɪ/ *n* spergiuro *m*

perk[1] /pɜːk/ *n* fam vantaggio *m*

perk[2] *vi* Am ⟨*coffee*⟩ passare
■ **perk up** ① *vt* tirare su
② *vi* tirarsi su

perky /'pɜːkɪ/ *adj* allegro

perm /pɜːm/ ① *n* permanente *f*
② *vt* ~ sb's hair fare la permanente a qno

permanent /'pɜːmənənt/ ① *adj* permanente; ⟨*job, address*⟩ stabile
② *n* Am = PERM

permanently /'pɜːmənəntlɪ/ *adv* stabilmente

permeable /'pɜːmɪəbl/ *adj* permeabile

permeate /'pɜːmɪeɪt/ *vt* impregnare

permissible /pə'mɪsəbl/ *adj* ammissibile

permission /pə'mɪʃn/ *n* permesso *m*

permissive /pə'mɪsɪv/ *adj* permissivo

permit[1] /pə'mɪt/ *vt* (pt/pp -**mitted**) permettere; ~ **somebody to do something** permettere a qualcuno di fare qualcosa

permit[2] /'pɜːmɪt/ *n* autorizzazione *f*

pernicious /pə'nɪʃəs/ *adj* pernicioso

pernickety /pə'nɪkətɪ/ *adj* Br fam puntiglioso, pignolo; (about food) difficile

peroxide blonde /pə'rɒksaɪd/ *n* bionda *f* ossigenata

perpendicular /pɜːpən'dɪkjʊlə(r)/ *adj* & *n* perpendicolare *f*

perpetrate /'pɜːpɪtreɪt/ *vt* perpetrare

perpetrator /'pɜːpɪtreɪtə(r)/ *n* autore, -trice *mf*

perpetual /pə'petjʊəl/ *adj* perenne

perpetually /pə'petjʊəlɪ/ *adv* perennemente

perpetuate /pə'petjʊeɪt/ *vt* perpetuare

perplex /pə'pleks/ *vt* lasciare perplesso

perplexed /pə'plekst/ *adj* perplesso

perplexity /pə'pleksɪtɪ/ *n* perplessità *f* inv

perquisite /'pɜːsɪkjuːt/ *n* fringe benefit *m* inv, beneficio *m* accessorio

per se /pɜː'seɪ/ *adv* in sé

persecute /'pɜːsɪkjuːt/ *vt* perseguitare

persecution /pɜːsɪ'kjuːʃn/ *n* persecuzione *f*

persecutor /'pɜːsɪkjuːtə(r)/ *n* persecutore, -trice *mf*

perseverance /pɜːsɪ'vɪərəns/ *n* perseveranza *f*

persevere /pɜːsɪ'vɪə(r)/ *vi* perseverare

persevering /pɜːsɪ'vɪərɪŋ/ *adj* assiduo

Persian /'pɜːʃn/ *adj* persiano

persist /pə'sɪst/ *vi* persistere; ~ **in doing something** persistere nel fare qualcosa

persistence /pə'sɪstəns/ *n* persistenza *f*

persistent /pə'sɪsənt/ *adj* persistente

persistently /pə'sɪstəntlɪ/ *adv* persistentemente

persistent offender *n* recidivo, -a *mf*

person /'pɜːsn/ *n* persona *f*; **in** ~ di persona

persona /pə'səʊnə/ *n* Psych individuo *m*; Theat personaggio *m*

personable /'pɜːsənəbl/ *adj* di bella presenza

personage /'pɜːsənɪdʒ/ *n* personaggio *m*

personal /'pɜːsənl/ *adj* personale

personal ad *n* annuncio *m* personale

personal allowance *n* (in taxation) quota *f* non imponibile

personal assistant *n* segretario, -a *mf* personale

personal belongings *npl* effetti *mpl* personali

personal column *n* rubrica *f* degli annunci personali

personal computer *n* personal computer *m* inv

personal hygiene *n* igiene *f* personale

personality /pɜːsə'nælətɪ/ *n* personalità *f* inv; (on TV) personaggio *m*

personalize /'pɜːsənəlaɪz/ *vt* personalizzare ⟨*stationery, clothing*⟩; mettere sul piano personale ⟨*issue, dispute*⟩

personal loan *n* prestito *m* a privato

personally /'pɜːsənəlɪ/ *adv* personalmente

personal organizer *n* Comput agenda *f* elettronica

personal stereo *n* walkman® *m* inv

personification /pəsɒnɪfɪ'keɪʃn/ *n* **the** ~ **of** la personificazione di

personify /pə'sɒnɪfaɪ/ *vt* (pt/pp -**ied**) personificare

personnel /pɜːsə'nel/ *n* personale *m*

personnel director *n* direttore, -trice *mf* del personale

personnel management *n* gestione *f* del personale

perspective /pə'spektɪv/ *n* prospettiva *f*

perspex® /'pɜːspeks/ *n* plexiglas® *m*

perspicacious /pɜːspɪ'keɪʃəs/ *adj* perspicace

perspiration /pɜːspɪ'reɪʃn/ *n* sudore *m*

perspire /pə'spaɪə(r)/ *vi* sudare

persuade /pə'sweɪd/ *vt* persuadere

persuasion /pə'sweɪʒn/ *n* persuasione *f*; (belief) convinzione *f*

persuasive /pə'sweɪsɪv/ *adj* persuasivo

persuasively /pə'sweɪsɪvlɪ/ *adv* in modo persuasivo

pert /pɜːt/ *adj* (lively) esuberante

pertinent /ˈpɜːtɪnənt/ *adj* pertinente (**to** a)

perturb /pəˈtɜːb/ *vt* perturbare

perturbing /pəˈtɜːbɪŋ/ *adj* conturbante

Peru /pəˈruː/ *n* Perù *m*

peruse /pəˈruːz/ *vt* leggere

Peruvian /pəˈruːvɪən/ *adj & n* peruviano, -a *mf*

pervade /pəˈveɪd/ *vt* pervadere

pervasive /pəˈveɪsɪv/ *adj* pervasivo

perverse /pəˈvɜːs/ *adj* perverso; (illogical) irragionevole

perversely /pəˈvɜːslɪ/ *adv* in modo perverso

perversion /pəˈvɜːʃn/ *n* perversione *f*

perversity /pəˈvɜːsɪtɪ/ *n* perversità *f*

pervert[1] /pəˈvɜːt/ *vt* deviare ‹*course of justice*›

pervert[2] /ˈpɜːvɜːt/ *n* pervertito, -a *mf*

perverted /pəˈvɜːtɪd/ *adj* perverso

pessary /ˈpesərɪ/ *n* candeletta *f*

pessimism /ˈpesɪmɪzm/ *n* pessimismo *m*

pessimist /ˈpesɪmɪst/ *n* pessimista *mf*

pessimistic /pesɪˈmɪstɪk/ *adj* pessimistico

pessimistically /pesɪˈmɪstɪklɪ/ *adv* in modo pessimistico

pest /pest/ *n* piaga *f*; (fam: person) peste *f*

pester /ˈpestə(r)/ *vt* molestare

pesticide /ˈpestɪsaɪd/ *n* pesticida *m*

pestilential /pestɪˈlenʃəl/ *adj* (hum: annoying) fastidiosissimo

pestle /ˈpesl/ *n* pestello *m*

pet /pet/ ① *n* animale *m* domestico; (favourite) cocco, -a *mf* ② *adj* (favourite) prediletto ③ *vt* (pt/pp **petted**) coccolare ④ *vi* ‹*couple*› praticare il petting

petal /ˈpetl/ *n* petalo *m*

peter /ˈpiːtə(r)/ *vi* ~ out finire

pet food *n* cibo *m* per animali

pet hate *n* Br bestia *f* nera

petite /pəˈtiːt/ *adj* minuto

petition /pəˈtɪʃn/ *n* petizione *f*

pet name *n* vezzeggiativo *m*

petrified /ˈpetrɪfaɪd/ *adj* (frightened) pietrificato

petrify /ˈpetrɪfaɪ/ *vt* (pt/pp **-ied**) pietrificare

petrochemical /petrəʊˈkemɪkl/ *n* petrolchimico *m*

petrodollar /ˈpetrəʊdɒlə(r)/ *n* petroldollaro *m*

petrol /ˈpetrəl/ *n* Br benzina *f*

petrol bomb *n* Br [bomba *f*] molotov *f inv*

petrol can *n* tanica *f* di benzina

petroleum /pɪˈtrəʊlɪəm/ *n* petrolio *m*

petroleum jelly *n* vaselina *f*

petrol-pump *n* Br pompa *f* di benzina

petrol station *n* Br stazione *f* di servizio

petrol tank *n* Br serbatoio *m* della benzina

pet shop *n* negozio *m* di animali

petticoat /ˈpetɪkəʊt/ *n* sottoveste *f*

pettifogging /ˈpetɪfɒgɪŋ/ *adj* pej cavilloso

petty /ˈpetɪ/ *adj* (**-ier**, **-iest**) insignificante; (mean) meschino

petty cash *n* cassa *f* per piccole spese

petty crime *n* piccola criminalità *f*

petty minded /-ˈmaɪndɪd/ *adj* meschino

petty officer *n* sottufficiale *m*

petty theft *n* furto *m* di minore entità

petulance /ˈpetjʊləns/ *n* petulanza *f*

petulant /ˈpetjʊlənt/ *adj* petulante

pew /pjuː/ *n* banco *m* (di chiesa)

pewter /ˈpjuːtə(r)/ *n* peltro *m*

PGCE *n abbr* Br (**postgraduate certificate in education**) diploma *m* di specializzazione nell'insegnamento

phallic /ˈfælɪk/ *adj* fallico

phallic symbol *n* simbolo *m* fallico

phallus /ˈfæləs/ *n* fallo *m*

phantom /ˈfæntəm/ *n* fantasma *m*

pharaoh /ˈfeərəʊ/ *n* faraone *m*

pharmaceutical /fɑːməˈsjuːtɪkl/ *adj* farmaceutico

pharmacist /ˈfɑːməsɪst/ *n* farmacista *mf*

pharmacy /ˈfɑːməsɪ/ *n* farmacia *f*

phase /feɪz/ ① *n* fase *f* ② *vt* ~ in/out introdurre/eliminare gradualmente

PhD *abbr* (**Doctor of Philosophy**) ≈ dottorato *m* di ricerca

pheasant /ˈfeznt/ *n* fagiano *m*

phenomenal /fɪˈnɒmɪnl/ *adj* fenomenale; (incredible) incredibile

phenomenally /fɪˈnɒmɪnəlɪ/ *adv* incredibilmente

phenomenon /fɪˈnɒmɪnən/ *n* (pl **-na**) fenomeno *m*

phew /fjuː/ *int* (when too hot, in relief) uff!; (in surprise) oh!

philanderer /fɪˈlændərə(r)/ *n* donnaiolo *m*

philanthropic /fɪlənˈθrɒpɪk/ *adj* filantropico

philanthropist /fɪˈlænθrəpɪst/ *adj* filantropo, -a *mf*

philatelist /fɪˈlætəlɪst/ *n* filatelico, -a *mf*

philately /fɪˈlætəlɪ/ *n* filatelia *f*

philharmonic /fɪhɑ:'mɒnɪk/ ① *n*
(orchestra) orchestra *f* filarmonica
② *adj* filarmonico
Philippines /'fɪlɪpi:nz/ *npl* Filippine *fpl*
philistine /'fɪlɪstaɪn/ *adj & n* filisteo, -a
mf
philology /fɪ'lɒlədʒɪ/ *n* filologia *f*
philosopher /fɪ'lɒsəfə(r)/ *n* filosofo, -a.
mf
philosophical /fɪlə'sɒfɪkl/ *adj* filosofico
philosophically /fɪlə'sɒfɪklɪ/ *adv* con
filosofia
philosophy /fɪ'lɒsəfɪ/ *n* filosofia *f*
phlebitis /flɪ'baɪtɪs/ *n* flebite *f*
phlegm /flem/ *n* Med flemma *f*
phlegmatic /fleg'mætɪk/ *adj*
flemmatico
phobia /'fəʊbɪə/ *n* fobia *f*
phobic /'fəʊbɪk/ *adj* fobico
phoenix /'fi:nɪks/ *n* fenice *f*
phone /fəʊn/ ① *n* telefono *m*; **be on the
~** avere il telefono; (be phoning) essere al
telefono
② *vt* telefonare a
■ **phone back** *vt* richiamare
■ **phone in** *vi* telefonare al lavoro; **he
~d in sick** ha telefonato [al lavoro] per
dire che è ammalato
■ **phone up** ① *vi* telefonare
② *vt* dare un colpo di telefono a
phone book *n* guida *f* del telefono
phone booth *n* cabina *f* telefonica
phone box *n* cabina *f* telefonica
phone call *n* telefonata *f*
phonecard *n* scheda *f* telefonica
phone-in *n* trasmissione *f* con chiamate
in diretta
phone link *n* phone link *m inv*
phoneme /'fəʊni:m/ *n* fonema *m*
phone number *n* numero *m* telefonico
phonetic /fə'netɪk/ *adj* fonetico
phonetics /fə'netɪks/ *n* fonetica *f*
phoney /'fəʊnɪ/ ① *adj* (**-ler**, **-iest**)
fasullo
② *n* ciarlatano, -a *mf*
phonology /fə'nɒlədʒɪ/ *n* fonologia *f*
phosphate /'fɒsfeɪt/ *n* fosfato *m*
phosphorus /'fɒsfərəs/ *n* fosforo *m*
photo /'fəʊtəʊ/ *n* foto *f*
photo album *n* album *m inv* di
fotografie
photo booth *n* macchina *f* fototessere
inv
photocall *n* photo opportunity *f*
photocell *n* fotocellula *f*
photocopier *n* fotocopiatrice *f*
photocopy ① *n* fotocopia *f*
② *vt* fotocopiare
photoengraving *n* fotoincisione *f*

photo finish *n* fotofinish *m*
photofit® *n* Br fotofit *m inv*
photogenic /fəʊtəʊ'dʒenɪk/ *adj*
fotogenico
photograph /'fəʊtəgrɑ:f/ ① *n* fotografia
f
② *vt* fotografare
photographer /fə'tɒgrəfə(r)/ *n*
fotografo, -a *mf*
photographic /fəʊtə'græfɪk/ *adj*
fotografico
photography /fə'tɒgrəfɪ/ *n* fotografia *f*
photojournalism *n* fotoreportage *m*
photojournalist *n* fotogiornalista *mf*
photomontage /fəʊtəʊmɒn'tɑ:ʒ/ *n*
fotomontaggio *m*
photo opportunity *n* photo
opportunity *f*
photosynthesis *n* fotosintesi *f*
phrase /freɪz/ ① *n* espressione *f*
② *vt* esprimere
phrase book *n* libro *m* di fraseologia
phut /fʌt/ *adv* fam **go ~** ⟨car, washing
machine etc⟩ scassarsi; ⟨plan⟩ andare in
fumo
physical /'fɪkl/ *adj* fisico
physical education *n* educazione *f*
fisica
physical fitness *n* forma *f* fisica
physically /'fɪzɪklɪ/ *adv* fisicamente
physically handicapped *adj*
handicappato fisicamente
physician /fɪ'zɪʃn/ *n* medico *m*
physicist /'fɪzɪsɪst/ *n* fisico, -a *mf*
physics /'fɪzɪks/ *n* fisica *f*
physio /'fɪzɪəʊ/ *n* Br fam (physiotherapist)
fisioterapista *mf*; (physiotherapy) fisioterapia
f
physiology /fɪzɪ'ɒlədʒɪ/ *n* fisiologia *f*
physiotherapist /fɪzɪəʊ'θerəpɪst/ *n*
fisioterapista *mf*
physiotherapy /fɪzɪəʊ'θerəpɪ/ *n*
fisioterapia *f*
physique /fɪ'zi:k/ *n* fisico *m*
pianist /'pɪənɪst/ *n* pianista *mf*
piano /pɪ'ænəʊ/ *n* piano *m*
pianola® /pɪə'nəʊlə/ *n* pianola® *f*
piazza /pɪ'ætsə/ *n* (public square) piazza *f*;
(Am: veranda) veranda *f*
pick[1] /pɪk/ *n* (tool) piccone *m*
pick[2] ① *n* scelta *f*; **take your ~** prendi
quello che vuoi
② *vt* (select) scegliere; cogliere ⟨flowers⟩;
scassinare ⟨lock⟩; borseggiare ⟨pockets⟩; **~
one's nose** mettersi le dita nel naso; **~ a
quarrel** attaccar briga; **~ holes in
something** (fam: criticize) criticare qualcosa
③ *vi* **~ and choose** fare il difficile
■ **pick at** *vt* piluccare ⟨food⟩; stuzzicare
⟨scab⟩

■ **pick off** *vt* (remove) togliere

■ **pick on** *vt* (fam: nag) assillare; **he always ∼s on me** ce l'ha con me

■ **pick out** *vt* (identify) individuare

■ **pick up** ① *vt* sollevare; raccogliere ⟨*fallen object, information*⟩; prendere in braccio ⟨*baby*⟩; prendere ⟨*passengers, habit*⟩; ⟨*police*⟩ arrestare ⟨*criminal*⟩; fam rimorchiare ⟨*girl*⟩; prendersi ⟨*illness*⟩; captare ⟨*signal*⟩; (buy) comprare; (learn) imparare; (collect) andare/venire a prendere; **∼ oneself up** riprendersi ② *vi* (improve) recuperare; ⟨*weather*⟩ rimettersi

pickaxe /'pɪkæks/ *n* piccone *m*

picker /'pɪkə(r)/ *n* raccoglitore, -trice *mf*

picket /'pɪkɪt/ ① *n* picchettista *mf* ② *vt* picchettare

picket line *n* picchetto *m*

pickings /'pɪkɪŋz/ *npl* **rich ∼** grossi guadagni

pickle /'pɪkl/ ① *n* ∼s *pl* sottaceti *mpl*; **in a ∼** fig nei pasticci ② *vt* mettere sottaceto

pick-me-up *n* (alcohol) cicchetto *m*; (medicine) tonico *m*

pickpocket /'pɪkpɒkɪt/ *n* borsaiolo *m*

pick-up *n* (truck) furgone *m*; (on record-player) pickup *m inv*

picky /'pɪkɪ/ *adj* (fam: choosy, fussy) difficile

picnic /'pɪknɪk/ ① *n* picnic *m* ② *vi* (pt/pp **-nicked**) fare un picnic

pictogram /'pɪktəgræm/ *n* (symbol) pittogramma *m*; (chart) tabella *f*

pictorial /pɪk'tɔ:rɪəl/ *adj* illustrato

picture /'pɪktʃə(r)/ ① *n* (painting) quadro *m*; (photo) fotografia *f*; (drawing) disegno *m*; (film) film *m inv*: **as pretty as a ∼** ⟨*girl*⟩ bella come una madonna; **put somebody in the ∼** fig mettere qualcuno al corrente; **the ∼s** Br fam il cinema ② *vt* (imagine) immaginare

picture [card] *n* (in pack of cards) figura *f*

picture messaging *n* Teleph picture messaging *m inv*

picturesque /pɪktʃə'resk/ *adj* pittoresco

piddle /'pɪdl/ *vi* fam fare pipì

pie /paɪ/ *n* torta *f*

piece /pi:s/ *n* pezzo *m*; (in game) pedina *f*; **a ∼ of bread/paper** un pezzo di pane/carta; **a ∼ of news/advice/junk** una notizia/un consiglio/una patacca; **take to ∼s** smontare

■ **piece together** *vt* montare; fig ricostruire

piecemeal /'pi:smi:l/ *adv* un po' alla volta

piecework /'pi:swɜ:k/ *n* lavoro *m* a cottimo

pie chart *n* grafico *f* a torta

Piedmont /'pi:dmɒnt/ *n* Piemonte *m*

pier /pɪə(r)/ molo *m*; (pillar) pilastro *m*

pierce /pɪəs/ *vt* perforare; **∼ a hole in something** fare un buco in qualcosa

piercing /'pɪəsɪŋ/ ① *adj* penetrante ② *n* (in body) piercing *m inv*

pig /pɪg/ *n* maiale *m* ■ **pig out** *vi* fam abbuffarsi; **∼ out on** abbuffarsi di

pigeon /'pɪdʒɪn/ *n* piccione *m*

pigeon-hole ① *n* casella *f* ② *vt* incasellare

pigeon-toed /-təʊd/ *adj* **be ∼** camminare con i piedi in dentro

piggery /'pɪgərɪ/ *n* (pigsty) porcile *m*; (fam: overeating) ingordigia *f*

piggyback /'pɪgɪbæk/ *n* **give somebody a ∼** portare qualcuno sulle spalle

piggy bank /'pɪgɪ/ *n* salvadanaio *m*

pig-headed /-'hedɪd/ *adj* fam cocciuto

piglet /'pɪglət/ *n* maialino *m*, porcellino *m*

pigment /'pɪgmənt/ *n* pigmento *m*

pigmentation /pɪgmən'teɪʃn/ *n* pigmentazione *f*

pigpen *n* Am = PIGSTY

pigskin /'pɪgskɪn/ *n* pelle *f* di cinghiale

pigsty *n* Br porcile *m*

pigtail /'pɪgteɪl/ *n* (plait) treccina *f*

pike /paɪk/ *n inv* (fish) luccio *m*

pilchard /'pɪtʃəd/ *n* sardina *f*

pile /paɪl/ ① *n* (heap) pila *f* ② *vt* **∼ something on to something** impilare qualcosa su qualcosa ■ **pile in** *vi* (enter, get on) entrare disordinatamente ■ **pile up** ① *vt* accatastare ② *vi* ammucchiarsi

piles /paɪlz/ *npl* emorroidi *fpl*

pile-up *n* tamponamento *m* a catena

pilfer /'pɪlfə(r)/ *vi/t* rubacchiare

pilfering /'pɪlfərɪŋ/ *n* piccoli furti *mpl*

pilgrim /'pɪlgrɪm/ *n* pellegrino, -a *mf*

pilgrimage /'pɪlgrɪmɪdʒ/ *n* pellegrinaggio *m*

pill /pɪl/ *n* pillola *f*

pillage /'pɪlɪdʒ/ *vt* saccheggiare

pillar /'pɪlə(r)/ *n* pilastro *m*

pillar box *n* buca *f* delle lettere

pillion /'pɪljən/ *n* sellino *m* posteriore; **ride ∼** viaggiare dietro

pillory /'pɪlərɪ/ *vt* (pt/pp **-ied**) fig mettere alla berlina

pillow /'pɪləʊ/ *n* guanciale *m*

pillowcase /'pɪləʊkeɪs/ *n* federa *f*

pilot /'paɪlət/ ① *n* pilota *mf* ② *vt* pilotare

pilot light *n* fiamma *f* di sicurezza

pilot scheme *n* progetto *m* pilota *inv*

pimp /pɪmp/ *n* protettore *m*

pimple /'pɪmpl/ n foruncolo m

pimply /'pɪmplɪ/ adj brufoloso

PIN /pɪn/ n abbr (**personal identification number**) [numero m di] codice m segreto

pin /pɪn/ ① n spillo m; electr spinotto m; Med chiodo m; **I have ∼s and needles in my leg** fam mi formicola una gamba
② vt (pt/pp **pinned**) appuntare (**to/on** su); (sewing) fissare con gli spilli; (hold down) immobilizzare; **∼ something on somebody** fam addossare a qualcuno la colpa di qualcosa
■ **pin down** vt (physically) immobilizzare; (to date) far fissare una data a ⟨somebody⟩; (identify) definire ⟨feeling, cause⟩
■ **pin up** vt appuntare; (on wall) affiggere

pinafore /'pɪnəfɔː(r)/ n grembiule m

pinafore dress n scamiciato m

pinball /'pɪnbɔːl/ n flipper m inv

pinball machine n flipper m inv

pincers /'pɪnsəz/ npl tenaglie fpl

pinch /pɪntʃ/ ① n pizzicotto m; (of salt) presa f; **at a ∼** fam in caso di bisogno
② vt pizzicare; (fam: steal) fregare
③ vi ⟨shoe⟩ stringere

pincushion /'pɪnkʊʃən/ n puntaspilli m inv

pine¹ /paɪn/ n (tree) pino m

pine² vi **she is pining for you** le manchi molto
■ **pine away** vi deperire

pineapple n ananas m inv

pine cone n pigna f

pine-needle n ago m di pino

pine nut n pinolo m

ping /pɪŋ/ n rumore m metallico

ping-pong n ping-pong m

pinhead /'pɪnhed/ n capocchia f di spillo; fam, pej testa f di rapa

pink /pɪŋk/ adj rosa inv

pinking shears, pinking scissors /'pɪŋkɪŋ/ npl forbici fpl a zigzag

pinnacle /'pɪnəkl/ n guglia f

PIN number n codice m segreto

pinpoint /'pɪnpɔɪnt/ vt definire con precisione

pinprick /'pɪnprɪk/ n puntura f di spillo; (fig: of jealousy, remorse) punta f

pinstripe /'pɪnstraɪp/ adj gessato

pint /'paɪntə/ n pinta f (Br = 0,57 l, Am = 0,47 l); **a ∼** fam una birra media

pin-up n ragazza f da copertina, pin-up f inv

pioneer /paɪə'nɪə(r)/ ① n pioniere, -a mf
② vt essere un pioniere di

pious /'paɪəs/ adj pio

pip¹ /pɪp/ n (seed) seme m

pip² n **the ∼s** il segnale orario; (telephone) il segnale telefonico

pip³ vt (pt/pp **pipped**) **be ∼ped at the post** essere battuto all'ultimo minuto

pipe /paɪp/ ① n tubo m; (for smoking) pipa f; **the ∼s** pl Mus la cornamusa
② vt far arrivare con tubature ⟨water, gas etc⟩; Culin mettere
■ **pipe down** vi fam abbassare la voce; (shut up) stare zitto
■ **pipe up** vi **∼ with a suggestion** venir fuori con una proposta

pipe-cleaner n scovolino m

piped music /paɪpt/ n musichetta f di sottofondo

pipe dream n illusione f

pipeline /'paɪplaɪn/ n conduttura f: **in the ∼** fam in cantiere

piper /'paɪpə(r)/ n suonatore m di cornamusa

piping /'paɪpɪŋ/ adj **∼ hot** bollente

pique /piːk/ n **in a fit of ∼** risentito

piracy /'paɪrəsɪ/ n pirateria f

piranha /pɪ'rɑːnə/ n piranha m

pirate /'paɪrət/ ① n pirata m
② vt pirateggiare

pirate copy n copia f pirata

pirated adj /'paɪrətɪd/ pirateggiato

pirate radio n radio f pirata

pirouette /pɪru:'et/ ① n piroetta f
② vi piroettare

Pisces /'paɪsiːz/ n Astr Pesci mpl

piss /pɪs/ sl ① n piscia f
② vi pisciare
■ **piss about, piss around** ① vi (waste time, play the fool) cazzeggiare
② vt **∼ somebody about** rompere le palle a qualcuno
■ **piss down** vi **it's ∼ing down** (raining heavily) piove a dirotto
■ **piss off** ① vt fare incacchiare; **that type of behaviour ∼es me off** questi comportamenti mi stanno sulle palle
② vi (leave) filarsela; **∼ off!** levati dalle palle!, va' a cagare!

pissed /pɪst/ adj sl sbronzo; **∼ as a newt** sbronzo come una cocuzza

pissed off adj sl scoglionato

pistachio [nut] /pɪ'stæʃɪəʊ/ n pistacchio m

pistol /'pɪstl/ n pistola f

piston /'pɪstn/ n Techn pistone m

pit /pɪt/ ① n fossa f; (mine) miniera f; (for orchestra) orchestra f; (of stomach) bocca f
② vt (pt/pp **pitted**) fig opporre (**against** a)

pit-a-pat /'pɪtəpæt/ n **go ∼** ⟨heart⟩ palpitare

pitbull [terrier] n pitbull m inv

pitch¹ /pɪtʃ/ ① n (tone) tono m; (level) altezza f; (in sport) campo m; (fig: degree) grado m
② vt montare ⟨tent⟩

pitch² n (substance) pece f

■ **pitch in** vi fam mettersi sotto

pitch-black adj nero come la pece; ⟨night⟩ buio pesto

pitch-dark adj buio pesto

pitcher /'pɪtʃə(r)/ n brocca f

pitchfork /'pɪtʃfɔːk/ n forca f

piteous /'pɪtɪəs/ adj pietoso

pitfall /'pɪtfɔːl/ n fig trabocchetto m

pith /pɪθ/ n (of lemon, orange) interno m della buccia; fig essenza f

pithy /'pɪθɪ/ adj (-ier, -iest) fig conciso

pitiable /'pɪtɪəbl/ adj pietoso

pitiful /'pɪtɪfl/ adj pietoso

pitifully /'pɪtɪfʊlɪ/ adv da far pietà

pitiless /'pɪtɪlɪs/ adj spietato

pitilessly /'pɪtɪlɪslɪ/ adv senza pietà

pittance /'pɪtns/ n miseria f

pitted /'pɪtɪd/ adj ⟨surface⟩ bucherellato; ⟨face, skin⟩ butterato; ⟨olive⟩ snocciolato

pituitary /pɪ'tjuːɪt(ə)rɪ/ adj pituitario

pituitary gland n ghiandola f pituitaria, ipofisi f

pity /'pɪtɪ/ **1** n pietà f; [what a] ~! che peccato!; **take** ~ **on** avere compassione di **2** vt aver pietà di

pivot /'pɪvət/ **1** n perno m; fig fulcro m **2** vi imperniarsi (**on** su)

pivotal /'pɪvətl/ adj ⟨role⟩ centrale; ⟨decision⟩ cruciale

pixel /'pɪksəl/ n pixel m inv

pixie /'pɪksɪ/ n folletto m

pizza /'piːtsə/ n pizza f

placard /'plækɑːd/ n cartellone m

placate /plə'keɪt/ vt placare

place /pleɪs/ **1** n posto m; (fam: house) casa f; (in book) segno m; **feel out of** ~ sentirsi fuori posto; **take** ~ aver luogo; **all over the** ~ dappertutto **2** vt collocare; (remember) identificare; ~ **an order** fare un'ordinazione; **be** ~**d** (in race) piazzarsi

placebo /plə'siːbəʊ/ n Med placebo m inv; fig contentino m

place mat n sottopiatto m

placement /'pleɪsmənt/ n (act: in accommodation) collocamento m; (Br: job) stage m inv

place name n toponimo m

placenta /plə'sentə/ n placenta f

placid /'plæsɪd/ adj placido

plagiarism /'pleɪdʒərɪzm/ n plagio m

plagiarist /'pleɪdʒərɪst/ n plagiario, -a mf

plagiarize /'pleɪdʒəraɪz/ vt plagiare

plague /pleɪg/ n peste f

plaice /pleɪs/ n inv platessa f

plaid /plæd/ **1** n (fabric) plaid m inv; (pattern) motivo m scozzese **2** attrib ⟨scarf, shirt⟩ scozzese

plain /pleɪn/ **1** adj chiaro; (simple) semplice; (not pretty) scialbo; (not patterned) in tinta unita; ⟨chocolate⟩ fondente; **in** ~ **clothes** in borghese **2** adv (simply) semplicemente **3** n pianura f

plain-clothes adj ⟨policeman etc⟩ in borghese

plainly /'pleɪnlɪ/ adv francamente; (simply) semplicemente; (obviously) chiaramente

plain paper fax n fax m inv a carta comune

plain-spoken adj franco

plaintiff /'pleɪntɪf/ n Jur parte f lesa

plaintive /'pleɪntɪv/ adj lamentoso

plaintively /'pleɪntɪvlɪ/ adv con aria lamentosa

plait /plæt/ **1** n treccia f **2** vt intrecciare

plan /plæn/ **1** n progetto m, piano m **2** vt (pt/pp **planned**) progettare; (intend) prevedere

■ **plan ahead** vi pianificare

plane[1] /pleɪn/ n (tree) platano m

plane[2] n aeroplano m; (in geometry) piano m

plane[3] **1** n (tool) pialla f **2** vt piallare

plane crash n incidente m aereo

planet /'plænɪt/ n pianeta m

plank /plæŋk/ n asse f

■ **plank down** vt (fam: put down) mollare

plankton /'plæŋktən/ n plancton m

planner /'plænə(r)/ n progettista mf; (in town planning) urbanista mf

planning /'plænɪŋ/ n pianificazione f

planning permission n licenza f edilizia

plant /plɑːnt/ **1** n pianta f; (machinery) impianto m; (factory) stabilimento m **2** vt piantare; ~ **oneself in front of somebody** piantarsi davanti a qualcuno

plantation /plæn'teɪʃn/ n piantagione f

planter /'plɑːntə(r)/ n (person) piantatore, -trice mf; (machine) piantatrice f

plant life n flora f

plaque /plɑːk/ n placca f

plasma /'plæzmə/ n plasma m

plaster /'plɑːstə(r)/ **1** n intonaco m; Med gesso m; (sticking ~) cerotto m; **in** ~ ingessato **2** vt intonacare ⟨wall⟩; (cover) ricoprire

plaster cast n ingessatura f

plastered /'plɑːstəd/ adj (sl: drunk) sbronzo

plasterer /'plɑːstərə(r)/ n intonacatore m

plaster of Paris n gesso m

plastic /'plæstɪk/ **1** n plastica f **2** adj plastico

Plasticine® /'plæstɪsiːn/ n Plastilina® f

plastic surgeon n chirurgo m plastico

plastic surgery n chirurgia f plastica

plate /pleɪt/ ① n piatto m; (flat sheet) placca f; (gold and silverware) argenteria f; (in book) tavola f fuori testo
② vt (cover with metal) placcare

plateau /ˈplætəʊ/ ① n (pl ~x /ˈplætəʊz/) altopiano m
② vi fig livellarsi

plate glass n lastra f di vetro

platform /ˈplætfɔːm/ n (stage) palco m; Rail marciapiede m; Pol piattaforma f; ~ **5** binario 5

platform shoes npl scarpe fpl con la zeppa

platinum /ˈplætɪnəm/ ① n platino m
② attrib di platino

platinum blonde n bionda f platinata

platitude /ˈplætɪtjuːd/ n luogo m comune

platonic /pləˈtɒnɪk/ adj platonico

platoon /pləˈtuːn/ n Mil plotone m

platter /ˈplætə(r)/ n piatto m da portata

platypus /ˈplætɪpəs/ n ornitorinco m

plausibility /plɔːzɪˈbɪlɪti/ n plausibilità f

plausible /ˈplɔːzəbl/ adj plausibile

play /pleɪ/ ① n gioco m; Theat, TV dramma m, opera f teatrale; (performance) rappresentazione f; Ratio sceneggiato m radiofonico; ~ **on words** gioco m di parole
② vt giocare a; (act) recitare; suonare ⟨instrument⟩; giocare ⟨card⟩
③ vi giocare; Mus suonare; ~ **by the rules** stare alle regole; ~ **with fire** scherzare col fuoco; ~ **dumb** fare lo gnorri; ~ **safe** non prendere rischi
■ **play along** vi ~ **along with somebody** (fam: cooperate) fare il gioco di qualcuno
■ **play around with** vt (meddle with) cincischiarsi con
■ **play back** vt riascoltare ⟨recording⟩
■ **play down** vt minimizzare
■ **play on** ① vi (continue to play) continuare a giocare
② vt (exploit) giocare su
■ **play out** vt vivere ⟨drama, fantasy⟩
■ **play up** vi fam fare i capricci

play-acting n commedia f

playboy /ˈpleɪbɔɪ/ n playboy m inv

player /ˈpleɪə(r)/ n giocatore, -trice mf

playful /ˈpleɪfʊl/ adj scherzoso

playfully /ˈpleɪfʊlɪ/ adv in modo scherzoso

playground /ˈpleɪɡraʊnd/ n Sch cortile m (per la ricreazione)

playgroup /ˈpleɪɡruːp/ n asilo m

playhouse n casetta f per i giochi

playing card /ˈpleɪɪŋ/ n carta f da gioco

playing field n campo m da gioco

playmate n compagno, -a mf di gioco

playpen n box m inv

play-off n play off m inv

playroom /ˈpleɪruːm/ n ludoteca f

plaything n giocattolo m

playtime n ricreazione f

playwright /ˈpleɪraɪt/ n drammaturgo, -a mf

plaza /ˈplɑːzə/ n (public square) piazza f; (shopping ~) centro m commerciale; (Am: services point) area f di servizio; (Am: toll point) casello m

plc abbr (**public limited company**) s.r.l.

plea /pliː/ n richiesta f; enter a ~ **of not guilty** Jur dichiararsi non colpevole; make a ~ **for** fare un appello a

plead /pliːd/ ① vi fare appello (for a); ~ **guilty** dichiararsi colpevole; ~ **with somebody** implorare qualcuno
② vt Jur perorare ⟨case⟩

pleasant /ˈpleznt/ adj piacevole

pleasantly /ˈplezntlɪ/ adv piacevolmente; ⟨say, smile⟩ cordialmente

pleasantry /ˈplezntrɪ/ n (joke) battuta f; **pleasantries** (pl: polite remarks) convenevoli mpl

please /pliːz/ ① adv per favore; ~ **do** prego
② vt far contento; ~ **oneself** fare il proprio comodo; ~ **yourself!** come vuoi!; pej fai come ti pare!

pleased /pliːzd/ adj lieto; ~ **with/about** contento di

pleasing /ˈpliːzɪŋ/ adj gradevole

pleasurable /ˈpleʒərəbl/ adj gradevole

pleasure /ˈpleʒə(r)/ n piacere m; with ~ con piacere, volentieri

pleat /pliːt/ ① n piega f
② vt pieghettare

pleated /ˈpliːtɪd/ adj a pieghe

pleb /pleb/ n fam plebeo, -a mf

plebby /ˈplebɪ/ adj fam plebeo

plebeian /plɪˈbiːən/ pej ① n plebeo, -a mf
② adj plebeo

plebiscite /ˈplebɪsaɪt/ n plebiscito m

pledge /pledʒ/ ① n pegno m; (promise) promessa f
② vt (pawn) impegnare; ~ **to do something** impegnarsi a fare qualcosa

plenary /ˈpliːnərɪ/ adj ⟨session⟩ plenario; ⟨powers⟩ pieno; ⟨authority⟩ assoluto

plentiful /ˈplentɪfl/ adj abbondante

plenty /ˈplentɪ/ n abbondanza f; ~ **of money** molti soldi; ~ **of people** molta gente; I've got ~ ne ho in abbondanza

pleurisy /ˈplʊərəsɪ/ n pleurite f

pliability /plaɪəˈbɪlɪtɪ/ n flessibilità f

pliable /ˈplaɪəbl/ adj flessibile

pliers /ˈplaɪəz/ npl pinze fpl

plight /plaɪt/ n triste condizione f

plimsolls /'plɪmsɒlz/ npl scarpe fpl da ginnastica

plinth /plɪnθ/ n plinto m

plod /plɒd/ vi (pt/pp **plodded**) trascinarsi; (work hard) sgobbare
■ **plod away** vi (work hard) sgobbare; ~ **away at** sgobbare su

plodder /'plɒdə(r)/ n sgobbone, -a mf

plonk[1] /plɒŋk/ n fam vino m; (poor wine) vinaccio m

plonk[2] vt (fam: put) sbattere

plop /plɒp/ [1] n plop m inv
[2] vi (pt/pp **plopped**) fare plop

plot /plɒt/ [1] n complotto m; (of novel) trama f; ~ **of land** appezzamento m [di terreno]
[2] vt/i (pt/pp **plotted**) complottare

plotter /'plɒtə(r)/ n (schemer) cospiratore, -trice mf; Comput plotter m inv, tracciatore m

plough /plaʊ/ [1] n aratro m
[2] vt/i arare
■ **plough back** vt Comm reinvestire
■ **plough into** vt (crash into) schiantarsi contro
■ **plough through** vt procedere a fatica in

ploughman /'plaʊmən/ n aratore m

ploughman's lunch n Br piatto m freddo a base di pane, formaggio e sottaceti

plow /plaʊ/ Am [1] n aratro m
[2] vt/i arare

ploy /plɔɪ/ n fam manovra f

pluck /plʌk/ [1] n fegato m
[2] vt strappare; depilare ⟨eyebrows⟩; spennare ⟨bird⟩; cogliere ⟨flower⟩
■ **pluck up** vt ~ **up courage** farsi coraggio

plucky /'plʌkɪ/ adj (**-ier, -iest**) coraggioso

plug /plʌg/ [1] n tappo m; Electr spina f; Auto candela f; (fam: advertisement) pubblicità f inv
[2] vt (pt/pp **plugged**) tappare; (fam: advertise) pubblicizzare
■ **plug away** vi (work hard) lavorare sodo
■ **plug in** vt Electr inserire la spina di

plug and play n Comput plug and play m inv

plughole /'plʌghəʊl/ n Br scarico m

plug-in adj con la spina

plum /plʌm/ n susina f; (tree) susino m

plumage /'pluːmɪdʒ/ n piumaggio m

plumb /plʌm/ [1] adj verticale
[2] adv esattamente
■ **plumb in** vt collegare

plumber /'plʌmə(r)/ n idraulico m

plumbing /'plʌmɪŋ/ n impianto m idraulico

plumb line n filo m a piombo

plume /pluːm/ n piuma f

plummet /'plʌmɪt/ vi precipitare; ⟨prices⟩ crollare

plump /plʌmp/ adj paffuto
■ **plump down** vt (put down) lasciare cadere
■ **plump for** vt scegliere

plumpness /'plʌmpnɪs/ n rotondità f

plunder /'plʌndə(r)/ [1] n (booty) bottino m
[2] vt saccheggiare

plunge /plʌndʒ/ [1] n tuffo m; **take the** ~ fam buttarsi
[2] vt tuffare; fig sprofondare; ~ **somebody into despair** piombare qualcuno nella disperazione
[3] vi tuffarsi

plunger /'plʌndʒə(r)/ n (tool) sturalavandini m inv; (handle) stantuffo m

plunging /'plʌndʒɪŋ/ adj ~ **neckline** scollatura f profonda

pluperfect /pluː'pɜːfɪkt/ n trapassato m prossimo

plural /'plʊərəl/ adj & n plurale m

plus /plʌs/ [1] prep più
[2] adj in più; **500** ~ più di 500
[3] n più m; (advantage) extra m inv

plush /plʌʃ/ adj ⟨hotel etc⟩ lussuoso

plus sign n (segno m) più m inv

Pluto /'pluːtəʊ/ n Plutone m

plutonium /pluː'təʊnɪəm/ n plutonio m

ply /plaɪ/ vt (pt/pp **plied**) esercitare ⟨trade⟩; ~ **somebody with drink** continuare ad offrire da bere a qualcuno

plywood /'plaɪwʊd/ n compensato m

PM abbr **Prime Minister**

p.m. abbr (**post meridiem**) del pomeriggio

PMS n abbr (**premenstrual syndrome**) sindrome f premestruale

PMT n abbr (**premenstrual tension**) tensione f premestruale

pneumatic /njuː'mætɪk/ adj pneumatico

pneumatic drill n martello m pneumatico

pneumonia /njuː'məʊnɪə/ n polmonite f

PO abbr (**Post Office**) ≈ P.T.; abbr (**postal order**) vaglia m inv postale

poach /pəʊtʃ/ vt Culin bollire; cacciare di frodo ⟨deer⟩; pescare di frodo ⟨salmon⟩; ~**ed egg** uovo m in camicia

poacher /'pəʊtʃə(r)/ n bracconiere m

PO Box n abbr (**Post Office Box**) C.P. f

pocket /'pɒkɪt/ [1] n tasca f; ~ **of resistance** sacca f di resistenza; **be out of** ~ rimetterci
[2] vt intascare

pocket-book n taccuino m; (wallet) portafoglio m

pocket-money n denaro m per le piccole spese

pock-marked /'pɒkmɑːkt/ adj butterato

pod /pɒd/ n baccello m

podgy /'pɒdʒɪ/ adj (-ier, -iest) grassoccio

podiatrist /pə'daɪətrɪst/ n Am pedicure mf inv

podium /'pəʊdɪəm/ n podio m

poem /'pəʊɪm/ n poesia f

poet /'pəʊɪt/ n poeta m

poetic /pəʊ'etɪk/ adj poetico

poetic licence n licenza f poetica

Poet Laureate /'lɔːrɪət/ n poeta m laureato

poetry /'pəʊɪtrɪ/ n poesia f

po-faced /pəʊ'feɪst/ adj Br fam look/be ~ avere un'aria di disapprovazione

poignancy /'pɔɪnjənsɪ/ n pregnanza f

poignant /'pɔɪnjənt/ adj pregnante

point /pɔɪnt/ ① n punto m; (sharp end) punta f; (meaning, purpose) senso m; Electr presa f; **what is the ~?** a che scopo?; **the ~ is** il fatto è; **I don't see the ~** non vedo il senso; **up to a ~** fino ad un certo punto; **be on the ~ of doing something** essere sul punto di fare qualcosa; **~s** pl Rail scambio m; **good/bad ~s** aspetti mpl positivi/negativi
② vt puntare (at verso)
③ vi (with finger) puntare il dito; **~ at/to** ⟨person⟩ mostrare col dito; ⟨indicator⟩ indicare; **~ and click** Comput punta e clicca
■ **point out** vt far notare ⟨fact⟩; **~ something out to somebody** far notare qualcosa a qualcuno

point-blank adj a bruciapelo

pointed /'pɔɪntɪd/ adj appuntito; ⟨question⟩ diretto

pointer /'pɔɪntə(r)/ n (piece of advice) consiglio m

pointillism /'pwæntɪlɪzm/ n divisionismo m

pointillist /'pwæntɪlɪst/ n divisionista mf

pointing /'pɔɪntɪŋ/ n Constr rifinitura f con la malta

pointing device n Comput dispositivo m di puntamento

pointless /'pɔɪntlɪs/ adj inutile

point of order n mozione f d'ordine

point of sale n (place) punto m di vendita; (promotional material) materiale m pubblicitario

point-of-sale promotion n promozione f punto vendita

point of view n punto m di vista

poise /pɔɪz/ n padronanza f

poised /pɔɪzd/ adj in equilibrio; (composed) padrone di sé; **~ to** sul punto di

poison /'pɔɪzn/ ① n veleno m
② vt avvelenare

poisoned /'pɔɪz(ə)nd/ adj avvelenato

poisoner /'pɔɪzənə(r)/ n avvelenatore, -trice mf

poisonous /'pɔɪzənəs/ adj velenoso

poison-pen letter n lettera f anonima diffamatoria

poke /pəʊk/ ① n spintarella f
② vt spingere; ⟨fire⟩ attizzare; (put) ficcare; **~ fun at** prendere in giro
■ **poke about**, **poke around** vi frugare
■ **poke out** vi (protrude) spuntare

poker¹ /'pəʊkə(r)/ n attizzatoio m

poker² n (Cards) poker m

poker-faced /-'feɪst/ adj ⟨person⟩ impassibile

poky /'pəʊkɪ/ adj (-ier, -iest) angusto

Poland /'pəʊlənd/ n Polonia f

polar /'pəʊlə(r)/ adj polare

polar bear n orso m bianco

polarity /pə'lærətɪ/ n Electr, Phys, fig polarità f inv

polarize /'pəʊləraɪz/ vt polarizzare

polarized adj polarizzato

Pole /pəʊl/ n polacco, -a mf

pole¹ n palo m

pole² n Geog, Electr polo m

polemic /pə'lemɪk/ n polemica f

polemical /pə'lemɪkl/ adj polemico

pole star n stella f polare

pole vault n salto m con l'asta

police /pə'liːs/ ① npl polizia f
② vt pattugliare ⟨area⟩; sorvegliare ⟨behaviour⟩

police car n gazzella f

police constable n agente mf di polizia

Police Department n Am dipartimento m di polizia

police force n polizia f

policeman n poliziotto m

police officer n agente mf di polizia

police state n stato m militarista

police station n commissariato m

policewoman n donna f poliziotto

policing /pə'liːsɪŋ/ n (maintaining law and order) mantenimento m dell'ordine pubblico; (of demonstration, match) organizzazione f del servizio d'ordine

policy¹ /'pɒlɪsɪ/ n politica f

policy² n (insurance) polizza f

policyholder n titolare mf della polizza

policy unit n Pol comitato m responsabile della linea politica

polio /'pəʊlɪəʊ/ n polio f

Polish /'pəʊlɪʃ/ *adj & n* polacco *m*

polish /'pɒlɪʃ/ **1** *n* (shine) lucentezza *f*; (substance) lucido *m*; (for nails) smalto *m*; fig raffinatezza *f*
2 *vt* lucidare; fig smussare
■ **polish off** *vt* fam finire; far fuori ⟨*food*⟩
■ **polish up** *vt* rispolverare ⟨*Italian*⟩

polished /'pɒlɪʃt/ *adj* ⟨*manner*⟩ raffinato; ⟨*performance*⟩ senza sbavature

polisher /'pɒləʃə(r)/ *n* (machine) lucidatrice *f*

polite /pə'laɪt/ *adj* cortese

politely /pə'laɪtlɪ/ *adv* cortesemente

politeness /pə'laɪtnɪs/ *n* cortesia *f*

politic /'pɒlɪtɪk/ *adj* prudente

political /pə'lɪtɪkl/ *adj* politico

politically /pə'lɪtɪklɪ/ *adv* dal punto di vista politico; ~ **correct** politicamente corretto

political prisoner *n* prigioniero, -a *mf* politico

politician /pɒlɪ'tɪʃn/ *n* politico *m*

politicize /pə'lɪtɪsaɪz/ *vt* politicizzare

politics /'pɒlɪtɪks/ *n* politica *f*

polka /'pɒlkə/ *n* polka *f*

polka dot **1** *n* pois *m inv*, pallino *m* **2** *attrib* a pois

poll /pəʊl/ **1** *n* votazione *f*; (election) elezioni *fpl*; [opinion] ~ sondaggio *m* d'opinione; **go to the** ~**s** andare alle urne **2** *vt* ottenere ⟨*votes*⟩

pollen /'pɒlən/ *n* polline *m*

polling booth /'pəʊlɪŋ/ *n* cabina *f* elettorale

polling day *n* giorno *m* delle elezioni

polling station *n* seggio *m* elettorale

pollster /'pəʊlstə(r)/ *n* (person) persona *f* che esegue un sondaggio d'opinione

poll tax *n* imposta *f* locale sulle persone fisiche

pollutant /pə'lu:tənt/ *n* sostanza *f* inquinante

pollute /pə'lu:t/ *vt* inquinare

polluted /pə'lu:tɪd/ *adj* inquinato

polluter /pə'lu:tə(r)/ *n* inquinatore, -trice *mf*

pollution /pə'lu:ʃn/ *n* inquinamento *m*

polo /'pəʊləʊ/ *n* polo *m*

polo neck *n* collo *m* alto

polo shirt *n* dolcevita *f*

poltergeist /'pɒltəgaɪst/ *n* poltergeist *m inv*

poly /'pɒlɪ/ *n* (Br fam: polytechnic) politecnico *m*

poly bag *n* sacchetto *m* di plastica

polyester /pɒlɪ'estə(r)/ *n* poliestere *m*

polygamous /pə'lɪgəməs/ *adj* poligamico

polygamy /pə'lɪgəmɪ/ *n* poligamia *f*

polymath /'pɒlɪmæθ/ *n* erudito, -a *mf*

polymer /'pɒlɪmə(r)/ *n* polimero *m*

polystyrene® /pɒlɪ'staɪri:n/ *n* polistirolo *m*

polytechnic /pɒlɪ'teknɪk/ *n* politecnico *m*

polythene /'pɒlɪθi:n/ *n* politene *m*

polythene bag *n* sacchetto *m* di plastica

polyunsaturates /pɒlɪʌn'sætjʊreɪts/ *npl* grassi *mpl* polinsaturi

pomade /pə'meɪd/ *n* pomata *f*

pomegranate /'pɒmɪgrænɪt/ *n* melagrana *f*

pomp /pɒmp/ *n* pompa *f*

pompom /'pɒmpɒm/, **pompon** *n* pompon *m*

pomposity /pɒm'pɒsətɪ/ *n* pomposità *f*

pompous /'pɒmpəs/ *adj* pomposo

pompously /'pɒmpəslɪ/ *adv* pomposamente

poncy /'pɒnsɪ/ *adj* fam da finocchio; ⟨*person*⟩ finocchio

pond /pɒnd/ *n* stagno *m*

ponder /'pɒndə(r)/ *vt/i* ponderare

ponderous /'pɒndərəs/ *adj* ponderoso; fig pesante

pong /pɒŋ/ **1** *n* fam puzza *f* **2** *vi* puzzare

pontiff /'pɒntɪf/ *n* pontefice *m*

pontificate /pɒn'tɪfɪkeɪt/ *vi* pontificare

pontoon /pɒn'tu:n/ *n* (float) galleggiante *m*; (pier) pontile *m*; (Br: game) ventuno *m*

pony /'pəʊnɪ/ *n* pony *m inv*

ponytail /'pəʊnɪteɪl/ *n* coda *f* di cavallo

pony-trekking /'pəʊnɪtrekɪŋ/ *n* escursioni *fpl* col pony

pooch /pu:tʃ/ *n* (fam: dog) cagnetto *m*

poodle /'pu:dl/ *n* barboncino *m*

poof /pʊf/, **poofter** /'pʊftə(r)/ *n* (Br fam: homosexual) finocchio *m*

pooh /pu:/ **1** *int* (scorn, disgust) puah! **2** *n* (Br: baby talk) popò *f inv*

pooh-pooh /pu:'pu:/ *vt* fam ridere di ⟨*suggestion*⟩

pool[1] /pu:l/ *n* (of water, blood) pozza *f*; [swimming] ~ piscina *f*

pool[2] **1** *n* (common fund) cassa *f* comune; (in cards) piatto *m*; (game) biliardo *m* a buca; ~**s** *pl* ≈ totocalcio *msg* **2** *vt* mettere insieme

pool table *n* tavolo *m* da biliardo

pooped /pu:pt/ *adj* fam be ~ [out] essere stanco morto

poor /pʊə(r)/ **1** *adj* povero; (not good) scadente; in ~ **health** in cattiva salute **2** *npl* the ~ i poveri

poorly /'pʊəlɪ/ **1** *adj* be ~ non stare bene

2 *adv* male
pop¹ /pɒp/ **1** *n* botto *m*; (drink) bibita *f* gasata
2 *vt* (pt/pp **popped**) (fam: put) mettere; (burst) far scoppiare
3 *vi* (burst) scoppiare
■ **pop in** *vi* fam fare un salto
■ **pop out** *vi* fam uscire; ∼ **out to the shop** fare un salto al negozio
■ **pop round** *vi* fam passare; ∼ **round to Ann's** passare da Ann
■ **pop up** *vi* (fam: appear unexpectedly) saltare fuori
pop² **1** *n* fam musica *f* pop
2 *attrib* pop *inv*
popcorn /'pɒpkɔːn/ *n* popcorn *m inv*
pope /pəʊp/ *n* papa *m*
poplar /'pɒplə(r)/ *n* pioppo *m*
poppy /'pɒpɪ/ *n* papavero *m*
pop sock *n* gambaletto *m*
populace /'pɒpjʊləs/ *n* popolo *m*
popular /'pɒpjʊlə(r)/ *adj* popolare; ⟨belief⟩ diffuso
popularity /pɒpjʊ'lærətɪ/ *n* popolarità *f*
popularize /'pɒpjʊləraɪz/ *vt* divulgare
populate /'pɒpjʊleɪt/ *vt* popolare
population /pɒpjʊ'leɪʃn/ *n* popolazione *f*
populist /'pɒpjʊlɪst/ *adj & n* populista *mf*
populous /'pɒpjʊləs/ *adj* popoloso
pop-up book *n* libro *m* con immagini tridimensionali
pop-up menu *n* Comput menu *m* a tendina
pop-up toaster *n* tostapane *m inv* a espulsione automatica
porcelain /'pɔːsəlɪn/ *n* porcellana *f*
porch /pɔːtʃ/ *n* portico *m*; Am veranda *f*
porcupine /'pɔːkjʊpaɪn/ *n* porcospino *m*
pore¹ /pɔː(r)/ *n* poro *m*
pore² *vi* ∼ **over** immergersi in
pork /pɔːk/ *n* carne *f* di maiale
porn /pɔːn/ *n* fam porno *m*
porno /'pɔːnəʊ/ *adj* fam porno *inv*
pornographic /pɔːnə'græfɪk/ *adj* pornografico
pornography /pɔː'nɒgrəfɪ/ *n* pornografia *f*
porous /'pɔːrəs/ *adj* poroso
porpoise /'pɔːpəs/ *n* focena *f*
porridge /'pɒrɪdʒ/ *n* farinata *f* di fiocchi d'avena
port¹ /pɔːt/ *n* porto *m*
port² *n* (Naut: side) babordo *m*
port³ *n* (wine) porto *m*
portable /'pɔːtəbl/ *adj & n* portatile *m*
Portakabin® /'pɔːtəkæbɪn/ *n* casotto *m* prefabbricato
portcullis /pɔː'tkʌlɪs/ *n* saracinesca *f*

portentous /pɔː'tentəs/ *adj* (significant) solenne; (ominous) infausto
porter /'pɔːtə(r)/ *n* portiere *m*; (for luggage) facchino *m*
portfolio /pɔːt'fəʊlɪəʊ/ *n* cartella *f*; Comm portafoglio *m*
porthole /'pɔːthəʊl/ *n* oblò *m inv*
portion /'pɔːʃn/ *n* parte *f*; (of food) porzione *f*
portly /'pɔːtlɪ/ *adj* (-ier, -iest) corpulento
portrait /'pɔːtrɪt/ *n* ritratto *m*
portrait painter *n* ritrattista *mf*
portray /pɔː'treɪ/ *vt* ritrarre; (represent) descrivere; ⟨actor⟩ impersonare
portrayal /pɔː'treɪəl/ *n* ritratto *m*; (by actor) caratterizzazione *f*
Portugal /'pɔːtjʊgl/ *n* Portogallo *m*
Portuguese /pɔːtjʊ'giːz/ *adj & n* portoghese *mf*; (language) portoghese *m*
pose /pəʊz/ **1** *n* posa *f*
2 *vt* porre ⟨problem, question⟩
3 *vi* (for painter) posare; ∼ **as** atteggiarsi a
poser /'pəʊzə(r)/ *n* fam (puzzle) rompicapo *m inv*; (person) montato, -a *mf*
posh /pɒʃ/ *adj* fam lussuoso; ⟨people⟩ danaroso
position /pə'zɪʃn/ **1** *n* posizione *f*; (job) posto *m*; (status) ceto *m* [sociale]
2 *vt* posizionare
positive /'pɒzɪtɪv/ **1** *adj* positivo; (certain) sicuro; (progress) concreto
2 *n* positivo *m*
positive discrimination *n* misure *fpl* antidiscriminatorie
positively /'pɒzɪtɪvlɪ/ *adv* positivamente; (decidedly) decisamente
posse /'pɒsɪ/ *n* gruppo *m* di volontari armati
possess /pə'zes/ *vt* possedere
possession /pə'zeʃn/ *n* possesso *m*; ∼**s** *pl* beni *mpl*
possessive /pə'zesɪv/ *adj* possessivo
possessiveness /pə'zesɪvnɪs/ *n* carattere *m* possessivo
possessor /pə'zesə(r)/ *n* possessore, -ditrice *mf*
possibility /pɒsə'bɪlətɪ/ *n* possibilità *f inv*
possible /'pɒsəbl/ *adj* possibile
possibly /'pɒsəblɪ/ *adv* possibilmente; **I couldn't** ∼ **accept** non mi è possibile accettare; **he can't** ∼ **be right** non è possibile che abbia ragione; **could you** ∼**...?** potrebbe per favore...?
possum /'pɒsəm/ *n* fam opossum *m inv*; **play** ∼ far finta di dormire; (pretend to be dead) fare il morto
post¹ /pəʊst/ **1** *n* (pole) palo *m*
2 *vt* affiggere ⟨notice⟩
post² **1** *n* (place of duty) posto *m*

2 *vt* appostare; (transfer) assegnare

post³ **1** *n* (mail) posta *f*; **by** ∼ per posta
2 *vt* spedire; (put in letter box) imbucare; (as opposed to fax) mandare per posta; **keep somebody** ∼**ed** tenere qualcuno al corrente

post+ *pref* post+

postage /'pəʊstɪdʒ/ *n* affrancatura *f*; ∼ **and packaging** spese *fpl* di posta

postage stamp *n* francobollo *m*

postal /'pəʊstl/ *adj* postale

postal order *n* vaglia *m inv* postale

postbox *n* cassetta *f* delle lettere

postcard *n* cartolina *f*

postcode *n* codice *m* postale

post-date *vt* postdatare

poster /'pəʊstə(r)/ *n* poster *m inv*; (advertising, election) cartellone *m*

posterior /pɒ'stɪərɪə(r)/ *n* fam posteriore *m*

posterity /pɒ'sterətɪ/ *n* posterità *f*

poster paint *n* pittura *f* a guazzo

postgraduate /pəʊs(t)'grædjʊət/ **1** *n* laureato, -a *mf* che continua gli studi
2 *adj* successivo alla laurea

posthumous /'pɒstjʊməs/ *adj* postumo

posthumously /'pɒstjʊməslɪ/ *adv* dopo la morte

posting /'pəʊstɪŋ/ *n* (job) incarico *m*; (Br: in mail) spedizione *f*; Comput posting *m inv*

postman /'pəʊstmən/ *n* postino *m*

postmark /'pəʊstmɑːk/ *n* timbro *m* postale

postmodern *adj* postmoderno

post-mortem /-'mɔːtəm/ *n* autopsia *f*

post-natal /-'neɪtl/ *adj* postnatale

post office *n* ufficio *m* postale

post office box *n* casella *f* postale

postpone /pəʊs(t)'pəʊn/ *vt* rimandare

postponement /pəʊs(t)'pəʊnmənt/ *n* rinvio *m*

postscript /'pəʊs(t)skrɪpt/ *n* post scriptum *m inv*

posture /'pɒstʃə(r)/ *n* posizione *f*

post-war *adj* del dopoguerra

pot /pɒt/ *n* vaso *m*; (for tea) teiera *f*; (for coffee) caffettiera *f*; (for cooking) pentola *f*; (sl: marijuana) erba *f*; ∼**s of money** fam un sacco di soldi; **go to** ∼ fam andare in malora

potash /'pɒtæʃ/ *n* potassa *f*

potassium /pə'tæsɪəm/ *n* potassio *m*

potato /pə'teɪtəʊ/ *n* (pl **-es**) patata *f*

potato chips Am, **potato crisps** Br *npl* patatine *fpl*

potato-peeler /-'piːlə(r)/ *n* pelapatate *m inv*

pot-bellied /'pɒtbelɪd/ *adj* panciuto

pot-belly /'pɒtbelɪ/ *n* fam pancione *m*

potent /'pəʊtənt/ *adj* potente

potentate /'pəʊtənteɪt/ *n* potentato *m*

potential /pə'tenʃl/ **1** *adj* potenziale
2 *n* potenziale *m*

potentially /pə'tenʃəlɪ/ *adv* potenzialmente

pothole *n* cavità *f inv*; (in road) buca *f*

potholer *n* speleologo, -a *mf*

potholing /'pɒthəʊlɪŋ/ *n* speleologia *f*

pot-luck *n* **take** ∼ affidarsi alla sorte

pot plant *n* pianta *f* da appartamento

pot-shot *n* **take a** ∼ **at** sparare a casaccio a

potted /'pɒtɪd/ *adj* conservato; (shortened) condensato

potted plant *n* pianta *f* da appartamento

potter¹ /'pɒtə(r)/ *vi* ∼ **[about]** gingillarsi

potter² *n* vasaio, -a *mf*

pottery /'pɒtərɪ/ *n* lavorazione *f* della ceramica; (articles) ceramiche *fpl*; (workshop) laboratorio *m* di ceramiche

potting compost /'pɒtɪŋ/ *n* terriccio *m*

potty /'pɒtɪ/ **1** *adj* (**-ier**, **-iest**) fam matto
2 *n* vasino *m*

pouch /paʊtʃ/ *n* marsupio *m*

pouffe /puːf/ *n* pouf *m inv*

poultry /'pəʊltrɪ/ *n* pollame *m*

pounce /paʊns/ *vi* balzare; ∼ **on** saltare su

pound¹ /paʊnd/ *n* libbra *f* (= 0,454 kg); (money) sterlina *f*

pound² **1** *vt* battere
2 *vi* ⟨heart⟩ battere forte; (run heavily) correre pesantemente

pound³ *n* (for cars) deposito *m* auto

pounding /'paʊndɪŋ/ **1** *n* martellio *m*
2 *adj* martellante

pour /pɔː(r)/ **1** *vt* versare
2 *vi* riversarsi; (with rain) piovere a dirotto
■ **pour away** *vi* svuotare
■ **pour in** *vi* ⟨people⟩ arrivare in massa; ⟨letters, money⟩ arrivare a valanghe; ⟨water⟩ entrare a fiotti
■ **pour out** **1** *vi* riversarsi fuori
2 *vt* versare ⟨drink⟩; sfogare ⟨troubles⟩

pout /paʊt/ **1** *vi* fare il broncio
2 *n* broncio *m*

poverty /'pɒvətɪ/ *n* povertà *f*

poverty line *n* soglia *f* di povertà

poverty-stricken *adj* indigente

POW *n abbr* (**prisoner of war**) prigioniero, -a *mf* di guerra

powder /'paʊdə(r)/ **1** *n* polvere *f*; (cosmetic) cipria *f*
2 *vt* polverizzare; (face) incipriare

powdered /'paʊdəd/ *adj* ⟨milk⟩ in polvere

powder room *n* euph toilette *f inv* per signore

powdery /'paʊdərɪ/ *adj* polveroso

power /'paʊə(r)/ *n* potere *m*; Electr corrente *f* [elettrica]; Math potenza *f*

powerboat *n* fuoribordo *m*

power cut *n* interruzione *f* di corrente

powered /'paʊəd/ *adj* ~ **by electricity** alimentato da corrente elettrica

powerful /'paʊfʊl/ *adj* potente

powerhouse /'paʊəhaʊs/ *n* (fig: person) persona *f* dinamica ed energica; **a** ~ **of ideas** un vulcano di idee

powerless /'paʊəlɪs/ *adj* impotente

power line *n* linea *f* elettrica

power of attorney *n* procura *f*

power-on light *n* spia *f* di accensione

power plant *n* centrale *f* elettrica

power sharing *n* condivisione *f* del potere

power station *n* centrale *f* elettrica

power steering *n* Auto servosterzo *m*

power switch *n* pulsante *m* di alimentazione

power unit *n* (of computer etc) alimentatore *m*

power-walk ① *n* camminata *f* a passo sostenuto
② *vi* camminare a passo sostenuto

power-walker *n* persona *f* che fa camminate a passo sostenuto

power-walking *n* camminate *fpl* a passo sostenuto (come esercizio fisico)

pow-wow /'paʊwaʊ/ *n* (of American Indians) raduno *m* tribale; (fam: discussion) discussione *f*

pp *abbr* (**pages**) pp.; *abbr* (**per procurationem**) pp.

PPP *abbr* (**public-private partnership**) partnership *f* tra un ente pubblico e un'impresa privata

PR *n abbr* (**proportional representation**) proporzionale *f*; *abbr* (**public relations**) pubbliche relazioni *fpl*

practicable /'præktɪkəbl/ *adj* praticabile

practical /'præktɪkl/ *adj* pratico

practicality /præktɪ'kælɪtɪ/ *n* praticità *f*

practical joke *n* scherzo *m* pratico

practically /'præktɪklɪ/ *adv* praticamente

practice /'præktɪs/ *n* pratica *f*; (custom) usanza *f*; (habit) abitudine *f*; (exercise) esercizio *m*; Sport allenamento *m*; **in** ~ (in reality) in pratica; **out of** ~ fuori esercizio; **put into** ~ mettere in pratica

practicing /'præktɪsɪŋ/ *adj* Am = PRACTISING

practise /'præktɪs/ ① *vt* fare pratica in; (carry out) mettere in pratica; esercitare ⟨profession⟩

② *vi* esercitarsi; ⟨doctor⟩ praticare

practised /'præktɪst/ *adj* esperto

practising /'præktɪsɪŋ/ *adj* Br praticante; **a** ~ **lawyer** un avvocato che esercita

pragmatic /præg'mætɪk/ *adj* pragmatico

pragmatism /'prægmətɪzm/ *n* pragmatismo *m*

pragmatist /'prægmətɪst/ *n* pragmatico, -a *mf*

prairie /'preərɪ/ *n* prateria *f*

praise /preɪz/ ① *n* lode *f*
② *vt* lodare

praiseworthy /'preɪzwɜːðɪ/ *adj* lodevole

pram /præm/ *n* carrozzella *f*

prance /prɑːns/ *vi* saltellare

prank /præŋk/ *n* tiro *m*

prattle /'prætl/ *vi* parlottare

prawn /prɔːn/ *n* gambero *m*

prawn cocktail *n* cocktail *m inv* di gamberetti

pray /preɪ/ *vi* pregare

prayer /preə(r)/ *n* preghiera *f*

preach /priːtʃ/ *vt/i* predicare

preacher /'priːtʃə(r)/ *n* predicatore, -trice *mf*

preamble /priː'æmbl/ *n* preambolo *m*

pre-arrange /priː-/ *vt* predisporre

precarious /prɪ'keərɪəs/ *adj* precario

precariously /prɪ'keərɪəslɪ/ *adv* in modo precario

precast /'priːkɑːst/ *adj* ⟨concrete⟩ prefabbricato

precaution /prɪ'kɔːʃn/ *n* precauzione *f*; **as a** ~ per precauzione

precautionary /prɪ'kɔːʃnərɪ/ *adj* preventivo

precede /prɪ'siːd/ *vt* precedere

precedence /'presɪdəns/ *n* precedenza *f*

precedent /'presɪdənt/ *n* precedente *m*

preceding /prɪ'siːdɪŋ/ *adj* precedente

preceptor /prɪ'septə(r)/ *n* Am Univ precettore *m*

precinct /'priːsɪŋkt/ *n* (traffic-free) zona *f* pedonale; (Am: district) circoscrizione *f*

precious /'preʃəs/ ① *adj* prezioso; ⟨style⟩ ricercato
② *adv* fam ~ **little** ben poco

precipice /'presɪpɪs/ *n* precipizio *m*

precipitate[1] /prɪ'sɪpɪtət/ *adj* precipitoso

precipitate[2] /prɪ'sɪpɪteɪt/ *vt* precipitare

precipitation /prɪsɪpɪ'teɪʃn/ *n* precipitazione *f*

précis /'preɪsiː/ *n* (pl **précis** /'preɪsiːz/) sunto *m*

precise /prɪ'saɪs/ *adj* preciso

precisely /prɪ'saɪslɪ/ *adv* precisamente

precision /prɪ'sɪʒn/ *n* precisione *f*

preclude /prɪ'klu:d/ *vt* precludere

precocious /prɪ'kəʊʃəs/ *adj* precoce

precociousness /prɪ'kəʊʃsnɪs/ *n* precocità *f*

preconceived /pri:kən'si:vd/ *adj* preconcetto

preconception /pri:kən'sepʃn/ *n* preconcetto *m*

precondition /pri:kən'dɪʃn/ **1** *n* presupposto *m* **2** *vt* Psych condizionare

precook /pri:'kʊk/ *vt* cuocere in anticipo

precursor /pri:'kɜ:sə(r)/ *n* precursore *m*

predate /pri:'deɪt/ *vt* retrodatare ⟨*cheque*⟩; ⟨*building, painting*⟩ essere antecedente a

predator /'predətə(r)/ *n* predatore, -trice *mf*

predatory /'predət(ə)rɪ/ *adj* rapace

predecessor /'pri:dɪsesə(r)/ *n* predecessore, -a *mf*

predetermine /pri:dɪ'tɜ:mɪn/ *vt* predeterminare

predicament /prɪ'dɪkəmənt/ *n* situazione *f* difficile

predicate /'predɪkət/ *n* Gram predicato *m*

predicative /prɪ'dɪkətɪv/ *adj* predicativo

predict /prɪ'dɪkt/ *vt* predire

predictable /prɪ'dɪktəbl/ *adj* prevedibile

prediction /prɪ'dɪkʃn/ *n* previsione *f*

predigested /pri:daɪ'dʒestɪd/ *adj* predigerito

predispose /pri:dɪ'spəʊz/ *vt* predisporre

predisposition /pri:dɪspə'zɪʃn/ *n* predisposizione *f*

predominant /prɪ'dɒmɪnənt/ *adj* predominante

predominantly /prɪ'dɒmɪnəntlɪ/ *adv* prevalentemente

predominate /prɪ'dɒmɪneɪt/ *vi* predominare

pre-eminent /pri:'emɪnənt/ *adj* preminente

pre-empt /pri:'empt/ *vt* (prevent) prevenire

pre-emptive /pri:'emptɪv/ *adj* preventivo

preen /pri:n/ *vt* lisciarsi; ~ **oneself** *fig* farsi bello

prefab /'pri:fæb/ *n* fam casa *f* prefabbricata

prefabricated /pri:'fæbrɪkeɪtɪd/ *adj* prefabbricato

preface /'prefɪs/ *n* prefazione *f*

prefatory /'prefət(ə)rɪ/ *adj* ⟨*comments*⟩ preliminare; ⟨*pages, notes*⟩ introduttivo

prefect /'pri:fekt/ *n* Schol studente, -tessa *mf* della scuola superiore con responsabilità disciplinari ecc

prefer /prɪ'fɜ:(r)/ *vt* (pt/pp **preferred**) preferire; **I ~ to walk** preferisco camminare

preferable /'prefərəbl/ *adj* preferibile (**to** a)

preferably /'prefərəblɪ/ *adv* preferibilmente

preference /'prefərəns/ *n* preferenza *f*

preferential /prefə'renʃl/ *adj* preferenziale

prefigure /pri:'fɪgə(r)/ *vt* preannunciare

prefix /'pri:fɪks/ *n* prefisso *m*

pregnancy /'pregnənsɪ/ *n* gravidanza *f*

pregnant /'pregnənt/ *adj* incinta

preheat /pri:'hi:t/ *vt* preriscaldare ⟨*oven*⟩

prehensile /pri:'hensaɪl/ *adj* prensile

prehistoric /pri:hɪs'tɒrɪk/ *adj* preistorico

pre-ignition /pri:ɪg'nɪʃn/ *n* preaccensione *f*

pre-installed /pri:ɪn'stɔ:ld/ *adj* preinstallato

prejudge /pri:'dʒʌdʒ/ *vt* giudicare prematuramente ⟨*issue*⟩

prejudice /'predʒʊdɪs/ **1** *n* pregiudizio *m* **2** *vt* influenzare (**against** contro); (harm) danneggiare

prejudiced /'predʒʊdɪst/ *adj* prevenuto

preliminary /prɪ'lɪmɪnərɪ/ *adj* preliminare

preloaded /pri:'ləʊdɪd/ *adj* precaricato

prelude /'prelju:d/ *n* preludio *m*

premarital /pri:'mærɪtl/ *adj* prematrimoniale

premarital sex *n* rapporti *mpl* prematrimoniali

premature /'premətjʊə(r)/ *adj* prematuro

premature birth *n* parto *m* prematuro

prematurely /'premətjʊəlɪ/ *adv* prematuramente

premeditated /pri:'medɪteɪtɪd/ *adj* premeditato

premeditation /pri:medɪ'teɪʃn/ *n* premeditazione *f*

premenstrual syndrome /pri:'menstrʊəl/ *n* sindrome *f* premestruale

premenstrual tension *n* tensione *f* premestruale

premier /'premɪə(r)/ **1** *adj* primario **2** *n* Pol primo ministro *m*, premier *m inv*

première /'premɪeə(r)/ *n* prima *f*

premiership /'premɪəʃɪp/ n Pol carica f di primo ministro nel Regno Unito; ≈ presidenza f del consiglio

premises /'premɪsɪz/ npl locali mpl; **on the ∼** sul posto

premium /'pri:mɪəm/ n premio m; **be at a ∼** essere una cosa rara

premium bond n obbligazione f a premio

premonition /premə'nɪʃn/ n presentimento m

prenatal /pri:'neɪtl/ adj esp Am prenatale

preoccupation /pri:ɒkjʊ'peɪʃn/ n preoccupazione f

preoccupied /pri:'ɒkjʊpaɪd/ adj preoccupato

preoperative /pri:'ɒp(ə)rətɪv/ adj preoperatorio

preordained /pri:ɔ:'deɪnd/ adj prestabilito; ⟨outcome⟩ predestinato

pre-owned /pri:'əʊnd/ adj ⟨video, game⟩ di seconda mano

prep /prep/ n Sch compiti mpl

pre-packed /pri:'pækt/ adj preconfezionato

prepaid /pri:'peɪd/ adj pagato in anticipo; ⟨envelope⟩ già affrancato

preparation /prepə'reɪʃn/ n preparazione f; **∼s** pl preparativi mpl

preparatory /prɪ'pærətrɪ/ adj preparatorio; **∼ to** come preparazione per

preparatory school n Br = PREP SCHOOL

prepare /prɪ'peə(r)/ ① vt preparare ② vi prepararsi (**for** per); **∼d to** disposto a

prepay /pri:'peɪ/ vt (pt/pp **-paid**) pagare in anticipo

preponderance /prɪ'pɒndərəns/ n preponderanza f

preponderantly /prɪ'pɒndərəntlɪ/ adv in modo preponderante

preponderate /prɪ'pɒndəreɪt/ vi predominare

preposition /prepə'zɪʃn/ n preposizione f

prepossessing /pri:pə'zesɪŋ/ adj attraente

preposterous /prɪ'pɒstərəs/ adj assurdo

pre-programmed /pri:'prəʊgræmd/ adj programmato; Comput preprogrammato

prep school n scuola f elementare privata

pre-recorded /-rɪ'kɔ:dɪd/ adj in differita

prerequisite /pri:'rekwɪzɪt/ n condizione f sine qua non

prerogative /prɪ'rɒgətɪv/ n prerogativa f

Pres. abbr (**President**) Pres.

Presbyterian /prezbɪ'tɪərɪən/ adj & n presbiteriano, -a mf

pre-school /'pri:sku:l/ ① n Am scuola f materna, asilo m ② adj ⟨child⟩ in età prescolastica; ⟨years⟩ prescolastico

prescribe /prɪ'skraɪb/ vt prescrivere

prescription /prɪ'skrɪpʃn/ n Med ricetta f

prescription charges npl Br ≈ ticket m inv sui medicinali

prescriptive /prɪ'skrɪptɪv/ adj normativo

presence /'prezns/ n presenza f

presence of mind n presenza f di spirito

present¹ /'preznt/ ① adj presente ② n presente m; **at ∼** attualmente

present² n (gift) regalo m; **give somebody something as a ∼** regalare qualcosa a qualcuno

present³ /prɪ'zent/ vt presentare; **∼ somebody with an award** consegnare un premio a qualcuno

presentable /prɪ'zentəbl/ adj **be ∼** essere presentabile

presentation /prezn'teɪʃn/ n presentazione f

present-day adj attuale

presenter /prɪ'zentə(r)/ n TV, Radio presentatore, -trice mf

presently /'prezntlɪ/ adv fra poco; (Am: now) attualmente

present perfect n passato m prossimo

preservation /prezə'veɪʃn/ n conservazione f

preservative /prɪ'zɜ:vətɪv/ n conservante m

preserve /prɪ'zɜ:v/ ① vt preservare; (maintain & Culin) conservare ② n (in hunting & fig) riserva f; (jam) marmellata f

pre-set /pri:'set/ vt programmare

pre-shrunk /pri:'ʃrʌŋk/ adj ⟨fabric⟩ irrestringibile

preside /prɪ'zaɪd/ vi presiedere (**over** a)

presidency /'prezɪdənsɪ/ n presidenza f

president /'prezɪdənt/ n presidente m

presidential /prezɪ'denʃl/ adj presidenziale

pre-soak /pri:'səʊk/ vt mettere in ammollo

press /pres/ ① n (machine) pressa f; (newspapers) stampa f ② vt premere; pressare ⟨flower⟩; (iron) stirare; (squeeze) stringere ③ vi (urge) incalzare

■ **press ahead** vi (continue) proseguire

■ **press for** vi fare pressione per; **be ∼ed for** (short of) essere a corto di

■ **press on** *vi* andare avanti

press agency *n* agenzia *f* di stampa

press conference *n* conferenza *f* stampa

press cutting *n* ritaglio *m* di giornale

press-gang *vt* forzare

pressing /'presɪŋ/ *adj* urgente

press release *n* comunicato *m* stampa

press stud *n* [bottone *m*] automatico *m*

press-up *n* flessione *f*

pressure /'preʃɪŋ/ ① *n* pressione *f*
② *vt* = PRESSURIZE

pressure-cooker *n* pentola *f* a pressione

pressure group *n* gruppo *m* di pressione

pressurize /'preʃə(r)/ *vt* far pressione su

pressurized /'preʃəraɪzd/ *adj* ⟨cabin⟩ pressurizzato

prestige /pre'stiːʒ/ *n* prestigio *m*

prestigious /pre'stɪdʒəs/ *adj* prestigioso

presumably /prɪ'zjuːməblɪ/ *adv* presumibilmente

presume /prɪ'zjuːm/ ① *vt* presumere; ∼ **to do something** permettersi di fare qualcosa
② *vi* ∼ **on** approfittare di

presumption /prɪ'zʌmpʃn/ *n* presunzione *f*; (boldness) impertinenza *f*

presumptuous /prɪ'zʌmptjʊəs/ *adj* impertinente

presuppose /priːsə'pəʊz/ *vt* presupporre

presupposition /priːsʌpə'zɪʃn/ *n* presupposizione *f*

pre-tax /'priːtæks/ *adj* al lordo d'imposta

pretence /prɪ'tens/ *n* finzione *f*; (pretext) pretesto *m*; **it's all** ∼ è tutta una scena

pretend /prɪ'tend/ ① *vt* fingere; (claim) pretendere
② *vi* fare finta

pretender /prɪ'tendə(r)/ *n* pretendente *mf*

pretension /prɪ'tenʃn/ *n* pretesa *f*

pretentious /prɪ'tenʃəs/ *adj* pretenzioso

preterite /'pretərɪt/ *n* preterito *m*

pretext /'priːtekst/ *n* pretesto *m*

pretty /'prɪtɪ/ ① *adj* (-ier, -iest) carino
② *adv* (fam: fairly) abbastanza

prevail /prɪ'veɪl/ *vi* prevalere; ∼ **upon somebody to do something** convincere qualcuno a fare qualcosa

prevailing /prɪ'veɪlɪŋ/ *adj* prevalente

prevalence /'prevələns/ *n* diffusione *f*

prevalent /'prevələnt/ *adj* diffuso

prevaricate /prɪ'værɪkeɪt/ *vi* tergiversare

prevent /prɪ'vent/ *vt* impedire; ∼ **somebody [from] doing something** impedire a qualcuno di fare qualcosa

preventable /prɪ'ventʃn/ *adj* evitabile

prevention /prɪ'venʃn/ *n* prevenzione *f*

preventive /prɪ'ventɪv/ *adj* preventivo

preview /'priːvjuː/ *n* anteprima *f*

previous /'priːvɪəs/ *adj* precedente

previously /'priːvɪəslɪ/ *adv* precedentemente

pre-war /priː'wɔː(r)/ *adj* anteguerra

pre-wash /'priːwɒʃ/ *n* prelavaggio *m*

prey /preɪ/ ① *n* preda *f*; **bird of** ∼ uccello *m* rapace
② *vi* ∼ **on** far preda di; ∼ **on sb's mind** attanagliare qualcuno

price /praɪs/ ① *n* prezzo *m*
② *vt* Comm fissare il prezzo di

price-conscious *adj* consapevole dell'andamento dei prezzi

price cut *n* riduzione *f* di prezzo

price cutting *n* taglio *m* dei prezzi

price freeze *n* congelamento *m* dei prezzi

price increase *n* aumento *m* di prezzo

priceless /'praɪslɪs/ *adj* inestimabile; (fam: amusing) spassosissimo

price list *n* listino *m* prezzi

price/performance ratio *n* rapporto *m* prezzo/prestazioni

price range *n* gamma *f* di prezzi

price rise *n* rialzo *m* dei prezzi

price tag *n* talloncino *m* del prezzo

price war *n* guerra *f* dei prezzi

pricey /'praɪsɪ/ *adj* fam caro

pricing policy /'praɪsɪŋ/ *n* politica *f* di determinazione dei prezzi

prick /prɪk/ ① *n* puntura *f*; vulg (penis) cazzo *m*; (person) stronzo *m*
② *vt* pungere
■ **prick up** *vt* ∼ **up one's ears** rizzare le orecchie

prickle /'prɪkl/ *n* spina *f*; (sensation) formicolio *m*

prickly /'prɪklɪ/ *adj* pungente; ⟨person⟩ irritabile

pride /praɪd/ ① *n* orgoglio *m*; (of lions) branco *m*; ∼ **of place** posizione *f* d'onore
② *vt* ∼ **oneself on** vantarsi di

priest /priːst/ *n* prete *m*

priesthood /'priːsthʊd/ *n* (clergy) clero *m*; (calling) sacerdozio *m*; **enter the** ∼ farsi prete

prig /prɪg/ *n* presuntuoso *m*

priggish /'prɪgɪʃ/ *adj* presuntuoso

prim /prɪm/ *adj* (**primmer, primmest**) perbenino

primacy /'praɪməsɪ/ *n* primato *m*; (of party, power) supremazia *f*; Relig carica *f* di primate

prima facie /praɪmə'feɪʃi/ ① adv (at first) a prima vista
② adj a prima vista legittimo

primal /'praɪməl/ adj ⟨quality, myth, feeling⟩ primitivo

primarily /'praɪmerɪlɪ/ adv in primo luogo

primary /'praɪmərɪ/ adj primario; (chief) principale

primary colour n colore m primario

primary school n scuola f elementare

primate /'praɪmeɪt/ n Zool, Relig primate m

prime[1] /praɪm/ ① adj principale, primo; (first-rate) eccellente
② n be in one's ∼ essere nel fiore degli anni

prime[2] vt preparare ⟨surface, person⟩

Prime Minister n Primo Ministro m

prime mover n promotore, -trice mf

primer /'praɪmə(r)/ n (paint) base f; (for detonating) innesco m

prime time ① n prime time m inv, fascia f di massimo ascolto
② attrib ⟨advertising, programme⟩ nella fascia di massimo ascolto

primeval /praɪ'miːvl/ adj primitivo

primitive /'prɪmɪtɪv/ adj primitivo

primordial /praɪ'mɔːdɪəl/ adj primordiale

primrose /'prɪmrəʊz/ n primula f

prince /prɪns/ n principe m

princely /'prɪnslɪ/ adj ⟨life, role⟩ da principe; ⟨amount, style⟩ principesco

princess /prɪn'ses/ n principessa f

principal /'prɪnsɪpl/ ① adj principale
② n Sch preside m

principality /prɪnsɪ'pælətɪ/ n principato m

principally /'prɪnsəplɪ/ adv principalmente

principle /'prɪnsəpl/ n principio m; in ∼ in teoria; on ∼ per principio; ∼s pl (fundamentals) fondamenti mpl

print /prɪnt/ ① n (mark, trace) impronta f; Phot copia f; (letters) stampatello m; (picture) stampa f; in ∼ (printed out) stampato; ⟨book⟩ in commercio; out of ∼ esaurito
② vt/i stampare; (write in capitals) scrivere in stampatello
■ **print off** vt stampare ⟨copies⟩
■ **print out** vt/i Comput stampare

printed matter /'prɪntɪd/ n stampe fpl

printer /'prɪntə(r)/ n stampante f; (person) tipografo, -a mf

printer port n porta f per la stampante

printing /'prɪntɪŋ/ n tipografia f

printout /'prɪntaʊt/ n Comput stampa f

print-preview vt Comput fare l'anteprima di stampa di

print speed n velocità f di stampa

prior /'praɪə(r)/ ① adj precedente
② prep ∼ to prima di

priority /praɪ'ɒrətɪ/ n precedenza f; (matter) priorità f inv

priory /'praɪərɪ/ n monastero m

prise /praɪz/ vt ∼ open/up forzare
■ **prise off** vt togliere facendo leva ⟨lid⟩

prism /'prɪzm/ n prisma f

prison /'prɪzn/ n prigione f

prison camp n campo m di prigionia

prisoner /'prɪz(ə)nə(r)/ n prigioniero, -a mf

prison officer n guardia f carceraria

prison sentence n pena f detentiva

prissy /'prɪsɪ/ adj ⟨person⟩ perbenista

pristine /'prɪstiːn/ adj originario; (unspoilt) intatto

privacy /'prɪvəsɪ/ n privacy f

private /'praɪvət/ ① adj privato; ⟨car, secretary, letter⟩ personale
② n Mil soldato m semplice; in ∼ in privato

private enterprise n iniziativa f privata

private eye n fam investigatore, -trice mf privato, -a

privately /'praɪvətlɪ/ adv ⟨funded, educated etc⟩ privatamente; (in secret) in segreto; (confidentially) in privato; (inwardly) interiormente

private property n proprietà f privata

privation /praɪ'veɪʃn/ n privazione f; ∼s pl stenti mpl

privatization /praɪvətaɪ'zeɪʃn/ n privatizzazione f

privatize /'praɪvətaɪz/ vt privatizzare

privilege /'prɪvəlɪdʒ/ n privilegio m

privileged /'prɪvəlɪdʒd/ adj privilegiato

privy /'prɪvɪ/ adj be ∼ to essere al corrente di

prize /praɪz/ ① n premio m
② adj (idiot etc) perfetto
③ vt apprezzare

prize draw n estrazione f a premi

prize-giving /'praɪzgɪvɪŋ/ n premiazione f

prize money n montepremi m

prizewinner n vincitore, -trice mf

prize-winning adj vincente

pro /prəʊ/ n (fam: professional) professionista mf; the ∼s and cons il pro e il contro

proactive /prəʊ'æktɪv/ adj ⟨approach⟩ proattivo

probability /prɒbə'bɪlətɪ/ n probabilità f inv

probable /'prɒbəbl/ adj probabile

probably /'prɒbəblɪ/ adv probabilmente

probate /'prəʊbeɪt/ n Jur omologazione f

probation /prə'beɪʃn/ n prova f; Jur libertà f vigilata

probationary /prə'beɪʃnəri/ adj in prova; ~ **period** periodo m di prova

probationer /prə'beɪʃnə(r)/ n (employee on trial) impiegato, -a mf in prova; (trainee) apprendista mf

probation officer n agente m addetto alla sorveglianza di chi si trova in regime di libertà vigilata

probe /prəʊb/ ① n sonda f; (fig: investigation) indagine f
② vt sondare; (investigate) esaminare a fondo

probing /'prəʊbɪŋ/ adj ⟨question⟩ penetrante

problem /'prɒbləm/ ① n problema m
② attrib difficile

problematic /prɒblə'mætɪk/ adj problematico

problem page n posta f del cuore

procedural /prə'si:dʒərəl/ adj ⟨detail, error⟩ procedurale

procedure /prə'si:dʒe(r)/ n procedimento m

proceed /prə'si:d/ ① vi procedere
② vt ~ to do something proseguire facendo qualcosa

proceedings /prə'si:dɪŋz/ npl (report) atti mpl; Jur azione fsg legale

proceeds /'prəʊsi:dz/ npl ricavato msg

process /'prəʊses/ ① n processo m; (procedure) procedimento m; **in the** ~ nel far ciò
② vt trattare; Admin occuparsi di; Phot sviluppare

processing /'prəʊsesɪŋ/ n trattamento m; **food** ~ l'industria alimentare

procession /prə'seʃn/ n processione f

processor /'prəʊsesə(r)/ n Comput processore m; (for food) tritatutto m inv

pro-choice /prəʊ'tʃɔɪs/ adj abortista

proclaim /prə'kleɪm/ vt proclamare

proclamation /prɒklə'meɪʃn/ n proclamazione f

proclivity /prə'klɪvəti/ n tendenza f

procrastinate /prə'kræstɪneɪt/ vi procrastinare

procrastination /prəkræstɪ'neɪʃn/ n procrastinazione f

procreate /'prəʊkrɪeɪt/ vi procreare

procreation /prəʊkrɪ'eɪʃn/ n procreazione f

procure /prə'kjʊə(r)/ vt ottenere

prod /prɒd/ ① n colpetto m
② vt (pt/pp **prodded**) punzecchiare; fig incitare

prodigal /'prɒdɪgl/ adj prodigo

prodigal son n figliol m prodigo

prodigious /prə'dɪdʒəs/ adj prodigioso

prodigy /'prɒdɪdʒɪ/ n **[infant]** ~ bambino m prodigio

produce[1] /'prɒdju:s/ n prodotti mpl; ~ **of Italy** prodotto in Italia

produce[2] /prə'dju:s/ vt produrre; (bring out) tirar fuori; (cause) causare; (fam: give birth to) fare

producer /prə'dju:sə(r)/ n produttore m

product /'prɒdʌkt/ n prodotto m

production /prə'dʌkʃn/ n produzione f; Theat spettacolo m

production control n controllo m della produzione

production director n direttore, -trice mf della produzione

production line n catena f di montaggio

production management n gestione f della produzione

production manager n direttore, -trice mf della produzione

productive /prə'dʌktɪv/ adj produttivo

productivity /prɒdʌk'tɪvətɪ/ n produttività f

product range n gamma f di prodotti

Prof. /prɒf/ abbr (**Professor**) Prof.

profane /prə'feɪn/ adj profano; (blasphemous) blasfemo

profanity /prə'fænəti/ n (oath) bestemmia f

profess /prə'fes/ vt (claim) dichiarare

professed /prə'fest/ adj (claiming to be) sedicente

profession /prə'feʃn/ n professione f

professional /prə'feʃnəl/ ① adj professionale; (not amateur) professionista; (piece of work) da professionista; ⟨man⟩ di professione
② n professionista mf

professionalism /prə'feʃnəlɪzm/ n (of person, organization, work) professionalità f; Sport professionismo m

professionally /prə'feʃnəlɪ/ adv professionalmente

professor /prə'fesə(r)/ n professore m [universitario]

professorial /prɒfə'sɔ:rɪəl/ adj ⟨duties, post, salary⟩ professorale

proffer /'prɒfə(r)/ vt (hold out) porgere; (fig: offer) offrire

proficiency /prə'fɪʃnsɪ/ n competenza f

proficient /prə'fɪʃnt/ adj competente (**in** in)

profile /'prəʊfaɪl/ n profilo m

profiling /'prəʊfaɪlɪŋ/ n profilo m; **genetic** ~ profilo genetico

profit /'prɒfɪt/ ① n profitto m
② vi ~ **from** trarre profitto da

profitable /'prɒfɪtəbl/ adj proficuo

profitably /'prɒfɪtəblɪ/ *adv* in modo
proficuo

profit and loss account *n* conto *m*
profitti e perdite

profiteer /prɒfɪ'tɪə(r)/ *n* profittatore,
-trice *mf*

profiterole /prə'fɪtərəʊl/ *n* profiterole *m*
inv

profit margin *n* margine *m* di profitto

profit-sharing *n* partecipazione *f* agli
utili

profligate /'prɒflɪgət/ *adj* (extravagant)
spendaccione; (dissolute) dissoluto; (spending)
eccessivo

pro forma invoice /'fɔ:mə/ *n* fattura *f*
proforma

profound /prə'faʊnd/ *adj* profondo

profoundly /prə'faʊndlɪ/ *adv*
profondamente

profuse /prə'fju:s/ *adj* ∼ apologies una
profusione di scuse

profusely /prə'fju:slɪ/ *adv* profusamente

profusion /prə'fju:ʒn/ *n* profusione *f*; in
∼ in abbondanza

progeny /'prɒdʒənɪ/ *n* progenie *f inv*

prognosis /prɒg'nəʊsɪs/ *n* (pl -**oses**)
(prediction) previsione *f*; Med prognosi *f inv*

prognosticate /prɒg'nɒstɪkeɪt/ *vt*
pronosticare

program /'prəʊgræm/ ① *n* Comput
programma *m*

② *vt* (pt/pp **programmed**) programmare

programme /'prəʊgræm/ *n* Br
programma *m*

programmer /'prəʊgræmə(r)/ *n* Comput
programmatore, -trice *mf*

programming /'prəʊgræmɪŋ/ *n*
programmazione *f*

progress[1] /'prəʊgres/ *n* progresso *m*; in
∼ in corso; **make** ∼ *fig* fare progressi

progress[2] /prə'gres/ *vi* progredire; *fig*
fare progressi

progression /prə'greʃn/ *n* (development)
progresso *m*; (improvement) evoluzione *f*;
(series) serie *f*

progressive /prə'gresɪv/ *adj*
progressivo; (reforming) progressista

progressively /prə'gresɪvlɪ/ *adv*
progressivamente

progress report *n* (on project) resoconto
sull'andamento del progetto; (on patient)
cartella *f* clinica

prohibit /prə'hɪbɪt/ *vt* proibire

prohibition /prəʊhɪ'bɪʃn/ *n* proibizione;
P∼ Am proibizionismo *m*

prohibitive /prə'hɪbɪtɪv/ *adj* proibitivo

prohibitively /prə'hɪbɪtɪvlɪ/ *adv*
⟨expensive⟩ in modo proibitivo

project[1] /'prɒdʒekt/ *n* progetto *m*; Sch
ricerca *f*

project[2] /prə'dʒekt/ ① *vt* proiettare
⟨film, image⟩

② *vi* (jut out) sporgere

projectile /prə'dʒektaɪl/ *n* proiettile *m*

projection /prə'dʒekʃn/ *n* (of figures)
proiezione *f*

project manager *n* project manager
mf inv

projector /prə'dʒektə(r)/ *n* proiettore *m*

proletarian /prəʊlə'teərɪən/ *adj* & *n*
proletario, -a *mf*

proletariat /prəʊlɪ'teərɪət/ *n*
proletariato *m*

pro-life /prəʊ'laɪf/ *adj* antiabortista

proliferate /prə'lɪfəreɪt/ *vi* proliferare

proliferation /prəlɪfə'reɪʃn/ *n*
proliferazione *f*

prolific /prə'lɪfɪk/ *adj* prolifico

prologue /'prəʊlɒg/ *n* prologo *m*

prolong /prə'lɒŋ/ *vt* prolungare

prom /prɒm/ *n* (Br fam: at seaside)
lungomare *m inv*; (Am fam: at high school)
ballo *m* studentesco

promenade /prɒmə'nɑːd/ *n* lungomare
m inv

prominence /'prɒmɪnəns/ *n* (of person,
issue) importanza *f*; (of object) sporgenza *f*;
(hill) rilievo *m*

prominent /'prɒmɪnənt/ *adj*
prominente; (conspicuous) di rilievo

promiscuity /prɒmɪ'skju:ətɪ/ *n*
promiscuità *f*

promiscuous /prə'mɪskjʊəs/ *adj*
promiscuo

promise /'prɒmɪs/ ① *n* promessa *f*

② *vt* promettere; ∼ somebody that
promettere a qualcuno che; I ∼d to l'ho
promesso

Promised Land /prɒmɪst'lænd/ *n*
Terra *f* Promessa

promising /'prɒmɪsɪŋ/ *adj* promettente

promo /'prəʊməʊ/ *n* (fam: of product)
campagna *f* promozionale; (video) video *m*
inv promozionale

promontory /'prɒmənt(ə)rɪ/ *n*
promontorio *m*

promote /prə'məʊt/ *vt* promuovere; be
∼d essere promosso

promoter /prə'məʊtə(r)/ *n* promotore,
-trice *mf*

promotion /prə'məʊʃn/ *n* promozione *f*

promotional /prə'məʊʃnəl/ *adj* Comm
promozionale

promotional video *n* video *m*
promozionale

prompt /prɒmpt/ ① *adj* immediato;
(punctual) puntuale

② *adv* in punto

③ *vt* incitare (**to** a); Theat suggerire a

④ *vi* suggerire

⑤ *n* Comput prompt *m inv*

prompter /'prɒmptə(r)/ n suggeritore, -trice mf

promptly /'prɒmptlɪ/ adv puntualmente

Proms /prɒmz/ npl rassegna f di concerti estivi di musica classica presso l'Albert Hall a Londra

prone /prəʊn/ adj prono; **be ~ to do something** essere incline a fare qualcosa

prong /prɒŋ/ n dente m

pronoun /'prəʊnaʊn/ n pronome m

pronounce /prə'naʊns/ vt pronunciare; (declare) dichiarare
■ **pronounce on** vt pronunciarsi su ⟨case, subject⟩

pronounced /prə'naʊnst/ adj (noticeable) pronunciato

pronouncement /prə'naʊnsmənt/ n dichiarazione f

pronunciation /prənʌnsɪ'eɪʃn/ n pronuncia f

proof /pru:f/ **1** n prova f; Typ bozza f, prova f; **12%** ~ 12° **2** adj ~ **against** a prova di

proof of purchase n ricevuta f d'acquisto

proof-read vt correggere le bozze di

proof-reader n correttore, -trice mf di bozze

proof-reading n revisione f di bozze

prop[1] /prɒp/ **1** n puntello m **2** vt (pt/pp **propped**) ~ **open** tenere aperto; ~ **against** (lean) appoggiare a
■ **prop up** vt sostenere

prop[2] n Theat, fam accessorio m di scena

propaganda /prɒpə'gændə/ n propaganda f

propagate /'prɒpəgeɪt/ vt propagare

propagator /'prɒpəgeɪtə(r)/ n propagatore m

propane /'prəʊpeɪn/ n propano m

propel /prə'pel/ vt (pt/pp **propelled**) spingere

propellant /prə'pelənt/ n (in aerosol) gas m inv propellente; (in rocket) propellente m

propeller /prə'pelə(r)/ n elica f

propelling pencil /prə'pelɪŋ/ n portamina m inv

propensity /prə'pensətɪ/ n tendenza f

proper /'prɒpə(r)/ adj corretto; (suitable) adatto; (fam: real) vero [e proprio]

properly /'prɒpəlɪ/ adv correttamente

proper name, **proper noun** n nome m proprio

property /'prɒpətɪ/ n proprietà f inv

property developer n impresa f edile; (person) impresario m edile

property market n mercato m immobiliare

prophecy /'prɒfəsɪ/ n profezia f

prophesy /'prɒfɪsaɪ/ vt (pt/pp **-ied**) profetizzare

prophet /'prɒfɪt/ n profeta m

prophetic /prə'fetɪk/ adj profetico

prophylactic /prɒfɪ'læktɪk/ **1** n (condom) profilattico m, preservativo m; (Med: treatment) misura f profilattica **2** adj profilattico

proponent /prə'pəʊnənt/ n fautore, -trice mf

proportion /prə'pɔ:ʃn/ n proporzione f; (share) parte f; **be in** ~ essere proporzionato (**to** a); **be out of** ~ essere sproporzionato; ~**s** pl (dimensions) proporzioni fpl

proportional /prə'pɔ:ʃnəl/ adj proporzionale

proportionally /prə'pɔ:ʃnəlɪ/ adv in proporzione

proportional representation n rappresentanza f proporzionale

proposal /prə'pəʊzl/ n proposta f; (of marriage) proposta f di matrimonio

propose /prə'pəʊz/ **1** vt proporre; (intend) proporsi **2** vi fare una proposta di matrimonio

proposition /prɒpə'zɪʃn/ n proposta f; (fam: task) impresa f

proprietor /prə'praɪətə(r)/ n proprietario, -a mf

propriety /prə'praɪətɪ/ n correttezza f; **the proprieties** pl l'etichetta f

propulsion /prə'pʌlʃn/ n propulsione f

pro rata /'rɑ:tə/ adj **on a** ~ ~ **basis** in proporzione

prosaic /prə'zeɪɪk/ adj prosaico

proscribe vt (exile) esiliare; (ban) bandire

prose /prəʊz/ n prosa f

prosecute /'prɒsɪkju:t/ vt intentare azione contro

prosecution /prɒsɪ'kju:ʃn/ n azione f giudiziaria; **the** ~ l'accusa f

prosecutor /'prɒsɪkju:tə(r)/ n [Public] **P~** Pubblico Ministero m

prospect[1] /'prɒspekt/ n (expectation) prospettiva f; (view) vista f

prospect[2] /prə'spekt/ vi ~ **for** cercare

prospective /prə'spektɪv/ adj (future) futuro; (possible) potenziale

prospector /prə'spektə(r)/ n cercatore m

prospectus /prə'spektəs/ n prospetto m

prosper /'prɒspə(r)/ vi prosperare; ⟨person⟩ stare bene finanziariamente

prosperity /prɒ'sperətɪ/ n prosperità f

prosperous /'prɒspərəs/ adj prospero

prostate /'prɒsteɪt/ n prostata f

prosthesis /prɒs'θi:sɪs/ n protesi f

prostitute /'prɒstɪtju:t/ **1** n prostituta f **2** vt fig prostituire

prostitution /prɒstɪˈtjuːʃn/ *n* prostituzione *f*

prostrate /ˈprɒstreɪt/ *adj* prostrato; ~ **with grief** fig prostrato dal dolore

protagonist /prəˈtægənɪst/ *n* protagonista *mf*

protect /prəˈtekt/ *vt* proteggere (**from** da)

protection /prəˈtekʃn/ *n* protezione *f*

protection factor *n* (of suntan lotion) fattore *m* di protezione

protection racket *n* racket *m inv* di protezione

protective /prəˈtektɪv/ *adj* protettivo

protector /prəˈtektə(r)/ *n* protettore, -trice *mf*

protégé /ˈprɒtɪʒeɪ/ *n* protetto *m*

protein /ˈprəʊtiːn/ *n* proteina *f*

protest[1] /ˈprəʊtest/ *n* protesta *f*

protest[2] /prəˈtest/ *vt/i* protestare

Protestant /ˈprɒtɪstənt/ *adj & n* protestante *mf*

Protestantism /ˈprɒtɪstəntɪzm/ *n* protestantesimo *m*

protestation /prɒtɪˈsteɪʃn/ *n* protesta *f*

protester /prəˈtestə(r)/ *n* contestatore, -trice *mf*; (at demonstration) dimostrante *mf*

protocol /ˈprəʊtəkɒl/ *n* protocollo *m*

prototype /ˈprəʊtətaɪp/ *n* prototipo *m*

protract /prəˈtrækt/ *vt* protrarre

protracted /prəˈtræktɪd/ *adj* prolungato

protractor /prəˈtræktə(r)/ *n* goniometro *m*

protrude /prəˈtruːd/ *vi* sporgere

protruding /prəˈtruːdɪŋ/ *adj* ⟨teeth, chin, ledge⟩ sporgente

protuberance /prəˈtuːbərəns/ *n* protuberanza *f*

proud /praʊd/ *adj* fiero (**of** di)

proudly /ˈpraʊdlɪ/ *adv* fieramente

prove /pruːv/ ① *vt* provare ② *vi* ~ **to be a lie** rivelarsi una bugia

proven /ˈpruːvən/ *adj* dimostrato

proverb /ˈprɒvɜːb/ *n* proverbio *m*

proverbial /prəˈvɜːbɪəl/ *adj* proverbiale

provide /prəˈvaɪd/ ① *vt* fornire; ~ **somebody with something** fornire qualcosa a qualcuno ② *vi* ~ **for** (allow for) tenere conto di; ⟨law⟩ prevedere

provided /prəˈvaɪdɪd/ *conj* ~ **[that]** purché

providence /ˈprɒvɪdəns/ *n* provvidenza *f*

provident /ˈprɒvɪdənt/ *adj* previdenziale

providential /prɒvɪˈdenʃl/ *adj* provvidenziale

provider /prəˈvaɪdə(r)/ *n* (in family) persona *f* che mantiene la famiglia

providing /prəˈvaɪdɪŋ/ *conj* = PROVIDED

province /ˈprɒvɪns/ *n* provincia *f*; fig campo *m*

provincial /prəˈvɪnʃl/ *adj* provinciale

provincialism /prəˈvɪnʃəlɪzm/ *n* provincialismo *m*

provision /prəˈvɪʒn/ *n* (of food, water) approvvigionamento *m* (**of** di); (of law) disposizione *f*; **make** ~ **for** ⟨law⟩ prevedere; ~**s** *pl* provviste *fpl*

provisional /prəˈvɪʒ(ə)nəl/ *adj* provvisorio

provisionally /prəˈvɪʒ(ə)nəlɪ/ *adv* provvisoriamente

proviso /prəˈvaɪzəʊ/ *n* condizione *f*

provocation /prɒvəˈkeɪʃn/ *n* provocazione *f*

provocative /prəˈvɒkətɪv/ *adj* provocatorio; (sexually) provocante

provocatively /prəˈvɒkətɪvlɪ/ *adv* in modo provocatorio; ⟨smile, be dressed⟩ in modo provocante

provoke /prəˈvəʊk/ *vt* provocare

prevost /ˈprɒvəst/ *n* Am Unlv decano *m*; Br Univ, Sch rettore *m*; (in Scotland) sindaco *m*

prow /praʊ/ *n* prua *f*

prowess /ˈpraʊɪs/ *n* abilità *f inv*

prowl /praʊl/ ① *vi* aggirarsi ② *n* **on the** ~ in cerca di preda

prowler /ˈpraʊlə(r)/ *n* tipo *m* sospetto

proximity /prɒkˈsɪmətɪ/ *n* prossimità *f*

proxy /ˈprɒksɪ/ *n* procura *f*; (person) persona *f* che agisce per procura

prude /pruːd/ *n* **be a** ~ essere eccessivamente pudico

prudence /ˈpruːdəns/ *n* prudenza *f*

prudent /ˈpruːdənt/ *adj* prudente; (wise) oculato *f*

prudently /ˈpruːdəntlɪ/ *adv* con prudenza

prudish /ˈpruːdɪʃ/ *adj* eccessivamente pudico

prudishness /ˈpruːdɪʃnɪs/ *n* eccessivo pudore *m*

prune[1] /pruːn/ *n* prugna *f* secca

prune[2] *vt* potare

pry /praɪ/ *vi* (*pt/pp* **pried**) ficcare il naso

prying /ˈpraɪɪŋ/ *adj* curioso

PS *n abbr* (**postscriptum**) PS *m inv*

psalm /sɑːm/ *n* salmo *m*

pseud /sjuːd/ *n fam* intellettualoide *mf*

pseudonym /ˈsjuːdənɪm/ *n* pseudonimo *m*

PSHE *n abbr* Br (**personal social and health education**) (school subject) studio *m* degli aspetti personali, sociali e sanitari dell'individuo in relazione alla collettività

PST *abbr* Am (**Pacific Standard Time**) tempo *m* medio della zona del Pacifico

psych /saɪk/ vt ~ **out** (fam: unnerve)
snervare ~ **up** vt (fam: prepare mentally)
preparare psicologicamente

psychedelic /saɪkə'delɪk/ adj
psichedelico

psychiatric /saɪkɪ'ætrɪk/ adj
psichiatrico

psychiatrist /saɪ'kaɪətrɪst/ n psichiatra
mf

psychiatry /saɪ'kaɪətrɪ/ n psichiatria f

psychic /'saɪkɪk/ ① n sensitivo, -a mf
② adj psichico; **I'm not** ~ non sono un
indovino

psychoanalyse /saɪkəʊ'ænəlaɪz/ vt
psicanalizzare

psychoanalysis /saɪkəʊə'nælɪsɪs/ n
psicanalisi f

psychoanalyst /saɪkəʊ'ænəlɪst/ n
psicanalista mf

psychological /saɪkə'lɒdʒɪkl/ adj
psicologico

psychologically /saɪkə'lɒdʒɪklɪ/ adv
psicologicamente

psychologist /saɪ'kɒlədʒɪst/ n
psicologo, -a mf

psychology /saɪ'kɒlədʒɪ/ n psicologia f

psychopath /'saɪkəpæθ/ n psicopatico,
-a mf

psychopathic /saɪkə'pæθɪk/ adj
psicopatico

psychosis /saɪ'kəʊsɪs/ n psicosi f inv

psychosomatic /saɪkəʊsə'mætɪk/ adj
psicosomatico

psychotherapist n psicoterapista mf,
psicoterapeuta mf

psychotic /saɪ'kɒtɪk/ adj & n psicotico,
-a mf

PT n abbr (**physical training**)
educazione f fisica

PTA n abbr (**Parent-Teacher
Association**) ≈ consiglio m d'istituto

PTO abbr (**please turn over**) vedi retro

pub /pʌb/ n fam pub m inv

puberty /'pju:bətɪ/ n pubertà f

pubic hair /'pju:bɪk/ n peli mpl del pube

public /'pʌblɪk/ ① adj pubblico; **make** ~
rendere pubblico
② n **the** ~ il pubblico; **in** ~ in pubblico

public address system n impianto
m di amplificazione

publican /'pʌblɪkən/ n gestore, -trice mf/
proprietario, -a mf di un pub

public assistance n Am assistenza f
pubblica

publication /pʌblɪ'keɪʃn/ n
pubblicazione f

public company n società f per azioni

public convenience n gabinetti mpl
pubblici

public holiday n festa f nazionale

public house n pub m inv

publicist /'pʌblɪsɪst/ n (press agent) press
agent mf inv, addetto, -a mf stampa

publicity /pʌb'lɪsətɪ/ n pubblicità f

publicity campaign n campagna f
pubblicitaria

publicity department n settore m
pubblicità

publicity director n direttore, -trice
mf della pubblicità

publicity stunt n trovata f
pubblicitaria

publicize /'pʌblɪsaɪz/ vt pubblicizzare

public library n biblioteca f pubblica

public limited company /'lɪmɪtɪd/ n
società f inv per azioni

publicly /'pʌblɪklɪ/ adv pubblicamente

public opinion n opinione f pubblica

public prosecutor n Pubblico
Ministero m

public relations npl pubbliche
relazioni fpl

public relations department n
ufficio m pubbliche relazioni

public relations officer n addetto, -a
mf alle pubbliche relazioni

public school n scuola f privata; Am
scuola f pubblica

public sector n settore m pubblico

public-spirited adj **be** ~ essere dotato
di senso civico

public transport n mezzi mpl pubblici

publish /'pʌblɪʃ/ vt pubblicare

publisher /'pʌblɪʃə(r)/ n editore m; (firm)
editore m, casa f editrice

publishing /'pʌblɪʃɪŋ/ n editoria f

puce /pju:s/ adj color bruno rossastro

puck /pʌk/ n (in ice-hockey) disco m; (sprite)
folletto m

pucker /'pʌkə(r)/ vi ⟨material⟩
arricciarsi

pudding /'pʊdɪŋ/ n dolce m cotto al
vapore; (course) dolce m

puddle /'pʌdl/ n pozzanghera f

pudgy /'pʌdʒɪ/ adj (-ier, -iest)
grassoccio

puerile /'pjʊəraɪl/ adj puerile

puff /pʌf/ ① n (of wind) soffio m; (of smoke)
tirata f; (for powder) piumino m
② vt sbuffare
■ **puff at** vt tirare boccate da ⟨pipe⟩
■ **puff out** vt lasciare senza fiato
⟨person⟩; spegnere ⟨candle⟩
■ **puff up** ① vi ⟨feathers⟩ arruffarsi; ⟨eye,
rice⟩ gonfiarsi
② vt arruffare ⟨feathers, fur⟩; ~**ed up**
with pride gonfio d'orgoglio

puffed /pʌft/ adj (out of breath) senza fiato

puff pastry n pasta f sfoglia

puff sleeve n manica f a palloncino

puffy /'pʌfɪ/ adj gonfio

pug /pʌg/ n (dog) carlino m

pugnacious /pʌg'neɪʃəs/ adj aggressivo

pull /pʊl/ **①** n trazione f; (fig: attraction) attrazione f; (fam: influence) influenza f **②** vt tirare; estrarre ⟨tooth⟩; stirarsi ⟨muscle⟩; ~ a fast one fam giocare un brutto tiro; ~ faces far boccacce; ~ oneself together ricomporsi; ~ one's weight mettercela tutta; ~ sb's leg fam prendere in giro qualcuno
- **pull ahead** vi (move in front) passare davanti
- **pull apart** vt (dismantle) smontare; (destroy) fare a pezzi
- **pull away** vi (increase one's lead) distanziarsi
- **pull back ①** vi ⟨soldiers⟩ ritirarsi; (not act) tirarsi indietro **②** vt far ritirare ⟨soldiers⟩
- **pull down** vt (demolish) demolire
- **pull in** vi Auto accostare
- **pull off** vt togliere; fam azzeccare
- **pull out ①** vt tirar fuori **②** vi Auto spostarsi; (of competition) ritirarsi
- **pull over** vi Aut accostare
- **pull through** vi (recover) farcela
- **pull together** vi (co-operate) sommare le forze
- **pull up ①** vt sradicare ⟨plant⟩; (reprimand) rimproverare **②** vi Auto fermarsi

pull-down menu n Comput menu m inv a discesa

pulley /'pʊlɪ/ n Techn puleggia f

pull-in n Br (lay-by) piazzuola f di sosta; (cafe) bar m inv sul bordo della strada

pullover /'pʊləʊvə(r)/ n pullover m inv

pulmonary /'pʌlmənərɪ/ adj polmonare

pulp /pʌlp/ n poltiglia f; (of fruit) polpa f; (for paper) pasta f

pulp fiction n letteratura f pulp

pulpit /pʌlpɪt/ n pulpito m

pulsar /'pʌlsɑ:(r)/ n pulsar m inv

pulsate /pʌl'seɪt/ vi pulsare

pulse /pʌls/ n polso m

pulse rate n polso m

pulses /'pʌlsɪz/ npl legumi mpl secchi

pulverize /'pʌlvəraɪz/ vt polverizzare

puma /'pju:mə/ n puma m inv

pumice /'pʌmɪs/ n pomice f

pummel /'pʌml/ vt (pt/pp **pummelled**) prendere a pugni

pump /pʌmp/ **①** n pompa f **②** vt pompare; fam cercare di estorcere informazioni da
- **pump up** vt (inflate) gonfiare

pumpkin /'pʌmpkɪn/ n zucca f

pun /pʌn/ n gioco m di parole

punch¹ /pʌntʃ/ **①** n pugno m; (device) pinza f per forare **②** vt dare un pugno a; forare ⟨ticket⟩; perforare ⟨hole⟩

punch² n (drink) punch m inv

Punch-and-Judy show n spettacolo m di burattini

punchbag n punching bag f inv

punch-drunk adj (in boxing) groggy inv; fig stordito

punchline n battuta f finale

punch-up n rissa f

punctual /'pʌŋktjʊəl/ adj puntuale

punctuality /pʌŋktjʊ'ælətɪ/ n puntualità f

punctually /'pʌŋktjʊəlɪ/ adv puntualmente

punctuate /'pʌŋktjʊeɪt/ vt punteggiare

punctuation /pʌŋktjʊ'eɪʃn/ n punteggiatura f

punctuation mark n segno m di interpunzione

puncture /'pʌŋktʃə(r)/ **①** n foro m: (tyre) foratura f **②** vt forare

pundit /'pʌndɪt/ n esperto m

pungency /'pʌndʒənsɪ/ n asprezza f

pungent /'pʌndʒənt/ adj acre

punish /'pʌnɪʃ/ vt punire

punishable /'pʌnɪʃəbl/ adj punibile

punishment /'pʌnɪʃmənt/ n punizione f

punitive /'pju:nɪtɪv/ adj punitivo

punk /pʌŋk/ n punk m inv

punk rock n punk rock m inv

punk rocker /'rɒkə(r)/ n punk mf inv

punnet /'pʌnɪt/ n cestello m

punt /pʌnt/ n (boat) barchino m

punter /'pʌntə(r)/ n (gambler) scommettitore, -trice mf; (fam: client) consumatore, -trice mf

puny /'pju:nɪ/ adj (-ier, -iest) striminzito

pup /pʌp/ n = PUPPY

pupil /'pju:pl/ n alunno, -a mf; (of eye) pupilla f

puppet /'pʌpɪt/ n marionetta f; (glove, fig) burattino m

puppy /'pʌpɪ/ n cucciolo m

purchase /'pɜ:tʃəs/ **①** n acquisto m; (leverage) presa f **②** vt acquistare

purchase invoice n fattura f di acquisto

purchase ledger n libro m mastro degli acquisti

purchase order n ordine m di acquisto

purchase price n prezzo m di acquisto

purchaser /'pɜ:tʃəsə(r)/ n acquirente mf

purchasing [department] /'pɜ:tʃəsɪŋ/ n ufficio m acquisti

P

purchasing power n potere m d'acquisto

purdah /'pɜːdə/ n reclusione f delle donne in alcune società musulmane e indù

pure /pjʊə(r)/ adj puro

pure-bred /-bred/ ① n (horse) purosangue m inv
② adj purosangue inv

purée /pjʊəreɪ/ ① n purè m inv
② vt passare

purely /'pjʊəlɪ/ adv puramente

purgatory /'pɜːgətrɪ/ n purgatorio m

purge /pɜːdʒ/ Pol ① n epurazione f
② vt epurare

purification /pjʊərɪfɪ'keɪʃn/ n purificazione f

purify /'pjʊərɪfaɪ/ vt (pt/pp -ied) purificare

purist /'pjʊərɪst/ adj & n purista mf

puritan /'pjʊərɪtən/ ① n puritano, -a mf
② adj fig puritano

puritanical /pjʊərɪ'tænɪkl/ adj puritano

purity /'pjʊərɪtɪ/ n purità f

purl /pɜːl/ ① n (Knitting) maglia f rovescia
② vt/i lavorare a rovescio

purple /'pɜːpl/ adj viola inv

purport /pə'pɔːt/ vt ∼ to be farsi passare per

purpose /'pɜːpəs/ n scopo m; (determination) fermezza f; on ∼ apposta

purpose-built /-'bɪlt/ adj costruito ad hoc

purposeful /'pɜːpəsfʊl/ adj deciso

purposefully /'pɜːpəsfʊlɪ/ adv con decisione

purposely /'pɜːpəslɪ/ adv apposta

purpose-made adj Br fatto appositamente

purr /pɜː(r)/ vi ⟨cat⟩ fare le fusa

purse /pɜːs/ ① n borsellino m; (Am: handbag) borsa f
② vt increspare ⟨lips⟩

purser /'pɜːsə(r)/ n commissario m di bordo

pursue /pə'sjuː/ vt inseguire; fig proseguire

pursuer /pə'sjuːə(r)/ n inseguitore, -trice mf

pursuit /pə'sjuːt/ n inseguimento m; (fig: of happiness) ricerca f; (pastime) attività f inv; in ∼ all'inseguimento

pus /pʌs/ n pus m

push /pʊʃ/ ① n spinta f; (fig: effort) sforzo m; (drive) iniziativa f; at a ∼ in caso di bisogno; get the ∼ fam essere licenziato
② vt spingere; premere ⟨button⟩; (pressurize) far pressione su; be ∼ed for time fam non avere tempo
③ vi spingere

■ **push around** vt (bully) fare il prepotente con

■ **push aside** vt scostare

■ **push back** vt respingere

■ **push for** vt fare pressione per ottenere ⟨reform⟩

■ **push in** ① vi (in queue) farsi largo spingendo
② vt spingere ⟨button⟩

■ **push off** ① vt togliere
② vi (fam: leave) levarsi dai piedi

■ **push on** vi (continue) continuare

■ **push over** vt (cause to fall) far cadere

■ **push through** vt (have accepted quickly) fare accettare

■ **push up** vt alzare ⟨price⟩

push-button n pulsante m

pushchair /'pʊʃtʃeə(r)/ n passeggino m

pusher /'pʊʃə(r)/ n (fam: of drugs) spacciatore, -trice mf [di droga]

pushover n fam bazzecola f

push start ① vt spingere (per far partire) ⟨vehicle⟩
② n give something a ∼ ∼ dare una spinta a qualcosa

push-up n flessione f

pushy /'pʊʃɪ/ adj fam troppo intraprendente

puss /pʊs/, **pussy** /'pʊsɪ/ n micio m

pussyfoot around /'pʊsɪfʊt/ vi fam tergiversare

pussyfooting /'pʊsɪfʊtɪŋ/ ① n fam tentennamento m
② adj fam ⟨attitude, behaviour⟩ tergiversante

put /pʊt/ ① vt (pt/pp put, pres p putting) mettere; ∼ the cost of something at £50 valutare il costo di qualcosa 50 sterline; ∼ an end to porre fine o termine a; ∼ in writing mettere per iscritto; ∼ into effect mettere in opera
② vi ∼ to sea salpare
③ adj stay ∼! rimani lì!

■ **put about** vt mettere in giro ⟨rumour⟩

■ **put across** vt raccontare ⟨joke⟩; esprimere ⟨message⟩

■ **put aside** vt mettere da parte

■ **put away** vt mettere via

■ **put back** vt rimettere; mettere indietro ⟨clock⟩

■ **put by** vt mettere da parte

■ **put down** vt mettere giù; (suppress) reprimere; (kill) sopprimere; (write) annotare; (criticize unfairly) sminuire; ∼ one's foot down fam essere fermo; Auto dare un'accelerata; ∼ down to (attribute) attribuire

■ **put forward** vt avanzare; mettere avanti ⟨clock⟩

■ **put in** ① vt (insert) introdurre; (submit) presentare
② vi ∼ in for far domanda di

■ **put off** vt spegnere ⟨light⟩; (postpone) rimandare; ∼ somebody off tenere a bada qualcuno; (deter) smontare qualcuno; (disconcert) distrarre qualcuno; ~ **somebody off something** (disgust) disgustare qualcuno di qualcosa

■ **put on** *vt* mettersi ‹*clothes*›; mettere ‹*brake*›; Culin mettere su; accendere ‹*light*› mettere in scena ‹*play*›; prendere ‹*accent*›; ~ **on weight** mettere su qualche chilo; he's just ~ting it on è solo una messa in scena

■ **put on to** *vt* (help find) indicare ‹*doctor, restaurant etc*›

■ **put out** *vt* spegnere ‹*fire, light*›; tendere ‹*hand*›; (inconvenience) creare degli inconvenienti a

■ **put through** *vt* far passare; Teleph I'll ~ **you through to him** glielo passo

■ **put to** *vt* ~ **somebody to trouble** scomodare qualcuno; I ~ **it to you that...** ritengo che...

■ **put together** *vt* montare ‹*machine*›; fare ‹*model, jigsaw*›

■ **put up** ➀ *vt* alzare; erigere ‹*building*›; montare ‹*tent*›; aprire ‹*umbrella*›; affiggere ‹*notice*›; aumentare ‹*price*›; ospitare ‹*guest*›; ~ **somebody up to something** mettere qualcosa in testa a qualcuno

➁ *vi* (at hotel) stare; ~ **up with** sopportare

put-down *n* commento *m* umiliante

putrefaction /pjuːtrɪˈfækʃn/ *n* putrefazione *f*

putrefy /ˈpjuːtrɪfaɪ/ *vi* (pt/pp -**ied**) putrefarsi

putrid /ˈpjuːtrɪd/ *adj* putrido

putt /pʌt/ ➀ *n* putt *m inv* ➁ *vi* colpire leggermente

putty /ˈpʌtɪ/ *n* mastice *m*

put-up job *n* fam truffa *f*

puzzle /ˈpʌzl/ ➀ *n* enigma *m*; (jigsaw) puzzle *m inv* ➁ *vt* lasciare perplesso ➂ *vi* ~ **over** scervellarsi su

■ **puzzle out** *vt* trovare ‹*solution*›

puzzled /ˈpʌzld/ *adj* perplesso

puzzling /ˈpʌzlɪŋ/ *adj* inspiegabile

PVC ➀ *n* PVC *m* ➁ *attrib* di PVC

pygmy /ˈpɪgmɪ/ *n* pigmeo, -a *mf*

pyjamas /pəˈdʒɑːməz/ *npl* pigiama *msg*

pylon /ˈpaɪlən/ *n* pilone *m*

pyramid /ˈpɪrəmɪd/ *n* piramide *f*

pyre /paɪə(r)/ *n* pira *f*

Pyrex® /ˈpaɪreks/ *n* Pyrex *m*

pyromaniac /paɪrəˈmeɪnɪæk/ *n* piromane *mf*

pyrotechnics /paɪrəˈtekniks/ *n* (display) fuochi *mpl* pirotecnici

python /ˈpaɪθn/ *n* pitone *m*

Qq

q, Q /kjuː/ *n* (letter) q, Q *f inv*

Qatar /ˈkætɑ(r)/ *n* Qatar *m*

QC *n* Br Jur avvocato *m* di rango superiore

QED *abbr* (**quod erat demonstrandum**) qed

quack[1] /kwæk/ ➀ *n* qua qua *m inv* ➁ *vi* fare qua qua

quack[2] *n* (doctor) ciarlatano *m*

quad /kwɒd/ *n* (fam: court) = QUADRANGLE; ~**s** *pl* fam = QUADRUPLETS

quadrangle /ˈkwɒdræŋgl/ *n* quadrangolo *m*; (court) cortile *m* quadrangolare

quadratic equation /kwɒˈdrætɪk/ *n* equazione *f* di secondo grado

quadriplegic /kwɒdrɪˈpliːdʒɪk/ *adj* quadriplegico

quadruped /ˈkwɒdrʊped/ *n* quadrupede *m*

quadruple /ˈkwɒdrʊpl/ ➀ *adj* quadruplo ➁ *vt* quadruplicare

➂ *vi* quadruplicarsi

quadruplets /kwɒdˈruːplɪts/ *npl* quattro gemelli *mpl*

quadruplicate /kwɒdˈruːplɪkət/ *n* in ~ in quattro copie

quagmire /ˈkwɒgmaɪə(r)/ *n* pantano *m*

quail /kweɪl/ *vi* farsi prendere dalla paura

quaint /kweɪnt/ *adj* pittoresco; (odd) bizzarro

quake /kweɪk/ ➀ *n* fam terremoto *m* ➁ *vi* tremare

Quaker /ˈkweɪkə(r)/ *n* quacchero, -a *mf*

qualification /kwɒlɪfɪˈkeɪʃn/ *n* qualifica *f*; (reservation) riserva *f*

qualified /ˈkwɒlɪfaɪd/ *adj* qualificato; (limited) con riserva

qualifier /ˈkwɒlɪfaɪə(r)/ *n* Sport concorrente *mf* qualificato, -a

qualify /ˈkwɒlɪfaɪ/ ➀ *vt* (pt/pp -**ied**) ‹*course*› dare la qualifica a (**as** di); ‹*entitle*› dare diritto a; ‹*limit*› precisare

2 *vi* ottenere la qualifica; Sport qualificarsi

qualitative /'kwɒlɪtətɪv/ *adj* qualitativo

quality /'kwɒlətɪ/ *n* qualità *f inv*

quality assurance *n* verifica *f* qualità

quality control *n* controllo *m* [di] qualità

quality controller *n* addetto, -a *mf* al controllo di qualità

qualm /kwɑːm/ *n* scrupolo *m*

quandary /'kwɒndərɪ/ *n* dilemma *m*

quango /'kwæŋgəʊ/ *n* Br organismo *m* autonomo ma finanziato dal governo

quantifiable /'kwɒntɪfaɪəbl/ *adj* quantificabile

quantify /'kwɒntɪfaɪ/ *vt* quantificare

quantitative /'kwɒntɪtətɪv/ *adj* quantitativo

quantity /'kwɒntətɪ/ *n* quantità *f inv*; in ∼ in grande quantità

quantity surveyor *n* geometra *mf* che calcola quantità e costo di materiali da costruzione

quantum leap /kwɒntəm'liːp/ *n* fig balzo *m* in avanti

quantum mechanics *n* meccanica *f* quantistica

quarantine /'kwɒrəntiːn/ *n* quarantena *f*

quarrel /'kwɒrəl/ **1** *n* lite *f* **2** *vi* (pt/pp **quarrelled**) litigare

quarrelsome /'kwɒrəlsəm/ *adj* litigioso

quarry[1] /'kwɒrɪ/ *n* (prey) preda *f*

quarry[2] *n* cava *f*

quarry tile *n* mattonella *f* grezza

quart /kwɔːt/ *n* = 1,14 litre

quarter /'kwɔːtə(r)/ **1** *n* quarto *m*; (of year) trimestre *m*; Am 25 centesimi *mpl*; ∼s *pl Mil* quartiere *msg*; **at [a]** ∼ **to six** alle sei meno un quarto; **from all** ∼s da tutti i lati **2** *vt* dividere in quattro

quarterdeck /'kwɔːtədek/ *n* Naut cassero *m*

quarter-final *n* quarto *m* di finale

quarterly /'kwɔːtəlɪ/ **1** *adj* trimestrale **2** *adv* trimestralmente

quartermaster /'kwɔːtəmɑːstə(r)/ *n* ‹in navy› timoniere *m*; ‹in army› furiere *m*

quartet /kwɔː'tet/ *n* quartetto *m*

quartz /kwɔːts/ *n* quarzo *m*; ∼ **watch** orologio *m* al quarzo

quash /kwɒʃ/ *vt* annullare; soffocare ‹rebellion›

quasi+ /'kweɪzaɪ/ *pref* semi+

quaver /'kweɪvə(r)/ **1** *n* Mus croma *f* **2** *vi* tremolare

quay /kiː/ *n* banchina *f*

quayside *n* banchina *f*

queasiness /'kwiːzɪnɪs/ *n* nausea *f*

queasy /'kwiːzɪ/ *adj* **I feel** ∼ **ho** la nausea

Quebec /kwɪ'bek/ *n* (province) Quebec *m*; (town) Quebec *f*

queen /kwiːn/ *n* regina *f*

queen bee *n* ape *f* regina; **she thinks she's the** ∼ ∼ fig si crede chissà chi

queenly /'kwiːnlɪ/ *adj* da regina

queen mother *n* regina *f* madre

Queen's Counsel *n* Br Jur avvocato *m* di rango superiore

Queen's English *n* Br **speak the** ∼ ∼ parlare un inglese corretto e senza accento

Queen's evidence *n* Br Jur **turn** ∼ ∼ deporre contro i propri complici

Queen's Regulations *npl* Br Mil codice *m* militare

queer /kwɪə(r)/ **1** *adj* strano; (dubious) sospetto; (fam: homosexual) finocchio **2** *n* fam finocchio *m*

quell /kwel/ *vt* reprimere

quench /kwentʃ/ *vt* ∼ **one's thirst** dissetarsi

querulous /'kwerələs/ *adj* lamentoso

query /'kwɪərɪ/ **1** *n* domanda *f*; (question mark) punto *m* interrogativo **2** *vt* (pt/pp **-ied**) interrogare; (doubt) mettere in dubbio

quest /kwest/ *n* ricerca *f* (**for** di)

question /'kwestʃən/ **1** *n* domanda *f*; (for discussion) questione *f*; **out of the** ∼ fuori discussione; **without** ∼ senza dubbio; **in** ∼ in questione **2** *vt* interrogare; (doubt) mettere in dubbio

questionable /'kwestʃ(ə)nəbl/ *adj* discutibile

questioner /'kwestʃ(ə)nə(r)/ *n* interrogante *mf*

questioning /'kwestʃ(ə)nɪŋ/ **1** *n* (of person) interrogatorio *m*; (of criteria) messa *f* in discussione **2** *adj* ‹look, tone› inquisitorio

question mark *n* punto *m* interrogativo

question master *n* presentatore, -trice *mf* di quiz

questionnaire /kwestʃə'neə(r)/ *n* questionario *m*

question tag *n* domanda *f* di conferma

queue /kjuː/ **1** *n* coda *f*, fila *f* **2** *vi* ∼ **[up]** mettersi in coda (**for** per)

queue-jump *vi* Br passare davanti alle altre persone in coda

quibble /'kwɪbl/ *vi* cavillare

quick /kwɪk/ **1** *adj* veloce; **be** ∼ sbrigati!; **have a** ∼ **meal** fare uno spuntino **2** *adv* in fretta

3 *n* be cut to the ∼ *fig* essere punto sul vivo

quick-assembly *adj* facile da montare

quicken /'kwɪkən/ **1** *vt* accelerare ⟨*pace*⟩
2 *vi* ⟨*pace*⟩ accelerarsi; ⟨*interest*⟩ intensificarsi

quick-fire *adj* ⟨*questions*⟩ a mitraglia

quick-freeze *vt* surgelare

quickie /'kwɪkɪ/ *n fam* (question) domanda *f* rapida; (drink) bicchierino *m* rapido; (film) cortometraggio *m*

quicklime /'kwɪklaɪm/ *n* calce *f* viva

quickly /'kwɪklɪ/ *adv* in fretta

quick march *n* Mil passo *m* di marcia veloce

quicksand *n* sabbie *fpl* mobili

quick-setting /-'setɪŋ/ *adj* a presa rapida

quicksilver *n* Chem argento *m* vivo, mercurio *m*

quick-tempered /-'tempəd/ *adj* collerico

quick time *n* Am marcia *f* veloce

quick-witted /-'wɪtɪd/ *adj* ⟨*reaction*⟩ pronto; ⟨*person*⟩ sveglio

quid /kwɪd/ *n inv fam* sterlina *f*

quid pro quo /kwɪdprəʊ'kwəʊ/ *n* contraccambio *m*

quiet /'kwaɪət/ **1** *adj* (calm) tranquillo; (silent) silenzioso; ⟨voice, music⟩ basso; **keep** ∼ **about** *fam* non raccontare a nessuno
2 *n* quiete *f*; **on the** ∼ di nascosto

quieten /'kwaɪətn/ *vt* calmare
■ **quieten down** **1** *vt* calmare
2 *vi* calmarsi

quietly /'kwaɪətlɪ/ *adv* (peacefully) tranquillamente; ⟨*say*⟩ a bassa voce

quietness /'kwaɪətnɪs/ *n* quiete *f*

quiff /kwɪf/ *n* (Br: hair) ciuffo *m*

quill /kwɪl/ *n* penna *f* d'uccello; (spine) spina *f*

quilt /kwɪlt/ *n* piumino *m*

quilted /'kwɪltɪd/ *adj* trapuntato

quilting /'kwɪltɪŋ/ *n* (fabric) matelassé *m inv*

quince /kwɪns/ *n* cotogna *f*; (tree) melo *m* cotogno

quinine /'kwɪniːn/ *n* chinino *m*

quins /kwɪnz/ *npl fam* = QUINTUPLETS

quintessential /kwɪntɪ'senʃl/ *adj* ⟨*quality*⟩ fondamentale

quintet /kwɪn'tet/ *n* quintetto *m*

quintuple /'kwɪntjʊpl/ **1** *vt* quintuplicare
2 *adj* quintuplo

quintuplets /'kwɪntjʊplɪts/ *npl* cinque gemelli *mpl*

quip /kwɪp/ **1** *n* battuta *f*
2 *vt* (pt/pp **quipped**) dire scherzando

quirk /kwɜːk/ *n* stranezza *f*

quisling /'kwɪzlɪŋ/ *n pej* collaborazionista *mf*

quit /kwɪt/ **1** *v* (pt/pp **-tted** or **quit**) *vt* lasciare; (give up) smettere (**doing** di fare); Comput uscire da
2 *vi* (fam: resign) andarsene; Comput uscire; **give somebody notice to** ∼ dare a qualcuno preavviso di sfratto

quite /kwaɪt/ *adv* (fairly) abbastanza; (completely) completamente; (really) veramente; ∼ **[so]!** proprio così!; ∼ **a few** parecchi

quits /kwɪts/ *adj* pari

quiver /'kwɪvə(r)/ *vi* tremare

quiz /kwɪz/ **1** *n* (game) quiz *m inv*
2 *vt* (pt/pp **quizzed**) interrogare

quiz game, **quiz show** *n* quiz *m inv*

quizzical /'kwɪzɪkl/ *adj* sardonico

quoit /kwɔɪt/ *n* anello *m* (del gioco)

quoits *n* (game) gioco *m* degli anelli

quorum /'kwɔːrəm/ *n* quorum *m inv*; **have a** ∼ avere il quorum

quota /'kwəʊtə/ *n* quota *f*

quotation /kwəʊ'teɪʃn/ *n* citazione *f*; (price) preventivo *m*; (of shares) quota *f*

quotation marks *npl* virgolette *fpl*

quote /kwəʊt/ **1** *n fam* = QUOTATION; **in** ∼**s** tra virgolette
2 *vt* citare; quotare ⟨*price*⟩; ∼**d on the Stock Exchange** quotato in Borsa

Rr

r¹, R /ɑː(r)/ *n* (letter) r, R *f inv*; **the three Rs** leggere, scrivere e contare

R² Br abbr (**regina**) regina *f*

R & B *n* rhythm and blues *m*

R & D *n* ricerca *f* e sviluppo *m*

rabbi /'ræbaɪ/ *n* rabbino *m*; (title) rabbi

rabbit /'ræbɪt/ *n* coniglio *m*
■ **rabbit on** *vi fam* what's he ∼ting on about now? cosa sta blaterando?

rabbit hutch *n* conigliera *f*

rabble/'ræbl/ *n* the ~ la plebaglia

rabble rouser /'raʊʒə(r)/ *n* agitatore, -trice *nmf*

rabble rousing *n* incitazione *f* alla violenza

rabid /'ræbɪd/ *adj* fig rabbioso

rabies /'reɪbiːz/ *n* rabbia *f*

RAC *n abbr* (**Royal Automobile Club**) ≈ ACI *f*

raccoon /rə'kuːn/ *n* procione *m*, orsetto *m* lavatore

race¹ /reɪs/ *n* (people) razza *f*

race² ① *n* corsa ⟨*f*⟩
② *vi* correre
③ *vt* gareggiare con; fare correre ⟨*horse*⟩

racecourse /'reɪskɔːs/ *n* ippodromo *m*

racehorse /'reɪshɔːs/ *n* cavallo *m* da corsa

racer /'reɪsə(r)/ *n* (bike) bicicletta *f* da corsa; (motorbike) motocicletta *f* da corsa; (car) automobile *f* da corsa; (runner, cyclist etc) corridore, -trice *mf*

race relations *npl* rapporti *mpl* tra le razze

race riots *npl* scontri *mpl* razziali

racetrack /'reɪstræk/ *n* pista *f*

racial /'reɪʃl/ *adj* razziale

racialism /'reɪʃəlɪzm/ *n* razzismo *m*

racially /'reɪʃ(ə)lɪ/ *adv* razzialmente

racing /'reɪsɪŋ/ *n* corse *fpl*; (horse-~) corse *fpl* dei cavalli

racing car *n* macchina *f* da corsa

racing driver *n* corridore *m* automobilistico

racism /'reɪsɪzm/ *n* razzismo *m*

racist /'reɪsɪst/ *adj* & *n* razzista *mf*

rack¹ /ræk/ ① *n* (for bikes) rastrelliera *f*; (for luggage) portabagagli *m inv*; (for plates) scolapiatti *m inv*
② *vt* ~ one's brains scervellarsi

rack² *n* go to ~ and ruin andare in rovina

racket¹ /'rækɪt/ *n* Sport racchetta *f*

racket² *n* (din) chiasso *m*; (swindle) truffa *f*; (crime) racket *m inv*, giro *m*

racketeer /rækɪ'tɪə(r)/ *n* trafficante *m*

racketeering /rækɪ'tɪərɪŋ/ *n* traffici *mpl* illeciti

racking /'rækɪŋ/ *adj* ⟨pain⟩ atroce

raconteur /'rækɒntɜː(r)/ *n* bravo narratore *m*, brava narratrice *f*

racquetball /'rækɪtbɔːl/ *n* Am = SQUASH

racy /'reɪsɪ/ *adj* (**-ier**, **-iest**) vivace; (risqué) osé *inv*, spinto

radar /'reɪdɑː(r)/ *n* radar *m*

radar trap *n* Auto tratto *m* di strada sul quale la polizia controlla la velocità dei veicoli

radial /'reɪdɪəl/ ① *n* (tyre) [pneumatico *m*] radiale *m*
② *adj* ⟨lines, roads⟩ radiale

radiance /'reɪdɪəns/ *n* radiosità *f*

radiant /'reɪdɪənt/ *adj* raggiante

radiate /'reɪdɪeɪt/ ① *vt* irradiare
② *vi* ⟨heat⟩ irradiarsi; ⟨roads⟩ partire

radiation /reɪdɪ'eɪʃn/ *n* radiazione *f*

radiation exposure *n* esposizione *f* a radiazioni

radiation sickness *n* patologia *f* da radiazioni

radiator /'reɪdɪeɪtə(r)/ *n* radiatore *m*

radical /'rædɪkl/ *adj* & *n* radicale *mf*

radicalism /'rædɪkəlɪzm/ *n* radicalismo *m*

radically /'rædɪklɪ/ *adv* radicalmente

radio /'reɪdɪəʊ/ ① *n* radio *f inv*
② *vt* mandare via radio ⟨message⟩

radioactive /reɪdɪəʊ'æktɪv/ *adj* radioattivo

radioactive waste *n* scorie *fpl* radioattive

radioactivity /reɪdɪəʊæk'tɪvətɪ/ *n* radioattività *f*

radio alarm *n* radiosveglia *f*

radio cassette player *n* radioregistratore *m*

radio-controlled *adj* radiocomandato

radiographer /reɪdɪ'ɒgrəfə(r)/ *n* radiologo, -a *mf*

radiography /reɪdɪ'ɒgrəfɪ/ *n* radiografia *f*

radio ham *n* radioamatore, -trice *mf*

radiologist /reɪdɪ'ɒlədʒɪst/ *n* radiologo, -a *mf*

radiology /reɪdɪ'ɒlədʒɪ/ *n* radiologia *f*

radio station *n* stazione *f* radiofonica

radiotherapy /reɪdɪəʊ'θerəpɪ/ *n* radioterapia *f*

radish /'rædɪʃ/ *n* ravanello *m*

radius /'reɪdɪəs/ *n* (pl **-dii** /'reɪdɪaɪ/) raggio *m*

RAF *n abbr* Br (**Royal Air Force**) aviazione *f* militare inglese

raffle /'ræfl/ ① *n* lotteria *f*
② *vt* mettere in palio

raft /rɑːft/ *n* zattera *f*

rafter /'rɑːftə(r)/ *n* trave *f*

rag¹ /ræg/ *n* straccio *m*; (pej: newspaper) giornalaccio *m*; in ~s stracciato

rag² ① *vt* (pt/pp **ragged**) fam fare scherzi a
② *n* Univ festa *f* di beneficenza organizzata da studenti universitari

ragamuffin /'rægəmʌfɪn/ *n* monellaccio *m*

rag-and-bone man *n* Br rigattiere *m*, straccivendolo *m*

ragbag /'rægbæg/ *n* fig accozzaglia *f*

rage /reɪdʒ/ **①** *n* rabbia *f*; **all the** ~ fam all'ultima moda

② *vi* infuriarsi; ⟨*storm*⟩ infuriare; ⟨*epidemic*⟩ imperversare

ragged /'rægɪd/ *adj* logoro; ⟨*edge*⟩ frastagliato

raging /'reɪdʒɪŋ/ *adj* ⟨*blizzard, sea*⟩ furioso; ⟨*thirst, pain*⟩ atroce; ⟨*passion, argument*⟩ acceso

raglan /'ræglən/ **①** *adj* raglan *inv* **②** *n* manica *f* raglan

rag trade *n* fam settore *m* dell'abbigliamento

rag week *n* Br Univ settimana *f* di manifestazioni a scopo benefico organizzata dagli studenti

raid /reɪd/ **①** *n* (by thieves) rapina *f*; Mil incursione *f*, raid *m inv*; (by police) irruzione *f*

② *vt* Mil fare un'incursione in; ⟨*police, thieves*⟩ fare irruzione in

raider /'reɪdə(r)/ *n* (of bank) rapinatore, -trice *mf*

rail[1] /reɪl/ *n* ringhiera *f*; ⟨*Rail*⟩ rotaia *f*; Naut parapetto *m*; **by** ~ per ferrovia

rail[2] *vi* ~ **against** *or* **at** inveire contro

railcard /'reɪlkɑːd/ *n* tessera *f* di riduzione ferroviaria

railings /'reɪlɪŋz/ *npl* ringhiera *f*

railroad /'reɪlrəʊd/ **①** *n* Am = RAILWAY **②** *vt* ~ **somebody into doing something** spingere qualcuno a fare qualcosa

railroad car *n* Am vagone *m* ferroviario

railroad schedule *n* Am orario *m* ferroviario

rail traffic *n* traffico *m* ferroviario

railway /'reɪlweɪ/ *n* ferrovia *f*

railway carriage *n* Br vagone *m* ferroviario

railwayman /'reɪlweɪmən/ *n* ferroviere *m*

railway station *n* stazione *f* ferroviaria

rain /reɪn/ **①** *n* pioggia *f*

② *vi* piovere; ~ **down on somebody** fig piovere addosso a qualcuno

③ *vt* ~ **blows on somebody** tempestare qualcuno di colpi

■ **rain off** *vt* **be** ~**ed off** essere annullato a causa della pioggia

rainbow *n* arcobaleno *m*

raincheck *n* Am **can I take a** ~? facciamo un'altra volta

raincoat *n* impermeabile *m*

raindrop *n* goccia *f* di pioggia

rainfall *n* precipitazione *f* [atmosferica]

rainforest *n* foresta *f* pluviale, foresta *f* equatoriale

rainstorm *n* temporale *m*

rain water *n* acqua *f* piovana

rainy /'reɪnɪ/ *adj* (**-ier,-iest**) piovoso

rainy day *n* **save something for a** ~ ~ fig mettere qualcosa in serbo per i tempi di magra

rainy season *n* stagione *f* delle piogge

raise /reɪz/ **①** *n* Am aumento *m* **②** *vt* alzare; levarsi ⟨*hat*⟩; allevare ⟨*children, animals*⟩; sollevare ⟨*question*⟩; ottenere ⟨*money*⟩; ~ **hell** indiavolarsi; ~ **a laugh** ⟨*joke, remark*⟩ far ridere; ~ **the stakes** rilanciare; ~ **one's voice** alzare la voce

raised /reɪzd/ *adj* ⟨*flowerbed, platform*⟩ soprelevato; ~ **voices** urla

raisin /'reɪzn/ *n* uvetta *f*; ~**s** *pl* uvetta *f*, uva *f* passa

Raj /rɑːʒ/ *n* governo *m* britannico in India

rake /reɪk/ **①** *n* rastrello *m* **②** *vt* rastrellare

■ **rake in** *vt* fam farsi ⟨*profits, money*⟩; **he's raking it in** sta facendo un sacco di soldi

■ **rake together** *vt* fig racimolare ⟨*money*⟩

■ **rake up** *vt* raccogliere col rastrello; fam rivangare

rake-off *n* fam parte *f*

rakish /'reɪkɪʃ/ *adj* (dissolute) dissoluto; (jaunty) disinvolto

rally /'rælɪ/ **①** *n* raduno *m*; Auto rally *m inv*; (Tennis) scambio *m*; (recovery) ripresa *f* **②** *vt* (pt/pp **-ied**) radunare **③** *vi* radunarsi; (recover strength) riprendersi

rallying cry /'rælɪŋ/, **rallying call** *n* slogan *m inv*

RAM /ræm/ *n* memoria *f* RAM

ram /ræm/ **①** *n* montone *m*; Astr Ariete *m* **②** *vt* (pt/pp **rammed**) cozzare contro

ramble /'ræmbl/ **①** *n* escursione *f* **②** *vi* gironzolare; (in speech) divagare

■ **ramble on** *vi* fam parlare/scrivere a ruota libera

rambler /'ræmblə(r)/ *n* escursionista *mf*; (rose) rosa *f* rampicante

rambling /'ræmblɪŋ/ *adj* (in speech) sconnesso; ⟨*club*⟩ escursionistico

ramification /ræmɪfɪ'keɪʃən/ *n* ramificazione *f*

ramify /'ræmɪfaɪ/ *vi* (pt/pp **-ied**) ramificarsi

ramp /ræmp/ *n* rampa *f*; Auto dosso *m*

rampage /'ræmpeɪdʒ/ **①** *n* **be/go on the** ~ scatenarsi

② *vi* ~ **through the streets** scatenarsi per le strade

rampant /'ræmpənt/ *adj* dilagante; (in heraldry) rampante

rampart /'ræmpɑːt/ *n* bastione *f*

ram raid *n* rapina *f* in un negozio con scasso della vetrina effettuato con un'auto

ram raider n rapinatore m che scassa la vetrina di un negozio con un'auto

ramshackle /'ræmʃækl/ adj sgangherato

ran /ræn/ ▶ RUN

ranch /rɑːntʃ/ n ranch m inv

rancher /'rɑːntʃə(r)/ n (worker) cow-boy m inv; (owner) proprietario m di ranch

rancid /'rænsɪd/ adj rancido

rancour /'ræŋkə(r)/ n rancore m

random /'rændəm/ ① adj casuale; ~ sample campione m a caso ② n at ~ a casaccio

random-access adj ad accesso casuale

random-access memory n memoria f viva

randy /'rændɪ/ adj (-ier, -iest) fam eccitato

rang /ræŋ/ ▶ RING²

range /reɪndʒ/ ① n serie f; Comm, Mus gamma f; (of mountains) catena f; (distance) raggio m; (for shooting) portata f; (stove) cucina f economica; **at a ~ of** ad una distanza di ② vi estendersi; ~ **from...to...** andare da...a...

ranger /'reɪndʒə(r)/ n guardia f forestale

rank¹ /ræŋk/ ① n (row) riga f; Mil grado m; (social position) rango m; **the ~ and file** la base; **the ~s** pl Mil i soldati mpl semplici ② vt (place) annoverare (**among** tra) ③ vi (be placed) collocarsi

rank² adj ⟨smell⟩ puzzolente; ⟨plants⟩ rigoglioso; fig vero e proprio

ranking /'ræŋkɪŋ/ n classificazione f

rankle /'ræŋkl/ vi fig bruciare; **it still ~s with him** gli brucia ancora

ransack /'rænsæk/ vt rovistare; (pillage) saccheggiare

ransom /'rænsəm/ n riscatto m; **hold somebody to ~** tenere qualcuno in ostaggio per il riscatto

rant /rænt/ vi ~ **[and rave]** inveire; **what's he ~ing on about?** cosa sta blaterando?

rap /ræp/ ① n colpo m secco; Mus rap m ② vt (pt/pp **rapped**) dare colpetti a; ~ **somebody over the knuckles** fig dare una tirata d'orecchie a qualcuno ③ vi ~ **at** bussare a

rape¹ /reɪp/ n Bot colza f

rape² ① n (sexual) stupro m ② vt violentare, stuprare

rape[seed] oil /'reɪp[siːd]/ n olio m [di semi] di colza

rapid /'ræpɪd/ adj rapido

rapidity /rə'pɪdətɪ/ n rapidità f

rapidly /'ræpɪdlɪ/ adv rapidamente

rapids /'ræpɪdz/ npl rapida fsg

rapist /'reɪpɪst/ n violentatore m

rapper /'ræpə(r)/ n (Br: door-knocker) battiporta m inv; Mus rapper mf inv

rapport /ræ'pɔː(r)/ n rapporto m di intesa

rapt /ræpt/ adj ⟨look⟩ rapito; ~ **in** assorto in

rapture /'ræptʃə(r)/ n estasi f

rapturous /'ræptʃərəs/ adj entusiastico

rapturously /'ræptʃərəslɪ/ adv entusiasticamente

rare¹ /reə(r)/ adj raro

rare² adj Culin al sangue

rarefied /'reərɪfaɪd/ adj rarefatto

rarely /'reəlɪ/ adv raramente

raring /'reərɪŋ/ adj fam **be ~ to** non vedere l'ora di

rarity /'reərətɪ/ n rarità f inv

rascal /'rɑːskl/ n mascalzone m

rash¹ /ræʃ/ n Med eruzione f

rash² adj avventato

rasher /'ræʃə(r)/ n fetta f di pancetta

rashly /'ræʃlɪ/ adv avventatamente

rashness /'ræʃnɪs/ n avventatezza f

rasp /rɑːsp/ n (noise) stridio m

raspberry /'rɑːzbərɪ/ n lampone m

rasping /'rɑːspɪŋ/ adj stridente

rat /ræt/ ① n topo m; (fam: person) carogna f; **smell a ~** fam sentire puzzo di bruciato ② vi (pt/pp **ratted**) fam ~ **on** far la spia a

rat-a-tat-tat /rætətæ(t)'tæt/ n toc toc m inv

rat-catcher n addetto, -a mf alla derattizzazione

ratchet /'rætʃɪt/ n (toothed rack) cremagliera f

rate /reɪt/ ① n (speed) velocità f inv; (of payment) tariffa f; (of exchange) tasso m; ~**s** pl (taxes) imposte fpl comunali sui beni immobili; **at any ~** in ogni caso; **at this ~** di questo passo ② vt stimare; ~ **among** annoverare tra ③ vt ~ **as** essere considerato

ratepayer /'reɪtpeɪə(r)/ n contribuente mf

rather /'rɑːðə(r)/ adv piuttosto; ~! eccome!; ~ **too...** un po' troppo...

ratification /rætɪfɪ'keɪʃn/ n ratifica f

ratify /'rætɪfaɪ/ vt (pt/pp -**ied**) ratificare

rating /'reɪtɪŋ/ n valutazione f; (class) livello m; (sailor) marinaio m semplice; ~**s** pl Radio, TV indice m d'ascolto, audience f inv

ratio /'reɪʃɪəʊ/ n rapporto m; **in a ~ of two to one** in [un] rapporto di due a uno

ration /'ræʃn/ ① n razione f ② vt razionare

rational /'ræʃənl/ adj razionale

rationale /ræʃə'nɑːl/ n (logic) base f logica; (reasons) ragioni fpl

rationalize /'ræ∫(ə)nəlaɪz/ *vt/i* razionalizzare

rationally /'ræ∫(ə)nəlɪ/ *adv* razionalmente

rationing /'ræ∫(ə)nɪŋ/ *n* razionamento *m*

rat race *n* fam corsa *f* al successo

rat run *n* scorciatoia *f* usata dagli automobilisti in zone residenziali

rattan /rə'tæn/ *n* (tree, material) malacca *f*

rattle /'rætl/ ① *n* tintinnio *m*; (toy) sonaglio *m*
② *vi* tintinnare
③ *vt* (shake) scuotere; fam innervosire
■ **rattle off** *vt* fam sciorinare
■ **rattle on** *vi* (talk at length) parlare ininterrottamente
■ **rattle through** *vt* (say quickly) dire velocemente; (do quickly) fare velocemente

rattlesnake /'rætlsneɪk/ *n* serpente *m* a sonagli

ratty /'rætɪ/ *adj* (Br fam: grumpy) irascibile; Am ⟨hair⟩ sudicio

raucous /'rɔ:kəs/ *adj* rauco

raunchy /'rɔ:nt∫ɪ/ *adj* fam ⟨performer, voice, song⟩ sexy *inv*; (bawdy) spinto

ravage /'rævɪdʒ/ *vt* devastare

ravages /'rævɪdʒɪz/ *npl* danni *mpl*

rave /reɪv/ *vi* vaneggiare; ∼ **about** andare in estasi per

raven /'reɪvn/ *n* corvo *m* imperiale

ravenous /'rævənəs/ *adj* ⟨person⟩ affamato

rave-up *n* Br fam festa *f* animata

ravine /rə'vi:n/ *n* gola *f*

raving /'reɪvɪŋ/ *adj* ∼ **mad** fam matto da legare

ravings /'reɪvɪŋz/ *npl* vaneggiamenti *mpl*

ravioli /rævɪ'əʊlɪ/ *n* ravioli *mpl*

ravishing /'rævɪ∫ɪŋ/ *adj* incantevole

raw /rɔ:/ *adj* crudo; (not processed) grezzo; ⟨weather⟩ gelido; (inexperienced) inesperto

raw deal *n* get a ∼ ∼ fam farsi fregare

rawhide *n* (leather) cuoio *m* grezzo

Rawlplug ® /'rɔ:lplʌg/ *n* tassello *m*

raw materials *npl* materie *fpl* prime

ray /reɪ/ *n* raggio *m*; ∼ **of hope** barlume *m* di speranza

rayon® /'reɪɒn/ *n* raion® *m*

raze /reɪz/ *vt* ∼ **to the ground** radere al suolo

razor /'reɪzə(r)/ *n* rasoio *m*

razor blade *n* lametta *f* da barba

razor-sharp *adj* affilatissimo

razzle /'ræzl/ *n* Br fam **go on the** ∼ andare a fare baldoria

razzle-dazzle *n* fam baldoria *f*

razzmatazz /ræzmə'tæz/ *n* fam clamore *m*

RC ① *n* (Roman Catholic) cattolico, -a *mf*
② *adj* cattolico

Rd. *abbr* (Road) Via

re /ri:/ *prep* con riferimento a

reach /ri:t∫/ ① *n* portata *f*; (of river) tratto *m*; **within** ∼ a portata di mano; **out of** ∼ of fuori dalla portata di; **within easy** ∼ facilmente raggiungibile
② *vt* arrivare a ⟨place, decision⟩; (contact) contattare; (pass) passare; **I can't** ∼ **it** non ci arrivo
③ *vi* arrivare (**to** a); **I can't** ∼ non ci arrivo; ∼ **for** allungare la mano per prendere

reaches /'ri:t∫ɪz/ *npl* (of river) **the upper/ lower** ∼ la parte superiore/inferiore

react /rɪ'ækt/ *vi* reagire

reaction /rɪ'æk∫n/ *n* reazione *f*

reactionary /rɪ'æk∫(ə)nərɪ/ *adj & n* reazionario, -a *mf*

reactor /rɪ'æktə(r)/ *n* reattore *m*

read /ri:d/ ① *vt* (pt/pp **read** /red/) leggere; Univ studiare
② *vi* leggere; ⟨instrument⟩ indicare
■ **read back** *vt* (say aloud) rileggere
■ **read on** *vi* (continue reading) continuare a leggere
■ **read out** *vt* leggere ad alta voce
■ **read up on** *vt* studiare a fondo

readable /'ri:dəbl/ *adj* piacevole a leggersi; (legible) leggibile

reader /'ri:də(r)/ *n* lettore, -trice *mf*; (book) antologia *f*

readership /'ri:də∫ɪp/ *n* numero *m* di lettori

read head *n* Comput testina *f* di lettura

readily /'redɪlɪ/ *adv* volentieri; (easily) facilmente

readiness /'redɪnɪs/ *n* disponibilità; *f*; **in** ∼ pronto

reading /'ri:dɪŋ/ *n* lettura *f*

readjust /ri:ə'dʒʌst/ ① *vt* regolare di nuovo
② *vi* riabituarsi (**to** a)

readjustment /ri:ə'dʒʌstmənt/ *n* riadattamento *m*

read-only memory *n* Comput memoria *f* di sola lettura

readvertise /'ri:ædvətaɪz/ *vt* far ripubblicare un'inserzione per ⟨position, item⟩

ready /'redɪ/ *adj* (**-ier, -iest**) pronto; (quick) veloce; **get** ∼ prepararsi

ready-made *adj* confezionato

ready-mixed *adj* già miscelato

ready money *n* contanti *mpl*

ready-to-wear *adj* prêt-à-porter

reaffirm /ri:ə'fɜ:m/ *vt* riaffermare

reafforestation /ri:əfɒrɪ'steɪ∫n/ *n* rimboschimento *m*

real /ri:l/ ① *adj* vero; ⟨increase⟩ reale

② *adv* Am fam veramente

real estate *n* beni *mpl* immobili

realign /riːəˈlaɪn/ ① *vt* riallineare
② *vi* fig formare nuove alleanze

realignment /riːəˈlaɪnmənt/ *n* Pol
formazione *f* di nuove alleanze; Fin
riallineamento *m*

realism /ˈrɪəlɪzm/ *n* realismo *m*

realist /ˈrɪəlɪst/ *n* realista *mf*

realistic /rɪəˈlɪstɪk/ *adj* realistico

realistically /rɪəˈlɪstɪklɪ/ *adv*
realisticamente

reality /rɪˈælətɪ/ *n* realtà *f inv*

realization /rɪəlaɪˈzeɪʃn/ *n* realizzazione
f

realize /ˈrɪəlaɪz/ *vt* realizzare

real life *n* realtà *f*: **in ∼ life** nella realtà

real-life *attrib* autentico

reallocate /riːˈæləkeɪt/ *vt* riassegnare

reallocation /riːæləˈkeɪʃn/ *n*
riassegnazione *f*

really /ˈrɪəlɪ/ *adv* davvero

realm /relm/ *n* regno *m*

real time ① *n* tempo *m* reale; **in ∼ ∼** in
tempo reale
② *adj* in tempo reale

realtor /ˈrɪəltə(r)/ *n* Am agente *mf*
immobiliare

realty /ˈrɪəltɪ/ *n* Am beni *mpl* immobili

reanimate /riːˈænɪmeɪt/ *vt* rianimare

reap /riːp/ *vt* mietere

reappear /riːəˈpɪə(r)/ *vi* riapparire

reappearance /riːəˈpɪərəns/ *n*
ricomparsa *f*

reapply /riːəˈplaɪ/ *vi* (pt/pp **-ied**)
ripresentare domanda

reappoint /riːəˈpɔɪnt/ *vt* riconfermare

reappraisal /riːəˈpreɪzl/ *n*
riconsiderazione *f*

reappraise /riːəˈpreɪz/ *vt* riesaminare
⟨question, policy⟩; rivalutare ⟨writer, work⟩

rear[1] /rɪə(r)/ *adj* posteriore; Auto di dietro

rear[2] ① *vt* allevare
② *vi* **∼ [up]** ⟨horse⟩ impennarsi
③ *n* **the ∼** (of building) il retro; (of bus, plane)
la parte posteriore; **from the ∼** da dietro

rear end *n* fam di dietro *m*

rearguard /ˈrɪəɡɑːd/ *n* Mil, fig
retroguardia *f*

rear light *n* luce *f* posteriore

rearm /riːˈɑːm/ ① *vt* riarmare
② *vi* riarmarsi

rearmament /riːˈɑːməmənt/ *n* riarmo
m

rearmost /ˈrɪəməʊst/ *adj* ultimo;
⟨carriage⟩ di coda

rearrange /riːəˈreɪndʒ/ *vt* cambiare la
disposizione di

rear-view mirror *n* Auto specchietto *m*
retrovisore

reason /ˈriːzn/ ① *n* ragione *f*; **within ∼**
nei limiti del ragionevole; **listen to ∼**
ascoltare la ragione
② *vi* ragionare; **∼ with** cercare di far
ragionare

reasonable /ˈriːznəbl/ *adj* ragionevole

reasonably /ˈriːznəblɪ/ *adv* (in reasonable
way, fairly) ragionevolmente

reasoning /ˈriːznɪŋ/ *n* ragionamento *m*

reassemble /riːəˈsemb(ə)l/ *vt*
riassemblare

reassembly /riːəˈsemblɪ/ *n*
riassemblaggio *m*

reassert /riːəˈsɜrt/ *vt* riaffermare
⟨authority⟩

reassess /riːəˈses/ *vt* riesaminare
⟨problem, situation⟩; riaccertare ⟨tax
liability⟩

reassessment /riːəˈsesmənt/ *n* (of
situation) riesame *m*; (of tax) nuovo
accertamento *m*

reassurance /riːəˈʃʊərəns/ *n*
rassicurazione *f*

reassure /riːəˈʃʊə(r)/ *vt* rassicurare; **∼**
somebody of something rassicurare
qualcuno su qualcosa

reassuring /riːəˈʃʊərɪŋ/ *adj*
rassicurante

reawaken /riːəˈweɪkn/ *vt* fig risvegliare
⟨interest⟩

rebate /ˈriːbeɪt/ *n* rimborso *m*; (discount)
deduzione *f*

rebel[1] /ˈrebl/ *n* ribelle *mf*

rebel[2] /rɪˈbel/ *vi* (pt/pp **rebelled**)
ribellarsi

rebellion /rɪˈbeljən/ *n* ribellione *f*

rebellious /rɪˈbeljəs/ *adj* ribelle

rebelliousness /rɪˈbeljəsnɪs/ *n* spirito
m di ribellione

rebirth "/riːbɜːθ/ *n* rinascita *f*

reboot /riːˈbuːt/ *vt* Comput reinizializzare

reborn /riːˈbɔːn/ *adj* Relig **be ∼** rinascere;
be ∼ as something rinascere come
qualcosa

rebound[1] /rɪˈbaʊnd/ *vi* rimbalzare; fig
ricadere

rebound[2] /ˈriːbaʊnd/ *n* rimbalzo *m*

rebuff /rɪˈbʌf/ ① *n* rifiuto *m*
② *vt* respingere

rebuild /riːˈbɪld/ *vt* (pt/pp **-built**)
ricostruire

rebuke /rɪˈbjuːk/ ① *n* rimprovero *m*
② *vt* rimproverare

rebut /rɪˈbʌt/ *vt* confutare

rebuttal /rɪˈbʌtl/ *n* rifiuto *m*

recalcitrant /rɪˈkælsɪtrənt/ *adj* fml
ricalcitrante

recalculate /riːˈkælkjʊleɪt/ vt ricalcolare

recall /rɪˈkɔːl/ **1** n richiamo m; **beyond** ~ irrevocabile
2 vt richiamare; riconvocare ⟨diplomat, parliament⟩; (remember) rievocare

recant /rɪˈkænt/ vi abiurare

recap /ˈriːkæp/ **1** vt/i fam = RECAPITULATE
2 n ricapitolazione f

recapitulate /riːkəˈpɪtjʊleɪt/ vt/i ricapitolare

recapture /riːˈkæptʃə(r)/ vt riconquistare; ricatturare ⟨person, animal⟩

recast /riːˈkɑːst/ vt rimaneggiare ⟨text, plan⟩; riformulare ⟨sentence⟩

recede /rɪˈsiːd/ vt allontanarsi

receding /rɪˈsiːdɪŋ/ adj ⟨forehead, chin⟩ sfuggente; **have** ~ **hair** essere stempiato

receipt /rɪˈsiːt/ n ricevuta f; (receiving) ricezione f; ~**s** pl Comm entrate fpl

receive /rɪˈsiːv/ vt ricevere

receiver /rɪˈsiːvə(r)/ n Teleph ricevitore m; Radio, TV, apparecchio m ricevente; (of stolen goods) ricettatore, -trice mf

receivership /rɪˈsiːvəʃɪp/ n Br **go into** ~ essere sottomesso all'amministrazione controllata

receiving /rɪˈsiːvɪŋ/ n (stolen goods) ricettazione f

receiving end n **be on the** ~ essere dall'altro lato della barricata

recent /ˈriːsnt/ adj recente

recently /ˈriːsəntlɪ/ adv recentemente

receptacle /rɪˈseptəkl/ n recipiente m

reception /rɪˈsepʃn/ n ricevimento m; (welcome) accoglienza f; Radio ricezione f; ~ **[desk]** (in hotel) reception f inv

receptionist /rɪˈsepʃənɪst/ n persona f alla reception

receptive /rɪˈseptɪv/ adj ricettivo

recess /rɪˈses/ n rientranza f; (holiday) vacanza f; Am Sch intervallo m

recession /rɪˈseʃn/ n recessione f

recharge /riːˈtʃɑːdʒ/ vt ricaricare

rechargeable /riːˈtʃɑːdʒəbl/ adj ⟨battery⟩ ricaricabile; ⟨costs⟩ addebitabile

recidivism /rɪˈsɪdɪvɪzm/ n recidività f

recidivist /rɪˈsɪdɪvɪst/ n recidivo, -a mf

recipe /ˈresəpɪ/ n ricetta f

recipe book n libro m di ricette

recipient /rɪˈsɪpɪənt/ n (of letter, parcel) destinatario, -a mf; (of money) beneficiario, -a mf

reciprocal /rɪˈsɪprəkl/ adj reciproco

reciprocate /rɪˈsɪprəkeɪt/ vt ricambiare

recital /rɪˈsaɪtl/ n recital m inv

recitation /resɪˈteɪʃn/ n recitazione f

recite /rɪˈsaɪt/ vt recitare; (list) elencare

reckless /ˈreklɪs/ adj ⟨action, decision⟩ sconsiderato; **be a** ~ **driver** guidare in modo spericolato

recklessly /ˈreklɪslɪ/ adv in modo sconsiderato

recklessness /ˈreklɪsnɪs/ n sconsideratezza f

reckon /ˈrekən/ vt calcolare; (consider) pensare; **be** ~**ed** essere considerato
■ **reckon on**, **reckon with** vt fare i conti con
■ **reckon without** vt fare i conti senza

reckoning /ˈrekənɪŋ/ n stima f, calcoli mpl; **by my/your etc** ~ secondo i miei/ tuoi ecc. calcoli

reclaim /rɪˈkleɪm/ vt reclamare; bonificare ⟨land⟩

reclaimable /rɪˈkleɪməbl/ adj ⟨expenses⟩ rimborsabile

recline /rɪˈklaɪn/ vi sdraiarsi

reclining /rɪˈklaɪnɪŋ/ adj ⟨seat⟩ reclinabile

recluse /rɪˈkluːs/ n recluso, -a mf

reclusive /rɪˈkluːsɪv/ adj solitario

recognition /rekəgˈnɪʃn/ n riconoscimento m; **in** ~ come riconoscimento (**of** per); **beyond** ~ irriconoscibile

recognizable /ˈrekəgnaɪzəbl/ adj riconoscibile

recognize /ˈrekəgnaɪz/ vt riconoscere

recoil[1] /ˈriːkɔɪl/ n (of gun) rinculo m

recoil[2] /rɪˈkɔɪl/ vi (in fear) indietreggiare

recollect /rekəˈlekt/ vt ricordare

recollection /rekəˈlekʃn/ n ricordo m

recommence /riːkəˈmens/ vt/i ricominciare

recommend /rekəˈmend/ vt raccomandare

recommendation /rekəmenˈdeɪʃn/ n raccomandazione f

recommended retail price /rekəˈmendɪd/ n Comm prezzo m di vendita raccomandato

recompense /ˈrekəmpens/ **1** n ricompensa f
2 vt ricompensare

reconcile /ˈrekənsaɪl/ vt riconciliare; conciliare ⟨facts⟩; far quadrare ⟨bank statement⟩; ~ **oneself to** rassegnarsi a

reconciliation /rekənsɪlɪˈeɪʃn/ n riconciliazione f

recondition /riːkənˈdɪʃn/ vt ripristinare; ~**ed engine** motore m che ha subito riparazioni

reconnaissance /rɪˈkɒnɪsns/ n Mil ricognizione f; **on** ~ in ricognizione

reconnoitre /rekəˈnɔɪtə(r)/ **1** vi (pres p -tring) fare una ricognizione
2 vt fare una ricognizione di

r

reconsider /ri:kən'sıdə(r)/ *vt* riconsiderare

reconstruct /ri:kən'strʌkt/ *vt* ricostruire

reconstruction /ri:kən'strʌkʃn/ *n* ricostruzione *f*

reconvene /ri:kən'vi:n/ *vi* riunirsi nuovamente

record[1] /rɪ'kɔ:d/ *vt* registrare; (make a note of) annotare

record[2] /'rekəd/ *n* (file) documentazione *f*: Mus disco *m*; Sport record *m inv*; ~s *pl* (files) schedario *msg*; **keep a** ~ **of** tener nota di; **off the** ~ in via ufficiosa; **have a [criminal]** ~ avere la fedina penale sporca

record book *n* libro *m* dei record

record-breaker /'rekɔ:dbreɪkə(r)/ *n* **be a** ~ battere un record

recorded /rɪ'kɔ:dɪd/ *adj* (on tape) ⟨message⟩ registrato; (in document) ⟨sighting, case⟩ documentato

recorded delivery *n* raccomandata *f*

recorder /rɪ'kɔ:də(r)/ *n* Mus flauto *m* dolce

record-holder *n* primatista *mf*

recording /rɪ'kɔ:dɪŋ/ *n* registrazione *f*

recording studio *n* sala *f* di registrazione

record player *n* giradischi *m inv*

recount /rɪ'kaʊnt/ *vt* raccontare

re-count[1] /ri:'kaʊnt/ *vt* ricontare

re-count[2] /'ri:kaʊnt/ *n* Pol nuovo conteggio *m*

recoup /rɪ'ku:p/ *vt* rifarsi di ⟨losses⟩

recourse /rɪ'kɔ:s/ *n* **have** ~ **to** ricorrere a

recover /rɪ'kʌvə(r)/ *vt/i* recuperare

re-cover /ri:'kʌvə(r)/ *vt* rifoderare

recovery /rɪ'kʌvəri/ *n* recupero *m*; (of health) guarigione *f*

recovery vehicle *n* autogrù *f*

recreate /ri:krɪ'eɪt/ *vt* ricreare

recreation /rekrɪ'eɪʃn/ *n* ricreazione *f*

recreational /rekrɪ'eɪʃənəl/ *adj* ricreativo

recreational drug *n* sostanza *f* stupefacente che si assume occasionalmente

recrimination /rɪkrɪmɪ'neɪʃn/ *n* recriminazione *f*

recruit /rɪ'kru:t/ ➊ *n* Mil recluta *f*; new ~ (member) nuovo, -a adepto, -a *mf*; (worker) neoassunto, -a *mf* ➋ *vt* assumere ⟨staff⟩

recruitment /rɪ'kru:tmənt/ *n* assunzione *f*

rectangle /'rektæŋgl/ *n* rettangolo *m*

rectangular /rek'tæŋgjʊlə(r)/ *adj* rettangolare

rectify /'rektɪfaɪ/ *vt* (pt/pp **-ied**) rettificare

rector /'rektə(r)/ *n* Univ rettore *m*

rectory /'rektəri/ *n* presbiterio *m*

rectum /'rektəm/ *n* retto *m*

recuperate /rɪ'kju:pəreit/ *vi* ristabilirsi

recur /rɪ'kɜ:(r)/ *vi* (pt/pp **recurred**) ricorrere; ⟨illness⟩ ripresentarsi

recurrence /rɪ'kʌrəns/ *n* ricorrenza *f* (of illness) ricomparsa *f*

recurrent /rɪ'kʌrənt/ *adj* ricorrente

recyclable /ri:'saɪkləbl/ *adj* riciclabile

recycle /ri:'saɪkl/ *vt* riciclare; ~d paper carta *f* riciclata

recycling /ri:'saɪklɪŋ/ *n* riciclaggio *m*

red /red/ ➊ *adj* (**redder, reddest**) rosso ➋ *n* rosso *m*; **be in the** ~ ⟨account⟩ essere scoperto; ⟨person⟩ avere il conto scoperto

red alert *n* allarme *m* rosso; **be on** ~ essere in stato di massima allerta

redbrick *adj* Univ di recente fondazione

Red Cross *n* Croce *f* Rossa

redcurrant *n* ribes *m* rosso

redden /'redn/ ➊ *vt* arrossare ➋ *vi* arrossire

reddish /'redɪʃ/ *adj* rossastro

redecorate /ri:'dekəreit/ *vt* ⟨paint⟩ ridipingere; (wallpaper) ritappezzare

redeem /rɪ'di:m/ *vt* (Relig, from pawnshop) riscattare; ~ing quality unico aspetto *m* positivo

redefine /ri:dɪ'faɪn/ *vt* ridefinire

redemption /rɪ'dempʃn/ *n* riscatto *m*

redeploy /ri:dɪ'plɔɪ/ *vt* ridistribuire

redevelop /'ri:dɪ'veləp/ *vt* risanare ⟨area, site⟩

red-faced *adj* also fig paonazzo

red-haired /-'heəd/ *adj* con i capelli rossi

red-handed /-'hændɪd/ *adj* **catch somebody** ~ cogliere qualcuno con le mani nel sacco

redhead *n* rosso, -a *mf* (di capelli)

red herring *n* diversione *f*

red-hot *adj* rovente

redial /ri:'daɪəl/ Teleph ➊ *vt* ricomporre ➋ *vi* ricomporre il numero

redial facility *n* Teleph funzione *f* di ricomposizione automatica dell'ultimo numero

redirect /ri:daɪ'rekt/ *vt* mandare al nuovo indirizzo ⟨letter⟩

rediscover /ri:dɪs'kʌvə(r)/ *vt* riscoprire

redistribute /ri:dɪs'trɪbju:t/ *vt* ridistribuire

redistribution /ri:dɪstrɪ'bju:ʃn/ *n* ridistribuzione *f*

red-letter day *n* giorno *m* memorabile

red light *n* Auto semaforo *m* rosso; go through a ~ ~ passare col rosso.

red light area, **red light district** *n* quartiere *m* a luci rosse

red meat *n* carne *f* rossa

redness /'rednɪs/ *n* rossore *m*

redo /riːˈduː/ *vt* (pt **-did**, pp **-done**) rifare

redolent /'redələnt/ *adj* profumato (**of** di)

redouble /riːˈdʌbl/ *vt* raddoppiare

red pepper *n* peperone *m* rosso

redraft /riːˈdrɑːft/ *vt* stendere nuovamente

redress /rɪˈdres/ **①** *n* riparazione *f* **②** *vt* ristabilire ⟨*balance*⟩

red tape *n* fam burocrazia *f*

reduce /rɪˈdjuːs/ *vt* ridurre; Culin far consumare

reductio ad absurdum /rɪdʌktɪəʊæedəbˈsɜːdəm/ *n* ragionamento *m* per assurdo

reduction /rɪˈdʌkʃn/ *n* riduzione *f*

redundancy /rɪˈdʌndənsɪ/ *n* licenziamento *m*; (payment) cassa *f* integrazione

redundant /rɪˈdʌndənt/ *adj* superfluo; make ~ licenziare; be made ~ essere licenziato

reed /riːd/ *n* Bot canna *f*

reedy /'riːdɪ/ *adj* ⟨*voice, tone*⟩ acuto

reef /riːf/ *n* scogliera *f*

reefer /'riːfə(r)/ *n* (jacket) giubbotto *m* a doppio petto; (fam: dope) spinello *m*

reef knot *n* nodo *m* piano

reek /riːk/ *vi* puzzare (**of** di)

reel /riːl/ **①** *n* bobina *f* **②** *vi* (stagger) vacillare

re-elect *vt* rieleggere

re-election *n* rielezione *f*

reel off *vt* fig snocciolare

re-emerge *vi* riemergere

re-emergence *n* ricomparsa *f*

re-enact /riːɪˈnækt/ *vt* ricostruire ⟨*crime*⟩; Jur rimettere in vigore; recitare nuovamente ⟨*role*⟩

re-enter /riːˈentə(r)/ *vt* rientrare in

re-entry *n* (of spacecraft) rientro *m*

re-establish *vt* ristabilire, ripristinare

re-establishment *n* ripristino *m*

re-examination *n* riesame *m*

re-examine *vt* riesaminare

ref /ref/ *n abbr* Br: fam (**referee**) arbitro *m*

refectory /rɪˈfektərɪ/ *n* refettorio *m*; Univ mensa *f* universitaria

refer /rɪˈfɜː(r)/ **①** *vt* (pt/pp **referred**) rinviare ⟨*matter*⟩; indirizzare ⟨*person*⟩

② *vi* ~ to fare allusione a; (consult) rivolgersi a ⟨*book*⟩; are you ~ring to me? alludi a me?

referee /refəˈriː/ **①** *n* arbitro *m*; (for job) garante *mf* **②** *vt/i* (pt/pp **refereed**) arbitrare

reference /'ref(ə)rəns/ *n* riferimento *m*; (in book) nota *f* bibliografica; (for job) referenza *f*; Comm 'your ~' 'riferimento'; with ~ to con riferimento a; make [a] ~ to fare riferimento a

reference book *n* libro *m* di consultazione

reference library *n* biblioteca *f* per la consultazione

reference number *n* numero *m* di riferimento

referendum /refəˈrendəm/ *n* referendum *m inv*

referral /rɪˈfɜːrəl/ *n* (of matter, problem) deferimento *m*; Med (act) invio *m* di un paziente a un altro medico; (person) paziente *mf* mandato da un medico a un altro

refill[1] /riːˈfɪl/ *vt* riempire di nuovo; ricaricare ⟨*pen, lighter*⟩

refill[2] /'riːfɪl/ *n* (for pen) ricambio *m*

refine /rɪˈfaɪn/ *vt* raffinare

refined /rɪˈfaɪnd/ *adj* raffinato

refinement /rɪˈfaɪnmənt/ *n* raffinatezza *f*

refinery /rɪˈfaɪnərɪ/ *n* raffineria *f*

refining /rɪˈfaɪnɪŋ/ *n* Techn raffinazione *f*

refit[1] /'riːfɪt/ *n* Naut raddobbo *m*; (of shop, factory etc) rinnovo *m*

refit[2] /riːˈfɪt/ *vt* raddobbare ⟨*ship*⟩ rinnovare ⟨*shop, factory etc*⟩

reflate /riːˈfleɪt/ *vt* reflazionare ⟨*economy*⟩

reflect /rɪˈflekt/ **①** *vt* riflettere; be ~ed in essere riflesso in **②** *vt* (think) riflettere (**on** su); ~ badly on somebody fig mettere in cattiva luce qualcuno

reflection /rɪˈflekʃn/ *n* riflessione *f*; ⟨*image*⟩ riflesso *m*; on ~ dopo riflessione

reflective /rɪˈflektɪv/ *adj* riflessivo

reflectively /rɪˈflektɪvlɪ/ *adv* in modo riflessivo

reflector /rɪˈflektə(r)/ *n* riflettore *m*

reflex /'riːfleks/ **①** *n* riflesso *m* **②** *attrib* di riflesso

reflexive /rɪˈfleksɪv/ *adj* riflessivo

reflexive verb *n* verbo *m* riflessivo

refloat /riːˈfləʊt/ *vt* Naut, Comm rimettere a galla

reforestation /riːfɒrɪˈsteɪʃn/ *n* rimboschimento *m*

reform /rɪˈfɔːm/ **①** *n* riforma *f* **②** *vt* riformare **③** *vi* correggersi.

reformat /riːˈfɔːmæt/ *vt* riformattare

Reformation /refəˈmeɪʃn/ *n* Relig Riforma *f*

reformer /rɪˈfɔːmə(r)/ *n* riformatore, -trice *mf*

refrain[1] /rɪˈfreɪn/ *n* ritornello *m*

refrain[2] *vi* astenersi (**from** da)

refresh /rɪˈfreʃ/ *vt* rinfrescare; Comput aggiornare

refresher course /rɪˈfreʃə(r)/ *n* corso *m* d'aggiornamento

refreshing /rɪˈfreʃɪŋ/ *adj* rinfrescante

refreshments /rɪˈfreʃmənts/ *npl* rinfreschi *mpl*

refrigerate /rɪˈfrɪdʒəreɪt/ *vt* conservare in frigo; Ind refrigerare

refrigerated lorry /rɪˈfrɪdʒəreɪtɪd/ *n* camion *m inv* frigorifero

refrigeration /rɪfrɪdʒəˈreɪʃn/ *n* Ind refrigerazione *f*

refrigerator /rɪˈfrɪdʒəreɪtə(r)/ *n* frigorifero *m*

refuel /riːˈfjʊəl/ ① *vt* (pt/pp **-fuelled**) rifornire di carburante ② *vi* fare rifornimento

refuge /ˈrefjuːdʒ/ *n* rifugio *m*; **take** ∼ rifugiarsi

refugee /refjʊˈdʒiː/ *n* rifugiato, -a *mf*

refugee camp *n* campo *m* profughi

refund[1] /ˈriːfʌnd/ *n* rimborso *m*

refund[2] /rɪˈfʌnd/ *vt* rimborsare

refurbish /riːˈfɜːbɪʃ/ *vt* rimettere a nuovo

refurbishment /riːˈfɜːbɪʃmənt/ *n* rinnovo *m*

refusal /rɪˈfjuːzl/ *n* rifiuto *m*

refuse[1] /rɪˈfjuːz/ *vt/i* rifiutare; ∼ **to do something** rifiutare di fare qualcosa

refuse[2] /ˈrefjuːs/ *n* rifiuti *mpl*

refuse collection *n* raccolta *f* dei rifiuti

refuse collector *n* Br spazzino, -a *mf*

refute /rɪˈfjuːt/ *vt* confutare

regain /rɪˈgeɪn/ *vt* riconquistare

regal /ˈriːgl/ *adj* regale

regale /rɪˈgeɪl/ *vt* ∼ **somebody with something** deliziare qualcuno con qualcosa

regalia /rɪˈgeɪlɪə/ *npl* insegne *fpl* reali

regard /rɪˈgɑːd/ ① *n* (heed) riguardo *m*; (respect) considerazione *f*; ∼**s** *pl*; saluti *mpl*; **send/give my** ∼**s to your brother** salutami tuo fratello; **with** ∼ **to** riguardo a ② *vt* (consider) considerare (**as** come); **as** ∼**s** riguardo a

regarding /rɪˈgɑːdɪŋ/ *prep* riguardo a

regardless /rɪˈgɑːdlɪs/ *adv* lo stesso; ∼ **of** senza badare a

regatta /rɪˈgætə/ *n* regata *f*

regency /ˈriːdʒənsiː/ *n* reggenza *f*

regenerate /rɪˈdʒenəreɪt/ ① *vt* rigenerare ② *vi* rigenerarsi

regent /ˈriːdʒənt/ *n* reggente *mf*

reggae /ˈregeɪ/ *n* reggae *m*

regime /reɪˈʒiːm/ *n* regime *m*

regiment[1] /ˈredʒɪmənt/ *n* reggimento *m*

regiment[2] /ˈredʒɪment/ *vt* irreggimentare

regimental /redʒɪˈmentl/ *adj* reggimentale

regimentation /redʒɪmənˈteɪʃn/ *n* irreggimentazione *f*

regimented /ˈredʒɪmentɪd/ *adj* irreggimentato

region /ˈriːdʒən/ *n* regione *f*; **in the** ∼ **of** fig approssimativamente

regional /ˈriːdʒənl/ *adj* regionale

register /ˈredʒɪstə(r)/ ① *n* registro *m* ② *vt* registrare; mandare tramite assicurata ⟨*letter, package*⟩; assicurare ⟨*luggage*⟩; immatricolare ⟨*motor vehicle*⟩; mostrare ⟨*feeling*⟩ ③ *vi* ⟨*instrument*⟩ funzionare; ⟨*student*⟩ iscriversi (**for** a); **it didn't** ∼ **with me** fig non ci ho fatto attenzione; ∼ **with** iscriversi nella lista di ⟨*doctor*⟩

registered /ˈredʒɪstəd/ *adj* ⟨*voter, student*⟩ iscritto; ⟨*vehicle*⟩ immatricolato

registered letter *n* lettera *f* assicurata

registered trademark *n* marchio *m* depositato

registrar /redʒɪˈstrɑː(r)/ *n* ufficiale *m* di stato civile

registration /redʒɪˈstreɪʃn/ *n* (of vehicle) immatricolazione *f*; (of letter, luggage) assicurazione *f*; (for course) iscrizione *f*

registration fee *n* tassa *f* d'iscrizione

registration number *n* Auto [numero *m* di] targa *f*

registry office /ˈredʒɪstrɪ/ *n* anagrafe *f*

regress /rɪˈgres/ *vi* Biol, Psych, fig regredire

regression /rɪˈgreʃən/ *n* regressione *f*

regressive /rɪˈgresɪv/ *adj* Biol, Psych regressivo

regret /rɪˈgret/ ① *n* rammarico *m* ② *vt* (pt/pp **regretted**) rimpiangere; **I** ∼ **that** mi rincresce che

regretfully /rɪˈgretfʊlɪ/ *adv* con rammarico

regrettable /rɪˈgretəbl/ *adj* spiacevole

regrettably /rɪˈgretəblɪ/ *adv* spiacevolmente; (before adjective) deplorevolmente

regroup /riːˈgruːp/ *vi* riorganizzarsi

regular /ˈregjʊlə(r)/ ① *adj* regolare; (usual) abituale ② *n* cliente *mf* abituale

regularity /regjʊˈlærətɪ/ n regolarità f

regularly /ˈregjʊləlɪ/ adv regolarmente

regulate /ˈregʊleɪt/ vt regolare

regulation /regjʊˈleɪʃn/ n (rule) regolamento m

regulator /ˈregjʊleɪtə(r)/ n (person) regolatore, -trice mf; (device) regolatore m

regurgitate /rɪˈgɜːdʒɪteɪt/ vt rigurgitare; fig pej ripetere meccanicamente

rehabilitate /riːhəˈbɪlɪteɪt/ vt riabilitare

rehabilitation /riːhəbɪlɪˈteɪʃn/ n riabilitazione f

rehabilitation centre Br, **rehabilitation center** Am n (after drug addiction, illness, prison) comunità f terapeutica

rehash¹ /riːˈhæʃ/ vt rimaneggiare

rehash² /ˈriːhæʃ/ n rimaneggiamento m

rehearsal /rɪˈhɜːsl/ n Theat prova f

rehearse /rɪˈhɜːs/ vt/i provare

reheat /riːˈhiːt/ vt scaldare di nuovo

rehouse /riːˈhaʊz/ vt rialloggiare

reign /reɪn/ ① n regno m
② vi regnare

reimburse /riːɪmˈbɜːs/ vt ∼ somebody for something rimborsare qualcosa a qualcuno

reimbursement /riːɪmˈbɜːsmənt/ n rimborso m

rein /reɪn/ n redine f

reincarnate /riːɪnˈkɑːneɪt/ vt be ∼d reincarnarsi

reincarnation /riːɪnkɑːˈneɪʃn/ n reincarnazione f

reindeer /ˈreɪndɪə(r)/ n inv renna f

reinforce /riːɪnˈfɔːs/ vt rinforzare

reinforced concrete n cemento m armato

reinforcement /riːɪnˈfɔːsmənt/ n rinforzo m; ∼s pl Mil rinforzi mpl

reinstall /ˈriːɪnstɔl/ vt Comput reinstallare ⟨software, program⟩

reinstate /riːɪnˈsteɪt/ vt reintegrare

reinstatement /riːɪnˈsteɪtmənt/ n reintegrazione f

reinterpret /riːɪntˈtɜːprɪt/ vt reinterpretare

reinterpretation /riːɪntˈtɜːprɪˈteɪʃn/ n reinterpretazione f

reintroduce /riːɪntrəˈdjuːs/ vt reintrodurre

reintroduction /riːɪntrəˈdʌkʃn/ n reintroduzione f

reiterate /riːˈɪtəreɪt/ vt reiterare

reiteration /riːɪtəˈreɪʃn/ n reiterazione f

reject /rɪˈdʒekt/ vt rifiutare

rejection /rɪˈdʒekʃn/ n rifiuto m; Med rigetto m

rejects /ˈriːdʒekts/ npl Comm scarti mpl

rejig /riːˈdʒɪg/ vt (pt/pp **rejigged**) Br riorganizzare

rejoice /rɪˈdʒɔɪs/ vi liter rallegrarsi

rejoicing /rɪˈdʒɔɪsɪŋ/ n gioia f

rejoin /rɪˈdʒɔɪn/ vt riassociarsi a ⟨club, party⟩; Mil reintegrarsi in ⟨regiment⟩; (answer) replicare

rejuvenate /rɪˈdʒuːvəneɪt/ vt rinnovare; ringiovanire ⟨person⟩

rejuvenation /rɪˈdʒuːvəneɪʃn/ n rinnovamento m; (of person) ringiovanimento m

rekindle /riːˈkɪndl/ vt riattizzare

relapse /rɪˈlæps/ ① n ricaduta f
② vi ricadere

relate /rɪˈleɪt/ vt (tell) riportare; (connect) collegare
■ **relate to** vt riferirsi a; identificarsi con ⟨person⟩

related /rɪˈleɪtɪd/ adj imparentato (to a); ⟨ideas etc⟩ affine

relation /rɪˈleɪʃn/ n rapporto m; (person) parente mf

relationship /rɪˈleɪʃnʃɪp/ n rapporto m; (blood tie) parentela f; (affair) relazione f

relative /ˈrelətɪv/ ① n parente mf
② adj relativo

relatively /ˈrelətɪvlɪ/ adv relativamente

relativity /reləˈtɪvətɪ/ n relatività f

relativity theory n Phys teoria f della relatività

relaunch¹ /ˈriːlɔːntʃ/ n rilancio m

relaunch² /riːˈlɔːntʃ/ vt rilanciare

relax /rɪˈlæks/ ① vt rilassare; allentare ⟨pace grip⟩
② vi rilassarsi

relaxation /riːlækˈseɪʃn/ n rilassamento m, relax m; (recreation) svago m

relaxed /rɪˈlækst/ adj rilassato

relaxing /rɪˈlæksɪŋ/ adj rilassante

relay¹ /riːˈleɪ/ vt (pt/pp **-layed**) trasmettere

relay² /ˈriːleɪ/ n Electr relais m inv; **work in** ∼**s** fare i turni

relay [race] /ˈriːleɪ/ n [corsa f a] staffetta f

release /rɪˈliːs/ ① n rilascio m; (of film) distribuzione f
② vt liberare; lasciare ⟨hand⟩; togliere ⟨brake⟩; distribuire ⟨film⟩; rilasciare ⟨information etc⟩

relegate /ˈrelɪgeɪt/ vt relegare; be ∼d Br Sport essere retrocesso

relegation /relɪˈgeɪʃn/ n relegazione f; Br Sport retrocessione f

relent /rɪˈlent/ vi cedere

relentless /rɪˈlentlɪs/ adj inflessibile; (unceasing) incessante

relentlessly /rɪˈlentlɪslɪ/ adv incessantemente

relevance /'reləvəns/ n pertinenza f

relevant /'reləvənt/ adj pertinente (**to** a)

reliability /rɪlaɪə'bɪlətɪ/ n affidabilità f

reliable /rɪ'laɪəbl/ adj affidabile

reliably /rɪ'laɪəblɪ/ adv in modo affidabile; be ∼ **informed** sapere da fonte certa

reliance /rɪ'laɪəns/ n fiducia f (**on** in)

reliant /rɪ'laɪənt/ adj fiducioso (**on** in)

relic /'relɪk/ n Relig reliquia f; ∼**s** pl resti mpl

relief /rɪ'li:f/ n sollievo m; (assistance) soccorso m; (distraction) diversivo m; (replacement) cambio m; (in art) rilievo m; **in** ∼ **in** rilievo

relief agency n organizzazione f umanitaria

relief map n carta f in rilievo

relief supplies npl soccorsi mpl, aiuti mpl umanitari

relief train n treno m supplementare

relief work n lavoro m presso un'organizzazione umanitaria

relief worker n persona f che lavora per un'organizzazione umanitaria

relieve /rɪ'li:v/ vt alleviare; (take over from) dare il cambio a; ∼ **of** liberare da ⟨burden⟩

religion /rɪ'lɪdʒən/ n religione f

religious /rɪ'lɪdʒəs/ adj religioso

religiously /rɪ'lɪdʒəslɪ/ adv (conscientiously) scrupolosamente

relinquish /rɪ'lɪŋkwɪʃ/ vt abbandonare; ∼ **something to somebody** rinunciare a qualcosa in favore di qualcuno

relish /'relɪʃ/ ① n gusto m; Culin salsa f ② vt fig apprezzare

relive /ri:'lɪv/ vt rivivere

reload /ri:'ləʊd/ vt ricaricare

relocate /ri:lə'keɪt/ ① vt trasferire ② vi trasferirsi

relocation /ri:lə'keɪʃn/ n (of employee, company) trasferimento m

relocation allowance n indennità f inv di trasferimento

reluctance /rɪ'lʌktəns/ n riluttanza f

reluctant /rɪ'lʌktənt/ adj riluttante

reluctantly /rɪ'lʌktəntlɪ/ adv con riluttanza, a malincuore

rely /rɪ'laɪ/ vi (pt/pp **-ied**) ∼ **on** dipendere da; (trust) contare su

remain /rɪ'meɪn/ vi restare

remainder /rɪ'meɪndə(r)/ ① n resto m; Comm rimanenza f ② vt Comm svendere

remaining /rɪ'meɪnɪŋ/ adj restante

remains /rɪ'meɪnz/ npl resti mpl; (dead body) spoglie fpl

remake /'ri:meɪk/ n (of film, recording) remake m inv

remand /rɪ'mɑ:nd/ ① n **on** ∼ in custodia cautelare ② vt ∼ **in custody** rinviare con detenzione provvisoria

remand centre n Br istituto m di carcerazione preventiva

remark /rɪ'mɑ:k/ ① n osservazione f ② vt osservare

remarkable /rɪ'mɑ:kəbl/ adj notevole

remarkably /rɪ'mɑ:kəblɪ/ adv notevolmente

remarry /ri:'mærɪ/ vi (pt/pp **-ied**) risposarsi

remaster /ri:'mɑ:stə(r)/ vt incidere di nuovo ⟨recording⟩

rematch /'ri:mætʃ/ n Sport partita f di ritorno; (in boxing) secondo incontro m

remedial /rɪ'mi:dɪəl/ adj correttivo; Med curativo

remedy /'remədɪ/ ① n rimedio m (**for** contro) ② vt (pt/pp **-ied**) rimediare a

remember /rɪ'membə(r)/ ① vt ricordare, ricordarsi; ∼ **to do something** ricordarsi di fare qualcosa; ∼ **me to him** salutamelo ② vi ricordarsi

Remembrance Day /rɪ'membrəns/ n commemorazione f dei caduti (11 novembre)

remind /rɪ'maɪnd/ vt ∼ **somebody of something** ricordare qualcosa a qualcuno

reminder /rɪ'maɪndə(r)/ n ricordo m; (memo) promemoria m inv; (letter) lettera f di sollecito; (to pay) sollecitazione f di pagamento

reminisce /remɪ'nɪs/ vi rievocare il passato

reminiscences /remɪ'nɪsənsɪz/ npl reminiscenze fpl

reminiscent /remɪ'nɪsənt/ adj be ∼ **of** richiamare alla memoria

remiss /rɪ'mɪs/ adj negligente

remission /rɪ'mɪʃn/ n remissione f; (of sentence) condono m

remit /rɪ'mɪt/ vt (pt/pp **remitted**) rimettere ⟨money⟩

remittance /rɪ'mɪtəns/ n rimessa f

remix¹ /ri:'mɪks/ vt Mus rimixare

remix² /'ri:mɪks/ n Mus rimixaggio m

remnant /'remnənt/ n resto m; (of material) scampolo m; (trace) traccia f

remonstrate /'remənstreɪt/ vi fare rimostranze (**with somebody** a qualcuno)

remorse /rɪ'mɔ:s/ n rimorso m

remorseful /rɪ'mɔ:sfʊl/ adj pieno di rimorso

remorsefully /rɪ'mɔ:sfʊlɪ/ adv con rimorso

remorseless /rɪ'mɔ:slɪs/ adj spietato

remorselessly /rɪ'mɔslɪslɪ/ *adv* senza pietà

remote /rɪ'məʊt/ *adj* remoto; (slight) minimo

remote access *n* Comput accesso *m* remoto

remote control *n* telecomando *m*

remote-controlled *adj* telecomandato

remotely /rɪ'məʊtlɪ/ *adv* lontanamente; be not ∼... non essere lontanamente...

remoteness /rɪ'məʊtnɪs/ *n* lontananza *f*

remould /'ri:məʊld/ *n* pneumatico *m* ricostruito

remount /ri:'maʊnt/ *vt* rimontare in sella a ⟨bike, horse⟩

removable /rɪ'mu:vəbl/ *adj* rimovibile

removal /rɪ'mu:vl/ *n* rimozione *f*; (from house) trasloco *m*

removal man *n* addetto *m* ai traslochi

removal van *n* camion *m* inv da trasloco

remove /rɪ'mu:v/ *vt* togliere; togliersi ⟨clothes⟩; eliminare ⟨stain, doubts⟩

removers /rɪ'mu:vəz/ *npl* fam traslocatori *mpl*

remuneration /rɪmju:nə'reɪʃn/ *n* rimunerazione *f*

remunerative /rɪ'mju:nərətɪv/ *adj* rimunerativo

renaissance /rɪ'neɪsɑns/ *n* rinascita *f*; R∼ Rinascimento *m*

renal /'ri:nəl/ *adj* renale

render /'rendə(r)/ *vt* rendere ⟨service⟩

rendering /'rend(ə)rɪŋ/ *n* Mus interpretazione *f*

rendezvous /'rɒndeɪvu:/ *vi esp* Mil incontrarsi

rendition /ren'dɪʃn/ *n* interpretazione *f*

renegade /'renɪgeɪd/ *n* rinnegato, -a *mf*

renege /rɪ'neɪg/ *vi* venire meno (on a)

renegotiate /ri:nɪ'gəʊʃɪeɪt/ *vt* rinegoziare

renegotiation /ri:nɪgəʊʃɪ'eɪʃn/ *n* rinegoziato *m*

renew /rɪ'nju:/ *vt* rinnovare ⟨contract⟩

renewable /rɪ'nju:əbl/ *adj* rinnovabile

renewal /rɪ'nju:əl/ *n* rinnovo *m*

renewed *adj* ⟨strength, interest⟩ rinnovato; ⟨attack⟩ nuovo

renounce /rɪ'naʊns/ *vt* rinunciare a

renovate /'renəveɪt/ *vt* rinnovare

renovation /renə'veɪʃn/ *n* rinnovo *m*

renown /rɪ'naʊn/ *n* fama *f*

renowned /rɪ'naʊnd/ *adj* rinomato

rent /rent/ ① *n* affitto *m*
② *vt* affittare; ∼ **[out]** dare in affitto

rental /'rentl/ *n* affitto *m*

rent boy *n* ragazzo *m* di vita

rent-free ① *adj* ⟨accommodation⟩ gratuito
② *adv* ⟨live, use⟩ senza pagare l'affitto

renunciation /rɪnʌnsɪ'eɪʃn/ *n* rinuncia *f*

reoffend /ri:'əfend/ *vi* recidivare

reopen /ri:'əʊpən/ *vt/i* riaprire

reorganization /ri:ɔ:gənaɪ'zeɪʃn/ *n* riorganizzazione *f*

reorganize /ri:'ɔ:gənaɪz/ *vt* riorganizzare

rep /rep/ *n* Comm fam rappresentante *mf*; Theat ≈ teatro *m* stabile

repackage /ri:'pækɪdʒ/ *vt* Comm cambiare la confezione di; (fig: change public image of) cambiare l'immagine pubblica di; cambiare i termini di ⟨proposal⟩

repaint /ri:'peɪnt/ *vt* ridipingere

repair /rɪ'peə(r)/ ① *n* riparazione *f*; in good/bad ∼ in buone/cattive condizioni
② *vt* riparare

repairman *n* tecnico *m* (delle riparazioni)

reparation /repə'reɪʃn/ *n* make ∼s for something risarcire qualcosa

repartee /repɑ:'ti:/ *n* botta e risposta *m* inv; piece of ∼ risposta *f* pronta

repatriate /ri:'pætrɪeɪt/ *vt* rimpatriare

repatriation /ri:pætrɪ'eɪʃn/ *n* rimpatrio *m*

repay /ri:'peɪ/ *vt* (pt/pp **-paid**) ripagare

repayment /ri:'peɪmənt/ *n* rimborso *m*

repeal /rɪ'pi:l/ ① *n* abrogazione *f*
② *vt* abrogare

repeat /rɪ'pi:t/ ① *n* TV replica *f*
② *vt/i* ripetere; ∼ **oneself** ripetersi

repeated /rɪ'pi:tɪd/ *adj* ripetuto

repeatedly /rɪ'pi:tɪdlɪ/ *adv* ripetutamente

repel /rɪ'pel/ *vt* (pt/pp **repelled**) respingere; fig ripugnare

repellent /rɪ'pelənt/ *adj* ripulsivo

repent /rɪ'pent/ *vi* pentirsi

repentance /rɪ'pentəns/ *n* pentimento *m*

repentant /rɪ'pentənt/ *adj* pentito

repercussions /ri:pə'kʌnz/ *npl* ripercussioni *fbl*

repertoire /'repətwɑ:(r)/ *n* repertorio *m*

repertory /'repətrɪ/ *n* ≈ teatro *m* stabile

repertory company *n* compagnia *f* di un teatro stabile

repetition /repɪ'tɪʃn/ *n* ripetizione *f*

repetitious /repɪ'tɪʃəs/, **repetitive** /rɪ'petɪtɪv/ *adj* ripetitivo

repetitive strain injury *n* patologia *f* da sforzo ripetuto

replace /rɪ'pleɪs/ *vt* (put back) rimettere a posto; (take the place of) sostituire; ∼ ⋯⋗

something with something sostituire
qualcosa con qualcosa
replacement /rɪ'pleɪsmənt/ n
sostituzione f; (person) sostituto, -a mf
replacement part n pezzo m di
ricambio
replant /ri:'plɑ:nt/ vt ripiantare
replay /'ri:pleɪ/ n Sport partita f ripetuta;
[action] ~ replay m inv
replenish /rɪ'plenɪʃ/ vt rifornire
⟨stocks⟩; (refill) riempire di nuovo
replete /rɪ'pli:t/ adj ~ with riempito di
replica /'replɪkə/ n copia f
replicate /'replɪkeɪt/ vt ripetere
⟨experiment⟩
reply /rɪ'plaɪ/ **1** n risposta f (to a)
2 vt (pt/pp **replied**) rispondere
reply-paid envelope n busta f
affrancata per rispondere
report /rɪ'pɔ:t/ **1** n rapporto m; TV, Radio
servizio m; Journ cronaca f; Sch pagella f;
(rumour) diceria f
2 vt riportare; ~ somebody to the police
denunciare qualcuno alla polizia
3 vi riportare; (present oneself) presentarsi
(to a)
report card n Am scheda f di
valutazione scolastica
reportedly /rɪ'pɔ:tɪdlɪ/ adv secondo
quanto si dice
reporter /rɪ'pɔ:tə(r)/ n cronista mf,
reporter mf inv
repose /rɪ'pəʊz/ n riposo m
repository /rɪ'pɒzɪt(ə)rɪ/ n (place)
deposito, m; (of secret, authority) depositario,
-a mf
repossess /ri:pə'zes/ vt riprendere
possesso di
repossession /ri:pə'zeʃn/ n esproprio
m
repot /ri:'pɒt/ vt rinvasare ⟨plant⟩
reprehensible /reprɪ'hensəbl/ adj
riprovevole
represent /reprɪ'zent/ vt rappresentare
representation /reprɪzen'teɪʃn/ n
rappresentazione f; **make ~s to** fare delle
rimostranze a
representative /reprɪ'zentətɪv/ **1** adj
rappresentativo
2 n rappresentante mf
repress /rɪ'pres/ vt reprimere
repression /rɪ'preʃn/ n repressione f
repressive /rɪ'presɪv/ adj repressivo
reprieve /rɪ'pri:v/ **1** n commutazione f
della pena capitale; (postponement)
sospensione f della pena capitale; fig
tregua f
2 vt sospendere la sentenza a; fig
risparmiare
reprimand /'reprɪmɑ:nd/ **1** n
rimprovero m

2 vt rimproverare
reprint[1] /'ri:prɪnt/ n ristampa f
reprint[2] /ri:'prɪnt/ vt ristampare
reprisal /rɪ'praɪzl/ n rappresaglia f; **in ~**
for per rappresaglia contro
reproach /rɪ'prəʊtʃ/ **1** n rimprovero m
2 vt rimproverare a (for doing something
di fare qualcosa)
reproachful /rɪ'prəʊtʃfʊl/ adj
riprovevole
reproachfully /rɪ'prəʊtʃfʊlɪ/ adv con
aria di rimprovero
reprocess /ri:'prəʊses/ vt trattare di
nuovo
reprocessing plant /ri:'prəʊsesɪŋ/ n
impianto m di rilavorazione (di scorie
nucleari)
reproduce /ri:prə'dju:s/ **1** vt
riprodurre
2 vi riprodursi
reproduction /ri:prə'dʌkʃn/ n
riproduzione f
reproduction furniture n
riproduzioni fpl di mobili antichi
reproductive /ri:prə'dʌktɪv/ adj
riproduttivo
reproof /rɪ'pru:f/ n rimprovero m
reprove /rɪ'pru:v/ vt rimproverare
reptile /'reptaɪl/ n rettile m
republic /rɪ'pʌblɪk/ n repubblica f
republican /rɪ'pʌblɪkn/ adj & n
repubblicano, -a mf
republish /ri:'pʌblɪʃ/ vt ripubblicare
repudiate /rɪ'pju:dɪeɪt/ vt ripudiare;
respingere ⟨view, suggestion⟩
repugnance /rɪ'pʌgnəns/ n ripugnanza
f
repugnant /rɪ'pʌgnənt/ adj ripugnante
repulse /rɪ'pʌls/ vt fml respingere
⟨attack⟩; rifiutare ⟨assistance⟩
repulsion /rɪ'pʌlʃn/ n repulsione f
repulsive /rɪ'pʌlsɪv/ adj ripugnante
reputable /'repjʊtəbl/ adj affidabile
reputation /repjʊ'teɪʃn/ n reputazione f
repute /rɪ'pju:t/ n reputazione f
reputed /rɪ'pju:tɪd/ adj presunto; **he is
~ to be** si presume che sia
reputedly /rɪ'pju:tɪdlɪ/ adv
presumibilmente
request /rɪ'kwest/ **1** n richiesta f
2 vt richiedere
request stop n fermata f a richiesta
requiem /'rekwɪəm/ n requiem m inv
require /rɪ'kwaɪə(r)/ vt (need) necessitare
di; (demand) esigere
required /rɪ'kwaɪəd/ adj richiesto
requirement /rɪ'kwaɪəmənt/ n esigenza
f; (condition) requisito m
requisite /'rekwɪzɪt/ **1** adj necessario

2 *n* toilet/travel ∼s *pl* articoli *mpl* da toilette/viaggio

requisition /rekwɪˈzɪʃn/ **1** *n* ∼ [order] [domanda *f* di] requisizione *f*
2 *vt* requisire

reread /riːˈriːd/ *vt* rileggere

re-release /riːrɪˈliːs/ **1** *n* (of film) nuova distribuzione *f*
2 *vt* ridistribuire ⟨*film*⟩

reroof /riːˈruːf/ *vt* rifare il tetto di ⟨*building*⟩

reroute /riːˈruːt/ *vt* dirottare ⟨*flight, traffic*⟩

rerun /ˈriːrʌn/ *n* (of film, play) replica *f*; (fig: repeat) ripetizione *f*

resale /riːˈseɪl/ *n* rivendita *f*

reschedule /riːˈʃedjuːl/ *vt* (change date of) cambiare la data di; (change time of) cambiare l'orario di; rinegoziare ⟨*debt*⟩

rescind /rɪˈsɪnd/ *vt* rescindere

rescue /ˈreskjuː/ **1** *n* salvataggio *m*
2 *vt* salvare

rescuer /ˈreskjʊə(r)/ *n* salvatore, -trice *mf*

rescue worker *n* soccorritore, -trice *mf*

research /rɪˈsɜːtʃ/ **1** *n* ricerca *f*
2 *vt* fare ricerche su; Journ fare un'inchiesta su
3 *vi* ∼ into fare ricerche su

research and development *n* ricerca *f* e sviluppo *m*

researcher /rɪˈsɜːtʃə(r)/ *n* ricercatore, -trice *mf*

research fellow *n* Br Univ ricercatore, -trice *mf*

resell /riːˈsel/ *vt* (pt/pp **resold**) rivendere

resemblance /rɪˈzembləns/ *n* rassomiglianza *f*

resemble /rɪˈzembl/ *vt* rassomigliare a

resent /rɪˈzent/ *vt* risentirsi per

resentful /rɪˈzentfʊl/ *adj* pieno di risentimento

resentfully /rɪˈzentfʊlɪ/ *adv* con risentimento

resentment /rɪˈzentmənt/ *n* risentimento *m*

reservation /rezəˈveɪʃn/ *n* (booking) prenotazione *f*; (doubt, enclosure) riserva *f*

reserve /rɪˈzɜːv/ **1** *n* riserva *f*; (shyness) riserbo *m*
2 *vt* riservare; riservarsi ⟨*right*⟩

reserved /rɪˈzɜːvd/ *adj* riservato

reservoir /ˈrezəvwɑː(r)/ *n* bacino *m* idrico

reset /riːˈset/ *vt* riprogrammare ⟨*clock*⟩; (zero) azzerare

reshape /riːˈʃeɪp/ *vt* ristrutturare

reshuffle /riːˈʃʌfl/ **1** Pol *n* rimpasto *m*

2 *vt* rimpastare

reside /rɪˈzaɪd/ *vi* risiedere

residence /ˈrezɪdəns/ *n* residenza *f*; (stay) soggiorno *m*

residence permit *n* permesso *m* di soggiorno

resident /ˈrezɪdənt/ *adj & n* residente *mf*

residential /rezɪˈdenʃl/ *adj* residenziale

residential area *n* quartiere *m* residenziale

residual /rɪˈzɪdjʊəl/ *adj* residuo

residue /ˈrezɪdjuː/ *n* residuo *m*

resign /rɪˈzaɪn/ **1** *vt* dimettersi da; ∼ oneself to rassegnarsi a
2 *vt* dare le dimissioni

resignation /rezɪgˈneɪʃn/ *n* rassegnazione *f*; (from job) dimissioni *fpl*

resigned /rɪˈzaɪnd/ *adj* rassegnato

resignedly /rɪˈzaɪnɪdlɪ/ *adv* con rassegnazione

resilient /rɪˈzɪlɪənt/ *adj* elastico; fig con buone capacità di ripresa

resin /ˈrezɪn/ *n* resina *f*

resist /rɪˈzɪst/ **1** *vt* resistere a
2 *vi* resistere

resistance /rɪˈzɪstəns/ *n* resistenza *f*

resistance fighter *n* combattente *mf* delle forze di resistenza

resistant /rɪˈzɪstənt/ *adj* resistente

resit /riːˈsɪt/ Br **1** *vt* (pt/pp **resat**) ridare ⟨*exam*⟩
2 *n* esame *m* di recupero

resize /riːˈsaɪz/ *vt* ridimensionare

reskill /riːˈskɪl/ *vt* riqualificare ⟨*workers*⟩

resolute /ˈrezəluːt/ *adj* risoluto

resolutely /ˈrezəluːtlɪ/ *adv* con risolutezza

resolution /rezəˈluːʃn/ *n* risolutezza *f*

resolve /rɪˈzɒlv/ **1** *n* risolutezza *f*; (decision) risoluzione *f*
2 *vt* (solve) risolvere; ∼ to do decidere di fare

resolved /rɪˈzɒlvd/ *adj* risoluto

resonance /ˈrezənəns/ *n* risonanza *f*

resonant /ˈrezɪnənt/ *adj* risonante

resonate /ˈrezəneɪt/ *vi* risuonare

resort /rɪˈzɔːt/ **1** *n* (place) luogo *m* di villeggiatura; **as a last** ∼ come ultima risorsa
2 *vi* ∼ **to** ricorrere a

resound /rɪˈzaʊnd/ *vi* risonare (with di)

resounding /rɪˈzaʊndɪŋ/ *adj* ⟨*success*⟩ risonante

resoundingly /rɪˈzaʊndɪŋlɪ/ *adv* in modo risonante

resource /rɪˈsɔːs/ *n* ∼s *pl* risorse *fpl*

resourceful /rɪˈsɔːsfʊl/ *adj* pieno di risorse; ⟨*solution*⟩ ingegnoso

resourcefulness /rɪ'sɔːsfʊlnɪs/ n
ingegnosità f

respect /rɪ'spekt/ ① n rispetto m;
(aspect) aspetto m; **with ~ to** per quanto
riguarda
② vt rispettare

respectability /rɪspektə'bɪlətɪ/ n
rispettabilità f

respectable /rɪ'spektəbl/ rispettabile

respectably /rɪ'spektəblɪ/ adv
rispettabilmente

respectful /rɪ'spektfʊl/ adj rispettoso

respectfully /rɪ'spektfʊlɪ/ adv
rispettosamente

respective /rɪ'spektɪv/ adj rispettivo

respectively /rɪ'spektɪvlɪ/ adv
rispettivamente

respiration /respɪ'reɪʃn/ n respirazione
f

respirator /'respɪreɪtə(r)/ n (apparatus)
respiratore m

respiratory /rɪ'spɪrətrɪ/ adj respiratorio

respite /'respaɪt/ n respiro m

resplendent /rɪ'splendənt/ adj
risplendente

respond /rɪ'spɒnd/ vi rispondere; (react)
reagire (**to** a); ⟨patient⟩ rispondere (**to** a)

respondent /rɪ'spɒndənt/ n Jur
convenuto, -a mf; (to questionnaire)
interrogato, -a mf

response /rɪ'spɒns/ n risposta f;
(reaction) reazione f

responsibility /rɪspɒnsɪ'bɪlətɪ/ n
responsabilità f inv

responsible /rɪ'spɒnsəbl/ adj
responsabile; (trustworthy) responsabile; (job)
impegnativo

responsibly /rɪ'spɒnsəblɪ/ adv in modo
responsabile

responsive /rɪ'spɒnsɪv/ adj **be ~**
⟨audience etc⟩ reagire; ⟨brakes⟩ essere
sensibile; **she wasn't very ~** non era
molto cooperativa

respray[1] /riː'spreɪ/ vt riverniciare
⟨vehicle⟩

respray[2] /'riːspreɪ/ n riverniciatura f;
it's had a ~ è stato riverniciato

rest[1] /rest/ ① n riposo m; Mus pausa f;
have a ~ riposarsi
② vt riposare; (lean, place) appoggiare (**on**
su)
③ vi riposarsi; ⟨elbows⟩ appoggiarsi;
⟨hopes⟩ riposare; **it ~s with you** sta a te
■ **rest up** vi riposarsi

rest[2] n **the ~** il resto; (people) gli altri

restart /riː'stɑːt/ vt rimettere in moto
⟨engine⟩; riprendere ⟨talks⟩; Comput
riavviare

restate /riː'steɪt/ vt (say differently)
riformulare; (say again) ribadire

restaurant /'restərɒnt/ n ristorante m

restaurant car n vagone m ristorante

restful /'restfl/ adj riposante

rest home n casa f di riposo

restitution /restɪ'tjuːʃn/ n restituzione f

restive /'restɪv/ adj irrequieto

restless /'restlɪs/ adj nervoso

restlessly /'restlɪslɪ/ adv nervosamente

restlessness /'restlɪsnɪs/ agitazione f

restock /riː'stɒk/ ① vt rifornire ⟨shelf,
shop⟩
② vi rifornirsi

restoration /restə'reɪʃn/ n
ristabilimento m; (of building) restauro m;
(of stolen property etc) restituzione f

restore /rɪ'stɔː(r)/ vt ristabilire;
restaurare ⟨building⟩; (give back) restituire

restorer /rɪ'stɔːrə(r)/ n (person)
restauratore, -trice mf

restrain /rɪ'streɪn/ vt trattenere; **~**
oneself controllarsi

restrained /rɪ'streɪnd/ adj controllato

restraint /rɪ'streɪnt/ n restrizione f;
(moderation) ritegno m

restrict /rɪ'strɪkt/ vt limitare (**to** a)

restricted /rɪ'strɪktɪd/ adj ⟨access,
parking⟩ riservato; ⟨growth, movement⟩
limitato; ⟨document, information⟩
confidenziale

restriction /rɪ'strɪkʃn/ n limite m;
(restraint) restrizione f

restrictive /rɪ'strɪktɪv/ adj limitativo

restring /riː'strɪŋ/ vt rinfilare ⟨necklace,
beads⟩; sostituire le corde di ⟨instrument,
racket⟩

restroom /'restruːm/ n Am toilette f inv

restructure /riː'strʌktʃə(r)/ vt
ristrutturare

restructuring /riː'strʌktʃərɪŋ/ n
ristrutturazione f

restyle /riː'staɪl/ vt cambiare il taglio di
⟨hair⟩; cambiare la linea di ⟨car⟩;
rimodernare ⟨shop⟩

resubmit /riːsʌb'mɪt/ vt ripresentare

result /rɪ'zʌlt/ ① n risultato m; **as a ~** di
conseguenza; **as a ~ of** a causa di
② vi **~ from** risultare da; **~ in** portare a

resume /rɪ'zjuːm/ vt/i riprendere

résumé /'rezjʊmeɪ/ n riassunto m; Am
curriculum m inv vitae

resumption /rɪ'zʌmpʃn/ n ripresa f

resurface /riː'sɜːfɪs/ ① vi ⟨sub, person,
rumour⟩ riemergere
② vt rifare la copertura di ⟨road⟩

resurgence /rɪ'sɜːdʒəns/ n rinascita f

resurrect /rezə'rekt/ vt fig risuscitare

resurrection /rezə'rekʃn/ n **the R~**
Relig la Risurrezione

resuscitate /rɪ'sʌsɪteɪt/ vt rianimare

resuscitation /rɪsʌsɪ'teɪʃn/ n
rianimazione f

retail /'ri:teɪl/ **1** *n* vendita *f* al minuto *o* al dettaglio
2 *adj & adv* al minuto
3 *vt* vendere al minuto
4 *vi* ~ **at** essere venduto al pubblico al prezzo di
retailer /'ri:teɪlə(r)/ *n* dettagliante *mf*
retail price *n* prezzo *m* al minuto
retail sales *npl* vendite *fpl* al dettaglio
retail trade *n* commercio *m* al dettaglio
retain /rɪ'teɪn/ *vt* conservare; (hold back) trattenere
retainer /rɪ'teɪnə(r)/ *n* (fee) anticipo *m*; (old: servant) servitore, -trice *mf*
retake¹ /ri:'teɪk/ *vt* Cinema girare di nuovo; Sch, Univ ridare; Mil riconquistare
retake² /'ri:teɪk/ *n* Cinema ulteriore ripresa *f*
retaliate /rɪ'tælɪeɪt/ *vi* vendicarsi
retaliation /rɪtælɪ'eɪʃn/ *n* rappresaglia *f*; in ~ **for** per rappresaglia contro
retarded /rɪ'tɑːdɪd/ *adj* ritardato
retch /retʃ/ *vi* avere conati di vomito
retention /rɪ'tenʃn/ *n* conservazione *f*; (of information) memorizzazione *f*; (of fluid) ritenzione *f*
retentive /rɪ'tentɪv/ *adj* ‹memory› buono
retentiveness /rɪ'tentɪvnɪs/ *n* capacità *f* di memorizzazione
rethink /ri:'θɪŋk/ **1** *vt* (pt/pp **rethought**) riconsiderare
2 *n* **have a** ~ riconsiderare la cosa
reticence /'retɪsəns/ *n* reticenza *f*
reticent /'retɪsənt/ *adj* reticente
retina /'retɪnə/ *n* retina *f*
retinue /'retɪmju:/ *n* seguito *m*
retire /rɪ'taɪə(r)/ **1** *vi* andare in pensione; (withdraw) ritirarsi
2 *vt* mandare in pensione ‹employee›
retired /rɪ'taɪəd/ *adj* in pensione
retirement /rɪ'taɪəmənt/ *n* pensione *f*; **since my** ~ da quando sono andato in pensione
retirement age *n* età *f* della pensione
retirement home *n* casa *f* di riposo
retiring /rɪ'taɪərɪŋ/ *adj* riservato
retort /rɪ'tɔːt/ **1** *n* replica *f*; Chem storta *f*
2 *vt* ribattere
retouch /ri:'tʌtʃ/ *vt* Phot ritoccare
retouching /ri:'tʌtʃɪŋ/ *n* Phot ritocco *m*
retrace /rɪ'treɪs/ *vt* ripercorrere; ~ **one's steps** ritornare sui propri passi
retract /rɪ'trækt/ **1** *vt* ritirare; ritrattare ‹statement, accusation›
2 *vi* ritrarsi
retractable /rɪ'træktəbl/ *adj* ‹landing gear› retrattile; ‹pen› con la punta retrattile
retraction /rɪ'trækʃn/ *n* ritiro *m*; (of statement, accusation) ritrattazione *f*

retrain /ri:'treɪn/ **1** *vt* riqualificare
2 *vi* riqualificarsi
retraining /ri:'treɪnɪŋ/ *n* riqualificazione *f*
retread /'ri:tred/ *n* pneumatico *m* ricostruito
retreat /rɪ'tri:t/ **1** *n* ritirata *f*; (place) ritiro *m*
2 *vi* ritirarsi; Mil battere in ritirata
retrench /rɪ'trentʃ/ *vi* ridurre le spese
retrenchment /rɪ'trentʃmənt/ *n* riduzione *f* delle spese
retrial /ri:'traɪəl/ *n* nuovo processo *m*
retribution /retrɪ'bju:ʃn/ *n* castigo *m*
retrievable /rɪ'tri:vəbl/ *adj* recuperabile
retrieval /rɪ'tri:vəl/ *n* recupero *m*
retrieve /rɪ'tri:v/ *vt* recuperare
retroactive /retrəʊ'æktɪv/ *adj* retroattivo
retroactively /retrəʊ'æktɪvlɪ/ *adv* retroattivamente
retrograde /'retrəgreɪd/ *adj* retrogrado
retrospect /'retrəspekt/ *n* **in** ~ guardando indietro
retrospective /retrə'spektɪv/ **1** *adj* ‹exhibit› retrospettivo; ‹legislation› retroattivo
2 *n* retrospettiva *f*
retrospectively /retrə'spektɪvlɪ/ *adv* retrospettivamente
retrovirus /'retrəʊvaɪrəs/ *n* retrovirus *m inv*
retry /ri:'traɪ/ *vt* Jur riprocessare; Comput riprovare
return /rɪ'tɜːn/ **1** *n* ritorno *m*; (giving back) restituzione *f*; Comm profitto *m*; (ticket) biglietto *m* di andata e ritorno; **by** ~ **[of post]** a stretto giro di posta; **in** ~ in cambio (**for** di); **many happy** ~**s!** cento di questi giorni!; ~ **on investment** utile *m* sul capitale investito
2 *vi* ritornare
3 *vt* (give back) restituire; ricambiare ‹affection, invitation›; (put back) rimettere; (send back) mandare indietro; (elect) eleggere
returnable /rɪ'tɜːnəbl/ *adj* restituibile
return flight *n* volo *m* di andata e ritorno
return match *n* rivincita *f*
return ticket *n* biglietto *m* di andata e ritorno
reunification /ri:ju:nɪfɪ'keɪʃn/ *n* riunificazione *f*
reunify /ri:'ju:nɪfaɪ/ *vt* riunificare
reunion /ri:'ju:njən/ *n* riunione *f*
reunite /ri:jʊ'naɪt/ *vt* riunire
reusable /ri:'ju:zəbl/ *adj* riutilizzabile
reuse /ri:'ju:z/ *vt* riutilizzare

rev /rev/ ① *n* Auto giro; ~**s per minute**
regime *m* di giri
② *vt* ~ **[up]** far andare su di giri
③ *vi* andare su di giri

revaluation /ˌriːˈvæljʊˈeɪʃn/ *n*
rivalutazione *f*

revalue /riːˈvæljuː/ *vt* Comm rivalutare

revamp /riːˈvæmp/ *vt* riorganizzare
⟨*company*⟩; rimodernare ⟨*building,
clothing*⟩

rev counter *n* contagiri *m*

Rev[d] *abbr* (**Reverend**) Reverendo

reveal /rɪˈviːl/ *vt* rivelare; ⟨*dress*⟩
scoprire

revealing /rɪˈviːlɪŋ/ *adj* rivelatore;
⟨*dress*⟩ osé *inv*

revel /ˈrevl/ *vi* (pt/pp **revelled**) ~ **in**
something godere di qualcosa

revelation /revəˈleɪʃn/ *n* rivelazione *f*

reveller /ˈrev(ə)lə(r)/ *n* festaiolo -a *mf*

revelry /ˈrev(ə)lrɪ/ *n* baldoria *f*

revenge /rɪˈvendʒ/ ① *n* vendetta *f*; Sport
rivincita *f*; **take** ~ vendicarsi (**on
somebody for something** di qualcuno per
qualcosa)
② *vt* vendicare

revenue /ˈrevənjuː/ *n* reddito *m*

reverberate /rɪˈvɜːbəreɪt/ *vi*
riverberare

reverberations /rɪvɜːbəˈreɪʃnz/ *npl* fig
ripercussione *f*

revere /rɪˈvɪə(r)/ *vt* riverire

reverence /ˈrevərəns/ *n* riverenza *f*

Reverend /ˈrevərənd/ *adj* Reverendo

reverent /ˈrevərənt/ *adj* riverente

reverential /revəˈrenʃ(ə)l/ *adj* riverente

reverently /ˈrevərəntlɪ/ *adv*
rispettosamente

reverie /ˈrevərɪ/ *n* sogno *m* ad occhi
aperti

reversal /rɪˈvɜːsl/ *n* inversione *f*

reverse /rɪˈvɜːs/ ① *adj* opposto; **in** ~
order in ordine inverso
② *n* contrario *m*; (back) rovescio *m*; Auto
marcia *m* indietro
③ *vt* invertire; ~ **the car into the garage**
entrare in garage a marcia indietro; ~
the charges Teleph fare una telefonata a
carico del destinatario
④ *vi* Auto fare marcia indietro

reverse charge [phone-]call *n*
telefonata *f* a carico del destinatario

reversible /rɪˈvɜːsɪbl/ *adj* ⟨*jacket*⟩
double-face; ⟨*procedure*⟩ reversibile

reversing lights /rɪˈvɜːsɪŋ/ *npl* luci *fpl*
di retromarcia

revert /rɪˈvɜːt/ *vi* ~ **to** tornare a

review /rɪˈvjuː/ ① *n* (survey) rassegna *f*;
(reexamination) riconsiderazione *f*; Mil rivista
f; (of book, play) recensione *f*

② *vt* riesaminare ⟨*situation*⟩; Mil passare
in rivista; recensire ⟨*book, play*⟩

reviewer /rɪˈvjuːə(r)/ *n* critico, -a *mf*

revile /rɪˈvaɪl/ *vt* ingiuriare

revise /rɪˈvaɪz/ *vt* rivedere; (for exam)
ripassare

revision /rɪˈvɪʒn/ *n* revisione *f*; (for exam)
ripasso *m*

revisionism /rɪˈvɪʒənɪzm/ *n*
revisionismo *m*

revisionist /rɪˈvɪʒənɪst/ *adj & n*
revisionista *mf*

revisit /riːˈvɪzɪt/ *vt* rivisitare ⟨*person,
museum etc*⟩

revitalization /riːvaɪtəlaɪˈzeɪʃn/ *n*
rivitalizzazione *f*

revitalize /riːˈvaɪtəlaɪz/ *vt* rivitalizzare

revival /rɪˈvaɪvl/ *n* ritorno *m*; (of patient)
recupero *m*; (from coma) risveglio *m*

revivalist /rɪˈvaɪvəlɪst/ *adj* Relig
revivalista

revive /rɪˈvaɪv/ ① *vt* resuscitare;
rianimare ⟨*person*⟩
② *vi* riprendersi; ⟨*person*⟩ rianimarsi

revocation /revəˈkeɪʃn/ *n* (of decision,
order) revoca *f*; (of law) abrogazione *f*; (of will)
annullamento *m*

revoke /rɪˈvəʊk/ *vt* revocare ⟨*decision,
order*⟩; abrogare ⟨*law*⟩; annullare ⟨*will*⟩

revolt /rɪˈvəʊlt/ ① *n* rivolta *f*
② *vi* ribellarsi
③ *vi* rivoltare

revolting /rɪˈvəʊltɪŋ/ *adj* rivoltante

revolution /revəˈluːʃn/ *n* rivoluzione *f*;
~**s per minute** Auto giri *mpl* al minuto

revolutionary /revəˈluːʃənərɪ/ *adj & n*
rivoluzionario, -a *mf*

revolutionize /revəˈluːʃənaɪz/ *vt*
rivoluzionare

revolve /rɪˈvɒlv/ *vi* ruotare; ~ **around**
girare intorno a

revolver /rɪˈvɒlvə(r)/ *n* rivoltella *f*,
revolver *m inv*

revolving /rɪˈvɒlvɪŋ/ *adj* ruotante

revolving doors *npl* porta *f* girevole

revue /rɪˈvjuː/ *n* rivista *f*

revulsion /rɪˈvʌlʃn/ *n* ripulsione *f*

reward /rɪˈwɔːd/ ① *n* ricompensa *f*
② *vt* ricompensare

reward card *n* = LOYALTY CARD

rewarding /rɪˈwɔːdɪŋ/ *adj* gratificante

rewind /riːˈwaɪnd/ *vt* riavvolgere ⟨*tape,
film*⟩

rewind button /ˈriːwaɪnd/ *n* tasto *m* di
riavvolgimento

rewire /riːˈwaɪə(r)/ *vt* rifare l'impianto
elettrico di

reword /riːˈwɜːd/ *vt* esprimere con parole
diverse

rework /riːˈwɜːk/ *vt* modificare

rewritable /riːˈraɪtəbl/ adj Comput ⟨CD-Rom⟩ riscrivibile

rewrite /riːˈraɪt/ vt (pt **rewrote**, pp **rewritten**) riscrivere

rhapsody /ˈræpsədɪ/ n rapsodia f

rhesus /ˈriːsəs/ n reso m

rhesus-negative adj Rh-negativo

rhesus-positive adj Rh-positivo

rhetoric /ˈretərɪk/ n retorica f

rhetorical /rɪˈtɒrɪkl/ adj retorico

rhetorically /rɪˈtɒrɪklɪ/ adv retoricamente

rhetorical question n domanda f retorica

rheumatic /rʊˈmætɪk/ adj reumatico

rheumatism /ˈruːmətɪzm/ n reumatismo m

rheumatoid arthritis /ˈruːmətɔɪd/ n periartrite f

Rhine /raɪn/ n Reno m

rhino /ˈraɪnəʊ/ n fam rinoceronte m

rhinoceros /raɪˈnɒsərəs/ n rinoceronte m

rhombus /ˈrɒmbəs/ n rombo m

rhubarb /ˈruːbɑːb/ n rabarbaro m

rhyme /raɪm/ ⓵ n rima f; (poem) filastrocca f
⓶ vi rimare; ∼ **with something** far rima con qualcosa

rhythm /ˈrɪðm/ n ritmo m

rhythmic[al] /ˈrɪðmɪk[l]/ adj ritmico

rhythmically /ˈrɪðmɪklɪ/ adv con ritmo

rhythm method n (of contraception) metodo m Ogino-Knauss

rib /rɪb/ ⓵ n costola f; ∼s pl Culin costata f
⓶ vt (pt/pp **ribbed**) fam punzecchiare

ribald /ˈrɪbld/ adj spinto

ribbon /ˈrɪbən/ n nastro m; **in** ∼s a brandelli

ribcage /ˈrɪbkeɪdʒ/ n gabbia f toracica, cassa f toracica

rice /raɪs/ n riso m

ricefield /ˈraɪsfiːld/ n risaia f

rice-paper n Culin carta f di riso

rich /rɪtʃ/ ⓵ adj ricco; ⟨food⟩ pesante
⓶ n **the** ∼ pl i ricchi; ∼**es** pl ricchezze fpl

richly /ˈrɪtʃlɪ/ adv riccamente; ⟨deserve⟩ largamente

richness /ˈrɪtʃnɪs/ n (of food) pesantezza f; (of furnishings) sfarzosità f; (of person, company) ricchezza f

Richter scale /ˈrɪktə(r)/ n scala f Richter

rick /rɪk/ vt Br ∼ **one's ankle** prendere una storta alla caviglia

rickets /ˈrɪkɪts/ n rachitismo m

rickety /ˈrɪkətɪ/ adj malfermo

rickshaw /ˈrɪkʃɔː/ n risciò m inv

ricochet /ˈrɪkəʃeɪ/ ⓵ vi rimbalzare
⓶ n rimbalzo m

rid /rɪd/ vt (pt/pp **rid**, pres p **ridding**) sbarazzare (**of** di); **get** ∼ **of** sbarazzarsi di

riddance /ˈrɪdns/ n **good** ∼! che liberazione!

ridden /ˈrɪdn/ ▶ RIDE

riddle /ˈrɪdl/ n enigma m

riddled /ˈrɪdld/ adj ∼ **with** crivellato di

ride /raɪd/ ⓵ n (on horse) cavalcata f; (in vehicle) giro m; (journey) viaggio m; **take somebody for a** ∼ fam prendere qualcuno in giro
⓶ vt (pt **rode**, pp **ridden**) montare ⟨horse⟩; andare su ⟨bicycle⟩
⓷ vi andare a cavallo; ⟨jockey, showjumper⟩ cavalcare; ⟨cyclist⟩ andare in bicicletta; (in vehicle) viaggiare
■ **ride out** vt superare ⟨storm, crisis⟩
■ **ride up** vt ⟨rider⟩ arrivare; ⟨skirt⟩ salire

rider /ˈraɪdə(r)/ n cavallerizzo, -a mf; (in race) fantino m; (on bicycle) ciclista mf; (in document) postilla f

ridge /rɪdʒ/ n spigolo m; (on roof) punta f; (of mountain) cresta f; (of high pressure) zona f ad alta pressione [atmosferica]

ridicule /ˈrɪdɪkjuːl/ ⓵ n ridicolo m
⓶ vt mettere in ridicolo

ridiculous /rɪˈdɪkjʊləs/ adj ridicolo

ridiculously /rɪˈdɪkjʊləslɪ/ adv in modo ridicolo; ∼ **expensive/easy** carissimo/facilissimo

riding /ˈraɪdɪŋ/ ⓵ n equitazione f
⓶ attrib d'equitazione

rife /raɪf/ adj **be** ∼ essere diffuso; ∼ **with** pieno di

riff-raff /ˈrɪfræf/ n marmaglia f

rifle /ˈraɪfl/ ⓵ n fucile m
⓶ vt ∼ **[through]** mettere a soqquadro

rifle-range n tiro m al bersaglio

rift /rɪft/ n fessura f; fig frattura f

rig[1] /rɪg/ n equipaggiamento m; (at sea) piattaforma f per trivellazioni subacquee

rig[2] vt (pt/pp **rigged**) manovrare ⟨election⟩
■ **rig out** vt equipaggiare; (with clothes) parare
■ **rig up** vt allestire

rigging /ˈrɪgɪŋ/ n Naut sartiame m; (of election, competition) broglio m

right /raɪt/ ⓵ adj giusto; (not left) destro; **be** ∼ ⟨person⟩ aver ragione; ⟨clock⟩ essere giusto; **put** ∼ mettere all'ora ⟨clock⟩; correggere ⟨person⟩; rimediare a ⟨situation⟩; **that's** ∼! proprio così! **do you have the** ∼ **time?** ha l'ora esatta?
⓶ adv (correctly) bene; (not left) a destra; (directly) proprio; (completely) completamente; **too** ∼! altroché!

3 *n* giusto *m*; (not left) destra *f*; (what is due) diritto *m*; **the R∼** Pol la destra; **on/to the ∼ a** destra; **be in the ∼** essere nel giusto; **by ∼s** secondo giustizia; **be within one's ∼s** avere tutti i diritti (**in doing something** di fare qualcosa)
4 *vt* raddrizzare; **∼ a wrong** fig riparare ad un torto

right angle *n* angolo *m* retto

right away *adv* subito

righteous /'raɪtʃəs/ *adj* virtuoso; (cause) giusto

rightful /'raɪtfl/ *adj* legittimo

rightfully /'raɪtfʊlɪ/ *adv* legittimamente

right-hand *adj* di destra; **on the ∼ side** sulla destra

right-hand drive *n* ⟨vehicle⟩ guida *f* a destra

right-handed /-'hændɪd/ *adj* che usa la mano destra

right-hand man *n* fig braccio *m* destro

rightly /'raɪtlɪ/ *adv* giustamente

right-minded /-'maɪndɪd/ *adj* sensato

right-of-centre *adj* Pol di centrodestra

right of way *n* diritto *m* di transito; (path) passaggio *m*; Auto precedenza *f*

right-on **1** *int* fam bene!
2 *adj* fam **they're very ∼** sono molto impegnati

rights issue *n* emissione *f* riservata agli azionisti

right-thinking *adj* sensato

right turn *n* svolta *f* a destra

right wing *n* Pol destra; Sport ala *f* destra

right-wing *adj* Pol di destra

right-winger *n* Pol persona *f* di destra; Sport ala *f* destra

rigid /'rɪdʒɪd/ *adj* rigido

rigidity /rɪ'dʒɪdətɪ/ *n* rigidità *f*

rigidly *adv* ⟨apply⟩ rigorosamente; ⟨oppose⟩ fermamente

rigmarole /'rɪgmərəʊl/ *n* trafila *f*; (story) tiritera *f*

rigor mortis /rɪgə'mɔːtɪs/ *n* rigidità *f* cadaverica

rigorous /'rɪgərəs/ *adj* rigoroso

rigorously /'rɪgərəslɪ/ *adv* rigorosamente

rigour /'rɪgə(r)/ *n* rigore *m*

rig-out *n* (fam: clothes) tenuta *f*

rile /raɪl/ *vt* fam irritare

rim /rɪm/ *n* bordo *m*; (of wheel) cerchione *m*

rind /raɪnd/ *n* (on cheese) crosta *f*; (on bacon) cotenna *f*

ring[1] /rɪŋ/ **1** *n* (circle) cerchio *m*; (on finger) anello *m*; (boxing) ring *m* inv; (for circus) pista *f*; **stand in a ∼** essere in cerchio
2 *vt* accerchiare; **∼ in red** fare un cerchio rosso intorno a

ring[2] **1** *n* suono *m*; **give somebody a ∼** Teleph dare un colpo di telefono a qualcuno
2 *vt* (pt **rang**, pp **rung**) suonare; Teleph telefonare a; **it ∼s a bell** fig mi dice qualcosa; **∼ the changes** fig cambiare
3 *vi* suonare; Teleph telefonare; **∼ true** aver l'aria di essere vero
▪ **ring back** *vt/i* Teleph richiamare
▪ **ring off** *vi* Teleph riattaccare
▪ **ring out** *vi* ⟨voice, shot etc⟩ risuonare chiaramente
▪ **ring round** *vi* Teleph fare un giro di telefonate
▪ **ring up** Teleph **1** *vt* telefonare a
2 *vi* telefonare

ring-binder /'rɪŋbaɪndə(r)/ *n* raccoglitore *m* ad anelli

ring finger *n* anulare *m*

ringing /'rɪŋɪŋ/ *n* (noise of bell, alarm) suono *m*; (in ears) fischio *m*

ringleader /'rɪŋliːdə(r)/ *n* capobanda *m*

ringlet /'rɪŋlɪt/ *n* boccolo *m*

ringmaster *n* direttore *m* di circo

ring-pull *n* linguetta *f*; **∼ can** *n* lattina *f* con linguetta

ring road *n* circonvallazione *f*

ringside *n* **at the ∼** in prima fila; **have a ∼ seat** fig essere in prima fila

ringtone *n* suoneria *f*

rink /rɪŋk/ *n* pista *f* di pattinaggio

rinse /rɪns/ **1** *n* risciacquo *m*; (hair colour) cachet *m* inv
2 *vt* sciacquare
▪ **rinse off** *vt* sciacquare via
▪ **rinse out** *vt* sciacquare ⟨cup, glass⟩; sciacquare via ⟨shampoo, soap⟩

riot /'raɪət/ **1** *n* rissa *f*; (of colour) accozzaglia *f*; **∼s** *pl* disordini *mpl*; **run ∼** impazzare
2 *vi* creare disordini

riot act *n* **read the ∼ to somebody** fig dare una lavata di capo a qualcuno

rioter /'raɪətə(r)/ *n* dimostrante *mf*

riot gear *n* tenuta *f* antisommossa

riotous /'raɪətəs/ *adj* sfrenato

riotously /'raɪətəslɪ/ *adv* **∼ funny** divertente da morire

riot police *n* DIGOS *f*, Divisione *f* Investigazioni Generali e Operazioni Speciali

RIP *abbr* (**rest in peace**) R.I.P.

rip /rɪp/ **1** *n* strappo *m*
2 *vt* (pt/pp **ripped**) strappare; **∼ open** aprire con uno strappo
3 *vi* strapparsi; **let ∼** scatenarsi
▪ **rip off** *vt* (remove) togliere; (fam: cheat) fregare
▪ **rip through** *vt* ⟨blast⟩ squaciare ⟨building⟩
▪ **rip up** *vt* stracciare ⟨letter⟩

ripcord /'rɪpkɔːd/ *n* cavo *m* di spiegamento

ripe /raɪp/ *adj* maturo; ⟨*cheese*⟩ stagionato

ripen /'raɪpn/ **[1]** *vi* maturare; ⟨*cheese*⟩ stagionarsi
[2] *vt* far maturare; stagionare ⟨*cheese*⟩

ripeness /'raɪpnɪs/ *n* maturazione *f*

rip-off *n* fam frode *f*; **these prices are a** ∼! questi prezzi sono un furto!

riposte /rɪ'pɒst/ *n* replica *f*

ripple /'rɪpl/ **[1]** *n* increspatura *f*; ⟨*sound*⟩ mormorio *m*
[2] *vt* increspare
[3] *vi* incresparsi

rip-roaring /'rɪprɔːrɪŋ/ *adj* (fam: success) travolgente

rise /raɪz/ **[1]** *n* (of sun) levata *f*; (fig: to fame, power) ascesa *f*; (increase) aumento *m*; **give** ∼ **to** dare adito a
[2] *vi* (pt **rose**, pp **risen**) alzarsi; ⟨*sun*⟩ sorgere; ⟨*dough*⟩ lievitare; ⟨*prices, water level*⟩ aumentare; (to power, position) arrivare (**to** a); (rebel) sollevarsi; ⟨*Parliament, court*⟩ aggiornare la seduta; (for holidays) sospendere i lavori
∎ **rise above** *vt* superare ⟨*difficulty*⟩

riser /'raɪzə(r)/ *n* **early** ∼ persona *f* mattiniera

rising /'raɪzɪŋ/ **[1]** *adj* ⟨*sun*⟩ levante; ∼ **generation** nuova generazione *f*
[2] *n* (revolt) sollevazione *f*

risk /rɪsk/ **[1]** *n* rischio *m*; **run the** ∼ **of** correre il rischio di; **at** ∼ in pericolo; **at one's own** ∼ a proprio rischio e pericolo; **at the** ∼ **of doing something** a costo di fare qualcosa
[2] *vt* rischiare

risky /'rɪskɪ/ *adj* (**-ier, -iest**) rischioso

risotto /rɪ'zɒtəʊ/ *n* risotto *m*

risqué /'rɪskeɪ/ *adj* spinto

rissole /'rɪsəʊl/ *n* crocchetta *f*

rite /raɪt/ *n* rito *m*; **last** ∼**s** *pl* estrema unzione *fsg*

ritual /'rɪtjʊəl/ *adj* & *n* rituale *m*

ritzy /'rɪtsɪ/ *adj* (fam: hotel, style, decoration) lussuoso

rival /'raɪvl/ **[1]** *adj* rivale
[2] *n* rivale *mf*; ∼**s** *pl* Comm concorrenti *mpl*
[3] *vt* (pt/pp **rivalled**) rivaleggiare con

rivalry /'raɪv(ə)lrɪ/ *n* rivalità *f inv*; Comm concorrenza *f*

river /'rɪvə(r)/ *n* fiume *m*

riverbank *n* riva *f* di fiume

river-bed *n* letto *m* del fiume

riverside **[1]** *n* lungofiume *m*
[2] *attrib* sul fiume

rivet /'rɪvɪt/ **[1]** *n* rivetto *m*
[2] *vt* rivettare; **be** ∼**ed by** fig essere avvinto da

riveting /'rɪvɪtɪŋ/ *adj* fig avvincente

Riviera /rɪvɪ'eərə/ *n* **the French** ∼ la Costa Azzurra; **the Italian** ∼ la riviera ligure

roach /rəʊtʃ/ *n* (fish) lasca *f*; (Am fam: insect) scarafaggio *m*

road /rəʊd/ *n* strada *f*, via *f*; **be on the** ∼ viaggiare

roadblock *n* blocco *m* stradale

road haulage *n* trasporto *m* su strada

road hog *n* fam pirata *m* della strada

road hump *n* dosso *m* di rallentamento

roadie /'rəʊdɪ/ *n* roadie *m inv*

road map *n* fig **a** ∼ **to peace** la roadmap per la pace

road safety *n* sicurezza *f* sulle strade

road sense *n* prudenza *f* (per strada)

roadshow *n* (play, show) spettacolo *m* di tournée; (publicity tour) giro *m* promozionale

roadside *n* bordo *m* della strada

road sign *n* cartello *m* stradale

road surface *n* fondo *m* stradale

road sweeper *n* (person) spazzino, -a *nmf*; (machine) autospazzatrice *f*

road tax *n* tassa *f* di circolazione

roadway *n* carreggiata *f*, corsia *f*

roadworks *npl* lavori *mpl* stradali

roadworthy *adj* sicuro

roam /rəʊm/ *vt/i* girovagare
∎ **roam around** *vi* girovagare

roar /rɔː(r)/ **[1]** *n* ruggito *m*; ∼**s of laughter** scroscio *msg* di risa
[2] *vi* ruggire; ⟨*lorry, thunder*⟩ rombare; ∼ **with laughter** ridere fragorosamente
∎ **roar out** *vt* gridare
∎ **roar past** *vi* ⟨*move noisily*⟩ passare rombando

roaring /'rɔːrɪŋ/ **[1]** *adj* **do a** ∼ **trade** fam fare affari d'oro
[2] *adv* ∼ **drunk** fam ubriaco fradicio

roast /rəʊst/ **[1]** *adj* arrosto; ∼ **pork** arrosto *m* di maiale
[2] *n* arrosto *m*
[3] *vt* arrostire ⟨*meat*⟩
[4] *vi* arrostirsi

roasting [hot] /'rəʊstɪŋ/ *adj* fam caldissimo

roasting pan *n* teglia *f* per arrosti

rob /rɒb/ *vt* (pt/pp **robbed**) derubare (**of** di); svaligiare ⟨*bank*⟩

robber /'rɒbə(r)/ *n* rapinatore, -trice *mf*

robbery /'rɒbərɪ/ *n* rapina *f*

robe /rəʊb/ *n* tunica *f*; (Am: bathrobe) accappatoio *m*

robin /'rɒbɪn/ *n* pettirosso *m*

robot /'rəʊbɒt/ *n* robot *m inv*

robotic /rəʊ'bɒtɪk/ *adj* ⟨*movement, voice*⟩ robotico; ⟨*tool, device, machine*⟩ robotizzato

robotics *n* robotica *f*

robust /rəʊ'bʌst/ *adj* robusto

rock[1] /rɒk/ n roccia f; (in sea) scoglio m; (sweet) zucchero m candito; **on the ∼s** ⟨ship⟩ incagliato; ⟨marriage⟩ finito; ⟨drink⟩ con ghiaccio

rock[2] ① vt cullare ⟨baby⟩; (shake) far traballare; (shock) scuotere ② vi dondolarsi

rock[3] n Mus rock m

rock and roll n rock and roll m

rock-bottom ① adj bassissimo ② n livello m più basso; **hit ∼** toccare il fondo

rock-climber n scalatore, -trice mf

rock-climbing n roccia f

rockery /'rɒkərɪ/ n giardino m roccioso

rocket /'rɒkɪt/ ① n razzo m; **give somebody a ∼** fam fare un cicchetto a qualcuno ② vi salire alle stelle

rocket launcher /'lɔːntʃə(r)/ n lanciarazzi m inv

rocket science n fam **it's not ∼** non ci vuole la laurea!

rock face n parete f rocciosa

rockfall n caduta f di massi

rocking chair /'rɒkɪŋ/ n sedia f a dondolo

rocking horse n cavallo m a dondolo

rock star n rock star mf inv

rocky /'rɒkɪ/ adj (**-ier, -iest**) roccioso; fig traballante

Rocky Mountains npl le Montagne fpl Rocciose

rod /rɒd/ n bacchetta f; (for fishing) canna f

rode /rəʊd/ ▶ RIDE

rodent /'rəʊdnt/ n roditore m

roe[1] /rəʊ/ n uova fpl di pesce; (soft) latte m di pesce

roe[2] n (pl **roe** or **roes**) **∼ [deer]** capriolo m

roebuck /'rəʊbʌk/ n capriolo m maschio

roger /'rɒdʒə(r)/ int Teleph ricevuto

rogue /rəʊg/ n farabutto m

role /rəʊl/ n ruolo m

role model n Psych modello m comportamentale

role-play, role-playing /'rəʊlpleɪɪŋ/ n Psych role playing m inv

roll /rəʊl/ ① n rotolo m; ⟨bread⟩ panino m; (list) lista f; ⟨of ship, drum⟩ rullio m ② vi rotolare; **be ∼ing in money** fam nuotare nell'oro ③ vt spianare ⟨lawn, pastry⟩; **∼ed into one** allo stesso tempo
■ **roll around, roll about** vi ⟨person, puppy⟩ rotolarsi; ⟨ball, marbles⟩ rotolare
■ **roll back** vt ridurre ⟨prices⟩
■ **roll down** vt srotolare ⟨blind, sleeves⟩
■ **roll in** vi (fam: arrive in large quantities) arrivare a valanghe; (arrive) arrivare

■ **roll on** vi **∼ on Friday!** non vedo l'ora che sia venerdì!
■ **roll over** vi rigirarsi; (fam: capitulate) arrendersi
■ **roll up** ① vt arrotolare; rimboccarsi ⟨sleeves⟩ ② vi fam arrivare

roll-call n appello m

roller /'rəʊlə(r)/ n rullo m; (for hair) bigodino m

rollerblade ① n pattino m a rotelle in linea ② vi pattinare (con pattini in linea)

roller blind n tapparella f

roller coaster n montagne fpl russe

roller skate n pattino m a rotelle

roller-skating n pattinaggio m a rotelle

rollicking /'rɒlɪkɪŋ/ adj **have a ∼ time** divertirsi da pazzi

rolling pin n mattarello m

rolling stock n materiale m rotabile

rolling stone n fig vagabondo, -a mf

rollneck n collo m alto; (whole sweater) dolcevita f

roll-on n (deodorant) deodorante m a sfera

roll-on roll-off ferry n traghetto m roll-on roll-off

ROM /rɒm/ n Comput Rom f inv

Roma /'rəʊmə/ npl i rom mpl

Roman /'rəʊmən/ ① adj (also print) romano ② n romano, -a mf

Roman Catholic adj & n cattolico, -a mf

romance /rəʊ'mæns/ n (love affair) storia f d'amore; (book) romanzo m rosa

Romania /rəʊ'meɪnɪə/ n Romania f

Romanian /rəʊ'meɪnɪən/ adj & n rumeno, -a mf; (language) rumeno m

roman numeral n numero m romano

romantic /rəʊ'mæntɪk/ adj romantico

romantically /rəʊ'mæntɪklɪ/ adv romanticamente

romanticism /rəʊ'mæntɪsɪzm/ n romanticismo m

romanticize /rəʊ'mæntɪsaɪz/ vt romantizzare

romanticized /rəʊ'mæntɪsaɪzd/ adj romanzato

Romany /'rəʊmənɪ/ n rom mf inv

Rome /rəʊm/ n Roma f

Romeo /'rəʊmɪəʊ/ n (fam: ladykiller) dongiovanni m inv

romp /rɒmp/ ① n gioco m rumoroso ② vi giocare rumorosamente
■ **romp home** vi (win easily) vincere senza difficoltà
■ **romp through** vt ① passare senza difficoltà ⟨exam⟩ ② vi riuscire senza difficoltà

rompers /'rɒmpəz/ *npl* pagliaccetto *msg*

roof /ru:f/ **1** *n* tetto *m*; (of mouth) palato *m*; **live under one** ∼ vivere sotto lo stesso tetto; **go through the** ∼ (fam: increase) andare alle stelle; (be very angry) andare su tutte le furie **2** *vt* mettere un tetto su

roof-rack *n* portabagagli *m inv*

rooftop /'ru:ftɒp/ *n* tetto *m*; **shout it from the** ∼**s** fig gridarlo ai quattro venti

rook /rʊk/ **1** *n* corvo *m*; (in chess) torre *f* **2** *vt* (fam: swindle) fregare

rookie /'rʊkɪ/ *n* Am fam novellino, -a *mf*

room /'ru:m/ *n* stanza *f*; (bedroom) camera *f*: (for functions) sala *f*: (space) spazio *m*

room-mate *n* (Am: flatmate) compagno, -a *mf* di appartamento; (in same room) compagno, -a *mf* di stanza

room service *n* servizio *m* in camera

room temperature *n* temperatura *f* ambiente

roomy /'ru:mɪ/ *adj* spazioso; ⟨clothes⟩ ampio

roost /ru:st/ **1** *n* posatoio *m* **2** *vi* appollaiarsi

rooster /'ru:stə(r)/ *n* gallo *m*

root[1] /ru:t/ **1** *n* radice *f*; **take** ∼ metter radici; **put down** ∼**s** fig metter radici **2** *vi* metter radici

root[2] /ru:t/ *vi* ∼ **for somebody** fam fare il tifo per qualcuno
■ **root about, root around** *vi* grufolare; ∼ **about for something** rovistare alla ricerca di qualcosa
■ **root out** *vt* fig scovare

rope /rəʊp/ *n* corda *f*; **know the** ∼**s** fam conoscere i trucchi del mestiere
■ **rope in** *vt* fam coinvolgere

rope ladder *n* scala *f* di corda

ropey /'rəʊpɪ/ *adj* Br fam scadente; **feel** ∼ sentirsi poco bene

rosary /'rəʊzərɪ/ *n* rosario *m*

rosé /'rəʊzeɪ/ *n* [vino *m*] rosé *m inv*

rose[1] /rəʊz/ *n* rosa *f*; (of watering-can) bocchetta *f*

rose[2] ▶ RISE

rosebud /'rəʊzbʌd/ *n* bocciolo *m* di rosa

rosehip /'rəʊzhɪp/ *n* frutto *m* della rosa canina

rosemary /'rəʊzmərɪ/ *n* rosmarino *m*

rose-tinted spectacles /'rəʊztɪntɪd/ *npl* wear ∼ ∼ vedere tutto rosa

rosette /rəʊ'zet/ *n* coccarda *f*

roster /'rɒstə(r)/ *n* tabella *f* dei turni

rostrum /'rɒstrəm/ *n* podio *m*

rosy /'rəʊzɪ/ *adj* (**-ier, -iest**) roseo

rot /rɒt/ **1** *n* marciume *m*; (fam: nonsense) sciocchezze *fpl* **2** *vi* (pt/pp **rotted**) marcire

rota /'rəʊtə/ *n* tabella *f* dei turni

rotary /'rəʊtərɪ/ *adj* rotante

rotate /rəʊ'teɪt/ **1** *vt* far ruotare; avvicendare ⟨crops⟩ **2** *vi* ruotare

rotation /rəʊ'teɪʃn/ *n* rotazione *f*; **in** ∼ a turno

rote /rəʊt/ *n* **by** ∼ meccanicamente

rotten /'rɒtn/ *adj* marcio; fam schifoso; ⟨person⟩ penoso

rotund /rəʊ'tʌnd/ *adj* paffuto

rotunda /rəʊ'tʌndə/ *n* rotonda *f*

rouble /'ru:bl/ *n* rublo *m*

rough /rʌf/ **1** *adj* (not smooth) ruvido; ⟨ground⟩ accidentato; ⟨behaviour⟩ rozzo; ⟨sport⟩ violento; ⟨area⟩ malfamato; ⟨crossing, time⟩ brutto; ⟨estimate⟩ approssimativo **2** *adv* ⟨play⟩ grossolanamente; **sleep** ∼ dormire sotto i ponti **3** *n* **do something in** ∼ far qualcosa alla bell'e meglio **4** *vi* ∼ **it** vivere senza confort
■ **rough out** *vt* abbozzare
■ **rough up** *vt* fam malmenare ⟨person⟩

roughage /'rʌfɪdʒ/ *n* fibre *fpl*

rough-and-ready *adj* ⟨person, manner⟩ sbrigativo; ⟨conditions, method⟩ rudimentale

rough-and-tumble *n* (rough play) zuffa *f*

rough copy *n* brutta copia *f*

rough draft *n* abbozzo *m*

roughen /'rʌfn/ *vt* rendere ruvido ⟨surface⟩

roughly /'rʌflɪ/ *adv* rozzamente; (more or less) pressappoco

roughness /'rʌfnɪs/ *n* ruvidità *f*; (of behaviour) rozzezza *f*

rough paper *n* carta *f* da brutta

roughshod /'rʌfʃɒd/ *adv* ride ∼ over infischiarsi di ⟨person, objection⟩; calpestare ⟨feelings⟩

roulette /ru:'let/ *n* roulette *f*

round /raʊnd/ **1** *adj* rotondo **2** *n* tondo *m*; (slice) fetta *f*; (of visits, drinks) giro *m*; (of competition) partita *f*; (boxing) ripresa *f*, round *m inv*; **do one's** ∼**s** ⟨doctor⟩ fare il giro delle visite **3** *prep* intorno a; **open** ∼ **the clock** aperto ventiquattr'ore **4** *adv* **all** ∼ tutt'intorno; **ask somebody** ∼ invitare qualcuno; **go/come** ∼ **to** (a friend etc) andare da; **turn/look** ∼ girarsi; ∼ **about** (approximately) intorno a **5** *vt* arrotondare; girare ⟨corner⟩
■ **round down** *vt* arrotondare (per difetto)
■ **round off** *vt* (end) terminare
■ **round on** *vt* aggredire
■ **round up** *vt* radunare; arrotondare ⟨prices⟩

roundabout /'raʊndəbaʊt/ **1** *adj* indiretto

r

2 n giostra f; (for traffic) rotonda f

round bracket n parentesi f tonda

rounders /'raʊndəz/ n Br Sport gioco m simile al baseball

round figure n cifra f tonda

round robin n petizione f

round-shouldered /-'ʃəʊldəd/ adj con le spalle curve

round table n tavola f rotonda

round the clock adv 24 ore su 24

round-the-clock adj ⟨Br: care, surveillance⟩ ventiquattr'ore su ventiquattro

round-the-world adj ⟨trip⟩ intorno al mondo

round trip n viaggio m di andata e ritorno

round-up n (of suspects) retata f; (of cattle) raduno m; (summary) riepilogo m

rouse /raʊz/ vt svegliare; risvegliare ⟨suspicion, interest⟩

rousing /'raʊzɪŋ/ adj ⟨speech⟩ che solleva il morale; ⟨music⟩ trionfale

rout /raʊt/ **1** vt Mil, fig sbaragliare **2** n disfatta f

route /ruːt/ n itinerario m; Naut, Aeron rotta f; (of bus) percorso m

routine /ruː'tiːn/ **1** adj di routine **2** n routine f inv; Theat numero m

routinely /ruː'tiːnlɪ/ adv d'ufficio

rove /rəʊv/ vi girovagare

roving /'rəʊvɪŋ/ adj ⟨reporter, ambassador⟩ itinerante

roving eye n have a ∼ essere sempre in cerca di avventure amorose

row¹ /rəʊ/ n (line) fila f; **three years in a** ∼ tre anni di fila

row² **1** vi (in boat) remare **2** vt ∼ **a boat** remare

row³ /raʊ/ **1** n fam (quarrel) litigata f; (noise) baccano m; **we've had a** ∼ abbiamo litigato **2** vi fam litigare

rowboat /'rəʊbəʊt/ n Am barca f a remi

rowdy /'raʊdɪ/ **1** adj (-ier, -iest) chiassoso **2** n attaccabrighe m inv

rower /'rəʊə(r)/ n rematore, -trice mf

rowing /'rəʊɪŋ/ n (sport) canottaggio m

rowing boat n barca f a remi

rowing machine n vogatore m

rowlock /'rɒlək/ n Br scalmo m

royal /'rɔɪəl/ **1** adj reale **2** n membro m della famiglia reale

royal blue n & adj blu m scuro

Royal Highness n His/Her ∼ Sua Altezza reale; Your ∼ Vostra Altezza

royally /'rɔɪəlɪ/ adv regalmente

royalties /'rɔɪəltɪz/ npl (payments) diritti mpl d'autore

royalty /'rɔɪəltɪ/ n appartenenza f alla famiglia reale; (persons) i membri della famiglia reale

rpm abbr (**revolutions per minute**) giri mpl al minuto

RSI abbr (**repetitive strain injury**) patologia f da sforzo ripetuto

RSVP abbr (**répondez s'il vous plaît = please reply**) SPR, si prega rispondere

rub /rʌb/ **1** n sfregata f **2** vt (pt/pp **rubbed**) sfregare; ∼ **one's hands** fregarsi le mani ■ **rub along** vi sopportarsi [a vicenda] ■ **rub down** vt frizionare ⟨person, body⟩; levigare ⟨wood⟩ ■ **rub in** vt far assorbire (massaggiando) ⟨cream⟩; **don't** ∼ **it in** fam non rigirare il coltello nella piaga ■ **rub off** **1** vt mandar via sfregando ⟨stain⟩; (from blackboard) cancellare **2** vi andar via; ∼ **off on** essere trasmesso a ■ **rub out** vt cancellare ■ **rub up** vt ∼ **somebody up the wrong way** prendere qualcuno per il verso sbagliato

rubber /'rʌbə(r)/ n gomma f; (eraser) gomma f [da cancellare]

rubber band n elastico m

rubber bullet n proiettile m di gomma

rubberneck n fam (onlooker) curioso, -a mf; (tourist) turista mf

rubber plant n ficus m inv

rubberstamp vt fig approvare senza discutere

rubber tree n albero m della gomma

rubbery /'rʌbərɪ/ adj gommoso

rubbish /'rʌbɪʃ/ **1** n immondizie fpl; (fam: nonsense) idiozie fpl; (fam: junk) robaccia f **2** vt fam fare a pezzi

rubbish bin n pattumiera f

rubbish dump n discarica f; (official) discarica f comunale

rubbishy /'rʌbɪʃɪ/ adj fam schifoso

rubble /'rʌbl/ n macerie fpl

rub-down n strofinata f

rubella /rʊ'belə/ n rosolia f

rubric /'ruːbrɪk/ n rubrica f

ruby /'ruːbɪ/ **1** n rubino m **2** attrib di rubini; ⟨lips⟩ scarlatto

rucksack /'rʌksæk/ n zaino m

ructions /'rʌkʃ(ə)nz/ npl fam finimondo msg; **there'll be** ∼ **if he finds out** se lo scopre succede il finimondo

rudder /'rʌdə(r)/ n timone m

ruddy /'rʌdɪ/ adj (-ier, -iest) rubicondo; fam maledetto

rude /ru:d/ *adj* scortese; (improper) spinto

rudely /'ru:dlɪ/ *adv* scortesemente

rudeness /'ru:dnɪs/ *n* scortesia *f*

rudimentary /ru:dɪ'mentərɪ/ *adj* rudimentale

rudiments /'ru:dɪmənts/ *npl* rudimenti *mpl*

rue[1] /ru:/ *vt* pentirsi di ⟨*decision*⟩; ~ **the day** maledire il giorno

rue[2] *n* Bot ruta *f*

rueful /'ru:fl/ *adj* rassegnato

ruefully /'ru:fʊlɪ/ *adv* con rassegnazione

ruff /rʌf/ *n* (of lace) colletto *m*; (of fur, feathers) collare *m*

ruffian /'rʌfɪən/ *n* farabutto *m*

ruffle /'rʌfl/ [1] *n* gala *f*
[2] *vt* scompigliare ⟨*hair*⟩

rug /rʌg/ *n* tappeto *m*; (blanket) coperta *f*

rugby /'rʌgbɪ/ *n* ~ **[football]** rugby *m*

rugby league *n* rugby *m* a tredici

rugby union *n* rugby *m* a quindici

rugged /'rʌgɪd/ *adj* ⟨*coastline*⟩ roccioso; ⟨*face, personality*⟩ duro

ruin /'ru:ɪn/ [1] *n* rovina *f*; **in** ~**s** in rovina
[2] *vt* rovinare

ruined /'ru:ɪnd/ *adj* ⟨*building, clothes*⟩ rovinato

ruinous /'ru:məs/ *adj* estremamente costoso

rule /ru:l/ [1] *n* regola *f*; (control) ordinamento *m*; (for measuring) metro *m*; ~**s** *pl* regolamento *msg*; **as a** ~ generalmente; **make it a** ~ **to do something** fare qualcosa sistematicamente
[2] *vt* governare; dominare ⟨*colony, behaviour*⟩; ~ **that** stabilire che
[3] *vi* governare
■ **rule out** *vt* escludere

ruled /ru:ld/ *adj* ⟨*paper*⟩ a righe

rule of thumb *n* principio *m* empirico

ruler /'ru:lə(r)/ *n* capo *m* di Stato; (sovereign) sovrano, -a *mf*; (measure) righello *m*, regolo *m*

ruling /'ru:lɪŋ/ [1] *adj* ⟨*class*⟩ dirigente; ⟨*party*⟩ di governo
[2] *n* decisione *f*

rum[1] /rʌm/ *n* rum *m inv*

rum[2] *adj* (fam: peculiar) curioso

rumble /'rʌmbl/ [1] *n* rombo *m*; (of stomach) brontolio *m*
[2] *vi* rombare; ⟨*stomach*⟩ brontolare

rumble strip *n* banda *f* rumorosa

rumbustious /rʌm'bʌstʃəs/ *adj* (noisy, very lively) chiassoso

ruminant /'ru:mɪnənt/ *n* ruminante *m*

ruminate /'ru:mɪneɪt/ *vi* ⟨*animals*⟩ ruminare; (think) rimuginare

rummage /'rʌmɪdʒ/ *vi* rovistare (**in/through** in)

rummy /'rʌmɪ/ *n* ramino *m*

rumour /'ru:mə(r)/ [1] *n* diceria *f*
[2] *vt* **it is** ~**ed that** si dice che

rumour-monger /'ru:məmʌŋgə(r)/ *n* persona *f* che sparge pettegolezzi

rump /rʌmp/ *n* natiche *fpl*

rumple /'rʌmpl/ *vt* sgualcire ⟨*clothes, sheets, papers*⟩; scompigliare ⟨*hair*⟩

rump steak *n* bistecca *f* di girello

rumpus /'rʌmpəs/ *n* fam baccano *m*

run /rʌn/ [1] *n* (on foot) corsa *f*; (distance to be covered) tragitto *m*; (outing) giro *m*; Theat rappresentazioni *fpl*; (in skiing) pista *f*; (Am: ladder) smagliatura *f* (in calze); **at a** ~ di corsa; ~ **of bad luck** periodo *m* sfortunato; **on the** ~ in fuga; **have the** ~ **of** avere a disposizione; **in the long** ~ a lungo termine
[2] *vi* (pt **ran**, pp **run**, pres p **running**) correre; ⟨*river*⟩ scorrere; ⟨*nose, makeup*⟩ colare; ⟨*bus*⟩ fare servizio; ⟨*play*⟩ essere in cartellone; ⟨*colours*⟩ sbiadire; (in election) presentarsi [come candidato]; ⟨*software*⟩ girare; ~ **aground** insabbiarsi; ~ **low on**, ~ **short of** essere a corto di
[3] *vt* (manage) dirigere; tenere ⟨*house*⟩; (drive) dare un passaggio a; correre ⟨*risk*⟩; Comput lanciare; Journ pubblicare ⟨*article*⟩; (pass) far scorrere ⟨*eyes, hand*⟩; ~ **a temperature** avere la febbre; ~ **a bath** far scorrere l'acqua per il bagno
■ **run about** *vi* ⟨*children*⟩ correre di qua e di là; (be busy) correre
■ **run across** *vt* imbattersi in
■ **run after** *vt* (chase) rincorrere; (romantically) andare dietro a
■ **run along** *vi* (go away) andare via
■ **run away** *vi* scappare [via], andare via di corsa; (from home) scappare di casa
■ **run away with** *vt* scappare con ⟨*lover, money*⟩; **she let her enthusiasm** ~ **away with her** si è lasciata trasportare dall'entusiasmo
■ **run back** [1] *vi* correre indietro
[2] *vt* (transport by car) riaccompagnare
■ **run back over** *vt* (review) rivedere
■ **run down** [1] *vi* ⟨*clock*⟩ scaricarsi; ⟨*stocks*⟩ esaurirsi
[2] *vt* Auto investire; (reduce) esaurire; (fam: criticize) denigrare
■ **run in** *vi* entrare di corsa
■ **run into** *vi* (meet) imbattersi in; (knock against) urtare
■ **run off** [1] *vi* scappare [via], andare via di corsa; (from home) scappare di casa
[2] *vt* stampare ⟨*copies*⟩
■ **run off with** *vt* = RUN AWAY WITH
■ **run on** *vi* ⟨*meeting*⟩ protrarsi; ⟨*person*⟩ chiacchierare senza sosta
■ **run out** *vi* uscire di corsa; ⟨*supplies, money*⟩ esaurirsi; ~ **out of** rimanere senza
■ **run over** [1] *vi* correre; (overflow) traboccare
[2] *vt* (review) dare una scorsa a; Auto investire

■ **run through** *vt* (use up) fare fuori; (be present in) pervadere; (review) dare una scorsa a

■ **run to** *vt* (be enough for) essere sufficiente per; (have enough money for) potersi permettere

■ **run up** **1** *vi* salire di corsa; (towards) arrivare di corsa
2 *vt* accumulare ⟨*debts, bill*⟩; (sew) cucire

■ **run up against** *vt* incontrare ⟨*difficulties*⟩

runabout *n* (vehicle) utilitaria *f*

run-around *n* he's giving me/her the ∼ mi/la sta menando per il naso

runaway **1** *n* fuggitivo, -a *mf*, fuggiasco, -a *mf*; (child) ragazzo, -a *mf* scappato, -a di casa
2 *adj* ⟨*person*⟩ in fuga; ⟨*child*⟩ scappato di casa; ⟨*inflation*⟩ galoppante; ⟨*success*⟩ eclatante

run-down **1** *adj* ⟨*area*⟩ in abbandono; ⟨*person*⟩ esaurito
2 *n* analisi *f inv*

rung[1] /rʌŋ/ *n* (of ladder) piolo *m*

rung[2] ▶ RING[2]

run-in *n* (fam: argument) lite *f*

runner /'rʌnə(r)/ *n* podista *mf*; (in race) corridore, -trice *mf*; (on sledge) pattino *f*; (carpet) guida *f*

runner bean *n* fagiolino *m*

runner-up *n* secondo, -a classificato, -a *mf*

running /'rʌnɪŋ/ **1** *adj* in corsa; ⟨*water*⟩ corrente; **four times** ∼ quattro volte di seguito
2 *n* corsa *f*; (management) direzione *f*; **be in the** ∼ essere in lizza

running battle *n* lotta *f* continua

running commentary *n* cronaca *f*

running total *n* totale *m* aggiornato

runny /'rʌnɪ/ *adj* semiliquido; ∼ **nose** naso *m* che cola

run-of-the-mill *adj* ordinario

runs /rʌnz/ *npl* the ∼ (fam: diarrhoea) la sciolta

runt /rʌnt/ *n* (of litter) cucciolo *m* più piccolo e debole di una figliata; (pej: weakling) mezza cartuccia *f*

run-through *n* prova *f* generale

run-up *n* Sport rincorsa *f*; the ∼ to il periodo precedente

runway /'rʌnweɪ/ *n* pista *f*

rupee /ruː'piː/ *n* rupia *f*

rupture /'rʌptʃə(r)/ **1** *n* rottura *f*; Med ernia *f*
2 *vt* rompere; ∼ **oneself** farsi venire l'ernia

3 *vi* rompersi

rural /'rʊərəl/ *adj* rurale

ruse /ruːz/ *n* astuzia *f*

rush[1] /rʌʃ/ *n* Bot giunco *m*

rush[2] **1** *n* fretta *f*; **in a** ∼ di fretta
2 *vi* precipitarsi
3 *vt* far premura a; ∼ **somebody to hospital** trasportare qualcuno di corsa all'ospedale

■ **rush away**, **rush off** *vi* andar via in fretta

■ **rush into** *vt* ∼ **into marriage** sposarsi senza riflettere; ∼ **into doing something** lanciarsi a fare qualcosa senza riflettere; ∼ **somebody into doing something** spingere qualcuno a fare qualcosa

■ **rush out** *vi* uscire di corsa

■ **rush through** *vt* svolgere in fretta ⟨*task*⟩; ∼ **something through** fare approvare qualcosa in fretta ⟨*legislation, order*⟩

rush hour **1** *n* ora *f* di punta
2 *attrib* delle ore di punta

rusk /rʌsk/ *n* biscotto *m*

russet /'rʌsɪt/ *adj* rossastro

Russia /'rʌʃə/ *n* Russia *f*

Russian /'rʌʃən/ *adj* & *n* russo, -a *mf*; (language) russo *m*

Russian roulette *n* roulette *f* russa

rust /rʌst/ **1** *n* ruggine *f*
2 *vi* arrugginirsi
3 *vt* arrugginire

rustic /'rʌstɪk/ *adj* rustico

rustle /'rʌsl/ **1** *vi* frusciare
2 *vt* far frusciare; Am rubare ⟨*cattle*⟩

■ **rustle up** *vt* fam fare ⟨*meal, cup of coffee*⟩

rustler /'rʌslə(r)/ *n* ladro *m* di bestiame

rustproof /'rʌstpruːf/ *adj* a prova di ruggine

rusty /'rʌstɪ/ *adj* (**-ier**, **-iest**) arrugginito

rut /rʌt/ *n* solco *m*; **in a** ∼ fam nella routine

ruthless /'ruːθlɪs/ *adj* spietato

ruthlessly /'ruːθlɪslɪ/ *adv* spietatamente

ruthlessness /'ruːθlɪsnɪs/ *n* spietatezza *f*

rutting /'rʌtɪŋ/ *n* accoppiamento *m*

rutting season *n* stagione *f* degli amori

RV *n abbr* Am (**recreational vehicle**) camper *m*

Rwanda /ruː'ændə/ *n* Rwanda *m*

rye /raɪ/ *n* segale *f*

rye bread *n* pane *m* di segale

Ss

s¹, S /es/ n (letter) s, S f inv

S² abbr **small**; abbr (**south**) S

sabbath /'sæbəθ/ n domenica f; (Jewish) sabato m

sabbatical /sə'bætɪkl/ n Univ anno m sabbatico

sable /'seɪbl/ n (animal, fur) zibellino m

sabotage /'sæbətɑːʒ/ **1** n sabotaggio m **2** vt sabotare

saboteur /sæbə'tɜː(r)/ n sabotatore, -trice mf

sabre /'seɪbə(r)/ n sciabola f

sac /sæk/ n Anat, Zool sacco m; Bot sacca f; **honey ~** cestella f

saccharin /'sækərɪn/ n saccarina f

sachet /'sæʃeɪ/ n bustina f; (scented) sacchetto m profumato

sack¹ /sæk/ vt (plunder) saccheggiare

sack² **1** n sacco m; **get the ~** fam essere licenziato; **give somebody the ~** licenziare qualcuno **2** vt fam licenziare

sackcloth /'sækklɒθ/ n tela f di sacco; **wear ~ and ashes** cospargersi il capo di cenere

sackful /'sækfʊl/ n sacco m (contenuto)

sacking /'sækɪŋ/ n tela f per sacchi; (fam: dismissal) licenziamento m

sackload /'sækləʊd/ n sacco m (contenuto)

sacrament /'sækrəmənt/ n sacramento m

sacred /'seɪkrɪd/ adj sacro

sacred cow /kaʊ/ n (institution) istituzione f intoccabile; (principle) principio m inderogabile; (person) mostro m sacro

sacrifice /'sækrɪfaɪs/ **1** n sacrificio m **2** vt sacrificare; **~ oneself** immolarsi

sacrificial /sækrɪ'fɪʃəl/ adj ⟨victim⟩ sacrificale

sacrilege /'sækrɪlɪdʒ/ n sacrilegio m

sacrilegious /sækrɪ'lɪdʒəs/ adj sacrilego

sacristy /'sækrɪstɪ/ n sagrestia f

sacrosanct /'sækrəʊsæŋkt/ adj sacrosanto

sacrum /'sækrʌm/ n Anat osso m sacro

SAD n abbr (**seasonal affective disorder**) Med disturbi mpl affettivi stagionali

sad /sæd/ adj (**sadder, saddest**) triste

sadden /'sædn/ vt rattristare

saddle /'sædl/ **1** n sella f; **be in the ~** fig tenere le redini **2** vt sellare; **I've been ~d with...** fig mi hanno affibbiato...

sadism /'seɪdɪzm/ n sadismo m

sadist /'seɪdɪst/ n sadico, -a mf

sadistic /sə'dɪstɪk/ adj sadico

sadistically /sə'dɪstɪklɪ/ adv sadicamente

sadly /'sædlɪ/ adv tristemente; (unfortunately) sfortunatamente

sadness /'sædnɪs/ n tristezza f

sadomasochism /seɪdəʊ'mæsəkɪzm/ n sadomasochismo m

sadomasochist /seɪdəʊ'mæsəkɪst/ n sadomasochista m

sadomasochistic /seɪdəʊ'mæsəkɪstɪk/ adj sadomasochistico

sae abbr **stamped addressed envelope**

safari /sə'fɑːrɪ/ n safari m inv

safari park n zoosafari m inv

safe /seɪf/ **1** adj sicuro; (out of danger) salvo; ⟨object⟩ al sicuro; **~ and sound** sano e salvo **2** n cassaforte f

safe bet n **it's a ~ ~ that he will come** è certo che verrà

safe-breaker n scassinatore, -trice mf

safe-conduct n salvacondotto m

safe-deposit box safety-deposit box n cassetta f di sicurezza

safeguard /'seɪfgɑːd/ **1** n protezione f **2** vt proteggere

safe house n rifugio m

safe keeping n custodia f; **for ~ ~** in custodia

safely /'seɪflɪ/ adv in modo sicuro; ⟨arrive⟩ senza incidenti; ⟨assume⟩ con certezza

safe sex n sesso m sicuro

safety /'seɪftɪ/ n sicurezza f

safety belt n cintura f di sicurezza

safety catch n sicura f

safety curtain n tagliafuoco m

safety-deposit box n = SAFE-DEPOSIT BOX

safety glass n vetro m di sicurezza

safety net n (for acrobat) rete f di protezione; fig protezione

safety pin n spilla f di sicurezza o da balia

safety razor n rasoio m di sicurezza

safety valve n valvola f di sicurezza; fig valvola f di sfogo

saffron /'sæfrən/ n zafferano m

sag /sæg/ vi (pt/pp **sagged**) abbassarsi

saga /'sɑːgə/ n saga f

sagacity /sə'gæsətɪ/ n sagacia f

sage[1] /seɪdʒ/ n (herb) salvia f

sage[2] adj & n saggio, -a mf

sagely /'seɪdʒlɪ/ adv ⟨reply, nod⟩ saggiamente

Sagittarius /sædʒɪ'teərɪəs/ n Sagittario m

sago /'seɪgəʊ/ n sagù m

Sahara /sə'hɑːrə/ n Sahara m

said /sed/ ▶SAY

sail /seɪl/ ① n vela f; (trip) giro m in barca a vela
② vi navigare; Sport praticare la vela; (leave) salpare
③ vt pilotare
■ **sail through** vt superare senza problemi ⟨exam⟩

sailboard /'seɪlbɔːd/ n tavola f da windsurf

sailboarder /'seɪlbɔːdə(r)/ n windsurfista mf

sailboarding /'seɪlbɔːdɪŋ/ n windsurf m inv

sailboat /'seɪlbəʊt/ n Am barca f a vela

sailing /'seɪlɪŋ/ n vela f

sailing boat n barca f a vela

sailing ship n veliero m

sailor /'seɪlə(r)/ n marinaio m

saint /seɪnt/ n santo, -a mf

sainthood /'seɪnthʊd/ n santità f

saintly /'seɪntlɪ/ adj da santo

sake /seɪk/ n for the ~ of ⟨person⟩ per il bene di; ⟨peace⟩ per amor di; for the ~ of it per il gusto di farlo

salacious /sə'leɪʃəs/ adj ⟨joke⟩ salace; ⟨book⟩ licenzioso; ⟨look⟩ lascivo

salad /'sæləd/ n insalata f

salad bar n tavola f fredda

salad bowl n insalatiera f

salad cream n salsa f per condire l'insalata

salad days npl anni mpl verdi

salad dressing n condimento m per insalata

salami /sə'lɑːmɪ/ n salame m

salaried /'sælərɪd/ adj stipendiato

salary /'sælərɪ/ n stipendio m

salary review n revisione f dello stipendio

salary scale n tabella f retributiva

sale /seɪl/ n vendita f; (at reduced prices) svendita f; for/on ~ in vendita; 'for ~' 'vendesi'

sale price n prezzo m scontato

sales and marketing n vendite fpl e marketing

sales and marketing department n ufficio m vendite e marketing

sales assistant n commesso, -a mf

sales director n capo mf dell'ufficio vendite

sales engineer n tecnico m commerciale

sales executive n direttore, -trice mf commerciale

sales figures npl volumi mpl d'affari

sales force n rappresentanti mpl

sales invoice n fattura f di vendita

sales ledger n partitario m vendite

salesman n venditore m; (traveller) rappresentante m

sales pitch n discorso m imbonitore

sales rep, **sales representative** n rappresentante mf di commercio

salesroom n (for auctions) sala f d'aste

sales team n team m inv vendite

saleswoman n venditrice f

salient /'seɪlɪənt/ adj saliente

saline /'seɪlaɪn/ adj salino

saliva /sə'laɪvə/ n saliva f

salivary glands /sə'laɪvərɪ/ npl ghiandole fpl salivari

salivate /'sælɪveɪt/ vi salivare; the smell of chicken roasting makes me ~ l'odore di pollo arrosto mi fa venire l'acquolina in bocca

sallow /'sæləʊ/ adj giallastro

sally /'sælɪ/ ① n (witty remark) battuta f; Mil sortita f
② vi saltar fuori

salmon /'sæmən/ n salmone m

salmonella /sælmə'nelə/ n salmonella f

salmon-pink adj [rosa inv] salmone inv

salmon trout n trota f salmonata

salon /'sælɒn/ n salone m

saloon /sə'luːn/ n Auto berlina f; (Am: bar) bar m

salsa /'sælsə/ n salsa f

salt /sɔːlt/ ① n sale m
② adj salato; ⟨fish, meat⟩ sotto sale
③ vt salare; ⟨cure⟩ mettere sotto sale

salt cellar n saliera f

saltiness /'sɔːltɪnɪs/ n salinità f

salt water n acqua f di mare

salt-water fish n pesce m d'acqua salata

salty /'sɔːltɪ/ adj salato

salubrious /sə'luːbrɪəs/ adj ⟨neighbourhood⟩ raccomandabile; it's not a very ~ area è una zona poco raccomandabile

salutary /'sæljʊtərɪ/ adj salutare

salute /səˈluːt/ Mil **1** *n* saluto *m*
2 *vt* salutare
3 *vi* fare il saluto

salvage /ˈsælvɪdʒ/ **1** *n* Naut recupero *m*
2 *vt* recuperare

salvation /sælˈveɪʃn/ *n* salvezza *f*

Salvation Army *n* Esercito *m* della
Salvezza

salve /sælv/ *vt* ~ one's conscience
mettersi la coscienza a posto

salver /ˈsælvə(r)/ *n* vassoio *m* (di
metallo)

salvo /ˈsælvəʊ/ *n* salva *f*

Samaritan /səmˈærɪtən/ *n* a good ~ un
buon samaritano; the ~s ≈ telefono *m*
amico

samba /ˈsæmbə/ *n* samba *f*

same /seɪm/ **1** *adj* stesso (as di)
2 *pron* the ~ lo stesso; be all the ~
essere tutti uguali
3 *adv* the ~ nello stesso modo; all the ~
(however) lo stesso; the ~ to you altrettanto

same-day *adj* ⟨service⟩ in giornata

same-day delivery *n* consegna *f* in
giornata

sample /ˈsɑːmpl/ **1** *n* campione *m*
2 *vt* testare

sanatorium /sænəˈtɔːrɪəm/ *n* casa *f* di
cura

sanctify /ˈsæŋktɪfaɪ/ *vt* (pt/pp **-fied**)
santificare

sanctimonious /sæŋktɪˈməʊnɪəs/ *adj*
moraleggiante

sanction /ˈsæŋkʃn/ **1** *n* (approval)
autorizzazione *f*; (penalty) sanzione *f*
2 *vt* autorizzare

sanctity /ˈsæŋktətɪ/ *n* santità *f*

sanctuary /ˈsæŋktjʊərɪ/ *n* Relig
santuario *m*; (refuge) asilo *m*; (for wildlife)
riserva *f*

sanctum /ˈsæŋktəm/ *n* (holy place)
santuario *m*; (private place) rifugio *m*; the
inner ~ Relig il Sancta Sanctorum

sand /sænd/ **1** *n* sabbia *f*
2 *vt* ~ [down] carteggiare

sandal /ˈsændl/ *n* sandalo *m*

sandbag *n* sacchetto *m* di sabbia

sandbank *n* banco *m* di sabbia

sandblast *vt* sabbiare

sandblasting *n* sabbiatura *f*

sandcastle *n* castello *m* di sabbia

sand dune *n* duna *f*

sander /ˈsændə(r)/ *n* (machine) levigatrice
f

Sandinista /sændɪˈniːstə/ *adj* & *n*
sandinista

sandpaper **1** *n* carta *f* vetrata
2 *vt* cartavetrare

sandpit *n* recinto *m* contenente sabbia
dove giocano i bambini

sandstone *n* arenaria *f*

sandstorm *n* tempesta *f* di sabbia

sandwich /ˈsænwɪdʒ/ **1** *n* tramezzino
m
2 *vt* ~ed **between** schiacciato tra

sandwich bar *n* locale *m* in cui si
comprano sandwich e panini pronti o su
ordinazione

sandwich course *n* corso *m* che
comprende dei periodi di tirocinio

sandwich-man *n* uomo *m* sandwich

sandy /ˈsændɪ/ *adj* (**-ier**, **-iest**) ⟨beach,
soil⟩ sabbioso; ⟨hair⟩ biondiccio

sane /seɪn/ *adj* (not mad) sano di mente;
(sensible) sensato

sang /sæŋ/ ▶ SING

sangria /sæŋˈgrɪə/ *n* sangria *f*

sanguine /ˈsæŋgwɪn/ *adj* ottimistico

sanitary /ˈsænɪtərɪ/ *adj* igienico;
⟨system⟩ sanitario

sanitary napkin *n* Am, **sanitary
towel** assorbente *m* igienico

sanitation /sænɪˈteɪʃn/ *n* impianti *mpl*
igienici

sanity /ˈsænətɪ/ *n* sanità *f* di mente;
(sensibleness) buon senso *m*

sank /sæŋk/ ▶ SINK

Santa [Claus] /ˈsæntə[klɔːz]/ *n* Babbo
m Natale

sap /sæp/ **1** *n* Bot linfa *f*
2 *vt* (pt/pp **sapped**) indebolire

sapling /ˈsæplɪŋ/ *n* alberello *m*

sapper /ˈsæpə(r)/ *n* Br Mil geniere *m*

sapphire /ˈsæfaɪə(r)/ **1** *n* zaffiro *m*
2 *attrib* blu zaffiro *inv*

sarcasm /ˈsɑːkæzm/ *n* sarcasmo *m*

sarcastic /sɑːˈkæstɪk/ *adj* sarcastico

sarcastically /sɑːˈkæstɪklɪ/ *adv*
sarcasticamente

sarcophagus /sɑːˈkɒfəgəs/ *n* sarcofago
m

sardine /sɑːˈdiːn/ *n* sardina *f*

Sardinia /sɑːˈdɪnɪə/ *n* Sardegna *f*

Sardinian /sɑːˈdɪnɪən/ *adj* & *n* sardo, -a
mf

sardonic /sɑːˈdɒnɪk/ *adj* sardonico

sardonically /sɑːˈdɒnɪklɪ/ *adv*
sardonicamente

sari /ˈsɑːrɪ/ *n* sari *m inv*

sarong /səˈrɒŋ/ *n* pareo *m*

SARS /sɑːz/ *n abbr* (**severe acute
respiratory syndrome**) SARS *f*

SAS *n* Br abbr (**Special Air Service**)
commando *mpl* britannico per operazioni
speciali

sash /sæʃ/ *n* fascia *f*; (for dress) fusciacca *f*

sashay /ˈsæʃeɪ/ *vi* fam (casually)
camminare in modo disinvolto; (seductively)
camminare in modo provocante

S

sassy /'sæsɪ/ adj Am fam (cheeky) sfacciato; (smart) chic inv

sat /sæt/ ▶ SIT

Satan /'seɪtən/ n Satana m

satanic /sə'tænɪk/ adj satanico

satchel /'sætʃl/ n cartella f

sated /'seɪtɪd/ adj ⟨person⟩ sazio; ⟨desire⟩ appagato; ⟨appetite⟩ soddisfatto

satellite /'sætəlaɪt/ n satellite m

satellite channel n rete f televisiva satellitare

satellite dish n antenna f parabolica

satellite television n televisione f satellitare

satiate /'seɪʃɪeɪt/ vt saziare ⟨person⟩; appagare ⟨desire⟩; soddisfare ⟨appetite⟩

satin /'sætɪn/ ① n raso m
② attrib di raso

satire /'sætaɪə(r)/ n satira f

satirical /sə'tɪrɪkl/ adj satirico

satirically /sə'tɪrɪklɪ/ adv satiricamente

satirist /'sætərɪst/ n scrittore, -trice mf satirico, -a; (comedian) comico, -a mf satirico, -a

satirize /'sætɪraɪz/ vt satireggiare

satisfaction /sætɪs'fækʃn/ n soddisfazione f; be to sb's ∼ soddisfare qualcuno

satisfactorily /sætɪs'fækt(ə)rɪlɪ/ adv in modo soddisfacente

satisfactory /sætɪs'fæktərɪ/ adj soddisfacente

satisfied /'sætɪsfaɪd/ adj (pleased) soddisfatto; ∼ with soddisfatto di; (convinced) convinto; ∼ that convinto che

satisfy /'sætɪsfaɪ/ vt (pt/pp -ied) soddisfare; (convince) convincere

satisfying /'sætɪsfaɪɪŋ/ adj soddisfacente

SATs /sæts/ npl abbr Br (**standard assessment tasks**) esami mpl sostenuti per tranche d'età allo scopo di testare la preparazione degli alunni

saturate /'sætʃəreɪt/ vt inzuppare (with di); Chem, fig saturare (with di)

saturated /'sætʃəreɪtɪd/ adj saturo

saturation /sætʃə'reɪʃn/ n reach ∼ point raggiungere il punto di saturazione

Saturday /'sætədeɪ/ n sabato m

Saturn /'sætən/ n Saturno m

sauce /sɔːs/ n salsa f; (cheek) impertinenza f

saucepan /'sɔːspən/ n pentola f

saucer /'sɔːsə(r)/ n piattino m

saucy /'sɔːsɪ/ adj (-ier, -iest) impertinente

Saudi /'saʊdɪ/ ① adj saudita
② n (person) saudita mf; (country) Arabia f Saudita

Saudi Arabia /ə'reɪbɪə/ n Arabia f Saudita

Saudi Arabian adj & n saudita mf

sauerkraut /'saʊəkraʊt/ n crauti mpl

sauna /'sɔːnə/ n sauna f

saunter /'sɔːntə(r)/ vi andare a spasso

sausage /'sɒsɪdʒ/ n salsiccia f; (dried) salame m

sausage dog /'sɒsɪdʒdɒg/ n fam bassotto m

sausage roll n involtino m di pasta sfoglia con salsiccia

sauté /'səʊteɪ/ ① vt rosolare
② adj rosolato

savage /'sævɪdʒ/ ① adj feroce; ⟨tribe, custom⟩ selvaggio
② n selvaggio, -a mf
③ vt fare a pezzi

savagely /'sævɪdʒlɪ/ adv ⟨attack⟩ selvaggiamente; ⟨criticize⟩ ferocemente

savagery /'sævɪdʒrɪ/ n ferocia f

save /seɪv/ ① n Sport parata f
② vt salvare (from da); (keep, collect) tenere; risparmiare ⟨time, money⟩; (avoid) evitare; Sport parare ⟨goal⟩; Comput salvare, memorizzare; ∼ face salvar la faccia
③ vi ∼ [up] risparmiare
④ prep salvo

saver /'seɪvə(r)/ n risparmiatore, -trice mf

saving grace /seɪvɪŋ'greɪs/ n that's his one ∼ ∼ si salva grazie a questo

savings /'seɪvɪŋz/ npl (money) risparmi mpl

savings account n libretto m di risparmio

savings and loan association n Am associazione f mutua di risparmi e prestiti

savings bank n cassa f di risparmio

saviour /'seɪvjə(r)/ n salvatore m

savoir faire /sævwɑː'feə(r)/ n (social) savoir-faire m

savory /'seɪvərɪ/ n Bot santoreggia f

savour /'seɪvə(r)/ ① n sapore m
② vt assaporare

savoury /'seɪvərɪ/ adj salato; fig rispettabile

saw[1] /sɔː/ ▶ SEE[1]

saw[2] ① n sega f
② vt (pt **sawed**, pp **sawn** or **sawed**) segare

sawdust /'sɔːdʌst/ n segatura f

sawmill /'sɔːmɪl/ n segheria f

sawn-off shotgun /'sɔːn/ n fucile m a canne mozze

Saxon /'sæksən/ adj & n sassone mf; (language) sassone m

saxophone /'sæksəfəʊn/ n sassofono m

saxophonist /sæk'sɒfənɪst/ *n* sassofonista *mf*

say /seɪ/ **1** *n* have one's ∼ dire la propria; have a ∼ avere voce in capitolo **2** *vt/i* (pt/pp **said**) dire; that is to ∼ cioè; that goes without ∼ing questo è ovvio; when all is said and done alla fine dei conti; ∼ yes/no dire di sì/no; just ∼ the word and I'll come tu chiama e io vengo; what more can I ∼? che altro dire?; some time next week ∼? la prossima settimana, diciamo?; the clock ∼s ten to six la sveglia fa le sei meno dieci; you can ∼ that again! puoi dirlo forte!; the tree is said to be very old a quanto pare l'albero è vecchissimo; he said you were to bring thè car ha detto che dovevi portare la macchina; it ∼s a lot for him that... il fatto che... la dice lunga sul suo conto; what have you got to ∼ for yourself? che scusa hai?; to ∼ nothing of... per non parlare di..., what would you ∼ to a new car? cosa ne diresti di una macchina nuova?

saying /'seɪŋ/ *n* proverbio *m*

scab /skæb/ *n* crosta *f*; pej crumiro *m*

scabby /'skæbɪ/ *adj* ⟨*plant*⟩ coperto di galle; ⟨*skin*⟩ coperto di croste; ⟨*animal*⟩ rognoso; (fam: nasty) schifoso

scaffold /'skæfəld/ *n* patibolo *m*

scaffolding /'skæfəldɪŋ/ *n* impalcatura *f*

scalar /'skeɪlə(r)/ *adj* scalare

scald /skɔːld/ **1** *vt* scottare; (milk) scaldare
2 *n* scottatura *f*

scalding /'skɔːldɪŋ/ *adj* bollente

scale¹ /skeɪl/ *n* (of fish) scaglia *f*

scale² **1** *n* scala *f*; on a grand ∼ su vasta scala; to ∼ in scala; ∼ of values scala *f* di valori
2 *vt* (climb) scalare
■ **scale down** *vt* diminuire

scale drawing *n* disegno *m* in scala

scale model *n* modello *m* in scala

scales /skeɪlz/ *npl* (for weighing) bilancia *fsg*

scallop /'skɒləp/ **1** *n* (in sewing) smerlo *m*, festone *m*; Zool pettine *m*; Culin cappasanta *f*
2 *vt* (in sewing) smerlare; ∼ed potatoes patate *fpl* gratinate

scalp /skælp/ **1** *n* cuoio *m* capelluto
2 *vt* scalpare

scalpel /'skælpl/ *n* bisturi *m inv*

scaly /'skeɪlɪ/ *adj* ⟨*wing, fish*⟩ squamoso; ⟨*plaster, wall*⟩ scrostato

scam /skæm/ *n* fam fregatura *f*

scamper /'skæmpə(r)/ *vi* ∼ away sgattaiolare via

scampi /'skæmpɪ/ *npl* scampi *mpl*

scan /skæn/ **1** *n* Med scanning *m inv*, scansioscintigrafia *f*
2 *vt* (pt/pp **scanned**) scrutare; (quickly) dare una scorsa a; Med fare uno scanning di; Comput scannerizzare
3 *vi* ⟨*poetry*⟩ scandire

scandal /'skændl/ *n* scandalo *m*; (gossip) pettegolezzi *mpl*

scandalize /'skændəlaɪz/ *vt* scandalizzare

scandalmonger /'skænd(ə)lmʌŋgə(r)/ *n* malalingua *f*

scandalous /'skændələs/ *adj* scandaloso

Scandinavia /skændɪ'neɪvɪə/ *n* Scandinavia *f*

Scandinavian /skændɪ'neɪvɪən/ *adj* & *n* scandinavo, -a *mf*

scanner /'skænə(r)/ *n* Med, Comput scanner *m inv*; (radar) antenna *f* radar; (for bar codes) lettore *m* di codice a barre

scanning /'skænɪŋ/ *n* Comput scannerizzazione *f*

scant /skænt/ *adj* scarso

scantily /'skæntɪlɪ/ *adv* scarsamente; ⟨*clothed*⟩ succintamente

scanty /'skæntɪ/ *adj* (**-ier**, **-iest**) scarso; ⟨*clothing*⟩ succinto

scapegoat /'skeɪpgəʊt/ *n* capro *m* espiatorio

scar /skɑː(r)/ **1** *n* cicatrice *f*
2 *vt* (pt/pp **scarred**) lasciare una cicatrice a

scarce /skeəs/ *adj* scarso; fig raro; make oneself ∼ fam svignarsela

scarcely /'skeəslɪ/ *adv* appena; ∼ anything quasi niente

scarcity /'skeəsətɪ/ *n* scarsezza *f*

scare /skeə(r)/ **1** *n* spavento *m*; (panic) panico *m*
2 *vt* spaventare; be ∼d aver paura (of di)
■ **scare away** *vt* far scappare

scarecrow /'skeəkrəʊ/ *n* spaventapasseri *m inv*

scaremonger /'skeəmʌŋgə(r)/ *n* allarmista *mf*

scaremongering /'skeəmʌŋgərɪŋ/ *n* allarmismo *m*

scarf /skɑːf/ *n* (*pl* **scarves**) sciarpa *f*; (square) foulard *m inv*

scarlet /'skɑːlət/ *adj* scarlatto

scarlet fever *n* scarlattina *f*

scarper /'skɑːpə(r)/ *vi* Br fam squagliarsela

scart connector /skɑːt/ *n* presa *f* scart *inv*

scar tissue *n* tessuto *m* di cicatrizzazione

scary /'skeərɪ/ *adj* be ∼ far paura

scathing /'skeɪðɪŋ/ *adj* mordace

scatter /'skætə(r)/ **1** *vt* spargere; (disperse) disperdere
2 *vi* dispersersi

s

scatterbrained /'skætəbreɪnd/ *adj* fam scervellato

scattered /'skætəd/ *adj* sparso

scatty /'skætɪ/ *adj* (**-ier, -iest**) fam svitato

scavenge /'skævɪndʒ/ *vi* frugare nella spazzatura

scavenger /'skævɪndʒə(r)/ *n* persona *f* che fruga nella spazzatura

scenario /sɪ'nɑːrɪəʊ/ *n* scenario *m*

scene /siːn/ *n* scena *f*; (quarrel) scenata *f*; **behind the** ∼**s** dietro le quinte

scene-of-crime *adj* ⟨*officer, team, investigation*⟩ della polizia scientifica

scenery /'siːnərɪ/ *n* scenario *m*

scenic /'siːnɪk/ *adj* panoramico

scent /sent/ *n* odore *m*; (trail) scia *f*; (perfume) profumo *m*

scented /'sentɪd/ *adj* profumato (**with** di)

sceptic /'skeptɪk/ *n* scettico, -a *mf*

sceptical /'skeptɪkl/ *adj* scettico

sceptically /'skeptɪklɪ/ *adv* in modo scettico

scepticism /'skeptɪsɪzm/ *n* scetticismo *m*

schedule /'ʃedjuːl/ ① *n* piano *m*, programma *m*; (of work) programma *m*; (Am: timetable) orario *m*; **behind** ∼ indietro; **on** ∼ nei tempi previsti; **according to** ∼ secondo i tempi previsti ② *vt* prevedere

scheduled flight /ʃedjuːld'flaɪt/ *n* volo *m* di linea

schematic /skɪ'mætɪk/ *adj* schematico

scheme /skiːm/ ① *n* (plan) piano *m*; (plot) macchinazione *f* ② *vi* pej macchinare

scheming /'skiːmɪŋ/ ① *n* pej macchinazioni *fpl*, intrighi *mpl* ② *adj* ⟨*person*⟩ intrigante

schism /'skɪzm/ *n* scisma *m*

schizophrenia /skɪtsə'friːnɪə/ *n* schizofrenia *f*

schizophrenic *adj* schizofrenico

schmaltzy /'ʃmɒltsɪ/ *adj* sdolcinato

scholar /'skɒlə(r)/ *n* studioso, -a *mf*

scholarly /'skɒləlɪ/ *adj* erudito

scholarship /'skɒləʃɪp/ *n* erudizione *f*; (grant) borsa *f* di studio

scholastic /skə'læstɪk/ *adj* scolastico

school /skuːl/ ① *n* scuola *f*; (in university) facoltà *f*; (of fish) banco *m* ② *vt* addestrare ⟨*animal*⟩

school age *n* **of** ∼ ∼ in età scolare

schoolbag *n* cartella *f* di scuola

schoolboy *n* scolaro *m*

schoolchild *n* scolaro, -a *mf*

schooldays *npl* tempi *mpl* della scuola

school fees *npl* tasse *fpl* scolastiche

schoolfriend *n* compagno, -a *mf* di scuola

schoolgirl *n* scolara *f*

schooling /'skuːlɪŋ/ *n* istruzione *f*

school leaver *n* ≈ neo diplomato, -a *mf*

school-leaving age *n* età *f* della scuola dell'obbligo

school lunch *n* pranzo *m* della mensa scolastica

schoolmaster *n* maestro *m*; (secondary) insegnante *m*

schoolmistress *n* maestra *f*; (secondary) insegnante *f*

school report *n* scheda *f* di valutazione scolastica

schoolteacher *n* insegnante *mf*

schoolwork *n* lavoro *m* scolastico

schooner /'skuːnə(r)/ *n* (Am: glass) boccale *m* da birra; (Br: glass) grande bicchiere *m* da sherry; (boat) goletta *f*

sciatica /saɪ'ætɪkə/ *n* sciatica *f*

science /'saɪəns/ *n* scienza *f*

science fiction *n* fantascienza *f*

scientific /saɪən'tɪfɪk/ *adj* scientifico

scientifically /saɪən'tɪfɪklɪ/ *adv* scientificamente

scientist /'saɪəntɪst/ *n* scienziato, -a *mf*

sci-fi /'saɪfaɪ/ *n* fam fantascienza *f*

scintillate /'sɪntɪleɪt/ *vi* fig brillare

scintillating /'sɪntɪleɪtɪŋ/ *adj* brillante

scissors /'sɪzəz/ *npl* forbici *fpl*

scoff[1] /skɒf/ *vi* ∼ **at** schernire

scoff[2] *vt* fam divorare

scold /skəʊld/ *vt* sgridare

scolding /'skəʊldɪŋ/ *n* sgridata *f*

scollop /'skɒləp/ = SCALLOP

scone /skɒn/ *n* pasticcino *m* da tè

scoop /skuːp/ *n* paletta *f*; Journ scoop *m inv*

■ **scoop out** *vt* svuotare

■ **scoop up** *vt* tirar su

scoot /skuːt/ *vi* fam filare

scooter /'skuːtə(r)/ *n* motoretta *f*

scope /skəʊp/ *n* portata *f*; (opportunity) opportunità *f inv*

scorch /skɔːtʃ/ *vt* bruciare

scorcher /'skɔːtʃə(r)/ *n* fam giornata *f* torrida

scorching /'skɔːtʃɪŋ/ *adj* caldissimo

score /skɔː(r)/ ① *n* punteggio *m*; Mus partitura *f*; (for film, play) musica *f*; **a** ∼ **[of]** (twenty) una ventina [di]; **keep [the]** ∼ tenere il punteggio; **on that** ∼ a questo proposito ② *vt* segnare ⟨*goal*⟩; (cut) incidere ③ *vi* far punti; (in football etc) segnare; (keep score) tenere il punteggio

■ **score out** *vt* cancellare

scoreboard *n* /'skɔ:bɔ:d/ tabellone *m* segnapunti

scorer /'skɔ:rə(r)/ *n* segnapunti *m inv*; (of goals) giocatore, -trice *mf* che segna; **top ~** cannoniere *m*

scorn /skɔ:n/ ① *n* disprezzo *m* ② *vt* disprezzare

scornful /'skɔ:nfʊl/ *adj* sprezzante

scornfully /'skɔ:nfʊlɪ/ *adv* sdegnosamente

Scorpio /'skɔ:pɪəʊ/ *n* Astr Scorpione *m*

scorpion /'skɔ:pɪən/ *n* scorpione *m*

Scot /skɒt/ *n* scozzese *mf*

Scotch /skɒtʃ/ ① *adj* scozzese ② *n* (whisky) whisky *m* [scozzese]

scotch /skɒtʃ/ *vt* far cessare

Scotch egg *n* Br polpetta *f* di salsiccia che racchiude un uovo sodo

Scotch tape *n* Am scotch® *m inv*

scot-free *adj* get off **~** cavarsela impunemente

Scotland /'skɒtlənd/ *n* Scozia *f*

Scots, Scottish /skɒts/, /'skɒtɪʃ/ *adj* scozzese

scoundrel /'skaʊndrəl/ *n* mascalzone *m*

scour[1] /'skaʊə(r)/ *vt* (search) perlustrare

scour[2] *vt* (clean) strofinare

scourer /'skaʊərə(r)/ *n* (pad) paglietta *f*

scourge /skɜ:dʒ/ *n* flagello *m*

scouring pad /'skaʊərɪŋ/ *n* paglietta *f* in lana d'acciaio

Scout *n* [Boy] **~** [boy]scout *m inv*

scout /skaʊt/ ① *n* Mil esploratore *m* ② *vi or* **scout around for** andare in cerca di

scowl /skaʊl/ ① *n* sguardo *m* torvo ② *vi* guardare storto

Scrabble® /'skræbl/ *n* Scarabeo® *m* ■ **scrabble around** *vi* (search) cercare a tastoni

scraggy /'skrægrɪ/ *adj* (**-ier, -iest**) pej scarno

scram /skræm/ *vi* fam levarsi dai piedi

scramble /'skræmbl/ ① *n* (climb) arrampicata *f* ② *vi* (clamber) arrampicarsi; **~ for** azzuffarsi per ③ *vt* Teleph creare delle interferenze in; (eggs) strapazzare

scrambled eggs /'skræmbəld/ *npl* uova *fpl* strapazzate

scrambler /'skræmblə(r)/ *n* (Br: motorcyclist) [moto]crossista *mf*

scrambling /'skræmblɪŋ/ *n* (sport) motocross *m*

scrap[1] /skræp/ *n* (fam: fight) litigio *m*

scrap[2] ① *n* pezzetto *m*; (metal) ferraglia *f*; **~s** *pl* (of food) avanzi *mpl* ② *vt* (pt/pp **scrapped**) buttare via

scrapbook /'skræpbʊk/ *n* album *m inv*

scrape /skreɪp/ *vt* raschiare; (damage) graffiare ■ **scrape by** *vi* (financially) sbarcare il lunario ■ **scrape in** *vi* (to university, school) entrare per il rotto della cuffia ■ **scrape out** *vt* (empty) svuotare ⟨bowl⟩; (clean) scrostare ⟨pan⟩ ■ **scrape through** *vi* passare per un pelo ■ **scrape together** *vt* racimolare

scraper /'skreɪpə(r)/ *n* raschietto *m*

scrap heap *n* be on the **~ ~** fig essere inutile

scrap iron *n* ferraglia *f*

scrap merchant *n* ferrovecchio *m*

scrap paper *n* carta *f* qualsiasi

scrappy /'skræpɪ/ *adj* frammentario

scrapyard /'skræpjɑ:d/ *n* deposito *m* di ferraglia; (for cars) cimitero *m* delle macchine

scratch /skrætʃ/ ① *n* graffio *m*; (to relieve itch) grattata *f*; **start from ~** partire da zero; **up to ~** ⟨work⟩ all'altezza ② *vt* graffiare; (to relieve itch) grattare ③ *vi* grattarsi

scratch card *n* gratta e vinci *m inv*

scratchy /'skrætʃɪ/ *adj* ⟨recording⟩ pieno di fruscii

scrawl /skrɔ:l/ ① *n* scarabocchio *m* ② *vt/i* scarabocchiare

scrawny /'skrɔ:nɪ/ *adj* (**-ier, -iest**) pej magro

scream /skri:m/ ① *n* strillo *m*; **be a ~** fam ⟨situation, film, person⟩ essere uno spasso ② *vt/i* strillare

scree /skri:/ *n* ghiaione *m*

screech /skri:tʃ/ ① *n* stridore *m*; **~ of tyres** sgommata *f* ② *vi* stridere ③ *vt* strillare

screen /skri:n/ ① *n* paravento *m*; Cinema, TV, Comput schermo *m* ② *vt* proteggere; (conceal) riparare; proiettare ⟨film⟩; passare al setaccio ⟨candidates⟩; Med sottoporre a visita medica

screening /'skri:nɪŋ/ *n* Med visita *f* medica; (of film) proiezione *f*

screenplay *n* sceneggiatura *f*

screen saver *n* Comput salvaschermo *m*

screen test *n* Cinema provino *m*

screen-writer *n* Cinema sceneggiatore, -trice *mf*

screw /skru:/ ① *n* vite *f* ② *vt* avvitare; vulg trombare; **~ something to something** avvitare qualcosa a qualcosa ■ **screw up** *vt* (crumple) accartocciare; strizzare ⟨eyes⟩; storcere ⟨face⟩; (sl: bungle) ⋯⋗

mandare all'aria; ~ **up one's courage**
prendere il coraggio a due mani

screwdriver /'skru:draɪvə(r)/ *n*
cacciavite *m inv*

screwed up /skru:d/ *adj* fam incasinato

screw top *n* tappo *m* a vite

screwy /'skru:ɪ/ *adj* (**-ier, -iest**) fam
svitato

scribble /'skrɪbl/ ① *n* scarabocchio *m*
② *vt/i* scarabocchiare

scrimmage /'skrɪmɪdʒ/ *n* (struggle) zuffa
f; (Am: in football) mischia *f*

scrimp /skrɪmp/ *vi* risparmiare; ~ **and**
save risparmiare fino all'osso; ~ **on**
something risparmiare su qualcosa

script /skrɪpt/ *n* scrittura *f*; (of film etc)
sceneggiatura *f*

Scriptures /'skrɪptʃəz/ *npl* Sacre
Scritture *fpl*

scriptwriter /'skrɪptraɪtə(r)/ *n*
sceneggiatore, -trice *mf*

scroll /skrəʊl/ ① *n* rotolo *m* (di
pergamena); (decoration) voluta *f*
② *vi* Comput far scorrere
■ **scroll down** Comput *vi* scorrere in giù
■ **scroll up** Comput *vi* scorrere in su

scroll bar *n* Comput barra *f* di
scorrimento

Scrooge /skru:dʒ/ *n* fam tirchio, -a *mf*

scrotum /'skrəʊtəm/ *n* scroto *m*

scrounge /skraʊndʒ/ *vt/i* scroccare

scrounger /'skraʊndʒə(r)/ *n* scroccone,
-a *mf*

scrub¹ /skrʌb/ *n* (land) boscaglia *f*

scrub² *vt/i* (pt/pp **scrubbed**) strofinare;
(fam: cancel) cancellare ⟨*plan*⟩
■ **scrub up** *vi* ⟨*doctor*⟩ lavarsi; fam ~ **up**
well fare un figurone

scrubbing brush /'skrʌbɪŋ/ *n*
spazzolone *m*

scruff /skrʌf/ *n* **by the** ~ **of the neck** per
la collottola

scruffy /'skrʌfɪ/ *adj* (**-ier, -iest**)
trasandato

scrum /skrʌm/ *n* (in rugby) mischia *f*

scrum half *n* mediano *m* di mischia

scrunch /skrʌntʃ/ ① *vi* ⟨*footsteps in*
snow, tyres⟩ scricchiolare
② *n* scricchiolio *m*
■ **scrunch up** *vt* accartocciare

scrunchie /'skrʌntʃɪ/ *n* fermacoda *m*
inv di stoffa

scruple /'skru:pl/ *n* scrupolo *m*; **have no**
~**s** essere senza scrupoli

scrupulous /'skru:pjʊləs/ *adj*
scrupoloso

scrupulously /'skru:pjʊləslɪ/ *adv*
scrupolosamente

scrutinize /'skru:tɪnaɪz/ *vt* scrutinare

scrutiny /'skru:tɪnɪ/ *n* (look) esame *m*
minuzioso

scuba diver /'sku:bə/ *n* sommozzatore,
-trice *mf*

scuba diving *n* immersione *f*
subacquea

scud /skʌd/ *vi* (pt/pp **scudded**) ⟨*clouds*⟩
muoversi velocemente

scuff /skʌf/ *vt* strascicare ⟨*one's feet*⟩

scuffle /'skʌfl/ *n* tafferuglio *m*

scull /skʌl/ ① *vi* (with two oars) vogare di
coppia; (with one oar) vogare a bratto
② *n* (boat) imbarcazione *f* da regata con
un vogatore

scullery /'skʌlərɪ/ *n* retrocucina *m inv*

sculpt /skʌlpt/ *vt/i* scolpire

sculptor /'skʌlptə(r)/ *n* scultore *m*

sculpture /'skʌlptʃə(r)/ *n* scultura *f*

scum /skʌm/ *n* schiuma *f*; (people) feccia *f*

scurrilous /'skʌrɪləs/ *adj* scurrile

scurry /'skʌrɪ/ *vi* (pt/pp **-ied**) affrettare
il passo

scuttle¹ /'skʌtl/ *n* secchio *m* per il
carbone

scuttle² *vt* affondare ⟨*ship*⟩

scuttle³ *vi* (hurry) ~ **away** correre via

scythe /saɪð/ *n* falce *f*

SE *abbr* (**south-east**) SE

sea /si:/ *n* mare *m*; **at** ~ in mare; fig
confuso; **by** ~ via mare; **by the** ~ sul
mare

seabed *n* fondale *m* marino

seabird *n* uccello *m* marino

seaboard *n* costiera *f*

seafaring *adj* ⟨*nation*⟩ marinaro

seafood *n* frutti *mpl* di mare

seafront *n* lungomare *m*

seagull *n* gabbiano *m*

sea horse *n* cavalluccio *m* marino

SEAL /si:l/ *n abbr* Am (**sea, air, land**)
reparti *mpl* speciali delle forze armate

seal¹ /si:l/ *n* Zool foca *f*

seal² ① *n* sigillo *m*; Techn chiusura *f*
ermetica
② *vt* sigillare; Techn chiudere
ermeticamente
■ **seal off** *vt* bloccare ⟨*area*⟩

sea level *n* livello *m* del mare; **above** ~
~ sopra il livello del mare

sealing wax /'si:lɪŋ/ *n* ceralacca *f*

sea lion *n* leone *m* marino

seam /si:m/ *n* cucitura *f*; (of coal) strato *m*

seaman /'si:mən/ *n* marinaio *m*

seamless /'si:mlɪs/ *adj* senza cucitura

seamy /'si:mɪ/ *adj* ⟨*scandal*⟩ sordido;
⟨*area*⟩ malfamato

seance /'seɪɑ:ns/ *n* seduta *f* spiritica

seaplane /'si:pleɪn/ *n* idrovolante *m*

seaport /'si:pə:t/ *n* porto *m* di mare

sear /sɪə(r)/ *vt* cauterizzare ⟨*wound*⟩; rosolare [a fuoco vivo] ⟨*meat*⟩; (scorch) bruciacchiare

search /sɜ:tʃ/ **1** *n* ricerca *f*; (official) perquisizione *f*; in ~ of alla ricerca di **2** *vt* frugare (**for** alla ricerca di); perlustrare ⟨*area*⟩; (officially) perquisire **3** *vi* ~ **for** cercare

search and replace *n* Comput ricerca *f* e sostituzione

search engine *n* Comput motore *m* di ricerca

searching /'sɜ:tʃɪŋ/ *adj* penetrante

searchlight *n* riflettore *m*

search party *n* squadra *f* di ricerca

search warrant *n* mandato *m* di perquisizione

searing /'sɪərɪŋ/ *adj* bruciante; ⟨*pace*⟩ travolgente; ⟨*pain*⟩ lancinante

sea salt *n* sale *m* marino

seascape *n* paesaggio *m* marino

seashell *n* conchiglia *f*

seashore *n* spiaggia *f*

seasick *adj* be/get ~ avere il mal di mare

seaside *n* at/to the ~ al mare

seaside resort *n* stazione *f* balneare

seaside town *n* città *f* di mare

season /'si:zn/ **1** *n* stagione *f*; In ~ ⟨*fruit*⟩ di stagione; ⟨*animal*⟩ in calore **2** *vt* (flavour) condire

seasonal /'si:zənəl/ *adj* stagionale

seasoned /'si:znd/ *adj* Culin ⟨*dish*⟩ condito; ⟨*timber*⟩ stagionato; ⟨*actor, politician*⟩ consumato; ⟨*leader*⟩ di provata capacità; ~ **traveller** persona *f* che ha viaggiato molto; ~ **soldier** veterano *m*

seasoning /'si:z(ə)nɪŋ/ *n* condimento *m*

season ticket *n* abbonamento *m*

seat /si:t/ **1** *n* (chair) sedia *f*; (in car) sedile *m*; (place to sit) posto *m* [a sedere]; (bottom) didietro *m*; (of government) sede *f*; take a ~ sedersi **2** *vt* mettere a sedere; (have seats for) aver posti [a sedere] per; **remain** ~**ed** mantenere il proprio posto

seat belt *n* cintura *f* di sicurezza; **fasten one's** ~ ~ allacciare la cintura di sicurezza

seating /'si:tɪŋ/ *n* (places) posti *mpl* a sedere; (arrangement) disposizione *f* dei posti a sedere

seating capacity *n* numero *m* dei posti a sedere

sea urchin *n* riccio *m* di mare

sea view *n* vista *f* sul mare

seaweed *n* alga *f* marina

seaworthy *adj* in stato di navigare

sec /sek/ *n* (fam: short instant) attimo *m*, secondo *m*; abbr (**second**) s

secateurs /sekə'tɜ:z/ *npl* cesoie *fpl*

secede /sɪ'si:d/ *vi* staccarsi

secession /sɪ'seʃn/ *n* secessione *f*

secluded /sɪ'klu:dɪd/ *adj* appartato

seclusion /sɪ'klu:ʒn/ *n* isolamento *m*

second[1] /sɪ'kɒnd/ *vt* (transfer) distaccare

second[2] /'sekənd/ **1** *adj* secondo; in ~ gear Auto in seconda; on ~ thoughts ripensandoci meglio; be having ~ thoughts ripensarci; **2** *n* secondo *m*; ~**s** *pl* (goods) merce *fsg* di seconda scelta; have ~**s** (at meal) fare il bis; John the S~ Giovanni Secondo **3** *adv* (in race) al secondo posto **4** *vt* assistere; appoggiare ⟨*proposal*⟩

secondary /'sekəndrɪ/ *adj* secondario

secondary school *n* ≈ scuola *f* media (inferiore e superiore)

second-best *adj* secondo dopo il migliore; be ~ pej essere un ripiego

second-class *adj* di seconda classe

second class *adv* ⟨*travel, send*⟩ in seconda classe

seconder /'sekəndə(r)/ *n* (of motion) persona *f* che appoggia una mozione

second-guess *vt* anticipare

second hand *n* (on watch, clock) lancetta *f* dei secondi

second-hand **1** *adj* ⟨*car, goods, news, information*⟩ di seconda mano; ⟨*clothes*⟩ usato; ⟨*market*⟩ dell'usato; ⟨*opinion*⟩ preso a prestito **2** *adv* ⟨*sell*⟩ di seconda mano

second in command *n* vice *mf inv*; Mil vicecomandante *m*

secondly /'sekəndlɪ/ *adv* in secondo luogo

secondment /sɪ'kɒndmənt/ *n* on ~ in trasferta

second name *n* (surname) cognome *m*; (middle name) secondo nome *m*

second-rate *adj* di second'ordine

secrecy /'si:krəsɪ/ *n* segretezza *f*; in ~ in segreto

secret /'si:krɪt/ **1** *adj* segreto **2** *n* segreto *m*; **make no** ~ **of something** non fare mistero di qualcosa

secret agent *n* agente *m* segreto

secretarial /sekrə'teərɪəl/ *adj* ⟨*work, staff*⟩ di segreteria

secretariat /sekrə'teərɪət/ *n* segretariato *m*

secretary /'sekrətərɪ/ *n* segretario, -a *mf*

Secretary of State *n* Segretario *m* di Stato; Am Pol ministro *m* degli Esteri

secret ballot *n* scrutinio *m* segreto, votazione *f* a scrutinio segreto

secrete /sɪ'kri:t/ vt secernere ⟨poison⟩

secretion /sɪ'kri:ʃn/ n secrezione f

secretive /'si:krətɪv/ adj riservato

secretly /'si:krɪtlɪ/ adv segretamente

secretness /'si:krɪtnɪs/ n riserbo m

secret police n polizia f segreta

secret service n servizi mpl segreti

secret society n società f segreta

secret weapon n arma f segreta

sect /sekt/ n setta f

sectarian /sek'teərɪən/ n & adj settario, -a mf

section /'sekʃn/ n sezione f

sector /'sektə(r)/ n settore m

secular /'sekjʊlə(r)/ adj secolare; ⟨education⟩ laico

secure /sɪ'kjʊə(r)/ **1** adj sicuro
2 vt proteggere; chiudere bene ⟨door⟩; rendere stabile ⟨ladder⟩; (obtain) assicurarsi

securely /sɪ'kjʊəlɪ/ adv saldamente

secure unit n (in psychiatric hospital, prison) reparto m di massima sicurezza

security /sɪ'kjʊərətɪ/ n sicurezza f; (for loan) garanzia f; **securities** pl titoli mpl

Security Council n (of the UN) Consiglio m di Sicurezza

security guard n guardia f giurata

security leak n fuga f di notizie

security risk n be a ~ ~ costituire un pericolo per la sicurezza

sedan /sɪ'dæn/ n Am berlina f

sedate[1] /sɪ'deɪt/ adj posato

sedate[2] vt somministrare sedativi a

sedately /sɪ'deɪtlɪ/ adv in modo posato

sedation /sɪ'deɪʃn/ n somministrazione f di sedativi; **be under** ~ essere sotto l'effetto di sedativi

sedative /'sedətɪv/ **1** adj sedativo
2 n sedativo m

sedentary /'sedəntərɪ/ adj sedentario

sediment /'sedɪmənt/ n sedimento m

seduce /sɪ'dju:s/ vt sedurre

seduction /sɪ'dʌkʃn/ n seduzione f

seductive /sɪ'dʌktɪv/ adj seducente

seductively /sɪ'dʌktɪvlɪ/ adv con aria seducente

see[1] /si:/ **1** vt (pt saw, pp seen) vedere; (understand) capire; (escort) accompagnare; **go and** ~ andare a vedere; (visit) andare a trovare; ~ **you!** ci vediamo!; ~ **you later!** a più tardi!; ~ing **that** visto che; ~ **somebody to the door** accompagnare qualcuno alla porta; **I can't** ~ **myself doing this forever** non mi ci vedo a farlo per sempre; **I can't think what she** ~s **in him** non capisco cosa trovi in lui; ~ **reason** ragionare; **you're** ~ing **things** hai le traveggole

2 vi vedere; (understand) capire; ~ **that** (make sure) assicurarsi che; **let me** ~ fammi pensare; **I** ~ (understand) ho capito
■ **see about** vt occuparsi di
■ **see off** vt salutare alla partenza; (chase away) mandar via
■ **see out** vt ~ **somebody out** accompagnare qualcuno alla porta
■ **see through** **1** vi vedere attraverso; fig non farsi ingannare da
2 vt portare a buon fine
■ **see to** vi occuparsi di

see[2] n Relig diocesi f inv

seed /si:d/ n seme m; Tennis testa f di serie; **go to** ~ fare seme; fig lasciarsi andare

seeded player /'si:dɪd/ n Tennis testa f di serie

seedless /'si:dlɪs/ adj senza semi

seedling /'si:dlɪŋ/ n pianticella f

seedy /'si:dɪ/ adj (-ier, -iest) squallido; **feel** ~ fam sentirsi poco bene

seek /si:k/ vt (pt/pp **sought**) cercare
■ **seek out** vt scovare

seeker /'si:kə(r)/ n ~ **after** or **for something** persona f che è alla ricerca di qualcosa; **gold** ~ cercatore, -trice mf d'oro

seem /si:m/ vi sembrare

seeming /'si:mɪŋ/ adj apparente

seemingly /'si:mɪŋlɪ/ adv apparentemente

seemly /'si:mlɪ/ adj decoroso

seen /si:n/ ▸ SEE[1]

seep /si:p/ vi filtrare

seepage /'si:pɪdʒ/ n (leak: from container) perdita f; Geol trasudamento m superficiale; (trickle) lenta fuoriuscita f; (into structure, soil) infiltrazione f

see-saw /'si:sɔ:/ n altalena f

seethe /si:ð/ vi ~ **with anger** ribollire di rabbia

see-through adj trasparente

segment /'segmənt/ n segmento m; (of orange) spicchio m

segregate /'segrɪgeɪt/ vt segregare

segregated /'segrɪgeɪtɪd/ adj segregazionistico

segregation /segrɪ'geɪʃn/ n segregazione f

seismic /'saɪzmɪk/ adj sismico

seismograph /'saɪzməgrɑ:f/ n sismografo m

seismology /saɪz'mɒlədʒɪ/ n sismologia f

seize /si:z/ vt afferrare; Jur confiscare; ~ **the opportunity** prendere la palla al balzo
■ **seize up** vi Techn bloccarsi

seizure /'si:ʒə(r)/ n Jur confisca f; Med colpo m [apoplettico]

seldom /'seldəm/ adv raramente

select /sɪ'lekt/ ① adj scelto; (exclusive) esclusivo
② vt scegliere; selezionare ‹team›
selection /sɪ'lekʃn/ n selezione f
selective /sɪ'lektɪv/ adj selettivo
selectively /sɪ'lektɪvlɪ/ adv con criterio
selector /sɪ'lektə(r)/ n Sport selezionatore, -trice mf
self /self/ n io m
self-addressed adj con il proprio indirizzo
self-addressed envelope n busta f affrancata con il proprio indirizzo
self-adhesive adj autoadesivo
self-analysis n autoanalisi f
self-assembly adj da montare
self-assurance n sicurezza f di sé
self-assured adj sicuro di sé
self-catering adj in appartamento attrezzato di cucina
self-centred adj egocentrico
self-cleaning adj ‹oven› autopulente
self-confessed adj dichiarato
self-confidence n fiducia f in se stesso
self-confident adj sicuro di sé
self-conscious adj impacciato
self-contained adj ‹flat› con ingresso indipendente
self-control n autocontrollo m
self-defence n autodifesa f; Jur legittima difesa f
self-denial n abnegazione f
self-destruct vi ‹missile, spacecraft› autodistruggersi
self-destruction n autodistruzione f, fig autolesionismo m
self-destructive adj autodistruttivo
self-determination n autodeterminazione f
self-discipline n autodisciplina f
self-disciplined adj disciplinato
self-effacing /-ɪ'feɪsɪŋ/ adj modesto, schivo
self-employed adj che lavora in proprio; **the ~** i lavoratori autonomi
self-esteem n stima f di sé
self-evident adj ovvio
self-explanatory adj **be ~** parlare da sé
self-expression n espressione f della propria personalità
self-financing /-faɪ'nænsɪŋ/ n autofinanziamento m
self-governing /-'gʌvənɪŋ/ adj autonomo
self-government n autogoverno m
self-harm n autolesionismo m
self-help n iniziativa f personale

self-image n immagine f di sé
self-important adj borioso
self-imposed /-ɪm'pəʊzd/ adj autoimposto
self-improvement n crescita f personale
self-induced /-ɪn'djusd/ adj autoindotto
self-indulgent adj indulgente con se stesso
self-inflicted adj **Anna's problems are ~** sono problemi che Anna si è creata da sé; **~ wound** autolesione f
self-interest n interesse m personale
self-interested adj interessato
selfish /'selfɪʃ/ adj egoista
selfishly /'selfɪʃlɪ/ adv egoisticamente
selfishness /'selfɪʃnɪs/ n egoismo m
selfless /'selflɪs/ adj disinteressato
selflessly /'selflɪslɪ/ adv disinteressatamente
selflessness /'selflɪsnɪs/ n disinteresse m
self-locking /-'lɒkɪŋ/ adj ‹door› a chiusura automatica
self-made adj che si è fatto da sé
self-pity n autocommiserazione f
self-portrait n autoritratto m
self-possessed /-pə'zest/ adj padrone di sé
self-preservation n istinto m di conservazione
self-raising flour Br, **self-rising flour** Am /'reɪzɪŋ/, /'raɪzɪŋ/ n farina f contenente lievito
self-reliant adj autosufficiente
self-respect n amor m proprio
self-respecting adj di rispetto
self-righteous adj presuntuoso
self-rising flour Am = SELF-RAISING FLOUR
self-rule n autogoverno m
self-sacrifice n abnegazione f
selfsame adj stesso
self-satisfied adj compiaciuto di sé
self-service ① n self-service m inv ② attrib self-service
self-styled adj sedicente
self-sufficiency n autosufficienza f
self-sufficient adj autosufficiente
self-supporting adj ‹person› indipendente (economicamente)
self-tan n autoabbronzante m
self-tanning /-'tænɪŋ/ adj autoabbronzante
self-taught /-'tɔːt/ adj ‹person› autodidatta
self-willed /-'wɪld/ adj ostinato

S

sell /sel/ **1** *vt* (pt/pp **sold**) vendere; be sold out essere esaurito; ~ somebody on the idea of... fam convincere qualcuno di... **2** *vi* vendersi
■ **sell off** *vt* liquidare
■ **sell out** *vt* (of tickets, goods) andare esaurito; **'sold out'** 'tutto esaurito'; ~ out of something esaurire qualcosa; (on one's principles) vendersi
■ **sell up** *vi* liquidare i propri beni

sell-by date *n* data *f* di scadenza per la vendita

seller /'selə(r)/ *n* venditore, -trice *mf*

sellers' market /'seləzmɑːkɪt/ *n* mercato *m* al rialzo

selling /'selɪŋ/ **1** *adj* ⟨price⟩ di vendita **2** *n* vendita *f*

selling price *n* prezzo *m* di vendita

Sellotape® /'seləʊteɪp/ *n* nastro *m* adesivo, scotch® *m*

sell-out *n* (fam: betrayal) tradimento *m*; be a ~ ⟨concert⟩ fare il tutto esaurito

selvage, selvedge /'selvɪdʒ/ *n* cimosa *f*

selves /selvz/ *pl of* self

semantic /sɪ'mæntɪk/ *adj* semantico

semantics /sɪ'mæntɪks/ *n* (subject) semantica *f*; **that's just** ~ sono solo sfumature di significato

semblance /'sembləns/ *n* parvenza *f*

semen /'siːmən/ *n* Anat liquido *m* seminale

semester /sɪ'mestə(r)/ *n* Am semestre *m*

semi /'semɪ/ *n* (Br: house) villetta *f* bifamiliare; Am Auto autoarticolato *m*

semi+ *pref* semi+

semi-automatic *adj* semiautomatico

semibreve *n* Mus semibreve *f*

semicircle *n* semicerchio *m*

semicircular *adj* semicircolare

semicolon *n* punto e virgola *m*

semiconscious *adj* semiincosciente

semi-darkness *n* semioscurità *f*

semi-detached **1** *adj* gemella **2** *n* casa *f* gemella

semi-final *n* semifinale *f*

semifinalist *n* semifinalista *mf*

seminal /'semɪnəl/ *adj* (major) determinante

seminar /'semɪnɑː(r)/ *n* seminario *m*

seminary /'semɪnərɪ/ *n* seminario *m*

semi-precious *adj* semiprezioso; ~ stone pietra *f* dura

semi-skilled /-'skɪld/ *adj* qualificato

semi-skimmed /-'skɪmd/ *adj* parzialmente scremato

semitone *n* Mus semitono *m*

semolina /semə'liːnə/ *n* semolino *m*

senate /'senət/ *n* senato *m*

senator /'senətə(r)/ *n* senatore *m*

send /send/ *vt/i* (pt/pp **sent**) mandare; (by mail) spedire
■ **send away for** *vt* farsi spedire ⟨information etc⟩
■ **send down** *vt* (send to prison) mandare in galera
■ **send for** *vt* mandare a chiamare ⟨person⟩; far venire ⟨thing⟩
■ **send in** *vt* presentare ⟨application⟩; far entrare ⟨person⟩
■ **send off** *vt* spedire ⟨letter, parcel⟩; espellere ⟨footballer⟩
■ **send on** *vt* spedire ⟨luggage, letter, parcel⟩
■ **send out** *vt* emettere ⟨light, heat⟩; mandare fuori della porta ⟨pupil⟩
■ **send up** *vt* fam parodiare

sender /'sendə(r)/ *n* mittente *mf*; **return to** ~ (on letter) rispedire al mittente

send-off *n* commiato *m*

send-up *n* Br: fam parodia *f*

Senegal /senɪ'gɔːl/ *n* Senegal *m*

senile /'siːnaɪl/ *adj* arteriosclerotico

senile dementia /dɪ'menʃə/ *n* demenza *f* senile

senility /sɪ'nɪlətɪ/ *n* senilismo *m*

senior /'siːnɪə(r)/ **1** *adj* più vecchio; (in rank) superiore **2** *n* (in rank) superiore *mf*; (in sport) senior *mf*; **she's two years my** ~ è più vecchia di me di due anni

senior citizen *n* anziano, -a *mf*

senior high school *n* Am ≈ scuola superiore

seniority /siːnɪ'ɒrətɪ/ *n* anzianità *f* di servizio

senior management *n* alta dirigenza *f*

sensation /sen'seɪʃn/ *n* sensazione *f*; **cause a** ~ fare scalpore

sensational /sen'seɪʃənəl/ *adj* sensazionale

sensationalist /sen'seɪʃənəlɪst/ *adj* ⟨headline, report⟩ sensazionalistico

sensationalize /sen'seɪʃənəlaɪz/ *vt* pej dare un tono scandalistico a

sensationally /sen'seɪʃənəlɪ/ *adv* in modo sensazionale

sense /sens/ **1** *n* senso *m*; (common ~) buon senso *m*; **in a** ~ in un certo senso; **make** ~ aver senso **2** *vt* sentire

senseless /'senslɪs/ *adj* insensato; (unconscious) privo di sensi

senselessly /'senslɪslɪ/ *adv* insensatamente

sensible /'sensəbl/ *adj* sensato; (suitable) appropriato

sensibly /'sensəblɪ/ *adv* in modo appropriato

sensitive /'sensətɪv/ adj sensibile; (touchy) suscettibile

sensitively /'sensətɪvlɪ/ adv con sensibilità

sensitivity /sensə'tɪvətɪ/ n sensibilità f inv

sensitize /'sensɪtaɪz/ vt **become** ∼**d to** (allergic to) diventare ipersensibile a

sensor /'sensə(r)/ n sensore m

sensory /'sensərɪ/ adj sensoriale

sensual /'sensjʊəl/ adj sensuale

sensuality /sensjʊ'ælətɪ/ n sensualità f inv

sensuous /'sensjʊəs/ adj voluttuoso

sent /sent/ ▶ SEND

sentence /'sentəns/ ① n frase f; Jur sentenza f; (punishment) condanna f ② vt ∼ **to** condannare a

sentiment /'sentɪmənt/ n sentimento m; (opinion) opinione f; (sentimentality) sentimentalismo m

sentimental /sentɪ'mentl/ adj sentimentale; pej sentimentalista

sentimentality /sentɪmen'tælətɪ/ n sentimentalità f inv

sentinel /'sentɪnəl/ n sentinella f

sentry /'sentrɪ/ n sentinella f

separable /'sepərəbl/ adj separabile

separate[1] /'sepərət/ adj separato

separate[2] /'sepəreɪt/ ① vt separare ② vi separarsi

separately /'sepərətlɪ/ adv separatamente

separates /'sepərəts/ npl [indumenti npl] coordinati npl

separation /sepə'reɪʃn/ n separazione f

separatist /'sepərətɪst/ n & adj separatista mf

sepia /'siːpɪə/ n (colour) seppia m

September /sep'tembə(r)/ n settembre m

septic /'septɪk/ adj settico; **go** ∼ infettarsi

septicaemia /septɪ'siːmɪə/ n setticemia f

septic tank n fossa f biologica

sequel /'siːkwəl/ n seguito m

sequence /'siːkwəns/ n sequenza f; **in** ∼ nell'ordine giusto

sequential /sɪ'kwenʃəl/ adj sequenziale

sequin /'siːkwɪn/ n lustrino m, paillette f inv

Serb /sɜːb/ adj & n serbo, -a mf

Serbia /'sɜːbɪə/ n Serbia f

Serbian /'sɜːbɪən/ ① n serbo, -a mf; (language) serbo m ② adj serbo

Serbo-Croat[ian] /sɜːbəʊ'krəʊæt/, /ˌsɜːbəʊkrəʊ'eɪʃən/ ① n (language) serbo-croato m ② adj serbo-croato

serenade /serə'neɪd/ ① n serenata f ② vt fare una serenata a

serene /sɪ'riːn/ adj sereno

serenely /sɪ'riːnlɪ/ adv serenamente

serenity /sɪ'renətɪ/ n serenità inv

sergeant /'sɑːdʒənt/ n sergente m

sergeant major n sergente m maggiore

serial /'sɪərɪəl/ ① n racconto m a puntate; TV sceneggiato m a puntate; Radio commedia f radiofonica a puntate ② adj Comput seriale

serialize /'sɪərɪəlaɪz/ vt pubblicare a puntate; Radio, TV trasmettere a puntate

serial killer n serial killer mf inv

serial number n numero m di serie

serial port n Comput porta f seriale

series /'sɪəriːz/ n serie f inv

serious /'sɪərɪəs/ adj serio; ⟨illness, error⟩ grave

seriously /'sɪərɪəslɪ/ adv seriamente; ⟨ill⟩ gravemente; **take** ∼ prendere sul serio

seriousness /'sɪərɪəsnɪs/ n serietà f; (of situation) gravità f

sermon /'sɜːmən/ n predica f

seropositive /sɪərəʊ'pɒzɪtɪv/ adj sieropositivo

serotonin /serə'təʊnɪn/ n serotonina f

serpent /'sɜːpənt/ n serpente m

serrated /se'reɪtɪd/ adj dentellato

serum /'sɪərəm/ n siero m

servant /'sɜːvənt/ n domestico, -a mf

serve /sɜːv/ ① n Tennis servizio m ② vt servire; Jur notificare ⟨writ⟩ (**on** somebody a qualcuno); scontare ⟨sentence⟩; ∼ **its purpose** servire al proprio scopo; **it** ∼**s you right!** ben ti sta!; ∼**s two** per due persone ③ vi prestare servizio; Tennis servire; ∼ **as** servire da

server /'sɜːvə(r)/ n (piece of cutlery) posata f da portata; (plate) piatto m da portata; (tray) vassoio m da portata; Sport giocatore, -trice mf che effettua il servizio; Comput server m inv

service /'sɜːvɪs/ ① n servizio m; Relig funzione f; (maintenance) revisione f; ∼**s** pl forze fpl armate; (on motorway) area f di servizio; **in** ∼ sotto le armi; **of** ∼ **to** utile a; **out of** ∼ ⟨machine⟩ guasto ② vt Techn revisionare

serviceable /'sɜːvɪsəbl/ adj utilizzabile; (hard-wearing) resistente; (practical) pratico

service area n area f di servizio

service centre Br, **service center** Am *n* (garage) officina *f*; (in shop) centro *m* di assistenza tecnica

service charge *n* servizio *m*

service company *n* compagnia *f* del settore terziario

service industry *n* industria *f* terziaria

serviceman *n* militare *m*

service provider *n* Comput fornitore *m* di servizi Internet

service road *n* strada *f* d'accesso

service station *n* stazione *f* di servizio

servicewoman *n* soldatessa *f*

serviette /sɜːvɪˈet/ *n* tovagliolo *m*

servile /ˈsɜːvaɪl/ *adj* servile

servility /səˈvɪlɪtɪ/ *n* servilismo *m*

serving /ˈsɜːvɪŋ/ ① *adj* ⟨officer⟩ di carriera
② *n* (helping) porzione *f*

serving dish *n* piatto *m* da portata

serving spoon *n* cucchiaio *m* da servizio

session /ˈseʃn/ *n* seduta *f*; Jur sessione *f*; Univ anno *m* accademico

set /set/ ① *n* serie *f inv*, set *m inv*; (of crockery, cutlery) servizio *m*; TV, Radio apparecchio *m*; Math insieme *m*; Theat scenario *m*; Cinema, Tennis set *m inv*; (of people) circolo *m*; (of hair) messa *f* in piega
② *adj* (ready) pronto; (rigid) fisso; ⟨book⟩ in programma; **be ⁓ on doing something** essere risoluto a fare qualcosa; **be ⁓ in one's ways** essere abitudinario
③ *vt* (pt/pp **set**, pres p **setting**) mettere, porre; mettere ⟨alarm clock⟩; assegnare ⟨task, homework⟩; fissare ⟨date, limit⟩; chiedere ⟨questions⟩; montare ⟨gem⟩; assestare ⟨bone⟩; apparecchiare ⟨table⟩; Typ comporre; **⁓ fire to** dare fuoco a; **⁓ free** liberare; **⁓ a good example** dare il buon esempio; **⁓ sail for** far vela per; **⁓ in motion** dare inizio a; **⁓ to music** musicare; **the film is ⁓ in Rome/the 18th century** il film è ambientato a Roma/nel XVIII secolo; **⁓ to music** musicare; **⁓ about doing something** mettersi a fare qualcosa
④ *vi* ⟨sun⟩ tramontare; ⟨jelly, concrete⟩ solidificarsi; **⁓ to work (on something)** mettersi al lavoro (su qualcosa)
■ **set apart** *vt* (distinguish) distinguere; **⁓ somebody** or **something apart from** distinguere qualcuno o qualcosa da
■ **set aside** *vt* mettere da parte ⟨money, time⟩; riservare ⟨room, area⟩
■ **set back** *vt* mettere indietro; (hold up) ritardare; (fam: cost) costare a
■ **set down** *vt* (establish) stabilire ⟨rules, conditions⟩; (write down) scrivere ⟨facts⟩
■ **set in** *vi* ⟨rain, infection, recession⟩ prendere piede
■ **set off** ① *vi* partire

② *vt* avviare; mettere ⟨alarm⟩; fare esplodere ⟨bomb⟩
■ **set on** *vt* **⁓ on somebody** (attack) aggredire qualcuno; **⁓ the dogs on somebody** aizzare i cani contro qualcuno
■ **set out** ① *vt* partire; **⁓ out to do something** proporsi di fare qualcosa
② *vt* disporre; (state) esporre
■ **set to** *vi* mettersi all'opera
■ **set up** *vt* fondare ⟨company⟩; istituire ⟨committee⟩

setback /ˈsetbæk/ *n* (hitch) contrattempo *m*; Mil sconfitta *f*, scacco *m*; Fin tracollo *m*; (in health) ricaduta *f*

set design *n* scenografia *f*

set designer *n* scenografo, -a *mf*

set meal *n* menù *m inv* fisso

settee /seˈtiː/ *n* divano *m*

setter /ˈsetə(r)/ *n* (dog) setter *m inv*

setting /ˈsetɪŋ/ *n* scenario *m*; (position) posizione *f*; (of sun) tramonto *m*; (of jewel) montatura *f*

setting-up *n* (of project, business) creazione *f*

settle /ˈsetl/ ① *vt* (decide) definire; risolvere ⟨argument⟩; fissare ⟨date⟩; calmare ⟨nerves⟩; saldare ⟨bill⟩; **that's ⁓d then** allora è deciso
② *vi* (live) stabilirsi; ⟨snow, dust, bird⟩ posarsi; (subside) assestarsi; ⟨sediment⟩ depositarsi
■ **settle down** *vi* sistemarsi; (stop making noise) calmarsi
■ **settle for** *vt* accontentarsi di
■ **settle in** *vi* (in new house, job) ambientarsi
■ **settle up** *vi* regolare i conti

settlement /ˈsetlmənt/ *n* (agreement) accordo *m*; (of bill) saldo *m*; Comm liquidazione *f*; (colony) insediamento *m*

settler /ˈsetlə(r)/ *n* colonizzatore, -trice *mf*

set-to *n* fam zuffa *f*; (verbal) battibecco *m*

set-top box *n* decoder *m inv*

set-up *n* situazione *f*

seven /ˈsevn/ *adj & n* sette *m*

seventeen /sevənˈtiːn/ *adj & n* diciassette *m*

seventeenth /sevənˈtiːn/ *adj & n* diciassettesimo, -a *mf*

seventh /ˈsevnθ/ *adj & n* settimo, -a *mf*

seventies /ˈsevntɪz/ *npl* (period) **the ⁓** gli anni Settanta *mpl*; (age) settant'anni *mpl*; ▸ *also* FORTIES

seventieth /ˈsevntɪɪθ/ *adj & n* settantesimo, -a *mf*

seventy /ˈsevntɪ/ *adj & n* settanta *m*

seven-year itch *n* fam crisi *f inv* del settimo anno

sever /ˈsevə(r)/ *vt* troncare ⟨relations⟩

several /ˈsevrəl/ *adj & pron* parecchi

severance /'sev(ə)rəns/ *n* ~ **pay** trattamento *m* di fine rapporto

severe /sɪ'vɪə(r)/ *adj* severo; ⟨*pain*⟩ violento; ⟨*illness*⟩ grave; ⟨*winter*⟩ rigido

severe acute respiratory syndrome *n* Med sindrome *f* respiratoria acuta severa

severely /sɪ'vɪəlɪ/ *adv* severamente; ⟨*ill*⟩ gravemente

severity /sɪ'verətɪ/ *n* severità *f*; (of pain) violenza *f*; (of illness) gravità *f*; (of winter) rigore *m*

sew /səʊ/ *vt/i* (pt **sewed**, pp **sewn** or **sewed**) cucire
■ **sew up** *vt* ricucire

sewage /'suːɪdʒ/ *n* acque *fpl* di scolo

sewer /'suːə(r)/ *n* fogna *f*

sewing /'səʊɪŋ/ *n* cucito *m*; (work) lavoro *m* di cucito

sewing machine *n* macchina *f* da cucire

sewn /səʊn/ ▶ SEW

sex /seks/ *n* sesso *m*; **have** ~ avere rapporti sessuali, fare l'amore

sex appeal *n* sex appeal *m*

sex change *n* have a ~ cambiare sesso

sex change operation *n* intervento *m* per il cambiamento di sesso

sex discrimination *n* discriminazione *f* sessuale

sex education *n* educazione *f* sessuale

sexism /'seksɪzm/ *n* sessismo *m*

sexist /'seksɪst/ *adj* sessista *mf*

sex life *n* vita *f* sessuale

sex maniac *n* maniaco *m* sessuale

sex object *n* oggetto *m* sessuale

sex offender *n* colpevole *mf* di delitti a sfondo sessuale

sextet /seks'tet/ *n* sestetto *m*

sex tourism *n* turismo *m* a scopo sessuale

sexual /'seksjʊəl/ *adj* sessuale

sexual abuse *n* abusi *mpl* sessuali

sexual assault *n* atti *mpl* di libidine violenta

sexual equality *n* parità *f* dei sessi

sexual harassment *n* molestie *fpl* sessuali

sexual intercourse *n* rapporti *mpl* sessuali

sexuality /seksjʊ'ælətɪ/ *n* sessualità *f*

sexually /'seksjʊəlɪ/ *adv* sessualmente; **be** ~ **assaulted** subire atti di libidine violenta

sexually transmitted disease /trænz'mɪtɪd/ *n* malattia *f* trasmissibile per via sessuale

sexy /'seksɪ/ *adj* (**-ier**, **-iest**) sexy *inv*

Seychelles /seɪ'ʃelz/ *npl* the ~ le Seychelles

sh /ʃ/ *int* silenzio!, sst!

shabbily /'ʃæbɪlɪ/ *adv* in modo scialbo; ⟨*treat*⟩ in modo meschino

shabbiness /'ʃæbɪnɪs/ *n* trasandatezza *f*; (of treatment) meschinità *f*

shabby /'ʃæbɪ/ *adj* (**-ier**, **-iest**) scialbo; ⟨*treatment*⟩ meschino

shack /ʃæk/ *n* catapecchia *f*

shackles /'ʃæklz/ *npl* catene *fpl*

shade /ʃeɪd/ **1** *n* ombra *f*; (of colour) sfumatura *f*; (for lamp) paralume *m*; (Am: for window) tapparella *f*; **a** ~ **better** un tantino meglio
2 *vt* riparare dalla luce; (draw lines on) ombreggiare

shades /ʃeɪdz/ *npl* fam occhiali *mpl* da sole

shading /'ʃeɪdɪŋ/ *n* (slight variation in colour) tonalità *f inv*; (to give effect of darkness) ombreggiature *fpl*

shadow /'ʃædəʊ/ **1** *n* ombra *f*
2 *vt* (follow) pedinare

shadow boxing *n* allenamento *m* di boxe con l'ombra

Shadow Cabinet *n* governo *m* ombra

shadowy /'ʃædəʊɪ/ *adj* (indistinct) confuso

shady /'ʃeɪdɪ/ *adj* (**-ier**, **-iest**) ombroso; (fam: disreputable) losco

shaft /ʃɑːft/ *n* Techn albero *m*; (of light) raggio *m*; (of lift, mine) pozzo *m*; ~**s** *pl* (of cart) stanghe *fpl*

shaggy /'ʃægɪ/ *adj* (**-ier**, **-iest**) irsuto; ⟨*animal*⟩ dal pelo arruffato

shaggy dog story *n* fam barzelletta *f* interminabile dal finale deludente

shake /ʃeɪk/ **1** *n* scrollata *f*
2 *vt* (pt **shook**, pp **shaken**) scuotere; agitare ⟨*bottle*⟩; far tremare ⟨*building*⟩; ~ **hands with** stringere la mano a; ~ **one's head** scuotere la testa
3 *vi* tremare
■ **shake off** *vt* scrollarsi di dosso
■ **shake up** *vt* agitare ⟨*bottle*⟩; ⟨*news, experience*⟩ scuotere ⟨*person*⟩

shaken [up] /'ʃeɪkən/ *adj* (after accident etc) scosso

shaker /'ʃeɪkə(r)/ *n* (for salad) centrifuga *f* [asciugaverdure]; (for dice) bicchiere *m*; (for cocktails) shaker *m inv*; (for pepper) pepaiola *f*; (for salt) saliera *f*

shake-up *n* Pol rimpasto *m*; Comm ristrutturazione *f*

shakily /'ʃeɪkɪlɪ/ *adv* ⟨*say something*⟩ con voce tremante; ⟨*walk*⟩ con passo esitante

shaky /'ʃeɪkɪ/ *adj* (**-ier**, **-iest**) tremante; ⟨*table etc*⟩ traballante; (unreliable) vacillante

shall /ʃæl/ *v aux* **I** ~ **go** andrò; **we** ~ **see** vedremo; **what** ~ **I do?** cosa faccio?; **I'll come too,** ~ **I?** vengo anch'io, no?; **thou shalt not kill** liter non uccidere; **passengers** ⋯▸

S

~ **remain seated** i passeggeri devono rimanere seduti

shallot /ʃəˈlɒt/ n scalogno m

shallow /ˈʃæləʊ/ adj basso, poco profondo; ⟨dish⟩ poco profondo; fig superficiale

shallows /ˈʃæləʊz/ npl secche fpl

sham /ʃæm/ ① adj falso
② n finzione f; (person) spaccone, -a mf
③ vt (pt/pp **shammed**) simulare

shambles /ˈʃæmblz/ n caos msg

shame /ʃeɪm/ n vergogna f; **it's a ~ that** è un peccato che; **what a ~!** che peccato!; ~ **on you!** vergognati!; **put somebody/ something to ~** far sfigurare qualcuno/ qualcosa

shamefaced /ʃeɪmˈfeɪst/ adj vergognoso

shameful /ˈʃeɪmfl/ adj vergognoso

shamefully /ˈʃeɪmfʊlɪ/ adv vergognosamente

shameless /ˈʃeɪmlɪs/ adj spudorato

shamelessly /ˈʃeɪmlɪslɪ/ adv spudoratamente

shampoo /ʃæmˈpuː/ ① n shampoo m inv; ~ **and set** shampoo m inv e messa in piega
② vt fare uno shampoo a ⟨carpet, person's hair etc⟩

shamrock /ˈʃæmrɒk/ n trifoglio m (simbolo dell'Irlanda)

shandy /ˈʃændɪ/ n bevanda f a base di birra e gassosa

shank /ʃæŋk/ n garretto m; (of knife) manico m; (of gold club) impugnatura f; (of screw) gambo m; (of anchor) fuso m; (of person) gamba f (dal ginocchio in giù)

shan't /ʃɑːnt/ = shall not

shanty /ˈʃæntɪ/ n (hut) baracca f; (song) marinaro

shanty town /ˈʃæntɪtaʊn/ n bidonville f inv, baraccopoli f inv

shape /ʃeɪp/ ① n forma f; (figure) ombra f; **take ~** prendere forma; **get back in ~** ritornare in forma; **be out of ~** non essere in forma
② vt dare forma a (**into** di)
③ vi ~ **[up]** mettere la testa a posto; ~ **up nicely** mettersi bene

shapeless /ˈʃeɪplɪs/ adj informe

shapely /ˈʃeɪplɪ/ adj (**-ier**, **-iest**) ben fatto

shard /ʃɑːd/ n frammento m; (of clay) coccio m

share /ʃeə(r)/ ① n porzione f; Comm azione f
② vt dividere; condividere ⟨views⟩
③ vi dividere; ~ **in** partecipare a
■ **share out** vt spartire; (including oneself) spartirsi

share capital n capitale m azionario

shared /ʃeəd/ adj ⟨house⟩ condiviso; ⟨bathroom⟩ in comune

share dealing n contrattazione f di azioni

shareholder n azionista mf

shareholding n titoli mpl azionari

share index n indice m azionario

share option scheme n partecipazione f agli utili dell'azienda tramite acquisto di azioni

shareware /ˈʃeəweə/ n Comput shareware m inv

shark /ʃɑːk/ n squalo m, pescecane m; fig truffatore, -trice mf

sharp /ʃɑːp/ ① adj ⟨knife etc⟩ tagliente; ⟨pencil⟩ appuntito; ⟨drop⟩ a picco; ⟨reprimand⟩ severo; ⟨outline⟩ marcato; (alert) acuto; (unscrupulous) senza scrupoli; ~ **pain** fitta f
② adv **at three o'clock** ~ alle tre in punto; **look ~!** sbrigati!
③ n Mus diesis m inv

sharpen /ˈʃɑːpn/ vt affilare ⟨knife⟩; appuntire ⟨pencil⟩

sharpener /ˈʃɑːpnə(r)/ n (for pencils) temperamatite m inv; (for knife) affilacoltelli m inv

sharply /ˈʃɑːplɪ/ adv ⟨turn, rise, fall⟩ bruscamente; ⟨speak⟩ in tono brusco

shatter /ˈʃætə(r)/ vt frantumare; fig mandare in frantumi

shattered /ˈʃætəd/ ① adj (fam: exhausted) a pezzi
② vi frantumarsi

shave /ʃeɪv/ ① n rasatura f; **have a ~** farsi la barba
② vt radere
③ vi radersi

shaver /ˈʃeɪvə(r)/ n rasoio m elettrico

shaving brush /ˈʃeɪvɪŋ/ n pennello m da barba

shaving foam n schiuma f da barba

shavings /ˈʃeɪvɪŋz/ npl (of wood, metal) trucioli mpl

shaving soap n sapone m da barba

shawl /ʃɔːl/ n scialle m

she /ʃiː/ pers pron lei; ~ **is tired** è stanca; **I'm going, but** ~ **is not** io vado, ma lei no

sheaf /ʃiːf/ n (pl **sheaves**) fascio m

shear /ʃɪə(r)/ vt (pt **sheared**, pp **shorn** or **sheared**) tosare

shears /ʃɪəz/ npl (for hedge) cesoie fpl

sheath /ʃiːθ/ n (pl ~**s** /ʃiːðz/) guaina f

sheathe /ʃiːð/ vt rifoderare; rivestire ⟨cable⟩

sheaves /ʃiːvz/ ▸ SHEAF

shed¹ /ʃed/ n baracca f; (for cattle) stalla f

shed² vt (pt/pp **shed**, pres p **shedding**) perdere; versare ⟨blood, tears⟩; ~ **light on** far luce su

shedload *n* Br: fam ∼s **of money** un sacco di soldi

sheen /ʃiːn/ *n* lucentezza *f*

sheep /ʃiːp/ *n inv* pecora *f*

sheepdog /'ʃiːpdɒg/ *n* cane *m* da pastore

sheepish /'ʃiːpɪʃ/ *adj* imbarazzato

sheepishly /'ʃiːpɪʃlɪ/ *adv* con aria imbarazzata

sheepskin /'ʃiːpskɪn/ *n* [pelle *f* di] montone *m*

sheer /ʃɪə(r)/ ① *adj* puro; (steep) a picco; (transparent) trasparente ② *adv* a picco

sheet /ʃiːt/ *n* lenzuolo *m*; (of paper) foglio *m*; (of glass, metal) lastra *f*

sheet lightning *n* bagliore *m* diffuso dei lampi; (without a storm) lampi *mpl* di calore

sheet metal *n* lamiera *f*

sheet music *n* spartiti *mpl*

sheikh /ʃeɪk/, **sheik** *n* sceicco *m*

shelf /ʃelf/ *n* (*pl* **shelves**) ripiano *m*; (set of shelves) scaffale *m*

shelf-life *n* (of product) durata *f* di conservazione; (fig: of technology, pop music) durata *f* di vita; (fig: of politician, star) periodo *m* di gloria

shell /ʃel/ ① *n* conchiglia *f*; (of egg, snail, tortoise) guscio *m*; (of crab) corazza *f*; (of unfinished building) ossatura *f*; Mil granata *f* ② *vt* sgusciare ⟨peas⟩; Mil bombardare ■ **shell out** *vi* fam sborsare

shellfish *n inv* mollusco *m*; Culin frutti *mpl* di mare

shell-shocked /'ʃelʃɒkt/ *adj* ⟨soldier⟩ traumatizzato da un bombardamento; fig in stato di shock

shell suit *n* tuta *f* di acetato

shelter /'ʃeltə(r)/ ① *n* rifugio *m*; (air raid ∼) rifugio *m* antiaereo; **take** ∼ rifugiarsi ② *vt* riparare (**from** da); fig mettere al riparo; (give lodging to) dare asilo a ③ *vi* rifugiarsi

sheltered /'ʃeltəd/ *adj* ⟨spot⟩ riparato; ⟨life⟩ ritirato

sheltered accommodation *n* residenza *f* protetta

shelve /ʃelv/ ① *vt* accantonare ⟨project⟩ ② *vi* ⟨slope⟩ scendere

shelves /ʃelvz/ ▸ SHELF

shelving /'ʃelvɪŋ/ *n* (shelves) ripiani *mpl*

shepherd /'ʃepəd/ ① *n* pastore *m* ② *vt* guidare

shepherdess /'ʃepədes/ *n* pastora *f*

shepherd's pie /ʃepədz'paɪ/ *n* pasticcio *m* di carne tritata e patate

sherbet /'sɜːbət/ *n* (Br: powder) polverina *f* effervescente al gusto di frutta; (Am: sorbet) sorbetto *m*

sheriff /'ʃerɪf/ *n* sceriffo *m*

Sherpa /'ʃɜːpə/ *n* scerpa *m*

sherry /'ʃerɪ/ *n* sherry *m inv*

shield /ʃiːld/ ① *n* scudo *m*; (for eyes) maschera *f*; Techn schermo *m* ② *vt* proteggere (**from** da)

shift /ʃɪft/ ① *n* cambiamento *m*; (in position) spostamento *m*; (at work) turno *m* ② *vt* spostare; (take away) togliere; riversare ⟨blame⟩ ③ *vi* spostarsi; ⟨wind⟩ cambiare; (fam: move quickly) darsi una mossa

shift key *n* tasto *m* delle maiuscole

shiftless /'ʃɪftlɪs/ *adj* privo di risorse

shift work *n* turni *mpl*

shift worker *n* turnista *mf*

shifty /'ʃɪftɪ/ *adj* (**-ier**, **-iest**) pej losco; ⟨eyes⟩ sfuggente

Shiite /'ʃiːaɪt/ *adj* & *n* sciita *mf*

shilling /'ʃɪlɪŋ/ *n* scellino *m*

shilly-shally /'ʃɪlɪʃælɪ/ *vi* titubare

shimmer /'ʃɪmə(r)/ ① *n* luccichio *m* ② *vi* luccicare

shin /ʃɪn/ ① *n* stinco *m* ② *vi* ∼ **up/down something** (climb) arrampicarsi su/scendere giù da qualcosa

shindig /'ʃɪndɪg/ *n* fam (party) baldoria *f*; (disturbance) pandemonio *m*

shindy /'ʃɪndɪ/ *n* fam (disturbance) pandemonio *m*; (party) baldoria *f*

shine /ʃaɪn/ ① *n* lucentezza *f*; **give something a** ∼ dare una lucidata a qualcosa ② *vi* (pt/pp **shone**) splendere; (reflect light) brillare; ⟨hair, shoes⟩ essere lucido ③ *vt* ∼ **a light on** puntare una luce su ■ **shine through** *vi* ⟨talent, ability⟩ trasparire

shingle /'ʃɪŋgl/ *n* (pebbles) ghiaia *f*

shingles /'ʃɪŋglz/ *n* Med fuoco *m* di Sant'Antonio

shin-guard *n* parastinchi *m inv*

shining /'ʃaɪnɪŋ/ *adj* ⟨eyes, jewel⟩ splendente; ⟨hair⟩ lucente **a** ∼ **example** un fulgido esempio

shiny /'ʃaɪnɪ/ *adj* (**-ier**, **-iest**) lucido

ship /ʃɪp/ ① *n* nave *f* ② *vt* (pt, pp **-pped**) spedire; (by sea) spedire via mare

shipbuilder /'ʃɪpbɪldə(r)/ *n* costruttore *m* navale

shipbuilding /'ʃɪpbɪldɪŋ/ *n* costruzione *f* di navi

shipment /'ʃɪpmənt/ *n* spedizione *f*; (consignment) carico *m*

shipowner /'ʃɪpəʊnə(r)/ *n* armatore *m*

shipper /'ʃɪpə(r)/ *n* spedizioniere *m*

shipping /'ʃɪpɪŋ/ *n* trasporto *m*; (traffic) imbarcazioni *fpl*

shipping agent *n* spedizioniere *m*

shipping company *n* compagnia *f* di spedizione

shipshape *adj & adv* in perfetto ordine

shipwreck *n* naufragio *m*

shipwrecked naufragato

shipyard *n* cantiere *m* navale

shire /ʃaɪə(r)/ *n* Br contea *f*

shire-horse *n* cavallo *m* da tiro

shirk /ʃɜːk/ *vt* scansare

shirker /ˈʃɜːkə(r)/ *n* scansafatiche *mf inv*

shirt /ʃɜːt/ *n* camicia *f*; in ~-sleeves in maniche di camicia

shirty /ˈʃɜːtɪ/ *adj* Br fam incavolato; get ~ with somebody incavolarsi con qualcuno

shish kebab /ʃɪʃkɪˈbæb/ *n* spiedino *m* di carne e verdure

shit /ʃɪt/ *vulg* ① *n & int* merda *f* ② *vi* (pt/pp **shit**) cagare

shit-scared *adj* vulg be ~ farsela sotto

shiver /ˈʃɪvə(r)/ ① *n* brivido *m* ② *vi* rabbrividire

shoal /ʃəʊl/ *n* (of fish) banco *m*

shock /ʃɒk/ ① *n* (impact) urto *m*; Electr scossa *f* [elettrica]; fig colpo *m*, shock *m inv*; Med shock *m inv*; get a ~ Electr prendere la scossa; in ~ Med in stato di shock ② *vt* scioccare

shock absorber *n* Auto ammortizzatore *m*

shocking /ˈʃɒkɪŋ/ *adj* scioccante; fam ⟨weather, handwriting etc⟩ tremendo

shockingly /ˈʃɒkɪŋlɪ/ *adv* ⟨behave⟩ in modo pessimo; ⟨expensive⟩ eccessivamente

shocking pink *n* rosa *m* shocking

shockproof *adj* antiurto

shock treatment *n* terapia *f* d'urto

shock wave *n* onda *f* d'urto

shod /ʃɒd/ ▶ SHOE

shoddily /ˈʃɒdɪlɪ/ *adv* in modo scadente

shoddy /ˈʃɒdɪ/ *adj* (-ier, -iest) scadente

shoe /ʃuː/ ① *n* scarpa *f*; (of horse) ferro *m* ② *vt* (pt/pp **shod**, pres p **shoeing**) ferrare ⟨horse⟩

shoehorn *n* calzante *m*

shoelace *n* laccio *m* da scarpa

shoemaker *n* calzolaio *m*

shoe rack *n* scarpiera *f*

shoe-shop *n* calzoleria *f*

shoestring *n* on a ~ fam con una miseria

shoe-tree *n* forma *f* da scarpa

shone /ʃɒn/ ▶ SHINE

shoo /ʃuː/ ① *vt* ~ away cacciar via ② *int* sciò!

shook /ʃʊk/ ▶ SHAKE

shoot /ʃuːt/ ① *n* Bot germoglio *m*; (hunt) battuta *f* di caccia

② *vt* (pt/pp **shot**) sparare, girare ⟨film⟩; ~ oneself in the foot fig darsi la zappa sui piedi

③ *vi* (hunt) andare a caccia

■ **shoot down** *vt* abbattere

■ **shoot out** *vi* (rush) precipitarsi fuori

■ **shoot up** *vi* (grow) crescere in fretta; ⟨prices⟩ salire di colpo

shooting /ˈʃuːtɪŋ/ ① *n* (pastime) caccia *f*; (killing) uccisione *f* ② *adj* ⟨pain⟩ lancinante

shooting range *n* poligono *m* di tiro

shooting star *n* stella *f* cadente

shoot-out *n* fam sparatoria *f*

shop /ʃɒp/ ① *n* negozio *m*; (workshop) officina *f*; talk ~ fam parlare di lavoro ② *vi* (pt/pp **shopped**, pres p **shopping**) far compere; go ~ping andare a fare compere

■ **shop around** *vi* confrontare i prezzi

shopaholic /ʃɒpəˈhɒlɪk/ *n* fanatico, -a *mf* dello shopping

shop assistant *n* commesso, -a *mf*

shop floor *n* problems on the ~ ~ problemi tra gli operai

shopkeeper *n* negoziante *mf*

shoplifter *n* taccheggiatore, -trice *mf*

shoplifting *n* taccheggio *m*

shopper /ˈʃɒpə(r)/ *n* compratore, -trice *mf*

shopping /ˈʃɒpɪŋ/ *n* compere *fpl*; (articles) acquisti *mpl*; do the ~ fare la spesa

shopping bag *n* borsa *f* per la spesa

shopping basket *n* (Comput: on web site) carrello *m* della spesa

shopping centre *n* centro *m* commerciale

shopping list *n* lista *f* della spesa

shopping mall *n* centro *m* commerciale

shopping trolley *n* carrello *m*

shop-soiled *adj* ⟨garment⟩ sporco (per lunga permanenza in negozio)

shop steward *n* rappresentante *mf* sindacale

shop window *n* vetrina *f*

shore /ʃɔː(r)/ *n* riva *f*

■ **shore up** *vt* puntellare ⟨building, wall⟩

shorn /ʃɔːn/ ▶ SHEAR

short /ʃɔːt/ ① *adj* corto; (not lasting) breve; ⟨person⟩ basso; (curt) brusco; a ~ time ago poco tempo fa; be ~ of essere a corto di; be in ~ supply essere scarso; fig essere raro; Mick is ~ for Michael Mick è il diminutivo di Michael; cut ~ interrompere ⟨holiday⟩; to cut a long story ~... per farla breve...; in the ~ term nell'immediato futuro, a breve termine

② *adv* bruscamente; in ~ in breve; ~ of doing a meno di fare; go ~ essere privato (of di); stop ~ of doing something non arrivare fino a fare qualcosa; **you're 10p** ~ mancano 10 pence

3 n (Cinema) cortometraggio m

shortage /'ʃɔ:tɪdʒ/ n scarsità f inv

shortbread n biscotto m di pasta frolla

short-change vt dare meno resto del dovuto a; (deliberately) imbrogliare sul resto; fig imbrogliare

short circuit **1** n corto m circuito

2 vt mandare in cortocircuito

3 vi causare un cortocircuito

shortcoming n difetto m

shortcrust pastry n pasta f frolla

short cut n scorciatoia f

shorten /'ʃɔ:tn/ vt abbreviare; accorciare ⟨garment⟩

shortfall n (in budget, accounts) deficit m inv

shorthand n stenografia f

short-handed /-'hændɪd/ adj a corto di personale

shorthand typist n stenodattilografo, -a mf

short list n lista f dei candidati selezionati per un lavoro

short-lived /-'lɪvd/ adj di breve durata

shortly /'ʃɔ:tlɪ/ adv presto; ~ before/after poco prima/dopo

shortness /'ʃɔ:tnɪs/ n brevità f inv; (of person) bassa statura f

short notice n at ~ ~ con poco preavviso

short-range adj di breve portata

shorts /ʃɔ:ts/ npl calzoncini mpl corti

short-sighted /-'saɪtɪd/ adj miope

short-sleeved /-'sli:vd/ adj a maniche corte

short-staffed /-'stɑ:ft/ adj a corto di personale

short story n racconto m, novella f

short-tempered /-'tempəd/ adj irascibile

short-term adj a breve termine

short time n be on ~ ~ ⟨worker⟩ fare orario ridotto

short wave n onde fpl corte

short wave radio n radio f inv a onde corte

shot /ʃɒt/ **1** ▸ SHOOT

2 n colpo m; (pellets) piombini mpl; (person) tiratore m; Phot foto f inv; (injection) puntura f; (fam: attempt) prova f; **like a** ~ fam come un razzo

shotgun n fucile m da caccia

shot put n (event) lancio m del peso

shot-putter n pesista mf

shot-putting n Sport lancio m del peso

should /ʃʊd/ v aux I ~ go dovrei andare; I ~ **have seen him** avrei dovuto vederlo; **you ~n't have said that** non avresti

dovuto dire questo; **I** ~ **like** mi piacerebbe; **this** ~ **be enough** questo dovrebbe bastare; **if he** ~ **come** se dovesse venire, se venisse

shoulder /'ʃəʊldə(r)/ **1** n spalla f; ~ **to** ~ gomito a gomito

2 vt mettersi in spalla; fig accollarsi

shoulder bag n borsa f a tracolla

shoulder blade n scapola f

shoulder-length adj ⟨hair⟩ lungo fino alle spalle

shoulder pad n spallina f

shoulder strap n spallina f; (of bag) tracolla f

shout /ʃaʊt/ **1** n grido m

2 vt/i gridare

■ **shout at** vi alzar la voce con

■ **shout down** vt azzittire gridando

shouting /'ʃaʊtɪŋ/ n grida fpl

shove /ʃʌv/ **1** n spintone m

2 vt spingere; (fam: put) ficcare

3 vi spingere

■ **shove off** vi fam togliersi di torno

■ **shove up** vi (fam: make room) farsi più in là

shovel /'ʃʌvl/ **1** n pala f

2 vt (pt/pp shovelled) spalare

show /ʃəʊ/ **1** n (display) manifestazione f; (exhibition) mostra f; (ostentation) ostentazione f; Theat, TV spettacolo m; (programme) programma m; **on** ~ esposto

2 vt (pt showed, pp shown) mostrare; (put on display) esporre; proiettare ⟨film⟩; ~ **somebody to the door** accompagnare qualcuno alla porta; ~ **somebody the door** mettere alla porta qualcuno

3 vi ⟨film⟩ essere proiettato; **your slip is** ~**ing** ti si vede la sottoveste

■ **show in** vt fare accomodare

■ **show off** **1** vi fam mettersi in mostra

2 vt mettere in mostra

■ **show out** vt ~ **somebody out** fare uscire qualcuno

■ **show round** vt ~ **somebody round** far visitare a qualcuno ⟨house, town⟩

■ **show up** **1** vi risaltare; (fam: arrive) farsi vedere

2 vt (fam: embarrass) far fare una brutta figura a

showbiz /'ʃəʊbɪz/ n fam mondo m dello spettacolo

show business n mondo m dello spettacolo

showcase **1** n also fig vetrina f

2 attrib ⟨village, prison⟩ modello

show-down n regolamento m dei conti

shower /'ʃaʊə(r)/ **1** n doccia f; (of rain) acquazzone m; **have a** ~ fare la doccia

2 vt ~ **with** coprire di

3 vi fare la doccia

shower-cap n cuffia f da doccia

shower-curtain n tenda f della doccia

shower-head n bocchetta f

S

showerproof *adj* impermeabile

showery /'ʃaʊərɪ/ *adj* it was ~ ci sono stati diversi acquazzoni

show house *n* casa *f* di nuova costruzione arredata per essere mostrata ad eventuali acquirenti

showjumper /'ʃəʊdʒʌmpə(r)/ *n* cavaliere *m*/cavallerizza *f* di salto ad ostacoli

showjumping /'ʃəʊdʒʌmpɪŋ/ *n* concorso *m* ippico

shown /ʃəʊn/ ▶ SHOW

show-off *n* esibizionista *mf*

show of hands *n* voto *m* per alzata di mano

showpiece *n* pezzo *m* forte

showplace *n* attrazione *f*

showroom *n* salone *m* [per] esposizioni

showy /'ʃəʊɪ/ *adj* appariscente

shrank /ʃræŋk/ ▶ SHRINK

shrapnel /'ʃræpnl/ *n* schegge *fpl* di granata, shrapnel *m*

shred /ʃred/ ① *n* brandello *m*; fig briciolo *m*
② *vt* (pt/pp **shredded**) fare a brandelli; Culin tagliuzzare

shredder /'ʃredə(r)/ *n* distruttore *m* di documenti

shrew /ʃruː/ *n* Zool toporagno *m*; (pej: woman) bisbetica *f*

shrewd /ʃruːd/ *adj* accorto

shrewdly /'ʃruːdlɪ/ *adv* con accortezza

shrewdness /'ʃruːdnɪs/ *n* accortezza *f*

shriek /ʃriːk/ ① *n* strillo *m*
② *vt/i* strillare

shrift /ʃrɪft/ *n* give somebody short ~ liquidare qualcuno rapidamente

shrill /ʃrɪl/ *adj* penetrante

shrillness /'ʃrɪlnɪs/ *n* acutezza *f*

shrilly /'ʃrɪlɪ/ *adv* in modo penetrante

shrimp /ʃrɪmp/ *n* gamberetto *m*

shrine /ʃraɪn/ *n* (place) santuario *m*

shrink /ʃrɪŋk/ ① *vi* (pt **shrank**, pp **shrunk**) restringersi; (draw back) ritrarsi (from da)
② *n* fam strizzacervelli *mf inv*

shrinkage /'ʃrɪŋkɪdʒ/ *n* (of fabric) restringimento *m*; (of area, company) rimpicciolimento *m*; (in a shop) perdite *fpl*; (of resources) diminuzione *f*

shrinking violet /ʃrɪŋkɪŋ'vaɪələt/ *n* hum mammoletta *f*

shrink-proof *adj* irrestringibile

shrink-resistant *adj* irrestringibile

shrink-wrap ① *vt* avvolgere nella pellicola trasparente
② *n* pellicola *f* trasparente

shrivel /'ʃrɪvl/ *vi* (pt/pp **shrivelled**) raggrinzare

shroud /ʃraʊd/ ① *n* sudario *m*; fig manto *m*
② *vt* ~ed in fig avvolto in

Shrove /ʃrəʊv/ *n* ~ **Tuesday** martedì *m* grasso

shrub /ʃrʌb/ *n* arbusto *m*

shrubbery /'ʃrʌbərɪ/ *n* (in garden) zona *f* piantata ad arbusti

shrug /ʃrʌg/ ① *n* scrollata *f* di spalle
② *vt/i* (pt/pp **shrugged**) ~ [one's shoulders] scrollare le spalle
■ **shrug off** *vt* ignorare

shrunk /ʃrʌŋk/ ▶ SHRINK.

shudder /'ʃʌdə(r)/ ① *n* fremito *m*
② *vi* fremere

shuffle /'ʃʌfl/ ① *vi* strascicare i piedi
② *vt* mescolare ⟨cards⟩
③ *n* strascicamento *m*; (at cards) mescolata *f*

shufty /'ʃʊftɪ/ *n* Br fam have a ~ at something dare un'occhiata a qualcosa

shun /ʃʌn/ *vt* (pt/pp **shunned**) rifuggire

shunt /ʃʌnt/ *vt* smistare

shush /ʃʊʃ/ *int* zitto!

shut /ʃʌt/ ① *vt* (pt/pp **shut**, pres p **shutting**) chiudere
② *vi* chiudersi; ⟨shop⟩ chiudere
■ **shut down** *vt/i* chiudere
■ **shut in** *vt* rinchiudere ⟨person, animal⟩
■ **shut off** *vt* chiudere ⟨water, gas⟩
■ **shut out** *vt* bloccare ⟨light⟩; impedire ⟨view⟩; scacciare ⟨memory⟩
■ **shut up** ① *vt* chiudere; fam far tacere
② *vi* fam stare zitto; ~ up! stai zitto!

shutdown /'ʃʌtdaʊn/ *n* chiusura *f*

shut-eye *n* (fam: short sleep) get some ~ fare un pisolino

shutter /'ʃʌtə(r)/ *n* serranda *f*; Phot otturatore *m*

shuttle /'ʃʌtl/ ① *n* navetta *f*
② *vi* far la spola

shuttlecock /'ʃʌtlkɒk/ *n* volano *m*

shuttle service *n* servizio *m* pendolare

shy /ʃaɪ/ ① *adj* (timid) timido
② *vi* (pt/pp **shied**) ⟨horse⟩ fare uno scarto
■ **shy away from** *vt* rifuggire da

shyly /'ʃaɪlɪ/ *adv* timidamente

shyness /'ʃaɪnɪs/ *n* timidezza *f*

Siamese /saɪə'miːz/ *adj* siamese

Siamese twins *npl* fratelli *mpl*/sorelle *fpl* siamesi

Siberia /saɪ'bɪərɪə/ *n* Siberia *f*

sibling /'sɪblɪŋ/ *n* (brother) fratello *m*; (sister) sorella *f*; ~s *pl* fratelli *mpl*

sibling rivalry *n* rivalità *f* tra fratelli

sibylline /'sɪbɪlaɪn/ *adj* sibillino

Sicilian /sɪ'sɪlɪən/ *adj* & *n* siciliano, -a *mf*

Sicily /'sɪsɪlɪ/ *n* Sicilia *f*

sick /sɪk/ *adj* ammalato; ⟨*humour*⟩ macabro; **be ∼** (vomit) vomitare; **be ∼ of something** fam essere stufo di qualcosa; **feel ∼** aver la nausea

sick bay *n* (in school) infermeria *f*

sick building syndrome *n* sindrome *f* da edifici malsani

sicken /'sɪkn/ ① *vt* disgustare ② *vi* **be ∼ing for something** covare qualche malanno

sickening /'sɪkənɪŋ/ *adj* disgustoso

sick leave *n* congedo *m* per malattia

sickly /'sɪklɪ/ *adj* (**-ier, -iest**) malaticcio

sickness /'sɪknɪs/ *n* malattia *f*; (vomiting) nausea *f*

sickness benefit *n* sussidio *m* di malattia

sick note *n* (from doctor) certificato *m* medico

sickpay *n* indennità *f* di malattia

sickroom /'sɪkru:m/ *n* camera *f* dell'ammalato

side /saɪd/ ① *n* lato *m*; (of person, mountain) fianco *m*; (of road) bordo *m*; **on the ∼** (as sideline) come attività secondaria; **∼ by ∼** fianco a fianco; **take ∼s** immischiarsi; **take sb's ∼** prendere le parti di qualcuno; **be on the safe ∼** andare sul sicuro ② *attrib* laterale ③ *vi* **∼ with** parteggiare per

sideboard *n* credenza *f*

sideboards /'saɪdbɔ:dz/ *npl* Br = SIDEBURNS

sideburns *npl* basette *fpl*

side effect *n* effetto *m* collaterale

side impact bars *npl* Auto barre *fpl* laterali antintrusione

sidekick *n* fam (companion) compare *mf*; (assistant) braccio *m* destro

sidelights *npl* luci *fpl* di posizione

sideline *n* attività *f inv* complementare

sidelong *adj* **∼ glance** sguincio *m*

side plate *n* piattino *m*

side road *n* strada *f* secondaria

side-saddle *adv* all'amazzone

sideshow *n* attrazione *f*

sidestep *vt* schivare

side street *n* strada *f* laterale

sidetrack *vt* sviare

sidewalk *n* Am marciapiede *m*

sideways *adv* obliquamente

siding /'saɪdɪŋ/ *n* binario *m* di raccordo

sidle /'saɪdl/ *vi* camminare furtivamente (up to verso)

siege /si:dʒ/ *n* assedio *m*

Sierra Leone /sɪeərəlɪ'əʊn/ *n* Sierra Leone *f*

siesta /sɪ'estə/ *n* siesta *f*; **take a ∼** fare una siesta

sieve /sɪv/ ① *n* setaccio *m* ② *vt* setacciare

sift /sɪft/ *vt* setacciare; **∼ [through]** fig passare al setaccio

sigh /saɪ/ ① *n* sospiro *m*; **give a ∼** sospirare ② *vi* sospirare

sight /saɪt/ ① *n* vista *f*; (on gun) mirino *m*; **the ∼s** *pl* le cose da vedere; **at first ∼** a prima vista; **be within/out of ∼** essere/ non essere in vista; **within ∼ of** vicino a; **lose ∼ of** perdere di vista; **know by ∼** conoscere di vista; **have bad ∼** vederci male ② *vt* avvistare

sightseeing /'saɪtsi:ɪŋ/ *n* **go ∼** andare a visitare posti

sightseer /'saɪtsi:ə(r)/ *n* turista *mf*

sign /saɪn/ ① *n* segno *m*; (notice) insegna *f* ② *vt/i* firmare
■ **sign for** *vt* firmare la ricevuta di ⟨*letter, parcel*⟩; firmare un contratto con ⟨*football club*⟩
■ **sign in** *vi* ⟨*hotel guest*⟩ firmare il registro
■ **sign on** *vi* (as unemployed) presentarsi all'ufficio di collocamento; Mil arruolarsi
■ **sign up** *vi* Mil arruolarsi; **∼ up for a course** iscriversi a un corso

signal /'sɪgnl/ ① *n* segnale *m* ② *vt* (pt/pp **signalled**) segnalare ③ *vi* fare segnali; **∼ to somebody** far segno a qualcuno (to di)

signal box *n* cabina *f* di segnalazione

signalman /'sɪgnəlmən/ *n* casellante *m*

signatory /'sɪgnət(ə)rɪ/ *n* firmatario, -a *mf*

signature /'sɪgnətʃə(r)/ *n* firma *f*

signature tune *n* sigla *f* [musicale]

signet ring /'sɪgnɪt/ *n* anello *m* con sigillo

significance /sɪg'nɪfɪkəns/ *n* significato *m*

significant /sɪg'nɪfɪkənt/ *adj* significativo

significantly /sɪg'nɪfɪkəntlɪ/ *adv* in modo significativo

signify /'sɪgnɪfaɪ/ *vt* (pt/pp **-ied**) indicare

signing /'saɪnɪŋ/ *n* (of treaty) firma *f*; (of footballer) ingaggio *m*; (footballer) nuovo acquisto *m*; (sign language) linguaggio *m* dei segni

sign language *n* linguaggio *m* dei segni

signpost /'saɪnpəʊst/ *n* segnalazione *f* stradale

Sikh /si:k/ ① *n* sikh *mf inv* ② *adj* sikh *inv*

silage /'saɪlɪdʒ/ *n* foraggio *m* conservato in silo

silence /'saɪləns/ ① *n* silenzio *m*; **in ∼** in silenzio

2 *vt* far tacere

silencer /'saɪlənsə(r)/ *n* (on gun) silenziatore *m*; Auto marmitta *f*

silent /'saɪlənt/ *adj* silenzioso; ⟨film⟩ muto; **remain ∼** rimanere in silenzio; **the ∼ majority** la maggioranza silenziosa

silently /'saɪləntlɪ/ *adv* silenziosamente

silhouette /sɪlʊ'et/ **1** *n* sagoma *f*, silhouette *f inv*
2 *vt* **be ∼d** profilarsi

silica gel /'sɪlɪkə/ *n* gel *m inv* di silice

silicon /'sɪlɪkən/ *n* silicio *m*

silicon chip *n* Comput chip *m inv* di silicio, piastrina *f* di silicio

silicone /'sɪlɪkəʊn/ *n* Chem silicone *m*

silicone varnish *n* vernice *f* siliconica

silk /sɪlk/ **1** *n* seta *f*
2 *attrib* di seta

silkworm /'sɪlkwɜːm/ *n* baco *m* da seta

silky /'sɪlkɪ/ *adj* (**-ier, -iest**) come la seta

sill /sɪl/ *n* davanzale *m*

silly /'sɪlɪ/ *adj* (**-ier, -iest**) sciocco

silo /'saɪləʊ/ *n* silo *m*

silt /sɪlt/ *n* melma *f*

silver /'sɪlvə(r)/ **1** *adj* d'argento; ⟨paper⟩ argentato
2 *n* argento *m*; (silverware) argenteria *f*

silver birch *n* betulla *f* bianca

silver foil *n* carta *f* stagnola, foglio *m* d'alluminio

silver-plated *adj* placcato d'argento

silver service *n* servizio *m* a tavola in cui il cameriere fa il giro dei commensali

silversmith *n* argentiere *m*

silverware *n* argenteria *f*

silver wedding *n* nozze *fpl* d'argento

silvery /'sɪlvərɪ/ *adj* argentino

similar /'sɪmɪlə(r)/ *adj* simile

similarity /sɪmɪ'lærətɪ/ *n* somiglianza *f*

similarly /'sɪmɪləlɪ/ *adv* in modo simile

simile /'sɪmɪlɪ/ *n* similitudine *f*

simmer /'sɪmə(r)/ **1** *vi* bollire lentamente
2 *vt* far bollire lentamente
■ **simmer down** *vi* calmarsi

simper /'sɪmpə(r)/ *vi* ostentare un sorriso

simpering /'sɪmp(ə)rɪŋ/ *adj* ⟨smile⟩ affettato; ⟨person⟩ smanceroso

simple /'sɪmpl/ *adj* semplice; ⟨person⟩ sempliciotto

simple-minded /-'maɪndɪd/ *adj* sempliciotto

simpleton /'sɪmpltən/ *n* sempliciotto, -a *mf*

simplicity /sɪm'plɪsətɪ/ *n* semplicità *f*

simplification /sɪmplɪfɪ'keɪʃn/ *n* semplificazione *f*

simplify /'sɪmplɪfaɪ/ *vt* (pt/pp **-ied**) semplificare

simplistic /sɪm'plɪstɪk/ *adj* semplicistico

simply /'sɪmplɪ/ *adv* semplicemente

simulate /'sɪmjʊleɪt/ *vt* simulare

simulation /sɪmjʊ'leɪʃn/ *n* simulazione *f*

simulator /'sɪmjʊleɪtə(r)/ *n* simulatore *m*

simulcast /'sɪməlkɑːst/ *vt* teleradiotrasmettere

simultaneous /sɪml'teɪnɪəs/ *adj* simultaneo

simultaneously /sɪməl'teɪnɪəslɪ/ *adv* simultaneamente

sin /sɪn/ **1** *n* peccato *m*
2 *vi* (pt/pp **sinned**) peccare

since /sɪns/ *prep* **1** da; **∼ when?** da quando in qua?
2 *adv* da allora
3 *conj* da quando; (because) siccome

sincere /sɪn'sɪə(r)/ *adj* sincero

sincerely /sɪn'sɪəlɪ/ *adv* sinceramente; **Yours ∼** Distinti saluti

sincerity /sɪn'serətɪ/ *n* sincerità *f*

sine /saɪn/ *n* Math seno *m*

sinew /'sɪnjuː/ *n* tendine *m*

sinful /'sɪnfl/ *adj* peccaminoso

sing /sɪŋ/ *vt/i* (pt **sang**, pp **sung**) cantare

singalong /'sɪŋəlɒŋ/ *n* **have a ∼** cantare [tutti] insieme

Singapore /sɪŋə'pɔː(r)/ *n* Singapore *f*

singe /sɪndʒ/ *vt* (pres p **-geing**) bruciacchiare

singer /'sɪŋə(r)/ *n* cantante *mf*

singer-songwriter /-'sɒŋraɪtə(r)/ *n* cantautore, -trice *mf*

singing /'sɪŋɪŋ/ *n* canto *m*

single /'sɪŋgl/ **1** *adj* solo; (not double) semplice; (unmarried) celibe; ⟨woman⟩ nubile; ⟨room⟩ singolo; ⟨bed⟩ a una piazza; **I haven't spoken to a ∼ person** non ho parlato con nessuno
2 *n* (ticket) biglietto *m* di sola andata; (record) singolo *m*
■ **single out** *vt* scegliere; (distinguish) distinguere

single-breasted /-'brestɪd/ *adj* ad un petto

single cream *n* panna *f* da cucina liquida

single currency *n* (in Europe) moneta *f* unica

single-decker /-'dekə(r)/ *n* autobus *m inv* (a un piano solo)

single file *adv* in fila indiana

single-handed /-'hændɪd/ *adj & adv* da solo

single-handedly /-'hændɪdlɪ/ *adv* da solo

single market *n* mercato *m* unico

single-minded /-'maɪndɪd/ *adj* risoluto

single mother *n* madre *f* single *inv*

single-parent *adj* ⟨family⟩ monoparentale

singles /'sɪŋglz/ *npl* Tennis singolo *m*; (people) single *mpl*; **the women's** ∼ il singolo femminile

singles bar *n* bar ritrovo *m* *inv* per single

singles charts *npl* classifica *f* *inv* dei singoli

single-sex *adj* (for boys) maschile; (for girls) femminile

single-storey *adj* ⟨house⟩ ad un piano

singlet /'sɪŋlɪt/ *n* Br canottiera *f*

singly /'sɪŋglɪ/ *adv* singolarmente

sing-song Br **1** *adj* ⟨voice, dialect⟩ che ha una sua particolare cadenza
2 *n* have a ∼ cantare [tutti] insieme

singular /'sɪŋgjʊlə(r)/ **1** *adj* Gram singolare; (uncommon) eccezionale
2 *n* singolare *m*

singularly /'sɪŋgjʊləlɪ/ *adv* singolarmente

sinister /'sɪnɪstə(r)/ *adj* sinistro

sink /sɪŋk/ **1** *n* lavandino *m*
2 *vi* (pt **sank**, pp **sunk**) affondare
3 *vt* affondare ⟨ship⟩; scavare ⟨shaft⟩; investire ⟨money⟩
■ **sink in** *vi* penetrare; **it took a while to** ∼ **in** (fam: be understood) c'è voluto un po' a capirlo

sinker /'sɪŋkə(r)/ *n* (in fishing) piombo *m*; Am Culin ≈ bombolone *m*

sinking /'sɪŋkɪŋ/ *n* affondamento *m*

sink unit *n* mobile *m* di cucina comprendente il lavandino

sinner /'sɪnə(r)/ *n* peccatore, -trice *mf*

sinuous /'sɪnjʊəs/ *adj* sinuoso

sinus /'saɪnəs/ *n* seno *m* paranasale

sinusitis /saɪnə'saɪtɪs/ *n* sinusite *f*

sip /sɪp/ **1** *n* sorso *m*
2 *vt* (pt/pp **sipped**) sorseggiare

siphon /'saɪfn/ *n* (bottle) sifone *m*
■ **siphon off** *vt* travasare (con sifone)

sir /sɜː(r)/ *n* signore *m*; **S**∼ (title) Sir *m*; **Dear S**∼ Egregio Signore; **Dear S**∼**s** Spettabile Ditta

sire /saɪə(r)/ *vt* generare

siren /'saɪrən/ *n* sirena *f*

sirloin /'sɜːlɔɪn/ *n* (of beef) controfiletto *m*

sirloin steak *n* bistecca *f* di controfiletto

sissy /'sɪsɪ/ *n* femminuccia *f*

sister /'sɪstə(r)/ *n* sorella *f*; (nurse) [infermiera *f*] caposala *f*

sisterhood /'sɪstəhʊd/ *n* Relig congregazione *f* religiosa femminile; (in feminism) solidarietà *f* *inv* femminile

sister-in-law *n* (*pl* ∼**s-in-law**) cognata *f*

sisterly /'sɪstəlɪ/ *adj* da sorella

Sistine Chapel /'sɪstiːn/ *n* Cappella *f* Sistina

sit /sɪt/ **1** *vi* (pt/pp **sat**, pres p **sitting**) essere seduto; (sit down) sedersi; ⟨committee⟩ riunirsi
2 *vt* sostenere ⟨exam⟩
■ **sit about**, **sit around** *vi* stare senza far niente
■ **sit back** *vi* fig starsene con le mani in mano
■ **sit by** *vi* starsene a guardare
■ **sit down** *vi* mettersi a sedere; **please** ∼ **down** si accomodi; ∼ **down!** siediti!
■ **sit for** *vi* posare per ⟨portrait⟩
■ **sit in** *vi* (observe) assistere; ∼ **in on a class** assistere (da osservatore) a una lezione
■ **sit on** *vt* far parte di ⟨committee⟩
■ **sit up** *vi* mettersi seduto; (not slouch) star seduto diritto; (stay up) stare alzato

sitcom /'sɪtkɒm/ *n* fam situation comedy *f* *inv*

sit-down *n* Br **have a** ∼ sedersi un momento

site /saɪt/ **1** *n* posto *m*; Archaeol sito *m*; (building ∼) cantiere *m*
2 *vt* collocare

sit-in /'sɪtɪn/ *n* occupazione *f* (di fabbrica ecc), sit-in *m* *inv*

sitter /'sɪtə(r)/ *n* (babysitter) baby-sitter *mf* *inv*; (for artist) modello *m*

sitting /'sɪtɪŋ/ *n* seduta *f*; (for meals) turno *m*

sitting duck *n* fam facile bersaglio *m*

sitting room *n* salotto *m*

sitting target *n* facile bersaglio *m*

sitting tenant *n* locatario *m* residente

situate /'sɪtjʊeɪt/ *vt* situare

situated /'sɪtjʊeɪtɪd/ *adj* situato

situation /sɪtjʊ'eɪʃn/ *n* situazione *f*; (location) posizione *f*; (job) posto *m*; '∼**s vacant**' 'offerte di lavoro'

situation report *n* quadro *m* della situazione

sit-ups *npl* addominali *mpl*

six /sɪks/ *adj* & *n* sei *m*

six-pack *n* confezione *f* da sei (di bottiglie o lattine)

sixteen /sɪks'tiːn/ *adj* & *n* sedici *m*

sixteenth /sɪks'tiːnθ/ *adj* & *n* sedicesimo, -a *mf*

sixteenth-century *adj* cinquecentesco

sixth /sɪksθ/ *adj* & *n* sesto, -a *mf*

sixth form *n* Sch ultimo biennio *m* facoltativo della scuola superiore

S

sixth form college n Br istituto m che prepara studenti dai 16 ai 18 anni agli esami di maturità

sixth sense n sesto senso m

sixties /'sɪkstɪz/ npl (period) **the ~** gli anni Sessanta mpl; (age) sessant'anni mpl; ▶ also FORTIES

sixtieth /'sɪkstɪɪθ/ adj & n sessantesimo, -a mf

sixty /'sɪkstɪ/ adj & n sessanta m

size /saɪz/ n dimensioni fpl; (of clothes) taglia f, misura f; (of shoes) numero m; **what ~ is the room?** che dimensioni ha la stanza?
- **size up** vt fam valutare

sizeable /'saɪzəbl/ adj piuttosto grande

sizzle /'sɪzl/ vi sfrigolare

skate[1] /skeɪt/ n inv (fish) razza f

skate[2] [1] n pattino m
[2] vi pattinare
- **skate over** vt fig glissare su

skateboard /'skeɪtbɔːd/ n skateboard m inv

skateboarder /'skeɪtbɔːdə(r)/ n persona f che va in skateboard

skateboarding /'skeɪtbɔːdɪŋ/ n skateboard m

skater /skeɪt/ n pattinatore, -trice mf

skating /'skeɪtɪŋ/ n pattinaggio m

skating rink n pista f di pattinaggio

skeletal /'skelɪtl/ adj also fig scheletrico; ⟨disease⟩ dello scheletro

skeleton /'skelɪtn/ n scheletro m

skeleton key n passe-partout m inv

skeleton staff n personale m ridotto

skeptic /'skeptɪk/ n Am = SCEPTIC

skeptical /'skeptɪkl/ adj Am = SCEPTICAL

skepticism /'skeptɪsɪzm/ n Am = SCEPTICISM

sketch /sketʃ/ [1] n schizzo m; Theat sketch m inv
[2] vt fare uno schizzo di
- **sketch out** vt delineare

sketchbook /'sketʃbʊk/ n (for sketching) album m inv per schizzi; (book of sketches) album m inv di schizzi

sketchily /'sketʃɪlɪ/ adv in modo abbozzato

sketchpad /'sketʃpæd/ n blocco m per schizzi

sketchy /'sketʃɪ/ adj (**-ier, -iest**) abbozzato

skew /skjuː/ vt alterare ⟨figures⟩

skewer /'skjuːə(r)/ n spiedo m

ski /skiː/ [1] n sci m inv
[2] vi (pt/pp **skied**, pres p **skiing**) sciare; **go ~ing** andare a sciare

ski boot n scarpone m da sci

skid /skɪd/ [1] n slittata f; **go into a ~** slittare

[2] vi (pt/pp **skidded**) slittare

skid mark n segno m di frenata

skier /'skiːə(r)/ n sciatore, -trice mf

skiing /'skiːɪŋ/ n sci m

ski instructor n maestro, -a mf di sci

ski jump n (competition) salto m con gli sci; (slope) trampolino m

ski jumping n salto m dal trampolino

skilful /'skɪlfl/ adj abile

skilfully /'skɪlfʊlɪ/ adv abilmente

ski lift n impianto m di risalita

skill /skɪl/ n abilità f inv

skilled /skɪld/ adj dotato; ⟨worker⟩ specializzato

skillet /'skɪlət/ n Am padella f

skim /skɪm/ vt (pt/pp **skimmed**) schiumare; scremare ⟨milk⟩
- **skim off** vt togliere
- **skim over** vt sfiorare ⟨surface, subject⟩
- **skim through** vt scorrere

skimmed milk /skɪmd/ n latte m scremato

skimp /skɪmp/ vi **~ on** lesinare su

skimpy /'skɪmpɪ/ adj (**-ier, -iest**) succinto

skin /skɪn/ [1] n pelle f; (on fruit) buccia f; **soaked to the ~** fradicio fino all'osso
[2] vt (pt/pp **skinned**) spellare

skin cancer n cancro m alla pelle

skincare n cura f della pelle

skin cream n crema f per la pelle

skin-deep adj superficiale

skin diver n sub mf inv

skin diving n nuoto m subacqueo

skinflint /'skɪnflɪnt/ n miserabile mf

skin graft n innesto m epidermico

skinhead /'skɪnhed/ n skinhead m inv

skinny /'skɪnɪ/ adj (**-ier, -iest**) molto magro

skint /skɪnt/ adj fam al verde

skintight /skɪn'taɪt/ adj aderente

skip[1] /skɪp/ n (container) benna f

skip[2] [1] n salto m
[2] vi (pt/pp **skipped**) saltellare; (with rope) saltare la corda
[3] vt omettere

ski pants npl pantaloni mpl da sci

ski pass n ski-pass m inv

ski pole n bastone m da sci

skipper /'skɪpə(r)/ n skipper m inv

skipping /'skɪpɪŋ/ n salto m della corda

skipping rope n corda f per saltare

ski rack n portasci m inv

ski resort n stazione f sciistica

skirmish /'skɜːmɪʃ/ n scaramuccia f

skirt /skɜːt/ [1] n gonna f
[2] vt costeggiare

skirting board /'skɜːtɪŋ/ n battiscopa m inv, zoccolo m

ski run n pista f da sci

ski slope n pista f da sci

ski stick n bastone m da sci

ski suit n tuta f da sci

skit /skɪt/ n bozzetto m comico

skittish /'skɪtɪʃ/ adj (difficult to handle) ombroso; (playful) giocherellone

skittle /'skɪtl/ n birillo m

skive /skaɪv/ vi fam fare lo scansafatiche

skivvy /'skɪvɪ/ n Br fam sguattera f

ski wax n sciolina f

skulduggery /skʌl'dʌgərɪ/ n fam imbrogli mpl

skulk /skʌlk/ vi aggirarsi furtivamente

skull /skʌl/ n cranio m

skunk /skʌŋk/ n moffetta f; (person) farabutto m

sky /skaɪ/ n cielo m

skydiving n paracadutismo m in caduta libera

sky-high ① adj (prices) alle stelle; (rates) esorbitante
② adv rise ∼ salire alle stelle

skyjacker /'skaɪdʒækə(r)/ n dirottatore, -trice mf aereo

skylight n lucernario m

skyline n (of city) profilo m

skyrocket vi (prices) andare alle stelle

skyscraper n grattacielo m

slab /slæk/ n lastra f; (slice) fetta f; (of chocolate) tavoletta f

slack /slæk/ ① adj lento; (person) fiacco
② vi fare lo scansafatiche
∎ **slack off** vi rilassarsi

slacken /'slækn/ ① vi allentare; ∼ [off] (trade) rallentare; (speed, rain) diminuire
② vt allentare; diminuire (speed)

slacker /'slækə(r)/ n lazzarone m

slacks /slæks/ npl pantaloni mpl sportivi

slag /slæg/ n scorie fpl
∎ **slag off** vt (pt/pp slagged) Br fam sparlare di

slain /sleɪn/ ▶ SLAY

slalom /'slɑːləm/ n slalom m inv

slam /slæm/ ① vt (pt/pp slammed) sbattere; (fam: criticize) stroncare
② vi sbattere

slammer /'slæmə(r)/ n (fam: prison) galera f

slander /'slɑːndə(r)/ ① n diffamazione f
② vt diffamare

slanderer /'slɑːndərə(r)/ n diffamatore, -trice mf

slanderous /'slɑːnd(ə)rəs/ adj diffamatorio

slang /slæŋ/ n gergo m

slangy /'slæŋɪ/ adj gergale

slant /slɑːnt/ ① n pendenza f; (point of view) angolazione f; **on the** ∼ in pendenza
② vt pendere; fig distorcere (report)
③ vi pendere

slanted /'slɑːntɪd/ adj fig (report) tendenzioso

slap /slæp/ ① n schiaffo m
② vt (pt/pp slapped) schiaffeggiare; (put) schiaffare
③ adv in pieno

slap bang adv fam **he went** ∼ ∼ **into the wall** è andato a sbattere in pieno contro il muro

slapdash adj fam frettoloso

slapstick n farsa f da torte in faccia

slap-up adj fam di prim'ordine

slash /slæʃ/ ① n taglio m; Typ barra f; Comput slash m inv
② vt tagliare; ridurre drasticamente (prices); ∼ **one's wrists** svenarsi

slat /slæt/ n stecca f

slate /sleɪt/ ① n ardesia f
② vt fam fare a pezzi

slater /'sleɪtə(r)/ n (roofer) addetto m alla ricopertura dei tetti con tegole di ardesia; Zool onisco m

slatted /'slætɪd/ adj (shutter) a stecche

slaughter /'slɔːtə(r)/ ① n macello m; (of people) massacro m
② vt macellare; massacrare (people)

slaughterhouse /'slɔːtəhaʊs/ n macello m

Slav /slɑːv/ ① adj slavo
② n slavo, -a mf

slave /sleɪv/ ① n schiavo, -a mf
② vi ∼ **[away]** lavorare come un negro

slave-driver n schiavista mf

slavery /'sleɪvərɪ/ n schiavitù f

Slavic /'slɑːvɪk/ adj slavo

slavish /'sleɪvɪʃ/ adj servile

slavishly /'sleɪvɪʃlɪ/ adv in modo servile

Slavonic /slə'vɒnɪk/ adj slavo

slaw /slɔː/ n Am = COLESLAW

slay /sleɪ/ vt (pt slew, pp slain) ammazzare

sleaze /sliːz/ n fam (pornography) pornografia f; (corruption) corruzione f

sleazy /'sliːzɪ/ adj (-ier, -iest) sordido

sled /sled/ ① n slitta f
② vi andare in slitta

sledge /sledʒ/ n slitta f

sledgehammer /'sledʒhæmə(r)/ n martello m

sleek /sliːk/ adj liscio, lucente; (well-fed) pasciuto

sleep /sliːp/ ① n sonno m; **go to** ∼ addormentarsi; **put to** ∼ far addormentare; **in my** ∼ nel sonno; **a good night's** ∼ una bella dormita

2 *vi* (*pt/pp* **slept**) dormire; ∼ **like a log** dormire come un ghiro; ∼ **on it** dormirci sopra; ∼ **with somebody** andare a letto con qualcuno

3 *vt* ∼**s six** ha sei posti letto

■ **sleep around** *vi* andare a letto con tutti

■ **sleep in** *vi* dormire più a lungo

sleeper /'sli:pə(r)/ *n* Rail treno *m* con vagoni letto; (compartment) vagone *m* letto; (on track) traversina *f*; **be a light/heavy** ∼ avere il sonno leggero/pesante

sleepily /'sli:pɪlɪ/ *adv* con aria assonnata

sleeping bag *n* sacco *m* a pelo

sleeping car *n* vagone *m* letto

sleeping partner *n* Br Comm socio *m* accomodante

sleeping pill *n* sonnifero *m*

sleeping policeman *n* dosso *m* di rallentamento

sleepless /'sli:plɪs/ *adj* insonne; **have a** ∼ **night** passare una notte insonne

sleeplessness /'sli:plɪsnɪs/ *n* insonnia *f*

sleepover /'sli:pəʊvə(r)/ *n* **the kids are having a** ∼ i bambini hanno invitato degli amichetti a dormire a casa

sleepsuit *n* tutina *f*

sleepwalk *vi* essere sonnambulo

sleepwalker *n* sonnambulo, -a *mf*

sleepwalking *n* sonnambulismo *m*

sleepy /'sli:pɪ/ *adj* (**-ier, -iest**) assonnato; **be** ∼ aver sonno

sleet /sli:t/ **1** *n* nevischio *m*

2 *vi* **it is** ∼**ing** nevischia

sleeve /sli:v/ *n* manica *f*; (for record) copertina *f*

sleeveless /'sli:vlɪs/ *adj* senza maniche

sleigh /sleɪ/ *n* slitta *f*

sleight /slaɪt/ *n* ∼ **of hand** gioco *m* di prestigio

slender /'slendə(r)/ *adj* snello; ⟨*fingers, stem*⟩ affusolato; fig scarso; ⟨*chance*⟩ magro

slept /slept/ ▶ SLEEP

sleuth /slu:θ/ *n* investigatore *m*, detective *m inv*

slew[1] /slu:/ *vi* girare

slew[2] ▶ SLAY

slice /slaɪs/ **1** *n* fetta *f*

2 *vt* affettare; ∼**d bread** pane *m* a cassetta

slick /slɪk/ **1** *adj* liscio; (cunning) astuto

2 *n* (of oil) chiazza *f* di petrolio

slide /slaɪd/ **1** *n* scivolata *f*; (in playground) scivolo *m*; (for hair) fermaglio *m* [per capelli]; Phot diapositiva *f*

2 *vi* (*pt/pp* **slid**) scivolare

3 *vt* far scivolare

slide projector *n* proiettore *m* per diapositive

slide rule *n* regolo *m* calcolatore

slide show *n* proiezione *f* di diapositive

sliding /'slaɪdɪŋ/ *adj* ⟨*door, seat*⟩ scorrevole

sliding scale *n* scala *f* mobile

slight /slaɪt/ **1** *adj* leggero; ⟨*importance*⟩ poco; (slender) esile; ∼**est** minimo; **not in the** ∼**est** niente affatto

2 *vt* offendere

3 *n* offesa *f*

slightly /'slaɪtlɪ/ *adv* leggermente

slim /slɪm/ **1** *adj* (**slimmer, slimmest**) snello; fig scarso; ⟨*chance*⟩ magro

2 *vi* dimagrire

slime /slaɪm/ *n* melma *f*

slimy /'slaɪmɪ/ *adj* melmoso; fig viscido

sling /slɪŋ/ **1** *n* Med benda *f* al collo

2 *vt* (*pt/pp* **slung**) fam lanciare

sling-back *n* sandalo *m* (chiuso davanti)

slingshot /'slɪŋʃɒt/ *n* fionda *f*

slink /slɪŋk/ *vi* (*pt/pp* **slunk**) entrare furtivamente

slinky /'slɪŋkɪ/ *adj* fam ⟨*dress*⟩ sexy *inv*, attillato

slip /slɪp/ **1** *n* scivolata *f*; (mistake) lieve errore *m*; (petticoat) sottoveste *f*; (for pillow) federa *f*; (paper) scontrino *m*; **give somebody the** ∼ fam sbarazzarsi di qualcuno; ∼ **of the tongue** lapsus *m inv*

2 *vi* (*pt/pp* **slipped**) scivolare; (go quickly) sgattaiolare; (decline) retrocedere; **let something** ∼ (reveal) lasciarsi sfuggire qualcosa

3 *vt* he ∼**ped it into his pocket** se l'è infilato in tasca; ∼ **sb's mind** sfuggire di mente a qualcuno

■ **slip away** *vi* sgusciar via; ⟨*time*⟩ sfuggire

■ **slip into** *vi* infilarsi ⟨*clothes*⟩

■ **slip on** *vt* infilarsi ⟨*jacket etc*⟩

■ **slip up** *vi* fam sbagliare

slip-knot *n* nodo *m* scorsoio

slip-on [shoe] *n* mocassino *m*

slipped disc /slɪpt'dɪsk/ *n* Med ernia *f* del disco

slipper /'slɪpə(r)/ *n* pantofola *f*

slippery /'slɪpərɪ/ *adj* scivoloso

slip road *n* bretella *f*

slipshod /'slɪpʃɒd/ *adj* trascurato

slip-up *n* fam sbaglio *m*

slit /slɪt/ **1** *n* spacco *m*; (tear) strappo *m*; (hole) fessura *f*

2 *vt* (*pt/pp* **slit**) tagliare

slither /'slɪðə(r)/ *vi* scivolare

sliver /'slɪvə(r)/ *n* scheggia *f*

slob /slɒb/ *n* fam (messy) maiale *m*; (lazy) pelandrone *m*

slobber /'slɒbə(r)/ *vi* sbavare

sloe /sləʊ/ *n* (fruit) prugnola *f*; (bush) prugnolo *m*

slog /slɒg/ ① n [hard] ~ sgobbata f
② vi (pt/pp **slogged**) (work) sgobbare

slogan /'sləʊgən/ n slogan m inv

slop /slɒp/ vt (pt/pp **slopped**) versare
■ **slop over** vi versarsi

slope /sləʊp/ ① n pendenza f; (ski ~)
pista f
② vi essere inclinato, inclinarsi
■ **slope off** vi scantonare

sloping /'sləʊpɪŋ/ adj in pendenza

sloppiness /'slɒpɪnɪs/ n (of work)
trascuratezza f

sloppy /'slɒpɪ/ adj (**-ier, -iest**) ⟨work⟩
trascurato; ⟨worker⟩ negligente; (in dress)
sciatto; (sentimental) sdolcinato

slosh /slɒʃ/ ① vi fam ⟨person, feet⟩
sguazzare; ⟨water⟩ scrosciare
② vt (fam: hit) colpire

sloshed /slɒʃt/ adj fam sbronzo

slot /slɒt/ ① n fessura f; (time- ~) spazio
m
② vt (pt/pp **slotted**) infilare
■ **slot in** vi incastrarsi
■ **slot together** vi ⟨pieces⟩ incastrarsi

sloth /sləʊθ/ n accidia f

slot machine n distributore m
automatico; (for gambling) slot-machine f inv

slouch /slaʊtʃ/ vi (in chair) stare
scomposto

Slovak /'sləʊvæk/ adj & n slovacco, -a
mf

Slovakia /sləʊ'vækɪə/ n Slovacchia f

Slovene /'sləʊviːn/ adj & n sloveno, -a
mf

Slovenia /sləʊ'viːnɪə/ n Slovenia f

slovenliness /'slʌvənlɪnɪs/ n sciatteria
f

slovenly /'slʌvnlɪ/ adj sciatto

slow /sləʊ/ ① adj lento; be ~ ⟨clock⟩
essere indietro; in ~ **motion** al
rallentatore
② adv lentamente
■ **slow down** vt/i rallentare
■ **slow up** vt/i rallentare

slowcoach /'sləʊkəʊtʃ/ n fam tartaruga
f

slowly /'sləʊlɪ/ adv lentamente

slow-moving adj ⟨film, river⟩ lento

slowness /'sləʊnɪs/ n lentezza f

slow puncture n foratura f

sludge /slʌdʒ/ n fanghiglia f

slug /slʌg/ n lumacone m; (bullet)
pallottola f

sluggish /'slʌgɪʃ/ adj lento

sluggishly /'slʌgɪʃnɪs/ adv lentamente

sluice /sluːs/ n chiusa f

sluice gate n saracinesca f (di chiusa)

slum /slʌm/ n (house) tugurio m; ~s pl
bassifondi mpl

slumber /'slʌmbə(r)/ ① n sonno m

② vi dormire

slump /slʌmp/ ① n crollo m; (economic)
depressione f
② vi crollare

slung /slʌŋ/ ▶ SLING

slunk /slʌŋk/ ▶ SLINK

slur /slɜː(r)/ ① n (discredit) calunnia f
② vt (pt/pp **slurred**) biascicare

slurp /slɜːp/ vt/i bere rumorosamente

slurry /'slʌrɪ/ n (waste from animals)
liquame m; (waste from factory) fanghiglia f
semiliquida; (of cement) impasto m
semiliquido

slush /slʌʃ/ n pantano m nevoso; fig
sdolcinatezza f

slush fund n fondi mpl neri

slushy /'slʌʃɪ/ adj fangoso; (sentimental)
sdolcinato

slut /slʌt/ n sgualdrina f

sly /slaɪ/ ① adj (**-ier, -iest**) scaltro
② n on the ~ di nascosto

slyly /'slaɪlɪ/ adv scaltramente

SM n abbr **sadomasochism**

smack¹ /smæk/ ① n (on face) schiaffo m;
(on bottom) sculaccione m
② vt (on face) schiaffeggiare; (on bottom)
sculacciare; ~ one's lips far schioccare le
labbra
③ adv fam in pieno

smack² vi ~ of fig sapere di

smacker /'smækə(r)/ n (fam: kiss) bacio
m; 500 ~s (£500) 500 sterline

small /smɔːl/ ① adj piccolo; be out/work
until the ~ hours fare le ore piccole
② adv chop up ~ fare a pezzettini
③ n the ~ of the back le reni

small ads npl annunci mpl
[commerciali]

small business n piccola impresa f

small change n spiccioli mpl

small-holding n piccola tenuta f

small hours npl ore fpl piccole

small letter n lettera f minuscola

small-minded /-'maɪndɪd/ adj
meschino

smallpox n vaiolo m

small print n caratteri mpl piccoli; **read
the ~ ~** fig leggere tutto fin nei minimi
particolari

small talk n chiacchiere fpl; make ~ ~
fare conversazione

smarmy /'smɑːmɪ/ adj (**-ier, -iest**) fam
untuoso

smart /smɑːt/ ① adj elegante; (clever)
intelligente; (brisk) svelto; be ~ (fam:
cheeky) fare il furbo
② vi (hurt) bruciare

smart alec[k] /'smɑːtælɪk/ n fam
sapientone m

smart bomb n bomba f intelligente

smart card *n* carta *f* intelligente

smarten /'smɑːt(ə)n/ *vt* ~ oneself up farsi bello

smartly /'smɑːtlɪ/ *adv* elegantemente; (cleverly) intelligentemente; (briskly) velocemente; (cheekily) sfacciatamente

smart money *n* fam the ~ ~ **was on Desert Orchid** gli esperti avevano puntato su Desert Orchid

smartphone *n* smartphone *m inv*

smash /smæʃ/ ① *n* fragore *m*; (collision) scontro *m*; Tennis schiacciata *f*
② *vt* spaccare; Tennis schiacciare
③ *vi* spaccarsi; (crash) schiantarsi (into contro)
■ **smash up** *vt* distruggere ⟨car, bar⟩

smash-and-grab *n* Br rapina *f* ad un negozio (con sfascio di vetrina)

smashed /smæʃt/ *adj* ⟨window⟩ in frantumi; ⟨vehicle⟩ sfasciato; ⟨limb⟩ fracassato; (fam: on drugs) fatto; (fam: on alcohol) ubriaco fradicio

smash [hit] *n* successo *m*

smashing /'smæʃɪŋ/ *adj* fam fantastico

smattering /'smætərɪŋ/ *n* infarinatura *f*

smear /smɪə(r)/ ① *n* macchia *f*; Med striscio *m*
② *vt* imbrattare; (coat) spalmare (with di); fig calunniare
③ *vi* sbavare

smear campaign *n* campagna *f* diffamatoria

smear test *n* Med striscio *m*, Pap test *m inv*

smell /smel/ ① *n* odore *m*; (sense) odorato *m*
② *vt* (pt/pp **smelt** or **smelled**) odorare (of di); that ~s good ha un buon odore

smelling salts /'smelɪŋ/ *npl* Med sali *mpl*

smelly /'smelɪ/ *adj* (-ier, -iest) puzzolente

smelt[1] /smelt/ ▶ SMELL

smelt[2] *vt* fondere

smidgeon /'smɪdʒɪn/ *n* (of something to eat) pizzico *m*; (of something to drink) goccio *m*

smile /smaɪl/ ① *n* sorriso *m*
② *vi* sorridere; ~ **at** sorridere a ⟨somebody⟩; sorridere di ⟨something⟩
■ **smile on** *vt* ⟨weather, fortune⟩ sorridere a ⟨person⟩

smiley /'smaɪlɪ/ *n* fam smiley *m inv*, faccina *f* sorridente

smirk /smɜːk/ ① *n* sorriso *m* compiaciuto
② *vi* sorridere con aria compiaciuta

smithereens /smɪðə'riːnz/ *npl* to/in ~ in mille pezzi

smithy /'smɪðɪ/ *n* fucina *f*

smitten /'smɪtn/ *adj* ~ with tutto preso da

smock /smɒk/ *n* grembiule *m*

smog /smɒg/ *n* smog *m inv*

smoke /sməʊk/ ① *n* fumo *m*
② *vt/i* fumare

smoke alarm *n* allarme *m* antifumo *inv*

smoked /sməʊkt/ *adj* affumicato

smoke-free zone *n* zona *f* non-fumatori; '~ ~' 'vietato fumare'

smokeless /'sməʊklɪs/ *adj* senza fumo; ⟨fuel⟩ che non fa fumo

smoker /'sməʊkə(r)/ *n* fumatore, -trice *mf*; Rail vagone *m* fumatori

smokescreen /'sməʊkskriːn/ *n* also fig cortina *f* di fumo

smoking /'sməʊkɪŋ/ *n* fumo *m*; 'no ~' 'vietato fumare'; '~ **or non-~?**' 'fumatori o non fumatori?'

smoking-related *adj* ⟨illness⟩ legato al fumo

smoky /'sməʊkɪ/ *adj* (-ier, -iest) fumoso; ⟨taste⟩ di fumo

smooch /smuːtʃ/ *vi* fam pomiciare

smooth /smuːð/ ① *adj* liscio; ⟨movement⟩ scorrevole; ⟨sea⟩ calmo; ⟨manners⟩ mellifluo
② *vt* lisciare; ~ **things over** sistemare le cose
■ **smooth out** *vt* lisciare

smoothly /'smuːðlɪ/ *adv* in modo scorrevole; go ~ andare liscio

smooth-running *adj* ⟨event, service⟩ ben organizzato

smooth-tongued /-'tʌŋd/ *adj* pej mellifluo

smother /'smʌðə(r)/ *vt* soffocare

smoulder /'sməʊldə(r)/ *vi* fumare; (with rage) consumarsi

SMS *n abbr* (**short message service**) SMS *m*

SMS message *n* sms *m inv*

smudge /smʌdʒ/ ① *n* macchia *f*
② *vt/i* imbrattare

smug /smʌg/ *adj* (**smugger, smuggest**) compiaciuto

smuggle /'smʌgl/ *vt* contrabbandare

smuggler /'smʌglə(r)/ *n* contrabbandiere, -a *mf*

smuggling /'smʌglɪŋ/ *n* contrabbando *m*

smugly /'smʌglɪ/ *adv* con aria compiaciuta

smugness /'smʌgnɪs/ *n* compiacimento *m*

smut /smʌt/ *n* macchia *f* di fuliggine; fig sconcezza *f*

smutty /'smʌtɪ/ *adj* (-ier, -iest) fuligginoso; fig sconcio

snack /snæk/ *n* spuntino *m*

snack-bar *n* snack bar *m inv*

snag[1] /snæg/ n (problem) intoppo m

snag[2] vt smagliarsi ⟨tights⟩ (on con)

snail /sneɪl/ n lumaca f; **at a ~'s pace** a passo di lumaca

snail mail n fam posta f tradizionale, così chiamata dagli utenti di email

snake /sneɪk/ n serpente m

snakebite n morso m di serpente

snake charmer n incantatore, -trice mf di serpenti

snakes and ladders n Br gioco m dell'oca

snap /snæp/ ① n colpo m secco; (photo) istantanea f
② attrib ⟨decision⟩ istantaneo
③ vi (pt/pp **snapped**) (break) spezzarsi
④ vt (break) spezzare; (say) dire seccamente; Phot fare un'istantanea di; schioccare ⟨fingers⟩
■ **snap at** ⟨dog⟩ cercare di azzannare; ⟨person⟩ parlare seccamente a
■ **snap off** vt ~ sb's head off fam aggredire qualcuno
■ **snap out** vi ~ out of it venirne fuori
■ **snap up** vt afferrare

snappy /'snæpɪ/ adj (-ier, -iest) scorbutico; (smart) elegante; **make it ~!** sbrigati!

snapshot /'snæpʃɒt/ n istantanea f

snare /sneə(r)/ n trappola f

snarl /snɑːl/ ① n ringhio m
② vi ringhiare

snarled-up /snɑːld'ʌp/ adj ⟨traffic⟩ bloccato

snarl-up n (in traffic, network) ingorgo m

snatch /snætʃ/ ① n strappo m; (fragment) brano m; (theft) scippo m; **make a ~ at something** cercare di afferrare qualcosa
② vt strappare [di mano] (**from** a); (steal) scippare; rapire ⟨child⟩

snazzy /'snæzɪ/ adj fam sciccoso

sneak /sniːk/ ① n (fam: devious person) tipo, -a mf subdolo, -a; (Br fam: telltale) spia f
② vt (fam: steal) fregare; rubare ⟨kiss⟩; **~ a glance at** dare una sbirciatina a
③ vi (Br fam: tell tales) fare la spia
④ attrib ⟨visit⟩ furtivo; **have a ~ preview of something** vedere qualcosa in anteprima
■ **sneak away** vi sgattaiolare via
■ **sneak in** vi sgattaiolare dentro
■ **sneak out** vi sgattaiolare fuori

sneakers /'sniːkəz/ npl Am scarpe fpl da ginnastica

sneaking /'sniːkɪŋ/ adj furtivo; ⟨suspicion⟩ vago

sneaky /'sniːkɪ/ adj sornione

sneer /snɪə(r)/ ① n ghigno m
② vi sogghignare; **~ at** (mock) ridere di

sneeze /sniːz/ ① n starnuto m
② vi starnutire; **it's not to be ~d at** non ci sputerei sopra

snide /snaɪd/ adj fam insinuante

sniff /snɪf/ ① n (of dog) annusata f; **give a ~** ⟨person⟩ tirare su col naso
② vi tirare su col naso
③ vt odorare ⟨flower⟩; sniffare ⟨glue⟩; ⟨dog⟩ annusare

sniffer dog /'snɪfə/ n cane m poliziotto (antidroga, antiterrorismo)

sniffle /'snɪfl/ ① n **have a ~** or **the ~s** (slight cold) avere un po' di raffreddore; **give a ~** tirar su col naso
② vi tirar su col naso

sniffy /'snɪfɪ/ adj (fam: haughty) con la puzza sotto il naso

snigger /'snɪgə(r)/ ① n risatina f soffocata
② vi ridacchiare

snip /snɪp/ ① n taglio m; (fam: bargain) affare m
② vt/t ~ [at] tagliare
■ **snip off** vt tagliare via ⟨corner, end⟩

snipe /snaɪp/ vi ~ at tirare su; fig sparare a zero su

sniper /'snaɪpə(r)/ n cecchino m

snippet /'snɪpɪt/ n **a ~ of information/ news** una breve notizia/informazione

snivel /'snɪvl/ vi (pt/pp **snivelled**) piagnucolare

snivelling /'snɪv(ə)lɪŋ/ adj piagnucoloso

snob /snɒb/ n snob mf inv

snobbery /'snɒbərɪ/ n snobismo m

snobbish /'snɒbɪʃ/ adj da snob; **be ~** ⟨person⟩ essere uno/una snob; ⟨club etc⟩ essere molto snob

snobbishness /'snɒbɪʃnɪs/ n snobismo m

snog /snɒg/ vi Br sl pomiciare

snooker /'snuːkə(r)/ ① n (game) snooker m; (shot) impallatura f
② vt Sport impallare; fig mettere in difficoltà

snoop /snuːp/ ① n spia f
② vi fam curiosare

snooper /'snuːpə(r)/ n ficcanaso mf

snooty /'snuːtɪ/ adj fam sdegnoso

snooze /snuːz/ ① n sonnellino m
② vi fare un sonnellino

snore /snɔː(r)/ vi russare

snoring /'snɔːrɪŋ/ n il russare

snorkel /'snɔːkl/ n respiratore m

snorkelling /'snɔːklɪŋ/ Br, **snorkeling** Am n snorkelling m inv

snort /snɔːt/ ① n sbuffo m
② vi sbuffare
③ vt fiutare ⟨cocaine⟩

snot /snɒt/ n (fam: mucus) moccolo m

snotty /'snɒtɪ/ adj fam ⟨nose⟩ moccioso; (disagreeable) sgradevole

snotty-nosed kid /-nəʊzd/ n moccioso, -a mf

S

snout /snaʊt/ *n* grugno *m*

snow /snəʊ/ **1** *n* neve *f*
2 *vi* nevicare; ~**ed under with** fig sommerso di

snowball **1** *n* palla *f* di neve
2 *vi* fig fare a palle di neve

snowboard **1** *n* snowboard *m inv*
2 *vi* fare snowboard

snowboarding /'snəʊ'bɔ:dɪŋ/ *n* snowboard *m inv*

snowdrift *n* cumulo *m* di neve

snowdrop *n* bucaneve *m inv*

snowfall *n* nevicata *f*

snowflake *n* fiocco *m* di neve

snowman *n* pupazzo *m* di neve

snowmobile /'snəʊməbi:l/ *n* gatto *m* delle nevi

snowplough *n* spazzaneve *m inv*

snowshoe *n* racchetta *f* da neve

snowstorm *n* tormenta *f*

snow tyres *npl* pneumatici *mpl* chiodati

snowy /'snəʊɪ/ *adj* nevoso

Snr *abbr* Senior

snub /snʌb/ **1** *n* sgarbo *m*
2 *vt* (pt/pp **snubbed**) snobbare

snub-nosed /'snʌbnəʊzd/ *adj* dal naso all'insù

snuff[1] /snʌf/ *n* tabacco *m* da fiuto

snuff[2] *vt* ~ **[out]** spegnere ‹candle›; ~ **it** fam tirare le cuoia

snug /snʌg/ *adj* (**snugger, snuggest**) comodo; (tight) aderente

snuggle /'snʌgl/ *vi* rannicchiarsi (**up to** accanto a)

so /səʊ/ **1** *adv* così; **so far** finora; **so am I** anch'io; **so I see** così pare; **you've left the door open –so I have!** hai lasciato la porta aperta –è vero!; **that is so** è così; **so much** così tanto; **so much the better** tanto meglio; **so it is** proprio così; **if so** se è così; **so as to** in modo da; **so long!** fam a presto!
2 *pron* **I hope/think/am afraid so** spero/penso/temo di sì; **I told you so** te l'ho detto; **because I say so** perché lo dico io; **I did so!** l'ho fatto!; **so saying/doing,...** così dicendo/facendo,...; **or so** circa; **very much so** sì, molto; **and so forth** or **on** e così via
3 *conj* (therefore) perciò; (in order that) così; **so that** affinché; **so there!** ecco!; **so what?** e allora?; **so where have you been?** allora, dove sei stato?

soak /səʊk/ **1** *vt* mettere a bagno
2 *vi* stare a bagno
■ **soak in** *vi* penetrare
■ **soak into** *vt* ‹liquid› penetrare
■ **soak up** *vt* assorbire

soaked /səʊkt/ *adj* fradicio; ~ **in** **something** impregnato di qualcosa

soaking /'səʊkɪŋ/ **1** *n* ammollo *m*

2 *adj & adv* ~ **[wet]** fam inzuppato

so-and-so *n* tal dei tali *mf*; (euphemism) specie *f* di imbecille

soap /səʊp/ *n* sapone *m*

soap opera *n* telenovela *f*, soap opera *f inv*

soap powder *n* detersivo *m* in polvere

soapy /'səʊpɪ/ *adj* (**-ier, -iest**) insaponato

soar /sɔ:(r)/ *vi* elevarsi; ‹prices› salire alle stelle

soaring /'sɔ:rɪŋ/ *adj* ‹costs, temperatures, inflation› in forte aumento

S.O.B. *n* Am *abbr* **son of a bitch**

sob /sɒb/ **1** *n* singhiozzo *m*
2 *vi* (pt/pp **sobbed**) singhiozzare

sobbing /'sɒbɪŋ/ *n* singhiozzi *mpl*

sober /'səʊbə(r)/ *adj* sobrio; (serious) serio
■ **sober up** *vi* ritornare sobrio

soberly /'səʊbəlɪ/ *adv* sobriamente; (seriously) con aria seria

sobriety /sə'braɪətɪ/ *n* (not drinking) sobrietà *f*; (seriousness) serietà *f*

sob story *n* storia *f* lacrimevole

so-called /'səʊkɔ:ld/ *adj* cosiddetto

soccer /'sɒkə(r)/ *n* calcio *m*

soccer pitch *n* campo *m* di calcio

soccer player *n* giocatore *m* di calcio

sociable /'səʊʃəbl/ *adj* socievole

social /'səʊʃl/ *adj* sociale; (sociable) socievole

social climber *n* arrampicatore, -trice *mf* sociale

social climbing *n* arrivismo *m* sociale

social club *n* circolo *m* sociale

socialism /'səʊʃəlɪzm/ *n* socialismo *m*

socialist /'səʊʃəlɪst/ **1** *adj* socialista
2 *n* socialista *mf*

socialite /'səʊʃəlaɪt/ *n* persona *f* che fa vita mondana

socialize /'səʊʃəlaɪz/ *vi* socializzare

socially /'səʊʃəlɪ/ *adv* socialmente; **know somebody** ~ frequentare qualcuno

social science *n* scienze *fpl* sociali

social security *n* previdenza *f* sociale

social services *npl* servizi *mpl* sociali

social work *n* assistenza *f* sociale

social worker *n* assistente *mf* sociale

society /sə'saɪətɪ/ *n* società *f inv*

socio-economic /səʊsɪəʊi:kə'nɒmɪk/ *adj* socioeconomico

sociological /səʊsɪə'lɒdʒɪkl/ *adj* sociologico

sociologist /səʊsɪ'ɒlədʒɪst/ *n* sociologo, -a *mf*

sociology /səʊsɪ'ɒlədʒɪ/ *n* sociologia *f*

sock[1] /sɒk/ *n* calzino *m*; (kneelength) calzettone *m*

sock² fam ① *n* pugno *m*
② *vt* dare un pugno a

socket /'sɒkɪt/ *n* (of eye) orbita *f*; (wall plug) presa *f* [di corrente]; (for bulb) portalampada *m inv*

sod /sɒd/ *n* fam stronzo *m*; **you lucky ∼!** che fortuna sfacciata!
■ **sod off** *vi* fam togliersi dai piedi

soda /'səʊdə/ *n* soda *f*; Am gazzosa *f*

soda water *n* seltz *m inv*

sodden /'sɒdn/ *adj* inzuppato

sodium /'səʊdɪəm/ *n* sodio *m*

sodium bicarbonate *n* bicarbonato *m* di sodio

Sod's Law /sɒdz/ *n* fam hum regola *f* per cui, se qualcosa può andare storto, va storto

sofa /'səʊfə/ *n* divano *m*

sofa bed *n* divano *m* letto

soft /sɒft/ *adj* morbido, soffice; ⟨voice⟩ sommesso; ⟨light, colour⟩ tenue; (not strict) indulgente; (fam: silly) stupido

soft-boiled /-'bɔɪld/ *adj* ⟨egg⟩ bazzotto

soft contact lenses *npl* lenti *fpl* a contatto morbide

soft drink *n* bibita *f* analcolica

soft drug *n* droga *f* leggera

soften /'sɒfn/ ① *vt* ammorbidire; fig attenuare
② *vi* ammorbidirsi
■ **soften up** *vi* ammorbidirsi *vt* ∼ somebody up ammorbidire qualcuno ⟨opponent, enemy, customer⟩

softener /'sɒf(ə)nə(r)/ *n* (for water) dolcificatore *m*; (substance) anti-calcare *m inv*; (for fabrics) ammorbidente *m*

soft furnishings *npl* tappeti *mpl* e tessuti *mpl* da arredamento

soft-hearted *adj* dal cuore tenero

soft ice-cream *n* mantecato *m*

softie /'sɒftɪ/ *n* fam = SOFTY

softly /'sɒftlɪ/ *adv* (say) sottovoce; ⟨treat⟩ con indulgenza; ⟨play music⟩ in sottofondo

soft option *n* take the ∼ ∼ scegliere la soluzione più semplice

soft-pedal *vt* fig minimizzare

soft porn *n* fam pornografia *f* soft[-core]

soft sell *n* metodo *m* di vendita basato sulla persuasione

soft soap *n* fig lusinghe *fpl*

soft-soap *vt* fig lusingare

soft-spoken *adj* dalla voce dolce

soft spot *n* have a ∼ ∼ for somebody fam avere un debole per qualcuno

soft-top *n* Auto decappottabile *f*

soft touch *n* be a ∼ ∼ lasciarsi spremere

soft toy *n* pupazzo *m* di peluche

software /'sɒftweə(r)/ *n* software *m*

software engineer *n* softwarista *mf*

software house *n* software house *f*

software package *n* pacchetto *m* software

software piracy *n* pirateria *f* informatica

software writer *n* scrittore, -trice *mf* di programmi

softy /'sɒftɪ/ *n* fam (weak person) pappamolle *mf inv*; (indulgent person) bonaccione, -a *mf*

soggy /'sɒgɪ/ *adj* (**-ier, -iest**) zuppo

soil¹ /sɔɪl/ *n* suolo *m*

soil² *vt* sporcare

soiled /sɔɪld/ *adj* sporco

solace /'sɒləs/ *n* sollievo *m*

solar /'səʊlə(r)/ *adj* solare

solar eclipse *n* eclissi *f inv* di sole

solar energy *n* energia *f* solare,

solar panel *n* pannello *m* solare

solar power *n* energia *f* solare

solar system *n* sistema *m* solare

sold /səʊld/ ▶ SELL

solder /'səʊldə(r)/ ① *n* lega *f* da saldatura
② *vt* saldare

soldier /'səʊldʒə(r)/ *n* soldato *m*
■ **soldier on** *vi* perseverare

sole¹ /səʊl/ *n* (of foot) pianta *f*; (of shoe) suola *f*

sole² *n* (fish) sogliola *f*

sole³ *adj* unico, solo

sole agency *n* rappresentanza *f* esclusiva

solecism /'sɒlɪsɪzm/ *n* (social) scorrettezza *f*; (linguistic) solecismo *m*

solely /'səʊllɪ/ *adv* unicamente

solemn /'sɒləm/ *adj* solenne

solemnity /sə'lemnɪtɪ/ *n* solennità *f inv*

solemnly /'sɒləmlɪ/ *adv* solennemente

sol-fa /'sɒlfɑː/ *n* solfeggio *m*

solicit /sə'lɪsɪt/ ① *vt* sollecitare
② *vi* ⟨prostitute⟩ adescare

soliciting /sə'lɪsɪtɪŋ/ *n* Jur adescamento *m*

solicitor /sə'lɪsɪtə(r)/ *n* avvocato *m*

solicitous /sə'lɪsɪtəs/ *adj* premuroso

solicitously /sə'lɪsɪtəslɪ/ *adv* premurosamente

solid /'sɒlɪd/ ① *adj* solido; ⟨oak, gold⟩ massiccio; **it took a ∼ hour** ci è voluta ben un'ora
② *n* (figure) solido *m*; ∼**s** *pl* (food) cibi *mpl* solidi

solidarity /sɒlɪ'dærətɪ/ *n* solidarietà *f inv*

solidify /sə'lɪdɪfaɪ/ *vi* (pt/pp **-ied**) solidificarsi

soliloquy /sə'lɪləkwɪ/ *n* soliloquio *m*

S

solitaire /sɒlɪ'teə(r)/ *n* solitario *m*

solitary /'sɒlɪtərɪ/ *adj* solitario; (sole) solo

solitary confinement *n* cella *f* di isolamento

solitude /'sɒlɪtjuːd/ *n* solitudine *f*

solo /'səʊləʊ/ [1] *n* Mus assolo *m*
[2] *adj* ⟨flight⟩ in solitario
[3] *adv* in solitario

soloist /'səʊləʊɪst/ *n* solista *mf*

solstice /'sɒlstɪs/ *n* solstizio *m*

soluble /'sɒljʊbl/ *adj* solubile

solution /sə'luːʃn/ *n* soluzione *f*

solvable /'sɒlvəbl/ *adj* risolvibile

solve /sɒlv/ *vt* risolvere

solvency /'sɒlvənsɪ/ *n* Fin solvibilità *f*

solvent /'sɒlvənt/ *adj & n* solvente *m*

solvent abuse *n* uso *m* di solventi come stupefacenti

Somali /sə'mɑːlɪ/ *adj & n* somalo, -a *mf*

Somalia /sə'mɑːlɪə/ *n* Somalia *f*

sombre /'sɒmbə(r)/ *adj* tetro; ⟨clothes⟩ scuro

some /sʌm/ [1] *adj* (a certain amount of) del; (a certain number of) alcuni, dei; ∼ **bread/ water** del pane/dell'acqua; ∼ **books/ oranges** dei libri/delle arance; **I need** ∼ **money/books** ho bisogno di soldi/libri; **do** ∼ **shopping** fare qualche acquisto; ∼ **day** un giorno o l'altro
[2] *pron* (a certain amount) un po'; (a certain number) alcuni; **I want** ∼ **ne voglio**; **would you like** ∼? ne vuoi?; ∼ **of the butter** una parte del burro; ∼ **of the apples/women** alcune delle mele/donne

somebody /'sʌmbədɪ/ [1] *pron* qualcuno *m*; ∼ **else will bring it** la porterà un altro
[2] *n* **he thinks he's** ∼ si crede chissà chi

somehow /'sʌmhaʊ/ *adv* in qualche modo; ∼ **or other** in un modo o nell'altro

someone /'sʌmwʌn/ *pron & n* = SOMEBODY

somersault /'sʌməsɔːlt/ [1] *n* capriola *f*; **turn a** ∼ fare una capriola
[2] *vi* fare una capriola

something /'sʌmθɪŋ/ *pron* qualche cosa, qualcosa; ∼ **different** qualcosa di diverso; ∼ **like** un po' come; (approximately) qualcosa come; **see** ∼ **of somebody** vedere qualcuno ogni tanto; **she is** ∼ **of an expert** è un'esperta

sometime /'sʌmtaɪm/ [1] *adv* un giorno o l'altro; ∼ **last summer** durante l'estate scorsa
[2] *adj* ex

sometimes /'sʌmtaɪmz/ *adv* qualche volta

somewhat /'sʌmwɒt/ *adv* piuttosto

somewhere /'sʌmweə(r)/ [1] *adv* da qualche parte

[2] *pron* ∼ **to eat** un posto in cui mangiare

son /sʌn/ *n* figlio *m*

sonar /'səʊnɑː(r)/ *n* sonar *m*

sonata /sə'nɑːtə/ *n* sonata *f*

song /sɒŋ/ *n* canzone *f*

song and dance *n* **make a** ∼ ∼ ∼ **about something** (fuss) far tante storie per qualcosa

songbird *n* uccello *m* canoro

songwriter *n* compositore, -trice *mf* di canzoni

sonic /'sɒnɪk/ *adj* sonico

sonic boom *n* bang *m inv* sonico

son-in-law *n* (*pl* ∼**s-in-law**) genero *m*

sonnet /'sɒnɪt/ *n* sonetto *m*

son of a bitch *n* fam figlio *m* di un cane

sonorous /'sɒnərəs/ *adj* sonoro; ⟨name⟩ altisonante

soon /suːn/ *adv* presto; (in a short time) tra poco; **as** ∼ **as** [non] appena; **as** ∼ **as possible** il più presto possibile; ∼**er or later** prima o poi; **the** ∼**er the better** prima è meglio è; **no** ∼**er had I arrived than...** ero appena arrivato quando...; **I would** ∼**er go** preferirei andare; ∼ **after** subito dopo

soot /sʊt/ *n* fuliggine *f*

soothe /suːð/ *vt* calmare

soothing /'suːðɪŋ/ *adj* calmante

sooty /'sʊtɪ/ *adj* fuligginoso

sop /sɒp/ *n* **throw a** ∼ **to** dare un contentino a

sophisticated /sə'fɪstɪkeɪtɪd/ *adj* sofisticato; (complex) complesso

sophistication /səfɪstɪ'keɪʃn/ *n* (elegance) sofisticatezza *f*, raffinatezza *f*; (complexity) complessità *f*

soporific /sɒpə'rɪfɪk/ *adj* soporifero

soppiness /'sɒpɪnɪs/ *n* fam svenevolezza *f*

sopping /'sɒpɪŋ/ *adj & adv* **be** ∼ **[wet]** essere bagnato fradicio

soppy /'sɒpɪ/ *adj* (**-ier, -iest**) fam svenevole

soprano /sə'prɑːnəʊ/ *n* soprano *m*

sorcerer /'sɔːsərə(r)/ *n* stregone *m*

sorceress /'sɔːsərɪs/ *n* strega *f*, maga *f*

sorcery /'sɔːsərɪ/ *n* (witchcraft) stregoneria *f*

sordid /'sɔːdɪd/ *adj* sordido

sordidness /'sɔːdɪdnɪs/ *n* sordidezza *f*

sore /sɔː(r)/ [1] *adj* dolorante; (Am: vexed) arrabbiato; **it's** ∼ **fa male**; **have a** ∼ **throat** avere mal di gola; **it's a** ∼ **point with her** è un punto delicato per lei
[2] *n* piaga *f*

sorely /'sɔːlɪ/ *adv* ⟨tempted⟩ seriamente

soreness /'sɔːnɪs/ *n* dolore *m*

sorrel /'sɒrəl/ *n* Bot acetosa *f*

sorrow /'sɒrəʊ/ n tristezza f

sorrowful /'sɒrəʊfʊl/ adj triste

sorrowfully /'sɒrəʊfʊlɪ/ adv tristemente

sorry /'sɒrɪ/ adj (**-ier, -iest**) (sad) spiacente; (wretched) pietoso; **you'll be** ∼! te ne pentirai!; **I am** ∼ mi dispiace; **be or feel** ∼ **for** provare compassione per; ∼! scusa!; (more polite) scusi!

sort /sɔːt/ [1] n tipo m; **it's a** ∼ **of fish** è un tipo di pesce; **be out of** ∼**s** (fam: unwell) stare poco bene

[2] vt classificare; fam sistemare ⟨problem, person⟩

■ **sort out** vt selezionare ⟨papers⟩; fig risolvere ⟨problem⟩; occuparsi di ⟨person⟩

sort code n Fin coordinate fpl bancarie

sorter /'sɔːtə(r)/ n (on photocopier) fascicolatrice f, fascicolatore m

SOS n SOS m; fig segnale m di soccorso

so-so adj & adv così così

sotto voce /sɒtəʊ'vəʊtʃeɪ/ adv ⟨say, add⟩ sottovoce

soufflé /'suːfleɪ/ n soufflé m

sought /sɔːt/ ▶ SEEK

sought-after adj ⟨job, brand, person⟩ richiesto

soul /səʊl/ n anima f; **poor** ∼ poveretto; **there was not a** ∼ **in sight** non c'era anima viva

soul-destroying /-dɪstrɔɪɪŋ/ adj ⟨job⟩ che abbruttisce

soulful /'səʊlfʊl/ adj sentimentale

soulmate n anima f gemella

soulsearching /-sɜːtʃɪŋ/ n esame m di coscienza

soul-stirring /-stɜːrɪŋ/ adj molto commovente

sound¹ /saʊnd/ [1] adj sano; (sensible) saggio; (secure) solido; ⟨thrashing⟩ clamoroso

[2] adv ∼ **asleep** profondamente addormentato

sound² /saʊnd/ [1] n suono m; (noise) rumore m; **I don't like the** ∼ **of it** fam non mi suona bene

[2] vi suonare; (seem) aver l'aria; **it** ∼**s to me as if...** mi sa che...

[3] vt (pronounce) pronunciare; Med auscultare ⟨chest⟩

■ **sound off** vi fare grandi discorsi

■ **sound out** vt fig sondare

sound barrier n muro m del suono

sound bite n breve frase f dal forte impatto mediatico

sound card n Comput scheda f audio

sound effect n effetto m sonoro

sound engineer n tecnico m del suono

soundless /'saʊndlɪs/ adj silenzioso

soundlessly /'saʊndlɪslɪ/ adv silenziosamente

soundly /'saʊndlɪ/ adv ⟨sleep⟩ profondamente; ⟨defeat⟩ clamorosamente

soundproof [1] adj impenetrabile al suono

[2] vt insonorizzare

sound system n (hifi) stereo m; (for disco etc) impianto m audio

soundtrack n colonna f sonora

soup /suːp/ n minestra f; **in the** ∼ fam nei pasticci

souped-up /suːpt'ʌp/ adj fam ⟨engine⟩ truccato

soup kitchen n mensa f dei poveri

soup plate n piatto m fondo

soup spoon n cucchiaio m da minestra

sour /'saʊə(r)/ adj agro; (not fresh & fig) acido

source /sɔːs/ n fonte f; **at** ∼ ⟨deducted⟩ alla fonte

source language n lingua f di partenza

sour cream n panna f acida

sourdough n lievito m

sour-faced /saʊə'feɪst/ adj ⟨person⟩ dall'espressione dura

sour grapes npl fam **it's just** ∼ ∼ [**on his part**] fa come la volpe con l'uva

south /saʊθ/ [1] n sud m; **to the** ∼ **of** a sud di

[2] adj del sud, meridionale

[3] adv a sud

South Africa n Sudafrica f

South African adj & n sudafricano, -a mf

South America n America f del Sud

South American adj & n sudamericano, -a mf

southbound adj ⟨traffic⟩ diretto a sud; ⟨carriageway⟩ sud

south-east /saʊθ'iːst/ n sud-est m

southerly /'sʌðəlɪ/ adj del sud

southern /'sʌðən/ adj del sud, meridionale; ∼ **Italy** il Mezzogiorno

southerner /'sʌðənə(r)/ n meridionale mf

South Korea n Corea f del Sud

southpaw /'saʊθpɔː/ n (in boxing) pugile m mancino

South Pole n polo m sud

southward[s] /'saʊθwəd[z]/ adv verso sud

south-west /saʊθ'west/ n sud-ovest m

south-western /saʊθ'westən/ adj sudoccidentale

souvenir /suːvə'nɪə(r)/ n ricordo m, souvenir m inv

sovereign /'sɒvrɪn/ adj & n sovrano, -a mf

sovereignty /'sɒvrɪntɪ/ n sovranità f inv

S

Soviet /'səʊvɪət/ *adj* sovietico

Soviet Union *n* Unione *f* Sovietica

sow[1] /saʊ/ *n* scrofa *f*

sow[2] /səʊ/ *vt* (pt **sowed**, pp **sown** or **sowed**) seminare

soya /'sɔɪə/ *n* soya *f*

soya bean *n* soia *f*

soy sauce /sɔɪ/, **soya sauce** *n* salsa *f* di soia

sozzled /'sɒzld/ *adj* fam sbronzo

spa /spɑː/ *n* stazione *f* termale

space /speɪs/ [1] *n* spazio *m*
[2] *adj* ⟨research etc⟩ spaziale
[3] *vt* ~ **[out]** distanziare

space age [1] *n* era *f* spaziale
[2] *attrib* dell'era spaziale

space bar *n* barra *f* spaziatrice

space cadet *n* fig fam allucinato, -a *mf*

space capsule *n* capsula *f* spaziale

spacecraft *n* navetta *f* spaziale

spaced out /speɪst'aʊt/ *adj* fam **he's completely ~ ~** è completamente fuori di testa

space-saving *adj* poco ingombrante

spaceship *n* astronave *f*

space shuttle *n* shuttle *m inv*

space station *n* stazione *f* spaziale

spacesuit *n* tuta *f* spaziale

space travel *n* viaggi *mpl* nello spazio

space walk *n* passeggiata *f* nello spazio

spacing /'speɪsɪŋ/ *n* distanziamento *m*; **single/double ~** interlinea *m* semplice/doppia

spacious /'speɪʃəs/ *adj* spazioso

spade /speɪd/ *n* vanga *f*; (for child) paletta *f*; **~s** *pl* (Cards) picche *fpl*; **call a ~ a ~** dire pane al pane e vino al vino

spadework /'speɪdwɜːk/ *n* fig lavoro *m* preparatorio

spaghetti /spə'ɡetɪ/ *n* spaghetti *mpl*

spaghetti bolognese /bɒlə'neɪz/ *n* spaghetti *mpl* al ragù

spaghetti junction *n* fam intricato raccordo *m* autostradale

Spain /speɪn/ *n* Spagna *f*

spam /spæm/ *n* Comput spam *m inv*

spamming /'spæmɪŋ/ *n* Comput invio *m* di spam

span[1] /spæn/ [1] *n* spanna *f*; (of arch) luce *f*; (of time) arco *m*; (of wings) apertura *f*
[2] *vt* (pt/pp **spanned**) estendersi su

span[2] ▶ SPICK

Spaniard /'spænjəd/ *n* spagnolo, -a *mf*

spaniel /'spænjəl/ *n* spaniel *m inv*

Spanish /'spænɪʃ/ [1] *adj* spagnolo
[2] *n* (language) spagnolo *m*; **the ~** *pl* gli spagnoli

spank /spæŋk/ *vt* sculacciare

spanking /'spæŋkɪŋ/ [1] *n* sculacciata *f*

[2] *adj* fam **at a ~ pace** con passo spedito
[3] *adv* fam **a ~ new car** una macchina nuova di zecca

spanner /'spænə(r)/ *n* chiave *f* inglese

spar /spɑː(r)/ *vi* (pt/pp **sparred**) (boxing) allenarsi; (argue) litigare

spare /speə(r)/ [1] *adj* (surplus) in più; (additional) di riserva; **go ~** (Br fam: be very angry) andare su tutte le furie
[2] *n* (part) ricambio *m*
[3] *vt* risparmiare; (do without) fare a meno di; **can you ~ five minutes?** avresti cinque minuti?; **no expense was ~d** non si è badato a spese; **to ~** (surplus) in eccedenza

spare part *n* pezzo *m* di ricambio

spare ribs *npl* costine *fpl*

spare room *n* stanza *f* degli ospiti

spare time *n* tempo *m* libero

spare tyre Br, **spare tire** Am *n* Auto gomma *f* di scorta; (fam: fat) trippa *f*

spare wheel *n* ruota *f* di scorta

sparing /'speərɪŋ/ *adj* parco (**with** di)

sparingly /'speərɪŋlɪ/ *adv* con parsimonia

spark /spɑːk/ *n* scintilla *f*
■ **spark off** *vt* far scoppiare

sparkle /'spɑːkl/ [1] *n* scintillio *m*
[2] *vi* scintillare

sparkler /'spɑːklə(r)/ *n* candela *f* magica

sparkling /'spɑːklɪŋ/ *adj* frizzante; ⟨wine⟩ spumante

spark-plug *n* Auto candela *f*

sparrow /'spærəʊ/ *n* passero *m*

sparse /spɑːs/ *adj* rado

sparsely /'spɑːslɪ/ *adv* scarsamente; **~ populated** ⟨area⟩ a bassa densità di popolazione

sparseness /'spɑːsnɪs/ *n* (of vegetation) radezza *f*

spartan /'spɑːtn/ *adj* spartano

spasm /'spæzm/ *n* spasmo *m*

spasmodic /spæz'mɒdɪk/ *adj* spasmodico

spasmodically /spæz'mɒdɪklɪ/ *adv* spasmodicamente

spastic /'spæstɪk/ [1] *adj* spastico
[2] *n* spastico, -a *mf*

spat /spæt/ ▶ SPIT[1]

spate /speɪt/ *n* (series) successione *f*; **be in full ~** essere in piena

spatial /'speɪʃl/ *adj* spaziale

spatio-temporal /speɪʃɪə'tempərəl/ *adj* spazio-temporale

spatter /'spætə(r)/ *vt/i* schizzare

spatula /'spætjʊlə/ *n* spatola *f*

spawn /spɔːn/ [1] *n* uova *fpl* (di pesci, rane ecc)
[2] *vi* deporre le uova
[3] *vt* fig generare

spay /speɪ/ vt sterilizzare

speak /spiːk/ ① vi (pt **spoke**, pp **spoken**) parlare (**to** a); ∼**ing!** Teleph sono io!

② vt dire; ∼ **one's mind** dire quello che si pensa

■ **speak for** vt parlare a nome di; ∼ **for yourself!** parla per te!

■ **speak of** vt ∼ **well/ill of somebody** parlare bene/male di qualcuno; **nothing to** ∼ **of** niente di speciale; (quantity) non un granché; ∼**ing of holidays...** a proposito di vacanze...

■ **speak out** vi (protest) parlare

■ **speak up** vi parlare più forte; ∼ **up for oneself** farsi valere

speaker /'spiːkə(r)/ n parlante mf; (in public) oratore, -trice mf; (of stereo) cassa f

speaking terms /'spiːkɪŋ/ npl **we are not on** ∼ ∼ non ci parliamo

spear /'spɪə(r)/ ① n lancia f
② vt trafiggere

spearhead /'spɪəhed/ vt fig essere l'iniziatore di

spearmint /'spɪəmɪnt/ n menta f verde

spec /spek/ n **on** ∼ fam ⟨take, use⟩ in prova; ⟨go somewhere⟩ per ispezione

special /'speʃl/ adj speciale

special correspondent n inviato, -a mf speciale

special delivery n espresso m

special effect ① n Cinema, TV effetto m speciale
② attrib ∼ ∼s ⟨specialist, team⟩ degli effetti speciali

special envoy n inviato, -a mf speciale

specialist /'speʃəlɪst/ n specialista mf

speciality /speʃɪ'ælətɪ/ n specialità f inv

specialize /'speʃəlaɪz/ vi specializzarsi

specially /'speʃəlɪ/ adv specialmente; (particularly) particolarmente

special needs npl difficoltà f d'apprendimento; **children with** ∼ ∼ bambini con difficoltà d'apprendimento

special offer n vendita f promozionale

special school n scuola f per bambini con difficoltà d'apprendimento

special treatment n trattamento m di riguardo

species /'spiːʃiːz/ n specie f inv

specific /spə'sɪfɪk/ adj specifico

specifically /spə'sɪfɪklɪ/ adv in modo specifico

specifications /spesɪfɪ'keɪʃnz/ npl descrizione f

specify /'spesɪfaɪ/ vt (pt/pp **-ied**) specificare

specimen /'spesɪmən/ n campione m

specious /'spiːʃəs/ adj ⟨argument, reasoning⟩ specioso

speck /spek/ n macchiolina f; (particle) granello m

speckled /'spekld/ adj picchiettato

specs /speks/ npl fam occhiali mpl

spectacle /'spektəkl/ n (show) spettacolo m

spectacles /'spektəklz/ npl occhiali mpl

spectacular /spek'tækjʊlə(r)/ adj spettacolare

spectacularly /spek'tækjʊləlɪ/ adv in modo spettacolare

spectator /spek'teɪtə(r)/ n spettatore, -trice mf

spectator sport n sport m inv di intrattenimento

spectre /'spektə(r)/ n spettro m

spectrum /'spektrəm/ n (pl **-tra**) spettro m; fig gamma f

speculate /'spekjʊleɪt/ vi speculare

speculation /spekjʊ'leɪʃn/ n speculazione f

speculative /'spekjʊlətɪv/ adj speculativo

speculator /'spekjʊleɪtə(r)/ n speculatore, -trice mf

sped /sped/ ▶ SPEED

speech /spiːtʃ/ n linguaggio m; (address) discorso m; **make/give a** ∼ fare un discorso

speech day n Sch giorno m della premiazione

speech impediment n difetto m di pronuncia

speechless /'spiːtʃlɪs/ adj senza parole

speech therapist n logoterapista mf

speech therapy n logoterapia f

speech-writer n persona f che scrive i discorsi di personaggi pubblici

speed /spiːd/ ① n velocità f inv; (gear) marcia f; **at** ∼ a tutta velocità
② vi (pt/pp **sped**) andare veloce
③ vi (pt/pp **speeded**) (go too fast) andare a velocità eccessiva

■ **speed up** (pt/pp **speeded up**) vt/i accelerare

speedboat n motoscafo m

speed bump n rallentatore m

speed camera n autovelox® m inv

speed hump n dosso m di rallentamento

speedily /'spiːdɪlɪ/ adv rapidamente

speeding /'spiːdɪŋ/ n eccesso m di velocità

speeding fine n multa f per eccesso di velocità

speed limit n limite m di velocità

speed merchant n fam fanatico, -a mf della velocità

speedometer /spi:'dɒmɪtə(r)/ n tachimetro m

speed skating n pattinaggio m di velocità

speed trap n Auto tratto m di strada sul quale la polizia controlla la velocità dei veicoli

speedy /'spi:dɪ/ adj (**-ier, -iest**) rapido

speleologist /spi:lɪ'ɒlədʒɪst/ n speleologo, -a mf

speleology /spi:lɪ'ɒlədʒɪ/ n speleologia f

spell[1] /spel/ n (turn) turno m; (of weather) periodo m

spell[2] [1] vt (pt/pp **spelled** or **spelt**) how do you ~...? come si scrive...?; could you ~ that for me? me lo può compitare?; ~ disaster fig essere disastroso [2] vi he can't ~ fa molti errori d'ortografia
■ **spell out** vt compitare; fig spiegare

spell[3] n (magic) incantesimo m

spellbound /'spelbaʊnd/ adj affascinato

spellcheck vt Comput fare il controllo ortografico di ⟨document⟩

spellchecker /'speltʃekə(r)/ n Comput correttore m ortografico

spelling /'spelɪŋ/ n ortografia f

spelt /spelt/ ▸ SPELL[2]

spend /spend/ vt/i (pt/pp **spent**) spendere; passare ⟨time⟩

spending cut n taglio m alla spesa

spending money /'spendɪŋ/ n soldi mpl per le piccole spese

spending power n potere m d'acquisto

spending spree n spese fpl folli

spendthrift /'spendθrɪft/ [1] adj spendaccione; ⟨habit, policy⟩ dispendioso [2] n spendaccione, -a mf

spent /spent/ ▸ SPEND

sperm /spɜːm/ n spermatozoo m; (semen) sperma m

sperm bank n banca f dello sperma

sperm count n conteggio m di spermatozoi

sperm donor n donatore m del seme

spermicidal /spɜːmɪ'saɪdl/ adj spermicida inv

spermicide /'spɜːmɪsaɪd/ n spermicida m

spew /spju:/ vt/i vomitare

sphere /sfɪə(r)/ n sfera f

sphere of influence n sfera f di influenza

spherical /'sferɪkl/ adj sferico

spice /spaɪs/ n spezia f; fig pepe m

spick /spɪk/ adj ~ **and span** lindo

spicy /'spaɪsɪ/ adj piccante

spider /'spaɪdə(r)/ n ragno m

spiderweb n Am = WEB

spiel /ʃpiəl/ n fam (sales pitch) imbonimento m; (long repetitive speech) tiritera f; he gave me some ~ about... mi ha raccontato un sacco di storie su...

spike /spaɪk/ n punta f; Bot, Zool spina f; (on shoe) chiodo m

spikes npl (shoes) scarpe fpl chiodate

spiky /'spaɪkɪ/ adj ⟨plant⟩ spinoso

spill /spɪl/ [1] vt (pt/pp **spilt** or **spilled**) versare ⟨blood⟩; ~ **the beans** fam vuotare il sacco [2] vi rovesciarsi
■ **spill over** vi ⟨water⟩ traboccare; ~ **over into** degenerare in ⟨violence, rioting⟩

spillage /'spɪlɪdʒ/ n (of oil, chemical) perdita f

spin /spɪn/ [1] vt (pt/pp **spun**, pres p **spinning**) far girare; filare ⟨wool⟩; centrifugare ⟨washing⟩ [2] vi girare; ⟨washing machine⟩ centrifugare [3] n rotazione f; (short drive) giretto m
■ **spin out** vt far durare
■ **spin round** [1] vi (turn quickly) girare vorticosamente; ⟨dancer, skater⟩ volteggiare; ⟨car⟩ fare un testa coda [2] vt ~ **somebody** or **something round** far girare qualcuno o qualcosa

spinach /'spɪnɪdʒ/ n spinaci mpl

spinal /'spaɪnl/ adj spinale

spinal column n colonna f vertebrale

spinal cord n midollo m spinale

spindle /'spɪndl/ n fuso m

spindly /'spɪndlɪ/ adj affusolato

spin doctor n persona f incaricata di presentare le scelte di un partito politico sotto una luce favorevole

spin-drier n centrifuga f

spine /spaɪn/ n spina f dorsale; (of book) dorso m; Bot, Zool spina f

spineless /'spaɪnlɪs/ adj fig smidollato

spinning /'spɪnɪŋ/ n filatura f

spinning wheel n filatoio m

spin-off n ricaduta f

spinster /'spɪnstə(r)/ n donna f nubile; (old maid, fam) zitella f

spiny /'spaɪnɪ/ adj ⟨plant, animal⟩ spinoso

spiral /'spaɪrəl/ [1] adj a spirale [2] n spirale f [3] vi (pt/pp **spiralled**) formare una spirale

spiral staircase n scala f a chiocciola

spire /'spaɪə(r)/ n guglia f

spirit /'spɪrɪt/ n spirito m; (courage) ardore m; ~**s** pl (alcohol) liquori mpl; in good ~**s** di buon umore; in low ~**s** abbattuto
■ **spirit away** vt far sparire

spirited /'spɪrɪtɪd/ adj vivace; (courageous) pieno d'ardore

spirit level *n* livella *f* a bolla d'aria

spirit stove *n* fornellino *m* [da campeggio]

spiritual /'spɪrɪtjʊəl/ **①** *adj* spirituale **②** *n* spiritual *m*

spiritualism /'spɪrɪtjʊəlɪzm/ *n* spiritismo *m*

spiritualist /'spɪrɪtjʊəlɪst/ *n* spiritista *mf*

spit¹ /spɪt/ *n* (for roasting) spiedo *m*

spit² **①** *n* sputo *m*
② *vt/i* (pt/pp **spat**, pres p **spitting**) sputare; ⟨cat⟩ soffiare; ⟨fat⟩ sfrigolare; **it's** ~**ting [with rain]** pioviggina; **the** ~**ting image of** il ritratto spiccicato di

spite /spaɪt/ **①** *n* dispetto *m*; **in** ~ **of** malgrado
② *vt* far dispetto a

spiteful /'spaɪtfʊl/ *adj* indispettito

spitefully /'spaɪtfʊlɪ/ *adv* con aria indispettita

spit out *vt* sputare ⟨food⟩; ~ **it out!** fam sputa l'osso!

spittle /'spɪtl/ *n* saliva *f*

splash /splæʃ/ **①** *n* schizzo *m*; (of colour) macchia *f*; (fam: drop) goccio *m*
② *vt* schizzare; ~ **somebody with something** schizzare qualcuno di qualcosa
③ *vi* schizzare
■ **splash about** *vi* schizzarsi
■ **splash down** *vi* ⟨spacecraft⟩ ammarare
■ **splash out** *vi* (spend freely) darsi alle spese folli

splashdown /'splæʃdaʊn/ *n* ammaraggio *m*

splatter /'splætə(r)/ **①** *vt* schizzare; ~ **somebody/something with something** schizzare qualcuno/qualcosa di qualcosa
② *vi* ~ **onto/over something** ⟨ink, paint⟩ schizzare su qualcosa

splay /spleɪ/ *vt* divaricare ⟨legs, feet, fingers⟩; svasare ⟨end of pipe etc⟩; strombare ⟨side of window, door⟩; ~**ed** ⟨feet, fingers, legs⟩ scartato

spleen /spli:n/ *n* Anat milza *f*

splendid /'splendɪd/ *adj* splendido

splendidly /'splendɪdlɪ/ *adv* splendidamente

splendour /'splendə(r)/ *n* splendore *m*

splice /splaɪs/ *vt* aggiuntare ⟨tape, film⟩

splint /splɪnt/ *n* Med stecca *f*

splinter /'splɪntə(r)/ **①** *n* scheggia *f*
② *vi* scheggiarsi

splinter group *n* gruppo *m* scissionista

split /splɪt/ **①** *n* fessura *f*; (quarrel) rottura *f*; (division) scissione *f*; (tear) strappo *m*
② *vt* (pt/pp **split**, pres p **splitting**) spaccare; (share, divide) dividere; (tear) strappare; ~ **hairs** spaccare il capello in quattro; ~ **one's sides** sbellicarsi dalle risa

③ *vi* spaccarsi; (tear) strapparsi; (divide) dividersi; ~ **on somebody** fam denunciare qualcuno
④ *adj* **a** ~ **second** una frazione di secondo
■ **split up** **①** *vt* dividersi
② *vi* ⟨couple⟩ separarsi

split ends *npl* (in hair) doppie punte *fpl*

split personality *n* sdoppiamento *m* della personalità

split screen *n* schermo *m* diviso

splitting /'splɪtɪŋ/ *adj* **have a** ~ **headache** avere un tremendo mal di testa

splutter /'splʌtə(r)/ *vi* farfugliare

spoil /spɔɪl/ **①** *n* ~**s** *pl* bottino *msg*
② *vt* (pt/pp **spoilt** or **spoiled**) rovinare; viziare ⟨person⟩
③ *vi* andare a male

spoiler /'spɔɪlə(r)/ *n* Auto, Aeron spoiler *m inv*

spoilsport /'spɔɪlspɔːt/ *n* guastafeste *mf inv*

spoilt /spɔɪlt/ *adj* ⟨child⟩ viziato; **be** ~ **for choice** non avere che l'imbarazzo della scelta

spoke¹ /spəʊk/ *n* raggio *m*

spoke² ▶ SPEAK

spoken /'spəʊkən/ **①** ▶ SPEAK
② *adj* ⟨language⟩ parlato; **be** ~ **for** essere messo da parte per qualcuno

spokesman /'spəʊksmən/ *n* portavoce *m inv*

spokesperson /'spəʊkspɜːsn/ *n* portavoce *mf*

spokeswoman /'spəʊkswʊmən/ *n* portavoce *f*

sponge /spʌndʒ/ **①** *n* spugna *f*
② *vt* pulire con la spugna
③ *vi* ~ **on** fam scroccare da

sponge bag *n* nécessaire *m inv*

sponge cake *n* pan *m* di Spagna

sponger /'spʌndʒə(r)/ *n* scroccone, -a *mf*

spongy /'spʌndʒɪ/ *adj* spugnoso

sponsor /'spɒnsə(r)/ **①** *n* garante *mf*; Radio, TV sponsor *m inv*; (god-parent) padrino *m*, madrina *f*; (for membership) socio, -a *mf* garante
② *vt* sponsorizzare

sponsorship /'spɒnsəʃɪp/ *n* sponsorizzazione *f*

sponsorship deal *n* accordo *m* con uno sponsor

spontaneity /spɒntə'neɪɪtɪ/ *n* spontaneità *f*

spontaneous /spɒn'teɪnɪəs/ *adj* spontaneo

spontaneously /spɒn'teɪnɪəslɪ/ *adv* spontaneamente

spoof /spuːf/ *n* fam parodia *f*

spook /spu:k/ fam **1** vt (haunt)
perseguitare; (frighten) spaventare
2 n (ghost) fantasma m; (Am: spy) spia f

spooky /'spu:kɪ/ adj (**-ier**, **-iest**) fam
sinistro

spool /spu:l/ n bobina f

spooling /'spu:lɪŋ/ n Comput spooling m

spoon /spu:n/ **1** n cucchiaio m
2 vt mettere col cucchiaio

spoonerism /'spu:nərɪzm/ n scambio m
delle iniziali di due parole con effetto
umoristico

spoon-feed vt (pt/pp **-fed**) fig imboccare

spoonful /'spu:nfʊl/ n cucchiaiata f

sporadic /spə'rædɪk/ adj sporadico

sporadically /spə'rædɪklɪ/ adv
sporadicamente

spore /spɔ:(r)/ n spora f

sporran /'spɒrə/n n borsa f di cuoio o
pelo portata alla cintura dagli scozzesi
insieme al kilt

sport /spɔ:t/ **1** n sport m inv; **be a
[good]** ∼**!** sii sportivo!
2 vt sfoggiare

sporting /'spɔ:tɪŋ/ adj sportivo

sporting calendar n calendario m
sportivo

sporting chance n possibilità f inv

sports car n automobile f sportiva

sports centre Br, **sports center** Am
n centro m polisportivo

sports club n club m sportivo

sports coat n, **sports jacket** n
giacca f sportiva

sports ground n (large) stadio m; (in
school) campo m sportivo

sports jacket n = SPORTS COAT

sportsman n sportivo m

sports star n star f inv dello sport

sportswear n abbigliamento m
sportivo

sportswoman n sportiva f

sports writer n giornalista mf
sportivo, -a

sporty /'spɔ:tɪ/ adj (**-ier**, **-iest**) sportivo

spot /spɒt/ **1** n macchia f; (pimple)
brufolo m; (place) posto m; (in pattern) pois
m inv; (of rain) goccia f; (of water) goccio m;
∼**s** pl (rash) sfogo msg; **a** ∼ **of** fam un po'
di; **a** ∼ **of bother** qualche problema; **on
the** ∼ sul luogo; (immediately)
immediatamente; **in a [tight]** ∼ fam in
difficoltà
2 vt (pt/pp **spotted**) macchiare; (fam:
notice) individuare

spot check n (without warning) controllo
m a sorpresa; **do a** ∼ ∼ **on something**
dare una controllata a qualcosa

spotless /'spɒtlɪs/ adj immacolato

spotlight n riflettore m; fig riflettori mpl

spot-on adj Br esatto

spot rate n Fin tasso m di cambio a vista

spotted /'spɒtɪd/ adj ⟨material⟩ a pois

spotty /'spɒtɪ/ adj (**-ier**, **-iest**) (pimply)
brufoloso

spot-weld vt saldare a punti

spouse /spaʊz/ n consorte mf

spout /spaʊt/ **1** n becco m; **up the** ∼
(fam: ruined) all'aria
2 vi zampillare (**from** da)

sprain /spreɪn/ **1** n slogatura f
2 vt slogare; ∼ **one's ankle** slogarsi la
caviglia

sprang /spræŋ/ ▶ SPRING[2]

sprat /spræt/ n spratto m

sprawl /sprɔ:l/ vi (in chair) stravaccarsi;
⟨city etc⟩ estendersi; **go** ∼**ing** (fall) cadere
disteso

sprawling /'sprɔ:lɪŋ/ adj ⟨suburb, city⟩
che si propaga disordinatamente;
⟨handwriting⟩ che occupa tutta la pagina

spray[1] /spreɪ/ n (of flowers) rametto m;
(bouquet) mazzolino m

spray[2] **1** n spruzzo m; (from sea) spruzzo
m; (preparation) spray m inv: (container)
spruzzatore m
2 vt spruzzare

spray can n bomboletta f spray inv

spray-gun n pistola f a spruzzo

spray-on adj ⟨conditioner, glitter⟩ spray
inv

spread /spred/ **1** n estensione f; (of
disease) diffusione f; (paste) crema f; (fam:
feast) banchetto m
2 vt (pt/pp **spread**) spargere; spalmare
⟨butter, jam⟩; stendere ⟨cloth, arms⟩;
diffondere ⟨news, disease⟩; dilazionare
⟨payments⟩; ∼ **something with** spalmare
qualcosa di
3 vi spargersi; ⟨butter⟩ spalmarsi;
⟨disease⟩ diffondersi
■ **spread out** **1** vt sparpagliare
2 vi sparpagliarsi

spread-eagled /-'i:gld/ adj a gambe e
braccia aperte

spreadsheet /'spredʃi:t/ n Comput foglio
m elettronico

spree /spri:/ n fam **go on a** ∼ far
baldoria; **go on a shopping** ∼ fare spese
folli

sprig /sprɪg/ n rametto m

sprightly /'spraɪtlɪ/ adj (**-ier**, **-iest**)
vivace

spring[1] /sprɪŋ/ **1** n primavera f; **in** ∼, **in
the** ∼ in primavera
2 attrib primaverile

spring[2] **1** n (jump) balzo m; (water)
sorgente f; (device) molla f; (elasticity)
elasticità f
2 vi (pt **sprang**, pp **sprung**) balzare;
(arise) provenire (**from** da); ∼ **to mind**
saltare in mente

3 *vt* he just sprang it on me me l'ha detto a cose fatte
■ **spring up** *vi* balzare; fig spuntare
springboard *n* trampolino *m*
spring chicken *n* Culin pollastrello *m*, pollastrella *f*; **she's no** ~ ~ fam non è una giovincella
spring-clean *vt* pulire a fondo
spring-cleaning *n* pulizie *fpl* di Pasqua
spring onion *n* cipollotto *m*
springtime *n* primavera *f*
springy /'sprɪŋɪ/ *adj* ⟨mattress, sofa⟩ molleggiato
sprinkle /'sprɪŋkl/ *vt* (scatter) spruzzare ⟨liquid⟩; spargere ⟨flour, cocoa⟩; ~ something with spruzzare qualcosa di ⟨liquid⟩; cospargere qualcosa di ⟨flour, cocoa⟩
sprinkler /'sprɪŋklə(r)/ *n* sprinkler *m inv*; (for garden) irrigatore *m*
sprinkling /'sprɪŋklɪŋ/ *n* (of liquid) spruzzatina *f*; (of pepper, salt) pizzico *m*; (of flour, sugar) spolveratina *f*; (of knowledge) infarinatura *f*; (of people) pugno *m*
sprint /sprɪnt/ **1** *n* sprint *m inv*
2 *vi* fare uno sprint; Sport sprintare
sprinter /'sprɪntə(r)/ *n* sprinter *mf inv*
sprite /spraɪt/ *n* folletto *m*
spritzer /'sprɪtsə(r)/ *n* spritz *m inv*, spritzer *m inv*
sprout /spraʊt/ **1** *n* germoglio *m*; [Brussels] ~s *pl* cavolini *mpl* di Bruxelles
2 *vi* germogliare
spruce /spru:s/ **1** *adj* elegante
2 *n* abete *m*
■ **spruce up** *vt* dare una ripulita a
sprung /sprʌŋ/ **1** ▸ SPRING²
2 *adj* molleggiato
spry /spraɪ/ *adj* (-er, -est) arzillo
spud /spʌd/ *n* fam patata *f*
spun /spʌn/ ▸ SPIN
spur /spɜ:(r)/ **1** *n* sperone *m*; (stimulus) stimolo *m*; (road) svincolo *m*; **on the** ~ **of the moment** su due piedi
2 *vt* (pt/pp **spurred**) ~ [**on**] fig spronare
spurious /'spjʊərɪəs/ *adj* falso
spuriously /'spjʊərɪəslɪ/ *adv* falsamente
spurn /spɜ:n/ *vt* sdegnare
spurt /spɜ:t/ **1** *n* getto *m*; Sport scatto *m*; **put on a** ~ fare uno scatto
2 *vi* sprizzare; (increase speed) scattare
sputter /'spʌtə(r)/ **1** *vi* ⟨engine⟩ scoppiettare
2 *n* colpi *mpl* irregolari del motore
spy /spaɪ/ **1** *n* spia *f*
2 *vi* spiare
3 *vt* (fam: see) spiare
■ **spy on** *vt* spiare
■ **spy out** *vt* esplorare
spying /'spaɪɪŋ/ *n* spionaggio *m*

squabble /'skwɒbl/ **1** *n* bisticcio *m*
2 *vi* bisticciare
squabbling /'skwɒblɪŋ/ *n* bisticci *mpl*
squad /skwɒd/ *n* squadra *f*
squad car *n* macchina *f* della volante
squaddie /'skwɒdɪ/ *n* Br fam soldato *m* semplice
squadron /'skwɒdrən/ *n* Mil squadrone *m*; Aeron, Naut squadriglia *f*
squalid /'skwɒlɪd/ *adj* squallido
squalidly /'skwɒlɪdlɪ/ *adv* squallidamente
squall /skwɔ:l/ **1** *n* (howl) strillo *m*; (storm) bufera *f*
2 *vi* strillare
squally /'skwɔ:lɪ/ *adj* burrascoso
squalor /'skwɒlə(r)/ *n* squallore *m*
squander /'skwɒndə(r)/ *vt* sprecare
square /skweə(r)/ **1** *adj* quadrato; ⟨meal⟩ sostanzioso; (fam: old-fashioned) vecchio stampo; **all** ~ fam pari
2 *n* quadrato *m*; (in city) piazza *f*; (on chessboard) riquadro *m*; **be back to** ~ **one** riessere al punto di partenza
3 *vt* (settle) far quadrare; Math elevare al quadrato
4 *vi* (agree) armonizzare
■ **square up** *vi* (settle accounts) saldare
■ **square up to** *vt* affrontare
square bracket *n* parentesi *f inv* quadra; **in** ~ ~s tra parentesi quadre
square dance *n* quadriglia *f*
squarely /'skweəlɪ/ *adv* direttamente
square root *n* radice *f* quadrata
squash /skwɒʃ/ **1** *n* calca *f*; (drink) spremuta *f*; (sport) squash *m*; (vegetable) zucca *f*
2 *vt* schiacciare; soffocare ⟨rebellion⟩
■ **squash up** *vi* (move closer together) stringersi
squashy /'skwɒʃɪ/ *adj* floscio
squat /skwɒt/ **1** *adj* tarchiato
2 *n* fam edificio *m* occupato abusivamente
3 *vi* (pt/pp **squatted**) accovacciarsi; ~ **in** occupare abusivamente
squatter /'skwɒtə(r)/ *n* occupante *mf* abusivo, -a
squaw /skwɔ:/ *n* squaw *f inv*
squawk /skwɔ:k/ **1** *n* gracchio *m*
2 *vi* gracchiare
squeak /skwi:k/ **1** *n* squittio *m*; (of hinge, brakes) cigolio *m*
2 *vi* squittire; ⟨hinge, brakes⟩ cigolare
squeaking /'skwi:kɪŋ/ *n* (of door, hinge) cigolio *m*
squeaky /'skwi:kɪ/ *adj* ⟨door, hinge⟩ cigolante
squeaky-clean *adj* fam ⟨glass, hair⟩ lucente; ⟨floor⟩ tirato a specchio; fig ⸬⸬▸

S

⟨person⟩ senza vizi; ⟨company⟩ al di sopra di ogni sospetto

squeal /skwiːl/ **1** n strillo m; (of brakes) cigolio m
2 vi strillare; sl spifferare

squeamish /ˈskwiːmɪʃ/ adj dallo stomaco delicato; (scrupulous) troppo scrupoloso

squeegee /ˈskwiːdʒiː/ n Phot rullo m asciugatore; (for glasses) lavavetri m inv

squeeze /skwiːz/ **1** n stretta f; (crush) pigia pigia m inv; **give sb's hand a ~** dare a qualcuno una stretta di mano
2 vt premere; (to get juice) spremere; stringere ⟨hand⟩; (force) stringere a forza; (fam: extort) estorcere (**out of** da)
  ■ **squeeze in/out** vi sgusciare dentro/fuori
  ■ **squeeze past** vi ⟨person, car⟩ passare
  ■ **squeeze up** vi stringersi

squelch /skweltʃ/ vi sguazzare

squib /skwɪb/ n petardo m

squid /skwɪd/ n calamaro m

squidgy /ˈskwɪdʒɪ/ adj (Br fam: squashy) molliccio

squiggle /ˈskwɪgl/ n scarabocchio m

squint /skwɪnt/ **1** n strabismo m
2 vi essere strabico

squire /ˈskwaɪə(r)/ n signorotto m di campagna

squirm /skwɜːm/ vi contorcersi; (feel embarrassed) sentirsi imbarazzato

squirrel /ˈskwɪrəl/ n scoiattolo m

squirt /skwɜːt/ **1** n spruzzo m; (fam: person) presuntuoso m
2 vt/i spruzzare

Sri Lanka /srɪˈlæŋkə/ n Sri Lanka m

St abbr (**Saint**) S; abbr **Street**

stab /stæb/ **1** n pugnalata f, coltellata f; (sensation) fitta f; (fam: attempt) tentativo m
2 vt (pt/pp **stabbed**) pugnalare, accoltellare

stability /stəˈbɪlətɪ/ n stabilità f inv

stabilization /steɪbɪlaɪˈzeɪʃn/ n stabilizzazione f

stabilize /ˈsteɪbɪlaɪz/ **1** vt stabilizzare
2 vi stabilizzarsi

stabilizer /ˈsteɪbɪlaɪzə(r)/ n stabilizzatore m; (on bike) rotella f; (in food) stabilizzante m

stable¹ /ˈsteɪbl/ adj stabile

stable² n stalla f; (establishment) scuderia f

staccato /stəˈkɑːtəʊ/ **1** adj Mus staccato; ⟨gasps, shots⟩ intermittente
2 adv ⟨play⟩ staccatamente

stack /stæk/ **1** n catasta f; (of chimney) comignolo m; (chimney) ciminiera f; (fam: large quantity) montagna f; **~s of** ⟨money, time, work⟩ un sacco di
2 vt accatastare

stadium /ˈsteɪdɪəm/ n stadio m

staff /stɑːf/ **1** n (stick) bastone m; (employees) personale m; (teachers) corpo m insegnante; Mil Stato m Maggiore
2 vt fornire di personale

staff meeting n riunione f del corpo insegnante

staffroom /ˈstɑːfruːm/ n Sch sala f insegnanti

stag /stæg/ n cervo m

stage /steɪdʒ/ **1** n palcoscenico m; (profession) teatro m; (in journey) tappa f; (in process) stadio m; **go on the ~** darsi al teatro; **by** or **in ~s** a tappe
2 vt mettere in scena; (arrange) organizzare

stagecoach n diligenza f

stage door n ingresso m degli artisti

stage fright n panico m da palcoscenico

stage-manage vt fig orchestrare

stage manager n direttore, -trice mf di scena

stage-struck /-strʌk/ adj appassionatissimo di teatro

stagger /ˈstægə(r)/ **1** vi barcollare
2 vt sbalordire; scaglionare ⟨holidays, payments etc⟩; **I was ~ed** sono rimasto sbalordito
3 n vacillamento m

staggering /ˈstægərɪŋ/ adj sbalorditivo

stagnant /ˈstægnənt/ adj stagnante

stagnate /stægˈneɪt/ vi fig [ri]stagnare

stagnation /stægˈneɪʃn/ n fig inattività f

stag night, **stag party** n addio m al celibato

staid /steɪd/ adj posato

stain /steɪn/ **1** n macchia f; (for wood) mordente m
2 vt macchiare; ⟨wood⟩ dare il mordente a

stained glass /steɪndˈglɑːs/ n vetro m colorato

stained-glass window n vetrata f colorata

stainless /ˈsteɪnlɪs/ adj senza macchia

stainless steel n acciaio m inossidabile

stain remover n smacchiatore m

stair /steə(r)/ n gradino m; **~s** pl scale fpl

staircase /ˈsteəkeɪs/ n scale fpl

stairlift n montascale m inv

stake /steɪk/ **1** n palo m; (wager) posta f; Comm partecipazione f; **at ~** in gioco
2 vt puntellare; (wager) scommettere; **~ a claim to something** rivendicare qualcosa
  ■ **stake out** vt mettere sotto sorveglianza ⟨building⟩

stake-out n fam sorveglianza f

stalactite /ˈstæləktaɪt/ n stalattite f

stalagmite /'stæləgmaɪt/ n stalagmite f

stale /steɪl/ adj stantio; ⟨air⟩ viziato; (uninteresting) trito [e ritrito]

stalemate /'steɪlmeɪt/ n (in chess) stallo m; (deadlock) situazione f di stallo

stalk¹ /stɔːk/ n gambo m

stalk² **1** vt inseguire
2 vi camminare impettito

stalker /'stɔːkə(r)/ n (of person) persona f che perseguita qualcuno per cui ha una fissazione maniacale

stalking /'stɔːkɪŋ/ n (of person) persecuzione f di una persona per cui si ha una fissazione maniacale

stall /stɔːl/ **1** n box m inv; (in market) bancarella f; ~s pl Theat platea f
2 vi ⟨engine⟩ spegnersi; fig temporeggiare
3 vt far spegnere ⟨engine⟩; tenere a bada ⟨person⟩

stallholder /'stɔːlhəʊldə(r)/ n bancarellista mf

stallion /'stæljən/ n stallone m

stalwart /'stɔːlwət/ **1** adj fedele
2 n sostenitore m fedele

stamina /'stæmɪnə/ n [capacità f di] resistenza f

stammer /'stæmə(r)/ **1** n balbettio m
2 vt/i balbettare

stamp /stæmp/ **1** n (postage ~) francobollo m; (instrument) timbro m; fig impronta f
2 vt affrancare ⟨letter⟩; timbrare ⟨bill⟩; battere ⟨feet⟩
■ **stamp out** vt spegnere; fig soffocare

stamp collecting n filatelia f

stamp collector n collezionista mf di francobolli

stamped addressed envelope busta f affrancata per la risposta

stampede /stæm'piːd/ **1** n fuga f precipitosa; fam fuggifuggi m inv
2 vi fuggire precipitosamente

stance /stɑːns/ n posizione f

stand /stænd/ **1** n (for bikes) rastrelliera f; (at exhibition) stand m inv; (in market) bancarella f; (in stadium) gradinata f; fig posizione f
2 vi (pt/pp **stood**) stare in piedi; (rise) alzarsi [in piedi]; (be) trovarsi; (be candidate) essere candidato (**for** a); (stay valid) rimanere valido; **I don't know where I** ~ non so qual è la mia posizione; ~ **still** non muoversi; ~ **firm** fig tener duro; ~ **on ceremony** formalizzarsi; ~ **together** essere solidali; ~ **to lose/gain** rischiare di perdere/vincere; ~ **one's ground** tener duro; ~ **the test of time** superare la prova del tempo; ~ **somebody a beer** offrire una birra a qualcuno
3 vt (withstand) resistere a; (endure) sopportare; (place) mettere; ~ **a chance** avere una possibilità; ~ **a beer**

■ **stand back** vi (withdraw) farsi da parte

■ **stand by** **1** vi stare a guardare; (be ready) essere pronto
2 vt (support) appoggiare

■ **stand down** vi (retire) ritirarsi

■ **stand for** vt (mean) significare; (tolerate) tollerare

■ **stand in for** vt sostituire

■ **stand out** vi spiccare

■ **stand up** vi alzarsi [in piedi]

■ **stand up for** vt prendere le difese di; ~ **up for oneself** farsi valere

■ **stand up to** vt affrontare

stand-alone adj Comput stand-alone

standard /'stændəd/ **1** adj standard; **be** ~ **practice** essere pratica corrente
2 n standard m inv; Techn norma f; (level) livello m; (quality) qualità f inv; (flag) stendardo m; ~s pl (morals) valori mpl

Standard Assessment Tasks n Br esami mpl sostenuti per tranche d'età allo scopo di testare la preparazione degli alunni

standardization /stændədaɪ'zeɪʃn/ n standardizzazione f

standardize /'stændədaɪz/ vt standardizzare

standard lamp n lampada f a stelo

standard of living n tenore m di vita

standby /'stændbaɪ/ **1** n (person) riserva f
2 attrib ⟨circuit, battery⟩ di emergenza; ⟨passenger⟩ in lista di attesa; ⟨ticket⟩ stand-by inv
3 adv ⟨fly⟩ con biglietto stand-by

stand-in n controfigura f

standing /'stændɪŋ/ **1** adj (erect) in piedi; (permanent) permanente
2 n posizione f; (duration) durata f

standing charge n canone m

standing order n ordine m permanente

standing ovation n give somebody a ~ alzarsi per applaudire qualcuno

standing room n posti mpl in piedi

stand-off n punto m morto

stand-offish /stænd'ɒfɪʃ/ adj scostante

standpoint n punto m di vista

standstill n come to a ~ fermarsi; at a ~ in un periodo di stasi

stand-up **1** adj ⟨buffet⟩ in piedi; ⟨argument⟩ accanito
2 n (comedy) recital m inv di un comico

stand-up comedian comico m che intrattiene il pubblico con barzellette

stank /stæŋk/ ▶STINK

Stanley knife® /'stænlɪ/ n cutter m inv

stanza /'stænzə/ n strofa f

staple¹ /'steɪpl/ n (product) prodotto m principale

staple² **1** n graffa f, pinzatrice f

2 *vt* pinzare

staple diet *n* a ~ ~ of una dieta basata principalmente su

staple gun *n* pistola *f* sparachiodi

stapler /'steɪplə(r)/ *n* pinzatrice *f*, cucitrice *f*

staple remover *n* levapunti *m inv*

star /stɑː(r)/ **1** *n* stella *f*; (asterisk) asterisco *m*; Theat, Cinema, Sport divo, -a *mf*, stella *f*
2 *vi* (pt/pp **starred**) essere l'interprete principale (**in** di)

starboard /'stɑːbəd/ *n* tribordo *m*

starch /stɑːtʃ/ **1** *n* amido *m*
2 *vt* inamidare

starchy /'stɑːtʃɪ/ *adj* ricco di amido; fig compito

stardom /'stɑːdəm/ *n* celebrità *f*

stare /steə(r)/ **1** *n* sguardo *m* fisso
2 *vi* it's rude to ~ è da maleducati fissare la gente; ~ **at** fissare; ~ **into space** guardare nel vuoto

starfish /'stɑːfɪʃ/ *n* stella *f* di mare

stark /stɑːk/ **1** *adj* austero; ⟨contrast⟩ forte
2 *adv* completamente; ~ **naked** completamente nudo

starlet /'stɑːlɪt/ *n* stellina *f*

starling /'stɑːlɪŋ/ *n* storno *m*

starlit /'stɑːlɪt/ *adj* stellato

starry /'stɑːrɪ/ *adj* stellato

starry-eyed /-'aɪd/ *adj* fam ingenuo

star sign *n* segno *m* zodiacale

star-struck /-strʌk/ *adj* ossessionato dalle celebrità

star-studded /-stʌdɪd/ *adj* ⟨cast, line-up⟩ con molti interpreti famosi; ⟨sky⟩ stellato

start /stɑːt/ **1** *n* inizio *m*; (departure) partenza *f*; (jump) sobbalzo *m*; **from the ~** [fin] dall'inizio; **for a ~** tanto per cominciare; **give somebody a ~** Sport dare un vantaggio a qualcuno
2 *vi* [in]cominciare; (set out) avviarsi; ⟨engine, car⟩ partire; (jump) trasalire; **to ~ with,...** tanto per cominciare,...
3 *vt* [in]cominciare; (cause) dare inizio a; (found) mettere su; mettere in moto ⟨car⟩; mettere in giro ⟨rumour⟩
■ **start off** *vi* (begin) cominciare
■ **start on** *vt* fam (attack) criticare; (nag) punzecchiare
■ **start out** *vi* (on journey) partire
■ **start over** *vi* (with task) ricominciare
■ **start up** *vt* mettere in funzione ⟨engine⟩; avviare ⟨business⟩

starter /'stɑːtə(r)/ *n* Culin primo *m* [piatto *m*]; (in race: giving signal) starter *m inv*; (participant) concorrente *mf*; Auto motorino *m* d'avviamento

starting point /'stɑːtɪŋ/ *n* punto *m* di partenza

starting salary *n* stipendio *m* iniziale

startle /'stɑːtl/ *vt* far trasalire; ⟨news⟩ sconvolgere

startling /'stɑːtlɪŋ/ *adj* sconvolgente

start-up capital *n* capitale *m* di avviamento

starvation /stɑː'veɪʃn/ *n* fame *f*

starve /stɑːv/ **1** *vi* morire di fame
2 *vt* far morire di fame

starving /'stɑːvɪŋ/ *adj* be ~ (dying of hunger) soffrire la fame; (fam: very hungry) morire di fame

stash /stæʃ/ *vt* fam ~ **[away]** nascondere

state /steɪt/ **1** *n* stato *m*; Pol Stato *m*; (grand style) pompa *f*; **be in a ~** ⟨person⟩ essere agitato; **lie in** ~ essere esposto
2 *attrib* di Stato; Sch pubblico; (with ceremony) di gala
3 *vt* dichiarare; (specify) precisare

state-aided /-'eɪdɪd/ *adj* sovvenzionato dallo Stato

State Department *n* Am Pol ministero *m* degli [affari] esteri

state-funded *adj* sovvenzionato dallo Stato

stateless /'steɪtlɪs/ *adj* apolide

stately /'steɪtlɪ/ *adj* (**-ier, -iest**) maestoso

stately home *n* dimora *f* signorile

statement /'steɪtmənt/ *n* dichiarazione *f*; Jur deposizione *f*; (from bank) estratto *m* conto; (account) rapporto *m*

state of emergency *n* stato *m* di emergenza

state of play *n* punteggio *m*

state of the art *adj* ⟨technology⟩ il più avanzato

stateside /'steɪtsaɪd/ **1** *adj* degli Stati Uniti
2 *adv* negli Stati Uniti

statesman /'steɪtsmən/ *n* statista *m*

static /'stætɪk/ *adj* statico

static electricity *n* elettricità *f* statica

station /'steɪʃn/ **1** *n* stazione *f*; (police) commissariato *m*
2 *vt* appostare ⟨guard⟩; **be ~ed in Germany** essere di stanza in Germania

stationary /'steɪʃənərɪ/ *adj* immobile

stationer /'steɪʃənə(r)/ *n* ~'**s [shop]** cartoleria *f*

stationery /'steɪʃənərɪ/ *n* cartoleria *f*

station wagon *n* Am station-wagon *f inv*

statistical /stə'tɪstɪkl/ *adj* statistico

statistically /stə'tɪstɪklɪ/ *adv* statisticamente

statistician /stætɪs'tɪʃn/ *n* esperto *m* di statistica

statistics /stə'tɪstɪks/ *n* (subject) statistica *f*; (pl: figures) statistiche *fpl*

statue /'stætʃu:/ n statua f

statuesque /stætʃʊ'esk/ adj statuario

stature /'stætʃə(r)/ n statura f

status /'steɪtəs/ n condizione f; (high rank) alto rango m

status bar n Comput barra f di stato

status quo /kwəʊ/ n statu quo m inv

status symbol n status symbol m inv

statute /'stætʃu:t/ n statuto m

statutory /'stætʃʊtərɪ/ adj statutario

staunch /stɔ:ntʃ/ adj fedele

staunchly /'stɔ:ntʃlɪ/ adv fedelmente

stave /steɪv/ vt ~ off tenere lontano

stay /steɪ/ ① n soggiorno m

② vi restare, rimanere; (reside) alloggiare; ~ the night passare la notte; ~ put non muoversi

③ vt ~ the course resistere fino alla fine

■ **stay away** vi stare lontano

■ **stay behind** vi non andare con gli altri

■ **stay in** vi (at home) stare in casa; Sch restare a scuola dopo le lezioni

■ **stay on** vi (remain) rimanere; ~ on at school continuare gli studi

■ **stay up** vi stare su; ⟨person⟩ stare alzato

staying power /'steɪɪŋ/ n capacità f di resistenza

STD abbr **sexually transmitted disease**

STD [area] code n Br prefisso m [di teleselezione]

stead /sted/ n in his ~ in sua vece; **stand somebody in good** ~ tornare utile a qualcuno

steadfast /'stedfɑ:st/ adj fedele; ⟨refusal⟩ fermo

steadily /'stedɪlɪ/ adv (continually) continuamente

steady /'stedɪ/ ① adj (-ier, -iest) saldo, fermo; ⟨breathing⟩ regolare; ⟨job, boyfriend⟩ fisso; (dependable) serio

② adv **be going** ~ ⟨couple⟩ fare coppia fissa

steak /steɪk/ n (for stew) spezzatino m; (for grilling, frying) bistecca f

steal /sti:l/ vt (pt **stole**, pp **stolen**) rubare (**from** da); ~ **the show** essere al centro dell'attenzione

■ **steal in/out** vi entrare/uscire furtivamente

stealth /stelθ/ n **by** ~ di nascosto

stealthily /'stelθɪlɪ/ adv furtivamente

stealthy /'stelθɪ/ adj furtivo

steam /sti:m/ ① n vapore m; **under one's own** ~ fam da solo; **let off** ~ fig sfogarsi

② vt Culin cucinare a vapore

③ vi fumare

■ **steam up** vi ⟨window⟩ appannarsi

steamed up /sti:md'ʌp/ adj **get** ~ **up** (angry) andare su tutte le furie

steam engine n locomotiva f

steamer /'sti:mə(r)/ n piroscafo m; (saucepan) pentola f a vapore

steam iron n ferro m [da stiro] a vapore

steamroller /'sti:mrəʊlə(r)/ n rullo m compressore

steamy /'sti:mɪ/ adj appannato; fig ⟨scene⟩ spinto

steel /sti:l/ ① n acciaio m

② vt ~ **oneself** temprarsi

steel wool n lana f d'acciaio

steelworks n acciaieria f

steely /'sti:lɪ/ adj d'acciaio

steep[1] /sti:p/ vt (soak) lasciare a bagno; ~**ed in** fig immerso in

steep[2] adj ripido; fam ⟨price⟩ esorbitante

steeple /'sti:pl/ n campanile m

steeplechase /'sti:pltʃeɪs/ n corsa f ippica a ostacoli

steeplejack /'sti:pldʒæk/ n persona f che ripara campanili e ciminiere

steeply /'sti:plɪ/ adv ripidamente

steer /stɪə(r)/ vt/i guidare; ~ **clear of** stare alla larga da

steering /'stɪərɪŋ/ n Auto sterzo m

steering column n Auto piantone m dello sterzo

steering committee n comitato m direttivo

steering lock n Auto bloccasterzo m; (turning circle) angolo m di massima sterzata

steering wheel n volante m

stem[1] /stem/ ① n stelo m; (of glass) gambo m; (of word) radice f

② vi (pt/pp **stemmed**) ~ **from** derivare da

stem[2] vt (pt/pp **stemmed**) contenere

stem ginger n zenzero m sciroppato

stench /stentʃ/ n fetore m

stencil /'stensl/ ① n stampino m; (decoration) stampo m

② vt (pt/pp **stencilled**) stampinare

stenographer /stɪ'nɒɡrəfə(r)/ n stenografo, -a mf

stenography /stɪ'nɒɡrəfɪ/ n stenografia f

step /step/ ① n passo m; (stair) gradino m; ~**s** pl (ladder) scaleo m; **in** ~ al passo; **be out of** ~ non stare al passo; ~ **by** ~ un passo alla volta

② vi (pt/pp **stepped**) ~ **into** entrare in; ~ **into sb's shoes** succedere a qualcuno; ~ **out of** uscire da; ~ **out of line** sgarrare

■ **step back** vi fare un passo indietro; ~ **back from something** fig prendere le distanze da qualcosa

■ **step down** vi fig dimettersi

■ **step forward** vi farsi avanti

S

■ **step in** vi fig intervenire
■ **step up** vt (increase) aumentare
step aerobics n step m inv
stepbrother n fratellastro m
stepchild n figliastro, -a mf
stepdaughter n figliastra f
stepfather n patrigno m
stepladder n scaleo m
stepmother n matrigna f
stepping stone /'stepɪŋ/ n pietra f per guadare; fig trampolino m
stepsister /'stepsɪstə(r)/ n sorellastra f
stepson /'stepsʌn/ n figliastro m
stereo /'sterɪəʊ/ n stereo m; **in** ~ in stereofonia
stereophonic /sterɪəʊ'fɒnɪk/ adj stereofonico
stereoscopic /sterɪəʊ'skɒɪk/ adj stereoscopico
stereotype /'sterɪətaɪp/ n stereotipo m
stereotyped /'sterɪətaɪpt/ adj stereotipato
sterile /'steraɪl/ adj sterile
sterility /stə'rɪlətɪ/ n sterilità f
sterilization /sterəlaɪ'zeɪʃn/ n sterilizzazione f
sterilize /'sterɪlaɪz/ vt sterilizzare
sterling /'stɜːlɪŋ/ ① adj fig apprezzabile ② n sterlina f
sterling silver n argento m pregiato
stern[1] /stɜːn/ adj severo
stern[2] n (of boat) poppa f
sternly /'stɜːnlɪ/ adv severamente
steroid /'sterɔɪd/ n steroide m
stet /stet/ (in proofreading) vive
stethoscope /'steθəskəʊp/ n stetoscopio m
stetson /'stetsən/ n cappello m da cowboy
stew /stjuː/ ① n stufato m; **in a** ~ fam agitato
② vt/i cuocere in umido; ~**ed fruit** frutta f cotta
steward /'stjuːəd/ n (at meeting) organizzatore, -trice mf; (on ship, aircraft) steward m inv
stewardess /stjuːə'des/ n hostess f inv
stick[1] /stɪk/ n bastone m; (of celery, rhubarb) gambo m; Sport mazza f
stick[2] ① vt (pt/pp **stuck**) (stab) conficcare; (glue) attaccare; (fam: put) mettere; (fam: endure) sopportare; **be stuck** ⟨vehicle, person⟩ essere bloccato; ⟨drawer⟩ essere incastrato; **stuck in a traffic jam** bloccato nel traffico; **be stuck for an answer** non saper cosa rispondere; **stuck on** fam attratto da; **be stuck with something** fam farsi incastrare con qualcosa

② vi (adhere) attaccarsi (**to** a); (jam) bloccarsi
■ **stick around** vi (fam: stay) rimanere
■ **stick at** vt ~ **at it** fam tener duro; ~ **at nothing** fam non fermarsi di fronte a niente
■ **stick by** vt (be faithful to) rimanere al fianco di ⟨somebody⟩
■ **stick down** vt incollare ⟨flap⟩; (fam: write down, put down) mettere
■ **stick out** ① vi (project) sporgere; (fam: catch the eye) risaltare
② vt fam fare ⟨tongue⟩; ~ **it out** (endure) tener duro; ~ **one's neck out** sbilanciarsi
■ **stick to** vt (keep to) attenersi a ⟨rules, facts⟩; mantenere ⟨story⟩; perseverare in ⟨task⟩; **I'll** ~ **to beer** continuo con la birra
■ **stick together** vi ⟨pages⟩ incollarsi; (be loyal) aiutarsi a vicenda; (not split up) rimanere uniti
■ **stick up** vi (project) sporgere
■ **stick up for** vt fam difendere
■ **stick with** vt (remain with) rimanere con ⟨somebody⟩
sticker /'stɪkə(r)/ n autoadesivo m
sticking plaster /'stɪkɪʃ/ n cerotto m
stick insect n insetto stecco m
stick-in-the-mud n retrogrado m
stickler /'stɪklə(r)/ n **be a** ~ **for** tenere molto a
stick-up n fam rapina f a mano armata
sticky /'stɪkɪ/ ① adj (**-ier, -iest**) appiccicoso; (adhesive) adesivo; (fig: difficult) difficile
② n fam post-it® m inv
sticky tape n fam nastro m adesivo
stiff /stɪf/ adj rigido; ⟨brush, task⟩ duro; ⟨person⟩ controllato; ⟨drink⟩ forte; ⟨penalty⟩ severo; ⟨price⟩ alto; **bored** ~ fam annoiato a morte; ~ **neck** torcicollo m
stiffen /'stɪfn/ ① vt irrigidire
② vi irrigidirsi
stiffly /'stɪflɪ/ adv rigidamente; ⟨smile, answer⟩ in modo controllato
stiffness /'stɪfnɪs/ n rigidità f
stifle /'staɪfl/ vt soffocare
stifling /'staɪflɪŋ/ adj soffocante
stigma /'stɪgmə/ n marchio m
stigmatize /'stɪgmətaɪz/ vt bollare
stile /staɪl/ n scaletta f
stiletto /stɪ'letəʊ/ n stiletto m; ~ **heels** tacchi mpl a spillo; ~**s** (pl: shoes) scarpe fpl coi tacchi a spillo
still[1] /stɪl/ n distilleria f
still[2] ① adj fermo; ⟨drink⟩ non gasato; **keep/stand** ~ stare fermo
② n quiete f; (photo) posa f
③ adv ancora; (nevertheless) nondimeno, comunque; **I'm** ~ **not sure** non sono ancora sicuro
stillborn /'stɪlbɔːn/ adj nato morto
still life n natura f morta

stilted /'stɪltɪd/ adj artificioso

stilts /stɪlts/ npl trampoli mpl

stimulant /'stɪmjʊlənt/ n eccitante m

stimulate /'stɪmjʊleɪt/ vt stimolare

stimulating /'stɪmjʊleɪtɪŋ/ adj stimolante

stimulation /stɪmjʊ'leɪʃn/ n stimolo m

stimulus /'stɪmjʊləs/ n (pl **-li** /'stɪmjʊlaɪ/) stimolo m

sting /stɪŋ/ ① n puntura f; (organ) pungiglione m
② vt (pt/pp **stung**) pungere; ⟨jellyfish⟩ pizzicare
③ vi ⟨insect⟩ pungere

stinging nettle /'stɪŋɪŋ/ n ortica f

stingy /'stɪndʒɪ/ adj (**-ier, -iest**) tirchio

stink /stɪŋk/ ① n puzza f
② vi (pt **stank**, pp **stunk**) puzzare

stink bomb n fialetta f puzzolente

stinker /'stɪŋkə(r)/ n (fam: difficult problem etc) rompicapo m

stinking /'stɪŋkɪŋ/ adv be ∼ **rich** fam essere ricco sfondato

stint /stɪnt/ ① n lavoro m; do one's ∼ fare la propria parte
② vt ∼ **on** lesinare su

stipend /'staɪpend/ n congrua f

stipulate /'stɪpjʊleɪt/ vt porre come condizione

stipulation /stɪpjʊ'leɪʃn/ n condizione f

stir /stɜː(r)/ ① n mescolata f; (commotion) trambusto m
② vt (pt/pp **stirred**) muovere; (mix) mescolare
③ vi muoversi
■ **stir up** vt fomentare ⟨hatred⟩

stir-fry ① vt saltare in padella
② n pietanza f saltata in padella

stirring /'stɜːrɪŋ/ adj ⟨speech, music⟩ commovente

stirrup /'stɪrəp/ n staffa f

stitch /stɪtʃ/ ① n punto m; (Knitting) maglia f; (pain) fitta f; have somebody in ∼es fam far ridere qualcuno a crepapelle
② vt cucire
■ **stitch up** vt ricucire ⟨wound⟩; the deal's ∼ed up l'affare è concluso

stoat /stəʊt/ n ermellino m

stock /stɒk/ ① n (for use or selling) scorta f, stock m inv; (livestock) bestiame m; (lineage) stirpe f; Fin titoli mpl; Culin brodo m; in ∼ disponibile; out of ∼ esaurito; take ∼ fig fare il punto
② adj solito
③ vt ⟨shop⟩ vendere; approvvigionare ⟨shelves⟩
■ **stock up** vi far scorta (with di)

stockbroker n agente m di cambio

stock car n (for racing) stock-car m inv

stock-car racing n corsa f di stock-car

stock cube n dado m [da brodo]

Stock Exchange n Borsa f Valori

Stockholm /'stɒkhəʊm/ n Stoccolma f

stocking /'stɒkɪŋ/ n calza f

stockist /'stɒkɪst/ n rivenditore m

stockmarket n mercato m azionario

stockpile ① vt fare scorta di
② n riserva f

stockroom n magazzino m

stock-still adj immobile

stocktaking n Comm inventario m

stocky /'stɒkɪ/ adj (**-ier, -iest**) tarchiato

stodge /stɒdʒ/ n (Br fam: food) ammazzafame m inv

stodgy /'stɒdʒɪ/ adj indigesto

stoic /'stəʊɪk/ n stoico, -a mf

stoical /'stəʊɪkl/ adj stoico

stoically /'stəʊɪklɪ/ adv stoicamente

stoicism /'stəʊɪsɪzm/ n stoicismo m

stoke /stəʊk/ vt alimentare

stole[1] /stəʊl/ n stola f

stole[2], **stolen** /'stəʊlən/ ▸ STEAL

stolid /'stɒlɪd/ adj apatico

stolidly /'stɒlɪdlɪ/ adv apaticamente

stomach /'stʌmək/ ① n pancia f; Anat stomaco m
② vt fam reggere

stomach-ache n mal m di pancia

stomp /stɒmp/ vi (walk heavily) camminare con passo pesante

stone /stəʊn/ ① n pietra f; (in fruit) nocciolo m; Med calcolo m; (weight) 6,348 kg; within a ∼'s throw of a un tiro di schioppo da
② adj di pietra
③ vt snocciolare ⟨fruit⟩

Stone Age n età f della pietra

stone circle n cromlech m inv

stone-cold adj gelido

stone-cold sober adj perfettamente sobrio

stoned /stəʊnd/ adj (fam: on drugs, drink) fatto

stone-deaf adj fam sordo come una campana

stonemason n scalpellino m

stonewall vi fare muro di gomma

stone-washed adj ⟨jeans, denim⟩ scolorito, stone-washed

stonework n lavoro m in muratura

stony /'stəʊnɪ/ adj pietroso; ⟨glare⟩ glaciale

stony-broke adj Br fam al verde

stood /stʊd/ ▸ STAND

stooge /stuːdʒ/ n Theat spalla f; (underling) tirapiedi mf inv

stool /stuːl/ n sgabello m

S

stool-pigeon *n* fam informatore, -trice *mf*

stoop /stuːp/ ① *n* curvatura *f*; **walk with a ~** camminare con la schiena curva ② *vi* stare curvo; (bend down) chinarsi; fig abbassarsi

stop /stɒp/ ① *n* (break) sosta *f*; (for bus, train) fermata *f*; Gram punto *m*; **come to a ~** fermarsi; **put a ~ to something** mettere fine a qualcosa ② *vt* (pt/pp **stopped**) fermare; arrestare ⟨machine⟩; (prevent) impedire; **~ somebody doing something** impedire a qualcuno di fare qualcosa; **~ doing something** smettere di fare qualcosa; **~ that!** smettila!; **~ a cheque** bloccare un assegno ③ *vi* fermarsi; ⟨rain⟩ smettere ④ *int* fermo!
■ **stop by** *vi* (make a brief visit) passare
■ **stop off** *vi* fare una sosta
■ **stop up** *vt* otturare ⟨sink⟩; tappare ⟨hole⟩
■ **stop with** *vi* (fam: stay with) fermarsi da

stopcock *n* rubinetto *m* di arresto

stopgap *n* palliativo *m*; (person) tappabuchi *m inv*

stop lights *npl* luci *fpl* di arresto

stop-off *n* sosta *f*

stopover *n* sosta *f*; Aeron scalo *m*

stoppage /ˈstɒpɪdʒ/ *n* ostruzione *f*; (strike) interruzione *f*; (deduction) trattenute *fpl*

stopper /ˈstɒpə(r)/ *n* tappo *m*

stop press *n* ultimissime *fpl*

stop sign *n* (segnale *m* di) stop *m inv*

stopwatch /ˈstɒpwɒtʃ/ *n* cronometro *m*

storage /ˈstɔːrɪdʒ/ *n* deposito *m*; (in warehouse) immagazzinaggio *m*; Comput memoria *f*

storage heater *n* caldaia *f* ad accumulo

store /stɔː(r)/ ① *n* (stock) riserva *f*; (shop) grande magazzino *m*; (depot) deposito *m*; **in ~** in deposito; **there's trouble in ~ for him** ci sono guai in vista per lui; **what the future has in ~ for me** cosa mi riserva il futuro; **set great ~ by** tenere in gran conto ② *vt* tenere; (in warehouse, Comput) immagazzinare
■ **store up** *vt* (accumulate) far scorte di

store card *n* carta *f* di credito di grandi magazzini

storekeeper *n* Am = SHOPKEEPER

storeroom /ˈstɔːruːm/ *n* magazzino *m*

storey /ˈstɔːrɪ/ *n* piano *m*

stork /stɔːk/ *n* cicogna *f*

storm /stɔːm/ ① *n* temporale *m*; (with thunder) tempesta *f* ② *vt* prendere d'assalto

stormy /ˈstɔːmɪ/ *adj* tempestoso

story /ˈstɔːrɪ/ *n* storia *f*; (in newspaper) articolo *m*

storybook /ˈstɔːrɪbʊk/ *n* libro *m* di racconti

storyteller /ˈstɔːrɪtelə(r)/ *n* (writer) narratore, -trice *mf*; (liar) contaballe *mf inv*

stout /staʊt/ ① *adj* ⟨shoes⟩ resistente; (fat) robusto; ⟨defence⟩ strenuo ② *n* birra *f* scura

stoutly /ˈstaʊtlɪ/ *adv* strenuamente

stove /stəʊv/ *n* cucina *f* [economica]; (for heating) stufa *f*

stow /stəʊ/ *vt* metter via
■ **stow away** *vi* Naut imbarcarsi clandestinamente

stowaway /ˈstəʊəweɪ/ *n* passeggero, -a *mf* clandestino, -a

straddle /ˈstrædl/ *vt* stare a cavalcioni su; (standing) essere a cavallo su

strafe /streɪf/ *vt* mitragliare da bassa quota

straggle /ˈstrægl/ *vi* crescere disordinatamente; (dawdle) rimanere indietro

straggler /ˈstræglə(r)/ *n* persona *f* che rimane indietro

straggly /ˈstræglɪ/ *adj* **have ~ hair** avere pochi capelli sottili

straight /streɪt/ ① *adj* diritto, dritto; ⟨answer, question, person⟩ diretto; (tidy) in ordine; ⟨drink, hair⟩ liscio; **three ~ wins** tre vittorie di seguito ② *adv* diritto, dritto; (directly) direttamente; **~ away** immediatamente; **~ on** or **ahead** diritto; **~ out** fig apertamente; **go ~** fam rigare diritto; **put something ~** mettere qualcosa in ordine; **sit/stand up ~** stare diritto; **let's get something ~** mettiamo una cosa in chiaro

straighten /ˈstreɪtn/ ① *vt* raddrizzare ② *vi* raddrizzarsi; **~ [up]** ⟨person⟩ mettersi diritto
■ **straighten out** *vt* fig chiarire ⟨situation⟩

straight face *n* **keep a ~ ~** restare serio

straight-faced /-ˈfeɪst/ *adj* con l'aria seria

straightforward *adj* franco; (simple) semplice

straight man *n* Theat spalla *f*

strain[1] /streɪn/ *n* (streak) vena *f*; Bot varietà *f inv*; (of virus) forma *f*

strain[2] ① *n* tensione *f*; (injury) stiramento *m*; **~s** *pl* (of music) note *fpl*; **put a ~ on** fig introdurre delle tensioni in; **under a lot of ~** estremamente sotto pressione ② *vt* tirare; sforzare ⟨eyes, voice⟩; stirarsi ⟨muscle⟩; Culin scolare ③ *vi* sforzarsi

strained /streɪnd/ *adj* ⟨relations⟩ teso

strainer /'streɪnə(r)/ *n* colino *m*

strait /streɪt/ *n* stretto *m*; **in dire ∼s** in serie difficoltà

straitjacket /'streɪtdʒækɪt/ *n* camicia *f* di forza

strait-laced /-'leɪst/ *adj* puritano

strand[1] /strænd/ *n* (of thread) gugliata *f*; (of beads) filo *m*; (of hair) capello *m*

strand[2] *vt* be ∼ed rimanere bloccato

strange /streɪndʒ/ *adj* strano; (not known) sconosciuto; (unaccustomed) estraneo

strangely /'streɪndʒlɪ/ *adv* stranamente; ∼ **enough** curiosamente

strangeness /'streɪndʒnəs/ *n* stranezza *f*

stranger /'streɪndʒə(r)/ *n* estraneo, -a *mf*

strangle /'stræŋgl/ *vt* strangolare; fig reprimere

stranglehold /'stræŋglhəʊld/ *n* (physical grip) presa *f* alla gola; (fig: powerful control) stretta *f* mortale; **have a ∼ on something** fig avere in pugno qualcosa

strangulation /stræŋgjʊ'leɪʃn/ *n* strangolamento *m*

strap /stræp/ ① *n* cinghia *f*; (to grasp in vehicle) maniglia *f*; (of watch) cinturino *m*; (shoulder ∼) bretella *f*, spallina *f* ② *vt* (pt/pp **strapped**) legare; ∼ **in/down** assicurare

strapless /'stræplɪs/ *adj* ⟨bra, dress⟩ senza spalline

strapped /stræpt/ *adj* fam be ∼ **for** essere a corto di

strapping /'stræpɪŋ/ *adj* robusto

strata /'strɑːtə/ ▶STRATUM

stratagem /'strætədʒəm/ *n* stratagemma *m*

strategic /strə'tiːdʒɪk/ *adj* strategico

strategically /strə'tiːdʒɪklɪ/ *adv* strategicamente

strategist /'strætədʒɪst/ *n* stratega *mf*

strategy /'strætədʒɪ/ *n* strategia *f*

stratosphere /'strætəsfɪə(r)/ *n* stratosfera *f*

stratum /'strɑːtəm/ *n* (*pl* **strata**) strato *m*

straw /strɔː/ *n* paglia *f*; (single piece) fuscello *m*; (for drinking) cannuccia *f*; **the last ∼** l'ultima goccia

strawberry /'strɔːbərɪ/ *n* fragola *f*

straw poll *n* Pol sondaggio *m* d'opinione non ufficiale

stray /streɪ/ ① *adj* (animal) randagio ② *n* randagio *m* ③ *vi* andarsene per conto proprio; (deviate) deviare (**from** da)

streak /striːk/ ① *n* striatura *f*; (fig: trait) vena *f*; ∼**s** (*pl*: in hair) mèche *fpl* ② *vi* (move fast) sfrecciare

streaky /'striːkɪ/ *adj* striato; ⟨bacon⟩ grasso

stream /striːm/ ① *n* ruscello *m*; (current) corrente *f*; (of blood, people) flusso *m*; Sch classe *f*; **come on ∼** (start operating) entrare in attività; ⟨oil⟩ cominciare a scorrere ② *vi* scorrere
■ **stream in** *vi* entrare a fiotti
■ **stream out** *vi* uscire a fiotti

streamer /'striːmə(r)/ *n* (paper) stella *f* filante; (flag) pennone *m*

streaming /'striːmɪŋ/ ① *adj* **a ∼ cold** raffreddore con naso che cola; Comput ⟨media, video⟩ in streaming ② *n* (in school) divisione *f* degli studenti in base alle loro capacità

streamline /'striːmlaɪn/ *vt* rendere aerodinamico; (simplify) snellire

streamlined /'striːmlaɪnd/ *adj* aerodinamico; (simplified) snellito

street /striːt/ *n* strada *f*

streetcar *n* Am tram *m inv*

street cred *n* fam immagine *f* pubblica

street lamp *n* lampione *m*

street market *n* mercato *m* all'aperto

street plan *n* stradario *m*

street value *n* (of drugs) valore *m* di mercato

streetwalker *n* passeggiatrice *f*

streetwise *adj* fam ⟨person⟩ che conosce tutti i trucchi per sopravvivere in una metropoli

strength /streŋθ/ *n* forza *f*; (of wall, bridge etc) solidità *f*; ∼**s** *pl* punti *mpl* forti; **on the ∼ of** grazie a

strengthen /'streŋθən/ *vt* rinforzare

strenuous /'strenjʊəs/ *adj* faticoso; ⟨attempt, denial⟩ energico

strenuously /'strenjʊəslɪ/ *adv* energicamente

stress /stres/ ① *n* (emphasis) insistenza *f*; Gram accento *m* tonico; (mental) stress *m inv*; Mech spinta *f* ② *vt* (emphasize) insistere su; Gram mettere l'accento (tonico) su
■ **stress out** *vt* ∼ **somebody out** stressare qualcuno

stressed /strest/ *adj* (mentally) ∼ [**out**] stressato

stressful /'stresfʊl/ *adj* stressante

stretch /stretʃ/ ① *n* stiramento *m*; (period) periodo *m* di tempo; (of road) tratto *m*; (elasticity) elasticità *f*; **at a ∼** di fila; **have a ∼** stirarsi ② *vt* tirare; allargare ⟨shoes, sweater, etc⟩; ∼ **one's legs** stendere le gambe; ∼ **a point** fare uno strappo alla regola ③ *vi* (become wider) allargarsi; (extend) estendersi; ⟨person⟩ stirarsi
■ **stretch out** ① *vt* allungare ⟨one's hand, legs⟩; allargare ⟨arms⟩ ② *vi* ⟨person⟩ sdraiarsi; ⟨land⟩ estendersi

stretcher /'stretʃə(r)/ *n* barella *f*

stretchy /'stretʃɪ/ *adj* elastico

S

strew /stru:/ vt (pt/pp **strewn** or **strewed**) sparpagliare; ∼n with coperto di

stricken /'strɪkn/ adj prostrato; ∼ with affetto da ⟨illness⟩

strict /strɪkt/ adj severo; (precise) preciso

strictly /'strɪktlɪ/ adv severamente; ∼ speaking in senso stretto

strictness /'strɪktnɪs/ n severità f

stricture /'strɪktʃə(r)/ n critica f; (constriction) restringimento m

stride /straɪd/ ① n [lungo] passo m; make great ∼s fig fare passi da gigante; take something in one's ∼ accettare qualcosa con facilità
② vi (pt **strode**, pp **stridden**) andare a gran passi

strident /'straɪdənt/ adj stridente; ⟨colour⟩ vistoso

stridently /'straɪdəntlɪ/ adv con voce stridente

strife /straɪf/ n conflitto m

strike /straɪk/ ① n sciopero m; Mil attacco m; on ∼ in sciopero
② vt (pt/pp **struck**) colpire; accendere ⟨match⟩; trovare ⟨oil, gold⟩; (delete) depennare; (occur to) venire in mente a; Mil attaccare; ∼ somebody a blow colpire qualcuno
③ vi ⟨lightning⟩ cadere; ⟨clock⟩ suonare; Mil attaccare; ⟨workers⟩ scioperare; ∼ lucky azzeccarla
■ **strike back** vi fare rappresaglia; (at critics) reagire
■ **strike off** vt eliminare; **be struck off [the register]** ⟨doctor⟩ essere radiato [dall'albo]
■ **strike out** vt eliminare
■ **strike up** vt fare ⟨friendship⟩; attaccare ⟨conversation⟩

strike-breaker n persona f che non aderisce a uno sciopero

strike-breaking n crumiraggio m

strike force n forze fpl d'intervento

striker /'straɪkə(r)/ n scioperante mf

striking /'straɪkɪŋ/ adj impressionante; (attractive) affascinante

string /strɪŋ/ ① n spago m; (of musical instrument, racket) corda f; (of pearls) filo m; (of lies) serie f; **the ∼s** pl Mus gli archi; **pull ∼s** fam usare le proprie conoscenze
② vt (pt/pp **strung**) (thread) infilare ⟨beads⟩
■ **string along** ① vt (fam: deceive) prendere in giro
② vi **I'll ∼ along** (come too) vengo anch'io; ∼ along with somebody andare/venire con qcno
■ **string out** ① vi (spread out) allinearsi
② vt disporre in fila; **be strung out** (sl: on drugs) essere fatto
■ **string together** vt mettere insieme ⟨words, remarks⟩

string bean n fagiolino m

stringed /strɪŋd/ adj ⟨instrument⟩ a corda

stringent /'strɪndʒnt/ adj rigido

stringy /'strɪŋɪ/ adj ⟨person, build⟩ asciutto; ⟨hair⟩ come spaghetti; Culin filaccioso

strip /strɪp/ ① n striscia f
② vt (pt/pp **stripped**) spogliare; togliere le lenzuola da ⟨bed⟩; scrostare ⟨wood, furniture⟩; smontare ⟨machine⟩; (deprive) privare (of di
③ vi (undress) spogliarsi
■ **strip down** vt smontare ⟨engine⟩

strip cartoon n striscia f

strip club n locale m di strip-tease

stripe /straɪp/ n striscia f; Mil gallone m

striped /straɪpt/ adj a strisce

stripey /'straɪpɪ/ adj a strisce, a righe

strip light n tubo m al neon

strip lighting n illuminazione f al neon

stripper /'strɪpə(r)/ n spogliarellista mf; (solvent) sverniciatore m

strip-search ① n perquisizione f (facendo spogliare qualcuno)
② vt perquisire (facendo spogliare)

striptease /'strɪpti:z/ n spogliarello m, strip-tease m inv

strive /straɪv/ vi (pt **strove**, pp **striven**) sforzarsi (to di); ∼ for sforzarsi di ottenere

strobe /strəʊb/ n luce f stroboscopica

strode /strəʊd/ ▶ STRIDE

stroke¹ /strəʊk/ n colpo m; (of pen) tratto m; (in swimming) bracciata f; Med ictus m inv; ∼ of luck colpo m di fortuna; put somebody off his ∼ far perdere il filo a qualcuno

stroke² ① vt accarezzare
② n carezza f

stroll /strəʊl/ ① n passeggiata f; **go for a ∼** andare a far due passi
② vi passeggiare

stroller /'strəʊlə(r)/ n (Am: push-chair) passeggino m

strong /strɒŋ/ adj (-er /'strɒŋgə(r)/, -est /'strɒŋgɪst/) forte; ⟨argument⟩ valido

strongbox /'strɒŋbɒks/ n cassaforte f

stronghold /'strɒŋhəʊld/ n roccaforte f

strong language n (forceful terms) linguaggio m incisivo; (swearing) linguaggio m offensivo

strongly /'strɒŋlɪ/ adv fortemente; **feel ∼ about something** avere molto a cuore qualcosa

strong-minded /-'maɪndɪd/ adj risoluto

strong point n punto m di forza

strongroom n camera f blindata

strong stomach n stomaco m di ferro

strong-willed /wɪld/ adj tenace

stroppiness ⋯⟩ stupefaction ⋯

stroppiness /'strɒpɪnɪs/ *n* scontrosità *f*

stroppy /'strɒpɪ/ *adj* fam scorbutico, scontroso

strove /strəʊv/ ▶ STRIVE

struck /strʌk/ ▶ STRIKE; ~ **on** *adj* fam entusiasta di

structural /'strʌktʃərəl/ *adj* strutturale

structural damage *n* danni *mpl* alla struttura portante

structurally /'strʌktʃərəlɪ/ *adv* strutturalmente

structure /'strʌktʃə(r)/ ① *n* struttura *f* ② *vt* strutturare

struggle /'strʌgl/ ① *n* lotta *f*; **with a** ~ con difficoltà
② *vi* lottare; ~ **for breath** respirare con fatica; ~ **to do something** fare fatica a fare qualcosa; ~ **to one's feet** alzarsi con fatica

struggling /'strʌglɪŋ/ *adj* **a** ~ **artist/ writer** un artista/uno scrittore che fatica ad affermarsi

strum /strʌm/ *vt/i* (pt/pp **strummed**) strimpellare

strung /strʌŋ/ ▶ STRING

strung out *adj* **be** ~ (from drugs) essere fatto; **be** ~ **on** essere dipendente da ⟨drugs⟩

strut[1] /strʌt/ *n* (component) puntello *m*

strut[2] *vi* (pt/pp **strutted**) camminare impettito

stub /stʌb/ ① *n* mozzicone *m*; (counterfoil) matrice *f*
② *vt* (pt/pp **stubbed**) ~ **one's toe** sbattere il dito del piede (on contro)
■ **stub out** *vt* spegnere ⟨cigarette⟩

stubble /'stʌbl/ *n* (on face) barba *f* ispida

stubbly /'stʌblɪ/ *adj* ispido

stubborn /'stʌbən/ *adj* testardo; ⟨refusal⟩ ostinato

stubbornly /'stʌbənlɪ/ *adv* testardamente; ⟨refuse⟩ ostinatamente

stubbornness /'stʌbənnɪs/ *n* (of person) testardaggine *f*

stubby /'stʌbɪ/ *adj* (-**ier**, -**iest**) tozzo

stucco /'stʌkəʊ/ *n* stucco *m*

stuck /stʌk/ ▶ STICK[2]

stuck-up *adj* fam snob *inv*

stud[1] /stʌd/ *n* (on boot) tacchetto *m*; (on jacket) borchia *f*; (for ear) orecchino *m* [a bottone]

stud[2] *n* (of horses) scuderia *f*

studded with /'stʌdɪd/ *adj* fig tempestato di

student /'stjuːdənt/ *n* studente *m*, studentessa *f*; (school child) scolaro, -a *mf*

student grant *n* borsa *f* di studio

student nurse *n* studente, -tessa *mf* infermiere, -a

student teacher *n* insegnante *mf* tirocinante

student union *n* (organization) organizzazione *f* studentesca; (building) casa *f* dello studente

stud-horse *n* stallone *m* [da monta]

studied /'stʌdɪd/ *adj* intenzionale; ⟨politeness⟩ studiato

studio /'stjuːdɪəʊ/ *n* studio *m*

studio apartment *n* Am monolocale *m*

studio flat *n* monolocale *m*

studious /'stjuːdɪəs/ *adj* studioso; ⟨attention⟩ studiato

studiously /'stjuːdɪəslɪ/ *adv* studiosamente; (carefully) attentamente

stud mare *n* giumenta *f* fattrice

study /'stʌdɪ/ ① *n* studio *m*
② *vt/i* (pt/pp -**ied**) studiare; ~ **for an exam** preparare un esame

study aid *n* sussidio *m* didattico

stuff /stʌf/ ① *n* materiale *m*; (fam: things) roba *f*
② *vt* riempire; (with padding) imbottire; Culin farcire; ~ **something into a drawer/one's pocket** ficcare qualcosa alla rinfusa in un cassetto/in tasca; ~ **oneself** ingozzarsi (with di); **get** ~**ed!** fam va' a quel paese!

stuffing /'stʌfɪŋ/ *n* (padding) imbottitura *f*; Culin ripieno *m*

stuffy /'stʌfɪ/ *adj* (-**ier**, -**iest**) che sa di chiuso; (old-fashioned) antiquato

stultifying /'stʌltɪfaɪɪŋ/ *adj* che abbruttisce

stumble /'stʌmbl/ *vi* inciampare; ~ **across** or **on** imbattersi in

stumbling block /'stʌmblɪŋ/ *n* ostacolo *m*

stump /stʌmp/ *n* ceppo *m*; (of limb) moncone *m*
■ **stump up** *vt/i* fam sganciare

stumped /stʌmpt/ *adj* fam perplesso

stumpy /'stʌmpɪ/ *adj* (-**ier**, -**iest**) ⟨person, legs⟩ tozzo

stun /stʌn/ *vt* (pt/pp **stunned**) stordire; (astonish) sbalordire

stung /stʌŋ/ ▶ STING

stunk /stʌŋk/ ▶ STINK

stunned /stʌnd/ *adj* ⟨expression⟩ sbalordito

stunning /'stʌnɪŋ/ *adj* fam favoloso; ⟨blow, victory⟩ sbalorditivo

stunt[1] /stʌnt/ *n* fam trovata *f* pubblicitaria

stunt[2] *vt* arrestare lo sviluppo di

stunted /'stʌntɪd/ *adj* stentato

stuntman /'stʌntmən/ *n* stuntman *m* *inv*, cascatore *m*

stuntwoman /'stʌntwʊmən/ *n* stuntwoman *f* *inv*

stupefaction /stjuːpɪ'fækʃn/ *n* stupore *m*

stupefy /'stjuːpɪfaɪ/ *vt* (pt/pp **-ied**) (astonish) stupire

stupefying /'stjuːpɪfaɪɪŋ/ *adj* stupefacente

stupendous /stjuːˈpendəs/ *adj* stupendo

stupendously /stjuːˈpendəslɪ/ *adv* stupendamente

stupid /'stjuːpɪd/ *adj* stupido

stupidity /stjuːˈpɪdətɪ/ *n* stupidità *f*

stupidly /'stjuːpɪdlɪ/ *adv* stupidamente

stupor /'stjuːpə(r)/ *n* torpore *m*

sturdy /'stɜːdɪ/ *adj* (**-ier**, **-iest**) robusto; ⟨*furniture*⟩ solido

stutter /'stʌtə(r)/ **1** *n* balbuzie *f*; **have a** ~ balbettare
2 *vt/i* balbettare

St Valentine's Day /'væləntaɪnz/ *n* san Valentino *m*

sty¹ /staɪ/ *n* (*pl* **sties**) porcile *m*

sty², **stye** *n* (*pl* **styes**) Med orzaiolo *m*

style /staɪl/ *n* stile *m*; (fashion) moda *f*; (sort) tipo *m*; (hair ~) pettinatura *f*; **in** ~ in grande stile

styling /'staɪlɪŋ/ **1** *adj* ⟨*gel, mousse*⟩ modellante
2 *n* (design) styling *m*; (in hairdressing) acconciatura *f*

stylish /'staɪlɪʃ/ *adj* elegante

stylishly /'staɪlɪʃlɪ/ *adv* con eleganza

stylist /'staɪlɪst/ *n* stilista *mf*; (hair ~) *n* parrucchiere, -a *mf*

stylistic /staɪˈlɪstɪk/ *adj* stilistico

stylistically /staɪˈlɪstɪklɪ/ *adv* stilisticamente

stylized /'staɪlaɪzd/ *adj* stilizzato

stylus /'staɪləs/ *n* (on record player) puntina *f*

styptic pencil /'stɪptɪk/ *n* matita *f* emostatica

suave /swɑːv/ *adj* dai modi garbati

sub-aqua /sʌbˈækwə/ *adj* ⟨*club*⟩ di sport subacquei

subcommittee /'sʌbkəmɪtɪ/ *n* sottocommissione *f*

subconscious /sʌbˈkɒnʃəs/ **1** *adj* subcosciente
2 *n* subcosciente *m*

subconsciously /sʌbˈkɒnʃəslɪ/ *adv* in modo inconscio

subcontinent /sʌbˈkɒntɪnənt/ *n* subcontinente *m*

subcontract /sʌbkənˈtrækt/ *vt* subappaltare (to a)

subcontractor /'sʌbkəntræktə(r)/ *n* subappaltatore, -trice *mf*

subdirectory /'sʌbdaɪrektərɪ/ *n* Comput sottodirectory *f inv*

subdivide /sʌbdɪˈvaɪd/ *vt* suddividere

subdivision /'sʌbdɪvɪʒn/ *n* suddivisione *f*

subdue /səbˈdjuː/ *vt* sottomettere; (make quieter) attenuare

subdued /səbˈdjuːd/ *adj* ⟨*light*⟩ attenuato; ⟨*person, voice*⟩ pacato

subheading /'sʌbhedɪŋ/ *n* sottotitolo *m*

subhuman /sʌbˈhjuːmən/ *adj* (cruel, not fit for humans) disumano; fam ⟨*appearance*⟩ da paleolitico

subject¹ /'sʌbdʒekt/ **1** *adj* ~ **to** soggetto a; (depending on) subordinato a; ~ **to availability** nei limiti della disponibilità
2 *n* soggetto *m*; (of ruler) suddito, -a *mf*; Sch materia *f*; **change the** ~ parlare di qualcos'altro

subject² /səbˈdʒekt/ *vt* (to attack, abuse) sottoporre; assoggettare ⟨*country*⟩

subjective /səbˈdʒektɪv/ *adj* soggettivo

subjectively /səbˈdʒektɪvlɪ/ *adv* soggettivamente

subjectiveness /səbˈdʒektɪvnɪs/ *n* soggetività *f*

subjugate /'sʌbdʒʊgeɪt/ *vt* soggiogare, sottomettere

subjugation /sʌbdʒəˈgeɪʃn/ *n* sottomissione *f*

subjunctive /səbˈdʒʌŋktɪv/ *adj & n* congiuntivo *m*

sub-let /sʌbˈlet/ *vt* (pt/pp **-let**, pres p **-letting**) subaffittare

sublime /səˈblaɪm/ *adj* sublime

sublimely /səˈblaɪmlɪ/ *adv* sublimamente

subliminal /səˈblɪmɪnl/ *adj* subliminale

sub-machine gun *n* mitraglietta *f*

submarine /'sʌbməriːn/ *n* sommergibile *m*

submerge /səbˈmɜːdʒ/ **1** *vt* immergere; **be** ~**d** essere sommerso
2 *vi* immergersi

submission /səbˈmɪʃn/ *n* sottomissione *f*

submissive /səbˈmɪsɪv/ *adj* sottomesso

submissively /səbˈmɪsɪvlɪ/ *adv* remissivamente

submissiveness /səbˈmɪsɪvnɪs/ *n* remissività *f*

submit /səbˈmɪt/ **1** *vt* (pt/pp **-mitted**, pres p **-mitting**) sottoporre
2 *vi* sottomettersi

subnormal /sʌbˈnɔːml/ *adj* ⟨*temperature*⟩ al di sotto della norma; ⟨*person*⟩ subnormale

subordinate¹ /səˈbɔːdɪnɪt/ *adj & n* subordinato, -a *mf*

subordinate² /səˈbɔːdɪneɪt/ *vt* subordinare (to a)

subpoena /səbˈpiːnə/ **1** *n* mandato *m* di comparizione
2 *vt* citare

subroutine /'sʌbruːtiːn/ *n* Comput subroutine *f*

subscribe /səb'skraɪb/ *vi* contribuire; ∼ to abbonarsi a ⟨*newspaper*⟩; sottoscrivere ⟨*fund*⟩; fig aderire a ⟨*theory*⟩

subscriber /səb'skraɪbə(r)/ *n* abbonato, -a *mf*

subscription /səb'skrɪpʃn/ *n* (to club) sottoscrizione *f*; (to newspaper) abbonamento *m*

subsequent /'sʌbsɪkwənt/ *adj* susseguente

subsequently /'sʌbsɪkwəntlɪ/ *adv* in seguito

subservience /səb'sɜːvɪəns/ *n* asservimento *m*

subservient /səb'sɜːvɪənt/ *adj* subordinato; (servile) servile

subserviently /səb'sɜːvɪəntlɪ/ *adv* servilmente

subset /'sʌbset/ *n* Math sottoinsieme *m*

subside /səb'saɪd/ *vi* sprofondare; ⟨*ground*⟩ avvallarsi; ⟨*storm*⟩ placarsi

subsidence /'sʌbsɪdəns/ *n* (of land) cedimento *m*

subsidiary /səb'sɪdɪərɪ/ **1** *adj* secondario
2 *n* ∼ **[company]** filiale *f*

subsidize /'sʌbsɪdaɪz/ *vt* sovvenzionare

subsidy /'sʌbsɪdɪ/ *n* sovvenzione *f*

subsist /səb'sɪst/ *vi* vivere (**on** di)

subsistence /səb'sɪstəns/ *n* sussistenza *f*

subsistence level *n* livello *m* di sussistenza

substance /'sʌbstəns/ *n* sostanza *f*

sub-standard /sʌb'stændəd/ *adj* di qualità inferiore

substantial /səb'stænʃl/ *adj* sostanziale; ⟨*meal*⟩ sostanzioso; (strong) solido

substantially /səb'stænʃəlɪ/ *adv* sostanzialmente; ⟨*built*⟩ solidamente

substantiate /səb'stænʃɪeɪt/ *vt* comprovare

substitute /'sʌbstɪtjuːt/ **1** *n* sostituto *m*
2 *vt* ∼ **A for B** sostituire B con A
3 *vi* ∼ **for somebody** sostituire qualcuno

substitution /sʌbstɪ'tjuːʃn/ *n* sostituzione *f*

subterfuge /'sʌbtəfjuːdʒ/ *n* sotterfugio *m*

subterranean /sʌbtə'reɪnɪən/ *adj* sotterraneo

subtext /'sʌbtekst/ *n* storia *f* secondaria; fig messaggio *m* implicito

subtitle /'sʌbtaɪtl/ **1** *n* sottotitolo *m*
2 *vt* sottotitolare

subtitled /'sʌbtaɪtld/ *adj* sottotitolato

subtle /'sʌtl/ *adj* sottile; ⟨*taste, perfume*⟩ delicato

subtlety /'sʌtltɪ/ *n* sottigliezza *f*

subtly /'sʌtlɪ/ *adv* sottilmente

subtotal /'sʌbtəʊtl/ *n* totale *m* parziale

subtract /səb'trækt/ *vt* sottrarre

subtraction /səb'trækʃn/ *n* sottrazione *f*

suburb /'sʌbɜːb/ *n* sobborgo *m*; **in the** ∼**s** in periferia

suburban /sə'bɜːbən/ *adj* suburbano

suburbia /sə'bɜːbɪə/ *n* sobborghi *mpl*

subversive /səb'vɜːsɪv/ *adj* sovversivo

subway /'sʌbweɪ/ *n* sottopassaggio *m*; (Am: railway) metropolitana *f*, metrò *m inv*

sub-zero /sʌb'zɪərəʊ/ *adj* sottozero *inv*

succeed /sək'siːd/ **1** *vi* riuscire (**in doing something** a fare qualcosa); (follow) succedere (**to** a)
2 *vt* succedere a ⟨*king*⟩

succeeding /sək'siːdɪŋ/ *adj* successivo

success /sək'ses/ *n* successo *m*; **be a** ∼ (in life) aver successo

successful /sək'sesfʊl/ *adj* riuscito; ⟨*businessman, artist etc*⟩ di successo

successfully /sək'sesfʊlɪ/ *adv* con successo

succession /sək'seʃn/ *n* successione *f*; **in** ∼ di seguito

successive /sək'sesɪv/ *adj* successivo

successively /sə'sesɪvlɪ/ *adv* successivamente

successor /sək'sesə(r)/ *n* successore *m*

success rate *n* percentuale *f* di promozioni

success story *n* successo *m*

succinct /sək'sɪŋkt/ *adj* succinto

succinctly /sək'sɪŋktlɪ/ *adv* succintamente

succour /'sʌkə(r)/ **1** *vt* soccorrere
2 *n* soccorso *m*

succulence /'sʌkjʊləns/ *n* succulenza *f*

succulent /'sʌkjʊlənt/ *adj* succulento

succumb /sə'kʌm/ *vi* soccombere (**to** a)

such /sʌtʃ/ **1** *adj* tale; ∼ **a book** un libro così; ∼ **a thing** una cosa del genere; ∼ **a long time ago** talmente tanto tempo fa; **there is no** ∼ **thing/person** non c'è una cosa/persona così
2 *pron* **as** ∼ in quanto tale; ∼ **as** come; **and** ∼ e simili; ∼ **as it is** per quel che vale; **if** ∼ **is the case** se questo è il caso

such and such *adj* tale; **for** ∼ ∼ **an amount** per un tot; **go on** ∼ ∼ **a day at** ∼ ∼ ∼ **a time** vai il tal giorno alla tal ora

suchlike /'sʌtʃlaɪk/ *pron* fam di tal genere

suck /sʌk/ *vt* succhiare
■ **suck up** *vt* assorbire
■ **suck up to** *vt* fam fare il lecchino con

sucker /'sʌkə(r)/ *n* Bot pollone *m*; (fam: person) credulone, -a *mf*

suckle /'sʌkl/ *vt* allattare

S

suction /'sʌkʃn/ n aspirazione f

suction pad n ventosa f

Sudan /sʊ'dæn/ n Sudan m

Sudanese /sʊdən'i:z/ adj & n sudanese mf

sudden /'sʌdn/ ➊ adj improvviso ➋ n all of a ~ all'improvviso

sudden death n (football) sudden death f

suddenly /'sʌdənlɪ/ adv improvvisamente

suds /sʌdz/ npl (foam) schiuma f; (soapy water) acqua f saponata

sue /su:/ ➊ vt (pres p **suing**) fare causa a (**for** per) ➋ vi fare causa

suede /sweɪd/ n pelle f scamosciata

suet /'su:ɪt/ n grasso m di rognone

suffer /'sʌfə(r)/ ➊ vi soffrire (**from** per) ➋ vt soffrire di ⟨pain⟩; subire ⟨loss etc⟩

sufferance /'sʌf(ə)rəns/ n you're here on ~ qui tu sei appena tollerato

sufferer /'sʌfərə(r)/ n malato, -a mf; **Aids** ~s malati di Aids

suffering /'sʌf(ə)rɪŋ/ n sofferenza f

suffice /sə'faɪs/ vi bastare

sufficient /sə'fɪʃənt/ adj sufficiente

sufficiently /sə'fɪʃəntlɪ/ adv sufficientemente

suffix /'sʌfɪks/ n suffisso m

suffocate /'sʌfəkeɪt/ vt/i soffocare

suffocating /'sʌfəkeɪtɪŋ/ adj ⟨heat⟩ soffocante

suffocation /sʌfə'keɪʃn/ n soffocamento m

suffrage /'sʌfrɪdʒ/ n (right) diritto m di voto; (system) suffragio m

suffragette /sʌfrə'dʒet/ n suffragetta f

sugar /'ʃʊgə(r)/ ➊ n zucchero m ➋ vt zuccherare; ~ **the pill** fig addolcire la pillola

sugar basin, sugar bowl n zuccheriera f

sugar beet n barbabietola f da zucchero

sugar cane n canna f da zucchero

sugar-coated /-'kəʊtɪd/ adj ricoperto di zucchero

sugar cube n zolletta f

sugar daddy n fam vecchio amante m danaroso

sugar-free adj senza zucchero

sugar lump n zolletta f

sugary /'ʃʊgərɪ/ adj zuccheroso; fig sdolcinato

suggest /sə'dʒest/ vt suggerire; (indicate, insinuate) fare pensare a

suggestible /sə'dʒestəbl/ adj suggestionabile

suggestion /sə'dʒestʃən/ n suggerimento m; (trace) traccia f

suggestive /sə'dʒestɪv/ adj allusivo; **be** ~ **of** fare pensare a

suggestively /sə'dʒestɪvlɪ/ adv in modo allusivo

suicidal /su:ɪ'saɪdl/ adj suicida

suicide /'su:ɪsaɪd/ n suicidio m; (person) suicida mf; **commit** ~ suicidarsi

suicide attempt n tentato suicidio m

suicide pact n patto m suicida

suit /su:t/ ➊ n vestito m; (woman's) tailleur m inv; (Cards) seme m; Jur causa f; **follow** ~ fig fare lo stesso ➋ vt andar bene a; (adapt) adattare (**to** a); (be convenient for) andare bene per; **be** ~**ed to** or **for** essere adatto a; ~ **yourself!** fa' come vuoi!

suitability /su:tə'bɪlɪtɪ/ n adeguatezza f

suitable /'su:təbl/ adj adatto

suitably /'su:təblɪ/ adv convenientemente

suitcase /'su:tkeɪs/ n valigia f

suite /swi:t/ n suite f inv; (of furniture) divano m e poltrone fpl assortiti

sulk /sʌlk/ vi fare il broncio

sulkily /'sʌlkɪlɪ/ adv con aria imbronciata

sulky /'sʌlkɪ/ adj imbronciato

sullen /'sʌlən/ adj svogliato

sullenly /'sʌlənlɪ/ adv svogliatamente

sulphur /'sʌlfə(r)/ n zolfo m

sulphur dioxide /daɪ'ɒksaɪd/ n anidride f solforosa

sulphuric acid /sʌl'fjʊərɪk/ n acido m solforico

sultana /sʌl'tɑ:nə/ n uva f sultanina

sultry /'sʌltrɪ/ adj (**-ier, -iest**) ⟨weather⟩ afoso; fig sensuale

sum /sʌm/ n somma f; Sch addizione f
■ **sum up** vi (pt/pp **summed**) ➊ riassumere ➋ vt valutare

summarily /sʌ'merɪlɪ/ adv sommariamente; ⟨dismissed⟩ sbrigativamente

summarize /'sʌməraɪz/ vt riassumere

summary /'sʌmərɪ/ ➊ n sommario m ➋ adj sommario; ⟨dismissal⟩ sbrigativo

summer /'sʌmə(r)/ n estate f; **in** ~, **in the** ~ in estate

summer camp n ≈ colonia f

summer holiday n vacanze fpl estive

summer house n padiglione m

summer school n corso m estivo

summertime n (season) estate f

summer time n (clock change) ora f legale

summery /'sʌmərɪ/ adj estivo

summing-up /sʌmɪŋ'ʌp/ *n* riepilogo *m*; Jur ricapitolazione *f* del processo

summit /'sʌmɪt/ *n* cima *f*

summit conference *n* vertice *m*

summon /'sʌmən/ *vt* convocare; Jur citare

■ **summon up** *vt* raccogliere ⟨strength⟩; rievocare ⟨memory⟩

summons /'sʌmənz/ ① *n* Jur citazione *f* ② *vt* citare in giudizio

sump /sʌmp/ *n* Auto coppa *f* dell'olio

sumptuous /'sʌmptjʊəs/ *adj* sontuoso

sumptuously /'sʌmptjʊəslɪ/ *adv* sontuosamente

sum total *n* totale *m*

sun /sʌn/ ① *n* sole *m* ② *vt* (pt/pp **sunned**) ~ oneself prendere il sole

sunbathe *vi* prendere il sole

sunbed *n* lettino *m* solare

sunblock *n* prodotto *m* solare a protezione totale

sunburn *n* scottatura *f* (solare)

sunburnt *adj* scottato (dal sole)

sun cream *n* crema *f* solare

sundae /'sʌndeɪ/ *n* gelato *m* guarnito

Sunday /'sʌndeɪ/ *n* domenica *f*

Sunday best *n* in one's ~ con l'abito della festa

Sunday trading *n* apertura *f* domenicale (dei negozi)

sundial /'sʌndaɪəl/ *n* meridiana *f*

sundress *n* prendisole *m*

sun-dried tomatoes /'sʌndraɪd/ *npl* pomodori *mpl* secchi

sundries /'sʌndrɪz/ *npl* articoli *mpl* vari

sundry /'sʌndrɪ/ *adj* svariati; **all and** ~ tutti quanti

sunflower /'sʌnflaʊə(r)/ *n* girasole *m*

sung /sʌŋ/ ▶ SING

sunglasses /'sʌnglɑːsɪz/ *npl* occhiali *mpl* da sole

sun hat *n* cappello *m* da sole

sunk /sʌŋk/ ▶ SINK

sunken /'sʌŋkn/ *adj* incavato

sunlamp /'sʌnlæmp/ *n* lampada *f* abbronzante

sunlight /'sʌnlaɪt/ *n* [luce *f* del] sole *m*

sunny /'sʌnɪ/ *adj* (**-ier, -iest**) assolato

sunrise *n* alba *f*

sunroof *n* Auto tettuccio *m* apribile

sunscreen *n* (to prevent sunburn) crema *f* solare protettiva

sunset *n* tramonto *m*

sunshade *n* parasole *m*

sunshine *n* [luce *f* del] sole *m*

sunshine roof *n* tettuccio *m* apribile

sunstroke *n* insolazione *f*

suntan *n* abbronzatura *f*

suntan lotion *n* lozione *f* solare

sun-tanned *adj* abbronzato

suntan oil *n* olio *m* solare

super /'suːpə(r)/ *adj* fam fantastico

superannuated /suːpər'ænjʊeɪtɪd/ *adj* fig che ha fatto il suo tempo

superannuation /suːpərænjʊ'eɪʃn/ *n* (contributions) contributi *mpl* pensionistici; (pension) pensione *f*

superannuation fund *n* fondo *m* pensione

superb /sʊ'pɜːb/ *adj* splendido

superbly /sʊ'pɜːblɪ/ *adv* splendidamente

supercilious /suːpə'sɪlɪəs/ *adj* altezzoso

superciliously /suːpə'sɪlɪəslɪ/ *adv* in modo altezzoso

superficial /suːpə'fɪʃl/ *adj* superficiale

superficiality /suːpəfɪʃɪ'ælɪtɪ/ *n* superficialità *f*

superficially /suːpə'fɪʃəlɪ/ *adv* superficialmente

superfluous /sʊ'pɜːflʊəs/ *adj* superfluo

superhighway /'suːpəhaɪweɪ/ *n* [information] ~ Comput autostrada *f* telematica

superhuman /suːpə'hjuːmən/ *adj* sovrumano

superimpose /suːpərɪm'pəʊz/ *vt* sovrapporre ⟨picture, soundtrack⟩ (on a); ~d title titolo *m* in sovrimpressione

superintendent /suːpərɪn'tendənt/ *n* (of police) commissario *m* di polizia

superior /suː'pɪərɪə(r)/ *adj* & *n* superiore *mf*

superiority /suːpɪərɪ'ɒrətɪ/ *n* superiorità *f*

superlative /suː'pɜːlətɪv/ ① *adj* eccellente ② *n* superlativo *m*

superlatively /suː'pɜːlətɪvlɪ/ *adv* ⟨perform⟩ in modo eccezionale; ⟨good⟩ estremamente

superman /'suːpəmæn/ *n* superuomo *m*

supermarket /'suːpəmɑːkɪt/ *n* supermercato *m*

supermodel /'suːpəmɒdl/ *n* top model *f* inv

supernatural /suːpə'nætʃrəl/ *adj* soprannaturale

superpower /'suːpəpaʊə(r)/ *n* superpotenza *f*

superscript /'suːpəskrɪpt/ *adj* ⟨number, letter⟩ all'esponente

supersede /suːpə'siːd/ *vt* rimpiazzare

supersonic /suːpə'sɒnɪk/ *adj* supersonico

superstar *n* superstar *mf*

superstition /suːpə'stɪʃn/ *n* superstizione *f*

S

superstitious /suːpəˈstɪʃəs/ *adj* superstizioso

superstitiously /suːpəˈstɪʃəslɪ/ *adv* in modo superstizioso

superstore /ˈsuːpəstɔː(r)/ *n* ipermercato *m*

superstructure /ˈsuːpəstrʌktʃə(r)/ *n* sovrastruttura *f*

supertax /ˈsuːpətæks/ *n* Fin soprattassa *f*

supervise /ˈsuːpəvaɪz/ *vt* supervisionare

supervision /suːpəˈvɪʒn/ *n* supervisione *f*

supervisor /ˈsuːpəvaɪzə(r)/ *n* supervisore *m*

supervisory /suːpəˈvaɪzərɪ/ *adj* di supervisione

superwoman /ˈsuːpəwʊmən/ *n* superdonna *f*

supper /ˈsʌpə(r)/ *n* cena *f*; **have ∼** cenare

supple /ˈsʌpl/ *adj* slogato

supplement /ˈsʌplɪmənt/ **1** *n* supplemento *m* **2** *vt* integrare

supplementary /sʌplɪˈmentərɪ/ *adj* supplementare

supplier /səˈplaɪə(r)/ *n* fornitore, -trice *mf*

supply /səˈplaɪ/ **1** *n* fornitura *f*; Econ offerta *f*; **be in short ∼** scarseggiare; **∼ and demand** domanda *f* e offerta *f*; **supplies** *pl* Mil approvvigionamenti *mpl* **2** *vt* (pt/pp **-ied**) fornire; **∼ somebody with something** fornire qualcosa a qualcuno

supply teacher *n* supplente *mf*

support /səˈpɔːt/ **1** *n* sostegno *m*; (base) supporto *m*; (keep) sostentamento *m* **2** *vt* sostenere; mantenere ⟨family⟩; (give money to) mantenere finanziariamente; Sport fare il tifo per; Comput supportare

supporter /səˈpɔːtə(r)/ *n* sostenitore, -trice *mf*; Sport tifoso, -a *mf*

support group *n* gruppo *m* di sostegno

supporting actor /səˈpɔːtɪŋ/ *n* attore *m* non protagonista

supporting actress *n* attrice *f* non protagonista

supportive /səˈpɔːtɪv/ *adj* incoraggiante; **be ∼ of somebody** dare tutto il proprio appoggio a qualcuno

support stockings *npl* calze *fpl* elastiche

suppose /səˈpəʊz/ *vt* (presume) supporre; (imagine) pensare; **be ∼d to do** dover fare; **not be ∼d to** non avere il permesso di; **I ∼ so** suppongo di sì

supposedly /səˈpəʊzɪdlɪ/ *adv* presumibilmente

supposing /səˈpəʊzɪŋ/ *conj* **∼ (that)** he agrees supponiamo che accetti

supposition /sʌpəˈzɪʃn/ *n* supposizione *f*

suppository /sʌˈpɒzɪtrɪ/ *n* supposta *f*

suppress /səˈpres/ *vt* sopprimere

suppressant /səˈpresənt/ *n* Med inibitore *m*

suppression /səˈpreʃn/ *n* soppressione *f*

suppurate /ˈsʌpjʊreɪt/ *vi* suppurare

supremacy /suːˈpreməsɪ/ *n* supremazia *f*

supreme /suːˈpriːm/ *adj* supremo

supremo /suːˈpriːməʊ/ *n* massima autorità *f inv*

Supt. *abbr* (**Superintendent**) commissario *m* di polizia

surcharge /ˈsɜːtʃɑːdʒ/ *n* supplemento *m*

sure /ʃʊə(r)/ **1** *adj* sicuro, certo; **make ∼** accertarsi; **be ∼ to do it** accertati di farlo **2** *adv* Am fam certamente; **∼ enough** infatti

sure-fire *adj* fam garantito

sure-footed /-ˈfʊtɪd/ *adj* agile

surely /ˈʃʊəlɪ/ *adv* certamente; (Am: gladly) volentieri

surety /ˈʃʊərətɪ/ *n* garanzia *f*; **stand ∼ for somebody/something** fare da garante a qualcuno/per qualcosa

surf /sɜːf/ **1** *n* schiuma *f* **2** *vt* **∼ the Net** navigare in Internet

surface /ˈsɜːfɪs/ **1** *n* superficie *f*; **on the ∼** *fig* in apparenza **2** *vi* (emerge) emergere

surface mail *n* **by ∼ ∼** per posta ordinaria

surface-to-air missile *n* missile *m* terra-aria

surfboard /ˈsɜːfbɔːd/ *n* tavola *f* da surf

surfeit /ˈsɜːfɪt/ *n* eccesso *m*

surfer /ˈsɜːfə(r)/ *n* surfista *mf*

surfing /ˈsɜːfɪŋ/ *n* surf *m*

surge /sɜːdʒ/ **1** *n* (of sea) ondata *f*; (of interest) aumento *m*; (in demand) impennata *f*; (of anger, pity) impeto *m* **2** *vi* riversarsi; **∼ forward** buttarsi in avanti

surgeon /ˈsɜːdʒən/ *n* chirurgo *m*

surgery /ˈsɜːdʒərɪ/ *n* chirurgia *f*; (place, consulting room) ambulatorio *m*; (hours) ore *fpl* di visita; **have ∼** subire un intervento [chirurgico]

surgical /ˈsɜːdʒɪkl/ *adj* chirurgico

surgically /ˈsɜːdʒɪklɪ/ *adv* chirurgicamente

surgical spirit *n* alcol *m* denaturato

Surinam /sʊərɪˈnæm/ *n* Suriname *m*

surliness /ˈsɜːlɪnɪs/ *n* scontrosità *f*

surly /ˈsɜːlɪ/ *adj* (**-ier, -iest**) scontroso

surmise /səˈmaɪz/ *vt* supporre

surmount /səˈmaʊnt/ *vt* sormontare

surname /'sɜːneɪm/ *n* cognome *m*

surpass /sə'pɑːs/ *vt* superare

surplus /'sɜːpləs/ **1** *adj* d'avanzo; **be ∼ to requirements** essere in eccedenza rispetto alle necessità **2** *n* sovrappiù *m*

surprise /sə'praɪz/ **1** *n* sorpreso *f* **2** *vt* sorprendere; **be ∼d** essere sorpreso (**at** da)

surprising /sə'praɪzɪŋ/ *adj* sorprendente

surprisingly /sə'praɪzɪŋlɪ/ *adv* sorprendentemente; **∼ enough** stranamente

surreal /sə'rɪəl/ *adj* surreale

surrealism /sə'rɪəlɪzm/ *n* surrealismo *m*

surrealist /sə'rɪəlɪst/ **1** *n* surrealista *mf* **2** *adj* surrealistico

surrender /sə'rendə(r)/ **1** *n* resa *f* **2** *vi* arrendersi **3** *vt* cedere

surreptitious /sʌrəp'tɪʃəs/ *adj* furtivo

surreptitiously /sʌrəp'tɪʃəslɪ/ *adv* furtivamente

surrogate /'sʌrəgət/ *n* surrogato *m*

surrogate mother *n* madre *f* surrogata

surround /sə'raʊnd/ *vt* circondare; **∼ed by** circondato da

surrounding /sə'raʊndɪŋ/ *adj* circostante

surroundings /sə'raʊndɪŋz/ *npl* dintorni *mpl*

surtax /'sɜːtæks/ *n* soprattassa *f*; (on income) imposta *f* supplementare

surveillance /sə'veɪləns/ *n* sorveglianza *f*; **under ∼** sotto sorveglianza

survey[1] /'sɜːveɪ/ *n* sguardo *m*; (poll) sondaggio *m*; (investigation) indagine *f*; (of land) rilevamento *m*; (of house) perizia *f*

survey[2] /sə'veɪ/ *vt* esaminare; fare un rilevamento di ⟨*land*⟩; fare una perizia di ⟨*building*⟩

surveyor /sə'veɪə(r)/ *n* perito *m*; (of land) topografo, -a *mf*

survival /sə'vaɪvl/ *n* sopravvivenza *f*; (relic) resto *m*

survive /sə'vaɪv/ **1** *vt* sopravvivere a **2** *vi* sopravvivere

surviving /sə'vaɪvɪŋ/ *adj* ⟨*relative*⟩ sopravvissuto

survivor /sə'vaɪvə(r)/ *n* superstite *mf*; **be a ∼** fam riuscire sempre a cavarsela

susceptible /sə'septəbl/ *adj* influenzabile; **∼ to** sensibile a

suspect[1] /sə'spekt/ *vt* sospettare; (assume) supporre

suspect[2] /'sʌspekt/ *adj* & *n* sospetto, -a *mf*

suspend /sə'spend/ *vt* appendere; (stop, from duty) sospendere

suspended sentence /sə'spendɪd/ *n* (sospensione *f*) condizionale *f* (della pena)

suspender belt /sə'spendə/ *n* reggicalze *m inv*

suspenders /sə'spendəz/ *npl* giarrettiere *fpl*; (Am: braces) bretelle *fpl*

suspense /sə'spens/ *n* tensione *f*; (in book etc) suspense *f*

suspension /sə'spenʃn/ *n* Auto sospensione *f*

suspension bridge *n* ponte *m* sospeso

suspicion /sə'spɪʃn/ *n* sospetto *m*; (trace) pizzico *m*; **under ∼** sospettato

suspicious /sə'spɪʃəs/ *adj* sospettoso; (arousing suspicion) sospetto

suspiciously /sə'spɪʃəslɪ/ *adv* sospettosamente; (arousing suspicion) in modo sospetto

suss *vt* **∼ out** Br fam intuire ⟨*person*⟩; capire ⟨*software, technique*⟩; **I've got you ∼ed [out]** ho scoperto il tuo piano

sustain /sə'steɪn/ *vt* sostenere; mantenere ⟨*life*⟩; subire ⟨*injury*⟩

sustainable /sə'steɪnəbl/ *adj* ⟨*development, growth*⟩ sostenibile; ⟨*resource, forest*⟩ rinnovabile

sustained /sə'steɪnd/ *adj* ⟨*effort*⟩ prolungato

sustenance /'sʌstɪnəns/ *n* nutrimento *m*

suture *n* /'suːtʃə(r)/ sutura *f*

SUV *n abbr* Am (**sports utility vehicle**) SUV *f inv*

SW *abbr* (**south-west**) SO

swab /swɒb/ *n* Med tampone *m*

swagger /'swægə(r)/ *vi* pavoneggiarsi

swallow[1] /'swɒləʊ/ *vt/i* inghiottire ■ **swallow up** *vt* divorare; ⟨*earth, crowd*⟩ inghiottire

swallow[2] *n* (bird) rondine *f*

swam /swæm/ ▶ SWIM

swamp /swɒmp/ **1** *n* palude *f* **2** *vt* fig sommergere

swampy /'swɒmpɪ/ *adj* paludoso

swan /swɒn/ *n* cigno *m*

swank /swæŋk/ *vi* fam darsi delle arie

swanky /'swæŋkɪ/ *adj* (fam: posh) snob *inv*

swap /swɒp/ **1** *n* fam scambio *m* **2** *vt* (pt/pp **swapped**) fam scambiare (**for** con) **3** *vi* fare cambio

swarm /swɔːm/ **1** *n* sciame *m* **2** *vi* sciamare; **be ∼ing with** fig brulicare di

swarthy /'swɔːðɪ/ *adj* (**-ier, -iest**) di carnagione scura

swashbuckling /'swɒʃbʌklɪŋ/ *adj* ⟨*hero, appearance*⟩ spericolato; ⟨*adventure, tale*⟩ di cappa e spada

S

swastika /'swɒstɪkə/ n svastica f

swat /swɒt/ vt (pt/pp **swatted**) schiacciare

swathe /sweɪð/ ① n (of grass, corn) falciata f; (land) larga striscia f
② vt (in bandages, silk) avvolgere

sway /sweɪ/ ① n fig influenza f
② vi oscillare; ⟨person⟩ ondeggiare
③ vt (influence) influenzare

Swaziland /'swɑːzɪlænd/ n Swaziland m

swear /sweə(r)/ ① vt (pt **swore**, pp **sworn**) giurare; **I could have sworn that...** avrei giurato che...
② vi giurare; (curse) dire parolacce; **I'd ~ to it!** ci potrei giurare!; **~ at somebody** imprecare contro qualcuno; **~ by** (believe in) credere ciecamente in
■ **swear in** vt prestare giuramento ⟨president⟩
■ **swear off** vt (fam: give up) smettere di

swear word n parolaccia f

sweat /swet/ ① n sudore m
② vi sudare
③ vt **~ blood** sudare sangue
■ **sweat out** vt **~ it out** (endure to the end) tener duro fino alla fine

sweatband /'swetbænd/ n fascia f per il sudore; (for wrist) polsino m

sweater /'swetə(r)/ n golf m inv

sweat pants npl Am pantaloni mpl della tuta

sweatshirt /'swetʃɜːt/ n felpa f

sweatshop n Br manifattura f in cui il personale viene sfruttato

sweaty /'swetɪ/ adj sudato

Swede /swiːd/ n svedese mf

swede n rapa f svedese

Sweden /'swiːdn/ n Svezia f

Swedish /'swiːdɪʃ/ adj & n svedese m

sweep /swiːp/ ① n scopata f, spazzata f; (curve) curva f; (movement) movimento m ampio; **make a clean ~** fig fare piazza pulita
② vt (pt/pp **swept**) scopare, spazzare; ⟨wind⟩ spazzare; **~ the board** fare piazza pulita
③ vi (go swiftly) andare rapidamente; ⟨wind⟩ soffiare
■ **sweep aside** vt ignorare ⟨objection⟩
■ **sweep away** vt fig spazzare via
■ **sweep up** vt spazzare

sweeper /'swiːpə(r)/ n (machine) spazzatrice f; (person) spazzino m; (in football) libero m

sweeping /'swiːpɪʃ/ adj ⟨gesture⟩ ampio; ⟨statement⟩ generico; ⟨changes⟩ radicale

sweet /swiːt/ ① adj dolce; **have a ~ tooth** essere goloso
② n caramella f; (dessert) dolce m

sweet and sour adj agrodolce

sweetbread n (veal) animella f di vitello; (lamb) animella di agnello

sweetcorn n mais m, granturco m

sweeten /'swiːtn/ vt addolcire
■ **sweeten up** vt raddolcire ⟨person⟩

sweetener /'swiːtnə(r)/ n dolcificante m; (fam: incentive) incentivo m; (fam: bribe) bustarella f

sweetheart /'swiːthɑːt/ n innamorato, -a mf; hi, **~** ciao, tesoro

sweetly /'swiːtlɪ/ adv dolcemente

sweetness /'swiːtnɪs/ n dolcezza f

sweet pea n pisello m odoroso

sweet potato n patata f americana

sweetshop n negozio m di dolciumi

sweet-talk vt **~ somebody into doing something** convincere qualcuno a fare qualcosa con tante belle parole

swell /swel/ ① n (of sea) mare m lungo
② vi (pt **swelled**, pp **swollen** or **swelled**) gonfiarsi; (increase) aumentare
③ vt gonfiare; (increase) far salire
④ adj fam eccellente

swelling /'swelɪŋ/ n gonfiore m

swelter /'sweltə(r)/ vi soffocare [dal caldo]

sweltering /'sweltərɪŋ/ adj torrido

swept /swept/ ▶ SWEEP

swerve /swɜːv/ vi deviare bruscamente

swift /swift/ adj rapido

swiftly /'swiftlɪ/ adv rapidamente

swiftness /'swiftnɪs/ n rapidità f

swig /swɪg/ fam ① n sorso m
② vt (pt/pp **swigged**) scolarsi

swill /swɪl/ ① n (for pigs) brodaglia f
② vt **~ [out]** risciacquare

swim /swɪm/ ① n **have a ~** fare una nuotata
② vi (pt **swam**, pp **swum**) nuotare; ⟨room⟩ girare; **go ~ming** andare a nuotare; **my head is ~ming** mi gira la testa
③ vt percorrere a nuoto ⟨distance⟩

swimmer /'swɪmə(r)/ n nuotatore, -trice mf

swimming /'swɪmɪŋ/ n nuoto m

swimming baths npl piscina fsg

swimming costume n costume m da bagno

swimmingly /'swɪmɪŋlɪ/ adv **go ~** andar liscio

swimming pool n piscina f

swimming trunks npl calzoncini mpl da bagno

swimsuit /'swɪmsuːt/ n costume m da bagno

swindle /'swɪndl/ ① n truffa f
② vt truffare

swindler /'swɪndlə(r)/ n truffatore, -trice mf

swine /swaɪn/ n fam porco m

swing /swɪʃ/ **1** n oscillazione f; (shift) cambiamento m; (seat) altalena f; Mus swing m; **in full** ~ in piena attività **2** vi (pt/pp **swung**) oscillare; (on swing, sway) dondolare; (dangle) penzolare; (turn) girare **3** vt oscillare; far deviare ‹vote›

swing-door n porta f a vento

swingeing /'swɪndʒɪŋ/ adj ‹increase› drastico

swingometer /swɪŋ'ɒmɪtə(r)/ n strumento m che permette di seguire l'andamento delle votazioni

swipe /swaɪp/ **1** n fam botta f **2** vt fam colpire; (fam: steal) rubare; far passare nella macchinetta ‹credit card›

swipe card n tessera f magnetica

swirl /swɜːl/ **1** n (of smoke, dust) turbine m **2** vt far girare **3** vi ‹water› fare mulinello

swish¹ /swɪʃ/ adj fam chic

swish² vi schioccare

Swiss /swɪs/ adj & n svizzero, -a mf; **the** ~ pl gli svizzeri

Swiss roll n rotolo m di pan di Spagna ripieno di marmellata

switch /swɪtʃ/ **1** n interruttore m; (change) mutamento m **2** vt cambiare; (exchange) scambiare **3** vi cambiare; ~ **to** passare a
■ **switch off** vt spegnere
■ **switch on** vt accendere
■ **switch over** vi TV cambiare [canale]; ~ **over to** passare a
■ **switch round** vt (change one for the other) scambiare

switchback n montagne fpl russe

switchblade n coltello m a scatto

switchboard n centralino m

switchboard operator n centralinista mf

switched line /swɪtʃt/ n Teleph linea f commutata

swither /'swɪðə(r)/ vi (fam: hesitate) tentennare

Switzerland /'swɪtsələnd/ n Svizzera f

swivel /'swɪvl/ **1** vt (pt/pp **swivelled**) girare **2** vi girarsi

swivel chair n sedia f girevole

swizz /swɪz/ n (fam: swindle) fregatura f

swollen /'swəʊlən/ **1** ▶ SWELL **2** adj gonfio

swollen-headed /-'hedɪd/ adj presuntuoso

swoon /swuːn/ vi svenire

swoop /swuːp/ **1** n (by police) incursione f **2** vi ~ **[down]** ‹bird› piombare; fig fare un'incursione

sword /sɔːd/ n spada f

swordfish /'sɔːdfɪʃ/ n pesce m spada inv

swore /swɔː(r)/ ▶ SWEAR

sworn /swɔːn/ ▶ SWEAR

sworn enemy n nemico m giurato

swot /swɒt/ **1** n fam sgobbone, -a mf **2** vt (pt/pp **swotted**) fam sgobbare (**for an exam** per un esame)

swum /swʌm/ ▶ SWIM

swung /swʌŋ/ ▶ SWING

sycamore /'sɪkəmɔː(r)/ n sicomoro m

sycophant /'sɪkəfænt/ n adulatore, -trice mf

sycophantic /sɪkə'fæntɪk/ adj adulatorio

syllable /'sɪləbl/ n sillaba f

syllabus /'sɪləbəs/ n programma m [dei corsi]

syllogism /'sɪlədʒɪzm/ n sillogismo m

sylph /sɪlf/ n silfide f

symbiosis /sɪmbaɪ'əʊsɪs/ n simbiosi f inv

symbiotic /sɪmbaɪ'ɒtɪk/ adj simbiotico

symbol /'sɪmbl/ n simbolo m (**of** di)

symbolic /sɪm'bɒlɪk/ adj simbolico

symbolically /sɪm'bɒlɪklɪ/ adv simbolicamente

symbolism /'sɪmbəlɪzm/ n simbolismo m

symbolist /'sɪmbəlɪst/ n simbolista mf

symbolize /'sɪmbəlaɪz/ vt simboleggiare

symmetrical /sɪ'metrɪkl/ adj simmetrico

symmetrically /sɪ'metrɪklɪ/ adv simmetricamente

symmetry /'sɪmətrɪ/ n simmetria f

sympathetic /sɪmpə'θetɪk/ adj (understanding) comprensivo; (showing pity) compassionevole

sympathetically /sɪmpə'θetɪklɪ/ adv con comprensione/compassione

sympathize /'sɪmpəθaɪz/ vi capire; (in grief) solidarizzare; ~ **with somebody** capire qualcuno/solidarizzare con qualcuno

sympathizer /'sɪmpəθaɪzə(r)/ n Pol simpatizzante mf

sympathy /'sɪmpəθɪ/ n comprensione f; (pity) compassione f; (condolences) condoglianze fpl; **in** ~ **with** ‹strike› per solidarietà con

symphonic /sɪm'fɒnɪk/ adj sinfonico

symphony /'sɪmfənɪ/ n sinfonia f

symphony orchestra n orchestra f sinfonica

symptom /'sɪmptəm/ n sintomo m

symptomatic /sɪmptə'mætɪk/ adj sintomatico (**of** di)

synagogue /'sɪnəgɒg/ n sinagoga f

sync[h] /sɪŋk/ n sincronia f; **be out of** ∼ essere sfasato; **be in** ∼ essere in sincronia; **be in** ∼ **with/out of** ∼ **with** essere sincronizzato/sfasato rispetto a

synchronize /'sɪŋkrənaɪz/ vt sincronizzare

synchronous /'sɪŋkrənəs/ adj sincrono

syndicate /'sɪndɪkət/ n gruppo m

syndrome /'sɪndrəʊm/ n sindrome f

synonym /'sɪnənɪm/ n sinonimo m

synonymous /sɪ'nɒnɪməs/ adj sinonimo

synopsis /sɪ'nɒpsɪs/ n (pl **-opses** /sɪ'nɒpsiːz/) (of opera, ballet) trama f; (of book) riassunto m

syntactic[al] /sɪn'tæktɪk[l]/ adj sintattico

syntax /'sɪntæks/ n sintassi f inv

synthesis /'sɪnθəsɪs/ n (pl **-theses** /'sɪnθəsiːz/) sintesi f inv

synthesize /'sɪnθəsaɪz/ vt sintetizzare

synthesizer /'sɪnθəsaɪzə(r)/ n Mus sintetizzatore m

synthetic /sɪn'θetɪk/ ① adj sintetico ② n fibra f sintetica

syphilis /'sɪfɪlɪs/ n sifilide f

Syria /'sɪrɪə/ n Siria f

Syrian /'sɪrɪən/ adj & n siriano, -a mf

syringe /sɪ'rɪndʒ/ ① n siringa f ② vt siringare

syrup /'sɪrəp/ n sciroppo m; Br tipo m di melassa

syrupy /'sɪrəpɪ/ adj sciropposo

system /'sɪstəm/ n sistema m

systematic /sɪstə'mætɪk/ adj sistematico

systematically /sɪstə'mætɪklɪ/ adv sistematicamente

systems analysis n analisi f dei sistemi

systems analyst n analista mf programmatore, -trice mf

systems design n progettazione f di sistemi

systems engineer n sistemista mf

Tt

t, T /tiː/ n (letter) t, T f inv

tab /tæb/ n linguetta f; (with name) etichetta f; **keep** ∼**s on** fam sorvegliare; **pick up the** ∼ fam pagare il conto

tabby /'tæbɪ/ n gatto m tigrato

tab key n tasto m tabulatore

table /'tæbɪ/ ① n tavolo m; (list) tavola f; **at [the]** ∼ a tavola ② vt proporre

table-cloth n tovaglia f

table lamp n lampada f da tavolo

table mat n sottopiatto m

table of contents tavola f delle materie

table salt n sale m fine

tablespoon n cucchiaio m da tavola

tablespoonful n cucchiaiata f

tablet /'tæblɪt/ n pastiglia f; (slab) lastra f; ∼ **of soap** saponetta f

table tennis n tennis m da tavolo; (everyday level) ping pong m

tabloid /'tæblɔɪd/ n tabloid m inv; pej giornale m scandalistico

taboo /tə'buː/ ① adj tabù inv ② n tabù m inv

tabulate /'tæbjʊleɪt/ vt tabulare

tabulation /tæbjʊ'leɪʃn/ n (of data, results) tabulazione f

tabulator /'tæbjʊleɪtə(r)/ n tabulatore m

tachograph /'tækəɡrɑːf/ n tachigrafo m

tachometer /tæ'kɒmɪtə(r)/ n tachimetro m

tacit /'tæsɪt/ adj tacito

tacitly /'tæsɪtlɪ/ adv tacitamente

taciturn /'tæsɪtɜːn/ adj taciturno

tack /tæk/ ① n (nail) chiodino m; (stitch) imbastitura f; Naut virata f; fig linea f di condotta ② vt inchiodare; (sew) imbastire ③ vi Naut virare ■ **tack on** (add later) vt aggiungere ⟨ending, paragraph⟩

tackle /'tækl/ ① n (equipment) attrezzatura f; (football etc) contrasto m, tackle m inv ② vt affrontare

tacky /'tækɪ/ adj ⟨paint⟩ non ancora asciutto; ⟨glue⟩ appiccicoso; fig pacchiano

tact /tækt/ n tatto m

tactful /'tæktfʊl/ adj pieno di tatto; ⟨remark⟩ delicato

tactfully /'tæktfʊlɪ/ adv con tatto

tactical /'tæktɪkl/ adj tattico

tactically /'tæktɪklɪ/ adv tatticamente

tactician /tæk'tɪʃn/ n stratega mf

tactics /'tæktɪks/ npl tattica fsg

tactile /'tæktaɪl/ *adj* tattile

tactless /'tæktlɪs/ *adj* privo di tatto

tactlessly /'tæktlɪslɪ/ *adv* senza tatto

tactlessness /'tæktlɪsnɪs/ *n* mancanza *f* di tatto; (of remark) indelicatezza *f*

tadpole /'tædpəʊl/ *n* girino *m*

tae kwon do /taɪ'kwɒndəʊ/ *n* tae-kwon-do *m*

taffeta /'tæfɪtə/ *n* taffettà *m*

tag[1] /tæg/ [1] *n* (label) etichetta *f*
[2] *vt* (pt/pp **tagged**) attaccare l'etichetta a

tag[2] *n* (game) acchiapparello *m*
■ **tag along** *vi* seguire passo passo
■ **tag on** *vt* (attach) aggiungere

tail /teɪl/ [1] *n* coda *f*; **~s** *pl* (tailcoat) frac *m inv*
[2] *vt* (fam: follow) pedinare
■ **tail off** *vi* diminuire

tailback *n* coda *f*

tall-end *n* parte *f* finale; (of train) coda *f*

tailgate *n* sponda *f* posteriore ribaltabile

tail light *n* fanalino *m* di coda

tail-off *n* diminuzione *f*

tailor /'teɪlə(r)/ [1] *n* sarto *m*
[2] *vt* **~ something to someone's needs** adattare qualcosa alle esigenze di qualcuno

tailor-made *adj* fatto su misura

tailspin /'teɪlspɪn/ *n* Aeron vite *f* di coda

tailwind /'teɪlwɪnd/ *n* vento *m* di coda

taint /teɪnt/ *vt* contaminare

Taiwan /taɪ'wɑːn/ *n* Taiwan *f*

Tajikistan /tədʒiːkɪ'stɑːn/ *n* Tajikistan *m*

take /teɪk/ [1] *n* (Cinema) ripresa *f*
[2] *vt* (pt **took**, pp **taken**) prendere; (to a place) portare ⟨*person, object*⟩; (contain) contenere ⟨*passengers etc*⟩; (endure) sopportare; (require) occorrere; (teach) insegnare; (study) studiare ⟨*subject*⟩; fare ⟨*exam, holiday, photograph, walk, bath*⟩; sentire ⟨*pulse*⟩; misurare ⟨*sb's temperature*⟩; **~ something to the cleaner's** portare qualcosa in lavanderia; **~ somebody home** (by car) portare qualcuno a casa; **~ somebody prisoner** fare prigioniero qualcuno; **be ~n ill** ammalarsi; **~ something calmly** prendere con calma qualcosa; **~ the dog for a walk** portare a spasso il cane; **~ one's time doing something** fare qualcosa con calma; **this will only ~ a minute** ci vuole solo un minuto; **I ~ it that...** (assume) presumo che... **~ it from me!** (believe me) dai retta a me!; **~ hold** ⟨*idea, disease*⟩ prendere piede; **~ part** prendere parte; **~ part in** prendere parte a; **~ place** svolgersi
[3] *vi* ⟨*plant*⟩ attecchire
■ **take aback** *vt* (surprise) cogliere di sorpresa
■ **take after** *vt* assomigliare a

■ **take against** *vt* (turn against) prendere in antipatia
■ **take apart** *vt* (dismantle) smontare
■ **take away** *vt* (with one) portare via; (remove) togliere; (subtract) sottrarre; **'to ~ away'** 'da asporto'
■ **take back** *vt* riprendere; ritirare ⟨*statement*⟩; (return) riportare [indietro]; **she took him back** (as husband, boyfriend) lo ha perdonato
■ **take down** *vt* portare giù; (remove) tirare giù; (write down) prendere nota di
■ **take in** *vt* (bring indoors) portare dentro; (to one's home) ospitare; (understand) capire; (deceive) ingannare; riprendere ⟨*garment*⟩; (include) includere; vedere ⟨*film etc*⟩
■ **take off** [1] *vt* togliersi ⟨*clothes*⟩; (deduct) togliere; (mimic) imitare; **~ time off** prendere delle vacanze; **~ oneself off** andarsene
[2] *vi* Aeron decollare; (fam: leave) andarsene; (become successful) decollare
■ **take on** *vt* farsi carico di; assumere ⟨*employee*⟩; (as opponent) prendersela con; **~ it on oneself to do something** arrogarsi il diritto di fare qualcosa
■ **take out** *vt* portare fuori; togliere ⟨*word, stain*⟩; (withdraw) ritirare ⟨*money, books*⟩; **~ out a subscription to something** abbonarsi a qualcosa; **she took a pen out of her pocket** ha preso una penna dalla tasca; **I'm taking my wife out tonight** esco con mia moglie stasera; **~ somebody out to dinner** portare a cena fuori qualcuno; **it'll ~ you out of yourself** (take your mind off things) servirà a distrarti; **~ it out on somebody** fam prendersela con qualcuno
■ **take over** [1] *vt* assumere il controllo di ⟨*firm*⟩
[2] *vi* **~ over from somebody** sostituire qualcuno; (permanently) succedere a qualcuno
■ **take to** *vt* (as a habit) darsi a; **I took to her** (liked) mi è piaciuta
■ **take up** [1] *vt* portare su; accettare ⟨*offer*⟩; intraprendere ⟨*profession*⟩; dedicarsi a ⟨*hobby*⟩; prendere ⟨*time*⟩; occupare ⟨*space*⟩; tirare su ⟨*floor-boards*⟩; accorciare ⟨*dress*⟩; **~ something up with somebody** discutere qualcosa con qualcuno; **~ somebody up on something** (question further) chiedere ulteriori chiarimenti a qualcuno su qualcosa; **I'll ~ you up on your offer** (accept) accetto la tua offerta
[2] *vi* **~ up with somebody** legarsi a qualcuno

takeaway /'teɪkəweɪ/ *n* (meal) piatto *m* da asporto; (restaurant) ristorante *m* che prepara piatti da asporto

take-home pay *n* stipendio *m* netto

taken /'teɪkən/ *adj* ⟨*room etc*⟩ occupato; **be very ~ with somebody/something** essere conquistato da qualcuno/qualcosa

take-off *n* Aeron decollo *m*

t

take-out *n* Am = TAKEAWAY

takeover *n* rilevamento *m*

takeover bid *n* offerta *f* pubblica di acquisto

takings /'teɪkɪŋz/ *npl* incassi *mpl*

talc /tælk/ *n* (boro)talco *m*

talcum /'tælkəm/ *n* ~ **[powder]** talco *m*

tale /teɪl/ *n* storia *f*; pej fandonia *f*; **tell** ~**s** fare la spia

talent /'tælənt/ *n* talento *m*

talent contest *n* concorso *m* per giovani talenti

talented /'tæləntɪd/ *adj* [ricco] di talento

talent scout *n* talent scout *mf inv*

talisman /'tælɪzmən/ *n* talismano *m*

talk /tɔːk/ ① *n* conversazione *f*; (lecture) conferenza *f*; (gossip) chiacchiere *fpl*; **make small** ~ parlare del più e del meno ② *vi* parlare ③ *vt* parlare di ‹*politics etc*›; ~ **somebody into something** convincere qualcuno di qualcosa

■ **talk about** *vt* parlare di; ~ **about bad luck!** e quando si dice la sfortuna!

■ **talk back** *vi* (reply defiantly) rispondere

■ **talk down to** *vt* (patronize) parlare con condiscendenza a

■ **talk of** *vt* parlare di; ~ing **of food...** a proposito di mangiare...

■ **talk over** *vt* discutere

■ **talk to** *vt* parlare con; (reprimand) fare un discorsetto a; ~ **to oneself** parlare da solo

talkative /'tɔːkətɪv/ *adj* loquace

talking /'tɔːkɪŋ/ *adj* ‹*doll, parrot*› parlante

talking book *n* audiolibro *m*

talking head *n* mezzobusto *m*

talking-to *n* sgridata *f*

talk show *n* talk show*m inv*

tall /tɔːl/ *adj* alto; **how** ~ **are you?** quanto sei alto?

tallboy *n* cassettone *m*

tall order *n* impresa *f* difficile

tall story *n* frottola *f*

tally /'tælɪ/ ① *n* conteggio *m*; **keep a** ~ **of** tenere il conto di ② *vi* coincidere

talon /'tælən/ *n* artiglio *m*

tambourine /tæmbə'riːn/ *n* tamburello *m*

tame /teɪm/ ① *adj* ‹*animal*› domestico; (dull) insulso ② *vt* domare

tamely /'teɪmlɪ/ *adv* docilmente

tamer /'teɪmə(r)/ *n* domatore, -trice *mf*

tamper /'tæmpə(r)/ *vi* ~ **with** manomettere

tampon /'tæmpɒn/ *n* tampone *m*

tan /tæn/ ① *adj* marrone rossiccio *inv*
② *n* marrone *m* rossiccio; (from sun) abbronzatura *f*
③ *vt* (pt/pp **tanned**) conciare ‹*hide*›
④ *vi* abbronzarsi

tandem /'tændəm/ *n* tandem *m inv*; **in** ~ in tandem

tang /tæŋ/ *n* sapore *m* forte; (smell) odore *m* penetrante

tanga /'tæŋɡə/ *n* tanga *m inv*

tangent /'tændʒənt/ *n* tangente *f*; **go off at a** ~ fam partire per la tangente

tangerine /tændʒə'riːn/ ① *n* (fruit) tipo *m* di mandarino; (colour) arancione *m*
② *adj* arancione

tangible /'tændʒɪbl/ *adj* tangibile

tangibly /'tændʒɪblɪ/ *adv* tangibilmente

tangle /'tæŋɡl/ ① *n* groviglio *m*; (in hair) nodo *m*
② *vt* ~ **[up]** aggrovigliare
③ *vi* aggrovigliarsi

tango /'tæŋɡəʊ/ *n* tango *m*

tangy /'tæŋɪ/ *adj* forte; ‹*smell*› penetrante

tank /tæŋk/ *n* contenitore *m*; (for petrol) serbatoio *m*; (fish ~) acquario *m*; Mil carro *m* armato

tankard /'tæŋkəd/ *n* boccale *m*

tanker /'tæŋkə(r)/ *n* nave *f* cisterna; (lorry) autobotte *f*

tank top *n* canottiera *f*

tanned /tænd/ *adj* abbronzato

tannin /'tænɪn/ *n* tannino *m*

Tannoy® /'tænɔɪ/ *n* Br sistema *m* di altoparlanti

tantalize /'tæntəlaɪz/ *vt* tormentare

tantalizing /'tæntəlaɪzɪŋ/ *adj* allettante; ‹*smell*› stuzzicante

tantamount /'tæntəmaʊnt/ *adj* ~ **to** equivalente a

tantrum /'tæntrəm/ *n* scoppio *m* d'ira; **throw a** ~ fare i capricci

Tanzania /tænzə'nɪə/ *n* Tanzania *f*

tap /tæp/ ① *n* rubinetto *m*; (knock) colpo *m*; **on** ~ a disposizione
② *vt* (pt/pp **tapped**) dare un colpetto a; sfruttare ‹*resources*›; mettere sotto controllo ‹*telephone*›
③ *vi* picchiettare

tap-dance ① *n* tip tap *m*
② *vi* ballare il tip tap

tap-dancer *n* ballerino, -a *mf* di tip tap

tape /teɪp/ ① *n* nastro *m*; (recording) cassetta *f*
② *vt* legare con nastro; (record) registrare

tape backup drive *n* Comput unità *f* di backup a nastro

tape deck *n* piastra *f*

tape-measure *n* metro *m* [a nastro]

taper /'teɪpə(r)/ ① *n* candela *f* sottile
② *vi* assottigliarsi

■ **taper off** *vi* assottigliarsi

tape-record *vt* registrare su nastro

tape recorder *n* registratore *m*

tape recording *n* registrazione *f*

tapered /'teɪpəd/ *adj* ⟨*trousers*⟩ affusolato

tape streamer *n* Comput unità *f* a nastro magnetico

tapestry /'tæpɪstrɪ/ *n* arazzo *m*

tapeworm /'teɪpwɜːm/ *n* verme *m* solitario, tenia *f*

tapping /'tæpɪŋ/ *n* (noise) picchiettio *m*

tap water *n* acqua *f* del rubinetto

tar /tɑː(r)/ **1** *n* catrame *m*
2 *vt* (pt/pp **tarred**) incatramare

tardy /'tɑːdɪ/ *adj* (**-ier, -iest**) tardivo

target /'tɑːgɪt/ **1** *n* bersaglio *m*; fig obiettivo *m*
2 *vt* stabilire come obiettivo ⟨*market*⟩

target language *n* lingua *f* d'arrivo

target market *n* mercato *m* obiettivo

target practice *n* tiro *m* al bersaglio

tariff /'tærɪf/ **1** *n* (price) tariffa *f*; (duty) dazio *m*
2 *adj* tariffario

Tarmac® /'tɑːmæk/ *n* macadam *m* al catrame

tarmac **1** *n* asfalto *m*; (Br: of airfield) pista *f*
2 *attrib* ⟨*road, footpath*⟩ asfaltato
3 *vt* asfaltare

tarnish /'tɑːnɪʃ/ **1** *vi* ossidarsi
2 *vt* ossidare; fig macchiare

tarpaulin /tɑː'pɔːlɪn/ *n* telone *m* impermeabile

tarragon /'tærəgən/ *n* dragoncello *m*

tart¹ /tɑːt/ *adj* aspro; fig acido

tart² *n* crostata *f*; (individual) crostatina *f*; (sl: prostitute) donnaccia *f*

■ **tart up** *vt* fam ~ **oneself up** agghindarsi

tartan /'tɑːtn/ **1** *n* tessuto *m* scozzese, tartan *m inv*
2 *attrib* di tessuto scozzese

tartar /'tɑːtə(r)/ *n* (on teeth) tartaro *m*

tartar sauce *n* salsa *f* tartara

task /tɑːsk/ *n* compito *m*; **take somebody to ~** riprendere qualcuno

task bar *n* Comput barra *f* delle applicazioni

task force *n* Pol commissione *f*; Mil taskforce *f inv*

taskmaster *n* tiranno *m*; **be a hard ~** essere molto esigente

tassel /'tæsl/ *n* nappa *f*

taste /teɪst/ **1** *n* gusto *m*; (sample) assaggio *m*; **get a ~ of something** fig assaporare il gusto di qualcosa; **in good/bad ~** di buongusto/di cattivo gusto

2 *vt* sentire il sapore di; (sample) assaggiare

3 *vi* sapere (of di); **it ~s lovely** è ottimo; **~ like something** sapere di qualcosa

taste buds *npl* papille *fpl* gustative

tasteful /'teɪs(t)fʊl/ *adj* di [buon] gusto

tastefully /'teɪs(t)fʊlɪ/ *adv* con gusto

tasteless /'teɪs(t)lɪs/ *adj* senza gusto

tastelessly /'teɪs(t)lɪslɪ/ *adv* con cattivo gusto

taster /'teɪstə(r)/ *n* (foretaste) assaggio *m*; (person) assaggiatore, -trice *mf*

tasty /'teɪstɪ/ *adj*(**-ier, -iest**) saporito

tat /tæt/ ▶ TIT²

tattered /'tætəd/ *adj* cencioso; ⟨*pages*⟩ stracciato

tatters /'tætəz/ *npl* **in ~** a brandelli

tattle /'tætl/ **1** *vi* spettegolare
2 *n* pettegolezzo *m*

tattoo¹ /tæ'tuː/ **1** *n* tatuaggio *m*
2 *vt* tatuare

tattoo² *n* Mil parata *f* militare

tatty /'tætɪ/ *adj* (**-ier, -iest**) ⟨*clothes, person*⟩ trasandato; ⟨*book*⟩ malandato

taught /tɔːt/ ▶ TEACH

taunt /tɔːnt/ **1** *n* scherno *m*
2 *vt* schernire

Taurus /'tɔːrəs/ *n* Astr Toro *m*

taut /tɔːt/ *adj* teso

tauten /'tɔːtən/ **1** *vt* tendere
2 *vi* tendersi

tautology /tɔː'tɒlədʒɪ/ *n* tautologia *f*

tavern /'tævən/ *n* liter taverna *f*

tawdry /'tɔːdrɪ/ *adj* (**-ier, -iest**) pacchiano

tawny /'tɔːnɪ/ *adj* fulvo

tax /tæks/ **1** *n* tassa *f*; (on income) imposte *fpl*; **before ~** ⟨*price*⟩ tasse escluse; ⟨*salary*⟩ lordo
2 *vt* tassare; fig mettere alla prova; **~ with** accusare di

taxable /'tæksəbl/ *adj* tassabile; **~ income** reddito *m* imponibile

tax allowance *n* detrazione *f* di imposta

taxation /tæk'seɪʃn/ *n* tasse *fpl*; **~ at source** ritenuta *f* alla fonte

tax avoidance *n* elusione *f* fiscale

tax bracket *n* scaglione *m* d'imposta

tax break *n* agevolazione *f* fiscale

tax burden *n* aggravio *m* fiscale

tax code *n* codice *m* fiscale

tax consultant *n* fiscalista *m*

tax-deductible *adj* detraibile

tax disc *n* Auto bollo *m*

tax evader *n* evasore *m* fiscale

tax evasion *n* evasione *f* fiscale

tax exile *n* (person) espatriato, -a *mf* per motivi fiscali

tax-free *adj* esentasse

tax haven *n* paradiso *m* fiscale

taxi /'tæksɪ/ ① *n* taxi *m inv*
② *vi* (pt/pp **taxied**, pres p **taxiing**)
⟨*aircraft*⟩ rullare

taxi driver *n* tassista *mf*

tax incentive *n* incentivo *m* fiscale

taxing /'tæksɪŋ/ *adj* (exhausting) sfiancante

tax inspector *n* ispettore *m* delle tasse

taxi rank *n* posteggio *m* per taxi

taxman /'tæksmæn/ *n* the ~ il fisco

tax office *n* ufficio *m* delle imposte

taxpayer *n* contribuente *mf*

tax rebate *n* rimborso *m* d'imposta

tax return *n* dichiarazione *f* dei redditi

tax shelter *n* paradiso *m* fiscale

tax system *n* regime *m* fiscale

TB *n abbr* (**tuberculosis**) TBC *f*

tbsp *abbr* (**tablespoon**)

tea /ti:/ *n* tè *m inv*

tea-bag *n* bustina *f* di tè

tea-break *n* intervallo *m* per il tè

teach /ti:tʃ/ *vt/i* (pt/pp **taught**)
insegnare; ~ **somebody something**
insegnare qualcosa a qualcuno; ~
somebody a lesson fig dare una lezione a
qualcuno

teacher /'ti:tʃə(r)/ *n* insegnante *mf*;
(primary) maestro, -a *mf*

teacher training *n* formazione *f*
professionale per insegnanti

teaching /'ti:tʃɪŋ/ *n* insegnamento *m*

teaching hospital *n* ≈ ospedale *m*
universitario

teacloth *n* (for drying) asciugapiatti *m inv*

tea cosy *n* copriteiera *f*

teacup *n* tazza *f* da tè

teak /ti:k/ *n* tek *m*

tea leaves *npl* tè *m inv* sfuso; (when
infused) fondi *mpl* di tè

team /ti:m/ *n* squadra *f*; fig équipe *f inv*
■ **team up** *vi* unirsi

team captain *n* caposquadra *mf*

team manager *n* direttore *m* sportivo

team-mate *n* compagno *m* di squadra

team player *n* persona *f* che dimostra
spirito di squadra

team spirit *n* spirito *m* di squadra

teamwork *n* lavoro *m* di squadra; fig
lavoro *m* d'équipe

teapot /'ti:pɒt/ *n* teiera *f*

tear[1] /teə(r)/ ① *n* strappo *m*
② *vt* (pt **tore**, pp **torn**) strappare; ~ **to
pieces** or **shreds** fare a pezzi; stroncare
⟨*book, film*⟩
③ *vi* strappare; ⟨*material*⟩ strapparsi;
(run) precipitarsi
■ **tear apart** *vt* (fig: criticize) fare a pezzi;
(separate) dividere

■ **tear away** *vt* ~ oneself away from
staccarsi da ⟨*television*⟩; abbandonare a
malincuore ⟨*party*⟩

■ **tear into** *vt* fam (reprimand) attaccare
duramente; (make a vigorous start on) dare
dentro a

■ **tear off** *vt* (carefully) staccare; (violently)
strappare

■ **tear open** *vt* aprire strappando

■ **tear out** *vt* staccare; ~ **one's hair out**
mettersi le mani nei capelli

■ **tear up** *vt* strappare; rompere
⟨*agreement*⟩

tear[2] /tɪə(r)/ *n* lacrima *f*

tearaway /'teərəweɪ/ *n* giovane teppista
mf

tearful /'tɪəfʊl/ *adj* ⟨*person*⟩ in lacrime;
⟨*farewell*⟩ lacrimevole

tearfully /'tɪəfʊlɪ/ *adv* in lacrime

tear gas /'tɪə/ *n* gas *m* lacrimogeno

tearing /'teərɪŋ/ *adj* be in a ~ hurry
avere una gran fretta

tear-jerker /'tɪədʒɜ:kə(r)/ *n* fam this film
is a real ~ è davvero un film
strappalacrime

tease /ti:z/ *vt* prendere in giro ⟨*person*⟩;
tormentare ⟨*animal*⟩

teasel /'ti:zl/ *n* Bot cardo *m*

teaset /'ti:set/ *n* servizio *m* da tè

tea shop *n* sala *f* da tè

teasing /'ti:zɪŋ/ *adj* canzonatorio

teaspoon *n* cucchiaino *m* [da tè]

teaspoon[ful] *n* cucchiaino *m*

tea-strainer *n* colino *m* per il tè

teat /ti:t/ *n* capezzolo *m*; (on bottle)
tettarella *f*

teatime *n* ora *f* del tè

tea towel *n* strofinaccio *m* [per i piatti]

technical /'teknɪkl/ *adj* tecnico

technical college *n* istituto *m* tecnico
professionale

technical drawing *n* (skill or process,
plan) disegno *m* tecnico

technical hitch *n* contrattempo *m*
tecnico

technicality /teknɪ'kælətɪ/ *n*
tecnicismo *m*; Jur cavillo *m* giuridico

technically /'teknɪklɪ/ *adv*
tecnicamente; (strictly) strettamente

technician /tek'nɪʃn/ *n* tecnico, -a *mf*

technique /tek'ni:k/ *n* tecnica *f*

techno /'teknəʊ/ *n* techno *f*

technocrat /'teknəkræt/ *n* tecnocrate *m*

technological /teknə'lɒdʒɪkl/ *adj*
tecnologico

technologically /teknə'lɒdʒɪklɪ/ *adv*
tecnologicamente

technology /tek'nɒlədʒɪ/ *n* tecnologia *f*

technophobe /'teknəfəʊb/ *n* tecnofobo,
-a *mf*

teddy /'tedɪ/ n ~ **[bear]** orsacchiotto m

tedious /'ti:dɪəs/ adj noioso

tedium /'ti:dɪəm/ n tedio m

tee /ti:/ n (Golf) tee m inv

teem /ti:m/ vi (rain) piovere a dirotto; **be ~ing with** (full of) pullulare di

teen /ti:n/ adj ⟨fashion, idol⟩ degli adolescenti

teenage /'ti:neɪdʒ/ adj per ragazzi; ~ **boy/girl** adolescente mf

teenager /'ti:neɪdʒə(r)/ n adolescente mf

teens /ti:nz/ npl **the ~** l'adolescenza fsg; **be in one's ~** essere adolescente

teeny /'ti:nɪ/ adj fam (**-ier, -iest**) piccolissimo

teeny-weeny /ti:nɪ'wi:nɪ/ adj fam minuscolo

tee-shirt n T-shirt f inv, maglietta f [a maniche corte]

teeter /'ti:tə(r)/ vi barcollare

teeth /ti:θ/ ▶ TOOTH

teethe /ti:ð/ vi mettere i primi denti

teething troubles /'ti:ðɪŋ/ npl fig difficoltà fpl iniziali

teetotal /ti:'təʊtl/ adj astemio

teetotaller /ti:'təʊt(ə)lə(r)/ n astemio, -a mf

TEFL /'tefl/ n insegnamento m dell'inglese come lingua straniera

tel. abbr (**telephone**) tel.

telebanking /'telɪbæŋkɪŋ/ n servizi mpl bancari telematici

telecast /'telɪkɑ:st/ ① n trasmissione f televisiva
② vt far vedere in televisione

telecomms /'telɪkɒmz/ npl telecomunicazioni fpl

telecommunications /telɪkəmju:nɪ'keɪʃnz/ npl telecomunicazioni fpl

telecommuter /telɪkə'mju:tə(r)/ n persona f che lavora da casa su computer

telecommuting /telɪkə'mju:tɪŋ/ n lavoro m su computer da casa

teleconference /'telɪkɒnf(ə)r(ə)ns/ n videoconferenza f

telegenic /telɪ'dʒenɪk/ adj telegenico

telegram /'telɪgræm/ n telegramma m

telegraph /'telɪgrɑ:f/ n telegrafo m

telegraphic /telɪ'græfɪk/ adj telegrafico

telegraph pole n palo m del telegrafo

telemarketing /'telɪmɑ:kətɪŋ/ n telemarketing m

telematics /telɪ'mætɪks/ n telematica f

telemessage /'telɪmesɪdʒ/ n Br telegramma m

telepathic /telɪ'pæθɪk/ adj telepatico

telepathy /tɪ'lepəθɪ/ n telepatia f; **by ~** per telepatia

telephone /'telɪfəʊn/ ① n telefono m; **be on the ~** avere il telefono; (be telephoning) essere al telefono
② vt telefonare a
③ vi telefonare

telephone answering service n segreteria f telefonica

telephone banking n servizi mpl bancari via telefono

telephone book n elenco m telefonico

telephone booking n prenotazione f telefonica

telephone booth n, **telephone box** n cabina f telefonica

telephone call n telefonata f

telephone conversation n conversazione f telefonica

telephone directory n elenco m telefonico

telephone helpline n servizio m telefonico

telephone message n messaggio m telefonico

telephone number n numero m di telefono

telephone operator n centralinista mf

telephone tapping n intercettazione f telefonica

telephonist /tɪ'lefənɪst/ n telefonista mf

telephoto /telɪ'fəʊtəʊ/ adj ~ **lens** teleobiettivo m

teleprinter /'telɪprɪntə(r)/ n telescrivente f

telerecording /'telɪrɪkɔ:dɪŋ/ n programma m [televisivo] registrato

telesales /'telɪseɪlz/ n vendita f per telefono

telescope /'telɪskəʊp/ n telescopio m

telescopic /telɪ'skɒpɪk/ adj telescopico

teleshopping /'telɪʃɒpɪŋ/ n acquisti mpl per telefono

teletext /'telɪtekst/ n televideo m

telethon /'telɪθɒn/ n telethon m inv

televise /'telɪvaɪz/ vt trasmettere per televisione

television /'telɪvɪʒn/ n televisione f; **watch ~** guardare la televisione; **on ~** alla televisione

television channel n rete f televisiva

television licence n abbonamento m alla televisione

television licence fee n costo m dell'abbonamento alla televisione

television programme n programma m televisivo

television screen n teleschermo m

television serial n sceneggiato m

television set n televisore m

televisual /telɪ'vɪʒʊəl/ adj televisivo

teleworking /'telɪwɜːkɪŋ/ n telelavoro m

telex /'teleks/ ① n telex m inv
② vt mandare via telex ‹message›; mandare un telex a ‹person›

tell /tel/ ① vt (pt/pp **told**) dire; raccontare ‹story›; (distinguish) distinguere (from da); ~ **somebody something** dire qualcosa a qualcuno; ~ **somebody to do something** dire a qualcuno di fare qualcosa; ~ **the time** dire l'ora; **I couldn't** ~ **why...** non sapevo perché...; **you're** ~**ing me!** a chi lo dici!
② vi (produce an effect) avere effetto; **time will** ~ il tempo ce lo dirà; **his age is beginning to** ~ l'età comincia a farsi sentire [per lui]; **don't** ~ **me** non dirmelo; **you mustn't** ~ non devi dire niente
■ **tell apart** vt distinguere
■ **tell off** vt sgridare
■ **tell on** vt (Sch: inform against) fare la spia a

teller /'telə(r)/ n (in bank) cassiere, -a mf

telling /'telɪŋ/ adj significativo; (argument) efficace

telling-off n cicchetto m

tell-tale ① n spione, -a mf
② adj rivelatore

telly /'telɪ/ n fam tv f inv, tele f inv

temerity /tɪ'merətɪ/ n audacia f

temp /temp/ fam ① n impiegato, -a mf temporaneo, -a
② vi lavorare come impiegato, -a temporaneo, -a

temper /'tempə(r)/ ① n (disposition) carattere m; (mood) umore m; (anger) collera f; **lose one's** ~ arrabbiarsi; **be in a** ~ essere arrabbiato; **keep one's** ~ mantenere la calma
② vt fig temperare

temperament /'temprəmənt/ n temperamento m

temperamental /temprə'mentl/ adj (moody) capriccioso

temperamentally /temprə'mentəlɪ/ adv **they are** ~ **unsuited** tra loro c'è incompatibilità di carattere

temperance /'tempərəns/ n (abstinence) astinenza f dal bere

temperate /'tempərət/ adj ‹climate› temperato

temperature /'temprətʃə(r)/ n temperatura f; **have** or **run a** ~ avere la febbre

tempest /'tempɪst/ n tempesta f

tempestuous /tem'pestjʊəs/ adj tempestoso

template /'templɪt/ n sagoma f

temple¹ /'templ/ n tempio m

temple² n Anat tempia f

tempo /'tempəʊ/ n ritmo m; Mus tempo m

temporal /'tempər(ə)l/ adj temporale

temporarily /tempə'rerɪlɪ/ adv temporaneamente; ‹introduced, erected› provvisoriamente

temporary /'tempərərɪ/ adj temporaneo; ‹measure, building› provvisorio

tempt /tempt/ vt tentare; sfidare ‹fate›; ~ **somebody to** indurre qualcuno a; **be** ~**ed** essere tentato (**to** di); **I am** ~**ed by the offer** l'offerta mi tenta

temptation /temp'teɪʃn/ n tentazione f

tempting /'temptɪŋ/ adj allettante; ‹food, drink› invitante

temptress /'temptrɪs/ n seduttrice f

ten /ten/ adj & n dieci m; **the T~ Commandments** i Dieci Comandamenti

tenable /'tenəbl/ adj fig sostenibile

tenacious /tɪ'neɪʃəs/ adj tenace

tenacity /tɪ'næsətɪ/ n tenacia f

tenancy /'tenənsɪ/ n locazione f

tenant /'tenənt/ n inquilino, -a mf; Comm locatario, -a mf

tend¹ /tend/ vt (look after) prendersi cura di

tend² vi ~ **to do something** tendere a far qualcosa

tendency /'tendənsɪ/ n tendenza f

tendentious /ten'denʃəs/ adj tendenzioso

tender¹ /'tendə(r)/ ① n Comm offerta f; **put out to** ~ dare in appalto; **be legal** ~ avere corso legale
② vt offrire; presentare ‹resignation›

tender² adj tenero; (painful) dolorante

tender-hearted /-hɑːtɪd/ adj dal cuore tenero

tenderize /'tendəraɪz/ vt rendere tenero ‹meat›

tenderly /'tendəlɪ/ adv teneramente

tenderness /'tendənɪs/ n tenerezza f; (painfulness) dolore m

tendon /'tendən/ n tendine m

tendril /'tendrɪl/ n (of plant) viticcio m

tenement /'tenəmənt/ n casamento m

tenet /'tenɪt/ n principio m

tenner /'tenə(r)/ n fam biglietto m da dieci sterline

tennis /'tenɪs/ n tennis m

tennis ball n palla f da tennis

tennis-court n campo m da tennis

tennis match n partita f di tennis

tennis player n tennista mf

tennis racket n racchetta f da tennis

tennis shoes npl scarpe fpl da tennis

tenor /'tenə(r)/ n tenore m

tenpin bowling Br, **tenpins** Am n bowling m

tense¹ /tens/ n Gram tempo m

tense² ① adj teso
② vt tendere ‹muscle›

■ **tense up** *vi* tendersi

tension /'tenʃn/ *n* tensione *f*

tent /tent/ *n* tenda *f*

tentacle /'tentəkl/ *n* tentacolo *m*

tentative /'tentətɪv/ *adj* provvisorio; ⟨smile, gesture⟩ esitante

tentatively /'tentətɪvlɪ/ *adv* timidamente; ⟨accept⟩ provvisoriamente

tent city *n* tendopoli *f inv*

tenterhooks /'tentəhʊks/ *npl* **be on ~** essere sulle spine

tenth /tenθ/ *adj* & *n* decimo, -a *mf*

tenuous /'tenjʊəs/ *adj* fig debole

tenure /'tenjə(r)/ *n* (period of office) permanenza *f* in carica; (Univ: job security) ruolo *m*; (of land, property) possesso *m*; **security of ~** (of land, property) diritto *m* di possesso

tepid /'tepɪd/ *adj* tiepido

tercentenary /tɜ:sen'ti:nərɪ/ *n* terzo centenario *m*

term /tɜ:m/ *n* periodo *m*; Sch Univ trimestre *m*; (in Italy) Sch quadrimestre *m*; Univ semestre *m*; (expression) termine *m*; **~s** *pl* (conditions) condizioni *fpl*; **~ of office** carica *f*; **in the short/long ~** a breve/lungo termine; **be on good/bad ~s** essere in buoni/cattivi rapporti; **come to ~s with** accettare ⟨past, fact⟩; **easy ~s** facilità *fpl* di pagamento; **~s of reference** *pl* (of committee) competenze *fpl*

terminal /'tɜ:mɪnl/ **1** *adj* finale; Med terminale

2 *n* Aeron terminal *m inv*; Rail stazione *f* di testa; (of bus) capolinea *m*; (on battery) morsetto *m*; Comput terminale *m*

terminally /'tɜ:mɪnəlɪ/ *adv* **be ~ ill** essere in fase terminale

terminate /'tɜ:mɪneɪt/ **1** *vt* terminare; rescindere ⟨contract⟩; interrompere ⟨pregnancy⟩

2 *vi* terminare; **~ in** finire in

termination /tɜ:mɪ'neɪʃn/ *n* termine *m*; Med interruzione *f* di gravidanza

terminologist /tɜ:mɪ'nɒlədʒɪst/ *n* linguista *mf* specializzato, -a in terminologia

terminology /tɜ:mɪ'nɒlədʒɪ/ *n* terminologia *f*

terminus /'tɜ:mɪnəs/ *n* (pl **-ni**) /'tɜ:mɪnaɪ/) (for bus) capolinea *m*; (for train) stazione *f* di testa

term-time *n* **during ~** durante il trimestre

terrace /'terəs/ *n* terrazza *f*; (houses) fila *f* di case a schiera; **the ~s** *pl* Sport le gradinate

terraced house /'terəsd/ *n* casa *f* a schiera

terracotta /terə'kɒtə/ *n* (earthenware) terracotta *f*; (colour) color *m* terracotta

terrain /te'reɪn/ *n* terreno *m*

terrestrial /tɪ'restrɪəl/ **1** *n* terrestre *mf*

2 *adj* terrestre; **~ television** televisione *f* terrestre

terrible /'terəbl/ *adj* terribile

terribly /'terəblɪ/ *adv* terribilmente; **I'm ~ sorry** sono infinitamente spiacente

terrier /'terɪə(r)/ *n* terrier *m inv*

terrific /tə'rɪfɪk/ *adj* fam (excellent) fantastico; (huge) enorme

terrifically /tə'rɪfɪklɪ/ *adv* fam terribilmente

terrify /'terɪfaɪ/ *vt* (pt/pp **-ied**) atterrire; **be terrified** essere terrorizzato

terrifying /'terɪfaɪɪŋ/ *adj* terrificante

territorial /terɪ'tɔ:rɪəl/ *adj* territoriale

territorial waters /wɔ:təz/ *npl* acque *fpl* territoriali

territory /'terɪtərɪ/ *n* territorio *m*

terror /'terə(r)/ *n* terrore *m*

terrorism /'terərɪzm/ *n* terrorismo *m*

terrorist /'terərɪst/ *n* terrorista *mf*

terrorize /'terəraɪz/ *vt* terrorizzare

terror-stricken *adj* terrorizzato

terry towelling /terɪ'taʊəlɪŋ/ Br, **terry cloth** Am *n* tessuto *m* di spugna

terse /tɜ:s/ *adj* conciso

tersely /'tɜ:slɪ/ *adv* concisamente

tertiary /'tɜ:ʃ(ə)rɪ/ *adj* ⟨era, industry, sector⟩ terziario; ⟨education, college⟩ superiore

Terylene® /'terɪli:n/ *n* terilene® *m*

test /test/ **1** *n* esame *m*; (in laboratory) esperimento *m*; (of friendship, machine) prova *f*; (of intelligence, aptitude) test *m inv*; **put to the ~** mettere alla prova; **pass one's ~** Auto passare l'esame di guida

2 *vt* esaminare; provare ⟨machine⟩

testament /'testəmənt/ *n* testamento *m*; **Old/New T~** Antico/Nuovo Testamento *m*

test ban *n* divieto *m* di test nucleari

test case *n* caso *m* giudiziario che fa giurisprudenza

test-drive 1 *vt* ⟨manufacturer⟩ collaudare; ⟨buyer⟩ provare

2 *n* collaudo *m*; prova *f*

tester /'testə(r)/ *n* (person) collaudatore, -trice *mf*; (device) tester *m inv*; (sample: of make-up, perfume) campione *m*

testicle /'testɪkl/ *n* testicolo *m*

testify /'testɪfaɪ/ *vt/i* (pt/pp **-ied**) testimoniare

testily /'testɪlɪ/ *adv* ⟨say, reply⟩ in modo scontroso

testimonial /testɪ'məʊnɪəl/ *n* lettera *f* di referenze

testimony /'testɪmənɪ/ *n* testimonianza *f*

testing /'testɪŋ/ n (of drug) test mpl; (of blood, water) analisi fpl; (of children) esami mpl

test market n mercato m di prova

test match n partita f internazionale

testosterone /tes'tɒstərəʊn/ n testosterone m

test pilot n pilota mf collaudatore, -trice

test tube n provetta f

test tube baby n fam bambino, -a mf in provetta

testy /'testɪ/ adj irascibile

tetanus /'tetənəs/ n tetano m

tetanus injection n antitetanica f

tetchy /'tetʃɪ/ adj facilmente irritabile

tether /'teðə(r)/ **1** n be at the end of one's ~ non poterne più
2 vt legare

Teutonic /tju:'tɒnɪk/ adj teutonico

text /tekst/ **1** n testo m; (on mobile phone) sms m inv
2 vi (on mobile phone) mandare sms
3 vt mandare sms a ⟨somebody⟩

textbook /'tekstbʊk/ n manuale m

textile /'tekstaɪl/ **1** adj tessile
2 n stoffa f

texting /'tekstɪŋ/ n fam scambio m di sms

text message n sms m inv, messaggio m di testo

text messaging /'mesɪdʒɪŋ/ n scambio m di sms

textual /'tekstjʊəl/ adj testuale

texture /'tekstʊə(r)/ n (of skin) grana f; (of food) consistenza f; **of a smooth ~** (to the touch) soffice al tatto

Thai /taɪ/ adj & n tailandese mf; (language) tailandese m

Thailand /'taɪlænd/ n Tailandia f

Thames /temz/ n Tamigi m

than /ðən/ stressed /ðæn/ conj che; (with numbers, names) di; **older ~ me** più vecchio di me

thank /θæŋk/ vt ringraziare; **~ you [very much]** grazie [mille]

thankful /'θæŋkfʊl/ adj grato

thankfully /'θæŋkfʊlɪ/ adv con gratitudine; (happily) fortunatamente

thankless /'θæŋklɪs/ adj ingrato

thanks /θæŋks/ npl ringraziamenti mpl; **~!** fam grazie!; **~ to** grazie a; **no ~ to you!** non certo grazie a te!

thank-you letter n lettera f di ringraziamento

that /ðæt/ **1** adj & pron (pl those) quel, quei pl; (before s + consonant, gn, ps, z) quello, quegli pl; (before vowel) quell' mf, quegli mpl, quelle fpl; **~ shop** quel negozio; **those shops** quei negozi; **~ mirror** quello specchio; **~ man/woman** quell'uomo/

quella donna; **those men/women** quegli uomini/quelle donne; **~ one** quello; **I don't like those** quelli non mi piacciono; **~ is** cioè; **is ~ you?** sei tu?; **who is ~?** chi è?; **what did you do after ~?** cosa hai fatto dopo?; **like ~** in questo modo, così; **a man like ~** un uomo così; **~ is why** ecco perché; **~ is the reason she gave me** questa è la ragione che mi ha dato; **~ is the easiest thing to do** è la cosa più facile da fare; **~'s it!** (you've understood) ecco!; (I've finished) ecco fatto!; (I've had enough) basta così!; (there's nothing more) tutto qui!; **~'s ~!** (with job) ecco fatto!; (with relationship) è tutto finito!; **and ~'s ~!** punto e basta!
2 adv così; **it wasn't ~ good** non era poi cosè buono
3 rel pron che; **the man ~ I spoke to** l'uomo con cui ho parlato; **the day ~ I saw him** il giorno in cui l'ho visto; **all ~ I know** tutto quello che so
4 conj che; **I think ~...** penso che...

thatch /θætʃ/ n tetto m di paglia

thatched /θætʃt/ adj coperto di paglia

thaw /θɔ:/ **1** n disgelo m
2 vt fare scongelare ⟨food⟩
3 vi ⟨food⟩ scongelarsi; **it's ~ing** sta sgelando

the /ðə/ **1** before a vowel /ðɪ/ def art il m, la f; i mpl, le fpl; (before s + consonant, gn, ps, z) lo m, gli mpl; (before vowel) l' mf, gli mpl, le fpl; **at ~ cinema/station** al cinema/alla stazione; **from ~ cinema/station** dal cinema/dalla stazione
2 adv ~ **more** ~ **better** più ce n'è meglio è; (with reference to pl) più ce ne sono meglio è; **all** ~ **better** tanto meglio

theatre /'θɪətə(r)/ n teatro m; Med sala f operatoria

theatregoer /'θɪətəgəʊə(r)/ n persona f che va a teatro

theatregoing /'θɪətəgəʊɪŋ/ n l'andare m a teatro

theatrical /θɪ'ætrɪkl/ adj teatrale; (showy) melodrammatico

theft /θeft/ n furto m

theft-proof adj antiscippo

their /ðeə(r)/ poss adj il loro m, la loro f, i loro mpl, le loro fpl; **~ mother/father** la loro madre/il loro padre

theirs /ðeəz/ poss pron il loro m, la loro f, i loro mpl, le loro fpl; **a friend of ~** un loro amico; **friends of ~** dei loro amici; **those are ~** quelli sono loro; (as opposed to ours) quelli sono i loro

them /ðem/ pers pron (direct object) li m, le f; (indirect object) gli, loro fml; (after prep: with people) loro; (after preposition: with things) essi; **we haven't seen ~** non li/le abbiamo visti/viste; **give ~ the money** dai loro o dagli i soldi; **give it to ~** daglielo; **I've spoken to ~** ho parlato con loro; **it's ~** sono loro

theme /θi:m/ n tema m

theme park *n* parco *m* a tema

theme song *n* motivo *m* conduttore

themselves /ðəm'selvz/ *pron* (reflexive) si; (emphatic) se stessi; **they poured ∼ a drink** si sono versati da bere; **they said so ∼** lo hanno detto loro stessi; **they kept it to ∼** se lo sono tenuti per sé; **by ∼** da soli

then /ðen/ ① *adv* allora; (next) poi; **by ∼** (in the past) ormai; (in the future) per allora; **since ∼** sin da allora; **before ∼** prima di allora; **from ∼ on** da allora in poi; **now and ∼** ogni tanto; **there and ∼** all'istante ② *adj* di allora

thence /ðens/ *adv* (from there) di là; (therefore) perciò

theologian /θɪə'ləʊdʒɪən/ *n* teologo, -a *mf*

theological /θɪə'lɒdʒɪkl/ *adj* teologico

theology /θɪ'ɒlədʒɪ/ *n* teologia *f*

theorem /'θɪərəm/ *n* teorema *m*

theoretical /θɪə'retɪkl/ *adj* teorico

theoretically /θɪə'retɪklɪ/ *adv* teoricamente

theorist /'θɪərɪst/ *n* teorico *m*

theorize /'θɪəraɪz/ *vi* teorizzare

theory /'θɪərɪ/ *n* teoria *f*; **in ∼** in teoria

therapeutic /θerə'pju:tɪk/ *adj* terapeutico

therapist /'θerəpɪst/ *n* terapista *mf*

therapy /'θerəpɪ/ *n* terapia *f*

there /ðeə(r)/ ① *adv* là, lì; **down/up ∼** laggiù/lassù; **∼ is/are** c'è/ci sono; **∼ he/ she is** eccolo/eccola ② *int* ∼, ∼! dai, su!

thereabouts /ðeərə'baʊts/ *adv* (roughly) all'incirca

thereafter *adv* dopo di che

thereby *adv* in tal modo

therefore /'ðeəfɔ:(r)/ *adv* perciò

therein *adv* ∼ **lies…** in ciò risiede…; **contained ∼** (Jur: in contract) contenuto nello stesso

thermal /'θɜ:ml/ *adj* termico; ⟨*treatment*⟩ termale

thermal imaging *n* termografia *f*

thermal paper *n* carta *f* termica

thermal printer *n* stampante *f* termica

thermal underwear *n* biancheria *f* che mantiene la temperatura corporea

thermometer /θə'mɒmɪtə(r)/ *n* termometro *m*

Thermos® /'θɜ:məs/ *n* ∼ **[flask]** termos *m inv*

thermostat /'θɜ:məstæt/ *n* termostato *m*

thesaurus /θɪ'sɔ:rəs/ *n* (of particular field) dizionario *m* specialistico; (of synonyms) dizionario *m* dei sinonimi

these /ði:z/ ▸ THIS

thesis /'θi:sɪs/ *n* (pl **-ses** /-si:z/) tesi *f inv*

they /ðeɪ/ *pers pron* loro; **∼ are tired** sono stanchi; **we're going, but ∼ are not** noi andiamo, ma loro no; **∼ say** (generalizing) si dice; **∼ are building a new road** stanno costruendo una nuova strada

thick /θɪk/ ① *adj* spesso; ⟨*forest*⟩ fitto; ⟨*liquid*⟩ denso; ⟨*hair*⟩ folto; (fam: stupid) ottuso; (fam: close) molto unito; **be 5 mm ∼** essere 5 mm di spessore; **give somebody a ∼ ear** fam dare uno schiaffone a qualcuno ② *adv* densamente ③ *n* **in the ∼ of** nel mezzo di

thicken /'θɪkn/ ① *vt* ispessire ⟨*sauce*⟩ ② *vi* ispessirsi; ⟨*fog*⟩ infittirsi

thicket /'θɪkɪt/ *n* boscaglia *f*

thickhead /'θɪkhed/ *n* fam zuccone *mf*

thickie /'θɪkɪ/ *n* fam zucca *f* vuota

thickly /'θɪklɪ/ *adv* densamente; ⟨*cut*⟩ a fette spesse

thickness /'θɪknɪs/ *n* spessore *m*

thicko /'θɪkəʊ/ *n* fam zucca *f* vuota

thickset /'θɪkset/ *adj* tozzo

thick-skinned /-'skɪnd/ *adj* fam insensibile

thief /θi:f/ *n* (pl **thieves**) ladro, -a *mf*

thieving /'θi:vɪŋ/ ① *adj* ladro ② *n* furti *mpl*

thigh /θaɪ/ *n* coscia *f*

thimble /'θɪmbl/ *n* ditale *m*

thimbleful /'θɪmbəlfʊl/ *n* (of wine etc) goccino *m*

thin /θɪn/ ① *adj* (**thinner, thinnest**) sottile; ⟨*shoes, sweater*⟩ leggero; ⟨*liquid*⟩ liquido; ⟨*person*⟩ magro; fig ⟨*excuse, plot*⟩ inconsistente; **be [going] ∼ on top** (be going bald) perdere i capelli; **vanish into ∼ air** volatilizzarsi ② *adv* ≈ thinly ③ *vt* (pt/pp **thinned**) diluire ⟨*liquid*⟩ ④ *vi* diradarsi ▪ **thin down** ① *vt* diluire ⟨*paint etc*⟩ ② *vi* (become slimmer) dimagrire ▪ **thin out** *vi* diradarsi

thing /θɪŋ/ *n* cosa *f*; **∼s** *pl* (belongings) roba *fsg*; **for one ∼** in primo luogo; **the right ∼** la cosa giusta; **just the ∼!** proprio quel che ci vuole!; **how are ∼s?** come vanno le cose?; **the latest ∼** fam l'ultima cosa; **the best ∼** would be la cosa migliore sarebbe; **poor ∼!** poveretto!; **have a ∼ about** (be frightened of) aver la fobia di; (be attracted to) avere un debole per

thingumabob /'θɪŋəməbɒb/ *n* fam coso *m*

thingumajig /'θɪŋəmədʒɪg/ *n* fam coso *m*

think /θɪŋk/ *vt/i* (pt/pp **thought**) pensare; (believe) credere; **I ∼ so** credo di sì; **what do you ∼?** (what is your opinion?) cosa ne pensi?; **∼ of/about** pensare a; **what do you ∼ of it?** cosa ne pensi di questo?; **∼ of doing something** pensare di ⋯✣

fare qualcosa; ∼ **better of it** ripensarci; ∼
for oneself pensare con la propria testa
■ **think again** vi pensarci su; **you can** ∼
again! sei matto!
■ **think ahead** vi pensare al futuro; ∼
ahead to something pensare in anticipo a
qualcosa
■ **think back** vi ∼ **back to something**
ripensare a qualcosa
■ **think out** vt mettere a punto ⟨strategy⟩
■ **think over** vt riflettere su
■ **think through** vt riflettere bene su
⟨problem⟩
■ **think up** vt escogitare; trovare ⟨name⟩
thinker /'θɪŋkə(r)/ n pensatore, -trice mf
thinking /'θɪŋkɪŋ/ n (opinion) opinione f
think-tank n gruppo m d'esperti
thinly /'θɪnlɪ/ adv ⟨populated⟩
scarsamente; ⟨disguised⟩ leggermente;
⟨cut⟩ a fette sottili
thinner /'θɪnə(r)/ n diluente m
thinness /'θɪnnɪs/ n (of person) magrezza
f; (of material) finezza f
thin-skinned /-'skɪnd/ adj (sensitive)
permaloso
third /θɜːd/ adj & n terzo, -a mf
third age n terza età f
third degree n **give somebody the** ∼ ∼
fare il terzo grado a qualcuno
third-degree burns npl ustioni fpl di
terzo grado
thirdly /'θɜːdlɪ/ adv terzo
third party n (in insurance, law) terzi mpl
third-party insurance n
assicurazione f contro terzi
third person n terzo m
third-rate adj scadente
Third World n Terzo Mondo m
thirst /θɜːst/ n sete f
thirstily /'θɜːstɪlɪ/ adv con sete
thirsty /'θɜːstɪ/ adj assetato; **be** ∼ aver
sete
thirteen /θɜː'tiːn/ adj & n tredici m
thirteenth /θɜː'tiːnθ/ adj & n
tredicesimo, -a mf
thirties /'θɜːtɪz/ npl (period) **the** ∼ gli anni
Trenta mpl; (age) trent'anni mpl; ▶also
FORTIES
thirtieth /'θɜːtɪɪθ/ adj & n trentesimo, -a
mf
thirty /'θɜːtɪ/ adj & n trenta m
thirty-something n trentenne mf
this /ðɪs/ **1** adj (pl **these**) questo; ∼
man/woman quest'uomo/questa donna;
these men/women questi uomini/queste
donne; ∼ **one** questo; ∼ **evening/morning**
stamattina/stasera
2 pron (pl **these**) questo; **we talked**
about ∼ **and that** abbiamo parlato del più
e del meno; **like** ∼ così; ∼ **is Peter** questo
è Peter; Teleph sono Peter; **who is** ∼**?** chi

è?; Teleph chi parla?; ∼ **is the happiest day**
of my life è il giorno più felice della mia
vita
3 adv così; ∼ **big** così grande
thistle /'θɪsl/ n cardo m
thong /θɒŋ/ n (on whip) cinghia f; (on shoe,
garment) laccetto m; (underwear) cache-sexe
m inv; ∼**s** (pl: sandals) infradito mpl or fpl
thorn /θɔːn/ n spina f
thorny /'θɔːnɪ/ adj spinoso
thorough /'θʌrə/ adj completo;
⟨knowledge⟩ profondo; ⟨clean, search,
training⟩ a fondo; ⟨person⟩ scrupoloso
thoroughbred n purosangue m inv
thoroughfare n via f principale; **'no** ∼**'**
'strada non transitabile'
thoroughly /'θʌrəlɪ/ adv ⟨clean, search,
know something⟩ a fondo; (extremely)
estremamente
thoroughness /'θʌrənɪs/ n completezza
f
those /ðəʊz/ ▶THAT
though /ðəʊ/ **1** conj sebbene; **as** ∼ come
se
2 adv fam tuttavia
thought /θɔːt/ **1** ▶THINK
2 n pensiero m; (idea) idea f; **I've given**
this some ∼ ci ho pensato su
thoughtful /'θɔːtfʊl/ adj pensieroso;
(considerate) premuroso
thoughtfully /'θɔːtfʊlɪ/ adv
pensierosamente; (considerately)
premurosamente
thoughtfulness /'θɔːtfʊlnɪs/ n (kindness)
considerazione f
thoughtless /'θɔːtlɪs/ adj (inconsiderate)
sconsiderato
thoughtlessly /'θɔːtlɪslɪ/ adv con
noncuranza
thoughtlessness /'θɔːtlɪsnɪs/ n
sconsideratezza f
thought-out adj **well/badly** ∼ ben/male
progettato
thought-provoking adj ⟨book, film
etc⟩ che fa riflettere
thousand /'θaʊznd/ **1** adj **one/a** ∼
mille m inv
2 n mille m inv; ∼**s of** migliaia fpl di
thousandth /'θaʊzndθ/ adj & n
millesimo
thrash /θræʃ/ vt picchiare; (defeat)
sconfiggere
■ **thrash about** vi dibattersi
■ **thrash out** vt mettere a punto
thrashing /'θræʃɪŋ/ n (defeat) sconfitta f;
give somebody a ∼ (beating) picchiare
qualcuno
thread /θred/ **1** n filo m; (of screw) filetto
m
2 vt infilare ⟨beads⟩; ∼ **one's way**
through farsi strada fra

threadbare /'θredbeə(r)/ adj logoro

threat /θret/ n minaccia f

threaten /'θretn/ ① vt minacciare (**to do** di fare)
② vi fig incalzare

threatening /'θretnɪŋ/ adj minaccioso; ⟨sky, atmosphere⟩ sinistro

threateningly /'θretnɪŋlɪ/ adv minacciosamente

three /θri:/ adj & n tre m

three-dimensional /-daɪ'menʃ(ə)nəl/ adj tridimensionale

threefold /'θri:fəʊld/ adj & adv triplo

3G adj abbr (**third generation**) ⟨technology, phone⟩ di terza generazione

three-legged /-'legɪd/ adj con tre gambe

three-piece suit n vestito m da uomo con panciotto

three-piece suite n insieme m di divano e due poltrone coordinati

three-quarter length adj ⟨portrait⟩ di tre quarti; ⟨sleeve⟩ a tre quarti

three-quarters adv ⟨empty, full, done⟩ per tre quarti

threesome /'θri:səm/ n trio m

three-wheeler /-'wi:lə(r)/ n (car) auto f inv a tre ruote

thresh /θreʃ/ vt trebbiare

threshold /'θreʃəʊld/ n soglia f

threw /θru:/ ▶ THROW

thrift /θrɪft/ n economia f

thrifty /'θrɪftɪ/ adj parsimonioso

thrill /θrɪl/ ① n emozione f; (of fear) brivido m
② vt entusiasmare; **be ∼ed with** essere entusiasta di

thriller /'θrɪlə(r)/ n (book) [romanzo m] giallo m; (film) [film m inv] giallo m

thrilling /'θrɪlɪŋ/ adj eccitante

thrive /θraɪv/ vi (pt **thrived or throve**, pp **thrived**) ⟨business⟩ prosperare; ⟨child, plant⟩ crescere bene; **I ∼ on pressure** mi piace essere sotto tensione

thriving /'θraɪvɪŋ/ adj fiorente

throat /θrəʊt/ n gola f; **sore ∼** mal m di gola

throaty /'θrəʊtɪ/ adj (husky) roco; (fam: with sore throat) rauco

throb /θrɒb/ ① n pulsazione f; (of heart) battito m
② vi (pt/pp **throbbed**) (vibrate) pulsare; ⟨heart⟩ battere

throbbing /'θrɒbɪŋ/ adj ⟨pain⟩ lancinante; ⟨music⟩ martellante

throes /θrəʊz/ npl **in the ∼ of** fig alle prese con

thrombosis /θrɒm'bəʊsɪs/ n trombosi f

throne /θrəʊn/ n trono m

throng /θrɒŋ/ n calca f

throttle /'θrɒtl/ ① n (on motorbike) manopola f di accelerazione
② vt strozzare

through /θru:/ ① prep attraverso; (during) durante; (by means of) tramite; (thanks to) grazie a; **Saturday ∼ Tuesday** Am da sabato a martedì incluso
② adv attraverso; **∼ and ∼** fino in fondo; **wet ∼** completamente bagnato; **read something ∼** dare una lettura a qualcosa; **let ∼** lasciar passare ⟨somebody⟩
③ adj ⟨train⟩ diretto; **be ∼** (finished) aver finito; Teleph avere la comunicazione

throughout /θru:'aʊt/ ① prep per tutto
② adv completamente; (time) per tutto il tempo

throughway n Am superstrada f

throve /θrəʊv/ ▶ THRIVE

throw /θrəʊ/ ① n tiro m
② vt (pt **threw**, pp **thrown**) lanciare; (throw away) gettare; azionare ⟨switch⟩; disarcionare ⟨rider⟩; (fam: disconcert) disorientare; fam dare ⟨party⟩
■ **throw about** vt spargere; **∼ one's money about** sbandierare i propri soldi
■ **throw away** vt gettare via
■ **throw back** vt ributtare in acqua ⟨fish⟩; rilanciare ⟨ball⟩
■ **throw in** vt (include at no extra cost) aggiungere [gratuitamente]; (in football) rimettere in gioco; **∼ in the towel** or **the sponge** fig abbandonare il campo
■ **throw off** vt seminare ⟨pursuers⟩; liberarsi di ⟨cold, infection etc⟩
■ **throw together** vt (assemble hastily) mettere insieme; improvvisare ⟨meal⟩; (bring into contact) fare incontrare
■ **throw out** vt gettare via; rigettare ⟨plan⟩; buttare fuori ⟨person⟩
■ **throw up** ① vt alzare
② vi (vomit) vomitare

throwaway adj ⟨remark⟩ buttato lì; ⟨paper cup⟩ usa e getta inv

throwback n Biol atavismo m; fig regressione f

throw-in n Sport rimessa f laterale

thrush /θrʌʃ/ n tordo m; Med mughetto m; (in woman) candida f

thrust /θrʌst/ ① n spinta f
② vt (pt/pp **thrust**) (push) spingere; (insert) conficcare; **∼ [up] on** imporre a

thud /θʌd/ n tonfo m

thug /θʌg/ n deliquente m

thuggish /'θʌgɪʃ/ adj violento

thumb /θʌm/ ① n pollice m; **as a rule of ∼** come regola generale; **under sb's ∼** succube di qualcuno
② vt **∼ a lift** fare l'autostop
■ **thumb through** vt sfogliare

thumb-index n indice m a rubrica

thumbnail sketch n breve descrizione f

thumbs down *n* fam get the ~ ~ non ottenere l'ok; **give somebody/something the ~ ~** non dare l'ok a qualcuno/qualcosa

thumbs up *n* fam get the ~ ~ ricevere l'ok; **give somebody/something the ~ ~** dare l'ok a qualcuno/qualcosa

thumbtack *n* Am cimice *f*, puntina *f* [da disegno]

thump /θʌmp/ **①** *n* colpo *m*; (noise) tonfo *m*
② *vt* battere su ⟨table, door⟩; battere ⟨fist⟩; colpire ⟨person⟩
③ *vi* battere (on su); ⟨heart⟩ battere forte
■ **thump about** *vi* camminare pesantemente

thumping /ˈθʌmpɪŋ/ *adj* (fam: very large) enorme; **a ~ headache** un mal di testa martellante

thunder /ˈθʌndə(r)/ **①** *n* tuono *m*: (loud noise) rimbombo *m*
② *vi* tuonare; (make loud noise) rimbombare

thunderbolt /ˈθʌndəbəʊlt/ *n* folgore *f*

thunderclap /ˈθʌndəklæp/ *n* rombo *m* di tuono

thundering /ˈθʌndərɪŋ/ *adj* (fam: very big or great) tremendo

thunderous /ˈθʌndərəs/ *adj* ⟨applause⟩ scrosciante

thunderstorm /ˈθʌndəstɔːm/ *n* temporale *m*

thunderstruck /ˈθʌndəstrʌk/ *adj* sbigottito

thundery /ˈθʌndərɪ/ *adj* temporalesco

Thursday /ˈθɜːzdeɪ/ *n* giovedì *m inv*

thus /ðʌs/ *adv* così

thwack /θwæk/ **①** *vt* colpire
② *n* colpo *m*

thwart /θwɔːt/ *vt* ostacolare

thyme /taɪm/ *n* timo *m*

thyroid /ˈθaɪrɔɪd/ *n* tiroide *f*

tiara /tɪˈɑːrə/ *n* diadema *m*

Tiber /ˈtaɪbə(r)/ *n* Tevere *m*

Tibet /tɪˈbet/ *n* Tibet *m*

tick¹ /tɪk/ *n* **on ~** fam a credito

tick² **①** *n* (sound) ticchettio *m*; (mark) segno *m*; (fam: instant) attimo *m*
② *vi* ticchettare
■ **tick off** *vt* spuntare; fam sgridare
■ **tick over** *vi* ⟨engine⟩ andare al minimo

ticket /ˈtɪkɪt/ *n* biglietto *m*; (for item deposited, library) tagliando *m*; (label) cartellino *m*; (fine) multa *f*

ticket barrier *n* cancelletto *m* di entrata e uscita

ticket-collector *n* controllore *m*

ticket-holder *n* persona *f* munita di biglietto

ticket-office *n* biglietteria *f*

ticket tout *n* Br bagarino *m*

ticket window *n* sportello *m* della biglietteria

tickle /ˈtɪkl/ **①** *n* solletico *m*
② *vt* fare il solletico a; (amuse) divertire
③ *vi* fare prurito

ticklish /ˈtɪklɪʃ/ *adj* che soffre il solletico; ⟨problem⟩ delicato

tidal /ˈtaɪdl/ *adj* ⟨river, harbour⟩ di marea

tidal wave *n* onda *f* di marea

tiddly /ˈtɪdlɪ/ *adj* (Br fam: drunk) brillo

tiddlywinks /ˈtɪdlɪwɪŋks/ *n* gioco *m* delle pulci

tide /taɪd/ *n* marea *f*; (of events) corso *m*; **the ~ is in/out** c'è alta/bassa marea
■ **tide over** *vt* **~ somebody over** aiutare qualcuno ad andare avanti

tidemark /ˈtaɪdmɑːk/ *n* linea *f* di marea; (Br fig: line of dirt) tracce *fpl* di sporco (nella vasca da bagno)

tidily /ˈtaɪdɪlɪ/ *adv* in modo ordinato

tidiness /ˈtaɪdɪnɪs/ *n* ordine *m*

tidy /ˈtaɪdɪ/ **①** *adj* (-ier, -iest) ordinato; fam ⟨amount⟩ bello
② *vt* ordinare
■ **tidy away** *vt* mettere a posto ⟨toys, books⟩
■ **tidy out** *vt* mettere in ordine ⟨drawer, cupboard⟩
■ **tidy up** *vt* ordinare; **~ oneself up** mettersi in ordine

tie /taɪ/ **①** *n* cravatta *f*; (cord) legaccio *m*; (fig: bond) legame *m*; (restriction) impedimento *m*; Sport pareggio *m*
② *vt* (pres p **tying**) legare; fare ⟨knot⟩ **be ~d** (in competition) essere in parità
③ *vi* pareggiare
■ **tie back** *vt* legare [dietro la nuca] ⟨hair⟩
■ **tie down** *vt* anche fig legare
■ **tie in with** *vi* corrispondere a
■ **tie on** *vt* attaccare
■ **tie up** *vt* legare; vincolare ⟨capital⟩ **be ~d up** (busy) essere occupato

tie-break[er] *n* Tennis tie-break *m inv*; (in quiz) spareggio *m*

tie-dye *vt* tingere annodando

tie-on *adj* ⟨label⟩ volante

tiepin *n* fermacravatta *m*

tier /tɪə(r)/ *n* fila *f*; (of cake) piano *m*; (in stadium) gradinata *f*

tiff /tɪf/ *n* battibecco *m*

tiger /ˈtaɪgə(r)/ *n* tigre *f*

tiger's-eye /ˈtaɪgəz/ *n* occhio *m* di tigre

tight /taɪt/ **①** *adj* stretto; (taut) teso; (fam: drunk) sbronzo; (fam: mean) spilorcio; **~ corner** fam brutta situazione *f*
② *adv* strettamente; ⟨hold⟩ forte; ⟨closed⟩ bene

tighten /ˈtaɪtn/ **①** *vt* stringere; avvitare ⟨screw⟩; intensificare ⟨control⟩; **~ one's belt** fig tirare la cinghia
② *vi* stringersi

■ **tighten up** *vt* stringere ⟨screw⟩; rendere più severo ⟨security⟩ *vi* (become stricter) diventare più severo

tight-fisted /-'fɪstɪd/ *adj* tirchio

tight-fitting /-'fɪtɪŋ/ *adj* attillato

tight-knit *adj* fig ⟨community, group⟩ unito

tight-lipped /-'lɪpt/ *adj* **they are remaining ~ about events** mantengono il riserbo sull'accaduto

tightly /'taɪtlɪ/ *adv* strettamente; ⟨hold⟩ forte; ⟨closed⟩ bene

tightrope /'taɪtrəʊp/ *n* fune *f* (da funamboli)

tightrope walker *n* equilibrista *mf*

tights /taɪts/ *npl* collant *m inv*

tigress /'taɪgrɪs/ *n* tigre *f* femmina

tile /taɪl/ ① *n* mattonella *f*; (on roof) tegola *f*

② *vt* rivestire di mattonelle ⟨wall⟩; coprire con tegole ⟨roof⟩; Comput affiancare

till¹ /tɪl/ *prep & conj* ≈ until

till² *n* cassa *f*

tiller /'tɪlə(r)/ *n* barra *f* del timone

tilt /tɪlt/ ① *n* inclinazione *f*; **at full ~** a tutta velocità
② *vt* inclinare
③ *vi* inclinarsi

timber /'tɪmbə(r)/ *n* legname *m*

time /taɪm/ ① *n* tempo *m*; (occasion) volta *f*; (by clock) ora *f*; **two ~s four** due volte quattro; **at any ~** in qualsiasi momento; **this ~** questa volta; **at ~s, from ~ to ~** ogni tanto; **~ and again** cento volte; **two at a ~** due alla volta; **on ~** in orario; **In ~** in tempo; (eventually) col tempo; **in no ~ at all** velocemente; **in a year's ~** fra un anno; **behind ~** in ritardo; **behind the ~s** antiquato; **for the ~ being** per il momento; **what is the ~?** che ora è?; **by the ~ we arrive** quando arriviamo; **do you have the ~?** (what is it?) hai l'ora?; **did you have a nice ~?** ti sei divertito?; **have a good ~!** divertiti!
② *vt* scegliere il momento per; cronometrare ⟨race⟩; **be well ~d** essere ben calcolato

time bomb *n* bomba *f* a orologeria

time-consuming *adj* che porta via molto tempo

time difference *n* differenza *f* di fuso orario

time-frame *n* arco *m* temporale

time-honoured /-ɒnəd/ *adj* venerando

timekeeper *n* Sport cronometrista *mf*; **be a good ~** (be punctual) essere sempre puntuale

time lag *n* intervallo *m* [di tempo]

timeless /'taɪmlɪs/ *adj* eterno

time limit *n* limite *m* di tempo

timely /'taɪmlɪ/ *adj* opportuno

time off *n* (leave) permesso *m*; **take some ~ ~** prendere delle ferie

time-out *n* (break) pausa *f*; Sport time out *m inv*

timer /'taɪmə(r)/ *n* timer *m inv*

timescale *n* periodo *m*

timeshare *n* (apartment) appartamento *m* in multiproprietà; (house) casa *f* in multiproprietà

time sheet *n* foglio *m* di presenza

time signal *n* segnale *m* orario

time span *n* arco *m* di tempo

time switch *n* interruttore *m* a tempo

timetable *n* orario *m*

time zone *n* fuso *m* orario

timid /'tɪmɪd/ *adj* (shy) timido; (fearful) timoroso

timidly /'tɪmɪdlɪ/ *adv* timidamente

timidness /'tɪmɪdnɪs/ *n* (shyness) timidezza *f*; (fear) paura *f*

timing /'taɪmɪŋ/ *n* Sport, Techn cronometraggio *m*; **the ~ of the election** il momento scelto per le elezioni; **have no sense of ~** non saper scegliere il momento opportuno

timorous /'tɪm(ə)rəs/ *adj* timoroso

timpani /'tɪmpənɪ/ *npl* timpani *mpl*

tin /tɪn/ ① *n* stagno *m*; (container) barattolo *m*
② *vt* (pt/pp **tinned**) inscatolare

tin can *n* lattina *f*, scatoletta *f*

tin foil *n* [carta *f*] stagnola *f*

tinge /tɪndʒ/ ① *n* sfumatura *f*
② *vt* **~d with** fig misto a

tingle /'tɪŋgl/ *vi* pizzicare

tinker /'tɪŋkə(r)/ *vi* armeggiare

tinkle /'tɪŋkl/ ① *n* tintinnio *m*; (fam: phone call) colpo *m* di telefono
② *vi* tintinnare

tinned /tɪnd/ *adj* in scatola

tinnitus /'tɪnɪtəs/ *n* Med ronzio *m* auricolare

tinny /'tɪnɪ/ *adj* ⟨sound, music⟩ metallico; (badly made) che sembra fatta di latta

tin-opener /-əʊpnə(r)/ *n* apriscatole *m inv*

tinpot /'tɪnpɒt/ *adj* pej ⟨firm⟩ da due soldi

tinsel /'tɪnsl/ *n* filo *m* d'argento

tint /tɪnt/ ① *n* tinta *f*
② *vt* tingersi ⟨hair⟩; **~ed glasses** occhiali *mpl* colorati

tiny /'taɪnɪ/ *adj* (**-ier, -iest**) minuscolo

tip¹ /tɪp/ *n* (point, top) punta *f*

tip² ① *n* (money) mancia *f*; (advice) consiglio *m*; (for rubbish) discarica *f*
② *vt* (pt/pp **tipped**) (tilt) inclinare; (overturn) capovolgere; (pour) versare; (reward) dare una mancia a
③ *vi* inclinarsi; (overturn) capovolgersi

t

■ **tip off** *vt* ~ somebody off (inform) fare una soffiata a qualcuno
■ **tip out** *vt* rovesciare
■ **tip over** *vt* capovolgere *vi* capovolgersi
■ **tip up** *vt* sollevare ‹seat›; (overturn) rovesciare

tip-off *n* soffiata *f*

tipped /tɪpt/ *adj* ‹cigarette› col filtro

tipple /'tɪpl/ **1** *vi* bere [alcool]
2 *n* have a ~ prendere un bicchierino; my favourite ~ il mio liquore preferito

tipster /'tɪpstə(r)/ *n* esperto *m* che dà suggerimenti su cavalli da corsa, azioni ecc

tipsy /'tɪpsɪ/ *adj* fam brillo

tiptoe /'tɪptəʊ/ *n* on ~ in punta di piedi

tip-top *adj* fam in condizioni perfette

tirade /taɪ'reɪd/ *n* filippica *f*

tire /'taɪə(r)/ **1** *vt* stancare
2 *vi* stancarsi
■ **tire out** *vt* (exhaust) sfinire

tired /'taɪəd/ *adj* stanco; ~ of stanco di; ~ out stanco morto

tiredness /'taɪədnɪs/ *n* stanchezza *f*

tireless /'taɪəlɪs/ *adj* instancabile

tirelessly /'taɪəlɪslɪ/ *adv* instancabilmente

tiresome /'taɪəsəm/ *adj* fastidioso

tiring /'taɪərɪŋ/ *adj* stancante

tissue /'tɪʃuː/ *n* tessuto *m*; (handkerchief) fazzolettino *m* di carta

tissue-paper *n* carta *f* velina

tit[1] /tɪt/ *n* (bird) cincia *f*

tit[2] *n* ~ for tat pan per focaccia

tit[3] *n* fam (breast) tetta *f*; (fool) stupido *m*

titbit /'tɪtbɪt/ *n* ghiottoneria *f*; (fig: of news) notizia *f* appetitosa

titillate /'tɪtɪleɪt/ *vt* titillare

titivate /'tɪtɪveɪt/ *vt* agghindare; ~ oneself agghindarsi

title /'taɪtl/ *n* titolo *m*

title bar *n* Comput barra *f* di titolo

title deed *n* atto *m* di proprietà

title-holder *n* detentore, -trice *mf* del titolo

title-page *n* frontespizio *m*

title role *n* ruolo *m* principale

titter /'tɪtə(r)/ **1** *vi* ridere nervosamente
2 *n* risatina *f* nervosa

tittle-tattle /'tɪtltætl/ *n* pettegolezzi *mpl*

titular /'tɪtjʊlə(r)/ *adj* nominale

tizzy /'tɪzɪ/ *n* fam in a ~ in grande agitazione

TLC *n abbr* fam (**tender loving care**) cura e gentilezza *f*

TM *abbr* (**trademark**) marchio *m* di fabbrica

to /tuː/, unstressed /tə/ **1** *prep* a; (to countries) in; (towards) verso; (up to, until) fino

a; I'm going to John's/the butcher's vado da John/dal macellaio; come/go to somebody venire/andare da qualcuno; to Italy/Switzerland in Italia/Svizzera; I've never been to Rome non sono mai stato a Roma; go to the market andare al mercato; to the toilet/my room in bagno/camera mia; to an exhibition ad una mostra; to university all'università; twenty/quarter to eight le otto meno venti/un quarto; 5 to 6 kilos da 5 a 6 chili; to the end alla fine; to this day fino a oggi; to the best of my recollection per quanto mi possa ricordare; give/say something to somebody dare/dire qualcosa a qualcuno; give it to me dammelo; there's nothing to it è una cosa da niente
2 verbal constructions to go andare; learn to swim imparare a nuotare; I want to/have to go voglio/devo andare; it's easy to forget è facile da dimenticare; too ill/tired to go troppo malato/stanco per andare; you have to devi; I don't want to non voglio; he wants to be a teacher vuole diventare un insegnante; to be 90 vivere fino a 90 anni; he was the last to arrive è stato l'ultimo ad arrivare; to be honest,... per essere sincero,...
3 *adv* pull to chiudere; to and fro avanti e indietro

toad /təʊd/ *n* rospo *m*

toadstool /'təʊdstuːl/ *n* fungo *m* velenoso

toady /'təʊdɪ/ *v*
■ **toady to** *vi* fare da leccapiedi a

toast /təʊst/ **1** *n* pane *m* tostato; (drink) brindisi *m inv*; be ~ fam essere fritto; if he finds out, we're ~ se lo scopre siamo fritti
2 *vt* tostare ‹bread›; (drink a ~ to) brindare a

toaster /'təʊstə(r)/ *n* tostapane *m inv*

toast rack /'təʊstræk/ *n* portatoast *m inv*

tobacco /tə'bækəʊ/ *n* tabacco *m*

tobacconist's [shop] /tə'bækənɪsts [ʃɒp]/ *n* tabaccheria *f*

toboggan /tə'bɒgən/ **1** *n* toboga *m inv*
2 *vi* andare in toboga

today /tə'deɪ/ *adj & adv* oggi *m*; a week ~ una settimana ad oggi; ~'s paper il giornale di oggi

toddle /'tɒdl/ *vi* ‹child› cominciare a camminare; ~ into town fam fare una passeggiata in centro; I must be toddling fam devo scappare

toddler /'tɒdlə(r)/ *n* bambino, -a *mf* piccolo, -a

toddy /'tɒdɪ/ *n* grog *m inv*

to-do /tə'duː/ *n* fam baccano *m*

toe /təʊ/ **1** *n* dito *m* del piede; (of footwear) punta *f*; on one's ~s fig pronto ad agire; big ~ alluce *m*; little ~ mignolo *m* [del piede]

2 *vt* ~ **the line** rigar diritto

toe-curling *adj* imbarazzante

toe-hold *n* punto *m* d'appoggio

toenail *n* unghia *f* del piede

toff /tɒf/ *n* fam elegantone, -a *mf*

toffee /'tɒfɪ/ *n* caramella *f* al mou

toffee apple *n* mela *f* caramellata

toffee-nosed *adj* Br fam con la puzza sotto il naso

together /tə'geðə(r)/ *adv* insieme; (at the same time) allo stesso tempo; ~ **with** insieme a

togetherness /tə'geðənɪs/ *n* intimità *f*

toggle /'tɒgl/ *n* (fastening) olivetta *f*

Togo /'təʊgəʊ/ *n* Togo *m*

toil /tɔɪl/ **1** *n* duro lavoro *m* **2** *vi* lavorare duramente

toilet /'tɔɪlɪt/ *n* (lavatory) gabinetto *m*

toilet bag *n* nécessaire *m inv*

toilet paper *n* carta *f* igienica

toiletries /'tɔɪlɪtrɪz/ *npl* articoli *mpl* da toilette

toilet roll *n* rotolo *m* di carta igienica

toilet soap *n* sapone *m*

toilet tissue *n* carta *f* igienica

toilet-train *vt* ~ **a child** insegnare ad un bambino ad usare il vasino

toilet water *n* acqua *f* di colonia

token /'təʊkən/ **1** *n* segno *m*; (counter) gettone *m*; (voucher) buono *m* **2** *attrib* simbolico

told /təʊld/ **1** ▶ TELL **2** *adj* **all** ~ in tutto

tolerable /'tɒl(ə)rəbl/ *adj* tollerabile; (not bad) discreto

tolerably /'tɒl(ə)rəblɪ/ *adv* discretamente

tolerance /'tɒl(ə)r(ə)ns/ *n* tolleranza *f*

tolerant /'tɒl(ə)r(ə)nt/ *adj* tollerante

tolerantly /'tɒl(ə)r(ə)ntlɪ/ *adv* con tolleranza

tolerate /'tɒləreɪt/ *vt* tollerare

toll¹ /təʊl/ *n* pedaggio *m*; **death** ~ numero *m* di morti; **take a heavy** ~ costare gravi perdite

toll² *vi* suonare a morto

toll-booth *n* casello *m*

toll call *n* Am chiamata *f* in teleselezione

toll-free number *n* Am Teleph numero *m* verde

toll motorway *n* autostrada *f* con pedaggio

tom /tɒm/ *n* (cat) gatto *m* maschio

tomato /tə'mɑːtəʊ/ *n* (pl **-es**) pomodoro *m*

tomato ketchup *n* ketchup *m*

tomato purée *n* concentrato *m* di pomodoro

tomato sauce *n* salsa *f* di pomodoro

tomb /tuːm/ *n* tomba *f*

tomboy /'tɒmbɔɪ/ *n* maschiaccio *m*

tombstone /'tuːmstəʊn/ *n* pietra *f* tombale

tom-cat *n* gatto *m* maschio

tome /təʊm/ *n* tomo *m*

tomfoolery /tɒm'fuːlərɪ/ *n* stupidaggini *fpl*

tomorrow /tə'mɒrəʊ/ *adj & adv* domani; ~ **morning** domani mattina; **the day after** ~ dopodomani; **see you** ~! a domani!

tom-tom *n* tamtam *m inv*

ton /tʌn/ *n* tonnellata *f* (= 1, 016 kg); ~**s of** fam un sacco di

tonal /'təʊnl/ *adj* tonale

tonality /təʊ'nælɪtɪ/ *n* tonalità *f inv*

tone /təʊn/ *n* tono *m*; (colour) tonalità *f inv*
  ■ **tone down** *vt* attenuare
  ■ **tone in** *vi* intonarsi
  ■ **tone up** *vt* tonificare ‹*muscles*›

tone-deaf *adj* **be** ~ non avere orecchio

toneless /'təʊnlɪs/ *adj* (unmusical) piatto

toner /'təʊnə(r)/ *n* toner *m*

Tonga /'tɒŋɡə/ *n* Tonga *f*

tongs /tɒŋz/ *npl* pinze *fpl*

tongue /tʌŋ/ *n* lingua *f*; ~ **in cheek** fam ‹*say*› ironicamente

tongue-lashing *n* (severe reprimand) strigliata *f*

tongue stud *n* piercing *m inv* nella lingua

tongue-tied *adj* senza parole

tongue-twister *n* scioglilingua *m inv*

tonic /'tɒnɪk/ *n* tonico *m*; (for hair) lozione *f* per i capelli; fig toccasana *m inv*; ~ **[water]** acqua *f* tonica

tonight /tə'naɪt/ **1** *adv* stanotte; (evening) stasera **2** *n* questa notte *f*; (evening) questa sera *f*

tonnage /'tʌnɪdʒ/ *n* stazza *f*

tonne /tʌn/ *n* tonnellata *f* metrica

tonsil /'tɒnsl/ *n* Anat tonsilla *f*; **have one's** ~**s out** operarsi di tonsille

tonsillitis /tɒnsə'laɪtɪs/ *n* tonsillite *f*; **have** ~ avere la tonsillite

too /tuː/ *adv* troppo; (also) anche; ~ **many** troppi; ~ **much** troppo; ~ **little** troppo poco

took /tʊk/ ▶ TAKE

tool /tuːl/ *n* attrezzo *m*

tool-bag *n* borsa *f* degli attrezzi

toolbar *n* Comput barra *f* degli strumenti

toolbox *n* cassetta *f* degli attrezzi

tool kit *n* astuccio *m* di attrezzi

toot /tuːt/ **1** *n* suono *m* di clacson **2** *vi* Auto clacsonare

tooth /tuːθ/ *n* (pl **teeth**) dente *m*

tooth ache /'tu:θeɪk/ n mal m di denti; **have** ~ avere mal di denti

toothbrush /'tu:θbrʌʃ/ n spazzolino m da denti

toothless /'tu:θlɪs/ adj sdentato

toothpaste /'tu:θpeɪst/ n dentifricio m

toothpick /'tu:θpɪk/ n stuzzicadenti m inv

toothy /'tu:θɪ/ adj **give a** ~ **grin** fare un sorriso a trentadue denti

top[1] /tɒp/ n (toy) trottola f

top[2] [1] n cima f; Sch primo, -a mf; (upper part or half) parte f superiore; (of page, list, street) inizio m; (upper surface) superficie f; (lid) coperchio m; (of bottle) tappo m; (garment) maglia f; (blouse) camicia f; Auto marcia f più alta; **at the** ~ fig al vertice; **at the** ~ **of one's voice** a squarciagola; **on** ~/**on** ~ **of** sopra; **on** ~ **of that** (besides) per di più; **from** ~ **to bottom** da cima a fondo; **blow one's** ~ fam perdere le staffe; **over the** ~ (fam: exaggerated, too much) eccessivo [2] adj in alto; ⟨official, floor of building⟩ superiore; ⟨pupil, musician etc⟩ migliore; ⟨speed⟩ massimo [3] vt (pt/pp **topped**) essere in testa a ⟨list⟩; (exceed) sorpassare; ~**ped with icecream** ricoperto di gelato; ~ **oneself** sl suicidarsi ■ **top up** vt riempire

topaz /'təʊpæz/ n topazio m

top brass n fam pezzi mpl grossi

topcoat n (of paint) strato m finale

top-end adj ⟨computer, model⟩ della fascia più alta

top floor n ultimo piano m

top gear n Auto marcia f più alta

top hat n cilindro m

top-heavy adj con la parte superiore sovraccarica

topic /'tɒpɪk/ n soggetto m; (of conversation) argomento m

topical /'tɒpɪkl/ adj d'attualità; **very** ~ di grande attualità

topless /'tɒplɪs/ adj & adv topless

top-level adj ad alto livello

top management n dirigenza f

topmost /'tɒpməʊst/ adj più alto

top-notch adj fam eccellente

top-of-the-range adj ⟨model⟩ della fascia più alta

topping /'tɒpɪŋ/ n **with a chocolate** ~ ricoperto di cioccolato; **pizza with a ham and mushroom** ~ pizza al prosciutto e funghi

topple /'tɒpl/ [1] vt rovesciare [2] vi rovesciarsi ■ **topple off** vi cadere

top-ranking adj ⟨official⟩ di massimo grado

top secret adj segretissimo, top secret inv

top security adj di massima sicurezza

top-shelf adj ⟨magazine⟩ pornografico

topsoil n strato m superficiale del terreno

topspin n topspin m inv

topsy-turvy /tɒpsɪ'tɜ:vɪ/ adj & adv sottosopra

top ten npl primi dieci mpl in classifica

top-up n **would you like a** ~? ti riempio il bicchiere/la tazza?

top-up card n ricarica f

torch /tɔ:tʃ/ n torcia f [elettrica]; (flaming) fiaccola f

torchlight procession /'tɔ:tʃlaɪt/ n fiaccolata f

tore /tɔ:(r)/ ▸ TEAR[1]

torment[1] /'tɔ:ment/ n tormento m

torment[2] /tɔ:'ment/ vt tormentare

tormentor /tɔ:'mentə(r)/ n tormentatore, -trice mf

torn /tɔ:n/ [1] ▸ TEAR[1] [2] adj bucato

tornado /tɔ:'neɪdəʊ/ n (pl **-es**) tornado m inv

torpedo /tɔ:'pi:dəʊ/ [1] n (pl **-es**) siluro m [2] vt silurare

torpid /'tɔ:pɪd/ adj intorpidito

torrent /'tɒrənt/ n torrente m

torrential /tə'renʃl/ adj ⟨rain⟩ torrenziale

torrid /'tɒrɪd/ adj torrido

torso /'tɔ:səʊ/ n torso m; (in art) busto m

tortoise /'tɔ:təs/ n tartaruga f

tortoiseshell /'tɔ:təsʃel/ n tartaruga f

tortuous /'tɔ:tʃʊəs/ adj tortuoso

tortuously /'tɔ:tʃʊəslɪ/ adv tortuosamente

torture /'tɔ:tʃə(r)/ [1] n tortura f [2] vt torturare

Tory /'tɔ:rɪ/ Br [1] n conservatore, -trice mf (appartenente al partito britannico conservatore) [2] adj del partito conservatore

toss /tɒs/ [1] vt gettare; (into the air) lanciare in aria; (shake) scrollare; ⟨horse⟩ disarcionare; mescolare ⟨salad⟩; rivoltare facendo saltare in aria ⟨pancake⟩; ~ **a coin** fare testa o croce [2] vi ~ **and turn** (in bed) rigirarsi; **let's** ~ **for it** facciamo testa o croce ■ **toss out** vt buttare via ⟨newspaper, rubbish⟩; **toss somebody out** buttare fuori qualcuno

toss-up n fam **let's have a** ~ **to decide** facciamo testa o croce

tot[1] /tɒt/ n bimbetto, -a mf; (fam: of liquor) goccio m

tot² *vt* (pt/pp **totted**) ∼ up fam fare la somma di

total /'təʊtl/ ① *adj* totale
② *n* totale *m*
③ *vt* (pt/pp **totalled**) ammontare a; (add up) sommare

totalitarian /təʊtælɪ'teərɪən/ *adj* totalitario

totally /'təʊtəlɪ/ *adv* totalmente

tote bag /təʊt/ *n* sporta *f*

totem /'təʊtəm/ *n* totem *m inv*

totem pole *n* totem *m inv*

totter /'tɒtə(r)/ *vi* barcollare; ⟨government⟩ vacillare

touch /tʌtʃ/ ① *n* tocco *m*; (sense) tatto *m*; (contact) contatto *m*; (trace) traccia *f*; (of irony, humour) tocco *m*; **get/be in** ∼ mettersi/ essere in contatto
② *vt* toccare; (lightly) sfiorare; (equal) eguagliare; (fig: move) commuovere
③ *vi* toccarsi
■ **touch down** *vi* Aeron atterrare
■ **touch off** *vi* fig scatenare
■ **touch on** *vt* fig accennare a
■ **touch up** *vt* ritoccare ⟨painting⟩; ∼ **somebody up** (sexually) allungare le mani su qualcuno

touch-and-go *adj* incerto

touchdown /'tʌtʃdaʊn/ *n* Aeron atterraggio *m*; Sport meta *f*

touché /tu:'ʃeɪ/ *int* fig touché!

touched /tʌtʃt/ *adj* (crazy) toccato

touching /'tʌtʃɪŋ/ *adj* commovente

touchingly /'tʌtʃɪŋlɪ/ *adv* in modo commovente

touchline *n* (in football) linea *f* laterale; (in rugby) touche *nf inv*

touchpad *n* Comput touchpad *m inv*

touch screen *n* Comput touch screen *m inv*, schermo *m* a sfioramento

touch[-sensitive] screen *n* Comput schermo *m* a sfioramento

touch-tone *adj* ⟨telephone⟩ a tastiera

touch-type *vi* dattilografare a tastiera cieca

touch-typing *n* dattilografia *f* a tastiera cieca

touch-up *n* (of paintwork) ritocco *m*

touchy /'tʌtʃɪ/ *adj* permaloso; ⟨subject⟩ delicato

tough /tʌf/ *adj* duro; (severe, harsh) severo; (durable) resistente; (resilient) forte; ∼! (fam: too bad) peggio per te/lui!

toughen /'tʌfn/ *vt* rinforzare
■ **toughen up** *vt* rendere più forte ⟨person⟩

toupee /'tu:peɪ/ *n* toupet *m inv*

tour /tʊə(r)/ ① *n* giro *m*; (of building, town) visita *f*; Theat, Sport tournée *f inv*; (of duty) servizio *m*
② *vt* visitare

③ *vi* fare un giro turistico; Theat essere in tournée

tour guide *n* guida *f* turistica

tourism /'tʊərɪzm/ *n* turismo *m*

tourist /'tʊərɪst/ ① *n* turista *mf*
② *attrib* turistico

tourist class *n* classe *f* turistica

tourist office *n* ufficio *m* turistico

tourist resort *n* località *f* turistica

tourist route *n* itinerario *m* turistico

tourist trap *n* locale *o* località per turisti dove i prezzi sono molto alti

touristy /'tʊərɪstɪ/ *adj* fam pej da turisti; it's too ∼ here è troppo turistico qui

tournament /'tʊənəmənt/ *n* torneo *m*

tourniquet /'tʊənɪkeɪ/ *n* laccio *m* emostatico

tour operator *n* tour operator *mf inv*, operatore, -trice *mf* turistico, -a

tousle /'taʊzl/ *vt* spettinare

tousled /'taʊzld/ *adj* ⟨hair⟩ arruffato; appearance scarmigliato

tout /taʊt/ ① *n* (ticket ∼) bagarino *m*; (horseracing) informatore *m*
② *vi* ∼ **for** sollecitare

tow /təʊ/ ① *n* rimorchio *m*; 'on ∼' 'a rimorchio'; in ∼ fam al seguito
② *vt* rimorchiare
■ **tow away** *vt* portare via col carro attrezzi

toward[s] /tə'wɔ:d(z)/ *prep* verso; (with respect to) nei riguardi di

tow bar *n* barra *f* di rimorchio

towel /'taʊəl/ *n* asciugamano *m*
■ **towel down** *vt* asciugare

towelling /'taʊəlɪŋ/ *n* spugna *f*

towelling robe *n* accappatoio *m*

towel rail *n* portasciugamano *m*

tower /'taʊə(r)/ ① *n* torre *f*; **be a** ∼ **of strength to somebody** essere di grande conforto per qualcuno
② *vi* ∼ **above** dominare

tower block *n* palazzone *m*

towering /'taʊərɪŋ/ *adj* torreggiante; ⟨rage⟩ violento

tow line *n* cavo *m* da rimorchio

town /taʊn/ *n* città *f inv*; in ∼ nel centro

town-and-country planning *n* pianificazione *f* territoriale

town centre *n* centro *m* della città

town council *n* municipalità *f inv*

town hall *n* municipio *m*

town house *n* casa *f* a schiera a tre o più piani

town planner *n* urbanista *mf*

town planning *n* urbanistica *f*

township *n* comune *m*; (in South Africa) township *f inv*

towpath /'təʊpɑ:θ/ *n* strada *f* alzaia

tow rope *n* cavo *m* da rimorchio

tow truck *n* carro *m* attrezzi *inv*

toxic /'tɒksɪk/ *adj* tossico

toxicity /tɒk'sɪsɪtɪ/ *n* tossicità *f*

toxicologist /tɒksɪ'kɒlədʒɪst/ *n* tossicologo, -a *mf*

toxicology /tɒksɪ'kɒlədʒɪ/ *n* tossicologia *f*

toxic waste *n* rifiuti *mpl* tossici

toxin /'tɒksɪn/ *n* tossina *f*

toy /tɔɪ/ *n* giocattolo *m*
- ■ **toy with** *vt* giocherellare con

toyboy /'tɔɪbɔɪ/ *n* Br fam uomo-oggetto *m*

toyshop /'tɔɪʃɒp/ *n* negozio *m* di giocattoli

trace /treɪs/ **①** *n* traccia *f*
② *vt* seguire le tracce di; (find) rintracciare; (draw) tracciare; (with tracing-paper) ricalcare
- ■ **trace back** *vt* trovare tracce di ⟨*family*⟩
- ■ **trace out** *vt* tracciare

tracer /'treɪsə(r)/ *n* Mil proiettile *m* tracciante

tracing /'treɪsɪŋ/ *n* ricalco *m*

tracing-paper *n* carta *f* da ricalco

track /træk/ **①** *n* traccia *f*; (path, Sport) pista *f*; Rail binario *m*; **keep ~ of** tenere d'occhio
② *vt* seguire le tracce di
- ■ **track down** *vt* scovare

trackball, tracker ball *n* Comput trackball *f inv*

tracker /'trækə(r)/ *n* (dog) segugio *m*

track record *n* fig background *m inv*

tracksuit /'træksu:t/ *n* tuta *f* da ginnastica

tract /trækt/ *n* (pamphlet) opuscolo *m*

tractable /'træktəbl/ *adj* trattabile; (docile) maneggevole

traction /'trækʃn/ *n* (of wheel) trazione *f*

traction engine *n* trattore *m*

tractor /'træktə(r)/ *n* trattore *m*

trade /treɪd/ **①** *n* commercio *m*; (line of business) settore *m*; (craft) mestiere *m*; **by ~** di mestiere
② *vt* commerciare; **~ something for something** scambiare qualcosa per qualcosa
③ *vi* commerciare
- ■ **trade in** *vt* (give in part exchange) dare in pagamento parziale
- ■ **trade off** *vt* scambiare
- ■ **trade on** *vt* approfittarsi di

trade deficit *n* bilancio *m* commerciale in deficit

trade discount *n* sconto *m* commerciale

trade fair *n* fiera *f* commerciale

trade-in *n* permuta *f* come pagamento parziale

trade mark *n* marchio *m* di fabbrica

trade-name *n* nome *m* despositato

trade-off *n* compromesso *m*

trade price *n* prezzo *m* all'ingrosso

trader /'treɪdə(r)/ *n* commerciante *mf*

trade secret *n* segreto *m* commerciale

tradesman /'treɪdzmən/ *n* (joiner etc) operaio *m*

tradesman's entrance *n* entrata *f* di servizio

Trades Union Congress *n* confederazione *f* dei sindacati britannici

trade union *n* sindacato *m*

trade unionist *n* sindacalista *mf*

trade union representative *n* rappresentante *mf* sindacale

trading /'treɪdɪŋ/ *n* commercio *m*

trading estate *n* zona *f* industriale

trading floor *n* Fin sala *f* delle contrattazioni

trading stamp *n* bollino *m* premio

tradition /trə'dɪʃŋ/ *n* tradizione *f*

traditional /trə'dɪʃnl/ *adj* tradizionale

traditionalist /trə'dɪʃn(ə)lɪst/ *n* tradizionalista *mf*

traditionally /trə'dɪʃn(ə)lɪ/ *adv* tradizionalmente

traffic /'træfɪk/ **①** *n* traffico *m*
② *vi* trafficare

traffic calming *n* misure *fpl* per rallentare la circolazione

traffic calming measures *npl* misure *fpl* per rallentare il traffico in città

traffic circle *n* Am isola *f* rotatoria

traffic cone *n* birillo *m*

traffic island *n* isola *f* spartitraffico

traffic jam *n* ingorgo *m*

trafficker /'træfɪkə(r)/ *n* trafficante *mf*

traffic lights *npl* semaforo *msg*

traffic offence *n* infrazione *f* al codice della strada

traffic warden *n* vigile *m* [urbano]; (woman) vigilessa *f*

tragedy /'trædʒədɪ/ *n* tragedia *f*

tragic /'trædʒɪk/ *adj* tragico

tragically /'trædʒɪklɪ/ *adv* tragicamente

trail /treɪl/ **①** *n* traccia *f*; (path) sentiero *m*
② *vi* strisciare; ⟨*plant*⟩ arrampicarsi; **~ [behind]** rimanere indietro; (in competition) essere in svantaggio
③ *vt* trascinare

trail bike *n* moto *f* fuoristrada

trailblazer /'treɪlbleɪzə(r)/ *n* pioniere, -a *mf*

trailblazing /'treɪlbleɪzɪŋ/ *adj* innovatore

trailer /'treɪlə(r)/ n Auto rimorchio m; (Am: caravan) roulotte f inv; (film) presentazione f (di un film)

trailer park n Am area f di sosta per roulotte

train /treɪn/ ① n treno m; (of dress) strascico m; by ~ in treno; ~ of thought filo m dei pensieri
② vt formare professionalmente; Sport allenare; (aim) puntare; educare ‹child›; addestrare ‹animal, soldier›; far crescere ‹plant›
③ vi fare il tirocinio; Sport allenarsi

trained /treɪnd/ adj ‹animal› addestrato (to do a fare)

trainee /treɪ'niː/ n apprendista mf

trainer /'treɪnə(r)/ n Sport allenatore, -trice mf; (in circus) domatore, -trice mf; (of dog, race-horse) addestratore, -trice mf; ~s (pl: shoes) scarpe fpl da ginnastica

training /'treɪnɪŋ/ n tirocinio m; Sport allenamento m; (of animal, soldier) addestramento m

training college n istituto m professionale

training course n corso m di formazione

train set n trenino m

train spotter /spɒtə(r)/ n appassionato, -a mf di treni

traipse /treɪps/ vi ~ around fam andare in giro

trait /treɪt/ n caratteristica f

traitor /'treɪtə(r)/ n traditore, -trice mf

trajectory /trə'dʒekt(ə)rɪ/ n traiettoria f

tram /træm/ n tram m inv

tram-lines npl rotaie fpl del tram

tramp /træmp/ ① n (hike) camminata f; (vagrant) barbone, -a mf; (of feet) calpestio m
② vi camminare con passo pesante; (hike) percorrere a piedi

trample /'træmpl/ v
■ **trample on** vt calpestare

trampoline /'træmpəliːn/ n trampolino m

trance /trɑːns/ n trance f inv

tranquil /'træŋkwɪl/ adj tranquillo

tranquillity /træŋ'kwɪlətɪ/ n tranquillità f

tranquillizer /'træŋkwɪlaɪzə(r)/ n tranquillante m

transact /træn'zækt/ vt trattare

transaction /træn'zækʃn/ n transazione f

transatlantic /trænzət'læntɪk/ adj ‹crossing, flight› transatlantico; ‹attitude, accent› americano

transceiver /træn'siːvə(r)/ n ricetrasmittente f

transcend /træn'send/ vt trascendere

transcontinental /trænzkɒntɪ'nent(ə)l/ adj transcontinentale

transcribe /træn'skraɪb/ vt trascrivere

transcript /'trænskrɪpt/ n trascrizione f

transcription /træn'skrɪpʃn/ n trascrizione f

transept /'trænsept/ n transetto m

transfer¹ /'trænsfɜː(r)/ n trasferimento m; Sport cessione f; (design) decalcomania f

transfer² /træns'fɜː(r)/ ① vt (pt/pp **transferred**) trasferire; Sport cedere; Comput trasferire
② vi trasferirsi; (when travelling) cambiare

transferable /træns'fɜːrəbl/ adj trasferibile

transfer fee n (for footballer) prezzo m d'acquisto

transfer list n (in football) lista f di giocatori da cedere

transferred charge call /træns'fɜːd/ n chiamata f a carico del destinatario

transfigure /træns'fɪgə(r)/ vt trasfigurare

transfix /træns'fɪks/ vt trafiggere; fig immobilizzare

transfixed /træns'fɪkst/ adj (with fascination) folgorato; (with horror) paralizzato

transform /træns'fɔːm/ vt trasformare

transformation /trænsfə'meɪʃn/ n trasformazione f

transformer /træns'fɔːmə(r)/ n trasformatore m

transfusion /træns'fjuːʒn/ n trasfusione f

transgression /træns'greʃn/ n Jur trasgressione f; Relig peccato m

transient /'trænzɪənt/ adj passeggero

transistor /træn'zɪstə(r)/ n transistor m inv; (radio) radiolina f a transistor

transit /'trænzɪt/ n transito m; in ~ (goods) in transito

transition /træn'zɪʃn/ n transizione f

transitional /træn'zɪʃənl/ adj di transizione

transitive /'trænzɪtɪv/ adj transitivo

transitively /'trænzɪtɪvlɪ/ adv transitivamente

transit lounge n sala f d'attesa transiti

transitory /'trænzɪtərɪ/ adj transitorio

transit passenger n passeggero m in transito

translate /trænz'leɪt/ vt tradurre

translation /trænz'leɪʃn/ n traduzione f

translation agency n agenzia f di traduzioni

translator /trænz'leɪtə(r)/ n traduttore, -trice mf

translucent /trænz'luːsnt/ adj liter traslucido

t

transmissible /trænz'mɪsəbl/ adj
trasmissibile

transmission /trænz'mɪʃn/ n
trasmissione f

transmit /trænz'mɪt/ vt (pt/pp
transmitted) trasmettere

transmitter /trænz'mɪtə(r)/ n
trasmettitore m

transparency /træn'spærənsɪ/ n Phot
diapositiva f

transparent /træn'spærənt/ adj
trasparente

transpire /træn'spaɪə(r)/ vi emergere;
(fam: happen) accadere

transplant¹ /'trænsplɑːnt/ n trapianto
m

transplant² /træns'plɑːnt/ vt
trapiantare

transport¹ /'trænspɔːt/ n trasporto m;
do you have ~? hai un mezzo di
trasporto?

transport² /træn'spɔːt/ vt trasportare

transportation /trænspɔː'teɪʃn/ n
trasporto m

transpose /træns'pəʊz/ vt trasporre

transsexual /trænz'seksʃʊəl/ ① n
transessuale mf
② adj transessuale

trans-shipment /trænz'ʃɪpmənt/ n
trasbordo m

transverse /trænz'vɜːs/ adj trasversale

transvestite /trænz'vestaɪt/ n
travestito, -a mf

trap /træp/ ① n trappola f; (fam: mouth)
boccaccia f; (carriage) calesse m
② vt (pt/pp **trapped**) intrappolare;
schiacciare ‹finger in door›; be ~ped
essere intrappolato

trapdoor /'træpdɔː(r)/ n botola f

trapeze /trə'piːz/ n trapezio m

trappings /'træpɪŋz/ npl (dress)
ornamenti mpl; the ~ of wealth/success i
segni esteriori della ricchezza/del
successo

traschcan /'træʃkæn/ n Am pattumiera
f, secchio m della spazzatura

trash /træʃ/ n robaccia f; (rubbish)
spazzatura f; (nonsense) schiocchezze fpl

trashy /'træʃɪ/ adj scadente

trauma /'trɔːmə/ n trauma m

traumatic /trɔː'mætɪk/ adj traumatico

traumatize /'trɔːmətaɪz/ vt
traumatizzare

travel /'trævl/ ① n viaggi mpl
② vi (pt/pp **travelled**) viaggiare; ‹to
work› andare
③ vt percorrere ‹distance›

travel agency n agenzia f di viaggi

travel agent n agente mf di viaggio

travel card n tessera f dei trasporti
pubblici

travel expenses npl spese fpl di
viaggio

traveller /'trævələ(r)/ n viaggiatore,
-trice mf; Comm commesso m viaggiatore;
~s pl (gypsies) zingari mpl

traveller's cheque n traveller's
cheque m inv

travelling /'trævəlɪŋ/ Br, **traveling** Am
adj ‹circus, theatre company› itinerante;
‹companion, conditions, expenses,
allowance› di viaggio

travelling salesman n commesso m
viaggiatore

travel news n informazioni fpl sulla
viabilità

travelogue /'trævəlɒg/ n (film)
documentario m di viaggio; (talk)
conferenza f su un viaggio

travel-sick adj be/get ~ (on plane)
soffrire il mal d'aria; (in car) soffrire il mal
d'auto; (on boat) soffrire il mal di mare

travel-sickness ① n (on plane) mal m
d'aria; (in car) mal m d'auto; (on boat) mal
m di mare
② attrib ‹pills› per il mal d'aria/d'auto/di
mare

traverse /trə'vɜːs/ vt traversare

travesty /'trævɪstɪ/ n (fig: farce) farsa f; a
~ of justice una presa in giro della
giustizia

trawler /'trɔːlə(r)/ n peschereccio m

tray /treɪ/ n vassoio m; (for baking) teglia f;
(for documents) vaschetta f; (of printer,
photocopier) vassoio m, cassetto m

treacherous /'tretʃərəs/ adj traditore;
‹weather, currents› pericoloso

treachery /'tretʃ(ə)rɪ/ n tradimento m

treacle /'triːkl/ n melassa f

tread /tred/ ① n andatura f; (step)
gradino m; (of tyre) battistrada m inv
② vi (pt **trod**, pp **trodden**) (walk)
camminare
■ **tread on** vt calpestare ‹grass›; pestare
‹foot›

treadmill /'tredmɪl/ n fig solito tran tran
m

treason /'triːzn/ n tradimento m

treasonable /'triːz(ə)nəbl/ adj
proditorio

treasure /'treʒə(r)/ ① n tesoro m
② vt tenere in gran conto

treasurer /'treʒərə(r)/ n tesoriere, -a mf

treasury /'treʒərɪ/ n the T~ il Ministero
del Tesoro

treat /triːt/ ① n piacere m; (present)
regalo m; give somebody a ~ fare una
sorpresa a qualcuno
② vt trattare; Med curare; ~ somebody to
something offrire qualcosa a qualcuno; ~

somebody for something Med sottoporre qualcuno ad una cura per qualcosa

treatise /'tri:tɪz/ n trattato m

treatment /'tri:tmənt/ n trattamento m; Med cura f

treaty /'tri:tɪ/ n trattato m

treble /'trebl/ ① adj triplo; ∼ **the amount** il triplo
② n Mus (voice) voce f bianca
③ vt triplicare
④ vi triplicarsi

treble clef n chiave f di violino

tree /tri:/ n albero m

tree house n capanna f su un albero

tree stump n ceppo m

treetop n cima f di un albero

tree trunk n tronco m d'albero

trek /trek/ ① n scarpinata f; (as holiday) trekking m inv
② vi (pt/pp **trekked**) farsi una scarpinata; (on holiday) fare trekking

trekking /'trekɪŋ/ n trekking m

trellis /'trelɪs/ n graticolato m

tremble /'trembl/ vi tremare **(with** di)

trembling /'tremblɪŋ/ adj tremante

tremendous /trɪ'mendəs/ adj (huge) enorme; (fam: excellent) formidabile

tremendously /trɪ'mendəslɪ/ adv (very) straordinariamente; (a lot) enormemente

tremor /'tremə(r)/ n tremito m; **[earth]** ∼ scossa f [sismica]

tremulous /'tremjʊləs/ adj tremulo

trench /trentʃ/ n fosso m; Mil trincea f

trenchant /'trentʃənt/ adj ⟨comment, criticism⟩ mordace

trench coat n trench m inv

trend /trend/ n tendenza f; (fashion) moda f

trend-setter n persona f che detta la moda

trend-setting adj che detta la moda

trendy /'trendɪ/ adj (**-ier, -iest**) fam di o alla moda

trepidation /trepɪ'deɪʃn/ n trepidazione f

trespass /'trespəs/ vi ∼ **on** introdursi abusivamente in; fig abusare di

trespasser /'trespəsə(r)/ n intruso, -a mf

trestle /'tresl/ n cavalletto m

trestle table n tavolo m a cavalletto

trial /'traɪəl/ n Jur processo m; (test, ordeal) prova f; **on** ∼ in prova; Jur in giudizio; **by** ∼ **and error** per tentativi

trial period n periodo m di prova

trial run n (preliminary test) prova f

triangle /'traɪæŋgl/ n triangolo m

triangular /traɪ'æŋgjʊlə(r)/ adj triangolare

tribal /'traɪbl/ adj tribale

tribe /traɪb/ n tribù f inv

tribulation /trɪbjʊ'leɪʃn/ n tribolazione f

tribunal /traɪ'bju:nl/ n tribunale m

tributary /'trɪbjʊtərɪ/ n affluente m

tribute /'trɪbju:t/ n tributo m; **pay** ∼ rendere omaggio

trice /traɪs/ n **in a** ∼ in un attimo

tricentenary /traɪsen'ti:nərɪ/ ① n terzo centenario m
② adj del terzo centenario

trick /trɪk/ ① n trucco m; (joke) scherzo m; (Cards) presa f; **do the** ∼ fam funzionare; **play a** ∼ **on** fare uno scherzo a
② vt imbrogliare; ∼ **of the trade** trucco m del mestiere
■ **trick into** vt ∼ **somebody into doing something** convincere qualcuno a fare qualcosa con l'inganno
■ **trick out** vt ∼ **somebody out of something** fregare qualcuno a qualcosa

trick cyclist n (sl: psychiatrist) psichiatra mf

trickle /'trɪkl/ vi colare
■ **trickle away** vi ⟨water⟩ uscire lentamente; ⟨people⟩ allontanarsi lentamente
■ **trickle in** vi fig entrare poco per volta
■ **trickle out** vi fig uscire poco per volta

trick question n domanda f trabocchetto inv

trickster /'trɪkstə(r)/ n imbroglione, -a mf

tricky /'trɪkɪ/ adj (**-ier, -iest**) adj ⟨operation⟩ complesso; ⟨situation⟩ delicato

tricolour /'trɪkələ(r)/ n tricolore m

tricycle /'traɪsɪkl/ n triciclo m

tried /traɪd/ ▶ TRY

tried and tested adj ⟨method⟩ sperimentato

trifle /'traɪfl/ n inezia f; Culin zuppa f inglese

trifling /'traɪflɪŋ/ adj insignificante

trig /trɪg/ n (fam: trigonometry) trigonometria f

trigger /'trɪgə(r)/ ① n grilletto m; fig causa f
② vt ∼ **[off]** scatenare

trigger-happy adj fam dalla pistola facile; fig impulsivo

trigonometry /trɪgə'nɒmɪtrɪ/ n trigonometria f

trilateral /traɪ'lætərəl/ adj trilaterale

trilby /'trɪlbɪ/ n cappello m di feltro

trill /trɪl/ n Mus trillo m

trilogy /'trɪlədʒɪ/ n trilogia f

trim /trɪm/ ① adj (**trimmer, trimmest**) curato; ⟨figure⟩ snello

2 *n* (of hair, hedge) spuntata *f*; (decoration) rifinitura *f*; **in good ~** in buono stato; ‹*person*› in forma
3 *vt* (pt/pp **trimmed**) spuntare ‹*hair etc*›; (decorate) ornare; Naut orientare
■ **trim off** *vt* tagliare via

trimming /ˈtrɪmɪŋ/ *n* bordo *m*; **~s** *pl* (of pastry) ritagli *mpl*; (decorations) guarnizioni *fpl*; **with all the ~s** Culin guarnito

Trinidad and Tobago /ˈtrɪnɪdæd, təˈbeɪɡəʊ/ *n* Trinidad e Tobago *m*

Trinity /ˈtrɪnɪtɪ/ *n* **the [Holy] ~** la [Santissima] Trinità

trinket /ˈtrɪŋkɪt/ *n* ninnolo *m*

trio /ˈtriːəʊ/ *n* trio *m*

trip /trɪp/ **1** *n* (excursion) gita *f*; (journey) viaggio *m*; (stumble) passo *m* falso
2 *vt* (pt/pp **tripped**) far inciampare
3 *vi* inciampare (**on/over** in)
■ **trip up** *vt* far inciampare

tripartite /traɪˈpɑːtaɪt/ *adj* tripartito

tripe /traɪp/ *n* trippa *f*; (sl: nonsense) fesserie *fpl*

triple /ˈtrɪpl/ **1** *adj* triplo
2 *vt* triplicare
3 *vi* triplicarsi

triplets /ˈtrɪplɪts/ *npl* tre gemelli *mpl*

triplicate /ˈtrɪplɪkət/ *n* **in ~** in triplice copia

tripod /ˈtraɪpɒd/ *n* treppiede *m inv*

tripper /ˈtrɪpə(r)/ *n* gitante *mf*

trite /traɪt/ *adj* banale

triteness /ˈtraɪtnɪs/ *n* banalità *f*

triumph /ˈtraɪʌmf/ **1** *n* trionfo *m*
2 *vi* trionfare (**over** su)

triumphant /traɪˈʌmf(ə)nt/ *adj* trionfante

triumphantly /traɪˈʌmf(ə)ntlɪ/ *adv* ‹*exclaim*› con tono trionfante

triumvirate /traɪˈʌmvɪrət/ *n* triumvirato *m*

trivia /ˈtrɪvɪə/ *npl* cose *fpl* secondarie

trivial /ˈtrɪvɪəl/ *adj* insignificante

triviality /trɪvɪˈælɪtɪ/ *n* banalità *f inv*

trivialize /ˈtrɪvɪəlaɪz/ *vt* sminuire

trod, **trodden** /trɒd/, /ˈtrɒdn/ ▶ TREAD

trolley /ˈtrɒlɪ/ *n* carrello *m*; (Am: tram) tram *m inv*

trolley bus *n* filobus *m inv*

trombone /trɒmˈbəʊn/ *n* trombone *m*

trombonist /trɒmˈbəʊnɪst/ *n* trombonista *mf*

troop /truːp/ **1** *n* gruppo *m*; **~s** *pl* truppe *fpl*
2 *vi* **~ in/out** entrare/uscire in gruppo

trooper /ˈtruːpə(r)/ *n* Mil soldato *m* di cavalleria; (Am: policeman) poliziotto *m*

trophy /ˈtrəʊfɪ/ *n* trofeo *m*

tropic /ˈtrɒpɪk/ *n* tropico *m*; **~s** *pl* tropici *mpl*

tropical /ˈtrɒpɪkl/ *adj* tropicale

tropical fruit *n* frutta *f inv* esotica

trot /trɒt/ **1** *n* trotto *m*
2 *vi* (pt/pp **trotted**) trottare
■ **trot out** *vt* (fam: produce) tirar fuori

trotter /ˈtrɒtə(r)/ *n* Culin piedino *m* di maiale

trouble /ˈtrʌbl/ **1** *n* guaio *m*; (difficulties) problemi *mpl*; (inconvenience, Med) disturbo *m*; (conflict) conflitto *m*; **be in ~** essere nei guai; ‹*swimmer, climber*› essere in difficoltà; **get into ~** finire nei guai; **get somebody into ~** mettere qualcuno nei guai; **take the ~ to do something** darsi la pena di far qualcosa; **it's no ~** nessun disturbo; **the ~ with you is...** il tuo problema è...
2 *vt* (worry) preoccupare; (inconvenience) disturbare; ‹*conscience, old wound*› tormentare
3 *vi* **don't ~!** non ti disturbare!

troubled /ˈtrʌbld/ *adj* ‹*mind*› inquieto; ‹*person, expression*› preoccupato; ‹*times, area*› difficile; ‹*waters, sleep*› agitato

troublefree *adj* senza problemi

troublemaker /ˈtrʌblmeɪkə(r)/ *n* **be a ~** seminare zizzania

troubleshooter *n* rilevatore e risolutore *m* di problemi

troublesome /ˈtrʌblsəm/ *adj* fastidioso

trouble spot *n* zona *f* calda

trough /trɒf/ *n* trogolo *m*; (atmospheric) depressione *f*

trounce /traʊns/ *vt* (in competition) schiacciare

troupe /truːp/ *n* troupe *f inv*

trouser press *n* stiracalzoni *m inv*

trousers /ˈtraʊzəz/ *npl* pantaloni *mpl*

trouser suit *n* tailleur *m inv* pantalone

trousseau /ˈtruːsəʊ/ *n* corredo *m*

trout /traʊt/ *n inv* trota *f*

trowel /ˈtraʊəl/ *n* (for gardening) paletta *f*; (for builder) cazzuola *f*

truancy /ˈtruːənsɪ/ *n* assenze *fpl* ingiustificate

truant /ˈtruːənt/ *n* **play ~** marinare la scuola

truce /truːs/ *n* tregua *f*

truck /trʌk/ *n* (lorry) camion *m inv*

truck driver *n* camionista *mf*

trucker /ˈtrʌkə(r)/ *n* (fam: lorry driver) camionista *mf*

truck farmer *n* Am ortofrutticoltore *m*, ortolano *m*

truculent /ˈtrʌkjʊlənt/ *adj* aggressivo

truculently /ˈtrʌkjʊləntlɪ/ *adv* aggressivamente

trudge /trʌdʒ/ **1** *n* camminata *f* faticosa
2 *vi* arrancare

true /truː/ *adj* vero; **come ~** avverarsi

true-life adj ⟨adventure, story⟩ vero

truffle /'trʌfl/ n tartufo m

truism /'truːɪzm/ n truismo m

truly /'truːlɪ/ adv veramente; **Yours** ∼ Distinti saluti

trump /trʌmp/ ① n (Cards) atout m inv ② vt prendere con l'atout
■ **trump up** vt fam inventare

trump card n fig asso m nella manica

trumped-up /'trʌmptʌp/ adj ⟨charges⟩ inventato

trumpet /'trʌmpɪt/ n tromba f

trumpeter /'trʌmpɪtə(r)/ n trombettista mf

truncate /trʌŋkeɪt/ vt tagliare ⟨text⟩; interrompere ⟨process, journey, event⟩

truncheon /'trʌntʃn/ n manganello m

trundle /'trʌndl/ ① vt far rotolare ② vi rotolare

trunk /trʌŋk/ n (of tree, body) tronco m; (of elephant) proboscide f; (for travelling, storage) baule m; (Am: of car) bagagliaio m, portabagagli m inv

trunk road n statale f

trunks /trʌŋks/ npl calzoncini mpl da bagno

truss /trʌs/ n Med cinto m erniario
■ **truss up** vt legare

trust /trʌst/ ① n fiducia f; (group of companies) trust m inv; (organization) associazione f; **on** ∼ sulla parola ② vt fidarsi di; (hope) augurarsi ③ vi ∼ **in** credere in; ∼ **to** affidarsi a

trust company n società f fiduciaria

trusted /'trʌstɪd/ adj fidato

trustee /trʌs'tiː/ n amministratore, -trice mf fiduciario, -a

trustful /'trʌstfʊl/ adj fiducioso

trustfully /'trʌstfʊlɪ/ adv fiduciosamente

trust fund n fondo m fiduciario

trusting /'trʌstɪŋ/ adj fiducioso

trustworthiness /'trʌstwɜːðɪnɪs/ n (of person) affidabilità f; (of source) attendibilità f

trustworthy /'trʌstwɜːðɪ/ adj fidato

trusty /'trʌstɪ/ adj fam fidato

truth /truːθ/ n (pl **-s** /truːðz/) verità f inv

truthful /'truːθfʊl/ adj ⟨person⟩ sincero; ⟨statement⟩ veritiero

truthfully /'truːθfʊlɪ/ adv sinceramente

truthfulness /'truːθfʊlnɪs/ n (of person) sincerità f; (of account) veridicità f

try /traɪ/ ① n tentativo m, prova f; (in rugby) meta f; **I'll give it a** ∼ faccio un tentativo
② vt (pt/pp **tried**) provare; (be a strain on) mettere a dura prova; Jur processare ⟨person⟩; discutere ⟨case⟩; ∼ **to do something** provare a fare qualcosa
③ vi provare

■ **try for** vi cercare di ottenere
■ **try on** vt provarsi ⟨garment⟩
■ **try out** vt provare

trying /'traɪɪŋ/ adj duro; ⟨person⟩ irritante

try-out n **give somebody a** ∼ mettere alla prova qualcuno

tsar /zɑː(r)/ n zar m inv

tsarina /tsɑː'riːnə/ n zarina f

tsarist /'tsɑːrɪst/ adj zarista

T-shirt n maglietta f

tsp abbr **teaspoonful**

tub /tʌb/ n tinozza f; (carton) vaschetta f; (bath) vasca f da bagno

tuba /'tjuːbə/ n Mus tuba f

tubby /'tʌbɪ/ adj (**-ier**, **-iest**) tozzo

tube /tjuːb/ n tubo m; (of toothpaste) tubetto m; Br Rail metro f

tuber /'tjuːbə(r)/ n tubero m

tuberculosis /tjuːbɜːkjʊ'ləʊsɪs/ n tubercolosi f

tubing /'tjuːbɪŋ/ n tubi mpl

tubular /'tjuːbjʊlə(r)/ adj tubolare

TUC n abbr Br (**Trades Union Congress**) confederazione f dei sindacati britannici

tuck /tʌk/ ① n piega f ② vt (put) infilare
■ **tuck away** vt (put in a safe place) mettere al sicuro; (eat) spolverare
■ **tuck in** ① vt rimboccare; ∼ **somebody in** rimboccare le coperte a qualcuno ② vi (fam: eat) mangiare con appetito
■ **tuck into** vt mangiare di gusto ⟨meal⟩; ∼ **something into one's pocket** infilarsi in tasca qualcosa; ∼ **somebody into bed** rimboccare le coperte a qualcuno
■ **tuck up** vt rimboccarsi ⟨sleeves⟩; (in bed) rimboccare le coperte a

Tuesday /'tjuːzdeɪ/ n martedì m inv

tuft /tʌft/ n ciuffo m

tug /tʌg/ ① n strattone m; Naut rimorchiatore m ② vt (pt/pp **tugged**) tirare ③ vi dare uno strattone

tug-of-love n disputa f tra i genitori per l'affidamento dei figli

tug of war n tiro m alla fune

tuition /tjuː'ɪʃn/ n lezioni fpl

tuition fees npl tasse fpl universitarie

tulip /'tjuːlɪp/ n tulipano m

tumble /'tʌmbl/ ① n ruzzolone m ② vi ruzzolare; ∼ **to something** (fam: realize) afferrare qualcosa
■ **tumble down** vi ⟨wall, building⟩ crollare

tumbledown /'tʌmbəldaʊn/ adj cadente

tumble-dry vt asciugare nell'asciugabiancheria

tumble-dryer, **tumble-drier** n asciugabiancheria m

tumbler /'tʌmblə(r)/ n bicchiere m (senza stelo)

tummy /'tʌmɪ/ n fam pancia f

tummy button n fam ombelico m

tumour /'tjuːmə(r)/ n tumore m

tumult /'tjuːmʌlt/ n tumulto m

tumultuous /tjuːˈmʌltjʊəs/ adj tumultuoso

tuna /'tjuːnə/ n tonno m

tune /tjuːn/ ❶ n motivo m; out of/in ~ ⟨instrument⟩ scordato/accordato; ⟨person⟩ stonato/intonato; to the ~ of fam per la modesta somma di
❷ vt accordare ⟨instrument⟩; sintonizzare ⟨radio, TV⟩; mettere a punto ⟨engine⟩
■ **tune in** ❶ vt sintonizzare
❷ vi sintonizzarsi (**to** su)
■ **tune up** vi ⟨orchestra⟩ accordare gli strumenti

tuneful /'tjuːnfl/ adj melodioso

tuner /'tjuːnə(r)/ n accordatore, -trice mf; Radio, TV sintonizzatore m

tune-up n (of engine) messa f a punto

tungsten /'tʌŋstən/ n tungsteno m

tunic /'tjuːnɪk/ n tunica f; Mil giacca f; Sch ≈ grembiule m

tuning-fork /'tjuːnɪŋ/ n diapason m inv

Tunisia /tjuːˈnɪzɪə/ n Tunisia f

Tunisian /tjuːˈnɪzɪən/ adj & n tunisino, -a mf

tunnel /'tʌnl/ ❶ n tunnel m inv
❷ vi (pt/pp **tunnelled**) scavare un tunnel

tunnel vision n Med restringimento m del campo visivo; fig paraocchi m inv

tuppence /'tʌpəns/ n due penny m

turban /'tɜːbən/ n turbante m

turbine /'tɜːbaɪn/ n turbina f

turbo /'tɜːbəʊ/ n turbo m inv

turbocharged /'tɜːbəʊtʃɑːdʒd/ adj con motore turbo

turbocharger /'tɜːbəʊtʃɑːdʒə(r)/ n turbocompressore m

turbot /'tɜːbət/ n rombo m gigante

turbulence /'tɜːbjʊləns/ n turbolenza f

turbulent /'tɜːbjʊlənt/ adj turbolento

turd /tɜːd/ n sl (excrement) stronzo m; (pej: person) stronzo, -a mf

tureen /tjʊˈriːn/ n zuppiera f

turf /tɜːf/ n erba f; (segment) zolla f erbosa
■ **turf out** vt fam buttar fuori

turf accountant n allibratore m

turgid /'tɜːdʒɪd/ adj ⟨style, water⟩ turgido

Turin /tjʊˈrɪn/ n Torino m

Turk /tɜːk/ n turco, -a mf

Turkey /'tɜːkɪ/ n Turchia f

turkey n tacchino m

Turkish /'tɜːkɪʃ/ adj turco

Turkish bath n bagno m turco

Turkish delight n cubetti mpl di gelatina ricoperti di zucchero a velo

Turkmenistan /tɜːkmenɪˈstɑːn/ n Turkmenistan m

turmeric /'tɜːmərɪk/ n (spice) curcumina f; (plant) curcuma f

turmoil /'tɜːmɔɪl/ n tumulto m

turn /tɜːn/ ❶ n (rotation, short walk) giro m; (in road) svolta f, curva f; (development) svolta f; Theat numero m; (fam: attack) crisi f inv; **a ~ for the better/worse** un miglioramento/peggioramento m; **do somebody a good ~** rendere un servizio a qualcuno; **take ~s** fare a turno; **in ~** a turno; **out of ~** ⟨speak⟩ a sproposito; **It's your ~** tocca a te
❷ vt girare; voltare ⟨back, eyes⟩; dirigere ⟨gun, attention⟩
❸ vi girare; ⟨person⟩ girarsi; ⟨leaves⟩ ingiallire; (become) diventare; ~ **right/left** girare a destra/sinistra; ~ **sour** inacidirsi; ~ **to somebody** girarsi verso qualcuno; fig rivolgersi a qualcuno
■ **turn against** ❶ vi diventare ostile a
❷ vt mettere contro
■ **turn around** ❶ vi ⟨person⟩ girarsi; ⟨car⟩ girare
❷ vt girare ⟨object⟩; risollevare ⟨company⟩
■ **turn away** ❶ vt mandare via ⟨people⟩; girare dall'altra parte ⟨head⟩
❷ vi girarsi dall'altra parte
■ **turn back** ❶ vi tornare indietro
❷ vt mandare indietro ⟨people⟩; ripiegare ⟨covers, sheet etc⟩
■ **turn down** vt piegare ⟨collar⟩; abbassare ⟨heat, gas, sound⟩; respingere ⟨person, proposal⟩
■ **turn in** ❶ vt ripiegare in dentro ⟨edges⟩; consegnare ⟨lost object⟩
❷ vi (fam: go to bed) andare a letto; ~ **in to the drive** entrare nel viale
■ **turn into** vt (become) diventare
■ **turn off** ❶ vt spegnere; chiudere ⟨tap, water⟩; ~ **somebody off** (fam: disgust) fare schifo a qualcuno
❷ vi ⟨car⟩ girare
■ **turn on** ❶ vt accendere; aprire ⟨tap, water⟩; (fam: attract) eccitare
❷ vi (attack) attaccare
■ **turn out** ❶ vt (expel) mandar via; spegnere ⟨light, gas⟩; (produce) produrre; (empty) svuotare ⟨room, cupboard⟩
❷ vi (transpire) risultare; (to see, do something) venire; ~ **out well/badly** ⟨cake, dress⟩ riuscire bene/male; ⟨situation⟩ andare bene/male
■ **turn over** ❶ vt girare; ~ **somebody over to the police** consegnare qualcuno alla polizia; **he ~ed the business over to her** le ha ceduto l'azienda
❷ vi girarsi; **please ~ over** vedi retro
■ **turn round** vi girarsi; ⟨car⟩ girare
■ **turn up** ❶ vt tirare su ⟨collar⟩; alzare ⟨heat, gas, sound, radio⟩
❷ vi farsi vedere

turn-about *n* (fig: change of direction) cambiamento *m*

turnaround *n* (in attitude) dietrofront *m inv*; (of fortune) capovolgimento *m*; (for the better) ripresa *f*

turncoat *n* voltagabbana *mf inv*

turning /'tɜːnɪŋ/ *n* svolta *f*

turning-point *n* svolta *f* decisiva

turnip /'tɜːnɪp/ *n* rapa *f*

turn-off *n* strada *f* laterale; **it's a real ∼** fam ti fa davvero passar la voglia

turn of mind *n* indole *f*

turn of phrase *n* espressione *f*

turn-on *n* fam **be a real ∼** essere veramente eccitante

turnout *n* (of people) affluenza *f*

turnover *n* Comm giro *m* d'affari, fatturato *m*; (of staff) ricambio *m*

turnpike *n* Am autostrada *f*

turnround *n* (in policy etc) cambiamento *m*

turnstile *n* cancelletto *m* girevole

turntable *n* piattaforma *f* girevole; (on record-player) piatto *m*

turn-up *n* (of trousers) risvolto *m*

turpentine /'tɜːpəntaɪn/ *n* trementina *f*

turquoise /'tɜːkwɔɪz/ ① *adj* (colour) turchese
② *n* turchese *m*

turret /'tʌrɪt/ *n* torretta *f*

turtle /'tɜːtl/ *n* tartaruga *f* acquatica

turtle-dove *n* tortora *f*

turtleneck /'tɜːtlnek/ *n* collo *m* a lupetto; (sweater) maglia *f* a lupetto

Tuscan /'tʌskən/ *adj* toscano

Tuscany /'tʌskənɪ/ *n* Toscana *f*

tusk /tʌsk/ *n* zanna *f*

tussle /'tʌsl/ ① *n* zuffa *f*
② *vi* azzuffarsi

tussock /'tʌsək/ *n* ciuffo *m* d'erba

tut /tʌt/ ① *vi* fare un'esclamazione di disapprovazione
② *int* ts!

tutor /'tjuːtə(r)/ *n* insegnante *mf* privato, -a; Univ insegnante *mf* universitario, -a che segue individualmente un ristretto numero di studenti

tutorial /tjuː'tɔːrɪəl/ *n* discussione *f* col tutor

tutorial package *n* Comput software *m* di autoapprendimento

tuxedo /tʌk'siːdəʊ/ *n* Am smoking *m inv*

TV *abbr* (**television**) tv *f inv*, tivù *f inv*

TV dinner *n* pasto *m* pronto

twaddle /'twɒdl/ *n* scemenze *fpl*

twain /tweɪn/ *npl* **the ∼** i due; **and never the ∼ shall meet** e mai i due si incontreranno

twang /twæŋ/ ① *n* (in voice) suono *m* nasale
② *vt* far vibrare

tweak /twiːk/ ① *vt* tirare ⟨ear, nose⟩; (adjust) apportare delle modifiche a
② *n* (adjustment) modifica *f*; **give sb's ears a ∼** dare una tirata d'orecchie a qualcuno

twee /twiː/ *adj* Br fam ⟨manner⟩ affettato

tweed /twiːd/ *n* tweed *m inv*

tweezers /'twiːzəz/ *npl* pinzette *f*

twelfth /twelfθ/ *adj & n* dodicesimo, -a *mf*

twelve /twelv/ *adj & n* dodici *m*

twenties /'twentɪz/ *npl* (period) **the ∼** gli anni Venti *mpl*; (age) vent'anni *mpl*;
▶ *also* FORTIES

twentieth /'twentɪθ/ *adj & n* ventesimo, -a *mf*

twenty /'twentɪ/ *adj & n* venti *m*

twerp /twɜːp/ *n* fam stupido, -a *mf*

twice /twaɪs/ *adv* due volte; **she's done ∼ as much as you** ha fatto il doppio di quanto hai fatto tu

twiddle /'twɪdl/ *vt* giocherellare con; **∼ one's thumbs** fig girarsi i pollici

twig¹ /twɪg/ *n* ramoscello *m*

twig² *vt/i* (pt/pp **twigged**) fam intuire

twilight /'twaɪlaɪt/ *n* crepuscolo *m*

twilight zone *n* (mysterious place or situation) zona *f* d'ombra

twill /twɪl/ *n* spigato *m*

twin /twɪn/ ① *n* gemello, -a *mf*
② *attrib* gemello

twin beds *npl* letti *mpl* gemelli

twine /twaɪn/ ① *n* spago *m*
② *vi* intrecciarsi; ⟨plant⟩ attorcigliarsi
③ *vt* intrecciare

twinge /twɪndʒ/ *n* fitta *f*; **∼ of conscience** rimorso *m* di coscienza

twinkle /'twɪŋkl/ ① *n* scintillio *m*
② *vi* scintillare

twinning /'twɪnɪŋ/ *n* (of companies) gemellaggio *m*

twin town *n* città *f inv* gemellata

twirl /twɜːl/ ① *vt* far roteare
② *vi* volteggiare
③ *n* piroetta *f*

twist /twɪst/ ① *n* torsione *f*; (curve) curva *f*; (in rope) attorcigliata *f*; (in book, plot) colpo *m* di scena; **round the ∼** (fam: crazy) ammattito
② *vt* attorcigliare ⟨rope⟩; torcere ⟨metal⟩; girare ⟨knob, cap⟩; (distort) distorcere; **∼ one's ankle** storcersi la caviglia
③ *vi* attorcigliarsi; ⟨road⟩ essere pieno di curve

twisted /'twɪstɪd/ *adj* ⟨wire, rope⟩ ritorto; ⟨ankle, wrist⟩ slogato; ⟨sense of humour, mind⟩ perverso

twister /'twɪstə(r)/ *n* fam imbroglione, -a *mf*; (tornado) tornado *m inv*

twit /twɪt/ n fam cretino, -a mf

twitch /twɪtʃ/ ① n tic m inv; (jerk) strattone m
② vi contrarsi

twitchy /'twɪtʃɪ/ adj (fam: nervous) nervosetto

twitter /'twɪtə(r)/ ① n cinguettio m; **in a ~** fam agitato
② vi cinguettare; ⟨person⟩ cianciare
■ **twitter on about** vt parlare incessantemente di

two /tuː/ adj & n due m; **put ~ and ~ together** fare due più due

two-faced /-'feɪst/ adj falso

twofold ① adj **a ~ increase** un raddoppio
② adv **to increase ~** raddoppiare

two-piece adj (swimsuit) due pezzi m inv; (suit) completo m

two-seater /-'siːtə(r)/ n biposto m inv

twosome /'tuːsəm/ n coppia f

two-tier adj ⟨system, health service⟩ a due velocità

two-time vt fam fare le corna a

two-tone adj (in colour) bicolore; (in sound) bitonale

two-way adj ⟨traffic⟩ a doppio senso di marcia

two-way mirror n specchio m unidirezionale

two-way radio n (radio f) ricetrasmittente f

tycoon /taɪ'kuːn/ n magnate m

tying /'taɪɪŋ/ ▶ TIE

type /taɪp/ ① n tipo m; (printing) carattere m [tipografico]
② vt/i scrivere a macchina

typecast ① vt Theat, fig far fare sempre la stessa parte a ⟨person⟩
② adj a ruolo fisso

typeface n carattere m tipografico

typeset vt comporre

typesetter n compositore m

typewriter n macchina f da scrivere

typewritten adj dattiloscritto

typhoid /'taɪfɔɪd/ n febbre f tifoidea

typhoon /taɪ'fuːn/ n tifone m

typical /'tɪpɪkl/ adj tipico

typically /'tɪpɪklɪ/ adv tipicamente; (as usual) come al solito

typify /'tɪpɪfaɪ/ vt (pt/pp **-ied**) essere tipico di

typing /'taɪpɪŋ/ n dattilografia f

typist /'taɪpɪst/ n dattilografo, -a mf

typo /'taɪpəʊ/ n errore m di stampa; (keying error) errore m di battitura

typography /taɪ'pɒɡrəfɪ/ n tipografia f

tyrannical /tɪ'rænɪkl/ adj tirannico

tyrannize /'tɪrənaɪz/ vt tiranneggiare

tyranny /'tɪrənɪ/ n tirannia f

tyrant /'taɪrənt/ n tiranno, -a mf

tyre /'taɪə(r)/ n gomma f, pneumatico m

tyre pressure n pressione f delle gomme

Tyrrhenian Sea /tɪ'riːnɪən/ n mar m Tirreno

tzar /zɑː(r)/ n zar m

tzarina /tsɑː'riːnə/ n zarina f

Uu

u¹, U /juː/ n (letter) u, U f inv

u² abbr Cinema (**universal**) per tutti

U-bend n (in pipe) gomito m; (in road) curva f a gomito

ubiquitous /juː'bɪkwɪtəs/ adj onnipresente

UCAS /'juːkæs/ abbr Br (**Universities and Colleges Admissions Service**) organismo m di valutazione delle ammissioni all'università

udder /'ʌdə(r)/ n mammella f (di vacca, capra ecc)

UEFA /juː'iːfə, -'eɪfə/ n abbr (**Union of European Football Associations**) UEFA f

UFO abbr (**unidentified flying object**) ufo m inv

Uganda /juː'ɡændə/ n Uganda f

Ugandan /juː'ɡændən/ adj & n ugandese mf

ugliness /'ʌɡlɪnɪs/ n bruttezza f

ugly /'ʌɡlɪ/ adj (**-ier, -iest**) brutto

UHF abbr (**ultra-high frequency**) UHF

UHT abbr (**ultra-heat-treated**) ⟨milk⟩ UHT

UK abbr **United Kingdom**

Ukraine /juː'kreɪn/ n Ucraina f

Ukrainian /juː'kreɪnɪən/ adj & n ucraino, -a mf; (language) ucraino m

ulcer /'ʌlsə(r)/ n ulcera f

ulterior /ʌl'tɪərɪə(r)/ adj **~ motive** secondo fine m

ultimate /'ʌltɪmət/ *adj* definitivo; (final) finale; (fundamental) fondamentale

ultimately /'ʌltɪmətlɪ/ *adv* alla fine

ultimatum /ʌltɪ'meɪtəm/ *n* ultimatum *m inv*

ultramarine /ʌltrəmə'ri:n/ ① *adj* oltremarino
② *n* azzurro *m* oltremarino

ultrasound /'ʌltrəsaʊnd/ *n* Med ecografia *f*

ultrasound scan *n* ecografia *m*

ultrasound scanner *n* scanner *m inv* per ecografia

ultraviolet /ʌltrə'vaɪələt/ *adj* ultravioletto

umbilical /ʌm'bɪlɪkl/ *adj* ∼ **cord** cordone *m* ombelicale

umbrage /'ʌmbrɪdʒ/ *n* **take** ∼ offendersi

umbrella /ʌm'brelə/ *n* ombrello *m*

umbrella stand *n* portaombrelli *m inv*

umpire /'ʌmpaɪə(r)/ ① *n* arbitro *m*
② *vt/i* arbitrare

umpteen /ʌmp'ti:n/ *adj* fam innumerevole

umpteenth /ʌmp'ti:nθ/ *adj* fam ennesimo; **for the** ∼ **time** per l'ennesima volta

UN *abbr* (**United Nations**) ONU *f*

unabashed /ʌnə'bæʃt/ *adj* spudorato

unabated /ʌnə'beɪtɪd/ *adj* ⟨enthusiasm⟩ inalterato; **continue** ∼ ⟨gales⟩ continuare con la stessa intensità

unable /ʌn'eɪbl/ *adj* **be** ∼ **to do something** non potere fare qualcosa; (not know how) non sapere fare qualcosa

unabridged /ʌnə'brɪdʒd/ *adj* integrale

unacceptable /ʌnək'septəbl/ *adj* ⟨proposal, suggestion⟩ inaccettabile

unaccompanied /ʌnə'kʌmpnɪd/ *adj* non accompagnato; ⟨luggage⟩ incustodito

unaccountable /ʌnə'kaʊntəbl/ *adj* inspiegabile

unaccountably /ʌnə'kaʊntəblɪ/ *adv* inspiegabilmente

unaccounted /ʌnə'kaʊntɪd/ *adj* **be** ∼ **for** (not explained) non avere spiegazione; (not found) mancare

unaccustomed /ʌnə'kʌstəmd/ *adj* insolito; **be** ∼ **to** non essere abituato a

unadorned /ʌnə'dɔ:nd/ *adj* ⟨walls⟩ disadorno

unadulterated /ʌnə'dʌltəreɪtɪd/ *adj* ⟨water⟩ puro; ⟨wine⟩ non sofisticato; fig assoluto

unadventurous /ʌnəd'ventʃ(ə)rəs/ *adj* ⟨person, production⟩ poco avventuroso; ⟨meal⟩ poco fantasioso

unaffected /ʌnə'fektɪd/ *adj* (natural) semplice ; **be** ∼ **by** non essere interessato da

unafraid /ʌnə'freɪd/ *adj* senza paura

unaided /ʌn'eɪdɪd/ *adj* senza aiuto

unalloyed /ʌnə'lɔɪd/ *adj* fig puro

unambiguous /ʌnæm'bɪgjʊəs/ *adj* inequivocabile

unanimity /ju:nə'nɪmətɪ/ *n* unanimità *f*

unanimous /ju:'nænɪməs/ *adj* unanime

unanimously /ju:'nænɪməslɪ/ *adv* all'unanimità

unannounced /ʌnə'naʊnst/ *adj* inaspettato

unanswerable /ʌn'ɑ:ns(ə)rəbl/ *adj* ⟨remark, case⟩ irrefutabile; ⟨question⟩ senza risposta

unanswered /ʌn'ɑ:nsəd/ *adj* ⟨question, letter⟩ senza risposta

unappealing /ʌnə'pi:lɪŋ/ *adj* poco attraente

unappetizing /ʌn'æpetaɪzɪŋ/ *adj* poco appetitoso

unappreciated /ʌnə'pri:ʃeɪtɪd/ *adj* ⟨work of art⟩ incompreso

unappreciative /ʌnə'pri:ʃ(ɪ)ətɪv/ *adj* ⟨audience⟩ indifferente; ⟨person⟩ ingrato

unapproachable /ʌnə'prəʊtʃəbl/ *adj* ⟨person⟩ inavvicinabile

unarmed /ʌn'ɑ:md/ *adj* disarmato

unarmed combat *n* lotta *f* senza armi

unashamedly /ʌnə'ʃeɪmd/ *adv* sfacciatamente

unasked /ʌn'ɑ:skt/ *adv* **he came** ∼ è venuto senza che nessuno glielo chiedesse

unassuming /ʌnə'sju:mɪŋ/ *adj* senza pretese

unattached /ʌnə'tætʃd/ *adj* staccato; ⟨person⟩ senza legami

unattainable /ʌnə'teɪnəbl/ *adj* irraggiungibile

unattended /ʌnə'tendɪd/ *adj* incustodito

unattractive /ʌnə'træktɪv/ *adj* ⟨person⟩ poco attraente; ⟨proposition⟩ poco allettante; ⟨characteristic⟩ sgradevole; ⟨building, furniture⟩ brutto

unauthorized /ʌn'ɔ:θəraɪzd/ *adj* non autorizzato

unavailable /ʌnə'veɪləbl/ *adj* non disponibile

unavoidable /ʌnə'vɔɪdəbl/ *adj* inevitabile

unavoidably /ʌnə'vɔɪdəblɪ/ *adv* inevitabilmente; **I was** ∼ **detained** sono stato trattenuto da cause di forza maggiore

unaware /ʌnə'weə(r)/ *adj* **be** ∼ **of something** non rendersi conto di qualcosa

unawares /ʌnə'weəz/ *adv* **catch somebody** ∼ prendere qualcuno alla sprovvista

u

unbalanced /ʌn'bælənst/ *adj* non equilibrato; (mentally) squilibrato

unbearable /ʌn'beərəbl/ *adj* insopportabile

unbearably /ʌn'beərəblɪ/ *adv* insopportabilmente

unbeatable /ʌn'biːtəbl/ *adj* imbattibile

unbeaten /ʌn'biːtən/ *adj* imbattuto

unbecoming /ʌnbɪ'kʌmɪŋ/ *adj* ‹garment› che non dona

unbeknown /ʌnbɪ'nəʊn/ *adj* fam ∼ **to me** a mia insaputa

unbelievable /ʌnbɪ'liːvəbl/ *adj* incredibile

unbend /ʌn'bend/ *vi* (pt/pp **-bent**) (relax) distendersi

unbending /ʌn'bendɪŋ/ *adj* (insistent) inflessibile

unbiased /ʌn'baɪəst/ *adj* obiettivo

unblock /ʌn'blɒk/ *vt* sbloccare

unbolt /ʌn'bəʊlt/ *vt* togliere il chiavistello di

unborn /ʌn'bɔːn/ *adj* non ancora nato

unbreakable /ʌn'breɪkəbl/ *adj* infrangibile

unbridled /ʌn'braɪdld/ *adj* sfrenato

unbroken /ʌn'brəʊk(ə)n/ *adj* ‹sequence, sleep, silence› ininterrotto

unbuckle /ʌn'bʌkl/ *vt* slacciare ‹belt›

unburden /ʌn'bɜːdən/ *vt* ∼ **oneself** fig sfogarsi (**to** con)

unbutton /ʌn'bʌtən/ *vt* sbottonare

uncalled-for /ʌn'kɔːldfɔː(r)/ *adj* fuori luogo

uncannily /ʌn'kænɪlɪ/ *adv* incredibilmente

uncanny /ʌn'kænɪ/ *adj* sorprendente; ‹silence, feeling› inquietante

uncared-for /ʌn'keədfɔː(r)/ *adj* ‹house, pet› trascurato

uncaring /ʌn'keərɪŋ/ *adj* ‹world› indifferente

unceasing /ʌn'siːsɪŋ/ *adj* incessante

uncensored /ʌn'sensəd/ *adj* ‹film, book› non censurato

unceremonious /ʌnserɪ'məʊnɪəs/ *adj* (abrupt) brusco

unceremoniously /ʌnserɪ'məʊnɪəslɪ/ *adv* senza tante cerimonie

uncertain /ʌn'sɜːtən/ *adj* incerto; ‹weather› instabile; **in no ∼ terms** senza mezzi termini

uncertainty /ʌn'sɜːtəntɪ/ *n* incertezza *f*

unchallenged /ʌn'tʃæləndʒd/ *adj* ‹statement, decision› incontestato; **I can't let that go ∼** non posso non contestarlo

unchanged /ʌn'tʃeɪndʒd/ *adj* invariato

uncharacteristic /ʌnkærəktə'rɪstɪk/ *adj* ‹generosity› insolito

uncharitable /ʌn'tʃærɪtəbl/ *adj* duro

unchecked /ʌn'tʃekt/ *adv* incontrollato; **go ∼** dilagare

uncivilized /ʌn'sɪvɪlaɪzd/ *adj* ‹people, nation› non civilizzato; ‹treatment, conditions› incivile

unclassified /ʌn'klæsɪfaɪd/ *adj* ‹document, information› non riservato; ‹road› non classificato

uncle /'ʌŋkl/ *n* zio *m*

unclear /ʌn'klɪːr/ *adj* ‹instructions, reason, voice, writing› non chiaro; ‹future› incerto; **be ∼ about something** ‹person› non aver ben chiaro qualcosa

unclog /ʌn'klɒg/ *vt* sturare ‹pipe›

uncoil /ʌn'kɔɪl/ *vt* srotolare

uncomfortable /ʌn'kʌmftəbl/ *adj* scomodo; imbarazzante ‹silence, situation›; **feel ∼** fig sentirsi a disagio

uncomfortably /ʌn'kʌmftəblɪ/ *adv* ‹sit› scomodamente; (causing alarm etc) spaventosamente

uncommon /ʌn'kɒmən/ *adj* insolito

uncommunicative /ʌnkə'mjuːnɪkətɪv/ *adj* poco comunicativo

uncomplimentary /ʌnkɒmplɪ'mentərɪ/ *adj* poco complimentoso

uncompromising /ʌn'kɒmprəmaɪzɪŋ/ *adj* intransigente

unconcerned /ʌnkən'sɜːnd/ *adj* indifferente

unconditional /ʌnkən'dɪʃ(ə)nl/ *adj* incondizionato

unconditionally /ʌnkən'dɪʃnəlɪ/ *adv* incondizionatamente

unconfirmed /ʌnkən'fɜːmd/ *adj* ‹report, sighting› non confermato

unconnected /ʌnkə'nektɪd/ *adj* ‹incidents, facts› senza alcun legame tra loro

unconscious /ʌn'kɒnʃəs/ *adj* privo di sensi; (unaware) inconsapevole; **be ∼ of something** non rendersi conto di qualcosa

unconsciously /ʌn'kɒnʃəslɪ/ *adv* inconsapevolmente

unconstitutional /ʌnkɒnstɪ'tjuːʃənl/ *adj* incostituzionale

uncontested /ʌnkʌn'testɪd/ *adj* Pol ‹seat› non disputato

uncontrollable /ʌnkən'trəʊləbl/ *adj* incontrollabile; ‹sobbing› irrefrenabile

uncontrollably /ʌnkən'trəʊləblɪ/ *adv* ‹increase› incontrollatamente; ‹laugh, sob› senza potersi controllare

unconventional /ʌnkən'venʃəl/ *adj* poco convenzionale

unconvincing /ʌnkən'vɪnsɪŋ/ *adj* poco convincente

uncooked /ʌn'kʊkt/ *adj* crudo

uncooperative /ʌnkəʊ'ɒpr(ə)tɪv/ *adj* poco cooperativo

uncoordinated /ʌnkəʊˈɔːdɪneɪtɪd/ *adj* ⟨*action, efforts*⟩ non coordinato; be ~ (person) essere scoordinato

uncork /ʌnˈkɔːk/ *vt* sturare

uncorroborated /ʌnkəˈrɒbəreɪtɪd/ *adj* non convalidato

uncouth /ʌnˈkuːθ/ *adj* zotico

uncover /ʌnˈkʌvə(r)/ *vt* scoprire; portare alla luce ⟨*buried object*⟩

uncritical /ʌnˈkrɪtɪkl/ *adj* poco critico

uncross /ʌnˈkrɒs/ *vt* disincrociare ⟨*legs, arms*⟩

unctuous /ˈʌŋktjʊəs/ *adj* untuoso

uncultivated /ʌnˈkʌltɪveɪtɪd/ *adj* incolto

uncut /ʌnˈkʌt/ *adj* ⟨*film*⟩ in versione integrale; ⟨*diamond*⟩ non tagliato

undamaged /ʌnˈdæmɪdʒd/ *adj* intatto

undaunted /ʌnˈdɔːntɪd/ *adj* imperterrito; ~ by something per nulla intimidito da qualcosa

undecided /ʌndɪˈsaɪdɪd/ *adj* indeciso; (not settled) incerto

undefined /ʌndɪˈfaɪnd/ *adj* ⟨*objective, nature*⟩ indeterminato

undelivered /ʌndɪˈlɪvəd/ *adj* ⟨*mail*⟩ non recapitato

undemanding /ʌndɪˈmɑːndɪŋ/ *adj* ⟨*job, course*⟩ poco impegnativo

undemocratic /ʌndeməˈkrætɪk/ *adj* antidemocratico

undemonstrative /ʌndɪˈmɒnstrətɪv/ *adj* poco espansivo

undeniable /ʌndɪˈnaɪəbl/ *adj* innegabile

undeniably /ʌndɪˈnaɪəblɪ/ *adv* innegabilmente

under /ˈʌndə(r)/ **1** *prep* sotto; (less than) al di sotto di; ~ there lì sotto; ~ repair/ construction in riparazione/costruzione; ~ way fig in corso; **2** *adv* (~ water) sott'acqua; (unconscious) sotto anestesia

underachieve /ʌndərəˈtʃiːv/ *vi* Sch restare al di sotto delle proprie possibilità

underachiever /ʌndərəˈtʃiːvə(r)/ *n* be an ~ non dare il meglio

underage /ʌndərˈeɪdʒ/ *adj* ~ drinking consumo di alcolici da parte dei minorenni; be ~ essere minorenne

underarm /ˈʌndərɑːm/ *adj* ⟨*deodorant*⟩ per le ascelle; ⟨*hair*⟩ sotto le ascelle; ⟨*service, throw*⟩ dal basso verso l'alto

undercarriage /ˈʌndəkærɪdʒ/ *n* Aeron carrello *m*

undercharge /ʌndəˈtʃɑːdʒ/ *vt* far pagare meno del dovuto a

underclass /ˈʌndəklɑːs/ *n* sottoproletariato *m*

underclothes /ˈʌndəkləʊðz/ *npl* biancheria *fsg* intima

undercoat /ˈʌndəkəʊt/ *n* prima mano *f*

undercook /ʌndəˈkʊk/ *vt* non cuocere abbastanza

undercover /ʌndəˈkʌvə(r)/ *adj* clandestino

undercurrent /ˈʌndəkʌrənt/ *n* corrente *f* sottomarina; fig sottofondo *m*

undercut /ʌndəˈkʌt/ *vt* (pt/pp **-cut**) Comm vendere a minor prezzo di

underdeveloped /ʌndədɪˈveləpt/ *adj* ⟨*country*⟩ sottosviluppato; Phot non completamente sviluppato

underdog /ˈʌndədɒg/ *n* perdente *m*

underdone /ʌndəˈdʌn/ *adj* ⟨*meat*⟩ al sangue

underemployed /ʌndərɪmˈplɔɪd/ *adj* ⟨*person*⟩ sottoccupato; ⟨*resources, equipment etc*⟩ non sfruttato completamente

underequipped /ʌndərɪˈkwɪpt/ *adj* ⟨*army, person*⟩ insufficientemente equipaggiato; ⟨*schools, gym*⟩ insufficientemente attrezzato

underestimate /ʌndərˈestɪmeɪt/ *vt* sottovalutare

underexpose /ʌndərɪksˈpəʊz/ *vt* Phot sottoesporre

underfed /ʌndəˈfed/ *adj* denutrito

underfloor /ˈʌndəflɔː(r)/ *adj* ⟨*pipes, wiring*⟩ sotto il pavimento

underfoot /ʌndəˈfʊt/ *adv* sotto i piedi; trample ~ calpestare

underfunded /ʌndəˈfʌndɪd/ *adj* insufficientemente finanziato

underfunding /ʌndəˈfʌndɪŋ/ *n* finanziamento *m* insufficiente

undergo /ʌndəˈgəʊ/ *vt* (pt **-went**, pp **-gone**) subire ⟨*operation, treatment*⟩; ~ repair essere in riparazione

undergraduate /ʌndəˈgrædʒʊət/ *n* studente, -tessa *mf* universitario, -a

underground[1] /ʌndəˈgraʊnd/ *adv* sottoterra

underground[2] /ˈʌndəgraʊnd/ **1** *adj* sotterraneo; (secret) clandestino **2** *n* (railway) metropolitana *f*

underground car park *n* parcheggio *m* sotterraneo

undergrowth /ˈʌndəgrəʊθ/ *n* sottobosco *m*

underhand /ˈʌndəhænd/ *adj* subdolo

underlay /ˈʌndəleɪ/ *n* strato *m* di gomma o feltro posto sotto la moquette

underlie /ʌndəˈlaɪ/ *vt* (pt **-lay**, pp **-lain**, pres p **-lying**) fig essere alla base di

underline /ʌndəˈlaɪn/ *vt* sottolineare

underling /ˈʌndəlɪŋ/ *n* pej subalterno, -a *mf*

underlying /ʌndəˈlaɪɪŋ/ *adj* fig fondamentale

undermanned /ʌndəˈmænd/ *adj* ⟨*factory*⟩ a corto di mano d'opera

undermentioned /ʌndə'menʃnd/ *adj* sottoindicato

undermine /ʌndə'maɪn/ *vt fig* minare

underneath /ʌndə'niːθ/ **1** *prep* sotto; ∼ it sotto
2 *adv* sotto

undernourished /ʌndə'nʌrɪʃt/ *adj* denutrito

underpaid /ʌndə'peɪd/ *adj* mal pagato

underpants /'ʌndəpænts/ *npl* mutande *fpl*

underpass /'ʌndəpɑːs/ *n* sottopassaggio *m*

underpay /ʌndə'peɪ/ *vt* sottopagare ⟨employee⟩

underpin /ʌndə'pɪn/ *vt* puntellare ⟨wall⟩; rafforzare ⟨currency, power, theory⟩; essere alla base di ⟨religion, society⟩

underpopulated /ʌndə'pɒpjʊleɪtɪd/ *adj* sottopopolato

underprivileged /ʌndə'prɪvɪlɪdʒd/ *adj* non abbiente

underrate /ʌndə'reɪt/ *vt* sottovalutare

underscore /ʌndə'skɔː(r)/ **1** *n* segno *m* di sottolineatura
2 *vt* sottolineare

underseal /'ʌndəsiːl/ *n* Auto antiruggine *m inv*

under-secretary /ʌndə'sekrət(ə)rɪ/ *n* Br Pol sottosegretario *m*

undersell /ʌndə'sel/ *vt* vendere a prezzo inferiore rispetto a ⟨competitor⟩; pubblicizzare poco ⟨product⟩

undersexed /ʌndə'sekst/ *adj* con scarsa libido

undershirt /'ʌndəʃɜːt/ *n* Am maglia *f* della salute

undersigned /ʌndə'saɪnd/ *adj* sottoscritto

undersized /ʌndə'saɪzd/ *adj* ⟨portion⟩ scarso; ⟨animal⟩ troppo piccolo; ⟨person⟩ di statura inferiore alla media

understaffed /ʌndə'stɑːft/ *adj* a corto di personale

understand /ʌndə'stænd/ **1** *vt* (pt/pp -stood) capire; I ∼ that... (have heard) mi risulta che...
2 *vi* capire

understandable /ʌndə'stændəbl/ *adj* comprensibile

understandably /ʌndə'stændəblɪ/ *adv* comprensibilmente

understanding /ʌndə'stændɪŋ/ **1** *adj* comprensivo
2 *n* comprensione *f*; (agreement) accordo *m*; reach an ∼ trovare un accordo; on the ∼ that a condizione che

understatement /'ʌndəsteɪtmʌnt/ *n* that's an ∼ non è dire abbastanza

understudy /'ʌndəstʌdɪ/ *n* Theat sostituto, a *mf*

undertake /ʌndə'teɪk/ *vt* (pt -took, pp -taken) intraprendere; ∼ to do something impegnarsi a fare qualcosa

undertaker /'ʌndəteɪkə(r)/ *n* impresario *m* di pompe funebri; [firm of] ∼s *n* impresa *f* di pompe funebri

undertaking /ʌndə'teɪkɪŋ/ *n* impresa *f*; (promise) promessa *f*

under-the-counter *adj* ⟨goods, supply, trade⟩ comprato/venduto sottobanco

undertone /'ʌndətəʊn/ *n fig* sottofondo *m*; in an ∼ sottovoce

undervalue /ʌndə'væljuː/ *vt* sottovalutare; the shares are ∼d le azioni si sono svalutate

underwater[1] /'ʌndəwɔːtə(r)/ *adj* subacqueo

underwater[2] /ʌndə'wɔːtə(r)/ *adv* sott'acqua

under way *adj* be ∼ ∼ ⟨vehicle⟩ essere in corsa; ⟨filming, talks⟩ essere in corso; get ∼ ∼ ⟨vehicle⟩ mettersi in viaggio; ⟨preparations, season⟩ avere inizio

underwear /'ʌndəweə(r)/ *n* biancheria *f* intima

underweight /ʌndə'weɪt/ *adj* sotto peso

underworld /'ʌndəwɜːld/ *n* (criminals) malavita *f*

underwriter /'ʌndəraɪtə(r)/ *n* assicuratore *m*

undeserved /ʌndɪ'zɜːvd/ *adj* ⟨praise, reward, win⟩ immeritato; ⟨blame, punish⟩ ingiusto

undeservedly /ʌndɪ'zɜːvɪdlɪ/ *adv* ⟨praise, reward, win⟩ immeritatamente; ⟨blame, punish⟩ ingiustamente

undesirable /ʌndɪ'zaɪərəbl/ *adj* indesiderato; ⟨person⟩ poco raccomandabile

undetected /ʌndɪ'tektɪd/ **1** *adj* ⟨crime, cancer⟩ non scoperto; ⟨flaw, movement, intruder⟩ non visto; go ∼ ⟨cancer, crime⟩ non essere scoperto; ⟨person⟩ passare inosservato
2 *adv* ⟨break in, listen⟩ senza essere scoperto

undeterred /ʌndɪ'tɜːd/ *adj* imperterrito

undeveloped /ʌndɪ'veləpt/ *adj* non sviluppato; ⟨land⟩ non sfruttato

undies /'ʌndɪz/ *npl fam* biancheria *f* intima (da donna)

undignified /ʌn'dɪgnɪfaɪd/ *adj* poco dignitoso

undisciplined /ʌn'dɪsɪplɪnd/ *adj* indisciplinato

undiscovered /ʌndɪs'kʌvəd/ *adj* ⟨secret⟩ non svelato; ⟨crime, document⟩ non scoperto; ⟨land⟩ inesplorato; ⟨species⟩ sconosciuto; ⟨talent⟩ non ancora scoperto

undiscriminating /ʌndɪs'krɪmɪneɪtɪŋ/ *adj* che non sa fare distinzioni

undisguised /ʌndɪs'gaɪzd/ *adj* evidente

undisputed /ʌndɪ'spjuːtɪd/ *adj* indiscusso

undisturbed /ʌndɪ'stɜːbd/ *adj* ‹*sleep, night*› indisturbato

undivided /ʌndɪ'vaɪdɪd/ *adj* ‹*loyalty, attention*› assoluto

undo /ʌn'duː/ *vt* (pt **-did**, pp **-done**) disfare; slacciare ‹*dress, shoes*›; sbottonare ‹*shirt*›; fig, Comput annullare

undone /ʌn'dʌn/ *adj* ‹*shirt, button*› sbottonato; ‹*shoes, dress*› slacciato; (not accomplished) non fatto; **leave ~** ‹*job*› tralasciare

undoubted /ʌn'daʊtɪd/ *adj* indubbio

undoubtedly /ʌn'daʊtɪdlɪ/ *adv* senza dubbio

undress /ʌn'dres/ ① *vt* spogliare; **get ~ed** spogliarsi ② *vi* spogliarsi

undrinkable /ʌn'drɪŋkəbl/ *adj* (unpleasant) imbevibile; (dangerous) non potabile

undue /ʌn'djuː/ *adj* eccessivo

undulating /'ʌndjʊleɪtɪŋ/ *adj* ondulato; ‹*country*› collinoso

unduly /ʌn'djuːlɪ/ *adv* eccessivamente

undying /ʌn'daɪɪŋ/ *adj* eterno

unearned /ʌn'ɜːnd/ *adj* immeritato; **~ income** rendita *f*

unearth /ʌn'ɜːθ/ *vt* dissotterrare; fig scovare; scoprire ‹*secret*›

unearthly /ʌn'ɜːθlɪ/ *adj* soprannaturale; **at an ~ hour** fam ad un'ora impossibile

unease /ʌn'iːz/ *n* disagio *m*

uneasily /ʌn'iːzɪlɪ/ *adv* a disagio

uneasiness /ʌn'iːzɪnəs/ *n* disagio *m*

uneasy /ʌn'iːzɪ/ *adj* a disagio; ‹*person*› inquieto; ‹*feeling*› inquietante; (truce) precario

uneatable /ʌn'iːtəbl/ *adj* immangiabile

uneconomic /ʌniːkə'nɒmɪk/ *adj* poco remunerativo

uneconomical /ʌniːkə'nɒmɪkl/ *adj* poco economico

uneducated /ʌn'edjʊkeɪtɪd/ *adj* ‹*person*› non istruito; ‹*tastes*› non raffinato; ‹*accent, speech*› da persona non istruita

unemotional /ʌnɪ'məʊʃənəl/ *adj* distaccato

unemployed /ʌnem'plɔɪd/ ① *adj* disoccupato ② *npl* **the ~** i disoccupati

unemployment /ʌnem'plɔɪmʌnt/ *n* disoccupazione *f*

unemployment benefit *n* sussidio *m* di disoccupazione

unemployment rate *n* tasso *m* di disoccupazione

unending /ʌn'endɪŋ/ *adj* senza fine

unenthusiastic /ʌnɪnθjuːzɪ'æstɪk/ *adj* poco entusiasta

unenviable /ʌn'envɪəbl/ *adj* ‹*position*› poco invidiabile

unequal /ʌn'iːkwəl/ *adj* disuguale; ‹*struggle*› impari; **be ~ to a task** non essere all'altezza di un compito

unequalled /ʌn'iːkwəld/ *adj* ‹*achievement, quality, record*› ineguagliato

unequally /ʌn'iːkwəlɪ/ *adv* in modo disuguale

unequivocal /ʌnə'kwɪvəkl/ *adj* inequivocabile; ‹*person*› esplicito

unequivocally /ʌnə'kwɪvəklɪ/ *adv* inequivocabilmente

unerring /ʌn'ɜːrɪŋ/ *adj* infallibile

unethical /ʌn'eθɪkl/ *adj* immorale

uneven /ʌn'iːvən/ *adj* irregolare; ‹*distribution*› ineguale; ‹*number*› dispari

unevenly /ʌn'iːvənlɪ/ *adv* irregolarmente; ‹*distributed*› inegualmente

uneventful /ʌnɪ'ventfʊl/ *adj* senza avvenimenti di rilievo

unexciting /ʌnɪk'saɪtɪŋ/ *adj* poco entusiasmante

unexpected /ʌnɪk'spektɪd/ *adj* inaspettato

unexpectedly /ʌnɪk'spektɪdlɪ/ *adv* inaspettatamente

unexplored /ʌnɪk'splɔːd/ *adj* inesplorato

unfailing /ʌn'feɪlɪŋ/ *adj* infallibile

unfair /ʌn'feə(r)/ *adj* ingiusto

unfair dismissal *n* licenziamento *m* ingiustificato

unfairly /ʌn'feəlɪ/ *adv* ingiustamente

unfairness /ʌn'feənəs/ *n* ingiustizia *f*

unfaithful /ʌn'feɪθfʊl/ *adj* infedele

unfamiliar /ʌnfə'mɪljə(r)/ *adj* sconosciuto; **be ~ with** non conoscere

unfashionable /ʌn'fæʃənəbl/ *adj* fuori moda

unfasten /ʌn'fɑːsn/ *vt* slacciare; (detach) staccare

unfathomable /ʌn'fæð(ə)məbl/ *adj* imperscrutabile

unfavourable /ʌn'feɪv(ə)rəbl/ *adj* sfavorevole; ‹*impression*› negativo

unfeeling /ʌn'fiːlɪŋ/ *adj* insensibile

unfinished /ʌn'fɪnɪʃt/ *adj* da finire; ‹*business*› in sospeso

unfit /ʌn'fɪt/ *adj* inadatto; (morally) indegno; Sport fuori forma; **~ for work** non in grado di lavorare; **~ for human consumption** non commestibile

unflappable /ʌn'flæpəbl/ *adj* fam calmo

unflattering /ʌn'flæt(ə)rɪŋ/ *adj* ‹*clothes, hairstyle*› che non dona; ‹*portrait, description*› poco lusinghiero

u

unflinching /ʌnˈflɪntʃɪŋ/ *adj* risoluto

unfold /ʌnˈfəʊld/ **1** *vt* spiegare; (spread out) aprire; fig rivelare **2** *vi* ⟨view⟩ spiegarsi

unforeseeable /ʌnfɔːˈsiːəbl/ *adj* imprevedibile

unforeseen /ʌnfɔːˈsiːn/ *adj* imprevisto

unforgettable /ʌnfəˈgetəbl/ *adj* indimenticabile

unforgivable /ʌnfəˈgɪvəbl/ *adj* imperdonabile

unforgiving /ʌnfəˈgɪvɪŋ/ *adj* che non perdona

unfortunate /ʌnˈfɔːtʃənət/ *adj* sfortunato; (regrettable) spiacevole; ⟨remark, choice⟩ infelice

unfortunately /ʌnˈfɔːtʃənətlɪ/ *adv* purtroppo

unfounded /ʌnˈfaʊndɪd/ *adj* infondato

unfriendly /ʌnˈfrendlɪ/ *adj* ⟨person, remark⟩ scortese, poco amichevole; ⟨place, climate, reception⟩ ostile; ⟨software⟩ difficile da usare

unfulfilled /ʌnfʊlˈfɪld/ *adj* ⟨prophecy⟩ non avverato; ⟨promise⟩ non mantenuto; ⟨ambition⟩ non realizzato; ⟨desire, need⟩ non soddisfatto; ⟨condition⟩ non rispettato; **feel ∼** essere insoddisfatto

unfurl /ʌnˈfɜːl/ **1** *vt* spiegare **2** *vi* spiegarsi

unfurnished /ʌnˈfɜːnɪʃt/ *adj* non ammobiliato

ungainly /ʌnˈgeɪnlɪ/ *adj* sgraziato

ungentlemanly /ʌnˈdʒentlmənlɪ/ *adj* non da gentiluomo

ungodly /ʌnˈgɒdlɪ/ *adj* empio; **∼ hour** fam ora *f* impossibile

ungracious /ʌnˈgreɪʃəs/ *adj* sgarbato

ungrammatical /ʌngrəˈmætɪkl/ *adj* sgrammaticato

ungrateful /ʌnˈgreɪtfʊl/ *adj* ingrato

ungratefully /ʌnˈgreɪtfʊlɪ/ *adv* senza riconoscenza

unhappily /ʌnˈhæpɪlɪ/ *adv* infelicemente; (unfortunately) purtroppo

unhappiness /ʌnˈhæpɪnəs/ *n* infelicità *f*

unhappy /ʌnˈhæpɪ/ *adj* infelice; (not content) insoddisfatto (**with** di)

unharmed /ʌnˈhɑːmd/ *adj* incolume

unhealthy /ʌnˈhelθɪ/ *adj* poco sano; (insanitary) malsano

unheard-of /ʌnˈhɜːdəv/ *adj* ⟨actor, brand⟩ mai sentito; ⟨levels, price⟩ incredibile

unheated /ʌnˈhiːtɪd/ *adj* senza riscaldamento

unheeded /ʌnˈhiːdɪd/ *adj* ignorato; **go ∼** ⟨warning, plea⟩ venir ignorato

unhelpful /ʌnˈhelpfʊl/ *adj* ⟨person, attitude⟩ poco disponibile; ⟨witness⟩ che non collabora; ⟨remark⟩ di poco aiuto

unhindered /ʌnˈhɪndəd/ *adj* senza intralci; **∼ by** senza essere ostacolato da ⟨rules, obstacles⟩

unholy /ʌnˈhəʊlɪ/ *adj* ⟨alliance, pact⟩ paradossale; fam ⟨mess, hour⟩ indecente

unhook /ʌnˈhʊk/ *vt* sganciare; staccare ⟨picture⟩

unhurried /ʌnˈhʌrɪd/ *adj* tranquillo

unhurt /ʌnˈhɜːt/ *adj* illeso

unhygienic /ʌnhaɪˈdʒiːnɪk/ *adj* non igienico

unicorn /ˈjuːnɪkɔːn/ *n* unicorno *m*

unidentified /ʌnaɪˈdentɪfaɪd/ *adj* non identificato

unification /juːnɪfɪˈkeɪʃn/ *n* unificazione *f*

uniform /ˈjuːnɪfɔːm/ **1** *adj* uniforme **2** *n* uniforme *f*

uniformly /ˈjuːnɪfɔːmlɪ/ *adv* uniformemente

unify /ˈjuːnɪfaɪ/ *vt* (pt/pp **-ied**) unificare

unilateral /juːnɪˈlæt(ə)rəl/ *adj* unilaterale

unilaterally /juːnɪˈlæt(ə)rəlɪ/ *adv* unilateralmente

unimaginable /ʌnɪˈmædʒɪnəbl/ *adj* inimmaginabile

unimaginative /ʌnɪˈmædʒɪnətɪv/ *adj* privo di fantasia

unimpeded /ʌnɪmˈpiːdɪd/ *adj* ⟨access⟩ libero

unimportant /ʌnɪmˈpɔːtənt/ *adj* irrilevante

unimpressed /ʌnɪmˈprest/ *adj* non impressionato

uninformed /ʌnɪnˈfɔːmd/ *adj* ⟨person⟩ disinformato

uninhabitable /ʌnɪnˈhæbɪtəbl/ *adj* inabitabile

uninhabited /ʌnɪnˈhæbɪtɪd/ *adj* disabitato

uninhibited /ʌnɪnˈhɪbɪtɪd/ *adj* ⟨person, attitude⟩ disinibito; ⟨performance, remarks⟩ disinvolto; **be ∼ about doing something** non avere problemi a fare qualcosa

uninitiated /ʌnɪˈnɪʃɪeɪtɪd/ **1** *adj* ⟨person⟩ non iniziato **2** *npl* **the ∼** i profani

uninjured /ʌnˈɪndʒəd/ *adj* illeso

uninspired /ʌnɪnˈspaɪəd/ *adj* privo di immaginazione; ⟨performance⟩ piatto; ⟨times⟩ banale

unintelligible /ʌnɪnˈtelɪdʒəbl/ *adj* incomprensibile

unintended /ʌnɪnˈtendɪd/ *adj* ⟨irony, consequence⟩ non voluto

unintentional /ʌnɪn'tenʃənl/ *adj* involontario

unintentionally /ʌnɪn'tenʃənəlɪ/ *adv* involontariamente

uninterested /ʌn'ɪntrəstɪd/ *adj* disinteressato

uninteresting /ʌn'ɪnt(ə)rəstɪŋ/ *adj* poco interessante

uninvited /ʌnɪn'vaɪtɪd/ *adj* ‹attentions› non richiesto; ~ **guest** ospite *mf* senza invito

uninviting /ʌnɪn'vaɪtɪŋ/ *adj* ‹room, food› poco invitante

union /'juːnɪən/ *n* unione *f*; (trade ~) sindacato *m*

Unionist /'juːnɪənɪst/ *n* unionista *mf*

Union Jack *n* bandiera *f* del Regno Unito

unique /juː'niːk/ *adj* unico

uniquely /juː'niːklɪ/ *adv* unicamente

unisex /'juːnɪseks/ *adj* unisex *inv*

unison /'juːnɪsn/ *n* **in** ~ all'unisono

unit /'juːnɪt/ *n* unità *f inv*; (department) reparto *m*; (of furniture) elemento *m*

unit cost *n* costo *m* unitario

unite /juː'naɪt/ **1** *vt* unire **2** *vi* unirsi

united /juː'naɪtɪd/ *adj* unito

United Arab Emirates /'emɪrəts/ *npl* **the** ~ gli Emirati Arabi Uniti

United Kingdom *n* Regno *m* Unito

United Nations *n* [Organizzazione *f* delle] Nazioni Unite *fpl*

United States [of America] *n* Stati *mpl* Uniti [d'America]

unit trust *n* Fin fondo *m* comune di investimento aperto

unity /'juːnɪtɪ/ *n* unità *f*; (agreement) accordo *m*

universal /juːnɪ'vɜːsl/ *adj* universale

universally /juːnɪ'vɜːsəlɪ/ *adv* universalmente

universe /'juːnɪvɜːs/ *n* universo *m*

university /juːnɪ'vɜːsətɪ/ **1** *n* università *f inv* **2** *attrib* universitario

unjust /ʌn'dʒʌst/ *adj* ingiusto

unjustifiable /ʌn'dʒʌstɪfaɪəbl/ *adj* ingiustificato

unjustifiably /ʌn'dʒʌstɪfaɪəblɪ/ *adv* ‹act› senza giustificazione

unjustified /ʌn'dʒʌstɪfaɪd/ *adj* ‹suspicion› ingiustificato

unjustly /ʌn'dʒʌstlɪ/ *adv* ingiustamente

unkempt /ʌn'kempt/ *adj* trasandato; ‹hair› arruffato

unkind /ʌn'kaɪnd/ *adj* scortese

unkindly /ʌn'kaɪndlɪ/ *adv* in modo scortese

unkindness /ʌn'kaɪndnɪs/ *n* mancanza *f* di gentilezza

unknown /ʌn'nəʊn/ *adj* sconosciuto

unlace /ʌn'leɪs/ *vt* slacciare ‹shoes›

unlawful /ʌn'lɔːfʊl/ *adj* illecito, illegale

unlawfully /ʌn'lɔːfʊlɪ/ *adv* illegalmente

unleaded /ʌn'ledɪd/ *adj* senza piombo

unleaded petrol *n* benzina *f* senza piombo *o* verde

unleash /ʌn'liːʃ/ *vt* fig scatenare

unleavened /ʌn'levnd/ *adj* ‹bread› non lievitato

unless /ʌn'les/ *conj* a meno che; ~ **I am mistaken** se non mi sbaglio

unlicensed /ʌn'laɪsnst/ *adj* ‹transmitter, activity› abusivo; ‹vehicle› senza bollo; ‹restaurant› non autorizzato a vendere alcolici

unlike /ʌn'laɪk/ **1** *adj* (not the same) diversi **2** *prep* diverso da; **that's** ~ **him** non è da lui; ~ **me, he...** diversamente da me, lui...

unlikely /ʌn'laɪklɪ/ *adj* improbabile

unlimited /ʌn'lɪmɪtɪd/ *adj* illimitato

unlined /ʌn'laɪnd/ *adj* ‹face› senza rughe; ‹paper› senza righe; ‹garment, curtain› senza fodera

unlit /ʌn'lɪt/ *adj* ‹cigarette, fire› spento; ‹room, street› non illuminato

unload /ʌn'ləʊd/ *vt* scaricare

unlock /ʌn'lɒk/ *vt* aprire (con chiave); sbloccare ‹mobile phone›

unloved /ʌn'lʌvd/ *adj* **feel** ~ ‹person› non sentirsi amato

unluckily /ʌn'lʌkɪlɪ/ *adv* sfortunatamente

unlucky /ʌn'lʌkɪ/ *adj* sfortunato; **It's** ~ **to...** porta sfortuna...

unmade /ʌn'meɪd/ *adj* ‹bed› sfatto

unmade-up *adj* ‹road› non asfaltato

unmanageable /ʌn'mænɪdʒəbl/ *adj* ‹number, company› difficile da gestire; ‹hair, child, animal› ribelle; ‹size› ingombrante

unmanly /ʌn'mænlɪ/ *adj* poco virile

unmanned /ʌn'mænd/ *adj* senza equipaggio

unmarked /ʌn'mɑːkt/ *adj* Sport smarcato; ‹skin› senza segni; ‹container› non contrassegnato; ~ **police car** [auto *f inv*] civetta *f*

unmarried /ʌn'mærɪd/ *adj* non sposato

unmarried mother *n* ragazza *f* madre

unmask /ʌn'mɑːsk/ *vt* fig smascherare

unmentionable /ʌn'menʃnəbl/ *adj* innominabile

unmistakable /ʌnmɪ'steɪkəbl/ *adj* inconfondibile

unmistakably /ʌnmɪ'steɪkəblɪ/ *adv* chiaramente

u

unmitigated /ʌnˈmɪtɪgeɪtɪd/ *adj*
assoluto

unmotivated /ʌnˈməʊtɪveɪtɪd/ *adj*
immotivato

unmoved /ʌnˈmuːvd/ *adj* fig impassibile

unnamed /ʌnˈneɪmd/ *adj* (not having a
name) senza nome; (name not divulged) di cui
non si conosce il nome; **the as yet ∼
winner...** il vincitore di cui ancora non si
conosce il nome...

unnatural /ʌnˈnætʃər(ə)l/ *adj*
innaturale; pej anormale

unnaturally /ʌnˈnætʃər(ə)lɪ/ *adv* in
modo innaturale; pej in modo anormale

unnecessarily /ʌnˈnesəs(ə)rɪlɪ/ *adv*
inutilmente

unnecessary /ʌnˈnesəs(ə)rɪ/ *adj* inutile

unnerve /ʌnˈnɜːv/ *vt* scuotere

unnerving /ʌnˈnɜːvɪŋ/ *adj* inquietante

unnoticed /ʌnˈnəʊtɪst/ *adj* inosservato

unobservant /ʌnəbˈzɜːvənt/ *adj* senza
spirito d'osservazione

unobserved /ʌnəbˈzɜːvd/ *adj*
inosservato; **go ∼** passare inosservato

unobstructed /ʌnəbˈstrʌktɪd/ *adj*
⟨view, path⟩ libero

unobtainable /ʌnəbˈteɪnəbl/ *adj*
⟨product⟩ introvabile; ⟨phone number⟩
non ottenibile

unobtrusive /ʌnəbˈtruːsɪf/ *adj* discreto

unobtrusively /ʌnəbˈtruːsɪvlɪ/ *adv* in
modo discreto

unoccupied /ʌnˈɒkjuːpaɪd/ *adj* ⟨house,
block, shop⟩ vuoto; ⟨table, seat⟩ libero

unofficial /ʌnəˈfɪʃl/ *adj* non ufficiale

unofficially /ʌnəˈfɪʃ(ə)lɪ/ *adv*
ufficiosamente

unopened /ʌnˈəʊpənd/ *adj* ⟨bottle,
packet⟩ chiuso; ⟨package⟩ ancora
incartato

unorthodox /ʌnˈɔːθədɒks/ *adj* poco
ortodosso

unpack /ʌnˈpæk/ **1** *vi* disfare le valigie
2 *vt* svuotare ⟨parcel⟩; spacchettare
⟨books⟩; **∼ one's case** disfare la valigia

unpaid /ʌnˈpeɪd/ *adj* da pagare; (work)
non retribuito

unpalatable /ʌnˈpælətəbl/ *adj*
sgradevole

unparalleled /ʌnˈpærəleld/ *adj* senza
pari

unpasteurized /ʌnˈpɑːstʃəraɪzd/ *adj*
non pastorizzato

unperturbed /ʌnpəˈtɜːbd/ *adj*
imperturbato

unpick /ʌnˈpɪk/ *vt* disfare

unplanned /ʌnˈplænd/ *adj* ⟨stoppage,
increase⟩ imprevisto

unpleasant /ʌnˈplezənt/ *adj* sgradevole;
⟨person⟩ maleducato

unpleasantly /ʌnˈplezəntlɪ/ *adv*
sgradevolmente; ⟨behave⟩
maleducatamente

unpleasantness /ʌnˈplezntnɪs/ *n* (bad
feeling) tensioni *fpl*

unplug /ʌnˈplʌg/ *vt* (pt/pp **-plugged**)
staccare

unpolluted /ʌnpəˈluːtɪd/ *adj* ⟨water⟩ non
inquinato; ⟨mind⟩ incontaminato

unpopular /ʌnˈpɒpjʊlə(r)/ *adj*
impopolare

unprecedented /ʌnˈpresɪdentɪd/ *adj*
senza precedenti

unpredictable /ʌnprɪˈdɪktəbl/ *adj*
imprevedibile

unprejudiced /ʌnˈpredʒʊdɪst/ *adj*
⟨person⟩ senza pregiudizi; ⟨opinion,
judgement⟩ imparziale

unpremeditated /ʌnpriːˈmedɪteɪtɪd/
adj involontario

unprepared /ʌnprɪˈpeəd/ *adj*
impreparato

unprepossessing /ʌnpriːpəˈzesɪŋ/ *adj*
poco attraente

unpretentious /ʌnprɪˈtenʃəs/ *adj* senza
pretese

unprincipled /ʌnˈprɪnsɪpəld/ *adj* senza
principi; ⟨behaviour⟩ scorretto

unproductive /ʌnprəˈdʌktɪv/ *adj*
⟨discussion, meeting⟩ poco produttivo

unprofessional /ʌnprəˈfeʃnl/ *adj* non
professionale; **it's ∼** è una mancanza di
professionalità

unprofitable /ʌnˈprɒfɪtəbl/ *adj* non
redditizio

unprompted /ʌnˈprɒm(p)tɪd/ *adj* ⟨offer⟩
spontaneo; ⟨answer⟩ non suggerito

unpronounceable /ʌnprəˈnaʊnsəbl/
adj impronunciabile

unprotected /ʌnprəˈtektɪd/ *adj* ⟨sex⟩
non protetto; ⟨person⟩ indifeso

unprovoked /ʌnprəˈvəʊkt/ *adj* ⟨attack,
aggression⟩ non provocato; **the attack was
∼** l'attacco è avvenuto senza
provocazione

unqualified /ʌnˈkwɒlɪfaɪd/ *adj* non
qualificato; (fig: absolute) assoluto

unquestionable /ʌnˈkwestʃənəbl/ *adj*
incontestabile

unquote /ʌnˈkwəʊt/ *vi* chiudere le
virgolette

unravel /ʌnˈrævl/ *vt* (pt/pp **-lled**)
districare; (in knitting) disfare

unreal /ʌnˈrɪəl/ *adj* irreale; fam
inverosimile

unrealistic /ʌnrɪəˈlɪstɪk/ *adj* ⟨character,
presentation⟩ poco realistico; ⟨expectation,
aim⟩ irrealistico; ⟨person⟩ poco realista

unreasonable /ʌnˈriːz(ə)nəbl/ *adj*
irragionevole

unrecognizable /ʌn'rekəgnaɪzəbl/ *adj*
irriconoscibile

unrecorded /ʌnrɪ'kɔːdɪd/ *adj* non
documentato; **go ~** non essere
documentato

unrefined /ʌnrɪ'faɪnd/ *adj* ‹*person,
manners, style*› rozzo; ‹*oil*› greggio; ‹*flour,
sugar*› non raffinato

unrehearsed /ʌnrɪ'hɜːst/ *adj* ‹*response,
action*› imprevisto; ‹*speech*› improvvisato

unrelated /ʌnrɪ'leɪtɪd/ *adj* ‹*facts*› senza
rapporto (**to** con); ‹*person*› non
imparentato (**to** con)

unrelenting /ʌnrɪ'lentɪŋ/ *adj* ‹*person*›
ostinato; ‹*stare*› insistente; ‹*pursuit*›
continuo; ‹*heat, zeal*› costante

unreliable /ʌnrɪ'laɪəbl/ *adj*
inattendibile; ‹*person*› inaffidabile, che
non dà affidamento

unremitting /ʌnrɪ'mɪtɪŋ/ *adj* costante;
‹*struggle*› continuo

unrepeatable /ʌnrɪ'piːtəbl/ *adj* ‹*offer,
bargain*› unico; **his comment was ~** il
commento che ha fatto è irripetibile

unrepentant /ʌnrɪ'pentənt/ *adj*
irriducibile; ‹*sinner*› impenitente

unrequited /ʌnrɪ'kwaɪtɪd/ *adj* non
corrisposto

unreservedly /ʌnrɪ'zɜːvɪdlɪ/ *adv* senza
riserve; (frankly) francamente

unresolved /ʌnrɪ'zɒlvd/ *adj* irrisolto

unrest /ʌn'rest/ *n* fermenti *mpl*

unrestricted /ʌnrɪ'strɪktɪd/ *adj* ‹*access,
view*› libero

unrewarding /ʌnrɪ'wɔːdɪŋ/ *adj* ‹*job*›
poco gratificante

unripe /ʌn'raɪp/ *adj* ‹*fruit*› acerbo;
‹*wheat*› non maturo

unrivalled /ʌn'raɪvəld/ *adj* ineguagliato

unroll /ʌn'rəʊl/ **1** *vt* srotolare
2 *vi* srotolarsi

unruffled /ʌn'rʌfld/ *adj* ‹*person*›
imperturbato; ‹*hair*› a posto; ‹*water*› non
mosso; **be ~** ‹*person*› rimanere
imperturbato; ‹*person, hair*› essere a
posto

unruly /ʌn'ruːlɪ/ *adj* indisciplinato

unsafe /ʌn'seɪf/ *adj* pericoloso

unsaid /ʌn'sed/ *adj* inespresso

unsalaried /ʌn'sælərɪd/ *adj* ‹*post*› non
stipendiato

unsalted /ʌn'sɔːltɪd/ *adj* non salato

unsatisfactory /ʌnsætɪs'fækt(ə)rɪ/ *adj*
poco soddisfacente

unsatisfied /ʌn'sætɪsfaɪd/ *adj* ‹*person,
need*› insoddisfatto

unsatisfying /ʌn'sætɪsfaɪɪŋ/ *adj* poco
soddisfacente

unsavoury /ʌn'seɪvərɪ/ *adj* equivoco

unscathed /ʌn'skeɪðd/ *adj* illeso

unscheduled /ʌn'ʃedjuːld/ *adj* ‹*flight*›
supplementare; ‹*appearance, speech*› fuori
programma; ‹*stop*› non programmato

unscramble /ʌn'skræmbl/ *vt* decifrare
‹*code, words*›; sbrogliare ‹*ideas, thoughts*›

unscrew /ʌn'skruː/ *vt* svitare

unscrupulous /ʌn'skruːpjʊləs/ *adj*
senza scrupoli

unseasoned /ʌn'siːznd/ *adj* ‹*wood*› non
stagionato; ‹*food*› scondito

unseat /ʌn'siːt/ *vt* disarcionare ‹*rider*›

unseemly /ʌn'siːmlɪ/ *adj* indecoroso

unseen /ʌn'siːn/ *adv* ‹*escape, slip away*›
senza essere visto

unselfconscious /ʌnselfkɒnʃəs/ *adj*
naturale

unselfish /ʌn'selfɪʃ/ *adj* disinteressato

unsentimental /ʌnsentɪ'mentl/ *adj*
poco sentimentale

unsettled /ʌn'setld/ *adj* in agitazione;
‹*weather*› variabile; ‹*bill*› non saldato

unsettling /ʌn'setlɪŋ/ *adj* ‹*experience,
novel*› inquietante

unshakeable /ʌn'ʃeɪkəbl/ *adj*
categorico

unshaken /ʌn'ʃeɪkən/ *adj* ‹*belief*› saldo

unshaven /ʌn'ʃeɪvn/ *adj* non rasato

unsightly /ʌn'saɪtlɪ/ *adj* brutto

unsinkable /ʌn'sɪŋkəbl/ *adj* ‹*ship,
object*› inaffondabile; hum ‹*personality*› che
non si deprime

unskilled /ʌn'skɪld/ *adj* non
specializzato

unskilled worker *n* manovale *m*

unsmiling /ʌn'smaɪlɪŋ/ *adj* ‹*person*›
serioso

unsociable /ʌn'səʊʃəbl/ *adj* scontroso

unsocial hours /ʌn'səʊʃl/ *npl* **to work
~** lavorare al di fuori degli orari
standard

unsolicited /ʌnsə'lɪsɪtɪd/ *adj* ‹*help,
advice*› non richiesto; ‹*job application*›
spontaneo

unsophisticated /ʌnsə'fɪstɪkeɪtɪd/ *adj*
semplice

unsound /ʌn'saʊnd/ *adj* ‹*building,
reasoning*› poco solido; ‹*advice*› poco
sensato; **of ~ mind** malato di mente

unspeakable /ʌn'spiːkəbl/ *adj*
indicibile

unspoiled /ʌn'spɔɪld/ *adj* ‹*town*› non
deturpato; ‹*landscape*› intatto; **she was ~
by fame** la fama non l'ha cambiata

unspoken /ʌn'spəʊkən/ *adj* (implicit)
tacito

unstable /ʌn'steɪbl/ *adj* instabile;
(mentally) squilibrato

unsteadily /ʌn'stedɪlɪ/ *adv* ‹*walk,
speak*› in modo malsicuro

unsteady /ʌn'stedɪ/ *adj* malsicuro

unstoppable /ʌnˈstɒpəbl/ *adj* ⟨*force, momentum*⟩ inarrestabile

unstressed /ʌnˈstrest/ *adj* ⟨*vowel, word*⟩ atono

unstuck /ʌnˈstʌk/ *adj* come ~ staccarsi; (fam: project) andare a monte

unsubstantiated /ʌnsəbˈstænʃɪeɪtɪd/ *adj* ⟨*report*⟩ non corroborato

unsuccessful /ʌnsəkˈsesfʊl/ *adj* fallimentare; be ~ (in attempt) non aver successo

unsuccessfully /ʌnsəkˈsesfʊlɪ/ *adv* senza successo

unsuitable /ʌnˈsuːtəbl/ *adj* (inappropriate) inadatto; (inconvenient) inopportuno

unsupervised /ʌnˈsuːpəvaɪzd/ *adj* ⟨*activity*⟩ non controllato

unsure /ʌnˈʃʊə(r)/ *adj* incerto; be ~ about non essere sicuro di; ~ of oneself essere insicuro

unsuspecting /ʌnsəˈspektɪŋ/ *adj* fiducioso

unsweetened /ʌnˈswiːtənd/ *adj* senza zucchero

unsympathetic /ʌnsɪmpəˈθetɪk/ *adj* ⟨*person, attitude, manner, tone*⟩ poco comprensivo; ⟨*person, character*⟩ antipatico; she is ~ to the cause non appoggia la causa

untamed /ʌnˈteɪmd/ *adj* ⟨*lion*⟩ non addomesticato; ⟨*passion, person*⟩ indomito

untangle /ʌnˈtæŋgl/ *vt* sbrogliare ⟨*threads*⟩; risolvere ⟨*difficulties, mystery*⟩

untaxed /ʌnˈtækst/ *adj* ⟨*goods*⟩ non imponibile; ⟨*income*⟩ esente da imposte

untenable /ʌnˈtenəbl/ *adj* ⟨*position, argument*⟩ insostenibile

unthinkable /ʌnˈθɪŋkəbl/ *adj* impensabile

unthought-of /ʌnˈθɔːtəv/ *adj* impensato; hitherto ~ finora impensato

untidily /ʌnˈtaɪdɪlɪ/ *adv* disordinatamente

untidiness /ʌnˈtaɪdɪnɪs/ *n* disordine *m*

untidy /ʌnˈtaɪdɪ/ *adj* disordinato

untie /ʌnˈtaɪ/ *vt* slegare

until /ʌnˈtɪl/ ① *prep* fino a; not ~ non prima di; ~ the evening fino alla sera; ~ his arrival fino al suo arrivo ② *conj* finché, fino a quando; not ~ you've seen it non prima che tu l'abbia visto

untimely /ʌnˈtaɪmlɪ/ *adj* inopportuno; (premature) prematuro

untiring /ʌnˈtaɪərɪŋ/ *adj* instancabile

untold /ʌnˈtəʊld/ *adj* ⟨*wealth*⟩ incalcolabile; ⟨*suffering*⟩ indescrivibile; ⟨*story*⟩ inedito

untouched /ʌnˈtʌtʃt/ *adj* (unchanged, undisturbed) intatto; (unscathed) incolume;

(unaffected) non toccato; leave one's dinner/a meal ~ non toccare cibo

untoward /ʌntəˈwɔːd/ *adj* if nothing ~ happens se non capita un imprevisto

untrained /ʌnˈtreɪnd/ *adj* ⟨*voice*⟩ non impostato; ⟨*eye, artist, actor*⟩ inesperto; be ~ ⟨*worker*⟩ non avere una formazione professionale

untranslatable /ʌntrænzˈleɪtəbl/ *adj* intraducibile

untreated /ʌnˈtriːtɪd/ *adj* ⟨*sewage, water*⟩ non depurato; ⟨*illness*⟩ non curato

untroubled /ʌnˈtrʌbld/ *adj* ⟨*sleep*⟩ tranquillo

untrue /ʌnˈtruː/ *adj* falso; that's ~ non è vero

untrustworthy /ʌnˈtrʌstwɜːðɪ/ *adj* ⟨*person*⟩ inaffidabile

unused[1] /ʌnˈjuːzd/ *adj* non usato

unused[2] /ʌnˈjuːst/ *adj* be ~ to non essere abituato a

unusual /ʌnˈjuːʒəl/ *adj* insolito

unusually /ʌnˈjuːʒəlɪ/ *adv* insolitamente

unveil /ʌnˈveɪl/ *vt* scoprire

unversed /ʌnˈvɜːst/ *adj* inesperto (in di)

unwanted /ʌnˈwɒntɪd/ *adj* ⟨*child, pet, visitor*⟩ indesiderato; ⟨*goods, produce*⟩ che non serve; feel ~ sentirsi respinto

unwarranted /ʌnˈwɒrəntɪd/ *adj* ingiustificato

unwelcome /ʌnˈwelkəm/ *adj* sgradito

unwell /ʌnˈwel/ *adj* indisposto

unwieldy /ʌnˈwiːldɪ/ *adj* ingombrante

unwilling /ʌnˈwɪlɪŋ/ *adj* riluttante

unwillingly /ʌnˈwɪlɪŋlɪ/ *adv* malvolentieri

unwillingness /ʌnˈwɪlɪŋnɪs/ *n* riluttanza

unwind /ʌnˈwaɪnd/ ① *vt* (pt/pp **unwound**) svolgere, srotolare ② *vi* svolgersi, srotolarsi; (fam: relax) rilassarsi

unwise /ʌnˈwaɪz/ *adj* imprudente

unwisely /ʌnˈwaɪzlɪ/ *adv* imprudentemente

unwitting /ʌnˈwɪtɪŋ/ *adj* involontario; ⟨*victim*⟩ inconsapevole

unwittingly /ʌnˈwɪtɪŋlɪ/ *adv* involontariamente

unworldly /ʌnˈwɜːldlɪ/ *adj* (not materialistic) poco materialista; (naive) ingenuo; (spiritual) non materialista

unworthy /ʌnˈwɜːðɪ/ *adj* non degno

unwrap /ʌnˈræp/ *vt* (pt/pp **-wrapped**) scartare ⟨*present, parcel*⟩

unwritten /ʌnˈrɪtn/ *adj* tacito

unyielding /ʌnˈjiːldɪŋ/ *adj* rigido

unzip /ʌnˈzɪp/ *vt* aprire [la cerniera di] ⟨*garment, bag*⟩

up /ʌp/ **1** *adv* su; (not in bed) alzato; ‹*road*› smantellato; ‹*theatre curtain, blinds*› alzato; ‹*shelves, tent*› montato; ‹*notice*› affisso; ‹*building*› costruito; **prices are up** i prezzi sono aumentati; **be up for sale** essere in vendita; **up here/there** quassù/ lassù; **time's up** tempo scaduto; **what's up?** fam cosa è successo?; **up to** (as far as) fino a; **be up to** essere all'altezza di ‹*task*›; **what's he up to?** fam cosa sta facendo?; (plotting) cosa sta combinando?; **I'm up to page 100** sono arrivato a pagina 100; **feel up to it** sentirsela; **be one up on somebody** fam essere in vantaggio su qualcuno; **go up** salire; **lift up** alzare; **up against** fig alle prese con **2** *prep* su; **the cat ran/is up the tree** il gatto è salito di corsa/è sull'albero; **further up this road** più avanti su questa strada; **row up the river** risalire il fiume; **go up the stairs** salire su per le scale; **be up the pub** fam essere al pub; **be up on** or **in something** essere bene informato su qualcosa **3** *npl* **ups and downs** alti *mpl* e bassi

up-and-coming *adj* promettente

upbeat /'ʌpbiːt/ *adj* ottimistico

upbringing /'ʌpbrɪŋɪŋ/ *n* educazione *f*

update /ʌp'deɪt/ *vt* aggiornare

upfront /ʌp'frʌnt/ **1** *adj* fam (frank) aperto; ‹*money*› anticipato **2** *adv* ‹*pay*› in anticipo

upgrade /ʌp'greɪd/ **1** *vt* promuovere ‹*person*›; modernizzare ‹*equipment*› **2** *n* aggiornamento *m*

upheaval /ʌp'hiːvl/ *n* scompiglio *m*

uphill /ʌp'hɪl/ **1** *adj* in salita; fig arduo **2** *adv* in salita

uphold /ʌp'həʊld/ *vt* (pt/pp **upheld**) sostenere ‹*principle*›; confermare ‹*verdict*›

upholster /ʌp'həʊlstə(r)/ *vt* tappezzare

upholsterer /ʌp'həʊlstərə(r)/ *n* tappezziere, -a *mf*

upholstery /ʌp'həʊlstərɪ/ *n* tappezzeria *f*

upkeep /'ʌpkiːp/ *n* mantenimento *m*

uplifting /ʌp'lɪftɪŋ/ *adj* (morally) edificante

upload /ʌp'ləʊd/ *vt* Comput fare l'upload di

up-market *adj* di qualità

upon /ə'pɒn/ *prep* su; ~ **arriving home** una volta arrivato a casa

upper /'ʌpə(r)/ **1** *adj* superiore **2** *n* (of shoe) tomaia *f*

upper-case *adj* maiuscolo

upper circle *n* seconda galleria *f*

upper class *n* alta borghesia *f*

upper crust *adj* hum aristocratico

upper hand *n* **have the** ~ ~ avere il sopravvento

upper middle class *n* ceto *m* medio-alto

uppermost /'ʌpəməʊst/ *adj* più alto; **that's** ~ **in my mind** è la mia preoccupazione principale

upright /'ʌpraɪt/ **1** *adj* dritto; ‹*piano*› verticale; (honest) retto **2** *n* montante *m*

upright freezer *n* freezer *m inv* verticale

uprising /'ʌpraɪzɪŋ/ *n* rivolta *f*

upriver /ʌp'rɪvə(r)/ *adv* ‹*lie*› a monte; ‹*sail*› controcorrente

uproar /'ʌprɔː(r)/ *n* tumulto *m*; **be in an** ~ essere in trambusto

uproot /ʌp'ruːt/ *vt* sradicare

upset[1] /ʌp'set/ *vt* (pt/pp **upset**, pres p **upsetting**) rovesciare; sconvolgere ‹*plan*›; (distress) turbare; **get** ~ **about something** prendersela per qualcosa; **be very** ~ essere sconvolto; **have an** ~ **stomach** avere l'intestino disturbato

upset[2] /'ʌpset/ *n* scombussolamento *m*

upsetting /ʌp'setɪŋ/ *adj* (distressing) sconvolgente; (annoying) fastidioso

upshot /'ʌpʃɒt/ *n* risultato *m*

upside down *adv* sottosopra; **turn** ~ ~ capovolgere

upstage /ʌp'steɪdʒ/ **1** *vt* Theat, fig distogliere l'attenzione del pubblico da **2** *adv* Theat ‹*stand*› al fondo del palcoscenico; ‹*move*› verso il fondo del palcoscenico

upstairs[1] /ʌp'steəz/ *adv* [al piano di] sopra

upstairs[2] /'ʌpsteəz/ *adj* del piano superiore

upstart /'ʌpstɑːt/ *n* arrivato, -a *mf*

upstream /ʌp'striːm/ *adv* controcorrente

upsurge /'ʌpsɜːdʒ/ *n* (in sales) aumento *m* improvviso; (of enthusiasm, crime) ondata *f*

uptake /'ʌpteɪk/ *n* **be slow on the** ~ essere lento nel capire; **be quick on the** ~ capire le cose al volo

uptight /ʌp'taɪt/ *adj* teso

up-to-date *adj* moderno; ‹*news*› ultimo; ‹*person, information, records*› aggiornato

up-to-the-minute *adj* ‹*information*› dell'ultimo minuto

uptown /'ʌptaʊn/ *adj* (Am: smart) dei quartieri alti

upturn /'ʌptɜːn/ *n* ripresa *f*

upward /'ʌpwəd/ **1** *adj* verso l'alto, in su; ~ **slope** salita *f* **2** *adv* ~[**s**] verso l'alto; ~**s of** oltre

upwardly mobile /ʌpwədlɪ'məʊbaɪl/ *adj* che sale nella scala sociale

uranium /jʊ'reɪnɪəm/ *n* uranio *m*

Uranus /'jʊərənəs/ *n* Urano *m*

urban /'ɜːbən/ *adj* urbano

urban blight, **urban decay** *n* degrado *m* urbano

urbane /ɜːˈbeɪn/ *adj* cortese

urban planning *n* urbanistica *f*

urchin /ˈɜːtʃɪn/ *n* riccio *m* di mare

Urdu /ˈʊəduː/ *n* urdu *m*

urge /ɜːdʒ/ ① *n* forte desiderio *m*
② *vt* esortare (**to** a)
■ **urge on** *vt* spronare

urgency /ˈɜːdʒənsɪ/ *n* urgenza *f*

urgent /ˈɜːdʒənt/ *adj* urgente

urgently /ˈɜːdʒəntlɪ/ *adv* urgentemente

urinal /jʊˈraɪnl/ *n* (fixture) orinale *m*; (place) vespasiano *m*

urinate /ˈjʊərɪneɪt/ *vi* urinare

urine /ˈjʊərɪn/ *n* urina *f*

URL *abbr* (**Unified Resource Locator**) URL *m*

urn /ɜːn/ *n* urna *f*; (for tea) contenitore *m* munito di rubinetto che si trova nei self-service, mense ecc

Uruguay /ˈjʊərəgwaɪ/ *n* Uruguay *m*

US *n abbr* (**United States**) U.S.A. *mpl*

us /ʌs/ *pers pron* ci; (after prep) noi; **they know us** ci conoscono; **give us the money** dateci i soldi; **give it to us** datecelo; **they showed it to us** ce l'hanno fatto vedere; **they meant us, not you** intendevano noi, non voi; **it's us** siamo noi; **she hates us** ci odia

USA *n abbr* (**United States of America**) U.S.A. *mpl*

usable /ˈjuːzəbl/ *adj* usabile

usage /ˈjuːsɪdʒ/ *n* uso *m*

use¹ /juːs/ *n* uso *m*; **be of ~** essere utile; **be of no ~** essere inutile; **make ~ of** usare; (exploit) sfruttare; **it is no ~** è inutile; **what's the ~?** a che scopo?

use² /juːz/ *vt* usare
■ **use up** *vt* consumare

used¹ /juːzd/ *adj* usato

used² /juːst/ *pt* **be ~ to something** essere abituato a qualcosa; **get ~ to** abituarsi a; **he ~ to say** diceva; **he ~ to live here** viveva qui

useful /ˈjuːsfl/ *adj* utile

usefulness /ˈjuːsflnɪs/ *n* utilità *f*

useless /ˈjuːslɪs/ *adj* inutile; fam ⟨person⟩ incapace; **you're ~!** sei un idiota!

user /ˈjuːzə(r)/ *n* utente *mf*

user-friendliness *n* facilità *f* d'uso

user-friendly *adj* facile da usare

user group *n* Comput gruppo *m* di utenti

user manual *n* manuale *m* d'uso

usher /ˈʌʃə(r)/ *n* Theat maschera *f*; Jur usciere *m*; (at wedding) persona *f* che accompagna gli invitati ad un matrimonio ai loro posti in chiesa
■ **usher in** *vt* fare entrare ⟨person⟩; inaugurare ⟨new age⟩

usherette /ʌʃəˈret/ *n* maschera *f*

USS *abbr* Am (**United States Ship**) nave *f* da guerra americana

USSR *n* URSS *f*

usual /ˈjuːʒəl/ *adj* usuale; **as ~** come al solito

usually /ˈjuːʒəlɪ/ *adv* di solito

usurp /jʊˈzɜːp/ *vt* usurpare

usurper /jʊˈzɜːpə(r)/ *n* usurpatore, -trice *mf*

utensil /jʊˈtensl/ *n* utensile *m*

uterus /ˈjuːtərəs/ *n* utero *m*

utilitarian /jʊtɪlɪˈteərɪən/ *adj* funzionale

utility /jʊˈtɪlətɪ/ *n* utilità *f*; (public) servizio *m*

utility company *n* servizio *m* pubblico

utility program *n* Comput [programma *m* di] utilità *f*

utility room *n* stanza *f* in casa privata per il lavaggio, la stiratura dei panni ecc

utilize /ˈjuːtɪlaɪz/ *vt* utilizzare

utmost /ˈʌtməʊst/ ① *adj* estremo
② *n* **one's ~** tutto il possibile

Utopia /juːˈtəʊpɪə/ *n* utopia *f*

Utopian /juːˈtəʊpɪən/ ① *n* utopista *mf*
② *adj* utopistico

utter¹ /ˈʌtə(r)/ *adj* totale

utter² *vt* emettere ⟨sigh, sound⟩; proferire ⟨word⟩

utterance /ˈʌtərəns/ *n* dichiarazione *f*

utterly /ˈʌtəlɪ/ *adv* completamente

U-turn *n* Auto inversione *f* a U; fig marcia *f* indietro

UV *abbr* (**ultraviolet**) UVA *mpl*

Uzbekistan /ʌzbekɪˈstɑːn/ *n* Uzbekistan *m*

Vv

v¹, V /viː/ *n* (letter) v, V *f inv*

v² *abbr* (**versus**) contro; *abbr* (**volt**) V *m*

vac /væk/ *n* Br *abbr* (**vacation**) vacanze *fpl*

vacancy /ˈveɪk(ə)nsɪ/ *n* (job) posto *m*

vacante; (room) stanza *f* disponibile

vacant /'veɪknt/ *adj* libero; ⟨position⟩ vacante; ⟨look⟩ assente

vacant possession *n* Br Jur bene *m* immobile libero

vacate /və'keɪt/ *vt* lasciare libero

vacation/və'keɪʃn/ *n* Univ & Am vacanza *f*

vacationer /və'keɪʃənə(r)/ *n* Am vacanziere, -a *mf*

vaccinate /'væksɪneɪt/ *vt* vaccinare

vaccination /væksɪ'neɪʃn/ *n* vaccinazione *f*

vaccine /'væksi:n/ *n* vaccino *m*

vacillate /'væsɪleɪt/ *vi* tentennare

vacuous /'vækjʊəs/ *adj* ⟨person, look, expression⟩ vacuo; ⟨person⟩ superficiale

vacuum /'vækjʊəm/ ①*n* vuoto *m*
② *vt* passare l'aspirapolvere in/su

vacuum cleaner *n* aspirapolvere *m inv*

vacuum flask *n* thermos *m inv*

vacuum-pack *vt* confezionare sotto vuoto ⟨food⟩

vacuum-packed *adj* confezionato sottovuoto

vagabond /'vægəbɒnd/ *n* vagabondo, -a *mf*

vagaries /'veɪgərɪz/ *npl* capricci *mpl*

vagina /və'dʒaɪnə/ *n* Anat vagina *f*

vagrancy /'veɪgrənsɪ/ *n* Jur vagabondaggio *m*

vagrant /'veɪgrənt/ *n* vagabondo, -a *mf*

vague /veɪg/ *adj* vago; ⟨outline⟩ impreciso; (absent-minded) distratto; **I'm still ∼ about it** non ho ancora le idee chiare in proposito

vaguely /'veɪglɪ/ *adv* vagamente

vagueness /'veɪgnɪs/ *n* (imprecision) vaghezza *f*; (of wording, proposals) indeterminatezza *f*; (of image) nebulosità *f*; (of thinking) imprecisione *f*

vain /veɪn/ *adj* vanitoso; ⟨hope, attempt⟩ vano; **in ∼** invano

vainly /'veɪnlɪ/ *adv* vanamente

valance /'væləns/ *n* (above curtains) mantovana *f*; (on bed base) balza *f*

vale /veɪl/ *n* liter valle *f*

valentine /'væləntaɪn/ *n* (card) biglietto *m* di San Valentino

Valentine's Day *n* giorno *m* di San Valentino

valet /'væleɪ/ *n* servitore *m* personale

valet parking *n* servizio *m* di parcheggio per clienti di alberghi e ristoranti

valiant /'vælɪənt/ *adj* valoroso

valiantly /'vælɪəntlɪ/ *adv* coraggiosamente

valid /'vælɪd/ *adj* valido

validate /'vælɪdeɪt/ *vt* (confirm) convalidare

validity /və'lɪdətɪ/ *n* validità *f*

valley /'vælɪ/ *n* valle *f*

valour /'vælə(r)/ *n* valore *m*

valuable /'væljʊəbl/ *adj* di valore; fig prezioso

valuables /'væljʊəblz/ *npl* oggetti *mpl* di valore

valuation /væljʊ'eɪʃn/ *n* valutazione *f*

value /'vælju:/ ①*n* valore *m*; (usefulness) utilità *f*
② *vt* valutare; (cherish) apprezzare

value added tax /'ædɪd/ *n* imposta *f* sul valore aggiunto

valued /'vælju:d/ *adj* (appreciated) apprezzato

valuer /'væljʊə(r)/ *n* stimatore, -trice *mf*

valve /vælv/ *n* valvola *f*

vamp /væmp/ *n* vamp *f inv*

vampire /'væmpaɪə(r)/ *n* vampiro *m*

van /væn/ *n* furgone *m*

vandal /'vændl/ *n* vandalo, -a *mf*

vandalism /'vænd(ə)lɪzm/ *n* vandalismo *m*

vandalize /'vænd(ə)laɪz/ *vt* vandalizzare

vane /veɪn/ *n* banduerola *f*

vanguard /'vængɑːd/ *n* avanguardia *f*; **in the ∼** all'avanguardia

vanilla /və'nɪlə/ *n* vaniglia *f*

vanish /'vænɪʃ/ *vi* svanire

vanishing cream *n* crema *f* base per il trucco

vanishing point *n* punto *m* di fuga

vanishing trick *n* trucco *m* da illusionista per far sparire un oggetto; **he's done his ∼ ∼ again** *fam* è sparito come al solito

vanity /'vænɪtɪ/ *n* vanità *f inv*

vanity bag, **vanity case** *n* beauty-case *m inv*

vanity mirror *n* Auto specchietto *m* di cortesia

vanquish /'væŋkwɪʃ/ *vt* sconfiggere ⟨enemy⟩

vantage point /'vɑːntɪdʒ/ *n* punto *m* d'osservazione; fig punto *m* di vista

vaporize /'veɪpəraɪz/ *vt* vaporizzare ⟨liquid⟩

vaporizer /'veɪpəraɪzə(r)/ *n* apparecchio *m* per aerosol

vapour /'veɪpə(r)/ *n* vapore *m*

vapour trail *n* scia *f*

variable /'veərɪəbl/ *adj* variabile; (adjustable) regolabile

variance /'veərɪəns/ *n* **be at ∼** essere in disaccordo

variant /'veərɪənt/ *n* variante *f*

variation /veərɪ'eɪʃn/ *n* variazione *f*

varicose /'værɪkəʊs/ adj ~ veins vene fpl varicose

varied /'veərɪd/ adj vario; ⟨diet⟩ diversificato; ⟨life⟩ movimentato

variegated /'veərɪəgeɪtɪd/ adj variegato

variety /və'raɪətɪ/ n varietà f inv

variety show n spettacolo m di varietà

varifocal /veərɪ'fəʊkl/ adj ⟨lens⟩ multifocale

varifocals /veərɪ'fəʊklz/ npl (glasses) occhiali mpl multifocali

various /'veərɪəs/ adj vario

variously /'veərɪəslɪ/ adv variamente

varnish /'vɑːnɪʃ/ **1** n vernice f; (for nails) smalto m
2 vt verniciare; ~ one's nails mettersi lo smalto

vary /'veərɪ/ vt/i (pt/pp -ied) variare

varying /'veərɪɪŋ/ adj variabile; (different) diverso

vascular /'væskjʊlə(r)/ adj Anat, Bot vascolare

vase /vɑːz/ n vaso m

vasectomy /və'sektəmɪ/ n vasectomia f

vast /vɑːst/ adj vasto; ⟨difference, amusement⟩ enorme

vastly /'vɑːstlɪ/ adv ⟨superior⟩ di gran lunga; ⟨different, amused⟩ enormemente

VAT /viːer'tiː/, /væt/ abbr (value added tax) I.V.A. f

vat /væt/ n tino m

Vatican /'vætɪkən/ n the ~ il Vaticano; ~ City la città del Vaticano

vaudeville /'vɔːdəvɪl/ n Theat varietà m

vault[1] /vɔːlt/ n (roof) volta f; (in bank) caveau m inv; (tomb) cripta f

vault[2] **1** n salto m
2 vt/i ~ [over] saltare

VCR abbr n (video cassette recorder) VCR m

VD abbr (venereal disease) malattia f venerea

VDU abbr (visual display unit) VDU m

veal /viːl/ **1** n carne f di vitello
2 attrib di vitello

vector /'vektə(r)/ n Biol, Math vettore m; Aeron rotta f

veer /vɪə(r)/ vi cambiare direzione; Naut, Auto virare

vegan /'viːgn/ **1** n vegetaliano, -a mf
2 adj vegetaliano

veganism /'viːgnɪzm/ n vegetalismo m

vegeburger /'vedʒɪbɜːgə(r)/ n = VEGGIE BURGER

vegetable /'vedʒtəbl/ **1** n (food) verdura f; (when growing) ortaggio m
2 attrib ⟨oil, fat⟩ vegetale

vegetarian /vedʒɪ'teərɪən/ adj & n vegetariano, -a mf

vegetarianism /vedʒɪ'teərɪənɪzm/ n vegetarianismo m

vegetate /'vedʒɪteɪt/ vi vegetare

vegetation /vedʒɪ'teɪʃn/ n vegetazione f

veggie burger /'vedʒɪbɜːgə(r)/ n hamburger m inv vegetariano

vehemence /'viːəməns/ n veemenza f

vehement /'viːəmənt/ adj veemente

vehemently /'viːəməntlɪ/ adv con veemenza

vehicle /'viːɪkl/ n veicolo m; (fig: medium) mezzo m

vehicular /vɪ'hɪkjʊlə(r)/ adj no ~ access, no ~ traffic circolazione vietata

veil /veɪl/ **1** n velo m
2 vt velare

veiled /veɪld/ adj ⟨woman⟩ velato, col velo; ⟨threat⟩ velato

vein /veɪn/ n vena f; (mood) umore m; (manner) tenore m

veined /veɪnd/ adj venato

Velcro® /'velkrəʊ/ n ~ fastening chiusura f con velcro

vellum /'veləm/ n pergamena f

velocity /vɪ'lɒsətɪ/ n velocità f inv

velvet /'velvɪt/ n velluto m

velvety /'velvətɪ/ adj vellutato

venal /'viːnl/ adj venale

vendetta /ven'detə/ n vendetta f

vending machine /'vendɪŋ/ n distributore m automatico

vendor /'vendə(r)/ n venditore, -trice mf

veneer /və'nɪə(r)/ n impiallacciatura f; fig vernice f

veneered /və'nɪərd/ adj impiallacciato

venerable /'venərəbl/ adj venerabile

veneration /venə'reɪʃn/ n venerazione f

venereal /vɪ'nɪərɪəl/ adj ~ disease malattia f venerea

Venetian /və'niːʃn/ adj & n veneziano, -a mf

Venetian blind n persiana f alla veneziana

Venezuela /venɪz'weɪlə/ n Venezuela m

Venezuelan /venɪz'weɪlən/ adj & n venezuelano, -a mf

vengeance /'vendʒəns/ n vendetta f; with a ~ fam a più non posso

Venice /'venɪs/ n Venezia f

venison /'venɪsn/ n Culin carne f di cervo

venom /'venəm/ n veleno m

venomous /'venəməs/ adj velenoso

vent[1] /vent/ **1** n presa f d'aria; give ~ to fig dar libero sfogo a
2 vt fig sfogare ⟨anger⟩

vent[2] n (in jacket) spacco m

ventilate /'ventɪleɪt/ vt ventilare

ventilation /ventɪ'leɪʃn/ n ventilazione f; (installation) sistema m di ventilazione

ventilator /'ventɪleɪtə(r)/ n ventilatore m

ventriloquist /ven'trɪləkwɪst/ n ventriloquo, -a mf

venture /'ventʃə(r)/ [1] n impresa f [2] vt azzardare [3] vi avventurarsi

venture capital n capitale m a rischio

venue /'venju:/ n luogo m (di convegno, concerto ecc)

Venus /'vi:nəs/ n Venere f

veraclty /və'ræsətɪ/ n veridicità f

veranda /və'rændə/ n veranda f

verb /vɜːb/ n verbo m

verbal /'vɜːbl/ adj verbale

verbally /'vɜːb(ə)lɪ/ adv verbalmente

verbatim /vɜː'beɪtɪm/ [1] adj letterale [2] adv parola per parola

verbose /vɜː'bəʊs/ adj prolisso

verdict /'vɜːdɪkt/ n verdetto m; (opinion) parere m

verdigris /'vɜːdɪgri:/ n verderame m

verge /vɜːdʒ/ n orlo m; be on the ∼ of doing something essere sul punto di fare qualcosa

■ **verge on** vt fig rasentare

verger /'vɜːdʒə(r)/ n sagrestano m

verification /verɪfɪ'keɪʃn/ n verifica f

verify /'verɪfaɪ/ vt (pt/pp **-led**) verificare; (confirm) confermare

veritable /'verɪtəbl/ adj vero

vermicelli /vɜːmɪ'tʃelɪ/ n (pasta) capelli mpl d'angelo; (chocolate) pezzettini mpl di cioccolato per decorazione

vermilion /və'məljɪn/ [1] n rosso m vermiglio [2] adj vermiglio

vermin /'vɜːmɪn/ n animali mpl nocivi

vermouth /'vɜːməθ/ n vermut m inv

vernacular /vɜː'nækjʊlə(r)/ n vernacolo m

verruca /və'ru:kə/ n verruca f

versatile /'vɜːsətaɪl/ adj versatile

versatility /vɜːsə'tɪlətə/ n versatilità f

verse /vɜːs/ n verso m; (of Bible) versetto m; (poetry) versi mpl

versed /vɜːst/ adj ∼ in versato in

versifier /'vɜːsɪfaɪə(r)/ n pej versificatore, -trice mf

version /'vɜːʃn/ n versione f; (translation) traduzione f

versus /'vɜːsəs/ prep contro

vertebra /'vɜːtɪbrə/ n (pl **-brae** /-bri:/) Anat vertebra f

vertebrate /'vɜːtɪbrət/ [1] n vertebrato m [2] adj vertebrato

vertex /'vɜːteks/ n Anat sommità f inv del capo; Math vertice m

vertical /'vɜːtɪkl/ adj & n verticale m

vertically /'vɜːtɪklɪ/ adv verticalmente

vertigo /'vɜːtɪgəʊ/ n Med vertigine f

verve /vɜːv/ n verve f

very /'verɪ/ [1] adv molto; ∼ much molto; ∼ little pochissimo; ∼ many moltissimi; ∼ few pochissimi; ∼ probably molto probabilmente; ∼ well benissimo; at the ∼ most tutt'al più; at the ∼ latest al più tardi [2] adj the ∼ first il primissimo; the ∼ thing proprio ciò che ci vuole; at the ∼ end/beginning proprio alla fine/all'inizio; that ∼ day proprio quel giorno; the ∼ thought la sola idea; only a ∼ little solo un pochino

vespers /'vespəz/ npl vespri mpl

vessel /'vesl/ n nave f; (receptacle) recipiente m; Anat vaso m

vest /vest/ [1] n maglia f della salute; (Am: waistcoat) gilè m inv [2] vt ∼ something in somebody investire qualcuno di qualcosa

vested interest /vestɪd'ɪntrəst/ n interesse m personale

vestige /'vestɪdʒ/ n (of past) vestigio m

vestment /'vestmənt/ n Relig paramento m

vestry /'vestrɪ/ n sagrestia f

vet /vet/ [1] n veterinario, -a mf [2] vt (pt/pp **vetted**) controllare minuziosamente

veteran /'vetərən/ n veterano, -a mf

veteran car n auto f inv d'epoca (costruita prima del 1916)

veterinarian /vetərɪ'neərɪən/ n Am = VET

veterinary /'vetərɪnərɪ/ adj veterinario

veterinary surgeon n medico m veterinario

veto /'vi:təʊ/ [1] n (pl **-es**) veto m [2] vt proibire

vetting /'vetɪŋ/ n verifica f del passato di un individuo

vex /veks/ vt irritare

vexation /vek'seɪʃn/ n irritazione f

vexatious /vek'seɪʃəs/ adj ⟨person⟩ fastidioso; ⟨situation⟩ spiacevole

vexed /vekst/ adj irritato; ∼ question questione f controversa

vexing /'veksɪŋ/ adj irritante

VHF abbr (**very high frequency**) VHF

via /'vaɪə/ prep via; (by means of) attraverso

viability /vaɪə'bɪlətɪ/ n probabilità f di sopravvivenza; (of proposition) attuabilità f

viable /'vaɪəbl/ adj ⟨life form, relationship, company⟩ in grado di sopravvivere; ⟨proposition⟩ attuabile

viaduct /'vaɪədʌkt/ n viadotto m

vibes /vaɪbz/ *npl* fam **I'm getting good/ bad ∼** provo una sensazione gradevole/ sgradevole

vibrant /'vaɪbrənt/ *adj* fig che sprizza vitalità

vibrate /vaɪ'breɪt/ *vi* vibrare

vibration /vaɪ'breʃn/ *n* vibrazione *f*

vicar /'vɪkə(r)/ *n* parroco *m* (protestante)

vicarage /'vɪkərɪdʒ/ *n* casa *f* parrocchiale

vicarious /vɪ'keərɪəs/ *adj* indiretto

vice¹ /vaɪs/ *n* vizio *m*

vice² *n* Techn morsa *f*

vice-captain *n* Sport vicecapitano *m*

vice-chairman *n* vicepresidente *mf*

vice-chancellor *n* Br Univ vicerettore *m*; Am Jur vicecancelliere *m*

vice-president *n* vicepresidente *mf*

vice-principal *n* (of senior school) vicepreside *mf*; (of junior school, college) vicedirettore, -trice *mf*

vice squad *n* buoncostume *f*

vice versa /vaɪsə'vɜːsə/ *adv* viceversa

vicinity /vɪ'sɪnətɪ/ *n* vicinanza *f*; **in the ∼ of** nelle vicinanze di

vicious /'vɪʃəs/ *adj* cattivo; ⟨*attack*⟩ brutale; ⟨*animal*⟩ pericoloso

vicious circle *n* circolo *m* vizioso

viciously /'vɪʃəslɪ/ *adv* ⟨*attack*⟩ brutalmente

victim /'vɪktɪm/ *n* vittima *f*

victimization /vɪktɪmaɪ'zeʃn/ *n* vittimizzazione *f*

victimize /'vɪktɪmaɪz/ *vt* vittimizzare

victor /'vɪktə(r)/ *n* vincitore *m*

Victorian /vɪk'tɔːrɪən/ **①** *n* persona *f* vissuta in epoca vittoriana
② *adj* ⟨*writer, poverty, age*⟩ vittoriano

victorious /vɪk'tɔːrɪəs/ *adj* vittorioso

victory /'vɪktərɪ/ *n* vittoria *f*

video /'vɪdɪəʊ/ **①** *n* video *m inv*; (cassette) videocassetta *f*; (recorder) videoregistratore *m*
② *attrib* video
③ *vt* registrare

video camera *n* videocamera *f*, telecamera *f*

video card *n* scheda *f* video

video cassette *n* videocassetta *f*

video clip *n* videoclip *m inv*

videoconference *n* videoconferenza *f*

videoconferencing /'kɒnfərənsɪŋ/ *n* videoconferenza *f*

videodisc *n* videodisco *m*

video game *n* videogioco *m*

video library *n* videoteca *f*

video nasty *n* film *m inv* con scene violente o pornografiche

videophone *n* videocitofono *m*

video recorder *n* videoregistratore *m*

video shop *n* negozio *m* che affitta o vende videocassette

video surveillance *n* videosorveglianza *f*

videotape *n* videocassetta *f*

vie /vaɪ/ *vi* (pres p **vying**) rivaleggiare

Vienna /vɪ'enə/ *n* Vienna *f*

Viennese /vɪə'niːz/ *adj* viennese

Vietnam /vɪet'næm/ *n* Vietnam *m*

Vietnamese /vɪetnæ'miːz/ *adj & n* vietnamita *mf*; (language) vietnamita *m*

view /vjuː/ **①** *n* vista *f*; (photographed, painted) veduta *f*; (opinion) visione *f*; **look at the ∼** guardare il panorama; **in my ∼** secondo me; **in ∼ of** in considerazione di; **on ∼** esposto; **with a ∼ to** con l'intenzione di
② *vt* visitare ⟨*house*⟩; consider considerare
③ *vi* TV guardare

viewer /'vjuːə(r)/ *n* TV telespettatore, -trice *mf*; Phot visore *m*

viewfinder /'vjuːfaɪndə(r)/ *n* Phot mirino *m*

viewing /'vjuːɪŋ/ **①** *n* TV programmi *mpl* della televisione; (of film) proiezione *f*; (of new range) presentazione *f*; (of exhibition, house) visita *f*; **it makes good ∼** TV vale la pena di vederlo; **what's tonight's ∼?** cosa danno alla tv stasera?
② *attrib* ⟨*habits, preferences*⟩ dei telespettatori; **the ∼ public** i telespettatori

view phone *n* videotelefono *m*

viewpoint /'vjuːpɔɪnt/ *n* punto *m* di vista

vigil /'vɪdʒɪl/ *n* veglia *f*

vigilance /'vɪdʒɪləns/ *n* vigilanza *f*

vigilant /'vɪdʒɪlənt/ *adj* vigile

vigilante /vdʒɪ'læntɪ/ *n* membro *m* di un'organizzazione privata per la prevenzione della criminalità

vigorous /'vɪg(ə)rəs/ *adj* vigoroso

vigorously /'vɪg(ə)rəslɪ/ *adv* vigorosamente

vigour /'vɪgə(r)/ *n* vigore *m*

vile /vaɪl/ *adj* disgustoso; ⟨*weather*⟩ orribile; ⟨*temper, mood*⟩ pessimo

vilification /vɪlɪfɪ'keɪʃn/ *n* denigrazione *f*

villa /'vɪlɪ/ *n* (for holidays) casa *f* di villeggiatura

village /'vɪlɪdʒ/ *n* paese *m*

village green *n* giardino *m* pubblico nel centro di un paese

village hall *n* sala *f* utilizzata per feste e altre attività

villager /'vɪlɪdʒə(r)/ *n* paesano, -a *mf*

villain /'vɪlɪn/ *n* furfante *m*; (in story) cattivo *m*

villainous /'vɪlənəs/ *adj* infame

vim /vɪm/ n fam energia f

vindicate /'vɪndɪkeɪt/ vt (from guilt) discolpare; **you are ∼d** ti sei dimostrato nel giusto

vindictive /vɪn'dɪktɪv/ adj vendicativo

vine /vaɪn/ n vite f

vinegar /'vɪnɪɡə(r)/ n aceto m

vinegary /'vɪnɪɡ(ə)rɪ/ adj agro

vineyard /'vɪnjɑːd/ n vigneto m

vintage /'vɪntɪdʒ/ ① adj ⟨wine⟩ d'annata ② n (year) annata f

vintage car n auto f inv d'epoca (costruita tra il 1917 e il 1930)

vintage year n also fig anno m memorabile

vinyl /'vaɪnɪl/ ① n vinile m ② attrib ⟨paint⟩ vinilico

viola /vɪ'əʊlə/ n Mus viola f

violate /'vaɪəleɪt/ vt violare

violation /vaɪə'leɪʃn/ n violazione f

violence /'vaɪələns/ n violenza f

violent /'vaɪələnt/ adj violento

violently /'vaɪələntlɪ/ adv violentemente

violet /'vaɪələt/ ① adj violetto ② n (flower) violetta f; (colour) violetto m

violin /vaɪə'lɪn/ n violino m

violinist /vaɪə'lɪnɪst/ n violinista mf

VIP n abbr (very important person) vip mf

viper /'vaɪpə(r)/ n vipera f

virgin /'vɜːdʒɪn/ ① adj vergine ② n vergine f

virginal /'vɜːdʒɪn(ə)l/ adj verginale

virginals /'vɜːdʒɪn(ə)lz/ npl Mus spinetta f

Virginia creeper /vədʒɪnɪə'kriːpə(r)/ n vite f del Canada

virginity /və'dʒɪnətɪ/ n verginità f

Virgo /'vɜːɡəʊ/ n Astr Vergine f

virile /'vɪraɪl/ adj virile

virility /vɪ'rɪlətɪ/ n virilità f

virologist /vaɪ'rɒlədʒɪst/ n virologo m

virtual /'vɜːtjʊəl/ adj effettivo

virtually /'vɜːtjʊəlɪ/ adv praticamente

virtual reality n realtà f virtuale

virtue /'vɜːtjuː/ n virtù f inv; (advantage) vantaggio m; **by** or **in ∼ of** a causa di

virtuoso /vɜːtʊ'əʊzəʊ/ n (pl -si /-ziː/) virtuoso m

virtuous /'vɜːtjʊəs/ adj virtuoso

virulent /'vɪrʊlənt/ adj virulento

virus /'vaɪərəs/ n virus m inv

virus checker n Comput (programma m) antivirus m inv

virus protection n Comput protezione f antivirus

visa /'viːzə/ n visto m

vis-à-vis /viːzɑː'viː/ prep rispetto a

visceral /'vɪs(ə)rəl/ adj ⟨power, performance⟩ viscerale

viscount /'vaɪkaʊnt/ n visconte m

viscous /'vɪskəs/ adj vischioso

visibility /vɪzə'bɪlətɪ/ n visibilità f

visible /'vɪzəbl/ adj visibile

visibly /'vɪzəblɪ/ adv visibilmente

vision /'vɪʒn/ n visione f; (sight) vista f

visionary /'vɪʒn(ə)rɪ/ adj & n visionario, -a mf

vision mixer n (person) tecnico m del mixaggio video; (equipment) mixaggio m video

visit /'vɪzɪt/ ① n visita f ② vt andare a trovare ⟨person⟩; andare da ⟨doctor etc⟩; visitare ⟨town, building⟩

visiting card n biglietto m da visita

visiting hours npl orario m delle visite

visiting lecturer n conferenziere, -a mf

visiting team n squadra f ospite

visiting time n orario m delle visite

visitor /'vɪzɪtə(r)/ n ospite mf; (of town, museum) visitatore, -trice mf; (in hotel) cliente mf

visitor centre n centro m di accoglienza e di informazione per i visitatori

visitors' book n (in exhibition) albo m dei visitatori; (in hotel) registro m dei clienti

visor /'vaɪzə(r)/ n visiera f; Auto parasole m

vista /'vɪstə/ n (view) panorama m

visual /'vɪzjʊəl/ adj visivo

visual aids npl supporto m visivo

visual arts npl arti fpl visive

visual display unit n visualizzatore m

visualize /'vɪzjʊəlaɪz/ vt visualizzare

visually /'vɪzjʊəlɪ/ adv visualmente; **∼ handicapped** non vedente

vital /'vaɪtl/ adj vitale

vitality /vaɪ'tælətɪ/ n vitalità f

vitally /'vaɪtəlɪ/ adv estremamente

vital statistics npl fam misure fpl

vitamin /'vɪtəmɪn/ n vitamina f

vitreous /'vɪtrɪəs/ adj vetroso; ⟨enamel⟩ vetrificato

vitriolic /vɪtrɪ'ɒlɪk/ adj Chem di vetriolo; fig al vetriolo

vituperative /vɪ'tjuːp(ə)rətɪv/ adj ingiurioso

viva /'vaɪvə/ n Br Univ [esame m] orale m

vivacious /vɪ'veɪʃəs/ adj vivace

vivaciously /vɪ'veɪʃəslɪ/ adv vivacemente

vivacity /vɪ'væsətɪ/ n vivacità f

vivid /'vɪvɪd/ adj vivido

vividly /'vɪvɪdlɪ/ adv in modo vivido

vivisect /'vɪvɪsekt/ vt vivisezionare

vivisection /vɪvɪ'sekʃn/ n vivisezione f

vixen /'vɪksn/ n volpe f femmina

viz /vɪz/ adv cioè

V-neck n (neckline) scollo m a V; (sweater) maglione m con scollo a V

vocabulary /və'kæbjʊlərɪ/ n vocabolario m; (list) glossario m

vocal /'vəʊkl/ adj vocale; (vociferous) eloquente

vocal cords npl corde fpl vocali

vocalist /'vəʊkəlɪst/ n vocalista mf

vocalize /'vəʊkəlaɪz/ vt (fig: express) esprimere a parole; articolare ⟨sound⟩

vocals /'vəʊklz/ npl do the ~ cantare

vocation /və'keɪʃn/ n vocazione f

vocational /və'keɪʃ(ə)nl/ adj di orientamento professionale

vocational course n corso m di formazione professionale

vociferous /və'sɪfərəs/ adj vociante

vodka /'vɒdkə/ n vodka f inv

vogue /vəʊg/ n moda f; in ~ in voga

voice /vɔɪs/ ①▸ n voce f
②▸ vt esprimere

voice box n Anat laringe f

voiceless /'vɔɪslɪs/ adj ⟨minority⟩ silenzioso; ⟨group⟩ privo del diritto di parola

voicemail /'vɔɪsmeɪl/ n posta f elettronica vocale

voice-over n voce f fuori campo

voice recognition n Comput riconoscimento m vocale

void /vɔɪd/ ①▸ adj (not valid) nullo; ~ of privo di
②▸ n vuoto m

vol /vɒl/ abbr (**volume**) vol.

volatile /'vɒlətaɪl/ adj volatile; ⟨person⟩ volubile

volcanic /vɒl'kænɪk/ adj vulcanico

volcano /vɒl'keɪnəʊ/ n vulcano m

volition /və'lɪʃn/ n of his own ~ di sua spontanea volontà

volley /'vɒlɪ/ n (of gunfire) raffica f; (Tennis) volée f inv

volleyball /'vɒlɪbɔːl/ n pallavolo f

volt /vəʊlt/ n volt m inv

voltage /'vəʊltɪdʒ/ n Electr voltaggio m

voluble /'vɒljʊbl/ adj loquace

volume /'vɒljuːm/ n volume m; (of work, traffic) quantità f inv

volume control n volume m

voluntarily /'vɒləntərɪlɪ/ adv volontariamente

voluntary /'vɒləntərɪ/ adj volontario

voluntary redundancy n Br dimissioni fpl volontarie

voluntary work n volontariato m

volunteer /vɒlən'tɪə(r)/ ①▸ n volontario, -a mf
②▸ vt offrire volontariamente ⟨information⟩
③▸ vi offrirsi volontario; Mil arruolarsi come volontario

voluptuous /və'lʌptjʊəs/ adj voluttuoso

vomit /'vɒmɪt/ ①▸ n vomito m
②▸ vt/i vomitare

voodoo /'vuːduː/ n vudu m inv

voracious /və'reɪʃəs/ adj vorace

vortex /'vɔːteks/ n vortice m; fig turbine m

vote /vəʊt/ ①▸ n voto m; (ballot) votazione f; (right) diritto m di voto; take a ~ on votare su
②▸ vi votare
③▸ vt ~ somebody president eleggere qualcuno presidente

■ **vote down** vt (reject by vote) bocciare ai voti

■ **vote in** vt (elect) eleggere

vote of confidence n Pol, fig voto m di fiducia

vote of thanks n discorso m di ringraziamento

voter /'vəʊtə(r)/ n elettore, -trice mf

voting /'vəʊtɪŋ/ n votazione f

voting age n età f inv per votare

voting booth n cabina f elettorale

vouch /vaʊtʃ/ vi ~ for garantire per

voucher /'vaʊtʃə(r)/ n buono m

vow /vaʊ/ ①▸ n voto m
②▸ vt giurare

vowel /'vaʊəl/ n vocale f

vox pop /vɒks'pɒp/ n TV, Radio opinione f pubblica

voyage /'vɔɪɪdʒ/ n viaggio m [marittimo]; (in space) viaggio m [nello spazio]

vs abbr (**versus**) contro

V-sign n (offensive gesture) gestaccio m; (victory sign) segno m di vittoria

VSO abbr (**Voluntary Service Overseas**) servizio m civile volontario nei paesi in via di sviluppo

vulgar /'vʌlgə(r)/ adj volgare

vulgar fraction n Math frazione f ordinaria

vulgarity /vʌl'gærətɪ/ n volgarità f inv

vulnerable /'vʌlnərəbl/ adj vulnerabile

vulture /'vʌltʃə(r)/ n avvoltoio m

vying /'vaɪɪŋ/ ▸ VIE

Ww

w¹, W /'dʌblju:/ *n* (letter) w, W *f inv*
W² *abbr* (West) O; *abbr* Electr (**watt**) w
wad /wɒd/ *n* batuffolo *m*; (bundle) rotolo *m*
wadding /'wɒdɪŋ/ *n* ovatta *f*
waddle /'wɒdl/ *vi* camminare ondeggiando
wade /weɪd/ *vi* guadare
■ **wade in** *vi* (fam: start working) mettersi al lavoro; (take part) prendere parte
■ **wade into** *vt* (attack) scagliarsi contro
■ **wade through** *vt* fam procedere faticosamente in ⟨book⟩
wader /'weɪdə(r)/ *n* Zool trampoliere *m*; ∼s (*pl*: boots) stivaloni *mpl* di gomma
wafer /'weɪfə(r)/ *n* cialda *f*, wafer *m inv*; Relig ostia *f*
wafer-thin *adj* sottilissimo
waffle¹ /'wɒfl/ *vi* fam blaterare
waffle² *n* Culin cialda *f*
waft /wɒft/ ① *vt* trasportare ② *vi* diffondersi
wag /wæg/ ① *vt* (pt/pp **wagged**) agitare ② *vi* agitarsi
wage¹ /weɪdʒ/ *vt* dichiarare ⟨war⟩ lanciare ⟨campaign⟩
wage² *n* & ∼s *pl* salario *msg*
wage earner *n* salariato, -a *mf*
wage packet *n* busta *f* paga
wager /'weɪdʒə(r)/ *n* scommessa *f*
wage slip *n* cedolino *m* dello stipendio
waggle /'wægl/ ① *vt* dimenare ② *vi* dimenarsi
wagon /'wægən/ *n* carro *m*; Rail vagone *m* merci; **be on the** ∼ *fam* astenersi dall'alcol
waif /weɪf/ *n* trovatello, -a *mf*
wail /weɪl/ ① *n* piagnucolio *m*; (of wind) lamento *m*; (of baby) vagito *m* ② *vi* piagnucolare; ⟨wind⟩ lamentarsi; ⟨baby⟩ vagire
Wailing Wall /'weɪlɪŋ/ *n* Muro *m* del pianto
waist /weɪst/ *n* vita *f*
waistband *n* cintura *f*
waistcoat *n* gilè *m inv*; (of man's suit) panciotto *m*
waistline *n* vita *f*
waist measurement *n* giro *m* vita
wait /weɪt/ ① *n* attesa *f*; **lie in** ∼ **for** appostarsi per sorprendere ② *vi* aspettare; ∼ **at table** servire ai tavoli; ∼ **for** aspettare

③ *vt* ∼ **one's turn** aspettare il proprio turno
■ **wait about**, **wait around** *vi* aspettare
■ **wait behind** *vi* trattenersi
■ **wait in** *vi* rimanere a casa ad aspettare
■ **wait on** *vt* servire
■ **wait up** *vi* rimanere alzato ad aspettare; **don't** ∼ **up for me** non mi aspettare alzato
waiter /'weɪtə(r)/ *n* cameriere *m*
waiter service *n* servizio *m* al tavolo
waiting game *n* **play a** ∼ ∼ *n* temporeggiare
waiting list *n* lista *f* d'attesa
waiting room *n* sala *f* d'aspetto
waitress /'weɪtrɪs/ *n* cameriera *f*
waive /weɪv/ *vt* rinunciare a ⟨claim⟩; non tener conto di ⟨rule⟩
waiver /'weɪvə(r)/ *n* Jur rinuncia *f*
wake¹ /weɪk/ ① *n* veglia *f* funebre ② *vt* (pt **woke**, pp **woken**) ∼ [**up**] svegliare ③ *vi* svegliarsi
■ **wake up to** *vt* ∼ **up to the fact that...** (realize) aprire gli occhi di fronte al fatto che...
wake² *n* Naut scia *f*; **in the** ∼ **of** fig nella scia di
wakeful /'weɪkfʊl/ *adj* ⟨night⟩ insonne
waken /'weɪkn/ ① *vt* svegliare ② *vi* svegliarsi
wake-up call *n* sveglia *f* telefonica
Wales /weɪlz/ *n* Galles *m*
walk /wɔːk/ ① *n* passeggiata *f*; (gait) andatura *f*; (path) sentiero *m*; **go for a** ∼ andare a fare una passeggiata; ∼ **of life** livello *m* sociale ② *vi* camminare; (as opposed to drive etc) andare a piedi; (ramble) passeggiare; '∼' Am (at crossing) 'avanti' ③ *vt* portare a spasso ⟨dog⟩; percorrere ⟨streets⟩
■ **walk away** *vi* (leave) allontanarsi; ∼ **away from** abbandonare ⟨place, person⟩; disinteressarsi di ⟨problem⟩; (survive unscathed) uscire illeso da ⟨accident⟩
■ **walk away with** *vt* (win easily) vincere senza difficoltà ⟨game, election, prize⟩
■ **walk back** *vi* ritornare a piedi
■ **walk in** *vi* entrare all'improvviso
■ **walk into** *vt* entrare in ⟨room⟩; andare a sbattere contro ⟨door, lamp post⟩; cadere in ⟨trap⟩; trovare facilmente ⟨job⟩
■ **walk off** *vi* (leave) andarsene

■ **walk off with** *vt* (win easily) riportare senza difficoltà; (take, steal) portarsi via

■ **walk out** *vi* ⟨husband, employee⟩ andarsene; ⟨workers⟩ scioperare

■ **walk out of** *vt* uscire da ⟨room⟩; abbandonare ⟨meeting⟩

■ **walk out on** *vt* lasciare

■ **walk over** *vt* ~ **all over somebody** (defeat) stracciare qualcuno; (treat badly) trattare qualcuno come una pezza da piedi

■ **walk through** *vt* superare senza difficoltà ⟨exam, interview⟩

■ **walk up** *vi* (as opposed to taking the lift) salire a piedi; (approach) avvicinarsi

walkabout /'wɔ:kəbaʊt/ *n* escursione *f* periodica degli aborigeni australiani nell'entroterra; (by royalty) incontro *m* con la folla; **go** ~ ⟨queen, politician⟩ camminare tra la folla

walker /'wɔ:kə(r)/ *n* camminatore, -trice *mf*; (rambler) escursionista *mf*

walkie-talkie /wɔ:kɪ'tɔ:kɪ/ *n* walkie-talkie *m inv*

walk-in *adj* ~ **closet** stanzino *m*

walking /'wɔ:kɪŋ/ *n* camminare *m*; (rambling) fare *m* delle escursioni

walking boots *npl* scarponi *mpl* [da trekking]

walking distance *n* **it's within** ~ ~ ci si arriva a piedi

walking frame *n* Med deambulatore *m*

walking pace *n* passo *m*

walking shoes *npl* scarpe *fpl* da passeggio

walking-stick *n* bastone *m* da passeggio

walking wounded *npl* feriti *mpl* in grado di camminare

Walkman® /'wɔ:kmən/ *n* Walkman® *m inv*

walk-on ① *n* Theat comparsa *f* ② *adj* ⟨role⟩ piccolo

walkout *n* sciopero *m*

walkover *n* fig vittoria *f* facile

walkway *n* passaggio *m* pedonale

wall /wɔ:l/ *n* muro *m*; **go to the** ~ fam andare a rotoli; **drive somebody up the** ~ fam far diventare matto qualcuno

■ **wall up** *vt* murare

wallchart /'wɔ:ltʃɑ:t/ *n* tabellone *m*

walled /wɔ:ld/ *adj* ⟨city⟩ fortificato

wallet /'wɒlɪt/ *n* portafoglio *m*

wallflower /'wɔ:lflaʊə(r)/ *n* violaciocca *f*

wall hanging *n* decorazione *f* murale

wallop /'wɒləp/ ① *n* fam colpo *m* ② *vt* (pt/pp **walloped**) fam colpire

walloping /'wɒləpɪŋ/ fam ① *adj* enorme ② *adv* ~ **great** (very big) enorme ③ *n* **give somebody a** ~ suonarle a qualcuno

wallow /'wɒləʊ/ *vi* sguazzare; (in self-pity, grief) crogiolarsi

wallpaper /'wɔ:lpeɪpə(r)/ ① *n* tappezzeria *f* ② *vt* tappezzare

wall-to-wall *adj* che copre tutto il pavimento

walnut /'wɔ:lnʌt/ *n* noce *f*

walrus /'wɔ:lrəs/ *n* tricheco *m*

waltz /wɔ:lts/ ① *n* valzer *m inv* ② *vi* ballare il valzer; **he came** ~**ing up and said...** fam è arrivato e ha detto con nonchalance...

■ **waltz off with** *vt* (fam: take, win) portarsi via

■ **waltz through** *vt* superare facilmente ⟨exam⟩

wan /wɒn/ *adj* esangue

wand /wɒnd/ *n* (magic ~) bacchetta *f* [magica]

wander /'wɒndə(r)/ *vi* girovagare; (fig: digress) divagare

■ **wander about** *vi* andare a spasso

■ **wander away** *vi* allontanarsi

■ **wander off** *vi* allontanarsi; **I'd better be** ~**ing off** fam è meglio che vada

wanderer /'wɒndərə(r)/ *n* vagabondo, -a *mf*

wanderlust /'wɒndəlʌst/ *n* smania *f* dei viaggi

wane /weɪn/ ① *n* **be on the** ~ essere in fase calante ② *vi* calare

wangle /'wæŋgl/ *vt* fam rimediare ⟨invitation, holiday⟩

waning /'weɪnɪŋ/ ① *n* (of moon) calare *m*; (weakening) declino *m* ② *adj* ⟨moon⟩ calante; ⟨popularity⟩ in declino

wannabee /'wɒnəbi:/ *n* fam persona *f* che sogna di diventare famosa

want /wɒnt/ ① *n* (hardship) bisogno *m*; (lack) mancanza *f* ② *vt* volere; (need) aver bisogno di; ~ **[to have] something** volere qualcosa; ~ **to do something** voler fare qualcosa; **we** ~ **to stay** vogliamo rimanere; **I** ~ **you to go** voglio che tu vada; **it** ~**s painting** ha bisogno d'essere dipinto; **you** ~ **to learn to swim** bisogna che impari a nuotare ③ *vi* ~ **for** mancare di

wanted /'wɒntɪd/ *adj* ricercato

wanted list *n* lista *f* dei ricercati

wanting /'wɒntɪŋ/ *adj* **be** ~ mancare; **be** ~ **in** mancare di

wanton /'wɒntən/ *adj* ⟨cruelty, neglect⟩ gratuito; (morally) debosciato

WAP /wæp/ *abbr* (**wireless application protocol**) WAP *m*; ~ **phone** telefonino WAP

WAP-enabled /ɪ'neɪbld/ *adj* ⟨device, system⟩ abilitato al WAP

war ⸱⸱⸱⸱⸳ washing machine ⸱⸱⸱

war /wɔ:(r)/ *n* guerra *f*; fig lotta *f* (**on** contro); **at** ~ **in** guerra

warble /'wɔ:bl/ *vt/i* trillare; ⟨*singer*⟩ gorgheggiare

war cabinet *n* consiglio *m* di guerra

war cry *n* grido *m* di guerra

ward /wɔ:d/ *n* (in hospital) reparto *m*; (child) minore *m* sotto tutela
  ■ **ward off** *vt* evitare; parare ⟨*blow*⟩

warden /'wɔ:dn/ *n* guardiano, -a *mf*

warder /'wɔ:də(r)/ *n* guardia *f* carceraria

wardrobe /'wɔ:drəʊb/ *n* guardaroba *m*

wardrobe assistant *n* costumista *mf*

ward round *n* Med giro *m* delle corsie

ward sister *n* Br Med caposala *f inv*

warehouse /'weəhaʊs/ *n* magazzino *m*

wares /weəz/ *npl* merci *mpl*

warfare /'wɔ:feə(r)/ *n* guerra *f*

war game *n* Mil simulazione *f* di scontro militare

warhead *n* testata *f*

warhorse *n* cavallo *m* da battaglia; (fig: campaigner) veterano *m*

warily /'weərɪlɪ/ *adv* cautamente

warlike /'wɔ:laɪk/ *adj* bellicoso

warm /wɔ:m/ ① *adj* caldo; ⟨*welcome*⟩ caloroso; **be** ~ ⟨*person*⟩ aver caldo; **it is** ~ ⟨*weather*⟩ fa caldo
  ② *vt* scaldare
  ■ **warm to** *vt* prendere in simpatia ⟨*person*⟩
  ■ **warm up** *vt* scaldare *vi* scaldarsi; fig animarsi

warm-blooded /-'blʌdɪd/ *adj* Zool con temperatura corporea costante

war memorial *n* monumento *m* ai caduti

warm-hearted /-'hɑ:tɪd/ *adj* espansivo

warmly /'wɔ:mlɪ/ *adv* ⟨*greet*⟩ calorosamente; ⟨*dress*⟩ in modo pesante

warmongering /'wɔ:mʌŋgərɪŋ/ ① *n* bellicismo *m*
  ② *adj* ⟨*article*⟩ bellicistico; ⟨*person*⟩ guerrafondaio

warmth /wɔ:mθ/ *n* calore *m*

warm-up *n* Sport riscaldamento *m*; (of musicians) prove *fpl*

warn /wɔ:n/ *vt* avvertire
  ■ **warn off** *vt* dare un avvertimento a

warning /'wɔ:nɪŋ/ *n* avvertimento *m*; (advance notice) preavviso *m*

warning light *n* spia *f* luminosa

warning shot *n* sparo *m* d'avvertimento

warning sign *n* (road sign) segnale *m* di pericolo; (of illness) segnale *m* d'allarme

warning triangle *n* triangolo *m* di segnalazione

warp /wɔ:p/ ① *vt* deformare; fig distorcere

② *vi* deformarsi

warpaint /'wɔ:peɪnt/ *n* Mil pitture *fpl* di guerra

warpath /'wɔ:pɑ:θ/ *n* **on the** ~ sul sentiero di guerra

warped /wɔ:pt/ *adj* deformato; ⟨*personality*⟩ contorto; ⟨*sexuality*⟩ deviato; ⟨*view*⟩ distorto

warplane /'wɔ:pleɪn/ *n* aereo *m* da guerra

warrant /'wɒrənt/ ① *n* (for arrest, search) mandato *m*
  ② *vt* (justify) giustificare; (guarantee) garantire

warranty /'wɒrəntɪ/ *n* garanzia *f*

warren /'wɒr(ə)n/ *n* (of rabbits) area *f* piena di tane di conigli; (building, maze of streets) labirinto *m*

warring /'wɔ:rɪŋ/ *adj* in guerra

warrior /'wɒrɪə(r)/ *n* guerriero, -a *mf*

Warsaw /'wɔ:sɔ:/ *n* Varsavia *f*

warship /'wɔ:ʃɪp/ *n* nave *f* da guerra

wart /wɔ:t/ *n* porro *m*

wartime /'wɔ:taɪm/ *n* tempo *m* di guerra

war-torn /'wɔ:tɔ:n/ *adj* logorato dalla guerra

wary /'weərɪ/ *adj* (**-ier, -iest**) (careful) cauto; (suspicious) diffidente

was /wɒz/ ▶ BE

wash /wɒʃ/ ① *n* lavata *f*; (clothes) bucato *m*; (in washing machine) lavaggio *m*; **have a** ~ darsi una lavata
  ② *vt* lavare; ⟨*sea*⟩ bagnare; ~ **one's hands** lavarsi le mani
  ③ *vi* lavarsi
  ■ **wash away** *vt* ⟨*rain*⟩ portare via; ⟨*sea, floodwaters*⟩ spazzare via
  ■ **wash off** ① *vt* lavar via ⟨*stain, mud*⟩
  ② *vi* andar via
  ■ **wash out** *vt* sciacquare ⟨*soap*⟩; sciacquarsi ⟨*mouth*⟩
  ■ **wash up** ① *vt* lavare
  ② *vi* lavare i piatti; Am lavarsi

washable /'wɒʃəbl/ *adj* lavabile

wash-and-wear *adj* che non si stira

wash bag *n* Br = TOILET BAG

washbasin *n* lavandino *m*

washbowl *n* Am = WASHBASIN

wash cloth *n* Am ≈ guanto *m* da bagno

washed out /wɒʃt'aʊt/ *adj* (faded) scolorito; (tired) spossato

washed up *adj* fam (finished) finito; (tired) distrutto

washer /'wɒʃə(r)/ *n* Techn guarnizione *f*; (machine) lavatrice *f*

washer-dryer /-'draɪə(r)/ *n* asciugabiancheria *m inv*

washing /'wɒʃɪŋ/ *n* bucato *m*

washing line *n* corda *f* per il bucato

washing machine *n* lavatrice *f*

washing powder n detersivo m

washing soda n soda f da bucato

washing-up n do the ~ lavare i piatti

washing-up bowl n bacinella f (per i piatti)

washing-up liquid n detersivo m per i piatti

washing-up water n rigovernatura f

wash load n carico m di lavatrice

wash-out n disastro m

washroom n bagno m

wash-stand n Am = WASHBASIN

WASP or **Wasp** /wɒsp/ n abbr Am (White Anglo-Saxon Protestant) WASP m

wasp /wɒsp/ n vespa f

waspish /'wɒspɪʃ/ adj pungente

wastage /'weɪstɪdʒ/ n perdita f

waste /weɪst/ ① n spreco m; (rubbish) rifiuto m; ~s pl distesa fsg desolata; ~ of time perdita f di tempo
② adj ⟨product⟩ di scarto; ⟨land⟩ desolato; lay ~ devastare
③ vt sprecare
∎ **waste away** vi deperire

wastebasket n cestino m della carta straccia

waste bin n (for paper) cestino m della carta straccia; (for rubbish) secchio m della spazzatura

wasted /'weɪstɪd/ adj ⟨energy, effort, life⟩ sprecato; ⟨limb⟩ atrofizzato; body scarnito

waste disposal n smaltimento m dei rifiuti

waste disposal unit n eliminatore m di rifiuti

wasteful /'weɪstfʊl/ adj dispendioso

wasteland n area f desolata

waste paper n carta f straccia

waste-paper basket n cestino m per la carta [straccia]

waste pipe n tubo m di scarico

watch /wɒtʃ/ ① n guardia f; (period of duty) turno m di guardia; (timepiece) orologio m; be on the ~ stare all'erta
② vt guardare ⟨film, match, television⟩; (be careful of, look after) stare attento a
③ vi guardare
∎ **watch out** vi (be careful) stare attento (for a)
∎ **watch out for** vt (look for) fare attenzione all'arrivo di ⟨person⟩
∎ **watch over** vt proteggere ⟨person⟩

watchband n Am = WATCH STRAP

watchdog /'wɒtʃdɒg/ n cane m da guardia

watchful /'wɒtʃfʊl/ adj attento

watchfully /'wɒtʃfʊl/ adv attentamente

watchmaker n orologiaio, -a mf

watchman n guardiano m

watch strap n cinturino m dell'orologio

watchtower n torre f di guardia

watchword n motto m

water /'wɔːtə(r)/ ① n acqua f; ~s pl acque fpl
② vt annaffiare ⟨garden, plant⟩; (dilute) annacquare; dare da bere a ⟨horse etc⟩
③ vi ⟨eyes⟩ lacrimare; my mouth was ~ing avevo l'acquolina in bocca
∎ **water down** vt diluire; fig attenuare

water authority n ente m dell'acqua

water bed n materasso m ad acqua

waterbird n uccello m acquatico

water birth n parto m in acqua

water bottle n borraccia f

water cannon n idrante m

watercolour n acquerello m

water company n società f inv dell'acqua

watercress n crescione m

water divining n rabdomanzia f

waterfall n cascata f

water filter n brocca f con filtro per l'acqua

waterfront n (by lakeside, riverside) riva f; (on harbour) zona f portuale

water-heater n scaldacqua m inv

waterhole n pozza f d'acqua

watering can /'wɔːtərɪŋ/ n annaffiatoio m

water jump n riviera f

water lily n ninfea f

waterline n linea f di galleggiamento

waterlogged adj inzuppato

water main n conduttura f dell'acqua

watermark n filigrana f

watermeadow n marcita f

watermelon n cocomero m, anguria f

watermill n mulino m ad acqua

water polo n pallanuoto f

water-power n energia f idraulica

waterproof ① adj ⟨coat⟩ impermeabile; ⟨make-up⟩ waterproof inv
② n impermeabile m

waterproofs npl sovrapantaloni mpl e giacca impermeabili

water rates mpl Br tariffe fpl dell'acqua

water-resistant adj ⟨sun cream⟩ resistente all'acqua; ⟨garment, watch⟩ impermeabile

watershed n spartiacque m inv; fig svolta f

waterside ① n riva f
② attrib ⟨cafe, hotel⟩ sulla riva

water-ski vi fare sci nautico

waterskiing n sci m nautico

water slide n acquascivolo m

water softener *n* (equipment) addolcitore *m*; (substance) anticalcare *m* inv

water-soluble *adj* idrosolubile

water sport *n* sport *m* inv acquatico

water-table *n* Geog superficie *f* freatica

watertight *adj* stagno; fig irrefutabile

water tower *n* serbatoio *m* idrico a torre

waterway *n* canale *m* navigabile

water-wheel *n* ruota *f* idraulica

water wings *npl* braccioli *mpl*

waterworks *n* impianto *m* idrico; **turn on the** ~ fam mettersi a piangere come una fontana

watery /'wɔːtərɪ/ *adj* acquoso; ⟨eyes⟩ lacrimoso

watt /wɒt/ *n* watt *m* inv

wattage /'wɒtɪdʒ/ *n* wattaggio *m*

wave /weɪv/ **①** *n* onda *f*; (gesture) cenno *m*; fig ondata *f*
② *vt* agitare; ~ **one's hand** agitare la mano
③ *vi* far segno; ⟨flag⟩ sventolare
■ **wave aside** *vt* respingere ⟨criticism⟩
■ **wave down** *vt* far segno di fermarsi a ⟨vehicle⟩

waveband /'weɪvbænd/ *n* gamma *f* d'onda

wavelength /'weɪvleŋθ/ *n* lunghezza *f* d'onda; **be on the same** ~ fig essere sulla stessa lunghezza d'onda

waver /'weɪvə(r)/ *vi* vacillare; (hesitate) esitare

wavy /'weɪvɪ/ *adj* ondulato

wax /wæks/ *vi* ⟨moon⟩ crescere; (fig: become) diventare

wax² **①** *n* cera *f*; (in ear) cerume *m*
② *vt* dare la cera a

waxed jacket /wækst/ *n* cerata *f*

waxwork /'wækswɜːk/ *n* statua *f* di cera

waxworks /'wækswɜːks/ *n* museo *m* delle cere

waxy /'wæksɪ/ *adj* ⟨skin, texture⟩ cereo

way /weɪ/ **①** *n* percorso *m*; (direction) direzione *f*; (manner, method) modo *m*; ~**s** *pl* (customs) abitudini *fpl*; **be in the** ~ essere in mezzo; **on the** ~ **to Rome** andando a Roma; **I'll do it on the** ~ lo faccio mentre vado; **it's on my** ~ è sul mio percorso; **a long** ~ **off** lontano; **this** ~ da questa parte; (like this) così; **by the** ~ a proposito; **by** ~ **of** come; (via) via; **either** ~ (whatever we do) in un modo o nell'altro; **in some** ~**s** sotto certi aspetti; **in a** ~ in un certo senso; **in a bad** ~ ⟨person⟩ molto grave; **out of the** ~ fuori mano; **under** ~ in corso; **lead the** ~ far strada; fig aprire la strada; **make** ~ far posto (**for** a); **give** ~ Auto dare la precedenza; **go out of one's** ~ fig scomodarsi (**to** per); **get one's [own]** ~ averla vinta

② *adv* ~ **behind** molto indietro

way in *n* entrata *f*

waylay /weɪ'leɪ/ *vt* (pt/pp -**laid**) aspettare al varco ⟨person⟩; intercettare ⟨letter⟩

way-out *adj* fam eccentrico

way out *n* uscita *f*; fig via *f* d'uscita

wayside /'weɪsaɪd/ *n* bordo *m*; **fall by the** ~ (morally) smarrire la retta via; (fail) fallire

wayward /'weɪwəd/ *adj* capriccioso

WC *abbr* WC; **the WC** il gabinetto

we /wiː/ *pers pron* noi; **we're the last** siamo gli ultimi; **they're going, but we're not** loro vanno, ma noi no

weak /wiːk/ *adj* debole; ⟨liquid⟩ leggero; **go** ~ **at the knees** fam sentirsi piegare le ginocchia

weaken /'wiːkn/ **①** *vt* indebolire
② *vi* indebolirsi

weakling /'wiːklɪŋ/ *n* smidollato, -a *mf*

weakly /'wiːklɪ/ *adv* debolmente

weak-minded /-'maɪndɪd/ *adj* (indecisive) debole; (simple) poco intelligente

weakness /'wiːknɪs/ *n* debolezza *f*; (liking) debole *m*

weak-willed /-'wɪld/ *adj* debole

weal /wiːl/ *n* piaga *f*

wealth /welθ/ *n* ricchezza *f*; fig gran quantità *f*

wealthy /'welθɪ/ *adj* (-**ier**, -**iest**) ricco

wean /wiːn/ *vt* svezzare

weapon /'wepən/ *n* arma *f*

weapon of mass destruction *n* arma *f* di distruzione di massa

weaponry /'wepənrɪ/ *n* armamento *m*

wear /weə(r)/ **①** *n* (clothing) abbigliamento *m*; **for everyday** ~ da portare tutti i giorni; ~ **[and tear]** usura *f*
② *vt* (pt **wore**, pp **worn**) portare; (damage) consumare; ~ **a hole in something** logorare qualcosa fino a fare un buco; **what shall I** ~? cosa mi metto?
③ *vi* consumarsi; (last) durare
■ **wear away** **①** *vt* consumare
② *vi* consumarsi
■ **wear down** *vt* estenuare ⟨opposition etc⟩
■ **wear off** *vi* scomparire; ⟨effect⟩ finire
■ **wear out** **①** *vt* consumare [fino in fondo]; (exhaust) estenuare
② *vi* estenuarsi
■ **wear through** *vi* ⟨elbow, knee, shoe⟩ bucarsi

wearable /'weərəbl/ *adj* portabile

wearily /'wɪərɪlɪ/ *adv* stancamente

weariness /'wɪərɪnɪs/ *n* stanchezza *f*

wearing /'weərɪŋ/ *adj* (tiring) faticoso; (irritating) fastidioso

weary /'wɪərɪ/ **①** *adj* (-**ier**, -**iest**) sfinito
② *vt* (pt/pp **wearied**) sfinire

❸ *vi* ~ **of** stancarsi di

weasel /'wi:zl/ *n* donnola *f*

weather /'weðə(r)/ ❶ *n* tempo *m*; **in this** ~ con questo tempo; **under the** ~ fam giù di corda
❷ *vt* sopravvivere a ‹storm›

weather balloon *n* pallone *m* sonda

weather-beaten /-bi:tn/ *adj* ‹face› segnato dalle intemperie

weathercock *n* gallo *m* segnavento

weather forecast *n* previsioni *fpl* del tempo

weatherman *n* TV meteorologo *m*

weatherproof *adj* ‹garment, shoe› impermeabile; ‹shelter, door› resistente alle intemperie

weather-vane *n* banderuola *f*

weave¹ /wi:v/ *vi* (pt/pp **weaved**) (move) zigzagare

weave² ❶ *n* (Tex) tessuto *m*
❷ *vt* (pt **wove**, pp **woven**) tessere; intrecciare ‹flowers etc›; intrecciare le fila di ‹story etc›

weaver /'wi:və(r)/ *n* tessitore, -trice *mf*

weaving /'wi:vɪŋ/ *n* tessitura *f*

web /web/ *n* rete *f*; Comput web *m*, rete *f*; (of spider) ragnatela *f*

web-based /beɪst/ *adj* ‹learning, software› basato sul web

webbed feet /webd'fi:t/ *npl* piedi *mpl* palmati

webbing /'webɪŋ/ *n* (material) cinghie *fpl*

web cam /kæm/ *n* Comput web cam *f inv*

web developer *n* Comput sviluppatore *m* web

weblog /'weblɒg/ *n* Comput = BLOG

weblogger /'weblɒgə(r)/ *n* Comput = BLOGGER

webmaster *n* Comput webmaster *mf inv*

web page *n* Comput pagina *f* web

web server *n* Comput server *m* web

web site *n* Comput sito *m* web

web space *n* Comput spazio *m* web

wed /wed/ ❶ *vt* (pt/pp **wedded**) sposare
❷ *vi* sposarsi

wedding /'wedɪŋ/ *n* matrimonio *m*

wedding anniversary *n* anniversario *m* di nozze

wedding bells *npl* fig marcia *f* nuziale

wedding breakfast *n* rinfresco *m* di nozze

wedding cake *n* torta *f* nuziale

wedding day *n* giorno *m* del matrimonio

wedding dress *n* vestito *m* da sposa

wedding march *n* marcia *f* nuziale

wedding night *n* prima notte *f* di nozze

wedding reception *n* ricevimento *m* di nozze

wedding ring *n* fede *f*

wedding vows *npl* voti *mpl* nuziali

wedge /wedʒ/ ❶ *n* zeppa *f*; (for splitting wood) cuneo *m*; (of cheese) fetta *f*
❷ *vt* (fix) fissare

wedlock /'wedlɒk/ *n* **born out of** ~ nato fuori dal matrimonio

Wednesday /'wenzdeɪ/ *n* mercoledì *m inv*

wee¹ /wi:/ *adj* fam piccolo

wee² ❶ *n* fam **do a** ~ fare la pipì
❷ *vi* fam fare la pipì

weed /wi:d/ ❶ *n* erbaccia *f*; (fam: person) mollusco *m*
❷ *vt* estirpare le erbacce da
❸ *vi* estirpare le erbacce
■ **weed out** *vt* fig eliminare

weedkiller /'wi:dkɪlə(r)/ *n* erbicida *m*

weedy /'wi:dɪ/ *adj* fam mingherlino

week /wi:k/ *n* settimana *f*

weekday /'wi:kdeɪ/ *n* giorno *m* feriale

weekend /'wi:kend/ *n* fine *m* settimana

weekend bag *n* piccola borsa *f* da viaggio

weekly /'wi:klɪ/ ❶ *adj* settimanale
❷ *n* settimanale *m*
❸ *adv* settimanalmente

weep /wi:p/ *vi* (pt/pp **wept**) piangere

weeping willow /wi:pɪŋ'wɪləʊ/ *n* salice *m* piangente

weepy /'wi:pɪ/ *adj* ‹film› strappalacrime *inv*

weigh /weɪ/ *vt/i* pesare; ~ **anchor** levare l'ancora
■ **weigh down** *vt* fig piegare
■ **weigh in** *vi* (fam: join in discussion) intromettersi
■ **weigh out** *vt* pesare ‹amount of flour etc›
■ **weigh up** *vt* fig soppesare; valutare ‹person›

weighing machine /'weɪɪŋ/ *n* bilancia *f*

weight /weɪt/ *n* peso *m*; **put on/lose** ~ ingrassare/dimagrire

weighting /'weɪtɪŋ/ *n* (allowance) indennità *f inv*

weightlessness /'weɪtlɪsnɪs/ *n* assenza *f* di gravità

weightlifter *n* sollevatore *m* di pesi

weightlifting *n* sollevamento *m* pesi

weight problem *n* problemi *mpl* di peso

weight training *n* **do** ~ ~ allenarsi con i pesi

weight-watcher *n* (in group) persona *f* che segue una dieta dimagrante

weighty /'weɪtɪ/ *adj* (**-ier**, **-iest**) pesante; (important) di un certo peso

weir /wɪə(r)/ n chiusa f

weird /wɪəd/ adj misterioso; (bizarre) bizzarro

welcome /'welkəm/ ① adj benvenuto; you're ~! prego!; you're ~ to have it/to come prendilo/vieni pure
② n accoglienza f
③ vt accogliere; (appreciate) gradire

welcoming /'welkəmɪŋ/ adj ⟨ceremony⟩ di benvenuto; ⟨committee, smile⟩ di accoglienza; ⟨house⟩ accogliente

weld /weld/ vt saldare

welder /'weldə(r)/ n saldatore m

welfare /'welfeə(r)/ n benessere m; (aid) assistenza f; Am previdenza f sociale

welfare services n servizi mpl sociali

Welfare State n Stato m assistenziale

welfare work n assistenza m sociale

well¹ /wel/ n pozzo m; (oil ~) pozzo m; (of staircase) tromba f

well² ① adv (better, best) bene; as ~ anche; as ~ as (in addition) oltre a; ~ done! bravo!; very ~ benissimo
② adj he is not ~ non sta bene; get ~ soon! guarisci presto!
③ int beh!; ~ I never! ma va'!

well-attended /-ə'tendɪd/ adj ben frequentato

well-balanced /'bælənst/ adj ⟨person, diet, meal⟩ equilibrato

well-behaved /-bɪ'heɪvd/ adj educato

well-being /'welbi:ɪŋ/ n benessere m

well-bred /wel'bred/ adj beneducato

well-defined /-dɪ'faɪnd/ adj ⟨role, boundary⟩ ben definito; ⟨outline, image⟩ netto

well-disposed /-dɪ'spəʊzd/ adj benevolo; be ~ towards essere bendisposto verso ⟨person⟩; essere favorevole a ⟨idea⟩

well done /dʌn/ adj ⟨task⟩ ben fatto; Culin ben cotto

well-educated adj istruito; (cultured) colto

well-founded /-'faʊndɪd/ adj fondato

well-heeled /-'hi:ld/ adj fam danaroso

well-informed /-ɪn'fɔ:md/ adj beninformato

wellingtons /'welɪŋtənz/ npl stivali mpl di gomma

well-judged /-'dʒʌdʒd/ adj ⟨performance⟩ molto intelligente; ⟨shot⟩ ben assestato; ⟨statement, phrase⟩ ben ponderato

well-kept /-'kept/ adj ⟨garden⟩ curato; ⟨secret⟩ ben custodito

well-known /-'nəʊn/ adj famoso

well-liked /-'laɪkt/ adj popolare

well-made /-'meɪd/ adj benfatto

well-mannered /-'mænəd/ adj educato

well-meaning adj con buone intenzioni

well-meant /-'ment/ adj con le migliori intenzioni

well-nigh /'welnaɪ/ adv quasi

well-off adj benestante

well-read /-'red/ adj colto

well-respected /rɪ'spektɪd/ adj molto rispettato

well-rounded /'raʊndɪd/ adj ⟨education, individual⟩ completo

well-spoken /-'spəʊkən/ adj ⟨person⟩ che parla bene

well-thought-of adj stimato

well-timed /'taɪmd/ adj tempestivo

well-to-do adj ricco

well-trodden /-'trɒdn/ adj also fig battuto

well-wisher /'welwɪʃə(r)/ n simpatizzante mf

well-worn /-'wɔ:n/ adj ⟨steps, floorboards⟩ consunto; ⟨carpet, garment⟩ logoro; fig ⟨argument⟩ trito e ritrito

Welsh /welʃ/ adj & n gallese mf; (language) gallese m; the ~ pl i gallesi

Welshman /'welʃmən/ n gallese m

Welsh rabbit n toast m inv al formaggio

welt /welt/ n (on shoe) rinforzo m; (on skin) segno m di frustata

welterweight /'weltəweɪt/ n pesi mpl welter

went /went/ ▶ GO

wept /wept/ ▶ WEEP

were /wɜ:(r)/ ▶ BE

west /west/ ① n ovest m; to the ~ of a ovest di; the W~ l'Occidente m
② adj occidentale
③ adv verso occidente; go ~ fam andare in malora

West Bank n Cisgiordania f

West Country n sud-ovest m dell'Inghilterra

West End n zona f di Londra con un'alta concentrazione di teatri e negozi di lusso

westerly /'westəlɪ/ adj verso ovest; occidentale ⟨wind⟩

western /'westən/ ① adj occidentale
② n western m inv

Westerner /'westənə(r)/ n occidentale mf

westernize /'westənaɪz/ vt occidentalizzare; become ~d occidentalizzarsi

Western Samoa /sə'məʊə/ n Samoa fpl Occidentali

West Germany n Germania f occidentale

West Indian adj & n antillese mf

West Indies /ˈɪndɪz/ npl Antille fpl

westward[s] /ˈwestwəd[z]/ adv verso ovest

wet /wet/ ① adj (**-tter, -test**) bagnato; fresco ⟨paint⟩; (rainy) piovoso; fam ⟨person⟩ smidollato; **get ~** bagnarsi
② vt (pt/pp **wet, wetted**) bagnare

wet blanket n guastafeste mf inv

wet fish n Br pesce m fresco

wet-look adj ⟨plastic, leather⟩ lucido

wet-nurse n balia f

wetsuit n muta f

whack /wæk/ ① n fam colpo m
② vt fam dare un colpo a

whacked /wæk/ adj fam stanco morto

whacking /ˈwækɪŋ/ ① adj (Br fam: enormous) enorme
② n fam sculacciata f

whacky /ˈwækɪ/ adj fam ⟨joke, person etc⟩ demenziale

whale /weɪl/ n balena f; **have a ~ of a time** fam divertirsi un sacco

whaling /ˈweɪlɪŋ/ n caccia f alla balena

wham /wæm/ int bum!

wharf /wɔːf/ n banchina f

what /wɒt/ ① pron che, [che] cosa; **~ for?** perché?; **~ is that for?** a che cosa serve?; **~ is it?** (what do you want) cosa c'è?; **~ is it like?** com'è?; **~ is your name?** come ti chiami?; **~ is the weather like?** com'è il tempo?; **~ is the film about?** di cosa parla il film?; **~ is he talking about?** di cosa sta parlando?; **he asked me ~ she had said** mi ha chiesto cosa ha detto; **~ about going to the cinema?** e se andassimo al cinema?; **~ about the children?** (what will they do) e i bambini?; **~ if it rains?** e se piove?
② adj quale, che; **take ~ books you want** prendi tutti i libri che vuoi; **~ kind of a** che tipo di; **at ~ time?** a che ora?
③ adv che; **~ a lovely day!** che bella giornata!
④ int **~!** [che] cosa!; **~?** [che] cosa?

what-d'yer-call-it /ˈwɒtdʒəkɔːlɪt/ n fam aggeggio m

whatever /wɒtˈevə(r)/ ① adj qualunque
② pron qualsiasi cosa; **~ is it?** cos'è?; **~ he does** qualsiasi cosa faccia; **~ happens** qualunque cosa succeda; **nothing ~** proprio niente

whatnot /ˈwɒtnɒt/ n coso m; (stand) scaffaletto m; **and ~** (and so on) e così via

what's-her-name /ˈwɒtzəneɪm/ n fam cosa f

what's-his-name /ˈwɒtsɪzneɪm/ n, fam, coso m

whatsit /ˈwɒtsɪt/ n fam aggeggio m, coso m

what's-its-name n fam coso, -a mf

whatsoever /wɒtsəʊˈevə(r)/ adj & pron = WHATEVER

wheat /wiːt/ n grano m, frumento m

wheatgerm /ˈwiːtdʒɜːm/ n germoglio m di grano

wheatmeal /ˈwiːtmiːl/ n farina f di frumento

wheedle /ˈwiːdl/ vt **~ something out of somebody** ottenere qualcosa da qualcuno con le lusinghe

wheel /wiːl/ ① n ruota f; (steering **~**) volante m; **at the ~** al volante
② vt (push) spingere
③ vi (circle) ruotare; **~ round** ruotare

wheelbarrow n carriola f

wheelchair n sedia f a rotelle

wheelchair access n accesso m disabili

wheel clamp n ceppo m bloccaruote

wheeler-dealer /wiːləˈdiːlə(r)/ n trafficone, -a mf

wheelie bin /ˈwiːlɪ/ n cassonetto m

wheeze /wiːz/ vi ansimare

wheezy /ˈwiːzɪ/ adj ⟨voice, cough⟩ dal respiro affannoso

when /wen/ adv & conj quando; **the day ~** il giorno in cui; **~ swimming/reading** nuotando/leggendo

whence /wens/ adv liter donde

whenever /wenˈevə(r)/ adv & conj in qualsiasi momento; (every time that) ogni volta che; **~ did it happen?** quando è successo?

where /weə(r)/ adv & conj dove; **the street ~ I live** la via in cui abito; **~ do you come from?** da dove vieni?

whereabouts[1] /weərəˈbaʊts/ adv dove

whereabouts[2] /ˈweərəbaʊts/ n **nobody knows his ~** nessuno sa dove si trovi

whereas /weərˈæz/ conj dal momento che; (in contrast) mentre

whereby /weəˈbaɪ/ adv attraverso il quale

whereupon /weərəˈpɒn/ adv dopo di che

wherever /weərˈevə(r)/ adv & conj dovunque; **~ is he?** dov'è mai?; **~ possible** dovunque sia possibile

wherewithal /ˈweəwɪðɔːl/ n mezzi mpl

whet /wet/ vt (pt/pp **whetted**) aguzzare ⟨appetite⟩

whether /ˈweðə(r)/ conj se; **~ you like it or not** che ti piaccia o no

whew /fjuː/ int (in relief) fiuu; (when hot) uff; (in surprise) wow

which /wɪtʃ/ ① adj & pron quale; **~ one?** quale?; **~ one of you?** chi di voi?; **~ way?** (direction) in che direzione?
② rel pron (object) che; **~ he does frequently** cosa che fa spesso; **after ~** dopo di che; **on/in ~** su/in cui

whichever /wɪtʃ'evə(r)/ *adj & pron* qualunque; ∼ **it is** qualunque sia; ∼ **one of you** chiunque tra voi

whiff /wɪf/ *n* zaffata *f*; **have a** ∼ **of something** odorare qualcosa

while /waɪl/ **1** *n* **a long** ∼ un bel po'; **a little** ∼ un po'
2 *conj* mentre; (as long as) finché; (although) sebbene; **he met her** ∼ **in exile** l'ha incontrata mentre era in esilio
■ **while away** *vt* passare ‹*time*›

whilst /waɪlst/ *conj* = WHILE

whim /wɪm/ *n* capriccio *m*

whimper /'wɪmpə(r)/ *vi* piagnucolare; ‹*dog*› mugolare

whimsical /'wɪmzɪkl/ *adj* capriccioso; ‹*story*› fantasioso

whine /waɪn/ **1** *n* lamento *m*; (of dog) guaito *m*
2 *vi* lamentarsi; ‹*dog*› guaire

whinge /wɪndʒ/ *vi* fam lagnarsi

whining /'waɪnɪŋ/ **1** *adj* ‹*voice, child*› lagnoso
2 *n* (complaints) lagne *fpl*; (of dog) guaiti *mpl*

whinny /'wɪnɪ/ **1** *n* nitrito *m*
2 *vi* ‹*horse*› nitrire

whip /wɪp/ **1** *n* frusta *f*; (Pol: person) parlamentare *mf* incaricato, -a di assicurarsi della presenza dei membri del suo partito alle votazioni
2 *vt* (pt/pp **whipped**) frustare; Culin sbattere; (snatch) afferrare; (fam: steal) fregare
■ **whip up** *vt* (incite) stimolare; fam improvvisare ‹*meal*›

whiplash injury /'wɪplæʃ/ *n* Med colpo *m* di frusta

whipped cream /wɪpt'kri:m/ *n* panna *f* montata

whipping boy /'wɪpɪŋ/ *n* capro *m* espiatorio

whip-round *n* fam colletta *f*; **have a** ∼ fare una colletta

whirl /wɜ:l/ **1** *n* (movement) rotazione *f*; **my mind's in a** ∼ ho le idee confuse
2 *vi* girare rapidamente
3 *vt* far girare rapidamente

whirlpool /'wɜ:lpu:l/ *n* vortice *m*

whirlpool bath *n* vasca *f* con idromassaggio

whirlwind /'wɜ:lwɪnd/ *n* turbine *m*

whirr /wɜ:(r)/ *vi* ronzare

whisk /wɪsk/ **1** *n* Culin frullino *m*
2 *vt* Culin frullare
■ **whisk away** *vt* portare via

whisker /'wɪskə(r)/ *n* ∼**s** *pl* (of cat) baffi *mpl*; (on man's cheek) basette *fpl*; **by a** ∼ per un pelo

whisky /'wɪskɪ/ *n* whisky *m inv*

whisper /'wɪspə(r)/ **1** *n* sussurro *m*; (rumour) diceria *f*

2 *vt/i* sussurrare

whispering gallery /'wɪspərɪŋ/ *n* galleria *f* acustica

whistle /'wɪsl/ **1** *n* fischio *m*; (instrument) fischietto *m*
2 *vt* fischiettare
3 *vi* fischiettare; ‹*referee*› fischiare

whistle-stop tour *n* Pol giro *m* elettorale

white /waɪt/ **1** *adj* bianco; **go** ∼ (pale) sbiancare
2 *n* bianco *m*; (of egg) albume *m*; (person) bianco, -a *mf*

whitebait *n* bianchetti *npl*

white-board *n* lavagna *f* bianca

white coffee *n* caffè *m inv* macchiato

white-collar worker *n* colletto *m* bianco

white elephant *n* (public project) progetto *m* dispendioso e di scarsa efficacia; (building) cattedrale *f* nel deserto; (item, knick-knack) oggetto *m* inutile

white goods *n* (linen) biancheria *f* per la casa; (appliances) elettrodomestici *mpl*

Whitehall *n* strada *f* di Londra sede degli uffici del governo britannico; fig amministrazione *f* britannica

white horses *npl* cavalloni *mpl*

white-hot *adj* ‹*metal*› arroventato

White House *n* the ∼ la Casa Bianca

white knight *n* Fin white knight *m inv*

white-knuckle ride *n* corsa *f* al cardiopalmo

white lie *n* bugia *f* pietosa

whiten /'waɪtn/ **1** *vt* imbiancare
2 *vi* sbiancare

whitener /'waɪt(ə)nə(r)/ *n* (for shoes) bianchetto *m*; (for clothes) sbiancante *m*; (for coffee, tea) surrogato *m* del latte

whiteness /'waɪtnɪs/ *n* bianchezza *f*

white spirit *n* acquaragia *f*

white tie *n* (tie) cravattino *m* bianco; (formal dress) frac *m inv*

whitewash *n* intonaco *m*; fig copertura *f* *vt* dare una mano d'intonaco a; fig coprire

white water *n* rapide *fpl*

white-water rafting /'rɑ:ftɪŋ/ *n* discesa *f* sulle rapide

white wedding *n* matrimonio *m* in bianco

whither /'wɪðə(r)/ *adv* liter dove

whiting /'waɪtɪŋ/ *n* (fish) merlano *m*

Whitsun /'wɪtsn/ *n* Pentecoste *f*

whittle /'wɪtl/ *v*
■ **whittle away** *vt* intaccare ‹*savings*›; ridurre ‹*lead in race*›
■ **whittle down** *vt* ridurre

Whit Sunday /wɪt/ *n* Pentecoste *f*

whiz[z] /wɪz/ *vi* (pt/pp **whizzed**) sibilare

whiz[z]-kid *n* fam giovane *m* prodigio

WHO *n abbr* (**World Health Organization**) OMS *f*

who /hu:/ ① *inter pron* chi
② *rel pron* che; **the children, ~ were all tired,...** i bambini che erano tutti stanchi,...

whodunnit /hu:'dʌnɪt/ *n* fam [romanzo *m*] giallo *m*

whoever /hu:'evə(r)/ *pron* chiunque; **~ he is** chiunque sia; **~ can that be?** chi può mai essere?

whole /həʊl/ ① *adj* tutto; (not broken) intatto; **the ~ truth** tutta la verità; **the ~ world** il mondo intero; **the ~ lot** (everything) tutto; (*pl*) tutti; **the ~ lot of you** tutti voi ② *n* tutto *m*; **as a ~** nell'insieme; **on the ~** tutto considerato; **the ~ of Italy** tutta l'Italia

wholefood *n* cibo *m* macrobiotico

wholehearted /'həʊlhɑ:tɪd/ *adj* di tutto cuore

wholeheartedly /həʊl'hɑ:tɪdlɪ/ *adv* ⟨agree, support⟩ senza riserve

wholemeal *adj* integrale

whole milk *n* latte *m* intero

whole number *n* numero *m* intero

wholesale /'həʊlseɪl/ *adj & adv* all'ingrosso; fig in massa

wholesaler /'həʊlseɪlə(r)/ *n* grossista *mf*

wholesome /'həʊlsəm/ *adj* sano

wholewheat *adj* = WHOLEMEAL

wholly /'həʊlɪ/ *adv* completamente

wholly-owned subsidiary *n* consociata *f* interamente controllata

whom /hu:m/ ① *rel pron* che; **the man ~ I saw** l'uomo che ho visto; **to/with ~ a/con cui** ② *inter pron* chi; **to ~ did you speak?** con chi hai parlato?

whoop /wu:p/ ① *n* (shout) grido *m* ② *vi* gridare

whoopee /'wʊpɪ/ ① *int* evviva! ② *n* hum **make ~** (have fun) fare baldoria; (make love) fare l'amore

whooping cough /'hu:pɪŋ/ *n* pertosse *f*

whoosh /wʊʃ/ *int* vuum!

whopper /'wɒpə(r)/ *n* fam (lie) balla *f*; **what a ~!** è veramente gigantesco!

whopping /'wɒpɪŋ/ *adj* fam enorme

whore /hɔ:(r)/ *n* puttana *f* vulg

whorl /wɔ:l/ *n* (of cream, chocolate etc) ghirigoro *m*; (of fingerprint) spirale *f*

whose /hu:z/ ① *rel pron* il cui; **people ~ name begins with D** le persone i cui nomi cominciano con la D ② *inter pron* di chi; **~ is that?** di chi è quello? ③ *adj* **~ car did you use?** di chi è la macchina che hai usato?

Who's Who *n* pubblicazione *f* annuale con l'elenco delle personalità di spicco

why /waɪ/ ① *adv* (inter) perché; **the reason ~** la ragione per cui; **that's ~** per questo ② *int* diamine!

WI *abbr* (**Women's Institute**); Am *abbr* Wisconsin

wick /wɪk/ *n* stoppino *m*

wicked /'wɪkɪd/ *adj* cattivo; (mischievous) malizioso

wicker /'wɪkə(r)/ ① *n* vimini *mpl* ② *attrib* di vimini

wicket /'wɪkɪt/ *n* (field gate) cancelletto *m*; Sport porta *f*; (Am: of ticket office etc) sportello *m*; **be on a sticky ~** fam essere in una situazione difficile

wide /waɪd/ ① *adj* largo; ⟨experience, knowledge⟩ vasto; ⟨difference⟩ profondo; (far from target) lontano; **10 cm ~** largo 10 cm; **how ~ is it?** quanto è largo? ② *adv* (off target) lontano dal bersaglio; **~ awake** del tutto sveglio; **~ open** spalancato; **open ~!** apri bene!; **far and ~** in lungo e in largo

wide-angle lens *n* grandangolo *m*

wide-eyed /-'aɪd/ *adj* ⟨person, innocence⟩ ingenuo; (with fear, surprise) con gli occhi sbarrati

widely /'waɪdlɪ/ *adv* largamente; ⟨known, accepted⟩ generalmente; ⟨different⟩ profondamente

widely read /red/ *adj* ⟨student⟩ colto; ⟨writer⟩ molto letto

widen /'waɪdn/ ① *vt* allargare; **~ the gap** fig accentuare il contrasto ② *vi* allargarsi

widening /'waɪdnɪŋ/ *adj* ⟨gap, division⟩ sempre più grande

wide open *adj* ⟨door, window, eyes⟩ spalancato

wide-ranging /'reɪndʒɪŋ/ *adj* ⟨interests, reforms, discussion⟩ di ampio respiro

wide screen *n* Cinema schermo *m* panoramico

wide-screen TV *n* televisore *m* con schermo panoramico

widespread /'waɪdspred/ *adj* diffuso

widow /'wɪdəʊ/ *n* vedova ⟨f⟩

widowed /'wɪdəʊd/ *adj* vedovo

widower /'wɪdəʊə(r)/ *n* vedovo *m*

width /wɪdθ/ *n* larghezza *f*; (of material) altezza *f*

widthways /'wɪdθweɪz/ *adv* trasversalmente

wield /wi:ld/ *vt* maneggiare; esercitare ⟨power⟩

wife /waɪf/ *n* (pl **wives**) moglie *f*

wife battering /'waɪfbæt(ə)rɪŋ/ *n* maltrattamento *m* della coniuge

wig /wɪg/ *n* parrucca *f*

wiggle /'wɪgl/ ① *vi* dimenarsi

2 vt dimenare

wild /waɪld/ **1** adj selvaggio; ⟨animal,
flower⟩ selvatico; (furious) furibondo;
⟨applause⟩ fragoroso; ⟨idea⟩ folle; (with joy)
pazzo; ⟨guess⟩ azzardato; **be ~ about** (keen
on) andare pazzo per
2 adv **run ~** crescere senza controllo
3 n **in the ~** allo stato naturale; **the ~s**
pl le zone sperdute

wild boar n cinghiale m

wild card n jolly m inv; Comput carattere
m jolly

wildcat strike n sciopero m selvaggio

wild dog n cane m randagio

wilderness /'wɪldənɪs/ n deserto m; (fig:
garden) giungla f

wild-eyed /-'aɪd/ adj (distressed) dall'aria
angosciata; (angry) dallo sguardo
minaccioso

wildfire n **spread like ~** allargarsi a
macchia d'olio

wild flower n flore m di campo

wildfowl n (bird) uccello m selvatico;
(birds collectively) uccelli mpl selvatici; (game)
selvaggina f di penna

wild-goose chase n ricerca f inutile

wildlife n animali mpl selvatici

wildlife park n parco m naturale

wildlife reserve n riserva f naturale

wildlife sanctuary n riserva f
naturale

wildly /'waɪldlɪ/ adv fig ⟨exaggerated⟩
estremamente; ⟨speak⟩ senza riflettere;
⟨applaud⟩ fragorosamente; ⟨hit out⟩
all'impazzata

Wild West n il far west m

wiles /waɪlz/ npl astuzie fpl

wilful /'wɪlfʊl/ adj intenzionale; ⟨person,
refusal⟩ ostinato

wilfully /'wɪlfʊlɪ/ adv intenzionalmente;
⟨refuse⟩ ostinatamente

will[1] /wɪl/ v aux **he ~ arrive tomorrow**
arriverà domani; **I won't tell him** non
glielo dirò; **you ~ be back soon, won't
you?** tornerai presto, no?; **he ~ be there,
won't he?** sarà là, no?; **she ~ be there by
now** sarà là ormai; **~ you go?** (do you
intend to go) pensi di andare?; **~ you go to
the baker's and buy...?** puoi andare dal
fornaio a comprare...?; **~ you be quiet!**
vuoi stare calmo!; **~ you have some
wine?** vuoi del vino?; **the engine won't
start** la macchina non parte

will[2] n volontà f inv; (document) testamento
m

willing /'wɪlɪŋ/ adj disposto; (eager)
volonteroso

willingly /'wɪlɪŋlɪ/ adv volentieri

willingness /'wɪlɪŋnɪs/ n buona volontà
f

willow /'wɪləʊ/ n salice m

willowy /'wɪləʊɪ/ adj ⟨person, figure⟩
slanciato

will-power n forza f di volontà

willy-nilly /wɪlɪ'nɪlɪ/ adv (at random) a
casaccio; (wanting to or not) volente o nolente

wilt /wɪlt/ vi appassire

wily /'waɪlɪ/ adj (-ier, -iest) astuto

wimp /wɪmp/ n rammollito, -a mf

wimpish /'wɪmpɪʃ/ adj fam ⟨behaviour⟩
da rammollito

wimpy /'wɪmpɪ/ adj fam ⟨person⟩
rammollito

win /wɪn/ **1** n vittoria f; **have a ~**
riportare una vittoria
2 vt (pt/pp **won**; pres p **winning**)
vincere; conquistare ⟨fame⟩
3 vi vincere
■ **win back** vt recuperare
■ **win over** vt convincere
■ **win through** vi (fam: be successful)
uscire vittorioso

wince /wɪns/ vi contrarre il viso

winch /wɪntʃ/ n argano m
■ **winch up** vt tirare con l'argano

wind[1] /wɪnd/ **1** n vento m; (breath) fiato
m; (fam: flatulence) aria f; **get/have the ~ up**
fam aver fifa; **get ~ of** aver sentore di; **in
the ~** nell'aria
2 vt **~ somebody** lasciare qualcuno
senza fiato; **~ a baby** far fare il ruttino ad
un neonato

wind[2] /waɪnd/ **1** vt (pt/pp **wound**) (wrap)
avvolgere; (move by turning) far girare;
⟨clock⟩ caricare
2 vi ⟨road⟩ serpeggiare
■ **wind down** vi (relax) rilassarsi;
(gradually come to an end) diminuire vt
(gradually bring to an end) metter fine in modo
graduale a
■ **wind up** vt caricare ⟨clock⟩; concludere
⟨proceedings⟩; fam sfottere ⟨somebody⟩ vi
(end up) **~ up doing something** finire per
fare qualcosa

windbreak n frangivento m

windcheater n Br giacca f a vento

windchill factor n fattore m di
raffreddamento da vento

wind chimes npl campane fpl eoliche

wind energy n forza f del vento

winder /'waɪndə(r)/ n (for car window)
manovella f alzacristalli; (for watch) bottone
m di carica

windfall n fig fortuna f inaspettata; **~s** pl
(fruit) frutta f abbattuta dal vento

winding /'waɪndɪŋ/ adj tortuoso

wind instrument /'wɪnd/ n strumento
m a fiato

windmill /'wɪn(d)mɪl/ n mulino m a
vento

window /'wɪndəʊ/ n finestra f; (of car)
finestrino m; (of shop) vetrina f

window box n cassetta f per i fiori

window cleaner n (person) lavavetri mf inv

window display n Comm esposizione f in vetrina

window dresser n vetrinista mf

window dressing n vetrinistica f; fig fumo m negli occhi

window envelope n busta f a finestra

window frame n telaio m di finestra

window ledge n davanzale m

window pane n vetro m

window seat n (in room) panca f sotto la finestra; (in plane, train) posto m accanto al finestrino

window-shopping n go ~ andare in giro a vedere le vetrine

window sill n davanzale m

windpipe n trachea f

windpower n energia f eolica

windscreen n, Am **windshield** n parabrezza m inv

windscreen washer n getto m d'acqua

windscreen-wiper n tergicristallo m

wind-sleeve n manica f a vento

wind-sock n manica f a vento

windsurf vi fare windsurf

windsurfer n (person) windsurfista mf; (board) windsurf m inv

windsurfing n windsurf m inv

windswept adj esposto al vento; ⟨person⟩ scompigliato

windy /'wɪndɪ/ adj (-ier, -iest) ventoso

wine /waɪn/ n vino m

wine bar n ≈ enoteca f

wine box n contenitore m di vino con rubinetto

wine cellar n cantina f

wine cooler n (ice bucket) secchiello m del ghiaccio; (Am: drink) bibita f leggermente alcolica

wineglass n bicchiere m da vino

wine grower /'grəʊə(r)/ n viticultore, -trice mf

wine growing /'grəʊɪŋ/ n viticultura f

wine list n carta f dei vini

wine merchant n commerciante mf di vini

wine producer n produttore, -trice mf di vini

wine rack n portabottiglie m inv

winery /'waɪnərɪ/ n Am vigneto m

wine tasting /'waɪnteɪstɪŋ/ n degustazione f di vini

wine vinegar n aceto m di vino

wine waiter n sommelier m inv

wing /wɪŋ/ n ala f; Auto parafango m; ~s pl Theat quinte fpl; under sb's ~ sotto l'ala [protettiva] di qualcuno

wing chair n poltrona f con ampio schienale

wing collar n colletto m rigido

wing commander n tenente m colonnello delle forze aeree

winger /'wɪŋə(r)/ n Sport ala f

wing-half n (in soccer) mediano m

wing mirror n Br specchietto m laterale

wing nut n dado m ad alette

wingspan n apertura f alare

wink /wɪŋk/ ① n strizzata f d'occhio; not sleep a ~ non chiudere occhio ② vi strizzare l'occhio; ⟨light⟩ lampeggiare

winner /'wɪnə(r)/ n vincitore, -trice mf

winning /'wɪnɪŋ/ adj vincente; ⟨smile⟩ accattivante

winning post n linea f d'arrivo

winnings /'wɪnɪŋz/ npl vincite fpl

winning streak n periodo m fortunato; be on a ~ essere in un periodo fortunato

winsome /'wɪnsəm/ adj accattivante

winter /'wɪntə(r)/ n inverno m

winter sports npl sport mpl invernali

wintertime /'wɪntətaɪm/ n inverno m

wintry /'wɪntrɪ/ adj invernale

wipe /waɪp/ ① n passata f; (to dry) asciugata f ② vt strofinare; (dry) asciugare ■ **wipe away** vt asciugare ⟨tears, sweat⟩; pulire ⟨dirt, mark⟩ ■ **wipe off** vt asciugare; (erase) cancellare ■ **wipe out** vt annientare; eliminare ⟨village⟩; estinguere ⟨debt⟩ ■ **wipe up** vt asciugare ⟨dishes⟩

wipe-clean adj ⟨surface, cover⟩ facile da pulire

wiper blade /'waɪpə/ n Auto bordo m gommato del tergicristallo

wire /'waɪə(r)/ n fil m di ferro; (electrical) filo m elettrico

wire brush n spazzola f metallica

wire-cutters npl tronchese msg

wire-haired /-'heəd/ adj dal pelo ispido

wireless /'waɪəlɪs/ n radio f inv

wire mesh n rete f metallica

wire netting n rete f metallica

wire wool n lana f d'acciaio

wiring /'waɪərɪŋ/ n impianto m elettrico

wiry /'waɪərɪ/ adj (-ier, -iest) ⟨person⟩ dal fisico asciutto; ⟨hair⟩ ispido

wisdom /'wɪzdəm/ n saggezza f; (of action) sensatezza f

wisdom tooth n dente m del giudizio

wise /waɪz/ adj saggio; (prudent) sensato ■ **wise up** fam ① vi (become more aware) aprire gli occhi ② vt aprire gli occhi a (to su)

wisecrack /'waɪzkræk/ fam **1** *n* battuta *f* salace
2 *vi* far battute salaci

wise guy *n* fam sapientone *m*

wisely /'waɪzlɪ/ *adv* saggiamente; ⟨act⟩ sensatamente

Wise Men *npl* Re Magi *mpl*

wish /wɪʃ/ **1** *n* desiderio *m*; **make a ~** esprimere un desiderio; **with best ~es** con i migliori auguri
2 *vt* desiderare; **~ somebody well** fare tanti auguri a qualcuno; **I ~ you every success** ti auguro buona fortuna; **I ~ you could stay** vorrei che tu potessi rimanere; **~ something on somebody** fam sbolognare qualcosa a qualcuno
3 *vi* **~ for something** desiderare qualcosa

wishbone /'wɪʃbəʊn/ *n* forcella *f* (di pollo o tacchino)

wishful /'wɪʃfʊl/ *adj* **~ thinking** illusione *f*

wishy-washy /'wɪʃɪwɒʃɪ/ *adj* ⟨colour⟩ spento; ⟨personality⟩ insignificante

wisp /wɪsp/ *n* (of hair) ciocca *f*; (of smoke) filo *m*; (of grass) ciuffo *m*

wispy /'wɪspɪ/ *adj* ⟨hair, beard⟩ a ciocche; ⟨clouds⟩ vaporoso

wisteria /wɪs'tɪərɪə/ *n* glicine *m*

wistful /'wɪstfʊl/ *adj* malinconico

wistfully /'wɪstfʊlɪ/ *adv* malinconicamente

wit /wɪt/ *n* spirito *m*; (person) persona *f* di spirito; **be at one's ~s' end** non saper che pesci pigliare; **scared out of one's ~s** spaventato a morte

witch /wɪtʃ/ *n* strega *f*

witchcraft *n* magia *f*

witch doctor *n* stregone *m*

witch-hunt *n* caccia *f* alle streghe

with /wɪð/ *prep* con; (fear, cold, jealousy etc) di; **I'm not ~ you** fam non ti seguo; **can I leave it ~ you?** (task) puoi occupartene tu?; **~ no regrets/money** senza rimpianti/ soldi; **be ~ it** fam essere al passo coi tempi; (alert) essere concentrato

withdraw /wɪð'drɔː/ **1** *vt* (pt **-drew**, pp **-drawn**) ritirare; prelevare ⟨money⟩
2 *vi* ritirarsi

withdrawal /wɪð'drɔː(ə)l/ *n* ritiro *m*; (of money) prelevamento *m*; (from drugs) crisi *f* *inv* di astinenza; Psych chiusura *f* in se stessi

withdrawal symptoms *npl* sintomi *mpl* da crisi di astinenza

withdrawn /wɪð'drɔːn/ **1** ▶ WITHDRAW
2 *adj* ⟨person⟩ chiuso in se stesso

wither /'wɪðə(r)/ *vi* ⟨flower⟩ appassire

withering /'wɪðərɪŋ/ *adj* ⟨look⟩ fulminante

withhold /wɪð'həʊld/ *vt* (pt/pp **-held**) rifiutare ⟨consent⟩ (**from** a); nascondere ⟨information⟩ (**from** a); trattenere ⟨smile⟩

within /wɪð'ɪn/ **1** *prep* in; (before the end of) entro; **~ the law** legale
2 *adv* all'interno

without /wɪð'aʊt/ *prep* senza; **~ stopping** senza fermarsi; **how could it have happened ~ you noticing it?** come è potuto succedere senza che tu lo notassi?

withstand /wɪð'stænd/ *vt* (pt/pp **-stood**) resistere a

witness /'wɪtnɪs/ **1** *n* testimone *mf*; **bear ~** portare testimonianza
2 *vt* autenticare ⟨signature⟩; essere testimone di ⟨accident⟩

witness box, Am **witness-stand** *n* banco *m* dei testimoni

witticism /'wɪtɪsɪzm/ *n* spiritosaggine *f*

wittingly /'wɪtɪŋlɪ/ *adv* consapevolmente

witty /'wɪtɪ/ *adj* (**-ier**, **-iest**) spiritoso

wives /waɪvz/ ▶ WIFE

wizard /'wɪzəd/ *n* mago *m*

wizardry /'wɪzədrɪ/ *n* stregoneria *f*

wizened /'wɪznd/ *adj* raggrinzito

wk *abbr* **week**

WMD *n* *abbr* (**weapon of mass destruction**) ADM *fpl*

wobble /'wɒbl/ *vi* traballare

wobbly /'wɒblɪ/ *adj* traballante

wodge /wɒdʒ/ *n* fam mucchio *m*

woe /wəʊ/ *n* afflizione *f*; **~ is me!** me meschino!

woeful /'wəʊfʊl/ *adj* ⟨story, sight⟩ triste; ⟨lack⟩ vergognoso

woke, **woken** /wəʊk/, /'wəʊkn/ ▶ WAKE[1]

wolf /wʊlf/ **1** *n* (pl **wolves** /wʊlvz/) lupo *m*; (fam: womanizer) donnaiolo *m*
2 *vt* **~ [down]** divorare

wolf cub *n* cucciolo *m* di lupo

wolfhound *n* Br cane *m* lupo

wolf whistle *n* fischio *m*
2 *vi* **~-whistle at somebody** fischiare dietro a qualcuno

woman /'wʊmən/ *n* (pl **women**) donna *f*

womanizer /'wʊmənaɪz(r)/ *n* donnaiolo *m*

womanly /'wʊmənlɪ/ *adj* femminile

womb /wuːm/ *n* utero *m*

women /'wɪmɪn/ ▶ WOMAN

Women's Institute *n* associazione *f* che si occupa dei problemi delle donne

Women's Libber /wɪmɪnz'lɪbə(r)/ *n* femminista *f*

Women's Liberation *n* movimento *m* femminista

women's movement *n* movimento *m* per l'emancipazione della donna

women's refuge *n* casa *f* rifugio *inv*

women's studies *npl* storia *f* dell'emancipazione femminile

won /wʌn/ ▸ WIN

wonder /'wʌndə(r)/ **①** *n* meraviglia *f*; (surprise) stupore *m*; **no ~!** non c'è da stupirsi!; **it's a ~ that...** è incredibile che... **②** *vi* restare in ammirazione; (be surprised) essere sorpreso; **I ~** è quello che mi chiedo; **I ~ whether she is ill** mi chiedo se è malata

wonderful /'wʌndəfʊl/ *adj* meraviglioso

wonderfully /'wʌndəfʊlɪ/ *adv* meravigliosamente

wonderland /'wʌndəlænd/ *n* paese *m* delle meraviglie

wonky /'wɒŋkɪ/ *adj* Br fam (faulty) difettoso; ‹furniture› traballante; (crooked) storto

wont /wəʊnt/ **①** *n* **as was his ~** come suo solito **②** *adj* **he was ~ to fall asleep** era solito addormentarsi

won't /wəʊnt/ = will not

woo /wuː/ *vt* corteggiare; fig cercare di accattivarsi ‹voters›; cercare di ottenere ‹fame, fortune›

wood /wʊd/ *n* legno *m*; (for burning) legna *f*; (forest) bosco *m*; **out of the ~** fig fuori pericolo; **touch ~!** tocca ferro!

woodcarving /'wʊdkɑːvɪŋ/ *n* scultura *f* di legno

wooded /'wʊdɪd/ *adj* boscoso

wooden /'wʊdn/ *adj* di legno; fig legnoso

wooden horse *n* cavallo *m* di Troia

wooden spoon *n* mestolo *m* di legno; fig premio *m* di consolazione

woodland *n* terreno *m* boschivo

woodlouse *n* onisco *m*

wood-pecker *n* picchio *m*

wood pigeon *n* colombaccio *m*

wood shavings *npl* trucioli *mpl*

woodshed *n* legnaia *f*

wood stove *n* stufa *f* a legna

woodwind *n* strumenti *mpl* a fiato

woodwork *n* (wooden parts) parti *fpl* in legno; (craft) falegnameria *f*

woodworm *n* tarlo *m*

woody /'wʊdɪ/ *adj* legnoso; ‹hill› boscoso

wool /wʊl/ **①** *n* lana *f*; **pull the ~ over sb's eyes** gettar fumo negli occhi a qualcuno **②** *attrib* di lana

woollen /'wʊlən/ *adj* di lana

woollens /'wʊlənz/ *npl* capi *mpl* di lana

woolly /'wʊlɪ/ *adj* (**-ier, -iest**) ‹sweater› di lana; fig confuso

woozy /'wuːzɪ/ *adj* intontito

word /wɜːd/ *n* parola *f*; (news) notizia *f*; **by ~ of mouth** a viva voce; **have a ~ with** dire due parole a; **have ~s** bisticciare; **in other ~s** in altre parole; **go back on one's ~** rimangiarsi la parola

word-for-word **①** *adj* ‹translation› letterale **②** *adv* parola per parola

wording /'wɜːdɪŋ/ *n* parole *fpl*

word-perfect *adj* che sa a memoria

word processing *n* Comput word processing *m*, elaborazione *f* testi

word processor *n* sistema *m* di videoscrittura, word processor *m* inv

wordy /'wɜːdɪ/ *adj* prolisso

wore /wɔː(r)/ ▸ WEAR

work /wɜːk/ **①** *n* lavoro *m*; (of art) opera *f*; **~s** *pl* (factory) fabbrica *fsg*; (mechanism) meccanismo *msg*; **at ~** al lavoro; **out of ~** disoccupato **②** *vi* lavorare; ‹machine, ruse› funzionare; (study) studiare **③** *vt* far funzionare ‹machine›; far lavorare ‹employee›; far studiare ‹student›; **~ one's way through something** (read) leggere attentamente

■ **work in** *vt* inserire ‹comment, fact›; Culin incorporare ‹butter›

■ **work off** *vt* sfogare ‹anger›; lavorare per estinguere ‹debt›; fare sport per smaltire ‹weight›

■ **work on** *vt* lavorare a ‹book, report›; occuparsi di ‹problem, case›; cercare ‹solution› *vi* (continue) continuare a lavorare

■ **work out** **①** *vt* elaborare ‹plan›; risolvere ‹problem›; calcolare ‹bill› **I ~ed out how he did it** ho capito come l'ha fatto **②** *vi* evolvere

■ **work up** *vt* **I've ~ed up an appetite** mi è venuto appetito; **don't get ~ed up** (anxious) non farti prendere dal panico; (angry) non arrabbiarti

workable /'wɜːkəbl/ *adj* (feasible) fattibile

workaday /'wɜːkədeɪ/ *adj* ‹clothes, life› ordinario

workaholic /wɜːkə'hɒlɪk/ *n* stacanovista *mf*

workbench *n* banco *m* da lavoro

workbook *n* (blank) quaderno *m*; (with exercises) libro *m* di esercizi

workday *n* giorno *m* lavorativo

worker /'wɜːkə(r)/ *n* lavoratore, -trice *mf*; (manual) operaio, -a *mf*

work experience *n* esperienza *f* professionale; (part of training programme) stage *m* inv

workforce *n* forza *f* lavoro

workhorse *n* fig lavoratore, -trice *mf* indefesso, -a

working /'wɜːkɪŋ/ *adj* ‹clothes etc› da lavoro; ‹day› feriale; **in ~ order** funzionante

working capital *n* capitale *m* netto di esercizio

working-class *adj* operaio; **be ~** appartenere alla classe operaia

working class *n* classe *f* operaia

workings /'wɜːkɪŋz/ *npl* meccanismi *mpl*

working week *n* settimana *f* lavorativa

workload *n* carico *m* di lavoro

workman *n* operaio *m*

workmanlike *adj* fatto con competenza

workmanship *n* lavorazione *f*

workmate *n* collega *mf*

work of art *n* opera *f* d'arte

workout *n* allenamento *m*

work permit *n* permesso *m* di lavoro

workplace *n* posto *m* di lavoro

work-sharing *n* divisione *f* di un posto di lavoro tra più persone

worksheet *n* foglio *m* degli esercizi

workshop *n* officina *f*; (discussion) dibattito *m*

work-shy *adj* pigro

workstation *n* stazione *f* di lavoro

work surface *n* piano *m* di lavoro

worktop *n* piano *m* di lavoro

work-to-rule *n* sciopero *m* bianco

world /wɜːld/ *n* mondo *m*; **a ~ of difference** una differenza abissale; **out of this ~** favoloso; **think the ~ of somebody** andare matto per qualcuno

world-class *adj* di livello internazionale

World Cup *n* (in football) Mondiali *mpl*

world-famous *adj* di fama mondiale

world leader *n* (politician, company) leader *m* mondiale; (athlete) campione, -essa *mf* mondiale

worldly /'wɜːldlɪ/ *adj* materiale; (person) materialista

worldly-wise *adj* vissuto

world music *n* world music *f*

world power *n* potenza *f* mondiale

worldview *n* visione *f* del mondo

world war *n* guerra *f* mondiale

worldwide /'wɜːldwaɪd/ ① *adj* mondiale
② *adv* mondialmente

World Wide Web *n* Comput World Wide Web *m*

worm /wɜːm/ ① *n* verme *m*
② *vt* ~ **one's way into sb's confidence** conquistarsi la fiducia di qualcuno in modo subdolo
■ **worm out** *vt* ~ **something out of somebody** carpire qualcosa a qualcuno

worm-eaten /'wɜːmiːtən/ *adj* (wood) tarlato; (fruit) bacato

wormhole /'wɜːmhəʊl/ *n* (in wood) buco *m* di tarlo; (in fruit, plant) buco *m* del verme

worn /wɔːn/ ① ▶ WEAR
② *adj* sciupato

worn-out *adj* consumato; (person) sfinito

worried /'wʌrɪd/ *adj* preoccupato

worrier /'wʌrɪə(r)/ *n* ansioso, -a *mf*; **he's a terrible ~** è ansioso da morire

worry /'wʌrɪ/ ① *n* preoccupazione *f*
② *vt* (pt/pp **worried**) preoccupare; (bother) disturbare
③ *vi* preoccuparsi
■ **worry at** *vt* (dog) rosicchiare (bone, toy); (person) sviscerare (problem)

worry beads *npl* rosario *m* per scaricare la tensione

worrying /'wʌrɪɪŋ/ *adj* preoccupante

worse /wɜːs/ ① *adj* peggiore
② *adv* peggio
③ *n* peggio *m*

worsen /'wɜːsn/ *vt/i* peggiorare

worsening /'wɜːsnɪŋ/ ① *adj* (situation, problem) sempre più grave
② *n* peggioramento *m*

worse off *adj* **be ~ ~ than** stare peggio di; **be £100 ~ ~** avere 100 sterline in meno

worship /'wɜːʃɪp/ ① *n* culto *m*; (service) funzione *f*; **Your/His W~** (to judge) signor giudice/il giudice
② *vt* (pt/pp **-shipped**) venerare
③ *vi* andare a messa

worshipper /'wɜːʃɪpə(r)/ *n* fedele *mf*

worst /wɜːst/ ① *adj* peggiore
② *adv* peggio
③ *n* **the ~** il peggio; **get the ~ of it** avere la peggio; **if the ~ comes to the ~** nella peggiore delle ipotesi

worsted /'wʊstɪd/ *n* lana *f* pettinata

worth /wɜːθ/ ① *n* valore *m*; **£10 ~ of petrol** 10 sterline di benzina
② *adj* **be ~** valere; **be ~ it** fig valerne la pena; **it is ~ trying** vale la pena provare; **it's ~ my while** mi conviene; **I'll make it ~ your while** te ne ricompenserò

worthless /'wɜːθlɪs/ *adj* senza valore

worthwhile /wɜːθ'waɪl/ *adj* che vale la pena; (cause) lodevole

worthy /'wɜːðɪ/ *adj* degno; (cause, motive) lodevole

would /wʊd/ *v aux* **I ~ do it** lo farei; **~ you go?** andresti?; **~ you mind if I opened the window?** ti dispiace se apro la finestra?; **he ~ come if he could** verrebbe se potesse; **he said he ~n't** ha detto di no; **he said he ~n't have** ha detto che non lo avrebbe fatto; **~ you like a drink?** vuoi qualcosa da bere?; **what ~ you like to drink?** cosa prendi da bere?; **you ~n't, ~ you?** non lo faresti, vero?

would-be *adj* pej (actor, singer) sedicente; (investor, buyer) aspirante

wound¹ /wuːnd/ ① *n* ferita *f*

2 *vt* ferire

wound² /waʊnd/ ▸WIND²

wove, woven /wəʊv/, /'wəʊvn/
▸WEAVE²

wow /waʊ/ **1** *n* (fam: success) successone
m; (in sound system) wow *m*
2 *vt* fam entusiasmare ⟨*person*⟩
3 *int* caspita!

WP *abbr* (**word processing**)
elaborazione *f* testi

wpm *abbr* (**words per minute**) parole
fpl al minuto

wrangle /'ræŋgl/ **1** *n* litigio *m*
2 *vi* litigare

wrap /ræp/ **1** *n* (shawl) scialle *m*
2 *vt* (pt/pp **wrapped**) ~ [**up**] avvolgere;
⟨*present*⟩ incartare; **be ~ped up in** fig
essere completamente preso da
3 *vi* ~ **up warmly** coprirsi bene

wraparound /'ræpəraʊnd/ *adj* ⟨*skirt*⟩ a
pareo; ⟨*window, windscreen*⟩ panoramico

wraparound sunglasses *npl*
occhiali *mpl* da sole avvolgenti

wrap-over *adj* ⟨*skirt, dress*⟩ a
portafoglio

wrapper /'ræpə(r)/ *n* (for sweet) carta *f* [di
caramella]

wrapping /'ræpɪŋ/ *n* materiale *m* da
imballaggio

wrapping paper *n* carta *f* da pacchi;
(for gift) carta *f* da regalo

wrath /rɒθ/ *n* ira *f*

wreak /ri:k/ *vt* ~ **havoc with something**
scombussolare qualcosa

wreath /ri:θ/ *n* (*pl* ~**s** /ri:ðz/) corona *f*

wreathed /ri:ðd/ *adj* ~ **in** avvolto in
⟨*mists*⟩; **her face was** ~ **in smiles** era
raggiante

wreck /rek/ **1** *n* (of ship) relitto *m*; (of car)
carcassa *f*; (person) rottame *m*
2 *vt* far naufragare; demolire ⟨*car*⟩

wreckage /'rekɪdʒ/ *n* rottami *mpl*; fig
brandelli *mpl*

wrecked /rekt/ *adj* ⟨*ship, car*⟩ distrutto;
⟨*building*⟩ demolito; (fig: exhausted)
distrutto

wren /ren/ *n* scricciolo *m*

wrench /rentʃ/ **1** *n* (injury) slogatura *f*;
(tool) chiave *f* inglese; (pull) strattone *m*; **it
was a ~ leaving home** fig è stato un passo
difficile andarsene da casa
2 *vt* (pull) strappare; slogarsi ⟨*wrist, ankle
etc*⟩

wrest /rest/ *vt* strappare (**from** a)

wrestle /'resl/ *vi* lottare corpo a corpo;
fig lottare

wrestler /'reslə(r)/ *n* lottatore, -trice *mf*

wrestling /'reslɪŋ/ *n* lotta *f* libera; (all-in)
catch *m*

wretch /retʃ/ *n* disgraziato, -a *mf*

wretched /'retʃɪd/ *adj* odioso; ⟨*weather*⟩
orribile; **feel ~** (unhappy) essere triste; (ill)
sentirsi malissimo

wriggle /'rɪgl/ **1** *n* contorsione *f*
2 *vi* contorcersi; (move forward) strisciare;
~ **out of something** fam sottrarsi a
qualcosa

wriggly /'rɪglɪ/ *adj* ⟨*person*⟩ che si
dimena; ⟨*snake, worm*⟩ che si contorce

wring /rɪŋ/ *vt* (pt/pp **wrung**) torcere
⟨*sb's neck*⟩; strizzare ⟨*clothes*⟩; ~ **one's
hands** torcersi le mani; ~ **something out
of somebody** fig estorcere qualcosa a
qualcuno; ~**ing wet** inzuppato

wrinkle /'rɪŋkl/ **1** *n* grinza *f*; (on skin)
ruga *f*
2 *vt/i* raggrinzire

wrinkled /'rɪŋkld/ *adj* ⟨*skin, face*⟩
rugoso; ⟨*clothes*⟩ raggrinzito

wrist /rɪst/ *n* polso *m*

wristband /'rɪs(t)bænd/ *n* polsino *m*; (on
watch) cinturino *m*

wristwatch /'rɪstwɒtʃ/ *n* orologio *m* da
polso

writ /rɪt/ *n* Jur mandato *m*

write /raɪt/ *vt/i* (pt **wrote**, pp **written**,
pres p **writing**) scrivere
■ **write away for** *vt* richiedere per
posta ⟨*information*⟩
■ **write back** *vi* rispondere
■ **write down** *vt* annotare
■ **write in** *vi* scrivere
■ **write off** *vt* cancellare ⟨*debt*⟩;
distruggere ⟨*car*⟩
■ **write out** *vt* fare ⟨*cheque, prescription*⟩;
(copy) ricopiare
■ **write up** *vt* redigere; aggiornare
⟨*diary*⟩; elaborare ⟨*notes*⟩

write-off *n* (car) rottame *m*

write-protect *vt* Comput proteggere da
sovrascrittura

writer /'raɪtə(r)/ *n* autore, -trice *mf*;
she's a ~ è una scrittrice

writer's block *n* blocco *m* dello
scrittore

write-up *n* (review) recensione *f*

writhe /raɪð/ *vi* contorcersi; ~ **with
embarrassment** vergognarsi a morte

writing /'raɪtɪŋ/ *n* (occupation) scrivere *m*;
(words) scritte *fpl*; (handwriting) scrittura *f*;
~**s** *pl* scritti *mpl*; **in** ~ per iscritto

writing desk *n* scrivania *f*

writing pad *n* (for notes) bloc-notes *m
inv*; (for letters) blocco *m* di carta da lettere

writing paper *n* carta *f* da lettere

written /'rɪtn/ ▸WRITE

wrong /rɒŋ/ **1** *adj* sbagliato; **be ~**
⟨*person*⟩ sbagliare; **what's ~?** cosa c'è che
non va?
2 *adv* ⟨*spelt*⟩ in modo sbagliato; **go ~**
⟨*person*⟩ sbagliare; ⟨*machine*⟩ funzionare

male; ⟨*plan*⟩ andar male; **don't get me** ∼ non fraintendermi

3 *n* ingiustizia *f*; **in the** ∼ dalla parte del torto; **know right from** ∼ distinguere il bene dal male

4 *vt* fare torto a

wrongdoer /'rɒŋduːə(r)/ *n* malfattore *m*

wrong-foot *vt* Sport, fig prendere in contropiede

wrongful /'rɒŋfʊl/ *adj* ingiusto

wrongfully /'rɒŋfʊlɪ/ *adv* ⟨*accuse*⟩ ingiustamente

wrongly /'rɒŋlɪ/ *adv* in modo sbagliato; ⟨*accuse, imagine*⟩ a torto; ⟨*informed*⟩ male

wrote /rəʊt/ ▶ WRITE

wrought iron /rɔːt'aɪən/ **1** *n* ferro *m* battuto

2 *attrib* di ferro battuto

wrung /rʌŋ/ ▶ WRING

wry /raɪ/ *adj* (**-er, -est**) ⟨*humour, smile*⟩ beffardo

WW1 *or* **WWI** *abbr* (**World War One**) prima guerra *f* mondiale

WW2 *or* **WWII** *abbr* (**World War Two**) seconda guerra *f* mondiale

WWW *abbr* (**World Wide Web**) WWW *m*

WYSIWYG /'wɪzɪwɪg/ *abbr* Comput (**what you see is what you get**) ciò che vedi è ciò che ottieni

x¹, **X** /eks/ *n* (letter) x, X *f inv*; (anonymous person, place etc) X

x² *n* Math *x f inv*

X certificate *adj* Br vietato ai minori di 18 anni

xenophobia /zenə'fəʊbɪə/ *n* xenofobia *f*

xerox® /'zɪərɒks/ **1** *vt* xerocopiare

2 *n* (machine) xerocopiatrice *f*; (document) xerocopia *f*

Xmas /'krɪsməs/ *n* fam Natale *m*

XML *abbr* (**extensible markup language**) Comput XML *m*

X-rated *adj* ⟨*film*⟩ vietato ai minori

X-ray **1** *n* (picture) radiografia *f*; **have an** ∼ farsi fare una radiografia

2 *vt* passare ai raggi X

X-ray machine *n* apparecchio *m* radiografico

X-ray unit *n* reparto *m* di radiologia

xxx *n* (at end of letter) baci *mpl*

y, Y /waɪ/ *n* (letter) y, Y *f inv*

yacht /jɒt/ *n* yacht *m inv*; (for racing) barca *f* a vela

yachting /'jɒtɪŋ/ *n* vela *f*

yachtsman /'jɒtsmən/ *n* diportista *m*

yak /jæk/ *n* Zool yak*m inv*

Yale® /jeɪl/ *n* (lock) serratura *f* di sicurezza

yam /jæm/ *n* (tropical) igname *m*; (Am: sweet potato) patata *f* dolce

Yank /jæŋk/ *n* fam americano, -a *mf*

yank /jæŋk/ *vt* fam tirare

Yankee /'jæŋkɪ/ *n* (pej: American) yankee *m inv*; (soldier) nordista *m*; (Am: of Northern USA) abitante *mf* degli USA settentrionali; (Am: inhabitant of New England) abitante *mf* della Nuova Inghilterra

yap /jæp/ *vi* (pt/pp **yapped**) ⟨*dog*⟩ guaire

yapping /'jæpɪŋ/ *n* (of dogs) guaiti *mpl*; (fam: of people) ciance *fpl*

yard¹ /jɑːd/ *n* cortile *m*; (for storage) deposito *m*; **the Y**∼ fam Scotland Yard *f* (polizia londinese)

yard² /jɑːd/ *n* iarda *f* (= 91,44 cm)

yardstick /'jɑːdstɪk/ *n* fig pietra *f* di paragone

yarn /jɑːn/ *n* filo *m*; (fam: tale) storia *f*

yashmak /'jæʃmæk/ *n* velo *m* (delle donne musulmane)

yawn /jɔːn/ **1** *n* sbadiglio *m*

2 *vi* sbadigliare

yawning /'jɔːnɪŋ/ *adj* ∼ **gap** sbadiglio *m*

yd *abbr* **yard**

yeah /je/ *adv* fam sì; **oh** ∼? ma davvero?

year /jɪə(r)/ *n* anno *m*; (of wine) annata *f*; **for** ∼s fam da secoli

yearbook /ˈjɪəbʊk/ n annuario m
yearlong adj ⟨stay⟩ di un anno
yearly /ˈjɪəlɪ/ ① adj annuale
  ② adv annualmente
yearn /jɜːn/ vi struggersi
yearning /ˈjɜːnɪŋ/ n desiderio m
struggente
year out n = GAP YEAR
year-round adj ⟨supply, source⟩
permanente
yeast /jiːst/ n lievito m
yell /jel/ ① n urlo m
  ② vi urlare
yelling /ˈjelɪŋ/ n urla fpl
yellow /ˈjeləʊ/ adj & n giallo m
yellow-belly n fam fifone m
yellow card n Sport cartellino m giallo
yellowish /ˈjeləʊɪʃ/ adj giallastro
yellow pages npl pagine fpl gialle
yellowy /ˈjeləʊɪ/ adj giallastro
yelp /jelp/ ① n (of dog) guaito m
  ② vi ⟨dog⟩ guaire
Yemen /ˈjemən/ n Yemen m
Yemeni /ˈjemənɪ/ adj & n yemenita mf
yen /jen/ n forte desiderio m (for di)
yeoman /ˈjəʊmən/ n Br piccolo
proprietario m terriero; Y~ of the Guard
guardiano m della Torre di Londra
yep /jep/ adv fam sì
yes /jes/ ① adv sì
  ② n sì m inv
yes-man n fam tirapiedi m inv
yesterday /ˈjestədeɪ/ n & adv ieri m
inv; ~'s paper il giornale di ieri; the day
before ~ l'altroieri; ~ afternoon ieri
pomeriggio; ~ evening ieri sera; ~
morning ieri mattina
yesteryear /ˈjestəjɪə(r)/ n lit passato m;
the music of ~ la musica del passato
yet /jet/ ① adv ancora; as ~ fino ad ora;
not ~ non ancora; the best ~ il migliore
finora
  ② conj eppure
yew /juː/ n tasso m (albero)
Y-fronts npl Br slip m inv da uomo con
apertura
YHA Br abbr (Youth Hostels Association)
associazione f degli ostelli della gioventù
Yiddish /ˈjɪdɪʃ/ n yiddish m
yield /jiːld/ ① n produzione f; ⟨profit⟩
reddito m
  ② vt produrre; fruttare ⟨profit⟩
  ③ vi cedere; Am Auto dare la precedenza
yielding /ˈjiːldɪŋ/ adj (submissive)
arrendevole; ⟨ground⟩ cedevole; ⟨person⟩
flessibile
YMCA abbr (Young Men's Christian
Association) Associazione f Cristiana dei
Giovani
yob /jɒb/, **yobbo** n Br: fam teppista mf

yodel /ˈjəʊdl/ vi (pt/pp **yodelled**)
cantare jodel
yoga /ˈjəʊgə/ n yoga m
yoghurt /ˈjɒgət/ n yogurt m inv
yoke /jəʊk/ n giogo m; (of garment) carré m
inv
yokel /ˈjəʊkl/ n zotico, -a mf
yolk /jəʊk/ n tuorlo m
yonder /ˈjɒndə(r)/ adv liter laggiù
yonks /jɒŋks/ npl fam I haven't seen him
for ~ è un secolo che non lo vedo
yore /jɔː(r)/ n in days of ~ un tempo
you /juː/ pers pron (subject) tu, voi pl;
(formal) lei, voi pl; (direct/indirect object) ti, vi
pl; (formal: direct object) la; (formal: indirect
object) le; (after prep) te, voi pl; (formal: after
prep) lei; ~ are very kind (sg) sei molto
gentile; (formal) è molto gentile; (pl & formal
pl) siete molto gentili; ~ can stay, but he
has to go (sg) tu puoi rimanere, ma lui
deve andarsene; (pl) voi potete rimanere,
ma lui deve andarsene; all of ~ tutti voi;
I'll give ~ the money (sg) ti darò i soldi;
(pl) vi darò i soldi; I'll give it to ~ (sg) te/
(pl) ve lo darò; it does ~ good (sg) ti/(pl)
vi fa bene; it was ~! (sg) eri tu!; (pl)
eravate voi!; ~ have to be careful these
days si deve fare attenzione di questi
tempi; ~ can't tell the difference non si
vede la differenza
you'd /juːd/ abbr you would; you had
you-know-what pron fam sai cosa
you-know-who pron fam sai chi
you'll /juːl/ abbr you will
young /jʌŋ/ ① adj giovane; ~ lady
signorina f; ~ man giovanotto m; her ~
man (boyfriend) il suo ragazzo
  ② npl (animals) piccoli mpl; the ~ (people) i
giovani
young blood n nuove leve fpl
youngish /ˈjʌŋɪʃ/ adj abbastanza
giovane
young-looking adj dall'aria giovanile
young offender n delinquente mf
minorenne
youngster /ˈjʌŋstə(r)/ n ragazzo, -a mf;
(child) bambino, -a mf
your /jɔː(r)/ poss adj tuo m, tua f, tuoi
mpl, tue fpl; (formal) suo m, sua f, suoi mpl,
sue fpl; (pl & formal pl) vostro m, vostra f,
vostri mpl, vostre fpl; ~ task/house il tuo
compito/la tua casa; (formal) il suo
compito/la sua casa; (pl & formal pl) il vostro
compito/la vostra casa; ~ mother/father
tua madre/tuo padre; (formal) sua madre/
suo padre; (pl & formal pl) vostra madre/
vostro padre
you're /jʊə(r)/ abbr you are
yours /jɔːz/ poss pron il tuo m, la tua f, i
tuoi mpl, le tue fpl; (formal) il suo m, la sua
f, i suoi mpl, le sue fpl; (pl & formal pl) il
vostro m, la vostra f, i vostri mpl, le

vostre *fpl*; **a friend of** ~ un tuo/suo/vostro amico; **friends of** ~ dei tuoi/vostri/suoi amici; **that is** ~ quello è tuo/vostro/suo; (as opposed to mine) quello è il tuo/il vostro/il suo

yourself /jɔːˈself/ *pers pron* (reflexive) ti; (formal) si; (emphatic) te stesso; (formal) sé, se stesso; **do pour** ~ **a drink** versati da bere; (formal) si versi da bere; **you said so** ~ lo hai detto tu stesso; (formal) lo ha detto lei stesso; **you can be proud of** ~ puoi essere fiero di te; (formal) può essere fiero di sé; **by** ~ da solo

yourselves /jɔːˈselvz/ *pers pron* (reflexive) vi; (emphatic) voi stessi; **do pour** ~ **a drink** versatevi da bere; **you said so** ~ lo avete detto voi stessi; **you can be proud of** ~ potete essere fieri di voi; **by** ~ da soli

youth /juːθ/ *n* (pl **youths** /juːðz/) gioventù *f inv*; (boy) giovanetto *m*; **the** ~ (young people) i giovani

youth club *n* club *m* per i giovani

youthful /ˈjuːθfʊl/ *adj* giovanile

youth hostel *n* ostello *m* [della gioventù]

youth hostelling *n* viaggiare *m* pernottando in ostelli della gioventù

youth work *n* lavoro *m* di educatore

youth worker *n* educatore, -trice *mf*

you've /juːv/ *abbr* **you have**

yowl /jaʊl/ *vi* ⟨dog⟩ ululare; ⟨cat⟩ miagolare; ⟨baby⟩ frignare

yo-yo® /ˈjəʊjəʊ/ ① *n* yo-yo *m inv* ② *vi* (prices, inflation) andare su e giù

yr *abbr* **year**

yuck /jʌk/ *int* Br: fam bleah

yucky /ˈjʌkɪ/ *adj* Br: fam schifoso

Yugoslav /ˈjuːɡəslaːv/ *adj & n* jugoslavo, -a *mf*

Yugoslavia /juːɡəˈslaːvɪə/ *n* Jugoslavia *f*

Yule log /juːl/ *n* tronchetto *m* natalizio

yummy /ˈjʌmɪ/ *fam* ① *adj* squisito ② *int* gnam gnam

yup /jʌp/ *adv* fam sì

yuppie /ˈjʌpɪ/ *n* yuppie *mf inv*

yuppie flu *n* sindrome *f* da affaticamento cronico

YWCA *abbr* (**Young Women's Christian Association**) Associazione *f* Cristiana delle Giovani

Zz

z, Z /zed/ *n* (letter) z, Z *f inv*

Zaire /zaːˈɪə(r)/ *n* Zaire *m*

Zambia /ˈzæmbɪə/ *n* Zambia *m*

zany /ˈzeɪnɪ/ *adj* (**-ier, -iest**) demenziale

zap /zæp/ ① *n* (fam: energy) energia *f* ② *vt* (pt/pp **zapped**) fam (destroy) distruggere ⟨town⟩; far fuori ⟨person, animal⟩; (fire at) fulminare; (Comput: delete) cancellare

zapper /ˈzæpə(r)/ *n* (fam: for TV) telecomando *m*

zeal /ziːl/ *n* zelo *m*

zealot /ˈzelət/ *n* fig fanatico *m*

zealous /ˈzeləs/ *adj* zelante

zealously /ˈzeləslɪ/ *adv* con zelo

zebra /ˈzebrə/ *n* zebra *f*

zebra crossing *n* passaggio *m* pedonale, zebre *fpl*

zenith /ˈzenɪθ/ *n* zenit *m inv*; fig apogeo *m*

zero /ˈzɪərəʊ/ *n* zero *m*

▪ **zero in on** *vt* concentrarsi su ⟨problem, person⟩; localizzare ⟨place⟩; Mil mirare ⟨target⟩

zero gravity *n* assenza *f* di gravità

zero hour *n* Mil, fig ora *f* zero

zero-rated /-ˈreɪtɪd/ *adj* Br esente [da] IVA

zest /zest/ *n* gusto *m*; (peel) scorza *f* (di agrumi)

zigzag /ˈzɪɡzæɡ/ ① *n* zigzag *m inv* ② *vi* (pt/pp **-zagged**) zigzagare

zilch /zɪltʃ/ *n* fam un tubo; **I understood** ~ non ho capito un tubo

Zimbabwe /zɪmˈbæbweɪ/ *n* Zimbabwe *m*

Zimmer® /ˈzɪmə(r)/ *n* Br deambulatore *m*

zinc /zɪŋk/ *n* zinco *m*

zinc oxide *n* ossido *m* di zinco

zing /zɪŋ/ ① *n* fam (energy) brio *m*; (sound) sibilo *m* ② *vt* (Am: criticize) stroncare

Zionism /ˈzaɪənɪzm/ *n* sionismo *m*

zip /zɪp/ ① *n* ~ **[fastener]** cerniera *f* [lampo] ② *vt* (pt/pp **zipped**) ~ **[up]** chiudere con la cerniera [lampo]

▪ **zip along** *vi* (move quickly) procedere velocemente

▪ **zip through** *vt* (do quickly) svolgere velocemente ⟨work⟩; (read quickly) leggere velocemente ⟨book⟩

■ **zip up** *vt* chiudere la cerniera di
⟨*jacket, bag*⟩ *vi* chiudersi con la cerniera

zip code *n* Am codice *m* [di avviamento]
postale, C.A.P. *m inv*

zipper /'zɪpə(r)/ *n* Am cerniera *f* [lampo]

zippy /'zɪpɪ/ *adj* fam ⟨*vehicle*⟩ scattante

zither /'zɪðə(r)/ *n* cetra *f*

zodiac /'zəʊdɪæk/ *n* zodiaco *m*

zombie /'zɒmbɪ/ *n* fam zombi *mf inv*

zone /zəʊn/ *n* zona *f*

zoning /'zəʊnɪŋ/ *n* zonazione *f*

zonked /zɒŋkt/ *adj* (fam: on drugs, drunk,
tired) fatto

zoo /zu:/ *n* zoo *m inv*

zoo keeper *n* guardiano, -a *mf* dello zoo

zoological /zəʊə'lɒdʒɪkl/ *adj* zoologico

zoologist /zəʊ'ɒlədʒɪst/ *n* zoologo, -a *mf*

zoology /zəʊ'ɒlədʒɪ/ *n* zoologia *f*

zoom /zu:m/ *vi* sfrecciare

zoom lens *n* zoom *m inv*

zucchini /zʊ'ki:nɪ/ *n* zucchino *m*,
zucchina *f*

z

Summary of Italian grammar

Nouns

Gender

All Italian nouns are either masculine feminine. As a general rule, nouns ending in -o are usually masculine.

il ragazzo boy	l'amico friend
lo sbaglio mistake	un albero tree
un treno train	uno specchio mirror

Nouns ending in -a are usually feminine.

la ragazza girl	la scuola school
l'arancia orange	un'amica friend
una sorella sister	una zia aunt

Nouns ending in -e can be either masculine or feminine.

il nome name	la stazione station
una ragione reason	un giornale newspaper

Plural forms

Masculine nouns ending in -o change to -i in the plural:

i ragazzi boys	gli amici friends
gli sbagli mistakes	

Feminine nouns ending in -a change to -e:

le ragazze girls	le scuole schools
le amiche friends	

All nouns ending in -e change to -i:

i genitori parents	le stazioni stations

Nouns ending in accented vowels do not change in the plural.

il caffè coffee	i caffè coffees
la città city	le città cities
la virtù virtue	le virtù virtues

Nouns ending in a consonant (imported from other languages) do not change in the plural.

il computer	i computer
lo sport	gli sport
l'autobus	gli autobus

The definite article

Masculine forms before:

	singular	plural	
most consonants	il	i	il treno, i treni
a, e, i, o, u	l'	gli	l'albero, gli alberi
gn, ps, z, s+ consonant	lo	gli	lo studente, gli studenti

Feminine forms before:

	singular	plural	
any consonant	la	le	la camera, le camere
a, e, i, o, u	l'	le	l'arancia, le arance

The indefinite article

Masculine forms before:

	singular	
vowel or most consonants	un	un ombrello, un caffè
gn, ps, z, s+consonant	uno	uno zoo

Feminine forms before:

	singular	
any consonant	una	una stanza
a, e, i, o, u	un'	un'aspirina

Adjectives

Adjectives agree in number and gender with the noun to which they refer.
Italian adjectives end in either -o or -e.

	singular	plural	
masculine	pigro	pigri	lazy
	felice	felici	happy
	singular	plural	
feminine	pigra	pigre	lazy
	felice	felici	happy

Summary of Italian grammar

When you have a mixture of masculine and feminine nouns, the adjective ending is masculine.

Max e Anna sono pigri/gentili.
Max and Anna are lazy/kind.

Position

Adjectives are usually placed after the noun they describe.

Ho letto un libro interessante.
I've read an interesting book.

There are, however, a few common adjectives, such as **bello, brutto, buono, cattivo, piccolo, grande, giovane, vecchio, nuovo**, which can be placed before the noun.

Ho visto un bel film.
I have seen a lovely film.

Possessive adjectives

In Italian, the possessive adjective agrees in gender and number with what is possessed and not with the possessor. The possessive adjective is generally preceded by the definite article: **il mio ufficio**.

	singular	
	masculine	feminine
my	il mio	la mia
your [*informal*]	il tuo	la tua
his/her; your [*formal*]	il suo	la sua
our	il nostro	la nostra
your [*plural*]	il vostro	la vostra
their	il loro	la loro

	plural	
	masculine	feminine
my	i miei	le mie
your [*informal*]	i tuoi	le tue
his/her; your [*formal*]	i suoi	le sue
our	i nostri	le nostre
your [*plural*]	i vostri	le vostre
their	i loro	le loro

Except with **loro**, the definite article is dropped when the noun refers to single immediate family members – **mia sorella, tuo fratello**, but **le mie sorelle, i tuoi fratelli; la loro sorella, i loro fratelli**.

Questo and *quello*

Questo and **quello** can be used both as adjectives ('this'/'that') and as pronouns ('this one'/'that one'). **Questo** takes the usual adjective endings (**-o/-a/-i/-e**) whether it is used as an adjective or a pronoun. **Quello** also takes these endings when used as a pronoun;

however, when it comes before a noun, it takes the same endings as the definite article.

singular	quel, quello, quell', quella	quella casa quell'amico
plural	quei, quegli, quelle	quegli amici quelle case

Subject pronouns

In Italian, subject pronouns are generally omitted (unless you want to place emphasis on them): the subject is shown in the verb ending.

io	I	noi	we
tu	you [*informal*]	voi	you [*plural*]
lui	he	loro	they
lei	she		
lei	you [*formal*]		

The **tu** form is used when speaking to a child or someone you know well;
the **lei** form when speaking to an adult you don't know well.

Object pronouns

Direct object pronouns

mi	me	ci	us
ti	you	vi	you
lo	him/it [*m*]	li	them [*m*]
la	her/it [*f*]	le	them [*f*]
la	you [*formal*]		

Indirect object pronouns

mi	to (etc.) me	ci	to us
ti	to you	vi	to you
gli	to him/to it [*m*]	gli	to them [*m/f*]
le	to her/to it [*f*]		
le	to you [*formal*]		

Indirect object pronouns are used with verbs which are normally followed by a preposition, such as **telefonare a** ('to telephone') and **dare a** ('to give to').

Anna telefona a Maria. Anna **le** telefona.
Anna telefona a Mario. Anna **gli** telefona.

The position of direct and indirect object pronouns

Both direct and indirect object pronouns come before the verb (or before **avere/essere** in the perfect tense). When both appear in a sentence, the indirect comes before the direct pronoun: the indirect pronoun may also change form (see below).

• •

Ti offro un caffè.
I'll buy you a coffee.

Le scrivo domani.
I'll write to her tomorrow.

Mi piacciono quegli stivali. **Li** compro!
I like those boots. I'll buy them!

Me lo avete comprato.
You bought it for me.

When there are two verbs, and the second is
an infinitive, the pronoun comes either
before the first verb or combines with the
infinitive.

Ti vorrei incontrare.
I'd like to meet you.

Vorrei incontra**rti**.
I'd like to meet you.

Before a direct object pronoun, the indirect
object pronouns **mi**, **ti**, **ci**, and **vi** change
respectively to **me**, **te**, **ce**, and **ve**.

Ti abbiamo già dato il libro.
We have already given the book to you.

Te lo abbiamo già dato.
We have already given it to you.

Vi mando la lettera domani.
I'll send the letter to you tomorrow.

Ve la mando domani.
I'll send it to you tomorrow.

The third person indirect pronouns – **le** and
gli – change to **glie**- and combine with **lo**, **la**, **li**,
and **le** to form one word.

Mando un biglietto d'auguri ai nonni. **Glielo** mando.
I'll send a card to our grandparents.
I'll send it to them.

These forms come before the verb or can be
joined to an infinitive.

Glielo dovrei dare.
I should give it to him/her/them.

Dovrei dar**glielo**.
I should give it to him/her/them.

Disjunctive pronouns

me	me	**noi**	us
te	you [*informal*]	**voi**	you [*plural*]
lui	him	**loro**	them
lei	her		
lei	you [*formal*]		

Disjunctive pronouns are used for emphasis
and after prepositions, such as **di**, **a**, **da**, **con**,
etc.:

Conosco **lui**.
I know him.

Mario gioca con **noi**.
Mario plays with us.

Lo fa per **me**.
He does it for me.

Viene con **te**?
Is he coming with you?

Possessive pronouns

These have the same form as the possessive
adjectives.

Questa è la mia bicicletta.
That's my bike.

E quella è **la mia**.
And that's mine.

The definite article is used with family
members in the singular.

Mia nonna abita a Roma.
My grandmother lives in Rome.

La mia abita a Napoli.
Mine lives in Naples.

ci

ci is used to refer to location. It is used to
mean 'here' or 'there', although in some
instances its meaning in English is
understood rather than translated.
It usually comes before the verb.

Siete mai stati a Parigi? Sì, **ci** siamo andati molte volte.
Have you ever been to Paris? Yes, we've been
there many times.

Quando andate a Roma? **Ci** andiamo venerdì.
When are you going to Rome? We're going
(there) on Friday.

ne

ne can mean 'of it/him/her', 'about
it/him/her', etc., or 'of them', 'about them',
etc. In some instances it isn't translated, but
it must be included.

Vorrei delle banane.
I would like some bananas.

Quante **ne** vuole?
How many (of them) do you want?

Maria parlerà delle sue vacanze.
Maria will talk about her holidays.

Maria **ne** parlerà.
Maria will talk about them.

Summary of Italian grammar

Prepositions

In addition to the general meanings of the prepositions the following uses are particularly worth noting.

a with cities

> Abito **a** Parma.
> I live in Parma.

> Vado **a** Parigi.
> I am going to Paris.

in with countries and regions

> Vivono **in** Italia – **in** Toscana.
> They live in Italy – in Tuscany.

di to express possession

> la mamma **di** Federica.
> Federica's mum

da + name of a person means 'to or at their house, shop, etc.'

> Vai **da** Paola?
> Are you going to Paola's?

> Andate **dal** giornalaio?
> Are you going to the newsagent's?

> Sei già stato **dal** dentista?
> Have you already been to the dentist's?

da + present tense to describe an action which began in the past and which continues in the present ('for', 'since')

> È malato **da** due giorni.
> He has been ill for two days.

> **Lavorano** qui **dal** 1975.
> They have worked here since 1975.

Prepositions and articles

When the prepositions **a** ('to'), **da** ('from'), **di** ('of'), **in** ('in'), and **su** ('on') are followed by the definite article, the words combine as follows.

	singular				plural		
	il	lo	l'	la	i	gli	le
a	al	allo	all'	alla	ai	agli	alle
da	dal	dallo	dall'	dalla	dai	dagli	dalle
di	del	dello	dell'	della	dei	degli	delle
in	nel	nello	nell'	nella	nei	negli	nelle
su	sul	sullo	sull'	sulla	sui	sugli	sulle

La sveglia è **sul** comodino.
The alarm clock is on the bedside cabinet.

I pantaloni sono **nell'**armadio.
The trousers are in the wardrobe.

Adverbs

Regular adverbs

Most adverbs are formed by adding **-mente** to the feminine form of the adjective.

lento slow	**lenta*mente*** slowly
vero true	**vera*mente*** truly

Adjectives ending in **–e** in the singular simply add **-mente**.

triste sad	**triste*mente*** sadly
semplice simple	**semplice*mente*** simply

However, if the adjective ends in **-re** or **-le**, the **-e** is dropped:

normale normal	**normal*mente*** normally
regolare regular	**regolar*mente*** regularly

The comparative and superlative

Comparative

più ... di	Lui è **più** giovane **di** lei.
	He is younger than she is.
meno ... di	Lui è **meno** vivace **di** lei.
	He is less lively than she is.
(tanto) ...	Lui è alto **quanto** lei.
quanto/come	He's as tall as she is.

Superlative

To say 'the most ...' in Italian is **il / la / i / le più**; 'the least ...' is **il / la / i / le meno**.

Mara è **la più** giovane.
Mara is the youngest.

Franco è **il più** alto.
Franco is the tallest.

After a superlative 'in' is translated by **di**.

È **la ragazza più** intelligente **della** classe.
She is the cleverest girl in her class.

È **l'albergo più** costoso **di** Venezia.
It is the most expensive hotel in Venice.

Irregular forms

Some adjectives have two different forms of the comparative and superlative. The distinctions in meaning are slight and best learnt in context.

	singular	plural
buono (good)	più buono / migliore	il/la più buono/a il/la migliore
cattivo (bad)	più cattivo / peggiore	il/la più cattivo/a il/la peggiore

Expressing quantities

di + article

Ordino **del** vino?
Shall I order some wine?

Preferisco **dell'**acqua.
I'd prefer some water.

Compra **dei** pomodori.
Buy some tomatoes.

Hai **delle** aspirine?
Do you have any aspirins®?

qualche

qualche is always followed by a singular noun.

Ho **qualche amico** a Roma.
I have some friends in Rome.

Asking questions

There are two ways of asking questions: (a) you keep the same wording as the sentence, but use a rising intonation; (b) you use a question word – then the verb and the subject change places.

È inglese?
Are you English?

Dove lavora Roberta?
Where does Roberta work?

Negatives

To make a sentence negative, you simply put **non** in front of the verb.

Sono americano.
I'm American.

Non sono americano.
I'm not American.

Numbers

1	uno	16	sedici
2	due	17	diciassette
3	tre	18	diciotto
4	quattro	19	diciannove
5	cinque	20	venti
6	sei	21	ventuno
7	sette	22	ventidue
8	otto	23	ventitré
9	nove	30	trenta
10	dieci	40	quaranta
11	undici	50	cinquanta
12	dodici	60	sessanta
13	tredici	70	settanta
14	quattordici	71	settantuno
15	quindici	72	settantadue
73	settantatré	101	centouno
74	settantaquattro, etc.	102	centodue
80	ottanta	200	duecento
81	ottantuno	202	duecentodue
82	ottantadue, etc.	999	novecentonovan-
90	novanta		tanove
91	novantuno	1000	mille
92	novantadue, etc.	2000	duemila
100	cento	2001	duemilauno

Verbs

The infinitive

Dictionaries and glossaries usually list verbs in the infinitive form, which in Italian has three different endings: **-are**, **-ere**, or **-ire** (apart from a few irregular forms in **-rre**). Regular verbs within each group take the same endings.

Reflexive verbs

Reflexive verbs can easily be identified by the additional **si** which appears at the end of the infinitive (**chiamarsi**): they end in **-arsi**, **-ersi**, or **-irsi**, taking the endings for **-are**, **-ere**, and **-ire** verbs respectively. They just add the reflexive pronouns **mi**, **ti**, **si**, **ci**, **vi**, and **si** in front of the verb.

	alzarsi – to get up	divertirsi – to enjoy oneself
(io)	*mi* alzo	*mi* diverto
(tu)	*ti* alzi	*ti* diverti
(lui/lei)	*si* alza	*si* diverte
(noi)	*ci* alziamo	*ci* divertiamo
(voi)	*vi* alzate	*vi* divertite
(loro)	*si* alzano	*si* divertono

Non **si alzano** mai prima delle otto.
They never get up before eight.

Si divertirà senz'altro.
He will definitely enjoy himself.

The imperative

The imperative is used to give orders, instructions, and advice. Irregular imperative forms are covered in the verb tables on pages 922–930.

The *tu* form of the imperative is used to address children or people you know well. The *voi* form is used to address a group of people. Except for the *tu form* of the **-are** verbs, the other forms are the same as the *tu form* of the present tense.

	parlare	credere	sentire	finire
(tu)	parla	credi	senti	finisci
(voi)	parlate	credete	sentite	finite

The imperative also has a *noi form*, translated 'let's …'. This is the same as the *noi form* of the present tense.

	parlare	credere	sentire	finire
(noi)	parliamo	crediamo	sentiamo	finiamo

The *lei form* of the imperative is used with adults you don't know.

	parlare	credere	sentire	finire
(lei)	parli	creda	senta	finisca

The imperative and object pronouns

Direct and indirect object pronouns come *before the lei imperative.*

La guardi meglio. È tutta sporca!
Look at it more closely. It's all dirty!

Non **lo ascolti!** Scherza.
Don't listen to him. He's joking.

However, they are added to the *end of the tu, voi, and noi imperatives.*

Telefonate**gli** al più presto.
Ring him very soon.

Alziamoci alle sette.
Let's get up at seven o'clock.

Non parliamo**ne** più.
Let's not speak about it any more.

When you add a pronoun to the *tu* imperative forms of **andare, fare, dare, dire,** and **stare,** the first letter of the pronoun is doubled. The only exception to this is **gli.**

Dimmi la verità!
Tell me the truth!

Da**lle** questo.
Give her this.

Digli che arrivo domani.
Tell him I'll be arriving tomorrow.

The negative imperative

tu form	non + infinitive	**Non fumare,** per favore. Please don't smoke.
other forms	non + imperative	**Non fumate,** per favore. Please don't smoke.

In the negative, object pronouns come *before the lei imperative.*

Non **lo dica!**
Don't say it!

They can either come before the *tu, voi,* and *noi* imperatives or be added on to the end of

it. In the negative **tu** form, the final **-e** of the infinitive is dropped when an object pronoun is added on.

Non **dirlo!**/Non **lo dire!**
Don't say it!

The present tense

The single present tense in Italian has a wider use than its English equivalent: **io lavoro** can be translated as either 'I work' or 'I am working', according to context. Besides expressing actions which relate to the immediate present, it can also be used to express:

– actions which are done regularly

Ogni mattina **faccio** una passeggiata.
Every morning I go for a walk.

– actions which relate to a future intention.

Fra un mese **andiamo** in Spagna.
In a month we're going to Spain.

For the forms of the present tense, see the verb tables on pages 922–930.

The progressive forms

The progressive forms are used to say what is or was happening at the moment of speaking. These forms are less common in Italian than in English, because it is perfectly normal to use the simple present tense to convey the same idea.

The progressives are formed by combining the verb **stare** with the gerund, the form of the verb which ends with **-ando** or **-endo**. The present tense and the imperfect tense of **stare** are used respectively to talk about the present and the past.

parlare	prendere	dormire
sto/ stavo parlando	sto/ stavo prendendo	sto/ stavo dormendo
stai/ stavi parlando	stai/ stavi prendendo	stai/ stavi dormendo
sta/ stava parlando	sta/ stava prendendo	sta/ stava dormendo
stiamo/ stavamo parlando	stiamo/ stavamo prendendo	stiamo/ stavamo dormendo
state/ stavate parlando	state/ stavate prendendo	state/ stavate dormendo

parlare	prendere	dormire
stanno/	stanno/	stanno/
stavano	stavano	stavano
parlando	prendendo	dormendo

Sta piovendo.
It is raining.

Che **stavi facendo**?
What were you doing?

The perfect tense

The perfect tense is used to describe a single completed event or action which took place in the past. It can be translated in one of two ways, depending on the context: for example, **ho parlato** can mean either 'I spoke' or 'I have spoken'. It is formed with the present tense of **avere** or **essere** + the past participle of the verb required. For regular verbs this is formed as follows: -**are** verbs → -**ato**, -**ere** verbs → -**uto**, and -**ire** verbs → -**ito**.

    parl**ato**   cred**uto**   sent**ito**

With avere

Most transitive verbs form the perfect tense with **avere**.

Ho mangiato troppo.
I've eaten too much.

Non **ha avuto** molta fortuna.
She didn't have much luck.

When **avere** is used, the past participle must agree with any direct object which comes before the verb. Note that **lo** and **la** shorten to **l'**; **li** and **le** don't.

Ho comprato una macchina. **L'**ho comprat**a** ieri.
I bought a car. I bought it yesterday.

Hai visto Maria e Carla? Sì, **le** ho vist**e** ieri.
Did you see Maria and Carla? Yes, I saw them yesterday.

With essere

Most intransitive verbs, all reflexive verbs, and a few others (such as **essere, piacere, sembrare**, etc.) form the perfect tense with **essere**. When this happens, the past participle acts like an adjective: it agrees with the subject in gender and number.

Maria **è andata** a Roma molte volte.
Maria has been to Rome many times.

Ci siamo annoiati molto.
We got really bored.

La serata **è stata** veramente piacevole.
The evening was very pleasant.

Irregular past participles

* indicates a verb forming the perfect with **essere**

infinitive	past participle
aprire (to open)	aperto
bere (to drink)	bevuto
chiedere (to ask)	chiesto
chiudere (to close)	chiuso
crescere* (to grow)	cresciuto
decidere (to decide)	deciso
dire (to say)	detto
essere* (to be)	stato
fare (to do)	fatto
leggere (to read)	letto
mettere (to put)	messo
morire* (to die)	morto
nascere* (to be born)	nato
perdere (to lose)	perso
piacere* (to please)	piaciuto
prendere (to take)	preso
rimanere* (to stay)	rimasto
scegliere (to choose)	scelto
scrivere (to write)	scritto
stare* (to stay, to be situated)	stato
succedere* (to happen)	successo
trascorrere (to spend)	trascorso
vedere (to see)	visto
venire* (to come)	venuto
vincere (to win)	vinto
vivere* (to live)	vissuto

The imperfect tense

The imperfect tense is used:

1 to describe something which used to happen frequently or regularly in the past.
   Andavamo a scuola a piedi.
   We walked/We used to walk to school.

2 to describe what was happening or what the situation was when something else happened.
   Dormivo quando Sergio **è arrivato**.
   I was sleeping when Sergio arrived.
   Aveva sei anni quando **è nata** Carla.
   He was six when Carla was born.

3 to express an emotional or physical state in the past and to refer to time, age, or the weather.
   Ieri sera Beatrice **era** stanca.
   Beatrice was tired.
   Aveva i capelli biondi.
   She had blonde hair.

· ·

Erano le sette.
It was seven o'clock.

Quando **eravamo** piccoli, ci piaceva andare al mare.
When we were little, we used to like going to the seaside.

Era una bella giornata.
It was a lovely day.

The imperfect tense is formed by adding the following endings to the stem.

	parlare	credere	sentire
(io)	parlavo	credevo	sentivo
(tu)	parlavi	credevi	sentivi
(lui/lei; lei)	parlava	credeva	sentiva
(noi)	parlavamo	credevamo	sentivamo
(voi)	parlavate	credevate	sentivate
(loro)	parlavano	credevano	sentivano

See the verb tables for details of verbs which are irregular in the imperfect.

Use of the perfect and the imperfect

The perfect is used to describe a completed or single action in the past; the imperfect describes a continuing, repeated, or habitual action. When they are used together, the imperfect is the tense that sets the scene, while the perfect is used to move the action forward.

Ho visto Marco giovedì.
I saw Marco on Thursday.

Andavo in piscina il giovedì.
I used to go swimming on Thursdays.

Poiché **faceva** caldo, **siamo andati** tutti al mare.
Because it was hot, we all went to the seaside.

The past historic tense

The past historic is a tense that refers to something that happened in the past, generally in the relatively distant past. It is formed by adding a set of endings to the verb. Before adding the endings, the infinitive ending (**-are**, **-ere**, or **-ire**) is dropped. For some **–ere** verbs there is a choice of endings for some forms; both sets of endings are commonly used. A large number of verbs form their past historic in irregular ways.

parlare	vendere	dormire
(io) parlai	vendei or **vendetti**	dormii
(tu) parlasti	vendesti	dormisti

(lui/lei; lei)	parlò	vendé or **vendette**	dormì
(noi)	parlammo	vendemmo	dormimmo
(voi)	parlaste	vendeste	dormiste
(loro)	parlarono	venderono or **vendettero**	dormirono

Pagò il conto e se ne andò.
He paid the bill and left.

La città **fu fondata** nel 500 a.C.
The city was founded in 500 BC.

The pluperfect tense

The pluperfect tense is used to talk about events that happened *before* the event that is the main focus of attention. Like the perfect tense, it uses a form of **avere** or **essere** with the past participle: the past tense of **avere** (or **essere** if the verb forms its compound tenses with **essere**) is followed by the past participle. If the verb uses **essere** as an auxiliary, the past participle agrees with the subject (see the section on the perfect tense).

Li **avevo visti** l'estate prima.
I had seen them the summer before.

Ci **eravamo** già **conosciuti**.
We had already met.

The future tense

In Italian, the future can be expressed in different ways.

1 You can use the present tense with an appropriate time expression when talking about plans (as in English):

   Non **sono** libero domani.
   I'm not/I won't be available tomorrow.

   Partiamo per le vacanze lunedì prossimo.
   We're going on holiday next Monday.

2 You can use the future tense – especially when making predictions (as in weather forecasts or horoscopes) or stating a fact about the future.

   Avrete molto successo.
   You will have great success.

   Balleranno tutta la notte.
   They'll dance all night.

   Domani **nevicherà**.
   Tomorrow it will snow.

The future tense is formed by dropping the final **-e** of the infinitive and adding the future endings. In **-are** verbs, the **a** in the infinitive changes to **e**.

	parlare	prendere	dormire
(io)	parlerò	prenderò	dormirò
(tu)	parlerai	prenderai	dormirai
(lui)	parlerà	prenderà	dormirà
(noi)	parleremo	prenderemo	dormiremo
(voi)	parlerete	prenderete	dormirete
(loro)	parleranno	prenderanno	dormiranno

Stasera Elio **parlerà** con il padre.
Tonight Elio will talk to his father.

Non lo **lascerà** mai.
She'll never leave him.

Verbs ending in **-care** and **-gare** add an **h** before
the endings to keep the hard sound of the
stem.

Gli spie**gheremo** tutto noi.
We will explain everything to him.

Cer**cherete** subito lavoro?
Will you be looking for work straight away?

*For irregular future forms, see the verb tables on pages
922–930.*

The conditional

In Italian the conditional is used for polite
requests and suggestions, and to express a
wish or a probable action. The endings are
the same for all conjugations and, like the
future tense, are added to the infinitive
minus the final **-e** (or, if irregular, to the same
stem used for the future tense).
As with the future, the **a** in **-are** verbs changes
to **e**. The rules affecting the
spelling of **cercare**, **spiegare**, etc. also apply:
see above.

	parlare	prendere	dormire
(io)	parlerei	prenderei	dormirei
(tu)	parleresti	prenderesti	dormiresti
(lui/lei; lei)	parlerebbe	prenderebbe	dormirebbe
(noi)	parleremmo	prenderemmo	dormiremmo
(voi)	parlereste	prendereste	dormireste
(loro)	parlerebbero	prenderebbero	dormirebbero

Potremmo venire con te.
We could come with you.

Dovresti andare a letto presto.
You should go to bed early.

Vorrebbe fare una partita a tennis?
Would you like to have a game of tennis?

Non **vivrebbero** mai all'estero.
They'd never live abroad.

Saresti il primo a saperlo.
You'd be the first to know.

The subjunctive

The subjunctive is a special form of the verb
that expresses doubt, unlikelihood, or desire.
The subjunctive is not very common in
modern English, and often forms with
let, *should*, etc. do the same job. In Italian the
subjunctive is very common, and is
obligatory in certain circumstances. The
subjunctive is commonly used to show that
what is being said is not a concrete fact, for
example to indicate doubt or necessity, or
after verbs of ordering, requiring, or
persuasion. It contrasts with the *indicative*,
the normal form of the verb, which always
implies a greater degree of certainty. The
subjunctive is sometimes translated by an
infinitive in English.

The present subjunctive is generally
used when the main verb in the sentence
is in the present; the past subjunctive is used
when the main verb is in the past,
or in order to talk about hypothetical
situations.

*For the forms of the subjunctive, see the verb tables on
pages 922-930.*

Credo che tu abbia ragione.
I think you're right.

Spero che questo problema si risolva.
I hope this problem is solved.

Bisogna che tu legga tutto.
It's necessary for you to read it all.

Voglio che tu mi aiuti.
I want you to help me.

Volevo che mi aiutassi.
I wanted you to help me.

. . . .

Regular verbs -are

parlare – to speak (past participle **parlato**)

	present	future	conditional	perfect	imperfect
io	parlo	parlerò	parlerei	ho parlato	parlavo
tu	parli	parlerai	parleresti	hai parlato	parlavi
lui/lei; lei	parla	parlerà	parlerebbe	ha parlato	parlava
noi	parliamo	parleremo	parleremmo	abbiamo parlato	parlavamo
voi	parlate	parlerete	parlereste	avete parlato	parlavate
loro	parlano	parleranno	parlerebbero	hanno parlato	parlavano

	pluperfect	past historic	present subjunctive	past subjunctive	imperative
io	avevo parlato	parlai	parli	parlassi	
tu	avevi parlato	parlasti	parli	parlassi	parla
lui/lei; lei	aveva parlato	parlò	parli	parlasse	parli
noi	avevamo parlato	parlammo	parliamo	parlassimo	parliamo
voi	avevate parlato	parlaste	parliate	parlaste	parlate
loro	avevano parlato	parlarono	parlino	parlassero	

Verbs ending in **-care** and **-gare**, such as **cercare**, ('to look for') or **spiegare** ('to explain'), add an **h** before **i** or **e**.

Cherchiamo un posto tranquillo. We're looking for a quiet place.

Ti spieghiamo tutto domani. We'll explain everything tomorrow.

Regular verbs -ere

credere – to believe (past participle **creduto**)

	present	future	conditional	perfect	imperfect
io	credo	crederò	crederei	ho creduto	credevo
tu	credi	crederai	crederesti	hai creduto	credevi
lui/lei; lei	crede	crederà	crederebbe	ha creduto	credeva
noi	crediamo	crederemo	crederemmo	abbiamo creduto	credevamo
voi	credete	crederete	credereste	avete creduto	credevate
loro	credono	crederanno	crederebbero	hanno creduto	credevano

	pluperfect	past historic	present subjunctive	past subjunctive	imperative
io	avevo creduto	credei *or* credetti	creda	credessi	
tu	avevi creduto	credesti	creda	credessi	credi
lui/lei; lei	aveva creduto	credé *or* credette	creda	credesse	creda
noi	avevamo creduto	credemmo	crediamo	credessimo	crediamo
voi	avevate creduto	credeste	crediate	credeste	credete
loro	avevano creduto	crederono *or* credettero	credano	credessero	

Regular verbs -ire (1)

sentire – to hear (past participle **sentito**)

	present	future	conditional	perfect	imperfect
io	sento	sentirò	sentirei	ho sentito	sentivo
tu	senti	sentirai	sentiresti	hai sentito	sentivi
lui/lei; lei	sente	sentirà	sentirebbe	ha sentito	sentiva
noi	sentiamo	sentiremo	sentiremmo	abbiamo sentito	sentivamo
voi	sentite	sentirete	sentireste	avete sentito	sentivate
loro	sentono	sentiranno	sentirebbero	hanno sentito	sentivano

	pluperfect	past historic	present subjunctive	past subjunctive	imperative
io	avevo sentito	sentii	senta	sentissi	
tu	avevi sentito	sentisti	senta	sentissi	senti
lui/lei; lei	aveva sentito	sentì	senta	sentisse	senta
noi	avevamo sentito	sentimmo	sentiamo	sentissimo	sentiamo
voi	avevate sentito	sentiste	sentiate	sentiste	sentite
loro	avevano sentito	sentirono	sentano	sentissero	

Regular verbs -ire (2)

Some verbs ending in **-ire** insert **-isc-** between the stem and the ending in the three singular forms and in the 3rd person plural form of the present tense.

finire – to finish (past participle **finito**)

	present	future	conditional	perfect	imperfect
io	finisco	finirò	finirei	ho finito	finivo
tu	finisci	finirai	finiresti	hai finito	finivi
lui/lei; lei	finisce	finirà	finirebbe	ha finito	finiva
noi	finiamo	finiremo	finiremmo	abbiamo finito	finivamo
voi	finite	finirete	finireste	avete finito	finivate
loro	finiscono	finiranno	finirebbero	hanno finito	finivano

	pluperfect	past historic	present subjunctive	past subjunctive	imperative
io	avevo finito	finii	finisca	finissi	
tu	avevi finito	finisti	finisca	finissi	finisci
lui/lei; lei	aveva finito	finì	finisca	finisse	finisca
noi	avevamo finito	finimmo	finiamo	finissimo	finiamo
voi	avevate finito	finiste	finiate	finiste	finite
loro	avevano finito	finirono	finiscano	finissero	

. . . .

Irregular verbs

---

avere – to have (past participle **avuto**)

	present	future	conditional	perfect	imperfect
io	ho	avrò	avrei	ho avuto	avevo
tu	hai	avrai	avresti	hai avuto	avevi
lui/lei; lei	ha	avrà	avrebbe	ha avuto	aveva
noi	abbiamo	avremo	avremmo	abbiamo avuto	avevamo
voi	avete	avrete	avreste	avete avuto	avevate
loro	hanno	avranno	avrebbero	hanno avuto	avevano

	pluperfect	past historic	present subjunctive	past subjunctive	imperative
io	avevo avuto	ebbi	abbia	avessi	
tu	avevi avuto	avesti	abbia	avessi	abbi
lui/lei; lei	aveva avuto	ebbe	abbia	avesse	abbia
noi	avevamo avuto	avemmo	abbiamo	avessimo	abbiamo
voi	avevate avuto	aveste	abbiate	aveste	abbiate
loro	avevano avuto	ebbero	abbiano	avessero	

---

essere* – to be (past participle **stato**)

	present	future	conditional	perfect	imperfect
io	sono	sarò	sarei	sono stato/stata	ero
tu	sei	sarai	saresti	sei stato/stata	eri
lui/lei; lei	è	sarà	sarebbe	è stato/stata	era
noi	siamo	saremo	saremmo	siamo stati/state	eravamo
voi	siete	sarete	sareste	siete stati/state	eravate
loro	sono	saranno	sarebbero	sono stati/state	erano

	pluperfect	past historic	present subjunctive	past subjunctive	imperative
io	ero stato/stata	fui	sia	fossi	
tu	eri stato/stata	fosti	sia	fossi	sii
lui/lei; lei	era stato/stata	fu	sia	fosse	sia
noi	eravamo stati/state	fummo	siamo	fossimo	siamo
voi	eravate stati/state	foste	siate	foste	siate
loro	erano stati/state	furono	siano	fossero	

. . . .

Irregular verbs cont.

andare* – to go (past participle **andato**)

	present	future	conditional	perfect	imperfect
io	vado	andrò	andrei	sono andato/andata	andavo
tu	vai	andrai	andresti	sei andato/andata	andavi
lui/lei; lei	va	andrà	andrebbe	è andato/andata	andava
noi	andiamo	andremo	andremmo	siamo andati/andate	andavamo
voi	andate	andrete	andreste	siete andati/andate	andavate
loro	vanno	andranno	andrebbero	sono andati/andate	andavano

	pluperfect	past historic	present subjunctive	past subjunctive	imperative
io	ero andato/andata	andai	vada	andassi	
tu	eri andato/andata	andasti	vada	andassi	va'
lui/lei; lei	era andato/andata	andò	vada	andasse	vada
noi	eravamo andati/andate	andammo	andiamo	andassimo	andiamo
voi	eravate andati/andate	andaste	andiate	andaste	andate
loro	erano andati/andate	andarono	vadano	andassero	

bere – to drink (past participle **bevuto**)

	present	future	conditional	perfect	imperfect
io	bevo	berrò	berrei	ho bevuto	bevevo
tu	bevi	berrai	berresti	hai bevuto	bevevi
lui/lei; lei	beve	berrà	berrebbe	ha bevuto	beveva
noi	beviamo	berremo	berremmo	abbiamo bevuto	bevevamo
voi	bevete	berrete	berreste	avete bevuto	bevevate
loro	bevono	berranno	berrebbero	hanno bevuto	bevevano

	pluperfect	past historic	present subjunctive	past subjunctive	imperative
io	avevo bevuto	bevvi *or* bevetti	beva	bevessi	
tu	avevi bevuto	bevesti	beva	bevessi	bevi
lui/lei; lei	aveva bevuto	bevve *or* bevette	beva	bevesse	beva
noi	avevamo bevuto	bevemmo	beviamo	bevessimo	beviamo
voi	avevate bevuto	beveste	beviate	beveste	bevete
loro	avevano bevuto	bevvero *or* bevettero	bevano	bevessero	

. . . .

Irregular verbs cont.

dare – to give (past participle **dato**)

	present	future	conditional	perfect	imperfect
io	do	darò	darei	ho dato	davo
tu	dai	darai	daresti	hai dato	davi
lui/lei; lei	dà	darà	darebbe	ha dato	dava
noi	diamo	daremo	daremmo	abbiamo dato	davamo
voi	date	darete	dareste	avete dato	davate
loro	danno	daranno	darebbero	hanno dato	davano

	pluperfect	past historic	present subjunctive	past subjunctive	imperative
io	avevo dato	diedi *or* detti	dia	dessi	
tu	avevi dato	desti	dia	dessi	da'
lui/lei; lei	aveva dato	diede *or* dette	dia	desse	dia
noi	avevamo dato	demmo	diamo	dessimo	diamo
voi	avevate dato	deste	diate	deste	date
loro	avevano dato	diedero *or* dettero	diano	dessero	

dire – to say (past participle **detto**)

	present	future	conditional	perfect	imperfect
io	dico	dirò	direi	ho detto	dicevo
tu	dici	dirai	diresti	hai detto	dicevi
lui/lei; lei	dice	dirà	direbbe	ha detto	diceva
noi	diciamo	diremo	diremmo	abbiamo detto	dicevamo
voi	dite	direte	direste	avete detto	dicevate
loro	dicono	diranno	direbbero	hanno detto	dicevano

	pluperfect	past historic	present subjunctive	past subjunctive	imperative
io	avevo detto	dissi	dica	dicessi	
tu	avevi detto	dicesti	dica	dicessi	di'
lui/lei; lei	aveva detto	disse	dica	dicesse	dica
noi	avevamo detto	dicemmo	diciamo	dicessimo	diciamo
voi	avevate detto	diceste	diciate	diceste	dite
loro	avevano detto	dissero	dicano	dicessero	

Irregular verbs cont.

dovere – to have to (past participle dovuto)

	present	future	conditional	perfect	imperfect
io	devo	dovrò	dovrei	ho dovuto	dovevo
tu	devi	dovrai	dovresti	hai dovuto	dovevi
lui/lei; lei	deve	dovrà	dovrebbe	ha dovuto	doveva
noi	dobbiamo	dovremo	dovremmo	abbiamo dovuto	dovevamo
voi	dovete	dovrete	dovreste	avete dovuto	dovevate
loro	devono	dovranno	dovrebbero	hanno dovuto	dovevano

	pluperfect	past historic	present subjunctive	past subjunctive
io	avevo dovuto	dovetti	deva	dovessi
tu	avevi dovuto	dovesti	deva	dovessi
lui/lei; lei	aveva dovuto	dovette	deva	dovesse
noi	avevamo dovuto	dovemmo	dobbiamo	dovessimo
voi	avevate dovuto	doveste	dobbiate	doveste
loro	avevano dovuto	dovettero	devano	dovessero

fare – to do, to make (past participle fatto)

	present	future	conditional	perfect	imperfect
io	faccio	farò	farei	ho fatto	facevo
tu	fai	farai	faresti	hai fatto	facevi
lui/lei; lei	fa	farà	farebbe	ha fatto	faceva
noi	facciamo	faremo	faremmo	abbiamo fatto	facevamo
voi	fate	farete	fareste	avete fatto	facevate
loro	fanno	faranno	farebbero	hanno fatto	facevano

	pluperfect	past historic	present subjunctive	past subjunctive	imperative
io	avevo fatto	feci	faccia	facessi	
tu	avevi fatto	facesti	faccia	facessi	fa'
lui/lei; lei	aveva fatto	fece	faccia	facesse	faccia
noi	avevamo fatto	facemmo	facciamo	facessimo	facciamo
voi	avevate fatto	faceste	facciate	faceste	fate
loro	avevano fatto	fecero	facciano	facessero	

. . . .

Irregular verbs cont.

potere – to be able to (past participle **potuto**)

	present	future	conditional	perfect	imperfect
io	posso	potrò	potrei	ho potuto	potevo
tu	puoi	potrai	potresti	hai potuto	potevi
lui/lei; lei	può	potrà	potrebbe	ha potuto	poteva
noi	possiamo	potremo	potremmo	abbiamo potuto	potevamo
voi	potete	potrete	potreste	avete potuto	potevate
loro	possono	potranno	potrebbero	hanno potuto	potevano

	pluperfect	past historic	present subjunctive	past subjunctive
io	avevo potuto	potei	possa	potessi
tu	avevi potuto	potesti	possa	potessi
lui/lei; lei	aveva potuto	poté	possa	potesse
noi	avevamo potuto	potemmo	possiamo	potessimo
voi	avevate potuto	poteste	possiate	poteste
loro	avevano potuto	poterono	possano	potessero

sapere – to know (a fact, how to do something) (past participle **saputo**)

	present	future	conditional	perfect	imperfect
io	so	saprò	saprei	ho saputo	sapevo
tu	sai	saprai	sapresti	hai saputo	sapevi
lui/lei; lei	sa	saprà	saprebbe	ha saputo	sapeva
noi	sappiamo	sapremo	sapremmo	abbiamo saputo	sapevamo
voi	sapete	saprete	sapreste	avete saputo	sapevate
loro	sanno	sapranno	saprebbero	hanno saputo	sapevano

	pluperfect	past historic	present subjunctive	past subjunctive	imperative
io	avevo saputo	seppi	sappia	sapessi	
tu	avevi saputo	sapesti	sappia	sapessi	sappi
lui/lei; lei	aveva saputo	seppe	sappia	sapesse	sappia
noi	avevamo saputo	sapemmo	sappiamo	sapessimo	sappiamo
voi	avevate saputo	sapeste	sappiate	sapeste	sappiate
loro	avevano saputo	seppero	sappiano	sapessero	

Irregular verbs cont.

stare* – to stay (past participle stato)

	present	future	conditional	perfect	imperfect
io	sto	starò	starei	sono stato/stata	stavo
tu	stai	starai	staresti	sei stato/stata	stavi
lui/lei; lei	sta	starà	starebbe	è stato/stata	stava
noi	stiamo	staremo	staremmo	siamo stati/state	stavamo
voi	state	starete	stareste	siete stati/state	stavate
loro	stanno	staranno	starebbero	sono stati/state	stavano

	pluperfect	past historic	present subjunctive	past subjunctive	imperative
io	ero stato/stata	stetti	stia	stessi	
tu	eri stato/stata	stesti	stia	stessi	sta'
lui/lei; lei	era stato/stata	stette	stia	stesse	stia
noi	eravamo stati/state	stemmo	stiamo	stessimo	stiamo
voi	eravate stati/state	steste	stiate	steste	state
loro	erano stati/state	stettero	stiano	stessero	

uscire* – to go out (past participle uscito)

	present	future	conditional	perfect	imperfect
io	esco	uscirò	uscirei	sono uscito/uscita	uscivo
tu	esci	uscirai	usciresti	sei uscito/uscita	uscivi
lui/lei; lei	esce	uscirà	uscirebbe	è uscito/uscita	usciva
noi	usciamo	usciremo	usciremmo	siamo usciti/uscite	uscivamo
voi	uscite	uscirete	uscireste	siete usciti/uscite	uscivate
loro	escono	usciranno	uscirebbero	sono usciti/uscite	uscivano

	pluperfect	past historic	present subjunctive	past subjunctive	imperative
io	ero uscito/uscita	uscii	esca	uscissi	
tu	eri uscito/uscita	uscisti	esca	uscissi	esci
lui/lei; lei	era uscito/uscita	uscì	esca	uscisse	esca
noi	eravamo usciti/uscite	uscimmo	usciamo	uscissimo	usciamo
voi	eravate usciti/uscite	usciste	usciate	usciste	uscite
loro	erano usciti/uscite	uscirono	escano	uscissero	

. . . .

Irregular verbs cont.

venire* – to come (past participle **venuto**)

	present	future	conditional	perfect	imperfect
io	vengo	verrò	verrei	sono venuto/venuta	venivo
tu	vieni	verrai	verresti	sei venuto/venuta	venivi
lui/lei; lei	viene	verrà	verrebbe	è venuto/venuta	veniva
noi	veniamo	verremo	verremmo	siamo venuti/venute	venivamo
voi	venite	verrete	verreste	siete venuti/venute	venivate
loro	vengono	verranno	verrebbero	sono venuti/venute	venivano

	pluperfect	past historic	present subjunctive	past subjunctive	imperative
io	ero venuto/venuta	venni	venga	venissi	
tu	eri venuto/venuta	venisti	venga	venissi	vieni
lui/lei; lei	era venuto/venuta	venne	venga	venisse	venga
noi	eravamo venuti/venute	venimmo	veniamo	venissimo	veniamo
voi	eravate venuti/venute	veniste	veniate	veniste	venite
loro	erano venuti/venute	vennero	vengano	venissero	

volere – to want (past participle **voluto**)

	present	future	conditional	perfect	imperfect
io	voglio	vorrò	vorrei	ho voluto	volevo
tu	vuoi	vorral	vorresti	hai voluto	volevi
lui/lei; lei	vuole	vorrà	vorrebbe	ha voluto	voleva
noi	vogliamo	vorremo	vorremmo	abbiamo voluto	volevamo
voi	volete	vorrete	vorreste	avete voluto	volevate
loro	vogliono	vorranno	vorrebbero	hanno voluto	volevano

	pluperfect	past historic	present subjunctive	past subjunctive
io	avevo voluto	volli	voglia	volessi
tu	avevi voluto	volesti	voglia	volessi
lui/lei; lei	aveva voluto	volle	voglia	volesse
noi	avevamo voluto	volemmo	vogliamo	volessimo
voi	avevate voluto	voleste	vogliate	voleste
loro	avevano voluto	vollero	vogliano	volessero

Note sulla grammatica inglese

Gli articoli

l'articolo indeterminativo

L'articolo indeterminativo è **a** davanti a una parola che comincia con consonante o con il suono 'i + vocal' (/j/):

a ball	**a girl**	**a union**
una palla	una ragazza	un'unione

È **an** davanti a vocale o h muta:

an apple	**an hour**
una mela	un'ora

L'uso dell'articolo indeterminativo è generalmente limitato ai nomi numerabili. Da notare i seguenti usi:

- con professione

She is a doctor.	**He is an engineer.**
È medico.	È ingegnere.

- dopo una preposizione

  She works as a tour guide.
  Fa la guida turistica.

  Anna has gone out without an umbrella.
  Anna è uscita senza ombrello.

- con senso generico

  A whale is larger than a frog.
  La balena è più grande della rana.

l'articolo determinativo

L'articolo determinativo è **the**, sia per i nomi singolari che per i plurali:

the cat	**the owls**
il gatto	le civette

L'articolo determinativo *non* viene generalmente usato con le parole che designano:

- istituzioni

  I don't go to church.
  Non vado in chiesa.

  He's starting school next week.
  Comincia la scuola la settimana prossima.

Quando ci si riferisce all'edificio, il nome viene invece accompagnato dall'articolo:
Turn right at the school (Alla scuola, gira a destra).

- pasti

  Breakfast is at 8.30.
  La colazione è alle 8.30.

  Dinner is ready!
  La cena è pronta!

- periodi del giorno, dopo una preposizione (eccetto **in** o **during**)

  I'm never out at night.
  Non esco mai di sera.

  They left in the morning.
  Sono partiti di mattina.

- cose astratte

  Hatred is a destructive force.
  L'odio è una forza distruttrice.

  The book is on English grammar.
  Il libro è sulla grammatica inglese.

- malattie

  She's got tonsillitis.
  Ha la tonsillite.

- stagioni

  Spring is here!
  È arrivata la primavera!

  It's like winter today.
  Oggi, sembra inverno.

- nazioni

  France la Francia
  England l'Inghilterra

- vie, parchi, ecc.

  a concert in Central Park
  un concerto a Central Park

  I work on Bath Street.
  Lavoro in Bath Street.

L'articolo è tuttavia utilizzato nei seguenti tipi di frasi:

The breakfast he served was awful.
La colazione che ha servito era orribile.

Le seguenti categorie di nomi prendono generalmente l'articolo determinativo:

- nomi geografici plurali

  the Netherlands i Paesi Bassi
  the United States gli Stati Uniti
  the Alps le Alpi

• nomi di fiumi e oceani

the Thames il Tamigi
the Pacific il Pacifico

• nomi di hotel, pub, teatri, musei, ecc.

the Hilton
the Fox and Hounds
the Odeon

Il plurale

Il plurale di un nome è di solito formato aggiungendo **-s** in fine di parola:

dog, dogs cane, cani
tape, tapes cassetta, cassette

-es viene aggiunto a parole che terminano in **-s, -ss, -sh, -ch, -x** o **-zz**:

dress, dresses vestito, vestiti
box, boxes scatola, scatole

Nomi che terminano in consonante + y:

baby, babies bambino, bambini

Nomi che terminano in vocale + y:

valley, valleys valle, valli

I nomi che terminano in **-o** talvolta prendono **-s**, talvolta **-es**:

potato, potatoes patata, patate
tomato, tomatoes pomodoro, pomodori
solo, solos assolo, assoli
zero, zeros zero, zeri

I plurali dei nomi terminanti in **-f(e)** sono di tre tipi:

life, lives vita, vite
dwarf, dwarfs/dwarves nano, nani
roof, roofs tetto, tetti

I plurali irregolari più frequenti includono:

child, children bambino, bambini
foot, feet piede, piedi
man, men uomo, uomini
mouse, mice topo, topi
tooth, teeth dente, denti
woman, women donna, donne

I nomi composti

I nomi composti possono avere diverse forme.

nome + nome:

summer dress abito estivo
tennis shoes scarpe da tennis
record collection collezione di dischi

nome + gerundio:

disco dancing ballo da discoteca
dressmaking cucito

gerundio + nome:

parking meter parchimetro
writing course corso di scrittura
boarding card carta di imbarco

Da notare la forma di composti quali **record collection**: a record collection (senza la s del plurale in **record**), ma **a collection of records** [una collezione di dischi]; **a photo album**, ma **an album of photos** [un album di fotografie].

Nel caso di nomi numerabili, la **s** del plurale va aggiunta al secondo elemento del composto: **summer dresses** [abiti estivi], **boarding cards** [carte di imbarco].

Il femminile

L'inglese ha un numero relativamente basso di forme femminili di parole. Pertanto, **cousin** = cugino o cugina; **friend** = amico o amica; **doctor** = dottore o dottoressa.

Dovendo specificare il sesso della persona alla quale ci si riferisce, si dirà, ad esempio, **a male student** (uno studente), **a woman doctor** (una dottoressa).

Il genitivo

Le regole sull'uso del genitivo – **s** preceduto dall'apostrofo (**'s**) o **s** seguito dall'apostrofo (**s'**) – sono le seguenti:

-'s viene aggiunto a nomi singolari:

the boy's book (il libro del ragazzo)

il solo apostrofo (**'**) viene aggiunto a nomi plurali terminanti in **-s**:

the boys' room (la camera dei ragazzi)
the boys' books (i libri dei ragazzi)

Se un nome plurale non termina in **-s** il genitivo si forma aggiungendo **-'s**:

the children's toys (i giocattoli dei bambini)

Con nomi propri terminanti in **-s** si possono trovare entrambe le forme **'s** e **s'**, benché **s'** sia più frequente: **Keats's poetry** o **Keats' poetry** [le poesie di Keats]. I nomi greci e romani terminanti in **s**, tuttavia, prendono in genere solo l'apostrofo: **Socrates' death** [la morte di Socrate], **Catullus' poetry** [le poesie di Catullo].

Il genitivo viene usato soprattutto con persone, animali (in particolare domestici) e paesi: **Andrew's house** [la casa di Andrew], **the lion's den** [la tana del leone], **America's foreign policy** [la politica estera dell'America].

Da notare i seguenti usi del genitivo:

We're going to Anne's.
Andiamo a casa di Anne.

We're going to Peter and Anne's.
Andiamo a casa di Peter e Anne. (Non, per lo più, **Peter's and Anne's** se Peter e Anne sono una coppia.)

Jane Austen's and George Orwell's novels
i romanzi di Jane Austen e quelli di George Orwell (Jane Austen e George Orwell sono ben distinti l'una dall'altro.)

I got it at the baker's/the chemist's.
L'ho preso dal panettiere/in farmacia. (Letteralmente, nel negozio del panettiere/del farmacista.)

Nell'inglese colloquiale il 'doppio genitivo' è frequente:

He's a friend of my brother's.
È un amico di mio fratello.

It was an idea of Anne's.
È stata un'idea di Anne.

Gli aggettivi

Gli aggettivi in inglese hanno un'unica forma, non concordano, cioè, né nel genere, né nel numero:

an old man
un uomo vecchio

three old women
tre donne vecchie

posizione dell'aggettivo

L'aggettivo può precedere il nome: **a long story** [una storia lunga] o seguire il verbo: **this story is long** [questa storia è lunga].

Alcuni aggettivi non possono essere usati davanti al nome: **The girl is upset.** [La ragazza è sconvolta.]; non si può dire **the upset girl.**

gradi comparativi

Ci sono tre gradi comparativi: la forma assoluta, il comparativo e il superlativo.

Gli aggettivi composti da una sola sillaba

formano il comparativo e il superlativo con l'aggiunta di **-(e)r** e **-(e)st**:

dull noioso
duller più noioso
dullest il più noioso

big grande
bigger
biggest

(Da notare che una consonante semplice in fine di parola viene raddoppiata.)

nice bello
nicer
nicest

Gli aggettivi di tre sillabe, per lo più, formano il comparativo e il superlativo con **more** e **most**:

generous generoso
more generous
most generous

Lo stesso vale per alcuni aggettivi di due sillabe, ad esempio **useful** [utile].

Non esistono tuttavia regole assolute per gli aggettivi bisillabici, benché **-er/-est** siano particolarmente frequenti con aggettivi terminanti in **-y, -le, -ow, -er**. Esempi:

pretty carino (da notare che **-y** diventa **-ie**)
prettier
prettiest

narrow stretto
narrower
narrowest

curious curioso
more curious
most curious

Per i participi presenti e passati si usa la forma con **more/most**:

boring noioso
more boring
most boring

bored annoiato
more bored
most bored

Most può essere inoltre usato come sinonimo di 'estremamente' o 'molto':
That was a most interesting story (Quella era una storia molto interessante).

alcuni aggettivi irregolari frequenti

bad cattivo
worse peggiore

worst il peggiore

good buono
better migliore
best il migliore

little poco
less meno
least il meno

many/much molti/molto
more più
most il più

far lontano
further
furthest (con riferimento a spazio, tempo, quantità, numero)

far lontano
farther
farthest (solo per distanza nello spazio)

old (1) vecchio
elder
eldest (usato solo per persone)

(1) Le forme regolari (**old, older, oldest** vecchio, più vecchio, il più vecchio) sono usate sia per persone che per cose.

Le comparazioni negative possono essere espresse dall'uso di **less/least**:

far lontano
less far meno lontano
least far il meno lontano

Gli aggettivi possono svolgere la funzione di nomi, in particolare quando si riferiscono a gruppi di persone: **the young** i giovani; **the old** i vecchi; **the unemployed** i disoccupati.

Gli aggettvi possessivi

Gli aggettivi possessivi sono:

my mio, mia, miei, mie
our nostro, nostra, nostri, nostre

your tuo, tua, tuoi, tue; suo,
your vostro, vostra, vostri, sua, suoi, sue vostre

his, her, its suo, sua, suoi, sue

their loro

Concordano con il possessore e non con la cosa posseduta:

his mother sua madre (la madre del ragazzo, ad esempio)

her mother sua madre (la madre della ragazza, ad esempio)

their mother la loro madre (la madre delle ragazze, o dei ragazzi, o dei ragazzi e delle ragazze)

Mantengono la stessa forma con nomi singolari e plurali:

my cat il mio gatto
my boots i miei stivali

Gli avverbi

Gli avverbi possono qualificare aggettivi:

The job was extremely dangerous.
Il lavoro era estremamente pericoloso.

verbi:

He finished quickly.
Ha finito in fretta.

altri avverbi:

very quickly
molto in fretta

Extremely, quickly e **very** sono avverbi.

Molti avverbi sono formati con il suffisso **-ly** aggiunto all'aggettivo: **sad, sadly** triste, tristemente; **brave, bravely** coraggioso, coraggiosamente; **beautiful, beautifully** bello, molto bene.

Possono tuttavia intervenire dei cambiamenti nell'ortografia: **true, truly** vero, veramente; **due, duly** dovuto, debitamente; **whole, wholly** intero, interamente.

Altri mutamenti fonetici regolari riguardano:

y in fine di parola: **ready, readily** pronto, prontamente

consonante in fine di parola + **le**: **gentle, gently** dolce, dolcemente.

Alcuni avverbi hanno forma identica all'aggettivo corrispondente; tra questi **back** dietro, **early** presto, **far** lontano, **fast** velocemente, **left** a sinistra, **little** poco, **long** a lungo, **more** più, **much** molto, **only** solo, **right** a destra, giustamente, **still** tranquillamente, **straight** dritto, **well** bene, **wrong** in modo sbagliato. Esempi:

a wrong answer (aggettivo)
una risposta sbagliata

He did it wrong. (avverbio)
L'ha fatto in modo sbagliato.

an early summer
un'estate precoce

Summer arrived early.
L'estate è arrivata in anticipo.

a straight road
una strada dritta

He came straight to the point.
È andato dritto al punto.

I pronomi

pronomi personali

soggetto	complemento
I io	me me, mi
you tu; lei	you te, ti; la, le
he egli, lui	him lo, gli
she essa, lei	her la, le
it esso, essa	it lo, la, gli, le
we noi	us ci
you voi	you vi
they essi, loro	them li, loro

Il soggetto di un verbo in inglese non è espresso dalla forma del verbo stesso; pertanto, la traduzione dell'italiano **vado**, ad esempio, è **I go** e non **go**.

I pronomi complemento sono usati come complemento oggetto:

Mary loves him.
Mary lo ama.

come complemento di termine:

John gave me a lift.
John mi ha dato un passaggio.

e dopo una preposizione:

The book is from her.
Il libro è da parte sua.

altri usi dei pronomi personali

he e she

Questi pronomi sono talvolta usati per indicare degli animali, specialmente domestici:

Poor Whiskers, we had to take him to the vet's.
Povero Whiskers, abbiamo dovuto portarlo dal veterinario.

it

• è usato in costruzioni impersonali:

It's sunny.
C'è il sole.

It's hard to know what to do.
È difficile sapere cosa fare.

It looks as though they were right.
Parrebbe che avessero ragione.

• in espressioni temporali e spaziali:

It's five o'clock.
Sono le cinque.

It's January the sixth.
È il sei gennaio.

How far is it to Edinburgh?
Quanto dista Edimburgo?

Va notato che **it's** è la forma contratta di **it is**, da non confondersi con il pronome possessivo **its**.

you

Rivolgendosi ad una persona, l'inglese non distingue l'uso del pronome **tu** dal pronome **lei** che vengono entrambi tradotti con **you**.

You è spesso usato in senso generico, per indicare la gente in generale:

You never know; it might be sunny this afternoon.
Non si sa mai; potrebbe esserci il sole oggi pomeriggio.

You can't buy cars like that any more.
Non si possono più comprare macchine così.

they

• è impiegato per riferirsi a un gruppo di persone sconosciute, specialmente se dotate di un qualche potere, autorità o abilità:

They don't make cars like that any more.
Non ne fanno più di macchine così.

They will have to find the murderer first.
Dovranno prima trovare l'assassino.

You'll have to get them to repair it.
Dovrai farglielo riparare.

• al posto di **he or she** (lui o lei)

The person appointed will be answerable to the director. They will be responsible for ...
La persona prescelta dovrà rispondere al direttore. Sarà responsabile di ...

A personal secretary will assist them. (= him/her)
Una segretaria personale lo/la assisterà.

• per rimandare ai pronomi indefiniti **somebody, someone** qualcuno; **anybody, anyone** chiunque; **everybody, everyone** tutti; **nobody, no one** nessuno:

If anyone has seen my pen, will they please tell
me.
Se qualcuno ha visto la mia penna, per
favore, me lo dica.

one

One è equivalente al pronome generico **you**,
ma è più formale:

**One needs to get a clearer picture of what one
wants.**
Bisogna avere un'idea più chiara di quello
che si vuole.

L'uso ripetuto di **one** viene di solito evitato.

pronomi riflessivi

myself mi	**ourselves** ci
yourself ti; si	**yourselves** vi
himself, herself, itself, oneself si	**themselves** si

Esempi dell'uso:

He burned himself badly. (complemento
  oggetto)
Si è bruciato seriamente.

I always buy myself a Christmas present.
  (complemento di termine)
Mi compro sempre un regalo di Natale.

She talks to herself. (dopo preposizione)
Parla da sola.

Do it yourself. (enfatico)
Fallo da te.

pronomi possessivi

mine il mio, la mia, i miei, le mie
yours il tuo, la tua, i tuoi, le tue
his, hers il suo, la sua, i suoi, le sue
ours il nostro, la nostra, i nostri, le nostre
yours il vostro, la vostra, i vostri, le vostre
theirs il loro, la loro, i loro, le loro

I pronomi possessivi concordano con il
possessore e non con la cosa posseduta:

Whose book is this? – It's hers.
Di chi è questo libro? – È suo.

Whose shoes are these? – They're hers.
Di chi sono queste scarpe? – Sono le sue.

Whose car is that? – It's theirs.
Di chi è questa macchina? – È la loro.

Gli aggettivi e i pronomi interrogativi

who chi
whom chi
whose di chi

which quale, quali
what quale, quali, che

Who è usato per persona con funzione di
soggetto:

Who is it? Chi è?

Whom è usato per persona con funzione di
complemento:

To whom did you send the letter?
A chi hai spedito la lettera?

Whom did you see?
Chi hai visto?

Whom è considerato piuttosto formale e
tende ad essere sostituito da **who**:

Who did you send the letter to?
A chi hai spedito la lettera?

Who did you see?
Chi hai visto?

Whose è la forma genitiva di **who**:

Whose are these?
Di chi sono questi?

Whose socks are these?
Di chi sono queste calze?

Which può designare sia persone che cose.
È usato con funzione di soggetto:

Which of you are going?
Chi di voi va?

Which is bigger?
Qual è più grande?

Which box is bigger?
Quale scatola è più grande?

e di complemento:

Which of the singers/pictures do you prefer?
Quale cantante/quadro preferisci?

Which dress should I wear?
Che vestito mi metto?

What è usato esclusivamente per cose. Può
avere funzione di soggetto:

What is this?
Cos'è questo?

What type of bird is that?
Che tipo di uccello è quello?

e di complemento:

What are you going to do?
Cosa farai?

What sort of books do you like?
Che tipo di libri ti piacciono?

What implica una gamma di possibilità più
estesa o meno definita rispetto a **which**.

I pronomi relativi

who, whom che   which che
that chi, che   whose il cui

I pronomi relativi rimandano normalmente ad un antecedente (cioè qualcosa che è già stato menzionato). In **She phoned the man who had contacted her** (Ha telefonato all'uomo che l'aveva contattata), il pronome relativo **who** (che) si riferisce a **the man** (l'uomo).

antecedente	soggetto	complemento
persone	who/that	whom/who/that
cose	which/that	which/that

persone: soggetto

Who è il pronome relativo generalmente usato in questo caso; anche **that** viene però usato:

There is a prize for the student who/that gets the highest mark.
C'è un premio per lo studente che ottiene il voto più alto.

persone: complemento

The man whom/who/that she met that night was a spy.
L'uomo che ha incontrato quella notte era una spia.

Whom viene considerato piuttosto formale ed è generalmente sostituito da **who** o **that**.

Il pronome relativo può anche essere omesso:

The man she met last night was a spy.
L'uomo che ha incontrato la notte scorsa era una spia.

cose: soggetto

The book, which is on the table, was a present.
Il libro che è sul tavolo è un regalo.

John gave me the book which/that is on the table.
John mi ha dato il libro che è sul tavolo.

cose: complemento

His latest film, which we went to see last week, was excellent.
Il suo ultimo film, che siamo andati a vedere la settimana scorsa, era ottimo.

The film which/that we went to see last week was excellent.
Il film che siamo andati a vedere la settimana scorsa era ottimo.

Nell'ultimo esempio, il pronome relativo può anche essere omesso:

The film we went to see last week was excellent.
Il film che siamo andati a vedere la settimana scorsa era ottimo.

Whose è la forma genitiva:

This is the boy whose dog has been killed.
Questo è il ragazzo il cui cane è stato ucciso.

La forma **of which** (il cui) è usata nel linguaggio più formale o tecnico per riferirsi a cose:

Water, the boiling point of which is 100°C, is a colourless liquid.
L'acqua, il cui punto di ebollizione è a 100°C, è un liquido incolore.

Si noti che **who's** è la forma contratta di **who is** (chi è), da non confondersi con il pronome relativo **whose** (il cui).

Gli aggettivi e i pronomi indefiniti

some/any

Come aggettivi, vengono usati con nomi plurali o non numerabili:

Take some biscuits.
Prendi dei biscotti.

Take some jam.
Prendi della marmellata.

Have you got any biscuits?
Hai dei biscotti?

Have you any jam?
Hai della marmellata?

Come pronomi, sostituiscono nomi plurali o non numerabili:

We haven't got any.
Non ne abbiamo.

Some (aggettivo e pronome) si usa in:

- frasi affermative

He bought some.
Ne ha comprato.

He bought some jam.
Ha comprato della marmellata.

He bought some biscuits.
Ha comprato dei biscotti.

- domande alle quali ci si aspetta una risposta affermativa

Can you lend me some money?
Mi puoi prestare dei soldi?

- offerte e richieste

Would you like some?
Ne vuoi?

Could you buy some onions for me?
Mi puoi comprare delle cipolle?

Any (aggettivo e pronome) si usa in:

- frasi negative

I haven't got any brothers or sisters.
Non ho né fratelli, né sorelle.

- domande

Have you got any bananas?
Hai delle banane?

I composti di **some** e **any** vengono usati in
modo simile. Esempi:

I saw something really strange today.
Ho visto qualcosa di veramente strano
oggi.

Did you meet anyone you knew?
Hai incontrato qualcuno che conoscevi?

We didn't see anything interesting.
Non abbiamo visto niente di interessante.

I verbi

L'infinito costituisce la radice o forma di
base. La forma intera dell'infinito
comprende **to**: **to live** vivere, **to die** morire, ecc.

Per una lista di verbi irregolari vedi p.948.

I verbi regolari vengono coniugati come
segue:

- infinito

want   love(1)   stop(2)   prefer(3)

participio presente/gerundio

wanting   loving   stopping   preferring

passato semplice/participio passato

wanted   loved   stopped   preferred

(1) infinito terminante in **-e**
(2) infinito monosillabico terminante in
    vocale + consonante semplice
(3) infinito terminante in vocale accentata
    + consonante semplice

Il gerundio è usato con funzione nominale:

I don't like swimming.
Non mi piace nuotare.

Dancing is fun.
Ballare è divertente.

I tempi

presente

to be essere	**to have** avere
I am sono	**I have** ho
you are sei	**you have** hai
he/she/it is è	**he/she/it has** ha
we are siamo	**we have** abbiamo
you are siete	**you have** avete
they are sono	**they have** hanno

Per gli altri verbi, la forma è la stessa della
radice, con l'eccezione della terza persona
singolare, che prende la desinenza **-s**:

to want (volere): **I want, you want, he/she/it
wants, we want, you want, they want**

to love (amare): **I love, you love, he/she/it loves,
we love, you love, they love**

La terza persona singolare dei verbi
terminanti in **-s**, **-ss**, **-sh**, **-ch**, **-x** o **-zz** è formata
con la desinenza **-es**:

to watch guardare: **he/she/it watches**
to kiss baciare: **he/she/it kisses**

Il presente esprime:

- azioni abituali, verità generalmente
  accettate ed enunciazioni di fatti:

He takes the 8 o'clock train to work.
Prende il treno delle 8 per andare al lavoro.

I work in publishing.
Lavoro nell'editoria.

- gusti e opinioni

I hate Monday mornings.
Odio i lunedì mattina.

He doesn't believe in God.
Non crede in Dio.

- percezioni sensoriali

It tastes delicious.
È squisito.

passato semplice

La forma è la stessa per tutte le persone, sia
singolari che plurali:

I/you/he/she/it/we/you/they wanted

È impiegato per descrivere azioni compiute
o avvenimenti del passato:

He flew to America last week.
Ha preso l'aereo per l'America la
settimana scorsa.

passato composto

È composto dal presente di **have** (avere) e il participio passato:

> **I/you have loved, he/she/it has loved, we/you/they have loved**

Descrive azioni passate o avvenimenti che hanno una qualche rilevanza per il presente.

Si può osservare la differenza tra il passato composto e il passato semplice confrontando le seguenti frasi:

> **Have you seen Peter this morning?**
> Hai visto Peter stamattina? (è sempre mattina)
> **Did you see Peter this morning?**
> Hai visto Peter stamattina? (è ora pomeriggio o sera)

Va notato il seguente uso del present perfect:

> **I have lived in Glasgow for three years.**
> Vivo a Glasgow da tre anni.

trapassato

È composto dal tempo passato di **have** (avere) e il participio passato:

> **I/you/he/she/it/we/you/they had wanted**

Descrive azioni o avvenimenti passati precedenti rispetto ad altre azioni o avvenimenti anch'essi passati:

> **She had already left home when I arrived.**
> Era già uscita di casa quando sono arrivato.

Le forme perifrastiche

Le forme perifrastiche sono formate dal verbo **be** (essere), nel tempo e persona richiesti, e dal participio presente.

presente progressivo

I am singing sto cantando, **you are singing**, ecc.

Descrive eventi, di solito temporanei, ancora in corso:

> **What are you doing? – I'm trying to fix the television.**
> Cosa stai facendo? – Sto cercando di riparare la televisione.
> **He always interrupts when I'm reading to the children.**

Mi interrompe sempre mentre sto leggendo per i bambini.

passato progressivo

I was singing stavo cantando, **you were singing**, ecc.

Descrive avvenimenti passati ancora in corso nel momento in cui un altro avvenimento passato ha luogo:

> **He rushed into my office while I was talking to the director.**
> Si è precipitato nel mio ufficio mentre stavo parlando al direttore.

Anche gli altri tempi verbali hanno una forma progressiva: **I have been living; I had been living; I will be living.**

Da notare il seguente uso del passato composto nella forma progressiva:

> **I have been living in Glasgow for three years.**
> Vivo a Glasgow da tre anni.

Il futuro

In inglese ci sono diversi modi per parlare del futuro.

- **will/shall**

Will può essere usato con tutte le persone; **shall** è usato esclusivamente con la prima persona singolare e plurale.

> **I will/shall go** andrò
> **we will/shall go** andremo
> **you will go** andrai
> **you will go** andrete
> **he/she/it will go** andrà
> **they will go** andranno

Will e le forme negative **will not** e **shall not** possono essere contratte:

> **You'll be angry.**
> Ti arrabbierai.
> **We won't/shan't stay long.**
> Non staremo a lungo.

- **going to**

Questa forma viene spesso usata per esprimere un'intenzione o per predire qualcosa che accadrà:

> **I'm going to go to London tomorrow.**
> Vado a Londra domani.
> **The boss is going to be furious when he hears.**
> Il capo si infurierà quando lo verrà a sapere.

Going to è spesso intercambiabile con **will**:

The boss will be furious when he hears.
Il capo si infurierà quando lo verrà a sapere.

I wonder whether the car is going to/will start.
Mi chiedo se la macchina partirà.

• il presente

Può essere usato per esprimere qualcosa che accadrà in un momento determinato, specialmente con riferimento ad un orario:

When does term finish?
Quando finisce il trimestre?

There is a train for London at 10 o'clock.
C'è un treno per Londra alle 10.

• il presente progressivo

Viene usato in modo simile a **going to** per esprimere un'intenzione:

I'm spending Christmas in Paris.
Passerò il Natale a Parigi.

Where are you going for your holidays?
Dove vai in vacanza?

L'imperativo

La radice del verbo è usata per impartire ordini:

Be quiet!
Fai silenzio!

Shut the door!
Chiudi la porta!

L'imperativo negativo viene formato con **don't**:

Don't forget to phone Alan!
Non dimenticarti di telefonare ad Alan!

Let's viene usato per la prima persona plurale per fare delle proposte:

Let's go.
Andiamo.

Don't let's go.
Non andiamo.

Let's not go.
Non andiamo.

La forma interrogativa

La forma interrogativa di frasi contenenti il presente e il passato semplice prevede l'uso del verbo **do**, accordato con il soggetto della frase:

Do you live here?
Vivi qui?

Did you live here?
Vivevi qui?

Se la frase contiene un verbo ausiliare (**have**, **be**) o modale, la forma interrogativa è realizzata invertendo il verbo e il soggetto:

Are they going to get married?
Si sposano?

Have they seen us?
Ci hanno visti?

Can John come at eight?
Può venire alle otto John?

Con i pronomi interrogativi, i modelli sono i seguenti:

Who came?
Chi è venuto?

Who fed the cat?
Chi ha dato da mangiare al gatto?

What have they done to you?
Che cosa ti hanno fatto?

What shall we write about?
Di cosa scriviamo?

In frasi negative **not** segue il soggetto, a meno che sia utilizzata la forma contratta:

Did they not say they would come?/
Didn't they say they would come?
Non avevano detto che sarebbero venuti?

Will the director not be there?/
Won't the director be there?
Non ci sarà il direttore?

Nell'inglese parlato, l'ordine delle parole nelle domande è spesso lo stesso che nelle affermazioni, ma l'intonazione è crescente:

He told you to leave?
Ti ha detto di andartene?

He left without saying a word?
Se ne è andato senza dire una parola?

Le domande di conferma

Si tratta di domande brevi, aggiunte alla fine di una frase, per chiedere una conferma di quanto si è detto.

Una frase affermativa è di solito seguita da una domanda negativa:

You smoke, don't you?
Fumi, no?

Da notare l'ausiliare **don't** che sostituisce nella domanda il verbo **smoke**.

Una frase negativa è invece generalmente seguita da una domanda in forma affermativa:

You don't smoke, do you?
Non fumi, vero?

Se la frase contiene un verbo ausiliare o modale, questo è ripetuto nella domanda:

You aren't going, are you?
Non ci vai, vero?

You will come, won't you?
Vieni, no?

You shouldn't say that, should you?
Non dovresti dire questo, vero?

Va notata la forma della domanda quando il verbo nell'affermazione è **am**:

I am lucky, aren't I?
Sono fortunato, no?

Il tempo verbale nella domanda è lo stesso che nella frase da cui dipende:

You wanted to go home, didn't you?
Volevi andare a casa, no?

Le risposte brevi

Nelle risposte non è necessario ripetere la forma intera del verbo; si può infatti semplicemente ripetere il verbo ausiliare (**be**, **have**, **do**) o modale contenuto nella domanda.

Is it raining? – Yes, it is./No, it isn't.
Piove? – Sì./No.

Do you like fish? – Yes, I do./No, I don't.
Ti piace il pesce? – Sì./No.

Can you drive? – Yes, I can./No, I can't.
Guidi? – Sì./No.

Le frasi negative

Le proposizioni negative sono formate con l'ausiliare **do** concordato con il soggetto + **not**. Le forme contratte sono **don't** e **doesn't** per il presente e **didn't** per il passato.

They do not/don't understand English.
Non capiscono l'inglese.

We did not/didn't go anywhere yesterday.
Non siamo andati da nessuna parte ieri.

Quando il verbo è impiegato con tono enfatico, viene utilizzata la forma non contratta:

I do not approve!
Non approvo!

I verbi modali

can, could; may, might; shall, should; will, would; must; ought

I verbi modali sono invariabili: **I can, you can, he can**, ecc.

La forma interrogativa si ottiene con l'inversione del soggetto e del verbo: **Can I go now?** (Posso andare ora?)

È facile trovare i modali nella forma contratta. **Will** e **shall** si contraggono in **'ll**: **I'll be going** (Andrò).

Would si contrae in **'d**: **I'd like a cup of tea** (Vorrei una tazza di tè).

La forma negativa dei verbi modali prevede l'uso di **not** (**would not, might not**, ecc.) È particolare la forma negativa di can: **cannot** (cioè un'unica parola nell'inglese britannico).

Le forme negative contratte sono: **can't, couldn't, mightn't, shan't, shouldn't, won't, wouldn't, mustn't, oughtn't**. (**Mayn't** non è frequente.)

can

- autorizzazione

  Can I leave the table, please?
  Posso alzarmi da tavola, per favore?

  I can have another sweet, daddy said so.
  Posso avere un'altra caramella, lo ha detto papà.

- capacità

  He can count to a hundred.
  Sa contare fino a cento.

  Can he drive?
  Sa guidare?

- possibilità

  Accidents can happen.
  Gli incidenti possono capitare.

- richieste

  Can you open the door for me, please?
  Mi puoi aprire la porta, per favore?

Note sulla grammatica inglese

could

Could è la forma passata di **can**. I suoi significati comprendono:

- autorizzazione, capacità, possibilità, richiesta, espresse nel passato

  Daddy said I could have another sweet.
  Papà ha detto che potevo avere un'altra caramella.

  By the time he was three, he could count to a hundred.
  A tre anni sapeva contare fino a cento.

  She asked if he could open the door for her.
  Gli ha chiesto se poteva aprirle la porta.

- richiesta formale

  Could I leave a message, please?
  Potrei lasciare un messaggio, per favore?

- possibilità

  I don't know where John is; I suppose he could be at Anne's.
  Non so dov'è John; forse potrebbe essere da Anne.

- indignazione

  You could have warned me!
  Avresti potuto avvertirmi!

may

- autorizzazione e richiesta formale

  May I use your phone, please?
  Potrei usare il suo telefono, per favore?

  You may not leave the examination hall until I give the sign.
  Non potete allontanarvi dalla sala d'esame prima che io abbia dato il segnale.

- possibilità

  We may get an extra day's holiday.
  Potremmo avere un giorno di vacanza in più.

  They may have left.
  Potrebbero essere andati via.

might

- possibilità

Might si differenzia da **may** in quanto spesso suggerisce che si tratta di una possibilità poco probabile:

  We might get a pay rise.
  Magari avremo un aumento di stipendio.
  (= è improbabile)

Viene usato anche nel passato:

  He was afraid he might have missed the train.
  Aveva paura di aver perso il treno.

- autorizzazione e richiesta formale

  Do you think I might have another whisky?
  Pensa che potrei avere un altro whisky?

- indignazione

  You might have phoned!
  Avresti potuto telefonare!

shall

Per l'uso di **shall** per esprimere il futuro vedi p. 939. **Shall** può essere inoltre usato per indicare:

- richieste di ordini o consigli

  Where shall we put the shopping?
  Dove mettiamo la spesa?

  What time shall I set the alarm for?
  Per che ora devo mettere la sveglia?

- offerte o suggerimenti

  Shall I make you a cup of tea?
  Ti preparo una tazza di tè?

  Shall we meet outside the station?
  Ci vediamo fuori dalla stazione?

should

Should è la forma passata di **shall** e viene inoltre impiegato per esprimere:

- convenienza o obbligo

  You shouldn't tell lies.
  Non dovresti dire le bugie.

  What do you think we should do?
  Cosa pensi che dovremmo fare?

- probabilità

  Once this job is finished, we should have more spare time.
  Una volta finito questo lavoro, dovremmo avere più tempo libero.

  They should be here by now.
  Dovrebbero essere qui ormai.

  The keys should be in that drawer. That's where I left them.
  Le chiavi dovrebbero essere in quel cassetto. È lì che le ho lasciate.

will

Per l'uso di **will** per esprimere il futuro, vedi p. 939. Per **will** in proposizioni condizionali, vedi p. 943.

Will può essere anche impiegato per esprimere:

- un comportamento tipico o una caratteristica innata

  The stadium will seat 4,000 people.
  Lo stadio ha 4 000 posti a sedere.

  Hot air will rise.
  L'aria calda sale verso l'alto.

- la volontà, un desiderio, il consenso

  Will you see to the post for me?
  Puoi occuparti della posta per me?

  I'll do what I can to help him.
  Farò quello che posso per aiutarlo.

- un'offerta

  Will you have another slice of cake?
  Prendi un'altra fetta di dolce?

- una forte probabilità o una deduzione

  There's someone at the door. That will be Kenneth.
  C'è qualcuno alla porta, sarà Kenneth.

- un ordine

  You will go and wash your hands immediately.
  Vai subito a lavarti le mani.

would

Per l'uso di **would** in frasi condizionali, vedi Sotto. **Would** è la forma passata di **will**. Può esprimere anche:

- il 'futuro nel passato', o un'intenzione passata

  He told me he would do it immediately.
  Mi ha detto che l'avrebbe fatto immediatamente.

  They said they wouldn't wait for me.
  Hanno detto che non mi avrebbero aspettato.

- abitudini nel passato

  He would always get up at 6 a.m.
  Si alzava sempre alle 6.

must

- obbligo

  You must make sure you lock up.
  Devi assicurarti di chiudere a chiave.

  I must check whether my neighbour is all right.
  Devo controllare se il mio vicino sta bene.

Da notare che **mustn't** significa che non si è autorizzati a fare qc:

You mustn't park there.
Non puoi parcheggiare qui. (= è vietato)

Se si vuole dire che non è necessario fare qualcosa, si può usare **don't have to** o **needn't** o **don't need to**.

You don't have to eat that./You needn't eat that./ You don't need to eat that.
Non sei obbligato a mangiarlo.

- probabilità

  They must be there by now.
  Devono essere là ormai.

  You must have been annoyed by the decision.
  La decisione deve averti seccato.

ought

- obbligo

  You ought to be leaving.
  Dovresti andare via.

  They ought to send him away.
  Lo dovrebbero mandare via.

- probabilità/attesa

  They ought to be there by now.
  Dovrebbero essere là ormai.

  Two kilos of potatoes. That ought to be enough.
  Due chili di patate. Dovrebbero bastare.

Le frasi ipotetiche con *if* (se)

I modelli di base sono:

if + presente, proposizione principale con **will**:

If we hurry, we'll catch the train./We'll catch the train if we hurry.
Se ci sbrighiamo, prenderemo il treno.

if + passato semplice, proposizione principale con **would**:

If I won the lottery, I would buy a new house./I would buy a new house if I won the lottery.
Se vincessi la lotteria, mi comprerei una casa nuova.

if + trapassato, proposizione principale con **would have**:

If Paolo hadn't lost the tickets, we would have arrived on time./We would have arrived on time if Paolo hadn't lost the tickets.
Se Paolo non avesse perso i biglietti, saremmo arrivati in orario.

I verbi frasali

Numerosi verbi possono combinarsi con una preposizione per formare i cosiddetti verbi frasali. La preposizione può cambiare il significato del verbo:

to take (prendere):

John took a book.
John ha preso un libro.

to take off:

He took off his boots./He took his boots off.
Si è tolto gli stivali.

The plane took off.
L'aereo ha decollato.

to take after:

He takes after his mother.
Assomiglia a sua madre.

Da notare che il complemento oggetto, nel primo esempio di **take off**, può trovarsi in due posizioni diverse: dopo la preposizione o tra il verbo e la preposizione.

Quando il complemento oggetto è un pronome, però, la sola posizione possibile è tra il verbo e la preposizione:

He looked it up in the dictionary.
Lo ha cercato nel dizionario.

They have put it off.
Lo hanno rimandato.

Italian verb tables

Regular verbs:

1. in **-are** (*eg* **compr | are**)

Present ~o, ~i, ~a, ~iamo, ~ate, ~ano
Imperfect ~avo, ~avi, ~ava, ~avamo, ~avate, ~avano
Past historic ~ai, ~asti, ~ò, ~ammo, ~aste, ~arono
Future ~erò, ~erai, ~erà, ~eremo, ~erete, ~eranno
Present subjunctive ~i, ~i, ~i, ~iamo, ~iate, ~ino
Past subjunctive ~assi, ~assi, ~asse, ~assimo, ~aste, ~assero
Present participle ~ando
Past participle ~ato
Imperative ~a (*fml* ~i), ~iamo, ~ate
Conditional ~erei, ~eresti, ~erebbe, ~eremmo, ~ereste, ~erebbero

2. in **-ere** (*eg* **vend | ere**)

Pres ~o, ~i, ~e, ~iamo, ~ete, ~ono
Impf ~evo, ~evi, ~eva, ~evamo, ~evate, ~evano
Past hist ~ei *or* ~etti, ~esti, ~è *or* ~ette, ~emmo, ~este, ~erono *or* ~ettero
Fut ~erò, ~erai, ~erà, ~eremo, ~erete, ~eranno
Pres sub ~a, ~a, ~a, ~iamo, ~iate, ~ano
Past sub ~essi, ~essi, ~esse, ~essimo, ~este, ~essero
Pres part ~endo
Past part ~uto
Imp ~i (*fml* ~a), ~iamo, ~ete
Cond ~erei, ~eresti, ~erebbe, ~eremmo, ~ereste, ~erebbero

3. in **-ire** (*eg* **dorm | ire**)

Pres ~o, ~i, ~e, ~iamo, ~ite, ~ono
Impf ~ivo, ~ivi, ~iva, ~ivamo, ~ivate, ~ivano
Past hist ~ii, ~isti, ~ì, ~immo, ~iste, ~irono
Fut ~irò, ~irai, ~irà, ~iremo, ~irete, ~iranno
Pres sub ~a, ~a, ~a, ~iamo, ~iate, ~ano
Past sub ~issi, ~issi, ~isse, ~issimo, ~iste, ~issero
Pres part ~endo
Past part ~ito
Imp ~i (*fml* ~a), ~iamo, ~ite
Cond ~irei, ~iresti, ~irebbe, ~iremmo, ~ireste, ~irebbero

Notes

- Many verbs in the third conjugation take *isc* between the stem and the ending in the first, second, and third person singular and in the third person plural of the present, the present subjunctive, and the imperative: fin | ire **Pres** ~isco, ~isci, ~isce, ~iscono. **Pres sub** ~isca, ~iscano **Imp** ~isci.

- The three forms of the imperative are the same as the corresponding forms of the present for the second and third conjugation. In the first conjugation the forms are also the same except for the second person singular: present *compri*, imperative *compra*. The negative form of the second person singular is formed by putting *non* before the infinitive for all conjugations: *non comprare*. In polite forms the third person of the present subjunctive is used instead for all conjugations: *compri*.

• •

Irregular verbs:

Certain forms of all irregular verbs are regular (except for *essere*). These are: the second person plural of the present, the past subjunctive, and the present participle. Forms not listed below can be derived from the parts given. Only those irregular verbs considered to be the most useful are shown in the tables.

accadere *as* cadere

accendere • **Past hist** accesi, accendesti • **Past part** acceso

affliggere • **Past hist** afflissi, affliggesti • **Past part** afflitto

ammettere *as* mettere

andare • **Pres** vado, vai, va, andiamo, andate, vanno • **Fut** andrò *etc* • **Pres sub** vada, vadano • **Imp** va', vada, vadano

apparire • **Pres** appaio *or* apparisco, appari *or* apparisci, appare *or* apparisce, appaiono *or* appariscono • **Past hist** apparvi *or* apparsi, apparisti, apparve *or* apparì *or* apparse, apparvero *or* apparirono *or* apparsero • **Pres sub** appaia *or* apparisca

aprire • **Pres** apro • **Past hist** aprii, apristi • **Pres sub** apra • **Past part** aperto

avere • **Pres** ho, hai, ha, abbiamo, hanno • **Past hist** ebbi, avesti, ebbe, avemmo, aveste, ebbero • **Fut** avrò *etc* • **Pres sub** abbia *etc* • **Imp** abbi, abbia, abbiate, abbiano

bere • **Pres** bevo *etc* • **Impf** bevevo *etc* • **Past hist** bevvi *or* bevetti, bevesti • **Fut** berrò *etc* • **Pres sub** beva *etc* • **Past sub** bevessi *etc* • **Pres part** bevendo • **Cond** berrei *etc*

cadere • **Past hist** caddi, cadesti • **Fut** cadrò *etc*

chiedere • **Past hist** chiesi, chiedesti • **Pres sub** chieda *etc* • **Past part** chiesto *etc*

chiudere • **Past hist** chiusi, chiudesti • **Past part** chiuso

cogliere • **Pres** colgo, colgono • **Past hist** colsi, cogliesti • **Pres sub** colga • **Past part** colto

correre • **Past hist** corsi, corresti • **Past part** corso

crescere • **Past hist** crebbi • **Past part** cresciuto

cuocere • **Pres** cuocio, cuociamo, cuociono • **Past hist** cossi, cocesti • **Past part** cotto

dare • **Pres** do, dai, da, diamo, danno • **Past hist** diedi *or* detti, desti • **Fut** darò *etc* • **Pres sub** dia *etc* • **Past sub** dessi *etc* • **Imp** da' (*fml* dia)

dire • **Pres** dico, dici, dice, diciamo, dicono • **Impf** dicevo *etc* • **Past hist** dissi, dicesti • **Fut** dirò *etc* • **Pres sub** dica, diciamo, diciate, dicano • **Past sub** dicessi *etc* • **Pres part** dicendo • **Past part** detto • **Imp** di' (*fml* dica)

dovere • **Pres** devo *or* debbo, devi, deve, dobbiamo, devono *or* debbono • **Fut** dovrò *etc* • **Pres sub** deva *or* debba, dobbiamo, dobbiate, devano *or* debbano • **Cond** dovrei *etc*

essere • **Pres** sono, sei, è, siamo, siete, sono • **Impf** ero, eri, era, eravamo, eravate, erano • **Past hist** fui, fosti, fu, fummo, foste, furono • **Fut** sarò *etc* • **Pres sub** sia *etc* • **Past sub** fossi, fossi, fosse, fossimo, foste, fossero • **Past part** stato • **Imp** sii (*fml* sia), siate • **Cond** sarei *etc*

fare • **Pres** faccio, fai, fa, facciamo, fanno • **Impf** facevo *etc* • **Past hist** feci, facesti • **Fut** farò *etc* • **Pres sub** faccia *etc* • **Past sub** facessi *etc* • **Pres part** facendo • **Past part** fatto • **Imp** fa' (*fml* faccia) • **Cond** farei *etc*

fingere • **Past hist** finsi, fingesti, finsero • **Past part** finto

giungere • **Past hist** giunsi, giungesti, giunsero • **Past part** giunto

leggere • **Past hist** lessi, leggesti • **Past part** letto

mettere • **Past hist** misi, mettesti • **Past part** messo

morire • **Pres** muoio, muori, muore, muoiono • **Fut** morirò *or* morrò *etc* • **Pres sub** muoia • **Past part** morto

muovere • **Past hist** mossi, movesti • **Past part** mosso

nascere • **Past hist** nacqui, nascesti • **Past part** nato

offrire • **Past hist** offersi *or* offrii, offristi • **Pres sub** offra • **Past part** offerto

parere • **Pres** paio, pari, pare, pariamo, paiono • **Past hist** parvi *or* parsi, paresti • **Fut** parrò *etc* • **Pres sub** paia, paiamo *or* pariamo, pariate, paiano • **Past part** parso

piacere • **Pres** piaccio, piaci, piace, piacciamo, piacciono • **Past hist** piacqui, piacesti, piacque, piacemmo, piaceste, piacquero • **Pres sub** piaccia *etc* • **Past part** piaciuto

porre • **Pres** pongo, poni, pone, poniamo, ponete, pongono • **Impf** ponevo *etc* • **Past hist** posi, ponesti • **Fut** porrò *etc* • **Pres sub** ponga, poniamo, poniate, pongano • **Past sub** ponessi *etc*

potere • **Pres** posso, puoi, può, possiamo, possono • **Fut** potrò *etc* • **Pres sub** possa, possiamo, possiate, possano • **Cond** potrei *etc*

prendere • **Past hist** presi, prendesti • **Past part** preso

ridere • **Past hist** risi, ridesti • **Past part** riso

rimanere • **Pres** rimango, rimani, rimane, rimaniamo, rimangono • **Past hist** rimasi, rimanesti • **Fut** rimarrò *etc* • **Pres sub** rimanga • **Past part** rimasto • **Cond** rimarrei

salire • **Pres** salgo, sali, sale, saliamo, salgono • **Pres sub** salga, saliate, salgano

sapere • **Pres** so, sai, sa, sappiamo, sanno • **Past hist** seppi, sapesti • **Fut** saprò *etc* • **Pres sub** sappia *etc* • **Imp** sappi (*fml* sappia), sappiate • **Cond** saprei *etc*

scegliere • **Pres** scelgo, scegli, sceglie, scegliamo, scelgono • **Past hist** scelsi, scegliesti *etc* • **Past part** scelto

scrivere • **Past hist** scrissi, scrivesti *etc* • **Past part** scritto

sedere • **Pres** siedo *or* seggo, siedi, siede, siedono • **Pres sub** sieda *or* segga

spegnere • **Pres** spengo, spengono • **Past hist** spensi, spegnesti • **Past part** spento

stare • **Pres** sto, stai, sta, stiamo, stanno • **Past hist** stetti, stesti • **Fut** starò *etc* • **Pres sub** stia *etc* • **Past sub** stessi *etc* • **Past part** stato • **Imp** sta' (*fml* stia)

tacere • **Pres** taccio, tacciono • **Past hist** tacqui, tacque, tacquero • **Pres sub** taccia

tendere • **Past hist** tesi • **Past part** teso

tenere • **Pres** tengo, tieni, tiene, tengono • **Past hist** tenni, tenesti • **Fut** terrò *etc* • **Pres sub** tenga

togliere • **Pres** tolgo, tolgono • **Past hist** tolsi, tolse, tolsero • **Pres sub** tolga, tolgano • **Past part** tolto • *Imp fml* tolga

trarre • **Pres** traggo, trai, trae, traiamo, traete, traggono • **Past hist** trassi, traesti • **Fut** trarrò *etc* • **Pres sub** tragga • **Past sub** traessi *etc* • **Past part** tratto

uscire • **Pres** esco, esci, esce, escono • **Pres sub** esca • **Imp** esci (*fml* esca)

valere • **Pres** valgo, valgono • **Past hist** valsi, valesti • **Fut** varrò *etc* • **Pres sub** valga, valgano • **Past part** valso • **Cond** varrei *etc*

vedere • **Past hist** vidi, vedesti • **Fut** vedrò *etc* • **Past part** visto *or* veduto • **Cond** vedrei *etc*

venire • **Pres** vengo, vieni, viene, vengono • **Past hist** venni, venisti • **Fut** verrò *etc*

vivere • **Past hist** vissi, vivesti • **Fut** vivrò *etc* • **Past part** vissuto • **Cond** vivrei *etc*

volere • **Pres** voglio, vuoi, vuole, vogliamo, volete, vogliono • **Past hist** volli, volesti • **Fut** vorrò *etc* • **Pres sub** voglia *etc* • **Imp** vogliate • **Cond** vorrei *etc*

Verbi inglesi

Infinitive	Past Tense	Past Participle	Infinitive	Past Tense	Past Participle
Infinito	*Passato*	*Participio passato*	*Infinito*	*Passato*	*Participio passato*
arise	arose	arisen	**fall**	fell	fallen
awake	awoke	awoken	**feed**	fed	fed
be	was	been	**feel**	felt	felt
bear	bore	borne	**fight**	fought	fought
beat	beat	beaten	**find**	found	found
become	became	become	**flee**	fled	fled
begin	began	begun	**fling**	flung	flung
behold	beheld	beheld	**fly**	flew	flown
bend	bent	bent	**forbid**	forbade	forbidden
beseech	beseeched, besought	beseeched, besought	**forget**	forgot	forgotten
			forgive	forgave	forgiven
bet	bet, betted	bet, betted	**forsake**	forsook	forsaken
			freeze	froze	frozen
bid	bade, bid	bidden, bid	**get**	got	got, gotten *Am*
bind	bound	bound	**give**	gave	given
bite	bit	bitten	**go**	went	gone
bleed	bled	bled	**grind**	ground	ground
blow	blew	blown	**grow**	grew	grown
break	broke	broken	**hang**	hung, hanged (*vt*)	hung, hanged
breed	bred	bred			
bring	brought	brought	**have**	had	had
build	built	built	**hear**	heard	heard
burn	burnt, burned	burnt, burned	**hew**	hewed	hewed, hewn
burst	burst	burst	**hide**	hid	hidden
bust	busted, bust	busted, bust	**hit**	hit	hit
			hold	held	held
buy	bought	bought	**hurt**	hurt	hurt
cast	cast	cast	**keep**	kept	kept
catch	caught	caught	**kneel**	knelt	knelt
choose	chose	chosen	**know**	knew	known
cling	clung	clung	**lay**	laid	laid
come	came	come	**lead**	led	led
cost	cost, costed (*vt*)	cost, costed	**lean**	leaned, leant	leaned, leant
creep	crept	crept	**leap**	leapt, leaped	leapt, leaped
cut	cut	cut			
deal	dealt	dealt	**learn**	learnt, learned	learnt, learned
dig	dug	dug			
do	did	done	**leave**	left	left
draw	drew	drawn	**lend**	lent	lent
dream	dreamt, dreamed	dreamt, dreamed	**let**	let	let
			lie	lay	lain
drink	drank	drunk	**light**	lit, lighted	lit, lighted
drive	drove	driven			
dwell	dwelt	dwelt	**lose**	lost	lost
eat	ate	eaten	**make**	made	made

Verbi inglesi

Infinitive	Past Tense	Past Participle	Infinitive	Past Tense	Past Participle
Infinito	*Passato*	*Participio passato*	*Infinito*	*Passato*	*Participio passato*
mean	meant	meant	**spell**	spelled, spelt	spelled, spelt
meet	met	met			
mow	mowed	mown, mowed	**spend**	spent	spent
			spill	spilt, spilled	spilt, spilled
overhang	overhung	overhung			
pay	paid	paid	**spin**	spun	spun
put	put	put	**spit**	spat	spat
quit	quitted, quit	quitted, quit	**split**	split	split
			spoil	spoilt, spoiled	spoilt, spoiled
read	read /red/	read /red/			
rid	rid	rid	**spread**	spread	spread
ride	rode	ridden	**spring**	sprang	sprung
ring	rang	rung	**stand**	stood	stood
rise	rose	risen	**steal**	stole	stolen
run	ran	run	**stick**	stuck	stuck
saw	sawed	sawn, sawed	**sting**	stung	stung
			stink	stank	stunk
say	said	said	**strew**	strewed	strewn, strewed
see	saw	seen			
seek	sought	sought	**stride**	strode	stridden
sell	sold	sold	**strike**	struck	struck
send	sent	sent	**string**	strung	strung
set	set	set	**strive**	strove	striven
sew	sewed	sewn, sewed	**swear**	swore	sworn
			sweep	swept	swept
shake	shook	shaken	**swell**	swelled	swollen, swelled
shear	sheared	shorn, sheared			
			swim	swam	swum
shed	shed	shed	**swing**	swung	swung
shine	shone	shone	**take**	took	taken
shit	shit	shit	**teach**	taught	taught
shoe	shod	shod	**tear**	tore	torn
shoot	shot	shot	**tell**	told	told
show	showed	shown	**think**	thought	thought
shrink	shrank	shrunk	**thrive**	thrived, throve	thrived, thriven
shut	shut	shut			
sing	sang	sung	**throw**	threw	thrown
sink	sank	sunk	**thrust**	thrust	thrust
sit	sat	sat	**tread**	trod	trodden
slay	slew	slain	**understand**	understood	understood
sleep	slept	slept	**undo**	undid	undone
slide	slid	slid	**wake**	woke	woken
sling	slung	slung	**wear**	wore	worn
slit	slit	slit	**weave**	wove	woven
smell	smelt, smelled	smelt, smelled	**weep**	wept	wept
			wet	wet, wetted	wet, wetted
sow	sowed	sown, sowed			
			win	won	won
speak	spoke	spoken	**wind**	wound	wound
speed	sped, speeded	sped, speeded	**wring**	wrung	wrung
			write	wrote	written